DATE DUE

DEMCO 38-296

THE
ENCYCLOPEDIA
OF THE
NCAA
BASKETBALL
TOURNAMENT

THE
ENCYCLOPEDIA
OF THE
NCAA
BASKETBALL
TOURNAMENT

The Complete
Independent Guide
to College Basketball's
Championship Event

JIM SAVAGE

A DELL HARDCOVER

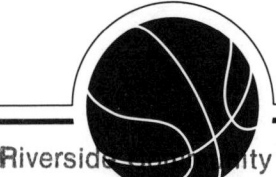

A DELL HARDCOVER

Published by
Dell Publishing
a division of
Bantam Doubleday Dell Publishing Group, Inc.
666 Fifth Avenue
New York, New York 10103

NCAA is a registered trademark of The National Collegiate Athletic Association. This book is not endorsed by or affiliated with the NCAA.

Throughout the book, the trade names and trademarks of some entities have been used, and no such uses are intended to convey endorsement or other affiliations with the book.

Design: Stanley S. Drate/Folio Graphics Co., Inc.

ISBN: 0-440-50362-0

Printed in the United States of America

Published simultaneously in Canada

December 1990

10   9   8   7   6   5   4   3   2

RRH

Dedication

To my wife, Nancy, and my sons, Jacob and Sam, for their patience. And to the thousands of men—players and coaches—who made the NCAA tournament the greatest continuing saga in American amateur sports.

Acknowledgments

This book could not have been done without the help and support of many people. First, my wife Nancy, who coordinated, compiled, and collected an immense amount of data, read and improved every word of my writing, and had the patience to bear with me every step of the way. Leslie Schnur, my editor at Dell, who believed in the project from day one and made it happen, on time, despite a million obstacles. Nick Egleson of Paladin Consulting, who programmed the extraordinary data base that's at the heart of the book, and made himself available to fine-tune it virtually whenever I called. Eric Wertzer, who scavenged libraries and tirelessly pored through microfilm to uncover the most obscure facts and figures. Kevin Smith and Jill Lamar at Dell, the former for providing his knowledge of the game, his enthusiasm, and an immense amount of energy to help me gather information, and the latter for her skill at juggling a thousand things at one time. My mother, Meta Savage, and my mother-in-law, Pearl Moskowitz, who tirelessly helped in the effort to ensure that every piece of data was correct and in the right place. Wayne Patterson of the Naismith Memorial Basketball Hall of Fame for his encouragement, advice, and the knowledge he shared so selflessly. Gary Johnson of the NCAA, who helped me find what I needed and pointed me in the right direction when I had no idea where to turn. Brian Zuckerman, Amanda Rosen, Joey Skoler, Sharon Herzfeld, and Ahron Balsam, all of whom contributed greatly to the gathering and accurate entry of information into the the data base. The people of *The Arkansas Gazette* and *The* (Salt Lake City) *Tribune* who opened up their morgues to send me decades-old articles I could not locate on my own. And, most especially, the Sports Information Directors, assistants, secretaries, librarians, and archivists at scores of colleges, who turned their offices upside down—often at a moment's notice—to provide me with facts, figures, and information that I could not have gotten anywhere else.

CONTENTS

INTRODUCTION by Denny Crum   xiii

FOREWORD   xvii

✪ PART 1 ✪

52 YEARS OF CHAMPIONSHIP BASKETBALL—YEAR-BY-YEAR:
The NCAA Men's Division I Basketball Tournament

- ✪ A Diagram of the Draw

- ✪ Tournament Highlights, Including Background on the Teams and Description of the Action

- ✪ Box Scores of Every Tournament Game

- ✪ All-Regional and All-Tournament Stars

- ✪ Records for Leading Individual and Team Performances in the Tournament

1939	3	1943	27
1940	9	1944	33
1941	15	1945	39
1942	21	1946	46

1947	52	1969	300
1948	59	1970	314
1949	66	1971	328
1950	73	1972	341
1951	81	1973	354
1952	90	1974	368
1953	99	1975	381
1954	111	1976	396
1955	123	1977	409
1956	135	1978	424
1957	147	1979	438
1958	161	1980	456
1959	173	1981	475
1960	186	1982	494
1961	199	1983	511
1962	212	1984	530
1963	225	1985	549
1964	238	1986	571
1965	250	1987	593
1966	264	1988	617
1967	276	1989	641
1968	288	1990	664

✪ PART 2 ✪

TWENTY TOURNAMENT GREATS—PROFILES AND ANALYSES OF THE MEN BEHIND THE STATISTICS

THE PLAYERS

Bob Kurland	691
Clyde Lovellette	692
Bill Russell	693
Bill Bradley	693
Gail Goodrich	695
Lew Alcindor (Kareem Abdul-Jabbar)	696
Austin Carr	697
Bill Walton	698
Earvin (Magic) Johnson	699
James Worthy	700

THE COACHES

Phog Allen	703
Branch McCracken	704
Adolph Rupp	705
John Wooden	707
Al McGuire	710
Dean Smith	712
Denny Crum	714
Bob Knight	715
John Thompson	718
Jerry Tarkanian	720

✪ PART 3 ✪

ALL-TIME TOURNAMENT RECORDS

COMPLETE SCHOOL-BY-SCHOOL RECORDS   725

A comprehensive list of all the schools that ever played in the tournament: coaches, appearances, won-lost records, championships, title game, Final Four, and Round of Eight appearances

ALL-TIME TOURNAMENT RECORDS   736

Individual Performances: single game, Final Four, championship game, tournament, and career leaders

Scoring 736
Field Goals 736
3-Point Field Goals 737
Free Throws 737

Rebounding 738
Assists 738
Blocked Shots, Steals, Turnovers 739

Team Performances: single game, Final Four, championship game, tournament, and all-time leaders

Scoring 740
Field Goals 740
Free Throws 742
3-Point Field Goals 743
Rebounding 743
Assists 744

Blocked Shots 744
Steals 744
Personal Fouls 744
Turnovers 745
Appearances/Wins 745

INTRODUCTION

The NCAA basketball tournament has truly become a national treasure, capturing the attention of every corner of the nation. Television exposure and the expansion to sixty-four teams (from the initial field of eight teams) has changed the tournament from a highly select small group into a very select large group. Every part of the country is represented by one or more teams, creating tremendous interest across every square mile of our nation.

I don't think there is any event creating as much interest nationwide over as long a time as the NCAA basketball tournament. The Super Bowl is one game. The World Series is no more than seven games. But it takes sixty-three games through the month of March to crown one national champion in college basketball. That is spectacular.

While I have been fortunate enough to coach in eighteen NCAA tournaments, I did not enter the world dribbling at birth. My first taste of basketball came in the eighth grade, when a friend across the street got me involved. My dad put up a goal for us in the yard, and my neighbor and I started playing. My friend was a couple years older and about eight inches taller than me, and I always had a tough time handling him. But that didn't deter me, and I have been involved in the game since.

I loved my high school coach, Vinnie Seekins, and thought he was a great person and an outstanding coach. I respected him so much that I decided I wanted to do the same with my life. The summer after tenth grade, I landed my first head coaching job in a spring-summer basketball league in San Fernando, California. Rules prohibited Coach Seekins from participating, so I coached and managed the team. Thirty-seven years later, I'm still a coach.

I feel a great deal of pride, satisfaction, and good fortune to have coached two NCAA championship teams in 1980 and 1986 at Louisville, and also to have been involved in three more titles as an assistant coach at UCLA, my alma mater. Six Final Four teams at Louisville, including an unmatched four appearances during the 1980s, and fifteen NCAA tournament showings have made the tournament a big part of my coaching career.

The first NCAA championship I was associated with at UCLA was great, but it was as if we were supposed to win. My first year as an assistant coach at UCLA was Kareem Abdul-Jabbar's senior year (he was then Lew Alcindor). After we won the title and he graduated, everyone thought that was the end of the UCLA dynasty. But we won it again my next couple of years with a new group.

There wasn't as much pressure on me to win at that time, since I was an assistant under John Wooden. I, like everyone else, just expected us to win. Then, when I came to Louisville, after having just been in three straight Final Fours with the Bruins, I went to yet another Final Four in my first year with the Cardinals. At first, I again thought that was the way it was supposed to be every year! Obviously, it doesn't always work out that way. At the time, though, I didn't know differently.

Ironically, we faced UCLA each time in my first three Final Fours at Louisville, and came away on the short end until 1980 when we won our first championship.

There was an enormous difference in my feelings toward winning the first championship at Louisville in 1980 and the second in 1986. During the first one, I felt pressure because we had been to two Final Fours and had come up short. I was not as relaxed then and did not enjoy the title as I probably should have. It was more of a feeling of relief when we won it. I had more fun with the second title in 1986 because the pressure had been lifted.

I was a mere two-year-old toddler when they tipped off the first NCAA basketball tournament in 1939. When Howard Hobson coached Oregon to a 46-33 victory over Ohio State in the first championship game, I was still nearly ten years away from my first association with the sport that would end up being my life.

And while I may have missed the early years of an event that has evolved into the nation's top sporting spectacle, Jim Savage has gathered a thoroughly complete history of the event. Every record, every box score, and information on the players, coaches, and teams are featured in this encyclopedia, one that is more than a simple reference guide.

Many of my coaching colleagues are featured within this historical volume. Despite a variance in styles, all have attained prosperity in the world of college basketball. But no one has achieved—or probably ever will achieve—the dominating presence of Coach Wooden and UCLA.

Having had the chance to play and coach under him, I thankfully give Coach Wooden a lot of the credit for any successes that I have had. My basic philosophy of the game—fundamentals, team play, conditioning, and mental preparation—was molded by his influence. The man taught me a lot.

Outstanding players from over the years are also featured. There have been so many dominant players that you could go season by season, make your list of the top players, and still leave out fifty guys that could make up a Who's Who of college basketball. You can go back and think of guys like Bill Russell, Oscar Robertson, Jerry West, Wilt Chamberlain, Elgin Baylor, Jerry Lucas, Bill Bradley, Kareem Abdul-Jabbar, and Bill Walton . . . but no matter how many you list, you'll always leave someone out. You'll enjoy reading about some of these superstars and other lesser lights.

Since the first eight teams competed for the NCAA championship over fifty years ago, the game continues to improve. Athletes today are better trained, conditioned, and taught.

They do things kids in the early days could not do or would not have dreamed of trying. Coaching has progressed over the years because so many of the top coaches have been willing to share their knowledge. There are not many secrets any more. Winning today comes down to teaching, preparation, chemistry, recruiting, and many other factors.

The numbers of talented players nationwide have vastly increased. The top players of previous eras could have played and probably dominated today as well, but there are just so many more of them now. Despite the fact that talent now is spread nearly uniformly across the country, nothing can detract from UCLA and Coach Wooden's successes. I do not think any other coach in history could have done what he did.

I think you will see very few changes in the tournament structure over the next ten years. One thing that we might see is a bigger piece of the financial pie distributed among more schools. A lot of people feel we need to spread the income out more. I have mixed feelings about that. On one hand, it would be beneficial to some of the lower-profile type programs. On the other hand, the American way is that the ones that do the best jobs reap the most rewards. I have sympathy for both sides.

Other than that, things are going so well now that I'd be surprised to see other changes. Interest is at a peak and we just have to maintain and fine tune it.

And so, while we contemplate the future, I hope you will enjoy reliving the past excitement of the NCAA tournament through *The Encyclopedia of the NCAA Basketball Tournament*. May it rekindle as many fond memories for you as it did for me.

DENNY CRUM

FOREWORD

These are the generations of the game of basketball. Dr. James Naismith, who begat Phog Allen, who begat Dean Smith, who in turn begat Michael Jordan. Four generations—from peach baskets in a Massachusetts YMCA to over-the-head reverse slam dunks in front of a national television audience—encompass the entire history of the game.

In basketball, unlike in other popular sports, every era has left an indelible mark. Every great player and coach has redefined the game's limitations, its strategies, and the skills needed to win.

If the inventor of basketball were to watch the game as it's played today, he would hardly recognize it. Naismith would have found the speed of Isiah Thomas mind-boggling; he could never have understood 6-9 Earvin Johnson's magic tricks with the ball, or believed that the high-flying acrobatics of the aforementioned Mr. Jordan were humanly possible. The man who told the young Phog Allen that basketball was a game to play, not to coach, would have been astounded by Dean Smith's seemingly infinite variety of defenses, and he would have been amazed by the strategic adjustments of Bob Knight.

In the 1930s, Dr. Naismith bitterly opposed the rule change that swept the game into the modern era. Despite his objections, the center jump after each basket was eliminated in 1938, and the game became forever faster, more competitive, and far more interesting to watch. The change also led to an explosion of popular interest in the sport that culminated in a New York sportswriters' group sponsoring a postseason national event, the National Invitational Tournament. The NIT captured the imagination of the public and filled Madison Square Garden to capacity with enthusiastic crowds who came to watch the new, modern game at its best.

The following year, the National Association of Basketball Coaches, picking up on the idea of a postseason elimination tourney, started a tournament of their own in collaboration with the National Collegiate Athletic Association: that event has since grown into the greatest competition in American amateur sports. That competition is the subject of this book.

The NCAA tournament has spanned virtually the entire modern era of basketball. From its humble beginnings in 1939 (with just eight teams and a shoestring budget), it has grown into the most exciting and widely followed eighteen days in American sports. The Men's Division I Basketball Tournament—March Madness—today brings together 64 teams representing colleges from all across the country. Tournament games are attended by hundreds of thousands of fans, and many millions more follow the action on television. It has become such a popular event that in 1990 CBS paid a billion dollars for the rights to televise all tournament games for the next seven years.

With such big money at stake, the NCAA tournament has also become a crucial revenue producer for participating schools as well as an increasingly important showcase for players. Tournament success can mean big endorsement contracts for coaches, provide the springboard for a player to enter the professional ranks, and bring an unknown college square into the public eye.

But it's the game that matters most to us. And nowhere—not in the NBA playoffs, not in the Super Bowl, not in the World Series—is the level of competition as consistently fierce as in the fight for the NCAA national championship.

Every year's tournament action brings something different and unexpected. Whether it's the school from the unknown conference that captures the imagination of the nation, or the hot middle-of-the-pack team from the Big East or the Big Ten or the ACC that thrusts itself into the spotlight, or the battle of titans that exceeds even the wildest expectations for a classic matchup, there is always something riveting and memorable when the 64 best teams in the country face off to decide who's No. 1. The tournament is the last-second first-round shot that leads, two weeks later, to a national championship, the sub who comes through in the clutch, the star who raises the level of his game yet another notch, the strategic move that turns the tide. It's the longest-running, widest-ranging, highest-flying hit show in the country.

This book is a labor of love, a chronicle of the tournament from its beginnings to the present day. It's a celebration—in words and statistics—of the teams, players, and coaches who've made the NCAA tournament the most thrilling eighteen days in American sports.

Welcome to March Madness.

PART 1

52 Years of Championship Basketball Year-by-Year:

The NCAA Men's Division I Basketball Tournament

NOTES

Part 1 is a complete year-by-year history of the NCAA Men's Division I Basketball Tournament. Included are:

- **A diagram of the draw.** This chart allows the reader to see the year's tournament results at a single glance.

- **Highlights of the action.** Since statistics don't tell the whole story (Bill Russell's domination of the 1956 tournament, for example, is not reflected in raw numbers), a short description of each year's tournament is included. These capsule essays spotlight important players and games, place the action in historical context, and describe the routes taken to the championship.

- **Box scores of every game.** The box scores that form the core of the statistics in the book have been compiled from every available source. Primary source material, specifically official records of games provided by participating institutions, has been used whenever possible. When school records have been incomplete or unavailable, dozens of newspapers from all over the country have served as a secondary source. Not all data is available for every game, even in the official school box scores; it has therefore at times been necessary to compile data from various sources in order to provide the most complete box score information. **Readers:** If you have primary source material pertaining to data missing from this edition, we would greatly appreciate your sending it to Dell Editorial, ATTN.: Basketball, 666 Fifth Ave., New York, N.Y. 10103, for inclusion in the next edition.

- **All-Regional and All-Tournament stars.** Wherever information is available, Most Outstanding Players and All-Stars (both for regionals and the tournament as a whole) have been included.

- **Individual and team performance leaders and records.** Box scores have been used to derive the leading performances—both individual and team—in every relevant statistical category. In order to make these records as accurate as possible, a category is included only if at least 80 percent of the year's box scores provides data for that specific category. In cases of percentages or averages, the requirement is more stringent; the data must be virtually complete for these categories to be included. Thus 1956 will not include rebound leaders, 1947 will not include leaders in field goal percentage, and 1962 will not include records for assists. Records are included wherever the minimum data is available, even if it precedes the time when the NCAA made the category an official statistic (e.g. the NCAA did not officially keep records for assists until 1984; this section includes assist leaders for over a decade before that date).

Following is a list of abbreviations used in box scores and other statistical material:

Min.	Minutes
FG	Field Goals
FGA	Field Goals Attempted
Reb.	Rebounds
O	Offensive
T	Total
A	Assists
TO	Turnovers
PF	Personal Fouls
S	Steals
Blk	Blocks
TP	Total Points
Pct.	Percentage
PPM	Points per minute

1939

REGIONAL SEMIFINAL	REGIONAL FINAL	NATIONAL CHAMPIONSHIP	REGIONAL FINAL	REGIONAL SEMIFINAL

WESTERN

EASTERN

Oregon 56

Villanova 42

Oregon 55

Villanova 36

Texas 41

Brown 30

Oregon 46
Ohio St. 33

Oklahoma 50

Wake Forest 52

Oklahoma 37

Ohio St. 53

Utah St. 39

Ohio St. 64

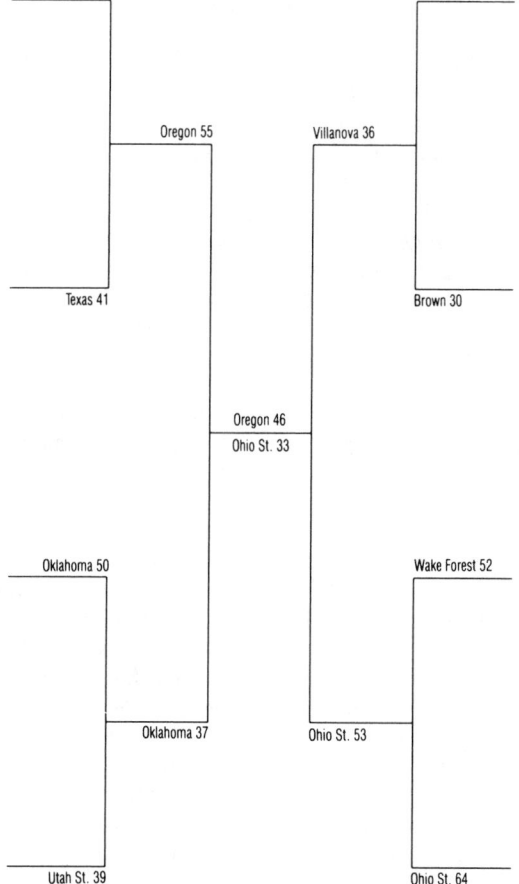

CONSOLATION GAME

Regional Third Place:

WESTERN:
Utah St. 51
Texas 49

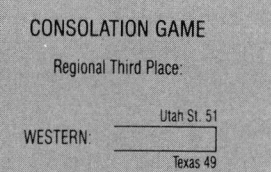

In the beginning, the NCAA tournament was a response to someone else's success. The previous year, New York's Metropolitan Basketball Writers Association had seized upon the surging popularity of the sport (largely a result of the abolition of the center jump after each score—a rules change that immeasurably sped up the action of the game) and hit upon the idea of a postseason National Invitational Tournament to be held in Madison Square Garden. The first NIT, held in March 1938, was both an artistic and financial triumph. A crowd of 14,497 fans watched an awesome, fast-breaking Temple team rout Colorado in the finals, 60–36.

The coaches and colleges wanted to get in on the act. Ohio State coach Harold Olsen proposed to the National Association of Basketball Coaches that the colleges themselves sponsor a national event. And NCAA president William B. Owens of Stanford authorized a championship basketball tournament to be held in March 1939. "It is entirely fitting," he stated, "that the 'prestige' of college basketball should be supported, and demonstrated to the nation, by the colleges themselves, rather than that this be left to private promotion and enterprise."

It would, nonetheless, be more than a decade before the NCAA surpassed the NIT to become the preeminent event in the sport.

The tournament started with eight teams in two divisions, East and West. The four Western teams were the fast-breaking Pacific Coast Conference champions, the Oregon Ducks (mistakenly called the "Webfeet" rather than "Webfoots" by some eastern commentators), also known as "the Tall Firs" because of their tall front line of 6-8 All-American Urgel (Slim) Wintermute, and two 6-4½ forwards, John Dick and Laddie Gale; the Southwest Conference champs, Texas, losers of only four of their 23 regular season games and known for their conservative play; Oklahoma of the Missouri Valley Conference, another fast-break-oriented team; and Utah State of the Rocky Mountain circuit. The Eastern fives, playing in the Palestra in Philadelphia, were a powerful Ohio State team, representing the Big Ten; the Southern champion Wake Forest Deacons; Philadelphia's own Villanova; and Brown, the Eastern League champs.

Back in 1939, college basketball was a regional affair. Different styles of play—and officiating—predominated in different regions of the country. Intersectional games were rare, and as a result few teams had the chance to adjust to other types of playing conditions. Under these circumstances, the team with the greatest intersectional experience had a distinct advantage in a national event. Oregon coach Howard "Hobby" Hobson certainly thought so; he considered his team's early season trip to the Madison Square Garden Invitational in New York the trial by fire that molded the Tall Firs into potential champions.

Many of the Oregon players had never been east of the Rockies before they got on the train to New York. Hobson later related that while his team was warming up for their Garden debut against Nat Holman's City College of New York (CCNY) team, a New York basketball official said, "Now, we aren't going to call every little brush a foul—that's okay with you, isn't it?" Hobson agreed, and as he tells it, his team was virtually mugged. Indeed, one New York sportswriter commented, "In the Northwest, the entire CCNY team would have been penalized off the floor." Following a two-point loss to CCNY, the barnstorming Ducks went on to Philadelphia, Buffalo, Cleveland, Detroit, Chicago, and points west. So when Oregon arrived back home in Eugene nearly three weeks after their trip began, they were seasoned travelers and ready for anything.

To qualify for the tournament, the Ducks had to win a Pacific Coast play-off series that ended just two days before the NCAA opening round. They then traveled to San Francisco, where, playing before 3,000 fans on Treasure Island, they opened the NCAA tournament by pulling away from Texas in the second half for a 56-41 victory. Then they routed Oklahoma.

After their fourth victory in six days, the Tall Firs got back on a train for the ride to Evanston, Illinois, and the first NCAA championship game with Ohio State. The Buckeyes, who had won the Eastern regionals easily, were playing close to home, but Oregon wore them down with constant pressure and a controlled fast-break run by their star guard Bobby Anet. Back in 1939 the rules forbade a coach from advising his players, either while the ball was in play or during a time-out, and the shifting defensive alignments run by the Webfoots confused the Big Ten champs. Meanwhile, Oregon captain Anet never called a time-out. When coach Hobson asked why, Anet replied, "You told me not to call one unless we were tired, and hell, we're still not tired." They won going away, dominating Ohio State as they had each of their NCAA opponents.

As the Tall Firs began their three-day train ride home from Chicago, the state of Oregon celebrated. In a town called The Dalles, citizens threatened to block the tracks unless the train stopped so they could honor their hometown hero John Dick. Folks celebrated in Portland, Salem, and Albany. "By the last stop," said Hobson, "they were literally hanging from the lampposts."

There were probably more people in the streets of Eugene when the Ducks arrived than there had been at all five tournament dates combined (only 15,025 people had attended the games). And when the National Association of Basketball Coaches finally counted the take, they had lost $2,531. Unable to cover the deficit, they asked the NCAA to take over. That was the beginning.

REGIONAL SEMIFINAL WESTERN

Oregon (56)   Coach: Howard Hobson

	Min.	Total FG / FGA	Pct.	FT / FTA	Pct.	Reb. O / T	A	TO	PF	S	Blk	TP	PPM
DICK, J.	-	6/ -	-	1/ -	-	-/ -	-	-	3	-	-	13	-
GALE, L.	-	2/ -	-	3/ -	-	-/ -	-	-	1	-	-	7	-
WINTERMUTE, S.	-	7/ -	-	0/ -	-	-/ -	-	-	0	-	-	14	-
ANET, B.	-	1/ -	-	2/ -	-	-/ -	-	-	0	-	-	4	-
JOHANSEN, W.	-	3/ -	-	1/ -	-	-/ -	-	-	2	-	-	7	-
SARPOLA, T.	-	0/ -	-	1/ -	-	-/ -	-	-	1	-	-	1	-
PAVALUNAS, M.	-	1/ -	-	1/ -	-	-/ -	-	-	1	-	-	3	-
MULLEN, F.	-	1/ -	-	1/ -	-	-/ -	-	-	0	-	-	3	-
SANDNESS, E.	-	1/ -	-	0/ -	-	-/ -	-	-	2	-	-	2	-
HARDY, B.	-	1/ -	-	0/ -	-	-/ -	-	-	1	-	-	2	-
Totals	200	23/ -	-	10/ -	-	-/ -	-	-	11	-	-	56	.280

Texas (41)   Coach: Jack Gray

	Min.	Total FG / FGA	Pct.	FT / FTA	Pct.	Reb. O / T	A	TO	PF	S	Blk	TP	PPM
HULL, T.	-	1/ -	-	4/ -	-	-/ -	-	-	4	-	-	6	-
GRANVILLE, C.	-	0/ -	-	2/ -	-	-/ -	-	-	2	-	-	2	-
SPEARS, G.	-	2/ -	-	1/ -	-	-/ -	-	-	4	-	-	5	-
TATE, W.	-	3/ -	-	1/ -	-	-/ -	-	-	3	-	-	7	-
MOERS, B.	-	3/ -	-	0/ -	-	-/ -	-	-	4	-	-	6	-
COOLEY	-	1/ -	-	1/ -	-	-/ -	-	-	0	-	-	3	-
FINLEY	-	2/ -	-	2/ -	-	-/ -	-	-	0	-	-	6	-
WIGGINS	-	1/ -	-	2/ -	-	-/ -	-	-	0	-	-	4	-
NELMS	-	1/ -	-	0/ -	-	-/ -	-	-	0	-	-	2	-
Totals	200	14/ -	-	13/ -	-	-/ -	-	-	17	-	-	41	.205

Disqualified: Texas—Hull, Spears, Moers.

	1st Half	2nd Half	Final
Oregon	19	37	56
Texas	16	25	41

Oklahoma (50)   Coach: Bruce Drake

	Min.	Total FG / FGA	Pct.	FT / FTA	Pct.	Reb. O / T	A	TO	PF	S	Blk	TP	PPM
MCNATT, J.	-	5/ -	-	2/ 3	.667	-/ -	-	-	3	-	-	12	-
CORBIN, G.	-	5/ -	-	2/ 3	.667	-/ -	-	-	2	-	-	12	-
SCHEFFLER, H.	-	1/ -	-	3/ 4	.750	-/ -	-	-	3	-	-	5	-
MESCH, M.	-	3/ -	-	1/ 1	1.000	-/ -	-	-	2	-	-	7	-
SNODGRASS, M.	-	3/ -	-	0/ 0	.000	-/ -	-	-	1	-	-	6	-
ROOP, G.	-	1/ -	-	3/ 4	.750	-/ -	-	-	1	-	-	5	-
KERR, B.	-	0/ -	-	1/ 1	1.000	-/ -	-	-	1	-	-	1	-
MULLEN, V.	-	0/ -	-	0/ 0	.000	-/ -	-	-	1	-	-	0	-
ZOLLER, M.	-	1/ -	-	0/ 1	.000	-/ -	-	-	1	-	-	2	-
WALKER, R.	-	0/ -	-	0/ 0	.000	-/ -	-	-	0	-	-	0	-
Totals	200	19/ -	-	12/16	.750	-/ -	-	-	15	-	-	50	.250

Utah State (39)   Coach: Dick Romney

	Min.	Total FG / FGA	Pct.	FT / FTA	Pct.	Reb. O / T	A	TO	PF	S	Blk	TP	PPM
BINGHAM, D.	-	1/ -	-	4/ 5	.800	-/ -	-	-	3	-	-	6	-
MORRIS, F.	-	6/ -	-	3/ 5	.600	-/ -	-	-	3	-	-	15	-
READING	-	4/ -	-	1/ 2	.500	-/ -	-	-	1	-	-	9	-
LINDQUIST, R.	-	1/ -	-	0/ 0	.000	-/ -	-	-	0	-	-	2	-
AGRICOLA, C.	-	0/ -	-	2/ 3	.667	-/ -	-	-	4	-	-	2	-
JAMES	-	1/ -	-	1/ 1	1.000	-/ -	-	-	0	-	-	3	-
MORRIS, C.	-	1/ -	-	0/ 1	.000	-/ -	-	-	1	-	-	2	-
JACOBSON	-	0/ -	-	0/ 0	.000	-/ -	-	-	0	-	-	0	-
Totals	200	14/ -	-	11/17	.647	-/ -	-	-	12	-	-	39	.195

Disqualified: Utah State—Agricola.

	1st Half	2nd Half	Final
Oklahoma	25	25	50
Utah State	14	25	39

REGIONAL SEMIFINAL EASTERN

Villanova (42)   Coach: Alex Severance

	Min.	Total FG / FGA	Pct.	FT / FTA	Pct.	Reb. O / T	A	TO	PF	S	Blk	TP	PPM
LAZORCHAK, M.	-	3/ -	-	0/ 1	.000	-/ -	-	-	2	-	-	6	-
ROBINSON, E.	-	0/ -	-	0/ 1	.000	-/ -	-	-	0	-	-	0	-
MONTGOMERY, J.	-	5/ -	-	2/ 3	.667	-/ -	-	-	0	-	-	12	-
SINNOTT, W.	-	1/ -	-	0/ 0	.000	-/ -	-	-	1	-	-	2	-
DUBINO, L.	-	2/ -	-	0/ 0	.000	-/ -	-	-	1	-	-	4	-
RICE, L.	-	0/ -	-	0/ 0	.000	-/ -	-	-	1	-	-	0	-
KRUTULIS, J.	-	6/ -	-	2/ 3	.667	-/ -	-	-	0	-	-	14	-
VIGILANTE, A.	-	1/ -	-	0/ 0	.000	-/ -	-	-	0	-	-	2	-
NUGENT, P.	-	1/ -	-	0/ 0	.000	-/ -	-	-	3	-	-	2	-
YUNG, C.	-	0/ -	-	0/ 0	.000	-/ -	-	-	2	-	-	0	-
Totals	200	19/ -	-	4/ 8	.500	-/ -	-	-	10	-	-	42	.210

Brown (30)   Coach: George Allen

	Min.	Total FG / FGA	Pct.	FT / FTA	Pct.	Reb. O / T	A	TO	PF	S	Blk	TP	PPM
PADDEN	-	2/ -	-	2/ 2	1.000	-/ -	-	-	3	-	-	6	-
WILSON	-	2/ -	-	1/ 4	.250	-/ -	-	-	0	-	-	5	-
CAMPBELL	-	0/ -	-	0/ 0	.000	-/ -	-	-	0	-	-	0	-
PLATT	-	3/ -	-	1/ 2	.500	-/ -	-	-	3	-	-	7	-
PERSON	-	3/ -	-	2/ 3	.667	-/ -	-	-	0	-	-	8	-
MULLEN	-	0/ -	-	1/ 1	1.000	-/ -	-	-	0	-	-	1	-
TRUMAN	-	0/ -	-	1/ 1	1.000	-/ -	-	-	1	-	-	1	-
FISHER	-	1/ -	-	0/ 0	.000	-/ -	-	-	0	-	-	2	-
Totals	200	11/ -	-	8/13	.615	-/ -	-	-	7	-	-	30	.150

Disqualified: None.

	1st Half	2nd Half	Final
Villanova	17	25	42
Brown	7	23	30

Wake Forest (52)   Coach: Murray Greason

	Min.	Total FG / FGA	Pct.	FT / FTA	Pct.	Reb. O / T	A	TO	PF	S	Blk	TP	PPM
WALLER, J.	-	5/ -	-	4/ 5	.800	-/ -	-	-	4	-	-	14	-
CONVERY	-	3/ -	-	1/ 1	1.000	-/ -	-	-	1	-	-	7	-
CARTER	-	0/ -	-	0/ 0	.000	-/ -	-	-	1	-	-	0	-
OWEN, B.	-	7/ -	-	5/ 9	.556	-/ -	-	-	0	-	-	19	-
FULLER	-	0/ -	-	0/ 1	.000	-/ -	-	-	0	-	-	0	-
APPLE	-	4/ -	-	2/ 2	1.000	-/ -	-	-	3	-	-	10	-
SWEEL	-	0/ -	-	1/ 3	.333	-/ -	-	-	4	-	-	1	-
YOUNG	-	0/ -	-	1/ 1	1.000	-/ -	-	-	3	-	-	1	-
Totals	200	19/ -	-	14/22	.636	-/ -	-	-	16	-	-	52	.260

Ohio State (64)   Coach: Harold Olsen

	Min.	Total FG / FGA	Pct.	FT / FTA	Pct.	Reb. O / T	A	TO	PF	S	Blk	TP	PPM
HULL, J.	-	7/ -	-	4/ 5	.800	-/ -	-	-	2	-	-	18	-
BAKER, R.	-	10/ -	-	5/ 7	.714	-/ -	-	-	1	-	-	25	-
MICKELSON, G.	-	1/ -	-	2/ 2	1.000	-/ -	-	-	3	-	-	4	-
SCHICK, J.	-	1/ -	-	0/ 1	.000	-/ -	-	-	3	-	-	2	-
SATTLER, W.	-	2/ -	-	0/ 4	.000	-/ -	-	-	3	-	-	4	-
BOUGHNER, R.	-	0/ -	-	0/ 0	.000	-/ -	-	-	2	-	-	0	-
MAAG, C.	-	0/ -	-	0/ 0	.000	-/ -	-	-	0	-	-	0	-
SCOTT, D.	-	0/ -	-	0/ 0	.000	-/ -	-	-	0	-	-	0	-
LYNCH, R.	-	2/ -	-	3/ 3	1.000	-/ -	-	-	1	-	-	7	-
DAWSON, J.	-	2/ -	-	0/ 1	.000	-/ -	-	-	4	-	-	4	-
MEES, J.	-	0/ -	-	0/ 0	.000	-/ -	-	-	0	-	-	0	-
Totals	200	25/ -	-	14/23	.609	-/ -	-	-	19	-	-	64	.320

Disqualified: Ohio State—Dawson; Wake Forest—Waller, Sweel

	1st Half	2nd Half	Final
Wake Forest	29	23	52
Ohio State	23	41	64

REGIONAL FINAL WESTERN

Oregon (55)   Coach: Howard Hobson

	Min.	Total FG/FGA	Pct.	FT/FTA	Pct.	Reb. O/T	A	TO	PF	S	Blk	TP	PPM
GALE, L.	-	3/ -	-	5/ 7	.714	-/ -	-	-	4	-	-	11	-
HARDY, B.	-	0/ -	-	3/ 3	1.000	-/ -	-	-	1	-	-	3	-
SARPOLA, T.	-	0/ -	-	0/ 0	.000	-/ -	-	-	0	-	-	0	-
MULLEN, F.	-	0/ -	-	1/ 2	.500	-/ -	-	-	0	-	-	1	-
DICK, J.	-	6/ -	-	2/ 2	1.000	-/ -	-	-	1	-	-	14	-
WINTERMUTE, S.	-	4/ -	-	2/ 2	1.000	-/ -	-	-	1	-	-	10	-
JOHANSEN, W.	-	4/ -	-	0/ 1	.000	-/ -	-	-	3	-	-	8	-
PAVALUNAS, M.	-	1/ -	-	0/ 0	.000	-/ -	-	-	1	-	-	2	-
ANET, B.	-	1/ -	-	4/ 5	.800	-/ -	-	-	2	-	-	6	-
Totals	200	19/ -	-	17/22	.773	-/ -	-	-	13	-	-	55	.275

Oklahoma (37)   Coach: Bruce Drake

	Min.	Total FG/FGA	Pct.	FT/FTA	Pct.	Reb. O/T	A	TO	PF	S	Blk	TP	PPM
MCNATT, J.	-	5/ -	-	2/ 3	.667	-/ -	-	-	1	-	-	12	-
ROOP, G.	-	1/ -	-	1/ 2	.500	-/ -	-	-	2	-	-	3	-
WALKER, R.	-	1/ -	-	0/ 1	.000	-/ -	-	-	0	-	-	2	-
CORBIN, G.	-	2/ -	-	0/ 0	.000	-/ -	-	-	3	-	-	4	-
SCHEFFLER, H.	-	1/ -	-	2/ 2	1.000	-/ -	-	-	4	-	-	4	-
MULLEN, V.	-	0/ -	-	0/ 0	.000	-/ -	-	-	1	-	-	0	-
KERR, B.	-	3/ -	-	3/ 3	1.000	-/ -	-	-	0	-	-	9	-
MESCH, M.	-	1/ -	-	0/ 1	.000	-/ -	-	-	4	-	-	2	-
ZOLLER, M.	-	0/ -	-	0/ 0	.000	-/ -	-	-	2	-	-	0	-
SNODGRASS, M.	-	0/ -	-	1/ 1	1.000	-/ -	-	-	1	-	-	1	-
Totals	200	14/ -	-	9/13	.692	-/ -	-	-	18	-	-	37	.185

Disqualified: Oregon—Gale; Oklahoma—Scheffler, Mesch.

	1st Half	2nd Half	Final
Oregon	21	34	55
Oklahoma	14	23	37

REGIONAL FINAL EASTERN

Villanova (36)   Coach: Alex Severance

	Min.	Total FG/FGA	Pct.	FT/FTA	Pct.	Reb. O/T	A	TO	PF	S	Blk	TP	PPM
LAZORCHAK, M.	-	2/ -	-	0/ 0	.000	-/ -	-	-	1	-	-	4	-
ROBINSON, E.	-	0/ -	-	0/ 0	.000	-/ -	-	-	0	-	-	0	-
MONTGOMERY, J.	-	1/ -	-	1/ 3	.333	-/ -	-	-	4	-	-	3	-
SINNOTT, W.	-	0/ -	-	0/ 0	.000	-/ -	-	-	0	-	-	0	-
DUBINO, L.	-	1/ -	-	0/ 3	.000	-/ -	-	-	3	-	-	2	-
RICE, L.	-	0/ -	-	0/ 0	.000	-/ -	-	-	0	-	-	0	-
KRUTULIS, J.	-	2/ -	-	1/ 1	1.000	-/ -	-	-	2	-	-	5	-
NUGENT, P.	-	7/ -	-	2/ 3	.667	-/ -	-	-	2	-	-	16	-
YUNG, C.	-	0/ -	-	0/ 0	.000	-/ -	-	-	0	-	-	0	-
DUZMINSKI, G.	-	2/ -	-	2/ 3	.667	-/ -	-	-	3	-	-	6	-
Totals	200	15/ -	-	6/13	.462	-/ -	-	-	15	-	-	36	.180

Ohio State (53)   Coach: Harold Olsen

	Min.	Total FG/FGA	Pct.	FT/FTA	Pct.	Reb. O/T	A	TO	PF	S	Blk	TP	PPM
HULL, J.	-	10/ -	-	8/ 8	1.000	-/ -	-	-	1	-	-	28	-
BAKER, R.	-	2/ -	-	0/ 0	.000	-/ -	-	-	2	-	-	4	-
MICKELSON, G.	-	1/ -	-	0/ 0	.000	-/ -	-	-	0	-	-	2	-
SCHICK, J.	-	3/ -	-	1/ 1	1.000	-/ -	-	-	3	-	-	7	-
SATTLER, W.	-	3/ -	-	2/ 3	.667	-/ -	-	-	1	-	-	8	-
BOUGHNER, R.	-	0/ -	-	0/ 0	.000	-/ -	-	-	0	-	-	0	-
MAAG, C.	-	0/ -	-	0/ 0	.000	-/ -	-	-	0	-	-	0	-
SCOTT, D.	-	0/ -	-	0/ 0	.000	-/ -	-	-	0	-	-	0	-
LYNCH, R.	-	0/ -	-	0/ 1	.000	-/ -	-	-	3	-	-	0	-
DAWSON, J.	-	1/ -	-	0/ 2	.000	-/ -	-	-	1	-	-	2	-
MEES, J.	-	0/ -	-	0/ 0	.000	-/ -	-	-	0	-	-	0	-
STAFFORD, R.	-	1/ -	-	0/ 0	.000	-/ -	-	-	0	-	-	2	-
Totals	200	21/ -	-	11/15	.733	-/ -	-	-	11	-	-	53	.265

Disqualified: Villanova—Montgomery.

	1st Half	2nd Half	Final
Villanova	10	26	36
Ohio State	25	28	53

CHAMPIONSHIP

Oregon (46)   Coach: Howard Hobson

	Min.	Total FG/FGA	Pct.	FT/FTA	Pct.	Reb. O/T	A	TO	PF	S	Blk	TP	PPM
GALE, L.	-	3/ -	-	4/ 5	.800	-/ -	-	-	0	-	-	10	-
DICK, J.	-	4/ -	-	5/ 5	1.000	-/ -	-	-	3	-	-	13	-
WINTERMUTE, S.	-	2/ -	-	0/ 1	.000	-/ -	-	-	1	-	-	4	-
ANET, B.	-	4/ -	-	2/ 3	.667	-/ -	-	-	3	-	-	10	-
JOHANSEN, W.	-	4/ -	-	1/ 2	.500	-/ -	-	-	1	-	-	9	-
PAVALUNAS, M.	-	0/ -	-	0/ 0	.000	-/ -	-	-	0	-	-	0	-
MULLEN, F.	-	0/ -	-	0/ 0	.000	-/ -	-	-	0	-	-	0	-
Totals	200	17/ -	-	12/16	.750	-/ -	-	-	8	-	-	46	.230

Ohio State (33)   Coach: Harold Olsen

	Min.	Total FG/FGA	Pct.	FT/FTA	Pct.	Reb. O/T	A	TO	PF	S	Blk	TP	PPM
HULL, J.	-	5/ -	-	2/ 4	.500	-/ -	-	-	2	-	-	12	-
BAKER, R.	-	0/ -	-	0/ 0	.000	-/ -	-	-	0	-	-	0	-
MICKELSON, G.	-	0/ -	-	0/ 0	.000	-/ -	-	-	2	-	-	0	-
SCHICK, J.	-	1/ -	-	0/ 0	.000	-/ -	-	-	1	-	-	2	-
SATTLER, W.	-	3/ -	-	1/ 2	.500	-/ -	-	-	0	-	-	7	-
BOUGHNER, R.	-	1/ -	-	0/ 0	.000	-/ -	-	-	0	-	-	2	-
MAAG, C.	-	0/ -	-	0/ 0	.000	-/ -	-	-	0	-	-	0	-
SCOTT, D.	-	0/ -	-	1/ 1	1.000	-/ -	-	-	1	-	-	1	-
LYNCH, R.	-	3/ -	-	1/ 3	.333	-/ -	-	-	3	-	-	7	-
DAWSON, J.	-	1/ -	-	0/ 0	.000	-/ -	-	-	4	-	-	2	-
STAFFORD, R.	-	0/ -	-	0/ 0	.000	-/ -	-	-	0	-	-	0	-
Totals	200	14/ -	-	5/10	.500	-/ -	-	-	13	-	-	33	.165

Disqualified: Ohio State—Dawson.

	1st Half	2nd Half	Final
Oregon	21	25	46
Ohio State	16	17	33

REGIONAL THIRD PLACE WESTERN

Utah State (51)   Coach: Dick Romney

	Min.	Total FG / FGA	Pct.	FT / FTA	Pct.	Reb. O / T	A	TO	PF	S	Blk	TP	PPM
BINGHAM, D.	-	9/ -	-	1/ 1	1.000	-/ -	-	-	3	-	-	19	-
MORRIS, F.	-	3/ -	-	2/ 2	1.000	-/ -	-	-	3	-	-	8	-
JAMES	-	0/ -	-	1/ 1	1.000	-/ -	-	-	2	-	-	1	-
READING	-	1/ -	-	1/ 2	.500	-/ -	-	-	2	-	-	3	-
MORRIS, C.	-	4/ -	-	1/ 1	1.000	-/ -	-	-	2	-	-	9	-
LINDQUIST, R.	-	1/ -	-	1/ 1	1.000	-/ -	-	-	4	-	-	3	-
AGRICOLA, C.	-	3/ -	-	2/ 3	.667	-/ -	-	-	4	-	-	8	-
WILKINS	-	0/ -	-	0/ 0	.000	-/ -	-	-	1	-	-	0	-
Totals	200	21/ -	-	9/11	.818	-/ -	-	-	21	-	-	51	.255

Texas (49)   Coach: Jack Gray

	Min.	Total FG / FGA	Pct.	FT / FTA	Pct.	Reb. O / T	A	TO	PF	S	Blk	TP	PPM
HULL, T.	-	3/ -	-	4/10	.400	-/ -	-	-	2	-	-	10	-
FINLEY	-	1/ -	-	0/ 0	.000	-/ -	-	-	0	-	-	2	-
GRANVILLE, C.	-	2/ -	-	3/ 4	.750	-/ -	-	-	4	-	-	7	-
TATE, W.	-	4/ -	-	2/ 3	.667	-/ -	-	-	2	-	-	10	-
COOLEY	-	2/ -	-	0/ 0	.000	-/ -	-	-	1	-	-	4	-
SPEARS, G.	-	1/ -	-	4/ 4	1.000	-/ -	-	-	0	-	-	6	-
WIGGINS	-	0/ -	-	2/ 4	.500	-/ -	-	-	0	-	-	2	-
MOERS, B.	-	0/ -	-	1/ 1	1.000	-/ -	-	-	3	-	-	1	-
NELMS	-	3/ -	-	1/ 1	1.000	-/ -	-	-	1	-	-	7	-
Totals	200	16/ -	-	17/27	.630	-/ -	-	-	13	-	-	49	.245

Disqualified: Utah State—Lindquist, Agricola; Texas—Granville.

	1st Half	2nd Half	Final
Utah State	25	26	51
Texas	25	24	49

✪ INDIVIDUAL RECORDS ✪

SCORING

Most points in a single game
1 JIMMY HULL, OHIO STATE (vs. VILLANOVA)   28
2 RICHARD BAKER, OHIO STATE (vs. WAKE FOREST)   25
3 DEL BINGHAM, UTAH STATE (vs. TEXAS)   19
3 BOYD OWEN, WAKE FOREST (vs. OHIO STATE) 19
5 JIMMY HULL, OHIO STATE (vs. WAKE FOREST)   18

Most total points in the tournament
1 JIMMY HULL, OHIO STATE   58
2 JOHN DICK, OREGON   40
3 RICHARD BAKER, OHIO STATE   29
4 SLIM WINTERMUTE, OREGON   28
4 LADDIE GALE, OREGON   28

Highest scoring average (minimum 2 games)
1 JIMMY HULL, OHIO STATE (58-3)   19.33
2 JOHN DICK, OREGON (40-3)   13.33
3 DEL BINGHAM, UTAH STATE (25-2)   12.50
4 JIMMY MCNATT, OKLAHOMA (24-2)   12.00
5 FLOYD MORRIS, UTAH STATE (23-2)   11.50

FIELD GOALS

Most field goals in a single game
1 JIMMY HULL, OHIO STATE (vs. VILLANOVA)   10
1 RICHARD BAKER, OHIO STATE (vs. WAKE FOREST)   10
3 DEL BINGHAM, UTAH STATE (vs. TEXAS)   9
4 4 tied for fourth place.

Most total field goals in the tournament
1 JIMMY HULL, OHIO STATE   22
2 JOHN DICK, OREGON   16
3 SLIM WINTERMUTE, OREGON   13
4 RICHARD BAKER, OHIO STATE   12
5 WALLY JOHANSEN, OREGON   11

FREE THROWS

Most free throws in a single game
1 JIMMY HULL, OHIO STATE (vs. VILLANOVA)   8
2 LADDIE GALE, OREGON (vs. OKLAHOMA)   5
2 JOHN DICK, OREGON (vs. OHIO STATE)   5
2 BOYD OWEN, WAKE FOREST (vs. OHIO STATE) 5
2 RICHARD BAKER, OHIO STATE (vs. WAKE FOREST)   5

Most total free throws in the tournament
1 JIMMY HULL, OHIO STATE   14
2 LADDIE GALE, OREGON   12
3 THURMON HULL, TEXAS   8
3 JOHN DICK, OREGON   8
3 BOBBY ANET, OREGON   8

Most free throws attempted in a single game
1 THURMON HULL, TEXAS (vs. UTAH)   10
2 BOYD OWEN, WAKE FOREST (vs. OHIO STATE)   9
3 JIMMY HULL, OHIO STATE (vs. VILLANOVA)   8
4 LADDIE GALE, OREGON (vs. OKLAHOMA)   7
4 RICHARD BAKER, OHIO STATE (vs. WAKE FOREST)   7

Highest free throw percentage in a single game (minimum 7 attempts)
1 JIMMY HULL, OHIO STATE (vs. VILLANOVA) (8-8)   1.000
2 LADDIE GALE, OREGON (vs. OKLAHOMA) (5-7)   .714
2 RICHARD BAKER, OHIO STATE (vs. WAKE FOREST) (5-7)   .714
4 BOYD OWEN, WAKE FOREST (vs. OHIO STATE) (5-9)   .556
5 THURMON HULL, TEXAS (vs. UTAH) (4-10)   .400

✪ TEAM RECORDS ✪

SCORING

Most points in a single game
1	OHIO STATE (vs. WAKE FOREST)	64
2	OREGON (vs. TEXAS)	56
3	OREGON (vs. OKLAHOMA)	55

Most total points in the tournament
1	OREGON	157
2	OHIO STATE	150
3	2 tied for third place.	

Highest scoring average (minimum 2 games)
1	OREGON (157-3)	52.33
2	OHIO STATE (150-3)	50.00
3	2 tied for third place.	

FIELD GOALS

Most field goals in a single game
1	OHIO STATE (vs. WAKE FOREST)	25
2	OREGON (vs. TEXAS)	23
3	2 tied for third place.	

Most total field goals in the tournament
1	OHIO STATE	60
2	OREGON	59
3	UTAH STATE	35

FREE THROWS

Most free throws in a single game
1	TEXAS (vs. UTAH STATE)	17
1	OREGON (vs. OKLAHOMA)	17
3	2 tied for third place.	

Most total free throws in the tournament
1	OREGON	39
2	TEXAS	30
2	OHIO STATE	30

Most free throws attempted in a single game
1	TEXAS (vs. UTAH STATE)	27
2	OHIO STATE (vs. WAKE FOREST)	23
3	2 tied for third place.	

Highest free throw percentage in a single game
1	UTAH STATE (vs. TEXAS) (9-11)	.818
2	OREGON (vs. OKLAHOMA) (17-22)	.773
3	2 tied for third place.	

Fewest free throws in a single game
1	VILLANOVA (vs. BROWN)	4
2	OHIO STATE (vs. OREGON)	5
3	VILLANOVA (vs. OHIO STATE)	6

Lowest free throw percentage in a single game
1	VILLANOVA (vs. OHIO STATE) (6-13)	.462
2	VILLANOVA (vs. BROWN) (4-8)	.500
3	OHIO STATE (vs. OREGON) (5-10)	.500

Lowest free throw percentage in the tournament (minimum 2 games)
1	VILLANOVA (10-21)	.476
2	OHIO STATE (30-48)	.625
3	UTAH STATE (20-28)	.714

1940

REGIONAL SEMIFINAL	REGIONAL FINAL	NATIONAL CHAMPIONSHIP	REGIONAL FINAL	REGIONAL SEMIFINAL

Indiana 48

USC 38

Indiana 39

USC 42

Springfield 24

Colorado 32

Indiana 60
Kansas 42

Duquesne 30

Rice 44

Duquesne 30

Kansas 43

Western Ky. 29

Kansas 50

CONSOLATION GAME

Regional Third Place:

Rice 60 (ot)

WESTERN:

Colorado 56

It was just like the tortoise and the hare in 1940, as Dr. Forrest C. "Phog" Allen's Kansas Jayhawks went up against Branch McCracken's Indiana Hoosiers for the NCAA championship . . . only this time the race belonged to the swift.

The game was a lot different back then. Indiana's tallest starter was 6-4 Bob Menke, and John Kline (at 6-2½) was the giant of the Kansas squad. The average height of both teams was just a shade over 6 feet.

Basketball was still earthbound. There was no such thing as a slam dunk—in fact nobody'd even thought of the jump shot yet.

Shooting in 1940 was truly a game of hit or miss. A shooting percentage of forty percent was almost unheard of. Much more often shooting statistics looked like these: In one early-round tournament game between Southern Cal and Colorado, the score at the half was tied at 20, and Colorado had hit 6 of 37 from the floor; Springfield shot even worse in their first-round match against Indiana, only 8 for 63 (12.7 percent) for the game. Even winning teams usually hit less than thirty percent of their shots.

Many of the best college teams practiced a deliberate, ball-control style of play. Kansas coach Phog Allen believed it was the only way to play. His small, quick team relied on good ball-handling and a patterned offense to spring loose the open man for a high percentage shot.

Kansas had finished in a three-way tie for the lead in the Big Six Conference. In the play-off, they drew a bye as Oklahoma defeated Missouri. Then, the night before the showdown between the Sooners and the Jayhawks, a dance was held on the playing floor. According to Allen, "the floor was still slick" when the Kansas squad got to the arena. So, Phog said, "Dean Nesmith (the Kansas trainer) and I put belt dressing—you know, tar and pitch—on the bottoms of their shoes. Our players had no trouble but the Sooners slid all over the place."

After the Jayhawks disposed of Oklahoma, they squeaked by Oklahoma A&M's Missouri Valley champs in overtime for the right to represent their region in the national tournament.

In the first round, Howard Engleman's season-high 21 points powered Kansas over Rice and its 6-6 center Bob Kinney. Then they met up with the powerful Trojans of Southern Cal, who had defeated the NIT champs from Colorado in their opener. USC was heavily favored, and they had a six point lead late in the game. But Kansas clawed their way back. Finally coach Allen's son Bob stole the ball and fed Engleman, whose shot from the corner with 16 seconds left gave the Jayhawks a one point victory. The star of the game was Dick Harp, who eventually replaced Allen as the Jayhawks' coach and led Kansas to

the 1957 NCAA final. In 1940, though, he led them into the final by holding USC ace Ralph Vaughn to six points while himself scoring a game high 15.

On the other side of the draw, the Hurryin' Hoosiers of Indiana under second-year coach Branch McCracken ran nonstop into the championship round. They overwhelmed Springfield in their opener and then raced to an early lead against the NIT's runner-up, Duquesne. The Iron Dukes rallied, but their comeback was cut off when McCracken's team put on the brakes and stalled out the final minutes to hand Duquesne only their third defeat of the season (the Hoosiers beat them the first time too).

Going into the championship game the Indiana squad had a better overall season record. On a neutral court they would have been the favorites, but the game was being held in the Jayhawks' backyard.

The previous year, Kansas's Phog Allen had been instrumental in starting the tournament, and when the NCAA took over its administration from the coaches in 1940, they asked Allen if he could manage the event and make money doing it. He thought he could, and he scheduled both the Western playoffs and the title game at the new Kansas City Municipal Auditorium, less than fifty miles from his home base of Lawrence.

Helped by the presence of the local favorites, the final game drew a sellout crowd. As he'd promised, Allen would make money for the NCAA (the final take was $22,228.65), and at first it looked like Kansas's home-court advantage would also carry them to the title. For eight minutes at the start of the game the Indiana fast break was unable to get into gear, and the Hoosiers didn't hit for a single basket. Then they caught fire and surged to a 32-19 halftime lead. They cleared the boards and threw long passes downcourt, where their streaking teammates put up shots before Kansas had the chance to set up their defense. Meanwhile Kansas remained in its deliberate style of play, even as they fell farther and farther behind. "Indiana finished in a whirlwind," reported the *Kansas City Star*, "amazing the crowd with its marvelous passes and amazing shooting . . . all accomplished while moving at unbelievable speed." The Hurryin' Hoosiers won going away.

Years later, Indiana forward Bob Dro remembered: "Someone, and I think it was Coach Allen, sent McCracken a letter after the championship game and said he thought Kansas was still the better club and should have won the game because they controlled the ball longer than Indiana did."

But even way back in 1940 the game was decided, not by who held the ball the longest, but on who put it in the hoop. Some things never change.

REGIONAL SEMIFINAL EASTERN

Indiana (48)   Coach: Branch McCracken

	Min.	Total FG/FGA	Pct.	FT/FTA	Pct.	Reb. O/T	A	TO	PF	S	Blk	TP	PPM
SCHAEFER, H.	24	6/15	.400	2/5	.400	-/-	-	-	0	-	-	14	.583
MCCREARY, J.	17	2/5	.400	0/1	.000	-/-	-	-	0	-	-	4	.235
ARMSTRONG, P.	16	2/10	.200	2/5	.400	-/-	-	-	1	-	-	6	.375
GRIDLEY, J.	16	1/4	.250	0/0	.000	-/-	-	-	1	-	-	2	.125
MENKE, BO.	17	0/1	.000	1/2	.500	-/-	-	-	0	-	-	1	.059
MENKE, BI.	17	2/3	.667	0/0	.000	-/-	-	-	2	-	-	4	.235
HUFFMAN, M.	26	2/5	.400	2/3	.667	-/-	-	-	1	-	-	6	.231
ZIMMER, A.	8	0/5	.000	0/1	.000	-/-	-	-	1	-	-	0	.000
DRO, B.	18	2/7	.286	1/1	1.000	-/-	-	-	2	-	-	5	.278
DORSEY, R.	15	1/6	.167	2/3	.667	-/-	-	-	2	-	-	4	.267
FRANCIS, C.	14	1/5	.200	0/0	.000	-/-	-	-	2	-	-	2	.143
FREY, W.	12	0/3	.000	0/0	.000	-/-	-	-	0	-	-	0	.000
Totals	200	19/69	.275	10/21	.476	-/-	-	-	12	-	-	48	.240

Springfield (24)   Coach: Ed Hickox

	Min.	Total FG/FGA	Pct.	FT/FTA	Pct.	Reb. O/T	A	TO	PF	S	Blk	TP	PPM
MORTENSON	16	1/8	.125	1/1	1.000	-/-	-	-	0	-	-	3	.188
MUNRO	15	0/1	.000	4/5	.800	-/-	-	-	4	-	-	4	.267
REDDING	35	3/15	.200	1/2	.500	-/-	-	-	3	-	-	7	.200
SCHMIDT	40	2/12	.167	0/2	.000	-/-	-	-	0	-	-	4	.100
WERNER	24	1/5	.200	0/1	.000	-/-	-	-	4	-	-	2	.083
MCVEAN	24	1/13	.077	1/1	1.000	-/-	-	-	0	-	-	3	.125
GRAY	21	0/3	.000	1/1	1.000	-/-	-	-	3	-	-	1	.048
KISTNER	13	0/4	.000	0/3	.000	-/-	-	-	1	-	-	0	.000
NOVER	6	0/0	.000	0/0	.000	-/-	-	-	1	-	-	0	.000
PANATIER	6	0/2	.000	0/0	.000	-/-	-	-	1	-	-	0	.000
Totals	200	8/63	.127	8/16	.500	-/-	-	-	17	-	-	24	.120

Disqualified: Springfield—Werner, Munro.

	1st Half	2nd Half	Final
Indiana	30	18	48
Springfield	11	13	24

Duquesne (30)   Coach: Chick Davies

	Min.	Total FG/FGA	Pct.	FT/FTA	Pct.	Reb. O/T	A	TO	PF	S	Blk	TP	PPM
KASPERIK, L.	-	1/-	-	0/0	.000	-/-	-	-	0	-	-	2	-
MILKOVICH, E.	-	2/-	-	2/3	.667	-/-	-	-	2	-	-	6	-
LACEY, B.	-	4/-	-	0/4	.000	-/-	-	-	2	-	-	8	-
DEBNAR, R.	-	3/-	-	1/2	.500	-/-	-	-	3	-	-	7	-
WIDOWITZ, P.	-	2/-	-	1/1	1.000	-/-	-	-	3	-	-	5	-
BECKER, M.	-	1/-	-	0/1	.000	-/-	-	-	3	-	-	2	-
Totals	200	13/-	-	4/11	.364	-/-	-	-	13	-	-	30	.150

Western Kentucky (29)   Coach: Ed Diddle

	Min.	Total FG/FGA	Pct.	FT/FTA	Pct.	Reb. O/T	A	TO	PF	S	Blk	TP	PPM
BALL, H.	-	1/-	-	2/3	.667	-/-	-	-	4	-	-	4	-
FULKS, K.	-	0/-	-	0/0	.000	-/-	-	-	2	-	-	0	-
TOWERY, C.	-	6/-	-	1/5	.200	-/-	-	-	4	-	-	13	-
WALTERS, J.	-	4/-	-	4/5	.800	-/-	-	-	0	-	-	12	-
DOWNING, H.	-	0/-	-	0/1	.000	-/-	-	-	1	-	-	0	-
SHELTON, E.	-	0/-	-	0/0	.000	-/-	-	-	0	-	-	0	-
WOODWARD, R.	-	0/-	-	0/0	.000	-/-	-	-	0	-	-	0	-
DOWNING, A.	-	0/-	-	0/0	.000	-/-	-	-	0	-	-	0	-
Totals	200	11/-	-	7/14	.500	-/-	-	-	11	-	-	29	.145

Disqualified: Western Ky.—Ball, Towery.

	1st Half	2nd Half	Final
Duquesne	14	16	30
Western Ky.	12	17	29

REGIONAL SEMIFINAL WESTERN

USC (38)   Coach: Sam Barry

	Min.	Total FG/FGA	Pct.	FT/FTA	Pct.	Reb. O/T	A	TO	PF	S	Blk	TP	PPM
VAUGHAN, R.	-	5/-	-	0/1	.000	-/-	-	-	0	-	-	10	-
MORRISON, J.	-	3/-	-	4/4	1.000	-/-	-	-	2	-	-	10	-
LAMBERT, K.	-	0/-	-	1/2	.500	-/-	-	-	2	-	-	1	-
SEARS, D.	-	2/-	-	0/1	.000	-/-	-	-	4	-	-	4	-
REISING, J.	-	2/-	-	1/2	.500	-/-	-	-	2	-	-	5	-
MCGARVIN, T.	-	0/-	-	0/1	.000	-/-	-	-	3	-	-	0	-
LUBER, J.	-	1/-	-	0/0	.000	-/-	-	-	2	-	-	2	-
LIPPERT, J.	-	2/-	-	2/3	.667	-/-	-	-	1	-	-	6	-
Totals	200	15/-	-	8/14	.571	-/-	-	-	16	-	-	38	.190

Colorado (32)   Coach: Frostey Cox

	Min.	Total FG/FGA	Pct.	FT/FTA	Pct.	Reb. O/T	A	TO	PF	S	Blk	TP	PPM
DOLL, B.	-	2/-	-	3/5	.600	-/-	-	-	2	-	-	7	-
HENDRICKS, D.	-	3/-	-	1/2	.500	-/-	-	-	1	-	-	7	-
GROVE, J.	-	0/-	-	0/1	.000	-/-	-	-	0	-	-	0	-
HARVEY, J.	-	1/-	-	3/4	.750	-/-	-	-	4	-	-	5	-
MCCLOUD, L.	-	1/-	-	1/1	1.000	-/-	-	-	0	-	-	3	-
THURMAN, D.	-	2/-	-	2/3	.667	-/-	-	-	0	-	-	6	-
HAMBURG, G.	-	2/-	-	0/0	.000	-/-	-	-	4	-	-	4	-
Totals	200	11/-	-	10/16	.625	-/-	-	-	11	-	-	32	.160

Disqualified: USC—Sears; Colorado—Harvey, Hamburg.

	1st Half	2nd Half	Final
USC	20	18	38
Colorado	20	12	32

Rice (44)   Coach: Buster Brannon

	Min.	Total FG/FGA	Pct.	FT/FTA	Pct.	Reb. O/T	A	TO	PF	S	Blk	TP	PPM
CRADDOCK, L.	-	1/-	-	0/0	.000	-/-	-	-	2	-	-	2	-
GOMEZ, P.	-	2/-	-	1/2	.500	-/-	-	-	1	-	-	5	-
PEPPER	-	2/-	-	0/0	.000	-/-	-	-	0	-	-	4	-
KINNEY, B.	-	8/-	-	2/6	.333	-/-	-	-	3	-	-	18	-
SELMAN, B.	-	0/-	-	0/0	.000	-/-	-	-	3	-	-	0	-
CARSWELL, F.	-	4/-	-	1/1	1.000	-/-	-	-	1	-	-	9	-
PALMER	-	3/-	-	0/0	.000	-/-	-	-	3	-	-	6	-
ZANDER	-	0/-	-	0/0	.000	-/-	-	-	0	-	-	0	-
Totals	200	20/-	-	4/9	.444	-/-	-	-	13	-	-	44	.220

Kansas (50)   Coach: Phog Allen

	Min.	Total FG/FGA	Pct.	FT/FTA	Pct.	Reb. O/T	A	TO	PF	S	Blk	TP	PPM
EBLING, D.	-	4/-	-	2/3	.667	-/-	-	-	0	-	-	10	-
HUNTER, T.	-	0/-	-	0/0	.000	-/-	-	-	1	-	-	0	-
ENGLEMAN, H.	-	10/-	-	1/1	1.000	-/-	-	-	1	-	-	21	-
HOGBEN, B.	-	0/-	-	0/0	.000	-/-	-	-	0	-	-	0	-
ALLEN, B.	-	0/-	-	0/1	.000	-/-	-	-	0	-	-	0	-
KLINE, J.	-	1/-	-	0/1	.000	-/-	-	-	4	-	-	2	-
MILLER, R.	-	3/-	-	4/8	.500	-/-	-	-	2	-	-	10	-
VORAN, B.	-	0/-	-	0/0	.000	-/-	-	-	0	-	-	0	-
HARP, D.	-	3/-	-	1/1	1.000	-/-	-	-	1	-	-	7	-
JOHNSON, B.	-	0/-	-	0/0	.000	-/-	-	-	0	-	-	0	-
Totals	200	21/-	-	8/15	.533	-/-	-	-	9	-	-	50	.250

Disqualified: Kansas—Kline.

	1st Half	2nd Half	Final
Rice	14	30	44
Kansas	24	26	50

REGIONAL FINAL EASTERN

Indiana (39) Coach: Branch McCracken

	Min.	Total FG / FGA	Pct.	FT / FTA	Pct.	Reb. O / T	A	TO	PF	S	Blk	TP	PPM
SCHAEFER, H.	34	2/ 8	.250	4/ 4	1.000	-/ -	-	-	3	-	-	8	.235
MCCREARY, J.	34	0/ 6	.000	0/ 2	.000	-/ -	-	-	3	-	-	0	.000
ARMSTRONG, P.	20	2/11	.182	3/ 4	.750	-/ -	-	-	0	-	-	7	.350
MENKE, Bl.	33	4/11	.364	2/ 3	.667	-/ -	-	-	4	-	-	10	.303
HUFFMAN, M.	26	2/ 8	.250	2/ 2	1.000	-/ -	-	-	3	-	-	6	.231
ZIMMER, A.	12	1/ 3	.333	1/ 1	1.000	-/ -	-	-	0	-	-	3	.250
DRO, B.	40	2/ 9	.222	1/ 3	.333	-/ -	-	-	2	-	-	5	.125
DORSEY, R.	1	0/ 0	.000	0/ 0	.000	-/ -	-	-	0	-	-	0	.000
Totals	200	13/56	.232	13/19	.684	-/ -	-	-	15	-	-	39	.195

Duquesne (30) Coach: Chick Davies

	Min.	Total FG / FGA	Pct.	FT / FTA	Pct.	Reb. O / T	A	TO	PF	S	Blk	TP	PPM
KASPERIK, L.	23	1/ 2	.500	1/ 4	.250	-/ -	-	-	1	-	-	3	.130
MILKOVICH, E.	39	4/11	.364	2/ 4	.500	-/ -	-	-	4	-	-	10	.256
LACEY, B.	19	1/ 6	.167	0/ 2	.000	-/ -	-	-	3	-	-	2	.105
DEBNAR, R.	40	0/ 1	.000	2/ 2	1.000	-/ -	-	-	2	-	-	2	.050
WIDOWITZ, P.	40	3/13	.231	1/ 1	1.000	-/ -	-	-	3	-	-	7	.175
BECKER, M.	38	2/14	.143	2/ 4	.500	-/ -	-	-	4	-	-	6	.158
REIBER, G.	1	0/ 0	.000	0/ 0	.000	-/ -	-	-	0	-	-	0	.000
Totals	200	11/47	.234	8/17	.471	-/ -	-	-	17	-	-	30	.150

Disqualified: Indiana—Menke; Duquesne—Becker, Milkovich.

	1st Half	2nd Half	Final
Indiana	25	14	39
Duquesne	13	17	30

REGIONAL FINAL WESTERN

USC (42) Coach: Sam Barry

	Min.	Total FG / FGA	Pct.	FT / FTA	Pct.	Reb. O / T	A	TO	PF	S	Blk	TP	PPM
VAUGHAN, R.	-	2/ -	-	2/ 5	.400	-/ -	-	-	2	-	-	6	-
MORRISON, J.	-	0/ -	-	0/ 0	.000	-/ -	-	-	3	-	-	0	-
LAMBERT, K.	-	0/ -	-	1/ 2	.500	-/ -	-	-	2	-	-	1	-
SEARS, D.	-	8/ -	-	3/ 4	.750	-/ -	-	-	2	-	-	19	-
MCGARVIN, T.	-	3/ -	-	0/ 0	.000	-/ -	-	-	4	-	-	6	-
LUBER, J.	-	1/ -	-	0/ 1	.000	-/ -	-	-	2	-	-	2	-
LIPPERT, J.	-	4/ -	-	0/ 1	.000	-/ -	-	-	3	-	-	8	-
Totals	200	18/ -	-	6/13	.462	-/ -	-	-	18	-	-	42	.210

Kansas (43) Coach: Phog Allen

	Min.	Total FG / FGA	Pct.	FT / FTA	Pct.	Reb. O / T	A	TO	PF	S	Blk	TP	PPM
EBLING, D.	-	2/ -	-	4/ 8	.500	-/ -	-	-	1	-	-	8	-
ENGLEMAN, H.	-	3/ -	-	0/ 0	.000	-/ -	-	-	1	-	-	6	-
ALLEN, B.	-	3/ -	-	2/ 2	1.000	-/ -	-	-	2	-	-	8	-
KLINE, J.	-	0/ -	-	0/ 0	.000	-/ -	-	-	0	-	-	0	-
MILLER, R.	-	2/ -	-	2/ 4	.500	-/ -	-	-	2	-	-	6	-
VORAN, B.	-	0/ -	-	0/ 1	.000	-/ -	-	-	0	-	-	0	-
HARP, D.	-	6/ -	-	3/ 4	.750	-/ -	-	-	3	-	-	15	-
Totals	200	16/ -	-	11/19	.579	-/ -	-	-	9	-	-	43	.215

Disqualified: USC—McGarvin.

	1st Half	2nd Half	Final
USC	21	21	42
Kansas	20	23	43

CHAMPIONSHIP

Indiana (60) Coach: Branch McCracken

	Min.	Total FG / FGA	Pct.	FT / FTA	Pct.	Reb. O / T	A	TO	PF	S	Blk	TP	PPM
SCHAEFER, H.	-	4/ -	-	1/ 1	1.000	-/ -	-	-	1	-	-	9	-
MCCREARY, J.	-	6/ -	-	0/ 0	.000	-/ -	-	-	2	-	-	12	-
ARMSTRONG, P.	-	4/ -	-	2/ 3	.667	-/ -	-	-	3	-	-	10	-
GRIDLEY, J.	-	0/ -	-	0/ 0	.000	-/ -	-	-	0	-	-	0	-
MENKE, BO.	-	0/ -	-	0/ 0	.000	-/ -	-	-	0	-	-	0	-
MENKE, Bl.	-	2/ -	-	1/ 2	.500	-/ -	-	-	3	-	-	5	-
HUFFMAN, M.	-	5/ -	-	2/ 3	.667	-/ -	-	-	4	-	-	12	-
ZIMMER, A.	-	2/ -	-	1/ 1	1.000	-/ -	-	-	1	-	-	5	-
DRO, B.	-	3/ -	-	1/ 1	1.000	-/ -	-	-	4	-	-	7	-
DORSEY, R.	-	0/ -	-	0/ 0	.000	-/ -	-	-	0	-	-	0	-
FRANCIS, C.	-	0/ -	-	0/ 0	.000	-/ -	-	-	1	-	-	0	-
Totals	200	26/ -	-	8/11	.727	-/ -	-	-	19	-	-	60	.300

Kansas (42) Coach: Phog Allen

	Min.	Total FG / FGA	Pct.	FT / FTA	Pct.	Reb. O / T	A	TO	PF	S	Blk	TP	PPM
EBLING, D.	-	1/ -	-	2/ 5	.400	-/ -	-	-	0	-	-	4	-
HUNTER, T.	-	0/ -	-	1/ 1	1.000	-/ -	-	-	0	-	-	1	-
ENGLEMAN, H.	-	5/ -	-	2/ 3	.667	-/ -	-	-	3	-	-	12	-
HOGBEN, B.	-	2/ -	-	0/ 0	.000	-/ -	-	-	0	-	-	4	-
ALLEN, B.	-	5/ -	-	3/ 4	.750	-/ -	-	-	3	-	-	13	-
KLINE, J.	-	0/ -	-	0/ 0	.000	-/ -	-	-	0	-	-	0	-
MILLER, R.	-	0/ -	-	2/ 2	1.000	-/ -	-	-	4	-	-	2	-
VORAN, B.	-	0/ -	-	1/ 2	.500	-/ -	-	-	0	-	-	1	-
HARP, D.	-	2/ -	-	1/ 3	.333	-/ -	-	-	1	-	-	5	-
SANDS, J.	-	0/ -	-	0/ 0	.000	-/ -	-	-	0	-	-	0	-
JOHNSON, B.	-	0/ -	-	0/ 0	.000	-/ -	-	-	0	-	-	0	-
Totals	200	15/ -	-	12/20	.600	-/ -	-	-	11	-	-	42	.210

Disqualified: Indiana—Dro, Huffman; Kansas—Miller. Technical fouls: Indiana—McCreary.

	1st Half	2nd Half	Final
Indiana	32	28	60
Kansas	19	23	42

1941

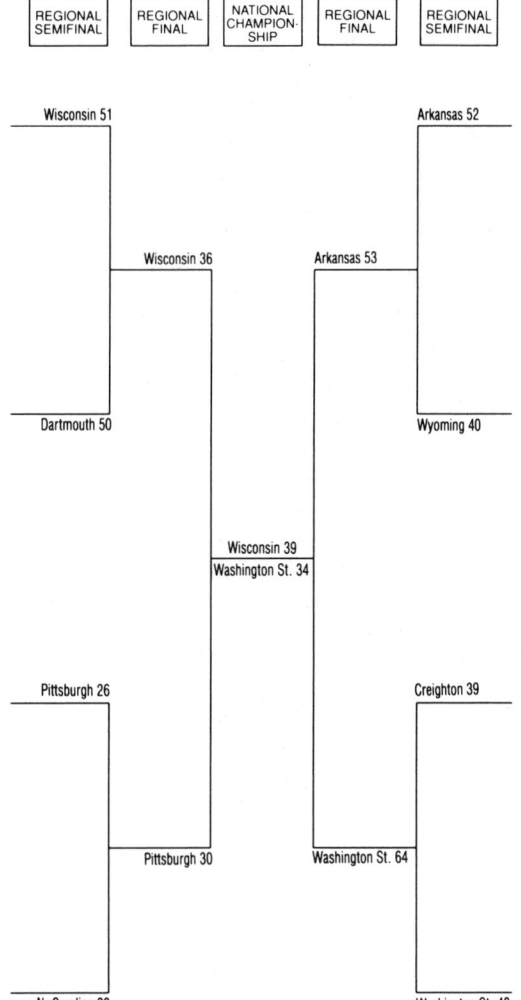

REGIONAL SEMIFINAL	REGIONAL FINAL	NATIONAL CHAMPION-SHIP	REGIONAL FINAL	REGIONAL SEMIFINAL

EASTERN

WESTERN

Wisconsin 51

Arkansas 52

Wisconsin 36

Arkansas 53

Dartmouth 50

Wyoming 40

Wisconsin 39
Washington St. 34

Pittsburgh 26

Creighton 39

Pittsburgh 30

Washington St. 64

N. Carolina 20

Washington St. 48

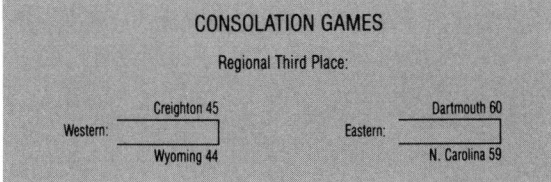

CONSOLATION GAMES

Regional Third Place:

Western:
Creighton 45
Wyoming 44

Eastern:
Dartmouth 60
N. Carolina 59

The Wisconsin Badgers finished ninth in the Big Ten in 1940, and at the beginning of the 1940–41 season, when they opened with a 44-27 loss to Minnesota, it looked like nothing much had changed. But as the season progressed, coach Harold E. (Bud) Foster's team became a well-oiled machine with every gear running smoothly.

By the time they went into the NCAA tournament, Wisconsin's Big Ten champions had won twelve straight games, including victories over two of the three teams that handed them early-season losses. Led by sophomore forward Johnny Kotz and center Gene Englund, their quick-cutting offense put plenty of points on the board. And their confidence had to be helped by the location of the Eastern regional games; they were playing at home in Madison.

Nonetheless, they barely survived their opening game against the Eastern League's Dartmouth Indians. In front of 11,500 cheering spectators (most of them Wisconsin partisans), the two teams fought to the wire in a brilliantly played, high-scoring contest. The Indians, led by forwards Gus Broberg and George Munroe, took a 2-point halftime lead, with most of their points coming on outside bombs. It was more of the same for most of the second half, but Wisconsin wouldn't give up and Dartmouth couldn't pull away. The Badgers pulled even at 44 and finally took the lead when Englund hit from underneath. After a Kotz free throw, Munroe brought Dartmouth back to within a point. But a hook by Englund and two free throws by Kotz sealed the Eastern champs' fate.

In the second round, Wisconsin faced Pittsburgh, the only team to hand them a regular season defeat with whom they had not yet evened the score. In the first half, to the dismay of the home crowd, it looked like Pitt would win again. The Panthers were up 18-14 at intermission, but again, largely as a result of the torrid shooting of Englund and Kotz, the Badgers stormed back. They won going away.

Almost as important as the victory was the mission of Wisconsin's assistant coach Fritz Wagner in Kansas City. Coach Foster had sent him ahead to scout the Western final between Washington State and Arkansas. Both the Cougars and the Razorbacks had won convincingly in the first round. Arkansas, led by the spectacular Johnny Adams, whose shooting style was described in an Associated Press dispatch as "an unusual jump, body-twist shot, flung in from the free-throw circle," had overwhelmed the Wyoming Cowboys and their one-handed shooting sophomore sensation Kenny Sailors by a dozen points. Meanwhile Washington State had demolished Creighton behind their bruising, 6-7, 230-pound center Paul Lindeman, who dominated under the boards and scored 26 points.

In the western final the Wisconsin scout observed that the one-man attack of Arkansas' jump-shooting Adams was no match for Lindeman's inside game and the Pacific Coast champions' balanced scoring attack. Shooting from the perimeter and utilizing the one-handed push shot first made famous by Stanford's great Hank Luisetti less than a decade earlier, the AP reported that Washington State "gave one of the greatest displays of shooting ever seen." Nonetheless, Wagner reported back to his boss that the Badgers had to stop Lindeman to win.

The strategy Foster devised was to double-team the big Cougar center and deny him the ball. It worked to perfection. From the opening tip, Englund played behind the Washington State pivot man, while a forward, either Kotz or Gene Charley Epperson, fronted him. With Lindeman's inside threat neutralized, the Washington State offense stalled. Midway through the first half, Wisconsin forged into the lead when they held the coast team scoreless for nine minutes. After intermission Washington State countered with a zone that helped them keep the game close until the final minutes. But it was an uphill battle all the way, and they never managed to get back into the lead. In the final minutes, Wisconsin put the game away with five straight points.

In the end Lindeman scored only 3 points, all on free throws, and he was ineffective off the boards. Washington State guard Kirk Gebert, who finished with 21, was the Cougars' only threat; the rest of the team connected on less than 10 percent of their shots and scored only 13 points. Wisconsin, led by Kotz (who was selected as the tournament's Most Outstanding Player) and Englund, won the strategic battle—and the national championship.

The tournament was also a rousing financial success. The 45,000 paying customers who saw the games in Madison and Kansas City paid $32,000 to fatten the NCAAs coffers. By the time the Wisconsin players took home the huge championship trophy, wrist watches, and gold and silver miniature basketballs that were awarded to them, it was more clear than ever that the tournament was here to stay.

REGIONAL SEMIFINAL EASTERN

Wisconsin (51) Coach: Bud Foster

	Min.	Total FG/FGA	Pct.	FT/FTA	Pct.	Reb. O/T	A	TO	PF	S	Blk	TP	PPM
KOTZ, J.	-	5/ -	-	5/ 9	.556	-/ -	-	-	0	-	-	15	-
EPPERSON, C.	-	4/ -	-	0/ 0	.000	-/ -	-	-	0	-	-	8	-
ENGLUND, G.	-	6/ -	-	6/ 7	.857	-/ -	-	-	3	-	-	18	-
TIMMERMAN, D.	-	0/ -	-	0/ 0	.000	-/ -	-	-	1	-	-	0	-
STRAIN, T.	-	0/ -	-	1/ 3	.333	-/ -	-	-	4	-	-	1	-
ALWIN, R.	-	0/ -	-	0/ 0	.000	-/ -	-	-	1	-	-	0	-
REHM, F.	-	2/ -	-	5/ 5	1.000	-/ -	-	-	2	-	-	9	-
Totals	200	17/ -	-	17/24	.708	-/ -	-	-	11	-	-	51	.255

Dartmouth (50) Coach: Ozzie Cowles

	Min.	Total FG/FGA	Pct.	FT/FTA	Pct.	Reb. O/T	A	TO	PF	S	Blk	TP	PPM
BROBERG, G.	-	9/ -	-	2/ 2	1.000	-/ -	-	-	1	-	-	20	-
MUNROE, G.	-	7/ -	-	1/ 2	.500	-/ -	-	-	2	-	-	15	-
OLSEN, J.	-	1/ -	-	0/ 1	.000	-/ -	-	-	4	-	-	2	-
SKAUG, S.	-	4/ -	-	2/ 2	1.000	-/ -	-	-	3	-	-	10	-
PEARSON, C.	-	0/ -	-	1/ 1	1.000	-/ -	-	-	4	-	-	1	-
ELSE	-	0/ -	-	0/ 0	.000	-/ -	-	-	2	-	-	0	-
SHAW, C.	-	0/ -	-	0/ 1	.000	-/ -	-	-	1	-	-	0	-
HORNER	-	0/ -	-	0/ 0	.000	-/ -	-	-	0	-	-	0	-
PARMER, W.	-	1/ -	-	0/ 0	.000	-/ -	-	-	3	-	-	2	-
Totals	200	22/ -	-	6/ 9	.667	-/ -	-	-	20	-	-	50	.250

Disqualified: Wisconsin—Strain; Dartmouth—Olsen, Pearson.

	1st Half	2nd Half	Final
Wisconsin	22	29	51
Dartmouth	24	26	50

Pittsburgh (26) Coach: Harold Carlson

	Min.	Total FG/FGA	Pct.	FT/FTA	Pct.	Reb. O/T	A	TO	PF	S	Blk	TP	PPM
STRALOSKI, E.	-	3/ -	-	0/ 2	.000	-/ -	-	-	1	-	-	6	-
PAFFRATH, L.	-	0/ -	-	0/ 0	.000	-/ -	-	-	3	-	-	0	-
KOCHERAN, G.	-	2/ -	-	2/ 2	1.000	-/ -	-	-	1	-	-	6	-
PORT, M.	-	0/ -	-	3/ 6	.500	-/ -	-	-	2	-	-	3	-
KLEIN, J.	-	0/ -	-	0/ 0	.000	-/ -	-	-	1	-	-	0	-
MALARKEY, T.	-	3/ -	-	1/ 1	1.000	-/ -	-	-	0	-	-	7	-
MILANOVICH, S.	-	1/ -	-	2/ 2	1.000	-/ -	-	-	1	-	-	4	-
Totals	200	9/ -	-	8/13	.615	-/ -	-	-	9	-	-	26	.130

North Carolina (20) Coach: Bill Lange

	Min.	Total FG/FGA	Pct.	FT/FTA	Pct.	Reb. O/T	A	TO	PF	S	Blk	TP	PPM
ROSE, B.	-	1/ -	-	0/ 1	.000	-/ -	-	-	1	-	-	2	-
PAINE, G.	-	0/ -	-	0/ 1	.000	-/ -	-	-	2	-	-	0	-
PESSAR, H.	-	1/ -	-	0/ 1	.000	-/ -	-	-	0	-	-	2	-
SEVERIN, P.	-	1/ -	-	1/ 1	1.000	-/ -	-	-	0	-	-	3	-
GLAMACK,	-	4/ -	-	1/ 2	.500	-/ -	-	-	4	-	-	9	-
HOWARD, J.	-	1/ -	-	0/ 0	.000	-/ -	-	-	2	-	-	2	-
GERSTEN, B.	-	0/ -	-	0/ 1	.000	-/ -	-	-	0	-	-	0	-
SUGGS, R.	-	1/ -	-	0/ 1	.000	-/ -	-	-	0	-	-	2	-
Totals	200	9/ -	-	2/ 8	.250	-/ -	-	-	9	-	-	20	.100

Disqualified: N. Carolina—Glamack.

	1st Half	2nd Half	Final
Pittsburgh	8	18	26
N. Carolina	12	8	20

REGIONAL SEMIFINAL WESTERN

Arkansas (52) Coach: Glen Rose

	Min.	Total FG/FGA	Pct.	FT/FTA	Pct.	Reb. O/T	A	TO	PF	S	Blk	TP	PPM
ADAMS, J.	-	11/ -	-	4/ 4	1.000	-/ -	-	-	0	-	-	26	-
CARPENTER, G.	-	3/ -	-	2/ 3	.667	-/ -	-	-	2	-	-	8	-
FREIBERGER, J.	-	2/ -	-	3/ 4	.750	-/ -	-	-	2	-	-	7	-
PITTS, R.	-	4/ -	-	0/ 0	.000	-/ -	-	-	4	-	-	8	-
WYNNE, C.	-	0/ -	-	0/ 0	.000	-/ -	-	-	2	-	-	0	-
HICKEY, H.	-	1/ -	-	1/ 2	.500	-/ -	-	-	4	-	-	3	-
ADAMS, O.	-	0/ -	-	0/ 0	.000	-/ -	-	-	0	-	-	0	-
Totals	200	21/ -	-	10/13	.769	-/ -	-	-	14	-	-	52	.260

Wyoming (40) Coach: Everet Shelton

	Min.	Total FG/FGA	Pct.	FT/FTA	Pct.	Reb. O/T	A	TO	PF	S	Blk	TP	PPM
KRPAN, N.	-	0/ -	-	1/ 2	.500	-/ -	-	-	2	-	-	1	-
BENTSON	-	1/ -	-	0/ 0	.000	-/ -	-	-	2	-	-	2	-
GOWDY, C.	-	0/ -	-	0/ 2	.000	-/ -	-	-	4	-	-	0	-
WEIR, J.	-	2/ -	-	0/ 1	.000	-/ -	-	-	2	-	-	4	-
MUIR, L.	-	0/ -	-	0/ 0	.000	-/ -	-	-	0	-	-	0	-
STRANNIGAN, B.	-	3/ -	-	2/ 2	1.000	-/ -	-	-	0	-	-	8	-
SAILORS, K.	-	6/ -	-	5/ 5	1.000	-/ -	-	-	2	-	-	17	-
BUTCHER, C.	-	0/ -	-	0/ 0	.000	-/ -	-	-	0	-	-	0	-
ROTHMAN, W.	-	3/ -	-	2/ 3	.667	-/ -	-	-	2	-	-	8	-
Totals	200	15/ -	-	10/15	.667	-/ -	-	-	14	-	-	40	.200

Disqualified: Arkansas—Pitts, Hickey; Wyoming—Gowdy.

	1st Half	2nd Half	Final
Arkansas	29	23	52
Wyoming	18	22	40

Creighton (39) Coach: Eddie Hickey

	Min.	Total FG/FGA	Pct.	FT/FTA	Pct.	Reb. O/T	A	TO	PF	S	Blk	TP	PPM
FLEMING	-	3/ -	-	1/ 2	.500	-/ -	-	-	1	-	-	7	-
JAQUAY	-	3/ -	-	1/ 2	.500	-/ -	-	-	0	-	-	7	-
BEISSER	-	4/ -	-	0/ 0	.000	-/ -	-	-	3	-	-	8	-
LANGER	-	0/ -	-	0/ 1	.000	-/ -	-	-	2	-	-	0	-
HALDEMAN	-	0/ -	-	0/ 1	.000	-/ -	-	-	3	-	-	0	-
THYNNE	-	1/ -	-	1/ 1	1.000	-/ -	-	-	1	-	-	3	-
NOLAN	-	5/ -	-	4/ 5	.800	-/ -	-	-	2	-	-	14	-
Totals	200	16/ -	-	7/12	.583	-/ -	-	-	12	-	-	39	.195

Washington State (48) Coach: Jack Friel

	Min.	Total FG/FGA	Pct.	FT/FTA	Pct.	Reb. O/T	A	TO	PF	S	Blk	TP	PPM
GENTRY, D.	-	1/ -	-	1/ 2	.500	-/ -	-	-	1	-	-	3	-
BUTTS, V.	-	4/ -	-	1/ 2	.500	-/ -	-	-	1	-	-	9	-
HOOPER, J.	-	0/ -	-	0/ 0	.000	-/ -	-	-	0	-	-	0	-
LINDEMAN, P.	-	12/ -	-	2/ 6	.333	-/ -	-	-	3	-	-	26	-
ZIMMERMAN, J.	-	1/ -	-	0/ 0	.000	-/ -	-	-	0	-	-	2	-
GEBERT, K.	-	2/ -	-	0/ 1	.000	-/ -	-	-	3	-	-	4	-
GILBERG, M.	-	0/ -	-	0/ 0	.000	-/ -	-	-	0	-	-	0	-
HUNT, O.	-	0/ -	-	0/ 0	.000	-/ -	-	-	0	-	-	0	-
SUNDQUIST, R.	-	2/ -	-	0/ 3	.000	-/ -	-	-	1	-	-	4	-
MAHAN, P.	-	0/ -	-	0/ 0	.000	-/ -	-	-	1	-	-	0	-
Totals	200	22/ -	-	4/14	.286	-/ -	-	-	10	-	-	48	.240

Disqualified: None.

	1st Half	2nd Half	Final
Creighton	14	25	39
Washington St.	25	23	48

REGIONAL FINAL EASTERN

Wisconsin (36)   Coach: Bud Foster

	Min.	Total FG/FGA	Pct.	FT/FTA	Pct.	Reb. O/T	A	TO	PF	S	Blk	TP	PPM
KOTZ, J.	-	3/ -	-	4/ 4	1.000	-/ -	-	-	1	-	-	10	-
EPPERSON, C.	-	2/ -	-	3/ 4	.750	-/ -	-	-	0	-	-	7	-
ENGLUND, G.	-	2/ -	-	7/ 8	.875	-/ -	-	-	4	-	-	11	-
TIMMERMAN, D.	-	0/ -	-	0/ 1	.000	-/ -	-	-	0	-	-	0	-
STRAIN, T.	-	2/ -	-	0/ 2	.000	-/ -	-	-	3	-	-	4	-
REHM, F.	-	1/ -	-	2/ 2	1.000	-/ -	-	-	0	-	-	4	-
Totals	200	10/ -	-	16/21	.762	-/ -	-	-	8	-	-	36	.180

Pittsburgh (30)   Coach: Harold Carlson

	Min.	Total FG/FGA	Pct.	FT/FTA	Pct.	Reb. O/T	A	TO	PF	S	Blk	TP	PPM
STRALOSKI, E.	-	6/ -	-	0/ 0	.000	-/ -	-	-	4	-	-	12	-
PAFFRATH, L.	-	1/ -	-	1/ 1	1.000	-/ -	-	-	0	-	-	3	-
KOCHERAN, G.	-	1/ -	-	2/ 2	1.000	-/ -	-	-	0	-	-	4	-
PORT, M.	-	1/ -	-	2/ 3	.667	-/ -	-	-	4	-	-	4	-
KLEIN, J.	-	0/ -	-	0/ 0	.000	-/ -	-	-	1	-	-	0	-
MALARKEY, T.	-	1/ -	-	1/ 1	1.000	-/ -	-	-	3	-	-	3	-
MILANOVICH, S.	-	2/ -	-	0/ 0	.000	-/ -	-	-	3	-	-	4	-
ZIOLKAUISKI, L.	-	0/ -	-	0/ 0	.000	-/ -	-	-	2	-	-	0	-
Totals	200	12/ -	-	6/ 7	.857	-/ -	-	-	17	-	-	30	.150

Disqualified: Wisconsin—Englund; Pittsburgh—Straloski, Port.

	1st Half	2nd Half	Final
Wisconsin	14	22	36
Pittsburgh	18	12	30

REGIONAL FINAL WESTERN

Arkansas (53)   Coach: Glen Rose

	Min.	Total FG/FGA	Pct.	FT/FTA	Pct.	Reb. O/T	A	TO	PF	S	Blk	TP	PPM
ADAMS, J.	-	10/ -	-	2/ 5	.400	-/ -	-	-	1	-	-	22	-
CARPENTER, G.	-	2/ -	-	1/ 3	.333	-/ -	-	-	2	-	-	5	-
FREIBERGER, J.	-	1/ -	-	3/ 4	.750	-/ -	-	-	3	-	-	5	-
PITTS, R.	-	5/ -	-	2/ 4	.500	-/ -	-	-	2	-	-	12	-
WYNNE, C.	-	0/ -	-	0/ 0	.000	-/ -	-	-	2	-	-	0	-
HICKEY, H.	-	1/ -	-	1/ 2	.500	-/ -	-	-	2	-	-	3	-
ADAMS, O.	-	2/ -	-	2/ 3	.667	-/ -	-	-	0	-	-	6	-
ROBBINS, N.	-	0/ -	-	0/ 1	.000	-/ -	-	-	3	-	-	0	-
Totals	200	21/ -	-	11/22	.500	-/ -	-	-	15	-	-	53	.265

Washington State (64)   Coach: Jack Friel

	Min.	Total FG/FGA	Pct.	FT/FTA	Pct.	Reb. O/T	A	TO	PF	S	Blk	TP	PPM
GENTRY, D.	-	4/ -	-	1/ 2	.500	-/ -	-	-	2	-	-	9	-
BUTTS, V.	-	5/ -	-	1/ 1	1.000	-/ -	-	-	1	-	-	11	-
HOOPER, J.	-	2/ -	-	0/ 0	.000	-/ -	-	-	4	-	-	4	-
LINDEMAN, P.	-	4/ -	-	6/ 9	.667	-/ -	-	-	2	-	-	14	-
ZIMMERMAN, J.	-	0/ -	-	0/ 0	.000	-/ -	-	-	2	-	-	0	-
GEBERT, K.	-	5/ -	-	2/ 2	1.000	-/ -	-	-	1	-	-	12	-
GILBERG, M.	-	3/ -	-	0/ 3	.000	-/ -	-	-	4	-	-	6	-
HUNT, O.	-	1/ -	-	0/ 0	.000	-/ -	-	-	3	-	-	2	-
SUNDQUIST, R.	-	2/ -	-	2/ 2	1.000	-/ -	-	-	2	-	-	6	-
ADKKINS, F.	-	0/ -	-	0/ 0	.000	-/ -	-	-	0	-	-	0	-
Totals	200	26/ -	-	12/19	.632	-/ -	-	-	21	-	-	64	.320

Disqualified: Washington St.—Gilberg, Hooper.

	1st Half	2nd Half	Final
Arkansas	25	28	53
Washington St.	37	27	64

CHAMPIONSHIP

Washington State (34)   Coach: Jack Friel

	Min.	Total FG/FGA	Pct.	FT/FTA	Pct.	Reb. O/T	A	TO	PF	S	Blk	TP	PPM
GENTRY, D.	-	0/ -	-	1/ 2	.500	-/ -	-	-	1	-	-	1	-
BUTTS, V.	-	1/ -	-	1/ 1	1.000	-/ -	-	-	1	-	-	3	-
HOOPER, J.	-	0/ -	-	0/ 0	.000	-/ -	-	-	0	-	-	0	-
LINDEMAN, P.	-	0/ -	-	3/ 4	.750	-/ -	-	-	1	-	-	3	-
ZIMMERMAN, J.	-	0/ -	-	0/ 0	.000	-/ -	-	-	0	-	-	0	-
GEBERT, K.	-	10/24	.417	1/ 2	.500	-/ -	-	-	1	-	-	21	-
HUNT, O.	-	0/ -	-	0/ 0	.000	-/ -	-	-	0	-	-	0	-
SUNDQUIST, R.	-	2/ -	-	0/ 1	.000	-/ -	-	-	3	-	-	4	-
GILBERG, M.	-	1/ -	-	0/ 2	.000	-/ -	-	-	1	-	-	2	-
Totals	200	14/65	.215	6/12	.500	-/ -	-	-	8	-	-	34	.170

Wisconsin (39)   Coach: Bud Foster

	Min.	Total FG/FGA	Pct.	FT/FTA	Pct.	Reb. O/T	A	TO	PF	S	Blk	TP	PPM
KOTZ, J.	-	5/ -	-	2/ 3	.667	-/ -	-	-	2	-	-	12	-
EPPERSON, C.	-	2/ -	-	0/ 0	.000	-/ -	-	-	3	-	-	4	-
ENGLUND, G.	-	5/ -	-	3/ 4	.750	-/ -	-	-	2	-	-	13	-
TIMMERMAN, D.	-	1/ -	-	0/ 0	.000	-/ -	-	-	1	-	-	2	-
STRAIN, T.	-	0/ -	-	2/ 2	1.000	-/ -	-	-	1	-	-	2	-
ALWIN, R.	-	1/ -	-	0/ 0	.000	-/ -	-	-	0	-	-	2	-
REHM, F.	-	2/ -	-	0/ 1	.000	-/ -	-	-	2	-	-	4	-
SCHRAGE, W.	-	0/ -	-	0/ 0	.000	-/ -	-	-	1	-	-	0	-
Totals	200	16/63	.254	7/10	.700	-/ -	-	-	12	-	-	39	.195

Disqualified: None.

	1st Half	2nd Half	Final
Washington St.	17	17	34
Wisconsin	21	18	39

1942

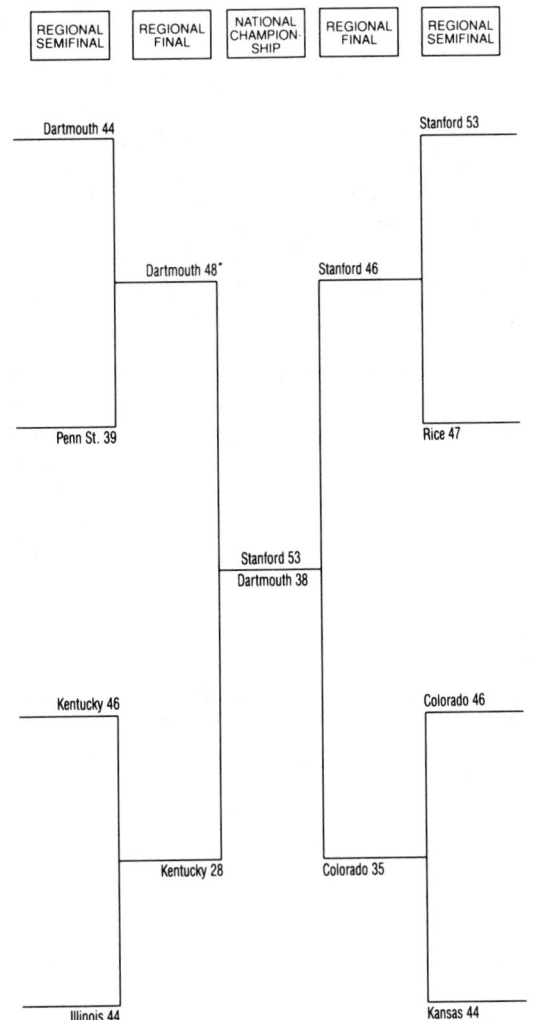

| REGIONAL SEMIFINAL | REGIONAL FINAL | NATIONAL CHAMPIONSHIP | REGIONAL FINAL | REGIONAL SEMIFINAL |

EASTERN

Dartmouth 44

Dartmouth 48*

Penn St. 39

Stanford 53
Dartmouth 38

Kentucky 46

Kentucky 28

Illinois 44

WESTERN

Stanford 53

Stanford 46

Rice 47

Colorado 46

Colorado 35

Kansas 44

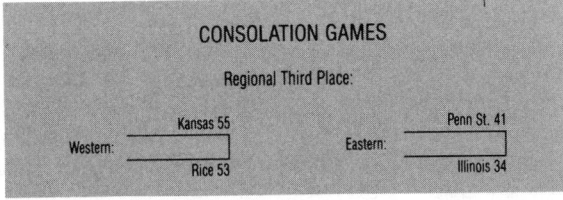

CONSOLATION GAMES

Regional Third Place:

Western:
Kansas 55
Rice 53

Eastern:
Penn St. 41
Illinois 34

*Official box of the game: 48-28. Associated Press dispatch shows score: 47-28. Official box shows Monroe (Dartmouth) scoring 21 points on 9 FG and 3/4 FT; AP has Monroe with 20 points on 2/4 FT.

When Ossie Cowles, coach of the Ivy League champion Dartmouth basketball team, announced to his players that the college's faculty senate had agreed to allow them to participate in the 1942 NCAA basketball tourney (despite serious misgivings about lost class time and fears that the trip would conflict with the college's accelerated wartime program), there were few who would have predicted that Cowles would eventually be facing his own mentor, Stanford's illustrious coach Everett Dean, in the tournament's championship game.

The Dartmouth faculty, if they read the New York papers, probably expected the Big Green team to return home rather quickly. Dartmouth was considered somewhat of a joke—not really on a par with the other squads selected for tournament play. The boys would be away from school for a few days at the most, even considering the long train ride to New Orleans. To make the event of a Dartmouth–Stanford match even more improbable, the Western half of the draw was virtually conceded to the rampaging Buffaloes of Colorado. Of course no one told Everett Dean or his Stanford team to stay home, so they packed their bags and went to Kansas City to play ball.

In the first half of their opener against Rice, Stanford played as though they were the tournament favorites, pulling out a 12-point lead at intermission. But Rice, behind the gutsy play of Chet Palmer, came back to tie. It wasn't until Stanford sophomore Jim Pollard (who was being hailed on the Coast as a second Hank Luisetti) took the game into his own hands that the Indians pulled away.

Colorado, meanwhile, barely survived a grudge match with Kansas. Frosty Cox, the Colorado coach, learned his basketball at Kansas, as a protege of Dr. F. C. "Phog" Allen. Allen had recently begun firing off salvos at his former student for persuading several Kansas boys—including four starters—to forsake the great plains of their home state for the Rockies. The Buffaloes surged to a 7-point halftime lead, with native Kansan Pete McCloud leading the way despite a stomach cramp that had him taking soda pills throughout the game. But Kansas came back to tie as the cavernous Kansas City municipal auditorium shook to the rafters with the shouts of Jayhawk partisans. The two teams pounded their way to the finish, with invincible Colorado finally—barely—prevailing by a score of 46-44.

The evening's events were not only a competitive success, but financially rewarding as well. Eight thousand two hundred spectators paid a total of $7,568.40 to see the doubleheader.

The next night, the Buffaloes took the floor against taller Stanford, and Colorado found themselves on the short end of a 19-7 score before they managed to warm up. "Seldom has such a velvet-actioned team such as Stanford been seen on the inlaid maples of this big auditorium," said *The Denver Post*. Stanford Coach Dean's smoothly switching defensive alignments, which alternated between a man-to-man and a zone, caused the Buffaloes no end of trouble. Stanford, led once again by the brilliant Pollard, breezed to victory.

Meanwhile, the Dartmouth players arrived in New Orleans on Friday morning, March 20th, following the long train ride from New England. They went directly to their French Quarter hotel and that evening faced the Penn State Nittany Lions, a team that had lost only two games all year. The score was tied early in the second half when the Ivy Leaguers' center, Jim Olsen, began to shoot, pass, and rebound like a man possessed. With two minutes remaining he fouled out, but by then his team had an insurmountable lead. The crowd of 3,000 gave Olsen a standing ovation. In the other Eastern first-round game, Phog Allen protégé Adolph Rupp coached his Kentucky squad to an upset victory over the Big Ten champions, Illinois.

In the Eastern final, Dartmouth again confounded expectations, as Kentucky, usually an excellent shooting team, couldn't hit the side of a barn. After taking an early 10-5 lead, the Wildcats connected on only six more field goals all night. Dartmouth won easily, 47-28.

Thus it was that the following weekend the Big Green Indians of Dartmouth traveled to Kansas City to take on Stanford's tall Indians. Stanford Coach Everett Dean knew a little about Dartmouth; he had sent an ace scout to watch the Eastern playoffs, and he fondly recalled that Dartmouth coach "Cowles was captain for me in 1922 at Carleton College in Northfield, Minnesota. He was one of the best guards I ever coached." Dean said there was no team in the country he would rather face.

Both teams were at less than full strength for the championship round: Dartmouth's Bob Myers was hampered by an ankle injury; after scoring eight points in the first half he was forced to leave the game. Stanford's sensational Jim Pollard missed the whole game; a sinus infection had forced him to stay in bed with a high fever the day before the title contest, and although he felt better by game time, Coach Dean wanted to take no chances with his 19-year-old sophomore and held him out of action.

Early in the second half, Dartmouth took a brief one point lead. But Stanford's Howie Dallmar, who would later be named the tourney MVP, began controlling the boards. In the final ten minutes, Stanford's fast break worked to perfection. They stung the nets for 23 points and won the cross-country confrontation easily.

As war raged halfway across the globe, the two teams returned to their respective campuses to resume their studies. Soon most of the players and their classmates would abandon the hallowed halls of academia to put on uniforms and pick up guns in the desperate struggle to save democracy.

REGIONAL SEMIFINAL EASTERN

Dartmouth (44)   Coach: Ozzie Cowles

	Min.	Total FG / FGA	Pct.	FT / FTA	Pct.	Reb. O / T	A	TO	PF	S	Blk	TP	PPM
MYERS, R.	-	3/ -	-	1/ 1	1.000	-/ -	-	-	3	-	-	7	-
MUNROE, G.	-	4/ -	-	0/ 0	.000	-/ -	-	-	1	-	-	8	-
OLSEN, J.	-	8/ -	-	3/ 4	.750	-/ -	-	-	4	-	-	19	-
SHAW, C.	-	0/ -	-	0/ 0	.000	-/ -	-	-	0	-	-	0	-
SKAUG, S.	-	2/ -	-	3/ 4	.750	-/ -	-	-	2	-	-	7	-
PEARSON, C.	-	1/ -	-	1/ 2	.500	-/ -	-	-	4	-	-	3	-
PARMER, W.	-	0/ -	-	0/ 1	.000	-/ -	-	-	0	-	-	0	-
Totals	200	18/ -	-	8/12	.667	-/ -	-	-	14	-	-	44	.220

Penn State (39)   Coach: John Lawther

	Min.	Total FG / FGA	Pct.	FT / FTA	Pct.	Reb. O / T	A	TO	PF	S	Blk	TP	PPM
GROSS	-	2/ -	-	3/ 3	1.000	-/ -	-	-	1	-	-	7	-
GENT	-	1/ -	-	0/ 0	.000	-/ -	-	-	0	-	-	2	-
BALTIMORE	-	3/ -	-	1/ 1	1.000	-/ -	-	-	0	-	-	7	-
RAMIN	-	0/ -	-	2/ 3	.667	-/ -	-	-	1	-	-	2	-
EGLI, J.	-	5/ -	-	2/ 4	.500	-/ -	-	-	4	-	-	12	-
GRIMES	-	0/ -	-	0/ 1	.000	-/ -	-	-	3	-	-	0	-
HORNSTEIN	-	3/ -	-	3/ 4	.750	-/ -	-	-	2	-	-	9	-
Totals	200	14/ -	-	11/16	.688	-/ -	-	-	11	-	-	39	.195

Disqualified: Dartmouth—Olsen, Pearson; Penn State—Egli.

	1st Half	2nd Half	Final
Dartmouth	22	22	44
Penn State	16	23	39

Kentucky (46)   Coach: Adolph Rupp

	Min.	Total FG / FGA	Pct.	FT / FTA	Pct.	Reb. O / T	A	TO	PF	S	Blk	TP	PPM
STAKER, C.	-	4/ -	-	1/ 2	.500	-/ -	-	-	3	-	-	9	-
ENGLAND, K.	-	1/ -	-	2/ 2	1.000	-/ -	-	-	3	-	-	4	-
AKERS, M.	-	4/ -	-	0/ 0	.000	-/ -	-	-	0	-	-	8	-
BREWER, M.	-	0/ -	-	1/ 1	1.000	-/ -	-	-	3	-	-	1	-
KING, J.	-	2/ -	-	2/ 4	.500	-/ -	-	-	1	-	-	6	-
ALLEN, E.	-	2/ -	-	0/ 0	.000	-/ -	-	-	2	-	-	4	-
TICCO, M.	-	6/ -	-	1/ 2	.500	-/ -	-	-	0	-	-	13	-
WHITE, W.	-	0/ -	-	1/ 1	1.000	-/ -	-	-	2	-	-	1	-
Totals	200	19/ -	-	8/12	.667	-/ -	-	-	14	-	-	46	.230

Illinois (44)   Coach: Doug Mills

	Min.	Total FG / FGA	Pct.	FT / FTA	Pct.	Reb. O / T	A	TO	PF	S	Blk	TP	PPM
MENKE	-	7/ -	-	1/ 1	1.000	-/ -	-	-	2	-	-	15	-
FOWLER	-	0/ -	-	0/ 0	.000	-/ -	-	-	1	-	-	0	-
SMILEY	-	5/ -	-	3/ 3	1.000	-/ -	-	-	2	-	-	13	-
HOCKING	-	0/ -	-	0/ 0	.000	-/ -	-	-	0	-	-	0	-
MATHISEN	-	0/ -	-	1/ 1	1.000	-/ -	-	-	0	-	-	1	-
WUKOVITZ	-	2/ -	-	0/ 4	.000	-/ -	-	-	3	-	-	4	-
PHILLIP	-	2/ -	-	2/ 4	.500	-/ -	-	-	0	-	-	6	-
VANCE	-	0/ -	-	0/ 0	.000	-/ -	-	-	3	-	-	0	-
SACHS	-	2/ -	-	1/ 2	.500	-/ -	-	-	2	-	-	5	-
Totals	200	18/ -	-	8/15	.533	-/ -	-	-	13	-	-	44	.220

Disqualified: None.

	1st Half	2nd Half	Final
Kentucky	20	26	46
Illinois	22	22	44

REGIONAL SEMIFINAL WESTERN

Stanford (53)   Coach: Everett Dean

	Min.	Total FG / FGA	Pct.	FT / FTA	Pct.	Reb. O / T	A	TO	PF	S	Blk	TP	PPM
DANA, J.	-	0/ -	-	0/ 1	.000	-/ -	-	-	0	-	-	0	-
LINARI, F.	-	0/ -	-	0/ 0	.000	-/ -	-	-	0	-	-	0	-
POLLARD, J.	-	12/ -	-	2/ 4	.500	-/ -	-	-	1	-	-	26	-
VOSS, E.	-	4/ -	-	7/ 8	.875	-/ -	-	-	3	-	-	15	-
COWDEN, B.	-	2/ -	-	2/ 4	.500	-/ -	-	-	3	-	-	6	-
DALLMAR, H.	-	3/ -	-	0/ 0	.000	-/ -	-	-	0	-	-	6	-
MCCAFFREY, L.	-	0/ -	-	0/ 0	.000	-/ -	-	-	0	-	-	0	-
Totals	200	21/ -	-	11/17	.647	-/ -	-	-	7	-	-	53	.265

Rice (47)   Coach: Buster Brannon

	Min.	Total FG / FGA	Pct.	FT / FTA	Pct.	Reb. O / T	A	TO	PF	S	Blk	TP	PPM
CLOSS	-	3/ -	-	2/ 3	.667	-/ -	-	-	4	-	-	8	-
ZANDER	-	0/ -	-	0/ 0	.000	-/ -	-	-	1	-	-	0	-
GOMEZ	-	2/ -	-	0/ 0	.000	-/ -	-	-	3	-	-	4	-
KINNEY	-	3/ -	-	2/ 3	.667	-/ -	-	-	4	-	-	8	-
MCDONALD	-	0/ -	-	1/ 2	.500	-/ -	-	-	0	-	-	1	-
PALMER, C.	-	8/ -	-	2/ 2	1.000	-/ -	-	-	3	-	-	18	-
LAMBERT	-	4/ -	-	0/ 0	.000	-/ -	-	-	0	-	-	8	-
Totals	200	20/ -	-	7/10	.700	-/ -	-	-	15	-	-	47	.235

Disqualified: Rice—Closs, Kinney.

	1st Half	2nd Half	Final
Stanford	33	20	53
Rice	21	26	47

Colorado (46)   Coach: Frosty Cox

	Min.	Total FG / FGA	Pct.	FT / FTA	Pct.	Reb. O / T	A	TO	PF	S	Blk	TP	PPM
MCCLOUD, L.	-	8/ -	-	3/ 4	.750	-/ -	-	-	0	-	-	19	-
NUCKOLLS, H.	-	1/ -	-	1/ 1	1.000	-/ -	-	-	2	-	-	3	-
DOLL, B.	-	2/ -	-	2/ 2	1.000	-/ -	-	-	4	-	-	6	-
HUGGINS, H.	-	2/ -	-	1/ 1	1.000	-/ -	-	-	4	-	-	5	-
HAMBURG, G.	-	4/ -	-	1/ 3	.333	-/ -	-	-	1	-	-	9	-
PUTNAM, D.	-	0/ -	-	0/ 0	.000	-/ -	-	-	0	-	-	0	-
KIRCHNER, B.	-	2/ -	-	0/ 0	.000	-/ -	-	-	3	-	-	4	-
Totals	200	19/ -	-	8/11	.727	-/ -	-	-	14	-	-	46	.230

Kansas (44)   Coach: Phog Allen

	Min.	Total FG / FGA	Pct.	FT / FTA	Pct.	Reb. O / T	A	TO	PF	S	Blk	TP	PPM
MILLER, R.	-	2/ -	-	1/ 2	.500	-/ -	-	-	4	-	-	5	-
BALLARD, J.	-	0/ -	-	0/ 0	.000	-/ -	-	-	0	-	-	0	-
BLACK, C.	-	6/ -	-	6/ 8	.750	-/ -	-	-	2	-	-	18	-
BUESCHER, J.	-	1/ -	-	3/ 4	.750	-/ -	-	-	2	-	-	5	-
HALL, V.	-	1/ -	-	0/ 0	.000	-/ -	-	-	1	-	-	2	-
EVANS, R.	-	5/ -	-	0/ 0	.000	-/ -	-	-	2	-	-	10	-
SOLLENBERGER, M.	-	1/ -	-	0/ 0	.000	-/ -	-	-	0	-	-	2	-
HUNTER, T.	-	1/ -	-	0/ 2	.000	-/ -	-	-	1	-	-	2	-
Totals	200	17/ -	-	10/16	.625	-/ -	-	-	12	-	-	44	.220

Disqualified: Colorado—Doll, Huggins; Kansas—Miller.

	1st Half	2nd Half	Final
Colorado	27	19	46
Kansas	20	24	44

REGIONAL FINAL EASTERN

Dartmouth (48)   Coach: Ozzie Cowles

	Min.	Total FG/FGA	Pct.	FT/FTA	Pct.	Reb. O/T	A	TO	PF	S	Blk	TP	PPM
MYERS, R.	-	4/ -		1/ 3	.333	-/ -			2			9	-
MUNROE, G.	-	9/ -		3/ 4	.750	-/ -			2			21	-
OLSEN, J.	-	5/ -		1/ 4	.250	-/ -			2			11	-
SHAW, C.	-	1/ -		0/ 0	.000	-/ -			0			2	-
SKAUG, S.	-	1/ -		0/ 1	.000	-/ -			4			2	-
PEARSON, C.	-	0/ -		3/ 3	1.000	-/ -			1			3	-
PARMER, W.	-	0/ -		0/ 1	.000	-/ -			2			0	-
Totals	200	20/ -		8/16	.500	-/ -			13			48	.240

Kentucky (28)   Coach: Adolph Rupp

	Min.	Total FG/FGA	Pct.	FT/FTA	Pct.	Reb. O/T	A	TO	PF	S	Blk	TP	PPM
STAKER, C.	-	0/ -		0/ 0	.000	-/ -			4			0	-
ENGLAND, K.	-	1/ -		0/ 0	.000	-/ -			0			2	-
AKERS, M.	-	5/ -		1/ 2	.500	-/ -			3			11	-
BREWER, M.	-	1/ -		2/ 4	.500	-/ -			1			4	-
KING, J.	-	1/ -		2/ 2	1.000	-/ -			0			4	-
ALLEN, E.	-	2/ -		2/ 4	.500	-/ -			2			6	-
TICCO, M.	-	0/ -		1/ 1	1.000	-/ -			1			1	-
WILLIAMS, L.	-	0/ -		0/ 0	.000	-/ -			2			0	-
RAMSEY, L.	-	0/ -		0/ 0	.000	-/ -			0			0	-
Totals	200	10/ -		8/13	.615	-/ -			13			28	.140

Disqualified: Dartmouth—Skaug; Kentucky—Staker.

	1st Half	2nd Half	Final
Dartmouth	23	25	48
Kentucky	13	15	28

REGIONAL FINAL WESTERN

Stanford (46)   Coach: Everett Dean

	Min.	Total FG/FGA	Pct.	FT/FTA	Pct.	Reb. O/T	A	TO	PF	S	Blk	TP	PPM
DANA, J.	-	3/ -		1/ 1	1.000	-/ -			1			7	-
LINARI, F.	-	0/ -		0/ 0	.000	-/ -			0			0	-
POLLARD, J.	-	8/ -		1/ 1	1.000	-/ -			2			17	-
VOSS, E.	-	4/ -		2/ 5	.400	-/ -			3			10	-
COWDEN, B.	-	2/ -		3/ 5	.600	-/ -			2			7	-
DALLMAR, H.	-	2/ -		1/ 1	1.000	-/ -			0			5	-
MCCAFFREY, L.	-	0/ -		0/ 0	.000	-/ -			0			0	-
OLIVER, F.	-	0/ -		0/ 0	.000	-/ -			0			0	-
MADDEN, M.	-	0/ -		0/ 0	.000	-/ -			0			0	-
EIKELMAN, J.	-	0/ -		0/ 0	.000	-/ -			1			0	-
Totals	200	19/ -		8/13	.615	-/ -			9			46	.230

Colorado (35)   Coach: Frosty Cox

	Min.	Total FG/FGA	Pct.	FT/FTA	Pct.	Reb. O/T	A	TO	PF	S	Blk	TP	PPM
MCCLOUD, L.	-	1/ -		1/ 2	.500	-/ -			2			3	-
NUCKOLLS, H.	-	0/ -		0/ 1	.000	-/ -			3			0	-
DOLL, B.	-	3/ -		5/ 5	1.000	-/ -			3			11	-
HUGGINS, H.	-	0/ -		0/ 0	.000	-/ -			0			0	-
HAMBURG, G.	-	3/ -		2/ 2	1.000	-/ -			2			8	-
PUTNAM, D.	-	3/ -		0/ 0	.000	-/ -			1			6	-
KIRCHNER, B.	-	3/ -		1/ 1	1.000	-/ -			0			7	-
Totals	200	13/ -		9/11	.818	-/ -			11			35	.175

Disqualified: None.

	1st Half	2nd Half	Final
Stanford	22	24	46
Colorado	15	20	35

CHAMPIONSHIP

Dartmouth (38)   Coach: Ozzie Cowles

	Min.	Total FG/FGA	Pct.	FT/FTA	Pct.	Reb. O/T	A	TO	PF	S	Blk	TP	PPM
MYERS, R.	29	4/ -		0/ 1	.000	-/ -			1			8	.276
MUNROE, G.	40	5/ -		2/ 2	1.000	-/ -			1			12	.300
OLSEN, J.	40	4/ -		0/ 1	.000	-/ -			0			8	.200
SKAUG, S.	40	1/ -		0/ 0	.000	-/ -			2			2	.050
PEARSON, C.	40	2/ -		2/ 2	1.000	-/ -			3			6	.150
PARMER, W.	11	1/ -		0/ 0	.000	-/ -			0			2	.182
Totals	200	17/ -		4/ 6	.667	-/ -			7			38	.190

Stanford (53)   Coach: Everett Dean

	Min.	Total FG/FGA	Pct.	FT/FTA	Pct.	Reb. O/T	A	TO	PF	S	Blk	TP	PPM
DANA, J.	40	7/ -		0/ 0	.000	-/ -			0			14	.350
LINARI, F.	31	3/ -		0/ 0	.000	-/ -			0			6	.194
VOSS, E.	40	6/ -		1/ 2	.500	-/ -			2			13	.325
COWDEN, B.	40	2/ -		1/ 1	1.000	-/ -			3			5	.125
DALLMAR, H.	40	6/ -		3/ 5	.600	-/ -			0			15	.375
BURNESS, D.	9	0/ -		0/ 0	.000	-/ -			0			0	.000
Totals	200	24/ -		5/ 8	.625	-/ -			5			53	.265

Disqualified: None.

	1st Half	2nd Half	Final
Dartmouth	22	16	38
Stanford	24	29	53

REGIONAL THIRD PLACE EASTERN

Penn State (41)   Coach: John Lawther

	Min.	Total FG/FGA	Pct.	FT/FTA	Pct.	Reb. O/T	A	TO	PF	S	Blk	TP	PPM
GROSS	-	0/ -	-	4/ 6	.667	-/ -	-	-	0	-	-	4	-
GENT	10/ -	10/ -	-	1/ 1	1.000	-/ -	-	-	1	-	-	21	-
BALTIMORE	5/ -	5/ -	-	0/ 0	.000	-/ -	-	-	2	-	-	10	-
RAMIN	-	0/ -	-	0/ 0	.000	-/ -	-	-	1	-	-	0	-
EGLI, J.	-	1/ -	-	2/ 3	.667	-/ -	-	-	4	-	-	4	-
GRIMES	-	0/ -	-	0/ 0	.000	-/ -	-	-	0	-	-	0	-
HORNSTEIN	-	1/ -	-	0/ 3	.000	-/ -	-	-	4	-	-	2	-
Totals	200	17/ -	-	7/13	.538	-/ -	-	-	12	-	-	41	.205

Illinois (34)   Coach: Doug Mills

	Min.	Total FG/FGA	Pct.	FT/FTA	Pct.	Reb. O/T	A	TO	PF	S	Blk	TP	PPM
MENKE	-	3/ -	-	2/ 2	1.000	-/ -	-	-	2	-	-	8	-
FOWLER	-	1/ -	-	0/ 0	.000	-/ -	-	-	0	-	-	2	-
SMILEY	-	2/ -	-	0/ 0	.000	-/ -	-	-	1	-	-	4	-
HOCKING	-	0/ -	-	0/ 0	.000	-/ -	-	-	1	-	-	0	-
MATHISEN	-	2/ -	-	4/ 4	1.000	-/ -	-	-	0	-	-	8	-
WUKOVITZ	-	1/ -	-	3/ 3	1.000	-/ -	-	-	2	-	-	5	-
PHILLIP	-	2/ -	-	1/ 2	.500	-/ -	-	-	1	-	-	5	-
VANCE	-	0/ -	-	0/ 0	.000	-/ -	-	-	1	-	-	0	-
SACHS	-	1/ -	-	0/ 0	.000	-/ -	-	-	3	-	-	2	-
PARKER	-	0/ -	-	0/ 0	.000	-/ -	-	-	1	-	-	0	-
Totals	200	12/ -	-	10/11	.909	-/ -	-	-	12	-	-	34	.170

Disqualified: Penn State—Egli, Hornstein.

	1st Half	2nd Half	Final
Penn State	26	15	41
Illinois	21	13	34

REGIONAL THIRD PLACE WESTERN

Kansas (55)   Coach: Phog Allen

	Min.	Total FG/FGA	Pct.	FT/FTA	Pct.	Reb. O/T	A	TO	PF	S	Blk	TP	PPM
MILLER, R.	-	4/ -	-	3/ 7	.429	-/ -	-	-	3	-	-	11	-
KISSELL	-	0/ -	-	0/ 0	.000	-/ -	-	-	0	-	-	0	-
BALLARD, J.	-	0/ -	-	0/ 0	.000	-/ -	-	-	4	-	-	0	-
WALKER	-	0/ -	-	0/ 0	.000	-/ -	-	-	0	-	-	0	-
BUESCHER, J.	-	7/ -	-	0/ 0	.000	-/ -	-	-	1	-	-	14	-
HALL, V.	-	0/ -	-	0/ 0	.000	-/ -	-	-	0	-	-	0	-
BLACK, C.	-	6/ -	-	4/ 6	.667	-/ -	-	-	4	-	-	16	-
HUNTER, T.	-	1/ -	-	0/ 0	.000	-/ -	-	-	3	-	-	2	-
EVANS, R.	-	5/ -	-	2/ 2	1.000	-/ -	-	-	4	-	-	12	-
SOLLENBERGER, M.	-	0/ -	-	0/ 0	.000	-/ -	-	-	0	-	-	0	-
Totals	200	23/ -	-	9/15	.600	-/ -	-	-	19	-	-	55	.275

Rice (53)   Coach: Buster Brannon

	Min.	Total FG/FGA	Pct.	FT/FTA	Pct.	Reb. O/T	A	TO	PF	S	Blk	TP	PPM
CLOSS	-	2/ -	-	5/ 9	.556	-/ -	-	-	2	-	-	9	-
GOMEZ	-	3/ -	-	0/ 1	.000	-/ -	-	-	3	-	-	6	-
ZANDER	-	0/ -	-	1/ 1	1.000	-/ -	-	-	2	-	-	1	-
KINNEY	-	2/ -	-	2/ 2	1.000	-/ -	-	-	4	-	-	6	-
MCDONALD	-	1/ -	-	0/ 0	.000	-/ -	-	-	0	-	-	2	-
PALMER, C.	-	11/ -	-	3/ 3	1.000	-/ -	-	-	1	-	-	25	-
LAMBERT	-	1/ -	-	2/ 3	.667	-/ -	-	-	1	-	-	4	-
Totals	200	20/ -	-	13/19	.684	-/ -	-	-	13	-	-	53	.265

Disqualified: Kansas—Ballard, Black, Evans; Rice—Kinney.

	1st Half	2nd Half	Final
Kansas	24	31	55
Rice	30	23	53

✪ INDIVIDUAL RECORDS ✪

SCORING

Most points in a single game
1 JIM POLLARD, STANFORD (vs. RICE) — 26
2 CHET PALMER, RICE (vs. KANSAS) — 25
3 LARRY GENT, PENN STATE (vs. ILLINOIS) — 21
3 GEORGE MUNROE, DARTMOUTH (vs. KENTUCKY) — 21
5 2 tied for fifth place.

Most total points in the tournament
1 JIM POLLARD, STANFORD — 43
1 CHET PALMER, RICE — 43
3 GEORGE MUNROE, DARTMOUTH — 41
4 ED VOSS, STANFORD — 38
4 JIM OLSEN, DARTMOUTH — 38

Highest scoring average (minimum 2 games)
1 JIM POLLARD, STANFORD (43-2) — 21.50
1 CHET PALMER, RICE (43-2) — 21.50
3 CHARLEY BLACK, KANSAS (34-2) — 17.00
4 GEORGE MUNROE, DARTMOUTH (41-3) — 13.67
5 2 tied for fifth place.

FIELD GOALS

Most field goals in a single game
1 JIM POLLARD, STANFORD (vs. RICE) — 12
2 CHET PALMER, RICE (vs. KANSAS) — 11
3 LARRY GENT, PENN STATE (vs. ILLINOIS) — 10
4 GEORGE MUNROE, DARTMOUTH (vs. KENTUCKY) — 9
5 4 tied for fifth place.

Most total field goals in the tournament
1 JIM POLLARD, STANFORD — 20
2 CHET PALMER, RICE — 19
3 GEORGE MUNROE, DARTMOUTH — 18
4 JIM OLSEN, DARTMOUTH — 17
5 ED VOSS, STANFORD — 14

FREE THROWS

Most free throws in a single game
1 ED VOSS, STANFORD (vs. RICE) — 7
2 CHARLEY BLACK, KANSAS (vs. COLORADO) — 6
3 CLOSS, RICE (vs. KANSAS) — 5
3 BOB DOLL, COLORADO (vs. STANFORD) — 5
5 3 tied for fifth place.

Most total free throws in the tournament
1 ED VOSS, STANFORD — 10
1 CHARLEY BLACK, KANSAS — 10
3 ELMER GROSS, PENN STATE — 7
3 BOB DOLL, COLORADO — 7
3 CLOSS, RICE — 7

Most free throws attempted in a single game
1 CLOSS, RICE (vs. KANSAS) — 9
2 ED VOSS, STANFORD (vs. RICE) — 8
2 CHARLEY BLACK, KANSAS (vs. COLORADO) — 8
4 RALPH MILLER, KANSAS (vs. RICE) — 7
5 2 tied for fifth place.

Most free throws attempted in the tournament
1 ED VOSS, STANFORD — 15
2 CHARLEY BLACK, KANSAS — 14
3 CLOSS, RICE — 12
4 BILL COWDEN, STANFORD — 10
5 3 tied for fifth place.

Highest free throw percentage in a single game (minimum 7 attempts)
1 ED VOSS, STANFORD (vs. RICE) (7-8) — .875
2 CHARLEY BLACK, KANSAS (vs. COLORADO) (6-8) — .750
3 CLOSS, RICE (vs. KANSAS) (5-9) — .556

Highest free throw percentage in the tournament (minimum 15 attempts)
1 ED VOSS, STANFORD (10-15) — .667

✪ TEAM RECORDS ✪

SCORING

Most points in a single game
1	KANSAS (vs. RICE)	55
2	3 tied for second place.	

Most total points in the tournament
1	STANFORD	152
2	DARTMOUTH	130
3	RICE	100

Highest scoring average (minimum 2 games)
1	STANFORD (152-3)	50.67
2	RICE (100-2)	50.00
3	KANSAS (99-2)	49.50

FIELD GOALS

Most field goals in a single game
1	STANFORD (vs. DARTMOUTH)	24
2	KANSAS (vs. RICE)	23
3	STANFORD (vs. RICE)	21

Most total field goals in the tournament
1	STANFORD	64
2	DARTMOUTH	55
3	2 tied for third place.	

FREE THROWS

Most free throws in a single game
1	RICE (vs. KANSAS)	13
2	STANFORD (vs. RICE)	11
2	PENN STATE (vs. DARTMOUTH)	11

Most total free throws in the tournament
1	STANFORD	24
2	RICE	20
2	DARTMOUTH	20

Most free throws attempted in a single game
1	RICE (vs. KANSAS)	19
2	STANFORD (vs. RICE)	17
3	KANSAS (vs. COLORADO)	16
3	DARTMOUTH (vs. KENTUCKY)	16
3	PENN STATE (vs. DARTMOUTH)	16

Most total free throws attempted in the tournament
1	STANFORD	38
2	DARTMOUTH	34
3	KANSAS	31

Highest free throw percentage in a single game
1	ILLINOIS (vs. PENN STATE) (10-11)	.909
2	COLORADO (vs. STANFORD) (9-11)	.818
3	COLORADO (vs. KANSAS) (8-11)	.727

Highest free throw percentage in the tournament (minimum 2 games)
1	COLORADO (17-22)	.773
2	ILLINOIS (18-26)	.692
3	RICE (20-29)	.690

Fewest free throws in a single game
1	DARTMOUTH (vs. STANFORD)	4
2	STANFORD (vs. DARTMOUTH)	5
3	2 tied for third place.	

Lowest free throw percentage in a single game
1	DARTMOUTH (vs. KENTUCKY) (8-16)	.500
2	ILLINOIS (vs. KENTUCKY) (8-15)	.533
3	PENN STATE (vs. ILLINOIS) (7-13)	.538

Lowest free throw percentage in the tournament (minimum 2 games)
1	DARTMOUTH (20-34)	.588
2	KANSAS (19-31)	.613
3	PENN STATE(18-29)	.621

1943

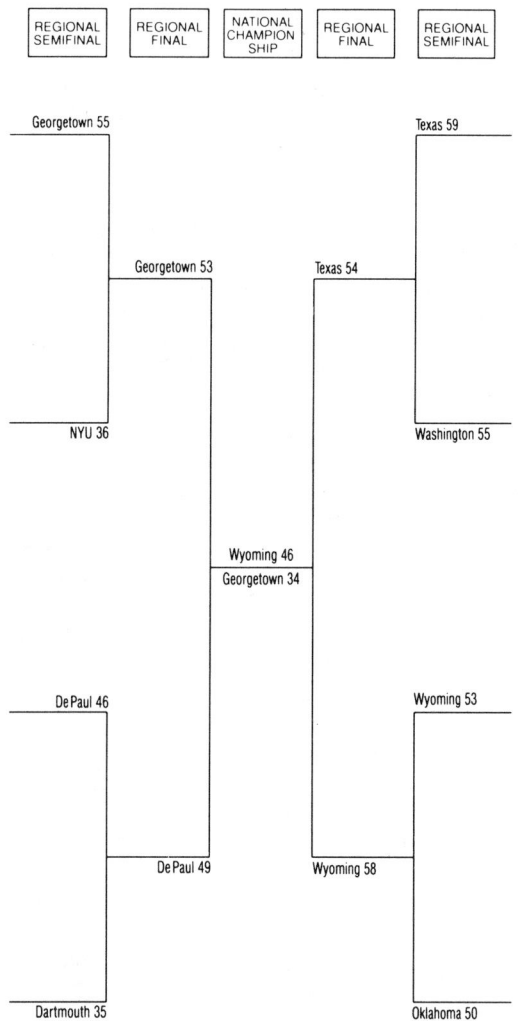

| REGIONAL SEMIFINAL | REGIONAL FINAL | NATIONAL CHAMPION SHIP | REGIONAL FINAL | REGIONAL SEMIFINAL |

EASTERN

WESTERN

Georgetown 55

Texas 59

Georgetown 53

Texas 54

NYU 36

Washington 55

Wyoming 46
Georgetown 34

De Paul 46

Wyoming 53

De Paul 49

Wyoming 58

Dartmouth 35

Oklahoma 50

CONSOLATION GAMES

Regional Third Place:

Western:
Oklahoma 48
Washington 43

Eastern:
Dartmouth 51
NYU 49

In March 1943, young men from all across America were joining up to fight against the Axis powers overseas. Kenny Sailors of Wyoming, the college Player of the Year and a member of the Reserve Officers' Training Corps, was scheduled to leave for Quantico, Virginia, and the Marines. Other key Cowboys due to report for duty included Jim Weir, Floyd Volker, and Jim Roney. (At 6-7, star center Milo Komenich was too tall to be accepted into the service.) And Wyoming wasn't alone; virtually every school was expecting players to enter the armed forces in the weeks following the tournament.

The war disrupted broadcasts, too, with Wyoming fans having to listen to a re-creation of their team's final contest by telegraph since coast-to-coast telephone lines had to be left open for more important communications. And because of the war, a post-tournament championship game was scheduled between the NIT and NCAA titleholders, as a benefit for the Red Cross.

Although the boys who took the floor for the 1943 NCAAs knew their competition was nothing like the life-and-death struggle that lay ahead of them, they still played fiercely and brilliantly.

In the opening round, the Rocky Mountain circuit champs from Wyoming, who had lost only one game, to Duquesne, during the regular season (Duquesne was decimated long before tournament time by enlistments), faced Oklahoma of the Big Six. At the start it looked like the Cowboys were fading into the sunset. Because while they were firing blanks, Oklahoma's big gun, center Gerald Tucker, was hot as a pistol. His fakes froze Wyoming's Komenich to the floor, as he went up and around the big Cowboy time and again to score. The Sooners surged to a 14-5 lead. But Wyoming fought back, and by the time Tucker fouled out with three minutes remaining in the first half, the Cowboys were down by only two. After the intermission, Wyoming's height told the tale, as the 6-7 Komenich and the 6-6 Weir combined for 25 points to overwhelm the undermanned Sooners.

In the second game of the opening round double-header, favored Washington took a 21-8 lead and looked like they would win in a walk over Texas. But the Longhorns started shaking their star John Hargis free, and they began to come back. It was a hard-fought, foul-plagued game, and seven men were disqualified. Finally, with three minutes left and Texas just one bucket behind, Longhorn coach Bully Gilstrap was forced to put in a little-used freshman guard, Roy Cox. The 17-year-old, 5-9 Cox came off the bench and let fly, scoring the tying 2-pointer. Hargis soon put Texas ahead with 2 of his 30 points, Cox hit for two more baskets, and the Longhorns stayed alive.

The next night the Texans took up where they left off. Hargis was again unstoppable, scoring 17 of the underdog Longhorns' first 26 points as they surged into a 13-point lead. But then Wyoming's All-American took over; Kenny Sailors hit for 5 of his team's 7 straight to lead the Cowboys back into the game. They continued their drive into the second half, and with substitute Jimmy Collins hitting three key baskets, they managed to survive.

Meanwhile in New York, Georgetown's dazzling ball handling and the inside shooting of Big John Mahnken crushed NYU by 19, and the bespectacled George Mikan of DePaul led his team both offensively and defensively to an easy victory over Dartmouth, as the inept Eastern leaguers missed their first 34 shots. Then in the regional final, Georgetown outlasted DePaul despite losing Mahnken on fouls.

It was power versus finesse in the finals, as the big, aggressive Cowboys of Wyoming finally wore down the Georgetown Hoyas to deliver a stunning knockout punch in the final minutes.

The outcome was in doubt almost to the very end. After Wyoming took an early lead, the Hoyas came back to forge ahead. But Georgetown soon got into foul trouble, and two starters, play-making guard Danny Kraus and forward Dan Gabbianelli, were forced to the bench with three fouls (it took four to foul out in 1943) for an extended period midway through the game. Wyoming scored the last 6 points of the first half, and regained the lead with a shot from near midcourt by Sailors with four seconds left.

Again Georgetown pulled ahead, passing with precision and patiently working the ball around for good shots against the taller Cowboys. With seven minutes remaining in the game, the Hoyas led 31-26. Then Wyoming flexed its muscles. With the speedy Sailors setting up the plays, the Cowboys ran the Hoyas into devastating picks and crashed the boards, throwing off the smaller Georgetown players like so many matchsticks. They scored 11 straight points, as Jimmy Collins sent them into the lead on a long set-shot and Komenich barreled in for a bruising follow of a missed free throw. Still, Georgetown held on. They narrowed the gap to 3, but in the final minute Sailors and his mates scored 9 points to turn a tight game—one in which the lead changed hands seven times and the score was tied ten times—into a rout.

In the Red Cross National Championship benefit game the following night, Wyoming took on the NIT winners from St. John's. It was still another tight contest for the Cowboys, one that took an overtime to decide. But in the end Wyoming once again came out ahead. They had survived four tough battles to win the national title.

Then they went to war.

REGIONAL SEMIFINAL EASTERN

Georgetown (55)   Coach: Elmer Ripley

	Min.	Total FG/FGA	Pct.	FT/FTA	Pct.	Reb. O/T	A	TO	PF	S	Blk	TP	PPM
GABBIANELLI, D.	-	2/ -	-	1/ 1	1.000	-/ -	-	-	3	-	-	5	-
REILLY, J.	-	1/ -	-	2/ 3	.667	-/ -	-	-	2	-	-	4	-
DUFFEY	-	1/ -	-	1/ 1	1.000	-/ -	-	-	0	-	-	3	-
POTOLICCHIO, L.	-	3/ -	-	0/ 0	.000	-/ -	-	-	0	-	-	6	-
FEENEY, B.	-	1/ -	-	0/ 0	.000	-/ -	-	-	0	-	-	2	-
FINNERTY	-	0/ -	-	0/ 0	.000	-/ -	-	-	0	-	-	0	-
MAHNKEN, J.	-	10/ -	-	0/ 1	.000	-/ -	-	-	1	-	-	20	-
HYDE, H.	-	0/ -	-	0/ 0	.000	-/ -	-	-	0	-	-	0	-
HASSETT, B.	-	2/ -	-	3/ 3	1.000	-/ -	-	-	1	-	-	7	-
KRAUS, D.	-	4/ -	-	0/ -	-	-/ -	-	-	1	-	-	8	-
Totals	200	24/ -	-	7/ 9	.778	-/ -	-	-	8	-	-	55	.275

NYU (36)   Coach: Howard Cann

	Min.	Total FG/FGA	Pct.	FT/FTA	Pct.	Reb. O/T	A	TO	PF	S	Blk	TP	PPM
FLEISHMAN	-	1/ -	-	0/ 0	.000	-/ -	-	-	1	-	-	2	-
GRENERT, A.	-	1/ -	-	2/ 4	.500	-/ -	-	-	1	-	-	4	-
MAHER, B.	-	4/ -	-	1/ 2	.500	-/ -	-	-	3	-	-	9	-
LEGGAT	-	1/ -	-	0/ 0	.000	-/ -	-	-	1	-	-	2	-
DANTO	-	5/ -	-	1/ 2	.500	-/ -	-	-	1	-	-	11	-
SIMMONS	-	1/ -	-	1/ 3	.333	-/ -	-	-	0	-	-	3	-
MELE	-	2/ -	-	1/ 1	1.000	-/ -	-	-	0	-	-	5	-
HEISER	-	0/ -	-	0/ 0	.000	-/ -	-	-	0	-	-	0	-
Totals	200	15/ -	-	6/12	.600	-/ -	-	-	7	-	-	36	.180

Disqualified: None.

	1st Half	2nd Half	Final
Georgetown	32	23	55
NYU	19	17	36

DePaul (46)   Coach: Ray Meyer

	Min.	Total FG/FGA	Pct.	FT/FTA	Pct.	Reb. O/T	A	TO	PF	S	Blk	TP	PPM
COMINSKY, J.	-	3/ -	-	3/ 4	.750	-/ -	-	-	3	-	-	9	-
JORGENSON, J.	-	5/ -	-	0/ 0	.000	-/ -	-	-	3	-	-	10	-
MIKAN, G.	-	7/ -	-	6/ 8	.750	-/ -	-	-	3	-	-	20	-
KELLY, T.	-	1/ -	-	2/ 2	1.000	-/ -	-	-	2	-	-	4	-
STARZYK, D.	-	0/ -	-	0/ 1	.000	-/ -	-	-	4	-	-	0	-
DONATO, B.	-	0/ -	-	0/ 0	.000	-/ -	-	-	0	-	-	0	-
FRAILEY, M.	-	0/ -	-	0/ 0	.000	-/ -	-	-	1	-	-	0	-
TRIPTOW, D.	-	0/ -	-	0/ 0	.000	-/ -	-	-	0	-	-	0	-
WISCONS, F.	-	0/ -	-	0/ 0	.000	-/ -	-	-	0	-	-	0	-
RYAN, B.	-	1/ -	-	1/ 2	.500	-/ -	-	-	2	-	-	3	-
CROWLEY, K.	-	0/ -	-	0/ 0	.000	-/ -	-	-	0	-	-	0	-
Totals	200	17/ -	-	12/17	.706	-/ -	-	-	18	-	-	46	.230

Dartmouth (35)   Coach: Ozzie Cowles

	Min.	Total FG/FGA	Pct.	FT/FTA	Pct.	Reb. O/T	A	TO	PF	S	Blk	TP	PPM
MUNROE, G.	-	3/ -	-	2/ 4	.500	-/ -	-	-	0	-	-	8	-
MYERS	-	1/ -	-	3/ 5	.600	-/ -	-	-	4	-	-	5	-
OLSEN, J.	-	2/ -	-	3/ 3	1.000	-/ -	-	-	4	-	-	7	-
SKAUG, S.	-	0/ -	-	2/ 3	.667	-/ -	-	-	3	-	-	2	-
COLEMAN	-	1/ -	-	1/ 1	1.000	-/ -	-	-	1	-	-	3	-
BRINDLEY, A.	-	5/ -	-	0/ 3	.000	-/ -	-	-	1	-	-	10	-
CARROLL	-	0/ -	-	0/ 0	.000	-/ -	-	-	0	-	-	0	-
MONAHAN, J.	-	0/ -	-	0/ 0	.000	-/ -	-	-	0	-	-	0	-
BRIGGS, J.	-	0/ -	-	0/ 0	.000	-/ -	-	-	0	-	-	0	-
Totals	200	12/ -	-	11/19	.579	-/ -	-	-	13	-	-	35	.175

Disqualified: DePaul—Starzyk; Dartmouth—Myers, Olsen.

	1st Half	2nd Half	Final
DePaul	26	20	46
Dartmouth	14	21	35

REGIONAL SEMIFINAL WESTERN

Texas (59)   Coach: H.C. Bully Gilstrap

	Min.	Total FG/FGA	Pct.	FT/FTA	Pct.	Reb. O/T	A	TO	PF	S	Blk	TP	PPM
OVERALL, B.	-	5/ -	-	5/ 6	.833	-/ -	-	-	4	-	-	15	-
GOSS	-	0/ -	-	0/ 0	.000	-/ -	-	-	0	-	-	0	-
HARGIS, J.	-	10/ -	-	10/12	.833	-/ -	-	-	3	-	-	30	-
LANGDON, J.	-	1/ -	-	0/ 0	.000	-/ -	-	-	4	-	-	2	-
WRIGHT, D.	-	0/ -	-	0/ 0	.000	-/ -	-	-	1	-	-	0	-
FITZGERALD, J.	-	1/ -	-	0/ 1	.000	-/ -	-	-	4	-	-	2	-
COX, R.	-	3/ -	-	0/ 0	.000	-/ -	-	-	0	-	-	6	-
BRAHANEY, F.	-	1/ -	-	2/ 3	.667	-/ -	-	-	4	-	-	4	-
KENT	-	0/ -	-	0/ 0	.000	-/ -	-	-	1	-	-	0	-
Totals	200	21/ -	-	17/22	.773	-/ -	-	-	21	-	-	59	.295

Washington (55)   Coach: Hec Edmunson

	Min.	Total FG/FGA	Pct.	FT/FTA	Pct.	Reb. O/T	A	TO	PF	S	Blk	TP	PPM
FORD, D.	-	3/ -	-	4/ 5	.800	-/ -	-	-	2	-	-	10	-
BIRD	-	3/ -	-	0/ 0	.000	-/ -	-	-	2	-	-	6	-
GILBERTSON, R.	-	2/ -	-	0/ 0	.000	-/ -	-	-	4	-	-	4	-
SHAEFER	-	0/ -	-	0/ 0	.000	-/ -	-	-	4	-	-	0	-
GILMER, C.	-	2/ -	-	1/ 3	.333	-/ -	-	-	4	-	-	5	-
NELSON	-	0/ -	-	0/ 3	.000	-/ -	-	-	1	-	-	0	-
MORRIS, B.	-	8/ -	-	6/ 9	.667	-/ -	-	-	2	-	-	22	-
GISSBERG	-	2/ -	-	2/ 2	1.000	-/ -	-	-	2	-	-	6	-
TAYLOR	-	1/ -	-	0/ 3	.000	-/ -	-	-	1	-	-	2	-
BROWN	-	0/ -	-	0/ 0	.000	-/ -	-	-	0	-	-	0	-
GRONSDALE	-	0/ -	-	0/ 0	.000	-/ -	-	-	0	-	-	0	-
Totals	200	21/ -	-	13/25	.520	-/ -	-	-	22	-	-	55	.275

Disqualified: Texas—Overall, Langdon, Fitzgerald, Brahaney; Washington—Gilbertson; Shaefer, Gilmer.

	1st Half	2nd Half	Final
Texas	28	31	59
Washington	33	22	55

Wyoming (53)   Coach: Everet Shelton

	Min.	Total FG/FGA	Pct.	FT/FTA	Pct.	Reb. O/T	A	TO	PF	S	Blk	TP	PPM
SAILORS, K.	-	4/ -	-	0/ 1	.000	-/ -	-	-	2	-	-	8	-
RAY, E.	-	0/ -	-	0/ 0	.000	-/ -	-	-	0	-	-	0	-
WEIR, J.	-	6/ -	-	2/ 2	1.000	-/ -	-	-	3	-	-	14	-
KOMENICH, M.	-	10/ -	-	2/ 3	.667	-/ -	-	-	2	-	-	22	-
VOLKER, F.	-	3/ -	-	0/ 0	.000	-/ -	-	-	4	-	-	6	-
WAITE, D.	-	0/ -	-	0/ 0	.000	-/ -	-	-	0	-	-	0	-
RONEY, L.	-	0/ -	-	1/ 1	1.000	-/ -	-	-	2	-	-	1	-
COLLINS, J.	-	1/ -	-	0/ 0	.000	-/ -	-	-	1	-	-	2	-
REESE, J.	-	0/ -	-	0/ 0	.000	-/ -	-	-	0	-	-	0	-
Totals	200	24/ -	-	5/ 7	.714	-/ -	-	-	14	-	-	53	.265

Oklahoma (50)   Coach: Bruce Drake

	Min.	Total FG/FGA	Pct.	FT/FTA	Pct.	Reb. O/T	A	TO	PF	S	Blk	TP	PPM
REICH, D.	-	5/ -	-	7/12	.583	-/ -	-	-	1	-	-	17	-
ROUSEY	-	0/ -	-	2/ 4	.500	-/ -	-	-	0	-	-	2	-
HEAP, P.	-	1/ -	-	1/ 1	1.000	-/ -	-	-	0	-	-	3	-
PUGHLEY	-	1/ -	-	0/ 0	.000	-/ -	-	-	0	-	-	2	-
TUCKER, G.	-	5/ -	-	1/ 1	1.000	-/ -	-	-	4	-	-	11	-
MCCURDY	-	0/ -	-	0/ 0	.000	-/ -	-	-	0	-	-	0	-
MARTENEY	-	1/ -	-	0/ 0	.000	-/ -	-	-	0	-	-	2	-
PAINE, A.	-	5/ -	-	1/ 1	1.000	-/ -	-	-	4	-	-	11	-
MITCHELL	-	1/ -	-	0/ 0	.000	-/ -	-	-	0	-	-	2	-
Totals	200	19/ -	-	12/19	.632	-/ -	-	-	9	-	-	50	.250

Disqualified: Wyoming—Volker; Oklahoma—Tucker, Paine.

	1st Half	2nd Half	Final
Wyoming	22	31	53
Oklahoma	25	25	50

REGIONAL FINAL EASTERN

Georgetown (53) Coach: Elmer Ripley

	Min.	Total FG/FGA	Pct.	FT/FTA	Pct.	Reb. O/T	A	TO	PF	S	Blk	TP	PPM
GABBIANELLI, D..	-	3/ -		0/ 0	.000	-/ -	-	-	1	-	-	6	-
REILLY, J.	-	0/ -		0/ 0	.000	-/ -	-	-	0	-	-	0	-
MAHNKEN, J.	-	8/ -		1/ 2	.500	-/ -	-	-	4	-	-	17	-
KRAUS, D.	-	1/ -		4/ 6	.667	-/ -	-	-	3	-	-	6	-
HASSETT, B.	-	2/ -		7/ 7	1.000	-/ -	-	-	0	-	-	11	-
FEENEY, B.	-	0/ -		0/ 0	.000	-/ -	-	-	2	-	-	0	-
DUFFEY	-	0/ -		0/ 0	.000	-/ -	-	-	0	-	-	0	-
POTOLICCHIO, L.	-	5/ -		1/ 2	.500	-/ -	-	-	1	-	-	11	-
HYDE, H.	-	1/ -		0/ 0	.000	-/ -	-	-	2	-	-	2	-
Totals	200	20/ -		13/17	.765	-/ -	-	-	13	-	-	53	.265

DePaul (49) Coach: Ray Meyer

	Min.	Total FG/FGA	Pct.	FT/FTA	Pct.	Reb. O/T	A	TO	PF	S	Blk	TP	PPM
COMINSKY, J.	-	5/ -		1/ 3	.333	-/ -	-	-	2	-	-	11	-
JORGENSON, J.	-	6/ -		2/ 3	.667	-/ -	-	-	2	-	-	14	-
MIKAN, G.	-	3/ -		5/ 7	.714	-/ -	-	-	1	-	-	11	-
KELLY, T.	-	2/ -		2/ 2	1.000	-/ -	-	-	4	-	-	6	-
STARZYK, D.	-	3/ -		1/ 1	1.000	-/ -	-	-	3	-	-	7	-
FRAILEY, M.	-	0/ -		0/ 0	.000	-/ -	-	-	0	-	-	0	-
RYAN, B.	-	0/ -		0/ 0	.000	-/ -	-	-	3	-	-	0	-
Totals	200	19/ -		11/16	.688	-/ -	-	-	15	-	-	49	.245

Disqualified: Georgetown—Mahnken; DePaul—Kelly.

	1st Half	2nd Half	Final
Georgetown	23	30	53
DePaul	28	21	49

REGIONAL FINAL WESTERN

Texas (54) Coach: H.C. Bully Gilstrap

	Min.	Total FG/FGA	Pct.	FT/FTA	Pct.	Reb. O/T	A	TO	PF	S	Blk	TP	PPM
OVERALL, B.	-	5/ -		4/ 7	.571	-/ -	-	-	3	-	-	14	-
HARGIS, J.	-	11/ -		7/12	.583	-/ -	-	-	3	-	-	29	-
LANGDON, J.	-	1/ -		2/ 3	.667	-/ -	-	-	2	-	-	4	-
WRIGHT, D.	-	1/ -		1/ 1	1.000	-/ -	-	-	2	-	-	3	-
FITZGERALD, J.	-	1/ -		0/ 0	.000	-/ -	-	-	4	-	-	2	-
COX, R.	-	0/ -		0/ 0	.000	-/ -	-	-	3	-	-	0	-
BRAHANEY, F.	-	1/ -		0/ 0	.000	-/ -	-	-	3	-	-	2	-
Totals	200	20/ -		14/23	.609	-/ -	-	-	20	-	-	54	.270

Wyoming (58) Coach: Everett Shelton

	Min.	Total FG/FGA	Pct.	FT/FTA	Pct.	Reb. O/T	A	TO	PF	S	Blk	TP	PPM
SAILORS, K.	-	4/ -		4/ 6	.667	-/ -	-	-	3	-	-	12	-
WEIR, J.	-	6/ -		1/ 1	1.000	-/ -	-	-	3	-	-	13	-
KOMENICH, M.	-	8/ -		1/ 4	.250	-/ -	-	-	2	-	-	17	-
VOLKER, F.	-	3/ -		1/ 3	.333	-/ -	-	-	4	-	-	7	-
WAITE, D.	-	0/ -		0/ 0	.000	-/ -	-	-	1	-	-	0	-
RONEY, L.	-	1/ -		2/ 3	.667	-/ -	-	-	3	-	-	4	-
COLLINS, J.	-	2/ -		1/ 2	.500	-/ -	-	-	2	-	-	5	-
Totals	200	24/ -		10/19	.526	-/ -	-	-	18	-	-	58	.290

Disqualified: Wyoming—Volker; Texas—Fitzgerald.

	1st Half	2nd Half	Final
Texas	33	21	54
Wyoming	27	31	58

CHAMPIONSHIP

Georgetown (34) Coach: Elmer Ripley

	Min.	Total FG/FGA	Pct.	FT/FTA	Pct.	Reb. O/T	A	TO	PF	S	Blk	TP	PPM
GABBIANELLI, D.	-	1/ -		2/ 3	.667	-/ -	-	-	3	-	-	4	-
REILLY, J.	-	1/ -		0/ 0	.000	-/ -	-	-	0	-	-	2	-
MAHNKEN, J.	-	2/ -		2/ 3	.667	-/ -	-	-	2	-	-	6	-
KRAUS, D.	-	2/ -		0/ 1	.000	-/ -	-	-	3	-	-	4	-
HASSETT, B.	-	3/ -		0/ 3	.000	-/ -	-	-	4	-	-	6	-
FEENEY, B.	-	4/ -		0/ 0	.000	-/ -	-	-	1	-	-	8	-
DUFFEY	-	0/ -		0/ 1	.000	-/ -	-	-	0	-	-	0	-
POTOLICCHIO, L.	-	1/ -		2/ 3	.667	-/ -	-	-	1	-	-	4	-
HYDE, H.	-	0/ -		0/ 0	.000	-/ -	-	-	0	-	-	0	-
Totals	200	14/ -		6/14	.429	-/ -	-	-	14	-	-	34	.170

Wyoming (46) Coach: Everett Shelton

	Min.	Total FG/FGA	Pct.	FT/FTA	Pct.	Reb. O/T	A	TO	PF	S	Blk	TP	PPM
SAILORS, K.	-	6/ -		4/ 6	.667	-/ -	-	-	2	-	-	16	-
WEIR, J.	-	2/ -		1/ 3	.333	-/ -	-	-	2	-	-	5	-
KOMENICH, M.	-	4/ -		1/ 4	.250	-/ -	-	-	2	-	-	9	-
VOLKER, F.	-	2/ -		1/ 2	.500	-/ -	-	-	3	-	-	5	-
WAITE, D.	-	0/ -		0/ 0	.000	-/ -	-	-	0	-	-	0	-
RONEY, L.	-	0/ -		1/ 2	.500	-/ -	-	-	1	-	-	1	-
COLLINS, J.	-	4/ -		0/ 1	.000	-/ -	-	-	1	-	-	8	-
REESE, J.	-	1/ -		0/ 0	.000	-/ -	-	-	0	-	-	2	-
Totals	200	19/ -		8/18	.444	-/ -	-	-	11	-	-	46	.230

Disqualified: Georgetown—Hassett.

	1st Half	2nd Half	Final
Georgetown	16	18	34
Wyoming	13	33	46

REGIONAL THIRD PLACE EASTERN

Dartmouth (51)   Coach: Ozzie Cowles

	Min.	Total FG / FGA	Pct.	FT / FTA	Pct.	Reb. O / T	A	TO	PF	S	Blk	TP	PPM
MUNROE, G.	-	2/ -	-	2/ 3	.667	-/ -	-	-	1	-	-	6	-
MYERS	-	11/ -	-	0/ 2	.000	-/ -	-	-	3	-	-	22	-
OLSEN, J.	-	1/ -	-	0/ 1	.000	-/ -	-	-	3	-	-	2	-
SKAUG, S.	-	2/ -	-	1/ 1	1.000	-/ -	-	-	4	-	-	5	-
COLEMAN	-	2/ -	-	2/ 2	1.000	-/ -	-	-	3	-	-	6	-
BRINDLEY, A.	-	3/ -	-	2/ 3	.667	-/ -	-	-	0	-	-	8	-
BRIGGS, J.	-	0/ -	-	1/ 1	1.000	-/ -	-	-	0	-	-	1	-
CARROLL	-	0/ -	-	1/ 2	.500	-/ -	-	-	0	-	-	1	-
Totals	200	21/ -	-	9/15	.600	-/ -	-	-	14	-	-	51	.255

NYU (49)   Coach: Howard Cann

	Min.	Total FG / FGA	Pct.	FT / FTA	Pct.	Reb. O / T	A	TO	PF	S	Blk	TP	PPM
FLEISHMAN	-	3/ -	-	0/ 0	.000	-/ -	-	-	4	-	-	6	-
GRENERT	-	3/ -	-	4/ 4	1.000	-/ -	-	-	4	-	-	10	-
LEGGAT	-	0/ -	-	1/ 2	.500	-/ -	-	-	0	-	-	1	-
MAHER, B.	-	3/ -	-	0/ 2	.000	-/ -	-	-	4	-	-	6	-
WEISSMAN	-	0/ -	-	0/ 0	.000	-/ -	-	-	0	-	-	0	-
DANTO	-	2/ -	-	1/ 1	1.000	-/ -	-	-	2	-	-	5	-
SIMMONS	-	3/ -	-	2/ 2	1.000	-/ -	-	-	0	-	-	8	-
MELE, S.	-	4/ -	-	5/ 6	.833	-/ -	-	-	2	-	-	13	-
Totals	200	18/ -	-	13/17	.765	-/ -	-	-	16	-	-	49	.245

Disqualified: Dartmouth—Skaug; NYU—Fleishman, Grenert, Maher.

	1st Half	2nd Half	Final
Dartmouth	25	26	51
NYU	19	30	49

REGIONAL THIRD PLACE WESTERN

Oklahoma (48)   Coach: Bruce Drake

	Min.	Total FG / FGA	Pct.	FT / FTA	Pct.	Reb. O / T	A	TO	PF	S	Blk	TP	PPM
HEAP, P.	-	2/ -	-	1/ 2	.500	-/ -	-	-	2	-	-	5	-
ROUSEY	-	0/ -	-	0/ 0	.000	-/ -	-	-	1	-	-	0	-
REICH, D.	-	6/ -	-	1/ 1	1.000	-/ -	-	-	2	-	-	13	-
PUGHLEY	-	0/ -	-	0/ 0	.000	-/ -	-	-	0	-	-	0	-
TUCKER, G.	-	6/ -	-	6/ 8	.750	-/ -	-	-	0	-	-	18	-
MARTENEY	-	1/ -	-	0/ 0	.000	-/ -	-	-	0	-	-	2	-
MCCURDY	-	0/ -	-	0/ 0	.000	-/ -	-	-	1	-	-	0	-
PAINE, A.	-	3/ -	-	4/ 4	1.000	-/ -	-	-	4	-	-	10	-
Totals	200	18/ -	-	12/15	.800	-/ -	-	-	10	-	-	48	.240

Washington (43)   Coach: Hec Edmunson

	Min.	Total FG / FGA	Pct.	FT / FTA	Pct.	Reb. O / T	A	TO	PF	S	Blk	TP	PPM
FORD, D.	-	1/ -	-	0/ 1	.000	-/ -	-	-	0	-	-	2	-
GISSBERG	-	3/ -	-	1/ 4	.250	-/ -	-	-	2	-	-	7	-
GILBERTSON, R.	-	3/ -	-	1/ 3	.333	-/ -	-	-	2	-	-	7	-
GILMER, C.	-	1/ -	-	0/ 0	.000	-/ -	-	-	4	-	-	2	-
MORRIS, B.	-	2/ -	-	1/ 2	.500	-/ -	-	-	4	-	-	5	-
BIRD	-	2/ -	-	0/ 0	.000	-/ -	-	-	0	-	-	4	-
TAYLOR	-	7/ -	-	2/ 2	1.000	-/ -	-	-	0	-	-	16	-
Totals	200	19/ -	-	5/12	.417	-/ -	-	-	12	-	-	43	.215

Disqualified: Oklahoma—Paine; Washington—Gilmer, Morris.

	1st Half	2nd Half	Final
Oklahoma	24	24	48
Washington	21	22	43

☉ INDIVIDUAL RECORDS ☉

SCORING

Most points in a single game
1 JOHN HARGIS, TEXAS (vs. WASHINGTON)   30
2 JOHN HARGIS, TEXAS (vs. WYOMING)   29
3 ROBERT MYERS, DARTMOUTH (vs. NYU)   22
3 BILL MORRIS, WASHINGTON (vs. TEXAS)   22
3 MILO KOMENICH, WYOMING (vs. OKLAHOMA)   22

Most total points in the tournament
1 JOHN HARGIS, TEXAS   59
2 MILO KOMENICH, WYOMING   48
3 JOHN MAHNKEN, GEORGETOWN   43
4 KENNY SAILORS, WYOMING   36
5 JIM WEIR, WYOMING   32

Highest scoring average (minimum 2 games)
1 JOHN HARGIS, TEXAS (59-2)   29.50
2 MILO KOMENICH, WYOMING (48-3)   16.00
3 GEORGE MIKAN, DEPAUL (31-2)   15.50
4 DICK REICH, OKLAHOMA (30-2)   15.00
5 2 tied for fifth place.

FIELD GOALS

Most field goals in a single game
1 ROBERT MYERS, DARTMOUTH (vs. NYU)   11
1 JOHN HARGIS, TEXAS (vs. WYOMING)   11
3 JOHN MAHNKEN, GEORGETOWN (vs. NYU)   10

3 JOHN HARGIS, TEXAS (vs. WASHINGTON)   10
3 MILO KOMENICH, WYOMING (vs. OKLAHOMA)   10

Most total field goals in the tournament
1 MILO KOMENICH, WYOMING   22
2 JOHN HARGIS, TEXAS   21
3 JOHN MAHNKEN, GEORGETOWN   20
4 JIM WEIR, WYOMING   14
4 KENNY SAILORS, WYOMING   14

FREE THROWS

Most free throws in a single game
1 JOHN HARGIS, TEXAS (vs. WASHINGTON)   10
2 JOHN HARGIS, TEXAS (vs. WYOMING)   7
2 DICK REICH, OKLAHOMA (vs. WYOMING)   7
2 BILL HASSETT, GEORGETOWN (vs. DEPAUL)   7
5 3 tied for fifth place.

Most total free throws in the tournament
1 JOHN HARGIS, TEXAS   17
2 GEORGE MIKAN, DEPAUL   11
3 BILL HASSETT, GEORGETOWN   10
4 BUCK OVERALL, TEXAS   9
5 2 tied for fifth place.

Most free throws attempted in a single game
1 JOHN HARGIS, TEXAS (vs. WYOMING)   12
1 JOHN HARGIS, TEXAS (vs. WASHINGTON)   12

1 DICK REICH, OKLAHOMA (vs. WYOMING)   12
4 BILL MORRIS, WASHINGTON (vs. TEXAS)   9
5 2 tied for fifth place.

Most free throws attempted in the tournament
1 JOHN HARGIS, TEXAS   24
2 GEORGE MIKAN, DEPAUL   15
3 4 tied for third place.

Highest free throw percentage in a single game (minimum 7 attempts)
1 BILL HASSETT, GEORGETOWN (vs. DEPAUL) (7-7)   1.000
2 JOHN HARGIS, TEXAS (vs. WASHINGTON) (10-12)   .833
3 GERALD TUCKER, OKLAHOMA (vs. WASHINGTON) (6-8)   .750
3 GEORGE MIKAN, DEPAUL (vs. DARTMOUTH) (6-8)   .750
5 GEORGE MIKAN, DEPAUL (vs. GEORGETOWN) (5-7)   .714

Highest free throw percentage in the tournament (minimum 15 attempts)
1 GEORGE MIKAN, DEPAUL (11-15)   .733
2 JOHN HARGIS, TEXAS (17-24)   .708

✪ TEAM RECORDS ✪

SCORING

Most points in a single game
1	TEXAS (vs. WASHINGTON)	59
2	WYOMING (vs. TEXAS)	58
3	2 tied for third place.	

Most total points in the tournament
1	WYOMING	157
2	GEORGETOWN	142
3	TEXAS	113

Highest scoring average (minimum 2 games)
1	TEXAS (113-2)	56.50
2	WYOMING (157-3)	52.33
3	2 tied for third place.	

FIELD GOALS

Most field goals in a single game
1	WYOMING (vs. TEXAS)	24
1	WYOMING (vs. OKLAHOMA)	24
1	GEORGETOWN (vs. NYU)	24

Most total field goals in the tournament
1	WYOMING	67
2	GEORGETOWN	58
3	TEXAS	41

FREE THROWS

Most free throws in a single game
1	TEXAS (vs. WASHINGTON)	17
2	TEXAS (vs. WYOMING)	14
3	NYU (vs. DARTMOUTH)	13
3	WASHINGTON (vs. TEXAS)	13
3	GEORGETOWN (vs. DEPAUL)	13

Most total free throws in the tournament
1	TEXAS	31
2	GEORGETOWN	26
3	OKLAHOMA	24

Most free throws attempted in a single game
1	WASHINGTON (vs. TEXAS)	25
2	TEXAS (vs. WYOMING)	23
3	TEXAS (vs. WASHINGTON)	22

Most total free throws attempted in the tournament
1	TEXAS	45
2	WYOMING	44
3	GEORGETOWN	40

Highest free throw percentage in a single game
1	OKLAHOMA (vs. WASHINGTON) (12-15)	.800
2	GEORGETOWN (vs. NYU) (7-9)	.778
3	TEXAS (vs. WASHINGTON) (17-22)	.773

Highest free throw percentage in the tournament (minimum 2 games)
1	OKLAHOMA (24-34)	.706
2	DEPAUL (23-33)	.697
3	TEXAS (31-45)	.689

Fewest free throws in a single game
1	WYOMING (vs. OKLAHOMA)	5
1	WASHINGTON (vs. OKLAHOMA)	5
3	2 tied for third place.	

Lowest free throw percentage in a single game
1	WASHINGTON (vs. OKLAHOMA) (5-12)	.417
2	GEORGETOWN (vs. WYOMING) (6-14)	.429
3	WYOMING (vs. GEORGETOWN) (8-18)	.444

Lowest free throw percentage in the tournament (minimum 2 games)
1	WASHINGTON (18-37)	.487
2	WYOMING (23-44)	.523
3	DARTMOUTH (20-34)	.588

1944

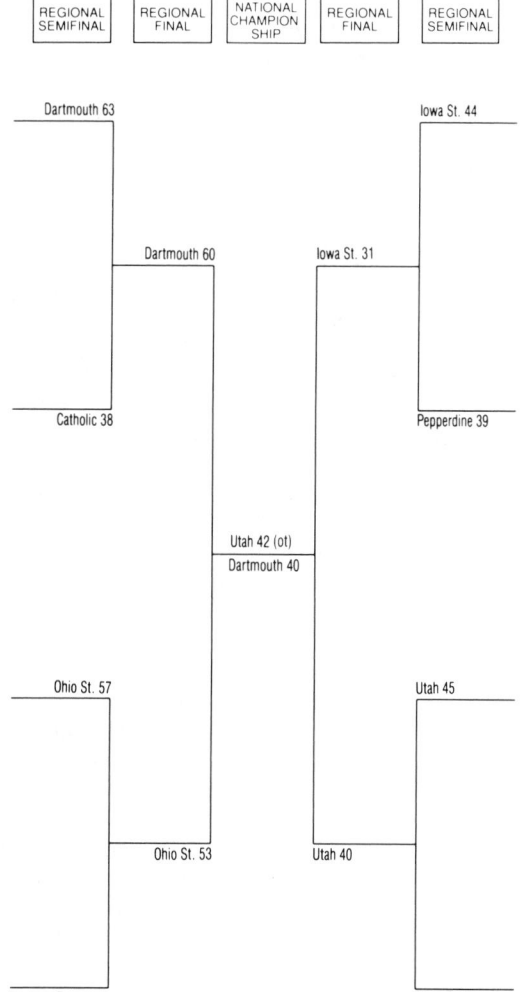

EASTERN

WESTERN

| REGIONAL SEMIFINAL | REGIONAL FINAL | NATIONAL CHAMPIONSHIP | REGIONAL FINAL | REGIONAL SEMIFINAL |

Dartmouth 63

Iowa St. 44

Dartmouth 60

Iowa St. 31

Catholic 38

Pepperdine 39

Utah 42 (ot)
Dartmouth 40

Ohio St. 57

Utah 45

Ohio St. 53

Utah 40

Temple 47

Missouri 35

CONSOLATION GAMES

Regional Third Place:

Western:
Missouri 61
Pepperdine 46

Eastern:
Temple 55
Catholic 35

It wasn't an ordinary tournament. Utah wasn't even supposed to be there. And with the war continuing, the Dartmouth players needed a naval commander's permission to play. But despite their odd routes into the tournament, both the Utes and the Hanover Indians stormed their way into the finals, where they fought down to the wire for the NCAA title.

At the end of the regular season, Utah received invitations to both the NCAA tournament and the NIT. When the New York invitational agreed to pay the Rocky Mountain team's expenses and the NCAA refused to match the offer, the Utes passed on the national event and headed for New York. But after they lost to Kentucky in the first round of the NIT they got another call from the NCAA. Arkansas, the team selected to replace the youthful Utes in the tournament, had been forced to withdraw because of injuries suffered by two of its players in a car crash. Would Utah consider coming to Kansas City, where the NCAA was holding its West regional?

Rather than go home in defeat, Utah accepted. They turned in their train tickets to the Rockies and headed for Kansas City. As it turned out they should have bought round-trip tickets, because they were soon headed back to New York and Madison Square Garden to play for the national championship.

The Utes had little trouble advancing to the final. Led by forward Arnold Ferrin, they took a 20-point lead early in the second half of their opener against Missouri, and coasted in for a 10-point victory. In the regional final against Iowa State, the Big Six Conference co-champs, Utah trailed only twice, after the Cyclones opened the scoring to take a 2-0 lead, and at the start of the second half, when Iowa State took a momentary 1-point lead.

On the other side of the draw, Dartmouth steamed full-speed ahead in sweeping through the Eastern regional. Although the Indians were seven-time winners of the Eastern League championship, they were helped considerably by a squad of new recruits who were stationed at Dartmouth as trainees for naval service. Three men in particular had been stars at other colleges during the regular season, before they were inducted into the Navy. There was Bob Gale, who earlier in the season was taking his shots for Cornell; Dick McGuire of St. John's, who just a day before the tournament began was awarded the Lieut. Frank C. Haggerty Memorial Award as New York City's Most Valuable Player (even without him the Redmen won the NIT); and Harry Leggatt of NYU. Plus, of course, Dartmouth had its own regular players, including Aud Brindley, the Eastern League's top scorer.

In their opener, the Indians simply outclassed Catholic University of Washington. Then they came up against the Buckeyes of Ohio State. The Big Ten champions, an explosive, hard-driving outfit, hoped to give their conference its third straight title, and at the outset they were favored to go all the way. But after an easy opening round victory over Temple, they were ambushed by the Indians. Dartmouth ran with them and shot with them. McGuire was unrelenting on defense, and Brindley was brilliant on offense. He exploded for 28 points, a Garden high for the year, and hit an amazing 65 percent of his shots from the floor as he broke the tournament field-goal record with 13.

It was on to Kansas City.

The showdown between Dartmouth and Utah was tight and tense from the opening tip to the final buzzer. Although both teams handled the ball like a hot potato, shot as though there was a lid on the basket, and in general played poorly, the title contest still provided a heart-stopping conclusion for a tournament which had not, up until that point, been highly competitive.

Neither team led by more than 4 points at any time during the game. Utah was ahead most of the way, but the Indians hung in. Still, with two minutes left Utah held a 4-point lead. Dartmouth was forced to foul to get the ball, but Utah, in a questionable strategic move, waived their foul shots. (The rules in 1944 permitted a team to either shoot the free throws or retain possession; in the end the Utah decision to hold on to the ball prevented them from building their lead and allowed Dartmouth to stay in the game.) Dartmouth cut the lead to 2, and with just seconds remaining, McGuire got the ball back. He raced downcourt, leading a three-man fast break. With three seconds left, he threw up a desperate set-shot. It dropped in, forcing an overtime.

The score was still tied when Brindley converted a feed from McGuire with less than two minutes left. The ball went back and forth until Utah took the ball out at their end of the floor with 20 seconds left. The Utes moved the ball quickly downcourt, but the Indians wouldn't give an inch. With the clock ticking away, guard Herb Wilkinson found himself with the ball far beyond the top of the key. With three seconds remaining and all his teammates covered, he was out of options—he had to shoot. He planted his feet, lofted a mortar shot, and watched as the ball hung on the rim for a moment before it fell through. Utah, first round losers in the NIT, were the champions of the NCAA.

Dartmouth's naval trainees returned to active duty, but the Utes stayed in New York. Two nights later they were back in Madison Square Garden, facing off against the NIT champs from St. John's in a game to benefit the Red Cross. The Utes won, and this time, when they got on the train for the long ride back home, it was not as first round losers, but as the undisputed national champions.

REGIONAL SEMIFINAL EASTERN

Dartmouth (63)   Coach: Earl Brown

	Min.	Total FG / FGA	Pct.	FT / FTA	Pct.	Reb. O / T	A	TO	PF	S	Blk	TP	PPM
LEGGAT, H.	27	7/ -	-	1/ 5	.200	-/ -	-	-	4	-	-	15	.556
GALE, B.	40	8/ -	-	1/ 1	1.000	-/ -	-	-	1	-	-	17	.425
BRINDLEY, A.	34	6/ -	-	1/ 1	1.000	-/ -	-	-	2	-	-	13	.382
MURPHY, F.	5	0/ -	-	0/ 0	.000	-/ -	-	-	0	-	-	0	.000
VANCISIN, J.	17	3/ -	-	0/ 0	.000	-/ -	-	-	2	-	-	6	.353
GOERING, V.	9	1/ -	-	0/ 0	.000	-/ -	-	-	0	-	-	2	.222
MERCER, W.	13	1/ -	-	0/ 0	.000	-/ -	-	-	1	-	-	2	.154
MCGUIRE, D.	40	4/ -	-	0/ 0	.000	-/ -	-	-	2	-	-	8	.200
WILSON, F.	1	0/ -	-	0/ 0	.000	-/ -	-	-	0	-	-	0	.000
MONAHAN, J.	14	0/ -	-	0/ 2	.000	-/ -	-	-	0	-	-	0	.000
Totals	200	30/ -	-	3/ 9	.333	-/ -	-	-	12	-	-	63	.315

Catholic (38)   Coach: John Long

	Min.	Total FG / FGA	Pct.	FT / FTA	Pct.	Reb. O / T	A	TO	PF	S	Blk	TP	PPM
SZKLARZ, G.	40	2/ -	-	2/ 5	.400	-/ -	-	-	1	-	-	6	.150
MERZAC	40	5/ -	-	2/ 3	.667	-/ -	-	-	0	-	-	12	.300
SCANLON, D.	40	4/ -	-	3/ 5	.600	-/ -	-	-	4	-	-	11	.275
CARLIN	40	1/ -	-	0/ 0	.000	-/ -	-	-	1	-	-	2	.050
RICE	31	3/ -	-	1/ 3	.333	-/ -	-	-	0	-	-	7	.226
KINGSBURY	9	0/ -	-	0/ 0	.000	-/ -	-	-	0	-	-	0	.000
Totals	200	15/ -	-	8/16	.500	-/ -	-	-	6	-	-	38	.190

Disqualified: Dartmouth—Leggat; Catholic—Scanlon.

	1st Half	2nd Half	Final
Dartmouth	28	35	63
Catholic	12	26	38

Ohio State (57)   Coach: Harold Olsen

	Min.	Total FG / FGA	Pct.	FT / FTA	Pct.	Reb. O / T	A	TO	PF	S	Blk	TP	PPM
GRATE, D.	-	8/ -	-	1/ 2	.500	-/ -	-	-	3	-	-	17	-
PLANK, E.	-	0/ -	-	0/ 0	.000	-/ -	-	-	0	-	-	0	-
DUGGER, J.	-	2/ -	-	0/ 0	.000	-/ -	-	-	0	-	-	4	-
CAUDILL, R.	-	3/ -	-	0/ 1	.000	-/ -	-	-	0	-	-	6	-
RISEN, A.	-	3/ -	-	1/ 3	.333	-/ -	-	-	3	-	-	7	-
BOWEN, R.	-	4/ -	-	2/ 5	.400	-/ -	-	-	3	-	-	10	-
FINK, J.	-	0/ -	-	1/ 4	.250	-/ -	-	-	0	-	-	1	-
HUSTON, P.	-	5/ -	-	2/ 2	1.000	-/ -	-	-	2	-	-	12	-
GUNTON, B.	-	0/ -	-	0/ 0	.000	-/ -	-	-	0	-	-	0	-
Totals	200	25/ -	-	7/17	.412	-/ -	-	-	11	-	-	57	.285

Temple (47)   Coach: Josh Cody

	Min.	Total FG / FGA	Pct.	FT / FTA	Pct.	Reb. O / T	A	TO	PF	S	Blk	TP	PPM
KOECHER	-	5/ -	-	2/ 3	.667	-/ -	-	-	4	-	-	12	-
JOYCE, J.	-	7/ -	-	2/ 6	.333	-/ -	-	-	0	-	-	16	-
BUDD	-	2/ -	-	0/ 0	.000	-/ -	-	-	3	-	-	4	-
BRAMBLE	-	3/ -	-	0/ 0	.000	-/ -	-	-	0	-	-	6	-
BURNS	-	0/ -	-	0/ 0	.000	-/ -	-	-	0	-	-	0	-
FOX	-	2/ -	-	5/ 6	.833	-/ -	-	-	3	-	-	9	-
COLLINS	-	0/ -	-	0/ 0	.000	-/ -	-	-	0	-	-	0	-
Totals	200	19/ -	-	9/15	.600	-/ -	-	-	10	-	-	47	.235

Disqualified: Temple—Koecher.

	1st Half	2nd Half	Final
Ohio State	26	31	57
Temple	23	24	47

REGIONAL SEMIFINAL WESTERN

Iowa State (44)   Coach: Louis Menze

	Min.	Total FG / FGA	Pct.	FT / FTA	Pct.	Reb. O / T	A	TO	PF	S	Blk	TP	PPM
WEHDE, RAY.	-	1/ -	-	2/ -	-	-/ -	-	-	-	-	-	4	-
WEHDE, ROY.	-	5/ -	-	2/ -	-	-/ -	-	-	-	-	-	12	-
MYERS, J.	-	5/ -	-	1/ -	-	-/ -	-	-	-	-	-	11	-
BROOKFIELD, P.	-	4/ -	-	2/ -	-	-/ -	-	-	-	-	-	10	-
OULMAN, G.	-	1/ -	-	0/ -	-	-/ -	-	-	-	-	-	2	-
BLOCK, W.	-	1/ -	-	0/ -	-	-/ -	-	-	-	-	-	2	-
SAUER, R.	-	0/ -	-	3/ -	-	-/ -	-	-	-	-	-	3	-
Totals	200	17/ -	-	10/ -	-	-/ -	-	-	-	-	-	44	.220

Pepperdine (39)   Coach: Al Duer

	Min.	Total FG / FGA	Pct.	FT / FTA	Pct.	Reb. O / T	A	TO	PF	S	Blk	TP	PPM
RUBY, L.	-	2/ -	-	1/ -	-	-/ -	-	-	-	-	-	5	-
WANDELL, L.	-	0/ -	-	0/ -	-	-/ -	-	-	-	-	-	0	-
NUNN, W.	-	2/ -	-	0/ -	-	-/ -	-	-	-	-	-	4	-
ASHER, R.	-	0/ -	-	0/ -	-	-/ -	-	-	-	-	-	0	-
BUZOLICH, N.	-	9/ -	-	4/ -	-	-/ -	-	-	-	-	-	22	-
WHALEY, B.	-	2/ -	-	1/ -	-	-/ -	-	-	-	-	-	5	-
WITECK, J.	-	1/ -	-	1/ -	-	-/ -	-	-	-	-	-	3	-
Totals	200	16/ -	-	7/ -	-	-/ -	-	-	-	-	-	39	.195

	1st Half	2nd Half	Final
Iowa State	0	0	44
Pepperdine	0	0	39

Utah (45)   Coach: Vadal Peterson

	Min.	Total FG / FGA	Pct.	FT / FTA	Pct.	Reb. O / T	A	TO	PF	S	Blk	TP	PPM
FERRIN, A.	-	5/ -	-	2/ 2	1.000	-/ -	-	-	1	-	-	12	-
SMUIN, D.	-	3/ -	-	1/ 2	.500	-/ -	-	-	3	-	-	7	-
NANCE, J.	-	0/ -	-	0/ 0	.000	-/ -	-	-	0	-	-	0	-
SHEFFIELD, F.	-	3/ -	-	1/ 1	1.000	-/ -	-	-	1	-	-	7	-
MISAKA, W.	-	2/ -	-	1/ 1	1.000	-/ -	-	-	4	-	-	5	-
LEWIS, F.	-	0/ -	-	0/ 1	.000	-/ -	-	-	1	-	-	0	-
WILKINSON, H.	-	3/ -	-	2/ 3	.667	-/ -	-	-	1	-	-	8	-
LEWIS, B.	-	3/ -	-	0/ 1	.000	-/ -	-	-	2	-	-	6	-
KINGSTON, R.	-	0/ -	-	0/ 0	.000	-/ -	-	-	0	-	-	0	-
Totals	200	19/ -	-	7/11	.636	-/ -	-	-	13	-	-	45	.225

Missouri (35)   Coach: George Edwards

	Min.	Total FG / FGA	Pct.	FT / FTA	Pct.	Reb. O / T	A	TO	PF	S	Blk	TP	PPM
CROWDER	36	3/ -	-	1/ 1	1.000	-/ -	-	-	3	-	-	7	.194
BROWN	4	1/ -	-	0/ 0	.000	-/ -	-	-	0	-	-	2	.500
MINX, C.	40	2/ -	-	1/ 3	.333	-/ -	-	-	2	-	-	5	.125
PIPPIN	38	3/ -	-	0/ 1	.000	-/ -	-	-	0	-	-	6	.158
TOAL	2	0/ -	-	0/ 1	.000	-/ -	-	-	0	-	-	0	.000
MINX, B.	40	2/ -	-	1/ 2	.500	-/ -	-	-	3	-	-	5	.125
COLLINS	35	4/ -	-	2/ 7	.286	-/ -	-	-	3	-	-	10	.286
HEINSOHN	5	0/ -	-	0/ 0	.000	-/ -	-	-	0	-	-	0	.000
Totals	200	15/ -	-	5/15	.333	-/ -	-	-	11	-	-	35	.175

Disqualified: Utah—Misaka.

	1st Half	2nd Half	Final
Utah	27	18	45
Missouri	14	21	35

REGIONAL FINAL EASTERN

Dartmouth (60) Coach: Earl Brown

	Min.	Total FG/FGA	Pct.	FT/FTA	Pct.	Reb. O/T	A	TO	PF	S	Blk	TP	PPM
LEGGAT, H.	40	5/ -	-	2/ 4	.500	-/ -	-	-	2	-	-	12	.300
GALE, B.	40	3/ -	-	1/ 1	1.000	-/ -	-	-	2	-	-	7	.175
BRINDLEY, A.	40	13/ -	-	2/ 3	.667	-/ -	-	-	3	-	-	28	.700
VANCISIN, J.	25	0/ -	-	0/ 0	.000	-/ -	-	-	2	-	-	0	.000
MCGUIRE, D.	40	4/ -	-	1/ 3	.333	-/ -	-	-	1	-	-	9	.225
MONAHAN, J.	15	2/ -	-	0/ 0	.000	-/ -	-	-	1	-	-	4	.267
Totals	200	27/ -	-	6/11	.545	-/ -	-	-	11	-	-	60	.300

Ohio State (53) Coach: Harold Olsen

	Min.	Total FG/FGA	Pct.	FT/FTA	Pct.	Reb. O/T	A	TO	PF	S	Blk	TP	PPM
GRATE, D.	40	3/ -	-	1/ 2	.500	-/ -	-	-	2	-	-	7	.175
DUGGER, J.	29	3/ -	-	2/ 6	.333	-/ -	-	-	4	-	-	8	.276
CAUDILL, R.	5	0/ -	-	0/ 0	.000	-/ -	-	-	1	-	-	0	.000
RISEN, A.	35	8/ -	-	5/ 6	.833	-/ -	-	-	0	-	-	21	.600
BOWEN, R.	34	3/ -	-	0/ 0	.000	-/ -	-	-	1	-	-	6	.176
FINK, J.	6	0/ -	-	0/ 0	.000	-/ -	-	-	0	-	-	0	.000
HUSTON, P.	40	5/ -	-	1/ 1	1.000	-/ -	-	-	3	-	-	11	.275
GUNTON, B.	11	0/ -	-	0/ 0	.000	-/ -	-	-	0	-	-	0	.000
Totals	200	22/ -	-	9/15	.600	-/ -	-	-	11	-	-	53	.265

Disqualified: Ohio State—Dugger.

	1st Half	2nd Half	Final
Dartmouth	31	29	60
Ohio State	28	25	53

REGIONAL FINAL WESTERN

Iowa State (31) Coach: Louis Menze

	Min.	Total FG/FGA	Pct.	FT/FTA	Pct.	Reb. O/T	A	TO	PF	S	Blk	TP	PPM
WEHDE, RAY.	-	2/ -	-	1/ -	-	-/ -	-	-	-	-	-	5	-
BLOCK, W.	-	2/ -	-	1/ -	-	-/ -	-	-	-	-	-	5	-
WEHDE, ROY.	-	2/ -	-	0/ -	-	-/ -	-	-	-	-	-	4	-
BROOKFIELD, P.	-	3/ -	-	0/ -	-	-/ -	-	-	-	-	-	6	-
EWOLDT, R.	-	0/ -	-	0/ -	-	-/ -	-	-	-	-	-	0	-
OULMAN, G.	-	2/ -	-	1/ -	-	-/ -	-	-	-	-	-	5	-
SAUER, R.	-	0/ -	-	2/ -	-	-/ -	-	-	-	-	-	2	-
MYERS, J.	-	2/ -	-	0/ -	-	-/ -	-	-	-	-	-	4	-
Totals	200	13/ -	-	5/ -	-	-/ -	-	-	-	-	-	31	.155

Utah (40) Coach: Vadal Peterson

	Min.	Total FG/FGA	Pct.	FT/FTA	Pct.	Reb. O/T	A	TO	PF	S	Blk	TP	PPM
FERRIN, A.	-	3/ -	-	0/ -	-	-/ -	-	-	-	-	-	6	-
SMUIN, D.	-	2/ -	-	1/ -	-	-/ -	-	-	-	-	-	5	-
SHEFFIELD, F.	-	4/ -	-	1/ -	-	-/ -	-	-	-	-	-	9	-
MISAKA, W.	-	4/ -	-	1/ -	-	-/ -	-	-	-	-	-	9	-
WILKINSON, H.	-	1/ -	-	2/ -	-	-/ -	-	-	-	-	-	4	-
LEWIS, B.	-	3/ -	-	1/ -	-	-/ -	-	-	-	-	-	7	-
Totals	200	17/ -	-	6/ -	-	-/ -	-	-	-	-	-	40	.200

	1st Half	2nd Half	Final
Iowa State	16	15	31
Utah	19	21	40

CHAMPIONSHIP

Dartmouth (40) Coach: Earl Brown

	Min.	Total FG/FGA	Pct.	FT/FTA	Pct.	Reb. O/T	A	TO	PF	S	Blk	TP	PPM
LEGGAT, H.	34	4/ -	-	0/ 0	.000	-/ -	-	-	1	-	-	8	.235
GALE, B.	37	5/ -	-	0/ 2	.000	-/ -	-	-	1	-	-	10	.270
NORDSTROM, E.	8	0/ -	-	0/ 0	.000	-/ -	-	-	0	-	-	0	.000
BRINDLEY, A.	39	5/ -	-	1/ 1	1.000	-/ -	-	-	3	-	-	11	.282
MURPHY, F.	17	0/ -	-	0/ 0	.000	-/ -	-	-	0	-	-	0	.000
VANCISIN, J.	19	2/ -	-	0/ 0	.000	-/ -	-	-	3	-	-	4	.211
GOERING, V.	14	0/ -	-	0/ 0	.000	-/ -	-	-	0	-	-	0	.000
MERCER, W.	19	0/ -	-	1/ 1	1.000	-/ -	-	-	3	-	-	1	.053
MCGUIRE, D.	38	3/ -	-	0/ 1	.000	-/ -	-	-	3	-	-	6	.158
Totals	225	19/ -	-	2/ 5	.400	-/ -	-	-	14	-	-	40	.178

Utah (42) Coach: Vadal Peterson

	Min.	Total FG/FGA	Pct.	FT/FTA	Pct.	Reb. O/T	A	TO	PF	S	Blk	TP	PPM
SMUIN, D.	45	0/ -	-	0/ 0	.000	-/ -	-	-	2	-	-	0	.000
FERRIN, A.	45	8/ -	-	6/ 7	.857	-/ -	-	-	0	-	-	22	.489
SHEFFIELD, F.	4	1/ -	-	0/ 0	.000	-/ -	-	-	1	-	-	2	.500
MISAKA, W.	41	2/ -	-	0/ 0	.000	-/ -	-	-	1	-	-	4	.098
WILKINSON, H.	45	3/ -	-	1/ 4	.250	-/ -	-	-	0	-	-	7	.156
LEWIS, B.	45	2/ -	-	3/ 3	1.000	-/ -	-	-	2	-	-	7	.156
Totals	225	16/ -	-	10/14	.714	-/ -	-	-	6	-	-	42	.187

Disqualified: None.

	1st Half	2nd Half	1st OT	Final
Dartmouth	18	18	4	40
Utah	17	19	6	42

REGIONAL THIRD PLACE EASTERN

Temple (55)   Coach: Josh Cody

	Min.	Total FG / FGA	Pct.	FT / FTA	Pct.	Reb. O / T	A	TO	PF	S	Blk	TP	PPM
KOECHER	-	3/ -	-	2/ 2	1.000	-/ -	-	-	4	-	-	8	-
JOYCE, J.	-	7/ -	-	1/ 2	.500	-/ -	-	-	1	-	-	15	-
BUDD	-	2/ -	-	0/ 1	.000	-/ -	-	-	2	-	-	4	-
BRAMBLE	-	3/ -	-	0/ 0	.000	-/ -	-	-	2	-	-	6	-
FOX	-	3/ -	-	0/ 0	.000	-/ -	-	-	1	-	-	6	-
BURNS	-	4/ -	-	0/ 1	.000	-/ -	-	-	2	-	-	8	-
ROSEN	-	3/ -	-	1/ 1	1.000	-/ -	-	-	1	-	-	7	-
COLLINS	-	0/ -	-	1/ 2	.500	-/ -	-	-	0	-	-	1	-
Totals	200	25/ -	-	5/ 9	.556	-/ -	-	-	13	-	-	55	.275

Catholic (35)   Coach: John Long

	Min.	Total FG / FGA	Pct.	FT / FTA	Pct.	Reb. O / T	A	TO	PF	S	Blk	TP	PPM
MERCAK	-	1/ -	-	1/ 1	1.000	·	-/ -	-	-	1	-	-	3	-
SZKLARZ, G.	-	5/ -	-	2/ 2	1.000	-/ -	-	-	0	-	-	12	-
SCANLON, D.	-	4/ -	-	4/ 9	.444	-/ -	-	-	3	-	-	12	-
KINGSBURY	-	0/ -	-	0/ 0	.000	-/ -	-	-	0	-	-	0	-
RICE	-	3/ -	-	1/ 1	1.000	-/ -	-	-	2	-	-	7	-
CARLIN	-	0/ -	-	1/ 4	.250	-/ -	-	-	2	-	-	1	-
Totals	200	13/ -	-	9/17	.529	-/ -	-	-	8	-	-	35	.175

Disqualified: Temple—Koecher.

	1st Half	2nd Half	Final
Temple	24	31	55
Catholic	21	14	35

REGIONAL THIRD PLACE WESTERN

Missouri (61)   Coach: George Edwards

	Min.	Total FG / FGA	Pct.	FT / FTA	Pct.	Reb. O / T	A	TO	PF	S	Blk	TP	PPM
CROWDER	30	2/ -	-	3/ 3	1.000	-/ -	-	-	2	-	-	7	.233
BROWN	12	3/ -	-	0/ 0	.000	-/ -	-	-	0	-	-	6	.500
MINX, C.	38	8/ -	-	5/ 7	.714	-/ -	-	-	1	-	-	21	.553
TOAL	2	0/ -	-	0/ 0	.000	-/ -	-	-	1	-	-	0	.000
PIPPIN	25	5/ -	-	2/ 4	.500	-/ -	-	-	4	-	-	12	.480
HEINSOHN	13	1/ -	-	0/ 2	.000	-/ -	-	-	3	-	-	2	.154
MINX, B.	38	1/ -	-	2/ 3	.667	-/ -	-	-	2	-	-	4	.105
DELLASTATIOUS	11	0/ -	-	0/ 0	.000	-/ -	-	-	0	-	-	0	.000
COLLINS	30	3/ -	-	3/ 6	.500	-/ -	-	-	2	-	-	9	.300
CLINKINGBEARD	1	0/ -	-	0/ 0	.000	-/ -	-	-	0	-	-	0	.000
Totals	200	23/ -	-	15/25	.600	-/ -	-	-	15	-	-	61	.305

Pepperdine (46)   Coach: Al Duer

	Min.	Total FG / FGA	Pct.	FT / FTA	Pct.	Reb. O / T	A	TO	PF	S	Blk	TP	PPM
RUBY, L.	-	2/ -	-	1/ 3	.333	-/ -	-	-	4	-	-	5	-
LEWIS, D.	-	0/ -	-	0/ 0	.000	-/ -	-	-	0	-	-	0	-
NUNN, W.	-	2/ -	-	0/ 0	.000	-/ -	-	-	4	-	-	4	-
ASHER, R.	-	2/ -	-	2/ 3	.667	-/ -	-	-	1	-	-	6	-
BUZOLICH, N.	-	8/ -	-	7/10	.700	-/ -	-	-	4	-	-	23	-
WANDELL, L.	-	1/ -	-	0/ 0	.000	-/ -	-	-	1	-	-	2	-
WHALEY, B.	-	3/ -	-	0/ 2	.000	-/ -	-	-	4	-	-	6	-
RICHARDSON, C.	-	0/ -	-	0/ 0	.000	-/ -	-	-	0	-	-	0	-
WITECK, J.	-	0/ -	-	0/ 0	.000	-/ -	-	-	2	-	-	0	-
LAWYER, R.	-	0/ -	-	0/ 0	.000	-/ -	-	-	0	-	-	0	-
Totals	200	18/ -	-	10/18	.556	-/ -	-	-	20	-	-	46	.230

Disqualified: Missouri—Pippin; Pepperdine—Ruby, Nunn, Buzolich, Whaley.

	1st Half	2nd Half	Final
Missouri	26	35	61
Pepperdine	21	25	46

✪ INDIVIDUAL RECORDS ✪

SCORING

Most points in a single game
1. AUD BRINDLEY, DARTMOUTH (vs. OHIO STATE)   28
2. NICK BUZOLICH, PEPPERDINE (vs. MISSOURI)   23
3. NICK BUZOLICH, PEPPERDINE (vs. IOWA STATE)   22
3. ARNOLD FERRIN, UTAH (vs. DARTMOUTH)   22
5. 2 tied for fifth place.

Most total points in the tournament
1. AUD BRINDLEY, DARTMOUTH   52
2. NICK BUZOLICH, PEPPERDINE   45
3. ARNOLD FERRIN, UTAH   40
4. HARRY LEGGAT, DARTMOUTH   35
5. BOB GALE, DARTMOUTH   34

Highest scoring average (minimum 2 games)
1. NICK BUZOLICH, PEPPERDINE (45-2)   22.50
2. AUD BRINDLEY, DARTMOUTH (52-3)   17.33
3. JIM JOYCE, TEMPLE (31-2)   15.50
4. ARNOLD RISEN, OHIO STATE (28-2)   14.00
5. ARNOLD FERRIN, UTAH (40-3)   13.33

FIELD GOALS

Most field goals in a single game
1. AUD BRINDLEY, DARTMOUTH (vs. OHIO STATE)   13
2. NICK BUZOLICH, PEPPERDINE (vs. IOWA STATE)   9
3. 6 tied for third place.

Most total field goals in the tournament
1. AUD BRINDLEY, DARTMOUTH   24
2. NICK BUZOLICH, PEPPERDINE   17
3. HARRY LEGGAT, DARTMOUTH   16
3. BOB GALE, DARTMOUTH   16
3. ARNOLD FERRIN, UTAH   16

FREE THROWS

Most free throws in a single game
1. NICK BUZOLICH, PEPPERDINE (vs. MISSOURI)   7
2. ARNOLD FERRIN, UTAH (vs. DARTMOUTH)   6
3. C. MINX, MISSOURI (vs. PEPPERDINE)   5
3. ARNOLD RISEN, OHIO STATE (vs. DARTMOUTH)   5
3. FOX, TEMPLE (vs. OHIO STATE)   5

Most total free throws in the tournament
1. NICK BUZOLICH, PEPPERDINE   11
2. ARNOLD FERRIN, UTAH   8
3. DICK SCANLON, CATHOLIC   7
4. ARNOLD RISEN, OHIO STATE   6
4. C. MINX, MISSOURI   6

Most free throws attempted in a single game
1. NICK BUZOLICH, PEPPERDINE (vs. MISSOURI)   10
2. DICK SCANLON, CATHOLIC (vs. TEMPLE)   9
3. COLLINS, MISSOURI (vs. UTAH)   7
3. C. MINX, MISSOURI (vs. PEPPERDINE)   7
3. ARNOLD FERRIN, UTAH (vs. DARTMOUTH)   7

Highest free throw percentage in a single game (minimum 7 attempts)
1. ARNOLD FERRIN, UTAH (vs. DARTMOUTH) (6-7)   .857
2. C. MINX, MISSOURI (vs. PEPPERDINE) (5-7)   .714
3. NICK BUZOLICH, PEPPERDINE (vs. MISSOURI) (7-10)   .700
4. DICK SCANLON, CATHOLIC (vs. TEMPLE) (4-9)   .444
5. COLLINS, MISSOURI (vs. UTAH) (2-7)   .286

❂ TEAM RECORDS ❂

SCORING

Most points in a single game

1	DARTMOUTH (vs. CATHOLIC)	63
2	MISSOURI (vs. PEPPERDINE)	61
3	DARTMOUTH (vs. OHIO STATE)	60

Most total points in the tournament

1	DARTMOUTH	163
2	UTAH	127
3	OHIO STATE	110

Highest scoring average (minimum 2 games)

1	OHIO STATE (110-2)	55.00
2	DARTMOUTH (163-3)	54.33
3	TEMPLE (102-2)	51.00

FIELD GOALS

Most field goals in a single game

1	DARTMOUTH (vs. CATHOLIC)	30
2	DARTMOUTH (vs. OHIO STATE)	27
3	2 tied for third place.	

Most total field goals in the tournament

1	DARTMOUTH	76
2	UTAH	52
3	OHIO STATE	47

FREE THROWS

Most free throws in a single game

1	MISSOURI (vs. PEPPERDINE)	15
2	3 tied for second place.	

Most total free throws in the tournament

1	UTAH	23
2	MISSOURI	20
3	2 tied for third place.	

Most free throws attempted in a single game

1	MISSOURI (vs. PEPPERDINE)	25
2	PEPPERDINE (vs. MISSOURI)	18
3	2 tied for third place.	

Highest free throw percentage in a single game

1	UTAH (vs. DARTMOUTH) (10-14)	.714
2	UTAH (vs. MISSOURI) (7-11)	.636
3	MISSOURI (vs. PEPPERDINE) (15-25)	.600

Fewest free throws in a single game

1	DARTMOUTH (vs. UTAH)	2
2	DARTMOUTH (vs. CATHOLIC)	3
3	MISSOURI (vs. UTAH)	5
3	IOWA STATE (vs. UTAH)	5
3	TEMPLE (vs. CATHOLIC)	5

Lowest free throw percentage in a single game

1	DARTMOUTH (vs. CATHOLIC) (3-9)	.333
2	MISSOURI (vs. UTAH) (5-15)	.333
3	DARTMOUTH (vs. UTAH) (2-5)	.400

1945

EASTERN

| REGIONAL SEMIFINAL | REGIONAL FINAL | NATIONAL CHAMPION- SHIP | REGIONAL FINAL | REGIONAL SEMIFINAL |

NYU 59

Arkansas 79

NYU 70 (ot)

Arkansas 41

Tufts 44

Oregon 76

Oklahoma A&M 49
NYU 45

Ohio St. 45

Oklahoma A&M 62

Ohio St. 65

Oklahoma A&M 68

Kentucky 37

Utah 37

WESTERN

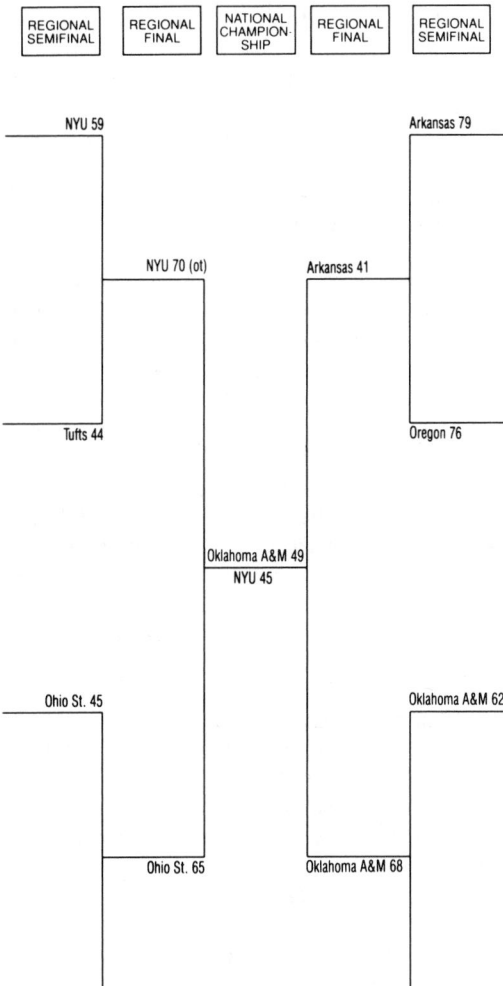

CONSOLATION GAMES

Regional Third Place:

Oregon 69

Kentucky 66

Western:

Eastern:

Utah 66

Tufts 56

At the end of the 1943 season, every member of the Oklahoma A&M basketball team was called up for active military duty. All except one, Bob Kurland. Nicknamed "Foothills," because he stood just a shade under 7-feet tall, the awkward freshman was too big to fit into a standard issue uniform. Opposing coaches, including Kansas's Phog Allen, ridiculed him as a freak of nature, too big to play basketball.

Despite the name calling, Kurland ws determined to prove himself. And his coach, Henry Iba, had no doubts that the big redhead would. Iba saw unlimited potential in Kurland and decided to build his team around the boy. The coach, always a stickler for conditioning and fundamentals, worked with Kurland on developing his technique and building his stamina. And he had the help of Floyd Burdette, a big, bruising, experienced post player, who was stationed at Oklahoma A&M with the Army Air Corps. Burdette set out to teach Kurland a few lessons about pivot play; he showed the younger man how to play with his back to the basket, how to use his size to gain position, and how to use his hands to push off.

During the course of the regular 1943–44 season, Iba's decision began to pay immediate dividends. With an offense designed to set up Kurland in the post, and a defense that positioned the 7-footer under the hoop where he could bat away opponents' shots, the Aggies lost only four games, all to service squads composed of ex-collegians called up for active duty. The Oklahomans were so successful that they received an NIT invitation, eventually losing to DePaul and their big center, George Mikan.

At the end of the season the NCAA rules committee declared Iba's goaltending defense illegal; no longer would A&M be able to station Kurland under the basket to swat away opponents' shots *on the way down* toward the hoop. But the new ruling didn't stop the big center from being a shot-blocking force; he was still mobile, aggressive, and intimidating, and when he jumped out at a shooter with his hands up he usually either blocked the shot or forced a change in trajectory.

The war decimated the A&M squad for the second straight year, leaving Kurland as the only returning letterman during the 1944–45 season. The new team took time to come together, and really only jelled after midseason, when they were able to add Cecil Hankins, a starring back on A&M's football team, and Doyle Parrack, a 1943 letterman who had been released from the service with a deferment because his family was involved in farming. The two new men helped the Aggies dominate their last eight regular season games, averaging 58 points a game to only 28 for their opponents. Kurland and the Aggies came into the NCAA tournament the most feared team in the nation.

But there were other good teams in the tournament field as well. In the Western regional there was Arkansas, with its own big, high-scoring center, 6-10 George Kok. In the east there was Ohio State, led by 6-9 Arnold Risen and guard Don Grate. And there was New York University, a balanced outfit anchored by Sid Tanenbaum and Frank Mangiapane and a promising freshman center, Adolph Schayes.

Oklahoma State, Arkansas, Ohio State, and NYU all won their first round games, and only the Arkansas contest with Oregon was close. The Razorbacks and Webfoots, both hard-driving, high-scoring teams, combined for 155 points, breaking—by an extraordinary 36 points—the previous NCAA two-team scoring record set by Dartmouth and North Carolina in 1941. Both teams also bettered the single-team scoring record, and Arkansas scored an unbelievable 47 points in the first half.

Then the Razorbacks came up against Henry Iba, Bob Kurland, and Oklahoma A&M. The Aggies, a defensive-minded, possession-oriented team, had easily defeated Utah, the defending national champions, in the first round. Kurland, as expected, led the way; he scored 28 points, many on his new "duffer" shot, in which he actually stuffed the ball *downward* through the hoop. But Kurland didn't need to score to help his team win. Against Arkansas, a team which A&M had already defeated two out of three times during the season, he was largely content to draw the defense around him and watch his teammates score. For although Big Bob had 6 first-half baskets, both Hankins and Parrack outscored him, combining for 38 points. At the other end of the court, meanwhile, Kurland was overwhelming. In describing his exploits, *The Arkansas Gazette* said the Razorbacks "were forced to shoot much of the time almost from mid-court, and it was a rare ball they took off the backboard after the repeatedly missed baskets." A&M held Arkansas to 41 points, less than they scored in the first half against Oregon.

While the Western final was a rout, the Eastern championship was a game so taut with excitement that it left the Madison Square Garden crowd of over 18,000 gasping. With two minutes remaining it seemed like no contest; Ohio State had a 10-point lead over the NYU Violets. They merely had to wait for the final buzzer to claim victory. But the Buckeyes' dominant center, Arnold Risen, was out of the game on fouls. And suddenly, a couple of Ohio State mistakes were turned into NYU baskets. Within 45 seconds, NYU had cut the lead to 4. Then, with 1:14 left on the clock, the Violets, desperately trying to regain possession, fouled.

Perhaps the Buckeyes remembered how Utah, in almost identical circumstances in the 1944 championship game, had waived their foul shots and allowed Dartmouth to get back into the game. Ohio State would not make the same mistake. They chose to shoot, and they missed. NYU rushed downcourt, but couldn't convert; Ohio State once more had the ball. Again NYU fouled, again Ohio State elected to shoot the clinching free throw, again they missed, and once more NYU came down with the ball. This time, though, Schayes tapped in a rebound. The lead stood at 2 when, with 36 seconds left, Ohio State was fouled again. Their strategy remained the same; they elected to shoot. For the third straight time, a Buckeye shooter missed the free throw. And this time, NYU tied the score. In a mere two minutes, a solid 10-point Ohio State lead had dissolved into dust.

The Buckeyes went into the overtime period stunned and demoralized by the NYU comeback, and five minutes later they walked off the floor a defeated team. NYU had won the privilege of facing Oklahoma A&M and their awesome 7-foot center in the NCAA championship game.

With Kurland in the lineup, NYU had no chance. The A&M offense revolved around the giant center, as the Aggies patiently waited for him to take his position in the post before running their set plays. He scored 22 points, but when NYU double-teamed, he kicked the ball back out to the open man. Kurland ran the floor, cut off NYU's inside game, and dominated both boards. The only way NYU stayed in the game at all was with a full-court press that forced turnovers and gave them the ball when the Aggies' big man was at the other end of the floor. "Foothills" Kurland, the game's most valuable player on both ends, was just too tall a mountain for the Violets to climb. For the NCAA tournament, the era of the big man had arrived.

REGIONAL SEMIFINAL EASTERN

NYU (59)   Coach: Howard Cann

	Min.	Total FG / FGA	Pct.	FT / FTA	Pct.	Reb. O / T	A	TO	PF	S	Blk	TP	PPM
GRENERT, A.	-	5/ -	-	2/ 4	.500	-/ -	-	-	0	-	-	12	-
FORMAN, D.	-	3/ -	-	0/ 2	.000	-/ -	-	-	1	-	-	6	-
SARATH, H.	-	0/ -	-	0/ 1	.000	-/ -	-	-	2	-	-	0	-
SCHAYES, A.	-	6/ -	-	1/ 3	.333	-/ -	-	-	1	-	-	13	-
MOST, A.	-	0/ -	-	3/ 3	1.000	-/ -	-	-	1	-	-	3	-
BENANTI, F.	-	0/ -	-	0/ 0	.000	-/ -	-	-	0	-	-	0	-
TANENBAUM, S.	-	7/ -	-	3/ 4	.750	-/ -	-	-	3	-	-	17	-
MANGIAPANE, F.	-	2/ -	-	2/ 5	.400	-/ -	-	-	3	-	-	6	-
WALSH, H.	-	1/ -	-	0/ 1	.000	-/ -	-	-	1	-	-	2	-
Totals	200	24/ -	-	11/23	.478	-/ -	-	-	12	-	-	59	.295

Tufts (44)   Coach: Richard Cochran

	Min.	Total FG / FGA	Pct.	FT / FTA	Pct.	Reb. O / T	A	TO	PF	S	Blk	TP	PPM
SKARDA, B.	-	7/ -	-	1/ 3	.333	-/ -	-	-	5	-	-	15	-
MORAN	-	0/ -	-	0/ 0	.000	-/ -	-	-	3	-	-	0	-
WALZ	-	2/ -	-	0/ 0	.000	-/ -	-	-	1	-	-	4	-
BURGBACHER	-	3/ -	-	2/ 2	1.000	-/ -	-	-	1	-	-	8	-
JOHNSON	-	1/ -	-	1/ 5	.200	-/ -	-	-	3	-	-	3	-
COONEY	-	0/ -	-	0/ 0	.000	-/ -	-	-	4	-	-	0	-
CUMISKEY, J.	-	6/ -	-	2/ 4	.500	-/ -	-	-	3	-	-	14	-
Totals	200	19/ -	-	6/14	.429	-/ -	-	-	20	-	-	44	.220

Disqualified: Tufts—Skarda.

NYU	1st Half	2nd Half	Final
NYU	27	32	59
Tufts	22	22	44

Ohio State (45)   Coach: Harold Olsen

	Min.	Total FG / FGA	Pct.	FT / FTA	Pct.	Reb. O / T	A	TO	PF	S	Blk	TP	PPM
GRATE, D.	-	5/ -	-	5/ 9	.556	-/ -	-	-	3	-	-	15	-
SIMS, J.	-	1/ -	-	0/ 0	.000	-/ -	-	-	0	-	-	2	-
DUGGER, J.	-	0/ -	-	0/ 1	.000	-/ -	-	-	2	-	-	0	-
CAUDILL, R.	-	5/ -	-	4/ 6	.667	-/ -	-	-	5	-	-	14	-
SNYDER, R.	-	0/ -	-	0/ 0	.000	-/ -	-	-	0	-	-	0	-
RISEN, A.	-	4/ -	-	1/ 3	.333	-/ -	-	-	5	-	-	9	-
HUSTON, P.	-	2/ -	-	1/ 1	1.000	-/ -	-	-	2	-	-	5	-
AMLING, W.	-	0/ -	-	0/ 4	.000	-/ -	-	-	4	-	-	0	-
Totals	200	17/ -	-	11/24	.458	-/ -	-	-	21	-	-	45	.225

Kentucky (37)   Coach: Adolph Rupp

	Min.	Total FG / FGA	Pct.	FT / FTA	Pct.	Reb. O / T	A	TO	PF	S	Blk	TP	PPM
TINGLE, J.	-	5/ -	-	1/ 2	.500	-/ -	-	-	0	-	-	11	-
SCHU, W.	-	2/ -	-	4/ 5	.800	-/ -	-	-	4	-	-	8	-
PARKER, E.	-	0/ -	-	0/ 3	.000	-/ -	-	-	0	-	-	0	-
CAMPBELL, K.	-	2/ -	-	2/ 5	.400	-/ -	-	-	4	-	-	6	-
VULICH, G.	-	0/ -	-	2/ 3	.667	-/ -	-	-	0	-	-	2	-
PARKINSON, J.	-	1/ -	-	5/ 6	.833	-/ -	-	-	4	-	-	7	-
STOUGH, J.	-	1/ -	-	1/ 3	.333	-/ -	-	-	4	-	-	3	-
STURGILL, W.	-	0/ -	-	0/ 0	.000	-/ -	-	-	3	-	-	0	-
Totals	200	11/ -	-	15/27	.556	-/ -	-	-	19	-	-	37	.185

Disqualified: Ohio State—Caudill, Risen.

Ohio State	1st Half	2nd Half	Final
Ohio State	21	24	45
Kentucky	15	22	37

REGIONAL SEMIFINAL WESTERN

Arkansas (79)   Coach: Eugene Lambert

	Min.	Total FG / FGA	Pct.	FT / FTA	Pct.	Reb. O / T	A	TO	PF	S	Blk	TP	PPM
RICHIE, O.	-	6/ -	-	1/ 1	1.000	-/ -	-	-	2	-	-	13	-
SCHUMCHYK, M.	-	7/ -	-	6/ 9	.667	-/ -	-	-	4	-	-	20	-
KEARNS, K.	-	0/ -	-	0/ 0	.000	-/ -	-	-	1	-	-	0	-
KOK, G.	-	9/ -	-	4/ 5	.800	-/ -	-	-	2	-	-	22	-
JOLLIFF, C.	-	0/ -	-	0/ 1	.000	-/ -	-	-	2	-	-	0	-
FLYNT, B.	-	4/ -	-	3/ 4	.750	-/ -	-	-	3	-	-	11	-
SCHUMCHYK, F.	-	0/ -	-	1/ 1	1.000	-/ -	-	-	0	-	-	1	-
WHEELER, E.	-	5/ -	-	2/ 3	.667	-/ -	-	-	0	-	-	12	-
Totals	200	31/ -	-	17/24	.708	-/ -	-	-	14	-	-	79	.395

Oregon (76)   Coach: Howard Hobson

	Min.	Total FG / FGA	Pct.	FT / FTA	Pct.	Reb. O / T	A	TO	PF	S	Blk	TP	PPM
SMITH	-	4/ -	-	3/ 4	.750	-/ -	-	-	3	-	-	11	-
BERG, R.	-	3/ -	-	2/ 3	.667	-/ -	-	-	4	-	-	8	-
WILKINS, D.	-	10/ -	-	3/ 3	1.000	-/ -	-	-	2	-	-	23	-
STAMPER	-	0/ -	-	0/ 0	.000	-/ -	-	-	2	-	-	0	-
HAYS, K.	-	3/ -	-	1/ 2	.500	-/ -	-	-	3	-	-	7	-
HAMILTON, B.	-	9/ -	-	2/ 3	.667	-/ -	-	-	2	-	-	20	-
BARTELT	-	3/ -	-	1/ 1	1.000	-/ -	-	-	5	-	-	7	-
Totals	200	32/ -	-	12/16	.750	-/ -	-	-	21	-	-	76	.380

Disqualified: Oregon—Bartelt.

Arkansas	1st Half	2nd Half	Final
Arkansas	47	32	79
Oregon	34	42	76

Oklahoma A&M (62)   Coach: Henry Iba

	Min.	Total FG / FGA	Pct.	FT / FTA	Pct.	Reb. O / T	A	TO	PF	S	Blk	TP	PPM
HANKINS, C.	-	5/ -	-	1/ -	-	-/ -	-	-	3	-	-	11	-
KERN, W.	-	2/ -	-	3/ -	-	-/ -	-	-	2	-	-	7	-
JOHNSON, B.	-	0/ -	-	0/ -	-	-/ -	-	-	0	-	-	0	-
KURLAND, B.	-	14/ -	-	0/ -	-	-/ -	-	-	2	-	-	28	-
HALBERT, J.	-	0/ -	-	0/ -	-	-/ -	-	-	1	-	-	0	-
PARRACK, D.	-	3/ -	-	0/ -	-	-/ -	-	-	2	-	-	6	-
WYLIE, J.	-	0/ -	-	0/ -	-	-/ -	-	-	1	-	-	0	-
WILLIAMS, B.	-	4/ -	-	0/ -	-	-/ -	-	-	3	-	-	8	-
PARKS, J.	-	1/ -	-	0/ -	-	-/ -	-	-	1	-	-	2	-
Totals	200	29/ -	-	4/10	-	-/ -	-	-	15	-	-	62	.310

Utah (37)   Coach: Vadal Peterson

	Min.	Total FG / FGA	Pct.	FT / FTA	Pct.	Reb. O / T	A	TO	PF	S	Blk	TP	PPM
HAMBLIN, L.	-	2/ -	-	1/ -	-	-/ -	-	-	3	-	-	5	-
HOWARD, D.	-	4/ -	-	3/ -	-	-/ -	-	-	2	-	-	11	-
SATTERFIELD, M.	-	4/ -	-	6/ -	-	-/ -	-	-	2	-	-	14	-
KELL, G.	-	0/ -	-	0/ -	-	-/ -	-	-	1	-	-	0	-
DORTON, D.	-	3/ -	-	1/ -	-	-/ -	-	-	0	-	-	7	-
BARNES, R.	-	0/ -	-	0/ -	-	-/ -	-	-	0	-	-	0	-
Totals	200	13/ -	-	11/19	-	-/ -	-	-	8	-	-	37	.185

Disqualified: None.

Oklahoma A&M	1st Half	2nd Half	Final
Oklahoma A&M	22	40	62
Utah	12	25	37

REGIONAL FINAL EASTERN

NYU (70) Coach: Howard Cann

	Min.	Total FG / FGA	Pct.	FT / FTA	Pct.	Reb. O / T	A	TO	PF	S	Blk	TP	PPM
GRENERT, A.	-	2/ -	-	2/ 5	.400	-/ -	-	-	3	-	-	6	-
BENANTI, F.	-	0/ -	-	0/ 0	.000	-/ -	-	-	1	-	-	0	-
FORMAN, D.	-	4/ -	-	2/ 2	1.000	-/ -	-	-	2	-	-	10	-
SCHAYES, A.	-	5/ -	-	4/ 8	.500	-/ -	-	-	4	-	-	14	-
WALSH, H.	-	2/ -	-	2/ 3	.667	-/ -	-	-	5	-	-	6	-
MOST, A.	-	1/ -	-	0/ 1	.000	-/ -	-	-	2	-	-	2	-
TANENBAUM, S.	-	5/ -	-	3/ 3	1.000	-/ -	-	-	2	-	-	13	-
MANGIAPANE, F.	-	7/ -	-	3/ 5	.600	-/ -	-	-	4	-	-	17	-
GOLDSTEIN, M.	-	1/ -	-	0/ 0	.000	-/ -	-	-	2	-	-	2	-
Totals	225	27/ -	-	16/27	.593	-/ -	-	-	25	-	-	70	.311

Ohio State (65) Coach: Harold Olsen

	Min.	Total FG / FGA	Pct.	FT / FTA	Pct.	Reb. O / T	A	TO	PF	S	Blk	TP	PPM
GRATE, D.	-	2/ -	-	2/ 3	.667	-/ -	-	-	4	-	-	6	-
SIMS, J.	-	2/ -	-	3/ 4	.750	-/ -	-	-	3	-	-	7	-
DUGGER, J.	-	1/ -	-	2/ 5	.400	-/ -	-	-	5	-	-	4	-
CAUDILL, R.	-	3/ -	-	1/ 1	1.000	-/ -	-	-	3	-	-	7	-
SNYDER, R.	-	0/ -	-	0/ 0	.000	-/ -	-	-	0	-	-	0	-
RISEN, A.	-	8/ -	-	10/13	.769	-/ -	-	-	5	-	-	26	-
HUSTON, P.	-	2/ -	-	1/ 3	.333	-/ -	-	-	5	-	-	5	-
AMLING, W.	-	5/ -	-	0/ 2	.000	-/ -	-	-	1	-	-	10	-
Totals	225	23/ -	-	19/31	.613	-/ -	-	-	26	-	-	65	.289

Disqualified: NYU—Walsh; Ohio State—Dugger, Risen, Huston.

	1st Half	2nd Half	1 OT	Final
NYU	34	28	8	70
Ohio State	36	26	3	65

REGIONAL FINAL WESTERN

Arkansas (41) Coach: Eugene Lambert

	Min.	Total FG / FGA	Pct.	FT / FTA	Pct.	Reb. O / T	A	TO	PF	S	Blk	TP	PPM
RICHIE, O.	-	2/ -	-	0/ -	-	-/ -	-	-	0	-	-	4	-
BYLES, T.	-	1/ -	-	0/ -	-	-/ -	-	-	1	-	-	2	-
SCHUMCHYK, M.	-	1/ -	-	2/ -	-	-/ -	-	-	3	-	-	4	-
SCHUMCHYK, F.	-	0/ -	-	0/ -	-	-/ -	-	-	1	-	-	0	-
KEARNS, K.	-	1/ -	-	1/ -	-	-/ -	-	-	2	-	-	3	-
KOK, G.	-	4/ -	-	4/ -	-	-/ -	-	-	2	-	-	12	-
JOLLIFF, C.	-	0/ -	-	0/ -	-	-/ -	-	-	3	-	-	0	-
FLYNT, B.	-	5/ -	-	1/ -	-	-/ -	-	-	2	-	-	11	-
COPELAND, J.	-	0/ -	-	1/ -	-	-/ -	-	-	0	-	-	1	-
WHEELER, E.	-	2/ -	-	0/ -	-	-/ -	-	-	3	-	-	4	-
Totals	200	16/ -	-	9/ -	-	-/ -	-	-	17	-	-	41	.205

Oklahoma A&M (68) Coach: Henry Iba

	Min.	Total FG / FGA	Pct.	FT / FTA	Pct.	Reb. O / T	A	TO	PF	S	Blk	TP	PPM
HANKINS, C.	-	8/ -	-	6/ -	-	-/ -	-	-	1	-	-	22	-
KERN, W.	-	3/ -	-	0/ -	-	-/ -	-	-	2	-	-	6	-
KURLAND, B.	-	6/ -	-	3/ -	-	-/ -	-	-	3	-	-	15	-
HALBERT, J.	-	0/ -	-	0/ -	-	-/ -	-	-	1	-	-	0	-
WILLIAMS, B.	-	2/ -	-	3/ -	-	-/ -	-	-	2	-	-	7	-
PARKS, J.	-	1/ -	-	0/ -	-	-/ -	-	-	1	-	-	2	-
PARRACK, D.	-	7/ -	-	2/ -	-	-/ -	-	-	1	-	-	16	-
WYLIE, J.	-	0/ -	-	0/ -	-	-/ -	-	-	0	-	-	0	-
Totals	200	27/ -	-	14/ -	-	-/ -	-	-	11	-	-	68	.340

Disqualified: None.

	1st Half	2nd Half	Final
Arkansas	17	24	41
Oklahoma A&M	36	32	68

CHAMPIONSHIP

NYU (45) Coach: Howard Cann

	Min.	Total FG / FGA	Pct.	FT / FTA	Pct.	Reb. O / T	A	TO	PF	S	Blk	TP	PPM
GRENERT, A.	-	5/ -	-	2/ 3	.667	-/ -	-	-	3	-	-	12	-
GOLDSTEIN, M.	-	0/ -	-	2/ 2	1.000	-/ -	-	-	0	-	-	2	-
FORMAN, D.	-	5/ -	-	1/ 1	1.000	-/ -	-	-	1	-	-	11	-
SCHAYES, A.	-	2/ -	-	2/ 6	.333	-/ -	-	-	2	-	-	6	-
TANENBAUM, S.	-	2/ -	-	0/ 0	.000	-/ -	-	-	2	-	-	4	-
WALSH, H.	-	0/ -	-	0/ 0	.000	-/ -	-	-	2	-	-	0	-
MANGIAPANE, F.	-	2/ -	-	2/ 2	1.000	-/ -	-	-	3	-	-	6	-
MOST, A.	-	1/ -	-	2/ 3	.667	-/ -	-	-	2	-	-	4	-
Totals	200	17/ -	-	11/17	.647	-/ -	-	-	15	-	-	45	.225

Oklahoma A&M (49) Coach: Henry Iba

	Min.	Total FG / FGA	Pct.	FT / FTA	Pct.	Reb. O / T	A	TO	PF	S	Blk	TP	PPM
HANKINS, C.	-	6/ -	-	3/ 6	.500	-/ -	-	-	3	-	-	15	-
KERN, W.	-	3/ -	-	0/ 4	.000	-/ -	-	-	3	-	-	6	-
KURLAND, B.	-	10/ -	-	2/ 3	.667	-/ -	-	-	3	-	-	22	-
PARRACK, D.	-	2/ -	-	0/ 1	.000	-/ -	-	-	3	-	-	4	-
PARKS, J.	-	0/ -	-	0/ 0	.000	-/ -	-	-	3	-	-	0	-
WILLIAMS, B.	-	1/ -	-	0/ 1	.000	-/ -	-	-	1	-	-	2	-
WYLIE, J.	-	0/ -	-	0/ 0	.000	-/ -	-	-	0	-	-	0	-
Totals	200	22/ -	-	5/15	.333	-/ -	-	-	16	-	-	49	.245

Disqualified: None.

	1st Half	2nd Half	Final
NYU	21	24	45
Oklahoma A&M	26	23	49

REGIONAL THIRD PLACE EASTERN

Kentucky (66)   Coach: Adolph Rupp

	Min.	Total FG / FGA	Pct.	FT / FTA	Pct.	Reb. O / T	A	TO	PF	S	Blk	TP	PPM
PARKER, E.	-	6/ -	-	2/ 5	.400	-/ -	-	-	4	-	-	14	-
ALLIN, E.	-	0/ -	-	0/ 0	.000	-/ -	-	-	0	-	-	0	-
SCHU, W.	-	10/ -	-	1/ 1	1.000	-/ -	-	-	3	-	-	21	-
TINGLE, J.	-	0/ -	-	0/ 0	.000	-/ -	-	-	0	-	-	0	-
CAMPBELL, K.	-	3/ -	-	1/ 2	.500	-/ -	-	-	0	-	-	7	-
VULICH, G.	-	4/ -	-	5/ 5	1.000	-/ -	-	-	2	-	-	13	-
PARKINSON, J.	-	4/ -	-	1/ 2	.500	-/ -	-	-	2	-	-	9	-
DURHAM, J.	-	0/ -	-	0/ 0	.000	-/ -	-	-	0	-	-	0	-
STOUGH, J.	-	0/ -	-	1/ 1	1.000	-/ -	-	-	1	-	-	1	-
STURGILL, W.	-	0/ -	-	1/ 2	.500	-/ -	-	-	5	-	-	1	-
Totals	200	27/ -	-	12/18	.667	-/ -	-	-	17	-	-	66	.330

Tufts (56)   Coach: Richard Cochran

	Min.	Total FG / FGA	Pct.	FT / FTA	Pct.	Reb. O / T	A	TO	PF	S	Blk	TP	PPM
SKARDA, B.	-	8/ -	-	4/ 6	.667	-/ -	-	-	1	-	-	20	-
MATTHEWS	-	0/ -	-	0/ 0	.000	-/ -	-	-	0	-	-	0	-
MORAN	-	4/ -	-	1/ 1	1.000	-/ -	-	-	2	-	-	9	-
WALZ	-	0/ -	-	1/ 1	1.000	-/ -	-	-	1	-	-	1	-
ANDREASON	-	0/ -	-	0/ 0	.000	-/ -	-	-	0	-	-	0	-
BURGBACHER	-	4/ -	-	2/ 5	.400	-/ -	-	-	2	-	-	10	-
JOHNSON	-	0/ -	-	1/ 4	.250	-/ -	-	-	2	-	-	1	-
CUMISKEY, J.	-	3/ -	-	2/ 3	.667	-/ -	-	-	1	-	-	8	-
COONEY	-	1/ -	-	5/ 7	.714	-/ -	-	-	4	-	-	7	-
BEERS	-	0/ -	-	0/ 0	.000	-/ -	-	-	0	-	-	0	-
GIORDANO	-	0/ -	-	0/ 0	.000	-/ -	-	-	0	-	-	0	-
WALKER	-	0/ -	-	0/ 0	.000	-/ -	-	-	0	-	-	0	-
DOUGHERTY	-	0/ -	-	0/ 0	.000	-/ -	-	-	0	-	-	0	-
Totals	200	20/ -	-	16/27	.593	-/ -	-	-	13	-	-	56	.280

Disqualified: Kentucky—Sturgill.

	1st Half	2nd Half	Final
Kentucky	24	42	66
Tufts	23	33	56

REGIONAL THIRD PLACE WESTERN

Oregon (69)   Coach: Howard Hobson

	Min.	Total FG / FGA	Pct.	FT / FTA	Pct.	Reb. O / T	A	TO	PF	S	Blk	TP	PPM
SMITH	-	0/ -	-	1/ 1	1.000	-/ -	-	-	0	-	-	1	-
BERG, R.	-	3/ -	-	3/ 4	.750	-/ -	-	-	5	-	-	9	-
WILKINS, D.	-	9/ -	-	3/ 4	.750	-/ -	-	-	3	-	-	21	-
STAMPER	-	1/ -	-	0/ 0	.000	-/ -	-	-	0	-	-	2	-
HAYS, K.	-	6/ -	-	2/ 2	1.000	-/ -	-	-	2	-	-	14	-
ALLEN	-	0/ -	-	0/ 0	.000	-/ -	-	-	0	-	-	0	-
HAMILTON, B.	-	3/ -	-	6/ 7	.857	-/ -	-	-	1	-	-	12	-
KOFTNIK	-	0/ -	-	0/ 0	.000	-/ -	-	-	0	-	-	0	-
HOFFINE, F.	-	4/ -	-	2/ 3	.667	-/ -	-	-	1	-	-	10	-
Totals	200	26/ -	-	17/21	.810	-/ -	-	-	12	-	-	69	.345

Utah (66)   Coach: Vadal Peterson

	Min.	Total FG / FGA	Pct.	FT / FTA	Pct.	Reb. O / T	A	TO	PF	S	Blk	TP	PPM
DORTON, D.	-	11/ -	-	2/ 4	.500	-/ -	-	-	4	-	-	24	-
HAMBLIN, L.	-	1/ -	-	3/ 3	1.000	-/ -	-	-	4	-	-	5	-
BARNES, R.	-	2/ -	-	0/ 0	.000	-/ -	-	-	2	-	-	4	-
SATTERFIELD, M.	-	9/ -	-	2/ 2	1.000	-/ -	-	-	3	-	-	20	-
KEIL	-	1/ -	-	2/ 3	.667	-/ -	-	-	2	-	-	4	-
HOWARD, D.	-	4/ -	-	1/ 1	1.000	-/ -	-	-	4	-	-	9	-
Totals	200	28/ -	-	10/13	.769	-/ -	-	-	19	-	-	66	.330

Disqualified: Oregon—Berg.

	1st Half	2nd Half	Final
Oregon	38	31	69
Utah	30	36	66

✪ INDIVIDUAL RECORDS ✪

SCORING

Most points in a single game
1. BOB KURLAND, OKLAHOMA A&M (vs. UTAH) — 28
2. ARNOLD RISEN, OHIO STATE (vs. NYU) — 26
3. DON DORTON, UTAH (vs. OREGON) — 24
4. DICK WILKINS, OREGON (vs. ARKANSAS) — 23
5. 3 tied for fifth place.

Most total points in the tournament
1. BOB KURLAND, OKLAHOMA A&M — 65
2. CECIL HANKINS, OKLAHOMA A&M — 48
3. DICK WILKINS, OREGON — 44
4. BOB SKARDA, TUFTS — 35
4. ARNOLD RISEN, OHIO STATE — 35

Highest scoring average (minimum 2 games)
1. DICK WILKINS, OREGON (44-2) — 22.00
2. BOB KURLAND, OKLAHOMA A&M (65-3) — 21.67
3. BOB SKARDA, TUFTS (35-2) — 17.50
3. ARNOLD RISEN, OHIO STATE (35-2) — 17.50
5. 2 tied for fifth place.

FIELD GOALS

Most field goals in a single game
1. BOB KURLAND, OKLAHOMA A&M (vs. UTAH) — 14
2. DON DORTON, UTAH (vs. OREGON) — 11

3. BOB KURLAND, OKLAHOMA A&M (vs. NYU) — 10
3. WILBER SCHU, KENTUCKY (vs. TUFTS) — 10
3. DICK WILKINS, OREGON (vs. ARKANSAS) — 10

Most total field goals in the tournament
1. BOB KURLAND, OKLAHOMA A&M — 30
2. DICK WILKINS, OREGON — 19
2. CECIL HANKINS, OKLAHOMA A&M — 19
4. BOB SKARDA, TUFTS — 15
5. 2 tied for fifth place.

FREE THROWS

Most free throws in a single game
1. ARNOLD RISEN, OHIO STATE (vs. NYU) — 10
2. CECIL HANKINS, OKLAHOMA A&M (vs. ARKANSAS) — 6
2. MURRAY SATTERFIELD, UTAH (vs. OKLAHOMA A&M) — 6
2. MIKE SCHUMCHYK, ARKANSAS (vs. OREGON) — 6
2. BOB HAMILTON, OREGON (vs. UTAH) — 6

Most total free throws in the tournament
1. ARNOLD RISEN, OHIO STATE — 11
2. CECIL HANKINS, OKLAHOMA A&M — 10
3. 4 tied for third place.

Most free throws attempted in a single game
1. ARNOLD RISEN, OHIO STATE (vs. NYU) — 13

2. MIKE SCHUMCHYK, ARKANSAS (vs. OREGON) — 9
2. DON GRATE, OHIO STATE (vs. KENTUCKY) — 9
4. ADOLPH SCHAYES, NYU (vs. OHIO STATE) — 8
5. 2 tied for fifth place.

Most free throws attempted in the tournament
1. ADOLPH SCHAYES, NYU — 17
2. ARNOLD RISEN, OHIO STATE — 16
3. FRANK MANGIAPANE, NYU — 12
3. AL GRENERT, NYU — 12
3. DON GRATE, OHIO STATE — 12

Highest free throw percentage in a single game (minimum 7 attempts)
1. BOB HAMILTON, OREGON (vs. UTAH) (6-7) — .857
2. ARNOLD RISEN, OHIO STATE (vs. NYU) (10-13) — .769
3. COONEY, TUFTS (vs. KENTUCKY) (5-7) — .714
4. MIKE SCHUMCHYK, ARKANSAS (vs. OREGON) (6-9) — .667
5. DON GRATE, OHIO STATE (vs. KENTUCKY) (5-9) — .556

Highest free throw percentage in the tournament (minimum 15 attempts)
1. ARNOLD RISEN, OHIO STATE (11-16) — .688
2. ADOLPH SCHAYES, NYU (7-17) — .412

✪ TEAM RECORDS ✪

SCORING

Most points in a single game
1	ARKANSAS (vs. OREGON)	79
2	OREGON (vs. ARKANSAS)	76
3	NYU (vs. OHIO STATE)	70

Most total points in the tournament
1	OKLAHOMA A&M	179
2	NYU	174
3	OREGON	145

Highest scoring average (minimum 2 games)
1	OREGON (145-2)	72.50
2	ARKANSAS (120-2)	60.00
3	OKLAHOMA A&M (179-3)	59.67

FIELD GOALS

Most field goals in a single game
1	OREGON (vs. ARKANSAS)	32
2	ARKANSAS (vs. OREGON)	31
3	OKLAHOMA A&M (vs. UTAH)	29

Most total field goals in the tournament
1	OKLAHOMA A&M	78
2	NYU	68
3	OREGON	58

FREE THROWS

Most free throws in a single game
1	OHIO STATE (vs. NYU)	19
2	OREGON (vs. UTAH)	17
2	ARKANSAS (vs. OREGON)	17

Most total free throws in the tournament
1	NYU	38
2	OHIO STATE	30
3	OREGON	29

Most free throws attempted in a single game
1	OHIO STATE (vs. NYU)	31
2	3 tied for second place.	

Highest free throw percentage in a single game
1	OREGON (vs. UTAH) (17-21)	.810
2	UTAH (vs. OREGON) (10-13)	.769
3	OREGON (vs. ARKANSAS) (12-16)	.750

Fewest free throws in a single game
1	OKLAHOMA A&M (vs. UTAH)	4
2	OKLAHOMA A&M (vs. NYU)	5
3	TUFTS (vs. NYU)	6

Lowest free throw percentage in a single game
1	OKLAHOMA A&M (vs. NYU) (5-15)	.333
2	OKLAHOMA A&M (vs. UTAH) (4-10)	.400
3	TUFTS (vs. NYU) (6-14)	.429

1946

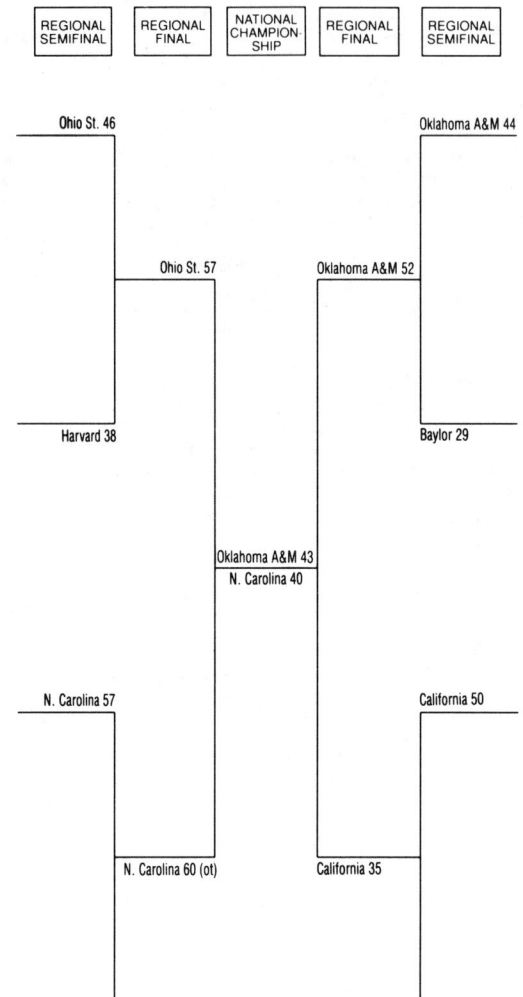

EASTERN

WESTERN

Ohio St. 46

Oklahoma A&M 44

Ohio St. 57

Oklahoma A&M 52

Harvard 38

Baylor 29

Oklahoma A&M 43
N. Carolina 40

N. Carolina 57

California 50

N. Carolina 60 (ot)

California 35

NYU 49

Colorado 44

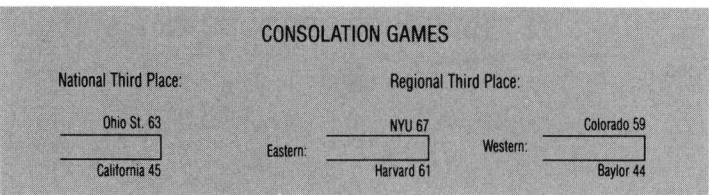

CONSOLATION GAMES

National Third Place:

Ohio St. 63

California 45

Regional Third Place:

Eastern:
NYU 67

Harvard 61

Western:
Colorado 59

Baylor 44

By tournament time 1946, World War II was over and the veterans were returning home to normal life. For some that meant going back to their families and their jobs. For some it meant picking up at school where they had left off. For some that meant playing college basketball. At Oklahoma A&M, for example, the five returning lettermen from the 1945 national championship team were joined by five former players who had just come home from the war. One of the vets was forward Sam Aubrey, who had been a starter in 1943 and a close friend of Bob Kurland's. When he was seriously wounded in battle, there had been a question as to whether he would ever walk again; Aubrey not only walked, he came home to play for the defending national champions.

The story in Stillwater, Oklahoma, was repeated on virtually every campus as America's heroes came home.

But even with the improved level of competition that came with the end of the war, one star shined brighter than ever. Bob Kurland dominated college basketball, and the NCAA tournament, even more than he had as a junior in 1945. In the first round, he scored 20 of A&M's 44 points while holding Baylor's high-scoring Jackie Robinson to a mere 5, and the Associated Press marveled that he "devoted at least half of his time to feeding the ball to his mates and grabbing the ball off the Baylor backboard." In the next round he was once again the difference, scoring 29 points in a rout of the California Golden Bears as the Aggies became the first team in the eight-year history of the tournament to repeat as Western regional titlists.

Meanwhile in the east, NYU was also making a second go at the regional crown. Before losing their regular season finale to CCNY, the Violets were ranked No. 1 in the nation, and they were still favored to win the Eastern title when they took the court for their first tournament game. But despite playing in the friendly confines of New York's Madison Square Garden, they were thoroughly outplayed by a talented North Carolina team led by the ambidextrous hook shot artist John Dillon and 6-6 center Horace "Bones" McKinney. In the end, the NYU coach Howard Cann could do nothing to stop the Tar Heels; he could only congratulate his former student, North Carolina coach Lieut. Bernie Carnevale, on a lesson well-learned. In the other first-round game, Ohio State won, as expected, against the Harvard Crimson.

For Ohio State, their second-round game aganst North Carolina was like being snakebit twice. In 1945, NYU had scored the last 10 points in regulation to tie Ohio State, and the Buckeyes had lost in overtime. In 1946, it was North Carolina's turn to break the Buckeyes' hearts.

The game started slowly, with neither team scoring a point in the first five minutes. Ohio State didn't hit their first field goal until just before the ten minute mark. Then North Carolina pulled ahead, scoring 11 straight points to turn a tie game into a 17-6 rout. But the Buckeyes came back strong behind the inside scoring of Jack Underman, and held a 34-27 lead early in the second half. When Carolina's Bones McKinney fouled out a little more than halfway through the period, it looked like the Tar Heels had run out of chances to come back.

But come back they did, finally closing to within 2 points. With 20 seconds left, North Carolina's Bob Paxton let fly from 30 feet, and for the second straight year Ohio State was forced into overtime. And once again, as in 1945, they lost.

In the finals, North Carolina threw waves of defensive players at Kurland. McKinney fouled out guarding the Aggie star, and his replacements, Paxton and Jim Jordan, had no better luck in stopping the great center. When the Tar Heels double-teamed Kurland, his teammates found the open man. And despite Dillon's hook shots and Carolina's tenacious pressing defense, whenever A&M needed their big man to score, he did. The last time the Tar Heels threatened, Kurland gave his most emphatic answer of all. North Carolina's running game had brought them from 13 back to within 3 points at 36-33 when Kurland took over. Calling for the ball, he took it straight for the hoop and jammed home a pair of monstrous dunks, one after the other. Within two minutes, the lead was up to 10 and the Aggies were back in command. And although the Carolinians made one more charge when A&M went into a freeze, it was too late.

By the end of Kurland's career at Oklahoma A&M, he had erased any doubts about whether a 7-footer could play basketball. In his senior year, he led the nation in scoring, and averaged over 25 points a game in his last twelve games. In his three 1946 tournament games, he netted 72 points, more than half his team's total. He dominated the boards in every contest, blocked or altered the direction of countless shots, and held Baylor's big gun, Jackie Robinson, and North Carolina's Bones McKinney to 5 points each. Most important of all, in leading his team to an unprecedented second straight NCAA championship, the big redhead proved that a good big man is the most valuable commodity in basketball. It's been that way ever since.

REGIONAL SEMIFINAL EASTERN

Ohio State (46)　Coach: Harold Olsen

	Min.	Total FG/FGA	Pct.	FT/FTA	Pct.	Reb. O/T	A	TO	PF	S	Blk	TP	PPM
BOWEN, R.	-	3/ -		0/ 0	.000	-/ -	-	-	4	-	-	6	-
SNYDER, R.	-	1/ -		1/ 2	.500	-/ -	-	-	4	-	-	3	-
WELLS, W.	-	2/ -		0/ 2	.000	-/ -	-	-	2	-	-	4	-
UNDERMAN, J.	-	5/ -		4/ 5	.800	-/ -	-	-	5	-	-	14	-
ELLIOTT, C.	-	0/ -		1/ 2	.500	-/ -	-	-	4	-	-	1	-
HUSTON, P.	-	3/ -		6/ 9	.667	-/ -	-	-	3	-	-	12	-
KUHN, C.	-	0/ -		0/ 0	.000	-/ -	-	-	0	-	-	0	-
AMLING, W.	-	3/ -		0/ 2	.000	-/ -	-	-	3	-	-	6	-
Totals	200	17/63	.270	12/22	.545	-/ -	-	-	25	-	-	46	.230

Harvard (38)　Coach: Floyd Stahl

	Min.	Total FG/FGA	Pct.	FT/FTA	Pct.	Reb. O/T	A	TO	PF	S	Blk	TP	PPM
GANTT	-	1/ -		2/ 2	1.000	-/ -	-	-	1	-	-	4	-
SWEGAN	-	1/ -		0/ 1	.000	-/ -	-	-	3	-	-	2	-
GRAY, W.	-	2/ -		7/ 9	.778	-/ -	-	-	3	-	-	11	-
CLARK	-	0/ -		0/ 0	.000	-/ -	-	-	0	-	-	0	-
DECSI	-	1/ -		5/ 8	.625	-/ -	-	-	4	-	-	7	-
DAVIS	-	0/ -		0/ 0	.000	-/ -	-	-	0	-	-	0	-
MARIASCHIN	-	5/ -		1/ 2	.500	-/ -	-	-	2	-	-	11	-
PETRILLO	-	0/ -		1/ 2	.500	-/ -	-	-	1	-	-	1	-
CHAMPION	-	0/ -		2/ 6	.333	-/ -	-	-	4	-	-	2	-
MCDANIEL	-	0/ -		0/ 0	.000	-/ -	-	-	0	-	-	0	-
Totals	200	10/72	.139	18/30	.600	-/ -	-	-	18	-	38	.190

Disqualified: Ohio State—Underman.

	1st Half	2nd Half	Final
Ohio State	26	20	46
Harvard	20	18	38

North Carolina (57)　Coach: Ben Carnevale

	Min.	Total FG/FGA	Pct.	FT/FTA	Pct.	Reb. O/T	A	TO	PF	S	Blk	TP	PPM
DILLON, J.	-	7/10	.700	1/ 4	.250	-/ -	-	-	5	-	-	15	-
ANDERSON, D.	-	1/ -		2/ 4	.500	-/ -	-	-	2	-	-	4	-
PAXTON, B.	-	6/ -		1/ 4	.250	-/ -	-	-	1	-	-	13	-
MCKINNEY, B.	-	4/ -		3/ 4	.750	-/ -	-	-	4	-	-	11	-
WHITE, J.	-	0/ -		0/ 0	.000	-/ -	-	-	5	-	-	0	-
THORNE, T.	-	2/ -		0/ 0	.000	-/ -	-	-	1	-	-	4	-
JORDAN, J.	-	4/ -		2/ 2	1.000	-/ -	-	-	5	-	-	10	-
SCHOLBE, R.	-	0/ -		0/ 0	.000	-/ -	-	-	0	-	-	0	-
Totals	200	24/52	.462	9/18	.500	-/ -	-	-	23	-	-	57	.285

NYU (49)　Coach: Howard Cann

	Min.	Total FG/FGA	Pct.	FT/FTA	Pct.	Reb. O/T	A	TO	PF	S	Blk	TP	PPM
FORMAN, D.	-	1/ -		3/ 4	.750	-/ -	-	-	2	-	-	5	-
SARATH	-	2/ -		0/ 2	.000	-/ -	-	-	1	-	-	4	-
GOLDSTEIN	-	0/ -		0/ 0	.000	-/ -	-	-	0	-	-	0	-
DEBONIS	-	5/ -		3/ 4	.750	-/ -	-	-	4	-	-	13	-
SCHAYES, D.	-	2/ -		5/ 6	.833	-/ -	-	-	1	-	-	9	-
KELLY, T.	-	0/ -		0/ 0	.000	-/ -	-	-	3	-	-	0	-
TANENBAUM, S.	-	1/ -		3/ 3	1.000	-/ -	-	-	3	-	-	5	-
DOLHON	-	1/ -		0/ 0	.000	-/ -	-	-	0	-	-	2	-
MANGIAPANE	-	4/ -		3/ 6	.500	-/ -	-	-	4	-	-	11	-
BENANTI	-	0/ -		0/ 0	.000	-/ -	-	-	0	-	-	0	-
Totals	200	16/ -		17/25	.680	-/ -	-	-	18	-	-	49	.245

Disqualified: N. Carolina—Dillon, White, Jordan.

	1st Half	2nd Half	Final
N. Carolina	29	28	57
NYU	22	27	49

REGIONAL SEMIFINAL WESTERN

Oklahoma A&M (44)　Coach: Henry Iba

	Min.	Total FG/FGA	Pct.	FT/FTA	Pct.	Reb. O/T	A	TO	PF	S	Blk	TP	PPM
AUBREY, S.	-	0/ -		0/ 0	.000	-/ -	-	-	0	-	-	0	-
BENNETT, A.	-	0/ -		0/ 0	.000	-/ -	-	-	0	-	-	0	-
KERN, W.	-	0/ -		3/ 5	.600	-/ -	-	-	2	-	-	3	-
BRADLEY, J.	-	3/ -		1/ 2	.500	-/ -	-	-	1	-	-	7	-
KURLAND, B.	-	7/13	.538	6/12	.500	-/ -	-	-	2	-	-	20	-
HALBERT, J.	-	0/ -		0/ 0	.000	-/ -	-	-	0	-	-	0	-
WILLIAMS, B.	-	1/ -		0/ 1	.000	-/ -	-	-	5	-	-	2	-
BELL, G.	-	0/ -		3/ 3	1.000	-/ -	-	-	1	-	-	3	-
PARKS, J.	-	4/ -		1/ 2	.500	-/ -	-	-	0	-	-	9	-
Totals	200	15/ -		14/25	.560	-/ -	-	-	11	-	-	44	.220

Baylor (29)　Coach: Bill Henderson

	Min.	Total FG/FGA	Pct.	FT/FTA	Pct.	Reb. O/T	A	TO	PF	S	Blk	TP	PPM
JOHNSON, B.	-	4/ -		2/ 3	.667	-/ -	-	-	4	-	-	10	-
GONZALES	-	0/ -		0/ 0	.000	-/ -	-	-	0	-	-	0	-
ROBINSON, J.	-	1/ -		3/ 4	.750	-/ -	-	-	4	-	-	5	-
MCCORMICK	-	0/ -		1/ 2	.500	-/ -	-	-	1	-	-	1	-
DEVEREAUX	-	1/ -		0/ 0	.000	-/ -	-	-	1	-	-	2	-
EDWARDS	-	0/ -		0/ 0	.000	-/ -	-	-	5	-	-	0	-
SHEARIN	-	0/ -		0/ 0	.000	-/ -	-	-	5	-	-	0	-
BELEW	-	2/ -		0/ 1	.000	-/ -	-	-	3	-	-	4	-
HAILEY, B.	-	3/ -		1/ 1	1.000	-/ -	-	-	2	-	-	7	-
Totals	200	11/ -		7/11	.636	-/ -	-	-	25	-	-	29	.145

Disqualified: Oklahoma A&M—Williams; Baylor—Edwards, Shearin.

	1st Half	2nd Half	Final
Oklahoma A&M	22	22	44
Baylor	17	12	29

California (50)　Coach: Nibs Price

	Min.	Total FG/FGA	Pct.	FT/FTA	Pct.	Reb. O/T	A	TO	PF	S	Blk	TP	PPM
LAFAILLE, M.	-	3/ -		2/ 2	1.000	-/ -	-	-	4	-	-	8	-
WOLFE, A.	-	8/ -		1/ 2	.500	-/ -	-	-	0	-	-	17	-
SMITH, J.	-	2/ -		0/ 3	.000	-/ -	-	-	4	-	-	4	-
WALKER, G.	-	2/ -		1/ 6	.167	-/ -	-	-	3	-	-	5	-
WRAY, J.	-	4/ -		0/ 2	.000	-/ -	-	-	2	-	-	8	-
HOGEBOOM, B.	-	3/ -		2/ 2	1.000	-/ -	-	-	0	-	-	8	-
Totals	200	22/ -		6/17	.353	-/ -	-	-	13	-	-	50	.250

Colorado (44)　Coach: Frosty Cox

	Min.	Total FG/FGA	Pct.	FT/FTA	Pct.	Reb. O/T	A	TO	PF	S	Blk	TP	PPM
WALSETH, R.	-	3/ -		1/ 1	1.000	-/ -	-	-	0	-	-	7	-
BEATTIE, H.	-	2/ -		1/ 1	1.000	-/ -	-	-	0	-	-	5	-
FULLER, E.	-	1/ -		0/ 0	.000	-/ -	-	-	2	-	-	2	-
ELLIS, C.	-	3/ -		0/ 0	.000	-/ -	-	-	0	-	-	6	-
HUNT, J.	-	0/ -		0/ 0	.000	-/ -	-	-	0	-	-	0	-
KNOCKE, H.	-	4/ -		1/ 1	1.000	-/ -	-	-	2	-	-	9	-
PUTNAM	-	2/ -		1/ 2	.500	-/ -	-	-	3	-	-	5	-
HUGGINS	-	2/ -		4/ 5	.800	-/ -	-	-	3	-	-	8	-
ROBBINS, L.	-	1/ -		0/ 3	.000	-/ -	-	-	5	-	-	2	-
ALLEN, B.	-	0/ -		0/ 0	.000	-/ -	-	-	0	-	-	0	-
Totals	200	18/ -		8/13	.615	-/ -	-	-	15	-	-	44	.220

Disqualified: Colorado—Robbins.

	1st Half	2nd Half	Final
California	23	27	50
Colorado	18	26	44

REGIONAL FINAL EASTERN

Ohio State (57)   Coach: Harold Olsen

	Min.	Total FG/FGA	Pct.	FT/FTA	Pct.	Reb. O/T	A	TO	PF	S	Blk	TP	PPM
BOWEN, R.	-	3/ -	-	6/ 6	1.000	-/ -	-	-	4	-	-	12	-
SNYDER, R.	-	4/ -	-	3/ 7	.429	-/ -	-	-	3	-	-	11	-
WELLS, W.	-	0/ -	-	0/ 2	.000	-/ -	-	-	4	-	-	0	-
UNDERMAN, J.	-	8/ -	-	7/ 8	.875	-/ -	-	-	4	-	-	23	-
HUSTON, P.	-	3/ -	-	3/ 6	.500	-/ -	-	-	5	-	-	9	-
AMLING, W.	-	1/ -	-	0/ 1	.000	-/ -	-	-	5	-	-	2	-
JOHNSTON, W.	-	0/ -	-	0/ 0	.000	-/ -	-	-	0	-	-	0	-
Totals	225	19/89	.213	19/30	.633	-/ -	-	-	25	-	-	57	.253

North Carolina (60)   Coach: Ben Carnevale

	Min.	Total FG/FGA	Pct.	FT/FTA	Pct.	Reb. O/T	A	TO	PF	S	Blk	TP	PPM
DILLON, J.	-	5/ -	-	6/13	.462	-/ -	-	-	4	-	-	16	-
ANDERSON, D.	-	3/ -	-	0/ 1	.000	-/ -	-	-	2	-	-	6	-
PAXTON, B.	-	4/ -	-	0/ 2	.000	-/ -	-	-	3	-	-	8	-
MCKINNEY, B.	-	4/ -	-	1/ 3	.333	-/ -	-	-	5	-	-	9	-
WHITE, J.	-	2/ -	-	3/ 4	.750	-/ -	-	-	4	-	-	7	-
THORNE, T.	-	1/ -	-	0/ 1	.000	-/ -	-	-	1	-	-	2	-
JORDAN, J.	-	4/ -	-	4/ 5	.800	-/ -	-	-	3	-	-	12	-
SCHOLBE, R.	-	0/ -	-	0/ 0	.000	-/ -	-	-	1	-	-	0	-
Totals	225	23/91	.253	14/29	.483	-/ -	-	-	23	-	-	60	.267

Disqualified: N. Carolina—McKinney; Ohio State—Huston, Amling.

	1st Half	2nd Half	1st OT	Final
Ohio State	20	34	3	57
N. Carolina	19	35	6	60

REGIONAL FINAL WESTERN

Oklahoma A&M (52)   Coach: Henry Iba

	Min.	Total FG/FGA	Pct.	FT/FTA	Pct.	Reb. O/T	A	TO	PF	S	Blk	TP	PPM
AUBREY, S.	-	0/ -	-	0/ 0	.000	-/ -	-	-	0	-	-	0	-
BENNETT, A.	-	1/ -	-	2/ 2	1.000	-/ -	-	-	1	-	-	4	-
KERN, W.	-	2/ -	-	0/ 0	.000	-/ -	-	-	1	-	-	4	-
BRADLEY, J.	-	1/ -	-	1/ 2	.500	-/ -	-	-	1	-	-	3	-
KURLAND, B.	-	12/ -	-	5/ 6	.833	-/ -	-	-	3	-	-	29	-
HALBERT, J.	-	0/ -	-	0/ 0	.000	-/ -	-	-	0	-	-	0	-
WILLIAMS, B.	-	1/ -	-	1/ 1	1.000	-/ -	-	-	0	-	-	3	-
BELL, G.	-	1/ -	-	2/ 2	1.000	-/ -	-	-	2	-	-	4	-
PARKS, J.	-	2/ -	-	1/ 1	1.000	-/ -	-	-	1	-	-	5	-
GEYMAN, P.	-	0/ -	-	0/ 0	.000	-/ -	-	-	0	-	-	0	-
STEINMEIER, L.	-	0/ -	-	0/ 0	.000	-/ -	-	-	0	-	-	0	-
Totals	200	20/ -	-	12/14	.857	-/ -	-	-	9	-	-	52	.260

California (35)   Coach: Nibs Price

	Min.	Total FG/FGA	Pct.	FT/FTA	Pct.	Reb. O/T	A	TO	PF	S	Blk	TP	PPM
LAFAILLE, M.	-	4/ -	-	2/ 2	1.000	-/ -	-	-	4	-	-	10	-
WOLFE, A.	-	7/ -	-	0/ 1	.000	-/ -	-	-	2	-	-	14	-
SMITH, J.	-	0/ -	-	1/ 3	.333	-/ -	-	-	3	-	-	1	-
WALKER, G.	-	2/ -	-	2/ 3	.667	-/ -	-	-	2	-	-	6	-
WRAY, J.	-	1/ -	-	0/ 0	.000	-/ -	-	-	2	-	-	2	-
HOGEBOOM, B.	-	0/ -	-	2/ 3	.667	-/ -	-	-	0	-	-	2	-
DEAN, L.	-	0/ -	-	0/ 0	.000	-/ -	-	-	0	-	-	0	-
LARNER, D.	-	0/ -	-	0/ 0	.000	-/ -	-	-	0	-	-	0	-
Totals	200	14/ -	-	7/12	.583	-/ -	-	-	13	-	-	35	.175

Disqualified: None.

	1st Half	2nd Half	Final
Oklahoma A&M	26	26	52
California	21	14	35

CHAMPIONSHIP

North Carolina (40)   Coach: Ben Carnevale

	Min.	Total FG/FGA	Pct.	FT/FTA	Pct.	Reb. O/T	A	TO	PF	S	Blk	TP	PPM
DILLON, J.	-	5/ -	-	6/ 6	1.000	-/ -	-	-	5	-	-	16	-
ANDERSON, D.	-	3/ -	-	2/ 3	.667	-/ -	-	-	3	-	-	8	-
PAXTON, B.	-	2/ -	-	0/ 0	.000	-/ -	-	-	4	-	-	4	-
MCKINNEY, B.	-	2/ -	-	1/ 3	.333	-/ -	-	-	5	-	-	5	-
WHITE, J.	-	0/ -	-	1/ 1	1.000	-/ -	-	-	0	-	-	1	-
THORNE, T.	-	1/ -	-	0/ 0	.000	-/ -	-	-	2	-	-	2	-
JORDAN, J.	-	0/ -	-	4/ 8	.500	-/ -	-	-	3	-	-	4	-
Totals	200	13/ -	-	14/21	.667	-/ -	-	-	22	-	-	40	.200

Oklahoma A&M (43)   Coach: Henry Iba

	Min.	Total FG/FGA	Pct.	FT/FTA	Pct.	Reb. O/T	A	TO	PF	S	Blk	TP	PPM
AUBREY, S.	-	0/ -	-	1/ 2	.500	-/ -	-	-	1	-	-	1	-
BENNETT, A.	-	3/ -	-	0/ 0	.000	-/ -	-	-	4	-	-	6	-
KERN, W.	-	3/ -	-	1/ 3	.333	-/ -	-	-	2	-	-	7	-
BRADLEY, J.	-	1/ -	-	1/ 2	.500	-/ -	-	-	1	-	-	3	-
KURLAND, B.	-	9/ -	-	5/ 9	.556	-/ -	-	-	5	-	-	23	-
HALBERT, J.	-	0/ -	-	0/ 0	.000	-/ -	-	-	0	-	-	0	-
WILLIAMS, B.	-	0/ -	-	2/ 4	.500	-/ -	-	-	2	-	-	2	-
BELL, G.	-	0/ -	-	1/ 1	1.000	-/ -	-	-	1	-	-	1	-
PARKS, J.	-	0/ -	-	0/ 1	.000	-/ -	-	-	2	-	-	0	-
Totals	200	16/ -	-	11/22	.500	-/ -	-	-	18	-	-	43	.215

Disqualified: Oklahoma A&M—Kurland; N. Carolina—Dillon, McKinney.

	1st Half	2nd Half	Final
N. Carolina	17	23	40
Oklahoma A&M	23	20	43

NATIONAL THIRD PLACE

Ohio State (63)   Coach: Harold Olsen

	Min.	Total FG/FGA	Pct.	FT/FTA	Pct.	Reb. O/T	A	TO	PF	S	Blk	TP	PPM
BOWEN, R.	-	6/ -	-	4/ 4	1.000	-/ -	-	-	2	-	-	16	-
WELLS, W.	-	0/ -	-	0/ 0	.000	-/ -	-	-	0	-	-	0	-
LOVETT, J.	-	0/ -	-	0/ 1	.000	-/ -	-	-	0	-	-	0	-
SNYDER, R.	-	3/ -	-	4/ 5	.800	-/ -	-	-	2	-	-	10	-
UNDERMAN, J.	-	6/ -	-	7/ 8	.875	-/ -	-	-	4	-	-	19	-
ELLIOTT, C.	-	1/ -	-	1/ 1	1.000	-/ -	-	-	1	-	-	3	-
HUSTON, P.	-	2/ -	-	1/ 2	.500	-/ -	-	-	3	-	-	5	-
JOHNSTON, W.	-	0/ -	-	0/ 0	.000	-/ -	-	-	0	-	-	0	-
AMLING, W.	-	5/ -	-	0/ 1	.000	-/ -	-	-	4	-	-	10	-
KUHN, C.	-	0/ -	-	0/ 0	.000	-/ -	-	-	0	-	-	0	-
Totals	200	23/ -	-	17/22	.773	-/ -	-	-	16	-	-	63	.315

California (45)   Coach: Nibs Price

	Min.	Total FG/FGA	Pct.	FT/FTA	Pct.	Reb. O/T	A	TO	PF	S	Blk	TP	PPM
LAFAILLE, M.	-	9/ -	-	4/ 4	1.000	-/ -	-	-	2	-	-	22	-
LARNER, D.	-	0/ -	-	0/ 0	.000	-/ -	-	-	0	-	-	0	-
WOLFE, A.	-	3/ -	-	0/ 0	.000	-/ -	-	-	1	-	-	6	-
ANDERSON, B.	-	0/ -	-	0/ 0	.000	-/ -	-	-	0	-	-	0	-
HOLCOMBE, L.	-	0/ -	-	1/ 1	1.000	-/ -	-	-	1	-	-	1	-
SMITH, J.	-	2/ -	-	0/ 0	.000	-/ -	-	-	4	-	-	4	-
WALKER, G.	-	1/ -	-	2/ 7	.286	-/ -	-	-	4	-	-	4	-
WRAY, D.	-	0/ -	-	1/ 2	.500	-/ -	-	-	1	-	-	1	-
BOWER	-	0/ -	-	1/ 1	1.000	-/ -	-	-	2	-	-	1	-
REMRE, C.	-	0/ -	-	0/ 0	.000	-/ -	-	-	1	-	-	0	-
HOGEBOOM, B.	-	2/ -	-	2/ 2	1.000	-/ -	-	-	1	-	-	6	-
DEAN, L.	-	0/ -	-	0/ 0	.000	-/ -	-	-	0	-	-	0	-
Totals	200	17/ -	-	11/17	.647	-/ -	-	-	17	-	-	45	.225

Disqualified: None.

	1st Half	2nd Half	Final
Ohio State	22	41	63
California	21	24	45

REGIONAL THIRD PLACE WESTERN

Colorado (59)   Coach: Frosty Cox

	Min.	Total FG/FGA	Pct.	FT/FTA	Pct.	Reb. O/T	A	TO	PF	S	Blk	TP	PPM
FULLER, E.	-	0/ -	-	0/ 1	.000	-/ -	-	-	0	-	-	-	-
WALSETH, R.	-	4/ -	-	3/ 3	1.000	-/ -	-	-	2	-	-	11	-
HUGGINS	-	6/ -	-	1/ 3	.333	-/ -	-	-	3	-	-	13	-
STARK	-	0/ -	-	0/ 0	.000	-/ -	-	-	0	-	-	0	-
ALLEN, B.	-	0/ -	-	0/ 0	.000	-/ -	-	-	1	-	-	0	-
KNOCKE, H.	-	1/ -	-	5/11	.455	-/ -	-	-	0	-	-	7	-
ROBBINS, L.	-	4/ -	-	3/ 5	.600	-/ -	-	-	1	-	-	11	-
PUTNAM	-	1/ -	-	1/ 2	.500	-/ -	-	-	3	-	-	3	-
BEATTIE, H.	-	1/ -	-	2/ 2	1.000	-/ -	-	-	3	-	-	4	-
RILEY	-	1/ -	-	0/ 0	.000	-/ -	-	-	0	-	-	2	-
ELLIS, C.	-	3/ -	-	2/ 3	.667	-/ -	-	-	4	-	-	8	-
HUNT, J.	-	0/ -	-	0/ 0	.000	-/ -	-	-	0	-	-	0	-
Totals	200	21/ -	-	17/30	.567	-/ -	-	-	17	-	-	59	.295

REGIONAL THIRD PLACE EASTERN

NYU (67)   Coach: Howard Cann

	Min.	Total FG/FGA	Pct.	FT/FTA	Pct.	Reb. O/T	A	TO	PF	S	Blk	TP	PPM
FORMAN, D.	-	0/ -	-	3/ 6	.500	-/ -	-	-	1	-	-	3	-
SARATH	-	0/ -	-	0/ 0	.000	-/ -	-	-	1	-	-	0	-
DEBONIS	-	7/ -	-	1/ 1	1.000	-/ -	-	-	3	-	-	15	-
GOLDSTEIN	-	0/ -	-	0/ 0	.000	-/ -	-	-	0	-	-	0	-
BENANTI	-	0/ -	-	0/ 0	.000	-/ -	-	-	1	-	-	0	-
SCHAYES, D.	-	1/ -	-	0/ 0	.000	-/ -	-	-	4	-	-	2	-
KELLY, T.	-	10/ -	-	2/ 5	.400	-/ -	-	-	5	-	-	22	-
REGAN	-	0/ -	-	0/ 0	.000	-/ -	-	-	0	-	-	0	-
TANENBAUM, S.	-	3/ -	-	4/ 4	1.000	-/ -	-	-	2	-	-	10	-
MANGIAPANE	-	6/ -	-	3/ 4	.750	-/ -	-	-	4	-	-	15	-
Totals	200	27/ -	-	13/20	.650	-/ -	-	-	21	-	-	67	.335

Harvard (61)   Coach: Floyd Stahl

	Min.	Total FG/FGA	Pct.	FT/FTA	Pct.	Reb. O/T	A	TO	PF	S	Blk	TP	PPM
GANTT	-	1/ -	-	2/ 3	.667	-/ -	-	-	4	-	-	4	-
SWEGAN	-	2/ -	-	2/ 4	.500	-/ -	-	-	1	-	-	6	-
GRAY, W.	-	9/ -	-	4/ 7	.571	-/ -	-	-	1	-	-	22	-
DECSI	-	5/ -	-	3/ 4	.750	-/ -	-	-	3	-	-	13	-
MARIASCHIN	-	2/ -	-	4/ 6	.667	-/ -	-	-	4	-	-	8	-
CHAMPION	-	3/ -	-	0/ 1	.000	-/ -	-	-	3	-	-	6	-
PETRILLO	-	1/ -	-	0/ 0	.000	-/ -	-	-	0	-	-	2	-
Totals	200	23/ -	-	15/25	.600	-/ -	-	-	16	-	-	61	.305

Disqualified: NYU—Kelly.

	1st Half	2nd Half	Final
NYU	40	27	67
Harvard	32	29	61

Baylor (44)   Coach: Bill Henderson

	Min.	Total FG/FGA	Pct.	FT/FTA	Pct.	Reb. O/T	A	TO	PF	S	Blk	TP	PPM
BELEW	-	6/ -	-	2/ 6	.333	-/ -	-	-	4	-	-	14	-
PULLEY	-	0/ -	-	0/ 0	.000	-/ -	-	-	1	-	-	0	-
JOHNSON, B.	-	3/ -	-	5/ 6	.833	-/ -	-	-	3	-	-	11	-
EDWARDS	-	0/ -	-	0/ 0	.000	-/ -	-	-	5	-	-	0	-
SHEARIN	-	0/ -	-	1/ 1	1.000	-/ -	-	-	5	-	-	1	-
HAILEY	-	0/ -	-	3/ 3	1.000	-/ -	-	-	4	-	-	3	-
DEVEREAUX	-	0/ -	-	0/ 0	.000	-/ -	-	-	1	-	-	0	-
ROBINSON, J.	-	5/ -	-	5/ 6	.833	-/ -	-	-	2	-	-	15	-
Totals	200	14/ -	-	16/22	.727	-/ -	-	-	25	-	-	44	.220

Disqualified: Baylor—Edwards, Shearin.

	1st Half	2nd Half	Final
Colorado	25	34	59
Baylor	22	22	44

✪ INDIVIDUAL RECORDS ✪

SCORING

Most points in a single game
1 BOB KURLAND, OKLAHOMA A&M (vs. CALIFORNIA) ... 29
2 JACK UNDERMAN, OHIO STATE (vs. N. CAROLINA) ... 23
2 BOB KURLAND, OKLAHOMA A&M (vs. N. CAROLINA) ... 23
4 3 tied for fourth place.

Most total points in the tournament
1 BOB KURLAND, OKLAHOMA A&M ... 72
2 JACK UNDERMAN, OHIO STATE ... 56
3 JOHN DILLON, N. CAROLINA ... 47
4 MERV LAFAILLE, CALIFORNIA ... 40
5 ANDY WOLFE, CALIFORNIA ... 37

Highest scoring average (minimum 2 games)
1 BOB KURLAND, OKLAHOMA A&M (72-3) ... 24.00
2 JACK UNDERMAN, OHIO STATE (56-3) ... 18.67
3 WYNDOL GRAY, HARVARD (33-2) ... 16.50
4 JOHN DILLON, N. CAROLINA (47-3) ... 15.67
5 DEBONIS, NYU (28-2) ... 14.00

FIELD GOALS

Most field goals in a single game
1 BOB KURLAND, OKLAHOMA A&M (vs. CALIFORNIA) ... 12
2 TOMMY KELLY, NYU (vs. HARVARD) ... 10
3 WYNDOL GRAY, HARVARD (vs. NYU) ... 9

3 MERV LAFAILLE, CALIFORNIA (vs. OHIO STATE)9
3 BOB KURLAND, OKLAHOMA A&M (vs. N. CAROLINA) ... 9

Most total field goals in the tournament
1 BOB KURLAND, OKLAHOMA A&M ... 28
2 JACK UNDERMAN, OHIO STATE ... 19
3 ANDY WOLFE, CALIFORNIA ... 18
4 JOHN DILLON, N. CAROLINA ... 17
5 MERV LAFAILLE, CALIFORNIA ... 16

FREE THROWS

Most free throws in a single game
1 JACK UNDERMAN, OHIO STATE (vs. CALIFORNIA) ... 7
1 WYNDOL GRAY, HARVARD (vs. OHIO STATE) ... 7
1 JACK UNDERMAN, OHIO STATE (vs. N. CAROLINA) ... 7
4 5 tied for fourth place.

Most total free throws in the tournament
1 JACK UNDERMAN, OHIO STATE ... 18
2 BOB KURLAND, OKLAHOMA A&M ... 16
3 JOHN DILLON, N. CAROLINA ... 13
4 WYNDOL GRAY, HARVARD ... 11
5 3 tied for fifth place.

Most free throws attempted in a single game
1 JOHN DILLON, N. CAROLINA (vs. OHIO STATE) ... 13

2 BOB KURLAND, OKLAHOMA A&M (vs. BAYLOR) ... 12
3 H. KNOCKE, COLORADO (vs. BAYLOR) ... 11
4 3 tied for fourth place.

Most free throws attempted in the tournament
1 BOB KURLAND, OKLAHOMA A&M ... 27
2 JOHN DILLON, N. CAROLINA ... 23
3 JACK UNDERMAN, OHIO STATE ... 21
4 PAUL HUSTON, OHIO STATE ... 17
5 2 tied for fifth place.

Highest free throw percentage in a single game (minimum 7 attempts)
1 JACK UNDERMAN, OHIO STATE (vs. CALIFORNIA) (7-8) ... .875
1 JACK UNDERMAN, OHIO STATE (vs. N. CAROLINA) (7-8) ... .875
3 WYNDOL GRAY, HARVARD (vs. OHIO STATE) (7-9) ... .778
4 PAUL HUSTON, OHIO STATE (vs. HARVARD) (6-9) ... .667
5 DECSI, HARVARD (vs. OHIO STATE) (5-8) ... .625

Highest free throw percentage in the tournament (minimum 15 attempts)
1 JACK UNDERMAN, OHIO STATE (18-21) ... .857
2 WYNDOL GRAY, HARVARD (11-16) ... .688
3 JIM JORDAN, N. CAROLINA (10-15) ... .667
4 BOB KURLAND, OKLAHOMA A&M (16-27) ... .593
5 PAUL HUSTON, OHIO STATE (10-17) ... .588

✪ TEAM RECORDS ✪

SCORING

Most points in a single game
1 NYU (vs. HARVARD) ... 67
2 OHIO STATE (vs. CALIFORNIA) ... 63
3 HARVARD (vs. NYU) ... 61

Most total points in the tournament
1 OHIO STATE ... 166
2 N. CAROLINA ... 157
3 OKLAHOMA A&M ... 139

Highest scoring average (minimum 2 games)
1 NYU (116-2) ... 58.00
2 OHIO STATE (166-3) ... 55.33
3 N. CAROLINA (157-3) ... 52.33

FIELD GOALS

Most field goals in a single game
1 NYU (vs. HARVARD) ... 27
2 N. CAROLINA (vs. NYU) ... 24
3 HARVARD (vs. NYU) ... 23
3 OHIO STATE (vs. CALIFORNIA) ... 23
3 N. CAROLINA (vs. OHIO STATE) ... 23

Most total field goals in the tournament
1 N. CAROLINA ... 60

2 OHIO STATE ... 59
3 CALIFORNIA ... 53

FREE THROWS

Most free throws in a single game
1 OHIO STATE (vs. N. CAROLINA) ... 19
2 HARVARD (vs. OHIO STATE) ... 18
3 COLORADO (vs. BAYLOR) ... 17
3 OHIO STATE (vs. CALIFORNIA) ... 17
3 NYU (vs. N. CAROLINA) ... 17

Most total free throws in the tournament
1 OHIO STATE ... 48
2 OKLAHOMA A&M ... 37
2 N. CAROLINA ... 37

Most free throws attempted in a single game
1 COLORADO (vs. BAYLOR) ... 30
1 OHIO STATE (vs. N. CAROLINA) ... 30
1 HARVARD (vs. OHIO STATE) ... 30

Most total free throws attempted in the tournament
1 OHIO STATE ... 74
2 N. CAROLINA ... 68
3 OKLAHOMA A&M ... 61

Highest free throw percentage in a single game
1 OKLAHOMA A&M (vs. CALIFORNIA) (12-14) ... .857
2 OHIO STATE (vs. CALIFORNIA) (17-22) ... .773
3 BAYLOR (vs. COLORADO) (16-22) ... .727

Highest free throw percentage in the tournament (minimum 2 games)
1 BAYLOR (23-33) ... .697
2 NYU (30-45) ... .667
3 OHIO STATE (48-74) ... .649

Fewest free throws in a single game
1 CALIFORNIA (vs. COLORADO) ... 6
2 BAYLOR (vs. OKLAHOMA A&M) ... 7
2 CALIFORNIA (vs. OKLAHOMA A&M) ... 7

Lowest free throw percentage in a single game
1 CALIFORNIA (vs. COLORADO) (6-17) ... .353
2 N. CAROLINA (vs. OHIO STATE) (14-29) ... .483
3 N. CAROLINA (vs. NYU) (9-18) ... .500

Lowest free throw percentage in the tournament (minimum 2 games)
1 CALIFORNIA (24-46) ... .522
2 N. CAROLINA (37-68) ... .544
3 COLORADO (25-43) ... .581

1947

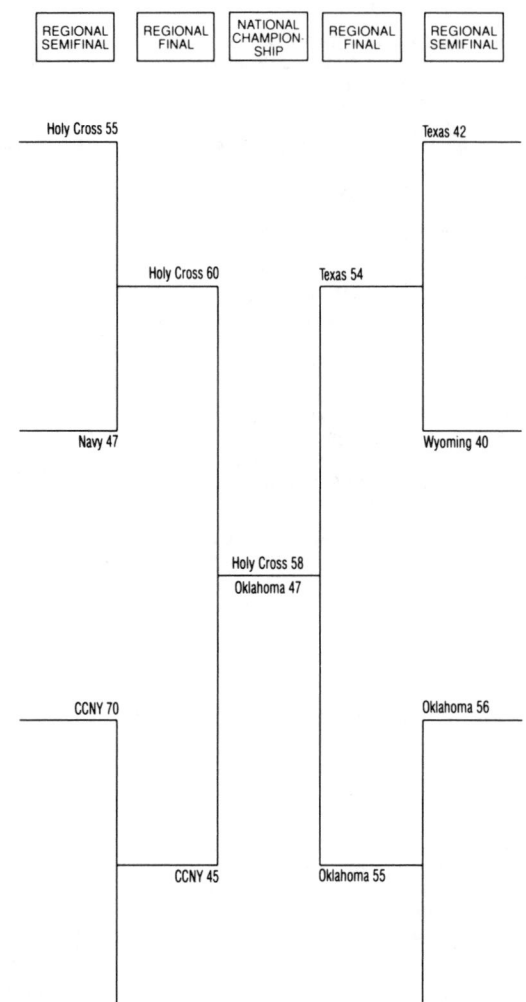

REGIONAL SEMIFINAL | REGIONAL FINAL | NATIONAL CHAMPION-SHIP | REGIONAL FINAL | REGIONAL SEMIFINAL

EASTERN

WESTERN

Holy Cross 55

Texas 42

Holy Cross 60

Texas 54

Navy 47

Wyoming 40

Holy Cross 58
Oklahoma 47

CCNY 70

Oklahoma 56

CCNY 45

Oklahoma 55

Wisconsin 56

Oregon St. 54

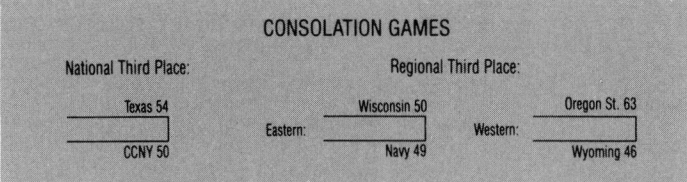

CONSOLATION GAMES

National Third Place:

Texas 54

CCNY 50

Regional Third Place:

Eastern:
Wisconsin 50
Navy 49

Western:
Oregon St. 63
Wyoming 46

By 1947 it was clear to everyone that basketball—at least the NCAA variety—was a game of wide-open spaces. In the tournament's first eight years, no school from east of the Great Lakes had won a title, while two championships had been brought back to each of four other regions: the West Coast, the Rocky Mountains, the Great Plains, and the Midwest. Although eastern teams had dominated Madison Square Garden's NIT, basketball, as it was played in the NCAA tournament, was a game to be learned on barn doors, not city streets.

In 1947, Holy Cross, a small Catholic college in Worcester, Massachusetts, fielded a team of New York City area boys that changed the perception of eastern basketball. The Crusaders' deadly combination of speed, guile, and ball-handling ability proved, once and for all, that the game was not just for tall westerners. It was a city game, too.

Doggie Julian's Crusaders opened the tournament against Navy. The Midshipmen had put together a 16-1 record, largely on the explosive scoring of their captain, little Kenny Shugart. Holy Cross had an impressive record of their own; they had won 20 straight games and taken 24 of 27 for the year, with Joe Mullaney's ball-handling wizardry and George Kaftan's inside scoring leading the high-speed Crusader attack. In their first round game, the Middies led by as much as 8 early on and stayed with Holy Cross until midway through the second half, when they trailed by only 2. But finally Mullaney's brilliance on both ends of the court (he scored 18 while holding Shugart to 9) and the Crusaders' superior depth wore down Ben Carnevale's Navy squad. The final score was 55-47.

City College of New York, the Crusaders' opponent in the regional final, had made a stirring comeback to win their opener against the Big Nine champion Wisconsin Badgers. The City College Beavers, down 26-10 midway through the first half, stormed back with a fast-breaking attack that left the Badgers floundering. City outscored Wisconsin 43-19 in the final twenty minutes to win 70-56.

CCNY started off against Holy Cross in the same high gear. They raced to a 23-12 lead, and it looked like the fast-moving Beavers would romp into the championship round. Holy Cross had other ideas, however. They regained their composure, cut off the City College fast break, and, with the Beavers concentrating on stopping Joe Mullaney, the Crusaders patiently worked the ball inside to their big, gum-chewing center, George Kaftan. Before intermission Holy Cross had come back all the way and taken a 2-point lead, with a spectacular Kaftan scoring 19 of their 27 points. Nine minutes into the second half

the score was tied at 38, but with Kaftan dominating the boards, Holy Cross finally began to pull away. They scored 8 points in the last 40 seconds to win 60-45.

In the West, meanwhile, the big, strong, defensive-minded Sooners of Oklahoma pulled off two stirring upsets to earn the right to meet Holy Cross for the national title. First they withstood a rally by the explosive Beavers of Oregon State to win 56-54, as center Gerald Tucker and forward Paul Courty paved the way with 17 points each. Next, in the regional finals, the Sooners came back from a 7-point halftime deficit to win a fierce, down-to-the-wire battle against Texas. Oklahoma's Tucker kept his team together against the fast-breaking Longhorns, pulling down rebounds, scoring from down low, and passing brilliantly from the high post. With less than ten seconds to play, Texas still held a 1-point lead. But Tucker whipped a pass out to Ken Pryor, who hit a spectacular long-range jump shot (his only 2 points of the night) to win the game. The Sooners were on their way to Madison Square Garden and a confrontation with Holy Cross.

In the title contest against Oklahoma, the Crusaders followed much the same script that they had used in the eastern regional games, falling behind early, fighting their way back into the game, and then roaring away at the end. Oklahoma's Gerald Tucker owned the first half. He needled Kaftan, calling the Holy Cross star a "hot shot," while putting in 15 points himself. The Sooners left the floor brimming with confidence and a 31-28 lead.

The Crusaders, on the other hand, had to do something different to turn the game around. And Coach Doggie Julian knew just what it was. During the halftime intermission, he told his players to speed up the tempo and run the fast break against the tall westerners. He assigned reserve Bob Curran to guard Tucker, and ordered Curran's teammates to sag off their men to double-team the big Sooner center. And he urged Kaftan to be more aggressive underneath. Five minutes into the second half, Julian's strategic adjustments were clearly working; Holy Cross led by 2, Tucker was invisible on offense, and Kaftan was beginning to assert himself. Twelve minutes later the game was still close, with the Crusaders clinging to a 48-45 lead. But Tucker had scored only one basket since halftime, and the Sooners were tiring from the quick Holy Cross pace. In the end, just as they had against Navy and CCNY, the Crusaders pulled away. The final score—58-47.

Holy Cross made history, became the first eastern team to win the national championship, and proved that city boys could play a little ball after all.

REGIONAL SEMIFINAL EASTERN

Holy Cross (55)   Coach: Doggie Julian

	Min.	Total FG/FGA	Pct.	FT/FTA	Pct.	Reb. O/T	A	TO	PF	S	Blk	TP	PPM
KAFTAN, G.	-	7/ -	-	1/ 7	.143	-/ -	-	-	2	-	-	15	-
O'CONNELL, D.	-	1/ -	-	0/ 0	.000	-/ -	-	-	1	-	-	2	-
OFTRING, F.	-	2/ -	-	1/ 1	1.000	-/ -	-	-	1	-	-	5	-
MULLANEY, J.	-	9/ -	-	0/ 0	.000	-/ -	-	-	4	-	-	18	-
HAGGERTY, K.	-	3/ -	-	1/ 1	1.000	-/ -	-	-	0	-	-	7	-
LASKA, A.	-	0/ -	-	0/ 0	.000	-/ -	-	-	0	-	-	0	-
COUSY, B.	-	3/ -	-	0/ 0	.000	-/ -	-	-	2	-	-	6	-
MCMULLEN, B.	-	0/ -	-	0/ 1	.000	-/ -	-	-	1	-	-	0	-
CURRAN, B.	-	0/ -	-	2/ 2	1.000	-/ -	-	-	4	-	-	2	-
Totals	200	25/ -	-	5/12	.417	-/ -	-	-	15	-	-	55	.275

Navy (47)   Coach: Ben Carnevale

	Min.	Total FG/FGA	Pct.	FT/FTA	Pct.	Reb. O/T	A	TO	PF	S	Blk	TP	PPM
ROBBINS	-	1/ -	-	1/ 1	1.000	-/ -	-	-	0	-	-	3	-
SHUGART, K.	-	3/ -	-	3/ 4	.750	-/ -	-	-	0	-	-	9	-
WALDROP	-	6/ -	-	3/ 4	.750	-/ -	-	-	3	-	-	15	-
BARROW, J.	-	5/ -	-	1/ 1	1.000	-/ -	-	-	4	-	-	11	-
DICK	-	0/ -	-	0/ 1	.000	-/ -	-	-	2	-	-	0	-
SEARLE	-	1/ -	-	2/ 3	.667	-/ -	-	-	0	-	-	4	-
DURHAM	-	0/ -	-	0/ 0	.000	-/ -	-	-	1	-	-	0	-
RENSBERGER	-	0/ -	-	0/ 1	.000	-/ -	-	-	0	-	-	0	-
SHEEHAN, C.	-	2/ -	-	1/ 3	.333	-/ -	-	-	0	-	-	5	-
Totals	200	18/ -	-	11/18	.611	-/ -	-	-	10	-	-	47	.235

Disqualified: None.

	1st Half	2nd Half	Final
Holy Cross	29	26	55
Navy	27	20	47

CCNY (70)   Coach: Nat Holman

	Min.	Total FG/FGA	Pct.	FT/FTA	Pct.	Reb. O/T	A	TO	PF	S	Blk	TP	PPM
TRUBOWITZ, S.	-	0/ -	-	0/ 0	.000	-/ -	-	-	1	-	-	0	-
DAMBROT, I.	-	6/ -	-	4/ 5	.800	-/ -	-	-	1	-	-	16	-
GALIBER, J.	-	0/ -	-	4/ 6	.667	-/ -	-	-	4	-	-	4	-
SHAPIRO, H.	-	0/ -	-	1/ 2	.500	-/ -	-	-	2	-	-	1	-
MALAMED, L.	-	6/ -	-	1/ 1	1.000	-/ -	-	-	3	-	-	13	-
JAMESON, S.	-	5/ -	-	0/ 0	.000	-/ -	-	-	1	-	-	10	-
FARBMAN, P.	-	2/ -	-	2/ 3	.667	-/ -	-	-	1	-	-	6	-
FINESTONE, E.	-	4/ -	-	1/ 1	1.000	-/ -	-	-	1	-	-	9	-
BRICKMAN, M.	-	0/ -	-	0/ 0	.000	-/ -	-	-	0	-	-	0	-
SCHMONES, P.	-	3/ -	-	1/ 2	.500	-/ -	-	-	3	-	-	7	-
FINGER, S.	-	2/ -	-	0/ 0	.000	-/ -	-	-	1	-	-	4	-
Totals	200	28/ -	-	14/20	.700	-/ -	-	-	18	-	-	70	.350

Wisconsin (56)   Coach: Bud Foster

	Min.	Total FG/FGA	Pct.	FT/FTA	Pct.	Reb. O/T	A	TO	PF	S	Blk	TP	PPM
COOK, B.	-	5/ -	-	3/ 4	.750	-/ -	-	-	4	-	-	13	-
MENZEL, E.	-	5/ -	-	5/ 8	.625	-/ -	-	-	3	-	-	15	-
MILLS	-	2/ -	-	2/ 3	.667	-/ -	-	-	4	-	-	6	-
LAUTENBACH	-	1/ -	-	0/ 0	.000	-/ -	-	-	2	-	-	2	-
SELBO	-	6/ -	-	0/ 0	.000	-/ -	-	-	3	-	-	12	-
MADER	-	0/ -	-	0/ 0	.000	-/ -	-	-	0	-	-	0	-
HERTZ	-	1/ -	-	0/ 0	.000	-/ -	-	-	0	-	-	2	-
REHFELDT	-	2/ -	-	0/ 2	.000	-/ -	-	-	1	-	-	4	-
HAARLOW	-	0/ -	-	1/ 1	1.000	-/ -	-	-	1	-	-	1	-
KRUEGER	-	0/ -	-	1/ 1	1.000	-/ -	-	-	0	-	-	1	-
FALLS	-	0/ -	-	0/ 0	.000	-/ -	-	-	0	-	-	0	-
POKRZYWINSKI	-	0/ -	-	0/ 0	.000	-/ -	-	-	0	-	-	0	-
Totals	200	22/ -	-	12/19	.632	-/ -	-	-	18	-	-	56	.280

Disqualified: None.

	1st Half	2nd Half	Final
CCNY	27	43	70
Wisconsin	37	19	56

REGIONAL SEMIFINAL WESTERN

Texas (42)   Coach: Jack Gray

	Min.	Total FG/FGA	Pct.	FT/FTA	Pct.	Reb. O/T	A	TO	PF	S	Blk	TP	PPM
HARGIS, J.	-	3/ -	-	3/ 4	.750	-/ -	-	-	1	-	-	9	-
HAMILTON, T.	-	0/ -	-	0/ 0	.000	-/ -	-	-	1	-	-	0	-
MARTIN, S.	-	4/ -	-	1/ 4	.250	-/ -	-	-	4	-	-	9	-
LANGDON, J.	-	4/ -	-	3/ 3	1.000	-/ -	-	-	3	-	-	11	-
COX, R.	-	1/ -	-	0/ 1	.000	-/ -	-	-	4	-	-	2	-
WAGNER, D.	-	3/ -	-	0/ 0	.000	-/ -	-	-	4	-	-	6	-
MADSEN, A.	-	1/ -	-	3/ 4	.750	-/ -	-	-	3	-	-	5	-
Totals	200	16/ -	-	10/16	.625	-/ -	-	-	20	-	-	42	.210

Wyoming (40)   Coach: Everett Shelton

	Min.	Total FG/FGA	Pct.	FT/FTA	Pct.	Reb. O/T	A	TO	PF	S	Blk	TP	PPM
REESE, J.	40	3/ -	-	4/ 7	.571	-/ -	-	-	4	-	-	10	.250
PEYTON, M.	32	1/ -	-	0/ 2	.000	-/ -	-	-	2	-	-	2	.063
TODOROVICH, M.	30	3/ -	-	3/ 4	.750	-/ -	-	-	3	-	-	9	.300
PILCH, J.	10	1/ -	-	0/ 1	.000	-/ -	-	-	1	-	-	2	.200
VOLKER, F.	40	5/ -	-	1/ 3	.333	-/ -	-	-	3	-	-	11	.275
COLLINS, J.	40	2/ -	-	2/ 2	1.000	-/ -	-	-	4	-	-	6	.150
ROGERS, T.	8	0/ -	-	0/ 0	.000	-/ -	-	-	0	-	-	0	.000
Totals	200	15/ -	-	10/19	.526	-/ -	-	-	17	-	-	40	.200

Disqualified: None.

	1st Half	2nd Half	Final
Texas	24	18	42
Wyoming	27	13	40

Oklahoma (56) Coach: Bruce Drake

	Min.	Total FG/FGA	Pct.	FT/FTA	Pct.	Reb. O/T	A	TO	PF	S	Blk	TP	PPM
REICH, D.	-	4/-		3/3	1.000	-/-	-	-	3	-	-	11	-
COURTY, P.	-	5/-		7/8	.875	-/-	-	-	4	-	-	17	-
JONES, B.	-	0/-		0/0	.000	-/-	-	-	0	-	-	0	-
TUCKER, G.	-	7/-		3/3	1.000	-/-	-	-	2	-	-	17	-
PAINE, A.	-	2/-		0/1	.000	-/-	-	-	4	-	-	4	-
WATERS, B.	-	2/-		1/4	.250	-/-	-	-	0	-	-	5	-
LANDON, J.	-	0/-		2/4	.500	-/-	-	-	3	-	-	2	-
MERCHANT, P.	-	0/-		0/0	.000	-/-	-	-	0	-	-	0	-
Totals	200	20/-		16/23	.696	-/-	-	-	16	-	-	56	.280

Oregon State (54) Coach: Amory "Slats" Gill

	Min.	Total FG/FGA	Pct.	FT/FTA	Pct.	Reb. O/T	A	TO	PF	S	Blk	TP	PPM
ANDERSON, E.	-	0/-		1/4	.250	-/-	-	-	2	-	-	1	-
SAMUEL	-	0/-		0/0	.000	-/-	-	-	1	-	-	0	-
CRANDALL, C.	-	3/-		2/2	1.000	-/-	-	-	5	-	-	8	-
CAREY	-	0/-		0/0	.000	-/-	-	-	0	-	-	0	-
TORREY	-	3/-		0/1	.000	-/-	-	-	1	-	-	6	-
ROCHA, R.	-	5/-		2/4	.500	-/-	-	-	3	-	-	12	-
PETERSON, A.	-	2/-		1/2	.500	-/-	-	-	4	-	-	5	-
BECK, L.	-	8/-		4/5	.800	-/-	-	-	2	-	-	20	-
SILVER	-	1/-		0/0	.000	-/-	-	-	1	-	-	2	-
ROELANDT	-	0/-		0/0	.000	-/-	-	-	1	-	-	0	-
Totals	200	22/-		10/18	.556	-/-	-	-	20	-	-	54	.270

Disqualified: Oregon State—Crandall.

	1st Half	2nd Half	Final
Oklahoma	32	24	56
Oregon State	27	27	54

REGIONAL FINAL EASTERN

Holy Cross (60) Coach: Doggie Julian

	Min.	Total FG/FGA	Pct.	FT/FTA	Pct.	Reb. O/T	A	TO	PF	S	Blk	TP	PPM
KAFTAN, G.	-	11/-		8/12	.667	-/-	-	-	2	-	-	30	-
O'CONNELL, D.	-	2/-		1/2	.500	-/-	-	-	1	-	-	5	-
CURRAN, B.	-	0/-		1/2	.500	-/-	-	-	2	-	-	1	-
OFTRING, F.	-	2/-		3/3	1.000	-/-	-	-	3	-	-	7	-
MULLANEY, J.	-	0/-		3/5	.600	-/-	-	-	2	-	-	3	-
HAGGERTY, K.	-	2/-		0/0	.000	-/-	-	-	3	-	-	4	-
COUSY, B.	-	2/-		1/2	.500	-/-	-	-	3	-	-	5	-
MCMULLEN, R.	-	1/-		1/3	.333	-/-	-	-	2	-	-	3	-
LASKA, A.	-	1/-		0/0	.000	-/-	-	-	1	-	-	2	-
Totals	200	21/-		18/29	.621	-/-	-	-	19	-	-	60	.300

CCNY (45) Coach: Nat Holman

	Min.	Total FG/FGA	Pct.	FT/FTA	Pct.	Reb. O/T	A	TO	PF	S	Blk	TP	PPM
TRUBOWITZ, S.	-	2/-		0/1	.000	-/-	-	-	1	-	-	4	-
DAMBROT, I.	-	5/-		4/7	.571	-/-	-	-	3	-	-	14	-
JAMESON, S.	-	1/-		1/1	1.000	-/-	-	-	5	-	-	3	-
FARBMAN, P.	-	0/-		1/1	1.000	-/-	-	-	1	-	-	1	-
GALIBER, J.	-	1/-		3/5	.600	-/-	-	-	3	-	-	5	-
BENSON, M.	-	0/-		0/0	.000	-/-	-	-	1	-	-	0	-
SHAPIRO, H.	-	2/-		1/1	1.000	-/-	-	-	3	-	-	5	-
MALAMED, L.	-	1/-		1/1	1.000	-/-	-	-	2	-	-	3	-
FINESTONE, E.	-	4/-		1/2	.500	-/-	-	-	4	-	-	9	-
SCHMONES, P.	-	0/-		1/1	1.000	-/-	-	-	1	-	-	1	-
Totals	200	16/-		13/20	.650	-/-	-	-	24	-	-	45	.225

Disqualified: CCNY—Jameson.

	1st Half	2nd Half	Final
Holy Cross	27	33	60
CCNY	25	20	45

REGIONAL FINAL WESTERN

Texas (54) Coach: Jack Gray

	Min.	Total FG/FGA	Pct.	FT/FTA	Pct.	Reb. O/T	A	TO	PF	S	Blk	TP	PPM
HARGIS, J.	-	3/-		3/4	.750	-/-	-	-	5	-	-	9	-
HAMILTON, T.	-	0/-		1/1	1.000	-/-	-	-	4	-	-	1	-
MARTIN, S.	-	8/-		2/2	1.000	-/-	-	-	2	-	-	18	-
LANGDON, J.	-	3/-		1/1	1.000	-/-	-	-	4	-	-	7	-
COX, R.	-	1/-		0/0	.000	-/-	-	-	0	-	-	2	-
WAGNER, D.	-	5/-		1/1	1.000	-/-	-	-	3	-	-	11	-
MADSEN, A.	-	1/-		4/5	.800	-/-	-	-	1	-	-	6	-
Totals	200	21/-		12/14	.857	-/-	-	-	19	-	-	54	.270

Oklahoma (55) Coach: Bruce Drake

	Min.	Total FG/FGA	Pct.	FT/FTA	Pct.	Reb. O/T	A	TO	PF	S	Blk	TP	PPM
REICH, D.	-	4/-		3/3	1.000	-/-	-	-	4	-	-	11	-
COURTY, P.	-	3/-		2/4	.500	-/-	-	-	4	-	-	8	-
TUCKER, G.	-	6/-		3/4	.750	-/-	-	-	0	-	-	15	-
PAINE, A.	-	4/-		0/0	.000	-/-	-	-	4	-	-	8	-
WATERS, B.	-	1/-		2/2	1.000	-/-	-	-	0	-	-	4	-
LANDON, J.	-	2/-		2/3	.667	-/-	-	-	4	-	-	6	-
PRYOR, K.	-	1/-		0/0	.000	-/-	-	-	0	-	-	2	-
MERCHANT, P.	-	0/-		1/1	1.000	-/-	-	-	2	-	-	1	-
Totals	200	21/-		13/17	.765	-/-	-	-	18	-	-	55	.275

Disqualified: Texas—Hargis.

	1st Half	2nd Half	Final
Texas	29	25	54
Oklahoma	22	33	55

CHAMPIONSHIP

Holy Cross (58)   Coach: Doggie Julian

	Min.	Total FG/FGA	Pct.	FT/FTA	Pct.	Reb. O/T	A	TO	PF	S	Blk	TP	PPM
KAFTAN, G.	-	7/-	-	4/5	.800	-/-	-	-	4	-	-	18	-
O'CONNELL, D.	-	7/-	-	2/4	.500	-/-	-	-	3	-	-	16	-
CURRAN, B.	-	0/-	-	0/1	.000	-/-	-	-	2	-	-	0	-
OFTRING, F.	-	6/-	-	2/3	.667	-/-	-	-	5	-	-	14	-
MULLANEY, J.	-	0/-	-	0/0	.000	-/-	-	-	2	-	-	0	-
HAGGERTY, K.	-	0/-	-	0/0	.000	-/-	-	-	0	-	-	0	-
COUSY, B.	-	0/-	-	2/2	1.000	-/-	-	-	1	-	-	2	-
MCMULLEN, R.	-	2/-	-	4/4	1.000	-/-	-	-	0	-	-	8	-
LASKA, A.	-	0/-	-	0/0	.000	-/-	-	-	0	-	-	0	-
BOLLINGER, C.	-	0/-	-	0/0	.000	-/-	-	-	0	-	-	0	-
GRAVER, C.	-	0/-	-	0/0	.000	-/-	-	-	0	-	-	0	-
RILEY, J.	-	0/-	-	0/0	.000	-/-	-	-	1	-	-	0	-
Totals	200	22/-	-	14/19	.737	-/-	-	-	18	-	-	58	.290

Oklahoma (47)   Coach: Bruce Drake

	Min.	Total FG/FGA	Pct.	FT/FTA	Pct.	Reb. O/T	A	TO	PF	S	Blk	TP	PPM
REICH, D.	-	3/-	-	2/2	1.000	-/-	-	-	3	-	-	8	-
COURTY, P.	-	3/-	-	2/3	.667	-/-	-	-	4	-	-	8	-
TUCKER, G.	-	6/-	-	10/12	.833	-/-	-	-	3	-	-	22	-
PAINE, A.	-	2/-	-	2/2	1.000	-/-	-	-	0	-	-	6	-
WATERS, B.	-	0/-	-	0/0	.000	-/-	-	-	0	-	-	0	-
MERCHANT, P.	-	0/-	-	0/0	.000	-/-	-	-	1	-	-	0	-
PRYOR, K.	-	0/-	-	1/1	1.000	-/-	-	-	1	-	-	1	-
LANDON, J.	-	1/-	-	0/1	.000	-/-	-	-	4	-	-	2	-
DAY, H.	-	0/-	-	0/0	.000	-/-	-	-	0	-	-	0	-
Totals	200	15/-	-	17/21	.810	-/-	-	-	16	-	-	47	.235

Disqualified: Holy Cross—Oftring.

	1st Half	2nd Half	Final
Holy Cross	28	30	58
Oklahoma	31	16	47

NATIONAL THIRD PLACE

Texas (54)   Coach: Jack Gray

	Min.	Total FG/FGA	Pct.	FT/FTA	Pct.	Reb. O/T	A	TO	PF	S	Blk	TP	PPM
HARGIS, J.	-	7/-	-	3/6	.500	-/-	-	-	3	-	-	17	-
HAMILTON, T.	-	0/-	-	0/1	.000	-/-	-	-	0	-	-	0	-
MARTIN, S.	-	7/-	-	0/2	.000	-/-	-	-	2	-	-	14	-
LANGDON, J.	-	4/-	-	1/2	.500	-/-	-	-	4	-	-	9	-
COX, R.	-	2/-	-	4/6	.667	-/-	-	-	2	-	-	8	-
WAGNER, D.	-	0/-	-	0/0	.000	-/-	-	-	1	-	-	0	-
MADSEN, A.	-	2/-	-	2/4	.500	-/-	-	-	3	-	-	6	-
Totals	200	22/-	-	10/21	.476	-/-	-	-	15	-	-	54	.270

CCNY (50)   Coach: Nat Holman

	Min.	Total FG/FGA	Pct.	FT/FTA	Pct.	Reb. O/T	A	TO	PF	S	Blk	TP	PPM
TRUBOWITZ, S.	-	0/-	-	0/0	.000	-/-	-	-	1	-	-	0	-
DAMBROT, I.	-	5/-	-	3/5	.600	-/-	-	-	3	-	-	13	-
JAMESON, S.	-	4/-	-	2/3	.667	-/-	-	-	2	-	-	10	-
FARBMAN, P.	-	0/-	-	1/2	.500	-/-	-	-	3	-	-	1	-
GALIBER, J.	-	1/-	-	0/1	.000	-/-	-	-	3	-	-	2	-
SHAPIRO, H.	-	1/-	-	0/0	.000	-/-	-	-	0	-	-	2	-
MALAMED, L.	-	3/-	-	0/3	.000	-/-	-	-	3	-	-	6	-
FINESTONE, E.	-	6/-	-	2/4	.500	-/-	-	-	3	-	-	14	-
SCHMONES, P.	-	1/-	-	0/0	.000	-/-	-	-	1	-	-	2	-
Totals	200	21/-	-	8/18	.444	-/-	-	-	19	-	-	50	.250

Disqualified: None.

	1st Half	2nd Half	Final
Texas	32	22	54
CCNY	28	22	50

REGIONAL THIRD PLACE EASTERN

Wisconsin (50)   Coach: Bud Foster

	Min.	Total FG/FGA	Pct.	FT/FTA	Pct.	Reb. O/T	A	TO	PF	S	Blk	TP	PPM
COOK, B.	-	10/-	-	1/1	1.000	-/-	-	-	2	-	-	21	-
MENZEL, E.	-	2/-	-	1/2	.500	-/-	-	-	3	-	-	5	-
MILLS	-	0/-	-	2/3	.667	-/-	-	-	3	-	-	2	-
REHFELDT	-	1/-	-	0/0	.000	-/-	-	-	0	-	-	2	-
SELBO	-	3/-	-	2/4	.500	-/-	-	-	1	-	-	8	-
LAUTENBACH	-	2/-	-	2/2	1.000	-/-	-	-	1	-	-	6	-
HAARLOW	-	2/-	-	2/4	.500	-/-	-	-	2	-	-	6	-
Totals	200	20/-	-	10/16	.625	-/-	-	-	12	-	-	50	.250

Navy (49)   Coach: Ben Carnevale

	Min.	Total FG/FGA	Pct.	FT/FTA	Pct.	Reb. O/T	A	TO	PF	S	Blk	TP	PPM
ROBBINS	-	4/-	-	0/0	.000	-/-	-	-	0	-	-	8	-
SHUGART, K.	-	5/-	-	2/2	1.000	-/-	-	-	1	-	-	12	-
SEARLE	-	3/-	-	1/3	.333	-/-	-	-	0	-	-	7	-
WOODS	-	0/-	-	0/0	.000	-/-	-	-	0	-	-	0	-
WALDROP	-	5/-	-	1/2	.500	-/-	-	-	3	-	-	11	-
RENSBERGER	-	0/-	-	0/1	.000	-/-	-	-	1	-	-	0	-
BARROW, J.	-	2/-	-	1/2	.500	-/-	-	-	3	-	-	5	-
DICK	-	0/-	-	1/1	1.000	-/-	-	-	4	-	-	1	-
SHEEHAN, C.	-	1/-	-	1/2	.500	-/-	-	-	1	-	-	3	-
ELIOPULOS	-	1/-	-	0/0	.000	-/-	-	-	0	-	-	2	-
Totals	200	21/-	-	7/13	.538	-/-	-	-	13	-	-	49	.245

Disqualified: None.

	1st Half	2nd Half	Final
Wisconsin	29	21	50
Navy	24	25	49

REGIONAL THIRD PLACE WESTERN

Oregon State (63)
Coach: Amory "Slats" Gill

	Min.	Total FG / FGA	Pct.	FT / FTA	Pct.	Reb. O / T	A	TO	PF	S	Blk	TP	PPM
ANDERSON, E.	-	4/ -	-	2/ 2	1.000	-/ -	-	-	4	-	-	10	-
CRANDALL, C.	-	2/ -	-	4/ 5	.800	-/ -	-	-	2	-	-	8	-
CAREY	-	0/ -	-	0/ 0	.000	-/ -	-	-	0	-	-	0	-
TORREY, D.	-	3/ -	-	0/ 0	.000	-/ -	-	-	0	-	-	6	-
ROCHA, R.	-	3/ -	-	3/ 5	.600	-/ -	-	-	5	-	-	9	-
BECK, L.	-	8/ -	-	4/ 5	.800	-/ -	-	-	1	-	-	20	-
SILVER	-	2/ -	-	0/ 0	.000	-/ -	-	-	2	-	-	4	-
MARTIN	-	0/ -	-	0/ 0	.000	-/ -	-	-	2	-	-	0	-
PETERSON, A.	-	3/ -	-	0/ 0	.000	-/ -	-	-	0	-	-	6	-
Totals	200	25/ -	-	13/17	.765	-/ -	-	-	16	-	-	63	.315

Wyoming (46)
Coach: Everett Shelton

	Min.	Total FG / FGA	Pct.	FT / FTA	Pct.	Reb. O / T	A	TO	PF	S	Blk	TP	PPM
REESE, J.	27	7/ -	-	3/ 3	1.000	-/ -	-	-	1	-	-	17	.630
PEYTON, M.	27	0/ -	-	1/ 1	1.000	-/ -	-	-	3	-	-	1	.037
TODOROVICH, M.	27	3/ -	-	5/ 6	.833	-/ -	-	-	2	-	-	11	.407
PILCH, J.	13	0/ -	-	1/ 2	.500	-/ -	-	-	0	-	-	1	.077
VOLKER, F.	40	4/ -	-	3/ 3	1.000	-/ -	-	-	4	-	-	11	.275
COLLINS, J.	30	2/ -	-	1/ 6	.167	-/ -	-	-	2	-	-	5	.167
ROGERS, T.	13	0/ -	-	0/ 0	.000	-/ -	-	-	0	-	-	0	.000
DOTY, L.	13	0/ -	-	0/ 0	.000	-/ -	-	-	2	-	-	0	.000
BLOOM, K.	10	0/ -	-	0/ 0	.000	-/ -	-	-	0	-	-	0	.000
Totals	200	16/ -	-	14/21	.667	-/ -	-	-	14	-	-	46	.230

Disqualified: Oregon State—Rocha.

	1st Half	2nd Half	Final
Oregon State	32	31	63
Wyoming	27	19	46

✪ INDIVIDUAL RECORDS ✪

SCORING

Most points in a single game
1 GEORGE KAFTAN, HOLY CROSS (vs. CCNY)   30
2 GERALD TUCKER, OKLAHOMA (vs. HOLY CROSS)   22
3 BOB COOK, WISCONSIN (vs. NAVY)   21
4 LEW BECK, OREGON STATE (vs. WYOMING)   20
4 LEW BECK, OREGON STATE (vs. OKLAHOMA)   20

Most total points in the tournament
1 GEORGE KAFTAN, HOLY CROSS   63
2 GERALD TUCKER, OKLAHOMA   54
3 IRWIN DAMBROT, CCNY   43
4 SLATER MARTIN, TEXAS   41
5 LEW BECK, OREGON STATE   40

Highest scoring average (minimum 2 games)
1 GEORGE KAFTAN, HOLY CROSS (63-3)   21.00
2 LEW BECK, OREGON STATE (40-2)   20.00
3 GERALD TUCKER, OKLAHOMA (54-3)   18.00
4 BOB COOK, WISCONSIN (34-2)   17.00
5 IRWIN DAMBROT, CCNY (43-3)   14.33

FIELD GOALS

Most field goals in a single game
1 GEORGE KAFTAN, HOLY CROSS (vs. CCNY)   11
2 BOB COOK, WISCONSIN (vs. NAVY)   10
3 JOE MULLANEY, HOLY CROSS (vs. NAVY)   9
4 3 tied for fourth place.

Most total field goals in the tournament
1 GEORGE KAFTAN, HOLY CROSS   25
2 GERALD TUCKER, OKLAHOMA   19
2 SLATER MARTIN, TEXAS   19
4 IRWIN DAMBROT, CCNY   16
4 LEW BECK, OREGON STATE   16

FREE THROWS

Most free throws in a single game
1 GERALD TUCKER, OKLAHOMA (vs. HOLY CROSS)   10
2 GEORGE KAFTAN, HOLY CROSS (vs. CCNY)   8
3 PAUL COURTY, OKLAHOMA (vs. OREGON STATE)   7
4 EXNER MENZEL, WISCONSIN (vs. CCNY)   5
4 MIKE TODOROVICH, WYOMING (vs. OREGON STATE)   5

Most total free throws in the tournament
1 GERALD TUCKER, OKLAHOMA   16
2 GEORGE KAFTAN, HOLY CROSS   13
3 IRWIN DAMBROT, CCNY   11
3 PAUL COURTY, OKLAHOMA   11
5 2 tied for fifth place.

Most free throws attempted in a single game
1 GERALD TUCKER, OKLAHOMA (vs. HOLY CROSS)   12
1 GEORGE KAFTAN, HOLY CROSS (vs. CCNY)   12

3 EXNER MENZEL, WISCONSIN (vs. CCNY)   8
3 PAUL COURTY, OKLAHOMA (vs. OREGON STATE)   8
5 3 tied for fifth place.

Most free throws attempted in the tournament
1 GEORGE KAFTAN, HOLY CROSS   24
2 GERALD TUCKER, OKLAHOMA   19
3 IRWIN DAMBROT, CCNY   17
4 PAUL COURTY, OKLAHOMA   15
5 JOHN HARGIS, TEXAS   14

Highest free throw percentage in a single game (minimum 7 attempts)
1 PAUL COURTY, OKLAHOMA (vs. OREGON STATE) (7-8)   .875
2 GERALD TUCKER, OKLAHOMA (vs. HOLY CROSS) (10-12)   .833
3 GEORGE KAFTAN, HOLY CROSS (vs. CCNY) (8-12)   .667
4 EXNER MENZEL, WISCONSIN (vs. CCNY) (5-8)   .625
5 2 tied for fifth place.

Highest free throw percentage in the tournament (minimum 15 attempts)
1 GERALD TUCKER, OKLAHOMA (16-19)   .842
2 PAUL COURTY, OKLAHOMA (11-15)   .733
3 IRWIN DAMBROT, CCNY (11-17)   .647

○ TEAM RECORDS ○

SCORING

Most points in a single game
1	CCNY (vs. WISCONSIN)	70
2	OREGON STATE (vs. WYOMING)	63
3	HOLY CROSS (vs. CCNY)	60

Most total points in the tournament
1	HOLY CROSS	173
2	CCNY	165
3	OKLAHOMA	158

Highest scoring average (minimum 2 games)
1	OREGON STATE (117-2)	58.50
2	HOLY CROSS (173-3)	57.67
3	CCNY (165-3)	55.00

FIELD GOALS

Most field goals in a single game
1	CCNY (vs. WISCONSIN)	28
2	OREGON STATE (vs. WYOMING)	25
2	HOLY CROSS (vs. NAVY)	25

Most total field goals in the tournament
1	HOLY CROSS	68
2	CCNY	65
3	TEXAS	59

FREE THROWS

Most free throws in a single game
1	HOLY CROSS (vs. CCNY)	18
2	OKLAHOMA (vs. HOLY CROSS)	17
3	OKLAHOMA (vs. OREGON STATE)	16

Most total free throws in the tournament
1	OKLAHOMA	46
2	HOLY CROSS	37
3	CCNY	35

Most free throws attempted in a single game
1	HOLY CROSS (vs. CCNY)	29
2	OKLAHOMA (vs. OREGON STATE)	23
3	WYOMING (vs. OREGON STATE)	21
3	TEXAS (vs. CCNY)	21
3	OKLAHOMA (vs. HOLY CROSS)	21

Most total free throws attempted in the tournament
1	OKLAHOMA	61
2	HOLY CROSS	60
3	CCNY	58

Highest free throw percentage in a single game
1	TEXAS (vs. OKLAHOMA) (12-14)	.857
2	OKLAHOMA (vs. HOLY CROSS) (17-21)	.810
3	2 tied for third place.	

Highest free throw percentage in the tournament (minimum 2 games)
1	OKLAHOMA (46-61)	.754
2	OREGON STATE (23-35)	.657
3	WISCONSIN (22-35)	.629

Fewest free throws in a single game
1	HOLY CROSS (vs. NAVY)	5
2	NAVY (vs. WISCONSIN)	7
3	CCNY (vs. TEXAS)	8

Lowest free throw percentage in a single game
1	HOLY CROSS (vs. NAVY) (5-12)	.417
2	CCNY (vs. TEXAS) (8-18)	.444
3	TEXAS (vs. CCNY) (10-21)	.476

Lowest free throw percentage in the tournament (minimum 2 games)
1	NAVY (18-31)	.581
2	WYOMING (24-40)	.600
3	CCNY (35-58)	.604

1948

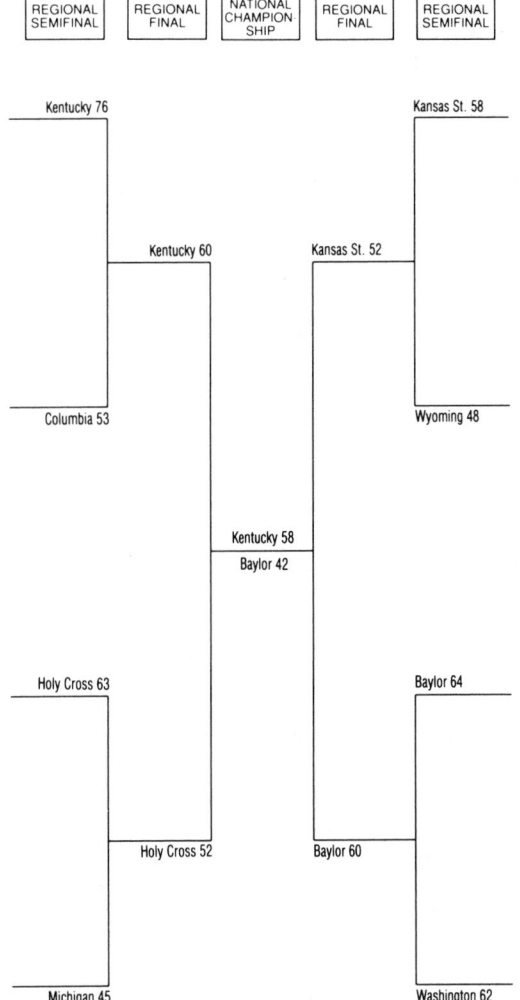

REGIONAL SEMIFINAL	REGIONAL FINAL	NATIONAL CHAMPIONSHIP	REGIONAL FINAL	REGIONAL SEMIFINAL

EASTERN

WESTERN

Kentucky 76

Kentucky 60

Columbia 53

Kansas St. 58

Kansas St. 52

Wyoming 48

Kentucky 58
Baylor 42

Holy Cross 63

Holy Cross 52

Michigan 45

Baylor 64

Baylor 60

Washington 62

CONSOLATION GAMES

National Third Place:

Holy Cross 60
Kansas St. 54

Regional Third Place:

Eastern:
Michigan 66
Columbia 49

Western:
Washington 57
Wyoming 47

They were known as "The Fabulous Five." They were big, strong, quick, and fiercely competitive, with a fast break like a runaway locomotive. They were a collection of stars who played *together*. Their coach, Adolph Rupp, called them "the greatest team ever assembled in college sport." They were the 1948 Kentucky Wildcats.

The squad that Rupp assembled came together partly on the basis of geography, partly as a result of world historic events, and partly because the Baron of the Bluegrass was a master at molding talented individuals into a cohesive unit.

The pieces of the puzzle that became The Fabulous Five started fitting together two seasons earlier, when, in the fall of 1945, Kentuckians Ralph Beard, Wallace "Wah Wah" Jones, and Joe Holland enrolled in Rupp's basketball factory. Because of the war, which had just ended (V-J Day was declared on August 14th), all three were eligible to play varsity ball in their freshman year. Each man became a starter on a squad that went 28 and 2 and won the 1946 NIT title.

The next fall Rupp had his pick of the most talented teenagers in the basketball crazy state of Kentucky. With the war over, he also had a strong contingent of graduates from the life-and-death school of combat. An extraordinary group of discharged veterans—Alex Groza, who had played on the Camp Hood, Texas, team while in the service, Cliff Barker, who, as a B-17 crewman had been shot down in Europe and wound up spending sixteen months working on his ball handling in a German POW camp, and Kenny Rollins, a Navy man—joined the already powerful Kentucky team. The gym in Lexington was packed with quality players—enough to field at least two very strong teams. Rollins, who would soon be elected team captain, recalled that when he first came onto the court and saw his future teammates he doubted his ability to compete with them. "Kenny," he said to himself, "you've come to the wrong place."

During the 1946–47 season, Rupp had his hands full just trying to keep all his players happy; many squad members, who would have been stars on lesser teams, were warming the bench for the Wildcats. Even though Kentucky reached the NIT finals and finished with a 34-3 record, there was plenty of grumbling over lack of playing time.

By the time the 1947–48 season rolled around, the Wildcats were an experienced, balanced, and deep squad. They combined height and power upfront with dazzling ball handling and blinding speed in the backcourt. They had two All-Americans: Ralph Beard, who was described in the UK yearbook as "the perfect Wheaties ad, the All-American boy," and Alex "The Nose" Groza, a prodigious 6-7 leaper. And they were, as expected, virtually unstop-pable all season, losing only to Temple (in Philadelphia, with Beard and Wah-Wah Jones injured) and to Notre Dame (in South Bend). They finished with a 31-2 regular season record, and as the most feared college team in the country they were solid favorites to win the NCAA championship.

When tournament time rolled around, Kentucky was selected for the Eastern regional and faced Columbia in the first round. *The New York Times* described the match-up, calling the Wildcats "awe-inspiring," with "assets the Columbians sadly lacked—speed, height, depth, experience, poise and scoring power from any spot on the floor." *The Times* estimation of the two teams' relative merits showed up clearly in the final score of 76-53.

The Wildcats next took on Holy Cross for the Eastern championship. Holy Cross came into the contest with a 19-game winning streak and had never lost in Madison Square Garden. The Crusaders were the defending NCAA titleholders, and they took the floor with most of their top players—including Bob Cousy, George Kaftan, and Frank Oftring—back from their championship season. But they were thoroughly outclassed by Kentucky. The Wildcats were bigger, stronger, faster, and better shooters than the Crusaders. Running the fast break to perfection, Rupp's boys built their lead to 14 points early in the second half. They hounded Cousy, holding the ball-handling wizard to a mere 5 points. On the other end Groza was unstoppable; he was electrifying under the boards, blowing by Kaftan for a number of spectacular tip-ins as he scored 23. Despite a late run by Holy Cross that momentarily cut the lead to 4, Kentucky won by 8.

In the finals, Kentucky came up against the Baylor Bears. The Texans—sparked by a no-holds-barred running attack and spectacular second-half shooting—had taken the Western crown with two spirited comebacks against heavily favored teams. But they were brought rudely back to reality when they took the floor against Rupp's Fabulous Five.

Baylor knew they would be outrebounded by the tall and talented Kentucky front line of Groza, Wah-Wah Jones, and Cliff Barker, so they went into the game with a strategy of working the ball around and making every shot count. But the Kentucky defense didn't allow any good shots, and as a result the Bears let fly only six times in the first seven and a half minutes. At that point they were trailing 13-1. Five minutes later, the Wildcat lead stood at 17 and the game was all but over. The Fabulous Five waltzed into the title.

After taking the NCAA crown, five Wildcats completed their dream season by qualifying for the United States Olympic Team and winning the world championship. It was a gold medal year all around for the Fabulous Five.

REGIONAL SEMIFINAL EASTERN

Kentucky (76)   Coach: Adolph Rupp

	Min.	Total FG/FGA	Pct.	FT/FTA	Pct.	Reb. O/T	A	TO	PF	S	Blk	TP	PPM
JONES, W.	-	9/ -	-	3/ 5	.600	-/ -	-	-	5	-	-	21	-
BARKER, C.	-	1/ -	-	0/ 1	.000	-/ -	-	-	3	-	-	2	-
LINE, J.	-	2/ -	-	1/ 1	1.000	-/ -	-	-	1	-	-	5	-
BARNSTABLE, D.	-	2/ -	-	1/ 3	.333	-/ -	-	-	0	-	-	5	-
DAY, R.	-	2/ -	-	0/ 0	.000	-/ -	-	-	1	-	-	4	-
TOWNES, G.	-	0/ -	-	0/ 0	.000	-/ -	-	-	0	-	-	0	-
GROZA, A.	-	7/ -	-	3/ 3	1.000	-/ -	-	-	2	-	-	17	-
HOLLAND, J.	-	2/ -	-	0/ 0	.000	-/ -	-	-	4	-	-	4	-
BEARD, R.	-	6/ -	-	3/ 5	.600	-/ -	-	-	1	-	-	15	-
ROLLINS, K.	-	0/ -	-	2/ 2	1.000	-/ -	-	-	3	-	-	2	-
STOUGH, J.	-	0/ -	-	0/ 1	.000	-/ -	-	-	0	-	-	0	-
JORDAN, J.	-	0/ -	-	1/ 1	1.000	-/ -	-	-	0	-	-	1	-
Totals	200	31/ -	-	14/22	.636	-/ -	-	-	20	-	-	76	.380

Holy Cross (63)   Coach: Doggie Julian

	Min.	Total FG/FGA	Pct.	FT/FTA	Pct.	Reb. O/T	A	TO	PF	S	Blk	TP	PPM
OFTRING, F.	-	5/ -	-	0/ 0	.000	-/ -	-	-	1	-	-	10	-
COUSY, B.	-	9/ -	-	5/ 9	.556	-/ -	-	-	3	-	-	23	-
O'CONNELL, D.	-	0/ -	-	1/ 1	1.000	-/ -	-	-	1	-	-	1	-
FORMON, M.	-	0/ -	-	0/ 1	.000	-/ -	-	-	0	-	-	0	-
GRAVER, C.	-	0/ -	-	0/ 1	.000	-/ -	-	-	0	-	-	0	-
DOLAN, B.	-	0/ -	-	0/ 0	.000	-/ -	-	-	0	-	-	0	-
KAFTAN, G.	-	7/ -	-	1/ 4	.250	-/ -	-	-	3	-	-	15	-
BOLLINGER, C.	-	1/ -	-	0/ 0	.000	-/ -	-	-	0	-	-	2	-
CURRAN, R.	-	2/ -	-	1/ 1	1.000	-/ -	-	-	1	-	-	5	-
MULLANEY, J.	-	2/ -	-	1/ 1	1.000	-/ -	-	-	0	-	-	5	-
MCMULLAN, R.	-	1/ -	-	0/ 0	.000	-/ -	-	-	1	-	-	2	-
LASKA, A.	-	0/ -	-	0/ 0	.000	-/ -	-	-	0	-	-	0	-
Totals	200	27/ -	-	9/18	.500	-/ -	-	-	10	-	-	63	.315

Columbia (53)   Coach: Gordon Ridings

	Min.	Total FG/FGA	Pct.	FT/FTA	Pct.	Reb. O/T	A	TO	PF	S	Blk	TP	PPM
VOGEL, A.	-	2/ -	-	2/ 4	.500	-/ -	-	-	2	-	-	6	-
GEHRKE, B.	-	2/ -	-	1/ 2	.500	-/ -	-	-	5	-	-	5	-
SKINNER	-	2/ -	-	5/ 6	.833	-/ -	-	-	2	-	-	9	-
MOSS	-	0/ -	-	0/ 0	.000	-/ -	-	-	0	-	-	0	-
LOCKWOOD	-	0/ -	-	0/ 0	.000	-/ -	-	-	0	-	-	0	-
BUDKO, W.	-	7/ -	-	3/ 4	.750	-/ -	-	-	5	-	-	17	-
HARWOOD	-	0/ -	-	0/ 0	.000	-/ -	-	-	2	-	-	0	-
MARSHALL, S.	-	1/ -	-	2/ 3	.667	-/ -	-	-	0	-	-	4	-
KAPLAN, A.	-	5/ -	-	2/ 5	.400	-/ -	-	-	2	-	-	12	-
OLSEN	-	0/ -	-	0/ 0	.000	-/ -	-	-	1	-	-	0	-
Totals	200	19/ -	-	15/24	.625	-/ -	-	-	19	-	-	53	.265

Disqualified: Kentucky—Jones; Columbia—Gehrke, Budko.

	1st Half	2nd Half	Final
Kentucky	38	38	76
Columbia	28	25	53

Michigan (45)   Coach: Ozzie Cowles

	Min.	Total FG/FGA	Pct.	FT/FTA	Pct.	Reb. O/T	A	TO	PF	S	Blk	TP	PPM
SUPRUNOWICZ	-	7/ -	-	0/ 0	.000	-/ -	-	-	1	-	-	14	-
MCINTOSH, D.	-	4/ -	-	2/ 2	1.000	-/ -	-	-	1	-	-	10	-
MCCASLIN	-	0/ -	-	0/ 0	.000	-/ -	-	-	1	-	-	0	-
MIKULICH	-	0/ -	-	0/ 0	.000	-/ -	-	-	0	-	-	0	-
WISNIEWSKI	-	0/ -	-	0/ 0	.000	-/ -	-	-	2	-	-	0	-
ROBERTS, B.	-	3/ -	-	4/ 4	1.000	-/ -	-	-	3	-	-	10	-
HARRISON	-	2/ -	-	3/ 5	.600	-/ -	-	-	0	-	-	7	-
ELLIOTT, P.	-	2/ -	-	0/ 0	.000	-/ -	-	-	5	-	-	4	-
MORRILL	-	0/ -	-	0/ 2	.000	-/ -	-	-	2	-	-	0	-
WIERDA	-	0/ -	-	0/ 0	.000	-/ -	-	-	0	-	-	0	-
BAUERLE	-	0/ -	-	0/ 0	.000	-/ -	-	-	0	-	-	0	-
STOTTLEBAUER	-	0/ -	-	0/ 0	.000	-/ -	-	-	0	-	-	0	-
Totals	200	18/ -	-	9/13	.692	-/ -	-	-	15	-	-	45	.225

Disqualified: Michigan—Elliott.

	1st Half	2nd Half	Final
Holy Cross	34	29	63
Michigan	27	18	45

REGIONAL SEMIFINAL WESTERN

Kansas State (58)   Coach: Jack Gardner

	Min.	Total FG/FGA	Pct.	FT/FTA	Pct.	Reb. O/T	A	TO	PF	S	Blk	TP	PPM
HARMAN, R.	-	5/ -	-	2/ 3	.667	-/ -	-	-	2	-	-	12	-
WEATHERBY, D.	-	1/ -	-	0/ 0	.000	-/ -	-	-	2	-	-	2	-
HOWEY, H.	-	1/ -	-	0/ 0	.000	-/ -	-	-	0	-	-	2	-
LANGTON, A.	-	0/ -	-	0/ 1	.000	-/ -	-	-	0	-	-	0	-
THORNTON, J.	-	0/ -	-	0/ 0	.000	-/ -	-	-	1	-	-	0	-
BRANNUM, C.	-	3/ -	-	2/ 3	.667	-/ -	-	-	5	-	-	8	-
CLARK, W.	-	3/ -	-	2/ 2	1.000	-/ -	-	-	0	-	-	8	-
DEAN, J.	-	5/ -	-	2/ 3	.667	-/ -	-	-	2	-	-	12	-
KRONE, L.	-	0/ -	-	0/ 1	.000	-/ -	-	-	0	-	-	0	-
SHANNON, H.	-	4/ -	-	6/ 6	1.000	-/ -	-	-	2	-	-	14	-
MAHONEY, K.	-	0/ -	-	0/ 0	.000	-/ -	-	-	1	-	-	0	-
THURSTON, B.	-	0/ -	-	0/ 0	.000	-/ -	-	-	0	-	-	0	-
Totals	200	22/ -	-	14/19	.737	-/ -	-	-	15	-	-	58	.290

Wyoming (48)   Coach: Everett Shelton

	Min.	Total FG/FGA	Pct.	FT/FTA	Pct.	Reb. O/T	A	TO	PF	S	Blk	TP	PPM
DOTY, L.	20	6/ -	-	1/ 3	.333	-/ -	-	-	3	-	-	13	.650
LARSON, L.	20	1/ -	-	1/ 2	.500	-/ -	-	-	1	-	-	3	.150
PEYTON, M.	40	9/ -	-	2/ 2	1.000	-/ -	-	-	2	-	-	20	.500
REED, G.	30	1/ -	-	1/ 2	.500	-/ -	-	-	5	-	-	3	.100
COTTON, J.	10	0/ -	-	0/ 0	.000	-/ -	-	-	0	-	-	0	.000
COLLINS, J.	10	0/ -	-	0/ 0	.000	-/ -	-	-	1	-	-	0	.000
PILCH, J.	40	1/ -	-	5/ 7	.714	-/ -	-	-	5	-	-	7	.175
BLOOM, K.	30	1/ -	-	0/ 0	.000	-/ -	-	-	2	-	-	2	.067
Totals	200	19/ -	-	10/16	.625	-/ -	-	-	19	-	-	48	.240

Disqualified: Kansas State—Brannum; Wyoming—Reed, Pilch.

	1st Half	2nd Half	Final
Kansas State	23	35	58
Wyoming	15	33	48

Baylor (64) Coach: Bill Henderson

	Min.	Total FG/FGA	Pct.	FT/FTA	Pct.	Reb. O/T	A	TO	PF	S	Blk	TP	PPM
OWENS, R.	-	3/-	-	6/7	.857	-/-	-	-	3	-	-	12	-
DEWITT, B.	-	0/-	-	0/0	.000	-/-	-	-	2	-	-	0	-
PRESTON, O.	-	1/-	-	0/0	.000	-/-	-	-	1	-	-	2	-
HICKMAN, B.	-	3/-	-	0/2	.000	-/-	-	-	2	-	-	6	-
HEATHINGTON, D.	-	4/-	-	4/8	.500	-/-	-	-	4	-	-	12	-
JOHNSON, B.	-	9/-	-	2/2	1.000	-/-	-	-	0	-	-	20	-
PULLEY, R.	-	0/-	-	0/0	.000	-/-	-	-	0	-	-	0	-
ROBINSON, J.	-	3/-	-	6/6	1.000	-/-	-	-	3	-	-	12	-
Totals	200	23/-	-	18/25	.720	-/-	-	-	15	-	-	64	.320

Washington (62) Coach: Art McLarney

	Min.	Total FG/FGA	Pct.	FT/FTA	Pct.	Reb. O/T	A	TO	PF	S	Blk	TP	PPM
VANDENBURGH	-	6/-	-	2/2	1.000	-/-	-	-	5	-	-	14	-
WHITE	-	4/-	-	3/5	.600	-/-	-	-	3	-	-	11	-
ARNASON	-	0/-	-	0/0	.000	-/-	-	-	1	-	-	0	-
MALLORY	-	0/-	-	0/0	.000	-/-	-	-	1	-	-	0	-
NICHOLS, J.	-	6/-	-	5/5	1.000	-/-	-	-	5	-	-	17	-
MILLIKAN	-	0/-	-	0/0	.000	-/-	-	-	0	-	-	0	-
OPACICH	-	1/-	-	4/4	1.000	-/-	-	-	3	-	-	6	-
JORGENSEN	-	3/-	-	0/0	.000	-/-	-	-	1	-	-	6	-
TAYLOR	-	3/-	-	2/2	1.000	-/-	-	-	2	-	-	8	-
BIRD	-	0/-	-	0/0	.000	-/-	-	-	1	-	-	0	-
ENGSTROM	-	0/-	-	0/0	.000	-/-	-	-	1	-	-	0	-
Totals	200	23/-	-	16/18	.889	-/-	-	-	23	-	-	62	.310

Disqualified: Washington—Vandenburgh, Nichols.

	1st Half	2nd Half	Final
Baylor	26	38	64
Washington	37	25	62

REGIONAL FINAL EASTERN

Kentucky (60) Coach: Adolph Rupp

	Min.	Total FG/FGA	Pct.	FT/FTA	Pct.	Reb. O/T	A	TO	PF	S	Blk	TP	PPM
JONES, W.	-	4/-	-	4/4	1.000	-/-	-	-	3	-	-	12	-
BARKER, C.	-	2/-	-	0/0	.000	-/-	-	-	4	-	-	4	-
LINE, J.	-	0/-	-	0/0	.000	-/-	-	-	1	-	-	0	-
GROZA, A.	-	10/-	-	3/5	.600	-/-	-	-	4	-	-	23	-
HOLLAND, J.	-	0/-	-	0/0	.000	-/-	-	-	0	-	-	0	-
BEARD, R.	-	6/-	-	1/5	.200	-/-	-	-	1	-	-	13	-
ROLLINS, K.	-	3/-	-	2/2	1.000	-/-	-	-	3	-	-	8	-
BARNSTABLE, D.	-	0/-	-	0/0	.000	-/-	-	-	2	-	-	0	-
Totals	200	25/-	-	10/16	.625	-/-	-	-	18	-	-	60	.300

Holy Cross (52) Coach: Doggie Julian

	Min.	Total FG/FGA	Pct.	FT/FTA	Pct.	Reb. O/T	A	TO	PF	S	Blk	TP	PPM
OFTRING, F.	-	4/-	-	4/4	1.000	-/-	-	-	2	-	-	12	-
COUSY, B.	-	1/-	-	4/5	.800	-/-	-	-	5	-	-	6	-
O'CONNELL, D.	-	3/-	-	3/4	.750	-/-	-	-	2	-	-	9	-
MCMULLAN, R.	-	0/-	-	0/0	.000	-/-	-	-	3	-	-	0	-
KAFTAN, G.	-	6/-	-	3/4	.750	-/-	-	-	2	-	-	15	-
BOLLINGER, C.	-	1/-	-	0/0	.000	-/-	-	-	0	-	-	2	-
CURRAN, R.	-	3/-	-	0/0	.000	-/-	-	-	5	-	-	6	-
MULLANEY, J.	-	0/-	-	0/0	.000	-/-	-	-	0	-	-	0	-
LASKA, A.	-	1/-	-	0/0	.000	-/-	-	-	1	-	-	2	-
FORMON, M.	-	0/-	-	0/0	.000	-/-	-	-	1	-	-	0	-
Totals	200	19/-	-	14/17	.824	-/-	-	-	21	-	-	52	.260

Disqualified: Holy Cross—Curran, Cousy.

	1st Half	2nd Half	Final
Kentucky	36	24	60
Holy Cross	28	24	52

REGIONAL FINAL WESTERN

Kansas State (52) Coach: Jack Gardner

	Min.	Total FG/FGA	Pct.	FT/FTA	Pct.	Reb. O/T	A	TO	PF	S	Blk	TP	PPM
HARMAN, R.	-	3/-	-	6/10	.600	-/-	-	-	4	-	-	12	-
WEATHERBY, D.	-	0/-	-	0/0	.000	-/-	-	-	2	-	-	0	-
HOWEY, H.	-	3/-	-	3/3	1.000	-/-	-	-	5	-	-	9	-
LANGTON, J.	-	1/-	-	1/1	1.000	-/-	-	-	3	-	-	3	-
BRANNUM, C.	-	3/-	-	1/1	1.000	-/-	-	-	5	-	-	7	-
CLARK, W.	-	1/-	-	3/3	1.000	-/-	-	-	5	-	-	5	-
DEAN, J.	-	3/-	-	2/2	1.000	-/-	-	-	4	-	-	8	-
KRONE, L.	-	0/-	-	2/2	1.000	-/-	-	-	0	-	-	2	-
SHANNON, H.	-	1/-	-	4/4	1.000	-/-	-	-	1	-	-	6	-
Totals	200	15/-	-	22/26	.846	-/-	-	-	29	-	-	52	.260

Baylor (60) Coach: Bill Henderson

	Min.	Total FG/FGA	Pct.	FT/FTA	Pct.	Reb. O/T	A	TO	PF	S	Blk	TP	PPM
OWENS, R.	-	3/-	-	2/3	.667	-/-	-	-	5	-	-	8	-
DEWITT, B.	-	3/-	-	0/1	.000	-/-	-	-	5	-	-	6	-
PRESTON, O.	-	1/-	-	3/4	.750	-/-	-	-	1	-	-	5	-
HICKMAN, B.	-	0/-	-	0/0	.000	-/-	-	-	2	-	-	0	-
HEATHINGTON, D.	-	3/-	-	9/10	.900	-/-	-	-	2	-	-	15	-
JOHNSON, B.	-	4/-	-	5/6	.833	-/-	-	-	3	-	-	13	-
PULLEY, R.	-	1/-	-	0/0	.000	-/-	-	-	0	-	-	2	-
ROBINSON, J.	-	5/-	-	1/1	1.000	-/-	-	-	4	-	-	11	-
Totals	200	20/-	-	20/25	.800	-/-	-	-	22	-	-	60	.300

Disqualified: Baylor—Owens, DeWitt; Kansas State—Howey, Brannum, Clark.

	1st Half	2nd Half	Final
Kansas State	32	20	52
Baylor	28	32	60

CHAMPIONSHIP

Kentucky (58)   Coach: Adolph Rupp

	Min.	Total FG / FGA	Pct.	FT / FTA	Pct.	Reb. O / T	A	TO	PF	S	Blk	TP	PPM
JONES, W.	-	4/ -	-	1/ 1	1.000	-/ -	-	-	3	-	-	9	-
BARKER, C.	-	2/ -	-	1/ 3	.333	-/ -	-	-	4	-	-	5	-
LINE, J.	-	3/ -	-	1/ 1	1.000	-/ -	-	-	3	-	-	7	-
GROZA, A.	-	6/ -	-	2/ 4	.500	-/ -	-	-	4	-	-	14	-
HOLLAND, J.	-	1/ -	-	0/ 0	.000	-/ -	-	-	1	-	-	2	-
BEARD, R.	-	4/ -	-	4/ 4	1.000	-/ -	-	-	1	-	-	12	-
ROLLINS, K.	-	3/ -	-	3/ 5	.600	-/ -	-	-	3	-	-	9	-
BARNSTABLE, D.	-	0/ -	-	0/ 1	.000	-/ -	-	-	0	-	-	0	-
Totals	200	23/83	.277	12/19	.632	-/ -	-	-	19	-	-	58	.290

Baylor (42)   Coach: Bill Henderson

	Min.	Total FG / FGA	Pct.	FT / FTA	Pct.	Reb. O / T	A	TO	PF	S	Blk	TP	PPM
OWENS, J.	-	2/ -	-	1/ 2	.500	-/ -	-	-	0	-	-	5	-
DEWITT, B.	-	3/ -	-	2/ 4	.500	-/ -	-	-	3	-	-	8	-
HICKMAN, B.	-	1/ -	-	0/ 0	.000	-/ -	-	-	0	-	-	2	-
PULLEY, R.	-	0/ -	-	1/ 1	1.000	-/ -	-	-	0	-	-	1	-
HEATHINGTON, D.	-	3/ -	-	2/ 4	.500	-/ -	-	-	5	-	-	8	-
PRESTON, O.	-	0/ -	-	0/ 2	.000	-/ -	-	-	2	-	-	0	-
JOHNSON, B.	-	3/ -	-	4/ 7	.571	-/ -	-	-	5	-	-	10	-
ROBINSON, J.	-	3/ -	-	2/ 4	.500	-/ -	-	-	4	-	-	8	-
SRACK, B.	-	0/ -	-	0/ 0	.000	-/ -	-	-	0	-	-	0	-
Totals	200	15/64	.234	12/24	.500	-/ -	-	-	19	-	-	42	.210

Disqualified: Baylor—Johnson, Heathington.

	1st Half	2nd Half	Final
Kentucky	29	29	58
Baylor	16	26	42

NATIONAL THIRD PLACE

Holy Cross (60)   Coach: Doggie Julian

	Min.	Total FG / FGA	Pct.	FT / FTA	Pct.	Reb. O / T	A	TO	PF	S	Blk	TP	PPM
COUSY, B.	-	2/ -	-	1/ 1	1.000	-/ -	-	-	2	-	-	5	-
O'CONNELL, D.	-	5/ -	-	0/ 0	.000	-/ -	-	-	2	-	-	10	-
OFTRING, F.	-	4/ -	-	3/ 4	.750	-/ -	-	-	2	-	-	11	-
KAFTAN, G.	-	4/ -	-	3/ 6	.500	-/ -	-	-	3	-	-	11	-
BOLLINGER, C.	-	1/ -	-	0/ 0	.000	-/ -	-	-	3	-	-	2	-
FORMON, M.	-	0/ -	-	0/ 0	.000	-/ -	-	-	1	-	-	0	-
CURRAN, R.	-	2/ -	-	1/ 2	.500	-/ -	-	-	4	-	-	5	-
MCMULLAN, R.	-	3/ -	-	0/ 0	.000	-/ -	-	-	2	-	-	6	-
MULLANEY, J.	-	3/ -	-	0/ 0	.000	-/ -	-	-	2	-	-	6	-
LASKA, A.	-	2/ -	-	0/ 0	.000	-/ -	-	-	0	-	-	4	-
DOLAN, B.	-	0/ -	-	0/ 0	.000	-/ -	-	-	0	-	-	0	-
Totals	200	26/ -	-	8/13	.615	-/ -	-	-	21	-	-	60	.300

Kansas State (54)   Coach: Jack Gardner

	Min.	Total FG / FGA	Pct.	FT / FTA	Pct.	Reb. O / T	A	TO	PF	S	Blk	TP	PPM
HARMAN, R.	-	3/ -	-	3/ 6	.500	-/ -	-	-	3	-	-	9	-
WEATHERBY, D.	-	0/ -	-	0/ 0	.000	-/ -	-	-	2	-	-	0	-
CLARK, W.	-	0/ -	-	0/ 0	.000	-/ -	-	-	0	-	-	0	-
HOWEY, H.	-	4/ -	-	2/ 6	.333	-/ -	-	-	1	-	-	10	-
MAHONEY, K.	-	0/ -	-	0/ 0	.000	-/ -	-	-	0	-	-	0	-
BRANNUM, C.	-	1/ -	-	2/ 6	.333	-/ -	-	-	3	-	-	4	-
THORNTON, J.	-	0/ -	-	0/ 0	.000	-/ -	-	-	0	-	-	0	-
DEAN, J.	-	5/ -	-	2/ 3	.667	-/ -	-	-	2	-	-	12	-
LANGTON, A.	-	0/ -	-	0/ 0	.000	-/ -	-	-	0	-	-	0	-
SHANNON, H.	-	6/ -	-	5/ 5	1.000	-/ -	-	-	1	-	-	17	-
KRONE, L.	-	1/ -	-	0/ 0	.000	-/ -	-	-	0	-	-	2	-
Totals	200	20/ -	-	14/26	.538	-/ -	-	-	12	-	-	54	.270

Disqualified: None.

	1st Half	2nd Half	Final
Holy Cross	36	24	60
Kansas State	24	30	54

REGIONAL THIRD PLACE EASTERN

Michigan (66)   Coach: Ozzie Cowles

	Min.	Total FG / FGA	Pct.	FT / FTA	Pct.	Reb. O / T	A	TO	PF	S	Blk	TP	PPM
SUPRUNOWICZ	-	7/ -	-	0/ 1	.000	-/ -	-	-	1	-	-	14	-
MCCASLIN	-	0/ -	-	1/ 1	1.000	-/ -	-	-	0	-	-	1	-
MCINTOSH, D.	-	7/ -	-	0/ 3	.000	-/ -	-	-	4	-	-	14	-
MIKULICH	-	0/ -	-	3/ 3	1.000	-/ -	-	-	0	-	-	3	-
STOTTLEBAUER	-	0/ -	-	0/ 0	.000	-/ -	-	-	1	-	-	0	-
ROBERTS, B.	-	1/ -	-	2/ 5	.400	-/ -	-	-	0	-	-	4	-
WISNIEWSKI	-	1/ -	-	0/ 0	.000	-/ -	-	-	3	-	-	2	-
HARRISON	-	4/ -	-	2/ 6	.333	-/ -	-	-	2	-	-	10	-
ELLIOTT, P.	-	5/ -	-	5/ 6	.833	-/ -	-	-	2	-	-	15	-
MORRILL	-	0/ -	-	0/ 0	.000	-/ -	-	-	1	-	-	0	-
WIERDA	-	1/ -	-	0/ 2	.000	-/ -	-	-	0	-	-	2	-
BAUERLE	-	0/ -	-	1/ 1	1.000	-/ -	-	-	1	-	-	1	-
Totals	200	26/ -	-	14/28	.500	-/ -	-	-	15	-	-	66	.330

Columbia (49)   Coach: Gordon Ridings

	Min.	Total FG / FGA	Pct.	FT / FTA	Pct.	Reb. O / T	A	TO	PF	S	Blk	TP	PPM
VOGEL, A.	-	7/ -	-	4/ 6	.667	-/ -	-	-	4	-	-	18	-
GEHRKE, B.	-	1/ -	-	2/ 3	.667	-/ -	-	-	0	-	-	4	-
SKINNER	-	1/ -	-	1/ 2	.500	-/ -	-	-	1	-	-	3	-
OLSEN	-	1/ -	-	1/ 1	1.000	-/ -	-	-	1	-	-	3	-
BUDKO, W.	-	3/ -	-	3/ 5	.600	-/ -	-	-	4	-	-	9	-
JOYDAT	-	0/ -	-	0/ 0	.000	-/ -	-	-	0	-	-	0	-
MARSHALL	-	2/ -	-	1/ 1	1.000	-/ -	-	-	3	-	-	5	-
KAPLAN, A.	-	2/ -	-	0/ 0	.000	-/ -	-	-	3	-	-	4	-
POCH	-	1/ -	-	0/ 0	.000	-/ -	-	-	3	-	-	2	-
MOSS	-	0/ -	-	0/ 0	.000	-/ -	-	-	1	-	-	0	-
LOCKWOOD	-	0/ -	-	1/ 2	.500	-/ -	-	-	0	-	-	1	-
Totals	200	18/ -	-	13/20	.650	-/ -	-	-	20	-	-	49	.245

Disqualified: None.

	1st Half	2nd Half	Final
Michigan	24	42	66
Columbia	21	28	49

REGIONAL THIRD PLACE WESTERN

Washington (57) Coach: Art McLarney

	Min.	Total FG/FGA	Pct.	FT/FTA	Pct.	Reb. O/T	A	TO	PF	S	Blk	TP	PPM
VANDENBURGH	-	1/ -	-	2/ 2	1.000	-/ -	-	-	5	-	-	4	-
CARNOVALE	-	0/ -	-	1/ 1	1.000	-/ -	-	-	0	-	-	1	-
WHITE	-	5/ -	-	4/ 5	.800	-/ -	-	-	1	-	-	14	-
ARNASON	-	0/ -	-	0/ 0	.000	-/ -	-	-	2	-	-	0	-
MALLORY	-	0/ -	-	0/ 0	.000	-/ -	-	-	0	-	-	0	-
NICHOLS, J.	-	7/ -	-	8/ 9	.889	-/ -	-	-	5	-	-	22	-
MILLIKAN	-	0/ -	-	0/ 0	.000	-/ -	-	-	2	-	-	0	-
OPACICH	-	3/ -	-	2/ 5	.400	-/ -	-	-	0	-	-	8	-
JORGENSEN	-	2/ -	-	0/ 0	.000	-/ -	-	-	0	-	-	4	-
TAYLOR	-	2/ -	-	0/ 0	.000	-/ -	-	-	3	-	-	4	-
Totals	200	20/ -	-	17/22	.773	-/ -	-	-	18	-	-	57	.285

Wyoming (47) Coach: Everett Shelton

	Min.	Total FG/FGA	Pct.	FT/FTA	Pct.	Reb. O/T	A	TO	PF	S	Blk	TP	PPM
DOTY, L.	20	6/ -	-	1/ 5	.200	-/ -	-	-	5	-	-	13	.650
LARSON, L.	20	0/ -	-	0/ 0	.000	-/ -	-	-	1	-	-	0	.000
PEYTON, M.	40	3/ -	-	1/ 1	1.000	-/ -	-	-	2	-	-	7	.175
MANKIN, J.	10	0/ -	-	0/ 1	.000	-/ -	-	-	1	-	-	0	.000
REED, G.	20	1/ -	-	0/ 0	.000	-/ -	-	-	5	-	-	2	.100
COTTON, J.	10	0/ -	-	0/ 0	.000	-/ -	-	-	0	-	-	0	.000
COLLINS, J.	20	0/ -	-	0/ 0	.000	-/ -	-	-	1	-	-	0	.000
FLINN, A.	10	0/ -	-	0/ 0	.000	-/ -	-	-	1	-	-	0	.000
PILCH, J.	30	8/ -	-	8/13	.615	-/ -	-	-	3	-	-	24	.800
BLOOM, K.	20	0/ -	-	1/ 1	1.000	-/ -	-	-	0	-	-	1	.050
Totals	200	18/ -	-	11/21	.524	-/ -	-	-	19	-	-	47	.235

Disqualified: Washington—Vandenburgh, Nichols; Wyoming—Doty, Reed.

	1st Half	2nd Half	Final
Washington	32	25	57
Wyoming	24	23	47

✪ INDIVIDUAL RECORDS ✪

SCORING

Most points in a single game
1 JOHN PILCH, WYOMING (vs. WASHINGTON) 24
2 ALEX GROZA, KENTUCKY (vs. HOLY CROSS) 23
2 BOB COUSY, HOLY CROSS (vs. MICHIGAN) 23
4 JACK NICHOLS, WASHINGTON (vs. WYOMING) 22
5 WALLACE JONES, KENTUCKY (vs. COLUMBIA) 21

Most total points in the tournament
1 ALEX GROZA, KENTUCKY 54
2 BILL JOHNSON, BAYLOR 43
3 WALLACE JONES, KENTUCKY 42
4 RALPH BEARD, KENTUCKY 40
5 JACK NICHOLS, WASHINGTON 39

Highest scoring average (minimum 2 games)
1 JACK NICHOLS, WASHINGTON (39-2) 19.50
2 ALEX GROZA, KENTUCKY (54-3) 18.00
3 JOHN PILCH, WYOMING (31-2) 15.50
4 BILL JOHNSON, BAYLOR (43-3) 14.33
5 WALLACE JONES, KENTUCKY (42-3) 14.00

FIELD GOALS

Most field goals in a single game
1 ALEX GROZA, KENTUCKY (vs. HOLY CROSS) 10
2 WALLACE JONES, KENTUCKY (vs. COLUMBIA) 9
2 BOB COUSY, HOLY CROSS (vs. MICHIGAN) 9
2 BILL JOHNSON, BAYLOR (vs. WASHINGTON) 9
2 MACK PEYTON, WYOMING (vs. KANSAS STATE) 9

Most total field goals in the tournament
1 ALEX GROZA, KENTUCKY 23
2 WALLACE JONES, KENTUCKY 17
3 BILL JOHNSON, BAYLOR 16
3 RALPH BEARD, KENTUCKY 16
5 SUPRUNOWICZ, MICHIGAN 14

FREE THROWS

Most free throws in a single game
1 DON HEATHINGTON, BAYLOR (vs. KANSAS STATE) 9
2 JOHN PILCH, WYOMING (vs. WASHINGTON) 8
2 JACK NICHOLS, WASHINGTON (vs. WYOMING) 8
4 4 tied for fourth place.

Most total free throws in the tournament
1 HOWARD SHANNON, KANSAS STATE 15
1 DON HEATHINGTON, BAYLOR 15
3 JOHN PILCH, WYOMING 13
3 JACK NICHOLS, WASHINGTON 13
5 2 tied for fifth place.

Most free throws attempted in a single game
1 JOHN PILCH, WYOMING (vs. WASHINGTON) 13
2 DON HEATHINGTON, BAYLOR (vs. KANSAS STATE) 10
2 RICK HARMAN, KANSAS STATE (vs. BAYLOR) 10
4 BOB COUSY, HOLY CROSS (vs. MICHIGAN) 9
4 JACK NICHOLS, WASHINGTON (vs. WYOMING) 9

Most free throws attempted in the tournament
1 DON HEATHINGTON, BAYLOR 22
2 JOHN PILCH, WYOMING 20
3 RICK HARMAN, KANSAS STATE 19
4 3 tied for fourth place.

Highest free throw percentage in a single game (minimum 7 attempts)
1 DON HEATHINGTON, BAYLOR (vs. KANSAS STATE) (9-10) .900
2 JACK NICHOLS, WASHINGTON (vs. WYOMING) (8-9) .889
3 JAMES OWENS, BAYLOR (vs. WASHINGTON) (6-7) .857
4 JOHN PILCH, WYOMING (vs. KANSAS STATE) (5-7) .714
5 JOHN PILCH, WYOMING (vs. WASHINGTON) (8-13) .615

Highest free throw percentage in the tournament (minimum 15 attempts)
1 HOWARD SHANNON, KANSAS STATE (15-15) 1.000
2 BILL JOHNSON, BAYLOR (11-15) .733
3 DON HEATHINGTON, BAYLOR (15-22) .682
4 BOB COUSY, HOLY CROSS (10-15) .667
5 JOHN PILCH, WYOMING (13-20) .650

❂ TEAM RECORDS ❂

SCORING

Most points in a single game
1 KENTUCKY (vs. COLUMBIA)   76
2 MICHIGAN (vs. COLUMBIA)   66
3 BAYLOR (vs. WASHINGTON)   64

Most total points in the tournament
1 KENTUCKY   194
2 HOLY CROSS   175
3 BAYLOR   166

Highest scoring average (minimum 2 games)
1 KENTUCKY (194-3)   64.67
2 WASHINGTON (119-2)   59.50
3 HOLY CROSS (175-3)   58.33

FIELD GOALS

Most field goals in a single game
1 KENTUCKY (vs. COLUMBIA)   31
2 HOLY CROSS (vs. MICHIGAN)   27
3 2 tied for third place.

Most total field goals in the tournament
1 KENTUCKY   79
2 HOLY CROSS   72
3 BAYLOR   58

FREE THROWS

Most free throws in a single game
1 KANSAS STATE (vs. BAYLOR)   22
2 BAYLOR (vs. KANSAS STATE)   20
3 BAYLOR (vs. WASHINGTON)   18

Most total free throws in the tournament
1 KANSAS STATE   50
1 BAYLOR   50
3 KENTUCKY   36

Most free throws attempted in a single game
1 MICHIGAN (vs. COLUMBIA)   28
2 KANSAS STATE (vs. HOLY CROSS)   26
2 KANSAS STATE (vs. BAYLOR)   26

Most total free throws attempted in the tournament
1 BAYLOR   74
2 KANSAS STATE   71
3 KENTUCKY   57

Highest free throw percentage in a single game
1 WASHINGTON (vs. BAYLOR) (16-18)   .889
2 KANSAS STATE (vs. BAYLOR) (22-26)   .846
3 HOLY CROSS (vs. KENTUCKY) (14-17)   .824

Highest free throw percentage in the tournament (minimum 2 games)
1 WASHINGTON (33-40)   .825
2 KANSAS STATE (50-71)   .704
3 BAYLOR (50-74)   .676

Fewest free throws in a single game
1 HOLY CROSS (vs. KANSAS STATE)   8
2 HOLY CROSS (vs. MICHIGAN)   9
2 MICHIGAN (vs. HOLY CROSS)   9

Lowest free throw percentage in a single game
1 HOLY CROSS (vs. MICHIGAN) (9-18)   .500
2 BAYLOR (vs. KENTUCKY) (12-24)   .500
3 MICHIGAN (vs. COLUMBIA) (14-28)   .500

Lowest free throw percentage in the tournament (minimum 2 games)
1 MICHIGAN (23-41)   .561
2 WYOMING (21-37)   .568
3 KENTUCKY (36-57)   .632

1949

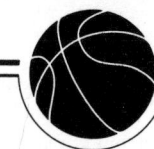

REGIONAL SEMIFINAL	REGIONAL FINAL	NATIONAL CHAMPIONSHIP	REGIONAL FINAL	REGIONAL SEMIFINAL

EASTERN

WESTERN

Illinois 71

Oklahoma A&M 40

Illinois 47

Oklahoma A&M 55

Yale 67

Wyoming 39

Kentucky 46
Oklahoma A&M 36

Kentucky 85

Oregon St. 56

Kentucky 76

Oregon St. 30

Villanova 72

Arkansas 38

CONSOLATION GAMES

National Third Place:

Illinois 57

Oregon St. 53

Regional Third Place:

Eastern:

Villanova 78

Yale 67

Western:

Arkansas 61

Wyoming 48

The 1949 Kentucky Wildcats could have been one of the greatest teams in the history of college basketball. Returning from the 1948 championship squad were starters Alex Groza, Ralph Beard, Wallace "Wah-Wah" Jones, and Cliff Barker, plus top subs Jim Line and Dale Barnstable. They were another year older and more experienced playing together against top-flight competition. The Wildcats appeared unbeatable—maybe even better than the previous year's "Fabulous Five"—except for occasional and inexplicable lapses in concentration.

Kentucky's only regular season loss came during the Sugar Bowl holiday tournament in St. Louis. The Wildcats were leading the St. Louis Bilikens by two points in the final seconds when a Kentucky guard bounced a dribble off his foot. St. Louis took the ball out of bounds and—with the Kentuckians just standing around on defense—St. Louis worked the ball inside and scored unmolested. After Kentucky was unable to break the tie, the ball went back to the Bilikens. With only seconds remaining, a foul sent a St. Louis player to the line. The free throw bounced harmlessly off the rim, but Kentucky failed to box out, thus allowing a winning tip-in at the buzzer.

As Kentucky Coach Adolph Rupp started off the floor, Burgess Carey, an ex-Wildcat All-American and a friend of Rupp's, stormed over and declared, "Coach, you just cost me $500!" Rupp denied that he was responsible for the lost wager, but when he entered the dressing room he in turn confronted Barnstable, who had missed a crucial shot late in the game. Later Rupp spoke about the breaks of the game, but his words didn't stop the rumblings about the unexpected Kentucky loss. It was all but forgotten, however, as they sailed into the post-season with only the one blemish on their perfect record.

Rupp, hoping for unprecedented sweep of the post-season tournaments, accepted bids from both the NIT and NCAA. But Rupp's express was derailed when the Wildcats were upset by Loyola of Chicago in the opening round of the NIT. Groza seemed to be backing away on defense all game, allowing Loyola pivotman Jack Kerris to shoot unchallenged. And when Kerris picked up his fourth foul early in the second half, Groza didn't fight for offensive position and Beard and Barker didn't even try to get him the ball. The Wildcats' loss shocked fans who had begun to think of their team as invincible.

The Kentucky team still had a chance to redeem itself in the NCAAs. But they fell behind Villanova and the Philadelphia school's star center, Paul Arizin, by a score of 15-10 before fighting their way back. At the half, with Groza controlling the boards, they were up by 11. In the end they broke the tournament scoring record and won 85-72, even though Beard was held without a field goal.

Kentucky was awesome in the Eastern championship against Illinois in Madison Square Garden. Louis Effrat wrote in *The New York Times* that they "were unrecogniz-

able alongside the squad that floundered so dismally against Loyola" in the NIT. Dominating on offense and defense, Groza scored 27 points in leading the Wildcats to a 29-point victory.

In the national final Kentucky played Oklahoma A&M. Henry Iba's squad, averaging 6-4 in height, was a perennial power. The Aggies were the only team ever to win two NCAA titles (in 1945 and 1946), and they came into the game against the Wildcats as the second-ranked club in the nation. It was a perfect matchup, featuring the nation's best running team (Kentucky) against the pre-eminent practitioners of ball control (A&M).

The Aggies had staged a spectacular comeback in their opening game against Wyoming, coming from 5 back in the last two minutes as forward Jack Shelton hit three straight shots, including the clincher with four seconds left. In the second round Oklahoma A&M completely dominated Oregon State, crushing the Pacific Coast champion Beavers by holding them to a mere 30 points.

The two best teams in America had survived the preliminary rounds, and were now ready to go head to head. It was thus an eagerly awaited final that took place in Seattle on March 26th.

At first the Oklahomans patiently worked the ball around, breaking through after a series of crisp passes for open lay-ups. But Rupp adjusted his game plan. The Kentucky defense became impregnable; it was so effective that at one point in the second half the Aggies didn't score a field goal for thirteen minutes.

On Kentucky's offensive end the story was all Alex Groza. Posting-up his lanky A&M counterpart, Bob Harris, Groza controlled the paint in scoring 15 first-half points. He even stole a pass and took the ball the length of the floor to score the basket that gave his team their first lead.

Only four minutes after the second half tap, A&M's Harris fouled out. Groza sat down, and played sparingly thereafter. In all, he was on court for less than thirty minutes. Still, when he was on the floor he was unstoppable. Groza finished with 25 points and was the unanimous choice of the sportswriters who selected him the Most Outstanding Player in the tournament for the second straight year. Kentucky was vindicated.

Two years later, Alex Groza, Ralph Beard, and Dale Barnstable admitted in sworn testimony that they had accepted $1,500 in bribes to throw the 1949 NIT game against Loyola. They also testified that they took money from gamblers to shave points in other key games during the 1948–49 season.

Groza, Beard, Barnstable, and their teammates could have been one of the greatest teams in history. And except for two losses that should never have happened, they would have been.

REGIONAL SEMIFINAL EASTERN

Illinois (71) Coach: Harry Combes

	Min.	Total FG/FGA	Pct.	FT/FTA	Pct.	Reb. O/T	A	TO	PF	S	Blk	TP	PPM
EDDLEMAN, D.	-	5/ -	-	1/ 1	1.000	-/ -	-	-	4	-	-	11	-
GATEWOOD, R.	-	0/ -	-	0/ 0	.000	-/ -	-	-	0	-	-	0	-
ANDERSON, V.	-	2/ -	-	0/ 0	.000	-/ -	-	-	1	-	-	4	-
KERSULIS, W.	-	3/ -	-	1/ 1	1.000	-/ -	-	-	3	-	-	7	-
BEACH, T.	-	0/ -	-	0/ 0	.000	-/ -	-	-	0	-	-	0	-
OSTERKORN, W.	-	5/ -	-	5/ 8	.625	-/ -	-	-	3	-	-	15	-
GREEN, F.	-	4/ -	-	2/ 2	1.000	-/ -	-	-	2	-	-	10	-
ERICKSON, B.	-	1/ -	-	3/ 6	.500	-/ -	-	-	3	-	-	5	-
SUNDERLAGE, D.	-	7/ -	-	1/ 3	.333	-/ -	-	-	5	-	-	15	-
FOLEY, D.	-	2/ -	-	0/ 0	.000	-/ -	-	-	1	-	-	4	-
COTTRELL, J.	-	0/ -	-	0/ 0	.000	-/ -	-	-	0	-	-	0	-
MARKS, J.	-	0/ -	-	0/ 0	.000	-/ -	-	-	1	-	-	0	-
Totals	200	29/ -	-	13/21	.619	-/ -	-	-	23	-	-	71	.355

Yale (67) Coach: Howard Hobson

	Min.	Total FG/FGA	Pct.	FT/FTA	Pct.	Reb. O/T	A	TO	PF	S	Blk	TP	PPM
LAVELLI, T.	-	10/ -	-	7/ 7	1.000	-/ -	-	-	3	-	-	27	-
ABERG	-	0/ -	-	0/ 0	.000	-/ -	-	-	0	-	-	0	-
ANDERSON, T.	-	7/ -	-	5/ 8	.625	-/ -	-	-	4	-	-	19	-
JOHNSON	-	0/ -	-	1/ 4	.250	-/ -	-	-	1	-	-	1	-
JOYCE	-	4/ -	-	1/ 1	1.000	-/ -	-	-	5	-	-	9	-
DECOURSEY	-	0/ -	-	0/ 0	.000	-/ -	-	-	0	-	-	0	-
OSBURN	-	1/ -	-	0/ 0	.000	-/ -	-	-	0	-	-	2	-
FITZGERALD, A.	-	1/ -	-	3/ 5	.600	-/ -	-	-	3	-	-	5	-
JACKSON	-	0/ -	-	0/ 0	.000	-/ -	-	-	0	-	-	0	-
NADHERNY	-	2/ -	-	0/ 2	.000	-/ -	-	-	2	-	-	4	-
UPJOHN	-	0/ -	-	0/ 0	.000	-/ -	-	-	0	-	-	0	-
BREEN	-	0/ -	-	0/ 0	.000	-/ -	-	-	0	-	-	0	-
Totals	200	25/ -	-	17/27	.630	-/ -	-	-	18	-	-	67	.335

Disqualified: Illinois—Sunderlage; Yale—Joyce.

	1st Half	2nd Half	Final
Illinois	31	40	71
Yale	35	32	67

Kentucky (85) Coach: Adolph Rupp

	Min.	Total FG/FGA	Pct.	FT/FTA	Pct.	Reb. O/T	A	TO	PF	S	Blk	TP	PPM
JONES, W.	-	0/ -	-	4/ -	-	-/ -	-	-	5	-	-	4	-
LINE, J.	-	9/ -	-	3/ -	-	-/ -	-	-	5	-	-	21	-
GROZA, A.	-	12/ -	-	6/ -	-	-/ -	-	-	4	-	-	30	-
BEARD, R.	-	0/ -	-	3/ -	-	-/ -	-	-	3	-	-	3	-
BARKER, C.	-	6/ -	-	6/ -	-	-/ -	-	-	3	-	-	18	-
HIRSCH, W.	-	1/ -	-	0/ -	-	-/ -	-	-	3	-	-	2	-
BARNSTABLE, D.	-	2/ -	-	1/ -	-	-/ -	-	-	2	-	-	5	-
DAY, R.	-	1/ -	-	0/ -	-	-/ -	-	-	1	-	-	2	-
Totals	200	31/ -	-	23/ -	-	-/ -	-	-	26	-	-	85	.425

Villanova (72) Coach: Alex Severance

	Min.	Total FG/FGA	Pct.	FT/FTA	Pct.	Reb. O/T	A	TO	PF	S	Blk	TP	PPM
RICCA, B.	-	6/ -	-	2/ -	-	-/ -	-	-	5	-	-	14	-
RAIKEN	-	3/ -	-	0/ -	-	-/ -	-	-	5	-	-	6	-
ARIZIN, P.	-	11/ -	-	8/ -	-	-/ -	-	-	5	-	-	30	-
WOLF, L.	-	0/ -	-	2/ -	-	-/ -	-	-	3	-	-	2	-
HANNAN, J.	-	3/ -	-	1/ -	-	-/ -	-	-	2	-	-	7	-
DELPURGATORIO	-	2/ -	-	0/ -	-	-/ -	-	-	2	-	-	4	-
GECKER	-	0/ -	-	0/ -	-	-/ -	-	-	0	-	-	0	-
WEGLICKI	-	2/ -	-	1/ -	-	-/ -	-	-	2	-	-	5	-
DOLAN	-	1/ -	-	0/ -	-	-/ -	-	-	0	-	-	2	-
CROSSIN	-	0/ -	-	2/ -	-	-/ -	-	-	1	-	-	2	-
Totals	200	28/ -	-	16/ -	-	-/ -	-	-	25	-	-	72	.360

Disqualified: Kentucky—Jones, Line; Villanova—Ricca, Raiken, Arizin.

	1st Half	2nd Half	Final
Kentucky	48	37	85
Villanova	37	35	72

REGIONAL SEMIFINAL WESTERN

Oklahoma A&M (40) Coach: Henry Iba

	Min.	Total FG/FGA	Pct.	FT/FTA	Pct.	Reb. O/T	A	TO	PF	S	Blk	TP	PPM
YATES, V.	-	1/ -	-	0/ 0	.000	-/ -	-	-	0	-	-	2	-
SHELTON, J.	-	5/ -	-	6/ 7	.857	-/ -	-	-	3	-	-	16	-
HARRIS, B.	-	2/ -	-	0/ 1	.000	-/ -	-	-	4	-	-	4	-
BRADLEY, J.	-	3/ -	-	2/ 4	.500	-/ -	-	-	2	-	-	8	-
PARKS, J.	-	2/ -	-	2/ 3	.667	-/ -	-	-	4	-	-	6	-
JACQUET, T.	-	1/ -	-	0/ 0	.000	-/ -	-	-	5	-	-	2	-
MCARTHUR, G.	-	1/ -	-	0/ 0	.000	-/ -	-	-	0	-	-	2	-
PILGRIM, N.	-	0/ -	-	0/ 1	.000	-/ -	-	-	1	-	-	0	-
HOBBS, J.	-	0/ -	-	0/ 0	.000	-/ -	-	-	1	-	-	0	-
Totals	200	15/ -	-	10/16	.625	-/ -	-	-	20	-	-	40	.200

Wyoming (39) Coach: Everett Shelton

	Min.	Total FG/FGA	Pct.	FT/FTA	Pct.	Reb. O/T	A	TO	PF	S	Blk	TP	PPM
DOTY	-	1/ -	-	4/10	.400	-/ -	-	-	4	-	-	6	-
BLOOM, K.	-	3/ -	-	3/ 5	.600	-/ -	-	-	1	-	-	9	-
LIVINGSTON, R.	-	4/ -	-	0/ 1	.000	-/ -	-	-	3	-	-	8	-
REED, G.	-	0/ -	-	0/ 0	.000	-/ -	-	-	0	-	-	0	-
PEYTON, M.	-	1/ -	-	0/ 1	.000	-/ -	-	-	1	-	-	2	-
PILCH, J.	-	6/ -	-	2/ 4	.500	-/ -	-	-	5	-	-	14	-
Totals	200	15/ -	-	9/21	.429	-/ -	-	-	14	-	-	39	.195

Disqualified: Oklahoma A&M—Jacquet; Wyoming—Pilch.

	1st Half	2nd Half	Final
Oklahoma A&M	22	18	40
Wyoming	25	14	39

Oregon State (56)   Coach: Amory "Slats" Gill

	Min.	Total FG / FGA	Pct.	FT / FTA	Pct.	Reb. O / T	A	TO	PF	S	Blk	TP	PPM
CRANDALL, C.	-	3/ -	-	7/ 7	1.000	-/ -	-	-	4	-	-	13	-
PETERSEN, A.	-	5/ -	-	0/ 1	.000	-/ -	-	-	1	-	-	10	-
RINEARSON, L.	-	0/ -	-	1/ 1	1.000	-/ -	-	-	2	-	-	1	-
SLIPER, P.	-	1/ -	-	0/ 0	.000	-/ -	-	-	0	-	-	2	-
SNYDER, R.	-	0/ -	-	0/ 0	.000	-/ -	-	-	1	-	-	0	-
WATT, H.	-	1/ -	-	0/ 0	.000	-/ -	-	-	2	-	-	2	-
FLEMING, E.	-	1/ -	-	0/ 1	.000	-/ -	-	-	3	-	-	2	-
HARPER, B.	-	2/ -	-	3/ 4	.750	-/ -	-	-	2	-	-	7	-
CATTERALL, J.	-	0/ -	-	0/ 0	.000	-/ -	-	-	1	-	-	0	-
BALLANTYNE, D.	-	2/ -	-	9/11	.818	-/ -	-	-	1	-	-	13	-
TORREY, D.	-	3/ -	-	0/ 2	.000	-/ -	-	-	4	-	-	6	-
HOLMAN, T.	-	0/ -	-	0/ 0	.000	-/ -	-	-	0	-	-	0	-
Totals	200	18/51	.353	20/27	.741	-/ -	-	-	21	-	-	56	.280

Arkansas (38)   Coach: Eugene Lambert

	Min.	Total FG / FGA	Pct.	FT / FTA	Pct.	Reb. O / T	A	TO	PF	S	Blk	TP	PPM
CATHCART	-	2/ -	-	2/ 4	.500	-/ -	-	-	5	-	-	6	-
HORTON, C.	-	4/ -	-	4/ 6	.667	-/ -	-	-	5	-	-	12	-
AMBLER	-	2/ -	-	0/ 5	.000	-/ -	-	-	1	-	-	4	-
COLEMAN	-	0/ -	-	2/ 2	1.000	-/ -	-	-	0	-	-	2	-
KEARNS, K.	-	1/ -	-	1/ 1	1.000	-/ -	-	-	4	-	-	3	-
WILLIAMS	-	0/ -	-	2/ 2	1.000	-/ -	-	-	2	-	-	2	-
RANKIN	-	2/ -	-	0/ 0	.000	-/ -	-	-	0	-	-	4	-
CAMPBELL	-	2/ -	-	1/ 3	.333	-/ -	-	-	3	-	-	5	-
ADAMS	-	0/ -	-	0/ 0	.000	-/ -	-	-	0	-	-	0	-
PRICE	-	0/ -	-	0/ 0	.000	-/ -	-	-	2	-	-	0	-
RUDSPETH	-	0/ -	-	0/ 0	.000	-/ -	-	-	2	-	-	0	-
Totals	200	13/63	.206	12/23	.522	-/ -	-	-	24	-	-	38	.190

Disqualified: Arkansas—Cathcart, Horton.

	1st Half	2nd Half	Final
Oregon State	21	35	56
Arkansas	17	21	38

REGIONAL FINAL EASTERN

Illinois (47)   Coach: Harry Combes

	Min.	Total FG / FGA	Pct.	FT / FTA	Pct.	Reb. O / T	A	TO	PF	S	Blk	TP	PPM
EDDLEMAN, D.	-	3/ -	-	0/ 2	.000	-/ -	-	-	1	-	-	6	-
GATEWOOD, R.	-	3/ -	-	0/ 0	.000	-/ -	-	-	0	-	-	6	-
ANDERSON, V.	-	0/ -	-	0/ 0	.000	-/ -	-	-	1	-	-	0	-
KERSULIS, W.	-	3/ -	-	3/ 3	1.000	-/ -	-	-	2	-	-	9	-
BEACH, T.	-	1/ -	-	0/ 0	.000	-/ -	-	-	0	-	-	2	-
OSTERKORN, W.	-	2/ -	-	1/ 2	.500	-/ -	-	-	5	-	-	5	-
GREEN, F.	-	3/ -	-	1/ 1	1.000	-/ -	-	-	2	-	-	7	-
ERICKSON, B.	-	2/ -	-	1/ 3	.333	-/ -	-	-	2	-	-	5	-
SUNDERLAGE, D.	-	0/ -	-	2/ 2	1.000	-/ -	-	-	2	-	-	2	-
FOLEY, D.	-	1/ -	-	1/ 1	1.000	-/ -	-	-	1	-	-	3	-
COTTRELL, J.	-	0/ -	-	0/ 0	.000	-/ -	-	-	1	-	-	0	-
MARKS, J.	-	1/ -	-	0/ 0	.000	-/ -	-	-	2	-	-	2	-
Totals	200	19/ -	-	9/14	.643	-/ -	-	-	19	-	-	47	.235

Kentucky (76)   Coach: Adolph Rupp

	Min.	Total FG / FGA	Pct.	FT / FTA	Pct.	Reb. O / T	A	TO	PF	S	Blk	TP	PPM
JONES, W.	-	4/ -	-	1/ 2	.500	-/ -	-	-	3	-	-	9	-
LINE, J.	-	6/ -	-	3/ 4	.750	-/ -	-	-	0	-	-	15	-
GROZA, A.	-	10/ -	-	7/10	.700	-/ -	-	-	4	-	-	27	-
BEARD, R.	-	4/ -	-	1/ 3	.333	-/ -	-	-	3	-	-	9	-
BARKER, C.	-	3/ -	-	2/ 3	.667	-/ -	-	-	2	-	-	8	-
BARNSTABLE, D.	-	1/ -	-	0/ 0	.000	-/ -	-	-	1	-	-	2	-
HIRSCH, W.	-	3/ -	-	0/ 0	.000	-/ -	-	-	1	-	-	6	-
DAY, R.	-	0/ -	-	0/ 0	.000	-/ -	-	-	0	-	-	0	-
STOUGH, J.	-	0/ -	-	0/ 0	.000	-/ -	-	-	0	-	-	0	-
Totals	200	31/ -	-	14/22	.636	-/ -	-	-	14	-	-	76	.380

Disqualified: Illinois—Osterkorn.

	1st Half	2nd Half	Final
Illinois	22	25	47
Kentucky	39	37	76

REGIONAL FINAL WESTERN

Oklahoma A&M (55)   Coach: Henry Iba

	Min.	Total FG / FGA	Pct.	FT / FTA	Pct.	Reb. O / T	A	TO	PF	S	Blk	TP	PPM
SHELTON, J.	-	3/ -	-	7/ 8	.875	-/ -	-	-	3	-	-	13	-
HOBBS, J.	-	0/ -	-	0/ 0	.000	-/ -	-	-	0	-	-	0	-
YATES, V.	-	0/ -	-	0/ 0	.000	-/ -	-	-	0	-	-	0	-
MCARTHUR, G.	-	0/ -	-	0/ 0	.000	-/ -	-	-	2	-	-	0	-
PILGRIM, N.	-	0/ -	-	0/ 0	.000	-/ -	-	-	4	-	-	0	-
HARRIS	-	8/ -	-	7/ 7	1.000	-/ -	-	-	1	-	-	23	-
BRADLEY, J.	-	3/ -	-	1/ 1	1.000	-/ -	-	-	1	-	-	7	-
JACQUET, T.	-	0/ -	-	0/ 0	.000	-/ -	-	-	0	-	-	0	-
ALLEN	-	0/ -	-	0/ 0	.000	-/ -	-	-	1	-	-	0	-
PARKS, J.	-	2/ -	-	4/ 6	.667	-/ -	-	-	2	-	-	8	-
SMITH, K.	-	1/ -	-	2/ 2	1.000	-/ -	-	-	1	-	-	4	-
HAYES, L.	-	0/ -	-	0/ 0	.000	-/ -	-	-	1	-	-	0	-
Totals	200	17/38	-	21/24	.875	-/ -	-	-	16	-	-	55	.275

Oregon State (30)   Coach: Amory "Slats" Gill

	Min.	Total FG / FGA	Pct.	FT / FTA	Pct.	Reb. O / T	A	TO	PF	S	Blk	TP	PPM
PETERSEN, A.	-	2/ -	-	0/ 3	.000	-/ -	-	-	5	-	-	4	-
CATTERALL, J.	-	0/ -	-	1/ 2	.500	-/ -	-	-	1	-	-	1	-
SLIPER, P.	-	0/ -	-	0/ 0	.000	-/ -	-	-	1	-	-	0	-
FLEMING, E.	-	1/ -	-	0/ 1	.000	-/ -	-	-	0	-	-	2	-
SNYDER, R.	-	1/ -	-	0/ 0	.000	-/ -	-	-	1	-	-	2	-
WATT, H.	-	0/ -	-	0/ 0	.000	-/ -	-	-	1	-	-	0	-
RINEARSON, L.	-	0/ -	-	0/ 0	.000	-/ -	-	-	2	-	-	0	-
CRANDALL, C.	-	4/ -	-	3/ 4	.750	-/ -	-	-	3	-	-	11	-
HARPER, B.	-	1/ -	-	0/ 1	.000	-/ -	-	-	1	-	-	2	-
BALLANTYNE, D.	-	1/ -	-	1/ 1	1.000	-/ -	-	-	2	-	-	3	-
TORREY, D.	-	0/ -	-	1/ 1	1.000	-/ -	-	-	1	-	-	1	-
HOLMAN, T.	-	1/ -	-	2/ 2	1.000	-/ -	-	-	1	-	-	4	-
Totals	200	11/ -	-	8/15	.533	-/ -	-	-	18	-	-	30	.150

Disqualified: Oregon State—Petersen.

	1st Half	2nd Half	Final
Oklahoma A&M	21	34	55
Oregon State	11	19	30

CHAMPIONSHIP

Kentucky (46)   Coach: Adolph Rupp

	Min.	Total FG / FGA	Pct.	FT / FTA	Pct.	Reb. O / T	A	TO	PF	S	Blk	TP	PPM
JONES, W.	-	1/ -	-	1/ 3	.333	-/ -	-	-	3	-	-	3	-
LINE, J.	-	2/ -	-	1/ 2	.500	-/ -	-	-	3	-	-	5	-
GROZA, A.	-	9/ -	-	7/ 8	.875	-/ -	-	-	5	-	-	25	-
BEARD, R.	-	1/ -	-	1/ 2	.500	-/ -	-	-	4	-	-	3	-
BARKER, C.	-	1/ -	-	3/ 3	1.000	-/ -	-	-	4	-	-	5	-
BARNSTABLE, D.	-	1/ -	-	1/ 1	1.000	-/ -	-	-	1	-	-	3	-
HIRSCH, W.	-	1/ -	-	0/ 0	.000	-/ -	-	-	1	-	-	2	-
Totals	200	16/ -	-	14/19	.737	-/ -	-	-	21	-	-	46	.230

Oklahoma A&M (36)   Coach: Henry Iba

	Min.	Total FG / FGA	Pct.	FT / FTA	Pct.	Reb. O / T	A	TO	PF	S	Blk	TP	PPM
YATES, V.	-	1/ -	-	0/ 0	.000	-/ -	-	-	1	-	-	2	-
SHELTON, J.	-	3/ -	-	6/ 7	.857	-/ -	-	-	4	-	-	12	-
HARRIS, B.	-	3/ -	-	1/ 1	1.000	-/ -	-	-	5	-	-	7	-
BRADLEY, J.	-	0/ -	-	3/ 6	.500	-/ -	-	-	3	-	-	3	-
PARKS, J.	-	2/ -	-	3/ 4	.750	-/ -	-	-	5	-	-	7	-
JACQUET, T.	-	0/ -	-	1/ 2	.500	-/ -	-	-	0	-	-	1	-
MCARTHUR, G.	-	0/ -	-	2/ 2	1.000	-/ -	-	-	1	-	-	2	-
PILGRIM, N.	-	0/ -	-	2/ 2	1.000	-/ -	-	-	1	-	-	2	-
SMITH, K.	-	0/ -	-	0/ 0	.000	-/ -	-	-	1	-	-	0	-
Totals	200	9/ -	-	18/24	.750	-/ -	-	-	21	-	-	36	.180

Disqualified: Kentucky—Groza; Oklahoma A&M—Harris, Parks.

	1st Half	2nd Half	Final
Kentucky	25	21	46
Oklahoma A&M	20	16	36

NATIONAL THIRD PLACE

Illinois (57)   Coach: Harry Combes

	Min.	Total FG / FGA	Pct.	FT / FTA	Pct.	Reb. O / T	A	TO	PF	S	Blk	TP	PPM
EDDLEMAN, D.	-	5/ -	-	1/ 2	.500	-/ -	-	-	5	-	-	11	-
GATEWOOD, R.	-	0/ -	-	0/ 0	.000	-/ -	-	-	0	-	-	0	-
ANDERSON, V.	-	0/ -	-	0/ 0	.000	-/ -	-	-	1	-	-	0	-
KERSULIS, W.	-	3/ -	-	1/ 4	.250	-/ -	-	-	2	-	-	7	-
BEACH, T.	-	0/ -	-	0/ 0	.000	-/ -	-	-	0	-	-	0	-
OSTERKORN, W.	-	6/ -	-	5/ 8	.625	-/ -	-	-	5	-	-	17	-
GREEN, F.	-	3/ -	-	1/ 1	1.000	-/ -	-	-	5	-	-	7	-
ERICKSON, B.	-	3/ -	-	0/ 2	.000	-/ -	-	-	4	-	-	6	-
SUNDERLAGE, D.	-	1/ -	-	0/ 0	.000	-/ -	-	-	0	-	-	2	-
FOLEY, D.	-	2/ -	-	3/ 6	.500	-/ -	-	-	4	-	-	7	-
COTTRELL, J.	-	0/ -	-	0/ 0	.000	-/ -	-	-	0	-	-	0	-
MARKS, J.	-	0/ -	-	0/ 0	.000	-/ -	-	-	0	-	-	0	-
Totals	200	23/ -	-	11/23	.478	-/ -	-	-	26	-	-	57	.285

Oregon State (53)   Coach: Amory "Slats" Gill

	Min.	Total FG / FGA	Pct.	FT / FTA	Pct.	Reb. O / T	A	TO	PF	S	Blk	TP	PPM
CRANDALL, C.	-	6/ -	-	6/ 8	.750	-/ -	-	-	4	-	-	18	-
PETERSEN, A.	-	3/ -	-	2/ 2	1.000	-/ -	-	-	1	-	-	8	-
RINEARSON, L.	-	1/ -	-	0/ 0	.000	-/ -	-	-	1	-	-	2	-
SLIPER, P.	-	0/ -	-	0/ 0	.000	-/ -	-	-	0	-	-	0	-
SNYDER, R.	-	1/ -	-	2/ 2	1.000	-/ -	-	-	2	-	-	4	-
WATT, H.	-	3/ -	-	0/ 5	.000	-/ -	-	-	2	-	-	6	-
FLEMING, E.	-	1/ -	-	3/ 4	.750	-/ -	-	-	4	-	-	5	-
HARPER, B.	-	1/ -	-	0/ 1	.000	-/ -	-	-	3	-	-	2	-
CATTERALL, J.	-	0/ -	-	0/ 0	.000	-/ -	-	-	0	-	-	0	-
BALLANTYNE, D.	-	3/ -	-	2/ 3	.667	-/ -	-	-	4	-	-	8	-
TORREY, D.	-	0/ -	-	0/ 0	.000	-/ -	-	-	1	-	-	0	-
HOLMAN, T.	-	0/ -	-	0/ 0	.000	-/ -	-	-	0	-	-	0	-
Totals	200	19/ -	-	15/25	.600	-/ -	-	-	22	-	-	53	.265

Disqualified: Illinois—Eddleman, Osterkorn, Green.

	1st Half	2nd Half	Final
Illinois	28	29	57
Oregon State	19	34	53

REGIONAL THIRD PLACE EASTERN

Villanova (78)   Coach: Alex Severance

	Min.	Total FG / FGA	Pct.	FT / FTA	Pct.	Reb. O / T	A	TO	PF	S	Blk	TP	PPM
RICCA, B.	-	5/ -	-	3/ -	-	-/ -	-	-	5	-	-	13	-
RAIKEN	-	6/ -	-	3/ -	-	-/ -	-	-	2	-	-	15	-
ARIZIN, P.	-	7/ -	-	8/ -	-	-/ -	-	-	3	-	-	22	-
WOLF, L.	-	0/ -	-	0/ -	-	-/ -	-	-	4	-	-	0	-
HANNAN, J.	-	12/ -	-	1/ -	-	-/ -	-	-	2	-	-	25	-
WEGLICKI	-	1/ -	-	1/ -	-	-/ -	-	-	0	-	-	3	-
Totals	200	31/ -	-	16/ -	-	-/ -	-	-	16	-	-	78	.390

Yale (67)   Coach: Howard Hobson

	Min.	Total FG / FGA	Pct.	FT / FTA	Pct.	Reb. O / T	A	TO	PF	S	Blk	TP	PPM
ANDERSON, T.	-	5/ -	-	2/ -	-	-/ -	-	-	4	-	-	12	-
LAVELLI, T.	-	1/ -	-	6/ -	-	-/ -	-	-	3	-	-	8	-
JOYCE	-	1/ -	-	1/ -	-	-/ -	-	-	4	-	-	3	-
FITZGERALD, A.	-	6/ -	-	0/ -	-	-/ -	-	-	0	-	-	12	-
NADHERNY	-	4/ -	-	0/ -	-	-/ -	-	-	1	-	-	8	-
JOHNSON	-	2/ -	-	0/ -	-	-/ -	-	-	1	-	-	4	-
OSBOURNE	-	0/ -	-	0/ -	-	-/ -	-	-	1	-	-	0	-
DECOURSEY	-	1/ -	-	1/ -	-	-/ -	-	-	2	-	-	3	-
JACKSON	-	2/ -	-	3/ -	-	-/ -	-	-	2	-	-	7	-
UPJOHN	-	5/ -	-	0/ -	-	-/ -	-	-	1	-	-	10	-
Totals	200	27/ -	-	13/ -	-	-/ -	-	-	19	-	-	67	.335

Disqualified: Villanova—Ricca.

	1st Half	2nd Half	Final
Villanova	33	45	78
Yale	31	36	67

REGIONAL THIRD PLACE WESTERN

Arkansas (61)   Coach: Eugene Lambert

	Min.	Total FG / FGA	Pct.	FT / FTA	Pct.	Reb. O / T	A	TO	PF	S	Blk	TP	PPM
CATHCART	-	4/ -	-	0/ 1	.000	-/ -	-	-	4	-	-	8	-
HORTON, C.	-	7/ -	-	2/ 5	.400	-/ -	-	-	4	-	-	16	-
AMBLER	-	5/ -	-	3/ 5	.600	-/ -	-	-	1	-	-	13	-
COLEMAN	-	1/ -	-	0/ 1	.000	-/ -	-	-	0	-	-	2	-
KEARNS, K.	-	7/ -	-	0/ 0	.000	-/ -	-	-	5	-	-	14	-
WILLIAMS	-	1/ -	-	0/ 0	.000	-/ -	-	-	1	-	-	2	-
RANKIN	-	0/ -	-	0/ 0	.000	-/ -	-	-	0	-	-	0	-
CAMPBELL	-	2/ -	-	2/ 2	1.000	-/ -	-	-	4	-	-	6	-
Totals	200	27/71	-	7/14	.500	-/ -	-	-	19	-	-	61	.305

Wyoming (48)   Coach: Everett Shelton

	Min.	Total FG / FGA	Pct.	FT / FTA	Pct.	Reb. O / T	A	TO	PF	S	Blk	TP	PPM
DOTY	-	1/ -	-	2/ 4	.500	-/ -	-	-	2	-	-	4	-
LARSON, L.	-	0/ -	-	0/ 1	.000	-/ -	-	-	0	-	-	0	-
BLOOM, K.	-	0/ -	-	3/ 3	1.000	-/ -	-	-	2	-	-	3	-
LIVINGSTON, R.	-	3/ -	-	0/ 3	.000	-/ -	-	-	3	-	-	6	-
REED, G.	-	2/ -	-	3/ 3	1.000	-/ -	-	-	3	-	-	7	-
PEYTON, M.	-	7/ -	-	2/ 3	.667	-/ -	-	-	0	-	-	16	-
PILCH, J.	-	4/ -	-	4/ 4	1.000	-/ -	-	-	3	-	-	12	-
Totals	200	17/61	-	14/21	.667	-/ -	-	-	13	-	-	48	.240

Disqualified: Arkansas—Kearns.

	1st Half	2nd Half	Final
Arkansas	33	28	61
Wyoming	23	25	48

⚙ INDIVIDUAL RECORDS ⚙

SCORING

Most points in a single game
1   PAUL ARIZIN, VILLANOVA (vs. KENTUCKY)   30
1   ALEX GROZA, KENTUCKY (vs. VILLANOVA)   30
3   ALEX GROZA, KENTUCKY (vs. ILLINOIS)   27
3   TONY LAVELLI, YALE (vs. ILLINOIS)   27
5   2 tied for fifth place.

Most total points in the tournament
1   ALEX GROZA, KENTUCKY   82
2   PAUL ARIZIN, VILLANOVA   52
3   CLIFF CRANDALL, OREGON STATE   42
4   JACK SHELTON, OKLAHOMA A&M   41
4   JAMES LINE, KENTUCKY   41

Highest scoring average (minimum 2 games)
1   ALEX GROZA, KENTUCKY (82-3)   27.33
2   PAUL ARIZIN, VILLANOVA (52-2)   26.00
3   TONY LAVELLI, YALE (35-2)   17.50
4   JOHN HANNAN, VILLANOVA (32-2)   16.00
5   TED ANDERSON, YALE (31-2)   15.50

FIELD GOALS

Most field goals in a single game
1   JOHN HANNAN, VILLANOVA (vs. YALE)   12
1   ALEX GROZA, KENTUCKY (vs. VILLANOVA)   12
3   PAUL ARIZIN, VILLANOVA (vs. KENTUCKY)   11
4   ALEX GROZA, KENTUCKY (vs. ILLINOIS)   10
4   TONY LAVELLI, YALE (vs. ILLINOIS)   10

Most total field goals in the tournament
1   ALEX GROZA, KENTUCKY   31
2   PAUL ARIZIN, VILLANOVA   18
3   JAMES LINE, KENTUCKY   17
4   JOHN HANNAN, VILLANOVA   15
5   4 tied for fifth place.

FREE THROWS

Most free throws in a single game
1   DICK BALLANTYNE, OREGON STATE (vs. ARKANSAS)   9
2   PAUL ARIZIN, VILLANOVA (vs. YALE)   8
2   PAUL ARIZIN, VILLANOVA (vs. KENTUCKY)   8
4   6 tied for fourth place.

Most total free throws in the tournament
1   ALEX GROZA, KENTUCKY   20
2   JACK SHELTON, OKLAHOMA A&M   19
3   CLIFF CRANDALL, OREGON STATE   16
3   PAUL ARIZIN, VILLANOVA   16
5   TONY LAVELLI, YALE   13

Most free throws attempted in a single game
1   DICK BALLANTYNE, OREGON STATE (vs. ARKANSAS)   11
2   ALEX GROZA, KENTUCKY (vs. ILLINOIS)   10
2   LOY DOTY, WYOMING (vs. OKLAHOMA A&M)   10
4   6 tied for fourth place.

Highest free throw percentage in a single game (minimum 7 attempts)
1   BOB HARRIS, OKLAHOMA A&M (vs. OREGON STATE) (7-7)   1.000
1   CLIFF CRANDALL, OREGON STATE (vs. ARKANSAS) (7-7)   1.000
1   TONY LAVELLI, YALE (vs. ILLINOIS) (7-7)   1.000
4   JACK SHELTON, OKLAHOMA A&M (vs. OREGON STATE) (7-8)   .875
4   ALEX GROZA, KENTUCKY (vs. OKLAHOMA A&M) (7-8)   .875

○ TEAM RECORDS ○

SCORING

Most points in a single game

1	KENTUCKY (vs. VILLANOVA)	85
2	VILLANOVA (vs. YALE)	78
3	KENTUCKY (vs. ILLINOIS)	76

Most total points in the tournament

1	KENTUCKY	207
2	ILLINOIS	175
3	VILLANOVA	150

Highest scoring average (minimum 2 games)

1	VILLANOVA (150-2)	75.00
2	KENTUCKY (207-3)	69.00
3	YALE (134-2)	67.00

FIELD GOALS

Most field goals in a single game

1	VILLANOVA (vs. YALE)	31
1	KENTUCKY (vs. ILLINOIS)	31
1	KENTUCKY (vs. VILLANOVA)	31

Most total field goals in the tournament

1	KENTUCKY	78
2	ILLINOIS	71
3	VILLANOVA	59

FREE THROWS

Most free throws in a single game

1	KENTUCKY (vs. VILLANOVA)	23
2	OKLAHOMA A&M (vs. OREGON STATE)	21
3	OREGON STATE (vs. ARKANSAS)	20

Most total free throws in the tournament

1	KENTUCKY	51
2	OKLAHOMA A&M	49
3	OREGON STATE	43

Most free throws attempted in a single game

1	OREGON STATE (vs. ARKANSAS)	27
1	YALE (vs. ILLINOIS)	27
3	OREGON STATE (vs. ILLINOIS)	25

Highest free throw percentage in a single game

1	OKLAHOMA A&M (vs. OREGON STATE) (21-24)	.875
2	OKLAHOMA A&M (vs. KENTUCKY) (18-24)	.750
3	OREGON STATE (vs. ARKANSAS) (20-27)	.741

Fewest free throws in a single game

1	ARKANSAS (vs. WYOMING)	7
2	OREGON STATE (vs. OKLAHOMA A&M)	8
3	2 tied for third place.	

Lowest free throw percentage in a single game

1	WYOMING (vs. OKLAHOMA A&M) (9-21)	.429
2	ILLINOIS (vs. OREGON STATE) (11-23)	.478
3	ARKANSAS (vs. WYOMING) (7-14)	.500

1950

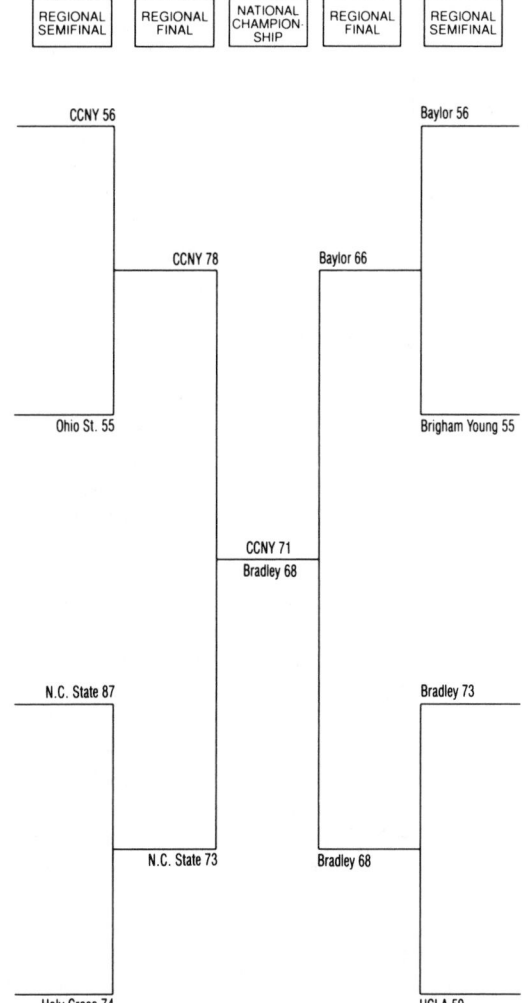

EASTERN

WESTERN

| REGIONAL SEMIFINAL | REGIONAL FINAL | NATIONAL CHAMPIONSHIP | REGIONAL FINAL | REGIONAL SEMIFINAL |

CCNY 56

Baylor 56

CCNY 78

Baylor 66

Ohio St. 55

Brigham Young 55

CCNY 71
Bradley 68

N.C. State 87

Bradley 73

N.C. State 73

Bradley 68

Holy Cross 74

UCLA 59

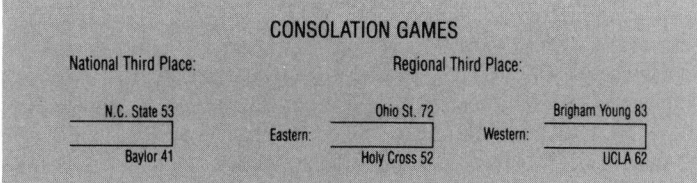

CONSOLATION GAMES

National Third Place:

N.C. State 53

Baylor 41

Regional Third Place:

Ohio St. 72

Eastern:

Holy Cross 52

Brigham Young 83

Western:

UCLA 62

ALLAGAROO
GAROO
GARA . . .

The City College of New York, Harvard of the Working Class, offering a free, public higher education to every citizen of the metropolis who qualified, went on a magic-carpet ride in March 1950 unlike anything ever seen in the history of college basketball.

The Beavers, whose players had hardly distinguished themselves before their remarkable March, and who would later be disgraced for their part in the most far-reaching game-fixing scandal ever, grabbed not one, but two gold rings in 1950—they were the only team to ever win both the NIT (National Invitational Tournament) and the NCAA in the same year. (It was not unusual back then for teams to receive invitations to both events.)

Led by their sagacious coach Nat Holman, they passed and ran and shot their way to the improbable double victory in the course of three incredible weeks.

As the season began the CCNY kiddie corps with its four sophomore starters was being touted as one of the nation's best teams, but they showed their inexperience and barely qualified for the NIT with a record of 17-5. In the tournament, though, they started out by dominating defending champion San Francisco, winning by 19. Next came the defending NCAA champ and SEC pacesetter Kentucky. Holman, trying to gain an immediate psychological advantage, started three black players—star forward Ed Warner, playmaker Floyd Lane, and 6-7 senior reserve Leroy Watkins at center—against Adolph Rupp's segregated Wildcats. When Watkins beat 7-footer Bill Spivey to the tap, the Beavers were off and running. After four and a half minutes they were up 13-1, and the score was 45-20 by halftime. In the end, Rupp was handed the worst defeat he had ever suffered (89-50), and the New York sportswriters were waxing euphoric over the City performance. Dana Mozley in the New York *Daily News* called it "An unparalleled exhibition of devastating speed, uncanny shooting, and precision defending." Everett Morris in the *Herald Tribune* wrote of a "team effort of such surpassing excellence that it defies description by normal adjectives." Even Lou Effrat in the usually staid *New York Times* wrote of Warner's "amazing shooting," Ed Roman's "flawless defense," and Layne's "incredibly successful" rebounding.

After an easy victory over Duquesne, City faced a Saturday night title showdown with the No. 1–ranked Bradley Braves. While the Beavers showed their nervousness in the early going, blowing layups and missing 7 of 8 from the line, Bradley played up to its billing and took a 29-18 lead after 14 minutes. Then Holman, who had left his sickbed with a temperature of 103 to coach the game, put in his outside-shooting specialist, World War II veteran

Norman Mager. By halftime the Beavers had cut the lead to three, and at the final buzzer the Garden erupted— "ALLAGAROO GAROO GARA!" CCNY had won the NIT by eight points.

Thursday was another day, another game, another tournament. The NCAA Eastern regionals were being held in Madison Square Garden, so the NIT champs came out before another highly partisan crowd to play Ohio State and their high-scoring All-American Dick Schnittker. The contest against the Western Conference champs made the entire NIT seem like a stroll in Central Park for the City College team. The Buckeyes' tight 3-2 zone bottled up City's inside pair of Warner and Roman, and Schnittker was devastating with his hook shots. But the outside shooting of Mager and Floyd Lane kept the Beavers in the game. The score was tied at 40 at the half. Then, with little over a minute remaining and City holding a two-point lead, Schnittker fouled out. In the last minute the CCNY big men turned the ball over twice, but when Ohio State missed with five seconds left, the Beavers held on for a 56-55 victory.

In the second round they faced North Carolina State, which had outclassed Bob Cousy's Holy Cross in their opener while breaking the all-time NCAA tournament scoring record. The explosive Wolfpack was led by All-Americans Sam Ranzino and Dick Dickey, who had combined for 57 points against the Crusaders. But a third key player, guard Vic Bubas, was hobbled by a sprained ankle suffered in the victory over Holy Cross. Again CCNY held on to win a close game despite fine individual performances by Ranzino and Dickey.

Meanwhile, in the Western play-offs, young Johnny Wooden's UCLA squad, making its first NCAA appearance, employed a strong running game to take a 57-50 lead over powerful Bradley with five minutes left in their first-round game. But then they stopped running, and the Braves took over. By the time the game ended, Bradley had outscored the Bruins 23-2. In the second round, the Braves held on to beat an inspired Baylor team by a basket. Bradley was coming back to the Garden for a rematch with the upstarts from City College.

This time Bradley coach Forddy Anderson came into town flatly predicting a more successful outcome. But Holman disagreed, saying, "I think we can beat anybody and that includes Bradley." Despite the predictions of the coaches, the game still had to be played on the Garden court.

Bradley opened in a zone, but City shot over it and hit from the outside. Just before the end of the first half, CCNY supersub Mager and Aaron Preece of Bradley were both knocked unconscious in a head-on collision. Mager was helped from the floor with blood streaming from a two-inch gash on his forehead. After being stitched up during halftime, Mager came back to start the second half with City in the lead 39-32. Their advantage had grown to 11 by the ten-minute mark, when Bradley switched to a man-to-man and started pressing full court. A minute later, City's Ed Roman fouled out. And Bradley clawed their way back into the game.

With just 57 seconds remaining, City still led 69-63. A six point deficit seemed almost insurmountable, particularly since a rule then in effect gave possession along with a free throw to a team fouled in the last two minutes. But Bradley didn't give up. After a Braves foul shot, their superb guard Gene Melchiorre hit a lay-up. Then he stole the ball and hit yet another two-pointer. The score was 69-68 with 30 seconds to go when Melchiorre stole another errant CCNY pass and headed for the basket. But this time he was met by Gene Dambrot, who blocked his shot, picked up the loose ball, and fired a floor-length pass to Mager, who hit the clincher with less than ten seconds left.

The Garden erupted with the City College cheer:

ALLAGAROO
GAROO
GARA
ALLAGAROO
GARA . . .

The unheralded kids from the sidewalks and public schools of New York had taken on six of the nation's Top Ten–ranked teams in the space of three weeks—and beaten them all. They were the undisputed kings of college basketball.

Eleven months later, seven members of the City College team were arrested on charges of taking bribes from gamblers to throw games. City was not the only school implicated: players from three other major New York City programs, LIU, NYU, and Manhattan, were also arrested; eight Bradley players, including Gene Melchiorre, confessed to the same charges, as did three stars of Kentucky's 1949 national champions. The scandal was widespread and devastated the integrity of the college game.

The NCAA responded by recommending a boycott of Madison Square Garden; in the four decades since there has never been another NCAA championship game held in New York City.

Nat Holman was forced out of his job in disgrace (albeit unjustly) by New York's Board of Higher Education for neglecting his duty. Two years later he was reinstated and vindicated of all wrongdoing, but it was too late for CCNY and for New York City basketball.

Despite all the revelations, it's still City College, the champs of 1950, who rose so high, and fell so far, so fast. The Cinderella kids.

REGIONAL SEMIFINAL EASTERN

CCNY (56)   Coach: Nat Holman

	Min.	Total FG/FGA	Pct.	FT/FTA	Pct.	Reb. O/T	A	TO	PF	S	Blk	TP	PPM
LAYNE, F.	-	7/11	.636	3/4	.750	-/-	4	-	2	-	-	17	-
WARNER, E.	-	3/16	.188	2/3	.667	-/-	1	-	1	-	-	8	-
ROMAN, E.	-	4/9	.444	0/2	.000	-/-	2	-	5	-	-	8	-
GALIBER, J.	-	0/4	.000	0/0	.000	-/-	0	-	1	-	-	0	-
WATKINS, L.	-	0/0	.000	0/0	.000	-/-	0	-	1	-	-	0	-
ROTH, A.	-	0/1	.000	0/0	.000	-/-	1	-	2	-	-	0	-
MAGER, N.	-	7/16	.438	1/2	.500	-/-	3	-	5	-	-	15	-
DAMBROT, I.	-	3/6	.500	2/4	.500	-/-	5	-	2	-	-	8	-
Totals	200	24/63	.381	8/15	.533	-/-	16	-	19	-	-	56	.280

Ohio State (55)   Coach: Tippy Dye

	Min.	Total FG/FGA	Pct.	FT/FTA	Pct.	Reb. O/T	A	TO	PF	S	Blk	TP	PPM
SCHNITTKER, D.	36	9/19	.474	8/11	.727	-/-	1	-	5	-	-	26	.722
ARMSTRONG	1	0/1	.000	0/0	.000	-/-	0	-	1	-	-	0	.000
REMINGTON, J.	1	0/1	.000	0/0	.000	-/-	0	-	0	-	-	0	.000
DONHAM, B.	35	4/9	.444	1/3	.333	-/-	5	-	5	-	-	9	.257
TAYLOR, F.	40	4/11	.364	0/2	.000	-/-	0	-	0	-	-	8	.200
BROWN	40	1/4	.250	1/1	1.000	-/-	2	-	1	-	-	3	.075
BURKHOLDER, B.	36	1/1	1.000	1/2	.500	-/-	6	-	1	-	-	3	.083
JACOBS, T.	11	2/5	.400	2/3	.667	-/-	0	-	2	-	-	6	.545
Totals	200	21/51	.412	13/22	.591	-/-	14	-	15	-	-	55	.275

Disqualified: CCNY—Roman, Mager; Ohio State—Schnittker, Donham.

	1st Half	2nd Half	Final
CCNY	40	16	56
Ohio State	40	15	55

North Carolina State (87)   Coach: Everett Case

	Min.	Total FG/FGA	Pct.	FT/FTA	Pct.	Reb. O/T	A	TO	PF	S	Blk	TP	PPM
RANZINO, S.	-	12/30	.400	8/10	.800	-/-	2	-	4	-	-	32	-
COOK, B.	-	1/3	.333	0/2	.000	-/-	0	-	0	-	-	2	-
DICKEY, D.	-	8/17	.471	9/13	.692	-/-	2	-	3	-	-	25	-
HORVATH, P.	-	0/2	.000	1/1	1.000	-/-	1	-	1	-	-	1	-
CARTIER, W.	-	5/9	.556	2/4	.500	-/-	5	-	4	-	-	12	-
HARAND, J.	-	1/3	.333	3/4	.750	-/-	7	-	2	-	-	5	-
BUBAS, V.	-	3/3	1.000	0/0	.000	-/-	1	-	2	-	-	6	-
TERRILL, L.	-	2/6	.333	0/4	.000	-/-	3	-	1	-	-	4	-
Totals	200	32/73	.438	23/38	.605	-/-	21	-	17	-	-	87	.435

Holy Cross (74)   Coach: Buster Sheary

	Min.	Total FG/FGA	Pct.	FT/FTA	Pct.	Reb. O/T	A	TO	PF	S	Blk	TP	PPM
COUSY, B.	-	11/38	.289	2/3	.667	-/-	5	-	3	-	-	24	-
MCDONOUGH	-	2/3	.667	0/1	.000	-/-	0	-	3	-	-	4	-
MCMULLAN, R.	-	0/4	.000	0/2	.000	-/-	2	-	5	-	-	0	-
MANN	-	0/1	.000	0/0	.000	-/-	1	-	0	-	-	0	-
FORMON, M.	-	7/10	.700	5/6	.833	-/-	2	-	1	-	-	19	-
DILLING	-	2/6	.333	2/2	1.000	-/-	2	-	2	-	-	6	-
O'NEILL	-	0/0	.000	0/0	.000	-/-	0	-	2	-	-	0	-
LASKA, A.	-	2/17	.118	2/2	1.000	-/-	2	-	1	-	-	6	-
OFTRING, F.	-	1/3	.333	1/2	.500	-/-	2	-	5	-	-	3	-
McLARNON	-	6/15	.400	0/1	.000	-/-	1	-	4	-	-	12	-
O'SHEA	-	0/0	.000	0/0	.000	-/-	0	-	4	-	-	0	-
DIEFFENBACH	-	0/4	.000	0/0	.000	-/-	0	-	2	-	-	0	-
Totals	200	31/101	.307	12/19	.632	-/-	17	-	32	-	-	74	.370

Disqualified: Holy Cross—McMullan, Oftring.

	1st Half	2nd Half	Final
N.C. State	44	43	87
Holy Cross	29	45	74

REGIONAL SEMIFINAL WESTERN

Baylor (56)   Coach: Bill Henderson

	Min.	Total FG/FGA	Pct.	FT/FTA	Pct.	Reb. O/T	A	TO	PF	S	Blk	TP	PPM
HICKMAN, B.	-	0/2	.000	2/2	1.000	-/-	-	-	4	-	-	2	-
COBB, G.	-	4/9	.444	4/4	1.000	-/-	-	-	3	-	-	12	-
HEATHINGTON, D.	-	7/16	.438	7/12	.583	-/-	-	-	3	-	-	21	-
HOVDE, H.	-	0/0	.000	0/0	.000	-/-	-	-	1	-	-	0	-
PRESTON, O.	-	0/7	.000	0/3	.000	-/-	-	-	1	-	-	0	-
CARINGTON, G.	-	0/0	.000	0/0	.000	-/-	-	-	0	-	-	0	-
DEWITT, B.	-	2/4	.500	3/3	1.000	-/-	-	-	5	-	-	7	-
JOHNSON, R.	-	0/0	.000	0/0	.000	-/-	-	-	0	-	-	0	-
SRACK, B.	-	6/14	.429	2/4	.500	-/-	-	-	1	-	-	14	-
MULLINS, N.	-	0/0	.000	0/0	.000	-/-	-	-	0	-	-	0	-
Totals	200	19/52	.365	18/30	.600	-/-	-	-	18	-	-	56	.280

Brigham Young (55)   Coach: Stan Watts

	Min.	Total FG/FGA	Pct.	FT/FTA	Pct.	Reb. O/T	A	TO	PF	S	Blk	TP	PPM
MINSON	-	8/23	.348	3/8	.375	-/-	-	-	2	-	-	19	-
NELSON, J.	-	5/23	.217	3/4	.750	-/-	-	-	4	-	-	13	-
HILLMAN	-	0/0	.000	0/0	.000	-/-	-	-	2	-	-	0	-
HUTCHINS, M.	-	8/22	.364	3/5	.600	-/-	-	-	3	-	-	19	-
JONES	-	1/4	.250	0/1	.000	-/-	-	-	2	-	-	2	-
ROMNEY	-	1/4	.250	0/1	.000	-/-	-	-	3	-	-	2	-
WHIPPLE	-	0/2	.000	0/1	.000	-/-	-	-	4	-	-	0	-
CRAIG	-	0/4	.000	0/0	.000	-/-	-	-	5	-	-	0	-
Totals	200	23/82	.280	9/20	.450	-/-	-	-	25	-	-	55	.275

Disqualified: Baylor—DeWitt; Brigham Young—Craig.

	1st Half	2nd Half	Final
Baylor	25	31	56
Brigham Young	26	29	55

Bradley (73)   Coach: Forddy Anderson

	Min.	Total FG/FGA	Pct.	FT/FTA	Pct.	Reb. O/T	A	TO	PF	S	Blk	TP	PPM
MANN, B.	-	2/ 6	.333	3/ 4	.750	-/ -	-	-	3	-	-	7	-
PREECE, A.	-	1/ 3	.333	1/ 2	.500	-/ -	-	-	1	-	-	3	-
CHIANAKAS, G.	-	2/ 4	.500	0/ 0	.000	-/ -	-	-	4	-	-	4	-
MELCHIORRE, G.	-	6/12	.500	7/ 8	.875	-/ -	-	-	4	-	-	19	-
SCHLICHTMAN, F.	-	0/ 1	.000	1/ 2	.500	-/ -	-	-	1	-	-	1	-
UNRUH, P.	-	5/14	.357	3/ 4	.750	-/ -	-	-	1	-	-	13	-
BEHNKE, E.	-	3/13	.231	4/ 7	.571	-/ -	-	-	2	-	-	10	-
KELLEY, J.	-	0/ 1	.000	0/ 0	.000	-/ -	-	-	1	-	-	0	-
GROVER, C.	-	7/14	.500	2/ 3	.667	-/ -	-	-	2	-	-	16	-
Totals	200	26/68	.382	21/30	.700	-/ -	-	-	19	-	-	73	.365

UCLA (59)   Coach: John Wooden

	Min.	Total FG/FGA	Pct.	FT/FTA	Pct.	Reb. O/T	A	TO	PF	S	Blk	TP	PPM
NORMAN	-	0/ 6	.000	0/ 0	.000	-/ -	-	-	3	-	-	0	-
JOECKEL, R.	-	5/13	.385	3/ 5	.600	-/ -	-	-	2	-	-	13	-
MATULICH	-	0/ 0	.000	0/ 0	.000	-/ -	-	-	0	-	-	0	-
SAWYER	-	7/21	.333	0/ 2	.000	-/ -	-	-	1	-	-	14	-
SAUNDERS	-	0/ 0	.000	0/ 1	.000	-/ -	-	-	1	-	-	0	-
KRAUSHAAR, C.	-	2/ 4	.500	1/ 1	1.000	-/ -	-	-	5	-	-	5	-
ALBA	-	0/ 8	.000	0/ 2	.000	-/ -	-	-	2	-	-	0	-
SHELDRAKE, E.	-	4/14	.286	3/ 5	.600	-/ -	-	-	5	-	-	11	-
SEIDEL	-	1/ 3	.333	0/ 0	.000	-/ -	-	-	2	-	-	2	-
JOHNSON	-	0/ 0	.000	0/ 0	.000	-/ -	-	-	0	-	-	0	-
STANICH, G.	-	6/12	.500	2/ 6	.333	-/ -	-	-	5	-	-	14	-
ALPER	-	0/ 0	.000	0/ 0	.000	-/ -	-	-	1	-	-	0	-
Totals	200	25/81	.309	9/22	.409	-/ -	-	-	27	-	-	59	.295

Disqualified: UCLA—Kraushaar, Sheldrake, Stanich.

	1st Half	2nd Half	Final
Bradley	33	40	73
UCLA	33	26	59

REGIONAL FINAL EASTERN

CCNY (78)   Coach: Nat Holman

	Min.	Total FG/FGA	Pct.	FT/FTA	Pct.	Reb. O/T	A	TO	PF	S	Blk	TP	PPM
DAMBROT, I.	-	5/14	.357	3/ 6	.500	-/ -	3	-	3	-	-	13	-
WARNER, E.	-	5/18	.278	7/11	.636	-/ -	2	-	3	-	-	17	-
ROMAN, E.	-	9/17	.529	3/ 4	.750	-/ -	1	-	5	-	-	21	-
GALIBER, J.	-	0/ 0	.000	0/ 0	.000	-/ -	0	-	1	-	-	0	-
NADELL, R.	-	2/ 2	1.000	0/ 1	.000	-/ -	0	-	2	-	-	4	-
ROTH, A.	-	2/ 6	.333	0/ 0	.000	-/ -	2	-	5	-	-	4	-
MAGER, N.	-	4/11	.364	1/ 2	.500	-/ -	3	-	5	-	-	9	-
LAYNE, F.	-	3/13	.231	4/ 5	.800	-/ -	9	-	2	-	-	10	-
COHEN, H.	-	0/ 0	.000	0/ 2	.000	-/ -	0	-	0	-	-	0	-
Totals	200	30/81	.370	18/31	.581	-/ -	20	-	26	-	-	78	.390

North Carolina State (73)   Coach: Everett Case

	Min.	Total FG/FGA	Pct.	FT/FTA	Pct.	Reb. O/T	A	TO	PF	S	Blk	TP	PPM
RANZINO, S.	-	9/30	.300	6/ 9	.667	-/ -	0	-	5	-	-	24	-
STINE, C.	-	1/ 2	.500	0/ 0	.000	-/ -	0	-	0	-	-	2	-
DICKEY, D.	-	7/19	.368	2/ 6	.333	-/ -	6	-	5	-	-	16	-
STOLL, J.	-	0/ 0	.000	0/ 0	.000	-/ -	0	-	0	-	-	0	-
HORVATH, P.	-	4/ 4	1.000	6/ 8	.750	-/ -	1	-	4	-	-	14	-
BUBAS, V.	-	0/ 2	.000	2/ 2	1.000	-/ -	0	-	4	-	-	2	-
HARAND, J.	-	0/ 0	.000	2/ 2	1.000	-/ -	5	-	2	-	-	2	-
CARTIER, W.	-	4/ 8	.500	3/ 4	.750	-/ -	4	-	5	-	-	11	-
COOK, B.	-	1/ 3	.333	0/ 0	.000	-/ -	0	-	0	-	-	2	-
Totals	200	26/68	.394	21/31	.677	-/ -	16	-	25	-	-	73	.365

Disqualified: CCNY—Roman, Roth, Mager; N.C. State—Ranzino, Dickey, Cartier.

	1st Half	2nd Half	Final
CCNY	38	40	78
N.C. State	37	36	73

REGIONAL FINAL WESTERN

Baylor (66)   Coach: Bill Henderson

	Min.	Total FG/FGA	Pct.	FT/FTA	Pct.	Reb. O/T	A	TO	PF	S	Blk	TP	PPM
HICKMAN, B.	-	3/ 7	.429	0/ 0	.000	-/ -	-	-	3	-	-	6	-
COBB, G.	-	3/ 8	.375	1/ 2	.500	-/ -	-	-	3	-	-	7	-
CARRINGTON	-	0/ 0	.000	0/ 0	.000	-/ -	-	-	0	-	-	0	-
HEATHINGTON, D.	-	10/20	.500	6/ 6	1.000	-/ -	-	-	5	-	-	26	-
FLEETWOOD, B.	-	0/ 0	.000	0/ 0	.000	-/ -	-	-	0	-	-	0	-
PRESTON, O.	-	4/11	.364	6/ 7	.857	-/ -	-	-	4	-	-	14	-
HOVDE, H.	-	0/ 0	.000	0/ 0	.000	-/ -	-	-	0	-	-	0	-
DEWITT, B.	-	1/ 6	.167	2/ 3	.667	-/ -	-	-	5	-	-	4	-
JOHNSON, R.	-	0/ 2	.000	0/ 0	.000	-/ -	-	-	0	-	-	0	-
SRACK, B.	-	3/ 7	.429	3/ 3	1.000	-/ -	-	-	3	-	-	9	-
Totals	200	24/61	.393	18/21	.857	-/ -	-	-	23	-	-	66	.330

Bradley (68)   Coach: Forddy Anderson

	Min.	Total FG/FGA	Pct.	FT/FTA	Pct.	Reb. O/T	A	TO	PF	S	Blk	TP	PPM
MANN, B.	-	4/ 7	.571	5/ 8	.625	-/ -	-	-	4	-	-	13	-
CHIANAKAS, G.	-	1/ 5	.200	0/ 0	.000	-/ -	-	-	0	-	-	2	-
SCHLICHTMAN, F.	-	0/ 0	.000	0/ 0	.000	-/ -	-	-	0	-	-	0	-
MELCHIORRE, G.	-	4/11	.364	3/ 3	1.000	-/ -	-	-	4	-	-	11	-
UNRUH, P.	-	2/11	.182	3/ 4	.750	-/ -	-	-	2	-	-	7	-
BEHNKE, E.	-	1/ 7	.143	0/ 1	.000	-/ -	-	-	0	-	-	2	-
PREECE, A.	-	4/ 6	.667	4/ 6	.667	-/ -	-	-	3	-	-	12	-
KELLEY, J.	-	3/ 7	.429	2/ 2	1.000	-/ -	-	-	2	-	-	8	-
GROVER, C.	-	6/14	.429	1/ 1	1.000	-/ -	-	-	2	-	-	13	-
Totals	200	25/68	.368	18/25	.720	-/ -	-	-	17	-	-	68	.340

Disqualified: Baylor—Heathington, DeWitt.

	1st Half	2nd Half	Final
Baylor	32	34	66
Bradley	35	33	68

CHAMPIONSHIP

CCNY (71)   Coach: Nat Holman

	Min.	Total FG/FGA	Pct.	FT/FTA	Pct.	Reb. O/T	A	TO	PF	S	Blk	TP	PPM
LAYNE, F.	-	3/ 7	.429	5/ 6	.833	-/ -	4	-	3	-	-	11	-
WARNER, E.	-	4/ 9	.444	6/14	.429	-/ -	3	-	2	-	-	14	-
ROMAN, E.	-	6/17	.353	0/ 2	.000	-/ -	1	-	5	-	-	12	-
GALIBER, J.	-	0/ 0	.000	0/ 0	.000	-/ -	0	-	1	-	-	0	-
ROTH, A.	-	2/ 7	.286	1/ 5	.200	-/ -	3	-	2	-	-	5	-
MAGER, N.	-	4/10	.400	6/ 6	1.000	-/ -	2	-	3	-	-	14	-
DAMBROT, I.	-	7/14	.500	1/ 2	.500	-/ -	2	-	0	-	-	15	-
NADELL, R.	-	0/ 0	.000	0/ 0	.000	-/ -	1	-	1	-	-	0	-
Totals	200	26/64	.406	19/35	.543	-/ -	16	-	17	-	-	71	.355

Bradley (68)   Coach: Forddy Anderson

	Min.	Total FG/FGA	Pct.	FT/FTA	Pct.	Reb. O/T	A	TO	PF	S	Blk	TP	PPM
GROVER, C.	-	0/10	.000	2/ 3	.667	-/ -	3	-	3	-	-	2	-
SCHLICHTMAN, F.	-	0/ 3	.000	0/ 0	.000	-/ -	0	-	2	-	-	0	-
UNRUH, P.	-	4/ 9	.444	0/ 0	.000	-/ -	2	-	5	-	-	8	-
BEHNKE, E.	-	3/10	.300	3/ 3	1.000	-/ -	2	-	4	-	-	9	-
KELLEY, J.	-	0/ 1	.000	0/ 2	.000	-/ -	0	-	0	-	-	0	-
MANN, B.	-	2/ 7	.286	5/ 5	1.000	-/ -	1	-	5	-	-	9	-
PREECE, A.	-	6/11	.545	0/ 0	.000	-/ -	0	-	5	-	-	12	-
MELCHIORRE, D.	-	0/ 0	.000	0/ 0	.000	-/ -	0	-	0	-	-	0	-
MELCHIORRE, G.	-	7/16	.438	2/ 4	.500	-/ -	5	-	4	-	-	16	-
CHIANAKAS, G.	-	5/ 7	.714	1/ 3	.333	-/ -	1	-	4	-	-	11	-
STOWELL, J.	-	0/ 0	.000	1/ 1	1.000	-/ -	0	-	0	-	-	1	-
Totals	200	27/74	.365	14/21	.667	-/ -	14	-	32	-	-	68	.340

Disqualified: CCNY—Roman; Bradley—Unruh, Mann, Preece.

	1st Half	2nd Half	Final
CCNY	39	32	71
Bradley	32	36	68

NATIONAL THIRD PLACE

North Carolina State (53)   Coach: Everett Case

	Min.	Total FG/FGA	Pct.	FT/FTA	Pct.	Reb. O/T	A	TO	PF	S	Blk	TP	PPM
RANZINO, S.	-	5/25	.200	11/15	.733	-/ -	0	-	2	-	-	21	-
DICKEY, D.	-	2/14	.143	2/ 3	.667	-/ -	2	-	3	-	-	6	-
HORVATH, P.	-	2/ 8	.250	1/ 3	.333	-/ -	0	-	2	-	-	5	-
CARTIER, W.	-	3/11	.273	3/ 4	.750	-/ -	0	-	3	-	-	9	-
HARAND, J.	-	1/ 3	.333	2/ 2	1.000	-/ -	0	-	1	-	-	4	-
BUBAS, V.	-	1/ 7	.143	4/ 6	.667	-/ -	5	-	4	-	-	6	-
TERRILL, L.	-	1/ 9	.111	0/ 2	.000	-/ -	2	-	0	-	-	2	-
Totals	200	15/77	.195	23/35	.657	-/ -	9	-	15	-	-	53	.265

Baylor (41)   Coach: Bill Henderson

	Min.	Total FG/FGA	Pct.	FT/FTA	Pct.	Reb. O/T	A	TO	PF	S	Blk	TP	PPM
DEWITT, B.	-	2/ 7	.286	2/ 3	.667	-/ -	0	-	5	-	-	6	-
COBB, G.	-	1/ 1	1.000	1/ 2	.500	-/ -	0	-	5	-	-	3	-
FLEETWOOD, B.	-	0/ 0	.000	0/ 0	.000	-/ -	0	-	1	-	-	0	-
SRACK, B.	-	5/17	.294	1/ 3	.333	-/ -	3	-	3	-	-	11	-
PRESTON, O.	-	1/ 7	.143	3/ 5	.600	-/ -	3	-	3	-	-	5	-
HARRIS	-	0/ 0	.000	0/ 0	.000	-/ -	0	-	2	-	-	0	-
HEATHINGTON, D.	-	3/14	.214	1/ 5	.200	-/ -	2	-	5	-	-	7	-
HICKMAN, B.	-	4/14	.286	0/ 0	.000	-/ -	1	-	1	-	-	8	-
JOHNSON, R.	-	0/ 0	.000	1/ 2	.500	-/ -	0	-	0	-	-	1	-
HOVDE, H.	-	0/ 0	.000	0/ 0	.000	-/ -	0	-	0	-	-	0	-
CARRINGTON, G.	-	0/ 0	.000	0/ 0	.000	-/ -	0	-	1	-	-	0	-
MULLINS, N.	-	0/ 0	.000	0/ 0	.000	-/ -	0	-	1	-	-	0	-
Totals	200	16/60	.267	9/20	.450	-/ -	9	-	27	-	-	41	.205

Disqualified: Baylor—Dewitt, Cobb, Heathington.

	1st Half	2nd Half	Final
N.C. State	21	32	53
Baylor	20	21	41

REGIONAL THIRD PLACE EASTERN

Ohio State (72)   Coach: Tippy Dye

	Min.	Total FG/FGA	Pct.	FT/FTA	Pct.	Reb. O/T	A	TO	PF	S	Blk	TP	PPM
SCHNITTKER, D.	24	6/10	.600	5/ 6	.833	-/ -	2	-	3	-	-	17	.708
ARMSTRONG	2	1/ 1	1.000	0/ 0	.000	-/ -	0	-	0	-	-	2	1.000
REMINGTON, J.	6	1/ 2	.500	1/ 2	.500	-/ -	0	-	2	-	-	3	.500
DONHAM, B.	34	4/11	.364	2/ 5	.400	-/ -	3	-	3	-	-	10	.294
TAYLOR, F.	36	5/15	.333	0/ 1	.000	-/ -	4	-	4	-	-	10	.278
BROWN	38	2/ 6	.333	1/ 2	.500	-/ -	2	-	2	-	-	5	.132
BURKHOLDER, B.	38	4/11	.364	5/ 5	1.000	-/ -	4	-	1	-	-	13	.342
JACOBS, T.	16	2/ 7	.286	6/ 9	.667	-/ -	0	-	2	-	-	10	.625
GIACOMELLI	2	0/ 1	.000	1/ 1	1.000	-/ -	0	-	0	-	-	1	.500
KARAFFA	2	0/ 0	.000	1/ 1	1.000	-/ -	0	-	0	-	-	1	.500
DAWE	2	0/ 0	.000	0/ 0	.000	-/ -	2	-	0	-	-	0	.000
Totals	200	25/64	.391	22/32	.688	-/ -	17	-	16	-	-	72	.360

Holy Cross (52)   Coach: Buster Sheary

	Min.	Total FG/FGA	Pct.	FT/FTA	Pct.	Reb. O/T	A	TO	PF	S	Blk	TP	PPM
COUSY, B.	-	6/23	.261	2/ 5	.400	-/ -	5	-	4	-	-	14	-
MCDONOUGH	-	3/ 9	.333	4/ 5	.800	-/ -	1	-	0	-	-	10	-
MCMULLAN, R.	-	0/ 0	.000	1/ 2	.500	-/ -	1	-	2	-	-	1	-
MANN	-	0/ 1	.000	0/ 0	.000	-/ -	0	-	0	-	-	0	-
FORMON, M.	-	1/12	.083	2/ 2	1.000	-/ -	0	-	4	-	-	4	-
DILLING	-	2/ 7	.286	2/ 2	1.000	-/ -	1	-	5	-	-	6	-
O'NEILL	-	0/ 1	.000	0/ 0	.000	-/ -	0	-	0	-	-	0	-
LASKA, A.	-	0/ 2	.000	0/ 0	.000	-/ -	0	-	1	-	-	0	-
OFTRING, F.	-	5/11	.455	1/ 2	.500	-/ -	3	-	2	-	-	11	-
MCLARNON	-	3/12	.250	0/ 0	.000	-/ -	2	-	4	-	-	6	-
O'SHEA	-	0/ 3	.000	0/ 0	.000	-/ -	0	-	3	-	-	0	-
DIEFFENBACH	-	0/ 1	.000	0/ 0	.000	-/ -	0	-	1	-	-	0	-
Totals	200	20/82	.244	12/18	.667	-/ -	13	-	26	-	-	52	.260

Disqualified: Holy Cross—Dilling.

	1st Half	2nd Half	Final
Ohio State	40	32	72
Holy Cross	24	28	52

REGIONAL THIRD PLACE WESTERN

Brigham Young (83)   Coach: Stan Watts

	Min.	Total FG/FGA	Pct.	FT/FTA	Pct.	Reb. O/T	A	TO	PF	S	Blk	TP	PPM
MINSON	-	5/11	.455	3/6	.500	-/-	-	-	2	-	-	13	-
NELSON, J.	-	12/25	.480	6/7	.857	-/-	-	-	1	-	-	30	-
HUTCHINS, M.	-	9/18	.500	3/6	.500	-/-	-	-	5	-	-	21	-
JONES	-	0/1	.000	1/2	.500	-/-	-	-	1	-	-	1	-
ROMNEY	-	0/0	.000	2/4	.500	-/-	-	-	2	-	-	2	-
WHIPPLE	-	2/3	.667	0/1	.000	-/-	-	-	3	-	-	4	-
CRAIG	-	0/2	.000	2/3	.667	-/-	-	-	1	-	-	2	-
BEEM	-	5/6	.833	0/1	.000	-/-	-	-	1	-	-	10	-
Totals	200	33/66	.500	17/30	.567	-/-	-	-	16	-	-	83	.415

UCLA (62)   Coach: John Wooden

	Min.	Total FG/FGA	Pct.	FT/FTA	Pct.	Reb. O/T	A	TO	PF	S	Blk	TP	PPM
JOEKEL, R.	-	1/4	.250	1/2	.500	-/-	-	-	4	-	-	3	-
NORMAN	-	0/4	.000	0/1	.000	-/-	-	-	2	-	-	0	-
SAUNDERS	-	2/6	.333	2/3	.667	-/-	-	-	1	-	-	6	-
SAWYER	-	7/22	.318	2/3	.667	-/-	-	-	4	-	-	16	-
MAUTLICH	-	0/0	.000	0/1	.000	-/-	-	-	0	-	-	0	-
KRAUSCHAAR	-	2/11	.182	2/3	.667	-/-	-	-	2	-	-	6	-
ALBA	-	0/7	.000	0/1	.000	-/-	-	-	2	-	-	0	-
JOHNSON	-	1/1	1.000	0/1	.000	-/-	-	-	0	-	-	2	-
SHELDRAKE, E.	-	9/17	.529	3/4	.750	-/-	-	-	2	-	-	21	-
STANICH, G.	-	1/16	.063	3/4	.750	-/-	-	-	5	-	-	5	-
ALPER	-	1/4	.250	1/2	.500	-/-	-	-	2	-	-	3	-
Totals	200	24/92	.293	14/25	.560	-/-	-	-	24	-	-	62	.310

Disqualified: Brigham Young—Hutchins; UCLA—Stanich.

	1st Half	2nd Half	Final
Brigham Young	37	46	83
UCLA	41	21	62

❂ INDIVIDUAL RECORDS ❂

SCORING

Most points in a single game
1 SAM RANZINO, N.C. STATE (vs. HOLY CROSS) 32
2 JOE NELSON, BRIGHAM YOUNG (vs. UCLA) 30
3 DON HEATHINGTON, BAYLOR (vs. BRADLEY) 26
3 DICK SCHNITTKER, OHIO STATE (vs. CCNY) 26
5 DICK DICKEY, N.C. STATE (vs. HOLY CROSS) 25

Most total points in the tournament
1 SAM RANZINO, N.C. STATE 77
2 DON HEATHINGTON, BAYLOR 54
3 DICK DICKEY, N.C. STATE 47
4 GENE MELCHIORRE, BRADLEY 46
5 2 tied for fifth place.

Highest scoring average (minimum 2 games)
1 SAM RANZINO, N.C. STATE (77-3) 25.67
2 DICK SCHNITTKER, OHIO STATE (43-2) 21.50
2 JOE NELSON, BRIGHAM YOUNG (43-2) 21.50
4 MEL HUTCHINS, BRIGHAM YOUNG (40-2) 20.00
5 BOB COUSY, HOLY CROSS (38-2) 19.00

FIELD GOALS

Most field goals in a single game
1 JOE NELSON, BRIGHAM YOUNG (vs. UCLA) 12
1 SAM RANZINO, N.C. STATE (vs. HOLY CROSS) 12
3 BOB COUSY, HOLY CROSS (vs. N.C. STATE) 11
4 DON HEATHINGTON, BAYLOR (vs. BRADLEY) 10
5 5 tied for fifth place.

Most total field goals in the tournament
1 SAM RANZINO, N.C. STATE 26
2 DON HEATHINGTON, BAYLOR 20
3 ED ROMAN, CCNY 19
4 5 tied for fourth place.

Most field goal attempts in a single game
1 BOB COUSY, HOLY CROSS (vs. N.C. STATE) 38
2 SAM RANZINO, N.C. STATE (vs. CCNY) 30
2 SAM RANZINO, N.C. STATE (vs. HOLY CROSS) 30

4 JOE NELSON, BRIGHAM YOUNG (vs. UCLA) 25
4 SAM RANZINO, N.C. STATE (vs. BAYLOR) 25

Most total field goal attempts in a tournament
1 SAM RANZINO, N.C. STATE 85
2 BOB COUSY, HOLY CROSS 61
3 DON HEATHINGTON, BAYLOR 50
3 DICK DICKEY, N.C. STATE 50
5 JOE NELSON, BRIGHAM YOUNG 48

Highest field goal percentage in a single game (minimum 10 attempts)
1 MATTHEW FORMON, HOLY CROSS (vs. N.C. STATE) (7-10) .700
2 FLOYD LAYNE, CCNY (vs. OHIO STATE) (7-11) .636
3 DICK SCHNITTKER, OHIO STATE (vs. HOLY CROSS) (6-10) .600
4 AARON PREECE, BRADLEY (vs. CCNY) (6-11) .545
5 2 tied for fifth place.

Highest field goal percentage in the tournament (minimum 15 attempts)
1 AARON PREECE, BRADLEY (11-20) .550
2 DICK SCHNITTKER, OHIO STATE (15-29) .517
3 GEORGE CHIANAKAS, BRADLEY (8-16) .500
4 GERALD COBB, BAYLOR (8-18) .444
5 ED ROMAN, CCNY (19-43) .442

FREE THROWS

Most free throws in a single game
1 SAM RANZINO, N.C. STATE (vs. BAYLOR) 11
2 DICK DICKEY, N.C. STATE (vs. HOLY CROSS) 9
3 SAM RANZINO, N.C. STATE (vs. HOLY CROSS) 8
3 DICK SCHNITTKER, OHIO STATE (vs. CCNY) 8
5 3 tied for fifth place.

Most total free throws in the tournament
1 SAM RANZINO, N.C. STATE 25

2 ED WARNER, CCNY 15
3 DON HEATHINGTON, BAYLOR 14
4 3 tied for fourth place.

Most free throws attempted in a single game
1 SAM RANZINO, N.C. STATE (vs. BAYLOR) 15
2 ED WARNER, CCNY (vs. BRADLEY) 14
3 DICK DICKEY, N.C. STATE (vs. HOLY CROSS) 13
4 DON HEATHINGTON, BAYLOR (vs. BRIGHAM YOUNG) 12
5 2 tied for fifth place.

Most free throws attempted in the tournament
1 SAM RANZINO, N.C. STATE 34
2 ED WARNER, CCNY 28
3 DON HEATHINGTON, BAYLOR 23
4 DICK DICKEY, N.C. STATE 2?
5 2 tied for fifth place.

Highest free throw percentage in a single game (minimum 7 attempts)
1 GENE MELCHIORRE, BRADLEY (vs. UCLA) (7-8) .875
2 ODELL PRESTON, BAYLOR (vs. BRADLEY) (6-7) .857
2 JOE NELSON, BRIGHAM YOUNG (vs. UCLA) (6-7) .857
4 SAM RANZINO, N.C. STATE (vs. HOLY CROSS) (8-10) .800
5 PAUL HORVATH, N.C. STATE (vs. CCNY) (6-8) .750

Highest free throw percentage in the tournament (minimum 15 attempts)
1 GENE MELCHIORRE, BRADLEY (12-15) .800
1 FLOYD LAYNE, CCNY (12-15) .800
3 DICK SCHNITTKER, OHIO STATE (13-17) .765
3 BILL MANN, BRADLEY (13-17) .765
5 SAM RANZINO, N.C. STATE (25-34) .735

✪ TEAM RECORDS ✪

SCORING

Most points in a single game
1. N.C. STATE (vs. HOLY CROSS)   87
2. BRIGHAM YOUNG (vs. UCLA)   83
3. CCNY (vs. N.C. STATE)   78

Most total points in the tournament
1. N.C. STATE   213
2. BRADLEY   209
3. CCNY   205

Highest scoring average (minimum 2 games)
1. N.C. STATE (213-3)   71.00
2. BRADLEY (209-3)   69.67
3. BRIGHAM YOUNG (138-2)   69.00

FIELD GOALS

Most field goals in a single game
1. BRIGHAM YOUNG (vs. UCLA)   33
2. N.C. STATE (vs. HOLY CROSS)   32
3. HOLY CROSS (vs. N.C. STATE)   31

Most total field goals in the tournament
1. CCNY   80
2. BRADLEY   78
3. N.C. STATE   73

Most field goals attempted in a single game
1. HOLY CROSS (vs. N.C. STATE)   101
2. UCLA (vs. BRIGHAM YOUNG)   92
3. 2 tied for third place.

Most total field goals attempted in the tournament
1. N.C. STATE   218
2. BRADLEY   210
3. CCNY   208

Highest field goal percentage in a single game
1. BRIGHAM YOUNG (vs. UCLA) (33-66)   .500
2. N.C. STATE (vs. HOLY CROSS) (32-73)   .438
3. OHIO STATE (vs. CCNY) (21-51)   .412

Highest field goal percentage in the tournament (minimum 2 games)
1. OHIO STATE (46-115)   .400
2. CCNY (80-208)   .385
3. BRIGHAM YOUNG (56-148)   .379

FREE THROWS

Most free throws in a single game
1. N.C. STATE (vs. BAYLOR)   23
1. N.C. STATE (vs. HOLY CROSS)   23
3. OHIO STATE (vs. HOLY CROSS)   22

Most total free throws in the tournament
1. N.C. STATE   67
2. BRADLEY   53
3. 2 tied for third place.

Most free throws attempted in a single game
1. N.C. STATE (vs. HOLY CROSS)   38
2. N.C. STATE (vs. BAYLOR)   35
2. CCNY (vs. BRADLEY)   35

Most total free throws attempted in the tournament
1. N.C. STATE   104
2. CCNY   81
3. BRADLEY   76

Highest free throw percentage in a single game
1. BAYLOR (vs. BRADLEY) (18-21)   .857
2. BRADLEY (vs. BAYLOR) (18-25)   .720
3. BRADLEY (vs. UCLA) (21-30)   .700

Highest free throw percentage in the tournament (minimum 2 games)
1. BRADLEY (53-76)   .697
2. HOLY CROSS (24-37)   .649
3. OHIO STATE (35-54)   .648

Fewest free throws in a single game
1. CCNY (vs. OHIO STATE)   8
2. 3 tied for second place.

Lowest free throw percentage in a single game
1. UCLA (vs. BRADLEY) (9-22)   .409
2. BRIGHAM YOUNG (vs. BAYLOR) (9-20)   .450
2. BAYLOR (vs. N.C. STATE) (9-20)   .450

Lowest free throw percentage in the tournament (minimum 2 games)
1. UCLA (23-47)   .489
2. BRIGHAM YOUNG (26-50)   .520
3. CCNY (45-81)   .556

1951

| FIRST ROUND | REGIONAL SEMIFINAL | REGIONAL FINAL | NATIONAL CHAMPIONSHIP | REGIONAL FINAL | REGIONAL SEMIFINAL | FIRST ROUND |

WEST

EAST

Kansas St. 61

Kansas St. 64

Arizona 59

Kansas St. 68

Brigham Young 68

Brigham Young 54

San Jose St. 61

Kentucky 68
Kansas St. 58

Oklahoma A&M 50

Oklahoma A&M 61

Montana St. 46

Oklahoma A&M 44

Washington 62

Washington 57

Texas A&M 40

Columbia 71

Illinois 84

Illinois 79

Illinois 74

N.C. State 67

N.C. State 70

Villanova 62

Kentucky 79

Kentucky 59

Louisville 68

Kentucky 76

St. John's 63

St. John's 43

U. Conn. 52

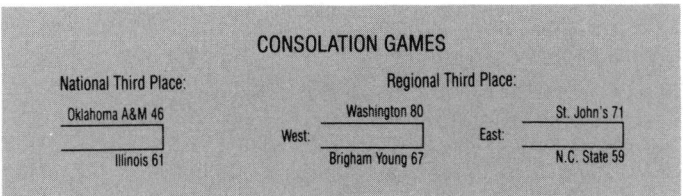

CONSOLATION GAMES

National Third Place:

Oklahoma A&M 46

Illinois 61

Regional Third Place:

Washington 80

West:

Brigham Young 67

St. John's 71

East:

N.C. State 59

In March of 1951, Adolph Rupp and his Kentucky Wildcats were living charmed lives. The scandal that was then engulfing college basketball had not yet reached the Baron's Lexington domain. The great man himself had been hospitalized in February with a variety of painful symptoms but he had recovered sufficiently to lead his charges into the post-season NCAA tournament. A combination of good fortune, clutch shooting, steel-cold nerves, and self-destructing opponents all contributed to Kentucky's march to Rupp's third title in four years.

It didn't matter that the tournament had doubled in size—to 16 teams—and that the Wildcats had to play an extra game before they could claim their crown. It didn't even matter that this was an entirely different roster from the 1948 and '49 champions. Groza and Beard might be gone, but there were plenty of able young men ready to put their bodies on the line in the service of the Bluegrass state's pre-eminent institution of human athletic endeavor (the Derby, remember, involved equine athletes).

The 1951 University of Kentucky Wildcat basketball team was led by the premier big man in the college game, 7-foot center Bill Spivey. His supporting cast included two future NBA stars, sophomores Frank Ramsey and Cliff Hagan, as well as the high-scoring forward Shelby Linville and the 5-10 sparkplug guard Bobby Watson. All in all, Rupp had assembled another deep and talented squad.

Kentucky came into the NCAAs with the No. 1 ranking. Unlike '48 and '49, however, when the Wildcats were head and shoulders above the competition, in 1951 they were first among equals—there were a number of excellent, competitive teams in the country. And once the tournament began nobody cared much about rankings anyway; the game had to be played on the hardwood floor.

In Raleigh, North Carolina, in the opening round, Kentucky was on the short end of a 64-60 score against feisty Louisville when, with 9:35 to go, Spivey fouled out. With Linville and Hagan also in foul trouble, things couldn't have looked much bleaker for the Wildcats. But instead of taking advantage of Spivey's absence and Linville's cautious play, the Cardinals went cold. Within two and a half minutes, Kentucky scored 10 straight to take a 6-point lead. It got worse from there; from the time Kentucky's star fouled out until the buzzer finally ended Louisville's ordeal, the Wildcats outscored the Cardinals 19 to 4.

The Wildcats next played St. John's in Madison Square Garden. Less than three weeks earlier, the NCAA had recommended a boycott of the famed arena, blaming the Garden for the proliferation of gambling and bribery in college basketball. But they had not gone so far as to reschedule the games already planned in New York for the upcoming championships. So it was that 14,214 fans—not all of them shouting for their team to beat the point spread—watched the Wildcats and Redmen square off in the Garden for their second round contest.

Despite missing more than a dozen easy lay-ups, the Redmen, led by their undersized center, Bob (Zeke) Zawoluk, stormed back from an 8-point deficit to tie the score at 43 with five and a half minutes left in the game. Once again Spivey was in foul trouble, playing tentatively to avoid fouling out. It appeared that Kentucky was ripe for the taking. St. John's should have known better: Shelby Linville hit a one-hander, Spivey scored from inside on a feed from Ramsey, and the Wildcats were off and running. By the time the weary Redmen trudged off, Kentucky had mopped the floor with them—the 'Cats had scored the final 16 points of the game to win 59-43.

The semifinal pitted the Wildcats against Illinois's Big Ten champs. The Fighting Illini had earned the privilege of meeting Kentucky by first coming from behind to defeat previously perfect Columbia and by following up that victory with a two-minute, 11-point, second-half burst that buried North Carolina State. But when they came up against Kentucky, they came up short, as Olympus once again smiled on Rupp's domain.

Illinois, boxing out brilliantly and outrebounding the taller Wildcats, held a 7-point lead at the half. But after intermission, Spivey became virtually invincible off both boards. By the time he fouled out with less than three minutes to go, he had scored 28 and nabbed 16 rebounds, both game highs. And though Kentucky held a 1 point lead, Illinois seemed to be in a great position to win. It still seemed that way when the Illini tied the score for the tenth time with fifty seconds left. And after Linville put Kentucky back in front twelve seconds later, Illinois' Don Sunderlage hit a lay-up to knot the score once more with the clock at 19:31. The ball came downcourt in Frank Ramsey's hands. He saw Linville all alone in the key, and he threaded the needle with a bullet pass. Linville hit a short jumper to put Kentucky back in front. There were still twelve seconds left. Sunderlage dribbled downcourt, penetrated, and fired. The Garden was suddenly quiet as the ball arced toward the hoop. It bounced off the rim and came down harmlessly onto the floor as the buzzer sounded.

The Kentucky 'Cats were on their way to a final showdown with the fourth-ranked Kansas State Wildcats, who were themselves brimming with confidence after their stunning victory over No. 2 Oklahoma A&M. The K Staters, who had defeated Illinois by 19 points in a pre-tournament post-season game, had left the Aggies begging for mercy after a 37-14 first half, and they were undaunted by Kentucky's reputation and record. At the end of the first half, Kansas State led by 2, largely because Kentucky's Spivey had been invisible. In the first ten minutes of the second half, however, Spivey scored six baskets and Kansas State went eight minutes without scoring a field goal. By then Kentucky led 56-40 and the celebration in Lexington was under way.

FIRST ROUND WEST

Kansas State (61)　　Coach: Jack Gardner

	Min.	Total FG / FGA	Pct.	FT / FTA	Pct.	Reb. O / T	A	TO	PF	S	Blk	TP	PPM
HEAD, E.	-	6/13	.462	1/ 2	.500	-/ 9	-	-	1	-	-	13	-
PECK, R.	-	1/ 2	.500	1/ 1	1.000	-/ 4	-	-	2	-	-	3	-
SCHUYLER, D.	-	0/ 0	.000	0/ 1	.000	-/ 1	-	-	1	-	-	0	-
STONE, J.	-	2/ 8	.250	2/ 3	.667	-/ 3	-	-	3	-	-	6	-
GIBSON, J.	-	0/ 0	.000	1/ 1	1.000	-/ 1	-	-	0	-	-	1	-
HITCH, L.	-	5/ 8	.625	2/ 6	.333	-/ 7	-	-	2	-	-	12	-
KNOSTMAN, R.	-	0/ 7	.000	2/ 3	.667	-/ 2	-	-	1	-	-	2	-
IVERSON, J.	-	4/11	.364	1/ 3	.333	-/ 5	-	-	1	-	-	9	-
UPSON, D.	-	0/ 1	.000	0/ 0	.000	-/ 0	-	-	1	-	-	0	-
BARRETT, E.	-	3/13	.231	1/ 1	1.000	-/ 8	-	-	1	-	-	7	-
ROUSEY, R.	-	3/10	.300	2/ 3	.667	-/ 2	-	-	1	-	-	8	-
Totals	200	24/73	.329	13/24	.542	-/42	-	-	14	-	-	61	.305

Arizona (59)　　Coach: Fred Enke

	Min.	Total FG / FGA	Pct.	FT / FTA	Pct.	Reb. O / T	A	TO	PF	S	Blk	TP	PPM
HONEA, R.	-	7/19	.368	1/ 1	1.000	-/ 5	-	-	4	-	-	15	-
SCHUFF, D.	-	3/ 5	.600	2/ 3	.667	-/ 4	-	-	5	-	-	8	-
CARROLL, A.	-	0/ 0	.000	0/ 0	.000	-/ 1	-	-	3	-	-	0	-
JOHNSON, L.	-	3/ 9	.333	3/ 3	1.000	-/ 2	-	-	4	-	-	9	-
DILLON, J.	-	2/ 8	.250	0/ 4	.000	-/ 3	-	-	3	-	-	4	-
HOWELL, J.	-	2/ 8	.250	0/ 0	.000	-/ 5	-	-	3	-	-	4	-
KEMMERIES, W.	-	2/ 4	.500	0/ 0	.000	-/ 0	-	-	0	-	-	4	-
JOHNSON, R.	-	6/17	.353	3/ 4	.750	-/ 8	-	-	4	-	-	15	-
Totals	200	25/70	.357	9/15	.600	-/28	-	-	26	-	-	59	.295

Team Rebounds: Kansas State 7; Arizona 5. Disqualified: Arizona—Schuff.

	1st Half	2nd Half	Final
Kansas State	36	25	61
Arizona	20	39	59

Brigham Young (68)　　Coach: Stan Watts

	Min.	Total FG / FGA	Pct.	FT / FTA	Pct.	Reb. O / T	A	TO	PF	S	Blk	TP	PPM
RICHEY	-	9/21	.429	0/ 3	.000	-/ 8	-	-	3	-	-	18	-
MINSON	-	5/11	.455	2/ 4	.500	-/ 4	-	-	5	-	-	12	-
HILLMAN	-	0/ 3	.000	2/ 5	.400	-/ 1	-	-	1	-	-	2	-
HUTCHINS, M.	-	10/23	.435	2/ 4	.500	-/12	-	-	1	-	-	22	-
JARMAN	-	1/ 1	1.000	0/ 0	.000	-/ 0	-	-	0	-	-	2	-
CHRISTENSEN	-	3/11	.273	1/ 2	.500	-/ 4	-	-	3	-	-	7	-
ROMNEY	-	1/11	.091	3/ 4	.750	-/ 7	-	-	2	-	-	5	-
JONES	-	0/ 1	.000	0/ 0	.000	-/ 0	-	-	0	-	-	0	-
Totals	200	29/82	.354	10/22	.455	-/36	-	-	15	-	-	68	.340

San Jose State (61)　　Coach: Walter McPherson

	Min.	Total FG / FGA	Pct.	FT / FTA	Pct.	Reb. O / T	A	TO	PF	S	Blk	TP	PPM
BAPTISTE	-	0/ 1	.000	0/ 1	.000	-/ 1	-	-	0	-	-	0	-
JENSEN	-	1/ 5	.200	0/ 0	.000	-/ 3	-	-	2	-	-	2	-
SCHORR	-	2/ 4	.500	1/ 1	1.000	-/ 0	-	-	1	-	-	5	-
GILES	-	7/23	.304	4/ 5	.800	-/10	-	-	2	-	-	18	-
DEMING	-	0/ 3	.000	0/ 1	.000	-/ 2	-	-	1	-	-	0	-
CLARK	-	3/11	.273	2/ 2	1.000	-/ 6	-	-	2	-	-	8	-
WILSON	-	1/ 3	.333	0/ 0	.000	-/ 7	-	-	2	-	-	2	-
CRAIG	-	5/ 9	.556	1/ 1	1.000	-/ 2	-	-	4	-	-	11	-
ENZENSPERGER	-	2/ 5	.400	0/ 1	.000	-/ 1	-	-	5	-	-	4	-
CRAMPTON	-	5/11	.455	0/ 0	.000	-/ 7	-	-	1	-	-	10	-
PRESCOTT	-	0/ 0	.000	1/ 1	1.000	-/ 0	-	-	0	-	-	1	-
Totals	200	26/75	.347	9/14	.643	-/39	-	-	20	-	-	61	.305

Team Rebounds: Brigham Young 8; San Jose 8. Disqualified: Brigham Young—Minson; San Jose St.—Enzensperger

	1st Half	2nd Half	Final
Brigham Young	43	25	68
San Jose St.	33	28	61

Oklahoma A&M (50)　　Coach: Henry Iba

	Min.	Total FG / FGA	Pct.	FT / FTA	Pct.	Reb. O / T	A	TO	PF	S	Blk	TP	PPM
JOHNSON, D.	-	4/22	.182	1/ 2	.500	-/ 6	-	-	1	-	-	9	-
SHEETS, K.	-	0/ 4	.000	0/ 0	.000	-/ 1	-	-	1	-	-	0	-
STOCKTON, G.	-	1/ 3	.333	0/ 0	.000	-/ 0	-	-	1	-	-	2	-
MILLER, J.	-	1/ 1	1.000	0/ 0	.000	-/ 1	-	-	0	-	-	2	-
ROGERS, H.	-	1/ 5	.200	2/ 2	1.000	-/ 4	-	-	4	-	-	4	-
AMAYA	-	1/ 1	1.000	0/ 0	.000	-/ 0	-	-	1	-	-	2	-
DARCEY, P.	-	1/ 2	.500	1/ 1	1.000	-/ 6	-	-	4	-	-	3	-
PAGER, B.	-	3/ 9	.333	3/ 3	1.000	-/ 5	-	-	3	-	-	9	-
MCARTHUR, G.	-	5/12	.417	1/ 3	.333	-/ 0	-	-	2	-	-	11	-
SMITH, K.	-	3/ 6	.500	2/ 4	.500	-/ 6	-	-	5	-	-	8	-
Totals	200	20/65	.308	10/15	.667	-/29	-	-	22	-	-	50	.250

Montana State (46)　　Coach: John Breeden

	Min.	Total FG / FGA	Pct.	FT / FTA	Pct.	Reb. O / T	A	TO	PF	S	Blk	TP	PPM
CURRY	-	5/13	.385	1/ 3	.333	-/ 0	-	-	0	-	-	11	-
MILLER	-	4/ 9	.444	0/ 0	.000	-/ 3	-	-	2	-	-	8	-
JOHNSON	-	0/ 3	.000	5/ 6	.833	-/ 6	-	-	5	-	-	5	-
MCCAHILL	-	0/ 3	.000	0/ 0	.000	-/ 5	-	-	1	-	-	0	-
MCKETHEN, J.	-	3/ 5	.600	9/14	.643	-/ 2	-	-	3	-	-	15	-
SAUNDERS	-	0/ 0	.000	0/ 0	.000	-/ 0	-	-	0	-	-	0	-
WARD	-	1/ 5	.200	0/ 1	.000	-/ 2	-	-	5	-	-	2	-
GLEASON	-	2/ 7	.286	1/ 1	1.000	-/ 2	-	-	0	-	-	5	-
Totals	200	15/45	.333	16/25	.640	-/20	-	-	16	-	-	46	.230

Team Rebounds: Oklahoma A&M 6; Montana St. 11. Disqualified: Oklahoma A&M—Smith; Montana St.—Ward, Johnson.

	1st Half	2nd Half	Final
Oklahoma A&M	25	25	50
Montana St.	21	25	46

Washington (62)　　Coach: Tippy Dye

	Min.	Total FG / FGA	Pct.	FT / FTA	Pct.	Reb. O / T	A	TO	PF	S	Blk	TP	PPM
GUISNESS	-	6/12	.500	4/ 8	.500	-/ 1	-	-	3	-	-	16	-
MCCLARY	-	4/14	.286	2/ 3	.667	-/13	-	-	2	-	-	10	-
ENOCHS	-	1/ 1	1.000	0/ 0	.000	-/ 5	-	-	1	-	-	2	-
HOUBREGS, B.	-	5/18	.278	1/ 2	.500	-/13	-	-	3	-	-	11	-
HENSON	-	5/ 6	.833	2/ 3	.667	-/ 1	-	-	3	-	-	12	-
MCCUTCHEN	-	2/ 7	.286	0/ 1	.000	-/ 6	-	-	3	-	-	4	-
CIPRIANO	-	0/ 1	.000	0/ 0	.000	-/ 1	-	-	1	-	-	0	-
SORIANO	-	2/ 8	.250	3/ 3	1.000	-/ 3	-	-	5	-	-	7	-
WARD	-	0/ 0	.000	0/ 0	.000	-/ 0	-	-	0	-	-	0	-
Totals	200	25/67	.373	12/20	.600	-/43	-	-	21	-	-	62	.310

Texas A&M (40)　　Coach: John Floyd

	Min.	Total FG / FGA	Pct.	FT / FTA	Pct.	Reb. O / T	A	TO	PF	S	Blk	TP	PPM
DEWITT	-	6/16	.375	2/ 2	1.000	-/ 8	-	-	3	-	-	14	-
MIKSCH	-	2/ 7	.286	1/ 4	.250	-/ 7	-	-	2	-	-	5	-
MARTIN	-	3/ 8	.375	0/ 0	.000	-/ 3	-	-	2	-	-	6	-
DAVIS	-	4/ 8	.500	1/ 4	.250	-/ 4	-	-	5	-	-	9	-
WILLIAMS	-	0/ 0	.000	0/ 1	.000	-/ 0	-	-	0	-	-	0	-
FARMER	-	0/ 0	.000	0/ 0	.000	-/ 1	-	-	0	-	-	0	-
WALKER	-	1/13	.077	1/ 1	1.000	-/ 3	-	-	3	-	-	3	-
CARPENTER	-	0/ 1	.000	0/ 0	.000	-/ 1	-	-	2	-	-	0	-
MCDOWELL	-	0/11	.000	1/ 1	1.000	-/ 0	-	-	5	-	-	1	-
HEFT	-	1/ 1	1.000	0/ 0	.000	-/ 0	-	-	0	-	-	2	-
Totals	200	17/65	.262	6/13	.462	-/28	-	-	22	-	-	40	.200

Team Rebounds: Washington 8; Texas A&M 6. Disqualified: Washington—Soriano; Texas A&M—Davis, McDowell.

	1st Half	2nd Half	Final
Washington	27	35	62
Texas A&M	15	25	40

FIRST ROUND EAST

Columbia (71) Coach: Lou Rossini

	Min.	Total FG/FGA	Pct.	FT/FTA	Pct.	Reb. O/T	A	TO	PF	S	Blk	TP	PPM
AZARY, J.	-	5/14	.357	3/3	1.000	-/9	6	-	2	-	-	13	-
REISS, B.	-	4/9	.444	1/1	1.000	-/2	2	-	3	-	-	9	-
MOLINAS, J.	-	8/19	.421	4/4	1.000	-/15	0	-	4	-	-	20	-
POWERS	-	4/12	.333	1/1	1.000	-/1	3	-	5	-	-	9	-
LEWIS	-	2/6	.333	4/5	.800	-/7	2	-	4	-	-	8	-
BRANDT	-	0/2	.000	1/2	.500	-/1	0	-	1	-	-	1	-
MARATOS	-	0/1	.000	0/0	.000	-/1	0	-	0	-	-	0	-
STEIN, A.	-	4/21	.190	1/1	1.000	-/4	4	-	4	-	-	9	-
GAITTAR	-	1/1	1.000	0/0	.000	-/0	0	-	1	-	-	2	-
ROHAN, J.	-	0/1	.000	0/0	.000	-/0	0	-	0	-	-	0	-
Totals	200	28/86	.326	15/17	.882	-/40	17	-	24	-	-	71	.355

Illinois (79) Coach: Harry Combes

	Min.	Total FG/FGA	Pct.	FT/FTA	Pct.	Reb. O/T	A	TO	PF	S	Blk	TP	PPM
FOLLMER, C.	-	1/6	.167	1/3	.333	-/3	3	-	3	-	-	3	-
BEMORAS, I.	-	2/7	.286	4/5	.800	-/8	4	-	2	-	-	8	-
PETERSON, B.	-	1/8	.125	3/3	1.000	-/8	0	-	5	-	-	5	-
FLETCHER, R.	-	6/18	.333	1/4	.250	-/12	5	-	3	-	-	13	-
SUNDERLAGE, D.	-	9/19	.474	7/10	.700	-/9	4	-	1	-	-	25	-
BEACH, T.	-	10/17	.588	2/2	1.000	-/2	3	-	1	-	-	22	-
BAUMGARDNER, M.	-	1/4	.250	1/1	1.000	-/2	1	-	0	-	-	3	-
Totals	200	30/79	.380	19/28	.679	-/44	20	-	15	-	-	79	.395

Disqualified: Illinois—Peterson; Columbia—Powers.

	1st Half	2nd Half	Final
Columbia	45	26	71
Illinois	38	41	79

North Carolina State (67) Coach: Everett Case

	Min.	Total FG/FGA	Pct.	FT/FTA	Pct.	Reb. O/T	A	TO	PF	S	Blk	TP	PPM
BRANDENBURG	-	3/6	.500	2/2	1.000	-/3	-	-	2	-	-	8	-
COOK, B.	-	0/2	.000	0/0	.000	-/2	-	-	1	-	-	0	-
KUKOY, B.	-	12/31	.387	3/4	.750	-/10	-	-	3	-	-	27	-
SPEIGHT, B.	-	5/16	.313	6/6	1.000	-/7	-	-	3	-	-	16	-
GOSS	-	1/12	.083	3/7	.429	-/17	-	-	5	-	-	5	-
TERRILL	-	3/8	.375	1/4	.250	-/8	-	-	2	-	-	7	-
YURIN, B.	-	1/8	.125	2/3	.667	-/9	-	-	2	-	-	4	-
Totals	200	25/83	.301	17/26	.654	-/56	-	-	18	-	-	67	.335

Villanova (62) Coach: Alex Severance

	Min.	Total FG/FGA	Pct.	FT/FTA	Pct.	Reb. O/T	A	TO	PF	S	Blk	TP	PPM
HENNESSEY	-	6/19	.316	4/5	.800	-/6	-	-	4	-	-	16	-
MOONEY	-	2/13	.154	4/4	1.000	-/9	-	-	3	-	-	8	-
GEPP	-	1/3	.333	1/1	1.000	-/7	-	-	3	-	-	3	-
STANKO	-	0/0	.000	0/0	.000	-/0	-	-	0	-	-	0	-
BRENNAN	-	4/12	.333	1/1	1.000	-/6	-	-	5	-	-	9	-
MAGUIRE, N.	-	0/1	.000	0/0	.000	-/1	-	-	1	-	-	0	-
GLASSMIRE	-	3/7	.429	1/3	.333	-/5	-	-	5	-	-	7	-
MAGUIRE, J.	-	0/2	.000	0/0	.000	-/0	-	-	0	-	-	0	-
STEWART, B.	-	8/21	.381	3/4	.750	-/15	-	-	5	-	-	19	-
Totals	200	24/78	.308	14/18	.778	-/49	-	-	26	-	-	62	.310

Disqualified: N. C. State—Goss; Villanova—Stewart, Glassmire, Brennan.

	1st Half	2nd Half	Final
N.C. State	32	35	67
Villanova	38	24	62

Kentucky (79) Coach: Adolph Rupp

	Min.	Total FG/FGA	Pct.	FT/FTA	Pct.	Reb. O/T	A	TO	PF	S	Blk	TP	PPM
HAGAN, C.	-	2/8	.250	4/4	1.000	-/12	-	-	4	-	-	8	-
LINVILLE, S.	-	9/26	.346	4/4	1.000	-/10	-	-	5	-	-	22	-
SPIVEY, B.	-	2/9	.222	6/6	1.000	-/7	-	-	5	-	-	10	-
TSIOROPOULOS, L.	-	1/5	.200	0/0	.000	-/9	-	-	1	-	-	2	-
WATSON, R.	-	3/9	.333	0/0	.000	-/2	-	-	1	-	-	6	-
RAMSEY, F.	-	4/17	.235	7/11	.636	-/15	-	-	3	-	-	15	-
WHITAKER, L.	-	8/15	.533	0/3	.000	-/1	-	-	2	-	-	16	-
Totals	200	29/89	.326	21/28	.750	-/56	-	-	21	-	-	79	.395

Louisville (68) Coach: Peck Hickman

	Min.	Total FG/FGA	Pct.	FT/FTA	Pct.	Reb. O/T	A	TO	PF	S	Blk	TP	PPM
BROWN, B.	-	7/26	.269	1/1	1.000	-/11	-	-	3	-	-	15	-
LOCHMUELLER, B.	-	6/23	.261	2/7	.286	-/18	-	-	4	-	-	14	-
FORD, L.	-	0/0	.000	0/0	.000	-/0	-	-	0	-	-	0	-
ROBISON, D.	-	5/10	.500	0/3	.000	-/3	-	-	5	-	-	10	-
LARRABEE, W.	-	2/5	.400	0/1	.000	-/6	-	-	3	-	-	4	-
DUNBAR, B.	-	0/1	.000	0/0	.000	-/1	-	-	0	-	-	0	-
NABER, B.	-	6/8	.750	3/5	.600	-/3	-	-	5	-	-	15	-
SULLIVAN, B.	-	3/6	.500	0/0	.000	-/4	-	-	2	-	-	6	-
RUBIN, R.	-	2/5	.400	0/1	.000	-/2	-	-	4	-	-	4	-
WELLMAN, B.	-	0/1	.000	0/0	.000	-/0	-	-	1	-	-	0	-
Totals	200	31/85	.365	6/18	.333	-/48	-	-	27	-	-	68	.340

Disqualified: Kentucky—Linville, Spivey; Louisville—Robison, Naber.

	1st Half	2nd Half	Final
Kentucky	44	35	79
Louisville	40	28	68

St. John's (63) Coach: Frank McGuire

	Min.	Total FG/FGA	Pct.	FT/FTA	Pct.	Reb. O/T	A	TO	PF	S	Blk	TP	PPM
DOMBROSKY	-	6/13	.462	5/5	1.000	-/10	1	-	0	-	-	17	-
O'SHEA	-	0/0	.000	0/0	.000	-/0	0	-	0	-	-	0	-
MCGUIRE, A.	-	0/0	.000	0/0	.000	-/4	1	-	2	-	-	0	-
MACGILVRAY, R.	-	2/8	.250	5/8	.625	-/13	1	-	3	-	-	9	-
MCCOOL	-	0/1	.000	0/0	.000	-/0	0	-	0	-	-	0	-
ZAWOLUK, Z.	-	7/18	.389	4/5	.800	-/18	2	-	3	-	-	18	-
GIANCONTIERI, F.	-	0/0	.000	0/0	.000	-/0	0	-	1	-	-	0	-
MCMAHON, J.	-	5/12	.417	0/0	.000	-/5	2	-	3	-	-	10	-
NOONAN	-	0/0	.000	0/0	.000	-/0	1	-	0	-	-	0	-
MULZOFF	-	2/7	.286	1/1	1.000	-/3	5	-	5	-	-	5	-
DUNN, D.	-	2/4	.500	0/0	.000	-/3	2	-	2	-	-	4	-
MCANDREWS	-	0/0	.000	0/0	.000	-/0	0	-	0	-	-	0	-
Totals	200	24/63	.381	15/20	.750	-/56	15	-	19	-	-	63	.315

U. Conn. (52) Coach: Hugh Greer

	Min.	Total FG/FGA	Pct.	FT/FTA	Pct.	Reb. O/T	A	TO	PF	S	Blk	TP	PPM
YOKABASKAS, V.	-	7/15	.467	8/11	.727	-/3	3	-	2	-	-	22	-
WIDHOLM	-	2/5	.400	3/3	1.000	-/6	3	-	5	-	-	7	-
SILVERSTEIN	-	0/1	.000	0/0	.000	-/0	0	-	0	-	-	0	-
DEMIR	-	0/0	.000	0/0	.000	-/0	0	-	1	-	-	0	-
EBEL	-	5/12	.417	2/3	.667	-/4	0	-	1	-	-	12	-
FLEISCHMAN	-	0/2	.000	0/0	.000	-/0	0	-	0	-	-	0	-
KLECKNER	-	1/3	.333	0/0	.000	-/3	4	-	1	-	-	2	-
CLARK	-	1/6	.167	0/1	.000	-/3	2	-	3	-	-	2	-
BROUKER	-	0/2	.000	0/0	.000	-/1	0	-	1	-	-	0	-
GATES, E.	-	3/17	.176	1/3	.333	-/1	3	-	2	-	-	7	-
Totals	200	19/63	.302	14/21	.667	-/21	15	-	16	-	-	52	.260

Disqualified: St. John's—Mulzoff; U. Conn.—Widholm.

	1st Half	2nd Half	Final
St. John's	34	29	63
U. Conn.	19	33	52

REGIONAL SEMIFINAL WEST

Kansas State (64) Coach: Jack Gardner

	Min.	Total FG / FGA	Pct.	FT / FTA	Pct.	Reb. O / T	A	TO	PF	S	Blk	TP	PPM
HEAD, E.	-	5/11	.455	1/ 2	.500	-/12	-	-	3	-	-	11	-
STONE, J.	-	4/13	.308	3/ 9	.333	-/ 6	-	-	1	-	-	11	-
GIBSON, J.	-	1/ 1	1.000	1/ 1	1.000	-/ 4	-	-	4	-	-	3	-
HITCH, L.	-	3/ 6	.500	0/ 1	.000	-/11	-	-	2	-	-	6	-
KNOSTMAN, R.	-	1/ 1	1.000	1/ 1	1.000	-/ 1	-	-	0	-	-	3	-
IVERSON, J.	-	3/ 9	.333	1/ 2	.500	-/ 2	-	-	0	-	-	7	-
BARRETT, E.	-	4/ 9	.444	2/ 2	1.000	-/ 4	-	-	5	-	-	10	-
ROUSEY, R.	-	5/ 9	.556	3/ 3	1.000	-/ 3	-	-	2	-	-	13	-
Totals	200	26/59	.441	12/21	.571	-/43	-	-	17	-	-	64	.320

Brigham Young (54) Coach: Stan Watts

	Min.	Total FG / FGA	Pct.	FT / FTA	Pct.	Reb. O / T	A	TO	PF	S	Blk	TP	PPM
RICHEY	-	6/15	.400	0/ 2	.000	-/ 7	-	-	3	-	-	12	-
MINSON	-	5/17	.294	2/ 3	.667	-/ 4	-	-	4	-	-	12	-
HILLMAN	-	4/10	.400	1/ 3	.333	-/ 1	-	-	5	-	-	9	-
HUTCHINS, M.	-	5/13	.385	0/ 1	.000	-/ 7	-	-	4	-	-	10	-
JARMAN	-	0/ 2	.000	1/ 1	1.000	-/ 1	-	-	0	-	-	1	-
CHRISTENSEN	-	0/ 0	.000	0/ 0	.000	-/ 1	-	-	3	-	-	0	-
ROMNEY	-	1/ 9	.111	6/ 8	.750	-/ 5	-	-	4	-	-	8	-
JONES	-	1/ 2	.500	0/ 0	.000	-/ 1	-	-	2	-	-	2	-
Totals	200	22/68	.324	10/18	.556	-/27	-	-	25	-	-	54	.270

Team Rebounds: Kansas State 3; Brigham Young 3. Disqualified: Kansas State—Barrett; Brigham Young—Hillman.

	1st Half	2nd Half	Final
Kansas State	39	25	64
Brigham Young	21	33	54

Oklahoma A&M (61) Coach: Henry Iba

	Min.	Total FG / FGA	Pct.	FT / FTA	Pct.	Reb. O / T	A	TO	PF	S	Blk	TP	PPM
JOHNSON, D.	-	7/11	.636	3/ 4	.750	-/ 5	-	-	5	-	-	17	-
ROGERS, H.	-	0/ 1	.000	0/ 0	.000	-/ 0	-	-	0	-	-	0	-
MILLER, J.	-	1/ 4	.250	2/ 4	.500	-/ 6	-	-	5	-	-	4	-
STOCKTON, G.	-	0/ 1	.000	1/ 1	1.000	-/ 4	-	-	1	-	-	1	-
SHEETS, K.	-	0/ 0	.000	0/ 0	.000	-/ 0	-	-	3	-	-	0	-
DARCEY, P.	-	1/ 2	.500	1/ 1	1.000	-/ 1	-	-	5	-	-	3	-
PAGER, B.	-	3/ 5	.600	1/ 1	1.000	-/ 3	-	-	4	-	-	7	-
MCARTHUR, G.	-	6/ 8	.750	5/ 6	.833	-/ 0	-	-	3	-	-	17	-
SMITH, K.	-	4/ 6	.667	4/ 5	.800	-/ 1	-	-	2	-	-	12	-
AMAYA	-	0/ 2	.000	0/ 0	.000	-/ 2	-	-	2	-	-	0	-
Totals	200	22/40	.550	17/22	.773	-/22	-	-	30	-	-	61	.305

Washington (57) Coach: Tippy Dye

	Min.	Total FG / FGA	Pct.	FT / FTA	Pct.	Reb. O / T	A	TO	PF	S	Blk	TP	PPM
GUISNESS	-	1/ 5	.200	2/ 3	.667	-/ 0	-	-	5	-	-	4	-
ENOCHS	-	3/ 6	.500	0/ 0	.000	-/ 1	-	-	2	-	-	6	-
MCCLARY	-	2/ 7	.286	4/ 4	1.000	-/10	-	-	3	-	-	8	-
WARD	-	0/ 0	.000	1/ 1	1.000	-/ 0	-	-	1	-	-	1	-
STEWART	-	0/ 0	.000	0/ 0	.000	-/ 0	-	-	0	-	-	0	-
HOUBREGS	-	6/18	.333	7/ 7	1.000	-/ 9	-	-	5	-	-	19	-
HENSEN	-	1/ 7	.143	0/ 2	.000	-/ 3	-	-	2	-	-	2	-
SORIANO	-	1/ 4	.250	1/ 1	1.000	-/ 1	-	-	4	-	-	3	-
MCCUTCHEN	-	3/ 7	.429	2/ 3	.667	-/ 5	-	-	2	-	-	8	-
CIPRIANO	-	3/ 8	.375	0/ 2	.000	-/ 0	-	-	4	-	-	6	-
Totals	200	20/62	.323	17/23	.739	-/27	-	-	29	-	-	57	.285

Team Rebounds: Oklahoma A&M 6; Washington 4. Disqualified: Oklahoma A&M—Johnson, Miller, Darcy; Washington—Guisness, Houbregs.

	1st Half	2nd Half	Final
Oklahoma A&M	36	25	61
Washington	23	34	57

REGIONAL SEMIFINAL EAST

Illinois (84) Coach: Harry Combes

	Min.	Total FG / FGA	Pct.	FT / FTA	Pct.	Reb. O / T	A	TO	PF	S	Blk	TP	PPM
FOLLMER, C.	-	2/ 8	.250	2/ 2	1.000	-/ 4	1	-	2	-	-	6	-
BEMORAS, I.	-	3/10	.300	1/ 1	1.000	-/12	2	-	2	-	-	7	-
PETERSON, B.	-	5/11	.455	0/ 1	.000	-/10	2	-	5	-	-	10	-
FLETCHER, R.	-	9/18	.500	1/ 2	.500	-/ 9	6	-	3	-	-	19	-
SUNDERLAGE, D.	-	9/17	.529	3/ 3	1.000	-/ 0	10	-	1	-	-	21	-
BEACH, T.	-	8/20	.400	1/ 1	1.000	-/ 5	3	-	1	-	-	17	-
BAUMGARDNER, M.	-	2/ 3	.667	0/ 0	.000	-/ 3	1	-	3	-	-	4	-
Totals	200	38/87	.437	8/10	.800	-/43	25	-	17	-	-	84	.420

North Carolina State (70) Coach: Everett Case

	Min.	Total FG / FGA	Pct.	FT / FTA	Pct.	Reb. O / T	A	TO	PF	S	Blk	TP	PPM
SPEIGHT, B.	-	7/20	.350	3/ 4	.750	-/10	5	-	2	-	-	17	-
KUKOY, B.	-	7/19	.368	6/ 8	.750	-/ 5	3	-	2	-	-	20	-
BRANDENBURG	-	4/ 5	.800	1/ 4	.250	-/ 3	1	-	0	-	-	9	-
GOSS	-	3/11	.273	2/ 3	.667	-/10	0	-	3	-	-	8	-
COOK, B.	-	1/ 4	.250	0/ 0	.000	-/ 2	0	-	0	-	-	2	-
YURIN, B.	-	0/ 1	.000	0/ 0	.000	-/ 1	0	-	0	-	-	0	-
MORRIS	-	1/ 4	.250	0/ 0	.000	-/ 9	2	-	1	-	-	2	-
JACKMOWSKI	-	2/ 2	1.000	0/ 0	.000	-/ 4	5	-	2	-	-	4	-
TERRILL, L.	-	4/14	.286	0/ 1	.000	-/ 4	3	-	0	-	-	8	-
Totals	200	29/80	.363	12/20	.600	-/48	19	-	10	-	-	70	.350

Disqualified: Illinois—Peterson.

	1st Half	2nd Half	Final
Illinois	40	44	84
N.C. State	29	41	70

Kentucky (59) Coach: Adolph Rupp

	Min.	Total FG/FGA	Pct.	FT/FTA	Pct.	Reb. O/T	A	TO	PF	S	Blk	TP	PPM
HAGAN, C.	-	1/8	.125	2/4	.500	-/11	1	-	3	-	-	4	-
LINVILLE, S.	-	4/9	.444	1/2	.500	-/5	3	-	2	-	-	9	-
SPIVEY, B.	-	5/9	.556	2/3	.667	-/11	1	-	4	-	-	12	-
TSIOROPOULOS, L.	-	1/5	.200	1/2	.500	-/4	1	-	2	-	-	3	-
LAYNE, R.	-	1/2	.500	0/1	.000	-/1	1	-	1	-	-	2	-
WATSON, R.	-	6/23	.261	0/0	.000	-/3	4	-	0	-	-	12	-
RAMSEY, F.	-	4/12	.333	5/5	1.000	-/12	4	-	5	-	-	13	-
WHITAKER, L.	-	2/4	.500	0/0	.000	-/2	1	-	1	-	-	4	-
Totals	200	24/72	.333	11/17	.647	-/49	16	-	18	-	-	59	.295

St. John's (43) Coach: Frank McGuire

	Min.	Total FG/FGA	Pct.	FT/FTA	Pct.	Reb. O/T	A	TO	PF	S	Blk	TP	PPM
DOMBROSKY	-	1/5	.200	2/3	.667	-/5	1	-	4	-	-	4	-
O'SHEA	-	0/0	.000	0/0	.000	-/0	0	-	0	-	-	0	-
MCGUIRE, A.	-	2/7	.286	1/4	.250	-/2	2	-	3	-	-	5	-
MACGILVRAY, R.	-	4/11	.364	2/4	.500	-/11	1	-	2	-	-	10	-
MCCOOL	-	0/0	.000	0/0	.000	-/0	0	-	0	-	-	0	-
ZAWOLUK, Z.	-	6/24	.250	3/5	.600	-/10	3	-	3	-	-	15	-
GIANCONTIERI, F.	-	1/3	.333	0/0	.000	-/1	0	-	0	-	-	2	-
MCMAHON, J.	-	2/16	.125	3/3	1.000	-/5	2	-	1	-	-	7	-
MULZOFF	-	0/4	.000	0/0	.000	-/4	2	-	3	-	-	0	-
DUNN, D.	-	0/0	.000	0/0	.000	-/0	0	-	0	-	-	0	-
MCANDREWS	-	0/0	.000	0/0	.000	-/0	0	-	0	-	-	0	-
Totals	200	16/70	.229	11/19	.579	-/38	11	-	16	-	-	43	.215

Disqualified: Kentucky—Ramsey.

	1st Half	2nd Half	Final
Kentucky	23	36	59
St. John's	23	20	43

REGIONAL FINAL WEST

Kansas State (68) Coach: Jack Gardner

	Min.	Total FG/FGA	Pct.	FT/FTA	Pct.	Reb. O/T	A	TO	PF	S	Blk	TP	PPM
HEAD, E.	-	4/9	.444	1/1	1.000	-/5	-	-	3	-	-	9	-
PECK, R.	-	0/1	.000	1/1	1.000	-/1	-	-	2	-	-	1	-
SCHUYLER, D.	-	2/4	.500	0/1	.000	-/0	-	-	1	-	-	4	-
STONE, J.	-	5/5	1.000	0/0	.000	-/1	-	-	2	-	-	10	-
GIBSON, J.	-	0/0	.000	0/0	.000	-/3	-	-	0	-	-	0	-
HITCH, L.	-	4/11	.364	4/6	.667	-/8	-	-	2	-	-	12	-
KNOSTMAN, R.	-	4/8	.500	3/6	.500	-/3	-	-	0	-	-	11	-
IVERSON, J.	-	3/4	.750	3/3	1.000	-/2	-	-	0	-	-	9	-
UPSON, D.	-	3/4	.750	0/0	.000	-/1	-	-	2	-	-	6	-
BARRETT, E.	-	1/7	.143	3/3	1.000	-/4	-	-	4	-	-	5	-
ROUSEY, R.	-	0/1	.000	1/4	.250	-/0	-	-	2	-	-	1	-
Totals	200	26/54	.481	16/27	.593	-/28	-	-	18	-	-	68	.340

Oklahoma A&M (44) Coach: Henry Iba

	Min.	Total FG/FGA	Pct.	FT/FTA	Pct.	Reb. O/T	A	TO	PF	S	Blk	TP	PPM
JOHNSON, D.	-	2/10	.200	3/3	1.000	-/5	-	-	4	-	-	7	-
MCAFEE, E.	-	0/1	.000	0/0	.000	-/0	-	-	3	-	-	0	-
MILLER, J.	-	0/2	.000	0/0	.000	-/2	-	-	3	-	-	0	-
STOCKTON, G.	-	0/0	.000	1/1	1.000	-/1	-	-	0	-	-	1	-
WARD, M.	-	1/2	.500	0/0	.000	-/0	-	-	1	-	-	2	-
DARCY, P.	-	2/5	.400	0/1	.000	-/1	-	-	4	-	-	4	-
PAGER, B.	-	5/10	.500	1/2	.500	-/2	-	-	3	-	-	11	-
SMITH, K.	-	0/0	.000	1/1	1.000	-/1	-	-	2	-	-	1	-
AMAYA	-	1/2	.500	0/0	.000	-/1	-	-	0	-	-	2	-
ROGERS, H.	-	2/5	.400	0/0	.000	-/0	-	-	2	-	-	4	-
MCARTHUR, G.	-	1/11	.091	5/5	1.000	-/2	-	-	2	-	-	7	-
SHEETS, K.	-	2/4	.500	1/1	1.000	-/0	-	-	1	-	-	5	-
Totals	200	16/52	.308	12/14	.857	-/15	-	-	25	-	-	44	.220

Team Rebounds: Kansas State 8; Oklahoma A&M 10. Disqualified: None.

	1st Half	2nd Half	Final
Kansas State	37	31	68
Oklahoma A&M	14	30	44

REGIONAL FINAL EAST

Illinois (74) Coach: Harry Combes

	Min.	Total FG/FGA	Pct.	FT/FTA	Pct.	Reb. O/T	A	TO	PF	S	Blk	TP	PPM
FOLLMER, C.	-	2/3	.667	2/3	.667	-/5	3	-	2	-	-	6	-
BEMORAS, I.	-	5/8	.625	2/3	.667	-/7	2	-	2	-	-	12	-
PETERSON, B.	-	3/11	.273	2/3	.667	-/5	0	-	5	-	-	8	-
FLETCHER, R.	-	8/19	.421	5/11	.455	-/10	1	-	0	-	-	21	-
SUNDERLAGE, D.	-	6/15	.400	8/11	.727	-/3	5	-	2	-	-	20	-
BEACH, T.	-	2/12	.167	3/3	1.000	-/6	4	-	1	-	-	7	-
BAUMGARDNER, M.	-	0/2	.000	0/1	.000	-/1	0	-	4	-	-	0	-
Totals	200	26/70	.371	22/35	.629	-/37	15	-	16	-	-	74	.370

Kentucky (76) Coach: Adolph Rupp

	Min.	Total FG/FGA	Pct.	FT/FTA	Pct.	Reb. O/T	A	TO	PF	S	Blk	TP	PPM
HAGAN, C.	-	3/9	.333	2/2	1.000	-/4	3	-	5	-	-	8	-
LINVILLE, S.	-	7/12	.583	0/0	.000	-/4	4	-	4	-	-	14	-
SPIVEY, B.	-	11/21	.524	6/10	.600	-/16	2	-	5	-	-	28	-
TSIOROPOULOS, L.	-	0/2	.000	1/2	.500	-/1	0	-	1	-	-	1	-
WATSON, R.	-	5/17	.294	0/0	.000	-/8	3	-	4	-	-	10	-
RAMSEY, F.	-	2/19	.105	1/3	.333	-/12	7	-	2	-	-	5	-
WHITAKER, L.	-	4/11	.364	2/4	.500	-/4	6	-	5	-	-	10	-
NEWTON, C.	-	0/0	.000	0/0	.000	-/0	0	-	1	-	-	0	-
Totals	200	32/91	.352	12/21	.571	-/49	25	-	27	-	-	76	.380

Disqualified: Kentucky—Hagan, Spivey, Whitaker; Illinois—Peterson.

	1st Half	2nd Half	Final
Illinois	39	35	74
Kentucky	32	44	76

NATIONAL CHAMPIONSHIP

Kansas State (58)   Coach: Jack Gardner

	Min.	Total FG/FGA	Pct.	FT/FTA	Pct.	Reb. O/T	A	TO	PF	S	Blk	TP	PPM
HEAD, E.	-	3/11	.273	2/2	1.000	-/3	-	-	2	-	-	8	-
SCHUYLER, D.	-	1/2	.500	0/0	.000	-/1	-	-	2	-	-	2	-
STONE, J.	-	3/8	.375	6/8	.750	-/6	-	-	2	-	-	12	-
GIBSON, J.	-	0/2	.000	1/1	1.000	-/1	-	-	5	-	-	1	-
KNOSTMAN, R.	-	1/4	.250	1/2	.500	-/3	-	-	1	-	-	3	-
IVERSON, J.	-	3/12	.250	1/2	.500	-/0	-	-	3	-	-	7	-
UPSON, D.	-	0/1	.000	0/0	.000	-/2	-	-	1	-	-	0	-
BARRETT, E.	-	2/12	.167	0/2	.000	-/3	-	-	1	-	-	4	-
ROUSEY, R.	-	2/10	.200	0/0	.000	-/2	-	-	3	-	-	4	-
HITCH, L.	-	6/15	.400	1/1	1.000	-/9	-	-	3	-	-	13	-
PECK, R.	-	2/3	.667	0/0	.000	-/0	-	-	0	-	-	4	-
Totals	200	23/80	.288	12/18	.667	-/30	-	-	23	-	-	58	.290

Kentucky (68)   Coach: Adolph Rupp

	Min.	Total FG/FGA	Pct.	FT/FTA	Pct.	Reb. O/T	A	TO	PF	S	Blk	TP	PPM
HAGAN, C.	-	5/6	.833	0/2	.000	-/4	-	-	5	-	-	10	-
LINVILLE, S.	-	2/7	.286	4/8	.500	-/8	-	-	5	-	-	8	-
SPIVEY, B.	-	9/29	.310	4/6	.667	-/21	-	-	2	-	-	22	-
TSIOROPOULOS, L.	-	1/4	.250	0/0	.000	-/3	-	-	1	-	-	2	-
WATSON, R.	-	3/8	.375	2/4	.500	-/3	-	-	3	-	-	8	-
RAMSEY, F.	-	4/10	.400	1/3	.333	-/4	-	-	5	-	-	9	-
WHITAKER, L.	-	4/5	.800	1/1	1.000	-/2	-	-	2	-	-	9	-
NEWTON, C.	-	0/0	.000	0/0	.000	-/0	-	-	0	-	-	0	-
Totals	200	28/69	.406	12/24	.500	-/45	-	-	23	-	-	68	.340

Disqualified: Kentucky—Linville, Ramsey, Hagan; Kansas State—Gibson.

	1st Half	2nd Half	Final
Kansas State	29	29	58
Kentucky	27	41	68

NATIONAL THIRD PLACE

Oklahoma A&M (46)   Coach: Henry Iba

	Min.	Total FG/FGA	Pct.	FT/FTA	Pct.	Reb. O/T	A	TO	PF	S	Blk	TP	PPM
JOHNSON, D.	-	4/20	.200	3/6	.500	-/7	-	-	3	-	-	11	-
STOCKTON, G.	-	0/3	.000	0/1	.000	-/0	-	-	3	-	-	0	-
DARCEY, P.	-	1/10	.100	0/1	.000	-/10	-	-	4	-	-	2	-
MCARTHUR, G.	-	7/16	.438	3/3	.000	-/2	-	-	4	-	-	17	-
SHEETS, K.	-	0/0	.000	0/0	.000	-/0	-	-	4	-	-	0	-
PAGER, B.	-	2/8	.250	2/4	.500	-/5	-	-	1	-	-	6	-
AMAYA	-	0/0	.000	0/0	.000	-/0	-	-	3	-	-	0	-
MILLER, J.	-	2/7	.286	2/3	.667	-/7	-	-	4	-	-	6	-
ROGERS, H.	-	2/7	.286	0/0	.000	-/7	-	-	4	-	-	4	-
WARD, M.	-	0/0	.000	0/0	.000	-/0	-	-	1	-	-	0	-
MCAFEE, E.	-	0/0	.000	0/0	.000	-/0	-	-	0	-	-	0	-
Totals	200	18/71	.254	10/19	.526	-/38	-	-	31	-	-	46	.230

Illinois (61)   Coach: Harry Combes

	Min.	Total FG/FGA	Pct.	FT/FTA	Pct.	Reb. O/T	A	TO	PF	S	Blk	TP	PPM
BEMORAS, I.	-	2/7	.286	1/2	.500	-/5	-	-	0	-	-	5	-
BEACH, T.	-	4/12	.333	4/4	1.000	-/4	-	-	2	-	-	12	-
PETERSON, B.	-	0/10	.000	4/5	.800	-/7	-	-	5	-	-	4	-
FLETCHER, R.	-	5/11	.455	4/8	.500	-/9	-	-	2	-	-	14	-
SUNDERLAGE, D.	-	4/11	.364	9/10	.900	-/6	-	-	4	-	-	17	-
FOLLMER, C.	-	0/2	.000	6/6	1.000	-/3	-	-	4	-	-	6	-
BAUMGARDNER, M.	-	0/2	.000	0/0	.000	-/0	-	-	2	-	-	0	-
MARKS, J.	-	0/1	.000	0/0	.000	-/0	-	-	0	-	-	0	-
BREDAR, J.	-	0/0	.000	0/0	.000	-/0	-	-	0	-	-	0	-
SCHULDT, J.	-	0/0	.000	0/0	.000	-/0	-	-	0	-	-	0	-
GERECKE, H.	-	1/1	1.000	1/1	1.000	-/0	-	-	0	-	-	3	-
FOLLMER, M.	-	0/0	.000	0/0	.000	-/0	-	-	0	-	-	0	-
Totals	200	16/57	.281	29/36	.806	-/34	-	-	19	-	-	61	.305

Disqualified: Illinois—Peterson.

	1st Half	2nd Half	Final
Oklahoma A&M	22	24	46
Illinois	31	30	61

REGIONAL THIRD PLACE EAST

St. John's (71)   Coach: Frank McGuire

	Min.	Total FG/FGA	Pct.	FT/FTA	Pct.	Reb. O/T	A	TO	PF	S	Blk	TP	PPM
DOMBROSKY	-	4/9	.444	0/0	.000	-/4	0	-	3	-	-	8	-
O'SHEA	-	0/0	.000	0/0	.000	-/0	0	-	0	-	-	0	-
MCGUIRE, A.	-	4/8	.500	8/12	.667	-/6	3	-	2	-	-	16	-
MACGILVRAY, R.	-	3/6	.500	2/2	1.000	-/4	4	-	0	-	-	8	-
MCCOOL	-	0/0	.000	0/0	.000	-/0	0	-	0	-	-	0	-
ZAWOLUK, Z.	-	4/9	.444	1/2	.500	-/9	1	-	3	-	-	9	-
GIANCONTIERI, F.	-	0/2	.000	0/0	.000	-/1	2	-	2	-	-	0	-
MCMAHON, J.	-	12/23	.522	0/0	.000	-/2	4	-	3	-	-	24	-
NOONAN	-	0/1	.000	0/0	.000	-/0	0	-	0	-	-	0	-
MULZOFF	-	0/4	.000	1/1	1.000	-/2	8	-	2	-	-	1	-
DUNN, D.	-	2/4	.500	1/2	.500	-/3	0	-	1	-	-	5	-
Totals	200	29/66	.439	13/19	.684	-/31	22	-	16	-	-	71	.355

North Carolina State (59)   Coach: Everett Case

	Min.	Total FG/FGA	Pct.	FT/FTA	Pct.	Reb. O/T	A	TO	PF	S	Blk	TP	PPM
SPEIGHT, B.	-	4/20	.200	4/4	1.000	-/9	2	-	2	-	-	12	-
KUKOY, B.	-	6/19	.316	10/10	1.000	-/5	1	-	4	-	-	22	-
BRANDENBURG	-	0/2	.000	1/1	1.000	-/1	1	-	0	-	-	1	-
GOSS	-	6/8	.750	1/2	.500	-/8	1	-	4	-	-	13	-
COOK, B.	-	0/2	.000	2/2	1.000	-/0	0	-	0	-	-	2	-
MORRIS	-	2/7	.286	0/0	.000	-/4	2	-	5	-	-	4	-
JACKMOWSKI	-	0/1	.000	0/0	.000	-/1	0	-	0	-	-	0	-
TERRILL, L.	-	2/8	.250	1/1	1.000	-/6	7	-	1	-	-	5	-
HOLT	-	0/0	.000	0/0	.000	-/0	0	-	0	-	-	0	-
Totals	200	20/67	.299	19/20	.950	-/37	14	-	14	-	-	59	.295

Disqualified: N.C. State—Morris.

	1st Half	2nd Half	Final
St. John's	33	38	71
N.C. State	33	26	59

REGIONAL THIRD PLACE WEST

Washington (80)   Coach: Tippy Dye

	Min.	Total FG/FGA	Pct.	FT/FTA	Pct.	Reb. O/T	A	TO	PF	S	Blk	TP	PPM
GUISNESS	-	4/11	.364	3/5	.600	-/4	-	-	5	-	-	11	-
WARD	-	1/3	.333	0/2	.000	-/1	-	-	0	-	-	2	-
MCCLARY	-	5/15	.333	2/2	1.000	-/7	-	-	3	-	-	12	-
ENOCHS	-	0/3	.000	0/0	.000	-/1	-	-	1	-	-	0	-
STEWART	-	0/1	.000	0/0	.000	-/0	-	-	0	-	-	0	-
HOUBREGS, B.	-	11/25	.440	1/4	.250	-/7	-	-	2	-	-	23	-
WADE	-	0/0	.000	0/0	.000	-/0	-	-	0	-	-	0	-
HENSON	-	3/9	.333	1/1	1.000	-/6	-	-	2	-	-	7	-
CIPRIANO	-	2/2	1.000	1/1	1.000	-/0	-	-	2	-	-	5	-
SARIANO	-	3/6	.500	2/2	1.000	-/0	-	-	2	-	-	8	-
MCCUTCHEN	-	6/12	.500	0/3	.000	-/10	-	-	4	-	-	12	-
JEFFERSON	-	0/0	.000	0/1	.000	-/0	-	-	0	-	-	0	-
Totals	200	35/87	.402	10/21	.476	-/36	-	-	21	-	-	80	.400

Brigham Young (67)   Coach: Stan Watts

	Min.	Total FG/FGA	Pct.	FT/FTA	Pct.	Reb. O/T	A	TO	PF	S	Blk	TP	PPM
HILLMAN	-	4/8	.500	2/4	.500	-/3	-	-	1	-	-	10	-
RICHEY	-	1/6	.167	1/2	.500	-/3	-	-	2	-	-	3	-
MINSON	-	7/23	.304	3/5	.600	-/5	-	-	3	-	-	17	-
MALMROSE	-	0/1	.000	0/0	.000	-/0	-	-	1	-	-	0	-
HUTCHINS, M.	-	3/8	.375	3/5	.600	-/7	-	-	3	-	-	9	-
CHRISTENSEN	-	3/5	.600	0/0	.000	-/0	-	-	0	-	-	6	-
JARMAN	-	0/2	.000	0/0	.000	-/0	-	-	0	-	-	0	-
CRAIG	-	1/2	.500	0/0	.000	-/3	-	-	2	-	-	2	-
DUNN	-	1/1	1.000	0/0	.000	-/1	-	-	1	-	-	2	-
JONES	-	4/9	.444	3/3	1.000	-/3	-	-	4	-	-	11	-
ROMNEY	-	1/5	.200	5/5	1.000	-/5	-	-	3	-	-	7	-
MONTGOMERY	-	0/0	.000	0/0	.000	-/0	-	-	0	-	-	0	-
Totals	200	25/70	.357	17/24	.708	-/30	-	-	20	-	-	67	.335

Team Rebounds: Washington 5; Brigham Young 6. Disqualified: Washington—Guisness.

	1st Half	2nd Half	Final
Washington	39	41	80
Brigham Young	39	28	67

○ INDIVIDUAL RECORDS ○

SCORING

Most points in a single game
1 BILL SPIVEY, KENTUCKY (vs. ILLINOIS)   28
2 BILL KUKOY, N.C. STATE (vs. VILLANOVA)   27
3 DON SUNDERLAGE, ILLINOIS (vs. COLUMBIA) 25
4 JACK MCMAHON, ST. JOHN'S (vs. N.C. STATE)   24
5 BOB HOUBREGS, WASHINGTON (vs. BRIGHAM YOUNG)   23

Most total points in the tournament
1 DON SUNDERLAGE, ILLINOIS   83
2 BILL SPIVEY, KENTUCKY   72
3 BILL KUKOY, N.C. STATE   69
4 ROD FLETCHER, ILLINOIS   67
5 TED BEACH, ILLINOIS   58

Highest scoring average (minimum 2 games)
1 BILL KUKOY, N.C. STATE (69-3)   23.00
2 DON SUNDERLAGE, ILLINOIS (83-4)   20.75
3 BILL SPIVEY, KENTUCKY (72-4)   18.00
4 BOB HOUBREGS, WASHINGTON (53-3)   17.67
5 ROD FLETCHER, ILLINOIS (67-4)   16.75

FIELD GOALS

Most field goals in a single game
1 BILL KUKOY, N.C. STATE (vs. VILLANOVA)   12
1 JACK MCMAHON, ST. JOHN'S (vs. N.C. STATE)   12
3 BOB HOUBREGS, WASHINGTON (vs. BRIGHAM YOUNG)   11
3 BILL SPIVEY, KENTUCKY (vs. ILLINOIS)   11
5 2 tied for fifth place.

Most total field goals in the tournament
1 DON SUNDERLAGE, ILLINOIS   28
1 ROD FLETCHER, ILLINOIS   28
3 BILL SPIVEY, KENTUCKY   27
4 BILL KUKOY, N.C. STATE   25
5 TED BEACH, ILLINOIS   24

Most field goal attempts in a single game
1 BILL KUKOY, N.C. STATE (vs. VILLANOVA)   31
2 BILL SPIVEY, KENTUCKY (vs. KANSAS STATE) 29
3 BOB BROWN, LOUISVILLE (vs. KENTUCKY)   26
3 SHELBY LINVILLE, KENTUCKY (vs. LOUISVILLE)   26
5 BOB HOUBREGS, WASHINGTON (vs. BRIGHAM YOUNG)   25

Most total field goal attempts in a tournament
1 BILL KUKOY, N.C. STATE   69
2 BILL SPIVEY, KENTUCKY   68
3 ROD FLETCHER, ILLINOIS   66
4 DON JOHNSON, OKLAHOMA A&M   63
5 DON SUNDERLAGE, ILLINOIS   62

Highest field goal percentage in a single game (minimum 10 attempts)
1 DON JOHNSON, OKLAHOMA A&M (vs. WASHINGTON) (7-11)   .636
2 TED BEACH, ILLINOIS (vs. COLUMBIA) (10-17)   .588
3 SHELBY LINVILLE, KENTUCKY (vs. ILLINOIS) (7-12)   .583
4 LUCIAN WHITAKER, KENTUCKY (vs. LOUISVILLE) (8-15)   .533
5 DON SUNDERLAGE, ILLINOIS (vs. N.C. STATE) (9-17)   .529

Highest field goal percentage in the tournament (minimum 20 attempts)
1 LUCIAN WHITAKER, KENTUCKY (18-35)   .514
2 DON SUNDERLAGE, ILLINOIS (28-62)   .452
3 LEW HITCH, KANSAS STATE (18-40)   .450
4 ROD FLETCHER, ILLINOIS (28-66)   .424
5 MIKE MCCUTCHEN, WASHINGTON (11-26)   .423

FREE THROWS

Most free throws in a single game
1 BILL KUKOY, N.C. STATE (vs. ST. JOHN'S)   10
2 DON SUNDERLAGE, ILLINOIS (vs. OKLAHOMA A&M)   9

2 JOE MCKETHEN, MONTANA ST. (vs. OKLAHOMA A&M)   9
4 3 tied for fourth place.

Most total free throws in the tournament
1 DON SUNDERLAGE, ILLINOIS   27
2 BILL KUKOY, N.C. STATE   19
3 BILL SPIVEY, KENTUCKY   18
4 3 tied for fourth place.

Most free throws attempted in a single game
1 JOE McKETHEN, MONTANA ST. (vs. OKLAHOMA A&M)   14
2 AL McGUIRE, ST. JOHN'S (vs. N.C. STATE)   12
3 4 tied for third place.

Most free throws attempted in the tournament
1 DON SUNDERLAGE, ILLINOIS   34
2 BILL SPIVEY, KENTUCKY   25
2 ROD FLETCHER, ILLINOIS   25
4 FRANK RAMSEY, KENTUCKY   22
4 BILL KUKOY, N.C. STATE   22

Highest free throw percentage in a single game (minimum 7 attempts)
1 BILL KUKOY, N.C. STATE (vs. ST. JOHN'S) (10-10)   1.000
2 BOB HOUBREGS, WASHINGTON (vs. OKLAHOMA A&M) (7-7)   1.000
3 DON SUNDERLAGE, ILLINOIS (vs. OKLAHOMA A&M) (9-10)   .900
4 3 tied for fourth place.

Highest free throw percentage in the tournament (minimum 15 attempts)
1 BILL KUKOY, N.C. STATE (19-22)   .864
2 JERRY ROMNEY, BRIGHAM YOUNG (14-17)   .824
3 DON SUNDERLAGE, ILLINOIS (27-34)   .794
4 BILL SPIVEY, KENTUCKY (18-25)   .720
5 DON JOHNSON, OKLAHOMA A&M (10-15)   .667

✪ TEAM RECORDS ✪

SCORING

Most points in a single game
1 ILLINOIS (vs. N.C. STATE)   84
2 WASHINGTON (vs. BRIGHAM YOUNG)   80
3 2 tied for third place.

Most total points in the tournament
1 ILLINOIS   298
2 KENTUCKY   282
3 KANSAS STATE   251

Highest scoring average (minimum 2 games)
1 ILLINOIS (298-4)   74.50
2 KENTUCKY (282-4)   70.50
3 WASHINGTON (199-3)   66.33

FIELD GOALS

Most field goals in a single game
1 ILLINOIS (vs. N.C. STATE)   38
2 WASHINGTON (vs. BRIGHAM YOUNG)   35
3 KENTUCKY (vs. ILLINOIS)   32

Most total field goals in the tournament
1 KENTUCKY   113
2 ILLINOIS   110
3 KANSAS STATE   99

Most field goals attempted in a single game
1 KENTUCKY (vs. ILLINOIS)   91
2 KENTUCKY (vs. LOUISVILLE)   89
3 2 tied for third place.

Most total field goals attempted in the tournament
1 KENTUCKY   321

2 ILLINOIS   293
3 KANSAS STATE   266

Highest field goal percentage in a single game
1 OKLAHOMA A&M (vs. WASHINGTON) (22-40)
                                           .550
2 KANSAS STATE (vs. OKLAHOMA A&M) (26-54)
                                           .482
3 KANSAS STATE (vs. BRIGHAM YOUNG) (26-59)
                                           .441

**Highest field goal percentage in the tournament
(minimum 2 games)**
1 ILLINOIS (110-293)   .376
2 KANSAS STATE (99-266)   .372
3 WASHINGTON (80-216)   .371

FREE THROWS

Most free throws in a single game
1 ILLINOIS (vs. OKLAHOMA A&M)   29
2 ILLINOIS (vs. KENTUCKY)   22
3 KENTUCKY (vs. LOUISVILLE)   21

Most total free throws in the tournament
1 ILLINOIS   78
2 KENTUCKY   56
3 KANSAS STATE   53

Most free throws attempted in a single game
1 ILLINOIS (vs. OKLAHOMA A&M)   36
2 ILLINOIS (vs. KENTUCKY)   35
3 2 tied for third place.

Most total free throws attempted in the tournament
1 ILLINOIS   109
2 KENTUCKY   90
2 KANSAS STATE   90

Highest free throw percentage in a single game
1 N.C. STATE (vs. ST. JOHN'S) (19-20)   .950
2 COLUMBIA (vs. ILLINOIS) (15-17)   .882
3 OKLAHOMA A&M (vs. KANSAS STATE) (12-14)
                                           .857

**Highest free throw percentage in the tournament
(minimum 2 games)**
1 OKLAHOMA A&M (49-67)   .731
2 N.C. STATE (48-66)   .727
3 ILLINOIS (78-109)   .716

Fewest free throws in a single game
1 TEXAS A&M (vs. WASHINGTON)   6
1 LOUISVILLE (vs. KENTUCKY)   6
3 ILLINOIS (vs. N.C. STATE)   8

Lowest free throw percentage in a single game
1 LOUISVILLE (vs. KENTUCKY) (6-18)   .333
2 BRIGHAM YOUNG (vs. SAN JOSE ST.) (10-22)
                                           .455
3 TEXAS A&M (vs. WASHINGTON) (6-13)   .462

**Lowest free throw percentage in the tournament
(minimum 2 games)**
1 BRIGHAM YOUNG (37-64)   .578
2 KANSAS STATE (53-90)   .589
3 WASHINGTON (39-64)   .609

1952

REGIONAL SEMIFINAL | REGIONAL FINAL | **FINAL FOUR** | REGIONAL FINAL | REGIONAL SEMIFINAL

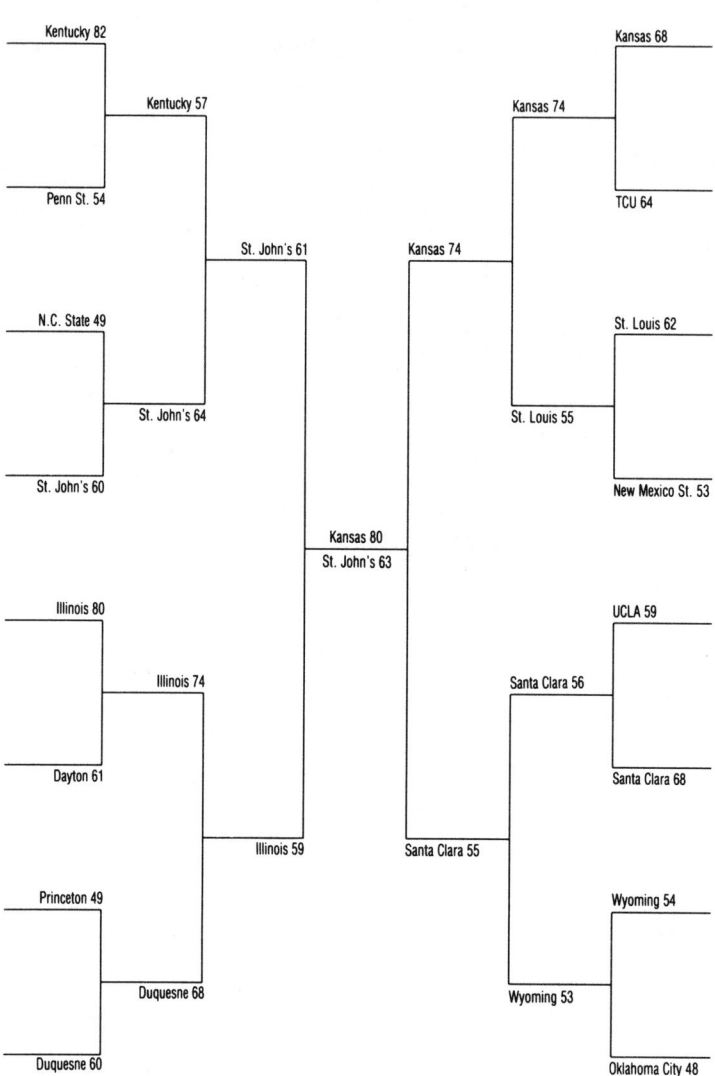

EAST

Kentucky 82
Kentucky 57
Penn St. 54
St. John's 61
N.C. State 49
St. John's 64
St. John's 60

Illinois 80
Illinois 74
Dayton 61
Illinois 59

Princeton 49
Duquesne 68
Duquesne 60

Kansas 80
St. John's 63

WEST

Kansas 68
Kansas 74
TCU 64
Kansas 74
St. Louis 62
St. Louis 55
New Mexico St. 53

UCLA 59
Santa Clara 56
Santa Clara 68
Santa Clara 55

Wyoming 54
Wyoming 53
Oklahoma City 48

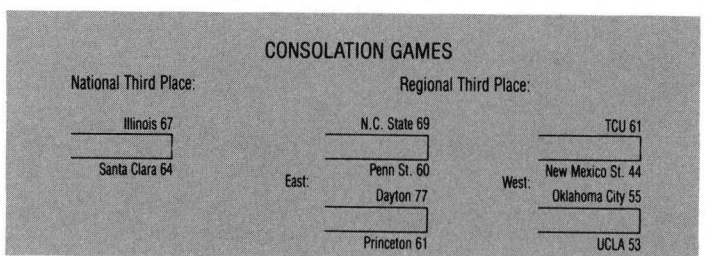

CONSOLATION GAMES

National Third Place: **Regional Third Place:**

Illinois 67
Santa Clara 64

East:
N.C. State 69
Penn St. 60
Dayton 77
Princeton 61

West:
TCU 61
New Mexico St. 44
Oklahoma City 55
UCLA 53

By 1952, University of Kansas coach Dr. F. C. "Phog" Allen, who had long had the reputation of being both a master strategist and a master of hot air, was well known for advocating raising the baskets to 12 feet in order to neutralize the big man's advantage. But that year he fell notably silent on the issue—and for good reason. Four years earlier Allen had bagged Indiana schoolboy Clyde Lovellette when he outrecruited his former student, Kentucky coach Adolph Rupp, as well as the boy's home-state Hoosiers. Now the 6-9, 240-pound Lovellette was clearly the most dominant big man in the game.

In the opening round, the third-ranked Jayhawks withstood a furious fourth-quarter rally, holding on to beat the Horned Frogs of Texas Christian University 68–64. Lovellette merely tied the all-time NCAA single-game scoring record with 31, after forcing TCU star George McLeod to foul out in the opening stanza.

Next, Cumulous Clyde wreaked his destruction on the unsuspecting St. Louis Billikens. St. Louis led 14-8 after the first quarter, but then Lovellette began raising his hands and calling for the ball in the low post and his teammates responded. By halftime Kansas had tied the score, and Lovellette had 19 points. But the Kansas juggernaut had just begun: in the second half the Jayhawk star added another 25 to finish with 44 points—carrying his team into the semifinals by a score of 74-55.

In the semis against Santa Clara, Clyde provided more of the same. The lightly regarded Broncos were everybody's favorite underdogs—they had already upset Western powers UCLA and Wyoming—but Clyde and the Jayhawks showed no mercy. Kansas's junior guards, defensive whiz Dean Kelley and lightning quick Charlie Hoag, each scored ten points, but again the big story was the big man. Lovellette scored 33 points and added 18 rebounds to pummel the Broncos and power Kansas into the title game.

The Jayhawks' opponent in the championship game was St. John's of Brooklyn. Cast in the role of giant killers, coach Frank McGuire's Redmen had already ended top-ranked Kentucky's 23-game winning streak behind their 6-6 center Joe Zawoluk's 32 points (avenging an early-season 81–40 thrashing in Lexington). They then outlasted second-ranked Illinois to get to the finals.

The Redmen beat No. 1 and No. 2, but they were no match for Big Clyde and his teammates. Despite an aggressive St. John's full-court press, Kansas led from start to finish en route to a final-game scoring record and an 80-63 victory. Zawoluk, who had carried the New Yorkers past Kentucky and Illinois, scored 20 points, but he, too, was overwhelmed, as Lovellette finished with 33. After the game Joe Zawoluk summed up the difference in three words: "He's too big."

On the broad back of his towering terror from Terre Haute, Phog Allen, the 66-year-old coach of Kansas, won his first—and only—NCAA title. Lovellette, meanwhile, single-handedly rewrote the tourney record books: he scored 141 points, breaking the old record of 83 (his per-game average of 35¼ points was easily higher than the previous single high game total); his 69 rebounds, 53 field goals, and 35 free throws were all new records; and he set single game marks for points (44), field goals (16), and free throws (12). After the tournament, Allen pronounced Lovellette the "greatest player the game has produced." For what may have been the first and last time in Allen's long career, no one argued.

REGIONAL SEMIFINAL EAST

Kentucky (82) Coach: Adolph Rupp

	Min.	Total FG/FGA	Pct.	FT/FTA	Pct.	Reb. O/T	A	TO	PF	S	Blk	TP	PPM
LINVILLE, S.	-	6/ -	-	0/ 0	.000	-/ -	-	-	1	-	-	12	-
TSIOROPOULOS, L.	-	2/ -	-	3/ 6	.500	-/ -	-	-	5	-	-	7	-
WHITAKER, L.	-	5/ -	-	0/ 0	.000	-/ -	-	-	5	-	-	10	-
NEFF	-	1/ -	-	0/ 0	.000	-/ -	-	-	0	-	-	2	-
EVANS, B.	-	2/ -	-	1/ 2	.500	-/ -	-	-	2	-	-	5	-
HAGAN, C.	-	9/ -	-	2/ 2	1.000	-/ -	-	-	3	-	-	20	-
CLARK	-	0/ -	-	0/ 2	.000	-/ -	-	-	0	-	-	0	-
ROSE, G.	-	2/ -	-	2/ 2	1.000	-/ -	-	-	0	-	-	6	-
RAMSEY, F.	-	4/ -	-	3/ 3	1.000	-/ -	-	-	3	-	-	11	-
ROUSE, W.	-	0/ -	-	1/ 2	.500	-/ -	-	-	2	-	-	1	-
WATSON, R.	-	4/ -	-	0/ 1	.000	-/ -	-	-	0	-	-	8	-
Totals	200	35/ -	-	12/20	.600	-/ -	-	-	21	-	-	82	.410

Penn State (54) Coach: Elmer Gross

	Min.	Total FG/FGA	Pct.	FT/FTA	Pct.	Reb. O/T	A	TO	PF	S	Blk	TP	PPM
WEIDENHAMMER, R.	-	1/ -	-	0/ 1	.000	-/ -	-	-	1	-	-	2	-
PIORKOWSKI	-	0/ -	-	1/ 1	1.000	-/ -	-	-	3	-	-	1	-
WILLIAMS	-	0/ -	-	2/ 5	.400	-/ -	-	-	0	-	-	2	-
SHERRY, J.	-	4/ -	-	2/ 4	.500	-/ -	-	-	3	-	-	10	-
MCMAHAN	-	1/ -	-	0/ 0	.000	-/ -	-	-	2	-	-	2	-
ARNELLE	-	8/ -	-	6/10	.600	-/ -	-	-	5	-	-	22	-
HAAG, E.	-	1/ -	-	1/ 2	.500	-/ -	-	-	1	-	-	3	-
SLEDZIK	-	4/ -	-	4/ 7	.571	-/ -	-	-	5	-	-	12	-
Totals	200	19/ -	-	16/30	.533	-/ -	-	-	20	-	-	54	.270

Disqualified: Kentucky—Tsioropolous, Whitaker; Penn State—Arnelle, Sledzik.

	1st Half	2nd Half	Final
Kentucky	43	39	82
Penn State	25	29	54

North Carolina State (49) Coach: Everett Case

	Min.	Total FG/FGA	Pct.	FT/FTA	Pct.	Reb. O/T	A	TO	PF	S	Blk	TP	PPM
TYLER, D.	-	3/ -	-	2/ 3	.667	-/ -	-	-	5	-	-	8	-
SPEIGHT, B.	-	1/ -	-	3/ 3	1.000	-/ -	-	-	3	-	-	5	-
BRANDENBURG	-	0/ -	-	1/ 2	.500	-/ -	-	-	0	-	-	1	-
KUKOY	-	1/ -	-	1/ 2	.500	-/ -	-	-	5	-	-	3	-
COOK, B.	-	1/ -	-	0/ 0	.000	-/ -	-	-	2	-	-	2	-
THOMPSON, M.	-	3/ -	-	0/ 1	.000	-/ -	-	-	3	-	-	6	-
KNAPP	-	1/ -	-	1/ 2	.500	-/ -	-	-	1	-	-	3	-
GOSS	-	0/ -	-	0/ 0	.000	-/ -	-	-	1	-	-	0	-
TERRILL, L.	-	4/ -	-	0/ 1	.000	-/ -	-	-	4	-	-	8	-
GOTKIN, D.	-	5/ -	-	3/ 3	1.000	-/ -	-	-	1	-	-	13	-
YURIN, B.	-	0/ -	-	0/ 2	.000	-/ -	-	-	1	-	-	0	-
APPLEBAUM	-	0/ -	-	0/ 0	.000	-/ -	-	-	1	-	-	0	-
Totals	200	19/ -	-	11/19	.579	-/ -	-	-	27	-	-	49	.245

St. John's (60) Coach: Frank McGuire

	Min.	Total FG/FGA	Pct.	FT/FTA	Pct.	Reb. O/T	A	TO	PF	S	Blk	TP	PPM
MCMAHON, J.	-	3/ -	-	5/ 8	.625	-/ -	-	-	5	-	-	11	-
DAVIS, J.	-	5/ -	-	0/ 2	.000	-/ -	-	-	4	-	-	10	-
PETERSON, C.	-	0/ -	-	0/ 0	.000	-/ -	-	-	0	-	-	0	-
GIANCONTIERI, F.	-	0/ -	-	1/ 2	.500	-/ -	-	-	0	-	-	1	-
ZAWOLUK, B.	-	5/ -	-	2/ 2	1.000	-/ -	-	-	3	-	-	12	-
WALSH, J.	-	1/ -	-	4/ 4	1.000	-/ -	-	-	3	-	-	6	-
WALKER, S.	-	1/ -	-	0/ 0	.000	-/ -	-	-	4	-	-	2	-
MACGILVRAY, R.	-	1/ -	-	5/ 6	.833	-/ -	-	-	3	-	-	7	-
DUCKETT, D.	-	5/ -	-	1/ 4	.250	-/ -	-	-	3	-	-	11	-
MCMORROW, J.	-	0/ -	-	0/ 0	.000	-/ -	-	-	0	-	-	0	-
Totals	200	21/ -	-	18/28	.643	-/ -	-	-	25	-	-	60	.300

Disqualified: St. John's—McMahon; N.C. State—Tyler, Kukoy.

	1st Qtr.	2nd Qtr.	3rd Qtr.	4th Qtr.	Final
N.C. State	10	15	8	16	49
St. John's	10	18	19	13	60

Illinois (80) Coach: Harry Combes

	Min.	Total FG/FGA	Pct.	FT/FTA	Pct.	Reb. O/T	A	TO	PF	S	Blk	TP	PPM
FOLLMER, C.	-	4/ -	-	3/ 5	.600	-/ -	-	-	1	-	-	11	-
BEMORAS, I.	-	4/ -	-	3/ 3	1.000	-/ -	-	-	4	-	-	11	-
KERR, J.	-	5/ -	-	3/ 9	.333	-/ -	-	-	2	-	-	13	-
BREDAR, J.	-	5/ -	-	9/11	.818	-/ -	-	-	2	-	-	19	-
FLETCHER, R.	-	4/ -	-	4/ 7	.571	-/ -	-	-	2	-	-	12	-
PETERSON, B.	-	1/ -	-	4/ 5	.800	-/ -	-	-	5	-	-	6	-
GERECKE, H.	-	0/ -	-	0/ 0	.000	-/ -	-	-	1	-	-	0	-
HOOPER, M.	-	1/ -	-	0/ 0	.000	-/ -	-	-	0	-	-	2	-
CHRISTIANSEN, D.	-	0/ -	-	0/ 0	.000	-/ -	-	-	0	-	-	0	-
FOLLMER, M.	-	0/ -	-	2/ 3	.667	-/ -	-	-	0	-	-	2	-
MAKOVSKY, E.	-	0/ -	-	4/ 4	1.000	-/ -	-	-	2	-	-	4	-
WRIGHT, J.	-	0/ -	-	0/ 0	.000	-/ -	-	-	1	-	-	0	-
Totals	200	24/ -	-	32/47	.681	-/ -	-	-	20	-	-	80	.400

Dayton (61) Coach: Tom Blackburn

	Min.	Total FG/FGA	Pct.	FT/FTA	Pct.	Reb. O/T	A	TO	PF	S	Blk	TP	PPM
GRIGSBY, C.	-	8/ -	-	5/ 6	.833	-/ -	-	-	5	-	-	21	-
HORAN, J.	-	4/ -	-	0/ 0	.000	-/ -	-	-	5	-	-	8	-
MEINEKE, D.	-	6/ -	-	6/ 8	.750	-/ -	-	-	5	-	-	18	-
BOYLE, P.	-	0/ -	-	1/ 2	.500	-/ -	-	-	5	-	-	1	-
NORRIS, L.	-	1/ -	-	1/ 1	1.000	-/ -	-	-	5	-	-	3	-
DONOHER, D.	-	2/ -	-	0/ 0	.000	-/ -	-	-	3	-	-	4	-
PAXSON, J.	-	3/ -	-	0/ 1	.000	-/ -	-	-	2	-	-	6	-
SALLEE, J.	-	0/ -	-	0/ 0	.000	-/ -	-	-	1	-	-	0	-
TAYLOR, B.	-	0/ -	-	0/ 0	.000	-/ -	-	-	2	-	-	0	-
WOYWOD, G.	-	0/ -	-	0/ 0	.000	-/ -	-	-	4	-	-	0	-
PEDICORD, L.	-	0/ -	-	0/ 0	.000	-/ -	-	-	1	-	-	0	-
HARRIS, C.	-	0/ -	-	0/ 0	.000	-/ -	-	-	3	-	-	0	-
Totals	200	24/ -	-	13/18	.722	-/ -	-	-	41	-	-	61	.305

Disqualified: Illinois—Peterson; Dayton—Grigsby, Horan, Meineke, Boyle, Norris.

	1st Qtr.	2nd Qtr.	3rd Qtr.	4th Qtr.	Final
Illinois	18	18	21	23	80
Dayton	14	23	12	12	61

Princeton (49) Coach: Franklin Cappon

	Min.	Total FG/FGA	Pct.	FT/FTA	Pct.	Reb. O/T	A	TO	PF	S	Blk	TP	PPM
SISLER, D.	-	3/ -	-	1/ 1	1.000	-/ -	-	-	2	-	-	7	-
TRITSCHLER, F.	-	1/ -	-	2/ 2	1.000	-/ -	-	-	2	-	-	4	-
EMERY, J.	-	0/ -	-	0/ 0	.000	-/ -	-	-	0	-	-	0	-
COOPER, F.	-	1/ -	-	2/ 3	.667	-/ -	-	-	4	-	-	4	-
DEVOE, C.	-	9/ -	-	5/ 8	.625	-/ -	-	-	2	-	-	23	-
ZURAVLEFF, P.	-	5/ -	-	1/ 2	.500	-/ -	-	-	5	-	-	11	-
Totals	200	19/ -	-	11/16	-	-/ -	-	-	15	-	-	49	.245

Duquesne (60) Coach: Dudey Moore

	Min.	Total FG/FGA	Pct.	FT/FTA	Pct.	Reb. O/T	A	TO	PF	S	Blk	TP	PPM
KENNEDY, J.	-	8/ -	-	0/ 0	.000	-/ -	-	-	3	-	-	16	-
RICKETTS, D.	-	6/ -	-	2/ 4	.500	-/ -	-	-	2	-	-	14	-
CERRA, H.	-	2/ -	-	0/ 0	.000	-/ -	-	-	0	-	-	4	-
TUCKER, J.	-	4/ -	-	3/ 3	1.000	-/ -	-	-	3	-	-	11	-
PACACHA, C.	-	3/ -	-	4/ 5	.800	-/ -	-	-	0	-	-	10	-
GARAY, S.	-	1/ -	-	2/ 2	1.000	-/ -	-	-	1	-	-	4	-
BAILEY, A.	-	0/ -	-	1/ 1	1.000	-/ -	-	-	4	-	-	1	-
Totals	200	24/ -	-	12/15	.800	-/ -	-	-	13	-	-	60	.300

Disqualified: Princeton—Zuravleff.

	1st Qtr.	2nd Qtr.	3rd Qtr.	4th Qtr.	Final
Princeton	14	10	14	11	49
Duquesne	16	12	11	21	60

REGIONAL SEMIFINAL WEST

Kansas (68) Coach: Phog Allen

	Min.	Total FG / FGA	Pct.	FT / FTA	Pct.	Reb. O / T	A	TO	PF	S	Blk	TP	PPM
KENNEY, R.	-	7/12	.583	3/ 7	.429	-/ -	-	-	2	-	-	17	-
LIENHARD, W.	-	1/ 3	.333	1/ 1	1.000	-/ -	-	-	5	-	-	3	-
DAVENPORT, L.	-	0/ 2	.000	0/ 0	.000	-/ -	-	-	0	-	-	0	-
KELLER, J.	-	1/ 7	.143	1/ 2	.500	-/ -	-	-	1	-	-	3	-
LOVELLETTE, C.	-	13/33	.394	5/ 7	.714	-/ -	-	-	4	-	-	31	-
BORN, B.	-	1/ 1	1.000	0/ 0	.000	-/ -	-	-	2	-	-	2	-
KELLEY, A.	-	0/ 0	-	0/ 1	1.000	-/ -	-	-	0	-	-	0	-
KELLEY, D.	-	1/ 4	.250	2/ 2	1.000	-/ -	-	-	2	-	-	4	-
HOAG, C.	-	2/ 8	.250	0/ 1	.000	-/ -	-	-	0	-	-	4	-
SMITH, D.	-	1/ 1	1.000	0/ 0	.000	-/ -	-	-	2	-	-	2	-
HOUGLAND, W.	-	1/ 1	1.000	0/ 0	.000	-/ -	-	-	1	-	-	2	-
HEITHOLT, B.	-	0/ 3	.000	0/ 1	.000	-/ -	-	-	0	-	-	0	-
Totals	200	28/75	.373	12/22	.545	-/ -	-	-	19	-	-	68	.340

UCLA (59) Coach: John Wooden

	Min.	Total FG / FGA	Pct.	FT / FTA	Pct.	Reb. O / T	A	TO	PF	S	Blk	TP	PPM
MOORE, J.	-	2/ 7	.286	2/ 2	1.000	-/ 3	0	-	5	-	-	6	-
NORMAN, J.	-	2/12	.167	0/ 0	.000	-/ 6	2	-	2	-	-	4	-
HIBLER, M.	-	3/ 8	.375	2/ 4	.500	-/ 8	0	-	5	-	-	8	-
JOHNSON, D.	-	2/16	.125	1/ 1	1.000	-/ 4	3	-	2	-	-	5	-
LIVINGSTON, R.	-	4/16	.250	6/ 6	1.000	-/ 4	3	-	1	-	-	14	-
PORTER, B.	-	0/ 6	.000	0/ 0	.000	-/ 2	1	-	0	-	-	0	-
BANE, R.	-	3/ 6	.500	7/ 8	.875	-/ 2	0	-	1	-	-	13	-
BRAGG, D.	-	3/10	.300	1/ 1	1.000	-/11	0	-	4	-	-	7	-
EVANS, J.	-	0/ 0	-	0/ 0	.000	-/ 0	0	-	0	-	-	0	-
DAVIDSON, J.	-	0/ 1	.000	0/ 0	.000	-/ 0	0	-	1	-	-	0	-
POUNDS, B.	-	0/ 2	.000	0/ 0	.000	-/ 0	0	-	1	-	-	0	-
COSTELLO, M.	-	1/ 1	1.000	0/ 0	.000	-/ 1	0	-	0	-	-	2	-
Totals	200	20/85	.235	19/22	.864	-/41	9	-	22	-	-	59	.295

TCU (64) Coach: Buster Brannon

	Min.	Total FG / FGA	Pct.	FT / FTA	Pct.	Reb. O / T	A	TO	PF	S	Blk	TP	PPM
FROMME	-	1/ 7	.143	1/ 3	.333	-/ -	-	-	5	-	-	3	-
KNOX	-	2/ 5	.400	0/ 0	.000	-/ -	-	-	1	-	-	4	-
REYNOLDS	-	3/12	.250	2/ 6	.333	-/ -	-	-	1	-	-	8	-
ALLEN	-	1/ 2	.500	0/ 2	.000	-/ -	-	-	2	-	-	2	-
MCLEOD, G.	-	3/ 7	.429	1/ 1	1.000	-/ -	-	-	5	-	-	7	-
OHLEN, H.	-	8/20	.400	4/ 6	.667	-/ -	-	-	2	-	-	20	-
ETHRIDGE, J.	-	4/13	.308	2/ 2	1.000	-/ -	-	-	1	-	-	10	-
SWAIN	-	3/ 5	.600	1/ 1	1.000	-/ -	-	-	2	-	-	7	-
KILPATRICK	-	1/ 7	.143	1/ 1	1.000	-/ -	-	-	5	-	-	3	-
CAMPBELL	-	0/ 0	.000	0/ 0	.000	-/ -	-	-	0	-	-	0	-
Totals	200	26/78	.333	12/22	.545	-/ -	-	-	24	-	-	64	.320

Disqualified: Kansas—Lienhard; TCU—Fromme, McLeod, Kilpatrick.

	1st Qtr.	2nd Qtr.	3rd Qtr.	4th Qtr.	Final
Kansas	20	14	24	10	68
TCU	13	11	18	22	64

Santa Clara (68) Coach: Bob Feerick

	Min.	Total FG / FGA	Pct.	FT / FTA	Pct.	Reb. O / T	A	TO	PF	S	Blk	TP	PPM
YOUNG, J.	-	7/16	.438	1/ 2	.500	-/ 5	2	-	1	-	-	15	-
SEARS, K.	-	3/12	.250	3/ 3	1.000	-/11	3	-	4	-	-	9	-
SCHOENSTEIN, H.	-	7/16	.438	4/ 8	.500	-/11	1	-	4	-	-	18	-
PETERS, B.	-	3/ 7	.429	1/ 2	.500	-/ 7	0	-	5	-	-	7	-
BROCK, D.	-	3/11	.273	0/ 1	.000	-/ 4	4	-	2	-	-	6	-
BENEDETTI, D.	-	1/ 5	.200	0/ 1	.000	-/ 2	0	-	0	-	-	2	-
GARIBALDI, D.	-	4/10	.400	1/ 4	.250	-/ 9	4	-	2	-	-	9	-
SOARES, D.	-	1/ 3	.333	0/ 0	.000	-/ 0	0	-	2	-	-	2	-
Totals	200	29/80	.363	10/21	.476	-/49	14	-	20	-	-	68	.340

Disqualified: Santa Clara—Peters; UCLA—Hibler, Moore. Techical fouls: Santa Clara—Soares; UCLA—Norman, Livingston.

	1st Half	2nd Half	Final
UCLA	35	24	59
Santa Clara	31	37	68

St. Louis (62) Coach: Eddie Hickey

	Min.	Total FG / FGA	Pct.	FT / FTA	Pct.	Reb. O / T	A	TO	PF	S	Blk	TP	PPM
KOVAR	-	1/ -	-	0/ 1	.000	-/ -	-	-	3	-	-	2	-
BOUSHKA	-	2/ -	-	4/ 5	.800	-/ -	-	-	2	-	-	8	-
LILLIS, H.	-	0/ -	-	0/ 0	.000	-/ -	-	-	1	-	-	0	-
SONNENBERG	-	1/ -	-	0/ 1	.000	-/ -	-	-	4	-	-	2	-
LILLIS, T.	-	3/ -	-	1/ 2	.500	-/ -	-	-	5	-	-	7	-
KOCH, J.	-	1/ -	-	0/ 0	.000	-/ -	-	-	3	-	-	2	-
KOCH, B.	-	1/ -	-	2/ 3	.667	-/ -	-	-	5	-	-	4	-
SHOCKLEY	-	2/ -	-	1/ 1	1.000	-/ -	-	-	1	-	-	5	-
STEINER	-	4/ -	-	2/ 3	.667	-/ -	-	-	2	-	-	10	-
MCKENNA	-	9/ -	-	4/ 6	.667	-/ -	-	-	3	-	-	22	-
PARTINGTON	-	0/ -	-	0/ 0	.000	-/ -	-	-	0	-	-	0	-
KLOSTMEYER	-	0/ -	-	0/ 0	.000	-/ -	-	-	0	-	-	0	-
Totals	200	24/ -	-	14/22	.636	-/ -	-	-	29	-	-	62	.310

New Mexico State (53) Coach: George McCarthy

	Min.	Total FG / FGA	Pct.	FT / FTA	Pct.	Reb. O / T	A	TO	PF	S	Blk	TP	PPM
PRIDDY	-	2/ -	-	2/ 4	.500	-/ -	-	-	3	-	-	6	-
TACKETT	-	8/ -	-	5/ 9	.556	-/ -	-	-	2	-	-	21	-
SVILAR	-	3/ -	-	3/ 4	.750	-/ -	-	-	5	-	-	9	-
BLEVINS	-	1/ -	-	1/ 2	.500	-/ -	-	-	5	-	-	3	-
CROUCH	-	2/ -	-	2/ 2	1.000	-/ -	-	-	3	-	-	6	-
COATS	-	0/ -	-	1/ 1	1.000	-/ -	-	-	1	-	-	1	-
CLEMENT	-	2/ -	-	1/ 1	1.000	-/ -	-	-	5	-	-	5	-
DUNN	-	1/ -	-	0/ 0	.000	-/ -	-	-	1	-	-	2	-
APODACA	-	0/ -	-	0/ 0	.000	-/ -	-	-	0	-	-	0	-
Totals	200	19/ -	-	15/23	.652	-/ -	-	-	25	-	-	53	.265

Disqualified: St. Louis—T. Lillis, B. Koch; New Mexico St.— Svilar, Blevins, Clement.

	1st Qtr.	2nd Qtr.	3rd Qtr.	4th Qtr.	Final
St. Louis	16	19	12	15	62
New Mexico St.	13	13	19	8	53

Wyoming (54) Coach: Everett Shelton

	Min.	Total FG / FGA	Pct.	FT / FTA	Pct.	Reb. O / T	A	TO	PF	S	Blk	TP	PPM
HAAG, R.	-	1/ -	-	0/ 1	.000	-/ -	-	-	0	-	-	2	-
ESAU, L.	-	4/ -	-	1/ 1	1.000	-/ -	-	-	2	-	-	9	-
FOWLER, P.	-	4/ -	-	0/ 0	.000	-/ -	-	-	2	-	-	8	-
ELIOPULOS, N.	-	0/ -	-	0/ 0	.000	-/ -	-	-	0	-	-	0	-
HUGHES, J.	-	1/ -	-	5/ 6	.833	-/ -	-	-	3	-	-	7	-
RIVERS, R.	-	4/ -	-	3/ 4	.750	-/ -	-	-	2	-	-	11	-
RADOVICH, G.	-	4/ -	-	5/ 6	.833	-/ -	-	-	2	-	-	13	-
SAMUELSON, M.	-	2/ -	-	0/ 0	.000	-/ -	-	-	4	-	-	4	-
BURNS, R.	-	0/ -	-	0/ 0	.000	-/ -	-	-	0	-	-	0	-
Totals	200	20/59	.339	14/18	.778	-/ -	-	-	15	-	-	54	.270

Oklahoma City (48) Coach: Doyle Parrack

	Min.	Total FG / FGA	Pct.	FT / FTA	Pct.	Reb. O / T	A	TO	PF	S	Blk	TP	PPM
LIKENS, A.	-	4/ -	-	2/ 2	1.000	-/ -	-	-	3	-	-	10	-
MAYFIELD, D.	-	2/ -	-	0/ 2	.000	-/ -	-	-	3	-	-	4	-
PENWELL, D.	-	8/ -	-	2/ 4	.500	-/ -	-	-	3	-	-	18	-
SHORT, A.	-	3/ -	-	2/ 3	.667	-/ -	-	-	0	-	-	8	-
ROSE, K.	-	3/ -	-	0/ 0	.000	-/ -	-	-	3	-	-	6	-
COUTS, B.	-	1/ -	-	0/ 1	.000	-/ -	-	-	3	-	-	2	-
THOMPSON, J.	-	0/ -	-	0/ 0	.000	-/ -	-	-	3	-	-	0	-
Totals	200	21/ -	-	6/12	.500	-/ -	-	-	18	-	-	48	.240

Disqualified: None.

	1st Qtr.	2nd Qtr.	3rd Qtr.	4th Qtr.	Final
Wyoming	16	13	17	8	54
Oklahoma City	12	9	13	14	48

REGIONAL FINAL EAST

Kentucky (57)   Coach: Adolph Rupp

	Min.	Total FG/FGA	Pct.	FT/FTA	Pct.	Reb. O/T	A	TO	PF	S	Blk	TP	PPM
TSIOROPOLOUS, L.	-	0/ -	-	0/ 0	.000	-/ -	-	-	5	-	-	0	-
WHITAKER, L.	-	3/ -	-	3/ 4	.750	-/ -	-	-	3	-	-	9	-
LINVILLE, S.	-	1/ -	-	2/ 3	.667	-/ -	-	-	3	-	-	4	-
ROUSE, W.	-	0/ -	-	0/ 0	.000	-/ -	-	-	0	-	-	0	-
HAGAN, C.	-	9/ -	-	4/ 5	.800	-/ -	-	-	5	-	-	22	-
ROSE, G.	-	1/ -	-	0/ 0	.000	-/ -	-	-	3	-	-	2	-
WATSON, R.	-	1/ -	-	2/ 2	1.000	-/ -	-	-	3	-	-	4	-
RAMSEY, F.	-	5/ -	-	4/ 6	.667	-/ -	-	-	5	-	-	14	-
EVANS, B.	-	1/ -	-	0/ 0	.000	-/ -	-	-	5	-	-	2	-
Totals	200	21/ -	-	15/20	.750	-/ -	-	-	32	-	-	57	.285

St. John's (64)   Coach: Frank McGuire

	Min.	Total FG/FGA	Pct.	FT/FTA	Pct.	Reb. O/T	A	TO	PF	S	Blk	TP	PPM
MCMAHON, J.	-	8/ -	-	2/ 5	.400	-/ -	-	-	2	-	-	18	-
DAVIS, J.	-	1/ -	-	0/ 1	.000	-/ -	-	-	2	-	-	2	-
ZAWOLUK, B.	-	12/ -	-	8/ 9	.889	-/ -	-	-	4	-	-	32	-
MACGILVRAY, R.	-	1/ -	-	3/ 4	.750	-/ -	-	-	1	-	-	5	-
DUCKETT, D.	-	1/ -	-	1/ 3	.333	-/ -	-	-	5	-	-	3	-
WALKER, S.	-	0/ -	-	0/ 1	.000	-/ -	-	-	4	-	-	0	-
WALSH, J.	-	1/ -	-	2/ 2	1.000	-/ -	-	-	5	-	-	4	-
Totals	200	24/ -	-	16/25	.640	-/ -	-	-	23	-	-	64	.320

Disqualified: St. John's—Walsh, Duckett; Kentucky—Tsioropolous, Hagan, Ramsey, Evans.

	1st Qtr.	2nd Qtr.	3rd Qtr.	4th Qtr.	Final
Kentucky	13	15	16	13	57
St. John's	21	13	20	10	64

Illinois (74)   Coach: Harry Combes

	Min.	Total FG/FGA	Pct.	FT/FTA	Pct.	Reb. O/T	A	TO	PF	S	Blk	TP	PPM
FOLLMER, C.	-	2/ -	-	8/ 9	.889	-/ -	-	-	4	-	-	12	-
BEMORAS, I.	-	7/ -	-	2/ 3	.667	-/ -	-	-	4	-	-	16	-
KERR, J.	-	3/ -	-	1/ 1	1.000	-/ -	-	-	3	-	-	7	-
PETERSON, B.	-	4/ -	-	0/ 2	.000	-/ -	-	-	3	-	-	8	-
BREDAR, J.	-	8/ -	-	0/ 1	.000	-/ -	-	-	1	-	-	16	-
FLETCHER, R.	-	5/ -	-	5/ 6	.833	-/ -	-	-	5	-	-	15	-
MAKOVSKY, E.	-	0/ -	-	0/ 0	.000	-/ -	-	-	1	-	-	0	-
Totals	200	29/ -	-	16/22	.727	-/ -	-	-	21	-	-	74	.370

Duquesne (68)   Coach: Dudey Moore

	Min.	Total FG/FGA	Pct.	FT/FTA	Pct.	Reb. O/T	A	TO	PF	S	Blk	TP	PPM
KENNEDY, J.	-	3/ -	-	2/ 2	1.000	-/ -	-	-	5	-	-	8	-
RICKETTS, D.	-	7/ -	-	8/ 9	.889	-/ -	-	-	4	-	-	22	-
RINGER, M.	-	0/ -	-	0/ 0	.000	-/ -	-	-	3	-	-	0	-
CERRA, H.	-	2/ -	-	0/ 2	.000	-/ -	-	-	5	-	-	4	-
NOSWORTHY, J.	-	1/ -	-	1/ 1	1.000	-/ -	-	-	0	-	-	3	-
TUCKER, J.	-	11/ -	-	7/ 7	1.000	-/ -	-	-	5	-	-	29	-
PACACHA, C.	-	1/ -	-	0/ 1	.000	-/ -	-	-	3	-	-	2	-
BAILEY, A.	-	0/ -	-	0/ 1	.000	-/ -	-	-	1	-	-	0	-
Totals	200	25/ -	-	18/23	.783	-/ -	-	-	26	-	-	68	.340

Disqualified: Illinois—Fletcher; Duquesne—Kennedy, Cerra, Tucker.

	1st Qtr.	2nd Qtr.	3rd Qtr.	4th Qtr.	Final
Illinois	21	16	19	18	74
Duquesne	19	15	18	16	68

REGIONAL FINAL WEST

Kansas (74)   Coach: Phog Allen

	Min.	Total FG/FGA	Pct.	FT/FTA	Pct.	Reb. O/T	A	TO	PF	S	Blk	TP	PPM
KELLER, J.	-	0/ -	-	1/ 2	.500	-/ -	-	-	1	-	-	1	-
KENNEY, R.	-	2/ -	-	2/ 3	.667	-/ -	-	-	4	-	-	6	-
DAVENPORT, L.	-	0/ -	-	0/ 0	.000	-/ -	-	-	0	-	-	0	-
LOVELLETTE, C.	-	16/ -	-	12/14	.857	-/ -	-	-	3	-	-	44	-
BORN, B.	-	0/ -	-	1/ 1	1.000	-/ -	-	-	0	-	-	1	-
HEITHOLT, B.	-	0/ -	-	0/ 0	.000	-/ -	-	-	0	-	-	0	-
HOUGLAND, W.	-	2/ -	-	1/ 1	1.000	-/ -	-	-	1	-	-	5	-
HOAG, C.	-	2/ -	-	3/ 3	1.000	-/ -	-	-	2	-	-	7	-
LIENHARD, W.	-	0/ -	-	0/ 0	.000	-/ -	-	-	1	-	-	0	-
KELLEY	-	4/ -	-	2/ 3	.667	-/ -	-	-	5	-	-	10	-
SMITH, D.	-	0/ -	-	0/ 0	.000	-/ -	-	-	0	-	-	0	-
SQUIRES, L.	-	0/ -	-	0/ 0	.000	-/ -	-	-	0	-	-	0	-
Totals	200	26/ -	-	22/27	.815	-/ -	-	-	17	-	-	74	.370

St. Louis (55)   Coach: Eddie Hickey

	Min.	Total FG/FGA	Pct.	FT/FTA	Pct.	Reb. O/T	A	TO	PF	S	Blk	TP	PPM
KOVAR	-	3/ -	-	4/ 5	.800	-/ -	-	-	2	-	-	10	-
KLOSTERMEYER	-	0/ -	-	0/ 0	.000	-/ -	-	-	1	-	-	0	-
PARTINGTON	-	1/ -	-	0/ 0	.000	-/ -	-	-	0	-	-	2	-
SONNENBERG	-	3/ -	-	2/ 3	.667	-/ -	-	-	2	-	-	8	-
BOUSHKA	-	0/ -	-	1/ 1	1.000	-/ -	-	-	2	-	-	1	-
SHOCKLEY	-	0/ -	-	0/ 0	.000	-/ -	-	-	1	-	-	0	-
KOCH, B.	-	1/ -	-	1/ 1	1.000	-/ -	-	-	5	-	-	3	-
LILLIS, T.	-	7/ -	-	0/ 2	.000	-/ -	-	-	5	-	-	14	-
LILLIS, H.	-	0/ -	-	0/ 0	.000	-/ -	-	-	0	-	-	0	-
STEINER	-	1/ -	-	0/ 1	.000	-/ -	-	-	3	-	-	2	-
KOCH, J.	-	2/ -	-	0/ 0	.000	-/ -	-	-	2	-	-	4	-
MCKENNA	-	4/ -	-	3/ 3	1.000	-/ -	-	-	4	-	-	11	-
Totals	200	22/ -	-	11/16	.688	-/ -	-	-	27	-	-	55	.275

Disqualified: Kansas—Kelley; St. Louis—B. Koch, T. Lillis.

	1st Qtr.	2nd Qtr.	3rd Qtr.	4th Qtr.	Final
Kansas	8	19	23	24	74
St. Louis	14	13	17	11	55

Santa Clara (56)   Coach: Bob Feerick

	Min.	Total FG/FGA	Pct.	FT/FTA	Pct.	Reb. O/T	A	TO	PF	S	Blk	TP	PPM
SEARS, K.	-	5/ -	-	4/ 4	1.000	-/ -	-	-	5	-	-	14	-
YOUNG, J.	-	5/ -	-	4/ 5	.800	-/ -	-	-	2	-	-	14	-
SOARES, D.	-	1/ -	-	2/ 2	1.000	-/ -	-	-	1	-	-	4	-
SHOENSTEIN, H.	-	5/ -	-	2/ 4	.500	-/ -	-	-	1	-	-	12	-
PETERS, B.	-	1/ -	-	1/ 1	1.000	-/ -	-	-	5	-	-	3	-
BROCK, D.	-	0/ -	-	0/ 3	.000	-/ -	-	-	3	-	-	0	-
GARIBALDI, D.	-	2/ -	-	1/ 2	.500	-/ -	-	-	3	-	-	5	-
BENEDETTI, D.	-	2/ -	-	0/ 1	.000	-/ -	-	-	2	-	-	4	-
Totals	200	21/57	.368	14/22	.636	-/ -	-	-	22	-	-	56	.280

Wyoming (53)   Coach: Everett Shelton

	Min.	Total FG/FGA	Pct.	FT/FTA	Pct.	Reb. O/T	A	TO	PF	S	Blk	TP	PPM
HAAG, R.	-	2/ -	-	0/ 0	.000	-/ -	-	-	5	-	-	4	-
BURNS, J.	-	1/ -	-	2/ 2	1.000	-/ -	-	-	3	-	-	4	-
FOWLER, P.	-	1/ -	-	0/ 1	.000	-/ -	-	-	4	-	-	2	-
ELIOPULOS, N.	-	0/ -	-	0/ 0	.000	-/ -	-	-	0	-	-	0	-
RIVERS, R.	-	2/ -	-	2/ 6	.333	-/ -	-	-	1	-	-	6	-
HUGHES, J.	-	0/ -	-	1/ 2	.500	-/ -	-	-	2	-	-	1	-
RADOVICH, G.	-	7/ -	-	4/ 5	.800	-/ -	-	-	2	-	-	18	-
SAMUELSON, M.	-	1/ -	-	3/ 3	1.000	-/ -	-	-	3	-	-	5	-
ESAU, L.	-	6/ -	-	1/ 3	.333	-/ -	-	-	5	-	-	13	-
RUTZ, L.	-	0/ -	-	0/ 0	.000	-/ -	-	-	1	-	-	0	-
Totals	200	20/75	.267	13/22	.591	-/ -	-	-	26	-	-	53	.265

Disqualified: Santa Clara—Sears, Peters; Wyoming—Haag, Esau.

	1st Qtr.	2nd Qtr.	3rd Qtr.	4th Qtr.	Final
Santa Clara	12	12	25	7	56
Wyoming	18	9	11	15	53

FINAL FOUR

St. John's (61) Coach: Frank McGuire

	Min.	Total FG / FGA	Pct.	FT / FTA	Pct.	Reb. O / T	A	TO	PF	S	Blk	TP	PPM
MCMAHON, J.	-	3/ -	-	3/ 3	1.000	-/ -	-	-	3	-	-	9	-
DAVIS, J.	-	1/ -	-	0/ 1	.000	-/ -	-	-	3	-	-	2	-
WALSH, J.	-	2/ -	-	0/ 1	.000	-/ -	-	-	4	-	-	4	-
PETERSON, C.	-	0/ -	-	0/ 0	.000	-/ -	-	-	0	-	-	0	-
ZAWOLUK, B.	-	9/ -	-	6/ 7	.857	-/ -	-	-	4	-	-	24	-
MACGILVRAY, R.	-	2/ -	-	2/ 3	.667	-/ -	-	-	2	-	-	6	-
DUCKETT, D.	-	4/ -	-	3/ 4	.750	-/ -	-	-	5	-	-	11	-
WALKER, S.	-	2/ -	-	1/ 1	1.000	-/ -	-	-	1	-	-	5	-
Totals	200	23/67	.343	15/20	.750	-/ -	-	-	22	-	-	61	.305

Illinois (59) Coach: Harry Combes

	Min.	Total FG / FGA	Pct.	FT / FTA	Pct.	Reb. O / T	A	TO	PF	S	Blk	TP	PPM
FOLLMER, C.	-	4/ -	-	2/ 4	.500	-/ -	-	-	3	-	-	10	-
BEMORAS, I.	-	1/ -	-	1/ 3	.333	-/ -	-	-	5	-	-	3	-
WRIGHT, J.	-	0/ -	-	0/ 0	.000	-/ -	-	-	2	-	-	0	-
PETERSON, B.	-	2/ -	-	0/ 3	.000	-/ -	-	-	4	-	-	4	-
KERR, J.	-	3/ -	-	2/ 5	.400	-/ -	-	-	1	-	-	8	-
BREDAR, J.	-	7/ -	-	0/ 1	.000	-/ -	-	-	1	-	-	14	-
FLETCHER, R.	-	5/ -	-	4/ 7	.571	-/ -	-	-	3	-	-	14	-
GERECKE, H.	-	3/ -	-	0/ 1	.000	-/ -	-	-	3	-	-	6	-
Totals	200	25/66	.379	9/24	.375	-/ -	-	-	22	-	-	59	.295

Disqualified: St. John's—Duckett; Illinois—Bemoras.

	1st Qtr.	2nd Qtr.	3rd Qtr.	4th Qtr.	Final
St. John's	18	15	10	18	61
Illinois	18	9	16	16	59

Kansas (74) Coach: Phog Allen

	Min.	Total FG / FGA	Pct.	FT / FTA	Pct.	Reb. O / T	A	TO	PF	S	Blk	TP	PPM
KENNEY, R.	-	3/11	.273	1/ 1	1.000	-/ -	-	-	0	-	-	7	-
LIENHARD, W.	-	0/ 1	.000	0/ 0	.000	-/ -	-	-	1	-	-	0	-
DAVENPORT, L.	-	0/ 2	.000	2/ 3	.667	-/ -	-	-	1	-	-	2	-
KELLER, J.	-	1/ 1	1.000	2/ 2	1.000	-/ -	-	-	2	-	-	4	-
LOVELLETTE, C.	-	12/22	.545	9/12	.750	-/ -	-	-	3	-	-	33	-
BORN, B.	-	1/ 1	1.000	2/ 3	.667	-/ -	-	-	1	-	-	4	-
KELLEY, A.	-	0/ 0	.000	0/ 0	.000	-/ -	-	-	0	-	-	0	-
KELLEY, D.	-	4/ 9	.444	2/ 4	.500	-/ -	-	-	0	-	-	10	-
HOAG, C.	-	4/ 5	.800	2/ 2	1.000	-/ -	-	-	0	-	-	10	-
SMITH, D.	-	0/ 0	.000	0/ 0	.000	-/ -	-	-	0	-	-	0	-
HEITHOLT, B.	-	2/ 4	.500	0/ 1	.000	-/ -	-	-	4	-	-	4	-
Totals	200	27/56	.482	20/28	.714	-/ -	-	-	12	-	-	74	.370

Santa Clara (55) Coach: Bob Feerick

	Min.	Total FG / FGA	Pct.	FT / FTA	Pct.	Reb. O / T	A	TO	PF	S	Blk	TP	PPM
YOUNG, J.	-	3/ 9	.333	2/ 3	.667	-/ -	-	-	1	-	-	8	-
SEARS, K.	-	0/ 3	.000	1/ 1	1.000	-/ -	-	-	5	-	-	1	-
SCHOENSTEIN, H.	-	6/18	.333	1/ 1	1.000	-/ -	-	-	4	-	-	13	-
PETERS, B.	-	1/ 4	.250	1/ 1	1.000	-/ -	-	-	1	-	-	3	-
BROCK, D.	-	3/ 6	.500	1/ 1	1.000	-/ -	-	-	2	-	-	7	-
BENEDETTI, D.	-	1/ 6	.167	0/ 0	.000	-/ -	-	-	1	-	-	2	-
GARIBALDI, D.	-	1/ 5	.200	0/ 0	.000	-/ -	-	-	4	-	-	2	-
SOARES, D.	-	7/12	.583	2/ 2	1.000	-/ -	-	-	3	-	-	16	-
SIMONI, J.	-	0/ 0	.000	0/ 1	.000	-/ -	-	-	0	-	-	0	-
GATZERT, G.	-	1/ 2	.500	1/ 2	.500	-/ -	-	-	2	-	-	3	-
Totals	200	23/65	.354	9/12	.750	-/ -	-	-	23	-	-	55	.275

Disqualified: Santa Clara—Sears.

	1st Qtr.	2nd Qtr.	3rd Qtr.	4th Qtr.	Final
Kansas	18	20	21	15	74
Santa Clara	10	15	14	16	55

NATIONAL CHAMPIONSHIP

St. John's (63) Coach: Frank McGuire

	Min.	Total FG / FGA	Pct.	FT / FTA	Pct.	Reb. O / T	A	TO	PF	S	Blk	TP	PPM
MCMAHON, J.	-	6/12	.500	1/ 4	.250	-/ 2	-	-	4	-	-	13	-
WALSH, J.	-	3/ 6	.500	0/ 0	.000	-/ 4	-	-	3	-	-	6	-
PETERSON, C.	-	0/ 1	.000	0/ 0	.000	-/ 0	-	-	0	-	-	0	-
ZAWOLUK, B.	-	7/12	.583	6/11	.545	-/ 9	-	-	5	-	-	20	-
MACGILVRAY, R.	-	3/ 8	.375	2/ 5	.400	-/10	-	-	3	-	-	8	-
DUCKETT, D.	-	2/ 5	.400	2/ 2	1.000	-/ 2	-	-	4	-	-	6	-
WALKER, S.	-	0/ 2	.000	0/ 0	.000	-/ 2	-	-	4	-	-	0	-
MCMORROW, J.	-	1/ 3	.333	0/ 0	.000	-/ 0	-	-	3	-	-	2	-
GIANCONTIERI, F.	-	0/ 0	.000	0/ 2	.000	-/ 1	-	-	0	-	-	0	-
SAGONA, P.	-	2/ 2	1.000	0/ 0	.000	-/ 0	-	-	5	-	-	4	-
DAVIS, J.	-	1/ 4	.250	2/ 3	.667	-/ 2	-	-	4	-	-	4	-
Totals	200	25/55	.455	13/27	.481	-/32	-	-	35	-	-	63	.315

Kansas (80) Coach: Phog Allen

	Min.	Total FG / FGA	Pct.	FT / FTA	Pct.	Reb. O / T	A	TO	PF	S	Blk	TP	PPM
KENNEY, R.	-	4/11	.364	4/ 6	.667	-/ 4	-	-	2	-	-	12	-
LIENHARD, W.	-	5/ 8	.625	2/ 2	1.000	-/ 4	-	-	4	-	-	12	-
DAVENPORT, L.	-	0/ 0	.000	0/ 0	.000	-/ 0	-	-	1	-	-	0	-
KELLER, J.	-	1/ 1	1.000	0/ 0	.000	-/ 4	-	-	2	-	-	2	-
LOVELLETTE, C.	-	12/25	.480	9/11	.818	-/17	-	-	4	-	-	33	-
BORN, B.	-	0/ 0	.000	0/ 0	.000	-/ 0	-	-	0	-	-	0	-
KELLEY, A.	-	0/ 2	.000	0/ 0	.000	-/ 1	-	-	0	-	-	0	-
KELLEY, D.	-	2/ 5	.400	3/ 6	.500	-/ 3	-	-	5	-	-	7	-
HOAG, C.	-	2/ 6	.333	5/ 7	.714	-/ 4	-	-	5	-	-	9	-
SMITH, D.	-	0/ 0	.000	0/ 0	.000	-/ -	-	-	0	-	-	0	-
HOUGLAND, W.	-	2/ 5	.400	1/ 3	.333	-/ 6	-	-	2	-	-	5	-
Totals	200	28/63	.444	24/35	.686	-/43	-	-	25	-	-	80	.400

Disqualified: Kansas—Hoag, D. Kelley; St. John's—Zawoluk, Sagona.

	1st Half	2nd Half	Final
St. John's	27	36	63
Kansas	41	39	80

NATIONAL THIRD PLACE

Illinois (67) Coach: Harry Combes

	Min.	Total FG/FGA	Pct.	FT/FTA	Pct.	Reb. O/T	A	TO	PF	S	Blk	TP	PPM
FOLLMER, C.	-	6/ -		5/ 5	1.000	-/ -	-	-	1	-	-	17	-
GERECKE, H.	-	2/ -		3/ 4	.750	-/ -	-	-	1	-	-	7	-
BEMORAS, I.	-	0/ -		3/ 4	.750	-/ -	-	-	0	-	-	3	-
PETERSON, B.	-	1/ -		3/ 5	.600	-/ -	-	-	0	-	-	5	-
KERR, J.	-	10/ -		6/ 7	.857	-/ -	-	-	3	-	-	26	-
FLETCHER, R.	-	1/ -		2/ 6	.333	-/ -	-	-	4	-	-	4	-
HOOPER, M.	-	1/ -		1/ 1	1.000	-/ -	-	-	3	-	-	3	-
BREDAR, J.	-	1/ -		0/ 0	.000	-/ -	-	-	5	-	-	2	-
WRIGHT, J.	-	0/ -		0/ 0	.000	-/ -	-	-	0	-	-	0	-
Totals	200	22/57	.386	23/32	.719	-/ -	-	-	17	-	-	67	.335

Santa Clara (64) Coach: Bob Feerick

	Min.	Total FG/FGA	Pct.	FT/FTA	Pct.	Reb. O/T	A	TO	PF	S	Blk	TP	PPM
SEARS, K.	-	4/ -		2/ 2	1.000	-/ -	-	-	4	-	-	10	
GATZERT, G.	-	1/ -		2/ 2	1.000	-/ -	-	-	4	-	-	4	
YOUNG, J.	-	6/ -		6/ 6	1.000	-/ -	-	-	4	-	-	18	
SCHOENSTEIN, H.	-	2/ -		4/ 4	1.000	-/ -	-	-	3	-	-	8	
SOARES, D.	-	2/ -		0/ 0	.000	-/ -	-	-	2	-	-	4	
PETERS, B.	-	4/ -		5/ 7	.714	-/ -	-	-	2	-	-	13	
BENEDETTI, D.	-	1/ -		0/ 0	.000	-/ -	-	-	0	-	-	2	
GARIBALDI, D.	-	0/ -		0/ 0	.000	-/ -	-	-	0	-	-	0	
BROCK, D.	-	2/ -		1/ 1	1.000	-/ -	-	-	2	-	-	5	
Totals	200	22/76	.289	20/22	.909	-/ -	-	-	21	-	-	64	.320

	1st Qtr.	2nd Qtr.	3rd Qtr.	4th Qtr.	Final
Illinois	12	20	20	15	67
Santa Clara	14	14	17	19	64

Disqualified: Illinois—Bredar

REGIONAL THIRD PLACE WEST

TCU (61) Coach: Buster Brannon

	Min.	Total FG/FGA	Pct.	FT/FTA	Pct.	Reb. O/T	A	TO	PF	S	Blk	TP	PPM
FROMME	-	4/ -		4/ 5	.800	-/ -	-	-	3	-	-	12	-
REYNOLDS	-	5/ -		1/ 3	.333	-/ -	-	-	4	-	-	11	-
ALLEN	-	0/ -		0/ 0	.000	-/ -	-	-	0	-	-	0	-
KNOX	-	0/ -		1/ 1	1.000	-/ -	-	-	3	-	-	1	-
MCLEOD, G.	-	4/ -		2/ 5	.400	-/ -	-	-	5	-	-	10	-
OHLEN, H.	-	2/ -		3/ 3	1.000	-/ -	-	-	1	-	-	7	-
ETHRIDGE, J.	-	3/ -		2/ 2	1.000	-/ -	-	-	4	-	-	8	-
SWAIN	-	2/ -		1/ 1	1.000	-/ -	-	-	3	-	-	5	-
TAYLOR, J.	-	0/ -		0/ 0	.000	-/ -	-	-	1	-	-	0	-
KILPATRICK	-	3/ -		1/ 1	1.000	-/ -	-	-	1	-	-	7	-
TAYLOR, T.	-	0/ -		0/ 0	.000	-/ -	-	-	0	-	-	0	-
Totals	200	23/ -		15/21	.714	-/ -	-	-	25	-	-	61	.305

New Mexico State (44) Coach: George McCarthy

	Min.	Total FG/FGA	Pct.	FT/FTA	Pct.	Reb. O/T	A	TO	PF	S	Blk	TP	PPM
PRIDDY	-	0/ -		1/ 2	.500	-/ -	-	-	2	-	-	1	-
VAUGHN	-	2/ -		0/ 0	.000	-/ -	-	-	0	-	-	4	-
COATS	-	1/ -		0/ 0	.000	-/ -	-	-	0	-	-	2	-
TACKETT	-	5/ -		4/ 5	.800	-/ -	-	-	0	-	-	14	-
SCOTT	-	3/ -		0/ 0	.000	-/ -	-	-	0	-	-	6	-
SVILAR	-	1/ -		3/ 5	.600	-/ -	-	-	3	-	-	5	-
CROUCH	-	2/ -		1/ 1	1.000	-/ -	-	-	4	-	-	5	-
DUNN	-	1/ -		0/ 0	.000	-/ -	-	-	3	-	-	2	-
BLEVINS	-	0/ -		0/ 0	.000	-/ -	-	-	4	-	-	0	-
APODACA	-	1/ -		1/ 2	.500	-/ -	-	-	1	-	-	3	-
CLEMENT	-	1/ -		0/ 1	.000	-/ -	-	-	2	-	-	2	-
Totals	200	17/ -		10/16	.625	-/ -	-	-	19	-	-	44	.220

Disqualified: TCU—McLeod

	1st Qtr.	2nd Qtr.	3rd Qtr.	4th Qtr.	Final
TCU	17	8	18	18	61
New Mexico St.	9	9	13	13	44

Oklahoma City (55) Coach: Doyle Parrack

	Min.	Total FG/FGA	Pct.	FT/FTA	Pct.	Reb. O/T	A	TO	PF	S	Blk	TP	PPM
LIKENS, A.	-	4/14	.286	2/ 2	1.000	-/12	4	-	2	-	-	10	-
SHORT, A.	-	7/14	.500	8/ 9	.889	-/ 7	4	-	2	-	-	22	-
PENWELL, D.	-	4/11	.364	3/ 5	.600	-/ 9	2	-	4	-	-	11	-
ROSE, K.	-	0/ 5	.000	2/ 3	.667	-/ 4	2	-	4	-	-	2	-
THOMPSON, J.	-	2/ 8	.250	4/ 5	.800	-/ 1	0	-	5	-	-	8	-
MAYFIELD, D.	-	0/ 3	.000	2/ 2	1.000	-/ 1	0	-	0	-	-	2	-
COUTS, B.	-	0/ 1	.000	0/ 0	.000	-/ 3	1	-	5	-	-	0	-
DALTON, D.	-	0/ 1	.000	0/ 0	.000	-/ 2	0	-	1	-	-	0	-
RICH, D.	-	0/ 0	.000	0/ 0	.000	-/ 0	0	-	0	-	-	0	-
BULLARD, G.	-	0/ 1	.000	0/ 1	.000	-/ 0	0	-	1	-	-	0	-
Totals	200	17/58	.293	21/27	.778	-/39	13	-	24	-	-	55	.275

UCLA (53) Coach: John Wooden

	Min.	Total FG/FGA	Pct.	FT/FTA	Pct.	Reb. O/T	A	TO	PF	S	Blk	TP	PPM
MOORE, J.	-	6/ 9	.667	3/ 4	.750	-/ 6	0	-	5	-	-	15	-
NORMAN, J.	-	3/11	.273	3/ 4	.750	-/ 7	3	-	5	-	-	9	-
HIBLER, M.	-	1/ 8	.125	2/ 5	.400	-/ 7	1	-	3	-	-	4	-
JOHNSON, D.	-	0/ 1	.000	1/ 2	.500	-/ 7	1	-	3	-	-	1	-
LIVINGSTON, R.	-	5/15	.333	3/ 4	.750	-/ 3	5	-	5	-	-	13	-
PORTER, B.	-	1/ 2	.500	1/ 2	.500	-/ 0	0	-	1	-	-	3	-
BANE, R.	-	1/ 2	.500	1/ 3	.333	-/ 3	0	-	1	-	-	3	-
BRAGG, D.	-	0/ 6	.000	1/ 2	.500	-/ 1	1	-	3	-	-	1	-
EVANS, J.	-	1/ 3	.333	0/ 1	.000	-/ 1	0	-	2	-	-	2	-
DAVIDSON, J.	-	1/ 2	.500	0/ 0	.000	-/ 2	0	-	3	-	-	2	-
POUNDS, B.	-	0/ 0	.000	0/ 0	.000	-/ 0	0	-	1	-	-	0	-
COSTELLO, M.	-	0/ 0	.000	0/ 0	.000	-/ 0	0	-	0	-	-	0	-
Totals	200	19/59	.322	15/27	.556	-/37	11	-	32	-	-	53	.265

Disqualified: Oklahoma City—Thompson, Couts; UCLA—Moore, Norman, Livingston.

	1st Qtr.	2nd Qtr.	3rd Qtr.	4th Qtr.	Final
Oklahoma City	16	19	12	8	55
UCLA	23	6	16	8	53

REGIONAL THIRD PLACE EAST

North Carolina State (69) Coach: Everett Case

	Min.	Total FG/FGA	Pct.	FT/FTA	Pct.	Reb. O/T	A	TO	PF	S	Blk	TP	PPM
TYLER, D.	-	2/ -		2/ 2	1.000	-/ -	-	-	4	-	-	6	-
SPEIGHT, B.	-	5/ -		5/ 7	.714	-/ -	-	-	4	-	-	15	-
KUKOY	-	1/ -		0/ 2	.000	-/ -	-	-	2	-	-	2	-
COOK, B.	-	1/ -		0/ 0	.000	-/ -	-	-	0	-	-	2	-
BRANDENBURG	-	0/ -		0/ 1	.000	-/ -	-	-	1	-	-	0	-
THOMPSON, M.	-	8/ -		5/ 9	.556	-/ -	-	-	3	-	-	21	-
KNAPP	-	1/ -		2/ 3	.667	-/ -	-	-	2	-	-	4	-
YURIN, B.	-	0/ -		3/ 4	.750	-/ -	-	-	3	-	-	3	-
TERRILL, L.	-	3/ -		2/ 3	.667	-/ -	-	-	2	-	-	8	-
GOTKIN	-	4/ -		0/ 0	.000	-/ -	-	-	2	-	-	8	-
APPLEBAUM	-	0/ -		0/ 0	.000	-/ -	-	-	0	-	-	0	-
Totals	200	25/ -		19/31	.613	-/ -	-	-	23	-	-	69	.345

Penn State (60) Coach: Elmer Gross

	Min.	Total FG/FGA	Pct.	FT/FTA	Pct.	Reb. O/T	A	TO	PF	S	Blk	TP	PPM
SHERRY, J.	-	3/ -		2/ 4	.500	-/ -	-	-	4	-	-	8	-
WEIDENHAMMER, R.	-	2/ -		0/ 0	.000	-/ -	-	-	5	-	-	4	-
WILLIAMS	-	2/ -		0/ 0	.000	-/ -	-	-	4	-	-	4	-
PFORKOWSKI	-	2/ -		1/ 1	1.000	-/ -	-	-	4	-	-	5	-
ARNELLE	-	8/ -		6/15	.400	-/ -	-	-	2	-	-	22	-
MCMAHON	-	1/ -		1/ 3	.333	-/ -	-	-	2	-	-	3	-
HAAG, E.	-	1/ -		1/ 1	1.000	-/ -	-	-	5	-	-	3	-
SLEDZIK	-	2/ -		1/ 1	1.000	-/ -	-	-	3	-	-	5	-
MAKAREWICZ	-	2/ -		2/ 2	1.000	-/ -	-	-	3	-	-	6	-
BLOCKER	-	0/ -		0/ 0	.000	-/ -	-	-	1	-	-	0	-
Totals	200	23/ -		14/27	.519	-/ -	-	-	33	-	-	60	.300

Disqualified: Penn State—Weidenhammer, Haag.

	1st Qtr.	2nd Qtr.	3rd Qtr.	4th Qtr.	Final
N.C. State	22	20	12	15	69
Penn State	17	19	9	15	60

Dayton (77) Coach: Tom Blackburn

	Min.	Total FG / FGA	Pct.	FT / FTA	Pct.	Reb. O / T	A	TO	PF	S	Blk	TP	PPM
GRIGSBY, C.	-	6/ -	-	2/ 7	.286	-/ -	-	-	4	-	-	14	-
HORAN, J.	-	3/ -	-	1/ 2	.500	-/ -	-	-	3	-	-	7	-
PAXSON, J.	-	2/ -	-	0/ 0	.000	-/ -	-	••	0	-	-	4	-
SALLEE, J.	-	0/ -	-	2/ 3	.667	-/ -	-	-	2	-	-	2	-
MEINEKE, D.	-	8/ -	-	10/11	.909	-/ -	-	-	5	-	-	26	-
DONOHER, D.	-	0/ -	-	1/ 1	1.000	-/ -	-	-	1	-	-	1	-
HARRIS, C.	-	1/ -	-	3/ 3	1.000	-/ -	-	-	1	-	-	5	-
BOYLE, P.	-	2/ -	-	1/ 2	.500	-/ -	-	-	3	-	-	5	-
NORRIS, L.	-	5/ -	-	3/ 3	1.000	-/ -	-	-	2	-	-	13	-
Totals	200	27/ -	-	23/32	.719	-/ -	-	-	21	-	-	77	.385

Princeton (61) Coach: Franklin Cappon

	Min.	Total FG / FGA	Pct.	FT / FTA	Pct.	Reb. O / T	A	TO	PF	S	Blk	TP	PPM
TRITSCHLER, F.	-	11/ -	-	0/ 5	.000	-/ -	-	-	3	-	-	22	-
SISLER, D.	-	4/ -	-	1/ 3	.333	-/ -	-	-	4	-	-	9	-
RIDGWAY	-	0/ -	-	0/ 0	.000	-/ -	-	-	3	-	-	0	-
MARSHALL, D.	-	0/ -	-	0/ 0	.000	-/ -	-	-	1	-	-	0	-
COOPER, F.	-	5/ -	-	1/ 3	.333	-/ -	-	-	5	-	-	11	-
HAUPTFUHRER	-	0/ -	-	1/ 1	1.000	-/ -	-	-	0	-	-	1	-
SARBANES	-	0/ -	-	1/ 2	.500	-/ -	-	-	1	-	-	1	-
EMERY, J.	-	1/ -	-	4/ 8	.500	-/ -	-	-	2	-	-	6	-
ZURAVLEFF, P.	-	2/ -	-	0/ 0	.000	-/ -	-	-	3	-	-	4	-
DEVOE, C.	-	2/ -	-	3/ 4	.750	-/ -	-	-	4	-	-	7	-
Totals	200	25/ -	-	11/26	.423	-/ -	-	-	26	-	-	61	.305

Disqualified: Dayton—Meineke; Princeton—Cooper.

	1st Qtr.	2nd Qtr.	3rd Qtr.	4th Qtr.	Final
Dayton	25	22	10	20	77
Princeton	15	18	14	14	61

⊙ ALL-STAR TEAMS ⊙

ALL TOURNAMENT

DEAN KELLEY	KANSAS
JOHN KERR	ILLINOIS
★ **CLYDE LOVELLETTE**	KANSAS
RON MACGILVRAY	ST. JOHN'S
BOB ZAWOLUK	ST. JOHN'S

★ Most Outstanding Player(s)

⊙ INDIVIDUAL RECORDS ⊙

SCORING

Most points in a single game
1 CLYDE LOVELLETTE, KANSAS (vs. ST. LOUIS) 44
2 CLYDE LOVELLETTE, KANSAS (vs. SANTA CLARA) 33
2 CLYDE LOVELLETTE, KANSAS (vs. ST. JOHN'S) 33
4 BOB ZAWOLUK, ST. JOHN'S (vs. KENTUCKY) 32
5 CLYDE LOVELLETTE, KANSAS (vs. TCU) 31

Most total points in the tournament
1 CLYDE LOVELLETTE, KANSAS 141
2 BOB ZAWOLUK, ST. JOHN'S 88
3 JIM YOUNG, SANTA CLARA 55
4 JOHN KERR, ILLINOIS 54
5 2 tied for fifth place.

Highest scoring average (minimum 2 games)
1 CLYDE LOVELLETTE, KANSAS (141-4) 35.25
2 BOB ZAWOLUK, ST. JOHN'S (88-4) 22.00
3 DON MEINEKE, DAYTON (44-2) 22.00
3 JESSE ARNELLE, PENN STATE (44-2) 22.00
5 CLIFF HAGAN, KENTUCKY (42-2) 21.00

FIELD GOALS

Most field goals in a single game
1 CLYDE LOVELLETTE, KANSAS (vs. ST. LOUIS) 16
2 CLYDE LOVELLETTE, KANSAS (vs. TCU) 13

3 BOB ZAWOLUK, ST. JOHN'S (vs. KENTUCKY) 12
3 CLYDE LOVELLETTE, KANSAS (vs. SANTA CLARA) 12
3 CLYDE LOVELLETTE, KANSAS (vs. ST. JOHN'S) 12

Most total field goals in the tournament
1 CLYDE LOVELLETTE, KANSAS 53
2 BOB ZAWOLUK, ST. JOHN'S 33
3 JIM YOUNG, SANTA CLARA 21
3 JOHN KERR, ILLINOIS 21
3 JIM BREDAR, ILLINOIS 21

FREE THROWS

Most free throws in a single game
1 CLYDE LOVELLETTE, KANSAS (vs. ST. LOUIS) 12
2 DON MEINEKE, DAYTON (vs. PRINCETON) 10
3 JIM BREDAR, ILLINOIS (vs. DAYTON) 9
3 CLYDE LOVELLETTE, KANSAS (vs. SANTA CLARA) 9
3 CLYDE LOVELLETTE, KANSAS (vs. ST. JOHN'S) 9

Most total free throws in the tournament
1 CLYDE LOVELLETTE, KANSAS 35
2 BOB ZAWOLUK, ST. JOHN'S 22
3 CLIVE FOLLMER, ILLINOIS 18
4 DON MEINEKE, DAYTON 16
5 ROD FLETCHER, ILLINOIS 15

Most free throws attempted in a single game
1 JESSE ARNELLE, PENN STATE (vs. N.C. STATE) 15
2 CLYDE LOVELLETTE, KANSAS (vs. ST. LOUIS) 14
3 CLYDE LOVELLETTE, KANSAS (vs. SANTA CLARA) 12
4 4 tied for fourth place.

Most free throws attempted in the tournament
1 CLYDE LOVELLETTE, KANSAS 44
2 BOB ZAWOLUK, ST. JOHN'S 29
3 ROD FLETCHER, ILLINOIS 26
4 JESSE ARNELLE, PENN STATE 25
5 CLIVE FOLLMER, ILLINOIS 23

Highest free throw percentage in a single game (minimum 7 attempts)
1 JIM TUCKER, DUQUESNE (vs. ILLINOIS) (7-7) 1.000
2 DON MEINEKE, DAYTON (vs. PRINCETON) (10-11) .909
3 4 tied for third place.

Highest free throw percentage in the tournament (minimum 15 attempts)
1 DON MEINEKE, DAYTON (16-19) .842
2 JIM YOUNG, SANTA CLARA (13-16) .813
3 CLYDE LOVELLETTE, KANSAS (35-44) .795
4 CLIVE FOLLMER, ILLINOIS (18-23) .783
5 BOB ZAWOLUK, ST. JOHN'S (22-29) .759

○ TEAM RECORDS ○

SCORING

Most points in a single game
1   KENTUCKY (vs. PENN STATE)   82
2   KANSAS (vs. ST. JOHN'S)   80
2   ILLINOIS (vs. DAYTON)   80

Most total points in the tournament
1   KANSAS   296
2   ILLINOIS   280
3   ST. JOHN'S   248

Highest scoring average (minimum 2 games)
1   KANSAS (296-4)   74.00
2   ILLINOIS (280-4)   70.00
3   KENTUCKY (139-2)   69.50

FIELD GOALS

Most field goals in a single game
1   KENTUCKY (vs. PENN STATE)   35
2   SANTA CLARA (vs. UCLA)   29
2   ILLINOIS (vs. DUQUESNE)   29

Most total field goals in the tournament
1   KANSAS   109
2   ILLINOIS   100
3   SANTA CLARA   95

FREE THROWS

Most free throws in a single game
1   ILLINOIS (vs. DAYTON)   32
2   KANSAS (vs. ST. JOHN'S)   24
3   2 tied for third place.

Most total free throws in the tournament
1   ILLINOIS   80
2   KANSAS   78
3   ST. JOHN'S   62

Most free throws attempted in a single game
1   ILLINOIS (vs. DAYTON)   47
2   KANSAS (vs. ST. JOHN'S)   35
3   2 tied for third place.

Most total free throws attempted in the tournament
1   ILLINOIS   125
2   KANSAS   112
3   ST. JOHN'S   100

Highest free throw percentage in a single game
1   SANTA CLARA (vs. ILLINOIS) (20-22)   .909
2   UCLA (vs. SANTA CLARA) (19-22)   .864
3   KANSAS (vs. ST. LOUIS) (22-27)   .815

Highest free throw percentage in the tournament (minimum 2 games)
1   DUQUESNE (30-38)   .790
2   DAYTON (36-50)   .720
3   KANSAS (78-112)   .697

Fewest free throws in a single game
1   OKLAHOMA CITY (vs. WYOMING)   6
2   ILLINOIS (vs. ST. JOHN'S)   9
2   SANTA CLARA (vs. KANSAS)   9

Lowest free throw percentage in a single game
1   ILLINOIS (vs. ST. JOHN'S) (9-24)   .375
2   PRINCETON (vs. DAYTON) (11-26)   .423
3   SANTA CLARA (vs. UCLA) (10-21)   .476

Lowest free throw percentage in the tournament (minimum 2 games)
1   PRINCETON (22-42)   .524
2   PENN STATE (30-57)   .526
3   N.C. STATE (30-50)   .600

1953

| FIRST ROUND | REGIONAL SEMIFINAL | REGIONAL FINAL | FINAL FOUR | REGIONAL FINAL | REGIONAL SEMIFINAL | FIRST ROUND |

EAST

WEST

Lebanon Valley 80
Lebanon Valley 76
Fordham 67
Louisiana St. 81
Louisiana St. 89

Holy Cross 87
Holy Cross 79
Navy 74
Holy Cross 73
(bye)
Wake Forest 71

Louisiana St. 67

Notre Dame 72
Notre Dame 69
Eastern Ky. 57
Notre Dame 66
(bye)
Pennsylvania 57

Indiana 80

DePaul 74
DePaul 80
Miami (Ohio) 72
Indiana 79
(bye)
Indiana 82

Indiana 69
Kansas 68

Washington 53

Kansas 79

Seattle 88
Seattle 70
Idaho St. 77
Washington 74
Washington 92
(bye)

Santa Clara 81
Santa Clara 67
Hardin-Simmons 56
Santa Clara 62
Wyoming 52
(bye)

TCU 54
(bye)
Oklahoma A&M 55
Oklahoma A&M 71
(bye)

Kansas 73
(bye)
Kansas 61
Oklahoma City 65
(bye)

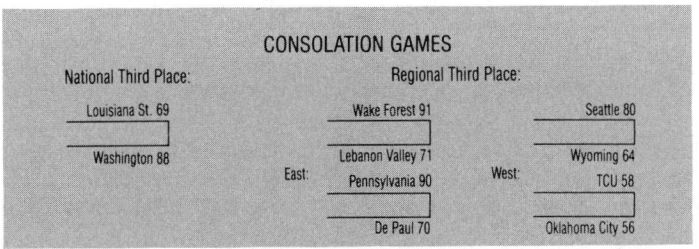

CONSOLATION GAMES

National Third Place:
Louisiana St. 69
Washington 88

Regional Third Place:

East:
Wake Forest 91
Lebanon Valley 71
Pennsylvania 90
De Paul 70

West:
Seattle 80
Wyoming 64
TCU 58
Oklahoma City 56

During the 1952–53 season, college basketball players found the hoop with unprecedented regularity. Eight teams broke the previous national scoring record of 82.5 points per game. And Henry Iba's Oklahoma A&M, as usual the stingiest defensive team in the nation, allowed an unusually generous 54 points a game. Despite college basketball's infusion of offense in 1953, six of the ten best defensive teams were selected for the NCAA tournament, while only two of the top ten offensive teams (Seattle and Indiana) were accorded the same level of respect.

Despite the selection committee's tilt toward defense, spectacular individual offensive shows garnered the headlines in the early rounds of the 1953 tournament. In Seattle's opener, little Johnny O'Brien scored 42 points to shoot holes in Idaho State's airtight defense. But in his next game, against crosstown rival Washington, O'Brien hit for only 24 and was outgunned by Washington's Bob Houbregs, who broke the single-game tournament scoring record with 45 points. Togo Palazzi's overhand push shots from every corner of the court accounted for a total of 62 markers in sparking his Holy Cross team past its first two opponents. LSU's smooth-shooting Bob Pettit averaged over 30 a game all tournament long. And Indiana's big center, Don Schlundt, poured in 41 against Notre Dame in leading the Hoosiers to the Final Four.

Even though the lid had been taken off the basket, one thing remained the same. The traditional basketball powers were still alive and well. Phog Allen's Kansas Jayhawks, the 1952 champions, returned to the field in 1953 despite the loss of Clyde Lovellette and almost all of his teammates. Only guard Dean Kelley remained from the previous year's starting five, while another Dean (Smith), was also back, warming the bench. Henry Iba's Oklahoma A&M Aggies also returned with their tenacious defense. And Branch McCracken was still teaching his Indiana Hoosiers to race downcourt well enough to earn them the No. 1 national ranking and a shot at the national title (last won by the Hoosiers in a showdown against Allen's Kansas squad in 1940). Among the perennial national powers, the most conspicuous absentee was Adolph Rupp's Kentucky Wildcats, who had reigned supreme in three of the previous five tournaments but whom the NCAA had banned from participating in intercollegiate basketball for a year as a result of recruiting violations and payments to players.

Kansas made it to the Final Four by defeating their old rival, Oklahoma A&M, in a bruising defensive battle that was tied ten times. Like two wily old pugilists, the Jayhawks and Aggies jabbed and feinted and punched each other to a virtual draw until Kansas's Dean Kelley broke the contest open with 10 points in the last five minutes of the third period, capping his efforts with a clean steal from Harold Rogers and a breakaway lay-up. Although Iba's

team got back onto their feet, even regaining the momentum for much of the final period, they were unable to take back the lead.

Kansas's opponent in the semis, the Washington Huskies, survived the regionals by riding Bob Houbregs' brilliant second-half shooting past Santa Clara. In the eastern half of the draw, Louisiana State, which lost only one game during the regular season, built an 18-point lead in their regional final against Holy Cross but had to fight for their lives as the Crusaders staged a desperate, and very nearly successful, fourth-quarter rally. And top-ranked Indiana, despite its All-American combination of Schlundt and guard Bob Leonard, barely survived De Paul before destroying Notre Dame.

In the semis, Kansas crushed Washington with an unrelenting, pressing, ball-hawking defense that turned virtually every Huskies mistake into a fast-break basket. Before 10,500 screaming Kansas partisans (the Final Four was being held in Kansas City), the Jayhawks stole the ball four times and forced three other turnovers before the Huskies even scored a point. When Bob Houbregs fouled out early in the third period, the game was all but over.

The other semi was also decided early, when the Hoosiers exploded for a 31-point opening quarter. In the end, only Pettit's 29 points kept the score respectable, as Indiana's "Mr. Inside and Mr. Outside," Schlundt and Leonard, combined for 51 points, even though neither played much more than half the game.

The final between Kansas and Indiana was a rematch of the 1940 title game. Unlike that earlier match, in which the Hurryin' Hoosiers left the Jayhawks in the dust, the 1953 championship duel was a fanatically contested encounter between two equally powerful heavyweight squads, each pummeling the other with neither being able to put the other down for even a second.

It was power against power, the fanatical Kansas press against Indiana's runaway fast break, an immovable object against an irresistible force. It was no holds barred from the very beginning, and it wasn't decided until the very end. There were ten ties, and neither team led at the end of any quarter by more than two points. There were individual duels between the star centers Don Schlundt and B. H. Born and the star guards Bob Leonard and Dean Kelley. And the game was played with elbows flying, tempers flaring, and a crowd that groaned with every Indiana point and roared with every Kansas counter.

It looked like Indiana would finally have a decisive advantage when Born barreled into the Hoosiers' Charlie Kraak with a minute to play in the third period and was whistled off the court with five fouls. But Kansas Coach Allen leaped up in protest, and the scorer changed his ruling: it was only Born's fourth personal, he decided. Now it was Indiana Coach McCracken's turn to protest.

"Your book shows five personals," he shouted as the crowd chanted "Four! Four!" "Born should be out. We're your guest and you're robbing us." The officials overlooked McCracken's rage (they had already called technicals on both Schlundt and Leonard for remarks they deemed offensive). Play resumed, and at the buzzer, as the two squads staggered off with Indiana holding a one-point lead, Born was still in the game.

Throughout the final period, the teams struggled for the lead, but neither could go up by more than 3 at any time during the quarter. With 5:36 left Born finally fouled out, finishing his night's work with 26 points. Still, Indiana could not take charge. With about two minutes left Kraak, jockeying for position, planted a vicious elbow in Kansas forward Harold Patterson's ribs and was called for a third Hoosier "T", along with a personal foul. Patterson made one of two, and then Al Kelley (Dean's younger brother) missed the technical. Kansas grabbed the rebound, and with a minute and five seconds to go, Dean Kelley drove to the hoop and tied the score, 68-68. With 27 seconds left in the game, Dean Kelley fouled Leonard in a scramble under the Kansas basket.

The noise from the crowd was deafening as Leonard stepped to the line. He composed himself, tried to concentrate—and missed. The crowd went wild. He calmed himself down, and the second shot went cleanly through the hoop.

It was 69-68 when Kansas called a time-out. Allen told his players not to hurry anything, that there was plenty of time to work the ball for a good shot. But they took a little too much time. Substitute Jerry Alberts, who had entered the game when Born fouled out, finally found himself holding the ball with only three seconds left on the clock. He fired up a jump shot from deep in the corner. When it came down, the Jayhawks were ex-champions. Thirteen years after their first championship battle against Kansas, Indiana won the rematch.

FIRST ROUND EAST

Lebanon Valley (80)   Coach: Rinso Marquette

	Min.	Total FG/FGA	Pct.	FT/FTA	Pct.	Reb. O/T	A	TO	PF	S	Blk	TP	PPM
FINKELSTEIN, H.	40	3/ -	-	3/ 5	.600	-/ -	-	-	0	-	-	9	.225
VOUGHT, W.	40	3/ -	-	2/ 3	.667	-/ -	-	-	2	-	-	8	.200
MILLER, L.	40	4/ -	-	4/ 7	.571	-/ -	-	-	3	-	-	12	.300
LANDA, H.	40	7/ -	-	7/ 8	.875	-/ -	-	-	2	-	-	21	.525
SORRENTINO, L.	40	9/ -	-	12/12	1.000	-/ -	-	-	3	-	-	30	.750
Totals	200	26/ -	-	28/35	.800	-/ -	-	-	10	-	-	80	.400

Fordham (67)   Coach: John Bach

	Min.	Total FG/FGA	Pct.	FT/FTA	Pct.	Reb. O/T	A	TO	PF	S	Blk	TP	PPM
LARKIN	-	7/ -	-	0/ 2	.000	-/ -	-	-	3	-	-	14	-
CUNNINGHAM	-	4/ -	-	0/ 0	.000	-/ -	-	-	4	-	-	8	-
BIGGIANO	-	1/ -	-	2/ 3	.667	-/ -	-	-	1	-	-	4	-
MCCABE	-	0/ -	-	1/ 2	.500	-/ -	-	-	2	-	-	1	-
CONLIN	-	7/ -	-	2/ 5	.400	-/ -	-	-	3	-	-	16	-
PARCHINSKI	-	8/ -	-	0/ 2	.000	-/ -	-	-	5	-	-	16	-
LYONS	-	4/ -	-	0/ 2	.000	-/ -	-	-	4	-	-	8	-
WOODS	-	0/ -	-	0/ 0	.000	-/ -	-	-	1	-	-	0	-
CONNORS	-	0/ -	-	0/ 0	.000	-/ -	-	-	0	-	-	0	-
Totals	200	31/ -	-	5/16	.313	-/ -	-	-	23	-	-	67	.335

Disqualified: Fordham—Parchinski.

	1st Qtr.	2nd Qtr.	3rd Qtr.	4th Qtr.	Final
Lebanon Valley	15	17	21	27	80
Fordham	18	14	17	18	67

Holy Cross (87)   Coach: Buster Sheary

	Min.	Total FG/FGA	Pct.	FT/FTA	Pct.	Reb. O/T	A	TO	PF	S	Blk	TP	PPM
SUPRUNOWICZ, W.	-	0/ -	-	2/ 4	.500	-/ -	-	-	0	-	-	2	-
PERRY, R.	-	5/ -	-	7/ 7	1.000	-/ -	-	-	3	-	-	17	-
PALAZZI, T.	-	11/ -	-	8/12	.667	-/ -	-	-	1	-	-	30	-
NANGLE, D.	-	1/ -	-	1/ 2	.500	-/ -	-	-	2	-	-	3	-
KIELLEY, J.	-	7/ -	-	0/ 0	.000	-/ -	-	-	4	-	-	14	-
MARKEY, E.	-	5/ -	-	7/14	.500	-/ -	-	-	3	-	-	17	-
MAGILLIGAN, R.	-	1/ -	-	1/ 1	1.000	-/ -	-	-	1	-	-	3	-
EARLY, J.	-	0/ -	-	0/ 0	.000	-/ -	-	-	0	-	-	0	-
CARROLL, J.	-	0/ -	-	1/ 2	.500	-/ -	-	-	1	-	-	1	-
CASEY, R.	-	0/ -	-	0/ 0	.000	-/ -	-	-	0	-	-	0	-
KASPRZAK, F.	-	0/ -	-	0/ 0	.000	-/ -	-	-	2	-	-	0	-
Totals	200	30/ -	-	27/42	.643	-/ -	-	-	17	-	-	87	.435

Navy (74)   Coach: Ben Carnevale

	Min.	Total FG/FGA	Pct.	FT/FTA	Pct.	Reb. O/T	A	TO	PF	S	Blk	TP	PPM
LANGE, D.	40	11/ -	-	6/ 9	.667	-/ -	-	-	2	-	-	28	.700
CLUNE, J.	35	9/ -	-	2/ 3	.667	-/ -	-	-	4	-	-	20	.571
HOGAN	20	1/ -	-	0/ 0	.000	-/ -	-	-	5	-	-	2	.100
MCCALLY	30	2/ -	-	1/ 1	1.000	-/ -	-	-	5	-	-	5	.167
VANSCOYOC	20	2/ -	-	1/ 2	.500	-/ -	-	-	0	-	-	5	.250
WIGLEY	25	0/ -	-	2/ 2	1.000	-/ -	-	-	0	-	-	2	.080
KNISS	14	3/ -	-	0/ 2	.000	-/ -	-	-	5	-	-	6	.429
CRAMER	2	0/ -	-	0/ 0	.000	-/ -	-	-	0	-	-	0	.000
WELLS	5	1/ -	-	2/ 2	1.000	-/ -	-	-	0	-	-	4	.800
HOOVER	4	0/ -	-	0/ 0	.000	-/ -	-	-	2	-	-	0	.000
SANDLIN	5	1/ -	-	0/ 2	.000	-/ -	-	-	3	-	-	2	.400
Totals	200	30/ -	-	14/23	.609	-/ -	-	-	26	-	-	74	.370

Disqualified: Navy—Hogan, Kniss, McCalley.

	1st Qtr.	2nd Qtr.	3rd Qtr.	4th Qtr.	Final
Holy Cross	23	21	18	25	87
Navy	20	17	14	23	74

Notre Dame (72)   Coach: John Jordan

	Min.	Total FG/FGA	Pct.	FT/FTA	Pct.	Reb. O/T	A	TO	PF	S	Blk	TP	PPM
ROSENTHAL, R.	-	6/ -	-	5/ 5	1.000	-/ -	-	-	4	-	-	17	-
BERTRAND, J.	-	8/ -	-	7/11	.636	-/ -	-	-	4	-	-	23	-
STEPHENS, J.	-	3/ -	-	2/ 5	.400	-/ -	-	-	1	-	-	8	-
SULLIVAN, W.	-	1/ -	-	0/ 0	.000	-/ -	-	-	2	-	-	2	-
MCCLOSKY, G.	-	4/ -	-	2/ 2	1.000	-/ -	-	-	1	-	-	10	-
GIBBONS, J.	-	0/ -	-	0/ 0	.000	-/ -	-	-	0	-	-	0	-
LEWINSKI, N.	-	4/ -	-	4/ 8	.500	-/ -	-	-	4	-	-	12	-
Totals	200	26/ -	-	20/31	.645	-/ -	-	-	16	-	-	72	.360

Eastern Kentucky (57)   Coach: Paul McBrayer

	Min.	Total FG/FGA	Pct.	FT/FTA	Pct.	Reb. O/T	A	TO	PF	S	Blk	TP	PPM
DAVIS	-	5/ -	-	1/ 3	.333	-/ -	-	-	5	-	-	11	-
MULCAHY	-	2/ -	-	0/ 0	.000	-/ -	-	-	3	-	-	4	-
BINGHAM	-	7/ -	-	6/11	.545	-/ -	-	-	2	-	-	20	-
FLOYD	-	0/ -	-	2/ 2	1.000	-/ -	-	-	3	-	-	2	-
STANFORD	-	0/ -	-	1/ 1	1.000	-/ -	-	-	1	-	-	1	-
GEYER	-	2/ -	-	3/ 5	.600	-/ -	-	-	3	-	-	7	-
KEARNS	-	0/ -	-	2/ 4	.500	-/ -	-	-	4	-	-	2	-
HOLBROOK	-	5/ -	-	0/ 0	.000	-/ -	-	-	0	-	-	10	-
Totals	200	21/ -	-	15/26	.577	-/ -	-	-	21	-	-	57	.285

Disqualified: Eastern Ky.—Davis.

	1st Qtr.	2nd Qtr.	3rd Qtr.	4th Qtr.	Final
Notre Dame	15	19	23	15	72
Eastern Ky.	16	13	16	12	57

DePaul (74)   Coach: Ray Meyer

	Min.	Total FG/FGA	Pct.	FT/FTA	Pct.	Reb. O/T	A	TO	PF	S	Blk	TP	PPM
LECOS, D.	-	2/ -	-	3/ 6	.500	-/ -	-	-	3	-	-	7	-
BLUM, F.	-	4/ -	-	2/ 2	1.000	-/ -	-	-	2	-	-	10	-
SCHYMAN, B.	-	0/ -	-	2/ 3	.667	-/ -	-	-	2	-	-	2	-
JOHNSON, R.	-	4/ -	-	5/ 7	.714	-/ -	-	-	2	-	-	13	-
FEIEREISEL, R.	-	6/ -	-	5/ 6	.833	-/ -	-	-	1	-	-	17	-
LAMKIN, J.	-	9/ -	-	7/ 9	.778	-/ -	-	-	4	-	-	25	-
Totals	200	25/77	-	24/33	.727	-/ -	-	-	14	-	-	74	.370

Miami (Ohio) (72)   Coach: Bill Rohr

	Min.	Total FG/FGA	Pct.	FT/FTA	Pct.	Reb. O/T	A	TO	PF	S	Blk	TP	PPM
GUNDERSON, E.	-	5/ -	-	5/ 6	.833	-/ -	-	-	5	-	-	15	-
KLITCH, D.	-	7/ -	-	2/ 4	.500	-/ -	-	-	4	-	-	16	-
GRIESINGER, B.	-	2/ -	-	3/ 3	1.000	-/ -	-	-	2	-	-	7	-
WALLS, D.	-	5/ -	-	4/ 7	.571	-/ -	-	-	5	-	-	14	-
YATES, J.	-	1/ -	-	0/ 0	.000	-/ -	-	-	1	-	-	2	-
DOLL, B.	-	1/ -	-	1/ 2	.500	-/ -	-	-	0	-	-	3	-
KNODEL, D.	-	4/ -	-	1/ 1	1.000	-/ -	-	-	2	-	-	9	-
HEDRIC, D.	-	1/ -	-	0/ 0	.000	-/ -	-	-	2	-	-	2	-
WELCH, M.	-	1/ -	-	0/ 0	.000	-/ -	-	-	1	-	-	2	-
BRYANT, T.	-	1/ -	-	0/ 2	.000	-/ -	-	-	1	-	-	2	-
Totals	200	28/94	-	16/25	.640	-/ -	-	-	23	-	-	72	.360

Disqualified: Miami (Ohio)—Gunderson, Walls.

	1st Qtr.	2nd Qtr.	3rd Qtr.	4th Qtr.	Final
DePaul	25	17	11	21	74
Miami (Ohio)	20	10	23	19	72

FIRST ROUND WEST

Seattle (88)   Coach: Al Brightman

	Min.	Total FG/FGA	Pct.	FT/FTA	Pct.	Reb. O/T	A	TO	PF	S	Blk	TP	PPM
MOSCATEL	-	3/ -	-	1/ 2	.500	-/ -	-	-	4	-	-	7	-
DOHERTY	-	3/ -	-	1/ 2	.500	-/ -	-	-	3	-	-	7	-
GLOWASKI	-	0/ -	-	1/ 1	1.000	-/ -	-	-	4	-	-	1	-
O'BRIEN, E.	-	8/ -	-	5/ 5	1.000	-/ -	-	-	5	-	-	21	-
O'BRIEN, J.	-	17/ -	-	8/ 9	.889	-/ -	-	-	2	-	-	42	-
SANFORD	-	3/ -	-	2/ 3	.667	-/ -	-	-	5	-	-	8	-
KELLY	-	0/ -	-	0/ 0	.000	-/ -	-	-	0	-	-	0	-
BISSETT	-	0/ -	-	0/ 0	.000	-/ -	-	-	0	-	-	0	-
PEHANICK	-	1/ -	-	0/ 0	.000	-/ -	-	-	0	-	-	2	-
MALONE	-	0/ -	-	0/ 0	.000	-/ -	-	-	0	-	-	0	-
HANSEN	-	0/ -	-	0/ 0	.000	-/ -	-	-	1	-	-	0	-
Totals	200	35/ -	-	18/22	.818	-/ -	-	-	24	-	-	88	.440

Idaho State (77)   Coach: Steve Belko

	Min.	Total FG/FGA	Pct.	FT/FTA	Pct.	Reb. O/T	A	TO	PF	S	Blk	TP	PPM
ROH, L.	-	7/ -	-	6/13	.462	-/ -	-	-	3	-	-	20	-
BECKHAM	-	8/ -	-	6/ 8	.750	-/ -	-	-	3	-	-	22	-
BAUER	-	6/ -	-	5/ 7	.714	-/ -	-	-	2	-	-	17	-
CONNOR	-	4/ -	-	2/ 4	.500	-/ -	-	-	2	-	-	10	-
HAYS	-	2/ -	-	3/ 3	1.000	-/ -	-	-	5	-	-	7	-
BELKEW	-	0/ -	-	0/ 0	.000	-/ -	-	-	0	-	-	0	-
DAKICH, R.	-	0/ -	-	1/ 1	1.000	-/ -	-	-	0	-	-	1	-
HARROCKS	-	0/ -	-	0/ 0	.000	-/ -	-	-	1	-	-	0	-
KOBZA	-	0/ -	-	0/ 0	.000	-/ -	-	-	0	-	-	0	-
Totals	200	27/ -	-	23/36	.639	-/ -	-	-	16	-	-	77	.385

Disqualified: Seattle—E. O'Brien, Sanford; Idaho State—Hays.

	1st Qtr.	2nd Qtr.	3rd Qtr.	4th Qtr.	Final
Seattle	23	20	20	25	88
Idaho State	19	16	21	21	77

Santa Clara (81)   Coach: Bob Feerick

	Min.	Total FG/FGA	Pct.	FT/FTA	Pct.	Reb. O/T	A	TO	PF	S	Blk	TP	PPM
SEARS, K.	-	3/ -	-	1/ 1	1.000	-/ -	-	-	5	-	-	7	-
YOUNG, J.	-	7/ -	-	3/ 6	.500	-/ -	-	-	1	-	-	17	-
GATZERT, G.	-	1/ -	-	1/ 2	.500	-/ -	-	-	2	-	-	3	-
SCHOENSTEIN, H.	-	1/ -	-	0/ 0	.000	-/ -	-	-	1	-	-	2	-
MOUNT, M.	-	4/ -	-	3/ 6	.500	-/ -	-	-	4	-	-	11	-
GARIBALDI, D.	-	3/ -	-	0/ 0	.000	-/ -	-	-	2	-	-	6	-
SOARES, D.	-	9/ -	-	3/ 3	1.000	-/ -	-	-	0	-	-	21	-
BENEDETTI, D.	-	3/ -	-	2/ 3	.667	-/ -	-	-	0	-	-	8	-
SIMONI, D.	-	1/ -	-	2/ 2	1.000	-/ -	-	-	0	-	-	4	-
DOYLE	-	0/ -	-	2/ 4	.500	-/ -	-	-	0	-	-	2	-
Totals	200	32/ -	-	17/27	.630	-/ -	-	-	15	-	-	81	.405

Hardin-Simmons (56)   Coach: Bill Scott

	Min.	Total FG/FGA	Pct.	FT/FTA	Pct.	Reb. O/T	A	TO	PF	S	Blk	TP	PPM
BRUNSON	-	2/ -	-	5/ 6	.833	-/ -	-	-	3	-	-	9	-
COVERT	-	2/ -	-	0/ 0	.000	-/ -	-	-	2	-	-	4	-
BURROUGHS	-	0/ -	-	0/ 2	.000	-/ -	-	-	2	-	-	0	-
GREEN	-	10/ -	-	7/12	.583	-/ -	-	-	2	-	-	27	-
ROBERTS	-	1/ -	-	1/ 1	1.000	-/ -	-	-	2	-	-	3	-
HIBLER	-	4/ -	-	0/ 0	.000	-/ -	-	-	1	-	-	8	-
BURKS	-	2/ -	-	1/ 1	1.000	-/ -	-	-	3	-	-	5	-
CROW	-	0/ -	-	0/ 0	.000	-/ -	-	-	3	-	-	0	-
Totals	200	21/ -	-	14/22	.636	-/ -	-	-	18	-	-	56	.280

Disqualified: Santa Clara—Sears.

	1st Qtr.	2nd Qtr.	3rd Qtr.	4th Qtr.	Final
Santa Clara	18	21	18	24	81
Hardin-Simmons	7	12	20	17	56

REGIONAL SEMIFINAL EAST

Lebanon Valley (76)   Coach: Rinso Marquette

	Min.	Total FG/FGA	Pct.	FT/FTA	Pct.	Reb. O/T	A	TO	PF	S	Blk	TP	PPM
VOUGHT, W.	-	1/ -	-	2/ 3	.667	-/ -	-	-	3	-	-	4	-
FINKELSTEIN, H.	-	7/ -	-	3/ 7	.429	-/ -	-	-	4	-	-	17	-
BLAKENEY, R.	-	0/ -	-	0/ 0	.000	-/ -	-	-	0	-	-	0	-
MILLER, L.	-	7/ -	-	12/17	.706	-/ -	-	-	3	-	-	26	-
LANDA, H.	-	5/ -	-	8/10	.800	-/ -	-	-	5	-	-	18	-
SORRENTINO, L.	-	3/ -	-	5/ 6	.833	-/ -	-	-	3	-	-	11	-
GLUNTZ, M.	-	0/ -	-	0/ 0	.000	-/ -	-	-	0	-	-	0	-
Totals	200	23/ -	-	30/43	.698	-/ -	-	-	18	-	-	76	.380

Louisiana State (89)   Coach: Harry Rabenhorst

	Min.	Total FG/FGA	Pct.	FT/FTA	Pct.	Reb. O/T	A	TO	PF	S	Blk	TP	PPM
BELCHER, D.	-	8/ -	-	1/ 3	.333	-/ -	-	-	2	-	-	17	-
CLARK, N.	-	2/ -	-	0/ 2	.000	-/ -	-	-	5	-	-	4	-
FRESHLEY, B.	-	0/ -	-	0/ 0	.000	-/ -	-	-	4	-	-	0	-
BRIDGES, K.	-	1/ -	-	2/ 3	.667	-/ -	-	-	4	-	-	4	-
PETTIT, B.	-	13/ -	-	2/ 7	.286	-/ -	-	-	4	-	-	28	-
MAGEE, N.	-	8/ -	-	7/ 8	.875	-/ -	-	-	5	-	-	23	-
MCARDLE, B.	-	6/ -	-	1/ 4	.250	-/ -	-	-	3	-	-	13	-
Totals	200	38/ -	-	13/27	.481	-/ -	-	-	27	-	-	89	.445

Disqualified: Louisiana St.—Clark, Magee; Lebanon Valley—Landa.

	1st Qtr.	2nd Qtr.	3rd Qtr.	4th Qtr.	Final
Lebanon Valley	24	19	15	18	76
Louisiana St.	24	25	14	26	89

Holy Cross (79)   Coach: Buster Sheary

	Min.	Total FG/FGA	Pct.	FT/FTA	Pct.	Reb. O/T	A	TO	PF	S	Blk	TP	PPM
SUPRUNOWICZ, W.	17	0/ 2	.000	0/ 0	.000	-/ 4	0	-	3	-	-	0	.000
PERRY, R.	36	5/ 7	.714	6/ 8	.750	-/ 5	4	-	2	-	-	16	.444
PALAZZI, T.	40	14/28	.500	4/ 6	.667	-/12	1	-	4	-	-	32	.800
NANGLE, D.	16	2/ 8	.250	2/ 4	.500	-/ 5	0	-	4	-	-	6	.375
KIELLEY, J.	24	2/ 5	.400	0/ 0	.000	-/ 1	1	-	5	-	-	4	.167
MARKEY, E.	29	5/15	.333	4/ 8	.500	-/11	1	-	4	-	-	14	.483
MAGILLIGAN, R.	38	2/ 3	.667	3/ 7	.429	-/ 3	6	-	4	-	-	7	.184
Totals	200	30/68	.441	19/33	.576	-/41	13	-	26	-	-	79	.395

Wake Forest (71)   Coach: Murray Greason

	Min.	Total FG/FGA	Pct.	FT/FTA	Pct.	Reb. O/T	A	TO	PF	S	Blk	TP	PPM
LYLES, B.	40	2/17	.118	1/ 1	1.000	-/ 4	5	-	3	-	-	5	.125
WILLIAMS, J.	40	6/14	.429	7/ 9	.778	-/14	2	-	4	-	-	19	.475
GEORGE, M.	13	1/ 3	.333	0/ 0	.000	-/ 0	0	-	5	-	-	2	.154
HEMRIC, D.	40	9/22	.409	11/16	.688	-/17	1	-	1	-	-	29	.725
DEPORTER, A.	34	1/ 4	.250	3/ 3	1.000	-/ 5	1	-	5	-	-	5	.147
LIPSTAS, R.	32	4/12	.333	3/10	.300	-/ 5	6	-	3	-	-	11	.344
KOCH, J.	1	0/ 0	.000	0/ 0	.000	-/ 0	0	-	0	-	-	0	.000
Totals	200	23/72	.319	25/39	.641	-/45	15	-	21	-	-	71	.355

Disqualified: Holy Cross—Kielly; Wake Forest—George, DePorter.

	1st Qtr.	2nd Qtr.	3rd Qtr.	4th Qtr.	Final
Holy Cross	24	19	13	23	79
Wake Forest	14	18	14	25	71

Notre Dame (69) Coach: John Jordan

	Min.	Total FG/FGA	Pct.	FT/FTA	Pct.	Reb. O/T	A	TO	PF	S	Blk	TP	PPM
ROSENTHAL, R.	-	3/ -	-	12/14	.857	-/ -	-	-	3	-	-	18	-
SULLIVAN, W.	-	1/ -	-	1/ 1	1.000	-/ -	-	-	0	-	-	3	-
BERTRAND, J.	-	5/ -	-	7/ 9	.778	-/ -	-	-	3	-	-	17	-
LEWINSKI, N.	-	3/ -	-	4/ 4	1.000	-/ -	-	-	2	-	-	10	-
GIBBONS, J.	-	0/ -	-	2/ 2	1.000	-/ -	-	-	2	-	-	2	-
STEPHENS, J.	-	8/ -	-	3/ 3	1.000	-/ -	-	-	3	-	-	19	-
MCGINN, E.	-	0/ -	-	0/ 0	.000	-/ -	-	-	0	-	-	0	-
Totals	200	20/ -	-	29/33	.879	-/ -	-	-	13	-	-	69	.345

Pennsylvania (57) Coach: Howie Dallmar

	Min.	Total FG/FGA	Pct.	FT/FTA	Pct.	Reb. O/T	A	TO	PF	S	Blk	TP	PPM
HEYLMUN	-	5/ -	-	3/ 6	.500	-/ -	-	-	4	-	-	13	-
MASTERS	-	0/ -	-	0/ 0	.000	-/ -	-	-	0	-	-	0	-
LEACH	-	1/ -	-	0/ 0	.000	-/ -	-	-	4	-	-	2	-
LAVIN	-	0/ -	-	0/ 0	.000	-/ -	-	-	3	-	-	0	-
BECK, E.	-	9/ -	-	7/ 9	.778	-/ -	-	-	2	-	-	25	-
VITETTA	-	0/ -	-	0/ 0	.000	-/ -	-	-	0	-	-	0	-
HOAGLAND	-	4/ -	-	1/ 1	1.000	-/ -	-	-	5	-	-	9	-
HARTER	-	0/ -	-	0/ 0	.000	-/ -	-	-	0	-	-	0	-
HOLT	-	2/ -	-	4/ 5	.800	-/ -	-	-	4	-	-	8	-
GRAMIGNA	-	0/ -	-	0/ 0	.000	-/ -	-	-	1	-	-	0	-
Totals	200	21/ -	-	15/21	.714	-/ -	-	-	23	-	-	57	.285

Disqualified: Pennsylvania—Hoagland.

	1st Qtr.	2nd Qtr.	3rd Qtr.	4th Qtr.	Final
Notre Dame	19	11	11	28	69
Pennsylvania	18	13	9	17	57

DePaul (80) Coach: Ray Meyer

	Min.	Total FG/FGA	Pct.	FT/FTA	Pct.	Reb. O/T	A	TO	PF	S	Blk	TP	PPM
LECOS, D.	-	0/ 5	.000	0/ 0	.000	-/ -	-	-	5	-	-	0	-
SCHYMAN, B.	-	4/ 9	.444	9/13	.692	-/ -	-	-	5	-	-	17	-
ROSE, D.	-	0/ 0	.000	0/ 0	.000	-/ -	-	-	0	-	-	0	-
JOHNSON, R.	-	4/ 7	.571	1/ 1	1.000	-/ -	-	-	5	-	-	9	-
BLUM, F.	-	4/12	.333	2/ 4	.500	-/ -	-	-	2	-	-	10	-
WYLDER, E.	-	0/ 0	.000	0/ 0	.000	-/ -	-	-	0	-	-	0	-
FEIEREISEL, R.	-	9/14	.643	9/12	.750	-/ -	-	-	4	-	-	27	-
LAMKIN, J.	-	6/20	.300	3/ 4	.750	-/ -	-	-	5	-	-	15	-
KIERES, D.	-	0/ 1	.000	2/ 2	1.000	-/ -	-	-	0	-	-	2	-
Totals	200	27/68	.397	26/36	.722	-/ -	-	-	26	-	-	80	.400

Indiana (82) Coach: Branch McCracken

	Min.	Total FG/FGA	Pct.	FT/FTA	Pct.	Reb. O/T	A	TO	PF	S	Blk	TP	PPM
FARLEY, R.	-	2/ 6	.333	8/11	.727	-/ -	-	-	4	-	-	12	-
KRAAK, C.	-	3/ 4	.750	0/ 0	.000	-/ -	-	-	5	-	-	6	-
WHITE, R.	-	3/ 9	.333	4/ 5	.800	-/ -	-	-	4	-	-	10	-
DEAKYNE, J.	-	1/ 3	.333	0/ 0	.000	-/ -	-	-	0	-	-	2	-
SCHLUNDT, D.	-	5/16	.313	13/17	.765	-/ -	-	-	3	-	-	23	-
SCOTT, B.	-	3/11	.273	0/ 0	.000	-/ -	-	-	5	-	-	6	-
POFF, P.	-	0/ 2	.000	1/ 2	.500	-/ -	-	-	3	-	-	1	-
LEONARD, R.	-	9/30	.300	4/ 9	.444	-/ -	-	-	1	-	-	22	-
Totals	200	26/81	.321	30/44	.682	-/ -	-	-	25	-	-	82	.410

Disqualified: Indiana—Kraak, Scott; DePaul—Schyman, Lamkin, Johnson, Lecos.

	1st Qtr.	2nd Qtr.	3rd Qtr.	4th Qtr.	Final
DePaul	16	17	22	25	80
Indiana	20	22	20	20	82

REGIONAL SEMIFINAL WEST

Seattle (70) Coach: Al Brightman

	Min.	Total FG/FGA	Pct.	FT/FTA	Pct.	Reb. O/T	A	TO	PF	S	Blk	TP	PPM
MOSCATEL	-	1/ -	-	0/ 0	.000	-/ -	-	-	3	-	-	2	-
DOHERTY	-	0/ -	-	0/ 0	.000	-/ -	-	-	1	-	-	0	-
JOHANSEN	-	2/ -	-	0/ 0	.000	-/ -	-	-	1	-	-	4	-
KELLY	-	2/ -	-	1/ 1	1.000	-/ -	-	-	2	-	-	5	-
SANFORD	-	1/ -	-	0/ 2	.000	-/ -	-	-	0	-	-	2	-
GLOWASKI	-	10/ -	-	2/ 4	.500	-/ -	-	-	1	-	-	22	-
PEHANICK	-	0/ -	-	2/ 3	.667	-/ -	-	-	2	-	-	2	-
O'BRIEN, E.	-	3/ -	-	3/ 4	.750	-/ -	-	-	4	-	-	9	-
O'BRIEN, J.	-	6/ -	-	12/14	.857	-/ -	-	-	2	-	-	24	-
Totals	200	25/ -	-	20/28	.714	-/ -	-	-	16	-	-	70	.350

Washington (92) Coach: Tippy Dye

	Min.	Total FG/FGA	Pct.	FT/FTA	Pct.	Reb. O/T	A	TO	PF	S	Blk	TP	PPM
MCCUTCHEN, M.	-	3/ -	-	4/ 4	1.000	-/ -	-	-	3	-	-	10	-
PARSONS, D.	-	1/ -	-	0/ 2	.000	-/ -	-	-	3	-	-	2	-
APELAND, D.	-	0/ -	-	0/ 0	.000	-/ -	-	-	0	-	-	0	-
MCCLARY, D.	-	5/ -	-	0/ 2	.000	-/ -	-	-	3	-	-	10	-
WARD, B.	-	0/ -	-	0/ 0	.000	-/ -	-	-	0	-	-	0	-
HOUBREGS, B.	-	20/ -	-	5/10	.500	-/ -	-	-	2	-	-	45	-
CIPRIANO, J.	-	4/ -	-	4/ 6	.667	-/ -	-	-	3	-	-	12	-
KOON, C.	-	6/ -	-	1/ 2	.500	-/ -	-	-	1	-	-	13	-
ELLIOTT, W.	-	0/ -	-	0/ 0	.000	-/ -	-	-	1	-	-	0	-
HALLE, R.	-	0/ -	-	0/ 0	.000	-/ -	-	-	0	-	-	0	-
Totals	200	39/ -	-	14/26	.538	-/ -	-	-	16	-	-	92	.460

Disqualified: None.

	1st Qtr.	2nd Qtr.	3rd Qtr.	4th Qtr.	Final
Seattle	11	21	16	22	70
Washington	24	23	21	24	92

Santa Clara (67) Coach: Bob Feerick

	Min.	Total FG/FGA	Pct.	FT/FTA	Pct.	Reb. O/T	A	TO	PF	S	Blk	TP	PPM
SEARS, K.	-	8/ -	-	3/ 4	.750	-/ -	-	-	3	-	-	19	-
YOUNG, J.	-	0/ -	-	3/ 5	.600	-/ -	-	-	3	-	-	3	-
GATZERT, G.	-	4/ -	-	1/ 2	.500	-/ -	-	-	3	-	-	9	-
SCHOENSTEIN, H.	-	4/ -	-	2/ 2	1.000	-/ -	-	-	1	-	-	10	-
MOUNT, M.	-	2/ -	-	4/ 7	.571	-/ -	-	-	3	-	-	8	-
GARIBALDI, D.	-	1/ -	-	6/ 6	1.000	-/ -	-	-	1	-	-	8	-
SOARES, D.	-	1/ -	-	0/ 0	.000	-/ -	-	-	3	-	-	2	-
BENEDETTI, D.	-	1/ -	-	6/ 6	1.000	-/ -	-	-	3	-	-	8	-
Totals	200	21/ -	-	25/32	.781	-/ -	-	-	20	-	-	67	.335

Wyoming (52) Coach: Everett Shelton

	Min.	Total FG/FGA	Pct.	FT/FTA	Pct.	Reb. O/T	A	TO	PF	S	Blk	TP	PPM
BURNS, R.	-	3/ -	-	1/ 1	1.000	-/ -	-	-	5	-	-	7	-
SHARP, W.	-	7/ -	-	9/ 9	1.000	-/ -	-	-	5	-	-	23	-
MOORE, R.	-	1/ -	-	0/ 2	.000	-/ -	-	-	0	-	-	2	-
RIVERS, R.	-	2/ -	-	0/ 2	.000	-/ -	-	-	1	-	-	4	-
JORGENSEN, H.	-	4/ -	-	5/ 8	.625	-/ -	-	-	2	-	-	13	-
WING, C.	-	0/ -	-	2/ 2	1.000	-/ -	-	-	4	-	-	2	-
MILVEHAL, J.	-	0/ -	-	1/ 1	1.000	-/ -	-	-	2	-	-	1	-
KUSKA, D.	-	0/ -	-	0/ 0	.000	-/ -	-	-	1	-	-	0	-
Totals	200	17/ -	-	18/25	.720	-/ -	-	-	20	-	-	52	.260

Disqualified: Wyoming—Burns, Sharp.

	1st Qtr.	2nd Qtr.	3rd Qtr.	4th Qtr.	Final
Santa Clara	20	6	23	18	67
Wyoming	17	7	15	13	52

TCU (54) Coach: Buster Brannon

	Min.	Total FG/FGA	Pct.	FT/FTA	Pct.	Reb. O/T	A	TO	PF	S	Blk	TP	PPM
WARREN	-	7/ -	-	8/10	.800	-/ -	-	-	1	-	-	22	-
WHITE	-	0/ -	-	1/ 3	.333	-/ -	-	-	2	-	-	1	-
ALLEN	-	2/ -	-	7/ 9	.778	-/ -	-	-	0	-	-	11	-
HOYT	-	0/ -	-	0/ 0	.000	-/ -	-	-	0	-	-	0	-
OHLEN	-	3/ -	-	2/ 3	.667	-/ -	-	-	5	-	-	8	-
BROWN	-	1/ -	-	0/ 0	.000	-/ -	-	-	1	-	-	2	-
LAMPKIN	-	0/ -	-	1/ 2	.500	-/ -	-	-	1	-	-	1	-
BRUMBLEY	-	1/ -	-	0/ 2	.000	-/ -	-	-	3	-	-	2	-
SWAIN	-	1/ -	-	1/ 1	1.000	-/ -	-	-	3	-	-	3	-
HILL	-	1/ -	-	2/ 4	.500	-/ -	-	-	2	-	-	4	-
Totals	200	16/ -	-	22/34	.647	-/ -	-	-	18	-	-	54	.270

Oklahoma A&M (71) Coach: Henry Iba

	Min.	Total FG/FGA	Pct.	FT/FTA	Pct.	Reb. O/T	A	TO	PF	S	Blk	TP	PPM
SHEETS, K.	-	6/ -	-	3/ 5	.600	-/ -	-	-	3	-	-	15	-
FULLER	-	0/ -	-	0/ 0	.000	-/ -	-	-	4	-	-	0	-
MALONEY	-	0/ -	-	0/ 0	.000	-/ -	-	-	0	-	-	0	-
STOCKTON, G.	-	1/ -	-	2/ 2	1.000	-/ -	-	-	3	-	-	4	-
HENDRICK	-	0/ -	-	0/ 0	.000	-/ -	-	-	1	-	-	0	-
HICKS	-	1/ -	-	2/ 2	1.000	-/ -	-	-	0	-	-	4	-
MATTICK, B.	-	13/ -	-	9/14	.643	-/ -	-	-	2	-	-	35	-
ROGERS, H.	-	3/ -	-	4/ 5	.800	-/ -	-	-	3	-	-	10	-
HASKINS	-	0/ -	-	0/ 0	.000	-/ -	-	-	0	-	-	0	-
ROARK	-	1/ -	-	1/ 1	1.000	-/ -	-	-	5	-	-	3	-
Totals	200	25/ -	-	21/29	.724	-/ -	-	-	21	-	-	71	.355

Disqualified: Oklahoma A&M—Roark; TCU—Ohlen.

	1st Qtr.	2nd Qtr.	3rd Qtr.	4th Qtr.	Final
TCU	14	15	13	12	54
Oklahoma A&M	15	13	18	25	71

Kansas (73) Coach: Phog Allen

	Min.	Total FG/FGA	Pct.	FT/FTA	Pct.	Reb. O/T	A	TO	PF	S	Blk	TP	PPM
KELLEY, A.	-	7/ -	-	3/ 4	.750	-/ -	-	-	4	-	-	17	-
SQUIRES, L.	-	0/ -	-	0/ 0	.000	-/ -	-	-	1	-	-	0	-
PATTERSON, H.	-	1/ -	-	7/ 8	.875	-/ -	-	-	1	-	-	9	-
BORN, B.	-	4/ -	-	3/ 4	.750	-/ -	-	-	4	-	-	11	-
KELLEY, D.	-	2/ -	-	3/ 5	.600	-/ -	-	-	5	-	-	7	-
DAVENPORT, L.	-	4/ -	-	0/ 0	.000	-/ -	-	-	1	-	-	8	-
REICH, G.	-	8/ -	-	4/ 6	.667	-/ -	-	-	4	-	-	20	-
SMITH, D.	-	0/ -	-	1/ 1	1.000	-/ -	-	-	0	-	-	1	-
ANDERSON, J.	-	0/ -	-	0/ 0	.000	-/ -	-	-	0	-	-	0	-
Totals	200	26/ -	-	21/28	.750	-/ -	-	-	20	-	-	73	.365

Oklahoma City (65) Coach: Doyle Parrack

	Min.	Total FG/FGA	Pct.	FT/FTA	Pct.	Reb. O/T	A	TO	PF	S	Blk	TP	PPM
SHORT	-	7/ -	-	3/ 3	1.000	-/ -	-	-	1	-	-	17	-
LIKENS	-	5/ -	-	4/ 4	1.000	-/ -	-	-	4	-	-	14	-
KEY	-	2/ -	-	8/10	.800	-/ -	-	-	2	-	-	12	-
ROSE	-	3/ -	-	5/ 7	.714	-/ -	-	-	3	-	-	11	-
COUTS	-	0/ -	-	1/ 1	1.000	-/ -	-	-	3	-	-	1	-
BOLIN	-	0/ -	-	0/ 2	.000	-/ -	-	-	1	-	-	0	-
NATH	-	2/ -	-	0/ 0	.000	-/ -	-	-	2	-	-	4	-
RICH	-	1/ -	-	1/ 1	1.000	-/ -	-	-	3	-	-	3	-
JONES	-	0/ -	-	0/ 0	.000	-/ -	-	-	1	-	-	0	-
BULLARD	-	1/ -	-	1/ 1	1.000	-/ -	-	-	1	-	-	3	-
Totals	200	21/ -	-	23/29	.793	-/ -	-	-	21	-	-	65	.325

Disqualified: Kansas—D. Kelley.

	1st Qtr.	2nd Qtr.	3rd Qtr.	4th Qtr.	Final
Kansas	24	23	17	9	73
Oklahoma City	13	13	20	19	65

REGIONAL FINAL EAST

Louisiana State (81) Coach: Harry Rabenhorst

	Min.	Total FG/FGA	Pct.	FT/FTA	Pct.	Reb. O/T	A	TO	PF	S	Blk	TP	PPM
CLARK, N.	-	2/ -	-	0/ 0	.000	-/ -	-	-	5	-	-	4	-
BELCHER, D.	-	6/ -	-	5/ 7	.714	-/ -	-	-	4	-	-	17	-
FRESHLEY, B.	-	0/ -	-	1/ 3	.333	-/ -	-	-	0	-	-	1	-
PETTIT, B.	-	12/ -	-	5/ 7	.714	-/ -	-	-	3	-	-	29	-
MCARDLE, B.	-	4/ -	-	5/ 8	.625	-/ -	-	-	5	-	-	13	-
MAGEE, N.	-	5/ -	-	5/ 7	.714	-/ -	-	-	3	-	-	15	-
BRIDGES, K.	-	1/ -	-	0/ 2	.000	-/ -	-	-	2	-	-	2	-
SCHULTZ, D.	-	0/ -	-	0/ 0	.000	-/ -	-	-	0	-	-	0	-
Totals	200	30/ -	-	21/34	.618	-/ -	-	-	22	-	-	81	.405

Holy Cross (73) Coach: Buster Sheary

	Min.	Total FG/FGA	Pct.	FT/FTA	Pct.	Reb. O/T	A	TO	PF	S	Blk	TP	PPM
PALAZZI, T.	-	1/ -	-	6/ 9	.667	-/ -	-	-	2	-	-	8	-
MAGILLIGAN, R.	-	2/ -	-	1/ 2	.500	-/ -	-	-	3	-	-	5	-
KASPRZAK, F.	-	0/ -	-	0/ 0	.000	-/ -	-	-	2	-	-	0	-
EARLY, J.	-	3/ -	-	0/ 0	.000	-/ -	-	-	4	-	-	6	-
CARROLL, J.	-	0/ -	-	0/ 0	.000	-/ -	-	-	0	-	-	0	-
CASEY, R.	-	0/ -	-	0/ 0	.000	-/ -	-	-	0	-	-	0	-
LEWIS, J.	-	1/ -	-	0/ 0	.000	-/ -	-	-	0	-	-	2	-
KIELLEY, J.	-	3/ -	-	1/ 2	.500	-/ -	-	-	3	-	-	7	-
NANGLE, D.	-	2/ -	-	4/ 4	1.000	-/ -	-	-	2	-	-	8	-
PERRY, R.	-	6/ -	-	5/ 5	1.000	-/ -	-	-	4	-	-	17	-
MARKEY, E.	-	5/ -	-	6/14	.429	-/ -	-	-	2	-	-	16	-
SUPRUNOWICZ, W.	-	2/ -	-	0/ 1	1.000	-/ -	-	-	1	-	-	4	-
Totals	200	25/ -	-	23/37	.622	-/ -	-	-	23	-	-	73	.365

Disqualified: Louisiana St.—Clark, McArdle.

	1st Qtr.	2nd Qtr.	3rd Qtr.	4th Qtr.	Final
Louisiana St.	18	23	23	17	81
Holy Cross	13	20	13	27	73

Notre Dame (66) Coach: John Jordan

	Min.	Total FG/FGA	Pct.	FT/FTA	Pct.	Reb. O/T	A	TO	PF	S	Blk	TP	PPM
ROSENTHAL, R.	-	6/17	.353	7/ 8	.875	-/ -	-	-	4	-	-	19	-
SULLIVAN, W.	-	1/ 2	.500	1/ 4	.250	-/ -	-	-	3	-	-	3	-
BERTRAND, J.	-	3/ 9	.333	2/ 4	.500	-/ -	-	-	4	-	-	8	-
LEWINSKI, N.	-	8/21	.381	3/ 3	1.000	-/ -	-	-	5	-	-	19	-
WISE, R.	-	0/ 3	.000	0/ 0	.000	-/ -	-	-	1	-	-	0	-
GIBBONS, J.	-	0/ 6	.000	2/ 3	.667	-/ -	-	-	5	-	-	2	-
REYNOLDS, J.	-	0/ 1	.000	1/ 2	.500	-/ -	-	-	1	-	-	1	-
STEPHENS, J.	-	5/15	.333	4/11	.364	-/ -	-	-	2	-	-	14	-
Totals	200	23/74	.311	20/35	.571	-/ -	-	-	25	-	-	66	.330

Indiana (79) Coach: Branch McCracken

	Min.	Total FG/FGA	Pct.	FT/FTA	Pct.	Reb. O/T	A	TO	PF	S	Blk	TP	PPM
FARLEY, R.	-	0/ 3	.000	2/ 2	1.000	-/ -	-	-	4	-	-	2	-
KRAAK, C.	-	2/ 6	.333	4/ 5	.800	-/ -	-	-	3	-	-	8	-
WHITE, R.	-	0/ 5	.000	1/ 1	1.000	-/ -	-	-	2	-	-	1	-
DEAKYNE, J.	-	0/ 0	.000	1/ 2	.500	-/ -	-	-	0	-	-	1	-
SCHLUNDT, D.	-	13/24	.542	15/18	.833	-/ -	-	-	5	-	-	41	-
SCOTT, B.	-	4/ 8	.500	2/ 2	1.000	-/ -	-	-	5	-	-	10	-
POFF, P.	-	1/ 3	.333	1/ 1	1.000	-/ -	-	-	1	-	-	3	-
LEONARD, R.	-	4/12	.333	3/ 4	.750	-/ -	-	-	4	-	-	11	-
BYERS, P.	-	1/ 1	1.000	0/ 2	.000	-/ -	-	-	1	-	-	2	-
Totals	200	25/62	.403	29/37	.784	-/ -	-	-	25	-	-	79	.395

Disqualified: Indiana—Schlundt, Scott; Notre Dame—Lewinski, Gibbons.

	1st Qtr.	2nd Qtr.	3rd Qtr.	4th Qtr.	Final
Notre Dame	18	14	16	18	66
Indiana	25	17	20	17	79

REGIONAL FINAL WEST

Washington (74) Coach: Tippy Dye

	Min.	Total FG/FGA	Pct.	FT/FTA	Pct.	Reb. O/T	A	TO	PF	S	Blk	TP	PPM
MCCUTCHEN, M.	-	2/ -	-	1/1	1.000	-/ -	-	-	3	-	-	5	-
MCCLARY, D.	-	2/ -	-	3/6	.500	-/ -	-	-	4	-	-	7	-
PARSONS, D.	-	1/ -	-	2/7	.286	-/ -	-	-	0	-	-	4	-
HOUBREGS, B.	-	12/ -	-	10/13	.769	-/ -	-	-	3	-	-	34	-
CIPRIANO, J.	-	6/ -	-	3/5	.600	-/ -	-	-	3	-	-	15	-
KOON, C.	-	3/ -	-	3/4	.750	-/ -	-	-	1	-	-	9	-
Totals	200	26/ -	-	22/36	.611	-/ -	-	-	14	-	-	74	.370

Santa Clara (62) Coach: Bob Feerick

	Min.	Total FG/FGA	Pct.	FT/FTA	Pct.	Reb. O/T	A	TO	PF	S	Blk	TP	PPM
SEARS, K.	-	7/ -	-	9/11	.818	-/ -	-	-	5	-	-	23	-
YOUNG, J.	-	3/ -	-	2/2	1.000	-/ -	-	-	5	-	-	8	-
GATZERT, G.	-	4/ -	-	0/0	.000	-/ -	-	-	3	-	-	8	-
MOUNT, M.	-	1/ -	-	3/4	.750	-/ -	-	-	4	-	-	5	-
SCHOENSTEIN, H.	-	2/ -	-	2/2	1.000	-/ -	-	-	3	-	-	6	-
GARIBALDI, D.	-	3/ -	-	0/0	.000	-/ -	-	-	2	-	-	6	-
SOARES, D.	-	2/ -	-	1/2	.500	-/ -	-	-	1	-	-	5	-
BENEDETTI, D.	-	0/ -	-	1/1	1.000	-/ -	-	-	1	-	-	1	-
Totals	200	22/ -	-	18/22	.818	-/ -	-	-	24	-	-	62	.310

Disqualified: Santa Clara—Sears, Young.

	1st Qtr.	2nd Qtr.	3rd Qtr.	4th Qtr.	Final
Washington	17	11	25	21	74
Santa Clara	16	14	21	11	62

Oklahoma A&M (55) Coach: Henry Iba

	Min.	Total FG/FGA	Pct.	FT/FTA	Pct.	Reb. O/T	A	TO	PF	S	Blk	TP	PPM
SHEETS, K.	-	0/ -	-	0/0	.000	-/ -	-	-	5	-	-	0	-
MALONEY	-	0/ -	-	0/0	.000	-/ -	-	-	0	-	-	0	-
HASKINS	-	0/ -	-	0/0	.000	-/ -	-	-	0	-	-	0	-
FULLER	-	1/ -	-	4/5	.800	-/ -	-	-	2	-	-	6	-
STOCKTON, G.	-	0/ -	-	0/0	.000	-/ -	-	-	0	-	-	0	-
MATTICK, B.	-	7/ -	-	8/16	.500	-/ -	-	-	3	-	-	22	-
HENDRICK	-	0/ -	-	1/1	1.000	-/ -	-	-	0	-	-	1	-
ROARK	-	3/ -	-	2/3	.667	-/ -	-	-	2	-	-	8	-
REAMES	-	4/ -	-	4/4	1.000	-/ -	-	-	5	-	-	12	-
HICKS	-	2/ -	-	2/2	1.000	-/ -	-	-	5	-	-	6	-
Totals	200	17/ -	-	21/31	.677	-/ -	-	-	22	-	-	55	.275

Kansas (61) Coach: Phog Allen

	Min.	Total FG/FGA	Pct.	FT/FTA	Pct.	Reb. O/T	A	TO	PF	S	Blk	TP	PPM
PATTERSON, H.	-	0/ -	-	4/6	.667	-/ -	-	-	5	-	-	4	-
KELLEY, A.	-	4/ -	-	5/8	.625	-/ -	-	-	4	-	-	13	-
BORN, B.	-	6/ -	-	6/6	1.000	-/ -	-	-	5	-	-	18	-
ALBERTS, J.	-	0/ -	-	1/1	1.000	-/ -	-	-	1	-	-	1	-
REICH, G.	-	2/ -	-	4/4	1.000	-/ -	-	-	3	-	-	8	-
SMITH, D.	-	0/ -	-	0/0	.000	-/ -	-	-	0	-	-	0	-
KELLEY, D.	-	6/ -	-	4/7	.571	-/ -	-	-	2	-	-	16	-
DAVENPORT, L.	-	0/ -	-	1/1	1.000	-/ -	-	-	1	-	-	1	-
Totals	200	18/ -	-	25/33	.758	-/ -	-	-	21	-	-	61	.305

Disqualified: Kansas—Patterson, Born; Oklahoma A&M—Sheets, Reames, Hicks.

	1st Qtr.	2nd Qtr.	3rd Qtr.	4th Qtr.	Final
Oklahoma A&M	15	13	14	13	55
Kansas	15	15	22	9	61

FINAL FOUR

Louisiana State (67) Coach: Harry Rabenhorst

	Min.	Total FG/FGA	Pct.	FT/FTA	Pct.	Reb. O/T	A	TO	PF	S	Blk	TP	PPM
BELCHER, D.	-	4/15	.267	2/3	.667	-/6	-	-	3	-	-	10	-
FRESHLEY, B.	-	0/1	.000	1/4	.250	-/0	-	-	4	-	-	1	-
MAGEE, N.	-	6/15	.400	5/8	.625	-/2	-	-	3	-	-	17	-
PETTIT, B.	-	10/24	.417	9/18	.500	-/15	-	-	4	-	-	29	-
MCARDLE, B.	-	1/6	.167	1/3	.333	-/1	-	-	5	-	-	3	-
CLARK, N.	-	0/7	.000	2/2	1.000	-/10	-	-	5	-	-	2	-
BRIDGES, K.	-	1/2	.500	3/6	.500	-/0	-	-	2	-	-	5	-
Totals	200	22/70	.314	23/44	.523	-/34	-	-	26	-	-	67	.335

Indiana (80) Coach: Branch McCracken

	Min.	Total FG/FGA	Pct.	FT/FTA	Pct.	Reb. O/T	A	TO	PF	S	Blk	TP	PPM
FARLEY, R.	-	4/5	.800	2/5	.400	-/7	-	-	4	-	-	10	-
KRAAK, C.	-	2/6	.333	5/7	.714	-/9	-	-	4	-	-	9	-
WHITE, R.	-	0/6	.000	3/4	.750	-/8	-	-	2	-	-	3	-
DEAKYNE, J.	-	0/0	.000	0/0	.000	-/0	-	-	0	-	-	0	-
SCHLUNDT, D.	-	8/15	.533	13/17	.765	-/5	-	-	4	-	-	29	-
SCOTT, B.	-	2/7	.286	3/4	.750	-/2	-	-	4	-	-	7	-
POFF, P.	-	0/2	.000	0/0	.000	-/1	-	-	2	-	-	0	-
LEONARD, R.	-	9/12	.750	4/5	.800	-/1	-	-	4	-	-	22	-
BYERS, P.	-	0/0	.000	0/0	.000	-/0	-	-	3	-	-	0	-
Totals	200	25/53	.472	30/42	.714	-/33	-	-	27	-	-	80	.400

Disqualified: Lousiana St.—Clark, McArdle.

	1st Qtr.	2nd Qtr.	3rd Qtr.	4th Qtr.	Final
Louisiana St.	20	21	15	11	67
Indiana	31	18	20	11	80

Washington (53)   Coach: Tippy Dye

	Min.	Total FG / FGA	Pct.	FT / FTA	Pct.	Reb. O / T	A	TO	PF	S	Blk	TP	PPM
MCCUTCHEN, M.	-	0/ 6	.000	3/ 6	.500	-/ -	-	-	2	-	-	3	-
MCCLARY, D.	-	2/ 8	.250	1/ 1	1.000	-/ -	-	-	4	-	-	5	-
PARSONS, D.	-	0/ 3	.000	1/ 4	.250	-/ -	-	-	3	-	-	1	-
HOUBREGS, B.	-	8/13	.615	2/ 2	1.000	-/ -	-	-	5	-	-	18	-
ELLIOTT, W.	-	1/ 3	.333	1/ 1	1.000	-/ -	-	-	0	-	-	3	-
CIPRIANO, J.	-	4/14	.286	3/ 5	.600	-/ -	-	-	1	-	-	11	-
APELAND, D.	-	1/ 2	.500	0/ 0	.000	-/ -	-	-	1	-	-	2	-
KOON, C.	-	3/12	.250	2/ 3	.667	-/ -	-	-	4	-	-	8	-
ROAKE, S.	-	0/ 1	.000	0/ 0	.000	-/ -	-	-	3	-	-	0	-
HALLE, R.	-	0/ 0	.000	2/ 6	.333	-/ -	-	-	0	-	-	2	-
WARD, B.	-	0/ 0	.000	0/ 0	.000	-/ -	-	-	0	-	-	0	-
Totals	200	19/62	.306	15/28	.536	-/ -	-	-	23	-	-	53	.265

Kansas (79)   Coach: Phog Allen

	Min.	Total FG / FGA	Pct.	FT / FTA	Pct.	Reb. O / T	A	TO	PF	S	Blk	TP	PPM
PATTERSON, H.	-	6/11	.545	4/ 7	.571	-/ -	-	-	2	-	-	16	-
SMITH, D.	-	0/ 1	.000	0/ 0	.000	-/ -	-	-	1	-	-	0	-
KELLEY, A.	-	5/16	.313	1/ 2	.500	-/ -	-	-	3	-	-	11	-
DAVENPORT, L.	-	0/ 1	.000	2/ 2	1.000	-/ -	-	-	0	-	-	2	-
BORN, B.	-	9/17	.529	7/ 9	.778	-/ -	-	-	4	-	-	25	-
KELLEY, D.	-	7/17	.412	2/ 4	.500	-/ -	-	-	4	-	-	16	-
REICH, G.	-	2/ 5	.400	2/ 2	1.000	-/ -	-	-	3	-	-	6	-
ALBERTS, J.	-	0/ 0	.000	0/ 0	.000	-/ -	-	-	0	-	-	0	-
BULLER, K.	-	0/ 0	.000	1/ 4	.250	-/ -	-	-	1	-	-	1	-
SQUIRES, L.	-	0/ 0	.000	0/ 0	.000	-/ -	-	-	0	-	-	0	-
HEITHOLT, B.	-	1/ 2	.500	0/ 0	.000	-/ -	-	-	0	-	-	2	-
ANDERSON, J.	-	0/ 0	.000	0/ 0	.000	-/ -	-	-	1	-	-	0	-
Totals	200	30/70	.429	19/30	.633	-/ -	-	-	19	-	-	79	.395

Disqualified: Washington—Houbregs.

	1st Qtr.	2nd Qtr.	3rd Qtr.	4th Qtr.	Final
Washington	20	14	10	9	53
Kansas	24	21	13	21	79

NATIONAL CHAMPIONSHIP

Indiana (69)   Coach: Branch McCracken

	Min.	Total FG / FGA	Pct.	FT / FTA	Pct.	Reb. O / T	A	TO	PF	S	Blk	TP	PPM
FARLEY, R.	-	1/ 8	.125	0/ 0	.000	-/ -	-	-	5	-	-	2	-
KRAAK, C.	-	5/ 8	.625	7/10	.700	-/ -	-	-	5	-	-	17	-
WHITE, R.	-	1/ 5	.200	0/ 0	.000	-/ -	-	-	2	-	-	2	-
DEAKYNE, J.	-	0/ 0	.000	0/ 0	.000	-/ -	-	-	1	-	-	0	-
SCHLUNDT, D.	-	11/26	.423	8/11	.727	-/ -	-	-	3	-	-	30	-
SCOTT, B.	-	2/ 4	.500	2/ 3	.667	-/ -	-	-	3	-	-	6	-
POFF, P.	-	0/ 1	.000	0/ 0	.000	-/ -	-	-	0	-	-	0	-
LEONARD, R.	-	5/15	.333	2/ 4	.500	-/ -	-	-	2	-	-	12	-
BYERS, P.	-	0/ 2	.000	0/ 0	.000	-/ -	-	-	0	-	-	0	-
Totals	200	25/69	.362	19/28	.679	-/ -	-	-	21	-	-	69	.345

Kansas (68)   Coach: Phog Allen

	Min.	Total FG / FGA	Pct.	FT / FTA	Pct.	Reb. O / T	A	TO	PF	S	Blk	TP	PPM
PATTERSON, H.	-	1/ 3	.333	7/ 8	.875	-/ -	-	-	3	-	-	9	-
SMITH, D.	-	0/ 0	.000	1/ 1	1.000	-/ -	-	-	1	-	-	1	-
KELLEY, A.	-	7/20	.350	6/ 8	.750	-/ -	-	-	3	-	-	20	-
DAVENPORT, L.	-	0/ 1	.000	0/ 0	.000	-/ -	-	-	0	-	-	0	-
BORN, B.	-	8/27	.296	10/12	.833	-/ -	-	-	5	-	-	26	-
KELLEY, D.	-	3/ 4	.750	2/ 4	.500	-/ -	-	-	2	-	-	8	-
REICH, G.	-	2/ 9	.222	0/ 0	.000	-/ -	-	-	2	-	-	4	-
ALBERTS, J.	-	0/ 1	.000	0/ 0	.000	-/ -	-	-	1	-	-	0	-
Totals	200	21/65	.323	26/33	.788	-/ -	-	-	17	-	-	68	.340

Disqualified: Indiana—Kraak, Farley; Kansas—Born. Technical fouls: Indiana—Kraak, Leonard, Schlundt.

	1st Qtr.	2nd Qtr.	3rd Qtr.	4th Qtr.	Final
Indiana	21	20	18	10	69
Kansas	19	22	17	10	68

NATIONAL THIRD PLACE

Louisiana State (69)   Coach: Harry Rabenhorst

	Min.	Total FG / FGA	Pct.	FT / FTA	Pct.	Reb. O / T	A	TO	PF	S	Blk	TP	PPM
BELCHER, D.	-	2/ -		2/ 2	1.000	-/ -	-	-	1	-	-	6	-
BRIDGES, K.	-	1/ -		0/ 0	.000	-/ -	-	-	2	-	-	2	-
CLARK, N.	-	5/ -		4/ 5	.800	-/ -	-	-	5	-	-	14	-
SCHULTZ, D.	-	2/ -		0/ 0	.000	-/ -	-	-	0	-	-	4	-
PETTIT, B.	-	14/ -		8/10	.800	-/ -	-	-	5	-	-	36	-
MCNEILLY, J.	-	0/ -		0/ 0	.000	-/ -	-	-	0	-	-	0	-
MAGEE, N.	-	0/ -		0/ 0	.000	-/ -	-	-	4	-	-	0	-
FRESHLEY, B.	-	0/ -		0/ 0	.000	-/ -	-	-	1	-	-	0	-
MCARDLE, B.	-	3/ -		1/ 1	1.000	-/ -	-	-	1	-	-	7	-
LOUGHMILLER, D.	-	0/ -		0/ 0	.000	-/ -	-	-	0	-	-	0	-
ROBERTS, C.	-	0/ -		0/ 0	.000	-/ -	-	-	0	-	-	0	-
Totals	200	27/ -		15/18	.833	-/ -	-	-	19	-	-	69	.345

Washington (88)   Coach: Tippy Dye

	Min.	Total FG / FGA	Pct.	FT / FTA	Pct.	Reb. O / T	A	TO	PF	S	Blk	TP	PPM
MCCUTCHEN, M.	-	1/ -		1/ 1	1.000	-/ -	-	-	0	-	-	3	-
WARD, B.	-	0/ -		0/ 2	.000	-/ -	-	-	0	-	-	0	-
MCCLARY, D.	-	1/ -		1/ 1	1.000	-/ -	-	-	2	-	-	3	-
ELLIOTT, W.	-	0/ -		1/ 2	.500	-/ -	-	-	0	-	-	1	-
HOUBREGS, B.	-	17/ -		8/10	.800	-/ -	-	-	0	-	-	42	-
ROAKE, S.	-	0/ -		4/ 4	1.000	-/ -	-	-	0	-	-	4	-
CIPRIANO, J.	-	11/ -		2/ 4	.500	-/ -	-	-	3	-	-	24	-
HALLE, R.	-	1/ -		1/ 1	1.000	-/ -	-	-	1	-	-	3	-
KOON, C.	-	1/ -		0/ 0	.000	-/ -	-	-	2	-	-	2	-
PARSONS, D.	-	2/ -		2/ 3	.667	-/ -	-	-	5	-	-	6	-
Totals	200	34/ -		20/28	.714	-/ -	-	-	13	-	-	88	.440

Disqualified: Washington—Parsons; Louisiana St.—Clark, Pettit.

	1st Qtr.	2nd Qtr.	3rd Qtr.	4th Qtr.	Final
Louisiana St.	14	12	19	24	69
Washington	18	21	27	22	88

REGIONAL THIRD PLACE EAST

Wake Forest (91)   Coach: Murray Greason

	Min.	Total FG / FGA	Pct.	FT / FTA	Pct.	Reb. O / T	A	TO	PF	S	Blk	TP	PPM
LYLES, B.	39	7/13	.538	3/ 6	.500	-/ 4	6	-	1	-	-	17	.436
WILLIAMS, J.	37	10/16	.625	3/ 3	1.000	-/13	1	-	5	-	-	23	.622
GEORGE, M.	31	4/ 7	.571	2/ 2	1.000	-/ 1	3	-	3	-	-	10	.323
HEMRIC, D.	39	11/23	.478	7/14	.500	-/18	5	-	4	-	-	29	.744
DEPORTER, A.	39	2/ 4	.500	6/ 9	.667	-/ 3	3	-	3	-	-	10	.256
LIPSTAS, R.	8	0/ 1	.000	0/ 0	.000	-/ 2	2	-	3	-	-	0	.000
KOCH, J.	1	0/ 1	.000	0/ 0	.000	-/ 0	0	-	1	-	-	0	.000
ALHEIM, B.	1	0/ 3	.000	0/ 0	.000	-/ 0	1	-	0	-	-	0	.000
PRESTON, T.	2	0/ 0	.000	0/ 2	.000	-/ 0	1	-	0	-	-	0	.000
HOWARD	1	1/ 1	1.000	0/ 0	.000	-/ 0	0	-	1	-	-	2	2.000
HOWELL	1	0/ 0	.000	0/ 0	.000	-/ 0	0	-	1	-	-	0	.000
DEVOS, J.	1	0/ 1	.000	0/ 0	.000	-/ 1	0	-	0	-	-	0	.000
Totals	200	35/70	.500	21/36	.583	-/42	22	-	22	-	-	91	.455

Lebanon Valley (71)   Coach: Rinso Marquette

	Min.	Total FG / FGA	Pct.	FT / FTA	Pct.	Reb. O / T	A	TO	PF	S	Blk	TP	PPM
GLUNTZ, M.	16	2/ 4	.500	1/ 1	1.000	-/ 0	0	-	1	-	-	5	.313
LANDA, H.	38	5/17	.294	3/ 4	.750	-/ 8	9	-	4	-	-	13	.342
HANDLEY, J.	2	0/ 0	.000	0/ 0	.000	-/ 1	0	-	0	-	-	0	.000
KOSIER, H.	4	0/ 0	.000	1/ 2	.500	-/ 0	0	-	2	-	-	1	.250
FINKLESTEIN, H.	40	6/10	.600	6/12	.500	-/ 9	1	-	1	-	-	18	.450
SORRENTINO, L.	26	5/15	.333	5/ 7	.714	-/ 4	2	-	4	-	-	15	.577
MILLER, L.	32	1/ 6	.167	4/ 7	.571	-/ 4	1	-	5	-	-	6	.188
BLAKENEY, R.	4	0/ 1	.000	0/ 0	.000	-/ 0	0	-	3	-	-	0	.000
VOUGHT, W.	38	6/18	.333	1/ 2	.500	-/ 9	1	-	3	-	-	13	.342
Totals	200	25/71	.352	21/35	.600	-/35	14	-	23	-	-	71	.355

Disqualified: Wake Forest—Williams; Lebanon Valley—Miller.

	1st Qtr.	2nd Qtr.	3rd Qtr.	4th Qtr.	Final
Wake Forest	26	23	18	24	91
Lebanon Valley	15	14	18	24	71

Pennsylvania (90)   Coach: Howie Dallmar

	Min.	Total FG / FGA	Pct.	FT / FTA	Pct.	Reb. O / T	A	TO	PF	S	Blk	TP	PPM
HEYLMUN	-	4/ -	-	3/ 4	.750	-/ -	-	-	3	-	-	11	-
MASTERS	-	0/ -	-	0/ 0	.000	-/ -	-	-	0	-	-	0	-
LEACH	-	10/ -	-	1/ 1	1.000	-/ -	-	-	4	-	-	21	-
LAVIN	-	0/ -	-	0/ 2	.000	-/ -	-	-	1	-	-	0	-
BECK, E.	-	9/ -	-	4/ 5	.800	-/ -	-	-	0	-	-	22	-
VITETTA	-	1/ -	-	5/ 6	.833	-/ -	-	-	2	-	-	7	-
HOAGLAND	-	8/ -	-	1/ 2	.500	-/ -	-	-	3	-	-	17	-
HARTER	-	0/ -	-	0/ 0	.000	-/ -	-	-	0	-	-	0	-
HOLT	-	3/ -	-	3/ 7	.429	-/ -	-	-	0	-	-	9	-
GRAMIGNA	-	1/ -	-	1/ 2	.500	-/ -	-	-	0	-	-	3	-
Totals	200	36/ -	-	18/29	.621	-/ -	-	-	13	-	-	90	.450

DePaul (70)   Coach: Ray Meyer

	Min.	Total FG / FGA	Pct.	FT / FTA	Pct.	Reb. O / T	A	TO	PF	S	Blk	TP	PPM
LECOS, D.	-	3/ -	-	0/ 2	.000	-/ -	-	-	1	-	-	6	-
SCHYMAN, B.	-	3/ -	-	3/ 5	.600	-/ -	-	-	4	-	-	9	-
JOHNSON, R.	-	1/ -	-	1/ 3	.333	-/ -	-	-	1	-	-	3	-
BLUM, F.	-	7/ -	-	0/ 0	.000	-/ -	-	-	2	-	-	14	-
WYLDER, E.	-	0/ -	-	0/ 0	.000	-/ -	-	-	0	-	-	0	-
FEIEREISEL, R.	-	7/ -	-	3/ 4	.750	-/ -	-	-	3	-	-	17	-
LAMKIN, J.	-	5/ -	-	5/ 7	.714	-/ -	-	-	5	-	-	15	-
KIERES, D.	-	3/ -	-	0/ 0	.000	-/ -	-	-	2	-	-	6	-
Totals	200	29/ -	-	12/21	.571	-/ -	-	-	18	-	-	70	.350

Disqualified: DePaul—Lankin.

	1st Qtr.	2nd Qtr.	3rd Qtr.	4th Qtr.	Final
Pennsylvania	28	16	22	24	90
DePaul	22	12	16	20	70

REGIONAL THIRD PLACE WEST

Seattle (80)   Coach: Al Brightman

	Min.	Total FG / FGA	Pct.	FT / FTA	Pct.	Reb. O / T	A	TO	PF	S	Blk	TP	PPM
MOSCATEL	-	1/ -	-	0/ 2	.000	-/ -	-	-	2	-	-	2	-
DOHERTY	-	1/ -	-	0/ 0	.000	-/ -	-	-	1	-	-	2	-
SANFORD	-	2/ -	-	2/ 2	1.000	-/ -	-	-	2	-	-	6	-
PEHANICK	-	0/ -	-	1/ 1	1.000	-/ -	-	-	1	-	-	1	-
BISSETT	-	2/ -	-	0/ 0	.000	-/ -	-	-	4	-	-	4	-
GLOWASKI	-	4/ -	-	4/ 6	.667	-/ -	-	-	3	-	-	12	-
KELLY	-	0/ -	-	0/ 0	.000	-/ -	-	-	2	-	-	0	-
O'BRIEN, E.	-	5/ -	-	6/ 7	.857	-/ -	-	-	4	-	-	16	-
O'BRIEN, J.	-	6/ -	-	18/22	.818	-/ -	-	-	4	-	-	30	-
MALONE	-	2/ -	-	1/ 2	.500	-/ -	-	-	0	-	-	5	-
JOHANSEN	-	1/ -	-	0/ 0	.000	-/ -	-	-	2	-	-	2	-
Totals	200	24/ -	-	32/42	.762	-/ -	-	-	25	-	-	80	.400

Wyoming (64)   Coach: Everett Shelton

	Min.	Total FG / FGA	Pct.	FT / FTA	Pct.	Reb. O / T	A	TO	PF	S	Blk	TP	PPM
JORGENSEN, H.	-	5/ -	-	7/10	.700	-/ -	-	-	5	-	-	17	-
MULVEHAL, J.	-	5/ -	-	4/12	.333	-/ -	-	-	4	-	-	14	-
BURNS, R.	-	1/ -	-	1/ 2	.500	-/ -	-	-	5	-	-	3	-
MOORE, W.	-	1/ -	-	0/ 0	.000	-/ -	-	-	4	-	-	2	-
RIVERS, R.	-	1/ -	-	1/ 2	.500	-/ -	-	-	1	-	-	3	-
WING, C.	-	5/ -	-	1/ 2	.500	-/ -	-	-	4	-	-	11	-
SHARP, W.	-	3/ -	-	8/10	.800	-/ -	-	-	4	-	-	14	-
Totals	200	21/ -	-	22/38	.579	-/ -	-	-	27	-	-	64	.320

Disqualified: Wyoming—Jorgensen, Burns.

	1st Qtr.	2nd Qtr.	3rd Qtr.	4th Qtr.	Final
Seattle	19	15	26	20	80
Wyoming	11	16	15	22	64

TCU (58)   Coach: Buster Brannon

	Min.	Total FG / FGA	Pct.	FT / FTA	Pct.	Reb. O / T	A	TO	PF	S	Blk	TP	PPM
ALLEN	-	2/ -	-	1/ -	-	-/ -	-	-	2	-	-	5	-
WARREN	-	3/ -	-	1/ -	-	-/ -	-	-	2	-	-	7	-
OHLEN	-	12/ -	-	4/ -	-	-/ -	-	-	2	-	-	28	-
WHITE	-	1/ -	-	1/ -	-	-/ -	-	-	3	-	-	3	-
SWAIN	-	2/ -	-	0/ -	-	-/ -	-	-	3	-	-	4	-
HILL	-	1/ -	-	3/ -	-	-/ -	-	-	3	-	-	5	-
LAMPKIN	-	1/ -	-	0/ -	-	-/ -	-	-	5	-	-	2	-
BRUMBLEY	-	0/ -	-	4/ -	-	-/ -	-	-	0	-	-	4	-
Totals	200	22/ -	-	14/ -	-	-/ -	-	-	20	-	-	58	.290

Oklahoma City (56)   Coach: Doyle Parrack

	Min.	Total FG / FGA	Pct.	FT / FTA	Pct.	Reb. O / T	A	TO	PF	S	Blk	TP	PPM
KEY	-	2/ -	-	6/10	.600	-/ -	-	-	4	-	-	10	-
NATH	-	0/ -	-	1/ 1	1.000	-/ -	-	-	3	-	-	1	-
LIKENS	-	9/ -	-	3/ 5	.600	-/ -	-	-	2	-	-	21	-
BOLIN	-	1/ -	-	0/ 0	.000	-/ -	-	-	3	-	-	2	-
ROSE	-	1/ -	-	3/ 4	.750	-/ -	-	-	0	-	-	5	-
BULLARD	-	0/ -	-	1/ 1	1.000	-/ -	-	-	1	-	-	1	-
COUTS	-	0/ -	-	1/ 1	1.000	-/ -	-	-	2	-	-	1	-
SHORT	-	5/ -	-	5/ 7	.714	-/ -	-	-	2	-	-	15	-
RICH	-	0/ -	-	0/ 0	.000	-/ -	-	-	1	-	-	0	-
Totals	200	18/ -	-	20/29	.690	-/ -	-	-	18	-	-	56	.280

Disqualified: TCU—Lampkin.

	1st Qtr.	2nd Qtr.	3rd Qtr.	4th Qtr.	Final
TCU	13	11	10	24	58
Oklahoma City	11	14	9	22	56

○ ALL-STAR TEAMS ○

ALL TOURNAMENT

★ B. H. BORN	KANSAS
BOB HOUBREGS	WASHINGTON
DEAN KELLEY	KANSAS
BOB LEONARD	INDIANA
DON SCHLUNDT	INDIANA

WESTERN REGIONAL (MANHATTAN, KS)

B. H. BORN	KANSAS
★ DEAN KELLEY	KANSAS
BOB MATTICK	OKLAHOMA A&M
GIL REICH	KANSAS
ARNOLD SHORT	OKLAHOMA CITY

★ Most Outstanding Player(s)

○ INDIVIDUAL RECORDS ○

SCORING

Most points in a single game
1. BOB HOUBREGS, WASHINGTON (vs. SEATTLE) 45
2. BOB HOUBREGS, WASHINGTON (vs. LOUISIANA ST.) 42
2. JOHNNY O'BRIEN, SEATTLE (vs. IDAHO STATE) 42
4. DON SCHLUNDT, INDIANA (vs. NOTRE DAME) 41
5. BOB PETTIT, LOUISIANA ST. (vs. WASHINGTON) 36

Most total points in the tournament
1. BOB HOUBREGS, WASHINGTON 139
2. DON SCHLUNDT, INDIANA 123
3. BOB PETTIT, LOUISIANA ST. 122
4. JOHNNY O'BRIEN, SEATTLE 96
5. B.H. BORN, KANSAS 80

Highest scoring average (minimum 2 games)
1. BOB HOUBREGS, WASHINGTON (139-4) 34.75
2. JOHNNY O'BRIEN, SEATTLE (96-3) 32.00
3. DON SCHLUNDT, INDIANA (123-4) 30.75
4. BOB PETTIT, LOUISIANA ST. (122-4) 30.50
5. DICK HEMRIC, WAKE FOREST (58-2) 29.00

FIELD GOALS

Most field goals in a single game
1. BOB HOUBREGS, WASHINGTON (vs. SEATTLE) 20
2. BOB HOUBREGS, WASHINGTON (vs. LOUISIANA ST.) 17
2. JOHNNY O'BRIEN, SEATTLE (vs. IDAHO STATE) 17

4. BOB PETTIT, LOUISIANA ST. (vs. WASHINGTON) 14
4. TOGO PALAZZI, HOLY CROSS (vs. WAKE FOREST) 14

Most total field goals in the tournament
1. BOB HOUBREGS, WASHINGTON 57
2. BOB PETTIT, LOUISIANA ST. 49
3. DON SCHLUNDT, INDIANA 37
4. JOHNNY O'BRIEN, SEATTLE 29
5. 2 tied for fifth place.

FREE THROWS

Most free throws in a single game
1. JOHNNY O'BRIEN, SEATTLE (vs. WYOMING) 18
2. DON SCHLUNDT, INDIANA (vs. NOTRE DAME) 15
3. DON SCHLUNDT, INDIANA (vs. LOUISIANA ST.) 13
3. DON SCHLUNDT, INDIANA (vs. DEPAUL) 13
5. 4 tied for fifth place.

Most total free throws in the tournament
1. DON SCHLUNDT, INDIANA 49
2. JOHNNY O'BRIEN, SEATTLE 38
3. B.H. BORN, KANSAS 26
4. BOB HOUBREGS, WASHINGTON 25
5. 2 tied for fifth place.

Most free throws attempted in a single game
1. JOHNNY O'BRIEN, SEATTLE (vs. WYOMING) 22
2. BOB PETTIT, LOUISIANA ST. (vs. INDIANA) 18
2. DON SCHLUNDT, INDIANA (vs. NOTRE DAME) 18
4. 3 tied for fourth place.

Most free throws attempted in the tournament
1. DON SCHLUNDT, INDIANA 63
2. JOHNNY O'BRIEN, SEATTLE 45
3. BOB PETTIT, LOUISIANA ST. 42
4. EARLE MARKEY, HOLY CROSS 36
5. BOB HOUBREGS, WASHINGTON 35

Highest free throw percentage in a single game (minimum 7 attempts)
1. LOUIS SORRENTINO, LEBANON VALLEY (vs. FORDHAM) (12-12) 1.000
2. WILLIAM SHARP, WYOMING (vs. SANTA CLARA) (9-9) 1.000
3. RONALD PERRY, HOLY CROSS (vs. NAVY) (7-7) 1.000
4. JOHNNY O'BRIEN, SEATTLE (vs. IDAHO STATE) (8-9) .889
5. 5 tied for fifth place.

Highest free throw percentage in the tournament (minimum 15 attempts)
1. RONALD PERRY, HOLY CROSS (18-20) .900
2. WILLIAM SHARP, WYOMING (17-19) .895
3. RICHARD ROSENTHAL, NOTRE DAME (24-27) .889
4. LOUIS SORRENTINO, LEBANON VALLEY (22-25) .880
5. EDDIE O'BRIEN, SEATTLE (14-16) .875

✪ TEAM RECORDS ✪

SCORING

Most points in a single game
1	WASHINGTON (vs. SEATTLE)	92
2	WAKE FOREST (vs. LEBANON VALLEY)	91
3	PENNSYLVANIA (vs. DE PAUL)	90

Most total points in the tournament
1	INDIANA	310
2	WASHINGTON	307
3	LOUISIANA ST.	306

Highest scoring average (minimum 2 games)
1	WAKE FOREST (162-2)	81.00
2	HOLY CROSS (239-3)	79.67
3	SEATTLE (238-3)	79.33

FIELD GOALS

Most field goals in a single game
1	WASHINGTON (vs. SEATTLE)	39
2	LOUISIANA ST. (vs. LEBANON VALLEY)	38
3	PENNSYLVANIA (vs. DE PAUL)	36

Most total field goals in the tournament
1	WASHINGTON	118
2	LOUISIANA ST.	117
3	INDIANA	101

FREE THROWS

Most free throws in a single game
1	SEATTLE (vs. WYOMING)	32
2	3 tied for second place.	

Most total free throws in the tournament
1	INDIANA	108
2	KANSAS	91
3	LEBANON VALLEY	79

Most free throws attempted in a single game
1	LOUISIANA ST. (vs. INDIANA)	44
1	INDIANA (vs. DEPAUL)	44
3	LEBANON VALLEY (vs. LOUISIANA ST.)	43

Most total free throws attempted in the tournament
1	INDIANA	151
2	KANSAS	124
3	LOUISIANA ST.	123

Highest free throw percentage in a single game
1	NOTRE DAME (vs. PENNSYLVANIA) (29-33)	.879
2	LOUISIANA ST. (vs. WASHINGTON) (15-18)	.833
3	2 tied for third place.	

Fewest free throws in a single game
1	FORDHAM (vs. LEBANON VALLEY)	5
2	DEPAUL (vs. PENNSYLVANIA)	12
3	LOUISIANA ST. (vs. LEBANON VALLEY)	13

Lowest free throw percentage in a single game
1	FORDHAM (vs. LEBANON VALLEY) (5-16)	.313
2	LOUISIANA ST. (vs. LEBANON VALLEY) (13-27)	.482
3	LOUISIANA ST. (vs. INDIANA) (23-44)	.523

Lowest free throw percentage in the tournament (minimum 2 games)
1	LOUISIANA ST. (72-123)	.585
2	WASHINGTON (71-118)	.602
3	WAKE FOREST (46-75)	.613

1954

EAST

WEST

Toledo 50

Penn St. 78

Penn St. 62

Penn St. 71

(bye)

Louisiana St. 70

Penn St. 54

Notre Dame 80

Notre Dame 65

Loyola N.O. 70

Notre Dame 63

(bye)

Indiana 64

Bradley 74

U. Conn. 80

Navy 69

Navy 85

Navy 48

(bye)

Cornell 67

La Salle 69

N.C. State 75

N.C. State 81

Geo. Wash. 73

La Salle 64

Fordham 74

La Salle 88

La Salle 76

Oklahoma City 55

Bradley 76

Bradley 61

Bradley 71

Colorado 64

(bye)

Rice 45

(bye)

Oklahoma A&M 57

Oklahoma A&M 51

(bye)

La Salle 92
Bradley 76

Idaho St. 77 (ot)

Idaho St. 59

Seattle 75

USC 66 (2 ot)

USC 73

(bye)

USC 72

Texas Tech 64

Santa Clara 73

Santa Clara 73

Santa Clara 65

Colorado A&M 50

(bye)

CONSOLATION GAMES

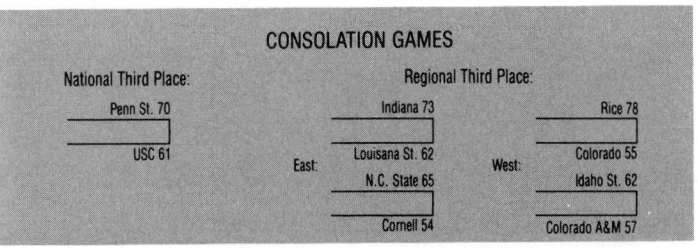

National Third Place:

Penn St. 70

USC 61

Regional Third Place:

East:

Indiana 73

Louisiana St. 62

N.C. State 65

Cornell 54

West:

Rice 78

Colorado 55

Idaho St. 62

Colorado A&M 57

In 1954 the NCAA tournament was a little like Alice in Wonderland—topsy turvy. None of the Final Four teams were ranked in the AP Top 10 writers' poll, and only La Salle even made it into the Top 20.

Among the top-ranked teams: unbeaten No. 1 Kentucky refused a tournament bid when its three "post-graduate" (fifth-year) stars—Cliff Hagan, Frank Ramsey and Lou Tsioropolos—were declared ineligible; the No. 2 defending champion Indiana Hoosiers were nipped in their opening tourney game by No. 6 Notre Dame, who lost the next night to Penn State; No. 3 Duquesne, No. 4 Western Kentucky, and No. 9 Holy Cross were all in the rival NIT; No. 5 Oklahoma A&M, playing at home in Stillwater, was beaten decisively by Bradley in the regional finals; No. 7 George Washington lost to No. 10 North Carolina State, who in turn lost to La Salle in the second round; and No. 8 Louisiana State, representing the SEC only because Kentucky refused the automatic bid, was whipped by Penn State in their opener.

The UPI coaches' poll selected two other teams for the Top 10: Kansas stood at No. 7, but they lost their final conference game to mediocre Missouri and were replaced as the Big Seven representatives; and Iowa, ranked No. 10 by the UPI, finished behind Indiana in the Big Ten and thus did not qualify for the tournament.

With all the favorites having fallen down the rabbit hole, it came down to which dark horse would win the March Hare's Kansas City tea party. The most likely candidate was La Salle. The explosive Explorers, led by All-American Tom Gola, had lost only four times all season. But they too almost bit the dust in their opening tournament game, as they were extended to the limit by Fordham before winning in overtime. With the score tied in the last three minutes of regulation, Fordham held for the final shot. When the Rams' Ed Parchinski's set shot bounded off the rim, Dan Lyons tipped it back in: Fordham led by 2 with eight seconds left. La Salle called time, quickly brought the ball across midcourt, and stopped the clock again. Everyone in the house knew the Explorers were going to try to get the ball into the pivot to All-American Tom Gola for the tying shot. Instead, La Salle coach Ken Loeffler called for the unexpected: Gola raced outside to get the inbounds pass, and whipped a bullet to Tom O'Malley, who was alone underneath. O'Malley's layup at the buzzer put the game into overtime.

In the regionals, played in Philadelphia's friendly Palestra, Gola was magnificent, averaging 24 points and 25 rebounds in victories over North Carolina State and Navy that put La Salle into the Final Four.

In the other eastern quarter of the draw, Penn State was a decided underdog. After finishing the regular season at 14-5, they beat Toledo and came up against Bob Pettit and Louisiana State in the regional semis. The Nittany Lions fell behind by 10 in the first half, but their zone defense finally declawed the cats from Baton Rouge. With its 78-70 victory, Penn State moved on to the regional final against red-hot Notre Dame, owners of an 18-game winning streak. Again the Nittany Lions confounded the experts; with center Jesse Arnelle doing yeoman service under the boards, guard Ed Haag hitting the target with three straight 30-foot set shots, and a pressing zone defense that forced the Irish to play their entire game at long range, Penn State beat Notre Dame by 8.

In the far west, Southern Cal advanced after a double-overtime victory over Santa Clara. Santa Clara had upset Seattle, the AP's 11th ranked team, in the opening round, but fell to the Trojans when USC hit a foul shot at the start of the second extra period, and the Broncos held for one last shot which they never got off.

Of all the outsiders at the party, the longest longshot of all was Bradley. The Braves from Peoria, with a 15-12 record, were clearly a desperation choice on the part of the committee that selected the tournament field. Nonetheless, they beat Oklahoma City and Colorado to advance to the regional finals, where they came up against Henry Iba's perennially powerful Aggies of Oklahoma A&M. The Braves sent the Aggies scurrying back to their dorms, whipping them 71-57 and piling up the highest score ever against Iba on his home court.

Thus it was that the Final Four opened in Kansas City with a motley assortment of unexpected guests. The Bradley Braves arrived and decided they liked the atmosphere just fine; they came back from a 10-point deficit to beat USC by 2 and win the hearts of the fans. In the other semi, Penn State held Gola to only 9 shots from the floor (his low for the year), but the La Salle All-American still scored 19 as the Explorers methodically picked apart the Nittany Lions' zone. Paul Unruh, an All-American from Bradley in 1950 and one of the most knowledgeable of the 10,500 in attendance, marveled at Gola's brilliance. "He makes plays a little man should make and then turns around and does things only a big man usually does." The rest of the crowd was not so positive: they booed lustily at the lack of action in the slow-moving contest.

Once La Salle had convinced midwestern basketball afficionados about the soporific quality of the eastern game, the Explorers turned around and blasted the Kansas City fans with as explosive a barrage of firepower as they'd ever seen. The Philadelphians spotted Bradley an early 7-point lead, and were down by a point at the half before breaking loose for a 30-point third quarter that buried the Braves, 92-76. Gola was only third high man for La Salle as sophomores Frank Blatcher and Charley Singley shared high-point honors with 23. The Explorer attack broke the previous championship-game scoring record (set by the hometown favorite Jayhawks in 1952) by a dozen points, and the two teams combined for the most points ever scored in a tournament game. If everyone else was a pretender, at least La Salle was for real.

FIRST ROUND EAST

Toledo (50)   Coach: Jerry Bush

	Min.	Total FG / FGA	Pct.	FT / FTA	Pct.	Reb. O/T	A	TO	PF	S	Blk	TP	PPM
MARTIN, P.	40	8/ -	-	7/ 8	.875	-/ -	-	-	3	-	-	23	.575
MAHER	40	1/ -	-	2/ 5	.400	-/ -	-	-	2	-	-	4	.100
SPICE	40	2/ -	-	7/10	.700	-/ -	-	-	3	-	-	11	.275
PADZIOR	40	2/ -	-	1/ 2	.500	-/ -	-	-	4	-	-	5	.125
RAY	40	1/ -	-	5/ 6	.833	-/ -	-	-	3	-	-	7	.175
Totals	200	14/50	-	22/31	.710	-/ -	-	-	15	-	-	50	.250

Penn State (62)   Coach: Elmer Gross

	Min.	Total FG / FGA	Pct.	FT / FTA	Pct.	Reb. O/T	A	TO	PF	S	Blk	TP	PPM
SHERRY, J.	-	2/ -	-	1/ 2	.500	-/ -	-	-	1	-	-	5	-
BLOCKER, J.	-	2/ -	-	0/ 0	.000	-/ -	-	-	2	-	-	4	-
ROHLAND, B.	-	2/ -	-	2/ 3	.667	-/ -	-	-	1	-	-	6	-
ARNELLE, J.	-	4/ -	-	5/ 5	1.000	-/ -	-	-	4	-	-	13	-
WEIDENHAMMER, R.	-	4/ -	-	2/ 2	1.000	-/ -	-	-	2	-	-	10	-
HAAG, E.	-	3/ -	-	2/ 2	1.000	-/ -	-	-	1	-	-	8	-
BREWER, J.	-	4/ -	-	3/ 7	.429	-/ -	-	-	2	-	-	11	-
FIELDS, E.	-	1/ -	-	3/ 3	1.000	-/ -	-	-	2	-	-	5	-
Totals	200	22/ -	-	18/24	.750	-/ -	-	-	15	-	-	62	.310

Disqualified: None.

	1st Qtr.	2nd Qtr.	3rd Qtr.	4th Qtr.	Final
Toledo	15	15	13	7	50
Penn State	18	9	16	19	62

Notre Dame (80)   Coach: John Jordan

	Min.	Total FG / FGA	Pct.	FT / FTA	Pct.	Reb. O/T	A	TO	PF	S	Blk	TP	PPM
FANNON, J.	40	5/ -	-	5/ 6	.833	-/ -	-	-	4	-	-	15	.375
BERTRAND, J.	40	6/ -	-	4/ 5	.800	-/ -	-	-	2	-	-	16	.400
ROSENTHAL, R.	40	12/ -	-	7/11	.636	-/ -	-	-	1	-	-	31	.775
STEPHENS, J.	40	3/ -	-	4/ 8	.500	-/ -	-	-	3	-	-	10	.250
SULLIVAN, W.	40	3/ -	-	2/ 2	1.000	-/ -	-	-	4	-	-	8	.200
Totals	200	29/77	-	22/32	.688	-/ -	-	-	14	-	-	80	.400

Loyola N.O. (70)   Coach: Jim McCafferty

	Min.	Total FG / FGA	Pct.	FT / FTA	Pct.	Reb. O/T	A	TO	PF	S	Blk	TP	PPM
BAER	-	1/ -	-	0/ 0	.000	-/ -	-	-	2	-	-	2	-
STACK	-	3/ -	-	1/ 2	.500	-/ -	-	-	3	-	-	7	-
REYNOLDS	-	3/ -	-	2/ 2	1.000	-/ -	-	-	2	-	-	8	-
GALLMANN	-	3/ -	-	4/ 7	.571	-/ -	-	-	1	-	-	10	-
CONRAD	-	1/ -	-	0/ 0	.000	-/ -	-	-	3	-	-	2	-
O'DONNELL, B.	-	12/ -	-	8/10	.800	-/ -	-	-	3	-	-	32	-
ROUZAN	-	4/ -	-	1/ 2	.500	-/ -	-	-	3	-	-	9	-
TOUHY	-	0/ -	-	0/ 0	.000	-/ -	-	-	0	-	-	0	-
Totals	200	27/59	-	16/23	.696	-/ -	-	-	17	-	-	70	.350

Disqualified: None.

	1st Qtr.	2nd Qtr.	3rd Qtr.	4th Qtr.	Final
Notre Dame	18	19	16	27	80
Loyola N.O.	8	16	19	27	70

U. Conn. (80)   Coach: Hugh Greer

	Min.	Total FG / FGA	Pct.	FT / FTA	Pct.	Reb. O/T	A	TO	PF	S	Blk	TP	PPM
PATTERSON	-	7/ -	-	7/ 8	.875	-/ -	-	-	5	-	-	21	-
AHEARN	-	2/ -	-	2/ 4	.500	-/ -	-	-	2	-	-	6	-
QUIMBY	-	8/ -	-	3/ 7	.429	-/ -	-	-	1	-	-	19	-
O'BRIEN	-	0/ -	-	0/ 0	.000	-/ -	-	-	1	-	-	0	-
ZIMA	-	2/ -	-	2/ 2	1.000	-/ -	-	-	1	-	-	6	-
WATSON	-	2/ -	-	2/ 2	1.000	-/ -	-	-	4	-	-	6	-
JONES	-	2/ -	-	1/ 1	1.000	-/ -	-	-	1	-	-	5	-
RUDDY	-	4/ -	-	4/ 5	.800	-/ -	-	-	2	-	-	12	-
BUSHWELL	-	2/ -	-	1/ 1	1.000	-/ -	-	-	5	-	-	5	-
BRAVERMAN	-	0/ -	-	0/ 0	.000	-/ -	-	-	0	-	-	0	-
Totals	200	29/ -	-	22/30	.733	-/ -	-	-	22	-	-	80	.400

Navy (85)   Coach: Ben Carnevale

	Min.	Total FG / FGA	Pct.	FT / FTA	Pct.	Reb. O/T	A	TO	PF	S	Blk	TP	PPM
LANGE, D.	35	8/ -	-	2/ 2	1.000	-/ -	-	-	4	-	-	18	.514
CLUNE, J.	32	16/ -	-	10/11	.909	-/ -	-	-	3	-	-	42	1.313
HOGAN, E.	39	5/ -	-	1/ 3	.333	-/ -	-	-	3	-	-	11	.282
HOOVER, W.	30	2/ -	-	1/ 3	.333	-/ -	-	-	2	-	-	5	.167
WIGLEY, L.	24	0/ -	-	6/ 7	.857	-/ -	-	-	4	-	-	6	.250
McCALLY, K.	3	0/ -	-	0/ 0	.000	-/ -	-	-	1	-	-	0	.000
SANDLIN, D.	11	0/ -	-	0/ 0	.000	-/ -	-	-	0	-	-	0	.000
SLATTERY, W.	5	0/ -	-	0/ 0	.000	-/ -	-	-	1	-	-	0	.000
WELLS, T.	12	0/ -	-	2/ 5	.400	-/ -	-	-	4	-	-	2	.167
McDONNELL, J.	1	0/ -	-	0/ 0	.000	-/ -	-	-	0	-	-	0	.000
THOMPSON, B.	5	0/ -	-	1/ 1	1.000	-/ -	-	-	0	-	-	1	.200
DEGROFF, J.	3	0/ -	-	0/ 0	.000	-/ -	-	-	0	-	-	0	.000
Totals	200	31/ -	-	23/32	.719	-/ -	-	-	22	-	-	85	.425

Disqualified: U. Conn.—Patterson, Bushwell.

	1st Qtr.	2nd Qtr.	3rd Qtr.	4th Qtr.	Final
U. Conn.	12	28	17	23	80
Navy	23	15	24	23	85

North Carolina State (75)   Coach: Everett Case

	Min.	Total FG / FGA	Pct.	FT / FTA	Pct.	Reb. O/T	A	TO	PF	S	Blk	TP	PPM
THOMPSON, M.	-	4/ -	-	6/ 9	.667	-/ -	-	-	2	-	-	14	-
TYLER, D.	-	5/ -	-	5/ 5	1.000	-/ -	-	-	4	-	-	15	-
DICKMAN	-	0/ -	-	1/ 2	.500	-/ -	-	-	0	-	-	1	-
SHAVLIK, R.	-	6/ -	-	8/ 9	.889	-/ -	-	-	2	-	-	20	-
DINARDO, P.	-	2/ -	-	0/ 0	.000	-/ -	-	-	2	-	-	4	-
MOLODET, V.	-	6/ -	-	0/ 0	.000	-/ -	-	-	5	-	-	12	-
APPLEBAUM	-	3/ -	-	3/ 5	.600	-/ -	-	-	5	-	-	9	-
BELL	-	0/ -	-	0/ 1	.000	-/ -	-	-	0	-	-	0	-
GOTKIN	-	0/ -	-	0/ 0	.000	-/ -	-	-	0	-	-	0	-
Totals	200	26/ -	-	23/31	.742	-/ -	-	-	20	-	-	75	.375

George Washington (73)   Coach: Bill Reinhart

	Min.	Total FG / FGA	Pct.	FT / FTA	Pct.	Reb. O/T	A	TO	PF	S	Blk	TP	PPM
KARVER	-	7/ -	-	7/14	.500	-/ -	-	-	5	-	-	21	-
HOLUP, J.	-	3/ -	-	1/ 1	1.000	-/ -	-	-	3	-	-	7	-
MORRISON	-	1/ -	-	0/ 0	.000	-/ -	-	-	2	-	-	2	-
HOLUP, J.	-	4/ -	-	5/ 6	.833	-/ -	-	-	4	-	-	13	-
CIRIELLO	-	0/ -	-	0/ 0	.000	-/ -	-	-	0	-	-	0	-
DEVLIN	-	6/ -	-	8/ 8	1.000	-/ -	-	-	2	-	-	20	-
KLEIN	-	1/ -	-	1/ 1	1.000	-/ -	-	-	2	-	-	3	-
CATINO	-	3/ -	-	1/ 2	.500	-/ -	-	-	3	-	-	7	-
Totals	200	25/ -	-	23/32	.719	-/ -	-	-	19	-	-	73	.365

Disqualified: N.C. State—Molodet, Applebaum; Geo. Wash.—Karver.

	1st Qtr.	2nd Qtr.	3rd Qtr.	4th Qtr.	Final
N.C. State	20	26	15	14	75
Geo. Wash.	18	21	23	11	73

Fordham (74)   Coach: John Bach

	Min.	Total FG/FGA	Pct.	FT/FTA	Pct.	Reb. O/T	A	TO	PF	S	Blk	TP	PPM
LYONS, D.	-	5/ -	-	2/ 4	.500	-/ -	-	-	5	-	-	12	-
REESE, B.	-	5/ -	-	2/ 3	.667	-/ -	-	-	4	-	-	12	-
VIGGIANO	-	0/ -	-	0/ 0	.000	-/ -	-	-	0	-	-	0	-
CONNORS	-	0/ -	-	0/ 0	.000	-/ -	-	-	1	-	-	0	-
CUNNINGHAM	-	1/ -	-	0/ 0	.000	-/ -	-	-	1	-	-	2	-
CONLIN, E.	-	10/ -	-	6/ 7	.857	-/ -	-	-	3	-	-	26	-
PARCHINSKI, E.	-	5/ -	-	4/ 4	1.000	-/ -	-	-	4	-	-	14	-
LARKIN	-	2/ -	-	4/ 5	.800	-/ -	-	-	2	-	-	8	-
Totals	225	28/ -	-	18/23	.783	-/ -	-	-	20	-	-	74	.329

La Salle (76)   Coach: Ken Loeffler

	Min.	Total FG/FGA	Pct.	FT/FTA	Pct.	Reb. O/T	A	TO	PF	S	Blk	TP	PPM
MAPLES, B.	-	1/ -	-	0/ 0	.000	-/ -	-	-	2	-	-	2	-
BLATCHER, F.	-	4/ -	-	2/ 3	.667	-/ -	-	-	4	-	-	10	-
O'MALLEY, F.	-	3/ -	-	7/ 9	.778	-/ -	-	-	1	-	-	13	-
GOLA, T.	-	12/ -	-	4/ 6	.667	-/ -	-	-	4	-	-	28	-
O'HARA, F.	-	2/ -	-	6/ 9	.667	-/ -	-	-	3	-	-	10	-
GREENBERG, C.	-	0/ -	-	2/ 3	.667	-/ -	-	-	0	-	-	2	-
SINGLEY, C.	-	5/ -	-	1/ 2	.500	-/ -	-	-	2	-	-	11	-
Totals	225	27/ -	-	22/32	.688	-/ -	-	-	16	-	-	76	.338

Disqualified: Fordham—Lyons.

Fordham	1st Qtr.	2nd Qtr.	3rd Qtr.	4th Qtr.	1st OT	Final
Fordham	23	12	18	15	6	74
La Salle	18	21	13	16	8	76

FIRST ROUND WEST

Oklahoma City (55)   Coach: Doyle Parrack

	Min.	Total FG/FGA	Pct.	FT/FTA	Pct.	Reb. O/T	A	TO	PF	S	Blk	TP	PPM
NATH	-	2/ -	-	0/ 0	.000	-/ -	-	-	-	-	-	4	-
SHORT	-	12/ -	-	5/ 5	1.000	-/ -	-	-	-	-	-	29	-
BOLIN	-	1/ -	-	5/ 7	.714	-/ -	-	-	-	-	-	7	-
COUTS	-	1/ -	-	0/ 0	.000	-/ -	-	-	-	-	-	2	-
COPP	-	4/ -	-	0/ 0	.000	-/ -	-	-	-	-	-	8	-
RICK	-	0/ -	-	2/ 2	1.000	-/ -	-	-	-	-	-	2	-
BULLARD	-	0/ -	-	2/ 3	.667	-/ -	-	-	-	-	-	2	-
JONES	-	0/ -	-	1/ 2	.500	-/ -	-	-	-	-	-	1	-
Totals	200	20/ -	-	15/19	.789	-/ -	-	-	-	-	-	55	.275

Bradley (61)   Coach: Forddy Anderson

	Min.	Total FG/FGA	Pct.	FT/FTA	Pct.	Reb. O/T	A	TO	PF	S	Blk	TP	PPM
PETERSEN, D.	-	1/ -	-	4/ 9	.444	-/ -	-	-	-	-	-	6	-
CARNEY, B.	-	9/ -	-	9/14	.643	-/ -	-	-	-	-	-	27	-
RILEY, J.	-	0/ -	-	0/ 0	.000	-/ -	-	-	-	-	-	0	-
ESTERGARD, D.	-	4/ -	-	3/ 3	1.000	-/ -	-	-	-	-	-	11	-
KING, E.	-	3/ -	-	3/ 4	.750	-/ -	-	-	-	-	-	9	-
KENT, J.	-	2/ -	-	1/ 1	1.000	-/ -	-	-	-	-	-	5	-
BABETCH, H.	-	0/ -	-	3/ 4	.750	-/ -	-	-	-	-	-	3	-
Totals	200	19/ -	-	23/35	.657	-/ -	-	-	-	-	-	61	.305

Disqualified: None.

Oklahoma City	1st Qtr.	2nd Qtr.	3rd Qtr.	4th Qtr.	Final
Oklahoma City	12	13	17	13	55
Bradley	12	15	15	19	61

Idaho State (77)   Coach: Steve Belko

	Min.	Total FG/FGA	Pct.	FT/FTA	Pct.	Reb. O/T	A	TO	PF	S	Blk	TP	PPM
BECKHAM, S.	-	6/ -	-	8/14	.571	-/ -	-	-	4	-	-	20	-
ROH, L.	-	8/ -	-	4/ 5	.800	-/ -	-	-	3	-	-	20	-
BAUER, R.	-	4/ -	-	4/ 4	1.000	-/ -	-	-	3	-	-	12	-
DAKICH, R.	-	3/ -	-	0/ 0	.000	-/ -	-	-	1	-	-	6	-
CONNOR, B.	-	3/ -	-	4/ 7	.571	-/ -	-	-	3	-	-	10	-
HAYS, B.	-	0/ -	-	0/ 0	.000	-/ -	-	-	0	-	-	0	-
BELKOW, J.	-	3/ -	-	3/ 5	.600	-/ -	-	-	1	-	-	9	-
Totals	225	27/ -	-	23/35	.657	-/ -	-	-	15	-	-	77	.342

Seattle (75)   Coach: Al Brightman

	Min.	Total FG/FGA	Pct.	FT/FTA	Pct.	Reb. O/T	A	TO	PF	S	Blk	TP	PPM
GLOWASKI	-	2/ -	-	4/ 6	.667	-/ -	-	-	3	-	-	8	-
KELLY	-	1/ -	-	2/ 3	.667	-/ -	-	-	5	-	-	4	-
PEMANICK	-	9/ -	-	2/ 7	.286	-/ -	-	-	2	-	-	20	-
BAUER	-	10/ -	-	2/ 3	.667	-/ -	-	-	2	-	-	22	-
MALONE	-	4/ -	-	2/ 2	1.000	-/ -	-	-	1	-	-	10	-
CASEY	-	0/ -	-	0/ 0	.000	-/ -	-	-	1	-	-	0	-
SANFORD	-	1/ -	-	1/ 1	1.000	-/ -	-	-	2	-	-	3	-
GILES	-	0/ -	-	0/ 0	.000	-/ -	-	-	1	-	-	0	-
GODES	-	2/ -	-	0/ 2	.000	-/ -	-	-	1	-	-	4	-
COX	-	0/ -	-	0/ 0	.000	-/ -	-	-	0	-	-	0	-
JOHANSEN	-	2/ -	-	0/ 0	.000	-/ -	-	-	4	-	-	4	-
Totals	225	31/ -	-	13/24	.542	-/ -	-	-	22	-	-	75	.333

Disqualified: Seattle—Kelly.

Idaho State	1st Qtr.	2nd Qtr.	3rd Qtr.	4th Qtr.	1st OT	Final
Idaho State	20	12	21	13	11	77
Seattle	19	22	11	14	9	75

Texas Tech (64)   Coach: Polk Robinson

	Min.	Total FG/FGA	Pct.	FT/FTA	Pct.	Reb. O/T	A	TO	PF	S	Blk	TP	PPM
BOLDING	-	2/ -	-	2/ 2	1.000	-/ -	-	-	-	-	-	6	-
REED	-	5/ -	-	3/ 5	.600	-/ -	-	-	-	-	-	13	-
BLACKSHEAR	-	1/ -	-	0/ 0	.000	-/ -	-	-	-	-	-	2	-
MCKIM	-	1/ -	-	0/ 2	.000	-/ -	-	-	-	-	-	2	-
WHATLEY	-	0/ -	-	0/ 0	.000	-/ -	-	-	-	-	-	0	-
CARPENTER	-	6/ -	-	9/11	.818	-/ -	-	-	-	-	-	21	-
BLACKMON, E.	-	3/ -	-	1/ 3	.333	-/ -	-	-	-	-	-	7	-
INCE	-	6/ -	-	1/ 3	.333	-/ -	-	-	-	-	-	13	-
SEXTON	-	0/ -	-	0/ 0	.000	-/ -	-	-	-	-	-	0	-
Totals	200	24/ -	-	16/26	.615	-/ -	-	-	-	-	-	64	.320

Santa Clara (73)   Coach: Bob Feerick

	Min.	Total FG/FGA	Pct.	FT/FTA	Pct.	Reb. O/T	A	TO	PF	S	Blk	TP	PPM
SEARS, K.	-	8/ -	-	5/ 7	.714	-/ -	-	-	-	-	-	21	-
YOUNG, J.	-	5/ -	-	2/ 2	1.000	-/ -	-	-	-	-	-	12	-
SIMONI, D.	-	2/ -	-	1/ 1	1.000	-/ -	-	-	-	-	-	5	-
BOUDREAU	-	0/ -	-	0/ 0	.000	-/ -	-	-	-	-	-	0	-
MOUNT, M.	-	1/ -	-	6/ 9	.667	-/ -	-	-	-	-	-	8	-
SCHOENSTEIN, H.	-	4/ -	-	3/ 3	1.000	-/ -	-	-	-	-	-	11	-
BENEDETTI, D.	-	3/ -	-	3/ 3	1.000	-/ -	-	-	-	-	-	9	-
GAZERT, G.	-	3/ -	-	1/ 1	1.000	-/ -	-	-	-	-	-	7	-
Totals	200	26/ -	-	21/26	.808	-/ -	-	-	-	-	-	73	.365

Disqualified: None.

Texas Tech	1st Qtr.	2nd Qtr.	3rd Qtr.	4th Qtr.	Final
Texas Tech	17	19	12	16	64
Santa Clara	17	18	21	17	73

REGIONAL SEMIFINAL EAST

Penn State (78) Coach: Elmer Gross

	Min.	Total FG/FGA	Pct.	FT/FTA	Pct.	Reb. O/T	A	TO	PF	S	Blk	TP	PPM
SHERRY, J.	-	1/10	.100	9/11	.818	-/2	-	-	3	-	-	11	-
ROHLAND, B.	-	0/4	.000	2/3	.667	-/2	-	-	4	-	-	2	-
ARNELLE, J.	-	10/25	.400	4/6	.667	-/14	-	-	2	-	-	24	-
HAAG, E.	-	4/10	.400	1/4	.250	-/2	-	-	2	-	-	9	-
WEIDENHAMMER, R.	-	4/12	.333	1/4	.250	-/4	-	-	2	-	-	9	-
BREWER, J.	-	2/11	.182	1/2	.500	-/4	-	-	2	-	-	5	-
FIELDS, E.	-	4/5	.800	1/1	1.000	-/3	-	-	2	-	-	9	-
BLOCKER, J.	-	4/5	.800	1/1	1.000	-/6	-	-	2	-	-	9	-
MARISA, R.	-	0/0	.000	0/0	.000	-/0	-	-	0	-	-	0	-
Totals	200	29/82	.354	20/32	.625	-/37	-	-	19	-	-	78	.390

Navy (69) Coach: Ben Carnevale

	Min.	Total FG/FGA	Pct.	FT/FTA	Pct.	Reb. O/T	A	TO	PF	S	Blk	TP	PPM
LANGE, D.	40	11/-	-	7/11	.636	-/-	-	-	2	-	-	29	.725
CLUNE, J.	40	7/-	-	7/8	.875	-/-	-	-	1	-	-	21	.525
HOGAN, E.	38	2/-	-	0/0	.000	-/-	-	-	1	-	-	4	.105
HOOVER, W.	31	2/-	-	1/1	1.000	-/-	-	-	3	-	-	5	.161
WIGLEY, L.	28	0/-	-	2/2	1.000	-/-	-	-	5	-	-	2	.071
MCCALLY, K.	4	1/-	-	0/0	.000	-/-	-	-	0	-	-	2	.500
SANDLIN, D.	8	1/-	-	0/0	.000	-/-	-	-	0	-	-	2	.250
SLATTERY, W.	2	0/-	-	0/0	.000	-/-	-	-	0	-	-	0	.000
WELLS, T.	9	1/-	-	2/5	.400	-/-	-	-	5	-	-	4	.444
Totals	200	25/-	-	19/27	.704	-/-	-	-	17	-	-	69	.345

Louisiana State (70) Coach: Harry Rabenhorst

	Min.	Total FG/FGA	Pct.	FT/FTA	Pct.	Reb. O/T	A	TO	PF	S	Blk	TP	PPM
BELCHER, D.	-	3/12	.250	0/0	.000	-/6	-	-	4	-	-	6	-
CLARK, N.	-	4/12	.333	2/5	.400	-/13	-	-	2	-	-	10	-
PETTIT, B.	-	13/21	.619	8/9	.889	-/24	-	-	3	-	-	34	-
MCARDLE, B.	-	2/10	.200	5/5	1.000	-/3	-	-	4	-	-	9	-
MAGEE, N.	-	3/7	.429	3/3	1.000	-/3	-	-	3	-	-	9	-
SEBASTIAN, D.	-	0/4	.000	0/0	.000	-/0	-	-	3	-	-	0	-
FRESHLEY, B.	-	0/0	.000	0/0	.000	-/1	-	-	1	-	-	0	-
MCNEILLY, J.	-	0/1	.000	2/2	1.000	-/1	-	-	0	-	-	2	-
JONES, L.	-	0/0	.000	0/0	.000	-/0	-	-	1	-	-	0	-
Totals	200	25/67	.373	20/24	.833	-/51	-	-	21	-	-	70	.350

Disqualified: None.

Cornell (67) Coach: Royner Greene

	Min.	Total FG/FGA	Pct.	FT/FTA	Pct.	Reb. O/T	A	TO	PF	S	Blk	TP	PPM
MACPHEE, W.	-	0/-	-	0/0	.000	-/-	-	-	0	-	-	0	-
ROLLES, C.	-	0/-	-	2/3	.667	-/-	-	-	1	-	-	2	-
BUNCOM, H.	-	0/-	-	1/1	1.000	-/-	-	-	2	-	-	1	-
MATTES, M.	-	2/-	-	3/3	1.000	-/-	-	-	3	-	-	7	-
WILENS, M.	-	1/-	-	3/5	.600	-/-	-	-	1	-	-	5	-
ZELEK, R.	-	4/-	-	0/2	.000	-/-	-	-	3	-	-	8	-
MORTON, L.	-	12/-	-	10/10	1.000	-/-	-	-	4	-	-	34	-
BRADFIELD, D.	-	5/-	-	0/0	.000	-/-	-	-	4	-	-	10	-
CODDINGTON	-	0/-	-	0/0	.000	-/-	-	-	0	-	-	0	-
Totals	200	24/-	-	19/24	.792	-/-	-	-	18	-	-	67	.335

Disqualified: Navy—Wigley, Wells.

	1st Qtr.	2nd Qtr.	3rd Qtr.	4th Qtr.	Final
Penn State	14	20	20	24	78
Louisiana St.	19	13	19	19	70

	1st Qtr.	2nd Qtr.	3rd Qtr.	4th Qtr.	Final
Navy	20	20	17	12	69
Cornell	18	14	25	10	67

Notre Dame (65) Coach: John Jordan

	Min.	Total FG/FGA	Pct.	FT/FTA	Pct.	Reb. O/T	A	TO	PF	S	Blk	TP	PPM
FANNON, J.	-	2/7	.286	0/0	.000	-/9	-	-	5	-	-	4	-
BERTRAND, J.	-	4/14	.286	3/5	.600	-/6	-	-	4	-	-	11	-
ROSENTHAL, R.	-	9/29	.310	7/8	.875	-/15	-	-	3	-	-	25	-
SULLIVAN, W.	-	4/10	.400	2/3	.667	-/8	-	-	2	-	-	10	-
STEPHENS, J.	-	2/6	.333	8/18	.444	-/4	-	-	3	-	-	12	-
WEIMAN, W.	-	0/1	.000	0/0	.000	-/0	-	-	4	-	-	0	-
MCGINN, E.	-	1/3	.333	1/3	.333	-/2	-	-	3	-	-	3	-
Totals	200	22/70	.314	21/37	.568	-/44	-	-	24	-	-	65	.325

Indiana (64) Coach: Branch McCracken

	Min.	Total FG/FGA	Pct.	FT/FTA	Pct.	Reb. O/T	A	TO	PF	S	Blk	TP	PPM
KRAAK, C.	-	2/5	.400	3/6	.500	-/8	-	-	3	-	-	7	-
FARLEY, R.	-	2/6	.333	9/13	.692	-/3	-	-	5	-	-	13	-
SCOTT, B.	-	9/16	.563	2/5	.400	-/9	-	-	5	-	-	20	-
LEONARD, B.	-	5/20	.250	1/2	.500	-/4	-	-	4	-	-	11	-
SCHLUNDT, D.	-	1/4	.250	8/8	1.000	-/6	-	-	4	-	-	10	-
CHOICE, W.	-	1/6	.167	1/2	.500	-/5	-	-	1	-	-	3	-
WHITE, R.	-	0/2	.000	0/2	.000	-/4	-	-	1	-	-	0	-
BYERS, P.	-	0/0	.000	0/0	.000	-/0	-	-	1	-	-	0	-
Totals	200	20/59	.339	24/38	.632	-/39	-	-	24	-	-	64	.320

Disqualified: Notre Dame—Fannon; Indiana—Farley, Scott.

North Carolina State (81) Coach: Everett Case

	Min.	Total FG/FGA	Pct.	FT/FTA	Pct.	Reb. O/T	A	TO	PF	S	Blk	TP	PPM
TYLER, D.	-	3/-	-	1/1	1.000	-/-	-	-	5	-	-	7	-
THOMPSON, M.	-	5/-	-	9/16	.563	-/-	-	-	1	-	-	19	-
DINARDO, P.	-	2/-	-	1/2	.500	-/-	-	-	2	-	-	5	-
SHAVLIK, R.	-	10/-	-	4/4	1.000	-/-	-	-	3	-	-	24	-
APPLEBAUM	-	4/-	-	1/1	1.000	-/-	-	-	4	-	-	9	-
MOLODET, V.	-	6/-	-	3/4	.750	-/-	-	-	2	-	-	15	-
BELL	-	0/-	-	0/0	.000	-/-	-	-	3	-	-	0	-
SCHEFFEL, R.	-	0/-	-	2/2	1.000	-/-	-	-	2	-	-	2	-
Totals	200	30/-	-	21/30	.700	-/-	-	-	22	-	-	81	.405

La Salle (88) Coach: Ken Loeffler

	Min.	Total FG/FGA	Pct.	FT/FTA	Pct.	Reb. O/T	A	TO	PF	S	Blk	TP	PPM
O'MALLEY, F.	-	5/-	-	3/5	.600	-/-	-	-	4	-	-	13	-
SINGLEY, C.	-	9/-	-	8/10	.800	-/-	-	-	4	-	-	26	-
GOLA, T.	-	6/-	-	14/18	.778	-/-	-	-	3	-	-	26	-
MAPLES, B.	-	2/-	-	0/0	.000	-/-	-	-	4	-	-	4	-
O'HARA, F.	-	3/-	-	3/4	.750	-/-	-	-	2	-	-	9	-
BLATCHER, F.	-	4/-	-	2/2	1.000	-/-	-	-	1	-	-	10	-
GREENBERG, C.	-	0/-	-	0/0	.000	-/-	-	-	0	-	-	0	-
Totals	200	29/-	-	30/39	.769	-/-	-	-	18	-	-	88	.440

Disqualified: N.C. State—Tyler.

	1st Qtr.	2nd Qtr.	3rd Qtr.	4th Qtr.	Final
Notre Dame	17	20	13	15	65
Indiana	16	16	16	16	64

	1st Qtr.	2nd Qtr.	3rd Qtr.	4th Qtr.	Final
N.C. State	13	22	15	31	81
La Salle	15	21	19	33	88

REGIONAL SEMIFINAL WEST

Bradley (76) Coach: Forddy Anderson

	Min.	Total FG/FGA	Pct.	FT/FTA	Pct.	Reb. O/T	A	TO	PF	S	Blk	TP	PPM
PETERSEN, D.	-	1/ -	-	0/ 0	.000	-/ -	-	-	5	-	-	2	-
CARNEY, B.	-	7/ -	-	23/26	.885	-/ -	-	-	4	-	-	37	-
BABETCH, H.	-	0/ -	-	2/ 2	1.000	-/ -	-	-	1	-	-	2	-
GOWER, J.	-	0/ -	-	0/ 0	.000	-/ -	-	-	2	-	-	0	-
HANSEN, J.	-	0/ -	-	1/ 1	1.000	-/ -	-	-	0	-	-	1	-
RILEY, J.	-	0/ -	-	0/ 0	.000	-/ -	-	-	0	-	-	0	-
KILCULLEN, B.	-	0/ -	-	1/ 1	1.000	-/ -	-	-	5	-	-	1	-
ESTERGARD, D.	-	1/ -	-	5/ 7	.714	-/ -	-	-	3	-	-	7	-
KING, E.	-	3/ -	-	3/ 3	1.000	-/ -	-	-	4	-	-	9	-
KENT, J.	-	7/ -	-	3/ 4	.750	-/ -	-	-	2	-	-	17	-
O'CONNELL, L.	-	0/ -	-	0/ 0	.000	-/ -	-	-	1	-	-	0	-
Totals	200	19/ -	-	38/44	.864	-/ -	-	-	27	-	-	76	.380

Colorado (64) Coach: Bebe Lee

	Min.	Total FG/FGA	Pct.	FT/FTA	Pct.	Reb. O/T	A	TO	PF	S	Blk	TP	PPM
JEANGERARD, R.	-	0/ -	-	4/ 4	1.000	-/ -	-	-	3	-	-	4	-
COFFMAN, M.	-	0/ -	-	2/ 2	1.000	-/ -	-	-	5	-	-	2	-
RANGLOS, J.	-	1/ -	-	3/ 5	.600	-/ -	-	-	3	-	-	5	-
WALTER, W.	-	1/ -	-	2/ 3	.667	-/ -	-	-	2	-	-	4	-
HALDORSON, B.	-	2/ -	-	7/13	.538	-/ -	-	-	5	-	-	11	-
HANNAH, G.	-	2/ -	-	3/ 3	1.000	-/ -	-	-	4	-	-	7	-
MOCK, C.	-	7/ -	-	3/ 4	.750	-/ -	-	-	5	-	-	17	-
HARROLD, T.	-	6/ -	-	1/ 2	.500	-/ -	-	-	5	-	-	13	-
PETERSON, B.	-	0/ -	-	1/ 1	1.000	-/ -	-	-	2	-	-	1	-
ABRAMES	-	0/ -	-	0/ 2	.000	-/ -	-	-	0	-	-	0	-
Totals	200	19/ -	-	26/39	.667	-/ -	-	-	34	-	-	64	.320

Disqualified: Bradley—Petersen, Kilcullen; Colorado—Coffman, Haldorson, Mock, Harrold.

	1st Qtr.	2nd Qtr.	3rd Qtr.	4th Qtr.	Final
Bradley	15	21	18	22	76
Colorado	16	19	12	17	64

Rice (45) Coach: Don Suman

	Min.	Total FG/FGA	Pct.	FT/FTA	Pct.	Reb. O/T	A	TO	PF	S	Blk	TP	PPM
BRYAN	-	0/ -	-	0/ 0	.000	-/ -	-	-	1	-	-	0	-
CHRISTENSEN	-	1/ -	-	0/ 0	.000	-/ -	-	-	0	-	-	2	-
LANCE	-	4/ -	-	1/ 1	1.000	-/ -	-	-	5	-	-	9	-
SCHWINGER	-	4/ -	-	3/ 4	.750	-/ -	-	-	1	-	-	11	-
DURRENBERGER	-	3/ -	-	4/ 8	.500	-/ -	-	-	5	-	-	10	-
BRASHEAR	-	3/ -	-	1/ 2	.500	-/ -	-	-	3	-	-	7	-
ROBICHEAUX	-	3/ -	-	0/ 0	.000	-/ -	-	-	3	-	-	6	-
BEAVERS	-	0/ -	-	0/ 0	.000	-/ -	-	-	2	-	-	0	-
Totals	200	18/ -	-	9/15	.600	-/ -	-	-	20	-	-	45	.225

Oklahoma A&M (51) Coach: Henry Iba

	Min.	Total FG/FGA	Pct.	FT/FTA	Pct.	Reb. O/T	A	TO	PF	S	Blk	TP	PPM
FULLER	-	2/ -	-	2/ 2	1.000	-/ -	-	-	1	-	-	6	-
CARTER	-	2/ -	-	3/ 8	.375	-/ -	-	-	2	-	-	7	-
BARNHOUSE	-	2/ -	-	2/ 4	.500	-/ -	-	-	2	-	-	6	-
MALONEY	-	0/ -	-	0/ 0	.000	-/ -	-	-	1	-	-	0	-
MATTICK	-	5/ -	-	1/ 4	.250	-/ -	-	-	4	-	-	11	-
HENDRICK	-	0/ -	-	0/ 2	.000	-/ -	-	-	0	-	-	0	-
BIGHAM	-	5/ -	-	2/ 3	.667	-/ -	-	-	0	-	-	12	-
BABB	-	2/ -	-	5/ 6	.833	-/ -	-	-	0	-	-	9	-
Totals	200	18/ -	-	15/29	.517	-/ -	-	-	10	-	-	51	.255

Disqualified: Rice—Lance, Durrenberger.

	1st Qtr.	2nd Qtr.	3rd Qtr.	4th Qtr.	Final
Rice	9	13	16	7	45
Oklahoma A&M	8	10	16	17	51

Idaho State (59) Coach: Steve Belko

	Min.	Total FG/FGA	Pct.	FT/FTA	Pct.	Reb. O/T	A	TO	PF	S	Blk	TP	PPM
ROH, L.	-	3/13	.231	7/ 8	.875	-/ 6	-	-	3	-	-	13	-
BECKHAM, S.	-	4/11	.364	4/ 5	.800	-/ 2	-	-	3	-	-	12	-
BAUER, R.	-	3/ 5	.600	2/ 3	.667	-/12	-	-	3	-	-	8	-
CONNOR, B.	-	3/ 7	.429	3/ 6	.500	-/ 5	-	-	1	-	-	9	-
DAKICH, R.	-	4/ 9	.444	2/ 3	.667	-/ 0	-	-	1	-	-	10	-
BELKOW, J.	-	2/ 6	.333	2/ 2	1.000	-/ 1	-	-	1	-	-	6	-
HAYS, B.	-	0/ 2	.000	1/ 2	.500	-/ 3	-	-	0	-	-	1	-
DETHLEFS, B.	-	0/ 0	.000	0/ 2	.000	-/ 1	-	-	1	-	-	0	-
Totals	200	19/53	.358	21/31	.677	-/30	-	-	12	-	-	59	.295

USC (73) Coach: Forrest Twogood

	Min.	Total FG/FGA	Pct.	FT/FTA	Pct.	Reb. O/T	A	TO	PF	S	Blk	TP	PPM
PSALTIS, T.	-	4/ 8	.500	3/ 4	.750	-/ 6	-	-	3	-	-	11	-
PAUSIG, R.	-	3/13	.231	0/ 0	.000	-/ 6	-	-	1	-	-	6	-
IRVIN, R.	-	9/19	.474	7/ 8	.875	-/ 3	-	-	2	-	-	25	-
WELSH, D.	-	3/ 8	.375	0/ 0	.000	-/ 1	-	-	4	-	-	6	-
HAMMER, D.	-	3/10	.300	1/ 1	1.000	-/ 8	-	-	2	-	-	7	-
CARR, C.	-	5/12	.417	1/ 3	.333	-/ 4	-	-	2	-	-	11	-
DUNNE, J.	-	3/ 7	.429	1/ 2	.500	-/ 3	-	-	0	-	-	7	-
LUDECKE, A.	-	0/ 0	.000	0/ 0	.000	-/ 2	-	-	3	-	-	0	-
FINDLEY, J.	-	0/ 0	.000	0/ 0	.000	-/ 0	-	-	0	-	-	0	-
NAGAI, D.	-	0/ 1	.000	0/ 0	.000	-/ 0	-	-	1	-	-	0	-
THOMPSON, P.	-	0/ 1	.000	0/ 0	.000	-/ 1	-	-	0	-	-	0	-
LOVRICH, J.	-	0/ 1	.000	0/ 0	.000	-/ 0	-	-	1	-	-	0	-
Totals	200	30/80	.375	13/18	.722	-/34	-	-	19	-	-	73	.365

Disqualified: None.

	1st Qtr.	2nd Qtr.	3rd Qtr.	4th Qtr.	Final
Idaho State	12	13	14	20	59
USC	18	15	16	24	73

Santa Clara (73) Coach: Bob Feerick

	Min.	Total FG/FGA	Pct.	FT/FTA	Pct.	Reb. O/T	A	TO	PF	S	Blk	TP	PPM
SEARS, K.	-	5/ -	-	1/ 2	.500	-/ -	-	-	2	-	-	11	-
YOUNG, J.	-	9/ -	-	2/ 2	1.000	-/ -	-	-	2	-	-	20	-
BOUDREAU	-	2/ -	-	0/ 0	.000	-/ -	-	-	0	-	-	4	-
ROBINSON	-	0/ -	-	0/ 0	.000	-/ -	-	-	0	-	-	0	-
MOUNT, M.	-	0/ -	-	1/ 1	1.000	-/ -	-	-	3	-	-	1	-
SCHOENSTEIN, H.	-	4/ -	-	5/ 5	1.000	-/ -	-	-	2	-	-	13	-
BENEDETTI, D.	-	3/ -	-	2/ 3	.667	-/ -	-	-	2	-	-	8	-
GATZERT, G.	-	3/ -	-	4/ 5	.800	-/ -	-	-	4	-	-	10	-
SIMONI, D.	-	2/ -	-	0/ 0	.000	-/ -	-	-	2	-	-	4	-
BALL, D.	-	0/ -	-	2/ 2	1.000	-/ -	-	-	1	-	-	2	-
Totals	200	28/ -	-	17/20	.850	-/ -	-	-	18	-	-	73	.365

Colorado A&M (50) Coach: Bill Strannigan

	Min.	Total FG/FGA	Pct.	FT/FTA	Pct.	Reb. O/T	A	TO	PF	S	Blk	TP	PPM
GREGORY, L.	-	0/ -	-	0/ 2	.000	-/ -	-	-	1	-	-	0	-
KINARD, H.	-	1/ -	-	2/ 2	1.000	-/ -	-	-	2	-	-	4	-
CAYLOR, R.	-	5/ -	-	1/ 1	1.000	-/ -	-	-	3	-	-	11	-
VANDERHOFF, C.	-	1/ -	-	0/ 0	.000	-/ -	-	-	0	-	-	2	-
BARTRAN, W.	-	0/ -	-	0/ 0	.000	-/ -	-	-	0	-	-	0	-
STUEHM, D.	-	6/ -	-	6/19	.316	-/ -	-	-	4	-	-	18	-
HIBBARD, G.	-	0/ -	-	0/ 0	.000	-/ -	-	-	2	-	-	0	-
PIVIC, S.	-	0/ -	-	1/ 2	.500	-/ -	-	-	1	-	-	1	-
BETZ, R.	-	2/ -	-	2/ 2	1.000	-/ -	-	-	2	-	-	6	-
BRYANT, J.	-	2/ -	-	2/ 2	1.000	-/ -	-	-	0	-	-	6	-
GATES, R.	-	0/ -	-	0/ 0	.000	-/ -	-	-	0	-	-	0	-
SAVIONI, J.	-	1/ -	-	0/ 0	.000	-/ -	-	-	0	-	-	2	-
Totals	200	18/ -	-	14/30	.467	-/ -	-	-	16	-	-	50	.250

Disqualified: None.

	1st Qtr.	2nd Qtr.	3rd Qtr.	4th Qtr.	Final
Santa Clara	19	25	16	13	73
Colorado A&M	17	10	13	10	50

REGIONAL FINAL EAST

Penn State (71) Coach: Elmer Gross

	Min.	Total FG / FGA	Pct.	FT / FTA	Pct.	Reb. O / T	A	TO	PF	S	Blk	TP	PPM
WEIDENHAMMER, R.	-	1/ -	-	1/ 2	.500	-/ -	-	-	3	-	-	3	-
SHERRY, J.	-	4/ -	-	6/ 7	.857	-/ -	-	-	5	-	-	14	-
BREWER, J.	-	3/ -	-	1/ 1	1.000	-/ -	-	-	1	-	-	7	-
ARNELLE, J.	-	7/ -	-	8/ 9	.889	-/ -	-	-	0	-	-	22	-
ROHLAND, B.	-	0/ -	-	0/ 0	.000	-/ -	-	-	1	-	-	0	-
HAAG, E.	-	4/ -	-	4/ 5	.800	-/ -	-	-	5	-	-	12	-
FIELDS, E.	-	0/ -	-	0/ 0	.000	-/ -	-	-	1	-	-	0	-
BLOCKER, J.	-	5/ -	-	3/ 6	.500	-/ -	-	-	3	-	-	13	-
Totals	200	24/ -	-	23/29	.793	-/ -	-	-	19	-	-	71	.355

Notre Dame (63) Coach: John Jordan

	Min.	Total FG / FGA	Pct.	FT / FTA	Pct.	Reb. O / T	A	TO	PF	S	Blk	TP	PPM
FANNON, J.	-	3/ -	-	2/ 3	.667	-/ -	-	-	4	-	-	8	-
BERTRAND, J.	-	3/ -	-	4/ 6	.667	-/ -	-	-	5	-	-	10	-
MCGINN, E.	-	0/ -	-	0/ 0	.000	-/ -	-	-	1	-	-	0	-
ROSENTHAL, R.	-	8/ -	-	4/ 5	.800	-/ -	-	-	4	-	-	20	-
SULLIVAN, N.	-	3/ -	-	3/ 4	.750	-/ -	-	-	3	-	-	9	-
STEPHENS, J.	-	4/ -	-	8/12	.667	-/ -	-	-	3	-	-	16	-
WEIMAN, W.	-	0/ -	-	0/ 0	.000	-/ -	-	-	0	-	-	0	-
Totals	200	21/ -	-	21/30	.700	-/ -	-	-	20	-	-	63	.315

Disqualified: Penn State—Sherry, Haag; Notre Dame—Bertrand.

	1st Qtr.	2nd Qtr.	3rd Qtr.	4th Qtr.	Final
Penn State	15	16	14	26	71
Notre Dame	15	13	14	21	63

Navy (48) Coach: Ben Carnevale

	Min.	Total FG / FGA	Pct.	FT / FTA	Pct.	Reb. O / T	A	TO	PF	S	Blk	TP	PPM
LANGE, D.	25	1/ -	-	1/ 2	.500	-/ -	-	-	5	-	-	3	.120
CLUNE, J.	35	7/ -	-	2/ 3	.667	-/ -	-	-	4	-	-	16	.457
HOGAN, E.	34	3/ -	-	1/ 3	.333	-/ -	-	-	3	-	-	7	.206
HOOVER, W.	34	3/ -	-	1/ 1	1.000	-/ -	-	-	0	-	-	7	.206
WIGLEY, L.	28	0/ -	-	4/ 5	.800	-/ -	-	-	3	-	-	4	.143
MCCALLY, K.	3	0/ -	-	0/ 0	.000	-/ -	-	-	3	-	-	0	.000
SANDLIN, D.	10	2/ -	-	2/ 2	1.000	-/ -	-	-	1	-	-	6	.600
SLATTERY, W.	4	0/ -	-	0/ 0	.000	-/ -	-	-	0	-	-	0	.000
WELLS, T.	7	0/ -	-	2/ 2	1.000	-/ -	-	-	1	-	-	2	.286
MCDONNELL, J.	2	0/ -	-	0/ 0	.000	-/ -	-	-	0	-	-	0	.000
THOMPSON, B.	16	1/ -	-	1/ 2	.500	-/ -	-	-	2	-	-	3	.188
DEGROFF, J.	2	0/ -	-	0/ 0	.000	-/ -	-	-	0	-	-	0	.000
Totals	200	17/ -	-	14/20	.700	-/ -	-	-	22	-	-	48	.240

La Salle (64) Coach: Ken Loeffler

	Min.	Total FG / FGA	Pct.	FT / FTA	Pct.	Reb. O / T	A	TO	PF	S	Blk	TP	PPM
GOLA, T.	-	8/ -	-	6/11	.545	-/ -	-	-	3	-	-	22	-
MAPLES, B.	-	5/ -	-	3/ 9	.333	-/ -	-	-	3	-	-	13	-
O'HARA, F.	-	0/ -	-	3/ 3	1.000	-/ -	-	-	2	-	-	3	-
BLATCHER, F.	-	2/ -	-	1/ 1	1.000	-/ -	-	-	1	-	-	5	-
SINGLEY, C.	-	5/ -	-	6/ 7	.857	-/ -	-	-	2	-	-	16	-
O'MALLEY, F.	-	1/ -	-	3/ 4	.750	-/ -	-	-	2	-	-	5	-
AMES, B.	-	0/ -	-	0/ 0	.000	-/ -	-	-	0	-	-	0	-
GREENBERG, C.	-	0/ -	-	0/ 0	.000	-/ -	-	-	0	-	-	0	-
YODSNUKIS, J.	-	0/ -	-	0/ 0	.000	-/ -	-	-	0	-	-	0	-
Totals	200	21/ -	-	22/35	.629	-/ -	-	-	13	-	-	64	.320

Disqualified: Navy—Lange.

	1st Qtr.	2nd Qtr.	3rd Qtr.	4th Qtr.	Final
Navy	14	7	8	19	48
La Salle	8	13	22	21	64

REGIONAL FINAL WEST

Bradley (71) Coach: Forddy Anderson

	Min.	Total FG / FGA	Pct.	FT / FTA	Pct.	Reb. O / T	A	TO	PF	S	Blk	TP	PPM
PETERSEN, D.	-	1/ -	-	2/ 4	.500	-/ -	-	-	5	-	-	4	-
CARNEY, B.	-	1/ -	-	4/ 4	1.000	-/ -	-	-	5	-	-	6	-
UTT, L.	-	0/ -	-	0/ 0	.000	-/ -	-	-	0	-	-	0	-
HANSEN, J.	-	0/ -	-	0/ 0	.000	-/ -	-	-	0	-	-	0	-
BABETCH, H.	-	0/ -	-	1/ 1	1.000	-/ -	-	-	0	-	-	1	-
RILEY, J.	-	0/ -	-	0/ 0	.000	-/ -	-	-	0	-	-	0	-
ESTERGARD, D.	-	5/ -	-	5/ 7	.714	-/ -	-	-	3	-	-	15	-
KILCULLEN, B.	-	0/ -	-	2/ 4	.500	-/ -	-	-	5	-	-	2	-
KING, E.	-	5/ -	-	13/16	.813	-/ -	-	-	1	-	-	23	-
KENT, J.	-	6/ -	-	0/ 1	.000	-/ -	-	-	3	-	-	12	-
GOWER, J.	-	2/ -	-	2/ 2	1.000	-/ -	-	-	1	-	-	6	-
O'CONNELL, L.	-	1/ -	-	0/ 0	.000	-/ -	-	-	0	-	-	2	-
Totals	200	21/ -	-	29/39	.744	-/ -	-	-	23	-	-	71	.355

Oklahoma A&M (57) Coach: Henry Iba

	Min.	Total FG / FGA	Pct.	FT / FTA	Pct.	Reb. O / T	A	TO	PF	S	Blk	TP	PPM
FULLER	-	1/ -	-	0/ 0	.000	-/ -	-	-	5	-	-	2	-
CARTER	-	1/ -	-	3/ 3	1.000	-/ -	-	-	5	-	-	5	-
MALONEY	-	2/ -	-	2/ 4	.500	-/ -	-	-	2	-	-	6	-
MATTICK	-	6/ -	-	7/11	.636	-/ -	-	-	5	-	-	19	-
HENDRICK	-	0/ -	-	3/ 3	1.000	-/ -	-	-	4	-	-	3	-
BARNHOUSE	-	3/ -	-	4/ 5	.800	-/ -	-	-	5	-	-	10	-
BABB	-	0/ -	-	0/ 0	.000	-/ -	-	-	3	-	-	0	-
REAMES	-	0/ -	-	0/ 0	.000	-/ -	-	-	0	-	-	0	-
BIGHAM	-	5/ -	-	2/ 4	.500	-/ -	-	-	1	-	-	12	-
Totals	200	18/ -	-	21/30	.700	-/ -	-	-	30	-	-	57	.285

Disqualified: Bradley—Petersen, Carney, Kilcullen; Oklahoma A&M— Fuller, Carter, Mattick, Barnhouse.

	1st Qtr.	2nd Qtr.	3rd Qtr.	4th Qtr.	Final
Bradley	16	15	16	24	71
Oklahoma A&M	16	12	16	13	57

USC (66) Coach: Forrest Twogood

	Min.	Total FG / FGA	Pct.	FT / FTA	Pct.	Reb. O / T	A	TO	PF	S	Blk	TP	PPM
PSALTIS, T.	-	6/ 9	.667	8/12	.667	-/ 2	-	-	2	-	-	20	-
PAUSIG, R.	-	0/ 1	.000	2/ 3	.667	-/ 4	-	-	3	-	-	2	-
IRVIN, R.	-	6/14	.429	3/ 3	1.000	-/ 4	-	-	4	-	-	15	-
WELSH, D.	-	3/11	.273	7/10	.700	-/ 8	-	-	2	-	-	13	-
HAMMER, D.	-	2/ 8	.250	1/ 1	1.000	-/ 5	-	-	3	-	-	5	-
CARR, C.	-	2/ 8	.250	5/ 7	.714	-/ 2	-	-	5	-	-	9	-
LUDECKE, A.	-	1/ 1	1.000	0/ 0	.000	-/ 1	-	-	0	-	-	2	-
Totals	250	20/52	.385	26/36	.722	-/26	-	-	19	-	-	66	.264

Santa Clara (65) Coach: Bob Feerick

	Min.	Total FG / FGA	Pct.	FT / FTA	Pct.	Reb. O / T	A	TO	PF	S	Blk	TP	PPM
SEARS, K.	-	6/16	.375	4/ 4	1.000	-/ 8	-	-	4	-	-	16	-
YOUNG, J.	-	8/13	.615	4/ 5	.800	-/ 4	-	-	5	-	-	20	-
MOUNT, M.	-	4/ 6	.667	7/10	.700	-/ 7	-	-	3	-	-	15	-
BENEDETTI, D.	-	1/ 7	.143	1/ 1	1.000	-/ 1	-	-	1	-	-	3	-
GATZERT, G.	-	1/ 6	.167	2/ 3	.667	-/ 4	-	-	5	-	-	4	-
SIMONI, D.	-	0/ 0	.000	0/ 0	.000	-/ 0	-	-	1	-	-	0	-
SCHOENSTEIN, H.	-	3/ 6	.500	1/ 3	.333	-/ 2	-	-	5	-	-	7	-
BALL, D.	-	0/ 0	.000	0/ 0	.000	-/ 0	-	-	1	-	-	0	-
Totals	250	23/54	.426	19/26	.731	-/26	-	-	25	-	-	65	.260

Disqualified: USC—Carr; Santa Clara—Young, Schoenstein, Gatzert. Technical fouls: Santa Clara—Mount.

	1st Qtr.	2nd Qtr.	3rd Qtr.	4th Qtr.	1st OT	2nd OT	Final
USC	13	15	19	10	8	1	66
Santa Clara	15	11	21	10	8	0	65

FINAL FOUR

Penn State (54) Coach: Elmer Gross

	Min.	Total FG / FGA	Pct.	FT / FTA	Pct.	Reb. O / T	A	TO	PF	S	Blk	TP	PPM
WEIDENHAMMER, R.	-	1/ -	-	1/ 2	.500	-/ -	-	-	2	-	-	3	-
FIELDS, E.	-	2/ -	-	1/ 1	1.000	-/ -	-	-	4	-	-	5	-
HAAG, E.	-	2/ -	-	0/ 0	.000	-/ -	-	-	4	-	-	4	-
BREWER, J.	-	3/ -	-	0/ 0	.000	-/ -	-	-	2	-	-	6	-
ARNELLE, J.	-	5/ -	-	8/10	.800	-/ -	-	-	2	-	-	18	-
ROHLAND, B.	-	2/ -	-	0/ 2	.000	-/ -	-	-	1	-	-	4	-
BLOCKER, J.	-	2/ -	-	0/ 2	.000	-/ -	-	-	1	-	-	4	-
SHERRY, J.	-	1/ -	-	4/ 7	.571	-/ -	-	-	4	-	-	6	-
EDWARDS, D.	-	2/ -	-	0/ 0	.000	-/ -	-	-	1	-	-	4	-
Totals	200	20/ -	-	14/24	.583	-/ -	-	-	21	-	-	54	.270

La Salle (69) Coach: Ken Loeffler

	Min.	Total FG / FGA	Pct.	FT / FTA	Pct.	Reb. O / T	A	TO	PF	S	Blk	TP	PPM
SINGLEY, C.	-	4/ -	-	2/ 3	.667	-/ -	-	-	4	-	-	10	-
MAPLES, B.	-	3/ -	-	1/ 1	1.000	-/ -	-	-	1	-	-	7	-
BLATCHER, F.	-	7/ -	-	5/ 7	.714	-/ -	-	-	2	-	-	19	-
GOLA, T.	-	5/ -	-	9/12	.750	-/ -	-	-	4	-	-	19	-
O'MALLEY, F.	-	3/ -	-	3/ 6	.500	-/ -	-	-	4	-	-	9	-
O'HARA, F.	-	2/ -	-	1/ 3	.333	-/ -	-	-	0	-	-	5	-
Totals	200	24/ -	-	21/32	.656	-/ -	-	-	15	-	-	69	.345

Disqualified: None.

	1st Qtr.	2nd Qtr.	3rd Qtr.	4th Qtr.	Final
Penn State	10	12	10	22	54
La Salle	15	18	12	24	69

Bradley (74) Coach: Forddy Anderson

	Min.	Total FG / FGA	Pct.	FT / FTA	Pct.	Reb. O / T	A	TO	PF	S	Blk	TP	PPM
PETERSEN, D.	-	1/ -	-	3/ 4	.750	-/ -	-	-	1	-	-	5	-
GOWER, J.	-	1/ -	-	0/ 0	.000	-/ -	-	-	3	-	-	2	-
KING, E.	-	6/ -	-	5/ 7	.714	-/ -	-	-	3	-	-	17	-
KILCULLEN, B.	-	0/ -	-	0/ 0	.000	-/ -	-	-	0	-	-	0	-
ESTERGARD, D.	-	7/ -	-	7/ 7	1.000	-/ -	-	-	2	-	-	21	-
UTT, L.	-	0/ -	-	0/ 0	.000	-/ -	-	-	0	-	-	0	-
CARNEY, B.	-	6/ -	-	8/ 9	.889	-/ -	-	-	4	-	-	20	-
O'CONNELL, L.	-	0/ -	-	0/ 0	.000	-/ -	-	-	0	-	-	0	-
KENT, J.	-	3/ -	-	1/ 5	.200	-/ -	-	-	3	-	-	7	-
BABETCH, H.	-	1/ -	-	0/ 0	.000	-/ -	-	-	0	-	-	2	-
Totals	200	25/ -	-	24/32	.750	-/ -	-	-	16	-	-	74	.370

USC (72) Coach: Forrest Twogood

	Min.	Total FG / FGA	Pct.	FT / FTA	Pct.	Reb. O / T	A	TO	PF	S	Blk	TP	PPM
PAUSIG, R.	-	5/ -	-	2/ 2	1.000	-/ -	-	-	3	-	-	12	-
CARR, C.	-	1/ -	-	1/ 2	.500	-/ -	-	-	1	-	-	3	-
PSALTIS, T.	-	2/ -	-	0/ 2	.000	-/ -	-	-	4	-	-	4	-
DUNNE, J.	-	1/ -	-	0/ 0	.000	-/ -	-	-	0	-	-	2	-
IRVIN, R.	-	9/ -	-	5/ 6	.833	-/ -	-	-	5	-	-	23	-
LUDECKE, A.	-	1/ -	-	0/ 0	.000	-/ -	-	-	0	-	-	2	-
HAMMER, D.	-	2/ -	-	3/ 3	1.000	-/ -	-	-	5	-	-	7	-
WELSH, D.	-	6/ -	-	7/11	.636	-/ -	-	-	2	-	-	19	-
Totals	200	27/ -	-	18/26	.692	-/ -	-	-	20	-	-	72	.360

Disqualified: USC—Irvin, Hammer.

	1st Qtr.	2nd Qtr.	3rd Qtr.	4th Qtr.	Final
Bradley	20	16	15	23	74
USC	26	16	16	14	72

NATIONAL CHAMPIONSHIP

La Salle (92)   Coach: Ken Loeffler

	Min.	Total FG / FGA	Pct.	FT / FTA	Pct.	Reb. O / T	A	TO	PF	S	Blk	TP	PPM
SINGLEY, C.	-	8/ -	-	7/10	.700	-/ -	-	-	4	-	-	23	-
GREENBERG, C.	-	2/ -	-	1/ 2	.500	-/ -	-	-	1	-	-	5	-
MAPLES, B.	-	2/ -	-	0/ 0	.000	-/ -	-	-	4	-	-	4	-
BLATCHER, F.	-	11/ -	-	1/ 2	.500	-/ -	-	-	4	-	-	23	-
GOLA, T.	-	7/ -	-	5/ 5	1.000	-/ -	-	-	5	-	-	19	-
O'MALLEY, F.	-	5/ -	-	1/ 1	1.000	-/ -	-	-	4	-	-	11	-
YODASNUKIS, J.	-	0/ -	-	0/ 0	.000	-/ -	-	-	5	-	-	0	-
O'HARA, F.	-	2/ -	-	3/ 4	.750	-/ -	-	-	1	-	-	7	-
Totals	200	37/ -	-	18/24	.750	-/ -	-	-	28	-	-	92	.460

Bradley (76)   Coach: Forddy Anderson

	Min.	Total FG / FGA	Pct.	FT / FTA	Pct.	Reb. O / T	A	TO	PF	S	Blk	TP	PPM
PETERSEN, D.	-	4/ -	-	2/ 2	1.000	-/ -	-	-	2	-	-	10	-
BABETCH, H.	-	0/ -	-	0/ 0	.000	-/ -	-	-	0	-	-	0	-
KING, E.	-	3/ -	-	6/ 7	.857	-/ -	-	-	4	-	-	12	-
GOWER, J.	-	0/ -	-	1/ 2	.500	-/ -	-	-	1	-	-	1	-
ESTERGARD, D.	-	3/ -	-	11/12	.917	-/ -	-	-	1	-	-	17	-
CARNEY, B.	-	3/ -	-	11/17	.647	-/ -	-	-	4	-	-	17	-
UTT, L.	-	0/ -	-	0/ 0	.000	-/ -	-	-	1	-	-	0	-
KENT, J.	-	8/ -	-	0/ 2	.000	-/ -	-	-	2	-	-	16	-
RILEY, J.	-	1/ -	-	1/ 2	.500	-/ -	-	-	1	-	-	3	-
Totals	200	22/ -	-	32/44	.727	-/ -	-	-	16	-	-	76	.380

Disqualified: La Salle—Gola, Yodasnukis.

	1st Qtr.	2nd Qtr.	3rd Qtr.	4th Qtr.	Final
La Salle	19	23	30	20	92
Bradley	22	21	14	19	76

NATIONAL THIRD PLACE

Penn State (70)   Coach: Elmer Gross

	Min.	Total FG / FGA	Pct.	FT / FTA	Pct.	Reb. O / T	A	TO	PF	S	Blk	TP	PPM
SHERRY, J.	-	2/ -	-	3/ 3	1.000	-/ -	-	-	5	-	-	7	-
ROHLAND, B.	-	1/ -	-	1/ 2	.500	-/ -	-	-	3	-	-	3	-
ARNELLE, J.	-	10/ -	-	5/ 6	.833	-/ -	-	-	5	-	-	25	-
HAAG, E.	-	4/ -	-	1/ 2	.500	-/ -	-	-	1	-	-	9	-
WEIDENHAMMER, R.	-	4/ -	-	4/ 4	1.000	-/ -	-	-	1	-	-	12	-
BREWER, J.	-	4/ -	-	0/ 0	.000	-/ -	-	-	3	-	-	8	-
FIELDS, E.	-	2/ -	-	0/ 0	.000	-/ -	-	-	1	-	-	4	-
BLOCKER, J.	-	0/ -	-	2/ 3	.667	-/ -	-	-	3	-	-	2	-
EDWARDS, D.	-	0/ -	-	0/ 0	.000	-/ -	-	-	1	-	-	0	-
Totals	200	27/ -	-	16/20	.800	-/ -	-	-	23	-	-	70	.350

USC (61)   Coach: Forrest Twogood

	Min.	Total FG / FGA	Pct.	FT / FTA	Pct.	Reb. O / T	A	TO	PF	S	Blk	TP	PPM
PSALTIS, T.	-	4/ -	-	3/ 3	1.000	-/ -	-	-	1	-	-	11	-
CARR, C.	-	1/ -	-	2/ 2	1.000	-/ -	-	-	3	-	-	4	-
THOMPSON, P.	-	0/ -	-	2/ 2	1.000	-/ -	-	-	0	-	-	2	-
PAUSIG, R.	-	2/ -	-	1/ 3	.333	-/ -	-	-	3	-	-	5	-
IRVIN, R.	-	5/ -	-	2/ 3	.667	-/ -	-	-	4	-	-	12	-
LUDECKE, A.	-	0/ -	-	1/ 3	.333	-/ -	-	-	0	-	-	1	-
HAMMER, D.	-	2/ -	-	4/ 7	.571	-/ -	-	-	3	-	-	8	-
DUNNE, J.	-	0/ -	-	0/ 0	.000	-/ -	-	-	0	-	-	0	-
WELSH, D.	-	3/ -	-	12/14	.857	-/ -	-	-	0	-	-	18	-
Totals	200	17/ -	-	27/37	.730	-/ -	-	-	14	-	-	61	.305

Disqualified: Penn State—Sherry, Arnelle.

	1st Qtr.	2nd Qtr.	3rd Qtr.	4th Qtr.	Final
Penn State	20	24	18	8	70
USC	13	13	21	14	61

REGIONAL THIRD PLACE WEST

Rice (78)   Coach: Don Suman

	Min.	Total FG / FGA	Pct.	FT / FTA	Pct.	Reb. O / T	A	TO	PF	S	Blk	TP	PPM
LANCE	-	9/15	.600	5/ 5	1.000	-/ -	-	-	2	-	-	23	-
DURRENBERGER	-	4/10	.400	6/11	.545	-/ -	-	-	3	-	-	14	-
SCHWINGER	-	6/15	.400	2/ 3	.667	-/ -	-	-	3	-	-	14	-
BRASHEAR	-	3/ 6	.500	0/ 0	.000	-/ -	-	-	3	-	-	6	-
ROBICHEAUX	-	6/14	.429	1/ 2	.500	-/ -	-	-	2	-	-	13	-
CHRISTENSEN	-	1/ 2	.500	0/ 0	.000	-/ -	-	-	0	-	-	2	-
PAHMETER	-	0/ 0	.000	0/ 2	.000	-/ -	-	-	0	-	-	0	-
TELLIGMAN	-	0/ 1	.000	0/ 0	.000	-/ -	-	-	1	-	-	0	-
BRYAN	-	0/ 1	.000	0/ 0	.000	-/ -	-	-	0	-	-	0	-
SMALL	-	1/ 2	.500	0/ 2	.000	-/ -	-	-	1	-	-	2	-
BEAVERS	-	2/ 7	.286	0/ 0	.000	-/ -	-	-	0	-	-	4	-
Totals	200	32/73	.438	14/25	.560	-/ -	-	-	15	-	-	78	.390

Colorado (55)   Coach: Bebe Lee

	Min.	Total FG / FGA	Pct.	FT / FTA	Pct.	Reb. O / T	A	TO	PF	S	Blk	TP	PPM
JEANGERARD, R.	-	5/16	.313	3/ 3	1.000	-/ -	-	-	4	-	-	13	-
COFFMAN, M.	-	1/ 4	.250	1/ 1	1.000	-/ -	-	-	4	-	-	3	-
HALDORSON, B.	-	3/ 5	.600	2/ 4	.500	-/ -	-	-	1	-	-	8	-
HARROLD, T.	-	4/11	.364	2/ 3	.667	-/ -	-	-	1	-	-	10	-
MOCK, C.	-	2/ 8	.250	2/ 3	.667	-/ -	-	-	2	-	-	6	-
RANGLOS, J.	-	4/ 9	.444	2/ 2	1.000	-/ -	-	-	1	-	-	10	-
WALTER, W.	-	1/ 2	.500	0/ 0	.000	-/ -	-	-	1	-	-	2	-
OWSLEY	-	0/ 0	.000	0/ 0	.000	-/ -	-	-	0	-	-	0	-
HANNAH, G.	-	0/ 3	.000	0/ 0	.000	-/ -	-	-	2	-	-	0	-
PETERSON, B.	-	0/ 0	.000	3/ 4	.750	-/ -	-	-	0	-	-	3	-
Totals	200	20/58	.345	15/20	.750	-/ -	-	-	16	-	-	55	.275

Disqualified: None.

	1st Qtr.	2nd Qtr.	3rd Qtr.	4th Qtr.	Final
Rice	14	22	26	16	78
Colorado	16	8	20	11	55

Idaho State (62)   Coach: Steve Belko

	Min.	Total FG/FGA	Pct.	FT/FTA	Pct.	Reb. O/T	A	TO	PF	S	Blk	TP	PPM
BECKHAM, S.	-	9/ -	-	3/ 5	.600	-/ -	-	-	5	-	-	21	-
ROH, L.	-	3/ -	-	9/11	.818	-/ -	-	-	0	-	-	15	-
BAUER, R.	-	1/ -	-	4/ 4	1.000	-/ -	-	-	3	-	-	6	-
BELKOW, J.	-	4/ -	-	0/ 0	.000	-/ -	-	-	1	-	-	8	-
DAKICH, R.	-	2/ -	-	1/ 1	1.000	-/ -	-	-	2	-	-	5	-
CONNOR, B.	-	1/ -	-	2/ 2	1.000	-/ -	-	-	1	-	-	4	-
HAYS, B.	-	1/ -	-	1/ 2	.500	-/ -	-	-	0	-	-	3	-
Totals	200	21/ -	-	20/25	.800	-/ -	-	-	12	-	-	62	.310

Colorado A&M (57)   Coach: Bill Strannigan

	Min.	Total FG/FGA	Pct.	FT/FTA	Pct.	Reb. O/T	A	TO	PF	S	Blk	TP	PPM
KINARD, H.	-	2/ -	-	1/ 1	1.000	-/ -	-	-	3	-	-	5	-
CAYLOR, R.	-	3/ -	-	0/ 0	.000	-/ -	-	-	3	-	-	6	-
BARTRAN, W.	-	2/ -	-	2/ 2	1.000	-/ -	-	-	1	-	-	6	-
VANDERHOFF, C.	-	1/ -	-	0/ 2	.000	-/ -	-	-	0	-	-	2	-
STUEHM, D.	-	4/ -	-	3/ 9	.333	-/ -	-	-	5	-	-	11	-
HIBBARD, G.	-	1/ -	-	0/ 2	.000	-/ -	-	-	2	-	-	2	-
PIVIC, S.	-	5/ -	-	3/ 4	.750	-/ -	-	-	1	-	-	13	-
BETZ, R.	-	2/ -	-	0/ 0	.000	-/ -	-	-	2	-	-	4	-
BRYANT, J.	-	2/ -	-	0/ 0	.000	-/ -	-	-	0	-	-	4	-
SAVIONI, J.	-	2/ -	-	0/ 0	.000	-/ -	-	-	0	-	-	4	-
GATES, R.	-	0/ -	-	0/ 0	.000	-/ -	-	-	0	-	-	0	-
Totals	200	24/ -	-	9/20	.450	-/ -	-	-	17	-	-	57	.285

Disqualified: Idaho State—Beckham; Colorado A&M—Stuehm.

	1st Qtr.	2nd Qtr.	3rd Qtr.	4th Qtr.	Final
Idaho State	10	16	17	19	62
Colorado A&M	6	15	13	23	57

REGIONAL THIRD PLACE EAST

Indiana (73)   Coach: Branch McCracken

	Min.	Total FG/FGA	Pct.	FT/FTA	Pct.	Reb. O/T	A	TO	PF	S	Blk	TP	PPM
KRAAK, C.	-	3/ 7	.429	4/ 5	.800	-/ 7	-	-	0	-	-	10	-
FARLEY, R.	-	0/ 4	.000	8/15	.533	-/16	-	-	2	-	-	8	-
SCOTT, L.	-	2/ 7	.286	1/ 1	1.000	-/ 2	-	-	2	-	-	5	-
SCOTT, B.	-	2/ 3	.667	4/ 5	.800	-/ 5	-	-	4	-	-	8	-
LEONARD, B.	-	3/13	.231	2/ 4	.500	-/ 3	-	-	3	-	-	8	-
SCHLUNDT, D.	-	9/21	.429	11/15	.733	-/ 3	-	-	4	-	-	29	-
CHOICE, W.	-	1/ 2	.500	3/ 4	.750	-/ 4	-	-	2	-	-	5	-
WHITE, R.	-	0/ 2	.000	0/ 0	.000	-/ 3	-	-	0	-	-	0	-
BYERS, P.	-	0/ 0	.000	0/ 0	.000	-/ 0	-	-	3	-	-	0	-
DEAKYNE, J.	-	0/ 1	.000	0/ 0	.000	-/ 0	-	-	1	-	-	0	-
POFF, P.	-	0/ 0	.000	0/ 0	.000	-/ 0	-	-	0	-	-	0	-
Totals	200	20/60	.333	33/49	.673	-/43	-	-	21	-	-	73	.365

North Carolina State (65)   Coach: Everett Case

	Min.	Total FG/FGA	Pct.	FT/FTA	Pct.	Reb. O/T	A	TO	PF	S	Blk	TP	PPM
TYLER, D.	-	2/ -	-	3/ 6	.500	-/ -	-	-	3	-	-	7	-
THOMPSON, M.	-	9/ -	-	8/16	.500	-/ -	-	-	0	-	-	26	-
GOTKIN	-	0/ -	-	0/ 0	.000	-/ -	-	-	0	-	-	0	-
SHAVLIK, D.	-	3/ -	-	2/ 5	.400	-/ -	-	-	3	-	-	8	-
APPLEBAUM	-	0/ -	-	6/ 8	.750	-/ -	-	-	2	-	-	6	-
MOLODET, V.	-	6/ -	-	6/ 7	.857	-/ -	-	-	3	-	-	18	-
STEVENSON	-	0/ -	-	0/ 0	.000	-/ -	-	-	0	-	-	0	-
Totals	200	20/ -	-	25/42	.595	-/ -	-	-	11	-	-	65	.325

Cornell (54)   Coach: Royner Greene

	Min.	Total FG/FGA	Pct.	FT/FTA	Pct.	Reb. O/T	A	TO	PF	S	Blk	TP	PPM
ROLLES, C.	-	3/ -	-	3/ 4	.750	-/ -	-	-	2	-	-	9	-
MACPHEE, W.	-	3/ -	-	3/ 3	1.000	-/ -	-	-	2	-	-	9	-
CODDINGTON	-	0/ -	-	0/ 0	.000	-/ -	-	-	2	-	-	0	-
MATTES, M.	-	1/ -	-	0/ 0	.000	-/ -	-	-	1	-	-	2	-
KNERR, W.	-	0/ -	-	0/ 0	.000	-/ -	-	-	0	-	-	0	-
ZELEK, R.	-	5/ -	-	2/ 3	.667	-/ -	-	-	5	-	-	12	-
BUNCOM, H.	-	1/ -	-	0/ 0	.000	-/ -	-	-	3	-	-	2	-
MORTON, L.	-	5/ -	-	1/ 1	1.000	-/ -	-	-	5	-	-	11	-
BRADFIELD, D.	-	2/ -	-	2/ 2	1.000	-/ -	-	-	3	-	-	6	-
WILENS, M.	-	1/ -	-	1/ 1	1.000	-/ -	-	-	3	-	-	3	-
Totals	200	21/ -	-	12/14	.857	-/ -	-	-	26	-	-	54	.270

Disqualified: Princeton—Zelek, Morton.

	1st Qtr.	2nd Qtr.	3rd Qtr.	4th Qtr.	Final
N.C. State	16	19	16	14	65
Cornell	15	14	14	11	54

Louisiana State (62)   Coach: Harry Rabenhorst

	Min.	Total FG/FGA	Pct.	FT/FTA	Pct.	Reb. O/T	A	TO	PF	S	Blk	TP	PPM
BELCHER, D.	-	4/11	.364	1/ 2	.500	-/ 4	-	-	4	-	-	9	-
CLARK, N.	-	2/ 9	.222	2/ 2	1.000	-/12	-	-	5	-	-	6	-
PETTIT, B.	-	10/24	.417	7/10	.700	-/12	-	-	4	-	-	27	-
MCARDLE, B.	-	0/ 0	.000	0/ 0	.000	-/ 0	-	-	1	-	-	0	-
MAGEE, N.	-	3/10	.300	3/ 6	.500	-/ 0	-	-	4	-	-	9	-
SEBASTIAN, D.	-	1/10	.100	7/ 8	.875	-/ 1	-	-	5	-	-	9	-
FRESHLEY, B.	-	0/ 4	.000	0/ 0	.000	-/ 6	-	-	5	-	-	0	-
MCNEILLY, J.	-	1/ 1	1.000	0/ 0	.000	-/ 1	-	-	2	-	-	2	-
LOUGHMILLER, D.	-	0/ 0	.000	0/ 0	.000	-/ 0	-	-	1	-	-	0	-
Totals	200	21/69	.304	20/28	.714	-/36	-	-	31	-	-	62	.310

Disqualified: Louisiana St.—Clark, Sebastian, Freshley.

	1st Qtr.	2nd Qtr.	3rd Qtr.	4th Qtr.	Final
Indiana	16	15	12	30	73
Louisiana St.	17	16	13	16	62

☉ ALL-STAR TEAMS ☉

ALL TOURNAMENT

JESSE ARNELLE	PENN STATE
BOB CARNEY	BRADLEY
★ **TOM GOLA**	LA SALLE
ROY IRVIN	USC
CHUCK SINGLEY	LA SALLE

EASTERN REGIONAL (PHILADELPHIA)

★ **TOM GOLA**	LA SALLE
DON LANGE	NAVY
VIC MOLODET	N.C. STATE
LEE MORTON	CORNELL
MEL THOMPSON	N.C. STATE

★ Most Outstanding Player(s)

☉ INDIVIDUAL RECORDS ☉

SCORING

Most points in a single game
1 JACK CLUNE, NAVY (vs. U. CONN.)   42
2 BOB CARNEY, BRADLEY (vs. COLORADO)   37
3 LEE MORTON, CORNELL (vs. NAVY)   34
3 BOB PETTIT, LOUISIANA ST. (vs. PENN STATE) 34
5 BOB O'DONNELL, LOYOLA N.O. (vs. NOTRE DAME)   32

Most total points in the tournament
1 TOM GOLA, LA SALLE   114
2 BOB CARNEY, BRADLEY   107
3 JESSE ARNELLE, PENN STATE   102
4 CHARLES SINGLEY, LA SALLE   86
5 JACK CLUNE, NAVY   79

Highest scoring average (minimum 2 games)
1 BOB PETTIT, LOUISIANA ST. (61-2)   30.50
2 JACK CLUNE, NAVY (79-3)   26.33
3 RICHARD ROSENTHAL, NOTRE DAME (76-3)   25.33
4 TOM GOLA, LA SALLE (114-5)   22.80
5 LEE MORTON, CORNELL (45-2)   22.50

FIELD GOALS

Most field goals in a single game
1 JACK CLUNE, NAVY (vs. U. CONN.)   16
2 BOB PETTIT, LOUISIANA ST. (vs. PENN STATE) 13
3 5 tied for third place.

Most total field goals in the tournament
1 TOM GOLA, LA SALLE   38
2 JESSE ARNELLE, PENN STATE   36
3 CHARLES SINGLEY, LA SALLE   31
4 JACK CLUNE, NAVY   30
5 2 tied for fifth place.

FREE THROWS

Most free throws in a single game
1 BOB CARNEY, BRADLEY (vs. COLORADO)   23
2 TOM GOLA, LA SALLE (vs. N.C. STATE)   14
3 EDDIE KING, BRADLEY (vs. OKLAHOMA A&M) 13
4 DICK WELSH, USC (vs. PENN STATE)   12
5 3 tied for fifth place.

Most total free throws in the tournament
1 BOB CARNEY, BRADLEY   55
2 TOM GOLA, LA SALLE   38
3 DICK ESTERGARD, BRADLEY   31
4 EDDIE KING, BRADLEY   30
4 JESSE ARNELLE, PENN STATE   30

Most free throws attempted in a single game
1 BOB CARNEY, BRADLEY (vs. COLORADO)   26
2 DENNY STUEHM, COLORADO STATE (vs. SANTA CLARA)   19
3 TOM GOLA, LA SALLE (vs. N.C. STATE)   18
3 JACK STEPHENS, NOTRE DAME (vs. INDIANA) 18
5 BOB CARNEY, BRADLEY (vs. LA SALLE)   17

Most free throws attempted in the tournament
1 BOB CARNEY, BRADLEY   70
2 TOM GOLA, LA SALLE   52
3 MEL THOMPSON, N.C. STATE   41
4 JACK STEPHENS, NOTRE DAME   38
5 EDDIE KING, BRADLEY   37

Highest free throw percentage in a single game (minimum 7 attempts)
1 LEE MORTON, CORNELL (vs. NAVY) (10-10)   1.000
2 DEVLIN, GEO. WASH. (vs. N.C. STATE) (8-8)   1.000
2 DON SCHLUNDT, INDIANA (vs. NOTRE DAME (8-8)   1.000
4 DICK ESTERGARD, BRADLEY (vs. USC) (7-7)   1.000
5 DICK ESTERGARD, BRADLEY (vs. LA SALLE) (11-12)   .917

Highest free throw percentage in the tournament (minimum 15 attempts)
1 JACK CLUNE, NAVY (19-22)   .864
2 DICK ESTERGARD, BRADLEY (31-36)   .861
3 ROY IRVIN, USC (17-20)   .850
4 JESSE ARNELLE, PENN STATE (30-36)   .833
5 LES ROH, IDAHO STATE (20-24)   .833

✪ TEAM RECORDS ✪

SCORING

Most points in a single game
1	LA SALLE (vs. BRADLEY)	92
2	LA SALLE (vs. N.C. STATE)	88
3	NAVY (vs. U. CONN.)	85

Most total points in the tournament
1	LA SALLE	389
2	BRADLEY	358
3	PENN STATE	335

Highest scoring average (minimum 2 games)
1	LA SALLE (389-5)	77.80
2	N.C. STATE (221-3)	73.67
3	BRADLEY (358-5)	71.60

FIELD GOALS

Most field goals in a single game
1	LA SALLE (vs. BRADLEY)	37
2	RICE (vs. COLORADO)	32
3	2 tied for third place.	

Most total field goals in the tournament
1	LA SALLE	138
2	PENN STATE	122
3	BRADLEY	106

FREE THROWS

Most free throws in a single game
1	BRADLEY (vs. COLORADO)	38
2	INDIANA (vs. LOUISIANA ST.)	33
3	BRADLEY (vs. LA SALLE)	32

Most total free throws in the tournament
1	BRADLEY	146
2	LA SALLE	113
3	PENN STATE	91

Most free throws attempted in a single game
1	INDIANA (vs. LOUISIANA ST.)	49
2	BRADLEY (vs. LA SALLE)	44
2	BRADLEY (vs. COLORADO)	44

Most total free throws attempted in the tournament
1	BRADLEY	194
2	LA SALLE	162
3	PENN STATE	129

Highest free throw percentage in a single game
1	BRADLEY (vs. COLORADO) (38-44)	.864
2	CORNELL (vs. N.C. STATE) (12-14)	.857
3	SANTA CLARA (vs. COLORADO STATE) (17-20)	
		.850

Highest free throw percentage in the tournament (minimum 2 games)
1	CORNELL (31-38)	.816
2	SANTA CLARA (57-72)	.792
3	LOUISIANA ST. (40-52)	.769

Fewest free throws in a single game
1	RICE (vs. OKLAHOMA A&M)	9
1	COLORADO STATE (vs. IDAHO STATE)	9
3	CORNELL (vs. N.C. STATE)	12

Lowest free throw percentage in a single game
1	COLORADO STATE (vs. IDAHO STATE) (9-20)	.450
2	COLORADO STATE (vs. SANTA CLARA) (14-30)	
		.467
3	OKLAHOMA A&M (vs. RICE) (15-29)	.517

Lowest free throw percentage in the tournament (minimum 2 games)
1	COLORADO STATE (23-50)	.460
2	RICE (23-40)	.575
3	OKLAHOMA A&M (36-59)	.610

1955

FIRST ROUND	REGIONAL SEMIFINAL	REGIONAL FINAL	**FINAL FOUR**	REGIONAL FINAL	REGIONAL SEMIFINAL	FIRST ROUND

EAST

Miami (Ohio) 79
Marquette 79
Marquette 90
Marquette 81
(bye)
Kentucky 71

Penn St. 59
Penn St. 53
Memphis St. 55
Iowa 86
(bye)
Iowa 82

Iowa 73

La Salle 95
La Salle 73
West Virginia 61
La Salle 99
(bye)
Princeton 46
La Salle 76

Williams 60
Canisius 73
Canisius 73
Canisius 64
Duke 73
Villanova 71
Villanova 74

San Francisco 77
La Salle 63

WEST

Oklahoma City 65
Bradley 81
Bradley 69
Bradley 81
(bye)
SMU 79

Colorado 50
Colorado 69
(bye)
Colorado 93
Tulsa 59
(bye)

Idaho St. 63
Seattle 71
Seattle 80
Oregon St. 56
Oregon St. 83
(bye)

San Francisco 62

West Texas St. 66
San Francisco 78
San Francisco 89
San Francisco 57
Utah 59
(bye)

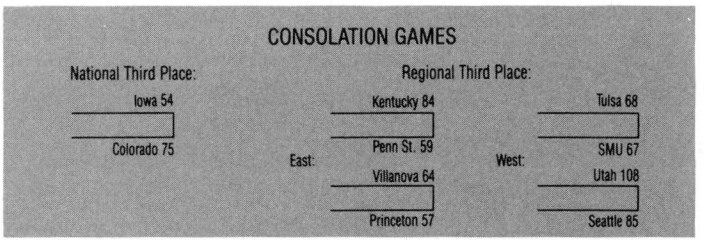

CONSOLATION GAMES

National Third Place:

Iowa 54
Colorado 75

Regional Third Place:

East:
Kentucky 84
Penn St. 59
Villanova 64
Princeton 57

West:
Tulsa 68
SMU 67
Utah 108
Seattle 85

When the University of San Francisco hired Phil Woolpert as the school's varsity basketball coach in 1950, he arrived at the small Jesuit college with very particular ideas about the game of basketball. "If your opponents can't shoot," he said, "they can't score." In an era of wide-open offensive play, when teams were regularly dropping in as many as 90 or even a hundred points in a game, Woolpert was passionate about defense. He wanted his guards to press, his forwards to fight through screens, and his center to block shots. But for his system to work, he needed players who were quick, intelligent, and athletic.

In 1952 Woolpert reached across San Francisco Bay and found a kindred spirit. Bill Russell, who had shot up to 6-6 in his senior year at Oakland's McClymonds High School, was an awkward ambidexterous stringbean of a teenager who couldn't shoot, pass or dribble. But he *was* hardworking, he could run and jump, and best of all, he could think. So when every major college coach passed on the skinny East Bay teenager, Woolpert took a chance that Russell could learn the game and offered him a scholarship.

That fall, Russell began to work under the guidance of Woolpert and freshman Coach Ross Giudice at the St. Ignatius High School gym, near the San Francisco campus. (The Dons, with no gym of their own, had to make do at the nearby Jesuit high school where Woolpert taught before moving up to the college ranks.) Soon a squad of quick, bright, ball-hawking players began to form around the charismatic young center.

By Russell's junior year Woolpert knew he had something special, although it was still a secret to the rest of the world. After losing to UCLA in the second week of the season, the Dons began to win. By early January the word was out and San Francisco broke into the national rankings. As they continued to beat all comers the buzz grew louder, until they found themselves perched at the No. 1 spot in the polls.

Russell (now 6-10), was gaining recognition for his uncanny rebounding, devastating tips and dunks, and demon shot-blocking. Like his coach, Russell found defense a joy. "Heck," he told *Sports Illustrated* soon after he and his team had begun to attract nationwide attention, "I'd rather block a shot any day than score." A master psychologist for one so young, the big center understood a blocked shot's effect as a morale booster for his own team and its devastating effect on the opposition.

Although some skeptics wondered what would happen when the Dons came up against an excellent all-around team like the defending national champions from La Salle, there were enough believers to install San Francisco as the 1955 NCAA tournament favorite. The Dons did not disap-

point their backers. In an easy first-round victory over West Texas State, Russell scored 29 points in 29 minutes. Against Utah Russell suffered from a cold, but he still slammed in his shots, according to the AP, "like he's stuffing clothes in a suitcase." With K. C. Jones and Hal Perry stealing the ball and Russell grabbing every rebound, San Francisco hit 9 of their first 10 shots and took a 20-6 lead in the first four minutes. The Dons qualified for the Final Four by squeaking past Oregon State and its 7-3 center Swede Halbrook, 57-56, as Russell scored 29.

Meanwhile, La Salle's defending champions were even more convincing than Phil Woolpert's squad as they swept through their regional. Despite a poor shooting night by All-American Tom Gola (whom many called the greatest all-around college basketball player ever), La Salle broke the single game tournament scoring record in their 95-61 victory over West Virginia. Next, the Explorers devastated Princeton. Finally, playing at home in the Palestra, they crushed Canisius, breaking their own four-day-old tournament scoring record in a 99-64 victory. Only a late freeze by Canisius prevented the Explorers from reaching the century mark.

In their semifinal against Iowa, La Salle continued setting records, this time breaking the all-time tournament mark for consecutive victories with nine. But unlike their three regional contests, which they won by an average of 32 points, they beat Iowa by only three, despite being in control most of the way.

San Francisco continued to be relentless in their semi against Colorado, hitting over 50 percent of their shots compared to the Buffaloes' 28.6 percent. Colorado's star center Burdette Haldorson, faced with the unenviable task of stopping Russell, fouled out with 14 minutes left; with 8 minutes to go the Dons led by 16. They coasted in.

The widely anticipated "Battle of All-Americans" between Gola of the defending national champions and Russell of the nation's No. 1 squad really didn't happen. In a surprise move, San Francisco Coach Woolpert assigned 6-1 K. C. Jones to guard the 6-7 Gola, and the strategy worked perfectly. Jones, with his cat-quick hands and feet and great jumping ability, made life miserable for the La Salle star, and Russell was free to stay near the boards to rebound and block the shots of any Explorer foolish enough to attempt to drive on him. Despite an injury to forward Jerry Mullen, the Dons—with Jones hitting from the outside and Russell scoring at will from underneath—had far too much firepower for the Explorers to overcome. Almost from the start, the outcome was a foregone conclusion—Russell and the Dons were as good as they were cracked up to be.

FIRST ROUND EAST

Miami (Ohio) (79) Coach: Bill Rohr

	Min.	Total FG/FGA	Pct.	FT/FTA	Pct.	Reb. O/T	A	TO	PF	S	Blk	TP	PPM
KENNON, W.	-	7/16	.438	1/4	.250	-/6	-	-	4	-	-	15	-
FOX, C.	-	1/5	.200	2/2	1.000	-/5	-	-	3	-	-	4	-
ELLIS, R.	-	4/16	.250	0/2	.000	-/13	-	-	3	-	-	8	-
BARNETTE, D.	-	9/19	.474	4/5	.800	-/4	-	-	0	-	-	22	-
BRYANT, T.	-	8/28	.286	4/5	.800	-/22	-	-	2	-	-	20	-
KLITCH, R.	-	3/7	.429	2/4	.500	-/6	-	-	2	-	-	8	-
ALBERS, R.	-	0/2	.000	0/1	.000	-/2	-	-	3	-	-	0	-
HEDRIC, D.	-	1/2	.500	0/0	.000	-/0	-	-	1	-	-	2	-
Totals	200	33/95	.347	13/23	.565	-/58	-	-	18	-	-	79	.395

Marquette (90) Coach: Jack Nagle

	Min.	Total FG/FGA	Pct.	FT/FTA	Pct.	Reb. O/T	A	TO	PF	S	Blk	TP	PPM
HOPFENSPERGER	-	1/-	-	0/0	.000	-/-	-	-	2	-	-	2	-
SCHULZ	-	0/-	-	2/2	1.000	-/-	-	-	1	-	-	2	-
RAND, T.	-	16/-	-	5/6	.833	-/-	-	-	2	-	-	37	-
WITTBERGER	-	2/-	-	2/7	.286	-/-	-	-	3	-	-	6	-
WALCZAK	-	4/-	-	8/8	1.000	-/-	-	-	1	-	-	16	-
BUGALSKI	-	7/-	-	4/7	.571	-/-	-	-	4	-	-	18	-
O'KEEFE	-	3/-	-	3/4	.750	-/-	-	-	2	-	-	9	-
Totals	200	33/-	-	24/34	.706	-/-	-	-	15	-	-	90	.450

Team Rebounds: Marquette 8; Miami (Ohio) 0. Disqualified: None.

	1st Half	2nd Half	Final
Miami (Ohio)	39	40	79
Marquette	29	61	90

Penn State (59) Coach: John Egli

	Min.	Total FG/FGA	Pct.	FT/FTA	Pct.	Reb. O/T	A	TO	PF	S	Blk	TP	PPM
BLOCKER, J.	-	3/6	.500	2/3	.667	-/14	-	-	3	-	-	8	-
EDWARDS, D.	-	2/8	.250	0/0	.000	-/7	-	-	1	-	-	4	-
HOFFMAN, B.	-	1/1	1.000	0/0	.000	-/2	-	-	2	-	-	2	-
ARNELLE, J.	-	6/19	.316	8/12	.667	-/22	-	-	3	-	-	20	-
WEIDENHAMMER, R.	-	4/11	.364	0/0	.000	-/2	-	-	1	-	-	8	-
FIELDS, E.	-	5/15	.333	7/8	.875	-/13	-	-	2	-	-	17	-
ROHLAND, B.	-	0/0	.000	0/0	.000	-/0	-	-	0	-	-	0	-
RAMSAY	-	0/0	.000	0/0	.000	-/1	-	-	0	-	-	0	-
Totals	200	21/60	.350	17/23	.739	-/61	-	-	12	-	-	59	.295

Memphis State (55) Coach: Eugene Lambert

	Min.	Total FG/FGA	Pct.	FT/FTA	Pct.	Reb. O/T	A	TO	PF	S	Blk	TP	PPM
SCOTT, H.	-	2/14	.143	1/2	.500	-/8	-	-	1	-	-	5	-
DAVIS, M.	-	4/16	.250	4/8	.500	-/10	-	-	4	-	-	12	-
JONES, D.	-	0/1	.000	0/0	.000	-/2	-	-	1	-	-	0	-
MCCLAIN, B.	-	2/6	.333	0/0	.000	-/2	-	-	0	-	-	4	-
BALLARD, J.	-	0/2	.000	0/0	.000	-/4	-	-	2	-	-	0	-
WINN, D.	-	1/2	.500	0/0	.000	-/0	-	-	0	-	-	2	-
ARNOLD, F.	-	5/15	.333	2/6	.333	-/10	-	-	4	-	-	12	-
FORTNER, E.	-	1/7	.143	0/1	.000	-/4	-	-	2	-	-	2	-
CALDWELL, K.	-	8/18	.444	2/2	1.000	-/4	-	-	1	-	-	18	-
Totals	200	23/81	.284	9/19	.474	-/44	-	-	15	-	-	55	.275

Team Rebounds: Penn State 1; Memphis State 3. Disqualified: None.

	1st Half	2nd Half	Final
Penn State	33	22	59
Memphis State	19	36	55

La Salle (95) Coach: Ken Loeffler

	Min.	Total FG/FGA	Pct.	FT/FTA	Pct.	Reb. O/T	A	TO	PF	S	Blk	TP	PPM
SINGLEY, C.	-	6/-	-	1/1	1.000	-/-	-	-	2	-	-	13	-
LEWIS, A.	-	9/-	-	4/8	.500	-/-	-	-	1	-	-	22	-
BLATCHER, F.	-	5/-	-	3/4	.750	-/-	-	-	0	-	-	13	-
AMES, B.	-	1/-	-	0/0	.000	-/-	-	-	0	-	-	2	-
GOLA, T.	-	7/20	.350	8/10	.800	-/-	-	-	4	-	-	22	-
FREDERICKS, W.	-	0/-	-	0/2	.000	-/-	-	-	0	-	-	0	-
O'MALLEY, F.	-	2/-	-	1/2	.500	-/-	-	-	2	-	-	5	-
GREENBERG, C.	-	6/-	-	0/0	.000	-/-	-	-	3	-	-	12	-
MAPLES, B.	-	3/-	-	0/2	.000	-/-	-	-	1	-	-	6	-
KRAEMER, B.	-	0/-	-	0/0	.000	-/-	-	-	0	-	-	0	-
GOLA, J.	-	0/-	-	0/0	.000	-/-	-	-	0	-	-	0	-
Totals	200	39/-	-	17/29	.586	-/-	-	-	13	-	-	95	.475

West Virginia (61) Coach: Fred Schaus

	Min.	Total FG/FGA	Pct.	FT/FTA	Pct.	Reb. O/T	A	TO	PF	S	Blk	TP	PPM
HUNDLEY, R.	-	8/-	-	1/2	.500	-/-	-	-	2	-	-	17	-
BERGINES	-	4/-	-	2/4	.500	-/-	-	-	1	-	-	10	-
MULLINS	-	1/-	-	0/0	.000	-/-	-	-	0	-	-	2	-
WITTING	-	0/-	-	3/4	.750	-/-	-	-	1	-	-	3	-
LANEVE	-	0/-	-	0/0	.000	-/-	-	-	0	-	-	0	-
WHITE, P.	-	7/-	-	5/8	.625	-/-	-	-	2	-	-	19	-
CONSTANTINE	-	0/-	-	0/0	.000	-/-	-	-	1	-	-	0	-
SPADAFORE	-	1/-	-	0/4	.000	-/-	-	-	3	-	-	2	-
KISHBAUGH	-	1/-	-	2/3	.667	-/-	-	-	4	-	-	4	-
HOLT	-	1/-	-	0/0	.000	-/-	-	-	3	-	-	2	-
BRENNAN	-	0/-	-	0/0	.000	-/-	-	-	0	-	-	0	-
KING	-	1/-	-	0/0	.000	-/-	-	-	0	-	-	2	-
Totals	200	24/-	-	13/25	.520	-/-	-	-	17	-	-	61	.305

Disqualified: None.

	1st Half	2nd Half	Final
La Salle	40	55	95
West Virginia	33	28	61

Williams (60) Coach: Alex Shaw

	Min.	Total FG/FGA	Pct.	FT/FTA	Pct.	Reb. O/T	A	TO	PF	S	Blk	TP	PPM
BUSS	-	1/-	-	3/5	.600	-/-	-	-	2	-	-	5	-
WHITE	-	0/-	-	0/1	.000	-/-	-	-	3	-	-	0	-
DUBROFF	-	0/-	-	0/0	.000	-/-	-	-	0	-	-	0	-
WILSON, R.	-	5/-	-	8/13	.615	-/-	-	-	2	-	-	18	-
SANTOS	-	0/-	-	0/0	.000	-/-	-	-	0	-	-	0	-
MORO, T.	-	9/-	-	9/12	.750	-/-	-	-	5	-	-	27	-
SYMONS	-	0/-	-	0/0	.000	-/-	-	-	0	-	-	0	-
CULLEN	-	3/-	-	0/0	.000	-/-	-	-	0	-	-	6	-
SMITH	-	0/-	-	0/0	.000	-/-	-	-	0	-	-	0	-
LEWIS	-	0/-	-	0/0	.000	-/-	-	-	0	-	-	0	-
JENSEN, W.	-	0/-	-	2/2	1.000	-/-	-	-	4	-	-	2	-
EVANS	-	1/-	-	0/0	.000	-/-	-	-	0	-	-	2	-
Totals	200	19/-	-	22/33	.667	-/-	-	-	16	-	-	60	.300

Canisius (73) Coach: Joseph Curran

	Min.	Total FG/FGA	Pct.	FT/FTA	Pct.	Reb. O/T	A	TO	PF	S	Blk	TP	PPM
ADAMS, R.	-	5/-	-	4/4	1.000	-/-	-	-	4	-	-	14	-
MARKEY, D.	-	0/-	-	0/0	.000	-/-	-	-	0	-	-	0	-
NOWAK, H.	-	3/-	-	7/7	1.000	-/-	-	-	2	-	-	13	-
COOGAN	-	0/-	-	0/0	.000	-/-	-	-	0	-	-	0	-
LEONE, J.	-	2/-	-	0/2	.000	-/-	-	-	5	-	-	4	-
ZATORSKI, J.	-	1/-	-	0/0	.000	-/-	-	-	0	-	-	2	-
MCCARTHY, JAMES	-	1/-	-	0/2	.000	-/-	-	-	2	-	-	2	-
KELLY, R.	-	7/-	-	1/4	.250	-/-	-	-	2	-	-	15	-
BRENNAN, G.	-	0/-	-	0/0	.000	-/-	-	-	0	-	-	0	-
MCCARTHY, JOHN	-	8/-	-	3/5	.600	-/-	-	-	1	-	-	19	-
CORCORAN, F.	-	2/-	-	0/0	.000	-/-	-	-	2	-	-	4	-
Totals	200	29/-	-	15/24	.625	-/-	-	-	18	-	-	73	.365

Disqualified: Canisius—Leone; Williams—Moro.

	1st Half	2nd Half	Final
Williams	25	35	60
Canisius	30	43	73

Duke (73)   Coach: Harold Bradley

	Min.	Total FG/FGA	Pct.	FT/FTA	Pct.	Reb. O/T	A	TO	PF	S	Blk	TP	PPM
MAYER, R.	-	2/ -		0/ 1	.000	-/ -			5			4	-
BELMONT, J.	-	5/ -		10/13	.769	-/ -			3			20	-
TURNER, H.	-	1/ -		0/ 0	.000	-/ -			0			2	-
MORGAN, J.	-	4/ -		5/10	.500	-/ -			4			13	-
DOHERTY, M.	-	0/ -		0/ 0	.000	-/ -			1			0	-
TOBIN, D.	-	10/ -		2/ 4	.500	-/ -			4			22	-
LAKATA, B.	-	0/ -		4/ 7	.571	-/ -			3			4	-
LAMLEY, H.	-	3/ -		2/ 3	.667	-/ -			2			8	-
KALBFUS, J.	-	0/ -		0/ 0	.000	-/ -			2			0	-
Totals	200	25/ -		23/38	.605	-/ -			24			73	.365

Villanova (74)   Coach: Alex Severance

	Min.	Total FG/FGA	Pct.	FT/FTA	Pct.	Reb. O/T	A	TO	PF	S	Blk	TP	PPM
CIRINO	-	3/ -		3/ 5	.600	-/ -			5			9	-
WEISSMAN, J.	-	1/ -		1/ 2	.500	-/ -			0			3	-
GRIFFITH	-	3/ -		1/ 2	.500	-/ -			3			7	-
DEVINE, J.	-	7/ -		3/ 4	.750	-/ -			4			17	-
SCHAEFER, B.	-	4/ -		14/20	.700	-/ -			4			22	-
SMITH	-	5/ -		5/ 7	.714	-/ -			5			15	-
POWERS	-	0/ -		1/ 2	.500	-/ -			1			1	-
Totals	200	23/ -		28/42	.667	-/ -			22			74	.370

Disqualified: Villanova—Cirino, Smith; Duke—Mayer.

	1st Half	2nd Half	Final
Duke	29	44	73
Villanova	39	35	74

FIRST ROUND WEST

Oklahoma City (65)   Coach: Doyle Parrack

	Min.	Total FG/FGA	Pct.	FT/FTA	Pct.	Reb. O/T	A	TO	PF	S	Blk	TP	PPM
LEE	-	4/ -		9/16	.563	-/ -			3			17	-
BRADSHAW	-	4/ -		5/ 7	.714	-/ -			4			13	-
DIERS	-	0/ -		0/ 0	.000	-/ -			1			0	-
HOLLOWAY	-	9/ -		2/ 3	.667	-/ -			3			20	-
NATH	-	0/ -		2/ 2	1.000	-/ -			3			2	-
BULLARD	-	0/ -		1/ 2	.500	-/ -			1			1	-
MAGANA	-	3/ -		2/ 3	.667	-/ -			0			8	-
JUBY	-	1/ -		2/ 2	1.000	-/ -			2			4	-
Totals	200	21/ -		23/35	.821	-/ -			17			65	.325

Idaho State (63)   Coach: Steve Belko

	Min.	Total FG/FGA	Pct.	FT/FTA	Pct.	Reb. O/T	A	TO	PF	S	Blk	TP	PPM
ROH, L.	-	7/ -		1/ 3	.333	-/ -			2			15	-
HICKS	-	3/ -		3/ 4	.750	-/ -			3			9	-
DETHLEFS, B.	-	0/ -		1/ 3	.333	-/ -			1			1	-
EASTERBROOKS, S.	-	1/ -		0/ 0	.000	-/ -			1			2	-
BAUER, R.	-	6/ -		1/ 2	.500	-/ -			5			13	-
HAYS, B.	-	2/ -		1/ 3	.333	-/ -			0			5	-
ARNOLD, F.	-	0/ -		0/ 0	.000	-/ -			0			0	-
CONNOR, B.	-	4/ -		10/13	.769	-/ -			4			18	-
Totals	200	23/ -		17/28	.607	-/ -			16			63	.315

Bradley (69)   Coach: Bob Vanatta

	Min.	Total FG/FGA	Pct.	FT/FTA	Pct.	Reb. O/T	A	TO	PF	S	Blk	TP	PPM
GOWER, J.	-	2/ -		6/ 7	.857	-/ -			5			10	-
HANSEN, J.	-	3/ -		0/ 0	.000	-/ -			3			6	-
BABETCH, H.	-	6/ -		9/11	.818	-/ -			3			21	-
PETERSEN, D.	-	2/ -		3/ 4	.750	-/ -			3			7	-
ALBECK, S.	-	2/ -		5/ 6	.833	-/ -			4			9	-
UTT, L.	-	6/ -		2/ 4	.500	-/ -			4			14	-
KENT, J.	-	1/ -		0/ 0	.000	-/ -			1			2	-
Totals	200	22/ -		25/32	.781	-/ -			23			69	.345

Disqualified: Bradley—Gower.

	1st Half	2nd Half	Final
Oklahoma City	31	34	65
Bradley	35	34	69

Seattle (80)   Coach: Al Brightman

	Min.	Total FG/FGA	Pct.	FT/FTA	Pct.	Reb. O/T	A	TO	PF	S	Blk	TP	PPM
GLOWASKI	-	7/ -		3/ 5	.600	-/ -			2			17	-
GODES	-	0/ -		0/ 0	.000	-/ -			0			0	-
VAUGHN	-	0/ -		0/ 0	.000	-/ -			1			0	-
KELLY	-	6/ -		1/ 3	.333	-/ -			2			13	-
FUHRER	-	1/ -		0/ 2	.000	-/ -			1			2	-
STRICKLIN, D.	-	9/ -		2/ 7	.286	-/ -			5			20	-
SANFORD	-	0/ -		0/ 0	.000	-/ -			0			0	-
BAUER, C.	-	6/ -		3/ 3	1.000	-/ -			3			15	-
COX	-	0/ -		2/ 2	1.000	-/ -			0			2	-
MALONE	-	3/ -		1/ 3	.333	-/ -			3			7	-
MARTIN	-	2/ -		0/ 0	.000	-/ -			0			4	-
Totals	200	34/ -		12/25	.480	-/ -			17			80	.400

Disqualified: Seattle—Stricklin; Idaho State—Bauer.

	1st Half	2nd Half	Final
Idaho State	27	36	63
Seattle	34	46	80

West Texas State (66)   Coach: Gus Mill

	Min.	Total FG / FGA	Pct.	FT / FTA	Pct.	Reb. O / T	A	TO	PF	S	Blk	TP	PPM
OVERCAST	-	0/ -	-	0/ 0	.000	-/ -	-	-	1	-	-	0	-
ROGERS	-	0/ -	-	0/ 0	.000	-/ -	-	-	0	-	-	0	-
NICHOL	-	0/ -	-	0/ 0	.000	-/ -	-	-	0	-	-	0	-
CLIFTON	-	2/ -	-	6/ 7	.857	-/ -	-	-	5	-	-	10	-
MCCLURE	-	1/ -	-	0/ 0	.000	-/ -	-	-	0	-	-	2	-
BURRIS	-	6/ -	-	0/ 0	.000	-/ -	-	-	4	-	-	12	-
GEORGE	-	1/ -	-	2/ 2	1.000	-/ -	-	-	0	-	-	4	-
ROBINSON	-	7/ -	-	0/ 0	.000	-/ -	-	-	2	-	-	14	-
KNOTT	-	0/ -	-	0/ 0	.000	-/ -	-	-	0	-	-	0	-
SCOTT	-	9/ -	-	6/ 8	.750	-/ -	-	-	2	-	-	24	-
Totals	200	26/ -	-	14/17	.824	-/ -	-	-	14	-	-	66	.330

San Francisco (89)   Coach: Phil Woolpert

	Min.	Total FG / FGA	Pct.	FT / FTA	Pct.	Reb. O / T	A	TO	PF	S	Blk	TP	PPM
MULLEN, J.	-	9/ -	-	2/ 6	.333	-/ -	-	-	2	-	-	20	-
LAWLESS, D.	-	0/ -	-	1/ 2	.500	-/ -	-	-	0	-	-	1	-
BUCHANAN, S.	-	4/ -	-	5/ 5	1.000	-/ -	-	-	2	-	-	13	-
KING, J.	-	1/ -	-	0/ 0	.000	-/ -	-	-	0	-	-	2	-
RUSSELL, B.	-	14/ -	-	1/ 6	.167	-/ -	-	-	2	-	-	29	-
WIEBUSCH, B.	-	0/ -	-	0/ 1	.000	-/ -	-	-	1	-	-	0	-
KIRBY, G.	-	1/ -	-	0/ 0	.000	-/ -	-	-	0	-	-	2	-
JONES, K.	-	6/ -	-	0/ 0	.000	-/ -	-	-	1	-	-	12	-
BAXTER, W.	-	1/ -	-	0/ 0	.000	-/ -	-	-	1	-	-	2	-
BUSH, B.	-	1/ -	-	0/ 0	.000	-/ -	-	-	0	-	-	2	-
PERRY, H.	-	1/ -	-	2/ 2	1.000	-/ -	-	-	0	-	-	4	-
ZANNINI, R.	-	1/ -	-	0/ 0	.000	-/ -	-	-	0	-	-	2	-
BALCHIOS, S.	-	0/ -	-	0/ 0	.000	-/ -	-	-	0	-	-	0	-
Totals	200	39/ -	-	11/22	.500	-/ -	-	-	9	-	-	89	.445

Disqualified: West Texas St.—Clifton.

	1st Half	2nd Half	Final
West Texas State	33	33	66
San Francisco	46	43	89

REGIONAL SEMIFINAL EAST

Marquette (79)   Coach: Jack Nagle

	Min.	Total FG / FGA	Pct.	FT / FTA	Pct.	Reb. O / T	A	TO	PF	S	Blk	TP	PPM
HOPFENSPERGER	-	3/ -	-	7/ 8	.875	-/ -	-	-	5	-	-	13	-
SCHULZ	-	5/ -	-	0/ 2	.000	-/ -	-	-	1	-	-	10	-
WITTBERGER	-	4/ -	-	10/12	.833	-/ -	-	-	1	-	-	18	-
RAND, T.	-	8/ -	-	3/ 5	.600	-/ -	-	-	4	-	-	19	-
BUGALSKI	-	6/ -	-	3/ 4	.750	-/ -	-	-	3	-	-	15	-
WALCZAK	-	2/ -	-	0/ 0	.000	-/ -	-	-	1	-	-	4	-
Totals	200	28/ -	-	23/31	.742	-/ -	-	-	15	-	-	79	.395

Kentucky (71)   Coach: Adolph Rupp

	Min.	Total FG / FGA	Pct.	FT / FTA	Pct.	Reb. O / T	A	TO	PF	S	Blk	TP	PPM
BREWER, J.	-	7/ -	-	2/ 3	.667	-/ -	-	-	2	-	-	16	-
BIRD, J.	-	2/ -	-	0/ 1	.000	-/ -	-	-	2	-	-	4	-
MILLS, R.	-	2/ -	-	0/ 1	.000	-/ -	-	-	5	-	-	4	-
BURROW, B.	-	6/ -	-	7/13	.538	-/ -	-	-	1	-	-	19	-
ROSE, G.	-	8/ -	-	4/ 6	.667	-/ -	-	-	3	-	-	20	-
CALVERT, G.	-	4/ -	-	0/ 1	.000	-/ -	-	-	5	-	-	8	-
ADKINS, E.	-	0/ -	-	0/ 0	.000	-/ -	-	-	1	-	-	0	-
CORUM	-	0/ -	-	0/ 0	.000	-/ -	-	-	0	-	-	0	-
Totals	200	29/ -	-	13/25	.520	-/ -	-	-	19	-	-	71	.355

Disqualified: Marquette—Hopfensperger; Kentucky—Mills, Calvert.

	1st Half	2nd Half	Final
Marquette	36	43	79
Kentucky	38	33	71

Penn State (53)   Coach: John Egli

	Min.	Total FG / FGA	Pct.	FT / FTA	Pct.	Reb. O / T	A	TO	PF	S	Blk	TP	PPM
BLOCKER, J.	-	2/ 9	.222	1/ 2	.500	-/ 7	-	-	0	-	-	5	-
EDWARDS, D.	-	0/ 0	.000	0/ 0	.000	-/ 1	-	-	0	-	-	0	-
HOFFMAN, J.	-	6/18	.333	2/ 2	1.000	-/ 3	-	-	1	-	-	14	-
ARNELLE, J.	-	3/15	.200	5/ 6	.833	-/10	-	-	2	-	-	11	-
WEIDENHAMMER, R.	-	2/ 7	.286	0/ 0	.000	-/ 1	-	-	2	-	-	4	-
FIELDS, E.	-	1/ 6	.167	1/ 1	1.000	-/ 5	-	-	1	-	-	3	-
ROHLAND, B.	-	0/ 0	.000	2/ 2	1.000	-/ 0	-	-	0	-	-	2	-
RAMSAY	-	1/ 3	.333	1/ 2	.500	-/ 2	-	-	4	-	-	3	-
MARISA, R.	-	3/ 7	.429	2/ 4	.500	-/ 6	-	-	2	-	-	8	-
HARTNETT	-	0/ 3	.000	0/ 0	.000	-/ 2	-	-	2	-	-	0	-
WATTS, C.	-	1/ 3	.333	0/ 0	.000	-/ 1	-	-	2	-	-	2	-
HALL	-	0/ 1	.000	1/ 2	.500	-/ 0	-	-	0	-	-	1	-
Totals	200	19/72	.264	15/21	.714	-/38	-	-	16	-	-	53	.265

Iowa (82)   Coach: Bucky O'Connor

	Min.	Total FG / FGA	Pct.	FT / FTA	Pct.	Reb. O / T	A	TO	PF	S	Blk	TP	PPM
DAVIS, M.	-	6/13	.462	7/ 9	.778	-/ 6	-	-	2	-	-	19	-
CAIN, C.	-	8/13	.615	5/ 6	.833	-/ 9	-	-	3	-	-	21	-
LOGAN, W.	-	4/14	.286	0/ 0	.000	-/ 5	-	-	1	-	-	8	-
SCHEUERMAN, M.	-	1/ 3	.333	0/ 0	.000	-/ 3	-	-	1	-	-	2	-
SEABERG, W.	-	6/ 8	.750	1/ 2	.500	-/ 2	-	-	1	-	-	13	-
JOHNSON, R.	-	0/ 1	.000	0/ 0	.000	-/ 1	-	-	0	-	-	0	-
SCHOOF, W.	-	2/ 4	.500	2/ 2	1.000	-/ 5	-	-	0	-	-	6	-
GEORGE, R.	-	3/ 5	.600	1/ 3	.333	-/ 4	-	-	1	-	-	7	-
RIDLEY, G.	-	1/ 4	.250	0/ 2	.000	-/ 4	-	-	1	-	-	2	-
MARTEL, A.	-	0/ 3	.000	1/ 2	.500	-/ 1	-	-	0	-	-	1	-
HAWTHORNE, L.	-	1/ 3	.333	1/ 2	.500	-/ 1	-	-	0	-	-	3	-
DUNCAN, D.	-	0/ 0	.000	0/ 1	.000	-/ 1	-	-	1	-	-	0	-
Totals	200	32/71	.451	18/29	.621	-/42	-	-	11	-	-	82	.410

Disqualified: None.

	1st Half	2nd Half	Final
Penn State	25	28	53
Iowa	39	43	82

La Salle (73) Coach: Ken Loeffler

	Min.	Total FG / FGA	Pct.	FT / FTA	Pct.	Reb. O / T	A	TO	PF	S	Blk	TP	PPM
SINGLEY, C.	-	4/ -	-	1/ 2	.500	-/ -	-	-	1	-	-	9	-
BLATCHER, F.	-	2/ -	-	3/ 4	.750	-/ -	-	-	0	-	-	7	-
LEWIS, A.	-	4/ -	-	1/ 5	.200	-/ -	-	-	2	-	-	9	-
AMES, B.	-	1/ -	-	0/ 0	.000	-/ -	-	-	0	-	-	2	-
GOLA, T.	-	9/ -	-	6/ 8	.750	-/ -	-	-	3	-	-	24	-
MAPLES, B.	-	1/ -	-	4/ 4	1.000	-/ -	-	-	0	-	-	6	-
GREENBERG, C.	-	4/ -	-	2/ 2	1.000	-/ -	-	-	1	-	-	10	-
KRAEMER, B.	-	0/ -	-	0/ 0	.000	-/ -	-	-	0	-	-	0	-
GOLA, J.	-	0/ -	-	0/ 0	.000	-/ -	-	-	1	-	-	0	-
O'MALLEY, F.	-	2/ -	-	2/ 3	.667	-/ -	-	-	3	-	-	6	-
FREDERICKS, W.	-	0/ -	-	0/ 0	.000	-/ -	-	-	1	-	-	0	-
Totals	200	27/82	.329	19/28	.679	-/ -	-	-	12	-	-	73	.365

Princeton (46) Coach: Franklin Cappon

	Min.	Total FG / FGA	Pct.	FT / FTA	Pct.	Reb. O / T	A	TO	PF	S	Blk	TP	PPM
HAABERSTAD, H.	-	6/ -	-	3/ 6	.500	-/ -	-	-	2	-	-	15	-
DEVOE, J.	-	3/ -	-	5/ 7	.714	-/ -	-	-	2	-	-	11	-
MACKENZIE, K.	-	1/ -	-	0/ 0	.000	-/ -	-	-	1	-	-	2	-
BATT, R.	-	1/ -	-	0/ 0	.000	-/ -	-	-	5	-	-	2	-
DAILEY, T.	-	0/ -	-	0/ 0	.000	-/ -	-	-	0	-	-	0	-
EASTON, J.	-	2/ -	-	2/ 4	.500	-/ -	-	-	4	-	-	6	-
BLANKLEY, W.	-	0/ -	-	0/ 0	.000	-/ -	-	-	0	-	-	0	-
DAVIDSON, D.	-	3/ -	-	2/ 3	.667	-/ -	-	-	3	-	-	8	-
Totals	200	16/76	.211	12/20	.600	-/ -	-	-	17	-	-	46	.230

Disqualified: Princeton—Batt. Tom Gola scored 1 field goal for Princeton.

	1st Half	2nd Half	Final
La Salle	33	40	73
Princeton	22	24	46

Canisius (73) Coach: Joseph Curran

	Min.	Total FG / FGA	Pct.	FT / FTA	Pct.	Reb. O / T	A	TO	PF	S	Blk	TP	PPM
KELLY, R.	-	2/ -	-	0/ 0	.000	-/ -	-	-	4	-	-	4	-
CORCORAN, F.	-	0/ -	-	0/ 0	.000	-/ -	-	-	0	-	-	0	-
NOWAK, H.	-	8/ -	-	11/15	.733	-/ -	-	-	3	-	-	27	-
LEONE, J.	-	1/ -	-	2/ 8	.250	-/ -	-	-	4	-	-	4	-
ZATORSKI, J.	-	0/ -	-	0/ 0	.000	-/ -	-	-	1	-	-	0	-
MCCARTHY, JOHN	-	7/ -	-	14/15	.933	-/ -	-	-	4	-	-	28	-
ADAMS, R.	-	4/ -	-	2/ 3	.667	-/ -	-	-	3	-	-	10	-
MCCARTHY, JAMES	-	0/ -	-	0/ 0	.000	-/ -	-	-	1	-	-	0	-
Totals	200	22/64	-	29/41	.707	-/ -	-	-	20	-	-	73	.365

Villanova (71) Coach: Alex Severance

	Min.	Total FG / FGA	Pct.	FT / FTA	Pct.	Reb. O / T	A	TO	PF	S	Blk	TP	PPM
CIRINO	-	1/ -	-	2/ 2	1.000	-/ -	-	-	5	-	-	4	-
DEVINE, J.	-	6/ -	-	15/17	.882	-/ -	-	-	5	-	-	27	-
MILLIGAN	-	0/ -	-	0/ 0	.000	-/ -	-	-	1	-	-	0	-
SCHAEFER, B.	-	8/ -	-	6/ 7	.857	-/ -	-	-	2	-	-	22	-
SMITH	-	1/ -	-	2/ 3	.667	-/ -	-	-	4	-	-	4	-
GRIFFITH	-	2/ -	-	4/ 4	1.000	-/ -	-	-	3	-	-	8	-
WEISSMAN, J.	-	3/ -	-	0/ 1	.000	-/ -	-	-	3	-	-	6	-
Totals	200	21/72	-	29/34	.853	-/ -	-	-	23	-	-	71	.355

Disqualified: Villanova—Cirino, Devine.

	1st Half	2nd Half	Final
Canisius	39	34	73
Villanova	39	32	71

REGIONAL SEMIFINAL WEST

Bradley (81) Coach: Bob Vanatta

	Min.	Total FG / FGA	Pct.	FT / FTA	Pct.	Reb. O / T	A	TO	PF	S	Blk	TP	PPM
HANSEN, J.	-	3/11	.273	0/ 0	.000	-/12	-	-	4	-	-	6	-
GOWER, J.	-	3/ 9	.333	2/ 3	.667	-/ 8	-	-	5	-	-	8	-
PETERSEN, D.	-	2/ 7	.286	4/ 5	.800	-/ 5	-	-	5	-	-	8	-
ALBECK, S.	-	5/12	.417	6/ 7	.857	-/ 4	-	-	2	-	-	16	-
BABETCH, H.	-	6/16	.375	6/11	.545	-/11	-	-	3	-	-	18	-
DICKMAN	-	0/ 1	.000	0/ 2	.000	-/ 2	-	-	0	-	-	0	-
KENT, J.	-	1/ 4	.250	1/ 2	.500	-/ 3	-	-	1	-	-	3	-
UTT, L.	-	8/14	.571	6/ 7	.857	-/ 7	-	-	3	-	-	22	-
Totals	200	28/74	.378	25/37	.676	-/52	-	-	23	-	-	81	.405

SMU (79) Coach: E.O. "Doc" Hayes

	Min.	Total FG / FGA	Pct.	FT / FTA	Pct.	Reb. O / T	A	TO	PF	S	Blk	TP	PPM
KROG, J.	-	5/17	.294	2/ 5	.400	-/11	-	-	4	-	-	12	-
MCGREGOR, B.	-	1/ 1	1.000	0/ 0	.000	-/ 0	-	-	3	-	-	2	-
SCHARFFENBERGER	-	1/ 3	.333	2/ 6	.333	-/ 0	-	-	1	-	-	4	-
SHOWALTER, L.	-	2/ 9	.222	0/ 0	.000	-/10	-	-	0	-	-	4	-
KREBS, J.	-	5/16	.313	9/11	.818	-/15	-	-	4	-	-	19	-
MILLER, T.	-	0/ 4	.000	2/ 3	.667	-/ 0	-	-	1	-	-	2	-
BARNES	-	8/20	.400	4/ 4	1.000	-/ 4	-	-	2	-	-	20	-
MILLS, B.	-	2/ 5	.400	3/ 4	.750	-/ 4	-	-	4	-	-	7	-
MORRIS, R.	-	3/ 7	.429	3/ 5	.600	-/ 1	-	-	3	-	-	9	-
Totals	200	27/82	.329	25/38	.658	-/45	-	-	22	-	-	79	.395

Team Rebounds: Bradley 5; SMU 3. Disqualified: Bradley—Gower, Petersen.

	1st Half	2nd Half	Final
Bradley	46	35	81
SMU	41	38	79

Colorado (69) Coach: Bebe Lee

	Min.	Total FG / FGA	Pct.	FT / FTA	Pct.	Reb. O / T	A	TO	PF	S	Blk	TP	PPM
COFFMAN, M.	-	3/ 5	.600	0/ 0	.000	-/ 5	-	-	2	-	-	6	-
JEANGERARD, B.	-	3/15	.200	1/ 2	.500	-/ 5	-	-	4	-	-	7	-
RANGLOS, J.	-	3/ 5	.600	1/ 2	.500	-/ 6	-	-	3	-	-	7	-
HALDORSON, B.	-	9/20	.450	10/12	.833	-/14	-	-	3	-	-	28	-
HANNAH, G.	-	0/ 0	.000	0/ 0	.000	-/ 0	-	-	0	-	-	0	-
HARROLD, T.	-	2/ 5	.400	6/ 9	.667	-/ 5	-	-	2	-	-	10	-
MANSFIELD, M.	-	0/ 1	.000	0/ 0	.000	-/ 0	-	-	1	-	-	0	-
MOCK, C.	-	4/ 7	.571	3/ 6	.500	-/ 5	-	-	1	-	-	11	-
Totals	200	24/58	.414	21/31	.677	-/40	-	-	16	-	-	69	.345

Tulsa (59) Coach: Clarence Iba

	Min.	Total FG / FGA	Pct.	FT / FTA	Pct.	Reb. O / T	A	TO	PF	S	Blk	TP	PPM
DUNCAN	-	1/ 1	1.000	1/ 2	.500	-/ 3	-	-	5	-	-	3	-
JOHNSTON	-	0/ 0	.000	0/ 0	.000	-/ 1	-	-	0	-	-	0	-
PATTERSON, B.	-	7/19	.368	7/ 8	.875	-/ 9	-	-	2	-	-	21	-
STOB	-	0/ 0	.000	0/ 0	.000	-/ 0	-	-	0	-	-	0	-
COURTER	-	2/ 9	.222	6/ 7	.857	-/10	-	-	2	-	-	10	-
KROUSE	-	0/ 0	.000	0/ 0	.000	-/ 0	-	-	0	-	-	0	-
YATES	-	0/ 0	.000	0/ 0	.000	-/ 0	-	-	0	-	-	0	-
BORN	-	3/10	.300	4/ 4	1.000	-/ 2	-	-	2	-	-	10	-
EVANS	-	0/ 1	.000	0/ 0	.000	-/ 0	-	-	1	-	-	0	-
HACKER	-	3/ 9	.333	7/ 8	.875	-/ 6	-	-	3	-	-	13	-
JOBE	-	0/ 0	.000	0/ 0	.000	-/ 0	-	-	0	-	-	0	-
STEWART	-	1/ 2	.500	0/ 0	.000	-/ 2	-	-	3	-	-	2	-
Totals	200	17/51	.333	25/29	.862	-/33	-	-	18	-	-	59	.295

Team Rebounds: Colorado 5; Tulsa 2. Disqualified: Tulsa—Duncan.

	1st Half	2nd Half	Final
Colorado	34	35	69
Tulsa	33	26	59

Seattle (71)   Coach: Al Brightman

	Min.	Total FG / FGA	Pct.	FT / FTA	Pct.	Reb. O / T	A	TO	PF	S	Blk	TP	PPM
GLOWASKI	-	4/ -	-	3/ 5	.600	-/ -	-	-	4	-	-	11	-
GODES	-	6/ -	-	4/ 6	.667	-/ -	-	-	3	-	-	16	-
KELLY	-	3/ -	-	0/ 1	.000	-/ -	-	-	2	-	-	6	-
VAUGHN	-	1/ -	-	0/ 0	.000	-/ -	-	-	1	-	-	2	-
STRICKLIN, D.	-	3/ -	-	8/11	.727	-/ -	-	-	1	-	-	14	-
FUHRER	-	2/ -	-	3/ 7	.429	-/ -	-	-	3	-	-	7	-
MALONE	-	3/ -	-	1/ 2	.500	-/ -	-	-	3	-	-	7	-
BAUER, C.	-	3/ -	-	2/ 2	1.000	-/ -	-	-	2	-	-	8	-
COX	-	0/ -	-	0/ 0	.000	-/ -	-	-	0	-	-	0	-
Totals	200	25/ -	-	21/34	.618	-/ -	-	-	19	-	-	71	.355

Oregon State (83)   Coach: Amory "Slats" Gill

	Min.	Total FG / FGA	Pct.	FT / FTA	Pct.	Reb. O / T	A	TO	PF	S	Blk	TP	PPM
VLASTELICA, T.	-	7/ -	-	0/ 0	.000	-/ -	-	-	0	-	-	14	-
WHITEMAN	-	3/ -	-	3/ 3	1.000	-/ -	-	-	3	-	-	9	-
DEAN	-	2/ -	-	3/ 4	.750	-/ -	-	-	2	-	-	7	-
PAULUS	-	0/ -	-	0/ 1	.000	-/ -	-	-	3	-	-	0	-
ALLORD	-	1/ -	-	0/ 1	.000	-/ -	-	-	0	-	-	2	-
HALBROOK, S.	-	9/ -	-	3/ 6	.500	-/ -	-	-	3	-	-	21	-
SHADOIN	-	5/ -	-	0/ 6	.000	-/ -	-	-	4	-	-	10	-
HALLIGAN	-	1/ -	-	2/ 2	1.000	-/ -	-	-	2	-	-	4	-
TOOLE	-	4/ -	-	2/ 3	.667	-/ -	-	-	3	-	-	10	-
JARBOE	-	0/ -	-	4/ 4	1.000	-/ -	-	-	3	-	-	4	-
FUNDINGSLAND	-	1/ -	-	0/ 0	.000	-/ -	-	-	0	-	-	2	-
Totals	200	33/ -	-	17/30	.567	-/ -	-	-	23	-	-	83	.415

Disqualified: None.

	1st Half	2nd Half	Final
Seattle	36	35	71
Oregon State	50	33	83

San Francisco (78)   Coach: Phil Woolpert

	Min.	Total FG / FGA	Pct.	FT / FTA	Pct.	Reb. O / T	A	TO	PF	S	Blk	TP	PPM
MULLEN, J.	-	7/ -	-	10/14	.714	-/ -	-	-	3	-	-	24	-
BUCHANAN, S.	-	1/ -	-	0/ 0	.000	-/ -	-	-	1	-	-	2	-
WIEBUSCH, B.	-	2/ -	-	0/ 1	.000	-/ -	-	-	2	-	-	4	-
LAWLESS, D.	-	0/ -	-	4/ 4	1.000	-/ -	-	-	1	-	-	4	-
KIRBY, G.	-	0/ -	-	0/ 0	.000	-/ -	-	-	0	-	-	0	-
RUSSELL, B.	-	5/ -	-	3/ 5	.600	-/ -	-	-	3	-	-	13	-
KING, J.	-	0/ -	-	0/ 0	.000	-/ -	-	-	0	-	-	0	-
JONES, K.	-	4/ -	-	5/13	.385	-/ -	-	-	2	-	-	13	-
PERRY, H.	-	6/ -	-	2/ 3	.667	-/ -	-	-	1	-	-	14	-
BAXTER, W.	-	1/ -	-	2/ 2	1.000	-/ -	-	-	1	-	-	4	-
ZANNINI, R.	-	0/ -	-	0/ 0	.000	-/ -	-	-	1	-	-	0	-
BUSH, B.	-	0/ -	-	0/ 0	.000	-/ -	-	-	0	-	-	0	-
Totals	200	26/50	-	26/42	.619	-/ -	-	-	15	-	-	78	.390

Utah (59)   Coach: Jack Gardner

	Min.	Total FG / FGA	Pct.	FT / FTA	Pct.	Reb. O / T	A	TO	PF	S	Blk	TP	PPM
BERGEN	-	5/ -	-	2/ 2	1.000	-/ -	-	-	5	-	-	12	-
BUCKWALTER	-	1/ -	-	6/ 6	1.000	-/ -	-	-	5	-	-	8	-
CONDIE	-	1/ -	-	0/ 0	.000	-/ -	-	-	2	-	-	2	-
MCCLEARY	-	1/ -	-	4/ 5	.800	-/ -	-	-	1	-	-	6	-
BUNTE	-	4/ -	-	4/ 5	.800	-/ -	-	-	1	-	-	12	-
LEWIS	-	1/ -	-	1/ 2	.500	-/ -	-	-	1	-	-	3	-
TONNESEN	-	0/ -	-	2/ 2	1.000	-/ -	-	-	2	-	-	2	-
JENSON	-	3/ -	-	0/ 2	.000	-/ -	-	-	2	-	-	6	-
CROWE	-	1/ -	-	0/ 0	.000	-/ -	-	-	4	-	-	2	-
PEPPLE	-	0/ -	-	0/ 0	.000	-/ -	-	-	1	-	-	0	-
BEINER	-	3/ -	-	0/ 0	.000	-/ -	-	-	2	-	-	6	-
Totals	200	20/70	-	19/24	.792	-/ -	-	-	26	-	-	59	.295

Disqualified: Utah—Buckwalter, Bergen.

	1st Half	2nd Half	Final
San Francisco	41	37	78
Utah	20	39	59

REGIONAL FINAL EAST

Marquette (81)   Coach: Jack Nagle

	Min.	Total FG / FGA	Pct.	FT / FTA	Pct.	Reb. O / T	A	TO	PF	S	Blk	TP	PPM
HOPFENSPERGER	-	5/11	.455	6/ 6	1.000	-/ 0	-	-	4	-	-	16	-
SCHULZ	-	5/11	.455	12/18	.667	-/ 9	-	-	4	-	-	22	-
RAND, T.	-	7/11	.636	3/ 3	1.000	-/12	-	-	5	-	-	17	-
BUGALSKI	-	0/ 5	.000	7/12	.583	-/ 6	-	-	4	-	-	7	-
WALCZAK	-	1/ 7	.143	1/ 2	.500	-/ 3	-	-	3	-	-	3	-
O'KEEFE	-	0/ 1	.000	0/ 0	.000	-/ 2	-	-	0	-	-	0	-
WITTBERGER	-	7/14	.500	2/ 3	.667	-/ 6	-	-	5	-	-	16	-
VANVOOREN	-	0/ 0	.000	0/ 0	.000	-/ 0	-	-	0	-	-	0	-
SEVCIK	-	0/ 0	.000	0/ 0	.000	-/ 1	-	-	1	-	-	0	-
Totals	200	25/60	.417	31/44	.705	-/39	-	-	26	-	-	81	.405

Iowa (86)   Coach: Bucky O'Connor

	Min.	Total FG / FGA	Pct.	FT / FTA	Pct.	Reb. O / T	A	TO	PF	S	Blk	TP	PPM
DAVIS, M.	-	2/11	.182	3/ 5	.600	-/ 4	-	-	2	-	-	7	-
CAIN, C.	-	5/14	.357	0/ 1	.000	-/ 8	-	-	4	-	-	10	-
LOGAN, W.	-	11/20	.550	9/14	.643	-/15	-	-	5	-	-	31	-
SCHEUERMAN, M.	-	3/ 8	.375	5/ 6	.833	-/ 7	-	-	2	-	-	11	-
SEABERG, W.	-	5/ 8	.625	2/ 4	.500	-/ 5	-	-	5	-	-	12	-
JOHNSON, R.	-	1/ 1	1.000	1/ 2	.500	-/ 0	-	-	0	-	-	3	-
SCHOOF, W.	-	3/ 8	.375	2/ 5	.400	-/ 7	-	-	5	-	-	8	-
GEORGE, R.	-	1/ 1	1.000	1/ 2	.500	-/ 0	-	-	1	-	-	3	-
HAWTHORNE, L.	-	0/ 0	.000	1/ 2	.500	-/ 0	-	-	0	-	-	1	-
Totals	200	31/71	.437	24/41	.585	-/46	-	-	24	-	-	86	.430

Disqualified: Iowa—Logan, Seaberg, Schoof; Marquette—Rand, Wittberger.

	1st Half	2nd Half	Final
Marquette	33	48	81
Iowa	46	40	86

La Salle (99)   Coach: Ken Loeffler

	Min.	Total FG / FGA	Pct.	FT / FTA	Pct.	Reb. O / T	A	TO	PF	S	Blk	TP	PPM
LEWIS, A.	-	7/ -	-	4/ 5	.800	-/ -	-	-	2	-	-	18	-
KRAEMER, B.	-	0/ -	-	0/ 0	.000	-/ -	-	-	0	-	-	0	-
SINGLEY, C.	-	5/ -	-	6/ 9	.667	-/ -	-	-	2	-	-	16	-
BLATCHER, F.	-	1/ -	-	0/ 0	.000	-/ -	-	-	4	-	-	2	-
AMES, B.	-	1/ -	-	2/ 2	1.000	-/ -	-	-	0	-	-	4	-
GOLA, T.	-	9/ -	-	12/12	1.000	-/25	-	-	4	-	-	30	-
FREDERICKS, W.	-	0/ -	-	0/ 0	.000	-/ -	-	-	1	-	-	0	-
GREENBERG, C.	-	5/ -	-	4/ 4	1.000	-/ -	-	-	1	-	-	14	-
GOLA, J.	-	1/ -	-	0/ 0	.000	-/ -	-	-	2	-	-	2	-
O'MALLEY, F.	-	2/ -	-	0/ 1	.000	-/ -	-	-	5	-	-	4	-
MAPLES, B.	-	1/ -	-	7/ 8	.875	-/ -	-	-	0	-	-	9	-
Totals	200	32/79	-	35/41	.854	-/ -	-	-	21	-	-	99	.495

Canisius (64)   Coach: Joseph Curran

	Min.	Total FG / FGA	Pct.	FT / FTA	Pct.	Reb. O / T	A	TO	PF	S	Blk	TP	PPM
KELLY, R.	-	0/ -	-	2/ 2	1.000	-/ -	-	-	5	-	-	2	-
MARKEY, D.	-	2/ -	-	11/13	.846	-/ -	-	-	2	-	-	15	-
NOWAK, H.	-	3/ -	-	4/ 5	.800	-/ -	-	-	3	-	-	10	-
COOGAN	-	2/ -	-	0/ 3	.000	-/ -	-	-	2	-	-	4	-
ZATORSKI, J.	-	0/ -	-	0/ 0	.000	-/ -	-	-	0	-	-	0	-
LEONE, J.	-	0/ -	-	0/ 0	.000	-/ -	-	-	0	-	-	0	-
CORCORAN, F.	-	0/ -	-	1/ 1	1.000	-/ -	-	-	3	-	-	1	-
MCCARTHY, JAMES	-	1/ -	-	2/ 2	1.000	-/ -	-	-	1	-	-	4	-
MCCARTHY, JOHN	-	5/ -	-	7/ 9	.778	-/ -	-	-	3	-	-	17	-
ADAMS, R.	-	4/ -	-	0/ 1	.000	-/ -	-	-	0	-	-	8	-
FLYNN, J.	-	1/ -	-	1/ 2	.500	-/ -	-	-	1	-	-	3	-
Totals	200	18/69	-	28/38	.737	-/ -	-	-	22	-	-	64	.320

Disqualified: La Salle—O'Malley; Canisius—Kelly.

	1st Half	2nd Half	Final
La Salle	43	56	99
Canisius	30	34	64

REGIONAL FINAL WEST

Bradley (81) Coach: Bob Vanatta

	Min.	Total FG / FGA	Pct.	FT / FTA	Pct.	Reb. O / T	A	TO	PF	S	Blk	TP	PPM
HANSEN, J.	-	2/ 6	.333	0/ 0	.000	-/ 3	-	-	5	-	-	4	-
GOWER, J.	-	3/ 6	.500	0/ 2	.000	-/ 4	-	-	1	-	-	6	-
PETERSEN, D.	-	5/12	.417	2/ 2	1.000	-/10	-	-	5	-	-	12	-
ALBECK, S.	-	6/15	.400	4/ 6	.667	-/ 3	-	-	5	-	-	16	-
BABETCH, H.	-	7/ 9	.778	8/ 9	.889	-/ ↵	-	-	5	-	-	22	-
DICKMAN	-	1/ 4	.250	0/ 0	.000	-/ 1	-	-	2	-	-	2	-
KENT, J.	-	2/ 6	.333	0/ 0	.000	-/ 3	-	-	1	-	-	4	-
UTT, L.	-	6/18	.333	3/ 4	.750	-/11	-	-	2	-	-	15	-
BURNHAM	-	0/ 0	.000	0/ 0	.000	-/ 1	-	-	1	-	-	0	-
Totals	200	32/76	.421	17/23	.739	-/39	-	-	27	-	-	81	.405

Colorado (93) Coach: Bebe Lee

	Min.	Total FG / FGA	Pct.	FT / FTA	Pct.	Reb. O / T	A	TO	PF	S	Blk	TP	PPM
COFFMAN, M.	-	0/ 0	.000	0/ 0	.000	-/ 0	-	-	1	-	-	0	-
JEANGERARD, B.	-	12/24	.500	5/ 6	.833	-/ 4	-	-	3	-	-	29	-
RANGLOS, J.	-	3/ 8	.375	4/ 5	.800	-/19	-	-	4	-	-	10	-
HALDORSON, B.	-	7/14	.500	9/12	.750	-/10	-	-	3	-	-	23	-
HANNAH, G.	-	0/ 0	.000	1/ 2	.500	-/ 1	-	-	0	-	-	1	-
HARROLD, T.	-	4/10	.400	10/15	.667	-/ 3	-	-	1	-	-	18	-
MANSFIELD, M.	-	1/ 1	1.000	2/ 3	.667	-/ 2	-	-	1	-	-	4	-
MOCK, C.	-	2/ 7	.286	2/ 4	.500	-/ 1	-	-	0	-	-	6	-
YARDLEY, B.	-	1/ 1	1.000	0/ 0	.000	-/ 1	-	-	0	-	-	2	-
GRANT, J.	-	0/ 0	.000	0/ 0	.000	-/ 0	-	-	0	-	-	0	-
PETERSON, B.	-	0/ 0	.000	0/ 0	.000	-/ 0	-	-	0	-	-	0	-
MOWBRAY, D.	-	0/ 0	.000	0/ 0	.000	-/ 0	-	-	0	-	-	0	-
Totals	200	30/65	.462	33/47	.702	-/41	-	-	13	-	-	93	.465

Team Rebounds: Colorado 6; Bradley 7. Disqualified: Bradley—Hansen, Petersen, Albeck, Babetch.

	1st Half	2nd Half	Final
Bradley	41	40	81
Colorado	49	44	93

Oregon State (56) Coach: Amory "Slats" Gill

	Min.	Total FG / FGA	Pct.	FT / FTA	Pct.	Reb. O / T	A	TO	PF	S	Blk	TP	PPM
HALLIGAN	-	2/ -	-	1/ 2	.500	-/ -	-	-	3	-	-	5	-
VLASTELICA, T.	-	6/ -	-	0/ 1	.000	-/ -	-	-	3	-	-	12	-
WHITEMAN	-	2/ -	-	7/ 8	.875	-/ -	-	-	2	-	-	11	-
SHADOIN	-	0/ -	-	0/ 0	.000	-/ -	-	-	0	-	-	0	-
HALBROOK, S.	-	7/ -	-	4/ 6	.667	-/ -	-	-	4	-	-	18	-
JARBOE	-	0/ -	-	0/ 0	.000	-/ -	-	-	2	-	-	0	-
TOOLE	-	2/ -	-	2/ 6	.333	-/ -	-	-	2	-	-	6	-
ROBINS	-	2/ -	-	0/ 0	.000	-/ -	-	-	3	-	-	4	-
Totals	200	21/ -	-	14/23	.609	-/ -	-	-	19	-	-	56	.280

San Francisco (57) Coach: Phil Woolpert

	Min.	Total FG / FGA	Pct.	FT / FTA	Pct.	Reb. O / T	A	TO	PF	S	Blk	TP	PPM
BUCHANAN, S.	-	2/ -	-	0/ 0	.000	-/ -	-	-	3	-	-	4	-
MULLEN, J.	-	0/ -	-	2/ 6	.333	-/ -	-	-	3	-	-	2	-
WIEBUSCH, B.	-	1/ -	-	4/ 5	.800	-/ -	-	-	0	-	-	6	-
RUSSELL, B.	-	11/ -	-	7/11	.636	-/ -	-	-	2	-	-	29	-
JONES, K.	-	2/ -	-	7/10	.700	-/ -	-	-	3	-	-	11	-
PERRY, H.	-	2/ -	-	0/ 0	.000	-/ -	-	-	1	-	-	4	-
BAXTER, W.	-	0/ -	-	1/ 2	.500	-/ -	-	-	0	-	-	1	-
ZANNINI, R.	-	0/ -	-	0/ 0	.000	-/ -	-	-	0	-	-	0	-
Totals	200	18/ -	-	21/34	.618	-/ -	-	-	12	-	-	57	.285

Disqualified: None.

	1st Half	2nd Half	Final
Oregon State	27	29	56
San Francisco	30	27	57

FINAL FOUR

Iowa (73) Coach: Bucky O'Connor

	Min.	Total FG / FGA	Pct.	FT / FTA	Pct.	Reb. O / T	A	TO	PF	S	Blk	TP	PPM
DAVIS, M.	-	1/ -	-	0/ 0	.000	-/ -	-	-	2	-	-	2	-
SCHOOF, W.	-	3/ -	-	0/ 1	.000	-/ -	-	-	4	-	-	6	-
CAIN, C.	-	8/ -	-	1/ 3	.333	-/ -	-	-	3	-	-	17	-
LOGAN, W.	-	7/ -	-	6/ 7	.857	-/ -	-	-	3	-	-	20	-
SEABERG, W.	-	5/ -	-	5/ 8	.625	-/ -	-	-	2	-	-	15	-
SCHEUERMAN, M.	-	1/ -	-	11/13	.846	-/ -	-	-	3	-	-	13	-
Totals	200	25/ -	-	23/32	.719	-/ -	-	-	17	-	-	73	.365

La Salle (76) Coach: Ken Loeffler

	Min.	Total FG / FGA	Pct.	FT / FTA	Pct.	Reb. O / T	A	TO	PF	S	Blk	TP	PPM
O'MALLEY, F.	-	1/ -	-	4/ 6	.667	-/ -	-	-	1	-	-	6	-
MAPLES, B.	-	1/ -	-	2/ 2	1.000	-/ -	-	-	0	-	-	4	-
SINGLEY, C.	-	5/ -	-	6/ 6	1.000	-/ -	-	-	2	-	-	16	-
BLATCHER, F.	-	2/ -	-	1/ 2	.500	-/ -	-	-	5	-	-	5	-
GOLA, T.	-	8/ -	-	7/ 7	1.000	-/ -	-	-	4	-	-	23	-
LEWIS, A.	-	5/ -	-	4/ 4	1.000	-/ -	-	-	3	-	-	14	-
GREENBERG, C.	-	4/ -	-	0/ 2	.000	-/ -	-	-	4	-	-	8	-
Totals	200	26/ -	-	24/29	.828	-/ -	-	-	19	-	-	76	.380

Disqualified: La Salle—Blatcher.

	1st Half	2nd Half	Final
Iowa	36	37	73
La Salle	45	31	76

Colorado (50)   Coach: Bebe Lee

	Min.	Total FG / FGA	Pct.	FT / FTA	Pct.	Reb. O / T	A	TO	PF	S	Blk	TP	PPM
COFFMAN, M.	-	1/ 1	1.000	2/ 2	1.000	-/ 1	-	-	2	-	-	4	-
JEANGERARD, B.	-	1/12	.083	2/ 3	.667	-/ 4	-	-	0	-	-	4	-
RANGLOS, J.	-	1/ 3	.333	2/ 2	1.000	-/ 8	-	-	1	-	-	4	-
HALDORSON, B.	-	3/11	.273	3/ 4	.750	-/ 6	-	-	5	-	-	9	-
HANNAH, G.	-	2/ 6	.333	5/ 7	.714	-/ 3	-	-	2	-	-	9	-
MANSFIELD, M.	-	0/ 3	.000	4/ 6	.667	-/ 1	-	-	1	-	-	4	-
MOCK, C.	-	2/ 6	.333	0/ 0	.000	-/ 6	-	-	5	-	-	4	-
PETERSON, B.	-	2/ 3	.667	2/ 2	1.000	-/ 3	-	-	1	-	-	6	-
YARDLEY, B.	-	1/ 2	.500	2/ 4	.500	-/ 1	-	-	0	-	-	4	-
GRANT, J.	-	1/ 2	.500	0/ 0	.000	-/ 0	-	-	0	-	-	2	-
Totals	200	14/49	.286	22/30	.733	-/33	-	-	17	-	-	50	.250

San Francisco (62)   Coach: Phil Woolpert

	Min.	Total FG / FGA	Pct.	FT / FTA	Pct.	Reb. O / T	A	TO	PF	S	Blk	TP	PPM
WIEBUSCH, B.	-	1/ 2	.500	0/ 0	.000	-/ 3	-	-	2	-	-	2	-
BUCHANAN, S.	-	0/ 4	.000	6/ 6	1.000	-/ 1	-	-	2	-	-	6	-
RUSSELL, B.	-	10/14	.714	4/10	.400	-/ 9	-	-	4	-	-	24	-
JONES, K.	-	3/ 9	.333	2/ 3	.667	-/ 5	-	-	3	-	-	8	-
PERRY, H.	-	5/ 8	.625	0/ 0	.000	-/ 4	-	-	1	-	-	10	-
BAXTER, W.	-	2/ 2	1.000	3/ 5	.600	-/ 1	-	-	0	-	-	7	-
MULLEN, J.	-	0/ 2	.000	0/ 0	.000	-/ 4	-	-	0	-	-	0	-
BUSH, B.	-	0/ 0	.000	1/ 2	.500	-/ 0	-	-	0	-	-	1	-
ZANNINI, R.	-	0/ 1	.000	0/ 0	.000	-/ 1	-	-	1	-	-	0	-
KING, J.	-	1/ 1	1.000	2/ 2	1.000	-/ 0	-	-	0	-	-	4	-
KIRBY, G.	-	0/ 0	.000	0/ 0	.000	-/ 0	-	-	1	-	-	0	-
Totals	200	22/43	.512	18/28	.643	-/28	-	-	14	-	-	62	.310

Disqualified: Colorado—Haldorson, Mock.

	1st Half	2nd Half	Final
Colorado	19	31	50
San Francisco	25	37	62

NATIONAL CHAMPIONSHIP

La Salle (63)   Coach: Ken Loeffler

	Min.	Total FG / FGA	Pct.	FT / FTA	Pct.	Reb. O / T	A	TO	PF	S	Blk	TP	PPM
O'MALLEY, F.	-	4/ -	-	2/ 3	.667	-/ -	-	-	1	-	-	10	-
SINGLEY, C.	-	8/ -	-	4/ 4	1.000	-/ -	-	-	1	-	-	20	-
GOLA, T.	-	6/ -	-	4/ 5	.800	-/ -	-	-	4	-	-	16	-
LEWIS, A.	-	1/ -	-	4/ 9	.444	-/ -	-	-	1	-	-	6	-
GREENBERG, C.	-	1/ -	-	1/ 2	.500	-/ -	-	-	4	-	-	3	-
BLATCHER, F.	-	4/ -	-	0/ 0	.000	-/ -	-	-	1	-	-	8	-
MAPLES, B.	-	0/ -	-	0/ 0	.000	-/ -	-	-	0	-	-	0	-
FREDERICKS, W.	-	0/ -	-	0/ 0	.000	-/ -	-	-	0	-	-	0	-
Totals	200	24/68	-	15/23	.652	-/ -	-	-	12	-	-	63	.315

San Francisco (77)   Coach: Phil Woolpert

	Min.	Total FG / FGA	Pct.	FT / FTA	Pct.	Reb. O / T	A	TO	PF	S	Blk	TP	PPM
MULLEN, J.	-	4/ -	-	2/ 5	.400	-/ -	-	-	5	-	-	10	-
BUCHANAN, S.	-	3/ -	-	2/ 2	1.000	-/ -	-	-	1	-	-	8	-
RUSSELL, B.	-	9/22	.409	5/ 7	.714	-/ -	-	-	1	-	-	23	-
JONES, K.	-	10/23	.435	4/ 4	1.000	-/ -	-	-	2	-	-	24	-
PERRY, H.	-	1/ -	-	2/ 2	1.000	-/ -	-	-	4	-	-	4	-
WIEBUSCH, B.	-	2/ -	-	0/ 0	.000	-/ -	-	-	0	-	-	4	-
ZANNINI, R.	-	1/ -	-	0/ 0	.000	-/ -	-	-	0	-	-	2	-
LAWLESS, D.	-	1/ -	-	0/ 0	.000	-/ -	-	-	0	-	-	2	-
KIRBY, G.	-	0/ -	-	0/ 0	.000	-/ -	-	-	1	-	-	0	-
Totals	200	31/83	-	15/20	.750	-/ -	-	-	14	-	-	77	.385

Disqualified: San Francisco—Mullen.

	1st Half	2nd Half	Final
La Salle	24	39	63
San Francisco	35	42	77

NATIONAL THIRD PLACE

Iowa (54)   Coach: Bucky O'Connor

	Min.	Total FG / FGA	Pct.	FT / FTA	Pct.	Reb. O / T	A	TO	PF	S	Blk	TP	PPM
DAVIS, M.	-	1/ -	-	0/ 2	.000	-/ -	-	-	3	-	-	2	-
SCHOOF, W.	-	2/ -	-	2/ 3	.667	-/ -	-	-	3	-	-	6	-
CAIN, C.	-	4/ -	-	6/ 6	1.000	-/ -	-	-	2	-	-	14	-
RIDLEY, G.	-	0/ -	-	0/ 0	.000	-/ -	-	-	0	-	-	0	-
DUNCAN, D.	-	0/ -	-	0/ 0	.000	-/ -	-	-	1	-	-	0	-
LOGAN, W.	-	5/ -	-	7/10	.700	-/ -	-	-	1	-	-	17	-
GEORGE, R.	-	0/ -	-	3/ 4	.750	-/ -	-	-	3	-	-	3	-
SEABERG, W.	-	1/ -	-	2/ 2	1.000	-/ -	-	-	1	-	-	4	-
JOHNSON, R.	-	0/ -	-	0/ 0	.000	-/ -	-	-	3	-	-	0	-
MARTEL, A.	-	1/ -	-	0/ 0	.000	-/ -	-	-	2	-	-	2	-
SCHEUERMAN, M.	-	2/ -	-	2/ 2	1.000	-/ -	-	-	3	-	-	6	-
HAWTHORNE, L.	-	0/ -	-	0/ 0	.000	-/ -	-	-	1	-	-	0	-
Totals	200	16/ -	-	22/29	.759	-/ -	-	-	23	-	-	54	.270

Colorado (75)   Coach: Bebe Lee

	Min.	Total FG / FGA	Pct.	FT / FTA	Pct.	Reb. O / T	A	TO	PF	S	Blk	TP	PPM
JEANGERARD, B.	-	5/ -	-	4/ 7	.571	-/ -	-	-	3	-	-	14	-
WALTER, W.	-	0/ -	-	0/ 0	.000	-/ -	-	-	0	-	-	0	-
RANGLOS, J.	-	6/ -	-	6/ 9	.667	-/ -	-	-	4	-	-	18	-
YARDLEY, B.	-	0/ -	-	0/ 0	.000	-/ -	-	-	0	-	-	0	-
HALDERSON, B.	-	4/ -	-	4/ 5	.800	-/ -	-	-	4	-	-	12	-
HANNAH, G.	-	1/ -	-	4/ 6	.667	-/ -	-	-	1	-	-	6	-
MOCK, C.	-	3/ -	-	7/ 9	.778	-/ -	-	-	3	-	-	13	-
MANSFIELD, M.	-	0/ -	-	0/ 0	.000	-/ -	-	-	0	-	-	0	-
PETERSON, B.	-	3/ -	-	4/ 4	1.000	-/ -	-	-	2	-	-	10	-
GRANT, J.	-	1/ -	-	0/ 0	.000	-/ -	-	-	0	-	-	2	-
Totals	200	23/ -	-	29/40	.725	-/ -	-	-	17	-	-	75	.375

Disqualified: None.

	1st Half	2nd Half	Final
Iowa	28	26	54
Colorado	35	40	75

REGIONAL THIRD PLACE EAST

Kentucky (84)   Coach: Adolph Rupp

	Min.	Total FG / FGA	Pct.	FT / FTA	Pct.	Reb. O / T	A	TO	PF	S	Blk	TP	PPM
BIRD, J.	-	8/ -	-	1/ 2	.500	-/ -	-	-	3	-	-	17	-
BREWER, J.	-	4/ -	-	3/ 4	.750	-/ -	-	-	2	-	-	11	-
MILLS, R.	-	3/ -	-	0/ 0	.000	-/ -	-	-	0	-	-	6	-
BURROW, B.	-	9/ -	-	4/ 5	.800	-/ -	-	-	3	-	-	22	-
ROSE, G.	-	3/ -	-	1/ 3	.333	-/ -	-	-	2	-	-	7	-
CALVERT, G.	-	7/ -	-	5/ 6	.833	-/ -	-	-	4	-	-	19	-
ADKINS, E.	-	1/ -	-	0/ 0	.000	-/ -	-	-	0	-	-	2	-
Totals	200	35/ -	-	14/20	.700	-/ -	-	-	14	-	-	84	.420

Penn State (59)   Coach: John Egli

	Min.	Total FG / FGA	Pct.	FT / FTA	Pct.	Reb. O / T	A	TO	PF	S	Blk	TP	PPM
WEIDENHAMMER, R.	-	5/ -	-	6/ 7	.857	-/ -	-	-	1	-	-	16	-
EDWARDS, D.	-	2/ -	-	0/ 0	.000	-/ -	-	-	2	-	-	4	-
HOFFMAN, B.	-	5/ -	-	0/ 0	.000	-/ -	-	-	3	-	-	10	-
ARNELLE, J.	-	8/ -	-	9/12	.750	-/ -	-	-	2	-	-	25	-
BLOCKER, J.	-	0/ -	-	1/ 2	.500	-/ -	-	-	1	-	-	1	-
ROHLAND, B.	-	0/ -	-	0/ 0	.000	-/ -	-	-	2	-	-	0	-
FIELDS, E.	-	0/ -	-	3/ 4	.750	-/ -	-	-	2	-	-	3	-
RAMSAY	-	0/ -	-	0/ 0	.000	-/ -	-	-	0	-	-	0	-
Totals	200	20/ -	-	19/25	.760	-/ -	-	-	13	-	-	59	.295

Disqualified: None.

	1st Half	2nd Half	Final
Kentucky	40	44	84
Penn State	28	31	59

Villanova (64)   Coach: Alex Severance

	Min.	Total FG / FGA	Pct.	FT / FTA	Pct.	Reb. O / T	A	TO	PF	S	Blk	TP	PPM
SCHAEFER, B.	-	6/ -	-	8/ 8	1.000	-/ -	-	-	2	-	-	20	-
MILLIGAN	-	0/ -	-	0/ 0	.000	-/ -	-	-	0	-	-	0	-
GRIFFITH	-	3/ -	-	0/ 1	.000	-/ -	-	-	1	-	-	6	-
CIRINO	-	2/ -	-	0/ 0	.000	-/ -	-	-	1	-	-	4	-
WEISSMAN, J.	-	3/ -	-	1/ 2	.500	-/ -	-	-	1	-	-	7	-
DEVINE, J.	-	4/ -	-	6/ 9	.667	-/ -	-	-	2	-	-	14	-
SMITH	-	5/ -	-	3/ 4	.750	-/ -	-	-	2	-	-	13	-
Totals	200	23/ -	-	18/24	.750	-/ -	-	-	9	-	-	64	.320

Princeton (57)   Coach: Franklin Cappon

	Min.	Total FG / FGA	Pct.	FT / FTA	Pct.	Reb. O / T	A	TO	PF	S	Blk	TP	PPM
HAABESTAD, H.	-	10/25	.400	3/ 4	.750	-/ -	-	-	4	-	-	23	-
ROBERTS, O.	-	0/ -	-	1/ 2	.500	-/ -	-	-	0	-	-	1	-
DAVIDSON, D.	-	4/ -	-	5/ 6	.833	-/ -	-	-	2	-	-	13	-
BATT, R.	-	3/ -	-	2/ 2	1.000	-/ -	-	-	2	-	-	8	-
DAILEY, T.	-	0/ -	-	0/ 0	.000	-/ -	-	-	0	-	-	0	-
DEVOE, J.	-	3/ -	-	0/ 1	.000	-/ -	-	-	2	-	-	6	-
MACKENZIE, K.	-	1/ -	-	0/ 0	.000	-/ -	-	-	1	-	-	2	-
KASTON	-	1/ -	-	2/ 2	1.000	-/ -	-	-	4	-	-	4	-
Totals	200	22/ -	-	13/17	.765	-/ -	-	-	15	-	-	57	.285

Disqualified: None.

	1st Half	2nd Half	Final
Villanova	32	32	64
Princeton	34	23	57

REGIONAL THIRD PLACE WEST

Tulsa (68)   Coach: Clarence Iba

	Min.	Total FG / FGA	Pct.	FT / FTA	Pct.	Reb. O / T	A	TO	PF	S	Blk	TP	PPM
DUNCAN	-	1/ 5	.200	3/ 4	.750	-/ 4	-	-	2	-	-	5	-
PATTERSON, B.	-	13/25	.520	10/12	.833	-/11	-	-	2	-	-	36	-
COURTER	-	4/10	.400	6/ 6	1.000	-/12	-	-	4	-	-	14	-
KROUSE	-	1/ 1	1.000	0/ 0	.000	-/ 1	-	-	0	-	-	2	-
YATES	-	2/ 3	.667	0/ 0	.000	-/ 2	-	-	3	-	-	4	-
BORN	-	2/ 9	.222	0/ 4	.000	-/ 2	-	-	2	-	-	4	-
EVANS	-	0/ 1	.000	0/ 0	.000	-/ 0	-	-	3	-	-	0	-
HACKER	-	1/ 8	.125	0/ 0	.000	-/ 3	-	-	3	-	-	2	-
STEWART	-	0/ 2	.000	1/ 3	.333	-/ 3	-	-	1	-	-	1	-
Totals	200	24/64	.375	20/29	.690	-/38	-	-	20	-	-	68	.340

SMU (67)   Coach: E.O. "Doc" Hayes

	Min.	Total FG / FGA	Pct.	FT / FTA	Pct.	Reb. O / T	A	TO	PF	S	Blk	TP	PPM
KROG, J.	-	3/ 6	.500	0/ 0	.000	-/11	-	-	0	-	-	6	-
MCGREGOR, B.	-	0/ 4	.000	2/ 4	.500	-/ 4	-	-	1	-	-	2	-
SCHARFFENBERGER	-	1/ 3	.333	0/ 1	.000	-/ 4	-	-	3	-	-	2	-
SHOWALTER, L.	-	0/ 2	.000	0/ 0	.000	-/ 2	-	-	1	-	-	0	-
KREBS, J.	-	5/15	.333	5/ 8	.625	-/10	-	-	4	-	-	15	-
MILLER, T.	-	6/11	.545	1/ 3	.333	-/ 5	-	-	2	-	-	13	-
BARNES	-	2/15	.133	5/ 6	.833	-/ 7	-	-	2	-	-	9	-
MILLS, B.	-	3/ 6	.500	4/ 4	1.000	-/ 1	-	-	0	-	-	10	-
MORRIS, R.	-	3/ 7	.429	4/ 8	.500	-/ 5	-	-	3	-	-	10	-
ALEXANDER	-	0/ 1	.000	0/ 0	.000	-/ 1	-	-	0	-	-	0	-
CLAYTON	-	0/ 2	.000	0/ 0	.000	-/ 3	-	-	1	-	-	0	-
LEE, P.	-	0/ 0	.000	0/ 0	.000	-/ 0	-	-	0	-	-	0	-
Totals	200	23/72	.319	21/34	.618	-/53	-	-	17	-	-	67	.335

Team Rebounds: Tulsa 3; SMU 1. Disqualified: None.

	1st Half	2nd Half	Final
Tulsa	43	25	68
SMU	33	34	67

Utah (108)   Coach: Jack Gardner

	Min.	Total FG / FGA	Pct.	FT / FTA	Pct.	Reb. O / T	A	TO	PF	S	Blk	TP	PPM
BUCKWALTER	-	2/ -	-	2/ 3	.667	-/ -	-	-	3	-	-	6	-
BERGEN	-	2/ -	-	3/ 4	.750	-/ -	-	-	5	-	-	7	-
BUNTE	-	13/ -	-	9/15	.600	-/ -	-	-	1	-	-	35	-
JENSEN	-	3/ -	-	4/ 5	.800	-/ -	-	-	0	-	-	10	-
TONNESEN	-	7/ -	-	2/ 3	.667	-/ -	-	-	3	-	-	16	-
CONDIE	-	2/ -	-	1/ 1	1.000	-/ -	-	-	3	-	-	5	-
CROWE	-	3/ -	-	0/ 0	.000	-/ -	-	-	5	-	-	6	-
MCCLEARY	-	6/ -	-	2/ 2	1.000	-/ -	-	-	4	-	-	14	-
BERNER	-	0/ -	-	1/ 2	.500	-/ -	-	-	0	-	-	1	-
PEPPLE	-	2/ -	-	0/ 2	.000	-/ -	-	-	2	-	-	4	-
LEWIS	-	2/ -	-	0/ 0	.000	-/ -	-	-	1	-	-	4	-
Totals	200	42/ -	-	24/37	.649	-/ -	-	-	27	-	-	108	.540

Seattle (85)   Coach: Al Brightman

	Min.	Total FG / FGA	Pct.	FT / FTA	Pct.	Reb. O / T	A	TO	PF	S	Blk	TP	PPM
KELLY	-	2/ -	-	2/ 4	.500	-/ -	-	-	3	-	-	6	-
GLOWASKI	-	5/ -	-	9/ 9	1.000	-/ -	-	-	3	-	-	19	-
STRICKLIN, D.	-	5/ -	-	4/ 7	.571	-/ -	-	-	1	-	-	14	-
BAUER, C.	-	7/ -	-	7/ 7	1.000	-/ -	-	-	1	-	-	21	-
MALONE	-	1/ -	-	7/ 8	.875	-/ -	-	-	2	-	-	9	-
GODES	-	1/ -	-	1/ 4	.250	-/ -	-	-	3	-	-	3	-
FUHRER	-	1/ -	-	5/ 7	.714	-/ -	-	-	2	-	-	7	-
COX	-	0/ -	-	4/ 4	1.000	-/ -	-	-	1	-	-	4	-
VAUGHAN	-	0/ -	-	0/ 0	.000	-/ -	-	-	3	-	-	0	-
MARTIN	-	0/ -	-	0/ 0	.000	-/ -	-	-	1	-	-	0	-
SANFORD	-	1/ -	-	0/ 1	.000	-/ -	-	-	1	-	-	2	-
Totals	200	23/ -	-	39/51	.765	-/ -	-	-	21	-	-	85	.425

Disqualified: Utah—Bergen, Crowe.

	1st Half	2nd Half	Final
Utah	58	50	108
Seattle	38	47	85

☢ ALL-STAR TEAMS ☢

ALL TOURNAMENT

CARL CAIN	IOWA
TOM GOLA	LA SALLE
K. C. JONES	SAN FRANCISCO
JIM RANGLOS	COLORADO
★ **BILL RUSSELL**	SAN FRANCISCO

★ Most Outstanding Player(s)

☢ INDIVIDUAL RECORDS ☢

SCORING

Most points in a single game
1 TERRY RAND, MARQUETTE (vs. MIAMI [OHIO])
    37
2 BOB PATTERSON, TULSA (vs. SMU) 36
3 ART BUNTE, UTAH (vs. SEATTLE) 35
4 BILL LOGAN, IOWA (vs. MARQUETTE) 31
5 TOM GOLA, LA SALLE (vs. CANISIUS) 30

Most total points in the tournament
1 BILL RUSSELL, SAN FRANCISCO 118
2 TOM GOLA, LA SALLE 115
3 BILL LOGAN, IOWA 76
4 CHARLES SINGLEY, LA SALLE 74
5 TERRY RAND, MARQUETTE 73

Highest scoring average (minimum 2 games)
1 BOB PATTERSON, TULSA (57-2) 28.50
2 TERRY RAND, MARQUETTE (73-3) 24.33
3 BILL RUSSELL, SAN FRANCISCO (118-5) 23.60
4 ART BUNTE, UTAH (47-2) 23.50
5 TOM GOLA, LA SALLE (115-5) 23.00

FIELD GOALS

Most field goals in a single game
1 TERRY RAND, MARQUETTE (vs. MIAMI [OHIO])
    16
2 BILL RUSSELL, SAN FRANCISCO (vs. WEST
    TEXAS ST.) 14

3 ART BUNTE, UTAH (vs. SEATTLE) 13
3 BOB PATTERSON, TULSA (vs. SMU) 13
5 BOB JEANGERARD, COLORADO (vs. BRADLEY)
    12

Most total field goals in the tournament
1 BILL RUSSELL, SAN FRANCISCO 49
2 TOM GOLA, LA SALLE 39
3 . TERRY RAND, MARQUETTE 31
4 CHARLES SINGLEY, LA SALLE 28
5 BILL LOGAN, IOWA 27

FREE THROWS

Most free throws in a single game
1 JACK DEVINE, VILLANOVA (vs. CANISIUS) 15
2 JOHN MCCARTHY, CANISIUS (vs. VILLANOVA) 14
2 BOB SCHAEFER, VILLANOVA (vs. DUKE) 14
4 TOM GOLA, LA SALLE (vs. CANISIUS) 12
4 SCHULZ, MARQUETTE (vs. IOWA) 12

Most total free throws in the tournament
1 TOM GOLA, LA SALLE 37
2 BOB SCHAEFER, VILLANOVA 28
3 JACK DEVINE, VILLANOVA 24
4 HARVEY BABETCH, BRADLEY 23
5 4 tied for fifth place.

Most free throws attempted in a single game
1 BOB SCHAEFER, VILLANOVA (vs. DUKE) 20
2 SCHULZ, MARQUETTE (vs. IOWA) 18

3 JACK DEVINE, VILLANOVA (vs. CANISIUS) 17
4 LYNDON LEE, OKLAHOMA CITY (vs. BRADLEY)
    16
5 4 tied for fifth place.

Most free throws attempted in the tournament
1 TOM GOLA, LA SALLE 42
2 BILL RUSSELL, SAN FRANCISCO 39
3 BOB SCHAEFER, VILLANOVA 35
4 4 tied for fourth place.

**Highest free throw percentage in a single game
(minimum 7 attempts)**
1 TOM GOLA, LA SALLE (vs. CANISIUS) (12-12)
    1.000
2 GLOWASKI, SEATTLE (vs. UTAH) (9-9) 1.000
3 WALCZAK, MARQUETTE (vs. MIAMI [OHIO]) (8-
    8) 1.000
3 BOB SCHAEFER, VILLANOVA (vs. PRINCETON)
    (8-8) 1.000
5 3 tied for fifth place.

**Highest free throw percentage in the tournament
(minimum 15 attempts)**
1 TOM GOLA, LA SALLE (37-42) .881
2 JOHN MCCARTHY, CANISIUS (21-24) .875
3 MILTON SCHEUERMAN, IOWA (18-21) .857
4 BOB PATTERSON, TULSA (17-20) .850
5 CHARLES SINGLEY, LA SALLE (18-22) .818

○ TEAM RECORDS ○

SCORING

Most points in a single game
1	UTAH (vs. SEATTLE)	108
2	LA SALLE (vs. CANISIUS)	99
3	LA SALLE (vs. WEST VIRGINIA)	95

Most total points in the tournament
1	LA SALLE	406
2	SAN FRANCISCO	363
3	IOWA	295

Highest scoring average (minimum 2 games)
1	UTAH (167-2)	83.50
2	MARQUETTE (250-3)	83.33
3	LA SALLE (406-5)	81.20

FIELD GOALS

Most field goals in a single game
1	UTAH (vs. SEATTLE)	42
2	SAN FRANCISCO (vs. WEST TEXAS ST.)	39
2	LA SALLE (vs. WEST VIRGINIA)	39

Most total field goals in the tournament
1	LA SALLE	148
2	SAN FRANCISCO	136
3	IOWA	104

FREE THROWS

Most free throws in a single game
1	SEATTLE (vs. UTAH)	39
2	LA SALLE (vs. CANISIUS)	35
3	COLORADO (vs. BRADLEY)	33

Most total free throws in the tournament
1	LA SALLE	110
2	COLORADO	105
3	SAN FRANCISCO	91

Most free throws attempted in a single game
1	SEATTLE (vs. UTAH)	51
2	COLORADO (vs. BRADLEY)	47
3	MARQUETTE (vs. IOWA)	44

Most total free throws attempted in the tournament
1	LA SALLE	150
2	COLORADO	148
3	SAN FRANCISCO	146

Highest free throw percentage in a single game
1	TULSA (vs. COLORADO) (25-29)	.862
2	LA SALLE (vs. CANISIUS) (35-41)	.854
3	VILLANOVA (vs. CANISIUS) (29-34)	.853

Highest free throw percentage in the tournament (minimum 2 games)
1	TULSA (45-58)	.776
2	VILLANOVA (75-100)	.750
3	PENN STATE (51-69)	.739

Fewest free throws in a single game
1	MEMPHIS STATE (vs. PENN STATE)	9
2	SAN FRANCISCO (vs. WEST TEXAS ST.)	11
3	2 tied for third place.	

Lowest free throw percentage in a single game
1	MEMPHIS STATE (vs. PENN STATE) (9-19)	.474
2	SEATTLE (vs. IDAHO STATE) (12-25)	.480
3	SAN FRANCISCO (vs. WEST TEXAS ST.) (11-22)	.500

Lowest free throw percentage in the tournament (minimum 2 games)
1	OREGON STATE (31-53)	.585
2	KENTUCKY (27-45)	.600
3	SAN FRANCISCO (91-146)	.623

1956

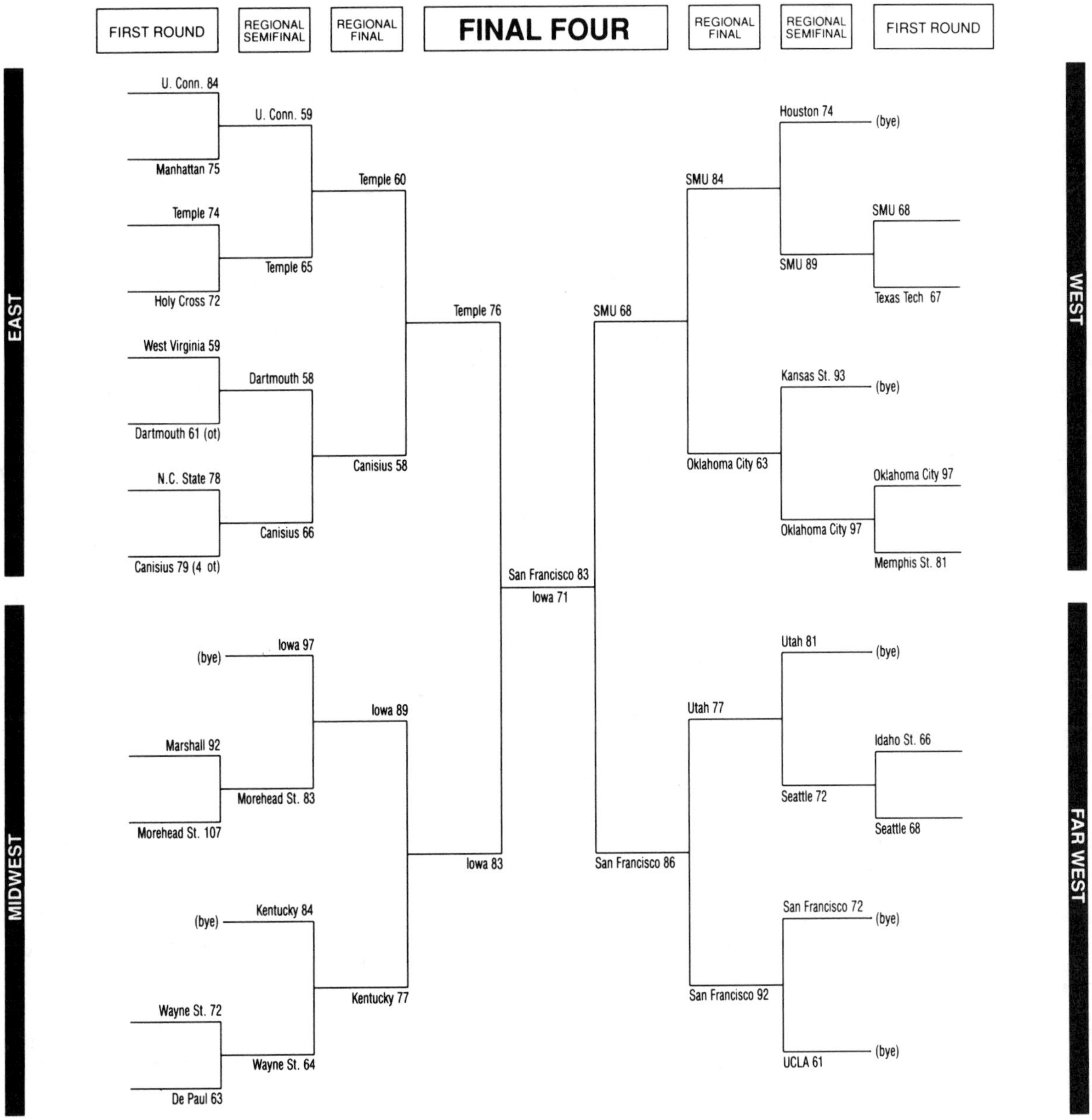

| FIRST ROUND | REGIONAL SEMIFINAL | REGIONAL FINAL | **FINAL FOUR** | REGIONAL FINAL | REGIONAL SEMIFINAL | FIRST ROUND |

EAST

U. Conn. 84
U. Conn. 59
Manhattan 75
Temple 60
Temple 74
Temple 65
Holy Cross 72
Temple 76
West Virginia 59
Dartmouth 58
Dartmouth 61 (ot)
Canisius 58
N.C. State 78
Canisius 66
Canisius 79 (4 ot)

SMU 68

WEST

Houston 74
(bye)
SMU 84
SMU 68
SMU 89
Texas Tech 67
Kansas St. 93
(bye)
Oklahoma City 63
Oklahoma City 97
Oklahoma City 97
Memphis St. 81

San Francisco 83
Iowa 71

MIDWEST

Iowa 97
(bye)
Iowa 89
Marshall 92
Morehead St. 83
Morehead St. 107
Iowa 83
(bye)
Kentucky 84
Kentucky 77
Wayne St. 72
Wayne St. 64
De Paul 63

San Francisco 86

FAR WEST

Utah 81
(bye)
Utah 77
Utah 77
Idaho St. 66
Seattle 72
Seattle 68
San Francisco 72
(bye)
San Francisco 92
UCLA 61
(bye)

CONSOLATION GAMES

National Third Place:
Temple 90
SMU 81

Regional Third Place:

East:
Dartmouth 85
U. Conn. 64

Midwest:
Morehead St. 95
Wayne St. 84

West:
Kansas St. 89
Houston 70

Far West:
UCLA 94
Seattle 70

An aura of invincibility hung from the bony shoulders of the San Francisco Dons' jumping-jack center Bill Russell as the 1956 NCAA tournament began. He and his talented teammates had finished the regular season undefeated—virtually untested—and their 51-game winning streak (including the previous year's NCAA title), was the longest in major college history. As they approached their opening tournament game with UCLA, Russell voiced his confidence. "We've been playing mighty sweet music for a long time," he said, "and I don't see any reason for it to get sour now."

For all intents and purposes, the tournament competition was on two rungs in 1956—there was San Francisco and there was everybody else.

As for everyone else: The most exciting action undoubtedly took place in the East regional. The Canisius Griffins started out the competition with an unbelievable quadruple overtime upset over No. 2 ranked North Carolina State, finally pulling out the victory when Fran (The Fireman) Corcoran scored his only 2-pointer of the night on a jump shot after 59 minutes and 56 seconds of action. In the second game of the same Madison Square Garden doubleheader, Temple's Fred Cohen put the Owls ahead of Holy Cross with six seconds to play. Tom Heinsohn, the Crusaders' star, came right back, but his basket was a second too late. With mayhem in mind, an incensed Holy Cross rooter charged at the official who made the call but was stopped in his felonious pursuit by Garden special police.

In the second round Canisius outlasted Dartmouth (which had won its opener over favored West Virginia on a last-second overtime shot of their own) and Temple beat Connecticut. Then the Griffins met the Owls and their fantastic backcourt combo of Hal (King) Lear and Guy Rodgers in the regional final played in Temple's own backyard, the Palestra. With five seconds left, Temple missed a shot and in the ensuing scramble under the boards a foul was called on Canisius. With two seconds left, Lear (who was held to 14 points by the Griffins' hard-nosed defensive zealot Johnny McCarthy) calmly sank two free throws. A last-second Canisius shot bounced off the rim, and Temple was in the Final Four.

Meanwhile, Iowa had little trouble getting through the Midwest quarter of the draw, and after an opening round squeaker over Texas Tech, SMU also breezed.

In the Far West, Johnny Wooden and his UCLA Bruins had the misfortune of being the Dons' first victims. UCLA had been the last team to defeat San Francisco, in the third game of the 1954–55 season. And the Dons had also been the last team to defeat the Bruins (back in December 1955). The Bruins, led by their fine center Willie Naulls, had since put together an 18-game streak of their own, but they had no chance against Russell and company. San Francisco came out of the blocks fired up, and held the fast-breaking UCLAns to only 5 of 25 from the floor in the first half; it may have been early but it was time to say good night.

Unlike the Bruins, Utah had a glimmer of hope in the regional final when they took a 49-48 lead over the Dons with 13 minutes to play. But Russell got down to business, pouring in 18 second-half points and leading the Dons to a 15-point victory, 92-77.

In the semis, San Francisco went back to its opening game strategy, putting SMU away early. Led by the shooting of 6-7 forward Mike Farmer, who finished with 26 points, the Dons took a 38-17 first-half lead before letting up and allowing the Mustangs (who had a 19-game winning streak of their own) back in the game. SMU managed to cut the lead to six early in the second half before the Dons returned to the matter at hand. The next day, San Francisco Coach Phil Woolpert said that Russell (who scored 17 points and pulled down 23 rebounds) wasn't at his best against SMU, "but you certainly can't be over-critical when you win by 18 points."

In the other semi, Iowa's all-Big Ten center, Carl Logan, scored 36 points in leading the Hawkeyes to victory over Temple, whose two star guards, Hal Lear and Guy Rodgers, accounted for all but 16 of the Owls' 76 points.

After Lear broke the tournament scoring record with 48 points in Temple's consolation game victory over SMU, the final between San Francisco and Iowa finally began. In the opening minutes, the Dons stood around like spectators as the Hawkeyes raced to a 15-4 lead. The crowd in Evanston, Illinois, cheered wildly for the Big Ten champs, and it looked like Phil Woolpert's team was in trouble. But in the next seven minutes, the Iowa lead dissolved under the onslaught of Russell's inside game and the shooting of guards Gene Brown and Hal Perry. "With the octopus-like Russell constantly knocking down shots," reported the Associated Press, "the Hawkeyes must have felt like they were looking into the mouth of a cannon." The Dons continued to pour it on until their lead reached 13 early in the second half. They cruised to victory.

After the game, the Iowa players tried to explain what it was like to play against Bill Russell. Bill Seaberg said "You'd shoot, and there Russell would be knocking the ball down your throat." And 6-7 center Carl Logan, who was held to 12 by Big Bill, said "You can jump as high as you can, and still you're only high enough to tap Russell on the shoulder."

Russell and his teammates had won each game by putting on a crushing spurt virtually at will. They had become only the third school to win two consecutive championships by extending their unbeaten streak to a record 55 games. The city by the bay would never see their likes again.

FIRST ROUND EAST

U. Conn. (84)   Coach: Hugh Greer

	Min.	Total FG / FGA	Pct.	FT / FTA	Pct.	Reb. O/T	A	TO	PF	S	Blk	TP	PPM
QUINN, F.	-	5/ -	-	2/ 2	1.000	-/ -	-	-	3	-	-	12	-
RUDDY	-	5/ -	-	3/ 5	.600	-/ -	-	-	3	-	-	13	-
NARRACCI	-	0/ -	-	0/ 0	.000	-/ -	-	-	0	-	-	0	-
KASPAR, P.	-	9/ -	-	5/ 8	.625	-/ -	-	-	2	-	-	23	-
O'LEARY	-	0/ -	-	0/ 0	.000	-/ -	-	-	0	-	-	0	-
BUSHWELL, R.	-	7/ -	-	10/10	1.000	-/ -	-	-	1	-	-	24	-
O'CONNOR	-	0/ -	-	0/ 0	.000	-/ -	-	-	1	-	-	0	-
OSBORN	-	4/ -	-	0/ 0	.000	-/ -	-	-	2	-	-	8	-
BURNS	-	2/ -	-	0/ 0	.000	-/ -	-	-	2	-	-	4	-
Totals	200	32/ -	-	20/25	.800	-/ -	-	-	14	-	-	84	.420

Manhattan (75)   Coach: Ken Norton

	Min.	Total FG / FGA	Pct.	FT / FTA	Pct.	Reb. O/T	A	TO	PF	S	Blk	TP	PPM
PAULSON	-	7/ -	-	5/ 5	1.000	-/ -	-	-	3	-	-	19	-
MURPHY	-	2/ -	-	2/ 4	.500	-/ -	-	-	0	-	-	6	-
MARTINSEN	-	3/ -	-	0/ 0	.000	-/ -	-	-	1	-	-	6	-
LOMBARDO, A.	-	4/ -	-	2/ 2	1.000	-/ -	-	-	5	-	-	10	-
JOSEPH	-	0/ -	-	1/ 2	.500	-/ -	-	-	1	-	-	1	-
POWERS, J.	-	12/ -	-	2/ 7	.286	-/ -	-	-	3	-	-	26	-
O'CONNOR	-	2/ -	-	0/ 0	.000	-/ -	-	-	1	-	-	4	-
CAVANAUGH	-	1/ -	-	1/ 5	.200	-/ -	-	-	0	-	-	3	-
Totals	200	31/ -	-	13/25	.520	-/ -	-	-	14	-	-	75	.375

Disqualified: Manhattan—Lombardo.

	1st Half	2nd Half	Final
U. Conn.	40	44	84
Manhattan	35	40	75

Temple (74)   Coach: Harry Litwack

	Min.	Total FG / FGA	Pct.	FT / FTA	Pct.	Reb. O/T	A	TO	PF	S	Blk	TP	PPM
REINFELD, H.	-	4/ 8	.500	0/ 0	.000	-/ 6	2	-	2	-	-	8	-
FLEMING, D.	-	1/ 3	.333	2/ 2	1.000	-/ 2	3	-	2	-	-	4	-
NORMAN, J.	-	1/ 1	1.000	0/ 1	.000	-/ 4	2	-	1	-	-	2	-
COHEN, F.	-	8/13	.615	0/ 1	.000	-/11	0	-	4	-	-	16	-
LEAR, H.	-	9/19	.474	8/12	.667	-/ 2	4	-	2	-	-	26	-
RODGERS, G.	-	6/12	.500	6/10	.600	-/ 8	8	-	1	-	-	18	-
Totals	200	29/56	.518	16/26	.615	-/33	19	-	12	-	-	74	.370

Holy Cross (72)   Coach: Roy Leening

	Min.	Total FG / FGA	Pct.	FT / FTA	Pct.	Reb. O/T	A	TO	PF	S	Blk	TP	PPM
HUGHES, J.	-	5/13	.385	3/ 5	.600	-/ 9	0	-	2	-	-	13	-
LIEBER, J.	-	10/20	.500	0/ 0	.000	-/ 5	4	-	2	-	-	20	-
HEINSOHN, T.	-	7/28	.250	12/12	1.000	-/20	2	-	3	-	-	26	-
PROHOVICH	-	2/ 7	.286	0/ 1	.000	-/ 8	5	-	4	-	-	4	-
WADDLETON	-	1/ 3	.333	0/ 0	.000	-/ 0	2	-	1	-	-	2	-
ANDREOLI	-	1/ 9	.111	2/ 2	1.000	-/ 4	2	-	3	-	-	4	-
RYAN, T.	-	1/ 1	1.000	1/ 2	.500	-/ 1	3	-	2	-	-	3	-
Totals	200	27/81	.333	18/22	.818	-/47	18	-	17	-	-	72	.360

Disqualified: None.

	1st Half	2nd Half	Final
Temple	40	34	74
Holy Cross	37	35	72

West Virginia (59)   Coach: Fred Schaus

	Min.	Total FG / FGA	Pct.	FT / FTA	Pct.	Reb. O/T	A	TO	PF	S	Blk	TP	PPM
GARDNER, J.	-	4/ -	-	3/ 6	.500	-/ -	-	-	0	-	-	11	-
HUNDLEY, R.	-	8/ -	-	2/ 5	.400	-/ -	-	-	3	-	-	18	-
SHARRAR, L.	-	3/ -	-	2/ 4	.500	-/ -	-	-	4	-	-	8	-
CONSTANTINE	-	1/ -	-	0/ 0	.000	-/ -	-	-	1	-	-	2	-
KISHBAUGH	-	6/ -	-	1/ 3	.333	-/ -	-	-	2	-	-	13	-
VINCENT, D.	-	1/ -	-	5/ 6	.833	-/ -	-	-	1	-	-	7	-
Totals	200	23/ -	-	13/24	.542	-/ -	-	-	11	-	-	59	.295

Dartmouth (61)   Coach: Doggie Julian

	Min.	Total FG / FGA	Pct.	FT / FTA	Pct.	Reb. O/T	A	TO	PF	S	Blk	TP	PPM
JUDSON, R.	-	7/ -	-	4/ 5	.800	-/ -	-	-	3	-	-	18	-
ERWIN	-	0/ -	-	0/ 0	.000	-/ -	-	-	0	-	-	0	-
MARKMAN	-	0/ -	-	0/ 0	.000	-/ -	-	-	0	-	-	0	-
CARRUTHERS, D.	-	2/ -	-	2/ 2	1.000	-/ -	-	-	3	-	-	6	-
FRASER	-	0/ -	-	0/ 0	.000	-/ -	-	-	0	-	-	0	-
FRANCIS, J.	-	9/ -	-	7/ 8	.875	-/ -	-	-	0	-	-	25	-
DONAHOE, T.	-	1/ -	-	0/ 0	.000	-/ -	-	-	0	-	-	2	-
JULIAN	-	0/ -	-	1/ 2	.500	-/ -	-	-	4	-	-	1	-
BLADES, L.	-	1/ -	-	2/ 2	1.000	-/ -	-	-	0	-	-	4	-
BOOTH	-	2/ -	-	1/ 2	.500	-/ -	-	-	4	-	-	5	-
JONES	-	0/ -	-	0/ 0	.000	-/ -	-	-	0	-	-	0	-
Totals	200	22/ -	-	17/21	.810	-/ -	-	-	14	-	-	61	.305

Disqualified: None.

	1st Half	2nd Half	Final
West Virginia	35	24	59
Dartmouth	33	28	61

North Carolina State (78)   Coach: Everett Case

	Min.	Total FG / FGA	Pct.	FT / FTA	Pct.	Reb. O/T	A	TO	PF	S	Blk	TP	PPM
DINARDO, P.	-	4/ -	-	5/ 8	.625	-/ -	-	-	3	-	-	13	-
HOPPER, T.	-	0/ -	-	0/ 0	.000	-/ -	-	-	0	-	-	0	-
KESSLER, M.	-	0/ -	-	0/ 0	.000	-/ -	-	-	0	-	-	0	-
DICKMAN, L.	-	2/ -	-	0/ 0	.000	-/ -	-	-	4	-	-	4	-
POND, N.	-	1/ -	-	2/ 2	1.000	-/ -	-	-	2	-	-	4	-
SEITZ, B.	-	0/ -	-	0/ 0	.000	-/ -	-	-	0	-	-	0	-
SHAVLIK, R.	-	10/ -	-	5/10	.500	-/ -	-	-	4	-	-	25	-
STEPANOVICH, G.	-	1/ -	-	2/ 4	.500	-/ -	-	-	2	-	-	4	-
MOLODET, V.	-	5/ -	-	4/ 6	.667	-/ -	-	-	5	-	-	14	-
MAGLIO, J.	-	5/ -	-	4/ 8	.500	-/ -	-	-	3	-	-	14	-
Totals	300	28/ -	-	22/38	.579	-/ -	-	-	23	-	-	78	.260

Canisius (79)   Coach: Joseph Curran

	Min.	Total FG / FGA	Pct.	FT / FTA	Pct.	Reb. O/T	A	TO	PF	S	Blk	TP	PPM
NOWAK, H.	-	8/ -	-	13/17	.765	-/ -	-	-	3	-	-	29	-
KELLY, R.	-	5/ -	-	4/ 7	.571	-/ -	-	-	5	-	-	14	-
BRITZ, G.	-	0/ -	-	0/ 0	.000	-/ -	-	-	0	-	-	0	-
LEONE, J.	-	2/ -	-	0/ 2	.000	-/ -	-	-	5	-	-	4	-
CORCORAN, F.	-	1/ -	-	2/ 2	1.000	-/ -	-	-	3	-	-	4	-
MCCARTHY, JAMES	-	0/ -	-	0/ 0	.000	-/ -	-	-	0	-	-	0	-
MCCARTHY, JOHN	-	5/ -	-	2/ 4	.500	-/ -	-	-	2	-	-	12	-
MCCARTHY, J.	-	5/ -	-	6/ 6	1.000	-/ -	-	-	5	-	-	16	-
Totals	300	26/ -	-	27/38	.711	-/ -	-	-	23	-	-	79	.263

Disqualified: Canisius—Kelly, Leone, John McCarthy; N.C. State— Molodet.

	1st Half	2nd Half	1st OT	2nd OT	3rd OT	4th OT	Final
N.C. State	34	31	4	2	0	7	78
Canisius	39	26	4	2	0	8	79

FIRST ROUND MIDWEST

Marshall (92)   Coach: Jule Rivlin

	Min.	Total FG/FGA	Pct.	FT/FTA	Pct.	Reb. O/T	A	TO	PF	S	Blk	TP	PPM
PRICE	-	11/ -	-	5/11	.455	-/ -	-	-	5	-	-	27	-
GREER	-	5/ -	-	2/ 3	.667	-/ -	-	-	4	-	-	12	-
ASHLEY	-	2/ -	-	2/ 3	.667	-/ -	-	-	5	-	-	6	-
KIRK	-	8/ -	-	2/ 2	1.000	-/ -	-	-	3	-	-	18	-
UNDERWOOD	-	9/ -	-	0/ 0	.000	-/ -	-	-	5	-	-	18	-
MAYFIELD	-	0/ -	-	0/ 0	.000	-/ -	-	-	2	-	-	0	-
FREEMAN	-	5/ -	-	1/ 2	.500	-/ -	-	-	2	-	-	11	-
Totals	200	40/ -	-	12/21	.571	-/ -	-	-	26	-	-	92	.460

Morehead State (107)   Coach: Robert Laughlin

	Min.	Total FG/FGA	Pct.	FT/FTA	Pct.	Reb. O/T	A	TO	PF	S	Blk	TP	PPM
HAMILTON, S.	-	9/ -	-	5/ 7	.714	-/ -	-	-	1	-	-	23	-
RICHARDS, B.	-	0/ -	-	0/ 0	.000	-/ -	-	-	0	-	-	0	-
KELEHER, D.	-	8/ -	-	0/ 2	.000	-/ -	-	-	5	-	-	16	-
JEWELL, J.	-	0/ -	-	2/ 2	1.000	-/ -	-	-	0	-	-	2	-
CARROLL, G.	-	0/ -	-	0/ 1	.000	-/ -	-	-	0	-	-	0	-
SWARTZ, D.	-	12/ -	-	15/17	.882	-/ -	-	-	4	-	-	39	-
SHIMFESSEL, B.	-	0/ -	-	0/ 0	.000	-/ -	-	-	0	-	-	0	-
TOLLE, H.	-	3/ -	-	2/ 5	.400	-/ -	-	-	1	-	-	8	-
THOMPSON, K.	-	0/ -	-	0/ 0	.000	-/ -	-	-	0	-	-	0	-
GAUNCE, D.	-	6/ -	-	7/10	.700	-/ -	-	-	2	-	-	19	-
Totals	200	38/ -	-	31/44	.705	-/ -	-	-	13	-	-	107	.535

Disqualified: Morehead State—Keleher; Marshall—Price, Ashley, Underwood.

	1st Half	2nd Half	Final
Marshall	46	46	92
Morehead State	51	56	107

Wayne State (72)   Coach: Joel Mason

	Min.	Total FG/FGA	Pct.	FT/FTA	Pct.	Reb. O/T	A	TO	PF	S	Blk	TP	PPM
PORTER	-	1/ -	-	2/ 2	1.000	-/ -	-	-	2	-	-	4	-
STRAUGHN, C.	-	9/ -	-	9/12	.750	-/ -	-	-	2	-	-	27	-
DUNCAN	-	1/ -	-	1/ 2	.500	-/ -	-	-	2	-	-	3	-
BROWN, G.	-	5/ -	-	3/ 4	.750	-/ -	-	-	3	-	-	13	-
KELLER	-	3/ -	-	0/ 0	.000	-/ -	-	-	3	-	-	6	-
WITTOCK	-	0/ -	-	0/ 0	.000	-/ -	-	-	0	-	-	0	-
KENDRICK, B.	-	4/ -	-	6/ 9	.667	-/ -	-	-	5	-	-	14	-
GREENBERG	-	0/ -	-	0/ 0	.000	-/ -	-	-	3	-	-	0	-
HARVEY	-	0/ -	-	3/ 4	.750	-/ -	-	-	0	-	-	3	-
LONDON	-	1/ -	-	0/ 0	.000	-/ -	-	-	0	-	-	2	-
Totals	200	24/55	.436	24/33	.727	-/32	-	-	20	-	-	72	.360

DePaul (63)   Coach: Ray Meyer

	Min.	Total FG/FGA	Pct.	FT/FTA	Pct.	Reb. O/T	A	TO	PF	S	Blk	TP	PPM
SUBHESZCZYK	-	6/15	.400	5/ 9	.556	-/11	-	-	4	-	-	17	-
HEISE	-	3/15	.200	4/ 4	1.000	-/ 6	-	-	1	-	-	10	-
JARSY	-	2/ 9	.222	6/ 7	.857	-/ 4	-	-	3	-	-	10	-
KROINZINE	-	6/18	.333	3/ 4	.750	-/ 3	-	-	2	-	-	15	-
CURTIN	-	1/ 5	.200	3/ 4	.750	-/ 4	-	-	3	-	-	5	-
HENRY	-	1/ 3	.333	4/ 7	.571	-/ 4	-	-	4	-	-	6	-
Totals	200	19/65	.292	25/35	.714	-/32	-	-	17	-	-	63	.315

Disqualified: Wayne State—Kendrick.

	1st Half	2nd Half	Final
Wayne State	37	35	72
DePaul	36	27	63

FIRST ROUND WEST

SMU (68)   Coach: E. O. "Doc" Hayes

	Min.	Total FG/FGA	Pct.	FT/FTA	Pct.	Reb. O/T	A	TO	PF	S	Blk	TP	PPM
SHOWALTER, L.	-	2/ 4	.500	0/ 0	.000	-/ 3	-	-	2	-	-	4	-
HERRSCHER, R.	-	0/ 0	.000	0/ 1	.000	-/ 0	-	-	2	-	-	0	-
KROG, J.	-	7/17	.412	5/ 5	1.000	-/12	-	-	1	-	-	19	-
MILLS, B.	-	4/ 8	.500	5/ 6	.833	-/ 1	-	-	2	-	-	13	-
MORRIS, R.	-	2/ 6	.333	2/ 3	.667	-/ 4	-	-	4	-	-	6	-
MILLER, T.	-	0/ 0	.000	4/ 4	1.000	-/ 1	-	-	1	-	-	4	-
KREBS, J.	-	10/17	.588	2/ 3	.667	-/ 6	-	-	4	-	-	22	-
Totals	200	25/52	.481	18/22	.818	-/27	-	-	16	-	-	68	.340

Texas Tech (67)   Coach: Polk Robinson

	Min.	Total FG/FGA	Pct.	FT/FTA	Pct.	Reb. O/T	A	TO	PF	S	Blk	TP	PPM
ELAM	-	0/ 0	.000	0/ 0	.000	-/ 0	-	-	0	-	-	0	-
CARPENTER, G.	-	10/24	.417	3/ 4	.750	-/ 5	-	-	4	-	-	23	-
SCALING	-	1/ 5	.200	4/ 6	.667	-/ 1	-	-	2	-	-	6	-
WILSON	-	3/ 7	.429	2/ 3	.667	-/ 4	-	-	1	-	-	8	-
CUMMINGS	-	5/ 7	.714	2/ 2	1.000	-/ 2	-	-	3	-	-	12	-
UNDERWOOD	-	3/ 6	.500	12/14	.857	-/ 3	-	-	4	-	-	18	-
Totals	200	22/49	.449	23/29	.793	-/15	-	-	14	-	-	67	.335

Disqualified: None.

	1st Half	2nd Half	Final
SMU	33	35	68
Texas Tech	35	32	67

Oklahoma City (97)   Coach: Abe Lemons

	Min.	Total FG/FGA	Pct.	FT/FTA	Pct.	Reb. O/T	A	TO	PF	S	Blk	TP	PPM
GRIFFIN, L.	-	7/11	.636	3/ 5	.600	-/ 3	-	-	4	-	-	17	-
BRADSHAW, L.	-	5/ 9	.556	1/ 2	.500	-/ 8	-	-	2	-	-	11	-
MAGANA, C.	-	3/ 8	.375	0/ 0	.000	-/ 3	-	-	2	-	-	6	-
WHEELER	-	0/ 0	.000	0/ 0	.000	-/ 0	-	-	1	-	-	0	-
LEE, L.	-	5/15	.333	5/ 8	.625	-/11	-	-	3	-	-	15	-
JUBY, T.	-	2/ 2	1.000	2/ 2	1.000	-/ 1	-	-	1	-	-	6	-
JETER, D.	-	2/ 5	.400	0/ 0	.000	-/ 0	-	-	1	-	-	4	-
HOLLOWAY, R.	-	1/ 8	.125	9/10	.900	-/11	-	-	4	-	-	11	-
REED, H.	-	10/14	.714	7/12	.583	-/ 7	-	-	5	-	-	27	-
Totals	200	35/72	.486	27/39	.692	-/44	-	-	23	-	-	97	.485

Memphis State (81)   Coach: Eugene Lambert

	Min.	Total FG/FGA	Pct.	FT/FTA	Pct.	Reb. O/T	A	TO	PF	S	Blk	TP	PPM
SWANDER, B.	-	3/13	.231	2/ 2	1.000	-/ 6	-	-	4	-	-	8	-
DOYLE, N.	-	0/ 2	.000	2/ 4	.500	-/ 0	-	-	1	-	-	2	-
SCOTT, H.	-	7/16	.438	9/11	.818	-/ 7	-	-	5	-	-	23	-
JONES, D.	-	1/ 1	1.000	0/ 0	.000	-/ 1	-	-	3	-	-	2	-
BALLARD, J.	-	1/ 4	.250	3/ 9	.333	-/ 5	-	-	4	-	-	5	-
FORTNER, E.	-	5/12	.417	5/ 8	.625	-/ 7	-	-	1	-	-	15	-
BUTCHER, J.	-	5/11	.455	0/ 3	.000	-/ 3	-	-	1	-	-	10	-
HAYS, M.	-	8/13	.615	0/ 1	.000	-/ 6	-	-	4	-	-	16	-
Totals	200	30/72	.417	21/38	.553	-/35	-	-	23	-	-	81	.405

Disqualified: Oklahoma City—Reed; Memphis State—Scott.

	1st Half	2nd Half	Final
Oklahoma City	33	64	97
Memphis State	41	40	81

FIRST ROUND FAR WEST

Idaho State (66)　Coach: Steve Belko

	Min.	Total FG / FGA	Pct.	FT / FTA	Pct.	Reb. O / T	A	TO	PF	S	Blk	TP	PPM
SIEMEN, G.	-	8/ -	-	0/ 0	.000	-/ -	-	-	4	-	-	16	-
HARRIS, L.	-	8/ -	-	0/ 0	.000	-/ -	-	-	5	-	-	16	-
ALLAIN, J.	-	2/ -	-	7/12	.583	-/ -	-	-	1	-	-	11	-
HICKS, J.	-	0/ -	-	1/ 2	.500	-/ -	-	-	5	-	-	1	-
HORROCKS, B.	-	3/ -	-	4/ 4	1.000	-/ -	-	-	2	-	-	10	-
DETHLEFS, B.	-	3/ -	-	2/ 2	1.000	-/ -	-	-	3	-	-	8	-
EASTERBROOKS, F.	-	1/ -	-	0/ 0	.000	-/ -	-	-	1	-	-	2	-
WELLS, C.	-	0/ -	-	2/ 2	1.000	-/ -	-	-	0	-	-	2	-
Totals	200	25/67	.373	16/22	.727	-/ -	-	-	21	-	-	66	.330

Seattle (68)　Coach: Al Brightman

	Min.	Total FG / FGA	Pct.	FT / FTA	Pct.	Reb. O / T	A	TO	PF	S	Blk	TP	PPM
SANFORD, L.	-	4/ -	-	2/ 2	1.000	-/ -	-	-	1	-	-	10	-
FUHRER, K.	-	2/ -	-	1/ 2	.500	-/ -	-	-	3	-	-	5	-
GODES, B.	-	4/ -	-	3/ 5	.600	-/ -	-	-	2	-	-	11	-
BAUER, C.	-	6/ -	-	8/13	.615	-/ -	-	-	3	-	-	20	-
HARNEY, J.	-	0/ -	-	0/ 1	.000	-/ -	-	-	0	-	-	0	-
JOCKEL	-	0/ -	-	0/ 1	.000	-/ -	-	-	1	-	-	0	-
FRIZZEL, J.	-	0/ -	-	1/ 2	.500	-/ -	-	-	0	-	-	1	-
STRICKLIN, D.	-	3/ -	-	2/ 3	.667	-/ -	-	-	2	-	-	8	-
MARKEY, C.	-	4/ -	-	5/ 6	.833	-/ -	-	-	0	-	-	13	-
Totals	200	23/64	.359	22/35	.629	-/ -	-	-	12	-	-	68	.340

Disqualified: Idaho State—Harris, Hicks.

	1st Half	2nd Half	Final
Idaho State	30	36	66
Seattle	37	31	68

REGIONAL SEMIFINAL EAST

U. Conn. (59)　Coach: Hugh Greer

	Min.	Total FG / FGA	Pct.	FT / FTA	Pct.	Reb. O / T	A	TO	PF	S	Blk	TP	PPM
OSBORN	-	4/14	.286	3/ 4	.750	-/15	2	-	0	-	-	11	-
RUDDY	-	8/23	.348	3/ 5	.600	-/ 9	0	-	1	-	-	19	-
O'CONNOR	-	0/ 1	.000	0/ 0	.000	-/ 1	0	-	1	-	-	0	-
KASPAR, P.	-	1/ 8	.125	2/ 5	.400	-/ 6	3	-	3	-	-	4	-
O'LEARY	-	0/ 1	.000	0/ 0	.000	-/ 2	0	-	1	-	-	0	-
CHEREPY	-	1/ 2	.500	0/ 1	.000	-/ 1	0	-	1	-	-	2	-
QUINN, F.	-	6/15	.400	4/ 5	.800	-/ 5	3	-	4	-	-	16	-
BUSHWELL, R.	-	2/14	.143	1/ 3	.333	-/ 7	1	-	2	-	-	5	-
BURNS	-	1/ 5	.200	0/ 1	.000	-/ 0	1	-	0	-	-	2	-
Totals	200	23/83	.277	13/24	.542	-/46	10	-	13	-	-	59	.295

Temple (65)　Coach: Harry Litwack

	Min.	Total FG / FGA	Pct.	FT / FTA	Pct.	Reb. O / T	A	TO	PF	S	Blk	TP	PPM
FLEMING, D.	-	0/ 4	.000	0/ 1	.000	-/ 9	0	-	2	-	-	0	-
REINFELD, H.	-	1/ 7	.143	0/ 1	.000	-/ 6	0	-	1	-	-	2	-
NORMAN, J.	-	2/ 6	.333	2/ 4	.500	-/10	1	-	5	-	-	6	-
COHEN, F.	-	5/21	.238	0/ 1	.000	-/34	3	-	3	-	-	10	-
VAN PATTON, T.	-	0/ 1	.000	0/ 0	.000	-/ 3	0	-	0	-	-	0	-
RODGERS, G.	-	1/15	.067	5/ 7	.714	-/ 5	13	-	3	-	-	7	-
LEAR, H.	-	18/27	.667	4/ 5	.800	-/ 9	1	-	2	-	-	40	-
Totals	200	27/81	.333	11/19	.579	-/76	18	-	16	-	-	65	.325

Disqualified: Temple—Norman.

	1st Half	2nd Half	Final
U. Conn.	27	32	59
Temple	38	27	65

Dartmouth (58)　Coach: Doggie Julian

	Min.	Total FG / FGA	Pct.	FT / FTA	Pct.	Reb. O / T	A	TO	PF	S	Blk	TP	PPM
JUDSON, R.	-	0/ 7	.000	6/ 6	1.000	-/ 5	2	-	2	-	-	6	-
CARRUTHERS, D.	-	7/19	.368	0/ 0	.000	-/ 3	2	-	2	-	-	14	-
DONOHOE, T.	-	2/ 5	.400	3/ 5	.600	-/ 5	1	-	3	-	-	7	-
ERWIN	-	0/ 1	.000	0/ 0	.000	-/ 1	0	-	0	-	-	0	-
FRASER	-	0/ 0	.000	0/ 0	.000	-/ 1	0	-	0	-	-	0	-
FRANCIS, J.	-	7/10	.700	5/ 6	.833	-/11	1	-	2	-	-	19	-
DOUGLAS	-	0/ 0	.000	0/ 0	.000	-/ 0	0	-	0	-	-	0	-
JULIAN	-	1/ 6	.167	0/ 0	.000	-/ 3	5	-	1	-	-	2	-
BOOTH	-	3/ 5	.600	0/ 0	.000	-/ 5	2	-	3	-	-	6	-
BLADES, L.	-	1/ 2	.500	0/ 1	.000	-/ 0	0	-	2	-	-	2	-
MARKMAN	-	0/ 0	.000	2/ 2	1.000	-/ 1	0	-	1	-	-	2	-
JONES	-	0/ 0	.000	0/ 0	.000	-/ 0	0	-	0	-	-	0	-
Totals	200	21/55	.382	16/20	.800	-/35	13	-	16	-	-	58	.290

Canisius (66)　Coach: Joseph Curran

	Min.	Total FG / FGA	Pct.	FT / FTA	Pct.	Reb. O / T	A	TO	PF	S	Blk	TP	PPM
KELLY, R.	-	6/10	.600	0/ 0	.000	-/ 7	2	-	3	-	-	12	-
NOWAK, H.	-	9/15	.600	11/15	.733	-/16	3	-	2	-	-	29	-
BRITZ, G.	-	0/ 0	.000	0/ 0	.000	-/ 0	0	-	0	-	-	0	-
COOGAN, J.	-	0/ 0	.000	0/ 0	.000	-/ 0	0	-	1	-	-	0	-
BARTKOWSKI, E.	-	0/ 0	.000	0/ 0	.000	-/ 0	0	-	1	-	-	0	-
LEONE, J.	-	2/ 7	.286	0/ 1	.000	-/ 4	0	-	4	-	-	4	-
MCCARTHY, JOHN	-	0/ 1	.000	0/ 0	.000	-/ 0	0	-	0	-	-	0	-
MCCARTHY, JAMES	-	2/18	.111	5/ 7	.714	-/ 5	7	-	0	-	-	9	-
CORCORAN, F.	-	4/10	.400	0/ 2	.000	-/ 5	0	-	1	-	-	8	-
MCCARTHY, J.	-	0/ 0	.000	0/ 0	.000	-/ 0	0	-	0	-	-	0	-
MARKEY, D.	-	2/10	.200	0/ 0	.000	-/ 5	2	-	1	-	-	4	-
Totals	200	25/71	.352	16/25	.640	-/42	14	-	12	-	-	66	.330

Disqualified: None.

	1st Half	2nd Half	Final
Dartmouth	30	28	58
Canisius	33	33	66

REGIONAL SEMIFINAL MIDWEST

Iowa (97)   Coach: Bucky O'Connor

	Min.	Total FG/FGA	Pct.	FT/FTA	Pct.	Reb. O/T	A	TO	PF	S	Blk	TP	PPM
CAIN, C.	-	8/25	.320	12/13	.923	-/14	-	-	3	-	-	28	-
SCHOOF, B.	-	5/13	.385	5/8	.625	-/11	-	-	3	-	-	15	-
LOGAN, B.	-	6/21	.286	5/8	.625	-/11	-	-	2	-	-	17	-
SEABERG, B.	-	4/12	.333	1/1	1.000	-/7	-	-	5	-	-	9	-
SCHEUERMAN, M.	-	6/10	.600	2/3	.667	-/5	-	-	5	-	-	14	-
GEORGE, B.	-	0/4	.000	3/8	.375	-/3	-	-	4	-	-	3	-
HAWTHORNE, L.	-	0/7	.000	4/4	1.000	-/0	-	-	4	-	-	4	-
MARTEL, A.	-	1/4	.250	0/2	.000	-/4	-	-	3	-	-	2	-
SEBOLT, F.	-	0/1	.000	0/1	.000	-/1	-	-	3	-	-	0	-
PAUL, N.	-	1/1	1.000	1/2	.500	-/1	-	-	0	-	-	3	-
MCCONNELL, J.	-	0/2	.000	0/0	.000	-/1	-	-	2	-	-	0	-
SCHROEDER, G.	-	0/0	.000	2/2	1.000	-/2	-	-	1	-	-	2	-
Totals	200	31/100	.310	35/52	.673	-/60	-	-	35	-	-	97	.485

Morehead State (83)   Coach: Robert Laughlin

	Min.	Total FG/FGA	Pct.	FT/FTA	Pct.	Reb. O/T	A	TO	PF	S	Blk	TP	PPM
KELEHER, D.	-	0/4	.000	3/4	.750	-/3	-	-	5	-	-	3	-
HAMILTON, S.	-	7/18	.389	5/6	.833	-/16	-	-	5	-	-	19	-
RICHARDS, B.	-	0/2	.000	0/0	.000	-/1	-	-	2	-	-	0	-
JEWELL, J.	-	0/2	.000	2/3	.667	-/4	-	-	1	-	-	2	-
THOMPSON, K.	-	1/2	.500	2/3	.667	-/3	-	-	1	-	-	4	-
SWARTZ, D.	-	8/23	.348	4/6	.667	-/12	-	-	5	-	-	20	-
SHIMFESSEL, B.	-	1/4	.250	1/3	.333	-/2	-	-	5	-	-	3	-
GAUNCE, D.	-	5/14	.357	14/24	.583	-/8	-	-	3	-	-	24	-
TOLLE, H.	-	2/8	.250	2/4	.500	-/4	-	-	4	-	-	6	-
CARROLL, G.	-	1/3	.333	0/0	.000	-/1	-	-	2	-	-	2	-
Totals	200	25/80	.313	33/53	.623	-/54	-	-	33	-	-	83	.415

Disqualified: Iowa—Seaberg, Scheuerman; Morehead State—Keleher, Hamilton, Shimfessel, Swartz.

	1st Half	2nd Half	Final
Iowa	54	43	97
Morehead State	35	48	83

Kentucky (84)   Coach: Adolph Rupp

	Min.	Total FG/FGA	Pct.	FT/FTA	Pct.	Reb. O/T	A	TO	PF	S	Blk	TP	PPM
BIRD, J.	-	5/-	-	0/2	.000	-/-	-	-	5	-	-	10	-
GRAWEMEYER, P.	-	3/-	-	1/3	.333	-/-	-	-	4	-	-	7	-
BURROW, B.	-	14/-	-	5/6	.833	-/-	-	-	5	-	-	33	-
BECK, E.	-	1/-	-	0/0	.000	-/-	-	-	0	-	-	2	-
CALVERT, G.	-	5/-	-	4/6	.667	-/-	-	-	1	-	-	14	-
HATTON, V.	-	4/-	-	2/2	1.000	-/-	-	-	2	-	-	10	-
BREWER, J.	-	1/-	-	0/0	.000	-/-	-	-	2	-	-	2	-
JOHNSON, P.	-	0/-	-	2/2	1.000	-/-	-	-	1	-	-	2	-
CASSADY, B.	-	1/-	-	1/4	.250	-/-	-	-	2	-	-	3	-
MILLS, R.	-	0/-	-	1/2	.500	-/-	-	-	1	-	-	1	-
Totals	200	34/-	-	16/27	.593	-/-	-	-	23	-	-	84	.420

Wayne State (64)   Coach: Joel Mason

	Min.	Total FG/FGA	Pct.	FT/FTA	Pct.	Reb. O/T	A	TO	PF	S	Blk	TP	PPM
KELLER	-	5/-	-	3/5	.600	-/-	-	-	2	-	-	13	-
DUNCAN	-	4/-	-	1/3	.333	-/-	-	-	0	-	-	9	-
KENDRICK, B.	-	2/-	-	10/18	.556	-/-	-	-	3	-	-	14	-
GREENBERG	-	0/-	-	0/0	.000	-/-	-	-	0	-	-	0	-
BROWN, G.	-	5/-	-	4/6	.667	-/-	-	-	5	-	-	14	-
LONDON	-	2/-	-	0/0	.000	-/-	-	-	0	-	-	4	-
STRAUGHN, C.	-	3/-	-	0/5	.000	-/-	-	-	3	-	-	6	-
HARVEY	-	0/-	-	0/0	.000	-/-	-	-	0	-	-	0	-
POTTER	-	2/-	-	0/0	.000	-/-	-	-	1	-	-	4	-
HALVERSON	-	0/-	-	0/0	.000	-/-	-	-	2	-	-	0	-
Totals	200	23/-	-	18/37	.486	-/-	-	-	16	-	-	64	.320

Disqualified: Kentucky—Bird, Burrow; Wayne State—Brown.

	1st Half	2nd Half	Final
Kentucky	32	52	84
Wayne State	34	30	64

REGIONAL SEMIFINAL WEST

Houston (74)   Coach: Alden Pasche

	Min.	Total FG/FGA	Pct.	FT/FTA	Pct.	Reb. O/T	A	TO	PF	S	Blk	TP	PPM
EVANS	-	4/9	.444	2/2	1.000	3/3	-	-	1	-	-	10	-
FOSTER	-	3/7	.429	2/5	.400	3/5	-	-	2	-	-	8	-
HELMS	-	3/18	.167	4/5	.800	5/10	-	-	5	-	-	10	-
TUCKER	-	3/7	.429	0/0	.000	3/8	-	-	3	-	-	6	-
BOLDEBUCK	-	4/15	.267	3/5	.600	2/7	-	-	5	-	-	11	-
BYRD	-	0/0	.000	0/0	.000	0/1	-	-	0	-	-	0	-
DOTSON	-	5/14	.357	0/1	.000	1/6	-	-	4	-	-	10	-
LOPEZ	-	1/1	1.000	0/0	.000	0/0	-	-	2	-	-	2	-
MCELWEEN	-	3/7	.429	0/3	.000	0/2	-	-	3	-	-	6	-
SELLS	-	2/4	.500	7/11	.636	2/5	-	-	2	-	-	11	-
Totals	200	28/82	.341	18/32	.563	19/47	-	-	27	-	-	74	.370

SMU (89)   Coach: E.O. "Doc" Hayes

	Min.	Total FG/FGA	Pct.	FT/FTA	Pct.	Reb. O/T	A	TO	PF	S	Blk	TP	PPM
SHOWALTER, L.	-	4/8	.500	1/4	.250	1/9	-	-	4	-	-	9	-
HERRSCHER, R.	-	0/3	.000	8/10	.800	1/3	-	-	0	-	-	8	-
KROG, J.	-	0/7	.000	8/10	.800	3/9	-	-	3	-	-	8	-
MILLS, B.	-	3/10	.300	5/6	.833	2/7	-	-	3	-	-	11	-
MORRIS, R.	-	4/10	.400	5/6	.833	1/6	-	-	2	-	-	13	-
MILLER, T.	-	3/3	1.000	1/2	.500	1/2	-	-	3	-	-	7	-
KREBS, J.	-	11/28	.393	5/7	.714	5/14	-	-	3	-	-	27	-
O'KELLEY, H.	-	0/1	.000	0/0	.000	0/0	-	-	1	-	-	0	-
SCHARFFENBERGER	-	2/2	1.000	0/0	.000	1/1	-	-	0	-	-	4	-
MCGREGOR, B.	-	1/1	1.000	0/1	.000	0/2	-	-	1	-	-	2	-
ELDRIDGE, B.	-	0/1	.000	0/0	.000	0/1	-	-	1	-	-	0	-
LEE, G.	-	0/0	.000	0/0	.000	0/0	-	-	0	-	-	0	-
Totals	200	28/74	.378	33/46	.717	15/54	-	-	21	-	-	89	.445

Team Rebounds: SMU 5; Houston 4. Disqualified: Houston—Helms, Boldebuck.

	1st Half	2nd Half	Final
Houston	31	43	74
SMU	47	42	89

Kansas State (93) Coach: Tex Winter

	Min.	Total FG / FGA	Pct.	FT / FTA	Pct.	Reb. O / T	A	TO	PF	S	Blk	TP	PPM
ABBOTT, J.	-	1/ 4	.250	0/ 0	.000	2/ 2	-	-	5	-	-	2	-
FISCHER, L.	-	0/ 1	.000	0/ 0	.000	0/ 1	-	-	1	-	-	0	-
POWELL, L.	-	0/ 2	.000	1/ 3	.333	0/ 2	-	-	1	-	-	1	-
STONE, F.	-	6/15	.400	2/ 2	1.000	5/ 7	-	-	1	-	-	14	-
PARR, J.	-	3/12	.250	13/19	.684	6/17	-	-	4	-	-	19	-
KIDDOO, C.	-	3/ 4	.750	3/ 4	.750	0/ 0	-	-	2	-	-	9	-
SCHNEIDER, F.	-	4/13	.308	2/ 2	1.000	4/ 8	-	-	5	-	-	10	-
VICENS, J.	-	4/10	.400	7/ 8	.875	1/ 3	-	-	5	-	-	15	-
WALLACE, H.	-	9/18	.500	5/ 6	.833	1/ 5	-	-	4	-	-	23	-
Totals	200	30/79	.380	33/44	.750	19/45	-	-	28	-	-	93	.465

Oklahoma City (97) Coach: Abe Lemons

	Min.	Total FG / FGA	Pct.	FT / FTA	Pct.	Reb. O / T	A	TO	PF	S	Blk	TP	PPM
GRIFFIN, L.	-	6/14	.429	8/ 9	.889	4/ 5	-	-	2	-	-	20	-
BRADSHAW, L.	-	3/ 7	.429	1/ 3	.333	1/ 9	-	-	5	-	-	7	-
MAGANA, C.	-	5/ 9	.556	6/ 6	1.000	2/ 6	-	-	1	-	-	16	-
LEE, L.	-	5/13	.385	10/15	.667	3/ 9	-	-	2	-	-	20	-
JUBY, T.	-	1/ 2	.500	0/ 1	.000	0/ 0	-	-	2	-	-	2	-
JETER, D.	-	0/ 0	.000	0/ 0	.000	0/ 1	-	-	0	-	-	0	-
HOLLOWAY, R.	-	5/ 9	.556	7/ 9	.778	2/ 7	-	-	5	-	-	17	-
REED, H.	-	6/11	.545	3/ 4	.750	2/ 4	-	-	5	-	-	15	-
DUNBAR, F.	-	0/ 0	.000	0/ 1	.000	0/ 1	-	-	1	-	-	0	-
Totals	200	31/65	.477	35/48	.729	14/42	-	-	23	-	-	97	.485

Team Rebounds: Oklahoma City 1; Kansas State 3. Disqualified: Oklahoma City—Holloway, Reed, Bradshaw; Kansas State—Abbott, Schneider, Vicens.

	1st Half	2nd Half	Final
Kansas State	43	50	93
Oklahoma City	47	50	97

REGIONAL SEMIFINAL FAR WEST

Utah (81) Coach: Jack Gardner

	Min.	Total FG / FGA	Pct.	FT / FTA	Pct.	Reb. O / T	A	TO	PF	S	Blk	TP	PPM
BUCKWALTER	-	3/ -	-	4/ -	-	-/ -	-	-	1	-	-	10	-
BERGEN	-	6/ -	-	4/ -	-	-/ -	-	-	4	-	-	16	-
KONCAR	-	0/ -	-	0/ -	-	-/ -	-	-	1	-	-	0	-
EILER	-	0/ -	-	0/ -	-	-/ -	-	-	1	-	-	0	-
BUNTE, A.	-	8/ -	-	8/ -	-	-/ -	-	-	3	-	-	24	-
MCCLEARY	-	1/ -	-	2/ -	-	-/ -	-	-	3	-	-	4	-
GAYTHWAITE	-	0/ -	-	0/ -	-	-/ -	-	-	0	-	-	0	-
HALE	-	3/ -	-	4/ -	-	-/ -	-	-	3	-	-	10	-
JENSEN, C.	-	6/ -	-	0/ -	-	-/ -	-	-	3	-	-	12	-
CROWE	-	2/ -	-	1/ -	-	-/ -	-	-	1	-	-	5	-
PASTRELL	-	0/ -	-	0/ -	-	-/ -	-	-	0	-	-	0	-
Totals	200	29/ -	-	23/28	.821	-/ -	-	-	20	-	-	81	.405

Seattle (72) Coach: Al Brightman

	Min.	Total FG / FGA	Pct.	FT / FTA	Pct.	Reb. O / T	A	TO	PF	S	Blk	TP	PPM
GODES, B.	-	4/ -	-	1/ -	-	-/ -	-	-	4	-	-	9	-
SANFORD, L.	-	1/ -	-	1/ -	-	-/ -	-	-	4	-	-	3	-
GOCKEL	-	0/ -	-	2/ -	-	-/ -	-	-	0	-	-	2	-
RAJCICH, B.	-	0/ -	-	0/ -	-	-/ -	-	-	2	-	-	0	-
STRICKLIN, D.	-	7/ -	-	2/ -	-	-/ -	-	-	2	-	-	16	-
FUHRER, K.	-	5/ -	-	5/ -	-	-/ -	-	-	3	-	-	15	-
MARKEY, C.	-	1/ -	-	2/ -	-	-/ -	-	-	0	-	-	4	-
BAUER, C.	-	3/ -	-	7/ -	-	-/ -	-	-	2	-	-	13	-
FRIZZELL, J.	-	5/ -	-	0/ -	-	-/ -	-	-	2	-	-	10	-
COX	-	0/ -	-	0/ -	-	-/ -	-	-	1	-	-	0	-
HARNEY, J.	-	0/ -	-	0/ -	-	-/ -	-	-	0	-	-	0	-
Totals	200	26/ -	-	20/33	.606	-/ -	-	-	20	-	-	72	.360

Disqualified: None

	1st Half	2nd Half	Final
Utah	44	37	81
Seattle	38	34	72

San Francisco (72) Coach: Phil Woolpert

	Min.	Total FG / FGA	Pct.	FT / FTA	Pct.	Reb. O / T	A	TO	PF	S	Blk	TP	PPM
BOLDT, C.	-	0/ 4	.000	0/ 0	.000	-/ 3	-	-	4	-	-	0	-
FARMER, M.	-	4/13	.308	7/ 8	.875	-/15	-	-	2	-	-	15	-
RUSSELL, B.	-	9/15	.600	3/ 4	.750	-/23	-	-	4	-	-	21	-
PERRY, H.	-	4/17	.235	2/ 2	1.000	-/ 0	-	-	2	-	-	10	-
BROWN, G.	-	9/16	.563	5/11	.455	-/ 5	-	-	3	-	-	23	-
PREASEAU, M.	-	1/ 6	.167	1/ 4	.250	-/ 1	-	-	5	-	-	3	-
BAXTER, W.	-	0/ 0	.000	0/ 0	.000	-/ 0	-	-	1	-	-	0	-
Totals	200	27/71	.380	18/29	.621	-/47	-	-	21	-	-	72	.360

UCLA (61) Coach: John Wooden

	Min.	Total FG / FGA	Pct.	FT / FTA	Pct.	Reb. O / T	A	TO	PF	S	Blk	TP	PPM
HERRING, A.	-	2/ 5	.400	3/ 6	.500	-/11	-	-	4	-	-	7	-
BURKE, C.	-	0/ 5	.000	2/ 2	1.000	-/ 3	-	-	1	-	-	2	-
NAULLS, W.	-	6/18	.333	4/ 4	1.000	-/ 8	-	-	4	-	-	16	-
TAFT, M.	-	6/23	.261	4/ 8	.500	-/12	-	-	2	-	-	16	-
BAMTON, D.	-	3/10	.300	7/ 7	1.000	-/ 3	-	-	2	-	-	13	-
HALSTEN, J.	-	1/ 3	.333	4/ 6	.667	-/ 2	-	-	1	-	-	6	-
ADAMS, C.	-	0/ 0	.000	0/ 0	.000	-/ 0	-	-	1	-	-	0	-
ARNOLD, J.	-	0/ 1	.000	0/ 0	.000	-/ 0	-	-	0	-	-	0	-
JOHNSON, N.	-	0/ 1	.000	1/ 2	.500	-/ 1	-	-	1	-	-	1	-
HUTCHINS, A.	-	0/ 0	.000	0/ 0	.000	-/ 0	-	-	0	-	-	0	-
Totals	200	18/66	.273	25/35	.714	-/40	-	-	16	-	-	61	.305

Disqualified: San Francisco—Preaseau.

	1st Half	2nd Half	Final
San Francisco	39	33	72
UCLA	21	40	61

REGIONAL FINAL EAST

Temple (60) Coach: Harry Litwack

	Min.	Total FG/FGA	Pct.	FT/FTA	Pct.	Reb. O/T	A	TO	PF	S	Blk	TP	PPM
REINFELD, H.	-	0/7	.000	1/2	.500	-/7	1	-	3	-	-	1	-
NORMAN, J.	-	3/5	.600	7/8	.875	-/10	2	-	4	-	-	13	-
FLEMING, D.	-	2/8	.250	0/0	.000	-/6	0	-	0	-	-	4	-
COHEN, F.	-	2/3	.667	0/0	.000	-/5	1	-	4	-	-	4	-
VAN PATTON, T.	-	1/5	.200	0/1	.000	-/5	0	-	3	-	-	2	-
LEAR, H.	-	4/14	.286	6/6	1.000	-/3	3	-	2	-	-	14	-
RODGERS, G.	-	9/22	.409	4/8	.500	-/8	4	-	3	-	-	22	-
Totals	200	21/64	.328	18/25	.720	-/44	11	-	19	-	-	60	.300

Canisius (58) Coach: Joseph Curran

	Min.	Total FG/FGA	Pct.	FT/FTA	Pct.	Reb. O/T	A	TO	PF	S	Blk	TP	PPM
KELLY, R.	-	5/11	.455	0/0	.000	-/8	2	-	2	-	-	10	
NOWAK, H.	-	3/11	.273	3/9	.333	-/9	4	-	2	-	-	9	
CORCORAN, F.	-	0/1	.000	0/0	.000	-/0	0	-	1	-	-	0	
LEONE, J.	-	5/10	.500	2/5	.400	-/9	0	-	3	-	-	12	
MARKEY, D.	-	7/7	1.000	3/5	.600	-/5	5	-	4	-	-	17	
MCCARTHY, JOHN	-	2/12	.167	6/9	.667	-/9	3	-	2	-	-	10	
Totals	200	22/52	.423	14/28	.500	-/40	14	-	14	-	-	58	.290

Disqualified: None.

	1st Half	2nd Half	Final
Temple	29	31	60
Canisius	30	28	58

REGIONAL FINAL MIDWEST

Iowa (89) Coach: Bucky O'Connor

	Min.	Total FG/FGA	Pct.	FT/FTA	Pct.	Reb. O/T	A	TO	PF	S	Blk	TP	PPM
CAIN, C.	-	12/21	.571	10/11	.909	-/9	-	-	2	-	-	34	-
SCHOOF, B.	-	2/6	.333	0/0	.000	-/3	-	-	3	-	-	4	-
MCCONNELL, J.	-	0/1	.000	0/0	.000	-/1	-	-	2	-	-	0	-
SEBOLT, F.	-	0/0	.000	0/0	.000	-/0	-	-	0	-	-	0	-
LOGAN, B.	-	6/18	.333	2/6	.333	-/13	-	-	3	-	-	14	-
SEABERG, B.	-	2/12	.167	5/5	1.000	-/11	-	-	1	-	-	9	-
SCHEUERMAN, M.	-	8/13	.615	6/9	.667	-/5	-	-	4	-	-	22	-
MARTEL, A.	-	0/0	.000	0/0	.000	-/0	-	-	0	-	-	0	-
HAWTHORNE, L.	-	0/0	.000	0/0	.000	-/0	-	-	0	-	-	0	-
PAUL, N.	-	0/2	.000	0/0	.000	-/2	-	-	0	-	-	0	-
GEORGE, B.	-	3/10	.300	0/1	.000	-/11	-	-	3	-	-	6	-
Totals	200	33/83	.398	23/32	.719	-/55	-	-	18	-	-	89	.445

Kentucky (77) Coach: Adolph Rupp

	Min.	Total FG/FGA	Pct.	FT/FTA	Pct.	Reb. O/T	A	TO	PF	S	Blk	TP	PPM
BIRD, J.	-	9/21	.429	5/9	.556	-/24	-	-	1	-	-	23	-
GRAWEMEYER, P.	-	2/10	.200	1/1	1.000	-/7	-	-	4	-	-	5	-
JOHNSON, P.	-	1/9	.111	1/3	.333	-/6	-	-	1	-	-	3	-
COLLINSWORTH, L.	-	0/0	.000	0/0	.000	-/0	-	-	1	-	-	0	-
BURROW, B.	-	13/23	.565	5/8	.625	-/12	-	-	3	-	-	31	-
CALVERT, G.	-	3/10	.300	1/1	1.000	-/6	-	-	3	-	-	7	-
HATTON, V.	-	2/4	.500	0/3	.000	-/1	-	-	2	-	-	4	-
BREWER, J.	-	2/5	.400	0/0	.000	-/1	-	-	4	-	-	4	-
Totals	200	32/82	.390	13/25	.520	-/57	-	-	19	-	-	77	.385

Disqualified: None.

	1st Half	2nd Half	Final
Iowa	49	40	89
Kentucky	38	39	77

REGIONAL FINAL WEST

SMU (84) Coach: E.O. "Doc" Hayes

	Min.	Total FG/FGA	Pct.	FT/FTA	Pct.	Reb. O/T	A	TO	PF	S	Blk	TP	PPM
SHOWALTER, L.	-	8/15	.533	4/4	1.000	-/6	-	-	1	-	-	20	-
HERRSCHER, R.	-	0/0	.000	2/2	1.000	-/0	-	-	0	-	-	2	-
KROG, J.	-	6/16	.375	10/13	.769	-/12	-	-	2	-	-	22	-
MILLS, B.	-	4/6	.667	6/7	.857	-/2	-	-	2	-	-	14	-
MORRIS, R.	-	4/5	.800	2/3	.667	-/5	-	-	3	-	-	10	-
MILLER, T.	-	1/1	1.000	6/8	.750	-/3	-	-	2	-	-	8	-
KREBS, J.	-	2/10	.200	3/4	.750	-/8	-	-	4	-	-	7	-
O'KELLEY, H.	-	0/0	.000	0/0	.000	-/1	-	-	1	-	-	0	-
SCHARFFENBERGER	-	0/1	.000	0/1	.000	-/1	-	-	1	-	-	0	-
MCGREGOR, B.	-	0/0	.000	0/0	.000	-/0	-	-	1	-	-	0	-
ELDRIDGE, B.	-	0/0	.000	0/0	.000	-/0	-	-	0	-	-	0	-
LEE, G.	-	0/1	.000	1/2	.500	-/0	-	-	0	-	-	1	-
Totals	200	25/56	.446	34/44	.773	-/39	-	-	17	-	-	84	.420

Oklahoma City (63) Coach: Abe Lemons

	Min.	Total FG/FGA	Pct.	FT/FTA	Pct.	Reb. O/T	A	TO	PF	S	Blk	TP	PPM
GRIFFIN, L.	-	7/14	.500	0/1	.000	-/3	-	-	3	-	-	14	-
BRADSHAW, L.	-	4/8	.500	0/0	.000	-/5	-	-	2	-	-	8	-
MAGANA, C.	-	0/1	.000	0/0	.000	-/7	-	-	3	-	-	0	-
WHEELER	-	1/3	.333	0/0	.000	-/0	-	-	2	-	-	2	-
LEE, L.	-	2/11	.182	4/7	.571	-/4	-	-	3	-	-	8	-
JUBY, T.	-	0/1	.000	0/0	.000	-/2	-	-	1	-	-	0	-
JETER, D.	-	0/4	.000	0/3	.000	-/2	-	-	3	-	-	0	-
HOLLOWAY, R.	-	3/7	.429	0/0	.000	-/5	-	-	1	-	-	6	-
REED, H.	-	7/20	.350	7/8	.875	-/9	-	-	4	-	-	21	-
DUNBAR, F.	-	0/2	.000	0/0	.000	-/0	-	-	2	-	-	0	-
GILBERT	-	1/1	1.000	2/2	1.000	-/1	-	-	0	-	-	4	-
Totals	200	25/72	.347	13/21	.619	-/38	-	-	24	-	-	63	.315

Team Rebounds: SMU 9; Oklahoma City 1. Disqualified: None.

	1st Half	2nd Half	Final
SMU	46	38	84
Oklahoma City	34	29	63

REGIONAL FINAL FAR WEST

Utah (77) Coach: Jack Gardner

	Min.	Total FG/FGA	Pct.	FT/FTA	Pct.	Reb. O/T	A	TO	PF	S	Blk	TP	PPM
McCLEARY	-	2/ -	-	0/ -	-	-/ -	-	-	3	-	-	4	-
BERGEN	-	2/ -	-	2/ -	-	-/ -	-	-	3	-	-	6	-
PASTRELL	-	0/ -	-	0/ -	-	-/ -	-	-	0	-	-	0	-
EILER	-	0/ -	-	0/ -	-	-/ -	-	-	0	-	-	0	-
MIRHNA	-	0/ -	-	0/ -	-	-/ -	-	-	0	-	-	0	-
BUNTE, A.	-	8/ -	-	7/ -	-	-/ -	-	-	2	-	-	23	-
BUCKWALTER	-	2/ -	-	7/ -	-	-/ -	-	-	4	-	-	11	-
JENSON, C.	-	9/ -	-	3/ -	-	-/ -	-	-	3	-	-	21	-
HALE	-	1/ -	-	6/ -	-	-/ -	-	-	3	-	-	8	-
CROWE	-	1/ -	-	0/ -	-	-/ -	-	-	2	-	-	2	-
GAYTHWAITE	-	1/ -	-	0/ -	-	-/ -	-	-	1	-	-	2	-
Totals	200	26/ -	-	25/35	.714	-/ -	-	-	21	-	-	77	.385

San Francisco (92) Coach: Phil Woolpert

	Min.	Total FG/FGA	Pct.	FT/FTA	Pct.	Reb. O/T	A	TO	PF	S	Blk	TP	PPM
BOLDT, C.	-	6/ -	-	1/ -	-	-/ -	-	-	3	-	-	13	-
FARMER, M.	-	5/ -	-	4/ -	-	-/ -	-	-	3	-	-	14	-
KING, J.	-	0/ -	-	0/ -	-	-/ -	-	-	0	-	-	0	-
PREASEAU, M.	-	3/ -	-	8/ -	-	-/ -	-	-	3	-	-	14	-
RUSSELL, B.	-	12/ -	-	3/ -	-	-/ -	-	-	4	-	-	27	-
NELSON, T.	-	0/ -	-	0/ -	-	-/ -	-	-	1	-	-	0	-
BROWN, G.	-	7/ -	-	4/ -	-	-/ -	-	-	3	-	-	18	-
PERRY, H.	-	2/ -	-	0/ -	-	-/ -	-	-	0	-	-	4	-
BAXTER, W.	-	1/ -	-	0/ -	-	-/ -	-	-	2	-	-	2	-
BUSH, B.	-	0/ -	-	0/ -	-	-/ -	-	-	1	-	-	0	-
BACHIOS, S.	-	0/ -	-	0/ -	-	-/ -	-	-	0	-	-	0	-
PAYNE, H.	-	0/ -	-	0/ -	-	-/ -	-	-	0	-	-	0	-
Totals	200	36/ -	-	20/32	.625	-/ -	-	-	20	-	-	92	.460

Disqualified: None.

	1st Half	2nd Half	Final
Utah	41	36	77
San Francisco	44	48	92

FINAL FOUR

Temple (76) Coach: Harry Litwack

	Min.	Total FG/FGA	Pct.	FT/FTA	Pct.	Reb. O/T	A	TO	PF	S	Blk	TP	PPM
NORMAN, J.	-	1/8	.125	0/2	.000	-/17	-	-	4	-	-	2	-
REINFELD, H.	-	1/6	.167	0/0	.000	-/2	-	-	2	-	-	2	-
FLEMING, D.	-	2/4	.500	0/0	.000	-/2	-	-	1	-	-	4	-
COHEN, F.	-	3/7	.429	0/1	.000	-/12	-	-	5	-	-	6	-
VAN PATTON, T.	-	1/4	.250	0/1	.000	-/5	-	-	4	-	-	2	-
LEAR, H.	-	15/30	.500	2/4	.500	-/2	-	-	4	-	-	32	-
RODGERS, G.	-	12/29	.414	4/9	.444	-/7	-	-	3	-	-	28	-
Totals	200	35/88	.398	6/17	.353	-/47	-	-	23	-	-	76	.380

Iowa (83) Coach: Bucky O'Connor

	Min.	Total FG/FGA	Pct.	FT/FTA	Pct.	Reb. O/T	A	TO	PF	S	Blk	TP	PPM
CAIN, C.	-	8/20	.400	4/9	.444	-/15	-	-	1	-	-	20	-
SCHOOF, B.	-	5/15	.333	8/9	.889	-/18	-	-	4	-	-	18	-
LOGAN, B.	-	13/21	.619	10/15	.667	-/8	-	-	2	-	-	36	-
SEABERG, B.	-	1/7	.143	0/0	.000	-/6	-	-	4	-	-	2	-
SCHEUERMAN, M.	-	1/3	.333	2/2	1.000	-/2	-	-	4	-	-	4	-
MARTEL, A.	-	1/4	.250	1/3	.333	-/2	-	-	0	-	-	3	-
Totals	200	29/70	.414	25/38	.658	-/51	-	-	15	-	-	83	.415

Disqualified: Temple—Cohen.

	1st Half	2nd Half	Final
Temple	36	40	76
Iowa	39	44	83

SMU (68) Coach: E.O. "Doc" Hayes

	Min.	Total FG/FGA	Pct.	FT/FTA	Pct.	Reb. O/T	A	TO	PF	S	Blk	TP	PPM
SHOWALTER, L.	-	4/ -	-	0/0	.000	-/ -	-	-	1	-	-	8	-
KROG, J.	-	3/ -	-	0/1	.000	-/ -	-	-	3	-	-	6	-
McGREGOR, B.	-	1/ -	-	1/2	.500	-/ -	-	-	0	-	-	3	-
KREBS, J.	-	10/ -	-	4/7	.571	-/ -	-	-	1	-	-	24	-
MILLER, T.	-	1/ -	-	0/0	.000	-/ -	-	-	2	-	-	2	-
MILLS, B.	-	1/ -	-	9/12	.750	-/ -	-	-	0	-	-	11	-
MORRIS, R.	-	4/ -	-	2/3	.667	-/ -	-	-	4	-	-	10	-
HERRSCHER, R.	-	1/ -	-	2/3	.667	-/ -	-	-	1	-	-	4	-
Totals	200	25/ -	-	18/28	.643	-/39	-	-	12	-	-	68	.340

San Francisco (86) Coach: Phil Woolpert

	Min.	Total FG/FGA	Pct.	FT/FTA	Pct.	Reb. O/T	A	TO	PF	S	Blk	TP	PPM
BOLDT, C.	-	3/ -	-	1/2	.500	-/ -	-	-	3	-	-	7	-
FARMER, M.	-	11/ -	-	4/6	.667	-/10	-	-	4	-	-	26	-
PREASEAU, M.	-	1/ -	-	0/0	.000	-/ -	-	-	2	-	-	2	-
KING, J.	-	0/ -	-	0/0	.000	-/ -	-	-	0	-	-	0	-
RUSSELL, B.	-	8/ -	-	1/2	.500	-/23	-	-	3	-	-	17	-
PERRY, H.	-	6/ -	-	2/3	.667	-/ -	-	-	1	-	-	14	-
BROWN, G.	-	5/ -	-	2/5	.400	-/ -	-	-	1	-	-	12	-
BAXTER, W.	-	4/ -	-	0/0	.000	-/ -	-	-	2	-	-	8	-
BUSH, B.	-	0/ -	-	0/0	.000	-/ -	-	-	0	-	-	0	-
Totals	200	38/82	.463	10/18	.556	-/49	-	-	16	-	-	86	.430

Disqualified: None.

	1st Half	2nd Half	Final
SMU	32	36	68
San Francisco	44	42	86

NATIONAL CHAMPIONSHIP

Iowa (71) Coach: Bucky O'Connor

	Min.	Total FG / FGA	Pct.	FT / FTA	Pct.	Reb. O / T	A	TO	PF	S	Blk	TP	PPM
CAIN, C.	-	7/ -	-	3/ 4	.750	-/12	-	-	1	-	-	17	-
SCHOOF, B.	-	5/ -	-	4/ 4	1.000	-/ -	-	-	3	-	-	14	-
LOGAN, B.	-	5/ -	-	2/ 2	1.000	-/15	-	-	3	-	-	12	-
GEORGE, B.	-	0/ -	-	0/ 0	.000	-/ -	-	-	0	-	-	0	-
SCHEUERMAN, M.	-	4/ -	-	3/ 4	.750	-/ -	-	-	2	-	-	11	-
SEABERG, B.	-	5/ -	-	7/10	.700	-/ -	-	-	1	-	-	17	-
MARTEL, A.	-	0/ -	-	0/ 0	.000	-/ -	-	-	0	-	-	0	-
McCONNELL, J.	-	0/ -	-	0/ 0	.000	-/ -	-	-	0	-	-	0	-
Totals	200	26/80	.325	19/24	.792	-/48	-	-	10	-	-	71	.355

San Francisco (83) Coach: Phil Woolpert

	Min.	Total FG / FGA	Pct.	FT / FTA	Pct.	Reb. O / T	A	TO	PF	S	Blk	TP	PPM
BOLDT, C.	-	7/ -	-	2/ 2	1.000	-/ -	-	-	4	-	-	16	-
FARMER, M.	-	0/ -	-	0/ 0	.000	-/12	-	-	2	-	-	0	-
PREASEAU, M.	-	3/ -	-	1/ 2	.500	-/ -	-	-	3	-	-	7	-
RUSSELL, B.	-	11/24	.458	4/ 5	.800	-/27	-	-	2	-	-	26	-
NELSON, T.	-	0/ -	-	0/ 0	.000	-/ -	-	-	0	-	-	0	-
PERRY, H.	-	6/ -	-	2/ 2	1.000	-/ -	-	-	2	-	-	14	-
BROWN, G.	-	6/ -	-	4/ 4	1.000	-/ -	-	-	0	-	-	16	-
BAXTER, W.	-	2/ -	-	0/ 0	.000	-/ -	-	-	0	-	-	4	-
Totals	200	35/87	.402	13/15	.867	-/60	-	-	13	-	-	83	.415

Disqualified: None.

	1st Half	2nd Half	Final
Iowa	33	38	71
San Francisco	38	45	83

NATIONAL THIRD PLACE

Temple (90) Coach: Harry Litwack

	Min.	Total FG / FGA	Pct.	FT / FTA	Pct.	Reb. O / T	A	TO	PF	S	Blk	TP	PPM
NORMAN, J.	-	8/ -	-	1/ 2	.500	-/ -	-	-	3	-	-	17	-
REINFELD, H.	-	0/ -	-	0/ 0	.000	-/ -	-	-	0	-	-	0	-
FLEMING, D.	-	2/ -	-	1/ 2	.500	-/ -	-	-	1	-	-	5	-
COHEN, F.	-	0/ -	-	0/ 0	.000	-/ -	-	-	1	-	-	0	-
VAN PATTON, T.	-	2/ -	-	2/ 2	1.000	-/ -	-	-	4	-	-	6	-
RODGERS, G.	-	6/ -	-	2/ 2	1.000	-/ -	-	-	4	-	-	14	-
LEAR, H.	-	17/ -	-	14/17	.824	-/ -	-	-	4	-	-	48	-
Totals	200	35/ -	-	20/25	.800	-/ -	-	-	17	-	-	90	.450

SMU (81) Coach: E.O. "Doc" Hayes

	Min.	Total FG / FGA	Pct.	FT / FTA	Pct.	Reb. O / T	A	TO	PF	S	Blk	TP	PPM
KROG, J.	-	4/ -	-	0/ 0	.000	-/ -	-	-	1	-	-	8	-
SHOWALTER, L.	-	4/ -	-	0/ 0	.000	-/ -	-	-	2	-	-	8	-
HERRSCHER, R.	-	2/ -	-	1/ 3	.333	-/ -	-	-	0	-	-	5	-
KREBS, J.	-	9/ -	-	11/12	.917	-/ -	-	-	1	-	-	29	-
MILLER, T.	-	0/ -	-	0/ 0	.000	-/ -	-	-	1	-	-	0	-
MORRIS, R.	-	2/ -	-	8/ 8	1.000	-/ -	-	-	4	-	-	12	-
MILLS, B.	-	6/ -	-	7/ 9	.778	-/ -	-	-	4	-	-	19	-
Totals	200	27/ -	-	27/32	.844	-/ -	-	-	13	-	-	81	.405

Disqualified: None.

	1st Half	2nd Half	Final
Temple	41	49	90
SMU	38	43	81

REGIONAL THIRD PLACE FAR WEST

UCLA (94) Coach: John Wooden

	Min.	Total FG / FGA	Pct.	FT / FTA	Pct.	Reb. O / T	A	TO	PF	S	Blk	TP	PPM
HERRING, A.	-	0/ 6	.000	0/ 0	.000	-/ 5	-	-	5	-	-	0	-
BURKE, C.	-	2/11	.182	1/ 2	.500	-/ 9	-	-	5	-	-	5	-
NAULLS, W.	-	14/28	.500	5/ 6	.833	-/14	-	-	5	-	-	33	-
TAFT, M.	-	5/20	.250	10/16	.625	-/ 9	-	-	4	-	-	20	-
BANTON, D.	-	3/ 5	.600	0/ 0	.000	-/ 6	-	-	4	-	-	6	-
HALSTEN, J.	-	5/10	.500	6/11	.545	-/ 7	-	-	4	-	-	16	-
ADAMS, C.	-	0/ 3	.000	0/ 0	.000	-/ 2	-	-	2	-	-	0	-
ARNOLD, J.	-	1/ 2	.500	0/ 0	.000	-/ 2	-	-	0	-	-	2	-
JOHNSON, N.	-	4/10	.400	4/ 5	.800	-/14	-	-	2	-	-	12	-
HUTCHINS, A.	-	0/ 0	.000	0/ 0	.000	-/ 1	-	-	2	-	-	0	-
EBLEN, B.	-	0/ 3	.000	0/ 0	.000	-/ 3	-	-	3	-	-	0	-
HARRISON, J.	-	0/ 2	.000	0/ 0	.000	-/ 0	-	-	0	-	-	0	-
Totals	200	34/100	.340	26/40	.650	-/72	-	-	36	-	-	94	.470

Seattle (70) Coach: Al Brightman

	Min.	Total FG / FGA	Pct.	FT / FTA	Pct.	Reb. O / T	A	TO	PF	S	Blk	TP	PPM
FRIZZELL, J.	-	8/23	.348	5/12	.417	-/15	-	-	1	-	-	21	-
SANFORD, L.	-	1/11	.091	3/ 6	.500	-/16	-	-	4	-	-	5	-
FUHRER, K.	-	3/ 8	.375	7/14	.500	-/ 9	-	-	4	-	-	13	-
MARKEY, C.	-	1/12	.083	6/ 8	.750	-/ 6	-	-	3	-	-	8	-
HARNEY, J.	-	3/ 9	.333	1/ 4	.250	-/ 4	-	-	4	-	-	7	-
GODES, B.	-	2/ 6	.333	2/ 2	1.000	-/ 4	-	-	4	-	-	6	-
BAUER, C.	-	3/ 9	.333	4/ 5	.800	-/ 2	-	-	4	-	-	10	-
STRICKLIN, D.	-	0/ 0	.000	0/ 0	.000	-/ 0	-	-	0	-	-	0	-
RAJCICH, B.	-	0/ 0	.000	0/ 1	.000	-/ 0	-	-	0	-	-	0	-
Totals	200	21/78	.269	28/52	.538	-/56	-	-	24	-	-	70	.350

Disqualified: UCLA—Herring, Burke, Naulls. Technical fouls: UCLA—Eblen (ejected); Seattle—Frizzell, Fuhrer.

	1st Half	2nd Half	Final
UCLA	40	54	94
Seattle	31	39	70

REGIONAL THIRD PLACE WEST

Kansas State (89)   Coach: Tex Winter

	Min.	Total FG/FGA	Pct.	FT/FTA	Pct.	Reb. O/T	A	TO	PF	S	Blk	TP	PPM
ABBOTT, J.	-	0/1	.000	0/0	.000	0/0	-	-	0	-	-	0	-
FISCHER, L.	-	0/1	.000	1/2	.500	0/1	-	-	0	-	-	1	-
POWELL, L.	-	0/0	.000	0/0	.000	0/0	-	-	0	-	-	0	-
STONE, F.	-	6/15	.400	8/8	1.000	2/10	-	-	2	-	-	20	-
PARR, J.	-	7/20	.350	7/10	.700	10/20	-	-	4	-	-	21	-
KIDDOO, C.	-	4/8	.500	3/3	1.000	2/3	-	-	2	-	-	11	-
SCHNEIDER, F.	-	2/4	.500	0/1	.000	1/2	-	-	1	-	-	4	-
VICENS, J.	-	4/11	.364	4/6	.667	2/8	-	-	3	-	-	12	-
WALLACE, H.	-	6/13	.462	4/6	.667	1/5	-	-	1	-	-	16	-
JEDWABNY, R.	-	2/5	.400	0/1	.000	2/4	-	-	4	-	-	4	-
PLAGGE, E.	-	0/0	.000	0/0	.000	0/0	-	-	0	-	-	0	-
RICHARDS, D.	-	0/1	.000	0/0	.000	0/1	-	-	0	-	-	0	-
Totals	200	31/79	.392	27/37	.730	20/54	-	-	17	-	-	89	.445

Houston (70)   Coach: Alden Pasche

	Min.	Total FG/FGA	Pct.	FT/FTA	Pct.	Reb. O/T	A	TO	PF	S	Blk	TP	PPM
EVANS	-	1/9	.111	0/0	.000	3/6	-	-	2	-	-	2	-
FOSTER	-	2/10	.200	0/0	.000	2/2	-	-	2	-	-	4	-
HELMS	-	4/10	.400	0/1	.000	3/6	-	-	5	-	-	8	-
TUCKER	-	2/3	.667	2/2	1.000	1/2	-	-	1	-	-	6	-
BOLDEBUCK	-	5/29	.172	11/17	.647	9/24	-	-	4	-	-	21	-
DOTSON	-	6/14	.429	2/2	1.000	4/6	-	-	3	-	-	14	-
LOPEZ	-	4/5	.800	1/2	.500	0/2	-	-	3	-	-	9	-
MCELWEEN	-	0/1	.000	0/0	.000	1/2	-	-	0	-	-	0	-
SELLS	-	1/4	.250	4/4	1.000	0/0	-	-	2	-	-	6	-
Totals	200	25/85	.294	20/29	.690	23/50	-	-	22	-	-	70	.350

Team Rebounds: Kansas State 5; Houston 3. Disqualified: Houston—Helms.

	1st Half	2nd Half	Final
Kansas State	40	49	89
Houston	37	33	70

REGIONAL THIRD PLACE MIDWEST

Morehead State (95)   Coach: Robert Laughlin

	Min.	Total FG/FGA	Pct.	FT/FTA	Pct.	Reb. O/T	A	TO	PF	S	Blk	TP	PPM
KELEHER, D.	-	3/-		4/-		-/-	-	-	5	-	-	10	-
HAMILTON, S.	-	6/-		0/-		-/-	-	-	5	-	-	12	-
RICHARDS, B.	-	2/-		2/-		-/-	-	-	2	-	-	6	-
JEWELL, J.	-	0/-		4/-		-/-	-	-	1	-	-	4	-
SHIMFESSEL, B.	-	4/-		0/-		-/-	-	-	3	-	-	8	-
SWARTZ, D.	-	13/-		6/-		-/-	-	-	5	-	-	32	-
GAUNCE, D.	-	2/-		6/-		-/-	-	-	4	-	-	10	-
TOLLE, H.	-	4/-		5/-		-/-	-	-	1	-	-	13	-
CARROLL, G.	-	0/-		0/-		-/-	-	-	1	-	-	0	-
Totals	200	34/-		27/-		-/-	-	-	27	-	-	95	.475

Wayne State (84)   Coach: Joel Mason

	Min.	Total FG/FGA	Pct.	FT/FTA	Pct.	Reb. O/T	A	TO	PF	S	Blk	TP	PPM
KELLER	-	9/-		2/-		-/-	-	-	4	-	-	20	-
GREENBERG	-	2/-		2/-		-/-	-	-	3	-	-	6	-
KENDRICK, B.	-	1/-		13/-		-/-	-	-	2	-	-	15	-
DUNCAN	-	5/-		4/-		-/-	-	-	4	-	-	14	-
BROWN, G.	-	9/-		1/-		-/-	-	-	1	-	-	19	-
LONDON	-	0/-		0/-		-/-	-	-	0	-	-	0	-
POTTER	-	1/-		0/-		-/-	-	-	0	-	-	2	-
HALVERSON	-	0/-		0/-		-/-	-	-	2	-	-	0	-
STRAUGHN, C.	-	3/-		0/-		-/-	-	-	1	-	-	6	-
HEDDEN	-	1/-		0/-		-/-	-	-	0	-	-	2	-
Totals	200	31/-		22/-		-/-	-	-	18	-	-	84	.420

Disqualified: Morehead State—Keleher, Hamilton, Swartz.

	1st Half	2nd Half	Final
Morehead State	48	47	95
Wayne State	39	45	84

REGIONAL THIRD PLACE EAST

Dartmouth (85)   Coach: Doggie Julian

	Min.	Total FG/FGA	Pct.	FT/FTA	Pct.	Reb. O/T	A	TO	PF	S	Blk	TP	PPM
JUDSON, R.	-	4/11	.364	0/0	.000	-/2	4	-	2	-	-	8	-
CARRUTHERS, D.	-	6/12	.500	4/5	.800	-/3	1	-	2	-	-	16	-
ERWIN	-	1/2	.500	2/2	1.000	-/3	0	-	1	-	-	4	-
FRASER	-	1/2	.500	0/0	.000	-/0	0	-	0	-	-	2	-
FRANCIS, J.	-	6/12	.500	2/3	.667	-/12	2	-	2	-	-	14	-
DONAHOE, T.	-	1/4	.250	0/0	.000	-/6	2	-	2	-	-	2	-
DOUGLAS	-	0/2	.000	2/2	1.000	-/3	0	-	1	-	-	2	-
BOOTH	-	7/11	.636	6/9	.667	-/8	6	-	1	-	-	20	-
JULIAN	-	3/5	.600	3/4	.750	-/6	1	-	3	-	-	9	-
BLADES, L.	-	3/5	.600	1/2	.500	-/1	2	-	1	-	-	7	-
JONES	-	0/0	.000	0/0	.000	-/1	0	-	0	-	-	0	-
MARKMAN	-	0/0	.000	1/3	.333	-/1	0	-	0	-	-	1	-
Totals	200	32/66	.485	21/30	.700	-/46	18	-	16	-	-	85	.425

U. Conn. (64)   Coach: Hugh Greer

	Min.	Total FG/FGA	Pct.	FT/FTA	Pct.	Reb. O/T	A	TO	PF	S	Blk	TP	PPM
OSBORN	-	1/7	.143	2/2	1.000	-/11	3	-	0	-	-	4	-
RUDDY	-	4/16	.250	7/10	.700	-/13	1	-	4	-	-	15	-
DUBE	-	0/3	.000	0/0	.000	-/1	1	-	1	-	-	0	-
KIERNAN	-	0/0	.000	0/0	.000	-/1	0	-	0	-	-	0	-
KASPAR, P.	-	4/8	.500	4/7	.571	-/4	0	-	4	-	-	12	-
CHEREPY	-	1/1	1.000	0/0	.000	-/1	0	-	0	-	-	2	-
O'LEARY	-	1/3	.333	1/2	.500	-/6	0	-	1	-	-	3	-
QUINN, F.	-	2/7	.286	1/3	.333	-/4	1	-	2	-	-	5	-
BUSHWELL, R.	-	3/14	.214	2/2	1.000	-/2	2	-	5	-	-	8	-
BURNS	-	5/12	.417	1/1	1.000	-/3	2	-	0	-	-	11	-
O'CONNOR	-	2/4	.500	0/1	.000	-/3	0	-	0	-	-	4	-
NARRACCI	-	0/2	.000	0/0	.000	-/0	0	-	1	-	-	0	-
Totals	200	23/77	.299	18/28	.643	-/49	10	-	18	-	-	64	.320

Disqualified: U. Conn.—Bushwell.

	1st Half	2nd Half	Final
Dartmouth	46	39	85
U. Conn.	34	30	64

✪ ALL-STAR TEAMS ✪

ALL TOURNAMENT

CARL CAIN	IOWA
★ **HAL LEAR**	TEMPLE
BILL LOGAN	IOWA
HAL PERRY	SAN FRANCISCO
BILL RUSSELL	SAN FRANCISCO

★ Most Outstanding Player(s)

✪ INDIVIDUAL RECORDS ✪

SCORING

Most points in a single game
1   HAL LEAR, TEMPLE (vs. SMU)   48
2   HAL LEAR, TEMPLE (vs. U. CONN.)   40
3   DAN SWARTZ, MOREHEAD STATE (vs.
    MARSHALL)   39
4   BILL LOGAN, IOWA (vs. TEMPLE)   36
5   CARL CAIN, IOWA (vs. KENTUCKY)   34

Most total points in the tournament
1   HAL LEAR, TEMPLE   160
2   JIM KREBS, SMU   109
3   CARL CAIN, IOWA   99
4   DAN SWARTZ, MOREHEAD STATE   91
4   BILL RUSSELL, SAN FRANCISCO   91

Highest scoring average (minimum 2 games)
1   HAL LEAR, TEMPLE (160-5)   32.00
2   BOB BURROW, KENTUCKY (64-2)   32.00
3   DAN SWARTZ, MOREHEAD STATE (91-3)   30.33
4   CARL CAIN, IOWA (99-4)   24.75
5   WILLIE NAULLS, UCLA (49-2)   24.50

FIELD GOALS

Most field goals in a single game
1   HAL LEAR, TEMPLE (vs. U. CONN.)   18

---

2   HAL LEAR, TEMPLE (vs. SMU)   17
3   HAL LEAR, TEMPLE (vs. IOWA)   15
4   BOB BURROW, KENTUCKY (vs. WAYNE STATE)   14
4   WILLIE NAULLS, UCLA (vs. SEATTLE)   14

Most total field goals in the tournament
1   HAL LEAR, TEMPLE   63
2   JIM KREBS, SMU   42
3   BILL RUSSELL, SAN FRANCISCO   40
4   CARL CAIN, IOWA   35
5   GUY RODGERS, TEMPLE   34

FREE THROWS

Most free throws in a single game
1   DAN SWARTZ, MOREHEAD STATE (vs.
    MARSHALL)   15
2   DONNIE GAUNCE, MOREHEAD STATE (vs. IOWA)
                                                   14
2   HAL LEAR, TEMPLE (vs. SMU)   14
4   3 tied for fourth place.

Most total free throws in the tournament
1   HAL LEAR, TEMPLE   34
2   BOBBY MILLS, SMU   32
3   BOB KENDRICK, WAYNE STATE   29
3   CARL CAIN, IOWA   29
5   2 tied for fifth place.

Most free throws attempted in a single game
1   DONNIE GAUNCE, MOREHEAD STATE
    (vs. IOWA)   24
2   JOHN PARR, KANSAS STATE (vs. OKLAHOMA
    CITY)   19
3   BOB KENDRICK, WAYNE STATE (vs. KENTUCKY)
                                                   18

4   4 tied for fourth place.

Most free throws attempted in the tournament
1   HAL LEAR, TEMPLE   44
2   HENRY NOWAK, CANISIUS   41
3   BOBBY MILLS, SMU   40
4   CARL CAIN, IOWA   37
5   GUY RODGERS, TEMPLE   36

**Highest free throw percentage in a single game
(minimum 7 attempts)**
1   TOM HEINSOHN, HOLY CROSS (vs. TEMPLE)
    (12-12)   1.000
2   RON BUSHWELL, U. CONN. (vs. MANHATTAN)
    (10-10)   1.000
3   RON MORRIS, SMU (vs. TEMPLE) (8-8)   1.000
3   FRANCIS STONE, KANSAS STATE (vs. HOUSTON)
    (8-8)   1.000
5   DICK BAMTON, UCLA (vs. SAN FRANCISCO)
    (7-7)   1.000

✪ TEAM RECORDS ✪

SCORING

Most points in a single game
1   MOREHEAD STATE (vs. MARSHALL)   107
2   3 tied for second place.

Most total points in the tournament
1   SMU   390
2   TEMPLE   365
3   IOWA   340

Highest scoring average (minimum 2 games)
1   MOREHEAD STATE (285-3)   95.00
2   KANSAS STATE (182-2)   91.00
3   OKLAHOMA CITY (257-3)   85.67

FIELD GOALS

Most field goals in a single game
1   MARSHALL (vs. MOREHEAD STATE)   40
2   SAN FRANCISCO (vs. SMU)   38
2   MOREHEAD STATE (vs. MARSHALL)   38

Most total field goals in the tournament
1   TEMPLE   147
2   SAN FRANCISCO   136
3   SMU   130

FREE THROWS

Most free throws in a single game
1   OKLAHOMA CITY (vs. KANSAS STATE)   35
1   IOWA (vs. MOREHEAD STATE)   35
3   SMU (vs. OKLAHOMA CITY)   34

Most total free throws in the tournament
1   SMU   130
2   IOWA   102
3   MOREHEAD STATE   91

Most free throws attempted in a single game
1   MOREHEAD STATE (vs. IOWA)   53
2   SEATTLE (vs. UCLA)   52
2   IOWA (vs. MOREHEAD STATE)   52

Most total free throws attempted in the tournament
1   SMU   172
2   IOWA   146
3   SEATTLE   120

Highest free throw percentage in a single game
1   SAN FRANCISCO (vs. IOWA) (13-15)   .867
2   SMU (vs. TEMPLE) (27-32)   .844
3   UTAH (vs. SEATTLE) (23-28)   .821

Fewest free throws in a single game
1   TEMPLE (vs. IOWA)   6
2   SAN FRANCISCO (vs. SMU)   10
3   TEMPLE (vs. U. CONN.)   11

Lowest free throw percentage in a single game
1   TEMPLE (vs. IOWA) (6-17)   .353
2   WAYNE STATE (vs. KENTUCKY) (18-37)   .487
3   CANISIUS (vs. TEMPLE) (14-28)   .500

1957

| FIRST ROUND | REGIONAL SEMIFINAL | REGIONAL FINAL | FINAL FOUR | REGIONAL FINAL | REGIONAL SEMIFINAL | FIRST ROUND |

EAST

(bye) — Lafayette 71

Syracuse 58

U. Conn. 76

Syracuse 75

Syracuse 82

N. Carolina 74 (3 ot)

West Virginia 56

Canisius 75

Canisius 64

N. Carolina 67

N. Carolina 90

N. Carolina 87

Yale 74

MIDWEST

St. Louis 66 — (bye)

Oklahoma City 61

Oklahoma City 76

Oklahoma City 75

Loyola N.O. 55

Kansas 80

Kansas 73 (ot) — (bye)

Kansas 81

(bye)

SMU 65

N. Carolina 54 (3 ot)
Kansas 53

MIDEAST

(bye) — Kentucky 98

Kentucky 68

Morehead St. 85

Pittsburgh 92

Pittsburgh 86

Michigan St. 70

Miami (Ohio) 77

Notre Dame 83

Notre Dame 89

Michigan St. 80

(bye)

Michigan St. 85

WEST

Brigham Young 59 — (bye)

California 46

(bye)

California 86

San Francisco 56

Idaho St. 68

Idaho St. 51

Hardin-Simmons 57

San Francisco 50

San Francisco 66 — (bye)

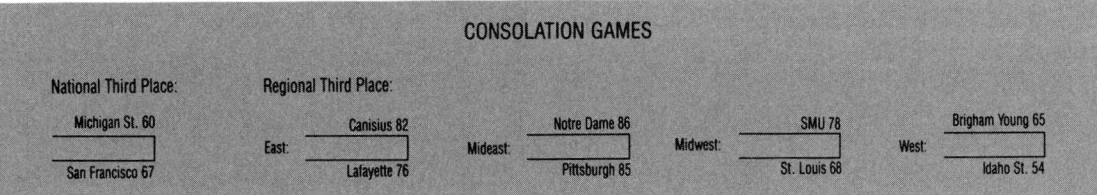

CONSOLATION GAMES

National Third Place:

Michigan St. 60
San Francisco 67

Regional Third Place:

East:
Canisius 82
Lafayette 76

Mideast:
Notre Dame 86
Pittsburgh 85

Midwest:
SMU 78
St. Louis 68

West:
Brigham Young 65
Idaho St. 54

Along about midnight on Saturday night, March 23rd, 1957, it was finally over. The cheering stopped, and a stunned crowd of Kansas diehards filed silently out of the Kansas City Municipal Arena. The North Carolina players raced back to their hotel to shower, trying to digest what they had just accomplished. Back in Chapel Hill, the celebration began.

That the two teams—the North Carolina Tar Heels and the Kansas Jayhawks—even existed was a miracle of modern basketball recruiting. North Carolina's coach Frank McGuire, who had grown up on the mean streets of New York's Greenwich Village, spent virtually his entire life in his hometown except for the war years when he was stationed in Chapel Hill, North Carolina. After leading his St. John's Redmen to the NCAA finals against Kansas in 1952, he was offered the head coaching job at the University of North Carolina. For personal reasons, he accepted and moved to Chapel Hill.

McGuire didn't give up his strong ties to New York, however. He had lots of friends back home, a number of whom, like Harry Gotkin, scoured the school gyms and playgrounds of the city on McGuire's behalf. In 1957, when the Tar Heels went undefeated, the team's entire starting five—Lennie Rosenbluth, Pete Brennan, Joe Quigg, Tommy Kearns, and Bobby Cunningham—came to Chapel Hill through McGuire's network, his "underground railroad." "New York is my personal territory," he said. "Duke can scout in Philadelphia, and North Carolina State can have the whole country. But if anybody wants to move into New York, they need a passport from me."

On the other side of the court stood Kansas's towering Wilt "the Stilt" Chamberlain. Two years earlier, the Big Dipper had been the most sought-after high school basketball player *ever*. Somehow the wily old Kansas coach Phog Allen had landed Chamberlain, persuading him to attend college in Lawrence, half a continent away from Philadelphia, where, as the overwhelming overlord of the Overbrook High School basketball team, he had attracted the attention of scouts from coast to coast. And though Allen begged university authorities to overlook the mandatory retirement age and allow him to coach Chamberlain for just one year on the varsity (he sensed that the tall young man would bring him his second NCAA title in his final game), rules were rules. Coaching Chamberlain to the championship was a task that fell to Allen's designated successor, Dick Harp.

Chamberlain's effect on opponents was uncanny. He was over seven feet tall, powerful, quick, and aggressive. All season long, he was challenged by double- and triple-teaming; he took a pounding from opponents, and Harp said, "He never got any breaks from the officials, but he never lost his composure." Although Wilt was looked upon in many quarters as superhuman, Kansas actually lost twice during the season, to defensive-minded Iowa State and Oklahoma A&M on the road.

Away from home, Wilt not only had to overcome the excessive physical play of opponents and the slow whistles of officials, he and his teammates often had to deal with hostile crowds and racial epithets as well. The Midwest regional was played in Dallas, where Southern Methodist University had won 36 straight starts. The partisan crowd hooted and hurled racial slurs at Chamberlain, but in the end he and the Jayhawks prevailed in overtime. The following night, the SMU crowd rooted for Oklahoma City. The Lawrence, Kansas, *Journal-World* described how "at least 7,000 fans fired verbal blasts, pillow seats and coins at Kansas." Despite the hostile crowd, Kansas won easily.

Upon their return to friendly Kansas City for the Final Four, the Jayhawks played San Francisco. Although the Dons' own intimidating center, Bill Russell, had graduated and gone on to the pros, Coach Phil Woolpert's squad remained the nation's top defensive team and a force to be reckoned with. But Chamberlain, from his emphatic opening block to his final thunderous dunk, put on an awesome display. The Jayhawks had little difficulty disposing of the Dons, and appeared, for all intents and purposes, invincible.

The team Chamberlain and his teammates met for the championship in Kansas City was undefeated, ranked No. 1, and given a snowball's chance in hell to win. The only question seemed to be how big a margin of victory Kansas would end up with. But the North Carolina Tar Heels had something intangible going for them; it wasn't simply that they hadn't lost all season, it was that they refused to lose.

In the fourth game of the season, down by three with 40 seconds left in overtime, Carolina had come back. Against Maryland midway through the season, the Tar Heels were down by four and Maryland had the ball with 40 seconds left to play when McGuire called time out. "Our winning streak had to end sometime," he said, "and this looks like it. So fellows, let's lose graciously. When the gun goes off, go right over and congratulate those Maryland boys." Again North Carolina won in overtime.

Playing against Wake Forest in the post-season ACC tournament, the Tar Heels came back in the last minute to win. And against Michigan State in the Final Four, they again escaped by an eyelash. With the score tied and time running out in regulation, the Spartans' Jumpin' Johnny Green picked off a rebound and quickly passed upcourt to Jack Quiggle, who threw up a 50 footer; it went in, but the refs said the shot was released after the buzzer. At the end of the first overtime, Michigan State led by two with six seconds remaining and Green on the line for a one-and-one. Tommy Kearns later recalled that his man walked over to him and said, grinning, "Thirty and one." But

Green missed and Pete Brennan got the rebound. He put his head down, dribbled all the way down the floor, and canned a twenty footer just before the buzzer. "I knew at the end of that first overtime that Michigan State was done," said McGuire. "Lady Luck was with us then." North Carolina won in three overtimes.

The Tar Heels had more than luck; they had chemistry. The Carolina Yankees worked hard in practice, worked out their problems off the court, and were all willing to walk through fire for McGuire. They felt they were just paying him back for his loyalty: When Lennie Rosenbluth's grades weren't up to North Carolina's admissions standards, McGuire made it clear there would be a place for him when he did qualify; Lennie's mother hocked her furs to pay his tuition at Staunton Military Academy in Virginia, and although other scouts came courting, Mrs. Rosenbluth kept her promise to McGuire. The Carolina coach first contacted Kearns when he was a sophomore substitute at New York's St. Ann's Academy for Boys; when he became good enough to be a prospect, Tommy remembered who was there first. Bobby Cunningham had been a brilliant scorer at All Hallows High, and was actively recruited by a number of schools. But after he fell through a glass door during his senior year and lost some of the sensation in his fingers, the other offers fell by the wayside. McGuire held to his promise. "I visited his home and told him he would have his scholarship whether or not he could play for us." McGuire had similar personal relationships with Brennan and Quigg, and he knew what made each of his players tick.

Early on the day of the championship game, little Tommy Kearns was hanging out in the lobby of Kansas City's Continental Hotel, talking to whoever would listen. When he was asked how the Tar Heels were planning to play Chamberlain, he replied, "We'll think of something." After a pause he continued, "We're a chilly club. I mean we just keep it cool. Chamberlain won't give us any jitters."

At game time, North Carolina's Governor Hodges plunked himself down next to McGuire on the bench. The coach suggested that the governor take a seat on the other end before his team went out for the opening tap.

McGuire sent Kearns—all 5 foot 11 of him—out to the center circle to jump against Chamberlain. The big man was bewildered as he watched Kearns crouch, acting for all the world as if he were ready to spring through the rafters to beat Chamberlain to the tap. "Wilt looked 10 feet tall towering over Tommy," McGuire later recalled, "but they made such a ridiculous picture together that Chamberlain must have felt no bigger than his thumb. At least that's the state of mind we wanted to get him into."

Although Chamberlain won the opening tap, he didn't hit a shot until nearly five minutes had elapsed, and by then North Carolina was leading 9-2. The Tar Heels collapsed around Wilt, daring his teammates to hit from outside. And Kansas opened in a box and one defense, which was ineffective against Rosenbluth and also left the other Carolina players free to shoot over the zone. By the time the period was half over, the score was 19-7 and the Tar Heels had not missed a single shot from the floor. Finally, the Jayhawks changed their defense to a man-to-man and began to come back. But at the half, it was still 29-22; Rosenbluth had 14 points and had missed only two shots, and Carolina as a whole was hitting 64.7 percent compared to Kansas's 27.3 percent.

In the second half, Wilt continued to lead Kansas back, and North Carolina started piling up fouls. With just over ten minutes to go, Chamberlain hit two free throws to put Kansas up 40-37. The Jayhawks had momentum and had the Tar Heels on the ropes; North Carolina was exhausted from their triple overtime victory the night before, and three of their key players were in foul trouble. North Carolina worked the ball around for a while, but the Jayhawks came up with a steal. And Kansas's Coach Harp called for a slowdown.

As the slowdown became a freeze, the Tar Heels sat back and caught their breath. The crowd went crazy; their beloved Jayhawks were giving North Carolina a taste of their own medicine. McGuire allowed Kansas to freeze until the five-minute mark, when he signaled for the Tar Heels defense to tighten. With 4:31 to play, Rosenbluth ran into Jayhawks' forward Ron Loneski and was charged with his fourth foul. Loneski missed the free throw and Rosenbluth hit on the other end. A long bomb by Brennan gave the Tar Heels the lead 41-40. But Chamberlain hit two free throws to put the Jayhawks back in front. With 1:45 to go Wilt made a beautiful pass to Gene Elstun, who made the shot while drawing Rosenbluth's fifth foul. After the free throw, Kansas was up by three and Carolina had lost its high scorer. Nonetheless, the Tar Heels fought back and tied the score on a foul shot by Kearns with twenty seconds left. It was 46-46 at the end of regulation.

In the first overtime, both teams played slowdown, each scored only one basket, and Chamberlain blocked a last second shot by Kearns. In the second overtime there was plenty of action. Carolina, almost punchy from fatigue, missed four straight foul shots. And the Tar Heels were leaning all over Chamberlain. At one point Cunningham fouled the Kansas center and Brennan grabbed him around the waist. Wilt threw the ball away and brought his elbow down on Brennan's head. Brennan charged at Chamberlain and for a moment before they were pulled apart it looked like all hell was going to break loose. Both benches cleared, although there is no report as to whether Governor Hodges joined in the fracas. McGuire claimed that during the melee a Kansas assistant came over to the Carolina bench and slugged him in the stomach. The crowd surged menacingly toward the court. Finally the police came on the floor to help the embattled game officials restore order. When the bedlam died down, neither team had scored; it was still 48-48 at the end of 50 minutes of play.

The scoring finally began to pick up in the third OT. Kearns hit a lay-up and both ends of a one-and-one to put the Tar Heels up by 4. Chamberlain made a 3-point play, and Maurice King and Elstun each hit a free throw. Kansas led 53-52. With 20 seconds left, Chamberlain batted away a shot by Kearns. The ball came to Quigg at the top of the key; he made a quick fake and drove on Wilt. Chamberlain blocked the shot cleanly, but King, coming over to help out, fouled Quigg with six seconds left. McGuire called for a time-out.

When the Tar Heels went into their huddle, McGuire began his talk by saying to Quigg, "Now Joe, as soon as you make 'em," before going on to talk about the Heels' defensive alignment. Quigg told his teammates he'd make the shots, then went to the line and coolly dropped them through the hoop. It was 54-53. Kansas tried to get the ball to Chamberlain, but Quigg knocked it away. With no more than a couple of ticks on the clock, Kearns picked the ball up, dribbled it once, and threw it straight up. The ball soared high in the air, far above even Chamberlain's reach. It didn't come down until the game was over.

While Kansas reacted to the outcome in stunned disbelief, there was rejoicing throughout the state of North Carolina. The celebrations went on all night, and reached a peak the following day when the team arrived at the Raleigh–Durham airport. Even the runway was filled with some of the 10,000 jubilant celebrants who came to welcome Frank McGuire's New Yorkers home to Carolina, and the well-wishers had to be moved away before the plane could land.

Basketball had always been popular in North Carolina, but with the Tar Heels' victory it became almost a religion; suddenly it didn't matter quite so much whether you were Baptist or Methodist or Catholic or Jew as long as you could put the ball in the hoop. Overnight college basketball—and the NCAA tournament—attained a new national stature; the Carolinians from New York and the Kansan from Philadelphia had captured the imagination of a new, previously untapped audience and had forever transformed the public perception of the game from a local phenomenon into a national event.

In the next decade, spurred by the pressure of outside events, the pace of change would speed up. On the border of the Mason-Dixon line, in Louisville, the color line was broken in 1963. Soon afterward the University of North Carolina, under Dean Smith, became the first school in the Deep South to recruit black players. Almost immediately, others followed suit. McGuire's New York ethnics, and their epic struggle against the great black Kansas center, helped pave the way for the world of college athletics to accept people who were different.

FIRST ROUND EAST

U. Conn. (76)   Coach: Hugh Greer.

	Min.	Total FG/FGA	Pct.	FT/FTA	Pct.	Reb. O/T	A	TO	PF	S	Blk	TP	PPM
QUINN	-	6/-	-	2/2	1.000	-/-	-	-	0	-	-	14	-
SCHMIDT	-	5/-	-	4/4	1.000	-/-	-	-	3	-	-	14	-
COOPER, A.	-	9/-	-	1/3	.333	-/-	-	-	3	-	-	19	-
DAVIS	-	0/-	-	0/1	.000	-/-	-	-	2	-	-	0	-
OSBORNE	-	1/-	-	6/8	.750	-/-	-	-	2	-	-	8	-
O'CONNOR, J.	-	8/-	-	5/6	.833	-/-	-	-	2	-	-	21	-
Totals	200	29/-	-	18/24	.750	-/-	-	-	12	-	-	76	.380

Syracuse (82)   Coach: Marc Guley

	Min.	Total FG/FGA	Pct.	FT/FTA	Pct.	Reb. O/T	A	TO	PF	S	Blk	TP	PPM
CLARK, G.	-	12/-	-	2/2	1.000	-/-	-	-	4	-	-	26	-
COHEN, V.	-	9/-	-	6/8	.750	-/-	-	-	3	-	-	24	-
SNYDER	-	4/-	-	3/6	.500	-/-	-	-	3	-	-	11	-
BRELAND	-	4/-	-	2/2	1.000	-/-	-	-	1	-	-	10	-
ALBANESE	-	1/-	-	2/4	.500	-/-	-	-	2	-	-	4	-
CINCEBOX	-	3/-	-	0/1	.000	-/-	-	-	1	-	-	6	-
LOUDIS	-	0/-	-	1/2	.500	-/-	-	-	0	-	-	1	-
Totals	200	33/-	-	16/25	.640	-/-	-	-	14	-	-	82	.410

Disqualified: None.

	1st Half	2nd Half	Final
U. Conn.	37	39	76
Syracuse	35	47	82

West Virginia (56)   Coach: Fred Schaus

	Min.	Total FG/FGA	Pct.	FT/FTA	Pct.	Reb. O/T	A	TO	PF	S	Blk	TP	PPM
HUNDLEY, R.	-	4/20	.200	9/9	1.000	-/7	-	-	1	-	-	17	-
SMITH	-	5/14	.357	0/2	.000	-/10	-	-	3	-	-	10	-
SHARRAR, L.	-	1/6	.167	1/2	.500	-/8	-	-	3	-	-	3	-
KISHBAUGH	-	5/11	.455	2/5	.400	-/5	-	-	1	-	-	12	-
VINCENT	-	3/9	.333	2/3	.667	-/7	-	-	1	-	-	8	-
GARDNER	-	1/5	.200	2/2	1.000	-/1	-	-	3	-	-	4	-
CLOUSSON, B.	-	1/2	.500	0/1	.000	-/5	-	-	3	-	-	2	-
SCHERTZINGER, H.	-	0/1	.000	0/0	.000	-/1	-	-	0	-	-	0	-
Totals	200	20/68	.294	16/24	.667	-/44	-	-	15	-	-	56	.280

Canisius (64)   Coach: Joseph Curran

	Min.	Total FG/FGA	Pct.	FT/FTA	Pct.	Reb. O/T	A	TO	PF	S	Blk	TP	PPM
NOWAK, H.	-	8/13	.615	3/6	.500	-/16	-	-	3	-	-	19	-
SPRINGER, J.	-	1/6	.167	0/0	.000	-/1	-	-	1	-	-	2	-
LEONE, J.	-	8/13	.615	2/2	1.000	-/12	-	-	4	-	-	18	-
COOGAN, J.	-	3/11	.273	0/1	.000	-/5	-	-	3	-	-	6	-
MARKEY, D.	-	2/13	.154	1/5	.200	-/8	-	-	1	-	-	5	-
MACKINNON, J.	-	1/2	.500	0/0	.000	-/1	-	-	0	-	-	2	-
BRITZ, G.	-	5/15	.333	2/3	.667	-/9	-	-	2	-	-	12	-
Totals	200	28/73	.384	8/17	.471	-/52	-	-	14	-	-	64	.320

Team Rebounds: Canisius 4; West Virginia 9. Disqualified: None.

	1st Half	2nd Half	Final
West Virginia	18	38	56
Canisius	34	30	64

North Carolina (90)   Coach: Frank McGuire

	Min.	Total FG/FGA	Pct.	FT/FTA	Pct.	Reb. O/T	A	TO	PF	S	Blk	TP	PPM
ROSENBLUTH, L.	-	11/19	.579	7/12	.583	-/19	-	-	4	-	-	29	-
YOUNG, B.	-	0/0	.000	0/0	.000	-/1	-	-	3	-	-	0	-
BRENNAN, P.	-	6/12	.500	8/11	.727	-/11	-	-	3	-	-	20	-
QUIGG, J.	-	5/8	.625	3/4	.750	-/1	-	-	2	-	-	13	-
KEARNS, T.	-	5/12	.417	6/9	.667	-/4	-	-	3	-	-	16	-
CUNNINGHAM, B.	-	4/7	.571	4/4	1.000	-/7	-	-	3	-	-	12	-
Totals	200	31/58	.534	28/40	.700	-/43	-	-	18	-	-	90	.450

Yale (74)   Coach: Joe Vancisin

	Min.	Total FG/FGA	Pct.	FT/FTA	Pct.	Reb. O/T	A	TO	PF	S	Blk	TP	PPM
LEE, J.	-	8/22	.364	9/9	1.000	-/4	-	-	5	-	-	25	-
BAIRD	-	0/4	.000	0/0	.000	-/4	-	-	3	-	-	0	-
DOWNS	-	5/15	.333	3/6	.500	-/9	-	-	5	-	-	13	-
BODMAN	-	1/1	1.000	0/0	.000	-/2	-	-	0	-	-	2	-
ROBINSON, E.	-	7/11	.636	6/9	.667	-/17	-	-	5	-	-	20	-
BAB	-	0/2	.000	0/0	.000	-/0	-	-	1	-	-	0	-
THOMPSON	-	3/5	.600	0/0	.000	-/2	-	-	3	-	-	6	-
SARGENT	-	3/6	.500	0/2	.000	-/0	-	-	5	-	-	6	-
MOLUMPHY	-	1/1	1.000	0/1	.000	-/0	-	-	1	-	-	2	-
Totals	200	28/67	.418	18/27	.667	-/38	-	-	28	-	-	74	.370

Disqualified: Yale—Lee, Downs, Robinson, Sargent.

	1st Half	2nd Half	Final
N. Carolina	40	50	90
Yale	40	34	74

FIRST ROUND MIDEAST

Morehead State (85)   Coach: Robert Laughlin

	Min.	Total FG / FGA	Pct.	FT / FTA	Pct.	Reb. O / T	A	TO	PF	S	Blk	TP	PPM
HAMILTON	-	5/ -	-	10/14	.714	-/ -	-	-	5	-	-	20	-
KELEHER	-	5/ -	-	6/ 6	1.000	-/ -	-	-	5	-	-	16	-
YENTES	-	0/ -	-	1/ 2	.500	-/ -	-	-	0	-	-	1	-
SCHIMFESSEL	-	2/ -	-	3/ 7	.429	-/ -	-	-	5	-	-	7	-
HILL	-	3/ -	-	2/ 4	.500	-/ -	-	-	2	-	-	8	-
THOMPSON	-	1/ -	-	5/ 9	.556	-/ -	-	-	2	-	-	7	-
TOLLE	-	5/ -	-	10/12	.833	-/ -	-	-	3	-	-	20	-
CARROLL	-	3/ -	-	0/ 0	.000	-/ -	-	-	3	-	-	6	-
Totals	200	24/ -	-	37/54	.685	-/ -	-	-	25	-	-	85	.425

Pittsburgh (86)   Coach: Bob Timmons

	Min.	Total FG / FGA	Pct.	FT / FTA	Pct.	Reb. O / T	A	TO	PF	S	Blk	TP	PPM
PEGUES	-	3/ -	-	8/11	.727	-/ -	-	-	4	-	-	14	-
RISER	-	6/ -	-	8/10	.800	-/ -	-	-	5	-	-	20	-
WOZNICKI	-	0/ -	-	0/ 1	.000	-/ -	-	-	0	-	-	0	-
BRAUTIGAM	-	2/ -	-	2/ 3	.667	-/ -	-	-	5	-	-	6	-
DORMAN	-	2/ -	-	2/ 3	.667	-/ -	-	-	5	-	-	6	-
MARKOVICH	-	0/ -	-	1/ 2	.500	-/ -	-	-	0	-	-	1	-
HURSH	-	2/ -	-	0/ 0	.000	-/ -	-	-	5	-	-	4	-
HENNON, D.	-	11/ -	-	9/11	.818	-/ -	-	-	4	-	-	31	-
SAWYER	-	0/ -	-	2/ 2	1.000	-/ -	-	-	2	-	-	2	-
LANEVE, J.	-	1/ -	-	0/ 0	.000	-/ -	-	-	1	-	-	2	-
Totals	200	27/ -	-	32/43	.744	-/ -	-	-	31	-	-	86	.430

Disqualified: Pittsburgh—Riser, Brautigam, Dorman, Hursh; Morehead State—Hamilton, Keleher, Schimfessel.

	1st Half	2nd Half	Final
Morehead State	44	41	85
Pittsburgh	46	40	86

Miami (Ohio) (77)   Coach: Bill Rohr

	Min.	Total FG / FGA	Pct.	FT / FTA	Pct.	Reb. O / T	A	TO	PF	S	Blk	TP	PPM
BROWN, B.	-	0/ -	-	0/ 0	.000	-/ -	-	-	1	-	-	0	-
ELLIS, R.	-	3/ -	-	1/ 2	.500	-/ -	-	-	4	-	-	7	-
WINGARD, E.	-	0/ -	-	2/ 3	.667	-/ -	-	-	1	-	-	2	-
MILLER, B.	-	0/ -	-	0/ 0	.000	-/ -	-	-	3	-	-	0	-
BABBS, K.	-	0/ -	-	1/ 2	.500	-/ -	-	-	2	-	-	1	-
EMBRY, W.	-	9/ -	-	7/12	.583	-/ -	-	-	2	-	-	25	-
ALBERS, R.	-	0/ -	-	0/ 0	.000	-/ -	-	-	0	-	-	0	-
THOMAS, J.	-	7/ -	-	1/ 2	.500	-/ -	-	-	1	-	-	15	-
POWELL, J.	-	10/ -	-	3/ 5	.600	-/ -	-	-	2	-	-	23	-
GENTRY, C.	-	1/ -	-	2/ 3	.667	-/ -	-	-	3	-	-	4	-
CRIST, L.	-	0/ -	-	0/ 0	.000	-/ -	-	-	1	-	-	0	-
KNOSHER, H.	-	0/ -	-	0/ 0	.000	-/ -	-	-	0	-	-	0	-
Totals	200	30/ -	-	17/29	.586	-/ -	-	-	20	-	-	77	.385

Notre Dame (89)   Coach: John Jordan

	Min.	Total FG / FGA	Pct.	FT / FTA	Pct.	Reb. O / T	A	TO	PF	S	Blk	TP	PPM
HAWKINS, T.	-	11/ -	-	3/ 5	.600	-/ -	-	-	4	-	-	25	-
SMYTH, J.	-	7/ -	-	9/11	.818	-/ -	-	-	4	-	-	23	-
MCCARTHY, J.	-	8/ -	-	6/ 6	1.000	-/ -	-	-	4	-	-	22	-
DUFFY, E.	-	2/ -	-	5/ 9	.556	-/ -	-	-	1	-	-	9	-
DEVINE, R.	-	4/ -	-	0/ 0	.000	-/ -	-	-	5	-	-	8	-
SULLIVAN, T.	-	0/ -	-	2/ 3	.667	-/ -	-	-	0	-	-	2	-
Totals	200	32/ -	-	25/34	.735	-/ -	-	-	18	-	-	89	.445

Disqualified: Notre Dame—Devine.

	1st Half	2nd Half	Final
Miami (Ohio)	31	46	77
Notre Dame	47	42	89

FIRST ROUND MIDWEST

Oklahoma City (76)   Coach: Abe Lemons

	Min.	Total FG / FGA	Pct.	FT / FTA	Pct.	Reb. O / T	A	TO	PF	S	Blk	TP	PPM
HOLLOWAY, R.	-	9/ -	-	0/ 1	.000	-/ -	-	-	2	-	-	18	-
LEE, L.	-	3/ -	-	3/ 7	.429	-/ -	-	-	4	-	-	9	-
REED, H.	-	9/ -	-	6/ 7	.857	-/ -	-	-	1	-	-	24	-
BRADSHAW, L.	-	2/ -	-	0/ 1	.000	-/ -	-	-	5	-	-	4	-
MAGANA, C.	-	1/ -	-	0/ 0	.000	-/ -	-	-	1	-	-	2	-
GRIFFIN	-	2/ -	-	4/ 4	1.000	-/ -	-	-	1	-	-	8	-
HILL, T.	-	3/ -	-	1/ 5	.200	-/ -	-	-	2	-	-	7	-
JETTER	-	0/ -	-	0/ 0	.000	-/ -	-	-	2	-	-	0	-
KELLEY, M.	-	1/ -	-	0/ 1	.000	-/ -	-	-	0	-	-	2	-
GARDNER, G.	-	0/ -	-	0/ 0	.000	-/ -	-	-	0	-	-	0	-
HANSON, B.	-	1/ -	-	0/ 0	.000	-/ -	-	-	1	-	-	2	-
MCCRAW, E.	-	0/ -	-	0/ 0	.000	-/ -	-	-	0	-	-	0	-
Totals	200	31/ -	-	14/26	.538	-/ -	-	-	19	-	-	76	.380

Loyola New Orleans (55)   Coach: Jim McCafferty

	Min.	Total FG / FGA	Pct.	FT / FTA	Pct.	Reb. O / T	A	TO	PF	S	Blk	TP	PPM
GAUDIN	-	10/ -	-	11/14	.786	-/ -	-	-	4	-	-	31	-
HALL	-	0/ -	-	2/ 5	.400	-/ -	-	-	1	-	-	2	-
DOLL	-	0/ -	-	0/ 0	.000	-/ -	-	-	1	-	-	0	-
VOGT	-	0/ -	-	0/ 3	.000	-/ -	-	-	2	-	-	0	-
SCHWEIBERGER	-	2/ -	-	0/ 0	.000	-/ -	-	-	4	-	-	4	-
LORIO	-	3/ -	-	2/ 5	.400	-/ -	-	-	5	-	-	8	-
MCLAUGHLIN	-	3/ -	-	2/ 2	1.000	-/ -	-	-	1	-	-	8	-
MURRET	-	0/ -	-	0/ 0	.000	-/ -	-	-	0	-	-	0	-
EXTERSTEIN	-	0/ -	-	0/ 0	.000	-/ -	-	-	0	-	-	0	-
HUGHES	-	1/ -	-	0/ 0	.000	-/ -	-	-	0	-	-	2	-
Totals	200	19/ -	-	17/29	.586	-/ -	-	-	18	-	-	55	.275

Disqualified: Oklahoma City—Bradshaw; Loyola N.O.—Lorio.

	1st Half	2nd Half	Final
Oklahoma City	38	38	76
Loyola N.O.	16	39	55

FIRST ROUND WEST

Idaho State (68)   Coach: John Grayson

	Min.	Total FG/FGA	Pct.	FT/FTA	Pct.	Reb. O/T	A	TO	PF	S	Blk	TP	PPM
SIEMEN	-	8/ -	-	5/ -	-	-/ -	-	-	2	-	-	21	-
HOGE, B.	-	0/ -	-	0/ -	-	-/ -	-	-	0	-	-	0	-
ADLEHARDT, R.	-	3/ -	-	3/ -	-	-/ -	-	-	3	-	-	9	-
ALLAIN, J.	-	1/ -	-	3/ -	-	-/ -	-	-	5	-	-	5	-
CHENEY, R.	-	0/ -	-	0/ -	-	-/ -	-	-	0	-	-	0	-
WELLS, C.	-	0/ -	-	0/ -	-	-/ -	-	-	1	-	-	0	-
DETMER, S.	-	0/ -	-	0/ -	-	-/ -	-	-	2	-	-	0	-
HICKS, J.	-	8/ -	-	7/ -	-	-/ -	-	-	2	-	-	23	-
EASTERBROOKS, S.	-	4/ -	-	2/ -	-	-/ -	-	-	4	-	-	10	-
MANLEY, R.	-	0/ -	-	0/ -	-	-/ -	-	-	0	-	-	0	-
Totals	200	24/ -	-	20/ -	-	-/ -	-	-	19	-	-	68	.340

Hardin-Simmons (57)   Coach: Bill Scott

	Min.	Total FG/FGA	Pct.	FT/FTA	Pct.	Reb. O/T	A	TO	PF	S	Blk	TP	PPM
EDMISTON	-	2/ -	-	2/ -	-	-/ -	-	-	4	-	-	6	-
MURRAY	-	0/ -	-	0/ -	-	-/ -	-	-	2	-	-	0	-
KNIGHT	-	0/ -	-	5/ -	-	-/ -	-	-	4	-	-	5	-
CARLSON	-	0/ -	-	0/ -	-	-/ -	-	-	1	-	-	0	-
CAPIN	-	0/ -	-	0/ -	-	-/ -	-	-	0	-	-	0	-
TREMAINE	-	3/ -	-	10/ -	-	-/ -	-	-	2	-	-	16	-
CUNNINGHAM	-	1/ -	-	0/ -	-	-/ -	-	-	1	-	-	2	-
KING	-	4/ -	-	0/ -	-	-/ -	-	-	2	-	-	8	-
GROOM	-	2/ -	-	2/ -	-	-/ -	-	-	4	-	-	6	-
BENTON	-	1/ -	-	0/ -	-	-/ -	-	-	4	-	-	2	-
LEWIS	-	4/ -	-	2/ -	-	-/ -	-	-	3	-	-	10	-
TRAVIS	-	1/ -	-	0/ -	-	-/ -	-	-	1	-	-	2	-
Totals	200	18/ -	-	21/ -	-	-/ -	-	-	28	-	-	57	.285

Disqualified: Idaho State—Allain.

	1st Half	2nd Half	Final
Idaho State	32	36	68
Hardin-Simmons	30	27	57

REGIONAL SEMIFINAL EAST

Lafayette (71)   Coach: George Davidson

	Min.	Total FG/FGA	Pct.	FT/FTA	Pct.	Reb. O/T	A	TO	PF	S	Blk	TP	PPM
GALTERE	-	1/ 9	.111	6/ 8	.750	-/11	-	-	3	-	-	8	-
STERLEIN	-	2/ 6	.333	0/ 1	.000	-/11	-	-	4	-	-	4	-
MANTZ	-	5/11	.455	6/ 7	.857	-/17	-	-	2	-	-	16	-
MURRAY	-	14/25	.560	2/ 5	.400	-/ 6	-	-	0	-	-	30	-
MACK	-	1/ 8	.125	6/ 9	.667	-/ 3	-	-	5	-	-	8	-
KOHLER	-	1/ 4	.250	1/ 2	.500	-/ 0	-	-	2	-	-	3	-
JONES	-	1/ 2	.500	0/ 0	.000	-/ 0	-	-	1	-	-	2	-
Totals	200	25/65	.385	21/32	.656	-/48	-	-	17	-	-	71	.355

Syracuse (75)   Coach: Marc Guley

	Min.	Total FG/FGA	Pct.	FT/FTA	Pct.	Reb. O/T	A	TO	PF	S	Blk	TP	PPM
CLARK, G.	-	13/20	.650	8/10	.800	-/13	-	-	3	-	-	34	-
COHEN, V.	-	3/15	.200	2/ 3	.667	-/ 4	-	-	3	-	-	8	-
SNYDER	-	6/10	.600	2/ 5	.400	-/14	-	-	4	-	-	14	-
BRELAND	-	0/ 7	.000	0/ 2	.000	-/ 7	-	-	3	-	-	0	-
ALBANESE	-	5/14	.357	2/ 3	.667	-/ 4	-	-	3	-	-	12	-
CINCEBOX	-	3/ 9	.333	1/ 4	.250	-/ 9	-	-	0	-	-	7	-
LOUDIS	-	0/ 0	.000	0/ 0	.000	-/ 2	-	-	1	-	-	0	-
Totals	200	30/75	.400	15/27	.556	-/53	-	-	17	-	-	75	.375

Disqualified: Lafayette—Mack.

	1st Half	2nd Half	Final
Lafayette	40	31	71
Syracuse	42	33	75

Canisius (75)   Coach: Joseph Curran

	Min.	Total FG/FGA	Pct.	FT/FTA	Pct.	Reb. O/T	A	TO	PF	S	Blk	TP	PPM
NOWAK, H.	-	8/11	.727	8/12	.667	-/ 9	-	-	4	-	-	24	-
SPRINGER, J.	-	2/ 4	.500	0/ 0	.000	-/ 1	-	-	1	-	-	4	-
LEONE, J.	-	3/10	.300	7/ 9	.778	-/ 6	-	-	5	-	-	13	-
COOGAN, J.	-	5/11	.455	0/ 2	.000	-/ 6	-	-	3	-	-	10	-
MARKEY, D.	-	5/11	.455	2/ 2	1.000	-/ 6	-	-	3	-	-	12	-
MACKINNON, J.	-	0/ 0	.000	0/ 0	.000	-/ 0	-	-	0	-	-	0	-
BRITZ, G.	-	2/15	.133	7/ 7	1.000	-/ 5	-	-	4	-	-	11	-
ROJEK, T.	-	0/ 0	.000	1/ 2	.500	-/ 0	-	-	2	-	-	1	-
RUSKA, J.	-	0/ 0	.000	0/ 0	.000	-/ 1	-	-	0	-	-	0	-
SHEA, J.	-	0/ 0	.000	0/ 0	.000	-/ 0	-	-	0	-	-	0	-
Totals	200	25/62	.403	25/34	.735	-/34	-	-	22	-	-	75	.375

North Carolina (87)   Coach: Frank McGuire

	Min.	Total FG/FGA	Pct.	FT/FTA	Pct.	Reb. O/T	A	TO	PF	S	Blk	TP	PPM
ROSENBLUTH, L.	-	15/30	.500	9/11	.818	-/10	-	-	2	-	-	39	-
YOUNG, B.	-	0/ 1	.000	0/ 0	.000	-/ 1	-	-	2	-	-	0	-
BRENNAN, P.	-	1/ 8	.125	4/ 4	1.000	-/13	-	-	5	-	-	6	-
QUIGG, J.	-	4/ 5	.800	0/ 2	.000	-/ 9	-	-	4	-	-	8	-
KEARNS, T.	-	8/11	.727	3/ 5	.600	-/ 4	-	-	2	-	-	19	-
CUNNINGHAM, B.	-	2/ 5	.400	11/15	.733	-/ 8	-	-	4	-	-	15	-
LOTZ, D.	-	0/ 0	.000	0/ 0	.000	-/ 0	-	-	0	-	-	0	-
SEARCY, R.	-	0/ 0	.000	0/ 0	.000	-/ 0	-	-	0	-	-	0	-
Totals	200	30/60	.500	27/37	.730	-/45	-	-	19	-	-	87	.435

Disqualified: N. Carolina—Brennan; Canisius—Leone.

	1st Half	2nd Half	Final
Canisius	25	50	75
N. Carolina	39	48	87

REGIONAL SEMIFINAL MIDEAST

Kentucky (98)   Coach: Adolph Rupp

	Min.	Total FG/FGA	Pct.	FT/FTA	Pct.	Reb. O/T	A	TO	PF	S	Blk	TP	PPM
COX, J.	-	7/-	-	12/14	.857	-/-	-	-	2	-	-	26	-
CRIGLER, J.	-	0/-	-	2/3	.667	-/-	-	-	5	-	-	2	-
MILLS, R.	-	4/-	-	1/3	.333	-/-	-	-	4	-	-	9	-
BECK, E.	-	3/-	-	3/6	.500	-/-	-	-	5	-	-	9	-
CALVERT, G.	-	9/-	-	0/0	.000	-/-	-	-	0	-	-	18	-
HATTON, V.	-	10/-	-	4/5	.800	-/-	-	-	1	-	-	24	-
BREWER, J.	-	1/-	-	8/8	1.000	-/-	-	-	1	-	-	10	-
Totals	200	34/-	-	30/39	.769	-/-	-	-	18	-	-	98	.490

Pittsburgh (92)   Coach: Bob Timmons

	Min.	Total FG/FGA	Pct.	FT/FTA	Pct.	Reb. O/T	A	TO	PF	S	Blk	TP	PPM
PEGUES	-	7/15	.467	1/1	1.000	-/7	-	-	4	-	-	15	-
RISER	-	7/13	.538	16/17	.941	-/13	-	-	5	-	-	30	-
BRAUTIGAM	-	4/11	.364	5/6	.833	-/5	-	-	1	-	-	13	-
DORMAN	-	2/3	.667	0/0	.000	-/2	-	-	5	-	-	4	-
MARKOVICH	-	1/2	.500	1/2	.500	-/4	-	-	0	-	-	3	-
HURSH	-	0/2	.000	1/2	.500	-/7	-	-	5	-	-	1	-
HENNON, D.	-	11/29	.379	2/2	1.000	-/5	-	-	4	-	-	24	-
SAWYER	-	1/1	1.000	0/0	.000	-/1	-	-	0	-	-	2	-
LANEVE, J.	-	0/0	.000	0/1	.000	-/1	-	-	0	-	-	0	-
Totals	200	33/76	.434	26/31	.839	-/45	-	-	24	-	-	92	.460

Disqualified: Kentucky—Beck, Crigler; Pittsburgh—Riser, Hursh, Dorman.

	1st Half	2nd Half	Final
Kentucky	50	48	98
Pittsburgh	42	50	92

Notre Dame (83)   Coach: John Jordan

	Min.	Total FG/FGA	Pct.	FT/FTA	Pct.	Reb. O/T	A	TO	PF	S	Blk	TP	PPM
MCCARTHY, J.	-	5/13	.385	11/12	.917	-/11	-	-	3	-	-	21	-
HAWKINS, T.	-	6/14	.429	7/7	1.000	-/11	-	-	3	-	-	19	-
MORELLI, J.	-	0/3	.000	0/0	.000	-/0	-	-	0	-	-	0	-
SMYTH, J.	-	11/22	.500	3/3	1.000	-/14	-	-	4	-	-	25	-
DUFFY, E.	-	3/4	.750	0/0	.000	-/1	-	-	5	-	-	6	-
DEVINE, R.	-	3/14	.214	4/5	.800	-/5	-	-	2	-	-	10	-
GLEASON, E.	-	1/3	.333	0/1	.000	-/0	-	-	3	-	-	2	-
SULLIVAN, T.	-	0/0	.000	0/0	.000	-/2	-	-	1	-	-	0	-
Totals	200	29/73	.397	25/28	.893	-/44	-	-	21	-	-	83	.415

Michigan State (85)   Coach: Forddy Anderson

	Min.	Total FG/FGA	Pct.	FT/FTA	Pct.	Reb. O/T	A	TO	PF	S	Blk	TP	PPM
FERGUSON, G.	-	8/20	.400	0/0	.000	-/10	-	-	4	-	-	16	-
HEDDEN, L.	-	4/16	.250	5/12	.417	-/11	-	-	3	-	-	13	-
GREEN, J.	-	8/21	.381	4/7	.571	-/27	-	-	3	-	-	20	-
QUIGGLE, J.	-	8/22	.364	2/3	.667	-/7	-	-	3	-	-	18	-
WILSON, P.	-	0/2	.000	0/0	.000	-/3	-	-	1	-	-	0	-
SCOTT, D.	-	1/2	.500	2/4	.500	-/3	-	-	0	-	-	4	-
ANDEREGG, B.	-	4/8	.500	6/8	.750	-/5	-	-	2	-	-	14	-
Totals	200	33/91	.363	19/34	.559	-/66	-	-	16	-	-	85	.425

Disqualified: Notre Dame—Duffy.

	1st Half	2nd Half	Final
Notre Dame	36	47	83
Michigan St.	37	48	85

REGIONAL SEMIFINAL MIDWEST

St. Louis (66)   Coach: Eddie Hickey

	Min.	Total FG/FGA	Pct.	FT/FTA	Pct.	Reb. O/T	A	TO	PF	S	Blk	TP	PPM
ALCORN	-	4/13	.308	8/9	.889	-/6	-	-	4	-	-	16	-
MIMLITZ	-	9/21	.429	2/3	.667	-/10	-	-	3	-	-	20	-
TODD	-	6/14	.429	2/2	1.000	-/2	-	-	2	-	-	14	-
SERKIN	-	3/9	.333	0/1	.000	-/11	-	-	5	-	-	6	-
BURNETT	-	0/4	.000	2/2	1.000	-/11	-	-	3	-	-	2	-
FERRY, R.	-	3/5	.600	0/0	.000	-/3	-	-	0	-	-	6	-
ROGERS	-	1/2	.500	0/0	.000	-/0	-	-	1	-	-	2	-
SMITH	-	0/0	.000	0/1	.000	-/0	-	-	1	-	-	0	-
FLOOD	-	0/1	.000	0/0	.000	-/0	-	-	0	-	-	0	-
Totals	200	26/69	.377	14/18	.778	-/43	-	-	19	-	-	66	.330

Oklahoma City (75)   Coach: Abe Lemons

	Min.	Total FG/FGA	Pct.	FT/FTA	Pct.	Reb. O/T	A	TO	PF	S	Blk	TP	PPM
HOLLOWAY, R.	-	4/11	.364	5/5	1.000	-/14	-	-	1	-	-	13	-
LEE, L.	-	7/19	.368	10/14	.714	-/12	-	-	1	-	-	24	-
REED, H.	-	12/26	.462	1/5	.200	-/12	-	-	3	-	-	25	-
BRADSHAW, L.	-	0/9	.000	2/3	.667	-/5	-	-	3	-	-	2	-
MAGANA, C.	-	4/13	.308	2/2	1.000	-/6	-	-	3	-	-	10	-
GRIFFIN	-	0/1	.000	0/0	.000	-/0	-	-	0	-	-	0	-
HILL, T.	-	0/0	.000	1/4	.250	-/1	-	-	0	-	-	1	-
JETTER	-	0/0	.000	0/0	.000	-/1	-	-	0	-	-	0	-
Totals	200	27/79	.342	21/33	.636	-/51	-	-	11	-	-	75	.375

Disqualified: St. Louis—Serkin.

	1st Half	2nd Half	Final
St. Louis	32	34	66
Oklahoma City	37	38	75

Kansas (73)   Coach: Dick Harp

	Min.	Total FG/FGA	Pct.	FT/FTA	Pct.	Reb. O/T	A	TO	PF	S	Blk	TP	PPM
ELSTUN, G.	-	4/12	.333	1/2	.500	-/8	-	-	1	-	-	9	-
LONESKI, R.	-	4/8	.500	0/0	.000	-/7	-	-	0	-	-	8	-
CHAMBERLAIN, W.	-	14/26	.538	8/13	.615	-/22	-	-	4	-	-	36	-
KING, M.	-	1/7	.143	2/4	.500	-/4	-	-	2	-	-	4	-
PARKER, J.	-	4/7	.571	0/0	.000	-/1	-	-	2	-	-	8	-
JOHNSON, L.	-	3/3	1.000	0/0	.000	-/2	-	-	2	-	-	6	-
BILLINGS, B.	-	0/3	.000	2/2	1.000	-/0	-	-	0	-	-	2	-
Totals	225	30/66	.455	13/21	.619	-/44	-	-	11	-	-	73	.324

SMU (65)   Coach: E.O. "Doc" Hayes

	Min.	Total FG/FGA	Pct.	FT/FTA	Pct.	Reb. O/T	A	TO	PF	S	Blk	TP	PPM
SHOWALTER, L.	-	4/9	.444	0/1	.000	-/5	-	-	4	-	-	8	-
HERRSCHER, R.	-	3/14	.214	6/6	1.000	-/14	-	-	3	-	-	12	-
KREBS, J.	-	8/28	.286	2/2	1.000	-/6	-	-	5	-	-	18	-
MILLS, B.	-	5/11	.455	0/2	.000	-/2	-	-	0	-	-	10	-
DUNCAN, N.	-	1/10	.100	4/4	1.000	-/0	-	-	1	-	-	6	-
MCGREGOR, B.	-	5/9	.556	1/2	.500	-/7	-	-	0	-	-	11	-
Totals	225	26/81	.321	13/17	.765	-/34	-	-	13	-	-	65	.289

Disqualified: SMU—Krebs.

	1st Half	2nd Half	1st OT	Final
Kansas	33	26	14	73
SMU	32	27	6	65

REGIONAL SEMIFINAL WEST

Brigham Young (59)   Coach: Stan Watts

	Min.	Total FG / FGA	Pct.	FT / FTA	Pct.	Reb. O / T	A	TO	PF	S	Blk	TP	PPM
BENSON, J.	-	7/15	.467	3/ 4	.750	-/ 6	-	-	1	-	-	17	-
ROWE, L.	-	3/ 7	.429	2/ 2	1.000	-/ 5	-	-	0	-	-	8	-
THACKER, R.	-	2/ 4	.500	1/ 2	.500	-/ 7	-	-	4	-	-	5	-
ANDERSON, H.	-	2/ 7	.286	1/ 3	.333	-/ 8	-	-	2	-	-	5	-
STEINKE, T.	-	6/17	.353	2/ 2	1.000	-/ 6	-	-	1	-	-	14	-
GUSTIN, J.	-	1/ 3	.333	2/ 2	1.000	-/ 3	-	-	1	-	-	4	-
JONES, R.	-	2/ 3	.667	0/ 0	.000	-/ 3	-	-	1	-	-	4	-
WILKES, M.	-	0/ 0	.000	2/ 2	1.000	-/ 0	-	-	0	-	-	2	-
JENSEN, H.	-	0/ 0	.000	0/ 0	.000	-/ 0	-	-	0	-	-	0	-
PETERSON, R.	-	0/ 1	.000	0/ 0	.000	-/ 0	-	-	1	-	-	0	-
Totals	200	23/57	.404	13/17	.765	-/38	-	-	11	-	-	59	.295

Idaho State (51)   Coach: John Grayson

	Min.	Total FG / FGA	Pct.	FT / FTA	Pct.	Reb. O / T	A	TO	PF	S	Blk	TP	PPM
EASTERBROOKS, S.	-	1/11	.091	3/ 6	.500	-/ 2	-	-	2	-	-	5	-
SIEMEN	-	4/ 8	.500	2/ 2	1.000	-/10	-	-	0	-	-	10	-
ALLAIN, J.	-	4/10	.400	4/ 8	.500	-/15	-	-	5	-	-	12	-
HICKS, J.	-	1/ 7	.143	4/ 4	1.000	-/ 4	-	-	5	-	-	6	-
WELLS, C.	-	5/10	.500	1/ 2	.500	-/ 3	-	-	3	-	-	11	-
ADLEHARDT, R.	-	2/ 2	1.000	1/ 5	.200	-/ 3	-	-	0	-	-	5	-
DETMER, S.	-	0/ 1	.000	2/ 4	.500	-/ 1	-	-	1	-	-	2	-
HOGE, B.	-	0/ 1	.000	0/ 0	.000	-/ 2	-	-	0	-	-	0	-
MANLEY, R.	-	0/ 0	.000	0/ 0	.000	-/ 0	-	-	0	-	-	0	-
CHENEY, R.	-	0/ 0	.000	0/ 0	.000	-/ 0	-	-	0	-	-	0	-
Totals	200	17/50	.340	17/31	.548	-/40	-	-	16	-	-	51	.255

California (86)   Coach: Pete Newell

	Min.	Total FG / FGA	Pct.	FT / FTA	Pct.	Reb. O / T	A	TO	PF	S	Blk	TP	PPM
FRIEND, L.	-	11/25	.440	3/ 6	.500	-/ 7	-	-	1	-	-	25	-
MCKEEN, E.	-	2/ 6	.333	1/ 2	.500	-/ 6	-	-	0	-	-	5	-
HAGLER, J.	-	3/ 8	.375	3/ 4	.750	-/ 5	-	-	3	-	-	9	-
ROBINSON, E.	-	8/14	.571	2/ 2	1.000	-/ 4	-	-	2	-	-	18	-
ARRILLAGA, G.	-	3/ 6	.500	0/ 1	.000	-/ 4	-	-	1	-	-	6	-
DIAZ, M.	-	0/ 4	.000	0/ 0	.000	-/ 0	-	-	1	-	-	0	-
GROUT, J.	-	3/ 4	.750	0/ 0	.000	-/ 3	-	-	0	-	-	6	-
MCINTOSH, D.	-	2/ 4	.500	0/ 0	.000	-/ 5	-	-	0	-	-	4	-
BUCH, A.	-	5/ 8	.625	2/ 3	.667	-/ 3	-	-	1	-	-	12	-
KAPP, J.	-	0/ 0	.000	0/ 0	.000	-/ 1	-	-	0	-	-	0	-
STERLING, G.	-	0/ 0	.000	1/ 2	.500	-/ 0	-	-	0	-	-	1	-
SIMPSON, B.	-	0/ 2	.000	0/ 0	.000	-/ 1	-	-	0	-	-	0	-
Totals	200	37/81	.457	12/20	.600	-/39	-	-	9	-	-	86	.430

Disqualified: None.

San Francisco (66)   Coach: Phil Woolpert

	Min.	Total FG / FGA	Pct.	FT / FTA	Pct.	Reb. O / T	A	TO	PF	S	Blk	TP	PPM
PREASEAU, M.	-	4/ 8	.500	4/ 4	1.000	-/ 3	-	-	2	-	-	12	-
FARMER, M.	-	5/13	.385	1/ 1	1.000	-/ 8	-	-	4	-	-	11	-
DAY, A.	-	4/13	.308	5/ 6	.833	-/ 7	-	-	4	-	-	13	-
BROWN, G.	-	6/14	.429	6/ 8	.750	-/ 8	-	-	3	-	-	18	-
DUNBAR, A.	-	2/ 4	.500	1/ 3	.333	-/ 5	-	-	0	-	-	5	-
MALLEN, B.	-	3/ 6	.500	0/ 0	.000	-/ 3	-	-	3	-	-	6	-
LILLEVAND, D.	-	0/ 3	.000	0/ 0	.000	-/ 0	-	-	0	-	-	0	-
RUSSELL, C.	-	0/ 1	.000	0/ 0	.000	-/ 2	-	-	0	-	-	0	-
KOLJIAN, J.	-	0/ 3	.000	1/ 3	.333	-/ 2	-	-	1	-	-	1	-
RADANOVICH, B.	-	0/ 2	.000	0/ 0	.000	-/ 2	-	-	0	-	-	0	-
MANCASOLA, R.	-	0/ 1	.000	0/ 0	.000	-/ 1	-	-	1	-	-	0	-
KING, J.	-	0/ 0	.000	0/ 0	.000	-/ 0	-	-	0	-	-	0	-
Totals	200	24/68	.353	18/25	.720	-/41	-	-	18	-	-	66	.330

Disqualified: Idaho State—Allain, Hicks.

	1st Half	2nd Half	Final
Brigham Young	35	24	59
California	40	46	86

	1st Half	2nd Half	Final
Idaho State	15	36	51
San Francisco	36	30	66

REGIONAL FINAL EAST

Syracuse (58)   Coach: Marc Guley

	Min.	Total FG / FGA	Pct.	FT / FTA	Pct.	Reb. O / T	A	TO	PF	S	Blk	TP	PPM
CLARK, G.	-	5/13	.385	1/ 2	.500	-/12	-	-	5	-	-	11	-
COHEN, V.	-	9/23	.391	7/11	.636	-/13	-	-	3	-	-	25	-
SNYDER	-	5/19	.263	0/ 2	.000	-/12	-	-	4	-	-	10	-
BRELAND	-	0/ 6	.000	0/ 2	.000	-/ 2	-	-	5	-	-	0	-
ALBANESE	-	1/ 2	.500	0/ 0	.000	-/ 0	-	-	0	-	-	2	-
CINCEBOX	-	0/ 5	.000	2/ 6	.333	-/15	-	-	5	-	-	2	-
LOUDIS	-	3/ 6	.500	0/ 0	.000	-/ 2	-	-	3	-	-	6	-
YOUMANS	-	0/ 0	.000	0/ 0	.000	-/ 1	-	-	0	-	-	0	-
SCHMELZER	-	1/ 1	1.000	0/ 0	.000	-/ 0	-	-	2	-	-	2	-
Totals	200	24/75	.320	10/23	.435	-/57	-	-	27	-	-	58	.290

North Carolina (67)   Coach: Frank McGuire

	Min.	Total FG / FGA	Pct.	FT / FTA	Pct.	Reb. O / T	A	TO	PF	S	Blk	TP	PPM
ROSENBLUTH, L.	-	8/18	.444	7/11	.636	-/ 9	-	-	2	-	-	23	-
BRENNAN, P.	-	3/ 9	.333	7/ 9	.778	-/15	-	-	4	-	-	13	-
QUIGG, J.	-	1/ 3	.333	4/ 4	1.000	-/ 8	-	-	4	-	-	6	-
KEARNS, T.	-	4/11	.364	14/19	.737	-/ 4	-	-	3	-	-	22	-
CUNNINGHAM, B.	-	1/ 4	.250	0/ 0	.000	-/ 5	-	-	3	-	-	2	-
LOTZ, D.	-	0/ 2	.000	1/ 2	.500	-/ 6	-	-	0	-	-	1	-
Totals	200	17/47	.362	33/45	.733	-/47	-	-	16	-	-	67	.335

Disqualified: Syracuse—Clark, Cincebox, Breland.

	1st Half	2nd Half	Final
Syracuse	28	30	58
N. Carolina	37	30	67

REGIONAL FINAL MIDEAST

Kentucky (68)　Coach: Adolph Rupp

	Min.	Total FG/FGA	Pct.	FT/FTA	Pct.	Reb. O/T	A	TO	PF	S	Blk	TP	PPM
COX, J.	-	3/12	.250	11/12	.917	-/ 4	-	-	5	-	-	17	-
CRIGLER, J.	-	5/11	.455	0/ 1	.000	-/ 9	-	-	2	-	-	10	-
MILLS, R.	-	0/ 2	.000	2/ 4	.500	-/ 4	-	-	2	-	-	2	-
COLLINSWORTH, L.	-	0/ 0	.000	0/ 0	.000	-/ 0	-	-	0	-	-	0	-
BECK, E.	-	2/10	.200	0/ 2	.000	-/16	-	-	2	-	-	4	-
CALVERT, G.	-	8/18	.444	2/ 4	.500	-/ 6	-	-	4	-	-	18	-
HATTON, V.	-	6/13	.462	3/ 5	.600	-/ 7	-	-	1	-	-	15	-
SMITH, A.	-	0/ 1	.000	2/ 3	.667	-/ 1	-	-	0	-	-	2	-
ADKINS, E.	-	0/ 0	.000	0/ 0	.000	-/ 0	-	-	2	-	-	0	-
Totals	200	24/67	.358	20/31	.645	-/47	-	-	18	-	-	68	.340

Michigan State (80)　Coach: Forddy Anderson

	Min.	Total FG/FGA	Pct.	FT/FTA	Pct.	Reb. O/T	A	TO	PF	S	Blk	TP	PPM
FERGUSON, G.	-	5/15	.333	5/ 6	.833	-/12	-	-	3	-	-	15	-
HEDDEN, L.	-	4/16	.250	2/ 6	.333	-/ 7	-	-	2	-	-	10	-
GREEN, J.	-	5/11	.455	4/ 6	.667	-/18	-	-	5	-	-	14	-
QUIGGLE, J.	-	9/22	.409	4/ 4	1.000	-/ 4	-	-	4	-	-	22	-
WILSON, P.	-	3/10	.300	0/ 0	.000	-/ 3	-	-	0	-	-	6	-
SCOTT, D.	-	1/ 3	.333	4/ 5	.800	-/ 0	-	-	0	-	-	6	-
ANDEREGG, B.	-	1/ 4	.250	0/ 0	.000	-/ 1	-	-	2	-	-	2	-
BENCIE, C.	-	2/ 5	.400	1/ 2	.500	-/ 5	-	-	1	-	-	5	-
MARKOVICH, T.	-	0/ 0	.000	0/ 0	.000	-/ 1	-	-	1	-	-	0	-
LUX, H.	-	0/ 1	.000	0/ 0	.000	-/ 0	-	-	0	-	-	0	-
Totals	200	30/87	.345	20/29	.690	-/51	-	-	18	-	-	80	.400

Disqualified: Michigan St.—Green; Kentucky—Cox.

	1st Half	2nd Half	Final
Kentucky	47	21	68
Michigan St.	35	45	80

REGIONAL FINAL MIDWEST

Oklahoma City (61)　Coach: Abe Lemons

	Min.	Total FG/FGA	Pct.	FT/FTA	Pct.	Reb. O/T	A	TO	PF	S	Blk	TP	PPM
HOLLOWAY, R.	-	1/ 7	.143	0/ 0	.000	-/10	-	-	5	-	-	2	-
LEE, L.	-	5/12	.417	9/12	.750	-/ 4	-	-	4	-	-	19	-
REED, H.	-	12/34	.353	2/ 3	.667	-/13	-	-	3	-	-	26	-
BRADSHAW, L.	-	0/ 5	.000	0/ 0	.000	-/ 3	-	-	3	-	-	0	-
MAGANA, C.	-	1/10	.100	0/ 0	.000	-/ 5	-	-	3	-	-	2	-
GRIFFIN	-	3/ 8	.375	0/ 0	.000	-/ 1	-	-	1	-	-	6	-
HILL, T.	-	0/ 1	.000	0/ 1	.000	-/ 2	-	-	0	-	-	0	-
GARDNER, G.	-	0/ 4	.000	0/ 2	.000	-/ 3	-	-	1	-	-	0	-
KELLEY, M.	-	0/ 0	.000	0/ 0	.000	-/ 0	-	-	0	-	-	0	-
WALLACE, J.	-	0/ 1	.000	0/ 0	.000	-/ 0	-	-	1	-	-	0	-
HANSON, B.	-	3/ 4	.750	0/ 0	.000	-/ 2	-	-	4	-	-	6	-
Totals	200	25/86	.291	11/18	.611	-/43	-	-	25	-	-	61	.305

Kansas (81)　Coach: Dick Harp

	Min.	Total FG/FGA	Pct.	FT/FTA	Pct.	Reb. O/T	A	TO	PF	S	Blk	TP	PPM
ELSTUN, G.	-	2/ 7	.286	2/ 3	.667	-/10	-	-	0	-	-	6	-
LONESKI, R.	-	3/ 8	.375	8/ 9	.889	-/ 4	-	-	0	-	-	14	-
CHAMBERLAIN, W.	-	8/17	.471	14/22	.636	-/15	-	-	2	-	-	30	-
KING, M.	-	5/12	.417	3/ 4	.750	-/ 3	-	-	3	-	-	13	-
PARKER, J.	-	4/ 4	1.000	2/ 2	1.000	-/ 0	-	-	0	-	-	10	-
JOHNSON, L.	-	1/ 5	.200	0/ 0	.000	-/ 9	-	-	1	-	-	2	-
BILLINGS, B.	-	0/ 0	.000	0/ 0	.000	-/ 0	-	-	0	-	-	0	-
HOLLINGER, B.	-	0/ 3	.000	0/ 0	.000	-/ 1	-	-	1	-	-	0	-
DATER, E.	-	2/ 3	.667	0/ 0	.000	-/ 2	-	-	2	-	-	4	-
JOHNSON, M.	-	0/ 0	.000	0/ 0	.000	-/ 0	-	-	0	-	-	0	-
GREEN, L.	-	0/ 0	.000	0/ 0	.000	-/ 2	-	-	1	-	-	0	-
KINDRED, L.	-	0/ 3	.000	2/ 2	1.000	-/ 1	-	-	0	-	-	2	-
Totals	200	25/62	.403	31/42	.738	-/51	-	-	10	-	-	81	.405

Disqualified: Oklahoma City—Holloway.

	1st Half	2nd Half	Final
Oklahoma City	24	37	61
Kansas	27	54	81

REGIONAL FINAL WEST

California (46)　Coach: Pete Newell

	Min.	Total FG/FGA	Pct.	FT/FTA	Pct.	Reb. O/T	A	TO	PF	S	Blk	TP	PPM
MCKEEN, E.	-	3/ 5	.600	0/ 1	.000	-/ 6	-	-	4	-	-	6	-
FRIEND, L.	-	5/13	.385	2/ 3	.667	-/ 6	-	-	1	-	-	12	-
HAGLER, J.	-	0/ 1	.000	0/ 2	.000	-/ 2	-	-	1	-	-	0	-
ROBINSON, E.	-	6/13	.462	4/ 4	1.000	-/ 6	-	-	3	-	-	16	-
ARRILLAGA, G.	-	0/ 2	.000	0/ 0	.000	-/ 1	-	-	1	-	-	0	-
MCINTOSH, D.	-	1/ 3	.333	2/ 2	1.000	-/ 2	-	-	2	-	-	4	-
DIAZ, M.	-	0/ 1	.000	4/ 5	.800	-/ 2	-	-	3	-	-	4	-
GROUT, J.	-	1/ 3	.333	0/ 1	.000	-/ 2	-	-	0	-	-	2	-
BUCH, A.	-	0/ 2	.000	2/ 2	1.000	-/ 1	-	-	1	-	-	2	-
KAPP, J.	-	0/ 0	.000	0/ 0	.000	-/ 0	-	-	1	-	-	0	-
Totals	200	16/43	.372	14/20	.700	-/28	-	-	17	-	-	46	.230

San Francisco (50)　Coach: Phil Woolpert

	Min.	Total FG/FGA	Pct.	FT/FTA	Pct.	Reb. O/T	A	TO	PF	S	Blk	TP	PPM
PREASEAU, M.	-	0/ 7	.000	5/ 6	.833	-/ 6	-	-	2	-	-	5	-
FARMER, M.	-	4/12	.333	3/ 4	.750	-/ 8	-	-	3	-	-	11	-
MALLEN, B.	-	0/ 0	.000	0/ 0	.000	-/ 0	-	-	0	-	-	0	-
DAY, A.	-	4/ 9	.444	1/ 5	.200	-/ 9	-	-	4	-	-	9	-
BROWN, G.	-	8/16	.500	4/ 5	.800	-/ 4	-	-	3	-	-	20	-
DUNBAR, A.	-	0/ 3	.000	5/ 8	.625	-/ 3	-	-	1	-	-	5	-
Totals	200	16/47	.340	18/28	.643	-/30	-	-	13	-	-	50	.250

Disqualified: None.

	1st Half	2nd Half	Final
California	22	24	46
San Francisco	27	23	50

FINAL FOUR

North Carolina (74)   Coach: Frank McGuire

	Min.	Total FG / FGA	Pct.	FT / FTA	Pct.	Reb. O / T	A	TO	PF	S	Blk	TP	PPM
ROSENBLUTH, L.	-	11/42	.262	7/ 9	.778	-/ 3	-	-	1	-	-	29	-
YOUNG, B.	-	1/ 3	.333	0/ 1	.000	-/ 2	-	-	1	-	-	2	-
BRENNAN, P.	-	6/16	.375	2/ 4	.500	-/17	-	-	5	-	-	14	-
QUIGG, J.	-	0/ 1	.000	2/ 3	.667	-/ 4	-	-	5	-	-	2	-
KEARNS, T.	-	1/ 8	.125	4/ 5	.800	-/ 6	-	-	4	-	-	6	-
CUNNINGHAM, B.	-	9/18	.500	3/ 5	.600	-/12	-	-	5	-	-	21	-
LOTZ, D.	-	0/ 0	.000	0/ 1	.000	-/ 4	-	-	1	-	-	0	-
SEARCY, R.	-	0/ 0	.000	0/ 0	.000	-/ 1	-	-	0	-	-	0	-
Totals	275	28/88	.318	18/28	.643	-/49	-	-	22	-	-	74	.269

Michigan State (70)   Coach: Forddy Anderson

	Min.	Total FG / FGA	Pct.	FT / FTA	Pct.	Reb. O / T	A	TO	PF	S	Blk	TP	PPM
FERGUSON, G.	-	4/ 8	.500	2/ 3	.667	-/ 1	-	-	5	-	-	10	-
HEDDEN, L.	-	4/20	.200	6/ 7	.857	-/15	-	-	5	-	-	14	-
GREEN, J.	-	4/12	.333	3/ 6	.500	-/19	-	-	2	-	-	11	-
QUIGGLE, J.	-	6/21	.286	8/10	.800	-/10	-	-	1	-	-	20	-
WILSON, P.	-	0/ 3	.000	2/ 2	1.000	-/ 5	-	-	1	-	-	2	-
SCOTT, D.	-	2/ 3	.667	0/ 2	.000	-/ 3	-	-	1	-	-	4	-
ANDEREGG, B.	-	2/ 7	.286	3/ 6	.500	-/ 3	-	-	2	-	-	7	-
BENCIE, C.	-	1/ 6	.167	0/ 0	.000	-/ 2	-	-	1	-	-	2	-
Totals	275	23/80	.288	24/36	.667	-/58	-	-	18	-	-	70	.255

Team Rebounds: N. Carolina 5; Michigan St. 7. Disqualified: N. Carolina—Cunningham, Brennan, Quigg; Michigan St.—Ferguson, Hedden.

	1st Half	2nd Half	1st OT	2nd OT	3rd OT	Final
N. Carolina	29	29	6	2	8	74
Michigan St.	29	29	6	2	4	70

Kansas (80)   Coach: Dick Harp

	Min.	Total FG / FGA	Pct.	FT / FTA	Pct.	Reb. O / T	A	TO	PF	S	Blk	TP	PPM
ELSTUN, G.	-	8/12	.667	0/ 0	.000	-/ 6	-	-	3	-	-	16	-
LONESKI, R.	-	2/ 6	.333	3/ 4	.750	-/ 1	-	-	2	-	-	7	-
CHAMBERLAIN, W.	-	12/22	.545	8/11	.727	-/11	-	-	0	-	-	32	-
KING, M.	-	6/ 8	.750	1/ 1	1.000	-/ 4	-	-	1	-	-	13	-
PARKER, J.	-	1/ 1	1.000	0/ 0	.000	-/ 3	-	-	0	-	-	2	-
JOHNSON, L.	-	1/ 3	.333	0/ 0	.000	-/ 8	-	-	0	-	-	2	-
BILLINGS, B.	-	0/ 1	.000	0/ 0	.000	-/ 0	-	-	0	-	-	0	-
HOLLINGER, B.	-	1/ 1	1.000	0/ 0	.000	-/ 0	-	-	0	-	-	2	-
DATER, E.	-	1/ 1	1.000	0/ 0	.000	-/ 0	-	-	2	-	-	2	-
GREEN, L.	-	1/ 1	1.000	0/ 0	.000	-/ 2	-	-	1	-	-	2	-
KINDRED, L.	-	0/ 0	.000	0/ 2	.000	-/ 2	-	-	0	-	-	0	-
JOHNSON, M.	-	1/ 1	1.000	0/ 0	.000	-/ 0	-	-	0	-	-	2	-
Totals	200	34/57	.596	12/19	.632	-/37	-	-	9	-	-	80	.400

San Francisco (56)   Coach: Phil Woolpert

	Min.	Total FG / FGA	Pct.	FT / FTA	Pct.	Reb. O / T	A	TO	PF	S	Blk	TP	PPM
DAY, A.	-	3/14	.214	3/ 8	.375	-/ 7	-	-	2	-	-	9	-
DUNBAR, A.	-	2/ 8	.250	0/ 0	.000	-/ 4	-	-	1	-	-	4	-
BROWN, G.	-	5/14	.357	0/ 0	.000	-/ 2	-	-	2	-	-	10	-
FARMER, M.	-	6/15	.400	2/ 2	1.000	-/ 4	-	-	2	-	-	14	-
PREASEAU, M.	-	5/ 8	.625	2/ 2	1.000	-/ 2	-	-	2	-	-	12	-
MALLEN, B.	-	0/ 2	.000	0/ 0	.000	-/ 1	-	-	1	-	-	0	-
LILLEVAND, D.	-	1/ 3	.333	0/ 0	.000	-/ 0	-	-	1	-	-	2	-
KOLJIAN, J.	-	0/ 1	.000	3/ 4	.750	-/ 0	-	-	0	-	-	3	-
KING, J.	-	0/ 3	.000	0/ 0	.000	-/ 0	-	-	1	-	-	0	-
RUSSELL, C.	-	0/ 0	.000	0/ 0	.000	-/ 5	-	-	0	-	-	0	-
RADANOVICH, B.	-	0/ 1	.000	0/ 0	.000	-/ 0	-	-	0	-	-	0	-
MANCASOLA, R.	-	1/ 2	.500	0/ 0	.000	-/ 0	-	-	1	-	-	2	-
Totals	200	23/71	.324	10/16	.625	-/25	-	-	13	-	-	56	.280

Team Rebounds: Kansas 1, San Francisco 5. Disqualified: None.

	1st Half	2nd Half	Final
Kansas	38	42	80
San Francisco	34	22	56

NATIONAL CHAMPIONSHIP

North Carolina (54)   Coach: Frank McGuire

	Min.	Total FG / FGA	Pct.	FT / FTA	Pct.	Reb. O / T	A	TO	PF	S	Blk	TP	PPM
ROSENBLUTH, L.	-	8/15	.533	4/ 4	1.000	-/ 5	-	-	5	-	-	20	-
YOUNG, B.	-	1/ 1	1.000	0/ 0	.000	-/ 3	-	-	1	-	-	2	-
BRENNAN, P.	-	4/ 8	.500	3/ 7	.429	-/11	-	-	3	-	-	11	-
QUIGG, J.	-	4/10	.400	2/ 3	.667	-/ 9	-	-	4	-	-	10	-
KEARNS, T.	-	4/ 8	.500	3/ 7	.429	-/ 1	-	-	4	-	-	11	-
CUNNINGHAM, B.	-	0/ 3	.000	0/ 1	.000	-/ 5	-	-	4	-	-	0	-
LOTZ, D.	-	0/ 0	.000	0/ 0	.000	-/ 2	-	-	0	-	-	0	-
Totals	275	21/45	.467	12/22	.545	-/36	-	-	21	-	-	54	.270

Kansas (53)   Coach: Dick Harp

	Min.	Total FG / FGA	Pct.	FT / FTA	Pct.	Reb. O / T	A	TO	PF	S	Blk	TP	PPM
ELSTUN, G.	-	4/12	.333	3/ 6	.500	-/ 4	-	-	2	-	-	11	-
LONESKI, R.	-	0/ 5	.000	2/ 3	.667	-/ 3	-	-	2	-	-	2	-
CHAMBERLAIN, W.	-	6/13	.462	11/16	.688	-/14	-	-	3	-	-	23	-
KING, M.	-	3/12	.250	5/ 6	.833	-/ 4	-	-	4	-	-	11	-
PARKER, J.	-	2/ 4	.500	0/ 0	.000	-/ 0	-	-	0	-	-	4	-
JOHNSON, L.	-	0/ 1	.000	2/ 2	1.000	-/ 0	-	-	1	-	-	2	-
BILLINGS, B.	-	0/ 0	.000	0/ 0	.000	-/ 0	-	-	2	-	-	0	-
Totals	275	15/47	.319	23/33	.697	-/25	-	-	14	-	-	53	.265

Disqualified: N. Carolina—Rosenbluth.

	1st Half	2nd Half	1 OT	2 OT	3 OT	Final
N. Carolina	29	17	2	0	6	54
Kansas	22	24	2	0	5	53

NATIONAL THIRD PLACE
Michigan State (60)   Coach: Forddy Anderson

	Min.	Total FG / FGA	Pct.	FT / FTA	Pct.	Reb. O / T	A	TO	PF	S	Blk	TP	PPM
FERGUSON, G.	-	4/11	.364	6/ 9	.667	-/11	-	-	2	-	-	14	-
HEDDEN, L.	-	4/10	.400	1/ 2	.500	-/ 5	-	-	5	-	-	9	-
GREEN, J.	-	4/ 9	.444	1/ 1	1.000	-/13	-	-	5	-	-	9	-
QUIGGLE, J.	-	2/ 6	.333	2/ 2	1.000	-/ 4	-	-	1	-	-	6	-
WILSON, P.	-	3/ 6	.500	0/ 1	.000	-/ 0	-	-	1	-	-	6	-
SCOTT, D.	-	2/ 6	.333	0/ 1	.000	-/ 3	-	-	1	-	-	4	-
ANDEREGG, B.	-	2/ 8	.250	3/ 4	.750	-/ 4	-	-	5	-	-	7	-
LUX, H.	-	2/ 2	1.000	1/ 1	1.000	-/ 3	-	-	2	-	-	5	-
BENCIE, C.	-	0/ 5	.000	0/ 0	.000	-/ 4	-	-	1	-	-	0	-
Totals	200	23/63	.365	14/21	.667	-/47	-	-	23	-	-	60	.300

San Francisco (67)   Coach: Phil Woolpert

	Min.	Total FG / FGA	Pct.	FT / FTA	Pct.	Reb. O / T	A	TO	PF	S	Blk	TP	PPM
DAY, A.	-	6/14	.429	0/ 3	.000	-/ 6	-	-	3	-	-	12	-
DUNBAR, A.	-	4/ 9	.444	1/ 4	.250	-/ 3	-	-	4	-	-	9	-
BROWN, G.	-	8/18	.444	6/11	.545	-/ 7	-	-	3	-	-	22	-
FARMER, M.	-	4/12	.333	8/ 9	.889	-/ 2	-	-	1	-	-	16	-
PREASEAU, M.	-	2/ 6	.333	4/ 4	1.000	-/ 6	-	-	4	-	-	8	-
MALLEN, B.	-	0/ 0	.000	0/ 0	.000	-/ 1	-	-	0	-	-	0	-
LILLEVAND, D.	-	0/ 1	.000	0/ 0	.000	-/ 1	-	-	0	-	-	0	-
KING, J.	-	0/ 2	.000	0/ 0	.000	-/ 0	-	-	2	-	-	0	-
Totals	200	24/62	.387	19/31	.613	-/26	-	-	17	-	-	67	.335

Team Rebounds: San Francisco 9; Michigan St. 13. Disqualified: Michigan St.—Green, Hedden, Anderegg.

	1st Half	2nd Half	Final
Michigan St.	30	30	60
San Francisco	33	34	67

REGIONAL THIRD PLACE EAST
Canisius (82)   Coach: Joseph Curran

	Min.	Total FG / FGA	Pct.	FT / FTA	Pct.	Reb. O / T	A	TO	PF	S	Blk	TP	PPM
NOWAK, H.	-	1/10	.100	13/16	.813	-/ 8	-	-	1	-	-	15	-
SHEA, J.	-	0/ 0	.000	0/ 0	.000	-/ 2	-	-	2	-	-	0	-
LEONE, J.	-	1/ 8	.125	2/ 2	1.000	-/ 4	-	-	5	-	-	4	-
COOGAN, J.	-	7/12	.583	0/ 0	.000	-/ 8	-	-	3	-	-	14	-
MARKEY, D.	-	6/15	.400	2/ 2	1.000	-/10	-	-	4	-	-	14	-
MACKINNON, J.	-	3/ 6	.500	2/ 2	1.000	-/ 2	-	-	1	-	-	8	-
BRITZ, G.	-	11/23	.478	3/ 7	.429	-/ 9	-	-	4	-	-	25	-
ROJEK, T.	-	1/ 2	.500	0/ 0	.000	-/ 2	-	-	0	-	-	2	-
Totals	200	30/76	.395	22/29	.759	-/45	-	-	20	-	-	82	.410

Lafayette (76)   Coach: George Davidson

	Min.	Total FG / FGA	Pct.	FT / FTA	Pct.	Reb. O / T	A	TO	PF	S	Blk	TP	PPM
GALTERE	-	4/13	.308	3/ 5	.600	-/13	-	-	3	-	-	11	-
STERLEIN	-	2/ 2	1.000	4/ 6	.667	-/ 7	-	-	2	-	-	8	-
MANTZ	-	8/15	.533	6/ 7	.857	-/20	-	-	3	-	-	22	-
MURRAY	-	7/20	.350	3/ 3	1.000	-/ 3	-	-	2	-	-	17	-
MACK	-	3/10	.300	9/14	.643	-/ 6	-	-	4	-	-	15	-
KOHLER	-	0/ 0	.000	0/ 0	.000	-/ 1	-	-	0	-	-	0	-
JONES	-	1/ 4	.250	1/ 2	.500	-/ 2	-	-	1	-	-	3	-
GUSTAFSON	-	0/ 0	.000	0/ 0	.000	-/ 1	-	-	1	-	-	0	-
Totals	200	25/64	.391	26/37	.703	-/53	-	-	16	-	-	76	.380

Disqualified: Canisius—Leone.

	1st Half	2nd Half	Final
Canisius	42	40	82
Lafayette	36	40	76

REGIONAL THIRD PLACE MIDEAST
Notre Dame (86)   Coach: John Jordan

	Min.	Total FG / FGA	Pct.	FT / FTA	Pct.	Reb. O / T	A	TO	PF	S	Blk	TP	PPM
HAWKINS, T.	40	8/20	.400	5/ 7	.714	-/14	-	-	1	-	-	21	.525
SMYTH, J.	40	8/20	.400	6/ 8	.750	-/23	-	-	3	-	-	22	.550
MCCARTHY, J.	40	5/15	.333	13/14	.929	-/ 9	-	-	4	-	-	23	.575
DUFFY, E.	40	3/ 4	.750	2/ 6	.333	-/ 3	-	-	3	-	-	8	.200
DEVINE, R.	40	3/15	.200	6/ 6	1.000	-/ 1	-	-	4	-	-	12	.300
Totals	200	27/74	.365	32/41	.780	-/50	-	-	15	-	-	86	.430

Pittsburgh (85)   Coach: Bob Timmons

	Min.	Total FG / FGA	Pct.	FT / FTA	Pct.	Reb. O / T	A	TO	PF	S	Blk	TP	PPM
PEGUES	-	4/12	.333	5/ 7	.714	-/ 7	-	-	5	-	-	13	-
RISER	-	14/22	.636	6/ 9	.667	-/10	-	-	4	-	-	34	-
BRAUTIGAM	-	2/10	.200	1/ 2	.500	-/ 5	-	-	4	-	-	5	-
DORMAN	-	0/ 0	.000	0/ 0	.000	-/ 0	-	-	0	-	-	0	-
MARKOVICH	-	2/ 3	.667	0/ 0	.000	-/ 2	-	-	2	-	-	4	-
HURSH	-	4/ 4	1.000	1/ 3	.333	-/ 9	-	-	4	-	-	9	-
HENNON, D.	-	7/16	.438	6/ 6	1.000	-/ 5	-	-	4	-	-	20	-
LANEVE, J.	-	0/ 0	.000	0/ 0	.000	-/ 0	-	-	1	-	-	0	-
Totals	200	33/67	.493	19/27	.704	-/38	-	-	24	-	-	85	.425

Disqualified: Pittsburgh—Pegues.

	1st Half	2nd Half	Final
Notre Dame	38	48	86
Pittsburgh	36	49	85

REGIONAL THIRD PLACE MIDWEST
SMU (78)   Coach: E.O. "Doc" Hayes

	Min.	Total FG / FGA	Pct.	FT / FTA	Pct.	Reb. O / T	A	TO	PF	S	Blk	TP	PPM
SHOWALTER, L.	-	1/ 7	.143	0/ 1	.000	-/ 6	-	-	0	-	-	2	-
HERRSCHER, R.	-	4/10	.400	6/ 6	1.000	-/ 7	-	-	5	-	-	14	-
KREBS, J.	-	9/24	.375	15/18	.833	-/ 9	-	-	3	-	-	33	-
MILLS, B.	-	6/15	.400	3/ 5	.600	-/ 5	-	-	1	-	-	15	-
DUNCAN, N.	-	4/ 7	.571	0/ 0	.000	-/ 4	-	-	0	-	-	8	-
MCGREGOR, B.	-	3/ 7	.429	0/ 3	.000	-/10	-	-	1	-	-	6	-
ELDRIDGE, B.	-	0/ 1	.000	0/ 0	.000	-/ 0	-	-	0	-	-	0	-
BROWN, A.	-	0/ 0	.000	0/ 0	.000	-/ 0	-	-	0	-	-	0	-
O'KELLEY, H.	-	0/ 0	.000	0/ 0	.000	-/ 2	-	-	0	-	-	0	-
MINTON, E.	-	0/ 0	.000	0/ 0	.000	-/ 0	-	-	1	-	-	0	-
BUDDENDORF, B.	-	0/ 0	.000	0/ 0	.000	-/ 0	-	-	0	-	-	0	-
KNAPP, B.	-	0/ 0	.000	0/ 0	.000	-/ 0	-	-	0	-	-	0	-
Totals	200	27/71	.380	24/33	.727	-/43	-	-	11	-	-	78	.390

St. Louis (68)   Coach: Eddie Hickey

	Min.	Total FG / FGA	Pct.	FT / FTA	Pct.	Reb. O / T	A	TO	PF	S	Blk	TP	PPM
ALCORN	-	10/19	.526	0/ 0	.000	-/ 6	-	-	5	-	-	20	-
MIMLITZ	-	6/17	.353	5/ 6	.833	-/ 3	-	-	2	-	-	17	-
TODD	-	6/14	.429	2/ 3	.667	-/ 4	-	-	1	-	-	14	-
SERKIN	-	1/ 5	.200	1/ 3	.333	-/ 6	-	-	4	-	-	3	-
BURNETT	-	0/ 3	.000	2/ 2	1.000	-/ 7	-	-	0	-	-	2	-
FERRY, R.	-	3/11	.273	0/ 1	.000	-/ 3	-	-	4	-	-	6	-
ROGERS	-	1/ 4	.250	0/ 0	.000	-/ 0	-	-	1	-	-	2	-
SMITH	-	0/ 1	.000	0/ 1	.000	-/ 4	-	-	3	-	-	0	-
FLOOD	-	0/ 3	.000	0/ 0	.000	-/ 2	-	-	0	-	-	0	-
HAKE	-	0/ 0	.000	0/ 1	.000	-/ 1	-	-	0	-	-	0	-
REDSHAW	-	1/ 1	1.000	0/ 0	.000	-/ 2	-	-	0	-	-	2	-
MCCARTNEY	-	1/ 1	1.000	0/ 0	.000	-/ 0	-	-	0	-	-	2	-
Totals	200	29/79	.367	10/17	.588	-/37	-	-	20	-	-	68	.340

Disqualified: SMU—Herrscher; St. Louis—Alcorn.

	1st Half	2nd Half	Final
SMU	36	42	78
St. Louis	28	40	68

REGIONAL THIRD PLACE WEST

Brigham Young (65) Coach: Stan Watts

	Min.	Total FG/FGA	Pct.	FT/FTA	Pct.	Reb. O/T	A	TO	PF	S	Blk	TP	PPM
BENSON, J.	-	6/12	.500	10/12	.833	-/ 3	-	-	4	-	-	22	-
ROWE, L.	-	1/ 6	.167	0/ 0	.000	-/11	-	-	0	-	-	2	-
THACKER, R.	-	3/ 8	.375	2/ 2	1.000	-/11	-	-	2	-	-	8	-
STEINKE, T.	-	2/13	.154	0/ 1	.000	-/ 4	-	-	5	-	-	4	-
ANDERSON, H.	-	9/16	.563	9/13	.692	-/ 2	-	-	3	-	-	27	-
JENSEN, H.	-	0/ 1	.000	0/ 0	.000	-/ 2	-	-	2	-	-	0	-
MILES	-	0/ 2	.000	2/ 2	1.000	-/ 1	-	-	0	-	-	2	-
GUSTIN, J.	-	0/ 1	.000	0/ 0	.000	-/ 0	-	-	0	-	-	0	-
CRAVENS, J.	-	0/ 0	.000	0/ 0	.000	-/ 2	-	-	0	-	-	0	-
WILKES, M.	-	0/ 0	.000	0/ 0	.000	-/ 1	-	-	1	-	-	0	-
Totals	200	21/59	.356	23/30	.767	-/37	-	-	17	-	-	65	.325

Idaho State (54) Coach: John Grayson

	Min.	Total FG/FGA	Pct.	FT/FTA	Pct.	Reb. O/T	A	TO	PF	S	Blk	TP	PPM
EASTERBROOKS, S.	-	2/10	.200	4/ 6	.667	-/ 3	-	-	4	-	-	8	-
ADELHARDT, R.	-	0/ 1	.000	0/ 0	.000	-/ 4	-	-	0	-	-	0	-
ALLAIN, J.	-	4/10	.400	2/ 3	.667	-/10	-	-	3	-	-	10	-
HICKS, J.	-	6/20	.300	0/ 2	.000	-/10	-	-	2	-	-	12	-
WELLS, C.	-	1/ 7	.143	16/19	.842	-/ 2	-	-	3	-	-	18	-
CHENEY, R.	-	0/ 2	.000	0/ 0	.000	-/ 4	-	-	1	-	-	0	-
DETMER, S.	-	1/ 3	.333	2/ 2	1.000	-/ 0	-	-	1	-	-	4	-
MANLEY, R.	-	0/ 0	.000	0/ 0	.000	-/ 0	-	-	2	-	-	0	-
HOGE, B.	-	1/ 4	.250	0/ 0	.000	-/ 1	-	-	0	-	-	2	-
Totals	200	15/57	.263	24/32	.750	-/34	-	-	16	-	-	54	.270

Disqualified: Brigham Young—Steinke. Technical fouls: Brigham Young—Steinke.

	1st Half	2nd Half	Final
Brigham Young	34	31	65
Idaho State	23	31	54

✪ ALL-STAR TEAMS ✪

ALL TOURNAMENT

PETE BRENNAN	N. CAROLINA
GENE BROWN	SAN FRANCISCO
★ WILT CHAMBERLAIN	KANSAS
JOHN GREEN	MICHIGAN STATE
LEN ROSENBLUTH	N. CAROLINA

★ Most Outstanding Player(s)

✪ INDIVIDUAL RECORDS ✪

SCORING

Most points in a single game
1 LENNIE ROSENBLUTH, N. CAROLINA (vs. CANISIUS) — 39
2 WILT CHAMBERLAIN, KANSAS (vs. SMU) — 36
3 RISER, PITTSBURGH (vs. NOTRE DAME) — 34
3 GARY CLARK, SYRACUSE (vs. LAFAYETTE) — 34
5 JIM KREBS, SMU (vs. ST. LOUIS) — 33

Most total points in the tournament
1 LENNIE ROSENBLUTH, N. CAROLINA — 140
2 WILT CHAMBERLAIN, KANSAS — 121
3 RISER, PITTSBURGH — 84
4 HUBERT REED, OKLAHOMA CITY — 75
4 DON HENNON, PITTSBURGH — 75

Highest scoring average (minimum 2 games)
1 WILT CHAMBERLAIN, KANSAS (121-4) — 30.25
2 LENNIE ROSENBLUTH, N. CAROLINA (140-5) — 28.00
3 RISER, PITTSBURGH (84-3) — 28.00
4 JIM KREBS, SMU (51-2) — 25.50
5 2 tied for fifth place.

FIELD GOALS

Most field goals in a single game
1 LENNIE ROSENBLUTH, N. CAROLINA (vs. CANISIUS) — 15
2 RISER, PITTSBURGH (vs. NOTRE DAME) — 14
2 WILT CHAMBERLAIN, KANSAS (vs. SMU) — 14
2 MURRAY, LAFAYETTE (vs. SYRACUSE) — 14
5 GARY CLARK, SYRACUSE (vs. LAFAYETTE) — 13

Most total field goals in the tournament
1 LENNIE ROSENBLUTH, N. CAROLINA — 53
2 WILT CHAMBERLAIN, KANSAS — 40
3 HUBERT REED, OKLAHOMA CITY — 33
4 GARY CLARK, SYRACUSE — 30
5 DON HENNON, PITTSBURGH — 29

Most field goal attempts in a single game
1 LENNIE ROSENBLUTH, N. CAROLINA (vs. MICHIGAN ST.) — 42
2 HUBERT REED, OKLAHOMA CITY (vs. KANSAS) — 34
3 LENNIE ROSENBLUTH, N. CAROLINA (vs. CANISIUS) — 30
4 DON HENNON, PITTSBURGH (vs. KENTUCKY) — 29
5 JIM KREBS, SMU (vs. KANSAS) — 28

Most total field goal attempts in tournament
1 LENNIE ROSENBLUTH, N. CAROLINA — 124
2 WILT CHAMBERLAIN, KANSAS — 78
3 JACK QUIGGLE, MICHIGAN ST. — 71
4 LARRY HEDDEN, MICHIGAN ST. — 62
4 GENE BROWN, SAN FRANCISCO — 62

Highest field goal percentage in a single game (minimum 10 attempts)
1 HENRY NOWAK, CANISIUS (vs. N. CAROLINA) (8-11) — .727
1 TOMMY KEARNS, N. CAROLINA (vs. CANISIUS) (8-11) — .727
3 GENE ELSTUN, KANSAS (vs. SAN FRANCISCO) (8-12) — .667
4 GARY CLARK, SYRACUSE (vs. LAFAYETTE) (13-20) — .650
5 RISER, PITTSBURGH (vs. NOTRE DAME) (14-22) — .636

FREE THROWS

Most free throws in a single game
1 RISER, PITTSBURGH (vs. KENTUCKY) — 16
1 CONRAD WELLS, IDAHO STATE (vs. BRIGHAM YOUNG) — 16
3 JIM KREBS, SMU (vs. ST. LOUIS) — 15
4 WILT CHAMBERLAIN, KANSAS (vs. OKLAHOMA CITY) — 14
4 TOMMY KEARNS, N. CAROLINA (vs. SYRACUSE) — 14

Most total free throws in the tournament
1 WILT CHAMBERLAIN, KANSAS — 41
2 LENNIE ROSENBLUTH, N. CAROLINA — 34
3 RISER, PITTSBURGH — 30
3 JOHN MCCARTHY, NOTRE DAME — 30
3 TOMMY KEARNS, N. CAROLINA — 30

Most free throws attempted in a single game
1	WILT CHAMBERLAIN, KANSAS (vs. OKLAHOMA CITY)	22
2	CONRAD WELLS, IDAHO STATE (vs. BRIGHAM YOUNG)	19
2	TOMMY KEARNS, N. CAROLINA (vs. SYRACUSE)	19
4	JIM KREBS, SMU (vs. ST. LOUIS)	18
5	RISER, PITTSBURGH (vs. KENTUCKY)	17

Most free throws attempted in the tournament
1	WILT CHAMBERLAIN, KANSAS	62
2	LENNIE ROSENBLUTH, N. CAROLINA	47
3	TOMMY KEARNS, N. CAROLINA	45
4	RISER, PITTSBURGH	36
5	PETE BRENNAN, N. CAROLINA	35

Highest free throw percentage in a single game (minimum 7 attempts)
1	JOHNNY LEE, YALE (vs. N. CAROLINA) (9-9)	1.000

1	ROD HUNDLEY, WEST VIRGINIA (vs. CANISIUS) (9-9)	1.000
3	JOHN BREWER, KENTUCKY (vs. PITTSBURGH) (8-8)	1.000
4	TOM HAWKINS, NOTRE DAME (vs. MICHIGAN ST.) (7-7)	1.000
4	GREGORY BRITZ, CANISIUS (vs. N. CAROLINA) (7-7)	1.000

REBOUNDS

Most rebounds in a single game
1	JOHN GREEN, MICHIGAN ST. (vs. NOTRE DAME)	27
2	JOHN SMYTH, NOTRE DAME (vs. PITTSBURGH)	23
3	WILT CHAMBERLAIN, KANSAS (vs. SMU)	22
4	MANTZ, LAFAYETTE (vs. CANISIUS)	20
5	2 tied for fifth place.	

Most total rebounds in the tournament
1	JOHN GREEN, MICHIGAN ST.	77
2	PETE BRENNAN, N. CAROLINA	67
3	WILT CHAMBERLAIN, KANSAS	62
4	LENNIE ROSENBLUTH, N. CAROLINA	46
5	LARRY HEDDEN, MICHIGAN ST.	38

Most rebounds per game (minimum 2 games)
1	JOHN GREEN, MICHIGAN ST. (77-4)	19.25
2	MANTZ, LAFAYETTE (37-2)	18.50
3	WILT CHAMBERLAIN, KANSAS (62-4)	15.50
4	PETE BRENNAN, N. CAROLINA (67-5)	13.40
5	JOHN SMYTH, NOTRE DAME (37-3)	12.33

✪ TEAM RECORDS ✪

SCORING

Most points in a single game
1	KENTUCKY (vs. PITTSBURGH)	98
2	PITTSBURGH (vs. KENTUCKY)	92
3	N. CAROLINA (vs. YALE)	90

Most total points in the tournament
1	N. CAROLINA	372
2	MICHIGAN ST.	295
3	KANSAS	287

Highest scoring average (minimum 2 games)
1	PITTSBURGH (263-3)	87.67
2	NOTRE DAME (258-3)	86.00
3	KENTUCKY (166-2)	83.00

FIELD GOALS

Most field goals in a single game
1	CALIFORNIA (vs. BRIGHAM YOUNG)	37
2	KANSAS (vs. SAN FRANCISCO)	34
2	KENTUCKY (vs. PITTSBURGH)	34

Most total field goals in the tournament
1	N. CAROLINA	127
2	MICHIGAN ST.	109
3	KANSAS	104

Most field goals attempted in a single game
1	MICHIGAN ST. (vs. NOTRE DAME)	91
2	N. CAROLINA (vs. MICHIGAN ST.)	88
3	MICHIGAN ST. (vs. KENTUCKY)	87

Most total field goals attempted in the tournament
1	MICHIGAN ST.	321
2	N. CAROLINA	298
3	SAN FRANCISCO	248

Highest field goal percentage in a single game
1	KANSAS (vs. SAN FRANCISCO) (34-57)	.597
2	N. CAROLINA (vs. YALE) (31-58)	.535
3	N. CAROLINA (vs. CANISIUS) (30-60)	.500

Highest field goal percentage in a tournament (minimum 2 games)
1	KENTUCKY (58-67)	.866
2	PITTSBURGH (93-143)	.650
3	NOTRE DAME (88-147)	.599

FREE THROWS

Most free throws in a single game
1	MOREHEAD STATE (vs. PITTSBURGH)	37
2	N. CAROLINA (vs. SYRACUSE)	33
3	2 tied for third place.	

Most total free throws in the tournament
1	N. CAROLINA	118
2	NOTRE DAME	82
3	KANSAS	79

Most free throws attempted in a single game
1	MOREHEAD STATE (vs. PITTSBURGH)	54
2	N. CAROLINA (vs. SYRACUSE)	45
3	PITTSBURGH (vs. MOREHEAD STATE)	43

Most total free throws attempted in the tournament
1	N. CAROLINA	172
2	MICHIGAN ST.	120
3	KANSAS	115

Highest free throw percentage in a single game
1	NOTRE DAME (vs. MICHIGAN ST.) (25-28)	.893
2	PITTSBURGH (vs. KENTUCKY) (26-31)	.839
3	NOTRE DAME (vs. PITTSBURGH) (32-41)	.781

Fewest free throws in a single game
1	CANISIUS (vs. WEST VIRGINIA)	8
2	3 tied for second place.	

Lowest free throw percentage in a single game
1	SYRACUSE (vs. N. CAROLINA) (10-23)	.435
2	CANISIUS (vs. WEST VIRGINIA) (8-17)	.471
3	OKLAHOMA CITY (vs. LOYOLA N.O.) (14-26)	.538

Lowest free throw percentage in the tournament (minimum 2 games)
1	SYRACUSE (41-75)	.547
2	OKLAHOMA CITY (46-77)	.597
3	MICHIGAN ST. (77-120)	.642

REBOUNDS

Most rebounds in a single game
1	MICHIGAN ST. (vs. NOTRE DAME)	66
2	MICHIGAN ST. (vs. N. CAROLINA)	58
3	SYRACUSE (vs. N. CAROLINA)	57

1958

| FIRST ROUND | REGIONAL SEMIFINAL | REGIONAL FINAL | **FINAL FOUR** | REGIONAL FINAL | REGIONAL SEMIFINAL | FIRST ROUND |

EAST

(bye) — Temple 71

Temple 69

Maryland 86

Boston College 63

Maryland 67

Temple 60

Manhattan 89

West Virginia 84

Manhattan 62

Dartmouth 50

Dartmouth 75

U. Conn. 64

Dartmouth 79

Kentucky 84
Seattle 72

MIDEAST

(bye) — Kentucky 94

Kentucky 89

Miami (Ohio) 82

Pittsburgh 77

Miami (Ohio) 70

Kentucky 61

Notre Dame 94

Tennessee Tech 61

Notre Dame 94

Notre Dame 56

(bye) — Indiana 87

MIDWEST

Arkansas 40 — (bye)

Oklahoma St. 57

Oklahoma St. 59

Oklahoma St. 65

Loyola N.O. 42

Kansas St. 51

Kansas St. 83 (ot) — (bye)

Kansas St. 69

Cincinnati 80 — (bye)

WEST

San Francisco 67 — (bye)

Seattle 66 (ot)

Seattle 88

Seattle 69

Wyoming 51

Seattle 73

Idaho St. 72

Idaho St. 43

Arizona St. 68

California 62

California 54 — (bye)

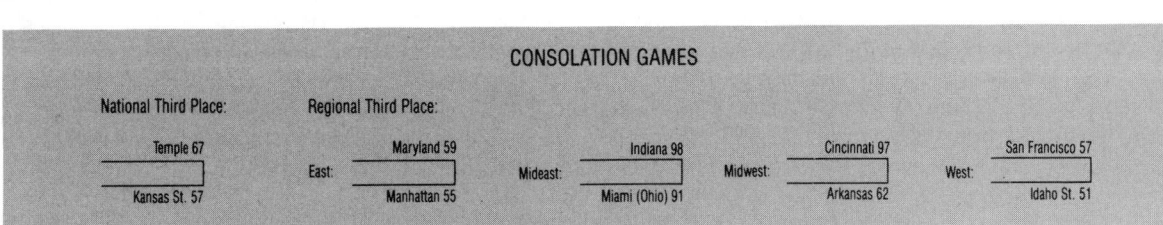

CONSOLATION GAMES

National Third Place:

Temple 67

Kansas St. 57

Regional Third Place:

East:
Maryland 59
Manhattan 55

Mideast:
Indiana 98
Miami (Ohio) 91

Midwest:
Cincinnati 97
Arkansas 62

West:
San Francisco 57
Idaho St. 51

When the University of Kentucky basketball team was banned from participating in intercollegiate competition in the 1952–1953 season, the ailing Baron of the Bluegrass, Adolph Rupp, swore he would not retire "until the man who said Kentucky can't play in the NCAA hands me the national championship trophy." The following year Rupp redoubled his vow when the three senior stars of his undefeated squad were declared ineligible for tournament play and a decimated Kentucky declined an NCAA bid. Years later, the Baron was still hoping to make good on his promise. But he was hardly predicting that the Wildcats' 1957–1958 squad would be the team to seal his victory vow. "They might be pretty good barnyard fiddlers," he said in the fall, "but we have a Carnegie Hall schedule, and it will take violinists to play that competition."

To be sure, there were a lot of virtuosos playing on college courts in 1957–58. There was little Guy Rodgers of Temple, one of the greatest floor generals the game has ever seen. There was Elgin Baylor of Seattle, whose fantastic solo performances often left audiences gasping. There was Cincinnati's splendid sophomore, Oscar Robertson, who had edged out Baylor for the national scoring title, and Jerry West of West Virginia, although "Mr. Clutch" had not yet come into his own. And of course Wilt Chamberlain was back at Kansas for another go-round before skipping to the Harlem Globetrotters. Very rarely in the history of the game have so many of basketball's all-time greats been plying their trade at the college level at the same time.

Compared to the competition, Rupp's "Fiddlin' Five"—Vernon Hatton, John Crigler, John Cox, Ed Beck, and Adrian Smith—looked like a bunch of beginners. They finished the regular season with six losses (at the time, no NCAA champion had ever been defeated so often), and were ranked ninth in the Associated Press poll and fourteenth by UPI. They had no height, no true playmaker and little speed. But as usual with Rupp-coached squads, they played as a *unit.*

The Wildcats were so lightly regarded near the end of the 1957–58 season that NCAA officials, doubting Kentucky would even qualify for the tournament, scheduled the Mideast regional in Lexington and the Final Four in nearby Louisville. Thus, when Kentucky did receive a bid, they were able to play all their games with a homecourt advantage. With that piece of good news in Baron Rupp's pocket, fortune again smiled on Kentucky when three of the country's top four teams bit the dust in their first tournament game: Top-ranked West Virginia (which had beaten UK in Lexington in December) fell to the unheralded, unknown, 15-8 Manhattan Jaspers; San Francisco

succumbed to Seattle when Elgin Baylor hit a 35-foot shot at the buzzer; and No. 2 Cincinnati, facing No. 3 Kansas State, lost in overtime after Robertson missed a free throw with one second left in regulation that would have given the Bearcats the victory.

Kentucky, playing in the regional with by far the weakest field, sailed through their opening games in Lexington with easy victories over Miami of Ohio and Notre Dame. A stone's throw away in Louisville, a highly partisan crowd of 18,586 watched the Wildcats' semifinal contest against the East regional champs, Temple and their All-American guard, Guy Rodgers. The Philadelphia team had lost only two games all season, but the first had been a triple overtime thriller to the Wildcats in Lexington. Again, the two teams went down to the wire. With less than a minute and a half left, Temple had the lead (59-55) and the ball. But the Owls' Bill (Pickle) Kennedy was called for charging and Adrian Smith hit two free throws to cut the margin in half. With 27 seconds left, Temple was up by one and Rodgers had the ball. He was fouled by Johnny Cox, but missed the front end of a one-and-one. After a Kentucky time-out, Cox fed Hatton, who drove and scored the winning basket with twelve seconds left.

In the Western half of the draw, Baylor was stupendous, his 23 points and 22 rebounds leading Seattle to an easy victory over favored Kansas State. After a showtime second half, in which Baylor performed an incredible variety of crowd pleasing moves and his teammate Charlie Brown actually *dribbled between his legs,* the Chieftains' coach Paul Castellani was asked how he planned to play Kentucky. "Baylor's my best strategy," he replied.

But in the end it was Rupp's game plan—and Castellani's inability to counter it effectively—that beat Seattle. Rupp, hoping to get Baylor in foul trouble, instructed his boys to drive at the Seattle star at every opportunity. In the first half, despite having painfully bruised ribs, Baylor played brilliantly—scoring, rebounding, and passing the Chieftains to an 11-point lead. But as Rupp had foreseen, he also started to pile up fouls. When he was called for his fourth personal with sixteen and a half minutes remaining in the game, Seattle held a 44-38 lead. Chieftains' Coach Castellani switched to a zone in an attempt to keep his big man from fouling out. But with a tentative Baylor becoming a spectator on defense, Kentucky came back on Johnny Cox's outside shooting and Vernon Hatton's scoring from the inside. By the end, Hatton and Cox had combined for 35 second-half points and the Baron had his revenge.

Rupp received his fourth championship trophy from the NCAA official who said Kentucky couldn't play in 1952, and he was finally satisfied. "Those boys certainly are not concert violinists," he said, "but they sure can fiddle."

FIRST ROUND EAST

Maryland (86) Coach: Bud Millikan

	Min.	Total FG / FGA	Pct.	FT / FTA	Pct.	Reb. O / T	A	TO	PF	S	Blk	TP	PPM
MCNEIL, C.	-	2/ 5	.400	2/ 3	.667	-/ 6	-	-	2	-	-	6	-
NACINCIK, J.	-	4/ 8	.500	6/ 7	.857	-/10	-	-	3	-	-	14	-
BUNGE, A.	-	4/ 9	.444	3/11	.273	-/12	-	-	4	-	-	11	-
DAVIS, N.	-	11/17	.647	2/ 4	.500	-/ 3	-	-	2	-	-	24	-
YOUNG, T.	-	3/ 5	.600	6/ 7	.857	-/ 4	-	-	4	-	-	12	-
HALLECK, J.	-	1/ 1	1.000	3/ 4	.750	-/ 2	-	-	3	-	-	5	-
MURPHY	-	1/ 2	.500	0/ 0	.000	-/ 1	-	-	2	-	-	2	-
DANKO	-	3/ 5	.600	0/ 0	.000	-/ 1	-	-	1	-	-	6	-
BECHTIE	-	1/ 2	.500	2/ 2	1.000	-/ 3	-	-	1	-	-	4	-
MOORE	-	0/ 1	.000	0/ 1	.000	-/ 1	-	-	0	-	-	0	-
KRUKAR	-	0/ 0	.000	0/ 0	.000	-/ 1	-	-	0	-	-	0	-
WEINGARTEN	-	0/ 0	.000	2/ 3	.667	-/ 2	-	-	1	-	-	2	-
Totals	200	30/55	.545	26/42	.619	-/46	-	-	23	-	-	86	.430

Boston College (63) Coach: Donald Martin

	Min.	Total FG / FGA	Pct.	FT / FTA	Pct.	Reb. O / T	A	TO	PF	S	Blk	TP	PPM
GIERSCH	-	2/12	.167	4/ 4	1.000	-/ 5	-	-	4	-	-	8	-
HARRINGTON	-	0/ 7	.000	7/10	.700	-/ 7	-	-	4	-	-	7	-
MCGRATH	-	2/ 9	.222	7/ 8	.875	-/ 6	-	-	3	-	-	11	-
MAGEE	-	3/15	.200	7/ 9	.778	-/ 7	-	-	3	-	-	13	-
LYONS	-	3/ 5	.600	0/ 0	.000	-/ 3	-	-	3	-	-	6	-
SCHOPPMEYER	-	0/ 2	.000	0/ 0	.000	-/ 1	-	-	4	-	-	0	-
POWER	-	4/13	.308	1/ 3	.333	-/ 9	-	-	1	-	-	9	-
LATKANY	-	2/ 4	.500	0/ 0	.000	-/ 1	-	-	2	-	-	4	-
VONBURG	-	0/ 0	.000	3/ 4	.750	-/ 4	-	-	2	-	-	3	-
BIGELOW	-	1/ 3	.333	0/ 0	.000	-/ 0	-	-	0	-	-	2	-
MANNING	-	0/ 0	.000	0/ 0	.000	-/ 0	-	-	1	-	-	0	-
Totals	200	17/70	.243	29/38	.763	-/43	-	-	27	-	-	63	.315

Disqualified: None.

	1st Half	2nd Half	Final
Maryland	41	45	86
Boston College	30	33	63

Manhattan (89) Coach: Ken Norton

	Min.	Total FG / FGA	Pct.	FT / FTA	Pct.	Reb. O / T	A	TO	PF	S	Blk	TP	PPM
MEALY, B.	-	5/ 9	.556	4/ 4	1.000	-/ 4	-	-	5	-	-	14	-
WILBUR, D.	-	3/11	.273	10/12	.833	-/11	-	-	5	-	-	16	-
BRUNONE, P.	-	2/ 2	1.000	2/ 5	.400	-/ 2	-	-	5	-	-	6	-
MCGORTY, D.	-	1/ 4	.250	2/ 4	.500	-/ 5	-	-	3	-	-	4	-
POWERS, J.	-	9/19	.474	11/15	.733	-/15	-	-	2	-	-	29	-
BURKOSKI, M.	-	5/ 8	.625	0/ 0	.000	-/ 2	-	-	5	-	-	10	-
KOENIG, C.	-	1/ 2	.500	4/ 7	.571	-/ 2	-	-	3	-	-	6	-
DOUGHERTY	-	1/ 2	.500	0/ 0	.000	-/ 1	-	-	1	-	-	2	-
QUARTO, F.	-	0/ 0	.000	2/ 2	1.000	-/ 1	-	-	0	-	-	2	-
Totals	200	27/57	.474	35/49	.714	-/43	-	-	29	-	-	89	.445

West Virginia (84) Coach: Fred Schaus

	Min.	Total FG / FGA	Pct.	FT / FTA	Pct.	Reb. O / T	A	TO	PF	S	Blk	TP	PPM
WEST, J.	-	5/12	.417	0/ 1	.000	-/ 4	-	-	5	-	-	10	-
AKERS, W.	-	2/ 3	.667	4/ 4	1.000	-/ 4	-	-	5	-	-	8	-
SHARRAR, L.	-	2/11	.182	10/16	.625	-/ 9	-	-	5	-	-	14	-
SMITH, B.	-	7/14	.500	4/ 5	.800	-/ 7	-	-	4	-	-	18	-
GARDNER, G.	-	5/15	.333	5/ 7	.714	-/ 4	-	-	5	-	-	15	-
RETTON, R.	-	3/ 8	.375	1/ 1	1.000	-/ 3	-	-	2	-	-	7	-
CLOUSSON, B.	-	0/ 0	.000	3/ 7	.429	-/ 2	-	-	3	-	-	3	-
BOLYARD, B.	-	4/ 7	.571	1/ 1	1.000	-/ 3	-	-	3	-	-	9	-
Totals	200	28/70	.400	28/42	.667	-/36	-	-	32	-	-	84	.420

Team Rebounds: Manhattan 11; West Virginia 10. Disqualified: Manhattan—Mealy, Wilbur, Brunone, Burkoski; West Virginia—West, Akers, Sharrar, Gardner. Technical Fouls: Manhattan—2.

	1st Half	2nd Half	Final
Manhattan	56	43	89
West Virginia	49	35	84

Dartmouth (75) Coach: Doggie Julian

	Min.	Total FG / FGA	Pct.	FT / FTA	Pct.	Reb. O / T	A	TO	PF	S	Blk	TP	PPM
CARRUTHERS, D.	-	2/ 5	.400	1/ 1	1.000	-/ 5	-	-	0	-	-	5	-
HANSON	-	1/ 1	1.000	0/ 0	.000	-/ 1	-	-	2	-	-	2	-
LARUSSO, R.	-	10/13	.769	4/ 5	.800	-/10	-	-	3	-	-	24	-
DOUGLAS	-	0/ 0	.000	0/ 1	.000	-/ 1	-	-	1	-	-	0	-
ALEY	-	4/ 9	.444	2/ 2	1.000	-/ 4	-	-	4	-	-	10	-
FARNSWORTH	-	0/ 1	.000	0/ 0	.000	-/ 2	-	-	0	-	-	0	-
KAUFMAN, C.	-	10/20	.500	4/10	.400	-/ 4	-	-	2	-	-	24	-
VANDEWEGHE, G.	-	1/ 3	.333	1/ 2	.500	-/ 5	-	-	3	-	-	3	-
HOBBIE	-	0/ 1	.000	0/ 0	.000	-/ 0	-	-	0	-	-	0	-
SOSNOWSKI, W.	-	2/ 6	.333	1/ 1	1.000	-/ 4	-	-	1	-	-	5	-
GAVITT, D.	-	1/ 8	.125	0/ 0	.000	-/ 4	-	-	0	-	-	2	-
JONES	-	0/ 0	.000	0/ 0	.000	-/ 0	-	-	0	-	-	0	-
Totals	200	31/67	.463	13/22	.591	-/40	-	-	16	-	-	75	.375

U. Conn. (64) Coach: Hugh Greer

	Min.	Total FG / FGA	Pct.	FT / FTA	Pct.	Reb. O / T	A	TO	PF	S	Blk	TP	PPM
PIPCZYNSKI	-	0/ 3	.000	2/ 2	1.000	-/ 5	-	-	1	-	-	2	-
KASPAR	-	8/19	.421	1/ 1	1.000	-/10	-	-	4	-	-	17	-
COOPER	-	1/ 7	.143	3/ 3	1.000	-/ 6	-	-	2	-	-	5	-
ROSE	-	7/18	.389	3/ 3	1.000	-/ 4	-	-	2	-	-	17	-
O'CONNOR	-	4/ 9	.444	1/ 3	.333	-/ 1	-	-	3	-	-	9	-
RISLEY	-	0/ 2	.000	0/ 0	.000	-/ 1	-	-	0	-	-	0	-
BROWN	-	0/ 2	.000	1/ 2	.500	-/ 0	-	-	0	-	-	1	-
CROSS	-	1/ 1	1.000	2/ 2	1.000	-/ 0	-	-	0	-	-	4	-
SCHMIDT	-	0/ 3	.000	2/ 4	.500	-/ 0	-	-	0	-	-	2	-
DAVIS	-	2/ 4	.500	1/ 2	.500	-/ 7	-	-	1	-	-	5	-
MARTIN	-	1/ 2	.500	0/ 0	.000	-/ 2	-	-	3	-	-	2	-
Totals	200	24/70	.343	16/22	.727	-/36	-	-	16	-	-	64	.320

Team Rebounds: Dartmouth 12; U. Conn. 8. Disqualified: None.

	1st Half	2nd Half	Final
Dartmouth	39	36	75
U. Conn.	38	26	64

FIRST ROUND MIDEAST

Miami (Ohio) (82) Coach: Dick Shrider

	Min.	Total FG/FGA	Pct.	FT/FTA	Pct.	Reb. O/T	A	TO	PF	S	Blk	TP	PPM
BROWN, B.	-	7/11	.636	3/ 4	.750	-/11	-	-	4	-	-	17	-
THOMAS	-	3/10	.300	4/ 5	.800	-/ 3	-	-	4	-	-	10	
EMBRY, W.	-	9/17	.529	3/10	.300	-/20	-	-	1	-	-	21	
HAMILTON, J.	-	3/10	.300	3/ 7	.429	-/ 2	-	-	3	-	-	9	
POWELL, J.	-	5/19	.263	5/ 7	.714	-/ 3	-	-	4	-	-	15	
WINGARD, E.	-	2/ 7	.286	1/ 2	.500	-/ 7	-	-	0	-	-	5	
CRIST, L.	-	1/ 1	1.000	3/ 4	.750	-/ 1	-	-	0	-	-	5	
ROWAN, H.	-	0/ 0	.000	0/ 0	.000	-/ 1	-	-	1	-	-	0	
Totals	200	30/75	.400	22/39	.629	-/48	-	-	17	-	-	82	.410

Pittsburgh (77) Coach: Bob Timmons

	Min.	Total FG/FGA	Pct.	FT/FTA	Pct.	Reb. O/T	A	TO	PF	S	Blk	TP	PPM
PEGUES	-	13/24	.542	5/ 9	.556	-/ 5	-	-	5	-	-	31	-
MILLS	-	0/ 0	.000	0/ 1	.000	-/ 1	-	-	5	-	-	0	
HENNON	-	12/33	.364	4/ 5	.800	-/ 7	-	-	4	-	-	28	
HURSH	-	2/ 4	.500	4/ 5	.800	-/ 9	-	-	2	-	-	8	
DORMAN	-	2/ 3	.667	3/ 3	1.000	-/ 7	-	-	4	-	-	7	
SIMPSON	-	0/ 2	.000	0/ 0	.000	-/ 2	-	-	2	-	-	0	
GOB	-	0/ 0	.000	0/ 0	.000	-/ 0	-	-	0	-	-	0	
MAURO	-	0/ 0	.000	0/ 0	.000	-/ 0	-	-	1	-	-	0	
SAWYER	-	1/ 4	.250	1/ 3	.333	-/13	-	-	4	-	-	3	
Totals	200	30/70	.429	17/26	.654	-/44	-	-	27	-	-	77	.385

Team Rebounds: Miami (Ohio) 8; Pittsburgh 4. Disqualified: Pittsburgh—Pegues, Mills.

	1st Half	2nd Half	Final
Miami (Ohio)	32	50	82
Pittsburgh	36	41	77

Notre Dame (94) Coach: John Jordan

	Min.	Total FG/FGA	Pct.	FT/FTA	Pct.	Reb. O/T	A	TO	PF	S	Blk	TP	PPM
HAWKINS, T.	-	12/22	.545	6/ 7	.857	-/14	-	-	2	-	-	30	
MCCARTHY, J.	-	6/16	.375	8/ 8	1.000	-/21	-	-	1	-	-	20	
WILLIAMS, J.	-	1/ 8	.125	0/ 0	.000	-/ 8	-	-	2	-	-	2	
IRELAND, M.	-	1/ 3	.333	0/ 0	.000	-/ 3	-	-	0	-	-	2	
GRANEY, M.	-	4/ 9	.444	4/ 5	.800	-/11	-	-	5	-	-	12	
REINHART, T.	-	2/ 8	.250	2/ 4	.500	-/ 9	-	-	1	-	-	6	
DEVINE, R.	-	5/16	.313	1/ 3	.333	-/ 9	-	-	2	-	-	11	
DUFFY, E.	-	3/10	.300	1/ 1	1.000	-/ 6	-	-	2	-	-	7	
BRADTKE, R.	-	0/ 2	.000	2/ 3	.667	-/ 1	-	-	1	-	-	2	
GLEASON, E.	-	1/ 1	1.000	0/ 0	.000	-/ 1	-	-	1	-	-	2	
Totals	200	35/95	.368	24/31	.774	-/83	-	-	17	-	-	94	.470

Tennessee Tech (61) Coach: Johnny Oldham

	Min.	Total FG/FGA	Pct.	FT/FTA	Pct.	Reb. O/T	A	TO	PF	S	Blk	TP	PPM
MCDONALD	-	5/17	.294	1/ 2	.500	-/ 9	-	-	4	-	-	11	
PUCKETT	-	0/ 0	.000	1/ 3	.333	-/ 3	-	-	5	-	-	1	
GILLEY	-	0/ 5	.000	1/ 2	.500	-/ 0	-	-	1	-	-	1	
SHEARER	-	4/ 6	.667	3/ 6	.500	-/ 2	-	-	1	-	-	11	
BRUKE	-	0/ 0	.000	0/ 0	.000	-/ 0	-	-	1	-	-	0	
HAGAN	-	3/18	.167	3/ 5	.600	-/ 9	-	-	5	-	-	9	
KELLER	-	3/ 9	.333	0/ 0	.000	-/ 1	-	-	1	-	-	6	
PHELPS	-	6/19	.316	4/ 4	1.000	-/10	-	-	4	-	-	16	
HERRON	-	2/ 5	.400	2/ 3	.667	-/ 2	-	-	1	-	-	6	
VAUGHN	-	0/ 5	.000	0/ 0	.000	-/ 3	-	-	0	-	-	0	
Totals	200	23/84	.274	15/25	.600	-/39	-	-	23	-	-	61	.305

Team Rebounds: Notre Dame 3; Tennessee Tech 5. Disqualified: Notre Dame—Graney; Tennessee Tech—Puckett, Hagan.

	1st Half	2nd Half	Final
Notre Dame	40	54	94
Tennessee Tech	28	33	61

FIRST ROUND MIDWEST

Oklahoma State (59) Coach: Henry Iba

	Min.	Total FG/FGA	Pct.	FT/FTA	Pct.	Reb. O/T	A	TO	PF	S	Blk	TP	PPM
SUTTON	-	3/ 6	.500	1/ 1	1.000	-/ 6	-	-	1	-	-	7	-
CRUTCHFIELD	-	2/ 6	.333	1/ 1	1.000	-/ 5	-	-	3	-	-	5	
CLARK	-	7/12	.583	12/12	1.000	-/14	-	-	3	-	-	26	
CARBERRY	-	0/ 5	.000	5/ 5	1.000	-/ 1	-	-	4	-	-	5	
ADAIR	-	6/12	.500	3/ 4	.750	-/ 1	-	-	2	-	-	15	
HALE	-	0/ 2	.000	1/ 1	1.000	-/ 3	-	-	2	-	-	1	
HEFFINGTON	-	0/ 2	.000	0/ 0	.000	-/ 0	-	-	0	-	-	0	
FLEMING	-	0/ 0	.000	0/ 0	.000	-/ 0	-	-	1	-	-	0	
Totals	200	18/45	.400	23/24	.958	-/30	-	-	16	-	-	59	.295

Loyola N.O. (42) Coach: Jim Harding

	Min.	Total FG/FGA	Pct.	FT/FTA	Pct.	Reb. O/T	A	TO	PF	S	Blk	TP	PPM
GAUDIN	-	5/15	.333	2/ 3	.667	-/ 8	-	-	3	-	-	12	-
HALL	-	1/ 7	.143	0/ 1	.000	-/ 9	-	-	4	-	-	2	
DOLL	-	3/ 7	.429	3/ 4	.750	-/ 9	-	-	5	-	-	9	
MCLAUGHLIN	-	2/ 4	.500	4/10	.400	-/ 4	-	-	2	-	-	8	
VOGT	-	5/11	.455	1/ 2	.500	-/ 4	-	-	2	-	-	11	
HENNEBERGER	-	0/ 1	.000	0/ 0	.000	-/ 0	-	-	0	-	-	0	
MORRIS	-	0/ 0	.000	0/ 0	.000	-/ 0	-	-	1	-	-	0	
Totals	200	16/45	.356	10/20	.500	-/34	-	-	17	-	-	42	.210

Team Rebounds: Oklahoma State 2; Loyola N.O. 1. Disqualified: Loyola N.O.—Doll.

	1st Half	2nd Half	Final
Oklahoma State	27	32	59
Loyola N.O.	20	22	42

FIRST ROUND WEST

Seattle (88)   Coach: John Castellani

	Min.	Total FG / FGA	Pct.	FT / FTA	Pct.	Reb. O / T	A	TO	PF	S	Blk	TP	PPM
FRIZZELL, J.	-	5/ -	-	2/ 2	1.000	-/ -	-	-	1	-	-	12	-
OGOREK, D.	-	5/ -	-	8/ 8	1.000	-/ -	-	-	1	-	-	18	-
BAYLOR, E.	-	10/ -	-	6/ 7	.857	-/ -	-	-	2	-	-	26	-
BROWN, C.	-	5/ -	-	1/ 1	1.000	-/ -	-	-	1	-	-	11	-
SAUNDERS, F.	-	1/ -	-	0/ 1	.000	-/ -	-	-	1	-	-	2	-
PIASECKI, D.	-	1/ -	-	0/ 1	.000	-/ -	-	-	2	-	-	2	-
KOOTNEKOFF, J.	-	2/ -	-	0/ 0	.000	-/ -	-	-	1	-	-	4	-
HUMPHRIES, T.	-	4/ -	-	1/ 4	.250	-/ -	-	-	2	-	-	9	-
PETRIE, J.	-	2/ -	-	0/ 3	.000	-/ -	-	-	1	-	-	4	-
Totals	200	35/ -	-	18/27	.667	-/ -	-	-	12	-	-	88	.440

Wyoming (51)   Coach: Everett Shelton

	Min.	Total FG / FGA	Pct.	FT / FTA	Pct.	Reb. O / T	A	TO	PF	S	Blk	TP	PPM
CARLSON, D.	-	0/ -	-	1/ 1	1.000	-/ -	-	-	3	-	-	1	-
BERTOLERO, J.	-	10/ -	-	2/ 2	1.000	-/ -	-	-	4	-	-	22	-
HADDEN, M.	-	5/ -	-	2/ 4	.500	-/ -	-	-	5	-	-	12	-
ECKHARDT, T.	-	2/ -	-	0/ 0	.000	-/ -	-	-	2	-	-	4	-
WINDIS, T.	-	3/ -	-	1/ 1	1.000	-/ -	-	-	1	-	-	7	-
BORA, R.	-	0/ -	-	1/ 1	1.000	-/ -	-	-	0	-	-	1	-
CAMPBELL, D.	-	1/ -	-	0/ 1	.000	-/ -	-	-	0	-	-	2	-
GARDNER, H.	-	0/ -	-	0/ 1	.000	-/ -	-	-	3	-	-	0	-
WHITEFOOT, H.	-	0/ -	-	2/ 2	1.000	-/ -	-	-	1	-	-	2	-
Totals	200	21/ -	-	9/13	.692	-/ -	-	-	19	-	-	51	.255

Disqualified: Wyoming—Hadden.

	1st Half	2nd Half	Final
Seattle	51	37	88
Wyoming	25	26	51

Idaho State (72)   Coach: John Grayson

	Min.	Total FG / FGA	Pct.	FT / FTA	Pct.	Reb. O / T	A	TO	PF	S	Blk	TP	PPM
CHRISTIAN, R.	-	2/ 3	.667	2/ 4	.500	-/12	-	-	4	-	-	6	-
SIEMEN, G.	-	7/16	.438	4/ 4	1.000	-/ 7	-	-	5	-	-	18	-
BACHER, L.	-	8/16	.500	5/10	.500	-/10	-	-	4	-	-	21	-
GERMAINE, J.	-	5/ 8	.625	6/ 6	1.000	-/ 4	-	-	2	-	-	16	-
RODGERS, J.	-	5/16	.313	1/ 3	.333	-/ 2	-	-	0	-	-	11	-
MORRIS, A.	-	0/ 1	.000	0/ 0	.000	-/ 0	-	-	0	-	-	0	-
ADELHARDT, R.	-	0/ 1	.000	0/ 0	.000	-/ 2	-	-	0	-	-	0	-
Totals	200	27/61	.443	18/27	.667	-/37	-	-	15	-	-	72	.360

Arizona State (68)   Coach: Ned Wulk

	Min.	Total FG / FGA	Pct.	FT / FTA	Pct.	Reb. O / T	A	TO	PF	S	Blk	TP	PPM
BURAU	-	2/12	.167	0/ 3	.000	-/ 7	-	-	2	-	-	4	-
NEALLY	-	6/14	.429	3/ 6	.500	-/ 5	-	-	2	-	-	15	-
WESTBROOKS	-	3/ 7	.429	1/ 1	1.000	-/ 8	-	-	4	-	-	7	-
NEWMAN, J.	-	8/16	.500	3/ 3	1.000	-/ 9	-	-	4	-	-	19	-
YOUREE, R.	-	7/17	.412	5/ 6	.833	-/ 5	-	-	4	-	-	19	-
BOWEN	-	0/ 0	.000	0/ 0	.000	-/ 0	-	-	0	-	-	0	-
OLSON	-	2/ 2	1.000	0/ 0	.000	-/ 0	-	-	3	-	-	4	-
DAUGHERTY	-	0/ 1	.000	0/ 0	.000	-/ 0	-	-	0	-	-	0	-
Totals	200	28/69	.406	12/19	.632	-/34	-	-	19	-	-	68	.340

Team Rebounds: Idaho State 5; Arizona St. 7. Disqualified: Idaho State—Siemen.

	1st Half	2nd Half	Final
Idaho State	40	32	72
Arizona St.	32	36	68

REGIONAL SEMIFINAL EAST

Temple (71)   Coach: Harry Litwack

	Min.	Total FG / FGA	Pct.	FT / FTA	Pct.	Reb. O / T	A	TO	PF	S	Blk	TP	PPM
BRODSKY, M.	-	4/ 8	.500	1/ 1	1.000	-/ 5	-	-	3	-	-	9	-
NORMAN, J.	-	6/12	.500	2/ 4	.500	-/14	-	-	3	-	-	14	-
VANPATTON, T.	-	3/10	.300	0/ 3	.000	-/11	-	-	4	-	-	6	-
KENNEDY, B.	-	8/11	.727	2/ 2	1.000	-/ 5	-	-	3	-	-	18	-
RODGERS, G.	-	7/25	.280	2/11	.182	-/ 6	-	-	3	-	-	16	-
FLEMING, D.	-	4/ 7	.571	0/ 0	.000	-/ 4	-	-	2	-	-	8	-
Totals	200	32/73	.438	7/21	.333	-/45	-	-	18	-	-	71	.355

Maryland (67)   Coach: Bud Millikan

	Min.	Total FG / FGA	Pct.	FT / FTA	Pct.	Reb. O / T	A	TO	PF	S	Blk	TP	PPM
MCNEIL, C.	-	8/19	.421	8/ 9	.889	-/13	-	-	2	-	-	24	-
NACINCIK, J.	-	1/ 4	.250	1/ 1	1.000	-/ 2	-	-	3	-	-	3	-
BUNGE, A.	-	2/ 8	.250	1/ 2	.500	-/ 6	-	-	3	-	-	5	-
DAVIS, N.	-	8/15	.533	2/ 2	1.000	-/ 2	-	-	1	-	-	18	-
YOUNG, T.	-	1/ 5	.200	6/ 8	.750	-/ 5	-	-	2	-	-	8	-
HALLECK, J.	-	0/ 1	.000	0/ 0	.000	-/ 4	-	-	2	-	-	0	-
MURPHY	-	0/ 2	.000	0/ 0	.000	-/ 0	-	-	2	-	-	0	-
DANKO	-	2/ 3	.667	5/ 6	.833	-/ 2	-	-	2	-	-	9	-
Totals	200	22/57	.386	23/28	.821	-/34	-	-	17	-	-	67	.335

Team Rebounds: Temple 1; Maryland 3. Disqualified: None.

	1st Half	2nd Half	Final
Temple	39	32	71
Maryland	32	35	67

Manhattan (62)   Coach: Ken Norton

	Min.	Total FG / FGA	Pct.	FT / FTA	Pct.	Reb. O / T	A	TO	PF	S	Blk	TP	PPM
QUARTO, F.	-	1/ 1	1.000	0/ 0	.000	-/ 1	-	-	1	-	-	2	-
WILBUR, D.	-	2/ 8	.250	2/ 3	.667	-/ 4	-	-	1	-	-	6	-
KOENIG, C.	-	3/ 4	.750	0/ 1	.000	-/ 1	-	-	3	-	-	6	-
SCHOENBERGER	-	0/ 1	.000	0/ 0	.000	-/ 0	-	-	0	-	-	0	-
POWERS	-	4/13	.308	4/ 7	.571	-/ 6	-	-	3	-	-	12	-
MCGORTY, D.	-	6/16	.375	0/ 3	.000	-/ 6	-	-	3	-	-	12	-
BURKOSKI, M.	-	3/ 7	.429	3/ 3	1.000	-/ 3	-	-	1	-	-	9	-
MEALY, B.	-	3/15	.200	1/ 5	.200	-/21	-	-	4	-	-	7	-
BRUNONE, P.	-	3/ 8	.375	2/ 3	.667	-/ 8	-	-	2	-	-	8	-
DOUGHERTY	-	0/ 3	.000	0/ 0	.000	-/ 1	-	-	1	-	-	0	-
Totals	200	25/76	.329	12/25	.480	-/51	-	-	19	-	-	62	.310

Dartmouth (79)   Coach: Doggie Julian

	Min.	Total FG / FGA	Pct.	FT / FTA	Pct.	Reb. O / T	A	TO	PF	S	Blk	TP	PPM
HOBBIE	-	0/ 0	.000	0/ 0	.000	-/ 0	-	-	0	-	-	0	-
FARNSWORTH	-	3/ 5	.600	0/ 1	.000	-/ 8	-	-	2	-	-	6	-
VANDEWEGHE, G.	-	1/ 5	.200	2/ 2	1.000	-/ 2	-	-	2	-	-	4	-
CARRUTHERS, D.	-	6/12	.500	0/ 0	.000	-/ 7	-	-	2	-	-	12	-
JONES	-	0/ 0	.000	0/ 0	.000	-/ 0	-	-	0	-	-	0	-
KAUFMAN, C.	-	8/20	.400	6/ 6	1.000	-/ 2	-	-	1	-	-	22	-
HANSON	-	0/ 2	.000	2/ 2	1.000	-/ 1	-	-	1	-	-	2	-
GAVITT, D.	-	0/ 1	.000	1/ 2	.500	-/ 5	-	-	1	-	-	1	-
SOSNOWSKI, W.	-	6/14	.429	1/ 5	.200	-/ 7	-	-	2	-	-	13	-
ALEY	-	2/ 8	.250	0/ 0	.000	-/ 3	-	-	3	-	-	4	-
DOUGLAS	-	0/ 0	.000	2/ 2	1.000	-/ 0	-	-	0	-	-	2	-
LARUSSO, R.	-	4/15	.267	5/ 6	.833	-/15	-	-	4	-	-	13	-
Totals	200	30/82	.366	19/26	.731	-/50	-	-	18	-	-	79	.395

Team Rebounds: Dartmouth 9; Manhattan 9. Disqualified: None.

	1st Half	2nd Half	Final
Manhattan	27	35	62
Dartmouth	38	41	79

REGIONAL SEMIFINAL MIDEAST

Kentucky (94) Coach: Adolph Rupp

	Min.	Total FG/FGA	Pct.	FT/FTA	Pct.	Reb. O/T	A	TO	PF	S	Blk	TP	PPM
COX, J.	-	9/25	.360	5/5	1.000	-/15	-	-	0	-	-	23	-
CRIGLER, J.	-	4/10	.400	0/0	.000	-/10	-	-	4	-	-	8	-
BECK, E.	-	2/7	.286	2/2	1.000	-/8	-	-	5	-	-	6	-
SMITH, A.	-	6/16	.375	6/8	.750	-/3	-	-	1	-	-	18	-
HATTON, V.	-	5/16	.313	4/5	.800	-/4	-	-	3	-	-	14	-
SMITH, B.	-	0/0	.000	0/0	.000	-/0	-	-	0	-	-	0	-
COLLINSWORTH, L.	-	2/4	.500	4/4	1.000	-/5	-	-	0	-	-	8	-
CASSADY, B.	-	1/1	1.000	0/0	.000	-/1	-	-	0	-	-	2	-
JOHNSON, P.	-	1/4	.250	0/0	.000	-/3	-	-	2	-	-	2	-
HOWE, D.	-	0/0	.000	0/0	.000	-/0	-	-	0	-	-	0	-
ADKINS, E.	-	1/2	.500	0/0	.000	-/0	-	-	0	-	-	2	-
MILLS, D.	-	4/14	.286	3/5	.600	-/12	-	-	4	-	-	11	-
Totals	200	35/99	.354	24/29	.828	-/61	-	-	19	-	-	94	.470

Miami (Ohio) (70) Coach: Dick Shrider

	Min.	Total FG/FGA	Pct.	FT/FTA	Pct.	Reb. O/T	A	TO	PF	S	Blk	TP	PPM
BROWN, B.	-	3/9	.333	1/1	1.000	-/9	-	-	4	-	-	7	-
THOMAS	-	5/17	.294	1/1	1.000	-/8	-	-	2	-	-	11	-
EMBRY, W.	-	8/22	.364	10/13	.769	-/15	-	-	4	-	-	26	-
POWELL	-	5/16	.313	2/3	.667	-/11	-	-	3	-	-	12	-
HAMILTON	-	3/7	.429	2/4	.500	-/1	-	-	2	-	-	8	-
WINGARD, E.	-	0/2	.000	2/2	1.000	-/6	-	-	2	-	-	2	-
BABBS, K.	-	0/0	.000	0/0	.000	-/0	-	-	0	-	-	0	-
ROWAN	-	0/1	.000	0/0	.000	-/1	-	-	0	-	-	0	-
HIGGINS, J.	-	2/3	.667	0/0	.000	-/0	-	-	2	-	-	4	-
MILLER, B.	-	0/0	.000	0/0	.000	-/0	-	-	1	-	-	0	-
CRIST, L.	-	0/1	.000	0/1	.000	-/0	-	-	0	-	-	0	-
Totals	200	26/78*	.333	18/25	.720	-/51	-	-	20	-	-	70	.350

Disqualified: Kentucky—Beck.

	1st Half	2nd Half	Final
Kentucky	50	44	94
Miami (Ohio)	35	35	70

Notre Dame (94) Coach: John Jordan

	Min.	Total FG/FGA	Pct.	FT/FTA	Pct.	Reb. O/T	A	TO	PF	S	Blk	TP	PPM
MCCARTHY, J.	-	12/26	.462	5/6	.833	-/11	-	-	1	-	-	29	-
HAWKINS, T.	-	10/24	.417	11/14	.786	-/11	-	-	3	-	-	31	-
GRANEY, M.	-	1/9	.111	0/0	.000	-/10	-	-	5	-	-	2	-
DUFFY, E.	-	2/4	.500	5/6	.833	-/2	-	-	4	-	-	9	-
DEVINE, R.	-	4/9	.444	6/8	.750	-/6	-	-	0	-	-	14	-
IRELAND, M.	-	0/2	.000	1/1	1.000	-/5	-	-	3	-	-	1	-
REINHART, T.	-	3/4	.750	2/2	1.000	-/5	-	-	5	-	-	8	-
WILLIAMS, J.	-	0/0	.000	0/0	.000	-/0	-	-	0	-	-	0	-
Totals	200	32/78	.410	30/37	.811	-/50	-	-	21	-	-	94	.470

Indiana (87) Coach: Branch McCracken

	Min.	Total FG/FGA	Pct.	FT/FTA	Pct.	Reb. O/T	A	TO	PF	S	Blk	TP	PPM
OBREMESKEY, P.	-	7/15	.467	4/6	.667	-/7	-	-	4	-	-	18	-
THOMPSON, J.	-	4/7	.571	1/1	1.000	-/3	-	-	4	-	-	9	-
DEES, A.	-	9/27	.333	10/11	.909	-/15	-	-	2	-	-	28	-
GEE, S.	-	2/5	.400	0/0	.000	-/2	-	-	3	-	-	4	-
WILKINSON, R.	-	7/14	.500	3/7	.429	-/3	-	-	5	-	-	17	-
SCHLEGELMILCH, A.	-	1/1	1.000	1/2	.500	-/0	-	-	1	-	-	3	-
HINDS, J.	-	3/4	.750	0/0	.000	-/6	-	-	3	-	-	6	-
RADOVICH, F.	-	1/7	.143	0/1	.000	-/6	-	-	4	-	-	2	-
Totals	200	34/80	.425	19/28	.679	-/42	-	-	26	-	-	87	.435

Disqualified: Notre Dame—Graney, Reinhart; Indiana—Wilkinson.

	1st Half	2nd Half	Final
Notre Dame	48	46	94
Indiana	37	50	87

REGIONAL SEMIFINAL MIDWEST

Arkansas (40) Coach: Glen Rose

	Min.	Total FG/FGA	Pct.	FT/FTA	Pct.	Reb. O/T	A	TO	PF	S	Blk	TP	PPM
THOMPSON	-	3/9	.333	1/1	1.000	-/6	-	-	1	-	-	7	-
DUNN	-	3/9	.333	2/3	.667	-/4	-	-	4	-	-	8	-
CARPENTER	-	2/2	1.000	0/1	.000	-/2	-	-	5	-	-	4	-
GRIM	-	5/16	.313	3/5	.600	-/5	-	-	2	-	-	13	-
GRISHAM	-	3/13	.231	0/1	.000	-/7	-	-	4	-	-	6	-
RANKIN	-	0/5	.000	0/0	.000	-/2	-	-	2	-	-	0	-
HANKINS	-	0/1	.000	0/0	.000	-/1	-	-	0	-	-	0	-
RITTMAN	-	0/2	.000	0/0	.000	-/0	-	-	1	-	-	0	-
STOLZER	-	1/2	.500	0/2	.000	-/2	-	-	1	-	-	2	-
BOSS	-	0/1	.000	0/0	.000	-/0	-	-	0	-	-	0	-
Totals	200	17/60	.283	6/13	.462	-/29	-	-	20	-	-	40	.200

Oklahoma State (65) Coach: Henry Iba

	Min.	Total FG/FGA	Pct.	FT/FTA	Pct.	Reb. O/T	A	TO	PF	S	Blk	TP	PPM
SUTTON	-	3/5	.600	2/2	1.000	-/5	-	-	1	-	-	8	-
CRUTCHFIELD	-	0/2	.000	1/1	1.000	-/1	-	-	1	-	-	1	-
CLARK, A.	-	4/7	.571	12/15	.800	-/13	-	-	2	-	-	20	-
CARBERRY	-	3/8	.375	5/7	.714	-/8	-	-	3	-	-	11	-
ADAIR	-	5/11	.455	1/1	1.000	-/5	-	-	2	-	-	11	-
HALE	-	3/8	.375	4/4	1.000	-/4	-	-	3	-	-	10	-
HEFFINGTON	-	1/1	1.000	0/0	.000	-/0	-	-	0	-	-	2	-
SOERGEL	-	0/0	.000	0/0	.000	-/0	-	-	0	-	-	0	-
WALKER	-	0/0	.000	0/0	.000	-/0	-	-	0	-	-	0	-
WADE	-	0/0	.000	0/0	.000	-/0	-	-	0	-	-	0	-
DEUTSCHENDORF	-	1/2	.500	0/0	.000	-/0	-	-	0	-	-	2	-
FLEMING	-	0/1	.000	0/0	.000	-/0	-	-	0	-	-	0	-
Totals	200	20/45	.444	25/30	.833	-/36	-	-	12	-	-	65	.325

Team Rebounds: Oklahoma State 2; Arkansas 3. Disqualified: Arkansas—Carpenter.

	1st Half	2nd Half	Final
Arkansas	23	17	40
Oklahoma State	37	28	65

Kansas State (83)   Coach: Tex Winter

	Min.	Total FG/FGA	Pct.	FT/FTA	Pct.	Reb. O/T	A	TO	PF	S	Blk	TP	PPM
ABBOTT, H.	-	0/ 1	.000	0/ 0	.000	-/ 2	-	-	3	-	-	0	-
BOOZER, B.	-	9/25	.360	6/11	.545	-/14	-	-	4	-	-	24	-
PARR, J.	-	7/22	.318	3/ 4	.750	-/12	-	-	4	-	-	17	-
DEWITZ, R.	-	4/10	.400	7/10	.700	-/ 9	-	-	1	-	-	15	-
MATUSZAK, D.	-	2/ 6	.333	5/ 7	.714	-/ 4	-	-	5	-	-	9	-
FRANK, W.	-	5/10	.500	2/ 2	1.000	-/ 5	-	-	5	-	-	12	-
FISCHER, L.	-	1/ 1	1.000	3/ 4	.750	-/ 2	-	-	2	-	-	5	
HOLWERDA, J.	-	0/ 0	.000	1/ 2	.500	-/ 0	-	-	0	-	-	1	-
Totals	225	28/75	.373	27/40	.675	-/48	-	-	24	-	-	83	.369

Cincinnati (80)   Coach: George Smith

	Min.	Total FG/FGA	Pct.	FT/FTA	Pct.	Reb. O/T	A	TO	PF	S	Blk	TP	PPM
STEVENS, W.	-	4/15	.267	5/ 7	.714	-/ 6	-	-	5	-	-	13	-
ROBERTSON, O.	-	12/20	.600	6/ 8	.750	-/14	-	-	5	-	-	30	-
DIERKING, C.	-	4/17	.235	10/13	.769	-/ 5	-	-	5	-	-	18	-
DAVIS, R.	-	4/12	.333	2/ 4	.500	-/ 2	-	-	3	-	-	10	-
MENDENHALL, M.	-	3/10	.300	3/ 3	1.000	-/ 3	-	-	2	-	-	9	-
HORNSBY, S.	-	0/ 0	.000	0/ 0	.000	-/ 0	-	-	0	-	-	0	-
DYKES, R.	-	0/ 2	.000	0/ 2	.000	-/ 1	-	-	4	-	-	0	-
WILLEY, L.	-	0/ 0	.000	0/ 1	.000	-/ 2	-	-	0	-	-	0	-
NALL, R.	-	0/ 0	.000	0/ 0	.000	-/ 0	-	-	1	-	-	0	-
WHITAKER, B.	-	0/ 0	.000	0/ 0	.000	-/ 0	-	-	1	-	-	0	-
Totals	225	27/76	.355	26/38	.684	-/33	-	-	26	-	-	80	.356

Team Rebounds: Kansas State 4; Cincinnati 4. Disqualified: Kansas State—Matuszak, Frank; Cincinnati—Stevens, Robertson, Dierking.

	1st Half	2nd Half	1st OT	Final
Kansas State	39	35	9	83
Cincinnati	40	34	6	80

REGIONAL SEMIFINAL WEST

San Francisco (67)   Coach: Phil Woolpert

	Min.	Total FG/FGA	Pct.	FT/FTA	Pct.	Reb. O/T	A	TO	PF	S	Blk	TP	PPM
FARMER	-	5/14	.357	0/ 1	.000	-/ 7	-	-	5	-	-	10	-
LACOUR	-	8/16	.500	4/ 4	1.000	-/ 4	-	-	4	-	-	20	-
DAY	-	4/14	.286	5/ 6	.833	-/10	-	-	1	-	-	13	-
BROWN	-	7/18	.389	5/ 6	.833	-/10	-	-	5	-	-	19	-
DUNBAR	-	1/ 7	.143	0/ 0	.000	-/ 2	-	-	1	-	-	2	-
LILLEVAND	-	1/ 2	.500	1/ 1	1.000	-/ 1	-	-	0	-	-	3	-
CUNNINGHAM	-	0/ 1	.000	0/ 1	.000	-/ 1	-	-	1	-	-	0	-
RUSSELL, C.	-	0/ 2	.000	0/ 0	.000	-/ 0	-	-	1	-	-	0	-
Totals	200	26/74	.351	15/19	.789	-/35	-	-	18	-	-	67	.335

Seattle (69)   Coach: John Castellani

	Min.	Total FG/FGA	Pct.	FT/FTA	Pct.	Reb. O/T	A	TO	PF	S	Blk	TP	PPM
FRIZZELL, J.	-	4/ 8	.500	0/ 0	.000	-/ 7	-	-	2	-	-	8	-
OGOREK, D.	-	2/10	.200	3/ 6	.500	-/ 8	-	-	4	-	-	7	-
BAYLOR, E.	-	11/20	.550	13/14	.929	-/14	-	-	3	-	-	35	-
BROWN	-	5/ 9	.556	3/ 7	.429	-/ 7	-	-	3	-	-	13	-
PIASECKI, D.	-	2/ 2	1.000	0/ 0	.000	-/ 5	-	-	0	-	-	4	-
HARVEY	-	1/ 3	.333	0/ 0	.000	-/ 2	-	-	0	-	-	2	-
Totals	200	25/52	.481	19/27	.704	-/43	-	-	12	-	-	69	.345

Team Rebounds: Seattle 2; San Francisco 4. Disqualified: San Francisco—Farmer, Brown.

	1st Half	2nd Half	Final
San Francisco	33	34	67
Seattle	31	38	69

Idaho State (43)   Coach: John Grayson

	Min.	Total FG/FGA	Pct.	FT/FTA	Pct.	Reb. O/T	A	TO	PF	S	Blk	TP	PPM
CHRISTIAN, R.	-	0/ 2	.000	2/ 2	1.000	-/ 7	-	-	4	-	-	2	-
SIEMEN, G.	-	7/14	.500	0/ 0	.000	-/ 9	-	-	2	-	-	14	-
BACHER, L.	-	5/13	.385	1/ 5	.200	-/10	-	-	4	-	-	11	-
GERMAINE, J.	-	3/ 5	.600	4/ 6	.667	-/ 2	-	-	4	-	-	10	-
RODGERS, J.	-	1/16	.063	0/ 0	.000	-/ 7	-	-	2	-	-	2	-
MORRIS, A.	-	1/ 2	.500	0/ 0	.000	-/ 0	-	-	2	-	-	2	-
ADELHARDT, R.	-	0/ 1	.000	0/ 0	.000	-/ 0	-	-	1	-	-	0	-
GRIFFIN, J.	-	1/ 2	.500	0/ 0	.000	-/ 0	-	-	0	-	-	2	-
KUGLER, D.	-	0/ 0	.000	0/ 0	.000	-/ 0	-	-	0	-	-	0	-
Totals	200	18/55	.327	7/13	.538	-/35	-	-	19	-	-	43	.215

California (54)   Coach: Pete Newell

	Min.	Total FG/FGA	Pct.	FT/FTA	Pct.	Reb. O/T	A	TO	PF	S	Blk	TP	PPM
DALTON, B.	-	4/ 7	.571	2/ 4	.500	-/ 8	-	-	0	-	-	10	-
STERLING, G.	-	2/ 7	.286	2/ 3	.667	-/ 6	-	-	1	-	-	6	-
MCINTOSH, D.	-	4/11	.364	2/ 2	1.000	-/14	-	-	3	-	-	10	-
BUCH, A.	-	2/11	.182	1/ 3	.333	-/ 0	-	-	0	-	-	5	-
ROBINSON, E.	-	5/11	.455	3/ 5	.600	-/ 9	-	-	2	-	-	13	-
FITZPATRICK, D.	-	1/ 3	.333	1/ 1	1.000	-/ 1	-	-	2	-	-	3	-
GROUT, J.	-	0/ 1	.000	0/ 0	.000	-/ 1	-	-	0	-	-	0	-
IMHOFF, D.	-	1/ 2	.500	1/ 1	1.000	-/ 2	-	-	2	-	-	3	-
RAPP	-	0/ 0	.000	0/ 1	.000	-/ 0	-	-	0	-	-	0	-
SCHNEIDER	-	1/ 1	1.000	2/ 2	1.000	-/ 0	-	-	0	-	-	4	-
Totals	200	20/54	.370	14/22	.636	-/41	-	-	10	-	-	54	.270

Team Rebounds: California 2; Idaho State 5. Disqualified: None.

	1st Half	2nd Half	Final
Idaho State	20	23	43
California	24	30	54

REGIONAL FINAL EAST

Temple (69) Coach: Harry Litwack

	Min.	Total FG / FGA	Pct.	FT / FTA	Pct.	Reb. O / T	A	TO	PF	S	Blk	TP	PPM
KENNEDY, B.	-	6/10	.600	1/ 1	1.000	-/ 3	-	-	3	-	-	13	-
RODGERS, G.	-	8/20	.400	1/ 6	.167	-/ 9	-	-	2	-	-	17	-
VANPATTON, T.	-	0/ 1	.000	2/ 3	.667	-/ 9	-	-	4	-	-	2	-
PEEPE, J.	-	0/ 0	.000	0/ 0	.000	-/ 0	-	-	1	-	-	0	-
BRODSKY, M.	-	6/12	.500	4/ 4	1.000	-/ 8	-	-	4	-	-	16	-
GOSS, P.	-	0/ 0	.000	0/ 0	.000	-/ 0	-	-	0	-	-	0	-
NORMAN, J.	-	6/14	.429	2/ 6	.333	-/ 9	-	-	3	-	-	14	-
FLEMING, D.	-	3/ 6	.500	1/ 1	1.000	-/ 4	-	-	2	-	-	7	-
FRANKLIN, O.	-	0/ 0	.000	0/ 0	.000	-/ 0	-	-	0	-	-	0	-
GOLDENBERG, J.	-	0/ 0	.000	0/ 0	.000	-/ 0	-	-	0	-	-	0	-
Totals	200	29/63	.460	11/21	.524	-/42	-	-	19	-	-	69	.345

Dartmouth (50) Coach: Doggie Julian

	Min.	Total FG / FGA	Pct.	FT / FTA	Pct.	Reb. O / T	A	TO	PF	S	Blk	TP	PPM
HOBBIE	-	0/ 0	.000	0/ 0	.000	-/ 0	-	-	0	-	-	0	-
FARNSWORTH	-	1/ 7	.143	0/ 3	.000	-/10	-	-	0	-	-	2	-
VANDEWEGHE, G.	-	4/12	.333	2/ 7	.286	-/ 6	-	-	3	-	-	10	-
CARRATHERS	-	0/ 3	.000	1/ 2	.500	-/ 1	-	-	2	-	-	1	-
JONES	-	0/ 1	.000	0/ 1	.000	-/ 1	-	-	0	-	-	0	-
KAUFMAN, C.	-	2/14	.143	5/ 6	.833	-/ 5	-	-	3	-	-	9	-
HANSON	-	0/ 0	.000	0/ 0	.000	-/ 0	-	-	0	-	-	0	-
GAVITT, D.	-	2/ 6	.333	0/ 0	.000	-/ 2	-	-	1	-	-	4	-
SOSNOWSKI, W.	-	1/10	.100	1/ 1	1.000	-/ 3	-	-	0	-	-	3	-
ALEY	-	1/ 2	.500	0/ 0	.000	-/ 2	-	-	2	-	-	2	-
DOUGLAS	-	0/ 0	.000	0/ 0	.000	-/ 1	-	-	0	-	-	0	-
LARUSSO, R.	-	7/22	.318	5/ 7	.714	-/21	-	-	5	-	-	19	-
Totals	200	18/77	.234	14/27	.519	-/52	-	-	16	-	-	50	.250

Team Rebounds: Temple 0; Dartmouth 9. Disqualified: Dartmouth—LaRusso.

	1st Half	2nd Half	Final
Temple	32	37	69
Dartmouth	22	28	50

REGIONAL FINAL MIDEAST

Kentucky (89) Coach: Adolph Rupp

	Min.	Total FG / FGA	Pct.	FT / FTA	Pct.	Reb. O / T	A	TO	PF	S	Blk	TP	PPM
COX, J.	-	6/18	.333	2/ 3	.667	-/13	-	-	2	-	-	14	-
CRIGLER, J.	-	4/10	.400	3/ 3	1.000	-/15	-	-	1	-	-	11	-
BECK, E.	-	4/ 8	.500	3/ 5	.600	-/12	-	-	3	-	-	11	-
HATTON, V.	-	11/22	.500	4/ 5	.800	-/ 9	-	-	2	-	-	26	-
SMITH, A.	-	4/10	.400	8/ 8	1.000	-/ 3	-	-	3	-	-	16	-
MILLS, D.	-	1/ 1	1.000	1/ 2	.500	-/ 0	-	-	0	-	-	3	-
COLLINSWORTH, L.	-	1/ 3	.333	0/ 0	.000	-/ 1	-	-	1	-	-	2	-
SMITH, B.	-	1/ 2	.500	0/ 0	.000	-/ 1	-	-	0	-	-	2	-
JOHNSON, P.	-	0/ 2	.000	0/ 0	.000	-/ 3	-	-	0	-	-	0	-
ADKINS, E.	-	0/ 1	.000	0/ 0	.000	-/ 1	-	-	0	-	-	0	-
ROSS, H.	-	0/ 0	.000	2/ 2	1.000	-/ 1	-	-	1	-	-	2	-
CASSADY, B.	-	0/ 1	.000	2/ 3	.667	-/ 1	-	-	1	-	-	2	-
Totals	200	32/78	.410	25/31	.806	-/60	-	-	14	-	-	89	.445

Notre Dame (56) Coach: John Jordan

	Min.	Total FG / FGA	Pct.	FT / FTA	Pct.	Reb. O / T	A	TO	PF	S	Blk	TP	PPM
MCCARTHY, J.	-	7/18	.389	3/ 3	1.000	-/ 8	-	-	2	-	-	17	-
HAWKINS, T.	-	7/24	.292	1/ 4	.250	-/16	-	-	4	-	-	15	-
GRANEY, M.	-	1/ 6	.167	2/ 3	.667	-/ 5	-	-	4	-	-	4	-
DUFFY, E.	-	0/ 3	.000	1/ 2	.500	-/ 0	-	-	4	-	-	1	-
DEVINE, R.	-	3/ 9	.333	1/ 1	1.000	-/ 1	-	-	1	-	-	7	-
AYOTTE, I.	-	0/ 0	.000	0/ 0	.000	-/ 0	-	-	1	-	-	0	-
WILLIAMS, J.	-	0/ 1	.000	0/ 0	.000	-/ 0	-	-	0	-	-	0	-
REINHART, T.	-	3/13	.231	0/ 0	.000	-/10	-	-	4	-	-	6	-
IRELAND, J.	-	0/ 0	.000	0/ 0	.000	-/ 0	-	-	1	-	-	0	-
BRADTKE, R.	-	0/ 0	.000	2/ 2	1.000	-/ 1	-	-	1	-	-	2	-
GLEASON, E.	-	1/ 4	.250	2/ 3	.667	-/ 0	-	-	0	-	-	4	-
Totals	200	22/78	.282	12/18	.667	-/41	-	-	22	-	-	56	.280

Disqualified: None.

	1st Half	2nd Half	Final
Kentucky	43	46	89
Notre Dame	31	25	56

REGIONAL FINAL MIDWEST

Oklahoma State (57) Coach: Henry Iba

	Min.	Total FG / FGA	Pct.	FT / FTA	Pct.	Reb. O / T	A	TO	PF	S	Blk	TP	PPM
SUTTON	-	2/ 2	1.000	1/ 1	1.000	-/ 0	-	-	1	-	-	5	-
CRUTCHFIELD	-	2/ 8	.250	2/ 2	1.000	-/ 1	-	-	3	-	-	6	-
CLARK, A.	-	8/22	.364	8/12	.667	-/ 8	-	-	4	-	-	24	-
CARBERRY	-	0/ 3	.000	2/ 2	1.000	-/ 0	-	-	2	-	-	2	-
ADAIR	-	2/10	.200	3/ 4	.750	-/ 5	-	-	0	-	-	7	-
HALE	-	4/ 9	.444	3/ 4	.750	-/ 5	-	-	3	-	-	11	-
HEFFINGTON	-	0/ 0	.000	0/ 0	.000	-/ 1	-	-	1	-	-	0	-
SOERGEL	-	0/ 1	.000	2/ 2	1.000	-/ 0	-	-	0	-	-	2	-
WALKER	-	0/ 0	.000	0/ 0	.000	-/ 0	-	-	0	-	-	0	-
Totals	200	18/55	.327	21/27	.778	-/20	-	-	14	-	-	57	.285

Kansas State (69) Coach: Tex Winter

	Min.	Total FG / FGA	Pct.	FT / FTA	Pct.	Reb. O / T	A	TO	PF	S	Blk	TP	PPM
ABBOTT, H.	-	0/ 1	.000	0/ 0	.000	-/ 0	-	-	0	-	-	0	-
BOOZER, B.	-	12/16	.750	2/ 5	.400	-/ 9	-	-	3	-	-	26	-
PARR, J.	-	5/14	.357	3/ 5	.600	-/10	-	-	4	-	-	13	-
DEWITZ, R.	-	3/ 6	.500	0/ 2	.000	-/ 2	-	-	4	-	-	6	-
MATUSZAK, D.	-	6/ 7	.857	2/ 2	1.000	-/ 5	-	-	4	-	-	14	-
FRANK, W.	-	4/11	.364	2/ 2	1.000	-/ 8	-	-	4	-	-	10	-
FISCHER, L.	-	0/ 0	.000	0/ 0	.000	-/ 0	-	-	0	-	-	0	-
HOLWERDA, J.	-	0/ 0	.000	0/ 1	.000	-/ 0	-	-	0	-	-	0	-
LONG, G.	-	0/ 0	.000	0/ 0	.000	-/ 0	-	-	0	-	-	0	-
BALLARD, S.	-	0/ 0	.000	0/ 0	.000	-/ 0	-	-	0	-	-	0	-
Totals	200	30/55	.545	9/17	.529	-/34	-	-	19	-	-	69	.345

Team Rebounds: Kansas State 2; Oklahoma State 1. Disqualified: None.

	1st Half	2nd Half	Final
Oklahoma State	31	26	57
Kansas State	38	31	69

REGIONAL FINAL WEST

Seattle (66)   Coach: John Castellani

	Min.	Total FG/FGA	Pct.	FT/FTA	Pct.	Reb. O/T	A	TO	PF	S	Blk	TP	PPM
OGOREK, D.	-	3/ 9	.333	2/ 2	1.000	-/ 7	-	-	4	-	-	8	-
FRIZZELL, J.	-	1/ 2	.500	1/ 1	1.000	-/ 1	-	-	3	-	-	3	-
BAYLOR, E.	-	9/25	.360	8/ 8	1.000	-/18	-	-	3	-	-	26	-
BROWN, C.	-	5/11	.455	0/ 0	.000	-/ 5	-	-	2	-	-	10	-
HARNEY, J.	-	2/ 7	.286	5/ 5	1.000	-/ 1	-	-	2	-	-	9	-
PIASECKI, D.	-	0/ 2	.000	0/ 0	.000	-/ 0	-	-	1	-	-	0	-
SAUNDERS, F.	-	4/ 7	.571	2/ 3	.667	-/ 8	-	-	1	-	-	10	-
Totals	225	24/63	.381	18/19	.947	-/40	-	-	16	-	-	66	.293

California (62)   Coach: Pete Newell

	Min.	Total FG/FGA	Pct.	FT/FTA	Pct.	Reb. O/T	A	TO	PF	S	Blk	TP	PPM
DALTON, B.	-	1/ 6	.167	1/ 2	.500	-/ 4	-	-	5	-	-	3	-
STERLING, G.	-	7/10	.700	1/ 2	.500	-/ 3	-	-	4	-	-	15	-
MCINTOSH, D.	-	7/14	.500	2/ 3	.667	-/10	-	-	1	-	-	16	-
BUCH, A.	-	4/10	.400	2/ 4	.500	-/ 7	-	-	2	-	-	10	-
ROBINSON, E.	-	6/18	.333	3/ 6	.500	-/ 6	-	-	2	-	-	15	-
GROUT, J.	-	1/ 1	1.000	0/ 0	.000	-/ 2	-	-	0	-	-	2	-
FITZPATRICK, D.	-	0/ 3	.000	1/ 1	1.000	-/ 0	-	-	0	-	-	1	-
Totals	225	26/62	.419	10/18	.556	-/32	-	-	14	-	-	62	.276

Team Rebounds: Seattle 7; California 3. Disqualified: California—Dalton.

	1st Half	2nd Half	1st OT	Final
Seattle	29	31	6	66
California	37	23	2	62

FINAL FOUR

Temple (60)   Coach: Harry Litwack

	Min.	Total FG/FGA	Pct.	FT/FTA	Pct.	Reb. O/T	A	TO	PF	S	Blk	TP	PPM
NORMAN, J.	-	7/17	.412	2/ 3	.667	-/ 6	-	-	3	-	-	16	-
BRODSKY, M.	-	2/ 5	.400	0/ 2	.000	-/14	-	-	2	-	-	4	-
VANPATTON, T.	-	1/ 1	1.000	1/ 2	.500	-/ 3	-	-	4	-	-	3	-
FLEMING, D.	-	3/ 7	.429	3/ 6	.500	-/ 5	-	-	1	-	-	9	-
RODGERS, G.	-	9/24	.375	4/ 6	.667	-/ 5	-	-	4	-	-	22	-
KENNEDY, B.	-	3/ 7	.429	0/ 1	.000	-/ 3	-	-	4	-	-	6	-
Totals	200	25/61	.410	10/20	.500	-/36	-	-	18	-	-	60	.300

Kentucky (61)   Coach: Adolph Rupp

	Min.	Total FG/FGA	Pct.	FT/FTA	Pct.	Reb. O/T	A	TO	PF	S	Blk	TP	PPM
CRIGLER, J.	-	3/11	.273	0/ 2	.000	-/ 9	-	-	4	-	-	6	-
COX, J.	-	6/17	.353	10/11	.909	-/13	-	-	4	-	-	22	-
COLLINSWORTH, L.	-	0/ 0	.000	0/ 0	.000	-/ 0	-	-	1	-	-	0	-
BECK, E.	-	3/ 9	.333	2/ 2	1.000	-/15	-	-	2	-	-	8	-
HATTON, V.	-	5/16	.313	3/ 4	.750	-/ 2	-	-	3	-	-	13	-
SMITH, A.	-	2/10	.200	8/ 9	.889	-/ 5	-	-	3	-	-	12	-
Totals	200	19/63	.302	23/28	.821	-/44	-	-	17	-	-	61	.305

Team Rebounds: Kentucky 5; Temple 5. Disqualified: None.

	1st Half	2nd Half	Final
Temple	31	29	60
Kentucky	31	30	61

Kansas State (51)   Coach: Tex Winter

	Min.	Total FG/FGA	Pct.	FT/FTA	Pct.	Reb. O/T	A	TO	PF	S	Blk	TP	PPM
ABBOTT, H.	-	0/ 4	.000	0/ 0	.000	-/ 2	-	0	1	-	-	0	-
BOOZER, B.	-	6/15	.400	3/ 5	.600	-/ 4	-	3	4	-	-	15	-
PARR, J.	-	2/11	.182	0/ 1	.000	-/ 8	-	0	1	-	-	4	-
DEWITZ, R.	-	2/ 7	.286	2/ 3	.667	-/ 0	-	2	2	-	-	6	-
MATUSZAK, D.	-	3/ 8	.375	1/ 3	.333	-/ 7	-	3	1	-	-	7	-
FRANK, W.	-	6/12	.500	3/ 4	.750	-/ 7	-	0	4	-	-	15	-
FISCHER, L.	-	0/ 1	.000	0/ 0	.000	-/ 0	-	0	1	-	-	0	-
HOLWERDA, J.	-	0/ 2	.000	0/ 0	.000	-/ 1	-	0	2	-	-	0	-
LONG, G.	-	2/ 6	.333	0/ 1	.000	-/ 4	-	0	2	-	-	4	-
Totals	200	21/66	.318	9/17	.529	-/33	-	8	18	-	-	51	.255

Seattle (73)   Coach: John Castellani

	Min.	Total FG/FGA	Pct.	FT/FTA	Pct.	Reb. O/T	A	TO	PF	S	Blk	TP	PPM
OGOREK, D.	-	3/ 9	.333	1/ 2	.500	-/ 4	-	0	4	-	-	7	-
FRIZZELL, J.	-	2/ 4	.500	6/ 7	.857	-/ 2	-	1	2	-	-	10	-
PETRIE, J.	-	0/ 0	.000	0/ 0	.000	-/ 0	-	0	0	-	-	0	-
BAYLOR, E.	-	9/21	.429	5/ 7	.714	-/22	-	1	3	-	-	23	-
HUMPHRIES, T.	-	0/ 0	.000	0/ 0	.000	-/ 0	-	0	0	-	-	0	-
HARNEY, J.	-	0/ 4	.000	0/ 0	.000	-/ 2	-	0	1	-	-	0	-
BROWN, C.	-	5/ 6	.833	4/ 5	.800	-/13	-	2	2	-	-	14	-
SAUNDERS, F.	-	5/11	.455	2/ 3	.667	-/ 8	-	2	1	-	-	12	-
PIASECKI, D.	-	1/ 1	1.000	3/ 4	.750	-/ 0	-	0	1	-	-	5	-
KOOTNEKOFF, J.	-	1/ 1	1.000	0/ 0	.000	-/ 0	-	0	0	-	-	2	-
Totals	200	26/57	.456	21/28	.750	-/51	-	6	14	-	-	73	.365

Team Rebounds: Seattle 5; Kansas State 1. Disqualified: None.

	1st Half	2nd Half	Final
Kansas State	32	19	51
Seattle	37	36	73

NATIONAL CHAMPIONSHIP

Kentucky (84)   Coach: Adolph Rupp

	Min.	Total FG / FGA	Pct.	FT / FTA	Pct.	Reb. O / T	A	TO	PF	S	Blk	TP	PPM
COX, J.	-	10/23	.435	4/ 4	1.000	-/16	-	-	3	-	-	24	-
CRIGLER, J.	-	5/12	.417	4/ 7	.571	-/14	-	-	4	-	-	14	-
BECK, E.	-	0/ 1	.000	0/ 1	.000	-/ 3	-	-	4	-	-	0	-
MILLS, D.	-	4/ 9	.444	1/ 4	.250	-/ 5	-	-	3	-	-	9	-
HATTON, V.	-	9/20	.450	12/15	.800	-/ 3	-	-	3	-	-	30	-
SMITH, A.	-	2/ 8	.250	3/ 5	.600	-/ 6	-	-	4	-	-	7	-
Totals	200	30/73	.411	24/36	.667	-/47	-	-	21	-	-	84	.420

Seattle (72)   Coach: John Castellani

	Min.	Total FG / FGA	Pct.	FT / FTA	Pct.	Reb. O / T	A	TO	PF	S	Blk	TP	PPM
FRIZZELL, J.	-	4/ 6	.667	8/11	.727	-/ 5	-	-	3	-	-	16	-
OGOREK, D.	-	4/ 7	.571	2/ 2	1.000	-/11	-	-	5	-	-	10	-
BAYLOR, E.	-	9/32	.281	7/ 9	.778	-/19	-	-	4	-	-	25	-
HARNEY, J.	-	2/ 5	.400	0/ 1	.000	-/ 1	-	-	1	-	-	4	-
BROWN, C.	-	6/17	.353	5/ 7	.714	-/ 5	-	-	5	-	-	17	-
SAUNDERS, F.	-	0/ 2	.000	0/ 0	.000	-/ 2	-	-	3	-	-	0	-
PIASECKI, D.	-	0/ 0	.000	0/ 0	.000	-/ 0	-	-	0	-	-	0	-
Totals	200	25/69	.362	22/30	.733	-/43	-	-	21	-	-	72	.360

Team Rebounds: Kentucky 8; Seattle 3. Disqualified: Seattle—Ogorek, Brown.

	1st Half	2nd Half	Final
Kentucky	36	48	84
Seattle	39	33	72

NATIONAL THIRD PLACE

Temple (67)   Coach: Harry Litwack

	Min.	Total FG / FGA	Pct.	FT / FTA	Pct.	Reb. O / T	A	TO	PF	S	Blk	TP	PPM
NORMAN, J.	-	1/11	.091	5/ 8	.625	-/13	-	3	3	-	-	7	-
BRODSKY, M.	-	4/13	.308	2/ 5	.400	-/12	-	1	3	-	-	10	-
VANPATTON, T.	-	1/ 6	.167	1/ 3	.333	-/12	-	1	5	-	-	3	-
FLEMING, D.	-	2/ 3	.667	3/ 3	1.000	-/ 6	-	3	4	-	-	7	-
KENNEDY, B.	-	8/16	.500	7/ 9	.778	-/ 0	-	6	0	-	-	23	-
RODGERS, G.	-	7/17	.412	3/ 3	1.000	-/ 4	-	3	2	-	-	17	-
Totals	200	23/66	.348	21/31	.677	-/47	-	17	17	-	-	67	.335

Kansas State (57)   Coach: Tex Winter

	Min.	Total FG / FGA	Pct.	FT / FTA	Pct.	Reb. O / T	A	TO	PF	S	Blk	TP	PPM
ABBOTT, H.	-	6/11	.545	2/ 2	1.000	-/ 3	-	1	3	-	-	14	-
BOOZER, B.	-	6/19	.316	7/ 9	.778	-/12	-	1	4	-	-	19	-
PARR, J.	-	1/13	.077	5/ 8	.625	-/10	-	4	2	-	-	7	-
DEWITZ, R.	-	3/12	.250	0/ 1	.000	-/ 4	-	2	1	-	-	6	-
MATUSZAK, D.	-	1/ 4	.250	1/ 3	.333	-/ 2	-	1	4	-	-	3	-
FRANK, W.	-	3/ 9	.333	2/ 3	.667	-/11	-	3	2	-	-	8	-
HOLWERDA, J.	-	0/ 1	.000	0/ 0	.000	-/ 0	-	0	2	-	-	0	-
BALLARD, S.	-	0/ 1	.000	0/ 0	.000	-/ 0	-	0	1	-	-	0	-
DOUGLAS, S.	-	0/ 1	.000	0/ 0	.000	-/ 1	-	1	3	-	-	0	-
Totals	200	20/71	.282	17/26	.654	-/43	-	13	22	-	-	57	.285

Team Rebounds: Temple 7; Kansas State 8. Disqualified: Temple—Van Patton.

	1st Half	2nd Half	Final
Temple	28	39	67
Kansas State	39	18	57

REGIONAL THIRD PLACE WEST

San Francisco (57)   Coach: Phil Woolpert

	Min.	Total FG / FGA	Pct.	FT / FTA	Pct.	Reb. O / T	A	TO	PF	S	Blk	TP	PPM
MALLEN, B.	-	4/ 7	.571	2/ 3	.667	-/ 3	-	-	1	-	-	10	-
RUSSELL, C.	-	2/ 8	.250	0/ 2	.000	-/ 7	-	-	0	-	-	4	-
FARMER, M.	-	4/11	.364	7/ 8	.875	-/ 5	-	-	3	-	-	15	-
DUNBAR, A.	-	0/ 3	.000	0/ 0	.000	-/ 4	-	-	3	-	-	0	-
BROWN, G.	-	3/ 8	.375	4/ 5	.800	-/ 5	-	-	0	-	-	10	-
CUNNINGHAM	-	3/ 4	.750	2/ 2	1.000	-/ 1	-	-	0	-	-	8	-
LACOUR	-	1/ 5	.200	1/ 1	1.000	-/ 0	-	-	2	-	-	3	-
DAY, A.	-	2/ 2	1.000	0/ 0	.000	-/ 1	-	-	2	-	-	4	-
LILLEVAND, D.	-	0/ 2	.000	1/ 2	.500	-/ 2	-	-	0	-	-	1	-
CONNOLLY	-	0/ 0	.000	0/ 0	.000	-/ 1	-	-	2	-	-	0	-
ROBINSON	-	0/ 0	.000	0/ 0	.000	-/ 1	-	-	0	-	-	0	-
RADANOVICH, B.	-	1/ 1	1.000	0/ 0	.000	-/ 1	-	-	1	-	-	2	-
Totals	200	20/51	.392	17/23	.739	-/31	-	-	14	-	-	57	.285

Idaho State (51)   Coach: John Grayson

	Min.	Total FG / FGA	Pct.	FT / FTA	Pct.	Reb. O / T	A	TO	PF	S	Blk	TP	PPM
CHRISTIAN, R.	-	0/ 0	.000	0/ 1	.000	-/ 2	-	-	5	-	-	0	-
SIEMEN, G.	-	7/14	.500	3/ 3	1.000	-/ 9	-	-	2	-	-	17	-
BACHER, L.	-	4/10	.400	4/ 5	.800	-/ 9	-	-	2	-	-	12	-
GERMAINE, J.	-	3/ 4	.750	3/ 3	1.000	-/ 1	-	-	3	-	-	9	-
RODGERS, J.	-	3/12	.250	1/ 1	1.000	-/ 3	-	-	4	-	-	7	-
MORRIS, A.	-	1/ 2	.500	1/ 1	1.000	-/ 0	-	-	1	-	-	3	-
ADELHARDT, R.	-	0/ 0	.000	0/ 0	.000	-/ 1	-	-	0	-	-	0	-
GRIFFIN, J.	-	0/ 0	.000	3/ 3	1.000	-/ 4	-	-	0	-	-	3	-
Totals	200	18/42	.429	15/17	.882	-/29	-	-	17	-	-	51	.255

Team Rebounds: San Francisco 3; Idaho State 4. Disqualified: Idaho State—Christian.

	1st Half	2nd Half	Final
San Francisco	26	31	57
Idaho State	20	31	51

REGIONAL THIRD PLACE MIDWEST
Cincinnati (97)   Coach: George Smith

	Min.	Total FG / FGA	Pct.	FT / FTA	Pct.	Reb. O / T	A	TO	PF	S	Blk	TP	PPM
STEVENS, W.	-	0/ 0	.000	1/ 1	1.000	-/ 4	-	-	2	-	-	1	-
ROBERTSON, O.	-	21/36	.583	14/16	.875	-/ 7	-	-	3	-	-	56	-
DIERKING, C.	-	5/11	.455	2/ 4	.500	-/16	-	-	1	-	-	12	-
DAVIS, R.	-	3/ 9	.333	1/ 1	1.000	-/ 2	-	-	5	-	-	7	-
MENDENHALL, M.	-	3/ 6	.500	9/10	.900	-/ 1	-	-	2	-	-	15	-
DYKES, R.	-	1/ 4	.250	0/ 0	.000	-/ 3	-	-	2	-	-	2	-
WILLEY, L.	-	1/ 2	.500	0/ 0	.000	-/ 2	-	-	2	-	-	2	-
NALL, R.	-	1/ 3	.333	0/ 1	.000	-/ 1	-	-	2	-	-	2	-
WHITAKER, B.	-	0/ 1	.000	0/ 0	.000	-/ 3	-	-	1	-	-	0	-
APKE, R.	-	0/ 0	.000	0/ 0	.000	-/ 2	-	-	0	-	-	0	-
Totals	200	35/72	.486	27/33	.818	-/41	-	-	20	-	-	97	.485

Arkansas (62)   Coach: Glen Rose

	Min.	Total FG / FGA	Pct.	FT / FTA	Pct.	Reb. O / T	A	TO	PF	S	Blk	TP	PPM
THOMPSON	-	6/13	.462	0/ 1	.000	-/ 2	-	-	3	-	-	12	-
DUNN	-	1/ 9	.111	1/ 2	.500	-/ 9	-	-	2	-	-	3	-
CARPENTER	-	3/11	.273	3/ 4	.750	-/ 9	-	-	4	-	-	9	-
GRIM	-	3/19	.158	10/10	1.000	-/ 3	-	-	2	-	-	16	-
GRISHAM	-	0/ 6	.000	1/ 1	1.000	-/ 4	-	-	3	-	-	1	-
RANKIN	-	3/10	.300	0/ 0	.000	-/ 1	-	-	1	-	-	6	-
HANKINS	-	3/ 6	.500	0/ 1	.000	-/ 3	-	-	5	-	-	6	-
RITTMAN	-	0/ 3	.000	0/ 0	.000	-/ 1	-	-	2	-	-	0	-
STOLZER	-	3/10	.300	3/ 8	.375	-/ 2	-	-	2	-	-	9	-
Totals	200	22/87	.253	18/27	.667	-/34	-	-	24	-	-	62	.310

Team Rebounds: Cincinnati 9; Arkansas 9. Disqualified: Cincinnati—Davis; Arkansas—Hankins.

	1st Half	2nd Half	Final
Cincinnati	51	46	97
Arkansas	29	33	62

REGIONAL THIRD PLACE EAST
Maryland (59)   Coach: Bud Millikan

	Min.	Total FG / FGA	Pct.	FT / FTA	Pct.	Reb. O / T	A	TO	PF	S	Blk	TP	PPM
MCNEIL, C.	-	2/ -	-	4/ 4	1.000	-/ -	-	-	1	-	-	8	-
NACINCIK, J.	-	1/ -	-	4/ 5	.800	-/ -	-	-	4	-	-	6	-
BUNGE, A.	-	2/ -	-	2/ 3	.667	-/ -	-	-	3	-	-	6	-
DAVIS, N.	-	5/ -	-	3/ 3	1.000	-/ -	-	-	2	-	-	13	-
YOUNG, T.	-	5/ -	-	8/10	.800	-/ -	-	-	3	-	-	18	-
HALLECK, J.	-	1/ -	-	4/ 4	1.000	-/ -	-	-	1	-	-	6	-
DANKO	-	0/ -	-	2/ 2	1.000	-/ -	-	-	2	-	-	2	-
BECHTIE	-	0/ -	-	0/ 0	.000	-/ -	-	-	0	-	-	0	-
MOORE	-	0/ -	-	0/ 0	.000	-/ -	-	-	0	-	-	0	-
Totals	200	16/ -	-	27/31	.871	-/ -	-	-	16	-	-	59	.295

REGIONAL THIRD PLACE MIDEAST
Indiana (98)   Coach: Branch McCracken

	Min.	Total FG / FGA	Pct.	FT / FTA	Pct.	Reb. O / T	A	TO	PF	S	Blk	TP	PPM
OBREMESKEY, P.	-	10/22	.455	0/ 1	.000	-/15	-	-	4	-	-	20	-
THOMPSON, J.	-	6/19	.316	3/ 4	.750	-/15	-	-	3	-	-	15	-
DEES, A.	-	8/15	.533	9/ 9	1.000	-/14	-	-	3	-	-	25	-
GEE, S.	-	2/10	.200	2/ 3	.667	-/ 2	-	-	4	-	-	6	-
WILKINSON, R.	-	8/20	.400	2/ 6	.333	-/ 8	-	-	4	-	-	18	-
SCHLEGELMILCH, A.	-	3/ 5	.600	0/ 0	.000	-/ 3	-	-	2	-	-	6	-
HINDS, J.	-	0/ 6	.000	0/ 0	.000	-/ 3	-	-	0	-	-	0	-
RADOVICH, F.	-	4/ 8	.500	0/ 0	.000	-/ 4	-	-	3	-	-	8	-
BALL, R.	-	0/ 1	.000	0/ 0	.000	-/ 1	-	-	0	-	-	0	-
Totals	200	41/106	.387	16/23	.696	-/65	-	-	23	-	-	98	.490

Miami (Ohio) (91)   Coach: Dick Shrider

	Min.	Total FG / FGA	Pct.	FT / FTA	Pct.	Reb. O / T	A	TO	PF	S	Blk	TP	PPM
BROWN, B.	-	2/10	.200	1/ 1	1.000	-/16	-	-	2	-	-	5	-
THOMAS, J.	-	5/ 9	.556	3/ 4	.750	-/ 5	-	-	3	-	-	13	-
EMBRY, W.	-	15/28	.536	6/10	.600	-/16	-	-	4	-	-	36	-
HAMILTON, J.	-	3/10	.300	3/ 5	.600	-/ 1	-	-	3	-	-	9	-
POWELL, J.	-	10/25	.400	5/ 6	.833	-/ 8	-	-	2	-	-	25	-
WINGARD, E.	-	0/ 3	.000	0/ 1	.000	-/ 8	-	-	1	-	-	0	-
CRIST, L.	-	1/ 2	.500	0/ 0	.000	-/ 3	-	-	0	-	-	2	-
HIGGINS, J.	-	0/ 1	.000	0/ 0	.000	-/ 0	-	-	0	-	-	0	-
MILLER, B.	-	0/ 0	.000	1/ 2	.500	-/ 0	-	-	0	-	-	1	-
Totals	200	36/88	.409	19/29	.655	-/57	-	-	15	-	-	91	.455

Disqualified: None.

	1st Half	2nd Half	Final
Indiana	56	42	98
Miami (Ohio)	45	46	91

Manhattan (55)   Coach: Ken Norton

	Min.	Total FG / FGA	Pct.	FT / FTA	Pct.	Reb. O / T	A	TO	PF	S	Blk	TP	PPM
MEALY, B.	-	3/ -	-	3/ 3	1.000	-/ -	-	-	3	-	-	9	-
WILBUR, D.	-	3/ -	-	2/ 2	1.000	-/ -	-	-	5	-	-	8	-
BRUNONE, P.	-	3/ -	-	6/ 8	.750	-/ -	-	-	1	-	-	12	-
MCGORTY, D.	-	5/ -	-	0/ 0	.000	-/ -	-	-	5	-	-	10	-
POWERS, J.	-	4/ -	-	4/ 4	1.000	-/ -	-	-	3	-	-	12	-
BURKOSKI, M.	-	0/ -	-	0/ 2	.000	-/ -	-	-	2	-	-	0	-
KOENIG, C.	-	0/ -	-	2/ 2	1.000	-/ -	-	-	1	-	-	2	-
QUARTO, F.	-	1/ -	-	0/ 0	.000	-/ -	-	-	2	-	-	2	-
Totals	200	19/ -	-	17/21	.810	-/ -	-	-	22	-	-	55	.275

Disqualified: Manhattan—Wilbur, McGorty.

	1st Half	2nd Half	Final
Maryland	28	31	59
Manhattan	32	23	55

○ ALL-STAR TEAMS ○

ALL TOURNAMENT

★ ELGIN BAYLOR	SEATTLE
CHARLEY BROWN	SEATTLE
JOHN COX	KENTUCKY
VERN HATTON	KENTUCKY
GUY RODGERS	TEMPLE

★ Most Outstanding Player(s)

✪ INDIVIDUAL RECORDS ✪

SCORING

Most points in a single game
1 OSCAR ROBERTSON. CINCINNATI (vs. ARKANSAS)   56
2 WAYNE EMBRY, MIAMI (OHIO) (vs. INDIANA) 36
3 ELGIN BAYLOR. SEATTLE (vs. SAN FRANCISCO) 35
4 TOM HAWKINS. NOTRE DAME (vs. INDIANA)   31
4 PEGUES. PITTSBURGH (vs. MIAMI [OHIO])   31

Most total points in the tournament
1 ELGIN BAYLOR. SEATTLE   135
2 OSCAR ROBERTSON. CINCINNATI   86
3 BOB BOOZER. KANSAS STATE   84
4 3 tied for fourth place.

Highest scoring average (minimum 2 games)
1 OSCAR ROBERTSON, CINCINNATI (86-2)   43.00
2 WAYNE EMBRY, MIAMI (OHIO) (83-3)   27.67
3 ELGIN BAYLOR. SEATTLE (135-5)   27.00
4 ARCHIE DEES, INDIANA (53-2)   26.50
5 TOM HAWKINS, NOTRE DAME (76-3)   25.33

FIELD GOALS

Most field goals in a single game
1 OSCAR ROBERTSON, CINCINNATI (vs. ARKANSAS)   21
2 WAYNE EMBRY, MIAMI (OHIO) (vs. INDIANA) 15
3 PEGUES, PITTSBURGH (vs. MIAMI ([OHIO])   13
4 5 tied for fourth place.

Most total field goals in the tournament
1 ELGIN BAYLOR, SEATTLE   48
2 OSCAR ROBERTSON, CINCINNATI   33
2 BOB BOOZER, KANSAS STATE   33
4 WAYNE EMBRY, MIAMI (OHIO)   32
5 2 tied for fifth place.

Most field goal attempts in a single game
1 OSCAR ROBERTSON, CINCINNATI (vs. ARKANSAS)   36
2 DON HENNON, PITTSBURGH (vs. MIAMI [OHIO])   33
3 ELGIN BAYLOR, SEATTLE (vs. KENTUCKY)   32
4 WAYNE EMBRY, MIAMI (OHIO) (vs. INDIANA) 28
5 ARCHIE DEES, INDIANA (vs. NOTRE DAME)   27

Highest field goal percentage in a single game (minimum 10 attempts)
1 RUDY LARUSSO, DARTMOUTH (vs. U. CONN.) (10-13)   .769
2 BOB BOOZER, KANSAS STATE (vs. OKLAHOMA STATE) (12-16)   .750
3 BILL KENNEDY, TEMPLE (vs. MARYLAND) (8-11)   .727
4 GEORGE STERLING, CALIFORNIA (vs. SEATTLE) (7-10)   .700
5 NICK DAVIS, MARYLAND (vs. BOSTON COLLEGE) (11-17)   .647

FREE THROWS

Most free throws in a single game
1 OSCAR ROBERTSON, CINCINNATI (vs. ARKANSAS)   14
2 ELGIN BAYLOR, SEATTLE (vs. SAN FRANCISCO)   13
3 VERNON HATTON, KENTUCKY (vs. SEATTLE)   12
3 ARLEN CLARK, OKLAHOMA STATE (vs. LOYOLA N.O.)   12
3 ARLEN CLARK, OKLAHOMA STATE (vs. ARKANSAS)   12

Most total free throws in the tournament
1 ELGIN BAYLOR, SEATTLE   39
2 ARLEN CLARK, OKLAHOMA STATE   32
3 ADRIAN SMITH, KENTUCKY   25
4 VERNON HATTON, KENTUCKY   23
5 JOHNNY COX, KENTUCKY   21

Most free throws attempted in a single game
1 OSCAR ROBERTSON, CINCINNATI (vs. ARKANSAS)   16
1 LLOYD SHARRAR, WEST VIRGINIA (vs. MANHATTAN)   16
3 VERNON HATTON, KENTUCKY (vs. SEATTLE)   15
3 ARLEN CLARK, OKLAHOMA STATE (vs. ARKANSAS)   15
3 JACK POWERS, MANHATTAN (vs. WEST VIRGINIA)   15

Highest free throw percentage in a single game (minimum 7 attempts)
1 ARLEN CLARK, OKLAHOMA STATE (vs. LOYOLA N.O.) (12-12)   1.000
2 GRIM, ARKANSAS (vs. CINCINNATI) (10-10)   1.000
3 ARCHIE DEES, INDIANA (vs. MIAMI [OHIO]) (9-9)   1.000
4 4 tied for fourth place.

REBOUNDS

Most rebounds in a single game
1 ELGIN BAYLOR, SEATTLE (vs. KANSAS STATE) 22
2 RUDY LARUSSO, DARTMOUTH (vs. TEMPLE)   21
2 BOB MEALY, MANHATTAN (vs. DARTMOUTH)   21
2 JOHN MCCARTHY, NOTRE DAME (vs. TENNESSEE TECH)   21
5 WAYNE EMBRY, MIAMI (OHIO) (vs. PITTSBURGH)   20

Most total rebounds in the tournament
1 ELGIN BAYLOR, SEATTLE   73
2 JOHNNY COX, KENTUCKY   57
3 WAYNE EMBRY, MIAMI (OHIO)   51
4 JOHN CRIGLER, KENTUCKY   48
5 RUDY LARUSSO, DARTMOUTH   46

✪ TEAM RECORDS ✪

SCORING

Most points in a single game
1 INDIANA (vs. MIAMI [OHIO])   98
2 CINCINNATI (vs. ARKANSAS)   97
3 NOTRE DAME (vs. INDIANA)   94
3 KENTUCKY (vs. MIAMI [OHIO])   94
3 NOTRE DAME (vs. TENNESSEE TECH)   94

Most total points in the tournament
1 SEATTLE   368
2 KENTUCKY   328
3 TEMPLE   267

Highest scoring average (minimum 2 games)
1 INDIANA (185-2)   92.50
2 CINCINNATI (177-2)   88.50
3 KENTUCKY (328-4)   82.00

FIELD GOALS

Most field goals in a single game
1 INDIANA (vs. MIAMI [OHIO])   41
2 MIAMI (OHIO) (vs. INDIANA)   36
3 4 tied for third place.

Most total field goals in the tournament
1 SEATTLE   135
2 KENTUCKY   116
3 TEMPLE   109

Most field goals attempted in a single game
1 INDIANA (vs. MIAMI [OHIO])   106
2 KENTUCKY (vs. MIAMI [OHIO])   99
3 NOTRE DAME (vs. TENNESSEE TECH)   95

Highest field goal percentage in a single game
1 KANSAS STATE (vs. OKLAHOMA STATE) (30-55) .546
1 MARYLAND (vs. BOSTON COLLEGE) (30-55) .546
3 CINCINNATI (vs. ARKANSAS) (35-72)   .486

FREE THROWS

Most free throws in a single game
1 MANHATTAN (vs. WEST VIRGINIA)   35
2 NOTRE DAME (vs. INDIANA)   30
3 BOSTON COLLEGE (vs. MARYLAND)   29

Most total free throws in the tournament
1 SEATTLE   98
2 KENTUCKY   96
3 MARYLAND   76

Most free throws attempted in a single game
1 MANHATTAN (vs. WEST VIRGINIA)   49
2 WEST VIRGINIA (vs. MANHATTAN)   42
2 MARYLAND (vs. BOSTON COLLEGE)   42

Highest free throw percentage in a single game
1 OKLAHOMA STATE (vs. LOYOLA N.O.) (23-24) .958
2 SEATTLE (vs. CALIFORNIA) (18-19)   .947
3 IDAHO STATE (vs. SAN FRANCISCO) (15-17) .882

Fewest free throws in a single game
1 ARKANSAS (vs. OKLAHOMA STATE)   6
2 TEMPLE (vs. MARYLAND)   7
2 IDAHO STATE (vs. CALIFORNIA)   7

Lowest free throw percentage in a single game
1 TEMPLE (vs. MARYLAND) (7-21)   .333
2 ARKANSAS (vs. OKLAHOMA STATE) (6-13)   .462
3 MANHATTAN (vs. DARTMOUTH) (12-25)   .480

REBOUNDS

Most rebounds in a single game
1 NOTRE DAME (vs. TENNESSEE TECH)   83
2 INDIANA (vs. MIAMI [OHIO])   65
3 KENTUCKY (vs. MIAMI [OHIO])   61

1959

| FIRST ROUND | REGIONAL SEMIFINAL | REGIONAL FINAL | **FINAL FOUR** | REGIONAL FINAL | REGIONAL SEMIFINAL | FIRST ROUND |

EAST

(bye)
St. Joseph's 92
West Virginia 86
West Virginia 82
Dartmouth 68
West Virginia 95
West Virginia 94
Boston Univ. 60
U. Conn. 58
Boston Univ. 62
Boston Univ. 82
Navy 76
N. Carolina 63
Navy 55

MIDWEST

Kansas St. 102
(bye)
Kansas St. 75
De Paul 57
De Paul 70
Portland 56
Cincinnati 58
Cincinnati 77
(bye)
Cincinnati 85
TCU 73
(bye)

California 71
West Virginia 70

MIDEAST

(bye)
Kentucky 61
Louisville 88
Louisville 77
Eastern Ky. 63
Louisville 76
Louisville 79
Marquette 89
Bowling Green 71
Marquette 69
Michigan St. 81
(bye)
Michigan St. 74

WEST

St. Mary's 80
(bye)
St. Mary's 46
Idaho St. 62
Idaho St. 71
New Mexico St. 61
California 64
California 71
(bye)
California 66
Utah 53
(bye)

CONSOLATION GAMES

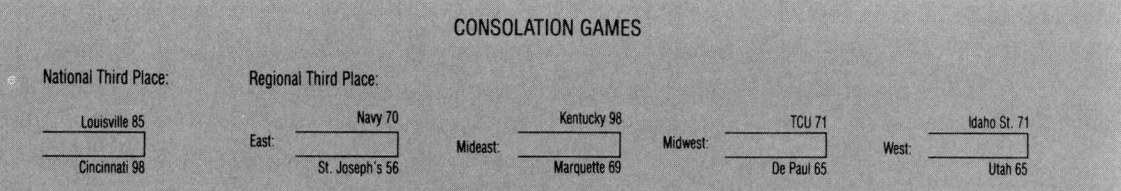

National Third Place:

Louisville 85
Cincinnati 98

Regional Third Place:

East:
Navy 70
St. Joseph's 56

Mideast:
Kentucky 98
Marquette 69

Midwest:
TCU 71
De Paul 65

West:
Idaho St. 71
Utah 65

In 1959, both Oscar Robertson and Jerry West led their teams into the Final Four, but both were ultimately neutralized by a towel-chewing, defensive-minded California coach who called the shots, dictated the tempo, and pushed the Golden Bears over the top.

Coach Pete Newell's California squad had come out of the West as the nation's top defensive team. But as everybody knew, low-scoring, deliberate-styled basketball was as much a West Coast regional characteristic as sun, sand, and surf. Virtually everybody west of the Rockies played the same way, so Cal's points-against-average was no indication of how they'd fare against a fast-moving, high-scoring team.

The Golden Bears had little trouble getting through the West regional, holding their two opponents to an average of just under 50 points a game. "When a player guards the man with the ball," Newell said, "the tendency is just to respond to his fakes and feints and try to stay with him. I try to teach my boys to take the initiative, to fake the man with the ball, to move him around instead of letting him move them around." Newell's philosophy—both on defense and offense—was, in short, to make the other guys play his game. And in the regional Cal did just that.

In the Midwest, the big story was "the Big O." Robertson, the nation's top regular season scorer and Player of the Year, had carried his team all year. But now he had to do even more: just before the tournament, Cincinnati's standout guard Mike Mendenhall was declared ineligible because he had played 16 minutes during the 1955–56 season (which technically made him a fourth-year varsity player). Losing Mendenhall was a serious blow to the Bearcats, who were already small (no starter stood taller than 6-6) and relatively nondescript except for Robertson. Oscar responded to the challenge by turning his game up another notch. In the opener against TCU, the Bearcats barely escaped in what their coach, George Smith, called "one of our worst games of the year." But Robertson scored 34, and took the reins every time the Southwest Conference champs threatened. In the second round Cincinnati came up against the towering, No. 1 ranked Kansas State Wildcats, who had thrashed DePaul, 102-70, in their opener.

Against Kansas State Robertson was constantly double- and triple-teamed, but he compensated, keeping the Bearcats in the game with his strong board-work and passing. A little less than four and a half minutes remained when, with Kansas State holding a one-point lead, Robertson took over. In the next minute and a half he scored four points and fed his teammates for two more baskets. With 2:04 to go, Cincinnati had a 75-74 lead and possession. As soon as the ball came to Robertson, three Wildcats converged on him. Without hesitating, he threaded

the needle, finding center Dave Tenwick alone under the basket for an easy lay-up. It was all over but the shouting.

If Robertson was great in the regional, Jerry West was, if anything, even more spectacular in leading the West Virginia Mountaineers to the Final Four. After an easy victory over Dartmouth, West Virginia was matched against St. Joseph's. With thirteen minutes left, the Hawks, who came in with a twelve-game winning streak, were making mincemeat out of the favored Mountaineers, leading 67-49. After guard Lee Patrone started the West Virginians on the comeback trail, West caught fire. In the last nine minutes he showed why he would soon be known as Mr. Clutch: he scored 21 points and led West Virginia into the victory column.

The next day he did it again. This time, Boston University was leading the Mountaineers with twelve minutes left when the kid from Cabin Creek took over. West scored 10 in a row in the next four minutes—and West Virginia never looked back.

West Virginia, Cal, and Cincinnati were all Top 10 teams, and while the Bearcats' victory over Kansas State in the Midwest regional was a mild upset, nobody was terribly surprised to see any of the three reach the Final Four. The same could hardly be said about Louisville in the Mideast.

The Cardinals came into the tournament unranked and overlooked with a 16-10 record. After a preliminary round victory over Eastern Kentucky, the Louisville squad traveled to Evanston, Illinois, where they met the fearsome Kentucky Wildcats. Kentucky, despite being the defending national champions and the second-ranked team in the country, had suffered both of their regular season losses in the SEC and had finished second in the conference (in 1959, only one team per conference received an invitation). But the SEC champ Mississippi State rejected the NCAA bid because, according to school president Ben Hilburn, "We cannot play in a tournament where our team might have to face teams that use Negro players." Mississippi State Coach Babe McCarthy supported the president's stand. "As a real true segregationist bred in Mississippi," he said, "I would not want to jeopardize the segregation cause in my state."

Thus Kentucky, which had played against integrated teams in Lexington as far back as 1951, came into the tournament through the backdoor—and as one of the heavy favorites to go all the way. From the start, the game between the Wildcats and Louisville looked like a mismatch; with nine minutes to play in the first half the Wildcats led 29-14. Then something remarkable happened; Louisville came back. They were down by eight at the half, and after a locker-room tirade from their coach, Peck Hickman, they came out in the second half loose as a goose and ready to roll. They won, 76-61. It was almost as if Louisville had died and gone to heaven; after so many years of playing second fiddle to the Wildcats in the basketball-crazy Bluegrass state, the Cardinals had finally overcome their nemesis. Still riding high, they next beat heavily favored Big Ten champions Michigan—and found themselves on their way back home to Louisville's Freedom Hall for a Final Four contest with West Virginia. Although they proved no match for the Mountaineers, they went home happy.

The other semi rested on whether high-scoring Cincinnati could set the tempo against defensive-minded Cal. Despite Robertson's best efforts, Pete Newell's Golden Bears didn't let the Bearcats play their game. They bottled up the Big O, slowed the game down to their pace, stopped the Cincinnati running game in its tracks, and played the favored Bearcats to a standstill. With three and a half minutes remaining the game was tied. Robertson drove, went up for a short jumper—and Cal's junior center, Darrall Imhoff, blocked it. The Golden Bears had the ball. They moved it around—ever so slowly—until Imhoff got it down low and scored on a hook shot with two minutes left. Again Robertson took the ball to the hoop, pulled up, and

shot—and Imhoff again rose to meet him. As the ball arced up toward the hoop, the Cal center got his hand on it and batted it away. The Bears were in the final.

The championship game was a down-to-the-last-shot thriller. West Virginia tore out to an early 10-point lead before Cal's press began to take its toll. The Mountaineers started turning the ball over and the Golden Bears, always working for the best possible shot, cashed in on virtually every West Virginia mistake. With ten minutes to play, the Golden Bears led by 12. But West Virginia, which had already come back twice in the tournament, put on its own smothering defense, and the Bears began to cough up the ball. West was everywhere, leading his team back on both ends of the floor. With just under a minute to play he put the ball up. Imhoff rose and batted it away—*on its way down;* the goaltending call pulled West Virginia to within a point. The Mountaineers kept up the pressure but Cal got the ball downcourt. It came to Imhoff. He shot and missed. But he immediately went back up for the follow, and when the ball came off the rim, Imhoff tapped it in.

West was wonderful and Oscar was outstanding, but Darrall was the difference.

FIRST ROUND EAST

West Virginia (82)   Coach: Fred Schaus

	Min.	Total FG / FGA	Pct.	FT / FTA	Pct.	Reb. O/T	A	TO	PF	S	Blk	TP	PPM
WEST, J.	-	11/17	.647	3/ 9	.333	-/15	5	-	3	-	-	25	-
AKERS, W.	-	3/ 8	.375	1/ 3	.333	-/ 6	1	-	2	-	-	7	-
CLOUSSON, B.	-	1/ 6	.167	4/ 5	.800	-/ 9	1	-	2	-	-	6	-
SMITH, B.	-	6/ 9	.667	2/ 2	1.000	-/ 6	3	-	3	-	-	14	-
BOLYARD, B.	-	1/ 9	.111	3/ 6	.500	-/ 9	1	-	1	-	-	5	-
POSCH, J.	-	0/ 1	.000	0/ 0	.000	-/ 0	0	-	1	-	-	0	-
RITCHIE, J.	-	5/ 7	.714	5/ 5	1.000	-/ 5	0	-	1	-	-	15	-
RETTON, R.	-	3/ 3	1.000	1/ 3	.333	-/ 1	3	-	0	-	-	7	-
PATRONE, L.	-	0/ 4	.000	3/ 3	1.000	-/ 3	1	-	1	-	-	3	-
GOODE, B.	-	0/ 0	.000	0/ 0	.000	-/ 0	0	-	1	-	-	0	-
VISNIC, N.	-	0/ 0	.000	0/ 0	.000	-/ 0	0	-	0	-	-	0	-
SCHERTZINGER, H.	-	0/ 0	.000	0/ 0	.000	-/ 0	0	-	0	-	-	0	-
Totals	200	30/64	.469	22/36	.611	-/54	15	-	15	-	-	82	.410

Dartmouth (68)   Coach: Doggie Julian

	Min.	Total FG / FGA	Pct.	FT / FTA	Pct.	Reb. O/T	A	TO	PF	S	Blk	TP	PPM
VANDEWEGHE, G.	-	6/17	.353	3/ 4	.750	-/ 8	3	-	5	-	-	15	-
LARUSSO, R.	-	5/13	.385	2/ 3	.667	-/ 7	2	-	5	-	-	12	-
FARNSWORTH	-	0/ 2	.000	0/ 0	.000	-/ 5	1	-	2	-	-	0	-
SOSNOWSKI, W.	-	6/ 8	.750	1/ 4	.250	-/ 3	6	-	4	-	-	13	-
KAUFMAN, C.	-	6/15	.400	1/ 1	1.000	-/ 1	3	-	4	-	-	13	-
GAVITT, D.	-	2/ 4	.500	0/ 0	.000	-/ 1	1	-	1	-	-	4	-
BARNES	-	3/ 7	.429	3/ 5	.600	-/ 1	1	-	0	-	-	9	-
BERRY	-	0/ 1	.000	0/ 0	.000	-/ 1	0	-	3	-	-	0	-
FAIRBANK	-	0/ 1	.000	2/ 2	1.000	-/ 1	0	-	0	-	-	2	-
Totals	200	28/68	.412	12/19	.632	-/28	17	-	24	-	-	68	.340

Team Rebounds: West Virginia 9; Dartmouth 6. Disqualified: Dartmouth—Vandeweghe, Larusso.

	1st Half	2nd Half	Final
West Virginia	35	47	82
Dartmouth	25	43	68

Boston Univ. (60)   Coach: Matt Zunic

	Min.	Total FG / FGA	Pct.	FT / FTA	Pct.	Reb. O/T	A	TO	PF	S	Blk	TP	PPM
CUMMINGS, B.	-	5/ -	-	5/ 6	.833	-/ -	-	-	2	-	-	15	-
GATES, B.	-	4/ -	-	2/ 2	1.000	-/ -	-	-	5	-	-	10	-
WASHINGTON, E.	-	1/ -	-	6/ 8	.750	-/ -	-	-	2	-	-	8	-
LEAMAN, J.	-	5/ -	-	5/ 8	.625	-/ -	-	-	4	-	-	15	-
STAGIS, T.	-	1/ -	-	2/ 2	1.000	-/ -	-	-	5	-	-	4	-
O'CONNELL, D.	-	1/ -	-	4/ 7	.571	-/ -	-	-	3	-	-	6	-
SUPRIANO, H.	-	1/ -	-	0/ 0	.000	-/ -	-	-	1	-	-	2	-
Totals	200	18/ -	-	24/33	.727	-/ -	-	-	22	-	-	60	.300

U. Conn. (58)   Coach: Hugh Greer

	Min.	Total FG / FGA	Pct.	FT / FTA	Pct.	Reb. O/T	A	TO	PF	S	Blk	TP	PPM
PIPCZYNSKI	-	2/ -	-	1/ 1	1.000	-/ -	-	-	2	-	-	5	-
DAVIS	-	3/ -	-	0/ 2	.000	-/ -	-	-	4	-	-	6	-
KELLY	-	0/ -	-	0/ 0	.000	-/ -	-	-	1	-	-	0	-
COOPER	-	7/ -	-	3/ 3	1.000	-/ -	-	-	4	-	-	17	-
ROSE, J.	-	5/ -	-	18/21	.857	-/ -	-	-	5	-	-	28	-
RISLEY	-	0/ -	-	0/ 0	.000	-/ -	-	-	1	-	-	0	-
COUNTRYMAN	-	1/ -	-	0/ 2	.000	-/ -	-	-	4	-	-	2	-
Totals	200	18/ -	-	22/29	.759	-/ -	-	-	21	-	-	58	.290

Disqualified: Boston Univ.—Gates, Stagis; U. Conn.—Rose.

	1st Half	2nd Half	Final
Boston Univ.	35	25	60
U. Conn.	35	23	58

Navy (76)   Coach: Ben Carnevale

	Min.	Total FG / FGA	Pct.	FT / FTA	Pct.	Reb. O/T	A	TO	PF	S	Blk	TP	PPM
BOWER	36	5/10	.500	3/ 5	.600	-/ 3	-	-	4	-	-	13	.361
BROWN	40	1/ 7	.143	1/ 3	.333	-/13	-	-	2	-	-	3	.075
METZLER, J.	35	7/10	.700	6/ 8	.750	-/12	-	-	4	-	-	20	.571
JOHNSON, D.	36	5/10	.500	6/ 9	.667	-/ 4	-	-	1	-	-	16	.444
DELANO, F.	17	2/ 7	.286	4/ 6	.667	-/ 4	-	-	0	-	-	8	.471
DOYLE	24	4/ 5	.800	3/ 4	.750	-/ 4	-	-	3	-	-	11	.458
EGAN	7	1/ 1	1.000	2/ 2	1.000	-/ 2	-	-	0	-	-	4	.571
LAND	5	0/ 1	.000	1/ 3	.333	-/ 1	-	-	0	-	-	1	.200
Totals	200	25/51	.490	26/40	.650	-/43	-	-	14	-	-	76	.380

North Carolina (63)   Coach: Frank McGuire

	Min.	Total FG / FGA	Pct.	FT / FTA	Pct.	Reb. O/T	A	TO	PF	S	Blk	TP	PPM
SHAFFER, L.	-	2/ 5	.400	2/ 2	1.000	-/ 3	-	-	5	-	-	6	-
MOE, D.	-	3/14	.214	1/ 5	.200	-/ 8	-	-	2	-	-	7	-
KEPLEY, D.	-	7/13	.538	2/ 3	.667	-/ 9	-	-	0	-	-	16	-
LARESE, Y.	-	3/15	.200	2/ 2	1.000	-/ 5	-	-	5	-	-	8	-
SALZ, H.	-	5/12	.417	4/ 4	1.000	-/ 5	-	-	5	-	-	14	-
STANLEY, R.	-	2/ 8	.250	2/ 2	1.000	-/ 9	-	-	2	-	-	6	-
LOTZ, D.	-	1/ 2	.500	3/ 3	1.000	-/ 5	-	-	3	-	-	5	-
BROWN, L.	-	0/ 0	.000	0/ 0	.000	-/ 0	-	-	0	-	-	0	-
CROTTY, J.	-	0/ 0	.000	1/ 2	.500	-/ 0	-	-	2	-	-	1	-
DONOHUE, H.	-	0/ 1	.000	0/ 0	.000	-/ 0	-	-	1	-	-	0	-
Totals	200	23/70	.329	17/23	.739	-/44	-	-	25	-	-	63	.315

Team Rebounds: Navy 4; N. Carolina 2. Disqualified: N. Carolina—Shaffer, Larese, Salz.

	1st Half	2nd Half	Final
Navy	34	42	76
N. Carolina	22	41	63

FIRST ROUND MIDEAST

Louisville (77) Coach: Peck Hickman

	Min.	Total FG / FGA	Pct.	FT / FTA	Pct.	Reb. O / T	A	TO	PF	S	Blk	TP	PPM
GOLDSTEIN, D.	-	10/17	.588	5/ 7	.714	-/13	-	-	2	-	-	25	-
TURNER, J.	-	3/ 8	.375	3/ 4	.750	-/ 9	-	-	5	-	-	9	-
SAWYER, F.	-	3/ 6	.500	2/ 4	.500	-/ 5	-	-	3	-	-	8	-
ANDREWS, H.	-	2/15	.133	3/ 7	.429	-/ 7	-	-	4	-	-	7	-
TIEMAN, R.	-	3/ 7	.429	1/ 5	.200	-/ 2	-	-	2	-	-	7	-
KITCHEN, J.	-	3/ 6	.500	2/ 3	.667	-/ 8	-	-	2	-	-	8	-
STACEY, H.	-	0/ 0	.000	0/ 0	.000	-/ 0	-	-	1	-	-	0	-
LEATHERS, B.	-	4/ 7	.571	5/ 7	.714	-/ 6	-	-	1	-	-	13	-
Totals	200	28/66	.424	21/37	.568	-/50	-	-	20	-	-	77	.385

Eastern Kentucky (63) Coach: Paul McBraver

	Min.	Total FG / FGA	Pct.	FT / FTA	Pct.	Reb. O / T	A	TO	PF	S	Blk	TP	PPM
UPCHURCH, J.	-	2/ 9	.222	1/ 3	.333	-/ 6	-	-	5	-	-	5	-
MOORE	-	3/13	.231	5/ 6	.833	-/ 7	-	-	5	-	-	11	-
KOTULA	-	3/ 7	.429	1/ 2	.500	-/ 2	-	-	3	-	-	7	-
WOOD, L.	-	2/ 8	.250	1/ 1	1.000	-/ 2	-	-	3	-	-	5	-
COLE, C.	-	4/15	.267	3/ 4	.750	-/ 5	-	-	3	-	-	11	-
WIERWILLE, R.	-	1/ 4	.250	5/ 8	.625	-/ 7	-	-	4	-	-	7	-
SPRINGATE	-	2/ 7	.286	3/ 3	1.000	-/ 4	-	-	2	-	-	7	-
VENCIL	-	3/ 7	.429	0/ 0	.000	-/ 3	-	-	3	-	-	6	-
SLAYBACK	-	0/ 0	.000	0/ 0	.000	-/ 0	-	-	0	-	-	0	-
ESTEPP	-	2/ 3	.667	0/ 1	.000	-/ 4	-	-	1	-	-	4	-
Totals	200	22/73	.301	19/28	.679	-/40	-	-	29	-	-	63	.315

Disqualified: Louisville—Turner; Eastern Ky.—Upchurch, Moore.

	1st Half	2nd Half	Final
Louisville	38	39	77
Eastern Ky.	31	32	63

Marquette (89) Coach: Eddie Hickey

	Min.	Total FG / FGA	Pct.	FT / FTA	Pct.	Reb. O / T	A	TO	PF	S	Blk	TP	PPM
MANGHAM, W.	-	6/12	.500	4/ 4	1.000	-/ 8	-	-	3	-	-	16	-
KOJIS, D.	-	5/ 9	.556	3/ 3	1.000	-/14	-	-	1	-	-	13	-
MORAN, M.	-	9/18	.500	4/ 8	.500	-/10	-	-	2	-	-	22	-
KOLLAR, J.	-	2/ 5	.400	4/ 5	.800	-/ 3	-	-	1	-	-	8	-
MCCOY, J.	-	4/11	.364	0/ 1	.000	-/ 8	-	-	3	-	-	8	-
SUPPELSA, G.	-	0/ 0	.000	0/ 0	.000	-/ 1	-	-	0	-	-	0	-
KAKUSKA, M.	-	1/ 2	.500	0/ 1	.000	-/ 1	-	-	2	-	-	2	-
RIPP, G.	-	1/ 6	.167	0/ 0	.000	-/ 0	-	-	1	-	-	2	-
PLINSKA, J.	-	3/ 8	.375	2/ 4	.500	-/ 6	-	-	2	-	-	8	-
KERSTEN, J.	-	1/ 5	.200	2/ 2	1.000	-/ 6	-	-	1	-	-	4	-
CARTER, E.	-	0/ 2	.000	2/ 2	1.000	-/ 1	-	-	0	-	-	2	-
ROGAN, T.	-	2/ 2	1.000	0/ 0	.000	-/ 0	-	-	0	-	-	4	-
Totals	200	34/80	.425	21/30	.700	-/58	-	-	16	-	-	89	.445

Bowling Green (71) Coach: Harold Anderson

	Min.	Total FG / FGA	Pct.	FT / FTA	Pct.	Reb. O / T	A	TO	PF	S	Blk	TP	PPM
MCCAMPBELL	-	2/11	.182	0/ 2	.000	-/ 7	-	-	1	-	-	4	-
LEACH	-	5/18	.278	4/ 5	.800	-/15	-	-	0	-	-	14	-
ROUTSON	-	0/ 3	.000	1/ 1	1.000	-/ 4	-	-	4	-	-	1	-
WADE	-	4/10	.400	0/ 2	.000	-/ 5	-	-	2	-	-	8	-
DARROW	-	12/24	.500	2/ 5	.400	-/ 2	-	-	3	-	-	26	-
PARSONS	-	1/ 4	.250	0/ 0	.000	-/ 5	-	-	4	-	-	2	-
ABELE	-	1/ 3	.333	0/ 0	.000	-/ 2	-	-	0	-	-	2	-
MCDONALD	-	4/11	.364	2/ 3	.667	-/ 3	-	-	4	-	-	10	-
KUZMA	-	0/ 3	.000	0/ 0	.000	-/ 0	-	-	0	-	-	0	-
WILLIAMS	-	0/ 1	.000	0/ 2	.000	-/ 1	-	-	1	-	-	0	-
BURMEISTER	-	0/ 0	.000	0/ 0	.000	-/ 0	-	-	0	-	-	0	-
HARLING	-	2/ 2	1.000	0/ 0	.000	-/ 2	-	-	0	-	-	4	-
Totals	200	31/90	.344	9/20	.450	-/46	-	-	19	-	-	71	.355

Disqualified: None.

	1st Half	2nd Half	Final
Marquette	45	44	89
Bowling Green	28	43	71

FIRST ROUND MIDWEST

DePaul (57) Coach: Ray Meyer

	Min.	Total FG / FGA	Pct.	FT / FTA	Pct.	Reb. O / T	A	TO	PF	S	Blk	TP	PPM
SALZINSKI	-	3/ -	-	1/ 1	1.000	-/ -	-	-	4	-	-	7	-
COWSEN, M.	-	3/ -	-	1/ 2	.500	-/ -	-	-	2	-	-	7	-
FLEMMING, J.	-	3/ -	-	2/ 2	1.000	-/ -	-	-	2	-	-	8	-
CARL, H.	-	6/ -	-	4/ 4	1.000	-/ -	-	-	4	-	-	16	-
HAIG	-	7/ -	-	5/ 7	.714	-/ -	-	-	1	-	-	19	-
RUBBY	-	0/ -	-	0/ 0	.000	-/ -	-	-	1	-	-	0	-
Totals	200	22/ -	-	13/16	.813	-/ -	-	-	14	-	-	57	.285

Portland (56) Coach: Al Negratti

	Min.	Total FG / FGA	Pct.	FT / FTA	Pct.	Reb. O / T	A	TO	PF	S	Blk	TP	PPM
O'DONNELL	-	0/ -	-	1/ 1	1.000	-/ -	-	-	0	-	-	1	-
JOLLEY	-	5/ -	-	2/ 2	1.000	-/ -	-	-	3	-	-	12	-
ALTENHOFEN	-	3/ -	-	2/ 4	.500	-/ -	-	-	2	-	-	8	-
PANEL	-	8/ -	-	1/ 3	.333	-/ -	-	-	2	-	-	17	-
ARMSTRONG	-	4/ -	-	0/ 1	.000	-/ -	-	-	4	-	-	8	-
BLOEDEL	-	4/ -	-	2/ 5	.400	-/ -	-	-	1	-	-	10	-
Totals	200	24/ -	-	8/16	.500	-/ -	-	-	12	-	-	56	.280

Disqualified: None.

	1st Half	2nd Half	Final
DePaul	33	24	57
Portland	29	27	56

FIRST ROUND WEST

Idaho State (62)   Coach: John Grayson

	Min.	Total FG / FGA	Pct.	FT / FTA	Pct.	Reb. O / T	A	TO	PF	S	Blk	TP	PPM
MORRIS, A.	-	0/ -	-	3/ 3	1.000	-/ -	-	-	1	-	-	3	-
CLOCK, N.	-	2/ -	-	1/ 1	1.000	-/ -	-	-	4	-	-	5	-
RODGERS, J.	-	3/ -	-	0/ 0	.000	-/ -	-	-	4	-	-	6	-
GRIFFITH, R.	-	11/ -	-	10/12	.833	-/ -	-	-	2	-	-	32	-
WATKINS, H.	-	1/ -	-	2/ 4	.500	-/ -	-	-	3	-	-	4	-
CHENEY, R.	-	4/ -	-	1/ 1	1.000	-/ -	-	-	4	-	-	9	-
MOULTON, D.	-	0/ -	-	1/ 3	.333	-/ -	-	-	1	-	-	1	-
	-	1/ -	-	0/ 2	.000	-/ -	-	-	2	-	-	2	-
Totals	200	22/ -	-	18/26	.692	-/ -	-	-	21	-	-	62	.310

New Mexico State (61)   Coach: Presley Askew

	Min.	Total FG / FGA	Pct.	FT / FTA	Pct.	Reb. O / T	A	TO	PF	S	Blk	TP	PPM
OLIVER	-	1/ -	-	0/ 0	.000	-/ -	-	-	1	-	-	2	-
KELLY, J.	-	3/ -	-	7/ 9	.778	-/ -	-	-	5	-	-	13	-
CLARK, C.	-	5/ -	-	2/ 3	.667	-/ -	-	-	5	-	-	12	-
PRICE	-	8/ -	-	2/ 6	.333	-/ -	-	-	2	-	-	18	-
BOWEN	-	1/ -	-	3/ 5	.600	-/ -	-	-	2	-	-	5	-
DAVIS	-	3/ -	-	5/ 6	.833	-/ -	-	-	1	-	-	11	-
Totals	200	21/ -	-	19/29	.655	-/ -	-	-	16	-	-	61	.305

Disqualified: New Mexico St.—Kelly, Clark.

	1st Half	2nd Half	Final
Idaho State	35	27	62
New Mexico St.	32	29	61

REGIONAL SEMIFINAL EAST

St. Joseph's (92)   Coach: Jack Ramsay

	Min.	Total FG / FGA	Pct.	FT / FTA	Pct.	Reb. O / T	A	TO	PF	S	Blk	TP	PPM
EGAN, J.	-	9/13	.692	2/ 2	1.000	-/ 8	0	-	5	-	-	20	-
SPRATT	-	6/10	.600	5/ 7	.714	-/10	1	-	5	-	-	17	-
CLARKE	-	6/ 9	.667	3/ 4	.750	-/13	1	-	5	-	-	15	-
GALLO	-	9/22	.409	4/ 4	1.000	-/ 4	4	-	4	-	-	22	-
MCNEILL	-	1/ 8	.125	5/ 6	.833	-/ 5	4	-	5	-	-	7	-
REILLY	-	1/ 4	.250	2/ 2	1.000	-/ 3	0	-	2	-	-	4	-
MAJEWSKI, F.	-	2/ 4	.500	0/ 2	.000	-/ 1	2	-	5	-	-	4	-
HOFFACKER	-	0/ 0	.000	1/ 2	.500	-/ 0	0	-	1	-	-	1	-
COOKE	-	1/ 1	1.000	0/ 0	.000	-/ 0	0	-	0	-	-	2	-
Totals	200	35/71	.493	22/29	.759	-/44	12	-	32	-	-	92	.460

West Virginia (95)   Coach: Fred Schaus

	Min.	Total FG / FGA	Pct.	FT / FTA	Pct.	Reb. O / T	A	TO	PF	S	Blk	TP	PPM
WEST, J.	-	12/22	.545	12/18	.667	-/15	1	-	1	-	-	36	-
AKERS, W.	-	3/10	.300	7/ 8	.875	-/ 6	0	-	4	-	-	13	-
CLOUSSON, B.	-	2/ 7	.286	0/ 0	.000	-/ 7	0	-	4	-	-	4	-
SMITH, B.	-	2/11	.182	3/ 4	.750	-/ 5	1	-	2	-	-	7	-
BOLYARD, B.	-	4/10	.400	2/ 4	.500	-/ 5	4	-	3	-	-	10	-
POSCH, J.	-	0/ 1	.000	0/ 0	.000	-/ 0	0	-	2	-	-	0	-
RITCHIE, J.	-	2/11	.182	4/ 7	.571	-/ 8	0	-	1	-	-	8	-
RETTON, R.	-	1/ 4	.250	2/ 2	1.000	-/ 2	1	-	2	-	-	4	-
PATRONE, L.	-	5/16	.313	3/ 7	.429	-/ 8	3	-	1	-	-	13	-
Totals	200	31/92	.337	33/50	.660	-/56	10	-	20	-	-	95	.475

Team Rebounds: West Virginia 9; St. Joseph's 11. Disqualified: St. Joseph's—Egan, Spratt, Clarke, McNeill, Majewski.

	1st Half	2nd Half	Final
St. Joseph's	48	44	92
West Virginia	42	53	95

Boston Univ. (62)   Coach: Matt Zunic

	Min.	Total FG / FGA	Pct.	FT / FTA	Pct.	Reb. O / T	A	TO	PF	S	Blk	TP	PPM
CUMINGS, B.	-	6/15	.400	2/ 3	.667	-/ 6	-	-	1	-	-	14	-
GATES, B.	-	3/ 9	.333	3/ 4	.750	-/ 3	-	-	2	-	-	9	-
WASHINGTON, E.	-	4/13	.308	6/ 7	.857	-/19	-	-	3	-	-	14	-
LEAMAN, J.	-	5/16	.313	3/ 4	.750	-/ 2	-	-	4	-	-	13	-
STAGIS, T.	-	3/13	.231	2/ 2	1.000	-/ 5	-	-	0	-	-	8	-
SUPRIANO, H.	-	0/ 0	.000	2/ 2	1.000	-/ 0	-	-	0	-	-	2	-
O'CONNELL, D.	-	1/ 3	.333	0/ 0	.000	-/ 0	-	-	1	-	-	2	-
Totals	225	22/69	.319	18/22	.818	-/35	-	-	11	-	-	62	.276

Navy (55)   Coach: Ben Carnevale

	Min.	Total FG / FGA	Pct.	FT / FTA	Pct.	Reb. O / T	A	TO	PF	S	Blk	TP	PPM
BOWER	43	1/11	.091	6/ 6	1.000	-/10	-	-	1	-	-	8	.186
BROWN	45	4/10	.400	0/ 0	.000	-/14	-	-	1	-	-	8	.178
METZLER, J.	38	8/14	.571	0/ 0	.000	-/ 8	-	-	5	-	-	16	.421
JOHNSON, D.	18	1/ 4	.250	0/ 0	.000	-/ 1	-	-	0	-	-	2	.111
DELANO, F.	22	2/ 2	1.000	4/ 6	.667	-/ 2	-	-	4	-	-	8	.364
DOYLE	23	1/ 3	.333	0/ 0	.000	-/ 2	-	-	2	-	-	2	.087
EGAN	5	0/ 0	.000	0/ 0	.000	-/ 1	-	-	0	-	-	0	.000
LAND	7	0/ 1	.000	0/ 0	.000	-/ 1	-	-	1	-	-	0	.000
BAGNARD	24	4/ 6	.667	3/ 3	1.000	-/ 1	-	-	2	-	-	11	.458
Totals	225	21/51	.412	13/15	.867	-/40	-	-	16	-	-	55	.244

Team Rebounds: Boston Univ. 5; Navy 3. Disqualified: Navy—Metzler.

	1st Half	2nd Half	1st OT	Final
Boston Univ.	32	20	10	62
Navy	30	22	3	55

REGIONAL SEMIFINAL MIDEAST

Kentucky (61) Coach: Adolph Rupp

	Min.	Total FG/FGA	Pct.	FT/FTA	Pct.	Reb. O/T	A	TO	PF	S	Blk	TP	PPM
COX, J.	-	3/15	.200	4/ 5	.800	-/ 7	-	-	5	-	-	10	-
LICKERT, B.	-	7/11	.636	2/ 3	.667	-/ 7	-	-	1	-	-	16	-
MILLS, D.	-	1/ 3	.333	4/ 5	.800	-/ 7	-	-	4	-	-	6	-
COFFMAN, B.	-	4/12	.333	5/ 6	.833	-/ 3	-	-	5	-	-	13	-
PARSONS, D.	-	2/ 9	.222	0/ 0	.000	-/ 2	-	-	3	-	-	4	-
JOHNSON, P.	-	2/ 4	.500	0/ 0	.000	-/ 4	-	-	0	-	-	4	-
COHEN, S.	-	2/ 7	.286	1/ 1	1.000	-/ 4	-	-	1	-	-	5	-
SLUSHER, B.	-	1/ 6	.167	1/ 1	1.000	-/ 3	-	-	3	-	-	3	-
Totals	200	22/67	.328	17/21	.810	-/37	-	-	22	-	-	61	.305

Louisville (76) Coach: Peck Hickman

	Min.	Total FG/FGA	Pct.	FT/FTA	Pct.	Reb. O/T	A	TO	PF	S	Blk	TP	PPM
GOLDSTEIN, D.	-	7/12	.583	5/ 7	.714	-/13	-	-	4	-	-	19	-
TURNER, J.	-	4/10	.400	5/ 7	.714	-/ 8	-	-	2	-	-	13	-
SAWYER, F.	-	2/10	.200	3/ 5	.600	-/10	-	-	2	-	-	7	-
ANDREWS, H.	-	5/ 9	.556	5/ 5	1.000	-/ 5	-	-	2	-	-	15	-
TIEMAN, R.	-	5/ 8	.625	3/ 4	.750	-/ 1	-	-	3	-	-	13	-
KITCHEN, J.	-	1/ 2	.500	5/ 5	1.000	-/ 2	-	-	2	-	-	7	-
LEATHERS, B.	-	1/ 4	.250	0/ 0	.000	-/ 7	-	-	1	-	-	2	-
Totals	200	25/55	.455	26/33	.788	-/46	-	-	16	-	-	76	.380

Disqualified: Kentucky—Cox, Coffman.

	1st Half	2nd Half	Final
Kentucky	36	25	61
Louisville	28	48	76

Marquette (69) Coach: Eddie Hickey

	Min.	Total FG/FGA	Pct.	FT/FTA	Pct.	Reb. O/T	A	TO	PF	S	Blk	TP	PPM
MANGHAM, W.	-	6/17	.353	3/ 7	.429	-/ 9	-	-	3	-	-	15	-
KOJIS, D.	-	7/17	.412	3/ 6	.500	-/21	-	-	3	-	-	17	-
MORAN, M.	-	3/15	.200	3/ 4	.750	-/ 5	-	-	4	-	-	9	-
KOLLAR, J.	-	6/11	.545	1/ 1	1.000	-/ 5	-	-	4	-	-	13	-
MCCOY, J.	-	6/18	.333	1/ 1	1.000	-/10	-	-	2	-	-	13	-
RIPP, G.	-	0/ 2	.000	0/ 0	.000	-/ 1	-	-	0	-	-	0	-
PLINSKA, J.	-	1/ 1	1.000	0/ 0	.000	-/ 0	-	-	1	-	-	2	-
KERSTEN, J.	-	0/ 0	.000	0/ 0	.000	-/ 0	-	-	0	-	-	0	-
Totals	200	29/81	.358	11/19	.579	-/51	-	-	17	-	-	69	.345

Michigan State (74) Coach: Forddy Anderson

	Min.	Total FG/FGA	Pct.	FT/FTA	Pct.	Reb. O/T	A	TO	PF	S	Blk	TP	PPM
RAND	-	1/ 5	.200	1/ 2	.500	-/ 5	-	-	2	-	-	3	-
ANDEREGG, B.	-	10/19	.526	3/ 7	.429	-/ 8	-	-	1	-	-	23	-
WALKER	-	9/21	.429	2/ 3	.667	-/ 8	-	-	2	-	-	20	-
GREEN	-	6/18	.333	2/ 4	.500	-/18	-	-	5	-	-	14	-
OLSON	-	1/ 7	.143	6/ 8	.750	-/ 4	-	-	4	-	-	8	-
FAHS	-	2/ 6	.333	0/ 1	.000	-/ 1	-	-	0	-	-	4	-
GOWENS	-	1/ 1	1.000	0/ 0	.000	-/ 1	-	-	0	-	-	2	-
Totals	200	30/77	.390	14/25	.560	-/45	-	-	14	-	-	74	.370

Team Rebounds: Michigan St. 6; Marquette 7. Disqualified: Michigan St.—Green.

	1st Half	2nd Half	Final
Marquette	34	35	69
Michigan St.	38	36	74

REGIONAL SEMIFINAL MIDWEST

Kansas State (102) Coach: Tex Winter

	Min.	Total FG/FGA	Pct.	FT/FTA	Pct.	Reb. O/T	A	TO	PF	S	Blk	TP	PPM
FRANK, W.	-	9/13	.692	5/ 6	.833	0/ 4	-	-	2	-	-	23	-
BOOZER, B.	-	7/21	.333	2/ 3	.667	6/12	-	-	1	-	-	16	-
PRICE, C.	-	3/13	.231	8/10	.800	3/ 8	-	-	2	-	-	14	-
MATUSZAK, D.	-	2/ 6	.333	2/ 3	.667	0/ 4	-	-	3	-	-	6	-
DOUGLAS, S.	-	7/ 8	.875	1/ 1	1.000	1/ 6	-	-	3	-	-	15	-
HEINZ, M.	-	1/ 5	.200	4/ 4	1.000	1/ 4	-	-	1	-	-	6	-
GUTHRIDGE, W.	-	2/ 4	.500	0/ 0	.000	0/ 1	-	-	1	-	-	4	-
LONG, G.	-	0/ 2	.000	1/ 2	.500	1/ 1	-	-	1	-	-	1	-
JOHNSON, J.	-	2/ 2	1.000	0/ 0	.000	1/ 3	-	-	1	-	-	4	-
HOLWERDA, J.	-	5/ 8	.625	1/ 1	1.000	0/ 2	-	-	3	-	-	11	-
BALDING, G.	-	0/ 0	.000	0/ 0	.000	0/ 2	-	-	0	-	-	0	-
GRAHAM, R.	-	1/ 1	1.000	0/ 0	.000	0/ 0	-	-	1	-	-	2	-
Totals	200	39/83	.470	24/30	.800	13/47	-	-	19	-	-	102	.510

DePaul (70) Coach: Ray Meyer

	Min.	Total FG/FGA	Pct.	FT/FTA	Pct.	Reb. O/T	A	TO	PF	S	Blk	TP	PPM
SALZINSKI	-	2/ 4	.500	2/ 2	1.000	0/ 1	-	-	3	-	-	6	-
COWSEN, M.	-	3/18	.167	1/ 3	.333	7/ 9	-	-	4	-	-	7	-
FLEMMING, J.	-	3/ 7	.429	2/ 4	.500	2/11	-	-	4	-	-	8	-
HAIG	-	3/11	.273	3/ 4	.750	0/ 5	-	-	2	-	-	9	-
CARL, H.	-	7/23	.304	8/10	.800	1/ 6	-	-	2	-	-	22	-
RUDDY	-	6/10	.600	6/ 7	.857	3/ 6	-	-	5	-	-	18	-
Totals	200	24/73	.329	22/30	.733	13/38	-	-	20	-	-	70	.350

Team Rebounds: Kansas State 15; DePaul 13. Disqualified: DePaul—Ruddy.

	1st Half	2nd Half	Final
Kansas State	49	53	102
DePaul	32	38	70

Cincinnati (77) Coach: George Smith

	Min.	Total FG/FGA	Pct.	FT/FTA	Pct.	Reb. O/T	A	TO	PF	S	Blk	TP	PPM
ROBERTSON, O.	40	12/24	.500	10/13	.769	4/10	7	-	4	-	-	34	.850
TENWICK, D.	19	2/ 7	.286	0/ 0	.000	0/ 1	0	-	4	-	-	4	.211
WHITAKER, B.	16	3/ 8	.375	0/ 1	.000	3/ 3	1	-	1	-	-	6	.375
WIESENHAHN, B.	40	5/ 8	.625	2/ 2	1.000	6/14	0	-	3	-	-	12	.300
DAVIS, R.	36	5/14	.357	0/ 3	.000	1/ 2	5	-	0	-	-	10	.278
BOULDIN, C.	27	2/ 4	.500	1/ 1	1.000	1/ 6	2	-	3	-	-	5	.185
WILLEY, L.	9	0/ 1	.000	0/ 0	.000	1/ 3	0	-	3	-	-	0	.000
LANDFRIED, M.	13	3/ 5	.600	0/ 0	.000	3/ 4	0	-	1	-	-	6	.462
Totals	200	32/71	.451	13/20	.650	19/43	15	21	19	-	-	77	.385

TCU (73) Coach: Buster Brannon

	Min.	Total FG/FGA	Pct.	FT/FTA	Pct.	Reb. O/T	A	TO	PF	S	Blk	TP	PPM
STEVENSON	-	4/16	.250	7/ 8	.875	9/12	-	-	5	-	-	15	-
NIPPERT	-	2/11	.182	5/ 5	1.000	2/ 5	-	-	0	-	-	9	-
KIRCHNER, H.	-	11/23	.478	3/ 7	.429	9/18	-	-	0	-	-	25	-
KING	-	1/ 6	.167	0/ 0	.000	1/ 1	-	-	5	-	-	2	-
BRUNSON	-	5/14	.357	0/ 0	.000	1/ 2	-	-	1	-	-	10	-
COBB	-	2/ 5	.400	0/ 0	.000	1/ 2	-	-	1	-	-	4	-
TYLER	-	3/ 8	.375	2/ 2	1.000	0/ 1	-	-	3	-	-	8	-
Totals	200	28/83	.337	17/22	.773	23/41	8	5	15	-	-	73	.365

Team Rebounds: Cincinnati 8; TCU 11. Disqualified: TCU—Stevenson, King.

	1st Half	2nd Half	Final
Cincinnati	38	39	77
TCU	37	36	73

REGIONAL SEMIFINAL WEST

St. Mary's (80)   Coach: James Weaver

	Min.	Total FG/FGA	Pct.	FT/FTA	Pct.	Reb. O/T	A	TO	PF	S	Blk	TP	PPM
SIGATY, D.	-	3/11	.273	0/2	.000	-/12	-	-	5	-	-	6	-
DOSS, L.	-	8/12	.667	5/5	1.000	-/5	-	-	1	-	-	21	-
MESCHERY, T.	-	8/14	.571	3/4	.750	-/13	-	-	3	-	-	19	-
BARRY, J.	-	4/6	.667	5/7	.714	-/2	-	-	2	-	-	13	-
DOLD, B.	-	4/10	.400	3/3	1.000	-/2	-	-	4	-	-	11	-
BRENNAN, L.	-	3/3	1.000	0/1	.000	-/0	-	-	0	-	-	6	-
WOMACK, G.	-	0/1	.000	2/2	1.000	-/1	-	-	0	-	-	2	-
DOLD, J.	-	0/0	.000	0/0	.000	-/0	-	-	0	-	-	0	-
TAMM, W.	-	0/1	.000	0/1	.000	-/1	-	-	0	-	-	0	-
CLAIBORNE	-	1/3	.333	0/0	.000	-/3	-	-	1	-	-	2	-
Totals	200	31/61	.508	18/25	.720	-/39	-	-	16	-	-	80	.400

Idaho State (71)   Coach: John Grayson

	Min.	Total FG/FGA	Pct.	FT/FTA	Pct.	Reb. O/T	A	TO	PF	S	Blk	TP	PPM
MORRIS, A.	-	4/9	.444	2/2	1.000	-/5	-	-	3	-	-	10	-
CLOCK, N.	-	1/6	.167	3/3	1.000	-/2	-	-	2	-	-	5	-
WATKINS, H.	-	5/7	.714	1/2	.500	-/4	-	-	5	-	-	11	-
RODGERS, J.	-	12/27	.444	5/6	.833	-/0	-	-	3	-	-	29	-
GRIFFITH, R.	-	1/2	.500	2/3	.667	-/5	-	-	2	-	-	4	-
GRIFFIN, J.	-	4/9	.444	0/2	.000	-/3	-	-	2	-	-	8	-
MOULTON, D.	-	2/3	.667	0/0	.000	-/5	-	-	1	-	-	4	-
CHENEY, R.	-	0/0	.000	0/1	.000	-/1	-	-	0	-	-	0	-
LINK, J.	-	0/0	.000	0/2	.000	-/1	-	-	0	-	-	0	-
Totals	200	29/63	.460	13/21	.619	-/26	-	-	18	-	-	71	.355

Team Rebounds: St. Mary's 3; Idaho State 5. Disqualified: St. Mary's—Sigaty; Idaho State—Watkins.

	1st Half	2nd Half	Final
St. Mary's	39	41	80
Idaho State	33	38	71

California (71)   Coach: Pete Newell

	Min.	Total FG/FGA	Pct.	FT/FTA	Pct.	Reb. O/T	A	TO	PF	S	Blk	TP	PPM
MCCLINTOCK, B.	-	4/-	-	1/3	.333	-/-	-	-	1	-	-	9	-
DALTON, B.	-	6/-	-	1/1	1.000	-/-	-	-	2	-	-	13	-
IMHOFF, D.	-	3/-	-	3/4	.750	-/-	-	-	4	-	-	9	-
FITZPATRICK, D.	-	4/-	-	4/4	1.000	-/-	-	-	3	-	-	12	-
BUCH, A.	-	7/-	-	1/2	.500	-/-	-	-	1	-	-	15	-
GROUT, J.	-	1/-	-	0/0	.000	-/-	-	-	2	-	-	2	-
SIMPSON, B.	-	1/-	-	0/0	.000	-/-	-	-	1	-	-	2	-
DOUGHTY, D.	-	3/-	-	0/0	.000	-/-	-	-	1	-	-	6	-
MANN, J.	-	0/-	-	0/0	.000	-/-	-	-	0	-	-	0	-
LANGLEY	-	0/-	-	0/0	.000	-/-	-	-	0	-	-	0	-
SCHULTZ, E.	-	0/-	-	1/2	.500	-/-	-	-	3	-	-	1	-
GILLIS, T.	-	1/-	-	0/0	.000	-/-	-	-	0	-	-	2	-
Totals	200	30/-	-	11/16	.688	-/-	-	-	18	-	-	71	.355

Utah (53)   Coach: Jack Gardner

	Min.	Total FG/FGA	Pct.	FT/FTA	Pct.	Reb. O/T	A	TO	PF	S	Blk	TP	PPM
RUFFELL	-	4/-	-	0/-	-	-/-	-	-	1	-	-	8	-
CHESTANG	-	3/-	-	3/-	-	-/-	-	-	2	-	-	9	-
POLLARD	-	4/-	-	1/-	-	-/-	-	-	2	-	-	9	-
CONDIE	-	4/-	-	0/-	-	-/-	-	-	0	-	-	8	-
SHORES	-	0/-	-	2/-	-	-/-	-	-	3	-	-	2	-
CRISLER	-	3/-	-	3/-	-	-/-	-	-	2	-	-	9	-
RHEAD	-	0/-	-	1/-	-	-/-	-	-	0	-	-	1	-
MORTON	-	1/-	-	2/-	-	-/-	-	-	1	-	-	4	-
ANCELL	-	0/-	-	0/-	-	-/-	-	-	1	-	-	0	-
CUTLER	-	0/-	-	0/-	-	-/-	-	-	1	-	-	0	-
VAN, W.	-	0/-	-	3/-	-	-/-	-	-	0	-	-	3	-
Totals	200	19/-	-	15/-	-	-/-	-	-	13	-	-	53	.265

Disqualified: None.

	1st Half	2nd Half	Final
California	42	29	71
Utah	27	26	53

REGIONAL FINAL EAST

West Virginia (86)   Coach: Fred Schaus

	Min.	Total FG/FGA	Pct.	FT/FTA	Pct.	Reb. O/T	A	TO	PF	S	Blk	TP	PPM
WEST, J.	-	12/24	.500	9/12	.750	-/17	3	-	4	-	-	33	-
AKERS, W.	-	3/13	.231	5/5	1.000	-/8	0	-	4	-	-	11	-
CLOUSSON, B.	-	2/4	.500	4/5	.800	-/6	0	-	4	-	-	8	-
SMITH, B.	-	6/11	.545	0/1	.000	-/1	2	-	0	-	-	12	-
BOLYARD, B.	-	2/11	.182	1/1	1.000	-/0	3	-	3	-	-	5	-
POSCH, J.	-	0/0	.000	0/0	.000	-/0	0	-	2	-	-	0	-
RITCHIE, J.	-	2/5	.400	8/10	.800	-/9	0	-	4	-	-	12	-
RETTON, R.	-	0/0	.000	1/3	.333	-/0	0	-	2	-	-	1	-
PATRONE, L.	-	1/4	.250	2/5	.400	-/5	3	-	1	-	-	4	-
Totals	200	28/72	.389	30/42	.714	-/46	11	-	24	-	-	86	.430

Boston Univ. (82)   Coach: Matt Zunic

	Min.	Total FG/FGA	Pct.	FT/FTA	Pct.	Reb. O/T	A	TO	PF	S	Blk	TP	PPM
CUMINGS, B.	-	9/17	.529	4/7	.571	-/13	1	-	1	-	-	22	-
GATES, B.	-	7/14	.500	4/6	.667	-/8	0	-	4	-	-	18	-
WASHINGTON, E.	-	2/5	.400	2/4	.500	-/10	1	-	5	-	-	6	-
LEAMAN, J.	-	3/9	.333	4/4	1.000	-/3	3	-	4	-	-	10	-
STAGIS, T.	-	5/15	.333	3/6	.500	-/7	5	-	5	-	-	13	-
SUPRIANO, H.	-	3/7	.429	2/5	.400	-/3	3	-	2	-	-	8	-
O'CONNELL, D.	-	1/7	.143	3/3	1.000	-/4	0	-	3	-	-	5	-
CHAMBERLAIN, T.	-	0/0	.000	0/0	.000	-/0	0	-	2	-	-	0	-
Totals	200	30/74	.405	22/35	.629	-/48	13	-	26	-	-	82	.410

Team Rebounds: West Virginia 9; Boston Univ. 10. Disqualified: Boston Univ.—Washington, Stagis.

	1st Half	2nd Half	Final
West Virginia	45	41	86
Boston Univ.	45	37	82

REGIONAL FINAL MIDEAST

Louisville (88) Coach: Peck Hickman

	Min.	Total FG/FGA	Pct.	FT/FTA	Pct.	Reb. O/T	A	TO	PF	S	Blk	TP	PPM
GOLDSTEIN, D.	-	7/15	.467	7/ 7	1.000	-/ 7	-	-	4	-	-	21	-
TURNER, J.	-	10/19	.526	2/ 3	.667	-/ 6	-	-	4	-	-	22	-
SAWYER, F.	-	6/12	.500	2/ 5	.400	-/15	-	-	4	-	-	14	-
ANDREWS, H.	-	5/ 9	.556	3/ 4	.750	-/ 4	-	-	5	-	-	13	-
TIEMAN, R.	-	0/ 6	.000	3/ 3	1.000	-/ 4	-	-	2	-	-	3	-
KITCHEN, J.	-	2/ 4	.500	1/ 1	1.000	-/ 4	-	-	1	-	-	5	-
LEATHERS, B.	-	3/10	.300	4/ 5	.800	-/ 3	-	-	3	-	-	10	-
Totals	200	33/75	.440	22/28	.786	-/43	-	-	23	-	-	88	.440

Michigan State (81) Coach: Forddy Anderson

	Min.	Total FG/FGA	Pct.	FT/FTA	Pct.	Reb. O/T	A	TO	PF	S	Blk	TP	PPM
RAND	-	1/ 7	.143	0/ 0	.000	-/ 2	-	-	3	-	-	2	-
ANDEREGG, B.	-	8/21	.381	6/10	.600	-/ 3	-	-	5	-	-	22	-
WALKER	-	1/ 9	.111	1/ 1	1.000	-/ 9	-	-	5	-	-	3	-
GREEN	-	11/21	.524	7/12	.583	-/23	-	-	3	-	-	29	-
OLSON	-	6/15	.400	4/ 4	1.000	-/ 3	-	-	3	-	-	16	-
FAHS	-	0/ 5	.000	0/ 1	.000	-/ 0	-	-	2	-	-	0	-
GOWENS	-	1/ 1	1.000	1/ 2	.500	-/ 0	-	-	0	-	-	3	-
STOUFFER	-	3/ 5	.600	0/ 0	.000	-/ 1	-	-	0	-	-	6	-
Totals	200	31/84	.369	19/30	.633	-/42	-	-	21	-	-	81	.405

Team Rebounds: Louisville 9; Michigan St. 8. Disqualified: Louisville—Andrews; Michigan St.—Anderegg, Walker.

	1st Half	2nd Half	Final
Louisville	40	48	88
Michigan St.	43	38	81

REGIONAL FINAL MIDWEST

Kansas State (75) Coach: Tex Winter

	Min.	Total FG/FGA	Pct.	FT/FTA	Pct.	Reb. O/T	A	TO	PF	S	Blk	TP	PPM
FRANK, W.	-	4/16	.250	2/ 4	.500	2/ 3	-	-	3	-	-	10	-
BOOZER, B.	-	11/26	.423	10/13	.769	7/13	-	-	5	-	-	32	-
PRICE, C.	-	1/ 6	.167	9/10	.900	0/ 5	-	-	5	-	-	11	-
MATUSZAK, D.	-	4/ 7	.571	0/ 0	.000	1/ 4	-	-	2	-	-	8	-
DOUGLAS, S.	-	1/ 5	.200	1/ 1	1.000	3/ 4	-	-	5	-	-	3	-
HEINZ, M.	-	1/ 6	.167	0/ 1	.000	4/ 8	-	-	1	-	-	2	-
GUTHRIDGE, W.	-	1/ 3	.333	1/ 2	.500	0/ 2	-	-	0	-	-	3	-
JOHNSON, J.	-	0/ 2	.000	0/ 0	.000	0/ 0	-	-	0	-	-	0	-
HOLWERDA, J.	-	3/11	.273	0/ 0	.000	1/ 3	-	-	2	-	-	6	-
Totals	200	26/82	.317	23/31	.742	18/42	12	11	23	-	-	75	.375

Cincinnati (85) Coach: George Smith

	Min.	Total FG/FGA	Pct.	FT/FTA	Pct.	Reb. O/T	A	TO	PF	S	Blk	TP	PPM
ROBERTSON, O.	40	8/19	.421	8/ 9	.889	5/17	13	-	4	-	-	24	.600
TENWICK, D.	40	5/16	.313	12/15	.800	3/ 9	0	-	4	-	-	22	.550
WHITAKER, B.	32	1/ 4	.250	2/ 3	.667	0/ 0	2	-	3	-	-	4	.125
WIESENHAHN, B.	21	6/12	.500	0/ 1	.000	5/ 9	0	-	5	-	-	12	.571
DAVIS, R.	40	6/16	.375	1/ 2	.500	1/ 2	2	-	3	-	-	13	.325
BOULDIN, C.	8	0/ 1	.000	0/ 0	.000	0/ 0	2	-	0	-	-	0	.000
LANDFRIED, M.	19	4/ 5	.800	2/ 3	.667	2/10	1	-	1	-	-	10	.526
Totals	200	30/73	.411	25/33	.758	16/47	20	16	20	-	-	85	.425

Team Rebounds: Cincinnati 5; Kansas State 13. Disqualified: Cincinnati—Wiesenhahn; Kansas State—Boozer, Price, Douglas.

	1st Half	2nd Half	Final
Kansas State	41	34	75
Cincinnati	39	46	85

REGIONAL FINAL WEST

St. Mary's (46) Coach: James Weaver

	Min.	Total FG/FGA	Pct.	FT/FTA	Pct.	Reb. O/T	A	TO	PF	S	Blk	TP	PPM
SIGATY, D.	-	2/ -	-	0/ 1	.000	-/ -	-	-	2	-	-	4	-
DOSS, L.	-	6/ -	-	2/ 2	1.000	-/ -	-	-	1	-	-	14	-
MESCHERY, T.	-	2/ -	-	1/ 3	.333	-/ -	-	-	2	-	-	5	-
DOLD, B.	-	1/ -	-	1/ 1	1.000	-/ -	-	-	3	-	-	3	-
BARRY, J.	-	6/ -	-	2/ 2	1.000	-/ -	-	-	4	-	-	14	-
BRENNAN, L.	-	2/ -	-	2/ 3	.667	-/ -	-	-	2	-	-	6	-
WOMACK, G.	-	0/ -	-	0/ 1	.000	-/ -	-	-	0	-	-	0	-
DOLD, J.	-	0/ -	-	0/ 0	.000	-/ -	-	-	0	-	-	0	-
TAMM, W.	-	0/ -	-	0/ 2	.000	-/ -	-	-	0	-	-	0	-
CLAIBORNE	-	0/ -	-	0/ 0	.000	-/ -	-	-	0	-	-	0	-
Totals	200	19/61	.311	8/15	.533	-/35	-	-	14	-	-	46	.230

California (66) Coach: Pete Newell

	Min.	Total FG/FGA	Pct.	FT/FTA	Pct.	Reb. O/T	A	TO	PF	S	Blk	TP	PPM
DALTON, B.	-	3/ -	-	7/ 7	1.000	-/ -	-	-	3	-	-	13	-
MCCLINTOCK, B.	-	4/ -	-	2/ 3	.667	-/ -	-	-	4	-	-	10	-
IMHOFF, D.	-	4/ -	-	2/ 2	1.000	-/15	-	-	1	-	-	10	-
FITZPATRICK, D.	-	9/ -	-	3/ 3	1.000	-/ -	-	-	2	-	-	21	-
BUCH, A.	-	2/ -	-	0/ 0	.000	-/ -	-	-	1	-	-	4	-
GROUT, J.	-	2/ -	-	0/ 0	.000	-/ -	-	-	1	-	-	4	-
SIMPSON, B.	-	0/ -	-	2/ 3	.667	-/ -	-	-	0	-	-	2	-
DOUGHTY, D.	-	0/ -	-	0/ 0	.000	-/ -	-	-	0	-	-	0	-
MANN, J.	-	0/ -	-	0/ 0	.000	-/ -	-	-	0	-	-	0	-
LANGLEY, J.	-	0/ -	-	0/ 0	.000	-/ -	-	-	0	-	-	0	-
GILLIS, T.	-	0/ -	-	0/ 0	.000	-/ -	-	-	1	-	-	0	-
SCHULTZ, E.	-	0/ -	-	2/ 2	1.000	-/ -	-	-	0	-	-	2	-
Totals	200	24/57	.421	18/20	.900	-/49	-	-	14	-	-	66	.330

Disqualified: None.

	1st Half	2nd Half	Final
St. Mary's	18	28	46
California	31	35	66

FINAL FOUR

West Virginia (94)   Coach: Fred Schaus

	Min.	Total FG/FGA	Pct.	FT/FTA	Pct.	Reb. O/T	A	TO	PF	S	Blk	TP	PPM
WEST, J.	-	12/21	.571	14/20	.700	-/15	-	-	3	-	-	38	-
AKERS, W.	-	2/5	.400	1/2	.500	-/8	-	-	5	-	-	5	-
CLOUSSON, B.	-	5/5	1.000	2/2	1.000	-/4	-	-	4	-	-	12	-
SMITH, B.	-	5/9	.556	2/4	.500	-/5	-	-	0	-	-	12	-
BOLYARD, J.	-	4/10	.400	5/7	.714	-/3	-	-	1	-	-	13	-
POSCH, J.	-	1/2	.500	0/0	.000	-/0	-	-	0	-	-	2	-
RITCHIE, J.	-	2/6	.333	0/2	.000	-/5	-	-	1	-	-	4	-
RETTON, R.	-	3/4	.750	0/0	.000	-/0	-	-	1	-	-	6	-
PATRONE, L.	-	1/4	.250	0/0	.000	-/1	-	-	0	-	-	2	-
GOODE, B.	-	0/0	.000	0/0	.000	-/0	-	-	0	-	-	0	-
VISNIC, N.	-	0/0	.000	0/0	.000	-/0	-	-	0	-	-	0	-
SCHERTZINGER, H.	-	0/0	.000	0/0	.000	-/0	-	-	0	-	-	0	-
Totals	200	35/66	.530	24/37	.649	-/41	-	-	15	-	-	94	.470

Louisville (79)   Coach: Peck Hickman

	Min.	Total FG/FGA	Pct.	FT/FTA	Pct.	Reb. O/T	A	TO	PF	S	Blk	TP	PPM
GOLDSTEIN, D.	-	6/10	.600	9/9	1.000	-/9	-	-	4	-	-	21	-
TURNER, J.	-	8/16	.500	2/5	.400	-/7	-	-	4	-	-	18	-
SAWYER, F.	-	2/6	.333	3/4	.750	-/2	-	-	5	-	-	7	-
ANDREWS, H.	-	9/15	.600	1/1	1.000	-/2	-	-	3	-	-	19	-
TIEMAN, R.	-	1/7	.143	1/1	1.000	-/0	-	-	0	-	-	3	-
KITCHEN, J.	-	3/7	.429	0/0	.000	-/5	-	-	4	-	-	6	-
STACEY, H.	-	0/0	.000	0/0	.000	-/2	-	-	1	-	-	0	-
LEATHERS, B.	-	2/8	.250	1/1	1.000	-/3	-	-	3	-	-	5	-
GEILING, B.	-	0/0	.000	0/0	.000	-/0	-	-	0	-	-	0	-
Totals	200	31/69	.449	17/21	.810	-/30	-	-	24	-	-	79	.395

Team Rebounds: West Virginia 8; Louisville 7. Disqualified: West Virginia—Akers; Louisville—Sawyer.

	1st Half	2nd Half	Final
West Virginia	48	46	94
Louisville	32	47	79

Cincinnati (58)   Coach: George Smith

	Min.	Total FG/FGA	Pct.	FT/FTA	Pct.	Reb. O/T	A	TO	PF	S	Blk	TP	PPM
ROBERTSON, O.	40	5/16	.313	9/11	.818	-/19	9	3	4	-	-	19	.475
TENWICK, D.	27	2/6	.333	1/1	1.000	-/4	0	1	1	-	-	5	.185
WHITAKER, B.	36	4/7	.571	0/2	.000	-/3	0	0	3	-	-	8	.222
WIESENHAHN, B.	25	5/11	.455	0/0	.000	-/3	0	0	1	-	-	10	.400
DAVIS, R.	40	6/15	.400	1/2	.500	-/2	2	1	2	-	-	13	.325
BOULDIN, C.	4	0/0	.000	0/1	.000	-/0	1	1	1	-	-	0	.000
LANDFRIED, M.	28	0/1	.000	3/5	.600	-/4	2	1	3	-	-	3	.107
Totals	200	22/56	.393	14/22	.636	-/35	14	7	15	-	-	58	.290

California (64)   Coach: Pete Newell

	Min.	Total FG/FGA	Pct.	FT/FTA	Pct.	Reb. O/T	A	TO	PF	S	Blk	TP	PPM
McCLINTOCK, B.	-	2/11	.182	2/4	.500	-/11	-	0	1	-	-	6	-
DALTON, B.	-	2/4	.500	3/4	.750	-/7	-	1	5	-	-	7	-
IMHOFF, D.	-	10/25	.400	2/5	.400	-/16	-	2	4	-	-	22	-
BUCH, A.	-	7/15	.467	4/6	.667	-/6	-	0	2	-	-	18	-
FITZPATRICK, D.	-	2/9	.222	0/0	.000	-/3	-	0	4	-	-	4	-
SIMPSON, B.	-	1/2	.500	0/0	.000	-/3	-	1	0	-	-	2	-
GROUT, J.	-	2/7	.286	1/2	.500	-/2	-	0	1	-	-	5	-
Totals	200	26/73	.356	12/21	.571	-/48	10	4	17	-	-	64	.320

Team Rebounds: California 8; Cincinnati 7. Disqualified: California—Dalton.

	1st Half	2nd Half	Final
Cincinnati	33	25	58
California	29	35	64

NATIONAL CHAMPIONSHIP

West Virginia (70)   Coach: Fred Schaus

	Min.	Total FG/FGA	Pct.	FT/FTA	Pct.	Reb. O/T	A	TO	PF	S	Blk	TP	PPM
WEST, J.	-	10/21	.476	8/12	.667	-/11	-	-	4	-	-	28	-
AKERS, W.	-	5/8	.625	0/1	.000	-/6	-	-	0	-	-	10	-
CLOUSSON, B.	-	4/7	.571	2/3	.667	-/4	-	-	4	-	-	10	-
SMITH, B.	-	2/5	.400	1/1	1.000	-/2	-	-	3	-	-	5	-
BOLYARD, B.	-	1/4	.250	4/4	1.000	-/3	-	-	4	-	-	6	-
RITCHIE, J.	-	1/4	.250	2/2	1.000	-/4	-	-	0	-	-	4	-
RETTON, R.	-	0/0	.000	2/2	1.000	-/0	-	-	0	-	-	2	-
PATRONE, L.	-	2/6	.333	1/2	.500	-/4	-	-	1	-	-	5	-
Totals	200	25/55	.455	20/27	.741	-/34	-	-	16	-	-	70	.350

California (71)   Coach: Pete Newell

	Min.	Total FG/FGA	Pct.	FT/FTA	Pct.	Reb. O/T	A	TO	PF	S	Blk	TP	PPM
McCLINTOCK, B.	-	4/13	.308	0/1	.000	-/10	-	-	1	-	-	8	-
DALTON, B.	-	6/11	.545	3/4	.750	-/2	-	-	4	-	-	15	-
IMHOFF, D.	-	4/13	.308	2/2	1.000	-/9	-	-	3	-	-	10	-
BUCH, A.	-	0/4	.000	2/2	1.000	-/2	-	-	3	-	-	2	-
FITZPATRICK, D.	-	8/13	.615	4/7	.571	-/2	-	-	1	-	-	20	-
SIMPSON, B.	-	0/1	.000	0/0	.000	-/2	-	-	2	-	-	0	-
GROUT, J.	-	4/5	.800	2/2	1.000	-/3	-	-	1	-	-	10	-
DOUGHTY, D.	-	3/6	.500	0/0	.000	-/1	-	-	3	-	-	6	-
Totals	200	29/66	.439	13/18	.722	-/31	-	-	18	-	-	71	.355

Team Rebounds: California 7; West Virginia 7. Disqualified: None.

	1st Half	2nd Half	Final
West Virginia	33	37	70
California	39	32	71

NATIONAL THIRD PLACE

Louisville (85)   Coach: Peck Hickman

	Min.	Total FG/FGA	Pct.	FT/FTA	Pct.	Reb. O/T	A	TO	PF	S	Blk	TP	PPM
GOLDSTEIN, D.	-	8/15	.533	5/6	.833	-/8	-	2	4	-	-	21	-
TURNER, J.	-	4/11	.364	1/2	.500	-/12	-	0	4	-	-	9	-
SAWYER, F.	-	0/5	.000	5/5	1.000	-/9	-	2	4	-	-	5	-
ANDREWS, H.	-	6/15	.400	6/6	1.000	-/4	-	2	3	-	-	18	-
TIEMAN, R.	-	10/18	.556	3/4	.750	-/1	-	7	4	-	-	23	-
KITCHEN, J.	-	1/2	.500	0/0	.000	-/3	-	0	2	-	-	2	-
STACEY, H.	-	0/0	.000	0/0	.000	-/0	-	0	0	-	-	0	-
LEATHERS, B.	-	2/4	.500	2/2	1.000	-/3	-	1	4	-	-	6	-
GEILING, B.	-	0/2	.000	1/1	1.000	-/0	-	0	0	-	-	1	-
MANTEL, A.	-	0/0	.000	0/0	.000	-/0	-	0	0	-	-	0	-
WATKINS, J.	-	0/0	.000	0/0	.000	-/0	-	0	0	-	-	0	-
Totals	200	31/72	.431	23/26	.885	-/40	14	14	25	-	-	85	.425

Cincinnati (98)   Coach: George Smith

	Min.	Total FG/FGA	Pct.	FT/FTA	Pct.	Reb. O/T	A	TO	PF	S	Blk	TP	PPM
ROBERTSON, O.	39	12/26	.462	15/19	.789	-/17	10	4	3	-		39	1.000
TENWICK, D.	36	2/8	.250	2/4	.500	-/6	1	1	2	-		6	.167
WHITAKER, B.	35	6/8	.750	3/6	.500	-/2	3	1	2	-		15	.429
WIESENHAHN, B.	33	4/9	.444	4/5	.800	-/10	1	0	3	-		12	.364
DAVIS, R.	39	11/25	.440	2/3	.667	-/3	6	1	3	-		24	.615
BOULDIN, C.	5	0/0	.000	0/0	.000	-/1	2	0	0	-		0	.000
WILLEY, L.		0/0	.000	0/0	.000	-/1	0	1	1	-		0	.000
LANDFRIED, M.	8	1/1	1.000	0/1	.000	-/5	1	0	2	-		2	.250
NALL, R.	2	0/0	.000	0/0	.000	-/0	0	0	1	-		0	.000
CETRONE, D.	1	0/0	.000	0/0	.000	-/0	0	0	1	-		0	.000
Totals	200	36/77	.468	26/38	.684	-/45	24	8	18	-	-	98	.490

Team Rebounds: Cincinnati 6; Louisville 6. Disqualified: None.

	1st Half	2nd Half	Final
Louisville	53	32	85
Cincinnati	49	49	98

REGIONAL THIRD PLACE WEST

Idaho State (71)   Coach: John Grayson

	Min.	Total FG/FGA	Pct.	FT/FTA	Pct.	Reb. O/T	A	TO	PF	S	Blk	TP	PPM
MORRIS, A.	-	8/17	.471	3/4	.750	-/5	-	-	5	-	-	19	-
CLOCK, N.	-	4/8	.500	1/3	.333	-/10	-	-	3	-	-	9	-
WATKINS, H.	-	5/7	.714	1/6	.167	-/14	-	-	4	-	-	11	-
RODGERS, J.	-	7/16	.438	5/6	.833	-/3	-	-	1	-	-	19	-
GRIFFITH, R.	-	0/1	.000	4/4	1.000	-/3	-	-	1	-	-	4	-
GRIFFIN, J.	-	4/14	.286	1/3	.333	-/7	-	-	0	-	-	9	-
MOULTON, D.	-	0/1	.000	0/0	.000	-/1	-	-	1	-	-	0	-
Totals	200	28/64	.438	15/26	.577	-/43	-	-	15	-	-	71	.355

Utah (65)   Coach: Jack Gardner

	Min.	Total FG/FGA	Pct.	FT/FTA	Pct.	Reb. O/T	A	TO	PF	S	Blk	TP	PPM
RUFFELL, R.	-	3/6	.500	1/1	1.000	-/3	-	-	1	-	-	7	-
CHESTANG	-	5/7	.714	3/4	.750	-/7	-	-	4	-	-	13	-
POLLARD, P.	-	8/16	.500	5/7	.714	-/10	-	-	4	-	-	21	-
CONDIE, D.	-	5/7	.714	1/2	.500	-/3	-	-	3	-	-	11	-
SHORES, D.	-	3/11	.273	0/0	.000	-/1	-	-	1	-	-	6	-
RHEAD, J.	-	0/3	.000	1/3	.333	-/1	-	-	1	-	-	1	-
CHISLER, C.	-	1/5	.200	1/1	1.000	-/1	-	-	0	-	-	3	-
ANCELL, K.	-	0/0	.000	0/0	.000	-/0	-	-	0	-	-	0	-
VANWAGENEN, D.	-	0/1	.000	2/2	1.000	-/2	-	-	1	-	-	2	-
THOMAS, J.	-	0/2	.000	0/0	.000	-/2	-	-	1	-	-	0	-
CUTLER, B.	-	0/0	.000	0/0	.000	-/1	-	-	0	-	-	0	-
MORTON, J.	-	0/1	.000	1/2	.500	-/0	-	-	1	-	-	1	-
Totals	200	25/59	.424	15/22	.682	-/31	-	-	17	-	-	65	.325

Team Rebounds: Idaho State 1; Utah 4. Disqualified: Idaho State—Morris.

	1st Half	2nd Half	Final
Idaho State	44	37	71
Utah	24	41	65

REGIONAL THIRD PLACE MIDWEST

TCU (71)   Coach: Buster Brannon

	Min.	Total FG/FGA	Pct.	FT/FTA	Pct.	Reb. O/T	A	TO	PF	S	Blk	TP	PPM
STEVENSON	-	7/16	.438	4/6	.667	-/14	-	-	2	-	-	18	-
NIPPERT	-	5/12	.417	3/5	.600	-/11	-	-	3	-	-	13	-
KIRCHNER, H.	-	10/33	.303	4/6	.667	-/24	-	-	2	-	-	24	-
KING	-	2/5	.400	1/1	1.000	-/1	-	-	1	-	-	5	-
BRUNSON	-	4/11	.364	1/1	1.000	-/0	-	-	2	-	-	9	-
COBB	-	0/1	.000	0/0	.000	-/1	-	-	0	-	-	0	-
TYLER	-	1/4	.250	0/0	.000	-/0	-	-	0	-	-	2	-
Totals	200	29/82	.354	13/19	.684	-/51	-	-	10	-	-	71	.355

DePaul (65)   Coach: Ray Meyer

	Min.	Total FG/FGA	Pct.	FT/FTA	Pct.	Reb. O/T	A	TO	PF	S	Blk	TP	PPM
SALZINSKI	-	6/19	.316	2/5	.400	-/6	-	-	1	-	-	14	-
COWSEN, M.	-	3/13	.231	0/1	.000	-/8	-	-	4	-	-	6	-
FLEMMING, J.	-	3/7	.429	1/1	1.000	-/7	-	-	5	-	-	7	-
HAIG	-	4/12	.333	1/2	.500	-/4	-	-	3	-	-	9	-
CARL, H.	-	10/18	.556	4/4	1.000	-/6	-	-	1	-	-	24	-
RUDDY	-	2/4	.500	1/1	1.000	-/3	-	-	3	-	-	5	-
Totals	200	28/73	.384	9/14	.643	-/34	-	-	17	-	-	65	.325

Team Rebounds: TCU 9; DePaul 12. Disqualified: DePaul—Flemming.

	1st Half	2nd Half	Final
TCU	37	34	71
DePaul	33	32	65

REGIONAL THIRD PLACE MIDEAST

Kentucky (98)   Coach: Adolph Rupp

	Min.	Total FG/FGA	Pct.	FT/FTA	Pct.	Reb. O/T	A	TO	PF	S	Blk	TP	PPM
COX, J.	-	5/9	.556	5/5	1.000	-/7	-	-	1	-	-	15	-
LICKERT, B.	-	5/13	.385	0/2	.000	-/8	-	-	3	-	-	10	-
MILLS, D.	-	11/19	.579	2/2	1.000	-/11	-	-	3	-	-	24	-
COFFMAN, B.	-	13/18	.722	2/3	.667	-/2	-	-	1	-	-	28	-
PARSONS, D.	-	3/6	.500	2/2	1.000	-/0	-	-	0	-	-	8	-
JOHNSON, P.	-	1/2	.500	1/2	.500	-/4	-	-	4	-	-	3	-
COHEN, S.	-	2/8	.250	0/0	.000	-/5	-	-	2	-	-	4	-
SLUSHER, B.	-	0/0	.000	0/0	.000	-/0	-	-	1	-	-	0	-
ROBINSON, A.	-	0/0	.000	0/0	.000	-/1	-	-	0	-	-	0	-
DARDEEN, H.	-	2/7	.286	0/0	.000	-/2	-	-	0	-	-	4	-
JENNINGS, N.	-	1/1	1.000	0/0	.000	-/1	-	-	1	-	-	2	-
Totals	200	43/83	.518	12/16	.750	-/41	-	-	16	-	-	98	.490

Marquette (69)   Coach: Eddie Hickey

	Min.	Total FG/FGA	Pct.	FT/FTA	Pct.	Reb. O/T	A	TO	PF	S	Blk	TP	PPM
MANGHAM, W.	-	2/13	.154	0/2	.000	-/13	-	-	1	-	-	4	-
KOJIS, D.	-	7/19	.368	1/2	.500	-/12	-	-	1	-	-	15	-
MORAN, M.	-	6/11	.545	6/10	.600	-/3	-	-	4	-	-	18	-
KOLLAR, J.	-	4/11	.364	2/2	1.000	-/4	-	-	0	-	-	10	-
MCCOY, J.	-	3/10	.300	1/2	.500	-/8	-	-	2	-	-	7	-
SUPPELSA, G.	-	0/0	.000	1/1	1.000	-/2	-	-	0	-	-	1	-
RIPP, G.	-	1/1	1.000	0/0	.000	-/0	-	-	0	-	-	2	-
PLINSKA, J.	-	5/10	.500	2/3	.667	-/3	-	-	4	-	-	12	-
KERSTEN, J.	-	0/0	.000	0/0	.000	-/0	-	-	0	-	-	0	-
CARTER, E.	-	0/0	.000	0/0	.000	-/0	-	-	0	-	-	0	-
Totals	200	28/75	.373	13/22	.591	-/45	-	-	12	-	-	69	.345

Team Rebounds: Kentucky 4; Marquette 4. Disqualified: None.

	1st Half	2nd Half	Final
Kentucky	54	44	98
Marquette	24	45	69

REGIONAL THIRD PLACE EAST

Navy (70)   Coach: Ben Carnevale

	Min.	Total FG/FGA	Pct.	FT/FTA	Pct.	Reb. O/T	A	TO	PF	S	Blk	TP	PPM
BOWER	40	3/ 7	.429	3/ 5	.600	-/ -	-	-	3	-	-	9	.225
BROWN	40	4/10	.400	3/ 3	1.000	-/ -	-	-	1	-	-	11	.275
METZLER, J.	30	7/17	.412	4/ 5	.800	-/ -	-	-	4	-	-	18	.600
DELANO, F.	24	1/ 4	.250	4/ 7	.571	-/ -	-	-	1	-	-	6	.250
DOYLE	16	2/ 4	.500	2/ 2	1.000	-/ -	-	-	0	-	-	6	.375
EGAN	13	5/ 7	.714	0/ 1	.000	-/ -	-	-	1	-	-	10	.769
LAND	10	1/ 2	.500	0/ 1	.000	-/ -	-	-	1	-	-	2	.200
BAGNARD	27	3/ 8	.375	2/ 5	.400	-/ -	-	-	1	-	-	8	.296
Totals	200	26/59	.441	18/29	.621	-/ -	-	-	12	-	-	70	.350

St. Joseph's (56)   Coach: Jack Ramsay

	Min.	Total FG/FGA	Pct.	FT/FTA	Pct.	Reb. O/T	A	TO	PF	S	Blk	TP	PPM
EGAN, J.	-	8/16	.500	2/ 3	.667	-/ -	-	-	4	-	-	18	-
SPRATT	-	4/ 7	.571	4/ 6	.667	-/ -	-	-	2	-	-	12	-
CLARKE	-	4/12	.333	3/ 4	.750	-/ -	-	-	3	-	-	11	-
GALLO	-	2/16	.125	2/ 2	1.000	-/ -	-	-	4	-	-	6	-
MCNEILL	-	2/ 9	.222	0/ 0	.000	-/ -	-	-	3	-	-	4	-
REILLY	-	0/ 1	.000	0/ 0	.000	-/ -	-	-	1	-	-	0	-
MAJEWSKI, F.	-	0/ 0	.000	1/ 1	1.000	-/ -	-	-	2	-	-	1	-
HOFFACKER	-	0/ 0	.000	0/ 0	.000	-/ -	-	-	0	-	-	0	-
COOKE	-	2/ 5	.400	0/ 0	.000	-/ -	-	-	1	-	-	4	-
COOLICAN	-	0/ 3	.000	0/ 0	.000	-/ -	-	-	0	-	-	0	-
Totals	200	22/69	.319	12/16	.750	-/ -	-	-	20	-	-	56	.280

Disqualified: None.

	1st Half	2nd Half	Final
Navy	32	38	70
St. Joseph's	19	37	56

✪ ALL-STAR TEAMS ✪

ALL TOURNAMENT

DENNY FITZPATRICK	CALIFORNIA
DON GOLDSTEIN	LOUISVILLE
DARRALL IMHOFF	CALIFORNIA
OSCAR ROBERTSON	CINCINNATI
★ **JERRY WEST**	WEST VIRGINIA

★ Most Outstanding Player(s)

✪ INDIVIDUAL RECORDS ✪

SCORING

Most points in a single game
1. OSCAR ROBERTSON, CINCINNATI (vs. LOUISVILLE) — 39
2. JERRY WEST, WEST VIRGINIA (vs. LOUISVILLE) — 38
3. JERRY WEST, WEST VIRGINIA (vs. ST. JOSEPH'S) — 36
4. OSCAR ROBERTSON, CINCINNATI (vs. TCU) — 34
5. JERRY WEST, WEST VIRGINIA (vs. BOSTON UNIV.) — 33

Most total points in the tournament
1. JERRY WEST, WEST VIRGINIA — 160
2. OSCAR ROBERTSON, CINCINNATI — 116
3. DON GOLDSTEIN, LOUISVILLE — 107
4. JIM RODGERS, IDAHO STATE — 80
5. HAROLD ANDREWS, LOUISVILLE — 72

Highest scoring average (minimum 2 games)
1. JERRY WEST, WEST VIRGINIA (160-5) — 32.00
2. OSCAR ROBERTSON, CINCINNATI (116-4) — 29.00
3. JIM RODGERS, IDAHO STATE (80-3) — 26.67
4. H.E. KIRCHNER, TCU (49-2) — 24.50
5. BOB BOOZER, KANSAS STATE (48-2) — 24.00

FIELD GOALS

Most field goals in a single game
1. BENNIE COFFMAN, KENTUCKY (vs. MARQUETTE) — 13
2. 7 tied for second place.

Most total field goals in the tournament
1. JERRY WEST, WEST VIRGINIA — 57
2. DON GOLDSTEIN, LOUISVILLE — 38
3. OSCAR ROBERTSON, CINCINNATI — 37
4. JIM RODGERS, IDAHO STATE — 30
5. JOHN TURNER, LOUISVILLE — 29

Most field goal attempts in a single game
1. H.E. KIRCHNER, TCU (vs. DEPAUL) — 33
2. JIM RODGERS, IDAHO STATE (vs. ST. MARY'S) — 27
3. OSCAR ROBERTSON, CINCINNATI (vs. LOUISVILLE) — 26
3. BOB BOOZER, KANSAS STATE (vs. CINCINNATI) — 26
5. 2 tied for fifth place.

Highest field goal percentage in a single game (minimum 10 attempts)
1. BENNIE COFFMAN, KENTUCKY (vs. MARQUETTE) (13-18) — .722
2. JAY METZLER, NAVY (vs. N. CAROLINA) (7-10) — .700

3. WALLY FRANK, KANSAS STATE (vs. DEPAUL) (9-13) — .692
3. JOHN EGAN, ST. JOSEPH'S (vs. WEST VIRGINIA) (9-13) — .692
5. LAROY DOSS, ST. MARY'S (vs. IDAHO STATE) (8-12) — .667

FREE THROWS

Most free throws in a single game
1. JACK ROSE, U. CONN. (vs. BOSTON UNIV.) — 18
2. OSCAR ROBERTSON, CINCINNATI (vs. LOUISVILLE) — 15
3. JERRY WEST, WEST VIRGINIA (vs. LOUISVILLE) — 14
4. DAVE TENWICK, CINCINNATI (vs. KANSAS STATE) — 12
4. JERRY WEST, WEST VIRGINIA (vs. ST. JOSEPH'S) — 12

Most total free throws in the tournament
1. JERRY WEST, WEST VIRGINIA — 46
2. OSCAR ROBERTSON, CINCINNATI — 42
3. DON GOLDSTEIN, LOUISVILLE — 31
4. JIM RODGERS, IDAHO STATE — 20
5. JIM RITCHIE, WEST VIRGINIA — 19

Most free throws attempted in a single game
1 JACK ROSE, U. CONN. (vs. BOSTON UNIV.) 21
2 JERRY WEST, WEST VIRGINIA (vs. LOUISVILLE) 20
3 OSCAR ROBERTSON, CINCINNATI (vs. LOUISVILLE) 19
4 JERRY WEST, WEST VIRGINIA (vs. ST. JOSEPH'S) 18
5 DAVE TENWICK, CINCINNATI (vs. KANSAS STATE) 15

Most free throws attempted in the tournament
1 JERRY WEST, WEST VIRGINIA 71
2 OSCAR ROBERTSON, CINCINNATI 52
3 DON GOLDSTEIN, LOUISVILLE 36
4 JIM RITCHIE, WEST VIRGINIA 26
5 JIM RODGERS, IDAHO STATE 24

Highest free throw percentage in a single game (minimum 7 attempts)
1 DON GOLDSTEIN, LOUISVILLE (vs. WEST VIRGINIA) (9-9) 1.000

2 BOB DALTON, CALIFORNIA (vs. ST. MARY'S) (7-7) 1.000
2 DON GOLDSTEIN, LOUISVILLE (vs. MICHIGAN ST.) (7-7) 1.000
4 CEDRIC PRICE, KANSAS STATE (vs. CINCINNATI) (9-10) .900
5 OSCAR ROBERTSON, CINCINNATI (vs. KANSAS STATE) (8-9) .889

Highest free throw percentage in the tournament (minimum 15 attempts)
1 HOWIE CARL, DEPAUL (16-18) .889
2 BOB DALTON, CALIFORNIA (14-16) .875
3 DON GOLDSTEIN, LOUISVILLE (31-36) .861
4 JACK ROSE, U. CONN. (18-21) .857
5 CEDRIC PRICE, KANSAS STATE (17-20) .850

REBOUNDS

Most rebounds in a single game
1 H.E. KIRCHNER, TCU (vs. DEPAUL) 24
2 JOHN GREEN, MICHIGAN ST. (vs. LOUISVILLE) 23

3 DON KOJIS, MARQUETTE (vs. MICHIGAN ST.) 21
4 OSCAR ROBERTSON, CINCINNATI (vs. CALIFORNIA) 19
4 EDWARD WASHINGTON, BOSTON UNIV. (vs. NAVY) 19

Most total rebounds in the tournament
1 JERRY WEST, WEST VIRGINIA 73
2 OSCAR ROBERTSON, CINCINNATI 63
3 DON GOLDSTEIN, LOUISVILLE 50
4 DON KOJIS, MARQUETTE 47
5 2 tied for fifth place.

Most rebounds per game (minimum 2 games)
1 H.E. KIRCHNER, TCU (42-2) 21.00
2 JOHN GREEN, MICHIGAN ST. (41-2) 20.50
3 OSCAR ROBERTSON, CINCINNATI (63-4) 15.75
4 DON KOJIS, MARQUETTE (47-3) 15.67
5 JERRY WEST, WEST VIRGINIA (73-5) 14.60

✪ TEAM RECORDS ✪

SCORING

Most points in a single game
1 KANSAS STATE (vs. DEPAUL) 102
2 CINCINNATI (vs. LOUISVILLE) 98
2 KENTUCKY (vs. MARQUETTE) 98

Most total points in the tournament
1 WEST VIRGINIA 427
2 LOUISVILLE 405
3 CINCINNATI 318

Highest scoring average (minimum 2 games)
1 KANSAS STATE (177-2) 88.50
2 WEST VIRGINIA (427-5) 85.40
3 LOUISVILLE (405-5) 81.00

FIELD GOALS

Most field goals in a single game
1 KENTUCKY (vs. MARQUETTE) 43
2 KANSAS STATE (vs. DEPAUL) 39
3 CINCINNATI (vs. LOUISVILLE) 36

Most total field goals in the tournament
1 WEST VIRGINIA 149
2 LOUISVILLE 148
3 CINCINNATI 120

Most field goals attempted in a single game
1 WEST VIRGINIA (vs. ST. JOSEPH'S) 92
2 BOWLING GREEN (vs. MARQUETTE) 90
3 MICHIGAN ST. (vs. LOUISVILLE) 84

Highest field goal percentage in a single game
1 WEST VIRGINIA (vs. LOUISVILLE) (35-66) .530
2 KENTUCKY (vs. MARQUETTE) (43-83) .518
3 ST. MARY'S (vs. IDAHO STATE) (31-61) .508

FREE THROWS

Most free throws in a single game
1 WEST VIRGINIA (vs. ST. JOSEPH'S) 33
2 WEST VIRGINIA (vs. BOSTON UNIV.) 30
3 CINCINNATI (vs. LOUISVILLE) 26
3 LOUISVILLE (vs. KENTUCKY) 26
3 NAVY (vs. N. CAROLINA) 26

Most total free throws in the tournament
1 WEST VIRGINIA 129
2 LOUISVILLE 109
3 CINCINNATI 78

Most free throws attempted in a single game
1 WEST VIRGINIA (vs. ST. JOSEPH'S) 50
2 WEST VIRGINIA (vs. BOSTON UNIV.) 42
3 NAVY (vs. N. CAROLINA) 40

Most total free throws attempted in the tournament
1 WEST VIRGINIA 192
2 LOUISVILLE 145
3 CINCINNATI 113

Highest free throw percentage in a single game
1 CALIFORNIA (vs. ST. MARY'S) (18-20) .900
2 LOUISVILLE (vs. CINCINNATI) (23-26) .885
3 NAVY (vs. BOSTON UNIV.) (13-15) .867

Fewest free throws in a single game
1 PORTLAND (vs. DEPAUL) 8
1 ST. MARY'S (vs. CALIFORNIA) 8
3 2 tied for third place.

Lowest free throw percentage in a single game
1 BOWLING GREEN (vs. MARQUETTE) (9-20) .450
2 PORTLAND (vs. DEPAUL) (8-16) .500
3 ST. MARY'S (vs. CALIFORNIA) (8-15) .533

REBOUNDS

Most rebounds in a single game
1 MARQUETTE (vs. BOWLING GREEN) 58
2 WEST VIRGINIA (vs. ST. JOSEPH'S) 56
3 WEST VIRGINIA (vs. DARTMOUTH) 54

1960

| FIRST ROUND | REGIONAL SEMIFINAL | REGIONAL FINAL | FINAL FOUR | REGIONAL FINAL | REGIONAL SEMIFINAL | FIRST ROUND |

EAST

(bye) — St. Joseph's 56

Duke 84
Princeton 60

Duke 58

Duke 59

West Virginia 94
Navy 86

West Virginia 81

NYU 54

NYU 74

NYU 78
U. Conn. 59

NYU 82 (ot)

MIDWEST

Cincinnati 99 — (bye)

Cincinnati 82

De Paul 59

De Paul 69
Air Force 63

Cincinnati 69

Kansas 90 — (bye)

Kansas 71

Texas 81 — (bye)

Ohio St. 75
California 55

MIDEAST

(bye) — Georgia Tech 57

Georgia Tech 69

Ohio 74
Notre Dame 66

Ohio 54

Ohio St. 76

Western Ky. 107
Miami (Fla.) 84

Western Ky. 79

Ohio St. 86

(bye) — Ohio St. 98

WEST

Santa Clara 49 — (bye)

California 70

California 69

California 71
Idaho St. 44

California 77

Oregon 65

New Mexico St. 60
Oregon 68

Oregon 49

USC 73

Utah 54

Utah 80

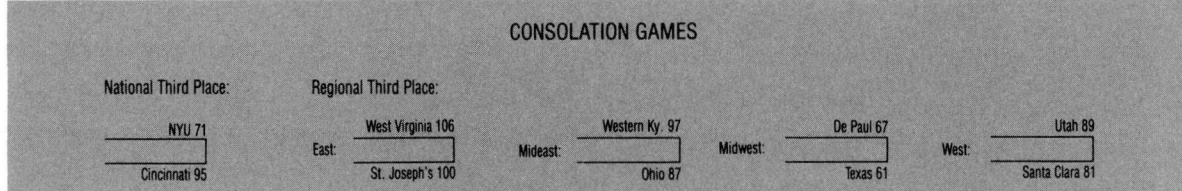

CONSOLATION GAMES

National Third Place:

NYU 71
Cincinnati 95

Regional Third Place:

East:
West Virginia 106
St. Joseph's 100

Mideast:
Western Ky. 97
Ohio 87

Midwest:
De Paul 67
Texas 61

West:
Utah 89
Santa Clara 81

Everything went pretty much according to form in 1960 until the end, when the defending champions from the University of California met the Ohio State Buckeyes on Cal's own home turf in San Francisco's Cow Palace.

The top three teams in the nation had sailed through their regionals. As usual, No. 1 Cal put a lid on the bucket; none of the Golden Bears' three opponents in the West regional cracked 50 points. In the Midwest, there was an Oscar-winning performance by the Big O. Approaching the end of his record-shattering college career, Robertson scored, rebounded, and handled the ball like a man among boys; he was, as he had been for three years, the Cincinnati Bearcats' leading man. In the Mideast, Ohio State's young Buckeyes, rated No. 3 in the nation on the basis of their dynamic, 91-plus points-per-game offense, raced away from the competition for easy victories. Only in the East was there a mild surprise, as the NYU Violets outlasted Jerry West and his cohorts from West Virginia before routing ACC champion Duke to qualify for the Final Four.

The four teams arrived in San Francisco with a composite record of 99 and 8, the best in tournament history. The first semi, pitting Ohio State against NYU, was no contest. The Buckeyes, despite having three sophomores in the line-up, were too tall, too fast, and too good for the Violets. They led from start to finish in overwhelming Tom "Satch" Sanders and his teammates from the Big Apple. Despite the rout, nobody was much impressed. NYU was obviously wound tight as a drum, and the experts believed that the Violets were blown out as much by the rarified atmosphere of the Final Four as they were by Jerry Lucas, John Havlicek, Larry Siegfried, and company.

The second game was a rematch of the 1959 semi, which Cal had won with an awesome display of ball-control and aggressive team defense. This time, though, Cincinnati came off the blocks with fire in their eyes. With Cal concentrating on stopping Robertson's scoring, Oscar's pinpoint passing pulled the Bearcats into a commanding nine-point lead midway through the first half, and it looked like the Bearcats were on the verge of running away with the game. But California Coach Pete Newell (who had recently announced that he would retire from coaching after the season) had taught his team well; they maintained their discipline and began to take advantage of their superior size and strength. Within three minutes they demolished the Cincinnati lead, and at intermission they were up by four. Midway through the second half, when Cincinnati's sophomore center, Paul Hogue, fouled out, the Bearcats had no one left to match up against Cal's Darrall Imhoff and Bill McClintock under the boards. The Golden Bears stepped up their defensive pressure a little more, but they still couldn't shake Cincinnati; Oscar had the ball on a string and his teammates hung in. With a minute and a half left, the Bearcats trailed by only three. But once

again—as in 1959—they fell short. Imhoff led all scorers with 25, and McClintock added 18 more. Robertson could counter with only 18—15 points below his average—but, according to California Coach Newell, he "must have passed off for at least 35."

The final was touted as a classic between the best defense and the best offense in the nation. The experts expected the defending champions from Berkeley to win. They were a veteran team whose coach instilled limitless discipline and self-confidence in his players. The Buckeyes, on the other hand, were young; their key man, Lucas, was just a sophomore, and their coach, 35-year-old Fred Taylor, was only in his second year in the big time. The Golden Bears not only had the edge in experience; they had just come through a trial by fire in overcoming tough Cincinnati. And they were playing in their own backyard.

What the experts didn't count on was the incredible accuracy of Ohio State's shooting or the Buckeyes' ability to beat Cal at its own game. From the opening tip, Ohio State conceded nothing, particularly to Imhoff. The only times Lucas gave Darrall any room was when he was far away from the basket, outside of his shooting range. Inside, Lucas fronted Imhoff; he pushed the Cal center out of position and consistently got in between him and the ball. On offense Ohio State was absolutely deadly; whether they were finishing fast breaks or popping long jumpers from behind picks, their shots were unerringly on target. They hit 16 for 19 in the first half, and went off the floor with an 18-point lead.

Cal had come from behind in the past, and the defending champs weren't about to give up. The Golden Bears started the second half with their vaunted full-court press, and at first it gave the Buckeyes problems. After a couple of Cal steals, it looked like the younger team might become rattled. But the Buckeyes regained their composure, and once they started breaking the press by finding the open man, the game was over.

The final stats showed that the Buckeye starters had hit 75 percent of their shots, and that all five finished in double figures. It also showed Lucas to be head and shoulders above Imhoff; he outscored the Cal star 16 to 8 and outrebounded his rival 10 to 5.

Ohio State coach Taylor was gracious in victory. "I went to Pete Newell last summer," he said, "to learn how to coach basketball. . . . He showed me everything. He confirmed some of my ideas, and he gave me the courage to try things I was afraid were too radical. Last year, our boys couldn't have caught Marilyn Monroe in a phone booth. Now look at them. I used many of Pete's ideas. And they paid off for us tonight."

For Ohio State, everything had come together. And it looked like they would stay that way for a long time to come.

FIRST ROUND EAST

Duke (84)   Coach: Vic Bubas

	Min.	Total FG/FGA	Pct.	FT/FTA	Pct.	Reb. O/T	A	TO	PF	S	Blk	TP	PPM
HURT, H.	-	8/ -		0/ 0	.000	-/ -	-	-	1	-	-	16	-
MEWHORT, B.	-	0/ -		0/ 2	.000	-/ -	-	-	1	-	-	0	-
KISTLER, D.	-	9/ -		8/11	.727	-/ -	-	-	3	-	-	26	-
BEAL, J.	-	1/ -		2/ 2	1.000	-/ -	-	-	0	-	-	4	-
BATEMAN, L.	-	1/ -		0/ 1	.000	-/ -	-	-	0	-	-	2	-
YOUNGKIN, C.	-	4/ -		1/ 2	.500	-/ -	-	-	2	-	-	9	-
KAST, F.	-	1/ -		0/ 0	.000	-/ -	-	-	1	-	-	2	-
ALBRIGHT, D.	-	0/ -		0/ 0	.000	-/ -	-	-	0	-	-	0	-
FRYE, J.	-	7/ -		1/ 1	1.000	-/ -	-	-	0	-	-	15	-
MORGAN, M.	-	2/ -		0/ 0	.000	-/ -	-	-	0	-	-	4	-
MULLEN, J.	-	2/ -		2/ 2	1.000	-/ -	-	-	1	-	-	6	-
CANTWELL, J.	-	0/ -		0/ 0	.000	-/ -	-	-	0	-	-	0	-
Totals	200	35/ -		14/21	.667	-/ -	-	-	9	-	-	84	.420

Princeton (60)   Coach: Franklin Cappon

	Min.	Total FG/FGA	Pct.	FT/FTA	Pct.	Reb. O/T	A	TO	PF	S	Blk	TP	PPM
CAMPBELL, P.	-	5/ -		1/ 3	.333	-/ -	-	-	0	-	-	11	-
HYLAND, D.	-	0/ -		0/ 1	.000	-/ -	-	-	0	-	-	0	-
BURTON, M.	-	3/ -		0/ 0	.000	-/ -	-	-	1	-	-	6	-
HIGGINS, A.	-	0/ -		1/ 1	1.000	-/ -	-	-	3	-	-	1	-
SWAN, D.	-	3/ -		1/ 3	.333	-/ -	-	-	2	-	-	7	-
PASALIS, J.	-	1/ -		1/ 2	.500	-/ -	-	-	1	-	-	3	-
BRANGAN, J.	-	8/ -		0/ 1	.000	-/ -	-	-	4	-	-	16	-
HOWSON, J.	-	0/ -		0/ 0	.000	-/ -	-	-	0	-	-	0	-
ADAMS, T.	-	6/ -		2/ 2	1.000	-/ -	-	-	4	-	-	14	-
BRENNAN, B.	-	1/ -		0/ 0	.000	-/ -	-	-	0	-	-	2	-
Totals	200	27/ -		6/13	.462	-/ -	-	-	15	-	-	60	.300

Disqualified: None.

	1st Half	2nd Half	Final
Duke	41	43	84
Princeton	26	34	60

West Virginia (94)   Coach: Fred Schaus

	Min.	Total FG/FGA	Pct.	FT/FTA	Pct.	Reb. O/T	A	TO	PF	S	Blk	TP	PPM
PATRONE, L.	-	3/ 4	.750	2/ 2	1.000	-/ 7	-	-	2	-	-	8	-
WARREN, J.	-	10/17	.588	2/ 2	1.000	-/ 5	-	-	0	-	-	22	-
AKERS, W.	-	2/ 6	.333	1/ 1	1.000	-/ 4	-	-	5	-	-	5	-
RITCHIE, J.	-	2/ 6	.333	3/ 4	.750	-/ 3	-	-	4	-	-	7	-
WEST, J.	-	12/21	.571	10/15	.667	-/15	-	-	2	-	-	34	-
POSCH, J.	-	4/ 5	.800	2/ 2	1.000	-/ 6	-	-	3	-	-	10	-
MILLER	-	3/ 7	.429	0/ 0	.000	-/ 0	-	-	2	-	-	6	-
POPOVICH	-	0/ 1	.000	0/ 0	.000	-/ 0	-	-	1	-	-	0	-
GOODE, B.	-	1/ 1	1.000	0/ 0	.000	-/ 1	-	-	1	-	-	2	-
WARD	-	0/ 0	.000	0/ 0	.000	-/ 2	-	-	0	-	-	0	-
Totals	200	37/68	.544	20/26	.769	-/43	-	-	20	-	-	94	.470

Navy (86)   Coach: Ben Carnevale

	Min.	Total FG/FGA	Pct.	FT/FTA	Pct.	Reb. O/T	A	TO	PF	S	Blk	TP	PPM
TREMAINE, D.	30	3/10	.300	2/ 2	1.000	-/ 4	-	-	4	-	-	8	.267
HUGUES, K.	30	4/11	.364	3/ 6	.500	-/ 3	-	-	3	-	-	11	.367
METZLER, J.	40	11/18	.611	5/ 9	.556	-/15	-	-	3	-	-	27	.675
BOWER, J.	35	5/15	.333	3/ 3	1.000	-/ 0	-	-	4	-	-	13	.371
BROWN, R.	40	7/12	.583	3/ 3	1.000	-/11	-	-	3	-	-	17	.425
DELANO, F.	5	2/ 3	.667	0/ 0	.000	-/ 1	-	-	0	-	-	4	.800
EGAN, H.	20	3/ 8	.375	0/ 2	.000	-/ 0	-	-	2	-	-	6	.300
Totals	200	35/77	.455	16/25	.640	-/34	-	-	19	-	-	86	.430

Team Rebounds: West Virginia 4; Navy 7. Disqualified: West Virginia—Akers.

	1st Half	2nd Half	Final
West Virginia	44	50	94
Navy	32	54	86

NYU (78)   Coach: Lou Rossini

	Min.	Total FG/FGA	Pct.	FT/FTA	Pct.	Reb. O/T	A	TO	PF	S	Blk	TP	PPM
BARDEN, A.	-	8/15	.533	7/ 8	.875	-/12	-	-	2	-	-	23	-
FILARDI, A.	-	0/ 3	.000	1/ 3	.333	-/ 4	-	-	2	-	-	1	-
SANDERS, T.	-	5/10	.500	1/ 2	.500	-/15	-	-	3	-	-	11	-
PAPROCKY, R.	-	5/12	.417	0/ 1	.000	-/ 2	-	-	2	-	-	10	-
CUNNINGHAM, R.	-	8/13	.615	2/ 2	1.000	-/ 6	-	-	2	-	-	18	-
REISS, J.	-	1/ 5	.200	6/ 6	1.000	-/ 8	-	-	2	-	-	8	-
LOCHE, A.	-	1/ 1	1.000	0/ 0	.000	-/ 0	-	-	2	-	-	2	-
MLODINOFF, B.	-	0/ 1	.000	0/ 0	.000	-/ 0	-	-	1	-	-	0	-
DINAPOLI, M.	-	0/ 0	.000	0/ 0	.000	-/ 1	-	-	1	-	-	0	-
MURPHY, L.	-	0/ 1	.000	0/ 0	.000	-/ 3	-	-	1	-	-	0	-
BIGELOW, B.	-	0/ 0	.000	0/ 0	.000	-/ 0	-	-	0	-	-	0	-
KEITH, R.	-	0/ 1	.000	0/ 0	.000	-/ 0	-	-	0	-	-	0	-
REGAN, B.	-	2/ 2	1.000	1/ 1	1.000	-/ 0	-	-	0	-	-	5	-
Totals	200	30/64	.469	18/23	.783	-/51	-	-	18	-	-	78	.390

U. Conn. (59)   Coach: Hugh Greer

	Min.	Total FG/FGA	Pct.	FT/FTA	Pct.	Reb. O/T	A	TO	PF	S	Blk	TP	PPM
SHELDON	-	2/11	.182	1/ 1	1.000	-/ 4	-	-	2	-	-	5	-
PIPCZNYSKI, J.	-	4/18	.222	2/ 3	.667	-/16	-	-	3	-	-	10	-
GRIFFIN, W.	-	2/10	.200	6/ 8	.750	-/ 9	-	-	4	-	-	10	-
ROSE, J.	-	6/20	.300	3/ 3	1.000	-/ 4	-	-	1	-	-	15	-
UHL	-	2/ 4	.500	3/ 3	1.000	-/ 3	-	-	4	-	-	7	-
MARTIN	-	1/ 3	.333	0/ 1	.000	-/ 1	-	-	0	-	-	2	-
COUNTRYMAN	-	1/ 2	.500	0/ 0	.000	-/ 0	-	-	0	-	-	2	-
MADISON	-	1/ 3	.333	0/ 0	.000	-/ 0	-	-	0	-	-	2	-
KING	-	1/ 2	.500	0/ 1	.000	-/ 2	-	-	1	-	-	2	-
RISLEY	-	1/ 1	1.000	2/ 2	1.000	-/ 0	-	-	0	-	-	4	-
KELLY	-	0/ 0	.000	0/ 0	.000	-/ 0	-	-	0	-	-	0	-
Totals	200	21/74	.284	17/22	.773	-/39	-	-	15	-	-	59	.295

Team Rebounds: NYU 6; U. Conn. 3. Disqualified: None.

	1st Half	2nd Half	Final
NYU	40	38	78
U. Conn.	31	28	59

FIRST ROUND MIDEAST

Ohio (74)   Coach: James Snyder

	Min.	Total FG/FGA	Pct.	FT/FTA	Pct.	Reb. O/T	A	TO	PF	S	Blk	TP	PPM
ADAMS, B.	-	2/9	.222	2/4	.500	-/10	-	-	2	-	-	6	-
KRUGER	-	8/16	.500	6/6	1.000	-/7	-	-	3	-	-	22	-
JOLLIFF, H.	-	11/19	.579	7/11	.636	-/16	-	-	4	-	-	29	-
WHALEY	-	3/10	.300	0/0	.000	-/2	-	-	4	-	-	6	-
BANDY	-	5/6	.833	1/1	1.000	-/3	-	-	2	-	-	11	-
KATZ	-	0/0	.000	0/0	.000	-/0	-	-	0	-	-	0	-
Totals	200	29/60	.483	16/22	.727	-/38	-	-	15	-	-	74	.370

Notre Dame (66)   Coach: John Jordan

	Min.	Total FG/FGA	Pct.	FT/FTA	Pct.	Reb. O/T	A	TO	PF	S	Blk	TP	PPM
McCARTHY, E.	-	4/12	.333	0/1	.000	-/3	-	-	2	-	-	8	-
GRANEY, M.	-	8/19	.421	4/5	.800	-/11	-	-	4	-	-	20	-
DEARIE, J.	-	9/18	.500	3/6	.500	-/6	-	-	4	-	-	21	-
CROSBY, W.	-	1/10	.100	0/2	.000	-/8	-	-	2	-	-	2	-
SCHNURR, E.	-	2/11	.182	5/6	.833	-/0	-	-	1	-	-	9	-
McGANN, D.	-	1/2	.500	0/0	.000	-/0	-	-	0	-	-	2	-
SKRZYCKI, R.	-	0/0	.000	0/0	.000	-/0	-	-	1	-	-	0	-
BEKELJA, M.	-	1/1	1.000	2/2	1.000	-/1	-	-	0	-	-	4	-
Totals	200	26/73	.356	14/22	.636	-/29	-	-	14	-	-	66	.330

Team Rebounds: Ohio 1; Notre Dame 2. Disqualified: None.

	1st Half	2nd Half	Final
Ohio	31	43	74
Notre Dame	32	34	66

Western Kentucky (107)   Coach: Ed Diddle

	Min.	Total FG/FGA	Pct.	FT/FTA	Pct.	Reb. O/T	A	TO	PF	S	Blk	TP	PPM
ELLISON, A.	-	7/17	.412	1/2	.500	-/14	-	-	2	-	-	15	-
TODD, H.	-	8/15	.533	5/6	.833	-/16	-	-	3	-	-	21	-
OSBORNE, C.	-	3/6	.500	4/4	1.000	-/8	-	-	3	-	-	10	-
RASCOE, B.	-	10/17	.588	7/11	.636	-/9	-	-	4	-	-	27	-
PARSONS, D.	-	3/7	.429	1/4	.250	-/1	-	-	1	-	-	7	-
SARAKATSANNIS, P.	-	2/4	.500	0/0	.000	-/2	-	-	3	-	-	4	-
TALBOTT, J.	-	5/9	.556	2/2	1.000	-/3	-	-	0	-	-	12	-
BICKNELL, D.	-	2/7	.286	2/3	.667	-/3	-	-	0	-	-	6	-
McDANIEL, R.	-	0/1	.000	0/0	.000	-/0	-	-	0	-	-	0	-
SMITH, D.	-	1/1	1.000	3/4	.750	-/6	-	-	2	-	-	5	-
WARREN, G.	-	0/1	.000	0/0	.000	-/0	-	-	1	-	-	0	-
BARNARD, B.	-	0/0	.000	0/0	.000	-/1	-	-	1	-	-	0	-
Totals	200	41/85	.482	25/36	.694	-/63	-	-	20	-	-	107	.535

Miami (Fla.) (84)   Coach: Bruce Hale

	Min.	Total FG/FGA	Pct.	FT/FTA	Pct.	Reb. O/T	A	TO	PF	S	Blk	TP	PPM
GODFREY	-	3/12	.250	2/3	.667	-/5	-	-	4	-	-	8	-
APPLEGATE	-	4/12	.333	5/7	.714	-/7	-	-	1	-	-	13	-
MANUSHAW	-	1/5	.200	2/4	.500	-/7	-	-	5	-	-	4	-
HICKOX	-	7/16	.438	3/4	.750	-/2	-	-	3	-	-	17	-
COHEN	-	2/8	.250	1/3	.333	-/1	-	-	3	-	-	5	-
HAMMOND	-	5/10	.500	5/5	1.000	-/3	-	-	0	-	-	15	-
STAVRETI	-	1/1	1.000	0/0	.000	-/0	-	-	0	-	-	2	-
LANDIS	-	0/0	.000	0/0	.000	-/1	-	-	0	-	-	0	-
SPISAK	-	4/6	.667	1/2	.500	-/6	-	-	2	-	-	9	-
NEBEL	-	3/7	.429	0/0	.000	-/3	-	-	1	-	-	6	-
SHAPIRO	-	1/2	.500	1/2	.500	-/0	-	-	2	-	-	3	-
SNIDER	-	0/0	.000	2/2	1.000	-/0	-	-	0	-	-	2	-
Totals	200	31/79	.392	22/32	.688	-/35	-	-	21	-	-	84	.420

Team Rebounds: Western Ky. 7; Miami (Fla.) 8. Disqualified: Miami (Fla.)—Manushaw.

	1st Half	2nd Half	Final
Western Ky.	51	56	107
Miami (Fla.)	40	44	84

FIRST ROUND MIDWEST

DePaul (69)   Coach: Ray Meyer

	Min.	Total FG/FGA	Pct.	FT/FTA	Pct.	Reb. O/T	A	TO	PF	S	Blk	TP	PPM
COWSEN, M.	-	4/9	.444	4/5	.800	-/10	-	-	3	-	-	12	-
SALZINSKI	-	2/8	.250	2/2	1.000	-/6	-	-	3	-	-	6	-
FLEMMING	-	6/8	.750	2/2	1.000	-/8	-	-	3	-	-	14	-
HAIG	-	3/8	.375	7/8	.875	-/2	-	-	3	-	-	13	-
CARL, H.	-	9/20	.450	6/6	1.000	-/2	-	-	1	-	-	24	-
RUDDY	-	0/2	.000	0/0	.000	-/4	-	-	0	-	-	0	-
Totals	200	24/55	.436	21/23	.913	-/32	-	-	13	-	-	69	.345

Air Force (63)   Coach: Bob Spear

	Min.	Total FG/FGA	Pct.	FT/FTA	Pct.	Reb. O/T	A	TO	PF	S	Blk	TP	PPM
NORRIS	-	1/3	.333	3/3	1.000	-/3	-	-	5	-	-	5	-
ULM, J.	-	9/15	.600	2/3	.667	-/5	-	-	2	-	-	20	-
VICELLIO	-	0/1	.000	0/0	.000	-/0	-	-	0	-	-	0	-
LONG	-	1/3	.333	3/3	1.000	-/2	-	-	4	-	-	5	-
WOLFSWINKEL	-	8/15	.533	2/2	1.000	-/3	-	-	4	-	-	18	-
STOVER	-	2/6	.333	0/0	.000	-/1	-	-	0	-	-	4	-
SCHAUMBERG	-	4/10	.400	1/2	.500	-/7	-	-	0	-	-	9	-
KNIPP	-	0/2	.000	0/1	.000	-/1	-	-	1	-	-	0	-
LAMMERS	-	1/1	1.000	0/1	.000	-/0	-	-	0	-	-	2	-
Totals	200	26/56	.464	11/15	.733	-/22	-	-	16	-	-	63	.315

Team Rebounds: DePaul 8; Air Force 5. Disqualified: Air Force—Norris.

	1st Half	2nd Half	Final
DePaul	43	26	69
Air Force	40	23	63

FIRST ROUND WEST

California (71) Coach: Pete Newell

	Min.	Total FG/FGA	Pct.	FT/FTA	Pct.	Reb. O/T	A	TO	PF	S	Blk	TP	PPM
MCCLINTOCK, B.	-	7/ -	-	1/3	.333	-/ -	-	-	1	-	-	15	-
GILLIS, T.	-	5/ -	-	0/1	.000	-/ -	-	-	3	-	-	10	-
IMHOFF, D.	-	7/ -	-	5/6	.833	-/ -	-	-	1	-	-	19	-
WENDELL, B.	-	3/ -	-	0/2	.000	-/ -	-	-	2	-	-	6	-
SHULTZ, E.	-	2/ -	-	0/0	.000	-/ -	-	-	1	-	-	4	-
DOUGHTY, D.	-	3/ -	-	0/0	.000	-/ -	-	-	3	-	-	6	-
MANN, J.	-	0/ -	-	2/2	1.000	-/ -	-	-	1	-	-	2	-
STAFFORD, D.	-	1/ -	-	4/5	.800	-/ -	-	-	0	-	-	6	-
ALEXANDER, B.	-	0/ -	-	3/4	.750	-/ -	-	-	0	-	-	3	-
MORRISON, S.	-	0/ -	-	0/0	.000	-/ -	-	-	2	-	-	0	-
PEARSON, E.	-	0/ -	-	0/0	.000	-/ -	-	-	1	-	-	0	-
AVERBUCK, N.	-	0/ -	-	0/0	.000	-/ -	-	-	0	-	-	0	-
Totals	200	28/ -	-	15/23	.652	-/ -	-	-	15	-	-	71	.355

Idaho State (44) Coach: John Evans

	Min.	Total FG/FGA	Pct.	FT/FTA	Pct.	Reb. O/T	A	TO	PF	S	Blk	TP	PPM
GRIFFITH, R.	-	0/2	.000	0/0	.000	-/3	-	-	4	-	-	0	-
GOODWIN, M.	-	4/16	.250	4/5	.800	-/8	-	-	1	-	-	12	-
WATKINS, H.	-	4/11	.364	5/9	.556	-/3	-	-	4	-	-	13	-
SWOPES, F.	-	3/10	.300	4/4	1.000	-/6	-	-	0	-	-	10	-
GERMAINE, J.	-	2/5	.400	0/0	.000	-/3	-	-	1	-	-	4	-
KUGLER, D.	-	1/2	.500	0/1	.000	-/3	-	-	2	-	-	2	-
KNACKSTEDT, L.	-	0/1	.000	0/0	.000	-/1	-	-	0	-	-	0	-
MCNELEY, R.	-	1/1	1.000	1/1	1.000	-/2	-	-	1	-	-	3	-
MOULTON, D.	-	0/0	.000	0/0	.000	-/0	-	-	3	-	-	0	-
Totals	200	15/48	.313	14/20	.700	-/29	-	-	16	-	-	44	.220

Team Rebounds: California 7. Disqualified: None.

	1st Half	2nd Half	Final
California	34	37	71
Idaho State	15	29	44

New Mexico State (60) Coach: Presley Askew

	Min.	Total FG/FGA	Pct.	FT/FTA	Pct.	Reb. O/T	A	TO	PF	S	Blk	TP	PPM
KNIGHTON	-	8/14	.571	6/9	.667	-/7	-	-	5	-	-	22	-
ROBISON	-	4/13	.308	3/3	1.000	-/3	-	-	3	-	-	11	-
PRICE	-	3/12	.250	5/7	.714	-/13	-	-	1	-	-	11	-
KNIGHT, V.	-	2/12	.167	4/4	1.000	-/9	-	-	4	-	-	8	-
BOWEN	-	2/6	.333	0/1	.000	-/6	-	-	3	-	-	4	-
CANADY	-	0/2	.000	0/0	.000	-/1	-	-	0	-	-	0	-
LOGBACK	-	0/1	.000	0/0	.000	-/1	-	-	2	-	-	0	-
CLARK	-	0/2	.000	1/1	1.000	-/3	-	-	0	-	-	1	-
BUSHMAIER	-	1/2	.500	1/4	.250	-/2	-	-	2	-	-	3	-
CASANOVA	-	0/0	.000	0/0	.000	-/0	-	-	0	-	-	0	-
Totals	200	20/64	.313	20/29	.690	-/45	-	-	20	-	-	60	.300

Oregon (68) Coach: Steve Belko

	Min.	Total FG/FGA	Pct.	FT/FTA	Pct.	Reb. O/T	A	TO	PF	S	Blk	TP	PPM
HERRON	-	4/11	.364	2/4	.500	-/6	-	-	4	-	-	10	-
SIMMONS	-	5/15	.333	1/3	.333	-/10	-	-	4	-	-	11	-
MOORE, G.	-	2/11	.182	1/3	.333	-/10	-	-	5	-	-	5	-
RASK, C.	-	4/12	.333	5/7	.714	-/6	-	-	2	-	-	13	-
STRICKLAND	-	4/8	.500	4/5	.800	-/6	-	-	2	-	-	12	-
WARREN	-	7/9	.778	1/2	.500	-/8	-	-	3	-	-	15	-
KNECHT	-	1/3	.333	0/1	.000	-/0	-	-	1	-	-	2	-
Totals	200	27/69	.391	14/25	.560	-/46	-	-	21	-	-	68	.340

Team Rebounds: Oregon 7; New Mexico St. 8. Disqualified: Oregon— Moore; New Mexico St.—Knighton.

	1st Half	2nd Half	Final
New Mexico St.	34	26	60
Oregon	27	41	68

USC (73) Coach: Forrest Twogood

	Min.	Total FG/FGA	Pct.	FT/FTA	Pct.	Reb. O/T	A	TO	PF	S	Blk	TP	PPM
RUDOMETKIN, J.	-	13/24	.542	5/9	.556	-/15	-	-	3	-	-	31	-
WHITE	-	5/13	.385	1/1	1.000	-/6	-	-	5	-	-	11	-
HANNA	-	0/0	.000	0/0	.000	-/1	-	-	4	-	-	0	-
PIMM	-	6/20	.300	4/5	.800	-/7	-	-	4	-	-	16	-
KEMP	-	3/15	.200	1/2	.500	-/3	-	-	4	-	-	7	-
HAMPTON	-	1/5	.200	0/1	.000	-/7	-	-	4	-	-	2	-
STANLEY	-	1/4	.250	0/0	.000	-/2	-	-	1	-	-	2	-
APPEL, C.	-	1/1	1.000	2/2	1.000	-/2	-	-	1	-	-	4	-
ASHBY	-	0/2	.000	0/0	.000	-/1	-	-	0	-	-	0	-
Totals	200	30/84	.357	13/20	.650	-/44	-	10	26	-	-	73	.365

Utah (80) Coach: Jack Gardner

	Min.	Total FG/FGA	Pct.	FT/FTA	Pct.	Reb. O/T	A	TO	PF	S	Blk	TP	PPM
RUFFEL	-	0/2	.000	0/0	.000	-/5	-	-	0	-	-	0	-
HOLMES, A.	-	5/18	.278	7/8	.875	-/17	-	-	2	-	-	17	-
MCGILL, B.	-	8/20	.400	11/18	.611	-/10	-	-	2	-	-	27	-
MORTON, J.	-	8/11	.727	2/3	.667	-/5	-	-	3	-	-	18	-
COWAN, B.	-	3/10	.300	1/2	.500	-/5	-	-	2	-	-	7	-
RHEAD, J.	-	4/12	.333	3/8	.375	-/14	-	-	3	-	-	11	-
Totals	200	28/73	.384	24/39	.615	-/56	-	15	12	-	-	80	.400

Team Rebounds: Utah 12; USC 9. Disqualified: USC—White.

	1st Half	2nd Half	Final
USC	34	39	73
Utah	44	36	80

REGIONAL SEMIFINAL EAST

St. Joseph's (56)   Coach: Jack Ramsay

	Min.	Total FG/FGA	Pct.	FT/FTA	Pct.	Reb. O/T	A	TO	PF	S	Blk	TP	PPM
CALLO	-	6/20	.300	2/2	1.000	-/5	-	-	5	-	-	14	-
CLARKE	-	7/15	.467	8/11	.727	-/15	-	-	4	-	-	22	-
MCNEIL	-	4/12	.333	0/0	.000	-/5	-	-	1	-	-	8	-
EGAN	-	2/12	.167	0/3	.000	-/6	-	-	2	-	-	4	-
KEMPTON	-	0/7	.000	2/2	1.000	-/14	-	-	2	-	-	2	-
MAJEWSKI	-	0/2	.000	0/0	.000	-/0	-	-	0	-	-	0	-
WESTHEAD	-	1/1	1.000	0/0	.000	-/1	-	-	3	-	-	2	-
REILY	-	2/5	.400	0/0	.000	-/1	-	-	1	-	-	4	-
BOOTH	-	0/0	.000	0/0	.000	-/0	-	-	0	-	-	0	-
Totals	200	22/74	.297	12/18	.667	-/47	-	-	18	-	-	56	.280

Duke (58)   Coach: Vic Bubas

	Min.	Total FG/FGA	Pct.	FT/FTA	Pct.	Reb. O/T	A	TO	PF	S	Blk	TP	PPM
MULLEN, J.	-	0/1	.000	5/7	.714	-/2	-	-	0	-	-	5	-
HURT, H.	-	7/14	.500	1/2	.500	-/6	-	-	2	-	-	15	-
YOUNGKIN, C.	-	9/15	.600	4/6	.667	-/12	-	-	5	-	-	22	-
FRYE, J.	-	2/9	.222	2/4	.500	-/3	-	-	0	-	-	6	-
KISTLER, D.	-	2/11	.182	2/4	.500	-/8	-	-	2	-	-	6	-
MEWHORT, B.	-	1/1	1.000	2/3	.667	-/2	-	-	2	-	-	4	-
Totals	200	21/51	.412	16/26	.615	-/33	-	-	11	-	-	58	.290

Team Rebounds: Duke 7; St. Joseph's 11. Disqualified: Duke—Youngkin; St. Joseph's—Callo.

	1st Half	2nd Half	Final
St. Joseph's	20	36	56
Duke	27	31	58

West Virginia (81)   Coach: Fred Schaus

	Min.	Total FG/FGA	Pct.	FT/FTA	Pct.	Reb. O/T	A	TO	PF	S	Blk	TP	PPM
PATRONE, L.	-	8/13	.615	3/5	.600	-/10	-	-	4	-	-	19	-
WARREN, J.	-	1/4	.250	0/0	.000	-/2	-	-	2	-	-	2	-
AKERS, W.	-	2/11	.182	4/5	.800	-/12	-	-	3	-	-	8	-
RITCHIE, J.	-	1/6	.167	3/6	.500	-/7	-	-	5	-	-	5	-
WEST, J.	-	11/28	.393	12/13	.923	-/16	-	-	2	-	-	34	-
POSCH, J.	-	0/1	.000	0/0	.000	-/0	-	-	1	-	-	0	-
POPOVICH	-	5/6	.833	0/0	.000	-/3	-	-	2	-	-	10	-
MILLER	-	1/3	.333	1/4	.250	-/1	-	-	4	-	-	3	-
Totals	200	29/72	.403	23/33	.697	-/51	-	-	23	-	-	81	.405

NYU (82)   Coach: Lou Rossini

	Min.	Total FG/FGA	Pct.	FT/FTA	Pct.	Reb. O/T	A	TO	PF	S	Blk	TP	PPM
SANDERS, T.	-	12/21	.571	4/7	.571	-/19	-	-	3	-	-	28	-
PAPROCKY, R.	-	5/13	.385	5/7	.714	-/5	-	-	2	-	-	15	-
FILARDI, A.	-	4/20	.200	5/9	.556	-/21	-	-	4	-	-	13	-
BARDEN, A.	-	1/4	.250	1/2	.500	-/6	-	-	5	-	-	3	-
CUNNINGHAM, R.	-	6/16	.375	4/8	.500	-/2	-	-	4	-	-	16	-
DINAPOLI, M.	-	1/6	.167	3/3	1.000	-/1	-	-	1	-	-	5	-
LOCHE, A.	-	0/2	.000	0/0	.000	-/1	-	-	0	-	-	0	-
REISS, J.	-	1/2	.500	0/0	.000	-/0	-	-	1	-	-	2	-
Totals	200	30/84	.357	22/36	.611	-/55	-	-	20	-	-	82	.410

Disqualified: NYU—Barden; West Virginia—Ritchie.

	1st Half	2nd Half	Final
West Virginia	41	40	81
NYU	40	42	82

REGIONAL SEMIFINAL MIDEAST

Georgia Tech (57)   Coach: Whack Hyder

	Min.	Total FG/FGA	Pct.	FT/FTA	Pct.	Reb. O/T	A	TO	PF	S	Blk	TP	PPM
DENTON, D.	-	7/18	.389	1/1	1.000	-/11	-	-	2	-	-	15	-
RICHARDS, W.	-	2/7	.286	0/1	.000	-/6	-	-	3	-	-	4	-
RILEY	-	0/0	.000	0/0	.000	-/0	-	-	3	-	-	0	-
DEWS, B.	-	1/3	.333	3/5	.600	-/4	-	-	3	-	-	5	-
KAISER, R.	-	7/22	.318	11/11	1.000	-/6	-	-	3	-	-	25	-
POWELL	-	0/1	.000	1/2	.500	-/2	-	-	0	-	-	1	-
HOFFMAN	-	0/1	.000	3/7	.429	-/5	-	-	1	-	-	3	-
POTEET	-	2/4	.500	0/0	.000	-/5	-	-	0	-	-	4	-
GHER	-	0/3	.000	0/0	.000	-/1	-	-	0	-	-	0	-
Totals	200	19/59	.322	19/27	.704	-/40	-	-	15	-	-	57	.285

Ohio (54)   Coach: James Snyder

	Min.	Total FG/FGA	Pct.	FT/FTA	Pct.	Reb. O/T	A	TO	PF	S	Blk	TP	PPM
ADAMS, B.	-	4/13	.308	3/9	.333	-/9	-	-	3	-	-	11	-
KRUGER	-	4/15	.267	2/2	1.000	-/8	-	-	3	-	-	10	-
JOLLIFF, H.	-	9/20	.450	2/7	.286	-/26	-	-	4	-	-	20	-
WHALEY	-	3/11	.273	3/3	1.000	-/1	-	-	1	-	-	9	-
BANDY	-	2/3	.667	0/0	.000	-/2	-	-	5	-	-	4	-
KATZ	-	0/2	.000	0/0	.000	-/0	-	-	2	-	-	0	-
Totals	200	22/64	.344	10/21	.476	-/46	-	-	18	-	-	54	.270

Team Rebounds: Georgia Tech 8; Ohio 8. Disqualified: Ohio—Bandy.

	1st Half	2nd Half	Final
Georgia Tech	23	34	57
Ohio	33	21	54

Western Kentucky (79)   Coach: Ed Diddle

	Min.	Total FG/FGA	Pct.	FT/FTA	Pct.	Reb. O/T	A	TO	PF	S	Blk	TP	PPM
TODD, H.	-	3/8	.375	0/0	.000	-/7	-	-	4	-	-	6	-
ELLISON, A.	-	8/21	.381	1/2	.500	-/7	-	-	4	-	-	17	-
OSBORNE, C.	-	6/11	.545	6/7	.857	-/9	-	-	1	-	-	18	-
RASCOE, B.	-	4/9	.444	8/11	.727	-/6	-	-	3	-	-	16	-
PARSONS, D.	-	6/11	.545	5/6	.833	-/6	-	-	2	-	-	17	-
TALBOTT, J.	-	0/2	.000	1/1	1.000	-/2	-	-	0	-	-	1	-
SARAKATSANNIS, P.	-	1/4	.250	0/0	.000	-/0	-	-	3	-	-	2	-
COLE	-	1/2	.500	0/0	.000	-/0	-	-	0	-	-	2	-
Totals	200	29/68	.426	21/27	.778	-/37	-	-	17	-	-	79	.395

Ohio State (98)   Coach: Fred Taylor

	Min.	Total FG/FGA	Pct.	FT/FTA	Pct.	Reb. O/T	A	TO	PF	S	Blk	TP	PPM
HAVILCEK, J.	-	7/15	.467	3/4	.750	-/8	-	-	1	-	-	17	-
ROBERTS, J.	-	2/4	.500	0/0	.000	-/3	-	-	1	-	-	4	-
LUCAS, J.	-	14/25	.560	8/10	.800	-/25	-	-	4	-	-	36	-
NOWELL, M.	-	6/11	.545	3/5	.600	-/0	-	-	2	-	-	15	-
SIEGFRIED, L.	-	6/15	.400	0/1	.000	-/7	-	-	2	-	-	12	-
GEARHART, G.	-	2/4	.500	0/0	.000	-/3	-	-	5	-	-	4	-
FURRY, R.	-	1/4	.250	0/0	.000	-/2	-	-	2	-	-	2	-
KNIGHT, B.	-	3/7	.429	0/0	.000	-/1	-	-	2	-	-	6	-
NOURSE, H.	-	1/1	1.000	0/0	.000	-/0	-	-	0	-	-	2	-
HOYT, R.	-	0/0	.000	0/0	.000	-/0	-	-	0	-	-	0	-
BARKER, D.	-	0/0	.000	0/0	.000	-/1	-	-	0	-	-	0	-
Totals	200	42/86	.488	14/20	.700	-/50	-	-	19	-	-	98	.490

Team Rebounds: Ohio State 2; Western Ky. 6. Disqualified: Ohio State—Gearhart.

	1st Half	2nd Half	Final
Western Ky.	43	36	79
Ohio State	37	61	98

REGIONAL SEMIFINAL MIDWEST

Cincinnati (99) Coach: George Smith

	Min.	Total FG/FGA	Pct.	FT/FTA	Pct.	Reb. O/T	A	TO	PF	S	Blk	TP	PPM
ROBERTSON, O.	-	12/25	.480	5/7	.714	-/9	-	-	2	-	-	29	-
WILLEY, L.	-	2/2	1.000	2/3	.667	-/5	-	-	3	-	-	6	-
HOGUE, P.	-	9/12	.750	0/3	.000	-/15	-	-	3	-	-	18	-
DAVIS, R.	-	7/13	.538	0/0	.000	-/2	-	-	0	-	-	14	-
BOULDIN, C.	-	4/6	.667	3/3	1.000	-/1	-	-	1	-	-	11	-
WIESENHAHN, B.	-	4/8	.500	1/3	.333	-/10	-	-	1	-	-	9	-
SIZER, T.	-	2/2	1.000	2/2	1.000	-/0	-	-	1	-	-	6	-
POMERANTZ, S.	-	2/7	.286	0/2	.000	-/3	-	-	1	-	-	4	-
CALHOUN, J.	-	1/2	.500	0/0	.000	-/1	-	-	0	-	-	2	-
BRYANT, J.	-	0/0	.000	0/0	.000	-/0	-	-	0	-	-	0	-
DIERKING, F.	-	0/1	.000	0/0	.000	-/0	-	-	0	-	-	0	-
REIS, R.	-	0/0	.000	0/0	.000	-/0	-	-	1	-	-	0	-
Totals	200	43/78	.551	13/23	.565	-/46	-	-	13	-	-	99	.495

DePaul (59) Coach: Ray Meyer

	Min.	Total FG/FGA	Pct.	FT/FTA	Pct.	Reb. O/T	A	TO	PF	S	Blk	TP	PPM
COWSEN, M.	-	4/11	.364	7/8	.875	-/6	-	-	4	-	-	15	-
SALZINSKI	-	2/6	.333	0/1	.000	-/4	-	-	3	-	-	4	-
FLEMMING	-	3/7	.429	0/0	.000	-/3	-	-	5	-	-	6	-
HAIG	-	3/7	.429	0/1	.000	-/2	-	-	0	-	-	6	-
CARL, H.	-	5/16	.313	2/5	.400	-/3	-	-	1	-	-	12	-
RUDDY	-	4/12	.333	2/2	1.000	-/6	-	-	2	-	-	10	-
MEIER	-	0/0	.000	0/2	.000	-/0	-	-	1	-	-	0	-
BAGLEY	-	3/3	1.000	0/0	.000	-/1	-	-	1	-	-	6	-
Totals	200	24/62	.387	11/19	.579	-/25	-	-	17	-	-	59	.295

Team Rebounds: Cincinnati 9; DePaul 11. Disqualified: DePaul—Flemming.

	1st Half	2nd Half	Final
Cincinnati	53	46	99
DePaul	23	36	59

Kansas (90) Coach: Dick Harp

	Min.	Total FG/FGA	Pct.	FT/FTA	Pct.	Reb. O/T	A	TO	PF	S	Blk	TP	PPM
HIGHTOWER, W.	-	13/26	.500	8/12	.667	-/9	-	-	3	-	-	34	-
GISEL, R.	-	2/6	.333	3/3	1.000	-/2	-	-	1	-	-	7	-
BRIDGES, B.	-	7/10	.700	3/7	.429	-/14	-	-	4	-	-	17	-
HICKMAN, R.	-	0/4	.000	11/11	1.000	-/6	-	-	2	-	-	11	-
GARDNER, J.	-	6/13	.462	1/2	.500	-/7	-	-	4	-	-	13	-
CORRELL, A.	-	2/3	.667	2/2	1.000	-/2	-	-	1	-	-	6	-
HOFFMAN, J.	-	0/0	.000	0/0	.000	-/1	-	-	0	-	-	0	-
MYERS	-	1/1	1.000	0/0	.000	-/0	-	-	1	-	-	2	-
Totals	200	31/63	.492	28/37	.757	-/41	-	-	16	-	-	90	.450

Texas (81) Coach: Harold Bradley

	Min.	Total FG/FGA	Pct.	FT/FTA	Pct.	Reb. O/T	A	TO	PF	S	Blk	TP	PPM
HUGHES	-	0/6	.000	2/3	.667	-/8	-	-	2	-	-	2	-
ALMANZA	-	7/13	.538	3/5	.600	-/6	-	-	3	-	-	17	-
BROWN	-	0/2	.000	1/1	1.000	-/4	-	-	5	-	-	1	-
ARNETTE, J.	-	16/31	.516	2/3	.667	-/7	-	-	4	-	-	34	-
LASITER	-	6/12	.500	2/3	.667	-/2	-	-	1	-	-	14	-
CLARK	-	2/6	.333	2/2	1.000	-/3	-	-	5	-	-	6	-
SKEETE	-	1/3	.333	0/1	.000	-/4	-	-	1	-	-	2	-
GRAHAM	-	0/2	.000	0/0	.000	-/0	-	-	3	-	-	0	-
WILSON	-	1/1	1.000	3/3	1.000	-/2	-	-	2	-	-	5	-
Totals	200	33/76	.434	15/21	.714	-/36	-	-	26	-	-	81	.405

Team Rebounds: Kansas 6; Texas 8. Disqualified: Texas—Brown, Clark.

	1st Half	2nd Half	Final
Kansas	36	54	90
Texas	42	39	81

REGIONAL SEMIFINAL WEST

Santa Clara (49) Coach: Bob Feerick

	Min.	Total FG/FGA	Pct.	FT/FTA	Pct.	Reb. O/T	A	TO	PF	S	Blk	TP	PPM
BACHICH, J.	-	2/3	.667	0/1	.000	-/3	-	-	1	-	-	4	-
SOBRERO, F.	-	2/8	.250	1/1	1.000	-/4	-	-	3	-	-	5	-
SHEAFF	-	2/5	.400	1/3	.333	-/6	-	-	3	-	-	5	-
RUSSI	-	7/18	.389	6/6	1.000	-/4	-	-	2	-	-	20	-
CRISTINA	-	0/3	.000	0/2	.000	-/0	-	-	0	-	-	0	-
MCGEE	-	2/8	.250	3/4	.750	-/2	-	-	2	-	-	7	-
LILLEVAND	-	1/3	.333	3/4	.750	-/3	-	-	1	-	-	5	-
KEISTER	-	1/2	.500	1/3	.333	-/0	-	-	0	-	-	3	-
MARSHALL	-	0/0	.000	0/0	.000	-/0	-	-	2	-	-	0	-
BUONOCRISTIANI	-	0/1	.000	0/0	.000	-/0	-	-	0	-	-	0	-
RAMM	-	0/1	.000	0/0	.000	-/0	-	-	1	-	-	0	-
Totals	200	17/52	.327	15/24	.625	-/22	-	-	15	-	-	49	.245

California (69) Coach: Pete Newell

	Min.	Total FG/FGA	Pct.	FT/FTA	Pct.	Reb. O/T	A	TO	PF	S	Blk	TP	PPM
GILLIS, T.	-	4/12	.333	3/3	1.000	-/3	-	-	2	-	-	11	-
MCCLINTOCK, B.	-	6/12	.500	1/2	.500	-/6	-	-	3	-	-	13	-
IMHOFF, D.	-	7/12	.583	2/2	1.000	-/12	-	-	2	-	-	16	-
WENDELL, B.	-	2/3	.667	1/1	1.000	-/2	-	-	3	-	-	5	-
SCHULTZ, E.	-	6/13	.462	4/5	.800	-/5	-	-	3	-	-	16	-
MANN, J.	-	0/0	.000	0/0	.000	-/0	-	-	0	-	-	0	-
DOUGHTY, D.	-	0/2	.000	2/2	1.000	-/0	-	-	1	-	-	2	-
STAFFORD, D.	-	1/1	1.000	0/0	.000	-/1	-	-	0	-	-	2	-
MORRISON, S.	-	1/1	1.000	1/4	.250	-/1	-	-	1	-	-	3	-
PEARSON, E.	-	0/0	.000	1/2	.500	-/0	-	-	3	-	-	1	-
ALEXANDER, B.	-	0/0	.000	0/0	.000	-/0	-	-	0	-	-	0	-
AVERBUCK, N.	-	0/0	.000	0/0	.000	-/0	-	-	0	-	-	0	-
Totals	200	27/56	.482	15/21	.714	-/30	-	-	18	-	-	69	.345

Team Rebounds: California 8; Santa Clara 10. Disqualified: None.

	1st Half	2nd Half	Final
Santa Clara	22	27	49
California	31	38	69

Oregon (65) Coach: Steve Belko

	Min.	Total FG/FGA	Pct.	FT/FTA	Pct.	Reb. O/T	A	TO	PF	S	Blk	TP	PPM
HERRON	-	3/ 6	.500	2/ 5	.400	-/ 5	-	-	4	-	-	8	-
SIMMONS	-	0/ 1	.000	3/ 6	.500	-/ 4	-	-	3	-	-	3	-
MOORE, G.	-	7/13	.538	5/ 9	.556	-/ 5	-	-	3	-	-	19	-
RASK, C.	-	6/13	.462	6/ 8	.750	-/ 8	-	-	4	-	-	18	-
STRICKLAND	-	3/ 7	.429	1/ 1	1.000	-/ 2	-	-	4	-	-	7	-
WARREN	-	2/ 3	.667	1/ 2	.500	-/ 1	-	-	2	-	-	5	-
KNECHT	-	0/ 0	.000	0/ 0	.000	-/ 0	-	-	1	-	-	0	-
KIMPTON, B.	-	0/ 2	.000	5/ 6	.833	-/ 2	-	-	0	-	-	5	-
ROBERTSON	-	0/ 0	.000	0/ 0	.000	-/ 0	-	-	0	-	-	0	-
HAYES	-	0/ 0	.000	0/ 0	.000	-/ 0	-	-	0	-	-	0	-
GRANATA	-	0/ 0	.000	0/ 1	.000	-/ 0	-	-	0	-	-	0	-
Totals	200	21/45	.467	23/38	.605	-/27	-	-	21	-	-	65	.325

Utah (54) Coach: Jack Gardner

	Min.	Total FG/FGA	Pct.	FT/FTA	Pct.	Reb. O/T	A	TO	PF	S	Blk	TP	PPM
RUFFEL	-	5/ 8	.625	0/ 0	.000	-/ 4	-	-	4	-	-	10	-
HOLMES, A.	-	1/ 2	.500	5/ 8	.625	-/ 1	-	-	3	-	-	7	-
MCGILL, B.	-	2/ 3	.667	2/ 3	.667	-/ 6	-	-	5	-	-	6	-
MORTON, J.	-	0/ 1	.000	4/ 6	.667	-/ 0	-	-	2	-	-	4	-
COWAN, B.	-	3/ 7	.429	2/ 2	1.000	-/ 1	-	-	1	-	-	8	-
RHEAD, J.	-	2/ 5	.400	5/ 8	.625	-/ 6	-	-	4	-	-	9	-
CRISLER	-	2/ 6	.333	2/ 2	1.000	-/ 1	-	-	4	-	-	6	-
CHESTANG	-	2/ 6	.333	0/ 0	.000	-/ 2	-	-	3	-	-	4	-
ANCELL, K.	-	0/ 2	.000	0/ 0	.000	-/ 0	-	-	0	-	-	0	-
AUFDERHEIDE, J.	-	0/ 1	.000	0/ 0	.000	-/ 2	-	-	1	-	-	0	-
LAMBERT	-	0/ 0	.000	0/ 0	.000	-/ 0	-	-	0	-	-	0	-
Totals	200	17/41	.415	20/29	.690	-/23	-	-	27	-	-	54	.270

Team Rebounds: Oregon 12; Utah 10. Disqualified: Utah—McGill.

	1st Half	2nd Half	Final
Oregon	26	39	65
Utah	19	35	54

REGIONAL FINAL EAST

Duke (59) Coach: Vic Bubas

	Min.	Total FG/FGA	Pct.	FT/FTA	Pct.	Reb. O/T	A	TO	PF	S	Blk	TP	PPM
MULLEN, J.	-	1/ 5	.200	0/ 1	.000	-/ 0	-	-	3	-	-	2	-
HURT, H.	-	3/ 9	.333	1/ 3	.333	-/ 6	-	-	3	-	-	7	-
YOUNGKIN, C.	-	2/ 5	.400	4/ 8	.500	-/ 8	-	-	2	-	-	8	-
FRYE, J.	-	5/11	.455	0/ 0	.000	-/ 2	-	-	3	-	-	10	-
KISTLER, D.	-	8/16	.500	4/ 5	.800	-/ 8	-	-	4	-	-	20	-
MEWHORT, B.	-	1/ 2	.500	1/ 2	.500	-/ 4	-	-	1	-	-	3	-
CANTWELL, J.	-	1/ 3	.333	1/ 2	.500	-/ 0	-	-	2	-	-	3	-
MORGAN, M.	-	1/ 2	.500	2/ 2	1.000	-/ 1	-	-	1	-	-	4	-
KAST, F.	-	0/ 2	.000	2/ 2	1.000	-/ 3	-	-	0	-	-	2	-
ALBRIGHT, D.	-	0/ 1	.000	0/ 0	.000	-/ 0	-	-	0	-	-	0	-
BATEMAN, L.	-	0/ 0	.000	0/ 0	.000	-/ 0	-	-	0	-	-	0	-
BEAL, J.	-	0/ 1	.000	0/ 0	.000	-/ 1	-	-	0	-	-	0	-
Totals	200	22/57	.386	15/25	.600	-/33	-	-	19	-	-	59	.295

NYU (74) Coach: Lou Rossini

	Min.	Total FG/FGA	Pct.	FT/FTA	Pct.	Reb. O/T	A	TO	PF	S	Blk	TP	PPM
SANDERS, T.	-	6/14	.429	10/12	.833	-/16	-	-	2	-	-	22	-
PADROCKY, R.	-	4/ 7	.571	3/ 5	.600	-/ 4	-	-	2	-	-	11	-
REISS, J.	-	1/ 4	.250	0/ 0	.000	-/ 1	-	-	3	-	-	2	-
BARDEN, A.	-	7/11	.636	0/ 0	.000	-/ 5	-	-	3	-	-	14	-
CUNNINGHAM, R.	-	4/ 6	.667	1/ 3	.333	-/ 3	-	-	1	-	-	9	-
LOCHE, A.	-	2/ 4	.500	1/ 3	.333	-/ 0	-	-	2	-	-	5	-
FILARDI, A.	-	4/ 6	.667	3/ 3	1.000	-/ 8	-	-	2	-	-	11	-
DINAPOLI, M.	-	0/ 0	.000	0/ 0	.000	-/ 0	-	-	0	-	-	0	-
MURPHY, L.	-	0/ 0	.000	0/ 0	.000	-/ 0	-	-	1	-	-	0	-
REGAN, B.	-	0/ 1	.000	0/ 0	.000	-/ 0	-	-	0	-	-	0	-
MLODINOFF, B.	-	0/ 0	.000	0/ 0	.000	-/ 0	-	-	0	-	-	0	-
Totals	200	28/53	.528	18/26	.692	-/37	-	-	16	-	-	74	.370

Team Rebounds: NYU 3; Duke 5. Disqualified: None.

	1st Half	2nd Half	Final
Duke	26	33	59
NYU	35	39	74

REGIONAL FINAL MIDEAST

Georgia Tech (69) Coach: Whack Hyder

	Min.	Total FG/FGA	Pct.	FT/FTA	Pct.	Reb. O/T	A	TO	PF	S	Blk	TP	PPM
DENTON, D.	-	5/17	.294	5/ 6	.833	-/ 6	-	-	4	-	-	15	-
RICHARDS, W.	-	2/ 8	.250	1/ 1	1.000	-/ 3	-	-	5	-	-	5	-
RILEY	-	2/ 5	.400	4/ 4	1.000	-/15	-	-	4	-	-	8	-
KAISER, R.	-	11/24	.458	5/ 6	.833	-/ 5	-	-	2	-	-	27	-
DEWS, B.	-	3/ 6	.500	3/ 6	.500	-/ 2	-	-	2	-	-	9	-
HOFFMAN	-	1/ 5	.200	1/ 4	.250	-/ 2	-	-	0	-	-	3	-
GHER	-	1/ 1	1.000	0/ 0	.000	-/ 1	-	-	0	-	-	2	-
POTEET	-	0/ 2	.000	0/ 0	.000	-/ 0	-	-	0	-	-	0	-
POWELL	-	0/ 0	.000	0/ 0	.000	-/ 1	-	-	0	-	-	0	-
Totals	200	25/68	.368	19/27	.704	-/35	-	-	17	-	-	69	.345

Ohio State (86) Coach: Fred Taylor

	Min.	Total FG/FGA	Pct.	FT/FTA	Pct.	Reb. O/T	A	TO	PF	S	Blk	TP	PPM
HAVILCEK, J.	-	7/14	.500	1/ 3	.333	-/10	-	-	3	-	-	15	-
ROBERTS, J.	-	8/13	.615	3/ 4	.750	-/ 9	-	-	2	-	-	19	-
LUCAS, J.	-	9/12	.750	7/10	.700	-/16	-	-	2	-	-	25	-
NOWELL, M.	-	3/ 6	.500	1/ 1	1.000	-/ 2	-	-	4	-	-	7	-
SIEGFRIED, L.	-	6/11	.545	2/ 2	1.000	-/ 4	-	-	4	-	-	14	-
GEARHART, G.	-	2/ 4	.500	0/ 3	.000	-/ 3	-	-	3	-	-	4	-
FURRY, J.	-	0/ 1	.000	0/ 0	.000	-/ 0	-	-	0	-	-	0	-
KNIGHT, B.	-	0/ 0	.000	0/ 0	.000	-/ 1	-	-	0	-	-	0	-
NOURSE, H.	-	0/ 1	.000	0/ 0	.000	-/ 1	-	-	0	-	-	0	-
BARKER, D.	-	1/ 2	.500	0/ 0	.000	-/ 0	-	-	0	-	-	2	-
CEDARGREN, J.	-	0/ 0	.000	0/ 0	.000	-/ 1	-	-	0	-	-	0	-
HOYT, R.	-	0/ 1	.000	0/ 0	.000	-/ 0	-	-	2	-	-	0	-
Totals	200	36/65	.554	14/23	.609	-/47	-	-	20	-	-	86	.430

Team Rebounds: Ohio State 5; Georgia Tech 2. Disqualified: Georgia Tech—Richards.

	1st Half	2nd Half	Final
Georgia Tech	35	34	69
Ohio State	41	45	86

REGIONAL FINAL MIDWEST

Cincinnati (82) Coach: George Smith

	Min.	Total FG/FGA	Pct.	FT/FTA	Pct.	Reb. O/T	A	TO	PF	S	Blk	TP	PPM
ROBERTSON, O.	-	19/30	.633	5/10	.500	-/14	-	-	2	-	-	43	-
WILLEY, L.	-	4/7	.571	0/0	.000	-/6	-	-	4	-	-	8	-
HOGUE, P.	-	5/10	.500	1/2	.500	-/10	-	-	4	-	-	11	-
DAVIS, R.	-	4/9	.444	0/1	.000	-/3	-	-	0	-	-	8	-
BOULDIN, C.	-	0/5	.000	2/3	.667	-/7	-	-	3	-	-	2	-
WIESENHAHN, B.	-	1/6	.167	5/5	1.000	-/8	-	-	3	-	-	7	-
SIZER, T.	-	0/0	.000	1/1	1.000	-/0	-	-	0	-	-	1	-
POMERANTZ, S.	-	1/1	1.000	0/0	.000	-/1	-	-	0	-	-	2	-
Totals	200	34/68	.500	14/22	.636	-/49	-	-	16	-	-	82	.410

Kansas (71) Coach: Dick Harp

	Min.	Total FG/FGA	Pct.	FT/FTA	Pct.	Reb. O/T	A	TO	PF	S	Blk	TP	PPM
HIGHTOWER, W.	-	8/24	.333	6/7	.857	-/9	-	-	3	-	-	22	-
GISEL, R.	-	1/8	.125	0/0	.000	-/3	-	-	0	-	-	2	-
BRIDGES, B.	-	8/14	.571	6/7	.857	-/9	-	-	4	-	-	22	-
HICKMAN, R.	-	1/5	.200	0/1	.000	-/3	-	-	3	-	-	2	-
GARDNER, J.	-	6/15	.400	0/1	.000	-/6	-	-	3	-	-	12	-
CORRELL, A.	-	4/5	.800	3/4	.750	-/3	-	-	5	-	-	11	-
Totals	200	28/71	.394	15/20	.750	-/33	-	-	18	-	-	71	.355

Team Rebounds: Cincinnati 6; Kansas 7. Disqualified: Kansas—Correl.

	1st Half	2nd Half	Final
Cincinnati	40	42	82
Kansas	42	29	71

REGIONAL FINAL WEST

California (70) Coach: Pete Newell

	Min.	Total FG/FGA	Pct.	FT/FTA	Pct.	Reb. O/T	A	TO	PF	S	Blk	TP	PPM
GILLIS, T.	-	2/6	.333	0/0	.000	-/1	-	-	4	-	-	4	-
MCCLINTOCK, B.	-	5/15	.333	2/6	.333	-/15	-	-	1	-	-	12	-
IMHOFF, D.	-	5/12	.417	8/9	.889	-/12	-	-	2	-	-	18	-
WENDELL, B.	-	1/6	.167	2/3	.667	-/3	-	-	2	-	-	4	-
SCHULTZ, E.	-	5/6	.833	1/2	.500	-/7	-	-	3	-	-	11	-
MANN, J.	-	2/3	.667	0/0	.000	-/1	-	-	1	-	-	4	-
DOUGHTY, D.	-	3/4	.750	4/5	.800	-/5	-	-	3	-	-	10	-
STAFFORD, D.	-	0/2	.000	5/9	.556	-/2	-	-	5	-	-	5	-
MORRISON, S.	-	1/1	1.000	0/0	.000	-/1	-	-	0	-	-	2	-
ALEXANDER, B.	-	0/0	.000	0/0	.000	-/0	-	-	0	-	-	0	-
Totals	200	24/55	.436	22/34	.647	-/47	-	-	21	-	-	70	.350

Oregon (49) Coach: Steve Belko

	Min.	Total FG/FGA	Pct.	FT/FTA	Pct.	Reb. O/T	A	TO	PF	S	Blk	TP	PPM
HERRON	-	3/12	.250	8/11	.727	-/6	-	-	4	-	-	14	-
SIMMONS	-	1/3	.333	0/1	.000	-/2	-	-	3	-	-	2	-
MOORE, G.	-	3/9	.333	3/3	1.000	-/1	-	-	3	-	-	9	-
RASK, C.	-	7/10	.700	1/4	.250	-/4	-	-	4	-	-	15	-
STRICKLAND	-	0/6	.000	0/0	.000	-/4	-	-	2	-	-	0	-
WARREN	-	1/7	.143	4/5	.800	-/8	-	-	4	-	-	6	-
KNECHT	-	0/0	.000	3/5	.600	-/0	-	-	1	-	-	3	-
KIMPTON, B.	-	0/1	.000	0/0	.000	-/0	-	-	1	-	-	0	-
ROBERTSON	-	0/0	.000	0/0	.000	-/1	-	-	1	-	-	0	-
HAYES	-	0/0	.000	0/0	.000	-/0	-	-	0	-	-	0	-
Totals	200	15/48	.313	19/29	.655	-/26	-	-	23	-	-	49	.245

Team Rebounds: California 7; Oregon 6. Disqualified: California—Stafford.

	1st Half	2nd Half	Final
California	32	38	70
Oregon	21	28	49

FINAL FOUR

NYU (54) Coach: Lou Rossini

	Min.	Total FG/FGA	Pct.	FT/FTA	Pct.	Reb. O/T	A	TO	PF	S	Blk	TP	PPM
BARDEN, A.	-	2/11	.182	4/4	1.000	-/8	-	-	2	-	-	8	-
FILARDI, A.	-	6/12	.500	0/1	.000	-/6	-	-	3	-	-	12	-
SANDERS, T.	-	4/13	.308	0/3	.000	-/22	-	-	2	-	-	8	-
CUNNINGHAM, R.	-	4/14	.286	6/8	.750	-/3	-	-	2	-	-	14	-
PAPROCKY, R.	-	4/17	.235	1/2	.500	-/0	-	-	3	-	-	9	-
LOCHE, A.	-	0/3	.000	1/1	1.000	-/0	-	-	0	-	-	1	-
DINAPOLI, M.	-	0/0	.000	0/0	.000	-/1	-	-	0	-	-	0	-
MURPHY, L.	-	1/1	1.000	0/1	.000	-/0	-	-	0	-	-	2	-
REISS, J.	-	0/0	.000	0/0	.000	-/0	-	-	1	-	-	0	-
REGAN, B.	-	0/1	.000	0/0	.000	-/0	-	-	1	-	-	0	-
KEITH, R.	-	0/1	.000	0/0	.000	-/0	-	-	0	-	-	0	-
MLODINOFF, B.	-	0/1	.000	0/0	.000	-/0	-	-	0	-	-	0	-
Totals	200	21/74	.284	12/20	.600	-/41	-	-	14	-	-	54	.270

Ohio State (76) Coach: Fred Taylor

	Min.	Total FG/FGA	Pct.	FT/FTA	Pct.	Reb. O/T	A	TO	PF	S	Blk	TP	PPM
HAVILCEK, J.	-	2/8	.250	2/2	1.000	-/10	-	-	0	-	-	6	-
ROBERTS, J.	-	3/6	.500	1/2	.500	-/7	-	-	0	-	-	7	-
LUCAS, J.	-	9/15	.600	1/1	1.000	-/13	-	-	2	-	-	19	-
NOWELL, M.	-	3/8	.375	0/0	.000	-/0	-	-	4	-	-	6	-
SIEGFRIED, L.	-	7/11	.636	5/5	1.000	-/3	-	-	3	-	-	19	-
GEARHART, G.	-	1/3	.333	1/1	1.000	-/1	-	-	3	-	-	3	-
FURRY, R.	-	4/7	.571	2/3	.667	-/7	-	-	2	-	-	10	-
KNIGHT, B.	-	0/0	.000	0/0	.000	-/1	-	-	0	-	-	0	-
NOURSE, H.	-	0/0	.000	0/0	.000	-/0	-	-	0	-	-	0	-
HOYT, R.	-	0/0	.000	2/2	1.000	-/0	-	-	0	-	-	2	-
BARKER, D.	-	1/1	1.000	0/0	.000	-/0	-	-	0	-	-	2	-
CEDARGREN, J.	-	1/1	1.000	0/0	.000	-/1	-	-	0	-	-	2	-
Totals	200	31/60	.517	14/16	.875	-/43	-	-	14	-	-	76	.380

Team Rebounds: Ohio State 5; NYU 3. Disqualified: None.

	1st Half	2nd Half	Final
NYU	28	26	54
Ohio State	37	39	76

Cincinnati (69) — Coach: George Smith

	Min.	Total FG/FGA	Pct.	FT/FTA	Pct.	Reb. O/T	A	TO	PF	S	Blk	TP	PPM
ROBERTSON, O.	-	4/16	.250	10/12	.833	-/10	-	-	4	-	-	18	-
WILLEY, L.	-	4/9	.444	1/2	.500	-/4	-	-	4	-	-	9	-
HOGUE, P.	-	5/9	.556	4/6	.667	-/11	-	-	5	-	-	14	-
DAVIS, R.	-	4/8	.500	2/2	1.000	-/2	-	-	1	-	-	10	-
BOULDIN, C.	-	4/7	.571	0/0	.000	-/0	-	-	4	-	-	8	-
WIESENHAHN, B.	-	5/8	.625	0/0	.000	-/9	-	-	3	-	-	10	-
SIZER, T.	-	0/0	.000	0/1	.000	-/1	-	-	0	-	-	0	-
POMERANTZ, S.	-	0/0	.000	0/0	.000	-/0	-	-	0	-	-	0	-
BRYANT, J.	-	0/1	.000	0/0	.000	-/1	-	-	3	-	-	0	-
Totals	200	26/58	.448	17/23	.739	-/38	-	14	24	-	-	69	.345

California (77) — Coach: Pete Newell

	Min.	Total FG/FGA	Pct.	FT/FTA	Pct.	Reb. O/T	A	TO	PF	S	Blk	TP	PPM
GILLIS, T.	-	5/10	.500	3/3	1.000	-/4	-	-	4	-	-	13	-
MCCLINTOCK, B.	-	5/12	.417	8/10	.800	-/10	-	-	3	-	-	18	-
IMHOFF, D.	-	10/21	.476	5/5	1.000	-/11	-	-	4	-	-	25	-
WENDELL, B.	-	0/4	.000	4/7	.571	-/3	-	-	2	-	-	4	-
SCHULTZ, E.	-	4/7	.571	3/5	.600	-/3	-	-	1	-	-	11	-
DOUGHTY, D.	-	1/3	.333	0/0	.000	-/2	-	-	1	-	-	2	-
STAFFORD, D.	-	1/4	.250	2/2	1.000	-/0	-	-	2	-	-	4	-
Totals	200	26/61	.426	25/32	.781	-/33	-	5	17	-	-	77	.385

Team Rebounds: California 7; Cincinnati 2. Disqualified: Cincinnati—Hogue.

	1st Half	2nd Half	Final
Cincinnati	30	39	69
California	34	43	77

NATIONAL CHAMPIONSHIP

Ohio State (75) — Coach: Fred Taylor

	Min.	Total FG/FGA	Pct.	FT/FTA	Pct.	Reb. O/T	A	TO	PF	S	Blk	TP	PPM
HAVILCEK, J.	-	4/8	.500	4/5	.800	-/6	-	-	2	-	-	12	-
ROBERTS, J.	-	5/6	.833	0/1	.000	-/5	-	-	1	-	-	10	-
LUCAS, J.	-	7/9	.778	2/2	1.000	-/10	-	-	2	-	-	16	-
NOWELL, M.	-	6/7	.857	3/3	1.000	-/4	-	-	2	-	-	15	-
SIEGFRIED, L.	-	5/6	.833	3/6	.500	-/1	-	-	2	-	-	13	-
GEARHART, G.	-	0/1	.000	0/0	.000	-/1	-	-	0	-	-	0	-
FURRY, R.	-	2/4	.500	0/0	.000	-/3	-	-	1	-	-	4	-
KNIGHT, B.	-	0/1	.000	0/0	.000	-/0	-	-	1	-	-	0	-
NOURSE, H.	-	2/3	.667	0/0	.000	-/3	-	-	1	-	-	4	-
HOYT, R.	-	0/1	.000	0/0	.000	-/0	-	-	0	-	-	0	-
BARKER, D.	-	0/0	.000	0/0	.000	-/0	-	-	0	-	-	0	-
CEDARGREN, J.	-	0/0	.000	1/2	.500	-/1	-	-	1	-	-	1	-
Totals	200	31/46	.674	13/19	.684	-/34	-	-	13	-	-	75	.375

California (55) — Coach: Pete Newell

	Min.	Total FG/FGA	Pct.	FT/FTA	Pct.	Reb. O/T	A	TO	PF	S	Blk	TP	PPM
MCCLINTOCK, B.	-	4/15	.267	2/3	.667	-/3	-	-	3	-	-	10	-
GILLIS, T.	-	4/9	.444	0/0	.000	-/1	-	-	1	-	-	8	-
IMHOFF, D.	-	3/9	.333	2/2	1.000	-/5	-	-	2	-	-	8	-
WENDELL, B.	-	0/6	.000	4/4	1.000	-/0	-	-	2	-	-	4	-
SCHULTZ, E.	-	2/8	.250	2/2	1.000	-/4	-	-	4	-	-	6	-
MANN, J.	-	3/5	.600	1/1	1.000	-/0	-	-	0	-	-	7	-
DOUGHTY, D.	-	4/5	.800	3/3	1.000	-/6	-	-	1	-	-	11	-
STAFFORD, D.	-	0/1	.000	1/2	.500	-/0	-	-	1	-	-	1	-
MORRISON, S.	-	0/0	.000	0/0	.000	-/1	-	-	1	-	-	0	-
AVERBUCK, N.	-	0/0	.000	0/1	.000	-/1	-	-	0	-	-	0	-
MORRISON, S.	-	0/1	.000	0/0	.000	-/0	-	-	0	-	-	0	-
ALEXANDER, B.	-	0/0	.000	0/0	.000	-/0	-	-	0	-	-	0	-
Totals	200	20/59	.339	15/18	.833	-/21	-	-	15	-	-	55	.275

Team Rebounds: Ohio State 1; California 7. Disqualified: None.

	1st Half	2nd Half	Final
Ohio State	37	38	75
California	19	36	55

NATIONAL THIRD PLACE

Cincinnati (95) — Coach: George Smith

	Min.	Total FG/FGA	Pct.	FT/FTA	Pct.	Reb. O/T	A	TO	PF	S	Blk	TP	PPM
ROBERTSON, O.	-	12/23	.522	8/11	.727	-/14	-	-	4	-	-	32	-
WILLEY, L.	-	5/8	.625	0/0	.000	-/5	-	-	4	-	-	10	-
HOGUE, P.	-	7/9	.778	1/5	.200	-/19	-	-	2	-	-	15	-
DAVIS, R.	-	3/9	.333	3/3	1.000	-/1	-	-	0	-	-	9	-
BOULDIN, C.	-	7/11	.636	0/1	.000	-/3	-	-	2	-	-	14	-
WIESENHAHN, B.	-	4/4	1.000	2/2	1.000	-/2	-	-	1	-	-	10	-
SIZER, T.	-	0/4	.000	1/2	.500	-/4	-	-	2	-	-	1	-
POMERANTZ, S.	-	1/2	.500	0/0	.000	-/0	-	-	0	-	-	2	-
BRYANT, J.	-	1/2	.500	0/0	.000	-/1	-	-	0	-	-	2	-
DIERKING, F.	-	0/2	.000	0/0	.000	-/2	-	-	0	-	-	0	-
REIS, R.	-	0/1	.000	0/0	.000	-/1	-	-	0	-	-	0	-
Totals	200	40/75	.533	15/24	.625	-/52	-	-	15	-	-	95	.475

NYU (71) — Coach: Lou Rossini

	Min.	Total FG/FGA	Pct.	FT/FTA	Pct.	Reb. O/T	A	TO	PF	S	Blk	TP	PPM
BARDEN, A.	-	3/12	.250	1/2	.500	-/13	-	-	4	-	-	7	-
FILARDI, A.	-	1/4	.250	1/1	1.000	-/4	-	-	0	-	-	3	-
SANDERS, T.	-	11/23	.478	5/6	.833	-/11	-	-	4	-	-	27	-
CUNNINGHAM, R.	-	4/9	.444	2/3	.667	-/0	-	-	2	-	-	10	-
PAPROCKY, R.	-	6/13	.462	3/4	.750	-/1	-	-	3	-	-	15	-
LOCHE, A.	-	1/2	.500	2/2	1.000	-/0	-	-	0	-	-	4	-
MURPHY, L.	-	0/4	.000	0/0	.000	-/2	-	-	0	-	-	0	-
REISS, J.	-	2/4	.500	1/2	.500	-/2	-	-	3	-	-	5	-
Totals	200	28/71	.394	15/20	.750	-/33	-	-	16	-	-	71	.355

Team Rebounds: Cincinnati 4; NYU 3. Disqualified: None.

	1st Half	2nd Half	Final
Cincinnati	39	56	95
NYU	25	46	71

REGIONAL THIRD PLACE EAST

West Virginia (106)   Coach: Fred Schaus

	Min.	Total FG / FGA	Pct.	FT / FTA	Pct.	Reb. O / T	A	TO	PF	S	Blk	TP	PPM
WEST, J.	-	12/28	.429	13/14	.929	-/16	-	-	3	-	-	37	-
RITCHIE, J.	-	3/7	.429	6/9	.667	-/10	-	-	1	-	-	12	-
AKERS, W.	-	2/13	.154	3/6	.500	-/12	-	-	2	-	-	7	-
PATRONE, L.	-	9/13	.692	5/9	.556	-/7	-	-	2	-	-	23	-
WARREN, J.	-	6/12	.500	2/2	1.000	-/4	-	-	1	-	-	14	-
GOODE, B.	-	0/0	.000	0/0	.000	-/0	-	-	1	-	-	0	-
POPOVICH	-	1/1	1.000	0/0	.000	-/1	-	-	0	-	-	2	-
POSCH, J.	-	1/4	.250	5/6	.833	-/6	-	-	1	-	-	7	-
VISNIC, N.	-	1/3	.333	0/0	.000	-/0	-	-	1	-	-	2	-
MILLER	-	1/3	.333	0/0	.000	-/0	-	-	2	-	-	2	-
BODE	-	0/1	.000	0/0	.000	-/0	-	-	0	-	-	0	-
Totals	200	36/85	.424	34/46	.739	-/56	-	-	14	-	-	106	.530

St. Joseph's (100)   Coach: Jack Ramsay

	Min.	Total FG / FGA	Pct.	FT / FTA	Pct.	Reb. O / T	A	TO	PF	S	Blk	TP	PPM
CLARKE	-	4/10	.400	1/1	1.000	-/6	-	-	5	-	-	9	-
MAJEWSKI	-	4/9	.444	4/4	1.000	-/6	-	-	3	-	-	12	-
GALLO	-	13/26	.500	3/4	.750	-/7	-	-	4	-	-	29	-
WESTHEAD	-	2/13	.154	4/5	.800	-/8	-	-	5	-	-	8	-
KEMPTON	-	4/10	.400	0/0	.000	-/10	-	-	5	-	-	8	-
EGAN	-	9/18	.500	2/2	1.000	-/10	-	-	5	-	-	20	-
MCNEILL	-	5/14	.357	4/4	1.000	-/4	-	-	2	-	-	14	-
REILLY	-	0/3	.000	0/0	.000	-/3	-	-	1	-	-	0	-
COOLICAN	-	0/0	.000	0/0	.000	-/0	-	-	0	-	-	0	-
Totals	200	41/103	.398	18/20	.900	-/54	-	-	30	-	-	100	.500

Team Rebounds: West Virginia 7; St. Joseph's 7. Disqualified: St. Joseph's—Clarke, Westhead, Kempton, Egan.

	1st Half	2nd Half	Final
West Virginia	51	55	106
St. Joseph's	59	41	100

REGIONAL THIRD PLACE MIDEAST

Western Kentucky (97)   Coach: Ed Diddle

	Min.	Total FG / FGA	Pct.	FT / FTA	Pct.	Reb. O / T	A	TO	PF	S	Blk	TP	PPM
ELLISON, A.	-	7/15	.467	4/5	.800	-/7	-	-	2	-	-	18	-
TODD, H.	-	5/9	.556	1/2	.500	-/6	-	-	5	-	-	11	-
OSBORNE, C.	-	7/11	.636	9/10	.900	-/12	-	-	2	-	-	23	-
RASCOE, B.	-	4/7	.571	10/12	.833	-/4	-	-	1	-	-	18	-
PARSONS, D.	-	8/13	.615	7/10	.700	-/1	-	-	4	-	-	23	-
SARAKATSANNIS, P.	-	2/4	.500	0/0	.000	-/1	-	-	1	-	-	4	-
TALBOTT, J.	-	0/1	.000	0/0	.000	-/1	-	-	1	-	-	0	-
Totals	200	33/60	.550	31/39	.795	-/32	-	-	16	-	-	97	.485

Ohio (87)   Coach: James Snyder

	Min.	Total FG / FGA	Pct.	FT / FTA	Pct.	Reb. O / T	A	TO	PF	S	Blk	TP	PPM
KRUGER	-	9/21	.429	0/1	.000	-/11	-	-	3	-	-	18	-
WITTE	-	2/7	.286	0/2	.000	-/5	-	-	3	-	-	4	-
JOLLIFF, H.	-	10/20	.500	3/6	.500	-/23	-	-	5	-	-	23	-
ADAMS, B.	-	11/20	.550	6/10	.600	-/10	-	-	4	-	-	28	-
FANDY	-	1/4	.250	1/2	.500	-/0	-	-	4	-	-	3	-
WHALEY	-	1/8	.125	1/2	.500	-/3	-	-	3	-	-	3	-
WILCOX	-	1/5	.200	0/0	.000	-/2	-	-	2	-	-	2	-
KATZ	-	3/7	.429	0/2	.000	-/0	-	-	2	-	-	6	-
Totals	200	38/92	.413	11/25	.440	-/54	-	-	26	-	-	87	.435

Team Rebounds: Western Ky. 0; Ohio 10. Disqualified: Western Ky.—Todd; Ohio—Joliff.

	1st Half	2nd Half	Final
Western Ky.	42	55	97
Ohio	43	44	87

REGIONAL THIRD PLACE MIDWEST

DePaul (67)   Coach: Ray Meyer

	Min.	Total FG / FGA	Pct.	FT / FTA	Pct.	Reb. O / T	A	TO	PF	S	Blk	TP	PPM
COWSEN, M.	-	4/11	.364	8/11	.727	-/17	-	-	2	-	-	16	-
RUDDY	-	1/3	.333	0/0	.000	-/3	-	-	1	-	-	2	-
FLEMMING	-	9/15	.600	0/0	.000	-/11	-	-	1	-	-	18	-
HAIG	-	2/7	.286	2/3	.667	-/2	-	-	4	-	-	6	-
CARL, H.	-	7/18	.389	5/5	1.000	-/5	-	-	1	-	-	19	-
SALZINSKI	-	2/4	.500	0/0	.000	-/1	-	-	5	-	-	4	-
FLAIZ	-	1/3	.333	0/0	.000	-/2	-	-	1	-	-	2	-
Totals	200	26/61	.426	15/19	.789	-/41	-	-	15	-	-	67	.335

Texas (61)   Coach: Harold Bradley

	Min.	Total FG / FGA	Pct.	FT / FTA	Pct.	Reb. O / T	A	TO	PF	S	Blk	TP	PPM
HUGHES	-	0/4	.000	0/0	.000	-/4	-	-	1	-	-	0	-
ALMANZA	-	2/13	.154	1/2	.500	-/11	-	-	3	-	-	5	-
CLARK	-	4/8	.500	3/5	.600	-/8	-	-	1	-	-	11	-
ARNETTE, J.	-	13/27	.481	3/6	.500	-/8	-	-	3	-	-	29	-
LASITER	-	3/16	.188	3/3	1.000	-/10	-	-	3	-	-	9	-
BROWN	-	0/2	.000	1/1	1.000	-/2	-	-	0	-	-	1	-
SKEETE	-	3/8	.375	0/0	.000	-/4	-	-	3	-	-	6	-
WILSON	-	0/1	.000	0/0	.000	-/1	-	-	1	-	-	0	-
Totals	200	25/79	.316	11/17	.647	-/48	-	-	15	-	-	61	.305

Team Rebounds: DePaul 5; Texas 5. Disqualified: DePaul—Salzinski.

	1st Half	2nd Half	Final
DePaul	39	28	67
Texas	37	24	61

REGIONAL THIRD PLACE WEST

Utah (89)   Coach: Jack Gardner

	Min.	Total FG / FGA	Pct.	FT / FTA	Pct.	Reb. O / T	A	TO	PF	S	Blk	TP	PPM
RUFFEL	-	7/14	.500	11/11	1.000	-/4	-	-	2	-	-	25	-
HOLMES, A.	-	3/10	.300	4/5	.800	-/4	-	-	2	-	-	10	-
MCGILL, B.	-	3/9	.333	8/10	.800	-/6	-	-	1	-	-	14	-
MORTON, J.	-	2/5	.400	6/7	.857	-/5	-	-	4	-	-	10	-
COWAN, B.	-	4/8	.500	2/2	1.000	-/4	-	-	2	-	-	10	-
RHEAD, J.	-	4/11	.364	4/7	.571	-/12	-	-	1	-	-	12	-
CRISTER	-	1/3	.333	4/4	1.000	-/5	-	-	3	-	-	6	-
CHESTANG	-	0/0	.000	2/2	1.000	-/0	-	-	1	-	-	2	-
ANCELL, K.	-	0/0	.000	0/0	.000	-/0	-	-	0	-	-	0	-
Totals	200	24/60	.400	41/48	.854	-/40	-	-	16	-	-	89	.445

Santa Clara (81)   Coach: Bob Feerick

	Min.	Total FG / FGA	Pct.	FT / FTA	Pct.	Reb. O / T	A	TO	PF	S	Blk	TP	PPM
BACHICH, J.	-	4/12	.333	1/1	1.000	-/3	-	-	2	-	-	9	-
SOBRERO, F.	-	3/10	.300	2/2	1.000	-/7	-	-	5	-	-	8	-
SHEAFF	-	5/11	.455	3/5	.600	-/4	-	-	5	-	-	13	-
RUSSI	-	6/18	.333	7/9	.778	-/8	-	-	3	-	-	19	-
CRISTINA	-	0/1	.000	0/0	.000	-/1	-	-	0	-	-	0	-
MCGEE	-	4/6	.667	2/2	1.000	-/1	-	-	5	-	-	10	-
LILLEVAND	-	6/8	.750	2/3	.667	-/3	-	-	5	-	-	14	-
KEISTER	-	2/5	.400	0/0	.000	-/2	-	-	2	-	-	4	-
MARSHALL	-	0/0	.000	0/0	.000	-/0	-	-	1	-	-	0	-
BUONOCRISTIANI	-	2/2	1.000	0/0	.000	-/0	-	-	1	-	-	4	-
RAMM	-	0/0	.000	0/0	.000	-/0	-	-	0	-	-	0	-
Totals	200	32/73	.438	17/22	.773	-/29	-	-	29	-	-	81	.405

Team Rebounds: Utah 10; Santa Clara 8. Disqualified: Santa Clara—Sobrero, Sheaff, McGee, Lillevand.

	1st Half	2nd Half	Final
Utah	45	44	89
Santa Clara	29	52	81

✪ ALL-STAR TEAMS ✪

ALL TOURNAMENT

DARRALL IMHOFF	CALIFORNIA
★ **JERRY LUCAS**	OHIO STATE
MEL NOWELL	OHIO STATE
OSCAR ROBERTSON	CINCINNATI
TOM SANDERS	NYU

★ Most Outstanding Player(s)

✪ INDIVIDUAL RECORDS ✪

SCORING

Most points in a single game
1 OSCAR ROBERTSON, CINCINNATI (vs. KANSAS) 43
2 JERRY WEST, WEST VIRGINIA (vs. ST. JOSEPH'S) 37
3 JERRY LUCAS, OHIO STATE (vs. WESTERN KY.) 36
4 4 tied for fourth place.

Most total points in the tournament
1 OSCAR ROBERTSON, CINCINNATI 122
2 JERRY WEST, WEST VIRGINIA 105
3 TOM SANDERS, NYU 96
3 JERRY LUCAS, OHIO STATE 96
5 DARRALL IMHOFF, CALIFORNIA 86

Highest scoring average (minimum 2 games)
1 JERRY WEST, WEST VIRGINIA (105-3) 35.00
2 JAY ARNETTE, TEXAS (63-2) 31.50
3 OSCAR ROBERTSON, CINCINNATI (122-4) 30.50
4 WAYNE HIGHTOWER, KANSAS (56-2) 28.00
5 ROGER KAISER, GEORGIA TECH (52-2) 26.00

FIELD GOALS

Most field goals in a single game
1 OSCAR ROBERTSON, CINCINNATI (vs. KANSAS) 19
2 JAY ARNETTE, TEXAS (vs. KANSAS) 16
3 JERRY LUCAS, OHIO STATE (vs. WESTERN KY.) 14
4 4 tied for fourth place.

Most total field goals in the tournament
1 OSCAR ROBERTSON, CINCINNATI 47
2 JERRY LUCAS, OHIO STATE 39
3 TOM SANDERS, NYU 38
4 JERRY WEST, WEST VIRGINIA 35
5 DARRALL IMHOFF, CALIFORNIA 32

Most field goal attempts in a single game
1 JAY ARNETTE, TEXAS (vs. KANSAS) 31
2 OSCAR ROBERTSON, CINCINNATI (vs. KANSAS) 30

3 JERRY WEST, WEST VIRGINIA (vs. ST. JOSEPH'S) 28
3 JERRY WEST, WEST VIRGINIA (vs. NYU) 28
5 JAY ARNETTE, TEXAS (vs. DEPAUL) 27

Highest field goal percentage in a single game (minimum 10 attempts)
1 PAUL HOGUE, CINCINNATI (vs. DEPAUL) (9-12) .750
1 JERRY LUCAS, OHIO STATE (vs. GEORGIA TECH) (9-12) .750
3 JOE MORTON, UTAH (vs. USC) (8-11) .727
4 CHUCK RASK, OREGON (vs. CALIFORNIA) (7-10) .700
4 BILL BRIDGES, KANSAS (vs. TEXAS) (7-10) .700

FREE THROWS

Most free throws in a single game
1 JERRY WEST, WEST VIRGINIA (vs. ST. JOSEPH'S) 13
2 JERRY WEST, WEST VIRGINIA (vs. NYU) 12
3 4 tied for third place.

Most total free throws in the tournament
1 JERRY WEST, WEST VIRGINIA 35
2 OSCAR ROBERTSON, CINCINNATI 28
3 BOBBY RASCOE, WESTERN KY. 25
4 DARRALL IMHOFF, CALIFORNIA 22
5 BILL MCGILL, UTAH 21

Most free throws attempted in a single game
1 BILL MCGILL, UTAH (vs. USC) 18
2 JERRY WEST, WEST VIRGINIA (vs. NAVY) 15
3 JERRY WEST, WEST VIRGINIA (vs. ST. JOSEPH'S) 14
4 JERRY WEST, WEST VIRGINIA (vs. NYU) 13
5 4 tied for fifth place.

Most free throws attempted in the tournament
1 JERRY WEST, WEST VIRGINIA 42
2 OSCAR ROBERTSON, CINCINNATI 40
3 BOBBY RASCOE, WESTERN KY. 34
4 BILL MCGILL, UTAH 31
5 TOM SANDERS, NYU 30

Highest free throw percentage in a single game (minimum 7 attempts)
1 ROGER KAISER, GEORGIA TECH (vs. OHIO) (11-11) 1.000
1 RICH RUFFELL, UTAH (vs. SANTA CLARA) (11-11) 1.000
1 R. HICKMAN, KANSAS (vs. TEXAS) (11-11) 1.000
4 JERRY WEST, WEST VIRGINIA (vs. ST. JOSEPH'S) (13-14) .929
5 JERRY WEST, WEST VIRGINIA (vs. NYU) (12-13) .923

Highest free throw percentage in the tournament (minimum 15 attempts)
1 ROGER KAISER, GEORGIA TECH (16-17) .941
2 DARRALL IMHOFF, CALIFORNIA (22-24) .917
3 CHARLIE OSBORNE, WESTERN KY. (19-21) .905
4 RUSSI, SANTA CLARA (13-15) .867
5 JERRY WEST, WEST VIRGINIA (35-42) .833

REBOUNDS

Most rebounds in a single game
1 HOWARD JOLLIFF, OHIO (vs. GEORGIA TECH) 26
2 JERRY LUCAS, OHIO STATE (vs. WESTERN KY.) 25
3 HOWARD JOLLIFF, OHIO (vs. WESTERN KY.) 23
4 TOM SANDERS, NYU (vs. OHIO STATE) 22
5 AL FILARDI, NYU (vs. WEST VIRGINIA) 21

Most total rebounds in the tournament
1 TOM SANDERS, NYU 83
2 HOWARD JOLLIFF, OHIO 65
3 JERRY LUCAS, OHIO STATE 64
4 PAUL HOGUE, CINCINNATI 55
5 2 tied for fifth place.

Most rebounds per game (minimum 2 games)
1 HOWARD JOLLIFF, OHIO (65-3) 21.67
2 TOM SANDERS, NYU (83-5) 16.60
3 JERRY LUCAS, OHIO STATE (64-4) 16.00
4 JERRY WEST, WEST VIRGINIA (47-3) 15.67
5 PAUL HOGUE, CINCINNATI (55-4) 13.75

✪ TEAM RECORDS ✪

SCORING

Most points in a single game
1 WESTERN KY. (vs. MIAMI [FLA.])   107
2 WEST VIRGINIA (vs. ST. JOSEPH'S)   106
3 ST. JOSEPH'S (vs. WEST VIRGINIA)   100

Most total points in the tournament
1 NYU   359
2 CINCINNATI   345
3 CALIFORNIA   342

Highest scoring average (minimum 2 games)
1 WESTERN KY. (283-3)   94.33
2 WEST VIRGINIA (281-3)   93.67
3 CINCINNATI (345-4)   86.25

FIELD GOALS

Most field goals in a single game
1 CINCINNATI (vs. DEPAUL)   43
2 OHIO STATE (vs. WESTERN KY.)   42
3 2 tied for third place.

Most total field goals in the tournament
1 CINCINNATI   143
2 OHIO STATE   140
3 NYU   137

Most field goals attempted in a single game
1 ST. JOSEPH'S (vs. WEST VIRGINIA)   103
2 OHIO (vs. WESTERN KY.)   92
3 OHIO STATE (vs. WESTERN KY.)   86

Highest field goal percentage in a single game
1 OHIO STATE (vs. CALIFORNIA) (31-46)   .674
2 OHIO STATE (vs. GEORGIA TECH) (36-65) .554
3 CINCINNATI (vs. DEPAUL) (43-78)   .551

FREE THROWS

Most free throws in a single game
1 UTAH (vs. SANTA CLARA)   41
2 WEST VIRGINIA (vs. ST. JOSEPH'S)   34
3 WESTERN KY. (vs. OHIO)   31

Most total free throws in the tournament
1 CALIFORNIA   92
2 UTAH   85
2 NYU   85

Most free throws attempted in a single game
1 UTAH (vs. SANTA CLARA)   48
2 WEST VIRGINIA (vs. ST. JOSEPH'S)   46
3 2 tied for third place.

Most total free throws attempted in the tournament
1 CALIFORNIA   128
2 NYU   125
3 UTAH   116

Highest free throw percentage in a single game
1 DEPAUL (vs. AIR FORCE) (21-23)   .913
2 ST. JOSEPH'S (vs. WEST VIRGINIA) (18-20) .900
3 OHIO STATE (vs. NYU) (14-16)   .875

Highest free throw percentage in the tournament (minimum 2 games)
1 ST. JOSEPH'S (30-38)   .790
2 DEPAUL (47-61)   .771
3 WESTERN KY. (77-102)   .755

Fewest free throws in a single game
1 PRINCETON (vs. DUKE)   6
2 OHIO (vs. GEORGIA TECH)   10
3 4 tied for third place.

Lowest free throw percentage in a single game
1 OHIO (vs. WESTERN KY.) (11-25)   .440
2 PRINCETON (vs. DUKE) (6-13)   .462
3 OHIO (vs. GEORGIA TECH) (10-21)   .476

Lowest free throw percentage in the tournament (minimum 2 games)
1 OHIO (37-68)   .544
2 OREGON (56-92)   .609
3 DUKE (45-72)   .625

REBOUNDS

Most rebounds in a single game
1 WESTERN KY. (vs. MIAMI [FLA.])   63
2 WEST VIRGINIA (vs. ST. JOSEPH'S)   56
2 UTAH (vs. USC)   56

1961

| FIRST ROUND | REGIONAL SEMIFINAL | REGIONAL FINAL | **FINAL FOUR** | REGIONAL FINAL | REGIONAL SEMIFINAL | FIRST ROUND |

EAST

(bye) — *St. Joseph's 72

*St. Joseph's 96

Princeton 84
Princeton 67
Geo. Wash. 67

*St. Joseph's 69

St. Bonaventure 86
St. Bonaventure 73
Rhode Island 76

Wake Forest 86

Wake Forest 97
Wake Forest 78
St. John's 74

MIDWEST

Kansas St. 75 — (bye)

Kansas St. 64

Houston 77
Houston 64
Marquette 61

Cincinnati 82

Cincinnati 78 — (bye)

Cincinnati 69

Texas Tech 55 — (bye)

Cincinnati 70 (ot)
Ohio St. 65

MIDEAST

(bye) — Ohio St. 56

Ohio St. 87

Louisville 76
Louisville 55
Ohio 70

Ohio St. 95

Morehead St. 71
Morehead St. 64
Xavier (Ohio) 66

Kentucky 74

(bye) — Kentucky 71

WEST

Arizona St. 72
Arizona St. 86
Seattle 70

Arizona St. 80

USC 81
USC 71
Oregon 79

Utah 67

Utah 91 — (bye)

Utah 88

Loyola Mymt. 75 — (bye)

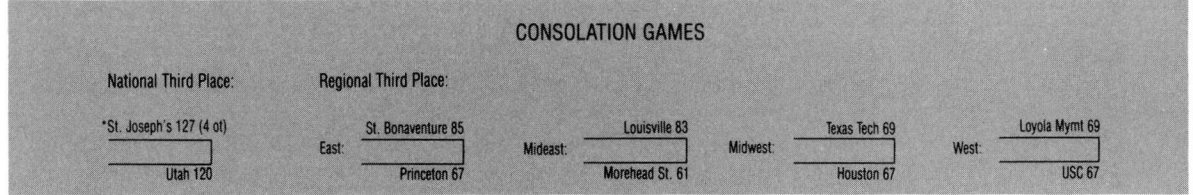

CONSOLATION GAMES

National Third Place:

*St. Joseph's 127 (4 ot)
Utah 120

Regional Third Place:

East:
St. Bonaventure 85
Princeton 67

Mideast:
Louisville 83
Morehead St. 61

Midwest:
Texas Tech 69
Houston 67

West:
Loyola Mymt 69
USC 67

*St. Joseph's participation in 1961 tournament vacated.

Ohio State was awesome. With stars Jerry Lucas, Larry Siegfried, and John Havlicek one year older and more experienced, the Buckeyes—who had lost only one starter from the team that had swept the NCAA's the previous year—dominated the competition throughout the regular season. Entering the 1961 tournament undefeated, they were the odds-on favorites to become the first team to repeat as NCAA champs since Bill Russell led San Francisco to the title in 1955 and 1956. They were also expected to become the first unbeaten titlists since North Carolina in 1957.

Meanwhile, a hundred miles from the Buckeyes' homecourt in Columbus, the University of Cincinnati was in a rebuilding year. The great Oscar Robertson, who had carried the Bearcats to third place finishes in both the 1959 and 1960 tourneys, had gone on to star for the Cincinnati Royals of the NBA, and two of the other three leading scorers from the 1960 team were also gone. To make matters even more uncertain, Coach George Smith, whose fast-break style had helped make the Bearcats one of the top-scoring teams in the nation, had moved upstairs to become athletic director and had appointed his assistant, Ed Jucker, as head coach.

Jucker looked at his squad and saw a rugged, hard-working bunch of role players who had the potential to be strong off the boards and hard-nosed on defense. But they had no standout star like Robertson; if they were to have a chance at a successful season they'd have to work together. Jucker immediately instituted a new style of play, featuring a tight, switching man-to-man defense, a ball-control, post-up offense, and aggressiveness under the boards. After losing three of their first eight games, the Bearcats jelled; exceeding everybody's expectations, they came into the tournament with 18 straight wins.

Eventually Ohio State and Cincinnati would meet in Kansas City to decide the national championship. But first, each of the Ohio teams had to win three times against out-of-state competition.

In its first tournament game, Ohio State had more trouble than anyone could have imagined when the unheralded Louisville Cardinals surrounded Jerry Lucas with three men and dared the Buckeyes to hit from the outside. The strategy worked almost to perfection as Lucas, who committed nine turnovers, was stopped cold. "I was guarded so tightly I felt like I was in jail," he said later. Meanwhile, the rest of the Buckeyes were unable to pick up the slack. Only Havlicek with 17 points and Siegfried with 14 made it to double figures. Starting forward Richie Hoyt scored only two, but his replacement, hard-nosed Bob Knight (the one and only), hit four of eight from the floor for eight points. Still, with less than three minutes left, Ohio State was trailing 54-49. But a Havlicek jumper and a steal by Siegfried that led to a three-point play tied

the score. After Havlicek was called for steps, he came back to force a turnover by Louisville star John Turner, and hit a 20-footer with only six seconds left. Turner then drove and was fouled with one second on the clock. The Cardinals' high scorer hit the front end of the one-and-one, but the second bounced off the rim, putting Ohio State into the regional final.

Having escaped with their lives in the opener, the Buckeyes took no chances against Kentucky, which for the second year in a row was in the tournament because of SEC champion Mississippi State's refusal to play against an integrated team. With 33 points and 30 rebounds (one more than the entire Kentucky squad), Lucas paid Kentucky back for his off night against Louisville. Moving on to Kansas City for the semis, the Ohio State starting five hit over 70 percent of their shots to crush St. Joseph's, the surprise winners of the Eastern regional.

On their way to the showdown with Ohio State, Cincinnati had a relatively easy time; they were tested only by Kansas State in the Midwest regional final. In the semis, they played their usual game, controlling the boards and closing down Utah's high-powered offense.

On March 25th, the two Ohio teams stood ready to fight it out for the national championship. First, however, a memorable preliminary was played to determine Third Place. It was a wide open, thrill-a-minute consolation game that featured four overtimes, 247 points, a wrong-way basket scored for Utah by St. Joseph's guard Bill Hoy off the first OT's opening tap, and 42 points by the Hawks' Captain Jack Egan.

Finally, the stage was set for the main event. Despite Cincinnati's 21 victories in a row, unbeaten Ohio State was the overwhelming favorite to take home the title and bragging rights to the state of Ohio. From the beginning, though, it was clear that the Bearcats were in the contest to stay. It was a bruising, physical match, with both teams playing near-flawless ball. Ohio State committed only eight turnovers all game, Cincinnati a remarkably low three. Bearcat center Paul Hogue spent all night keeping Lucas away from the boards, and Lucas responded by hitting his shots from the outside. Cincinnati outrebounded the fearsome Buckeyes, but Ohio State outshot the Bearcats. With 1:41 left to play, Ohio State had the ball, trying to work it around for a good shot against a tenacious Bearcat defense. Buckeye Bob Knight found an opening; he drove in for a lay-up that tied the game. Less than a minute remained when Cincinnati got possession. They took the ball inside, where Tom Thacker put up a shot with five seconds left. It fell short, and Lucas grabbed the rebound. Time out, Ohio State.

When play resumed, the Buckeyes took the ball out from underneath their own basket, 80 feet from the winning hoop. A long pass downcourt took one second, and brought Ohio State within striking distance. Coach Fred Taylor stopped the clock again. After the huddle, Havlicek took the ball out; he lofted a pass toward the bucket, Lucas went up for an alley-oop, and Cincinnati batted the ball away. Time ran out with the score tied at 61. After twelve ties and twelve lead changes, the title contest was going into overtime.

Soon after the extra period began, Hogue was fouled by Lucas. The big Bearcat center had hit only 7 of 19 from the charity stripe since the tournament began, but this time he hit 2. Ohio State never got even again. The Bearcats of Cincinnati—without Oscar Robertson—won the national championship.

Less than a month after the 1961 tournament, three of St. Joseph's key players—Captain Jack Egan, center Vince Kempton, and forward Frank Majewski—were among those implicated in a game-fixing scandal that finally became as widespread and damaging to college basketball as the 1951 scandal. The gamblers who had bought the players' services knew who they were recruiting: Egan was the father of two young children and his wife had suffered a miscarriage just before the season began; Majewski's father, a Jersey City printer, had died during his sophomore year, the next year his mother had a heart attack which left Frank as the family's sole support, and a hernia had limited his earning power the summer before his senior season; Kempton also needed money desperately. The three, all seniors, were expelled from school and lost their chances for degrees. Egan and Kempton, both drafted by the NBA, forfeited the opportunity to play pro ball. St. Joseph's had to return their third-place trophy.

FIRST ROUND EAST

Princeton (84)   Coach: Jake McCandless

	Min.	Total FG / FGA	Pct.	FT / FTA	Pct.	Reb. O / T	A	TO	PF	S	Blk	TP	PPM
WHITEHOUSE, J.	-	3/ 9	.333	0/ 4	.000	-/ 8	-	-	5	-	-	6	-
KAEMMERLEN, A.	-	6/11	.545	4/ 7	.571	-/10	-	-	2	-	-	16	-
CAMPBELL, P.	-	11/18	.611	5/ 7	.714	-/ 4	-	-	3	-	-	27	-
HYLAND, A.	-	6/ 7	.857	4/ 5	.800	-/ 9	-	-	3	-	-	16	-
BURTON, M.	-	2/ 6	.333	1/ 3	.333	-/ 5	-	-	1	-	-	5	-
ADAMS, T.	-	1/ 1	1.000	3/ 3	1.000	-/ 2	-	-	1	-	-	5	-
HYLAND, D.	-	0/ 0	.000	0/ 0	.000	-/ 0	-	-	0	-	-	0	-
PASALIS, J.	-	0/ 0	.000	0/ 0	.000	-/ 0	-	-	0	-	-	0	-
BRENNAN, B.	-	0/ 1	.000	1/ 2	.500	-/ 0	-	-	0	-	-	1	-
HAARLOW, A.	-	0/ 0	.000	0/ 0	.000	-/ 0	-	-	0	-	-	0	-
SWAN, D.	-	0/ 0	.000	1/ 2	.500	-/ 0	-	-	0	-	-	1	-
HIGGINS, A.	-	3/ 6	.500	1/ 5	.200	-/ 5	-	-	5	-	-	7	-
Totals	200	32/59	.542	20/38	.526	-/43	-	20	-	-	84	.420

George Washington (67)   Coach: Bill Reinhart

	Min.	Total FG / FGA	Pct.	FT / FTA	Pct.	Reb. O / T	A	TO	PF	S	Blk	TP	PPM
MARKOWITZ, D.	-	8/16	.500	9/14	.643	-/11	-	-	4	-	-	25	-
ARDELL	-	0/ 3	.000	1/ 3	.333	-/ 3	-	-	4	-	-	1	-
INGRAM, B.	-	6/16	.375	0/ 0	.000	-/ 4	-	-	2	-	-	12	-
FELDMAN	-	5/22	.227	1/ 5	.200	-/ 5	-	-	3	-	-	11	-
NORTON	-	3/ 7	.429	4/ 4	1.000	-/ 1	-	-	4	-	-	10	-
SCHWEICKHARDT	-	1/ 3	.333	2/ 2	1.000	-/ 6	-	-	2	-	-	4	-
HERRON	-	1/ 2	.500	0/ 0	.000	-/ 1	-	-	0	-	-	2	-
LOCKMAN	-	0/ 1	.000	2/ 2	1.000	-/ 4	-	-	4	-	-	2	-
WICLINE	-	0/ 0	.000	0/ 0	.000	-/ 0	-	-	0	-	-	0	-
Totals	200	24/70	.343	19/30	.633	-/35	-	23	-	-	67	.335

Disqualified: Princeton—Whitehouse, Higgins.

	1st Half	2nd Half	Final
Princeton	41	43	84
Geo. Wash.	34	33	67

St. Bonaventure (86)   Coach: Eddie Donovan

	Min.	Total FG / FGA	Pct.	FT / FTA	Pct.	Reb. O / T	A	TO	PF	S	Blk	TP	PPM
CRAWFORD, F.	-	16/ -		2/ 3	.667	-/ -	-	-	4	-	-	34	-
STITH, T.	-	11/ -		7/ 9	.778	-/ -	-	-	0	-	-	29	-
MCCULLY, B.	-	2/ -		2/ 5	.400	-/ -	-	-	4	-	-	6	-
FITZMAURICE, T.	-	0/ -		0/ 0	.000	-/ -	-	-	0	-	-	0	-
HERBERT, B.	-	0/ -		0/ 0	.000	-/ -	-	-	2	-	-	0	-
MARTIN, W.	-	8/ -		1/ 1	1.000	-/ -	-	-	4	-	-	17	-
JIRELE, O.	-	0/ -		0/ 0	.000	-/ -	-	-	0	-	-	0	-
HANNON, T.	-	0/ -		0/ 0	.000	-/ -	-	-	1	-	-	0	-
Totals	200	37/ -		12/18	.667	-/ -	-	-	15	-	-	86	.430

Rhode Island (76)   Coach: Ernie Calverley

	Min.	Total FG / FGA	Pct.	FT / FTA	Pct.	Reb. O / T	A	TO	PF	S	Blk	TP	PPM
LEE, C.	-	8/ -		5/ 5	1.000	-/ -	-	-	1	-	-	21	-
RICERETO	-	2/ -		2/ 3	.667	-/ -	-	-	3	-	-	6	-
WEISS	-	1/ -		1/ 2	.500	-/ -	-	-	1	-	-	3	-
SMITH	-	0/ -		0/ 0	.000	-/ -	-	-	0	-	-	0	-
KOENIG	-	3/ -		3/ 3	1.000	-/ -	-	-	5	-	-	9	-
LOGAN	-	1/ -		0/ 0	.000	-/ -	-	-	0	-	-	2	-
MULTER, B.	-	9/ -		5/ 5	1.000	-/ -	-	-	3	-	-	23	-
SCHACHTER, S.	-	6/ -		0/ 2	.000	-/ -	-	-	0	-	-	12	-
STENHOUSE	-	0/ -		0/ 0	.000	-/ -	-	-	0	-	-	0	-
Totals	200	30/ -		16/20	.800	-/ -	-	-	13	-	-	76	.380

Disqualified: Rhode Island—Koenig.

	1st Half	2nd Half	Final
St. Bonaventure	38	48	86
Rhode Island	43	33	76

Wake Forest (97)   Coach: Bones McKinney

	Min.	Total FG / FGA	Pct.	FT / FTA	Pct.	Reb. O / T	A	TO	PF	S	Blk	TP	PPM
HULL, B.	-	3/ 4	.750	1/ 3	.333	-/ 6	1	-	5	-	-	7	-
STEELE	-	0/ 1	.000	0/ 1	.000	-/ 1	0	-	1	-	-	0	-
CHAPPELL, L.	-	9/21	.429	13/17	.765	-/20	3	-	4	-	-	31	-
HART, A.	-	12/17	.706	4/ 6	.667	-/12	9	-	2	-	-	28	-
PACKER, B.	-	1/10	.100	3/ 4	.750	-/ 3	5	-	2	-	-	5	-
WIEDEMAN, D.	-	8/18	.444	6/ 8	.750	-/ 7	1	-	3	-	-	22	-
WOOLLARD, B.	-	2/ 2	1.000	0/ 0	.000	-/ 1	0	-	1	-	-	4	-
FENNELL, W.	-	0/ 0	.000	0/ 0	.000	-/ 0	0	-	1	-	-	0	-
KOEHLER, A.	-	0/ 0	.000	0/ 1	.000	-/ 1	0	-	2	-	-	0	-
CALDWELL, P.	-	0/ 1	.000	0/ 0	.000	-/ 0	0	-	0	-	-	0	-
MCCOY, T.	-	0/ 0	.000	0/ 0	.000	-/ 0	0	-	0	-	-	0	-
ZAWACKI, T.	-	0/ 0	.000	0/ 0	.000	-/ 0	0	-	0	-	-	0	-
Totals	200	35/74	.473	27/40	.675	-/51	19	-	21	-	-	97	.485

St. John's (74)   Coach: Joel Lapchick

	Min.	Total FG / FGA	Pct.	FT / FTA	Pct.	Reb. O / T	A	TO	PF	S	Blk	TP	PPM
HALL, W.	-	7/22	.318	2/ 3	.667	-/10	0	-	5	-	-	16	-
JACKSON, T.	-	9/15	.600	8/ 8	1.000	-/ 6	1	-	1	-	-	26	-
ELLIS, L.	-	5/14	.357	2/ 4	.500	-/16	0	-	4	-	-	12	-
LOUGHERY, K.	-	4/11	.364	4/ 6	.667	-/ 4	6	-	5	-	-	12	-
KOVAC	-	2/ 6	.333	3/ 4	.750	-/ 2	2	-	3	-	-	7	-
MAROZAS	-	0/ 0	.000	0/ 1	.000	-/ 2	0	-	2	-	-	0	-
BURKS	-	0/ 7	.000	1/ 3	.333	-/ 2	1	-	4	-	-	1	-
O'SULLIVAN	-	0/ 0	.000	0/ 0	.000	-/ 1	0	-	1	-	-	0	-
EDELMAN	-	0/ 0	.000	0/ 0	.000	-/ 0	0	-	0	-	-	0	-
LARRANAGA	-	0/ 0	.000	0/ 0	.000	-/ 0	0	-	0	-	-	0	-
Totals	200	27/75	.360	20/29	.690	-/43	10	-	25	-	-	74	.370

Team Rebounds: Wake Forest 10; St. John's 5. Disqualified: Wake Forest— Hull; St John's—Hall, Loughery.

	1st Half	2nd Half	Final
Wake Forest	36	61	97
St. John's	46	28	74

FIRST ROUND MIDEAST

Louisville (76)   Coach: Peck Hickman

	Min.	Total FG / FGA	Pct.	FT / FTA	Pct.	Reb. O / T	A	TO	PF	S	Blk	TP	PPM
TURNER, J.	-	7/20	.350	10/11	.909	-/ 8	-	3	0	-	-	24	-
SAWYER, F.	-	1/ 6	.167	1/ 1	1.000	-/ 7	-	2	1	-	-	3	-
OLSEN, B.	-	8/15	.533	2/ 5	.400	-/10	-	1	3	-	-	18	-
STACEY, H.	-	3/ 7	.429	5/ 8	.625	-/ 3	-	2	4	-	-	11	-
FRAZIER, J.	-	3/ 4	.750	0/ 0	.000	-/ 4	-	0	3	-	-	6	-
RUBENSTEIN, R.	-	4/ 7	.571	4/ 6	.667	-/ 4	-	3	3	-	-	12	-
LEATHERS, B.	-	0/ 1	.000	0/ 0	.000	-/ 1	-	0	0	-	-	0	-
ARMSTRONG, J.	-	0/ 1	.000	0/ 0	.000	-/ 0	-	0	2	-	-	0	-
RAY, J.	-	1/ 1	1.000	0/ 0	.000	-/ 1	-	0	0	-	-	2	-
Totals	200	27/62	.435	22/31	.710	-/38	-	11	16	-	-	76	.380

Ohio (70)   Coach: James Snyder

	Min.	Total FG / FGA	Pct.	FT / FTA	Pct.	Reb. O / T	A	TO	PF	S	Blk	TP	PPM
ADAMS	-	7/13	.538	1/ 2	.500	-/10	-	2	4	-	-	15	-
KRUGER, L.	-	11/20	.550	2/ 4	.500	-/ 8	-	1	4	-	-	24	-
BUNTON	-	3/ 7	.429	1/ 1	1.000	-/ 5	-	4	5	-	-	7	-
KATZ	-	2/ 8	.250	0/ 0	.000	-/ 4	-	0	2	-	-	4	-
WHALEY	-	5/12	.417	10/13	.769	-/ 4	-	5	3	-	-	20	-
BOLEN	-	0/ 0	.000	0/ 1	.000	-/ 1	-	0	1	-	-	0	-
WILCOX	-	0/ 1	.000	0/ 1	.000	-/ 2	-	2	0	-	-	0	-
Totals	200	28/61	.459	14/22	.636	-/34	-	14	19	-	-	70	.350

Disqualified: Ohio—Bunton.

	1st Half	2nd Half	Final
Louisville	30	46	76
Ohio	30	40	70

Morehead State (71)   Coach: Robert Laughlin

	Min.	Total FG / FGA	Pct.	FT / FTA	Pct.	Reb. O / T	A	TO	PF	S	Blk	TP	PPM
GIBSON, J.	-	2/ 5	.400	1/ 3	.333	-/ 4	-	0	2	-	-	5	-
POKLEY, N.	-	3/ 7	.429	2/ 5	.400	-/11	-	5	2	-	-	8	-
NOE, E.	-	8/16	.500	5/ 7	.714	-/15	-	0	3	-	-	21	-
THOMPSON, H.	-	3/13	.231	10/12	.833	-/ 8	-	2	1	-	-	16	-
WILLIAMS, G.	-	9/23	.391	3/ 8	.375	-/ 6	-	2	2	-	-	21	-
COLE, A.	-	0/ 3	.000	0/ 0	.000	-/ 3	-	0	1	-	-	0	-
Totals	200	25/67	.373	21/35	.600	-/47	-	9	11	-	-	71	.355

Xavier (Ohio) (66)   Coach: Jim McCafferty

	Min.	Total FG / FGA	Pct.	FT / FTA	Pct.	Reb. O / T	A	TO	PF	S	Blk	TP	PPM
NICOLAI, R.	-	2/ 7	.286	1/ 3	.333	-/ 9	-	1	5	-	-	5	-
MCDERMOTT, L.	-	6/19	.316	3/ 6	.500	-/12	-	2	3	-	-	15	-
THOBE, J.	-	9/16	.563	1/ 3	.333	-/ 8	-	2	4	-	-	19	-
KIRVIN, B.	-	7/18	.389	0/ 2	.000	-/ 6	-	1	4	-	-	14	-
ENRIGHT, J.	-	5/13	.385	0/ 1	.000	-/ 2	-	3	3	-	-	10	-
TEPE, E.	-	1/ 2	.500	1/ 1	1.000	-/ 4	-	0	2	-	-	3	-
Totals	200	30/75	.400	6/16	.375	-/41	-	9	21	-	-	66	.330

Team Rebounds: Morehead State 10; Xavier 9. Disqualified: Xavier—Nicolai.

	1st Half	2nd Half	Final
Morehead State	33	38	71
Xavier (Ohio)	33	33	66

FIRST ROUND MIDWEST

Houston (77)   Coach: Guy Lewis

	Min.	Total FG / FGA	Pct.	FT / FTA	Pct.	Reb. O / T	A	TO	PF	S	Blk	TP	PPM
THOMPSON, J.	-	0/ 4	.000	3/ 4	.750	-/ 2	-	-	1	-	-	3	-
LEMMON, J.	-	1/ 3	.333	0/ 0	.000	-/ 0	-	-	1	-	-	2	-
LUCKENBILL, T.	-	8/15	.533	7/ 8	.875	-/16	-	-	5	-	-	23	-
THOMSON, T.	-	6/10	.600	1/ 3	.333	-/ 7	-	-	1	-	-	13	-
HARGER, L.	-	0/ 0	.000	0/ 0	.000	-/ 1	-	-	1	-	-	0	-
PHILLIPS, G.	-	12/19	.632	3/ 5	.600	-/ 6	-	-	4	-	-	27	-
THURMAN, R.	-	0/ 1	.000	0/ 0	.000	-/ 2	-	-	1	-	-	0	-
TUFFLI, N.	-	0/ 0	.000	1/ 2	.500	-/ 3	-	-	0	-	-	1	-
MOLCHANY, R.	-	4/ 6	.667	0/ 0	.000	-/ 3	-	-	2	-	-	8	-
BISHOP, D.	-	0/ 0	.000	0/ 0	.000	-/ 1	-	-	0	-	-	0	-
Totals	200	31/58	.534	15/22	.682	-/41	-	-	16	-	-	77	.385

Marquette (61)   Coach: Eddie Hickey

	Min.	Total FG / FGA	Pct.	FT / FTA	Pct.	Reb. O / T	A	TO	PF	S	Blk	TP	PPM
KOJIS, D.	-	5/13	.385	3/ 5	.600	-/10	-	-	3	-	-	13	-
GLASER, R.	-	1/12	.083	6/ 8	.750	-/ 5	-	-	1	-	-	8	-
ERICKSON, D.	-	3/ 8	.375	3/ 4	.750	-/ 7	-	-	3	-	-	9	-
NIXON, D.	-	4/12	.333	0/ 0	.000	-/ 2	-	-	4	-	-	8	-
HORNAK, B.	-	5/10	.500	2/ 4	.500	-/ 4	-	-	4	-	-	12	-
JEFFERSON, L.	-	0/ 3	.000	1/ 2	.500	-/ 3	-	-	1	-	-	1	-
SCANLON, J.	-	3/ 6	.500	0/ 0	.000	-/ 2	-	-	1	-	-	6	-
CHMIELEWSKI, B.	-	2/ 3	.667	0/ 0	.000	-/ 0	-	-	0	-	-	4	-
KEIDEL	-	0/ 0	.000	0/ 0	.000	-/ 0	-	-	0	-	-	0	-
Totals	200	23/67	.343	15/23	.652	-/33	-	-	17	-	-	61	.305

Team Rebounds: Houston 4; Marquette 8. Disqualified: Houston—Luckenbill.

	1st Half	2nd Half	Final
Houston	42	35	77
Marquette	18	43	61

FIRST ROUND WEST

Arizona State (72)   Coach: Ned Wulk

	Min.	Total FG / FGA	Pct.	FT / FTA	Pct.	Reb. O / T	A	TO	PF	S	Blk	TP	PPM
CERKVENIK, T.	-	4/ 7	.571	7/ 9	.778	-/ 9	-	-	1	-	-	15	-
PAYNE, O.	-	8/27	.296	2/ 4	.500	-/ 9	-	-	4	-	-	18	-
HAHN, G.	-	5/10	.500	3/ 6	.500	-/12	-	-	2	-	-	13	-
ARMSTRONG, L.	-	6/21	.286	0/ 0	.000	-/ 7	-	-	5	-	-	12	-
DISARUFINO, R.	-	3/10	.300	1/ 2	.500	-/10	-	-	4	-	-	7	-
MCCONNELL, M.	-	3/ 5	.600	1/ 1	1.000	-/ 3	-	-	0	-	-	7	-
DERNOVICH, R.	-	0/ 1	.000	0/ 0	.000	-/ 3	-	-	1	-	-	0	-
Totals	200	29/81	.358	14/22	.636	-/53	-	-	17	-	-	72	.360

Seattle (70)   Coach: Vince Cazzetta

	Min.	Total FG / FGA	Pct.	FT / FTA	Pct.	Reb. O / T	A	TO	PF	S	Blk	TP	PPM
DUNSTON	-	5/ 8	.625	0/ 0	.000	-/ 6	-	-	4	-	-	10	-
MILLS	-	10/19	.526	2/ 6	.333	-/15	-	-	4	-	-	22	-
BRENNAN	-	1/ 4	.250	0/ 0	.000	-/ 6	-	-	3	-	-	2	-
MILES, E.	-	8/21	.381	8/ 9	.889	-/ 3	-	-	2	-	-	24	-
SHAULES, T.	-	2/ 4	.500	3/ 5	.600	-/ 2	-	-	3	-	-	7	-
STEPAN	-	1/ 2	.500	0/ 0	.000	-/ 0	-	-	0	-	-	2	-
BURTON	-	0/ 0	.000	0/ 0	.000	-/ 0	-	-	1	-	-	0	-
PRESTON, J.	-	1/ 2	.500	1/ 2	.500	-/ 4	-	-	0	-	-	3	-
STAUTZ	-	0/ 1	.000	0/ 0	.000	-/ 0	-	-	0	-	-	0	-
Totals	200	28/61	.459	14/22	.636	-/36	-	-	17	-	-	70	.350

Team Rebounds: Arizona St. 4; Seattle 3. Disqualified: Arizona St.—Armstrong.

	1st Half	2nd Half	Final
Arizona St.	28	44	72
Seattle	39	31	70

USC (81)   Coach: Forrest Twogood

	Min.	Total FG / FGA	Pct.	FT / FTA	Pct.	Reb. O / T	A	TO	PF	S	Blk	TP	PPM
STANLEY, K.	-	4/ 9	.444	9/12	.750	-/ 8	-	-	5	-	-	17	-
ASHBY, V.	-	1/ 3	.333	0/ 2	.000	-/ 4	-	-	3	-	-	2	-
RUDOMETKIN, J.	-	9/18	.500	6/ 6	1.000	-/11	-	-	5	-	-	24	-
APPEL, C.	-	3/10	.300	2/ 7	.286	-/ 8	-	-	5	-	-	8	-
EDWARDS, N.	-	5/ 7	.714	0/ 0	.000	-/ 5	-	-	1	-	-	10	-
SLONIGER, W.	-	0/ 0	.000	2/ 2	1.000	-/ 0	-	-	0	-	-	2	-
MARTIN, G.	-	5/10	.500	4/ 5	.800	-/ 5	-	-	3	-	-	14	-
HILLMAN, P.	-	2/ 2	1.000	0/ 1	.000	-/ 0	-	-	1	-	-	4	-
Totals	200	29/59	.492	23/35	.657	-/41	-	-	23	-	-	81	.405

Oregon (79)   Coach: Steve Belko

	Min.	Total FG / FGA	Pct.	FT / FTA	Pct.	Reb. O / T	A	TO	PF	S	Blk	TP	PPM
SIMMONS, B.	-	6/13	.462	4/ 5	.800	-/ 7	-	-	3	-	-	16	-
WARREN, C.	-	8/14	.571	5/ 7	.714	-/ 7	-	-	5	-	-	21	-
MOORE, G.	-	5/11	.455	2/ 7	.286	-/10	-	-	5	-	-	12	-
HAYES, L.	-	1/ 6	.167	1/ 1	1.000	-/ 4	-	-	1	-	-	3	-
STRICKLAND, D.	-	7/12	.583	5/ 9	.556	-/ 7	-	-	3	-	-	19	-
MACK, J.	-	0/ 1	.000	0/ 0	.000	-/ 1	-	-	3	-	-	0	-
KIMPTON, B.	-	3/ 6	.500	2/ 2	1.000	-/ 2	-	-	3	-	-	8	-
JONES, R.	-	0/ 2	.000	0/ 1	.000	-/ 1	-	-	1	-	-	0	-
Totals	200	30/65	.462	19/32	.594	-/39	-	-	24	-	-	79	.395

Team Rebounds: USC 6; Oregon 6. Disqualified: USC—Stanley, Rudometkin, Appel; Oregon—Warren, Moore.

	1st Half	2nd Half	Final
USC	27	54	81
Oregon	36	43	79

REGIONAL SEMIFINAL EAST

St. Joseph's (72)   Coach: Jack Ramsay

	Min.	Total FG / FGA	Pct.	FT / FTA	Pct.	Reb. O / T	A	TO	PF	S	Blk	TP	PPM
LYNAM, J.	-	4/ 9	.444	3/ 4	.750	-/ 7	1	-	3	-	-	11	-
HOY, W.	-	2/ 5	.400	6/ 8	.750	-/ 4	0	-	3	-	-	10	-
MAJEWSKI, P.	-	0/10	.000	2/ 2	1.000	-/ 8	1	-	5	-	-	2	-
EGAN, J.	-	7/21	.333	5/ 7	.714	-/13	2	-	0	-	-	19	-
KEMPTON, V.	-	9/15	.600	3/ 4	.750	-/10	1	-	3	-	-	21	-
WYNNE, T.	-	1/10	.100	1/ 2	.500	-/10	1	-	5	-	-	3	-
BOOTH, H.	-	0/ 1	.000	2/ 3	.667	-/ 1	0	-	0	-	-	2	-
GORMLEY, R.	-	2/ 3	.667	0/ 0	.000	-/ 3	0	-	2	-	-	4	-
Totals	200	25/74	.338	22/30	.733	-/56	6	-	21	-	-	72	.360

Princeton (67)   Coach: Jake McCandless

	Min.	Total FG / FGA	Pct.	FT / FTA	Pct.	Reb. O / T	A	TO	PF	S	Blk	TP	PPM
CAMPBELL, P.	-	6/15	.400	12/13	.923	-/ 2	0	-	5	-	-	24	-
HYLAND, A.	-	3/ 9	.333	1/ 1	1.000	-/ 7	0	-	5	-	-	7	-
HIGGINS, A.	-	0/ 2	.000	0/ 0	.000	-/ 0	0	-	3	-	-	0	-
KAEMMERLEN, A.	-	7/11	.636	4/ 5	.800	-/ 9	0	-	3	-	-	18	-
WHITEHOUSE, J.	-	3/10	.300	2/ 7	.286	-/13	1	-	0	-	-	8	-
ADAMS, T.	-	0/ 6	.000	1/ 3	.333	-/ 4	0	-	2	-	-	1	-
HYLAND, D.	-	2/ 4	.500	1/ 2	.500	-/ 1	0	-	1	-	-	5	-
BURTON, N.	-	2/ 4	.500	0/ 0	.000	-/ 2	0	-	2	-	-	4	-
HAARLOW, A.	-	0/ 0	.000	0/ 0	.000	-/ 0	0	-	0	-	-	0	-
Totals	200	23/61	.377	21/31	.677	-/38	1	-	21	-	-	67	.335

Team Rebounds: St. Joseph's 5; Princeton 6. Disqualified: St. Joseph's—Majewski, Wynne; Princeton—Campbell, Hyland, A.

	1st Half	2nd Half	Final
St. Joseph's	29	43	72
Princeton	28	39	67

St. Bonaventure (73)   Coach: Eddie Donovan

	Min.	Total FG / FGA	Pct.	FT / FTA	Pct.	Reb. O / T	A	TO	PF	S	Blk	TP	PPM
JIRELE, O.	37	2/ 4	.500	1/ 1	1.000	-/ 3	2	-	4	-	-	5	.135
MCCULLY, B.	31	1/ 7	.143	2/ 6	.333	-/ 8	1	-	2	-	-	4	.129
MARTIN, W.	26	3/10	.300	1/ 1	1.000	-/ 6	1	-	5	-	-	7	.269
STITH, T.	40	8/21	.381	13/16	.813	-/12	5	-	2	-	-	29	.725
CRAWFORD, F.	40	9/20	.450	1/ 6	.167	-/10	1	-	4	-	-	19	.475
FITZMAURICE, T.	9	1/ 2	.500	3/ 4	.750	-/ 3	0	-	5	-	-	5	.556
HANNON, T.	17	2/ 3	.667	0/ 0	.000	-/ 1	2	-	1	-	-	4	.235
Totals	200	26/67	.388	21/34	.618	-/43	12	-	23	-	-	73	.365

Wake Forest (78)   Coach: Bones McKinney

	Min.	Total FG / FGA	Pct.	FT / FTA	Pct.	Reb. O / T	A	TO	PF	S	Blk	TP	PPM
HULL, B.	21	3/ 5	.600	0/ 0	.000	-/ 6	0	-	4	-	-	6	.286
CHAPPELL, L.	40	7/20	.350	10/12	.833	-/15	1	-	4	-	-	24	.600
HART, A.	33	5/11	.455	0/ 1	.000	-/ 2	0	-	2	-	-	10	.303
PACKER, B.	25	3/ 8	.375	1/ 1	1.000	-/ 0	5	-	3	-	-	7	.280
WIEDEMAN, D.	39	4/14	.286	6/ 9	.667	-/ 7	1	-	4	-	-	14	.359
WOOLLARD, B.	19	2/ 4	.500	6/ 7	.857	-/11	3	-	4	-	-	10	.526
KOEHLER, A.	3	1/ 1	1.000	0/ 0	.000	-/ 0	1	-	2	-	-	2	.667
MCCOY, T.	20	1/ 4	.250	3/ 4	.750	-/ 4	1	-	0	-	-	5	.250
Totals	200	26/67	.388	26/34	.765	-/45	12	-	23	-	-	78	.390

Team Rebounds: Wake Forest 11; St. Bonaventure 4. Disqualified: St. Bonaventure—Martin, Fitzmaurice.

	1st Half	2nd Half	Final
St. Bonaventure	37	36	73
Wake Forest	36	42	78

REGIONAL SEMIFINAL MIDEAST

Ohio State (56)   Coach: Fred Taylor

	Min.	Total FG / FGA	Pct.	FT / FTA	Pct.	Reb. O / T	A	TO	PF	S	Blk	TP	PPM
HAVILCEK, J.	-	8/13	.615	1/ 2	.500	-/ 8	-	-	4	-	-	17	-
HOYT, R.	-	1/ 4	.250	0/ 0	.000	-/ 0	-	-	1	-	-	2	-
LUCAS, J.	-	2/ 7	.286	5/ 7	.714	-/18	-	-	1	-	-	9	-
SIEGFRIED, L.	-	6/12	.500	2/ 2	1.000	-/ 5	-	-	1	-	-	14	-
NOWELL, M.	-	1/ 8	.125	0/ 1	.000	-/ 5	-	-	4	-	-	2	-
KNIGHT, B.	-	4/ 8	.500	0/ 0	.000	-/ 3	-	-	3	-	-	8	-
GEARHART, G.	-	2/ 4	.500	0/ 0	.000	-/ 2	-	-	3	-	-	4	-
Totals	200	24/56	.429	8/12	.667	-/41	-	-	17	-	-	56	.280

Louisville (55)   Coach: Peck Hickman

	Min.	Total FG / FGA	Pct.	FT / FTA	Pct.	Reb. O / T	A	TO	PF	S	Blk	TP	PPM
TURNER, J.	-	9/20	.450	7/ 8	.875	-/15	-	-	1	-	-	25	-
SAWYER, F.	-	1/ 6	.167	2/ 5	.400	-/ 7	-	-	4	-	-	4	-
OLSEN, B.	-	2/12	.167	2/ 3	.667	-/ 9	-	-	2	-	-	6	-
STACEY, H.	-	6/15	.400	3/ 6	.500	-/ 1	-	-	2	-	-	15	-
FRAZIER, J.	-	1/ 7	.143	1/ 3	.333	-/ 3	-	-	0	-	-	3	-
RUBENSTEIN, R.	-	1/ 3	.333	0/ 0	.000	-/ 2	-	-	1	-	-	2	-
Totals	200	20/63	.317	15/25	.600	-/37	-	-	10	-	-	55	.275

Team Rebounds: Ohio State 1; Louisville 4. Disqualified: None.

	1st Half	2nd Half	Final
Ohio State	26	30	56
Louisville	25	30	55

Morehead State (64)   Coach: Robert Laughlin

	Min.	Total FG / FGA	Pct. ·	FT / FTA	Pct.	Reb. O / T	A	TO	PF	S	Blk	TP	PPM
GIBSON, J.	-	4/ 8	.500	6/ 7	.857	-/ 4	-	-	3	-	-	14	-
POKLEY, N.	-	2/ 2	1.000	1/ 3	.333	-/15	-	-	3	-	-	5	-
NOE, E.	-	4/10	.400	5/ 5	1.000	-/11	-	-	5	-	-	13	-
THOMPSON, H.	-	3/15	.200	4/ 5	.800	-/ 4	-	-	4	-	-	10	-
WILLIAMS, G.	-	7/22	.318	6/ 7	.857	-/ 4	-	-	4	-	-	20	-
COLE, A.	-	1/ 1	1.000	0/ 0	.000	-/ 1	-	-	2	-	-	2	-
Totals	200	21/58	.362	22/27	.815	-/39	-	-	21	-	-	64	.320

Kentucky (71)   Coach: Adolph Rupp

	Min.	Total FG / FGA	Pct.	FT / FTA	Pct.	Reb. O / T	A	TO	PF	S	Blk	TP	PPM
NEWMAN, R.	-	5/14	.357	4/10	.400	-/ 8	-	-	4	-	-	14	-
LICKERT, B.	-	11/23	.478	6/ 7	.857	-/16	-	-	1	-	-	28	-
JENNINGS, N.	-	2/ 8	.250	0/ 0	.000	-/ 1	-	-	5	-	-	4	-
PURSIFUL, L.	-	2/10	.200	2/ 2	1.000	-/ 7	-	-	3	-	-	6	-
PARSONS, D.	-	2/ 7	.286	3/ 3	1.000	-/ 4	-	-	5	-	-	7	-
BURCHETT, C.	-	2/ 7	.286	8/10	.800	-/ 7	-	-	1	-	-	12	-
FELDHAUS, A.	-	0/ 0	.000	0/ 0	.000	-/ 0	-	-	0	-	-	0	-
BAESLER, S.	-	0/ 0	.000	0/ 0	.000	-/ 0	-	-	1	-	-	0	-
Totals	200	24/69	.348	23/32	.719	-/43	-	-	20	-	-	71	.355

Team Rebounds: Kentucky 11; Morehead State 3. Disqualified: Kentucky—Jennings, Parsons; Morehead State—Noe.

	1st Half	2nd Half	Final
Morehead State	35	29	64
Kentucky	40	31	71

REGIONAL SEMIFINAL MIDWEST

Kansas State (75)   Coach: Tex Winter

	Min.	Total FG / FGA	Pct.	FT / FTA	Pct.	Reb. O / T	A	TO	PF	S	Blk	TP	PPM
COMLEY, L.	-	7/15	.467	4/ 5	.800	6/12	-	-	3	-	-	18	-
MCKENZIE, P.	-	3/ 7	.429	1/ 3	.333	2/ 4	-	-	1	-	-	7	-
PRICE, C.	-	2/ 6	.333	8/11	.727	4/12	-	-	3	-	-	12	-
EWY, R.	-	2/ 3	.667	0/ 0	.000	0/ 0	-	-	4	-	-	4	-
PEITHMAN, A.	-	1/ 8	.125	2/ 2	1.000	1/ 1	-	-	3	-	-	4	-
NELSON, D.	-	1/ 5	.200	4/ 4	1.000	4/ 4	-	-	1	-	-	6	-
BROWN, W.	-	1/ 2	.500	4/ 4	1.000	0/ 1	-	-	1	-	-	6	-
HEITMEYER, J.	-	2/ 3	.667	1/ 1	1.000	1/ 3	-	-	2	-	-	5	-
WROBLEWSKI, M.	-	3/ 4	.750	1/ 2	.500	0/ 3	-	-	3	-	-	7	-
DAVIDSON, G.	-	2/ 2	1.000	2/ 2	1.000	0/ 1	-	-	4	-	-	6	-
ROY, J.	-	0/ 0	.000	0/ 0	.000	0/ 0	-	-	1	-	-	0	-
BAXTER, J.	-	0/ 0	.000	0/ 0	.000	1/ 1	-	-	0	-	-	0	-
Totals	200	24/55	.436	27/35	.771	19/42	-	-	26	-	-	75	.375

Houston (64)   Coach: Guy Lewis

	Min.	Total FG / FGA	Pct.	FT / FTA	Pct.	Reb. O / T	A	TO	PF	S	Blk	TP	PPM
THOMPSON, J.	-	1/ 5	.200	6/ 9	.667	0/ 0	-	-	1	-	-	8	-
LEMMON, J.	-	1/ 2	.500	0/ 0	.000	0/ 0	-	-	0	-	-	2	-
LUCKENBILL, T.	-	1/ 7	.143	3/ 3	1.000	1/ 7	-	-	5	-	-	5	-
THOMSON, T.	-	5/12	.417	4/ 5	.800	2/ 5	-	-	2	-	-	14	-
HARGER, L.	-	2/ 5	.400	1/ 4	.250	2/ 6	-	-	4	-	-	5	-
PHILLIPS, G.	-	6/14	.429	10/11	.909	1/ 6	-	-	2	-	-	22	-
THURMAN, R.	-	2/ 4	.500	0/ 2	.000	1/ 2	-	-	2	-	-	4	-
TUFFLI, N.	-	0/ 0	.000	1/ 1	1.000	1/ 2	-	-	2	-	-	1	-
MOLCHANY, R.	-	1/ 1	1.000	1/ 1	1.000	1/ 1	-	-	3	-	-	3	-
BISHOP, D.	-	0/ 0	.000	0/ 0	.000	0/ 0	-	-	1	-	-	0	-
POLLAN, B.	-	0/ 1	.000	0/ 0	.000	0/ 1	-	-	0	-	-	0	-
BROWN, B.	-	0/ 0	.000	0/ 0	.000	0/ 0	-	-	0	-	-	0	-
Totals	200	19/51	.373	26/36	.722	9/30	-	-	22	-	-	64	.320

Team Rebounds: Kansas State 6; Houston 9. Disqualified: Houston—Luckenbill.

	1st Half	2nd Half	Final
Kansas State	33	42	75
Houston	29	35	64

Cincinnati (78)   Coach: Ed Jucker

	Min.	Total FG / FGA	Pct.	FT / FTA	Pct.	Reb. O / T	A	TO	PF	S	Blk	TP	PPM
WIESENHAHN, B.	-	9/21	.429	3/ 5	.600	7/18	-	-	2	-	-	21	-
THACKER, T.	-	3/10	.300	0/ 2	.000	3/14	-	-	2	-	-	6	-
HOGUE, P.	-	10/17	.588	4/ 5	.800	6/ 8	-	-	3	-	-	24	-
BOULDIN, C.	-	6/12	.500	0/ 0	.000	0/ 0	-	-	3	-	-	12	-
YATES, T.	-	2/ 4	.500	0/ 0	.000	0/ 5	-	-	0	-	-	4	-
HEIDOTTING, D.	-	2/ 5	.400	0/ 0	.000	2/ 3	-	-	3	-	-	4	-
SIZER, T.	-	2/ 3	.667	0/ 1	.000	0/ 2	-	-	1	-	-	4	-
DIERKING, F.	-	0/ 3	.000	1/ 1	1.000	1/ 2	-	-	1	-	-	1	-
SHINGLETON, L.	-	1/ 2	.500	0/ 0	.000	0/ 1	-	-	0	-	-	2	-
ALTENAU, M.	-	0/ 1	.000	0/ 1	.000	0/ 0	-	-	2	-	-	0	-
CALHOUN, J.	-	0/ 2	.000	0/ 0	.000	0/ 1	-	-	0	-	-	0	-
REIS, R.	-	0/ 0	.000	0/ 1	.000	0/ 0	-	-	1	-	-	0	-
Totals	200	35/80	.438	8/16	.500	19/54	-	-	18	-	-	78	.390

Texas Tech (55)   Coach: Polk Robinson

	Min.	Total FG / FGA	Pct.	FT / FTA	Pct.	Reb. O / T	A	TO	PF	S	Blk	TP	PPM
HENNIG, R.	-	3/11	.273	1/ 3	.333	1/ 2	-	-	2	-	-	7	-
HUDGENS	-	9/20	.450	8/10	.800	2/ 6	-	-	1	-	-	26	-
PERCIVAL, M.	-	3/ 7	.429	0/ 3	.000	1/ 9	-	-	4	-	-	6	-
MOUNTS, D.	-	2/11	.182	3/ 5	.600	0/ 2	-	-	0	-	-	7	-
GINDORF	-	0/ 1	.000	0/ 0	.000	0/ 2	-	-	1	-	-	0	-
MICKEY	-	0/ 0	.000	2/ 3	.667	0/ 0	-	-	0	-	-	2	-
LEMMONS	-	2/ 2	1.000	1/ 1	1.000	0/ 0	-	-	1	-	-	5	-
PERKINS	-	1/ 2	.500	0/ 0	.000	0/ 1	-	-	0	-	-	2	-
VARNELL	-	0/ 1	.000	0/ 0	.000	0/ 0	-	-	1	-	-	0	-
PATTY	-	0/ 5	.000	0/ 0	.000	0/ 3	-	-	3	-	-	0	-
Totals	200	20/60	.333	15/25	.600	4/25	-	-	13	-	-	55	.275

Team Rebounds: Cincinnati 14; Texas Tech 10. Disqualified: None.

	1st Half	2nd Half	Final
Cincinnati	37	41	78
Texas Tech	20	35	55

REGIONAL SEMIFINAL WEST

Arizona State (86)   Coach: Ned Wulk

	Min.	Total FG/FGA	Pct.	FT/FTA	Pct.	Reb. O/T	A	TO	PF	S	Blk	TP	PPM
CERKVENIK, T.	-	2/6	.333	3/3	1.000	-/18	-	-	4	-	-	7	-
PAYNE, O.	-	4/11	.364	1/3	.333	-/6	-	-	4	-	-	9	-
HAHN, G.	-	9/17	.529	2/4	.500	-/14	-	-	3	-	-	20	-
ARMSTRONG, L.	-	12/27	.444	3/6	.500	-/4	-	-	1	-	-	27	-
DISARUFINO, R.	-	3/11	.273	0/1	.000	-/5	-	-	3	-	-	6	-
MCCONNELL, M.	-	4/7	.571	1/1	1.000	-/8	-	-	2	-	-	9	-
DERNOVICH, R.	-	0/0	.000	1/2	.500	-/1	-	-	1	-	-	1	-
PRYOR, B.	-	3/6	.500	1/3	.333	-/6	-	-	2	-	-	7	-
DAUGHERTY, J.	-	0/1	.000	0/0	.000	-/0	-	-	0	-	-	0	-
ENGBRETSTON, L.	-	0/0	.000	0/0	.000	-/0	-	-	0	-	-	0	-
Totals	200	37/86	.430	12/23	.522	-/62	-	-	20	-	-	86	.430

USC (71)   Coach: Forrest Twogood

	Min.	Total FG/FGA	Pct.	FT/FTA	Pct.	Reb. O/T	A	TO	PF	S	Blk	TP	PPM
STANLEY, K.	-	4/12	.333	3/6	.500	-/8	-	-	1	-	-	11	-
ASHBY, V.	-	0/2	.000	0/0	.000	-/1	-	-	1	-	-	0	-
RUDOMETKIN, J.	-	7/23	.304	7/8	.875	-/13	-	-	2	-	-	21	-
APPEL, C.	-	4/11	.364	2/2	1.000	-/4	-	-	4	-	-	10	-
EDWARDS, N.	-	3/5	.600	0/4	.000	-/5	-	-	1	-	-	6	-
SLONIGER, W.	-	0/5	.000	4/4	1.000	-/2	-	-	2	-	-	4	-
MARTIN, G.	-	7/17	.412	1/1	1.000	-/6	-	-	4	-	-	15	-
HILLMAN, P.	-	1/1	1.000	0/0	.000	-/0	-	-	2	-	-	2	-
BENNEDETTI, B.	-	1/1	1.000	0/0	.000	-/0	-	-	0	-	-	2	-
PARSONS, B.	-	0/0	.000	0/0	.000	-/0	-	-	0	-	-	0	-
LEDGER, B.	-	0/0	.000	0/0	.000	-/1	-	-	0	-	-	0	-
CARLETON, W.	-	0/1	.000	0/0	.000	-/0	-	-	1	-	-	0	-
Totals	200	27/78	.346	17/25	.680	-/40	-	-	18	-	-	71	.355

Team Rebounds: Arizona St. 8; USC 9. Disqualified: None.

	1st Half	2nd Half	Final
Arizona St.	42	44	86
USC	32	39	71

Utah (91)   Coach: Jack Gardner

	Min.	Total FG/FGA	Pct.	FT/FTA	Pct.	Reb. O/T	A	TO	PF	S	Blk	TP	PPM
RHEAD, J.	-	8/12	.667	7/7	1.000	-/20	-	-	2	-	-	23	-
RUFFELL, R.	-	7/15	.467	6/8	.750	-/8	-	-	3	-	-	20	-
MCGILL, B.	-	12/21	.571	5/8	.625	-/13	-	-	3	-	-	29	-
MORTON, J.	-	3/7	.429	2/2	1.000	-/3	-	-	3	-	-	8	-
ROWE, E.	-	1/7	.143	0/0	.000	-/2	-	-	0	-	-	2	-
AUFDERHEIDE, J.	-	2/2	1.000	0/0	.000	-/5	-	-	0	-	-	4	-
CRAIN, B.	-	2/3	.667	1/2	.500	-/2	-	-	0	-	-	5	-
THOMAS, J.	-	0/1	.000	0/0	.000	-/1	-	-	0	-	-	0	-
JENSON, N.	-	0/0	.000	0/0	.000	-/0	-	-	0	-	-	0	-
COZBY, B.	-	0/0	.000	0/0	.000	-/0	-	-	0	-	-	0	-
Totals	200	35/68	.515	21/27	.778	-/54	-	-	11	-	-	91	.455

Loyola Marymount (75)   Coach: John Arndt

	Min.	Total FG/FGA	Pct.	FT/FTA	Pct.	Reb. O/T	A	TO	PF	S	Blk	TP	PPM
KRALLMAN, T.	-	4/10	.400	1/2	.500	-/5	-	-	4	-	-	9	-
RYAN, T.	-	6/15	.400	3/3	1.000	-/9	-	-	3	-	-	15	-
BENTO, E.	-	7/11	.636	1/2	.500	-/3	-	-	5	-	-	15	-
QUINN, B.	-	8/20	.400	1/1	1.000	-/3	-	-	0	-	-	17	-
GROTE, J.	-	5/11	.455	0/2	.000	-/5	-	-	2	-	-	10	-
BOWLER	-	3/4	.750	1/2	.500	-/0	-	-	3	-	-	7	-
SIMEON, O.	-	1/4	.250	0/1	.000	-/3	-	-	0	-	-	2	-
SENSKE, J.	-	0/1	.000	0/0	.000	-/0	-	-	0	-	-	0	-
Totals	200	34/76	.447	7/13	.538	-/28	-	-	17	-	-	75	.375

Team Rebounds: Utah 5; Loyola Mymt. 2. Disqualified: Loyola Mymt.—Bento.

	1st Half	2nd Half	Final
Utah	49	42	91
Loyola Mymt.	42	33	75

REGIONAL FINAL EAST

St. Joseph's (96)   Coach: Jack Ramsay

	Min.	Total FG/FGA	Pct.	FT/FTA	Pct.	Reb. O/T	A	TO	PF	S	Blk	TP	PPM
LYNAM, J.	39	3/11	.273	9/12	.750	-/2	5	-	4	-	-	15	.385
MAJEWSKI, F.	39	8/13	.615	3/4	.750	-/9	2	-	4	-	-	19	.487
HOY, W.	39	6/13	.462	8/11	.727	-/6	1	-	1	-	-	20	.513
EGAN, J.	35	6/15	.400	2/3	.667	-/9	3	-	4	-	-	14	.400
KEMPTON, V.	22	6/11	.545	0/1	.000	-/2	1	-	5	-	-	12	.545
WYNNE, T.	22	7/10	.700	2/2	1.000	-/4	0	-	4	-	-	16	.727
WESTHEAD, P.	2	0/0	.000	0/0	.000	-/0	0	-	0	-	-	0	.000
BOOTH, H.	2	0/0	.000	0/0	.000	-/1	0	-	0	-	-	0	.000
Totals	200	36/73	.493	24/33	.727	-/33	12	-	22	-	-	96	.480

Wake Forest (86)   Coach: Bones McKinney

	Min.	Total FG/FGA	Pct.	FT/FTA	Pct.	Reb. O/T	A	TO	PF	S	Blk	TP	PPM
HULL, B.	32	4/10	.400	1/2	.500	-/12	2	-	2	-	-	9	.281
CHAPPELL, L.	40	11/18	.611	10/14	.714	-/16	3	-	3	-	-	32	.800
HART, A.	33	5/11	.455	6/6	1.000	-/3	4	-	5	-	-	16	.485
PACKER, B.	24	2/6	.333	0/1	.000	-/1	1	-	5	-	-	4	.167
WIEDEMAN, D.	35	5/13	.385	1/4	.250	-/5	0	-	3	-	-	11	.314
WOOLLARD, B.	5	0/1	.000	0/0	.000	-/0	0	-	0	-	-	0	.000
FENNELL, W.	3	0/0	.000	0/0	.000	-/0	0	-	0	-	-	0	.000
KOEHLER, A.	7	0/2	.000	0/0	.000	-/3	0	-	1	-	-	0	.000
CALDWELL, P.	1	0/1	.000	0/0	.000	-/0	0	-	1	-	-	0	.000
MCCOY, T.	20	6/6	1.000	2/2	1.000	-/3	3	-	3	-	-	14	.700
Totals	200	33/68	.485	20/29	.690	-/43	13	-	23	-	-	86	.430

Team Rebounds: St. Joseph's 4; Wake Forest 10. Disqualified: St Joseph's—Kempton; Wake Forest—Hart, Packer.

	1st Half	2nd Half	Final
St. Joseph's	48	48	96
Wake Forest	28	58	86

REGIONAL FINAL MIDEAST

Ohio State (87)   Coach: Fred Taylor

	Min.	Total FG/FGA	Pct.	FT/FTA	Pct.	Reb. O/T	A	TO	PF	S	Blk	TP	PPM
HAVILCEK, J.	-	2/10	.200	4/5	.800	-/10	-	-	2	-	-	8	-
HOYT, R.	-	1/3	.333	0/0	.000	-/2	-	-	2	-	-	2	-
LUCAS, J.	-	14/18	.778	5/12	.417	-/30	-	-	4	-	-	33	-
SIEGFRIED, L.	-	8/14	.571	4/7	.571	-/3	-	-	3	-	-	20	-
NOWELL, M.	-	5/7	.714	3/5	.600	-/1	-	-	3	-	-	13	-
KNIGHT, B.	-	3/4	.750	1/1	1.000	-/1	-	-	4	-	-	7	-
GEARHART, G.	-	1/2	.500	0/0	.000	-/0	-	-	2	-	-	2	-
MCDONALD, D.	-	0/0	.000	0/1	.000	-/2	-	-	2	-	-	0	-
REASBECK, R.	-	0/0	.000	0/0	.000	-/0	-	-	1	-	-	0	-
MILLER, N.	-	1/1	1.000	0/0	.000	-/0	-	-	1	-	-	2	-
LEE, K.	-	0/0	.000	0/0	.000	-/0	-	-	0	-	-	0	-
Totals	200	35/59	.593	17/31	.548	-/49	-	-	24	-	-	87	.435

Kentucky (74)   Coach: Adolph Rupp

	Min.	Total FG/FGA	Pct.	FT/FTA	Pct.	Reb. O/T	A	TO	PF	S	Blk	TP	PPM
LICKERT, B.	-	6/16	.375	5/6	.833	-/3	-	-	1	-	-	17	-
NEWMAN, R.	-	7/12	.583	17/22	.773	-/7	-	-	1	-	-	31	-
JENNINGS, N.	-	1/3	.333	2/2	1.000	-/4	-	-	5	-	-	4	-
PURSIFUL, L.	-	4/16	.250	2/2	1.000	-/2	-	-	5	-	-	10	-
PARSONS, D.	-	2/10	.200	2/2	1.000	-/3	-	-	3	-	-	6	-
BURCHETT, C.	-	1/4	.250	0/0	.000	-/2	-	-	5	-	-	2	-
FELDHAUS, A.	-	1/3	.333	1/2	.500	-/1	-	-	2	-	-	3	-
MCDONALD, J.	-	0/3	.000	1/2	.500	-/4	-	-	1	-	-	1	-
BAESLER, S.	-	0/2	.000	0/1	.000	-/0	-	-	0	-	-	0	-
Totals	200	22/69	.319	30/39	.769	-/26	-	-	23	-	-	74	.370

Team Rebounds: Ohio State 2; Kentucky 3. Disqualified: Kentucky—Jennings, Pursiful, Burchett.

	1st Half	2nd Half	Final
Ohio State	36	51	87
Kentucky	28	46	74

REGIONAL FINAL MIDWEST

Kansas State (64)   Coach: Tex Winter

	Min.	Total FG/FGA	Pct.	FT/FTA	Pct.	Reb. O/T	A	TO	PF	S	Blk	TP	PPM
COMLEY, L.	-	7/19	.368	2/2	1.000	2/9	-	-	4	-	-	16	-
MCKENZIE, P.	-	1/4	.250	1/1	1.000	3/5	-	-	5	-	-	3	-
PRICE, C.	-	3/8	.375	4/6	.667	1/6	-	-	4	-	-	10	-
EWY, R.	-	3/5	.600	1/4	.250	0/1	-	-	5	-	-	7	-
PEITHMAN, A.	-	5/11	.455	0/0	.000	0/1	-	-	4	-	-	10	-
NELSON, D.	-	1/5	.200	2/2	1.000	3/3	-	-	0	-	-	4	-
HEITMEYER, J.	-	0/1	.000	1/2	.500	0/1	-	-	2	-	-	1	-
DAVIDSON, G.	-	0/0	.000	2/2	1.000	0/0	-	-	0	-	-	2	-
MATUSZAK, E.	-	0/0	.000	0/0	.000	0/0	-	-	0	-	-	0	-
WROBLEWSKI, M.	-	3/7	.429	5/5	1.000	2/2	-	-	2	-	-	11	-
Totals	200	23/60	.383	18/24	.750	11/28	-	-	26	-	-	64	.320

Cincinnati (69)   Coach: Ed Jucker

	Min.	Total FG/FGA	Pct.	FT/FTA	Pct.	Reb. O/T	A	TO	PF	S	Blk	TP	PPM
WIESENHAHN, B.	-	8/12	.667	6/9	.667	8/12	-	-	2	-	-	22	-
THACKER, T.	-	5/11	.455	6/10	.600	3/12	-	-	4	-	-	16	-
HOGUE, P.	-	3/6	.500	2/6	.333	2/7	-	-	5	-	-	8	-
BOULDIN, C.	-	4/16	.250	2/4	.500	0/2	-	-	0	-	-	10	-
YATES, T.	-	1/5	.200	6/7	.857	1/4	-	-	1	-	-	8	-
HEIDOTTING, D.	-	2/4	.500	1/1	1.000	3/5	-	-	5	-	-	5	-
SIZER, T.	-	0/0	.000	0/0	.000	0/0	-	-	0	-	-	0	-
DIERKING, F.	-	0/1	.000	0/0	.000	1/1	-	-	0	-	-	0	-
Totals	200	23/55	.418	23/37	.622	18/43	-	-	17	-	-	69	.345

Team Rebounds: Cincinnati 8; Kansas State 8. Disqualified: Cincinnati—Hogue, Heidotting; Kansas State—Ewy. McKenzie.

	1st Half	2nd Half	Final
Kansas State	33	31	64
Cincinnati	33	36	69

REGIONAL FINAL WEST

Arizona State (80)   Coach: Ned Wulk

	Min.	Total FG/FGA	Pct.	FT/FTA	Pct.	Reb. O/T	A	TO	PF	S	Blk	TP	PPM
CERKVENIK, T.	-	3/6	.500	1/3	.333	-/7	-	-	0	-	-	7	-
PAYNE, O.	-	6/17	.353	0/0	.000	-/4	-	-	2	-	-	12	-
HAHN, G.	-	6/15	.400	2/3	.667	-/11	-	-	5	-	-	14	-
ARMSTRONG, L.	-	13/23	.565	1/2	.500	-/6	-	-	4	-	-	27	-
DISARUFINO, R.	-	5/12	.417	2/4	.500	-/4	-	-	1	-	-	12	-
PRYOR, B.	-	0/1	.000	0/1	.000	-/3	-	-	0	-	-	0	-
MCCONNELL, M.	-	4/10	.400	0/0	.000	-/6	-	-	3	-	-	8	-
Totals	200	37/84	.440	6/13	.462	-/41	-	-	15	-	-	80	.400

Utah (88)   Coach: Jack Gardner

	Min.	Total FG/FGA	Pct.	FT/FTA	Pct.	Reb. O/T	A	TO	PF	S	Blk	TP	PPM
RHEAD, J.	-	5/10	.500	7/9	.778	-/10	-	-	3	-	-	17	-
RUFFELL, R.	-	12/17	.706	0/0	.000	-/8	-	-	1	-	-	24	-
MCGILL, B.	-	12/27	.444	7/8	.875	-/18	-	-	3	-	-	31	-
MORTON, J.	-	4/15	.267	1/2	.500	-/6	-	-	0	-	-	9	-
ROWE, E.	-	1/3	.333	0/0	.000	-/4	-	-	2	-	-	2	-
COZBY, B.	-	0/1	.000	0/0	.000	-/1	-	-	1	-	-	0	-
AUFDERHEIDE, J.	-	1/4	.250	1/1	1.000	-/2	-	-	1	-	-	3	-
CRAIN, B.	-	1/4	.250	0/0	.000	-/2	-	-	0	-	-	2	-
THOMAS, J.	-	0/1	.000	0/0	.000	-/2	-	-	0	-	-	0	-
Totals	200	36/82	.439	16/20	.800	-/53	-	-	11	-	-	88	.440

Team Rebounds: Utah 2; Arizona St. 6. Disqualified: Arizona St.—Hahn.

	1st Half	2nd Half	Final
Arizona St.	28	52	80
Utah	46	42	88

FINAL FOUR

St. Joseph's (69)   Coach: Jack Ramsay

	Min.	Total FG/FGA	Pct.	FT/FTA	Pct.	Reb. O/T	A	TO	PF	S	Blk	TP	PPM
LYNAM, J.	-	2/ 5	.400	3/ 4	.750	-/ 0	-	-	0	-	-	7	-
MAJEWSKI, F.	-	4/12	.333	5/ 7	.714	-/ 4	-	-	1	-	-	13	-
HOY, W.	-	6/17	.353	1/ 1	1.000	-/ 2	-	-	2	-	-	13	-
EGAN, J.	-	3/15	.200	2/ 3	.667	-/ 5	-	-	2	-	-	8	-
KEMPTON, V.	-	5/ 9	.556	8/ 8	1.000	-/ 8	-	-	3	-	-	18	-
WYNNE, T.	-	1/ 9	.111	2/ 2	1.000	-/ 2	-	-	4	-	-	4	-
WESTHEAD, P.	-	0/ 1	.000	0/ 1	.000	-/ 2	-	-	0	-	-	0	-
BOOTH, H.	-	0/ 3	.000	2/ 2	1.000	-/ 2	-	-	3	-	-	2	-
GORMLEY, B.	-	1/ 5	.200	2/ 2	1.000	-/ 1	-	-	3	-	-	4	-
DICKEY, B.	-	0/ 0	.000	0/ 0	.000	-/ 0	-	-	0	-	-	0	-
BUGEY, D.	-	0/ 0	.000	0/ 0	.000	-/ 1	-	-	0	-	-	0	-
Totals	200	22/76	.289	25/30	.833	-/27	-	-	18	-	-	69	.345

Cincinnati (82)   Coach: Ed Jucker

	Min.	Total FG/FGA	Pct.	FT/FTA	Pct.	Reb. O/T	A	TO	PF	S	Blk	TP	PPM
WIESENHAHN, B.	-	5/ 7	.714	4/ 6	.667	-/ 5	-	-	4	-	-	14	-
THACKER, T.	-	1/ 7	.143	5/ 6	.833	-/ 6	-	-	3	-	-	7	-
HOGUE, P.	-	9/16	.563	0/ 4	.000	-/14	-	-	4	-	-	18	-
BOULDIN, C.	-	7/14	.500	7/ 8	.875	-/ 3	-	-	0	-	-	21	-
YATES, T.	-	4/ 6	.667	5/ 7	.714	-/ 5	-	-	2	-	-	13	-
HEIDOTTING, D.	-	3/ 8	.375	1/ 1	1.000	-/ 6	-	-	1	-	-	7	-
SIZER, T.	-	1/ 1	1.000	0/ 0	.000	-/ 0	-	-	0	-	-	2	-
DIERKING, F.	-	0/ 0	.000	0/ 0	.000	-/ 1	-	-	1	-	-	0	-
SHINGLETON, L.	-	0/ 0	.000	0/ 0	.000	-/ 0	-	-	0	-	-	0	-
ALTENAU, M.	-	0/ 0	.000	0/ 0	.000	-/ 0	-	-	0	-	-	0	-
CALHOUN, J.	-	0/ 0	.000	0/ 0	.000	-/ 0	-	-	0	-	-	0	-
Totals	200	30/59	.508	22/32	.688	-/40	-	20	15	-	-	82	.410

Ohio State (95)   Coach: Fred Taylor

	Min.	Total FG/FGA	Pct.	FT/FTA	Pct.	Reb. O/T	A	TO	PF	S	Blk	TP	PPM
HAVILCEK, J.	-	5/ 6	.833	1/ 2	.500	-/ 9	-	-	2	-	-	11	-
HOYT, R.	-	2/ 6	.333	0/ 0	.000	-/ 1	-	-	3	-	-	4	-
LUCAS, J.	-	10/11	.909	9/10	.900	-/13	-	-	2	-	-	29	-
SIEGFRIED, L.	-	8/11	.727	5/ 7	.714	-/ 9	-	-	4	-	-	21	-
NOWELL, M.	-	7/11	.636	1/ 1	1.000	-/ 0	-	-	2	-	-	15	-
KNIGHT, B.	-	2/ 5	.400	1/ 2	.500	-/ 3	-	-	2	-	-	5	-
GEARHART, G.	-	0/ 2	.000	2/ 2	1.000	-/ 1	-	-	2	-	-	2	-
MCDONALD, D.	-	1/ 4	.250	0/ 0	.000	-/ 2	-	-	1	-	-	2	-
REASBECK, R.	-	0/ 1	.000	0/ 1	.000	-/ 1	-	-	1	-	-	0	-
MILLER, N.	-	0/ 0	.000	0/ 0	.000	-/ 0	-	-	0	-	-	0	-
LEE, K.	-	1/ 1	1.000	0/ 0	.000	-/ 2	-	-	0	-	-	2	-
LANDES, J.	-	2/ 2	1.000	0/ 0	.000	-/ 0	-	-	1	-	-	4	-
Totals	200	38/60	.633	19/25	.760	-/41	-	-	20	-	-	95	.475

Team Rebounds: Ohio State 9; St. Joseph's 9. Disqualified: None.

	1st Half	2nd Half	Final
St. Joseph's	28	41	69
Ohio State	45	50	95

Utah (67)   Coach: Jack Gardner

	Min.	Total FG/FGA	Pct.	FT/FTA	Pct.	Reb. O/T	A	TO	PF	S	Blk	TP	PPM
RUFFELL, R.	-	6/11	.545	2/ 2	1.000	-/ 5	-	-	4	-	-	14	-
RHEAD, J.	-	2/ 5	.400	4/ 6	.667	-/10	-	-	4	-	-	8	-
MCGILL, B.	-	11/31	.355	3/ 4	.750	-/ 8	-	-	4	-	-	25	-
MORTON, J.	-	3/ 9	.333	1/ 1	1.000	-/ 1	-	-	4	-	-	7	-
ROWE, E.	-	1/ 3	.333	0/ 0	.000	-/ 1	-	-	2	-	-	2	-
CRAIN, B.	-	2/ 5	.400	0/ 1	.000	-/ 5	-	-	4	-	-	4	-
AUFDERHEIDE, J.	-	2/ 3	.667	2/ 2	1.000	-/ 3	-	-	1	-	-	6	-
COZBY, B.	-	0/ 0	.000	0/ 0	.000	-/ 0	-	-	0	-	-	0	-
THOMAS, J.	-	0/ 0	.000	1/ 2	.500	-/ 0	-	-	0	-	-	1	-
JENSON, N.	-	0/ 0	.000	0/ 0	.000	-/ 0	-	-	0	-	-	0	-
Totals	200	27/67	.403	13/18	.722	-/33	-	21	23	-	-	67	.335

Team Rebounds: Cincinnati 5; Utah 6. Disqualified: None.

	1st Half	2nd Half	Final
Cincinnati	35	47	82
Utah	20	47	67

NATIONAL CHAMPIONSHIP

Ohio State (65)   Coach: Fred Taylor

	Min.	Total FG/FGA	Pct.	FT/FTA	Pct.	Reb. O/T	A	TO	PF	S	Blk	TP	PPM
HAVILCEK, J.	-	1/ 5	.200	2/ 2	1.000	-/ 4	-	-	2	-	-	4	-
HOYT, R.	-	3/ 5	.600	1/ 1	1.000	-/ 1	-	-	3	-	-	7	-
LUCAS, J.	-	10/17	.588	7/ 7	1.000	-/12	-	-	4	-	-	27	-
SIEGFRIED, L.	-	6/10	.600	2/ 3	.667	-/ 3	-	-	2	-	-	14	-
NOWELL, M.	-	3/ 9	.333	3/ 3	1.000	-/ 3	-	-	1	-	-	9	-
KNIGHT, B.	-	1/ 3	.333	0/ 0	.000	-/ 1	-	-	1	-	-	2	-
GEARHART, G.	-	1/ 1	1.000	0/ 0	.000	-/ 0	-	-	1	-	-	2	-
Totals	225	25/50	.500	15/16	.938	-/24	-	8	14	-	-	65	.289

Cincinnati (70)   Coach: Ed Jucker

	Min.	Total FG/FGA	Pct.	FT/FTA	Pct.	Reb. O/T	A	TO	PF	S	Blk	TP	PPM
WIESENHAHN, B.	-	8/15	.533	1/ 1	1.000	-/ 9	-	-	3	-	-	17	-
THACKER, T.	-	7/21	.333	1/ 4	.250	-/ 7	-	-	0	-	-	15	-
HOGUE, P.	-	3/ 8	.375	3/ 6	.500	-/ 7	-	-	3	-	-	9	-
BOULDIN, C.	-	7/12	.583	2/ 3	.667	-/ 4	-	-	4	-	-	16	-
YATES, T.	-	4/ 8	.500	5/ 5	1.000	-/ 2	-	-	3	-	-	13	-
HEIDOTTING, D.	-	0/ 0	.000	0/ 0	.000	-/ 0	-	-	0	-	-	0	-
SIZER, T.	-	0/ 0	.000	0/ 0	.000	-/ 1	-	-	0	-	-	0	-
Totals	225	29/64	.453	12/19	.632	-/30	-	3	13	-	-	70	.311

Team Rebounds: Cincinnati 6; Ohio State 8. Disqualified: None.

	1st Half	2nd Half	1st OT	Final
Ohio State	39	22	4	65
Cincinnati	38	23	9	70

NATIONAL THIRD PLACE
St. Joseph's (127)　　Coach: Jack Ramsay

	Min.	Total FG / FGA	Pct.	FT / FTA	Pct.	Reb. O / T	A	TO	PF	S	Blk	TP	PPM
MAJEWSKI, F.	-	5/ 9	.556	1/ 2	.500	-/11	-	-	3	-	-	11	-
EGAN, J.	-	17/33	.515	8/ 8	1.000	-/16	-	-	5	-	-	42	-
KEMPTON, V.	-	7/12	.583	2/ 3	.667	-/10	-	-	5	-	-	16	-
LYNAM, J.	-	9/18	.500	13/14	.929	-/ 2	-	-	2	-	-	31	-
HOY, W.	-	3/14	.214	4/ 4	1.000	-/ 3	-	-	1	-	-	10	-
WYNNE, T.	-	4/12	.333	7/ 9	.778	-/10	-	-	5	-	-	15	-
GORMLEY, B.	-	0/ 2	.000	0/ 0	.000	-/ 1	-	-	0	-	-	0	-
BOOTH, H.	-	0/ 0	.000	2/ 2	1.000	-/ 1	-	-	0	-	-	2	-
WESTHEAD, P.	-	0/ 0	.000	0/ 0	.000	-/ 0	-	-	0	-	-	0	-
DICKEY, B.	-	0/ 1	.000	0/ 0	.000	-/ 2	-	-	3	-	-	0	-
Totals	300	45/101	.446	37/42	.881	-/56	-	-	24	-	-	127	.423

Utah (120)　　Coach: Jack Gardner

	Min.	Total FG / FGA	Pct.	FT / FTA	Pct.	Reb. O / T	A	TO	PF	S	Blk	TP	PPM
RHEAD, J.	-	12/20	.600	4/10	.400	-/11	-	-	4	-	-	28	-
RUFFELL, R.	-	7/14	.500	0/ 0	.000	-/ 5	-	-	3	-	-	14	-
MCGILL, B.	-	14/23	.609	6/ 9	.667	-/14	-	-	5	-	-	34	-
MORTON, J.	-	3/11	.273	5/ 9	.556	-/ 6	-	-	3	-	-	11	-
ROWE, E.	-	3/ 8	.375	0/ 0	.000	-/ 3	-	-	4	-	-	6	-
CRAIN, B.	-	5/13	.385	3/ 3	1.000	-/ 8	-	-	5	-	-	13	-
THOMAS, J.	-	3/ 7	.429	0/ 0	.000	-/ 3	-	-	0	-	-	6	-
AUFDERHEIDE, J.	-	1/ 4	.250	0/ 1	.000	-/ 3	-	-	3	-	-	2	-
COZBY, B.	-	2/ 3	.667	2/ 2	1.000	-/ 3	-	-	1	-	-	6	-
JENSON, N.	-	0/ 0	.000	0/ 0	.000	-/ 0	-	-	0	-	-	0	-
Totals	300	50/103	.485	20/34	.588	-/56	-	-	28	-	-	120	.400

Team Rebounds: St. Joseph's 7; Utah 9. Disqualified: St. Joseph's—Egan, Kempton, Wynne; Utah—McGill, Crain. McGill credited with field goal scored for Utah by St. Joseph's Hoy.

	1st Half	2nd Half	1st OT	2nd OT	3rd OT	4th OT	Final
St. Joseph's	48	41	8	4	11	15	127
Utah	41	48	8	4	11	8	120

REGIONAL THIRD PLACE EAST
St. Bonaventure (85)　　Coach: Eddie Donovan

	Min.	Total FG / FGA	Pct.	FT / FTA	Pct.	Reb. O / T	A	TO	PF	S	Blk	TP	PPM
CRAWFORD, F.	-	7/14	.500	2/ 3	.667	-/ 7	-	-	3	-	-	16	-
STITH, T.	-	10/17	.588	9/11	.818	-/ 5	-	-	1	-	-	29	-
MCCULLY, B.	-	2/ 4	.500	0/ 0	.000	-/ 9	-	-	4	-	-	4	-
MARTIN, W.	-	5/ 9	.556	0/ 0	.000	-/ 4	-	-	2	-	-	10	-
JIRELE, O.	-	5/ 7	.714	1/ 1	1.000	-/ 2	-	-	1	-	-	11	-
HANNON, T.	-	7/12	.583	1/ 4	.250	-/ 6	-	-	2	-	-	15	-
FITZMAURICE, T.	-	0/ 1	.000	0/ 0	.000	-/ 0	-	-	1	-	-	0	-
HERBERT, B.	-	0/ 3	.000	0/ 0	.000	-/ 3	-	-	1	-	-	0	-
PETROVICK, E.	-	0/ 0	.000	0/ 0	.000	-/ 0	-	-	0	-	-	0	-
ORMSBY, J.	-	0/ 1	.000	0/ 0	.000	-/ 0	-	-	0	-	-	0	-
Totals	200	36/68	.529	13/19	.684	-/36	-	-	15	-	-	85	.425

Princeton (67)　　Coach: Jake McCandless

	Min.	Total FG / FGA	Pct.	FT / FTA	Pct.	Reb. O / T	A	TO	PF	S	Blk	TP	PPM
BURTON, M.	-	3/ 7	.429	1/ 1	1.000	-/ 6	-	-	3	-	-	7	-
WHITEHOUSE, J.	-	3/ 8	.375	1/ 4	.250	-/ 4	-	-	2	-	-	7	-
KAEMMERLEN, A.	-	4/11	.364	5/ 5	1.000	-/18	-	-	2	-	-	13	-
HYLAND, A.	-	5/12	.417	3/ 3	1.000	-/ 3	-	-	2	-	-	13	-
CAMPBELL, P.	-	11/25	.440	2/ 2	1.000	-/ 2	-	-	1	-	-	24	-
HIGGINS, A.	-	0/ 2	.000	1/ 2	.500	-/ 1	-	-	1	-	-	1	-
ADAMS, T.	-	1/ 2	.500	0/ 1	.000	-/ 2	-	-	2	-	-	2	-
HYLAND, D.	-	0/ 0	.000	0/ 0	.000	-/ 0	-	-	0	-	-	0	-
Totals	200	27/67	.403	13/18	.722	-/36	-	-	13	-	-	67	.335

Team Rebounds: St. Bonaventure 5; Princeton 6. Disqualified: None.

	1st Half	2nd Half	Final
St. Bonaventure	31	54	85
Princeton	42	25	67

REGIONAL THIRD PLACE MIDEAST
Louisville (83)　　Coach: Peck Hickman

	Min.	Total FG / FGA	Pct.	FT / FTA	Pct.	Reb. O / T	A	TO	PF	S	Blk	TP	PPM
LEATHERS, B.	-	0/ 4	.000	0/ 1	.000	-/ 0	-	1	0	-	-	0	-
ARMSTRONG, J.	-	0/ 0	.000	0/ 0	.000	-/ 1	-	3	1	-	-	0	-
RAY, J.	-	0/ 0	.000	0/ 0	.000	-/ 2	-	1	1	-	-	0	-
TURNER, J.	-	13/25	.520	2/ 2	1.000	-/13	-	2	3	-	-	28	-
SAWYER, F.	-	7/11	.636	2/ 3	.667	-/13	-	1	4	-	-	16	-
OLSEN, J.	-	9/21	.429	2/ 3	.667	-/12	-	2	3	-	-	20	-
STACEY, H.	-	4/ 9	.444	0/ 1	.000	-/ 1	-	1	1	-	-	8	-
FRAZIER, J.	-	3/ 6	.500	1/ 3	.333	-/ 2	-	4	2	-	-	7	-
RUBENSTEIN, R.	-	1/ 1	1.000	0/ 0	.000	-/ 1	-	1	1	-	-	2	-
PELOFF, D.	-	0/ 2	.000	0/ 0	.000	-/ 0	-	4	3	-	-	0	-
WATKINS, J.	-	1/ 2	.500	0/ 0	.000	-/ 0	-	1	0	-	-	2	-
Totals	200	38/81	.469	7/13	.538	-/49	-	17	19	-	-	83	.415

Morehead State (61)　　Coach: Robert Laughlin

	Min.	Total FG / FGA	Pct.	FT / FTA	Pct.	Reb. O / T	A	TO	PF	S	Blk	TP	PPM
GIBSON, J.	-	1/ 3	.333	0/ 0	.000	-/ 1	-	1	0	-	-	2	-
POKLEY, N.	-	3/10	.300	1/ 5	.200	-/11	-	2	4	-	-	7	-
NOE, E.	-	7/21	.333	6/ 9	.667	-/10	-	2	3	-	-	20	-
THOMPSON, H.	-	5/13	.385	3/ 4	.750	-/ 6	-	2	3	-	-	13	-
WILLIAMS, J.	-	1/ 4	.250	0/ 1	.000	-/ 1	-	3	0	-	-	2	-
COLE, A.	-	0/ 1	.000	0/ 1	.000	-/ 1	-	0	0	-	-	0	-
MARTIN	-	1/ 3	.333	1/ 2	.500	-/ 3	-	2	2	-	-	3	-
MORGAN	-	1/ 3	.333	0/ 0	.000	-/ 1	-	0	1	-	-	2	-
GREENE	-	0/ 0	.000	2/ 2	1.000	-/ 3	-	2	0	-	-	2	-
ELLIS	-	0/ 3	.000	0/ 0	.000	-/ 1	-	1	0	-	-	0	-
THOMPSON, W.	-	5/ 8	.625	0/ 2	.000	-/ 5	-	1	0	-	-	10	-
Totals	200	24/69	.348	13/26	.500	-/43	-	16	13	-	-	61	.305

Team Rebounds: Louisville 2; Morehead State 2. Disqualified: None.

	1st Half	2nd Half	Final
Louisville	47	36	83
Morehead State	23	38	61

REGIONAL THIRD PLACE MIDWEST
Texas Tech (69)　　Coach: Polk Robinson

	Min.	Total FG / FGA	Pct.	FT / FTA	Pct.	Reb. O / T	A	TO	PF	S	Blk	TP	PPM
PATTY	-	4/ -	-	0/ 3	.000	-/ -	-	-	0	-	-	8	-
HENNIG, R.	-	2/ -	-	7/ 8	.875	-/ -	-	-	4	-	-	11	-
HUDGENS	-	11/ -	-	2/ 4	.500	-/ -	-	-	4	-	-	24	-
PERCIVAL, M.	-	5/ -	-	0/ 7	.000	-/ -	-	-	2	-	-	10	-
MOUNTS, D.	-	2/ -	-	8/11	.727	-/ -	-	-	3	-	-	12	-
GINDORF	-	2/ -	-	0/ 0	.000	-/ -	-	-	0	-	-	4	-
Totals	200	26/ -	-	17/33	.515	-/ -	-	-	13	-	-	69	.345

Houston (67)　　Coach: Guy Lewis

	Min.	Total FG / FGA	Pct.	FT / FTA	Pct.	Reb. O / T	A	TO	PF	S	Blk	TP	PPM
THOMSON, T.	-	2/ -	-	0/ 0	.000	-/ -	-	-	3	-	-	4	-
LUCKENBILL, T.	-	6/ -	-	3/ 5	.600	-/ -	-	-	1	-	-	15	-
HARGER, L.	-	2/ -	-	1/ 2	.500	-/ -	-	-	4	-	-	5	-
PHILLIPS, G.	-	5/ -	-	2/ 4	.500	-/ -	-	-	1	-	-	12	-
THOMPSON, J.	-	2/ -	-	0/ 0	.000	-/ -	-	-	3	-	-	4	-
MOLCHANY, R.	-	0/ -	-	0/ 0	.000	-/ -	-	-	3	-	-	0	-
TUFFLI, N.	-	1/ -	-	0/ 0	.000	-/ -	-	-	2	-	-	2	-
THURMAN, R.	-	1/ -	-	2/ 3	.667	-/ -	-	-	1	-	-	4	-
LEMMON, J.	-	5/ -	-	1/ 2	.500	-/ -	-	-	2	-	-	11	-
BISHOP, D.	-	0/ -	-	0/ 0	.000	-/ -	-	-	2	-	-	0	-
POLLAN, B.	-	5/ -	-	0/ 0	.000	-/ -	-	-	0	-	-	10	-
Totals	200	29/ -	-	9/16	.563	-/ -	-	-	22	-	-	67	.335

Disqualified: None.

	1st Half	2nd Half	Final
Texas Tech	36	33	69
Houston	27	40	67

REGIONAL THIRD PLACE WEST

Loyola Marymount (69)   Coach: John Arndt

	Min.	Total FG/FGA	Pct.	FT/FTA	Pct.	Reb. O/T	A	TO	PF	S	Blk	TP	PPM
KRALLMAN, T.	-	3/6	.500	2/2	1.000	-/8	-	-	5	-	-	8	-
RYAN, T.	-	4/11	.364	2/2	1.000	-/12	-	1	-	1	-	10	-
BENTO, E.	-	11/21	.524	10/16	.625	-/7	-	-	4	-	-	32	-
QUINN, B.	-	3/10	.300	2/3	.667	-/2	-	-	2	-	-	8	-
GROTE, J.	-	2/7	.286	7/8	.875	-/3	-	-	5	-	-	11	-
SENSKE, J.	-	0/0	.000	0/0	.000	-/1	-	-	0	-	-	0	-
SIMEON, O.	-	0/0	.000	0/0	.000	-/3	-	-	0	-	-	0	-
Totals	200	23/55	.418	23/31	.742	-/36	-	-	17	-	-	69	.345

USC (67)   Coach: Forrest Twogood

	Min.	Total FG/FGA	Pct.	FT/FTA	Pct.	Reb. O/T	A	TO	PF	S	Blk	TP	PPM
STANLEY, K.	-	0/3	.000	0/0	.000	-/7	-	-	5	-	-	0	-
ASHBY, V.	-	0/0	.000	1/2	.500	-/3	-	-	1	-	-	1	-
RUDOMETKIN, J.	-	8/15	.533	8/10	.800	-/12	-	-	2	-	-	24	-
APPEL, C.	-	10/22	.455	2/4	.500	-/4	-	-	3	-	-	22	-
EDWARDS, N.	-	0/0	.000	0/0	.000	-/0	-	-	0	-	-	0	-
SLONIGER, W.	-	0/5	.000	4/5	.800	-/2	-	-	2	-	-	4	-
MARTIN, G.	-	4/8	.500	3/4	.750	-/5	-	-	3	-	-	11	-
HILLMAN, P.	-	0/0	.000	0/0	.000	-/0	-	-	2	-	-	0	-
CARLETON, W.	-	0/0	.000	0/0	.000	-/0	-	-	0	-	-	0	-
PARSONS, B.	-	2/6	.333	1/2	.500	-/4	-	-	3	-	-	5	-
Totals	200	24/59	.407	19/27	.704	-/37	-	-	21	-	-	67	.335

Team Rebounds: Loyola Mymt. 5; USC 7. Disqualified: Loyola Mymt.—Krallman, Grote; USC—Stanley.

	1st Half	2nd Half	Final
Loyola Mymt.	34	35	69
USC	33	34	67

○ ALL-STAR TEAMS ○

ALL TOURNAMENT

CARL BOULDIN	CINCINNATI
JOHN EGAN	ST. JOSEPH'S
★ JERRY LUCAS	OHIO STATE
LARRY SIEGFRIED	OHIO STATE
BOB WIESENHAHN	CINCINNATI

MIDWEST REGIONAL

★ LARRY COMLEY	KANSAS STATE
HAROLD HUDGENS	TEXAS TECH
GARY PHILLIPS	HOUSTON
TOM THACKER	CINCINNATI
★ BOB WIESENHAHN	CINCINNATI

★ Most Outstanding Player(s)

○ INDIVIDUAL RECORDS ○

SCORING

Most points in a single game
1 JOHN EGAN, ST. JOSEPH'S (vs. UTAH)   42
2 FRED CRAWFORD, ST. BONAVENTURE (vs. RHODE ISLAND)   34
2 BILL MCGILL, UTAH (vs. ST. JOSEPH'S)   34
4 JERRY LUCAS, OHIO STATE (vs. KENTUCKY)   33
5 2 tied for fifth place.

Most total points in the tournament
1 BILL MCGILL, UTAH   119
2 JERRY LUCAS, OHIO STATE   98
3 TOM STITH, ST. BONAVENTURE   87
3 LEN CHAPPELL, WAKE FOREST   87
5 JOHN EGAN, ST. JOSEPH'S   83

Highest scoring average (minimum 2 games)
1 BILL MCGILL, UTAH (119-4)   29.75
2 TOM STITH, ST. BONAVENTURE (87-3)   29.00
2 LEN CHAPPELL, WAKE FOREST (87-3)   29.00

4 JOHN TURNER, LOUISVILLE (77-3)   25.67
5 PETER CAMPBELL, PRINCETON (75-3)   25.00

FIELD GOALS

Most field goals in a single game
1 JOHN EGAN, ST. JOSEPH'S (vs. UTAH)   17
2 FRED CRAWFORD, ST. BONAVENTURE (vs. RHODE ISLAND)   16
3 BILL MCGILL, UTAH (vs. ST. JOSEPH'S)   14
3 JERRY LUCAS, OHIO STATE (vs. KENTUCKY)   14
5 2 tied for fifth place.

Most total field goals in the tournament
1 BILL MCGILL, UTAH   49
2 JERRY LUCAS, OHIO STATE   36
3 JOHN EGAN, ST. JOSEPH'S   33
4 RICH RUFFELL, UTAH   32
4 FRED CRAWFORD, ST. BONAVENTURE   32

Most field goal attempts in a single game
1 JOHN EGAN, ST. JOSEPH'S (vs. UTAH)   33
2 BILL MCGILL, UTAH (vs. CINCINNATI)   31
3 BILL MCGILL, UTAH (vs. ARIZONA ST.)   27
3 OLLIE PAYNE, ARIZONA ST. (vs. SEATTLE)   27
3 LARRY ARMSTRONG, ARIZONA ST. (vs. USC)   27

Most total field goal attempts in the tournament
1 BILL MCGILL, UTAH   102
2 JOHN EGAN, ST. JOSEPH'S   84
3 LARRY ARMSTRONG, ARIZONA ST.   71
4 JOHN TURNER, LOUISVILLE   65
5 LEN CHAPPELL, WAKE FOREST   59

Highest field goal percentage in a single game (minimum 10 attempts)
1 JERRY LUCAS, OHIO STATE (vs. ST. JOSEPH'S) (10-11)   .909
2 JERRY LUCAS, OHIO STATE (vs. KENTUCKY) (14-18)   .778

3 LARRY SIEGFRIED, OHIO STATE (vs. ST.
   JOSEPH'S) (8-11)   .727
4 RICH RUFFELL, UTAH (vs. ARIZONA ST.) (12-17)
                                            .706
4 ALLEY HART, WAKE FOREST (vs. ST. JOHN'S)
   (12-17)   .706

FREE THROWS

Most free throws in a single game
1 ROGER NEWMAN, KENTUCKY (vs. OHIO STATE)
                                            17
2 JAMES LYNAM, ST. JOSEPH'S (vs. UTAH)   13
2 TOM STITH, ST. BONAVENTURE (vs. WAKE
   FOREST)   13
2 LEN CHAPPELL, WAKE FOREST (vs. ST. JOHN'S)
                                            13
5 PETER CAMPBELL, PRINCETON (vs. ST.
   JOSEPH'S)   12

Most total free throws in the tournament
1 LEN CHAPPELL, WAKE FOREST   33
2 TOM STITH, ST. BONAVENTURE   29
3 JAMES LYNAM, ST. JOSEPH'S   28
4 JERRY LUCAS, OHIO STATE   26
5 JIM RHEAD, UTAH   22

Most free throws attempted in a single game
1 ROGER NEWMAN, KENTUCKY (vs. OHIO STATE)
                                            22

2 LEN CHAPPELL, WAKE FOREST (vs. ST. JOHN'S)
                                            17
3 ED BENTO, LOYOLA MYMT. (vs. USC)   16
3 TOM STITH, ST. BONAVENTURE (vs. WAKE
   FOREST)   16
5 3 tied for fifth place.

Most free throws attempted in the tournament
1 LEN CHAPPELL, WAKE FOREST   43
2 TOM STITH, ST. BONAVENTURE   36
2 JERRY LUCAS, OHIO STATE   36
4 JAMES LYNAM, ST. JOSEPH'S   34
5 2 tied for fifth place.

**Highest free throw percentage in a single game
(minimum 7 attempts)**
1 JOHN EGAN, ST. JOSEPH'S (vs. UTAH) (8-8)
                                            1.000
1 VINCENT KEMPTON, ST. JOSEPH'S (vs. OHIO
   STATE) (8-8)   1.000
1 TONY JACKSON, ST. JOHN'S (vs. WAKE FOREST)
   (8-8)   1.000
4 JIM RHEAD, UTAH (vs. LOYOLA MYMT.) (7-7)
                                            1.000
4 JERRY LUCAS, OHIO STATE (vs. CINCINNATI) (7-
   7)   1.000

**Highest free throw percentage in the tournament
(minimum 15 attempts)**
1 JOHN TURNER, LOUISVILLE (19-21)   .905

2 JOHN RUDOMETKIN, USC (21-24)   .875
3 PETER CAMPBELL, PRINCETON (19-22)   .864
4 TONY YATES, CINCINNATI (16-19)   .842
5 JAMES LYNAM, ST. JOSEPH'S (28-34)   .824

REBOUNDS

Most rebounds in a single game
1 JERRY LUCAS, OHIO STATE (vs. KENTUCKY) 30
2 JIM RHEAD, UTAH (vs. LOYOLA MYMT.)   20
2 LEN CHAPPELL, WAKE FOREST (vs. ST. JOHN'S)
                                            20
4 5 tied for fourth place.

Most total rebounds in the tournament
1 JERRY LUCAS, OHIO STATE   73
2 BILL MCGILL, UTAH   53
3 JIM RHEAD, UTAH   51
3 LEN CHAPPELL, WAKE FOREST   51
5 BOB WIESENHAHN, CINCINNATI   44

Most rebounds per game (minimum 2 games)
1 JERRY LUCAS, OHIO STATE (73-4)   18.25
2 LEN CHAPPELL, WAKE FOREST (51-3)   17.00
3 ALFRED KAEMMERLEN, PRINCETON (28-2)14.00
4 BILL MCGILL, UTAH (53-4)   13.25
5 JIM RHEAD, UTAH (51-4)   12.75

✪ TEAM RECORDS ✪

SCORING

Most points in a single game
1 ST. JOSEPH'S (vs. UTAH)   127
2 UTAH (vs. ST. JOSEPH'S)   120
3 WAKE FOREST (vs. ST. JOHN'S)   97

Most total points in the tournament
1 UTAH   366
2 ST. JOSEPH'S   364
3 OHIO STATE   303

Highest scoring average (minimum 2 games)
1 UTAH (366-4)   91.50
2 ST. JOSEPH'S (364-4)   91.00
3 WAKE FOREST (261-3)   87.00

FIELD GOALS

Most field goals in a single game
1 UTAH (vs. ST. JOSEPH'S)   50
2 ST. JOSEPH'S (vs. UTAH)   45
3 2 tied for third place.

Most total field goals in the tournament
1 UTAH   148
2 ST. JOSEPH'S   128
3 OHIO STATE   122

Most field goals attempted in a single game
1 UTAH (vs. ST. JOSEPH'S)   103
2 ST. JOSEPH'S (vs. UTAH)   101
3 ARIZONA ST. (vs. USC)   86

Most total field goals attempted in the tournament
1 ST. JOSEPH'S   324
2 UTAH   320
3 CINCINNATI   258

Highest field goal percentage in a single game
1 OHIO STATE (vs. ST. JOSEPH'S) (38-60)   .633
2 OHIO STATE (vs. KENTUCKY) (35-59)   .593
3 PRINCETON (vs. GEO. WASH.) (32-59)   .542

FREE THROWS

Most free throws in a single game
1 ST. JOSEPH'S (vs. UTAH)   37
2 KENTUCKY (vs. OHIO STATE)   30
3 2 tied for third place.

Most total free throws in the tournament
1 ST. JOSEPH'S   108
2 WAKE FOREST   73
3 UTAH   70

Most free throws attempted in a single game
1 ST. JOSEPH'S (vs. UTAH)   42
2 WAKE FOREST (vs. ST. JOHN'S)   40
3 KENTUCKY (vs. OHIO STATE)   39

Most total free throws attempted in the tournament
1 ST. JOSEPH'S   135
2 CINCINNATI   104
3 WAKE FOREST   103

Highest free throw percentage in a single game
1 OHIO STATE (vs. CINCINNATI) (15-16)   .938
2 ST. JOSEPH'S (vs. UTAH) (37-42)   .881
3 ST. JOSEPH'S (vs. OHIO STATE) (25-30)   .833

**Highest free throw percentage in the tournament
(minimum 2 games)**
1 ST. JOSEPH'S (108-135)   .800
2 KANSAS STATE (45-59)   .763
3 KENTUCKY (53-71)   .747

Fewest free throws in a single game
1 XAVIER (OHIO) (vs. MOREHEAD STATE)   6
1 ARIZONA ST. (vs. UTAH)   6
3 2 tied for third place.

Lowest free throw percentage in a single game
1 XAVIER (OHIO) (vs. MOREHEAD STATE) (6-16)
                                            .375
2 ARIZONA ST. (vs. UTAH) (6-13)   .462
3 CINCINNATI (vs. TEXAS TECH) (8-16)   .500

REBOUNDS

Most rebounds in a single game
1 ARIZONA ST. (vs. USC)   62
2 3 tied for second place.

1962

FIRST ROUND	REGIONAL SEMIFINAL	REGIONAL FINAL	**FINAL FOUR**	REGIONAL FINAL	REGIONAL SEMIFINAL	FIRST ROUND

EAST

(bye) — St. Joseph's 85

Wake Forest 92 (ot)

Yale 82

Wake Forest 96

Wake Forest 79

U. Mass. 50

NYU 70

NYU 76

West Virginia 75

Villanova 90

Villanova 79

Villanova 69

Wake Forest 68

MIDEAST

(bye) — Kentucky 81

Bowling Green 55

Butler 56

Butler 60

Kentucky 64

Western Ky. 90

Detroit 81

Western Ky. 73

(bye)

Ohio St. 93

Ohio St. 74

Ohio St. 84

Cincinnati 72

Cincinnati 71
Ohio St. 59

MIDWEST

Colorado 67 — (bye)

Texas Tech 68

Air Force 66

Texas Tech 60

Colorado 46

Creighton 87

Memphis St. 83

Creighton 46

Cincinnati 73

Cincinnati 66 — (bye)

WEST

Pepperdine 67 — (bye)

Oregon St. 69 (ot)

Seattle 65

Oregon St. 69

Oregon St. 69

UCLA 70

Utah St. 78

Arizona St. 73

Utah St. 62

UCLA 73 — (bye)

UCLA 88

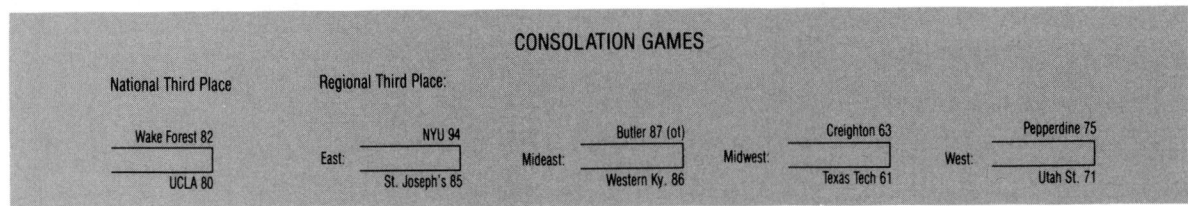

CONSOLATION GAMES

National Third Place

Wake Forest 82

UCLA 80

Regional Third Place:

East: NYU 94 / St. Joseph's 85

Mideast: Butler 87 (ot) / Western Ky. 86

Midwest: Creighton 63 / Texas Tech 61

West: Pepperdine 75 / Utah St. 71

The Ohio, navigable for virtually its entire course, is one of the most important commercial waterways in middle America. But along a 200-mile stretch of river, from Columbus in the northeast to Louisville in the southwest, the talk in March 1962 was not about commerce—but of war!

The trouble had been brewing for almost two years, since the sophomore-dominated 1960 Ohio State Buckeyes had flexed their muscles and, by winning the national championship, had also supplanted the Oscar Robertson-led Cincinnati Bearcats as Ohio's best college basketball team. In 1961 the rivalry grew hotter when Cincinnati (this time without Robertson) squeaked by previously unbeaten Ohio State to win the national title. At the close of the 1961–62 regular season, the Bearcats were still demanding the respect they thought they deserved. Cincinnati had lost only 14 games in five years, but Ohio State was ranked No. 1—unanimously—in both major wire service polls. Ohio State's All-American Jerry Lucas was everybody's college Player of the Year for the second straight year. And Ohio State's Fred Taylor had been selected Coach of the Year, for the second consecutive time, defeating Cincinnati's sophomore coach Ed Jucker.

Ohio State had its own score to settle. They wanted to prove—once and for all—that Cincinnati's victory in the previous year's title game had been a fluke—that they were indeed No. 1.

As far back as January, partisans of the two sides had been anticipating the showdown. Tickets for the Final Four went on sale on January 15th, at 12:01 A.M.—and within hours every seat in Louisville's 17,865-seat Freedom Hall was sold out. And as the expectation of the Cincinnati–Ohio State rematch came closer to reality, the excitement grew to a fever pitch. Finally, during the tournament, an NCAA official estimated that 100,000 tickets could have been sold for the Finals. As the Final Four began, half the state of Ohio seemed to cross the river to converge on Louisville. Scalpers hawking their wares on the grounds of the Kentucky Fair and Exposition Center commanded more than twenty times the price printed on the tickets. Bearcat vendors were doing a brisk business in "Hate State" buttons, and Buckeye entrepreneurs made a bundle on "Go Go Ohio" bibs. The stage was set for the final confrontation.

In the Midwest regional, 46 was Cincinnati's magic number. After beating Missouri Valley rival Bradley 61-46 to qualify for the tournament, they held Creighton to the same number (30 points below Creighton's season average) while outscoring them by 20 points. Then the Bearcats beat Colorado 73-46.

In Louisville, Cincinnati's semifinal opponent was UCLA. Coach John Wooden had never brought his Bruins so far in his 14 years at the coast school, and his underdog team started the tournament with the second worst record in the entire field. After Wooden's brash young Bruins had run and passed their way into the semis and into the role of sentimental favorites, the coach quietly came over to each player and said, "I'm proud of you." "We're proud of you, too," one of his players replied. Everyone, though, expected the tall, talented, disciplined Cincinnati Bearcats to eat the Bruins alive. "I don't think we can beat Cincinnati at their slow-down game," commented Wooden, "and I don't much think we can beat them at our fast one either." After five and a half minutes of the Cincinnati-UCLA semifinal, it seemed like a good time for Wooden to throw in the towel and go home. The Bearcats had scored on every possession, gotten every rebound, and led 18-4. But somehow, UCLA fought their way back. With 10 seconds left the score was tied at 70 and Ed Jucker called a time-out. Paul Hogue, who towered over the UCLA front line, had scored the last 14 Cincinnati points, and the play was once again designed to get the ball to the big man. It failed to materialize, however, and guard Tom Thacker, a less than spectacular outside shooter who had not scored a point all game, was forced to put up a 25-footer with three seconds to go. It went in.

Ohio State won their two Mideast regional games easily, despite a cold and hot performance by Jerry Lucas. In the opener against Western Kentucky he scored a mere nine points (tying his lowest total ever) but the Buckeyes won by 20. The next night against Kentucky, while Ohio State's defensive specialist John Havlicek was shutting down Kentucky's All-American Cotton Nash, Lucas scored 25 first-half points, including three consecutive 3-point plays in one devastating minute. The Buckeyes coasted home by 10.

In their semi against Wake Forest, the hope of the Confederacy had no hope against the Ohio regulars. Again Havlicek buried the opposition's All-American (in this case it was Len Chappell), and again the Buckeyes were breezing along to an easy victory. But with 6:19 left disaster struck the Ohioans. After going up for a rebound, Lucas came down off-balance and fell to the floor in agony. He was helped to the dressing room, and his knee was immediately wrapped in ice. Lucas's wife sent a message into the locker room asking if Jerry would play against Cincinnati. "Will the sun come up in the east?" responded Lucas. For the next twenty hours, a quorum of doctors, trainers, and medicine men worked on Lucas's knee.

The Buckeyes' general would lead them into battle come hell or high water. When he finally took the floor to jump against Paul Hogue he walked with no discernible limp, although his left leg was tightly taped. Buoyed by Lucas's presence, in the first minutes the Buckeyes stayed close. Hogue and George Wilson swept the boards for Cincinnati, but Lucas's shooting offset the Bearcats' rebounding advantage. After five minutes it was 11-8 Ohio State. But Ohio State's All-American, usually a great rebounder, couldn't compete with Hogue underneath, and a brilliant strategic move by Ed Jucker, pulling Havlicek's man Ron Bonham far away from his usual position inside, meant that the Buckeyes' other top board man was consistently out of rebounding range. With Cincinnati controlling the boards, the Buckeyes' fearsome fast break totally disappeared and Ohio State was forced into playing the Bearcats' slowdown game. Cincinnati inexorably pulled away.

A jubilant Cincinnati crowd chanted "We're No. 1! We're No. 1!" Ed Jucker, who had led his team to national championships in his first two years as a head coach, finally felt vindicated. "Does this prove it?" he asked. "Aren't we the best?" Two years in a row Cincinnati had beaten No. 1 Ohio State, handing Lucas and his senior teammates Havlicek and Mel Nowell one-third of the six defeats they suffered in their three years as Buckeyes. "They can't overlook us now," said Jucker. The war within the state was over. Ohio State was No. 2.

FIRST ROUND EAST

Wake Forest (92)   Coach: Bones McKinney

	Min.	Total FG/FGA	Pct.	FT/FTA	Pct.	Reb. O/T	A	TO	PF	S	Blk	TP	PPM
CHAPPELL, L.	-	8/13	.615	9/15	.600	-/18	0	-	5	-	-	25	-
CHRISTIE, F.	-	2/5	.400	0/0	.000	-/4	1	-	2	-	-	4	-
WOOLLARD, B.	-	2/8	.250	4/5	.800	-/11	0	-	3	-	-	8	-
WIEDEMAN, D.	-	9/20	.450	4/5	.800	-/6	1	-	2	-	-	22	-
PACKER, B.	-	5/14	.357	5/7	.714	-/3	8	-	0	-	-	15	-
MCCOY, T.	-	6/12	.500	3/4	.750	-/6	1	-	1	-	-	15	-
HULL, B.	-	1/1	1.000	1/3	.333	-/3	1	-	2	-	-	3	-
Totals	225	33/73	.452	26/39	.667	-/51	12	-	15	-	-	92	.409

Yale (82)   Coach: Joe Vancisin

	Min.	Total FG/FGA	Pct.	FT/FTA	Pct.	Reb. O/T	A	TO	PF	S	Blk	TP	PPM
EVANS, D.	-	5/11	.455	2/3	.667	-/10	2	-	4	-	-	12	-
KAMINSKY, R.	-	10/18	.556	3/4	.750	-/10	4	-	5	-	-	23	-
GOULDING	-	1/3	.333	2/2	1.000	-/2	0	-	5	-	-	4	-
MADDEN	-	5/10	.500	4/6	.667	-/1	3	-	3	-	-	14	-
LYNCH	-	5/14	.357	2/3	.667	-/2	2	-	2	-	-	12	-
SCHUMACHER, D.	-	2/5	.400	1/2	.500	-/5	0	-	3	-	-	5	-
DERBY	-	2/7	.286	0/0	.000	-/3	1	-	2	-	-	4	-
POLINSKY	-	3/3	1.000	0/0	.000	-/4	0	-	1	-	-	6	-
LUDLUM	-	1/1	1.000	0/0	.000	-/0	0	-	0	-	-	2	-
Totals	225	34/72	.472	14/20	.700	-/37	12	-	25	-	-	82	.364

Team Rebounds: Wake Forest 5; Yale 4. Disqualified: Wake Forest—Chappell; Yale—Kaminsky, Goulding.

	1st Half	2nd Half	1st OT	Final
Wake Forest	46	30	16	92
Yale	42	34	6	82

U. Mass. (50)   Coach: Matt Zunic

	Min.	Total FG/FGA	Pct.	FT/FTA	Pct.	Reb. O/T	A	TO	PF	S	Blk	TP	PPM
LESLIE, K.	-	3/10	.300	1/1	1.000	-/6	1	-	5	-	-	7	-
TWITCHELL, R.	-	0/10	.000	2/4	.500	-/10	1	-	4	-	-	2	-
BLACK	-	3/7	.429	4/8	.500	-/6	0	-	5	-	-	10	-
BERNARD, P.	-	6/18	.333	1/4	.250	-/7	1	-	1	-	-	13	-
MOLE, M.	-	3/16	.188	5/7	.714	-/4	5	-	5	-	-	11	-
FOHLIN, C.	-	2/6	.333	3/4	.750	-/14	0	-	5	-	-	7	-
JOHNSON, R.	-	0/1	.000	0/0	.000	-/1	0	-	0	-	-	0	-
JOHNSON, M.	-	0/0	.000	0/0	.000	-/1	0	-	0	-	-	0	-
GVENTER	-	0/0	.000	0/0	.000	-/2	0	-	0	-	-	0	-
Totals	200	17/68	.250	16/28	.571	-/51	8	-	25	-	-	50	.250

NYU (70)   Coach: Lou Rossini

	Min.	Total FG/FGA	Pct.	FT/FTA	Pct.	Reb. O/T	A	TO	PF	S	Blk	TP	PPM
KRAMER, B.	-	4/16	.250	7/10	.700	-/7	3	-	3	-	-	15	-
HAIRSTON, H.	-	3/7	.429	1/4	.250	-/9	1	-	4	-	-	7	-
GAILLARD	-	2/3	.667	5/9	.556	-/8	0	-	3	-	-	9	-
REINER, M.	-	2/12	.167	2/2	1.000	-/8	3	-	2	-	-	6	-
BOOSE, T.	-	5/11	.455	4/6	.667	-/11	3	-	3	-	-	14	-
O'NEILL, N.	-	0/0	.000	0/0	.000	-/2	4	-	4	-	-	0	-
WILLIAMS, B.	-	3/7	.429	0/0	.000	-/3	1	-	1	-	-	6	-
FILARDI, A.	-	1/1	1.000	5/6	.833	-/2	0	-	3	-	-	7	-
BLAHA	-	3/5	.600	0/2	.000	-/3	0	-	2	-	-	6	-
JORDAN	-	0/1	.000	0/0	.000	-/2	0	-	0	-	-	0	-
FRONTERA	-	0/0	.000	0/0	.000	-/0	0	-	0	-	-	0	-
PATTON	-	0/1	.000	0/0	.000	-/1	0	-	0	-	-	0	-
Totals	200	23/64	.359	24/39	.615	-/56	15	-	25	-	-	70	.350

Team Rebounds: NYU 3; U. Mass. 9. Disqualified: U. Mass.—Leslie, Black, Mole, Fohlin.

	1st Half	2nd Half	Final
U. Mass.	28	22	50
NYU	32	38	70

West Virginia (75)   Coach: George King

	Min.	Total FG/FGA	Pct.	FT/FTA	Pct.	Reb. O/T	A	TO	PF	S	Blk	TP	PPM
WARD	-	4/12	.333	1/2	.500	-/8	7	-	5	-	-	9	-
CATLETT	-	5/16	.313	2/3	.667	-/7	2	-	4	-	-	12	-
LOWRY	-	7/13	.538	2/2	1.000	-/13	2	-	2	-	-	16	-
THORN, R.	-	11/21	.524	1/3	.333	-/13	2	-	2	-	-	23	-
WEIR	-	3/6	.500	1/2	.500	-/5	1	-	1	-	-	7	-
WOLFE	-	0/4	.000	0/0	.000	-/2	0	-	0	-	-	0	-
DUBOIS	-	2/2	1.000	2/2	1.000	-/0	0	-	0	-	-	6	-
SHUCK	-	0/1	.000	2/2	1.000	-/1	0	-	1	-	-	2	-
BODE	-	0/1	.000	0/0	.000	-/0	0	-	1	-	-	0	-
Totals	200	32/76	.421	11/16	.688	-/49	14	-	16	-	-	75	.375

Villanova (90)   Coach: Jack Kraft

	Min.	Total FG/FGA	Pct.	FT/FTA	Pct.	Reb. O/T	A	TO	PF	S	Blk	TP	PPM
JONES, W.	-	13/17	.765	1/2	.500	-/5	2	-	0	-	-	27	-
LEFTWICH, G.	-	4/17	.235	0/0	.000	-/3	0	-	4	-	-	8	-
MCMONAGLE	-	6/12	.500	4/5	.800	-/11	2	-	4	-	-	16	-
O'BRIEN	-	4/14	.286	3/3	1.000	-/8	2	-	2	-	-	11	-
WHITE, H.	-	11/21	.524	6/10	.600	-/10	2	-	2	-	-	28	-
WALSH	-	0/0	.000	0/0	.000	-/0	0	-	0	-	-	0	-
MCGILL	-	0/0	.000	0/0	.000	-/2	1	-	2	-	-	0	-
WINTERBOTTOM, W.	-	0/0	.000	0/0	.000	-/0	0	-	1	-	-	0	-
BROKARS	-	0/0	.000	0/0	.000	-/1	0	-	0	-	-	0	-
MORRIS	-	0/0	.000	0/0	.000	-/0	0	-	0	-	-	0	-
Totals	200	38/81	.469	14/20	.700	-/40	9	-	15	-	-	90	.450

Team Rebounds: Villanova 4; West Virginia 5. Disqualified: West Virginia—Ward.

	1st Half	2nd Half	Final
West Virginia	42	33	75
Villanova	39	51	90

FIRST ROUND MIDEAST

Bowling Green (55)   Coach: Harold Anderson

	Min.	Total FG/FGA	Pct.	FT/FTA	Pct.	Reb. O/T	A	TO	PF	S	Blk	TP	PPM
CHATMAN	-	1/6	.167	2/2	1.000	-/8	-	-	0	-	-	4	-
GILBERT	-	3/12	.250	0/0	.000	-/9	-	-	2	-	-	6	-
THURMOND, N.	-	10/18	.556	1/3	.333	-/14	-	-	4	-	-	21	-
KOMIVES, H.	-	5/15	.333	1/1	1.000	-/1	-	-	4	-	-	11	-
DAWSON	-	4/10	.400	1/3	.333	-/2	-	-	2	-	-	9	-
BAKER	-	1/3	.333	0/1	.000	-/3	-	-	1	-	-	2	-
CARBAUGH	-	0/2	.000	2/3	.667	-/4	-	-	1	-	-	2	-
REYNOLDS	-	0/0	.000	0/0	.000	-/0	-	-	0	-	-	0	-
KNEPPER	-	0/0	.000	0/0	.000	-/0	-	-	0	-	-	0	-
Totals	200	24/66	.364	7/13	.538	-/41	-		14	-		55	.275

Butler (56)   Coach: Tony Hinkle

	Min.	Total FG/FGA	Pct.	FT/FTA	Pct.	Reb. O/T	A	TO	PF	S	Blk	TP	PPM
BOWMAN	-	7/22	.318	4/6	.667	-/11	-	-	1	-	-	18	-
FREEMAN	-	1/4	.250	0/0	.000	-/7	-	-	4	-	-	2	-
BLUE	-	4/8	.500	8/11	.727	-/12	-	-	2	-	-	16	-
WILLIAMS, J.	-	5/13	.385	3/3	1.000	-/5	-	-	4	-	-	13	-
HASLAM	-	3/9	.333	1/1	1.000	-/8	-	-	1	-	-	7	-
SHOOK	-	0/1	.000	0/0	.000	-/1	-	-	0	-	-	0	-
Totals	200	20/57	.351	16/21	.762	-/44	-		12	-		56	.280

Team Rebounds: Butler 1; Bowling Green 4. Disqualified: None.

	1st Half	2nd Half	Final
Bowling Green	25	30	55
Butler	28	28	56

Western Kentucky (90)   Coach: Ed Diddle

	Min.	Total FG/FGA	Pct.	FT/FTA	Pct.	Reb. O/T	A	TO	PF	S	Blk	TP	PPM
DUNN, J.	-	7/15	.467	5/7	.714	-/10	0	-	4	-	-	19	-
JACKSON, B.	-	2/8	.250	2/2	1.000	-/9	1	-	3	-	-	6	-
TODD, H.	-	2/5	.400	6/6	1.000	-/17	-	-	5	-	-	10	-
CARRIER, D.	-	11/17	.647	4/5	.800	-/3	1	-	3	-	-	26	-
RASCOE, B.	-	9/19	.474	7/8	.875	-/5	2	-	3	-	-	25	-
SMITH, D.	-	1/4	.250	2/2	1.000	-/3	1	-	3	-	-	4	-
Totals	200	32/68	.471	26/30	.867	-/47	6	-	21	-	-	90	.450

Detroit (81)   Coach: Robert Calihan

	Min.	Total FG/FGA	Pct.	FT/FTA	Pct.	Reb. O/T	A	TO	PF	S	Blk	TP	PPM
MUNSON	-	4/13	.308	5/6	.833	-/12	1	-	1	-	-	13	-
DEBUSSCHERE, D.	-	14/33	.424	10/13	.769	-/19	4	-	5	-	-	38	-
DZIK	-	6/18	.333	0/1	.000	-/16	0	-	5	-	-	12	-
CHICKOWSKI	-	0/9	.000	2/3	.667	-/1	1	-	3	-	-	2	-
CECH	-	6/21	.286	2/2	1.000	-/4	2	-	3	-	-	14	-
MCDANIEL	-	0/0	.000	2/2	1.000	-/3	0	-	2	-	-	2	-
JOHNSON	-	0/1	.000	0/0	.000	-/2	0	-	1	-	-	0	-
SCHOENHERR	-	0/1	.000	0/0	.000	-/1	0	-	1	-	-	0	-
BARNES	-	0/0	.000	0/0	.000	-/0	0	-	0	-	-	0	-
Totals	200	30/96	.313	21/27	.778	-/58	8	-	21	-	-	81	.405

Team Rebounds: Western Ky. 4; Detroit 3. Disqualified: Western Ky.—Todd; Detroit—DeBusschere, Dzik.

	1st Half	2nd Half	Final
Western Ky.	43	47	90
Detroit	39	42	81

FIRST ROUND MIDWEST

Texas Tech (68)   Coach: Gene Gibson

	Min.	Total FG/FGA	Pct.	FT/FTA	Pct.	Reb. O/T	A	TO	PF	S	Blk	TP	PPM
MOUNTS, D.	-	5/10	.500	6/7	.857	-/3	-	-	4	-	-	16	-
PERCIVAL	-	3/9	.333	2/4	.500	-/8	-	-	5	-	-	8	-
HUDGENS, H.	-	4/13	.308	2/6	.333	-/12	-	-	3	-	-	10	-
GINDORF	-	8/18	.444	4/4	1.000	-/6	-	-	2	-	-	20	-
HENNIG	-	5/8	.625	0/1	.000	-/4	-	-	5	-	-	10	-
WALL	-	1/2	.500	2/3	.667	-/1	-	-	0	-	-	4	-
FARLEY	-	0/1	.000	0/0	.000	-/1	-	-	0	-	-	0	-
Totals	200	26/61	.426	16/25	.640	-/35	-		19	-		68	.340

Air Force (66)   Coach: Bob Spear

	Min.	Total FG/FGA	Pct.	FT/FTA	Pct.	Reb. O/T	A	TO	PF	S	Blk	TP	PPM
ZOELLER	-	2/11	.182	4/4	1.000	-/7	-	-	1	-	-	8	-
JUDD	-	1/5	.200	0/0	.000	-/2	-	-	3	-	-	2	-
KNIPP	-	7/16	.438	5/6	.833	-/4	-	-	2	-	-	19	-
SCHAUMBERG	-	3/11	.273	4/5	.800	-/7	-	-	1	-	-	10	-
VICCELLIO	-	3/3	1.000	7/7	1.000	-/7	-	-	5	-	-	13	-
HINMAN	-	1/8	.125	2/2	1.000	-/2	-	-	3	-	-	4	-
DIFFENDORFER	-	5/8	.625	0/2	.000	-/5	-	-	3	-	-	10	-
HEAD	-	0/3	.000	0/0	.000	-/1	-	-	0	-	-	0	-
Totals	200	22/65	.338	22/26	.846	-/35	-		18	-		66	.330

Team Rebounds: Texas Tech 11; Air Force 10. Disqualified: Texas Tech—Percival, Hennig; Air Force—Viccellio.

	1st Half	2nd Half	Final
Texas Tech	41	27	68
Air Force	31	35	66

Creighton (87)   Coach: Red McManus

	Min.	Total FG/FGA	Pct.	FT/FTA	Pct.	Reb. O/T	A	TO	PF	S	Blk	TP	PPM
BAKOS, J.	-	7/14	.500	6/8	.750	-/11	-	-	5	-	-	20	-
MILLARD, H.	-	2/7	.286	0/1	.000	-/2	-	-	5	-	-	4	-
OFFICER, C.	-	3/7	.429	2/2	1.000	-/8	-	-	5	-	-	8	-
SILAS, P.	-	11/31	.355	5/10	.500	-/24	-	-	3	-	-	27	-
MCMANAMON, P.	-	6/9	.667	5/8	.625	-/2	-	-	1	-	-	17	-
DOWLING, T.	-	0/1	.000	0/0	.000	-/0	-	-	0	-	-	0	-
SILVESTRINI, C.	-	0/0	.000	0/1	.000	-/0	-	-	0	-	-	0	-
WAGNER, L.	-	4/16	.250	3/5	.600	-/5	-	-	5	-	-	11	-
JIMENES, S.	-	0/3	.000	0/0	.000	-/0	-	-	1	-	-	0	-
FOREHAND, H.	-	0/0	.000	0/0	.000	-/0	-	-	0	-	-	0	-
SWASSING, J.	-	0/0	.000	0/0	.000	-/2	-	-	1	-	-	0	-
Totals	200	33/88	.375	21/35	.600	-/54	-	-	26	-	-	87	.435

Memphis State (83)   Coach: Bob Vanatta

	Min.	Total FG/FGA	Pct.	FT/FTA	Pct.	Reb. O/T	A	TO	PF	S	Blk	TP	PPM
BECKMANN, H.	-	7/12	.583	5/6	.833	-/5	-	-	4	-	-	19	-
NEUMANN, B.	-	7/16	.438	9/12	.750	-/8	-	-	5	-	-	23	-
RANDOLPH, D.	-	0/0	.000	2/2	1.000	-/0	-	-	1	-	-	2	-
GARBER, L.	-	5/16	.313	3/4	.750	-/4	-	-	3	-	-	13	-
HORTON, J.	-	3/9	.333	2/2	1.000	-/2	-	-	3	-	-	8	-
KIRK, G.	-	5/9	.556	5/6	.833	-/6	-	-	5	-	-	15	-
PARRISH, J.	-	1/9	.111	1/2	.500	-/4	-	-	3	-	-	3	-
WEAVER, T.	-	0/0	.000	0/0	.000	-/1	-	-	1	-	-	0	-
DREWEL, D.	-	0/0	.000	0/1	.000	-/0	-	-	0	-	-	0	-
Totals	200	28/71	.394	27/35	.771	-/30	-	-	25	-	-	83	.415

Team Rebounds: Creighton 30; Memphis State 15. Disqualified: Creighton—Bakos, Millard, Officer, Wagner; Memphis State—Neumann, Kirk.

	1st Half	2nd Half	Final
Creighton	44	43	87
Memphis State	47	36	83

FIRST ROUND WEST

Oregon State (69)   Coach: Amory "Slats" Gill

	Min.	Total FG / FGA	Pct.	FT / FTA	Pct.	Reb. O / T	A	TO	PF	S	Blk	TP	PPM
CARTY	-	8/15	.533	11/12	.917	-/11	-	-	0	-	-	27	-
JACOBSON	-	0/ 0	.000	0/ 0	.000	-/ 5	-	-	1	-	-	0	-
COUNTS. M.	-	6/19	.316	8/ 9	.889	-/15	-	-	4	-	-	20	-
BAKER, T.	-	2/ 8	.250	0/ 1	.000	-/ 0	-	-	4	-	-	4	-
PAULY, S.	-	5/18	.278	1/ 1	1.000	-/10	-	-	3	-	-	11	-
TORGERSON, R.	-	0/ 0	.000	0/ 0	.000	-/ 1	-	-	1	-	-	0	-
CAMPBELL, T.	-	0/ 1	.000	0/ 0	.000	-/ 2	-	-	0	-	-	0	-
HAYWARD, D.	-	2/ 6	.333	3/ 3	1.000	-/ 0	-	-	3	-	-	7	-
Totals	200	23/67	.343	23/26	.885	-/44	-	16	-	-	69	.345

Seattle (65)   Coach: Vince Cazzetta

	Min.	Total FG / FGA	Pct.	FT / FTA	Pct.	Reb. O / T	A	TO	PF	S	Blk	TP	PPM
BUTLER	-	4/ 8	.500	0/ 1	.000	-/ 7	-	-	2	-	-	8	-
DUNSTON	-	3/10	.300	1/ 3	.333	-/ 4	-	-	5	-	-	7	-
TRESVANT	-	2/ 3	.667	0/ 1	.000	-/ 3	-	-	4	-	-	4	-
MILES	-	10/14	.714	6/ 8	.750	-/ 6	-	-	1	-	-	26	-
SHAULES	-	6/17	.353	4/ 6	.667	-/ 4	-	-	4	-	-	16	-
BRENNAN	-	0/ 0	.000	2/ 2	1.000	-/ 2	-	-	0	-	-	2	-
PRESTON	-	1/ 1	1.000	0/ 0	.000	-/ 1	-	-	4	-	-	2	-
SMITHER	-	0/ 0	.000	0/ 0	.000	-/ 0	-	-	0	-	-	0	-
STAUTZ	-	0/ 0	.000	0/ 0	.000	-/ 0	-	-	0	-	-	0	-
Totals	200	26/53	.491	13/21	.619	-/27	-	20	-	-	65	.325

Team Rebounds: Oregon State 4; Seattle 5. Disqualified: Seattle—Dunston.

	1st Half	2nd Half	Final
Oregon State	23	46	69
Seattle	29	36	65

Utah State (78)   Coach: Ladell Anderson

	Min.	Total FG / FGA	Pct.	FT / FTA	Pct.	Reb. O / T	A	TO	PF	S	Blk	TP	PPM
GREEN, C.	-	9/ -	-	9/11	.818	-/ -	-	-	2	-	-	27	-
JOHNSON	-	7/ -	-	2/ 5	.400	-/ -	-	-	4	-	-	16	-
HANEY	-	6/ -	-	3/ 4	.750	-/ -	-	-	4	-	-	15	-
GOLDSBERRY	-	1/ -	-	0/ 0	.000	-/ -	-	-	2	-	-	2	-
HANSEN	-	7/ -	-	0/ 1	.000	-/ -	-	-	5	-	-	14	-
NATE	-	1/ -	-	0/ 1	.000	-/ -	-	-	1	-	-	2	-
HOLMAN	-	0/ -	-	2/ 2	1.000	-/ -	-	-	0	-	-	2	-
Totals	200	31/ -	-	16/24	.667	-/ -	-	-	18	-	-	78	.390

Arizona State (73)   Coach: Ned Wulk

	Min.	Total FG / FGA	Pct.	FT / FTA	Pct.	Reb. O / T	A	TO	PF	S	Blk	TP	PPM
ARMSTRONG, L.	-	4/ -	-	5/ 6	.833	-/ -	-	-	2	-	-	13	-
DISARUFINO	-	1/ -	-	0/ 0	.000	-/ -	-	-	1	-	-	2	-
HAHN	-	4/ -	-	0/ 2	.000	-/ -	-	-	4	-	-	8	-
CERKVENICK	-	6/ -	-	2/ 3	.667	-/ -	-	-	3	-	-	14	-
CALDWELL, J.	-	6/ -	-	4/ 4	1.000	-/ -	-	-	4	-	-	16	-
PAYNE	-	3/ -	-	0/ 0	.000	-/ -	-	-	4	-	-	6	-
SENITZA	-	2/ -	-	2/ 2	1.000	-/ -	-	-	1	-	-	6	-
HOWARD	-	0/ -	-	0/ 0	.000	-/ -	-	-	0	-	-	0	-
BECKER	-	1/ -	-	0/ 3	.000	-/ -	-	-	0	-	-	2	-
MCCONNELL	-	3/ -	-	0/ 0	.000	-/ -	-	-	0	-	-	6	-
Totals	200	30/ -	-	13/20	.650	-/ -	-	-	19	-	-	73	.365

Disqualified: Utah State—Hansen.

	1st Half	2nd Half	Final
Utah State	35	43	78
Arizona St.	36	37	73

REGIONAL SEMIFINAL EAST

St. Joseph's (85)   Coach: Jack Ramsay

	Min.	Total FG / FGA	Pct.	FT / FTA	Pct.	Reb. O / T	A	TO	PF	S	Blk	TP	PPM
BOYLE	-	6/13	.462	4/ 4	1.000	-/ 7	0	-	4	-	-	16	-
WYNNE, T.	-	10/26	.385	9/ 9	1.000	-/ 7	0	-	2	-	-	29	-
DICKEY, B.	-	2/ 8	.250	1/ 2	.500	-/ 4	1	-	5	-	-	5	-
HOY, B.	-	1/ 6	.167	4/ 5	.800	-/ 9	1	-	3	-	-	6	-
LYNAM, J.	-	6/12	.500	3/ 3	1.000	-/ 3	0	-	2	-	-	15	-
GORMLEY, B.	-	5/ 6	.833	0/ 0	.000	-/ 0	0	-	3	-	-	10	-
HOFFMAN	-	0/ 1	.000	3/ 6	.500	-/ 5	0	-	5	-	-	3	-
TILLER	-	0/ 0	.000	0/ 0	.000	-/ 0	0	-	0	-	-	0	-
BOOTH, H.	-	0/ 2	.000	1/ 2	.500	-/ 1	0	-	1	-	-	1	-
COURTIN	-	0/ 0	.000	0/ 0	.000	-/ 0	0	-	0	-	-	0	-
Totals	225	30/74	.405	25/31	.806	-/36	2	-	25	-	-	85	.378

Wake Forest (96)   Coach: Bones McKinney

	Min.	Total FG / FGA	Pct.	FT / FTA	Pct.	Reb. O / T	A	TO	PF	S	Blk	TP	PPM
CHAPPELL, L.	-	9/17	.529	16/20	.800	-/18	4	-	4	-	-	34	-
CHRISTIE, F.	-	5/10	.500	0/ 1	.000	-/10	0	-	3	-	-	10	-
WOOLLARD, B.	-	4/ 8	.500	4/ 4	1.000	-/11	0	-	5	-	-	12	-
WIEDEMAN, D.	-	5/12	.417	5/ 6	.833	-/ 4	1	-	3	-	-	15	-
PACKER, B.	-	8/14	.571	1/ 2	.500	-/ 1	2	-	2	-	-	17	-
MCCOY, T.	-	3/ 5	.600	2/ 2	1.000	-/ 4	1	-	1	-	-	8	-
HULL, B.	-	0/ 3	.000	0/ 0	.000	-/ 4	0	-	1	-	-	0	-
CARMICHAEL, R.	-	0/ 0	.000	0/ 0	.000	-/ 0	0	-	0	-	-	0	-
HASSELL, B.	-	0/ 0	.000	0/ 0	.000	-/ 0	0	-	0	-	-	0	-
Totals	225	34/69	.493	28/35	.800	-/52	8	-	19	-	-	96	.427

Team Rebounds: Wake Forest 1; St. Joseph's 3. Disqualified: Wake Forest—Woollard; St. Joseph's—Dickey, Hoffman.

	1st Half	2nd Half	1st OT	Final
St. Joseph's	41	33	11	85
Wake Forest	36	38	22	96

NYU (76)   Coach: Lou Rossini

	Min.	Total FG / FGA	Pct.	FT / FTA	Pct.	Reb. O / T	A	TO	PF	S	Blk	TP	PPM
BOOSE, T.	-	4/ 6	.667	3/ 4	.750	-/ 4	0	-	4	-	-	11	-
HAIRSTON, H.	-	7/14	.500	7/ 9	.778	-/12	0	-	4	-	-	21	-
KRAMER, B.	-	10/15	.667	6/ 6	1.000	-/10	1	-	4	-	-	26	-
O'NEILL, N.	-	3/ 5	.600	0/ 2	.000	-/ 1	2	-	1	-	-	6	-
REINER, M.	-	5/ 8	.625	2/ 2	1.000	-/ 5	4	-	4	-	-	12	-
WILLIAMS, B.	-	0/ 0	.000	0/ 0	.000	-/ 0	0	-	0	-	-	0	-
FILARDI, A.	-	0/ 1	.000	0/ 0	.000	-/ 0	0	-	0	-	-	0	-
BLAHA	-	0/ 0	.000	0/ 0	.000	-/ 0	0	-	0	-	-	0	-
JORDAN	-	0/ 0	.000	0/ 0	.000	-/ 1	0	-	0	-	-	0	-
Totals	200	29/49	.592	18/23	.783	-/33	7	-	17	-	-	76	.380

Villanova (79)   Coach: Jack Kraft

	Min.	Total FG / FGA	Pct.	FT / FTA	Pct.	Reb. O / T	A	TO	PF	S	Blk	TP	PPM
JONES, W.	-	6/15	.400	2/ 3	.667	-/ 4	0	-	1	-	-	14	-
LEFTWICH, G.	-	3/13	.231	3/ 5	.600	-/ 2	1	-	2	-	-	9	-
MCMONAGLE	-	5/10	.500	3/ 3	1.000	-/ 8	0	-	3	-	-	13	-
O'BRIEN	-	6/13	.462	0/ 0	.000	-/10	2	-	5	-	-	12	-
WHITE, H.	-	11/19	.579	9/12	.750	-/ 6	1	-	4	-	-	31	-
WALSH	-	0/ 1	.000	0/ 0	.000	-/ 1	0	-	1	-	-	0	-
Totals	200	31/71	.437	17/23	.739	-/31	4	-	16	-	-	79	.395

Team Rebounds: Villanova 5; NYU 2. Disqualified: Villanova—O'Brien.

	1st Half	2nd Half	Final
NYU	42	34	76
Villanova	40	39	79

REGIONAL SEMIFINAL MIDEAST

Kentucky (81)   Coach: Adolph Rupp

	Min.	Total FG / FGA	Pct.	FT / FTA	Pct.	Reb. O / T	A	TO	PF	S	Blk	TP	PPM
BURCHETT, C.	-	6/11	.545	0/ 0	.000	-/ 9	-	-	4	-	-	12	-
ROBERTS, R.	-	2/ 4	.500	3/ 5	.600	-/ 6	-	-	2	-	-	7	-
NASH, C.	-	11/24	.458	1/ 1	1.000	-/10	-	-	5	-	-	23	-
PURSIFUL, L.	-	12/21	.571	2/ 2	1.000	-/ 6	-	-	1	-	-	26	-
BAESLER, S.	-	3/ 9	.333	0/ 1	.000	-/ 4	-	-	1	-	-	6	-
FELDHAUS, A.	-	2/ 4	.500	1/ 2	.500	-/ 3	-	-	3	-	-	5	-
MCDONALD, J.	-	0/ 2	.000	0/ 0	.000	-/ 0	-	-	0	-	-	0	-
DEEKEN, T.	-	0/ 1	.000	0/ 0	.000	-/ 0	-	-	0	-	-	0	-
ISHMAEL, C.	-	1/ 1	1.000	0/ 0	.000	-/ 1	-	-	1	-	-	2	-
RUPP, H.	-	0/ 1	.000	0/ 0	.000	-/ 0	-	-	0	-	-	0	-
Totals	200	37/78	.474	7/11	.636	-/39	-	-	17	-	-	81	.405

Butler (60)   Coach: Tony Hinkle

	Min.	Total FG / FGA	Pct.	FT / FTA	Pct.	Reb. O / T	A	TO	PF	S	Blk	TP	PPM
BOWMAN	-	4/11	.364	1/ 1	1.000	-/ 2	-	-	1	-	-	9	-
FREEMAN	-	2/ 3	.667	0/ 0	.000	-/ 3	-	-	1	-	-	4	-
BLUE	-	7/14	.500	5/ 8	.625	-/11	-	-	2	-	-	19	-
WILLIAMS, J.	-	9/20	.450	2/ 3	.667	-/ 3	-	-	2	-	-	20	-
HASLAM	-	1/ 9	.111	1/ 1	1.000	-/ 6	-	-	3	-	-	3	-
SHOOK	-	0/ 1	.000	0/ 1	.000	-/ 1	-	-	0	-	-	0	-
ENGLE	-	1/ 8	.125	3/ 3	1.000	-/ 2	-	-	4	-	-	5	-
Totals	200	24/66	.364	12/17	.706	-/28	-	-	13	-	-	60	.300

Team Rebounds: Kentucky 2; Butler 0. Disqualified: Kentucky—Nash.

	1st Half	2nd Half	Final
Kentucky	37	44	81
Butler	36	24	60

Western Kentucky (73)   Coach: Ed Diddle

	Min.	Total FG / FGA	Pct.	FT / FTA	Pct.	Reb. O / T	A	TO	PF	S	Blk	TP	PPM
DUNN, J.	-	5/13	.385	2/ 2	1.000	-/11	-	-	3	-	-	12	-
JACKSON, B.	-	4/ 9	.444	3/ 3	1.000	-/ 7	-	-	4	-	-	11	-
TODD, H.	-	4/ 9	.444	4/ 7	.571	-/ 8	-	-	3	-	-	12	-
CARRIER, D.	-	4/13	.308	0/ 0	.000	-/ 2	-	-	3	-	-	8	-
RASCOE, B.	-	8/23	.348	10/12	.833	-/ 7	-	-	3	-	-	26	-
RIDLEY, M.	-	1/ 1	1.000	0/ 0	.000	-/ 2	-	-	0	-	-	2	-
SMITH, D.	-	1/ 1	1.000	0/ 0	.000	-/ 0	-	-	1	-	-	2	-
DAY, D.	-	0/ 0	.000	0/ 0	.000	-/ 0	-	-	1	-	-	0	-
CAINES, W.	-	0/ 0	.000	0/ 0	.000	-/ 0	-	-	1	-	-	0	-
CASTLE, L.	-	0/ 0	.000	0/ 0	.000	-/ 0	-	-	0	-	-	0	-
Totals	200	27/69	.391	19/24	.792	-/37	-	-	19	-	-	73	.365

Ohio State (93)   Coach: Fred Taylor

	Min.	Total FG / FGA	Pct.	FT / FTA	Pct.	Reb. O / T	A	TO	PF	S	Blk	TP	PPM
HAVLICEK, J.	-	7/ 9	.778	3/ 3	1.000	-/ 5	-	-	4	-	-	17	-
MCDONALD, D.	-	9/14	.643	3/ 6	.500	-/ 5	-	-	0	-	-	21	-
LUCAS, J.	-	4/13	.308	1/ 1	1.000	-/13	-	-	4	-	-	9	-
NOWELL, M.	-	3/ 9	.333	4/ 6	.667	-/ 4	-	-	2	-	-	10	-
REASBECK, R.	-	6/11	.545	0/ 0	.000	-/ 1	-	-	3	-	-	12	-
DOUGHTY, J.	-	1/ 4	.250	1/ 2	.500	-/ 1	-	-	0	-	-	3	-
BRADDS, G.	-	3/ 7	.429	4/ 5	.800	-/ 7	-	-	0	-	-	10	-
TAYLOR, R.	-	1/ 2	.500	0/ 0	.000	-/ 0	-	-	0	-	-	2	-
FLATT, D.	-	0/ 0	.000	0/ 0	.000	-/ 1	-	-	0	-	-	0	-
FRAZIER, L.	-	0/ 1	.000	0/ 1	.000	-/ 0	-	-	1	-	-	0	-
KNIGHT, B.	-	1/ 6	.167	0/ 0	.000	-/ 1	-	-	2	-	-	2	-
GEARHART, G.	-	3/ 7	.429	1/ 2	.500	-/ 2	-	-	2	-	-	7	-
LANE, G.	-	0/ 0	.000	0/ 0	.000	-/ 0	-	-	0	-	-	0	-
Totals	200	38/83	.458	17/26	.654	-/40	-	-	18	-	-	93	.465

Disqualified: None. Technical fouls: Ohio State—1.

	1st Half	2nd Half	Final
Western Ky.	30	43	73
Ohio State	43	50	93

REGIONAL SEMIFINAL MIDWEST

Colorado (67)   Coach: Sox Walseth

	Min.	Total FG / FGA	Pct.	FT / FTA	Pct.	Reb. O / T	A	TO	PF	S	Blk	TP	PPM
GILMORE, W.	-	4/ 8	.500	3/ 4	.750	-/ 9	-	-	2	-	-	11	-
CHARLTON, K.	-	9/21	.429	0/ 0	.000	-/ 6	-	-	0	-	-	18	-
DAVIS, J.	-	8/11	.727	1/ 5	.200	-/ 9	-	-	4	-	-	17	-
LEE, E.	-	3/ 7	.429	2/ 4	.500	-/ 8	-	-	3	-	-	8	-
WHISSEN, G.	-	2/ 4	.500	1/ 3	.333	-/ 4	-	-	2	-	-	5	-
SPARKS, G.	-	0/ 1	.000	1/ 2	.500	-/ 1	-	-	1	-	-	1	-
MUELLER, M.	-	2/ 5	.400	1/ 1	1.000	-/ 5	-	-	2	-	-	5	-
MELTON, L.	-	1/ 4	.250	0/ 0	.000	-/ 1	-	-	0	-	-	2	-
Totals	200	29/61	.475	9/19	.474	-/43	-	-	14	-	-	67	.335

Texas Tech (60)   Coach: Gene Gibson

	Min.	Total FG / FGA	Pct.	FT / FTA	Pct.	Reb. O / T	A	TO	PF	S	Blk	TP	PPM
PERCIVAL	-	3/ 6	.500	1/ 2	.500	-/ 5	-	-	3	-	-	7	-
GINDORF	-	4/ 7	.571	3/ 3	1.000	-/ 1	-	-	3	-	-	11	-
HUDGENS, H.	-	5/13	.385	2/ 3	.667	-/10	-	-	1	-	-	12	-
MOUNTS, D.	-	7/20	.350	5/ 6	.833	-/ 3	-	-	2	-	-	19	-
HENNIG	-	1/ 6	.167	3/ 3	1.000	-/ 5	-	-	5	-	-	5	-
WALL	-	3/ 6	.500	0/ 0	.000	-/ 0	-	-	2	-	-	6	-
Totals	200	23/58	.397	14/17	.824	-/24	-	-	16	-	-	60	.300

Team Rebounds: Colorado 3; Texas Tech 10. Disqualified: Texas Tech—Hennig.

	1st Half	2nd Half	Final
Colorado	43	24	67
Texas Tech	32	28	60

Creighton (46)   Coach: Red McManus

	Min.	Total FG / FGA	Pct.	FT / FTA	Pct.	Reb. O / T	A	TO	PF	S	Blk	TP	PPM
BAKOS, J.	-	2/14	.143	3/ 4	.750	-/12	-	-	5	-	-	7	-
MILLARD, H.	-	2/13	.154	1/ 2	.500	-/ 4	-	-	4	-	-	5	-
OFFICER, C.	-	2/ 9	.222	0/ 0	.000	-/ 1	-	-	1	-	-	4	-
SILAS, P.	-	3/14	.214	9/12	.750	-/ 7	-	-	4	-	-	15	-
MCMANAMON, P.	-	1/ 8	.125	2/ 4	.500	-/ 8	-	-	5	-	-	4	-
SILVESTRINI, C.	-	2/ 3	.667	0/ 0	.000	-/ 3	-	-	1	-	-	4	-
WAGNER, L.	-	2/11	.182	3/ 4	.750	-/ 3	-	-	4	-	-	7	-
Totals	200	14/72	.194	18/26	.692	-/38	-	-	24	-	-	46	.230

Cincinnati (66)   Coach: Ed Jucker

	Min.	Total FG / FGA	Pct.	FT / FTA	Pct.	Reb. O / T	A	TO	PF	S	Blk	TP	PPM
BONHAM, R.	-	4/10	.400	6/ 7	.857	-/ 5	-	-	2	-	-	14	-
WILSON, G.	-	0/ 3	.000	3/ 6	.500	-/ 1	-	-	4	-	-	3	-
HOGUE, P.	-	10/14	.714	4/ 5	.800	-/19	-	-	4	-	-	24	-
THACKER, T.	-	5/ 8	.625	2/ 3	.667	-/13	-	-	1	-	-	12	-
YATES, T.	-	0/ 7	.000	2/ 3	.667	-/ 5	-	-	1	-	-	2	-
SIZER, T.	-	1/ 3	.333	4/ 6	.667	-/ 1	-	-	3	-	-	6	-
DIERKING, F.	-	1/ 3	.333	0/ 0	.000	-/ 2	-	-	1	-	-	2	-
HEIDOTTING, D.	-	0/ 1	.000	0/ 2	.000	-/ 1	-	-	1	-	-	0	-
SHINGLETON, L.	-	0/ 1	.000	1/ 2	.500	-/ 1	-	-	0	-	-	1	-
CALHOUN, J.	-	1/ 1	1.000	0/ 0	.000	-/ 1	-	-	0	-	-	2	-
Totals	200	22/51	.431	22/34	.647	-/49	-	-	17	-	-	66	.330

Team Rebounds: Cincinnati 10; Creighton 10. Disqualified: Creighton—McMannamon, Bakos.

	1st Half	2nd Half	Final
Creighton	18	28	46
Cincinnati	29	37	66

REGIONAL SEMIFINAL WEST

Pepperdine (67)　　Coach: Duck Dowell

	Min.	Total FG / FGA	Pct.	FT / FTA	Pct.	Reb. O / T	A	TO	PF	S	Blk	TP	PPM
DINNEL, H.	-	3/10	.300	2/ 8	.250	-/ 9	-	-	4	-	-	8	-
SMITH, N.	-	4/ 9	.444	0/ 0	.000	-/ 4	-	-	3	-	-	8	-
TIFT, T.	-	6/11	.545	3/ 7	.429	-/ 9	-	-	3	-	-	15	-
TINSLEY, L.	-	6/15	.400	1/ 2	.500	-/ 3	-	-	3	-	-	13	-
WARLICK, B.	-	9/21	.429	5/ 6	.833	-/13	-	-	4	-	-	23	-
BRIDGES, T.	-	0/ 1	.000	0/ 0	.000	-/ 2	-	-	0	-	-	0	-
DOUGAN, D.	-	0/ 1	.000	0/ 1	.000	-/ 1	-	-	3	-	-	0	-
Totals	200	28/68	.412	11/24	.458	-/41	-	-	20	-	-	67	.335

Oregon State (69)　　Coach: Amory "Slats" Gill

	Min.	Total FG / FGA	Pct.	FT / FTA	Pct.	Reb. O / T	A	TO	PF	S	Blk	TP	PPM
CARTY	-	4/15	.267	6/ 6	1.000	-/ 6	-	-	1	-	-	14	-
PAULY, S.	-	7/18	.389	1/ 2	.500	-/ 7	-	-	1	-	-	15	-
COUNTS, M.	-	4/18	.222	7/ 8	.875	-/21	-	-	5	-	-	15	-
BAKER, T.	-	6/14	.429	3/ 5	.600	-/ 3	-	-	4	-	-	15	-
HAYWARD, D.	-	0/ 2	.000	0/ 0	.000	-/ 0	-	-	0	-	-	0	-
JACOBSEN	-	4/ 9	.444	2/ 2	1.000	-/ 6	-	-	5	-	-	10	-
TORGERSON, R.	-	0/ 0	.000	0/ 1	.000	-/ 4	-	-	1	-	-	0	-
CAMPBELL, T.	-	0/ 0	.000	0/ 0	.000	-/ 0	-	-	0	-	-	0	-
Totals	200	25/76	.329	19/24	.792	-/47	-	-	17	-	-	69	.345

Team Rebounds: Oregon State 15; Pepperdine 6. Disqualified: Oregon State—Counts, Jacobsen.

	1st Half	2nd Half	Final
Pepperdine	30	37	67
Oregon State	35	34	69

Utah State (62)　　Coach: Ladell Anderson

	Min.	Total FG / FGA	Pct.	FT / FTA	Pct.	Reb. O / T	A	TO	PF	S	Blk	TP	PPM
GREEN, C.	-	9/20	.450	8/12	.667	-/16	-	-	4	-	-	26	-
JOHNSON	-	4/ 9	.444	2/ 6	.333	-/15	-	-	2	-	-	10	-
HANEY	-	4/16	.250	4/ 9	.444	-/14	-	-	4	-	-	12	-
HANSEN	-	5/15	.333	0/ 1	.000	-/ 0	-	-	4	-	-	10	-
GOLDSBERRY	-	1/ 3	.333	0/ 0	.000	-/ 2	-	-	4	-	-	2	-
NATE	-	0/ 0	.000	0/ 0	.000	-/ 0	-	-	2	-	-	0	-
HOLMAN	-	1/ 6	.167	0/ 1	.000	-/ 0	-	-	2	-	-	2	-
Totals	200	24/69	.348	14/29	.483	-/47	-	10	22	-	-	62	.310

UCLA (73)　　Coach: John Wooden

	Min.	Total FG / FGA	Pct.	FT / FTA	Pct.	Reb. O / T	A	TO	PF	S	Blk	TP	PPM
BLACKMAN, P.	-	3/ 8	.375	2/ 2	1.000	-/ 2	-	-	4	-	-	8	-
CUNNINGHAM, G.	-	9/18	.500	3/ 4	.750	-/ 7	-	-	4	-	-	21	-
SLAUGHTER, F.	-	5/ 7	.714	0/ 0	.000	-/ 9	-	-	5	-	-	10	-
GREEN, J.	-	3/15	.200	5/ 8	.625	-/ 7	-	-	2	-	-	11	-
HAZZARD, W.	-	4/12	.333	5/ 8	.625	-/ 8	-	-	0	-	-	13	-
WAXMAN, D.	-	0/ 2	.000	0/ 0	.000	-/ 1	-	-	1	-	-	0	-
STEWART, K.	-	2/ 5	.400	4/ 6	.667	-/ 7	-	-	4	-	-	8	-
HICKS, B.	-	1/ 2	.500	0/ 0	.000	-/ 0	-	-	2	-	-	2	-
ROSVALL, J.	-	0/ 0	.000	0/ 0	.000	-/ 0	-	-	0	-	-	0	-
Totals	200	27/69	.391	19/28	.679	-/41	-	7	22	-	-	73	.365

Team Rebounds: UCLA 12; Utah State 9. Disqualified: UCLA—Slaughter.

	1st Half	2nd Half	Final
Utah State	30	32	62
UCLA	43	30	73

REGIONAL FINAL EAST

Wake Forest (79)　　Coach: Bones McKinney

	Min.	Total FG / FGA	Pct.	FT / FTA	Pct.	Reb. O / T	A	TO	PF	S	Blk	TP	PPM
CHAPPELL, L.	-	9/23	.391	4/ 6	.667	-/21	0	-	2	-	-	22	-
CHRISTIE, F.	-	2/ 4	.500	2/ 3	.667	-/ 3	0	-	2	-	-	6	-
WOOLLARD, B.	-	9/15	.600	1/ .1	1.000	-/18	2	-	1	-	-	19	-
WIEDEMAN, D.	-	5/12	.417	2/ 4	.500	-/ 3	1	-	2	-	-	12	-
PACKER, B.	-	7/15	.467	4/ 4	1.000	-/ 1	0	-	2	-	-	18	-
MCCOY, T.	-	1/ 2	.500	0/ 0	.000	-/ 2	0	-	1	-	-	2	-
HULL, B.	-	0/ 0	.000	0/ 0	.000	-/ 0	0	-	0	-	-	0	-
Totals	200	33/71	.465	13/18	.722	-/48	3	-	10	-	-	79	.395

Villanova (69)　　Coach: Jack Kraft

	Min.	Total FG / FGA	Pct.	FT / FTA	Pct.	Reb. O / T	A	TO	PF	S	Blk	TP	PPM
JONES, W.	-	11/18	.611	3/ 3	1.000	-/ 5	0	-	2	-	-	25	-
LEFTWICH, G.	-	4/13	.308	2/ 6	.333	-/ 8	0	-	2	-	-	10	-
MCMONAGLE	-	3/11	.273	0/ 1	.000	-/ 6	0	-	4	-	-	6	-
O'BRIEN	-	7/10	.700	0/ 0	.000	-/10	0	-	3	-	-	14	-
WHITE, H.	-	6/25	.240	2/ 4	.500	-/14	1	-	2	-	-	14	-
WALSH	-	0/ 0	.000	0/ 0	.000	-/ 0	0	-	1	-	-	0	-
MCGILL	-	0/ 0	.000	0/ 0	.000	-/ 0	0	-	0	-	-	0	-
WINTERBOTTOM, W.	-	0/ 0	.000	0/ 0	.000	-/ 0	0	-	0	-	-	0	-
STEFANIC	-	0/ 0	.000	0/ 0	.000	-/ 0	0	-	0	-	-	0	-
Totals	200	31/77	.403	7/14	.500	-/43	1	-	14	-	-	69	.345

Team Rebounds: Wake Forest 2; Villanova 3. Disqualified: None.

	1st Half	2nd Half	Final
Wake Forest	42	37	79
Villanova	44	25	69

REGIONAL FINAL MIDEAST

Kentucky (64)   Coach: Adolph Rupp

	Min.	Total FG/FGA	Pct.	FT/FTA	Pct.	Reb. O/T	A	TO	PF	S	Blk	TP	PPM
BURCHETT, C.	-	3/9	.333	2/4	.500	-/3	-	-	5	-	-	8	-
ROBERTS, R.	-	4/8	.500	0/0	.000	-/0	-	-	5	-	-	8	-
NASH, C.	-	5/19	.263	4/6	.667	-/9	-	-	1	-	-	14	-
PURSIFUL, L.	-	8/17	.471	5/5	1.000	-/4	-	-	4	-	-	21	-
BAESLER, S.	-	2/10	.200	3/4	.750	-/9	-	-	4	-	-	7	-
FELDHAUS, A.	-	1/4	.250	0/2	.000	-/2	-	-	2	-	-	2	-
MCDONALD, J.	-	2/2	1.000	0/0	.000	-/1	-	-	0	-	-	4	-
DEEKEN, T.	-	0/0	.000	0/0	.000	-/0	-	-	0	-	-	0	-
Totals	200	25/69	.362	14/21	.667	-/28	-	-	21	-	-	64	.320

Ohio State (74)   Coach: Fred Taylor

	Min.	Total FG/FGA	Pct.	FT/FTA	Pct.	Reb. O/T	A	TO	PF	S	Blk	TP	PPM
HAVLICEK, J.	-	5/15	.333	3/4	.750	-/10	-	-	3	-	-	13	-
MCDONALD, D.	-	0/0	.000	0/0	.000	-/0	-	-	1	-	-	0	-
LUCAS, J.	-	12/21	.571	9/10	.900	-/15	-	-	3	-	-	33	-
NOWELL, M.	-	1/5	.200	3/4	.750	-/3	-	-	2	-	-	5	-
REASBECK, R.	-	4/11	.364	0/0	.000	-/3	-	-	3	-	-	8	-
DOUGHTY, J.	-	4/12	.333	0/0	.000	-/2	-	-	2	-	-	8	-
BRADDS, G.	-	0/0	.000	0/1	.000	-/0	-	-	0	-	-	0	-
TAYLOR, R.	-	0/0	.000	0/0	.000	-/0	-	-	0	-	-	0	-
FLATT, D.	-	0/0	.000	0/0	.000	-/0	-	-	0	-	-	0	-
KNIGHT, B.	-	0/0	.000	0/0	.000	-/0	-	-	0	-	-	0	-
GEARHART, G.	-	1/1	1.000	5/7	.714	-/4	-	-	0	-	-	7	-
Totals	200	27/65	.415	20/26	.769	-/37	-	-	14	-	-	74	.370

Disqualified: Kentucky—Burchett, Roberts.

	1st Half	2nd Half	Final
Kentucky	37	27	64
Ohio State	41	33	74

REGIONAL FINAL MIDWEST

Colorado (46)   Coach: Sox Walseth

	Min.	Total FG/FGA	Pct.	FT/FTA	Pct.	Reb. O/T	A	TO	PF	S	Blk	TP	PPM
GILMORE, W.	-	5/6	.833	5/6	.833	-/7	-	-	3	-	-	15	-
CHARLTON, K.	-	4/16	.250	3/6	.500	-/7	-	-	3	-	-	11	-
DAVIS, J.	-	3/8	.375	0/0	.000	-/4	-	-	2	-	-	6	-
LEE, E.	-	2/5	.400	0/0	.000	-/1	-	-	4	-	-	4	-
WHISSEN, G.	-	2/6	.333	0/0	.000	-/0	-	-	0	-	-	4	-
SPARKS, G.	-	0/1	.000	0/1	.000	-/1	-	-	0	-	-	0	-
MUELLER, M.	-	0/1	.000	2/2	1.000	-/2	-	-	1	-	-	2	-
MELTON, L.	-	0/0	.000	0/0	.000	-/0	-	-	0	-	-	0	-
MILLIES, W.	-	2/4	.500	0/1	.000	-/4	-	-	1	-	-	4	-
WOODWARD, T.	-	0/0	.000	0/2	.000	-/0	-	-	0	-	-	0	-
ZYZDA	-	0/0	.000	0/0	.000	-/0	-	-	0	-	-	0	-
MCCANN, T.	-	0/0	.000	0/0	.000	-/0	-	-	0	-	-	0	-
Totals	200	18/47	.383	10/18	.556	-/26	-	-	14	-	-	46	.230

Cincinnati (73)   Coach: Ed Jucker

	Min.	Total FG/FGA	Pct.	FT/FTA	Pct.	Reb. O/T	A	TO	PF	S	Blk	TP	PPM
BONHAM, R.	-	8/20	.400	1/2	.500	-/7	-	-	3	-	-	17	-
WILSON, G.	-	7/12	.583	5/8	.625	-/7	-	-	2	-	-	19	-
HOGUE, P.	-	9/17	.529	4/4	1.000	-/12	-	-	3	-	-	22	-
THACKER, T.	-	3/8	.375	0/1	.000	-/4	-	-	0	-	-	6	-
YATES, T.	-	1/8	.125	3/3	1.000	-/6	-	-	1	-	-	5	-
SIZER, T.	-	1/1	1.000	0/0	.000	-/1	-	-	2	-	-	2	-
HEIDOTTING, D.	-	0/0	.000	0/0	.000	-/0	-	-	1	-	-	0	-
DIERKING, F.	-	0/0	.000	0/0	.000	-/0	-	-	0	-	-	0	-
SHINGLETON, L.	-	0/1	.000	0/0	.000	-/1	-	-	0	-	-	0	-
CALHOUN, J.	-	1/1	1.000	0/0	.000	-/0	-	-	1	-	-	2	-
REIS, R.	-	0/0	.000	0/0	.000	-/1	-	-	0	-	-	0	-
Totals	200	30/68	.441	13/18	.722	-/39	-	-	13	-	-	73	.365

Team Rebounds: Cincinnati 6, Colorado 9. Disqualified: None.

	1st Half	2nd Half	Final
Colorado	29	17	46
Cincinnati	41	32	73

REGIONAL FINAL WEST

Oregon State (69)   Coach: Amory "Slats" Gill

	Min.	Total FG/FGA	Pct.	FT/FTA	Pct.	Reb. O/T	A	TO	PF	S	Blk	TP	PPM
CARTY	-	4/8	.500	1/5	.200	-/5	-	-	2	-	-	9	-
JACOBSEN	-	2/3	.667	1/2	.500	-/5	-	-	1	-	-	5	-
COUNTS, M.	-	11/25	.440	2/2	1.000	-/17	-	-	2	-	-	24	-
BAKER, T.	-	2/10	.200	2/3	.667	-/2	-	-	4	-	-	6	-
PAULY, S.	-	4/8	.500	2/5	.400	-/2	-	-	3	-	-	10	-
ROSSI, G.	-	1/4	.250	0/0	.000	-/2	-	-	3	-	-	2	-
BENNER, R.	-	0/3	.000	0/0	.000	-/3	-	-	2	-	-	0	-
HAYWARD, D.	-	3/9	.333	0/0	.000	-/2	-	-	1	-	-	6	-
CAMPBELL, T.	-	0/1	.000	0/0	.000	-/2	-	-	1	-	-	0	-
BASTER	-	1/3	.333	1/1	1.000	-/0	-	-	2	-	-	3	-
TORGERSON, R.	-	2/3	.667	0/0	.000	-/2	-	-	0	-	-	4	-
Totals	200	30/77	.390	9/18	.500	-/42	-	12	21	-	-	69	.345

UCLA (88)   Coach: John Wooden

	Min.	Total FG/FGA	Pct.	FT/FTA	Pct.	Reb. O/T	A	TO	PF	S	Blk	TP	PPM
BLACKMAN, P.	-	3/9	.333	1/1	1.000	-/5	-	-	1	-	-	7	-
CUNNINGHAM, G.	-	4/9	.444	4/4	1.000	-/11	-	-	4	-	-	12	-
SLAUGHTER, F.	-	2/8	.250	3/5	.600	-/10	-	-	0	-	-	7	-
GREEN, J.	-	5/16	.313	13/16	.813	-/3	-	-	3	-	-	23	-
HAZZARD, W.	-	6/9	.667	5/5	1.000	-/4	-	-	5	-	-	17	-
WAXMAN, D.	-	5/8	.625	2/2	1.000	-/5	-	-	0	-	-	12	-
STEWART, K.	-	1/2	.500	0/0	.000	-/1	-	-	1	-	-	2	-
HICKS, B.	-	2/2	1.000	0/1	.000	-/2	-	-	0	-	-	4	-
ROSVALL, J.	-	1/2	.500	0/0	.000	-/0	-	-	0	-	-	2	-
GOWER, L.	-	0/0	.000	2/2	1.000	-/1	-	-	0	-	-	2	-
MILHORN, J.	-	0/1	.000	0/0	.000	-/0	-	-	0	-	-	0	-
HUGGINS, M.	-	0/0	.000	0/1	.000	-/0	-	-	0	-	-	0	-
Totals	200	29/66	.439	30/37	.811	-/42	-	9	14	-	-	88	.440

Team Rebounds: UCLA 8; Oregon State 8. Disqualified: UCLA—Hazzard.

	1st Half	2nd Half	Final
Oregon State	30	39	69
UCLA	44	44	88

FINAL FOUR

Wake Forest (68) Coach: Bones McKinney

	Min.	Total FG / FGA	Pct.	FT / FTA	Pct.	Reb. O / T	A	TO	PF	S	Blk	TP	PPM
CHAPPELL, L.	-	10/24	.417	7/11	.636	-/18	-	-	5	-	-	27	-
CHRISTIE, F.	-	0/ 2	.000	1/ 1	1.000	-/ 4	-	-	2	-	-	1	-
WOOLLARD, B.	-	1/ 3	.333	1/ 2	.500	-/ 3	-	-	2	-	-	3	-
WIEDEMAN, D.	-	5/16	.313	3/ 6	.500	-/ 8	-	-	0	-	-	13	-
PACKER, B.	-	8/14	.571	1/ 2	.500	-/ 5	-	-	3	-	-	17	-
MCCOY, T.	-	0/ 1	.000	2/ 2	1.000	-/ 1	-	-	1	-	-	2	-
HULL, B.	-	0/ 2	.000	0/ 0	.000	-/ 2	-	-	2	-	-	0	-
CARMICHAEL, R.	-	0/ 0	.000	0/ 0	.000	-/ 1	-	-	1	-	-	0	-
HASSELL, B.	-	1/ 2	.500	0/ 0	.000	-/ 0	-	-	0	-	-	2	-
ZAWACKI, T.	-	0/ 0	.000	1/ 3	.333	-/ 0	-	-	0	-	-	1	-
KOEHLER, A.	-	0/ 1	.000	0/ 0	.000	-/ 0	-	-	0	-	-	0	-
BROOKS, B.	-	0/ 1	.000	2/ 2	1.000	-/ 1	-	-	1	-	-	2	-
Totals	200	25/66	.379	18/29	.621	-/43	-	-	17	-	-	68	.340

Ohio State (84) Coach: Fred Taylor

	Min.	Total FG / FGA	Pct.	FT / FTA	Pct.	Reb. O / T	A	TO	PF	S	Blk	TP	PPM
HAVLICEK, J.	-	9/16	.563	7/ 9	.778	-/16	-	-	3	-	-	25	-
MCDONALD, D.	-	5/10	.500	1/ 2	.500	-/ 5	-	-	3	-	-	11	-
LUCAS, J.	-	8/16	.500	3/ 4	.750	-/16	-	-	1	-	-	19	-
NOWELL, M.	-	2/11	.182	0/ 0	.000	-/ 2	-	-	2	-	-	4	-
REASBECK, R.	-	5/ 7	.714	0/ 0	.000	-/ 3	-	-	4	-	-	10	-
DOUGHTY, J.	-	2/ 4	.500	4/ 4	1.000	-/ 5	-	-	1	-	-	8	-
BRADDS, G.	-	0/ 0	.000	0/ 1	.000	-/ 4	-	-	3	-	-	0	-
TAYLOR, R.	-	0/ 0	.000	0/ 0	.000	-/ 0	-	-	1	-	-	0	-
FLATT, D.	-	0/ 0	.000	1/ 2	.500	-/ 0	-	-	0	-	-	1	-
FRAZIER, L.	-	1/ 1	1.000	0/ 0	.000	-/ 0	-	-	0	-	-	2	-
KNIGHT, B.	-	0/ 2	.000	0/ 0	.000	-/ 2	-	-	2	-	-	0	-
GEARHART, G.	-	2/ 5	.400	0/ 0	.000	-/ 0	-	-	4	-	-	4	-
Totals	200	34/72	.472	16/22	.727	-/53	-	-	24	-	-	84	.420

Disqualified: Wake Forest—Chappell.

	1st Half	2nd Half	Final
Wake Forest	34	34	68
Ohio State	46	38	84

Cincinnati (72) Coach: Ed Jucker

	Min.	Total FG / FGA	Pct.	FT / FTA	Pct.	Reb. O / T	A	TO	PF	S	Blk	TP	PPM
BONHAM, R.	-	8/14	.571	3/ 6	.500	-/ 2	-	2	4	-	-	19	-
WILSON, G.	-	1/ 6	.167	1/ 2	.500	-/ 4	-	1	1	-	-	3	-
HOGUE, P.	-	12/18	.667	12/17	.706	-/19	-	0	3	-	-	36	-
THACKER, T.	-	1/ 7	.143	0/ 0	.000	-/ 4	-	2	3	-	-	2	-
YATES, T.	-	4/10	.400	2/ 3	.667	-/ 3	-	0	3	-	-	10	-
SIZER, T.	-	1/ 3	.333	0/ 0	.000	-/ 1	-	1	3	-	-	2	-
Totals	200	27/58	.466	18/28	.643	-/33	-	6	17	-	-	72	.360

UCLA (70) Coach: John Wooden

	Min.	Total FG / FGA	Pct.	FT / FTA	Pct.	Reb. O / T	A	TO	PF	S	Blk	TP	PPM
BLACKMAN, P.	-	2/ 3	.667	0/ 0	.000	-/ 2	-	1	5	-	-	4	-
CUNNINGHAM, G.	-	8/14	.571	3/ 3	1.000	-/ 9	-	2	2	-	-	19	-
SLAUGHTER, F.	-	1/ 4	.250	0/ 0	.000	-/ 7	-	1	5	-	-	2	-
GREEN, J.	-	9/16	.563	9/11	.818	-/ 7	-	3	1	-	-	27	-
HAZZARD, W.	-	5/10	.500	2/ 3	.667	-/ 6	-	3	2	-	-	12	-
WAXMAN, D.	-	2/ 3	.667	2/ 3	.667	-/ 3	-	1	1	-	-	6	-
STEWART, K.	-	0/ 0	.000	0/ 0	.000	-/ 1	-	0	2	-	-	0	-
Totals	200	27/50	.540	16/20	.800	-/35	-	11	18	-	-	70	.350

Disqualified: UCLA—Blackman, Slaughter.

	1st Half	2nd Half	Final
Cincinnati	37	35	72
UCLA	37	33	70

NATIONAL CHAMPIONSHIP

Ohio State (59) Coach: Fred Taylor

	Min.	Total FG / FGA	Pct.	FT / FTA	Pct.	Reb. O / T	A	TO	PF	S	Blk	TP	PPM
HAVLICEK, J.	-	5/14	.357	1/ 2	.500	-/ 9	-	1	1	-	-	11	-
MCDONALD, D.	-	0/ 1	.000	3/ 3	1.000	-/ 1	-	0	2	-	-	3	-
LUCAS, J.	-	5/17	.294	1/ 2	.500	-/16	-	1	3	-	-	11	-
NOWELL, M.	-	4/16	.250	1/ 1	1.000	-/ 6	-	1	2	-	-	9	-
REASBECK, R.	-	4/ 6	.667	0/ 0	.000	-/ 0	-	2	4	-	-	8	-
DOUGHTY, J.	-	0/ 1	.000	0/ 0	.000	-/ 2	-	0	2	-	-	0	-
BRADDS, G.	-	5/ 7	.714	5/ 6	.833	-/ 4	-	2	2	-	-	15	-
GEARHART, G.	-	1/ 4	.250	0/ 0	.000	-/ 4	-	2	3	-	-	2	-
Totals	200	24/66	.364	11/14	.786	-/42	-	9	19	-	-	59	.295

Cincinnati (71) Coach: Ed Jucker

	Min.	Total FG / FGA	Pct.	FT / FTA	Pct.	Reb. O / T	A	TO	PF	S	Blk	TP	PPM
BONHAM, R.	-	3/12	.250	4/ 4	1.000	-/ 6	-	3	3	-	-	10	-
WILSON, G.	-	1/ 6	.167	4/ 4	1.000	-/11	-	2	2	-	-	6	-
HOGUE, P.	-	11/18	.611	0/ 2	.000	-/19	-	2	2	-	-	22	-
THACKER, T.	-	6/14	.429	9/11	.818	-/ 6	-	1	2	-	-	21	-
YATES, T.	-	4/ 8	.500	4/ 7	.571	-/ 1	-	0	1	-	-	12	-
SIZER, T.	-	0/ 0	.000	0/ 0	.000	-/ 0	-	0	0	-	-	0	-
Totals	200	25/58	.431	21/28	.750	-/43	-	8	10	-	-	71	.355

Disqualified: None.

	1st Half	2nd Half	Final
Ohio State	29	30	59
Cincinnati	37	34	71

NATIONAL THIRD PLACE
Wake Forest (82)   Coach: Bones McKinney

	Min.	Total FG / FGA	Pct.	FT / FTA	Pct.	Reb. O / T	A	TO	PF	S	Blk	TP	PPM
CHAPPELL, L.	-	9/13	.692	8/10	.800	-/11	-	2	5	-	-	26	-
CHRISTIE, F.	-	1/ 8	.125	0/ 0	.000	-/ 2	-	1	3	-	-	2	-
WOOLLARD, B.	-	4/ 6	.667	1/ 3	.333	-/12	-	1	3	-	-	9	-
WIEDEMAN, D.	-	7/13	.538	4/ 6	.667	-/ 1	-	1	4	-	-	18	-
PACKER, B.	-	10/19	.526	2/ 2	1.000	-/ 5	-	2	1	-	-	22	-
McCOY, T.	-	0/ 1	.000	0/ 0	.000	-/ 2	-	0	3	-	-	3	-
HULL, B.	-	0/ 0	.000	0/ 1	.000	-/ 2	-	0	1	-	-	0	-
BROOKS, B.	-	0/ 0	.000	0/ 0	.000	-/ 0	-	0	0	-	-	0	-
HASSELL, B.	-	1/ 1	1.000	0/ 0	.000	-/ 0	-	2	0	-	-	2	-
Totals	200	32/61	.525	18/25	.720	-/35	-	9	20	-	-	82	.410

UCLA (80)   Coach: John Wooden

	Min.	Total FG / FGA	Pct.	FT / FTA	Pct.	Reb. O / T	A	TO	PF	S	Blk	TP	PPM
BLACKMAN, P.	-	4/10	.400	3/ 4	.750	-/ 8	-	1	2	-	-	11	-
CUNNINGHAM, G.	-	5/17	.294	7/ 8	.875	-/11	-	1	5	-	-	17	-
SLAUGHTER, F.	-	8/11	.727	1/ 1	1.000	-/10	-	0	1	-	-	17	-
GREEN, J.	-	3/12	.250	1/ 3	.333	-/ 4	-	2	5	-	-	7	-
HAZZARD, W.	-	5/17	.294	5/ 5	1.000	-/10	-	2	3	-	-	15	-
WAXMAN, D.	-	1/ 3	.333	5/ 6	.833	-/ 8	-	2	0	-	-	7	-
STEWART, K.	-	1/ 2	.500	0/ 0	.000	-/ 1	-	0	2	-	-	2	-
MILHORN, J.	-	0/ 1	.000	0/ 0	.000	-/ 0	-	0	0	-	-	0	-
HICKS, B.	-	2/ 4	.500	0/ 1	.000	-/ 3	-	0	1	-	-	4	-
Totals	200	29/77	.377	22/28	.786	-/55	-	8	19	-	-	80	.400

Disqualified: Wake Forest—Chappell; UCLA—Cunningham, Green.

	1st Half	2nd Half	Final
Wake Forest	38	44	82
UCLA	36	44	80

REGIONAL THIRD PLACE EAST
NYU (94)   Coach: Lou Rossini

	Min.	Total FG / FGA	Pct.	FT / FTA	Pct.	Reb. O / T	A	TO	PF	S	Blk	TP	PPM
KRAMER, B.	-	4/11	.364	4/ 7	.571	-/12	-	-	5	-	-	12	-
O'NEILL, N.	-	4/ 6	.667	5/ 8	.625	-/ 3	-	-	3	-	-	13	-
HAIRSTON, H.	-	10/15	.667	5/ 6	.833	-/ 8	-	-	2	-	-	25	-
BOOSE, T.	-	4/15	.267	8/12	.667	-/18	-	-	4	-	-	16	-
REINER, M.	-	5/10	.500	7/ 7	1.000	-/ 1	-	-	3	-	-	17	-
BLAHA	-	1/ 3	.333	2/ 3	.667	-/ 3	-	-	5	-	-	4	-
GAILLARD	-	0/ 1	.000	4/ 4	1.000	-/ 4	-	-	4	-	-	4	-
WILLIAMS, B.	-	1/ 1	1.000	0/ 0	.000	-/ 1	-	-	2	-	-	2	-
FILARDI, A.	-	0/ 1	.000	1/ 2	.500	-/ 1	-	-	0	-	-	1	-
JORDAN	-	0/ 0	.000	0/ 0	.000	-/ 0	-	-	0	-	-	0	-
PATTON	-	0/ 0	.000	0/ 0	.000	-/ 0	-	-	0	-	-	0	-
FRONTERA	-	0/ 0	.000	0/ 0	.000	-/ 0	-	-	0	-	-	0	-
Totals	200	29/63	.460	36/49	.735	-/51	-	-	28	-	-	94	.470

St. Joseph's (85)   Coach: Jack Ramsay

	Min.	Total FG / FGA	Pct.	FT / FTA	Pct.	Reb. O / T	A	TO	PF	S	Blk	TP	PPM
BOYLE	-	3/ 6	.500	3/ 4	.750	-/ 5	-	-	5	-	-	9	-
WYNNE, T.	-	8/18	.444	8/11	.727	-/ 8	-	-	5	-	-	24	-
DICKEY, B.	-	0/ 2	.000	0/ 0	.000	-/ 5	-	-	5	-	-	0	-
HOY, B.	-	7/15	.467	4/ 4	1.000	-/ 7	-	-	1	-	-	18	-
LYNAM, J.	-	1/ 1	1.000	0/ 1	.000	-/ 0	-	-	3	-	-	2	-
HOFFMAN	-	2/11	.182	5/12	.417	-/19	-	-	1	-	-	9	-
BOOTH, H.	-	2/ 8	.250	3/ 4	.750	-/ 0	-	-	1	-	-	7	-
GORMLEY, B.	-	5/11	.455	2/ 2	1.000	-/ 4	-	-	3	-	-	12	-
KELLY	-	0/ 1	.000	0/ 0	.000	-/ 0	-	-	2	-	-	0	-
COURTIN	-	1/ 6	.167	0/ 0	.000	-/ 0	-	-	3	-	-	2	-
TILLER	-	1/ 3	.333	0/ 2	.000	-/ 4	-	-	1	-	-	2	-
Totals	200	30/82	.366	25/40	.625	-/52	-	-	30	-	-	85	.425

Team Rebounds: NYU 6; St. Joseph's 5. Disqualified: NYU—Kramer, Blaha; St. Joseph's—Boyle, Wynne, Dickey.

	1st Half	2nd Half	Final
NYU	51	43	94
St. Joseph's	40	45	85

REGIONAL THIRD PLACE MIDEAST
Butler (87)   Coach: Tony Hinkle

	Min.	Total FG / FGA	Pct.	FT / FTA	Pct.	Reb. O / T	A	TO	PF	S	Blk	TP	PPM
BOWMAN	-	9/18	.500	3/ 3	1.000	-/ 7	-	-	0	-	-	21	-
FREEMAN	-	4/ 8	.500	0/ 0	.000	-/ 5	-	-	2	-	-	8	-
BLUE	-	8/14	.571	2/ 4	.500	-/ 8	-	-	0	-	-	18	-
WILLIAMS, J.	-	9/20	.450	5/ 8	.625	-/ 3	-	-	2	-	-	23	-
HASLAM	-	4/ 8	.500	1/ 1	1.000	-/ 4	-	-	2	-	-	9	-
ENGLE	-	4/ 5	.800	0/ 0	.000	-/ 0	-	-	1	-	-	8	-
POPE	-	0/ 2	.000	0/ 0	.000	-/ 0	-	-	1	-	-	0	-
Totals	200	38/75	.507	11/16	.688	-/27	-	-	8	-	-	87	.435

Western Kentucky (86)   Coach: Ed Diddle

	Min.	Total FG / FGA	Pct.	FT / FTA	Pct.	Reb. O / T	A	TO	PF	S	Blk	TP	PPM
DUNN, J.	40	9/15	.600	1/ 1	1.000	-/ 9	-	-	3	-	-	19	.475
JACKSON, B.	40	5/16	.313	4/ 4	1.000	-/ 4	-	-	1	-	-	14	.350
CARRIER, D.	40	11/20	.550	0/ 1	.000	-/ 8	-	-	4	-	-	22	.550
RASCOE, B.	40	14/22	.636	1/ 1	1.000	-/ 5	-	-	3	-	-	29	.725
SMITH, D.	40	1/ 4	.250	0/ 0	.000	-/ 5	-	-	4	-	-	2	.050
Totals	200	40/77	.519	6/ 7	.857	-/31	-	-	15	-	-	86	.430

Disqualified: None.

	1st Half	2nd Half	Final
Butler	39	48	87
Western Ky.	40	46	86

REGIONAL THIRD PLACE MIDWEST
Creighton (63)   Coach: Red McManus

	Min.	Total FG / FGA	Pct.	FT / FTA	Pct.	Reb. O / T	A	TO	PF	S	Blk	TP	PPM
McMANAMON, P.	-	8/19	.421	2/ 4	.500	-/ -	-	-	2	-	-	18	-
BAKOS, J.	-	5/12	.417	0/ 2	.000	-/ -	-	-	5	-	-	10	-
SILAS, P.	-	3/16	.188	6/ 8	.750	-/ -	-	-	4	-	-	12	-
MILLARD, H.	-	3/10	.300	6/ 7	.857	-/ -	-	-	4	-	-	12	-
WAGNER, L.	-	2/ 7	.286	1/ 1	1.000	-/ -	-	-	3	-	-	5	-
OFFICER, C.	-	1/ 3	.333	0/ 1	.000	-/ -	-	-	3	-	-	2	-
SIVESTRINI, C.	-	2/ 7	.286	0/ 0	.000	-/ -	-	-	1	-	-	4	-
SWASSING, J.	-	0/ 1	.000	0/ 0	.000	-/ -	-	-	1	-	-	0	-
Totals	200	24/75	.320	15/24	.625	-/ -	-	-	23	-	-	63	.315

Texas Tech (61)   Coach: Gene Gibson

	Min.	Total FG / FGA	Pct.	FT / FTA	Pct.	Reb. O / T	A	TO	PF	S	Blk	TP	PPM
PERCIVAL	-	4/14	.286	1/ 3	.333	-/ -	-	-	3	-	-	9	-
GINDORF	-	1/ 3	.333	0/ 0	.000	-/ -	-	-	5	-	-	2	-
HUDGENS, H.	-	5/11	.455	2/ 5	.400	-/ -	-	-	5	-	-	12	-
MOUNTS, D.	-	6/16	.375	12/14	.857	-/ -	-	-	1	-	-	24	-
HENNIG	-	4/ 7	.571	2/ 4	.500	-/ -	-	-	4	-	-	10	-
WALL	-	1/ 6	.167	2/ 4	.500	-/ -	-	-	3	-	-	4	-
FARLEY	-	0/ 1	.000	0/ 1	.000	-/ -	-	-	0	-	-	0	-
MICKEY	-	0/ 0	.000	0/ 0	.000	-/ -	-	-	0	-	-	0	-
Totals	200	21/58	.362	19/31	.613	-/ -	-	-	21	-	-	61	.305

Disqualified: Creighton—Bakos; Texas Tech—Gindorf, Hudgens.

	1st Half	2nd Half	Final
Creighton	34	29	63
Texas Tech	30	31	61

REGIONAL THIRD PLACE WEST

Pepperdine (75) Coach: Duck Dowell

	Min.	Total FG / FGA	Pct.	FT / FTA	Pct.	Reb. O / T	A	TO	PF	S	Blk	TP	PPM
DINNEL, H.	-	4/10	.400	3/ 5	.600	-/ 6	-	-	1	-	-	11	-
SMITH, N.	-	1/ 6	.167	2/ 4	.500	-/ 6	-	-	2	-	-	4	-
TIFT, T.	-	10/17	.588	2/ 5	.400	-/ 5	-	-	3	-	-	22	-
TINSLEY, L.	-	9/20	.450	1/ 1	1.000	-/ 6	-	-	4	-	-	19	-
WARLICK, B.	-	4/16	.250	3/ 5	.600	-/12	-	-	5	-	-	11	-
BRIDGES, T.	-	3/ 9	.333	0/ 2	.000	-/ 9	-	-	3	-	-	6	-
DOUGAN, D.	-	1/ 3	.333	0/ 0	.000	-/ 6	-	-	1	-	-	2	-
Totals	200	32/81	.395	11/22	.500	-/50	-	-	19	-	-	75	.375

Utah State (71) Coach: Ladell Anderson

	Min.	Total FG / FGA	Pct.	FT / FTA	Pct.	Reb. O / T	A	TO	PF	S	Blk	TP	PPM
JOHNSON	-	1/ 6	.167	1/ 1	1.000	-/ 3	-	-	4	-	-	3	-
GREEN, C.	-	6/17	.353	8/13	.615	-/ 7	-	-	3	-	-	20	-
HANEY	-	9/16	.563	1/ 1	1.000	-/ 8	-	-	2	-	-	19	-
HANSEN	-	1/ 4	.250	2/ 2	1.000	-/ 1	-	-	2	-	-	4	-
GOLDSBERRY	-	0/ 0	.000	0/ 0	.000	-/ 1	-	-	2	-	-	0	-
HOLMAN	-	6/13	.462	1/ 1	1.000	-/ 1	-	-	1	-	-	13	-
GARN	-	3/ 6	.500	2/ 2	1.000	-/ 4	-	-	0	-	-	8	-
NATE	-	1/ 6	.167	0/ 2	.000	-/ 4	-	-	1	-	-	2	-
CASEY	-	0/ 1	.000	0/ 1	.000	-/ 2	-	-	3	-	-	0	-
PUZEY	-	1/ 1	1.000	0/ 0	.000	-/ 0	-	-	0	-	-	2	-
WATTS	-	0/ 0	.000	0/ 0	.000	-/ 0	-	-	0	-	-	0	-
Totals	200	28/70	.400	15/23	.652	-/31	-	-	18	-	-	71	.355

Team Rebounds: Pepperdine 14; Utah State 15. Disqualified: Pepperdine—Warlick.

	1st Half	2nd Half	Final
Pepperdine	42	33	75
Utah State	36	35	71

○ ALL-STAR TEAMS ○

ALL TOURNAMENT

LEN CHAPPELL	WAKE FOREST
JOHN HAVLICEK	OHIO STATE
★ **PAUL HOGUE**	CINCINNATI
JERRY LUCAS	OHIO STATE
TOM THACKER	CINCINNATI

MIDWEST REGIONAL

KEN CHARLTON	COLORADO
DEL RAY MOUNTS	TEXAS TECH
★ **PAUL HOGUE**	CINCINNATI
TOM THACKER	CINCINNATI
GEORGE WILSON	CINCINNATI

★ Most Outstanding Player(s)

○ INDIVIDUAL RECORDS ○

SCORING

Most points in a single game
1. DAVE DEBUSSCHERE, DETROIT (vs. WESTERN KY.) 38
2. PAUL HOGUE, CINCINNATI (vs. UCLA) 36
3. LEN CHAPPELL, WAKE FOREST (vs. ST. JOSEPH'S) 34
4. JERRY LUCAS, OHIO STATE (vs. KENTUCKY) 33
5. HUBIE WHITE, VILLANOVA (vs. NYU) 31

Most total points in the tournament
1. LEN CHAPPELL, WAKE FOREST 134
2. PAUL HOGUE, CINCINNATI 104
3. BILLY PACKER, WAKE FOREST 89
4. DAVE WIEDEMAN, WAKE FOREST 80
4. BOBBY RASCOE, WESTERN KY. 80

Highest scoring average (minimum 2 games)
1. LEN CHAPPELL, WAKE FOREST (134-5) 26.80
2. BOBBY RASCOE, WESTERN KY. (80-3) 26.67
3. PAUL HOGUE, CINCINNATI (104-4) 26.00
4. HUBIE WHITE, VILLANOVA (73-3) 24.33
4. CORNELL GREEN, UTAH STATE (73-3) 24.33

FIELD GOALS

Most field goals in a single game
1. BOBBY RASCOE, WESTERN KY. (vs. BUTLER) 14
1. DAVE DEBUSSCHERE, DETROIT (vs. WESTERN KY.) 14
3. WALLY JONES, VILLANOVA (vs. WEST VIRGINIA) 13
4. 3 tied for fourth place.

Most total field goals in the tournament
1. LEN CHAPPELL, WAKE FOREST 45
2. PAUL HOGUE, CINCINNATI 42
3. BILLY PACKER, WAKE FOREST 38
4. DAVE WIEDEMAN, WAKE FOREST 31
4. BOBBY RASCOE, WESTERN KY. 31

Most field goal attempts in a single game
1. DAVE DEBUSSCHERE, DETROIT (vs. WESTERN KY.) 33
2. PAUL SILAS, CREIGHTON (vs. MEMPHIS STATE) 31
3. TOM WYNNE, ST. JOSEPH'S (vs. WAKE FOREST) 26
4. MEL COUNTS, OREGON STATE (vs. UCLA) 25
4. HUBIE WHITE, VILLANOVA (vs. WAKE FOREST) 25

Most total field goal attempts in the tournament
1. LEN CHAPPELL, WAKE FOREST 90
2. BILLY PACKER, WAKE FOREST 76
3. DAVE WIEDEMAN, WAKE FOREST 73
4. JERRY LUCAS, OHIO STATE 67
4. PAUL HOGUE, CINCINNATI 67

Highest field goal percentage in a single game (minimum 10 attempts)
1 WALLY JONES, VILLANOVA (vs. WEST VIRGINIA) (13-17) .765
2 FRED SLAUGHTER, UCLA (vs. WAKE FOREST) (8-11) .727
2 JIM DAVIS, COLORADO (vs. TEXAS TECH) (8-11) .727
4 EDDIE MILES, SEATTLE (vs. OREGON STATE) (10-14) .714
4 PAUL HOGUE, CINCINNATI (vs. CREIGHTON) (10-14) .714

FREE THROWS

Most free throws in a single game
1 LEN CHAPPELL, WAKE FOREST (vs. ST. JOSEPH'S) 16
2 JOHN GREEN, UCLA (vs. OREGON STATE) 13
3 DELRAY MOUNTS, TEXAS TECH (vs. CREIGHTON) 12
3 PAUL HOGUE, CINCINNATI (vs. UCLA) 12
5 CARTY, OREGON STATE (vs. SEATTLE) 11

Most total free throws in the tournament
1 LEN CHAPPELL, WAKE FOREST 44
2 JOHN GREEN, UCLA 28
3 CORNELL GREEN, UTAH STATE 25
4 DELRAY MOUNTS, TEXAS TECH 23
5 2 tied for fifth place.

Most free throws attempted in a single game
1 LEN CHAPPELL, WAKE FOREST (vs. ST. JOSEPH'S) 20
2 PAUL HOGUE, CINCINNATI (vs. UCLA) 17
3 JOHN GREEN, UCLA (vs. OREGON STATE) 16
4 LEN CHAPPELL, WAKE FOREST (vs. YALE) 15
5 DELRAY MOUNTS, TEXAS TECH (vs. CREIGHTON) 14

Most free throws attempted in the tournament
1 LEN CHAPPELL, WAKE FOREST 62
2 JOHN GREEN, UCLA 38
3 CORNELL GREEN, UTAH STATE 36
4 PAUL SILAS, CREIGHTON 30
5 PAUL HOGUE, CINCINNATI 28

Highest free throw percentage in a single game (minimum 7 attempts)
1 TOM WYNNE, ST. JOSEPH'S (vs. WAKE FOREST) (9-9) 1.000
2 MARK REINER, NYU (vs. ST. JOSEPH'S) (7-7) 1.000
2 VICCELLIO, AIR FORCE (vs. TEXAS TECH) (7-7) 1.000
4 CARTY, OREGON STATE (vs. SEATTLE) (11-12) .917
5 JERRY LUCAS, OHIO STATE (vs. KENTUCKY) (9-10) .900

Highest free throw percentage in the tournament (minimum 15 attempts)
1 GARY CUNNINGHAM, UCLA (17-19) .895
1 MEL COUNTS, OREGON STATE (17-19) .895
3 BOBBY RASCOE, WESTERN KY. (18-21) .857
4 DELRAY MOUNTS, TEXAS TECH (23-27) .852
5 JERRY LUCAS, OHIO STATE (14-17) .824

REBOUNDS

Most rebounds in a single game
1 PAUL SILAS, CREIGHTON (vs. MEMPHIS STATE) 24
2 MEL COUNTS, OREGON STATE (vs. PEPPERDINE) 21
2 LEN CHAPPELL, WAKE FOREST (vs. VILLANOVA) 21
4 5 tied for fourth place.

Most total rebounds in the tournament
1 LEN CHAPPELL, WAKE FOREST 86
2 PAUL HOGUE, CINCINNATI 69
3 JERRY LUCAS, OHIO STATE 60
4 BOB WOOLLARD, WAKE FOREST 55
5 MEL COUNTS, OREGON STATE 53

Most rebounds per game (minimum 2 games)
1 MEL COUNTS, OREGON STATE (53-3) 17.67
2 PAUL HOGUE, CINCINNATI (69-4) 17.25
3 LEN CHAPPELL, WAKE FOREST (86-5) 17.20
4 JERRY LUCAS, OHIO STATE (60-4) 15.00
5 2 tied for fifth place.

○ TEAM RECORDS ○

SCORING

Most points in a single game
1 WAKE FOREST (vs. ST. JOSEPH'S) 96
2 NYU (vs. ST. JOSEPH'S) 94
3 OHIO STATE (vs. WESTERN KY.) 93

Most total points in the tournament
1 WAKE FOREST 417
2 UCLA 311
3 OHIO STATE 310

Highest scoring average (minimum 2 games)
1 ST. JOSEPH'S (170-2) 85.00
2 WAKE FOREST (417-5) 83.40
3 WESTERN KY. (249-3) 83.00

FIELD GOALS

Most field goals in a single game
1 WESTERN KY. (vs. BUTLER) 40
2 3 tied for second place.

Most total field goals in the tournament
1 WAKE FOREST 157
2 OHIO STATE 123
3 UCLA 112

Most field goals attempted in a single game
1 DETROIT (vs. WESTERN KY.) 96
2 CREIGHTON (vs. MEMPHIS STATE) 88
3 OHIO STATE (vs. WESTERN KY.) 83

Most total field goals attempted in the tournament
1 WAKE FOREST 340
2 OHIO STATE 286
3 UCLA 262

Highest field goal percentage in a single game
1 NYU (vs. VILLANOVA) (29-49) .592
2 UCLA (vs. CINCINNATI) (27-50) .540
3 WAKE FOREST (vs. UCLA) (32-61) .525

FREE THROWS

Most free throws in a single game
1 NYU (vs. ST. JOSEPH'S) 36
2 UCLA (vs. OREGON STATE) 30
3 WAKE FOREST (vs. ST. JOSEPH'S) 28

Most total free throws in the tournament
1 WAKE FOREST 103
2 UCLA 87
3 NYU 78

Most free throws attempted in a single game
1 NYU (vs. ST. JOSEPH'S) 49
2 ST. JOSEPH'S (vs. NYU) 40
3 2 tied for third place.

Most total free throws attempted in the tournament
1 WAKE FOREST 146
2 UCLA 113
3 NYU 111

Highest free throw percentage in a single game
1 OREGON STATE (vs. SEATTLE) (23-26) .885
2 WESTERN KY. (vs. DETROIT) (26-30) .867
3 WESTERN KY. (vs. BUTLER) (6-7) .857

Highest free throw percentage in the tournament (minimum 2 games)
1 WESTERN KY. (51-61) .836
2 UCLA (87-113) .770
3 OREGON STATE (51-68) .750

Fewest free throws in a single game
1 WESTERN KY. (vs. BUTLER) 6
2 3 tied for second place.

Lowest free throw percentage in a single game
1 PEPPERDINE (vs. OREGON STATE) (11-24) .458
2 COLORADO (vs. TEXAS TECH) (9-19) .474
3 UTAH STATE (vs. UCLA) (14-29) .483

Lowest free throw percentage in the tournament (minimum 2 games)
1 PEPPERDINE (22-46) .478
2 COLORADO (19-37) .514
3 UTAH STATE (45-76) .592

REBOUNDS

Most rebounds in a single game
1 DETROIT (vs. WESTERN KY.) 58
2 NYU (vs. U. MASS.) 56
3 UCLA (vs. WAKE FOREST) 55

1963

| FIRST ROUND | REGIONAL SEMIFINAL | REGIONAL FINAL | FINAL FOUR | REGIONAL FINAL | REGIONAL SEMIFINAL | FIRST ROUND |

EAST

(bye) — Duke 81

Duke 73

NYU 93

NYU 76

Pittsburgh 83

Duke 75

West Virginia 77

West Virginia 88

U. Conn. 71

St. Joseph's 59

St. Joseph's 82

St. Joseph's 97

Princeton 81

MIDWEST

Colorado 78 — (bye)

Colorado 60

Colorado St. 67

Oklahoma City 72

Oklahoma City 70

Cincinnati 80

Texas 64

Texas 68

Texas Western 47

Cincinnati 67

(bye)

Cincinnati 73

Loyola-Chicago 60 (ot)

Cincinnati 58

MIDEAST

(bye) — Illinois 70

Illinois 64

Bowling Green 77

Bowling Green 67

Notre Dame 72

Loyola-Chicago 94

Tennessee Tech 42

Loyola-Chicago 61

Loyola-Chicago 111

Loyola-Chicago 79

(bye) — Mississippi St. 51

WEST

UCLA 79 — (bye)

Arizona St. 65

Arizona St. 79 (ot)

Arizona St. 93

Utah St. 75

Oregon St. 46

Seattle 66

Oregon St. 65

Oregon St. 70

Oregon St. 83

San Francisco 61 — (bye)

CONSOLATION GAMES

National Third Place:

Duke 85

Oregon St. 63

Regional Third Place:

| | East: | Mideast: | Midwest: | West: |

West Virginia 83

NYU 73

East:

Mississippi St. 65

Bowling Green 60

Mideast:

Texas 90

Oklahoma City 83

Midwest:

San Francisco 76

UCLA 75

West:

In 1959, in 1961, and again in 1962, the Mississippi State basketball team won the Southeastern Conference title and thus received an automatic bid to the NCAA tournament; each time they turned it down. The reason was simple: the all-white team from Clarksville would not take the court against black players. In the fall of 1962, when the federal government intervened and forced the desegregation of State's sister institution, the University of Mississippi, President John F. Kennedy appealed for the state's voices of moderation to be heard. But the day James Meredith enrolled in Ole' Miss, the college town of Oxford exploded in violence.

In 1963, Mississippi State won the SEC title again. But this time a voice of moderation spoke out loud and clear. On March 2nd, Dr. Dean W. Colvard, president of the university, announced that sixth-ranked Mississippi State would accept the invitation to the tournament and an almost certain second-round pairing with third-ranked Loyola of Chicago, a team with four black starters. On March 13th, a state senator obtained an injunction prohibiting the State team from leaving Mississippi. That same night, before Colvard or another school official could be formally served with the order, Colvard called the school's athletic director and told him to take the team and leave the state. The university president then went to Alabama where he had a speaking engagement, and athletic director Wade Walker, his assistant Ralph Brown, and basketball coach Babe McCarthy drove across the border into Tennessee. The next morning the players quietly boarded a plane at a private airfield and flew to Nashville.

When Babe McCarthy saw Loyola beat Tennessee Tech 111-42 in their tourney opener, he said "I wish I'd stayed home. It was useless to come here. Nobody can beat a team like that."

Loyola, the highest scoring team in the nation, played a racehorse style of basketball, and their coach, George Ireland, particularly loved to pile up the points against segregated southern teams. (Many years later Ireland would tell *Sports Illustrated,* "I wanted them to wake up and smell the coffee.")

Four nights after witnessing the Tennessee Tech massacre, Babe McCarthy brought his Mississippi State Maroons out to meet Loyola first-hand in the regional semifinals in East Lansing, Michigan. The place was an armed camp, but the boys just came out to play some ball. The players shook hands and the game began. McCarthy knew that to trade baskets with the explosive Loyola contingent would be suicide, so he slowed the pace. The boys from State made a game of it; they scored the first 7 points and held Loyola scoreless for the first 5:49. Eventually, though, the Ramblers' strength off the backboard proved decisive, and Loyola pulled away to win 61-51.

After the game, Coach McCarthy was asked what he

expected to happen when his Maroon team returned to Mississippi. "I don't think they're going to shoot us down," he replied. Indeed, after Mississippi State star Leland Mitchell shook hands with Bowling Green's great black center Nate Thurmond following the Maroons' consolation game victory, the team returned home without incident.

The night after beating Mississippi State, Loyola returned to the same East Lansing court and took apart another Top 10 team, Illinois. The Big Ten co-champions were murdered under the boards, forced into turnovers by the Ramblers' pressing defense, and devastated by the quickness of Loyola All-American Jerry Harkness, who scored 33 points. Loyola of Chicago, in their first NCAA appearance ever, was in the national semifinals, playing against second-ranked Duke.

On the other side of the draw, inexorably, there was Cincinnati. The fearsome Bearcats, No. 1 in the nation and defeated only once (and that by a single point), were gunning for their third consecutive title. They were a veteran team, extremely skilled at playing the disciplined style instituted by Coach Ed Jucker two years earlier, and used to winning. (Neither Jucker nor any of his players had ever *not* won the national championship.) They were known for playing a virtually error-free brand of basketball, and their smothering defense was the best in the nation.

Unlike Loyola, though, Cincinnati struggled in their regional. They had to come back from an early 8-point Texas lead to make it through the opening round. The Longhorns outshot the Bearcats, 55 percent to 39 percent, and were only 2 points behind with 2:30 to play. But in the end Cincinnati prevailed. Against Colorado, whose Buffaloes had survived a bench-clearing opening-game brawl against Oklahoma City, Cincinnati came back from a 5-point second half deficit to win.

In the semis, both Cincinnati and Loyola breezed. The Bearcats led Oregon State by only 3 at the half, but when OSU's 7-foot center Mel Counts picked up his fourth foul, Cincinnati pulled away. They put on a clinic, outscoring Oregon State 50-19 in the second half. Cincinnati center George Wilson outplayed the heralded Counts, and Tony Yates held Terry Baker (the Heisman trophy-winning quarterback and second leading scorer on Oregon State's basketball team) scoreless. Meanwhile all five Cincinnati starters finished in double figures.

In their semi, Loyola played another all-white southern team—second-ranked Duke and their All-Americans Art Heyman and Jeff Mullins. The Ramblers moved the ball well against Duke's zone, getting the ball inside to their 6-7 center Les Hunter often enough for him to score 29 points. After a Duke comeback led by Heyman, the Ramblers led by only 3 with 4:19 to play. Then Loyola turned on the turbojets. By the end of the game, the Ramblers had put 20 more points on the board, while the

Blue Devils scored only 4. Like Cincinnati's win over Oregon State, it was a team victory all the way, as each of the five Loyola starters scored in double figures.

The two teams playing for the title couldn't have been more different. Loyola played a wide-open, freelancing, racehorse style of basketball. They pressed on defense, hit the boards with abandon, and fired the ball at the hoop at every opportunity. Cincinnati, on the other hand, played a tight, disciplined game. They relied on a superior switching man-to-man defense, great ball control, and had a reputation for never taking a bad shot. The team that controlled the tempo would more than likely win the game.

For the first 26 minutes it was all Cincinnati. The Bearcats kept Loyola away from the boards, shutting off their running game. They moved the ball with precision and made every shot count. And they completely shut down the high-powered Loyola offense: for one nine-minute stretch in the first half, the Ramblers didn't connect on a single field goal, and the ferocious in-your-face defense of Tom Thacker prevented Loyola's star, Jerry Harkness, from canning his first two-pointer until less than five minutes remained in the game.

With 13:56 left, Ron Bonham hit his third straight basket to put the Bearcats in the lead 45-30. The game appeared to be over. Cincinnati, the most disciplined team in the country, simply couldn't lose a 15-point lead. With everything perfectly in place for an unprecedented third straight title, Jucker called for a stall. Soon everything started going wrong for Cincinnati. The team that rarely fouled began getting into foul trouble. With 10:21 left and the score 45-33, center George Wilson was called for his fourth and sat down briefly. Within minutes, Thacker and Tony Yates also picked up number four. Loyola put on its full-court press, and the team that never got rattled started turning the ball over. Cincinnati still refused to shoot.

With 4:41 remaining, Jerry Harkness finally scored a bucket for Loyola. Within seconds, he picked off a pass and drove in for another one. The score was 48-45 Cincinnati with 4:26 remaining when Cincinnati called a time-out. When play resumed, Jucker was still in the stall. With 3:42 left Loyola's Vic Rouse committed his fourth foul and Ron Bonham sank two free throws to make the score 50-45. Harkness brought the Ramblers back to 50-48 with 2:41 left.

Cincinnati continued to freeze. After a couple of Loyola fouls and a disputed goaltending call against George Wilson, Cincinnati finally moved the ball downcourt quickly and Thacker scored on a fast break. Following a Loyola tip-in by Les Hunter, Harkness fouled Cincinnati's Larry Shingleton, who stepped to the line with 12 seconds left and a 1-point lead. He hit the first shot, but after a Loyola time-out he missed the second. With four seconds remaining, Harkness tied the score for the first time in 37 minutes.

In the overtime, the two teams traded baskets and the score was still tied when, with 1:21 left, Shingleton tied up Loyola's John Egan. The two smallest men on the court, both 5-10, jumped . . . and the Ramblers controlled the ball. They held for the last shot. With seven seconds left, Harkness went up—but Ron Bonham got his hand on the ball and the Loyola star was forced to pass it to Les Hunter near the free-throw line. Hunter's shot was off target, but Rouse leaped high and rerouted it into the hoop just before the buzzer sounded. Loyola ended Cincinnati's dream of three consecutive championships. They came back, all the way from nowhere, to win it all.

The game was one of the most thrilling in NCAA history. In the end, two players—Hunter and Rouse—whom George Ireland had recruited to come to the north side of Chicago from segregated Pearl High School in Nashville, combined to take home the championship. The Tennesseans and their teammates, two other young black men from the Bronx and an Irish-American from Chicago, had played the entire 45 minutes for Loyola. And Cincinnati, except for the few minutes George Wilson sat on the bench with four fouls, had also played their starters—three black and two white—for the entire heart-stopping game.

There had been black players in the NCAAs before—both CCNY's 1950 champions and San Francisco's 1955 team used three black players in key roles, and Wilt Chamberlain, Elgin Baylor, and Cincinnati's own Oscar Robertson and Paul Hogue had all starred in the tournament. But something was different this time. For the first time in basketball history, a *majority* of black men walked onto the court for the 1963 NCAA finals. And by the time they walked off, the game of basketball was changed forever.

FIRST ROUND EAST

NYU (93) Coach: Lou Rossini

	Min.	Total FG/FGA	Pct.	FT/FTA	Pct.	Reb. O/T	A	TO	PF	S	Blk	TP	PPM
KRAMER, B.	-	13/23	.565	11/14	.786	-/9	6	-	1	-	-	37	-
HAIRSTON, H.	-	11/17	.647	7/9	.778	-/10	0	-	4	-	-	29	-
WILLIAMS, B.	-	5/10	.500	1/2	.500	-/16	1	-	1	-	-	11	-
O'NEILL, N.	-	0/3	.000	2/6	.333	-/2	4	-	5	-	-	2	-
PATTON, B.	-	1/4	.250	0/0	.000	-/6	1	-	4	-	-	2	-
JORDAN, S.	-	1/2	.500	0/0	.000	-/3	0	-	1	-	-	2	-
BLAHA, D.	-	1/2	.500	6/7	.857	-/0	2	-	4	-	-	8	-
GROOTHUIS	-	0/1	.000	2/5	.400	-/0	0	-	0	-	-	2	-
Totals	200	32/62	.516	29/43	.674	-/46	14	-	20	-	-	93	.465

Pittsburgh (83) Coach: Bob Timmons

	Min.	Total FG/FGA	Pct.	FT/FTA	Pct.	Reb. O/T	A	TO	PF	S	Blk	TP	PPM
JINKS	-	8/14	.571	1/2	.500	-/6	1	-	4	-	-	17	-
GENERALOVICH, B.	-	5/16	.313	3/6	.500	-/4	0	-	5	-	-	13	-
GRGURICH	-	2/5	.400	1/1	1.000	-/2	3	-	2	-	-	5	-
ROMAN	-	6/19	.316	4/4	1.000	-/6	2	-	3	-	-	16	-
RUBY	-	2/3	.667	0/0	.000	-/4	0	-	4	-	-	4	-
SHEFFIELD	-	6/8	.750	8/8	1.000	-/4	2	-	1	-	-	20	-
SAVER	-	2/5	.400	3/4	.750	-/1	1	-	4	-	-	7	-
KRIEGER, P.	-	0/1	.000	1/1	1.000	-/1	0	-	5	-	-	1	-
Totals	200	31/71	.437	21/27	.778	-/28	9	-	28	-	-	83	.415

Team Rebounds: NYU 8; Pittsburgh 8. Disqualified: NYU—O'Neill; Pittsburgh—Generalovich, Krieger.

	1st Half	2nd Half	Final
NYU	44	49	93
Pittsburgh	34	49	83

West Virginia (77) Coach: George King

	Min.	Total FG/FGA	Pct.	FT/FTA	Pct.	Reb. O/T	A	TO	PF	S	Blk	TP	PPM
CATLETT, G.	-	3/5	.600	1/1	1.000	-/3	0	-	4	-	-	7	-
WOLFE, M.	-	0/3	.000	1/1	1.000	-/1	3	-	0	-	-	1	-
LOWRY, T.	-	7/11	.636	5/7	.714	-/13	1	-	3	-	-	19	-
MCCORMICK, J.	-	6/11	.545	3/3	1.000	-/5	3	-	4	-	-	15	-
THORN, R.	-	8/17	.471	1/3	.333	-/7	2	-	0	-	-	17	-
LENTZ, M.	-	0/1	.000	2/2	1.000	-/6	2	-	3	-	-	2	-
MAPHIS, B.	-	2/7	.286	1/3	.333	-/4	1	-	0	-	-	5	-
SHUCK, D.	-	1/2	.500	0/1	.000	-/2	0	-	2	-	-	2	-
RAY, R.	-	1/4	.250	7/8	.875	-/2	0	-	2	-	-	9	-
WEIR, D.	-	0/0	.000	0/0	.000	-/0	0	-	1	-	-	0	-
Totals	200	28/61	.459	21/29	.724	-/43	12	-	19	-	-	77	.385

U. Conn. (71) Coach: George Wigton

	Min.	Total FG/FGA	Pct.	FT/FTA	Pct.	Reb. O/T	A	TO	PF	S	Blk	TP	PPM
MANNING	-	4/13	.308	1/2	.500	-/10	2	-	2	-	-	9	-
KIMBALL	-	8/14	.571	3/7	.429	-/19	1	-	4	-	-	19	-
SLOMCENSKI, E.	-	1/6	.167	0/1	.000	-/9	0	-	5	-	-	2	-
PERNO	-	4/14	.286	8/10	.800	-/4	4	-	2	-	-	16	-
CZUCHRY	-	0/2	.000	2/2	1.000	-/0	1	-	0	-	-	2	-
COMEY	-	8/17	.471	1/3	.333	-/1	0	-	3	-	-	17	-
HAINES	-	0/3	.000	0/0	.000	-/3	0	-	1	-	-	0	-
HULTEEN	-	1/6	.167	4/4	1.000	-/3	0	-	3	-	-	6	-
Totals	200	26/75	.347	19/29	.655	-/49	8	-	20	-	-	71	.355

Team Rebounds: West Virginia 3; U. Conn. 5. Disqualified: U. Conn.—Slomcenski.

	1st Half	2nd Half	Final
West Virginia	42	35	77
U. Conn.	40	31	71

St. Joseph's (82) Coach: Jack Ramsay

	Min.	Total FG/FGA	Pct.	FT/FTA	Pct.	Reb. O/T	A	TO	PF	S	Blk	TP	PPM
WYNNE, T.	-	5/16	.313	4/7	.571	-/7	0	-	4	-	-	14	-
BOYLE, J.	-	6/13	.462	4/4	1.000	-/5	1	-	4	-	-	16	-
HOFFMAN, L.	-	0/1	.000	0/1	.000	-/3	0	-	1	-	-	0	-
LYNAM, J.	-	8/16	.500	2/3	.667	-/4	4	-	3	-	-	18	-
COURTIN, S.	-	9/19	.474	3/3	1.000	-/6	1	-	5	-	-	21	-
TILLER, J.	-	2/3	.667	4/6	.667	-/10	0	-	1	-	-	8	-
KELLY, J.	-	2/6	.333	0/0	.000	-/1	1	-	1	-	-	4	-
HOY, B.	-	0/3	.000	1/3	.333	-/0	0	-	1	-	-	1	-
Totals	225	32/77	.416	18/27	.667	-/36	7	-	20	-	-	82	.364

Princeton (81) Coach: B. Van Breda Kolff

	Min.	Total FG/FGA	Pct.	FT/FTA	Pct.	Reb. O/T	A	TO	PF	S	Blk	TP	PPM
HAARLOW, B.	-	5/9	.556	0/1	.000	-/4	0	-	1	-	-	10	-
BERLING, C.	-	1/1	1.000	0/0	.000	-/0	0	-	1	-	-	2	-
HOWARD, W.	-	2/2	1.000	3/4	.750	-/7	0	-	4	-	-	7	-
BRADLEY, B.	-	12/21	.571	16/16	1.000	-/16	3	-	5	-	-	40	-
HYLAND, A.	-	8/16	.500	4/4	1.000	-/7	7	-	3	-	-	20	-
ROTH, D.	-	0/2	.000	2/2	1.000	-/5	1	-	5	-	-	0	-
JOHNSTON, R.	-	1/2	.500	0/0	.000	-/1	0	-	1	-	-	2	-
NIEMANN, D.	-	0/1	.000	0/0	.000	-/1	0	-	2	-	-	0	-
KINGSTON, W.	-	0/0	.000	0/0	.000	-/0	0	-	0	-	-	0	-
Totals	225	29/54	.537	23/27	.852	-/41	11	-	22	-	-	81	.360

Team Rebounds: St. Joseph's 2; Princeton 4. Disqualified: St. Joseph's—Courtin; Princeton—Bradley, Roth.

	1st Half	2nd Half	1st OT	Final
St. Joseph's	31	46	5	82
Princeton	33	44	4	81

FIRST ROUND MIDEAST

Bowling Green (77) Coach: Harold Anderson

	Min.	Total FG/FGA	Pct.	FT/FTA	Pct.	Reb. O/T	A	TO	PF	S	Blk	TP	PPM
GILBERT	-	1/ 5	.200	2/ 2	1.000	-/ 5	-	-	4	-	-	4	-
JUNIOR	-	4/ 9	.444	0/ 0	.000	-/ 7	-	-	1	-	-	8	-
THURMOND. N.	-	5/16	.313	6/ 9	.667	-/20	-	-	4	-	-	16	-
HALEY	-	4/ 7	.571	0/ 1	.000	-/ 2	-	-	1	-	-	8	-
KOMIVES. H.	-	10/25	.400	14/15	.933	-/ 7	-	-	2	-	-	34	-
CHATMAN. E.	-	1/ 2	.500	1/ 1	1.000	-/ 2	-	-	2	-	-	3	-
REYNOLDS	-	2/ 4	.500	0/ 0	.000	-/ 2	-	-	0	-	-	4	-
Totals	200	27/68	.397	23/28	.821	-/45	-	-	14	-	-	77	.385

Notre Dame (72) Coach: John Jordan

	Min.	Total FG/FGA	Pct.	FT/FTA	Pct.	Reb. O/T	A	TO	PF	S	Blk	TP	PPM
MILLER. J.	-	1/ 7	.143	1/ 1	1.000	-/ 5	-	-	3	-	-	3	-
SAHM. W.	-	7/13	.538	0/ 0	.000	-/15	-	-	3	-	-	14	-
JESEWITZ. L.	-	1/ 8	.125	4/ 7	.571	-/10	-	-	4	-	-	6	-
ANDREOLI. J.	-	7/22	.318	3/ 3	1.000	-/ 3	-	-	2	-	-	17	-
MATTHEWS. J.	-	9/19	.474	5/ 7	.714	-/ 3	-	-	5	-	-	23	-
ERLENBAUGH. R.	-	1/ 3	.333	3/ 3	1.000	-/ 4	-	-	2	-	-	5	-
SKARICH. S.	-	2/ 4	.500	0/ 0	.000	-/ 5	-	-	0	-	-	4	-
Totals	200	28/76	.368	16/21	.762	-/45	-	-	19	-	-	72	.360

Team Rebounds: Bowling Green 4; Notre Dame 5. Disqualified: Notre Dame—Matthews.

	1st Half	2nd Half	Final
Bowling Green	42	35	77
Notre Dame	40	32	72

Tennessee Tech (42) Coach: Johnny Oldham

	Min.	Total FG/FGA	Pct.	FT/FTA	Pct.	Reb. O/T	A	TO	PF	S	Blk	TP	PPM
CARDWELL	-	4/ 6	.667	0/ 0	.000	-/ 4	-	-	4	-	-	8	-
YOUNG	-	6/21	.286	2/ 3	.667	-/ 3	-	-	1	-	-	14	-
ADAMS	-	0/ 1	.000	1/ 1	1.000	-/ 2	-	-	3	-	-	1	-
RYCHENER	-	2/10	.200	0/ 0	.000	-/ 4	-	-	5	-	-	4	-
MASON	-	4/15	.267	2/ 2	1.000	-/ 2	-	-	4	-	-	10	-
DAVENPORT	-	0/ 1	.000	0/ 0	.000	-/ 1	-	-	2	-	-	0	-
NICHOLS	-	0/ 5	.000	0/ 0	.000	-/ 2	-	-	2	-	-	0	-
SEXTON	-	2/ 9	.222	0/ 0	.000	-/ 8	-	-	1	-	-	4	-
WRIGHT	-	0/ 6	.000	0/ 0	.000	-/ 8	-	-	1	-	-	0	-
HAYS	-	0/ 2	.000	1/ 1	1.000	-/ 1	-	-	4	-	-	1	-
UNDERHILL	-	0/ 1	.000	0/ 0	.000	-/ 1	-	-	0	-	-	0	-
WOOD	-	0/ 5	.000	0/ 1	.000	-/ 2	-	-	0	-	-	0	-
Totals	200	18/82	.220	6/ 8	.750	-/38	-	-	27	-	-	42	.210

Loyola-Chicago (111) Coach: George Ireland

	Min.	Total FG/FGA	Pct.	FT/FTA	Pct.	Reb. O/T	A	TO	PF	S	Blk	TP	PPM
HARKNESS. J.	-	9/17	.529	1/ 4	.250	-/12	-	-	1	-	-	19	-
ROUSE. V.	-	7/ 9	.778	4/ 5	.800	-/14	-	-	2	-	-	18	-
HUNTER. L.	-	6/ 8	.750	5/ 5	1.000	-/ 6	-	-	1	-	-	17	-
EGAN. J.	-	5/13	.385	8/10	.800	-/ 5	-	-	2	-	-	18	-
MILLER. R.	-	7/14	.500	7/ 8	.875	-/ 7	-	-	0	-	-	21	-
WOOD. C.	-	2/ 3	.667	2/ 2	1.000	-/ 5	-	-	1	-	-	6	-
CONNAUGHTON. D.	-	2/ 2	1.000	2/ 4	.500	-/ 3	-	-	0	-	-	6	-
REARDON. J.	-	1/ 3	.333	0/ 0	.000	-/ 4	-	-	0	-	-	2	-
ROCHELLE. R.	-	1/ 3	.333	2/ 3	.667	-/ 4	-	-	0	-	-	4	-
Totals	200	40/72	.556	31/41	.756	-/60	-	-	7	-	-	111	.555

Team Rebounds: Loyola-Chicago 6; Tennessee Tech 4. Disqualified: Tennessee Tech—Rychener.

	1st Half	2nd Half	Final
Tennessee Tech	20	22	42
Loyola-Chicago	61	50	111

FIRST ROUND MIDWEST

Colorado State (67) Coach: Jim Williams

	Min.	Total FG/FGA	Pct.	FT/FTA	Pct.	Reb. O/T	A	TO	PF	S	Blk	TP	PPM
ETHERIDGE. B.	-	1/ 8	.125	2/ 2	1.000	-/15	-	-	4	-	-	4	-
SIGAFOOS. D.	-	6/10	.600	0/ 1	.000	-/ 4	-	-	4	-	-	12	-
GREEN. W.	-	6/15	.400	7/ 8	.875	-/12	-	-	5	-	-	19	-
MATTHEWS. T.	-	8/13	.615	1/ 3	.333	-/ 4	-	-	1	-	-	17	-
ANDERSON	-	5/10	.500	0/ 1	.000	-/ 4	-	-	1	-	-	10	-
ELLIS. H.	-	2/ 4	.500	1/ 1	1.000	-/ 2	-	-	1	-	-	5	-
FOSTER. D.	-	0/ 0	.000	0/ 1	.000	-/ 1	-	-	2	-	-	0	-
Totals	200	28/60	.467	11/17	.647	-/41	-	-	18	-	-	67	.335

Oklahoma City (70) Coach: Abe Lemons

	Min.	Total FG/FGA	Pct.	FT/FTA	Pct.	Reb. O/T	A	TO	PF	S	Blk	TP	PPM
JACKSON. E.	-	4/10	.400	2/ 6	.333	-/10	-	-	3	-	-	10	-
MILLER. J.	-	2/ 3	.667	0/ 0	.000	-/ 3	-	-	1	-	-	4	-
JOHNSTON. B.	-	4/12	.333	3/ 5	.600	-/ 9	-	-	3	-	-	11	-
KOPER. B.	-	8/21	.381	1/ 1	1.000	-/ 6	-	-	1	-	-	17	-
HILL. G.	-	8/13	.615	3/ 7	.429	-/ 0	-	-	4	-	-	19	-
GIBBON	-	0/ 0	.000	1/ 2	.500	-/ 1	-	-	0	-	-	1	-
STEPHENS. E.	-	0/ 1	.000	0/ 1	.000	-/ 2	-	-	4	-	-	0	-
WHITE	-	3/ 7	.429	0/ 2	.000	-/ 3	-	-	0	-	-	6	-
HEUSMAN	-	1/ 3	.333	0/ 0	.000	-/ 0	-	-	2	-	-	2	-
HOPKINS	-	0/ 0	.000	0/ 0	.000	-/ 0	-	-	0	-	-	0	-
Totals	200	30/70	.429	10/24	.417	-/34	-	-	18	-	-	70	.350

Team Rebounds: Oklahoma City 10; Colorado State 7. Disqualified: Colorado State—Green.

	1st Half	2nd Half	Final
Colorado State	42	25	67
Oklahoma City	31	39	70

Texas (65) Coach: Harold Bradley

	Min.	Total FG/FGA	Pct.	FT/FTA	Pct.	Reb. O/T	A	TO	PF	S	Blk	TP	PPM
FRANKS. L.	-	4/ 6	.667	1/ 1	1.000	-/ 6	-	-	3	-	-	9	-
FULTZ. J.	-	7/10	.700	2/ 3	.667	-/ 5	-	-	3	-	-	16	-
HUMPHREY	-	8/11	.727	2/ 4	.500	-/10	-	-	2	-	-	18	-
GILBERT. J.	-	2/ 8	.250	7/ 7	1.000	-/ 0	-	-	2	-	-	11	-
PURYEAR	-	1/ 2	.500	4/ 5	.800	-/ 1	-	-	3	-	-	6	-
HELLER	-	1/ 1	1.000	1/ 1	1.000	-/ 2	-	-	1	-	-	3	-
FISHER	-	0/ 1	.000	0/ 1	.000	-/ 2	-	-	5	-	-	0	-
CLARK	-	0/ 2	.000	0/ 0	.000	-/ 0	-	-	0	-	-	0	-
WEEKS	-	0/ 1	.000	0/ 0	.000	-/ 2	-	-	0	-	-	0	-
DUGAN	-	1/ 1	1.000	0/ 0	.000	-/ 1	-	-	4	-	-	2	-
SMITH	-	0/ 0	.000	0/ 0	.000	-/ 0	-	-	0	-	-	0	-
CARTER	-	0/ 0	.000	0/ 0	.000	-/ 0	-	-	0	-	-	0	-
Totals	200	24/43	.558	17/22	.773	-/29	-	-	23	-	-	65	.325

Texas Western (47) Coach: Don Haskins

	Min.	Total FG/FGA	Pct.	FT/FTA	Pct.	Reb. O/T	A	TO	PF	S	Blk	TP	PPM
TORREN. T.	-	1/ 2	.500	3/ 4	.750	-/ 0	-	-	3	-	-	5	-
RICHARDSON. N.	-	2/ 7	.286	0/ 1	.000	-/ 2	-	-	4	-	-	4	-
BARNES. J.	-	2/ 4	.500	6/ 9	.667	-/ 6	-	-	5	-	-	10	-
LESLEY. B.	-	3/12	.250	2/ 2	1.000	-/ 5	-	-	2	-	-	8	-
BROWN	-	6/15	.400	3/ 4	.750	-/ 2	-	-	2	-	-	15	-
VAUGHN. D.	-	0/ 2	.000	1/ 1	1.000	-/ 2	-	-	1	-	-	1	-
CAMPBELL	-	1/ 2	.500	2/ 3	.667	-/ 5	-	-	2	-	-	4	-
Totals	200	15/44	.341	17/24	.708	-/22	-	-	19	-	-	47	.235

Team Rebounds: Texas 5; Texas Western 4. Disqualified: Texas—Fisher; Texas Western—Barnes.

	1st Half	2nd Half	Final
Texas	25	40	65
Texas Western	25	22	47

FIRST ROUND WEST

Arizona State (79) — Coach: Ned Wulk

	Min.	Total FG/FGA	Pct.	FT/FTA	Pct.	Reb. O/T	A	TO	PF	S	Blk	TP	PPM
CALDWELL, J.	-	13/22	.591	5/6	.833	-/9	-	-	4	-	-	31	-
BECKER, A.	-	8/18	.444	1/2	.500	-/19	-	-	4	-	-	17	-
CERKVENIK, T.	-	1/5	.200	5/7	.714	-/10	-	-	3	-	-	7	-
SENITZA	-	5/13	.385	2/3	.667	-/2	-	-	0	-	-	12	-
DAIRMAN	-	4/15	.267	0/0	.000	-/8	-	-	3	-	-	8	-
HOWARD	-	1/2	.500	1/4	.250	-/0	-	-	0	-	-	3	-
DISARUFINO	-	0/0	.000	1/2	.500	-/0	-	-	0	-	-	1	-
Totals	225	32/75	.427	15/24	.625	-/48	-	-	14	-	-	79	.351

Utah State (75) — Coach: Ladell Anderson

	Min.	Total FG/FGA	Pct.	FT/FTA	Pct.	Reb. O/T	A	TO	PF	S	Blk	TP	PPM
ESTES, W.	-	12/22	.545	8/8	1.000	-/9	-	-	4	-	-	32	-
JOHNSON	-	7/13	.538	1/2	.500	-/7	-	-	5	-	-	15	-
COLLIER	-	2/12	.167	4/4	1.000	-/11	-	-	4	-	-	8	-
HASEN, M.	-	6/12	.500	0/0	.000	-/2	-	-	5	-	-	12	-
GOLDSBERRY	-	2/6	.333	0/1	.000	-/5	-	-	3	-	-	4	-
ANGLE	-	2/5	.400	0/0	.000	-/2	-	-	1	-	-	4	-
WATTS	-	0/0	.000	0/0	.000	-/0	-	-	0	-	-	0	-
CASEY	-	0/0	.000	0/0	.000	-/0	-	-	0	-	-	0	-
Totals	225	31/70	.443	13/15	.867	-/36	-	-	22	-	-	75	.333

Team Rebounds: Arizona St. 5; Utah State 4. Disqualified: Utah State—Johnson, Hasen.

	1st Half	2nd Half	1st OT	Final
Arizona St.	35	32	12	79
Utah State	41	26	8	75

Seattle (66) — Coach: Clair Markey

	Min.	Total FG/FGA	Pct.	FT/FTA	Pct.	Reb. O/T	A	TO	PF	S	Blk	TP	PPM
DUNSTON, E.	-	2/7	.286	1/2	.500	-/6	-	-	4	-	-	5	-
SMITHER, B.	-	4/9	.444	1/1	1.000	-/6	-	-	2	-	-	9	-
TRESVANT	-	6/11	.545	4/4	1.000	-/8	-	-	3	-	-	16	-
MILES, E.	-	11/19	.579	6/9	.667	-/5	-	-	3	-	-	28	-
WILLIAMS, C.	-	4/8	.500	0/0	.000	-/2	-	-	3	-	-	8	-
PRESTON, J.	-	0/1	.000	0/0	.000	-/0	-	-	0	-	-	0	-
Totals	200	27/55	.491	12/16	.750	-/27	-	-	15	-	-	66	.330

Oregon State (70) — Coach: Amory "Slats" Gill

	Min.	Total FG/FGA	Pct.	FT/FTA	Pct.	Reb. O/T	A	TO	PF	S	Blk	TP	PPM
PAULY, S.	-	6/10	.600	1/3	.333	-/5	-	-	3	-	-	13	-
KRAUS, J.	-	1/1	1.000	0/0	.000	-/1	-	-	0	-	-	2	-
COUNTS, M.	-	13/21	.619	4/5	.800	-/11	-	-	3	-	-	30	-
PETERS, F.	-	3/6	.500	2/2	1.000	-/3	-	-	3	-	-	8	-
BAKER, T.	-	2/8	.250	5/7	.714	-/3	-	-	4	-	-	9	-
JARVIS, J.	-	3/7	.429	0/0	.000	-/2	-	-	0	-	-	6	-
ROSSI, G.	-	0/0	.000	0/0	.000	-/0	-	-	1	-	-	0	-
HAYWARD, D.	-	1/3	.333	0/0	.000	-/1	-	-	1	-	-	2	-
Totals	200	29/56	.518	12/17	.706	-/26	-	-	15	-	-	70	.350

Team Rebounds: Oregon State 5; Seattle 7. Disqualified: None.

	1st Half	2nd Half	Final
Seattle	29	37	66
Oregon State	35	35	70

REGIONAL SEMIFINAL EAST

Duke (81) — Coach: Vic Bubas

	Min.	Total FG/FGA	Pct.	FT/FTA	Pct.	Reb. O/T	A	TO	PF	S	Blk	TP	PPM
HEYMAN, A.	-	6/21	.286	10/14	.714	-/13	-	-	2	-	-	22	-
MULLINS, J.	-	10/16	.625	5/7	.714	-/7	-	-	0	-	-	25	-
BUCKLEY, J.	-	4/8	.500	2/5	.400	-/16	-	-	5	-	-	10	-
HARRISON, B.	-	2/2	1.000	0/0	.000	-/0	-	-	4	-	-	4	-
SCHMIDT, F.	-	6/10	.600	0/0	.000	-/0	-	-	3	-	-	12	-
HERBSTER, R.	-	3/3	1.000	0/0	.000	-/1	-	-	2	-	-	6	-
TISON, H.	-	1/2	.500	0/0	.000	-/4	-	-	3	-	-	2	-
FERGUSON, D.	-	0/2	.000	0/0	.000	-/1	-	-	0	-	-	0	-
Totals	200	32/64	.500	17/26	.654	-/42	-	-	19	-	-	81	.405

NYU (76) — Coach: Lou Rossini

	Min.	Total FG/FGA	Pct.	FT/FTA	Pct.	Reb. O/T	A	TO	PF	S	Blk	TP	PPM
KRAMER, B.	-	12/26	.462	10/11	.909	-/4	-	-	4	-	-	34	-
WILLIAMS, B.	-	2/4	.500	1/2	.500	-/3	-	-	2	-	-	5	-
HAIRSTON, H.	-	8/13	.615	2/4	.500	-/11	-	-	4	-	-	18	-
O'NEILL, N.	-	3/9	.333	0/0	.000	-/4	-	-	3	-	-	6	-
PATTON, B.	-	2/5	.400	0/1	.000	-/5	-	-	4	-	-	4	-
BLAHA, D.	-	3/9	.333	3/6	.500	-/4	-	-	1	-	-	9	-
JORDAN, S.	-	0/1	.000	0/0	.000	-/1	-	-	0	-	-	0	-
Totals	200	30/67	.448	16/24	.667	-/32	-	-	18	-	-	76	.380

Disqualified: Duke—Buckley.

	1st Half	2nd Half	Final
Duke	32	49	81
NYU	27	49	76

West Virginia (88) — Coach: George King

	Min.	Total FG/FGA	Pct.	FT/FTA	Pct.	Reb. O/T	A	TO	PF	S	Blk	TP	PPM
CATLETT, G.	-	2/5	.400	1/1	1.000	-/2	1	-	5	-	-	5	-
WOLFE, M.	-	2/5	.400	1/1	1.000	-/7	0	-	5	-	-	5	-
LOWRY, T.	-	1/3	.333	1/1	1.000	-/5	0	-	3	-	-	3	-
MCCORMICK, J.	-	10/18	.556	3/5	.600	-/2	2	-	3	-	-	23	-
THORN, R.	-	16/28	.571	12/15	.800	-/6	1	-	3	-	-	44	-
SHUCK, D.	-	1/1	1.000	0/0	.000	-/3	0	-	1	-	-	2	-
WEIR, D.	-	0/1	.000	0/0	.000	-/0	0	-	1	-	-	0	-
MAPHIS, J.	-	1/6	.167	0/0	.000	-/3	1	-	2	-	-	2	-
RAY, R.	-	1/2	.500	2/2	1.000	-/2	0	-	3	-	-	4	-
Totals	200	34/69	.493	20/25	.800	-/30	5	-	26	-	-	88	.440

St. Joseph's (97) — Coach: Jack Ramsay

	Min.	Total FG/FGA	Pct.	FT/FTA	Pct.	Reb. O/T	A	TO	PF	S	Blk	TP	PPM
BOYLE, J.	-	9/11	.818	5/6	.833	-/8	7	-	4	-	-	23	-
WYNNE, T.	-	10/19	.526	3/5	.600	-/7	2	-	3	-	-	23	-
HOFFMAN, L.	-	4/9	.444	1/7	.143	-/11	0	-	3	-	-	9	-
LYNAM, J.	-	6/8	.750	8/12	.667	-/7	3	-	3	-	-	20	-
COURTIN, S.	-	7/13	.538	3/4	.750	-/4	2	-	5	-	-	17	-
TILLER, J.	-	2/3	.667	1/2	.500	-/1	0	-	1	-	-	5	-
HOY, B.	-	0/0	.000	0/1	.000	-/1	1	-	1	-	-	0	-
KELLY, J.	-	0/0	.000	0/0	.000	-/1	0	-	0	-	-	0	-
Totals	200	38/63	.603	21/37	.568	-/34	15	-	20	-	-	97	.485

Team Rebounds: St. Joseph's 8; West Virginia 9. Disqualified: St. Joseph's—Courtin; West Virginia—Catlett, Wolfe.

	1st Half	2nd Half	Final
West Virginia	37	51	88
St. Joseph's	58	39	97

REGIONAL SEMIFINAL MIDEAST

Illinois (70)   Coach: Harry Combes

	Min.	Total FG/FGA	Pct.	FT/FTA	Pct.	Reb. O/T	A	TO	PF	S	Blk	TP	PPM
DOWNEY, D.	-	7/20	.350	6/9	.667	-/12	-	-	4	-	-	20	-
STARNES, B.	-	1/7	.143	1/2	.500	-/2	-	-	1	-	-	3	-
BURWELL, B.	-	8/16	.500	5/9	.556	-/11	-	-	1	-	-	21	-
SMALL, B.	-	4/14	.286	5/5	1.000	-/2	-	-	1	-	-	13	-
BRODY, T.	-	1/2	.500	1/1	1.000	-/0	-	-	4	-	-	3	-
THOREN, S.	-	5/9	.556	0/0	.000	-/12	-	-	2	-	-	10	-
EDWARDS, B.	-	0/0	.000	0/0	.000	-/1	-	-	2	-	-	0	-
Totals	200	26/68	.382	18/26	.692	-/40	-	-	15	-	-	70	.350

Bowling Green (67)   Coach: Harold Anderson

	Min.	Total FG/FGA	Pct.	FT/FTA	Pct.	Reb. O/T	A	TO	PF	S	Blk	TP	PPM
JUNIOR	-	6/17	.353	2/2	1.000	-/8	-	-	4	-	-	14	-
GILBERT	-	2/8	.250	0/0	.000	-/6	-	-	4	-	-	4	-
THURMOND, N.	-	6/19	.316	2/3	.667	-/19	-	-	3	-	-	14	-
HALEY	-	1/3	.333	3/3	1.000	-/4	-	-	3	-	-	5	-
KOMIVES, H.	-	8/21	.381	9/10	.900	-/8	-	-	5	-	-	25	-
CHATMAN, E.	-	2/5	.400	1/1	1.000	-/3	-	-	3	-	-	5	-
REYNOLDS	-	0/1	.000	0/0	.000	-/0	-	-	0	-	-	0	-
Totals	200	25/74	.338	17/19	.895	-/48	-	-	22	-	-	67	.335

Team Rebounds: Illinois 9; Bowling Green 3. Disqualified: Bowling Green—Komives.

	1st Half	2nd Half	Final
Illinois	35	35	70
Bowling Green	37	30	67

Loyola-Chicago (61)   Coach: George Ireland

	Min.	Total FG/FGA	Pct.	FT/FTA	Pct.	Reb. O/T	A	TO	PF	S	Blk	TP	PPM
HARKNESS, J.	-	7/11	.636	6/7	.857	-/9	-	-	1	-	-	20	-
ROUSE, V.	-	8/24	.333	0/0	.000	-/19	-	-	4	-	-	16	-
HUNTER, L.	-	3/13	.231	6/7	.857	-/10	-	-	3	-	-	12	-
EGAN, J.	-	1/9	.111	0/1	.000	-/1	-	-	5	-	-	2	-
MILLER, R.	-	5/9	.556	1/1	1.000	-/4	-	-	1	-	-	11	-
WOOD, C.	-	0/0	.000	0/0	.000	-/1	-	-	3	-	-	0	-
Totals	200	24/66	.364	13/16	.813	-/44	-	-	17	-	-	61	.305

Mississippi State (51)   Coach: Babe McCarthy

	Min.	Total FG/FGA	Pct.	FT/FTA	Pct.	Reb. O/T	A	TO	PF	S	Blk	TP	PPM
MITCHELL, L.	-	6/10	.600	2/5	.400	-/11	-	-	5	-	-	14	-
GOLD, J.	-	3/9	.333	5/7	.714	-/3	-	-	3	-	-	11	-
BRINKER	-	3/6	.500	3/5	.600	-/7	-	-	4	-	-	9	-
HUTTON	-	5/9	.556	0/2	.000	-/1	-	-	0	-	-	10	-
STROUD, W.	-	3/15	.200	1/1	1.000	-/3	-	-	2	-	-	7	-
NICHOLS, A.	-	0/0	.000	0/0	.000	-/0	-	-	0	-	-	0	-
Totals	200	20/49	.408	11/20	.550	-/25	-	-	14	-	-	51	.255

Team Rebounds: Loyola-Chicago 4; Mississippi St. 10. Disqualified: Loyola-Chicago—Egan; Mississippi St.—Mitchell.

	1st Half	2nd Half	Final
Loyola-Chicago	26	35	61
Mississippi St.	19	32	51

REGIONAL SEMIFINAL MIDWEST

Colorado (78)   Coach: Sox Walseth

	Min.	Total FG/FGA	Pct.	FT/FTA	Pct.	Reb. O/T	A	TO	PF	S	Blk	TP	PPM
MUELLER, M.	-	4/6	.667	3/5	.600	2/5	-	-	3	-	-	11	-
CHARLTON, K.	-	9/14	.643	8/10	.800	3/12	-	-	0	-	-	26	-
DAVIS, J.	-	8/13	.615	0/4	.000	5/17	-	-	3	-	-	16	-
LEE, E.	-	8/19	.421	1/4	.250	5/6	-	-	0	-	-	17	-
PARSONS, G.	-	0/6	.000	5/7	.714	2/5	-	-	2	-	-	5	-
MELTON	-	1/3	.333	1/2	.500	1/1	-	-	1	-	-	3	-
SPARKS, G.	-	0/1	.000	0/0	.000	0/0	-	-	1	-	-	0	-
JOYCE, B.	-	0/0	.000	0/0	.000	0/0	-	-	1	-	-	0	-
Totals	200	30/62	.484	18/32	.563	18/46	-	16	11	-	-	78	.390

Oklahoma City (72)   Coach: Abe Lemons

	Min.	Total FG/FGA	Pct.	FT/FTA	Pct.	Reb. O/T	A	TO	PF	S	Blk	TP	PPM
JACKSON, E.	-	5/11	.455	1/2	.500	5/11	-	-	3	-	-	11	-
MILLER, J.	-	0/3	.000	2/2	1.000	1/2	-	-	2	-	-	2	-
JOHNSTON, B.	-	1/3	.333	2/3	.667	2/6	-	-	2	-	-	4	-
KOPER, B.	-	11/28	.393	4/4	1.000	1/1	-	-	2	-	-	26	-
HILL, G.	-	7/15	.467	1/1	1.000	1/2	-	-	5	-	-	15	-
GIBBON	-	0/0	.000	0/0	.000	0/0	-	-	0	-	-	0	-
STEPHENS, E.	-	0/2	.000	2/3	.667	2/4	-	-	4	-	-	2	-
WHITE	-	4/10	.400	0/0	.000	1/2	-	-	0	-	-	8	-
HEUSMAN	-	2/3	.667	0/0	.000	0/2	-	-	2	-	-	4	-
SNIDER	-	0/1	.000	0/0	.000	0/0	-	-	0	-	-	0	-
Totals	200	30/76	.395	12/15	.800	13/30	-	12	20	-	-	72	.360

Team Rebounds: Colorado 7; Oklahoma City 10. Disqualified: Oklahoma City—Hill.

	1st Half	2nd Half	Final
Colorado	37	41	78
Oklahoma City	34	38	72

Texas (68)   Coach: Harold Bradley

	Min.	Total FG/FGA	Pct.	FT/FTA	Pct.	Reb. O/T	A	TO	PF	S	Blk	TP	PPM
FRANKS, L.	-	8/13	.615	2/2	1.000	2/6	-	-	5	-	-	18	-
FULTZ, J.	-	6/9	.667	1/2	.500	0/8	-	-	4	-	-	13	-
HUMPHREY	-	4/4	1.000	1/1	1.000	0/5	-	-	4	-	-	9	-
GILBERT, J.	-	4/10	.400	5/5	1.000	0/1	-	-	2	-	-	13	-
PURYEAR	-	4/8	.500	1/1	1.000	0/5	-	-	1	-	-	9	-
HELLER	-	0/1	.000	0/0	.000	0/0	-	-	1	-	-	0	-
FISHER	-	2/6	.333	0/0	.000	2/3	-	-	2	-	-	4	-
CLARK	-	0/0	.000	1/1	1.000	0/0	-	-	1	-	-	1	-
WEEKS	-	0/0	.000	0/0	.000	0/0	-	-	0	-	-	0	-
DUGAN	-	0/0	.000	1/1	1.000	0/2	-	-	3	-	-	1	-
SMITH	-	0/0	.000	0/0	.000	0/0	-	-	1	-	-	0	-
Totals	200	28/51	.549	12/13	.923	4/30	-	17	23	-	-	68	.340

Cincinnati (73)   Coach: Ed Jucker

	Min.	Total FG/FGA	Pct.	FT/FTA	Pct.	Reb. O/T	A	TO	PF	S	Blk	TP	PPM
BONHAM, R.	-	9/23	.391	6/11	.545	3/4	-	-	1	-	-	24	-
THACKER, T.	-	5/11	.455	4/7	.571	4/7	-	-	1	-	-	14	-
WILSON, G.	-	8/20	.400	9/12	.750	9/12	-	-	2	-	-	25	-
YATES, T.	-	2/6	.333	3/3	1.000	1/2	-	-	4	-	-	7	-
HEIDOTTING, D.	-	1/1	1.000	0/0	.000	0/0	-	-	1	-	-	2	-
SHINGLETON, L.	-	0/3	.000	1/2	.500	2/4	-	-	2	-	-	1	-
Totals	200	25/64	.391	23/35	.657	19/29	-	8	11	-	-	73	.365

Team Rebounds: Cincinnati 11; Texas 4. Disqualified: Texas—Franks.

	1st Half	2nd Half	Final
Texas	34	34	68
Cincinnati	36	37	73

REGIONAL SEMIFINAL WEST

UCLA (79) — Coach: John Wooden

	Min.	Total FG/FGA	Pct.	FT/FTA	Pct.	Reb. O/T	A	TO	PF	S	Blk	TP	PPM
HIRSCH, J.	-	8/17	.471	3/4	.750	-/4	-	-	5	-	-	19	-
GOSS, F.	-	3/10	.300	2/3	.667	-/5	-	-	0	-	-	8	-
SLAUGHTER, F.	-	4/9	.444	6/7	.857	-/5	-	-	4	-	-	14	-
HAZZARD, W.	-	4/11	.364	5/7	.714	-/5	-	-	2	-	-	13	-
GOODRICH, G.	-	1/8	.125	1/2	.500	-/1	-	-	0	-	-	3	-
ERICKSON, K.	-	0/6	.000	2/2	1.000	-/2	-	-	0	-	-	2	-
STEWART, K.	-	5/15	.333	3/4	.750	-/11	-	-	2	-	-	13	-
WAXMAN, D.	-	2/5	.400	1/3	.333	-/1	-	-	2	-	-	5	-
MILHORN, J.	-	1/5	.200	0/0	.000	-/3	-	-	3	-	-	2	-
Totals	200	28/86	.326	23/32	.719	-/37	-	-	18	-	-	79	.395

Arizona State (93) — Coach: Ned Wulk

	Min.	Total FG/FGA	Pct.	FT/FTA	Pct.	Reb. O/T	A	TO	PF	S	Blk	TP	PPM
CERKVENIK, T.	-	9/12	.750	0/1	.000	-/13	-	-	2	-	-	18	-
CALDWELL, J.	-	10/18	.556	2/3	.667	-/12	-	-	2	-	-	22	-
SENITZA	-	5/7	.714	3/4	.750	-/1	-	-	3	-	-	13	-
BECKER, A.	-	9/14	.643	5/6	.833	-/13	-	-	3	-	-	23	-
DAIRMAN	-	6/10	.600	1/4	.250	-/3	-	-	3	-	-	13	-
HOWARD	-	1/5	.200	0/1	.000	-/1	-	-	2	-	-	2	-
RISARUFINA	-	0/4	.000	0/0	.000	-/2	-	-	4	-	-	0	-
ORR	-	0/1	.000	0/2	.000	-/2	-	-	2	-	-	0	-
JONES	-	1/6	.167	0/0	.000	-/0	-	-	2	-	-	2	-
OWENS	-	0/1	.000	0/0	.000	-/1	-	-	1	-	-	0	-
STURGEON	-	0/1	.000	0/0	.000	-/0	-	-	1	-	-	0	-
Totals	200	41/79	.519	11/21	.524	-/48	-	-	25	-	-	93	.465

Team Rebounds: Arizona St. 17; UCLA 12. Disqualified: UCLA—Hirsch.

	1st Half	2nd Half	Final
UCLA	31	48	79
Arizona St.	62	31	93

Oregon State (65) — Coach: Amory "Slats" Gill

	Min.	Total FG/FGA	Pct.	FT/FTA	Pct.	Reb. O/T	A	TO	PF	S	Blk	TP	PPM
KRAUS, J.	-	1/3	.333	1/2	.500	-/9	-	-	4	-	-	3	-
BAKER, T.	-	10/17	.588	1/1	1.000	-/0	-	-	0	-	-	21	-
COUNTS, M.	-	9/22	.409	4/5	.800	-/4	-	-	5	-	-	22	-
PAULY, S.	-	1/3	.333	0/2	.000	-/4	-	-	2	-	-	2	-
PETERS, F.	-	2/4	.500	5/7	.714	-/3	-	-	2	-	-	9	-
JARVIS, J.	-	3/5	.600	2/2	1.000	-/3	-	-	2	-	-	8	-
CAMPBELL, T.	-	0/1	.000	0/0	.000	-/0	-	-	1	-	-	0	-
Totals	200	26/55	.473	13/19	.684	-/23	-	-	16	-	-	65	.325

San Francisco (61) — Coach: Peter Peletta

	Min.	Total FG/FGA	Pct.	FT/FTA	Pct.	Reb. O/T	A	TO	PF	S	Blk	TP	PPM
THOMAS	-	8/10	.800	5/7	.714	-/8	-	-	4	-	-	21	-
LEE	-	4/14	.286	4/4	1.000	-/9	-	-	4	-	-	12	-
JOHNSON, O.	-	5/11	.455	5/6	.833	-/10	-	-	3	-	-	15	-
MOFFATT	-	2/4	.500	0/1	.000	-/1	-	-	1	-	-	4	-
BROVELLI	-	3/7	.429	1/2	.500	-/4	-	-	5	-	-	7	-
BRAINARD	-	1/4	.250	0/0	.000	-/1	-	-	1	-	-	2	-
THOMAS	-	0/1	.000	0/2	.000	-/0	-	-	0	-	-	0	-
BELLUOMINI	-	0/0	.000	0/0	.000	-/1	-	-	0	-	-	0	-
Totals	200	23/51	.451	15/22	.682	-/34	-	-	18	-	-	61	.305

Team Rebounds: Oregon State 7; San Francisco 6. Disqualified: Oregon State—Counts; San Francisco—Brovelli.

	1st Half	2nd Half	Final
Oregon State	35	30	65
San Francisco	30	31	61

REGIONAL FINAL EAST

Duke (73) — Coach: Vic Bubas

	Min.	Total FG/FGA	Pct.	FT/FTA	Pct.	Reb. O/T	A	TO	PF	S	Blk	TP	PPM
HEYMAN, A.	-	3/14	.214	10/15	.667	-/10	3	-	2	-	-	16	-
MULLINS, J.	-	10/16	.625	4/4	1.000	-/5	2	-	1	-	-	24	-
BUCKLEY, J.	-	4/9	.444	2/3	.667	-/18	0	-	2	-	-	10	-
HARRISON, B.	-	0/3	.000	1/2	.500	-/2	0	-	0	-	-	1	-
SCHMIDT, F.	-	9/16	.563	2/2	1.000	-/5	0	-	0	-	-	20	-
HERBSTER, R.	-	0/2	.000	2/2	1.000	-/0	0	-	1	-	-	2	-
TISON, H.	-	0/1	.000	0/0	.000	-/1	0	-	0	-	-	0	-
Totals	200	26/61	.426	21/28	.750	-/41	5	-	6	-	-	73	.365

St. Joseph's (59) — Coach: Jack Ramsay

	Min.	Total FG/FGA	Pct.	FT/FTA	Pct.	Reb. O/T	A	TO	PF	S	Blk	TP	PPM
BOYLE, J.	-	2/17	.118	0/1	.000	-/10	2	-	5	-	-	4	-
WYNNE, T.	-	13/23	.565	3/3	1.000	-/9	0	-	2	-	-	29	-
HOFFMAN, J.	-	1/5	.200	0/0	.000	-/4	0	-	4	-	-	2	-
COURTIN, S.	-	7/16	.438	0/0	.000	-/4	0	-	1	-	-	14	-
LYNAM, J.	-	4/7	.571	0/1	.000	-/5	1	-	4	-	-	8	-
TILLER, J.	-	0/2	.000	2/2	1.000	-/5	0	-	3	-	-	2	-
KELLY, J.	-	0/2	.000	0/0	.000	-/1	0	-	1	-	-	0	-
Totals	200	27/72	.375	5/7	.714	-/38	3	-	20	-	-	59	.295

Team Rebounds: Duke 5; St. Joseph's 5. Disqualified: St. Joseph's—Boyle.

	1st Half	2nd Half	Final
Duke	34	39	73
St. Joseph's	33	26	59

REGIONAL FINAL MIDEAST

Illinois (64)   Coach: Harry Combes

	Min.	Total FG / FGA	Pct.	FT / FTA	Pct.	Reb. O / T	A	TO	PF	S	Blk	TP	PPM
DOWNEY, D.	31	9/22	.409	2/ 5	.400	-/ 6	-	-	4	-	-	20	.645
STARNES, B.	20	1/ 6	.167	0/ 0	.000	-/ 4	-	-	2	-	-	2	.100
BURWELL, B.	37	5/15	.333	0/ 1	.000	-/ 7	-	-	4	-	-	10	.270
SMALL, B.	37	3/ 9	.333	3/ 3	1.000	-/ 4	-	-	3	-	-	9	.243
BRODY, T.	22	3/ 8	.375	0/ 1	.000	-/ 5	-	-	3	-	-	6	.273
THOREN, S.	23	4/11	.364	0/ 2	.000	-/ 7	-	-	3	-	-	8	.348
EDWARDS, B.	12	2/ 4	.500	1/ 2	.500	-/ 0	-	-	2	-	-	5	.417
REDMON, B.	9	0/ 1	.000	0/ 0	.000	-/ 2	-	-	1	-	-	0	.000
MCKEOWN, B.	9	1/ 4	.250	2/ 3	.667	-/ 0	-	-	1	-	-	4	.444
Totals	200	28/80	.350	8/17	.471	-/35	-	20	23	-	-	64	.320

Loyola-Chicago (79)   Coach: George Ireland

	Min.	Total FG / FGA	Pct.	FT / FTA	Pct.	Reb. O / T	A	TO	PF	S	Blk	TP	PPM
HARKNESS, J.	40	13/23	.565	7/11	.636	-/ 7	-	-	3	-	-	33	.825
ROUSE, V.	40	3/17	.176	0/ 0	.000	-/19	-	-	2	-	-	6	.150
HUNTER, L.	40	4/ 9	.444	4/ 4	1.000	-/15	-	-	4	-	-	12	.300
EGAN, J.	39	3/11	.273	7/ 8	.875	-/ 4	-	-	3	-	-	13	.333
MILLER, R.	40	6/15	.400	3/ 4	.750	-/11	-	-	2	-	-	15	.375
WOOD, C.	1	0/ 1	.000	0/ 0	.000	-/ 1	-	-	0	-	-	0	.000
Totals	200	29/76	.382	21/27	.778	-/57	-	14	14	-	-	79	.395

Team Rebounds: Loyola-Chicago 8; Illinois 14. Disqualified: None.

	1st Half	2nd Half	Final
Illinois	30	34	64
Loyola-Chicago	38	41	79

REGIONAL FINAL MIDWEST

Colorado (60)   Coach: Sox Walseth

	Min.	Total FG / FGA	Pct.	FT / FTA	Pct.	Reb. O / T	A	TO	PF	S	Blk	TP	PPM
MUELLER, M.	-	3/10	.300	3/ 6	.500	4/14	-	-	4	-	-	9	-
CHARLTON, K.	-	9/17	.529	5/ 5	1.000	5/12	-	-	3	-	-	23	-
DAVIS, J.	-	5/ 9	.556	1/ 4	.250	5/12	-	-	3	-	-	11	-
LEE, E.	-	2/ 7	.286	0/ 1	.000	0/ 0	-	-	2	-	-	4	-
PARSONS, G.	-	4/11	.364	1/ 5	.200	0/ 0	-	-	3	-	-	9	-
MELTON	-	2/ 2	1.000	0/ 0	.000	0/ 0	-	-	2	-	-	4	-
SPARKS, G.	-	0/ 0	.000	0/ 0	.000	0/ 0	-	-	1	-	-	0	-
JOYCE, G.	-	0/ 0	.000	0/ 0	.000	0/ 0	-	-	1	-	-	0	-
WOODWARD, T.	-	0/ 0	.000	0/ 0	.000	0/ 0	-	-	0	-	-	0	-
PRICE, E.	-	0/ 0	.000	0/ 0	.000	0/ 0	-	-	0	-	-	0	-
SPONHOLTZ, G.	-	0/ 0	.000	0/ 0	.000	0/ 0	-	-	0	-	-	0	-
SAUNDERS, N.	-	0/ 0	.000	0/ 0	.000	0/ 0	-	-	0	-	-	0	-
Totals	200	25/56	.446	10/21	.476	14/38	-	13	19	-	-	60	.300

Cincinnati (67)   Coach: Ed Jucker

	Min.	Total FG / FGA	Pct.	FT / FTA	Pct.	Reb. O / T	A	TO	PF	S	Blk	TP	PPM
BONHAM, R.	-	8/18	.444	6/ 7	.857	0/ 2	-	-	3	-	-	22	-
THACKER, T.	-	7/13	.538	4/ 5	.800	4/13	-	-	1	-	-	18	-
WILSON, G.	-	6/11	.545	3/ 7	.429	3/10	-	-	3	-	-	15	-
YATES, T.	-	2/11	.182	1/ 3	.333	3/ 4	-	-	4	-	-	5	-
SHINGLETON, L.	-	1/ 2	.500	2/ 4	.500	0/ 0	-	-	1	-	-	4	-
HEIDOTTING, D.	-	1/ 1	1.000	1/ 1	1.000	1/ 1	-	-	3	-	-	3	.000
Totals	200	25/56	.446	17/27	.630	11/30	-	7	15	-	-	67	.335

Team Rebounds: Cincinnati 10; Colorado 5. Disqualified: None.

	1st Half	2nd Half	Final
Colorado	32	28	60
Cincinnati	31	36	67

REGIONAL FINAL WEST

Arizona State (65)   Coach: Ned Wulk

	Min.	Total FG / FGA	Pct.	FT / FTA	Pct.	Reb. O / T	A	TO	PF	S	Blk	TP	PPM
CALDWELL, J.	-	6/19	.316	5/10	.500	-/ 7	-	-	3	-	-	17	-
CERKVENIK, T.	-	5/12	.417	6/10	.600	-/ 7	-	-	5	-	-	16	-
BECKER, A.	-	6/16	.375	1/ 3	.333	-/16	-	-	3	-	-	13	-
DAIRMAN	-	2/ 4	.500	2/ 3	.667	-/ 2	-	-	2	-	-	6	-
SENITZA	-	4/15	.267	0/ 2	.000	-/ 1	-	-	3	-	-	8	-
HOWARD	-	0/ 2	.000	3/ 3	1.000	-/ 4	-	-	3	-	-	3	-
DISARUFINA	-	1/ 1	1.000	0/ 0	.000	-/ 0	-	-	3	-	-	2	-
Totals	200	24/69	.348	17/31	.548	-/37	-	-	22	-	-	65	.325

Oregon State (83)   Coach: Amory "Slats" Gill

	Min.	Total FG / FGA	Pct.	FT / FTA	Pct.	Reb. O / T	A	TO	PF	S	Blk	TP	PPM
KRAUS, J.	-	0/ 0	.000	0/ 0	.000	-/ 2	-	-	2	-	-	0	-
PAULY, S.	-	9/14	.643	3/ 6	.500	-/ 6	-	-	3	-	-	21	-
COUNTS, M.	-	11/20	.550	4/ 4	1.000	-/13	-	-	3	-	-	26	-
PETERS, F.	-	4/ 7	.571	6/ 6	1.000	-/ 5	-	-	4	-	-	14	-
BAKER, T.	-	6/ 9	.667	3/ 3	1.000	-/ 1	-	-	4	-	-	15	-
JARVIS, J.	-	1/ 3	.333	3/ 3	1.000	-/ 1	-	-	5	-	-	5	-
ROSSI, G.	-	0/ 1	.000	2/ 3	.667	-/ 0	-	-	3	-	-	2	-
TORGERSON, R.	-	0/ 0	.000	0/ 2	.000	-/ 0	-	-	0	-	-	0	-
Totals	200	31/54	.574	21/27	.778	-/28	-	-	24	-	-	83	.415

Team Rebounds: Oregon State 13; Arizona St. 10. Disqualified: Oregon State—Jarvis; Arizona St.—Cerkvenik.

	1st Half	2nd Half	Final
Arizona St.	38	27	65
Oregon State	43	40	83

FINAL FOUR

Duke (75) Coach: Vic Bubas

	Min.	Total FG/FGA	Pct.	FT/FTA	Pct.	Reb. O/T	A	TO	PF	S	Blk	TP	PPM
HEYMAN, A.	-	11/30	.367	7/9	.778	-/12	-	-	5	-	-	29	-
MULLINS, J.	-	10/20	.500	1/3	.333	-/9	-	-	4	-	-	21	-
BUCKLEY, J.	-	4/10	.400	2/4	.500	-/13	-	-	3	-	-	10	-
SCHMIDT, F.	-	0/2	.000	0/0	.000	-/2	-	-	3	-	-	0	-
HARRISON, B.	-	0/3	.000	2/3	.667	-/3	-	-	0	-	-	2	-
TISON, H.	-	5/12	.417	1/3	.333	-/8	-	-	3	-	-	11	-
HERBSTER, R.	-	0/2	.000	0/0	.000	-/0	-	-	1	-	-	0	-
FERGUSON, D.	-	1/2	.500	0/0	.000	-/0	-	-	1	-	-	2	-
JAMIESON, B.	-	0/0	.000	0/0	.000	-/0	-	-	0	-	-	0	-
COX, R.	-	0/0	.000	0/0	.000	-/0	-	-	0	-	-	0	-
MANN, T.	-	0/1	.000	0/0	.000	-/0	-	-	0	-	-	0	-
Totals	200	31/82	.378	13/22	.591	-/47	-	-	20	-	-	75	.375

Cincinnati (80) Coach: Ed Jucker

	Min.	Total FG/FGA	Pct.	FT/FTA	Pct.	Reb. O/T	A	TO	PF	S	Blk	TP	PPM
BONHAM, R.	30	3/12	.250	8/9	.889	-/5	0	1	3	-	-	14	.467
THACKER, T.	35	5/8	.625	4/8	.500	-/11	1	6	3	-	-	14	.400
WILSON, G.	34	8/9	.889	8/12	.667	-/13	0	4	2	-	-	24	.706
YATES, T.	32	5/9	.556	2/3	.667	-/5	3	2	1	-	-	12	.375
SHINGLETON, L.	32	1/2	.500	0/0	.000	-/2	0	2	1	-	-	2	.063
HEIDOTTING, D.	8	0/0	.000	1/2	.500	-/2	0	1	1	-	-	1	.125
CUNNINGHAM, K.	8	2/3	.667	0/0	.000	-/0	0	0	1	-	-	4	.500
MEYER, F.	8	1/1	1.000	1/2	.500	-/1	1	0	1	-	-	3	.375
SMITH, G.	6	1/3	.333	0/2	.000	-/1	0	0	1	-	-	2	.333
ELSASSER, L.	5	1/2	.500	0/1	.000	-/1	0	0	0	-	-	2	.400
ABERNETHY, B.	2	1/2	.500	0/0	.000	-/3	0	0	0	-	-	2	1.000
Totals	200	28/51	.549	24/39	.615	-/44	5	16	14	-	-	80	.400

Loyola-Chicago (94) Coach: George Ireland

	Min.	Total FG/FGA	Pct.	FT/FTA	Pct.	Reb. O/T	A	TO	PF	S	Blk	TP	PPM
HARKNESS, J.	-	7/18	.389	6/9	.667	-/11	-	-	3	-	-	20	-
ROUSE, V.	-	6/12	.500	1/2	.500	-/6	-	-	4	-	-	13	-
HUNTER, L.	-	11/20	.550	7/9	.778	-/18	-	-	3	-	-	29	-
EGAN, J.	-	4/9	.444	6/7	.857	-/3	-	-	2	-	-	14	-
MILLER, R.	-	8/11	.727	2/2	1.000	-/5	-	-	4	-	-	18	-
WOOD, C.	-	0/1	.000	0/0	.000	-/3	-	-	0	-	-	0	-
ROCHELLE, R.	-	0/0	.000	0/0	.000	-/0	-	-	0	-	-	0	-
REARDON, J.	-	0/0	.000	0/0	.000	-/0	-	-	0	-	-	0	-
CONNAUGHTON, D.	-	0/0	.000	0/0	.000	-/0	-	-	0	-	-	0	-
Totals	200	36/71	.507	22/29	.759	-/46	-	-	16	-	-	94	.470

Team Rebounds: Loyola-Chicago 5; Duke 5. Disqualified: Duke—Heyman.

Oregon State (46) Coach: Amory "Slats" Gill

	Min.	Total FG/FGA	Pct.	FT/FTA	Pct.	Reb. O/T	A	TO	PF	S	Blk	TP	PPM
KRAUS, J.	22	1/6	.167	1/1	1.000	-/3	0	1	3	-	-	3	.136
BAKER, T.	27	0/9	.000	0/1	.000	-/2	0	6	0	-	-	0	.000
COUNTS, M.	27	8/14	.571	4/4	1.000	-/9	0	2	5	-	-	20	.741
PAULY, S.	26	2/8	.250	0/1	.000	-/3	0	1	5	-	-	4	.154
PETERS, F.	29	1/5	.200	2/2	1.000	-/4	1	1	4	-	-	4	.138
JARVIS, J.	27	1/6	.167	3/4	.750	-/0	0	1	3	-	-	5	.185
CAMPBELL, T.	6	0/2	.000	1/1	1.000	-/2	0	1	2	-	-	1	.167
ROSSI, G.	13	1/3	.333	0/0	.000	-/0	0	3	1	-	-	2	.154
TORGERSON, R.	1	1/2	.500	0/0	.000	-/0	0	0	0	-	-	2	2.000
HAYWARD, D.	12	0/2	.000	1/1	1.000	-/2	0	0	3	-	-	1	.083
BENNER, R.	10	2/2	1.000	0/0	.000	-/1	0	2	0	-	-	4	.400
Totals	200	17/59	.288	12/15	.800	-/26	1	18	26	-	-	46	.230

Team Rebounds: Cincinnati 6; Oregon State 7. Disqualified: Oregon State—Pauly, Counts.

	1st Half	2nd Half	Final
Duke	31	44	75
Loyola-Chicago	44	50	94

	1st Half	2nd Half	Final
Cincinnati	30	50	80
Oregon State	27	19	46

NATIONAL CHAMPIONSHIP

Loyola-Chicago (60) Coach: George Ireland

	Min.	Total FG/FGA	Pct.	FT/FTA	Pct.	Reb. O/T	A	TO	PF	S	Blk	TP	PPM
ROUSE, V.	45	6/22	.273	3/4	.750	-/12	0	1	4	-	-	15	.333
HUNTER, L.	45	6/22	.273	4/4	1.000	-/11	1	1	3	-	-	16	.356
EGAN, J.	45	3/8	.375	3/5	.600	-/3	0	1	3	-	-	9	.200
MILLER, R.	45	3/14	.214	0/0	.000	-/2	0	0	3	-	-	6	.133
HARKNESS, J.	45	5/18	.278	4/8	.500	-/6	0	0	4	-	-	14	.311
Totals	225	23/84	.274	14/21	.667	-/34	1	3	17	-	-	60	.267

Cincinnati (58) Coach: Ed Jucker

	Min.	Total FG/FGA	Pct.	FT/FTA	Pct.	Reb. O/T	A	TO	PF	S	Blk	TP	PPM
BONHAM, R.	45	8/16	.500	6/6	1.000	-/4	0	1	3	-	-	22	.489
THACKER, T.	45	5/12	.417	3/4	.750	-/15	3	7	4	-	-	13	.289
WILSON, G.	41	4/8	.500	2/3	.667	-/13	0	2	4	-	-	10	.244
YATES, T.	45	4/6	.667	1/4	.250	-/8	1	3	4	-	-	9	.200
SHINGLETON, L.	45	1/3	.333	2/3	.667	-/4	0	3	0	-	-	4	.089
HEIDOTTING, D.	4	0/0	.000	0/0	.000	-/1	0	0	2	-	-	0	.000
Totals	225	22/45	.489	14/20	.700	-/45	4	16	17	-	-	58	.258

Team Rebounds: Loyola-Chicago 11; Cincinnati 7. Disqualified: None.

	1st Half	2nd Half	1st OT	Final
Loyola-Chicago	21	33	6	60
Cincinnati	29	25	4	58

NATIONAL THIRD PLACE

Duke (85) Coach: Vic Bubas

	Min.	Total FG/FGA	Pct.	FT/FTA	Pct.	Reb. O/T	A	TO	PF	S	Blk	TP	PPM
TISON, H.	-	4/ 9	.444	3/ 5	.600	-/11	-	-	3	-	-	11	-
MULLINS, J.	-	4/13	.308	6/ 8	.750	-/10	-	-	2	-	-	14	-
BUCKLEY, J.	-	2/ 5	.400	2/ 5	.400	-/ 7	-	-	4	-	-	6	-
SCHMIDT, F.	-	10/15	.667	0/ 0	.000	-/ 4	-	-	1	-	-	20	-
HEYMAN, A.	-	7/14	.500	8/13	.615	-/ 7	-	-	3	-	-	22	-
HARRISON, B.	-	4/ 8	.500	1/ 2	.500	-/ 5	-	-	1	-	-	9	-
HERBSTER, R.	-	0/ 0	.000	1/ 2	.500	-/ 0	-	-	0	-	-	1	-
MANN, T.	-	0/ 0	.000	0/ 0	.000	-/ 0	-	-	0	-	-	0	-
FERGUSON, D.	-	1/ 1	1.000	0/ 0	.000	-/ 0	-	-	0	-	-	2	-
KITCHING, B.	-	0/ 0	.000	0/ 0	.000	-/ 0	-	-	0	-	-	0	-
JAMIESON, B.	-	0/ 0	.000	0/ 0	.000	-/ 0	-	-	2	-	-	0	-
COX, R.	-	0/ 0	.000	0/ 0	.000	-/ 0	-	-	0	-	-	0	-
Totals	200	32/65	.492	21/35	.600	-/44	-	16	-	-	-	85	.425

Oregon State (63) Coach: Amory "Slats" Gill

	Min.	Total FG/FGA	Pct.	FT/FTA	Pct.	Reb. O/T	A	TO	PF	S	Blk	TP	PPM
POULY, S.	-	5/15	.333	2/ 2	1.000	-/11	-	-	4	-	-	12	-
JARVIS, J.	-	3/12	.250	1/ 1	1.000	-/ 6	-	-	5	-	-	7	-
COUNTS, M.	-	9/30	.300	7/10	.700	-/18	-	-	2	-	-	25	-
PETERS, F.	-	3/ 9	.333	2/ 2	1.000	-/ 6	-	-	4	-	-	8	-
BAKER, T.	-	3/11	.273	1/ 1	1.000	-/ 3	-	-	2	-	-	7	-
KRAUS, J.	-	0/ 3	.000	0/ 1	.000	-/ 8	-	-	3	-	-	0	-
BENNER, R.	-	0/ 1	.000	0/ 0	.000	-/ 0	-	-	1	-	-	0	-
HAYWARD, D.	-	2/ 6	.333	0/ 0	.000	-/ 1	-	-	3	-	-	4	-
TORGERSON, R.	-	0/ 0	.000	0/ 0	.000	-/ 1	-	-	0	-	-	0	-
Totals	200	25/87	.287	13/17	.765	-/54	-	24	-	-	-	63	.315

Team Rebounds: Duke 6; Oregon State 8. Disqualified: Oregon State—Jarvis.

	1st Half	2nd Half	Final
Duke	34	51	85
Oregon State	23	40	63

REGIONAL THIRD PLACE WEST

San Francisco (76) Coach: Peter Peletta

	Min.	Total FG/FGA	Pct.	FT/FTA	Pct.	Reb. O/T	A	TO	PF	S	Blk	TP	PPM
THOMAS	-	5/14	.357	5/ 6	.833	-/ 9	-	-	4	-	-	15	-
LEE	-	1/ 4	.250	3/ 4	.750	-/ 3	-	-	3	-	-	5	-
JOHNSON, O.	-	7/16	.438	6/ 9	.667	-/20	-	-	1	-	-	20	-
MOFFATT	-	4/10	.400	3/ 6	.500	-/ 8	-	-	4	-	-	11	-
BROVELLI	-	4/ 7	.571	5/ 5	1.000	-/ 0	-	-	3	-	-	13	-
BRAINARD	-	0/ 2	.000	4/ 6	.667	-/ 1	-	-	2	-	-	4	-
THOMAS	-	1/ 2	.500	6/ 6	1.000	-/ 1	-	-	0	-	-	8	-
Totals	200	22/55	.400	32/42	.762	-/42	-	12	17	-	-	76	.380

UCLA (75) Coach: John Wooden

	Min.	Total FG/FGA	Pct.	FT/FTA	Pct.	Reb. O/T	A	TO	PF	S	Blk	TP	PPM
HIRSCH, J.	-	2/ 9	.222	2/ 3	.667	-/ 8	-	-	4	-	-	6	-
GOSS, F.	-	4/ 8	.500	2/ 2	1.000	-/ 2	-	-	0	-	-	10	-
SLAUGHTER, F.	-	2/ 6	.333	0/ 2	.000	-/11	-	-	5	-	-	4	-
HAZZARD, W.	-	4/11	.364	5/ 5	1.000	-/ 4	-	-	4	-	-	13	-
GOODRICH, G.	-	6/ 9	.667	5/ 7	.714	-/ 3	-	-	5	-	-	17	-
ERICKSON, K.	-	1/ 2	.500	0/ 0	.000	-/ 2	-	-	1	-	-	2	-
STEWART, K.	-	1/ 4	.250	0/ 0	.000	-/ 3	-	-	4	-	-	2	-
WAXMAN, D.	-	6/16	.375	1/ 2	.500	-/ 8	-	-	2	-	-	13	-
MILHORN, J.	-	3/10	.300	0/ 0	.000	-/ 1	-	-	1	-	-	6	-
HUGGINS, M.	-	0/ 0	.000	2/ 2	1.000	-/ 1	-	-	3	-	-	2	-
Totals	200	29/75	.387	17/23	.739	-/43	-	10	29	-	-	75	.375

Team Rebounds: San Francisco 7; UCLA 3. Disqualified: UCLA—Slaughter, Goodrich.

	1st Half	2nd Half	Final
San Francisco	30	46	76
UCLA	35	40	75

REGIONAL THIRD PLACE MIDWEST

Texas (90) Coach: Harold Bradley

	Min.	Total FG/FGA	Pct.	FT/FTA	Pct.	Reb. O/T	A	TO	PF	S	Blk	TP	PPM
FRANKS, L.	-	5/ 8	.625	2/ 3	.667	1/ 4	-	-	5	-	-	12	-
FULTZ, J.	-	4/ 6	.667	1/ 3	.333	4/ 6	-	-	5	-	-	9	-
HUMPHREY	-	4/ 7	.571	8/10	.800	3/10	-	-	4	-	-	16	-
GILBERT, J.	-	5/10	.500	7/11	.636	4/ 6	-	-	3	-	-	17	-
PURYEAR	-	5/11	.455	3/ 4	.750	1/ 4	-	-	4	-	-	13	-
HELLER	-	6/ 7	.857	0/ 1	.000	1/ 3	-	-	2	-	-	12	-
FISHER	-	0/ 2	.000	0/ 1	.000	0/ 1	-	-	1	-	-	0	-
CLARK	-	0/ 1	.000	0/ 0	.000	0/ 0	-	-	0	-	-	0	-
WEEKS	-	0/ 1	.000	1/ 1	1.000	0/ 1	-	-	1	-	-	1	-
DUGAN	-	3/ 5	.600	4/ 6	.667	3/ 6	-	-	5	-	-	10	-
Totals	200	32/58	.552	26/40	.650	17/41	-	11	30	-	-	90	.450

Oklahoma City (83) Coach: Abe Lemons

	Min.	Total FG/FGA	Pct.	FT/FTA	Pct.	Reb. O/T	A	TO	PF	S	Blk	TP	PPM
JACKSON, E.	-	2/ 8	.250	3/ 3	1.000	8/13	-	-	5	-	-	7	-
MILLER, J.	-	2/ 3	.667	4/ 6	.667	1/ 4	-	-	2	-	-	8	-
JOHNSTON, B.	-	1/ 6	.167	3/ 3	1.000	2/ 2	-	-	2	-	-	5	-
KOPER, B.	-	10/18	.556	5/ 9	.556	4/ 5	-	-	1	-	-	25	-
HILL, G.	-	8/19	.421	5/ 8	.625	3/ 4	-	-	4	-	-	21	-
GIBBON	-	0/ 1	.000	0/ 0	.000	0/ 0	-	-	1	-	-	0	-
STEPHENS, E.	-	4/ 6	.667	3/ 4	.750	0/ 2	-	-	5	-	-	11	-
WHITE	-	1/ 3	.333	1/ 2	.500	1/ 2	-	-	2	-	-	3	-
HEUSMAN	-	0/ 2	.000	1/ 2	.500	1/ 2	-	-	2	-	-	1	-
HOPKINS	-	1/ 1	1.000	0/ 2	.000	0/ 2	-	-	2	-	-	2	-
NYGARD	-	0/ 0	.000	0/ 1	.000	0/ 1	-	-	1	-	-	0	-
SNIDER	-	0/ 0	.000	0/ 0	.000	0/ 0	-	-	0	-	-	0	-
Totals	200	29/67	.433	25/40	.625	20/37	-	9	27	-	-	83	.415

Team Rebounds: Texas 7; Oklahoma City 8. Disqualified: Texas—Franks, Fultz, Dugan; Oklahoma City—Stephens, Jackson.

	1st Half	2nd Half	Final
Texas	50	40	90
Oklahoma City	44	39	83

REGIONAL THIRD PLACE MIDEAST

Mississippi State (65) Coach: Babe McCarthy

	Min.	Total FG/FGA	Pct.	FT/FTA	Pct.	Reb. O/T	A	TO	PF	S	Blk	TP	PPM
MITCHELL, L.	-	5/14	.357	13/16	.813	-/ 8	-	-	4	-	-	23	-
BRINKER	-	2/ 6	.333	3/ 3	1.000	-/10	-	-	4	-	-	7	-
SHOWS	-	2/ 5	.400	1/ 3	.333	-/ 7	-	-	5	-	-	5	-
HUTTON	-	5/11	.455	4/ 7	.571	-/ 3	-	-	1	-	-	14	-
STROUD, W.	-	5/13	.385	3/ 3	1.000	-/ 2	-	-	2	-	-	13	-
WILLIAMS	-	0/ 5	.000	1/ 2	.500	-/ 6	-	-	4	-	-	1	-
POSEY	-	0/ 1	.000	0/ 0	.000	-/ 2	-	-	0	-	-	0	-
NICHOLS, A.	-	1/ 1	1.000	0/ 1	.000	-/ 4	-	-	0	-	-	2	-
Totals	200	20/56	.357	25/35	.714	-/42	-	20	-	-	-	65	.325

Bowling Green (60) Coach: Harold Anderson

	Min.	Total FG/FGA	Pct.	FT/FTA	Pct.	Reb. O/T	A	TO	PF	S	Blk	TP	PPM
JUNIOR	-	3/12	.250	3/ 3	1.000	-/ 5	-	-	3	-	-	9	-
CHATMAN, E.	-	0/ 2	.000	0/ 1	.000	-/ 6	-	-	3	-	-	0	-
THURMOND, N.	-	6/22	.273	7/10	.700	-/31	-	-	3	-	-	19	-
HALEY	-	1/ 1	1.000	0/ 0	.000	-/ 1	-	-	1	-	-	2	-
KOMIVES, H.	-	7/26	.269	6/ 7	.857	-/ 3	-	-	3	-	-	20	-
REYNOLDS	-	0/ 3	.000	0/ 0	.000	-/ 0	-	-	1	-	-	0	-
GILBERT	-	1/ 3	.333	2/ 3	.667	-/ 2	-	-	3	-	-	4	-
CHAPMAN	-	0/ 3	.000	0/ 0	.000	-/ 3	-	-	3	-	-	0	-
PEPIN	-	2/ 3	.667	0/ 0	.000	-/ 1	-	-	4	-	-	4	-
BAKER	-	1/ 5	.200	0/ 0	.000	-/ 1	-	-	3	-	-	2	-
Totals	200	21/80	.263	18/24	.750	-/52	-	27	-	-	-	60	.300

Team Rebounds: Mississippi St. 9; Bowling Green 8. Disqualified: Mississippi St.—Shows.

	1st Half	2nd Half	Final
Mississippi St.	34	31	65
Bowling Green	26	34	60

REGIONAL THIRD PLACE EAST

West Virginia (83) Coach: George King

	Min.	Total FG / FGA	Pct.	FT / FTA	Pct.	Reb. O / T	A	TO	PF	S	Blk	TP	PPM
CATLETT, G.	-	1/ 3	.333	0/ 0	.000	-/ 2	-	-	4	-	-	2	-
WOLFE, M.	-	1/ 2	.500	4/ 4	1.000	-/ 0	-	-	1	-	-	6	-
SHUCK, D.	-	1/ 3	.333	2/ 4	.500	-/ 2	-	-	2	-	-	4	-
McCORMICK, J.	-	1/ 3	.333	0/ 0	.000	-/ 0	-	-	4	-	-	2	-
THORN, R.	-	13/24	.542	7/ 7	1.000	-/ 9	-	-	0	-	-	33	-
LOWRY, T.	-	2/ 8	.250	8/11	.727	-/ 3	-	-	4	-	-	12	-
LENTZ, M.	-	6/ 9	.667	0/ 1	.000	-/10	-	-	3	-	-	12	-
MAPHIS, B.	-	3/ 8	.375	1/ 1	1.000	-/ 6	-	-	5	-	-	7	-
WEIR, D.	-	2/ 8	.250	1/ 2	.500	-/ 2	-	-	0	-	-	5	-
Totals	200	30/68	.441	23/30	.767	-/34	-	-	23	-	-	83	.415

NYU (73) Coach: Lou Rossini

	Min.	Total FG / FGA	Pct.	FT / FTA	Pct.	Reb. O / T	A	TO	PF	S	Blk	TP	PPM
KRAMER, B.	-	6/13	.462	17/20	.850	-/14	-	-	4	-	-	29	-
HAIRSTON, H.	-	5/13	.385	7/ 9	.778	-/ 7	-	-	5	-	-	17	-
WILLIAMS, B.	-	3/ 8	.375	1/ 1	1.000	-/ 3	-	-	3	-	-	7	-
O'NEILL, N.	-	3/ 7	.429	2/ 2	1.000	-/ 3	-	-	1	-	-	8	-
PATTON, B.	-	3/ 5	.600	0/ 0	.000	-/11	-	-	5	-	-	6	-
JORDAN, S.	-	0/ 2	.000	0/ 0	.000	-/ 3	-	-	1	-	-	0	-
BLAHA, D.	-	3/ 4	.750	0/ 0	.000	-/ 4	-	-	2	-	-	6	-
FRONTERA, J.	-	0/ 0	.000	0/ 0	.000	-/ 0	-	-	0	-	-	0	-
Totals	200	23/52	.442	27/32	.844	-/45	-	-	21	-	-	73	.365

Disqualified: West Virginia—Maphis; NYU—Hairston, Patton.

	1st Half	2nd Half	Final
West Virginia	39	44	83
NYU	36	37	73

✪ ALL-STAR TEAMS ✪

ALL TOURNAMENT

RON BONHAM	CINCINNATI
★ ART HEYMAN	DUKE
LES HUNTER	LOYOLA-CHICAGO
TOM THACKER	CINCINNATI
GEORGE WILSON	CINCINNATI

MIDEAST REGIONAL

DAVE DOWNEY	ILLINOIS
★ JERRY HARKNESS	LOYOLA-CHICAGO
HOWARD KOMIVES	BOWLING GREEN
LELAND MITCHELL	MISSISSIPPI ST.
NATE THURMOND	BOWLING GREEN

MIDWEST REGIONAL

★ KEN CHARLTON	COLORADO

★ Most Outstanding Player(s)

✪ INDIVIDUAL RECORDS ✪

SCORING

Most points in a single game
1 ROD THORN, WEST VIRGINIA (vs. ST. JOSEPH'S) 44
2 BILL BRADLEY, PRINCETON (vs. ST. JOSEPH'S) 40
3 BARRY KRAMER, NYU (vs. PITTSBURGH) 37
4 HOWARD KOMIVES, BOWLING GREEN (vs. NOTRE DAME) 34
4 BARRY KRAMER, NYU (vs. DUKE) 34

Most total points in the tournament
1 MEL COUNTS, OREGON STATE 123
2 JERRY HARKNESS, LOYOLA-CHICAGO 106
3 BARRY KRAMER, NYU 100
4 ROD THORN, WEST VIRGINIA 94
5 ART HEYMAN, DUKE 89

Highest scoring average (minimum 2 games)
1 BARRY KRAMER, NYU (100-3) 33.33
2 ROD THORN, WEST VIRGINIA (94-3) 31.33
3 HOWARD KOMIVES, BOWLING GREEN (79-3) 26.33
4 MEL COUNTS, OREGON STATE (123-5) 24.60
5 KEN CHARLTON, COLORADO (49-2) 24.50

FIELD GOALS

Most field goals in a single game
1 ROD THORN, WEST VIRGINIA (vs. ST. JOSEPH'S) 16
2 6 tied for second place.

Most total field goals in the tournament
1 MEL COUNTS, OREGON STATE 50
2 JERRY HARKNESS, LOYOLA-CHICAGO 41
3 ROD THORN, WEST VIRGINIA 37
4 JEFF MULLINS, DUKE 34
5 BARRY KRAMER, NYU 31

Most field goal attempts in a single game
1 MEL COUNTS, OREGON STATE (vs. DUKE) 30
1 ART HEYMAN, DUKE (vs. LOYOLA-CHICAGO) 30
3 ROD THORN, WEST VIRGINIA (vs. ST. JOSEPH'S) 28
3 BUD KOPER, OKLAHOMA CITY (vs. COLORADO) 28
5 2 tied for fifth place.

Most total field goal attempts in the tournament
1 MEL COUNTS, OREGON STATE 107
2 JERRY HARKNESS, LOYOLA-CHICAGO 87
3 VIC ROUSE, LOYOLA-CHICAGO 84
4 ART HEYMAN, DUKE 79
5 2 tied for fifth place.

Highest field goal percentage in a single game (minimum 10 attempts)
1 JIM BOYLE, ST. JOSEPH'S (vs. WEST VIRGINIA) (9-11) .818

2 ED THOMAS, SAN FRANCISCO (vs. OREGON STATE) (8-10) .800
3 TONY CERKVENIK, ARIZONA ST. (vs. UCLA) (9-12) .750
4 RON MILLER, LOYOLA-CHICAGO (vs. DUKE) (8-11) .727
4 HUMPHREY, TEXAS (vs. TEXAS WESTERN) (8-11) .727

Highest field goal percentage in the tournament (minimum 20 attempts)
1 HUMPHREY, TEXAS (16-22) .727
2 JOHN FULTZ, TEXAS (17-25) .680
3 LARRY FRANKS, TEXAS (17-27) .630
4 JIM DAVIS, COLORADO (13-22) .591
5 FRED SCHMIDT, DUKE (25-43) .581

FREE THROWS

Most free throws in a single game
1 BARRY KRAMER, NYU (vs. WEST VIRGINIA) 17
2 BILL BRADLEY, PRINCETON (vs. ST. JOSEPH'S) 16
3 HOWARD KOMIVES, BOWLING GREEN (vs. NOTRE DAME) 14
4 LELAND MITCHELL, MISSISSIPPI ST. (vs. BOWLING GREEN) 13
5 ROD THORN, WEST VIRGINIA (vs. ST. JOSEPH'S) 12

Most total free throws in the tournament
1 BARRY KRAMER, NYU 38
2 ART HEYMAN, DUKE 35

3 HOWARD KOMIVES, BOWLING GREEN 29
4 LES HUNTER, LOYOLA-CHICAGO 26
4 RON BONHAM, CINCINNATI 26

Most free throws attempted in a single game
1 BARRY KRAMER, NYU (vs. WEST VIRGINIA) 20
2 LELAND MITCHELL, MISSISSIPPI ST. (vs. BOWLING GREEN) 16
2 BILL BRADLEY, PRINCETON (vs. ST. JOSEPH'S) 16
4 3 tied for fourth place.

Most free throws attempted in the tournament
1 ART HEYMAN, DUKE 51
2 BARRY KRAMER, NYU 45
3 JERRY HARKNESS, LOYOLA-CHICAGO 39
4 GEORGE WILSON, CINCINNATI 34
5 RON BONHAM, CINCINNATI 33

Highest free throw percentage in a single game (minimum 7 attempts)
1 BILL BRADLEY, PRINCETON (vs. ST. JOSEPH'S) (16-16) 1.000
2 WAYNE ESTES, UTAH STATE (vs. ARIZONA ST.) (8-8) 1.000
2 SHEFFIELD, PITTSBURGH (vs. NYU) (8-8) 1.000
4 ROD THORN, WEST VIRGINIA (vs. NYU) (7-7) 1.000
4 JIMMY GILBERT, TEXAS (vs. TEXAS WESTERN) (7-7) 1.000

Highest free throw percentage in the tournament (minimum 15 attempts)
1 BILL BRADLEY, PRINCETON (16-16) 1.000
2 HOWARD KOMIVES, BOWLING GREEN (29-32) .906
3 LES HUNTER, LOYOLA-CHICAGO (26-29) .897
4 FRANK PETERS, OREGON STATE (17-19) .895
5 2 tied for fifth place.

REBOUNDS

Most rebounds in a single game
1 NATE THURMOND, BOWLING GREEN (vs. MISSISSIPPI ST.) 31
2 NATE THURMOND, BOWLING GREEN (vs. NOTRE DAME) 20
2 OLLIE JOHNSON, SAN FRANCISCO (vs. UCLA) 20
4 5 tied for fourth place.

Most total rebounds in the tournament
1 NATE THURMOND, BOWLING GREEN 70
1 VIC ROUSE, LOYOLA-CHICAGO 70
3 LES HUNTER, LOYOLA-CHICAGO 60
4 MEL COUNTS, OREGON STATE 55
5 JAY BUCKLEY, DUKE 54

Most rebounds per game (minimum 2 games)
1 NATE THURMOND, BOWLING GREEN (70-3) 23.33
2 ART BECKER, ARIZONA ST. (48-3) 16.00
3 OLLIE JOHNSON, SAN FRANCISCO (30-2) 15.00
4 JIM DAVIS, COLORADO (29-2) 14.50
5 VIC ROUSE, LOYOLA-CHICAGO (70-5) 14.00

✪ TEAM RECORDS ✪

SCORING

Most points in a single game
1 LOYOLA-CHICAGO (vs. TENNESSEE TECH) 111
2 ST. JOSEPH'S (vs. WEST VIRGINIA) 97
3 LOYOLA-CHICAGO (vs. DUKE) 94

Most total points in the tournament
1 LOYOLA-CHICAGO 405
2 OREGON STATE 327
3 DUKE 314

Highest scoring average (minimum 2 games)
1 WEST VIRGINIA (248-3) 82.67
2 LOYOLA-CHICAGO (405-5) 81.00
3 NYU (242-3) 80.67

FIELD GOALS

Most field goals in a single game
1 ARIZONA ST. (vs. UCLA) 41
2 LOYOLA-CHICAGO (vs. TENNESSEE TECH) 40
3 ST. JOSEPH'S (vs. WEST VIRGINIA) 38

Most total field goals in the tournament
1 LOYOLA-CHICAGO 152
2 OREGON STATE 128
3 DUKE 121

Most field goals attempted in a single game
1 OREGON STATE (vs. DUKE) 87
2 UCLA (vs. ARIZONA ST.) 86
3 LOYOLA-CHICAGO (vs. CINCINNATI) 84

Most total field goals attempted in the tournament
1 LOYOLA-CHICAGO 369
2 OREGON STATE 311
3 DUKE 272

Highest field goal percentage in a single game
1 ST. JOSEPH'S (vs. WEST VIRGINIA) (38-63) .603
2 OREGON STATE (vs. ARIZONA ST.) (31-54) .574
3 TEXAS (vs. TEXAS WESTERN) (24-43) .558

Highest field goal percentage in the tournament (minimum 2 games)
1 TEXAS (84-152) .553
2 PRINCETON (29-54) .537
3 SEATTLE (27-55) .491

FREE THROWS

Most free throws in a single game
1 SAN FRANCISCO (vs. UCLA) 32
2 LOYOLA-CHICAGO (vs. TENNESSEE TECH) 31
3 NYU (vs. PITTSBURGH) 29

Most total free throws in the tournament
1 LOYOLA-CHICAGO 101
2 CINCINNATI 78
3 2 tied for third place.

Most free throws attempted in a single game
1 NYU (vs. PITTSBURGH) 43
2 SAN FRANCISCO (vs. UCLA) 42
3 LOYOLA-CHICAGO (vs. TENNESSEE TECH) 41

Most total free throws attempted in the tournament
1 LOYOLA-CHICAGO 134
2 CINCINNATI 121
3 DUKE 111

Highest free throw percentage in a single game
1 TEXAS (vs. CINCINNATI) (12-13) .923
2 BOWLING GREEN (vs. ILLINOIS) (17-19) .895
3 UTAH STATE (vs. ARIZONA ST.) (13-15) .867

Highest free throw percentage in the tournament (minimum 2 games)
1 BOWLING GREEN (58-71) .817
2 WEST VIRGINIA (64-84) .762
3 LOYOLA-CHICAGO (101-134) .754

Fewest free throws in a single game
1 ST. JOSEPH'S (vs. DUKE) 5
2 TENNESSEE TECH (vs. LOYOLA-CHICAGO) 6
3 ILLINOIS (vs. LOYOLA-CHICAGO) 8

Lowest free throw percentage in a single game
1 OKLAHOMA CITY (vs. COLORADO STATE) (10-24) .417
2 ILLINOIS (vs. LOYOLA-CHICAGO) (8-17) .471
3 COLORADO (vs. CINCINNATI) (10-21) .476

Lowest free throw percentage in the tournament (minimum 2 games)
1 COLORADO (28-53) .528
2 ARIZONA ST. (43-76) .566
3 OKLAHOMA CITY (47-79) .595

REBOUNDS

Most rebounds in a single game
1 LOYOLA-CHICAGO (vs. TENNESSEE TECH) 60
2 LOYOLA-CHICAGO (vs. ILLINOIS) 57
3 OREGON STATE (vs. DUKE) 54

1964

| FIRST ROUND | REGIONAL SEMIFINAL | REGIONAL FINAL | **FINAL FOUR** | REGIONAL FINAL | REGIONAL SEMIFINAL | FIRST ROUND |

EAST

(bye) — Duke 87

Duke 101

Villanova 77

Villanova 73

Providence 66

Duke 91

Temple 48

U. Conn. 52

U. Conn. 53

U. Conn. 54

VMI 60

Princeton 50

Princeton 86

MIDWEST

Wichita St. 84 — (bye)

Wichita St. 86

Oklahoma City 78

Creighton 68

Creighton 89

Kansas St. 84

Texas A&M 62

Texas Western 60

Texas Western 68

Kansas St. 94

Kansas St. 64 — (bye)

UCLA 98
Duke 83

MIDEAST

(bye) — Kentucky 69

Ohio 57

Ohio 71

Ohio 85

Louisville 69

Michigan 80

Murray St. 91

Loyola-Chicago 80

Loyola-Chicago 101

Michigan 69

(bye) — Michigan 84

WEST

UCLA 95 — (bye)

UCLA 76

Oregon St. 57

Seattle 90

Seattle 61

UCLA 90

Arizona St. 90

Utah St. 58

Utah St. 92

San Francisco 72

San Francisco 64 — (bye)

CONSOLATION GAMES

National Third Place:

Michigan 100

Kansas St. 90

Regional Third Place:

East:
Villanova 74
Princeton 62

Mideast:
Loyola-Chicago 100
Kentucky 91

Midwest:
Texas Western 63
Creighton 52

West:
Seattle 88
Utah St. 78

In 1964, in the 26th year of the NCAA tournament, John Wooden and his UCLA Bruins won their first title. By that March, UCLA's veteran coach had been in Westwood for 16 of them, so when his team finally won, no bells chimed, no alarms went off, nobody said, "Let's pack it away, this man is going to own this thing for the forseeable future." It just seemed as if a very good, disciplined, well-coached team with an explosive fast break and a superb full-court zone press beat everybody they played on the way to the championship.

Even though UCLA had finished the regular season without a loss, nobody thought they were awesome. The Bruins were lightning-fast, there was no doubt about that, but they were also small, with no starter taller than 6-5. On the strength of their unbeaten record they were on top of the polls. But most everybody believed they were just one of a number of very good teams in the tournament field.

Defending champion Loyola of Chicago was back, but without the sizzle of their 1963 scoring star Jerry Harkness. Duke was another returnee from the 1963 Final Four, and although the Blue Devils had lost All-American Art Heyman, they still had smooth Jeff Mullins and two 6-10 starters up front. The Michigan Wolverines were young, but with lots of muscle and sophomore of the year Cazzie Russell, they were among the favorites. And you couldn't count out Adolph Rupp's Kentucky Wildcats, with All-American sharpshooter Cotton Nash, or tall, fast-breaking Wichita State, with high-scoring Dave Stallworth, or defensive-minded San Francisco, or Big Eight champion Kansas State. As for UCLA, Coach Wooden called his Bruins "a truly great team," but nobody else thought so.

UCLA played four games on their way to the title, and in every one the Bruins' "mighty midgets" looked eminently beatable. But they were never defeated. What UCLA had, along with Player of the Year Walt Hazzard and a healthy dose of team chemistry, was an impeccable fast break and a full-court zone press that—in the wink of an eye—caused opponents to break down and beg for mercy.

Wooden and his staff called his team's penchant for an instantaneous turnaround "the two-minute explosion," and in the 1964 tournament it was as inevitable as night following day. It came late in the second half against Seattle, when, with UCLA holding a 1-point lead, Gail Goodrich zinged in a strike to sophomore Kenny Washington for a 3-point play and then stole a pass off the press for a breakaway lay-up. "I thought we'd beat them," said Seattle Coach Bob Boyd. Didn't happen, though.

Things looked even more precarious for the Bruins in their regional final against San Francisco. The Dons came in with their own 19-game winning streak, and for most of the first half their ball-control offense and tight defense, anchored by 6-8 center Ollie Johnson, worked to perfection. San Francisco led by 13 late in the half, and went into the intermission with an 8-point advantage. Wooden, noting that his team had shot a pitiful 9 for 29 from the floor, remained confident. "We'll be all right as soon as our shots start dropping," he said. In less than five-and-a-half second-half minutes, UCLA outscored San Francisco 17-8 to take the lead. The Bruins were on their way to the Final Four.

UCLA's semifinal opponent was Kansas State, the only regional non-favorite to make it to the championship rounds. With 7:28 to play, K State scored and took a 75-70 lead. With two starters on the bench in foul trouble, many teams would have packed it up and gone home. Instead the Bruins turned up the pressure. Led by Keith Erickson, Kenny Washington, and Walt Hazzard, UCLA turned its press into a lethal weapon. In less than three minutes, the score was 81-75 UCLA.

In the final the Bruins were matched up against Duke. The Blue Devils were tall, disciplined, and experienced, and despite UCLA's No. 1 ranking and unblemished record, the ACC champions were favored to win the title after their convincing victory over tough Michigan in the semis.

Through most of the first half, the game went according to form. The two teams, playing at a fast pace, traded baskets, with Mullins leading Duke to a 3-point lead after thirteen minutes. Wooden started his usual line-up, but within minutes he brought in two sophomores—Doug McIntosh and Kenny Washington—to replace veterans Fred Slaughter and Jack Hirsch up front. Later in the half Keith Erickson, the team's best defensive player, got into foul trouble and Hirsch got back in. With 7:07 left in the half, the UCLA line-up of Hazzard, Goodrich, Hirsch, Washington, and McIntosh exploded. Suddenly the Bruins attacked the taller Blue Devils like a swarm of enraged mosquitoes—everywhere Duke turned, there were UCLA bodies in the way, UCLA hands reaching for the ball. Under the relentless Bruin pressure, the Blue Devils suddenly lost their composure. They threw the ball away, and their turnovers became easy UCLA fast breaks. When they didn't lose the ball in the backcourt they rushed their shots, and the small, quick UCLA front line got inside to pick off the rebounds. After two minutes and thirty-three seconds of sheer hell, the Blue Devils looked around and found themselves down by 13. The game was over, and the Blue Devils—like all the other UCLA victims—were left wondering what had happened to them.

The Bruins went back to California as the first undefeated national champions since North Carolina turned the trick in 1957. They were very good indeed. But they were surely not invincible, particularly with Walt Hazzard graduating. Around the country, there was hope for the future. UCLA may have won, but all the also-rans went home saying wait till next year.

FIRST ROUND EAST

Villanova (77)   Coach: Jack Kraft

	Min.	Total FG / FGA	Pct.	FT / FTA	Pct.	Reb. O / T	A	TO	PF	S	Blk	TP	PPM
MOORE, R.	-	12/24	.500	1/ 1	1.000	-/ 8	5	-	1	-	-	25	-
SALLEE, A.	-	1/ 5	.200	0/ 0	.000	-/ 7	1	-	3	-	-	2	-
WASHINGTON, J.	-	5/13	.385	4/ 7	.571	-/19	0	-	1	-	-	14	-
JONES, W.	-	7/22	.318	3/ 3	1.000	-/ 6	7	-	0	-	-	17	-
MELCHIONNI, B.	-	6/11	.545	1/ 1	1.000	-/ 2	5	-	1	-	-	13	-
SCHAFFER, B.	-	1/ 3	.333	1/ 1	1.000	-/ 5	0	-	3	-	-	3	-
LEFTWICH, G.	-	0/ 2	.000	3/ 4	.750	-/ 2	1	-	1	-	-	3	-
ERICKSON, E.	-	0/ 0	.000	0/ 0	.000	-/ 0	0	-	0	-	-	0	-
WINTERBOTTOM, W.	-	0/ 0	.000	0/ 0	.000	-/ 0	0	-	0	-	-	0	-
IORIO	-	0/ 0	.000	0/ 0	.000	-/ 0	0	-	0	-	-	0	-
Totals	200	32/80	.400	13/17	.765	-/49	19	-	10	-	-	77	.385

Providence (66)   Coach: Joe Mullaney

	Min.	Total FG / FGA	Pct.	FT / FTA	Pct.	Reb. O / T	A	TO	PF	S	Blk	TP	PPM
STONE	-	5/12	.417	4/ 4	1.000	-/ 4	0	-	0	-	-	14	-
KOVALSKI	-	4/ 9	.444	0/ 0	.000	-/ 9	0	-	5	-	-	8	-
THOMPSON, J.	-	7/13	.538	4/ 8	.500	-/ 3	1	-	5	-	-	18	-
BENEDICT	-	8/14	.571	0/ 0	.000	-/ 4	3	-	2	-	-	16	-
AHERN	-	1/ 3	.333	0/ 0	.000	-/ 4	6	-	1	-	-	2	-
BLAIR	-	3/ 5	.600	1/ 1	1.000	-/ 1	2	-	0	-	-	7	-
DUTTON	-	0/ 0	.000	0/ 0	.000	-/ 4	0	-	0	-	-	0	-
LASHER	-	0/ 0	.000	1/ 3	.333	-/ 0	0	-	0	-	-	1	-
STEIN	-	0/ 0	.000	0/ 0	.000	-/ 0	0	-	0	-	-	0	-
Totals	200	28/56	.500	10/16	.625	-/29	12	-	13	-	-	66	.330

Team Rebounds: Villanova 4; Providence 4. Disqualified: Providence—Kovalski, Thompson.

	1st Half	2nd Half	Final
Villanova	34	43	77
Providence	28	38	66

Temple (48)   Coach: Harry Litwack

	Min.	Total FG / FGA	Pct.	FT / FTA	Pct.	Reb. O / T	A	TO	PF	S	Blk	TP	PPM
FITZGERALD, D.	-	5/13	.385	0/ 1	.000	-/ 9	1	-	2	-	-	10	-
RICHARDSON, V.	-	3/10	.300	0/ 0	.000	-/ 7	1	-	2	-	-	6	-
WILLIAMS, J.	-	4/15	.267	3/ 4	.750	-/20	1	-	3	-	-	11	-
KELLEY, B.	-	7/14	.500	2/ 2	1.000	-/ 4	2	-	3	-	-	16	-
HARRINGTON, B.	-	1/10	.100	3/ 4	.750	-/ 0	1	-	2	-	-	5	-
BISHOP, F.	-	0/ 0	.000	0/ 0	.000	-/ 1	1	-	1	-	-	0	-
SNETHEN, E.	-	0/ 0	.000	0/ 0	.000	-/ 0	0	-	0	-	-	0	-
Totals	200	20/62	.323	8/11	.727	-/41	7	-	13	-	-	48	.240

U. Conn. (53)   Coach: Fred Shabel

	Min.	Total FG / FGA	Pct.	FT / FTA	Pct.	Reb. O / T	A	TO	PF	S	Blk	TP	PPM
HESFORD, D.	-	5/12	.417	4/ 5	.800	-/ 6	5	-	1	-	-	14	-
KIMBALL, T.	-	6/21	.286	0/ 4	.000	-/17	0	-	1	-	-	12	-
SLOMCENSKI, E.	-	5/11	.455	3/ 4	.750	-/14	1	-	2	-	-	13	-
PERNO, D.	-	0/ 8	.000	0/ 1	.000	-/ 1	3	-	2	-	-	0	-
RITTER, A.	-	0/ 1	.000	0/ 0	.000	-/ 1	0	-	0	-	-	0	-
DELLASALA, W.	-	7/13	.538	0/ 1	.000	-/ 8	2	-	1	-	-	14	-
WHITNEY, K.	-	0/ 0	.000	0/ 0	.000	-/ 0	0	-	0	-	-	0	-
Totals	200	23/66	.348	7/15	.467	-/47	11	-	7	-	-	53	.265

Team Rebounds: U. Conn. 3; Temple 5. Disqualified: None.

	1st Half	2nd Half	Final
Temple	26	22	48
U. Conn.	24	29	53

VMI (60)   Coach: Weenie Miller

	Min.	Total FG / FGA	Pct.	FT / FTA	Pct.	Reb. O / T	A	TO	PF	S	Blk	TP	PPM
SCHMAUS, C.	-	2/ 7	.286	1/ 1	1.000	-/ 5	0	-	3	-	-	5	-
GAUSEPOHL	-	0/ 2	.000	1/ 2	.500	-/ 3	0	-	1	-	-	1	-
WATSON, B.	-	2/10	.200	5/ 5	1.000	-/ 5	0	-	5	-	-	9	-
KRUSZEWSKI, J.	-	8/17	.471	3/ 4	.750	-/ 5	2	-	4	-	-	19	-
BLAIR, B.	-	6/20	.300	8/12	.667	-/ 4	5	-	4	-	-	20	-
GUY	-	1/ 2	.500	2/ 3	.667	-/ 5	0	-	1	-	-	4	-
PROSSER	-	0/ 0	.000	0/ 0	.000	-/ 0	0	-	0	-	-	0	-
HARTUNG	-	0/ 1	.000	0/ 0	.000	-/ 0	0	-	0	-	-	0	-
COOPER	-	1/ 1	1.000	0/ 0	.000	-/ 0	0	-	0	-	-	2	-
Totals	200	20/60	.333	20/27	.741	-/27	7	-	18	-	-	60	.300

Princeton (86)   Coach: B. Van Breda Kolff

	Min.	Total FG / FGA	Pct.	FT / FTA	Pct.	Reb. O / T	A	TO	PF	S	Blk	TP	PPM
BRADLEY, B.	-	12/22	.545	10/11	.909	-/12	8	-	3	-	-	34	-
HAARLOW, B.	-	7/17	.412	1/ 1	1.000	-/ 7	1	-	1	-	-	15	-
NIEMANN, D.	-	1/ 1	1.000	0/ 0	.000	-/ 3	0	-	1	-	-	2	-
ROTH, D.	-	0/ 1	.000	1/ 1	1.000	-/ 4	4	-	4	-	-	1	-
HOWARD, B.	-	3/ 6	.500	5/ 6	.833	-/10	0	-	3	-	-	11	-
STEUBE, E.	-	1/ 3	.333	1/ 2	.500	-/ 2	2	-	4	-	-	3	-
KINGSTON, W.	-	0/ 0	.000	0/ 0	.000	-/ 3	0	-	0	-	-	0	-
RODENBACH, D.	-	4/12	.333	2/ 2	1.000	-/ 3	0	-	3	-	-	10	-
KITCH, P.	-	1/ 1	1.000	0/ 0	.000	-/ 0	0	-	0	-	-	2	-
WRIGHT, R.	-	2/ 2	1.000	0/ 0	.000	-/ 0	0	-	0	-	-	4	-
UHLE, W.	-	1/ 1	1.000	0/ 0	.000	-/ 1	0	-	0	-	-	2	-
BERLING	-	1/ 1	1.000	0/ 0	.000	-/ 0	1	-	1	-	-	2	-
Totals	200	33/67	.493	20/23	.870	-/45	16	-	20	-	-	86	.430

Disqualified: VMI—Watson.

	1st Half	2nd Half	Final
VMI	36	24	60
Princeton	35	51	86

FIRST ROUND MIDEAST

Ohio (71)   Coach: James Snyder

	Min.	Total FG / FGA	Pct.	FT / FTA	Pct.	Reb. O / T	A	TO	PF	S	Blk	TP	PPM
HILT, D.	-	5/ 8	.625	4/10	.400	-/15	-	-	4	-	-	14	-
HALEY, M.	-	6/12	.500	5/ 5	1.000	-/ 5	-	-	3	-	-	17	-
STOREY, P.	-	5/13	.385	3/ 5	.600	-/ 6	-	-	2	-	-	13	-
GILL	-	2/ 3	.667	1/ 2	.500	-/ 4	-	-	3	-	-	5	-
JACKSON, J.	-	5/14	.357	5/ 8	.625	-/ 4	-	-	0	-	-	15	-
DAVIS	-	2/ 4	.500	0/ 0	.000	-/ 4	-	-	3	-	-	4	-
WEIRICH	-	1/ 1	1.000	1/ 1	1.000	-/ 2	-	-	0	-	-	3	-
Totals	225	26/55	.473	19/31	.613	-/40	-	-	15	-	-	71	.316

Louisville (69)   Coach: Peck Hickman

	Min.	Total FG / FGA	Pct.	FT / FTA	Pct.	Reb. O / T	A	TO	PF	S	Blk	TP	PPM
HAWLEY, R.	-	3/ 7	.429	3/ 3	1.000	-/ 7	-	-	4	-	-	9	-
REUTHER, JOHN	-	11/22	.500	5/ 7	.714	-/ 7	-	-	4	-	-	27	-
ROTHMAN, J.	-	3/ 8	.375	2/ 3	.667	-/12	-	-	4	-	-	8	-
ROOKS, R.	-	2/ 7	.286	1/ 1	1.000	-/ 1	-	-	3	-	-	5	-
CREAMER, E.	-	6/16	.375	0/ 0	.000	-/ 2	-	-	4	-	-	12	-
FINNEGAN, T.	-	2/ 7	.286	0/ 0	.000	-/ 0	-	-	0	-	-	4	-
CLIFFORD, D.	-	1/ 3	.333	2/ 3	.667	-/ 7	-	-	2	-	-	4	-
HOUSTON, W.	-	0/ 1	.000	0/ 0	.000	-/ 0	-	-	2	-	-	0	-
Totals	225	28/71	.394	13/17	.765	-/36	-	-	23	-	-	69	.307

Team Rebounds: Ohio 3; Louisville 2. Disqualified: None.

	1st Half	2nd Half	1 OT	Final
Ohio	32	33	6	71
Louisville	37	28	4	69

Murray State (91)   Coach: Cal Luther

	Min.	Total FG / FGA	Pct.	FT / FTA	Pct.	Reb. O / T	A	TO	PF	S	Blk	TP	PPM
JENNINGS	-	8/21	.381	8/ 9	.889	-/19	-	-	3	-	-	24	-
VARNAS	-	10/15	.667	1/ 1	1.000	-/10	-	-	3	-	-	21	-
JOHNSON	-	9/23	.391	0/ 0	.000	-/ 6	-	-	5	-	-	18	-
PENDLETON	-	7/15	.467	1/ 1	1.000	-/ 4	-	-	3	-	-	15	-
SCHLOSSER	-	2/ 4	.500	0/ 2	.000	-/ 4	-	-	5	-	-	4	-
GOHEEN	-	3/ 5	.600	1/ 1	1.000	-/ 2	-	-	4	-	-	7	-
GOEBEL	-	0/ 0	.000	0/ 0	.000	-/ 0	-	-	2	-	-	0	-
WALKER	-	1/ 3	.333	0/ 0	.000	-/ 2	-	-	1	-	-	2	-
Totals	200	40/86	.465	11/14	.786	-/47	-	-	26	-	-	91	.455

Loyola-Chicago (101)   Coach: George Ireland

	Min.	Total FG / FGA	Pct.	FT / FTA	Pct.	Reb. O / T	A	TO	PF	S	Blk	TP	PPM
ROUSE, V.	-	6/14	.429	4/ 8	.500	-/11	-	-	4	-	-	16	-
MILLER, R.	-	10/16	.625	1/ 4	.250	-/ 6	-	-	2	-	-	21	-
HUNTER, L.	-	5/10	.500	3/ 6	.500	-/22	-	-	4	-	-	13	-
COLEMAN, J.	-	9/13	.692	9/12	.750	-/ 6	-	-	3	-	-	27	-
EGAN, J.	-	9/26	.346	6/ 9	.667	-/ 4	-	-	2	-	-	24	-
WOOD, C.	-	0/ 1	.000	0/ 0	.000	-/ 0	-	-	0	-	-	0	-
MANZKE	-	0/ 0	.000	0/ 0	.000	-/ 0	-	-	0	-	-	0	-
Totals	200	39/80	.488	23/39	.590	-/49	-	-	15	-	-	101	.505

Team Rebounds: Loyola-Chicago 4; Murray State 6. Disqualified: Murray State—Johnson, Schlosser.

	1st Half	2nd Half	Final
Murray State	43	48	91
Loyola-Chicago	54	47	101

FIRST ROUND MIDWEST

Oklahoma City (78)   Coach: Abe Lemons

	Min.	Total FG / FGA	Pct.	FT / FTA	Pct.	Reb. O / T	A	TO	PF	S	Blk	TP	PPM
MILLER	-	2/ 6	.333	2/ 3	.667	-/ 2	-	-	4	-	-	6	-
HUNTER	-	4/ 9	.444	1/ 1	1.000	-/ 1	-	-	5	-	-	9	-
JACKSON, E.	-	5/10	.500	2/ 3	.667	-/24	-	-	3	-	-	12	-
KOPER, B.	-	9/18	.500	8/11	.727	-/ 4	-	-	2	-	-	26	-
WELLS, J.	-	9/15	.600	1/ 4	.250	-/ 6	-	-	5	-	-	19	-
WARE	-	1/ 4	.250	0/ 3	.000	-/ 5	-	-	1	-	-	2	-
BAGBY	-	2/ 4	.500	0/ 0	.000	-/ 2	-	-	0	-	-	4	-
SNIDER	-	0/ 2	.000	0/ 0	.000	-/ 1	-	-	1	-	-	0	-
HARRIS	-	0/ 0	.000	0/ 0	.000	-/ 0	-	-	0	-	-	0	-
Totals	200	32/68	.471	14/25	.560	-/45	-	-	21	-	-	78	.390

Creighton (89)   Coach: Red McManus

	Min.	Total FG / FGA	Pct.	FT / FTA	Pct.	Reb. O / T	A	TO	PF	S	Blk	TP	PPM
POINTER, F.	-	10/21	.476	3/ 3	1.000	-/ 7	-	-	3	-	-	23	-
MCGRIFF, E.	-	10/15	.667	5/ 8	.625	-/10	-	-	5	-	-	25	-
SILAS, P.	-	7/15	.467	1/ 6	.167	-/27	-	-	4	-	-	15	-
BROWN, C.	-	4/12	.333	1/ 1	1.000	-/ 0	-	-	2	-	-	9	-
OFFICER, C.	-	1/10	.100	1/ 1	1.000	-/ 7	-	-	0	-	-	3	-
FOREHAND	-	3/ 6	.500	6/ 8	.750	-/ 5	-	-	2	-	-	12	-
APKE	-	0/ 3	.000	0/ 0	.000	-/ 4	-	-	3	-	-	0	-
MILES	-	1/ 3	.333	0/ 1	.000	-/ 2	-	-	0	-	-	2	-
Totals	200	36/85	.424	17/28	.607	-/62	-	-	19	-	-	89	.445

Disqualified: Creighton—McGriff; Oklahoma City—Hunter, Wells.

	1st Half	2nd Half	Final
Oklahoma City	38	40	78
Creighton	47	42	89

Texas A&M (62)   Coach: Shelby Metcalf

	Min.	Total FG / FGA	Pct.	FT / FTA	Pct.	Reb. O / T	A	TO	PF	S	Blk	TP	PPM
GASWAY	-	1/ 2	.500	0/ 0	.000	-/ 5	-	-	3	-	-	2	-
ROBINETTE	-	1/ 4	.250	1/ 2	.500	-/ 4	-	-	2	-	-	3	-
BEASLEY	-	6/12	.500	1/ 1	1.000	-/ 4	-	-	3	-	-	13	-
LENOX, B.	-	11/25	.440	2/ 2	1.000	-/ 1	-	-	1	-	-	24	-
TIMMINS	-	3/ 7	.429	0/ 0	.000	-/ 1	-	-	2	-	-	6	-
FERGUSON	-	0/ 0	.000	0/ 0	.000	-/ 0	-	-	2	-	-	0	-
STRINGFELLOW	-	2/ 3	.667	1/ 1	1.000	-/ 2	-	-	2	-	-	5	-
NORMAN	-	3/ 5	.600	2/ 3	.667	-/ 1	-	-	3	-	-	8	-
TIMMERMAN	-	0/ 1	.000	1/ 1	1.000	-/ 0	-	-	0	-	-	1	-
Totals	200	27/59	.458	8/10	.800	-/18	-	-	18	-	-	62	.310

Texas Western (68)   Coach: Don Haskins

	Min.	Total FG / FGA	Pct.	FT / FTA	Pct.	Reb. O / T	A	TO	PF	S	Blk	TP	PPM
STOGLIN, A.	-	6/14	.429	0/ 1	.000	-/10	-	-	3	-	-	12	-
BANKS, C.	-	1/ 4	.250	0/ 0	.000	-/ 1	-	-	1	-	-	2	-
BARNES, J.	16/23	16/23	.696	10/13	.769	-/19	-	-	3	-	-	42	-
ARTIS, O.	-	2/ 7	.286	3/ 4	.750	-/ 2	-	-	1	-	-	7	-
TREDENNICK, S.	-	0/ 1	.000	0/ 0	.000	-/ 0	-	-	1	-	-	0	-
DIBLER, B.	-	0/ 1	.000	0/ 1	.000	-/ 1	-	-	0	-	-	0	-
FLOURNOY, H.	-	1/ 3	.333	3/ 3	1.000	-/ 3	-	-	1	-	-	5	-
Totals	200	26/53	.491	16/23	.696	-/36	-	-	10	-	-	68	.340

Team Rebounds: Texas Western 6; Texas A&M 8. Disqualified: None.

	1st Half	2nd Half	Final
Texas A&M	35	27	62
Texas Western	32	36	68

FIRST ROUND WEST

Oregon State (57)   Coach: Amory "Slats" Gill

	Min.	Total FG / FGA	Pct.	FT / FTA	Pct.	Reb. O / T	A	TO	PF	S	Blk	TP	PPM
EATON	-	3/ 6	.500	2/ 5	.400	-/ 4	-	-	4	-	-	8	-
DREISEWERD	-	2/ 3	.667	0/ 1	.000	-/ 1	-	-	3	-	-	4	-
COUNTS, M.	-	6/17	.353	15/18	.833	-/19	-	-	4	-	-	27	-
JARVIS, J.	-	4/ 9	.444	0/ 2	.000	-/ 2	-	-	5	-	-	8	-
PETERS, F.	-	3/11	.273	0/ 1	.000	-/ 7	-	-	5	-	-	6	-
KRAUS	-	1/ 4	.250	0/ 0	.000	-/ 7	-	-	1	-	-	2	-
BAXTER	-	0/ 0	.000	0/ 0	.000	-/ 0	-	-	1	-	-	0	-
BENNER	-	0/ 0	.000	0/ 0	.000	-/ 0	-	-	0	-	-	0	-
WHELAN	-	1/ 2	.500	0/ 0	.000	-/ 1	-	-	5	-	-	2	-
Totals	200	20/52	.385	17/27	.630	-/41	-	-	28	-	-	57	.285

Seattle (61)   Coach: Bob Boyd

	Min.	Total FG / FGA	Pct.	FT / FTA	Pct.	Reb. O / T	A	TO	PF	S	Blk	TP	PPM
VERMILLION, G.	-	3/ 7	.429	7/10	.700	-/ 4	-	-	3	-	-	13	-
TURNEY, R.	-	0/ 6	.000	1/ 2	.500	-/ 3	-	-	3	-	-	1	-
TRESVANT, J.	-	1/ 8	.125	3/ 5	.600	-/ 7	-	-	4	-	-	5	-
WILLIAMS, C.	-	3/11	.273	6/ 8	.750	-/ 2	-	-	2	-	-	12	-
HEYWARD, R.	-	5/ 9	.556	4/ 8	.500	-/ 4	-	-	4	-	-	14	-
GRIFFIN	-	0/ 0	.000	0/ 0	.000	-/ 1	-	-	1	-	-	0	-
WHEELER, L.	-	2/ 7	.286	5/ 6	.833	-/ 5	-	-	3	-	-	9	-
PHILLIPS, P.	-	2/ 8	.250	3/ 4	.750	-/ 6	-	-	2	-	-	7	-
TEBBS, J.	-	0/ 0	.000	0/ 0	.000	-/ 0	-	-	0	-	-	0	-
Totals	200	16/56	.286	29/43	.674	-/32	-	-	22	-	-	61	.305

Team Rebounds: Seattle 16; Oregon State 7. Disqualified: Oregon State—Jarvis, Peters, Whelan.

	1st Half	2nd Half	Final
Oregon State	34	23	57
Seattle	31	30	61

Arizona State (90)   Coach: Ned Wulk

	Min.	Total FG / FGA	Pct.	FT / FTA	Pct.	Reb. O / T	A	TO	PF	S	Blk	TP	PPM
DAIRMAN, D.	-	0/ 6	.000	4/ 5	.800	-/ 6	-	-	5	-	-	4	-
CALDWELL, J.	-	10/16	.625	5/ 5	1.000	-/15	-	-	5	-	-	25	-
BECKER, A.	-	13/24	.542	3/ 6	.500	-/ 9	-	-	4	-	-	29	-
SENITZA, G.	-	2/ 9	.222	3/ 4	.750	-/ 4	-	-	5	-	-	7	-
COPPOLA, R.	-	5/ 8	.625	3/ 5	.600	-/ 2	-	-	0	-	-	13	-
MYERS, J.	-	3/ 6	.500	2/ 2	1.000	-/ 5	-	-	2	-	-	8	-
HAMILTON, T.	-	2/12	.167	0/ 0	.000	-/10	-	-	4	-	-	4	-
JONES, G.	-	0/ 0	.000	0/ 0	.000	-/ 0	-	-	0	-	-	0	-
HARPER, L.	-	0/ 0	.000	0/ 0	.000	-/ 0	-	-	0	-	-	0	-
Totals	200	35/81	.432	20/27	.741	-/51	-	10	25	-	-	90	.450

Utah State (92)   Coach: Ladell Anderson

	Min.	Total FG / FGA	Pct.	FT / FTA	Pct.	Reb. O / T	A	TO	PF	S	Blk	TP	PPM
WALKER, L.	-	7/16	.438	4/ 6	.667	-/ 8	-	-	3	-	-	18	-
ESTES, W.	-	14/29	.483	10/11	.909	-/ 8	-	-	3	-	-	38	-
COLLIER, T.	-	9/21	.429	4/ 5	.800	-/13	-	-	5	-	-	22	-
WATTS, G.	-	5/ 8	.625	1/ 4	.250	-/ 2	-	-	4	-	-	11	-
LONG, B.	-	1/ 3	.333	1/ 2	.500	-/ 1	-	-	1	-	-	3	-
HANSON, R.	-	0/ 2	.000	0/ 0	.000	-/ 0	-	-	0	-	-	0	-
DITTEBRAND, M.	-	0/ 0	.000	0/ 1	.000	-/ 0	-	-	2	-	-	0	-
ANGLE, L.	-	0/ 5	.000	0/ 0	.000	-/ 2	-	-	0	-	-	0	-
Totals	200	36/84	.429	20/29	.690	-/34	-	6	18	-	-	92	.460

Team Rebounds: Utah State 13; Arizona St. 12. Disqualified: Utah State—Collier; Arizona St.—Dairman, Caldwell, Senitza. Technical fouls: Utah State—Walker.

	1st Half	2nd Half	Final
Arizona St.	48	42	90
Utah State	43	49	92

REGIONAL SEMIFINAL EAST

Duke (87)   Coach: Vic Bubas

	Min.	Total FG / FGA	Pct.	FT / FTA	Pct.	Reb. O / T	A	TO	PF	S	Blk	TP	PPM
FERGUSON, D.	32	0/ 3	.000	0/ 0	.000	-/ 2	1	-	4	-	-	0	.000
BUCKLEY, J.	40	3/ 8	.375	3/ 6	.500	-/12	2	-	0	-	-	9	.225
TISON, H.	31	3/ 6	.500	7/ 8	.875	-/ 6	3	-	5	·	-	13	.419
HARRISON, B.	13	1/ 8	.125	0/ 0	.000	-/ 1	1	-	2	-	-	2	.154
MULLINS, J.	40	19/28	.679	5/ 6	.833	-/12	1	-	1	-	-	43	1.075
VACENDAK, S.	25	3/ 5	.600	2/ 3	.667	-/ 6	2	-	0	-	-	8	.320
HERBSTER, R.	10	2/ 3	.667	0/ 0	.000	-/ 0	0	-	0	·	-	4	.400
MARIN, J.	9	2/ 5	.400	4/ 6	.667	-/ 5	0	-	1	-	-	8	.889
Totals	200	33/66	.500	21/29	.724	-/44	10	-	13	-	-	87	.435

Villanova (73)   Coach: Jack Kraft

	Min.	Total FG / FGA	Pct.	FT / FTA	Pct.	Reb. O / T	A	TO	PF	S	Blk	TP	PPM
MELCHIONNI, B.	36	9/17	.529	0/ 2	.000	-/ 3	1	-	4	-	-	18	.500
JONES, W.	40	6/20	.300	6/ 7	.857	-/ 6	3	-	3	-	-	18	.450
MOORE, R.	35	4/12	.333	0/ 0	.000	-/ 3	2	-	3	-	-	8	.229
WASHINGTON, J.	27	2/ 7	.286	4/ 4	1.000	-/11	0	-	5	-	-	8	.296
SALLEE, A.	34	3/ 7	.429	0/ 0	.000	-/ 6	1	-	1	-	-	6	.176
ERICKSON, B.	12	5/ 7	.714	0/ 2	.000	-/ 2	0	-	2	-	-	10	.833
SCHAFFER, B.	14	2/ 4	.500	1/ 1	1.000	-/ 4	0	-	3	-	-	5	.357
LEFTWICH, G.	2	0/ 1	.000	0/ 0	.000	-/ 0	0	-	1	-	-	0	.000
Totals	200	31/75	.413	11/16	.688	-/35	7	-	22	-	-	73	.365

Team Rebounds: Duke 5; Villanova 6. Disqualified: Duke—Tison; Villanova—Washington.

	1st Half	2nd Half	Final
Duke	49	38	87
Villanova	33	40	73

U. Conn. (52)   Coach: Fred Shabel

	Min.	Total FG / FGA	Pct.	FT / FTA	Pct.	Reb. O / T	A	TO	PF	S	Blk	TP	PPM
HISFORD, D.	27	1/ 2	.500	1/ 1	1.000	-/ 1	0	-	4	-	-	3	.111
PERNO, D.	40	4/15	.267	4/ 5	.800	-/ 3	3	-	2	-	-	12	.300
RITTER, A.	37	5/ 9	.556	0/ 0	.000	-/ 0	0	-	1	-	-	10	.270
KIMBALL, T.	40	6/11	.545	4/ 8	.500	-/13	0	-	2	-	-	16	.400
SLOMCENSKI, E.	40	1/ 4	.250	5/ 5	1.000	-/ 8	1	-	1	-	-	7	.175
DELLASALA, W.	16	2/ 3	.667	0/ 0	.000	-/ 3	0	-	1	-	-	4	.250
Totals	200	19/44	.432	14/19	.737	-/28	4	-	11	-	-	52	.260

Princeton (50)   Coach: B. Van Breda Kolff

	Min.	Total FG / FGA	Pct.	FT / FTA	Pct.	Reb. O / T	A	TO	PF	S	Blk	TP	PPM
RODENBACH, D.	25	3/ 6	.500	0/ 0	.000	-/ 0	0	-	0	-	-	6	.240
HAARLOW, B.	40	5/13	.385	0/ 0	.000	-/ 7	0	-	0	-	-	10	.250
ROTH, D.	10	0/ 0	.000	0/ 0	.000	-/ 0	0	-	1	-	-	0	.000
BRADLEY, B.	40	6/15	.400	10/11	.909	-/10	1	-	3	-	-	22	.550
UHLE, W.	30	2/ 5	.400	0/ 0	.000	-/ 4	1	-	1	-	-	4	.133
HOWARD, B.	19	1/ 3	.333	0/ 0	.000	-/ 3	0	-	3	-	-	2	.105
STEUBE, E.	13	1/ 4	.250	0/ 0	.000	-/ 0	0	-	2	-	-	2	.154
KINGSTON, W.	2	1/ 1	1.000	0/ 0	.000	-/ 0	0	-	1	-	-	2	1.000
NIEMANN, D.	21	1/ 1	1.000	0/ 0	.000	-/ 1	1	-	2	-	-	2	.095
Totals	200	20/48	.417	10/11	.909	-/25	3	-	13	-	-	50	.250

Team Rebounds: U. Conn. 3; Princeton 3. Disqualified: None.

	1st Half	2nd Half	Final
U. Conn.	27	25	52
Princeton	28	22	50

REGIONAL SEMIFINAL MIDEAST

Kentucky (69) Coach: Adolph Rupp

	Min.	Total FG/FGA	Pct.	FT/FTA	Pct.	Reb. O/T	A	TO	PF	S	Blk	TP	PPM
DEEKEN, T.	-	5/17	.294	0/ 1	.000	-/14	-	-	4	-	-	10	-
CONLEY, L.	-	7/16	.438	3/ 3	1.000	-/ 5	-	-	5	-	-	17	-
NASH, C.	-	4/14	.286	2/ 3	.667	-/ 9	-	-	3	-	-	10	-
MOBLEY, T.	-	8/13	.615	1/ 1	1.000	-/ 5	-	-	3	-	-	17	-
KRON, T.	-	0/ 1	.000	0/ 0	.000	-/ 1	-	-	0	-	-	0	-
ISHMAEL, C.	-	1/ 5	.200	0/ 0	.000	-/ 1	-	-	1	-	-	2	-
ADAMS, J.	-	0/ 0	.000	0/ 0	.000	-/ 0	-	-	1	-	-	0	-
EMBRY, R.	-	5/12	.417	1/ 3	.333	-/ 2	-	-	2	-	-	11	-
HARPER, S.	-	1/ 2	.500	0/ 1	.000	-/ 1	-	-	1	-	-	2	-
Totals	200	31/80	.388	7/12	.583	-/38	-	-	20	-	-	69	.345

Ohio (85) Coach: James Snyder

	Min.	Total FG/FGA	Pct.	FT/FTA	Pct.	Reb. O/T	A	TO	PF	S	Blk	TP	PPM
HALEY, M.	-	7/14	.500	1/ 1	1.000	-/ 7	-	-	1	-	-	15	-
HILT, D.	-	4/ 9	.444	6/ 7	.857	-/ 9	-	-	4	-	-	14	-
STOREY, P.	-	8/15	.533	3/ 6	.500	-/ 9	-	-	0	-	-	19	-
JACKSON, J.	-	11/22	.500	3/ 5	.600	-/11	-	-	1	-	-	25	-
GILL	-	1/ 1	1.000	1/ 3	.333	-/ 5	-	-	3	-	-	3	-
DAVIS	-	1/ 5	.200	5/ 7	.714	-/ 3	-	-	2	-	-	7	-
WEIRICH	-	0/ 0	.000	0/ 0	.000	-/ 0	-	-	0	-	-	0	-
BARRY	-	0/ 0	.000	0/ 0	.000	-/ 0	-	-	0	-	-	0	-
BUCK	-	0/ 0	.000	0/ 0	.000	-/ 0	-	-	0	-	-	0	-
SCHOON	-	0/ 0	.000	0/ 0	.000	-/ 0	-	-	0	-	-	0	-
BROWN	-	1/ 2	.500	0/ 0	.000	-/ 1	-	-	0	-	-	2	-
Totals	200	33/68	.485	19/29	.655	-/45	-	-	11	-	-	85	.425

Disqualified: Kentucky—Conley.

	1st Half	2nd Half	Final
Kentucky	24	45	69
Ohio	40	45	85

Loyola-Chicago (80) Coach: George Ireland

	Min.	Total FG/FGA	Pct.	FT/FTA	Pct.	Reb. O/T	A	TO	PF	S	Blk	TP	PPM
MILLER, R.	-	7/26	.269	2/ 5	.400	-/ 7	-	-	2	-	-	16	-
ROUSE, V.	-	5/13	.385	2/ 3	.667	-/14	-	-	2	-	-	12	-
HUNTER, L.	-	11/18	.611	3/ 6	.500	-/ 6	-	-	5	-	-	25	-
EGAN, J.	-	3/15	.200	4/ 5	.800	-/ 3	-	-	5	-	-	10	-
COLEMAN, J.	-	7/14	.500	3/ 4	.750	-/ 6	-	-	3	-	-	17	-
WOOD, C.	-	0/ 1	.000	0/ 0	.000	-/ 1	-	-	1	-	-	0	-
MANZKE	-	0/ 1	.000	0/ 0	.000	-/ 0	-	-	0	-	-	0	-
Totals	200	33/88	.375	14/23	.609	-/37	-	-	18	-	-	80	.400

Michigan (84) Coach: Dave Strack

	Min.	Total FG/FGA	Pct.	FT/FTA	Pct.	Reb. O/T	A	TO	PF	S	Blk	TP	PPM
TREGONING, L.	-	7/15	.467	0/ 0	.000	-/14	-	-	5	-	-	14	-
DARDEN, O.	-	4/10	.400	1/ 1	1.000	-/ 6	-	-	4	-	-	9	-
BUNTIN, B.	-	9/23	.391	8/10	.800	-/13	-	-	4	-	-	26	-
CANTRELL, B.	-	3/ 6	.500	6/ 8	.750	-/ 3	-	-	2	-	-	12	-
RUSSELL, C.	-	8/15	.533	5/ 8	.625	-/ 7	-	-	2	-	-	21	-
POMEY, G.	-	0/ 0	.000	0/ 0	.000	-/ 1	-	-	1	-	-	0	-
MYERS, J.	-	1/ 4	.250	0/ 0	.000	-/ 3	-	-	1	-	-	2	-
Totals	200	32/73	.438	20/27	.741	-/47	-	-	19	-	-	84	.420

Disqualified: Michigan—Tregoning; Loyola-Chicago—Hunter, Egan.

	1st Half	2nd Half	Final
Loyola-Chicago	36	44	80
Michigan	43	41	84

REGIONAL SEMIFINAL MIDWEST

Wichita State (84) Coach: Ralph Miller

	Min.	Total FG/FGA	Pct.	FT/FTA	Pct.	Reb. O/T	A	TO	PF	S	Blk	TP	PPM
STALLWORTH, D.	-	7/17	.412	8/ 9	.889	-/23	-	-	3	-	-	22	-
BOWMAN, N.	-	5/10	.500	6/ 9	.667	-/ 8	-	-	4	-	-	16	-
LEACH, D.	-	3/ 5	.600	8/10	.800	-/ 3	-	-	3	-	-	14	-
PETE, K.	-	4/ 7	.571	3/ 4	.750	-/ 7	-	-	5	-	-	11	-
CRISS, J.	-	1/ 6	.167	0/ 0	.000	-/ 1	-	-	5	-	-	2	-
SMITH, V.	-	1/ 5	.200	7/ 7	1.000	-/ 5	-	-	3	-	-	9	-
NOSICH, L.	-	4/ 5	.800	0/ 1	.000	-/ 2	-	-	3	-	-	8	-
DAVIS, G.	-	1/ 1	1.000	0/ 0	.000	-/ 0	-	-	1	-	-	2	-
ROWLAND	-	0/ 0	.000	0/ 0	.000	-/ 0	-	-	0	-	-	0	-
REIMOND	-	0/ 0	.000	0/ 1	.000	-/ 1	-	-	0	-	-	0	-
Totals	200	26/56	.464	32/41	.780	-/50	-	-	27	-	-	84	.420

Creighton (68) Coach: Red McManus

	Min.	Total FG/FGA	Pct.	FT/FTA	Pct.	Reb. O/T	A	TO	PF	S	Blk	TP	PPM
SILAS, P.	-	5/12	.417	12/15	.800	-/17	-	-	2	-	-	22	-
POINTER, F.	-	3/10	.300	1/ 1	1.000	-/ 5	-	-	5	-	-	7	-
OFFICER, C.	-	10/25	.400	1/ 3	.333	-/ 3	-	-	4	-	-	21	-
MCGRIFF, E.	-	1/ 7	.143	4/ 9	.444	-/ 6	-	-	5	-	-	6	-
BROWN, C.	-	1/ 8	.125	1/ 3	.333	-/ 2	-	-	2	-	-	3	-
FOREHAND	-	1/ 2	.500	0/ 0	.000	-/ 0	-	-	2	-	-	2	-
APKE	-	0/ 1	.000	0/ 1	.000	-/ 3	-	-	4	-	-	0	-
JAMES	-	0/ 0	.000	0/ 2	.000	-/ 0	-	-	1	-	-	0	-
MILES	-	3/ 6	.500	1/ 2	.500	-/ 4	-	-	3	-	-	7	-
Totals	200	24/71	.338	20/36	.556	-/40	-	-	28	-	-	68	.340

Team Rebounds: Wichita State 2; Creighton 9. Disqualified: Wichita State—Pete, Criss; Creighton—Pointer, McGriff.

	1st Half	2nd Half	Final
Wichita State	38	46	84
Creighton	28	40	68

Texas Western (60) Coach: Don Haskins

	Min.	Total FG/FGA	Pct.	FT/FTA	Pct.	Reb. O/T	A	TO	PF	S	Blk	TP	PPM
BARNES, J.	-	1/ 5	.200	2/ 3	.667	5/ 9	1	-	5	-	-	4	-
ARTIS, O.	-	1/12	.083	0/ 1	.000	2/ 4	4	-	2	-	-	2	-
TREDENNICK, S.	-	0/ 1	.000	0/ 0	.000	0/ 0	-	-	0	-	-	0	-
STOGLIN, A.	-	5/12	.417	2/ 2	1.000	3/ 5	1	-	5	-	-	12	-
FLOURNOY, H.	-	3/ 5	.600	1/ 1	1.000	2/ 5	3	-	3	-	-	7	-
BANKS, C.	-	8/16	.500	4/ 6	.667	3/ 6	1	-	2	-	-	20	-
DIBLER, B.	-	6/15	.400	1/ 1	1.000	0/ 4	3	-	1	-	-	13	-
SHOCKLEY	-	1/ 2	.500	0/ 0	.000	0/ 0	0	-	1	-	-	2	-
Totals	200	25/68	.368	10/14	.714	15/33	13	-	19	-	-	60	.300

Kansas State (64) Coach: Tex Winter

	Min.	Total FG/FGA	Pct.	FT/FTA	Pct.	Reb. O/T	A	TO	PF	S	Blk	TP	PPM
MOSS, M.	-	0/ 3	.000	2/ 2	1.000	1/ 4	4	-	0	-	-	2	-
MURRELL, W.	-	9/24	.375	6/ 8	.750	4/11	1	-	2	-	-	24	-
ROBINSON, S.	-	5/ 6	.833	4/ 6	.667	1/ 4	1	-	1	-	-	14	-
SUTTNER, R.	-	5/10	.500	6/ 8	.750	4/13	0	-	4	-	-	16	-
SIMONS, J.	-	2/ 7	.286	2/ 3	.667	2/ 4	4	-	2	-	-	6	-
WILLIAMS, G.	-	1/ 2	.500	0/ 0	.000	0/ 0	0	-	2	-	-	2	-
Totals	200	22/52	.423	20/27	.741	12/36	10	-	11	-	-	64	.320

Team Rebounds: Kansas State 10; Texas Western 7. Disqualified: Texas Western—Barnes, Stoglin.

	1st Half	2nd Half	Final
Texas Western	21	39	60
Kansas State	23	41	64

REGIONAL SEMIFINAL WEST

UCLA (95)   Coach: John Wooden

	Min.	Total FG/FGA	Pct.	FT/FTA	Pct.	Reb. O/T	A	TO	PF	S	Blk	TP	PPM
ERICKSON, K.	-	3/13	.231	1/4	.250	-/13	-	-	5	-	-	7	-
HIRSCH, J.	-	8/12	.667	5/5	1.000	-/13	-	-	5	-	-	21	-
SLAUGHTER, F.	-	6/10	.600	1/3	.333	-/13	-	-	5	-	-	13	-
GOODRICH, G.	-	6/22	.273	7/11	.636	-/6	-	-	4	-	-	19	-
HAZZARD, W.	-	9/14	.643	8/11	.727	-/7	-	-	3	-	-	26	-
MCINTOSH, D.	-	1/1	1.000	0/1	.000	-/1	-	-	1	-	-	2	-
STEWART, K.	-	0/1	.000	0/0	.000	-/0	-	-	2	-	-	0	-
WASHINGTON, K.	-	3/4	.750	1/4	.250	-/3	-	-	4	-	-	7	-
HUGGINS, M.	-	0/0	.000	0/0	.000	-/0	-	-	0	-	-	0	-
HOFFMAN, V.	-	0/0	.000	0/0	.000	-/0	-	-	0	-	-	0	-
DARROW, C.	-	0/0	.000	0/0	.000	-/0	-	-	0	-	-	0	-
Totals	200	36/77	.468	23/39	.590	-/56	-	-	29	-	-	95	.475

Seattle (90)   Coach: Bob Boyd

	Min.	Total FG/FGA	Pct.	FT/FTA	Pct.	Reb. O/T	A	TO	PF	S	Blk	TP	PPM
TRESVANT, J.	-	5/15	.333	10/16	.625	-/20	-	-	3	-	-	20	-
VERMILLION, G.	-	6/9	.667	3/3	1.000	-/5	-	-	5	-	-	15	-
WHEELER, L.	-	7/16	.438	6/11	.545	-/8	-	-	4	-	-	20	-
WILLIAMS, C.	-	5/20	.250	2/4	.500	-/13	-	-	5	-	-	12	-
HEYWARD, R.	-	3/8	.375	3/5	.600	-/4	-	-	4	-	-	9	-
PHILLIPS, P.	-	2/8	.250	2/2	1.000	-/4	-	-	4	-	-	6	-
TURNEY, R.	-	2/6	.333	4/4	1.000	-/2	-	-	5	-	-	8	-
TEBBS, J.	-	0/0	.000	0/0	.000	-/0	-	-	1	-	-	0	-
Totals	200	30/82	.366	30/45	.667	-/56	-	-	31	-	-	90	.450

Team Rebounds: UCLA 6; Seattle 6. Disqualified: UCLA—Erickson, Hirsch, Slaughter; Seattle—Verillion, Williams, Turney.

	1st Half	2nd Half	Final
UCLA	49	46	95
Seattle	39	51	90

Utah State (58)   Coach: Ladell Anderson

	Min.	Total FG/FGA	Pct.	FT/FTA	Pct.	Reb. O/T	A	TO	PF	S	Blk	TP	PPM
WALKER, L.	-	7/16	.438	1/2	.500	-/4	-	-	3	-	-	15	-
ESTES, W.	-	6/19	.316	9/9	1.000	-/11	-	-	4	-	-	21	-
COLLIER, T.	-	9/18	.500	4/6	.667	-/14	-	-	3	-	-	22	-
WATTS, G.	-	0/4	.000	0/0	.000	-/1	-	-	5	-	-	0	-
LONG, B.	-	0/6	.000	0/0	.000	-/3	-	-	0	-	-	0	-
DITTEBRAND, M.	-	0/2	.000	0/0	.000	-/3	-	-	0	-	-	0	-
Totals	200	22/65	.338	14/17	.824	-/36	-	-	15	-	-	58	.290

San Francisco (64)   Coach: Peter Peletta

	Min.	Total FG/FGA	Pct.	FT/FTA	Pct.	Reb. O/T	A	TO	PF	S	Blk	TP	PPM
LEE, D.	-	1/3	.333	1/1	1.000	-/2	-	-	5	-	-	3	-
MUELLER, E.	-	4/8	.500	0/2	.000	-/4	-	-	5	-	-	8	-
JOHNSON, W.	-	9/13	.692	8/9	.889	-/17	-	-	3	-	-	26	-
BROVELLI, J.	-	4/8	.500	0/0	.000	-/1	-	-	0	-	-	8	-
ELLIS, J.	-	6/13	.462	3/4	.750	-/4	-	-	1	-	-	15	-
THOMAS, E.	-	1/4	.250	0/2	.000	-/1	-	-	3	-	-	2	-
BRAINARD, D.	-	1/4	.250	0/2	.000	-/4	-	-	1	-	-	2	-
GUMINA, R.	-	0/0	.000	0/0	.000	-/0	-	-	0	-	-	0	-
Totals	200	26/53	.491	12/20	.600	-/33	-	-	18	-	-	64	.320

Team Rebounds: San Francisco 6; Utah State 6. Disqualified: San Francisco—Lee, Mueller; Utah State—Watts.

	1st Half	2nd Half	Final
Utah State	25	33	58
San Francisco	29	35	64

REGIONAL FINAL EAST

Duke (101)   Coach: Vic Bubas

	Min.	Total FG/FGA	Pct.	FT/FTA	Pct.	Reb. O/T	A	TO	PF	S	Blk	TP	PPM
FERGUSON, D.	22	3/4	.750	0/0	.000	-/1	6	5	1	-	-	6	.273
BUCKLEY, J.	30	5/7	.714	2/3	.667	-/6	2	0	3	-	-	12	.400
TISON, H.	27	4/8	.500	6/7	.857	-/8	2	2	3	-	-	14	.519
HARRISON, B.	23	2/6	.333	1/1	1.000	-/2	1	0	0	-	-	5	.217
MULLINS, J.	33	14/23	.609	2/2	1.000	-/8	5	3	1	-	-	30	.909
MARIN, J.	9	2/3	.667	0/0	.000	-/0	1	0	5	-	-	4	.444
VACENDAK, S.	16	7/7	1.000	0/0	.000	-/3	1	0	1	-	-	14	.875
HERBSTER, R.	14	2/3	.667	0/1	.000	-/2	2	0	3	-	-	4	.286
KITCHING, B.	9	1/6	.167	0/1	.000	-/2	0	0	1	-	-	2	.222
HARSCHER, F.	6	2/3	.667	1/1	1.000	-/3	0	2	2	-	-	5	.833
MANN, T.	6	0/3	.000	2/3	.667	-/5	0	0	0	-	-	2	.333
COX, R.	5	1/2	.500	1/2	.500	-/1	2	0	1	-	-	3	.600
Totals	200	43/75	.573	15/21	.714	-/41	22	12	21	-	-	101	.505

U. Conn. (54)   Coach: Fred Shabel

	Min.	Total FG/FGA	Pct.	FT/FTA	Pct.	Reb. O/T	A	TO	PF	S	Blk	TP	PPM
HESFORD, D.	22	3/6	.500	1/1	1.000	-/3	1	3	2	-	-	7	.318
PERNO, J.	32	2/7	.286	1/3	.333	-/3	3	3	2	-	-	5	.156
RITTER, A.	25	4/8	.500	0/0	.000	-/0	0	4	1	-	-	8	.320
KIMBALL, T.	36	6/21	.286	6/8	.750	-/14	1	5	3	-	-	18	.500
SLOMCENSKI, E.	25	1/5	.200	1/2	.500	-/6	1	2	1	-	-	3	.120
WHITNEY, K.	12	0/3	.000	1/3	.333	-/0	0	1	1	-	-	1	.083
DELLASALA, W.	12	3/5	.600	1/1	1.000	-/1	2	0	3	-	-	7	.583
WITCOMB, C.	12	1/4	.250	0/1	.000	-/1	0	1	0	-	-	2	.167
LIBERTOFF, K.	9	0/5	.000	1/3	.333	-/2	1	1	2	-	-	1	.111
CAPIGA, T.	8	1/4	.250	0/0	.000	-/1	0	1	3	-	-	2	.250
TALBOTT, C.	4	0/1	.000	0/0	.000	-/1	0	1	0	-	-	0	.000
STANEK, D.	3	0/0	.000	0/1	.000	-/0	0	0	0	-	-	0	.000
Totals	200	21/69	.304	12/23	.522	-/32	9	22	18	-	-	54	.270

Team Rebounds: Duke 19; U. Conn. 15. Disqualified: Duke—Marin.

	1st Half	2nd Half	Final
Duke	62	39	101
U. Conn.	27	27	54

REGIONAL FINAL MIDEAST

Ohio (57) Coach: James Snyder

	Min.	Total FG/FGA	Pct.	FT/FTA	Pct.	Reb. O/T	A	TO	PF	S	Blk	TP	PPM
HALEY, M.	-	4/16	.250	2/ 6	.333	-/11	-	-	3	-	-	10	-
HILT, D.	-	8/15	.533	2/ 3	.667	-/ 9	-	-	1	-	-	18	-
STOREY, P.	-	6/12	.500	0/ 0	.000	-/ 3	-	-	2	-	-	12	-
JACKSON, J.	-	6/14	.429	1/ 2	.500	-/ 7	-	-	2	-	-	13	-
GILL	-	1/ 5	.200	0/ 0	.000	-/ 3	-	-	4	-	-	2	-
DAVIS	-	0/ 1	.000	0/ 0	.000	-/ 0	-	-	0	-	-	0	-
WEIRICH	-	0/ 2	.000	0/ 0	.000	-/ 0	-	-	1	-	-	0	-
LASHLEY	-	0/ 0	.000	0/ 0	.000	-/ 0	-	-	1	-	-	0	-
SCHOON	-	0/ 0	.000	0/ 0	.000	-/ 0	-	-	1	-	-	0	-
BARRY	-	0/ 0	.000	2/ 2	1.000	-/ 0	-	-	0	-	-	2	-
BUCK	-	0/ 0	.000	0/ 0	.000	-/ 0	-	-	0	-	-	0	-
Totals	200	25/65	.385	7/13	.538	-/33	-	-	15	-	-	57	.285

Michigan (69) Coach: Dave Strack

	Min.	Total FG/FGA	Pct.	FT/FTA	Pct.	Reb. O/T	A	TO	PF	S	Blk	TP	PPM
TREGONING, L.	-	1/ 3	.333	1/ 2	.500	-/ 3	-	-	2	-	-	3	-
DARDEN, O.	-	3/ 5	.600	0/ 0	.000	-/ 7	-	-	3	-	-	6	-
BUNTIN, B.	-	6/17	.353	3/ 3	1.000	-/10	-	-	4	-	-	15	-
RUSSELL, C.	-	9/20	.450	7/ 7	1.000	-/ 6	-	-	0	-	-	25	-
CANTRELL, B.	-	2/ 2	1.000	2/ 2	1.000	-/ 1	-	-	2	-	-	6	-
POMEY, G.	-	3/ 7	.429	0/ 0	.000	-/ 2	-	-	1	-	-	6	-
MYERS, J.	-	2/10	.200	2/ 2	1.000	-/ 7	-	-	1	-	-	6	-
HERNER, D.	-	0/ 1	.000	2/ 3	.667	-/ 0	-	-	0	-	-	2	-
Totals	200	26/65	.400	17/19	.895	-/36	-	-	13	-	-	69	.345

Disqualified: None.

	1st Half	2nd Half	Final
Ohio	27	30	57
Michigan	32	37	69

REGIONAL FINAL MIDWEST

Wichita State (86) Coach: Ralph Miller

	Min.	Total FG/FGA	Pct.	FT/FTA	Pct.	Reb. O/T	A	TO	PF	S	Blk	TP	PPM
STALLWORTH, D.	-	14/22	.636	9/12	.750	7/16	1	-	3	-	-	37	-
BOWMAN, N.	-	4/ 6	.667	4/ 5	.800	3/ 8	1	-	5	-	-	12	-
LEACH, D.	-	3/10	.300	1/ 1	1.000	0/ 5	3	-	5	-	-	7	-
CRISS, J.	-	4/ 9	.444	1/ 1	1.000	0/ 1	6	-	5	-	-	9	-
SMITH, V.	-	2/ 3	.667	0/ 0	.000	0/ 3	1	-	4	-	-	4	-
NOSICH, L.	-	0/ 0	.000	0/ 0	.000	0/ 0	0	-	0	-	-	0	-
DAVIS, G.	-	0/ 1	.000	0/ 0	.000	0/ 2	0	-	1	-	-	0	-
ROWLAND	-	0/ 0	.000	0/ 0	.000	0/ 0	0	-	0	-	-	0	-
PETE, K.	-	7/12	.583	3/ 3	1.000	3/ 5	2	-	2	-	-	17	-
Totals	200	34/63	.540	18/22	.818	13/40	14	25	25	-	-	86	.430

Kansas State (94) Coach: Tex Winter

	Min.	Total FG/FGA	Pct.	FT/FTA	Pct.	Reb. O/T	A	TO	PF	S	Blk	TP	PPM
MOSS, M.	-	4/ 8	.500	3/ 5	.600	1/ 2	2	-	1	-	-	11	-
MURRELL, W.	-	11/24	.458	6/10	.600	6/10	2	-	1	-	-	28	-
ROBINSON, S.	-	2/ 7	.286	7/10	.700	1/ 7	5	-	3	-	-	11	-
SUTTNER, R.	-	7/11	.636	2/ 4	.500	4/ 6	1	-	5	-	-	16	-
SIMONS, J.	-	6/14	.429	2/ 3	.667	3/ 6	3	-	5	-	-	14	-
WILLIAMS, G.	-	3/ 3	1.000	2/ 2	1.000	6/ 6	1	-	4	-	-	8	-
PARADIS, R.	-	2/ 2	1.000	2/ 3	.667	1/ 1	0	-	1	-	-	6	-
Totals	200	35/69	.507	24/37	.649	22/38	14	15	20	-	-	94	.470

Team Rebounds: Kansas State 2; Wichita State 0. Disqualified: Kansas State—Suttner, Simons; Wichita State—Bowman, Leach, Criss.

	1st Half	2nd Half	Final
Wichita State	33	53	86
Kansas State	46	48	94

REGIONAL FINAL WEST

UCLA (76) Coach: John Wooden

	Min.	Total FG/FGA	Pct.	FT/FTA	Pct.	Reb. O/T	A	TO	PF	S	Blk	TP	PPM
ERICKSON, K.	-	3/10	.300	1/ 6	.167	-/10	-	-	4	-	-	7	-
HIRSCH, J.	-	5/11	.455	4/ 5	.800	-/ 7	-	-	3	-	-	14	-
SLAUGHTER, F.	-	4/ 9	.444	1/ 4	.250	-/ 8	-	-	4	-	-	9	-
GOODRICH, G.	-	6/18	.333	3/ 5	.600	-/ 4	-	-	1	-	-	15	-
HAZZARD, W.	-	9/19	.474	5/ 5	1.000	-/ 3	-	-	3	-	-	23	-
MCINTOSH, D.	-	0/ 1	.000	3/ 5	.600	-/ 4	-	-	1	-	-	3	-
WASHINGTON, K.	-	2/ 4	.500	1/ 4	.250	-/ 3	-	-	1	-	-	5	-
Totals	200	29/72	.403	18/34	.529	-/39	-	-	17	-	-	76	.380

San Francisco (72) Coach: Peter Peletta

	Min.	Total FG/FGA	Pct.	FT/FTA	Pct.	Reb. O/T	A	TO	PF	S	Blk	TP	PPM
LEE, D.	-	2/ 5	.400	2/ 2	1.000	-/ 4	-	-	4	-	-	6	-
MUELLER, E.	-	6/12	.500	3/ 5	.600	-/ 7	-	-	4	-	-	15	-
JOHNSON, W.	-	6/ 9	.667	10/11	.909	-/13	-	-	2	-	-	22	-
BROVELLI, J.	-	5/ 8	.625	1/ 1	1.000	-/ 2	-	-	4	-	-	11	-
ELLIS, J.	-	5/14	.357	1/ 2	.500	-/10	-	-	3	-	-	11	-
THOMAS, E.	-	0/ 0	.000	0/ 0	.000	-/ 2	-	-	2	-	-	0	-
BRAINARD, D.	-	2/ 8	.250	1/ 2	.500	-/ 4	-	-	5	-	-	5	-
GUMINA, R.	-	1/ 1	1.000	0/ 0	.000	-/ 1	-	-	1	-	-	2	-
Totals	200	27/57	.474	18/23	.783	-/43	-	-	25	-	-	72	.360

Team Rebounds: UCLA 9; San Francisco 3. Disqualified: San Francisco—Brainard. Technical fouls: San Francisco—Brovelli.

	1st Half	2nd Half	Final
UCLA	28	48	76
San Francisco	36	36	72

FINAL FOUR

Duke (91)   Coach: Vic Bubas

	Min.	Total FG/FGA	Pct.	FT/FTA	Pct.	Reb. O/T	A	TO	PF	S	Blk	TP	PPM
TISON, H.	-	3/10	.300	6/10	.600	-/13	-	-	4	-	-	12	-
MULLINS, J.	-	8/19	.421	5/6	.833	-/8	-	-	1	-	-	21	-
BUCKLEY, J.	-	11/16	.688	3/5	.600	-/14	-	-	4	-	-	25	-
FERGUSON, D.	-	6/11	.545	0/1	.000	-/0	-	-	0	-	-	12	-
HARRISON, B.	-	6/15	.400	2/3	.667	-/2	-	-	2	-	-	14	-
MARIN, J.	-	1/2	.500	0/0	.000	-/2	-	-	1	-	-	2	-
VACENDAK, S.	-	2/5	.400	1/2	.500	-/2	-	-	1	-	-	5	-
HERBSTER, R.	-	0/0	.000	0/0	.000	-/0	-	-	0	-	-	0	-
Totals	200	37/78	.474	17/27	.630	-/41	-	-	13	-	-	91	.455

Michigan (80)   Coach: Dave Strack

	Min.	Total FG/FGA	Pct.	FT/FTA	Pct.	Reb. O/T	A	TO	PF	S	Blk	TP	PPM
TREGONING, L.	-	3/11	.273	2/2	1.000	-/6	-	-	4	-	-	8	-
DARDEN, O.	-	2/6	.333	1/1	1.000	-/9	-	-	5	-	-	5	-
BUNTIN, B.	-	8/18	.444	3/3	1.000	-/9	-	-	5	-	-	19	-
RUSSELL, C.	-	13/19	.684	5/6	.833	-/8	-	-	5	-	-	31	-
CANTRELL, B.	-	6/10	.600	0/0	.000	-/4	-	-	2	-	-	12	-
MYERS, J.	-	2/5	.400	0/0	.000	-/5	-	-	2	-	-	4	-
POMEY, G.	-	0/1	.000	1/2	.500	-/0	-	-	0	-	-	1	-
HERNER, D.	-	0/1	.000	0/0	.000	-/0	-	-	0	-	-	0	-
Totals	200	34/71	.479	12/14	.857	-/41	-	-	23	-	-	80	.400

Team Rebounds: Duke 5; Michigan 4. Disqualified: Michigan—Buntin, Russell, Darden.

	1st Half	2nd Half	Final
Duke	48	43	91
Michigan	39	41	80

Kansas State (84)   Coach: Tex Winter

	Min.	Total FG/FGA	Pct.	FT/FTA	Pct.	Reb. O/T	A	TO	PF	S	Blk	TP	PPM
MOSS, M.	-	3/9	.333	1/1	1.000	2/5	4	4	3	-	-	7	-
MURRELL, W.	-	13/22	.591	3/5	.600	6/13	2	5	3	-	-	29	-
ROBINSON, S.	-	2/7	.286	0/1	.000	0/5	2	0	4	-	-	4	-
SUTTNER, R.	-	3/9	.333	0/5	.000	4/10	0	2	2	-	-	6	-
SIMONS, J.	-	10/17	.588	4/6	.667	2/7	2	2	3	-	-	24	-
WILLIAMS, G.	-	1/1	1.000	2/3	.667	1/1	1	0	2	-	-	4	-
PARADIS, R.	-	5/9	.556	0/0	.000	0/1	2	0	0	-	-	10	-
NELSON, D.	-	0/1	.000	0/0	.000	0/0	0	0	1	-	-	0	-
GOTTFRID, J.	-	0/0	.000	0/0	.000	0/0	0	0	1	-	-	0	-
BARNARD, D.	-	0/1	.000	0/0	.000	0/0	1	0	0	-	-	0	-
Totals	200	37/76	.487	10/21	.476	15/42	14	13	19	-	-	84	.420

UCLA (90)   Coach: John Wooden

	Min.	Total FG/FGA	Pct.	FT/FTA	Pct.	Reb. O/T	A	TO	PF	S	Blk	TP	PPM
ERICKSON, K.	-	10/21	.476	8/9	.889	3/10	1	2	2	-	-	28	-
HIRSCH, J.	-	2/11	.182	0/0	.000	1/1	0	1	4	-	-	4	-
SLAUGHTER, F.	-	2/6	.333	0/0	.000	3/5	0	0	4	-	-	4	-
GOODRICH, G.	-	7/18	.389	0/0	.000	3/6	2	3	3	-	-	14	-
HAZZARD, W.	-	7/10	.700	5/7	.714	1/7	9	3	2	-	-	19	-
MCINTOSH, D.	-	3/5	.600	2/3	.667	4/10	1	1	3	-	-	8	-
WASHINGTON, K.	-	5/11	.455	3/4	.750	4/6	0	0	1	-	-	13	-
Totals	200	36/82	.439	18/23	.783	19/45	13	10	19	-	-	90	.450

Team Rebounds: UCLA 8; Kansas State 6. Disqualified: None.

	1st Half	2nd Half	Final
Kansas State	41	43	84
UCLA	43	47	90

NATIONAL CHAMPIONSHIP

Duke (83)   Coach: Vic Bubas

	Min.	Total FG/FGA	Pct.	FT/FTA	Pct.	Reb. O/T	A	TO	PF	S	Blk	TP	PPM
FERGUSON, D.	-	2/6	.333	0/1	.000	0/1	4	0	3	-	-	4	-
BUCKLEY, J.	-	5/8	.625	8/12	.667	6/9	0	3	4	-	-	18	-
TISON, H.	-	3/8	.375	1/1	1.000	1/1	2	4	2	-	-	7	-
HARRISON, B.	-	1/1	1.000	0/0	.000	0/1	1	1	2	-	-	2	-
MULLINS, J.	-	9/21	.429	4/4	1.000	1/4	1	6	5	-	-	22	-
VACENDAK, S.	-	2/7	.286	3/3	1.000	1/6	0	4	4	-	-	7	-
HERBSTER, R.	-	1/4	.250	0/2	.000	0/0	0	3	0	-	-	2	-
MARIN, J.	-	8/16	.500	0/1	.000	8/10	1	3	3	-	-	16	-
KITCHING, B.	-	1/1	1.000	0/0	.000	0/1	0	0	0	-	-	2	-
MANN, T.	-	0/0	.000	3/4	.750	0/2	0	0	1	-	-	3	-
HARSCHER, F.	-	0/0	.000	0/0	.000	0/0	0	0	0	-	-	0	-
COX, R.	-	0/0	.000	0/0	.000	0/0	0	0	0	-	-	0	-
Totals	200	32/72	.444	19/28	.679	17/35	9	24	24	-	-	83	.415

UCLA (98)   Coach: John Wooden

	Min.	Total FG/FGA	Pct.	FT/FTA	Pct.	Reb. O/T	A	TO	PF	S	Blk	TP	PPM
ERICKSON, K.	-	2/7	.286	4/4	1.000	3/5	1	1	5	-	-	8	-
HIRSCH, J.	-	5/9	.556	3/5	.600	3/6	6	2	3	-	-	13	-
SLAUGHTER, F.	-	0/1	.000	0/0	.000	1/1	2	0	0	-	-	0	-
GOODRICH, G.	-	9/18	.500	9/9	1.000	1/3	1	4	1	-	-	27	-
HAZZARD, W.	-	4/10	.400	3/5	.600	1/3	8	5	5	-	-	11	-
MCINTOSH, D.	-	4/9	.444	0/0	.000	3/11	1	3	2	-	-	8	-
STEWART, K.	-	0/1	.000	0/0	.000	0/0	0	0	1	-	-	0	-
WASHINGTON, K.	-	11/16	.688	4/4	1.000	8/12	1	3	4	-	-	26	-
HUGGINS, M.	-	0/1	.000	0/1	.000	0/1	2	0	2	-	-	0	-
HOFFMAN, V.	-	1/2	.500	0/0	.000	0/0	0	0	0	-	-	2	-
DARROW, C.	-	0/1	.000	3/4	.750	0/1	0	1	2	-	-	3	-
LEVIN, R.	-	0/1	.000	0/0	.000	0/0	0	0	0	-	-	0	-
Totals	200	36/76	.474	26/32	.813	20/43	22	19	25	-	-	98	.490

Team Rebounds: UCLA 8; Duke 9. Disqualified: UCLA—Hazzard, Erickson; Duke—Mullins.

	1st Half	2nd Half	Final
Duke	38	45	83
UCLA	50	48	98

NATIONAL THIRD PLACE
Michigan (100) Coach: Dave Strack

	Min.	Total FG / FGA	Pct.	FT / FTA	Pct.	Reb. O / T	A	TO	PF	S	Blk	TP	PPM
BUNTIN, B.	-	9/18	.500	15/17	.882	7/14	1	4	2	-	-	33	-
CANTRELL, B.	-	8/17	.471	4/5	.800	2/3	2	4	2	-	-	20	-
HERNER, D.	-	0/3	.000	0/0	.000	0/1	10	4	3	-	-	0	-
TREGONING, L.	-	6/13	.462	4/5	.800	3/8	1	2	1	-	-	16	-
DARDEN, O.	-	8/16	.500	1/3	.333	6/14	2	2	3	-	-	17	-
MYERS, J.	-	3/10	.300	1/2	.500	3/6	2	1	1	-	-	7	-
POMEY, G.	-	2/4	.500	0/0	.000	1/2	0	2	1	-	-	4	-
CLAWSON, J.	-	1/3	.333	1/2	.500	2/2	0	0	0	-	-	3	-
Totals	200	37/84	.440	26/34	.765	24/50	18	19	13	-	-	100	.500

Kansas State (90) Coach: Tex Winter

	Min.	Total FG / FGA	Pct.	FT / FTA	Pct.	Reb. O / T	A	TO	PF	S	Blk	TP	PPM
MOSS, M.	-	4/9	.444	3/3	1.000	1/3	6	2	5	-	-	11	-
MURRELL, W.	-	10/19	.526	0/0	.000	3/10	1	5	2	-	-	20	-
ROBINSON, S.	-	6/11	.545	0/0	.000	2/6	1	0	2	-	-	12	-
SUTTNER, R.	-	7/15	.467	6/8	.750	2/5	6	0	4	-	-	20	-
SIMONS, J.	-	4/8	.500	3/3	1.000	1/3	5	2	3	-	-	11	-
WILLIAMS, G.	-	2/4	.500	0/1	.000	0/2	0	1	0	-	-	4	-
NELSON, D.	-	2/6	.333	1/1	1.000	0/2	0	3	2	-	-	5	-
PARADIS, R.	-	1/4	.250	3/4	.750	0/0	0	1	0	-	-	5	-
GOTTFRID, J.	-	1/1	1.000	0/0	.000	2/2	1	0	3	-	-	2	-
BARNARD, D.	-	0/1	.000	0/0	.000	1/3	0	1	1	-	-	0	-
POMA, L.	-	0/1	.000	0/0	.000	0/1	0	0	1	-	-	0	-
HOFFMAN, J.	-	0/0	.000	0/0	.000	0/0	0	0	0	-	-	0	-
Totals	200	37/79	.468	16/20	.800	12/37	20	15	23	-	-	90	.450

Team Rebounds: Michigan 9; Kansas State 5. Disqualified: Kansas State—Moss.

	1st Half	2nd Half	Final
Michigan	52	48	100
Kansas State	47	43	90

REGIONAL THIRD PLACE EAST
Villanova (74) Coach: Jack Kraft

	Min.	Total FG / FGA	Pct.	FT / FTA	Pct.	Reb. O / T	A	TO	PF	S	Blk	TP	PPM
MELCHIONNI, B.	39	8/20	.400	1/2	.500	-/9	1	0	2	-	-	17	.436
JONES, W.	40	16/29	.552	2/3	.667	-/7	2	1	1	-	-	34	.850
MOORE, R.	8	1/2	.500	2/2	1.000	-/0	0	2	1	-	-	4	.500
WASHINGTON, J.	33	1/9	.111	2/2	1.000	-/13	1	1	3	-	-	4	.121
SALLEE, A.	7	0/0	.000	0/0	.000	-/0	0	0	2	-	-	0	.000
ERICKSON, E.	28	2/6	.333	0/1	.000	-/4	0	1	0	-	-	4	.143
SCHAFFER, B.	30	1/4	.250	0/2	.000	-/8	2	0	1	-	-	2	.067
LEFTWICH, G.	14	4/11	.364	1/1	1.000	-/4	0	0	0	-	-	9	.643
WINTERBOTTOM, W.	1	0/1	.000	0/0	.000	-/0	0	0	0	-	-	0	.000
Totals	200	33/82	.402	8/13	.615	-/45	6	5	10	-	-	74	.370

Princeton (62) Coach: B. Van Breda Kolff

	Min.	Total FG / FGA	Pct.	FT / FTA	Pct.	Reb. O / T	A	TO	PF	S	Blk	TP	PPM
RODENBACH, D.	18	1/5	.200	0/0	.000	-/0	1	1	3	-	-	2	.111
HAARLOW, B.	25	3/7	.429	2/3	.667	-/4	0	2	1	-	-	8	.320
ROTH, D.	3	0/0	.000	0/0	.000	-/1	0	0	0	-	-	0	.000
BRADLEY, B.	40	13/23	.565	4/6	.667	-/13	4	6	3	-	-	30	.750
UHLE, W.	19	2/3	.667	0/0	.000	-/0	1	0	1	-	-	4	.211
HOWARD, B.	13	0/2	.000	2/3	.667	-/4	0	1	0	-	-	2	.154
STEUBE, E.	22	2/5	.400	2/2	1.000	-/2	2	2	0	-	-	6	.273
KINGSTON, B.	18	0/1	.000	0/0	.000	-/3	1	1	2	-	-	0	.000
NIEMANN, D.	27	2/5	.400	0/1	.000	-/4	0	1	2	-	-	4	.148
WRIGHT, R.	14	3/6	.500	0/0	.000	-/4	2	0	1	-	-	6	.429
KITCH, P.	1	0/0	.000	0/0	.000	-/0	0	1	0	-	-	0	.000
Totals	200	26/57	.456	10/15	.667	-/35	11	15	13	-	-	62	.310

Team Rebounds: Villanova 5; Princeton 5. Disqualified: None.

	1st Half	2nd Half	Final
Villanova	42	32	74
Princeton	30	32	62

REGIONAL THIRD PLACE MIDEAST
Loyola-Chicago (100) Coach: George Ireland

	Min.	Total FG / FGA	Pct.	FT / FTA	Pct.	Reb. O / T	A	TO	PF	S	Blk	TP	PPM
MILLER, R.	-	8/16	.500	3/6	.500	-/5	-	-	2	-	-	19	-
ROUSE, V.	-	2/8	.250	4/4	1.000	-/4	-	-	0	-	-	8	-
HUNTER, L.	-	10/22	.455	7/7	1.000	-/18	-	-	2	-	-	27	-
EGAN, J.	-	4/11	.364	5/5	1.000	-/4	-	-	5	-	-	13	-
COLEMAN, J.	-	3/12	.250	14/17	.824	-/8	-	-	3	-	-	20	-
WOOD, C.	-	0/1	.000	0/0	.000	-/0	-	-	0	-	-	0	-
MANZKE	-	4/9	.444	3/3	1.000	-/2	-	-	2	-	-	11	-
CONNAUGHTON	-	0/2	.000	2/2	1.000	-/1	-	-	2	-	-	2	-
Totals	200	31/81	.383	38/44	.864	-/42	-	-	16	-	-	100	.500

Kentucky (91) Coach: Adolph Rupp

	Min.	Total FG / FGA	Pct.	FT / FTA	Pct.	Reb. O / T	A	TO	PF	S	Blk	TP	PPM
DEEKEN, T.	-	5/11	.455	2/2	1.000	-/2	-	-	5	-	-	12	-
CONLEY, L.	-	6/13	.462	3/5	.600	-/7	-	-	4	-	-	15	-
NASH, C.	-	11/27	.407	1/3	.333	-/11	-	-	5	-	-	23	-
MOBLEY, T.	-	8/13	.615	5/5	1.000	-/4	-	-	5	-	-	21	-
EMBRY, R.	-	0/4	.000	0/0	.000	-/3	-	-	2	-	-	0	-
ISHMAEL, C.	-	3/7	.429	0/0	.000	-/7	-	-	1	-	-	6	-
KRON, T.	-	2/4	.500	1/2	.500	-/2	-	-	4	-	-	5	-
ADAMS, J.	-	4/5	.800	1/1	1.000	-/2	-	-	1	-	-	9	-
HARPER, S.	-	0/0	.000	0/0	.000	-/0	-	-	1	-	-	0	-
Totals	200	39/84	.464	13/20	.650	-/38	-	-	28	-	-	91	.455

Disqualified: Loyola-Chicago—Egan; Kentucky—Deeken, Nash, Mobley.

	1st Half	2nd Half	Final
Loyola-Chicago	53	47	100
Kentucky	45	46	91

REGIONAL THIRD PLACE MIDWEST
Texas Western (63) Coach: Don Haskins

	Min.	Total FG / FGA	Pct.	FT / FTA	Pct.	Reb. O / T	A	TO	PF	S	Blk	TP	PPM
BARNES, J.	-	6/15	.400	3/4	.750	-/10	-	-	5	-	-	15	-
ARTIS, O.	-	3/11	.273	3/3	1.000	-/13	-	-	1	-	-	9	-
TREDENNICK, S.	-	0/1	.000	0/0	.000	-/0	-	-	1	-	-	0	-
STOGLIN, A.	-	1/8	.125	8/8	1.000	-/6	-	-	1	-	-	10	-
FLOURNOY, H.	-	0/2	.000	2/3	.667	-/4	-	-	3	-	-	2	-
BANKS, C.	-	4/12	.333	5/8	.625	-/6	-	-	1	-	-	13	-
DIBLER, B.	-	7/18	.389	0/2	.000	-/3	-	-	0	-	-	14	-
Totals	200	21/67	.313	21/28	.750	-/42	-	-	12	-	-	63	.315

Creighton (52) Coach: Red McManus

	Min.	Total FG / FGA	Pct.	FT / FTA	Pct.	Reb. O / T	A	TO	PF	S	Blk	TP	PPM
SILAS, P.	-	6/15	.400	2/3	.667	-/13	-	-	5	-	-	14	-
POINTER, F.	-	4/9	.444	0/1	.000	-/4	-	-	3	-	-	8	-
OFFICER, C.	-	5/13	.385	1/2	.500	-/5	-	-	2	-	-	11	-
McGRIFF, E.	-	5/11	.455	2/7	.286	-/8	-	-	5	-	-	12	-
BROWN, C.	-	0/2	.000	0/0	.000	-/1	-	-	1	-	-	0	-
FOREHAND	-	2/8	.250	1/1	1.000	-/6	-	-	0	-	-	5	-
APKE	-	0/2	.000	0/0	.000	-/2	-	-	3	-	-	0	-
JAMES	-	0/0	.000	0/0	.000	-/0	-	-	0	-	-	0	-
MILES	-	0/0	.000	2/2	1.000	-/0	-	-	0	-	-	2	-
Totals	200	22/60	.367	8/16	.500	-/39	-	-	19	-	-	52	.260

Team Rebounds: Texas Western 8; Creighton 10. Disqualified: Texas Western—Barnes; Creighton—Silas, McGriff.

	1st Half	2nd Half	Final
Texas Western	26	37	63
Creighton	32	20	52

REGIONAL THIRD PLACE WEST

Seattle (88) Coach: Bob Boyd

	Min.	Total FG/FGA	Pct.	FT/FTA	Pct.	Reb. O/T	A	TO	PF	S	Blk	TP	PPM
WHEELER, L.	-	3/11	.273	2/3	.667	-/12	-	-	5	-	-	8	-
VERMILLION, G.	-	8/15	.533	10/11	.909	-/13	-	-	3	-	-	26	-
TRESVANT, J.	-	8/14	.571	2/4	.500	-/19	-	-	5	-	-	18	-
HEYWARD, R.	-	3/4	.750	0/2	.000	-/1	-	-	5	-	-	6	-
WILLIAMS, C.	-	3/16	.188	8/9	.889	-/7	-	-	3	-	-	14	-
PHILLIPS, P.	-	1/2	.500	0/0	.000	-/1	-	-	0	-	-	2	-
TURNEY, R.	-	2/4	.500	0/0	.000	-/8	-	-	0	-	-	4	-
TEBBS, J.	-	4/9	.444	1/2	.500	-/1	-	-	0	-	-	9	-
GRIFFIN	-	0/0	.000	0/0	.000	-/1	-	-	0	-	-	0	-
MATTHEWS	-	0/0	.000	1/2	.500	-/2	-	-	0	-	-	1	-
Totals	200	32/75	.427	24/33	.727	-/65	-	-	21	-	-	88	.440

Utah State (78) Coach: Ladell Anderson

	Min.	Total FG/FGA	Pct.	FT/FTA	Pct.	Reb. O/T	A	TO	PF	S	Blk	TP	PPM
ESTES, W.	-	6/18	.333	2/3	.667	-/6	-	-	2	-	-	14	-
WALKER, L.	-	9/21	.429	3/3	1.000	-/5	-	-	4	-	-	21	-
COLLIER, T.	-	8/20	.400	6/8	.750	-/8	-	-	2	-	-	22	-
WATTS, G.	-	3/8	.375	0/5	.000	-/5	-	-	4	-	-	6	-
LONG, B.	-	1/1	1.000	0/0	.000	-/1	-	-	1	-	-	2	-
DITTEBRAND, M.	-	3/9	.333	1/4	.250	-/8	-	-	5	-	-	7	-
HANSON, R.	-	1/2	.500	0/0	.000	-/1	-	-	1	-	-	2	-
ANGLE, L.	-	1/2	.500	0/0	.000	-/1	-	-	1	-	-	2	-
HUNSAKER	-	1/3	.333	0/0	.000	-/2	-	-	2	-	-	2	-
WILDMER	-	0/1	.000	0/0	.000	-/0	-	-	0	-	-	0	-
JONES	-	0/0	.000	0/0	.000	-/1	-	-	0	-	-	0	-
LYONS	-	0/1	.000	0/0	.000	-/0	-	-	1	-	-	0	-
Totals	200	33/86	.384	12/23	.522	-/38	-	-	23	-	-	78	.390

Team Rebounds: Seattle 7; Utah State 6. Disqualified: Seattle—Wheeler, Tresvant, Heyward; Utah State—Dittebrand.

	1st Half	2nd Half	Final
Seattle	41	47	88
Utah State	35	43	78

✪ ALL-STAR TEAMS ✪

ALL TOURNAMENT

BILL BUNTIN	MICHIGAN
GAIL GOODRICH	UCLA
★ **WALT HAZZARD**	UCLA
JEFF MULLINS	DUKE
WILLIE MURRELL	KANSAS STATE

WEST REGIONAL

TROY COLLIER	UTAH STATE
GAIL GOODRICH	UCLA
★ **WALT HAZZARD**	UCLA
OLLIE JOHNSON	SAN FRANCISCO
JOHN TRESVANT	SEATTLE

★ Most Outstanding Player(s)

✪ INDIVIDUAL RECORDS ✪

SCORING

Most points in a single game
1. JEFF MULLINS, DUKE (vs. VILLANOVA) — 43
2. JIM BARNES, TEXAS WESTERN (vs. TEXAS A&M) — 42
3. WAYNE ESTES, UTAH STATE (vs. ARIZONA ST.) — 38
4. DAVE STALLWORTH, WICHITA STATE (vs. KANSAS STATE) — 37
5. 2 tied for fifth place.

Most total points in the tournament
1. JEFF MULLINS, DUKE — 116
2. WILLIE MURRELL, KANSAS STATE — 101
3. BILL BUNTIN, MICHIGAN — 93
4. BILL BRADLEY, PRINCETON — 86
5. WALT HAZZARD, UCLA — 79

Highest scoring average (minimum 2 games)
1. DAVE STALLWORTH, WICHITA STATE (59-2) — 29.50
2. JEFF MULLINS, DUKE (116-4) — 29.00
3. BILL BRADLEY, PRINCETON (86-3) — 28.67
4. CAZZIE RUSSELL, MICHIGAN (77-3) — 25.67
5. WILLIE MURRELL, KANSAS STATE (101-4) — 25.25

FIELD GOALS

Most field goals in a single game
1. JEFF MULLINS, DUKE (vs. VILLANOVA) — 19
2. JIM BARNES, TEXAS WESTERN (vs. TEXAS A&M) — 16
2. WALLY JONES, VILLANOVA (vs. PRINCETON) — 16
4. 3 tied for fourth place.

Most total field goals in the tournament
1. JEFF MULLINS, DUKE — 50
2. WILLIE MURRELL, KANSAS STATE — 43
3. BILL BUNTIN, MICHIGAN — 32
4. BILL BRADLEY, PRINCETON — 31
5. CAZZIE RUSSELL, MICHIGAN — 30

Most field goal attempts in a single game
1. WAYNE ESTES, UTAH STATE (vs. ARIZONA ST.) — 29
1. WALLY JONES, VILLANOVA (vs. PRINCETON) — 29
3. JEFF MULLINS, DUKE (vs. VILLANOVA) — 28
4. COTTON NASH, KENTUCKY (vs. LOYOLA-CHICAGO) — 27
5. 2 tied for fifth place.

Most total field goal attempts in the tournament
1. JEFF MULLINS, DUKE — 91
2. WILLIE MURRELL, KANSAS STATE — 89
3. GAIL GOODRICH, UCLA — 76
3. BILL BUNTIN, MICHIGAN — 76
5. WALLY JONES, VILLANOVA — 71

Highest field goal percentage in a single game (minimum 10 attempts)
1. WALT HAZZARD, UCLA (vs. KANSAS STATE) (7-10) — .700

2 JIM BARNES, TEXAS WESTERN (vs. TEXAS
   A&M) (16-23)   .696
3 JIM COLEMAN, LOYOLA-CHICAGO (vs. MURRAY
   STATE) (9-13)   .692
3 WILLIE JOHNSON, SAN FRANCISCO (vs. UTAH
   STATE) (9-13)   .692
5 2 tied for fifth place.

**Highest field goal percentage in the tournament
(minimum 20 attempts)**
1 WILLIE JOHNSON, SAN FRANCISCO (15-22) .682
2 JAY BUCKLEY, DUKE (24-39)   .615
3 TERRY MOBLEY, KENTUCKY (16-26)   .615
4 KEN WASHINGTON, UCLA (21-35)   .600
5 WILLIAM DELLASALA, U. CONN. (12-21)   .571

FREE THROWS

Most free throws in a single game
1 MEL COUNTS, OREGON STATE (vs. SEATTLE) 15
1 BILL BUNTIN, MICHIGAN (vs. KANSAS STATE) 15
3 JIM COLEMAN, LOYOLA-CHICAGO (vs.
   KENTUCKY)   14
4 PAUL SILAS, CREIGHTON (vs. WICHITA STATE)
                                                    12
5 7 tied for fifth place.

Most total free throws in the tournament
1 BILL BUNTIN, MICHIGAN   29
2 JIM COLEMAN, LOYOLA-CHICAGO   26
3 BILL BRADLEY, PRINCETON   24

4 WALT HAZZARD, UCLA   21
4 WAYNE ESTES, UTAH STATE   21

Most free throws attempted in a single game
1 MEL COUNTS, OREGON STATE (vs. SEATTLE) 18
2 JIM COLEMAN, LOYOLA-CHICAGO (vs.
   KENTUCKY)   17
2 BILL BUNTIN, MICHIGAN (vs. KANSAS STATE) 17
4 JOHN TRESVANT, SEATTLE (vs. UCLA)   16
5 PAUL SILAS, CREIGHTON (vs. WICHITA STATE)
                                                    15

Most free throws attempted in the tournament
1 JIM COLEMAN, LOYOLA-CHICAGO   33
1 BILL BUNTIN, MICHIGAN   33
3 WALT HAZZARD, UCLA   28
3 BILL BRADLEY, PRINCETON   28
5 2 tied for fifth place.

**Highest free throw percentage in a single game
(minimum 7 attempts)**
1 WAYNE ESTES, UTAH STATE (vs. SAN
   FRANCISCO) (9-9)   1.000
1 GAIL GOODRICH, UCLA (vs. DUKE) (9-9)   1.000
3 ANDY STOGLIN, TEXAS WESTERN (vs.
   CREIGHTON) (8-8)   1.000
4 3 tied for fourth place.

**Highest free throw percentage in the tournament
(minimum 15 attempts)**
1 WAYNE ESTES, UTAH STATE (21-23)   .913
2 WILLIE JOHNSON, SAN FRANCISCO (18-20) .900

3 JEFF MULLINS, DUKE (16-18)   .889
4 BILL BUNTIN, MICHIGAN (29-33)   .879
5 BILL BRADLEY, PRINCETON (24-28)   .857

REBOUNDS

Most rebounds in a single game
1 PAUL SILAS, CREIGHTON (vs. OKLAHOMA CITY)
                                                    27
2 EDDIE JACKSON, OKLAHOMA CITY (vs.
   CREIGHTON)   24
3 DAVE STALLWORTH, WICHITA STATE (vs.
   CREIGHTON)   23
4 LES HUNTER, LOYOLA-CHICAGO (vs. MURRAY
   STATE)   22
5 2 tied for fifth place.

Most total rebounds in the tournament
1 PAUL SILAS, CREIGHTON   57
2 JOHN TRESVANT, SEATTLE   46
2 LES HUNTER, LOYOLA-CHICAGO   46
2 BILL BUNTIN, MICHIGAN   46
5 2 tied for fifth place.

Most rebounds per game (minimum 2 games)
1 DAVE STALLWORTH, WICHITA STATE (39-2)
                                                 19.50
2 PAUL SILAS, CREIGHTON (57-3)   19.00
3 JOHN TRESVANT, SEATTLE (46-3)   15.33
3 LES HUNTER, LOYOLA-CHICAGO (46-3)   15.33
5 WILLIE JOHNSON, SAN FRANCISCO (30-2) 15.00

❂ TEAM RECORDS ❂

SCORING

Most points in a single game
1 LOYOLA-CHICAGO (vs. MURRAY STATE)   101
1 DUKE (vs. U. CONN.)   101
3 2 tied for third place.

Most total points in the tournament
1 DUKE   362
2 UCLA   359
3 MICHIGAN   333

Highest scoring average (minimum 2 games)
1 LOYOLA-CHICAGO (281-3)   93.67
2 DUKE (362-4)   90.50
3 UCLA (359-4)   89.75

FIELD GOALS

Most field goals in a single game
1 DUKE (vs. U. CONN.)   43
2 MURRAY STATE (vs. LOYOLA-CHICAGO)   40
3 2 tied for third place.

Most total field goals in the tournament
1 DUKE   145
2 UCLA   137
3 KANSAS STATE   131

Most field goals attempted in a single game
1 LOYOLA-CHICAGO (vs. MICHIGAN)   88
2 UTAH STATE (vs. SEATTLE)   86
2 MURRAY STATE (vs. LOYOLA-CHICAGO)   86

Most total field goals attempted in the tournament
1 UCLA   307
2 MICHIGAN   293
3 DUKE   291

Highest field goal percentage in a single game
1 DUKE (vs. U. CONN.) (43-75)   .573
2 WICHITA STATE (vs. KANSAS STATE) (34-63)
                                                   .540
3 KANSAS STATE (vs. WICHITA STATE) (35-69)
                                                   .507

Highest field goal percentage in a single game
1 DUKE (vs. U. CONN.) (43-75)   .573
2 WICHITA STATE (vs. KANSAS STATE) (34-63)
                                                   .540
3 KANSAS STATE (vs. WICHITA STATE) (35-69)
                                                   .507

**Highest field goal percentage in the tournament
(minimum 2 games)**
1 WICHITA STATE (60-119)   .504
2 PROVIDENCE (28-56)   .500
3 DUKE (145-291)   .499

FREE THROWS

Most free throws in a single game
1 LOYOLA-CHICAGO (vs. KENTUCKY)   38
2 WICHITA STATE (vs. CREIGHTON)   32
3 SEATTLE (vs. UCLA)   30

Most total free throws in the tournament
1 UCLA   85
2 SEATTLE   83
3 2 tied for third place.

Most free throws attempted in a single game
1 SEATTLE (vs. UCLA)   45
2 LOYOLA-CHICAGO (vs. KENTUCKY)   44
3 SEATTLE (vs. OREGON STATE)   43

Most total free throws attempted in the tournament
1 UCLA   128
2 SEATTLE   121
3 LOYOLA-CHICAGO   106

Highest free throw percentage in a single game
1 PRINCETON (vs. U. CONN.) (10-11)   .909
2 MICHIGAN (vs. OHIO) (17-19)   .895
3 PRINCETON (vs. VMI) (20-23)   .870

**Highest free throw percentage in the tournament
(minimum 2 games)**
1 PRINCETON (40-49)   .816
2 MICHIGAN (75-94)   .798
3 WICHITA STATE (50-63)   .794

Fewest free throws in a single game
1 U. CONN. (vs. TEMPLE)   7
1 KENTUCKY (vs. OHIO)   7
1 OHIO (vs. MICHIGAN)   7

Lowest free throw percentage in a single game
1 U. CONN. (vs. TEMPLE) (7-15)   .467
2 KANSAS STATE (vs. UCLA) (10-21)   .476
3 CREIGHTON (vs. TEXAS WESTERN) (8-16) .500

**Lowest free throw percentage in the tournament
(minimum 2 games)**
1 CREIGHTON (45-80)   .563
2 U. CONN. (33-57)   .579
3 OHIO (45-73)   .617

REBOUNDS

Most rebounds in a single game
1 SEATTLE (vs. UTAH STATE)   65
2 CREIGHTON (vs. OKLAHOMA CITY)   62
3 2 tied for third place.

1965

FIRST ROUND	REGIONAL SEMIFINAL	REGIONAL FINAL	FINAL FOUR	REGIONAL FINAL	REGIONAL SEMIFINAL	FIRST ROUND

EAST

(bye)

N.C. State 48

Princeton 109

Princeton 60

Princeton 66

Penn St. 58

Princeton 76

St. Joseph's 67

St. Joseph's 73

U. Conn. 61

Providence 69

West Virginia 67

Providence 81 (ot)

Providence 91

MIDEAST

(bye)

Michigan 98

Michigan 87

Ohio 65

Dayton 71

Dayton 66

Michigan 93

Eastern Ky. 52

De Paul 78

De Paul 99

Vanderbilt 85

(bye)

Vanderbilt 83 (ot)

MIDWEST

Oklahoma St. 75

(bye)

Oklahoma St. 46

Houston 99

Houston 60

Notre Dame 98

Wichita St. 89

SMU 81

(bye)

Wichita St. 54

(bye)

Wichita St. 86

WEST

San Francisco 91

(bye)

San Francisco 93

Oklahoma City 70

Oklahoma City 67

Colorado St. 68

UCLA 108

Brigham Young 76

(bye)

UCLA 101

(bye)

UCLA 100

UCLA 91
Michigan 80

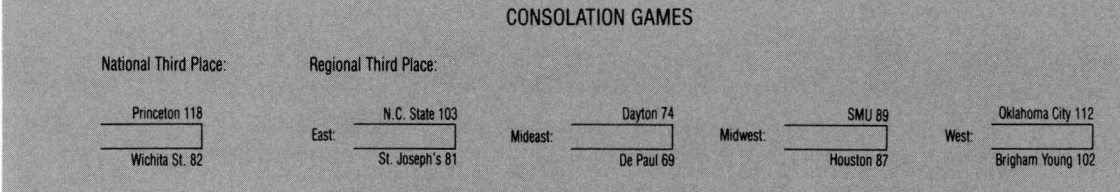

CONSOLATION GAMES

National Third Place:

Princeton 118

Wichita St. 82

Regional Third Place:

East:

N.C. State 103

St. Joseph's 81

Mideast:

Dayton 74

De Paul 69

Midwest:

SMU 89

Houston 87

West:

Oklahoma City 112

Brigham Young 102

Before the action began in the 1965 tournament, all the talk was about the big, bad No. 1–ranked Wolverines of Michigan. But by the time it ended, two individuals of uncommon brilliance shared the spotlight with a second straight UCLA championship team.

Going into the tournament, the second-ranked Bruins were considered to be a class below Michigan. Indeed, in its pre-tournament feature, *Sports Illustrated* predicted that Brigham Young, playing at home in Provo, Utah, would defeat UCLA. But John Wooden had other ideas. A Brigham Young scout, who came to see UCLA in their last regular-season contest against USC, went home disappointed; for the first time in nearly two years the Bruins played an entire game without employing their chief weapon, the full-court zone press. "We simply didn't want to show off everything to the scouts," explained the UCLA coach about his surprising game plan. "Let these people get their information second-hand."

In the regional opener, Brigham Young was holding a scant 30-29 lead after fifteen minutes of play when UCLA gave the Provo squad a first-hand demonstration of the press and its effects. Keith Erickson hit for three baskets in 45 seconds, and after Edgar Lacey scored another for UCLA, Erickson popped in three more. The score was suddenly 43-34. At the beginning of the second half, Gail Goodrich keyed a second blitz: after six and a half minutes, UCLA had a 22-point margin, with Goodrich scoring 16 points in an 18-7 UCLA run. So much for Brigham Young.

Next UCLA came up against San Francisco. The Dons' 6-8 Ollie Johnson had scored 24 points in the first half against Oklahoma City, and he was ably abetted by 6-8 Erwin Mueller and 6-6 Joe Ellis; together the three had accounted for 43 rebounds in a rout of the Chiefs. The Dons were far from an easy touch. In fact, with five and a half minutes remaining in their game against UCLA, San Francisco led, 83-82. Then the Bruins shifted gears. Mike Lynn hit a free throw to tie the game, and with the press working to perfection, Kenny Washington stole the ball and fed Goodrich, who hit a lay-up and was fouled. After Lynn hit a jumper with 4:05 left, the score was 89-83. Goodrich finished with 8 points in the final five minutes, and the Bruins won, 101-93.

In the Midwest, the depleted Wichita State Shockers (Dave Stallworth had used up his eligibility and 6-11 Nate Bowman was ineligible for academic reasons) surprised everyone by winning against a relatively weak field. But in the semis, they were crushed by the UCLA press. The Bruins took a 27-point lead into the locker room at halftime. In the second half, Wooden substituted freely, pulling out Goodrich for good twelve and a half minutes before the final gun.

Meanwhile Michigan moved through its regional toward what appeared like a certain showdown with UCLA.

They ripped Dayton, 98-71 but barely got past No. 5–ranked Vanderbilt, 87-85, as Cazzie Russell's 11 points down the stretch offset a 28-point, 20-rebound performance by Vandy's Clyde Lee.

Yet despite the appearance of an inevitable Michigan-UCLA confrontation, the Wolverines were not the popular favorite to face UCLA in the title game. The people's choice was Princeton of the Ivy League, whose tweedy Tigers were carried into the Final Four by the charismatic All-American, Bill Bradley. Although the Tigers had taken Michigan to the limit in December, losing to the Wolverines only after Bradley fouled out, the experts believed they were hardly to be taken seriously as threats for the title. Surely the Eastern regional representative would be either St. Joseph's or Providence. Still, Princeton managed to squeeze past Penn State's terrific zone with a clutch, down-the-stretch performance by Bradley, and they roared past the favored ACC champions from North Carolina State. After Providence squeaked by St. Joe's in overtime, Princeton met Providence for the regional championship. In one of the most stunning victories ever by an Ivy League team, Princeton blew Providence all the way back to Rhode Island. With Bradley leading the way with 41 points, Princeton won 109-69. The Tigers hit 68.3 percent of their shots for the game, and for one twelve-minute second-half stretch, they didn't miss a single shot. Maybe, just maybe, Bradley and the Tigers could become the first Ivy League team ever to win it all.

But first they had to get by Michigan. In describing the Wolverines, one writer commented that if you put a ball-carrier behind them, they'd look like an offensive line. Another pointed out that 6-4, 195-pound defensive specialist George Pomey was the shrimp of the bunch—and the only one who was outweighed by heavyweight champion Mohammed Ali. Led by Cazzie Russell and Bill Buntin, Michigan scored, rebounded, intimidated, and invariably came out in front.

Using their size to full advantage, the Wolverines dominated the boards against Princeton, outrebounding the Tigers 56-32. They still might have lost if Bradley hadn't gotten into foul trouble, but he picked up his third with Princeton holding a 5-point lead in the first half, and he drew his fourth soon after intermission. When he finally fouled out, Michigan led by 8; the margin quickly rose to 17. After a post-game interview, a *Los Angeles Times* reporter called Bradley "too good to be true."

He was even better than that. Against Wichita State in the consolation game, he had the entire crowd on its feet, roaring with every point, as he took aim at Oscar Robertson's single-game tournament-scoring record and—hitting nothing but net for the final three and a half minutes of his college career—he scored 39 points in the second half and finally surpassed the Big O, scoring 58 points before leaving to a standing ovation. It seemed that after Bradley's performance, the championship showdown between UCLA and Michigan would be an anticlimax.

No way. The Bruins, led by an electrifying Gail Goodrich, were stupendous. And they did it the way they always did, by pressing the giant Wolverines into submission. In the first few minutes of the game, Michigan looked unbeatable—they swept the boards, moved the ball where they wanted to, and shot unerringly. With Keith Erickson hobbled by a pulled muscle, Michigan's 20-13 lead was starting to look mighty big indeed. Then UCLA struck. With Goodrich leading the charge, they stole the ball, forced Michigan to kick it away, and started hitting their shots. Less than three minutes later, the Bruins were up 26-24. The Wolverines regained their equilibrium—temporarily, as it turned out—and each team scored 9 points to make it 35-33. Again, UCLA struck. In less than two minutes the Bruins scored 10 more to the Wolverines' 1. At the half, the score was 47-34.

In the second half, Michigan's big, brawny players chased Goodrich—all 6-1, 170 pounds of him (soaking wet after a big meal)—all over the court, but to no avail. He dribbled through them, he dribbled around them, he shot over them, he shot under them, he passed to his teammates for easy lay-ups—the only way the Wolverines could get near the wispy Bruin guard was to foul him. In one 39-second span, Michigan's entire front line fouled out chasing him. By then the score was 89-69, and Goodrich had 42 points.

Bradley won the award as the tournament's outstanding player, although there were plenty of dissenters on the UCLA side of the court who felt Goodrich deserved the honor. On one incredible March night in 1965, both players—Bradley and Goodrich—lifted the game to a level of brilliance rarely seen in tournament history. As for the best team, there was no dissent: UCLA proved, beyond a shadow of a doubt, who was No. 1.

FIRST ROUND EAST

Princeton (60)   Coach: B. Van Breda Kolff

	Min.	Total FG / FGA	Pct.	FT / FTA	Pct.	Reb. O / T	A	TO	PF	S	Blk	TP	PPM
BRADLEY, B.	-	7/22	.318	8/ 9	.889	-/ 9	6	-	2	-	-	22	-
HAARLOW, B.	-	5/13	.385	1/ 2	.500	-/ 9	1	-	2	-	-	11	-
BROWN, R.	-	0/ 4	.000	0/ 0	.000	-/ 5	1	-	1	-	-	0	-
RODENBACH, D.	-	5/11	.455	2/ 3	.667	-/ 5	1	-	3	-	-	12	-
WALTERS, G.	-	3/ 7	.429	0/ 0	.000	-/ 2	3	-	2	-	-	6	-
HUMMER, E.	-	4/ 5	.800	1/ 3	.333	-/13	1	-	1	-	-	9	-
Totals	200	24/62	.387	12/17	.706	-/43	13	-	11	-	-	60	.300

Penn State (58)   Coach: John Egli

	Min.	Total FG / FGA	Pct.	FT / FTA	Pct.	Reb. O / T	A	TO	PF	S	Blk	TP	PPM
AVILION	-	5/11	.455	1/ 2	.500	-/ 8	0	-	4	-	-	11	-
SAUNDERS	-	3/ 5	.600	0/ 0	.000	-/ 6	0	-	2	-	-	6	-
CLINTON, C.	-	5/21	.238	2/ 5	.400	-/16	2	-	4	-	-	12	-
WEISS, J.	-	5/16	.313	3/ 4	.750	-/ 5	8	-	2	-	-	13	-
REED, J.	-	7/15	.467	2/ 3	.667	-/ 6	0	-	2	-	-	16	-
MICKEY	-	0/ 1	.000	0/ 0	.000	-/ 3	0	-	1	-	-	0	-
Totals	200	25/69	.362	8/14	.571	-/44	10	-	15	-	-	58	.290

Team Rebounds: Princeton 5; Penn State 1. Disqualified: None.

	1st Half	2nd Half	Final
Princeton	31	29	60
Penn State	28	30	58

St. Joseph's (67)   Coach: Jack Ramsay

	Min.	Total FG / FGA	Pct.	FT / FTA	Pct.	Reb. O / T	A	TO	PF	S	Blk	TP	PPM
FORD	-	6/14	.429	2/ 3	.667	-/ 4	-	1	4	-	-	14	-
DUFF	-	5/11	.455	0/ 1	.000	-/ 6	-	1	1	-	-	10	-
ANDERSON	-	5/15	.333	2/ 3	.667	-/12	-	3	2	-	-	12	-
OAKES	-	3/ 9	.333	0/ 1	.000	-/ 3	-	3	4	-	-	6	-
GOUKAS, M.	-	7/12	.583	5/ 5	1.000	-/ 5	-	6	2	-	-	19	-
McKENNA	-	2/ 2	1.000	2/ 2	1.000	-/ 4	-	2	1	-	-	6	-
CHAPMAN	-	0/ 0	.000	0/ 0	.000	-/ 0	-	0	0	-	-	0	-
Totals	200	28/63	.444	11/15	.733	-/34	-	16	14	-	-	67	.335

U. Conn. (61)   Coach: Fred Shabel

	Min.	Total FG / FGA	Pct.	FT / FTA	Pct.	Reb. O / T	A	TO	PF	S	Blk	TP	PPM
HESFORD	-	7/12	.583	0/ 1	.000	-/ 6	-	4	1	-	-	14	-
RITTER	-	3/10	.300	1/ 2	.500	-/ 2	-	3	2	-	-	7	-
KIMBALL	-	9/15	.600	3/ 3	1.000	-/29	-	2	3	-	-	21	-
CURRAN	-	0/ 0	.000	0/ 1	.000	-/ 0	-	0	2	-	-	0	-
BIALOSUKNIA	-	5/18	.278	3/ 4	.750	-/ 1	-	1	3	-	-	13	-
PENDERS	-	2/ 6	.333	2/ 5	.400	-/ 4	-	0	2	-	-	6	-
THOMPSON	-	0/ 2	.000	0/ 0	.000	-/ 1	-	1	0	-	-	0	-
Totals	200	26/63	.413	9/16	.563	-/43	-	11	13	-	-	61	.305

Team Rebounds: St. Joseph's 3; U. Conn. 3. Disqualified: None

	1st Half	2nd Half	Final
St. Joseph's	26	41	67
U. Conn.	33	28	61

West Virginia (67)   Coach: George King

	Min.	Total FG / FGA	Pct.	FT / FTA	Pct.	Reb. O / T	A	TO	PF	S	Blk	TP	PPM
MAPHIS	-	10/18	.556	1/ 5	.200	-/11	2	-	5	-	-	21	-
CAMP	-	0/10	.000	0/ 1	.000	-/11	3	-	5	-	-	0	-
LENTZ	-	5/13	.385	0/ 0	.000	-/11	4	-	2	-	-	10	-
QUERTINMONT	-	4/10	.400	5/ 7	.714	-/ 2	1	-	3	-	-	13	-
LESHER	-	4/ 8	.500	4/ 4	1.000	-/ 9	2	-	1	-	-	12	-
SHAFFER	-	3/ 8	.375	1/ 2	.500	-/ 1	2	-	2	-	-	7	-
BENFIELD	-	0/ 0	.000	0/ 0	.000	-/ 0	0	-	1	-	-	0	-
RYCZAI	-	0/ 1	.000	0/ 0	.000	-/ 2	0	-	0	-	-	0	-
PALMER	-	1/ 2	.500	2/ 2	1.000	-/ 2	0	-	1	-	-	4	-
Totals	200	27/70	.386	13/21	.619	-/49	14	-	20	-	-	67	.335

Providence (91)   Coach: Joe Mullaney

	Min.	Total FG / FGA	Pct.	FT / FTA	Pct.	Reb. O / T	A	TO	PF	S	Blk	TP	PPM
BLAIR	-	5/11	.455	8/ 9	.889	-/ 9	3	-	4	-	-	18	-
RIORDAN, M.	-	4/ 9	.444	5/ 5	1.000	-/ 7	3	-	3	-	-	13	-
WESTBROOK	-	8/15	.533	2/ 4	.500	-/14	2	-	4	-	-	18	-
BENEDICT, J.	-	10/18	.556	1/ 1	1.000	-/ 2	1	-	1	-	-	21	-
WALKER, J.	-	6/13	.462	2/ 2	1.000	-/ 3	5	-	5	-	-	14	-
KINSKI	-	1/ 2	.500	1/ 1	1.000	-/ 1	1	-	2	-	-	3	-
LASHER	-	0/ 1	.000	0/ 0	.000	-/ 1	0	-	0	-	-	0	-
AHERN	-	1/ 2	.500	0/ 0	.000	-/ 1	1	-	0	-	-	2	-
DUTTON	-	0/ 1	.000	0/ 0	.000	-/ 1	1	-	0	-	-	0	-
SARATOPOLOUS	-	1/ 2	.500	0/ 0	.000	-/ 0	0	-	0	-	-	2	-
COX	-	0/ 1	.000	0/ 0	.000	-/ 1	0	-	0	-	-	0	-
McLAUGHLIN	-	0/ 0	.000	0/ 0	.000	-/ 0	0	-	0	-	-	0	-
Totals	200	36/75	.480	19/22	.864	-/40	17	-	19	-	-	91	.455

Team Rebounds: Providence 2; West Virginia 2. Disqualified: Providence—Walker; West Virginia—Maphis, Camp.

	1st Half	2nd Half	Final
West Virginia	29	38	67
Providence	49	42	91

FIRST ROUND MIDEAST

Ohio (65) Coach: James Snyder

	Min.	Total FG/FGA	Pct.	FT/FTA	Pct.	Reb. O/T	A	TO	PF	S	Blk	TP	PPM
HALEY, M.	-	4/9	.444	3/5	.600	-/5	1	1	3	-	-	11	-
HILT, D.	-	6/10	.600	7/11	.636	-/8	0	3	3	-	-	19	-
SCHROEDER, J.	-	5/9	.556	6/8	.750	-/7	1	2	3	-	-	16	-
HAMMOND, M.	-	6/12	.500	3/4	.750	-/7	2	3	1	-	-	15	-
DAVIS, T.	-	0/3	.000	0/0	.000	-/3	0	2	0	-	-	0	-
BROWN, D.	-	2/5	.400	0/1	.000	-/0	0	3	3	-	-	4	-
BUCK, L.	-	0/2	.000	0/0	.000	-/2	0	0	2	-	-	0	-
Totals	200	23/50	.460	19/29	.655	-/32	4	14	15	-	-	65	.325

Dayton (66) Coach: Don Donoher

	Min.	Total FG/FGA	Pct.	FT/FTA	Pct.	Reb. O/T	A	TO	PF	S	Blk	TP	PPM
SULLIVAN, B.	-	3/12	.250	3/3	1.000	-/5	1	2	4	-	-	9	-
CASSIDY, B.	-	2/9	.222	5/5	1.000	-/11	0	2	3	-	-	9	-
FINKEL, H.	-	10/13	.769	7/9	.778	-/11	0	4	5	-	-	27	-
PAPP, D.	-	6/16	.375	5/6	.833	-/6	1	1	1	-	-	17	-
KLAUS, G.	-	2/8	.250	0/0	.000	-/2	0	3	2	-	-	4	-
WANNEMACHER, J.	-	0/1	.000	0/0	.000	-/0	0	0	4	-	-	0	-
WARRELL, J.	-	0/4	.000	0/0	.000	-/1	0	1	1	-	-	0	-
Totals	200	23/63	.365	20/23	.870	-/36	2	13	20	-	-	66	.330

Team Rebounds: Dayton 7; Ohio 5. Disqualified: Dayton—Finkel.

	1st Half	2nd Half	Final
Ohio	29	36	65
Dayton	30	36	66

Eastern Kentucky (52) Coach: Jim Baechtold

	Min.	Total FG/FGA	Pct.	FT/FTA	Pct.	Reb. O/T	A	TO	PF	S	Blk	TP	PPM
BODKIN	-	8/17	.471	5/5	1.000	-/6	-	-	3	-	-	21	-
BRADLEY	-	1/9	.111	0/0	.000	-/2	-	-	4	-	-	2	-
TOLAN	-	4/8	.500	3/6	.500	-/5	-	-	3	-	-	11	-
LEMOS	-	2/12	.167	0/1	.000	-/4	-	-	1	-	-	4	-
WALTON	-	3/7	.429	3/3	1.000	-/1	-	-	2	-	-	9	-
BISBEY	-	2/5	.400	0/0	.000	-/7	-	-	1	-	-	4	-
CLEMONS	-	0/2	.000	0/0	.000	-/1	-	-	1	-	-	0	-
CARR	-	0/0	.000	0/0	.000	-/0	-	-	0	-	-	0	-
WESTERFIELD	-	0/1	.000	0/1	.000	-/0	-	-	1	-	-	0	-
GRABOWSKI	-	0/2	.000	0/0	.000	-/0	-	-	0	-	-	0	-
KING	-	0/2	.000	1/1	1.000	-/0	-	-	1	-	-	1	-
CLARK	-	0/3	.000	0/0	.000	-/3	-	-	0	-	-	0	-
Totals	200	20/68	.294	12/17	.706	-/29	-	-	17	-	-	52	.260

DePaul (99) Coach: Ray Meyer

	Min.	Total FG/FGA	Pct.	FT/FTA	Pct.	Reb. O/T	A	TO	PF	S	Blk	TP	PPM
PALMER	-	4/5	.800	3/3	1.000	-/13	-	-	2	-	-	11	-
SWANSON, D.	-	7/13	.538	1/1	1.000	-/9	-	-	3	-	-	15	-
MILLS, D.	-	9/10	.900	3/6	.500	-/6	-	-	2	-	-	21	-
MEYER	-	9/16	.563	2/2	1.000	-/7	-	-	2	-	-	20	-
MURPHY, J.	-	6/16	.375	4/4	1.000	-/6	-	-	3	-	-	16	-
MODESTES	-	0/1	.000	0/0	.000	-/4	-	-	0	-	-	0	-
BIRGELLS	-	1/1	1.000	0/0	.000	-/1	-	-	1	-	-	2	-
FLANAGAN	-	1/1	1.000	0/0	.000	-/1	-	-	1	-	-	2	-
GULLEY	-	2/2	1.000	2/3	.667	-/0	-	-	0	-	-	6	-
NORRIS	-	2/4	.500	2/2	1.000	-/1	-	-	0	-	-	6	-
ODISHOO	-	0/0	.000	0/0	.000	-/0	-	-	1	-	-	0	-
ORTOLANO	-	0/1	.000	0/0	.000	-/0	-	-	0	-	-	0	-
Totals	200	41/70	.586	17/21	.810	-/48	-	-	15	-	-	99	.495

Team Rebounds: DePaul 7; Eastern Ky. 2. Disqualified: None.

	1st Half	2nd Half	Final
Eastern Ky.	33	19	52
De Paul	43	56	99

FIRST ROUND MIDWEST

Houston (99) Coach: Guy Lewis

	Min.	Total FG/FGA	Pct.	FT/FTA	Pct.	Reb. O/T	A	TO	PF	S	Blk	TP	PPM
BALLARD, W.	-	8/20	.400	6/6	1.000	-/6	-	-	4	-	-	22	-
JONES	-	4/10	.400	3/4	.750	-/9	-	-	5	-	-	11	-
LENTZ, L.	-	6/7	.857	6/11	.545	-/12	-	-	3	-	-	18	-
HAMOOD	-	5/15	.333	4/5	.800	-/4	-	-	5	-	-	14	-
MARGENTHALER	-	6/10	.600	1/2	.500	-/2	-	-	2	-	-	13	-
APOLSKIS	-	3/3	1.000	4/6	.667	-/4	-	-	5	-	-	10	-
PERRY	-	2/2	1.000	1/2	.500	-/2	-	-	2	-	-	5	-
GRIDER	-	0/0	.000	0/0	.000	-/0	-	-	0	-	-	0	-
WINCH	-	0/3	.000	2/2	1.000	-/0	-	-	1	-	-	2	-
NEUMANN	-	2/4	.500	0/0	.000	-/1	-	-	1	-	-	4	-
Totals	200	36/74	.486	27/38	.711	-/40	-	-	28	-	-	99	.495

Notre Dame (98) Coach: Johnny Dee

	Min.	Total FG/FGA	Pct.	FT/FTA	Pct.	Reb. O/T	A	TO	PF	S	Blk	TP	PPM
MILLER, J.	-	6/16	.375	6/11	.545	-/8	-	-	3	-	-	18	-
SAHM, W.	-	6/11	.545	5/7	.714	-/10	-	-	5	-	-	17	-
JESEWITZ, L.	-	6/16	.375	5/6	.833	-/20	-	-	5	-	-	17	-
SHEFFIELD, L.	-	8/15	.533	1/2	.500	-/3	-	-	4	-	-	17	-
REED, R.	-	7/25	.280	2/4	.500	-/15	-	-	5	-	-	16	-
MCGANN, J.	-	5/9	.556	3/3	1.000	-/3	-	-	3	-	-	13	-
HARDY, K.	-	0/0	.000	0/1	.000	-/0	-	-	1	-	-	0	-
MONAHAN, J.	-	0/0	.000	0/0	.000	-/0	-	-	1	-	-	0	-
Totals	200	38/92	.413	22/34	.647	-/59	-	-	27	-	-	98	.490

Team Rebounds: Houston 9; Notre Dame 7. Disqualified: Houston—Jones, Hamood, Apolskis; Notre Dame—Sahm, Jesewitz, Reed.

	1st Half	2nd Half	Final
Houston	40	59	99
Notre Dame	49	49	98

FIRST ROUND WEST

Oklahoma City (70) Coach: Abe Lemons

	Min.	Total FG/FGA	Pct.	FT/FTA	Pct.	Reb. O/T	A	TO	PF	S	Blk	TP	PPM
HOPKINS	-	1/7	.143	5/7	.714	-/9	-	-	4	-	-	7	-
HUNTER, C.	-	10/17	.588	4/4	1.000	-/11	-	-	0	-	-	24	-
WARE	-	3/13	.231	0/1	.000	-/17	-	-	3	-	-	6	-
GRAY	-	9/20	.450	2/4	.500	-/2	-	-	1	-	-	20	-
WELLS	-	4/10	.400	5/7	.714	-/5	-	-	2	-	-	13	-
Totals	200	27/67	.403	16/23	.696	-/44	-	-	10	-	-	70	.350

Colorado State (68) Coach: Jim Williams

	Min.	Total FG/FGA	Pct.	FT/FTA	Pct.	Reb. O/T	A	TO	PF	S	Blk	TP	PPM
WRIGHT, L.	-	4/14	.286	0/0	.000	-/4	-	-	4	-	-	8	-
KEY, W.	-	1/2	.500	0/0	.000	-/4	-	-	1	-	-	2	-
BUSTION, S.	-	13/26	.500	4/6	.667	-/20	-	-	2	-	-	30	-
VIDAKOVICH, T.	-	6/13	.462	1/1	1.000	-/1	-	-	4	-	-	13	-
FOSTER	-	1/4	.250	1/4	.250	-/3	-	-	2	-	-	3	-
DAVIDSON	-	0/2	.000	0/0	.000	-/3	-	-	1	-	-	0	-
WESTOBY, W.	-	6/9	.667	0/0	.000	-/1	-	-	2	-	-	12	-
Totals	200	31/70	.443	6/11	.545	-/36	-	-	16	-	-	68	.340

Disqualified: None.

	1st Half	2nd Half	Final
Oklahoma City	36	34	70
Colorado State	32	36	68

REGIONAL SEMIFINAL EAST

North Carolina State (48) Coach: Press Maravich

	Min.	Total FG/FGA	Pct.	FT/FTA	Pct.	Reb. O/T	A	TO	PF	S	Blk	TP	PPM
COKER, P.	-	4/10	.400	0/3	.000	-/8	0	2	3	-	-	8	-
MATTOCKS, T.	-	3/14	.214	1/2	.500	-/4	1	2	2	-	-	7	-
LAKINS, L.	-	2/10	.200	3/5	.600	-/2	0	3	5	-	-	7	-
MOFFITT, B.	-	0/2	.000	4/6	.667	-/3	1	3	3	-	-	4	-
BIEDENBACH, E.	-	1/7	.143	0/2	.000	-/3	1	1	1	-	-	2	-
WORSLEY, L.	-	5/15	.333	4/5	.800	-/13	0	0	2	-	-	14	-
GEALY	-	0/0	.000	0/0	.000	-/1	0	0	0	-	-	0	-
HODGDON, R.	-	0/0	.000	0/0	.000	-/0	0	0	0	-	-	0	-
MOORE	-	0/3	.000	2/2	1.000	-/2	0	0	3	-	-	2	-
TAYLOR, P.	-	0/1	.000	0/0	.000	-/1	0	0	0	-	-	0	-
BLONDEAU	-	1/3	.333	0/0	.000	-/1	0	2	1	-	-	2	-
HALE	-	1/1	1.000	0/0	.000	-/0	0	0	0	-	-	2	-
Totals	200	17/66	.258	14/25	.560	-/38	5	11	20	-	-	48	.240

Princeton (66) Coach: B. Van Breda Kolff

	Min.	Total FG/FGA	Pct.	FT/FTA	Pct.	Reb. O/T	A	TO	PF	S	Blk	TP	PPM
BRADLEY, B.	-	10/18	.556	7/9	.778	-/14	8	2	4	-	-	27	-
HAARLOW, B.	-	4/9	.444	2/2	1.000	-/3	2	1	4	-	-	10	-
BROWN, R.	-	2/6	.333	0/2	.000	-/13	0	1	3	-	-	4	-
RODENBACH, D.	-	3/6	.500	2/2	1.000	-/4	0	2	2	-	-	8	-
WALTERS, G.	-	0/3	.000	0/0	.000	-/2	1	3	2	-	-	0	-
HUMMER, E.	-	5/12	.417	3/4	.750	-/10	1	3	3	-	-	13	-
ROTH, D.	-	1/1	1.000	0/0	.000	-/2	0	1	0	-	-	2	-
KINGSTON, B.	-	0/0	.000	0/0	.000	-/0	0	0	0	-	-	0	-
KOCH, W.	-	1/4	.250	0/2	.000	-/3	0	1	0	-	-	2	-
SHANK, K.	-	0/1	.000	0/1	.000	-/2	0	0	0	-	-	0	-
ADLER, A.	-	0/0	.000	0/0	.000	-/1	0	0	0	-	-	0	-
Totals	200	26/60	.433	14/22	.636	-/54	12	14	18	-	-	66	.330

Disqualified: N.C. State—Lakins.

	1st Half	2nd Half	Final
N.C. State	16	32	48
Princeton	27	39	66

St. Joseph's (73) Coach: Jack Ramsay

	Min.	Total FG/FGA	Pct.	FT/FTA	Pct.	Reb. O/T	A	TO	PF	S	Blk	TP	PPM
FORD	-	5/14	.357	3/5	.600	-/12	-	-	2	-	-	13	-
DUFF	-	3/10	.300	5/6	.833	-/11	-	-	5	-	-	11	-
ANDERSON	-	5/14	.357	5/6	.833	-/12	-	-	5	-	-	15	-
GOUKAS, M.	-	7/11	.636	0/1	.000	-/6	-	-	4	-	-	14	-
OAKES	-	6/17	.353	0/2	.000	-/4	-	-	3	-	-	12	-
MCKENNA	-	4/10	.400	0/3	.000	-/10	-	-	1	-	-	8	-
CHAPMAN	-	0/0	.000	0/0	.000	-/0	-	-	2	-	-	0	-
Totals	200	30/76	.395	13/23	.565	-/55	-	-	22	-	-	73	.365

Providence (81) Coach: Joe Mullaney

	Min.	Total FG/FGA	Pct.	FT/FTA	Pct.	Reb. O/T	A	TO	PF	S	Blk	TP	PPM
WESTBROOK	-	6/13	.462	4/10	.400	-/17	-	-	5	-	-	16	-
WALKER, J.	-	6/16	.375	8/10	.800	-/3	-	-	2	-	-	20	-
BLAIR	-	3/9	.333	1/1	1.000	-/7	-	-	3	-	-	7	-
BENEDICT, J.	-	11/17	.647	0/0	.000	-/3	-	-	2	-	-	22	-
RIORDAN, M.	-	5/11	.455	6/8	.750	-/6	-	-	4	-	-	16	-
LASHER	-	0/1	.000	0/0	.000	-/0	-	-	0	-	-	0	-
Totals	200	31/67	.463	19/29	.655	-/36	-	-	16	-	-	81	.405

Disqualified: Providence—Westbrook; St. Joseph's—Duff, Anderson.

	1st Half	2nd Half	Final
St. Joseph's	40	33	73
Providence	34	47	81

REGIONAL SEMIFINAL MIDEAST

Michigan (98)   Coach: Dave Strack

	Min.	Total FG/FGA	Pct.	FT/FTA	Pct.	Reb. O/T	A	TO	PF	S	Blk	TP	PPM
TREGONING, L.	-	6/10	.600	0/0	.000	-/7	-	-	1	-	-	12	-
DARDEN, O.	-	7/12	.583	3/3	1.000	-/9	-	-	0	-	-	17	-
BUNTIN, B.	-	12/21	.571	2/5	.400	-/11	-	-	1	-	-	26	-
RUSSELL, C.	-	5/14	.357	4/4	1.000	-/9	-	-	2	-	-	14	-
POMEY, G.	-	4/7	.571	3/3	1.000	-/4	-	-	1	-	-	11	-
MYERS, J.	-	1/2	.500	3/4	.750	-/4	-	-	0	-	-	5	-
THOMPSON, J.	-	1/2	.500	0/0	.000	-/2	-	-	1	-	-	2	-
CLAWSON, J.	-	1/6	.167	1/1	1.000	-/4	-	-	0	-	-	3	-
LUDWIG, T.	-	0/3	.000	0/0	.000	-/3	-	-	1	-	-	0	-
BROWN	-	0/1	.000	0/0	.000	-/1	-	-	0	-	-	0	-
BANKEY	-	0/0	.000	0/0	.000	-/0	-	-	0	-	-	0	-
DILL, C.	-	4/9	.444	0/1	.000	-/2	-	-	1	-	-	8	-
Totals	200	41/87	.471	16/21	.762	-/56	-	-	8	-	-	98	.490

Dayton (71)   Coach: Don Donoher

	Min.	Total FG/FGA	Pct.	FT/FTA	Pct.	Reb. O/T	A	TO	PF	S	Blk	TP	PPM
SULLIVAN, B.	-	6/14	.429	1/1	1.000	-/3	-	-	2	-	-	13	-
CASSIDY, B.	-	4/15	.267	2/2	1.000	-/8	-	-	4	-	-	10	-
FINKEL, H.	-	11/18	.611	0/0	.000	-/12	-	-	4	-	-	22	-
PAPP, D.	-	7/16	.438	1/1	1.000	-/4	-	-	0	-	-	15	-
KLAUS, G.	-	1/3	.333	0/0	.000	-/0	-	-	1	-	-	2	-
WANNEMACHER, J.	-	2/4	.500	0/0	.000	-/2	-	-	2	-	-	4	-
WARRELL, J.	-	1/3	.333	0/0	.000	-/0	-	-	2	-	-	2	-
JOHNSTON, F.	-	1/2	.500	0/0	.000	-/1	-	-	0	-	-	2	-
HRCKA, D.	-	0/0	.000	0/0	.000	-/0	-	-	0	-	-	0	-
BROOKS, T.	-	0/0	.000	1/1	1.000	-/0	-	-	0	-	-	1	-
SEMANICH, J.	-	0/0	.000	0/0	.000	-/0	-	-	0	-	-	0	-
INDERRIEDEN, D.	-	0/0	.000	0/0	.000	-/0	-	-	0	-	-	0	-
Totals	200	33/75	.440	5/7	.714	-/30	-	-	15	-	-	71	.355

Team Rebounds: Michigan 5; Dayton 4. Disqualified: None.

	1st Half	2nd Half	Final
Michigan	44	54	98
Dayton	27	44	71

DePaul (78)   Coach: Ray Meyer

	Min.	Total FG/FGA	Pct.	FT/FTA	Pct.	Reb. O/T	A	TO	PF	S	Blk	TP	PPM
PALMER	-	10/18	.556	8/11	.727	-/19	-	-	5	-	-	28	-
SWANSON, D.	-	4/8	.500	1/1	1.000	-/8	-	-	5	-	-	9	-
MILLS, D.	-	3/4	.750	1/2	.500	-/5	-	-	5	-	-	7	-
MURPHY, J.	-	9/25	.360	3/4	.750	-/7	-	-	2	-	-	21	-
MEYER	-	5/11	.455	1/3	.333	-/4	-	-	2	-	-	11	-
FLANAGAN	-	0/3	.000	0/0	.000	-/1	-	-	4	-	-	0	-
BIRGELLS	-	1/3	.333	0/0	.000	-/2	-	-	1	-	-	2	-
NORRIS	-	0/3	.000	0/0	.000	-/1	-	-	0	-	-	0	-
Totals	225	32/75	.427	14/21	.667	-/47	-	16	24	-	-	78	.347

Vanderbilt (83)   Coach: Roy Skinner

	Min.	Total FG/FGA	Pct.	FT/FTA	Pct.	Reb. O/T	A	TO	PF	S	Blk	TP	PPM
GRACE, B.	-	4/9	.444	3/3	1.000	-/4	-	-	5	-	-	11	-
TAYLOR, W.	-	0/2	.000	2/3	.667	-/7	-	-	1	-	-	2	-
LEE, C.	-	8/20	.400	8/10	.800	-/15	-	-	5	-	-	24	-
MILLER, J.	-	5/13	.385	6/10	.600	-/1	-	-	1	-	-	16	-
THOMAS, K.	-	7/10	.700	4/4	1.000	-/6	-	-	0	-	-	18	-
CALVERT, W.	-	6/8	.750	0/1	.000	-/4	-	-	4	-	-	12	-
GREEN, R.	-	0/2	.000	0/0	.000	-/5	-	-	3	-	-	0	-
GIBBS, K.	-	0/0	.000	0/0	.000	-/0	-	-	0	-	-	0	-
Totals	225	30/64	.469	23/31	.742	-/42	-	15	18	-	-	83	.369

Team Rebounds: Vanderbilt 1; DePaul 2. Disqualified: Vanderbilt—Grace, Lee; DePaul—Palmer, Swanson, Mills.

	1st Half	2nd Half	1st OT	Final
DePaul	32	44	2	78
Vanderbilt	39	37	7	83

REGIONAL SEMIFINAL MIDWEST

Oklahoma State (75)   Coach: Henry Iba

	Min.	Total FG/FGA	Pct.	FT/FTA	Pct.	Reb. O/T	A	TO	PF	S	Blk	TP	PPM
HAUSMANN	-	9/20	.450	0/0	.000	-/7	-	-	3	-	-	18	-
KING	-	3/6	.500	4/4	1.000	-/11	-	-	2	-	-	10	-
JOHNSON, G.	-	11/17	.647	3/5	.600	-/13	-	-	4	-	-	25	-
HAWK	-	2/9	.222	2/3	.667	-/6	-	-	3	-	-	6	-
IBA	-	2/3	.667	3/5	.600	-/3	-	-	4	-	-	7	-
MOULDER	-	1/2	.500	1/1	1.000	-/1	-	-	0	-	-	3	-
LABRUE	-	2/2	1.000	2/2	1.000	-/0	-	-	0	-	-	6	-
TEAMSTER	-	0/0	.000	0/0	.000	-/1	-	-	0	-	-	0	-
Totals	200	30/59	.508	15/20	.750	-/42	-	-	16	-	-	75	.375

Houston (60)   Coach: Guy Lewis

	Min.	Total FG/FGA	Pct.	FT/FTA	Pct.	Reb. O/T	A	TO	PF	S	Blk	TP	PPM
BALLARD	-	3/12	.250	0/1	.000	-/5	-	-	4	-	-	6	-
JONES	-	2/8	.250	2/4	.500	-/8	-	-	3	-	-	6	-
LENTZ, L.	-	3/9	.333	0/0	.000	-/9	-	-	1	-	-	6	-
HAMOOD	-	8/24	.333	1/1	1.000	-/7	-	-	1	-	-	17	-
MARGENTHALER	-	3/8	.375	1/1	1.000	-/1	-	-	1	-	-	7	-
APOLSKIS	-	3/5	.600	2/5	.400	-/1	-	-	3	-	-	8	-
PERRY	-	1/1	1.000	0/0	.000	-/2	-	-	1	-	-	2	-
GRIDER	-	0/1	.000	2/3	.667	-/1	-	-	0	-	-	2	-
WINCH	-	2/4	.500	1/1	1.000	-/0	-	-	2	-	-	5	-
PALMQUIST	-	0/1	.000	1/3	.333	-/2	-	-	0	-	-	1	-
ARNING	-	0/0	.000	0/0	.000	-/0	-	-	1	-	-	0	-
Totals	200	25/73	.342	10/19	.526	-/36	-	-	17	-	-	60	.300

Team Rebounds: Oklahamo State 7; Houston 6. Disqualified: None.

	1st Half	2nd Half	Final
Oklahoma State	33	42	75
Houston	22	38	60

SMU (81) Coach: E. O. "Doc" Hayes

	Min.	Total FG/FGA	Pct.	FT/FTA	Pct.	Reb. O/T	A	TO	PF	S	Blk	TP	PPM
SMITH, J.	-	3/6	.500	0/0	.000	-/3	-	-	0	-	-	6	-
WARD, B.	-	3/6	.500	4/7	.571	-/5	-	-	5	-	-	10	-
HOOSER, C.	-	9/16	.563	2/3	.667	-/9	-	-	5	-	-	20	-
HOLMAN, D.	-	3/10	.300	2/2	1.000	-/5	-	-	5	-	-	8	-
BEASLEY, C.	-	7/16	.438	4/4	1.000	-/6	-	-	3	-	-	18	-
BEGERT, B.	-	5/8	.625	6/10	.600	-/9	-	-	4	-	-	16	-
WENDORF, H.	-	1/3	.333	1/2	.500	-/2	-	-	3	-	-	3	-
CARPENTER, B.	-	0/0	.000	0/0	.000	-/1	-	-	0	-	-	0	-
Totals	200	31/65	.477	19/28	.679	-/40	-	-	25	-	-	81	.405

Wichita State (86) Coach: Gary Thompson

	Min.	Total FG/FGA	Pct.	FT/FTA	Pct.	Reb. O/T	A	TO	PF	S	Blk	TP	PPM
SMITH, V.	-	3/9	.333	3/3	1.000	-/4	-	-	4	-	-	9	-
THOMPSON, J.	-	8/22	.364	2/3	.667	-/7	-	-	3	-	-	18	-
LEACH, D.	-	4/13	.308	3/6	.500	-/8	-	-	4	-	-	11	-
PETE, K.	-	12/16	.750	7/12	.583	-/12	-	-	4	-	-	31	-
CRISS, J.	-	4/6	.667	1/1	1.000	-/2	-	-	4	-	-	9	-
REED, M.	-	2/4	.500	3/5	.600	-/7	-	-	3	-	-	7	-
DAVIS, G.	-	0/0	.000	1/1	1.000	-/0	-	-	0	-	-	1	-
NOSICH, L.	-	0/2	.000	0/0	.000	-/1	-	-	1	-	-	0	-
Totals	200	33/72	.458	20/31	.645	-/41	-	-	23	-	-	86	.430

Team Rebounds: Wichita State 6; SMU 6. Disqualified: SMU—Ward, Hooser, Holman.

	1st Half	2nd Half	Final
SMU	41	40	81
Wichita State	43	43	86

REGIONAL SEMIFINAL WEST

San Francisco (91) Coach: Peter Peletta

	Min.	Total FG/FGA	Pct.	FT/FTA	Pct.	Reb. O/T	A	TO	PF	S	Blk	TP	PPM
GUMINA	-	6/10	.600	0/2	.000	-/5	-	-	5	-	-	12	-
MUELLER	-	5/14	.357	3/4	.750	-/12	-	-	4	-	-	13	-
JOHNSON, O.	-	17/27	.630	1/2	.500	-/16	-	-	0	-	-	35	-
THOMAS, H.	-	1/4	.250	1/1	1.000	-/2	-	-	4	-	-	3	-
ELLIS	-	6/18	.333	0/0	.000	-/14	-	-	3	-	-	12	-
JAMES, C.	-	0/3	.000	0/0	.000	-/2	-	-	2	-	-	0	-
BLUM	-	7/11	.636	1/2	.500	-/1	-	-	0	-	-	15	-
ESTERS	-	0/2	.000	0/0	.000	-/0	-	-	1	-	-	0	-
GALE	-	0/1	.000	1/1	1.000	-/1	-	-	0	-	-	1	-
Totals	200	42/90	.467	7/12	.583	-/53	-	-	19	-	-	91	.455

Oklahoma City (67) Coach: Abe Lemons

	Min.	Total FG/FGA	Pct.	FT/FTA	Pct.	Reb. O/T	A	TO	PF	S	Blk	TP	PPM
HOPKINS	-	2/6	.333	1/1	1.000	-/8	-	-	1	-	-	5	-
HUNTER, C.	-	5/16	.313	2/2	1.000	-/3	-	-	1	-	-	12	-
WARE	-	6/18	.333	5/6	.833	-/22	-	-	3	-	-	17	-
WELLS	-	4/15	.267	5/7	.714	-/6	-	-	3	-	-	13	-
GRAY	-	8/15	.533	4/6	.667	-/0	-	-	5	-	-	20	-
BOLEN	-	0/1	.000	0/0	.000	-/1	-	-	0	-	-	0	-
CASTLEBERRY	-	0/1	.000	0/0	.000	-/0	-	-	0	-	-	0	-
MORRISON	-	0/0	.000	0/0	.000	-/0	-	-	0	-	-	0	-
Totals	200	25/72	.347	17/22	.773	-/40	-	-	13	-	-	67	.335

Team Rebounds: San Francisco 6; Oklahoma City 5. Disqualified: San Francisco—Gumina; Oklahoma City—Gray.

	1st Half	2nd Half	Final
San Francisco	29	62	91
Oklahoma City	29	38	67

Brigham Young (76) Coach: Stan Watts

	Min.	Total FG/FGA	Pct.	FT/FTA	Pct.	Reb. O/T	A	TO	PF	S	Blk	TP	PPM
KRAMER	-	5/7	.714	0/1	.000	-/4	-	-	2	-	-	10	-
ROBERTS	-	2/11	.182	3/4	.750	-/6	-	-	0	-	-	7	-
FAIRCHILD	-	8/17	.471	7/8	.875	-/13	-	-	2	-	-	23	-
GARDNER	-	5/10	.500	4/4	1.000	-/4	-	-	4	-	-	14	-
NEMELKA	-	2/11	.182	1/5	.200	-/1	-	-	2	-	-	5	-
HILL	-	2/5	.400	0/3	.000	-/7	-	-	4	-	-	4	-
QUINNEY	-	1/5	.200	2/2	1.000	-/4	-	-	0	-	-	4	-
CONGDON	-	2/5	.400	0/1	.000	-/1	-	-	1	-	-	4	-
STANLEY	-	2/3	.667	0/1	.000	-/4	-	-	0	-	-	4	-
RAYMOND	-	0/2	.000	1/2	.500	-/4	-	-	1	-	-	1	-
JIMAS	-	0/1	.000	0/0	.000	-/0	-	-	0	-	-	0	-
JAMES	-	0/3	.000	0/1	.000	-/1	-	-	0	-	-	0	-
Totals	200	29/80	.363	18/32	.563	-/49	-	-	16	-	-	76	.380

UCLA (100) Coach: John Wooden

	Min.	Total FG/FGA	Pct.	FT/FTA	Pct.	Reb. O/T	A	TO	PF	S	Blk	TP	PPM
LACEY, E.	-	7/11	.636	1/3	.333	-/13	-	-	3	-	-	15	-
ERICKSON, K.	-	14/22	.636	0/1	.000	-/9	-	-	4	-	-	28	-
MCINTOSH, D.	-	1/6	.167	0/2	.000	-/9	-	-	3	-	-	2	-
GOODRICH, G.	-	16/27	.593	8/9	.889	-/5	-	-	2	-	-	40	-
GOSS, F.	-	2/10	.200	0/0	.000	-/2	-	-	5	-	-	4	-
WASHINGTON, K.	-	0/5	.000	1/1	1.000	-/4	-	-	5	-	-	1	-
LYNN, M.	-	3/9	.333	2/2	1.000	-/10	-	-	3	-	-	8	-
HOFFMAN, V.	-	0/1	.000	0/1	.000	-/2	-	-	0	-	-	0	-
CHAMBERS, B.	-	0/1	.000	0/0	.000	-/1	-	-	0	-	-	0	-
LYONS, J.	-	1/2	.500	0/0	.000	-/0	-	-	0	-	-	2	-
LEVIN, R.	-	0/0	.000	0/0	.000	-/0	-	-	1	-	-	0	-
Totals	200	44/94	.468	12/19	.632	-/55	-	-	26	-	-	100	.500

Team Rebounds: UCLA 11; Brigham Young 7. Disqualified: UCLA—Goss, Washington.

	1st Half	2nd Half	Final
Brigham Young	40	36	76
UCLA	51	49	100

REGIONAL FINAL EAST

Princeton (109)   Coach: B. Van Breda Kolff

	Min.	Total FG/FGA	Pct.	FT/FTA	Pct.	Reb. O/T	A	TO	PF	S	Blk	TP	PPM
BRADLEY, B.	-	14/20	.700	13/13	1.000	-/10	-	-	3	-	-	41	-
HAARLOW, B.	-	7/10	.700	4/5	.800	-/7	-	-	2	-	-	18	-
BROWN, R.	-	5/10	.500	4/5	.800	-/11	-	-	3	-	-	14	-
RODENBACH, D.	-	3/4	.750	0/0	.000	-/1	-	-	4	-	-	6	-
WALTERS, G.	-	2/4	.500	0/0	.000	-/0	-	-	3	-	-	4	-
HUMMER, E.	-	4/4	1.000	5/5	1.000	-/9	-	-	3	-	-	13	-
ROTH, D.	-	1/1	1.000	0/0	.000	-/0	-	-	0	-	-	2	-
KINGSTON, W.	-	1/2	.500	1/3	.333	-/1	-	-	1	-	-	3	-
KOCH, W.	-	1/1	1.000	0/0	.000	-/2	-	-	0	-	-	2	-
SHANK, C.	-	1/2	.500	0/0	.000	-/1	-	-	1	-	-	2	-
NIEMANN, D.	-	2/2	1.000	0/0	.000	-/0	-	-	0	-	-	4	-
ADLER, A.	-	0/0	.000	0/0	.000	-/0	-	-	0	-	-	0	-
Totals	200	41/60	.683	27/31	.871	-/42	-	-	20	-	-	109	.545

Providence (69)   Coach: Joe Mullaney

	Min.	Total FG/FGA	Pct.	FT/FTA	Pct.	Reb. O/T	A	TO	PF	S	Blk	TP	PPM
WESTBROOK	-	6/12	.500	1/5	.200	-/8	-	-	4	-	-	13	-
WALKER, J.	-	8/19	.421	11/13	.846	-/4	-	-	5	-	-	27	-
BLAIR	-	0/0	.000	0/0	.000	-/1	-	-	5	-	-	0	-
BENEDICT, J.	-	4/17	.235	2/2	1.000	-/3	-	-	1	-	-	10	-
RIORDAN, M.	-	4/8	.500	1/2	.500	-/5	-	-	2	-	-	9	-
LASHER	-	1/4	.250	4/4	1.000	-/3	-	-	1	-	-	6	-
MCLAUGHLIN	-	0/0	.000	0/0	.000	-/0	-	-	0	-	-	0	-
KINSKI	-	0/0	.000	0/0	.000	-/0	-	-	2	-	-	0	-
AHERN	-	1/4	.250	0/1	.000	-/0	-	-	0	-	-	2	-
DUTTON	-	0/3	.000	0/0	.000	-/1	-	-	1	-	-	0	-
SARANTOPOLOU	-	1/2	.500	0/0	.000	-/0	-	-	0	-	-	2	-
COX	-	0/0	.000	0/0	.000	-/1	-	-	0	-	-	0	-
Totals	200	25/69	.362	19/27	.704	-/26	-	-	21	-	-	69	.345

Team Rebounds: Princeton 4; Providence 3. Disqualified: Providence—Walker, Blair.

	1st Half	2nd Half	Final
Princeton	47	62	109
Providence	34	35	69

REGIONAL FINAL MIDEAST

Michigan (87)   Coach: Dave Strack

	Min.	Total FG/FGA	Pct.	FT/FTA	Pct.	Reb. O/T	A	TO	PF	S	Blk	TP	PPM
TREGONING, L.	-	5/9	.556	1/3	.333	-/6	-	-	1	-	-	11	-
DARDEN, O.	-	6/14	.429	2/6	.333	-/12	-	-	4	-	-	14	-
BUNTIN, B.	-	11/25	.440	4/7	.571	-/14	-	-	5	-	-	26	-
RUSSELL, C.	-	9/19	.474	8/10	.800	-/8	-	-	2	-	-	26	-
POMEY, G.	-	3/4	.750	0/2	.000	-/3	-	-	4	-	-	6	-
MYERS, J.	-	2/3	.667	0/0	.000	-/2	-	-	1	-	-	4	-
DILL, C.	-	0/0	.000	0/1	.000	-/0	-	-	0	-	-	0	-
Totals	200	36/74	.486	15/29	.517	-/45	-	10	17	-	-	87	.435

Vanderbilt (85)   Coach: Roy Skinner

	Min.	Total FG/FGA	Pct.	FT/FTA	Pct.	Reb. O/T	A	TO	PF	S	Blk	TP	PPM
GRACE, B.	-	2/4	.500	3/5	.600	-/12	-	-	4	-	-	7	-
TAYLOR, W.	-	3/7	.429	0/1	.000	-/6	-	-	3	-	-	6	-
LEE, C.	-	11/22	.500	6/7	.857	-/20	-	-	4	-	-	28	-
MILLER, J.	-	8/16	.500	1/2	.500	-/3	-	-	2	-	-	17	-
THOMAS, K.	-	9/18	.500	3/3	1.000	-/3	-	-	5	-	-	21	-
CALVERT, W.	-	1/2	.500	0/0	.000	-/0	-	-	3	-	-	2	-
GREEN, R.	-	1/2	.500	2/2	1.000	-/3	-	-	0	-	-	4	-
GIBBS, K.	-	0/2	.000	0/1	.000	-/2	-	-	2	-	-	0	-
Totals	200	35/73	.479	15/21	.714	-/49	-	15	23	-	-	85	.425

Team Rebounds: Michigan 2; Vanderbilt 1. Disqualified: Michigan—Buntin; Vanderbilt—Thomas.

	1st Half	2nd Half	Final
Michigan	38	49	87
Vanderbilt	39	46	85

REGIONAL FINAL MIDWEST

Oklahoma State (46)   Coach: Henry Iba

	Min.	Total FG/FGA	Pct.	FT/FTA	Pct.	Reb. O/T	A	TO	PF	S	Blk	TP	PPM
HAUSMANN	-	4/9	.444	1/1	1.000	-/1	-	-	5	-	-	9	-
KING	-	2/3	.667	2/2	1.000	-/5	-	-	2	-	-	6	-
JOHNSON, G.	-	3/8	.375	3/3	1.000	-/3	-	-	3	-	-	9	-
IBA	-	2/2	1.000	1/2	.500	-/2	-	-	3	-	-	5	-
HAWK	-	2/6	.333	3/4	.750	-/4	-	-	1	-	-	7	-
MOULDER	-	3/10	.300	0/1	.000	-/4	-	-	2	-	-	6	-
LABRUE	-	2/4	.500	0/0	.000	-/1	-	-	1	-	-	4	-
Totals	200	18/42	.429	10/13	.769	-/20	-	-	17	-	-	46	.230

Wichita State (54)   Coach: Gary Thompson

	Min.	Total FG/FGA	Pct.	FT/FTA	Pct.	Reb. O/T	A	TO	PF	S	Blk	TP	PPM
SMITH, V.	40	2/2	1.000	8/9	.889	-/4	-	-	4	-	-	12	.300
THOMPSON, J.	40	2/4	.500	3/3	1.000	-/2	-	-	2	-	-	7	.175
LEACH, D.	40	5/8	.625	1/3	.333	-/2	-	-	4	-	-	11	.275
CRISS, J.	40	2/6	.333	1/1	1.000	-/3	-	-	3	-	-	5	.125
PETE, K.	40	6/9	.667	7/9	.778	-/9	-	-	0	-	-	19	.475
Totals	200	17/29	.586	20/25	.800	-/20	-	-	13	-	-	54	.270

Team Rebounds: Wichita State 2; Oklahoma State 2. Disqualified: Oklahoma State—Hausmann.

	1st Half	2nd Half	Final
Oklahoma State	22	24	46
Wichita State	31	23	54

REGIONAL FINAL WEST

San Francisco (93)   Coach: Peter Peletta

	Min.	Total FG / FGA	Pct.	FT / FTA	Pct.	Reb. O / T	A	TO	PF	S	Blk	TP	PPM
GUMINA	-	6/12	.500	4/ 5	.800	-/ 4	-	-	2	-	-	16	-
MUELLER	-	4/ 6	.667	4/ 5	.800	-/ 4	-	-	5	-	-	12	-
JOHNSON, O.	-	15/20	.750	7/10	.700	-/21	-	-	4	-	-	37	-
ELLIS	-	7/13	.538	2/ 4	.500	-/11	-	-	3	-	-	16	-
THOMAS, H.	-	3/ 4	.750	2/ 2	1.000	-/ 0	-	-	1	-	-	8	-
JAMES, C.	-	1/ 5	.200	0/ 0	.000	-/ 0	-	-	2	-	-	2	-
BLUM	-	1/ 4	.250	0/ 0	.000	-/ 1	-	-	2	-	-	2	-
ESTERS	-	0/ 1	.000	0/ 1	.000	-/ 2	-	-	1	-	-	0	-
Totals	200	37/65	.569	19/27	.704	-/43	-	-	20	-	-	93	.465

UCLA (101)   Coach: John Wooden

	Min.	Total FG / FGA	Pct.	FT / FTA	Pct.	Reb. O / T	A	TO	PF	S	Blk	TP	PPM
LACEY, E.	-	7/13	.538	1/ 2	.500	-/ 7	-	-	4	-	-	15	-
ERICKSON, K.	-	13/26	.500	3/ 6	.500	-/11	-	-	4	-	-	29	-
MCINTOSH, D.	-	2/ 3	.667	1/ 1	1.000	-/ 6	-	-	1	-	-	5	-
GOODRICH, G.	-	10/18	.556	10/11	.909	-/ 3	-	-	3	-	-	30	-
GOSS, F.	-	6/15	.400	1/ 1	1.000	-/ 0	-	-	1	-	-	13	-
WASHINGTON, K.	-	1/ 4	.250	0/ 1	.000	-/ 1	-	-	2	-	-	2	-
LYNN, M.	-	2/ 3	.667	3/ 4	.750	-/ 1	-	-	4	-	-	7	-
Totals	200	41/82	.500	19/26	.731	-/29	-	-	19	-	-	101	.505

Team Rebounds: UCLA 9; San Francisco 3. Disqualified: San Fransisco—Mueller.

	1st Half	2nd Half	Final
San Francisco	46	47	93
UCLA	51	50	101

FINAL FOUR

Princeton (76)   Coach: B. Van Breda Kolff

	Min.	Total FG / FGA	Pct.	FT / FTA	Pct.	Reb. O / T	A	TO	PF	S	Blk	TP	PPM
BRADLEY, B.	-	12/25	.480	5/ 5	1.000	-/ 7	-	-	5	-	-	29	-
HAARLOW, B.	-	4/10	.400	1/ 4	.250	-/ 3	-	-	1	-	-	9	-
BROWN, R.	-	2/ 6	.333	0/ 0	.000	-/ 3	-	-	5	-	-	4	-
WALTERS, G.	-	5/10	.500	1/ 2	.500	-/ 3	-	-	1	-	-	11	-
RODENBACH, D.	-	2/ 5	.400	2/ 2	1.000	-/ 1	-	-	3	-	-	6	-
HUMMER, E.	-	4/10	.400	4/ 5	.800	-/ 9	-	-	4	-	-	12	-
KOCH, W.	-	1/ 4	.250	1/ 2	.500	-/ 4	-	-	1	-	-	3	-
KINGSTON, W.	-	0/ 1	.000	2/ 2	1.000	-/ 2	-	-	1	-	-	2	-
Totals	200	30/71	.423	16/22	.727	-/32	-	-	21	-	-	76	.380

Michigan (93)   Coach: Dave Strack

	Min.	Total FG / FGA	Pct.	FT / FTA	Pct.	Reb. O / T	A	TO	PF	S	Blk	TP	PPM
TREGONING, L.	-	6/ 9	.667	1/ 1	1.000	-/10	-	-	2	-	-	13	-
DARDEN, O.	-	6/13	.462	1/ 3	.333	-/ 9	-	-	3	-	-	13	-
BUNTIN, B.	-	7/13	.538	8/10	.800	-/14	-	-	4	-	-	22	-
RUSSELL, C.	-	10/21	.476	8/ 9	.889	-/10	-	-	0	-	-	28	-
POMEY, G.	-	2/ 8	.250	2/ 2	1.000	-/ 3	-	-	4	-	-	6	-
MYERS, J.	-	1/ 4	.250	0/ 0	.000	-/ 4	-	-	1	-	-	2	-
DILL, C.	-	0/ 0	.000	3/ 4	.750	-/ 1	-	-	2	-	-	3	-
LUDWIG, T.	-	0/ 0	.000	0/ 0	.000	-/ 0	-	-	1	-	-	0	-
CLAWSON, J.	-	2/ 2	1.000	0/ 1	.000	-/ 1	-	-	0	-	-	4	-
THOMPSON, J.	-	0/ 1	.000	2/ 2	1.000	-/ 0	-	-	0	-	-	2	-
Totals	200	34/71	.479	25/32	.781	-/52	-	-	17	-	-	93	.465

Team Rebounds: Michigan 4; Princeton 2. Disqualified: Princeton—Bradley, Brown.

	1st Half	2nd Half	Final
Princeton	36	40	76
Michigan	40	53	93

Wichita State (89)   Coach: Gary Thompson

	Min.	Total FG / FGA	Pct.	FT / FTA	Pct.	Reb. O / T	A	TO	PF	S	Blk	TP	PPM
SMITH, V.	-	4/11	.364	0/ 1	.000	-/ 2	-	-	3	-	-	8	-
THOMPSON, J.	-	13/19	.684	10/11	.909	-/ 6	-	-	2	-	-	36	-
LEACH, D.	-	6/14	.429	0/ 1	.000	-/10	-	-	3	-	-	12	-
PETE, K.	-	6/11	.545	5/ 5	1.000	-/ 6	-	-	5	-	-	17	-
CRISS, J.	-	4/13	.308	0/ 0	.000	-/ 4	-	-	4	-	-	8	-
REED, M.	-	2/ 3	.667	1/ 1	1.000	-/ 4	-	-	4	-	-	5	-
DAVIS, G.	-	1/ 2	.500	0/ 0	.000	-/ 1	-	-	0	-	-	2	-
TROPE, A.	-	0/ 1	.000	0/ 0	.000	-/ 0	-	-	0	-	-	0	-
NOSICH, L.	-	0/ 0	.000	1/ 3	.333	-/ 0	-	-	0	-	-	1	-
REIMOND, G.	-	0/ 1	.000	0/ 0	.000	-/ 1	-	-	0	-	-	0	-
Totals	200	36/75	.480	17/22	.773	-/34	-	-	21	-	-	89	.445

UCLA (108)   Coach: John Wooden

	Min.	Total FG / FGA	Pct.	FT / FTA	Pct.	Reb. O / T	A	TO	PF	S	Blk	TP	PPM
LACEY, E.	-	9/13	.692	6/10	.600	-/13	-	-	2	-	-	24	-
ERICKSON, K.	-	1/ 6	.167	0/ 0	.000	-/ 5	-	-	2	-	-	2	-
MCINTOSH, D.	-	4/ 5	.800	3/ 4	.750	-/ 4	-	-	2	-	-	11	-
GOODRICH, G.	-	11/21	.524	6/ 8	.750	-/ 5	-	-	2	-	-	28	-
GOSS, F.	-	8/13	.615	3/ 4	.750	-/ 9	-	-	2	-	-	19	-
WASHINGTON, K.	-	4/13	.308	2/ 4	.500	-/ 7	-	-	1	-	-	10	-
LYNN, M.	-	5/ 9	.556	0/ 0	.000	-/ 8	-	-	2	-	-	10	-
HOFFMAN, V.	-	0/ 0	.000	0/ 0	.000	-/ 0	-	-	0	-	-	0	-
CHAMBERS, B.	-	0/ 5	.000	0/ 0	.000	-/ 2	-	-	1	-	-	0	-
LYONS, J.	-	2/ 3	.667	0/ 0	.000	-/ 1	-	-	2	-	-	4	-
LEVIN, R.	-	0/ 1	.000	0/ 0	.000	-/ 1	-	-	1	-	-	0	-
GALBRAITH, J.	-	0/ 0	.000	0/ 0	.000	-/ 0	-	-	1	-	-	0	-
Totals	200	44/89	.494	20/29	.690	-/55	-	-	18	-	-	108	.540

Team Rebounds: UCLA 5; Wichita State 4. Disqualified: Wichita State—Pete.

	1st Half	2nd Half	Final
Wichita State	38	51	89
UCLA	65	43	108

NATIONAL CHAMPIONSHIP

Michigan (80) Coach: Dave Strack

	Min.	Total FG / FGA	Pct.	FT / FTA	Pct.	Reb. O / T	A	TO	PF	S	Blk	TP	PPM
TREGONING, L.	-	2/ 7	.286	1/ 1	1.000	-/ 5	0	-	5	-	-	5	-
DARDEN, O.	-	8/10	.800	1/ 1	1.000	-/ 4	0	-	5	-	-	17	-
BUNTIN, B.	-	6/14	.429	2/ 4	.500	-/ 6	1	-	5	-	-	14	-
RUSSELL, C.	-	10/16	.625	8/ 9	.889	-/ 5	1	-	2	-	-	28	-
POMEY, G.	-	2/ 5	.400	0/ 0	.000	-/ 2	0	-	2	-	-	4	-
MYERS, J.	-	0/ 4	.000	0/ 0	.000	-/ 3	0	-	2	-	-	0	-
DILL, C.	-	1/ 2	.500	2/ 2	1.000	-/ 1	0	-	1	-	-	4	-
BROWN, D.	-	0/ 0	.000	0/ 0	.000	-/ 0	0	-	0	-	-	0	-
LUDWIG, T.	-	1/ 2	.500	0/ 0	.000	-/ 0	0	-	0	-	-	2	-
THOMPSON, J.	-	0/ 0	.000	0/ 0	.000	-/ 0	0	-	0	-	-	0	-
CLAWSON, J.	-	3/ 4	.750	0/ 0	.000	-/ 0	0	-	2	-	-	6	-
Totals	200	33/64	.516	14/17	.824	-/26	2	-	24	-	-	80	.400

UCLA (91) Coach: John Wooden

	Min.	Total FG / FGA	Pct.	FT / FTA	Pct.	Reb. O / T	A	TO	PF	S	Blk	TP	PPM
LACEY, E.	-	5/ 7	.714	1/ 2	.500	-/ 7	0	-	3	-	-	11	-
ERICKSON, K.	-	1/ 1	1.000	1/ 2	.500	-/ 1	1	-	1	-	-	3	-
MCINTOSH, D.	-	1/ 2	.500	1/ 2	.500	-/ 0	0	-	2	-	-	3	-
GOODRICH, G.	-	12/22	.545	18/20	.900	-/ 4	1	-	4	-	-	42	-
GOSS, F.	-	4/12	.333	0/ 0	.000	-/ 3	0	-	1	-	-	8	-
WASHINGTON, K.	-	7/ 9	.778	3/ 4	.750	-/ 5	0	-	2	-	-	17	-
LYNN, M.	-	2/ 3	.667	1/ 2	.500	-/ 6	2	-	1	-	-	5	-
HOFFMAN, V.	-	1/ 1	1.000	0/ 0	.000	-/ 1	0	-	0	-	-	2	-
CHAMBERS, B.	-	0/ 0	.000	0/ 1	.000	-/ 0	0	-	0	-	-	0	-
LYONS, J.	-	0/ 0	.000	0/ 0	.000	-/ 0	0	-	1	-	-	0	-
LEVIN, R.	-	0/ 1	.000	0/ 0	.000	-/ 1	0	-	0	-	-	0	-
GALBRAITH, J.	-	0/ 0	.000	0/ 0	.000	-/ 0	0	-	0	-	-	0	-
Totals	200	33/58	.569	25/33	.758	-/28	4	-	15	-	-	91	.455

Team Rebounds: UCLA 4; Michigan 7. Disqualified: Michigan—Darden, Buntin, Tregoning.

	1st Half	2nd Half	Final
Michigan	34	46	80
UCLA	47	44	91

NATIONAL THIRD PLACE

Princeton (118) Coach: B. Van Breda Kolff

	Min.	Total FG / FGA	Pct.	FT / FTA	Pct.	Reb. O / T	A	TO	PF	S	Blk	TP	PPM
BRADLEY, B.	-	22/29	.759	14/15	.933	-/17	4	-	4	-	-	58	-
HAARLOW, B.	-	4/ 7	.571	2/ 3	.667	-/ 0	1	-	3	-	-	10	-
BROWN, R.	-	3/ 5	.600	1/ 1	1.000	-/11	0	-	4	-	-	7	-
RODENBACH, D.	-	7/14	.500	2/ 2	1.000	-/ 1	0	-	2	-	-	16	-
WALTERS, G.	-	3/ 5	.600	0/ 0	.000	-/ 3	2	-	1	-	-	6	-
HUMMER, E.	-	3/ 4	.750	3/ 3	1.000	-/ 4	2	-	3	-	-	9	-
KINGSTON, W.	-	0/ 1	.000	0/ 1	.000	-/ 1	0	-	1	-	-	0	-
SHANK, K.	-	1/ 2	.500	0/ 0	.000	-/ 2	0	-	0	-	-	2	-
KOCH, W.	-	5/ 6	.833	0/ 3	.000	-/ 3	1	-	1	-	-	10	-
NIEMANN, D.	-	0/ 1	.000	0/ 0	.000	-/ 1	0	-	2	-	-	0	-
ROTH, D.	-	0/ 0	.000	0/ 0	.000	-/ 2	0	-	0	-	-	0	-
ADLER, A.	-	0/ 1	.000	0/ 0	.000	-/ 0	0	-	0	-	-	0	-
Totals	200	48/75	.640	22/28	.786	-/45	10	-	21	-	-	118	.590

Wichita State (82) Coach: Gary Thompson

	Min.	Total FG / FGA	Pct.	FT / FTA	Pct.	Reb. O / T	A	TO	PF	S	Blk	TP	PPM
SMITH, V.	-	3/ 6	.500	7/ 9	.778	-/ 5	0	-	4	-	-	13	-
THOMPSON, J.	-	6/15	.400	6/ 7	.857	-/ 3	0	-	4	-	-	18	-
LEACH, D.	-	5/10	.500	0/ 0	.000	-/ 2	0	-	5	-	-	10	-
PETE, K.	-	6/11	.545	9/13	.692	-/ 8	0	-	2	-	-	21	-
CRISS, J.	-	5/ 9	.556	0/ 0	.000	-/ 1	1	-	5	-	-	10	-
REED, M.	-	2/ 7	.286	0/ 0	.000	-/ 3	0	-	1	-	-	4	-
NOSICH, L.	-	1/ 3	.333	2/ 2	1.000	-/ 1	0	-	0	-	-	4	-
DAVIS, G.	-	1/ 4	.250	0/ 1	.000	-/ 0	0	-	0	-	-	2	-
ZAFIROS, M.	-	0/ 1	.000	0/ 0	.000	-/ 0	0	-	0	-	-	0	-
TROPE	-	0/ 0	.000	0/ 0	.000	-/ 0	0	-	0	-	-	0	-
REIMOND, G.	-	0/ 0	.000	0/ 0	.000	-/ 0	0	-	0	-	-	0	-
Totals	200	29/66	.439	24/32	.750	-/23	1	-	21	-	-	82	.410

Team Rebounds: Princeton 4; Wichita State 8. Disqualified: Wichita State—Leach, Criss.

	1st Half	2nd Half	Final
Princeton	53	65	118
Wichita State	39	43	82

REGIONAL THIRD PLACE EAST

North Carolina State (103) Coach: Press Maravich

	Min.	Total FG / FGA	Pct.	FT / FTA	Pct.	Reb. O / T	A	TO	PF	S	Blk	TP	PPM
COKER	-	2/ 5	.400	3/ 5	.600	-/ 4	4	1	1	-	-	7	-
MATTOCKS	-	6/12	.500	2/ 2	1.000	-/ 9	8	2	2	-	-	14	-
LAKINS, L.	-	12/22	.545	9/11	.818	-/14	1	3	4	-	-	33	-
MOFFIT	-	5/ 9	.556	5/ 6	.833	-/ 3	2	3	2	-	-	15	-
BIEDENBACH	-	5/ 7	.714	4/ 6	.667	-/ 2	5	4	-	-	-	14	-
WORSLEY, L.	-	6/11	.545	0/ 2	.000	-/ 6	5	2	3	-	-	12	-
BLONDEAU	-	1/ 3	.333	0/ 0	.000	-/ 1	0	1	0	-	-	2	-
GEALY	-	0/ 0	.000	0/ 0	.000	-/ 0	0	0	0	-	-	0	-
HALE	-	0/ 0	.000	0/ 0	.000	-/ 0	0	0	0	-	-	0	-
HODGDON	-	1/ 2	.500	0/ 0	.000	-/ 0	0	0	0	-	-	2	-
MOORE	-	2/ 4	.500	0/ 0	.000	-/ 3	0	0	1	-	-	4	-
TAYLOR, P.	-	0/ 0	.000	0/ 0	.000	-/ 1	0	0	1	-	-	0	-
Totals	200	40/75	.533	23/32	.719	-/43	22	17	18	-	-	103	.515

St. Joseph's (81) Coach: Jack Ramsay

	Min.	Total FG / FGA	Pct.	FT / FTA	Pct.	Reb. O / T	A	TO	PF	S	Blk	TP	PPM
FORD	-	8/20	.400	5/ 5	1.000	-/ 7	0	-	3	-	-	21	-
DUFF	-	1/ 4	.250	1/ 1	1.000	-/ 6	2	-	5	-	-	3	-
ANDERSON	-	12/22	.545	2/ 6	.333	-/23	2	-	4	-	-	26	-
GOUKAS, M.	-	5/12	.417	4/ 5	.800	-/ 2	7	-	4	-	-	14	-
OAKES	-	3/14	.214	2/ 3	.667	-/ 1	1	-	3	-	-	8	-
MCKENNA	-	1/ 3	.333	1/ 1	1.000	-/ 3	0	-	0	-	-	3	-
CHAPMAN	-	0/ 2	.000	0/ 0	.000	-/ 0	1	-	0	-	-	0	-
JULIA, D.	-	1/ 2	.500	0/ 0	.000	-/ 0	0	-	3	-	-	2	-
BRENNER	-	1/ 2	.500	0/ 0	.000	-/ 3	0	-	1	-	-	2	-
GRUNDY	-	1/ 1	1.000	0/ 0	.000	-/ 0	0	-	0	-	-	2	-
MCFADDEN	-	0/ 0	.000	0/ 1	.000	-/ 1	0	-	0	-	-	0	-
Totals	200	33/82	.402	15/24	.625	-/45	14	-	23	-	-	81	.405

Team Rebounds: N.C. State 7; St. Joseph's 7. Disqualified: St. Joseph's—Duff.

	1st Half	2nd Half	Final
N.C. State	48	55	103
St. Joseph's	37	44	81

REGIONAL THIRD PLACE MIDEAST

Dayton (75)   Coach: Don Donoher

	Min.	Total FG/FGA	Pct.	FT/FTA	Pct.	Reb. O/T	A	TO	PF	S	Blk	TP	PPM
SULLIVAN, B.	-	2/ 8	.250	4/ 4	1.000	-/12	-	-	0	-	-	8	-
CASSIDY, B.	-	3/ 9	.333	2/ 2	1.000	-/ 6	-	-	4	-	-	8	-
FINKEL, H.	-	11/16	.688	4/ 6	.667	-/12	-	-	5	-	-	26	-
PAPP, D.	-	3/ 9	.333	5/ 5	1.000	-/ 2	-	-	2	-	-	11	-
KLAUS, G.	-	4/ 8	.500	4/ 6	.667	-/ 6	-	-	3	-	-	12	-
WANNEMACHER, J.	-	4/ 7	.571	2/ 4	.500	-/ 3	-	-	1	-	-	10	-
Totals	200	27/57	.474	21/27	.778	-/41	-	-	15	-	-	75	.375

DePaul (69)   Coach: Ray Meyer

	Min.	Total FG/FGA	Pct.	FT/FTA	Pct.	Reb. O/T	A	TO	PF	S	Blk	TP	PPM
PALMER	-	4/10	.400	5/ 6	.833	-/18	-	-	4	-	-	13	-
SWANSON, D.	-	6/16	.375	3/ 4	.750	-/ 7	-	-	3	-	-	15	-
MILLS, D.	-	4/ 7	.571	4/ 6	.667	-/ 7	-	-	3	-	-	12	-
MEYER	-	6/18	.333	1/ 1	1.000	-/ 1	-	-	3	-	-	13	-
MURPHY, J.	-	5/15	.333	5/ 5	1.000	-/ 5	-	-	2	-	-	15	-
ODISHOU	-	0/ 2	.000	1/ 1	1.000	-/ 0	-	-	2	-	-	1	-
Totals	200	25/68	.368	19/23	.826	-/38	-	-	17	-	-	69	.345

Disqualified: Dayton—Finkel.

		1st Half	2nd Half	Final
Dayton		39	36	75
DePaul		34	35	69

REGIONAL THIRD PLACE MIDWEST

SMU (89)   Coach: E. O. "Doc" Hayes

	Min.	Total FG/FGA	Pct.	FT/FTA	Pct.	Reb. O/T	A	TO	PF	S	Blk	TP	PPM
SMITH, J.	-	4/ 9	.444	4/ 5	.800	-/ 9	-	-	3	-	-	12	-
WARD, B.	-	4/13	.308	3/ 7	.429	-/ 9	-	-	4	-	-	11	-
HOOSER, C.	-	11/18	.611	5/ 8	.625	-/22	-	-	5	-	-	27	-
HOLMAN, D.	-	3/ 8	.375	2/ 3	.667	-/ 4	-	-	4	-	-	8	-
BEASLEY, C.	-	6/13	.462	7/ 8	.875	-/ 3	-	-	0	-	-	19	-
BEGERT, B.	-	1/ 2	.500	6/10	.600	-/ 5	-	-	5	-	-	8	-
WENDORF, H.	-	0/ 1	.000	0/ 1	.000	-/ 0	-	-	1	-	-	0	-
CARPENTER, B.	-	1/ 2	.500	0/ 0	.000	-/ 0	-	-	1	-	-	2	-
JONES, B.	-	0/ 0	.000	0/ 0	.000	-/ 0	-	-	0	-	-	0	-
RAMSAY, J.	-	0/ 0	.000	0/ 0	.000	-/ 0	-	-	0	-	-	0	-
MARSH	-	1/ 3	.333	0/ 0	.000	-/ 0	-	-	1	-	-	2	-
Totals	200	31/69	.449	27/42	.643	-/52	-	-	24	-	-	89	.445

Houston (87)   Coach: Guy Lewis

	Min.	Total FG/FGA	Pct.	FT/FTA	Pct.	Reb. O/T	A	TO	PF	S	Blk	TP	PPM
BALLARD, W.	-	7/16	.438	0/ 1	.000	-/ 4	-	-	4	-	-	14	-
JONES	-	3/ 7	.429	1/ 1	1.000	-/ 7	-	-	5	-	-	7	-
LENTZ, L.	-	2/ 8	.250	2/ 3	.667	-/ 9	-	-	3	-	-	6	-
HAMOOD	-	10/22	.455	3/ 5	.600	-/ 5	-	-	1	-	-	23	-
MARGENTHALER	-	8/15	.533	1/ 2	.500	-/ 3	-	-	4	-	-	17	-
APOLSKIS	-	2/ 7	.286	6/ 8	.750	-/ 8	-	-	5	-	-	10	-
PERRY	-	0/ 0	.000	2/ 2	1.000	-/ 1	-	-	0	-	-	2	-
GRIDER	-	1/ 2	.500	0/ 1	.000	-/ 2	-	-	0	-	-	2	-
WINCH	-	1/ 4	.250	0/ 0	.000	-/ 3	-	-	1	-	-	2	-
PALMQUIST	-	0/ 2	.000	4/ 7	.571	-/ 1	-	-	4	-	-	4	-
ARNING	-	0/ 0	.000	0/ 0	.000	-/ 0	-	-	1	-	-	0	-
Totals	200	34/83	.410	19/30	.633	-/43	-	-	28	-	-	87	.435

Team Rebounds: SMU 7; Houston 11. Disqualified: SMU—Hooser, Begert; Houston—Jones, Apolskis.

		1st Half	2nd Half	Final
SMU		47	42	89
Houston		50	37	87

REGIONAL THIRD PLACE WEST

Oklahoma City (112)   Coach: Abe Lemons

	Min.	Total FG/FGA	Pct.	FT/FTA	Pct.	Reb. O/T	A	TO	PF	S	Blk	TP	PPM
HOPKINS	-	5/ 7	.714	2/ 3	.667	-/ 6	-	-	4	-	-	12	-
HUNTER, C.	-	8/22	.364	1/ 2	.500	-/12	-	-	3	-	-	17	-
WARE	-	6/12	.500	6/ 6	1.000	-/16	-	-	5	-	-	18	-
WELLS	-	10/20	.500	11/12	.917	-/ 5	-	-	3	-	-	31	-
GRAY	-	12/22	.545	8/ 9	.889	-/ 2	-	-	3	-	-	32	-
CASTLEBERRY	-	1/ 1	1.000	0/ 0	.000	-/ 0	-	-	1	-	-	2	-
Totals	200	42/84	.500	28/32	.875	-/41	-	-	19	-	-	112	.560

Brigham Young (102)   Coach: Stan Watts

	Min.	Total FG/FGA	Pct.	FT/FTA	Pct.	Reb. O/T	A	TO	PF	S	Blk	TP	PPM
QUINNEY	-	10/18	.556	4/ 4	1.000	-/ 9	-	-	3	-	-	24	-
KRAMER	-	8/11	.727	2/ 2	1.000	-/10	-	-	4	-	-	18	-
FAIRCHILD	-	4/19	.211	8/12	.667	-/21	-	-	0	-	-	16	-
GARDNER	-	5/15	.333	6/ 7	.857	-/ 5	-	-	3	-	-	16	-
NEMELKA	-	9/23	.391	2/ 3	.667	-/ 6	-	-	4	-	-	20	-
ROBERTS	-	0/ 2	.000	0/ 0	.000	-/ 0	-	-	1	-	-	0	-
CONGDON	-	1/ 6	.167	0/ 1	.000	-/ 1	-	-	5	-	-	2	-
HILL	-	2/ 4	.500	0/ 0	.000	-/ 3	-	-	1	-	-	4	-
JIMAS	-	1/ 1	1.000	0/ 0	.000	-/ 0	-	-	1	-	-	2	-
Totals	200	40/99	.404	22/29	.759	-/55	-	-	22	-	-	102	.510

Team Rebounds: Oklahoma City 9; Brigham Young 7. Disqualified: Oklahoma City—Ware; Brigham Young—Congdon.

		1st Half	2nd Half	Final
Oklahoma City		62	50	112
Brigham Young		46	56	102

✪ ALL-STAR TEAMS ✪

ALL TOURNAMENT

★ BILL BRADLEY	PRINCETON
GAIL GOODRICH	UCLA
EDGAR LACEY	UCLA
CAZZIE RUSSELL	MICHIGAN
KENNY WASHINGTON	UCLA

MIDEAST REGIONAL

BILL BUNTIN	MICHIGAN
★ CLYDE LEE	VANDERBILT
ERROL PALMER	DEPAUL
CAZZIE RUSSELL	MICHIGAN
KEITH THOMAS	VANDERBILT

WEST REGIONAL

JOE ELLIS	SAN FRANCISCO
KEITH ERICKSON	UCLA
GAIL GOODRICH	UCLA
GARY GRAY	OKLAHOMA CITY
★ OLLIE JOHNSON	SAN FRANCISCO

★ Most Outstanding Player(s)

✪ INDIVIDUAL RECORDS ✪

SCORING

Most points in a single game
1 BILL BRADLEY, PRINCETON (vs. WICHITA STATE) 58
2 GAIL GOODRICH, UCLA (vs. MICHIGAN) 42
3 BILL BRADLEY, PRINCETON (vs. PROVIDENCE) 41
4 GAIL GOODRICH, UCLA (vs. BRIGHAM YOUNG) 40
5 OLLIE JOHNSON, SAN FRANCISCO (vs. UCLA) 37

Most total points in the tournament
1 BILL BRADLEY, PRINCETON 177
2 GAIL GOODRICH, UCLA 140
3 CAZZIE RUSSELL, MICHIGAN 96
4 KELLY PETE, WICHITA STATE 88
4 BILL BUNTIN, MICHIGAN 88

Highest scoring average (minimum 2 games)
1 OLLIE JOHNSON, SAN FRANCISCO (72-2) 36.00
2 BILL BRADLEY, PRINCETON (177-5) 35.40
3 GAIL GOODRICH, UCLA (140-4) 35.00
4 CLYDE LEE, VANDERBILT (52-2) 26.00
5 HENRY FINKEL, DAYTON (75-3) 25.00

FIELD GOALS

Most field goals in a single game
1 BILL BRADLEY, PRINCETON (vs. WICHITA STATE) 22
2 OLLIE JOHNSON, SAN FRANCISCO (vs. OKLAHOMA CITY) 17
3 GAIL GOODRICH, UCLA (vs. BRIGHAM YOUNG) 16
4 OLLIE JOHNSON, SAN FRANCISCO (vs. UCLA) 15
5 2 tied for fifth place.

Most total field goals in the tournament
1 BILL BRADLEY, PRINCETON 65
2 GAIL GOODRICH, UCLA 49
3 BILL BUNTIN, MICHIGAN 36
4 CAZZIE RUSSELL, MICHIGAN 34
5 2 tied for fifth place.

Most field goal attempts in a single game
1 BILL BRADLEY, PRINCETON (vs. WICHITA STATE) 29
2 OLLIE JOHNSON, SAN FRANCISCO (vs. OKLAHOMA CITY) 27
2 GAIL GOODRICH, UCLA (vs. BRIGHAM YOUNG) 27
4 SONNY BUSTION, COLORADO STATE (vs. OKLAHOMA CITY) 26
4 KEITH ERICKSON, UCLA (vs. SAN FRANCISCO) 26

Most total field goal attempts in the tournament
1 BILL BRADLEY, PRINCETON 114
2 GAIL GOODRICH, UCLA 88
3 BILL BUNTIN, MICHIGAN 73
4 CAZZIE RUSSELL, MICHIGAN 70
5 JOE HAMOOD, HOUSTON 61

Highest field goal percentage in a single game (minimum 10 attempts)
1 DAVE MILLS, DEPAUL (vs. EASTERN KY.) (9-10) .900
2 OLIVER DARDEN, MICHIGAN (vs. UCLA) (8-10) .800
3 HENRY FINKEL, DAYTON (vs. OHIO) (10-13) .769
4 BILL BRADLEY, PRINCETON (vs. WICHITA STATE) (22-29) .759
5 OLLIE JOHNSON, SAN FRANCISCO (vs. UCLA) (15-20) .750

Highest field goal percentage in the tournament (minimum 20 attempts)
1 DAVE MILLS, DEPAUL (16-21) .762
2 OLLIE JOHNSON, SAN FRANCISCO (32-47) .681
2 HENRY FINKEL, DAYTON (32-47) .681
4 KELLY PETE, WICHITA STATE (30-47) .638
5 EDGAR LACEY, UCLA (28-44) .636

FREE THROWS

Most free throws in a single game
1 GAIL GOODRICH, UCLA (vs. MICHIGAN) 18
2 BILL BRADLEY, PRINCETON (vs. WICHITA STATE) 14
3 BILL BRADLEY, PRINCETON (vs. PROVIDENCE) 13
4 JIM WALKER, PROVIDENCE (vs. PRINCETON) 11
4 JERRY WELLS, OKLAHOMA CITY (vs. BRIGHAM YOUNG) 11

Most total free throws in the tournament
1 BILL BRADLEY, PRINCETON 47
2 GAIL GOODRICH, UCLA 42
3 CAZZIE RUSSELL, MICHIGAN 28
3 KELLY PETE, WICHITA STATE 28
5 3 tied for fifth place.

Most free throws attempted in a single game
1 GAIL GOODRICH, UCLA (vs. MICHIGAN) 20
2 BILL BRADLEY, PRINCETON (vs. WICHITA STATE) 15
3 JIM WALKER, PROVIDENCE (vs. PRINCETON) 13
3 BILL BRADLEY, PRINCETON (vs. PROVIDENCE) 13
3 KELLY PETE, WICHITA STATE (vs. PRINCETON) 13

Most free throws attempted in the tournament
1 BILL BRADLEY, PRINCETON   51
2 GAIL GOODRICH, UCLA   48
3 KELLY PETE, WICHITA STATE   39
4 CAZZIE RUSSELL, MICHIGAN   32
5 2 tied for fifth place.

Highest free throw percentage in a single game
(minimum 7 attempts)
1 BILL BRADLEY, PRINCETON (vs. PROVIDENCE)
   (13-13)   1.000
2 BILL BRADLEY, PRINCETON (vs. WICHITA STATE)
   (14-15)   .933
3 JERRY WELLS, OKLAHOMA CITY (vs. BRIGHAM
   YOUNG) (11-12)   .917
4 JAMIE THOMPSON, WICHITA STATE (vs. UCLA)
   (10-11)   .909
4 GAIL GOODRICH, UCLA (vs. SAN FRANCISCO)
   (10-11)   .909

Highest free throw percentage in the tournament
(minimum 15 attempts)
1 BILL BRADLEY, PRINCETON (47-51)   .922
2 GAIL GOODRICH, UCLA (42-48)   .875
3 CAZZIE RUSSELL, MICHIGAN (28-32)   .875
4 JAMIE THOMPSON, WICHITA STATE (21-24) .875
5 JIM WALKER, PROVIDENCE (21-25)   .840

REBOUNDS

Most rebounds in a single game
1 THOMAS KIMBALL, U. CONN.
   (vs. ST. JOSEPH'S)   29
2 CLIFFORD ANDERSON, ST. JOSEPH'S (vs. N.C.
   STATE)   23
3 JAMES WARE, OKLAHOMA CITY (vs. SAN
   FRANCISCO)   22
3 CARROLL HOOSER, SMU (vs. HOUSTON)   22
5 2 tied for fifth place.

Most total rebounds in the tournament
1 BILL BRADLEY, PRINCETON   57
2 JAMES WARE, OKLAHOMA CITY   55
3 ERROL PALMER, DEPAUL   50
4 CLIFFORD ANDERSON, ST. JOSEPH'S   47
5 2 tied for fifth place.

Most rebounds per game (minimum 2 games)
1 OLLIE JOHNSON, SAN FRANCISCO (37-2)   18.50
2 JAMES WARE, OKLAHOMA CITY (55-3)   18.33
3 CLYDE LEE, VANDERBILT (35-2)   17.50
4 FAIRCHILD, BRIGHAM YOUNG (34-2)   17.00
5 ERROL PALMER, DEPAUL (50-3)   16.67

○ TEAM RECORDS ○

SCORING

Most points in a single game
1 PRINCETON (vs. WICHITA STATE)   118
2 OKLAHOMA CITY (vs. BRIGHAM YOUNG)   112
3 PRINCETON (vs. PROVIDENCE)   109

Most total points in the tournament
1 PRINCETON   429
2 UCLA   400
3 MICHIGAN   358

Highest scoring average (minimum 2 games)
1 UCLA (400-4)   100.00
2 SAN FRANCISCO (184-2)   92.00
3 MICHIGAN (358-4)   89.50

FIELD GOALS

Most field goals in a single game
1 PRINCETON (vs. WICHITA STATE)   48
2 UCLA (vs. WICHITA STATE)   44
2 UCLA (vs. BRIGHAM YOUNG)   44

Most total field goals in the tournament
1 PRINCETON   169
2 UCLA   162
3 MICHIGAN   144

Most field goals attempted in a single game
1 BRIGHAM YOUNG (vs. OKLAHOMA CITY)   99
2 UCLA (vs. BRIGHAM YOUNG)   94
3 NOTRE DAME (vs. HOUSTON)   92

Most total field goals attempted in the tournament
1 PRINCETON   328
2 UCLA   323
3 MICHIGAN   296

Highest field goal percentage in a single game
1 PRINCETON (vs. PROVIDENCE) (41-60)   .683
2 PRINCETON (vs. WICHITA STATE) (48-75) .640
3 WICHITA STATE (vs. OKLAHOMA STATE) (17-29)
                                          .586

Highest field goal percentage in the tournament
(minimum 2 games)
1 PRINCETON (169-328)   .516
2 SAN FRANCISCO (79-155)   .510
3 UCLA (162-323)   .502

FREE THROWS

Most free throws in a single game
1 OKLAHOMA CITY (vs. BRIGHAM YOUNG)   28
2 3 tied for second place.

Most total free throws in the tournament
1 PRINCETON   91
2 WICHITA STATE   81
3 UCLA   76

Most free throws attempted in a single game
1 SMU (vs. HOUSTON)   42
2 HOUSTON (vs. NOTRE DAME)   38
3 NOTRE DAME (vs. HOUSTON)   34

Most total free throws attempted in the tournament
1 PRINCETON   120
2 WICHITA STATE   110
3 UCLA   107

Highest free throw percentage in a single game
1 OKLAHOMA CITY (vs. BRIGHAM YOUNG) (28-32)
                                          .875
2 PRINCETON (vs. PROVIDENCE) (27-31)   .871
3 DAYTON (vs. OHIO) (20-23)   .870

Highest free throw percentage in the tournament
(minimum 2 games)
1 DAYTON (46-57)   .807
2 OKLAHOMA CITY (61-77)   .792
3 DEPAUL (50-65)   .769

Fewest free throws in a single game
1 DAYTON (vs. MICHIGAN)   5
2 COLORADO STATE (vs. OKLAHOMA CITY)   6
3 SAN FRANCISCO (vs. OKLAHOMA CITY)   7

Lowest free throw percentage in a single game
1 MICHIGAN (vs. VANDERBILT) (15-29)   .517
2 HOUSTON (vs. OKLAHOMA STATE) (10-19)   .526
3 COLORADO STATE (vs. OKLAHOMA CITY) (6-11)
                                          .545

Lowest free throw percentage in the tournament
(minimum 2 games)
1 ST. JOSEPH'S (39-62)   .629
2 HOUSTON (56-87)   .644
3 N.C. STATE (37-57)   .649

REBOUNDS

Most rebounds in a single game
1 NOTRE DAME (vs. HOUSTON)   59
2 MICHIGAN (vs. DAYTON)   56
3 4 tied for third place.

Most rebounds per game (minimum 2 games)
1 BRIGHAM YOUNG (104-2)   52.00
2 SAN FRANCISCO (96-2)   48.00
3 SMU (92-2)   46.00

1966

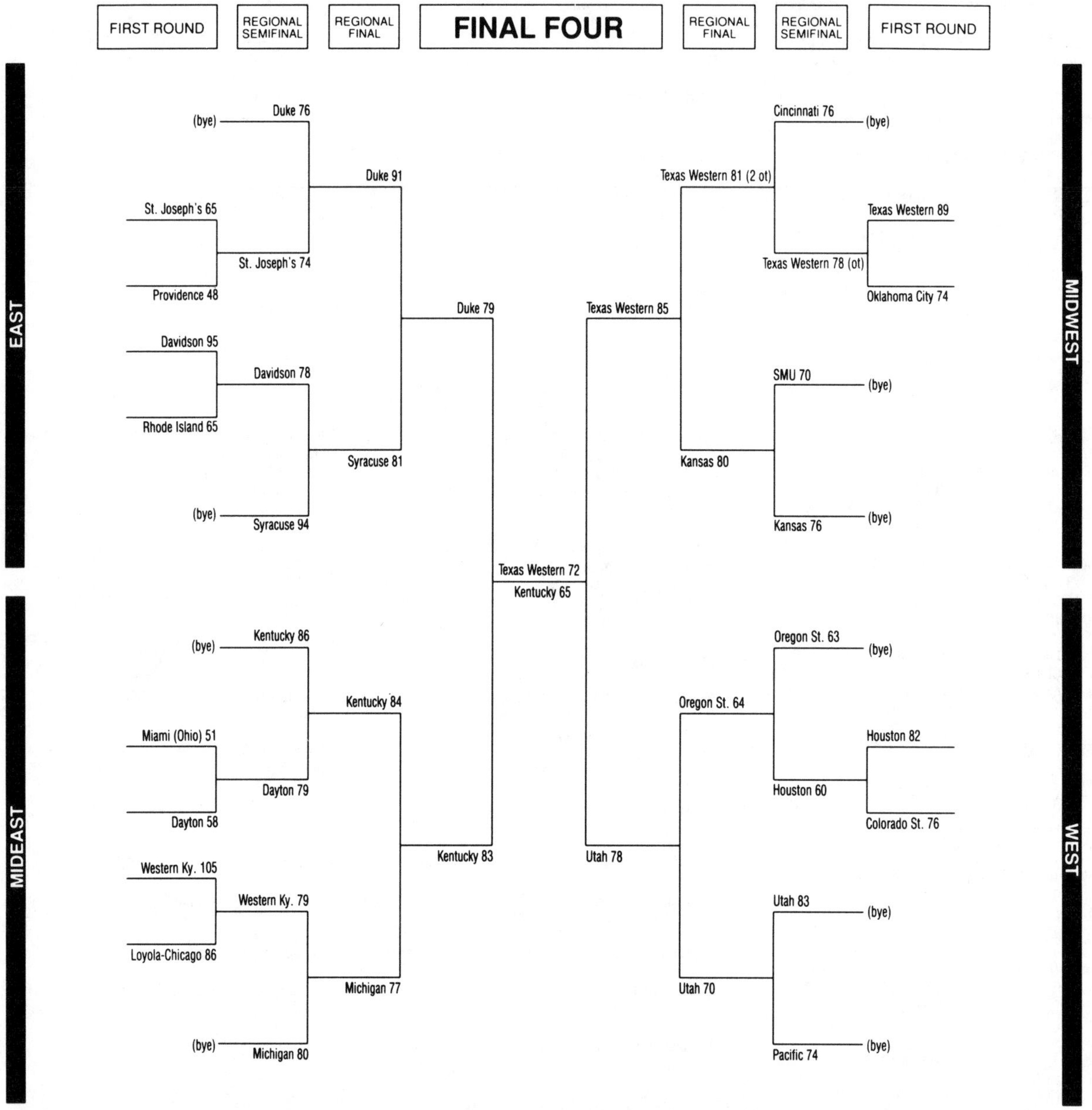

| FIRST ROUND | REGIONAL SEMIFINAL | REGIONAL FINAL | **FINAL FOUR** | REGIONAL FINAL | REGIONAL SEMIFINAL | FIRST ROUND |

EAST

(bye) — Duke 76

Duke 91

St. Joseph's 65

St. Joseph's 74

Providence 48

Duke 79

Davidson 95

Davidson 78

Rhode Island 65

Syracuse 81

(bye) — Syracuse 94

Texas Western 72
Kentucky 65

MIDEAST

(bye) — Kentucky 86

Kentucky 84

Miami (Ohio) 51

Dayton 79

Dayton 58

Kentucky 83

Western Ky. 105

Western Ky. 79

Loyola-Chicago 86

Michigan 77

(bye) — Michigan 80

MIDWEST

Cincinnati 76 — (bye)

Texas Western 81 (2 ot)

Texas Western 89

Texas Western 78 (ot)

Oklahoma City 74

Texas Western 85

SMU 70 — (bye)

Kansas 80

Kansas 76 — (bye)

WEST

Oregon St. 63 — (bye)

Oregon St. 64

Houston 82

Houston 60

Colorado St. 76

Utah 78

Utah 83 — (bye)

Utah 70

Pacific 74 — (bye)

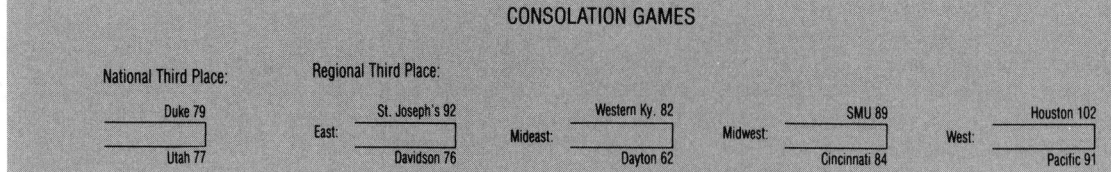

CONSOLATION GAMES

National Third Place:

Duke 79
Utah 77

Regional Third Place:

East:
St. Joseph's 92
Davidson 76

Mideast:
Western Ky. 82
Dayton 62

Midwest:
SMU 89
Cincinnati 84

West:
Houston 102
Pacific 91

They said it couldn't be done. But in 1966 a small college in El Paso, founded as a mining school, gave the no-names of the nation a name—and a national championship.

Even Bobby Joe Hill, the 5-9 sparkplug of the Texas Western Miners, had never heard of the school before its young coach, Don Haskins, recruited him to play there. Haskins, in his fifth year as Miner coach, plucked Hill out of Detroit in a nationwide search for the right combination of players to fit the aggressive, defensive style he had learned as an undergraduate at Oklahoma A&M from the legendary Henry Iba. All of Haskins's top seven players were black, and all but one (Dave Lattin, a native of Houston) came to El Paso from the inner cities of the industrial north—New York, Detroit, and Gary, Indiana. Haskins was remarkably adept at both finding and teaching talented players; he went into the 1966 tournament with a career record of 106-26.

The Miners, according to Haskins, were a team that "wouldn't do more than they had to. This could drive you crazy." And if they drove their coach to distraction, they sent their opponents up the wall. They attacked mercilessly on defense: Their big men threw their weight around while their little men used their quick hands to pick the pockets of opposing guards. One coach respectfully observed that the Miners "don't let you play the way you want to."

In the 1966 NCAAs, the Miners' penchant for close games was enough to keep Haskins awake nights gobbling aspirins for tension headaches. In the first round, Texas Western spotted Oklahoma City and their heralded center James (Weasel) Ware to a 20-9 lead before they got their wake-up call. Led by their own imposing center, David (Big Daddy D) Lattin, the Miners stormed back. Eight minutes later the score was 33-27 Texas Western and the Chiefs never threatened again.

In the regional semis, the rough, tough Miners battled Cincinnati. Forward Nevil (Shadow) Shed even landed a right to a Bearcat jaw (for which he was booted out of the game). Shed's replacement, Willie Cager, scored 6 points in overtime to lead Texas Western to victory.

In the regional final, the powerful Kansas Jayhawks were favored to beat the Miners. Kansas hadn't lost since January and had outscored the opposition by 30 points a game since Jo Jo White became eligible on February 12th. Again the game went down to the wire, with Kansas sending the game into overtime on a last-minute 3-point play. When the game resumed, the Jayhawks' 6-11 All-American, Walt Wesley, and Lattin each scored a basket. With seven seconds remaining Jo Jo White took the ball deep into the corner and hit a 25-footer, apparently giving Kansas the game. But the referee ruled he was out of bounds. Texas Western pulled ahead in a second overtime, finally winning by one, 81-80.

In the national semis, the Miners beat Utah 85-78, but Coach Haskins was unhappy. "Our defense looked bad," he said, no doubt distressed by the 38 points scored by Utah star Jerry Chambers. And he was no happier with the offense. All in all, he considered his team fortunate to have come away with a win. Big Daddy D Lattin and Shadow Shed, on the other hand, both blamed the officials for the relatively close outcome. "The officials called it like a girls' game," said Lattin. "They called baby fouls," contended Shed.

While the Miners were digging their way to a shot at the title, all the experts concluded that the national championship would surely be decided in the semi between No. 1 Kentucky and No. 2 Duke. The Kentucky five, affectionately known in Bluegrass country as "Rupp's Runts," were among the smallest, fastest, and best-shooting squads in the country. Against the taller, excellent shooting Blue Devils, Kentucky Coach Rupp opened in a 1-3-1 zone, but Duke shot over it and the Wildcats were forced to return to a man-to-man.

Both Kentucky starter Larry Conley and Duke's top scorer, Bob Verga, came out of their sick beds to play in the tightly fought game. Verga was totally ineffective, but Conley starred in the Wildcats' late surge. He hit two free throws to give them a 73-71 lead, and then broke away for the clincher with a minute to play.

So it was that the old legend, Baron Adolph Rupp and his No. 1–ranked, tradition-soaked, all-white Kentucky Wildcats went after a record fifth national crown against Don Haskins, a self-described "young punk," and his upstart squad of inner-city blacks from no-name Texas Western.

Don Haskins, after observing the Duke-Kentucky game, reckoned that the Miners would also see Kentucky's 1-3-1 zone. To counter both the zone and the small and speedy Kentucky starting five, he decided to play three guards—5-foot-9 Bobby Joe Hill, 6-1 Orsten Artis, and 5-6 Willie Worsley—along with the 6-7, 245-pound Lattin and forward Harry Fluornoy. Fluornoy was injured early in the game and Haskins replaced him with Nevil Shed and later with Willie Cager. But each of the three guards, including Worsley, who ordinarily came in off the bench, played every minute of the game.

From the start, the Miners showed themselves to be an aggressive, intimidating defensive team, but they were as ineffective offensively as they were effective defensively. After seven minutes, Kentucky led 7-5. A few minutes later, with Texas Western holding a 10-9 lead, Bobby Joe Hill sent an emphatic message to Kentucky. He made a spectacular steal from Wildcat guard Tommy Kron and took it in for an easy lay-up. Ten seconds later, he cleanly picked off a Louie Dampier dribble and broke away for another lay-up and a 14-9 Miner advantage. Kentucky never again took the lead.

Throughout the game, the score remained close, but

every time Kentucky threatened to pull ahead, Texas Western responded with a quick burst. The Wildcats, described by Rupp as "the greatest bunch of shooters I've ever had," fired blanks. They made only 3 of their first 16 shots and finished with a 38.6 shooting percentage. The Texas Western pressure also forced 18 turnovers from the usually sure-handed Wildcats. The final score, 72-65, was hardly a true reflection of the Miner's superiority.

Kentucky's appearance in the final turned out to be Rupp's last shot at the championship; he retired six years later without ever again taking a Wildcat team past the second round. It was also the last time a segregated southern school mounted a serious challenge for the NCAA title. Within the next few years, "white" colleges throughout the south began to actively recruit black players. Kentucky's intrastate rival Louisville already had black players, and in the fall of 1966 black stars arrived as freshmen at both the University of North Carolina and Davidson. Rupp himself integrated his Kentucky team before his retirement.

Meanwhile, the no-name national champions from the school founded as the Texas School of Mines but known (albeit temporarily) as Texas Western had their moment of glory. The next fall, the south Texas school once again became known by a new name, the University of Texas at El Paso, or UTEP. Their young punk of a coach stuck around and eventually joined Kentucky's great Adolph Rupp as one of the most consistently successful coaches in basketball history.

Looking ahead to 1967, when UCLA freshman Lew Alcindor would be promoted to the Bruin varsity, *Sports Illustrated* called 1966 the "Tournament of the Last Chance." How right they were. For a large part of the next decade, UCLA would rule college basketball as no other school ever had. It was indeed the end of an era when anyone—even an unheralded state school from a town along the border—could cross the river and win it all.

FIRST ROUND EAST

St. Joseph's (65)   Coach: Jack Ramsay

	Min.	Total FG/FGA	Pct.	FT/FTA	Pct.	Reb. O/T	A	TO	PF	S	Blk	TP	PPM
ANDERSON, C.	-	4/12	.333	3/7	.429	-/14	1	-	1	-	-	11	-
DUFF, T.	-	7/13	.538	5/5	1.000	-/11	1	-	2	-	-	19	-
FORD, M.	-	1/4	.250	2/3	.667	-/6	0	-	2	-	-	4	-
GUOKAS, M.	-	5/9	.556	1/1	1.000	-/5	1	-	2	-	-	11	-
OAKES, W.	-	7/16	.438	4/5	.800	-/2	1	-	1	-	-	18	-
MCKENNA, C.	-	1/3	.333	0/1	.000	-/3	0	-	1	-	-	2	-
Totals	200	25/57	.439	15/22	.682	-/41	4	-	9	-	-	65	.325

Providence (48)   Coach: Joe Mullaney

	Min.	Total FG/FGA	Pct.	FT/FTA	Pct.	Reb. O/T	A	TO	PF	S	Blk	TP	PPM
BLAIR	-	3/8	.375	3/3	1.000	-/3	1	-	4	-	-	9	-
BENEDICT	-	5/14	.357	0/0	.000	-/4	0	-	2	-	-	10	-
WALKER	-	8/16	.500	3/6	.500	-/6	2	-	4	-	-	19	-
LASHER	-	2/8	.250	0/0	.000	-/6	0	-	1	-	-	4	-
RIORDAN	-	2/7	.286	2/3	.667	-/10	4	-	4	-	-	6	-
MCLAUGHLIN	-	0/1	.000	0/0	.000	-/0	0	-	0	-	-	0	-
Totals	200	20/54	.370	8/12	.667	-/29	7	-	15	-	-	48	.240

Team Rebounds: St. Joseph's 4; Providence 3. Disqualified: None.

	1st Half	2nd Half	Final
St. Joseph's	31	34	65
Providence	29	19	48

Davidson (95)   Coach: Lefty Driesell

	Min.	Total FG/FGA	Pct.	FT/FTA	Pct.	Reb. O/T	A	TO	PF	S	Blk	TP	PPM
SNYDER, D.	-	3/6	.500	5/5	1.000	-/5	-	-	4	-	-	11	-
SQUIER, P.	-	1/5	.200	0/1	.000	-/4	-	-	1	-	-	2	-
KNOWLES, R.	-	15/27	.556	9/11	.818	-/20	-	-	3	-	-	39	-
LANE, B.	-	7/14	.500	2/3	.667	-/4	-	-	2	-	-	16	-
YOUNGDALE, T.	-	5/8	.625	1/2	.500	-/8	-	-	4	-	-	11	-
HATCHER, S.	-	4/6	.667	1/2	.500	-/5	-	-	1	-	-	9	-
LEIGHT, G.	-	1/3	.333	1/2	.500	-/4	-	-	1	-	-	3	-
STONE, R.	-	2/4	.500	0/0	.000	-/1	-	-	0	-	-	4	-
HYDER	-	0/0	.000	0/0	.000	-/1	-	-	0	-	-	0	-
CLIFTON, C.	-	0/0	.000	0/0	.000	-/0	-	-	0	-	-	0	-
Totals	200	38/73	.521	19/26	.731	-/52	-	-	16	-	-	95	.475

Rhode Island (65)   Coach: Ernie Calverley

	Min.	Total FG/FGA	Pct.	FT/FTA	Pct.	Reb. O/T	A	TO	PF	S	Blk	TP	PPM
STEPHENSON	-	1/6	.167	1/2	.500	-/4	-	-	4	-	-	3	-
FITZGERALD	-	4/10	.400	2/2	1.000	-/6	-	-	3	-	-	10	-
CHUBIN	-	5/20	.250	13/14	.929	-/10	-	-	3	-	-	23	-
CAREY	-	3/13	.231	0/0	.000	-/2	-	-	1	-	-	6	-
CYMBALE	-	8/14	.571	3/4	.750	-/3	-	-	2	-	-	19	-
BOEHM	-	1/4	.250	0/0	.000	-/1	-	-	5	-	-	2	-
JOHNSON	-	1/3	.333	0/1	.000	-/2	-	-	2	-	-	2	-
GRANAT	-	0/1	.000	0/0	.000	-/0	-	-	0	-	-	0	-
Totals	200	23/71	.324	19/23	.826	-/28	-	-	20	-	-	65	.325

Team Rebounds: Davidson 7; Rhode Island 7. Disqualified: Rhode Island—Boehm.

	1st Half	2nd Half	Final
Davidson	37	58	95
Rhode Island	28	37	65

FIRST ROUND MIDEAST

Miami (Ohio) (51)   Coach: Dick Shrider

	Min.	Total FG/FGA	Pct.	FT/FTA	Pct.	Reb. O/T	A	TO	PF	S	Blk	TP	PPM
PEIRSON	-	4/7	.571	1/2	.500	-/4	-	-	4	-	-	9	-
CHAMBERLAIN	-	2/4	.500	1/2	.500	-/2	-	-	2	-	-	5	-
PATTERSON	-	1/2	.500	2/2	1.000	-/3	-	-	5	-	-	4	-
FISHER	-	2/4	.500	1/2	.500	-/6	-	-	1	-	-	5	-
SNOW, P.	-	8/17	.471	2/2	1.000	-/2	-	-	1	-	-	18	-
HALLIHAN	-	1/1	1.000	1/3	.333	-/0	-	-	0	-	-	3	-
FOSTER	-	1/4	.250	0/1	.000	-/0	-	-	1	-	-	2	-
LUKACS	-	0/1	.000	1/1	1.000	-/0	-	-	0	-	-	1	-
JACKSON	-	2/2	1.000	0/0	.000	-/2	-	-	0	-	-	4	-
Totals	200	21/42	.500	9/15	.600	-/19	-	-	14	-	-	51	.255

Dayton (58)   Coach: Don Donoher

	Min.	Total FG/FGA	Pct.	FT/FTA	Pct.	Reb. O/T	A	TO	PF	S	Blk	TP	PPM
MAY, S.	-	3/11	.273	6/7	.857	-/7	-	-	1	-	-	12	-
TORAIN, G.	-	2/6	.333	0/0	.000	-/6	-	-	2	-	-	4	-
FINKEL, H.	-	9/15	.600	7/7	1.000	-/17	-	-	4	-	-	25	-
WATERMAN, R.	-	5/16	.313	3/5	.600	-/4	-	-	3	-	-	13	-
HOOPER, B.	-	1/2	.500	2/2	1.000	-/3	-	-	3	-	-	4	-
KLAUS, G.	-	0/0	.000	0/0	.000	-/1	-	-	0	-	-	0	-
Totals	200	20/50	.400	18/21	.857	-/38	-	-	13	-	-	58	.290

Team Rebounds: Dayton 3; Miami (Ohio) 0. Disqualified: Miami (Ohio)—Patterson.

	1st Half	2nd Half	Final
Miami (Ohio)	25	26	51
Dayton	32	26	58

Western Kentucky (105)   Coach: Johnny Oldham

	Min.	Total FG/FGA	Pct.	FT/FTA	Pct.	Reb. O/T	A	TO	PF	S	Blk	TP	PPM
SMITH, D.	-	12/21	.571	5/6	.833	-/5	0	-	3	-	-	29	-
SMITH, G.	-	9/14	.643	1/1	1.000	-/15	0	-	4	-	-	19	-
HASKINS, C.	-	11/17	.647	3/5	.600	-/9	4	-	2	-	-	25	-
CUNNINGHAM, C.	-	7/14	.500	2/2	1.000	-/8	0	-	4	-	-	16	-
CHAPMAN, W.	-	2/6	.333	2/2	1.000	-/5	1	-	4	-	-	6	-
KAUFMAN, B.	-	4/8	.500	2/3	.667	-/1	0	-	0	-	-	10	-
BUTLER, J.	-	0/1	.000	0/1	.000	-/0	0	-	0	-	-	0	-
Totals	200	45/81	.556	15/20	.750	-/43	5	-	17	-	-	105	.525

Loyola-Chicago (86)   Coach: George Ireland

	Min.	Total FG/FGA	Pct.	FT/FTA	Pct.	Reb. O/T	A	TO	PF	S	Blk	TP	PPM
WARDLAW	-	9/18	.500	2/3	.667	-/5	-	-	4	-	-	20	-
COLEMAN, J.	-	5/14	.357	0/0	.000	-/10	-	-	4	-	-	10	-
BELL, C.	-	9/22	.409	6/8	.750	-/6	-	-	4	-	-	24	-
PEREZ, F.	-	1/2	.500	1/2	.500	-/0	-	-	0	-	-	3	-
TILLMAN	-	1/4	.250	1/2	.500	-/3	-	-	2	-	-	3	-
MANZKE	-	0/0	.000	0/0	.000	-/0	-	-	0	-	-	0	-
HOGAN	-	0/0	.000	0/0	.000	-/0	-	-	0	-	-	0	-
SMITH, B.	-	8/11	.727	9/9	1.000	-/16	-	-	3	-	-	25	-
BUKOVSKY	-	0/0	.000	0/0	.000	-/0	-	-	0	-	-	0	-
Totals	200	33/71	.465	20/24	.833	-/40	-	-	17	-	-	86	.430

Team Rebounds: Western Ky 0; Loyola-Chicago 0. Disqualified: None.

	1st Half	2nd Half	Final
Western Ky.	49	56	105
Loyola-Chicago	43	43	86

FIRST ROUND MIDWEST

Texas Western (89)   Coach: Don Haskins

	Min.	Total FG/FGA	Pct.	FT/FTA	Pct.	Reb. O/T	A	TO	PF	S	Blk	TP	PPM
HILL	-	8/18	.444	8/14	.571	-/4	-	-	3	-	-	24	-
LATTIN	-	8/15	.533	4/5	.800	-/15	-	-	3	-	-	20	-
ARTIS	-	5/14	.357	4/4	1.000	-/7	-	-	1	-	-	14	-
WORSLEY	-	4/7	.571	6/8	.750	-/2	-	-	3	-	-	14	-
FLOURNOY	-	4/7	.571	1/3	.333	-/7	-	-	5	-	-	9	-
SHED	-	2/4	.500	0/0	.000	-/6	-	-	4	-	-	4	-
ARMSTRONG	-	0/1	.000	0/0	.000	-/0	-	-	0	-	-	0	-
MYERS	-	0/0	.000	0/0	.000	-/0	-	-	1	-	-	0	-
CAGER	-	1/3	.333	2/4	.500	-/6	-	-	4	-	-	4	-
Totals	200	32/69	.464	25/38	.658	-/47	-	-	24	-	-	89	.445

Oklahoma City (74)   Coach: Abe Lemons

	Min.	Total FG/FGA	Pct.	FT/FTA	Pct.	Reb. O/T	A	TO	PF	S	Blk	TP	PPM
HUNTER	-	9/15	.600	3/4	.750	-/6	-	-	5	-	-	21	-
WELLS	-	7/19	.368	4/7	.571	-/0	-	-	5	-	-	18	-
GRAY	-	4/10	.400	3/3	1.000	-/0	-	-	5	-	-	11	-
WARE	-	3/7	.429	4/5	.800	-/12	-	-	5	-	-	10	-
LAWRENCE	-	1/2	.500	7/7	1.000	-/1	-	-	2	-	-	9	-
KOPER, R.	-	1/1	1.000	0/0	.000	-/2	-	-	2	-	-	2	-
O'BRIEN	-	1/2	.500	0/0	.000	-/4	-	-	2	-	-	2	-
KOPER, B.	-	0/3	.000	1/1	1.000	-/1	-	-	1	-	-	1	-
BOLEN	-	0/0	.000	0/0	.000	-/0	-	-	1	-	-	0	-
Totals	200	26/59	.441	22/27	.815	-/26	-	-	28	-	-	74	.370

Team Rebounds: Texas Western 8; Oklahoma City 6. Disqualified: Texas Western—Flournoy; Oklahoma City—Hunter, Wells, Gray, Ware.

	1st Half	2nd Half	Final
Texas Western	43	46	89
Oklahoma City	37	37	74

FIRST ROUND WEST

Houston (82)   Coach: Guy Lewis

	Min.	Total FG/FGA	Pct.	FT/FTA	Pct.	Reb. O/T	A	TO	PF	S	Blk	TP	PPM
BALLARD	30	4/7	.571	5/5	1.000	2/3	2	-	1	-	-	13	.433
HAMOOD, J.	40	9/17	.529	5/7	.714	1/1	9	-	1	-	-	23	.575
HAYES, E.	36	8/15	.533	2/5	.400	4/12	0	-	5	-	-	18	.500
LENTZ, L.	26	3/11	.273	3/4	.750	5/6	0	-	2	-	-	9	.346
GRIDER, B.	14	2/2	1.000	0/1	.000	0/3	2	-	0	-	-	4	.286
KRUSE, D.	17	4/9	.444	0/0	.000	1/5	1	-	1	-	-	8	.471
CHANEY, D.	36	3/12	.250	1/2	.500	6/11	2	-	1	-	-	7	.194
APOLSKIS	1	0/1	.000	0/3	.000	2/2	0	-	0	-	-	0	.000
Totals	200	33/74	.452	16/27	.593	21/43	16	12	11	-	-	82	.410

Colorado State (76)   Coach: Jim Williams

	Min.	Total FG/FGA	Pct.	FT/FTA	Pct.	Reb. O/T	A	TO	PF	S	Blk	TP	PPM
VIDAKOVICH, T.	-	7/12	.583	0/0	.000	2/5	6	-	4	-	-	14	-
WRIGHT, L.	-	8/16	.500	1/2	.500	1/6	2	-	4	-	-	17	-
RULE, B.	-	7/18	.389	4/6	.667	3/7	5	-	5	-	-	18	-
SCHLUETER, D.	-	3/7	.429	4/5	.800	3/19	1	-	4	-	-	10	-
FINES, R.	-	5/6	.833	1/1	1.000	1/1	5	-	4	-	-	11	-
GREEN, D.	-	1/2	.500	0/0	.000	0/0	0	-	0	-	-	2	-
GOOD, M.	-	1/2	.500	0/0	.000	0/2	2	-	0	-	-	2	-
MONTEL, G.	-	1/5	.200	0/0	.000	1/1	0	-	0	-	-	2	-
ROBINSON	-	0/0	.000	0/0	.000	0/0	1	-	0	-	-	0	-
Totals	200	33/68	.485	10/14	.714	11/41	22	16	21	-	-	76	.380

Team Rebounds: Houston 4; Colorado State 2. Disqualified: Houston—Hayes; Colorado State—Rule.

	1st Half	2nd Half	Final
Houston	44	38	82
Colorado State	35	41	76

REGIONAL SEMIFINAL EAST

Duke (76)   Coach: Vic Bubas

	Min.	Total FG/FGA	Pct.	FT/FTA	Pct.	Reb. O/T	A	TO	PF	S	Blk	TP	PPM
VERGA, B.	-	8/17	.471	6/6	1.000	-/4	0	-	1	-	-	22	-
REIDY, B.	-	1/5	.200	3/5	.600	-/5	1	-	3	-	-	5	-
MARIN, J.	-	6/16	.375	6/8	.750	-/15	0	-	2	-	-	18	-
VACENDAK, S.	-	6/14	.429	1/2	.500	-/7	2	-	2	-	-	13	-
LEWIS, M.	-	6/12	.500	2/2	1.000	-/15	0	-	4	-	-	14	-
CHAPMAN, W.	-	1/3	.333	2/3	.667	-/5	0	-	4	-	-	4	-
WENDELIN, R.	-	0/0	.000	0/0	.000	-/0	0	-	1	-	-	0	-
Totals	200	28/67	.418	20/26	.769	-/51	3	-	17	-	-	76	.380

St. Joseph's (74)   Coach: Jack Ramsay

	Min.	Total FG/FGA	Pct.	FT/FTA	Pct.	Reb. O/T	A	TO	PF	S	Blk	TP	PPM
OAKES, W.	-	4/18	.222	0/0	.000	-/1	0	-	1	-	-	8	-
FORD, M.	-	2/5	.400	2/4	.500	-/6	0	-	1	-	-	6	-
GUOKAS, M.	-	7/15	.467	5/5	1.000	-/4	2	-	5	-	-	19	-
ANDERSON, C.	-	6/15	.400	8/10	.800	-/15	1	-	4	-	-	20	-
DUFF, T.	-	7/22	.318	3/5	.600	-/8	1	-	3	-	-	17	-
MCKENNA, C.	-	1/8	.125	2/2	1.000	-/13	0	-	3	-	-	4	-
CHAPMAN, S.	-	0/1	.000	0/0	.000	-/0	0	-	0	-	-	0	-
Totals	200	27/84	.321	20/26	.769	-/47	4	-	17	-	-	74	.370

Team Rebounds: Duke 5; St. Joseph's 0. Disqualified: St. Joseph's—Guokas.

	1st Half	2nd Half	Final
Duke	37	39	76
St. Joseph's	33	41	74

Davidson (78) Coach: Lefty Driesell

	Min.	Total FG/FGA	Pct.	FT/FTA	Pct.	Reb. O/T	A	TO	PF	S	Blk	TP	PPM
SNYDER, D.	-	9/22	.409	7/9	.778	-/8	-	-	4	-	-	25	-
YOUNGDALE, T.	-	3/9	.333	4/6	.667	-/9	-	-	5	-	-	10	-
LANE, B.	-	1/7	.143	3/3	1.000	-/3	-	-	3	-	-	5	-
SQUIER, P.	-	2/11	.182	1/1	1.000	-/3	-	-	1	-	-	5	-
KNOWLES, R.	-	9/24	.375	7/9	.778	-/11	-	-	3	-	-	25	-
LEIGHT, G.	-	1/4	.250	0/1	.000	-/4	-	-	1	-	-	2	-
HATCHER, S.	-	2/4	.500	2/4	.500	-/5	-	-	1	-	-	6	-
Totals	200	27/81	.333	24/33	.727	-/43	-	-	18	-	-	78	.390

Syracuse (94) Coach: Fred Lewis

	Min.	Total FG/FGA	Pct.	FT/FTA	Pct.	Reb. O/T	A	TO	PF	S	Blk	TP	PPM
PENCEAL, S.	-	4/5	.800	0/1	.000	-/0	-	-	0	-	-	8	-
BING, D.	-	9/20	.450	2/2	1.000	-/12	-	-	2	-	-	20	-
BOEHEIM, J.	-	7/9	.778	0/0	.000	-/3	-	-	3	-	-	14	-
HARPER, V.	-	0/2	.000	1/2	.500	-/2	-	-	4	-	-	1	-
DEAN, R.	-	5/13	.385	2/2	1.000	-/12	-	-	4	-	-	12	-
HICKEY, G.	-	9/14	.643	4/6	.667	-/8	-	-	2	-	-	22	-
CORNWALL, R.	-	4/7	.571	1/1	1.000	-/3	-	-	1	-	-	9	-
GOLDSMITH, N.	-	2/4	.500	0/0	.000	-/2	-	-	3	-	-	4	-
NICOLETTI, F.	-	0/0	.000	0/0	.000	-/3	-	-	2	-	-	0	-
REID	-	1/3	.333	0/3	.000	-/5	-	-	1	-	-	2	-
ABLEMAN	-	0/1	.000	0/0	.000	-/0	-	-	1	-	-	0	-
TROBRIDGE	-	0/1	.000	2/2	1.000	-/2	-	-	2	-	-	2	-
Totals	200	41/79	.519	12/19	.632	-/52	-	-	25	-	-	94	.470

Team Rebounds: Syracuse 7; Davidson 6. Disqualified: Davidson—Youngdale.

	1st Half	2nd Half	Final
Davidson	27	51	78
Syracuse	43	51	94

REGIONAL SEMIFINAL MIDEAST

Kentucky (86) Coach: Adolph Rupp

	Min.	Total FG/FGA	Pct.	FT/FTA	Pct.	Reb. O/T	A	TO	PF	S	Blk	TP	PPM
DAMPIER, L.	-	14/23	.609	6/7	.857	-/6	-	-	1	-	-	34	-
KRON, T.	-	1/6	.167	1/1	1.000	-/6	-	-	3	-	-	3	-
CONLEY, L.	-	0/5	.000	1/1	1.000	-/3	-	-	1	-	-	1	-
RILEY, P.	-	11/18	.611	7/8	.875	-/8	-	-	3	-	-	29	-
JARACZ, T.	-	7/9	.778	3/3	1.000	-/7	-	-	3	-	-	17	-
LEMASTER, J.	-	0/2	.000	0/0	.000	-/1	-	-	0	-	-	0	-
BERGER, C.	-	1/3	.333	0/0	.000	-/0	-	-	4	-	-	2	-
Totals	200	34/66	.515	18/20	.900	-/31	-	-	15	-	-	86	.430

Western Kentucky (79) Coach: Johnny Oldham

	Min.	Total FG/FGA	Pct.	FT/FTA	Pct.	Reb. O/T	A	TO	PF	S	Blk	TP	PPM
SMITH, D.	-	3/10	.300	1/2	.500	-/2	0	-	5	-	-	7	-
SMITH, G.	-	4/11	.364	1/3	.333	-/13	0	-	4	-	-	9	-
HASKINS, C.	-	5/16	.313	5/7	.714	-/12	4	-	3	-	-	15	-
CUNNINGHAM, C.	-	11/21	.524	2/4	.500	-/6	0	-	0	-	-	24	-
CHAPMAN, W.	-	11/23	.478	0/1	.000	-/6	3	-	4	-	-	22	-
KAUFMAN, B.	-	1/2	.500	0/0	.000	-/0	0	-	0	-	-	2	-
Totals	200	35/83	.479	9/17	.529	-/39	7	-	16	-	-	79	.395

Michigan (80) Coach: Dave Strack

	Min.	Total FG/FGA	Pct.	FT/FTA	Pct.	Reb. O/T	A	TO	PF	S	Blk	TP	PPM
THOMPSON, J.	-	4/9	.444	0/0	.000	-/5	-	-	3	-	-	8	-
RUSSELL, C.	-	7/15	.467	10/12	.833	-/6	-	-	3	-	-	24	-
CLAWSON, J.	-	8/12	.667	2/2	1.000	-/2	-	-	2	-	-	18	-
MYERS, J.	-	4/15	.267	2/3	.667	-/10	-	-	3	-	-	10	-
DARDEN, O.	-	7/16	.438	4/5	.800	-/12	-	-	1	-	-	18	-
BANKEY, D.	-	0/0	.000	0/0	.000	-/0	-	-	0	-	-	0	-
DILL, C.	-	1/2	.500	0/0	.000	-/1	-	-	1	-	-	2	-
Totals	200	31/69	.449	18/22	.818	-/36	-	-	13	-	-	80	.400

Team Rebounds: Michigan 7; Western Ky. 5. Disqualified: Western Ky.—D. Smith.

	1st Half	2nd Half	Final
Western Ky.	47	32	79
Michigan	41	39	80

Dayton (79) Coach: Don Donoher

	Min.	Total FG/FGA	Pct.	FT/FTA	Pct.	Reb. O/T	A	TO	PF	S	Blk	TP	PPM
FINKEL, H.	-	15/26	.577	6/7	.857	-/13	-	-	4	-	-	36	-
MAY, D.	-	6/16	.375	4/5	.800	-/3	-	-	3	-	-	16	-
WATERMAN, R.	-	6/13	.462	2/4	.500	-/9	-	-	3	-	-	14	-
HOOPER, B.	-	2/7	.286	1/2	.500	-/7	-	-	3	-	-	5	-
TORAIN, G.	-	2/10	.200	2/2	1.000	-/4	-	-	3	-	-	6	-
KLAUS, G.	-	1/1	1.000	0/0	.000	-/0	-	-	1	-	-	2	-
CASSIDY, B.	-	0/0	.000	0/0	.000	-/0	-	-	0	-	-	0	-
Totals	200	32/73	.438	15/20	.750	-/36	-	-	17	-	-	79	.395

Team Rebounds: Kentucky 3; Dayton 2. Disqualified: None.

	1st Half	2nd Half	Final
Kentucky	38	48	86
Dayton	40	39	79

REGIONAL SEMIFINAL MIDWEST

Cincinnati (76) Coach: Tay Baker

	Min.	Total FG/FGA	Pct.	FT/FTA	Pct.	Reb. O/T	A	TO	PF	S	Blk	TP	PPM
ROLFES, D.	-	3/9	.333	4/6	.667	-/4	1	-	2	-	-	10	-
HOWARD, J.	-	1/9	.111	3/3	1.000	-/6	4	-	4	-	-	5	-
KRICK, R.	-	9/12	.750	0/0	.000	-/9	0	-	4	-	-	18	-
WEST, R.	-	7/12	.583	5/6	.833	-/11	0	-	5	-	-	19	-
FOSTER, D.	-	5/9	.556	1/2	.500	-/2	6	-	2	-	-	11	-
ROLF, M.	-	4/8	.500	1/1	1.000	-/7	0	-	1	-	-	9	-
CALLOWAY, K.	-	2/3	.667	0/0	.000	-/1	0	-	0	-	-	4	-
WEIDNER, P.	-	0/0	.000	0/0	.000	-/1	0	-	0	-	-	0	-
Totals	225	31/62	.500	14/18	.778	-/41	11	-	18	-	-	76	.338

Texas Western (78) Coach: Don Haskins

	Min.	Total FG/FGA	Pct.	FT/FTA	Pct.	Reb. O/T	A	TO	PF	S	Blk	TP	PPM
FLOURNOY, H.	-	1/5	.200	0/0	.000	-/7	0	-	2	-	-	2	-
LATTIN, D.	-	10/15	.667	9/10	.900	-/8	0	-	3	-	-	29	-
HILL, B.	-	7/18	.389	3/6	.500	-/5	1	-	1	-	-	17	-
ARTIS, O.	-	4/8	.500	3/3	1.000	-/1	1	-	4	-	-	11	-
CAGER, W.	-	5/5	1.000	5/6	.833	-/2	0	-	2	-	-	15	-
WORSLEY, W.	-	1/10	.100	2/2	1.000	-/2	3	-	3	-	-	4	-
SHED, N.	-	0/2	.000	0/0	.000	-/2	0	-	0	-	-	0	-
Totals	225	28/63	.000	22/27	.815	-/27	5	-	15	-	-	78	.347

Team Rebounds: Texas Western 5; Cincinnati 2. Disqualified: Cincinnati—West.

	1st Half	2nd Half	1st OT	Final
Cincinnati	42	27	7	76
Texas Western	36	33	9	78

SMU (70)   Coach: E. O. "Doc" Hayes

	Min.	Total FG/FGA	Pct.	FT/FTA	Pct.	Reb. O/T	A	TO	PF	S	Blk	TP	PPM
BEGERT, B.	-	4/10	.400	4/7	.571	-/9	-	-	4	-	-	12	-
BEASLEY, C.	-	5/13	.385	7/9	.778	-/9	-	-	2	-	-	17	-
HOOSER, C.	-	10/20	.500	2/4	.500	-/7	-	-	4	-	-	22	-
HOLMAN, D.	-	3/8	.375	0/1	.000	-/10	-	-	1	-	-	6	-
JONES, B.	-	2/3	.667	0/0	.000	-/0	-	-	1	-	-	4	-
RAMSAY, J.	-	2/5	.400	1/1	1.000	-/3	-	-	2	-	-	5	-
HIGGENBOTHAM, J.	-	1/2	.500	2/2	1.000	-/1	-	-	0	-	-	4	-
Totals	200	27/61	.443	16/24	.667	-/39	-	-	14	-	-	70	.350

Kansas (76)   Coach: Ted Owens

	Min.	Total FG/FGA	Pct.	FT/FTA	Pct.	Reb. O/T	A	TO	PF	S	Blk	TP	PPM
FRANZ, R.	-	9/15	.600	1/2	.500	-/5	-	-	5	-	-	19	-
LOPES, A.	-	4/10	.400	3/3	1.000	-/5	-	-	5	-	-	11	-
WESLEY, W.	-	9/17	.529	5/8	.625	-/12	-	-	2	-	-	23	-
WHITE, J.	-	4/17	.235	2/2	1.000	-/7	-	-	4	-	-	10	-
LEWIS, D.	-	4/12	.333	1/1	1.000	-/7	-	-	1	-	-	9	-
BOHNENSTIEHL, R.	-	1/6	.167	0/0	.000	-/7	-	-	1	-	-	2	-
LOCHMANN, R.	-	1/4	.250	0/1	.000	-/6	-	-	2	-	-	2	-
Totals	200	32/81	.395	12/17	.706	-/49	-	-	20	-	-	76	.380

Team Rebounds: Kansas 4; SMU 4. Disqualified: Kansas—Franz, Lopes.

	1st Half	2nd Half	Final
SMU	46	24	70
Kansas	46	30	76

REGIONAL SEMIFINAL WEST

Oregon State (63)   Coach: Paul Valenti

	Min.	Total FG/FGA	Pct.	FT/FTA	Pct.	Reb. O/T	A	TO	PF	S	Blk	TP	PPM
PETERSEN	-	6/8	.750	1/2	.500	-/10	-	-	5	-	-	13	-
EATON	-	2/5	.400	2/2	1.000	-/1	-	-	1	-	-	6	-
FREDENBURG, E.	-	3/6	.500	4/7	.571	-/5	-	-	2	-	-	10	-
WHITE	-	4/9	.444	2/4	.500	-/8	-	-	1	-	-	10	-
WHELAN	-	11/14	.786	2/5	.400	-/6	-	-	3	-	-	24	-
GUNNER	-	0/0	.000	0/0	.000	-/2	-	-	2	-	-	0	-
Totals	200	26/42	.619	11/20	.550	-/32	-	-	14	-	-	63	.315

Houston (60)   Coach: Guy Lewis

	Min.	Total FG/FGA	Pct.	FT/FTA	Pct.	Reb. O/T	A	TO	PF	S	Blk	TP	PPM
BALLARD	20	1/8	.125	0/0	.000	-/2	1	-	1	-	-	2	.100
HAMOOD, J.	40	6/18	.333	6/8	.750	-/4	3	-	3	-	-	18	.450
HAYES, E.	40	6/13	.462	2/4	.500	-/10	0	-	4	-	-	14	.350
LENTZ, L.	20	1/7	.143	1/1	1.000	-/3	1	-	2	-	-	3	.150
GRIDER, B.	20	2/5	.400	2/2	1.000	-/6	2	-	2	-	-	6	.300
KRUSE, D.	17	4/10	.400	0/2	.000	-/2	1	-	2	-	-	8	.471
CHANEY, D.	34	2/8	.250	2/2	1.000	-/9	1	-	3	-	-	6	.176
APOLSKIS	9	0/1	.000	3/3	1.000	-/1	1	-	2	-	-	3	.333
Totals	200	22/70	.314	16/22	.727	-/37	10	-	19	-	-	60	.300

Utah (83)   Coach: Jack Gardner

	Min.	Total FG/FGA	Pct.	FT/FTA	Pct.	Reb. O/T	A	TO	PF	S	Blk	TP	PPM
MACKAY	-	4/8	.500	2/5	.400	-/9	-	-	3	-	-	10	-
CHAMBERS, J.	-	17/30	.567	6/8	.750	-/11	-	-	1	-	-	40	-
OCKEL, J.	-	3/6	.500	4/7	.571	-/10	-	-	4	-	-	10	-
TATE, R.	-	3/12	.250	1/3	.333	-/9	-	-	1	-	-	7	-
JACKSON	-	5/9	.556	0/2	.000	-/4	-	-	4	-	-	10	-
BLACK	-	1/3	.333	0/0	.000	-/1	-	-	0	-	-	2	-
LAKE	-	1/4	.250	2/2	1.000	-/1	-	-	1	-	-	4	-
Totals	200	34/72	.472	15/27	.556	-/45	-	-	14	-	-	83	.415

Pacific (74)   Coach: Dick Edwards

	Min.	Total FG/FGA	Pct.	FT/FTA	Pct.	Reb. O/T	A	TO	PF	S	Blk	TP	PPM
ODALE, D.	-	3/9	.333	1/2	.500	-/4	-	-	3	-	-	7	-
KRULISH, B.	-	8/18	.444	3/4	.750	-/10	-	-	5	-	-	19	-
SWAGERTY, K.	-	6/22	.273	4/6	.667	-/19	-	-	3	-	-	16	-
FOX, D.	-	5/16	.313	1/2	.500	-/6	-	-	4	-	-	11	-
PARSONS, B.	-	7/13	.538	3/5	.600	-/9	-	-	3	-	-	17	-
GILBERT, A.	-	0/0	.000	0/0	.000	-/0	-	-	1	-	-	0	-
SELIM, R.	-	2/4	.500	0/0	.000	-/1	-	-	0	-	-	4	-
Totals	200	31/82	.378	12/19	.632	-/49	-	-	19	-	-	74	.370

Team Rebounds: Oregon State 3; Houston 7. Disqualified: Oregon State—Petersen.

Team Rebounds: Utah 7; Pacific 7. Disqualified: Pacific—Krulish.

	1st Half	2nd Half	Final
Oregon State	28	35	63
Houston	30	30	60

	1st Half	2nd Half	Final
Utah	49	34	83
Pacific	41	33	74

REGIONAL FINAL EAST

Duke (91)   Coach: Vic Bubas

	Min.	Total FG/FGA	Pct.	FT/FTA	Pct.	Reb. O/T	A	TO	PF	S	Blk	TP	PPM
VERGA, B.	40	10/13	.769	1/3	.333	-/1	1	4	2	-	-	21	.525
RIEDY, B.	30	3/6	.500	6/8	.750	-/10	1	1	4	-	-	12	.400
MARIN, J.	40	7/14	.500	8/10	.800	-/9	1	2	1	-	-	22	.550
VACENDAK, S.	40	7/15	.467	5/7	.714	-/3	3	6	3	-	-	19	.475
LEWIS, M.	31	4/10	.400	8/8	1.000	-/13	0	3	3	-	-	16	.516
CHAPMAN, W.	10	0/0	.000	1/1	1.000	-/2	0	0	2	-	-	1	.100
LICCARDO, T.	9	0/2	.000	0/0	.000	-/0	0	0	0	-	-	0	.000
Totals	200	31/60	.517	29/37	.784	-/38	6	16	15	-	-	91	.455

Syracuse (81)   Coach: Fred Lewis

	Min.	Total FG/FGA	Pct.	FT/FTA	Pct.	Reb. O/T	A	TO	PF	S	Blk	TP	PPM
PENCEAL, S.	6	0/1	.000	0/0	.000	-/0	0	1	0	-	-	0	.000
BING, D.	36	4/14	.286	2/2	1.000	-/8	3	6	4	-	-	10	.278
BOEHEIM, J.	34	6/10	.600	3/4	.750	-/1	1	1	3	-	-	15	.441
HARPER, V.	33	5/12	.417	3/3	1.000	-/10	3	2	5	-	-	13	.394
DEAN, R.	39	4/8	.500	8/9	.889	-/7	1	1	4	-	-	16	.410
HICKEY, G.	30	7/20	.350	3/3	1.000	-/7	0	1	4	-	-	17	.567
CORNWALL, R.	18	5/10	.500	0/0	.000	-/1	1	2	1	-	-	10	.556
GOLDSMITH, N.	3	0/0	.000	0/0	.000	-/0	0	0	0	-	-	0	.000
NICOLETTI, F.	1	0/0	.000	0/0	.000	-/0	0	0	2	-	-	0	.000
Totals	200	31/75	.413	19/21	.905	-/34	9	14	23	-	-	81	.405

Team Rebounds: Duke 5; Syracuse 6. Disqualified: Syracuse—Harper.

	1st Half	2nd Half	Final
Duke	44	47	91
Syracuse	37	44	81

REGIONAL FINAL MIDEAST

Kentucky (84) Coach: Adolph Rupp

	Min.	Total FG/FGA	Pct.	FT/FTA	Pct.	Reb. O/T	A	TO	PF	S	Blk	TP	PPM
DAMPIER, L.	-	6/12	.500	3/4	.750	-/6	-	-	3	-	-	15	-
KRON, T.	-	6/14	.429	2/5	.400	-/9	-	-	4	-	-	14	-
CONLEY, L.	-	6/11	.545	2/6	.333	-/8	-	-	4	-	-	14	-
RILEY, P.	-	13/27	.481	3/4	.750	-/5	-	-	2	-	-	29	-
JARACZ, T.	-	6/8	.750	0/0	.000	-/7	-	-	2	-	-	12	-
PORTER, T.	-	0/0	.000	0/0	.000	-/0	-	-	0	-	-	0	-
Totals	200	37/72	.514	10/19	.526	-/35	-	-	15	-	-	84	.420

Michigan (77) Coach: Dave Strack

	Min.	Total FG/FGA	Pct.	FT/FTA	Pct.	Reb. O/T	A	TO	PF	S	Blk	TP	PPM
THOMPSON, J.	-	2/6	.333	2/4	.500	-/3	-	-	2	-	-	6	-
RUSSELL, C.	-	10/25	.400	9/9	1.000	-/11	-	-	2	-	-	29	-
CLAWSON, J.	-	5/14	.357	1/2	.500	-/5	-	-	3	-	-	11	-
MYERS, J.	-	5/19	.263	0/0	.000	-/11	-	-	3	-	-	10	-
DARDEN, O.	-	8/16	.500	1/3	.333	-/12	-	-	5	-	-	17	-
BANKEY, D.	-	1/1	1.000	0/0	.000	-/0	-	-	1	-	-	2	-
DILL, C.	-	1/3	.333	0/0	.000	-/0	-	-	0	-	-	2	-
BROWN, D.	-	0/1	.000	0/0	.000	-/0	-	-	1	-	-	0	-
Totals	200	32/85	.376	13/18	.722	-/42	-	-	17	-	-	77	.385

Team Rebounds: Kentucky 7; Michigan 4. Disqualified: Michigan—Darden.

	1st Half	2nd Half	Final
Kentucky	42	42	84
Michigan	32	45	77

REGIONAL FINAL MIDWEST

Texas Western (81) Coach: Don Haskins

	Min.	Total FG/FGA	Pct.	FT/FTA	Pct.	Reb. O/T	A	TO	PF	S	Blk	TP	PPM
ARMSTRONG, J.	-	0/0	.000	0/0	.000	-/1	-	-	0	-	-	0	-
FLOURNOY, H.	-	3/7	.429	5/6	.833	-/8	-	-	5	-	-	11	-
LATTIN, D.	-	7/16	.438	1/2	.500	-/17	-	-	4	-	-	15	-
HILL, B.	-	7/20	.350	8/13	.615	-/4	-	-	3	-	-	22	-
ARTIS, O.	-	5/12	.417	2/3	.667	-/7	-	-	3	-	-	12	-
CAGER, W.	-	3/7	.429	0/1	.000	-/4	-	-	4	-	-	6	-
WORSLEY, W.	-	1/4	.250	1/1	1.000	-/1	-	-	0	-	-	3	-
SHED, N.	-	3/5	.600	6/9	.667	-/4	-	-	2	-	-	12	-
Totals	250	29/71	.408	23/35	.657	-/46	-	-	21	-	-	81	.324

Kansas (80) Coach: Ted Owens

	Min.	Total FG/FGA	Pct.	FT/FTA	Pct.	Reb. O/T	A	TO	PF	S	Blk	TP	PPM
FRANZ, R.	-	5/8	.625	2/3	.667	-/4	-	-	5	-	-	12	-
LOPES, A.	-	7/15	.467	3/4	.750	-/6	-	-	4	-	-	17	-
WESLEY, W.	-	9/23	.391	6/12	.500	-/15	-	-	5	-	-	24	-
WHITE, J.	-	7/14	.500	5/6	.833	-/11	-	-	4	-	-	19	-
LEWIS, D.	-	1/3	.333	4/4	1.000	-/1	-	-	5	-	-	6	-
BOHNENSTIEHL, R.	-	1/3	.333	0/0	.000	-/2	-	-	1	-	-	2	-
LOCHMANN, R.	-	0/0	.000	0/0	.000	-/3	-	-	1	-	-	0	-
WILSON, R.	-	0/0	.000	0/0	.000	-/0	-	-	0	-	-	0	-
Totals	250	30/66	.455	20/29	.690	-/42	-	-	25	-	-	80	.320

Team Rebounds: Texas Western 5; Kansas 6. Disqualified: Texas Western—Flournoy; Kansas—Franz, Wesley, Lewis. Techical fouls: Texas Western—Lattin.

	1st Half	2nd Half	1st OT	2nd OT	Final
Texas Western	38	31	2	10	81
Kansas	35	34	2	9	80

REGIONAL FINAL WEST

Oregon State (64) Coach: Paul Valenti

	Min.	Total FG/FGA	Pct.	FT/FTA	Pct.	Reb. O/T	A	TO	PF	S	Blk	TP	PPM
PETERSON	-	2/13	.154	1/1	1.000	-/4	-	-	4	-	-	5	-
EATON	-	6/13	.462	1/1	1.000	-/5	-	-	3	-	-	13	-
FREDENBURG, E.	-	7/14	.500	1/1	1.000	-/9	-	-	2	-	-	15	-
WHITE	-	9/18	.500	2/2	1.000	-/14	-	-	4	-	-	20	-
WHELAN	-	5/14	.357	0/0	.000	-/1	-	-	1	-	-	10	-
GUNNER	-	0/4	.000	1/2	.500	-/3	-	-	2	-	-	1	-
CARLISLE	-	0/4	.000	0/0	.000	-/2	-	-	2	-	-	0	-
Totals	200	29/80	.363	6/7	.857	-/38	-	-	18	-	-	64	.320

Utah (70) Coach: Jack Gardner

	Min.	Total FG/FGA	Pct.	FT/FTA	Pct.	Reb. O/T	A	TO	PF	S	Blk	TP	PPM
MACKAY	-	1/8	.125	2/2	1.000	-/9	-	-	0	-	-	4	-
CHAMBERS	-	13/31	.419	7/8	.875	-/10	-	-	4	-	-	33	-
OCKEL	-	2/6	.333	1/2	.500	-/14	-	-	1	-	-	5	-
TATE	-	5/14	.357	6/10	.600	-/7	-	-	0	-	-	16	-
JACKSON	-	5/10	.500	0/1	.000	-/11	-	-	3	-	-	10	-
BLACK	-	1/2	.500	0/0	.000	-/3	-	-	1	-	-	2	-
Totals	200	27/71	.380	16/23	.696	-/54	-	-	9	-	-	70	.350

Team Rebounds: Utah 7; Oregon State 4. Disqualified: None.

	1st Half	2nd Half	Final
Oregon State	24	40	64
Utah	41	29	70

FINAL FOUR

Duke (79) Coach: Vic Bubas

	Min.	Total FG/FGA	Pct.	FT/FTA	Pct.	Reb. O/T	A	TO	PF	S	Blk	TP	PPM
MARIN, J.	-	11/18	.611	7/10	.700	-/ 7	-	-	2	-	-	29	-
RIEDY, B.	-	2/ 7	.286	2/ 2	1.000	-/ 8	-	-	3	-	-	6	-
LEWIS, M.	-	9/13	.692	3/ 3	1.000	-/ 6	-	-	3	-	-	21	-
VERGA, B.	-	2/ 7	.286	0/ 0	.000	-/ 3	-	-	1	-	-	4	-
VACENDAK, S.	-	7/16	.438	3/ 3	1.000	-/ 3	-	-	5	-	-	17	-
WENDELIN, R.	-	1/ 4	.250	0/ 1	.000	-/ 2	-	-	4	-	-	2	-
LICCARDO, T.	-	0/ 1	.000	0/ 0	.000	-/ 0	-	-	0	-	-	0	-
BARONE, T.	-	0/ 0	.000	0/ 0	.000	-/ 0	-	-	1	-	-	0	-
Totals	200	32/66	.485	15/19	.789	-/29	-	-	19	-	-	79	.395

Kentucky (83) Coach: Adolph Rupp

	Min.	Total FG/FGA	Pct.	FT/FTA	Pct.	Reb. O/T	A	TO	PF	S	Blk	TP	PPM
CONLEY, L.	-	3/ 5	.600	4/ 4	1.000	-/ 1	-	-	0	-	-	10	-
RILEY, P.	-	8/17	.471	3/ 4	.750	-/ 8	-	-	5	-	-	19	-
JARACZ, T.	-	3/ 5	.600	2/ 3	.667	-/ 4	-	-	5	-	-	8	-
DAMPIER, L.	-	11/20	.550	1/ 2	.500	-/ 4	-	-	3	-	-	23	-
KRON, T.	-	5/13	.385	2/ 2	1.000	-/10	-	-	1	-	-	12	-
TALENT, B.	-	1/ 2	.500	2/ 2	1.000	-/ 1	-	-	0	-	-	4	-
BERGER, C.	-	1/ 4	.250	5/ 6	.833	-/ 5	-	-	1	-	-	7	-
GAMBLE, G.	-	0/ 0	.000	0/ 1	.000	-/ 0	-	-	1	-	-	0	-
Totals	200	32/66	.485	19/24	.792	-/33	-	-	16	-	-	83	.415

Team Rebounds: Kentucky 8; Duke 7. Disqualified: Kentucky—Riley, Jaracz; Duke—Vacendak.

	1st Half	2nd Half	Final
Duke	42	37	79
Kentucky	41	42	83

Texas Western (85) Coach: Don Haskins

	Min.	Total FG/FGA	Pct.	FT/FTA	Pct.	Reb. O/T	A	TO	PF	S	Blk	TP	PPM
ARTIS	-	10/20	.500	2/ 3	.667	-/ 5	-	-	2	-	-	22	-
HILL	-	5/20	.250	8/10	.800	-/11	-	-	4	-	-	18	-
WORSLEY	-	5/ 8	.625	2/ 3	.667	-/ 5	-	-	3	-	-	12	-
LATTIN	-	5/ 7	.714	1/ 1	1.000	-/ 4	-	-	3	-	-	11	-
SHED	-	2/ 3	.667	5/ 6	.833	-/ 3	-	-	5	-	-	9	-
FLOURNOY	-	3/ 6	.500	2/ 2	1.000	-/ 9	-	-	5	-	-	8	-
CAGER	-	2/ 5	.400	1/ 1	1.000	-/ 0	-	-	3	-	-	5	-
ARMSTRONG	-	0/ 2	.000	0/ 1	.000	-/ 3	-	-	2	-	-	0	-
Totals	200	32/71	.451	21/27	.778	-/40	-	-	27	-	-	85	.425

Utah (78) Coach: Jack Gardner

	Min.	Total FG/FGA	Pct.	FT/FTA	Pct.	Reb. O/T	A	TO	PF	S	Blk	TP	PPM
TATE	-	0/ 4	.000	1/ 3	.333	-/ 2	-	-	5	-	-	1	-
JACKSON	-	3/ 9	.333	2/ 2	1.000	-/ 2	-	-	1	-	-	8	-
MACKAY	-	4/10	.400	6/ 9	.667	-/ 7	-	-	2	-	-	14	-
OCKEL	-	1/ 1	1.000	3/ 3	1.000	-/ 9	-	-	3	-	-	5	-
CHAMBERS	-	14/31	.452	10/12	.833	-/17	-	-	3	-	-	38	-
BLACK	-	3/ 8	.375	2/ 4	.500	-/ 2	-	-	3	-	-	8	-
LAKE	-	1/ 1	1.000	0/ 0	.000	-/ 0	-	-	3	-	-	2	-
DAY	-	1/ 2	.500	0/ 0	.000	-/ 0	-	-	0	-	-	2	-
Totals	200	27/66	.409	24/33	.727	-/39	-	-	20	-	-	78	.390

Disqualified: Texas Western—Shed, Flournoy; Utah—Tate.

	1st Half	2nd Half	Final
Texas Western	42	43	85
Utah	39	39	78

NATIONAL CHAMPIONSHIP

Kentucky (65) Coach: Adolph Rupp

	Min.	Total FG/FGA	Pct.	FT/FTA	Pct.	Reb. O/T	A	TO	PF	S	Blk	TP	PPM
DAMPIER, L.	-	7/18	.389	5/ 5	1.000	-/ 9	-	-	4	-	-	19	-
KRON, T.	-	3/ 6	.500	0/ 0	.000	-/ 7	-	-	2	-	-	6	-
CONLEY, L.	-	4/ 9	.444	2/ 2	1.000	-/ 8	-	-	5	-	-	10	-
RILEY, P.	-	8/22	.364	3/ 4	.750	-/ 4	-	-	4	-	-	19	-
JARACZ, T.	-	3/ 8	.375	1/ 2	.500	-/ 5	-	-	5	-	-	7	-
LEMASTER, J.	-	0/ 1	.000	0/ 0	.000	-/ 0	-	-	1	-	-	0	-
BERGER, C.	-	2/ 3	.667	0/ 0	.000	-/ 0	-	-	0	-	-	4	-
GAMBLE, G.	-	0/ 0	.000	0/ 0	.000	-/ 0	-	-	1	-	-	0	-
TALLENT, B.	-	0/ 3	.000	0/ 0	.000	-/ 0	-	-	1	-	-	0	-
Totals	200	27/70	.386	11/13	.846	-/33	-	-	23	-	-	65	.325

Texas Western (72) Coach: Don Haskins

	Min.	Total FG/FGA	Pct.	FT/FTA	Pct.	Reb. O/T	A	TO	PF	S	Blk	TP	PPM
FLOURNOY, H.	-	1/ 1	1.000	0/ 0	.000	-/ 2	-	-	0	-	-	2	-
LATTIN, D.	-	5/10	.500	6/ 6	1.000	-/ 9	-	-	4	-	-	16	-
HILL, B.	-	7/17	.412	6/ 9	.667	-/ 3	-	-	3	-	-	20	-
ARTIS, O.	-	5/13	.385	5/ 5	1.000	-/ 8	-	-	1	-	-	15	-
CAGER, W.	-	1/ 3	.333	6/ 7	.857	-/ 6	-	-	3	-	-	8	-
WORSLEY, W.	-	2/ 4	.500	4/ 6	.667	-/ 4	-	-	0	-	-	8	-
SHED, N.	-	1/ 1	1.000	1/ 1	1.000	-/ 3	-	-	1	-	-	3	-
Totals	200	22/49	.449	28/34	.824	-/35	-	-	12	-	-	72	.360

Disqualified: Kentucky—Conley, Jaracz.

	1st Half	2nd Half	Final
Kentucky	31	34	65
Texas Western	34	38	72

NATIONAL THIRD PLACE

Duke (79) Coach: Vic Bubas

	Min.	Total FG/FGA	Pct.	FT/FTA	Pct.	Reb. O/T	A	TO	PF	S	Blk	TP	PPM
VERGA, B.	-	7/13	.538	1/1	1.000	-/3	-	-	2	-	-	15	-
RIEDY, B.	-	2/5	.400	0/0	.000	-/2	-	-	5	-	-	4	-
MARIN, J.	-	9/26	.346	5/5	1.000	-/8	-	-	4	-	-	23	-
VACENDAK, S.	-	5/13	.385	1/4	.250	-/4	-	-	3	-	-	11	-
LEWIS, M.	-	5/7	.714	4/5	.800	-/11	-	-	1	-	-	14	-
CHAPMAN, W.	-	2/8	.250	0/1	.000	-/4	-	-	1	-	-	4	-
LICCARDO, T.	-	0/2	.000	0/2	.000	-/3	-	-	0	-	-	0	-
WENDELIN, R.	-	2/4	.500	0/2	.000	-/0	-	-	1	-	-	4	-
KENNEDY, J.	-	0/0	.000	0/0	.000	-/1	-	-	0	-	-	0	-
BARONE, T.	-	1/2	.500	0/0	.000	-/1	-	-	1	-	-	2	-
KOLODZIEJ, T.	-	1/1	1.000	0/0	.000	-/0	-	-	1	-	-	2	-
Totals	200	34/81	.420	11/20	.550	-/37	-	-	19	-	-	79	.395

Utah (77) Coach: Jack Gardner

	Min.	Total FG/FGA	Pct.	FT/FTA	Pct.	Reb. O/T	A	TO	PF	S	Blk	TP	PPM
MACKAY	-	4/10	.400	5/6	.833	-/8	-	-	4	-	-	13	-
CHAMBERS, J.	-	11/16	.688	10/12	.833	-/18	-	-	3	-	-	32	-
OCKEL, J.	-	5/9	.556	0/0	.000	-/5	-	-	3	-	-	10	-
TATE, R.	-	1/8	.125	2/5	.400	-/2	-	-	1	-	-	4	-
JACKSON	-	6/12	.500	2/2	1.000	-/5	-	-	0	-	-	14	-
BLACK	-	2/5	.400	0/1	.000	-/3	-	-	3	-	-	4	-
DAY	-	0/1	.000	0/0	.000	-/0	-	-	0	-	-	0	-
Totals	200	29/61	.475	19/26	.731	-/41	-	-	14	-	-	77	.385

Team Rebounds: Duke 0; Utah 1. Disqualified: Duke—Riedy.

	1st Half	2nd Half	Final
Duke	41	38	79
Utah	37	40	77

REGIONAL THIRD PLACE WEST

Houston (102) Coach: Guy Lewis

	Min.	Total FG/FGA	Pct.	FT/FTA	Pct.	Reb. O/T	A	TO	PF	S	Blk	TP	PPM
BALLARD	26	7/13	.538	2/4	.500	-/7	1	-	3	-	-	16	.615
HAMOOD, J.	26	9/20	.450	0/1	.000	-/2	6	-	3	-	-	18	.692
HAYES, E.	39	11/26	.423	9/12	.750	-/28	1	-	4	-	-	31	.795
LENTZ, L.	24	6/12	.500	0/0	.000	-/6	1	-	2	-	-	12	.500
GRIDER, B.	14	3/7	.429	4/5	.800	-/3	5	-	2	-	-	10	.714
KRUSE, D.	16	0/1	.000	0/0	.000	-/1	2	-	1	-	-	0	.000
CHANEY, D.	26	3/12	.250	0/0	.000	-/10	2	-	4	-	-	6	.231
APOLSKIS	14	3/5	.600	1/2	.500	-/1	2	-	0	-	-	7	.500
OZUG	14	1/3	.333	0/0	.000	-/3	1	-	0	-	-	2	.143
PERRY	1	0/1	.000	0/0	.000	-/0	0	-	0	-	-	0	.000
Totals	200	43/100	.430	16/24	.667	-/61	21	-	19	-	-	102	.510

Pacific (91) Coach: Dick Edwards

	Min.	Total FG/FGA	Pct.	FT/FTA	Pct.	Reb. O/T	A	TO	PF	S	Blk	TP	PPM
ODALE, D.	-	4/13	.308	4/7	.571	-/8	-	-	2	-	-	12	-
KRULISH, B.	-	7/19	.368	3/3	1.000	-/7	-	-	3	-	-	17	-
SWAGERTY, K.	-	11/23	.478	4/5	.800	-/23	-	-	4	-	-	26	-
FOX, D.	-	2/10	.200	5/7	.714	-/5	-	-	5	-	-	9	-
PARSONS, B.	-	9/19	.474	3/3	1.000	-/11	-	-	4	-	-	21	-
GILBERT, A.	-	1/3	.333	0/0	.000	-/1	-	-	1	-	-	2	-
SELIM, R.	-	2/7	.286	0/1	.000	-/8	-	-	0	-	-	4	-
MICHELSON, S.	-	0/0	.000	0/0	.000	-/0	-	-	0	-	-	0	-
Totals	200	36/94	.277	19/26	.731	-/63	-	-	19	-	-	91	.455

Team Rebounds: Houston 2; Pacific 4. Disqualified: Pacific—Fox.

	1st Half	2nd Half	Final
Houston	47	55	102
Pacific	43	48	91

REGIONAL THIRD PLACE MIDWEST

SMU (89) Coach: E. O. "Doc" Hayes

	Min.	Total FG/FGA	Pct.	FT/FTA	Pct.	Reb. O/T	A	TO	PF	S	Blk	TP	PPM
BEGERT, B.	-	7/11	.636	4/5	.800	-/7	1	-	4	-	-	18	-
BEASLEY, C.	-	2/12	.167	4/5	.800	-/3	8	-	0	-	-	8	-
HOOSER, C.	-	8/11	.727	5/6	.833	-/8	3	-	4	-	-	21	-
HOLMAN, D.	-	12/13	.923	1/1	1.000	-/2	1	-	0	-	-	25	-
JONES, B.	-	0/1	.000	0/0	.000	-/0	0	-	3	-	-	0	-
RAMSAY, J.	-	2/5	.400	1/1	1.000	-/6	1	-	2	-	-	5	-
HIGGENBOTHAM, J.	-	4/9	.444	4/4	1.000	-/9	0	-	2	-	-	12	-
Totals	200	35/62	.565	19/22	.864	-/35	14	-	15	-	-	89	.445

Cincinnati (84) Coach: Tay Baker

	Min.	Total FG/FGA	Pct.	FT/FTA	Pct.	Reb. O/T	A	TO	PF	S	Blk	TP	PPM
ROLFES, D.	-	6/15	.400	6/7	.857	-/6	7	-	2	-	-	18	-
HOWARD, J.	-	5/9	.556	1/2	.500	-/7	1	-	3	-	-	11	-
KRICK, R.	-	1/1	1.000	0/0	.000	-/1	0	-	2	-	-	2	-
WEST, R.	-	4/17	.235	4/6	.667	-/12	3	-	2	-	-	12	-
FOSTER, D.	-	5/10	.500	0/0	.000	-/3	6	-	0	-	-	10	-
ROLF, M.	-	2/5	.400	3/4	.750	-/2	0	-	2	-	-	7	-
COUZINS, J.	-	1/3	.333	0/0	.000	-/0	0	-	1	-	-	2	-
CALLOWAY, K.	-	6/7	.857	0/0	.000	-/3	1	-	3	-	-	12	-
WEIDNER, P.	-	3/5	.600	0/0	.000	-/0	0	-	3	-	-	6	-
BIEDENHARN, T.	-	2/2	1.000	0/0	.000	-/1	0	-	0	-	-	4	-
Totals	200	35/74	.473	14/19	.737	-/35	18	-	18	-	-	84	.420

Team Rebounds: SMU 2; Cincinnati 2. Disqualified: None.

	1st Half	2nd Half	Final
SMU	50	39	89
Cincinnati	41	43	84

REGIONAL THIRD PLACE MIDEAST

Western Kentucky (82) Coach: Johnny Oldham

	Min.	Total FG/FGA	Pct.	FT/FTA	Pct.	Reb. O/T	A	TO	PF	S	Blk	TP	PPM
SMITH, D.	-	1/14	.071	9/12	.750	-/11	0	-	3	-	-	11	-
SMITH, G.	-	4/6	.667	3/7	.429	-/13	0	-	5	-	-	11	-
HASKINS, C.	-	7/18	.389	6/6	1.000	-/17	3	-	1	-	-	20	-
CUNNINGHAM, C.	-	8/15	.533	4/4	1.000	-/12	0	-	1	-	-	20	-
CHAPMAN, W.	-	6/16	.375	6/8	.750	-/8	2	-	3	-	-	18	-
HICKS, P.	-	1/6	.167	0/0	.000	-/1	0	-	2	-	-	2	-
Totals	200	27/75	.360	28/37	.757	-/62	5	-	15	-	-	82	.410

Dayton (68) Coach: Don Donoher

	Min.	Total FG/FGA	Pct.	FT/FTA	Pct.	Reb. O/T	A	TO	PF	S	Blk	TP	PPM
FINKEL, H.	-	13/20	.650	5/7	.714	-/18	-	-	5	-	-	31	-
MAY, D.	-	6/25	.240	3/8	.375	-/11	-	-	4	-	-	15	-
WATERMAN, R.	-	3/10	.300	1/1	1.000	-/5	-	-	4	-	-	7	-
HOOPER, B.	-	2/7	.286	0/0	.000	-/2	-	-	3	-	-	4	-
TORAIN, G.	-	4/15	.267	1/1	1.000	-/3	-	-	2	-	-	9	-
KLAUS, G.	-	1/7	.143	0/0	.000	-/2	-	-	1	-	-	2	-
CASSIDY, B.	-	0/4	.000	0/0	.000	-/2	-	-	4	-	-	0	-
BROOKS, T.	-	0/1	.000	0/0	.000	-/1	-	-	1	-	-	0	-
Totals	200	29/89	.326	10/17	.588	-/44	-	-	24	-	-	68	.340

Team Rebounds: Western Ky. 4; Dayton 4. Disqualified: Western Ky.—G. Smith; Dayton—Finkel.

	1st Half	2nd Half	Final
Western Ky.	41	41	82
Dayton	29	39	68

REGIONAL THIRD PLACE EAST

St. Joseph's (92) Coach: Jack Ramsay

	Min.	Total FG/FGA	Pct.	FT/FTA	Pct.	Reb. O/T	A	TO	PF	S	Blk	TP	PPM
FORD, M.	30	7/15	.467	3/4	.750	-/7	2	0	1	-	-	17	.567
GUOKAS, M.	34	6/16	.375	2/2	1.000	-/9	3	1	2	-	-	14	.412
ANDERSON, C.	34	5/11	.455	10/12	.833	-/10	3	5	1	-	-	20	.588
DUFF, T.	30	6/16	.375	5/6	.833	-/8	1	1	2	-	-	17	.567
MCKENNA, C.	18	2/9	.222	0/1	.000	-/7	0	0	3	-	-	4	.222
OAKES, W.	26	2/5	.400	2/3	.667	-/2	0	1	1	-	-	6	.231
CHAPMAN, S.	10	2/6	.333	3/3	1.000	-/1	0	1	0	-	-	7	.700
BRENNER, R.	6	1/4	.250	0/0	.000	-/2	0	0	1	-	-	2	.333
DONCHES, S.	4	2/3	.667	0/0	.000	-/2	0	0	2	-	-	4	1.000
GRUNDY, A.	4	0/2	.000	1/3	.333	-/1	1	0	0	-	-	1	.250
DEARGELIS, W.	4	0/0	.000	0/0	.000	-/0	0	0	2	-	-	0	.000
Totals	200	33/87	.379	26/34	.765	-/49	10	9	15	-	-	92	.460

Davidson (76) Coach: Lefty Driesell

	Min.	Total FG/FGA	Pct.	FT/FTA	Pct.	Reb. O/T	A	TO	PF	S	Blk	TP	PPM
SNYDER, D.	32	3/14	.214	0/0	.000	-/10	4	2	5	-	-	6	.188
YOUNGDALE, T.	25	3/3	1.000	2/2	1.000	-/1	1	4	5	-	-	8	.320
LANE, B.	39	5/10	.500	4/4	1.000	-/4	2	4	1	-	-	14	.359
SQUIER, P.	31	4/10	.400	0/1	.000	-/2	1	5	2	-	-	8	.258
KNOWLES, R.	39	10/19	.526	8/11	.727	-/10	1	4	4	-	-	28	.718
LEIGHT, G.	16	1/2	.500	0/0	.000	-/1	1	1	4	-	-	2	.125
HATCHER, S.	11	1/1	1.000	2/2	1.000	-/4	0	3	0	-	-	4	.364
CLIFTON, C.	5	1/3	.333	2/2	1.000	-/2	1	3	0	-	-	4	.800
STONE, R.	2	0/1	.000	2/2	1.000	-/0	0	0	0	-	-	2	1.000
Totals	200	28/63	.444	20/24	.833	-/34	11	26	21	-	-	76	.380

Team Rebounds: St. Joseph's 9; Davidson 9. Disqualified: Davidson—Snyder, Youngdale.

	1st Half	2nd Half	Final
St. Joseph's	43	49	92
Davidson	35	41	76

○ ALL-STAR TEAMS ○

ALL TOURNAMENT

★ JERRY CHAMBERS	UTAH
LOUIE DAMPIER	KENTUCKY
BOBBY JOE HILL	TEXAS WESTERN
JACK MARIN	DUKE
PAT RILEY	KENTUCKY

★ Most Outstanding Player(s)

○ INDIVIDUAL RECORDS ○

SCORING

Most points in a single game
1. JERRY CHAMBERS, UTAH (vs. PACIFIC) — 40
2. RODNEY KNOWLES, DAVIDSON (vs. RHODE ISLAND) — 39
3. JERRY CHAMBERS, UTAH (vs. TEXAS WESTERN) — 38
4. HENRY FINKEL, DAYTON (vs. KENTUCKY) — 36
5. LOUIE DAMPIER, KENTUCKY (vs. DAYTON) — 34

Most total points in the tournament
1. JERRY CHAMBERS, UTAH — 143
2. BOBBY JOE HILL, TEXAS WESTERN — 101
3. PAT RILEY, KENTUCKY — 96
4. 3 tied for fourth place.

Highest scoring average (minimum 2 games)
1. JERRY CHAMBERS, UTAH (143-4) — 35.75
2. RODNEY KNOWLES, DAVIDSON (92-3) — 30.67
2. HENRY FINKEL, DAYTON (92-3) — 30.67
4. CAZZIE RUSSELL, MICHIGAN (53-2) — 26.50
5. PAT RILEY, KENTUCKY (96-4) — 24.00

FIELD GOALS

Most field goals in a single game
1. JERRY CHAMBERS, UTAH (vs. PACIFIC) — 17
2. RODNEY KNOWLES, DAVIDSON (vs. RHODE ISLAND) — 15

2. HENRY FINKEL, DAYTON (vs. KENTUCKY) — 15
4. JERRY CHAMBERS, UTAH (vs. TEXAS WESTERN) — 14
4. LOUIE DAMPIER, KENTUCKY (vs. DAYTON) — 14

Most total field goals in the tournament
1. JERRY CHAMBERS, UTAH — 55
2. PAT RILEY, KENTUCKY — 40
3. LOUIE DAMPIER, KENTUCKY — 38
4. HENRY FINKEL, DAYTON — 37
5. DAVID LATTIN, TEXAS WESTERN — 35

Most field goal attempts in a single game
1. JERRY CHAMBERS, UTAH (vs. OREGON STATE) — 31
1. JERRY CHAMBERS, UTAH (vs. TEXAS WESTERN) — 31
3. JERRY CHAMBERS, UTAH (vs. PACIFIC) — 30
4. RODNEY KNOWLES, DAVIDSON (vs. RHODE ISLAND) — 27
4. PAT RILEY, KENTUCKY (vs. MICHIGAN) — 27

Most total field goal attempts in the tournament
1. JERRY CHAMBERS, UTAH — 108
2. BOBBY JOE HILL, TEXAS WESTERN — 93
3. PAT RILEY, KENTUCKY — 84
4. JACK MARIN, DUKE — 74
5. LOUIE DAMPIER, KENTUCKY — 73

Highest field goal percentage in a single game (minimum 10 attempts)
1. DENNY HOLMAN, SMU (vs. CINCINNATI) (12-13) — .923
2. RICK WHELAN, OREGON STATE (vs. HOUSTON) (11-14) — .786
3. BOB VERGA, DUKE (vs. SYRACUSE) (10-13) — .769
4. RON KRICK, CINCINNATI (vs. TEXAS WESTERN) (9-12) — .750
5. 2 tied for fifth place.

Highest field goal percentage in the tournament (minimum 20 attempts)
1. DENNY HOLMAN, SMU (15-21) — .714
2. THAD JARACZ, KENTUCKY (19-30) — .633
3. RON FRANZ, KANSAS (14-23) — .609
4. HENRY FINKEL, DAYTON (37-61) — .607
5. CARROLL HOOSER, SMU (18-31) — .581

FREE THROWS

Most free throws in a single game
1. CHUBIN, RHODE ISLAND (vs. DAVIDSON) — 13
2. JERRY CHAMBERS, UTAH (vs. TEXAS WESTERN) — 10
2. CLIFFORD ANDERSON, ST. JOSEPH'S (vs. DAVIDSON) — 10
2. JERRY CHAMBERS, UTAH (vs. DUKE) — 10
2. CAZZIE RUSSELL, MICHIGAN (vs. WESTERN KY.) — 10

Most total free throws in the tournament

1	BOBBY JOE HILL, TEXAS WESTERN	33
1	JERRY CHAMBERS, UTAH	33
3	JACK MARIN, DUKE	26
4	RODNEY KNOWLES, DAVIDSON	24
5	2 tied for fifth place.	

Most free throws attempted in a single game

1	CHUBIN, RHODE ISLAND (vs. DAVIDSON)	14
1	BOBBY JOE HILL, TEXAS WESTERN (vs. OKLAHOMA CITY)	14
3	BOBBY JOE HILL, TEXAS WESTERN (vs. KANSAS)	13
4	7 tied for fourth place.	

Most free throws attempted in the tournament

1	BOBBY JOE HILL, TEXAS WESTERN	52
2	JERRY CHAMBERS, UTAH	40
3	JACK MARIN, DUKE	33
4	RODNEY KNOWLES, DAVIDSON	31
5	CLIFFORD ANDERSON, ST. JOSEPH'S	29

Highest free throw percentage in a single game (minimum 7 attempts)

1	CAZZIE RUSSELL, MICHIGAN (vs. KENTUCKY) (9-9)	1.000
1	BILLY SMITH, LOYOLA-CHICAGO (vs. WESTERN KY.) (9-9)	1.000
3	MIKE LEWIS, DUKE (vs. SYRACUSE) (8-8)	1.000
4	LAWRENCE, OKLAHOMA CITY (vs. TEXAS WESTERN) (7-7)	1.000
4	HENRY FINKEL, DAYTON (vs. MIAMI [OHIO]) (7-7)	1.000

Highest free throw percentage in the tournament (minimum 15 attempts)

1	MIKE LEWIS, DUKE (17-18)	.944
2	CAZZIE RUSSELL, MICHIGAN (19-21)	.905
3	ORSTEN ARTIS, TEXAS WESTERN (16-18)	.889
4	DAVID LATTIN, TEXAS WESTERN (21-24)	.875
5	HENRY FINKEL, DAYTON (18-21)	.857

REBOUNDS

Most rebounds in a single game

1	ELVIN HAYES, HOUSTON (vs. PACIFIC)	28
2	KEITH SWAGERTY, PACIFIC (vs. HOUSTON)	23
3	RODNEY KNOWLES, DAVIDSON (vs. RHODE ISLAND)	20
4	KEITH SWAGERTY, PACIFIC (vs. UTAH)	19
4	DALE SCHLUETER, COLORADO STATE (vs. HOUSTON)	19

Most total rebounds in the tournament

1	JERRY CHAMBERS, UTAH	56
2	DAVID LATTIN, TEXAS WESTERN	53
3	ELVIN HAYES, HOUSTON	50
4	HENRY FINKEL, DAYTON	48
5	MIKE LEWIS, DUKE	45

Most rebounds per game (minimum 2 games)

1	KEITH SWAGERTY, PACIFIC (42-2)	21.00
2	ELVIN HAYES, HOUSTON (50-3)	16.67
3	HENRY FINKEL, DAYTON (48-3)	16.00
4	JERRY CHAMBERS, UTAH (56-4)	14.00
5	2 tied for fifth place.	

❂ TEAM RECORDS ❂

SCORING

Most points in a single game

1	WESTERN KY. (vs. LOYOLA-CHICAGO)	105
2	HOUSTON (vs. PACIFIC)	102
3	DAVIDSON (vs. RHODE ISLAND)	95

Most total points in the tournament

1	TEXAS WESTERN	405
2	DUKE	325
3	KENTUCKY	318

Highest scoring average (minimum 2 games)

1	WESTERN KY. (266-3)	88.67
2	SYRACUSE (175-2)	87.50
3	DAVIDSON (249-3)	83.00

FIELD GOALS

Most field goals in a single game

1	WESTERN KY. (vs. LOYOLA-CHICAGO)	45
2	HOUSTON (vs. PACIFIC)	43
3	SYRACUSE (vs. DAVIDSON)	41

Most total field goals in the tournament

1	TEXAS WESTERN	143
2	KENTUCKY	130
3	DUKE	125

Most field goals attempted in a single game

1	HOUSTON (vs. PACIFIC)	100
2	PACIFIC (vs. HOUSTON)	94
3	DAYTON (vs. WESTERN KY.)	89

Most total field goals attempted in the tournament

1	TEXAS WESTERN	323
2	KENTUCKY	274
2	DUKE	274

Highest field goal percentage in a single game

1	OREGON STATE (vs. HOUSTON) (26-42)	.619
2	SMU (vs. CINCINNATI) (35-62)	.565
3	WESTERN KY. (vs. LOYOLA-CHICAGO) (45-81)	.556

Highest field goal percentage in the tournament (minimum 2 games)

1	SMU (62-123)	.504
2	CINCINNATI (66-136)	.485
3	KENTUCKY (130-274)	.475

FREE THROWS

Most free throws in a single game

1	DUKE (vs. SYRACUSE)	29
2	WESTERN KY. (vs. DAYTON)	28
2	TEXAS WESTERN (vs. KENTUCKY)	28

Most total free throws in the tournament

1	TEXAS WESTERN	119
2	DUKE	75
3	UTAH	74

Most free throws attempted in a single game

1	TEXAS WESTERN (vs. OKLAHOMA CITY)	38
2	WESTERN KY. (vs. DAYTON)	37
2	DUKE (vs. SYRACUSE)	37

Most total free throws attempted in the tournament

1	TEXAS WESTERN	161
2	UTAH	109
3	DUKE	102

Highest free throw percentage in a single game

1	SYRACUSE (vs. DUKE) (19-21)	.905
2	KENTUCKY (vs. DAYTON) (18-20)	.900
3	SMU (vs. CINCINNATI) (19-22)	.864

Highest free throw percentage in the tournament (minimum 2 games)

1	SYRACUSE (31-40)	.775
1	MICHIGAN (31-40)	.775
3	KENTUCKY (58-76)	.763

Fewest free throws in a single game

1	OREGON STATE (vs. UTAH)	6
2	PROVIDENCE (vs. ST. JOSEPH'S)	8
3	2 tied for third place.	

Lowest free throw percentage in a single game

1	KENTUCKY (vs. MICHIGAN) (10-19)	.526
2	WESTERN KY. (vs. MICHIGAN) (9-17)	.529
3	2 tied for third place.	

Lowest free throw percentage in the tournament (minimum 2 games)

1	OREGON STATE (17-27)	.630
2	HOUSTON (48-73)	.658
3	UTAH (74-109)	.679

REBOUNDS

Most rebounds in a single game

1	PACIFIC (vs. HOUSTON)	63
2	WESTERN KY. (vs. DAYTON)	62
3	HOUSTON (vs. PACIFIC)	61

Most rebounds per game (minimum 2 games)

1	PACIFIC (112-2)	56.00
2	WESTERN KY. (144-3)	48.00
3	HOUSTON (141-3)	47.00

1967

FIRST ROUND	REGIONAL SEMIFINAL	REGIONAL FINAL	FINAL FOUR	REGIONAL FINAL	REGIONAL SEMIFINAL	FIRST ROUND

EAST

(bye)

N. Carolina 78 (ot)

N. Carolina 96

Princeton 68

Princeton 70

West Virginia 57

N. Carolina 62

St. John's 57

St. John's 62

Temple 53

Boston College 48

Boston College 80

Boston College 63

U. Conn. 42

MIDEAST

(bye)

Tennessee 52

Dayton 71 (ot)

Dayton 69 (ot)

Dayton 53

Western Ky. 67

Dayton 76

Virginia Tech 82

Virginia Tech 79

Toledo 76

Virginia Tech 66

(bye)

Indiana 70

MIDWEST

Kansas 53

(bye)

Houston 83

Houston 59

Houston 66

New Mexico St. 58

Houston 58

SMU 83

(bye)

SMU 75

Louisville 81

(bye)

WEST

Pacific 72

(bye)

Pacific 64

Texas Western 62

Texas Western 63

Seattle 54

UCLA 73

UCLA 109

(bye)

UCLA 80

Wyoming 60

(bye)

UCLA 79
Dayton 64

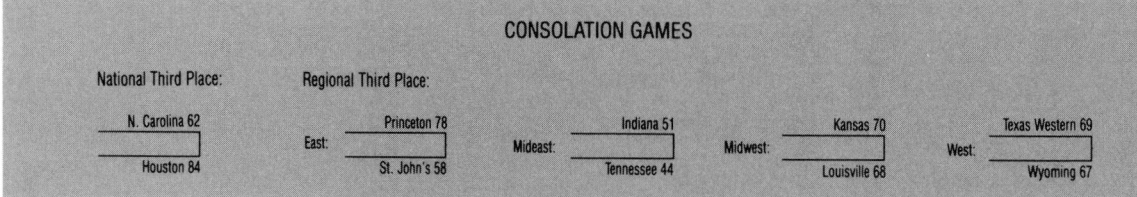

CONSOLATION GAMES

National Third Place:

N. Carolina 62

Houston 84

Regional Third Place:

East:

Princeton 78

St. John's 58

Mideast:

Indiana 51

Tennessee 44

Midwest:

Kansas 70

Louisville 68

West:

Texas Western 69

Wyoming 67

In the spring of 1965, soon after UCLA had won its second consecutive national title, John Wooden carried out the recruiting coup of the decade: Lew Alcindor, a senior at New York's Power Memorial High School and the most ballyhooed big man to come down the pike since Wilt Chamberlain, decided to attend UCLA the following fall. With the arrival of Alcindor and a bumper crop of supporting players, it became apparent that in the next four years, barring the unforeseen, Wooden and UCLA would eclipse every previous record of success in big-time college basketball. UCLA had the makings of a dynasty.

At the tip-off of the 1965–1966 season, many basketball pundits, as well as the coaches of the nation's top teams, assumed it would be the last year in the decade that anyone else would have much of a chance to win. This perception became even more deeply ingrained in the public psyche when the UCLA varsity, with a preseason No. 1 ranking, was blown off the court by a squad of Bruin freshmen.

The UCLA team that brought the Bruins back into the tournament in 1967 after a one-year hiatus consisted of four sophomores and a junior. They came into the NCAAs undefeated, with 26 straight victories. Unlike the 1964 and 1965 champions, this was a team with size as well as speed, and a defense that not only picked the pockets of opposing players but also knocked their shots back in their faces. The reason for the difference was Alcindor.

As a sophomore, he was already being described as a cross between Chamberlain and Russell. And he was a consummate team player: If the ball came into big Lew and he was double- or triple-teamed, he'd simply pass it off to the open man. And the open men—particularly the Bruin backcourt—were extraordinarily talented, probably the college game's best backcourt tandem since UCLA's own Walt Hazzard and Gail Goodrich. Sophomore Lucius Allen was lightning quick and an exceptional shot, and the brilliant junior playmaker Mike Warren had great court sense and intelligence to go with his physical skills. The forwards, Kenny Heitz and Lynn Shackelford, were both solid players, and Shackelford, when called upon, could also score. Plus the Bruins had a bench.

Going into the tournament, UCLA's edge appeared insurmountable. Phil Elderkin of *The Christian Science Monitor* later wrote that the letters NCAA had taken on a new meaning—"No Chance Against Alcindor." And Coach Wooden, alluding to his big man's role in the UCLA team defense, said, "We have a tough psychological barrier back there." Of course not everyone was convinced that UCLA was invincible. Houston Coach Guy Lewis said all year that "UCLA will lose sometime during the season." And there were others who felt that the Bruins' inexperience would finally, at some point, cause them to lose their

edge. But even those who felt the Bruins could be beaten believed it would require the fortuitous combination of a bad game from UCLA and a brilliant one from their opponents. They were that good.

The Bruins came into the tournament ready to play. After taking a 12-6 lead over Wyoming in their opener, they scored 18 straight points. At the half the score was 55-18; even before intermission, Wooden started emptying his bench.

UCLA's toughest test of the tournament was in the regional final. The University of the Pacific Tigers, who had upset the defending champs of UTEP in their opener, were determined to show the nation that their 21-game winning streak was more than a mirage. They banged around the UCLA big man and stayed close. The game was tied at 21 after fourteen minutes, before UCLA exploded for a 10-point splurge, keyed by a Mike Warren steal and breakaway lay-up off the press. The Tigers refused to fold; they trailed by only 7 with seven and a half minutes left to play. Four minutes later it was still only 69-60. But Alcindor, who had been knocked to the floor several times during the course of the game, finally had enough of the rough stuff under the boards; he lost his temper and threw an elbow at Pacific's Robbie DeWitt. In short order, an Alcindor stuff, a Lucius Allen fast-break lay-up, and a second stuff on a 3-point play made it 76-60. It was a tough game, the kind of contest opposing coaches hoped UCLA would lose. The Bruins needed a top performance from Alcindor to prevail, and they got it: he scored 38 points (his high for the tournament), blocked half a dozen shots, and led all rebounders with 14.

In the Final Four, UCLA was matched against sixth-ranked Houston, the surprise winners of the Midwest regional. The Cougars, led by Elvin Hayes and Don Chaney, had averaged 92.9 points per game during the regular season, but they squeaked through their opener against New Mexico State 59-58, and even that margin wasn't secure until a charging call gave them possession with three seconds left. In the regional semis, the Cougars played favored Kansas on the Jayhawks' homecourt in Lawrence; a pressure zone employed by Houston gave them the victory. Next, the Cougars beat SMU. Southern Methodist had come back from a late 8-point deficit to knock out No. 2 Louisville (the team experts believed was most likely to defeat UCLA) in their regional semi. But Houston's height and strength were too much for them.

And UCLA was too much for Houston. The Cougars led the Bruins 19-18 midway through the first half; they were holding their own on the boards, stopping Alcindor and breaking the press. But as usual the UCLA press keyed an explosion—the Bruins scored 11 straight points and were never again seriously challenged. And although Alcindor had only 19 points, the Houston strategy of triple-teaming him allowed his teammates—particularly Shackelford, Allen, and Warren, who combined for 53 points—to shoot unmolested.

After the game, Hayes, who had outrebounded and outscored Alcindor (although he took 20 more shots than Big Lew) said his teammates "choked." He also criticized his UCLA rival for not being aggressive enough on the boards and for just standing around on defense. "He's not all they really put him up to be," concluded the Big E about Big Lew.

In the final, UCLA met the improbable Dayton Flyers. Unranked Dayton had soared through the tournament in a series of upsets: First they beat seventh-ranked Western Kentucky in overtime after trailing by 10 at the half; next they topped Tennessee by a point; then they came back from a 62-52 second-half deficit to overcome Virginia Tech in overtime; and finally their star forward, Scott May, was unstoppable in carrying them over Dean Smith's first North Carolina Final Four team in the national semis.

But against UCLA, the Flyers crash landed. The score was only 5-0 after 3:24; it was still only 8-4 after 7 minutes. Four minutes later, with the score 20-4, Dayton finally got its third field goal when Alcindor was called for goaltending (he already had four clean blocks to his credit). The score was 76-47 UCLA when the last Bruin starter went to the bench, allowing the Flyers to close the margin to a respectable 79-64 by the end of the game.

UCLA became the fourth team in NCAA history to finish a championship season undefeated, the second to win three national championships in four years (Kentucky in 1948, '49 and '51), and their victory tied Kentucky's record of 12 straight tournament wins.

The Bruins were so totally dominating (they won 26 of their 30 games by 15 points or more) that after the tourney Elvin Hayes was one of the few who held out any hope of an Alcindor-led UCLA team ever losing a game. UCLA, as advertised, was a dynasty.

FIRST ROUND EAST

Princeton (68) Coach: B. Van Breda Kolff

	Min.	Total FG/FGA	Pct.	FT/FTA	Pct.	Reb. O/T	A	TO	PF	S	Blk	TP	PPM
HEISER, J.	-	12/22	.545	2/2	1.000	-/5	0	4	3	-	-	26	-
WALTERS, G.	-	0/5	.000	0/0	.000	-/3	1	5	1	-	-	0	-
THOMFORDE, C.	-	2/2	1.000	10/11	.909	-/6	3	3	4	-	-	14	-
HAARLOW, J.	-	8/23	.348	2/2	1.000	-/11	0	1	3	-	-	18	-
HUMMER, E.	-	1/5	.200	4/4	1.000	-/13	1	2	4	-	-	6	-
BROWN, R.	-	0/2	.000	0/2	.000	-/6	0	4	5	-	-	0	-
LAWYER, D.	-	0/0	.000	0/0	.000	-/1	0	0	0	-	-	0	-
LUCCHINO, L.	-	2/2	1.000	0/0	.000	-/0	0	0	0	-	-	4	-
Totals	200	25/61	.410	18/21	.857	-/45	5	19	20	-	-	68	.340

West Virginia (57) Coach: Bucky Waters

	Min.	Total FG/FGA	Pct.	FT/FTA	Pct.	Reb. O/T	A	TO	PF	S	Blk	TP	PPM
HOLMES, N.	-	1/4	.250	1/2	.500	-/6	0	3	2	-	-	3	-
WILLIAMS, R.	-	9/18	.500	3/4	.750	-/3	0	5	3	-	-	21	-
HEAD, C.	-	9/16	.563	2/6	.333	-/4	0	2	5	-	-	20	-
REASER, D.	-	1/7	.143	1/2	.500	-/1	0	0	4	-	-	3	-
BENFIELD, B.	-	2/10	.200	3/9	.333	-/14	0	4	5	-	-	7	-
LUDWIG, G.	-	1/3	.333	1/2	.500	-/2	0	0	0	-	-	3	-
GRIMM, W.	-	0/0	.000	0/0	.000	-/1	0	0	0	-	-	0	-
PENROD, D.	-	0/1	.000	0/0	.000	-/0	0	0	0	-	-	0	-
HALE, L.	-	0/0	.000	0/0	.000	-/0	0	0	0	-	-	0	-
HARVARD, E.	-	0/0	.000	0/0	.000	-/0	0	0	0	-	-	0	-
Totals	200	23/59	.390	11/25	.440	-/31	0	14	19	-	-	57	.285

Team Rebounds: Princeton 5; West Virginia 8. Disqualified: Princeton—Brown; West Virginia—Head, Benfield.

	1st Half	2nd Half	Final
Princeton	29	39	68
West Virginia	21	36	57

St. John's (57) Coach: Lou Carnesecca

	Min.	Total FG/FGA	Pct.	FT/FTA	Pct.	Reb. O/T	A	TO	PF	S	Blk	TP	PPM
SWARTZ, A.	-	0/7	.000	2/4	.500	-/3	-	-	0	-	-	2	-
CALZONETTI, C.	-	3/4	.750	0/0	.000	-/3	-	-	1	-	-	6	-
BOGAD, R.	-	5/12	.417	4/5	.800	-/6	-	-	2	-	-	14	-
WARREN, J.	-	4/8	.500	4/4	1.000	-/9	-	-	3	-	-	12	-
DOVE, S.	-	7/17	.412	7/9	.778	-/13	-	-	3	-	-	21	-
BRUNNER, J.	-	0/0	.000	0/0	.000	-/0	-	-	1	-	-	0	-
JACKSON, R.	-	1/1	1.000	0/0	.000	-/0	-	-	0	-	-	2	-
HILL, B.	-	0/1	.000	0/0	.000	-/0	-	-	0	-	-	0	-
Totals	200	20/50	.400	17/22	.773	-/34	-	-	10	-	-	57	.285

Temple (53) Coach: Harry Litwack

	Min.	Total FG/FGA	Pct.	FT/FTA	Pct.	Reb. O/T	A	TO	PF	S	Blk	TP	PPM
BAUM, J.	-	4/9	.444	2/2	1.000	-/4	-	-	4	-	-	10	-
CROMER	-	3/6	.500	0/0	.000	-/7	-	-	4	-	-	6	-
BROCCHI	-	4/11	.364	2/2	1.000	-/6	-	-	2	-	-	10	-
BROOKINS, C.	-	9/14	.643	3/6	.500	-/3	-	-	0	-	-	21	-
KEFALOS	-	1/8	.125	2/3	.667	-/2	-	-	0	-	-	4	-
KEHOE	-	0/1	.000	0/0	.000	-/0	-	-	5	-	-	0	-
MAST	-	1/1	1.000	0/0	.000	-/0	-	-	1	-	-	2	-
Totals	200	22/50	.440	9/13	.692	-/22	-	-	16	-	-	53	.265

Team Rebounds: St. John's 8; Temple 4. Disqualified: Temple—Kehoe.

	1st Half	2nd Half	Final
St. John's	28	29	57
Temple	24	29	53

Boston College (48)　Coach: Bob Cousey

	Min.	Total FG/FGA	Pct.	FT/FTA	Pct.	Reb. O/T	A	TO	PF	S	Blk	TP	PPM
KISSANE, J.	-	4/5	.800	2/3	.667	-/4	-	-	2	-	-	10	-
EVANS, B.	-	1/3	.333	3/6	.500	-/0	-	-	3	-	-	5	-
KVANCZ, J.	-	3/3	1.000	2/4	.500	-/1	-	-	4	-	-	8	-
ADELMAN, S.	-	5/7	.714	6/7	.857	-/1	-	-	1	-	-	16	-
DRISCOLL	-	0/2	.000	2/3	.667	-/2	-	-	2	-	-	2	-
WOLTERS, W.	-	3/5	.600	1/2	.500	-/4	-	-	3	-	-	7	-
KELLEHER	-	0/1	.000	0/0	.000	-/1	-	-	0	-	-	0	-
Totals	200	16/26	.615	16/25	.640	-/13	-	-	15	-	-	48	.240

U. Conn. (42)　Coach: Fred Shabel

	Min.	Total FG/FGA	Pct.	FT/FTA	Pct.	Reb. O/T	A	TO	PF	S	Blk	TP	PPM
PENDERS	-	2/3	.667	1/1	1.000	-/0	-	-	5	-	-	5	-
CORLEY	-	3/3	1.000	0/0	.000	-/3	-	-	5	-	-	6	-
HOLOWATY, B.	-	3/6	.500	2/2	1.000	-/4	-	-	2	-	-	8	-
RITTER	-	2/4	.500	0/0	.000	-/0	-	-	0	-	-	4	-
BIALOSUKNIA	-	5/15	.333	5/5	1.000	-/2	-	-	3	-	-	15	-
THOMPSON	-	1/2	.500	2/3	.667	-/2	-	-	1	-	-	4	-
CURRAN	-	0/0	.000	0/0	.000	-/0	-	-	1	-	-	0	-
Totals	200	16/33	.485	10/11	.909	-/11	-	-	17	-	-	42	.210

Team Rebounds: Boston College 8; U. Conn. 5. Disqualified: U. Conn.—Penders, Corley.

	1st Half	2nd Half	Final
Boston College	14	34	48
U. Conn.	13	29	42

FIRST ROUND MIDEAST

Dayton (69)　Coach: Don Donoher

	Min.	Total FG/FGA	Pct.	FT/FTA	Pct.	Reb. O/T	A	TO	PF	S	Blk	TP	PPM
MAY, D.	45	10/18	.556	6/9	.667	-/20	1	-	3	-	-	26	.578
SADLIER, D.	37	3/6	.500	0/0	.000	-/4	0	-	3	-	-	6	.162
OBROVAC, D.	20	0/4	.000	1/2	.500	-/6	1	-	1	-	-	1	.050
KLAUS, G.	17	0/3	.000	1/1	1.000	-/0	1	-	4	-	-	1	.059
HOOPER, B.	44	2/5	.400	5/5	1.000	-/1	2	-	1	-	-	9	.205
WATERMAN, R.	30	6/14	.429	4/7	.571	-/3	3	-	5	-	-	16	.533
TORAIN, G.	32	4/10	.400	2/4	.500	-/8	0	-	0	-	-	10	.313
Totals	225	25/60	.417	19/28	.679	-/42	8	12	13	-	-	69	.307

Western Kentucky (67)　Coach: Johnny Oldham

	Min.	Total FG/FGA	Pct.	FT/FTA	Pct.	Reb. O/T	A	TO	PF	S	Blk	TP	PPM
CHAPMAN, W.	26	5/10	.500	2/3	.667	-/3	1	-	5	-	-	12	.462
HASKINS, C.	39	3/14	.214	2/5	.400	-/7	2	-	1	-	-	8	.205
SMITH, G.	30	3/6	.500	1/3	.333	-/11	2	-	4	-	-	7	.233
SMITH, D.	45	7/12	.583	4/7	.571	-/5	3	-	2	-	-	18	.400
KAUFMAN, W.	45	8/19	.421	1/1	1.000	-/8	3	-	3	-	-	17	.378
HICKS, P.	2	0/0	.000	0/0	.000	-/0	0	-	0	-	-	0	.000
WEAVER, N.	24	2/5	.400	1/1	1.000	-/4	0	-	4	-	-	5	.208
FAWCETT, M.	14	0/1	.000	0/0	.000	-/0	0	-	2	-	-	0	.000
Totals	225	28/67	.418	11/20	.550	-/38	11	8	21	-	-	67	.298

Virginia Tech (82)　Coach: Howard Shannon

	Min.	Total FG/FGA	Pct.	FT/FTA	Pct.	Reb. O/T	A	TO	PF	S	Blk	TP	PPM
PERRY, R.	-	5/12	.417	2/2	1.000	-/6	5	-	3	-	-	12	-
TALLEY, K.	-	10/15	.667	4/7	.571	-/19	1	-	3	-	-	24	-
WARE, T.	-	8/11	.727	1/2	.500	-/9	3	-	4	-	-	17	-
COMBS, G.	-	7/20	.350	4/5	.800	-/3	0	-	4	-	-	18	-
ELLIS, C.	-	2/6	.333	1/3	.333	-/7	1	-	3	-	-	5	-
BROWN, D.	-	3/7	.429	0/0	.000	-/7	0	-	3	-	-	6	-
MALLARD, W.	-	0/2	.000	0/0	.000	-/0	0	-	0	-	-	0	-
ALAUDER, R.	-	0/0	.000	0/0	.000	-/0	0	-	0	-	-	0	-
Totals	200	35/73	.479	12/19	.632	-/51	10	-	20	-	-	82	.410

Toledo (76)　Coach: Bob Nichols

	Min.	Total FG/FGA	Pct.	FT/FTA	Pct.	Reb. O/T	A	TO	PF	S	Blk	TP	PPM
BACKENSTO, B.	27	1/6	.167	1/2	.500	-/6	2	-	2	-	-	3	.111
BRISKER, J.	27	7/17	.412	1/1	1.000	-/10	0	-	0	-	-	15	.556
MIX, S.	40	5/16	.313	8/11	.727	-/14	0	-	3	-	-	18	.450
BABIONE, W.	32	4/9	.444	0/0	.000	-/5	1	-	4	-	-	8	.250
RUDLEY, J.	40	6/9	.667	1/4	.250	-/3	1	-	3	-	-	13	.325
MILLER, B.	26	6/15	.400	7/9	.778	-/7	0	-	1	-	-	19	.731
WHITE, D.	8	0/4	.000	0/0	.000	-/0	1	-	1	-	-	0	.000
Totals	200	29/76	.382	18/27	.667	-/45	5	-	14	-	-	76	.380

Team Rebounds: Dayton 7; Western Ky. 5. Disqualified: Dayton—Waterman; Western Ky.—Chapman.

	1st Half	2nd Half	1 OT	Final
Dayton	25	37	7	69
Western Ky.	35	27	5	67

Team Rebounds: Virginia Tech 3; Toledo 2. Disqualified: None.

	1st Half	2nd Half	Final
Virginia Tech	43	39	82
Toledo	46	30	76

FIRST ROUND MIDWEST

Houston (59)　Coach: Guy Lewis

	Min.	Total FG/FGA	Pct.	FT/FTA	Pct.	Reb. O/T	A	TO	PF	S	Blk	TP	PPM
HAYES, E.	40	12/20	.600	6/10	.600	-/14	0	-	2	-	-	30	.750
BELL, M.	34	5/10	.500	0/2	.000	-/6	4	-	3	-	-	10	.294
CHANEY, D.	33	5/17	.294	1/2	.500	-/1	2	-	5	-	-	11	.333
GRIDER, B.	34	2/3	.667	2/3	.667	-/0	1	-	2	-	-	6	.176
KRUSE, D.	17	0/4	.000	0/0	.000	-/1	3	-	2	-	-	0	.000
LENTZ, L.	17	1/3	.333	0/1	.000	-/3	2	-	1	-	-	2	.118
SPAIN, K.	10	0/0	.000	0/0	.000	-/2	1	-	0	-	-	0	.000
LEWIS, V.	15	0/0	.000	0/0	.000	-/0	3	-	2	-	-	0	.000
Totals	200	25/57	.439	9/19	.474	-/27	16	7	17	-	-	59	.295

New Mexico State (58)　Coach: Lou Henson

	Min.	Total FG/FGA	Pct.	FT/FTA	Pct.	Reb. O/T	A	TO	PF	S	Blk	TP	PPM
TURNER	-	2/5	.400	3/4	.750	-/4	-	-	3	-	-	7	-
GAMBILL	-	6/13	.462	2/2	1.000	-/7	-	-	3	-	-	14	-
EVANS, B.	-	5/10	.500	4/5	.800	-/1	-	-	4	-	-	14	-
LANDIS	-	0/1	.000	2/2	1.000	-/0	-	-	1	-	-	2	-
COLLINS, J.	-	7/13	.538	5/6	.833	-/10	-	-	4	-	-	19	-
MOREHEAD	-	0/0	.000	0/0	.000	-/1	-	-	2	-	-	0	-
HARRIS	-	1/2	.500	0/1	.000	-/2	-	-	0	-	-	2	-
FRANCO, R.	-	0/1	.000	0/0	.000	-/0	-	-	0	-	-	0	-
Totals	200	21/45	.467	16/20	.800	-/25	-	12	17	-	-	58	.290

Team Rebounds: Houston 8; New Mexico St. 10. Disqualified: Houston—Chaney.

	1st Half	2nd Half	Final
Houston	23	36	59
New Mexico St.	25	33	58

FIRST ROUND WEST

Texas Western (62)   Coach: Don Haskins

	Min.	Total FG/FGA	Pct.	FT/FTA	Pct.	Reb. O/T	A	TO	PF	S	Blk	TP	PPM
LATTIN, D.	-	4/6	.667	9/13	.692	-/14	-	-	4	-	-	17	-
WORSLEY, W.	-	6/14	.429	12/12	1.000	-/0	-	-	1	-	-	24	-
CAGER, W.	-	3/10	.300	5/6	.833	-/9	-	-	3	-	-	11	-
PALACIO, D.	-	1/7	.143	5/8	.625	-/6	-	-	4	-	-	7	-
JOHN, K.	-	0/2	.000	0/0	.000	-/0	-	-	0	-	-	0	-
HARRIS, P.	-	1/6	.167	1/1	1.000	-/3	-	-	2	-	-	3	-
CARR, F.	-	0/4	.000	0/0	.000	-/1	-	-	2	-	-	0	-
MYERS, D.	-	0/0	.000	0/1	.000	-/0	-	-	0	-	-	0	-
Totals	200	15/49	.306	32/41	.780	-/33	-	-	16	-	-	62	.310

Seattle (54)   Coach: Lionel Purcell

	Min.	Total FG/FGA	Pct.	FT/FTA	Pct.	Reb. O/T	A	TO	PF	S	Blk	TP	PPM
WORKMAN, T.	-	5/8	.625	3/6	.500	-/4	-	-	0	-	-	13	-
STRONG	-	2/6	.333	4/5	.800	-/3	-	-	5	-	-	8	-
LOTT	-	2/7	.286	2/4	.500	-/7	-	-	4	-	-	6	-
LOONEY, S.	-	7/18	.389	1/1	1.000	-/4	-	-	4	-	-	15	-
WILKINS	-	1/4	.250	0/0	.000	-/6	-	-	4	-	-	2	-
LACOUR	-	2/6	.333	2/3	.667	-/5	-	-	4	-	-	6	-
KREIGER	-	0/0	.000	0/0	.000	-/1	-	-	2	-	-	0	-
ACRES	-	0/0	.000	0/0	.000	-/0	-	-	2	-	-	0	-
BEIL	-	2/5	.400	0/0	.000	-/2	-	-	3	-	-	4	-
JACKSON	-	0/1	.000	0/0	.000	-/0	-	-	0	-	-	0	-
WORKMAN, J.	-	0/0	.000	0/0	.000	-/0	-	-	0	-	-	0	-
O'BRIEN	-	0/0	.000	0/0	.000	-/0	-	-	0	-	-	0	-
Totals	200	21/55	.382	12/19	.632	-/32	-	-	28	-	-	54	.270

Team Rebounds: Texas Western 9; Seattle 10. Disqualified: Seattle—Strong.

	1st Half	2nd Half	Final
Texas Western	20	42	62
Seattle	23	31	54

REGIONAL SEMIFINAL EAST

North Carolina (78)   Coach: Dean Smith

	Min.	Total FG/FGA	Pct.	FT/FTA	Pct.	Reb. O/T	A	TO	PF	S	Blk	TP	PPM
MILLER, L.	44	7/17	.412	2/2	1.000	-/10	3	3	4	-	-	16	.364
BUNTING, B.	35	4/8	.500	1/2	.500	-/9	1	1	0	-	-	9	.257
CLARK, R.	28	3/10	.300	7/9	.778	-/9	0	2	5	-	-	13	.464
GRUBAR, D.	43	2/5	.400	12/16	.750	-/7	3	3	4	-	-	16	.372
LEWIS, B.	43	4/17	.235	6/9	.667	-/10	1	2	3	-	-	14	.326
TUTTLE, G.	19	0/0	.000	3/4	.750	-/0	1	0	1	-	-	3	.158
GAUNTLETT, T.	5	1/3	.333	0/0	.000	-/2	0	1	0	-	-	2	.400
BROWN, J.	8	2/4	.500	1/1	1.000	-/5	1	1	0	-	-	5	.625
Totals	225	23/64	.359	32/43	.744	-/52	10	13	17	-	-	78	.347

Princeton (70)   Coach: B. Van Breda Kolff

	Min.	Total FG/FGA	Pct.	FT/FTA	Pct.	Reb. O/T	A	TO	PF	S	Blk	TP	PPM
HEISER, J.	45	8/20	.400	2/3	.667	-/8	1	2	4	-	-	18	.400
WALTERS, G.	31	1/5	.200	0/4	.000	-/4	4	4	5	-	-	2	.065
THOMFORDE, C.	24	6/17	.353	2/2	1.000	-/7	1	0	5	-	-	14	.583
HAARLOW, J.	17	1/4	.250	0/1	.000	-/2	1	1	1	-	-	2	.118
HUMMER, E.	45	6/18	.333	2/5	.400	-/9	1	2	4	-	-	14	.311
BROWN, R.	20	3/8	.375	2/4	.500	-/7	0	1	2	-	-	8	.400
LAWYER, D.	23	3/9	.333	2/2	1.000	-/4	1	0	5	-	-	8	.348
LUCCHINO, L.	20	2/4	.500	0/0	.000	-/1	0	0	2	-	-	4	.200
Totals	225	30/85	.353	10/21	.476	-/42	9	10	28	-	-	70	.311

Team Rebounds: N. Carolina 12; Princeton 10. Disqualified: N. Carolina—Clark; Princeton—Walters, Lawyer, Thomforde.

	1st Half	2nd Half	1 OT	Final
N. Carolina	29	34	15	78
Princeton	28	35	7	70

St. John's (62)   Coach: Lou Carnesecca

	Min.	Total FG/FGA	Pct.	FT/FTA	Pct.	Reb. O/T	A	TO	PF	S	Blk	TP	PPM
BOGAD, R.	-	7/16	.438	7/8	.875	-/16	-	-	4	-	-	21	-
WARREN, J.	-	2/8	.250	0/0	.000	-/4	-	-	4	-	-	4	-
DOVE, S.	-	6/11	.545	3/4	.750	-/10	-	-	5	-	-	15	-
SWARTZ, A.	-	2/5	.400	0/1	.000	-/3	-	-	3	-	-	4	-
CALZONETTI, C.	-	5/9	.556	2/2	1.000	-/4	-	-	1	-	-	12	-
BRUNNER, J.	-	2/3	.667	0/0	.000	-/3	-	-	2	-	-	4	-
HILL, B.	-	1/1	1.000	0/0	.000	-/0	-	-	5	-	-	2	-
Totals	200	25/53	.472	12/15	.800	-/40	-	-	24	-	-	62	.310

Boston College (63)   Coach: Bob Cousey

	Min.	Total FG/FGA	Pct.	FT/FTA	Pct.	Reb. O/T	A	TO	PF	S	Blk	TP	PPM
ADELMAN, S.	-	5/14	.357	7/7	1.000	-/4	-	-	1	-	-	17	-
KISSANE, J.	-	1/8	.125	5/6	.833	-/5	-	-	3	-	-	7	-
WOLTERS, W.	-	2/9	.222	5/5	1.000	-/7	-	-	3	-	-	9	-
KVANCZ, J.	-	2/7	.286	3/3	1.000	-/1	-	-	1	-	-	7	-
EVANS, B.	-	2/7	.286	6/9	.667	-/3	-	-	0	-	-	10	-
DRISCOLL	-	2/8	.250	1/2	.500	-/8	-	-	3	-	-	5	-
HICE	-	1/1	1.000	4/4	1.000	-/1	-	-	3	-	-	6	-
KELLEHER	-	1/1	1.000	0/0	.000	-/0	-	-	1	-	-	2	-
Totals	200	16/55	.291	31/36	.861	-/29	-	-	15	-	-	63	.315

Team Rebounds: Boston College 2; St. John's 4. Disqualified: St. John's—Dove, Hill.

	1st Half	2nd Half	Final
St. John's	24	38	62
Boston College	22	41	63

REGIONAL SEMIFINAL MIDEAST

Tennessee (52) Coach: Ray Mears

	Min.	Total FG / FGA	Pct.	FT / FTA	Pct.	Reb. O / T	A	TO	PF	S	Blk	TP	PPM
WIDBY, R.	-	7/20	.350	6/ 7	.857	-/ 4	-	-	2	-	-	20	-
HENDRIX, T.	-	5/11	.455	0/ 0	.000	-/ 1	-	-	2	-	-	10	-
BOERWINKLE, T.	-	4/ 7	.571	2/ 3	.667	-/ 9	-	-	5	-	-	10	-
JUSTUS, B.	-	4/ 9	.444	2/ 3	.667	-/ 5	-	-	2	-	-	10	-
HANN, B.	-	0/ 4	.000	1/ 1	1.000	-/ 2	-	-	0	-	-	1	-
COFFMAN, W.	-	0/ 0	.000	0/ 0	.000	-/ 0	-	-	0	-	-	0	-
BELL, D.	-	0/ 1	.000	1/ 2	.500	-/ 2	-	-	0	-	-	1	-
Totals	200	20/52	.385	12/16	.750	-/23	-	-	11	-	-	52	.260

Dayton (53) Coach: Don Donoher

	Min.	Total FG / FGA	Pct.	FT / FTA	Pct.	Reb. O / T	A	TO	PF	S	Blk	TP	PPM
MAY, D.	-	2/10	.200	5/ 5	1.000	-/14	-	-	2	-	-	9	-
SADLIER, D.	-	4/ 4	1.000	2/ 2	1.000	-/ 1	-	-	4	-	-	10	-
OBROVAC, D.	-	1/ 2	.500	1/ 2	.500	-/ 4	-	-	2	-	-	3	-
KLAUS, G.	-	5/ 7	.714	2/ 2	1.000	-/ 0	-	-	0	-	-	12	-
HOOPER, B.	-	6/ 7	.857	2/ 2	1.000	-/ 2	-	-	0	-	-	14	-
WATERMAN, R.	-	2/ 3	.667	0/ 0	.000	-/ 0	-	-	0	-	-	4	-
TORAIN, G.	-	0/ 2	.000	1/ 1	1.000	-/ 3	-	-	2	-	-	1	-
Totals	200	20/35	.571	13/14	.929	-/24	-	-	10	-	-	53	.265

Team Rebounds: Dayton 1; Tennessee 4. Disqualified: Tennessee—Boerwinkle.

	1st Half	2nd Half	Final
Tennessee	25	27	52
Dayton	36	17	53

Virginia Tech (79) Coach: Howard Shannon

	Min.	Total FG / FGA	Pct.	FT / FTA	Pct.	Reb. O / T	A	TO	PF	S	Blk	TP	PPM
PERRY, R.	-	2/12	.167	3/ 5	.600	-/13	-	-	5	-	-	7	-
TALLEY, K.	-	6/10	.600	4/ 4	1.000	-/11	-	-	2	-	-	16	-
WARE, T.	-	1/ 4	.250	5/ 8	.625	-/ 8	-	-	4	-	-	7	-
COMBS, G.	-	11/24	.458	7/10	.700	-/ 4	-	-	2	-	-	29	-
ELLIS, C.	-	4/ 9	.444	0/ 0	.000	-/ 7	-	-	5	-	-	8	-
BROWN, D.	-	2/ 4	.500	4/ 4	1.000	-/ 7	-	-	4	-	-	8	-
MALLARD, W.	-	1/ 1	1.000	2/ 2	1.000	-/ 0	-	-	0	-	-	4	-
Totals	200	27/64	.422	25/33	.758	-/50	-	15	22	-	-	79	.395

Indiana (70) Coach: Lou Watson

	Min.	Total FG / FGA	Pct.	FT / FTA	Pct.	Reb. O / T	A	TO	PF	S	Blk	TP	PPM
JOYNER, H.	-	6/18	.333	2/ 7	.286	-/10	-	-	4	-	-	14	-
JOHNSON, J.	-	6/15	.400	3/ 4	.750	-/14	-	-	3	-	-	15	-
DEHEER, W.	-	2/ 5	.400	1/ 1	1.000	-/11	-	-	3	-	-	5	-
PAYNE, V.	-	7/19	.368	4/ 8	.500	-/ 4	-	-	5	-	-	18	-
RUSSELL, W.	-	4/17	.235	3/ 7	.429	-/ 7	-	-	3	-	-	11	-
STENBERG, W.	-	1/ 1	1.000	1/ 1	1.000	-/ 0	-	-	1	-	-	3	-
SCHNEIDER, E.	-	0/ 3	.000	0/ 0	.000	-/ 2	-	-	3	-	-	0	-
PFAFF, V.	-	2/ 3	.667	0/ 1	.000	-/ 0	-	-	3	-	-	4	-
TURPEN, L.	-	0/ 0	.000	0/ 0	.000	-/ 0	-	-	0	-	-	0	-
OLIVERIO, G.	-	0/ 3	.000	0/ 0	.000	-/ 2	-	-	0	-	-	0	-
Totals	200	28/84	.333	14/29	.483	-/50	-	9	25	-	-	70	.350

Team Rebounds: Virginia Tech 5; Indiana 11. Disqualified: Virginia Tech—Perry, Ellis; Indiana—Payne.

	1st Half	2nd Half	Final
Virginia Tech	35	44	79
Indiana	31	39	70

REGIONAL SEMIFINAL MIDWEST

Kansas (53) Coach: Ted Owens

	Min.	Total FG / FGA	Pct.	FT / FTA	Pct.	Reb. O / T	A	TO	PF	S	Blk	TP	PPM
FRANZ, R.	-	3/11	.273	0/ 0	.000	-/ 2	-	4	4	-	-	6	-
BOHNENSTIEHL, R.	-	5/13	.385	2/ 3	.667	-/ 8	-	2	1	-	-	12	-
VANOY, V.	-	4/ 5	.800	5/ 6	.833	-/ 9	-	3	1	-	-	13	-
WHITE, J.	-	9/24	.375	0/ 0	.000	-/ 3	-	1	4	-	-	18	-
SLOAN, B.	-	0/ 1	.000	0/ 0	.000	-/ 0	-	0	2	-	-	0	-
HARMON, P.	-	2/ 9	.222	0/ 0	.000	-/ 3	-	2	4	-	-	4	-
ARNDT, H.	-	0/ 0	.000	0/ 0	.000	-/ 0	-	0	0	-	-	0	-
Totals	200	23/63	.365	7/ 9	.778	-/25	-	12	16	-	-	53	.265

Houston (66) Coach: Guy Lewis

	Min.	Total FG / FGA	Pct.	FT / FTA	Pct.	Reb. O / T	A	TO	PF	S	Blk	TP	PPM
HAYES, E.	40	9/18	.500	1/ 2	.500	-/14	-	1	3	-	-	19	.475
BELL, M.	31	5/11	.455	1/ 4	.250	-/ 8	-	1	0	-	-	11	.355
CHANEY, D.	40	8/16	.500	4/ 4	1.000	-/ 5	-	2	0	-	-	20	.500
GRIDER, B.	36	1/ 2	.500	2/ 5	.400	-/ 5	-	2	0	-	-	4	.111
KRUSE, D.	20	2/ 4	.500	2/ 3	.667	-/ 7	-	1	4	-	-	6	.300
LENTZ, L.	22	2/ 6	.333	2/ 3	.667	-/ 4	-	1	0	-	-	6	.273
SPAIN, K.	7	0/ 1	.000	0/ 0	.000	-/ 1	-	0	0	-	-	0	.000
LEWIS, V.	4	0/ 3	.000	0/ 0	.000	-/ 0	-	1	0	-	-	0	.000
Totals	200	27/61	.443	12/21	.571	-/44	-	9	7	-	-	66	.330

Team Rebounds: Houston 10; Kansas 6. Disqualified: None.

	1st Half	2nd Half	Final
Kansas	29	24	53
Houston	32	34	66

SMU (83) Coach: E. O. "Doc" Hayes

	Min.	Total FG / FGA	Pct.	FT / FTA	Pct.	Reb. O / T	A	TO	PF	S	Blk	TP	PPM
BEGERT, B.	-	7/10	.700	2/ 2	1.000	-/ 9	-	1	2	-	-	16	-
BEASLEY, C.	-	4/13	.308	1/ 2	.500	-/ 4	-	1	3	-	-	9	-
PHILLIPS, L.	-	8/14	.571	2/ 8	.250	-/ 6	-	2	0	-	-	18	-
JONES, B.	-	3/ 6	.500	0/ 0	.000	-/ 1	-	1	2	-	-	6	-
HOLMAN, D.	-	13/21	.619	4/ 4	1.000	-/ 5	-	2	2	-	-	30	-
VOIGHT, B.	-	2/ 6	.333	0/ 0	.000	-/ 4	-	1	2	-	-	4	-
Totals	200	37/70	.529	9/16	.563	-/29	-	8	11	-	-	83	.415

Louisville (81) Coach: Peck Hickman

	Min.	Total FG / FGA	Pct.	FT / FTA	Pct.	Reb. O / T	A	TO	PF	S	Blk	TP	PPM
KING, J.	-	10/13	.769	0/ 2	.000	-/ 8	-	5	3	-	-	20	-
BEARD, B.	-	6/15	.400	2/ 7	.286	-/ 9	-	5	2	-	-	14	-
UNSELD, W.	-	8/14	.571	2/ 2	1.000	-/12	-	2	4	-	-	18	-
GILBERT, D.	-	2/ 8	.250	0/ 0	.000	-/ 3	-	2	1	-	-	4	-
HOLDEN, F.	-	11/17	.647	1/ 2	.500	-/ 3	-	4	2	-	-	23	-
DEEKEN, D.	-	1/ 1	1.000	0/ 1	.000	-/ 1	-	0	0	-	-	2	-
LIEDTKE, J.	-	0/ 0	.000	0/ 0	.000	-/ 0	-	0	1	-	-	0	-
Totals	200	38/68	.559	5/14	.357	-/36	-	18	13	-	-	81	.405

Team Rebounds: SMU 4; Louisville 7. Disqualified: None.

	1st Half	2nd Half	Final
SMU	44	39	83
Louisville	45	36	81

REGIONAL SEMIFINAL WEST

Pacific (72) Coach: Dick Edwards

	Min.	Total FG/FGA	Pct.	FT/FTA	Pct.	Reb. O/T	A	TO	PF	S	Blk	TP	PPM
KRULISH, B.	-	10/14	.714	4/ 5	.800	-/ 3	-	-	2	-	-	24	-
JONES, B.	-	0/ 1	.000	0/ 0	.000	-/ 1	-	-	1	-	-	0	-
SWAGERTY, K.	-	5/ 9	.556	9/12	.750	-/ 8	-	-	4	-	-	19	-
FOX, D.	-	7/15	.467	0/ 2	.000	-/ 4	-	-	3	-	-	14	-
PARSONS, B.	-	4/ 9	.444	2/ 4	.500	-/ 4	-	-	2	-	-	10	-
DEWITT, R.	-	0/ 0	.000	0/ 0	.000	-/ 1	-	-	1	-	-	0	-
FOLEY, P.	-	1/ 6	.167	3/ 5	.600	-/ 8	-	-	2	-	-	5	-
Totals	200	27/54	.500	18/28	.643	-/29	-	4	15	-	-	72	.360

Texas Western (63) Coach: Don Haskins

	Min.	Total FG/FGA	Pct.	FT/FTA	Pct.	Reb. O/T	A	TO	PF	S	Blk	TP	PPM
LATTIN, D.	-	6/13	.462	1/ 1	1.000	-/ 5	-	-	5	-	-	13	-
WORSLEY, W.	-	6/22	.273	1/ 4	.250	-/ 4	-	-	4	-	-	13	-
CAGER, W.	-	5/15	.333	3/ 3	1.000	-/10	-	-	3	-	-	13	-
PALACIO, D.	-	1/ 7	.143	0/ 0	.000	-/ 3	-	-	1	-	-	2	-
JOHN, K.	-	0/ 1	.000	0/ 0	.000	-/ 0	-	-	0	-	-	0	-
HARRIS, P.	-	3/ 4	.750	2/ 2	1.000	-/ 9	-	-	4	-	-	8	-
CARR, F.	-	5/ 8	.625	2/ 6	.333	-/12	-	-	0	-	-	12	-
MYERS, D.	-	1/ 1	1.000	0/ 0	.000	-/ 2	-	-	2	-	-	2	-
Totals	200	27/71	.380	9/16	.563	-/45	-	11	19	-	-	63	.315

Team Rebounds: Pacific 7; Texas Western 4. Disqualified: Texas Western—Lattin. Technical fouls: Texas Western—bench.

	1st Half	2nd Half	Final
Pacific	36	36	72
Texas Western	33	30	63

UCLA (109) Coach: John Wooden

	Min.	Total FG/FGA	Pct.	FT/FTA	Pct.	Reb. O/T	A	TO	PF	S	Blk	TP	PPM
HEITZ, K.	-	3/ 3	1.000	0/ 0	.000	-/ 0	-	-	5	-	-	6	-
SHACKELFORD, L.	-	5/ 8	.625	0/ 0	.000	-/ 7	-	-	2	-	-	10	-
ALCINDOR, L.	-	12/17	.706	5/ 5	1.000	-/10	-	-	1	-	-	29	-
ALLEN, L.	-	6/11	.545	3/ 3	1.000	-/ 5	-	-	1	-	-	15	-
WARREN, M.	-	4/11	.364	2/ 4	.500	-/ 5	-	-	0	-	-	10	-
CHRISMAN, J.	-	2/ 2	1.000	2/ 3	.667	-/ 0	-	-	3	-	-	6	-
NIELSEN, J.	-	4/ 6	.667	0/ 0	.000	-/ 5	-	-	1	-	-	8	-
SANER, N.	-	2/ 3	.667	0/ 0	.000	-/ 4	-	-	1	-	-	4	-
SWEEK, B.	-	4/ 6	.667	0/ 2	.000	-/ 5	-	-	2	-	-	8	-
LYNN, D.	-	0/ 1	.000	0/ 0	.000	-/ 0	-	-	1	-	-	0	-
SUTHERLAND, G.	-	2/ 4	.500	1/ 2	.500	-/ 1	-	-	1	-	-	5	-
SAFFER, D.	-	4/ 6	.667	0/ 0	.000	-/ 2	-	-	0	-	-	8	-
Totals	200	48/78	.615	13/19	.684	-/44	-	10	18	-	-	109	.545

Wyoming (60) Coach: Bill Strannigan

	Min.	Total FG/FGA	Pct.	FT/FTA	Pct.	Reb. O/T	A	TO	PF	S	Blk	TP	PPM
HALL, H.	-	6/16	.375	7/11	.636	-/ 5	-	-	2	-	-	19	-
ASBURY, T.	-	8/20	.400	4/ 6	.667	-/10	-	-	2	-	-	20	-
VONKROSIGK, G.	-	1/ 7	.143	2/ 4	.500	-/ 8	-	-	4	-	-	4	-
WILSON, B.	-	2/ 6	.333	1/ 1	1.000	-/ 3	-	-	3	-	-	5	-
EBERLE, M.	-	6/12	.500	0/ 1	.000	-/ 5	-	-	4	-	-	12	-
NELSON, C.	-	0/ 2	.000	0/ 0	.000	-/ 2	-	-	1	-	-	0	-
Totals	200	23/63	.365	14/23	.609	-/33	-	19	16	-	-	60	.300

Team Rebounds: UCLA 1; Wyoming 7. Disqualified: UCLA—Heitz.

	1st Half	2nd Half	Final
UCLA	55	54	109
Wyoming	18	42	60

REGIONAL FINAL EAST

North Carolina (96) Coach: Dean Smith

	Min.	Total FG/FGA	Pct.	FT/FTA	Pct.	Reb. O/T	A	TO	PF	S	Blk	TP	PPM
MILLER, L.	-	6/16	.375	10/12	.833	-/ 5	-	-	2	-	-	22	-
BUNTING, B.	-	5/10	.500	2/ 3	.667	-/ 4	-	-	4	-	-	12	-
CLARK, R.	-	7/10	.700	4/ 5	.800	-/18	-	-	3	-	-	18	-
GRUBAR, D.	-	1/ 2	.500	1/ 1	1.000	-/ 3	-	-	3	-	-	3	-
LEWIS, B.	-	11/18	.611	9/10	.900	-/ 3	-	-	1	-	-	31	-
GAUNTLETT, T.	-	1/ 1	1.000	0/ 0	.000	-/ 0	-	-	0	-	-	2	-
TUTTLE, G.	-	1/ 1	1.000	0/ 0	.000	-/ 0	-	-	1	-	-	2	-
BROWN, J.	-	2/ 4	.500	0/ 0	.000	-/ 3	-	-	2	-	-	4	-
MOE	-	0/ 0	.000	0/ 0	.000	-/ 0	-	-	0	-	-	0	-
FRYE	-	1/ 1	1.000	0/ 1	.000	-/ 0	-	-	0	-	-	2	-
FLETCHER	-	0/ 0	.000	0/ 0	.000	-/ 0	-	-	0	-	-	0	-
BOSTICK	-	0/ 0	.000	0/ 0	.000	-/ 0	-	-	0	-	-	0	-
Totals	200	35/63	.556	26/32	.813	-/36	-	-	16	-	-	96	.480

Boston College (80) Coach: Bob Cousey

	Min.	Total FG/FGA	Pct.	FT/FTA	Pct.	Reb. O/T	A	TO	PF	S	Blk	TP	PPM
ADELMAN, S.	-	4/12	.333	1/ 2	.500	-/ 6	-	-	2	-	-	9	-
KISSANE, J.	-	5/15	.333	5/ 5	1.000	-/10	-	-	3	-	-	15	-
WOLTERS, W.	-	2/ 8	.250	2/ 2	1.000	-/ 7	-	-	4	-	-	6	-
KVANCZ, J.	-	5/ 8	.625	1/ 1	1.000	-/ 1	-	-	4	-	-	11	-
EVANS, B.	-	3/ 8	.375	2/ 5	.400	-/ 3	-	-	2	-	-	8	-
DRISCOLL	-	7/17	.412	3/ 4	.750	-/10	-	-	2	-	-	17	-
HICE	-	3/ 7	.429	0/ 1	.000	-/ 2	-	-	4	-	-	6	-
KELLEHER	-	0/ 1	.000	0/ 0	.000	-/ 0	-	-	0	-	-	0	-
KING	-	1/ 2	.500	0/ 0	.000	-/ 1	-	-	1	-	-	2	-
ROONEY	-	0/ 1	.000	0/ 0	.000	-/ 0	-	-	0	-	-	0	-
PACYNSKI	-	3/ 3	1.000	0/ 0	.000	-/ 2	-	-	1	-	-	6	-
GALLUP	-	0/ 0	.000	0/ 0	.000	-/ 0	-	-	1	-	-	0	-
Totals	200	33/82	.402	14/20	.700	-/42	-	-	24	-	-	80	.400

Team Rebounds: N. Carolina 5; Boston College 6. Disqualified: None.

	1st Half	2nd Half	Final
N. Carolina	44	52	96
Boston College	42	38	80

REGIONAL FINAL MIDEAST

Dayton (71)   Coach: Don Donoher

	Min.	Total FG / FGA	Pct.	FT / FTA	Pct.	Reb. O / T	A	TO	PF	S	Blk	TP	PPM
MAY, D.	-	9/24	.375	10/11	.909	-/16	-	-	1	-	-	28	-
SADLIER, D.	-	3/ 6	.500	0/ 1	.000	-/ 7	-	-	4	-	-	6	-
OBROVAC, D.	-	1/ 2	.500	1/ 1	1.000	-/ 0	-	-	3	-	-	3	-
KLAUS, G.	-	0/ 1	.000	0/ 0	.000	-/ 0	-	-	1	-	-	0	-
HOOPER, B.	-	5/10	.500	2/ 2	1.000	-/ 1	-	-	0	-	-	12	-
WATERMAN, R.	-	4/12	.333	1/ 2	.500	-/ 4	-	-	2	-	-	9	-
TORAIN, G.	-	5/11	.455	3/ 3	1.000	-/ 9	-	-	4	-	-	13	-
Totals	225	27/66	.409	17/20	.850	-/37	-	12	15	-	-	71	.316

Virginia Tech (66)   Coach: Howard Shannon

	Min.	Total FG / FGA	Pct.	FT / FTA	Pct.	Reb. O / T	A	TO	PF	S	Blk	TP	PPM
PERRY, R.	-	6/12	.500	2/ 5	.400	-/ 2	-	-	5	-	-	14	-
TALLEY, K.	-	4/ 5	.800	1/ 1	1.000	-/10	-	-	4	-	-	9	-
WARE, T.	-	3/ 7	.429	2/ 3	.667	-/ 8	-	-	4	-	-	8	-
COMBS, G.	-	7/23	.304	2/ 3	.667	-/ 8	-	-	0	-	-	16	-
ELLIS, C.	-	5/11	.455	1/ 1	1.000	-/ 4	-	-	4	-	-	11	-
BROWN, D.	-	2/ 4	.500	0/ 0	.000	-/ 3	-	-	1	-	-	4	-
MALLARD, W.	-	1/ 2	.500	2/ 2	1.000	-/ 2	-	-	0	-	-	4	-
Totals	225	28/64	.438	10/15	.667	-/37	-	14	18	-	-	66	.293

Team Rebounds: Dayton 7; Virginia Tech 2. Disqualified: Virginia Tech—Perry.

	1st Half	2nd Half	1 OT	Final
Dayton	28	36	7	71
Virginia Tech	27	37	2	66

REGIONAL FINAL MIDWEST

Houston (83)   Coach: Guy Lewis

	Min.	Total FG / FGA	Pct.	FT / FTA	Pct.	Reb. O / T	A	TO	PF	S	Blk	TP	PPM
HAYES, E.	39	14/27	.519	3/ 6	.500	-/11	2	2	3	-	-	31	.795
BELL, M.	25	5/11	.455	1/ 2	.500	-/ 8	2	4	4	-	-	11	.440
CHANEY, D.	40	3/15	.200	4/ 4	1.000	-/10	9	5	2	-	-	10	.250
GRIDER, B.	35	3/ 4	.750	3/ 5	.600	-/ 2	8	1	2	-	-	9	.257
KRUSE, D.	15	1/ 1	1.000	2/ 2	1.000	-/ 1	2	1	3	-	-	4	.267
LENTZ, L.	27	3/ 5	.600	2/ 4	.500	-/10	3	3	3	-	-	8	.296
SPAIN, K.	14	4/ 4	1.000	2/ 3	.667	-/ 6	0	4	3	-	-	10	.714
LEWIS, V.	5	0/ 1	.000	0/ 0	.000	-/ 0	1	2	0	-	-	0	.000
Totals	200	33/68	.485	17/26	.654	-/48	27	22	20	-	-	83	.415

SMU (75)   Coach: E. O. ''Doc'' Hayes

	Min.	Total FG / FGA	Pct.	FT / FTA	Pct.	Reb. O / T	A	TO	PF	S	Blk	TP	PPM
BEGERT, B.	-	3/11	.273	5/ 5	1.000	-/15	-	2	3	-	-	11	-
BEASLEY, C.	-	8/16	.500	2/ 2	1.000	-/ 4	-	1	3	-	-	18	-
PHILLIPS, L.	-	1/ 4	.250	4/ 7	.571	-/ 7	-	3	4	-	-	6	-
JONES, B.	-	5/ 9	.556	0/ 0	.000	-/ 1	-	1	1	-	-	10	-
HOLMAN, D.	-	5/14	.357	6/ 7	.857	-/ 0	-	5	4	-	-	16	-
VOIGHT, B.	-	4/10	.400	6/ 8	.750	-/ 4	-	2	2	-	-	14	-
HIGGINBOTHAM, J.	-	0/ 0	.000	0/ 1	.000	-/ 0	-	0	0	-	-	0	-
Totals	200	26/64	.406	23/30	.767	-/31	-	14	17	-	-	75	.375

Team Rebounds: Houston 3; SMU 7. Disqualified: None.

	1st Half	2nd Half	Final
Houston	39	44	83
SMU	33	42	75

REGIONAL FINAL WEST

Pacific (64)   Coach: Dick Edwards

	Min.	Total FG / FGA	Pct.	FT / FTA	Pct.	Reb. O / T	A	TO	PF	S	Blk	TP	PPM
KRULISH, B.	-	5/12	.417	2/ 2	1.000	-/ 7	-	-	3	-	-	12	-
JONES, B.	-	0/ 1	.000	0/ 0	.000	-/ 0	-	-	1	-	-	0	-
SWAGERTY, K.	-	5/12	.417	1/ 5	.200	-/ 8	-	-	4	-	-	11	-
FOX, D.	-	6/18	.333	5/ 7	.714	-/ 6	-	-	4	-	-	17	-
PARSONS, B.	-	1/ 3	.333	5/ 6	.833	-/ 6	-	-	2	-	-	7	-
DEWITT, R.	-	3/ 9	.333	0/ 3	.000	-/13	-	-	2	-	-	6	-
FOLEY, P.	-	4/ 6	.667	1/ 2	.500	-/ 4	-	-	4	-	-	9	-
FERGUSON, J.	-	1/ 3	.333	0/ 0	.000	-/ 0	-	-	1	-	-	2	-
Totals	200	25/64	.391	14/25	.560	-/44	-	10	21	-	-	64	.320

UCLA (80)   Coach: John Wooden

	Min.	Total FG / FGA	Pct.	FT / FTA	Pct.	Reb. O / T	A	TO	PF	S	Blk	TP	PPM
HEITZ, K.	-	4/ 6	.667	1/ 1	1.000	-/ 3	-	-	3	-	-	9	-
SHACKELFORD, L.	-	3/12	.250	0/ 1	.000	-/ 4	-	-	2	-	-	6	-
ALCINDOR, L.	-	13/20	.650	12/14	.857	-/14	-	-	4	-	-	38	-
ALLEN, L.	-	5/ 8	.625	3/ 6	.500	-/ 6	-	-	3	-	-	13	-
WARREN, M.	-	4/ 8	.500	4/ 6	.667	-/ 2	-	-	1	-	-	12	-
SWEEK, B.	-	1/ 4	.250	0/ 0	.000	-/ 0	-	-	4	-	-	2	-
SAFFER, D.	-	0/ 0	.000	0/ 0	.000	-/ 0	-	-	0	-	-	0	-
Totals	200	30/58	.517	20/28	.714	-/29	-	9	17	-	-	80	.400

Team Rebounds: UCLA 6; Pacific 6. Disqualified: None.

	1st Half	2nd Half	Final
Pacific	27	37	64
UCLA	37	43	80

FINAL FOUR

North Carolina (62)　Coach: Dean Smith

	Min.	Total FG/FGA	Pct.	FT/FTA	Pct.	Reb. O/T	A	TO	PF	S	Blk	TP	PPM
MILLER, L.	40	6/18	.333	1/1	1.000	-/13	0	-	4	-	-	13	.325
BUNTING, B.	22	1/3	.333	1/1	1.000	-/5	2	-	4	-	-	3	.136
CLARK, R.	37	8/14	.571	3/5	.600	-/11	0	-	4	-	-	19	.514
LEWIS, B.	37	5/18	.278	1/1	1.000	-/3	0	-	3	-	-	11	.297
GRUBAR, D.	36	2/7	.286	3/3	1.000	-/2	2	-	4	-	-	7	.194
GAUNTLETT, T.	8	1/4	.250	0/0	.000	-/3	0	-	0	-	-	2	.250
BROWN, J.	6	0/3	.000	0/0	.000	-/0	0	-	0	-	-	0	.000
TUTTLE, G.	14	3/5	.600	1/1	1.000	-/1	3	-	3	-	-	7	.500
Totals	200	26/72	.361	10/12	.833	-/38	7	-	22	-	-	62	.310

Dayton (76)　Coach: Don Donoher

	Min.	Total FG/FGA	Pct.	FT/FTA	Pct.	Reb. O/T	A	TO	PF	S	Blk	TP	PPM
MAY, D.	39	16/22	.727	2/6	.333	-/15	3	-	2	-	-	34	.872
SADLIER, D.	40	4/7	.571	0/1	.000	-/0	0	-	0	-	-	8	.200
OBROVAC, D.	4	0/0	.000	0/0	.000	-/1	0	-	1	-	-	0	.000
KLAUS, G.	40	3/6	.500	9/10	.900	-/8	2	-	4	-	-	15	.375
HOOPER, B.	40	1/7	.143	3/4	.750	-/4	3	-	1	-	-	5	.125
TORAIN, G.	34	4/14	.286	6/8	.750	-/11	4	-	5	-	-	14	.412
WANNEMACHER, J.	2	0/0	.000	0/2	.000	-/0	0	-	0	-	-	0	.000
WATERMAN, R.	1	0/0	.000	0/0	.000	-/0	0	-	0	-	-	0	.000
Totals	200	28/56	.500	20/31	.645	-/39	12	-	13	-	-	76	.380

Team Rebounds: Dayton 4; N. Carolina 5. Disqualified: Dayton—Torain.

	1st Half	2nd Half	Final
N. Carolina	23	39	62
Dayton	29	47	76

Houston (58)　Coach: Guy Lewis

	Min.	Total FG/FGA	Pct.	FT/FTA	Pct.	Reb. O/T	A	TO	PF	S	Blk	TP	PPM
HAYES, E.	40	12/31	.387	1/2	.500	-/24	1	-	4	-	-	25	.625
BELL, M.	30	3/11	.273	4/7	.571	-/11	1	-	4	-	-	10	.333
CHANEY, D.	40	3/11	.273	0/2	.000	-/4	1	-	4	-	-	6	.150
GRIDER, B.	32	2/7	.286	0/0	.000	-/2	2	-	2	-	-	4	.125
KRUSE, D.	14	2/5	.400	1/1	1.000	-/0	0	-	2	-	-	5	.357
LENTZ, L.	18	1/2	.500	0/3	.000	-/4	0	-	1	-	-	2	.111
SPAIN, K.	12	1/5	.200	0/0	.000	-/4	0	-	2	-	-	2	.167
LEWIS, V.	8	0/0	.000	0/1	.000	-/0	0	-	1	-	-	0	.000
LEE, T.	6	2/3	.667	0/0	.000	-/1	0	-	0	-	-	4	.667
Totals	200	26/75	.347	6/16	.375	-/50	5	-	20	-	-	58	.290

UCLA (73)　Coach: John Wooden

	Min.	Total FG/FGA	Pct.	FT/FTA	Pct.	Reb. O/T	A	TO	PF	S	Blk	TP	PPM
HEITZ, K.	7	0/0	.000	1/1	1.000	-/0	0	-	1	-	-	1	.143
SHACKELFORD, L.	40	11/19	.579	0/1	.000	-/8	1	-	1	-	-	22	.550
ALCINDOR, L.	40	6/11	.545	7/13	.538	-/20	0	-	1	-	-	19	.475
ALLEN, L.	40	6/15	.400	5/5	1.000	-/9	1	-	2	-	-	17	.425
WARREN, M.	40	4/10	.400	6/7	.857	-/9	1	-	0	-	-	14	.350
NIELSEN, J.	19	0/3	.000	0/0	.000	-/3	0	-	5	-	-	0	.000
SWEEK, B.	12	0/4	.000	0/0	.000	-/1	0	-	2	-	-	0	.000
SAFFER, D.	2	0/0	.000	0/0	.000	-/0	0	-	0	-	-	0	.000
Totals	200	27/62	.435	19/27	.704	-/50	3	-	12	-	-	73	.365

Team Rebounds: UCLA 6; Houston 6. Disqualified: UCLA—Nielsen.

	1st Half	2nd Half	Final
Houston	28	30	58
UCLA	39	34	73

NATIONAL CHAMPIONSHIP

Dayton (64)　Coach: Don Donoher

	Min.	Total FG/FGA	Pct.	FT/FTA	Pct.	Reb. O/T	A	TO	PF	S	Blk	TP	PPM
MAY, D.	40	9/23	.391	3/4	.750	-/17	3	-	4	-	-	21	.525
SADLIER, D.	26	2/5	.400	1/2	.500	-/7	0	-	5	-	-	5	.192
OBROVAC, D.	5	0/2	.000	0/0	.000	-/2	1	-	1	-	-	0	.000
KLAUS, G.	22	4/7	.571	0/0	.000	-/0	0	-	1	-	-	8	.364
HOOPER, B.	34	2/7	.286	2/4	.500	-/5	2	-	2	-	-	6	.176
WATERMAN, R.	23	4/11	.364	2/3	.667	-/1	2	-	3	-	-	10	.435
TORAIN, G.	23	3/14	.214	0/0	.000	-/4	0	-	3	-	-	6	.261
SHARPENTER, N.	23	2/5	.400	4/5	.800	-/5	0	-	1	-	-	8	.348
SAMANICH, J.	1	0/2	.000	0/0	.000	-/2	0	-	0	-	-	0	.000
BECKMAN, T.	1	0/0	.000	0/0	.000	-/0	0	-	0	-	-	0	.000
INDERRIEDEN, D.	1	0/0	.000	0/0	.000	-/0	0	-	0	-	-	0	.000
WANNEMACHER, J.	1	0/0	.000	0/0	.000	-/0	0	-	0	-	-	0	.000
Totals	200	26/76	.342	12/18	.667	-/43	8	-	20	-	-	64	.320

UCLA (79)　Coach: John Wooden

	Min.	Total FG/FGA	Pct.	FT/FTA	Pct.	Reb. O/T	A	TO	PF	S	Blk	TP	PPM
HEITZ, K.	27	2/7	.286	0/0	.000	-/6	1	-	2	-	-	4	.148
SHACKELFORD, L.	35	5/10	.500	0/2	.000	-/3	1	-	1	-	-	10	.286
ALCINDOR, L.	35	8/12	.667	4/11	.364	-/18	3	-	0	-	-	20	.571
ALLEN, L.	36	7/15	.467	5/8	.625	-/9	2	-	2	-	-	19	.528
WARREN, M.	35	8/16	.500	1/1	1.000	-/7	0	-	1	-	-	17	.486
CHRISMAN, J.	4	0/0	.000	1/2	.500	-/1	0	-	2	-	-	1	.250
NIELSEN, J.	4	0/1	.000	0/1	.000	-/1	0	-	3	-	-	0	.000
SANER, N.	5	1/1	1.000	0/0	.000	-/2	0	-	2	-	-	2	.400
SWEEK, B.	8	1/1	1.000	0/0	.000	-/0	0	-	1	-	-	2	.250
LYNN, D.	2	0/1	.000	0/0	.000	-/0	0	-	0	-	-	0	.000
SUTHERLAND, G.	4	0/0	.000	0/0	.000	-/0	0	-	0	-	-	0	.000
SAFFER, D.	5	2/5	.400	0/0	.000	-/0	0	-	1	-	-	4	.800
Totals	200	34/69	.493	11/25	.440	-/47	7	-	15	-	-	79	.395

Team Rebounds: UCLA 7; Dayton 8. Disqualified: Dayton—Sadlier.

	1st Half	2nd Half	Final
Dayton	20	44	64
UCLA	38	41	79

NATIONAL THIRD PLACE
North Carolina (62)   Coach: Dean Smith

	Min.	Total FG/FGA	Pct.	FT/FTA	Pct.	Reb. O/T	A	TO	PF	S	Blk	TP	PPM
MILLER, L.	36	5/20	.250	2/4	.500	-/11	1	-	0	-	-	12	.333
BUNTING, B.	24	1/8	.125	2/7	.286	-/4	1	-	2	-	-	4	.167
CLARK, R.	23	3/6	.500	3/4	.750	-/10	2	-	5	-	-	9	.391
GRUBAR, D.	27	1/7	.143	0/0	.000	-/4	1	-	2	-	-	2	.074
LEWIS, B.	35	9/23	.391	5/6	.833	-/11	2	-	3	-	-	23	.657
TUTTLE, G.	9	1/4	.250	0/0	.000	-/1	1	-	2	-	-	2	.222
GAUNTLETT, T.	18	2/7	.286	2/3	.667	-/1	1	-	2	-	-	6	.333
BROWN, J.	16	0/5	.000	0/1	.000	-/1	0	-	2	-	-	0	.000
FLETCHER, R.	4	1/3	.333	0/0	.000	-/2	0	-	1	-	-	2	.500
FRYE, J.	2	0/1	.000	0/0	.000	-/0	0	-	0	-	-	0	.000
BOSTICK, J.	2	1/1	1.000	0/0	.000	-/1	0	-	0	-	-	2	1.000
MOE, D.	4	0/0	.000	0/0	.000	-/0	1	-	0	-	-	0	.000
Totals	200	24/85	.282	14/25	.560	-/46	10	-	19	-	-	62	.310

Houston (84)   Coach: Guy Lewis

	Min.	Total FG/FGA	Pct.	FT/FTA	Pct.	Reb. O/T	A	TO	PF	S	Blk	TP	PPM
HAYES, E.	38	10/23	.435	3/5	.600	-/16	1	-	3	-	-	23	.605
BELL, M.	8	0/2	.000	0/2	.000	-/7	0	-	2	-	-	0	.000
CHANEY, D.	38	6/13	.462	7/8	.875	-/8	0	-	0	-	-	19	.500
GRIDER, B.	30	2/6	.333	2/3	.667	-/3	2	-	1	-	-	6	.200
KRUSE, D.	7	2/5	.400	0/0	.000	-/2	1	-	5	-	-	4	.571
LENTZ, L.	33	3/10	.300	0/1	.000	-/17	1	-	3	-	-	6	.182
SPAIN, K.	26	9/14	.643	6/9	.667	-/14	1	-	3	-	-	24	.923
LEWIS, V.	9	0/1	.000	0/0	.000	-/0	0	-	1	-	-	0	.000
LEE, T.	6	0/1	.000	0/1	.000	-/5	0	-	1	-	-	0	.000
HAMOOD, N.	2	1/1	1.000	0/0	.000	-/0	0	-	0	-	-	2	1.000
BENSON, A.	2	0/1	.000	0/0	.000	-/0	0	-	0	-	-	0	.000
MCVAY, E.	1	0/1	.000	0/0	.000	-/0	0	-	0	-	-	0	.000
Totals	200	33/78	.423	18/29	.621	-/72	6	-	19	-	-	84	.420

Team Rebounds: Houston 4; N. Carolina 6. Disqualified: Houston—Kruse; N. Carolina—Clark.

	1st Half	2nd Half	Final
N. Carolina	23	39	62
Houston	42	42	84

REGIONAL THIRD PLACE WEST
Texas Western (69)   Coach: Don Haskins

	Min.	Total FG/FGA	Pct.	FT/FTA	Pct.	Reb. O/T	A	TO	PF	S	Blk	TP	PPM
LATTIN, D.	-	11/20	.550	12/13	.923	-/13	-	-	1	-	-	34	-
WORSLEY, W.	-	3/9	.333	2/6	.333	-/3	-	-	3	-	-	8	-
CAGER, W.	-	2/4	.500	2/5	.400	-/2	-	-	3	-	-	6	-
PALACIO, D.	-	4/14	.286	1/3	.333	-/4	-	-	4	-	-	9	-
HARRIS, P.	-	1/4	.250	2/2	1.000	-/5	-	-	1	-	-	4	-
CARR, F.	-	4/5	.800	0/0	.000	-/5	-	-	5	-	-	8	-
MYERS, D.	-	0/0	.000	0/0	.000	-/0	-	-	1	-	-	0	-
Totals	200	25/56	.446	19/29	.655	-/32	-	8	18	-	-	69	.345

Wyoming (67)   Coach: Bill Strannigan

	Min.	Total FG/FGA	Pct.	FT/FTA	Pct.	Reb. O/T	A	TO	PF	S	Blk	TP	PPM
HALL, H.	-	8/14	.571	5/8	.625	-/6	-	-	1	-	-	21	-
ASBURY, T.	-	3/8	.375	0/1	.000	-/6	-	-	5	-	-	6	-
VONKROSIGK, G.	-	3/6	.500	4/6	.667	-/9	-	-	3	-	-	10	-
WILSON, B.	-	2/3	.667	0/0	.000	-/3	-	-	5	-	-	4	-
EBERLE, M.	-	4/15	.267	5/5	1.000	-/8	-	-	4	-	-	13	-
NELSON, C.	-	5/14	.357	3/3	1.000	-/2	-	-	2	-	-	13	-
JOHNSON, K.	-	0/0	.000	0/0	.000	-/1	-	-	0	-	-	0	-
Totals	200	25/60	.417	17/23	.739	-/35	-	15	20	-	-	67	.335

Team Rebounds: Texas Western 4; Wyoming 11. Disqualified: Texas Western—Carr; Wyoming—Asbury, Wilson.

	1st Half	2nd Half	Final
Texas Western	35	34	69
Wyoming	31	36	67

REGIONAL THIRD PLACE MIDWEST
Kansas (70)   Coach: Ted Owens

	Min.	Total FG/FGA	Pct.	FT/FTA	Pct.	Reb. O/T	A	TO	PF	S	Blk	TP	PPM
FRANZ, R.	-	4/9	.444	0/0	.000	-/5	-	1	5	-	-	8	-
BOHNENSTIEHL, R.	-	5/9	.556	3/3	1.000	-/6	-	1	2	-	-	13	-
VANOY, V.	-	4/10	.400	2/4	.500	-/10	-	3	2	-	-	10	-
WHITE, J.	-	11/22	.500	0/0	.000	-/5	-	2	2	-	-	22	-
SLOAN, B.	-	0/3	.000	2/2	1.000	-/0	-	0	1	-	-	2	-
HARMON, P.	-	5/9	.556	3/4	.750	-/2	-	0	1	-	-	13	-
ARNDT, H.	-	1/3	.333	0/0	.000	-/4	-	1	1	-	-	2	-
Totals	200	30/65	.462	10/13	.769	-/32	-	8	14	-	-	70	.350

Louisville (68)   Coach: Peck Hickman

	Min.	Total FG/FGA	Pct.	FT/FTA	Pct.	Reb. O/T	A	TO	PF	S	Blk	TP	PPM
KING, J.	-	6/12	.500	3/4	.750	-/5	-	0	3	-	-	15	-
BEARD, B.	-	7/17	.412	3/5	.600	-/6	-	3	2	-	-	17	-
UNSELD, W.	-	6/14	.429	4/6	.667	-/17	-	1	2	-	-	16	-
GILBERT, D.	-	3/5	.600	0/2	.000	-/2	-	4	2	-	-	6	-
HOLDEN, F.	-	6/9	.667	2/3	.667	-/2	-	3	3	-	-	14	-
LIEDTKE, J.	-	0/0	.000	0/0	.000	-/0	-	0	0	-	-	0	-
Totals	200	28/57	.491	12/20	.600	-/32	-	11	12	-	-	68	.340

Team Rebounds: Kansas 3; Louisville 8. Disqualified: Kansas—Franz.

	1st Half	2nd Half	Final
Kansas	39	31	70
Louisville	38	30	68

REGIONAL THIRD PLACE MIDEAST
Indiana (51)   Coach: Lou Watson

	Min.	Total FG/FGA	Pct.	FT/FTA	Pct.	Reb. O/T	A	TO	PF	S	Blk	TP	PPM
JOYNER, H.	-	5/10	.500	0/2	.000	-/8	-	-	3	-	-	10	-
JOHNSON, J.	-	2/7	.286	5/5	1.000	-/7	-	-	4	-	-	9	-
DEHEER, W.	-	4/8	.500	5/8	.625	-/16	-	-	3	-	-	13	-
PAYNE, V.	-	2/6	.333	4/5	.800	-/2	-	-	3	-	-	8	-
RUSSELL, W.	-	3/11	.273	4/4	1.000	-/5	-	-	2	-	-	10	-
SCHNEIDER, E.	-	0/0	.000	0/0	.000	-/0	-	-	1	-	-	0	-
PFAFF, V.	-	0/1	.000	1/1	1.000	-/1	-	-	1	-	-	1	-
Totals	200	16/43	.372	19/25	1.160	-/39	-	15	17	-	-	51	.255

Tennessee (44)   Coach: Ray Mears

	Min.	Total FG/FGA	Pct.	FT/FTA	Pct.	Reb. O/T	A	TO	PF	S	Blk	TP	PPM
WIDBY, R.	-	8/19	.421	7/9	.778	-/9	-	-	4	-	-	23	-
HENDRIX, T.	-	2/7	.286	0/2	.000	-/1	-	-	5	-	-	4	-
BOERWINKLE, T.	-	1/5	.200	0/1	.000	-/7	-	-	4	-	-	2	-
JUSTUS, B.	-	3/12	.250	7/7	1.000	-/4	-	-	2	-	-	13	-
HANN, B.	-	0/1	.000	2/2	1.000	-/1	-	-	0	-	-	2	-
COFFMAN, W.	-	0/1	.000	0/0	.000	-/0	-	-	1	-	-	0	-
BELL, D.	-	0/1	.000	0/0	.000	-/0	-	-	1	-	-	0	-
Totals	200	14/46	.304	16/21	.762	-/22	-	10	17	-	-	44	.220

Team Rebounds: Indiana 4; Tennessee 5. Disqualified: Tennessee—Hendrix.

	1st Half	2nd Half	Final
Indiana	21	30	51
Tennessee	21	23	44

REGIONAL THIRD PLACE EAST

Princeton (78) Coach: B. Van Breda Kolff

	Min.	Total FG/FGA	Pct.	FT/FTA	Pct.	Reb. O/T	A	TO	PF	S	Blk	TP	PPM
HEISER, J.	24	6/11	.545	2/2	1.000	-/1	0	2	1	-	-	14	.583
WALTERS, G.	27	4/9	.444	2/3	.667	-/4	1	3	2	-	-	10	.370
THOMFORDE, C.	32	9/14	.643	4/6	.667	-/15	6	5	2	-	-	22	.688
HUMMER, E.	38	3/8	.375	1/1	1.000	-/7	3	2	1	-	-	7	.184
BROWN, R.	8	0/3	.000	0/0	.000	-/2	0	0	2	-	-	0	.000
LAWYER, D.	4	0/0	.000	1/2	.500	-/2	0	0	1	-	-	1	.250
LUCCHINO, L.	28	3/12	.250	0/0	.000	-/1	1	0	2	-	-	6	.214
PAJCIC, S.	1	1/2	.500	0/0	.000	-/0	0	0	0	-	-	2	2.000
ADLER, A.	19	5/7	.714	0/0	.000	-/8	2	1	5	-	-	10	.526
KOCH, B.	18	2/6	.333	0/0	.000	-/3	1	0	2	-	-	4	.222
DODD, J.	1	1/1	1.000	0/0	.000	-/1	0	0	0	-	-	2	2.000
Totals	200	34/73	.466	10/14	.714	-/44	14	13	18	-	-	78	.390

St. John's (58) Coach: Lou Carnesecca

	Min.	Total FG/FGA	Pct.	FT/FTA	Pct.	Reb. O/T	A	TO	PF	S	Blk	TP	PPM
BOGAD, R.	40	7/18	.389	3/4	.750	-/11	2	3	2	-	-	17	.425
WARREN, J.	26	1/5	.200	5/5	1.000	-/6	0	4	0	-	-	7	.269
DOVE, S.	36	4/11	.364	4/7	.571	-/2	1	7	2	-	-	12	.333
SWARTZ, A.	22	2/4	.500	0/0	.000	-/5	1	2	2	-	-	4	.182
CALZONETTI, C.	30	4/8	.500	0/0	.000	-/1	1	3	0	-	-	8	.267
BRUNNER, J.	6	0/1	.000	1/2	.500	-/2	0	0	1	-	-	1	.167
HILL, B.	3	1/2	.500	0/0	.000	-/0	0	0	0	-	-	2	.667
JACKSON, R.	20	2/6	.333	1/1	1.000	-/0	1	2	1	-	-	5	.250
ROWLAND, M.	9	1/1	1.000	0/1	.000	-/3	1	1	2	-	-	2	.222
FREY, K.	5	0/1	.000	0/1	.000	-/0	0	0	0	-	-	0	.000
BETTRIDGE	3	0/0	.000	0/0	.000	-/0	0	1	1	-	-	0	.000
Totals	200	22/57	.386	14/21	.667	-/38	7	23	11	-	-	58	.290

Team Rebounds: Princeton 0; St. John's 3. Disqualified: Princeton—Adler.

	1st Half	2nd Half	Final
Princeton	32	46	78
St. John's	28	30	58

○ ALL-STAR TEAMS ○

ALL TOURNAMENT

★ LEW ALCINDOR	UCLA
LUCIUS ALLEN	UCLA
ELVIN HAYES	HOUSTON
DON MAY	DAYTON
MIKE WARREN	UCLA

WEST REGIONAL

★ LEW ALCINDOR	UCLA
LUCIUS ALLEN	UCLA
DAVE FOX	PACIFIC
DAVID LATTIN	UTEP
MIKE WARREN	UCLA

★ Most Outstanding Player(s)

○ INDIVIDUAL RECORDS ○

SCORING

Most points in a single game
1 LEW ALCINDOR, UCLA (vs. PACIFIC) — 38
2 DON MAY, DAYTON (vs. N. CAROLINA) — 34
2 DAVID LATTIN, TEXAS WESTERN (vs. WYOMING) — 34
4 BOBBY LEWIS, N. CAROLINA (vs. BOSTON COLLEGE) — 31
4 ELVIN HAYES, HOUSTON (vs. SMU) — 31

Most total points in the tournament
1 ELVIN HAYES, HOUSTON — 128
2 DON MAY, DAYTON — 118
3 LEW ALCINDOR, UCLA — 106
4 BOBBY LEWIS, N. CAROLINA — 79
5 DON CHANEY, HOUSTON — 66

Highest scoring average (minimum 2 games)
1 LEW ALCINDOR, UCLA (106-4) — 26.50
2 ELVIN HAYES, HOUSTON (128-5) — 25.60

3 DON MAY, DAYTON (118-5) — 23.60
4 DENNY HOLMAN, SMU (46-2) — 23.00
5 RON WIDBY, TENNESSEE (43-2) — 21.50

FIELD GOALS

Most field goals in a single game
1 DON MAY, DAYTON (vs. N. CAROLINA) — 16
2 ELVIN HAYES, HOUSTON (vs. SMU) — 14
3 LEW ALCINDOR, UCLA (vs. PACIFIC) — 13
3 DENNY HOLMAN, SMU (vs. LOUISVILLE) — 13
5 4 tied for fifth place.

Most total field goals in the tournament
1 ELVIN HAYES, HOUSTON — 57
2 DON MAY, DAYTON — 46
3 LEW ALCINDOR, UCLA — 39
4 BOBBY LEWIS, N. CAROLINA — 29
5 J. HEISER, PRINCETON — 26

Most field goal attempts in a single game
1 ELVIN HAYES, HOUSTON (vs. UCLA) — 31
2 ELVIN HAYES, HOUSTON (vs. SMU) — 27
3 DON MAY, DAYTON (vs. VIRGINIA TECH) — 24
3 JO JO WHITE, KANSAS (vs. HOUSTON) — 24
3 GLEN COMBS, VIRGINIA TECH (vs. INDIANA) — 24

Most total field goal attempts in the tournament
1 ELVIN HAYES, HOUSTON — 119
2 DON MAY, DAYTON — 97
3 BOBBY LEWIS, N. CAROLINA — 76
4 DON CHANEY, HOUSTON — 72
5 LARRY MILLER, N. CAROLINA — 71

Highest field goal percentage in a single game (minimum 10 attempts)
1 JERRY KING, LOUISVILLE (vs. SMU) (10-13) — .769
2 DON MAY, DAYTON (vs. N. CAROLINA) (16-22) — .727
3 TED WARE, VIRGINIA TECH (vs. TOLEDO) (8-11) — .727

4 BOB KRULISH, PACIFIC (vs. TEXAS WESTERN)
   (10-14)   .714
5 LEW ALCINDOR, UCLA (vs. WYOMING) (12-17)
                                                      .706

**Highest field goal percentage in the tournament
(minimum 20 attempts)**
1 KEN TALLEY, VIRGINIA TECH (20-30)   .667
2 FRED HOLDEN, LOUISVILLE (17-26)   .654
3 LEW ALCINDOR, UCLA (39-60)   .650
4 JERRY KING, LOUISVILLE (16-25)   .640
5 KEN SPAIN, HOUSTON (14-24)   .583

FREE THROWS

Most free throws in a single game
1 DAVID LATTIN, TEXAS WESTERN (vs.
   WYOMING)   12
1 LEW ALCINDOR, UCLA (vs. PACIFIC)   12
1 DICK GRUBAR, N. CAROLINA (vs. PRINCETON)
                                             12
1 WILLIE WORSLEY, TEXAS WESTERN (vs.
   SEATTLE)   12
5 3 tied for fifth place.

Most total free throws in the tournament
1 LEW ALCINDOR, UCLA   28
2 DON MAY, DAYTON   26
3 DAVID LATTIN, TEXAS WESTERN   22
4 BOBBY LEWIS, N. CAROLINA   21
5 RUSTY CLARK, N. CAROLINA   17

Most free throws attempted in a single game
1 DICK GRUBAR, N. CAROLINA (vs. PRINCETON)
                                             16
2 LEW ALCINDOR, UCLA (vs. PACIFIC)   14
3 DAVID LATTIN, TEXAS WESTERN (vs.
   WYOMING)   13
3 LEW ALCINDOR, UCLA (vs. HOUSTON)   13
3 DAVID LATTIN, TEXAS WESTERN (vs. SEATTLE)
                                             13

Most free throws attempted in the tournament
1 LEW ALCINDOR, UCLA   43
2 DON MAY, DAYTON   35
3 DAVID LATTIN, TEXAS WESTERN   27
4 BOBBY LEWIS, N. CAROLINA   26
5 ELVIN HAYES, HOUSTON   25

**Highest free throw percentage in a single game
(minimum 7 attempts)**
1 WILLIE WORSLEY, TEXAS WESTERN (vs.
   SEATTLE) (12-12)   1.000
2 STEVE ADELMAN, BOSTON COLLEGE (vs. ST.
   JOHN'S) (7-7)   1.000
2 BILL JUSTUS, TENNESSEE (vs. INDIANA) (7-7)
                                          1.000
4 DAVID LATTIN, TEXAS WESTERN (vs.
   WYOMING) (12-13)   .923
5 2 tied for fifth place.

**Highest free throw percentage in the tournament
(minimum 15 attempts)**
1 STEVE ADELMAN, BOSTON COLLEGE (14-16)
                                           .875
2 CHRIS THOMFORDE, PRINCETON (16-19)   .842
3 BOBBY JO HOOPER, DAYTON (14-17)   .824
3 RUDY BOGAD, ST. JOHN'S (14-17)   .824
5 DAVID LATTIN, TEXAS WESTERN (22-27)   .815

REBOUNDS

Most rebounds in a single game
1 ELVIN HAYES, HOUSTON (vs. UCLA)   24
2 LEW ALCINDOR, UCLA (vs. HOUSTON)   20
2 DON MAY, DAYTON (vs. WESTERN KY.)   20
4 KEN TALLEY, VIRGINIA TECH (vs. TOLEDO)   19
5 2 tied for fifth place.

Most total rebounds in the tournament
1 DON MAY, DAYTON   82
2 ELVIN HAYES, HOUSTON   79
3 LEW ALCINDOR, UCLA   62
4 RUSTY CLARK, N. CAROLINA   48
5 2 tied for fifth place.

Most rebounds per game (minimum 2 games)
1 DON MAY, DAYTON (82-5)   16.40
2 ELVIN HAYES, HOUSTON (79-5)   15.80
3 LEW ALCINDOR, UCLA (62-4)   15.50
4 WES UNSELD, LOUISVILLE (29-2)   14.50
5 WILLIAM DEHEER, INDIANA (27-2)   13.50

✪ TEAM RECORDS ✪

SCORING

Most points in a single game
1 UCLA (vs. WYOMING)   109
2 N. CAROLINA (vs. BOSTON COLLEGE)   96
3 HOUSTON (vs. N. CAROLINA)   84

Most total points in the tournament
1 HOUSTON   350
2 UCLA   341
3 DAYTON   333

Highest scoring average (minimum 2 games)
1 UCLA (341-4)   85.25
2 SMU (158-2)   79.00
3 VIRGINIA TECH (227-3)   75.67

FIELD GOALS

Most field goals in a single game
1 UCLA (vs. WYOMING)   48
2 LOUISVILLE (vs. SMU)   38
3 SMU (vs. LOUISVILLE)   37

Most total field goals in the tournament
1 HOUSTON   144
2 UCLA   139
3 DAYTON   126

Most field goals attempted in a single game
1 N. CAROLINA (vs. HOUSTON)   85
1 PRINCETON (vs. N. CAROLINA)   85
3 INDIANA (vs. VIRGINIA TECH)   84

Most total field goals attempted in the tournament
1 HOUSTON   339
2 DAYTON   293
3 N. CAROLINA   284

Highest field goal percentage in a single game
1 UCLA (vs. WYOMING) (48-78)   .615
2 BOSTON COLLEGE (vs. U. CONN.) (16-26)   .615
3 DAYTON (vs. TENNESSEE) (20-35)   .571

**Highest field goal percentage in the tournament
(minimum 2 games)**
1 LOUISVILLE (66-125)   .528
2 UCLA (139-267)   .521
3 SMU (63-134)   .470

FREE THROWS

Most free throws in a single game
1 TEXAS WESTERN (vs. SEATTLE)   32
1 N. CAROLINA (vs. PRINCETON)   32
3 BOSTON COLLEGE (vs. ST. JOHN'S)   31

Most total free throws in the tournament
1 N. CAROLINA   82
2 DAYTON   81
3 UCLA   63

Most free throws attempted in a single game
1 N. CAROLINA (vs. PRINCETON)   43
2 TEXAS WESTERN (vs. SEATTLE)   41
3 BOSTON COLLEGE (vs. ST. JOHN'S)   36

Most total free throws attempted in the tournament
1 N. CAROLINA   112
2 HOUSTON   111
3 DAYTON   111

Highest free throw percentage in a single game
1 DAYTON (vs. TENNESSEE) (13-14)   .929
2 U. CONN. (vs. BOSTON COLLEGE) (10-11)   .909
3 BOSTON COLLEGE (vs. ST. JOHN'S) (31-36) .861

**Highest free throw percentage in the tournament
(minimum 2 games)**
1 KANSAS (17-22)   .773
2 TENNESSEE (28-37)   .757
3 BOSTON COLLEGE (61-81)   .753

Fewest free throws in a single game
1 LOUISVILLE (vs. SMU)   5
2 HOUSTON (vs. UCLA)   6
3 KANSAS (vs. HOUSTON)   7

Lowest free throw percentage in a single game
1 LOUISVILLE (vs. SMU) (5-14)   .357
2 HOUSTON (vs. UCLA) (6-16)   .375
3 2 tied for third place.

**Lowest free throw percentage in the tournament
(minimum 2 games)**
1 LOUISVILLE (17-34)   .500
2 HOUSTON (62-111)   .559
3 PACIFIC (32-53)   .604

REBOUNDS

Most rebounds in a single game
1 HOUSTON (vs. N. CAROLINA)   72
2 N. CAROLINA (vs. PRINCETON)   52
3 VIRGINIA TECH (vs. TOLEDO)   51

Most rebounds per game (minimum 2 games)
1 HOUSTON (241-5)   48.20
2 VIRGINIA TECH (138-3)   46.00
3 INDIANA (89-2)   44.50

1968

FIRST ROUND	REGIONAL SEMIFINAL	REGIONAL FINAL	FINAL FOUR	REGIONAL FINAL	REGIONAL SEMIFINAL	FIRST ROUND

EAST

(bye)
N. Carolina 91

N. Carolina 70

St. Bonaventure 102

St. Bonaventure 72

Boston College 93

N. Carolina 80

Davidson 79

Davidson 61 (ot)

St. John's 70

Davidson 66

Columbia 83

Columbia 59

La Salle 69

MIDWEST

Houston 94

Houston 91

Loyola-Chicago 76

Houston 103

Houston 69

(bye)

Louisville 75

TCU 77

(bye)

TCU 68

Kansas St. 72

(bye)

MIDEAST

(bye)
Ohio St. 79

Ohio St. 82

East Tenn. St. 79

East Tenn. St. 72

Florida St. 69

Ohio St. 66

Kentucky 107

(bye)

Kentucky 81

Marquette 72

Marquette 89

Bowling Green 71

FINAL FOUR

UCLA 78
N. Carolina 55

WEST

UCLA 58

(bye)

UCLA 87

New Mexico St. 68

New Mexico St. 49

Weber St. 57

UCLA 101

Santa Clara 86

(bye)

Santa Clara 66

New Mexico 73

(bye)

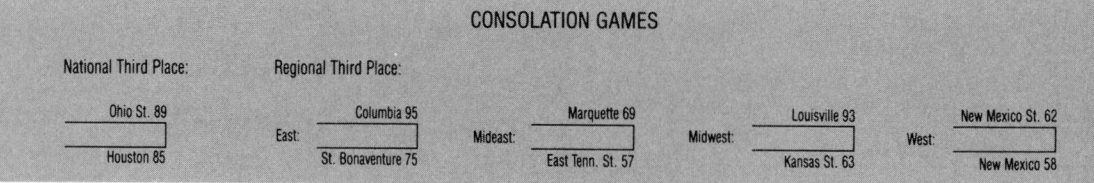

CONSOLATION GAMES

National Third Place:

Ohio St. 89

Houston 85

Regional Third Place:

East:
Columbia 95

St. Bonaventure 75

Mideast:
Marquette 69

East Tenn. St. 57

Midwest:
Louisville 93

Kansas St. 63

West:
New Mexico St. 62

New Mexico 58

On January 20th, 1968, the University of Houston defeated UCLA in a nationally televised game from the Astrodome. The unbeaten Cougars, paced by the Big E—Elvin Hayes—proved that UCLA was not invincible after all.

Eight days earlier Lew Alcindor had been scratched in his left cornea. For three days he lay in a hospital room; the lights were dimmed and a patch placed over his eye. When he was finally released, Alcindor suffered from double vision, his depth perception was off, and he had lost the edge of fitness he needed to play competitive basketball. Still, he took the court with his teammates against Houston. Hayes ate Alcindor up alive. The Big E scored 29 points in the first half, and Big Lew shot a pitiful 4 for 18 for the game. Meanwhile Edgar Lacey, the Bruins' second-best rebounder and third-highest scorer, spent the night sitting in Coach John Wooden's doghouse. Houston won by 2 points.

The king is dead, proclaimed the polls. Long live the king. Houston had deposed UCLA and was now No. 1, while UCLA was No. 2. They remained that way until tournament time.

In March, the Final Four was almost a carbon copy of the previous year's lineup: the semifinals matched 31-0 Houston against UCLA and North Carolina against an underdog team from the state of Ohio (in 1968 it was Ohio State instead of Dayton).

The Buckeyes had sneaked past Adolph Rupp's favored Kentucky Wildcats (in Lexington, no less!), but this time Dean Smith promised that his Tar Heels would not be looking ahead to the final—they would take the Big Ten champs seriously. And in the opening semifinal, North Carolina, a stronger team in 1968 than 1967 because of the development of center Rusty Clark and the arrival of their first black player, 6-5 playmaking guard Charlie Scott, had little trouble with the Buckeyes.

After their victory, the Tar Heels took their seats to watch the main event. The psychological warfare between Houston and UCLA started long before the two teams took the court. UCLA Coach John Wooden mused, "I'm surprised nobody has stalled against them. Maybe that's the best way to play them." On the other side the Big E said, "I am a more settled player than I was last year at Louisville, when Alcindor forced me out of my normal game. I won't be forced out of it this time even though I know Alcindor will be much stronger physically than he was at Houston." He predicted an easy victory over UCLA.

One thing was clear: Hayes would be hard to stop. In his first three tournament games, he had scored 123 points and grabbed 76 rebounds, prompting Joe Jares of *Sports Illustrated* to write, "Without leg irons or an anchor,

UCLA probably is not going to be able to hold down Elvin Hayes."

The rematch was in Los Angeles on March 22nd. It was quite simply one of the greatest team performances in the history of basketball.

UCLA did not stall, but Coach Wooden and his assistant Jerry Norman did devise a special defense to shackle Hayes. Along with the usual Bruin full-court zone press that forced turnovers in the backcourt, once Houston crossed midcourt UCLA moved into a diamond-and-one alignment, with Alcindor underneath and Lynn Shackelford assigned to stick to Hayes. At first it looked like it would be the fight to the finish everyone expected. After the Bruins raced to an early lead, the Cougars came back, and the score was 20-19 UCLA. Then UCLA went into high gear: in the next four minutes and nineteen seconds, they outscored Houston 17-5. The Cougars were finding it increasingly difficult to get the ball across the midcourt line, and even when they did, they couldn't get it to their main man. By halftime, UCLA led 53-31.

In the second half, Houston's nightmare grew even worse. The UCLA lead ballooned to 44 before Wooden started removing his starters. When Alcindor, the last of the UCLA starters to leave, was taken out with just over two minutes remaining, he raised his finger to indicate that UCLA was No. 1.

Alcindor, with 19 points, shared the scoring lead with Mike Lynn and Lucius Allen. Shackelford added 17 and Mike Warren 14 in the balanced UCLA attack. Hayes, the college basketball Player of the Year, was held to 10 points and 5 rebounds.

Coach Guy Lewis of Houston, who only hours before had been named Coach of the Year, wiped his eyes and said, "That was the greatest exhibition of basketball I've ever seen in my life. They could have beaten anybody—I mean anybody."

The next night North Carolina played UCLA for the national championship. But the Tar Heels had watched in awe as UCLA dismantled mighty Houston, and they were virtually beaten before they took the floor. In the first few minutes, Alcindor blocked half a dozen North Carolina shots. The Tar Heels' attempt to stall was thwarted by the quick hands of Mike Warren and Lucius Allen. By halftime, UCLA led 32-22, and North Carolina had to play at the Bruins' pace. But nobody could run with UCLA, and by the end the Bruins had the most decisive victory in championship game history.

North Carolina Coach Smith said, "UCLA has got to be the greatest college basketball team ever assembled. They are even better this year than last."

Did somebody say wait til next year?

FIRST ROUND EAST

St. Bonaventure (102) Coach: Larry Weise

	Min.	Total FG/FGA	Pct.	FT/FTA	Pct.	Reb. O/T	A	TO	PF	S	Blk	TP	PPM
KALBAUGH, B.	40	2/ 5	.400	4/ 5	.800	-/ 0	-	-	0	-	-	8	.200
BUTLER, B.	40	12/19	.632	10/13	.769	-/11	-	-	4	-	-	34	.850
SATALIN, J.	40	4/12	.333	1/ 1	1.000	-/ 2	-	-	4	-	-	9	.225
LANIER, B.	40	12/15	.800	8/12	.667	-/15	-	-	4	-	-	32	.800
HAYES, J.	40	7/12	.583	5/ 8	.625	-/ 4	-	-	2	-	-	19	.475
Totals	200	37/63	.587	28/39	.718	-/32	-	-	14	-	-	102	.510

Boston College (93) Coach: Bob Cousey

	Min.	Total FG/FGA	Pct.	FT/FTA	Pct.	Reb. O/T	A	TO	PF	S	Blk	TP	PPM
ADELMAN, L.	-	3/ 7	.429	0/ 1	.000	-/ 2	-	-	2	-	-	6	-
DUKIET, B.	-	5/ 6	.833	2/ 4	.500	-/ 3	-	-	5	-	-	12	-
DRISCOLL, T.	-	10/21	.476	4/ 8	.500	-/13	-	-	4	-	-	24	-
KISSANE, J.	-	3/ 7	.429	1/ 1	1.000	-/ 5	-	-	4	-	-	7	-
KVANCZ, J.	-	6/12	.500	0/ 0	.000	-/ 2	-	-	1	-	-	12	-
EVANS, B.	-	3/ 6	.500	1/ 1	1.000	-/ 1	-	-	3	-	-	7	-
KELLEHER, S.	-	5/10	.500	0/ 0	.000	-/ 3	-	-	3	-	-	10	-
VERRONEAU, T.	-	0/ 0	.000	0/ 0	.000	-/ 0	-	-	1	-	-	0	-
LAGACE, R.	-	1/ 2	.500	0/ 0	.000	-/ 0	-	-	1	-	-	2	-
PACYNSKI, T.	-	6/ 8	.750	1/ 3	.333	-/ 5	-	-	4	-	-	13	-
Totals	200	42/79	.532	9/18	.500	-/34	-	-	28	-	-	93	.465

Team Rebounds: St. Bonaventure 9; Boston College 8. Disqualified: Boston College—Dukiet.

	1st Half	2nd Half	Final
St. Bonaventure	54	48	102
Boston College	46	47	93

Davidson (79) Coach: Lefty Driesell

	Min.	Total FG/FGA	Pct.	FT/FTA	Pct.	Reb. O/T	A	TO	PF	S	Blk	TP	PPM
MOSER, D.	-	1/ 7	.143	1/ 1	1.000	-/ 1	-	-	1	-	-	3	-
HUCKEL, W.	-	2/ 8	.250	2/ 5	.400	-/ 4	-	-	1	-	-	6	-
MALOY, M.	-	9/12	.750	5/ 7	.714	-/10	-	-	1	-	-	23	-
COOK, D.	-	5/ 7	.714	6/ 9	.667	-/ 3	-	-	4	-	-	16	-
KROLL, J.	-	4/ 9	.444	8/ 9	.889	-/ 7	-	-	3	-	-	16	-
O'NEILL, M.	-	1/ 2	.500	2/ 2	1.000	-/ 3	-	-	1	-	-	4	-
KNOWLES, R.	-	4/13	.308	3/ 3	1.000	-/ 6	-	-	2	-	-	11	-
Totals	200	26/58	.448	27/36	.750	-/34	-	-	13	-	-	79	.395

St. John's (70) Coach: Lou Carnesecca

	Min.	Total FG/FGA	Pct.	FT/FTA	Pct.	Reb. O/T	A	TO	PF	S	Blk	TP	PPM
WARREN, J.	-	10/18	.556	4/ 6	.667	-/ 9	-	-	2	-	-	24	-
BOGAD, R.	-	6/10	.600	2/ 2	1.000	-/ 8	-	-	5	-	-	14	-
CORNELIUS, D.	-	0/ 1	.000	0/ 1	.000	-/ 1	-	-	5	-	-	0	-
CALZONETTI, C.	-	4/ 8	.500	0/ 0	.000	-/ 0	-	-	2	-	-	8	-
DE, P.	-	4/ 9	.444	5/ 5	1.000	-/10	-	-	4	-	-	13	-
SMYTH, J.	-	1/ 1	1.000	0/ 0	.000	-/ 1	-	-	0	-	-	2	-
FREY, K.	-	1/ 3	.333	1/ 2	.500	-/ 2	-	-	2	-	-	3	-
ROWLAND, M.	-	0/ 1	.000	0/ 0	.000	-/ 0	-	-	0	-	-	0	-
ABRAHAM, R.	-	3/ 8	.375	0/ 2	.000	-/ 5	-	-	3	-	-	6	-
Totals	200	29/59	.492	12/18	.667	-/36	-	-	23	-	-	70	.350

Team Rebounds: Davidson 3; St. John's 4. Disqualified: St. John's—Bogad, Cornelius.

	1st Half	2nd Half	Final
Davidson	40	39	79
St. John's	34	36	70

Columbia (83) Coach: Jack Rohan

	Min.	Total FG/FGA	Pct.	FT/FTA	Pct.	Reb. O/T	A	TO	PF	S	Blk	TP	PPM
MCMILLIAN, J.	38	7/16	.438	3/ 4	.750	-/ 8	3	2	0	-	-	17	.447
WALASZEK, R.	39	5/11	.455	7/ 7	1.000	-/ 6	0	1	5	-	-	17	.436
NEWMARK, D.	30	5/11	.455	3/ 4	.750	-/ 7	1	0	2	-	-	13	.433
DOTSON, H.	39	10/14	.714	12/14	.857	-/10	3	5	5	-	-	32	.821
AMES, W.	32	1/ 6	.167	0/ 1	.000	-/ 3	2	2	1	-	-	2	.063
BORGER, L.	10	0/ 0	.000	0/ 0	.000	-/ 0	0	0	2	-	-	0	.000
METZ, B.	7	0/ 0	.000	0/ 0	.000	-/ 1	1	0	0	-	-	0	.000
THOMAS, G.	1	0/ 0	.000	0/ 1	.000	-/ 0	0	0	0	-	-	0	.000
GARNEVICUS, T.	1	0/ 0	.000	0/ 0	.000	-/ 0	0	0	0	-	-	0	.000
SCHILLER, J.	2	1/ 1	1.000	0/ 0	.000	-/ 0	0	0	0	-	-	2	1.000
BROWN	1	0/ 0	.000	0/ 0	.000	-/ 0	0	0	0	-	-	0	.000
Totals	200	29/59	.492	25/31	.806	-/35	10	10	15	-	-	83	.415

La Salle (69) Coach: Jim Harding

	Min.	Total FG/FGA	Pct.	FT/FTA	Pct.	Reb. O/T	A	TO	PF	S	Blk	TP	PPM
CANNON, L.	40	6/17	.353	2/ 4	.500	-/ 3	3	3	3	-	-	14	.350
SZCZESNY, E.	39	7/10	.700	4/ 5	.800	-/ 9	0	1	1	-	-	18	.462
WLODARCZYK, S.	24	2/ 6	.333	3/ 5	.600	-/ 7	1	2	4	-	-	7	.292
WILLIAMS, B.	35	9/17	.529	6/ 6	1.000	-/ 4	0	2	3	-	-	24	.686
TAYLOR, R.	32	1/ 4	.250	0/ 0	.000	-/ 5	7	2	2	-	-	2	.063
ERVIN, D.	13	1/ 2	.500	0/ 0	.000	-/ 0	0	0	5	-	-	2	.154
DUMPHY, F.	14	1/ 2	.500	0/ 2	.000	-/ 2	1	1	2	-	-	2	.143
MARKMANN, J.	1	0/ 0	.000	0/ 0	.000	-/ 0	0	0	0	-	-	0	.000
DUGAN, J.	2	0/ 0	.000	0/ 0	.000	-/ 0	0	0	1	-	-	0	.000
Totals	200	27/58	.466	15/22	.682	-/30	12	11	21	-	-	69	.345

Team Rebounds: Columbia 5; La Salle 4. Disqualified: Columbia—Walaszek, Dotson; La Salle—Ervin.

	1st Half	2nd Half	Final
Columbia	45	38	83
La Salle	34	35	69

FIRST ROUND MIDEAST

East Tennessee State (79)   Coach: J. Madison Brooks

	Min.	Total FG/FGA	Pct.	FT/FTA	Pct.	Reb. O/T	A	TO	PF	S	Blk	TP	PPM
FISHER, L.	-	7/12	.583	5/6	.833	-/12	-	-	2	-	-	19	-
KRETZER, M.	-	4/8	.500	0/0	.000	-/4	-	-	5	-	-	8	-
SIMS, E.	-	2/9	.222	1/1	1.000	-/8	-	-	2	-	-	5	-
ARNOLD, R.	-	6/9	.667	4/4	1.000	-/4	-	-	1	-	-	16	-
SWIFT, H.	-	7/23	.304	8/8	1.000	-/10	-	-	2	-	-	22	-
WARD, W.	-	2/5	.400	1/1	1.000	-/6	-	-	3	-	-	5	-
FLEMING, T.	-	2/3	.667	0/1	.000	-/0	-	-	0	-	-	4	-
Totals	200	30/69	.435	19/21	.905	-/44	-	-	15	-	-	79	.395

Florida State (69)   Coach: Hugh Durham

	Min.	Total FG/FGA	Pct.	FT/FTA	Pct.	Reb. O/T	A	TO	PF	S	Blk	TP	PPM
DANFORD, D.	-	1/3	.333	1/3	.333	-/4	-	-	1	-	-	3	-
GIES, J.	-	4/8	.500	5/5	1.000	-/6	-	-	1	-	-	13	-
COWENS, D.	-	5/12	.417	1/1	1.000	-/4	-	-	5	-	-	11	-
HOGAN, J.	-	4/11	.364	2/2	1.000	-/4	-	-	2	-	-	10	-
STEWART, D.	-	6/13	.462	0/0	.000	-/3	-	-	4	-	-	12	-
CABLE, R.	-	1/5	.200	1/1	1.000	-/0	-	-	0	-	-	3	-
KLAY, D.	-	4/7	.571	1/1	1.000	-/1	-	-	3	-	-	9	-
DEPATHY, B.	-	3/5	.600	2/3	.667	-/3	-	-	0	-	-	8	-
Totals	200	28/64	.438	13/16	.813	-/25	-	-	16	-	-	69	.345

Team Rebounds: East Tenn. St. 5; Florida State 6. Disqualified: East Tenn. St.—Kretzer; Florida State—Cowens.

	1st Half	2nd Half	Final
East Tenn. St.	37	42	79
Florida State	30	39	69

Marquette (72)   Coach: Al McGuire

	Min.	Total FG/FGA	Pct.	FT/FTA	Pct.	Reb. O/T	A	TO	PF	S	Blk	TP	PPM
THOMPSON, G.	-	12/19	.632	9/14	.643	-/10	-	-	4	-	-	33	-
BRUNKHORST, B.	-	8/20	.400	4/7	.571	-/14	-	-	4	-	-	20	-
SMITH, P.	-	0/1	.000	0/3	.000	-/4	-	-	5	-	-	0	-
BURKE, J.	-	5/7	.714	1/1	1.000	-/1	-	-	1	-	-	11	-
LUCHINI, B.	-	3/9	.333	2/3	.667	-/5	-	-	4	-	-	8	-
SIMMONS, B.	-	0/1	.000	0/0	.000	-/0	-	-	1	-	-	0	-
THOMAS, J.	-	0/0	.000	0/0	.000	-/1	-	-	1	-	-	0	-
Totals	200	28/57	.491	16/28	.571	-/35	-	-	20	-	-	72	.360

Bowling Green (71)   Coach: Bob Fitch

	Min.	Total FG/FGA	Pct.	FT/FTA	Pct.	Reb. O/T	A	TO	PF	S	Blk	TP	PPM
PIATKOWSKI, W.	-	13/21	.619	1/3	.333	-/5	-	-	4	-	-	27	-
HENDERSON, J.	-	0/1	.000	1/2	.500	-/0	-	-	3	-	-	1	-
DIXON, A.	-	1/7	.143	4/6	.667	-/10	-	-	4	-	-	6	-
HAIRSTON, A.	-	7/14	.500	4/4	1.000	-/2	-	-	1	-	-	18	-
RUDGERS, D.	-	3/13	.231	3/4	.750	-/7	-	-	2	-	-	9	-
ASSENHEIMER, C.	-	5/7	.714	0/0	.000	-/5	-	-	5	-	-	10	-
HEFT, J.	-	0/0	.000	0/2	.000	-/0	-	-	0	-	-	0	-
HOFFMAN, M.	-	0/0	.000	0/0	.000	-/0	-	-	1	-	-	0	-
Totals	200	29/63	.460	13/21	.619	-/29	-	-	20	-	-	71	.355

Team Rebounds: Marquette 10; Bowling Green 9. Disqualified: Marquette—Smith; Bowling Green—Assenheimer.

	1st Half	2nd Half	Final
Marquette	39	33	72
Bowling Green	34	37	71

FIRST ROUND MIDWEST

Houston (94)   Coach: Guy Lewis

	Min.	Total FG/FGA	Pct.	FT/FTA	Pct.	Reb. O/T	A	TO	PF	S	Blk	TP	PPM
CHANEY, D.	38	4/10	.400	4/4	1.000	-/3	4	3	3	-	-	12	.316
LEWIS, V.	40	2/6	.333	1/3	.333	-/1	6	1	3	-	-	5	.125
HAYES, E.	40	20/28	.714	9/15	.600	-/27	1	1	1	-	-	49	1.225
SPAIN, K.	38	5/14	.357	5/9	.556	-/15	5	2	2	-	-	15	.395
LEE, T.	38	4/10	.400	5/9	.556	-/6	5	2	2	-	-	13	.342
BELL, C.	2	0/0	.000	0/2	.000	-/2	0	0	0	-	-	0	.000
HAMOOD, N.	2	0/1	.000	0/0	.000	-/0	0	0	0	-	-	0	.000
GRIBBEN, T.	2	0/1	.000	0/0	.000	-/2	0	0	0	-	-	0	.000
Totals	200	35/70	.500	24/42	.571	-/56	21	9	11	-	-	94	.470

Loyola-Chicago (76)   Coach: George Ireland

	Min.	Total FG/FGA	Pct.	FT/FTA	Pct.	Reb. O/T	A	TO	PF	S	Blk	TP	PPM
ROBERTSON, W.	-	5/13	.385	1/4	.250	-/4	-	2	4	-	-	11	-
WARDLAW, D.	-	2/9	.222	2/2	1.000	-/3	-	1	4	-	-	6	-
TILLMAN, J.	-	5/11	.455	0/0	.000	-/7	-	0	3	-	-	10	-
BELL, C.	-	8/15	.533	2/2	1.000	-/7	-	0	5	-	-	18	-
FULLER, W.	-	7/16	.438	2/4	.500	-/11	-	2	5	-	-	16	-
OATES, A.	-	1/3	.333	0/0	.000	-/2	-	0	3	-	-	2	-
CANNON, C.	-	0/8	.000	1/1	1.000	-/7	-	0	4	-	-	1	-
BAUMGARTNER, B.	-	0/1	.000	2/2	1.000	-/1	-	0	1	-	-	2	-
MILLER, A.	-	2/8	.250	0/0	.000	-/1	-	1	0	-	-	4	-
HOGAN, M.	-	3/5	.600	0/0	.000	-/2	-	0	1	-	-	6	-
Totals	200	33/89	.371	10/15	.667	-/45	-	6	30	-	-	76	.380

Team Rebounds: Houston 7; Loyola-Chicago 7. Disqualified: Loyola-Chicago—Bell, Fuller.

	1st Half	2nd Half	Final
Houston	53	41	94
Loyola-Chicago	34	42	76

FIRST ROUND WEST

New Mexico State (68) Coach: Lou Henson

	Min.	Total FG/FGA	Pct.	FT/FTA	Pct.	Reb. O/T	A	TO	PF	S	Blk	TP	PPM
LANDIS, P.	-	0/0	.000	0/3	.000	-/2	-	0	2	-	-	0	-
EVANS, R.	-	3/6	.500	1/1	1.000	-/7	-	3	1	-	-	7	-
LACEY, S.	-	8/13	.615	4/8	.500	-/18	-	0	3	-	-	20	-
COLLINS, J.	-	8/19	.421	5/8	.625	-/8	-	1	2	-	-	21	-
COLLINS, R.	-	7/16	.438	4/6	.667	-/9	-	0	2	-	-	18	-
BURGESS, J.	-	0/1	.000	0/0	.000	-/1	-	0	3	-	-	0	-
MURPHY, H.	-	0/2	.000	2/3	.667	-/2	-	0	1	-	-	2	-
LAS, T.	-	0/0	.000	0/0	.000	-/1	-	0	1	-	-	0	-
Totals	200	26/57	.456	16/29	.552	-/48	-	4	15	-	-	68	.340

Weber State (57) Coach: Dick Motta

	Min.	Total FG/FGA	Pct.	FT/FTA	Pct.	Reb. O/T	A	TO	PF	S	Blk	TP	PPM
THIGPEN, J.	-	2/9	.222	2/3	.667	-/1	-	0	1	-	-	6	-
VRENON, M.	-	5/10	.500	2/2	1.000	-/2	-	2	4	-	-	12	-
SPARKS, D.	-	3/6	.500	3/7	.429	-/12	-	0	5	-	-	9	-
ARCHIBALD, N.	-	4/6	.667	6/8	.750	-/11	-	1	4	-	-	14	-
BERGH, L.	-	3/8	.375	0/0	.000	-/2	-	0	3	-	-	6	-
BRYANT, T.	-	2/6	.333	0/1	.000	-/3	-	1	1	-	-	4	-
REID, R.	-	2/4	.500	0/0	.000	-/1	-	1	1	-	-	4	-
NIELSON, R.	-	1/1	1.000	0/1	.000	-/1	-	0	2	-	-	2	-
STRONG, G.	-	0/0	.000	0/0	.000	-/0	-	1	0	-	-	0	-
CHATMON, G.	-	0/0	.000	0/0	.000	-/0	-	0	0	-	-	0	-
Totals	200	22/50	.440	13/22	.591	-/33	-	6	21	-	-	57	.285

Team Rebounds: New Mexico St. 3; Weber St. 3. Disqualified: Weber St.—Sparks.

	1st Half	2nd Half	Final
New Mexico St.	36	32	68
Weber St.	28	29	57

REGIONAL SEMIFINAL EAST

North Carolina (91) Coach: Dean Smith

	Min.	Total FG/FGA	Pct.	FT/FTA	Pct.	Reb. O/T	A	TO	PF	S	Blk	TP	PPM
GRUBAR, D.	26	4/7	.571	1/1	1.000	-/3	2	1	4	-	-	9	.346
BUNTING, B.	27	1/5	.200	2/3	.667	-/8	1	4	2	-	-	4	.148
SCOTT, C.	35	9/13	.692	3/4	.750	-/3	2	3	3	-	-	21	.600
CLARK, R.	34	9/13	.692	0/0	.000	-/10	2	5	3	-	-	18	.529
MILLER, L.	37	9/18	.500	9/14	.643	-/16	2	3	4	-	-	27	.730
BROWN, J.	15	2/5	.400	0/1	.000	-/5	1	2	4	-	-	4	.267
FOSTER, E.	13	2/5	.400	0/0	.000	-/0	2	1	0	-	-	4	.308
TUTTLE, G.	8	0/2	.000	0/0	.000	-/0	1	2	1	-	-	0	.000
DELANY, J.	1	0/0	.000	0/0	.000	-/0	1	0	0	-	-	0	.000
FRYE, J.	1	0/0	.000	0/0	.000	-/1	0	0	1	-	-	0	.000
WHITEHEAD, G.	1	0/0	.000	0/0	.000	-/0	0	0	0	-	-	0	.000
FLETCHER, R.	2	1/3	.333	2/3	.667	-/2	0	0	0	-	-	4	2.000
Totals	200	37/71	.521	17/26	.654	-/48	14	21	22	-	-	91	.455

St. Bonaventure (72) Coach: Larry Weise

	Min.	Total FG/FGA	Pct.	FT/FTA	Pct.	Reb. O/T	A	TO	PF	S	Blk	TP	PPM
KALBAUGH, B.	40	1/3	.333	1/2	.500	-/1	5	7	3	-	-	3	.075
BUTLER, B.	40	10/22	.455	3/5	.600	-/12	1	0	3	-	-	23	.575
SATALIN, J.	31	2/11	.182	3/4	.750	-/5	1	5	5	-	-	7	.226
LANIER, B.	39	10/24	.417	3/5	.600	-/9	2	4	5	-	-	23	.590
HAYES, J.	35	4/8	.500	2/2	1.000	-/7	1	7	4	-	-	10	.286
MARTIN, V.	14	0/1	.000	2/5	.400	-/4	2	1	1	-	-	2	.143
FAHEY, G.	1	1/3	.333	2/2	1.000	-/1	0	0	0	-	-	4	4.000
Totals	200	28/72	.389	16/25	.640	-/39	12	24	21	-	-	72	.360

Team Rebounds: N. Carolina 5; St. Bonaventure 4. Disqualified: St. Bonaventure—Satalin, Lanier.

	1st Half	2nd Half	Final
N. Carolina	40	51	91
St. Bonaventure	30	42	72

Davidson (61) Coach: Lefty Driesell

	Min.	Total FG/FGA	Pct.	FT/FTA	Pct.	Reb. O/T	A	TO	PF	S	Blk	TP	PPM
MOSER, D.	45	4/8	.500	0/0	.000	-/8	3	3	0	-	-	8	.178
HUCKEL, W.	37	3/14	.214	4/5	.800	-/2	1	5	4	-	-	10	.270
MALOY, M.	45	4/8	.500	3/4	.750	-/10	1	0	1	-	-	11	.244
COOK, D.	10	1/2	.500	2/2	1.000	-/2	0	1	1	-	-	4	.400
KROLL, J.	30	2/7	.286	1/4	.250	-/4	1	5	3	-	-	5	.167
KNOWLES, R.	22	7/13	.538	0/0	.000	-/7	1	3	5	-	-	14	.636
O'NEILL, M.	31	3/7	.429	3/6	.500	-/8	1	0	2	-	-	9	.290
YOUNGSDALE, J.	5	0/0	.000	0/0	.000	-/0	0	0	1	-	-	0	.000
Totals	225	24/59	.407	13/21	.619	-/41	8	17	17	-	-	61	.271

Columbia (59) Coach: Jack Rohan

	Min.	Total FG/FGA	Pct.	FT/FTA	Pct.	Reb. O/T	A	TO	PF	S	Blk	TP	PPM
MCMILLIAN, J.	44	6/15	.400	2/3	.667	-/12	1	5	4	-	-	14	.318
DOTSON, H.	38	4/6	.667	7/7	1.000	-/3	0	5	5	-	-	15	.395
WALASZEK, R.	32	0/5	.000	1/3	.333	-/3	1	1	2	-	-	1	.031
AMES, B.	28	2/4	.500	0/2	.000	-/1	0	0	4	-	-	4	.143
NEWMARK, D.	44	8/20	.400	3/3	1.000	-/9	2	4	1	-	-	19	.432
METZ, B.	24	1/1	1.000	0/1	.000	-/2	0	2	0	-	-	2	.083
BORGER, L.	15	2/2	1.000	0/0	.000	-/2	0	3	1	-	-	4	.267
Totals	225	23/53	.434	13/19	.684	-/32	4	20	17	-	-	59	.262

Team Rebounds: Davidson 4; Columbia 2. Disqualified: Davidson—Knowles; Columbia—Dotson.

	1st Half	2nd Half	1st OT	Final
Davidson	32	23	6	61
Columbia	28	27	4	59

REGIONAL SEMIFINAL MIDEAST

Ohio State (79)   Coach: Fred Taylor

	Min.	Total FG/FGA	Pct.	FT/FTA	Pct.	Reb. O/T	A	TO	PF	S	Blk	TP	PPM
HOWELL, S.	-	10/17	.588	2/3	.667	-/8	-	-	2	-	-	22	-
HOSKET, B.	-	7/13	.538	4/7	.571	-/20	-	-	5	-	-	18	-
SORENSON, D.	-	7/9	.778	0/0	.000	-/6	-	-	4	-	-	14	-
MEADORS, D.	-	4/11	.364	4/7	.571	-/3	-	-	3	-	-	12	-
SCHNABEL, B.	-	4/8	.500	1/1	1.000	-/1	-	-	3	-	-	9	-
FINNEY, J.	-	0/0	.000	0/0	.000	-/1	-	-	0	-	-	0	-
SMITH, E.	-	2/5	.400	0/0	.000	-/5	-	-	0	-	-	4	-
ANDREAS, D.	-	0/0	.000	0/0	.000	-/0	-	-	0	-	-	0	-
Totals	200	34/63	.540	11/18	.611	-/44	-	-	17	-	-	79	.395

East Tennessee State (72)   Coach: J. Madison Brooks

	Min.	Total FG/FGA	Pct.	FT/FTA	Pct.	Reb. O/T	A	TO	PF	S	Blk	TP	PPM
FISHER, L.	-	6/16	.375	1/1	1.000	-/4	-	-	1	-	-	13	-
KRETZER, M.	-	10/15	.667	3/4	.750	-/9	-	-	3	-	-	23	-
SIMS, E.	-	2/9	.222	1/7	.143	-/18	-	-	1	-	-	5	-
SWIFT, H.	-	7/21	.333	7/7	1.000	-/6	-	-	4	-	-	21	-
ARNOLD	-	2/10	.200	2/2	1.000	-/1	-	-	3	-	-	6	-
WOODS, L.	-	0/1	.000	2/2	1.000	-/2	-	-	1	-	-	2	-
WARD, W.	-	0/2	.000	0/0	.000	-/3	-	-	1	-	-	0	-
WALLING, G.	-	1/2	.500	0/0	.000	-/0	-	-	0	-	-	2	-
HALL	-	0/1	.000	0/0	.000	-/0	-	-	1	-	-	0	-
FLEMING, T.	-	0/1	.000	0/0	.000	-/0	-	-	1	-	-	0	-
Totals	200	28/78	.359	16/23	.696	-/43	-	-	16	-	-	72	.360

Team Rebounds: Ohio State 1; East Tenn. St. 4. Disqualified: Ohio State—Hosket.

	1st Half	2nd Half	Final
Ohio State	37	42	79
East Tenn. St.	27	45	72

Kentucky (107)   Coach: Adolph Rupp

	Min.	Total FG/FGA	Pct.	FT/FTA	Pct.	Reb. O/T	A	TO	PF	S	Blk	TP	PPM
PRATT, M.	-	8/13	.615	2/2	1.000	-/6	-	-	3	-	-	18	-
JARACZ, T.	-	1/4	.250	0/0	.000	-/2	-	-	1	-	-	2	-
ISSEL, D.	-	14/18	.778	8/10	.800	-/13	-	-	2	-	-	36	-
CASEY, M.	-	8/19	.421	3/4	.750	-/6	-	-	2	-	-	19	-
CLEVENGER, S.	-	2/4	.500	2/2	1.000	-/1	-	-	3	-	-	6	-
LEMASTER, J.	-	2/3	.667	2/3	.667	-/2	-	-	2	-	-	6	-
GAMBLE, G.	-	3/3	1.000	2/3	.667	-/4	-	-	4	-	-	8	-
PORTER, T.	-	4/5	.800	0/2	.000	-/3	-	-	0	-	-	8	-
POOL, R.	-	1/1	1.000	0/0	.000	-/2	-	-	3	-	-	2	-
LAIB, A.	-	0/0	.000	0/0	.000	-/0	-	-	1	-	-	0	-
BUSEY, B.	-	0/0	.000	0/0	.000	-/0	-	-	0	-	-	0	-
ARGENTO, P.	-	0/0	.000	2/2	1.000	-/0	-	-	1	-	-	2	-
Totals	200	43/70	.614	21/28	.750	-/36	-	-	22	-	-	107	.535

Marquette (89)   Coach: Al McGuire

	Min.	Total FG/FGA	Pct.	FT/FTA	Pct.	Reb. O/T	A	TO	PF	S	Blk	TP	PPM
THOMPSON, G.	-	4/7	.571	5/5	1.000	-/2	-	-	5	-	-	13	-
BRUNKHORST, B.	-	6/14	.429	11/12	.917	-/7	-	-	2	-	-	23	-
SMITH, P.	-	0/0	.000	0/2	.000	-/5	-	-	4	-	-	0	-
BURKE, J.	-	7/13	.538	2/2	1.000	-/1	-	-	1	-	-	16	-
LUCHINI, B.	-	6/11	.545	7/8	.875	-/1	-	-	5	-	-	19	-
THOMAS, J.	-	5/10	.500	0/2	.000	-/7	-	-	3	-	-	10	-
RAHN, R.	-	2/5	.400	0/0	.000	-/3	-	-	2	-	-	4	-
SEWELL, J.	-	1/1	1.000	2/2	1.000	-/0	-	-	0	-	-	4	-
CURRAN, M.	-	0/1	.000	0/1	.000	-/1	-	-	0	-	-	0	-
Totals	200	31/62	.500	27/34	.794	-/27	-	-	22	-	-	89	.445

Team Rebounds: Kentucky 4; Marquette 5. Disqualified: Marquette—Thompson, Luchini.

	1st Half	2nd Half	Final
Kentucky	53	54	107
Marquette	40	49	89

REGIONAL SEMIFINAL MIDWEST

Houston (91)   Coach: Guy Lewis

	Min.	Total FG/FGA	Pct.	FT/FTA	Pct.	Reb. O/T	A	TO	PF	S	Blk	TP	PPM
CHANEY, D.	40	7/12	.583	3/6	.500	2/3	3	-	4	-	-	17	.425
LEWIS, V.	38	4/7	.571	1/1	1.000	0/3	10	-	3	-	-	9	.237
HAYES, E.	40	16/31	.516	3/8	.375	8/24	1	-	1	-	-	35	.875
SPAIN, K.	40	4/15	.267	4/5	.800	8/11	3	-	2	-	-	12	.300
LEE, T.	40	9/21	.429	0/2	.000	5/9	2	-	4	-	-	18	.450
HAMOOD, N.	2	0/0	.000	0/0	.000	0/0	0	-	0	-	-	0	.000
Totals	200	40/86	.465	11/22	.500	23/50	19	15	14	-	-	91	.455

Louisville (75)   Coach: John Dromo

	Min.	Total FG/FGA	Pct.	FT/FTA	Pct.	Reb. O/T	A	TO	PF	S	Blk	TP	PPM
UNSELD, W.	-	9/16	.563	5/9	.556	11/22	3	-	4	-	-	23	-
KING, J.	-	5/13	.385	0/1	.000	0/1	3	-	2	-	-	10	-
SELVY, M.	-	0/2	.000	0/0	.000	1/1	0	-	0	-	-	0	-
BEARD, B.	-	9/23	.391	3/5	.600	4/7	6	-	5	-	-	21	-
HOLDEN, F.	-	4/11	.364	1/1	1.000	1/1	4	-	2	-	-	9	-
LINONIS, E.	-	0/4	.000	1/2	.500	0/4	0	-	0	-	-	1	-
DEEKEN, D.	-	1/2	.500	0/0	.000	0/0	0	-	0	-	-	2	-
GROSSO, M.	-	2/7	.286	1/1	1.000	3/12	3	-	3	-	-	5	-
MINNER, G.	-	0/0	.000	0/0	.000	0/0	0	-	0	-	-	0	-
GORIUS, B.	-	2/2	1.000	0/0	.000	1/2	0	-	0	-	-	4	-
Totals	200	32/80	.400	11/19	.579	21/50	19	22	16	-	-	75	.375

Team Rebounds: Houston 9; Louisville 4. Disqualified: Louisville—Beard.

	1st Half	2nd Half	Final
Houston	45	46	91
Louisville	32	43	75

TCU (77)   Coach: Johnny Swaim

	Min.	Total FG/FGA	Pct.	FT/FTA	Pct.	Reb. O/T	A	TO	PF	S	Blk	TP	PPM
MCCARTY, M.	-	8/23	.348	1/1	1.000	4/15	1	-	3	-	-	17	-
SWIFT, T.	-	6/12	.500	1/1	1.000	2/4	1	-	5	-	-	13	-
CASH, J.	-	5/9	.556	0/0	.000	0/5	2	-	2	-	-	10	-
WITTENBRAKER, R.	-	6/14	.429	6/8	.750	2/6	4	-	1	-	-	18	-
SWANSON, B.	-	0/4	.000	1/2	.500	1/5	4	-	0	-	-	1	-
SLOAN, C.	-	0/2	.000	5/5	1.000	1/3	2	-	2	-	-	5	-
SECHRIST, M.	-	1/3	.333	0/1	.000	2/6	0	-	1	-	-	2	-
HARP, J.	-	3/5	.600	5/6	.833	1/1	0	-	2	-	-	11	-
KERTH, R.	-	0/3	.000	0/1	.000	1/1	0	-	2	-	-	0	-
Totals	200	29/75	.387	19/25	.760	14/46	14	10	18	-	-	77	.385

Kansas State (72)   Coach: Tex Winter

	Min.	Total FG/FGA	Pct.	FT/FTA	Pct.	Reb. O/T	A	TO	PF	S	Blk	TP	PPM
HONEYCUTT, S.	-	7/17	.412	5/5	1.000	2/4	1	-	5	-	-	19	-
WEBB, J.	-	4/12	.333	3/6	.500	1/12	4	-	4	-	-	11	-
PINO, N.	-	7/21	.333	1/5	.200	2/8	1	-	2	-	-	15	-
SEYFERT, E.	-	4/9	.444	2/5	.400	4/9	2	-	3	-	-	10	-
WILLIAMS, E.	-	5/9	.556	2/2	1.000	4/10	4	-	1	-	-	12	-
ARNOLD, F.	-	0/1	.000	0/0	.000	0/0	0	-	1	-	-	0	-
WILLS, R.	-	0/2	.000	0/0	.000	1/2	0	-	0	-	-	0	-
LIFTON, K.	-	2/3	.667	1/1	1.000	0/2	0	-	1	-	-	5	-
SHUPE, C.	-	0/0	.000	0/0	.000	0/0	0	-	0	-	-	0	-
Totals	200	29/74	.392	14/24	.583	14/47	12	18	17	-	-	72	.360

Team Rebounds: TCU 8; Kansas State 6. Disqualified: TCU—Swift; Kansas State—Honeycutt.

	1st Half	2nd Half	Final
TCU	37	40	77
Kansas State	41	31	72

REGIONAL SEMIFINAL WEST

UCLA (58)   Coach: John Wooden

	Min.	Total FG/FGA	Pct.	FT/FTA	Pct.	Reb. O/T	A	TO	PF	S	Blk	TP	PPM
ALCINDOR, L.	-	9/13	.692	10/16	.625	-/23	-	-	3	-	-	28	-
LYNN, M.	-	2/7	.286	0/0	.000	-/4	-	-	3	-	-	4	-
ALLEN, L.	-	3/11	.273	0/0	.000	-/3	-	-	5	-	-	6	-
WARREN, M.	-	4/6	.667	2/2	1.000	-/3	-	-	1	-	-	10	-
SHACKELFORD, L.	-	2/7	.286	3/3	1.000	-/6	-	-	3	-	-	7	-
HEITZ, K.	-	1/7	.143	1/3	.333	-/2	-	-	4	-	-	3	-
NIELSEN, J.	-	0/1	.000	0/0	.000	-/0	-	-	0	-	-	0	-
SWEEK, B.	-	0/0	.000	0/0	.000	-/0	-	-	1	-	-	0	-
Totals	200	21/52	.404	16/24	.667	-/41	-	-	20	-	-	58	.290

New Mexico State (49)   Coach: Lou Henson

	Min.	Total FG/FGA	Pct.	FT/FTA	Pct.	Reb. O/T	A	TO	PF	S	Blk	TP	PPM
LANDIS, P.	-	1/4	.250	2/5	.400	-/3	-	-	0	-	-	4	-
EVANS, R.	-	4/13	.308	6/10	.600	-/3	-	-	4	-	-	14	-
LACEY, S.	-	3/12	.250	0/0	.000	-/5	-	-	5	-	-	6	-
COLLINS, J.	-	7/16	.438	2/5	.400	-/6	-	-	1	-	-	16	-
COLLINS, R.	-	2/6	.333	1/2	.500	-/11	-	-	5	-	-	5	-
BURGESS, J.	-	2/5	.400	0/3	.000	-/5	-	-	4	-	-	4	-
MURPHY, H.	-	0/1	.000	0/0	.000	-/0	-	-	0	-	-	0	-
LAS, T.	-	0/0	.000	0/0	.000	-/1	-	-	2	-	-	0	-
MOREHEAD, W.	-	0/1	.000	0/1	.000	-/1	-	-	0	-	-	0	-
Totals	200	19/58	.328	11/26	.423	-/35	-	-	21	-	-	49	.245

Team Rebounds: UCLA 9; New Mexico St. 7. Disqualified: UCLA—Allen; New Mexico St.—R. Collins, Lacey.

	1st Half	2nd Half	Final
UCLA	28	30	58
New Mexico St.	28	21	49

Santa Clara (86)   Coach: Dick Garibaldi

	Min.	Total FG/FGA	Pct.	FT/FTA	Pct.	Reb. O/T	A	TO	PF	S	Blk	TP	PPM
O'BRIEN, T.	-	7/7	1.000	4/5	.800	-/10	-	-	3	-	-	18	-
HEANEY, B.	-	3/7	.429	1/1	1.000	-/6	-	-	1	-	-	7	-
OGDEN, B.	-	9/13	.692	4/7	.571	-/7	-	-	4	-	-	22	-
DIFFLEY, J.	-	1/2	.500	5/9	.556	-/5	-	-	2	-	-	7	-
AWTREY, D.	-	5/11	.455	3/5	.600	-/5	-	-	5	-	-	13	-
EAGLESON, K.	-	0/2	.000	0/2	.000	-/1	-	-	4	-	-	0	-
DEMPSEY, C.	-	4/5	.800	0/0	.000	-/3	-	-	2	-	-	8	-
OGDEN, R.	-	5/9	.556	1/3	.333	-/7	-	.*	3	-	-	11	-
Totals	200	34/56	.607	18/32	.563	-/44	-	-	24	-	-	86	.430

New Mexico (73)   Coach: Bob King

	Min.	Total FG/FGA	Pct.	FT/FTA	Pct.	Reb. O/T	A	TO	PF	S	Blk	TP	PPM
NELSON, R.	-	9/19	.474	2/3	.667	-/1	-	-	5	-	-	20	-
SANFORD, R.	-	3/9	.333	2/3	.667	-/3	-	-	5	-	-	8	-
BECKER, R.	-	7/15	.467	4/5	.800	-/4	-	-	5	-	-	18	-
GRIMES, H.	-	3/7	.429	0/3	.000	-/7	-	-	4	-	-	6	-
SHROPSHIRE, S.	-	0/2	.000	1/2	.500	-/0	-	-	0	-	-	1	-
GRIFFITH, K.	-	1/4	.250	0/0	.000	-/1	-	-	1	-	-	2	-
JONES, L.	-	1/3	.333	0/1	.000	-/3	-	-	1	-	-	2	-
LOPEZ, L.	-	2/4	.500	3/5	.600	-/4	-	-	3	-	-	7	-
SCHAASFMA, T.	-	0/2	.000	0/0	.000	-/0	-	-	1	-	-	0	-
CULVER, D.	-	1/2	.500	5/7	.714	-/6	-	-	3	-	-	7	-
MAES, G.	-	1/1	1.000	0/0	.000	-/0	-	-	1	-	-	2	-
Totals	200	28/68	.412	17/29	.586	-/29	-	-	29	-	-	73	.365

Team Rebounds: Santa Clara 5; New Mexico 10. Disqualified: Santa Clara—Awtrey; New Mexico—Becker, Nelson, Sanford.

	1st Half	2nd Half	Final
Santa Clara	45	41	86
New Mexico	34	39	73

REGIONAL FINAL EAST

North Carolina (70)   Coach: Dean Smith

	Min.	Total FG/FGA	Pct.	FT/FTA	Pct.	Reb. O/T	A	TO	PF	S	Blk	TP	PPM
GRUBAR, D.	36	3/8	.375	5/6	.833	-/1	1	3	5	-	-	11	.306
BUNTING, B.	20	1/4	.250	0/0	.000	-/4	0	0	4	-	-	2	.100
SCOTT, C.	39	8/15	.533	2/2	1.000	-/6	0	2	2	-	-	18	.462
CLARK, R.	37	8/17	.471	6/7	.857	-/17	3	6	3	-	-	22	.595
MILLER, L.	40	7/14	.500	2/5	.400	-/6	4	1	2	-	-	16	.400
FOGLER, E.	10	0/3	.000	1/2	.500	-/0	3	1	0	-	-	1	.100
BROWN, J.	5	0/1	.000	0/0	.000	-/1	0	1	0	-	-	0	.000
TUTTLE, R.	13	0/0	.000	0/1	.000	-/2	1	0	0	-	-	0	.000
Totals	200	27/62	.435	16/23	.696	-/37	12	14	16	-	-	70	.350

Davidson (66)   Coach: Lefty Driesell

	Min.	Total FG/FGA	Pct.	FT/FTA	Pct.	Reb. O/T	A	TO	PF	S	Blk	TP	PPM
MOSER, D.	40	0/7	.000	2/2	1.000	-/7	2	5	4	-	-	2	.050
HUCKEL, W.	31	4/8	.500	4/5	.800	-/5	0	5	0	-	-	12	.387
MALOY, M.	40	6/13	.462	6/6	1.000	-/13	2	3	1	-	-	18	.450
KROLL, J.	28	5/13	.385	6/6	1.000	-/5	1	0	5	-	-	16	.571
KNOWLES, R.	39	5/17	.294	1/2	.500	-/12	0	3	4	-	-	11	.282
O'NEILL, M.	22	3/7	.429	1/1	1.000	-/5	0	3	2	-	-	7	.318
Totals	200	23/65	.354	20/22	.909	-/47	5	19	16	-	-	66	.330

Team Rebounds: N. Carolina 1; Davidson 1. Disqualified: N. Carolina—Grubar; Davidson—Kroll.

	1st Half	2nd Half	Final
N. Carolina	28	42	70
Davidson	34	32	66

REGIONAL FINAL MIDEAST

Ohio State (82) — Coach: Fred Taylor

	Min.	Total FG / FGA	Pct.	FT / FTA	Pct.	Reb. O / T	A	TO	PF	S	Blk	TP	PPM
HOWELL, S.	-	8/16	.500	2/ 2	1.000	-/ 7	-	-	2	-	-	18	-
HOSKET, B.	-	8/14	.571	5/ 5	1.000	-/12	-	-	4	-	-	21	-
SORENSON, D.	-	11/17	.647	2/ 5	.400	-/ 7	-	-	1	-	-	24	-
MEADORS, D.	-	3/ 6	.500	0/ 0	.000	-/ 2	-	-	1	-	-	6	-
SCHNABEL, B.	-	0/ 0	.000	0/ 0	.000	-/ 0	-	-	0	-	-	0	-
FINNEY, J.	-	4/ 9	.444	1/ 1	1.000	-/ 7	-	-	2	-	-	9	-
SMITH, E.	-	2/ 5	.400	0/ 1	.000	-/ 4	-	-	0	-	-	4	-
Totals	200	36/67	.537	10/14	.714	-/39	-	-	10	-	-	82	.410

Kentucky (81) — Coach: Adolph Rupp

	Min.	Total FG / FGA	Pct.	FT / FTA	Pct.	Reb. O / T	A	TO	PF	S	Blk	TP	PPM
PRATT, M.	-	6/18	.333	2/ 3	.667	-/ 7	-	-	2	-	-	14	-
JARACZ, T.	-	6/ 8	.750	1/ 1	1.000	-/ 7	-	-	3	-	-	13	-
ISSEL, D.	-	7/18	.389	5/ 6	.833	-/ 8	-	-	2	-	-	19	-
CASEY, M.	-	8/18	.444	0/ 0	.000	-/ 8	-	-	4	-	-	16	-
CLEVENGER, S.	-	7/12	.583	1/ 2	.500	-/ 3	-	-	1	-	-	15	-
LEMASTER, J.	-	1/ 4	.250	0/ 1	.000	-/ 0	-	-	0	-	-	2	-
GAMBLE, G.	-	1/ 1	1.000	0/ 0	.000	-/ 1	-	-	0	-	-	2	-
Totals	200	36/79	.456	9/13	.692	-/34	-	-	12	-	-	81	.405

Team Rebounds: Ohio State 5; Kentucky 4. Disqualified: None.

	1st Half	2nd Half	Final
Ohio State	44	38	82
Kentucky	40	41	81

REGIONAL FINAL MIDWEST

Houston (103) — Coach: Guy Lewis

	Min.	Total FG / FGA	Pct.	FT / FTA	Pct.	Reb. O / T	A	TO	PF	S	Blk	TP	PPM
CHANEY, D.	29	4/11	.364	4/ 5	.800	4/ 6	1	-	4	-	-	12	.414
LEWIS, V.	31	0/ 5	.000	3/ 5	.600	1/ 3	2	-	1	-	-	3	.097
HAYES, E.	38	17/34	.500	5/10	.500	7/25	0	-	2	-	-	39	1.026
SPAIN, K.	38	5/11	.455	6/ 7	.857	3/16	3	-	2	-	-	16	.421
LEE, T.	31	7/14	.500	2/ 3	.667	4/ 7	3	-	2	-	-	16	.516
BELL, C.	9	2/ 4	.500	3/ 4	.750	2/ 3	0	-	0	-	-	7	.778
HAMOOD, N.	9	2/ 4	.500	0/ 0	.000	0/ 2	1	-	1	-	-	4	.444
GRIBBEN, T.	11	2/ 6	.333	2/ 2	1.000	1/ 5	0	-	4	-	-	6	.545
COOPER, L.	2	0/ 0	.000	0/ 0	.000	0/ 0	0	-	0	-	-	0	.000
TAYLOR, K.	2	0/ 0	.000	0/ 0	.000	0/ 0	0	-	1	-	-	0	.000
Totals	200	39/89	.438	25/36	.694	22/67	10	16	17	-	-	103	.515

TCU (68) — Coach: Johnny Swaim

	Min.	Total FG / FGA	Pct.	FT / FTA	Pct.	Reb. O / T	A	TO	PF	S	Blk	TP	PPM
MCCARTY, M.	-	3/12	.250	2/ 4	.500	0/ 7	2	-	2	-	-	8	-
SWIFT, T.	-	3/14	.214	3/ 3	1.000	2/ 7	1	-	4	-	-	9	-
CASH, J.	-	4/ 8	.500	0/ 0	.000	4/14	3	-	3	-	-	8	-
WITTENBRAKER, R.	-	2/12	.167	3/ 5	.600	3/ 6	3	-	3	-	-	7	-
SWANSON, B.	-	2/10	.200	0/ 1	.000	0/ 3	0	-	1	-	-	4	-
SLOAN, C.	-	1/ 7	.143	2/ 3	.667	3/ 4	0	-	1	-	-	4	-
SECHRIST, M.	-	0/ 1	.000	1/ 1	1.000	0/ 1	0	-	3	-	-	1	-
HARP, J.	-	4/11	.364	0/ 0	.000	1/ 1	0	-	2	-	-	8	-
KERTH, R.	-	2/ 2	1.000	1/ 1	1.000	1/ 2	1	-	0	-	-	5	-
NEES, R.	-	1/ 4	.250	0/ 0	.000	0/ 1	0	-	1	-	-	2	-
CHAMBERS, J.	-	0/ 1	.000	1/ 1	1.000	0/ 0	0	-	0	-	-	1	-
GOWAN, T.	-	5/ 9	.556	1/ 1	1.000	2/ 2	0	-	1	-	-	11	-
Totals	200	27/91	.297	14/20	.700	16/48	10	19	23	-	-	68	.340

Team Rebounds: Houston 9; TCU 7. Disqualified: None.

	1st Half	2nd Half	Final
Houston	59	44	103
TCU	26	42	68

REGIONAL FINAL WEST

UCLA (87) — Coach: John Wooden

	Min.	Total FG / FGA	Pct.	FT / FTA	Pct.	Reb. O / T	A	TO	PF	S	Blk	TP	PPM
ALCINDOR, L.	-	6/ 8	.750	10/17	.588	-/18	-	2	2	-	-	22	-
LYNN, M.	-	5/ 9	.556	0/ 1	.000	-/ 5	-	1	4	-	-	10	-
ALLEN, L.	-	7/15	.467	7/ 7	1.000	-/ 8	-	1	3	-	-	21	-
WARREN, M.	-	6/14	.429	3/ 3	1.000	-/ 5	-	1	3	-	-	15	-
SHACKELFORD, L.	-	1/ 8	.125	2/ 2	1.000	-/ 6	-	0	0	-	-	4	-
HEITZ, K.	-	3/ 8	.375	1/ 1	1.000	-/ 3	-	1	1	-	-	7	-
NIELSEN, J.	-	2/ 4	.500	0/ 0	.000	-/ 3	-	0	4	-	-	4	-
SWEEK, B.	-	1/ 2	.500	0/ 0	.000	-/ 1	-	1	3	-	-	2	-
SUTHERLAND, G.	-	0/ 3	.000	0/ 0	.000	-/ 1	-	1	0	-	-	0	-
SANER, N.	-	1/ 3	.333	0/ 0	.000	-/ 1	-	0	3	-	-	2	-
Totals	200	32/74	.432	23/31	.742	-/51	-	8	23	-	-	87	.435

Santa Clara (66) — Coach: Dick Garibaldi

	Min.	Total FG / FGA	Pct.	FT / FTA	Pct.	Reb. O / T	A	TO	PF	S	Blk	TP	PPM
O'BRIEN, T.	-	3/ 6	.500	1/ 1	1.000	-/ 2	-	0	3	-	-	7	-
HEANEY, B.	-	2/10	.200	0/ 1	.000	-/ 1	-	1	2	-	-	4	-
OGDEN, B.	-	4/ 7	.571	5/10	.500	-/ 9	-	3	3	-	-	13	-
DIFFLEY, J.	-	0/ 3	.000	2/ 2	1.000	-/ 0	-	0	2	-	-	2	-
AWTREY, D.	-	7/12	.583	3/ 4	.750	-/10	-	2	4	-	-	17	-
EAGLESON, K.	-	0/ 1	.000	2/ 3	.667	-/ 0	-	1	4	-	-	2	-
STUCKEY, B.	-	1/ 5	.200	3/ 4	.750	-/ 2	-	1	0	-	-	5	-
DONAHUE, K.	-	0/ 0	.000	0/ 0	.000	-/ 1	-	1	0	-	-	0	-
PAULSON, K.	-	0/ 3	.000	0/ 0	.000	-/ 1	-	0	1	-	-	0	-
DEMPSEY, C.	-	0/ 4	.000	1/ 2	.500	-/ 4	-	0	1	-	-	1	-
OGDEN, R.	-	5/11	.455	1/ 1	1.000	-/ 3	-	0	2	-	-	11	-
THOMAS, R.	-	2/ 3	.667	0/ 1	.000	-/ 2	-	0	2	-	-	4	-
Totals	200	24/65	.369	18/29	.621	-/35	-	9	24	-	-	66	.330

Team Rebounds: UCLA 6; Santa Clara 10. Disqualified: None.

	1st Half	2nd Half	Final
UCLA	51	36	87
Santa Clara	34	32	66

FINAL FOUR

North Carolina (80)   Coach: Dean Smith

	Min.	Total FG / FGA	Pct.	FT / FTA	Pct.	Reb. O / T	A	TO	PF	S	Blk	TP	PPM
MILLER, L.	-	10/23	.435	0/ 1	.000	-/ 6	-	-	2	-	-	20	-
BUNTING, B.	-	4/ 7	.571	9/10	.900	-/12	-	-	2	-	-	17	-
CLARK, R.	-	7/ 9	.778	1/ 1	1.000	-/11	-	-	4	-	-	15	-
SCOTT, C.	-	6/16	.375	1/ 4	.250	-/ 5	-	-	3	-	-	13	-
GRUBAR, D.	-	4/ 9	.444	3/ 3	1.000	-/ 6	-	-	0	-	-	11	-
FOGLER, E.	-	1/ 2	.500	0/ 0	.000	-/ 0	-	-	1	-	-	2	-
BROWN, J.	-	0/ 4	.000	0/ 0	.000	-/ 4	-	-	2	-	-	0	-
TUTTLE, G.	-	1/ 1	1.000	0/ 1	.000	-/ 0	-	-	0	-	-	2	-
Totals	200	33/71	.465	14/20	.700	-/44	-	-	14	-	-	80	.400

Ohio State (66)   Coach: Fred Taylor

	Min.	Total FG / FGA	Pct.	FT / FTA	Pct.	Reb. O / T	A	TO	PF	S	Blk	TP	PPM
HOWELL, S.	-	6/17	.353	1/ 2	.500	-/ 3	-	-	2	-	-	13	-
HOSKET, B.	-	4/11	.364	6/ 9	.667	-/ 9	-	-	5	-	-	14	-
SORENSON, D.	-	5/17	.294	1/ 3	.333	-/11	-	-	3	-	-	11	-
MEADORS, D.	-	3/13	.231	2/ 2	1.000	-/ 3	-	-	3	-	-	8	-
SCHNABEL, B.	-	0/ 1	.000	0/ 0	.000	-/ 2	-	-	1	-	-	0	-
FINNEY, J.	-	8/13	.615	0/ 2	.000	-/ 4	-	-	2	-	-	16	-
SMITH, E.	-	2/ 6	.333	0/ 0	.000	-/ 5	-	-	1	-	-	4	-
ANDREAS, D.	-	0/ 0	.000	0/ 0	.000	-/ 0	-	-	0	-	-	0	-
BARCLAY, C.	-	0/ 1	.000	0/ 0	.000	-/ 0	-	-	0	-	-	0	-
GEDDES, J.	-	0/ 0	.000	0/ 0	.000	-/ 1	-	-	1	-	-	0	-
Totals	200	28/79	.354	10/18	.556	-/38	-	-	18	-	-	66	.330

Team Rebounds: N. Carolina 9; Ohio State 11. Disqualified: Ohio State—Hosket.

	1st Half	2nd Half	Final
N. Carolina	34	46	80
Ohio State	27	39	66

Houston (69)   Coach: Guy Lewis

	Min.	Total FG / FGA	Pct.	FT / FTA	Pct.	Reb. O / T	A	TO	PF	S	Blk	TP	PPM
CHANEY, D.	33	5/13	.385	5/ 7	.714	-/ 7	2	4	2	-	-	15	.455
LEWIS, V.	33	2/ 8	.250	2/ 2	1.000	-/ 5	3	0	0	-	-	6	.182
HAYES, E.	39	3/10	.300	4/ 7	.571	-/ 5	0	3	4	-	-	10	.256
SPAIN, K.	39	4/12	.333	7/10	.700	-/13	2	6	1	-	-	15	.385
LEE, T.	21	2/15	.133	0/ 0	.000	-/ 4	2	4	4	-	-	4	.190
BELL, C.	7	3/ 8	.375	3/ 4	.750	-/ 5	0	2	0	-	-	9	1.286
HAMOOD, N.	14	3/ 5	.600	4/ 6	.667	-/ 0	0	2	2	-	-	10	.714
GRIBBEN, T.	12	0/ 5	.000	0/ 1	.000	-/ 5	3	3	1	-	-	0	.000
TAYLOR, K.	1	0/ 0	.000	0/ 0	.000	-/ 0	0	0	0	-	-	0	.000
COOPER, L.	1	0/ 2	.000	0/ 0	.000	-/ 1	0	0	0	-	-	0	.000
Totals	200	22/78	.282	25/37	.676	-/45	12	24	14	-	-	69	.345

UCLA (101)   Coach: John Wooden

	Min.	Total FG / FGA	Pct.	FT / FTA	Pct.	Reb. O / T	A	TO	PF	S	Blk	TP	PPM
ALCINDOR, L.	38	7/14	.500	5/ 6	.833	-/18	0	6	3	-	-	19	.500
LYNN, M.	30	8/10	.800	3/ 3	1.000	-/ 8	2	2	4	-	-	19	.633
ALLEN, L.	35	9/18	.500	1/ 2	.500	-/ 9	12	5	1	-	-	19	.543
WARREN, M.	33	7/18	.389	0/ 0	.000	-/ 5	9	4	3	-	-	14	.424
SHACKELFORD, L.	24	6/10	.600	5/ 5	1.000	-/ 3	0	0	4	-	-	17	.708
HEITZ, K.	12	3/ 6	.500	1/ 1	1.000	-/ 1	1	1	1	-	-	7	.583
NIELSEN, J.	12	2/ 3	.667	0/ 0	.000	-/ 1	0	0	4	-	-	4	.333
SWEEK, B.	7	1/ 1	1.000	0/ 1	.000	-/ 0	0	2	0	-	-	2	.286
SUTHERLAND, G.	5	0/ 1	.000	0/ 0	.000	-/ 0	2	0	1	-	-	0	.000
SANER, N.	4	0/ 2	.000	0/ 0	.000	-/ 1	0	3	2	-	-	0	.000
Totals	200	43/83	.518	15/18	.833	-/46	26	23	23	-	-	101	.505

Team Rebounds: UCLA 11; Houston 8. Disqualified: None.

	1st Half	2nd Half	Final
Houston	31	38	69
UCLA	53	48	101

NATIONAL CHAMPIONSHIP

North Carolina (55)   Coach: Dean Smith

	Min.	Total FG / FGA	Pct.	FT / FTA	Pct.	Reb. O / T	A	TO	PF	S	Blk	TP	PPM
MILLER, L.	37	5/13	.385	4/ 6	.667	-/ 6	3	7	3	-	-	14	.378
BUNTING, B.	15	1/ 3	.333	1/ 2	.500	-/ 2	1	1	5	-	-	3	.200
CLARK, R.	37	4/12	.333	1/ 3	.333	-/ 8	1	3	3	-	-	9	.243
SCOTT, C.	35	6/17	.353	0/ 1	.000	-/ 3	2	7	3	-	-	12	.343
GRUBAR, D.	35	2/ 5	.400	1/ 2	.500	-/ 0	1	3	2	-	-	5	.143
FOGLER, E.	16	1/ 4	.250	2/ 2	1.000	-/ 0	2	0	0	-	-	4	.250
BROWN, J.	13	2/ 5	.400	2/ 2	1.000	-/ 5	0	0	1	-	-	6	.462
TUTTLE, G.	2	0/ 0	.000	0/ 0	.000	-/ 0	1	0	0	-	-	0	.000
FRYE, J.	3	1/ 2	.500	0/ 1	.000	-/ 1	0	0	0	-	-	2	.667
WHITEHEAD, G.	1	0/ 0	.000	0/ 0	.000	-/ 0	0	0	0	-	-	0	.000
DELANY, J.	3	0/ 1	.000	0/ 0	.000	-/ 0	2	0	0	-	-	0	.000
FLETCHER, R.	3	0/ 1	.000	0/ 0	.000	-/ 0	0	0	0	-	-	0	.000
Totals	200	22/63	.349	11/19	.579	-/25	11	23	17	-	-	55	.275

UCLA (78)   Coach: John Wooden

	Min.	Total FG / FGA	Pct.	FT / FTA	Pct.	Reb. O / T	A	TO	PF	S	Blk	TP	PPM
ALCINDOR, L.	37	15/21	.714	4/ 4	1.000	-/16	1	6	3	-	-	34	.919
LYNN, M.	22	1/ 7	.143	5/ 7	.714	-/ 6	4	4	3	-	-	7	.318
ALLEN, L.	35	3/ 7	.429	5/ 7	.714	-/ 5	5	3	0	-	-	11	.314
WARREN, M.	35	3/ 7	.429	1/ 1	1.000	-/ 3	1	6	2	-	-	7	.200
SHACKELFORD, L.	26	3/ 5	.600	0/ 1	.000	-/ 2	4	1	0	-	-	6	.231
HEITZ, K.	20	3/ 6	.500	1/ 1	1.000	-/ 2	2	2	3	-	-	7	.350
NIELSEN, J.	10	1/ 1	1.000	0/ 0	.000	-/ 1	0	1	1	-	-	2	.200
SWEEK, B.	5	0/ 1	.000	0/ 0	.000	-/ 0	0	0	1	-	-	0	.000
SUTHERLAND, G.	5	1/ 2	.500	0/ 0	.000	-/ 2	1	2	1	-	-	2	.400
SANER, N.	5	1/ 3	.333	0/ 0	.000	-/ 2	1	1	2	-	-	2	.400
Totals	200	31/60	.517	16/21	.762	-/39	19	26	16	-	-	78	.390

Team Rebounds: UCLA 9; N. Carolina 10. Disqualified: N. Carolina—Bunting.

	1st Half	2nd Half	Final
N. Carolina	22	33	55
UCLA	32	46	78

NATIONAL THIRD PLACE

Ohio State (89) Coach: Fred Taylor

	Min.	Total FG/FGA	Pct.	FT/FTA	Pct.	Reb. O/T	A	TO	PF	S	Blk	TP	PPM
HOWELL, S.	40	12/26	.462	2/ 2	1.000	-/13	2	-	4	-	-	26	.650
HOSKET, B.	38	5/11	.455	9/11	.818	-/17	5	-	4	-	-	19	.500
SORENSON, D.	39	8/13	.615	3/ 4	.750	-/ 9	3	-	2	-	-	19	.487
MEADORS, D.	40	3/11	.273	3/ 4	.750	-/ 5	4	-	0	-	-	9	.225
FINNEY, J.	28	5/11	.455	3/ 3	1.000	-/ 3	5	-	3	-	-	13	.464
SMITH, E.	3	0/ 2	.000	1/ 2	.500	-/ 1	0	-	0	-	-	1	.333
SWAIN, M.	12	1/ 3	.333	0/ 0	.000	-/ 2	1	-	1	-	-	2	.167
Totals	200	34/77	.442	21/26	.808	-/50	20	-	14	-	-	89	.445

Houston (85) Coach: Guy Lewis

	Min.	Total FG/FGA	Pct.	FT/FTA	Pct.	Reb. O/T	A	TO	PF	S	Blk	TP	PPM
CHANEY, D.	39	4/15	.267	0/ 1	.000	-/ 8	1	-	5	-	-	8	.205
LEWIS, V.	35	3/ 7	.429	0/ 1	.000	-/ 3	14	-	3	-	-	6	.171
HAYES, E.	39	14/34	.412	6/ 8	.750	-/16	1	-	4	-	-	34	.872
SPAIN, K.	40	4/12	.333	2/ 4	.500	-/12	1	-	4	-	-	10	.250
LEE, T.	40	13/26	.500	1/ 2	.500	-/ 8	4	-	0	-	-	27	.675
BELL, C.	1	0/ 0	.000	0/ 0	.000	-/ 0	0	-	1	-	-	0	.000
HAMOOD, N.	5	0/ 1	.000	0/ 0	.000	-/ 0	1	-	1	-	-	0	.000
GRIBBEN, T.	1	0/ 0	.000	0/ 0	.000	-/ 0	0	-	1	-	-	0	.000
Totals	200	38/95	.400	9/16	.563	-/47	22	-	19	-	-	85	.425

Team Rebounds: Ohio State 8; Houston 7. Disqualified: Houston—Chaney.

	1st Half	2nd Half	Final
Ohio State	46	43	89
Houston	42	43	85

REGIONAL THIRD PLACE MIDEAST

Marquette (69) Coach: Al McGuire

	Min.	Total FG/FGA	Pct.	FT/FTA	Pct.	Reb. O/T	A	TO	PF	S	Blk	TP	PPM
THOMPSON, G.	-	7/13	.538	6/ 8	.750	-/ 5	-	-	1	-	-	20	-
BRUNKHORST, B.	-	1/ 3	.333	3/ 3	1.000	-/ 4	-	-	4	-	-	5	-
SMITH, P.	-	2/ 2	1.000	4/ 6	.667	-/ 4	-	-	2	-	-	8	-
BURKE, J.	-	3/ 6	.500	4/ 5	.800	-/ 2	-	-	3	-	-	10	-
LUCHINI, B.	-	7/13	.538	4/ 5	.800	-/ 6	-	-	1	-	-	18	-
THOMAS, J.	-	4/ 6	.667	0/ 0	.000	-/ 3	-	-	1	-	-	8	-
RAHN, R.	-	0/ 0	.000	0/ 0	.000	-/ 1	-	-	0	-	-	0	-
BURKE, J.	-	0/ 0	.000	0/ 0	.000	-/ 0	-	-	0	-	-	0	-
CURRAN, M.	-	0/ 0	.000	0/ 0	.000	-/ 0	-	-	0	-	-	0	-
LANGENKAMP, J.	-	0/ 0	.000	0/ 0	.000	-/ 0	-	-	0	-	-	0	-
Totals	200	24/43	.558	21/27	.778	-/25	-	-	12	-	-	69	.345

East Tennessee State (57) Coach: J. Madison Brooks

	Min.	Total FG/FGA	Pct.	FT/FTA	Pct.	Reb. O/T	A	TO	PF	S	Blk	TP	PPM
FISHER, L.	-	3/ 7	.429	1/ 2	.500	-/ 3	-	-	2	-	-	7	-
KRETZER, M.	-	11/17	.647	4/ 6	.667	-/ 5	-	-	4	-	-	26	-
SIMS, E.	-	3/ 5	.600	1/ 2	.500	-/ 9	-	-	5	-	-	7	-
SWIFT, H.	-	3/ 8	.375	3/ 3	1.000	-/ 0	-	-	3	-	-	9	-
ARNOLD	-	2/ 8	.250	1/ 1	1.000	-/ 2	-	-	3	-	-	5	-
WOODS, L.	-	0/ 0	.000	1/ 2	.500	-/ 1	-	-	1	-	-	1	-
WARD, W.	-	1/ 1	1.000	0/ 0	.000	-/ 0	-	-	0	-	-	2	-
WALLING, G.	-	0/ 0	.000	0/ 0	.000	-/ 1	-	-	2	-	-	0	-
HALL	-	0/ 1	.000	0/ 0	.000	-/ 0	-	-	0	-	-	0	-
FLEMING, T.	-	0/ 0	.000	0/ 0	.000	-/ 0	-	-	0	-	-	0	-
NICKERSON, W.	-	0/ 2	.000	0/ 0	.000	-/ 0	-	-	0	-	-	0	-
Totals	200	23/49	.469	11/16	.688	-/21	-	-	20	-	-	57	.285

Team Rebounds: Marquette 4; East Tenn. St. 2. Disqualified: East Tenn. St.—Sims.

	1st Half	2nd Half	Final
Marquette	42	27	69
East Tenn. St.	26	31	57

REGIONAL THIRD PLACE EAST

Columbia (95) Coach: Jack Rohan

	Min.	Total FG/FGA	Pct.	FT/FTA	Pct.	Reb. O/T	A	TO	PF	S	Blk	TP	PPM
MCMILLIAN, J.	39	7/13	.538	5/ 7	.714	-/14	1	2	1	-	-	19	.487
DOTSON, H.	33	8/ 8	1.000	4/ 7	.571	-/ 3	1	5	4	-	-	20	.606
WALASZEK, R.	26	1/ 4	.250	1/ 2	.500	-/ 6	0	2	3	-	-	3	.115
AMES, W.	30	6/10	.600	3/ 3	1.000	-/ 7	2	1	1	-	-	15	.500
NEWMARK, D.	26	5/ 8	.625	6/ 8	.750	-/ 7	1	4	5	-	-	16	.615
METZ, B.	14	1/ 5	.200	0/ 0	.000	-/ 1	0	3	2	-	-	2	.143
SCHILLER, J.	13	1/ 1	1.000	0/ 1	.000	-/ 3	2	0	2	-	-	2	.154
BORGER, L.	13	3/ 4	.750	4/ 5	.800	-/ 2	0	0	0	-	-	10	.769
BROWN, K.	3	0/ 0	.000	2/ 3	.667	-/ 0	0	0	1	-	-	2	.667
FOGEL, B.	1	0/ 0	.000	4/ 4	1.000	-/ 3	1	0	0	-	-	4	4.000
THOMAS, G.	1	1/ 1	1.000	0/ 0	.000	-/ 1	0	1	1	-	-	2	2.000
GARNEVICUS, T.	1	0/ 0	.000	0/ 0	.000	-/ 0	0	2	2	-	-	0	.000
Totals	200	33/54	.611	29/40	.725	-/47	8	20	22	-	-	95	.475

St. Bonaventure (75) Coach: Larry Weise

	Min.	Total FG/FGA	Pct.	FT/FTA	Pct.	Reb. O/T	A	TO	PF	S	Blk	TP	PPM
KALBAUGH, B.	39	4/17	.235	0/ 1	.000	-/ 3	2	3	4	-	-	8	.205
BUTLER, B.	39	6/13	.462	4/ 5	.800	-/11	1	3	4	-	-	16	.410
SATALIN, J.	36	3/12	.250	2/ 2	1.000	-/ 4	2	2	5	-	-	8	.222
LANIER, B.	29	8/22	.364	2/ 4	.500	-/13	1	2	5	-	-	18	.621
HAYES, J.	38	5/11	.455	5/ 6	.833	-/10	1	3	5	-	-	15	.395
MARTIN, V.	11	0/ 3	.000	7/ 8	.875	-/ 1	0	2	1	-	-	7	.636
FAHEY, G.	4	0/ 3	.000	3/ 4	.750	-/ 2	0	0	3	-	-	3	.750
ULASEWIEZ, D.	2	0/ 1	.000	0/ 0	.000	-/ 0	0	0	1	-	-	0	.000
GAGNIER, J.	1	0/ 0	.000	0/ 0	.000	-/ 0	0	1	0	-	-	0	.000
WISNIOWSKI, P.	1	0/ 0	.000	0/ 0	.000	-/ 0	0	0	0	-	-	0	.000
Totals	200	26/82	.317	23/30	.767	-/44	7	16	28	-	-	75	.375

Team Rebounds: Columbia 1; St. Bonaventure 3. Disqualified: Columbia—Newmark; St. Bonaventure—Satalin, Lanier, Hayes.

	1st Half	2nd Half	Final
Columbia	46	49	95
St. Bonaventure	36	39	75

REGIONAL THIRD PLACE MIDWEST

Louisville (93)　Coach: John Dromo

	Min.	Total FG/FGA	Pct.	FT/FTA	Pct.	Reb. O/T	A	TO	PF	S	Blk	TP	PPM
UNSELD, W.	-	9/14	.643	7/10	.700	4/19	8	-	1	-	-	25	-
KING, J.	-	6/13	.462	0/0	.000	1/5	1	-	3	-	-	12	-
SELVY, M.	-	4/6	.667	0/1	.000	3/5	3	-	2	-	-	8	-
BEARD, B.	-	9/13	.692	3/3	1.000	2/5	1	-	4	-	-	21	-
HOLDEN, F.	-	6/10	.600	4/4	1.000	1/4	6	-	1	-	-	16	-
LINONIS, E.	-	1/1	1.000	0/2	.000	0/1	0	-	1	-	-	2	-
DEEKEN, D.	-	1/5	.200	1/1	1.000	1/2	0	-	1	-	-	3	-
GROSSO, M.	-	2/6	.333	2/2	1.000	1/4	0	-	3	-	-	6	-
MINNER, G.	-	0/1	.000	0/1	.000	0/0	1	-	0	-	-	0	-
GORIUS, B.	-	0/0	.000	0/0	.000	0/1	0	-	2	-	-	0	-
HOLLAND, G.	-	0/0	.000	0/0	.000	0/0	0	-	0	-	-	0	-
CALLAHAN, P.	-	0/0	.000	0/0	.000	0/0	0	-	0	-	-	0	-
Totals	200	38/69	.551	17/24	.708	13/46	20	12	18	-	-	93	.465

Kansas State (63)　Coach: Tex Winter

	Min.	Total FG/FGA	Pct.	FT/FTA	Pct.	Reb. O/T	A	TO	PF	S	Blk	TP	PPM
HONEYCUTT, S.	-	8/22	.364	2/4	.500	2/4	2	-	4	-	-	18	-
WEBB, J.	-	2/7	.286	0/2	.000	3/5	3	-	1	-	-	4	-
SEYFERT, E.	-	4/11	.364	0/1	.000	1/4	2	-	4	-	-	8	-
WILLIAMS, E.	-	1/3	.333	4/4	1.000	2/4	2	-	1	-	-	6	-
ARNOLD, F.	-	0/1	.000	0/0	.000	0/0	0	-	0	-	-	0	-
WILLS, R.	-	1/7	.143	0/1	.000	2/4	2	-	2	-	-	2	-
LIFTON, K.	-	0/1	.000	0/0	.000	0/1	0	-	1	-	-	0	-
SHUPE, G.	-	0/1	.000	0/0	.000	0/1	0	-	0	-	-	0	-
DICKERSON, G.	-	1/7	.143	0/0	.000	2/2	1	-	1	-	-	2	-
BARBER, M.	-	7/13	.538	3/8	.375	6/10	2	-	3	-	-	17	-
PEITHMAN, L.	-	0/1	.000	0/0	.000	0/0	0	-	0	-	-	0	-
THIRD, M.	-	2/6	.333	2/4	.500	6/7	1	-	0	-	-	6	-
Totals	200	26/80	.325	11/24	.458	24/42	15	-	17	-	-	63	.315

Team Rebounds: Louisville 9; Kansas State 7. Disqualified: None.

	1st Half	2nd Half	Final
Louisville	42	51	93
Kansas State	33	30	63

REGIONAL THIRD PLACE WEST

New Mexico State (62)　Coach: Lou Henson

	Min.	Total FG/FGA	Pct.	FT/FTA	Pct.	Reb. O/T	A	TO	PF	S	Blk	TP	PPM
LANDIS, P.	-	5/7	.714	2/4	.500	-/2	-	-	1	-	-	12	-
EVANS, R.	-	4/10	.400	2/2	1.000	-/5	-	-	3	-	-	10	-
LACEY, S.	-	1/9	.111	3/3	1.000	-/7	-	-	5	-	-	5	-
COLLINS, J.	-	6/11	.545	5/6	.833	-/1	-	-	2	-	-	17	-
COLLINS, R.	-	2/7	.286	2/2	1.000	-/7	-	-	2	-	-	6	-
BURGESS, J.	-	3/3	1.000	5/6	.833	-/1	-	-	2	-	-	11	-
MURPHY, H.	-	0/2	.000	1/1	1.000	-/1	-	-	1	-	-	1	-
Totals	200	21/49	.429	20/24	.833	-/24	-	-	16	-	-	62	.310

New Mexico (58)　Coach: Bob King

	Min.	Total FG/FGA	Pct.	FT/FTA	Pct.	Reb. O/T	A	TO	PF	S	Blk	TP	PPM
NELSON, R.	-	9/23	.391	8/8	1.000	-/2	-	-	0	-	-	26	-
SANFORD, R.	-	11/17	.647	1/4	.250	-/8	-	-	3	-	-	23	-
BECKER, R.	-	1/2	.500	1/2	.500	-/3	-	-	4	-	-	3	-
GRIMES, H.	-	1/4	.250	2/5	.400	-/9	-	-	5	-	-	4	-
SHROPSHIRE, S.	-	1/1	1.000	0/1	.000	-/1	-	-	4	-	-	2	-
GRIFFITH, K.	-	0/0	.000	0/0	.000	-/0	-	-	1	-	-	0	-
JONES, L.	-	0/3	.000	0/0	.000	-/1	-	-	2	-	-	0	-
LOPEZ, L.	-	0/4	.000	0/0	.000	-/4	-	-	2	-	-	0	-
Totals	200	23/54	.426	12/20	.600	-/28	-	-	21	-	-	58	.290

Team Rebounds: New Mexico St. 11; New Mexico 8. Disqualified: New Mexico St.—Lacey; New Mexico—Grimes.

	1st Half	2nd Half	Final
New Mexico St.	29	33	62
New Mexico	30	28	58

✪ ALL-STAR TEAMS ✪

ALL TOURNAMENT

★ LEW ALCINDOR	UCLA
LUCIUS ALLEN	UCLA
LARRY MILLER	N. CAROLINA
LYNN SHACKELFORD	UCLA
MIKE WARREN	UCLA

★ Most Outstanding Player(s)

✪ INDIVIDUAL RECORDS ✪

SCORING

Most points in a single game
1 ELVIN HAYES, HOUSTON (vs. LOYOLA-CHICAGO)   49
2 ELVIN HAYES, HOUSTON (vs. TCU)   39
3 DAN ISSEL, KENTUCKY (vs. MARQUETTE)   36
4 ELVIN HAYES, HOUSTON (vs. LOUISVILLE)   35
5 3 tied for fifth place.

Most total points in the tournament
1 ELVIN HAYES, HOUSTON   167
2 LEW ALCINDOR, UCLA   103
3 STEVE HOWELL, OHIO STATE   79
4 THEODIS LEE, HOUSTON   78
5 LARRY MILLER, N. CAROLINA   77

Highest scoring average (minimum 2 games)
1 ELVIN HAYES, HOUSTON (167-5)   33.40
2 DAN ISSEL, KENTUCKY (55-2)   27.50
3 LEW ALCINDOR, UCLA (103-4)   25.75
4 BOB LANIER, ST. BONAVENTURE (73-3)   24.33
4 BILL BUTLER, ST. BONAVENTURE (73-3)   24.33

FIELD GOALS

Most field goals in a single game
1 ELVIN HAYES, HOUSTON (vs. LOYOLA-CHICAGO)   20
2 ELVIN HAYES, HOUSTON (vs. TCU)   17
3 ELVIN HAYES, HOUSTON (vs. LOUISVILLE)   16
4 LEW ALCINDOR, UCLA (vs. N. CAROLINA)   15
5 2 tied for fifth place.

Most total field goals in the tournament
1 ELVIN HAYES, HOUSTON   70
2 LEW ALCINDOR, UCLA   37
3 STEVE HOWELL, OHIO STATE   36
4 THEODIS LEE, HOUSTON   35
5 2 tied for fifth place.

Most field goal attempts in a single game
1 ELVIN HAYES, HOUSTON (vs. OHIO STATE)   34
1 ELVIN HAYES, HOUSTON (vs. TCU)   34
3 ELVIN HAYES, HOUSTON (vs. LOUISVILLE)   31
4 ELVIN HAYES, HOUSTON (vs. LOYOLA-CHICAGO)   28
5 2 tied for fifth place.

Most total field goal attempts in tournament
1 ELVIN HAYES, HOUSTON   137

2	THEODIS LEE, HOUSTON	86
3	STEVE HOWELL, OHIO STATE	76
4	LARRY MILLER, N. CAROLINA	68
5	KEN SPAIN, HOUSTON	64

Highest field goal percentage in a single game (minimum 10 attempts)
1. BOB LANIER, ST. BONAVENTURE (vs. BOSTON COLLEGE) (12-15) .800
2. MIKE LYNN, UCLA (vs. HOUSTON) (8-10) .800
3. DAN ISSEL, KENTUCKY (vs. MARQUETTE) (14-18) .778
4. MIKE MALOY, DAVIDSON (vs. ST. JOHN'S) (9-12) .750
5. ELVIN HAYES, HOUSTON (vs. LOYOLA-CHICAGO) (20-28) .714

Highest field goal percentage in the tournament (minimum 20 attempts)
1. HEYWARD DOTSON, COLUMBIA (22-28) .786
2. LEW ALCINDOR, UCLA (37-56) .661
3. BUD OGDEN, SANTA CLARA (13-20) .650
4. MIKE KRETZER, EAST TENN. ST. (25-40) .625
5. WALT PIATKOWSKI, BOWLING GREEN (13-21) .619

FREE THROWS

Most free throws in a single game
1. HEYWARD DOTSON, COLUMBIA (vs. LA SALLE) 12
2. BRIAN BRUNKHORST, MARQUETTE (vs. KENTUCKY) 11
3. BILL BUTLER, ST. BONAVENTURE (vs. BOSTON COLLEGE) 10
3. LEW ALCINDOR, UCLA (vs. SANTA CLARA) 10

3. LEW ALCINDOR, UCLA (vs. NEW MEXICO ST.) 10

Most total free throws in the tournament
1. LEW ALCINDOR, UCLA 29
2. ELVIN HAYES, HOUSTON 27
3. KEN SPAIN, HOUSTON 24
3. BILL HOSKET, OHIO STATE 24
5. HEYWARD DOTSON, COLUMBIA 23

Most free throws attempted in a single game
1. LEW ALCINDOR, UCLA (vs. SANTA CLARA) 17
2. LEW ALCINDOR, UCLA (vs. NEW MEXICO ST.) 16
3. ELVIN HAYES, HOUSTON (vs. LOYOLA-CHICAGO) 15
4. 3 tied for fourth place.

Most free throws attempted in the tournament
1. ELVIN HAYES, HOUSTON 48
2. LEW ALCINDOR, UCLA 43
3. KEN SPAIN, HOUSTON 35
4. BILL HOSKET, OHIO STATE 32
5. HEYWARD DOTSON, COLUMBIA 28

Highest free throw percentage in a single game (minimum 7 attempts)
1. HARLEY SWIFT, EAST TENN. ST. (vs. FLORIDA STATE) (8-8) 1.000
1. RON NELSON, NEW MEXICO (vs. NEW MEXICO ST.) (8-8) 1.000
3. 4 tied for third place.

Highest free throw percentage in the tournament (minimum 15 attempts)
1. HARLEY SWIFT, EAST TENN. ST. (18-18) 1.000
2. MIKE MALOY, DAVIDSON (14-17) .824
3. HEYWARD DOTSON, COLUMBIA (23-28) .821

4. BRIAN BRUNKHORST, MARQUETTE (18-22) .818
5. 3 tied for fifth place.

REBOUNDS

Most rebounds in a single game
1. ELVIN HAYES, HOUSTON (vs. LOYOLA-CHICAGO) 27
2. ELVIN HAYES, HOUSTON (vs. TCU) 25
3. ELVIN HAYES, HOUSTON (vs. LOUISVILLE) 24
4. LEW ALCINDOR, UCLA (vs. NEW MEXICO ST.) 23
5. WES UNSELD, LOUISVILLE (vs. HOUSTON) 22

Most total rebounds in the tournament
1. ELVIN HAYES, HOUSTON 97
2. LEW ALCINDOR, UCLA 75
3. KEN SPAIN, HOUSTON 67
4. BILL HOSKET, OHIO STATE 58
5. RUSTY CLARK, N. CAROLINA 46

Most rebounds per game (minimum 2 games)
1. WES UNSELD, LOUISVILLE (41-2) 20.50
2. ELVIN HAYES, HOUSTON (97-5) 19.40
3. LEW ALCINDOR, UCLA (75-4) 18.75
4. BILL HOSKET, OHIO STATE (58-4) 14.50
5. KEN SPAIN, HOUSTON (67-5) 13.40

ASSISTS

Most assists in a single game
1. VERN LEWIS, HOUSTON (vs. OHIO STATE) 14
2. LUCIUS ALLEN, UCLA (vs. HOUSTON) 12
3. VERN LEWIS, HOUSTON (vs. LOUISVILLE) 10
4. MIKE WARREN, UCLA (vs. HOUSTON) 9
5. WES UNSELD, LOUISVILLE (vs. KANSAS STATE) 8

○ TEAM RECORDS ○

SCORING

Most points in a single game
1. KENTUCKY (vs. MARQUETTE) 107
2. HOUSTON (vs. TCU) 103
3. ST. BONAVENTURE (vs. BOSTON COLLEGE) 102

Most total points in the tournament
1. HOUSTON 442
2. UCLA 324
3. OHIO STATE 316

Highest scoring average (minimum 2 games)
1. KENTUCKY (188-2) 94.00
2. HOUSTON (442-5) 88.40
3. LOUISVILLE (168-2) 84.00

FIELD GOALS

Most field goals in a single game
1. UCLA (vs. HOUSTON) 43
1. KENTUCKY (vs. MARQUETTE) 43
3. BOSTON COLLEGE (vs. ST. BONAVENTURE) 42

Most total field goals in the tournament
1. HOUSTON 174
2. OHIO STATE 132
3. UCLA 127

Most field goals attempted in a single game
1. HOUSTON (vs. OHIO STATE) 95
2. TCU (vs. HOUSTON) 91
3. 2 tied for third place.

Most total field goals attempted in the tournament
1. HOUSTON 418
2. OHIO STATE 286
3. UCLA 269

Highest field goal percentage in a single game
1. KENTUCKY (vs. MARQUETTE) (43-70) .614
2. COLUMBIA (vs. ST. BONAVENTURE) (33-54) .611
3. SANTA CLARA (vs. NEW MEXICO) (34-56) .607

Highest field goal percentage in the tournament (minimum 2 games)
1. KENTUCKY (79-149) .530
2. MARQUETTE (83-162) .513
3. COLUMBIA (85-166) .512

FREE THROWS

Most free throws in a single game
1. COLUMBIA (vs. ST. BONAVENTURE) 29
2. ST. BONAVENTURE (vs. BOSTON COLLEGE) 28
3. 2 tied for third place.

Most total free throws in the tournament
1. HOUSTON 94
2. UCLA 70
3. 2 tied for third place.

Most free throws attempted in a single game
1. HOUSTON (vs. LOYOLA-CHICAGO) 42
2. COLUMBIA (vs. ST. BONAVENTURE) 40
3. ST. BONAVENTURE (vs. BOSTON COLLEGE) 39

Most total free throws attempted in the tournament
1. HOUSTON 153
2. UCLA 94
2. ST. BONAVENTURE 94

Highest free throw percentage in a single game
1. DAVIDSON (vs. N. CAROLINA) (20-22) .909
2. EAST TENN. ST. (vs. FLORIDA STATE) (19-21) .905

3. NEW MEXICO ST. (vs. NEW MEXICO) (20-24) .833

Highest free throw percentage in the tournament (minimum 2 games)
1. EAST TENN. ST. (46-60) .767
2. DAVIDSON (60-79) .760
3. UCLA (70-94) .745

Fewest free throws in a single game
1. BOSTON COLLEGE (vs. ST. BONAVENTURE) 9
1. KENTUCKY (vs. OHIO STATE) 9
1. HOUSTON (vs. OHIO STATE) 9

Lowest free throw percentage in a single game
1. NEW MEXICO ST. (vs. UCLA) (11-26) .423
2. KANSAS STATE (vs. LOUISVILLE) (11-24) .458
3. BOSTON COLLEGE (vs. ST. BONAVENTURE) (9-18) .500

Lowest free throw percentage in the tournament (minimum 2 games)
1. KANSAS STATE (25-48) .521
2. SANTA CLARA (36-61) .590
3. NEW MEXICO (29-49) .592

REBOUNDS

Most rebounds in a single game
1. HOUSTON (vs. TCU) 67
2. HOUSTON (vs. LOYOLA-CHICAGO) 56
3. UCLA (vs. SANTA CLARA) 51

Most rebounds per game (minimum 2 games)
1. HOUSTON (265-5) 53.00
2. LOUISVILLE (96-2) 48.00
3. TCU (94-2) 47.00

1969

FIRST ROUND	REGIONAL SEMIFINAL	REGIONAL FINAL	**FINAL FOUR**	REGIONAL FINAL	REGIONAL SEMIFINAL	FIRST ROUND

EAST

(bye) — N. Carolina 79

N. Carolina 87

Duquesne 74 — Duquesne 78

St. Joseph's 52

N. Carolina 65

Davidson 75 — Davidson 79

Villanova 61

Davidson 85

St. John's 72 — St. John's 69

Princeton 63

MIDEAST

(bye) — Purdue 91

Purdue 75 (ot)

Miami (Ohio) 63 — Miami (Ohio) 71

Notre Dame 60

Purdue 92

Marquette 82 — Marquette 81

Murray St. 62

Marquette 73

(bye) — Kentucky 74

UCLA 92 / Purdue 72

Drake 82

UCLA 85

MIDWEST

Drake 81 — (bye)

Drake 84

Texas A&M 81 — Texas A&M 63

Trinity 66

Colorado St. 52 — Colorado St. 64

Dayton 50

Colorado St. 77

Colorado 56 — (bye)

WEST

UCLA 53 — (bye)

UCLA 90

New Mexico St. 74 — New Mexico St. 38

Brigham Young 62

Santa Clara 63 — (bye)

Santa Clara 52

Weber St. 75 — Weber St. 59

Seattle 73

CONSOLATION GAMES

National Third Place:

Drake 104
N. Carolina 84

Regional Third Place:

East:
Duquesne 75
St. John's 72

Mideast:
Kentucky 72
Miami (Ohio) 71

Midwest:
Colorado 97
Texas A&M 82

West:
Weber St. 58
New Mexico St. 56

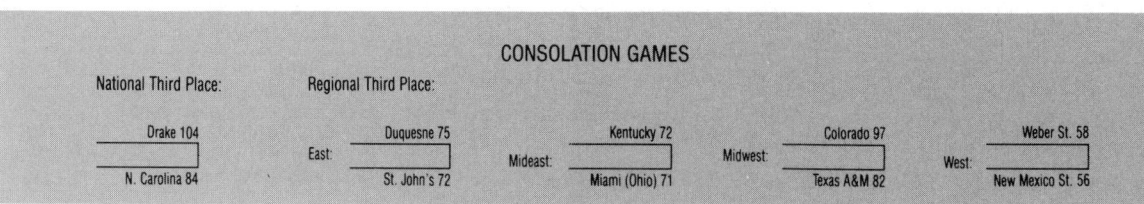

After Lew Alcindor led UCLA to its second consecutive title in 1968, almost everybody thought three in a row was a foregone conclusion. But the following season, UCLA just wasn't the same. Sure, they still had Big Lew as the master of the middle, but the supporting cast had changed, and they simply didn't dominate the way they did in 1967 and '68.

Their fallibility was never clearer than in the final week of the regular season. Although UCLA had survived some close calls earlier in the year, they were still 23-0 when they came up against conference foe California in Berkeley. The Bruins trailed by 12 in the second half before rallying to beat the Golden Bears. A few days later, the Bruins started a home and home series against their crosstown rival USC. Playing on the Trojans' court, they went to double overtime before pulling out a 61-55 victory. The next night in Pauley Pavilion, UCLA finally lost (after 41 straight victories) when the Trojans stalled their way to a 46-44 decision.

The UCLA defeat gave 24 other teams a ray of hope as the NCAA tournament began. The 1969 Bruins had at last shown that they could be taken.

Although a stall had brought the UCLA winning streak to an end, it wasn't the only strategy opposing coaches thought might beat John Wooden's team. Without Mike Warren and Lucius Allen, the quicksilver guards who had keyed the press and run the break in '67 and '68, the Bruins were no longer faster than everybody else. They could even lose a running game.

But in UCLA's tournament opener, the Bruins pulled away in the second half to beat ninth-ranked New Mexico State's sticky zone defense and slow motion offense, 53-38. Next they came up with their best performance of the season in crushing fourth-ranked Santa Clara for the western crown. UCLA's full-court press was as powerful as ever as the Bruins took a 7-0 lead before Santa Clara could get the ball across midcourt; a few minutes later the score was 18-2. Every member of the 12-man Bruin squad scored in the 90-52 blowout. The mighty Bruins once again seemed unbeatable.

Play in the other three regionals was in stark contrast to the Bruins' domination of the West. In the Midwest, high-scoring guard Willie McCarter led Drake, the Missouri Valley Conference champions and the surprise team of the tournament, as they zipped past the tall Texas A&M Aggies before pulling away from Colorado State in the last three minutes to win the regional final 84-77.

Dean Smith led his North Carolina team to the Final Four for the third straight year—but barely. The Tar Heels had plenty of height, but without their super swingman Charlie Scott they would have been sent packing back to Chapel Hill twice. They were in desperate straits against strong Duquesne, and led by only a single point after the

Dukes' charged back from 14 down. With 27 seconds left, Scott took the ball out from under his own backboard and threw an 85-foot strike to 6-10 Lee Dedmon, who was basket-hanging at the other end. The Dukes' Barry Nelson slammed into Dedmon and blocked the shot; Nelson was called for goaltending and a foul. But Dedmon missed the free throw, and Duquesne came back to score with 16 seconds to go. Scott took the ball out but couldn't find anyone to throw in to; he was forced to call time to avert a five-second violation. When play resumed, Eddie Fogler took the ball out. He in-bounded to Scott, who dribbled through the Dukes to the hoop; when Scott was double-teamed he fed Dedmon for an easy lay-up. Scott continued his heroics in the regional final against Davidson, capping off a 32-point performance (23 in the second half) by hitting a 20-footer with two seconds left to give North Carolina an 87-85 victory and an appointment with Big Ten and Mideast regional champs Purdue in the Final Four.

The Boilermakers were making their first tournament appearance ever; they had won the conference title in 1940, but turned down an NCAA invitation because they had lost twice during the season to Indiana, the eventual national champs. In Purdue's regional final, against Marquette, Warrior Ric Cobb went to the line with a chance to win with two seconds left in the game. He hit the first shot and smiled; then his second bounced off the rim and out. With the score tied and two seconds left in overtime, Purdue's All-American guard Rick Mount let fly from deep in the right corner—and found nothing but net.

In the Final Four, Purdue surprised North Carolina with a sticky defense that never let Charlie Scott get started and an exceptional show of firepower by Mount (the nation's second leading scorer) and his backcourt partner Bill Keller. The two combined for 56 points, and the Boilermakers beat the Tar Heels 92-65.

In the UCLA-Drake semi, the Bruins once again proved they were mortal. Drake's Bulldogs more than lived up to their name with their tenacious play. Their guards, Willie McCarter and Willie Wise, had no trouble breaking the Bruins' famous press. The Bulldogs' big men took turns on Alcindor, and although they didn't stop him, they slowed him down and made him work for his points. Five minutes into the second half, Drake led by 1, when they made the mistake of challenging big Lew down low. Three times in a row they took the ball to the hoop, and three times Alcindor came up with blocks. The Bruins, keyed by guard John Vallely's pinpoint shooting, started to pull away. With 3:48 to go, UCLA led by 12 and the TV commentators were talking about the upcoming UCLA-Purdue final. But in an amazing turnaround, Drake, taking a page out of UCLA's book, put on full-court pressure and UCLA started to turn the ball over. With 1:12 to go, UCLA still led 83-74. But Drake, led by McCarter, scored

8 straight points. With seven seconds remaining, UCLA had the ball and a scant 1-point lead. Drake desperately tried to get the ball, but Alcindor, holding the ball high above his head, hit Lynn Shackelford with a pass at midcourt. UCLA was saved. Curt Gowdy on NBC said the Bulldogs were "the most underrated team ever to play in the final round." And John Wooden breathed a sigh of relief. "I feel like I've had a reprieve," he said.

For three seasons, Lew Alcindor had made the Bruins virtually invincible; they had lost only two games out of 89, to Houston in the Astrodome in January 1968 (when big Lew was recovering from a serious eye injury), and to USC just before the 1969 tournament. Alcindor always made everyone around him better. And he always came through in the clutch with whatever his team needed to win.

Still, after the Drake game, there were questions about UCLA's will, or ability, to win another title. Purdue, with its two fine guards, was fully expected to give UCLA as much trouble as Drake had.

Despite the predictions, the Bruins dominated virtually from start to finish. Big Lew was spectacular, with 37 points (24 in the first half) and 20 rebounds. And his fellow senior Kenny Heitz hounded deadeye Rick Mount into missing 14 straight shots.

Alcindor was selected the tournament's Most Outstanding Player for an unprecedented third straight year as UCLA broke the records for consecutive titles (three), total championships (five), and consecutive tournament victories (20). The big man went out the same way he came in—as a winner.

FIRST ROUND EAST

Duquesne (74)   Coach: Red Manning

	Min.	Total FG/FGA	Pct.	FT/FTA	Pct.	Reb. O/T	A	TO	PF	S	Blk	TP	PPM
ABRAHAM, L.	-	0/0	.000	0/0	.000	-/0	0	0	0	-	-	0	-
BARR, M.	-	2/7	.286	0/0	.000	-/7	1	2	4	-	-	4	-
BRADLEY, T.	-	0/0	.000	0/0	.000	-/0	0	0	0	-	-	0	-
CONNOLLEY, R.	-	1/1	1.000	0/1	.000	-/0	0	1	1	-	-	2	-
DURHAM, J.	-	9/13	.692	1/1	1.000	-/8	1	3	4	-	-	19	-
GILBERT, G.	-	0/0	.000	0/0	.000	-/0	0	0	0	-	-	0	-
HINES, W.	-	1/4	.250	3/3	1.000	-/1	3	0	2	-	-	5	-
MAJOR, G.	-	2/10	.200	4/4	1.000	-/7	2	6	4	-	-	8	-
NELSON, G.	-	7/14	.500	3/7	.429	-/18	2	1	4	-	-	17	-
ZOPF, B.	-	5/9	.556	0/0	.000	-/6	2	2	3	-	-	10	-
NELSON, B.	-	0/1	.000	7/9	.778	-/5	2	3	4	-	-	7	-
ZINN, W.	-	0/0	.000	2/2	1.000	-/0	0	2	1	-	-	2	-
MCHUGH, S.	-	0/1	.000	0/0	.000	-/0	0	0	0	-	-	0	-
Totals	200	27/60	.450	20/27	.741	-/52	13	20	27	-	-	74	.370

St. Joseph's (52)   Coach: Jack McKinney

	Min.	Total FG/FGA	Pct.	FT/FTA	Pct.	Reb. O/T	A	TO	PF	S	Blk	TP	PPM
CONNOLLY, J.	-	1/5	.200	1/1	1.000	-/4	0	3	2	-	-	3	-
DIGNAZIO, M.	-	1/3	.333	0/1	.000	-/0	0	1	1	-	-	2	-
HAVER, M.	-	3/10	.300	8/12	.667	-/4	0	6	3	-	-	14	-
KELLY, D.	-	6/15	.400	4/5	.800	-/3	0	2	1	-	-	16	-
LEONARCZYK, E.	-	0/2	.000	1/2	.500	-/3	0	1	2	-	-	1	-
LYNCH, T.	-	0/0	.000	0/0	.000	-/0	0	0	2	-	-	0	-
MARKS, B.	-	0/3	.000	0/1	.000	-/3	0	0	0	-	-	0	-
MCLAUGHLIN, F.	-	0/1	.000	0/0	.000	-/3	0	0	1	-	-	0	-
MITCHELL, E.	-	2/3	.667	2/2	1.000	-/5	0	0	3	-	-	6	-
PFAHLER, D.	-	1/4	.250	1/6	.167	-/6	1	5	5	-	-	3	-
SNYDER, J.	-	3/11	.273	1/1	1.000	-/1	1	1	2	-	-	7	-
Totals	200	17/57	.298	18/31	.581	-/32	2	19	22	-	-	52	.260

Team Rebounds: Duquesne 5; St. Joseph's 4. Disqualified: St. Joseph's—Pfahler.

	1st Half	2nd Half	Final
Duquesne	29	45	74
St. Joseph's	21	31	52

Davidson (75)   Coach: Lefty Driesell

	Min.	Total FG/FGA	Pct.	FT/FTA	Pct.	Reb. O/T	A	TO	PF	S	Blk	TP	PPM
MOSER, D.	35	3/5	.600	4/5	.800	-/5	3	2	4	-	-	10	.286
HUCKEL, W.	29	2/4	.500	3/3	1.000	-/3	1	1	1	-	-	7	.241
MALOY, M.	39	11/19	.579	9/13	.692	-/17	1	1	1	-	-	31	.795
COOK, D.	39	7/15	.467	2/3	.667	-/5	4	0	3	-	-	16	.410
KROLL, J.	29	3/10	.300	1/1	1.000	-/6	1	0	2	-	-	7	.241
O'NEILL, M.	20	2/4	.500	0/0	.000	-/0	2	2	0	-	-	4	.200
STELZER, R.	4	0/0	.000	0/0	.000	-/0	2	0	0	-	-	0	.000
POSTMA, D.	1	0/0	.000	0/0	.000	-/0	0	0	0	-	-	0	.000
CROSSWHITE, R.	1	0/0	.000	0/0	.000	-/0	0	0	0	-	-	0	.000
ORSBON, T.	1	0/0	.000	0/0	.000	-/0	0	0	0	-	-	0	.000
KIRLEY, S.	1	0/0	.000	0/0	.000	-/0	0	0	0	-	-	0	.000
POSTMA, J.	1	0/0	.000	0/0	.000	-/0	0	0	0	-	-	0	.000
Totals	200	28/57	.491	19/25	.760	-/36	14	6	11	-	-	75	.375

Villanova (61)   Coach: Jack Kraft

	Min.	Total FG/FGA	Pct.	FT/FTA	Pct.	Reb. O/T	A	TO	PF	S	Blk	TP	PPM
GILLEN, F.	39	1/5	.200	1/1	1.000	-/4	1	2	3	-	-	3	.077
O'HANLON, F.	39	3/11	.273	4/4	1.000	-/3	2	0	5	-	-	10	.256
JONES, J.	39	7/19	.368	1/3	.333	-/6	2	2	2	-	-	15	.385
MCINTOSH, E.	39	4/5	.800	2/2	1.000	-/8	0	0	3	-	-	10	.256
PORTER, H.	31	10/20	.500	3/4	.750	-/10	0	1	4	-	-	23	.742
WOJOLOWSKI, L.	3	0/0	.000	0/0	.000	-/0	0	1	0	-	-	0	.000
MCCALL, F.	3	0/1	.000	0/0	.000	-/0	0	0	0	-	-	0	.000
SIMS, S.	3	0/0	.000	0/0	.000	-/0	0	0	1	-	-	0	.000
SMITH, C.	1	0/1	.000	0/0	.000	-/1	0	0	0	-	-	0	.000
WALTERS, J.	1	0/0	.000	0/0	.000	-/0	0	0	0	-	-	0	.000
MELCHIONNI, R.	1	0/1	.000	0/0	.000	-/0	0	0	0	-	-	0	.000
FOX, J.	1	0/0	.000	0/0	.000	-/0	0	0	0	-	-	0	.000
Totals	200	25/63	.397	11/14	.786	-/32	5	6	18	-	-	61	.305

Team Rebounds: Davidson 4; Villanova 4. Disqualified: Villanova—O'Hanlon.

	1st Half	2nd Half	Final
Davidson	35	40	75
Villanova	37	24	61

St. John's (72)   Coach: Lou Carnesecca

	Min.	Total FG/FGA	Pct.	FT/FTA	Pct.	Reb. O/T	A	TO	PF	S	Blk	TP	PPM
CALZONETTI, C.	-	5/10	.500	2/2	1.000	-/2	-	-	0	-	-	12	-
ABRAHAM, R.	-	3/4	.750	4/5	.800	-/10	-	-	4	-	-	10	-
WARREN, J.	-	7/11	.636	4/4	1.000	-/3	-	-	0	-	-	18	-
CORNELIUS, D.	-	3/7	.429	3/3	1.000	-/3	-	-	3	-	-	9	-
DEPRE, J.	-	7/15	.467	4/5	.800	-/3	-	-	4	-	-	18	-
PAULTZ, B.	-	2/4	.500	1/1	1.000	-/3	-	-	4	-	-	5	-
SMYTH, J.	-	0/3	.000	0/0	.000	-/0	-	-	0	-	-	0	-
GILKES, R.	-	0/0	.000	0/1	.000	-/1	-	-	1	-	-	0	-
Totals	200	27/54	.500	18/21	.857	-/25	-	-	16	-	-	72	.360

Princeton (63)   Coach: Pete Carril

	Min.	Total FG/FGA	Pct.	FT/FTA	Pct.	Reb. O/T	A	TO	PF	S	Blk	TP	PPM
STANCZAK, E.	-	1/2	.500	4/6	.667	-/6	-	-	4	-	-	6	-
THOMFORDE, C.	-	5/16	.313	2/3	.667	-/14	-	-	4	-	-	12	-
SICKLER, W.	-	0/2	.000	2/2	1.000	-/2	-	-	0	-	-	2	-
HUMMER, J.	-	13/16	.813	2/5	.400	-/10	-	-	4	-	-	28	-
PETRIE, G.	-	5/19	.263	5/5	1.000	-/6	-	-	4	-	-	15	-
ARBOGAST, J.	-	0/0	.000	0/0	.000	-/3	-	-	0	-	-	0	-
Totals	200	24/55	.436	15/21	.714	-/41	-	-	16	-	-	63	.315

Team Rebounds: St. John's 1; Princeton 0. Disqualified: None.

	1st Half	2nd Half	Final
St. John's	37	35	72
Princeton	33	30	63

FIRST ROUND MIDEAST

Miami (Ohio) (63)   Coach: Tates Locke

	Min.	Total FG / FGA	Pct.	FT / FTA	Pct.	Reb. O / T	A	TO	PF	S	Blk	TP	PPM
PRYOR, G.	-	2/ 5	.400	3/ 3	1.000	-/ 8	0	-	4	-	-	7	-
WILLIAMS, W.	-	7/21	.333	1/ 1	1.000	-/ 7	1	-	2	-	-	15	-
LOUCKS, R.	-	3/ 8	.375	3/ 5	.600	-/14	1	-	4	-	-	9	-
LUKACS, F.	-	4/12	.333	1/ 1	1.000	-/ 4	1	-	2	-	-	9	-
BURKHART, G.	-	2/ 4	.500	3/ 4	.750	-/ 1	1	-	2	-	-	7	-
WREN, M.	-	2/ 6	.333	12/13	.923	-/ 1	0	-	3	-	-	16	-
Totals	200	20/56	.357	23/27	.852	-/35	4	17	17	-	-	63	.315

Notre Dame (60)   Coach: Johnny Dee

	Min.	Total FG / FGA	Pct.	FT / FTA	Pct.	Reb. O / T	A	TO	PF	S	Blk	TP	PPM
ARNZEN, B.	-	4/10	.400	3/ 4	.750	-/11	0	-	1	-	-	11	-
MURPHY, D.	-	4/ 9	.444	3/ 4	.750	-/ 6	0	-	5	-	-	11	-
WHITMORE, B.	-	5/15	.333	3/ 6	.500	-/ 6	0	-	4	-	-	13	-
MEEHAN, J.	-	1/ 2	.500	0/ 0	.000	-/ 2	1	-	1	-	-	2	-
CARR, A.	-	1/ 6	.167	4/ 6	.667	-/ 3	0	-	1	-	-	6	-
O'CONNELL, M.	-	4/ 6	.667	0/ 1	.000	-/ 2	0	-	3	-	-	8	-
SINNOTT, T.	-	2/ 3	.667	0/ 0	.000	-/ 1	0	-	3	-	-	4	-
JONES, C.	-	1/ 5	.200	3/ 5	.600	-/ 3	0	-	1	-	-	5	-
CATLETT, S.	-	0/ 1	.000	0/ 1	.000	-/ 3	0	-	0	-	-	0	-
PLEICK, J.	-	0/ 0	.000	0/ 0	.000	-/ 0	0	-	0	-	-	0	-
Totals	200	22/57	.386	16/27	.593	-/37	1	14	19	-	-	60	.300

Team Rebounds: Miami (Ohio) 10; Notre Dame 7. Disqualified: Notre Dame—Murphy.

	1st Half	2nd Half	Final
Miami (Ohio)	34	29	63
Notre Dame	31	29	60

Marquette (82)   Coach: Al McGuire

	Min.	Total FG / FGA	Pct.	FT / FTA	Pct.	Reb. O / T	A	TO	PF	S	Blk	TP	PPM
THOMPSON, G.	-	9/20	.450	5/ 5	1.000	-/ 5	0	-	2	-	-	23	-
THOMAS, J.	-	4/ 8	.500	1/ 1	1.000	-/ 6	1	-	0	-	-	9	-
COBB, R.	-	4/ 6	.667	2/ 9	.222	-/ 8	1	-	2	-	-	10	-
SEWELL, J.	-	8/11	.727	1/ 2	.500	-/ 4	0	-	5	-	-	17	-
MEMINGER, D.	-	6/11	.545	3/ 4	.750	-/ 5	2	-	1	-	-	15	-
RAHN, R.	-	0/ 1	.000	0/ 0	.000	-/ 0	0	-	0	-	-	0	-
BURKE, J.	-	1/ 2	.500	0/ 0	.000	-/ 0	1	-	2	-	-	2	-
SMITH, P.	-	0/ 0	.000	0/ 1	.000	-/ 0	0	-	0	-	-	0	-
REIDER, J.	-	0/ 0	.000	0/ 0	.000	-/ 0	0	-	0	-	-	0	-
BLACK, B.	-	0/ 0	.000	1/ 2	.500	-/ 0	0	-	0	-	-	1	-
CURRAN, M.	-	0/ 0	.000	1/ 2	.500	-/ 1	0	-	0	-	-	1	-
MCMAHON, H.	-	2/ 2	1.000	0/ 0	.000	-/ 2	0	-	0	-	-	4	-
Totals	200	34/61	.557	14/26	.538	-/31	5	7	12	-	-	82	.410

Murray State (62)   Coach: Cal Luther

	Min.	Total FG / FGA	Pct.	FT / FTA	Pct.	Reb. O / T	A	TO	PF	S	Blk	TP	PPM
VIRDEN, C.	-	8/17	.471	1/ 1	1.000	-/10	1	-	4	-	-	17	-
BLONDETT, H.	-	7/10	.700	1/ 1	1.000	-/ 3	2	-	3	-	-	15	-
JOHNSON, R.	-	4/ 7	.571	2/ 3	.667	-/ 4	0	-	4	-	-	10	-
YOUNG, J.	-	3/ 7	.429	1/ 1	1.000	-/ 2	0	-	0	-	-	7	-
STREETY, F.	-	0/ 4	.000	2/ 2	1.000	-/ 1	2	-	2	-	-	2	-
STOCKS, J.	-	3/ 5	.600	3/ 4	.750	-/ 3	0	-	5	-	-	9	-
ROMANI, R.	-	0/ 0	.000	0/ 0	.000	-/ 0	0	-	0	-	-	0	-
RILEY, S.	-	1/ 1	1.000	0/ 1	.000	-/ 1	0	-	0	-	-	2	-
WILSON, G.	-	0/ 0	.000	0/ 0	.000	-/ 0	0	-	0	-	-	0	-
STEVERSON, G.	-	0/ 1	.000	0/ 0	.000	-/ 0	0	-	0	-	-	0	-
Totals	200	26/52	.500	10/13	.769	-/24	5	18	18	-	-	62	.310

Team Rebounds: Marquette 6; Murray State 7. Disqualified: Marquette—Sewell; Murray State—Stocks.

	1st Half	2nd Half	Final
Marquette	42	40	82
Murray State	32	30	62

FIRST ROUND MIDWEST

Texas A&M (81)   Coach: Shelby Metcalf

	Min.	Total FG / FGA	Pct.	FT / FTA	Pct.	Reb. O / T	A	TO	PF	S	Blk	TP	PPM
PERET, R.	-	2/ 5	.400	6/ 8	.750	-/ 8	-	-	4	-	-	10	-
BARNETT, B.	-	4/ 7	.571	4/ 5	.800	-/11	-	-	4	-	-	12	-
NILES, S.	-	6/ 6	1.000	5/ 6	.833	-/16	-	-	2	-	-	17	-
BENEFIELD, S.	-	10/19	.526	5/ 7	.714	-/ 3	-	-	1	-	-	25	-
HEITMANN, M.	-	2/ 7	.286	5/ 5	1.000	-/ 3	-	-	2	-	-	9	-
BROWN, B.	-	0/ 0	.000	1/ 2	.500	-/ 0	-	-	1	-	-	1	-
COOKSEY, B.	-	3/ 6	.500	1/ 3	.333	-/ 3	-	-	1	-	-	7	-
BOSTIC, H.	-	0/ 0	.000	0/ 0	.000	-/ 2	-	-	1	-	-	0	-
SMITH, C.	-	0/ 0	.000	0/ 0	.000	-/ 2	-	-	0	-	-	0	-
Totals	200	27/50	.540	27/36	.750	-/48	-	-	16	-	-	81	.405

Trinity (66)   Coach: Bob Polk

	Min.	Total FG / FGA	Pct.	FT / FTA	Pct.	Reb. O / T	A	TO	PF	S	Blk	TP	PPM
JEFFRIES, L.	-	6/18	.333	2/ 4	.500	-/ 6	-	-	3	-	-	14	-
FISHER, T.	-	3/ 9	.333	2/ 2	1.000	-/ 3	-	-	1	-	-	8	-
BOWLES, J.	-	3/ 7	.429	1/ 4	.250	-/ 8	-	-	5	-	-	7	-
STOKES, B.	-	4/11	.364	0/ 1	.000	-/ 4	-	-	5	-	-	8	-
LYNCH, J.	-	4/16	.250	2/ 2	1.000	-/ 1	-	-	3	-	-	10	-
THRUSTON, F.	-	6/ 9	.667	2/ 2	1.000	-/ 7	-	-	4	-	-	14	-
SUMMERS, B.	-	2/ 6	.333	1/ 2	.500	-/ 3	-	-	4	-	-	5	-
WATTAN, T.	-	0/ 1	.000	0/ 0	.000	-/ 1	-	-	2	-	-	0	-
Totals	200	28/77	.364	10/17	.588	-/33	-	-	27	-	-	66	.330

Team Rebounds: Texas A&M 4; Trinity 3. Disqualified: Trinity—Bowles, Stokes.

	1st Half	2nd Half	Final
Texas A&M	42	39	81
Trinity	34	32	66

Colorado State (52)   Coach: Jim Williams

	Min.	Total FG / FGA	Pct.	FT / FTA	Pct.	Reb. O / T	A	TO	PF	S	Blk	TP	PPM
SHEGOGG, C.	-	4/12	.333	4/ 4	1.000	-/ 7	-	-	3	-	-	12	-
WEEMS, J.	-	2/ 6	.333	1/ 1	1.000	-/ 5	-	-	5	-	-	5	-
DAVIS, M.	-	2/ 4	.500	0/ 2	.000	-/ 9	-	-	5	-	-	4	-
KERR, L.	-	6/16	.375	5/ 7	.714	-/ 4	-	-	0	-	-	17	-
KERR, F.	-	3/ 7	.429	5/ 7	.714	-/ 8	-	-	0	-	-	11	-
MEEKER, T.	-	0/ 0	.000	0/ 0	.000	-/ 1	-	-	0	-	-	0	-
ASH, J.	-	1/ 3	.333	0/ 0	.000	-/ 1	-	-	2	-	-	2	-
PEDEN, W.	-	0/ 0	.000	0/ 0	.000	-/ 0	-	-	0	-	-	0	-
STOCKHAM, J.	-	0/ 0	.000	1/ 2	.500	-/ 0	-	-	1	-	-	1	-
Totals	200	18/48	.375	16/23	.696	-/35	-	13	16	-	-	52	.260

Dayton (50)   Coach: Don Donoher

	Min.	Total FG / FGA	Pct.	FT / FTA	Pct.	Reb. O / T	A	TO	PF	S	Blk	TP	PPM
MAY, K.	-	6/10	.600	1/ 3	.333	-/ 5	-	-	2	-	-	13	-
SADLIER, D.	-	6/14	.429	2/ 4	.500	-/ 6	-	-	3	-	-	14	-
OBROVAC, D.	-	5/ 6	.833	2/ 7	.286	-/ 9	-	-	4	-	-	12	-
GOTTSCHALL, JI..	-	0/ 2	.000	0/ 0	.000	-/ 1	-	-	2	-	-	0	-
GOTTSCHALL, JE..	-	1/ 7	.143	0/ 0	.000	-/ 2	-	-	3	-	-	2	-
JANKY, G.	-	1/ 3	.333	1/ 2	.500	-/ 5	-	-	3	-	-	3	-
TURNWALD, S.	-	3/ 7	.429	0/ 0	.000	-/ 2	-	-	2	-	-	6	-
CROSSWHITE, T.	-	0/ 1	.000	0/ 0	.000	-/ 1	-	-	0	-	-	0	-
Totals	200	22/50	.440	6/16	.375	-/31	-	11	19	-	-	50	.250

Team Rebounds: Colorado State 3; Dayton 6. Disqualified: Colorado State—Weems, Davis.

	1st Half	2nd Half	Final
Colorado State	27	25	52
Dayton	23	27	50

FIRST ROUND WEST

New Mexico State (74) Coach: Lou Henson

	Min.	Total FG / FGA	Pct.	FT / FTA	Pct.	Reb. O / T	A	TO	PF	S	Blk	TP	PPM
COLLINS, J.	-	9/22	.409	0/ 0	.000	-/ 3	1	-	3	-	-	18	-
MURPHY, H.	-	1/ 2	.500	2/ 2	1.000	-/ 2	1	-	1	-	-	4	-
BURGESS, J.	-	1/ 2	.500	3/ 3	1.000	-/14	5	-	1	-	-	5	-
SMITH, J.	-	6/ 9	.667	1/ 7	.143	-/13	2	-	4	-	-	13	-
LACEY, S.	-	6/16	.375	4/ 6	.667	-/13	5	-	5	-	-	16	-
REYES, C.	-	6/16	.375	6/ 8	.750	-/ 9	2	-	1	-	-	18	-
BOWEN, H.	-	0/ 1	.000	0/ 0	.000	-/ 0	0	-	0	-	-	0	-
Totals	200	29/68	.426	16/26	.615	-/54	16	13	15	-	-	74	.370

Brigham Young (62) Coach: Stan Watts

	Min.	Total FG / FGA	Pct.	FT / FTA	Pct.	Reb. O / T	A	TO	PF	S	Blk	TP	PPM
PARSONS, L.	-	4/ 8	.500	1/ 1	1.000	-/ 3	5	-	1	-	-	9	-
HOCHID, D.	-	5/16	.313	2/ 2	1.000	-/ 1	3	-	0	-	-	12	-
LIIMO, K.	-	7/15	.467	4/ 5	.800	-/ 9	2	-	3	-	-	18	-
LITHGOE, M.	-	2/ 7	.286	0/ 0	.000	-/ 0	1	-	3	-	-	4	-
RIFFNER, D.	-	4/13	.308	3/ 4	.750	-/13	0	-	5	-	-	11	-
MILLER, J.	-	0/ 0	.000	0/ 0	.000	-/ 0	0	-	1	-	-	0	-
WHINER, S.	-	3/ 9	.333	2/ 5	.400	-/ 4	1	-	4	-	-	8	-
VAINIO, C.	-	0/ 0	.000	0/ 0	.000	-/ 1	0	-	1	-	-	0	-
Totals	200	25/68	.368	12/17	.706	-/31	12	7	18	-	-	62	.310

Team Rebounds: New Mexico St. 8; Brigham Young 5. Disqualified: New Mexico St.—Lacey; Brigham Young—Riffner.

	1st Half	2nd Half	Final
New Mexico St.	37	37	74
Brigham Young	33	29	62

Weber State (75) Coach: Phil Johnson

	Min.	Total FG / FGA	Pct.	FT / FTA	Pct.	Reb. O / T	A	TO	PF	S	Blk	TP	PPM
CHATMON, G.	-	1/ 4	.250	1/ 4	.250	-/ 7	1	0	2	-	-	3	-
BERGH, L.	-	8/13	.615	0/ 1	.000	-/10	4	1	4	-	-	16	-
SOJOURNER, W.	-	7/11	.636	8/10	.800	-/12	0	3	3	-	-	22	-
THIGPEN, S.	-	7/12	.583	0/ 0	.000	-/ 2	2	5	4	-	-	14	-
HARLAN, S.	-	6/ 9	.667	3/ 5	.600	-/ 4	1	7	4	-	-	15	-
STRONG, G.	-	0/ 4	.000	1/ 3	.333	-/ 4	0	0	1	-	-	1	-
NIELSEN, R.	-	0/ 2	.000	4/ 5	.800	-/ 1	3	2	2	-	-	4	-
SACKOLWITZ, D.	-	0/ 0	.000	0/ 0	.000	-/ 0	0	0	0	-	-	0	-
Totals	200	29/55	.527	17/28	.607	-/40	11	18	20	-	-	75	.375

Seattle (73) Coach: Morris Buckwalter

	Min.	Total FG / FGA	Pct.	FT / FTA	Pct.	Reb. O / T	A	TO	PF	S	Blk	TP	PPM
LITTLE, T.	-	7/22	.318	5/10	.500	-/ 6	0	2	5	-	-	19	-
WEST, L.	-	3/10	.300	5/ 9	.556	-/ 7	1	2	2	-	-	11	-
PIERCE, S.	-	6/16	.375	3/ 4	.750	-/ 6	0	2	3	-	-	15	-
EDWARDS, D.	-	0/ 0	.000	1/ 1	1.000	-/ 5	4	4	3	-	-	1	-
JONES, B.	-	3/ 6	.500	2/ 2	1.000	-/ 9	0	0	3	-	-	8	-
GARDNER, J.	-	7/11	.636	3/ 4	.750	-/12	2	2	3	-	-	17	-
GILES, T.	-	1/ 4	.250	0/ 0	.000	-/ 1	0	0	1	-	-	2	-
O'BRIEN	-	0/ 0	.000	0/ 0	.000	-/ 0	0	0	0	-	-	0	-
Totals	200	27/69	.391	19/30	.633	-/46	7	12	20	-	-	73	.365

Team Rebounds: Weber St. 2; Seattle 2. Disqualified: Seattle—Little.

	1st Half	2nd Half	Final
Weber St.	39	36	75
Seattle	35	38	73

REGIONAL SEMIFINAL EAST

North Carolina (79) Coach: Dean Smith

	Min.	Total FG / FGA	Pct.	FT / FTA	Pct.	Reb. O / T	A	TO	PF	S	Blk	TP	PPM
BUNTING, B.	28	6/ 8	.750	2/ 2	1.000	-/ 9	1	1	5	-	-	14	.500
SCOTT, C.	40	9/19	.474	4/ 7	.571	-/ 9	6	5	2	-	-	22	.550
CLARK, R.	38	5/ 9	.556	5/ 6	.833	-/ 8	1	3	2	-	-	15	.395
FOGLER, E.	31	3/ 8	.375	3/ 3	1.000	-/ 2	4	3	2	-	-	9	.290
TUTTLE, G.	9	0/ 2	.000	0/ 1	.000	-/ 1	1	0	0	-	-	0	.000
DELANY, J.	13	0/ 1	.000	5/ 5	1.000	-/ 0	0	2	1	-	-	5	.385
DEDMON, L.	27	4/10	.400	2/ 5	.400	-/ 6	1	3	3	-	-	10	.370
BROWN, J.	14	1/ 4	.250	2/ 4	.500	-/ 2	0	3	0	-	-	4	.286
Totals	200	28/61	.459	23/33	.697	-/37	14	20	15	-	-	79	.395

Duquesne (78) Coach: Red Manning

	Min.	Total FG / FGA	Pct.	FT / FTA	Pct.	Reb. O / T	A	TO	PF	S	Blk	TP	PPM
BARR, M.	-	8/16	.500	1/ 3	.333	-/ 9	3	1	1	-	-	17	-
DURHAM, J.	-	9/16	.563	3/ 3	1.000	-/ 5	6	5	3	-	-	21	-
HINES, W.	-	2/ 4	.500	0/ 1	.000	-/ 3	2	1	1	-	-	4	-
MAJOR, G.	-	2/ 5	.400	1/ 6	.167	-/ 5	1	1	4	-	-	5	-
NELSON, G.	-	5/ 9	.556	2/ 2	1.000	-/ 5	1	0	5	-	-	12	-
ZOPF, B.	-	6/11	.545	1/ 2	.500	-/ 5	3	6	3	-	-	13	-
NELSON, B.	-	3/ 8	.375	0/ 0	.000	-/ 5	0	1	3	-	-	6	-
Totals	200	35/69	.507	8/17	.471	-/37	16	15	20	-	-	78	.390

Team Rebounds: N. Carolina 6; Duquesne 6. Disqualified: N. Carolina—Bunting; Duquesne—G. Nelson.

	1st Half	2nd Half	Final
N. Carolina	48	31	79
Duquesne	41	37	78

Davidson (79) Coach: Lefty Driesell

	Min.	Total FG / FGA	Pct.	FT / FTA	Pct.	Reb. O / T	A	TO	PF	S	Blk	TP	PPM
COOK, D.	-	6/10	.600	7/ 9	.778	-/ 5	-	-	3	-	-	19	-
KROLL, J.	-	3/ 8	.375	5/ 6	.833	-/10	-	-	3	-	-	11	-
MALOY, M.	-	11/19	.579	13/13	1.000	-/12	-	-	3	-	-	35	-
HUCKEL, W.	-	1/ 3	.333	0/ 2	.000	-/ 0	-	-	0	-	-	2	-
KIRLEY, S.	-	0/ 0	.000	0/ 0	.000	-/ 0	-	-	0	-	-	0	-
MOSER, D.	-	2/ 7	.286	5/ 6	.833	-/ 7	-	-	2	-	-	9	-
O'NEILL, M.	-	1/ 2	.500	1/ 2	.500	-/ 1	-	-	1	-	-	3	-
Totals	200	24/49	.490	31/38	.816	-/35	-	-	12	-	-	79	.395

St. John's (69) Coach: Lou Carnesecca

	Min.	Total FG / FGA	Pct.	FT / FTA	Pct.	Reb. O / T	A	TO	PF	S	Blk	TP	PPM
CALZONETTI, C.	-	1/ 4	.250	1/ 1	1.000	-/ 0	-	-	2	-	-	3	-
ABRAHAM, R.	-	2/ 7	.286	3/ 3	1.000	-/ 9	-	-	4	-	-	7	-
WARREN, J.	-	9/20	.450	0/ 1	.000	-/ 5	-	-	4	-	-	18	-
CORNELIUS, D.	-	2/ 4	.500	3/ 3	1.000	-/ 5	-	-	4	-	-	7	-
DEPRE, J.	-	8/15	.533	0/ 1	.000	-/ 1	-	-	4	-	-	16	-
PAULTZ, B.	-	2/ 3	.667	0/ 1	.000	-/ 4	-	-	5	-	-	4	-
SMYTH, J.	-	4/10	.400	0/ 0	.000	-/ 2	-	-	2	-	-	8	-
GILKES, R.	-	2/ 2	1.000	2/ 2	1.000	-/ 2	-	-	2	-	-	6	-
Totals	200	30/65	.462	9/11	.818	-/28	-	-	27	-	-	69	.345

Team Rebounds: Davidson 3; St. John's 3. Disqualified: St. John's—Paultz.

	1st Half	2nd Half	Final
Davidson	44	35	79
St. John's	43	26	69

REGIONAL SEMIFINAL MIDEAST

Purdue (91)   Coach: George King

	Min.	Total FG/FGA	Pct.	FT/FTA	Pct.	Reb. O/T	A	TO	PF	S	Blk	TP	PPM
WEATHERFORD, L.	-	3/9	.333	1/2	.500	-/7	-	-	1	-	-	7	-
FAERBER, G.	-	8/8	1.000	0/2	.000	-/14	-	-	1	-	-	16	-
BAVIS, C.	-	1/1	1.000	0/0	.000	-/1	-	-	4	-	-	2	-
MOUNT, R.	-	12/20	.600	8/8	1.000	-/1	-	-	0	-	-	32	-
KELLER, B.	-	9/15	.600	1/1	1.000	-/6	-	-	2	-	-	19	-
BEDFORD, T.	-	2/5	.400	0/0	.000	-/5	-	-	3	-	-	4	-
JOHNSON, J.	-	2/2	1.000	1/1	1.000	-/5	-	-	4	-	-	5	-
KAUFMAN, F.	-	0/1	.000	3/4	.750	-/4	-	-	0	-	-	3	-
TAYLOR, R.	-	0/0	.000	0/0	.000	-/0	-	-	0	-	-	0	-
LONGFELLOW, S.	-	1/1	1.000	0/0	.000	-/1	-	-	0	-	-	2	-
REASONER, T.	-	0/0	.000	1/2	.500	-/0	-	-	0	-	-	1	-
Totals	200	38/62	.613	15/20	.750	-/44	-	-	15	-	-	91	.455

Miami (Ohio) (71)   Coach: Tates Locke

	Min.	Total FG/FGA	Pct.	FT/FTA	Pct.	Reb. O/T	A	TO	PF	S	Blk	TP	PPM
PRYOR, G.	-	4/5	.800	1/1	1.000	-/2	-	-	1	-	-	9	-
WILLIAMS, W.	-	4/15	.267	3/3	1.000	-/5	-	-	1	-	-	11	-
LOUCKS, R.	-	0/3	.000	1/1	1.000	-/3	-	-	1	-	-	1	-
LUKACS, F.	-	4/10	.400	0/0	.000	-/2	-	-	3	-	-	8	-
BURKHART, G.	-	0/2	.000	1/2	.500	-/2	-	-	1	-	-	1	-
WREN, M.	-	6/13	.462	4/4	1.000	-/1	-	-	2	-	-	16	-
SNYDER, R.	-	0/3	.000	3/4	.750	-/2	-	-	3	-	-	3	-
SLATER, T.	-	0/1	.000	0/0	.000	-/0	-	-	0	-	-	0	-
SEARS, G.	-	2/8	.250	0/0	.000	-/0	-	-	0	-	-	4	-
MARTIN, T.	-	8/15	.533	2/4	.500	-/10	-	-	2	-	-	18	-
STRAUCH, B.	-	0/0	.000	0/0	.000	-/0	-	-	1	-	-	0	-
Totals	200	28/75	.373	15/19	.789	-/27	-	-	15	-	-	71	.355

Team Rebounds: Purdue 5; Miami (Ohio) 4. Disqualified: None.

	1st Half	2nd Half	Final
Purdue	49	42	91
Miami (Ohio)	34	37	71

Marquette (81)   Coach: Al McGuire

	Min.	Total FG/FGA	Pct.	FT/FTA	Pct.	Reb. O/T	A	TO	PF	S	Blk	TP	PPM
THOMPSON, G.	-	7/16	.438	8/13	.615	-/4	-	-	1	-	-	22	-
THOMAS, J.	-	3/6	.500	0/0	.000	-/2	-	-	5	-	-	6	-
COBB, R.	-	7/8	.875	3/7	.429	-/14	-	-	1	-	-	17	-
MEMINGER, D.	-	6/15	.400	8/13	.615	-/6	-	-	2	-	-	20	-
SEWELL, J.	-	7/9	.778	1/2	.500	-/3	-	-	5	-	-	15	-
BURKE, J.	-	0/1	.000	1/2	.500	-/0	-	-	2	-	-	1	-
SMITH, P.	-	0/1	.000	0/1	.000	-/1	-	-	2	-	-	0	-
RAHN, R.	-	0/1	.000	0/0	.000	-/1	-	-	1	-	-	0	-
Totals	200	30/57	.526	21/38	.553	-/31	-	-	19	-	-	81	.405

Kentucky (74)   Coach: Adolph Rupp

	Min.	Total FG/FGA	Pct.	FT/FTA	Pct.	Reb. O/T	A	TO	PF	S	Blk	TP	PPM
STEELE, L.	-	1/6	.167	2/2	1.000	-/2	-	-	5	-	-	4	-
PRATT, M.	-	6/13	.462	5/6	.833	-/5	-	-	5	-	-	17	-
ISSEL, D.	-	4/8	.500	5/7	.714	-/16	-	-	2	-	-	13	-
ARGENTO, P.	-	8/15	.533	0/0	.000	-/2	-	-	5	-	-	16	-
CASEY, M.	-	7/14	.500	10/10	1.000	-/5	-	-	5	-	-	24	-
MCCOWAN, B.	-	0/2	.000	0/0	.000	-/1	-	-	4	-	-	0	-
DINWIDDIE, J.	-	0/6	.000	0/0	.000	-/0	-	-	0	-	-	0	-
MILLS, T.	-	0/0	.000	0/0	.000	-/0	-	-	0	-	-	0	-
Totals	200	26/64	.406	22/25	.880	-/31	-	-	26	-	-	74	.370

Team Rebounds: Marquette 15; Kentucky 8. Disqualified: Marquette—Thomas, Sewell; Kentucky—Steele, Pratt, Argento, Casey.

	1st Half	2nd Half	Final
Marquette	36	45	81
Kentucky	33	41	74

REGIONAL SEMIFINAL MIDWEST

Drake (81)   Coach: Maurice John

	Min.	Total FG/FGA	Pct.	FT/FTA	Pct.	Reb. O/T	A	TO	PF	S	Blk	TP	PPM
PULLIAM, D.	-	4/8	.500	1/1	1.000	-/6	-	-	4	-	-	9	-
WILLIAMS, A.	-	1/3	.333	3/4	.750	-/3	-	-	4	-	-	5	-
WISE, W.	-	2/15	.133	6/9	.667	-/16	-	-	3	-	-	10	-
MCCARTER, W.	-	12/24	.500	0/0	.000	-/3	-	-	1	-	-	24	-
DRAPER, D.	-	6/16	.375	1/1	1.000	-/3	-	-	2	-	-	13	-
ODOM, J.	-	2/2	1.000	4/8	.500	-/12	-	-	2	-	-	8	-
ZELLER, G.	-	3/6	.500	2/2	1.000	-/0	-	-	3	-	-	8	-
GWIN, R.	-	2/2	1.000	0/0	.000	-/1	-	-	1	-	-	4	-
WANAMAKER, R.	-	0/0	.000	0/0	.000	-/0	-	-	0	-	-	0	-
SAKYS, A.	-	0/0	.000	0/0	.000	-/0	-	-	0	-	-	0	-
MAST, B.	-	0/0	.000	0/0	.000	-/0	-	-	0	-	-	0	-
Totals	200	32/76	.421	17/25	.680	-/44	-	-	20	-	-	81	.405

Texas A&M (63)   Coach: Shelby Metcalf

	Min.	Total FG/FGA	Pct.	FT/FTA	Pct.	Reb. O/T	A	TO	PF	S	Blk	TP	PPM
HEITMAN, M.	-	3/12	.250	6/8	.750	-/4	-	-	1	-	-	12	-
PARET, R.	-	1/5	.200	2/4	.500	-/9	-	-	5	-	-	4	-
NILES, S.	-	5/10	.500	2/3	.667	-/9	-	-	5	-	-	12	-
BARNETT, B.	-	2/8	.250	2/4	.500	-/11	-	-	2	-	-	6	-
BENEFIELD, S.	-	2/14	.143	4/4	1.000	-/2	-	-	1	-	-	8	-
SMITH, C.	-	5/12	.417	0/1	.000	-/11	-	-	4	-	-	10	-
COOKSEY, B.	-	4/8	.500	3/4	.750	-/6	-	-	2	-	-	11	-
BROWN, B.	-	0/2	.000	0/0	.000	-/0	-	-	0	-	-	0	-
BOSTIC, H.	-	0/0	.000	0/0	.000	-/0	-	-	1	-	-	0	-
Totals	200	22/71	.310	19/28	.679	-/52	-	-	21	-	-	63	.315

Team Rebounds: Drake 10; Texas A&M 0. Disqualified: Texas A&M—Paret, Niles.

	1st Half	2nd Half	Final
Drake	32	49	81
Texas A&M	26	37	63

Colorado State (64)   Coach: Jim Williams

	Min.	Total FG/FGA	Pct.	FT/FTA	Pct.	Reb. O/T	A	TO	PF	S	Blk	TP	PPM
SHEGOGG, C.	-	9/18	.500	2/3	.667	-/9	-	-	4	-	-	20	-
WEEMS, J.	-	0/2	.000	0/0	.000	-/4	-	-	4	-	-	0	-
DAVIS, M.	-	3/5	.600	4/6	.667	-/13	-	-	5	-	-	10	-
KERR, L.	-	4/17	.235	4/8	.500	-/9	-	-	1	-	-	12	-
KERR, F.	-	4/6	.667	6/9	.667	-/3	-	-	1	-	-	14	-
MEEKER, T.	-	1/3	.333	1/3	.333	-/3	-	-	1	-	-	3	-
PEDEN, W.	-	0/0	.000	2/3	.667	-/0	-	-	0	-	-	2	-
STOCKHAM, J.	-	1/1	1.000	1/2	.500	-/0	-	-	2	-	-	3	-
Totals	200	22/52	.423	20/34	.588	-/41	-	18	18	-	-	64	.320

Colorado (56)   Coach: Sox Walseth

	Min.	Total FG/FGA	Pct.	FT/FTA	Pct.	Reb. O/T	A	TO	PF	S	Blk	TP	PPM
WEDGEWORTH, T.	-	1/9	.111	2/2	1.000	-/10	-	-	2	-	-	4	-
COLEMAN, M.	-	0/5	.000	1/7	.143	-/9	-	-	0	-	-	1	-
MEELY, C.	-	11/26	.423	10/14	.714	-/11	-	-	4	-	-	32	-
TOPE, G.	-	1/6	.167	1/1	1.000	-/0	-	-	5	-	-	3	-
MITCHELL, D.	-	5/16	.313	0/0	.000	-/2	-	-	3	-	-	10	-
ERFERT, T.	-	2/4	.500	0/0	.000	-/4	-	-	2	-	-	4	-
RICHARDSON, T.	-	1/3	.333	0/0	.000	-/3	-	-	3	-	-	2	-
KERN, M.	-	0/0	.000	0/0	.000	-/1	-	-	4	-	-	0	-
HUTCHINSON	-	0/0	.000	0/0	.000	-/0	-	-	0	-	-	0	-
JAMESON, T.	-	0/1	.000	0/0	.000	-/0	-	-	0	-	-	0	-
SMITH, S.	-	0/0	.000	0/0	.000	-/0	-	-	1	-	-	0	-
MAULSBY, R.	-	0/0	.000	0/0	.000	-/0	-	-	0	-	-	0	-
Totals	200	21/70	.300	14/24	.583	-/40	-	13	24	-	-	56	.280

Team Rebounds: Colorado State 9; Colorado 13. Disqualified: Colorado State—Davis; Colorado—Tope.

	1st Half	2nd Half	Final
Colorado State	28	36	64
Colorado	27	29	56

REGIONAL SEMIFINAL WEST

UCLA (53)   Coach: John Wooden

	Min.	Total FG/FGA	Pct.	FT/FTA	Pct.	Reb. O/T	A	TO	PF	S	Blk	TP	PPM
ROWE, C.	-	3/12	.250	2/2	1.000	-/7	-	-	2	-	-	8	-
SHACKELFORD, L.	-	4/10	.400	0/0	.000	-/3	-	-	0	-	-	8	-
ALCINDOR, L.	-	8/15	.533	0/5	.000	-/16	-	-	3	-	-	16	-
HEITZ, K.	-	4/6	.667	1/1	1.000	-/4	-	-	3	-	-	9	-
VALLELY, J.	-	5/12	.417	0/0	.000	-/5	-	-	1	-	-	10	-
WICKS, S.	-	0/2	.000	0/0	.000	-/0	-	-	0	-	-	0	-
SWEEK, B.	-	1/1	1.000	0/2	.000	-/0	-	-	1	-	-	2	-
PATTERSON, S.	-	0/0	.000	0/0	.000	-/0	-	-	1	-	-	0	-
SCHOFIELD, T.	-	0/0	.000	0/0	.000	-/0	-	-	0	-	-	0	-
Totals	200	25/58	.431	3/10	.300	-/35	-	-	11	-	-	53	.265

New Mexico State (38)   Coach: Lou Henson

	Min.	Total FG/FGA	Pct.	FT/FTA	Pct.	Reb. O/T	A	TO	PF	S	Blk	TP	PPM
COLLINS, J.	-	4/17	.235	3/3	1.000	-/4	-	-	1	-	-	11	-
MURPHY, H.	-	1/2	.500	0/0	.000	-/1	-	-	1	-	-	2	-
BURGESS, J.	-	0/3	.000	0/1	.000	-/2	-	-	0	-	-	0	-
SMITH, J.	-	2/4	.500	3/3	1.000	-/8	-	-	3	-	-	7	-
LACEY, S.	-	5/16	.313	1/1	1.000	-/11	-	-	4	-	-	11	-
REYES, C.	-	2/5	.400	1/2	.500	-/2	-	-	0	-	-	5	-
BOWEN, H.	-	1/1	1.000	0/0	.000	-/0	-	-	0	-	-	2	-
Totals	200	15/48	.313	8/10	.800	-/28	-	-	9	-	-	38	.190

Team Rebounds: UCLA 7; New Mexico St. 5. Disqualified: None.

	1st Half	2nd Half	Final
UCLA	21	32	53
New Mexico St.	17	21	38

Santa Clara (63)   Coach: Dick Garibaldi

	Min.	Total FG/FGA	Pct.	FT/FTA	Pct.	Reb. O/T	A	TO	PF	S	Blk	TP	PPM
OGDEN, R.	-	4/13	.308	1/1	1.000	-/6	-	-	3	-	-	9	-
OGDEN, B.	-	7/13	.538	4/7	.571	-/13	-	-	2	-	-	18	-
AWTREY, D.	-	9/17	.529	1/1	1.000	-/7	-	-	5	-	-	19	-
EAGELSON, K.	-	2/2	1.000	1/3	.333	-/2	-	-	4	-	-	5	-
O'BRIEN, T.	-	1/3	.333	3/3	1.000	-/1	-	-	4	-	-	5	-
DEMPSEY, C.	-	1/2	.500	3/5	.600	-/8	-	-	0	-	-	5	-
DIFFLEY, J.	-	1/5	.200	0/1	.000	-/5	-	-	0	-	-	2	-
Totals	225	25/55	.455	13/21	.619	-/42	-	-	18	-	-	63	.280

Weber State (59)   Coach: Phil Johnson

	Min.	Total FG/FGA	Pct.	FT/FTA	Pct.	Reb. O/T	A	TO	PF	S	Blk	TP	PPM
CHATMON, G.	-	0/1	.000	0/0	.000	-/3	-	-	3	-	-	0	-
BERGH, L.	-	3/5	.600	2/2	1.000	-/1	-	-	5	-	-	8	-
SOJOURNER, W.	-	2/14	.143	8/9	.889	-/18	-	-	3	-	-	12	-
THIGPEN, J.	-	7/16	.438	2/4	.500	-/2	-	-	1	-	-	16	-
HARLAN, S.	-	4/10	.400	3/4	.750	-/5	-	-	1	-	-	11	-
STRONG, G.	-	4/10	.400	0/2	.000	-/6	-	-	1	-	-	8	-
NIELSEN, R.	-	0/2	.000	0/0	.000	-/0	-	-	0	-	-	0	-
SACKOLWITZ, D.	-	1/2	.500	2/5	.400	-/3	-	-	5	-	-	4	-
Totals	225	21/60	.350	17/26	.654	-/38	-	-	19	-	-	59	.262

Team Rebounds: Santa Clara 2; Weber St. 4. Disqualified: Santa Clara—Awtrey; Weber St.—Bergh, Sackolwitz.

	1st Half	2nd Half	1 OT	Final
Santa Clara	29	26	8	63
Weber St.	19	36	4	59

REGIONAL FINAL EAST

North Carolina (87)   Coach: Dean Smith

	Min.	Total FG/FGA	Pct.	FT/FTA	Pct.	Reb. O/T	A	TO	PF	S	Blk	TP	PPM
BUNTING, B.	39	7/12	.583	8/9	.889	-/8	4	4	2	-	-	22	.564
SCOTT, C.	40	14/21	.667	4/5	.800	-/6	4	4	1	-	-	32	.800
CLARK, R.	26	8/9	.889	0/1	.000	-/6	2	3	4	-	-	16	.615
FOGLER, E.	31	4/8	.500	0/1	.000	-/1	3	2	2	-	-	8	.258
DEDMON, L.	12	1/2	.500	0/0	.000	-/3	0	0	5	-	-	2	.167
DELANY, J.	33	0/6	.000	3/4	.750	-/2	2	1	2	-	-	3	.091
TUTTLE, G.	9	1/3	.333	0/0	.000	-/2	0	0	2	-	-	2	.222
BROWN, J.	10	0/4	.000	2/2	1.000	-/4	1	2	0	-	-	2	.200
Totals	200	35/65	.538	17/22	.773	-/32	16	16	18	-	-	87	.435

Davidson (85)   Coach: Lefty Driesell

	Min.	Total FG/FGA	Pct.	FT/FTA	Pct.	Reb. O/T	A	TO	PF	S	Blk	TP	PPM
COOK, D.	25	7/13	.538	4/4	1.000	-/6	2	1	5	-	-	18	.720
KROLL, J.	23	6/15	.400	4/4	1.000	-/2	0	3	5	-	-	16	.696
MALOY, M.	40	10/23	.435	5/7	.714	-/13	0	5	3	-	-	25	.625
HUCKEL, W.	27	3/10	.300	1/1	1.000	-/8	5	0	1	-	-	7	.259
KIRLEY, S.	15	2/3	.667	0/0	.000	-/5	0	0	2	-	-	4	.267
MOSER, D.	37	2/6	.333	0/0	.000	-/3	5	3	3	-	-	4	.108
O'NEILL, M.	30	3/9	.333	4/7	.571	-/1	2	1	2	-	-	10	.333
STELZER, R.	3	0/0	.000	1/2	.500	-/1	0	1	0	-	-	1	.333
Totals	200	33/79	.418	19/25	.760	-/39	14	14	21	-	-	85	.425

Team Rebounds: N. Carolina 5; Davidson 11. Disqualified: N. Carolina—Dedmon; Davidson—Cook, Kroll.

	1st Half	2nd Half	Final
N. Carolina	47	40	87
Davidson	46	39	85

REGIONAL FINAL MIDEAST

Purdue (75)   Coach: George King

	Min.	Total FG/FGA	Pct.	FT/FTA	Pct.	Reb. O/T	A	TO	PF	S	Blk	TP	PPM
WEATHERFORD, L.	-	5/14	.357	3/3	1.000	-/3	-	2	0	-	-	13	-
FAERBER, G.	-	3/5	.600	2/3	.667	-/8	-	0	4	-	-	8	-
GILLIAM, H.	-	2/3	.667	3/3	1.000	-/3	-	2	2	-	-	7	-
MOUNT, R.	-	11/32	.344	4/5	.800	-/2	-	5	2	-	-	26	-
KELLER, B.	-	6/11	.545	5/5	1.000	-/2	-	1	5	-	-	17	-
BEDFORD, T.	-	0/1	.000	0/0	.000	-/3	-	0	2	-	-	0	-
JOHNSON, J.	-	2/6	.333	0/1	.000	-/16	-	0	3	-	-	4	-
KAUFMAN, F.	-	0/0	.000	0/0	.000	-/0	-	0	3	-	-	0	-
Totals	200	29/72	.403	17/20	.850	-/37	-	10	21	-	-	75	.375

Marquette (73)   Coach: Al McGuire

	Min.	Total FG/FGA	Pct.	FT/FTA	Pct.	Reb. O/T	A	TO	PF	S	Blk	TP	PPM
THOMPSON, G.	-	9/17	.529	10/11	.909	-/8	-	4	1	-	-	28	-
THOMAS, J.	-	5/13	.385	1/2	.500	-/13	-	3	3	-	-	11	-
COBB, R.	-	2/10	.200	3/7	.429	-/9	-	0	4	-	-	7	-
MEMINGER, D.	-	5/14	.357	2/6	.333	-/14	-	5	1	-	-	12	-
SEWELL, J.	-	3/9	.333	2/2	1.000	-/2	-	1	4	-	-	8	-
BURKE, J.	-	3/5	.600	1/1	1.000	-/2	-	0	3	-	-	7	-
Totals	200	27/68	.397	19/29	.655	-/48	-	13	16	-	-	73	.365

Team Rebounds: Purdue 5; Marquette 7. Disqualified: Purdue—Keller.

	1st Half	2nd Half	Final
Purdue	35	40	75
Marquette	30	43	73

REGIONAL FINAL MIDWEST

Drake (84)   Coach: Maurice John

	Min.	Total FG/FGA	Pct.	FT/FTA	Pct.	Reb. O/T	A	TO	PF	S	Blk	TP	PPM
PULLIAM, D.	-	5/14	.357	3/4	.750	-/3	-	-	4	-	-	13	-
WILLIAMS, A.	-	2/8	.250	0/0	.000	-/5	-	-	3	-	-	4	-
WISE, W.	-	4/11	.364	8/12	.667	-/7	-	-	4	-	-	16	-
MCCARTER, W.	-	9/23	.391	3/3	1.000	-/5	-	-	4	-	-	21	-
DRAPPER, D.	-	5/11	.455	1/1	1.000	-/4	-	-	4	-	-	11	-
ODOM, G.	-	4/5	.800	2/3	.667	-/6	-	-	1	-	-	10	-
ZELLER, G.	-	4/5	.800	1/2	.500	-/3	-	-	2	-	-	9	-
GWIN, R.	-	0/1	.000	0/0	.000	-/1	-	-	0	-	-	0	-
Totals	200	33/78	.423	18/25	.720	-/34	-	6	22	-	-	84	.420

Colorado State (77)   Coach: Jim Williams

	Min.	Total FG/FGA	Pct.	FT/FTA	Pct.	Reb. O/T	A	TO	PF	S	Blk	TP	PPM
SHEGOGG, C.	-	1/7	.143	6/6	1.000	-/2	-	-	5	-	-	8	-
WEEMS, J.	-	2/7	.286	0/0	.000	-/9	-	-	4	-	-	4	-
DAVIS, M.	-	2/4	.500	9/10	.900	-/16	-	-	4	-	-	13	-
KERR, L.	-	5/15	.333	2/2	1.000	-/8	-	-	2	-	-	12	-
KERR, F.	-	8/17	.471	5/7	.714	-/6	-	-	4	-	-	21	-
MEEKER, T.	-	0/0	.000	0/0	.000	-/0	-	-	1	-	-	0	-
PEDEN, W.	-	7/10	.700	5/6	.833	-/1	-	-	2	-	-	19	-
STOCKHAM, J.	-	0/0	.000	0/0	.000	-/0	-	-	0	-	-	0	-
Totals	200	25/60	.417	27/31	.871	-/42	-	17	22	-	-	77	.385

Team Rebounds: Drake 8; Colorado State 10. Disqualified: Colorado State—Shegogg.

	1st Half	2nd Half	Final
Drake	38	46	84
Colorado State	37	40	77

REGIONAL FINAL WEST

UCLA (90)   Coach: John Wooden

	Min.	Total FG/FGA	Pct.	FT/FTA	Pct.	Reb. O/T	A	TO	PF	S	Blk	TP	PPM
ROWE, C.	-	3/6	.500	1/2	.500	-/5	-	-	1	-	-	7	-
SHACKELFORD, L.	-	3/7	.429	0/1	.000	-/3	-	-	1	-	-	6	-
ALCINDOR, L.	-	8/14	.571	1/3	.333	-/7	-	-	2	-	-	17	-
HEITZ, K.	-	3/6	.500	0/0	.000	-/1	-	-	2	-	-	6	-
VALLELY, J.	-	5/5	1.000	1/2	.500	-/3	-	-	2	-	-	11	-
WICKS, S.	-	3/4	.750	5/8	.625	-/2	-	-	1	-	-	11	-
SWEEK, B.	-	4/7	.571	4/5	.800	-/1	-	-	1	-	-	12	-
PATTERSON, S.	-	4/6	.667	1/1	1.000	-/5	-	-	4	-	-	9	-
SCHOFIELD, T.	-	1/6	.167	0/0	.000	-/2	-	-	0	-	-	2	-
ECKER, J.	-	2/2	1.000	1/1	1.000	-/1	-	-	0	-	-	5	-
SEIBERT, B.	-	0/0	.000	2/2	1.000	-/3	-	-	1	-	-	2	-
FARMER, G.	-	1/2	.500	0/0	.000	-/0	-	-	0	-	-	2	-
Totals	200	37/65	.569	16/25	.615	-/33	-	-	15	-	-	90	.450

Santa Clara (52)   Coach: Dick Garibaldi

	Min.	Total FG/FGA	Pct.	FT/FTA	Pct.	Reb. O/T	A	TO	PF	S	Blk	TP	PPM
OGDEN, R.	-	1/13	.077	2/4	.500	-/7	-	-	2	-	-	4	-
OGDEN, B.	-	3/10	.300	3/3	1.000	-/5	-	-	4	-	-	9	-
AWTREY, D.	-	5/9	.556	4/6	.667	-/8	-	-	4	-	-	14	-
EAGELSON, K.	-	0/0	.000	0/1	.000	-/3	-	-	3	-	-	0	-
O'BRIEN, T.	-	0/2	.000	0/1	.000	-/1	-	-	2	-	-	0	-
DEMPSEY, C.	-	2/3	.667	1/1	1.000	-/2	-	-	2	-	-	5	-
DIFFLEY, J.	-	1/4	.250	0/0	.000	-/2	-	-	2	-	-	2	-
PAULSON, K.	-	2/4	.500	1/3	.333	-/1	-	-	0	-	-	5	-
TOBIN, B.	-	1/2	.500	0/0	.000	-/4	-	-	2	-	-	2	-
SCHERER, T.	-	2/5	.400	0/0	.000	-/1	-	-	0	-	-	4	-
GRAVES, G.	-	1/1	1.000	1/1	1.000	-/1	-	-	1	-	-	3	-
CHAMP, M.	-	2/3	.667	0/0	.000	-/2	-	-	3	-	-	4	-
Totals	200	20/56	.357	12/20	.600	-/37	-	-	25	-	-	52	.260

Team Rebounds: UCLA 6; Santa Clara 5. Disqualified: None.

	1st Half	2nd Half	Final
UCLA	46	44	90
Santa Clara	25	27	52

FINAL FOUR

North Carolina (65)   Coach: Dean Smith

	Min.	Total FG/FGA	Pct.	FT/FTA	Pct.	Reb. O/T	A	TO	PF	S	Blk	TP	PPM
BUNTING, B.	37	7/13	.538	5/7	.714	3/7	2	4	2	-	-	19	.514
SCOTT, C.	36	6/19	.316	4/6	.667	1/6	6	2	3	-	-	16	.444
CLARK, R.	37	7/9	.778	6/10	.600	2/9	1	3	2	-	-	20	.541
FOGLER, E.	27	1/4	.250	0/0	.000	2/2	1	5	2	-	-	2	.074
TUTTLE, G.	20	2/4	.500	0/1	.000	1/3	1	7	3	-	-	4	.200
DELANY, J.	13	0/2	.000	0/0	.000	1/1	2	1	4	-	-	0	.000
DEDMON, L.	16	0/1	.000	0/1	.000	0/4	2	3	2	-	-	0	.000
BROWN, J.	6	1/4	.250	0/0	.000	0/1	0	1	0	-	-	2	.333
GIPPLE, D.	4	0/3	.000	0/0	.000	1/1	0	0	0	-	-	0	.000
CHADWICK, D.	2	1/2	.500	0/0	.000	1/2	0	0	0	-	-	2	1.000
TUTTLE, R.	1	0/1	.000	0/0	.000	0/0	0	0	0	-	-	0	.000
EGGLESTON, D.	1	0/0	.000	0/0	.000	0/0	0	0	0	-	-	0	.000
Totals	200	25/62	.403	15/25	.600	12/36	15	26	18	-	-	65	.325

Purdue (92)   Coach: George King

	Min.	Total FG/FGA	Pct.	FT/FTA	Pct.	Reb. O/T	A	TO	PF	S	Blk	TP	PPM
WEATHERFORD, L.	11	3/6	.500	1/1	1.000	0/2	0	2	1	-	-	7	.636
FAERBER, G.	31	3/3	1.000	2/2	1.000	2/9	0	3	3	-	-	8	.258
YOUNG, G.	2	0/0	.000	0/0	.000	0/0	0	0	0	-	-	0	.000
MOUNT, R.	33	14/28	.500	8/9	.889	0/4	3	3	0	-	-	36	1.091
KELLER, B.	32	9/19	.474	2/3	.667	4/5	5	2	3	-	-	20	.625
BEDFORD, T.	17	3/3	1.000	0/0	.000	2/5	1	0	4	-	-	6	.353
JOHNSON, J.	13	2/5	.400	1/3	.333	3/5	0	1	4	-	-	5	.385
KAUFMAN, F.	26	0/1	.000	2/3	.667	3/6	1	0	4	-	-	2	.077
TAYLOR, R.	2	1/1	1.000	0/1	.000	2/3	0	0	0	-	-	2	1.000
LONGFELLOW, S.	4	0/1	.000	0/0	.000	0/2	0	1	0	-	-	0	.000
REASONER, T.	2	0/0	.000	0/0	.000	0/0	0	0	1	-	-	0	.000
GILLIAM, H.	27	3/11	.273	0/0	.000	2/8	7	3	0	-	-	6	.222
Totals	200	38/78	.487	16/22	.727	18/49	17	15	20	-	-	92	.460

Team Rebounds: Purdue 2; N. Carolina 1. Disqualified: None.

	1st Half	2nd Half	Final
N. Carolina	35	30	65
Purdue	39	53	92

Drake (82)   Coach: Maurice John

	Min.	Total FG/FGA	Pct.	FT/FTA	Pct.	Reb. O/T	A	TO	PF	S	Blk	TP	PPM
PULLIAM, D.	-	4/14	.286	4/5	.800	-/5	6	-	4	-	-	12	-
WILLIAMS, A.	-	0/1	.000	0/0	.000	-/1	0	-	4	-	-	0	-
WISE, W.	-	5/7	.714	3/4	.750	-/16	1	-	3	-	-	13	-
MCCARTER, W.	-	10/27	.370	4/4	1.000	-/1	2	-	3	-	-	24	-
DRAPER, D.	-	5/13	.385	2/2	1.000	-/1	1	-	2	-	-	12	-
ODOM, G.	-	0/2	.000	0/1	.000	-/2	0	-	4	-	-	0	-
ZELLER, G.	-	4/12	.333	4/6	.667	-/3	1	-	3	-	-	12	-
GWIN, R.	-	0/0	.000	0/1	.000	-/1	0	-	1	-	-	0	-
WANAMAKER, R.	-	4/7	.571	1/1	1.000	-/7	1	-	4	-	-	9	-
Totals	200	32/83	.386	18/24	.750	-/37	12	-	30	-	-	82	.410

UCLA (85)   Coach: John Wooden

	Min.	Total FG/FGA	Pct.	FT/FTA	Pct.	Reb. O/T	A	TO	PF	S	Blk	TP	PPM
ROWE, C.	-	6/9	.667	2/2	1.000	-/13	3	-	2	-	-	14	-
SHACKELFORD, L.	-	2/5	.400	2/3	.667	-/2	3	-	4	-	-	6	-
ALCINDOR, L.	-	8/14	.571	9/16	.563	-/21	3	-	3	-	-	25	-
HEITZ, K.	-	3/6	.500	1/3	.333	-/1	3	-	5	-	-	7	-
VALLELY, J.	-	9/11	.818	11/14	.786	-/6	5	-	5	-	-	29	-
WICKS, S.	-	0/2	.000	0/0	.000	-/1	0	-	1	-	-	0	-
SWEEK, B.	-	0/0	.000	0/0	.000	-/0	0	-	1	-	-	0	-
PATTERSON, S.	-	0/0	.000	2/2	1.000	-/0	0	-	0	-	-	2	-
SCHOFIELD, T.	-	0/3	.000	2/4	.500	-/0	1	-	0	-	-	2	-
Totals	200	28/50	.560	29/44	.659	-/44	18	-	21	-	-	85	.425

Team Rebounds: UCLA 4; Drake 4. Disqualified: UCLA—Heitz, Vallely.

	1st Half	2nd Half	Final
Drake	39	43	82
UCLA	41	44	85

NATIONAL CHAMPIONSHIP

Purdue (72)   Coach: George King

	Min.	Total FG / FGA	Pct.	FT / FTA	Pct.	Reb. O/T	A	TO	PF	S	Blk	TP	PPM
WEATHERFORD, L.	15	1/ 5	.200	2/ 2	1.000	1/ 1	0	0	3	-	-	4	.267
FAERBER, G.	17	1/ 2	.500	0/ 0	.000	2/ 3	0	1	5	-	-	2	.118
MOUNT, R.	37	12/36	.333	4/ 5	.800	0/ 1	0	0	3	-	-	28	.757
KELLER, B.	32	4/17	.235	3/ 4	.750	3/ 4	3	2	5	-	-	11	.344
BEDFORD, T.	25	3/ 8	.375	1/ 3	.333	4/ 8	0	0	3	-	-	7	.280
JOHNSON, J.	27	4/ 9	.444	3/ 4	.750	5/ 9	0	0	2	-	-	11	.407
KAUFMAN, F.	13	0/ 0	.000	2/ 2	1.000	1/ 5	0	0	5	-	-	2	.154
TAYLOR, R.	1	0/ 0	.000	0/ 0	.000	0/ 0	0	0	0	-	-	0	.000
REASONER, T.	1	0/ 1	.000	0/ 1	.000	1/ 1	0	0	2	-	-	0	.000
GILLIAM, H.	32	2/14	.143	3/ 3	1.000	3/11	3	1	2	-	-	7	.219
Totals	200	27/92	.293	18/24	.750	20/43	6	4	30	-	-	72	.360

UCLA (92)   Coach: John Wooden

	Min.	Total FG / FGA	Pct.	FT / FTA	Pct.	Reb. O/T	A	TO	PF	S	Blk	TP	PPM
ROWE, C.	37	4/10	.400	4/ 4	1.000	5/12	3	2	2	-	-	12	.324
SHAKELFORD, L.	35	3/ 8	.375	5/ 8	.625	2/ 9	0	2	3	-	-	11	.314
ALCINDOR, L.	36	15/20	.750	7/ 9	.778	5/20	0	2	2	-	-	37	1.028
HEITZ, K.	34	0/ 3	.000	0/ 1	.000	1/ 3	4	4	4	-	-	0	.000
VALLELY, J.	31	4/ 9	.444	7/10	.700	0/ 4	0	4	3	-	-	15	.484
WICKS, S.	6	0/ 1	.000	3/ 6	.500	0/ 4	1	1	1	-	-	3	.500
SWEEK, B.	10	3/ 3	1.000	0/ 1	.000	1/ 1	0	1	3	-	-	6	.600
PATTERSON, S.	5	1/ 1	1.000	2/ 2	1.000	1/ 2	0	1	0	-	-	4	.800
SEIBERT, B.	1	0/ 0	.000	0/ 0	.000	0/ 1	0	0	0	-	-	0	.000
FARMER, G.	1	0/ 0	.000	0/ 0	.000	0/ 0	0	1	1	-	-	0	.000
ECKER, J.	1	1/ 1	1.000	0/ 0	.000	0/ 0	0	0	0	-	-	2	2.000
SCHOFIELD, T.	3	1/ 2	.500	0/ 0	.000	0/ 0	0	1	0	-	-	2	.667
Totals	200	32/58	.552	28/41	.683	15/56	8	19	19	-	-	92	.460

Team Rebounds: UCLA 5; Purdue 5. Disqualified: Purdue—Faerber, Keller, Kaufman.

	1st Half	2nd Half	Final
Purdue	31	41	72
UCLA	42	50	92

NATIONAL THIRD PLACE

Drake (104)   Coach: Maurice John

	Min.	Total FG / FGA	Pct.	FT / FTA	Pct.	Reb. O/T	A	TO	PF	S	Blk	TP	PPM
PULLIAM, D.	32	4/10	.400	2/ 3	.667	1/ 3	1	3	4	-	-	10	.313
WILLIAMS, A.	34	8/13	.615	0/ 1	.000	4/ 8	1	3	4	-	-	16	.471
WISE, W.	29	6/ 9	.667	4/ 4	1.000	2/ 9	0	7	3	-	-	16	.552
MCCARTER, W.	39	12/20	.600	4/ 5	.800	1/ 6	11	5	3	-	-	28	.718
DRAPER, D.	19	3/ 8	.375	0/ 0	.000	0/ 0	2	2	1	-	-	6	.316
ZELLER, G.	20	3/ 9	.333	1/ 1	1.000	1/ 3	1	2	0	-	-	7	.350
ODOM, G.	11	2/ 2	1.000	0/ 0	.000	1/ 3	0	0	3	-	-	4	.364
WANAMAKER, R.	11	5/ 6	.833	1/ 2	.500	4/ 4	0	0	2	-	-	11	1.000
GWIN, R.	2	1/ 2	.500	2/ 2	1.000	0/ 0	0	1	1	-	-	4	2.000
MAST, B.	1	0/ 0	.000	0/ 0	.000	0/ 0	0	0	1	-	-	0	.000
TEETER, D.	1	1/ 1	1.000	0/ 0	.000	0/ 0	0	0	0	-	-	2	2.000
O'DEA, J.	1	0/ 0	.000	0/ 0	.000	0/ 0	0	0	0	-	-	0	.000
Totals	200	45/80	.563	14/18	.778	14/36	16	23	22	-	-	104	.520

North Carolina (84)   Coach: Dean Smith

	Min.	Total FG / FGA	Pct.	FT / FTA	Pct.	Reb. O/T	A	TO	PF	S	Blk	TP	PPM
BUNTING, B.	33	3/ 6	.500	1/ 2	.500	4/ 9	0	2	5	-	-	7	.212
SCOTT, C.	35	16/26	.615	3/ 6	.500	0/ 4	1	4	2	-	-	35	1.000
CLARK, R.	39	2/ 9	.222	8/10	.800	5/12	3	3	1	-	-	12	.308
FOGLER, E.	32	3/ 7	.429	1/ 3	.333	1/ 4	5	11	1	-	-	7	.219
DEDMON, L.	31	5/10	.500	1/ 2	.500	7/10	2	9	3	-	-	11	.355
TUTTLE, G.	6	1/ 3	.333	2/ 2	1.000	0/ 0	0	2	1	-	-	4	.667
BROWN, J.	9	0/ 2	.000	0/ 0	.000	2/ 2	0	1	1	-	-	0	.000
DELANY, J.	10	0/ 2	.000	2/ 2	1.000	0/ 1	1	3	2	-	-	2	.200
GIPPLE, D.	2	0/ 0	.000	1/ 2	.500	0/ 0	0	0	1	-	-	1	.500
CHADWICK, D.	1	1/ 2	.500	0/ 0	.000	2/ 2	0	1	0	-	-	2	2.000
EGGLESTON, D.	1	0/ 0	.000	0/ 0	.000	0/ 0	0	0	0	-	-	0	.000
TUTTLE, R.	1	1/ 1	1.000	1/ 2	.500	1/ 1	0	0	0	-	-	3	3.000
Totals	200	32/68	.471	20/31	.645	22/45	12	36	17	-	-	84	.420

Team Rebounds: Drake 1; N. Carolina 2. Disqualified: N. Carolina—Bunting.

	1st Half	2nd Half	Final
Drake	50	54	104
N. Carolina	39	45	84

REGIONAL THIRD PLACE WEST

Weber State (58)   Coach: Phil Johnson

	Min.	Total FG / FGA	Pct.	FT / FTA	Pct.	Reb. O/T	A	TO	PF	S	Blk	TP	PPM
CHATMON, G.	-	3/ 6	.500	0/ 0	.000	-/11	-	-	0	-	-	6	-
BERGH, L.	-	6/15	.400	1/ 1	1.000	-/ 4	-	-	2	-	-	13	-
SOJOURNER, W.	-	4/ 9	.444	4/ 6	.667	-/11	-	-	3	-	-	12	-
THIGPEN, J.	-	6/19	.316	2/ 2	1.000	-/ 2	-	-	2	-	-	14	-
HARLAN, S.	-	3/ 8	.375	0/ 2	.000	-/ 3	-	-	2	-	-	6	-
STRONG, R.	-	1/ 2	.500	0/ 0	.000	-/ 2	-	-	0	-	-	2	-
NIELSEN, R.	-	0/ 2	.000	3/ 4	.750	-/ 2	-	-	0	-	-	3	-
SACKOLWITZ, D.	-	0/ 1	.000	2/ 2	1.000	-/ 1	-	-	1	-	-	2	-
Totals	200	23/62	.371	12/17	.706	-/36	-	-	10	-	-	58	.290

New Mexico State (56)   Coach: Lou Henson

	Min.	Total FG / FGA	Pct.	FT / FTA	Pct.	Reb. O/T	A	TO	PF	S	Blk	TP	PPM
COLLINS, J.	-	8/15	.533	3/ 4	.750	-/ 6	-	-	3	-	-	19	-
BURGESS, J.	-	3/10	.300	0/ 1	.000	-/11	-	-	1	-	-	6	-
SMITH, J.	-	2/ 5	.400	0/ 0	.000	-/ 9	-	-	3	-	-	4	-
LACEY, S.	-	3/10	.300	2/ 3	.667	-/13	-	-	2	-	-	8	-
REYES, C.	-	4/12	.333	1/ 1	1.000	-/ 4	-	-	2	-	-	9	-
LEONARD, L.	-	5/ 9	.556	0/ 0	.000	-/ 2	-	-	1	-	-	10	-
BANKS, M.	-	0/ 1	.000	0/ 0	.000	-/ 0	-	-	0	-	-	0	-
Totals	200	25/62	.403	6/12	.500	-/45	-	-	12	-	-	56	.280

Team Rebounds: Weber St. 4; New Mexico St. 2. Disqualified: None.

	1st Half	2nd Half	Final
Weber St.	23	35	58
New Mexico St.	29	27	56

REGIONAL THIRD PLACE MIDWEST

Colorado (97)   Coach: Sox Walseth

	Min.	Total FG / FGA	Pct.	FT / FTA	Pct.	Reb. O / T	A	TO	PF	S	Blk	TP	PPM
MEELY, C.	-	12/23	.522	2/ 4	.500	-/ 5	-	-	4	-	-	26	-
HUTCHINSON, L.	-	2/ 3	.667	3/ 3	1.000	-/ 5	-	-	5	-	-	7	-
ERFERT, T.	-	2/ 6	.333	0/ 2	.000	-/ 7	-	-	5	-	-	4	-
TOPE, G.	-	11/14	.786	2/ 2	1.000	-/ 3	-	-	1	-	-	24	-
KERN, M.	-	0/ 1	.000	2/ 2	1.000	-/ 1	-	-	2	-	-	2	-
MITCHELL, D.	-	6/ 9	.667	0/ 1	.000	-/ 1	-	-	0	-	-	12	-
WEDGEWORTH, T.	-	3/ 7	.429	1/ 2	.500	-/ 7	-	-	2	-	-	7	-
RICHARDSON, T.	-	2/ 5	.400	3/ 4	.750	-/ 4	-	-	2	-	-	7	-
COLEMAN, M.	-	2/ 2	1.000	2/ 5	.400	-/ 3	-	-	4	-	-	6	-
SMITH, S.	-	1/ 1	1.000	0/ 1	.000	-/ 2	-	-	0	-	-	2	-
MAULSBY, R.	-	0/ 0	.000	0/ 0	.000	-/ 0	-	-	1	-	-	0	-
JAMESON, T.	-	0/ 1	.000	0/ 0	.000	-/ 0	-	-	1	-	-	0	-
Totals	200	41/72	.569	15/26	.577	-/38	-	-	27	-	-	97	.485

Texas A&M (82)   Coach: Shelby Metcalf

	Min.	Total FG / FGA	Pct.	FT / FTA	Pct.	Reb. O / T	A	TO	PF	S	Blk	TP	PPM
HEITMAN, M.	-	6/14	.429	5/ 6	.833	-/ 4	-	-	3	-	-	17	-
BARNETT, B.	-	8/14	.571	2/ 5	.400	-/ 8	-	-	5	-	-	18	-
NILES, S.	-	2/ 8	.250	5/13	.385	-/12	-	-	4	-	-	9	-
BENEFIELD, S.	-	5/10	.500	2/ 2	1.000	-/ 3	-	-	3	-	-	12	-
PERET, R.	-	7/15	.467	7/ 9	.778	-/12	-	-	3	-	-	1	-
SMITH, C.	-	0/ 2	.000	1/ 2	.500	-/ 2	-	-	1	-	-	1	-
COOKSEY, B.	-	1/ 4	.250	2/ 2	1.000	-/ 0	-	-	0	-	-	4	-
BROWN, B.	-	0/ 0	.000	0/ 0	.000	-/ 0	-	-	1	-	-	0	-
MCALPINE, R.	-	0/ 1	.000	0/ 0	.000	-/ 0	-	-	1	-	-	0	-
Totals	200	29/68	.426	24/39	.615	-/41	-	-	21	-	-	82	.410

Team Rebounds: Colorado 5; Texas A&M 12. Disqualified: Colorado—Hutchinson; Erfert; Texas A&M—Barnett.

	1st Half	2nd Half	Final
Colorado	51	46	97
Texas A&M	31	51	82

REGIONAL THIRD PLACE MIDEAST

Kentucky (72)   Coach: Adolph Rupp

	Min.	Total FG / FGA	Pct.	FT / FTA	Pct.	Reb. O / T	A	TO	PF	S	Blk	TP	PPM
STEELE, L.	-	5/10	.500	2/ 3	.667	-/ 6	-	-	3	-	-	12	-
PRATT, M.	-	3/ 8	.375	2/ 5	.400	-/ 6	-	-	2	-	-	8	-
ISSEL, D.	-	12/17	.706	12/12	1.000	-/10	-	-	4	-	-	36	-
ARGENTO, P.	-	0/ 4	.000	3/ 3	1.000	-/ 2	-	-	2	-	-	3	-
CASEY, M.	-	1/ 6	.167	3/ 4	.750	-/ 4	-	-	3	-	-	5	-
MCCOWAN, B.	-	3/ 5	.600	2/ 2	1.000	-/ 2	-	-	2	-	-	8	-
POOL, R.	-	0/ 2	.000	0/ 0	.000	-/ 0	-	-	0	-	-	0	-
Totals	200	24/52	.462	24/29	.828	-/30	-	-	16	-	-	72	.360

Miami (Ohio) (71)   Coach: Tates Locke

	Min.	Total FG / FGA	Pct.	FT / FTA	Pct.	Reb. O / T	A	TO	PF	S	Blk	TP	PPM
PRYOR, G.	-	2/10	.200	7/ 8	.875	-/10	-	-	3	-	-	11	-
SNYDER, R.	-	0/ 6	.000	1/ 3	.333	-/ 5	-	-	4	-	-	1	-
MARTIN, T.	-	4/13	.308	2/ 4	.500	-/ 9	-	-	4	-	-	10	-
BURKHARDT, G.	-	4/10	.400	2/ 2	1.000	-/ 4	-	-	3	-	-	10	-
LUKACAS, F.	-	2/ 4	.500	0/ 0	.000	-/ 3	-	-	2	-	-	4	-
WILLIAMS, W.	-	2/ 4	.500	0/ 0	.000	-/ 1	-	-	0	-	-	4	-
SLATER, L.	-	1/ 1	1.000	1/ 2	.500	-/ 1	-	-	0	-	-	3	-
WREN, M.	-	11/15	.733	0/ 2	.000	-/ 5	-	-	2	-	-	22	-
LOUCKS, R.	-	3/ 5	.600	0/ 0	.000	-/ 2	-	-	2	-	-	6	-
Totals	200	29/68	.426	13/21	.619	-/40	-	-	20	-	-	71	.355

Team Rebounds: Kentucky 6; Miami (Ohio) 4. Disqualified: None.

	1st Half	2nd Half	Final
Kentucky	38	34	72
Miami (Ohio)	33	38	71

REGIONAL THIRD PLACE EAST

Duquesne (75)   Coach: Red Manning

	Min.	Total FG / FGA	Pct.	FT / FTA	Pct.	Reb. O / T	A	TO	PF	S	Blk	TP	PPM
BARR, M.	30	3/10	.300	1/ 2	.500	-/ 5	3	0	1	-	-	7	.233
DURHAM, J.	40	8/ 9	.889	8/10	.800	-/ 3	1	2	4	-	-	24	.600
HINES, W.	10	1/ 2	.500	0/ 1	.000	-/ 2	0	1	0	-	-	2	.200
MAJOR, G.	33	5/10	.500	3/ 5	.600	-/ 5	0	0	4	-	-	13	.394
NELSON, G.	28	3/ 9	.333	0/ 0	.000	-/ 6	1	0	2	-	-	6	.214
ZOPF, B.	40	9/15	.600	5/ 6	.833	-/ 8	11	2	3	-	-	23	.575
NELSON, B.	19	0/ 2	.000	0/ 1	.000	-/ 2	2	0	3	-	-	0	.000
Totals	200	29/57	.509	17/25	.680	-/31	18	5	17	-	-	75	.375

St. John's (72)   Coach: Lou Carnesecca

	Min.	Total FG / FGA	Pct.	FT / FTA	Pct.	Reb. O / T	A	TO	PF	S	Blk	TP	PPM
CALZONETTI, C.	11	2/ 2	1.000	1/ 1	1.000	-/ 0	0	0	0	-	-	5	.455
ABRAHAM, R.	15	0/ 2	.000	3/ 3	1.000	-/ 2	1	0	1	-	-	3	.200
WARREN, J.	28	6/13	.462	1/ 1	1.000	-/ 2	6	1	4	-	-	13	.464
CORNELIUS, D.	5	0/ 1	.000	0/ 0	.000	-/ 2	0	1	0	-	-	0	.000
DEBRE, J.	38	4/12	.333	5/ 6	.833	-/ 6	4	4	2	-	-	13	.342
PAULTZ, B.	35	9/16	.563	6/ 6	1.000	-/12	3	0	3	-	-	24	.686
SMYTH, J.	29	4/ 9	.444	2/ 3	.667	-/ 4	3	1	2	-	-	10	.345
GILKES, R.	25	1/ 4	.250	2/ 2	1.000	-/ 3	0	0	2	-	-	4	.160
DEVASTO, J.	2	0/ 1	.000	0/ 0	.000	-/ 0	0	1	1	-	-	0	.000
LAMANTIA, P.	4	0/ 0	.000	0/ 0	.000	-/ 0	0	0	0	-	-	0	.000
LEVANE, N.	8	0/ 1	.000	0/ 0	.000	-/ 0	1	0	0	-	-	0	.000
Totals	200	26/61	.426	20/22	.909	-/31	18	9	15	-	-	72	.360

Team Rebounds: Duquesne 4; St. John's 7. Disqualified: None.

	1st Half	2nd Half	Final
Duquesne	31	44	75
St. John's	35	37	72

✪ ALL-STAR TEAMS ✪

ALL TOURNAMENT

★ **LEW ALCINDOR**	UCLA
WILLIE MCCARTER	DRAKE
RICK MOUNT	PURDUE
CHARLIE SCOTT	N. CAROLINA
JOHN VALLELY	UCLA

★ Most Outstanding Player(s)

✪ INDIVIDUAL RECORDS ✪

SCORING

Most points in a single game
1	LEW ALCINDOR, UCLA (vs. PURDUE)	37
2	DAN ISSEL, KENTUCKY (vs. MIAMI [OHIO])	36
2	RICK MOUNT, PURDUE (vs. N. CAROLINA)	36
4	MIKE MALOY, DAVIDSON (vs. ST. JOHN'S)	35
4	CHARLIE SCOTT, N. CAROLINA (vs. DRAKE)	35

Most total points in the tournament
1	RICK MOUNT, PURDUE	122
2	CHARLIE SCOTT, N. CAROLINA	105
3	WILLIE MCCARTER, DRAKE	97
4	LEW ALCINDOR, UCLA	95
5	MIKE MALOY, DAVIDSON	91

Highest scoring average (minimum 2 games)
1	RICK MOUNT, PURDUE (122-4)	30.50
2	MIKE MALOY, DAVIDSON (91-3)	30.33
3	CLIFF MEELY, COLORADO (58-2)	29.00
4	CHARLIE SCOTT, N. CAROLINA (105-4)	26.25
5	DAN ISSEL, KENTUCKY (49-2)	24.50

FIELD GOALS

Most field goals in a single game
1	CHARLIE SCOTT, N. CAROLINA (vs. DRAKE)	16
2	LEW ALCINDOR, UCLA (vs. PURDUE)	15
3	CHARLIE SCOTT, N. CAROLINA (vs. DAVIDSON)	14
3	RICK MOUNT, PURDUE (vs. N. CAROLINA)	14
5	JOHN HUMMER, PRINCETON (vs. ST. JOHN'S)	13

Most total field goals in the tournament
1	RICK MOUNT, PURDUE	49
2	CHARLIE SCOTT, N. CAROLINA	45
3	WILLIE MCCARTER, DRAKE	43
4	LEW ALCINDOR, UCLA	39
5	MIKE MALOY, DAVIDSON	32

Most field goal attempts in a single game
1	RICK MOUNT, PURDUE (vs. UCLA)	36
2	RICK MOUNT, PURDUE (vs. MARQUETTE)	32
3	RICK MOUNT, PURDUE (vs. N. CAROLINA)	28
4	WILLIE MCCARTER, DRAKE (vs. UCLA)	27
5	2 tied for fifth place.	

Most total field goal attempts in tournament
1	RICK MOUNT, PURDUE	116
2	WILLIE MCCARTER, DRAKE	94
3	CHARLIE SCOTT, N. CAROLINA	85

4	LEW ALCINDOR, UCLA	63
5	BILL KELLER, PURDUE	62

Highest field goal percentage in a single game (minimum 10 attempts)
1	JOHN VALLELY, UCLA (vs. DRAKE) (9-11)	.818
2	JOHN HUMMER, PRINCETON (vs. ST. JOHN'S) (13-16)	.813
3	GORDON TOPE, COLORADO (vs. TEXAS A&M) (11-14)	.786
4	LEW ALCINDOR, UCLA (vs. PURDUE) (15-20)	.750
5	MIKE WREN, MIAMI (OHIO) (vs. KENTUCKY) (11-15)	.733

Highest field goal percentage in the tournament (minimum 20 attempts)
1	JARRETT DURHAM, DUQUESNE (26-38)	.684
2	DAN ISSEL, KENTUCKY (16-25)	.640
3	JOHN VALLELY, UCLA (23-37)	.622
4	JEFF SEWELL, MARQUETTE (18-29)	.621
5	LEW ALCINDOR, UCLA (39-63)	.619

FREE THROWS

Most free throws in a single game
1	MIKE MALOY, DAVIDSON (vs. ST. JOHN'S)	13
2	DAN ISSEL, KENTUCKY (vs. MIAMI [OHIO])	12
2	MIKE WREN, MIAMI (OHIO) (vs. NOTRE DAME)	12
4	JOHN VALLELY, UCLA (vs. DRAKE)	11
5	3 tied for fifth place.	

Most total free throws in the tournament
1	MIKE MALOY, DAVIDSON	27
2	RICK MOUNT, PURDUE	24
3	GEORGE THOMPSON, MARQUETTE	23
4	WILLIE WISE, DRAKE	21
5	WILLIE SOJOURNER, WEBER ST.	20

Most free throws attempted in a single game
1	LEW ALCINDOR, UCLA (vs. DRAKE)	16
2	JOHN VALLELY, UCLA (vs. DRAKE)	14
2	CLIFF MEELY, COLORADO (vs. COLORADO STATE)	14
4	6 tied for fourth place.	

Most free throws attempted in the tournament
1	MIKE MALOY, DAVIDSON	33
1	LEW ALCINDOR, UCLA	33

3	WILLIE WISE, DRAKE	29
3	GEORGE THOMPSON, MARQUETTE	29
5	2 tied for fifth place.	

Highest free throw percentage in a single game (minimum 7 attempts)
1	MIKE MALOY, DAVIDSON (vs. ST. JOHN'S) (13-13)	1.000
2	DAN ISSEL, KENTUCKY (vs. MIAMI [OHIO]) (12-12)	1.000
3	MIKE CASEY, KENTUCKY (vs. MARQUETTE) (10-10)	1.000
4	RICK MOUNT, PURDUE (vs. MIAMI [OHIO]) (8-8)	1.000
5	MIKE WREN, MIAMI (OHIO) (vs. NOTRE DAME) (12-13)	.923

Highest free throw percentage in the tournament (minimum 15 attempts)
1	DAN ISSEL, KENTUCKY (17-19)	.895
2	RICK MOUNT, PURDUE (24-27)	.889
3	MIKE WREN, MIAMI (OHIO) (16-19)	.842
4	MIKE MALOY, DAVIDSON (27-33)	.818
5	DOUG COOK, DAVIDSON (13-16)	.813

REBOUNDS

Most rebounds in a single game
1	LEW ALCINDOR, UCLA (vs. DRAKE)	21
2	LEW ALCINDOR, UCLA (vs. PURDUE)	20
3	WILLIE SOJOURNER, WEBER ST. (vs. SANTA CLARA)	18
3	GARRY NELSON, DUQUESNE (vs. ST. JOSEPH'S)	18
5	MIKE MALOY, DAVIDSON (vs. VILLANOVA)	17

Most total rebounds in the tournament
1	LEW ALCINDOR, UCLA	64
2	WILLIE WISE, DRAKE	48
3	MIKE MALOY, DAVIDSON	42
4	WILLIE SOJOURNER, WEBER ST.	41
5	MIKE DAVIS, COLORADO STATE	38

Most rebounds per game (minimum 2 games)
1	LEW ALCINDOR, UCLA (64-4)	16.00
2	MIKE MALOY, DAVIDSON (42-3)	14.00
3	WILLIE SOJOURNER, WEBER ST. (41-3)	13.67
4	DAN ISSEL, KENTUCKY (26-2)	13.00
5	MIKE DAVIS, COLORADO STATE (38-3)	12.67

○ TEAM RECORDS ○

SCORING

Most points in a single game
1   DRAKE (vs. N. CAROLINA)   104
2   COLORADO (vs. TEXAS A&M)   97
3   2 tied for third place.

Most total points in the tournament
1   DRAKE   351
2   PURDUE   330
3   UCLA   320

Highest scoring average (minimum 2 games)
1   DRAKE (351-4)   87.75
2   PURDUE (330-4)   82.50
3   UCLA (320-4)   80.00

FIELD GOALS

Most field goals in a single game
1   DRAKE (vs. N. CAROLINA)   45
2   COLORADO (vs. TEXAS A&M)   41
3   2 tied for third place.

Most total field goals in the tournament
1   DRAKE   142
2   PURDUE   132
3   UCLA   122

Most field goals attempted in a single game
1   PURDUE (vs. UCLA)   92
2   DRAKE (vs. UCLA)   83
3   DRAKE (vs. N. CAROLINA)   80

Most total field goals attempted in the tournament
1   DRAKE   317
2   PURDUE   304
3   N. CAROLINA   256

Highest field goal percentage in a single game
1   PURDUE (vs. MIAMI [OHIO]) (38-62)   .613
2   COLORADO (vs. TEXAS A&M) (41-72)   .570
3   UCLA (vs. SANTA CLARA) (37-65)   .569

Highest field goal percentage in the tournament (minimum 2 games)
1   UCLA (122-231)   .528
2   MARQUETTE (91-186)   .489
2   DUQUESNE (91-186)   .489

FREE THROWS

Most free throws in a single game
1   DAVIDSON (vs. ST. JOHN'S)   31
2   UCLA (vs. DRAKE)   29
3   UCLA (vs. PURDUE)   28

Most total free throws in the tournament
1   UCLA   76
2   N. CAROLINA   75
3   TEXAS A&M   70

Most free throws attempted in a single game
1   UCLA (vs. DRAKE)   44
2   UCLA (vs. PURDUE)   41
3   TEXAS A&M (vs. COLORADO)   39

Most total free throws attempted in the tournament
1   UCLA   120
2   N. CAROLINA   111
3   TEXAS A&M   103

Highest free throw percentage in a single game
1   ST. JOHN'S (vs. DUQUESNE) (20-22)   .909
2   KENTUCKY (vs. MARQUETTE) (22-25)   .880
3   COLORADO STATE (vs. DRAKE) (27-31)   .871

Highest free throw percentage in the tournament (minimum 2 games)
1   ST. JOHN'S (47-54)   .870
2   KENTUCKY (46-54)   .852
3   DAVIDSON (69-88)   .784

Fewest free throws in a single game
1   UCLA (vs. NEW MEXICO ST.)   3
2   DAYTON (vs. COLORADO STATE)   6
3   NEW MEXICO ST. (vs. WEBER ST.)   6

Lowest free throw percentage in a single game
1   UCLA (vs. NEW MEXICO ST.) (3-10)   .300
2   DAYTON (vs. COLORADO STATE) (6-16)   .375
3   DUQUESNE (vs. N. CAROLINA) (8-17)   .471

Lowest free throw percentage in the tournament (minimum 2 games)
1   COLORADO (29-50)   .580
2   MARQUETTE (54-93)   .581
3   SANTA CLARA (25-41)   .610

REBOUNDS

Most rebounds in a single game
1   UCLA (vs. PURDUE)   56
2   NEW MEXICO ST. (vs. BRIGHAM YOUNG)   54
3   2 tied for third place.

Most rebounds per game (minimum 2 games)
1   TEXAS A&M (141-3)   47.00
2   PURDUE (173-4)   43.25
3   NEW MEXICO ST. (127-3)   42.33

1970

| FIRST ROUND | REGIONAL SEMIFINAL | REGIONAL FINAL | FINAL FOUR | REGIONAL FINAL | REGIONAL SEMIFINAL | FIRST ROUND |

EAST

St. Bonaventure 85
Davidson 72
St. Bonaventure 80
St. Bonaventure 97
(bye)
N.C. State 68

St. Bonaventure 83

Villanova 77
Temple 69
Villanova 98
Villanova 74
Niagara 79
Pennsylvania 69
Niagara 73

MIDEAST

Jacksonville 109
Western Ky. 96
Jacksonville 104
Jacksonville 106
(bye)
Iowa 103

Jacksonville 91

(bye)
Kentucky 109
Kentucky 100
Notre Dame 112
Notre Dame 99
Ohio 82

UCLA 80
Jacksonville 69

MIDWEST

New Mexico 101
New Mexico 70
Rice 77
New Mexico 87
Kansas St. 66
(bye)

New Mexico 77

Drake 92
(bye)
Drake 78
Houston 71
Houston 87
Dayton 64

WEST

UCLA 88
(bye)
UCLA 101
Long Beach St. 92
Long Beach St. 65
Weber St. 73

UCLA 93

Utah St. 81
Utah St. 69
UTEP 81
Utah St. 79
Santa Clara 68
(bye)

CONSOLATION GAMES

National Third Place:

New Mexico 79
St. Bonaventure 73

Regional Third Place:

East:
N.C. State 108
Niagara 88

Mideast:
Iowa 121
Notre Dame 106

Midwest:
Kansas St. 107
Houston 98

West:
Santa Clara 89
Long Beach St. 86

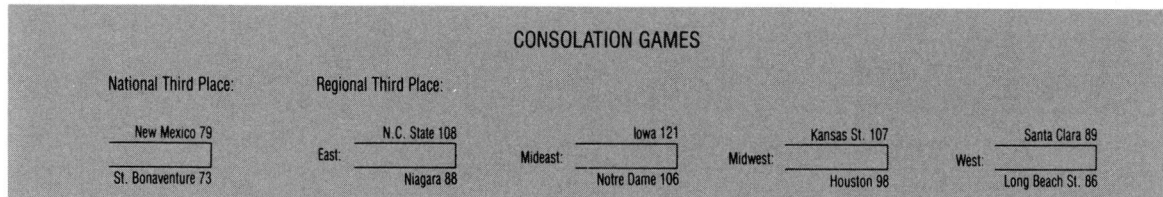

In 1970, John Wooden's UCLA Bruins had to defend their title without Lew Alcindor.

Jacksonville had a dominant big man, Artis Gilmore, a 7-2 goateed giant with a penchant for ramming shots down a shooter's throat.

St. Bonaventure had Bob Lanier, who at 6-11 and 275 pounds was both wide and agile; he also had a beautiful soft touch on his jump shot.

Kentucky had high-scoring Dan Issel; at 6-8½ he was no giant, but he had quickness, court sense, a nose for the net, and an excellent outside shot.

New Mexico State had 6-10 Sam Lacey, an aggressive tower of strength under the boards.

When Lew Alcindor graduated, Steve Patterson took over the middle for the Bruins. As a sophomore, Patterson had been Big Lew's backup. Now as a junior, he was the starter: a solid 6-9 team man with good basic skills. He was not expected to be the equal of his illustrious predecessor, nor did he try to be. The stars of UCLA in 1970, were the men on the wings: 6-8 Sidney Wicks and 6-6 Curtis Rowe. They combined speed, strength, and shooting ability to form the best forward tandem in the country. At guard the Bruins had Henry Bibby to run the fast break, hit from the outside, and key the press, and John Vallely, a fine shooter and good defensive player. Vallely and Rowe were the only two returning starters from the 1969 championship team.

UCLA was a favorite, but the team many observers felt was the nation's best wasn't even in the NCAA field. Frank McGuire's third-ranked South Carolina Gamecocks went into the ACC playoffs with a 14-0 conference record (five games better than their closest rival). But the ACC chose its representative to the NCAAs through its own tournament (which detached observers noted was staged primarily to fatten the coffers of conference teams). And in the ACC final, South Carolina was outscored by North Carolina State in double overtime due to a Wolfpack stall, a Gamecock fall, a controversial call, and a stolen ball. South Carolina thus ended their season before the NCAA competition began. North Carolina State, by winning the ACC playoff, earned the right to be eliminated in the NCAA Eastern regional by big Bob Lanier and powerful St. Bonaventure.

In the Mideast a high-caliber collection of gunners let loose awesome barrages of postseason firepower. (The six Mideast regional contests finally produced a total of 1247 points.) Jacksonville, utilizing Artis Gilmore's large hand as the regional's only effective antiaircraft weapon, bombarded Western Kentucky and its 7-footer, Jim McDaniels, 109-96; Gilmor scored 30, grabbed 19 boards and turned away 9 shots. Notre Dame's Austin Carr, meanwhile, broke the single-game tournament scoring record with 61 in a rout of Ohio University.

Following Carr's record-breaking performance, Notre Dame met Kentucky, the No. 1–ranked team in the nation. After five minutes Dan Issel, the Wildcats' bread and butter, had yet to take a shot, and the venerable Kentucky mentor, Adolph Rupp, saw trouble brewing. Rupp called time out, and, according to *The* (Louisville) *Courier-Journal,* told his other four starters, "Look, fellows, I don't know whether you realize it or not but this boy [Issel] has on a Kentucky shirt . . . Now it would humor me greatly in my advancing years if you would hereafter let him in on our little act." Issel scored four baskets in the next two minutes, on his way to a total of 44. He was outscored by Notre Dame superstar Austin Carr (who peppered the net for 52), but a Kentucky second-half zone finally gave the Wildcats the lead in the last five and a half minutes, and Kentucky went on to win 109-99.

Rupp's dream of a fifth championship for Kentucky (and a tie with Wooden of UCLA) ended when his Wildcats came up against big, bad Artis Gilmore and the Jacksonville Dolphins. Jacksonville had themselves come into the regional final as the fortunate survivors of a 104-103 shoot-em-up with Iowa (they won when their *other* 7-footer, Pembrook Burrows, put in a teammate's miss with three seconds left). Against the Dolphins, four Wildcat starters—including Issel—fouled out. And with Issel on the bench Kentucky, though valiant in defeat, couldn't handle Gilmore inside. Jacksonville moved on to the Final Four with a 106-100 decision.

In the East, after sailing through against North Carolina, St. Bonaventure's chances to bring home all the marbles disappeared when their big man, Bob Lanier, tore a knee ligament in a freak accident after the Bonnies had clinched their contest with Villanova. In the Midwest, New Mexico State outlasted Kansas State and Drake behind the one-on-one brilliance of Jimmy Collins and the rebounding strength of Sam Lacey. And in the West, inevitably, there was UCLA.

"What might have been" was St. Bonaventure's lament as they fought tooth and nail with huge Jacksonville without their main man, Lanier. With no one over 6-5 to counter Gilmore and company, the Bonnies still sped out to an early lead and were within 4 only two minutes from the end. But four Bonnies fouled out, and a Jacksonville parade to the free throw line enabled the Dolphins to win, 91-83.

Smoothly running UCLA, meanwhile, rolled over New Mexico State, reminding everyone that John Wooden had won with small fast teams in the era before Alcindor. The Bruins had every gear working, and their five starters combined for 91 points, too much for Jimmy Collins and his Aggie teammates to contend with.

Before the final, Wooden told forward Sidney Wicks that he would be guarding Gilmore. The Bruins opened as though they were the outsiders: they turned the ball over, missed free throws, and Wicks drew two fouls and even lost 2 points when he dunked the ball in violation of the antidunking rule passed in response to Alcindor's dominance after his sophomore year. With Gilmore doing virtually what he pleased, Jacksonville took a 24-15 lead.

Wooden adjusted. He moved Wicks behind Gilmore, and slacked off the pressure on the passer, instead sloughing Patterson off to front the Jacksonville center. Thus sandwiched, Artis quickly became invisible. With Jacksonville leading 36-32, UCLA exploded. They ripped off 9 straight points, and led at the half, 41-36.

In the second half, UCLA's high-speed patterned offense worked to perfection. Wicks terrorized the taller Gilmore, outrebounding him and actually blocking five of the giant's shots. The pressure defense of all five Bruin starters, playing as a unit for the first 38 minutes, stopped the Dolphins cold. Jacksonville, which had averaged well over 100 points per game all season, finished on the short end of an 80-69 score.

"When I had Lewis," Wooden said, "it changed my game. I feel I know what we do now a little better." What UCLA did in 1970 was to prove once again that basketball is a five-man game.

FIRST ROUND EAST

St. Bonaventure (85)   Coach: Larry Weise

	Min.	Total FG/FGA	Pct.	FT/FTA	Pct.	Reb. O/T	A	TO	PF	S	Blk	TP	PPM
LANIER, B.	-	13/24	.542	2/3	.667	-/15	-	-	5	-	-	28	-
KALBAUGH, B.	-	8/11	.727	1/1	1.000	-/3	-	-	3	-	-	17	-
GANTT, M.	-	8/17	.471	3/4	.750	-/16	-	-	4	-	-	19	-
HOFFMAN, P.	-	1/4	.250	3/4	.750	-/6	-	-	1	-	-	5	-
GARY, G.	-	4/8	.500	5/5	1.000	-/4	-	-	4	-	-	13	-
KULL, M.	-	1/4	.250	1/1	1.000	-/0	-	-	2	-	-	3	-
Totals	200	35/68	.515	15/18	.833	-/44	-	16	19	-	-	85	.425

Davidson (72)   Coach: Terry Holland

	Min.	Total FG/FGA	Pct.	FT/FTA	Pct.	Reb. O/T	A	TO	PF	S	Blk	TP	PPM
ADRIAN, B.	-	12/26	.462	4/5	.800	-/7	-	-	3	-	-	28	-
COOK, D.	-	6/12	.500	3/6	.500	-/6	-	-	2	-	-	15	-
MALOY, M.	-	5/12	.417	3/6	.500	-/12	-	-	3	-	-	13	-
KROLL, J.	-	4/10	.400	4/5	.800	-/2	-	-	4	-	-	12	-
KIRLEY, S.	-	0/4	.000	2/2	1.000	-/2	-	-	2	-	-	2	-
MINKIN, E.	-	1/3	.333	0/2	.000	-/3	-	-	0	-	-	2	-
STELZER, R.	-	0/0	.000	0/0	.000	-/0	-	-	0	-	-	0	-
Totals	200	28/67	.418	16/26	.615	-/32	-	10	14	-	-	72	.360

Team Rebounds: St. Bonaventure 5; Davidson 4. Disqualified: St. Bonaventure—Lanier.

	1st Half	2nd Half	Final
St. Bonaventure	34	51	85
Davidson	36	36	72

Villanova (77)   Coach: Jack Kraft

	Min.	Total FG/FGA	Pct.	FT/FTA	Pct.	Reb. O/T	A	TO	PF	S	Blk	TP	PPM
SMITH, C.	-	5/13	.385	2/5	.400	-/13	1	-	1	-	-	12	-
SIMS, S.	-	5/12	.417	2/6	.333	-/8	0	-	3	-	-	12	-
PORTER, H.	-	7/15	.467	4/6	.667	-/14	1	-	5	-	-	18	-
O'HANLON, F.	-	5/19	.263	4/6	.667	-/7	9	-	4	-	-	14	-
FORD, C.	-	6/16	.375	7/8	.875	-/7	8	-	1	-	-	19	-
SIEMIONTKOWSKI, H	-	1/1	1.000	0/0	.000	-/0	0	-	0	-	-	2	-
WOJOLOWSKI, L.	-	0/0	.000	0/0	.000	-/0	0	-	0	-	-	0	-
Totals	200	29/76	.382	19/31	.613	-/49	19	17	14	-	-	77	.385

Temple (69)   Coach: Harry Litwack

	Min.	Total FG/FGA	Pct.	FT/FTA	Pct.	Reb. O/T	A	TO	PF	S	Blk	TP	PPM
JOHNSON, O.	-	3/15	.200	0/1	.000	-/10	0	-	1	-	-	6	-
RICHARDSON, J.	-	9/15	.600	4/6	.667	-/14	1	-	4	-	-	22	-
TRESS, L.	-	7/21	.333	6/8	.750	-/21	2	-	4	-	-	20	-
WIECZERAK, T.	-	5/15	.333	0/0	.000	-/1	3	-	5	-	-	10	-
COLLINS, P.	-	4/10	.400	1/2	.500	-/6	8	-	4	-	-	9	-
NOLAN, D.	-	0/0	.000	0/0	.000	-/1	0	-	3	-	-	0	-
FENELI	-	1/3	.333	0/0	.000	-/2	0	-	1	-	-	2	-
Totals	200	29/79	.367	11/17	.647	-/55	14	13	22	-	-	69	.345

Team Rebounds: Villanova 5; Temple 6. Disqualified: Villanova—Porter; Temple—Wieczerak.

	1st Half	2nd Half	Final
Villanova	39	38	77
Temple	36	33	69

Niagara (79)   Coach: Frank Layden

	Min.	Total FG/FGA	Pct.	FT/FTA	Pct.	Reb. O/T	A	TO	PF	S	Blk	TP	PPM
WINGATE, M.	-	2/3	.667	1/4	.250	-/4	-	-	1	-	-	5	-
MURPHY, C.	-	13/24	.542	9/10	.900	-/5	-	-	3	-	-	35	-
SCHAFER, S.	-	3/8	.375	1/3	.333	-/6	-	-	5	-	-	7	-
SAMUEL, M.	-	4/8	.500	1/1	1.000	-/3	-	-	1	-	-	9	-
CHURCHWELL, B.	-	6/12	.500	2/3	.667	-/14	-	-	4	-	-	14	-
BROWN, M.	-	0/1	.000	6/7	.857	-/4	-	-	2	-	-	6	-
JONES, W.	-	1/3	.333	1/2	.500	-/5	-	-	2	-	-	3	-
Totals	200	29/59	.492	21/30	.700	-/41	-	-	18	-	-	79	.395

Pennsylvania (69)   Coach: Dick Harter

	Min.	Total FG/FGA	Pct.	FT/FTA	Pct.	Reb. O/T	A	TO	PF	S	Blk	TP	PPM
WOHL, D.	-	5/15	.333	1/1	1.000	-/5	-	-	5	-	-	11	-
BILSKY, S.	-	7/16	.438	8/9	.889	-/2	-	-	4	-	-	22	-
CALHOUN, C.	-	5/17	.294	5/7	.714	-/13	-	-	3	-	-	15	-
MORSE, J.	-	5/18	.278	0/0	.000	-/2	-	-	1	-	-	10	-
WOLF, J.	-	1/7	.143	1/4	.250	-/10	-	-	4	-	-	3	-
MURPHY, J.	-	0/0	.000	0/0	.000	-/0	-	-	1	-	-	0	-
ROBBINS, C.	-	0/0	.000	1/3	.333	-/3	-	-	2	-	-	1	-
KOLLER, J.	-	0/2	.000	0/0	.000	-/1	-	-	0	-	-	0	-
COTLER, A.	-	3/5	.600	1/1	1.000	-/2	-	-	1	-	-	7	-
Totals	200	26/80	.325	17/25	.680	-/38	-	-	21	-	-	69	.345

Team Rebounds: Niagara 11; Pennsylvania 10. Disqualified: Niagara—Schafer; Pennsylvania—Wohl.

	1st Half	2nd Half	Final
Niagara	34	45	79
Pennsylvania	35	34	69

FIRST ROUND MIDEAST

Jacksonville (109)   Coach: Joe Williams

	Min.	Total FG/FGA	Pct.	FT/FTA	Pct.	Reb. O/T	A	TO	PF	S	Blk	TP	PPM
BLEVINS, M.	-	2/5	.400	0/1	.000	-/2	0	1	0	-	-	4	-
BURROWS, P.	-	2/4	.500	0/2	.000	-/3	1	0	3	-	-	4	-
GILMORE, A.	-	11/20	.550	8/13	.615	-/19	4	7	2	-	-	30	-
MORGAN, R.	-	7/12	.583	10/13	.769	-/6	7	2	1	-	-	24	-
WEDEKING, V.	-	9/15	.600	1/2	.500	-/4	4	1	0	-	-	19	-
DUBLIN, C.	-	4/4	1.000	1/1	1.000	-/4	3	3	4	-	-	9	-
NELSON, G.	-	3/3	1.000	5/7	.714	-/7	2	2	2	-	-	11	-
MCINTYRE, R.	-	1/3	.333	4/4	1.000	-/3	0	2	3	-	-	6	-
BALDWIN, R.	-	1/1	1.000	0/0	.000	-/0	0	1	1	-	-	2	-
KRUER, C.	-	0/1	.000	0/0	.000	-/0	0	0	0	-	-	0	-
SELKE, K.	-	0/2	.000	0/0	.000	-/3	0	3	0	-	-	0	-
Totals	200	40/70	.571	29/43	.674	-/51	21	22	16	-	-	109	.545

Western Kentucky (96)   Coach: Johnny Oldham

	Min.	Total FG/FGA	Pct.	FT/FTA	Pct.	Reb. O/T	A	TO	PF	S	Blk	TP	PPM
PERRY, J.	-	6/15	.400	0/0	.000	-/7	3	5	3	-	-	12	-
GLOVER, C.	-	3/12	.250	1/2	.500	-/6	0	0	4	-	-	7	-
MCDANIELS, J.	-	13/22	.591	3/4	.750	-/7	0	2	5	-	-	29	-
SUNDMACKER, G.	-	3/7	.429	2/2	1.000	-/1	2	1	1	-	-	8	-
ROSE, J.	-	6/11	.545	4/4	1.000	-/3	1	0	2	-	-	16	-
BANKS, W.	-	1/4	.250	1/1	1.000	-/2	1	2	5	-	-	3	-
JOHNSON, D.	-	3/5	.600	2/2	1.000	-/6	4	3	3	-	-	8	-
BRIGHT, W.	-	1/4	.250	0/0	.000	-/6	0	1	5	-	-	2	-
HASKINS, P.	-	3/4	.750	4/4	1.000	-/1	1	1	1	-	-	10	-
DAVIS, T.	-	0/2	.000	0/0	.000	-/1	0	0	0	-	-	0	-
EATON, S.	-	0/3	.000	1/2	.500	-/0	1	0	0	-	-	1	-
Totals	200	39/89	.438	18/21	.857	-/40	13	15	29	-	-	96	.480

Team Rebounds: Jacksonville 5; Western Ky. 6. Disqualified: Western Ky.—McDaniels, Bright, Banks.

	1st Half	2nd Half	Final
Jacksonville	53	56	109
Western Ky.	47	49	96

Notre Dame (112)   Coach: Johnny Dee

	Min.	Total FG/FGA	Pct.	FT/FTA	Pct.	Reb. O/T	A	TO	PF	S	Blk	TP	PPM
CARR, A.	-	25/44	.568	11/14	.786	-/6	3	1	1	-	-	61	-
JONES, C.	-	9/19	.474	6/6	1.000	-/17	1	0	4	-	-	24	-
MEGHAN, J.	-	0/1	.000	2/2	1.000	-/2	17	6	0	-	-	2	-
GALLAGER, J.	-	4/8	.500	1/2	.500	-/2	0	1	1	-	-	9	-
ZIZNEWSKI, J.	-	5/12	.417	0/1	.000	-/10	0	2	2	-	-	10	-
CATLETT, S.	-	0/1	.000	0/0	.000	-/11	0	2	3	-	-	0	-
SINNOTT, T.	-	2/4	.500	0/1	.000	-/6	7	3	2	-	-	4	-
HINGA, J.	-	1/1	1.000	0/0	.000	-/0	0	0	0	-	-	2	-
Totals	200	46/90	.511	20/26	.769	-/54	28	15	13	-	-	112	.560

Ohio (82)   Coach: James Snyder

	Min.	Total FG/FGA	Pct.	FT/FTA	Pct.	Reb. O/T	A	TO	PF	S	Blk	TP	PPM
MCDIVITT, G.	-	2/13	.154	4/8	.500	-/11	3	3	2	-	-	8	-
GROFF, D.	-	7/13	.538	3/7	.429	-/5	0	0	3	-	-	17	-
LOVE, C.	-	4/12	.333	0/0	.000	-/13	1	1	4	-	-	8	-
CANINE, J.	-	12/29	.414	0/0	.000	-/4	2	2	3	-	-	24	-
KOWALL, K.	-	3/7	.429	1/2	.500	-/0	0	1	3	-	-	7	-
PARKER, D.	-	1/4	.250	2/2	1.000	-/4	0	1	1	-	-	4	-
CORDE, T.	-	2/6	.333	0/1	.000	-/3	2	1	0	-	-	4	-
WOLF, G.	-	3/5	.600	0/0	.000	-/6	0	2	1	-	-	6	-
HUNTER, L.	-	1/3	.333	0/0	.000	-/3	1	2	3	-	-	2	-
MILLER, M.	-	1/1	1.000	0/0	.000	-/0	0	0	0	-	-	2	-
RUMPKE, B.	-	0/0	.000	0/0	.000	-/0	0	0	0	-	-	0	-
GLANEY, J.	-	0/1	.000	0/0	.000	-/0	0	0	0	-	-	0	-
Totals	200	36/94	.383	10/20	.500	-/49	9	13	20	-	-	82	.410

Team Rebounds: Notre Dame 8; Ohio 7. Disqualified: None.

	1st Half	2nd Half	Final
Notre Dame	54	58	112
Ohio	41	41	82

FIRST ROUND MIDWEST

New Mexico State (101)   Coach: Lou Henson

	Min.	Total FG/FGA	Pct.	FT/FTA	Pct.	Reb. O/T	A	TO	PF	S	Blk	TP	PPM
COLLINS, J.	-	10/17	.588	2/3	.667	-/2	-	-	2	-	-	22	-
CRISS, C.	-	2/6	.333	3/3	1.000	-/3	-	-	3	-	-	7	-
LACEY, S.	-	9/20	.450	1/1	1.000	-/20	-	-	0	-	-	19	-
BURGESS, J.	-	1/6	.167	0/1	.000	-/7	-	-	2	-	-	2	-
SMITH, J.	-	8/13	.615	2/2	1.000	-/7	-	-	2	-	-	18	-
HORNE, M.	-	3/5	.600	0/1	.000	-/1	-	-	2	-	-	6	-
NEAL, C.	-	3/8	.375	1/3	.333	-/6	-	-	1	-	-	7	-
REYES, C.	-	5/10	.500	1/1	1.000	-/7	-	-	2	-	-	11	-
MOORE, B.	-	2/3	.667	0/0	.000	-/1	-	-	0	-	-	4	-
LEFEVRE, L.	-	1/2	.500	0/1	.000	-/3	-	-	3	-	-	2	-
MCCARTHY, T.	-	0/1	.000	3/4	.750	-/0	-	-	1	-	-	3	-
FRANCO, R.	-	0/0	.000	0/0	.000	-/1	-	-	0	-	-	0	-
Totals	200	44/91	.484	13/20	.650	-/58	-	18	18	-	-	101	.505

Rice (77)   Coach: Don Knodel

	Min.	Total FG/FGA	Pct.	FT/FTA	Pct.	Reb. O/T	A	TO	PF	S	Blk	TP	PPM
MELADY, T.	-	0/2	.000	1/1	1.000	-/5	-	-	1	-	-	1	-
SNYDER, D.	-	0/2	.000	2/2	1.000	-/0	-	-	1	-	-	2	-
WENDEL, S.	-	1/6	.167	0/0	.000	-/12	-	-	0	-	-	2	-
REIST, G.	-	7/23	.304	4/4	1.000	-/1	-	-	3	-	-	18	-
MEYER, T.	-	10/23	.435	1/1	1.000	-/3	-	-	4	-	-	21	-
NAPLES, J.	-	5/8	.625	3/3	1.000	-/6	-	-	2	-	-	13	-
STURR, D.	-	3/10	.300	2/3	.667	-/10	-	-	1	-	-	8	-
TIMMERMAN, T.	-	0/1	.000	0/1	.000	-/5	-	-	1	-	-	0	-
NELSON, C.	-	0/2	.000	0/1	.000	-/2	-	-	1	-	-	0	-
MCQUIRE, D.	-	2/7	.286	2/2	1.000	-/1	-	-	1	-	-	6	-
MARION, L.	-	0/1	.000	1/2	.500	-/6	-	-	1	-	-	1	-
JOHNSON, D.	-	1/1	1.000	3/3	1.000	-/0	-	-	2	-	-	5	-
Totals	200	29/86	.337	19/23	.826	-/51	-	15	18	-	-	77	.385

Team Rebounds: New Mexico St. 3; Rice 3. Disqualified: None.

	1st Half	2nd Half	Final
New Mexico St.	52	49	101
Rice	30	47	77

Houston (71) Coach: Guy Lewis

	Min.	Total FG/FGA	Pct.	FT/FTA	Pct.	Reb. O/T	A	TO	PF	S	Blk	TP	PPM
BELL. M.	-	0/2	.000	2/2	1.000	-/3	2	0	0	-	-	2	-
TAYLOR	-	7/18	.389	12/14	.857	-/6	2	6	2	-	-	26	-
DAVIS. D.	-	9/20	.450	1/1	1.000	-/14	1	2	3	-	-	19	-
GRIBBEN. T.	-	4/9	.444	0/0	.000	-/6	1	4	2	-	-	8	-
WELCH. P.	-	3/4	.750	1/1	1.000	-/2	5	3	2	-	-	7	-
HICKMAN. J.	-	0/5	.000	0/0	.000	-/4	2	0	1	-	-	0	-
HALL. B.	-	4/4	1.000	1/1	1.000	-/3	0	0	0	-	-	9	-
Totals	200	27/62	.435	17/19	.895	-/38	13	15	10	-	-	71	.355

Dayton (64) Coach: Don Donoher

	Min.	Total FG/FGA	Pct.	FT/FTA	Pct.	Reb. O/T	A	TO	PF	S	Blk	TP	PPM
MURNEN. P.	-	1/7	.143	1/2	.500	-/1	5	3	2	-	-	3	-
JACKSON. G.	-	2/6	.333	1/3	.333	-/11	0	0	0	-	-	5	-
JANKY. G.	-	3/7	.429	2/3	.667	-/9	2	3	3	-	-	8	-
MAY. K.	-	8/18	.444	0/0	.000	-/9	2	0	4	-	-	16	-
GOTTSCHALL. J.	-	9/17	.529	2/2	1.000	-/0	6	3	2	-	-	20	-
TURNWALD. S.	-	0/0	.000	0/0	.000	-/1	2	2	1	-	-	0	-
CROSSWHITE. T.	-	5/11	.455	0/0	.000	-/4	1	3	3	-	-	10	-
BERTKE. A.	-	1/3	.333	0/0	.000	-/0	2	1	1	-	-	2	-
Totals	200	29/69	.420	6/10	.600	-/35	20	15	16	-	-	64	.320

Team Rebounds: Houston 5; Dayton 3. Disqualified: None.

	1st Half	2nd Half	Final
Houston	32	39	71
Dayton	34	30	64

FIRST ROUND WEST

Long Beach State (92) Coach: Jerry Tarkanian

	Min.	Total FG/FGA	Pct.	FT/FTA	Pct.	Reb. O/T	A	TO	PF	S	Blk	TP	PPM
ROBINSON. S.	-	4/10	.400	2/2	1.000	-/14	-	-	4	-	-	10	-
JANKANS. B.	-	7/8	.875	2/3	.667	-/6	-	-	4	-	-	16	-
TRAPP. G.	-	7/11	.636	3/3	1.000	-/6	-	-	3	-	-	17	-
GRITTON. R.	-	4/10	.400	0/0	.000	-/0	-	-	0	-	-	8	-
JOHNSON. S.	-	7/11	.636	2/2	1.000	-/3	-	-	1	-	-	16	-
MCLUCAS. D.	-	3/4	.750	0/0	.000	-/8	-	-	2	-	-	6	-
MONTGOMERY. A.	-	2/6	.333	1/2	.500	-/4	-	-	1	-	-	5	-
TAYLOR. G.	-	2/5	.400	8/10	.800	-/1	-	-	4	-	-	12	-
WILLIAMS. B.	-	0/2	.000	2/2	1.000	-/0	-	-	2	-	-	2	-
SULLIVAN	-	0/1	.000	0/0	.000	-/1	-	-	0	-	-	0	-
Totals	200	36/68	.529	20/24	.833	-/43	-	16	21	-	-	92	.460

Utah State (91) Coach: Ladell Anderson

	Min.	Total FG/FGA	Pct.	FT/FTA	Pct.	Reb. O/T	A	TO	PF	S	Blk	TP	PPM
WILLIAMS. N.	-	14/21	.667	3/4	.750	-/10	-	-	5	-	-	31	-
ROBERTS. M.	-	11/20	.550	8/9	.889	-/16	-	-	4	-	-	30	-
TOLLESTRUP. T.	-	5/9	.556	4/6	.667	-/9	-	-	3	-	-	14	-
TEBBS. J.	-	0/2	.000	1/2	.500	-/4	-	-	3	-	-	1	-
JEPPESEN. P.	-	1/6	.167	2/3	.667	-/3	-	-	2	-	-	4	-
EPPS. R.	-	0/0	.000	0/0	.000	-/0	-	-	2	-	-	0	-
HATCH. R.	-	2/4	.500	3/4	.750	-/2	-	-	1	-	-	7	-
ERICKSEN. J.	-	1/1	1.000	0/0	.000	-/0	-	-	5	-	-	2	-
WAKEFIELD. T.	-	1/2	.500	0/0	.000	-/0	-	-	0	-	-	2	-
WADE. D.	-	0/0	.000	0/0	.000	-/0	-	-	0	-	-	0	-
BEAN. C.	-	0/0	.000	0/0	.000	-/0	-	-	0	-	-	0	-
Totals	200	35/65	.538	21/28	.750	-/44	-	-	25	-	-	91	.455

Weber State (73) Coach: Phil Johnson

	Min.	Total FG/FGA	Pct.	FT/FTA	Pct.	Reb. O/T	A	TO	PF	S	Blk	TP	PPM
ROSS. K.	-	3/12	.250	2/6	.333	-/4	-	-	1	-	-	8	-
KNOBLE. F.	-	4/14	.286	3/4	.750	-/9	-	-	4	-	-	11	-
SOJOURNER. W.	-	5/11	.455	3/6	.500	-/9	-	-	4	-	-	13	-
HARLAN. S.	-	4/10	.400	7/10	.700	-/6	-	-	2	-	-	15	-
NIELSEN. R.	-	2/8	.250	0/1	.000	-/1	-	-	2	-	-	4	-
SACKOLWITZ. D.	-	1/6	.167	0/0	.000	-/3	-	-	0	-	-	2	-
ORR. B.	-	3/7	.429	0/1	.000	-/0	-	-	0	-	-	6	-
PLUIM. H.	-	0/0	.000	0/0	.000	-/1	-	-	1	-	-	0	-
NATIONS. C.	-	4/9	.444	0/0	.000	-/0	-	-	2	-	-	8	-
SIVULICH. J.	-	1/1	1.000	0/0	.000	-/1	-	-	2	-	-	2	-
CAMAC. R.	-	2/3	.667	0/0	.000	-/2	-	-	0	-	-	4	-
DELLA. P.	-	0/0	.000	0/0	.000	-/0	-	-	1	-	-	0	-
Totals	200	29/81	.358	15/28	.536	-/36	-	7	19	-	-	73	.365

Team Rebounds: Long Beach St. 12; Weber St. 10. Disqualified: None.

	1st Half	2nd Half	Final
Long Beach St.	37	55	92
Weber St.	28	45	73

UTEP (81) Coach: Don Haskins

	Min.	Total FG/FGA	Pct.	FT/FTA	Pct.	Reb. O/T	A	TO	PF	S	Blk	TP	PPM
DOYLE. B.	-	3/11	.273	0/1	.000	-/2	-	-	2	-	-	6	-
GIBBS. D.	-	2/10	.200	3/4	.750	-/10	-	-	1	-	-	7	-
SWITZER. M.	-	5/13	.385	8/10	.800	-/8	-	-	5	-	-	18	-
VANN. P.	-	1/6	.167	2/4	.500	-/4	-	-	4	-	-	4	-
ARCHIBALD. N.	-	13/21	.619	10/11	.909	-/3	-	-	2	-	-	36	-
ENGLISH. S.	-	0/1	.000	0/2	.000	-/0	-	-	0	-	-	0	-
STEWART	-	3/7	.429	2/2	1.000	-/3	-	-	3	-	-	8	-
RUDD. J.	-	1/2	.500	0/0	.000	-/0	-	-	3	-	-	2	-
Totals	200	28/71	.394	25/34	.735	-/30	-		20	-	-	81	.405

Team Rebounds: Utah State 7; UTEP 8. Disqualified: Utah State—Williams, Ericksen; UTEP—Switzer.

	1st Half	2nd Half	Final
Utah State	45	46	91
UTEP	33	48	81

REGIONAL SEMIFINAL EAST

St. Bonaventure (80) Coach: Larry Weise

	Min.	Total FG / FGA	Pct.	FT / FTA	Pct.	Reb. O / T	A	TO	PF	S	Blk	TP	PPM
GANTT, M.	36	7/18	.389	1/ 4	.250	-/11	0	1	5	-	-	15	.417
GARY, G.	36	6/11	.545	0/ 1	.000	-/11	1	2	0	-	-	12	.333
LANIER, B.	39	10/23	.435	4/ 5	.800	-/19	0	3	4	-	-	24	.615
HOFFMAN, P.	33	6/ 9	.667	0/ 1	.000	-/ 9	0	3	1	-	-	12	.364
KALBAUGH, B.	37	4/ 8	.500	5/ 6	.833	-/ 2	1	3	3	-	-	13	.351
KULL, M.	16	1/ 4	.250	2/ 3	.667	-/ 0	2	0	2	-	-	4	.250
BALDWIN, T.	3	0/ 1	.000	0/ 0	.000	-/ 0	0	0	1	-	-	0	.000
Totals	200	34/74	.459	12/20	.600	-/52	4	12	16	-	-	80	.400

North Carolina State (68) Coach: Norm Sloan

	Min.	Total FG / FGA	Pct.	FT / FTA	Pct.	Reb. O / T	A	TO	PF	S	Blk	TP	PPM
CODER, P.	40	8/14	.571	0/ 1	.000	-/ 6	0	0	3	-	-	16	.400
WILLIFORD, V.	40	13/22	.591	9/13	.692	-/12	3	0	3	-	-	35	.875
ANHEUSER, R.	40	3/ 6	.500	1/ 2	.500	-/10	5	3	4	-	-	7	.175
LEFTWICH, E.	35	4/13	.308	0/ 1	.000	-/ 5	0	4	3	-	-	8	.229
DUNNING, J.	36	0/ 7	.000	2/ 2	1.000	-/ 3	4	1	3	-	-	2	.056
HEARTEY, A.	9	0/ 1	.000	0/ 1	.000	-/ 1	0	0	0	-	-	0	.000
Totals	200	28/63	.444	12/20	.600	-/37	12	8	16	-	-	68	.340

Team Rebounds: St. Bonaventure 1; N.C. State 1. Disqualified: St. Bonaventure—Gantt.

	1st Half	2nd Half	Final
St. Bonaventure	41	39	80
N.C. State	31	37	68

Villanova (98) Coach: Jack Kraft

	Min.	Total FG / FGA	Pct.	FT / FTA	Pct.	Reb. O / T	A	TO	PF	S	Blk	TP	PPM
SMITH, C.	37	6/ 9	.667	1/ 1	1.000	-/12	1	2	1	-	-	13	.351
SIMS, S.	27	8/15	.533	3/ 5	.600	-/14	0	1	1	-	-	19	.704
PORTER, H.	38	13/22	.591	3/ 3	1.000	-/18	0	3	3	-	-	29	.763
O'HANLON, F.	34	5/11	.455	4/ 4	1.000	-/ 7	4	9	4	-	-	14	.412
FORD, C.	31	3/ 8	.375	5/ 8	.625	-/ 2	6	4	4	-	-	11	.355
SIEMIONTKOWSKI, H	13	2/ 6	.333	0/ 0	.000	-/ 1	0	0	1	-	-	4	.308
WOJOLOWSKI, L.	2	0/ 1	.000	0/ 0	.000	-/ 0	0	0	0	-	-	0	.000
GOLIL, B.	6	1/ 1	1.000	0/ 3	.000	-/ 1	1	1	0	-	-	2	.333
FOX, J.	6	1/ 3	.333	0/ 0	.000	-/ 2	0	1	0	-	-	2	.333
McDOWELL, J.	3	1/ 1	1.000	0/ 0	.000	-/ 0	0	0	1	-	-	2	.667
DALY, M.	3	1/ 1	1.000	0/ 0	.000	-/ 0	0	0	1	-	-	2	.667
Totals	200	41/78	.526	16/24	.667	-/57	12	21	16	-	-	98	.490

Niagara (73) Coach: Frank Layden

	Min.	Total FG / FGA	Pct.	FT / FTA	Pct.	Reb. O / T	A	TO	PF	S	Blk	TP	PPM
WINGATE, M.	17	3/ 9	.333	5/ 7	.714	-/ 7	1	2	0	-	-	11	.647
MURPHY, C.	39	8/22	.364	2/ 3	.667	-/ 7	1	4	4	-	-	18	.462
SCHAFER, S.	22	3/ 9	.333	0/ 0	.000	-/ 7	1	2	2	-	-	6	.273
SAMUEL, M.	13	1/ 5	.200	0/ 0	.000	-/ 2	0	6	1	-	-	2	.154
CHURCHWELL, B.	36	2/ 9	.222	6/ 6	1.000	-/ 4	0	1	3	-	-	10	.278
BROWN, M.	31	3/ 6	.500	1/ 2	.500	-/ 1	1	5	3	-	-	7	.226
JONES, W.	38	7/19	.368	3/ 3	1.000	-/ 8	1	0	3	-	-	17	.447
AIELLO, P.	1	0/ 0	.000	0/ 0	.000	-/ 0	0	1	0	-	-	0	.000
ADOMANIS, J.	1	1/ 1	1.000	0/ 0	.000	-/ 0	0	0	0	-	-	2	2.000
HARRISON, O.	1	0/ 0	.000	0/ 0	.000	-/ 0	0	0	0	-	-	0	.000
THORNTON, P.	1	0/ 0	.000	0/ 0	.000	-/ 0	0	0	0	-	-	0	.000
Totals	200	28/80	.350	17/21	.810	-/36	5	21	16	-	-	73	.365

Team Rebounds: Villanova 7; Niagara 5. Disqualified: None.

	1st Half	2nd Half	Final
Villanova	46	52	98
Niagara	29	44	73

REGIONAL SEMIFINAL MIDEAST

Jacksonville (104) Coach: Joe Williams

	Min.	Total FG / FGA	Pct.	FT / FTA	Pct.	Reb. O / T	A	TO	PF	S	Blk	TP	PPM
BLEVINS, M.	-	0/ 1	.000	0/ 0	.000	-/ 1	-	-	3	-	-	0	-
BURROWS, P.	-	11/12	.917	1/ 2	.500	-/ 9	-	-	3	-	-	23	-
GILMORE, A.	-	13/24	.542	4/ 7	.571	-/17	-	-	5	-	-	30	-
WEDEKING, V.	-	2/ 8	.250	1/ 3	.333	-/ 4	-	-	1	-	-	5	-
MORGAN, R.	-	9/14	.643	5/ 9	.556	-/ 4	-	-	4	-	-	23	-
DUBLIN, C.	-	2/ 8	.250	0/ 0	.000	-/ 2	-	-	5	-	-	4	-
NELSON, G.	-	6/ 7	.857	6/ 6	1.000	-/ 9	-	-	1	-	-	18	-
McINTYRE, R.	-	0/ 1	.000	1/ 2	.500	-/ 1	-	-	0	-	-	1	-
BALDWIN, R.	-	0/ 1	.000	0/ 0	.000	-/ 0	-	-	1	-	-	0	-
Totals	200	43/76	.566	18/29	.621	-/47	-	-	23	-	-	104	.520

Iowa (103) Coach: Ralph Miller

	Min.	Total FG / FGA	Pct.	FT / FTA	Pct.	Reb. O / T	A	TO	PF	S	Blk	TP	PPM
VIDNOVIC, G.	-	8/13	.615	8/11	.727	-/ 8	-	-	3	-	-	24	-
JOHNSON, J.	-	9/19	.474	1/ 3	.333	-/ 8	-	-	3	-	-	19	-
JENSEN, D.	-	1/ 8	.125	2/ 3	.667	-/ 4	-	-	3	-	-	4	-
BROWN, F.	-	13/23	.565	1/ 2	.500	-/ 4	-	-	3	-	-	27	-
CALABRIA, C.	-	7/12	.583	7/ 8	.875	-/ 8	-	-	4	-	-	21	-
McGILMER, B.	-	4/ 8	.500	0/ 2	.000	-/ 3	-	-	4	-	-	8	-
GRABINSKI, K.	-	0/ 0	.000	0/ 2	.000	-/ 2	-	-	0	-	-	0	-
Totals	200	42/83	.506	19/31	.613	-/37	-	-	20	-	-	103	.515

Team Rebounds: Jacksonville 4; Iowa 9. Disqualified: Jacksonville—Gilmore, Dublin.

	1st Half	2nd Half	Final
Jacksonville	50	54	104
Iowa	49	54	103

Kentucky (109) Coach: Adolph Rupp

	Min.	Total FG / FGA	Pct.	FT / FTA	Pct.	Reb. O / T	A	TO	PF	S	Blk	TP	PPM
PARKER, T.	-	4/ 7	.571	4/ 5	.800	-/ 6	-	-	4	-	-	12	-
PRATT, M.	-	7/15	.467	0/ 2	.000	-/ 4	-	-	5	-	-	14	-
ISSEL, D.	-	17/28	.607	10/14	.714	-/11	-	-	4	-	-	44	-
HOLLENBECK, K.	-	3/ 5	.600	1/ 3	.333	-/ 4	-	-	3	-	-	7	-
DINWIDDIE, J.	-	5/ 7	.714	1/ 1	1.000	-/ 2	-	-	1	-	-	11	-
MILLS, T.	-	5/ 7	.714	3/ 5	.600	-/ 5	-	-	3	-	-	13	-
KEY, S.	-	0/ 0	.000	0/ 0	.000	-/ 0	-	-	0	-	-	0	-
STEELE, L.	-	2/ 3	.667	4/ 4	1.000	-/ 6	-	-	4	-	-	8	-
Totals	200	43/72	.597	23/34	.676	-/38	-	-	24	-	-	109	.545

Notre Dame (99) Coach: Johnny Dee

	Min.	Total FG / FGA	Pct.	FT / FTA	Pct.	Reb. O / T	A	TO	PF	S	Blk	TP	PPM
CARR, A.	-	22/35	.629	8/ 8	1.000	-/ 8	-	-	2	-	-	52	-
JONES, C.	-	9/17	.529	4/10	.400	-/ 9	-	-	5	-	-	22	-
CATLETT, S.	-	0/ 2	.000	0/ 1	.000	-/ 5	-	-	5	-	-	0	-
GALLAGHER, J.	-	2/ 7	.286	1/ 2	.500	-/ 5	-	-	2	-	-	5	-
ZIZNEWSKI, J.	-	1/ 3	.333	1/ 1	1.000	-/ 6	-	-	4	-	-	3	-
MEEHAN, J.	-	3/ 6	.500	1/ 2	.500	-/ 0	-	-	0	-	-	7	-
SINNOTT, T.	-	1/ 2	.500	2/ 2	1.000	-/ 4	-	-	5	-	-	4	-
O'CONNELL	-	1/ 3	.333	4/ 5	.800	-/ 0	-	-	2	-	-	6	-
HINGA, J.	-	0/ 0	.000	0/ 1	.000	-/ 0	-	-	1	-	-	0	-
Totals	200	39/75	.520	21/32	.656	-/37	-	-	26	-	-	99	.495

Team Rebounds: Kentucky 6; Notre Dame 6. Disqualified: Kentucky—Pratt; Notre Dame—Jones, Catlett, Sinnott.

	1st Half	2nd Half	Final
Kentucky	48	61	109
Notre Dame	53	46	99

REGIONAL SEMIFINAL MIDWEST

New Mexico State (70) Coach: Lou Henson

	Min.	Total FG / FGA	Pct.	FT / FTA	Pct.	Reb. O / T	A	TO	PF	S	Blk	TP	PPM
COLLINS, J.	-	8/19	.421	7/ 9	.778	-/ 6	-	8	2	-	-	23	-
CRISS, C.	-	4/ 9	.444	5/ 7	.714	-/ 4	-	3	3	-	-	13	-
LACEY, S.	-	5/12	.417	5/ 7	.714	-/11	-	1	3	-	-	15	-
BURGESS, J.	-	0/ 4	.000	3/ 3	1.000	-/10	-	2	3	-	-	3	-
SMITH, J.	-	3/10	.300	2/ 3	.667	-/ 7	-	2	4	-	-	8	-
HORNE, M.	-	0/ 0	.000	0/ 0	.000	-/ 1	-	1	1	-	-	0	-
NEAL, R.	-	1/ 1	1.000	0/ 1	.000	-/ 2	-	1	5	-	-	2	-
REYES, C.	-	2/ 3	.667	2/ 2	1.000	-/ 2	-	3	1	-	-	6	-
MOORE, B.	-	0/ 0	.000	0/ 0	.000	-/ 1	-	0	0	-	-	0	-
Totals	200	23/58	.397	24/32	.750	-/44	-	21	22	-	-	70	.350

Kansas State (66) Coach: Cotton Fitzsimmons

	Min.	Total FG / FGA	Pct.	FT / FTA	Pct.	Reb. O / T	A	TO	PF	S	Blk	TP	PPM
ZENDER, R.	-	3/10	.300	1/ 2	.500	-/ 9	-	1	2	-	-	7	-
VENABLE, J.	-	12/30	.400	2/ 8	.250	-/14	-	2	3	-	-	26	-
HALL, D.	-	5/16	.313	6/11	.545	-/21	-	3	5	-	-	16	-
WEBB, J.	-	4/17	.235	0/ 0	.000	-/ 1	-	4	4	-	-	8	-
HUGHES, W.	-	2/ 7	.286	2/ 4	.500	-/ 3	-	4	4	-	-	6	-
SNIDER, T.	-	1/ 4	.250	0/ 0	.000	-/ 6	-	1	4	-	-	2	-
THOMAS, J.	-	0/ 0	.000	0/ 1	.000	-/ 0	-	0	0	-	-	0	-
LAWRENCE, D.	-	0/ 1	.000	1/ 3	.333	-/ 4	-	1	0	-	-	1	-
SMITH, E.	-	0/ 0	.000	0/ 0	.000	-/ 0	-	1	0	-	-	0	-
Totals	200	27/85	.318	12/29	.414	-/58	-	17	22	-	-	66	.330

Team Rebounds: New Mexico St. 7; Kansas State 9. Disqualified: New Mexico St.—Neal; Kansas State—Hall.

	1st Half	2nd Half	Final
New Mexico St.	35	35	70
Kansas State	27	39	66

Drake (92) Coach: Maurice John

	Min.	Total FG / FGA	Pct.	FT / FTA	Pct.	Reb. O / T	A	TO	PF	S	Blk	TP	PPM
WILLIAMS, A.	-	10/19	.526	4/ 7	.571	-/17	-	3	3	-	-	24	-
HALLIBURTEN, J.	-	3/ 8	.375	5/ 6	.833	-/ 7	-	6	4	-	-	11	-
BUSH, T.	-	3/ 6	.500	1/ 2	.500	-/ 7	-	7	4	-	-	7	-
JONES, B.	-	7/15	.467	1/ 2	.500	-/ 5	-	6	2	-	-	15	-
ZELLER, G.	-	7/16	.438	5/ 7	.714	-/ 3	-	4	3	-	-	19	-
WANAMAKER, R.	-	4/10	.400	0/ 1	.000	-/10	-	0	0	-	-	8	-
SALYERS, C.	-	4/ 4	1.000	0/ 1	.000	-/ 0	-	1	3	-	-	8	-
Totals	200	38/78	.487	16/26	.615	-/49	-	27	19	-	-	92	.460

Houston (87) Coach: Guy Lewis

	Min.	Total FG / FGA	Pct.	FT / FTA	Pct.	Reb. O / T	A	TO	PF	S	Blk	TP	PPM
BELL, M.	-	0/ 0	.000	0/ 1	.000	-/ 0	0	0	0	-	-	0	-
TAYLOR	-	6/12	.500	3/ 5	.600	-/ 9	2	5	3	-	-	15	-
DAVIS, D.	-	9/19	.474	6/ 8	.750	-/10	1	5	4	-	-	24	-
GRIBBEN, T.	-	2/ 9	.222	1/ 2	.500	-/ 7	1	5	5	-	-	5	-
WELCH, P.	-	9/18	.500	4/ 4	1.000	-/ 3	3	8	3	-	-	22	-
HICKMAN, J.	-	7/11	.636	2/ 3	.667	-/ 4	5	0	3	-	-	16	-
HALL, B.	-	1/ 2	.500	0/ 0	.000	-/ 2	0	0	2	-	-	2	-
WILLIS, S.	-	0/ 3	.000	0/ 1	.000	-/ 2	0	0	1	-	-	0	-
EVANS, M.	-	1/ 1	1.000	1/ 2	.500	-/ 2	0	0	1	-	-	3	-
Totals	200	35/75	.467	17/26	.654	-/39	12	23	22	-	-	87	.435

Team Rebounds: Drake 6; Houston 4. Disqualified: Houston—Gribben.

	1st Half	2nd Half	Final
Drake	45	47	92
Houston	32	55	87

REGIONAL SEMIFINAL WEST

UCLA (88)   Coach: John Wooden

	Min.	Total FG / FGA	Pct.	FT / FTA	Pct.	Reb. O / T	A	TO	PF	S	Blk	TP	PPM
WICKS, S.	-	8/14	.571	4/ 7	.571	-/11	3	-	3	-	-	20	-
ROWE, C.	-	5/11	.455	5/ 9	.556	-/11	6	-	1	-	-	15	-
PATTERSON, S.	-	6/14	.429	1/ 1	1.000	-/12	4	-	4	-	-	13	-
VALLELY, J.	-	6/15	.400	2/ 5	.400	-/ 5	4	-	2	-	-	14	-
BIBBY, H.	-	8/13	.615	4/ 5	.800	-/ 6	3	-	2	-	-	20	-
BOOKER, K.	-	0/ 1	.000	0/ 0	.000	-/ 0	1	-	1	-	-	0	-
ECKER, J.	-	1/ 2	.500	0/ 0	.000	-/ 1	0	-	0	-	-	2	-
SCHOFIELD, T.	-	1/ 2	.500	0/ 0	.000	-/ 1	1	-	0	-	-	2	-
SEIBERT, B.	-	0/ 1	.000	0/ 0	.000	-/ 0	0	-	0	-	-	0	-
CHAPMAN, J.	-	1/ 1	1.000	0/ 0	.000	-/ 1	1	-	0	-	-	2	-
Totals	200	36/74	.486	16/27	.593	-/48	23	-	13	-	-	88	.440

Long Beach State (65)   Coach: Jerry Tarkanian

	Min.	Total FG / FGA	Pct.	FT / FTA	Pct.	Reb. O / T	A	TO	PF	S	Blk	TP	PPM
ROBINSON, S.	-	7/13	.538	4/ 6	.667	-/ 7	4	-	2	-	-	18	-
JANKANS, B.	-	2/10	.200	1/ 3	.333	-/ 7	2	-	5	-	-	5	-
TRAPP, G.	-	10/18	.556	0/ 1	.000	-/ 4	3	-	3	-	-	20	-
GRITTON, R.	-	0/ 2	.000	0/ 0	.000	-/ 1	4	-	1	-	-	0	-
JOHNSON, S.	-	5/12	.417	3/ 3	1.000	-/ 4	1	-	0	-	-	13	-
MCLUCAS, D.	-	0/ 0	.000	0/ 0	.000	-/ 1	0	-	0	-	-	0	-
TAYLOR, D.	-	1/ 7	.143	1/ 2	.500	-/ 0	1	-	3	-	-	3	-
MONTGOMERY, A.	-	3/ 4	.750	0/ 0	.000	-/ 1	0	-	5	-	-	6	-
WILLIAMS, B.	-	0/ 1	.000	0/ 0	.000	-/ 1	0	-	2	-	-	0	-
Totals	200	28/67	.418	9/15	.600	-/26	15	-	21	-	-	65	.325

Team Rebounds: UCLA 6; Long Beach St. 8. Disqualified: Long Beach St.—Jankans, Montgomery.

	1st Half	2nd Half	Final
UCLA	42	46	88
Long Beach St.	29	36	65

Utah State (69)   Coach: Ladell Anderson

	Min.	Total FG / FGA	Pct.	FT / FTA	Pct.	Reb. O / T	A	TO	PF	S	Blk	TP	PPM
WILLIAMS, N.	-	10/22	.455	4/ 5	.800	-/ 4	1	2	3	-	-	24	-
ROBERTS, M.	-	5/14	.357	6/ 9	.667	-/16	0	2	1	-	-	16	-
TOLLESTRUP, T.	-	3/11	.273	1/ 2	.500	-/13	2	0	5	-	-	7	-
TEBBS, J.	-	1/ 8	.125	1/ 1	1.000	-/ 4	3	5	2	-	-	3	-
JEPPESEN, P.	-	2/ 8	.250	4/ 4	1.000	-/ 3	2	3	5	-	-	8	-
EPPS, R.	-	3/ 5	.600	3/ 3	1.000	-/ 2	1	3	1	-	-	9	-
HATCH, R.	-	1/ 4	.250	0/ 0	.000	-/ 3	1	0	3	-	-	2	-
ERICKSEN, J.	-	0/ 0	.000	0/ 0	.000	-/ 1	0	0	1	-	-	0	-
BEAN, C.	-	0/ 1	.000	0/ 0	.000	-/ 0	0	1	0	-	-	0	-
Totals	200	25/73	.342	19/24	.792	-/46	10	16	21	-	-	69	.345

Santa Clara (68)   Coach: Dick Garibaldi

	Min.	Total FG / FGA	Pct.	FT / FTA	Pct.	Reb. O / T	A	TO	PF	S	Blk	TP	PPM
OGDEN, R.	-	5/15	.333	2/ 7	.286	-/ 4	2	4	3	-	-	12	-
BOCHTE, B.	-	1/ 3	.333	2/ 4	.500	-/ 8	1	3	4	-	-	4	-
AWTREY, D.	-	9/16	.563	6/ 8	.750	-/11	3	3	4	-	-	24	-
EAGLESON, K.	-	2/ 5	.400	1/ 2	.500	-/ 3	7	4	2	-	-	5	-
SPIGHT, J.	-	8/16	.500	5/ 7	.714	-/ 9	7	2	4	-	-	21	-
PETERSEN, M.	-	1/ 3	.333	0/ 0	.000	-/ 2	0	1	3	-	-	2	-
PAULSON, K.	-	0/ 1	.000	0/ 0	.000	-/ 0	2	1	0	-	-	0	-
Totals	200	26/59	.441	16/28	.571	-/37	22	18	20	-	-	68	.340

Team Rebounds: Utah State 3; Santa Clara 12. Disqualified: Utah State—Tollestrup, Jeppesen.

	1st Half	2nd Half	Final
Utah State	31	38	69
Santa Clara	35	33	68

REGIONAL FINAL EAST

St. Bonaventure (97)   Coach: Larry Weise

	Min.	Total FG / FGA	Pct.	FT / FTA	Pct.	Reb. O / T	A	TO	PF	S	Blk	TP	PPM
GANTT, M.	40	7/20	.350	5/ 8	.625	-/18	1	3	3	-	-	19	.475
GARY, G.	36	10/17	.588	0/ 1	.000	-/11	0	4	1	-	-	20	.556
LANIER, B.	31	11/22	.500	4/ 4	1.000	-/14	0	2	2	-	-	26	.839
KALBAUGH, B.	40	5/ 9	.556	5/ 5	1.000	-/ 3	3	4	1	-	-	15	.375
HOFFMAN, P.	23	3/ 6	.500	0/ 1	.000	-/ 4	0	0	3	-	-	6	.261
KULL, M.	30	4/ 6	.667	3/ 3	1.000	-/ 2	2	3	2	-	-	11	.367
Totals	200	40/80	.500	17/22	.773	-/52	6	16	12	-	-	97	.485

Villanova (74)   Coach: Jack Kraft

	Min.	Total FG / FGA	Pct.	FT / FTA	Pct.	Reb. O / T	A	TO	PF	S	Blk	TP	PPM
SMITH, C.	19	1/ 8	.125	0/ 0	.000	-/ 4	0	1	1	-	-	2	.105
SIMS, S.	24	1/ 5	.200	3/ 5	.600	-/ 7	0	0	1	-	-	5	.208
PORTER, H.	33	6/14	.429	2/ 2	1.000	-/ 9	0	1	5	-	-	14	.424
O'HANLON, F.	36	10/15	.667	0/ 2	.000	-/ 4	3	6	5	-	-	20	.556
FORD, C.	34	7/14	.500	1/ 2	.500	-/ 4	1	3	3	-	-	15	.441
SIEMIONTKOWSKI, H	28	3/13	.231	4/ 4	1.000	-/ 3	0	2	2	-	-	10	.357
WOJOLOWSKI, L.	2	0/ 0	.000	0/ 0	.000	-/ 0	0	0	0	-	-	0	.000
MCDOWELL, J.	14	3/ 7	.429	0/ 1	.000	-/ 3	1	0	2	-	-	6	.429
FOX, J.	6	1/ 2	.500	0/ 0	.000	-/ 0	0	0	0	-	-	2	.333
GOHL, B.	4	0/ 1	.000	0/ 0	.000	-/ 0	0	0	1	-	-	0	.000
Totals	200	32/79	.405	10/16	.625	-/34	5	13	20	-	-	74	.370

Team Rebounds: St. Bonaventure 6; Villanova 0. Disqualified: Villanova—Porter, O'Hanlon.

	1st Half	2nd Half	Final
St. Bonaventure	46	51	97
Villanova	30	44	74

REGIONAL FINAL MIDEAST

Jacksonville (106)   Coach: Joe Williams

	Min.	Total FG/FGA	Pct.	FT/FTA	Pct.	Reb. O/T	A	TO	PF	S	Blk	TP	PPM
BURROWS	-	3/ 4	.750	2/ 2	1.000	-/ 4	-	-	3	-	-	8	-
BLEVINS	-	0/ 1	.000	0/ 0	.000	-/ 3	-	-	2	-	-	0	-
GILMORE, A.	-	10/20	.500	4/ 7	.571	-/20	-	-	4	-	-	24	-
MORGAN, R.	-	10/14	.714	8/ 9	.889	-/ 3	-	-	4	-	-	28	-
WEDEKING	-	4/13	.308	4/ 5	.800	-/ 3	-	-	0	-	-	12	-
DUBLIN	-	6/ 8	.750	7/ 8	.875	-/ 2	-	-	4	-	-	19	-
NELSON	-	5/ 7	.714	3/ 5	.600	-/ 6	-	-	1	-	-	13	-
MCINTYRE	-	1/ 2	.500	0/ 0	.000	-/ 3	-	-	2	-	-	2	-
Totals	200	39/69	.565	28/36	.778	-/44	-	-	20	-	-	106	.530

Kentucky (100)   Coach: Adolph Rupp

	Min.	Total FG/FGA	Pct.	FT/FTA	Pct.	Reb. O/T	A	TO	PF	S	Blk	TP	PPM
PARKER, T.	-	8/18	.444	5/ 5	1.000	-/ 4	-	-	2	-	-	21	-
PRATT, M.	-	4/13	.308	6/ 9	.667	-/13	-	-	5	-	-	14	-
ISSEL, D.	-	13/25	.520	2/ 2	1.000	-/10	-	-	5	-	-	28	-
DINWIDDIE, J.	-	1/ 2	.500	0/ 1	.000	-/ 0	-	-	0	-	-	2	-
HOLLENBECK, K.	-	4/ 8	.500	2/ 2	1.000	-/ 7	-	-	3	-	-	10	-
KEY, S.	-	0/ 2	.000	0/ 0	.000	-/ 1	-	-	1	-	-	0	-
MILLS, T.	-	7/11	.636	4/ 4	1.000	-/ 3	-	-	5	-	-	18	-
STEELE, L.	-	1/ 4	.250	1/ 1	1.000	-/ 2	-	-	5	-	-	3	-
SODERBERG, M.	-	2/ 5	.400	0/ 0	.000	-/ 3	-	-	0	-	-	4	-
NOLL, R.	-	0/ 1	.000	0/ 0	.000	-/ 0	-	-	0	-	-	0	-
Totals	200	40/89	.449	20/24	.833	-/43	-	-	26	-	-	100	.500

Team Rebounds: Jacksonville 3; Kentucky 1. Disqualified: Kentucky—Pratt, Issel, Mills, Steele.

	1st Half	2nd Half	Final
Jacksonville	52	54	106
Kentucky	45	55	100

REGIONAL FINAL MIDWEST

New Mexico State (87)   Coach: Lou Henson

	Min.	Total FG/FGA	Pct.	FT/FTA	Pct.	Reb. O/T	A	TO	PF	S	Blk	TP	PPM
COLLINS, J.	-	9/18	.500	8/10	.800	-/ 3	-	4	3	-	-	26	-
CRISS, C.	-	5/10	.500	4/ 7	.571	-/ 0	-	3	4	-	-	14	-
LACEY, S.	-	7/12	.583	6/10	.600	-/24	-	2	2	-	-	20	-
BURGESS, J.	-	0/ 0	.000	0/ 0	.000	-/ 7	-	1	2	-	-	0	-
SMITH, J.	-	2/ 4	.500	1/ 3	.333	-/ 3	-	2	5	-	-	5	-
HORNE, M.	-	3/ 6	.500	7/ 9	.778	-/ 0	-	4	4	-	-	13	-
NEAL, R.	-	2/ 2	1.000	3/ 4	.750	-/ 4	-	1	1	-	-	7	-
REYES, C.	-	0/ 1	.000	2/ 2	1.000	-/ 5	-	0	1	-	-	2	-
Totals	200	28/53	.528	31/45	.689	-/46	-	17	22	-	-	87	.435

Drake (78)   Coach: Maurice John

	Min.	Total FG/FGA	Pct.	FT/FTA	Pct.	Reb. O/T	A	TO	PF	S	Blk	TP	PPM
WILLIAMS, A.	-	4/15	.267	1/ 3	.333	-/14	-	0	5	-	-	9	-
HALLIBURTEN, J.	-	8/18	.444	8/ 8	1.000	-/ 9	-	4	3	-	-	24	-
BUSH, T.	-	6/ 8	.750	1/ 6	.167	-/ 7	-	1	5	-	-	13	-
JONES, B.	-	5/ 8	.625	0/ 0	.000	-/ 1	-	1	5	-	-	10	-
ZELLER, G.	-	4/15	.267	1/ 1	1.000	-/ 1	-	3	5	-	-	9	-
WANAMAKER, R.	-	1/ 4	.250	1/ 2	.500	-/ 3	-	0	3	-	-	3	-
SALYERS, C.	-	3/ 5	.600	0/ 0	.000	-/ 0	-	0	1	-	-	6	-
ALLEN, L.	-	1/ 3	.333	0/ 0	.000	-/ 0	-	0	2	-	-	2	-
TEETER, D.	-	0/ 1	.000	0/ 0	.000	-/ 1	-	0	0	-	-	0	-
SAKYS, A.	-	0/ 2	.000	2/ 4	.500	-/ 1	-	0	3	-	-	2	-
Totals	200	32/79	.405	14/24	.583	-/37	-	9	32	-	-	78	.390

Team Rebounds: New Mexico St. 8; Drake 5. Disqualified: New Mexico St.—Smith; Drake—Williams, Bush, Zeller, Jones.

	1st Half	2nd Half	Final
New Mexico St.	47	40	87
Drake	35	43	78

REGIONAL FINAL WEST

UCLA (101)   Coach: John Wooden

	Min.	Total FG/FGA	Pct.	FT/FTA	Pct.	Reb. O/T	A	TO	PF	S	Blk	TP	PPM
WICKS, S.	-	10/14	.714	6/ 7	.857	-/ 8	3	-	4	-	-	26	-
ROWE, C.	-	9/17	.529	8/ 8	1.000	-/16	4	-	3	-	-	26	-
PATTERSON, S.	-	4/12	.333	1/ 2	.500	-/ 9	6	-	2	-	-	9	-
VALLELY, J.	-	5/13	.385	4/ 7	.571	-/ 3	3	-	1	-	-	14	-
BIBBY, H.	-	4/ 8	.500	7/ 9	.778	-/ 7	5	-	4	-	-	15	-
BOOKER, K.	-	2/ 4	.500	0/ 1	.000	-/ 1	0	-	2	-	-	4	-
ECKER, J.	-	0/ 0	.000	1/ 2	.500	-/ 2	1	-	1	-	-	1	-
SCHOFIELD, T.	-	0/ 0	.000	0/ 0	.000	-/ 0	0	-	0	-	-	0	-
SEIBERT, B.	-	1/ 1	1.000	2/ 2	1.000	-/ 1	0	-	1	-	-	4	-
CHAPMAN, J.	-	0/ 2	.000	0/ 0	.000	-/ 3	0	-	0	-	-	0	-
BETCHLEY, R.	-	1/ 2	.500	0/ 0	.000	-/ 0	0	-	0	-	-	2	-
HILL, A.	-	0/ 0	.000	0/ 0	.000	-/ 0	0	-	0	-	-	0	-
Totals	200	36/73	.493	29/38	.763	-/50	22	-	18	-	-	101	.505

Utah State (79)   Coach: Ladell Anderson

	Min.	Total FG/FGA	Pct.	FT/FTA	Pct.	Reb. O/T	A	TO	PF	S	Blk	TP	PPM
WILLIAMS, N.	-	7/24	.292	0/ 0	.000	-/11	3	-	4	-	-	14	-
ROBERTS, M.	-	14/35	.400	5/ 7	.714	-/15	0	-	4	-	-	33	-
TOLLESTRUP, T.	-	1/ 4	.250	4/ 6	.667	-/10	3	-	4	-	-	6	-
TEBBS, J.	-	0/ 4	.000	0/ 0	.000	-/ 2	4	-	4	-	-	0	-
JEPPESEN, P.	-	4/ 6	.667	4/ 4	1.000	-/ 1	0	-	4	-	-	12	-
EPPS, R.	-	6/13	.462	0/ 1	.000	-/ 6	2	-	3	-	-	12	-
HATCH, R.	-	0/ 4	.000	2/ 2	1.000	-/ 2	0	-	2	-	-	2	-
ERICKSEN, J.	-	0/ 0	.000	0/ 0	.000	-/ 0	0	-	0	-	-	0	-
WAKEFIELD, T.	-	0/ 0	.000	0/ 0	.000	-/ 0	0	-	1	-	-	0	-
WADE, D.	-	0/ 1	.000	0/ 0	.000	-/ 1	1	-	0	-	-	0	-
BEAN, C.	-	0/ 0	.000	0/ 0	.000	-/ 1	0	-	0	-	-	0	-
Totals	200	32/91	.352	15/20	.750	-/49	13	-	26	-	-	79	.395

Team Rebounds: UCLA 6; Utah State 5. Disqualified: None.

	1st Half	2nd Half	Final
UCLA	51	50	101
Utah State	44	35	79

FINAL FOUR

St. Bonaventure (83)   Coach: Larry Weise

	Min.	Total FG / FGA	Pct.	FT / FTA	Pct.	Reb. O / T	A	TO	PF	S	Blk	TP	PPM
KALBAUGH, B.	-	5/ 8	.625	2/ 2	1.000	-/ 4	-	-	3	-	-	12	-
HOFFMAN, P.	-	4/14	.286	2/ 4	.500	-/ 6	-	-	3	-	-	10	-
GARY, G.	-	2/ 7	.286	5/ 8	.625	-/13	-	-	5	-	-	9	-
BALDWIN, T.	-	2/10	.200	1/ 2	.500	-/ 4	-	-	5	-	-	5	-
GANTT, M.	-	8/17	.471	0/ 0	.000	-/ 8	-	-	5	-	-	16	-
KULL, M.	-	4/ 7	.571	0/ 0	.000	-/ 0	-	-	5	-	-	8	-
THOMAS, V.	-	7/17	.412	1/ 2	.500	-/ 4	-	-	3	-	-	15	-
GRYS, P.	-	1/ 5	.200	2/ 2	1.000	-/ 1	-	-	2	-	-	4	-
TEPAS, D.	-	0/ 0	.000	2/ 2	1.000	-/ 1	-	-	0	-	-	2	-
FAHEY, G.	-	1/ 1	1.000	0/ 0	.000	-/ 0	-	-	1	-	-	2	-
Totals	200	34/86	.395	15/22	.682	-/41	-	-	32	-	-	83	.415

Jacksonville (91)   Coach: Joe Williams

	Min.	Total FG / FGA	Pct.	FT / FTA	Pct.	Reb. O / T	A	TO	PF	S	Blk	TP	PPM
WEDEKING, V.	-	7/15	.467	1/ 1	1.000	-/ 6	-	-	4	-	-	15	-
MORGAN, R.	-	6/15	.400	5/ 6	.833	-/ 5	-	-	3	-	-	17	-
BURROWS, P.	-	2/ 4	.500	1/ 1	1.000	-/ 4	-	-	4	-	-	5	-
MCINTYRE, R.	-	0/ 3	.000	0/ 0	.000	-/ 3	-	-	1	-	-	0	-
GILMORE, A.	-	9/14	.643	11/15	.733	-/21	-	-	2	-	-	29	-
DUBLIN, C.	-	1/ 3	.333	9/ 9	1.000	-/ 2	-	-	2	-	-	11	-
NELSON, G.	-	1/ 7	.143	10/12	.833	-/ 7	-	-	3	-	-	12	-
BLEVINS, M.	-	1/ 1	1.000	0/ 0	.000	-/ 0	-	-	1	-	-	2	-
BALDWIN, R.	-	0/ 1	.000	0/ 1	.000	-/ 0	-	-	1	-	-	0	-
Totals	200	27/63	.429	37/45	.822	-/48	-	-	21	-	-	91	.455

Team Rebounds: Jacksonville 4; St. Bonaventure 6. Disqualified: St. Bonaventure—Gary, Baldwin, Gantt, Kull.

	1st Half	2nd Half	Final
St. Bonaventure	34	49	83
Jacksonville	42	49	91

New Mexico State (77)   Coach: Lou Henson

	Min.	Total FG / FGA	Pct.	FT / FTA	Pct.	Reb. O / T	A	TO	PF	S	Blk	TP	PPM
COLLINS, J.	35	13/23	.565	2/ 3	.667	-/ 0	2	1	3	-	-	28	.800
CRISS, C.	33	6/16	.375	7/ 9	.778	-/ 2	1	6	5	-	-	19	.576
LACEY, S.	31	3/ 9	.333	2/ 3	.667	-/16	0	1	3	-	-	8	.258
BURGESS, J.	25	1/ 6	.167	0/ 0	.000	-/ 2	0	0	2	-	-	2	.080
SMITH, J.	28	4/11	.364	2/ 3	.667	-/ 7	0	0	5	-	-	10	.357
HORNE, M.	7	0/ 4	.000	2/ 2	1.000	-/ 1	2	1	2	-	-	2	.286
NEAL, R.	19	2/ 4	.500	0/ 0	.000	-/ 6	0	1	2	-	-	4	.211
REYES, C.	14	1/ 6	.167	0/ 0	.000	-/ 4	0	2	2	-	-	2	.143
MOORE, B.	5	1/ 1	1.000	0/ 0	.000	-/ 1	0	0	0	-	-	2	.400
LEFEVRE, L.	1	0/ 0	.000	0/ 0	.000	-/ 1	0	0	0	-	-	0	.000
MCCARTHY, T.	1	0/ 0	.000	0/ 0	.000	-/ 0	0	1	0	-	-	0	.000
FRANCO, R.	1	0/ 0	.000	0/ 0	.000	-/ 0	0	0	0	-	-	0	.000
Totals	200	31/80	.388	15/20	.750	-/40	5	13	24	-	-	77	.385

UCLA (93)   Coach: John Wooden

	Min.	Total FG / FGA	Pct.	FT / FTA	Pct.	Reb. O / T	A	TO	PF	S	Blk	TP	PPM
WICKS, S.	39	10/12	.833	2/ 5	.400	-/16	2	4	3	-	-	22	.564
ROWE, C.	39	4/ 7	.571	7/11	.636	-/15	1	3	0	-	-	15	.385
PATTERSON, S.	38	5/ 9	.556	2/ 2	1.000	-/ 6	7	1	3	-	-	12	.316
VALLELY, J.	35	7/19	.368	9/10	.900	-/ 4	1	3	3	-	-	23	.657
BIBBY, H.	34	8/13	.615	3/ 3	1.000	-/ 2	0	6	5	-	-	19	.559
BOOKER, K.	7	0/ 1	.000	0/ 0	.000	-/ 0	0	1	2	-	-	0	.000
ECKER, J.	3	0/ 0	.000	0/ 0	.000	-/ 0	0	0	0	-	-	0	.000
SCHOFIELD, T.	1	0/ 0	.000	0/ 0	.000	-/ 0	0	2	1	-	-	0	.000
SEIBERT, B.	1	0/ 1	.000	0/ 0	.000	-/ 1	1	0	0	-	-	0	.000
CHAPMAN, J.	1	1/ 1	1.000	0/ 0	.000	-/ 1	0	0	0	-	-	2	2.000
BETCHLEY, R.	1	0/ 0	.000	0/ 0	.000	-/ 0	0	0	0	-	-	0	.000
HILL, A.	1	0/ 0	.000	0/ 1	.000	-/ 0	0	0	1	-	-	0	.000
Totals	200	35/63	.556	23/32	.719	-/45	12	20	18	-	-	93	.465

Team Rebounds: UCLA 0; New Mexico St. 5. Disqualified: UCLA—Bibby; New Mexico St.—Criss, Smith.

	1st Half	2nd Half	Final
New Mexico St.	41	36	77
UCLA	48	45	93

NATIONAL CHAMPIONSHIP

Jacksonville (69)   Coach: Joe Williams

	Min.	Total FG / FGA	Pct.	FT / FTA	Pct.	Reb. O / T	A	TO	PF	S	Blk	TP	PPM
BLEVINS, M.	19	1/ 2	.500	1/ 2	.500	-/ 0	1	2	1	-	-	3	.158
BURROWS, P.	24	6/ 9	.667	0/ 0	.000	-/ 6	0	0	1	-	-	12	.500
GILMORE, A.	38	9/29	.310	1/ 1	1.000	-/16	1	4	5	-	-	19	.500
MORGAN, R.	37	5/11	.455	0/ 0	.000	-/ 4	11	8	5	-	-	10	.270
WEDEKING, V.	37	6/11	.545	0/ 0	.000	-/ 2	3	1	2	-	-	12	.324
DUBLIN, C.	18	0/ 5	.000	2/ 2	1.000	-/ 1	1	2	4	-	-	2	.111
NELSON, G.	16	3/ 9	.333	2/ 2	1.000	-/ 5	0	1	1	-	-	8	.500
MCINTYRE, R.	6	1/ 3	.333	0/ 0	.000	-/ 3	0	0	3	-	-	2	.333
BALDWIN, R.	2	0/ 0	.000	0/ 0	.000	-/ 0	0	0	0	-	-	0	.000
HAWKINS, D.	2	0/ 1	.000	1/ 1	1.000	-/ 1	0	1	1	-	-	1	.500
SELKE, K.	1	0/ 0	.000	0/ 0	.000	-/ 0	0	0	0	-	-	0	.000
Totals	200	31/80	.388	7/ 8	.875	-/38	17	18	23	-	-	69	.345

UCLA (80)   Coach: John Wooden

	Min.	Total FG / FGA	Pct.	FT / FTA	Pct.	Reb. O / T	A	TO	PF	S	Blk	TP	PPM
BETCHLEY, R.	1	0/ 0	.000	0/ 1	.000	-/ 0	0	0	0	-	-	0	.000
HILL, A.	1	0/ 0	.000	0/ 1	.000	-/ 0	0	0	0	-	-	0	.000
WICKS, S.	38	5/ 9	.556	7/10	.700	-/18	3	6	3	-	-	17	.447
ROWE, C.	38	7/15	.467	5/ 5	1.000	-/ 8	1	6	4	-	-	19	.500
PATTERSON, S.	38	8/15	.533	1/ 4	.250	-/11	2	1	1	-	-	17	.447
VALLELY, J.	38	5/10	.500	5/ 7	.714	-/ 7	5	7	2	-	-	15	.395
BIBBY, H.	38	2/11	.182	4/ 4	1.000	-/ 4	2	1	1	-	-	8	.211
BOOKER, K.	1	0/ 0	.000	2/ 3	.667	-/ 0	0	1	0	-	-	2	2.000
ECKER, J.	2	1/ 1	1.000	0/ 0	.000	-/ 0	0	0	0	-	-	2	1.000
SCHOFIELD, T.	1	0/ 0	.000	0/ 0	.000	-/ 0	0	0	0	-	-	0	.000
SEIBERT, B.	2	0/ 1	.000	0/ 0	.000	-/ 1	0	1	1	-	-	0	.000
CHAPMAN, J.	2	0/ 1	.000	0/ 0	.000	-/ 1	0	0	0	-	-	0	.000
Totals	200	28/63	.444	24/35	.686	-/50	13	23	12	-	-	80	.400

Team Rebounds: UCLA 3; Jacksonville 2. Disqualified: Jacksonville—Morgan, Gilmore.

	1st Half	2nd Half	Final
Jacksonville	36	33	69
UCLA	41	39	80

NATIONAL THIRD PLACE
New Mexico State (79) Coach: Lou Henson

	Min.	Total FG / FGA	Pct.	FT / FTA	Pct.	Reb. O / T	A	TO	PF	S	Blk	TP	PPM
COLLINS, J.	-	9/22	.409	0/ 0	.000	-/ 3	2	5	2	-	-	18	-
CRISS, C.	-	4/16	.250	2/ 2	1.000	-/ 7	4	4	3	-	-	10	-
LACEY, S.	-	7/17	.412	4/ 6	.667	-/19	1	2	0	-	-	18	-
BURGESS, J.	-	1/ 2	.500	0/ 0	.000	-/ 9	0	2	1	-	-	2	-
SMITH, J.	-	2/ 5	.400	3/ 6	.500	-/ 5	1	1	4	-	-	7	-
HORNE, M.	-	1/ 1	1.000	0/ 0	.000	-/ 0	2	1	1	-	-	2	-
NEAL, R.	-	5/ 7	.714	2/ 2	1.000	-/ 7	0	1	1	-	-	12	-
REYES, C.	-	4/ 7	.571	2/ 2	1.000	-/ 5	2	0	0	-	-	10	-
MOORE, B.	-	0/ 0	.000	0/ 0	.000	-/ 0	0	0	0	-	-	0	-
Totals	200	33/77	.429	13/18	.722	-/55	12	16	12	-	-	79	.395

St. Bonaventure (73) Coach: Larry Weise

	Min.	Total FG / FGA	Pct.	FT / FTA	Pct.	Reb. O / T	A	TO	PF	S	Blk	TP	PPM
GANTT, M.	-	6/16	.375	2/ 5	.400	-/10	0	5	2	-	-	14	-
GARY, G.	-	8/14	.571	6/ 7	.857	-/11	2	2	4	-	-	22	-
KALBAUGH, B.	-	3/ 9	.333	0/ 0	.000	-/ 3	5	3	1	-	-	6	-
HOFFMAN, P.	-	2/ 5	.400	0/ 1	.000	-/ 4	2	1	3	-	-	4	-
KULL, M.	-	7/17	.412	0/ 0	.000	-/ 2	2	2	2	-	-	14	-
TEPAS, D.	-	0/ 1	.000	0/ 0	.000	-/ 0	0	0	0	-	-	0	-
THOMAS, V.	-	3/ 7	.429	2/ 2	1.000	-/ 1	0	0	2	-	-	8	-
BALDWIN, T.	-	1/ 1	1.000	1/ 1	1.000	-/ 0	1	0	0	-	-	3	-
GRYS, P.	-	1/ 1	1.000	0/ 0	.000	-/ 1	0	0	0	-	-	2	-
Totals	200	31/71	.437	11/16	.688	-/32	12	13	14	-	-	73	.365

Team Rebounds: New Mexico St. 2; St. Bonaventure 2. Disqualified: None.

	1st Half	2nd Half	Final
New Mexico St.	36	43	79
St. Bonaventure	30	43	73

REGIONAL THIRD PLACE EAST
North Carolina State (108) Coach: Norm Sloan

	Min.	Total FG / FGA	Pct.	FT / FTA	Pct.	Reb. O / T	A	TO	PF	S	Blk	TP	PPM
WILLIFORD, V.	40	11/24	.458	14/16	.875	-/11	1	1	1	-	-	36	.900
ANHEUSER, R.	37	12/15	.800	4/ 6	.667	-/10	2	4	2	-	-	28	.757
CODER, P.	40	10/20	.500	4/ 8	.500	-/13	0	2	2	-	-	24	.600
DUNNING, J.	35	2/ 3	.667	2/ 4	.500	-/ 7	1	2	3	-	-	6	.171
LEFTWICH, E.	23	4/ 8	.500	2/ 3	.667	-/ 2	4	1	4	-	-	10	.435
HEARTLEY, A.	22	1/ 5	.200	2/ 4	.500	-/ 6	4	1	2	-	-	4	.182
RISINGER, J.	3	0/ 1	.000	0/ 0	.000	-/ 1	0	0	1	-	-	0	.000
Totals	200	40/76	.526	28/41	.683	-/50	12	11	15	-	-	108	.540

Niagara (88) Coach: Frank Layden

	Min.	Total FG / FGA	Pct.	FT / FTA	Pct.	Reb. O / T	A	TO	PF	S	Blk	TP	PPM
SCHAFER, S.	21	3/ 6	.500	1/ 3	.333	-/ 5	0	2	4	-	-	7	.333
JONES, W.	38	10/20	.500	0/ 1	.000	-/12	0	2	1	-	-	20	.526
CHURCHWELL, B.	36	1/12	.083	0/ 0	.000	-/10	0	1	5	-	-	2	.056
BROWN, M.	38	7/14	.500	5/ 5	1.000	-/ 4	1	6	5	-	-	19	.500
MURPHY, C.	36	13/26	.500	9/ 9	1.000	-/ 7	0	4	5	-	-	35	.972
WINGATE, M.	13	1/ 2	.500	3/ 3	1.000	-/ 4	0	1	3	-	-	5	.385
SAMUEL, M.	3	0/ 2	.000	0/ 0	.000	-/ 0	0	1	0	-	-	0	.000
HARRISON, O.	9	0/ 0	.000	0/ 0	.000	-/ 1	1	1	0	-	-	0	.000
THORNTON, P.	5	0/ 1	.000	0/ 0	.000	-/ 0	0	1	3	-	-	0	.000
ADOMANIS	1	0/ 0	.000	0/ 0	.000	-/ 0	0	0	0	-	-	0	.000
Totals	200	35/83	.422	18/21	.857	-/43	2	19	26	-	-	88	.440

Team Rebounds: N.C. State 3; Niagara 4. Disqualified: Niagara—Churchwell, Brown, Murphy.

	1st Half	2nd Half	Final
N.C. State	57	51	108
Niagara	48	40	88

REGIONAL THIRD PLACE MIDEAST
Iowa (121) Coach: Ralph Miller

	Min.	Total FG / FGA	Pct.	FT / FTA	Pct.	Reb. O / T	A	TO	PF	S	Blk	TP	PPM
VIDNOVIC, G.	-	7/14	.500	10/10	1.000	-/11	-	-	1	-	-	24	-
JOHNSON, J.	-	14/31	.452	3/ 3	1.000	-/ 9	-	-	3	-	-	31	-
JENSEN, D.	-	2/ 2	1.000	1/ 1	1.000	-/ 7	-	-	1	-	-	5	-
BROWN, F.	-	8/16	.500	0/ 0	.000	-/ 6	-	-	3	-	-	16	-
CALABRIA, C.	-	15/22	.682	1/ 2	.500	-/ 8	-	-	3	-	-	31	-
MCGILMER, B.	-	6/ 9	.667	0/ 0	.000	-/ 6	-	-	3	-	-	12	-
SCHULZE, T.	-	0/ 1	.000	0/ 0	.000	-/ 0	-	-	0	-	-	0	-
HODGE, J.	-	0/ 0	.000	2/ 2	1.000	-/ 0	-	-	0	-	-	2	-
GRABINSKI, K.	-	0/ 1	.000	0/ 1	.000	-/ 0	-	-	1	-	-	0	-
HAZLEY, O.	-	0/ 1	.000	0/ 0	.000	-/ 1	-	-	0	-	-	0	-
MILLER, T.	-	0/ 1	.000	0/ 0	.000	-/ 1	-	-	0	-	-	0	-
Totals	200	52/98	.531	17/19	.895	-/49	-	-	15	-	-	121	.605

Notre Dame (106) Coach: Johnny Dee

	Min.	Total FG / FGA	Pct.	FT / FTA	Pct.	Reb. O / T	A	TO	PF	S	Blk	TP	PPM
CARR, A.	-	21/39	.538	3/ 4	.750	-/10	-	-	2	-	-	45	-
JONES, C.	-	12/24	.500	0/ 0	.000	-/ 8	-	-	3	-	-	24	-
MEGHAN, J.	-	1/ 3	.333	1/ 1	1.000	-/ 1	-	-	0	-	-	3	-
GALLAGER, J.	-	1/ 2	.500	0/ 0	.000	-/ 2	-	-	0	-	-	2	-
ZIZNEWSKI, J.	-	2/ 6	.333	3/ 4	.750	-/10	-	-	2	-	-	7	-
CATLETT, S.	-	3/10	.300	1/ 1	1.000	-/ 6	-	-	2	-	-	7	-
SINNOTT, T.	-	2/ 5	.400	6/ 6	1.000	-/ 3	-	-	2	-	-	10	-
HINGA, J.	-	2/ 5	.400	2/ 2	1.000	-/ 2	-	-	1	-	-	6	-
O'CONNELL, M.	-	1/ 3	.333	0/ 0	.000	-/ 0	-	-	1	-	-	2	-
Totals	200	45/97	.464	16/18	.889	-/42	-	-	13	-	-	106	.530

Team Rebounds: Iowa 3; Notre Dame 8. Disqualified: None.

	1st Half	2nd Half	Final
Iowa	75	46	121
Notre Dame	42	64	106

REGIONAL THIRD PLACE MIDWEST
Kansas State (107) Coach: Cotton Fitzsimmons

	Min.	Total FG / FGA	Pct.	FT / FTA	Pct.	Reb. O / T	A	TO	PF	S	Blk	TP	PPM
ZENDER, R.	-	7/13	.538	1/ 3	.333	-/10	-	3	3	-	-	15	-
VENABLE, J.	-	11/26	.423	2/ 4	.500	-/10	-	3	5	-	-	24	-
HALL, D.	-	12/19	.632	1/ 3	.333	-/19	-	1	4	-	-	25	-
WEBB, J.	-	7/13	.538	0/ 0	.000	-/ 6	-	6	2	-	-	14	-
HUGHES, W.	-	4/ 8	.500	1/ 2	.500	-/ 5	-	4	5	-	-	9	-
SNIDER, T.	-	2/ 4	.500	3/ 5	.600	-/ 1	-	6	3	-	-	7	-
THOMAS, J.	-	0/ 0	.000	1/ 1	1.000	-/ 1	-	1	1	-	-	1	-
LAWRENCE, D.	-	2/ 4	.500	2/ 6	.333	-/ 5	-	1	3	-	-	6	-
SMITH, E.	-	2/ 6	.333	2/ 2	1.000	-/ 7	-	2	0	-	-	6	-
BARBER, M.	-	0/ 0	.000	0/ 0	.000	-/ 0	-	0	0	-	-	0	-
LIFTON, K.	-	0/ 1	.000	0/ 0	.000	-/ 1	-	0	0	-	-	0	-
Totals	200	47/94	.500	13/26	.500	-/65	-	27	26	-	-	107	.535

Houston (98) Coach: Guy Lewis

	Min.	Total FG / FGA	Pct.	FT / FTA	Pct.	Reb. O / T	A	TO	PF	S	Blk	TP	PPM
BELL, M.	-	0/ 0	.000	0/ 0	.000	-/ 0	0	1	1	-	-	0	-
TAYLOR	-	10/18	.556	6/11	.545	-/13	3	7	3	-	-	26	-
DAVIS, D.	-	7/14	.500	2/ 3	.667	-/ 9	0	5	4	-	-	16	-
GRIBBEN, T.	-	6/16	.375	5/ 9	.556	-/10	4	3	5	-	-	17	-
WELCH, P.	-	5/18	.278	4/ 5	.800	-/ 5	8	2	4	-	-	14	-
HICKMAN, J.	-	7/12	.583	2/ 2	1.000	-/ 6	1	3	3	-	-	16	-
HALL, B.	-	2/ 5	.400	0/ 0	.000	-/ 4	0	1	1	-	-	4	-
WILLIS, O.	-	0/ 3	.000	1/ 3	.333	-/ 0	1	1	0	-	-	1	-
EVANS, M.	-	0/ 2	.000	0/ 0	.000	-/ 0	1	2	3	-	-	0	-
YOUNGDALE, J.	-	2/ 2	1.000	0/ 0	.000	-/ 0	0	0	0	-	-	4	-
Totals	200	39/90	.433	20/33	.606	-/47	18	25	24	-	-	98	.490

Team Rebounds: Kansas State 6; Houston 6. Disqualified: Kansas State—Venable, Hughes; Houston—Gribben.

	1st Half	2nd Half	Final
Kansas State	51	56	107
Houston	46	52	98

REGIONAL THIRD PLACE WEST

Santa Clara (89)   Coach: Dick Garibaldi

	Min.	Total FG/FGA	Pct.	FT/FTA	Pct.	Reb. O/T	A	TO	PF	S	Blk	TP	PPM
OGDEN, R.	-	9/28	.321	3/4	.750	-/7	-	-	4	-	-	21	-
TOBIN, B.	-	2/4	.500	0/0	.000	-/6	-	-	1	-	-	4	-
AWTREY, D.	-	15/17	.882	7/11	.636	-/13	-	-	2	-	-	37	-
EAGLESON, K.	-	0/2	.000	2/3	.667	-/3	-	-	4	-	-	2	-
PAULSON, K.	-	1/3	.333	0/0	.000	-/2	-	-	1	-	-	2	-
PETERSEN, M.	-	1/2	.500	0/0	.000	-/0	-	-	0	-	-	2	-
SPIGHT, J.	-	4/8	.500	3/3	1.000	-/4	-	-	3	-	-	11	-
LUNCEFORD, T.	-	0/1	.000	0/0	.000	-/3	-	-	0	-	-	0	-
BOCHTE, B.	-	4/5	.800	2/2	1.000	-/1	-	-	3	-	-	10	-
Totals	200	36/70	.514	17/23	.739	-/39	-	-	18	-	-	89	.445

Long Beach State (86)   Coach: Jerry Tarkanian

	Min.	Total FG/FGA	Pct.	FT/FTA	Pct.	Reb. O/T	A	TO	PF	S	Blk	TP	PPM
ROBINSON, S.	-	6/15	.400	3/4	.750	-/6	-	-	2	-	-	15	-
MONTGOMERY, A.	-	1/6	.167	3/3	1.000	-/9	-	-	3	-	-	5	-
TRAPP, G.	-	6/16	.375	5/6	.833	-/10	-	-	5	-	-	17	-
GRITTON, R.	-	5/13	.385	3/3	1.000	-/3	-	-	0	-	-	13	-
JOHNSON, S.	-	6/19	.316	3/3	1.000	-/8	-	-	1	-	-	15	-
MCLUCAS, D.	-	2/2	1.000	0/0	.000	-/5	-	-	3	-	-	4	-
JANKANS, B.	-	7/12	.583	1/2	.500	-/5	-	-	4	-	-	15	-
TAYLOR, D.	-	0/1	.000	2/2	1.000	-/1	-	-	1	-	-	2	-
Totals	200	33/84	.393	20/23	.870	-/47	-	-	19	-	-	86	.430

Team Rebounds: Santa Clara 5; Long Beach St. 3. Disqualified: Long Beach St.—Trapp.

	1st Half	2nd Half	Final
Santa Clara	51	38	89
Long Beach St.	50	36	86

✪ ALL-STAR TEAMS ✪

ALL TOURNAMENT		MIDEAST REGIONAL		MIDWEST REGIONAL	
JIMMY COLLINS	NEW MEXICO ST.	FRED BROWN	IOWA	★ JIMMY COLLINS	NEW MEXICO ST.
ARTIS GILMORE	JACKSONVILLE	★ AUSTIN CARR	NOTRE DAME	DAVID HALL	KANSAS STATE
CURTIS ROWE	UCLA	ARTIS GILMORE	JACKSONVILLE	SAM LACEY	NEW MEXICO ST.
JOHN VALLELY	UCLA	DAN ISSEL	KENTUCKY	JERRY VENABLE	KANSAS STATE
★ SIDNEY WICKS	UCLA	REX MORGAN	JACKSONVILLE	AL WILLIAMS	DRAKE

★ Most Outstanding Player(s)

✪ INDIVIDUAL RECORDS ✪

SCORING

Most points in a single game
1 AUSTIN CARR, NOTRE DAME (vs. OHIO) — 61
2 AUSTIN CARR, NOTRE DAME (vs. KENTUCKY) — 52
3 AUSTIN CARR, NOTRE DAME (vs. IOWA) — 45
4 DAN ISSEL, KENTUCKY (vs. NOTRE DAME) — 44
5 DENNIS AWTREY, SANTA CLARA (vs. LONG BEACH ST.) — 37

Most total points in the tournament
1 AUSTIN CARR, NOTRE DAME — 158
2 ARTIS GILMORE, JACKSONVILLE — 132
3 JIMMY COLLINS, NEW MEXICO ST. — 117
4 REX MORGAN, JACKSONVILLE — 102
5 CALVIN MURPHY, NIAGARA — 88

Highest scoring average (minimum 2 games)
1 AUSTIN CARR, NOTRE DAME (158-3) — 52.67
2 DAN ISSEL, KENTUCKY (72-2) — 36.00
3 VANN WILLIFORD, N.C. STATE (71-2) — 35.50
4 DENNIS AWTREY, SANTA CLARA (61-2) — 30.50
5 CALVIN MURPHY, NIAGARA (88-3) — 29.33

FIELD GOALS

Most field goals in a single game
1 AUSTIN CARR, NOTRE DAME (vs. OHIO) — 25
2 AUSTIN CARR, NOTRE DAME (vs. KENTUCKY) — 22
3 AUSTIN CARR, NOTRE DAME (vs. IOWA) — 21
4 DAN ISSEL, KENTUCKY (vs. NOTRE DAME) — 17
5 2 tied for fifth place.

Most total field goals in the tournament
1 AUSTIN CARR, NOTRE DAME — 68
2 ARTIS GILMORE, JACKSONVILLE — 52
3 JIMMY COLLINS, NEW MEXICO ST. — 49
4 REX MORGAN, JACKSONVILLE — 37
5 MATT GANTT, ST. BONAVENTURE — 36

Most field goal attempts in a single game
1 AUSTIN CARR, NOTRE DAME (vs. OHIO) — 44
2 AUSTIN CARR, NOTRE DAME (vs. IOWA) — 39
3 AUSTIN CARR, NOTRE DAME (vs. KENTUCKY) — 35
3 MARVIN ROBERTS, UTAH STATE (vs. UCLA) — 35
5 JOHN JOHNSON, IOWA (vs. NOTRE DAME) — 31

Most total field goal attempts in tournament
1 AUSTIN CARR, NOTRE DAME — 118
2 ARTIS GILMORE, JACKSONVILLE — 107
3 JIMMY COLLINS, NEW MEXICO ST. — 99
4 MATT GANTT, ST. BONAVENTURE — 88
5 CALVIN MURPHY, NIAGARA — 72

Highest field goal percentage in a single game (minimum 10 attempts)
1 PEMBROOK BURROWS, JACKSONVILLE (vs. IOWA) (11-12) — .917
2 DENNIS AWTREY, SANTA CLARA (vs. LONG BEACH ST.) (15-17) — .882
3 SIDNEY WICKS, UCLA (vs. NEW MEXICO ST.) (10-12) — .833
4 RICK ANHEUSER, N.C. STATE (vs. NIAGARA) (12-15) — .800
5 BILL KALBAUGH, ST. BONAVENTURE (vs. DAVIDSON) (8-11) — .727

Highest field goal percentage in the tournament (minimum 20 attempts)
1 PEMBROOK BURROWS, JACKSONVILLE (24-33) — .727
1 DENNIS AWTREY, SANTA CLARA (24-33) — .727
3 RICK ANHEUSER, N.C. STATE (15-21) — .714
4 SIDNEY WICKS, UCLA (33-49) — .674
5 CHAD CALABRIA, IOWA (22-34) — .647

FREE THROWS

Most free throws in a single game
1 VANN WILLIFORD, N.C. STATE (vs. NIAGARA) — 14
2 OLLIE TAYLOR, HOUSTON (vs. DAYTON) — 12
3 ARTIS GILMORE, JACKSONVILLE (vs. ST. BONAVENTURE) — 11
3 AUSTIN CARR, NOTRE DAME (vs. OHIO) — 11
5 5 tied for fifth place.

Most total free throws in the tournament
1 REX MORGAN, JACKSONVILLE — 28
1 ARTIS GILMORE, JACKSONVILLE — 28
3 GREG NELSON, JACKSONVILLE — 26
4 CURTIS ROWE, UCLA — 25
5 VANN WILLIFORD, N.C. STATE — 23

Most free throws attempted in a single game
1 VANN WILLIFORD, N.C. STATE (vs. NIAGARA) — 16
2 ARTIS GILMORE, JACKSONVILLE (vs. ST. BONAVENTURE) — 15
3 DAN ISSEL, KENTUCKY (vs. NOTRE DAME) — 14
3 AUSTIN CARR, NOTRE DAME (vs. OHIO) — 14
3 OLLIE TAYLOR, HOUSTON (vs. DAYTON) — 14

Most free throws attempted in the tournament

1. ARTIS GILMORE, JACKSONVILLE — 43
2. REX MORGAN, JACKSONVILLE — 37
3. CURTIS ROWE, UCLA — 33
4. GREG NELSON, JACKSONVILLE — 32
5. OLLIE TAYLOR, HOUSTON — 30

Highest free throw percentage in a single game (minimum 7 attempts)

1. GLENN VIDNOVIC, IOWA (vs. NOTRE DAME) (10-10) — 1.000
2. CHIP DUBLIN, JACKSONVILLE (vs. ST. BONAVENTURE) (9-9) — 1.000
2. CALVIN MURPHY, NIAGARA (vs. N.C. STATE) (9-9) — 1.000
4. 3 tied for fourth place.

Highest free throw percentage in the tournament (minimum 15 attempts)

1. CHIP DUBLIN, JACKSONVILLE (19-20) — .950
2. CALVIN MURPHY, NIAGARA (20-22) — .909
3. GLENN VIDNOVIC, IOWA (18-21) — .857
3. HENRY BIBBY, UCLA (18-21) — .857
5. AUSTIN CARR, NOTRE DAME (22-26) — .846

REBOUNDS

Most rebounds in a single game

1. SAM LACEY, NEW MEXICO ST. (vs. DRAKE) — 24
2. ARTIS GILMORE, JACKSONVILLE (vs. ST. BONAVENTURE) — 21
2. LEE TRESS, TEMPLE (vs. VILLANOVA) — 21

2. DAVID HALL, KANSAS STATE (vs. NEW MEXICO ST.) — 21
5. 2 tied for fifth place.

Most total rebounds in the tournament

1. ARTIS GILMORE, JACKSONVILLE — 93
2. SAM LACEY, NEW MEXICO ST. — 90
3. MATT GANTT, ST. BONAVENTURE — 63
4. SIDNEY WICKS, UCLA — 53
5. 2 tied for fifth place.

Most rebounds per game (minimum 2 games)

1. DAVID HALL, KANSAS STATE (40-2) — 20.00
2. ARTIS GILMORE, JACKSONVILLE (93-5) — 18.60
3. SAM LACEY, NEW MEXICO ST. (90-5) — 18.00
4. BOB LANIER, ST. BONAVENTURE (48-3) — 16.00
5. MARVIN ROBERTS, UTAH STATE (47-3) — 15.67

✪ TEAM RECORDS ✪

SCORING

Most points in a single game

1. IOWA (vs. NOTRE DAME) — 121
2. NOTRE DAME (vs. OHIO) — 112
3. 2 tied for third place.

Most total points in the tournament

1. JACKSONVILLE — 479
2. ST. BONAVENTURE — 418
3. NEW MEXICO ST. — 414

Highest scoring average (minimum 2 games)

1. IOWA (224-2) — 112.00
2. NOTRE DAME (317-3) — 105.67
3. KENTUCKY (209-2) — 104.50

FIELD GOALS

Most field goals in a single game

1. IOWA (vs. NOTRE DAME) — 52
2. KANSAS STATE (vs. HOUSTON) — 47
3. NOTRE DAME (vs. OHIO) — 46

Most total field goals in the tournament

1. JACKSONVILLE — 180
2. ST. BONAVENTURE — 174
3. NEW MEXICO ST. — 159

Most field goals attempted in a single game

1. IOWA (vs. NOTRE DAME) — 98
2. NOTRE DAME (vs. IOWA) — 97
3. 2 tied for third place.

Most total field goals attempted in the tournament

1. ST. BONAVENTURE — 379
2. NEW MEXICO ST. — 359
3. JACKSONVILLE — 358

Highest field goal percentage in a single game

1. KENTUCKY (vs. NOTRE DAME) (43-72) — .597
2. JACKSONVILLE (vs. WESTERN KY.) (40-70) — .571
3. JACKSONVILLE (vs. IOWA) (43-76) — .566

Highest field goal percentage in the tournament (minimum 2 games)

1. IOWA (94-181) — .520
2. KENTUCKY (83-161) — .516
3. JACKSONVILLE (180-358) — .503

FREE THROWS

Most free throws in a single game

1. JACKSONVILLE (vs. ST. BONAVENTURE) — 37
2. NEW MEXICO ST. (vs. DRAKE) — 31
3. 2 tied for third place.

Most total free throws in the tournament

1. JACKSONVILLE — 119
2. NEW MEXICO ST. — 96
3. UCLA — 92

Most free throws attempted in a single game

1. JACKSONVILLE (vs. ST. BONAVENTURE) — 45
1. NEW MEXICO ST. (vs. DRAKE) — 45
3. JACKSONVILLE (vs. WESTERN KY.) — 43

Most total free throws attempted in the tournament

1. JACKSONVILLE — 161
2. NEW MEXICO ST. — 135
3. UCLA — 132

Highest free throw percentage in a single game

1. IOWA (vs. NOTRE DAME) (17-19) — .895
1. HOUSTON (vs. DAYTON) (17-19) — .895
3. NOTRE DAME (vs. IOWA) (16-18) — .889

Highest free throw percentage in the tournament (minimum 2 games)

1. LONG BEACH ST. (49-62) — .790
2. NIAGARA (56-72) — .778
3. UTAH STATE (55-72) — .764

Fewest free throws in a single game

1. DAYTON (vs. HOUSTON) — 6
2. JACKSONVILLE (vs. UCLA) — 7
3. LONG BEACH ST. (vs. UCLA) — 9

Lowest free throw percentage in a single game

1. KANSAS STATE (vs. NEW MEXICO ST.) (12-29) — .414
2. OHIO (vs. NOTRE DAME) (10-20) — .500
3. KANSAS STATE (vs. HOUSTON) (13-26) — .500

Lowest free throw percentage in the tournament (minimum 2 games)

1. KANSAS STATE (25-55) — .455
2. DRAKE (30-50) — .600
3. VILLANOVA (45-71) — .634

REBOUNDS

Most rebounds in a single game

1. KANSAS STATE (vs. HOUSTON) — 65
2. KANSAS STATE (vs. NEW MEXICO ST.) — 58
2. NEW MEXICO ST. (vs. RICE) — 58

Most rebounds per game (minimum 2 games)

1. KANSAS STATE (123-2) — 61.50
2. NEW MEXICO ST. (243-5) — 48.60
3. UCLA (193-4) — 48.25

1971

FIRST ROUND | REGIONAL SEMIFINAL | REGIONAL FINAL | **FINAL FOUR** | REGIONAL FINAL | REGIONAL SEMIFINAL | FIRST ROUND

EAST

*Villanova 93
St. Joseph's 75
*Villanova 85

Fordham 105
Furman 74
Fordham 75

*Villanova 90

Pennsylvania 70
Duquesne 65
Pennsylvania 79

Pennsylvania 47

(bye)
S. Carolina 64

*Villanova 92 (2 ot)

MIDEAST

*Western Ky. 74
Jacksonville 72
*Western Ky. 107

(bye)
Kentucky 83

*Western Ky. 81 (ot)

(bye)
Ohio St. 60

Ohio St. 78

Marquette 62
Miami (Ohio) 47
Marquette 59

*Western Ky. 89

MIDWEST

Kansas 78
(bye)

Houston 72
New Mexico St. 69
Houston 77

Kansas 73

Drake 79 (ot)
(bye)

Notre Dame 102
TCU 94
Notre Dame 72

Drake 71

Kansas 60

WEST

UCLA 91
(bye)

Brigham Young 91
Utah St. 82
Brigham Young 73

UCLA 57

*Long Beach St. 77
Weber St. 66
*Long Beach St. 78

Pacific 65
(bye)

*Long Beach St. 55

UCLA 68

Kansas 60

UCLA 68
*Villanova 62

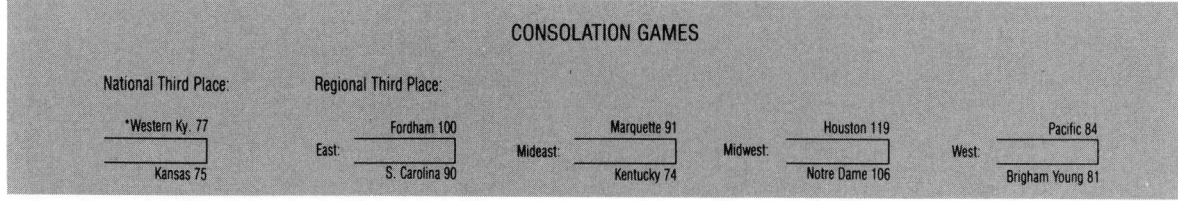
*Villanova's, Western Kentucky's, and Long Beach State's participation in 1971 tournament vacated.

They beat you with the fast break, they beat you with the press. They beat you with hot shooting, and with defense. They beat you with their lightning-quick guards, with a dominating center, with powerful, versatile forwards. By 1971, opposing coaches were at the point of wondering "what else can Wooden come up with to beat us with?"

In 1971 the prophet of the press, the guru of the fast break, the Wizard of Westwood, stalled.

Unlike the 1964 Bruins, with their blinding speed, or the 1967 team, so physically dominant that they won all but four of their games by 15 points or more, the 1971 UCLA squad won as much on heart as on talent. They went 29-1, but eight of their victories were by five points or less. They were a bunch of scrappers. Still, they were UCLA, and after six titles in seven years, one would have been hard-pressed to bet against them.

The Bruins may not have been the powerhouse of years past, but they were still the favorites. The year's Final Four newcomers, on the other hand, were Villanova and Western Kentucky. Kansas, with its long basketball tradition, rounded out the semifinal round.

The Western Kentucky Hilltoppers, in their half-century of varsity basketball, had not only never reached the NCAA semifinal round, they had also always been regarded as big-time Kentucky's poor country cousins—Rupp's Wildcats had never even deigned to put Western on their schedule. But after the Hilltoppers' 7-footer Jim McDaniels outplayed Jacksonville's Artis Gilmore, and Western overcame a 14-point halftime deficit to qualify for the Mideast regional semi against Kentucky, Rupp had no choice but to play the upstarts from Bowling Green. In a victory made even sweeter by a half century of disdain, the Hilltoppers sent their hifalutin' opponents back to Lexington with a 107-83 thrashing.

The favorite to win the Mideast regional, Marquette, had entered the tournament undefeated. But with five minutes left and a 5-point lead against Ohio State, their All-American guard, Dean "The Dream" Meminger fouled out. With seven seconds remaining, Marquette still had a 1-point lead and the ball, but Allie McGuire (Coach Al McGuire's son) stepped on the end line on an in-bounds play. After the turnover, he fouled Buckeye Allen Hornyak, who calmly sank the game-winning free throws and sent Ohio State into the regional final with Western Kentucky. The Buckeyes' luck ran out when the Hilltoppers pulled out an overtime victory.

In the East, the unbeaten, No. 3–ranked Penn Quakers were humiliated by Villanova 90-47 in the regional final. In the Final Four, the Philadelphians had a much harder time getting past Western Kentucky. After 39 minutes and 56 seconds of action, Villanova's Hank Siemiontkowski, who had scored 31 points, picked up his fifth personal foul, sending the Hilltoppers' Jerry Dunn to the line with a chance to break a 74-74 deadlock. Dunn didn't do it, and two overtimes later Villanova became the first northeastern team in 16 years to qualify for the championship game.

Their opponent was, as expected, UCLA. None of the Bruins' previous championship teams had ever averaged less than 80 points a game in the tournament, but the 1971 edition averaged only 69 in their four NCAA games. Against Jerry Tarkanian's Long Beach State 49ers, the Bruins faced an 11-point deficit and shot an unbelievably low 29 percent from the floor. Still they managed to win 57-55 when the 49ers' star sophomore Ed Ratleff fouled out with more than five minutes remaining and Sidney Wicks hit four free throws in the last 25 seconds to provide the final margin of victory. The Kansas Jayhawks, who had barely gotten by Drake in their regional final, were then efficiently disposed of by UCLA.

In the final UCLA came up against an excellent, effective Villanova zone. Wooden wanted the Wildcats in a man-to-man, so he ordered a tactic to force them out of the zone—a stall. UCLA held the ball while a big Astrodome crowd booed and Villanova's players taunted the usually fast-moving Bruins, urging them to "play ball."

But John Wooden didn't become the game's most successful coach by doing what others wanted him to do; he won by forcing the opposition to play his game. And at the end of the 1971 tournament he did it again. His Bruins controlled the tempo, taking only 12 second-half shots and making 8, while limiting Villanova to a mere eight second-half rebounds. Once they were forced into playing man-to-man, the Wildcats actually—unexpectedly—became more effective. They cut into the UCLA lead and were down by only 3 with 1:53 left to play. But UCLA knew how to win. Steve Patterson, in his final college game, bettered his career best by 7 points with 29 (he had 20 at the half on 9 for 13 shooting), and Sidney Wicks, the Bruins' star forward, took only seven shots all game and was outscored by Villanova's Howard Porter 25 to 7, but he contributed seven assists and nine rebounds to help insure the Bruins' 68-62 victory.

After accepting his seventh championship trophy in eight years, John Wooden looked ahead to the following season, when he would lose six of his top seven players. "I expect to have a good basketball team next year," said a confident Wizard of Westwood. "Certainly we'll have to go with youngsters."

FIRST ROUND EAST

Villanova (93) Coach: Jack Kraft

	Min.	Total FG/FGA	Pct.	FT/FTA	Pct.	Reb. O/T	A	TO	PF	S	Blk	TP	PPM
PORTER, H.	-	9/20	.450	8/11	.727	-/18	1	-	4	-	-	26	-
SMITH, C.	-	5/12	.417	3/ 4	.750	-/ 9	1	-	3	-	-	13	-
SIEMIONTKOSKI, H.	-	9/20	.450	5/ 5	1.000	-/11	1	-	5	-	-	23	-
FORD, C.	-	2/ 9	.222	3/ 3	1.000	-/ 9	10	-	4	-	-	7	-
INGLESBY, T.	-	6/ 9	.667	8/12	.667	-/ 3	5	-	0	-	-	20	-
MCDOWELL, J.	-	0/ 0	.000	0/ 1	.000	-/ 5	0	-	1	-	-	0	-
GOHL, B.	-	1/ 1	1.000	0/ 1	.000	-/ 1	1	-	0	-	-	2	-
FOX, J.	-	1/ 1	1.000	0/ 0	.000	-/ 0	0	-	1	-	-	2	-
DALY, M.	-	0/ 0	.000	0/ 0	.000	-/ 0	0	-	0	-	-	0	-
Totals	200	33/72	.458	27/37	.730	-/56	19	-	18	-	-	93	.465

St. Joseph's (75) Coach: Jack McKinney

	Min.	Total FG/FGA	Pct.	FT/FTA	Pct.	Reb. O/T	A	TO	PF	S	Blk	TP	PPM
CONNOLLY, J.	-	6/10	.600	3/ 3	1.000	-/ 5	1	-	5	-	-	15	-
MCFARLAND, P.	-	6/20	.300	2/ 3	.667	-/ 2	5	-	2	-	-	14	-
BANTOM, M.	-	7/15	.467	6/ 8	.750	-/14	1	-	4	-	-	20	-
SNYDER, J.	-	4/ 6	.667	2/ 2	1.000	-/ 2	3	-	4	-	-	10	-
MOODY, M.	-	1/ 6	.167	2/ 3	.667	-/ 5	7	-	4	-	-	4	-
MCCOLLUM, J.	-	2/ 9	.222	2/ 3	.667	-/ 2	1	-	5	-	-	6	-
MITCHELL, E.	-	3/ 5	.600	0/ 1	.000	-/ 3	0	-	2	-	-	6	-
MARKS, B.	-	0/ 0	.000	0/ 0	.000	-/ 0	0	-	0	-	-	0	-
SABUL, B.	-	0/ 2	.000	0/ 0	.000	-/ 1	0	-	0	-	-	0	-
HAAS, B.	-	0/ 0	.000	0/ 0	.000	-/ 0	0	-	0	-	-	0	-
KRUTSICK, J.	-	0/ 0	.000	0/ 0	.000	-/ 0	0	-	0	-	-	0	-
Totals	200	29/73	.397	17/23	.739	-/34	18	-	26	-	-	75	.375

Team Rebounds: Villanova 3; St. Joseph's 6. Disqualified: Villanova—Siemiontkoski; St. Joseph's—Connolly, McCollum.

	1st Half	2nd Half	Final
Villanova	49	44	93
St. Joseph's	38	37	75

Pennsylvania (70) Coach: Dick Harter

	Min.	Total FG/FGA	Pct.	FT/FTA	Pct.	Reb. O/T	A	TO	PF	S	Blk	TP	PPM
MORSE, B.	40	10/22	.455	4/ 6	.667	-/16	0	-	3	-	-	24	.600
HANKINSON, P.	15	2/ 3	.667	0/ 0	.000	-/ 3	1	-	0	-	-	4	.267
WOLF, J.	18	1/ 1	1.000	0/ 0	.000	-/ 4	0	-	3	-	-	2	.111
CALHOUN, C.	40	4/ 9	.444	3/ 3	1.000	-/ 5	1	-	3	-	-	11	.275
LITTLEPAGE, C.	16	0/ 3	.000	0/ 2	.000	-/ 4	0	-	0	-	-	0	.000
BILSKY, S.	31	2/ 8	.250	6/ 6	1.000	-/ 3	5	-	3	-	-	10	.323
WOHL, D.	40	7/17	.412	5/ 8	.625	-/ 1	1	-	2	-	-	19	.475
Totals	200	26/63	.413	18/25	.720	-/36	8	5	14	-	-	70	.350

Fordham (105) Coach: Digger Phelps

	Min.	Total FG/FGA	Pct.	FT/FTA	Pct.	Reb. O/T	A	TO	PF	S	Blk	TP	PPM
YELVERTON, C.	-	11/24	.458	8/14	.571	-/19	-	-	2	-	-	30	-
MAINOR, W.	-	8/15	.533	3/ 4	.750	-/ 6	-	-	2	-	-	19	-
CHARLES, K.	-	8/16	.500	2/ 7	.286	-/10	-	-	3	-	-	18	-
WOYTOWICZ, B.	-	9/14	.643	0/ 0	.000	-/13	-	-	4	-	-	18	-
ZAMBETTI, G.	-	3/ 3	1.000	0/ 0	.000	-/ 1	-	-	1	-	-	6	-
SULLIVAN, T.	-	0/ 2	.000	2/ 2	1.000	-/ 2	-	-	4	-	-	2	-
BURIK, J.	-	2/ 4	.500	0/ 1	.000	-/ 2	-	-	4	-	-	4	-
PIPICH, T.	-	1/ 2	.500	2/ 2	1.000	-/ 0	-	-	0	-	-	4	-
LARBES, R.	-	2/ 3	.667	0/ 0	.000	-/ 0	-	-	1	-	-	4	-
CAIN, S.	-	0/ 2	.000	0/ 0	.000	-/ 0	-	-	0	-	-	0	-
CARLESIMO, P.	-	0/ 0	.000	0/ 0	.000	-/ 0	-	-	0	-	-	0	-
GRISWOLD, P.	-	0/ 0	.000	0/ 0	.000	-/ 0	-	-	0	-	-	0	-
Totals	200	44/85	.518	17/30	.567	-/53	-	-	21	-	-	105	.525

Furman (74) Coach: Joe Williams

	Min.	Total FG/FGA	Pct.	FT/FTA	Pct.	Reb. O/T	A	TO	PF	S	Blk	TP	PPM
JACKSON, D.	-	4/12	.333	3 5	.600	-/ 2	-	-	3	-	-	11	-
COLLIER, B.	-	4/ 8	.500	3/ 4	.750	-/ 3	-	-	1	-	-	11	-
MARTIN, J.	-	2/ 6	.333	1/ 2	.500	-/ 2	-	-	3	-	-	5	-
THOMAS, L.	-	10/20	.500	1/ 4	.250	-/14	-	-	1	-	-	21	-
SELVY, C.	-	4/ 6	.667	1/ 3	.333	-/ 2	-	-	2	-	-	9	-
COCKRUM, S.	-	4/10	.400	5/ 8	.625	-/10	-	-	3	-	-	13	-
DOUGHERTY, S.	-	0/ 3	.000	2/ 3	.667	-/ 3	-	-	5	-	-	2	-
WHITNER, D.	-	0/ 0	.000	0/ 0	.000	-/ 1	-	-	1	-	-	0	-
EHLMAN, S.	-	0/ 0	.000	0/ 0	000	-/ 1	-	-	0	-	-	0	-
CAMPBELL, J.	-	1/ 2	.500	0/ 0	.000	-/ 0	-	-	0	-	-	2	-
Totals	200	29/67	.433	16/29	.552	-/38	-	-	19	-	-	74	.370

Team Rebounds: Fordham 7; Furman 7. Disqualified: Furman—Dougherty.

	1st Half	2nd Half	Final
Fordham	50	55	105
Furman	30	44	74

Duquesne (65) Coach: Red Manning

	Min.	Total FG/FGA	Pct.	FT/FTA	Pct.	Reb. O/T	A	TO	PF	S	Blk	TP	PPM
DAVIS, M.	40	7/16	.438	2/ 4	.500	-/12	4	-	3	-	-	16	.400
NELSON, B.	23	3/ 6	.500	0/ 0	.000	-/ 3	1	-	3	-	-	6	.261
NELSON, G.	36	4/ 9	.444	3/ 5	.600	-/13	2	-	3	-	-	11	.306
DURHAM, J.	40	3/11	.273	4/ 7	.571	-/ 6	1	-	3	-	-	10	.250
BARR, J.	23	1/ 2	.500	0/ 0	.000	-/ 2	0	-	3	-	-	2	.087
MCHUGH, S.	17	5/ 7	.714	2/ 2	1.000	-/ 3	0	-	3	-	-	12	.706
WOJDOWSKI, J.	21	4/ 6	.667	0/ 0	.000	-/ 1	1	-	2	-	-	8	.381
Totals	200	27/57	.474	11/18	.611	-/40	9	14	20	-	-	65	.325

Team Rebounds: Pennsylvania 2; Duquesne 3. Disqualified: None.

	1st Half	2nd Half	Final
Pennsylvania	32	38	70
Duquesne	28	37	65

FIRST ROUND MIDEAST

Western Kentucky (74)   Coach: Johnny Oldham

	Min.	Total FG / FGA	Pct.	FT / FTA	Pct.	Reb. O / T	A	TO	PF	S	Blk	TP	PPM
ROSE, J.	-	6/17	.353	1/ 2	.500	-/ 7	5	2	2	-	-	13	-
BAILEY, R.	-	3/ 7	.429	0/ 1	.000	-/ 6	5	4	3	-	-	6	-
McDANIELS, J.	-	11/28	.393	1/ 4	.250	-/13	1	1	4	-	-	23	-
DUNN, J.	-	5/16	.313	1/ 4	.250	-/10	2	4	5	-	-	11	-
GLOVER, C.	-	8/21	.381	0/ 1	.000	-/17	3	4	2	-	-	16	-
SUDMACKER, G.	-	0/ 0	.000	0/ 0	.000	-/ 2	0	2	1	-	-	0	-
WITT, C.	-	2/ 7	.286	1/ 1	1.000	-/ 0	2	0	1	-	-	5	-
Totals	200	35/96	.365	4/13	.308	-/55	18	17	18	-	-	74	.370

Jacksonville (72)   Coach: Tom Wasdin

	Min.	Total FG / FGA	Pct.	FT / FTA	Pct.	Reb. O / T	A	TO	PF	S	Blk	TP	PPM
DUBLIN, C.	-	2/ 5	.400	1/ 2	.500	-/ 3	3	4	2	-	-	5	-
FOX, H.	-	9/18	.500	1/ 1	1.000	-/ 6	6	6	2	-	-	19	-
GILMORE, A.	-	3/10	.300	6/10	.600	-/22	2	7	1	-	-	12	-
BURROWS, P.	-	0/ 6	.000	1/ 3	.333	-/ 8	2	5	3	-	-	1	-
FLEMING, E.	-	8/15	.533	2/ 2	1.000	-/ 8	0	3	4	-	-	18	-
WEDEKING, V.	-	3/ 8	.375	1/ 3	.333	-/ 3	5	6	0	-	-	7	-
BALDWIN, R.	-	0/ 0	.000	0/ 0	.000	-/ 0	0	0	0	-	-	0	-
BLEVINS, M.	-	3/ 3	1.000	0/ 0	.000	-/ 2	1	1	2	-	-	6	-
NELSON, G.	-	2/ 2	1.000	0/ 0	.000	-/ 0	0	1	3	-	-	4	-
Totals	200	30/67	.448	12/21	.571	-/52	19	33	17	-	-	72	.360

Team Rebounds: Western Ky. 6; Jacksonville 3. Disqualified: Western Ky.—Dunn.

	1st Half	2nd Half	Final
Western Ky.	30	44	74
Jacksonville	44	28	72

Marquette (62)   Coach: Al McGuire

	Min.	Total FG / FGA	Pct.	FT / FTA	Pct.	Reb. O / T	A	TO	PF	S	Blk	TP	PPM
LACKEY, B.	-	4/ 8	.500	0/ 1	.000	-/12	-	-	4	-	-	8	-
BRELL, G.	-	0/ 2	.000	0/ 0	.000	-/ 2	-	-	1	-	-	0	-
CHONES, J.	-	9/13	.692	3/ 6	.500	-/14	-	-	0	-	-	21	-
McGUIRE, A.	-	4/ 6	.667	0/ 1	.000	-/ 1	-	-	2	-	-	8	-
MEMINGER, D.	-	6/ 9	.667	9/12	.750	-/ 2	-	-	2	-	-	21	-
SPYCHALLA, K.	-	0/ 0	.000	0/ 0	.000	-/ 0	-	-	0	-	-	0	-
LAM, G.	-	0/ 1	.000	0/ 0	.000	-/ 0	-	-	0	-	-	0	-
GRZESK, G.	-	0/ 0	.000	0/ 0	.000	-/ 1	-	-	0	-	-	0	-
McMAHON, H.	-	1/ 3	.333	0/ 1	.000	-/ 6	-	-	4	-	-	2	-
FRAZIER, G.	-	1/ 1	1.000	0/ 0	.000	-/ 3	-	-	1	-	-	2	-
MILLS, M.	-	0/ 0	.000	0/ 1	.000	-/ 0	-	-	0	-	-	0	-
Totals	200	25/43	.581	12/22	.545	-/42	-	18	14	-	-	62	.310

Miami (Ohio) (47)   Coach: Darrell Hedric

	Min.	Total FG / FGA	Pct.	FT / FTA	Pct.	Reb. O / T	A	TO	PF	S	Blk	TP	PPM
SEARS, J.	-	4/ 8	.500	8/ 9	.889	-/ 3	-	-	2	-	-	16	-
MEYER, T.	-	0/ 5	.000	0/ 0	.000	-/ 1	-	-	3	-	-	0	-
ROBERTS, T.	-	3/ 6	.500	0/ 1	.000	-/ 5	-	-	1	-	-	6	-
DUNLAP, D.	-	1/ 6	.167	3/ 3	1.000	-/ 2	-	-	2	-	-	5	-
NEIKAMP, R.	-	4/10	.400	0/ 0	.000	-/ 5	-	-	2	-	-	8	-
WREN, M.	-	1/ 5	.200	1/ 3	.333	-/ 0	-	-	2	-	-	3	-
HANDY, S.	-	4/ 9	.444	1/ 2	.500	-/ 4	-	-	4	-	-	9	-
HILGEMAN, H.	-	0/ 0	.000	0/ 0	.000	-/ 0	-	-	0	-	-	0	-
BYRD, K.	-	0/ 1	.000	0/ 0	.000	-/ 1	-	-	0	-	-	0	-
Totals	200	17/50	.340	13/18	.722	-/21	-	13	16	-	-	47	.235

Team Rebounds: Marquette 1; Miami (Ohio) 2. Disqualified: None.

	1st Half	2nd Half	Final
Marquette	23	39	62
Miami (Ohio)	21	26	47

FIRST ROUND MIDWEST

Houston (72)   Coach: Guy Lewis

	Min.	Total FG / FGA	Pct.	FT / FTA	Pct.	Reb. O / T	A	TO	PF	S	Blk	TP	PPM
BONNEY, J.	34	1/ 5	.200	0/ 0	.000	-/ 3	3	0	0	0	-	2	.059
WILLIS, S.	7	0/ 1	.000	0/ 1	.000	-/ 0	0	0	1	0	-	0	.000
BROWN, L.	13	0/ 3	.000	0/ 0	.000	-/ 1	3	4	1	2	-	0	.000
WELCH, P.	40	9/18	.500	5/ 7	.714	-/ 4	7	6	1	2	-	23	.575
DAVIS, D.	38	11/19	.579	8/10	.800	-/ 8	3	0	5	1	-	30	.789
HALL, B.	33	4/ 7	.571	4/ 5	.800	-/13	2	3	3	0	-	12	.364
NEWSOME, S.	35	2/11	.182	1/ 1	1.000	-/10	2	3	4	1	-	5	.143
Totals	200	27/64	.422	18/24	.750	-/39	20	16	15	6	-	72	.360

New Mexico State (69)   Coach: Lou Henson

	Min.	Total FG / FGA	Pct.	FT / FTA	Pct.	Reb. O / T	A	TO	PF	S	Blk	TP	PPM
GREEN, E.	4	0/ 2	.000	0/ 0	.000	-/ 1	0	0	0	0	-	0	.000
MOORE, B.	27	0/ 2	.000	0/ 0	.000	-/ 0	1	2	4	0	-	0	.000
SCOTT, A.	34	13/22	.591	1/ 2	.500	-/ 6	9	2	4	1	-	27	.794
DAVIS, C.	14	1/ 3	.333	0/ 2	.000	-/ 1	0	2	2	1	-	2	.143
SMITH, J.	24	3/ 9	.333	2/ 2	1.000	-/ 5	2	4	3	0	-	8	.333
NEAL, R.	30	2/ 4	.500	2/ 4	.500	-/ 2	2	1	1	0	-	6	.200
WARD, H.	28	8/22	.364	5/ 8	.625	-/10	2	3	3	1	-	21	.750
REYES, C.	39	2/ 6	.333	1/ 1	1.000	-/10	5	4	2	2	-	5	.128
Totals	200	29/70	.414	11/19	.579	-/35	21	18	19	5	-	69	.345

Team Rebounds: Houston 11; New Mexico St. 7. Disqualified: Houston—Davis.

	1st Half	2nd Half	Final
Houston	28	44	72
New Mexico St.	36	33	69

Notre Dame (102)   Coach: Johnny Dee

	Min.	Total FG / FGA	Pct.	FT / FTA	Pct.	Reb. O / T	A	TO	PF	S	Blk	TP	PPM
EGART, J.	1	0/ 0	.000	0/ 0	.000	-/ 0	0	0	0	0	-	0	.000
SINNOTT, T.	2	0/ 0	.000	2/ 2	1.000	-/ 0	0	1	1	0	-	2	1.000
CARR, A.	40	20/34	.588	12/15	.800	-/ 6	6	1	1	5	-	52	1.300
MEEHAN, J.	40	4/ 8	.500	0/ 1	.000	-/ 1	11	2	2	2	-	8	.200
HINGA, B.	1	0/ 0	.000	0/ 0	.000	-/ 0	0	0	0	0	-	0	.000
JONES, C.	36	10/19	.526	6/ 8	.750	-/11	4	4	5	0	-	26	.722
CATLETT, S.	38	3/ 8	.375	1/ 1	1.000	-/ 9	3	4	4	0	-	7	.184
GEMMELL, D.	2	0/ 1	.000	0/ 0	.000	-/ 0	0	0	0	0	-	0	.000
SILENSKI, J.	1	0/ 0	.000	0/ 0	.000	-/ 0	0	0	0	0	-	0	.000
PLEICK, J.	38	3/ 6	.500	1/ 3	.333	-/ 8	1	3	5	0	-	7	.184
HINGA, J.	1	0/ 0	.000	0/ 0	.000	-/ 0	0	0	0	0	-	0	.000
Totals	200	40/76	.526	22/30	.733	-/35	25	15	18	7	-	102	.510

TCU (94)   Coach: Johnny Swaim

	Min.	Total FG / FGA	Pct.	FT / FTA	Pct.	Reb. O / T	A	TO	PF	S	Blk	TP	PPM
WILLIAMS, J.	31	8/12	.667	2/ 2	1.000	-/ 2	2	2	5	1	-	18	.581
FERGUSON, J.	40	4/10	.400	3/ 4	.750	-/ 4	11	5	3	2	-	11	.275
HURDLE, J.	1	0/ 0	.000	0/ 0	.000	-/ 0	0	0	0	0	-	0	.000
PARKER, J.	1	1/ 1	1.000	0/ 0	.000	-/ 0	0	0	0	0	-	2	2.000
HALL, R.	38	8/12	.667	2/ 3	.667	-/ 4	5	6	4	0	-	18	.474
VILLARREAL, C.	4	0/ 1	.000	0/ 0	.000	-/ 1	0	0	0	0	-	0	.000
SMITH, S.	1	0/ 0	.000	0/ 0	.000	-/ 0	0	0	0	0	-	0	.000
DEGRATE, S.	36	9/16	.563	4/ 7	.571	-/ 9	2	2	2	1	-	22	.611
ROYAL, E.	9	0/ 1	.000	0/ 0	.000	-/ 0	1	0	3	1	-	0	.000
HOUGH, K.	1	0/ 0	.000	0/ 0	.000	-/ 1	0	0	0	0	-	0	.000
STONE, M.	1	0/ 0	.000	0/ 0	.000	-/ 0	0	0	0	0	-	0	.000
KENNEDY, E.	37	10/20	.500	3/ 3	1.000	-/16	3	5	4	1	-	23	.622
Totals	200	40/73	.548	14/19	.737	-/37	24	20	21	6	-	94	.470

Team Rebounds: Notre Dame 3; TCU 8. Disqualified: Notre Dame—Jones, Pleick; TCU—Williams.

	1st Half	2nd Half	Final
Notre Dame	56	46	102
TCU	42	52	94

FIRST ROUND WEST

Brigham Young (91)   Coach: Stan Watts

	Min.	Total FG / FGA	Pct.	FT / FTA	Pct.	Reb. O / T	A	TO	PF	S	Blk	TP	PPM
FRYER, B.	-	6/ 8	.750	13/15	.867	-/ 5	2	3	2	-	-	25	-
KRESIMIR, C.	-	10/19	.526	10/12	.833	-/11	4	5	4	-	-	30	-
KELLY, S.	-	7/10	.700	4/ 5	.800	-/ 1	3	3	5	-	-	18	-
MILLER, J.	-	1/ 3	.333	4/ 8	.500	-/ 6	3	4	4	-	-	6	-
TOLLESTRUP, P.	-	4/ 9	.444	2/ 4	.500	-/ 2	5	1	3	-	-	10	-
BUNKER, J.	-	1/ 2	.500	0/ 0	.000	-/ 1	0	0	1	-	-	2	-
SARKALAHTI, K.	-	0/ 0	.000	0/ 0	.000	-/ 0	0	0	1	-	-	0	-
BAILEY, D.	-	0/ 0	.000	0/ 0	.000	-/ 0	0	0	0	-	-	0	-
BAKER, C.	-	0/ 0	.000	0/ 0	.000	-/ 1	0	0	0	-	-	0	-
JORGENSEN, C.	-	0/ 0	.000	0/ 0	.000	-/ 0	0	1	0	-	-	0	-
VAINIO, V.	-	0/ 0	.000	0/ 0	.000	-/ 0	0	0	0	-	-	0	-
Totals	200	29/51	.569	33/44	.750	-/27	17	17	20	-	-	91	.455

Long Beach State (77)   Coach: Jerry Tarkanian

	Min.	Total FG / FGA	Pct.	FT / FTA	Pct.	Reb. O / T	A	TO	PF	S	Blk	TP	PPM
TRAPP, G.	-	8/13	.615	5/ 5	1.000	-/ 5	3	5	5	-	-	21	-
RATLEFF, E.	-	10/15	.667	11/12	.917	-/13	1	3	1	-	-	31	-
TERRY, C.	-	1/ 6	.167	1/ 1	1.000	-/ 6	3	3	5	-	-	3	-
McWILLIAMS, E.	-	0/ 1	.000	1/ 2	.500	-/ 3	1	0	1	-	-	1	-
LYNN, R.	-	4/10	.400	4/ 5	.800	-/ 6	2	1	3	-	-	12	-
WILLIAMS, B.	-	2/ 6	.333	3/ 3	1.000	-/ 4	3	6	4	-	-	7	-
TAYLOR, D.	-	0/ 1	.000	2/ 2	1.000	-/ 0	1	2	1	-	-	2	-
McLUCAS, D.	-	0/ 0	.000	0/ 0	.000	-/ 0	0	0	0	-	-	0	-
EWASKY, R.	-	0/ 0	.000	0/ 0	.000	-/ 0	0	1	0	-	-	0	-
MILLER, R.	-	0/ 0	.000	0/ 0	.000	-/ 0	0	1	0	-	-	0	-
Totals	200	25/52	.481	27/30	.900	-/37	14	22	20	-	-	77	.385

Utah State (82)   Coach: Ladell Anderson

	Min.	Total FG / FGA	Pct.	FT / FTA	Pct.	Reb. O / T	A	TO	PF	S	Blk	TP	PPM
WILLIAMS, N.	-	11/21	.524	7/ 8	.875	-/ 6	1	2	5	-	-	29	-
WAKEFIELD, T.	-	2/ 6	.333	0/ 0	.000	-/ 1	2	3	5	-	-	4	-
LOVE, J.	-	3/ 6	.500	1/ 2	.500	-/ 7	0	2	4	-	-	7	-
LAURISKI, R.	-	9/16	.563	2/ 2	1.000	-/ 8	1	4	4	-	-	20	-
ROBERTS, M.	-	2/ 6	.333	3/ 4	.750	-/ 3	1	1	5	-	-	7	-
EPPS, E.	-	2/ 4	.500	3/ 3	1.000	-/ 2	2	4	1	-	-	7	-
TEBBS, J.	-	0/ 2	.000	0/ 0	.000	-/ 0	3	3	2	-	-	0	-
PAVLISH, B.	-	0/ 0	.000	0/ 0	.000	-/ 0	1	0	0	-	-	0	-
COOLEY, P.	-	0/ 0	.000	0/ 0	.000	-/ 0	0	0	0	-	-	0	-
BEES, W.	-	0/ 0	.000	0/ 0	.000	-/ 0	0	0	0	-	-	0	-
HATCH, R.	-	2/ 3	.667	2/ 2	1.000	-/ 1	0	1	2	-	-	6	-
THOMPSON, K.	-	1/ 1	1.000	0/ 0	.000	-/ 1	1	2	1	-	-	2	-
Totals	200	32/65	.492	18/21	.857	-/29	12	22	29	-	-	82	.410

Team Rebounds: Brigham Young 7; Utah State 6. Disqualified: Brigham Young—Kelly; Utah State—Williams, Wakefield, Roberts.

	1st Qtr.	2nd Qtr.	3rd Qtr.	4th Qtr.	Final
Brigham Young	22	23	23	23	91
Utah State	21	19	16	26	82

Weber State (66)   Coach: Phil Johnson

	Min.	Total FG / FGA	Pct.	FT / FTA	Pct.	Reb. O / T	A	TO	PF	S	Blk	TP	PPM
SOJOURNER, W.	-	4/10	.400	1/ 1	1.000	-/10	0	2	5	-	-	9	-
DAVIS, B.	-	3/16	.188	0/ 1	.000	-/ 9	2	2	3	-	-	6	-
SMALL, B.	-	2/16	.125	2/ 2	1.000	-/ 2	6	2	3	-	-	6	-
KNOBLE, B.	-	3/ 8	.375	5/ 9	.556	-/ 5	0	2	4	-	-	11	-
COOPER, R.	-	5/11	.455	5/ 5	1.000	-/ 5	0	2	4	-	-	15	-
ROSS, K.	-	7/13	.538	3/ 4	.750	-/ 5	0	1	1	-	-	17	-
SOTER, G.	-	0/ 2	.000	0/ 0	.000	-/ 0	1	0	0	-	-	0	-
ORR, B.	-	0/ 1	.000	2/ 2	1.000	-/ 0	0	0	0	-	-	2	-
Totals	200	24/77	.312	18/24	.750	-/36	9	11	19	-	-	66	.330

Team Rebounds: Long Beach St. 5; Weber St. 11. Disqualified: Long Beach St.—Trapp, Terry; Weber St.—Sojourner.

	1st Qtr.	2nd Qtr.	3rd Qtr.	4th Qtr.	Final
Long Beach St.	21	17	17	22	77
Weber St.	12	13	22	19	66

REGIONAL SEMIFINAL EAST

Villanova (85)   Coach: Jack Kraft

	Min.	Total FG/FGA	Pct.	FT/FTA	Pct.	Reb. O/T	A	TO	PF	S	Blk	TP	PPM
INGLESBY, T.	-	4/9	.444	4/4	1.000	-/8	6	-	2	-	-	12	-
SIEMIONTKOSKI, H.	-	7/9	.778	5/5	1.000	-/8	0	-	3	-	-	19	-
FORD, C.	-	5/10	.500	2/4	.500	-/5	9	-	3	-	-	12	-
SMITH, C.	-	5/11	.455	1/1	1.000	-/10	0	-	4	-	-	11	-
PORTER, H.	-	11/17	.647	3/3	1.000	-/8	0	-	5	-	-	25	-
MCDOWELL, J.	-	3/4	.750	0/0	.000	-/0	0	-	0	-	-	6	-
FOX, J.	-	0/0	.000	0/0	.000	-/0	0	-	0	-	-	0	-
DALY, M.	-	0/0	.000	0/0	.000	-/0	0	-	0	-	-	0	-
GOHL, B.	-	0/1	.000	0/0	.000	-/0	0	-	0	-	-	0	-
Totals	200	35/61	.574	15/17	.882	-/39	15	-	17	-	-	85	.425

Fordham (75)   Coach: Digger Phelps

	Min.	Total FG/FGA	Pct.	FT/FTA	Pct.	Reb. O/T	A	TO	PF	S	Blk	TP	PPM
MAINOR, W.	-	4/15	.267	2/2	1.000	-/2	0	-	4	-	-	10	-
BURIK, J.	-	2/6	.333	2/2	1.000	-/5	2	-	1	-	-	6	-
YELVERTON, C.	-	12/28	.429	8/8	1.000	-/9	1	-	3	-	-	32	-
CHARLES, K.	-	2/8	.250	2/2	1.000	-/8	0	-	3	-	-	6	-
WOYTOWICZ, B.	-	5/17	.294	5/6	.833	-/8	0	-	4	-	-	15	-
SULLIVAN, T.	-	2/5	.400	2/7	.286	-/6	1	-	3	-	-	6	-
PIPICH, T.	-	0/1	.000	0/0	.000	-/0	0	-	0	-	-	0	-
LARBES, R.	-	0/0	.000	0/0	.000	-/0	0	-	0	-	-	0	-
CARLESIMO, P.	-	0/0	.000	0/0	.000	-/0	0	-	0	-	-	0	-
GRISWOLD, P.	-	0/0	.000	0/0	.000	-/1	0	-	0	-	-	0	-
CAIN, S.	-	0/0	.000	0/0	.000	-/0	0	-	0	-	-	0	-
ZAMBETTIS, G.	-	0/0	.000	0/0	.000	-/0	0	-	0	-	-	0	-
Totals	200	27/80	.338	21/27	.778	-/39	4	-	14	-	-	75	.375

Team Rebounds: Villanova 0; Fordham 9. Disqualified: Villanova—Porter.

	1st Half	2nd Half	Final
Villanova	47	38	85
Fordham	36	39	75

Pennsylvania (79)   Coach: Dick Harter

	Min.	Total FG/FGA	Pct.	FT/FTA	Pct.	Reb. O/T	A	TO	PF	S	Blk	TP	PPM
MORSE, B.	39	10/18	.556	8/10	.800	-/5	0	2	3	-	-	28	.718
HANKINSON, P.	23	2/6	.333	2/2	1.000	-/7	0	1	1	-	-	6	.261
WOLF, J.	29	1/2	.500	4/4	1.000	-/10	1	1	4	-	-	6	.207
CALHOUN, C.	39	3/8	.375	4/4	1.000	-/7	1	1	3	-	-	10	.256
LITTLEPAGE, C.	11	0/0	.000	0/0	.000	-/3	0	0	2	-	-	0	.000
BILSKY, S.	16	3/8	.375	2/2	1.000	-/1	1	3	1	-	-	8	.500
WOHL, D.	39	5/15	.333	10/11	.909	-/3	2	4	3	-	-	20	.513
KOLLER, J.	1	0/1	.000	0/0	.000	-/0	0	0	0	-	-	0	.000
COTLER, A.	1	0/0	.000	1/2	.500	-/0	0	0	0	-	-	1	1.000
HANEY, J.	1	0/0	.000	0/0	.000	-/0	0	0	0	-	-	0	.000
WALTERS, B.	1	0/0	.000	0/0	.000	-/0	0	0	0	-	-	0	.000
Totals	200	24/58	.414	31/35	.886	-/36	5	12	17	-	-	79	.395

South Carolina (64)   Coach: Frank McGuire

	Min.	Total FG/FGA	Pct.	FT/FTA	Pct.	Reb. O/T	A	TO	PF	S	Blk	TP	PPM
ROCHE, J.	39	5/18	.278	4/5	.800	-/5	6	4	2	-	-	14	.359
CARVER, B.	13	2/5	.400	0/0	.000	-/1	0	0	1	-	-	4	.308
AYDLETT, R.	24	3/5	.600	2/2	1.000	-/3	1	2	5	-	-	8	.333
OWENS, T.	39	6/14	.429	4/7	.571	-/10	1	5	2	-	-	16	.410
RIKER, T.	20	3/15	.200	4/4	1.000	-/9	0	2	2	-	-	10	.500
RIBOCK, J.	20	1/2	.500	0/1	.000	-/3	0	5	5	-	-	2	.100
JOYCE, K.	30	3/8	.375	2/2	1.000	-/9	1	2	4	-	-	8	.267
TRAYLOR, D.	12	1/2	.500	0/0	.000	-/3	0	1	1	-	-	2	.167
MANNING, C.	1	0/0	.000	0/0	.000	-/1	0	0	0	-	-	0	.000
POWELL, J.	1	0/0	.000	0/0	.000	-/0	0	0	0	-	-	0	.000
POWELL, D.	1	0/0	.000	0/0	.000	-/0	0	0	0	-	-	0	.000
Totals	200	24/69	.348	16/21	.762	-/44	9	15	22	-	-	64	.320

Team Rebounds: Pennsylvania 5; S. Carolina 3. Disqualified: S. Carolina—Aydlett, Ribock.

	1st Half	2nd Half	Final
Pennsylvania	36	43	79
S. Carolina	37	27	64

REGIONAL SEMIFINAL MIDEAST

Western Kentucky (107)   Coach: Johnny Oldham

	Min.	Total FG/FGA	Pct.	FT/FTA	Pct.	Reb. O/T	A	TO	PF	S	Blk	TP	PPM
ROSE, J.	-	12/21	.571	1/1	1.000	-/3	3	-	3	-	-	25	-
BAILEY, R.	-	3/10	.300	3/4	.750	-/2	3	-	2	-	-	9	-
MCDANIELS, J.	-	12/21	.571	11/11	1.000	-/11	1	-	4	-	-	35	-
DUNN, J.	-	3/8	.375	3/5	.600	-/7	4	-	4	-	-	9	-
GLOVER, C.	-	8/16	.500	2/5	.400	-/17	8	-	2	-	-	18	-
SUDMACKER, G.	-	2/2	1.000	1/2	.500	-/1	1	-	3	-	-	5	-
WITT, C.	-	2/4	.500	0/0	.000	-/4	1	-	0	-	-	4	-
JOHNSON, D.	-	0/0	.000	2/2	1.000	-/0	3	-	1	-	-	2	-
DAVIS, T.	-	0/0	.000	0/0	.000	-/0	0	-	0	-	-	0	-
KIEYCAMP, R.	-	0/0	.000	0/0	.000	-/0	0	-	0	-	-	0	-
EATON, S.	-	0/1	.000	0/0	.000	-/0	1	-	0	-	-	0	-
Totals	200	42/83	.506	23/30	.767	-/42	24	-	19	-	-	107	.535

Kentucky (83)   Coach: Adolph Rupp

	Min.	Total FG/FGA	Pct.	FT/FTA	Pct.	Reb. O/T	A	TO	PF	S	Blk	TP	PPM
PARKER, T.	-	11/18	.611	1/1	1.000	-/5	2	-	4	-	-	23	-
STEELE, L.	-	1/5	.200	2/3	.667	-/1	2	-	5	-	-	4	-
PAINE, T.	-	7/18	.389	1/3	.333	-/10	0	-	2	-	-	15	-
DINWIDDIE, J.	-	2/7	.286	0/0	.000	-/2	3	-	2	-	-	4	-
CASEY, M.	-	4/11	.364	4/5	.800	-/4	2	-	2	-	-	12	-
HOLLENBECK, K.	-	2/2	1.000	3/4	.750	-/0	1	-	5	-	-	7	-
ANDREWS, J.	-	3/5	.600	2/4	.500	-/6	1	-	0	-	-	8	-
MILLS, T.	-	0/2	.000	4/5	.800	-/1	3	-	1	-	-	4	-
KEY, S.	-	3/4	.750	0/0	.000	-/2	0	-	2	-	-	6	-
STAMPER, L.	-	0/2	.000	0/0	.000	-/2	0	-	0	-	-	0	-
Totals	200	33/74	.446	17/25	.680	-/36	16	-	23	-	-	83	.415

Team Rebounds: Western Ky. 9; Kentucky 10. Disqualified: Kentucky—Steele, Hollenbeck.

	1st Half	2nd Half	Final
Western Ky.	51	56	107
Kentucky	38	45	83

Ohio State (60)
Coach: Fred Taylor

	Min.	Total FG/FGA	Pct.	FT/FTA	Pct.	Reb. O/T	A	TO	PF	S	Blk	TP	PPM
WAGAR, M.	-	0/ 2	.000	1/ 3	.333	-/ 2	0	-	1	-	-	1	-
MINOR, M.	-	1/ 5	.200	0/ 2	.000	-/ 3	3	-	2	-	-	2	-
WITTE, L.	-	5/13	.385	3/ 4	.750	-/11	1	-	3	-	-	13	-
HORNYAK, A.	-	4/15	.267	3/ 3	1.000	-/ 4	1	-	4	-	-	11	-
CLEAMONS, J.	-	7/13	.538	7/ 8	.875	-/ 4	4	-	2	-	-	21	-
SEIKMANN, R.	-	4/ 5	.800	2/ 2	1.000	-/ 4	4	-	4	-	-	10	-
MERCHANT, D.	-	1/ 3	.333	0/ 0	.000	-/ 1	0	-	1	-	-	2	-
Totals	200	22/56	.393	16/22	.727	-/29	13	-	17	-	-	60	.300

Marquette (59)
Coach: Al McGuire

	Min.	Total FG/FGA	Pct.	FT/FTA	Pct.	Reb. O/T	A	TO	PF	S	Blk	TP	PPM
LACKEY, B.	-	1/ 9	.111	6/ 8	.750	-/ 9	1	-	4	-	-	8	-
BRELL, G.	-	5/10	.500	0/ 0	.000	-/ 8	8	-	0	-	-	10	-
CHONES, J.	-	9/19	.474	0/ 2	.000	-/10	0	-	3	-	-	18	-
MCGUIRE, A.	-	5/11	.455	2/ 3	.667	-/ 0	0	-	4	-	-	12	-
MEMINGER, D.	-	4/11	.364	3/ 7	.429	-/ 3	5	-	5	-	-	11	-
GRZESK, G.	-	0/ 0	.000	0/ 0	.000	-/ 1	0	-	0	-	-	0	-
FRAZIER, G.	-	0/ 1	.000	0/ 1	.000	-/ 0	0	-	0	-	-	0	-
MCMAHON, H.	-	0/ 1	.000	0/ 0	.000	-/ 2	0	-	3	-	-	0	-
Totals	200	24/62	.387	11/21	.524	-/33	14	-	19	-	-	59	.295

Team Rebounds: Ohio State 13; Marquette 13. Disqualified: Marquette—Meminger.

	1st Half	2nd Half	Final
Ohio State	27	33	60
Marquette	31	28	59

REGIONAL SEMIFINAL MIDWEST

Kansas (78)
Coach: Ted Owens

	Min.	Total FG/FGA	Pct.	FT/FTA	Pct.	Reb. O/T	A	TO	PF	S	Blk	TP	PPM
STALLWORTH, B.	-	10/21	.476	5/ 7	.714	-/ 8	1	4	2	-	-	25	-
NASH, A.	-	4/ 7	.571	1/ 3	.333	-/ 1	3	1	4	-	-	9	-
BROWN, R.	-	1/ 9	.111	1/ 2	.500	-/ 7	1	1	4	-	-	3	-
ROBISCH, D.	-	10/23	.435	9/14	.643	-/16	2	0	3	-	-	29	-
RUSSELL, P.	-	3/10	.300	0/ 0	.000	-/ 4	2	2	3	-	-	6	-
KIVISTO, B.	-	0/ 1	.000	2/ 3	.667	-/ 0	2	1	0	-	-	2	-
DOUGLAS, G.	-	0/ 1	.000	0/ 0	.000	-/ 1	0	0	0	-	-	0	-
CANFIELD, R.	-	2/ 3	.667	0/ 0	.000	-/ 4	0	0	3	-	-	4	-
Totals	200	30/75	.400	18/29	.621	-/41	11	9	19	-	-	78	.390

Houston (77)
Coach: Guy Lewis

	Min.	Total FG/FGA	Pct.	FT/FTA	Pct.	Reb. O/T	A	TO	PF	S	Blk	TP	PPM
BONNEY, J.	-	1/ 2	.500	2/ 2	1.000	-/ 1	1	4	2	-	-	4	-
WILLIS, S.	-	1/ 3	.333	0/ 1	.000	-/ 1	1	0	2	-	-	2	-
BROWN, L.	-	0/ 1	.000	0/ 0	.000	-/ 0	0	1	1	-	-	0	-
WELCH, P.	-	13/22	.591	2/ 2	1.000	-/ 5	3	5	4	-	-	28	-
DAVIS, D.	-	5/18	.278	9/14	.643	-/10	3	7	5	-	-	19	-
HALL, B.	-	5/ 8	.625	3/ 5	.600	-/17	1	3	2	-	-	13	-
NEWSOME, S.	-	4/13	.308	2/ 2	1.000	-/11	0	1	4	-	-	10	-
BODDEN, G.	-	0/ 1	.000	1/ 3	.333	-/ 3	0	0	2	-	-	1	-
Totals	200	29/68	.426	19/29	.655	-/48	9	21	22	-	-	77	.385

Team Rebounds: Kansas 8; Houston 10. Disqualified: Houston—Davis.

	1st Half	2nd Half	Final
Kansas	36	42	78
Houston	37	40	77

Drake (79)
Coach: Maurice John

	Min.	Total FG/FGA	Pct.	FT/FTA	Pct.	Reb. O/T	A	TO	PF	S	Blk	TP	PPM
SAKYS, A.	-	7/13	.538	1/ 1	1.000	-/ 8	1	0	5	-	-	15	-
JONES, B.	-	5/16	.313	1/ 2	.500	-/ 9	3	3	0	-	-	11	-
BUSH, T.	-	7/11	.636	5/10	.500	-/16	3	5	4	-	-	19	-
HUFF, L.	-	7/19	.368	1/ 3	.333	-/12	2	1	5	-	-	15	-
HALLIBURTON, J.	-	5/21	.238	2/ 3	.667	-/11	3	6	5	-	-	12	-
WICKLUND, D.	-	0/ 0	.000	0/ 0	.000	-/ 0	0	0	0	-	-	0	-
SALYERS, C.	-	1/ 2	.500	2/ 2	1.000	-/ 0	0	0	0	-	-	4	-
NORDRUM, J.	-	1/ 3	.333	1/ 3	.333	-/ 5	0	0	0	-	-	3	-
JOHNSON, T.	-	0/ 1	.000	0/ 2	.000	-/ 2	0	0	0	-	-	0	-
Totals	225	33/86	.384	13/26	.500	-/63	12	15	19	-	-	79	.351

Notre Dame (72)
Coach: Johnny Dee

	Min.	Total FG/FGA	Pct.	FT/FTA	Pct.	Reb. O/T	A	TO	PF	S	Blk	TP	PPM
SINNOTT, T.	-	1/ 2	.500	1/ 2	.500	-/ 2	0	1	1	-	-	3	-
CARR, A.	-	11/27	.407	4/ 5	.800	-/ 8	0	4	4	-	-	26	-
MEEHAN, J.	-	4/ 8	.500	3/ 4	.750	-/ 4	6	9	5	-	-	11	-
JONES, C.	-	7/26	.269	5/ 7	.714	-/16	1	2	4	-	-	19	-
CATLETT, S.	-	2/11	.182	3/ 3	1.000	-/17	4	1	2	-	-	7	-
GEMMELL, D.	-	1/ 4	.250	0/ 1	.000	-/ 6	2	0	2	-	-	2	-
PLEICK, J.	-	2/ 4	.500	0/ 0	.000	-/ 4	1	3	5	-	-	4	-
Totals	225	28/82	.341	16/22	.727	-/57	14	20	23	-	-	72	.320

Team Rebounds: Drake 3; Notre Dame 3. Disqualified: Drake—Sakys, Huff, Halliburton; Notre Dame—Meehan, Plecik.

	1st Half	2nd Half	1st OT	Final
Drake	39	23	17	79
Notre Dame	32	30	10	72

REGIONAL SEMIFINAL WEST

UCLA (91)
Coach: John Wooden

	Min.	Total FG/FGA	Pct.	FT/FTA	Pct.	Reb. O/T	A	TO	PF	S	Blk	TP	PPM
ROWE, C.	-	5/11	.455	3/ 6	.500	-/ 9	6	-	0	-	-	13	-
WICKS, S.	-	6/16	.375	2/ 5	.400	-/20	1	-	1	-	-	14	-
PATTERSON, S.	-	6/13	.462	1/ 3	.333	-/11	4	-	4	-	-	13	-
BIBBY, H.	-	6/13	.462	3/ 3	1.000	-/ 9	4	-	3	-	-	15	-
BOOKER, K.	-	2/ 6	.333	0/ 0	.000	-/ 1	1	-	2	-	-	4	-
SCHOFIELD, T.	-	6/13	.462	0/ 2	.000	-/ 6	3	-	3	-	-	12	-
FARMER, L.	-	5/ 9	.556	1/ 3	.333	-/ 6	1	-	0	-	-	11	-
ECKER, J.	-	1/ 3	.333	0/ 0	.000	-/ 0	0	-	0	-	-	2	-
BETCHLEY, R.	-	3/ 4	.750	1/ 1	1.000	-/ 0	0	-	0	-	-	7	-
Totals	200	40/88	.455	11/23	.478	-/62	20	-	13	-	-	91	.455

Brigham Young (73)
Coach: Stan Watts

	Min.	Total FG/FGA	Pct.	FT/FTA	Pct.	Reb. O/T	A	TO	PF	S	Blk	TP	PPM
FRYER, B.	-	8/19	.421	2/ 6	.333	-/ 4	6	-	3	-	-	18	-
KELLY, S.	-	9/16	.563	6/ 6	1.000	-/ 5	2	-	1	-	-	24	-
MILLER, J.	-	4/11	.364	2/ 5	.400	-/ 5	1	-	3	-	-	10	-
TOLLESTRUP, P.	-	0/ 3	.000	1/ 2	.500	-/ 1	2	-	2	-	-	1	-
BUNKER, J.	-	1/ 3	.333	0/ 0	.000	-/ 5	4	-	4	-	-	2	-
SARKALAHTI, K.	-	0/ 0	.000	0/ 0	.000	-/ 0	0	-	0	-	-	0	-
BAILEY, D.	-	0/ 1	.000	0/ 0	.000	-/ 0	0	-	1	-	-	0	-
JORGENSEN, C.	-	0/ 1	.000	0/ 0	.000	-/ 1	0	-	0	-	-	0	-
COSIC, K.	-	8/18	.444	2/ 2	1.000	-/23	5	-	3	-	-	18	-
Totals	200	30/72	.417	13/21	.619	-/44	20	-	17	-	-	73	.365

Team Rebounds: UCLA 2; Brigham Young 2. Disqualified: None.

	1st Half	2nd Half	Final
UCLA	41	50	91
Brigham Young	32	41	73

Long Beach State (78) Coach: Jerry Tarkanian

	Min.	Total FG / FGA	Pct.	FT / FTA	Pct.	Reb. O / T	A	TO	PF	S	Blk	TP	PPM
TRAPP, G.	-	8/18	.444	7/10	.700	-/ 6	4	-	3	-	-	23	-
RATLEFF, E.	-	5/13	.385	3/ 5	.600	-/10	6	-	2	-	-	13	-
TERRY, C.	-	9/19	.474	0/ 0	.000	-/ 9	1	-	3	-	-	18	-
MCWILLIAMS, E.	-	3/ 6	.500	1/ 1	1.000	-/ 2	1	-	5	-	-	7	-
LYNN, B.	-	3/ 9	.333	0/ 1	.000	-/ 7	1	-	4	-	-	6	-
WILLIAMS, B.	-	0/ 3	.000	0/ 2	.000	-/ 4	3	-	2	-	-	0	-
TAYLOR, D.	-	3/ 5	.600	5/ 6	.833	-/ 3	7	-	2	-	-	11	-
Totals	200	31/73	.425	16/25	.640	-/41	23	-	21	-	-	78	.390

Pacific (65) Coach: Dick Edwards

	Min.	Total FG / FGA	Pct.	FT / FTA	Pct.	Reb. O / T	A	TO	PF	S	Blk	TP	PPM
MCCARGO, J.	-	3/ 9	.333	5/ 9	.556	-/10	0	-	5	-	-	11	-
DULANEY, B.	-	2/ 9	.222	0/ 1	.000	-/ 6	3	-	3	-	-	4	-
GIANELLI, J.	-	5/ 9	.556	6/ 8	.750	-/17	1	-	4	-	-	16	-
THOMASON, B.	-	7/22	.318	5/ 6	.833	-/ 3	7	-	2	-	-	19	-
SPERRING, R.	-	4/ 4	1.000	5/ 6	.833	-/ 4	6	-	2	-	-	13	-
SCHEIDEGGER, P.	-	1/ 3	.333	0/ 0	.000	-/ 2	0	-	1	-	-	2	-
JOSHUA, J.	-	0/ 0	.000	0/ 0	.000	-/ 1	1	-	0	-	-	0	-
JENSEN, P.	-	0/ 0	.000	0/ 0	.000	-/ 1	0	-	2	-	-	0	-
NOBLE, O.	-	0/ 0	.000	0/ 0	.000	-/ 0	0	-	0	-	-	0	-
DOUGLASS, P.	-	0/ 1	.000	0/ 0	.000	-/ 0	0	-	1	-	-	0	-
Totals	200	22/57	.386	21/30	.700	-/44	18	-	20	-	-	65	.325

Team Rebounds: Long Beach St. 5; Pacific 5. Disqualified: Long Beach St.—McWiliams; Pacific—McCargo.

	1st Half	2nd Half	Final
Long Beach St.	31	47	78
Pacific	44	21	65

REGIONAL FINAL EAST

Villanova (90) Coach: Jack Kraft

	Min.	Total FG / FGA	Pct.	FT / FTA	Pct.	Reb. O / T	A	TO	PF	S	Blk	TP	PPM
INGELSBY, T.	37	1/ 3	.333	6/ 7	.857	-/ 4	7	4	2	-	-	8	.216
SIEMIONTKOWSKI, H	38	10/15	.667	0/ 0	.000	-/ 7	1	2	3	-	-	20	.526
FORD, C.	35	2/ 4	.500	5/ 9	.556	-/ 5	4	4	0	-	-	9	.257
SMITH, C.	36	7/11	.636	1/ 2	.500	-/ 8	1	2	0	-	-	15	.417
PORTER, H.	39	16/24	.667	3/ 4	.750	-/15	0	0	2	-	-	35	.897
MCDOWELL, J.	6	0/ 1	.000	0/ 0	.000	-/ 1	1	0	0	-	-	0	.000
FOX, J.	5	0/ 1	.000	1/ 1	1.000	-/ 0	0	0	0	-	-	1	.200
GOHL, B.	3	1/ 1	1.000	0/ 0	.000	-/ 1	0	1	1	-	-	2	.667
DALY, M.	1	0/ 0	.000	0/ 0	.000	-/ 0	0	0	0	-	-	0	.000
Totals	200	37/60	.617	16/23	.696	-/41	14	13	8	-	-	90	.450

Pennsylvania (47) Coach: Dick Harter

	Min.	Total FG / FGA	Pct.	FT / FTA	Pct.	Reb. O / T	A	TO	PF	S	Blk	TP	PPM
MORSE, B.	22	2/ 8	.250	2/ 2	1.000	-/ 2	0	2	1	-	-	6	.273
HANKINSON, P.	26	4/ 9	.444	0/ 0	.000	-/ 4	0	2	1	-	-	8	.308
WOLF, J.	19	3/ 8	.375	1/ 1	1.000	-/ 8	0	1	3	-	-	7	.368
CALHOUN, C.	38	1/ 7	.143	0/ 0	.000	-/ 5	0	6	2	-	-	2	.053
LITTLEPAGE, C.	20	1/ 7	.143	3/ 5	.600	-/ 4	0	0	2	-	-	5	.250
BILSKY, S.	14	1/ 4	.250	0/ 0	.000	-/ 0	0	2	2	-	-	2	.143
WOHL, D.	33	3/10	.300	0/ 0	.000	-/ 0	0	3	2	-	-	6	.182
COTLER, A.	8	2/ 7	.286	0/ 0	.000	-/ 2	0	1	2	-	-	4	.500
KOLLER, J.	13	2/ 4	.500	0/ 0	.000	-/ 1	0	0	0	-	-	4	.308
HANEY, J.	6	0/ 2	.000	0/ 0	.000	-/ 2	0	1	0	-	-	0	.000
WALTERS, B.	1	1/ 1	1.000	1/ 1	1.000	-/ 1	0	0	1	-	-	3	3.000
Totals	200	20/67	.299	7/ 9	.778	-/29	0	18	16	-	-	47	.235

Team Rebounds: Villanova 3; Pennsylvania 5. Disqualified: None.

	1st Half	2nd Half	Final
Villanova	43	47	90
Pennsylvania	22	25	47

REGIONAL FINAL MIDEAST

Western Kentucky (81) Coach: Johnny Oldham

	Min.	Total FG / FGA	Pct.	FT / FTA	Pct.	Reb. O / T	A	TO	PF	S	Blk	TP	PPM
ROSE, J.	-	6/13	.462	1/ 1	1.000	-/ 6	3	-	4	-	-	13	-
BAILEY, R.	-	7/ 9	.778	0/ 1	.000	-/ 0	4	-	2	-	-	14	-
MCDANIELS, J.	-	14/35	.400	3/ 6	.500	-/ 6	0	-	4	-	-	31	-
DUNN, J.	-	5/14	.357	2/ 5	.400	-/15	3	-	4	-	-	12	-
GLOVER, C.	-	2/ 9	.222	7/ 9	.778	-/22	2	-	2	-	-	11	-
WITT, C.	-	0/ 1	.000	0/ 0	.000	-/ 1	0	-	0	-	-	0	-
JOHNSON, D.	-	0/ 1	.000	0/ 0	.000	-/ 0	1	-	1	-	-	0	-
Totals	225	34/82	.415	13/22	.591	-/50	13	17	17	-	-	81	.360

Ohio State (78) Coach: Fred Taylor

	Min.	Total FG / FGA	Pct.	FT / FTA	Pct.	Reb. O / T	A	TO	PF	S	Blk	TP	PPM
WAGAR, M.	-	2/ 6	.333	3/ 4	.750	-/ 3	3	-	5	-	-	7	-
MINOR, M.	-	3/ 8	.375	1/ 1	1.000	-/ 3	6	-	4	-	-	7	-
WITTE, L.	-	10/19	.526	3/ 5	.600	-/17	1	-	4	-	-	23	-
HORNYAK, A.	-	11/21	.524	4/ 4	1.000	-/ 3	2	-	1	-	-	26	-
CLEAMONS, J.	-	4/ 9	.444	4/ 6	.667	-/ 7	4	-	4	-	-	12	-
SEIKMANN, R.	-	1/ 2	.500	1/ 1	1.000	-/ 2	0	-	0	-	-	3	-
MERCHANT, D.	-	0/ 2	.000	0/ 0	.000	-/ 0	0	-	0	-	-	0	-
Totals	225	31/67	.463	16/21	.762	-/35	16	17	18	-	-	78	.347

Team Rebounds: Western Ky. 6; Ohio State 7. Disqualified: Ohio State—Wagar.

	1st Half	2nd Half	1st OT	Final
Western Ky.	34	35	12	81
Ohio State	40	29	9	78

REGIONAL FINAL MIDWEST

Kansas (73) Coach: Ted Owens

	Min.	Total FG/FGA	Pct.	FT/FTA	Pct.	Reb. O/T	A	TO	PF	S	Blk	TP	PPM
STALLWORTH, B.	-	6/13	.462	1/ 3	.333	-/ 3	0	3	5	-	-	13	-
NASH, A.	-	2/ 4	.500	2/ 3	.667	-/ 3	1	3	4	-	-	6	-
BROWN, R.	-	6/10	.600	3/ 5	.600	-/ 9	1	1	1	-	-	15	-
ROBISCH, D.	-	10/18	.556	7/ 9	.778	-/10	3	2	3	-	-	27	-
RUSSELL, P.	-	0/ 3	.000	3/ 5	.600	-/ 5	2	4	5	-	-	3	-
KIVISTO, B.	-	2/ 4	.500	5/ 8	.625	-/ 2	3	4	0	-	-	9	-
CANFIELD, R.	-	0/ 0	.000	0/ 0	.000	-/ 1	0	1	2	-	-	0	-
MATHEWS, M.	-	0/ 0	.000	0/ 1	.000	-/ 0	0	0	0	-	-	0	-
Totals	200	26/52	.500	21/34	.618	-/33	10	18	20	-	-	73	.365

Drake (71) Coach: Maurice John

	Min.	Total FG/FGA	Pct.	FT/FTA	Pct.	Reb. O/T	A	TO	PF	S	Blk	TP	PPM
SAKYS, A.	-	2/ 4	.500	0/ 1	.000	-/ 5	2	4	5	-	-	4	-
JONES, B.	-	5/14	.357	0/ 0	.000	-/ 5	2	6	3	-	-	10	-
BUSH, T.	-	6/ 9	.667	4/ 6	.667	-/15	0	1	5	-	-	16	-
HUFF, L.	-	8/14	.571	4/ 5	.800	-/ 4	0	1	5	-	-	20	-
HALLIBURTON, J.	-	8/20	.400	1/ 4	.250	-/ 7	5	6	3	-	-	17	-
WICKLUND, D.	-	0/ 1	.000	1/ 1	1.000	-/ 2	1	1	0	-	-	1	-
NORDRUM, J.	-	1/ 1	1.000	0/ 0	.000	-/ 1	0	0	2	-	-	2	-
JOHNSON, T.	-	0/ 1	.000	1/ 2	.500	-/ 0	1	0	0	-	-	1	-
Totals	200	30/64	.469	11/19	.579	-/39	11	19	23	-	-	71	.355

Team Rebounds: Kansas 4; Drake 5. Disqualified: Kansas—Stallworth, Russell; Drake—Sakys, Bush, Huff.

	1st Half	2nd Half	Final
Kansas	30	43	73
Drake	38	33	71

REGIONAL FINAL WEST

UCLA (57) Coach: John Wooden

	Min.	Total FG/FGA	Pct.	FT/FTA	Pct.	Reb. O/T	A	TO	PF	S	Blk	TP	PPM
ROWE, C.	-	3/ 6	.500	6/12	.500	-/12	1	-	2	-	-	12	-
WICKS, S.	-	5/13	.385	8/12	.667	-/15	0	-	4	-	-	18	-
PATTERSON, S.	-	2/ 8	.250	1/ 1	1.000	-/ 5	2	-	2	-	-	5	-
BIBBY, H.	-	4/18	.222	3/ 3	1.000	-/ 1	0	-	4	-	-	11	-
BOOKER, K.	-	0/ 4	.000	0/ 0	.000	-/ 2	0	-	0	-	-	0	-
SCHOFIELD, T.	-	3/ 9	.333	0/ 0	.000	-/ 3	1	-	1	-	-	6	-
FARMER, L.	-	0/ 3	.000	1/ 2	.500	-/ 4	1	-	2	-	-	1	-
BETCHLEY, R.	-	1/ 1	1.000	2/ 2	1.000	-/ 0	1	-	0	-	-	4	-
ECKER, J.	-	0/ 0	.000	0/ 0	.000	-/ 0	0	-	1	-	-	0	-
Totals	200	18/62	.290	21/32	.656	-/47	7	-	16	-	-	57	.285

Long Beach State (55) Coach: Jerry Tarkanian

	Min.	Total FG/FGA	Pct.	FT/FTA	Pct.	Reb. O/T	A	TO	PF	S	Blk	TP	PPM
TRAPP, G.	-	5/13	.385	5/ 6	.833	-/16	5	-	3	-	-	15	-
RATLEFF, E.	-	8/14	.571	2/ 4	.500	-/ 4	2	-	5	-	-	18	-
TERRY, C.	-	4/ 4	1.000	3/ 4	.750	-/ 6	7	-	3	-	-	11	-
MCWILLIAMS, E.	-	0/ 1	.000	0/ 0	.000	-/ 2	2	-	2	-	-	0	-
LYNN, B.	-	3/10	.300	1/ 3	.333	-/ 5	0	-	4	-	-	7	-
WILLIAMS, B.	-	1/ 7	.143	0/ 0	.000	-/ 4	1	-	3	-	-	2	-
TAYLOR, D.	-	0/ 2	.000	2/ 4	.500	-/ 2	0	-	2	-	-	2	-
Totals	200	21/51	.412	13/21	.619	-/39	17	-	22	-	-	55	.275

Team Rebounds: UCLA 4; Long Beach St. 2. Disqualified: Long Beach St.—Ratleff.

	1st Half	2nd Half	Final
UCLA	27	30	57
Long Beach St.	31	24	55

FINAL FOUR

Villanova (92) Coach: Jack Kraft

	Min.	Total FG/FGA	Pct.	FT/FTA	Pct.	Reb. O/T	A	TO	PF	S	Blk	TP	PPM
INGELSBY, T.	50	5/10	.500	4/ 7	.571	-/ 4	3	5	1	-	-	14	.280
SIEMIONTKOWSKI, H	36	11/20	.550	9/10	.900	-/15	3	4	5	-	-	31	.861
FORD, C.	50	3/ 6	.500	2/ 2	1.000	-/ 1	7	7	4	-	-	8	.160
SMITH, C.	50	5/14	.357	3/ 6	.500	-/11	3	3	1	-	-	13	.260
PORTER, H.	50	10/20	.500	2/ 3	.667	-/16	1	0	4	-	-	22	.440
MCDOWELL, J.	14	2/ 3	.667	0/ 3	.000	-/ 3	1	3	1	-	-	4	.286
Totals	250	36/73	.493	20/31	.645	-/50	18	22	16	-	-	92	.368

Western Kentucky (89) Coach: Johnny Oldham

	Min.	Total FG/FGA	Pct.	FT/FTA	Pct.	Reb. O/T	A	TO	PF	S	Blk	TP	PPM
GLOVER, C.	50	5/15	.333	2/ 4	.500	-/20	0	4	4	-	-	12	.240
DUNN, J.	50	11/33	.333	3/ 6	.500	-/ 8	6	6	5	-	-	25	.500
MCDANIELS, J.	44	10/24	.417	2/ 4	.500	-/17	2	3	5	-	-	22	.500
ROSE, J.	50	8/21	.381	2/ 3	.667	-/ 8	1	4	2	-	-	18	.360
BAILEY, R.	47	5/11	.455	2/ 3	.667	-/ 8	7	3	1	-	-	12	.255
WITT, C.	5	0/ 1	.000	0/ 0	.000	-/ 0	0	0	3	-	-	0	.000
SUNDMAKER, G.	4	0/ 0	.000	0/ 0	.000	-/ 0	1	0	1	-	-	0	.000
Totals	250	39/105	.371	11/20	.550	-/61	17	20	21	-	-	89	.356

Team Rebounds: Villanova 4; Western Ky. 8. Disqualified: Villanova—Siemiontkowski; Western Ky.—McDaniels, Dunn.

	1st Half	2nd Half	1st OT	2nd OT	Final
Villanova	39	35	11	7	92
Western Ky.	36	38	11	4	89

Kansas (60)   Coach: Ted Owens

	Min.	Total FG / FGA	Pct.	FT / FTA	Pct.	Reb. O / T	A	TO	PF	S	Blk	TP	PPM
STALLWORTH, B.	35	5/10	.500	2/ 4	.500	-/ 5	3	2	5	-	-	12	.343
NASH, A.	32	3/ 9	.333	1/ 2	.500	-/ 3	2	3	1	-	-	7	.219
BROWN, R.	33	3/ 8	.375	1/ 3	.333	-/ 9	2	1	4	-	-	7	.212
ROBISCH, D.	38	7/19	.368	3/ 6	.500	-/ 6	4	2	3	-	-	17	.447
RUSSELL, P.	34	5/12	.417	2/ 2	1.000	-/ 4	1	2	4	-	-	12	.353
KIVISTO, B.	19	1/ 1	1.000	1/ 4	.250	-/ 1	4	1	2	-	-	3	.158
DOUGLAS, G.	2	0/ 0	.000	0/ 0	.000	-/ 1	0	0	0	-	-	0	.000
CANFIELD, R.	2	0/ 0	.000	0/ 0	.000	-/ 0	2	0	1	-	-	0	.000
WILLIAMS, M.	3	0/ 1	.000	2/ 2	1.000	-/ 0	0	0	2	-	-	2	.667
MATHEWS, M.	2	0/ 0	.000	0/ 0	.000	-/ 0	0	0	0	-	-	0	.000
Totals	200	24/60	.400	12/23	.522	-/29	18	11	22	-	-	60	.300

UCLA (68)   Coach: John Wooden

	Min.	Total FG / FGA	Pct.	FT / FTA	Pct.	Reb. O / T	A	TO	PF	S	Blk	TP	PPM
ROWE, C.	38	7/10	.700	2/ 4	.500	-/15	1	3	2	-	-	16	.421
WICKS, S.	38	5/ 9	.556	11/13	.846	-/ 8	3	4	2	-	-	21	.553
PATTERSON, S.	37	3/11	.273	0/ 0	.000	-/ 6	2	4	2	-	-	6	.162
BIBBY, H.	37	6/ 9	.667	6/ 6	1.000	-/ 4	1	1	3	-	-	18	.486
BOOKER, K.	20	1/ 2	.500	1/ 2	.500	-/ 5	6	5	3	-	-	3	.150
SCHOFIELD, T.	17	1/ 3	.333	0/ 1	.000	-/ 0	0	4	3	-	-	2	.118
FARMER, L.	3	0/ 2	.000	0/ 1	.000	-/ 2	0	1	-	-	-	0	.000
ECKER, J.	2	0/ 1	.000	2/ 2	1.000	-/ 1	0	0	0	-	-	2	1.000
BETCHLEY, R.	4	0/ 0	.000	0/ 1	.000	-/ 0	0	0	0	-	-	0	.000
HILL, A.	2	0/ 0	.000	0/ 0	.000	-/ 0	0	2	0	-	-	0	.000
CHAPMAN, J.	2	0/ 0	.000	0/ 0	.000	-/ 1	0	1	2	-	-	0	.000
Totals	200	23/47	.489	22/30	.733	-/42	13	24	18	-	-	68	.340

Team Rebounds: UCLA 5; Kansas 3. Disqualified: Kansas—Stallworth.

	1st Half	2nd Half	Final
Kansas	25	35	60
UCLA	32	36	68

NATIONAL CHAMPIONSHIP

Villanova (62)   Coach: Jack Kraft

	Min.	Total FG / FGA	Pct.	FT / FTA	Pct.	Reb. O / T	A	TO	PF	S	Blk	TP	PPM
INGELSBY, T.	40	3/ 9	.333	1/ 1	1.000	-/ 4	7	0	2	-	-	7	.175
SIEMIONTKOWSKI, H	37	9/16	.563	1/ 2	.500	-/ 6	0	1	3	-	-	19	.514
FORD, C.	40	0/ 4	.000	2/ 3	.667	-/ 5	10	7	4	-	-	2	.050
SMITH, C.	40	4/11	.364	1/ 1	1.000	-/ 2	0	1	1	-	-	9	.225
PORTER, H.	40	10/21	.476	5/ 6	.833	-/ 8	0	1	1	-	-	25	.625
MCDOWELL, J.	3	0/ 1	.000	0/ 0	.000	-/ 2	1	0	0	-	-	0	.000
Totals	200	26/62	.419	10/13	.769	-/27	18	10	14	-	-	62	.310

UCLA (68)   Coach: John Wooden

	Min.	Total FG / FGA	Pct.	FT / FTA	Pct.	Reb. O / T	A	TO	PF	S	Blk	TP	PPM
ROWE, C.	40	2/ 3	.667	4/ 5	.800	-/ 8	2	4	0	-	-	8	.200
WICKS, S.	40	3/ 7	.429	1/ 1	1.000	-/ 9	7	3	2	-	-	7	.175
PATTERSON, S.	40	13/18	.722	3/ 5	.600	-/ 8	4	3	1	-	-	29	.725
BIBBY, H.	40	6/12	.500	5/ 5	1.000	-/ 2	3	1	1	-	-	17	.425
BOOKER, K.	5	0/ 0	.000	0/ 0	.000	-/ 0	0	1	0	-	-	0	.000
SCHOFIELD, T.	26	3/ 9	.333	0/ 0	.000	-/ 1	4	0	4	-	-	6	.231
BETCHLEY, R.	9	0/ 0	.000	1/ 2	.500	-/ 1	0	1	1	-	-	1	.111
Totals	200	27/49	.551	14/18	.778	-/29	20	13	9	-	-	68	.340

Team Rebounds: UCLA 5; Villanova 4. Disqualified: None.

	1st Half	2nd Half	Final
Villanova	37	25	62
UCLA	45	23	68

NATIONAL THIRD PLACE

Western Kentucky (77)   Coach: Johnny Oldham

	Min.	Total FG / FGA	Pct.	FT / FTA	Pct.	Reb. O / T	A	TO	PF	S	Blk	TP	PPM
GLOVER, C.	26	3/ 8	.375	4/ 5	.800	-/13	3	2	5	-	-	10	.385
DUNN, J.	29	3/13	.231	4/ 6	.667	-/10	4	3	3	-	-	10	.345
MCDANIELS, J.	33	14/30	.467	8/10	.800	-/19	1	3	4	-	-	36	1.091
ROSE, J.	39	4/12	.333	3/ 4	.750	-/ 2	3	4	3	-	-	11	.282
BAILEY, R.	40	3/11	.273	1/ 2	.500	-/ 5	7	3	2	-	-	7	.175
SUNDMACKER, G.	12	1/ 1	1.000	0/ 1	.000	-/ 1	0	1	1	-	-	2	.167
WITT, C.	16	0/ 1	.000	0/ 1	.000	-/ 1	0	0	3	-	-	0	.000
EATON, S.	4	0/ 0	.000	1/ 2	.500	-/ 0	0	1	0	-	-	1	.250
JOHNSON, D.	1	0/ 0	.000	0/ 0	.000	-/ 1	0	2	0	-	-	0	.000
Totals	200	28/76	.368	21/31	.677	-/52	18	19	21	-	-	77	.385

Kansas (75)   Coach: Ted Owens

	Min.	Total FG / FGA	Pct.	FT / FTA	Pct.	Reb. O / T	A	TO	PF	S	Blk	TP	PPM
ROBISCH, D.	38	9/21	.429	5/ 8	.625	-/ 9	1	3	4	-	-	23	.605
RUSSELL, P.	30	4/10	.400	0/ 1	.000	-/ 7	5	2	1	-	-	8	.267
BROWN, R.	30	7/16	.438	2/ 3	.667	-/16	1	4	3	-	-	16	.533
STALLWORTH, B.	32	3/13	.231	4/ 8	.500	-/14	2	6	4	-	-	10	.313
NASH, A.	40	4/14	.286	2/ 3	.667	-/ 7	4	5	3	-	-	10	.250
KIVISTO, B.	20	2/ 3	.667	0/ 1	.000	-/ 2	4	3	1	-	-	4	.200
CANFIELD, R.	10	1/ 6	.167	2/ 3	.667	-/ 5	0	1	5	-	-	4	.400
Totals	200	30/83	.361	15/27	.556	-/60	17	24	21	-	-	75	.375

Team Rebounds: Western Ky. 4; Kansas 7. Disqualified: Western Ky.—Glover; Kansas—Canfield.

	1st Half	2nd Half	Final
Western Ky.	38	39	77
Kansas	37	38	75

REGIONAL THIRD PLACE EAST

Fordham (100)   Coach: Digger Phelps

	Min.	Total FG / FGA	Pct.	FT / FTA	Pct.	Reb. O / T	A	TO	PF	S	Blk	TP	PPM
YELVERTON, C.	39	11/23	.478	3/ 3	1.000	-/10	0	0	5	-	-	25	.641
CHARLES, K.	39	9/24	.375	4/ 4	1.000	-/10	1	1	4	-	-	22	.564
WOYTOWICZ, B.	18	0/ 2	.000	1/ 1	1.000	-/ 3	0	0	2	-	-	1	.056
MANIOR, W.	39	9/19	.474	5/ 5	1.000	-/ 6	1	1	4	-	-	23	.590
BURIK, J.	39	8/14	.571	7/ 7	1.000	-/ 2	1	1	0	-	-	23	.590
SULLIVAN, T.	21	2/ 6	.333	2/ 2	1.000	-/ 6	0	1	5	-	-	6	.286
PIPICH, T.	1	0/ 0	.000	0/ 0	.000	-/ 0	0	1	0	-	-	0	.000
CARLESIMO, P.	1	0/ 0	.000	0/ 0	.000	-/ 0	0	0	0	-	-	0	.000
LARBES, R.	1	0/ 0	.000	0/ 0	.000	-/ 0	0	0	0	-	-	0	.000
CAIN, S.	1	0/ 0	.000	0/ 0	.000	-/ 0	0	0	0	-	-	0	.000
CAMBETTI	1	0/ 0	.000	0/ 0	.000	-/ 0	0	0	0	-	-	0	.000
Totals	200	39/88	.443	22/22	1.000	-/37	3	5	20	-	-	100	.500

South Carolina (90)   Coach: Frank McGuire

	Min.	Total FG / FGA	Pct.	FT / FTA	Pct.	Reb. O / T	A	TO	PF	S	Blk	TP	PPM
OWENS, T.	40	5/11	.455	3/ 5	.600	-/13	1	7	4	-	-	13	.325
RIKER, T.	40	18/26	.692	3/ 5	.600	-/11	1	5	2	-	-	39	.975
ROCHE, J.	37	2/ 9	.222	4/ 6	.667	-/ 0	3	5	5	-	-	8	.216
CARVER, D.	26	1/ 3	.333	0/ 1	.000	-/ 3	3	2	2	-	-	2	.077
JOYCE, K.	40	5/10	.500	8/ 8	1.000	-/ 8	3	4	3	-	-	18	.450
AYDLETT, R.	17	4/11	.364	2/ 2	1.000	-/ 6	0	2	3	-	-	10	.588
Totals	200	35/70	.500	20/27	.741	-/41	11	25	19	-	-	90	.450

Team Rebounds: Fordham 4; S. Carolina 9. Disqualified: Fordham—Yelverton, Sullivan; S. Carolina—Roche.

	1st Half	2nd Half	Final
Fordham	42	58	100
S. Carolina	48	42	90

REGIONAL THIRD PLACE MIDEAST

Marquette (91)   Coach: Al McGuire

	Min.	Total FG/FGA	Pct.	FT/FTA	Pct.	Reb. O/T	A	TO	PF	S	Blk	TP	PPM
BRELL, G.	-	3/9	.333	1/2	.500	-/9	-	-	2	-	-	7	-
LACKEY, B.	-	4/7	.571	2/3	.667	-/12	-	-	3	-	-	10	-
CHONES, J.	-	11/16	.688	5/7	.714	-/12	-	-	0	-	-	27	-
MEMINGER, D.	-	8/12	.667	14/17	.824	-/4	-	-	4	-	-	30	-
MCGUIRE, A.	-	3/10	.300	1/2	.500	-/1	-	-	5	-	-	7	-
FRAZIER, G.	-	1/2	.500	1/2	.500	-/4	-	-	1	-	-	3	-
OSTRAND, M.	-	1/1	1.000	0/0	.000	-/0	-	-	0	-	-	2	-
GRZESK, G.	-	0/0	.000	2/2	1.000	-/0	-	-	4	-	-	2	-
MILLS, M.	-	0/0	.000	1/2	.500	-/0	-	-	0	-	-	1	-
LAM, G.	-	0/1	.000	0/0	.000	-/0	-	-	0	-	-	0	-
SPYCHALLA, K.	-	1/1	1.000	0/0	.000	-/0	-	-	0	-	-	2	-
Totals	200	32/59	.542	27/37	.730	-/42	-	-	19	-	-	91	.455

Kentucky (74)   Coach: Adolph Rupp

	Min.	Total FG/FGA	Pct.	FT/FTA	Pct.	Reb. O/T	A	TO	PF	S	Blk	TP	PPM
PARKER, T.	-	5/12	.417	0/1	.000	-/3	-	-	4	-	-	10	-
STEELE, L.	-	7/11	.636	6/9	.667	-/2	-	-	4	-	-	20	-
PAYNE, T.	-	0/1	.000	1/1	1.000	-/2	-	-	5	-	-	1	-
DINWIDDIE, J.	-	0/1	.000	0/0	.000	-/0	-	-	1	-	-	0	-
CASEY, M.	-	2/8	.250	4/4	1.000	-/1	-	-	2	-	-	8	-
HOLLENBECK, K.	-	5/8	.625	4/4	1.000	-/0	-	-	3	-	-	14	-
ANDREWS, J.	-	6/9	.667	2/2	1.000	-/5	-	-	0	-	-	14	-
KEY, S.	-	0/1	.000	1/2	.500	-/1	-	-	2	-	-	1	-
MILLS, T.	-	1/1	1.000	0/2	.000	-/1	-	-	2	-	-	2	-
STAMPER, L.	-	2/3	.667	0/0	.000	-/0	-	-	0	-	-	4	-
WHEELER, C.	-	0/0	.000	0/0	.000	-/0	-	-	0	-	-	0	-
PENHORWOOD, S.	-	0/0	.000	0/0	.000	-/0	-	-	0	-	-	0	-
Totals	200	28/55	.509	18/25	.720	-/15	-	-	23	-	-	74	.370

Team Rebounds: Marquette 6; Kentucky 8. Disqualified: Marquette—McGuire; Kentucky—Payne.

	1st Half	2nd Half	Final
Marquette	43	48	91
Kentucky	43	31	74

REGIONAL THIRD PLACE MIDWEST

Houston (119)   Coach: Guy Lewis

	Min.	Total FG/FGA	Pct.	FT/FTA	Pct.	Reb. O/T	A	TO	PF	S	Blk	TP	PPM
WELCH, P.	-	13/30	.433	12/18	.667	-/4	7	3	3	-	-	38	-
DAVIS, D.	-	8/14	.571	2/2	1.000	-/13	5	5	4	-	-	18	-
NEWSOME, S.	-	12/16	.750	5/9	.556	-/8	3	2	5	-	-	29	-
HALL, B.	-	9/16	.563	2/3	.667	-/15	1	3	2	-	-	20	-
BONNEY, J.	-	4/6	.667	0/1	.000	-/4	3	2	3	-	-	8	-
WILLIS, S.	-	0/0	.000	2/3	.667	-/1	0	0	1	-	-	2	-
BODDEN, G.	-	1/2	.500	2/2	1.000	-/3	0	2	4	-	-	4	-
Totals	200	47/84	.560	25/38	.658	-/48	19	17	22	-	-	119	.595

Notre Dame (106)   Coach: Johnny Dee

	Min.	Total FG/FGA	Pct.	FT/FTA	Pct.	Reb. O/T	A	TO	PF	S	Blk	TP	PPM
CARR, A.	-	17/40	.425	13/17	.765	-/12	2	2	3	-	-	47	-
MEEHAN, J.	-	1/7	.143	0/1	.000	-/1	1	3	5	-	-	2	-
CATLETT, S.	-	7/11	.636	2/3	.667	-/10	3	2	1	-	-	16	-
JONES, C.	-	8/17	.471	9/9	1.000	-/22	0	7	4	-	-	25	-
PLEICK, J.	-	1/9	.111	2/2	1.000	-/5	0	1	3	-	-	4	-
GEMMEL, D.	-	3/10	.300	1/1	1.000	-/3	0	0	4	-	-	7	-
EGART, J.	-	1/1	1.000	0/0	.000	-/0	0	0	0	-	-	2	-
SINNOTT, T.	-	1/7	.143	1/3	.333	-/6	1	3	5	-	-	3	-
Totals	200	39/102	.382	28/36	.778	-/59	7	18	25	-	-	106	.530

Team Rebounds: Houston 7; Notre Dame 7. Disqualified: Houston—Newsome; Notre Dame—Meehan, Sinnott.

	1st Half	2nd Half	Final
Houston	62	57	119
Notre Dame	50	56	106

REGIONAL THIRD PLACE WEST

Pacific (84)   Coach: Dick Edwards

	Min.	Total FG/FGA	Pct.	FT/FTA	Pct.	Reb. O/T	A	TO	PF	S	Blk	TP	PPM
DULANEY, B.	-	4/5	.800	1/1	1.000	-/1	0	-	3	-	-	9	-
MCCARGO, J.	-	2/5	.400	4/6	.667	-/11	4	-	4	-	-	8	-
GIANELLI, J.	-	10/17	.588	4/6	.667	-/13	1	-	5	-	-	24	-
THOMASON, B.	-	4/10	.400	3/5	.600	-/2	3	-	2	-	-	11	-
SCHEIDEGGER, P.	-	2/6	.333	6/8	.750	-/5	1	-	1	-	-	10	-
DOUGLASS, P.	-	4/5	.800	6/6	1.000	-/3	1	-	1	-	-	14	-
JOSHUA, J.	-	0/1	.000	0/0	.000	-/1	2	-	0	-	-	0	-
JENSEN, P.	-	0/0	.000	0/0	.000	-/3	0	-	1	-	-	0	-
SPERRING, R.	-	3/4	.750	2/4	.500	-/2	2	-	3	-	-	8	-
Totals	200	29/53	.547	26/36	.722	-/41	14	-	20	-	-	84	.420

Brigham Young (81)   Coach: Stan Watts

	Min.	Total FG/FGA	Pct.	FT/FTA	Pct.	Reb. O/T	A	TO	PF	S	Blk	TP	PPM
KELLY, S.	-	6/21	.286	4/6	.667	-/7	6	-	4	-	-	16	-
TOLLESTRUP, P.	-	2/7	.286	4/4	1.000	-/1	2	-	4	-	-	8	-
COSIC, K.	-	6/9	.667	2/3	.667	-/13	4	-	4	-	-	14	-
FRYER, B.	-	6/15	.400	5/5	1.000	-/3	2	-	4	-	-	17	-
MILLER, J.	-	7/14	.500	0/4	.000	-/11	5	-	4	-	-	14	-
BUNKER, J.	-	4/7	.571	0/1	.000	-/6	4	-	5	-	-	8	-
SARKALAHTI, K.	-	2/2	1.000	0/0	.000	-/1	2	-	1	-	-	4	-
Totals	200	33/75	.440	15/23	.652	-/42	25	-	26	-	-	81	.405

Team Rebounds: Pacific 1; Brigham Young 3. Disqualified: Pacific—Gianelli; Brigham Young—Bunker.

	1st Half	2nd Half	Final
Pacific	48	36	84
Brigham Young	37	44	81

✪ ALL-STAR TEAMS ✪

ALL TOURNAMENT

★ JIM MCDANIELS	WESTERN KY.
STEVE PATTERSON	UCLA
HOWARD PORTER	VILLANOVA
HANK SIEMIONTKOWSKI	VILLANOVA
SIDNEY WICKS	UCLA

★ Most Outstanding Player(s)

✪ INDIVIDUAL RECORDS ✪

SCORING

Most points in a single game
1	AUSTIN CARR, NOTRE DAME (vs. TCU)	52
2	AUSTIN CARR, NOTRE DAME (vs. HOUSTON)	47
3	TOM RIKER, S. CAROLINA (vs. FORDHAM)	39
4	POO WELCH, HOUSTON (vs. NOTRE DAME)	38
5	JIM MCDANIELS, WESTERN KY. (vs. KANSAS)	36

Most total points in the tournament
1	JIM MCDANIELS, WESTERN KY.	147
2	HOWARD PORTER, VILLANOVA	133
3	AUSTIN CARR, NOTRE DAME	125
4	HANK SIEMIONTKOWSKI, VILLANOVA	112
5	DAVE ROBISCH, KANSAS	96

Highest scoring average (minimum 2 games)
1	AUSTIN CARR, NOTRE DAME (125-3)	41.67
2	POO WELCH, HOUSTON (89-3)	29.67
3	JIM MCDANIELS, WESTERN KY. (147-5)	29.40
4	CHARLES YELVERTON, FORDHAM (87-3)	29.00
5	HOWARD PORTER, VILLANOVA (133-5)	26.60

FIELD GOALS

Most field goals in a single game
1	AUSTIN CARR, NOTRE DAME (vs. TCU)	20
2	TOM RIKER, S. CAROLINA (vs. FORDHAM)	18
3	AUSTIN CARR, NOTRE DAME (vs. HOUSTON)	17
4	HOWARD PORTER, VILLANOVA (vs. PENNSYLVANIA)	16
5	2 tied for fifth place.	

Most total field goals in the tournament
1	JIM MCDANIELS, WESTERN KY.	61
2	HOWARD PORTER, VILLANOVA	56
3	AUSTIN CARR, NOTRE DAME	48
4	HANK SIEMIONTKOWSKI, VILLANOVA	46
5	DAVE ROBISCH, KANSAS	36

Most field goal attempts in a single game
1	AUSTIN CARR, NOTRE DAME (vs. HOUSTON)	40
2	JIM MCDANIELS, WESTERN KY. (vs. OHIO STATE)	35
3	AUSTIN CARR, NOTRE DAME (vs. TCU)	34
4	JIM DUNN, WESTERN KY. (vs. VILLANOVA)	33
5	2 tied for fifth place.	

Most total field goal attempts in tournament
1	JIM MCDANIELS, WESTERN KY.	138
2	HOWARD PORTER, VILLANOVA	102
3	AUSTIN CARR, NOTRE DAME	101
4	JIM DUNN, WESTERN KY.	84
5	DAVE ROBISCH, KANSAS	81

Highest field goal percentage in a single game (minimum 10 attempts)
1	STEVE NEWSOME, HOUSTON (vs. NOTRE DAME) (12-16)	.750
2	STEVE PATTERSON, UCLA (vs. VILLANOVA) (13-18)	.722

3	CURTIS ROWE, UCLA (vs. KANSAS) (7-10)	.700
3	STEVE KELLY, BRIGHAM YOUNG (vs. UTAH STATE) (7-10)	.700
5	TOM RIKER, S. CAROLINA (vs. FORDHAM) (18-26)	.692

Highest field goal percentage in the tournament (minimum 20 attempts)
1	TOM BUSH, DRAKE (13-20)	.650
2	JIM CHONES, MARQUETTE (29-48)	.604
3	ALEX SCOTT, NEW MEXICO ST. (13-22)	.591
4	BOB HALL, HOUSTON (18-31)	.581
5	JOHN GIANELLI, PACIFIC (15-26)	.577

FREE THROWS

Most free throws in a single game
1	DEAN MEMINGER, MARQUETTE (vs. KENTUCKY)	14
2	AUSTIN CARR, NOTRE DAME (vs. HOUSTON)	13
2	BERNIE FRYER, BRIGHAM YOUNG (vs. UTAH STATE)	13
4	POO WELCH, HOUSTON (vs. NOTRE DAME)	12
4	AUSTIN CARR, NOTRE DAME (vs. TCU)	12

Most total free throws in the tournament
1	AUSTIN CARR, NOTRE DAME	29
2	DEAN MEMINGER, MARQUETTE	26
3	JIM MCDANIELS, WESTERN KY.	25
4	DAVE ROBISCH, KANSAS	24
5	TOM INGELSBY, VILLANOVA	23

Most free throws attempted in a single game
1	POO WELCH, HOUSTON (vs. NOTRE DAME)	18
2	DEAN MEMINGER, MARQUETTE (vs. KENTUCKY)	17
2	AUSTIN CARR, NOTRE DAME (vs. HOUSTON)	17
4	AUSTIN CARR, NOTRE DAME (vs. TCU)	15
4	BERNIE FRYER, BRIGHAM YOUNG (vs. UTAH STATE)	15

Most free throws attempted in the tournament
1	DAVE ROBISCH, KANSAS	37
1	AUSTIN CARR, NOTRE DAME	37
3	DEAN MEMINGER, MARQUETTE	36
4	JIM MCDANIELS, WESTERN KY.	35
5	2 tied for fifth place.	

Highest free throw percentage in a single game (minimum 7 attempts)
1	JIM MCDANIELS, WESTERN KY. (vs. KENTUCKY) (11-11)	1.000
2	COLLIS JONES, NOTRE DAME (vs. HOUSTON) (9-9)	1.000
3	CHARLES YELVERTON, FORDHAM (vs. VILLANOVA) (8-8)	1.000
3	KEVIN JOYCE, S. CAROLINA (vs. FORDHAM) (8-8)	1.000
5	JOHN BURIK, FORDHAM (vs. S. CAROLINA) (7-7)	1.000

Highest free throw percentage in the tournament (minimum 15 attempts)
1	HENRY BIBBY, UCLA (17-17)	1.000
2	HANK SIEMIONTKOWSKI, VILLANOVA (20-22)	.909
3	COLLIS JONES, NOTRE DAME (20-24)	.833
4	STEVE KELLY, BRIGHAM YOUNG (14-17)	.824
4	KRESIMIR COSIC, BRIGHAM YOUNG (14-17)	.824

REBOUNDS

Most rebounds in a single game
1	KRESIMIR COSIC, BRIGHAM YOUNG (vs. UCLA)	23
2	COLLIS JONES, NOTRE DAME (vs. HOUSTON)	22
2	CLARENCE GLOVER, WESTERN KY. (vs. OHIO STATE)	22
2	ARTIS GILMORE, JACKSONVILLE (vs. WESTERN KY.)	22
5	2 tied for fifth place.	

Most total rebounds in the tournament
1	CLARENCE GLOVER, WESTERN KY.	89
2	JIM MCDANIELS, WESTERN KY.	66
3	HOWARD PORTER, VILLANOVA	65
4	SIDNEY WICKS, UCLA	52
5	JIM DUNN, WESTERN KY.	50

Most rebounds per game (minimum 2 games)
1	CLARENCE GLOVER, WESTERN KY. (89-5)	17.80
2	COLLIS JONES, NOTRE DAME (49-3)	16.33
3	KRESIMIR COSIC, BRIGHAM YOUNG (47-3)	15.67
4	TOM BUSH, DRAKE (31-2)	15.50
5	BOB HALL, HOUSTON (45-3)	15.00

ASSISTS

Most assists in a single game
1	JACKIE MEEHAN, NOTRE DAME (vs. TCU)	11
1	JIM FERGUSON, TCU (vs. NOTRE DAME)	11
3	CHRIS FORD, VILLANOVA (vs. ST. JOSEPH'S)	10
3	CHRIS FORD, VILLANOVA (vs. UCLA)	10
5	2 tied for fifth place.	

Most total assists in the tournament
1	CHRIS FORD, VILLANOVA	40
2	TOM INGELSBY, VILLANOVA	28
3	REX BAILEY, WESTERN KY.	26
4	JIM DUNN, WESTERN KY.	19
5	JACKIE MEEHAN, NOTRE DAME	18

Most assists per game (minimum 2 appearances)
1	CHRIS FORD, VILLANOVA (40-5)	8.00
2	JACKIE MEEHAN, NOTRE DAME (18-3)	6.00
3	POO WELCH, HOUSTON (17-3)	5.67
4	TOM INGELSBY, VILLANOVA (28-5)	5.60
5	REX BAILEY, WESTERN KY. (26-5)	5.20

✪ TEAM RECORDS ✪

SCORING

Most points in a single game
1	HOUSTON (vs. NOTRE DAME)	119
2	WESTERN KY. (vs. KENTUCKY)	107
3	NOTRE DAME (vs. HOUSTON)	106

Most total points in the tournament
1	WESTERN KY.	428
2	VILLANOVA	422
3	KANSAS	286

Highest scoring average (minimum 2 games)
1	NOTRE DAME (280-3)	93.33
1	FORDHAM (280-3)	93.33
3	HOUSTON (268-3)	89.33

FIELD GOALS

Most field goals in a single game
1	HOUSTON (vs. NOTRE DAME)	47
2	FORDHAM (vs. FURMAN)	44
3	WESTERN KY. (vs. KENTUCKY)	42

Most total field goals in the tournament
1	WESTERN KY.	178
2	VILLANOVA	167
3	2 tied for third place.	

Most field goals attempted in a single game
1	WESTERN KY. (vs. VILLANOVA)	105
2	NOTRE DAME (vs. HOUSTON)	102
3	WESTERN KY. (vs. JACKSONVILLE)	96

Most total field goals attempted in the tournament
1	WESTERN KY.	442
2	VILLANOVA	328
3	KANSAS	270

Highest field goal percentage in a single game
1	VILLANOVA (vs. PENNSYLVANIA) (37-60)	.617
2	MARQUETTE (vs. MIAMI [OHIO]) (25-43)	.581
3	VILLANOVA (vs. FORDHAM) (35-61)	.574

Highest field goal percentage in the tournament (minimum 2 games)
1	VILLANOVA (167-328)	.509
2	MARQUETTE (81-164)	.494
3	HOUSTON (103-216)	.477

FREE THROWS

Most free throws in a single game
1	BRIGHAM YOUNG (vs. UTAH STATE)	33
2	PENNSYLVANIA (vs. S. CAROLINA)	31
3	NOTRE DAME (vs. HOUSTON)	28

Most total free throws in the tournament
1	VILLANOVA	88
2	WESTERN KY.	72
3	UCLA	68

Most free throws attempted in a single game
1	BRIGHAM YOUNG (vs. UTAH STATE)	44
2	HOUSTON (vs. NOTRE DAME)	38
3	2 tied for third place.	

Most total free throws attempted in the tournament
1	VILLANOVA	121
2	WESTERN KY.	116
3	KANSAS	113

Highest free throw percentage in a single game
1	FORDHAM (vs. S. CAROLINA) (22-22)	1.000
2	LONG BEACH ST. (vs. WEBER ST.) (27-30)	.900
3	PENNSYLVANIA (vs. S. CAROLINA) (31-35)	.886

Highest free throw percentage in the tournament (minimum 2 games)
1	PENNSYLVANIA (56-69)	.812
2	FORDHAM (60-79)	.760
3	NOTRE DAME (66-88)	.750

Fewest free throws in a single game
1	WESTERN KY. (vs. JACKSONVILLE)	4
2	PENNSYLVANIA (vs. VILLANOVA)	7
3	VILLANOVA (vs. UCLA)	10

Lowest free throw percentage in a single game
1	WESTERN KY. (vs. JACKSONVILLE) (4-13)	.308
2	UCLA (vs. BRIGHAM YOUNG) (11-23)	.478
3	DRAKE (vs. NOTRE DAME) (13-26)	.500

Lowest free throw percentage in the tournament (minimum 2 games)
1	DRAKE (24-45)	.533
2	KANSAS (66-113)	.584
3	WESTERN KY. (72-116)	.621

REBOUNDS

Most rebounds in a single game
1	DRAKE (vs. NOTRE DAME)	63
2	UCLA (vs. BRIGHAM YOUNG)	62
3	WESTERN KY. (vs. VILLANOVA)	61

Most rebounds per game (minimum 2 games)
1	WESTERN KY. (260-5)	52.00
2	DRAKE (102-2)	51.00
3	NOTRE DAME (151-3)	50.33

ASSISTS

Most assists in a single game
1	BRIGHAM YOUNG (vs. PACIFIC)	25
1	NOTRE DAME (vs. TCU)	25
3	2 tied for third place.	

Most assists per game (minimum 2 games)
1	BRIGHAM YOUNG (62-3)	20.67
2	WESTERN KY. (90-5)	18.00
3	LONG BEACH ST. (54-3)	18.00

1972

| FIRST ROUND | REGIONAL SEMIFINAL | REGIONAL FINAL | FINAL FOUR | REGIONAL FINAL | REGIONAL SEMIFINAL | FIRST ROUND |

MIDEAST

Florida St. 83
Florida St. 70
Eastern Ky. 81
Florida St. 73
(bye)
*Minnesota 56
Florida St. 79
Kentucky 85
(bye)
Kentucky 54
Marquette 73
Marquette 69
Ohio 49

UCLA 81
Florida St. 76

EAST

(bye)
N. Carolina 92
N. Carolina 73
S. Carolina 53
S. Carolina 69
Temple 51
N. Carolina 75
Pennsylvania 76
Pennsylvania 78
Providence 60
Pennsylvania 59
Villanova 85
Villanova 67
East Carolina 70

MIDWEST

Louisville 88
(bye)
Louisville 72
*S'western La. 112
*S'western La. 84
Marshall 101
Louisville 77
Kansas St. 66
(bye)
Kansas St. 65
Texas 85
Texas 55
Houston 74

WEST

UCLA 90
(bye)
UCLA 73
Weber St. 91
Weber St. 58
Hawaii 64
UCLA 96
*Long Beach St. 95 (ot)
*Long Beach St. 75
Brigham Young 90
*Long Beach St. 57
San Francisco 55
(bye)

CONSOLATION GAMES

National Third Place:

N. Carolina 105
Louisville 91

Regional Third Place:

East:
S. Carolina 90
Villanova 78

Mideast:
*Minnesota 77
Marquette 72

Midwest:
*S'western La. 100
Texas 70

West:
San Francisco 74
Weber St. 64

*Southwestern Louisiana's, Long Beach State's, and Minnesota's participation in 1972 tournament vacated.

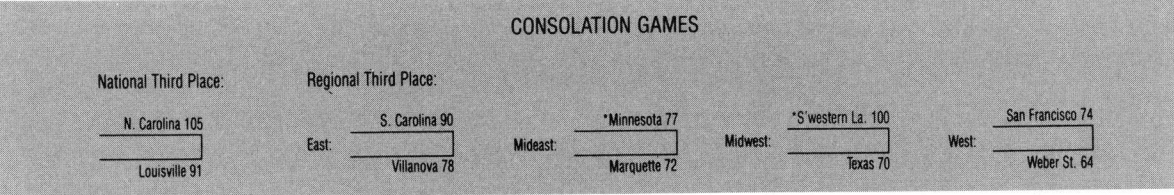

The 1971–72 season marked the arrival of a new UCLA nucleus: joining upperclassmen Henry Bibby, Larry Farmer, and Larry Hollyfield was a remarkable group of sophomores, including the smooth as silk 18-year-old forward Keith Wilkes and guards Greg Lee and Tommy Curtis. The center of attention, though, was 6-11 Bill Walton. From the moment he stepped onto the court for the Bruin varsity, Walton was college basketball's most dominant player since Lew Alcindor hung up his UCLA uniform.

In 1972 the Bruins won the NCAA championship—again. They went undefeated—again. And they accomplished it all so efficiently, so methodically, so automatically, that at times the most exciting action was off the court.

After it was disclosed that the stars of both the 1971 second- and third-place teams—Villanova and Western Kentucky—had signed pro contracts before the tournament, the NCAA Executive Committee vacated the teams' records and ordered the two schools to return their trophies and prize money. In 1972 the bidding war for top college players between the rival ABA and NBA pro leagues (which had precipitated the signings of Villanova's Howard Porter and Western Kentucky's Jim McDaniels the previous year) continued unabated, but under heavier NCAA scrutiny. Al McGuire's Marquette Warriors, who had gone through much of the season undefeated and were widely regarded as the team most likely to give UCLA a run for its money, had their chance for a championship severely damaged when their big man, Jim Chones, signed a professional contract in February. NCAA investigators, hoping to avoid another embarrassing disclosure, demanded that ten players from six schools sign lengthy affidavits attesting to their continued amateur status. When Marquette Coach McGuire advised Bob Lackey to refuse to sign the affidavit without first consulting with a lawyer, the Warriors were ruled ineligible to compete in the tournament (even though they had already won their first-round game).

After receiving legal advice, Lackey signed a statement that he had not retained the services of an agent and was thus still an amateur. Marquette was reinstated. But in their next game, they held a 6-point second-half lead over Kentucky when forward George Frazier was forced off the court with an ankle injury. The decimated Warriors finally succumbed to Adolph Rupp's Wildcats.

In the Mideast regional final, Kentucky was routed by Florida State, whose Seminoles were in their first year of eligibility after three years of NCAA probation for recruiting violations. Florida State then went on to meet heavily favored North Carolina, whose Tar Heels were in their fourth Final Four in six years. The Seminoles were not impressed. They outran North Carolina, breaking the Tar Heels' usually powerful press with ease. The smallest man on the court, 5-7 Otto Perry, time and again raced past the taller but slower Carolinians, finally forcing Coach Dean Smith to set up in a half-court defense. North Carolina, with Bob McAdoo leading the charge both on offense and off the boards, mounted a furious second-half comeback. But McAdoo fouled out, and the Seminoles held on for a 79-75 victory.

Soon after Florida State qualified to play UCLA in the final (the Bruins having routed three opponents, including Louisville and the Cardinals' rookie coach, former Wooden assistant Denny Crum, in their semi), Bill Wall, the president of the National Association of Basketball Coaches, referring to the Seminoles' presence in the tournament, declared that "our coaches are amazed, disgusted, and disillusioned." He said "I resent the fact that they are here and a lot of coaches feel the same." Wall, the coach of MacMurray College in Illinois, remarked that Florida State had "twice been on probation" and that their coach Hugh Durham "got what he wanted [the players] and the institution got the instant recognition." An NCAA spokesman disavowed Wall's comments, stating that the school had served its probation and had every right to be in the tournament. And Dr. Stanley Marshall, the president of Florida State University, responded to Wall by calling the N.A.B.C. president's remarks "very damaging, inaccurate, and totally untrue," and threatened a lawsuit.

Out of the courts and on the court, the Seminoles faced the Bruins of UCLA for the national championship. Florida State, by virtue of excellent long-range shooting, raced out to an early 21-14 advantage. But UCLA, led by Walton, Wilkes, and Bibby, stormed back to go ahead 50-39 at the half. The Bruins built their lead to 16 as substitute guard Tommy Curtis (a Tallahassee native who was heavily recruited by his hometown school Florida State) penetrated and fed Walton inside. But Walton picked up his fourth foul and was forced to sit down for six minutes, and the hot shooting of Florida State's Ron King led a Seminole comeback. When Walton returned, the Bruins slowed the pace, and although the final margin was just 5 (81-76) the outcome was never in doubt.

Despite all the controversy that swirled around college basketball in 1972, the mighty Bruins just kept rolling along.

FIRST ROUND MIDEAST

Florida State (83)   Coach: Hugh Durham

	Min.	Total FG / FGA	Pct.	FT / FTA	Pct.	Reb. O / T	A	TO	PF	S	Blk	TP	PPM
GARRETT, R.	-	3/11	.273	0/ 2	.000	-/10	1	-	4	-	-	6	-
ROYALS, R.	-	4/ 6	.667	4/ 6	.667	-/ 8	1	-	5	-	-	12	-
MCCRAY, L.	-	4/ 5	.800	3/ 4	.750	-/ 4	2	-	4	-	-	11	-
KING, R.	-	3/13	.231	4/ 7	.571	-/ 2	2	-	2	-	-	10	-
SAMUEL, G.	-	0/ 0	.000	0/ 0	.000	-/ 1	3	-	0	-	-	0	-
HARRIS, R.	-	5/11	.455	3/ 4	.750	-/ 8	0	-	1	-	-	13	-
PETTY, O.	-	5/ 8	.625	5/ 6	.833	-/ 2	3	-	3	-	-	15	-
GAY, L.	-	3/ 3	1.000	0/ 1	.000	-/ 3	0	-	0	-	-	6	-
COLE, O.	-	3/ 9	.333	4/ 6	.667	-/ 7	1	-	0	-	-	10	-
Totals	200	30/66	.455	23/36	.639	-/45	13	-	19	-	-	83	.415

Eastern Kentucky (81)   Coach: Guy Strong

	Min.	Total FG / FGA	Pct.	FT / FTA	Pct.	Reb. O / T	A	TO	PF	S	Blk	TP	PPM
DUNAGAN, D.	-	3/10	.300	8/10	.800	-/15	5	-	3	-	-	14	-
MITCHELL, C.	-	10/18	.556	3/ 5	.600	-/ 4	0	-	4	-	-	23	-
ARGABRIGHT, D.	-	7/10	.700	0/ 1	.000	-/ 2	1	-	5	-	-	14	-
BRYANT, G.	-	4/16	.250	3/ 4	.750	-/ 4	6	-	3	-	-	11	-
BURTON, B.	-	2/ 3	.667	1/ 2	.500	-/ 4	5	-	5	-	-	5	-
BROOKS, R.	-	1/ 2	.500	1/ 3	.333	-/ 2	0	-	1	-	-	3	-
UPCHURCH, W.	-	1/ 2	.500	1/ 2	.500	-/ 1	0	-	1	-	-	3	-
NEWELL, B.	-	1/ 2	.500	0/ 0	.000	-/ 0	0	-	1	-	-	2	-
WORTHINGTON, C.	-	0/ 0	.000	2/ 2	1.000	-/ 1	0	-	1	-	-	2	-
BRUNKER, C.	-	2/ 7	.286	0/ 0	.000	-/ 1	0	-	3	-	-	4	-
Totals	200	31/70	.443	19/29	.655	-/34	17	-	27	-	-	81	.405

Team Rebounds: Florida State 12; Eastern Ky. 7. Disqualified: Florida State—Royals; Eastern Ky.—Argabright, Burton.

	1st Half	2nd Half	Final
Florida State	50	33	83
Eastern Ky.	42	39	81

Marquette (73)   Coach: Al McGuire

	Min.	Total FG / FGA	Pct.	FT / FTA	Pct.	Reb. O / T	A	TO	PF	S	Blk	TP	PPM
FRAZIER, G.	-	6/ 8	.750	3/ 4	.750	-/ 7	-	-	3	-	-	15	-
LACKEY, B.	-	8/16	.500	4/ 4	1.000	-/ 7	-	-	3	-	-	20	-
MCNEILL, L.	-	9/16	.563	4/ 4	1.000	-/ 9	-	-	4	-	-	22	-
WASHINGTON, M.	-	2/ 7	.286	0/ 2	.000	-/ 4	-	-	2	-	-	4	-
MCGUIRE, A.	-	3/ 7	.429	0/ 0	.000	-/ 4	-	-	2	-	-	6	-
SPYCHALIA, K.	-	1/ 2	.500	0/ 1	.000	-/ 0	-	-	0	-	-	2	-
OSTRAND, M.	-	1/ 2	.500	0/ 0	.000	-/ 0	-	-	0	-	-	2	-
GRZESK, G.	-	0/ 0	.000	0/ 0	.000	-/ 0	-	-	1	-	-	0	-
MILLS, M.	-	1/ 1	1.000	0/ 0	.000	-/ 2	-	-	0	-	-	2	-
Totals	200	31/59	.525	11/15	.733	-/33	-	-	15	-	-	73	.365

Ohio (49)   Coach: James Snyder

	Min.	Total FG / FGA	Pct.	FT / FTA	Pct.	Reb. O / T	A	TO	PF	S	Blk	TP	PPM
RICCARDI, T.	-	2/11	.182	1/ 1	1.000	-/ 4	-	-	2	-	-	5	-
BROWN, B.	-	4/ 6	.667	2/ 2	1.000	-/ 4	-	-	1	-	-	10	-
BALL, D.	-	2/ 7	.286	0/ 0	.000	-/ 2	-	-	1	-	-	4	-
CORDE, T.	-	2/ 7	.286	1/ 3	.333	-/ 2	-	-	1	-	-	5	-
LALICH, T.	-	4/ 8	.500	2/ 4	.500	-/ 6	-	-	4	-	-	10	-
HOWELL, B.	-	3/ 9	.333	1/ 2	.500	-/ 0	-	-	2	-	-	7	-
RUSCH, D.	-	1/ 5	.200	6/ 7	.857	-/ 7	-	-	4	-	-	8	-
THOMPSON, D.	-	0/ 1	.000	0/ 0	.000	-/ 0	-	-	0	-	-	0	-
Totals	200	18/54	.333	13/19	.684	-/25	-	-	14	-	-	49	.245

Team Rebounds: Marquette 7; Ohio 8. Disqualified: None.

	1st Half	2nd Half	Final
Marquette	38	35	73
Ohio	20	29	49

FIRST ROUND EAST

South Carolina (53)   Coach: Frank McGuire

	Min.	Total FG / FGA	Pct.	FT / FTA	Pct.	Reb. O / T	A	TO	PF	S	Blk	TP	PPM
AYDLETT, R.	-	1/ 6	.167	1/ 1	1.000	-/ 1	3	2	1	-	-	3	-
RIKER, T.	-	9/14	.643	5/ 8	.625	-/ 5	2	6	2	-	-	23	-
TRAYLOR, D.	-	5/ 5	1.000	1/ 3	.333	-/10	1	3	4	-	-	11	-
CARVER, B.	-	2/ 3	.667	0/ 0	.000	-/ 2	3	2	1	-	-	4	-
JOYCE, K.	-	6/14	.429	0/ 1	.000	-/ 7	4	4	1	-	-	12	-
MOUSA, R.	-	0/ 0	.000	0/ 0	.000	-/ 0	0	0	0	-	-	0	-
WINTERS, B.	-	0/ 3	.000	0/ 0	.000	-/ 1	1	0	2	-	-	0	-
Totals	200	23/45	.511	7/13	.538	-/26	14	17	11	-	-	53	.265

Temple (51)   Coach: Harry Litwack

	Min.	Total FG / FGA	Pct.	FT / FTA	Pct.	Reb. O / T	A	TO	PF	S	Blk	TP	PPM
JOHNSON, O.	-	7/16	.438	2/ 4	.500	-/ 8	2	2	1	-	-	16	-
JONES, M.	-	4/ 8	.500	1/ 2	.500	-/ 7	2	1	2	-	-	9	-
NEWMAN, J.	-	3/13	.231	2/ 3	.667	-/ 5	0	6	4	-	-	8	-
TRUDEAU, R.	-	2/ 5	.400	1/ 2	.500	-/ 3	5	4	0	-	-	5	-
KNEIB, J.	-	3/ 8	.375	3/ 3	1.000	-/ 4	5	1	1	-	-	9	-
COLLINS, P.	-	1/ 2	.500	0/ 0	.000	-/ 1	1	1	0	-	-	2	-
TRESS, L.	-	1/ 5	.200	0/ 0	.000	-/ 3	0	1	4	-	-	2	-
Totals	200	21/57	.368	9/14	.643	-/31	15	16	12	-	-	51	.255

Team Rebounds: S. Carolina 4; Temple 8. Disqualified: None.

	1st Half	2nd Half	Final
S. Carolina	25	28	53
Temple	29	22	51

Pennsylvania (76)   Coach: Chuck Daly

	Min.	Total FG / FGA	Pct.	FT / FTA	Pct.	Reb. O / T	A	TO	PF	S	Blk	TP	PPM
CALHOUN, C.	-	8/ 9	.889	3/ 6	.500	-/ 6	5	4	1	-	-	19	-
HANKINSON, P.	-	6/11	.545	2/ 2	1.000	-/ 4	6	3	3	-	-	14	-
MORSE, B.	-	9/16	.563	1/ 1	1.000	-/ 9	3	2	3	-	-	19	-
COTLER, A.	-	3/ 4	.750	0/ 0	.000	-/ 1	6	6	2	-	-	6	-
LITTLEPAGE, C.	-	4/ 5	.800	3/ 4	.750	-/ 2	1	0	1	-	-	11	-
JABLONSKI, J.	-	1/ 1	1.000	0/ 1	.000	-/ 0	0	1	0	-	-	2	-
BILLINGSLEA, R.	-	2/ 3	.667	0/ 0	.000	-/ 2	2	1	0	-	-	4	-
FINGER, B.	-	0/ 0	.000	1/ 2	.500	-/ 0	0	0	0	-	-	1	-
VARGA, W.	-	0/ 0	.000	0/ 0	.000	-/ 0	0	1	0	-	-	0	-
Totals	200	33/49	.673	10/16	.625	-/24	23	18	10	-	-	76	.380

Providence (60)   Coach: Dave Gavitt

	Min.	Total FG / FGA	Pct.	FT / FTA	Pct.	Reb. O / T	A	TO	PF	S	Blk	TP	PPM
DIGREGORIO, E.	-	8/15	.533	1/ 2	.500	-/ 2	4	3	2	-	-	17	-
BARNES, M.	-	3/10	.300	1/ 2	.500	-/ 6	1	4	2	-	-	7	-
CRAWFORD, C.	-	2/ 3	.667	1/ 1	1.000	-/ 6	0	1	3	-	-	5	-
LEWIS, D.	-	4/ 8	.500	0/ 0	.000	-/ 3	4	4	2	-	-	8	-
KING, N.	-	1/ 4	.250	0/ 0	.000	-/ 2	1	1	0	-	-	2	-
COSTELLO, F.	-	8/18	.444	4/ 5	.800	-/ 4	2	1	4	-	-	20	-
KETVIRTIS, L.	-	0/ 1	.000	1/ 3	.333	-/ 4	0	0	1	-	-	1	-
WALTERS, T.	-	0/ 0	.000	0/ 0	.000	-/ 0	1	1	0	-	-	0	-
Totals	200	26/59	.441	8/13	.615	-/27	13	15	13	-	-	60	.300

Team Rebounds: Pennsylvania 7; Providence 2. Disqualified: None.

	1st Half	2nd Half	Final
Pennsylvania	31	45	76
Providence	27	33	60

Villanova (85)   Coach: Jack Kraft

	Min.	Total FG/FGA	Pct.	FT/FTA	Pct.	Reb. O/T	A	TO	PF	S	Blk	TP	PPM
HASTINGS, E.	-	2/7	.286	5/7	.714	-/5	4	1	3	-	-	9	-
INGELSBY, T.	-	8/18	.444	2/2	1.000	-/5	2	0	2	-	-	18	-
SIEMIONTKOWSKI, H	-	6/15	.400	0/0	.000	-/8	6	3	2	-	-	12	-
FORD, C.	-	11/19	.579	2/5	.400	-/4	7	0	1	-	-	24	-
MOODY, L.	-	8/13	.615	4/5	.800	-/10	0	0	4	-	-	20	-
GOHL, B.	-	0/0	.000	2/2	1.000	-/0	0	0	0	-	-	2	-
JENTZ	-	0/0	.000	0/0	.000	-/0	0	0	0	-	-	0	-
ALSTON, D.	-	0/1	.000	0/0	.000	-/0	0	0	0	-	-	0	-
DALY, M.	-	0/0	.000	0/0	.000	-/0	0	0	0	-	-	0	-
MCDOWELL, J.	-	0/1	.000	0/0	.000	-/0	0	0	1	-	-	0	-
GASPAR, J.	-	0/1	.000	0/0	.000	-/0	0	0	0	-	-	0	-
BOYLAN	-	0/0	.000	0/0	.000	-/0	0	0	0	-	-	0	-
Totals	200	35/75	.467	15/21	.714	-/32	19	4	13	-	-	85	.425

East Carolina (70)   Coach: Tom Quinn

	Min.	Total FG/FGA	Pct.	FT/FTA	Pct.	Reb. O/T	A	TO	PF	S	Blk	TP	PPM
FABER, A.	-	5/11	.455	1/1	1.000	-/14	1	4	2	-	-	11	-
FAIRLEY, J.	-	5/10	.500	6/9	.667	-/9	4	8	3	-	-	16	-
FRANKLIN, D.	-	9/15	.600	1/3	.333	-/5	1	1	1	-	-	19	-
OWENS, J.	-	5/10	.500	3/3	1.000	-/2	4	3	2	-	-	13	-
QUASH, E.	-	2/6	.333	1/2	.500	-/2	2	1	3	-	-	5	-
WHITE, N.	-	2/7	.286	0/0	.000	-/2	1	0	2	-	-	4	-
POPE, E.	-	0/1	.000	0/0	.000	-/1	0	1	0	-	-	0	-
CROUSE	-	0/2	.000	0/0	.000	-/1	1	0	0	-	-	0	-
PESZKO, R.	-	0/1	.000	2/2	1.000	-/1	0	0	0	-	-	2	-
MCNEILL	-	0/0	.000	0/0	.000	-/0	0	0	0	-	-	0	-
BJORBJEVIZH	-	0/0	.000	0/0	.000	-/0	0	0	0	-	-	0	-
MCKENZIE	-	0/0	.000	0/0	.000	-/0	0	0	0	-	-	0	-
Totals	200	28/63	.444	14/20	.700	-/37	14	18	13	-	-	70	.350

Team Rebounds: Villanova 8; East Carolina 10. Disqualified: None.

	1st Half	2nd Half	Final
Villanova	38	47	85
East Carolina	36	34	70

FIRST ROUND MIDWEST

Southwestern Louisiana (112)   Coach: Beryl Shipley

	Min.	Total FG/FGA	Pct.	FT/FTA	Pct.	Reb. O/T	A	TO	PF	S	Blk	TP	PPM
LAMAR, D.	-	12/31	.387	11/15	.733	-/5	11	-	0	-	-	35	-
GREEN, S.	-	0/1	.000	0/0	.000	-/1	1	-	1	-	-	0	-
BRISBANO, J.	-	7/12	.583	5/7	.714	-/7	5	-	3	-	-	19	-
HANEY, M.	-	0/0	.000	1/2	.500	-/3	2	-	4	-	-	1	-
HERBERT, W.	-	1/1	1.000	0/0	.000	-/0	0	-	0	-	-	2	-
SAUNDERS, F.	-	0/1	.000	3/4	.750	-/9	2	-	5	-	-	3	-
TOWNSEND, P.	-	3/6	.500	3/5	.600	-/5	0	-	2	-	-	9	-
LOFTIN, W.	-	5/6	.833	0/1	.000	-/11	3	-	4	-	-	10	-
EBRON, R.	-	14/22	.636	5/7	.714	-/20	1	-	3	-	-	33	-
Totals	200	42/80	.525	28/41	.683	-/61	25	-	22	-	-	112	.560

Marshall (101)   Coach: Carl Tacy

	Min.	Total FG/FGA	Pct.	FT/FTA	Pct.	Reb. O/T	A	TO	PF	S	Blk	TP	PPM
D'ANTONI, M.	-	9/22	.409	8/11	.727	-/9	10	-	3	-	-	26	-
GANES, B.	-	4/14	.286	0/0	.000	-/6	4	-	3	-	-	8	-
COLLINS, T.	-	4/18	.222	3/3	1.000	-/6	3	-	3	-	-	11	-
DRISCOLL, B.	-	2/7	.286	3/6	.500	-/7	0	-	3	-	-	7	-
ORSINI, G.	-	2/3	.667	0/4	.000	-/4	0	-	5	-	-	4	-
NOLL, R.	-	10/19	.526	1/3	.333	-/16	3	-	5	-	-	21	-
SARK, J.	-	0/0	.000	0/0	.000	-/1	0	-	0	-	-	0	-
LEE, R.	-	11/29	.379	2/3	.667	-/16	2	-	4	-	-	24	-
Totals	200	42/112	.375	17/30	.567	-/65	22	-	26	-	-	101	.505

Team Rebounds: S'western La. 5; Marshall 3. Disqualified: S'western La.—Saunders; Marshall—Orsini, Noll.

	1st Half	2nd Half	Final
S'western La.	55	57	112
Marshall	52	49	101

Texas (85)   Coach: Leon Black

	Min.	Total FG/FGA	Pct.	FT/FTA	Pct.	Reb. O/T	A	TO	PF	S	Blk	TP	PPM
GROSCURTH, E.	30	3/6	.500	4/5	.800	5/11	1	3	4	-	-	10	.333
LENOX, J.	35	4/11	.364	8/12	.667	0/2	6	4	3	-	-	16	.457
BROSTERHOUS, B.	39	6/13	.462	1/1	1.000	7/12	4	6	3	-	-	13	.333
LARRABEE, H.	38	3/6	.500	9/11	.818	0/5	7	4	2	-	-	15	.395
ROBINSON, L.	35	9/16	.563	5/6	.833	3/14	0	4	2	-	-	23	.657
LOUIS, J.	15	3/5	.600	0/1	.000	1/1	1	2	5	-	-	6	.400
BLACKLOCK, J.	7	0/0	.000	2/2	1.000	0/1	0	1	0	-	-	2	.286
HOWDEN, L.	1	0/0	.000	0/0	.000	0/0	0	0	1	-	-	0	.000
Totals	200	28/57	.491	29/38	.763	16/46	19	24	20	-	-	85	.425

Houston (74)   Coach: Guy Lewis

	Min.	Total FG/FGA	Pct.	FT/FTA	Pct.	Reb. O/T	A	TO	PF	S	Blk	TP	PPM
HAYES, D.	28	2/6	.333	0/0	.000	0/0	2	0	4	-	-	4	.143
BONNEY, J.	29	1/7	.143	1/2	.500	1/2	4	0	4	-	-	3	.103
JONES, D.	35	3/10	.300	2/5	.400	6/9	2	0	4	-	-	8	.229
DAVIS, D.	38	11/22	.500	3/7	.429	3/7	3	8	5	-	-	25	.658
NEWSOME, S.	39	10/22	.455	6/8	.750	9/17	5	5	4	-	-	26	.667
KIGHTL, R.	1	0/0	.000	0/0	.000	0/0	0	1	1	-	-	0	.000
WILLIS, S.	6	1/2	.500	0/0	.000	0/1	0	1	2	-	-	2	.333
HOSTER, C.	5	1/2	.500	0/0	.000	0/0	0	0	1	-	-	2	.400
BROWN, L.	4	0/1	.000	1/2	.500	0/0	1	0	2	-	-	1	.250
WORRELL, D.	5	0/2	.000	0/0	.000	1/1	0	0	2	-	-	0	.000
EDWARDS, S.	10	1/3	.333	1/2	.500	0/1	2	2	0	-	-	3	.300
Totals	200	30/77	.390	14/26	.538	20/38	19	17	25	-	-	74	.370

Team Rebounds: Texas 5; Houston 8. Disqualified: Texas—Louis; Houston—Davis.

	1st Half	2nd Half	Final
Texas	45	40	85
Houston	33	41	74

FIRST ROUND WEST

Weber State (91)   Coach: Gene Visscher

	Min.	Total FG / FGA	Pct.	FT / FTA	Pct.	Reb. O / T	A	TO	PF	S	Blk	TP	PPM
SMALL, B.	-	6/11	.545	9/10	.900	-/ 5	8	-	1	-	-	21	-
DAVIS, B.	-	12/22	.545	8/10	.800	-/13	1	-	3	-	-	32	-
KNOBLE, J.	-	4/14	.286	6/10	.600	-/14	1	-	3	-	-	14	-
COOPER, R.	-	2/ 5	.400	4/ 7	.571	-/ 9	0	-	1	-	-	8	-
VANDYKE, W.	-	2/ 4	.500	1/ 3	.333	-/ 3	2	-	4	-	-	5	-
MCGARRY, K.	-	0/ 0	.000	0/ 1	.000	-/ 1	0	-	0	-	-	0	-
WILLIAMS	-	0/ 0	.000	1/ 3	.333	-/ 0	0	-	0	-	-	1	-
SOTER, G.	-	1/ 2	.500	2/ 3	.667	-/ 0	0	-	1	-	-	4	-
GUBLER, K.	-	0/ 1	.000	0/ 0	.000	-/ 0	0	-	0	-	-	0	-
CAMAC, R.	-	0/ 1	.000	2/ 4	.500	-/ 5	1	-	1	-	-	2	-
WIMBERLEY, R.	-	1/ 3	.333	0/ 1	.000	-/ 2	1	-	1	-	-	2	-
MUIRBROOK, D.	-	1/ 2	.500	0/ 0	.000	-/ 1	0	-	1	-	-	2	-
Totals	200	29/65	.446	33/52	.635	-/53	14	-	16	-	-	91	.455

Hawaii (64)   Coach: Red Rocha

	Min.	Total FG / FGA	Pct.	FT / FTA	Pct.	Reb. O / T	A	TO	PF	S	Blk	TP	PPM
HOLIDAY, D.	-	6/13	.462	2/ 3	.667	-/ 6	1	-	5	-	-	14	-
FREEMAN, J.	-	3/13	.231	5/ 5	1.000	-/ 5	1	-	4	-	-	11	-
PENEBACKER, J.	-	3/ 9	.333	0/ 4	.000	-/ 7	0	-	5	-	-	6	-
DAVIS, A.	-	5/13	.385	4/ 5	.800	-/ 7	0	-	5	-	-	14	-
NASH, R.	-	3/16	.188	1/ 4	.250	-/10	0	-	5	-	-	7	-
KENDALL, M.	-	0/ 1	.000	2/ 2	1.000	-/ 1	0	-	3	-	-	2	-
SKILLICORN, M.	-	0/ 1	.000	0/ 0	.000	-/ 2	0	-	0	-	-	0	-
WILSON, A.	-	0/ 2	.000	0/ 0	.000	-/ 1	0	-	0	-	-	0	-
BRADSHAW, T.	-	2/ 3	.667	0/ 0	.000	-/ 3	0	-	3	-	-	4	-
BLACKSHIRE, M.	-	0/ 3	.000	2/ 2	1.000	-/ 1	0	-	1	-	-	2	-
HUBER, T.	-	1/ 1	1.000	0/ 0	.000	-/ 3	0	-	4	-	-	2	-
WIENSTROER	-	0/ 0	.000	0/ 0	.000	-/ 0	0	-	0	-	-	0	-
WILLIAMS, C.	-	1/ 3	.333	0/ 0	.000	-/ 2	0	-	0	-	-	2	-
Totals	200	24/78	.308	16/25	.640	-/48	2	-	35	-	-	64	.320

Team Rebounds: Weber St. 10; Hawaii 7. Disqualified: Hawaii—Holiday, Penebacker, Davis, Nash.

	1st Half	2nd Half	Final
Weber St.	37	54	91
Hawaii	30	34	64

Long Beach State (95)   Coach: Jerry Tarkanian

	Min.	Total FG / FGA	Pct.	FT / FTA	Pct.	Reb. O / T	A	TO	PF	S	Blk	TP	PPM
MCWILLIAMS, E.	-	8/14	.571	0/ 0	.000	-/ 8	0	-	5	-	-	16	-
MCDONALD, G.	-	7/14	.500	1/ 1	1.000	-/ 7	0	-	0	-	-	15	-
TERRY, C.	-	4/10	.400	4/ 5	.800	-/ 4	5	-	3	-	-	12	-
RATLEFF, E.	-	8/16	.500	5/ 6	.833	-/ 5	6	-	2	-	-	21	-
GRAY, L.	-	2/16	.125	3/ 5	.600	-/11	3	-	3	-	-	7	-
KING, L.	-	7/ 8	.875	2/ 2	1.000	-/ 4	2	-	4	-	-	16	-
STEPHENS, N.	-	3/10	.300	2/ 4	.500	-/10	0	-	4	-	-	8	-
Totals	225	39/88	.443	17/23	.739	-/49	16	-	21	-	-	95	.422

Brigham Young (90)   Coach: Stan Watts

	Min.	Total FG / FGA	Pct.	FT / FTA	Pct.	Reb. O / T	A	TO	PF	S	Blk	TP	PPM
COSIC, K.	-	9/20	.450	9/ 9	1.000	-/13	-	-	3	-	-	27	-
RICHARDS, D.	-	9/10	.900	6/ 6	1.000	-/ 7	-	-	2	-	-	24	-
AMBROZICH, B.	-	4/10	.400	3/ 4	.750	-/13	-	-	3	-	-	11	-
FRYER, B.	-	6/19	.316	3/ 5	.600	-/ 3	-	-	2	-	-	15	-
TOLLESTRUP, P.	-	6/15	.400	1/ 1	1.000	-/ 5	-	-	5	-	-	13	-
ANDERSON, B.	-	0/ 1	.000	0/ 0	.000	-/ 1	-	-	0	-	-	0	-
SARKALAHTI, K.	-	0/ 0	.000	0/ 1	.000	-/ 0	-	-	0	-	-	0	-
Totals	225	34/75	.453	22/26	.846	-/42	-	-	15	-	-	90	.400

Team Rebounds: Long Beach St. 5; Brigham Young 4. Disqualified: Long Beach St.—McWilliams; Brigham Young— Tollestrup.

	1st Half	2nd Half	1st OT	Final
Long Beach St.	39	40	16	95
Brigham Young	49	30	11	90

REGIONAL SEMIFINAL MIDEAST

Florida State (70)   Coach: Hugh Durham

	Min.	Total FG / FGA	Pct.	FT / FTA	Pct.	Reb. O / T	A	TO	PF	S	Blk	TP	PPM
SAMUEL, G.	17	0/ 1	.000	1/ 1	1.000	-/ 0	4	2	1	-	-	1	.059
GARRETT, R.	36	11/19	.579	1/ 1	1.000	-/11	0	1	3	-	-	23	.639
ROYALS, R.	32	4/ 9	.444	3/ 6	.500	-/11	2	1	4	-	-	11	.344
KING, R.	27	5/11	.455	1/ 3	.333	-/ 5	2	1	1	-	-	11	.407
MCCRAY, L.	24	1/ 2	.500	0/ 1	.000	-/ 8	0	0	1	-	-	2	.083
HARRIS, R.	28	5/ 7	.714	0/ 1	.000	-/ 2	1	2	0	-	-	10	.357
PETTY, O.	23	0/ 8	.000	2/ 3	.667	-/ 1	6	2	1	-	-	2	.087
COLE, O.	13	3/ 5	.600	4/ 4	1.000	-/ 1	2	1	1	-	-	10	.769
Totals	200	29/62	.468	12/20	.600	-/39	17	10	12	-	-	70	.350

Minnesota (56)   Coach: Bill Musselman

	Min.	Total FG / FGA	Pct.	FT / FTA	Pct.	Reb. O / T	A	TO	PF	S	Blk	TP	PPM
NIX, B.	40	1/12	.083	4/ 5	.800	-/ 1	2	0	2	-	-	6	.150
YOUNG, K.	27	3/12	.250	1/ 1	1.000	-/ 5	2	4	5	-	-	7	.259
WINFIELD, D.	40	2/ 8	.250	4/ 5	.800	-/ 8	0	3	3	-	-	8	.200
TURNER, C.	40	8/17	.471	3/ 4	.750	-/12	2	2	3	-	-	19	.475
BREWER, J.	40	5/11	.455	0/ 0	.000	-/14	3	1	1	-	-	10	.250
MURPHY, B.	13	3/ 6	.500	0/ 0	.000	-/ 3	1	0	2	-	-	6	.462
Totals	200	22/66	.333	12/15	.800	-/43	8	12	16	-	-	56	.280

Team Rebounds: Florida State 3; Minnesota 3. Disqualified: Minnesota—Young.

	1st Half	2nd Half	Final
Florida State	35	35	70
Minnesota	29	27	56

Kentucky (85) Coach: Adolph Rupp

	Min.	Total FG/FGA	Pct.	FT/FTA	Pct.	Reb. O/T	A	TO	PF	S	Blk	TP	PPM
PARKER, T.	-	3/5	.600	6/8	.750	-/9	-	-	3	-	-	12	-
LYONS, R.	-	6/16	.375	7/8	.875	-/1	-	-	2	-	-	19	-
STAMPER, L.	-	7/10	.700	3/5	.600	-/11	-	-	2	-	-	17	-
KEY, S.	-	4/5	.800	6/6	1.000	-/5	-	-	0	-	-	14	-
ANDREWS, J.	-	5/11	.455	7/7	1.000	-/16	-	-	3	-	-	17	-
MCCOWAN, B.	-	0/0	.000	0/0	.000	-/0	-	-	1	-	-	0	-
DREWITZ, R.	-	3/4	.750	0/0	.000	-/2	-	-	2	-	-	6	-
Totals	200	28/51	.549	29/34	.853	-/44	-	-	13	-	-	85	.425

Marquette (69) Coach: Al McGuire

	Min.	Total FG/FGA	Pct.	FT/FTA	Pct.	Reb. O/T	A	TO	PF	S	Blk	TP	PPM
MCGUIRE, A.	-	3/15	.200	2/2	1.000	-/1	-	-	0	-	-	8	-
MCNEILL, L.	-	3/10	.300	3/4	.750	-/8	-	-	5	-	-	9	-
LACKEY, B.	-	8/14	.571	5/7	.714	-/6	-	-	4	-	-	21	-
FRAZIER, G.	-	4/5	.800	0/0	.000	-/6	-	-	3	-	-	8	-
WASHINGTON, M.	-	6/24	.250	2/4	.500	-/4	-	-	5	-	-	14	-
MILLS, M.	-	3/5	.600	1/1	1.000	-/7	-	-	1	-	-	7	-
OSTRAND, M.	-	0/0	.000	0/0	.000	-/0	-	-	1	-	-	0	-
SPYCHALLA, K.	-	1/3	.333	0/0	.000	-/3	-	-	5	-	-	2	-
LAM, G.	-	0/2	.000	0/0	.000	-/0	-	-	0	-	-	0	-
Totals	200	28/78	.359	13/18	.722	-/35	-	-	24	-	-	69	.345

Team Rebounds: Kentucky 2; Marquette 2. Disqualified: Marquette—McNeill, Washington, Spychalla.

	1st Half	2nd Half	Final
Kentucky	33	52	85
Marquette	34	35	69

REGIONAL SEMIFINAL EAST

North Carolina (92) Coach: Dean Smith

	Min.	Total FG/FGA	Pct.	FT/FTA	Pct.	Reb. O/T	A	TO	PF	S	Blk	TP	PPM
CHAMBERLAIN, B.	25	3/6	.500	4/5	.800	-/4	0	-	1	-	-	10	.400
WUYCIK, D.	27	4/11	.364	8/10	.800	-/5	3	-	3	-	-	16	.593
MCADOO, B.	32	4/14	.286	3/6	.500	-/13	3	-	3	-	-	11	.344
PREVIS, S.	29	5/8	.625	3/4	.750	-/5	4	-	4	-	-	13	.448
KARL, G.	23	8/12	.667	2/3	.667	-/3	3	-	4	-	-	18	.783
HUBAND, G.	19	2/5	.400	4/4	1.000	-/4	0	-	3	-	-	8	.421
JONES, B.	22	1/3	.333	3/4	.750	-/9	2	-	2	-	-	5	.227
HITE, R.	6	2/2	1.000	0/0	.000	-/1	0	-	1	-	-	4	.667
JOHNSTON, D.	7	0/1	.000	0/0	.000	-/2	2	-	0	-	-	0	.000
CORSON, C.	5	0/0	.000	0/0	.000	-/0	1	-	2	-	-	0	.000
CHAMBERS, D.	5	2/3	.667	3/4	.750	-/1	1	-	0	-	-	7	1.400
Totals	200	31/65	.477	30/40	.750	-/47	19	18	22	-	-	92	.460

South Carolina (69) Coach: Frank McGuire

	Min.	Total FG/FGA	Pct.	FT/FTA	Pct.	Reb. O/T	A	TO	PF	S	Blk	TP	PPM
RIKER, T.	38	4/13	.308	2/4	.500	-/10	1	-	4	-	-	10	.263
AYDLETT, R.	25	2/4	.500	2/2	1.000	-/4	0	-	4	-	-	6	.240
TRAYLOR, D.	24	3/6	.500	3/4	.750	-/2	0	-	4	-	-	9	.375
JOYCE, K.	32	6/18	.333	9/9	1.000	-/7	1	-	5	-	-	21	.656
CARVER, B.	24	2/6	.333	2/2	1.000	-/2	2	-	3	-	-	6	.250
WINTERS, B.	20	4/11	.364	1/1	1.000	-/3	0	-	5	-	-	9	.450
MOUSA, R.	11	1/4	.250	1/4	.250	-/4	1	-	1	-	-	3	.273
MANNING, J.	21	0/3	.000	3/3	1.000	-/2	0	-	0	-	-	3	.143
POWELL, J.	3	0/2	.000	0/0	.000	-/1	0	-	0	-	-	0	.000
GRIMES, B.	2	1/1	1.000	0/1	.000	-/1	0	-	0	-	-	2	1.000
Totals	200	23/68	.338	23/30	.767	-/36	5	19	26	-	-	69	.345

Team Rebounds: N. Carolina 5; S. Carolina 8. Disqualified: S. Carolina—Joyce, Winters.

	1st Half	2nd Half	Final
N. Carolina	51	41	92
S. Carolina	32	37	69

Pennsylvania (78) Coach: Chuck Daly

	Min.	Total FG/FGA	Pct.	FT/FTA	Pct.	Reb. O/T	A	TO	PF	S	Blk	TP	PPM
CALHOUN, C.	31	8/11	.727	5/5	1.000	-/7	2	-	4	-	-	21	.677
HANKINSON, P.	40	10/19	.526	2/2	1.000	-/6	2	-	2	-	-	22	.550
MORSE, B.	40	8/18	.444	4/4	1.000	-/9	2	-	0	-	-	20	.500
COTLER, A.	39	3/7	.429	3/4	.750	-/1	6	-	3	-	-	9	.231
LITTLEPAGE, C.	29	2/4	.500	2/3	.667	-/4	2	-	4	-	-	6	.207
JABLONSKI, J.	9	0/2	.000	0/2	.000	-/0	0	-	2	-	-	0	.000
BILLINGSLEA, R.	11	0/1	.000	0/0	.000	-/1	0	-	2	-	-	0	.000
VARGA, W.	1	0/0	.000	0/0	.000	-/0	0	-	0	-	-	0	.000
Totals	200	31/62	.500	16/20	.800	-/28	14	10	17	-	-	78	.390

Villanova (67) Coach: Jack Kraft

	Min.	Total FG/FGA	Pct.	FT/FTA	Pct.	Reb. O/T	A	TO	PF	S	Blk	TP	PPM
HASTINGS, E.	30	3/3	1.000	0/0	.000	-/2	1	-	4	-	-	6	.200
INGELSBY, T.	39	8/19	.421	5/5	1.000	-/6	2	-	2	-	-	21	.538
SIEMIONTKOWSKI, H	40	6/11	.545	10/12	.833	-/11	1	-	1	-	-	22	.550
FORD, C.	40	6/11	.545	2/3	.667	-/4	3	-	3	-	-	14	.350
MOODY, L.	32	2/4	.500	0/1	.000	-/3	0	-	4	-	-	4	.125
GOHL, B.	10	0/0	.000	0/0	.000	-/0	2	-	1	-	-	0	.000
MCDOWELL, J.	9	0/1	.000	0/0	.000	-/0	0	-	1	-	-	0	.000
Totals	200	25/49	.510	17/21	.810	-/26	9	14	16	-	-	67	.335

Team Rebounds: Pennsylvania 5; Villanova 4. Disqualified: None.

	1st Half	2nd Half	Final
Pennsylvania	38	40	78
Villanova	31	36	67

REGIONAL SEMIFINAL MIDWEST

Louisville (88)   Coach: Denny Crum

	Min.	Total FG / FGA	Pct.	FT / FTA	Pct.	Reb. O / T	A	TO	PF	S	Blk	TP	PPM
BACON, H.	-	5/ 9	.556	1/ 2	.500	-/ 6	-	-	0	-	-	11	-
THOMAS, R.	-	8/12	.667	3/10	.300	-/13	-	-	4	-	-	19	-
VILCHECK, A.	-	5/ 6	.833	3/ 6	.500	-/10	-	-	3	-	-	13	-
PRICE, J.	-	10/15	.667	5/ 6	.833	-/ 2	-	-	2	-	-	25	-
LAWHON, M.	-	2/ 6	.333	6/ 6	1.000	-/ 2	-	-	3	-	-	10	-
BRADLEY, K.	-	2/ 6	.333	2/ 2	1.000	-/ 5	-	-	1	-	-	6	-
CARTER, L.	-	2/ 6	.333	0/ 1	.000	-/ 1	-	-	2	-	-	4	-
Totals	200	34/60	.567	20/33	.606	-/39	-	-	15	-	-	88	.440

Southwestern Louisiana (84)   Coach: Beryl Shipley

	Min.	Total FG / FGA	Pct.	FT / FTA	Pct.	Reb. O / T	A	TO	PF	S	Blk	TP	PPM
LOFTIN, W.	-	5/ 7	.714	2/ 2	1.000	-/10	-	-	4	-	-	12	-
SAUNDERS, F.	-	2/10	.200	0/ 1	.000	-/11	-	-	4	-	-	4	-
EBRON, R.	-	3/10	.300	5/ 5	1.000	-/12	-	-	4	-	-	11	-
LAMAR, D.	-	14/42	.333	1/ 3	.333	-/ 0	-	-	2	-	-	29	-
BISBANO, J.	-	6/13	.462	3/ 4	.750	-/ 5	-	-	4	-	-	15	-
TOWNSEND, P.	-	4/ 6	.667	2/ 3	.667	-/ 7	-	-	3	-	-	10	-
HANEY, M.	-	1/ 5	.200	1/ 2	.500	-/ 6	-	-	2	-	-	3	-
GREENE, S.	-	0/ 1	.000	0/ 0	.000	-/ 1	-	-	1	-	-	0	-
Totals	200	35/94	.372	14/20	.700	-/52	-	-	24	-	-	84	.420

Disqualified: None.

	1st Half	2nd Half	Final
Louisville	44	44	88
S'western La.	39	45	84

Kansas State (66)   Coach: Jack Hartman

	Min.	Total FG / FGA	Pct.	FT / FTA	Pct.	Reb. O / T	A	TO	PF	S	Blk	TP	PPM
KUSNYER, E.	-	5/ 9	.556	2/ 5	.400	-/ 6	-	-	3	-	-	12	-
ZENDER, R.	-	2/ 6	.333	2/ 2	1.000	-/ 9	-	-	2	-	-	6	-
HALL, D.	-	4/ 6	.667	5/ 6	.833	-/12	-	-	3	-	-	13	-
KRUGER, L.	-	4/ 9	.444	3/ 4	.750	-/ 3	-	-	1	-	-	11	-
BEARD, D.	-	8/18	.444	4/ 7	.571	-/ 2	-	-	1	-	-	20	-
WILLIAMS, L.	-	1/ 4	.250	0/ 0	.000	-/ 4	-	-	2	-	-	2	-
MITCHELL, S.	-	1/ 2	.500	0/ 0	.000	-/ 2	-	-	2	-	-	2	-
Totals	200	25/54	.463	16/24	.667	-/38	-	-	14	-	-	66	.330

Texas (55)   Coach: Leon Black

	Min.	Total FG / FGA	Pct.	FT / FTA	Pct.	Reb. O / T	A	TO	PF	S	Blk	TP	PPM
GROSCURTH, E.	-	0/ 5	.000	0/ 1	.000	-/ 5	-	-	2	-	-	0	-
LENOX, J.	-	6/12	.500	2/ 3	.667	-/ 2	-	-	4	-	-	14	-
BROSTERHOUS, B.	-	4/ 8	.500	2/ 5	.400	-/ 4	-	-	4	-	-	10	-
LARRABEE, H.	-	2/10	.200	1/ 1	1.000	-/ 8	-	-	5	-	-	5	-
ROBINSON, L.	-	10/14	.714	2/ 3	.667	-/ 3	-	-	3	-	-	22	-
LOUIS, J.	-	2/ 5	.400	0/ 1	.000	-/ 5	-	-	1	-	-	4	-
BLACKLOCK, J.	-	0/ 0	.000	0/ 0	.000	-/ 0	-	-	0	-	-	0	-
Totals	200	24/54	.444	7/14	.500	-/27	-	-	19	-	-	55	.275

Team Rebounds: Kansas State 5; Texas 4. Disqualified: Texas—Larrabee.

	1st Half	2nd Half	Final
Kansas State	36	30	66
Texas	25	30	55

REGIONAL SEMIFINAL WEST

UCLA (90)   Coach: John Wooden

	Min.	Total FG / FGA	Pct.	FT / FTA	Pct.	Reb. O / T	A	TO	PF	S	Blk	TP	PPM
FARMER, L.	27	7/15	.467	1/ 1	1.000	-/ 7	1	-	1	-	-	15	.556
WILKES, J.	25	4/12	.333	2/ 2	1.000	-/13	2	-	4	-	-	10	.400
WALTON, B.	20	1/ 1	1.000	2/ 5	.400	-/12	0	-	4	-	-	4	.200
LEE, G.	17	3/ 8	.375	0/ 0	.000	-/ 4	6	-	1	-	-	6	.353
BIBBY, H.	30	7/18	.389	2/ 2	1.000	-/ 3	1	-	2	-	-	16	.533
CURTIS, T.	21	3/ 7	.429	1/ 1	1.000	-/ 3	6	-	2	-	-	7	.333
HOLLYFIELD, L.	13	2/ 9	.222	0/ 0	.000	-/ 5	2	-	2	-	-	4	.308
NATER, S.	20	5/ 9	.556	2/ 4	.500	-/ 8	0	-	2	-	-	12	.600
CARSON, V.	9	0/ 3	.000	0/ 1	.000	-/ 5	2	-	2	-	-	0	.000
CHAPMAN, J.	7	1/ 1	1.000	0/ 0	.000	-/ 2	0	-	1	-	-	2	.286
HILL, A.	6	3/ 4	.750	4/ 4	1.000	-/ 1	1	-	2	-	-	10	1.667
FRANKLIN, G.	5	2/ 2	1.000	0/ 0	.000	-/ 2	0	-	0	-	-	4	.800
Totals	200	38/89	.427	14/21	.667	-/65	21	12	23	-	-	90	.450

Weber State (58)   Coach: Gene Visscher

	Min.	Total FG / FGA	Pct.	FT / FTA	Pct.	Reb. O / T	A	TO	PF	S	Blk	TP	PPM
SMALL, B.	34	1/12	.083	2/ 3	.667	-/ 2	3	-	0	-	-	4	.118
DAVIS, B.	28	4/14	.286	8/13	.615	-/ 6	2	-	4	-	-	16	.571
KNOBLE, J.	32	3/ 8	.375	3/ 8	.375	-/ 9	2	-	4	-	-	9	.281
COOPER, R.	31	2/10	.200	4/ 6	.667	-/12	0	-	4	-	-	8	.258
VANDYKE, W.	37	2/11	.182	0/ 1	.000	-/ 1	1	-	3	-	-	4	.108
MCGARRY, K.	0	0/ 0	.000	0/ 0	.000	-/ 0	1	-	0	-	-	0	-
WILLIAMS, R.	0	0/ 1	.000	0/ 0	.000	-/ 0	0	-	0	-	-	0	-
SOTER, G.	5	0/ 0	.000	1/ 2	.500	-/ 0	0	-	0	-	-	1	.200
GUBLER, K.	5	1/ 2	.500	0/ 0	.000	-/ 1	0	-	2	-	-	2	.400
CAMAC, R.	4	0/ 0	.000	0/ 0	.000	-/ 0	0	-	0	-	-	0	.000
WIMBERLEY, R.	22	7/15	.467	0/ 0	.000	-/ 5	0	-	0	-	-	14	.636
MUIRBROOK, D.	2	0/ 0	.000	0/ 0	.000	-/ 0	0	-	0	-	-	0	.000
Totals	200	20/73	.274	18/33	.545	-/36	9	16	17	-	-	58	.290

Team Rebounds: UCLA 11; Weber St. 18. Disqualified: None. Players who played 0 min. played less than 1 min. each.

	1st Half	2nd Half	Final
UCLA	42	48	90
Weber St.	25	33	58

Long Beach State (75)   Coach: Jerry Tarkanian

	Min.	Total FG / FGA	Pct.	FT / FTA	Pct.	Reb. O / T	A	TO	PF	S	Blk	TP	PPM
TERRY, C.	-	6/14	.429	4/ 4	1.000	-/ 4	2	-	1	-	-	16	-
MCWILLIAMS, E.	-	4/10	.400	3/ 5	.600	-/12	0	-	4	-	-	11	-
GRAY, L.	-	3/ 7	.429	0/ 0	.000	-/ 4	5	-	3	-	-	6	-
RATLEFF, E.	-	7/17	.412	2/ 3	.667	-/ 5	6	-	0	-	-	16	-
MCDONALD, G.	-	3/10	.300	2/ 3	.667	-/ 5	2	-	2	-	-	8	-
STEPHENS, N.	-	2/ 4	.500	0/ 1	.000	-/ 3	1	-	1	-	-	4	-
KING, L.	-	2/ 4	.500	2/ 4	.500	-/ 1	1	-	3	-	-	6	-
LYNN, B.	-	4/ 4	1.000	0/ 0	.000	-/ 5	0	-	0	-	-	8	-
MOTLEY, T.	-	0/ 0	.000	0/ 0	.000	-/ 0	1	-	1	-	-	0	-
MILLER, R.	-	0/ 1	.000	0/ 0	.000	-/ 0	1	-	0	-	-	0	-
Totals	200	31/71	.437	13/20	.650	-/39	19	-	15	-	-	75	.375

San Francisco (55)   Coach: Bob Gaillard

	Min.	Total FG / FGA	Pct.	FT / FTA	Pct.	Reb. O / T	A	TO	PF	S	Blk	TP	PPM
BURKS, J.	-	3/10	.300	1/ 1	1.000	-/ 9	0	-	3	-	-	7	-
JONES, B.	-	1/ 6	.167	2/ 4	.500	-/11	0	-	3	-	-	4	-
RESTANI, K.	-	4/16	.250	1/ 5	.200	-/17	1	-	4	-	-	9	-
SMITH, P.	-	3/10	.300	2/ 2	1.000	-/ 9	1	-	2	-	-	8	-
QUICK, M.	-	7/17	.412	5/ 6	.833	-/ 0	3	-	2	-	-	19	-
BORO, J.	-	3/ 9	.333	0/ 0	.000	-/ 3	3	-	2	-	-	6	-
LEWIS, A.	-	0/ 1	.000	0/ 0	.000	-/ 2	0	-	1	-	-	0	-
HANCOCK, J.	-	0/ 3	.000	0/ 0	.000	-/ 0	0	-	0	-	-	0	-
CENTERWALL, R.	-	1/ 1	1.000	0/ 0	.000	-/ 1	0	-	0	-	-	2	-
Totals	200	22/73	.301	11/18	.611	-/52	8	-	17	-	-	55	.275

Team Rebounds: Long Beach St. 8; San Francisco 6. Disqualified: None.

	1st Half	2nd Half	Final
Long Beach St.	33	42	75
San Francisco	22	33	55

REGIONAL FINAL MIDEAST

Florida State (73)   Coach: Hugh Durham

	Min.	Total FG/FGA	Pct.	FT/FTA	Pct.	Reb. O/T	A	TO	PF	S	Blk	TP	PPM
SAMUEL, G.	8	1/2	.500	1/1	1.000	-/1	2	0	0	-	-	3	.375
GARRETT, R.	21	2/4	.500	1/1	1.000	-/3	2	2	2	-	-	5	.238
ROYALS, R.	40	4/13	.308	4/5	.800	-/12	1	2	3	-	-	12	.300
KING, R.	33	9/19	.474	4/4	1.000	-/8	0	1	0	-	-	22	.667
MCCRAY, L.	31	6/13	.462	0/2	.000	-/5	0	4	3	-	-	12	.387
HARRIS, R.	28	3/7	.429	0/0	.000	-/5	2	3	3	-	-	6	.214
PETTY, O.	32	2/5	.400	9/9	1.000	-/6	8	1	2	-	-	13	.406
COLE, O.	7	0/1	.000	0/0	.000	-/0	0	0	0	-	-	0	.000
Totals	200	27/64	.422	19/22	.864	-/40	15	13	13	-	-	73	.365

Kentucky (54)   Coach: Adolph Rupp

	Min.	Total FG/FGA	Pct.	FT/FTA	Pct.	Reb. O/T	A	TO	PF	S	Blk	TP	PPM
PARKER, T.	35	5/13	.385	0/1	.000	-/6	1	2	3	-	-	10	.286
LYONS, R.	33	5/13	.385	0/0	.000	-/2	3	3	3	-	-	10	.303
STAMPER, L.	40	2/6	.333	5/7	.714	-/9	1	2	2	-	-	9	.225
KEY, S.	17	1/4	.250	0/0	.000	-/1	2	5	3	-	-	2	.118
ANDREWS, J.	40	7/14	.500	3/3	1.000	-/11	1	1	1	-	-	17	.425
MCCOWAN, B.	30	2/4	.500	1/1	1.000	-/2	7	9	4	-	-	5	.167
DREWITZ, R.	5	0/0	.000	1/1	1.000	-/0	1	0	0	-	-	1	.200
Totals	200	22/54	.407	10/13	.769	-/31	16	22	16	-	-	54	.270

Team Rebounds: Florida State 2; Kentucky 2. Disqualified: None.

	1st Half	2nd Half	Final
Florida State	34	39	73
Kentucky	28	26	54

REGIONAL FINAL EAST

North Carolina (73)   Coach: Dean Smith

	Min.	Total FG/FGA	Pct.	FT/FTA	Pct.	Reb. O/T	A	TO	PF	S	Blk	TP	PPM
CHAMBERLAIN, B.	26	2/6	.333	3/3	1.000	-/2	0	-	1	-	-	7	.269
WUYCIK, D.	30	7/12	.583	4/5	.800	-/4	2	-	4	-	-	18	.600
MCADOO, B.	38	5/10	.500	7/10	.700	-/9	0	-	0	-	-	17	.447
PREVIS, S.	34	1/3	.333	0/0	.000	-/5	4	-	1	-	-	2	.059
KARL, G.	19	5/9	.556	6/7	.857	-/1	1	-	4	-	-	16	.842
HUBAND, K.	19	2/3	.667	3/3	1.000	-/2	1	-	4	-	-	7	.368
HITE, R.	4	0/0	.000	0/0	.000	-/0	0	-	1	-	-	0	.000
JONES, B.	20	2/4	.500	0/1	.000	-/6	5	-	3	-	-	4	.200
CORSON, C.	2	0/0	.000	0/0	.000	-/1	0	-	0	-	-	0	.000
JOHNSTON, D.	4	0/0	.000	0/0	.000	-/1	0	-	0	-	-	0	.000
CHAMBERS, B.	4	1/1	1.000	0/0	.000	-/2	0	-	0	-	-	2	.500
Totals	200	25/48	.521	23/29	.793	-/33	13	-	18	-	-	73	.365

Pennsylvania (59)   Coach: Chuck Daly

	Min.	Total FG/FGA	Pct.	FT/FTA	Pct.	Reb. O/T	A	TO	PF	S	Blk	TP	PPM
CALHOUN, C.	39	3/8	.375	1/2	.500	-/7	3	-	2	-	-	7	.179
HANKINSON, P.	39	5/19	.263	2/2	1.000	-/9	2	-	5	-	-	12	.308
MORSE, B.	34	5/14	.357	4/6	.667	-/6	0	-	4	-	-	14	.412
COTLER, A.	33	2/7	.286	6/6	1.000	-/1	3	-	4	-	-	10	.303
LITTLEPAGE, C.	19	1/1	1.000	2/4	.500	-/4	0	-	4	-	-	4	.211
JABLONSKI, J.	2	0/0	.000	0/0	.000	-/0	0	-	0	-	-	0	.000
BILLINGSLEA, R.	25	5/7	.714	2/3	.667	-/3	1	-	4	-	-	12	.480
VARGA, W.	9	0/0	.000	0/0	.000	-/1	1	-	0	-	-	0	.000
Totals	200	21/56	.375	17/23	.739	-/31	10	-	23	-	-	59	.295

Team Rebounds: N. Carolina 2; Pennsylvania 4. Disqualified: Pennsylvania—Hankinson.

	1st Half	2nd Half	Final
N. Carolina	37	36	73
Pennsylvania	35	24	59

REGIONAL FINAL MIDWEST

Louisville (72)   Coach: Denny Crum

	Min.	Total FG/FGA	Pct.	FT/FTA	Pct.	Reb. O/T	A	TO	PF	S	Blk	TP	PPM
BACON, H.	-	4/10	.400	0/3	.000	-/5	-	-	3	-	-	8	-
THOMAS, R.	-	6/10	.600	6/10	.600	-/14	-	-	4	-	-	18	-
VILCHECK, A.	-	4/9	.444	0/0	.000	-/7	-	-	5	-	-	8	-
PRICE, J.	-	11/16	.688	3/4	.750	-/0	-	-	1	-	-	25	-
LAWHON, M.	-	3/8	.375	4/5	.800	-/7	-	-	1	-	-	10	-
BRADLEY, K.	-	0/2	.000	0/0	.000	-/0	-	-	0	-	-	0	-
CARTER, L.	-	0/1	.000	0/0	.000	-/0	-	-	1	-	-	0	-
BUNTON, B.	-	1/2	.500	1/1	1.000	-/6	-	-	1	-	-	3	-
Totals	200	29/58	.500	14/23	.609	-/39	-	19	16	-	-	72	.360

Kansas State (65)   Coach: Jack Hartman

	Min.	Total FG/FGA	Pct.	FT/FTA	Pct.	Reb. O/T	A	TO	PF	S	Blk	TP	PPM
KUSNYER, E.	-	4/6	.667	5/5	1.000	-/6	-	-	4	-	-	13	-
ZENDER, R.	-	2/6	.333	0/1	.000	-/4	-	-	1	-	-	4	-
HALL, D.	-	4/9	.444	0/2	.000	-/10	-	-	3	-	-	8	-
KRUGER, L.	-	3/8	.375	8/9	.889	-/2	-	-	4	-	-	14	-
BEARD, D.	-	4/9	.444	0/1	.000	-/2	-	-	4	-	-	8	-
WILLIAMS, L.	-	6/8	.750	0/1	.000	-/3	-	-	1	-	-	12	-
MITCHELL, S.	-	3/7	.429	0/0	.000	-/5	-	-	1	-	-	6	-
CHIPMAN, B.	-	0/1	.000	0/2	.000	-/0	-	-	1	-	-	0	-
WHITE, L.	-	0/2	.000	0/0	.000	-/0	-	-	0	-	-	0	-
Totals	200	26/56	.464	13/21	.619	-/32	-	18	19	-	-	65	.325

Disqualified: Louisville—Vilcheck.

	1st Half	2nd Half	Final
Louisville	42	30	72
Kansas State	26	39	65

REGIONAL FINAL WEST

UCLA (73)   Coach: John Wooden

	Min.	Total FG / FGA	Pct.	FT / FTA	Pct.	Reb. O/T	A	TO	PF	S	Blk	TP	PPM
FARMER, L.	36	2/ 7	.286	1/ 3	.333	-/ 3	2	-	3	-	-	5	.139
WILKES, J.	34	4/10	.400	6/ 7	.857	-/ 6	2	-	3	-	-	14	.412
WALTON, B.	37	7/10	.700	5/ 7	.714	-/11	1	-	3	-	-	19	.514
LEE, G.	32	2/ 6	.333	2/ 3	.667	-/ 3	4	-	0	-	-	6	.188
BIBBY, H.	38	10/17	.588	3/ 4	.750	-/ 4	4	-	2	-	-	23	.605
CURTIS, T.	6	0/ 0	.000	0/ 0	.000	-/ 0	1	-	1	-	-	0	.000
HOLLYFIELD, L.	6	0/ 1	.000	0/ 0	.000	-/ 0	0	-	2	-	-	0	.000
NATER, S.	3	2/ 2	1.000	1/ 2	.500	-/ 1	0	-	0	-	-	5	1.667
CARSON, V.	3	0/ 0	.000	0/ 0	.000	-/ 1	0	-	1	-	-	0	.000
CHAPMAN, J.	2	0/ 0	.000	0/ 0	.000	-/ 0	0	-	0	-	-	0	.000
HILL, A.	2	0/ 0	.000	1/ 3	.333	-/ 0	1	-	0	-	-	1	.500
FRANKLIN, G.	1	0/ 0	.000	0/ 0	.000	-/ 0	0	-	0	-	-	0	.000
Totals	200	27/53	.509	19/29	.655	-/29	15	-	15	-	-	73	.365

Long Beach State (57)   Coach: Jerry Tarkanian

	Min.	Total FG / FGA	Pct.	FT / FTA	Pct.	Reb. O/T	A	TO	PF	S	Blk	TP	PPM
MCWILLIAMS, E.	25	2/ 4	.500	3/ 3	1.000	-/ 5	1	-	4	-	-	7	.280
MCDONALD, G.	31	3/ 3	1.000	2/ 2	1.000	-/ 5	2	-	0	-	-	8	.258
TERRY, C.	40	2/ 6	.333	2/ 2	1.000	-/ 4	3	-	4	-	-	6	.150
RATLEFF, E.	38	7/19	.368	3/ 6	.500	-/ 3	3	-	3	-	-	17	.447
GRAY, L.	18	2/ 5	.400	3/ 4	.750	-/ 3	0	-	4	-	-	7	.389
KING, L.	11	2/ 2	1.000	0/ 0	.000	-/ 0	0	-	2	-	-	4	.364
STEPHENS, N.	14	1/ 5	.200	0/ 0	.000	-/ 3	0	-	1	-	-	2	.143
LYNN, B.	23	2/ 6	.333	2/ 2	1.000	-/ 8	0	-	2	-	-	6	.261
Totals	200	21/50	.420	15/19	.789	-/31	9	-	20	-	-	57	.285

Team Rebounds: UCLA 7; Long Beach St. 2. Disqualified: None.

	1st Half	2nd Half	Final
UCLA	34	39	73
Long Beach St.	23	34	57

FINAL FOUR

Florida State (79)   Coach: Hugh Durham

	Min.	Total FG / FGA	Pct.	FT / FTA	Pct.	Reb. O/T	A	TO	PF	S	Blk	TP	PPM
GARRETT, R.	34	4/ 8	.500	3/ 7	.429	-/ 5	1	6	4	-	-	11	.324
ROYALS, R.	32	6/ 8	.750	6/ 7	.857	-/10	4	3	5	-	-	18	.563
MCCRAY, L.	26	3/ 6	.500	3/ 6	.500	-/ 9	1	3	3	-	-	9	.346
SAMUEL, G.	13	2/ 4	.500	1/ 4	.250	-/ 1	0	3	0	-	-	5	.385
HARRIS, R.	26	1/ 6	.167	2/ 2	1.000	-/ 4	2	2	2	-	-	4	.154
PETTY, O.	27	3/ 5	.600	4/ 7	.571	-/ 1	6	5	5	-	-	10	.370
COLE, O.	3	0/ 0	.000	0/ 0	.000	-/ 0	0	1	0	-	-	0	.000
GAY, L.	1	0/ 1	.000	0/ 0	.000	-/ 0	0	0	0	-	-	0	.000
KING, R.	38	6/17	.353	10/10	1.000	-/ 5	2	4	1	-	-	22	.579
Totals	200	25/55	.455	29/43	.674	-/35	16	27	20	-	-	79	.395

North Carolina (75)   Coach: Dean Smith

	Min.	Total FG / FGA	Pct.	FT / FTA	Pct.	Reb. O/T	A	TO	PF	S	Blk	TP	PPM
JONES, B.	31	4/ 8	.500	1/ 1	1.000	-/ 9	2	4	3	-	-	9	.290
WUYCIK, D.	34	7/16	.438	6/ 6	1.000	-/ 6	0	4	4	-	-	20	.588
MCADOO, B.	28	10/19	.526	4/ 5	.800	-/15	1	4	5	-	-	24	.857
PREVIS, S.	32	1/ 5	.200	3/ 6	.500	-/ 3	8	5	4	-	-	5	.156
KARL, G.	30	5/14	.357	1/ 3	.333	-/ 6	5	5	3	-	-	11	.367
HUBAND, K.	11	0/ 1	.000	0/ 0	.000	-/ 2	0	0	2	-	-	0	.000
HITE, R.	1	0/ 0	.000	0/ 0	.000	-/ 0	1	1	0	-	-	0	.000
CHAMBERLAIN, B.	23	2/ 5	.400	2/ 3	.667	-/10	3	3	4	-	-	6	.261
CORSON, C.	1	0/ 0	.000	0/ 0	.000	-/ 0	0	0	0	-	-	0	.000
JOHNSTON, D.	6	0/ 1	.000	0/ 0	.000	-/ 0	0	0	1	-	-	0	.000
CHAMBERS, B.	3	0/ 1	.000	0/ 1	.000	-/ 0	0	0	1	-	-	0	.000
Totals	200	29/70	.414	17/25	.680	-/51	20	26	27	-	-	75	.375

Team Rebounds: Florida State 6; N. Carolina 1. Disqualified: Florida State—Royals, Petty; N. Carolina—McAdoo.

	1st Half	2nd Half	Final
Florida State	45	34	79
N. Carolina	32	43	75

Louisville (77)   Coach: Denny Crum

	Min.	Total FG / FGA	Pct.	FT / FTA	Pct.	Reb. O/T	A	TO	PF	S	Blk	TP	PPM
BACON, H.	32	5/11	.455	5/ 7	.714	-/ 4	4	-	0	-	-	15	.469
THOMAS, R.	21	2/ 4	.500	0/ 0	.000	-/ 3	1	-	5	-	-	4	.190
VILCHECK, A.	25	3/ 6	.500	0/ 0	.000	-/ 1	0	-	5	-	-	6	.240
PRICE, J.	38	11/23	.478	8/ 9	.889	-/ 5	2	-	3	-	-	30	.789
LAWHON, M.	22	0/ 7	.000	1/ 2	.500	-/ 3	0	-	3	-	-	1	.045
BRADLEY, K.	5	1/ 3	.333	0/ 0	.000	-/ 2	2	-	1	-	-	2	.400
CARTER, L.	20	4/ 8	.500	0/ 0	.000	-/ 2	2	-	0	-	-	8	.400
COOPER, T.	3	0/ 1	.000	2/ 2	1.000	-/ 1	0	-	1	-	-	2	.667
PRY, P.	2	2/ 3	.667	0/ 0	.000	-/ 1	0	-	1	-	-	4	2.000
MEIMAN, J.	2	0/ 1	.000	0/ 0	.000	-/ 1	0	-	0	-	-	0	.000
STALLINGS, R.	7	1/ 2	.500	0/ 1	.000	-/ 1	0	-	2	-	-	2	.286
BUNTON, B.	23	1/ 5	.200	1/ 1	1.000	-/ 4	0	-	1	-	-	3	.130
Totals	200	30/74	.405	17/22	.773	-/28	11	-	22	-	-	77	.385

UCLA (96)   Coach: John Wooden

	Min.	Total FG / FGA	Pct.	FT / FTA	Pct.	Reb. O/T	A	TO	PF	S	Blk	TP	PPM
FARMER, L.	27	6/12	.500	3/ 5	.600	-/ 4	1	-	2	-	-	15	.556
WILKES, J.	31	5/11	.455	2/ 2	1.000	-/ 6	2	-	0	-	-	12	.387
WALTON, B.	36	11/13	.846	11/12	.917	-/21	1	-	2	-	-	33	.917
LEE, G.	30	3/ 6	.500	4/ 6	.667	-/ 4	8	-	1	-	-	10	.333
BIBBY, H.	21	1/ 5	.200	0/ 0	.000	-/ 3	2	-	5	-	-	2	.095
CURTIS, T.	22	4/ 5	.800	0/ 0	.000	-/ 2	3	-	2	-	-	8	.364
HOLLYFIELD, L.	14	3/ 6	.500	0/ 0	.000	-/ 4	1	-	1	-	-	6	.429
NATER, S.	4	0/ 0	.000	2/ 4	.500	-/ 1	0	-	1	-	-	2	.500
CARSON, V.	4	1/ 1	1.000	0/ 0	.000	-/ 0	0	-	1	-	-	2	.500
CHAPMAN, J.	3	0/ 0	.000	0/ 1	.000	-/ 1	1	-	0	-	-	0	.000
HILL, A.	5	1/ 1	1.000	4/ 4	1.000	-/ 0	0	-	1	-	-	6	1.200
FRANKLIN, G.	3	0/ 1	.000	0/ 0	.000	-/ 2	0	-	0	-	-	0	.000
Totals	200	35/61	.574	26/34	.765	-/48	19	-	16	-	-	96	.480

Team Rebounds: UCLA 3; Louisville 4. Disqualified: UCLA—Bibby; Louisville—Thomas, Vilcheck.

	1st Half	2nd Half	Final
Louisville	31	46	77
UCLA	39	57	96

NATIONAL CHAMPIONSHIP

Florida State (76)   Coach: Hugh Durham

	Min.	Total FG/FGA	Pct.	FT/FTA	Pct.	Reb. O/T	A	TO	PF	S	Blk	TP	PPM
ROYALS, R.	33	5/7	.714	5/6	.833	-/10	2	-	5	-	-	15	.455
GARRETT, L.	37	1/9	.111	1/1	1.000	-/5	0	-	1	-	-	3	.081
MCCRAY, L.	23	3/6	.500	2/5	.400	-/6	3	-	4	-	-	8	.348
KING, R.	31	12/20	.600	3/3	1.000	-/6	1	-	1	-	-	27	.871
SAMUEL, G.	31	3/10	.300	0/0	.000	-/1	7	-	1	-	-	6	.194
HARRIS, R.	26	7/13	.538	2/3	.667	-/6	1	-	1	-	-	16	.615
PETTY, O.	9	0/0	.000	1/1	1.000	-/0	2	-	1	-	-	1	.111
COLE, O.	10	0/2	.000	0/0	.000	-/2	1	-	1	-	-	0	.000
Totals	200	31/67	.463	14/19	.737	-/36	17	-	15	-	-	76	.380

UCLA (81)   Coach: John Wooden

	Min.	Total FG/FGA	Pct.	FT/FTA	Pct.	Reb. O/T	A	TO	PF	S	Blk	TP	PPM
FARMER, L.	33	2/6	.333	0/0	.000	-/6	0	-	2	-	-	4	.121
WILKES, J.	38	11/16	.688	1/2	.500	-/10	3	-	4	-	-	23	.605
WALTON, B.	34	9/17	.529	6/11	.545	-/20	2	-	4	-	-	24	.706
LEE, G.	16	0/0	.000	0/0	.000	-/2	4	-	0	-	-	0	.000
BIBBY, H.	40	8/17	.471	2/3	.667	-/3	1	-	2	-	-	18	.450
CURTIS, T.	24	4/14	.286	0/1	.000	-/4	6	-	1	-	-	8	.333
HOLLYFIELD, L.	9	1/6	.167	0/0	.000	-/2	3	-	2	-	-	2	.222
NATER, S.	6	1/2	.500	0/1	.000	-/1	0	-	0	-	-	2	.333
Totals	200	36/78	.462	9/18	.500	-/48	19	-	15	-	-	81	.405

Team Rebounds: UCLA 2; Florida State 6. Disqualified: Florida State—Royals.

	1st Half	2nd Half	Final
Florida State	39	37	76
UCLA	50	31	81

NATIONAL THIRD PLACE

North Carolina (105)   Coach: Dean Smith

	Min.	Total FG/FGA	Pct.	FT/FTA	Pct.	Reb. O/T	A	TO	PF	S	Blk	TP	PPM
CHAMBERLAIN, B.	18	4/6	.667	1/1	1.000	-/4	5	-	5	-	-	9	.500
WUYCIK, D.	34	8/12	.667	11/16	.688	-/8	2	-	2	-	-	27	.794
MCADOO, R.	37	12/20	.600	6/6	1.000	-/19	2	-	1	-	-	30	.811
PREVIS, S.	33	2/5	.400	3/5	.600	-/4	7	-	4	-	-	7	.212
KARL, G.	28	6/8	.750	4/5	.800	-/2	3	-	5	-	-	16	.571
HUBAND, K.	12	0/0	.000	0/0	.000	-/2	1	-	1	-	-	0	.000
JONES, B.	21	4/8	.500	3/4	.750	-/4	5	-	5	-	-	11	.524
JOHNSTON,	4	0/0	.000	0/0	.000	-/0	0	-	0	-	-	0	.000
CORSON, C.	2	0/0	.000	0/0	.000	-/2	0	-	0	-	-	0	.000
HITE, R.	7	0/0	.000	1/3	.333	-/1	0	-	1	-	-	1	.143
CHAMBERS, B.	3	0/0	.000	4/4	1.000	-/0	0	-	0	-	-	4	1.333
ELSTON,	1	0/0	.000	0/0	.000	-/0	0	-	0	-	-	0	.000
Totals	200	36/59	.610	33/44	.750	-/46	25	-	24	-	-	105	.525

Louisville (91)   Coach: Denny Crum

	Min.	Total FG/FGA	Pct.	FT/FTA	Pct.	Reb. O/T	A	TO	PF	S	Blk	TP	PPM
BACON, H.	31	3/8	.375	6/8	.750	-/4	4	-	3	-	-	12	.387
THOMAS, R.	32	5/11	.455	4/6	.667	-/10	0	-	4	-	-	14	.438
VILCHECK, A.	19	3/5	.600	2/3	.667	-/5	1	-	3	-	-	8	.421
PRICE, J.	36	9/17	.529	5/7	.714	-/4	4	-	5	-	-	23	.639
LAWHON, M.	27	4/10	.400	5/6	.833	-/2	2	-	3	-	-	13	.481
BRADLEY, H.	6	1/4	.250	0/0	.000	-/4	3	-	2	-	-	2	.333
CARTER, L.	6	1/5	.200	0/0	.000	-/0	0	-	0	-	-	2	.333
BUNTON, B.	18	2/4	.500	1/2	.500	-/5	0	-	2	-	-	5	.278
COOPER, T.	11	2/5	.400	4/5	.800	-/0	2	-	4	-	-	8	.727
MEIMAN, J.	6	0/2	.000	0/0	.000	-/1	1	-	3	-	-	0	.000
STALLINGS, R.	4	1/5	.200	0/0	.000	-/2	0	-	2	-	-	2	.500
PRY, P.	4	1/2	.500	0/0	.000	-/1	0	-	0	-	-	2	.500
Totals	200	32/78	.410	27/37	.730	-/38	17	-	31	-	-	91	.455

Team Rebounds: N. Carolina 1; Louisville 5. Disqualified: N. Carolina—Chamberlain, Karl, Jones; Louisville—Price.

	1st Half	2nd Half	Final
N. Carolina	51	54	105
Louisville	34	57	91

REGIONAL THIRD PLACE EAST

South Carolina (90)   Coach: Frank McGuire

	Min.	Total FG/FGA	Pct.	FT/FTA	Pct.	Reb. O/T	A	TO	PF	S	Blk	TP	PPM
RIKER, T.	40	14/22	.636	8/11	.727	-/16	0	-	1	-	-	36	.900
AYDLETT, R.	26	2/8	.250	3/3	1.000	-/3	3	-	4	-	-	7	.269
TRAYLOR, D.	38	7/12	.583	1/6	.167	-/7	2	-	4	-	-	15	.395
JOYCE, K.	39	6/12	.500	7/8	.875	-/7	9	-	1	-	-	19	.487
CARVER, B.	33	3/10	.300	3/3	1.000	-/1	5	-	2	-	-	9	.273
WINTERS, B.	13	1/2	.500	0/0	.000	-/0	0	-	2	-	-	2	.154
MANNING, C.	9	1/1	1.000	0/0	.000	-/0	0	-	0	-	-	2	.222
MOUSA, R.	2	0/0	.000	0/0	.000	-/0	0	-	1	-	-	0	.000
Totals	200	34/60	.567	22/31	.710	-/34	19	12	15	-	-	90	.450

Villanova (78)   Coach: Jack Kraft

	Min.	Total FG/FGA	Pct.	FT/FTA	Pct.	Reb. O/T	A	TO	PF	S	Blk	TP	PPM
HASTINGS, E.	33	3/5	.600	1/1	1.000	-/5	3	-	4	-	-	7	.212
INGELSBY, T.	38	5/12	.417	1/3	.333	-/6	1	-	3	-	-	11	.289
SIEMIONTKOWSKI, H	40	11/22	.500	4/5	.800	-/10	5	-	2	-	-	26	.650
FORD, C.	40	7/19	.368	5/8	.625	-/6	6	-	4	-	-	19	.475
MOODY, L.	33	4/8	.500	1/2	.500	-/9	0	-	4	-	-	9	.273
GOHL, B.	7	1/3	.333	0/0	.000	-/3	0	-	1	-	-	2	.286
DALY, M.	2	0/0	.000	0/0	.000	-/1	0	-	1	-	-	0	.000
MCDOWELL, J.	7	2/2	1.000	0/0	.000	-/1	0	-	2	-	-	4	.571
Totals	200	33/71	.465	12/19	.632	-/41	15	12	21	-	-	78	.390

Team Rebounds: S. Carolina 3; Villanova 2. Disqualified: None.

	1st Half	2nd Half	Final
S. Carolina	38	52	90
Villanova	43	35	78

REGIONAL THIRD PLACE MIDEAST

Minnesota (77)   Coach: Bill Musselman

	Min.	Total FG/FGA	Pct.	FT/FTA	Pct.	Reb. O/T	A	TO	PF	S	Blk	TP	PPM
TURNER, C.	39	12/25	.480	1/ 3	.333	-/ 5	0	-	4	-	-	25	.641
WINFIELD, D.	36	4/ 7	.571	8/11	.727	-/ 9	1	-	1	-	-	16	.444
BREWER, J.	38	5/12	.417	4/ 4	1.000	-/22	2	-	4	-	-	14	.368
NIX, B.	39	1/ 3	.333	2/ 2	1.000	-/ 3	3	-	2	-	-	4	.103
YOUNG, K.	40	8/15	.533	2/ 2	1.000	-/ 6	1	-	2	-	-	18	.450
MURPHY, B.	8	0/ 2	.000	0/ 0	.000	-/ 0	1	-	0	-	-	0	.000
Totals	200	30/64	.469	17/22	.773	-/45	8	-	13	-	-	77	.385

Marquette (72)   Coach: Al McGuire

	Min.	Total FG/FGA	Pct.	FT/FTA	Pct.	Reb. O/T	A	TO	PF	S	Blk	TP	PPM
MCGUIRE, A.	39	5/11	.455	0/ 0	.000	-/ 4	3	-	2	-	-	10	.256
MCNEILL, L.	39	10/21	.476	4/ 4	1.000	-/10	0	-	4	-	-	24	.615
LACKEY, B.	40	3/15	.200	7/ 8	.875	-/12	3	-	4	-	-	13	.325
WASHINGTON, M.	36	9/21	.429	0/ 0	.000	-/ 8	3	-	0	-	-	18	.500
MILLS, M.	37	2/ 8	.250	3/ 5	.600	-/ 9	1	-	3	-	-	7	.189
OSTRAND, M.	2	0/ 1	.000	0/ 0	.000	-/ 0	0	-	0	-	-	0	.000
SPYCHALLA, K.	5	0/ 1	.000	0/ 0	.000	-/ 0	1	-	1	-	-	0	.000
LAM, G.	1	0/ 0	.000	0/ 0	.000	-/ 1	0	-	0	-	-	0	.000
GRZESK, G.	1	0/ 0	.000	0/ 0	.000	-/ 0	0	-	0	-	-	0	.000
Totals	200	29/78	.372	14/17	.824	-/44	11	-	14	-	-	72	.360

Team Rebounds: Minnesota 2; Marquette 3. Disqualified: None.

	1st Half	2nd Half	Final
Minnesota	47	30	77
Marquette	39	33	72

REGIONAL THIRD PLACE MIDWEST

Southwestern Louisiana (100)   Coach: Beryl Shipley

	Min.	Total FG/FGA	Pct.	FT/FTA	Pct.	Reb. O/T	A	TO	PF	S	Blk	TP	PPM
LOFTIN, W.	-	6/10	.600	1/ 1	1.000	-/ 9	-	-	4	-	-	13	-
SAUNDERS, F.	-	1/ 5	.200	1/ 1	1.000	-/ 7	-	-	2	-	-	3	-
EBRON, R.	-	8/12	.667	3/ 4	.750	-/12	-	-	2	-	-	19	-
LAMAR, D.	-	15/32	.469	6/ 7	.857	-/ 2	-	-	1	-	-	36	-
BISBANO, J.	-	7/10	.700	0/ 2	.000	-/ 7	-	-	3	-	-	14	-
TOWNSEND, P.	-	3/ 3	1.000	1/ 1	1.000	-/ 7	-	-	1	-	-	7	-
HANEY, M.	-	0/ 1	.000	0/ 1	.000	-/ 5	-	-	2	-	-	0	-
GREENE, S.	-	1/ 4	.250	3/ 3	1.000	-/ 2	-	-	2	-	-	5	-
WRIGHT, D.	-	1/ 2	.500	1/ 1	1.000	-/ 1	-	-	2	-	-	3	-
CALDWELL, S.	-	0/ 0	.000	0/ 0	.000	-/ 0	-	-	2	-	-	0	-
MARSH, K.	-	0/ 0	.000	0/ 0	.000	-/ 0	-	-	0	-	-	0	-
Totals	200	42/79	.519	16/21	.762	-/52	-	21	21	-	-	100	.500

Texas (70)   Coach: Leon Black

	Min.	Total FG/FGA	Pct.	FT/FTA	Pct.	Reb. O/T	A	TO	PF	S	Blk	TP	PPM
GROSCURTH, E.	-	6/11	.545	9/10	.900	-/ 9	-	-	3	-	-	21	-
LENOX, J.	-	5/17	.294	5/ 6	.833	-/ 1	-	-	3	-	-	15	-
BROSTERHOUS, B.	-	5/13	.385	4/ 6	.667	-/18	-	-	4	-	-	14	-
LARRABEE, H.	-	1/ 4	.250	2/ 4	.500	-/ 4	-	-	1	-	-	4	-
LOUIS, J.	-	1/ 7	.143	2/ 6	.333	-/ 4	-	-	0	-	-	4	-
BLACKLOCK, J.	-	3/ 5	.600	1/ 3	.333	-/ 6	-	-	3	-	-	7	-
SLATON, S.	-	1/ 3	.333	1/ 1	1.000	-/ 0	-	-	3	-	-	3	-
BROOKS, J.	-	0/ 1	.000	0/ 0	.000	-/ 0	-	-	0	-	-	0	-
STACY, G.	-	0/ 0	.000	2/ 2	1.000	-/ 0	-	-	0	-	-	2	-
Totals	200	22/61	.361	26/38	.684	-/42	-	24	17	-	-	70	.350

Disqualified: None. Technical fouls: S'Western La.—Lamar.

	1st Half	2nd Half	Final
S'Western La.	43	57	100
Texas	29	41	70

REGIONAL THIRD PLACE WEST

San Francisco (74)   Coach: Bob Gaillard

	Min.	Total FG/FGA	Pct.	FT/FTA	Pct.	Reb. O/T	A	TO	PF	S	Blk	TP	PPM
BURKS, J.	23	4/11	.364	2/ 2	1.000	-/ 3	0	-	5	-	-	10	.435
JONES, B.	36	5/ 5	1.000	0/ 1	.000	-/ 7	3	-	4	-	-	10	.278
RESTANI, K.	32	1/ 7	.143	1/ 2	.500	-/ 4	1	-	3	-	-	3	.094
SMITH, P.	37	6/13	.462	5/ 7	.714	-/ 0	4	-	2	-	-	17	.459
QUICK, M.	40	8/13	.615	8/10	.800	-/ 2	5	-	2	-	-	24	.600
BORO, J.	28	3/ 7	.429	4/ 7	.571	-/ 7	4	-	2	-	-	10	.357
CENTERWALL, R.	4	0/ 0	.000	0/ 0	.000	-/ 0	0	-	2	-	-	0	.000
Totals	200	27/56	.482	20/29	.690	-/23	17	-	20	-	-	74	.370

Weber State (64)   Coach: Gene Visscher

	Min.	Total FG/FGA	Pct.	FT/FTA	Pct.	Reb. O/T	A	TO	PF	S	Blk	TP	PPM
SMALL, B.	32	4/ 8	.500	1/ 1	1.000	-/ 3	5	-	2	-	-	9	.281
DAVIS, B.	36	8/15	.533	5/ 7	.714	-/11	1	-	3	-	-	21	.583
KNOBLE, J.	31	6/13	.462	2/ 3	.667	-/ 6	0	-	4	-	-	14	.452
COOPER, R.	38	3/12	.250	1/ 2	.500	-/10	1	-	4	-	-	7	.184
VANDYKE, W.	35	2/ 4	.500	3/ 4	.750	-/ 1	2	-	4	-	-	7	.200
SOTER, G.	13	0/ 2	.000	0/ 0	.000	-/ 0	2	-	0	-	-	0	.000
WIMBERLEY, R.	15	2/ 8	.250	2/ 3	.667	-/ 5	2	-	1	-	-	6	.400
Totals	200	25/62	.403	14/20	.700	-/36	13	-	18	-	-	64	.320

Team Rebounds: San Francisco 14; Weber St. 6. Disqualified: San Francisco—Burks.

	1st Half	2nd Half	Final
San Francisco	36	38	74
Weber St.	31	33	64

○ ALL-STAR TEAMS ○

ALL TOURNAMENT

RON KING	FLORIDA STATE
ROBERT MCADOO	N. CAROLINA
JIM PRICE	LOUISVILLE
★ **BILL WALTON**	UCLA
KEITH WILKES	UCLA

WEST REGIONAL

HENRY BIBBY	UCLA
BOB DAVIS	WEBER ST.
MIKE QUICK	SAN FRANCISCO
ED RATLEFF	LONG BEACH ST.
★ **BILL WALTON**	UCLA

★ Most Outstanding Player(s)

○ INDIVIDUAL RECORDS ○

SCORING

Most points in a single game
1. DWIGHT LAMAR, S'WESTERN LA. (vs. TEXAS) 36
1. TOM RIKER, S. CAROLINA (vs. VILLANOVA) 36
3. DWIGHT LAMAR, S'WESTERN LA. (vs. MARSHALL) 35
4. ROY EBRON, S'WESTERN LA. (vs. MARSHALL) 33
4. BILL WALTON, UCLA (vs. LOUISVILLE) 33

Most total points in the tournament
1. JIM PRICE, LOUISVILLE 103
2. DWIGHT LAMAR, S'WESTERN LA. 100
3. RON KING, FLORIDA STATE 92
4. BOB MCADOO, N. CAROLINA 82
5. DENNIS WUYCIK, N. CAROLINA 81

Highest scoring average (minimum 2 games)
1. DWIGHT LAMAR, S'WESTERN LA. (100-3) 33.33
2. JIM PRICE, LOUISVILLE (103-4) 25.75
3. TOM RIKER, S. CAROLINA (69-3) 23.00
3. BOB DAVIS, WEBER ST. (69-3) 23.00
5. LARRY ROBINSON, TEXAS (45-2) 22.50

FIELD GOALS

Most field goals in a single game
1. DWIGHT LAMAR, S'WESTERN LA. (vs. TEXAS) 15
2. ROY EBRON, S'WESTERN LA. (vs. MARSHALL) 14
2. TOM RIKER, S. CAROLINA (vs. VILLANOVA) 14
2. DWIGHT LAMAR, S'WESTERN LA. (vs. LOUISVILLE) 14
5. 5 tied for fifth place.

Most total field goals in the tournament
1. JIM PRICE, LOUISVILLE 41
1. DWIGHT LAMAR, S'WESTERN LA. 41
3. RON KING, FLORIDA STATE 35
4. BOB MCADOO, N. CAROLINA 31
5. BILL WALTON, UCLA 28

Most field goal attempts in a single game
1. DWIGHT LAMAR, S'WESTERN LA. (vs. LOUISVILLE) 42
2. DWIGHT LAMAR, S'WESTERN LA. (vs. TEXAS) 32
3. DWIGHT LAMAR, S'WESTERN LA. (vs. MARSHALL) 31
4. RUSSELL LEE, MARSHALL (vs. S'WESTERN LA.) 29
5. CLYDE TURNER, MINNESOTA (vs. MARQUETTE) 25

Most total field goal attempts in tournament
1. DWIGHT LAMAR, S'WESTERN LA. 105
2. RON KING, FLORIDA STATE 80
3. JIM PRICE, LOUISVILLE 71
4. BOB MCADOO, N. CAROLINA 63
5. HENRY BIBBY, UCLA 57

Highest field goal percentage in a single game (minimum 10 attempts)
1. DOUG RICHARDS, BRIGHAM YOUNG (vs. LONG BEACH ST.) (9-10) .900
2. BILL WALTON, UCLA (vs. LOUISVILLE) (11-13) .846
3. CORKY CALHOUN, PENNSYLVANIA (vs. VILLANOVA) (8-11) .727
4. LARRY ROBINSON, TEXAS (vs. KANSAS STATE) (10-14) .714
5. 4 tied for fifth place.

Highest field goal percentage in the tournament (minimum 20 attempts)
1. WILBERT LOFTIN, S'WESTERN LA. (16-23) .696
2. BILL WALTON, UCLA (28-41) .683
3. CORKY CALHOUN, PENNSYLVANIA (19-28) .679
4. DANNY TRAYLOR, S. CAROLINA (15-23) .652
5. LARRY ROBINSON, TEXAS (19-30) .633

FREE THROWS

Most free throws in a single game
1. DWIGHT LAMAR, S'WESTERN LA. (vs. MARSHALL) 11

1. DENNIS WUYCIK, N. CAROLINA (vs. LOUISVILLE) 11
1. BILL WALTON, UCLA (vs. LOUISVILLE) 11
4. RON KING, FLORIDA STATE (vs. N. CAROLINA) 10
4. HANK SIEMIONTKOWSKI, VILLANOVA (vs. PENNSYLVANIA) 10

Most total free throws in the tournament
1. DENNIS WUYCIK, N. CAROLINA 29
2. BILL WALTON, UCLA 24
3. REGGIE ROYALS, FLORIDA STATE 22
3. RON KING, FLORIDA STATE 22
5. 3 tied for fifth place.

Most free throws attempted in a single game
1. DENNIS WUYCIK, N. CAROLINA (vs. LOUISVILLE) 16
2. DWIGHT LAMAR, S'WESTERN LA. (vs. MARSHALL) 15
3. BOB DAVIS, WEBER ST. (vs. UCLA) 13
4. 3 tied for fourth place.

Most free throws attempted in the tournament
1. DENNIS WUYCIK, N. CAROLINA 37
2. BILL WALTON, UCLA 35
3. REGGIE ROYALS, FLORIDA STATE 30
3. BOB DAVIS, WEBER ST. 30
5. 2 tied for fifth place.

Highest free throw percentage in a single game (minimum 7 attempts)
1. RON KING, FLORIDA STATE (vs. N. CAROLINA) (10-10) 1.000
2. OTTO PETTY, FLORIDA STATE (vs. KENTUCKY) (9-9) 1.000
2. KEVIN JOYCE, S. CAROLINA (vs. N. CAROLINA) (9-9) 1.000
2. KRESIMIR COSIC, BRIGHAM YOUNG (vs. LONG BEACH ST.) (9-9) 1.000
5. JIM ANDREWS, KENTUCKY (vs. MARQUETTE) (7-7) 1.000

Highest free throw percentage in the tournament (minimum 15 attempts)
1 KEVIN JOYCE, S. CAROLINA (16-18) .889
2 MIKE LAWHON, LOUISVILLE (16-19) .842
2 BOB LACKEY, MARQUETTE (16-19) .842
4 HANK SIEMIONTKOWSKI, VILLANOVA (14-17) .824
5 RON KING, FLORIDA STATE (22-27) .815

REBOUNDS

Most rebounds in a single game
1 JIM BREWER, MINNESOTA (vs. MARQUETTE) 22
2 BILL WALTON, UCLA (vs. LOUISVILLE) 21
3 ROY EBRON, S'WESTERN LA. (vs. MARSHALL) 20
3 BILL WALTON, UCLA (vs. FLORIDA STATE) 20
5 BOB MCADOO, N. CAROLINA (vs. LOUISVILLE) 19

Most total rebounds in the tournament
1 BILL WALTON, UCLA 64
2 BOB MCADOO, N. CAROLINA 56
3 REGGIE ROYALS, FLORIDA STATE 51
4 ROY EBRON, S'WESTERN LA. 44
5 RON THOMAS, LOUISVILLE 40

Most rebounds per game (minimum 2 games)
1 JIM BREWER, MINNESOTA (36-2) 18.00
2 BILL WALTON, UCLA (64-4) 16.00
3 ROY EBRON, S'WESTERN LA. (44-3) 14.67
4 BOB MCADOO, N. CAROLINA (56-4) 14.00
5 JIM ANDREWS, KENTUCKY (27-2) 13.50

ASSISTS

Most assists in a single game
1 DWIGHT LAMAR, S'WESTERN LA. (vs. MARSHALL) 11

2 MIKE D'ANTONI, MARSHALL (vs. S'WESTERN LA.) 10
3 KEVIN JOYCE, S. CAROLINA (vs. VILLANOVA) 9
4 4 tied for fourth place.

Most total assists in the tournament
1 OTTO PETTY, FLORIDA STATE 25
2 STEVE PREVIS, N. CAROLINA 23
3 GREG LEE, UCLA 22
4 4 tied for fourth place.

Most assists per game (minimum 2 appearances)
1 STEVE PREVIS, N. CAROLINA (23-4) 5.75
2 GREG LEE, UCLA (22-4) 5.50
3 BRADY SMALL, WEBER ST. (16-3) 5.33
3 CHRIS FORD, VILLANOVA (16-3) 5.33
5 OTTO PETTY, FLORIDA STATE (25-5) 5.00

✪ TEAM RECORDS ✪

SCORING

Most points in a single game
1 S'WESTERN LA.(vs. MARSHALL) 112
2 N. CAROLINA (vs. LOUISVILLE) 105
3 MARSHALL (vs. S'WESTERN LA.) 101

Most total points in the tournament
1 FLORIDA STATE 381
2 N. CAROLINA 345
3 UCLA 340

Highest scoring average (minimum 2 games)
1 S'WESTERN LA. (296-3) 98.67
2 N. CAROLINA (345-4) 86.25
3 UCLA (340-4) 85.00

FIELD GOALS

Most field goals in a single game
1 S'WESTERN LA.(vs. TEXAS) 42
1 MARSHALL (vs. S'WESTERN LA.) 42
1 S'WESTERN LA. (vs. MARSHALL) 42

Most total field goals in the tournament
1 FLORIDA STATE 142
2 UCLA 136
3 LOUISVILLE 125

Most field goals attempted in a single game
1 MARSHALL (vs. S'WESTERN LA.) 112
2 S'WESTERN LA. (vs. LOUISVILLE) 94
3 UCLA (vs. WEBER ST.) 89

Most total field goals attempted in the tournament
1 FLORIDA STATE 314
2 UCLA 281
3 LOUISVILLE 270

Highest field goal percentage in a single game
1 PENNSYLVANIA (vs. PROVIDENCE) (33-49) .674

2 N. CAROLINA (vs. LOUISVILLE) (36-59) .610
3 UCLA (vs. LOUISVILLE) (35-61) .574

Highest field goal percentage in the tournament (minimum 2 games)
1 PENNSYLVANIA (85-167) .509
2 N. CAROLINA (121-242) .500
3 UCLA (136-281) .484

FREE THROWS

Most free throws in a single game
1 N. CAROLINA (vs. LOUISVILLE) 33
1 WEBER ST. (vs. HAWAII) 33
3 N. CAROLINA (vs. S. CAROLINA) 30

Most total free throws in the tournament
1 N. CAROLINA 103
2 FLORIDA STATE 97
3 LOUISVILLE 78

Most free throws attempted in a single game
1 WEBER ST. (vs. HAWAII) 52
2 N. CAROLINA (vs. LOUISVILLE) 44
3 FLORIDA STATE (vs. N. CAROLINA) 43

Most total free throws attempted in the tournament
1 FLORIDA STATE 140
2 N. CAROLINA 138
3 LOUISVILLE 115

Highest free throw percentage in a single game
1 FLORIDA STATE (vs. KENTUCKY) (19-22) .864
2 KENTUCKY (vs. MARQUETTE) (29-34) .853
3 BRIGHAM YOUNG (vs. LONG BEACH ST.) (22-26) .846

Highest free throw percentage in the tournament (minimum 2 games)
1 KENTUCKY (39-47) .830

2 MINNESOTA (29-37) .784
3 MARQUETTE (38-50) .760

Fewest free throws in a single game
1 S. CAROLINA (vs. TEMPLE) 7
1 TEXAS (vs. KANSAS STATE) 7
3 PROVIDENCE (vs. PENNSYLVANIA) 8

Lowest free throw percentage in a single game
1 TEXAS (vs. KANSAS STATE) (7-14) .500
2 UCLA (vs. FLORIDA STATE) (9-18) .500
3 S. CAROLINA (vs. TEMPLE) (7-13) .538

Lowest free throw percentage in the tournament (minimum 2 games)
1 WEBER ST. (65-105) .619
2 KANSAS STATE (29-45) .644
3 SAN FRANCISCO (31-47) .660

REBOUNDS

Most rebounds in a single game
1 UCLA (vs. WEBER ST.) 65
1 MARSHALL (vs. S'WESTERN LA.) 65
3 S'WESTERN LA. (vs. MARSHALL) 61

Most rebounds per game (minimum 2 games)
1 S'WESTERN LA. (165-3) 55.00
2 UCLA (190-4) 47.50
3 N. CAROLINA (177-4) 44.25

Most assists in a single game
1 N. CAROLINA (vs. LOUISVILLE) 25
1 S'WESTERN LA. (vs. MARSHALL) 25
3 PENNSYLVANIA (vs. PROVIDENCE) 23

Most assists per game (minimum 2 games)
1 N. CAROLINA (77-4) 19.25
2 UCLA (74-4) 18.50
3 PENNSYLVANIA (47-3) 15.67

1973

FIRST ROUND	REGIONAL SEMIFINAL	REGIONAL FINAL	**FINAL FOUR**	REGIONAL FINAL	REGIONAL SEMIFINAL	FIRST ROUND

MIDWEST

(bye)
Memphis St. 90

Memphis St. 92

S. Carolina 78

S. Carolina 76

Texas Tech 70

Memphis St. 98

(bye)
Kansas St. 66

Kansas St. 72

*S'western La. 102

*S'western La. 63

Houston 89

EAST

Providence 89

Providence 87

St. Joseph's 76

Providence 103

Pennsylvania 62

Pennsylvania 65

St. John's 61

Providence 85

(bye)
Maryland 91

Maryland 89

Syracuse 83

Syracuse 75

Furman 82

MIDEAST

Indiana 75
(bye)

Indiana 72

Marquette 77

Marquette 69

Miami (Ohio) 62

Indiana 59

Kentucky 106 (ot)
(bye)

Kentucky 65

*Austin Peay 77

*Austin Peay 100

Jacksonville 75

WEST

UCLA 98
(bye)

UCLA 54

Arizona St. 103

Arizona St. 81

Oklahoma City 78

UCLA 70

San Francisco 77
(bye)

San Francisco 39

*Long Beach St. 88

*Long Beach St. 67

Weber St. 75

Memphis St. 98 — Indiana 59

UCLA 87
Memphis St. 66

CONSOLATION GAMES

National Third Place:

Indiana 97

Providence 79

Regional Third Place:

Midwest:	S. Carolina 90	
	*S'western La. 85	

East:	Syracuse 69	
	Pennsylvania 68	

Mideast:	Marquette 88	
	*Austin Peay 73	

West:	*Long Beach St. 84	
	Arizona St. 80	

*Southwestern Louisiana's, Long Beach State's, and Austin Peay's participation in 1973 tournament vacated.

By the end of the 1972–73 season, many observers were calling UCLA's Walton gang the greatest college basketball team ever assembled. And who could argue?

The Bruins had not lost in over two years, since late in the 1971 season (before Bill Walton, Keith Wilkes, and company graduated to the varsity). On January 28th, they broke the Bill Russell–led San Francisco Dons' 1956 record of 60 consecutive victories by destroying a strong Notre Dame team in South Bend by 19 points. By the start of the 1973 tournament, they had accumulated ten more wins, and finished the regular season with an average victory margin of over 22 points in their 26 games; no UCLA opponent had ended within 6 points of the Bruins. UCLA was deep, strong, and fast, and they never seemed to lose their poise. They were as close to unbeatable as any team had ever been.

The West regional eliminations did nothing to dispel the UCLA image of invincibility. After beating over-matched Arizona State by 17, they played San Francisco in the West regional final. The Dons' coach, Bob Gaillard, terming it "suicidal to run against UCLA," slowed the pace, sagged inside on Walton, and forced UCLA to hit their outside shots. San Francisco led 14-9 when Wooden inserted Tommy Curtis into the game. Curtis swished three straight long bombs, and the Dons had to come out to guard him. This opened up the inside for Walton. By intermission, UCLA had a 1-point lead. The Bruins, ignited by a pair of spectacular Walton rebounds, broke the game open in the second half to win 54-39.

In the East, two excellent teams battled it out for a Final Four spot. Maryland Coach Lefty Dreisell had boasted that his team would soon become the "UCLA of the East." The Terrapins were strong up front with Tom McMillen and Len Elmore, and had the brilliant freshman John Lucas as the team quarterback. Their opponent, Providence, was only six deep: ball-handling wizard Ernie DiGregorio and big Marvin Barnes, one of the nation's toughest centers, were joined by a formidable supporting cast—high-scoring off-guard Kevin Stacom, Fran Costello, Charles Crawford, and Nehru King. Despite an early season 101-77 loss to UCLA on the Bruins' home court, Providence was given as good a chance as anybody of ultimately defeating the defending champions.

Against Maryland, after scoring 30 points to put the Friars in the lead, DiGregorio fouled out (all on offensive fouls) with 11:37 left in the game. But Stacom took over and popped for two quick baskets; he finished with 24 and Providence held on for a 103-89 victory.

The Friars' semifinal opponent was Memphis State. The Tigers were tall (6-9, 6-8, and 6-8 in the front line), and fast. Led by guard Larry Finch and forward Larry Kenon, they dominated the Midwest region on their way to the Final Four.

Providence jumped out to an early 24-16 lead, with Barnes controlling the boards and Ernie D leading a sizzling fast break. Just under seven and a half minutes into the game, Barnes jumped to block a shot by Memphis State's Ronnie Robinson. Barnes's face collided with Robinson's shoulder and big Marvin hit the floor hard, bleeding from the nose. When he tried to get up, his knee buckled under him. It was dislocated. Still Providence led at the half 49-40. Finally the Tigers' height started to take its toll; Kenon had 28 points and 22 rebounds, Robinson 24 points and 16 rebounds—and Memphis State rolled to victory, 98-95.

Indiana, the Mideast regional champion, was a young, enthusiastic, and disciplined team coached by 32-year-old Bob Knight. In only his second season at the Hoosiers' helm, he had already taken Indiana further than it had been for twenty years (since Branch McCracken won the 1953 national title). Despite his objections to the new freshman eligibility rule, Knight took full advantage of the change by inserting the extraordinarily poised 6-5 fresh-man Quinn Buckner into the starting line-up. The move paid off when Buckner excelled in Indiana's regional victo-ries over Marquette and Kentucky. Knight hoped that his patient, ball-control style, considered by many to be the best way of confronting UCLA, would be as effective in their Final Four matchup with the Bruins.

In their semi, the Hoosiers built a 20-17 lead before the Bruins got their wake-up call. Walton, angry at being whistled for a foul, threw a towel to the UCLA bench, accidentally hitting the Wizard in his face. Wooden inserted instant-offense Tommy Curtis and scrambling Dave Mey-ers and UCLA stormed back; Walton's rebounding and outlet passes ignited a run of 18 unanswered points. UCLA went into the intermission leading 40-22. Three minutes after play resumed, UCLA was up by 20 when Walton asked his coach to take off the press. When Wooden complied with the redhead's suggestion, Walton picked up two quick fouls (bringing his total to four) and earned a seat on the bench. The Bruins suddenly fell apart, and the Hoosiers reeled off 17 straight points. It was, said Wooden, the first time all season his team had lost their poise.

Walton came back, and immediately took the ball to the hoop. He ran into Indiana's high-scoring center Steve Downing. The whistle blew, and the call went against the Hoosier. A minute later, Downing picked up his fifth and was gone. And so were Indiana's hopes.

Before the final against Memphis State, Walton seemed to be, according to his coach, more emotionally prepared to play than he'd ever been. His performance reflected his state of mind: he had the greatest game ever by an individual in a championship contest. The Tigers came out in a man-to-man, with Kenon on Walton, and from the start, UCLA guards Greg Lee and Larry Hollyfield fed the big man inside. Whenever and wherever he got the ball, it went into the hoop. When Kenon picked up a couple of quick fouls, Memphis State coach Gene Bartow switched into a zone and the Tigers clawed their way back into the game. With 4:14 to go and UCLA holding a 37-31 lead, Walton picked up his third foul and Wooden took him out. By halftime, Memphis State had tied the score.

In the second half, the UCLA press started to rattle Memphis State, and Walton remained unstoppable. Within nine minutes he had scored 14 points and UCLA had built a 10-point lead. Then Walton picked up his fourth foul. This time Wooden kept him in, and he kept going up and around the Tigers to score. With just under three minutes remaining and the UCLA lead at 15, Walton fell to the floor. He limped off with the help of the Tigers' Billy Buford. As Memphis State's Larry Finch embraced his opponent, the crowd roared its appreciation. Walton left with a championship game record 44 points. He shot an astonishing 21 of 22 from the floor, and still had time to lead both teams in rebounds with 13.

When the cheering died down, the Bruins had their 75th consecutive victory, their 28th straight tournament win, their seventh straight championship and their ninth trophy in ten years. Wooden, who had always avoided comparing his clubs, was finally moved to say, "I've never had a greater team." As for Walton, no superlatives could suffice.

FIRST ROUND MIDWEST

South Carolina (78) Coach: Frank McGuire

	Min.	Total FG/FGA	Pct.	FT/FTA	Pct.	Reb. O/T	A	TO	PF	S	Blk	TP	PPM
ENGLISH, A.	40	7/11	.636	1/1	1.000	-/15	1	5	3	1	3	15	.375
WINTERS, B.	20	4/5	.800	1/1	1.000	-/3	0	1	5	1	0	9	.450
TRAYLOR, D.	34	8/13	.615	0/0	.000	-/16	2	5	5	1	2	16	.471
DUNLEAVY, M.	31	5/10	.500	1/2	.500	-/1	2	4	0	1	0	11	.355
JOYCE, K.	40	6/16	.375	9/10	.900	-/1	4	3	2	2	0	21	.525
MATHIAS, B.	7	0/0	.000	0/0	.000	-/2	1	1	0	0	0	0	.000
MANNING, C.	13	1/2	.500	0/0	.000	-/1	0	0	0	0	0	2	.154
GREINER, M.	15	2/3	.667	0/1	.000	-/4	0	2	1	1	0	4	.267
Totals	200	33/60	.550	12/15	.800	-/43	10	21	16	7	5	78	.390

Texas Tech (70) Coach: Gerald Myers

	Min.	Total FG/FGA	Pct.	FT/FTA	Pct.	Reb. O/T	A	TO	PF	S	Blk	TP	PPM
JOHNSON, W.	14	2/5	.400	2/2	1.000	-/5	1	1	1	0	0	6	.429
RICHARDSON, R.	28	8/11	.727	1/2	.500	-/6	0	3	3	2	0	17	.607
WAKEFIELD, E.	37	6/12	.500	4/4	1.000	-/7	3	3	1	2	0	16	.432
BULLOCK	38	8/18	.444	3/5	.600	-/7	1	7	3	1	1	19	.500
LITTLE, R.	37	3/11	.273	0/0	.000	-/0	9	2	5	4	0	6	.162
BAILEY, P.	13	3/5	.600	0/0	.000	-/1	1	0	0	0	0	6	.462
DERKOWSKI, J.	1	0/0	.000	0/0	.000	-/0	1	1	0	1	0	0	.000
KABERLINE, G.	3	0/0	.000	0/0	.000	-/0	0	1	1	0	0	0	.000
MANK, B.	1	0/0	.000	0/0	.000	-/0	0	0	0	0	0	0	.000
MOORE, D.	28	0/2	.000	0/0	.000	-/0	3	2	2	0	0	0	.000
Totals	200	30/64	.469	10/13	.769	-/25	19	20	16	10	1	70	.350

Team Rebounds: S. Carolina 0; Texas Tech 0. Disqualified: S. Carolina—Winters, Traylor; Texas Tech—Little. Technical fouls: None.

	1st Half	2nd Half	Final
S. Carolina	30	48	78
Texas Tech	30	40	70

Southwestern Louisiana (102) Coach: Beryl Shipley

	Min.	Total FG/FGA	Pct.	FT/FTA	Pct.	Reb. O/T	A	TO	PF	S	Blk	TP	PPM
LAMAR, D.	-	15/34	.441	5/6	.833	-/3	3	2	1	2	0	35	-
BISBANO, J.	-	4/9	.444	3/3	1.000	-/4	7	4	3	1	0	11	-
SAUNDERS, F.	-	2/7	.286	0/0	.000	-/8	3	2	5	0	1	4	-
WILSON, R.	-	3/11	.273	4/4	1.000	-/7	3	1	2	2	1	10	-
FOGLE, L.	-	5/9	.556	7/10	.700	-/9	5	3	1	0	0	17	-
EBRON, R.	-	10/15	.667	3/4	.750	-/11	1	2	4	1	0	23	-
WELLS, P.	-	1/1	1.000	0/0	.000	-/0	1	0	1	0	0	2	-
Totals	200	40/86	.465	22/27	.815	-/42	23	14	17	6	2	102	.510

Houston (89) Coach: Guy Lewis

	Min.	Total FG/FGA	Pct.	FT/FTA	Pct.	Reb. O/T	A	TO	PF	S	Blk	TP	PPM
JONES, D.	40	6/11	.545	6/7	.857	-/14	3	3	3	0	2	18	.450
BONNEY, J.	23	3/9	.333	0/2	.000	-/4	3	4	1	1	0	6	.261
DUNBAR, L.	40	11/26	.423	5/7	.714	-/4	3	1	4	0	1	27	.675
NEWSOME, S.	35	6/15	.400	2/4	.500	-/9	5	4	5	3	0	14	.400
PRESLEY, M.	20	2/3	.667	0/0	.000	-/8	0	0	3	1	2	4	.200
EDWARDS, S.	20	5/9	.556	0/0	.000	-/8	0	5	1	2	0	10	.500
HAYES, D.	18	5/11	.455	0/0	.000	-/0	5	3	4	2	0	10	.556
MARRS, D.	4	0/0	.000	0/0	.000	-/0	1	0	0	0	0	0	.000
Totals	200	38/84	.452	13/20	.650	-/47	20	20	21	9	5	89	.445

Team Rebounds: S'western La. 9; Houston 6. Disqualified: S'western La.—Saunders; Houston—Newsome. Technical fouls: None.

	1st Half	2nd Half	Final
S'western La.	46	56	102
Houston	39	50	89

FIRST ROUND EAST

Providence (89) Coach: Dave Gavitt

	Min.	Total FG/FGA	Pct.	FT/FTA	Pct.	Reb. O/T	A	TO	PF	S	Blk	TP	PPM
DIGREGORIO, E.	40	14/21	.667	3/4	.750	-/2	6	4	4	2	0	31	.775
CRAWFORD, C.	31	2/4	.500	0/1	.000	-/5	1	1	1	0	0	4	.129
BARNES, M.	40	10/21	.476	1/2	.500	-/17	2	3	4	1	4	21	.525
STACOM, K.	40	5/11	.455	2/2	1.000	-/3	2	3	2	0	1	12	.300
COSTELLO, F.	36	4/8	.500	1/2	.500	-/11	2	1	2	1	0	9	.250
KING, N.	13	4/8	.500	4/4	1.000	-/2	0	1	0	1	0	12	.923
Totals	200	39/73	.534	11/15	.733	-/40	13	13	13	5	5	89	.445

St. Joseph's (76) Coach: Jack McKinney

	Min.	Total FG/FGA	Pct.	FT/FTA	Pct.	Reb. O/T	A	TO	PF	S	Blk	TP	PPM
BANTOM, M.	33	10/19	.526	3/4	.750	-/13	1	4	4	2	5	23	.697
FUREY, K.	37	3/9	.333	5/8	.625	-/8	1	4	1	0	1	11	.297
KELLY, C.	19	2/4	.500	1/2	.500	-/1	0	0	0	1	0	5	.263
McFARLAND, P.	40	8/13	.615	0/1	.000	-/7	4	0	1	0	0	16	.400
O'BRIEN, J.	35	3/8	.375	1/2	.500	-/2	3	3	1	0	0	7	.200
MOODY, M.	17	4/6	.667	0/0	.000	-/2	1	4	5	1	0	8	.471
SABOL, B.	8	1/2	.500	0/0	.000	-/1	0	0	0	1	0	2	.250
PELTZER, L.	6	1/4	.250	0/0	.000	-/1	0	0	0	0	0	2	.333
RAFFERTY, F.	5	1/1	1.000	0/0	.000	-/1	0	1	0	0	0	2	.400
Totals	200	33/66	.500	10/17	.588	-/36	10	16	11	6	6	76	.380

Team Rebounds: Providence 4; St. Joseph's 0. Disqualified: St. Joseph's—Moody. Technical fouls: St. Joseph's—bench.

	1st Half	2nd Half	Final
Providence	36	53	89
St. Joseph's	29	47	76

Pennsylvania (62) Coach: Chuck Daly

	Min.	Total FG/FGA	Pct.	FT/FTA	Pct.	Reb. O/T	A	TO	PF	S	Blk	TP	PPM
HANKINSON, B.	-	8/16	.500	0/0	.000	-/10	1	2	2	1	1	16	-
HAIGLER, R.	-	7/16	.438	6/6	1.000	-/6	2	3	1	2	2	20	-
BEECROFT, J.	-	3/8	.375	2/3	.667	-/3	3	3	2	3	0	8	-
BIGELOW, J.	-	3/10	.300	2/2	1.000	-/4	1	3	3	3	0	8	-
LITTLEPAGE, C.	-	0/1	.000	0/0	.000	-/4	0	0	5	1	0	0	-
FINGER, B.	-	0/0	.000	0/0	.000	-/0	0	0	0	0	0	0	-
VARGA, W.	-	0/0	.000	0/0	.000	-/1	0	0	0	0	1	0	-
LEWIS, L.	-	1/2	.500	0/0	.000	-/1	0	1	0	0	0	2	-
JABLONSKI, J.	-	3/5	.600	2/3	.667	-/4	0	4	0	0	0	8	-
Totals	200	25/58	.431	12/14	.857	-/33	7	11	18	10	4	62	.310

St. John's (61) Coach: Frank Mulzoff

	Min.	Total FG/FGA	Pct.	FT/FTA	Pct.	Reb. O/T	A	TO	PF	S	Blk	TP	PPM
SCHAEFFER, B.	38	8/19	.421	0/0	.000	-/8	0	0	3	0	0	16	.421
PRINCE, T.	32	1/3	.333	0/0	.000	-/7	1	1	2	0	0	2	.063
SEARCY, E.	40	6/12	.500	7/8	.875	-/10	0	1	1	0	1	19	.475
UTLEY, M.	29	2/9	.222	2/4	.500	-/5	2	7	5	1	0	6	.207
CLUESS, K.	29	3/8	.375	0/0	.000	-/4	2	2	0	1	0	6	.207
JENKINS, L.	2	0/0	.000	0/0	.000	-/0	0	0	0	0	0	0	.000
ALAGIA, F.	22	4/10	.400	4/6	.667	-/0	1	1	3	1	0	12	.545
SMITH, B.	8	0/2	.000	0/0	.000	-/2	0	1	2	1	0	0	.000
Totals	200	24/63	.381	13/18	.722	-/36	6	13	16	4	1	61	.305

Team Rebounds: Pennsylvania 5; St. John's 5. Disqualified: Pennsylvania—Littlepage; St. John's—Utley. Technical fouls: None.

	1st Half	2nd Half	Final
Pennsylvania	38	24	62
St. John's	32	29	61

Syracuse (83) Coach: Roy Danforth

	Min.	Total FG/FGA	Pct.	FT/FTA	Pct.	Reb. O/T	A	TO	PF	S	Blk	TP	PPM
LEE, M.	-	9/16	.563	4/5	.800	-/4	-	-	3	-	-	22	-
DOOMS, B.	-	5/10	.500	0/4	.000	-/9	-	-	5	-	-	10	-
HACKETT, R.	-	5/13	.385	2/4	.500	-/18	-	-	1	-	-	12	-
DUVAL, D.	-	9/22	.409	0/0	.000	-/3	-	-	4	-	-	18	-
WADACH, M.	-	3/8	.375	1/2	.500	-/3	-	-	3	-	-	7	-
LEE, J.	-	1/4	.250	4/5	.800	-/0	-	-	0	-	-	6	-
STUNDIS, T.	-	2/2	1.000	4/4	1.000	-/1	-	-	0	-	-	8	-
Totals	200	34/75	.453	15/24	.625	-/38	-	-	16	-	-	83	.415

Furman (82) Coach: Joe Williams

	Min.	Total FG/FGA	Pct.	FT/FTA	Pct.	Reb. O/T	A	TO	PF	S	Blk	TP	PPM
MAYES, C.	-	5/13	.385	1/1	1.000	-/11	-	-	4	-	-	11	-
SIMPSON, R.	-	7/15	.467	2/3	.667	-/7	-	-	2	-	-	16	-
LEONARD, F.	-	5/14	.357	0/0	.000	-/11	-	-	4	-	-	10	-
HILL, B.	-	3/5	.600	0/0	.000	-/0	-	-	2	-	-	6	-
HUNT, R.	-	1/2	.500	0/0	.000	-/1	-	-	0	-	-	2	-
LYNCH, C.	-	6/11	.545	0/0	.000	-/7	-	-	3	-	-	12	-
KELLEY, E.	-	3/10	.300	3/3	1.000	-/2	-	-	4	-	-	9	-
CLARK, G.	-	1/3	.333	2/3	.667	-/2	-	-	0	-	-	4	-
BIERLY, B.	-	3/4	.750	2/2	1.000	-/5	-	-	1	-	-	8	-
BRENIZER, T.	-	2/3	.667	0/0	.000	-/3	-	-	3	-	-	4	-
Totals	200	36/80	.450	10/12	.833	-/49	-	-	23	-	-	82	.410

Team Rebounds: Syracuse 5; Furman 3. Disqualified: Syracuse—Dooms. Technical fouls: None.

	1st Half	2nd Half	Final
Syracuse	43	40	83
Furman	37	45	82

FIRST ROUND MIDEAST

Marquette (77) Coach: Al McGuire

	Min.	Total FG/FGA	Pct.	FT/FTA	Pct.	Reb. O/T	A	TO	PF	S	Blk	TP	PPM
MCGUIRE, A.	-	3/8	.375	2/3	.667	-/2	-	-	1	-	-	8	-
LUCAS, M.	-	8/16	.500	8/9	.889	-/12	-	-	3	-	-	24	-
MCNEILL, L.	-	5/16	.313	1/2	.500	-/5	-	-	5	-	-	11	-
FRAZIER, G.	-	9/12	.750	2/3	.667	-/8	-	-	2	-	-	20	-
WASHINGTON, M.	-	2/5	.400	0/0	.000	-/2	-	-	0	-	-	4	-
DELSMAN, D.	-	1/1	1.000	2/2	1.000	-/0	-	-	1	-	-	4	-
MILLS, M.	-	0/0	.000	0/0	.000	-/1	-	-	1	-	-	0	-
VOLLMER, P.	-	0/1	.000	0/0	.000	-/0	-	-	0	-	-	0	-
TATUM, W.	-	2/3	.667	0/0	.000	-/2	-	-	0	-	-	4	-
HOMAN, J.	-	0/0	.000	0/0	.000	-/0	-	-	0	-	-	0	-
DANIELS, E.	-	1/3	.333	0/0	.000	-/0	-	-	5	-	-	2	-
Totals	200	31/65	.477	15/19	.789	-/32	-	-	18	-	-	77	.385

Miami (Ohio) (62) Coach: Darrel Hedric

	Min.	Total FG/FGA	Pct.	FT/FTA	Pct.	Reb. O/T	A	TO	PF	S	Blk	TP	PPM
LUMPKIN, P.	-	4/12	.333	0/0	.000	-/0	-	-	2	-	-	8	-
GARLOCH, L.	-	2/7	.286	0/0	.000	-/8	-	-	5	-	-	4	-
HAMPTON, R.	-	9/18	.500	3/3	1.000	-/6	-	-	2	-	-	21	-
DEES, G.	-	2/4	.500	0/0	.000	-/1	-	-	3	-	-	4	-
ELMER, D.	-	4/4	1.000	2/2	1.000	-/10	-	-	4	-	-	10	-
FIELDS, S.	-	3/5	.600	0/0	.000	-/2	-	-	2	-	-	6	-
DORSEY, W.	-	1/5	.200	4/4	1.000	-/3	-	-	0	-	-	6	-
ESSENBURG, K.	-	0/1	.000	0/0	.000	-/0	-	-	1	-	-	0	-
DIERINGER, R.	-	0/0	.000	3/4	.750	-/0	-	-	0	-	-	3	-
FREYTAG, J.	-	0/0	.000	0/0	.000	-/0	-	-	0	-	-	0	-
DEMOSS, G.	-	0/0	.000	0/0	.000	-/0	-	-	0	-	-	0	-
HANDY, S.	-	0/0	.000	0/0	.000	-/0	-	-	0	-	-	0	-
Totals	200	25/56	.446	12/13	.923	-/30	-	-	19	-	-	62	.310

Team Rebounds: Marquette 3; Miami (Ohio) 2. Disqualified: Marquette—McNeill, Daniels; Miami (Ohio)—Garloch. Technical fouls: None.

	1st Half	2nd Half	Final
Marquette	38	39	77
Miami (Ohio)	31	31	62

Austin Peay (77) Coach: Lake Kelly

	Min.	Total FG/FGA	Pct.	FT/FTA	Pct.	Reb. O/T	A	TO	PF	S	Blk	TP	PPM
ODUMS, D.	-	2/9	.222	2/2	1.000	-/9	-	-	2	-	-	6	-
HOWARD, P.	-	4/11	.364	2/4	.500	-/5	-	-	5	-	-	10	-
CHILDRESS, E.	-	5/10	.500	0/0	.000	-/1	-	-	4	-	-	10	-
WILLIAMS, J.	-	12/26	.462	2/2	1.000	-/5	-	-	3	-	-	26	-
JACKSON, H.	-	4/6	.667	0/2	.000	-/4	-	-	3	-	-	8	-
WANSTRATH, J.	-	1/2	.500	2/2	1.000	-/1	-	-	3	-	-	4	-
TURNER, R.	-	2/4	.500	1/2	.500	-/6	-	-	2	-	-	5	-
JIMMERSON, R.	-	4/7	.571	0/1	.000	-/5	-	-	3	-	-	8	-
HAMPTON, K.	-	0/0	.000	0/0	.000	-/0	-	-	0	-	-	0	-
Totals	200	34/75	.453	9/15	.600	-/36	-	-	25	-	-	77	.385

Jacksonville (75) Coach: Tom Wasdin

	Min.	Total FG/FGA	Pct.	FT/FTA	Pct.	Reb. O/T	A	TO	PF	S	Blk	TP	PPM
WILLIAMS, H.	-	6/17	.353	3/4	.750	-/6	-	-	2	-	-	15	-
BENBOW, L.	-	6/13	.462	6/8	.750	-/3	-	-	3	-	-	18	-
STEWARD, A.	-	3/7	.429	2/5	.400	-/13	-	-	2	-	-	8	-
CLARK, J.	-	4/6	.667	0/0	.000	-/3	-	-	3	-	-	8	-
TAYLOR, B.	-	6/9	.667	8/10	.800	-/16	-	-	3	-	-	20	-
STOWERS, D.	-	0/0	.000	0/0	.000	-/0	-	-	3	-	-	0	-
COLEMAN, R.	-	2/6	.333	0/0	.000	-/1	-	-	1	-	-	4	-
NYLAN, B.	-	1/1	1.000	0/0	.000	-/1	-	-	2	-	-	2	-
Totals	200	28/59	.475	19/27	.704	-/43	-	-	19	-	-	75	.375

Team Rebounds: Austin Peay 5; Jacksonville 3. Disqualified: Austin Peay—Howard.

	1st Half	2nd Half	Final
Austin Peay	47	30	77
Jacksonville	32	43	75

FIRST ROUND WEST

Arizona State (103) Coach: Ned Wulk

	Min.	Total FG/FGA	Pct.	FT/FTA	Pct.	Reb. O/T	A	TO	PF	S	Blk	TP	PPM
GRAY, K.	-	2/ 6	.333	1/ 1	1.000	-/ 5	3	1	1	-	-	5	-
CONTRERAS, M.	-	10/14	.714	1/ 2	.500	-/ 7	3	2	4	-	-	21	-
OWENS, J.	-	8/16	.500	0/ 0	.000	-/ 2	1	2	3	-	-	16	-
KENNEDY, R.	-	4/11	.364	2/ 2	1.000	-/ 8	1	1	5	-	-	10	-
WASLEY, M.	-	4/ 6	.667	0/ 0	.000	-/ 6	1	2	4	-	-	8	-
WHITE, R.	-	6/10	.600	7/ 8	.875	-/ 6	5	3	1	-	-	19	-
BROWN, J.	-	3/ 5	.600	1/ 4	.250	-/ 6	1	2	1	-	-	7	-
JACKSON, G.	-	2/ 5	.400	3/ 6	.500	-/ 3	3	1	5	-	-	7	-
SCHRADER, J.	-	4/ 4	1.000	2/ 4	.500	-/ 4	0	0	4	-	-	10	-
MOON, M.	-	0/ 5	.000	0/ 1	.000	-/ 3	0	1	0	-	-	0	-
Totals	200	43/82	.524	17/28	.607	-/50	18	15	28	-	-	103	.515

Oklahoma City (78) Coach: Abe Lemons

	Min.	Total FG/FGA	Pct.	FT/FTA	Pct.	Reb. O/T	A	TO	PF	S	Blk	TP	PPM
EDWARDS, O.	-	13/28	.464	5/ 5	1.000	-/ 9	0	2	4	-	-	31	-
WASHINGTON, J.	-	4/13	.308	3/ 5	.600	-/ 8	1	1	3	-	-	11	-
BROWN	-	1/ 8	.125	3/ 6	.500	-/ 8	1	2	3	-	-	5	-
RICH, M.	-	6/22	.273	4/ 6	.667	-/ 9	0	3	5	-	-	16	-
TOSEE, M.	-	3/ 6	.500	0/ 1	.000	-/ 2	1	1	2	-	-	6	-
RUSSELL, N.	-	2/ 5	.400	1/ 2	.500	-/ 5	1	0	1	-	-	5	-
LANIER, L.	-	0/ 1	.000	4/ 5	.800	-/ 1	0	3	3	-	-	4	-
GILKEY, H.	-	0/ 3	.000	0/ 0	.000	-/ 3	0	0	1	-	-	0	-
POLANSKY, M.	-	0/ 1	.000	0/ 0	.000	-/ 0	0	0	0	-	-	0	-
LACKEY, J.	-	0/ 0	.000	0/ 0	.000	-/ 0	0	2	1	-	-	0	-
TRIBBLE	-	0/ 0	.000	0/ 0	.000	-/ 0	0	0	0	-	-	0	-
BEATLY	-	0/ 0	.000	0/ 0	.000	-/ 0	0	0	0	-	-	0	-
Totals	200	29/87	.333	20/30	.667	-/45	4	14	23	-	-	78	.390

Team Rebounds: Arizona St. 13; Oklahoma City 10. Disqualified: Arizona St.—Kennedy, Jackson; Oklahoma City— Rich. Technical fouls: None.

	1st Half	2nd Half	Final
Arizona St.	42	61	103
Oklahoma City	40	38	78

Long Beach State (88) Coach: Jerry Tarkanian

	Min.	Total FG/FGA	Pct.	FT/FTA	Pct.	Reb. O/T	A	TO	PF	S	Blk	TP	PPM
ABEREGG, R.	-	1/ 6	.167	2/ 2	1.000	-/ 2	3	5	3	-	-	4	-
MCDONALD, G.	-	1/ 5	.200	2/ 2	1.000	-/ 2	3	0	1	-	-	4	-
RATLEFF, E.	-	9/13	.692	7/ 7	1.000	-/ 6	3	1	2	-	-	25	-
GRAY, L.	-	11/18	.611	3/ 3	1.000	-/ 7	2	2	3	-	-	25	-
STEPHENS, N.	-	5/ 9	.556	2/ 4	.500	-/ 5	0	2	5	-	-	12	-
PONDEXTER, R.	-	5/11	.455	2/ 2	1.000	-/ 8	0	2	3	-	-	12	-
DOUSE, E.	-	2/ 3	.667	2/ 5	.400	-/ 5	1	3	4	-	-	6	-
KING, L.	-	0/ 3	.000	0/ 0	.000	-/ 0	0	0	1	-	-	0	-
Totals	250	34/68	.500	20/25	.800	-/35	12	15	22	-	-	88	.352

Weber State (75) Coach: Gene Visscher

	Min.	Total FG/FGA	Pct.	FT/FTA	Pct.	Reb. O/T	A	TO	PF	S	Blk	TP	PPM
DION, D.	-	0/ 6	.000	0/ 0	.000	-/ 2	2	2	0	-	-	0	-
SMALL, B.	-	8/17	.471	2/ 2	1.000	-/ 3	4	2	1	-	-	18	-
GUBLER, K.	-	3/ 7	.429	4/ 4	1.000	-/ 2	1	2	4	-	-	10	-
FLEMING, S.	-	6/11	.545	4/ 6	.667	-/ 9	3	3	4	-	-	16	-
COOPER, R.	-	2/ 5	.400	0/ 0	.000	-/ 5	3	2	5	-	-	4	-
WATTS, J.	-	5/ 5	1.000	1/ 2	.500	-/ 3	1	4	4	-	-	11	-
WIMBERLY, R.	-	4/10	.400	0/ 1	.000	-/ 5	2	0	5	-	-	8	-
TAUSHECK, B.	-	0/ 0	.000	0/ 0	.000	-/ 1	0	0	1	-	-	0	-
DEVITA, T.	-	0/ 2	.000	0/ 0	.000	-/ 1	0	0	0	-	-	0	-
MUIRBROOK, D.	-	0/ 0	.000	0/ 1	.000	-/ 1	0	0	0	-	-	0	-
CHILDS, F.	-	0/ 1	.000	0/ 0	.000	-/ 0	0	0	0	-	-	0	-
VAN, D.	-	3/ 5	.600	2/ 2	1.000	-/ 3	1	0	1	-	-	8	-
Totals	250	31/69	.449	13/18	.722	-/35	17	15	25	-	-	75	.300

Team Rebounds: Long Beach St. 7; Weber St. 5. Disqualified: Long Beach St.—Stephens; Weber St.—Cooper, Wimberly. Technical fouls: None.

	1st Half	2nd Half	1st OT	2nd OT	Final
Long Beach St.	22	19	19	28	88
Weber St.	16	23	24	12	75

REGIONAL SEMIFINAL MIDWEST

Memphis State (90) Coach: Gene Bartow

	Min.	Total FG/FGA	Pct.	FT/FTA	Pct.	Reb. O/T	A	TO	PF	S	Blk	TP	PPM
BUFORD, B.	-	5/ 7	.714	0/ 0	.000	-/10	4	2	3	3	1	10	-
ROBINSON, R.	-	5/16	.313	1/ 4	.250	-/17	3	1	2	2	0	11	-
KENON, L.	-	16/30	.533	2/ 6	.333	-/20	4	2	4	1	4	34	-
LAURIE, B.	-	0/ 1	.000	6/ 7	.857	-/ 1	4	4	2	0	6	6	-
FINCH, L.	-	8/17	.471	9/10	.900	-/ 1	4	4	4	0	0	25	-
MCKINNEY, D.	-	0/ 0	.000	0/ 0	.000	-/ 0	0	1	1	0	0	0	-
WESTFALL, W.	-	0/ 1	.000	0/ 0	.000	-/ 0	0	0	0	0	0	0	-
COOK, B.	-	2/ 5	.400	0/ 0	.000	-/ 0	1	1	1	0	4	4	-
Totals	200	36/77	.468	18/27	.667	-/49	20	13	19	8	5	90	.450

South Carolina (76) Coach: Frank McGuire

	Min.	Total FG/FGA	Pct.	FT/FTA	Pct.	Reb. O/T	A	TO	PF	S	Blk	TP	PPM
ENGLISH, A.	38	9/15	.600	1/ 1	1.000	-/ 8	0	3	5	1	0	19	.500
WINTERS, B.	36	5/11	.455	4/ 4	1.000	-/ 8	4	0	5	0	1	14	.389
TRAYLOR, D.	37	5/12	.417	0/ 4	.000	-/ 6	1	2	3	0	3	10	.270
DUNLEAVY, M.	36	4/10	.400	4/ 4	1.000	-/ 0	1	1	3	1	1	12	.333
JOYCE, K.	39	8/21	.381	2/ 2	1.000	-/ 2	6	5	2	2	1	18	.462
WALSH, J.	1	0/ 0	.000	0/ 0	.000	-/ 0	0	1	0	0	0	0	.000
MATHIAS, B.	1	1/ 1	1.000	0/ 0	.000	-/ 1	0	1	0	0	1	2	2.000
MANNING, C.	7	0/ 0	.000	0/ 0	.000	-/ 0	0	0	4	1	0	0	.000
GREINER, M.	4	0/ 0	.000	0/ 0	.000	-/ 1	0	0	0	0	0	0	.000
COX, T.	1	0/ 0	.000	1/ 2	.500	-/ 1	0	0	0	0	0	1	1.000
Totals	200	32/70	.457	12/17	.706	-/27	12	13	22	7	7	76	.380

Team Rebounds: Memphis State 11; S. Carolina 6. Disqualified: S. Carolina—English, Winters. Technical fouls: None.

	1st Half	2nd Half	Final
Memphis State	39	51	90
S. Carolina	24	52	76

Kansas State (66) Coach: Jack Hartman

	Min.	Total FG / FGA	Pct.	FT / FTA	Pct.	Reb. O / T	A	TO	PF	S	Blk	TP	PPM
KRUGER, L.	38	6/11	.545	4/ 6	.667	-/ 2	4	5	2	-	-	16	.421
CHIPMAN, B.	40	4/ 6	.667	3/ 5	.600	-/ 2	6	4	1	-	-	11	.275
WILLIAMS, L.	24	2/ 8	.250	0/ 0	.000	-/ 7	0	2	2	-	-	4	.167
KUSNYER, E.	36	7/15	.467	1/ 3	.333	-/ 7	3	5	4	-	-	15	.417
MITCHELL, S.	17	4/ 7	.571	0/ 0	.000	-/ 5	1	3	5	-	-	8	.471
BEARD, D.	6	0/ 1	.000	0/ 0	.000	-/ 1	0	0	0	-	-	0	.000
THRUSTON, J.	16	1/ 3	.333	1/ 2	.500	-/ 3	3	2	2	-	-	3	.188
MCVEY, G.	23	4/ 5	.800	1/ 4	.250	-/ 3	1	2	2	-	-	9	.391
Totals	200	28/56	.500	10/20	.500	-/30	18	23	18	-	-	66	.330

Southwestern Louisiana (63) Coach: Beryl Shipley

	Min.	Total FG / FGA	Pct.	FT / FTA	Pct.	Reb. O / T	A	TO	PF	S	Blk	TP	PPM
LAMAR, D.	39	8/21	.381	2/ 2	1.000	-/ 4	3	4	2	-	-	18	.462
BISBANO, J.	38	2/ 7	.286	0/ 0	.000	-/ 2	1	2	5	-	-	4	.105
SAUNDERS, F.	28	4/ 8	.500	0/ 0	.000	-/ 7	2	2	4	-	-	8	.286
WILSON, R.	24	3/ 7	.429	1/ 2	.500	-/ 6	0	1	2	-	-	7	.292
FOGLE, L.	29	4/14	.286	2/ 3	.667	-/ 7	0	3	3	-	-	10	.345
EBRON, R.	37	5/15	.333	6/ 7	.857	-/12	2	6	4	-	-	16	.432
WELLS, P.	2	0/ 0	.000	0/ 0	.000	-/ 0	1	0	0	-	-	0	.000
BROWN, A.	3	0/ 0	.000	0/ 0	.000	-/ 1	0	0	1	-	-	0	.000
Totals	200	26/72	.361	11/14	.786	-/39	9	18	21	-	-	63	.315

Team Rebounds: Kansas State 11; S'western La. 6. Disqualified: Kansas State—Mitchell; S'western La.—Bisbano. Technical fouls: None.

	1st Half	2nd Half	Final
Kansas State	38	28	66
S'western La.	26	37	63

REGIONAL SEMIFINAL EAST

Providence (87) Coach: Dave Gavitt

	Min.	Total FG / FGA	Pct.	FT / FTA	Pct.	Reb. O / T	A	TO	PF	S	Blk	TP	PPM
DIGREGORIO, E.	-	9/21	.429	0/ 0	.000	-/ 3	10	5	2	-	-	18	-
STACOM, K.	-	7/ 9	.778	2/ 2	1.000	-/ 5	5	3	0	-	-	16	-
COSTELLO, F.	-	1/ 3	.333	0/ 0	.000	-/ 4	4	2	4	-	-	2	-
CRAWFORD, C.	-	6/ 6	1.000	0/ 0	.000	-/ 3	0	4	1	-	-	12	-
BARNES, M.	-	10/10	1.000	0/ 0	.000	-/13	0	0	3	-	-	20	-
KING, N.	-	7/11	.636	4/ 4	1.000	-/ 6	1	0	2	-	-	18	-
BELLO, G.	-	0/ 0	.000	0/ 0	.000	-/ 0	0	0	0	-	-	0	-
MODEST, D.	-	0/ 0	.000	0/ 0	.000	-/ 0	0	1	0	-	-	0	-
BAKER, A.	-	0/ 1	.000	0/ 0	.000	-/ 3	0	0	0	-	-	0	-
DUNPHY, R.	-	0/ 0	.000	1/ 2	.500	-/ 1	0	0	0	-	-	1	-
Totals	200	40/61	.656	7/ 8	.875	-/38	20	15	12	-	-	87	.435

Maryland (91) Coach: Lefty Driesell

	Min.	Total FG / FGA	Pct.	FT / FTA	Pct.	Reb. O / T	A	TO	PF	S	Blk	TP	PPM
LUCAS, J.	-	9/17	.529	3/ 4	.750	-/ 5	-	-	2	-	-	21	-
BODELL, B.	-	5/11	.455	2/ 2	1.000	-/ 1	-	-	1	-	-	12	-
ELMORE, L.	-	5/10	.500	0/ 0	.000	-/14	-	-	2	-	-	10	-
MCMILLEN, T.	-	8/10	.800	2/ 2	1.000	-/ 6	-	-	2	-	-	18	-
O'BRIEN, J.	-	8/14	.571	6/ 7	.857	-/ 6	-	-	2	-	-	22	-
BROWN, D.	-	3/ 4	.750	0/ 1	.000	-/ 4	-	-	2	-	-	6	-
WHITE, H.	-	0/ 0	.000	0/ 0	.000	-/ 1	-	-	1	-	-	0	-
BROWN, O.	-	0/ 0	.000	0/ 0	.000	-/ 1	-	-	1	-	-	0	-
ROY, T.	-	0/ 0	.000	0/ 0	.000	-/ 1	-	-	1	-	-	0	-
HOWARD, M.	-	1/ 1	1.000	0/ 0	.000	-/ 0	-	-	0	-	-	2	-
PORAC, R.	-	0/ 1	.000	0/ 0	.000	-/ 0	-	-	0	-	-	0	-
HAHN, B.	-	0/ 0	.000	0/ 0	.000	-/ 0	-	-	0	-	-	0	-
Totals	200	39/68	.574	13/16	.813	-/39	-	-	14	-	-	91	.455

Pennsylvania (65) Coach: Chuck Daly

	Min.	Total FG / FGA	Pct.	FT / FTA	Pct.	Reb. O / T	A	TO	PF	S	Blk	TP	PPM
HANKINSON, B.	-	9/29	.310	1/ 3	.333	-/ 9	2	2	1	-	-	19	-
HAIGLER, R.	-	7/15	.467	4/ 4	1.000	-/12	0	1	4	-	-	18	-
BEECROFT, J.	-	1/ 6	.167	0/ 0	.000	-/ 1	4	1	0	-	-	2	-
BIGELOW, B.	-	5/19	.263	0/ 0	.000	-/ 6	6	1	3	-	-	10	-
LITTLEPAGE, C.	-	1/ 1	1.000	0/ 0	.000	-/ 0	0	0	3	-	-	2	-
FINGER, B.	-	0/ 1	.000	0/ 0	.000	-/ 0	1	0	0	-	-	0	-
VARGA, W.	-	5/ 9	.556	0/ 0	.000	-/ 2	2	1	1	-	-	10	-
LEWIS, L.	-	1/ 6	.167	0/ 0	.000	-/ 5	0	0	1	-	-	2	-
JABLONSKI, J.	-	0/ 0	.000	0/ 0	.000	-/ 0	0	0	0	-	-	0	-
HANSEN, K.	-	1/ 1	1.000	0/ 0	.000	-/ 0	0	0	1	-	-	2	-
FRANK, B.	-	0/ 1	.000	0/ 0	.000	-/ 0	0	1	0	-	-	0	-
BATORY, S.	-	0/ 1	.000	0/ 0	.000	-/ 0	0	0	0	-	-	0	-
Totals	200	30/89	.337	5/ 7	.714	-/35	15	7	14	-	-	65	.325

Team Rebounds: Providence 6; Pennsylvania 5. Disqualified: None. Technical fouls: None.

	1st Half	2nd Half	Final
Providence	36	51	87
Pennsylvania	29	36	65

Syracuse (75) Coach: Roy Danforth

	Min.	Total FG / FGA	Pct.	FT / FTA	Pct.	Reb. O / T	A	TO	PF	S	Blk	TP	PPM
LEE, M.	-	8/13	.615	1/ 2	.500	-/ 3	-	-	4	-	-	17	-
DOOMS, B.	-	3/ 5	.600	0/ 0	.000	-/ 4	-	-	2	-	-	6	-
HACKETT, R.	-	4/10	.400	1/ 3	.333	-/ 5	-	-	3	-	-	9	-
DUVAL, D.	-	11/17	.647	0/ 0	.000	-/ 2	-	-	0	-	-	22	-
WADACH, M.	-	3/ 6	.500	2/ 2	1.000	-/ 3	-	-	4	-	-	8	-
LEE, J.	-	3/ 6	.500	3/ 4	.750	-/ 1	-	-	2	-	-	9	-
STUNDIS, T.	-	0/ 1	.000	0/ 0	.000	-/ 0	-	-	1	-	-	0	-
SUPRUNOWICZ, B.	-	1/ 1	1.000	0/ 0	.000	-/ 0	-	-	0	-	-	2	-
STAPLETON, S.	-	0/ 0	.000	0/ 1	.000	-/ 1	-	-	0	-	-	0	-
SHAW, S.	-	0/ 0	.000	0/ 0	.000	-/ 0	-	-	1	-	-	0	-
BEGNER, D.	-	1/ 2	.500	0/ 0	.000	-/ 0	-	-	0	-	-	2	-
WICKMAN, C.	-	0/ 0	.000	0/ 0	.000	-/ 1	-	-	0	-	-	0	-
BARTHOLOMEW, B.	-	0/ 0	.000	0/ 0	.000	-/ 0	-	-	0	-	-	0	-
Totals	200	34/61	.557	7/12	.583	-/20	-	-	17	-	-	75	.375

Team Rebounds: Maryland 3; Syracuse 3. Disqualified: None. Technical fouls: None.

	1st Half	2nd Half	Final
Maryland	35	56	91
Syracuse	34	41	75

REGIONAL SEMIFINAL MIDEAST

Indiana (75)   Coach: Bob Knight

	Min.	Total FG/FGA	Pct.	FT/FTA	Pct.	Reb. O/T	A	TO	PF	S	Blk	TP	PPM
GREEN, S.	40	8/15	.533	0/1	.000	-/6	7	1	3	1	0	16	.400
RITTER, J.	32	5/9	.556	4/4	1.000	-/6	2	2	0	0	0	14	.438
DOWNING, S.	40	12/17	.706	5/11	.455	-/10	0	4	2	2	0	29	.725
CREWS, J.	24	3/4	.750	0/0	.000	-/1	2	3	1	0	0	6	.250
BUCKNER, Q.	40	2/6	.333	0/2	.000	-/7	4	3	3	5	1	4	.100
LASKOWSKI, J.	24	1/2	.500	4/4	1.000	-/1	1	2	1	0	1	6	.250
Totals	200	31/53	.585	13/22	.591	-/31	16	15	12	8	2	75	.375

Marquette (69)   Coach: Al McGuire

	Min.	Total FG/FGA	Pct.	FT/FTA	Pct.	Reb. O/T	A	TO	PF	S	Blk	TP	PPM
MCNEILL, L.	38	5/9	.556	2/2	1.000	-/12	1	4	4	3	1	12	.316
FRAZIER, G.	39	4/7	.571	0/0	.000	-/2	1	2	5	0	1	8	.205
LUCAS, M.	35	6/15	.400	0/0	.000	-/5	2	2	4	0	1	12	.343
MCGUIRE, A.	31	6/9	.667	3/3	1.000	-/1	4	3	2	0	0	15	.484
WASHINGTON, M.	33	10/15	.667	0/0	.000	-/5	2	5	3	3	0	20	.606
DELSMAN, D.	12	1/1	1.000	0/0	.000	-/0	2	1	1	0	0	2	.167
DANIELS, E.	6	0/1	.000	0/0	.000	-/1	0	1	1	0	1	0	.000
MILLS, M.	4	0/0	.000	0/0	.000	-/0	0	0	0	0	0	0	.000
TATUM, W.	2	0/1	.000	0/0	.000	-/0	0	0	0	1	0	0	.000
Totals	200	32/58	.552	5/5	1.000	-/26	12	18	20	7	4	69	.345

Team Rebounds: Indiana 5; Marquette 0. Disqualified: Marquette—Frazier. Technical fouls: Indiana—Coach Knight.

	1st Half	2nd Half	Final
Indiana	35	40	75
Marquette	38	31	69

Kentucky (106)   Coach: Joe Hall

	Min.	Total FG/FGA	Pct.	FT/FTA	Pct.	Reb. O/T	A	TO	PF	S	Blk	TP	PPM
ANDREWS, J.	-	15/19	.789	0/0	.000	-/14	2	-	1	-	-	30	-
CONNER, J.	-	4/7	.571	1/1	1.000	-/2	3	-	4	-	-	9	-
GREVEY, K.	-	10/24	.417	1/2	.500	-/13	6	-	4	-	-	21	-
FLYNN, M.	-	3/8	.375	4/6	.667	-/6	6	-	5	-	-	10	-
LYONS, R.	-	6/16	.375	0/0	.000	-/4	3	-	0	-	-	12	-
GUYETTE, B.	-	4/9	.444	0/0	.000	-/8	1	-	1	-	-	8	-
LOCHMUELLER, S.	-	2/2	1.000	0/0	.000	-/1	0	-	1	-	-	4	-
EDELMAN, R.	-	1/3	.333	0/0	.000	-/0	0	-	0	-	-	2	-
DREWITZ, R.	-	0/0	.000	0/0	.000	-/0	0	-	0	-	-	0	-
HALE, J.	-	0/0	.000	0/0	.000	-/1	0	-	0	-	-	0	-
STAMPER, L.	-	5/9	.556	0/0	.000	-/7	2	-	0	-	-	10	-
Totals	225	50/97	.515	6/9	.667	-/56	23	-	16	-	-	106	.471

Austin Peay (100)   Coach: Lake Kelly

	Min.	Total FG/FGA	Pct.	FT/FTA	Pct.	Reb. O/T	A	TO	PF	S	Blk	TP	PPM
WILLIAMS, J.	35	13/31	.419	0/0	.000	-/6	1	-	4	-	-	26	.743
CHILDRESS, E.	42	10/19	.526	2/2	1.000	-/5	2	-	3	-	-	22	.524
HOWARD, P.	29	7/10	.700	0/0	.000	-/9	0	-	4	-	-	14	.483
ODUMS, D.	42	5/10	.500	1/1	1.000	-/2	5	-	2	-	-	11	.262
JACKSON, H.	41	10/19	.526	3/7	.429	-/18	3	-	2	-	-	23	.561
WANSTRATH, J.	21	0/3	.000	2/2	1.000	-/4	1	-	0	-	-	2	.095
HAMPTON, K.	3	1/3	.333	0/0	.000	-/2	1	-	0	-	-	2	.667
TURNER, R.	6	0/2	.000	0/0	.000	-/1	0	-	0	-	-	0	.000
JIMMERSON, R.	6	0/2	.000	0/0	.000	-/0	0	-	0	-	-	0	.000
Totals	225	46/99	.465	8/12	.667	-/47	13	-	15	-	-	100	.444

Disqualified: Kentucky—Flynn.

	1st Half	2nd Half	1 OT	Final
Kentucky	43	49	14	106
Austin Peay	47	45	8	100

REGIONAL SEMIFINAL WEST

UCLA (98)   Coach: John Wooden

	Min.	Total FG/FGA	Pct.	FT/FTA	Pct.	Reb. O/T	A	TO	PF	S	Blk	TP	PPM
WILKES, J.	-	6/14	.429	0/0	.000	-/10	1	-	2	-	-	12	-
FARMER, L.	-	5/10	.500	0/0	.000	-/4	0	-	2	-	-	10	-
WALTON, B.	-	13/18	.722	2/2	1.000	-/14	6	-	3	-	-	28	-
LEE, G.	-	1/2	.500	1/1	1.000	-/0	4	-	0	-	-	3	-
HOLLYFIELD, L.	-	9/16	.563	2/2	1.000	-/5	6	-	3	-	-	20	-
CURTIS, T.	-	2/3	.667	3/3	1.000	-/1	5	-	2	-	-	7	-
MEYERS, D.	-	2/3	.667	2/3	.667	-/5	4	-	1	-	-	6	-
NATER, S.	-	2/5	.400	0/2	.000	-/2	0	-	2	-	-	4	-
FRANKLIN, G.	-	1/2	.500	0/0	.000	-/2	1	-	0	-	-	2	-
CARSON, V.	-	0/0	.000	0/2	.000	-/1	1	-	0	-	-	0	-
WEBB, B.	-	0/2	.000	0/0	.000	-/0	0	-	2	-	-	0	-
CORLISS, C.	-	0/0	.000	2/2	1.000	-/0	0	-	1	-	-	2	-
DROLLINGER, R.	-	0/0	.000	0/0	.000	-/0	0	-	1	-	-	0	-
TRGOVICH, P.	-	2/5	.400	0/0	.000	-/2	1	-	0	-	-	4	-
Totals	200	43/80	.538	12/17	.706	-/46	29	-	19	-	-	98	.490

Arizona State (81)   Coach: Ned Wulk

	Min.	Total FG/FGA	Pct.	FT/FTA	Pct.	Reb. O/T	A	TO	PF	S	Blk	TP	PPM
GRAY, K.	-	2/4	.500	0/1	.000	-/2	2	-	0	-	-	4	-
WASLEY, M.	-	3/8	.375	0/0	.000	-/10	1	-	1	-	-	6	-
KENNEDY, R.	-	2/7	.286	5/6	.833	-/8	5	-	5	-	-	9	-
CONTRERAS, M.	-	9/20	.450	0/0	.000	-/4	1	-	3	-	-	18	-
OWENS, J.	-	8/20	.400	6/8	.750	-/4	1	-	2	-	-	22	-
WHITE, R.	-	3/6	.500	0/0	.000	-/2	0	-	0	-	-	6	-
JACKSON, G.	-	3/8	.375	4/6	.667	-/4	1	-	3	-	-	10	-
BROWN, J.	-	2/6	.333	2/3	.667	-/6	0	-	2	-	-	6	-
SCHRADER, J.	-	0/1	.000	0/0	.000	-/3	1	-	1	-	-	0	-
MOON, M.	-	0/2	.000	0/0	.000	-/1	0	-	0	-	-	0	-
Totals	200	32/82	.390	17/24	.708	-/44	12	-	17	-	-	81	.405

Team Rebounds: UCLA 5; Arizona St. 4. Disqualified: Arizona St.—Kennedy. Technical fouls: None.

	1st Half	2nd Half	Final
UCLA	51	47	98
Arizona St.	37	44	81

San Francisco (77)   Coach: Bob Gaillard

	Min.	Total FG/FGA	Pct.	FT/FTA	Pct.	Reb. O/T	A	TO	PF	S	Blk	TP	PPM
RESTANI, K.	-	8/15	.533	2/3	.667	-/9	7	-	2	-	-	18	-
JONES, S.	-	0/3	.000	0/0	.000	-/4	1	-	1	-	-	0	-
FERNSTEN, E.	-	4/14	.286	0/0	.000	-/17	2	-	2	-	-	8	-
SMITH, P.	-	5/11	.455	10/14	.714	-/6	8	-	2	-	-	20	-
QUICK, M.	-	12/18	.667	1/2	.500	-/6	3	-	3	-	-	25	-
BORO, J.	-	2/2	1.000	2/3	.667	-/2	4	-	0	-	-	6	-
LEWIS, A.	-	0/1	.000	0/0	.000	-/0	0	-	0	-	-	0	-
Totals	200	31/64	.484	15/22	.682	-/44	25	-	10	-	-	77	.385

Long Beach State (67)   Coach: Jerry Tarkanian

	Min.	Total FG/FGA	Pct.	FT/FTA	Pct.	Reb. O/T	A	TO	PF	S	Blk	TP	PPM
RATLEFF, E.	-	4/18	.222	4/4	1.000	-/7	7	-	3	-	-	12	-
GRAY, L.	-	4/6	.667	2/2	1.000	-/8	5	-	2	-	-	10	-
STEPHENS, N.	-	9/20	.450	0/1	.000	-/16	1	-	1	-	-	18	-
MCDONALD, G.	-	2/9	.222	0/0	.000	-/2	0	-	1	-	-	4	-
ABEREGG, R.	-	4/10	.400	0/0	.000	-/1	9	-	5	-	-	8	-
PONDEXTER, R.	-	5/14	.357	1/2	.500	-/6	1	-	3	-	-	11	-
DOUSE, E.	-	2/5	.400	0/0	.000	-/4	0	-	2	-	-	4	-
KING, L.	-	0/0	.000	0/0	.000	-/0	0	-	2●	-	-	0	-
Totals	200	30/82	.366	7/9	.778	-/44	23	-	19	-	-	67	.335

Team Rebounds: San Francisco 4; Long Beach St. 2. Disqualified: Long Beach St.—Aberegg. Technical fouls: San Francisco—Coach Gaillard; Long Beach St.—Aberegg.

	1st Half	2nd Half	Final
San Francisco	37	40	77
Long Beach St.	31	36	67

REGIONAL FINAL MIDWEST

Memphis State (92)   Coach: Gene Bartow

	Min.	Total FG/FGA	Pct.	FT/FTA	Pct.	Reb. O/T	A	TO	PF	S	Blk	TP	PPM
BUFORD, B.	14	2/5	.400	0/0	.000	-/3	1	0	4	1	0	4	.286
KENON, L.	27	7/12	.583	0/0	.000	-/7	1	2	4	1	1	14	.519
ROBINSON, R.	38	7/10	.700	0/0	.000	-/16	2	2	3	1	1	14	.368
LAURIE, B.	39	2/4	.500	4/4	1.000	-/3	11	4	2	1	0	8	.205
FINCH, L.	39	10/16	.625	12/12	1.000	-/2	3	5	2	1	0	32	.821
COOK, B.	18	3/6	.500	2/2	1.000	-/3	3	4	0	0	0	8	.444
WESTFALL, W.	18	5/6	.833	0/0	.000	-/6	0	0	5	0	0	10	.556
JONES, C.	3	0/0	.000	0/0	.000	-/0	0	0	1	0	0	0	.000
TETZLAFF, J.	1	0/1	.000	0/2	.000	-/2	0	0	0	0	0	0	.000
LISS, J.	1	1/1	1.000	0/0	.000	-/0	0	0	0	0	0	2	2.000
ANDREWS, K.	1	0/0	.000	0/0	.000	-/0	0	0	1	0	0	0	.000
MCKINNEY, D.	1	0/1	.000	0/0	.000	-/0	1	0	0	1	0	0	.000
Totals	200	37/62	.597	18/20	.900	-/42	22	17	22	6	2	92	.460

Kansas State (72)   Coach: Jack Hartman

	Min.	Total FG/FGA	Pct.	FT/FTA	Pct.	Reb. O/T	A	TO	PF	S	Blk	TP	PPM
KRUGER, L.	40	6/12	.500	3/3	1.000	-/5	4	3	3	3	0	15	.375
CHIPMAN, B.	25	1/4	.250	1/2	.500	-/2	2	0	1	2	1	3	.120
WILLIAMS, L.	23	2/8	.250	0/0	.000	-/5	0	3	2	1	1	4	.174
KUSNYER, E.	33	8/19	.421	5/10	.500	-/5	2	2	4	1	1	21	.636
MITCHELL, S.	24	6/14	.429	0/1	.000	-/6	0	2	3	1	0	12	.500
BEARD, D.	15	0/3	.000	1/2	.500	-/1	2	1	1	2	0	1	.067
THRUSTON, J.	17	2/3	.667	0/2	.000	-/1	1	0	2	2	0	4	.235
MCVEY, G.	16	4/7	.571	4/4	1.000	-/4	1	1	1	0	0	12	.750
SNIDER, D.	7	0/3	.000	0/0	.000	-/0	0	0	2	2	0	0	.000
Totals	200	29/73	.397	14/24	.583	-/29	12	12	19	14	3	72	.360

Team Rebounds: Memphis State 5; Kansas State 5. Disqualified: Memphis State—Westfall. Technical fouls: None.

	1st Half	2nd Half	Final
Memphis State	49	43	92
Kansas State	34	38	72

REGIONAL FINAL EAST

Providence (103)   Coach: Dave Gavitt

	Min.	Total FG/FGA	Pct.	FT/FTA	Pct.	Reb. O/T	A	TO	PF	S	Blk	TP	PPM
DIGREGORIO, E.	27	14/21	.667	2/2	1.000	-/3	5	5	5	-	-	30	1.111
STACOM, K.	40	10/17	.588	4/5	.800	-/2	1	4	3	-	-	24	.600
COSTELLO, F.	28	2/5	.400	4/4	1.000	-/6	2	2	4	-	-	8	.286
CRAWFORD, C.	40	2/4	.500	3/3	1.000	-/5	0	2	2	-	-	7	.175
BARNES, M.	40	8/18	.444	3/5	.600	-/15	0	3	2	-	-	19	.475
KING, N.	25	7/9	.778	1/3	.333	-/7	2	1	1	-	-	15	.600
Totals	200	43/74	.581	17/22	.773	-/38	10	17	17	-	-	103	.515

Maryland (89)   Coach: Lefty Driesell

	Min.	Total FG/FGA	Pct.	FT/FTA	Pct.	Reb. O/T	A	TO	PF	S	Blk	TP	PPM
LUCAS, J.	-	9/20	.450	2/2	1.000	-/6	4	2	5	-	-	20	-
BODELL, B.	-	2/8	.250	0/0	.000	-/7	3	0	3	-	-	4	-
ELMORE, L.	-	7/11	.636	0/1	.000	-/10	0	4	5	-	-	14	-
MCMILLEN, T.	-	10/16	.625	5/5	1.000	-/6	0	6	4	-	-	25	-
O'BRIEN, J.	-	3/9	.333	2/2	1.000	-/3	2	2	1	-	-	8	-
BROWN, J.	-	1/3	.333	0/0	.000	-/1	3	0	0	-	-	2	-
WHITE, H.	-	0/1	.000	0/0	.000	-/0	0	0	0	-	-	0	-
BROWN, O.	-	2/4	.500	0/0	.000	-/1	0	0	0	-	-	4	-
ROY, T.	-	4/5	.800	0/2	.000	-/5	0	3	3	-	-	8	-
HOWARD, M.	-	2/6	.333	0/0	.000	-/0	1	0	1	-	-	4	-
Totals	200	40/83	.482	9/12	.750	-/39	13	17	22	-	-	89	.445

Team Rebounds: Providence 3; Maryland 3. Disqualified: Providence—DiGregorio; Maryland—Lucas, Elmore. Technical fouls: None.

	1st Half	2nd Half	Final
Providence	50	53	103
Maryland	51	38	89

REGIONAL FINAL MIDEAST

Indiana (72) Coach: Bob Knight

	Min.	Total FG / FGA	Pct.	FT / FTA	Pct.	Reb. O / T	A	TO	PF	S	Blk	TP	PPM
BUCKNER, Q.	39	8/21	.381	0/ 1	.000	-/11	5	7	3	3	0	16	.410
DOWNING, S.	40	10/22	.455	3/ 4	.750	-/13	0	6	3	3	0	23	.575
GREEN, S.	32	5/13	.385	4/ 4	1.000	-/ 6	2	2	3	3	2	14	.438
RITTER, J.	38	4/ 5	.800	1/ 1	1.000	-/ 2	1	0	2	0	0	9	.237
CREWS, J.	25	0/ 2	.000	0/ 0	.000	-/ 1	2	1	0	0	0	0	.000
ABERNETHY, T.	2	0/ 0	.000	0/ 0	.000	-/ 1	0	0	0	0	0	0	.000
LASKOWSKI, J.	24	4/ 5	.800	2/ 4	.500	-/ 6	3	1	1	1	0	10	.417
Totals	200	31/68	.456	10/14	.714	-/40	13	17	12	10	2	72	.360

Kentucky (65) Coach: Joe Hall

	Min.	Total FG / FGA	Pct.	FT / FTA	Pct.	Reb. O / T	A	TO	PF	S	Blk	TP	PPM
LYONS, R.	23	3/ 7	.429	2/ 2	1.000	-/ 2	3	1	0	1	0	8	.348
CONNER, J.	37	1/ 6	.167	0/ 0	.000	-/10	6	0	2	0	0	2	.054
FLYNN, M.	36	4/10	.400	0/ 0	.000	-/ 2	2	2	4	0	0	8	.222
GREVEY, K.	36	7/14	.500	0/ 0	.000	-/ 8	3	2	4	0	0	14	.389
ANDREWS, J.	37	11/20	.550	1/ 2	.500	-/10	3	9	3	1	6	23	.622
EDELMAN, R.	2	0/ 0	.000	0/ 0	.000	-/ 0	1	1	0	0	0	0	.000
STAMPER, L.	5	0/ 0	.000	0/ 0	.000	-/ 0	0	2	0	0	0	0	.000
HALE, J.	5	0/ 1	.000	0/ 0	.000	-/ 0	0	1	0	0	0	0	.000
LOCHMUELLER, S.	3	2/ 3	.667	0/ 0	.000	-/ 1	0	0	3	0	0	4	1.333
GUYETTE, B.	16	3/ 4	.750	0/ 0	.000	-/ 3	0	0	1	1	2	6	.375
Totals	200	31/65	.477	3/ 4	.750	-/36	18	18	17	3	8	65	.325

Team Rebounds: Indiana 0; Kentucky 0. Disqualified: None. Technical fouls: None.

	1st Half	2nd Half	Final
Indiana	45	27	72
Kentucky	32	33	65

REGIONAL FINAL WEST

UCLA (54) Coach: John Wooden

	Min.	Total FG / FGA	Pct.	FT / FTA	Pct.	Reb. O / T	A	TO	PF	S	Blk	TP	PPM
WILKES, J.	-	6/13	.462	0/ 0	.000	-/ 1	1	-	0	-	-	12	-
FARMER, L.	-	5/10	.500	3/ 3	1.000	-/ 4	1	-	0	-	-	13	-
WALTON, B.	-	4/ 7	.571	1/ 2	.500	-/14	2	-	0	-	-	9	-
LEE, G.	-	1/ 4	.250	0/ 0	.000	-/ 1	0	-	0	-	-	2	-
HOLLYFIELD, L.	-	0/ 3	.000	0/ 0	.000	-/ 1	0	-	0	-	-	0	-
CURTIS, T.	-	6/ 9	.667	0/ 1	.000	-/ 1	4	-	1	-	-	12	-
MEYERS, D.	-	1/ 3	.333	0/ 0	.000	-/ 3	1	-	3	-	-	2	-
NATER, S.	-	0/ 2	.000	0/ 0	.000	-/ 1	0	-	0	-	-	0	-
FRANKLIN, G.	-	1/ 2	.500	0/ 0	.000	-/ 2	0	-	0	-	-	2	-
CARSON, V.	-	0/ 0	.000	0/ 0	.000	-/ 1	0	-	1	-	-	0	-
WEBB, B.	-	0/ 1	.000	0/ 0	.000	-/ 0	0	-	1	-	-	0	-
TRGOVICH, P.	-	1/ 2	.500	0/ 0	.000	-/ 0	0	-	0	-	-	2	-
Totals	200	25/56	.446	4/ 6	.667	-/29	9	4	6	-	-	54	.270

San Francisco (39) Coach: Bob Gaillard

	Min.	Total FG / FGA	Pct.	FT / FTA	Pct.	Reb. O / T	A	TO	PF	S	Blk	TP	PPM
RESTANI, K.	40	4/11	.364	0/ 0	.000	-/ 9	2	-	0	-	-	8	.200
SMITH, P.	40	8/13	.615	1/ 1	1.000	-/ 3	1	-	0	-	-	17	.425
FERNSTEN, E.	40	2/ 5	.400	0/ 0	.000	-/ 8	0	-	3	-	-	4	.100
QUICK, M.	40	4/ 9	.444	0/ 0	.000	-/ 2	1	-	1	-	-	8	.200
BORO, J.	40	0/ 3	.000	2/ 2	1.000	-/ 0	1	-	3	-	-	2	.050
Totals	200	18/41	.439	3/ 3	1.000	-/22	5	13	7	-	-	39	.195

Team Rebounds: UCLA 1; San Francisco 4. Disqualified: None. Technical fouls: None.

	1st Half	2nd Half	Final
UCLA	23	31	54
San Francisco	22	17	39

FINAL FOUR

Memphis State (98) Coach: Gene Bartow

	Min.	Total FG / FGA	Pct.	FT / FTA	Pct.	Reb. O / T	A	TO	PF	S	Blk	TP	PPM
BUFORD, B.	25	3/ 7	.429	0/ 0	.000	-/ 3	4	1	2	0	1	6	.240
KENON, L.	40	14/27	.519	0/ 4	.000	-/22	4	3	1	0	3	28	.700
ROBINSON, R.	40	11/17	.647	2/ 3	.667	-/16	1	0	2	2	0	24	.600
LAURIE, B.	25	1/ 3	.333	2/ 3	.667	-/ 1	3	1	4	2	0	4	.160
FINCH, L.	34	7/16	.438	7/ 9	.778	-/ 6	5	5	4	1	0	21	.618
COOK, B.	21	3/ 6	.500	2/ 3	.667	-/ 1	5	1	2	0	0	8	.381
WESTFALL, W.	13	2/ 3	.667	3/ 4	.750	-/ 2	2	0	0	0	1	7	.538
JONES, C.	2	0/ 1	.000	0/ 0	.000	-/ 0	0	0	0	0	0	0	.000
Totals	200	41/80	.513	16/26	.615	-/51	24	11	15	5	5	98	.490

Providence (85) Coach: Dave Gavitt

	Min.	Total FG / FGA	Pct.	FT / FTA	Pct.	Reb. O / T	A	TO	PF	S	Blk	TP	PPM
CRAWFORD, C.	38	5/12	.417	0/ 0	.000	-/15	1	0	3	1	0	10	.263
COSTELLO, F.	38	5/ 5	1.000	1/ 1	1.000	-/ 8	3	3	5	0	0	11	.289
BARNES, M.	11	5/ 7	.714	2/ 3	.667	-/ 3	1	0	4	0	0	12	1.091
DIGREGORIO, E.	39	15/36	.417	2/ 2	1.000	-/ 2	7	3	4	1	0	32	.821
STACOM, K.	37	6/15	.400	3/ 3	1.000	-/ 5	3	2	5	1	1	15	.405
KING, N.	30	2/ 6	.333	0/ 0	.000	-/ 1	0	2	1	1	0	4	.133
BAKER, A.	3	0/ 0	.000	0/ 0	.000	-/ 1	0	0	0	0	0	0	.000
DUNPHY, R.	3	0/ 1	.000	1/ 2	.500	-/ 1	0	0	0	0	0	1	.333
BELLO, G.	1	0/ 0	.000	0/ 0	.000	-/ 0	0	0	0	0	0	0	.000
Totals	200	38/82	.463	9/11	.818	-/36	15	10	22	4	1	85	.425

Team Rebounds: Memphis State 3; Providence 3. Disqualified: Providence—Costello, Stacom. Technical fouls: Memphis St—Robinson.

	1st Half	2nd Half	Final
Memphis State	40	58	98
Providence	49	36	85

Indiana (59)   Coach: Bob Knight

	Min.	Total FG/FGA	Pct.	FT/FTA	Pct.	Reb. O/T	A	TO	PF	S	Blk	TP	PPM
RITTER, J.	-	6/10	.600	1/1	1.000	-/2	6	-	3	-	-	13	-
GREEN, S.	-	1/7	.143	0/0	.000	-/5	2	-	2	-	-	2	-
DOWNING, S.	-	12/20	.600	2/4	.500	-/5	2	-	5	-	-	26	-
BUCKNER, Q.	-	3/10	.300	0/1	.000	-/5	4	-	2	-	-	6	-
CREWS, J.	-	4/10	.400	0/0	.000	-/2	2	-	3	-	-	8	-
LASKOWSKI, J.	-	1/8	.125	0/0	.000	-/4	1	-	0	-	-	2	-
ABERNETHY, T.	-	0/1	.000	0/0	.000	-/1	0	-	1	-	-	0	-
SMOCK, T.	-	0/0	.000	0/0	.000	-/0	0	-	0	-	-	0	-
NOORT, D.	-	0/0	.000	0/0	.000	-/1	0	-	0	-	-	0	-
WILSON, F.	-	0/0	.000	0/0	.000	-/0	0	-	0	-	-	0	-
MORRIS, C.	-	0/0	.000	0/0	.000	-/0	0	-	0	-	-	0	-
AHLFELD, S.	-	0/0	.000	0/0	.000	-/0	1	-	0	-	-	0	-
ALLEN, D.	-	1/1	1.000	0/0	.000	-/0	0	-	0	-	-	2	-
MEMERING, J.	-	0/0	.000	0/0	.000	-/0	0	-	0	-	-	0	-
Totals	200	28/67	.418	3/6	.500	-/25	18	-	16	-	-	59	.295

	1st Half	2nd Half	Final
Indiana	22	37	59
UCLA	40	30	70

UCLA (70)   Coach: John Wooden

	Min.	Total FG/FGA	Pct.	FT/FTA	Pct.	Reb. O/T	A	TO	PF	S	Blk	TP	PPM
WILKES, J.	-	5/10	.500	3/4	.750	-/6	1	-	3	-	-	13	-
FARMER, L.	-	3/6	.500	1/2	.500	-/3	0	-	4	-	-	7	-
WALTON, B.	-	7/12	.583	0/0	.000	-/17	9	-	4	-	-	14	-
LEE, G.	-	0/1	.000	0/0	.000	-/0	1	-	0	-	-	0	-
HOLLYFIELD, L.	-	5/6	.833	0/0	.000	-/2	2	-	1	-	-	10	-
CURTIS, T.	-	9/15	.600	4/7	.571	-/2	4	-	2	-	-	22	-
MEYERS, D.	-	2/3	.667	0/0	.000	-/5	0	-	1	-	-	4	-
NATER, S.	-	0/0	.000	0/0	.000	-/0	0	-	1	-	-	0	-
Totals	200	31/53	.585	8/13	.615	-/35	17	-	16	-	-	70	.350

Team Rebounds: UCLA 3; Indiana 4. Disqualified: Indiana—Downing. Technical fouls: UCLA—Meyers; Indiana—Coach Knight.

NATIONAL CHAMPIONSHIP

Memphis State (66)   Coach: Gene Bartow

	Min.	Total FG/FGA	Pct.	FT/FTA	Pct.	Reb. O/T	A	TO	PF	S	Blk	TP	PPM
BUFORD, B.	38	3/7	.429	1/2	.500	-/3	1	0	1	0	0	7	.184
KENON, L.	34	8/16	.500	4/4	1.000	-/8	3	2	3	0	1	20	.588
ROBINSON, R.	33	3/6	.500	0/1	.000	-/7	1	1	4	0	0	6	.182
LAURIE, B.	21	0/1	.000	0/0	.000	-/0	2	0	0	0	0	0	.000
FINCH, B.	38	9/21	.429	11/13	.846	-/1	2	2	2	0	0	29	.763
COOK, B.	18	1/4	.250	2/2	1.000	-/0	2	2	1	0	0	4	.222
WESTFALL, W.	10	0/1	.000	0/0	.000	-/0	0	1	5	0	0	0	.000
JONES, C.	4	0/0	.000	0/0	.000	-/0	0	0	0	0	0	0	.000
TETZLAFF, J.	1	0/0	.000	0/2	.000	-/0	0	0	1	0	0	0	.000
LISS, J.	1	0/1	.000	0/0	.000	-/0	0	0	0	0	0	0	.000
ANDREWS, K.	1	0/0	.000	0/0	.000	-/0	0	0	0	0	0	0	.000
MCKINNEY, D.	1	0/0	.000	0/0	.000	-/0	0	0	0	0	0	0	.000
Totals	200	24/57	.421	18/24	.750	-/19	11	8	17	0	1	66	.330

	1st Half	2nd Half	Final
Memphis State	39	27	66
UCLA	39	48	87

UCLA (87)   Coach: John Wooden

	Min.	Total FG/FGA	Pct.	FT/FTA	Pct.	Reb. O/T	A	TO	PF	S	Blk	TP	PPM
WILKES, J.	39	8/14	.571	0/0	.000	-/7	1	4	2	1	0	16	.410
FARMER, L.	33	1/4	.250	0/0	.000	-/2	0	2	2	0	1	2	.061
WALTON, B.	33	21/22	.955	2/5	.400	-/13	2	6	4	0	1	44	1.333
LEE, G.	34	1/1	1.000	3/3	1.000	-/3	14	3	2	0	0	5	.147
HOLLYFIELD, L.	30	4/7	.571	0/0	.000	-/3	9	0	4	1	1	8	.267
CURTIS, T.	11	1/4	.250	2/2	1.000	-/3	0	0	1	0	2	4	.364
MEYERS, D.	10	2/7	.286	0/0	.000	-/3	0	2	1	0	0	4	.400
NATER, S.	7	1/1	1.000	0/0	.000	-/3	0	0	2	0	0	2	.286
FRANKLIN, G.	1	1/2	.500	0/1	.000	-/1	0	0	0	0	0	2	2.000
CARSON, V.	1	0/0	.000	0/0	.000	-/0	0	0	0	0	0	0	.000
WEBB, B.	1	0/0	.000	0/0	.000	-/0	0	0	0	0	0	0	.000
Totals	200	40/62	.645	7/11	.636	-/38	26	17	18	2	5	87	.435

Team Rebounds: UCLA 2; Memphis State 2. Disqualified: Memphis State—Westfall. Technical fouls: UCLA—Hollyfield; Memphis State—Kenon.

NATIONAL THIRD PLACE

Indiana (97)   Coach: Bob Knight

	Min.	Total FG/FGA	Pct.	FT/FTA	Pct.	Reb. O/T	A	TO	PF	S	Blk	TP	PPM
RITTER, J.	27	8/15	.533	5/8	.625	-/7	2	-	5	-	-	21	.778
GREEN, S.	33	8/13	.615	0/1	.000	-/7	7	-	4	-	-	16	.485
DOWNING, S.	39	10/17	.588	1/1	1.000	-/14	2	-	3	-	-	21	.538
BUCKNER, Q.	34	5/9	.556	5/5	1.000	-/8	8	-	3	-	-	15	.441
CREWS, J.	32	3/10	.300	0/1	.000	-/4	3	-	3	-	-	6	.188
LASKOWSKI, J.	17	4/7	.571	0/0	.000	-/5	0	-	3	-	-	8	.471
ABERNETHY, T.	5	1/1	1.000	0/0	.000	-/1	0	-	1	-	-	2	.400
SMOCK, T.	1	0/0	.000	0/0	.000	-/0	1	-	0	-	-	0	.000
NOORT, D.	1	0/0	.000	0/0	.000	-/0	0	-	0	-	-	0	.000
WILSON, F.	1	1/1	1.000	0/1	.000	-/1	0	-	0	-	-	2	2.000
MORRIS, C.	1	0/0	.000	0/0	.000	-/0	0	-	0	-	-	0	.000
AHLFELD, S.	7	1/2	.500	4/4	1.000	-/1	1	-	2	-	-	6	.857
ALLEN, D.	1	0/1	.000	0/0	.000	-/0	0	-	0	-	-	0	.000
MEMERING, J.	1	0/0	.000	0/0	.000	-/1	0	-	0	-	-	0	.000
Totals	200	41/76	.539	15/21	.714	-/49	24	-	24	-	-	97	.485

	1st Half	2nd Half	Final
Indiana	51	46	97
Providence	42	37	79

Providence (79)   Coach: Dave Gavitt

	Min.	Total FG/FGA	Pct.	FT/FTA	Pct.	Reb. O/T	A	TO	PF	S	Blk	TP	PPM
CRAWFORD, C.	20	1/4	.250	2/3	.667	-/5	0	-	4	-	-	4	.200
COSTELLO, F.	35	8/15	.533	3/4	.750	-/4	0	-	3	-	-	19	.543
DIGREGORIO, E.	38	7/22	.318	3/4	.750	-/7	7	-	4	-	-	17	.447
STACOM, K.	40	10/21	.476	9/10	.900	-/7	2	-	3	-	-	29	.725
KING, N.	28	2/10	.200	0/0	.000	-/5	0	-	3	-	-	4	.143
BAKER, A.	28	0/2	.000	2/2	1.000	-/7	0	-	0	-	-	2	.071
DUNPHY, R.	5	0/1	.000	4/4	1.000	-/1	0	-	3	-	-	4	.800
BELLO, G.	2	0/1	.000	0/0	.000	-/0	0	-	0	-	-	0	.000
MCANDREW, M.	3	0/1	.000	0/0	.000	-/1	0	-	0	-	-	0	.000
MODEST, D.	1	0/1	.000	0/0	.000	-/0	0	-	0	-	-	0	.000
Totals	200	28/78	.359	23/27	.852	-/37	9	-	20	-	-	79	.395

Team Rebounds: Indiana 4; Providence 1. Disqualified: Indiana—Ritter. Technical fouls: None.

REGIONAL THIRD PLACE MIDWEST

South Carolina (90)   Coach: Frank McGuire

	Min.	Total FG/FGA	Pct.	FT/FTA	Pct.	Reb. O/T	A	TO	PF	S	Blk	TP	PPM
ENGLISH, A.	33	9/18	.500	4/4	1.000	-/10	1	4	3	1	4	22	.667
WINTERS, B.	34	4/12	.333	2/2	1.000	-/3	6	2	0	4	0	10	.294
TRAYLOR, D.	40	8/15	.533	0/2	.000	-/16	3	0	3	1	6	16	.400
DUNLEAVY, M.	19	4/8	.500	3/4	.750	-/0	2	3	2	0	1	11	.579
JOYCE, K.	35	1/13	.077	10/13	.769	-/6	8	4	1	3	0	12	.343
WALSH, J.	2	0/0	.000	0/0	.000	-/0	1	1	0	0	0	0	.000
MATHIAS, B.	5	0/0	.000	0/0	.000	-/1	0	0	1	0	0	0	.000
MANNING, C.	21	6/10	.600	1/2	.500	-/3	0	0	1	1	0	13	.619
GREINER, M.	9	2/2	1.000	0/0	.000	-/2	0	0	2	0	0	4	.444
COX, T.	2	1/2	.500	0/0	.000	-/1	0	0	0	0	0	2	1.000
Totals	200	35/80	.438	20/27	.741	-/42	21	14	13	10	11	90	.450

Southwestern Louisiana (85)   Coach: Beryl Shipley

	Min.	Total FG/FGA	Pct.	FT/FTA	Pct.	Reb. O/T	A	TO	PF	S	Blk	TP	PPM
SAUNDERS, F.	34	8/16	.500	3/6	.500	-/16	0	4	3	3	1	19	.559
FOGLE, L.	26	6/17	.353	0/1	.000	-/14	1	2	2	1	0	12	.462
EBRON, R.	32	9/17	.529	2/3	.667	-/10	0	2	5	1	3	20	.625
LAMAR, D.	40	11/27	.407	0/0	.000	-/8	4	5	4	1	0	22	.550
BISBANO, J.	28	1/6	.167	1/2	.500	-/3	3	2	3	0	0	3	.107
BROWN, A.	6	1/3	.333	1/2	.500	-/2	0	0	1	0	0	3	.500
HANEY, M.	3	0/0	.000	0/0	.000	-/0	0	0	1	0	0	0	.000
WILSON, R.	19	2/5	.400	0/0	.000	-/4	0	0	3	2	1	4	.211
WRIGHT, D.	12	1/3	.333	0/0	.000	-/1	2	0	1	0	0	2	.167
Totals	200	39/94	.415	7/14	.500	-/58	10	15	23	8	5	85	.425

Team Rebounds: S. Carolina 8; S'western La. 6. Disqualified: S'western La.—Ebron. Technical fouls: None.

	1st Half	2nd Half	Final
S. Carolina	33	57	90
S'western La.	39	46	85

REGIONAL THIRD PLACE MIDEAST

Marquette (88)   Coach: Al McGuire

	Min.	Total FG/FGA	Pct.	FT/FTA	Pct.	Reb. O/T	A	TO	PF	S	Blk	TP	PPM
FRAZIER, G.	21	1/4	.250	2/3	.667	-/5	0	-	5	-	-	4	.190
MCNEILL, L.	37	12/17	.706	3/5	.600	-/15	2	-	5	-	-	27	.730
LUCAS, M.	39	9/18	.500	2/3	.667	-/19	2	-	2	-	-	20	.513
MCGUIRE, A.	38	7/24	.292	3/3	1.000	-/4	8	-	2	-	-	17	.447
WASHINGTON, M.	33	2/12	.167	2/3	.667	-/5	3	-	3	-	-	6	.182
CAMPBELL, R.	10	3/8	.375	0/1	.000	-/4	0	-	3	-	-	6	.600
DELSMAN, D.	7	0/2	.000	2/2	1.000	-/1	1	-	1	-	-	2	.286
MILLS, M.	4	0/0	.000	0/0	.000	-/0	0	-	0	-	-	0	.000
HOMAN, J.	1	0/0	.000	0/0	.000	-/0	2	-	0	-	-	0	.000
DANIELS, E.	4	0/1	.000	0/0	.000	-/1	0	-	0	-	-	0	.000
TATUM, W.	6	2/3	.667	2/2	1.000	-/2	0	-	0	-	-	6	1.000
Totals	200	36/89	.404	16/22	.727	-/56	18	-	21	-	-	88	.440

Austin Peay (73)   Coach: Lake Kelly

	Min.	Total FG/FGA	Pct.	FT/FTA	Pct.	Reb. O/T	A	TO	PF	S	Blk	TP	PPM
JACKSON, H.	39	8/15	.533	6/7	.857	-/17	0	-	3	-	-	22	.564
WILLIAMS, J.	20	9/18	.500	4/4	1.000	-/2	0	-	1	-	-	22	1.100
CHILDRESS, E.	32	3/13	.231	2/2	1.000	-/3	2	-	5	-	-	8	.250
HOWARD, P.	15	0/1	.000	2/4	.500	-/7	1	-	2	-	-	2	.133
ODUMS, D.	23	2/3	.667	0/0	.000	-/3	4	-	2	-	-	4	.174
WANSTRATH, J.	14	1/2	.500	0/0	.000	-/3	0	-	5	-	-	2	.143
TURNER, R.	22	1/3	.333	2/3	.667	-/2	6	-	1	-	-	4	.182
JIMMERSON, R.	17	0/1	.000	0/0	.000	-/2	0	-	1	-	-	0	.000
HAMPTON, K.	12	2/7	.286	1/1	1.000	-/0	0	-	1	-	-	5	.417
HIGDON	1	0/0	.000	2/2	1.000	-/2	0	-	0	-	-	2	2.000
JACKSON, L.	3	1/1	1.000	0/0	.000	-/0	0	-	2	-	-	2	.667
FISHER, M.	1	0/0	.000	0/0	.000	-/1	1	-	0	-	-	0	.000
SEWELL	1	0/0	.000	0/0	.000	-/0	0	-	0	-	-	0	.000
Totals	200	27/64	.422	19/23	.826	-/42	14	-	23	-	-	73	.365

Team Rebounds: Marquette 0; Austin Peay 1. Disqualified: Marquette—Frazier, McNeill; Austin Peay—Childress, Wanstrath.

	1st Half	2nd Half	Final
Marquette	57	31	88
Austin Peay	42	31	73

REGIONAL THIRD PLACE WEST

Long Beach State (84)   Coach: Jerry Tarkanian

	Min.	Total FG/FGA	Pct.	FT/FTA	Pct.	Reb. O/T	A	TO	PF	S	Blk	TP	PPM
ABEREGG, R.	-	3/5	.600	6/6	1.000	-/2	6	-	3	-	-	12	-
MCDONALD, G.	-	1/7	.143	0/0	.000	-/8	2	-	1	-	-	2	-
RATLEFF, E.	-	6/14	.429	4/5	.800	-/13	2	-	3	-	-	16	-
GRAY, L.	-	3/7	.429	3/4	.750	-/2	3	-	4	-	-	9	-
STEPHENS, N.	-	7/15	.467	3/4	.750	-/7	1	-	1	-	-	17	-
PONDEXTER, R.	-	7/11	.636	3/6	.500	-/10	2	-	1	-	-	17	-
DOUSE, E.	-	3/8	.375	3/7	.429	-/4	2	-	0	-	-	9	-
KING, L.	-	1/1	1.000	0/0	.000	-/1	0	-	1	-	-	2	-
Totals	200	31/68	.456	22/32	.688	-/47	18	-	14	-	-	84	.420

Arizona State (80)   Coach: Ned Wulk

	Min.	Total FG/FGA	Pct.	FT/FTA	Pct.	Reb. O/T	A	TO	PF	S	Blk	TP	PPM
GRAY, K.	-	6/11	.545	0/0	.000	-/14	0	-	3	-	-	12	-
WASLEY, M.	-	5/9	.556	0/1	.000	-/4	1	-	3	-	-	10	-
KENNEDY, K.	-	4/9	.444	1/1	1.000	-/9	3	-	4	-	-	9	-
CONTRERAS, M.	-	10/18	.556	1/1	1.000	-/1	5	-	3	-	-	21	-
OWENS, J.	-	7/17	.412	2/2	1.000	-/3	5	-	3	-	-	16	-
WHITE, R.	-	2/7	.286	0/0	.000	-/3	1	-	2	-	-	4	-
JACKSON, G.	-	2/7	.286	2/2	1.000	-/1	0	-	2	-	-	6	-
SCHRADER, J.	-	1/2	.500	0/0	.000	-/2	0	-	2	-	-	2	-
Totals	200	37/80	.463	6/7	.857	-/38	15	-	22	-	-	80	.400

Team Rebounds: Long Beach St. 4; Arizona St. 4. Disqualified: None. Technical fouls: Long Beach St.—Gray.

	1st Half	2nd Half	Final
Long Beach St.	42	42	84
Arizona St.	42	38	80

REGIONAL THIRD PLACE EAST

Syracuse (69)   Coach: Roy Danforth

	Min.	Total FG/FGA	Pct.	FT/FTA	Pct.	Reb. O/T	A	TO	PF	S	Blk	TP	PPM
LEE, M.	-	2/10	.200	2/3	.667	-/3	-	-	4	-	-	6	-
DOOMS, B.	-	6/8	.750	0/0	.000	-/9	-	-	4	-	-	12	-
HACKETT, R.	-	9/17	.529	2/3	.667	-/15	-	-	0	-	-	20	-
DUVAL, D.	-	10/24	.417	0/0	.000	-/7	-	-	2	-	-	20	-
WADACH, M.	-	3/8	.375	0/0	.000	-/4	-	-	5	-	-	6	-
LEE, J.	-	0/4	.000	3/4	.750	-/3	-	-	1	-	-	3	-
STUNDIS, T.	-	0/1	.000	0/1	.000	-/1	-	-	1	-	-	0	-
STAPLETON, S.	-	1/5	.200	0/0	.000	-/2	-	-	1	-	-	2	-
Totals	200	31/77	.403	7/11	.636	-/44	-	-	18	-	-	69	.345

Pennsylvania (68)   Coach: Chuck Daly

	Min.	Total FG/FGA	Pct.	FT/FTA	Pct.	Reb. O/T	A	TO	PF	S	Blk	TP	PPM
BEECROFT, J.	-	3/6	.500	4/4	1.000	-/1	-	-	2	-	-	10	-
LITTLEPAGE, C.	-	1/2	.500	2/3	.667	-/5	-	-	2	-	-	4	-
BIGELOW, B.	-	4/6	.667	0/0	.000	-/4	-	-	4	-	-	8	-
HAIGLER, R.	-	9/16	.563	0/0	.000	-/5	-	-	4	-	-	18	-
HANKINSON, P.	-	6/12	.500	5/5	1.000	-/6	-	-	1	-	-	17	-
JABLONSKI, J.	-	0/1	.000	0/0	.000	-/2	-	-	1	-	-	0	-
LEWIS, L.	-	4/8	.500	1/2	.500	-/1	-	-	2	-	-	9	-
VARGA, W.	-	0/2	.000	0/0	.000	-/1	-	-	0	-	-	0	-
FINGER, B.	-	1/1	1.000	0/0	.000	-/2	-	-	1	-	-	2	-
BATORY, S.	-	0/2	.000	0/0	.000	-/0	-	-	0	-	-	0	-
Totals	200	28/56	.500	12/14	.857	-/27	-	-	17	-	-	68	.340

Team Rebounds: Syracuse 2; Pennsylvania 5. Disqualified: Syracuse—Wadach. Technical fouls: Syracuse—bench, Dooms, Lee.

	1st Half	2nd Half	Final
Syracuse	29	40	69
Pennsylvania	35	33	68

✪ ALL-STAR TEAMS ✪

ALL TOURNAMENT

ERNIE DIGREGORIO	PROVIDENCE
STEVE DOWNING	INDIANA
LARRY FINCH	MEMPHIS STATE
LARRY KENON	MEMPHIS STATE
★ BILL WALTON	UCLA

EAST REGIONAL

MARVIN BARNES	PROVIDENCE
★ ERNIE DIGREGORIO	PROVIDENCE
DENNIS DUVAL	SYRACUSE
TOM MCMILLEN	MARYLAND
KEVIN STACOM	PROVIDENCE

MIDEAST REGIONAL

JIM ANDREWS	KENTUCKY
QUINN BUCKNER	INDIANA
★ STEVE DOWNING	INDIANA
HOWARD JACKSON	AUSTIN PEAY
LARRY MCNEIL	MARQUETTE

MIDWEST REGIONAL

ALEX ENGLISH	S. CAROLINA
★ LARRY FINCH	MEMPHIS STATE
LARRY KENON	MEMPHIS STATE
DWIGHT LAMAR	S'WESTERN LA.
RONNIE ROBINSON	MEMPHIS STATE

WEST REGIONAL

MIKE CONTRERAS	ARIZONA ST.
TOMMY CURTIS	UCLA
MIKE QUICK	SAN FRANCISCO
PHIL SMITH	SAN FRANCISCO
★ BILL WALTON	UCLA

★ Most Outstanding Player(s)

✪ INDIVIDUAL RECORDS ✪

SCORING

Most points in a single game
1 BILL WALTON, UCLA (vs. MEMPHIS STATE) 44
2 DWIGHT LAMAR, S'WESTERN LA. (vs. HOUSTON) 35
3 LARRY KENON, MEMPHIS STATE (vs. S. CAROLINA) 34
4 LARRY FINCH, MEMPHIS STATE (vs. KANSAS STATE) 32
4 ERNIE DIGREGORIO, PROVIDENCE (vs. MEMPHIS STATE) 32

Most total points in the tournament
1 ERNIE DIGREGORIO, PROVIDENCE 128
2 LARRY FINCH, MEMPHIS STATE 107
3 STEVE DOWNING, INDIANA 99
4 KEVIN STACOM, PROVIDENCE 96
4 LARRY KENON, MEMPHIS STATE 96

Highest scoring average (minimum 2 games)
1 LARRY FINCH, MEMPHIS STATE (107-4) 26.75
2 JIM ANDREWS, KENTUCKY (53-2) 26.50
3 ERNIE DIGREGORIO, PROVIDENCE (128-5) 25.60
4 DWIGHT LAMAR, S'WESTERN LA. (75-3) 25.00
5 STEVE DOWNING, INDIANA (99-4) 24.75

FIELD GOALS

Most field goals in a single game
1 BILL WALTON, UCLA (vs. MEMPHIS STATE) 21
2 LARRY KENON, MEMPHIS STATE (vs. S. CAROLINA) 16
3 JIM ANDREWS, KENTUCKY (vs. AUSTIN PEAY) 15
3 DWIGHT LAMAR, S'WESTERN LA. (vs. HOUSTON) 15
3 ERNIE DIGREGORIO, PROVIDENCE (vs. MEMPHIS STATE) 15

Most total field goals in the tournament
1 ERNIE DIGREGORIO, PROVIDENCE 59
2 BILL WALTON, UCLA 45
2 LARRY KENON, MEMPHIS STATE 45
4 STEVE DOWNING, INDIANA 44
5 KEVIN STACOM, PROVIDENCE 38

FREE THROWS

Most free throws in a single game
1 LARRY FINCH, MEMPHIS STATE (vs. KANSAS STATE) 12
2 LARRY FINCH, MEMPHIS STATE (vs. UCLA) 11
3 PHIL SMITH, SAN FRANCISCO (vs. LONG BEACH ST.) 10

Most field goal attempts in a single game
1 ERNIE DIGREGORIO, PROVIDENCE (vs. MEMPHIS STATE) 36
2 DWIGHT LAMAR, S'WESTERN LA. (vs. HOUSTON) 34
3 JAMES WILLIAMS, AUSTIN PEAY (vs. KENTUCKY) 31
4 LARRY KENON, MEMPHIS STATE (vs. S. CAROLINA) 30
5 PHIL HANKINSON, PENNSYLVANIA (vs. PROVIDENCE) 29

Most total field goal attempts in the tournament
1 ERNIE DIGREGORIO, PROVIDENCE 121
2 LARRY KENON, MEMPHIS STATE 85
3 DWIGHT LAMAR, S'WESTERN LA. 82
4 STEVE DOWNING, INDIANA 76
5 JAMES WILLIAMS, AUSTIN PEAY 75

Highest field goal percentage in a single game (minimum 10 attempts)
1 MARVIN BARNES, PROVIDENCE (vs. PENNSYLVANIA) (10-10) 1.000
2 BILL WALTON, UCLA (vs. MEMPHIS STATE) (21-22) .955
3 TOM MCMILLEN, MARYLAND (vs. SYRACUSE) (8-10) .800
4 JIM ANDREWS, KENTUCKY (vs. AUSTIN PEAY) (15-19) .789
5 GEORGE FRAZIER, MARQUETTE (vs. MIAMI (OHIO)) (9-12) .750

Highest field goal percentage in the tournament (minimum 20 attempts)
1 BILL WALTON, UCLA (45-59) .763
2 TOM MCMILLEN, MARYLAND (18-26) .692
3 JIM ANDREWS, KENTUCKY (26-39) .667
4 GEORGE FRAZIER, MARQUETTE (14-23) .609
4 BOB DOOMS, SYRACUSE (14-23) .609

Most free throws in the tournament
3 KEVIN JOYCE, S. CAROLINA (vs. S'WESTERN LA.) 10
5 3 tied for fifth place.

Most total free throws in the tournament
1 LARRY FINCH, MEMPHIS STATE 39
2 KEVIN JOYCE, S. CAROLINA 21
3 KEVIN STACOM, PROVIDENCE 20
4 ED RATLEFF, LONG BEACH ST. 15
5 BILL LAURIE, MEMPHIS STATE 12

Most free throws attempted in a single game
1 PHIL SMITH, SAN FRANCISCO (vs. LONG BEACH ST.) 14
2 KEVIN JOYCE, S. CAROLINA (vs. S'WESTERN LA.) 13
2 LARRY FINCH, MEMPHIS STATE (vs. UCLA) 13
4 LARRY FINCH, MEMPHIS STATE (vs. KANSAS STATE) 12
5 STEVE DOWNING, INDIANA (vs. MARQUETTE) 11

Most free throws attempted in the tournament
1 LARRY FINCH, MEMPHIS STATE 44
2 KEVIN JOYCE, S. CAROLINA 25
3 KEVIN STACOM, PROVIDENCE 22
4 STEVE DOWNING, INDIANA 20
5 2 tied for fifth place.

Highest free throw percentage in a single game (minimum 7 attempts)
1 LARRY FINCH, MEMPHIS STATE (vs. KANSAS STATE) (12-12) 1.000
2 ED RATLEFF, LONG BEACH ST. (vs. WEBER ST.) (7-7) 1.000
3 LARRY FINCH, MEMPHIS STATE (vs. S. CAROLINA) (9-10) .900
3 KEVIN JOYCE, S. CAROLINA (vs. TEXAS TECH) (9-10) .900
3 KEVIN STACOM, PROVIDENCE (vs. INDIANA) (9-10) .900

Highest free throw percentage in the tournament (minimum 15 attempts)
1 ED RATLEFF, LONG BEACH ST. (15-16) .938
2 KEVIN STACOM, PROVIDENCE (20-22) .909
3 LARRY FINCH, MEMPHIS STATE (39-44) .886
4 KEVIN JOYCE, S. CAROLINA (21-25) .840
5 PHIL SMITH, SAN FRANCISCO (11-15) .733

REBOUNDS

Most rebounds in a single game
1. LARRY KENON, MEMPHIS STATE (vs. PROVIDENCE) — 22
2. LARRY KENON, MEMPHIS STATE (vs. S. CAROLINA) — 20
3. MAURICE LUCAS, MARQUETTE (vs. AUSTIN PEAY) — 19
4. HOWARD JACKSON, AUSTIN PEAY (vs. KENTUCKY) — 18
4. RUDY HACKETT, SYRACUSE (vs. FURMAN) — 18

Most total rebounds in the tournament
1. BILL WALTON, UCLA — 58
2. LARRY KENON, MEMPHIS STATE — 57
3. RONNIE ROBINSON, MEMPHIS STATE — 56

4. MARVIN BARNES, PROVIDENCE — 48
5. STEVE DOWNING, INDIANA — 42

Most rebounds per game (minimum 2 games)
1. BILL WALTON, UCLA (58-4) — 14.50
2. LARRY KENON, MEMPHIS STATE (57-4) — 14.25
3. RONNIE ROBINSON, MEMPHIS STATE (56-4) — 14.00
4. HOWARD JACKSON, AUSTIN PEAY (39-3) — 13.00
5. 2 tied for fifth place.

ASSISTS

Most assists in a single game
1. GREG LEE, UCLA (vs. MEMPHIS STATE) — 14
2. BILL LAURIE, MEMPHIS STATE (vs. KANSAS STATE) — 11

3. ERNIE DIGREGORIO, PROVIDENCE (vs. PENNSYLVANIA) — 10
4. 4 tied for fourth place.

Most total assists in the tournament
1. ERNIE DIGREGORIO, PROVIDENCE — 35
2. QUINN BUCKNER, INDIANA — 21
3. BILL LAURIE, MEMPHIS STATE — 20
4. BILL WALTON, UCLA — 19
4. GREG LEE, UCLA — 19

Most assists per game (minimum 2 appearances)
1. ERNIE DIGREGORIO, PROVIDENCE (35-5) — 7.00
2. KEVIN JOYCE, S. CAROLINA (18-3) — 6.00
2. RICK ABEREGG, LONG BEACH ST. (18-3) — 6.00
4. QUINN BUCKNER, INDIANA (21-4) — 5.25
5. BILL LAURIE, MEMPHIS STATE (20-4) — 5.00

⚬ TEAM RECORDS ⚬

SCORING

Most points in a single game
1. KENTUCKY (vs. AUSTIN PEAY) — 106
2. ARIZONA ST. (vs. OKLAHOMA CITY) — 103
2. PROVIDENCE (vs. MARYLAND) — 103

Most total points in the tournament
1. PROVIDENCE — 443
2. MEMPHIS STATE — 346
3. UCLA — 309

Highest scoring average (minimum 2 games)
1. MARYLAND (180-2) — 90.00
2. PROVIDENCE (443-5) — 88.60
3. ARIZONA ST. (264-3) — 88.00

FIELD GOALS

Most field goals in a single game
1. KENTUCKY (vs. AUSTIN PEAY) — 50
2. AUSTIN PEAY (vs. KENTUCKY) — 46
3. UCLA (vs. ARIZONA ST.) — 43
3. ARIZONA ST. (vs. OKLAHOMA CITY) — 43
3. PROVIDENCE (vs. MARYLAND) — 43

Most total field goals in the tournament
1. PROVIDENCE — 188
2. UCLA — 139
3. MEMPHIS STATE — 138

Most field goals attempted in a single game
1. AUSTIN PEAY (vs. KENTUCKY) — 99
2. KENTUCKY (vs. AUSTIN PEAY) — 97
3. S'WESTERN LA. (vs. S. CAROLINA) — 94

Most total field goals attempted in the tournament
1. PROVIDENCE — 368
2. MEMPHIS STATE — 276
3. INDIANA — 264

Highest field goal percentage in a single game
1. PROVIDENCE (vs. PENNSYLVANIA) (40-61) — .656

2. UCLA (vs. MEMPHIS STATE) (40-62) — .645
3. MEMPHIS STATE (vs. KANSAS STATE) (37-62) — .597

Highest field goal percentage in the tournament (minimum 2 games)
1. UCLA (139-251) — .554
2. MARYLAND (79-151) — .523
3. PROVIDENCE (188-368) — .511

FREE THROWS

Most free throws in a single game
1. PROVIDENCE (vs. INDIANA) — 23
2. LONG BEACH ST. (vs. ARIZONA ST.) — 22
2. S'WESTERN LA. (vs. HOUSTON) — 22

Most total free throws in the tournament
1. MEMPHIS STATE — 70
2. PROVIDENCE — 67
3. LONG BEACH ST. — 49

Most free throws attempted in a single game
1. LONG BEACH ST. (vs. ARIZONA ST.) — 32
2. OKLAHOMA CITY (vs. ARIZONA ST.) — 30
3. ARIZONA ST. (vs. OKLAHOMA CITY) — 28

Most total free throws attempted in the tournament
1. MEMPHIS STATE — 97
2. PROVIDENCE — 83
3. LONG BEACH ST. — 66

Highest free throw percentage in a single game
1. MARQUETTE (vs. INDIANA) (5-5) — 1.000
2. SAN FRANCISCO (vs. UCLA) (3-3) — 1.000
3. MIAMI (OHIO) (vs. MARQUETTE) (12-13) — .923

Highest free throw percentage in the tournament (minimum 2 games)
1. PENNSYLVANIA (29-35) — .829
2. PROVIDENCE (67-83) — .807
3. MARYLAND (22-28) — .786

Fewest free throws in a single game
1. KENTUCKY (vs. INDIANA) — 3
1. SAN FRANCISCO (vs. UCLA) — 3
1. INDIANA (vs. UCLA) — 3

Lowest free throw percentage in a single game
1. INDIANA (vs. UCLA) (3-6) — .500
2. S'WESTERN LA. (vs. S. CAROLINA) (7-14) — .500
3. KANSAS STATE (vs. S'WESTERN LA.) (10-20) — .500

Lowest free throw percentage in the tournament (minimum 2 games)
1. KANSAS STATE (24-44) — .545
2. SYRACUSE (29-47) — .617
3. INDIANA (41-63) — .651

REBOUNDS

Most rebounds in a single game
1. S'WESTERN LA. (vs. S. CAROLINA) — 58
2. MARQUETTE (vs. AUSTIN PEAY) — 56
2. KENTUCKY (vs. AUSTIN PEAY) — 56

Most rebounds per game (minimum 2 games)
1. S'WESTERN LA. (139-3) — 46.33
2. KENTUCKY (92-2) — 46.00
3. ARIZONA ST. (132-3) — 44.00

ASSISTS

Most assists in a single game
1. UCLA (vs. ARIZONA ST.) — 29
2. UCLA (vs. MEMPHIS STATE) — 26
3. SAN FRANCISCO (vs. LONG BEACH ST.) — 25

Most assists per game (minimum 2 games)
1. KENTUCKY (41-2) — 20.50
2. UCLA (81-4) — 20.25
3. MEMPHIS STATE (77-4) — 19.25

1974

| FIRST ROUND | REGIONAL SEMIFINAL | REGIONAL FINAL | FINAL FOUR | REGIONAL FINAL | REGIONAL SEMIFINAL | FIRST ROUND |

EAST

(bye) — N.C. State 92

N.C. State 100

Providence 84

Providence 78

Pennsylvania 69

N.C. State 80 (2 ot)

Pittsburgh 54

Pittsburgh 81

St. Joseph's 42

Pittsburgh 72

Furman 75

Furman 78

S. Carolina 67

MIDEAST

Marquette 85

Marquette 69

Ohio 59

Marquette 72

Vanderbilt 61

(bye)

Marquette 64

Michigan 77

(bye)

Michigan 70

Austin Peay 66

Notre Dame 68

Notre Dame 108

N.C. State 76
Marquette 64

WEST

(bye) — UCLA 111 (3 ot)

UCLA 83

Dayton 88

Dayton 100

Cal. St. LA 80

UCLA 77

(bye) — San Francisco 64

San Francisco 60

New Mexico 73

New Mexico 61

Idaho St. 65

MIDWEST

Kansas 55

(bye)

Kansas 93 (ot)

Creighton 77

Creighton 54

Texas 61

Kansas 51

Oral Roberts 86 (ot)

Oral Roberts 96

Syracuse 82

Oral Roberts 90

(bye)

Louisville 93

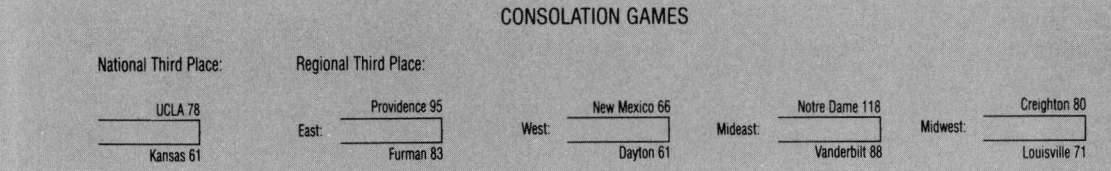

It had to happen sometime. But nobody expected it to happen to this UCLA team: the Bill Walton-led squad, that just a few months earlier was hailed as the greatest ever, finally lost. Early in the 1973–74 season it looked for all the world like these Bruins would roll to another undefeated season. But in 1974 UCLA lost—one game, two games, three games, and finally, the national championship.

Maybe the law of averages caught up with them. Maybe they really weren't that much better than everyone else, and the wizard of Westwood's psychological voodoo finally ran its course. Or maybe they just lost the fire in the belly that had always enabled them to deal the crushing blow to the opposition. Whatever the cause, UCLA's downfall began on January 19th, 1974, when Notre Dame came back from an 11-point deficit in the final 3:32 to beat them. After 88 straight wins, the Bruins crashed to earth.

By the time the NCAA tournament rolled around, UCLA was no longer No. 1. North Carolina State, led by the brilliant David Thompson, was the nation's top-ranked team. The Wolfpack had lost only once all year (to UCLA in December by 18 points); but their defeat came before the Bruins' fall from grace, and along with UCLA's descent from Olympus, Norm Sloan's State squad got stronger as the year progressed.

Against Purdue in January and Maryland in the ACC tournament finals, they erased big deficits to win. They did it with Thompson, their spectacular main man, and with an overall team effort. The 'Pack had no weak links: their starters included one of the nation's best big men, 7-4 Tom Burleson, and one of the best (and smallest) little men, 5-5½ Monte Towe. The solid, steady, two-way players Mo Rivers and Tim Stoddard rounded out an exceptionally well-balanced team that knew how to win.

Thompson carried North Carolina State past Providence in their tournament opener, scoring 40 points on a succession of spectacular backdoor alley-oops. Meanwhile the Friars' Marvin Barnes, the nation's top rebounder, was outplayed under the boards by Burleson. The Wolfpack capped their 92-78 victory with an awe-inspiring play: with six seconds left Towe took a long outlet pass from Burleson and threw a no-look, over-the-head lob toward the hoop; with a man hanging on him, Thompson took off into the stratosphere and banked the ball home.

In the regional final against Pitt, the 'Pack showed what they were made of. With his team leading by 7 in the tenth minute of play, Thompson leaped to make a block. Cartwheeling over the shoulders of teammate Phil Spence, Thompson landed with a sickening thud on the back of his head. "I thought he was dead," said Spence. "His eyes rolled back in his head and he seemed to quit breathing. . . . I just wanted to give up." Minutes later, after Thompson regained consciousness, he was carried off the court and taken to a nearby hospital. His emotionally charged teammates responded: Burleson scored 11 points in the next four minutes, Towe cut through the Pitt press easily, and Rivers shot better than he had in weeks. With 7:40 left and State in command, Thompson, his head wrapped in a bandage, returned to the Wolfpack bench. He had suffered a mild concussion and needed 15 stitches, but he would be ready for UCLA.

The question was would UCLA be ready for him? The Bruins had lucked out in their regional semi against unheralded Dayton, blowing a 17-point lead and surviving only because Flyer coach Don Donoher called a timeout just before the Ohio team's Donald Smith hit a jump shot that would have won the game. It took three overtimes before UCLA finally subdued the 20-point underdog Flyers.

Despite being ranked No. 1 and playing the Final Four in friendly Greensboro, North Carolina State was the underdog in their semifinal against UCLA. After all, the Bruins still hadn't lost a game that counted for eight years.

Early in the second half, it looked like the oddsmakers would be proven right. N.C. State seemed to be coming apart at the seams while UCLA could do no wrong in building an 11-point lead. With 10:53 remaining, the Bruins appeared to have the game in hand, but then, astoundingly, they went four minutes without scoring. At the end, the Wolfpack had the best chance to win, but Tim Stoddard missed an open jumper, sending the game into overtime.

The extra period resolved nothing. Early in the second OT, UCLA's Walton and Wilkes combined for 7 unanswered points. Suddenly, the tide turned. UCLA guard Tommy Curtis charged a pressing Monte Towe in the backcourt and Towe hit two free throws. After Curtis hit one of two on the other end, Thompson scored to cut the Bruin lead to 4. Towe missed from the corner, and Burleson and Walton went up for the rebound. It went in off Walton's hands. Mo Rivers and Stoddard stole the ball. Burleson, fouled by Walton, hit the first of two, but missed the second. Stoddard rebounded but Towe missed again. UCLA's David Meyers missed a foul shot, Thompson cleared the boards, and canned a jumper over Wilkes. UCLA came downcourt and missed; Wilkes pushed off on the rebound, fouling out and sending Thompson to the line for two. He hit them both. Towe hit two more less than half a minute later.

State scored 11 points in a row to win the game. The spell was finally broken. The king was dead. UCLA, with its newfound penchant for blowing leads, threw away a big one when it most counted. And David Thompson and the Wolfpack, with icewater running through their veins, proved themselves to be the right team in the right place at the right time to beat UCLA.

The next night they beat Marquette to win the championship.

FIRST ROUND EAST

Providence (84)　　Coach: Dave Gavitt

	Min.	Total FG/FGA	Pct.	FT/FTA	Pct.	Reb. O/T	A	TO	PF	S	Blk	TP	PPM
BELLO, G.	40	6/11	.545	5/5	1.000	-/3	8	2	1	3	0	17	.425
MCANDREW, M.	32	1/9	.111	0/0	.000	-/14	6	2	3	0	0	2	.063
BARNES, M.	39	11/20	.550	4/4	1.000	-/17	4	4	3	4	4	26	.667
STACOM, K.	39	8/17	.471	0/0	.000	-/2	3	2	1	0	0	16	.410
COOPER, B.	19	7/11	.636	0/0	.000	-/8	0	0	2	0	1	14	.737
BAKER, A.	19	2/3	.667	2/2	1.000	-/2	1	1	2	1	0	6	.316
HASSETT, J.	8	0/5	.000	0/0	.000	-/1	2	0	0	0	0	0	.000
SANTOS, R.	3	1/1	1.000	0/0	.000	-/2	0	0	1	0	0	2	.667
DUNPHY, R.	1	0/1	.000	1/2	.500	-/0	0	0	1	0	0	1	1.000
Totals	200	36/78	.462	12/13	.923	-/49	24	11	14	8	5	84	.420

Pennsylvania (69)　　Coach: Chuck Daly

	Min.	Total FG/FGA	Pct.	FT/FTA	Pct.	Reb. O/T	A	TO	PF	S	Blk	TP	PPM
VARGA, W.	32	4/7	.571	0/0	.000	-/2	5	1	2	2	0	8	.250
HAIGLER, R.	34	8/21	.381	3/4	.750	-/9	3	3	2	0	0	19	.559
ENGLES, J.	31	12/21	.571	3/4	.750	-/10	4	6	4	0	1	27	.871
BIGELOW, B.	38	2/5	.400	0/0	.000	-/4	2	1	1	0	0	4	.105
BEECROFT, J.	28	1/9	.111	2/2	1.000	-/1	3	0	1	1	0	4	.143
FINGER, B.	7	0/1	.000	0/0	.000	-/1	1	2	0	2	0	0	.000
STESANSKI, E.	9	1/1	1.000	0/0	.000	-/0	0	4	2	0	0	2	.222
JABLONSKI, J.	3	1/2	.500	0/1	.000	-/1	0	1	0	1	0	2	.667
JOHNSON, H.	15	1/2	.500	0/0	.000	-/4	1	0	2	0	0	2	.133
ENOCH, E.	2	0/0	.000	0/0	.000	-/0	0	0	0	0	0	0	.000
JONES, B.	1	0/0	.000	1/2	.500	-/1	0	0	0	0	0	1	1.000
Totals	200	30/69	.435	9/13	.692	-/33	19	18	14	6	1	69	.345

Team Rebounds: Providence 2; Pennsylvania 1. Disqualified: None.

	1st Half	2nd Half	Final
Providence	39	45	84
Pennsylvania	34	35	69

Pittsburgh (54)　　Coach: Buzz Ridl

	Min.	Total FG/FGA	Pct.	FT/FTA	Pct.	Reb. O/T	A	TO	PF	S	Blk	TP	PPM
KNIGHT, B.	-	5/16	.313	1/2	.500	-/7	-	-	3	-	-	11	-
MARTIN, M.	-	6/12	.500	0/2	.000	-/5	-	-	3	-	-	12	-
BOLLA, J.	-	1/2	.500	0/2	.000	-/2	-	-	2	-	-	2	-
BRUCE, K.	-	1/6	.167	1/1	1.000	-/2	-	-	0	-	-	3	-
RICHARDS, T.	-	2/7	.286	1/2	.500	-/3	-	-	1	-	-	5	-
WAGONER, K.	-	0/0	.000	0/0	.000	-/1	-	-	0	-	-	0	-
HILL, L.	-	4/6	.667	1/2	.500	-/4	-	-	3	-	-	9	-
STARR, K.	-	4/8	.500	2/2	1.000	-/1	-	-	3	-	-	10	-
KELLY, W.	-	1/1	1.000	0/0	.000	-/0	-	-	1	-	-	2	-
ABRAMS, M.	-	0/1	1.000	0/0	.000	-/0	-	-	0	-	-	0	-
Totals	200	24/59	.407	6/13	.462	-/25	-	11	16	-	-	54	.270

St. Joseph's (42)　　Coach: Jack McKinney

	Min.	Total FG/FGA	Pct.	FT/FTA	Pct.	Reb. O/T	A	TO	PF	S	Blk	TP	PPM
RIGHTER, R.	-	7/14	.500	3/5	.600	-/10	-	-	3	-	-	17	-
PRYBELLA, E.	-	1/7	.143	0/0	.000	-/4	-	-	1	-	-	2	-
FUREY, K.	-	2/3	.667	2/3	.667	-/8	-	-	4	-	-	6	-
MOODY, M.	-	2/8	.250	3/5	.600	-/7	-	-	3	-	-	7	-
O'BRIEN, J.	-	2/7	.286	1/1	1.000	-/1	-	-	4	-	-	5	-
RAFFERTY,	-	1/3	.333	0/0	.000	-/0	-	-	1	-	-	2	-
KELLY, C.	-	1/2	.500	1/1	1.000	-/1	-	-	1	-	-	3	-
Totals	200	16/44	.364	10/15	.667	-/31	-	22	17	-	-	42	.210

Team Rebounds: Pittsburgh 5; St. Joseph's 5. Disqualified: None.

	1st Half	2nd Half	Final
Pittsburgh	25	29	54
St. Joseph's	16	26	42

Furman (75)　　Coach: Joe Williams

	Min.	Total FG/FGA	Pct.	FT/FTA	Pct.	Reb. O/T	A	TO	PF	S	Blk	TP	PPM
LYNCH, C.	40	6/17	.353	2/2	1.000	-/8	4	2	1	0	0	14	.350
MAYES, C.	39	9/13	.692	3/3	1.000	-/16	0	0	1	3	5	21	.538
LEONARD, F.	19	4/9	.444	3/4	.750	-/2	0	2	4	0	3	11	.579
KELLEY, J.	36	4/7	.571	2/3	.667	-/4	5	1	2	1	0	10	.278
GRIMM, B.	36	8/18	.444	3/5	.600	-/2	2	5	2	0	0	19	.528
BIERLY, B.	22	0/4	.000	0/0	.000	-/5	0	2	2	1	0	0	.000
CLARK, G.	4	0/2	.000	0/0	.000	-/2	0	0	0	0	0	0	.000
HILL, B.	4	0/0	.000	0/0	.000	-/1	1	0	0	0	0	0	.000
Totals	200	31/70	.443	13/17	.765	-/40	12	12	12	5	8	75	.375

South Carolina (67)　　Coach: Frank McGuire

	Min.	Total FG/FGA	Pct.	FT/FTA	Pct.	Reb. O/T	A	TO	PF	S	Blk	TP	PPM
DAVIS, N.	38	8/19	.421	0/0	.000	-/13	0	2	4	0	1	16	.421
ENGLISH, A.	40	5/15	.333	1/2	.500	-/11	2	0	4	0	4	11	.275
MATHIAS, B.	28	2/6	.333	0/1	.000	-/8	1	0	4	2	0	4	.143
DUNLEAVY, M.	40	5/14	.357	2/2	1.000	-/4	4	3	0	2	0	12	.300
WINTERS, B.	39	11/27	.407	0/0	.000	-/1	2	3	5	2	0	22	.564
GREINER, M.	14	1/2	.500	0/2	.000	-/7	0	1	2	0	0	2	.143
WALSH, J.	1	0/1	.000	0/0	.000	-/0	0	0	0	0	0	0	.000
Totals	200	32/84	.381	3/7	.429	-/44	9	9	19	6	5	67	.335

Team Rebounds: Furman 10; S. Carolina 5. Disqualified: S. Carolina—Winters.

	1st Half	2nd Half	Final
Furman	39	36	75
S. Carolina	38	29	67

FIRST ROUND WEST

Dayton (88)   Coach: Don Donoher

	Min.	Total FG/FGA	Pct.	FT/FTA	Pct.	Reb. O/T	A	TO	PF	S	Blk	TP	PPM
SMITH, D.	40	9/17	.529	4/4	1.000	-/3	3	3	3	0	1	22	.550
DAVIS, J.	39	8/15	.533	6/6	1.000	-/4	4	2	4	0	0	22	.564
SYLVESTER, M.	40	13/20	.650	4/4	1.000	-/11	0	5	2	1	0	30	.750
VON, L.	28	1/2	.500	2/4	.500	-/5	2	2	2	0	0	4	.143
ELIJAH, A.	23	2/4	.500	0/1	.000	-/9	0	2	3	0	0	4	.174
FISHER, J.	12	2/2	1.000	2/2	1.000	-/7	1	0	1	0	0	6	.500
TEATERMAN, J.	17	0/0	.000	0/0	.000	-/0	0	0	0	0	1	0	.000
COLEMAN, B.	0	0/0	.000	0/0	.000	-/0	0	0	0	0	0	0	
MOULTON, L.	1	0/0	.000	0/0	.000	-/0	0	0	0	0	0	0	.000
Totals	200	35/60	.583	18/21	.857	-/39	10	14	15	1	2	88	.440

California State LA (80)   Coach: Bob Miller

	Min.	Total FG/FGA	Pct.	FT/FTA	Pct.	Reb. O/T	A	TO	PF	S	Blk	TP	PPM
BRIGHAM, A.	33	6/16	.375	0/1	.000	-/2	3	1	1	0	0	12	.364
TAYLOR, B.	12	4/7	.571	0/0	.000	-/2	0	0	2	1	0	8	.667
TATE, T.	26	1/4	.250	0/1	.000	-/4	1	0	3	2	0	2	.077
LINSEY, T.	39	9/15	.600	4/4	1.000	-/8	3	5	2	1	1	22	.564
MALLORY, B.	33	7/14	.500	0/1	.000	-/4	0	1	5	1	0	14	.424
JACKSON, W.	26	5/8	.625	2/3	.667	-/1	2	2	3	1	0	12	.462
SLAUGHTER, D.	19	3/6	.500	0/0	.000	-/1	0	3	5	0	0	6	.316
BAILEY, D.	12	2/4	.500	0/0	.000	-/3	2	0	2	0	0	4	.333
Totals	200	37/74	.500	6/10	.600	-/25	11	12	23	6	1	80	.400

Team Rebounds: Dayton 1; Cal. St. LA 4. Disqualified: Cal. St. LA—Mallory, Slaughter. Technical fouls: None. Played who played 0 min. played less than 1 min.

	1st Half	2nd Half	Final
Dayton	46	42	88
Cal. St. LA	44	36	80

New Mexico (73)   Coach: Norm Ellenberger

	Min.	Total FG/FGA	Pct.	FT/FTA	Pct.	Reb. O/T	A	TO	PF	S	Blk	TP	PPM
NAVA, G.	36	3/12	.250	0/0	.000	-/2	0	3	2	0	2	6	.167
TAYLOR, W.	10	1/4	.250	0/0	.000	-/2	2	3	4	0	0	2	.200
HARDIN, B.	34	8/22	.364	3/3	1.000	-/6	0	0	2	0	1	19	.559
KING, P.	26	2/5	.400	0/1	.000	-/1	3	0	1	0	0	4	.154
TOPPERT, B.	4	0/1	.000	0/0	.000	-/0	1	0	2	0	0	0	.000
BATTLE, B.	14	2/6	.333	0/0	.000	-/3	1	3	0	0	0	4	.286
SAIERS, M.	34	8/15	.533	2/2	1.000	-/14	6	3	1	0	0	18	.529
POKORSKI, R.	6	1/1	1.000	0/0	.000	-/4	0	1	3	0	0	2	.333
PATTERSON, M.	1	0/0	.000	0/0	.000	-/0	0	0	0	0	0	0	.000
HAGINS, B.	31	6/8	.750	2/2	1.000	-/10	0	3	3	0	1	14	.452
KRUSE, P.	3	1/1	1.000	0/0	.000	-/3	0	2	1	0	1	2	.667
DAVIS, D.	1	1/1	1.000	0/0	.000	-/0	0	0	0	0	0	2	2.000
Totals	200	33/76	.434	7/8	.875	-/45	13	18	19	0	4	73	.365

Idaho State (65)   Coach: Jim Killingsworth

	Min.	Total FG/FGA	Pct.	FT/FTA	Pct.	Reb. O/T	A	TO	PF	S	Blk	TP	PPM
HOYT, K.	39	7/18	.389	0/0	.000	-/5	3	3	0	1	0	14	.359
STRANNIGAN, M.	11	1/5	.200	2/2	1.000	-/0	0	2	3	0	0	4	.364
GREEN, D.	4	0/1	.000	1/2	.500	-/1	0	0	0	0	0	1	.250
GIBBONS, L.	28	3/7	.429	0/0	.000	-/10	3	1	4	0	3	6	.214
KRAHN, F.	4	0/0	.000	0/0	.000	-/0	0	0	1	0	0	0	.000
ANDERSON, J.	32	6/14	.429	1/1	1.000	-/9	1	3	2	1	0	13	.406
RODRIGUEZ, G.	26	0/3	.000	2/2	1.000	-/2	6	7	4	2	0	2	.077
SPINDLER, D.	25	6/9	.667	2/3	.667	-/5	0	0	1	0	0	14	.560
KRUIDHOF, R.	6	0/2	.000	0/0	.000	-/1	0	1	0	0	0	0	.000
HAYES, S.	16	3/5	.600	3/4	.750	-/1	0	2	2	0	0	9	.563
DOOS, P.	9	1/2	.500	0/0	.000	-/2	0	0	0	0	0	2	.222
Totals	200	27/66	.409	11/14	.786	-/36	13	19	17	4	3	65	.325

Team Rebounds: New Mexico 5; Idaho State 2. Disqualified: None. Technical fouls: New Mexico—Coach Ellenberger.

	1st Half	2nd Half	Final
New Mexico	39	34	73
Idaho State	34	31	65

FIRST ROUND MIDEAST

Marquette (85)   Coach: Al McGuire

	Min.	Total FG/FGA	Pct.	FT/FTA	Pct.	Reb. O/T	A	TO	PF	S	Blk	TP	PPM
ELLIS, M.	33	8/11	.727	0/0	.000	-/9	2	-	2	0	1	16	.485
TATUM, E.	30	8/15	.533	0/0	.000	-/6	1	-	4	4	1	16	.533
LUCAS, M.	34	9/18	.500	0/0	.000	-/15	1	-	4	0	2	18	.529
WALTON, L.	28	6/13	.462	0/0	.000	-/3	4	-	2	3	0	12	.429
WASHINGTON, M.	23	3/8	.375	1/2	.500	-/1	3	-	1	0	0	7	.304
DANIELS, E.	15	0/2	.000	2/2	1.000	-/2	3	-	2	0	0	2	.133
CAMPBELL, R.	17	3/6	.500	2/5	.400	-/3	0	-	3	0	0	8	.471
HOMAN, J.	9	2/4	.500	0/0	.000	-/1	0	-	0	0	0	4	.444
DELSMAN, D.	7	1/1	1.000	0/0	.000	-/1	0	-	1	1	0	2	.286
VOLLMER, P.	2	0/0	.000	0/0	.000	-/0	0	-	0	0	0	0	.000
JOHNSON, G.	2	0/2	.000	0/0	.000	-/2	0	-	0	0	0	0	.000
Totals	200	40/80	.500	5/9	.556	-/43	14	9	19	8	4	85	.425

Ohio (59)   Coach: James Snyder

	Min.	Total FG/FGA	Pct.	FT/FTA	Pct.	Reb. O/T	A	TO	PF	S	Blk	TP	PPM
BROWN	30	5/12	.417	3/3	1.000	-/4	0	-	1	1	2	13	.433
GREEN	27	4/10	.400	3/5	.600	-/12	3	-	2	1	1	11	.407
BALL	30	0/2	.000	0/1	.000	-/1	0	-	3	0	0	0	.000
SLAPPY	25	1/5	.200	2/2	1.000	-/2	2	-	0	0	0	4	.160
LUCKETT	38	7/15	.467	0/0	.000	-/4	2	-	1	2	4	14	.368
PAYNE	23	3/8	.375	1/2	.500	-/2	2	-	0	1	0	7	.304
THOMPSON	9	1/2	.500	0/0	.000	-/0	1	-	1	1	0	2	.222
HESTER	6	0/1	.000	0/0	.000	-/0	0	-	1	0	0	0	.000
CORDE	6	2/2	1.000	4/4	1.000	-/1	1	-	0	0	0	8	1.333
JAUCH	2	0/0	.000	0/0	.000	-/0	0	-	0	0	0	0	.000
TALBERT	2	0/0	.000	0/0	.000	-/0	0	-	0	0	0	0	.000
STRACK	2	0/0	.000	0/0	.000	-/0	0	-	0	0	0	0	.000
Totals	200	23/57	.404	13/17	.765	-/26	11	18	11	6	7	59	.295

Disqualified: None. Technical fouls: Marquette—Coach McGuire.

	1st Half	2nd Half	Final
Marquette	37	48	85
Ohio	28	31	59

Austin Peay (66)   Coach: Lake Kelly

	Min.	FG/FGA	Pct.	FT/FTA	Pct.	Reb. O/T	A	TO	PF	S	Blk	TP	PPM
WILLIAMS, J.	34	13/31	.419	0/0	.000	-/5	1	6	3	2	0	26	.765
TURNER, R.	28	2/6	.333	0/0	.000	-/3	2	1	2	0	0	4	.143
HOWARD, P.	18	1/6	.167	0/0	.000	-/7	2	2	3	0	0	2	.111
ODUMS, D.	28	2/5	.400	3/4	.750	-/3	1	4	0	0	0	7	.250
FISHER, M.	9	0/0	.000	0/0	.000	-/0	1	1	1	0	0	0	.000
JIMMERSON, R.	19	3/5	.600	1/2	.500	-/6	0	1	2	0	0	7	.368
JOHNSON, J.	20	1/5	.200	1/4	.250	-/3	0	1	4	2	0	3	.150
GARNER, R.	8	0/2	.000	0/0	.000	-/0	0	1	0	0	1	0	.000
HAMPTON, K.	2	0/1	.000	0/0	.000	-/1	0	0	0	0	0	0	.000
LEE, F.	8	0/2	.000	2/2	1.000	-/0	2	0	0	0	0	2	.250
REID, J.	4	1/1	1.000	4/4	1.000	-/0	0	1	1	0	0	6	1.500
EPLEY, R.	7	2/4	.500	1/1	1.000	-/2	0	1	1	2	0	5	.714
SMITH, J.	10	0/1	.000	3/4	.750	-/1	0	0	0	0	0	3	.300
MAIER, G.	5	0/1	.000	1/3	.333	-/1	0	1	0	0	0	1	.200
Totals	200	25/70	.357	16/24	.667	-/32	7	22	17	6	1	66	.330

Notre Dame (108)   Coach: Digger Phelps

	Min.	FG/FGA	Pct.	FT/FTA	Pct.	Reb. O/T	A	TO	PF	S	Blk	TP	PPM
DANTLEY, A.	29	9/16	.563	4/4	1.000	-/10	3	1	2	0	1	22	.759
NOVAK, G.	30	6/10	.600	0/1	.000	-/8	3	1	1	0	2	12	.400
SHUMATE, J.	33	10/14	.714	2/2	1.000	-/10	5	2	3	2	1	22	.667
BROKAW, G.	33	12/21	.571	1/2	.500	-/6	4	1	3	2	0	25	.758
CLAY, D.	26	4/6	.667	0/0	.000	-/0	9	4	3	3	0	8	.308
PATERNO, B.	12	2/5	.400	0/0	.000	-/4	1	2	3	2	0	4	.333
MARTIN, R.	13	2/3	.667	0/0	.000	-/1	3	2	1	2	0	4	.308
CROTTY, P.	8	1/1	1.000	0/0	.000	-/3	2	2	0	0	0	2	.250
KUZMICZ, D.	6	3/4	.750	0/0	.000	-/0	2	3	0	0	0	6	1.000
KNIGHT, T.	6	1/2	.500	0/0	.000	-/4	0	0	1	2	0	2	.333
SCHUCKMAN, M.	4	0/1	.000	1/2	.500	-/1	0	1	1	0	1	1	.250
Totals	200	50/83	.602	8/11	.727	-/47	30	18	21	13	5	108	.540

Team Rebounds: Notre Dame 4; Austin Peay 5. Disqualified: None.

	1st Half	2nd Half	Final
Austin Peay	34	32	66
Notre Dame	54	54	108

FIRST ROUND MIDWEST

Creighton (77)   Coach: Eddie Sutton

	Min.	FG/FGA	Pct.	FT/FTA	Pct.	Reb. O/T	A	TO	PF	S	Blk	TP	PPM
HARMON, G.	35	11/17	.647	0/0	.000	-/6	2	2	2	0	1	22	.629
BROOKINS, D.	34	7/14	.500	2/2	1.000	-/9	0	3	2	1	0	16	.471
HECK, M.	16	2/5	.400	2/2	1.000	-/3	1	0	1	0	0	6	.375
BOBIK, R.	38	3/3	1.000	1/2	.500	-/6	12	9	1	1	0	7	.184
BUTLER, C.	35	6/11	.545	0/0	.000	-/4	0	2	3	1	0	12	.343
WEUBBEN, T.	24	5/10	.500	1/2	.500	-/2	3	0	1	2	0	11	.458
ANDERSON, T.	10	0/0	.000	1/3	.333	-/0	1	0	0	0	0	1	.100
SMITH, R.	5	0/1	.000	0/0	.000	-/0	1	0	0	0	0	0	.000
PIETRO, B.	2	1/1	1.000	0/0	.000	-/0	0	0	1	0	0	2	1.000
MASSIE, J.	1	0/0	.000	0/0	.000	-/0	0	0	0	0	0	0	.000
Totals	200	35/62	.565	7/11	.636	-/30	20	16	11	5	1	77	.385

Texas (61)   Coach: Leon Black

	Min.	FG/FGA	Pct.	FT/FTA	Pct.	Reb. O/T	A	TO	PF	S	Blk	TP	PPM
JOHNSON, E.	38	7/11	.636	2/4	.500	-/7	0	2	1	0	1	16	.421
ROBINSON, L.	38	10/25	.400	0/0	.000	-/8	2	8	5	0	2	20	.526
PARSON, R.	24	0/3	.000	0/0	.000	-/5	3	1	4	1	0	0	.000
KRUEGGER, D.	38	4/10	.400	0/0	.000	-/1	4	0	4	4	0	8	.211
LARRABEE, H.	38	7/12	.583	1/1	1.000	-/4	2	1	1	1	0	15	.395
WEILERT, T.	5	0/0	.000	0/0	.000	-/0	0	1	1	0	0	0	.000
JOHNSON, T.	9	0/0	.000	0/0	.000	-/1	2	2	2	0	1	0	.000
BAKER, B.	2	0/0	.000	0/0	.000	-/0	0	1	0	0	0	0	.000
DAVIS, P.	2	0/1	.000	0/0	.000	-/0	0	0	1	0	0	0	.000
VOEGELE, C.	2	1/1	1.000	0/0	.000	-/1	0	0	1	0	0	2	1.000
BAUERSCHLER, H.	2	0/0	.000	0/0	.000	-/0	0	1	0	0	0	0	.000
PRICE, J.	2	0/0	.000	0/0	.000	-/0	0	0	0	0	0	0	.000
Totals	200	29/63	.460	3/5	.600	-/27	13	16	15	7	4	61	.305

Team Rebounds: Creighton 4; Texas 6. Disqualified: Texas—Robinson.

	1st Half	2nd Half	Final
Creighton	43	34	77
Texas	35	26	61

Oral Roberts (86)   Coach: Ken Trickey

	Min.	FG/FGA	Pct.	FT/FTA	Pct.	Reb. O/T	A	TO	PF	S	Blk	TP	PPM
FOX, D.	35	7/15	.467	0/2	.000	-/10	2	0	4	1	2	14	.400
WOODS, E.	42	4/10	.400	3/5	.600	-/11	1	0	5	1	2	11	.262
MCDOUGALD, G.	36	3/11	.273	2/3	.667	-/8	3	3	4	2	1	8	.222
MCCANTS, S.	45	10/27	.370	5/6	.833	-/8	7	5	2	1	0	25	.556
BOSWELL, A.	45	8/17	.471	1/2	.500	-/8	2	3	4	3	0	17	.378
ROBERTS, A.	17	4/6	.667	1/2	.500	-/3	0	0	1	0	0	9	.529
COLLINS, W.	5	0/0	.000	2/2	1.000	-/0	0	0	0	0	0	2	.400
Totals	225	36/86	.419	14/22	.636	-/48	15	11	20	8	5	86	.382

Syracuse (82)   Coach: Roy Danforth

	Min.	FG/FGA	Pct.	FT/FTA	Pct.	Reb. O/T	A	TO	PF	S	Blk	TP	PPM
SAUNDERS, F.	29	4/8	.500	1/2	.500	-/11	3	2	5	1	0	9	.310
HACKETT, R.	45	6/16	.375	0/6	.000	-/14	3	3	2	1	1	12	.267
DOOMS, B.	38	6/10	.600	0/1	.000	-/9	0	2	1	0	0	12	.316
LEE, J.	45	7/14	.500	3/4	.750	-/1	2	1	1	0	0	17	.378
DUVAL, D.	44	13/26	.500	2/4	.500	-/5	2	4	5	1	0	28	.636
SEASE, C.	13	0/1	.000	0/0	.000	-/1	0	1	3	1	0	0	.000
STUNDE, T.	5	1/1	1.000	0/0	.000	-/0	0	0	2	0	0	2	.400
KING, K.	5	1/2	.500	0/1	.000	-/1	2	0	2	0	0	2	.400
WILLIAMS, J.	1	0/0	.000	0/0	.000	-/0	0	0	0	0	0	0	.000
Totals	225	38/78	.487	6/18	.333	-/42	12	13	21	4	1	82	.364

Team Rebounds: Oral Roberts 10; Syracuse 10. Disqualified: Oral Roberts—Woods; Syracuse—Saunders, DuVal.

	1st Half	2nd Half	1st OT	Final
Oral Roberts	43	31	12	86
Syracuse	41	33	8	82

REGIONAL SEMIFINAL EAST

North Carolina State (92) Coach: Norm Sloan

	Min.	Total FG/FGA	Pct.	FT/FTA	Pct.	Reb. O/T	A	TO	PF	S	Blk	TP	PPM
RIVERS, M.	36	3/16	.188	5/6	.833	-/3	2	2	3	4	0	11	.306
BURLESON, T.	31	7/19	.368	2/5	.400	-/24	0	0	3	0	2	16	.516
TOWE, M.	35	5/14	.357	5/6	.833	-/4	2	3	3	2	0	15	.429
STODDARD, T.	29	1/6	.167	0/0	.000	-/3	7	1	4	1	0	2	.069
THOMPSON, D.	40	16/29	.552	8/10	.800	-/10	1	2	2	4	1	40	1.000
SPENCE, P.	11	1/2	.500	0/0	.000	-/2	2	1	2	0	0	2	.182
NUCE, S.	9	1/2	.500	4/4	1.000	-/4	1	0	2	0	0	6	.667
MOELLER, M.	9	0/0	.000	0/0	.000	-/2	0	0	0	1	0	0	.000
Totals	200	34/88	.386	24/31	.774	-/52	15	9	19	12	3	92	.460

Providence (78) Coach: Dave Gavitt

	Min.	Total FG/FGA	Pct.	FT/FTA	Pct.	Reb. O/T	A	TO	PF	S	Blk	TP	PPM
BELLO, G.	36	4/10	.400	1/2	.500	-/3	3	4	1	2	0	9	.250
MCANDREW, M.	13	2/2	1.000	0/0	.000	-/0	0	0	2	0	0	4	.308
BARNES, M.	39	5/14	.357	4/7	.571	-/13	2	4	5	0	5	14	.359
STACOM, K.	33	8/17	.471	2/2	1.000	-/4	2	5	5	1	0	18	.545
COOPER, B.	26	7/13	.538	3/4	.750	-/10	3	3	2	1	2	17	.654
BAKER, A.	14	1/3	.333	0/1	.000	-/3	0	0	4	0	0	2	.143
SANTOS, R.	20	3/5	.600	0/0	.000	-/3	0	1	5	1	0	6	.300
HASSETT, J.	18	4/11	.364	0/0	.000	-/1	0	0	2	1	0	8	.444
DUNPHY, R.	1	0/0	.000	0/0	.000	-/0	0	0	0	0	0	0	.000
Totals	200	34/75	.453	10/16	.625	-/37	10	17	26	6	7	78	.390

Team Rebounds: N.C. State 6; Providence 7. Disqualified: Providence—Barnes, Stacom, Santos.

	1st Half	2nd Half	Final
N.C. State	44	48	92
Providence	39	39	78

Pittsburgh (81) Coach: Buzz Ridl

	Min.	Total FG/FGA	Pct.	FT/FTA	Pct.	Reb. O/T	A	TO	PF	S	Blk	TP	PPM
KNIGHT, B.	40	12/20	.600	10/11	.909	-/7	2	8	4	1	0	34	.850
MARTIN, M.	33	5/14	.357	0/0	.000	-/4	0	2	4	0	0	10	.303
BOLLA, J.	14	0/1	.000	0/0	.000	-/0	0	1	0	0	0	0	.000
BRUCE, K.	22	6/9	.667	0/0	.000	-/6	0	4	2	0	0	12	.545
RICHARDS, T.	25	3/5	.600	0/0	.000	-/1	2	1	3	0	0	6	.240
WAGONER, K.	12	1/1	1.000	0/0	.000	-/2	1	0	1	0	0	2	.167
HILL, L.	25	6/13	.462	0/2	.000	-/1	0	3	2	1	0	12	.480
STARR, K.	21	1/4	.250	1/3	.333	-/4	3	1	3	1	0	3	.143
KELLY, W.	8	1/2	.500	0/0	.000	-/2	0	0	2	0	2	2	.250
Totals	200	35/69	.507	11/16	.688	-/27	8	20	21	3	2	81	.405

Furman (78) Coach: Joe Williams

	Min.	Total FG/FGA	Pct.	FT/FTA	Pct.	Reb. O/T	A	TO	PF	S	Blk	TP	PPM
KELLEY, E.	31	3/7	.429	3/4	.750	-/0	3	6	4	2	0	9	.290
LEONARD, F.	33	7/13	.538	3/3	1.000	-/5	1	3	5	0	0	17	.515
MAYES, C.	40	6/11	.545	0/1	.000	-/8	3	4	2	1	1	12	.300
LYNCH, C.	28	3/6	.500	0/0	.000	-/4	2	2	2	0	1	6	.214
GRIMM, B.	38	9/18	.500	9/11	.818	-/6	3	3	4	1	0	27	.711
BIERLY, B.	17	1/3	.333	1/1	1.000	-/4	0	2	4	2	0	3	.176
HILL, B.	10	1/2	.500	2/2	1.000	-/1	0	4	1	0	0	4	.400
HALL, J.	1	0/0	.000	0/0	.000	-/0	0	0	0	0	0	0	.000
CLARK, G.	2	0/0	.000	0/0	.000	-/0	0	1	0	0	0	0	.000
Totals	200	30/60	.500	18/22	.818	-/28	12	25	22	6	2	78	.390

Team Rebounds: Pittsburgh 8; Furman 6. Disqualified: Furman—Leonard.

	1st Half	2nd Half	Final
Pittsburgh	38	43	81
Furman	34	44	78

REGIONAL SEMIFINAL WEST

UCLA (111) Coach: John Wooden

	Min.	Total FG/FGA	Pct.	FT/FTA	Pct.	Reb. O/T	A	TO	PF	S	Blk	TP	PPM
MEYERS, D.	-	13/25	.520	2/4	.500	-/14	-	-	5	-	-	28	-
WILKES, J.	-	7/15	.467	0/1	.000	-/7	-	-	5	-	-	14	-
WALTON, B.	-	13/23	.565	1/3	.333	-/19	-	-	2	-	-	27	-
CURTIS, T.	-	0/0	.000	0/0	.000	-/0	-	-	1	-	-	0	-
LEE, G.	-	6/10	.600	0/0	.000	-/3	-	-	3	-	-	12	-
TRGOVICH, P.	-	2/6	.333	0/0	.000	-/0	-	-	2	-	-	4	-
MCCARTER, A.	-	4/8	.500	2/3	.667	-/1	-	-	2	-	-	10	-
FRANKLIN, G.	-	1/1	1.000	0/1	.000	-/0	-	-	1	-	-	2	-
JOHNSON, M.	-	5/8	.625	4/5	.800	-/5	-	-	2	-	-	14	-
WASHINGTON, R.	-	0/1	.000	0/1	.000	-/1	-	-	0	-	-	0	-
Totals	275	51/97	.526	9/18	.500	-/50	-	19	23	-	-	111	.404

Dayton (100) Coach: Don Donoher

	Min.	Total FG/FGA	Pct.	FT/FTA	Pct.	Reb. O/T	A	TO	PF	S	Blk	TP	PPM
SYLVESTER, M.	-	12/21	.571	12/13	.923	-/13	-	-	4	-	-	36	-
ELIJAH, A.	-	1/4	.250	0/0	.000	-/4	-	-	4	-	-	2	-
VON, L.	-	1/4	.250	0/0	.000	-/0	-	-	1	-	-	2	-
SMITH, D.	-	12/23	.522	2/2	1.000	-/4	-	-	2	-	-	26	-
DAVIS, J.	-	7/13	.538	3/7	.429	-/4	-	-	4	-	-	17	-
FISHER, J.	-	6/6	1.000	3/3	1.000	-/5	-	-	4	-	-	15	-
TESTERMAN, J.	-	1/3	.333	0/0	.000	-/3	-	-	4	-	-	2	-
Totals	275	40/74	.541	20/25	.800	-/33	-	19	23	-	-	100	.364

Team Rebounds: UCLA 6; Dayton 5. Disqualified: UCLA—Meyers, Wilkes.

	1st Half	2nd Half	1st OT	2nd CT	3rd OT	Final
UCLA	48	32	8	10	13	111
Dayton	36	44	8	10	2	100

San Francisco (64) Coach: Bob Gaillard

	Min.	Total FG/FGA	Pct.	FT/FTA	Pct.	Reb. O/T	A	TO	PF	S	Blk	TP	PPM
RANDELL, J.	-	3/9	.333	2/2	1.000	-/6	-	-	3	-	-	8	-
RESTANI, K.	-	7/12	.583	0/0	.000	-/4	-	-	2	-	-	14	-
FERNSTEN, E.	-	3/5	.600	1/1	1.000	-/3	-	-	3	-	-	7	-
BORO, J.	-	1/1	1.000	2/2	1.000	-/3	-	-	2	-	-	4	-
SMITH, P.	-	3/13	.231	1/2	.500	-/1	-	-	2	-	-	7	-
COLEMAN, R.	-	2/3	.667	0/0	.000	-/1	-	-	5	-	-	4	-
SMITH, H.	-	8/12	.667	2/2	1.000	-/3	-	-	0	-	-	18	-
QUANSTROM, B.	-	1/1	1.000	0/0	.000	-/1	-	-	1	-	-	2	-
Totals	200	28/56	.500	8/9	.889	-/22	-	22	18	-	-	64	.320

New Mexico (61) Coach: Norm Ellenberger

	Min.	Total FG/FGA	Pct.	FT/FTA	Pct.	Reb. O/T	A	TO	PF	S	Blk	TP	PPM
HARDIN, B.	-	7/14	.500	2/3	.667	-/7	-	-	3	-	-	16	-
SAIERS, M.	-	6/7	.857	0/0	.000	-/5	-	-	3	-	-	12	-
HAGINS, B.	-	4/6	.667	1/2	.500	-/4	-	-	0	-	-	9	-
NAVA, G.	-	2/8	.250	0/0	.000	-/2	-	-	3	-	-	4	-
TAYLOR, W.	-	4/8	.500	2/2	1.000	-/2	-	-	0	-	-	10	-
POKORSKI, R.	-	0/1	.000	0/0	.000	-/0	-	-	0	-	-	0	-
TOPPERT, S.	-	0/1	.000	0/0	.000	-/0	-	-	0	-	-	0	-
KING, P.	-	3/3	1.000	4/4	1.000	-/1	-	-	2	-	-	10	-
BATTLE, B.	-	0/1	.000	0/0	.000	-/1	-	-	0	-	-	0	-
PATTERSON, M.	-	0/0	.000	0/0	.000	-/1	-	-	1	-	-	0	-
Totals	200	26/49	.531	9/11	.818	-/23	-	26	12	-	-	61	.305

Team Rebounds: San Francisco 4; New Mexico 5. Disqualified: San Francisco—Coleman.

	1st Half	2nd Half	Final
San Francisco	28	36	64
New Mexico	24	37	61

REGIONAL SEMIFINAL MIDEAST

Marquette (69) Coach: Al McGuire

	Min.	Total FG/FGA	Pct.	FT/FTA	Pct.	Reb. O/T	A	TO	PF	S	Blk	TP	PPM
ELLIS, M.	35	7/10	.700	2/2	1.000	-/9	1	-	2	1	1	16	.457
TATUM, E.	23	7/10	.700	0/0	.000	-/5	1	-	5	1	2	14	.609
LUCAS, M.	39	5/18	.278	5/6	.833	-/11	3	-	1	0	1	15	.385
WALTON, L.	39	5/5	1.000	4/4	1.000	-/2	4	-	3	0	0	14	.359
WASHINGTON, M.	23	2/6	.333	0/0	.000	-/3	0	-	2	0	0	4	.174
DANIELS, E.	12	2/3	.667	2/2	1.000	-/0	0	-	2	1	0	6	.500
CAMPBELL, R.	20	0/0	.000	0/0	.000	-/3	1	-	2	0	0	0	.000
DELSMAN, D.	5	0/2	.000	0/0	.000	-/1	1	-	1	0	0	0	.000
VOLLMER, P.	1	0/0	.000	0/0	.000	-/0	0	-	0	0	0	0	.000
JOHNSON, G.	1	0/0	.000	0/0	.000	-/0	0	-	0	0	0	0	.000
BRYANT, J.	1	0/0	.000	0/0	.000	-/0	0	-	0	0	0	0	.000
HOMAN, J.	1	0/0	.000	0/0	.000	-/0	0	-	0	0	0	0	.000
Totals	200	28/54	.519	13/14	.929	-/34	11	12	18	3	4	69	.345

Vanderbilt (61) Coach: Roy Skinner

	Min.	Total FG/FGA	Pct.	FT/FTA	Pct.	Reb. O/T	A	TO	PF	S	Blk	TP	PPM
FOSNES, J.	39	6/15	.400	2/2	1.000	-/4	0	-	2	2	1	14	.359
FORD, J.	40	5/8	.625	3/4	.750	-/1	3	-	2	0	0	13	.325
VAN, B.	40	2/5	.400	4/4	1.000	-/10	3	-	3	0	1	8	.200
FEHER, B.	37	3/12	.250	4/4	1.000	-/4	0	-	2	1	0	10	.270
COMPTON, T.	34	4/13	.308	4/4	1.000	-/5	0	-	2	1	0	12	.353
FOWLER, L.	7	0/2	.000	4/4	1.000	-/0	0	-	3	0	0	4	.571
LIGON, B.	3	0/2	.000	0/0	.000	-/2	0	-	0	0	0	0	.000
Totals	200	20/57	.351	21/22	.955	-/26	6	10	14	4	2	61	.305

Team Rebounds: Marquette 2; Vanderbilt 3. Disqualified: Marquette—Tatum.

	1st Half	2nd Half	Final
Marquette	40	29	69
Vanderbilt	30	31	61

Michigan (77) Coach: Johnny Orr

	Min.	Total FG/FGA	Pct.	FT/FTA	Pct.	Reb. O/T	A	TO	PF	S	Blk	TP	PPM
JOHNSON, J.	40	1/5	.200	3/4	.750	-/2	2	2	1	3	0	5	.125
GROTE, S.	30	2/7	.286	0/0	.000	-/4	1	5	5	1	0	4	.133
KUPEC, C.	36	5/16	.313	2/2	1.000	-/8	4	3	5	0	0	12	.333
BRITT, W.	39	9/16	.563	0/2	.000	-/7	4	3	5	1	2	18	.462
RUSSELL, R.	40	16/32	.500	4/7	.571	-/18	1	2	1	0	0	36	.900
ROGERS, C.	4	0/0	.000	1/2	.500	-/2	0	2	1	0	0	1	.250
WORRELL, L.	10	0/1	.000	1/2	.500	-/2	0	0	1	0	0	1	.100
WHITTEN, J.	1	0/0	.000	0/0	.000	-/0	0	0	0	0	0	0	.000
Totals	200	33/77	.429	11/19	.579	-/43	12	17	19	5	2	77	.385

Notre Dame (68) Coach: Digger Phelps

	Min.	Total FG/FGA	Pct.	FT/FTA	Pct.	Reb. O/T	A	TO	PF	S	Blk	TP	PPM
DANTLEY, A.	27	1/7	.143	0/0	.000	-/6	0	1	3	0	1	2	.074
NOVAK, G.	33	5/15	.333	1/2	.500	-/12	1	3	3	0	1	11	.333
SHUMATE, J.	40	14/22	.636	6/8	.750	-/17	2	5	3	2	0	34	.850
BROKAW, G.	40	4/16	.250	2/4	.500	-/3	3	5	3	3	0	10	.250
CLAY, D.	39	3/10	.300	0/0	.000	-/2	8	4	4	0	0	6	.154
PATERNO, B.	13	2/5	.400	1/2	.500	-/4	1	0	3	0	0	5	.385
MARTIN, R.	8	0/0	.000	0/0	.000	-/0	0	2	2	0	0	0	.000
Totals	200	29/75	.387	10/16	.625	-/44	15	20	21	5	2	68	.340

Team Rebounds: Michigan 10; Notre Dame 5. Disqualified: Michigan—Grote, Kupec, Britt.

	1st Half	2nd Half	Final
Michigan	34	43	77
Notre Dame	29	39	68

REGIONAL SEMIFINAL MIDWEST

Kansas (55) Coach: Ted Owens

	Min.	Total FG/FGA	Pct.	FT/FTA	Pct.	Reb. O/T	A	TO	PF	S	Blk	TP	PPM
COOK, N.	-	4/7	.571	3/4	.750	-/7	3	-	1	-	-	11	-
MORNINGSTAR, R.	-	9/19	.474	0/0	.000	-/5	1	-	3	-	-	18	-
KNIGHT, D.	-	1/4	.250	0/0	.000	-/1	2	-	0	-	-	2	-
KIVISTO, T.	-	2/8	.250	2/2	1.000	-/3	10	-	3	-	-	6	-
GREENLEE, D.	-	2/8	.250	0/1	.000	-/4	3	-	1	-	-	4	-
SUTTLE, R.	-	5/13	.385	0/0	.000	-/6	0	-	2	-	-	10	-
SMITH, T.	-	2/3	.667	0/0	.000	-/1	0	-	1	-	-	4	-
Totals	200	25/62	.403	5/7	.714	-/27	19	-	11	-	-	55	.275

Creighton (54) Coach: Eddie Sutton

	Min.	Total FG/FGA	Pct.	FT/FTA	Pct.	Reb. O/T	A	TO	PF	S	Blk	TP	PPM
HARMON, G.	-	7/13	.538	2/2	1.000	-/6	4	-	0	-	-	16	-
BROOKINS, D.	-	5/14	.357	0/0	.000	-/15	2	-	0	-	-	10	-
HECK, M.	-	2/3	.667	0/0	.000	-/1	0	-	2	-	-	4	-
BOBIK, R.	-	2/7	.286	4/5	.800	-/1	0	-	2	-	-	8	-
BUTLER, C.	-	2/2	1.000	0/0	.000	-/2	0	-	1	-	-	4	-
WEUBBEN, T.	-	3/7	.429	0/1	.000	-/3	1	-	5	-	-	6	-
ANDERSON, T.	-	2/2	1.000	0/0	.000	-/1	1	-	0	-	-	4	-
SMITH, R.	-	1/1	1.000	0/0	.000	-/0	1	-	0	-	-	2	-
Totals	200	24/49	.490	6/8	.750	-/29	9	-	10	-	-	54	.270

Team Rebounds: Kansas 4; Creighton 6. Disqualified: Creighton—Weubben.

	1st Half	2nd Half	Final
Kansas	30	25	55
Creighton	33	21	54

Oral Roberts (96) Coach: Ken Trickey

	Min.	Total FG/FGA	Pct.	FT/FTA	Pct.	Reb. O/T	A	TO	PF	S	Blk	TP	PPM
FOX, D.	-	0/1	.000	0/0	.000	-/1	0	-	4	-	-	0	-
WOODS, E.	-	6/9	.667	1/2	.500	-/6	0	-	5	-	-	13	-
MCDOUGALD, G.	-	7/16	.438	0/0	.000	-/9	1	-	4	-	-	14	-
MCCANTS, S.	-	11/33	.333	8/10	.800	-/8	10	-	0	-	-	30	-
BOSWELL, M.	-	10/26	.385	3/5	.600	-/9	3	-	4	-	-	23	-
ROBERTS, A.	-	6/12	.500	2/2	1.000	-/14	0	-	1	-	-	14	-
COLLINS, W.	-	1/2	.500	0/0	.000	-/1	0	-	1	-	-	2	-
Totals	200	41/99	.414	14/19	.737	-/48	14	-	19	-	-	96	.480

Louisville (93) Coach: Denny Crum

	Min.	Total FG/FGA	Pct.	FT/FTA	Pct.	Reb. O/T	A	TO	PF	S	Blk	TP	PPM
MURPHY, A.	-	12/21	.571	2/2	1.000	-/10	2	-	4	-	-	26	-
BUTLER, B.	-	5/7	.714	1/2	.500	-/7	2	-	2	-	-	11	-
COX, W.	-	5/13	.385	12/12	1.000	-/9	3	-	1	-	-	22	-
HOWARD, T.	-	3/7	.429	1/2	.500	-/1	0	-	2	-	-	7	-
BRIDGEMAN, J.	-	1/5	.200	2/4	.500	-/3	0	-	5	-	-	4	-
WHITFIELD, I.	-	4/6	.667	1/4	.250	-/2	0	-	2	-	-	9	-
BUNTON, S.	-	0/0	.000	0/0	.000	-/0	0	-	0	-	-	0	-
HARMON, B.	-	0/0	.000	0/0	.000	-/0	0	-	0	-	-	0	-
BROWN, D.	-	7/10	.700	0/0	.000	-/3	3	-	2	-	-	14	-
Totals	200	37/69	.536	19/26	.731	-/35	10	-	18	-	-	93	.465

Team Rebounds: Oral Roberts 9; Louisville 10. Disqualified: Oral Roberts—Woods; Louisville—Bridgeman.

	1st Half	2nd Half	Final
Oral Roberts	51	45	96
Louisville	51	42	93

REGIONAL FINAL EAST

North Carolina State (100) Coach: Norm Sloan

	Min.	Total FG/FGA	Pct.	FT/FTA	Pct.	Reb. O/T	A	TO	PF	S	Blk	TP	PPM
STODDARD, T.	22	3/9	.333	1/2	.500	-/6	1	2	3	1	0	7	.318
THOMPSON, D.	10	3/4	.750	2/3	.667	-/2	0	0	0	0	0	8	.800
BURLESON, T.	31	9/19	.474	8/8	1.000	-/12	0	3	4	1	3	26	.839
RIVERS, M.	37	8/12	.667	1/4	.250	-/8	3	4	2	1	0	17	.459
TOWE, M.	36	6/17	.353	7/7	1.000	-/4	6	3	2	3	0	19	.528
SPENCE, P.	31	4/10	.400	2/3	.667	-/14	4	0	3	1	0	10	.323
HAWKINS, G.	12	1/4	.250	5/6	.833	-/1	1	1	2	0	0	7	.583
MOELLER, M.	4	0/0	.000	0/0	.000	-/0	0	3	0	0	0	0	.000
NUCE, S.	12	1/4	.250	2/2	1.000	-/2	1	1	2	0	0	4	.333
LAKE, B.	1	0/0	.000	2/2	1.000	-/0	0	0	0	0	0	2	2.000
JOHNSON, D.	1	0/0	.000	0/0	.000	-/0	0	0	0	0	0	0	.000
KUZMAUL, C.	1	0/0	.000	0/0	.000	-/0	0	0	0	0	0	0	.000
BUURMA, M.	1	0/0	.000	0/0	.000	-/0	0	0	0	0	0	0	.000
DAYHUFF, B.	1	0/0	.000	0/0	.000	-/0	0	0	0	0	0	0	.000
Totals	200	35/79	.443	30/37	.811	-/49	16	17	18	7	3	100	.500

Pittsburgh (72) Coach: Buzz Ridl

	Min.	Total FG/FGA	Pct.	FT/FTA	Pct.	Reb. O/T	A	TO	PF	S	Blk	TP	PPM
KNIGHT, B.	39	9/19	.474	1/2	.500	-/10	4	5	2	0	1	19	.487
MARTIN, M.	36	6/13	.462	0/0	.000	-/2	0	0	3	0	0	12	.333
BOLLA, J.	6	2/3	.667	0/0	.000	-/0	0	0	2	0	0	4	.667
BRUCE, K.	21	0/5	.000	3/4	.750	-/1	1	2	3	0	0	3	.143
RICHARDS, T.	26	3/7	.429	4/4	1.000	-/2	1	4	3	0	0	10	.385
WAGONER, K.	8	0/0	.000	0/0	.000	-/0	1	1	5	0	0	0	.000
HILL, L.	24	5/12	.417	0/1	.000	-/3	0	1	3	0	0	10	.417
STARR, K.	17	2/7	.286	0/0	.000	-/2	0	1	1	0	0	4	.235
KELLY, W.	10	1/3	.333	1/2	.500	-/2	0	4	0	0	0	3	.300
ABRAMS, M.	3	2/3	.667	0/0	.000	-/1	0	1	2	1	0	4	1.333
FLEMING, S.	5	1/1	1.000	1/3	.333	-/1	0	1	1	0	0	3	.600
SHREWSBURY, B.	3	0/2	.000	0/0	.000	-/0	1	1	1	1	0	0	.000
MCBRIDE, G.	1	0/1	.000	0/0	.000	-/0	0	0	0	0	0	0	.000
DISCO, M.	1	0/0	.000	0/0	.000	-/2	0	0	1	0	0	0	.000
Totals	200	31/76	.408	10/16	.625	-/26	8	17	31	2	1	72	.360

Team Rebounds: N.C. State 11; Pittsburgh 8. Disqualified: Pittsburgh—Wagoner. Technical fouls: N.C. State—Stoddard; Pittsburgh—Bruce. Team Turnovers: N.C. State 1.

	1st Half	2nd Half	Final
N.C. State	47	53	100
Pittsburgh	41	31	72

REGIONAL FINAL WEST

UCLA (83) Coach: John Wooden

	Min.	Total FG/FGA	Pct.	FT/FTA	Pct.	Reb. O/T	A	TO	PF	S	Blk	TP	PPM
MEYERS, D.	25	6/11	.545	0/0	.000	-/2	1	-	3	-	-	12	.480
WILKES, J.	34	13/28	.464	1/1	1.000	-/8	3	-	0	-	-	27	.794
WALTON, B.	36	7/12	.583	3/5	.600	-/9	4	-	3	-	-	17	.472
CURTIS, T.	24	3/7	.429	0/0	.000	-/2	0	-	0	-	-	6	.250
LEE, G.	35	3/6	.500	2/2	1.000	-/4	5	-	0	-	-	8	.229
TRGOVICH, P.	4	0/0	.000	0/0	.000	-/1	1	-	0	-	-	0	.000
MCCARTER, A.	14	1/2	.500	0/1	.000	-/2	2	-	2	-	-	2	.143
FRANKLIN, G.	4	1/1	1.000	0/0	.000	-/0	0	-	0	-	-	2	.500
JOHNSON, M.	14	2/3	.667	1/2	.500	-/5	0	-	1	-	-	5	.357
DROLLINGER, R.	4	0/2	.000	0/0	.000	-/2	1	-	0	-	-	0	.000
WASHINGTON, R.	3	2/2	1.000	0/0	.000	-/1	0	-	1	-	-	4	1.333
WEBB, B.	3	0/0	.000	0/0	.000	-/1	0	-	0	-	-	0	.000
Totals	200	38/74	.514	7/11	.636	-/37	17	-	10	-	-	83	.415

San Francisco (60) Coach: Bob Gaillard

	Min.	Total FG/FGA	Pct.	FT/FTA	Pct.	Reb. O/T	A	TO	PF	S	Blk	TP	PPM
RANDELL, J.	29	0/6	.000	2/2	1.000	-/7	0	-	3	-	-	2	.069
RESTANI, K.	37	10/13	.769	0/0	.000	-/7	0	-	1	-	-	20	.541
FERNSTEN, E.	28	1/3	.333	1/2	.500	-/5	0	-	5	-	-	3	.107
SMITH, P.	37	9/20	.450	0/0	.000	-/4	3	-	3	-	-	18	.486
SMITH, H.	25	3/4	.750	3/3	1.000	-/3	0	-	5	-	-	9	.360
BORO, J.	12	0/3	.000	0/0	.000	-/3	1	-	1	-	-	0	.000
COLEMAN, R.	17	0/2	.000	0/0	.000	-/1	2	-	1	-	-	0	.000
QUANSTROM, B.	7	3/4	.750	0/0	.000	-/2	1	-	0	-	-	6	.857
REDMOND, M.	4	1/3	.333	0/0	.000	-/0	0	-	0	-	-	2	.500
STYLES, T.	4	0/2	.000	0/0	.000	-/1	0	-	0	-	-	0	.000
Totals	200	27/60	.450	6/7	.857	-/31	9	-	19	-	-	60	.300

Team Rebounds: UCLA 4; San Francisco 2. Disqualified: San Francisco—Fernsten, H. Smith.

	1st Half	2nd Half	Final
UCLA	35	48	83
San Francisco	23	37	60

REGIONAL FINAL MIDEAST

Marquette (72) Coach: Al McGuire

	Min.	Total FG/FGA	Pct.	FT/FTA	Pct.	Reb. O/T	A	TO	PF	S	Blk	TP	PPM
ELLIS, M.	38	6/10	.600	3/4	.750	-/10	1	-	2	0	2	15	.395
TATUM, E.	31	4/8	.500	0/2	.000	-/5	1	-	2	2	2	8	.258
LUCAS, M.	29	4/10	.400	0/0	.000	-/7	0	-	5	0	0	8	.276
WALTON, L.	37	6/10	.600	1/2	.500	-/2	2	-	4	2	0	13	.351
WASHINGTON, M.	27	7/16	.438	3/5	.600	-/2	0	-	3	2	0	17	.630
DANIELS, E.	4	0/0	.000	0/0	.000	-/0	0	-	0	1	0	0	.000
CAMPBELL, R.	9	1/1	1.000	1/1	1.000	-/0	1	-	2	0	0	3	.333
HOMAN, J.	18	1/4	.250	2/2	1.000	-/7	0	-	2	0	0	4	.222
DELSMAN, D.	7	0/0	.000	4/4	1.000	-/1	0	-	1	0	0	4	.571
Totals	200	29/59	.492	14/20	.700	-/34	5	14	21	7	4	72	.360

Michigan (70) Coach: Johnny Orr

	Min.	Total FG/FGA	Pct.	FT/FTA	Pct.	Reb. O/T	A	TO	PF	S	Blk	TP	PPM
JOHNSON, J.	40	4/8	.500	0/0	.000	-/1	6	-	1	1	0	8	.200
GROTE, S.	32	5/13	.385	5/6	.833	-/3	1	-	5	1	0	15	.469
KUPEC, C.	40	3/10	.300	6/8	.750	-/7	1	-	3	0	1	12	.300
BRITT, W.	40	5/15	.333	2/2	1.000	-/9	6	-	4	1	0	12	.300
RUSSELL, R.	40	7/18	.389	7/9	.778	-/14	0	-	3	0	1	21	.525
WORRELL, L.	8	0/0	.000	2/2	1.000	-/2	1	-	2	0	0	2	.250
Totals	200	24/64	.375	22/27	.815	-/36	15	20	18	3	2	70	.350

Disqualified: Marquette—Lucas; Michigan—Grote. Technical fouls: Marquette—Coach McGuire 2.

	1st Half	2nd Half	Final
Marquette	37	35	72
Michigan	39	31	70

REGIONAL FINAL MIDWEST

Kansas (93)   Coach: Ted Owens

	Min.	Total FG/FGA	Pct.	FT/FTA	Pct.	Reb. O/T	A	TO	PF	S	Blk	TP	PPM
COOK, N.	-	5/7	.714	0/1	.000	-/7	3	0	2	0	1	10	-
MORNINGSTAR, R.	-	6/8	.750	4/5	.800	-/6	1	0	4	0	0	16	-
KNIGHT, D.	-	9/16	.563	1/2	.500	-/8	1	3	4	0	1	19	-
KIVISTO, T.	-	5/12	.417	3/4	.750	-/1	10	4	3	1	0	13	-
GREENLEE, D.	-	8/14	.571	2/2	1.000	-/2	8	3	3	0	0	18	-
SUTTLE, R.	-	5/10	.500	2/2	1.000	-/6	2	2	4	0	1	12	-
SMITH, T.	-	2/6	.333	1/2	.500	-/5	3	1	1	0	0	5	-
Totals	225	40/73	.548	13/18	.722	-/35	28	13	21	1	3	93	.413

Oral Roberts (90)   Coach: Ken Trickey

	Min.	Total FG/FGA	Pct.	FT/FTA	Pct.	Reb. O/T	A	TO	PF	S	Blk	TP	PPM
FOX, D.	-	4/8	.500	0/0	.000	-/5	1	0	4	0	0	8	-
WOODS, E.	-	4/7	.571	3/5	.600	-/6	0	0	5	0	0	11	-
MCDOUGALD, G.	-	5/11	.455	3/4	.750	-/6	1	3	4	0	0	13	-
MCCANTS, S.	-	8/24	.333	8/11	.727	-/10	7	5	2	0	0	24	-
BOSWELL, A.	-	7/23	.304	4/4	1.000	-/3	6	1	4	0	0	18	-
ROBERTS, A.	-	6/9	.667	0/0	.000	-/6	2	0	0	0	0	12	-
COLLINS, W.	-	2/6	.333	0/0	.000	-/7	0	0	3	0	0	4	-
Totals	225	36/88	.409	18/24	.750	-/43	17	9	22	0	0	90	.400

Team Rebounds: Kansas 9; Oral Roberts 9. Disqualified: Oral Roberts—Woods. Technical fouls: Kansas—bench.

	1st Half	2nd Half	1 OT	Final
Kansas	45	36	12	93
Oral Roberts	44	37	9	90

FINAL FOUR

North Carolina State (80)   Coach: Norm Sloan

	Min.	Total FG/FGA	Pct.	FT/FTA	Pct.	Reb. O/T	A	TO	PF	S	Blk	TP	PPM
STODDARD, T.	41	4/11	.364	1/2	.500	-/9	5	2	5	3	0	9	.220
THOMPSON, D.	45	12/25	.480	4/6	.667	-/10	2	5	3	1	2	28	.622
BURLESON, T.	42	9/20	.450	2/6	.333	-/14	0	3	4	2	2	20	.476
RIVERS, M.	50	3/8	.375	1/2	.500	-/2	4	1	3	0	0	7	.140
TOWE, M.	50	4/10	.400	4/4	1.000	-/2	3	2	4	0	0	12	.240
SPENCE, P.	19	2/3	.667	0/0	.000	-/5	1	0	0	0	0	4	.211
HAWKINS, G.	3	0/0	.000	0/0	.000	-/0	0	0	0	0	0	0	.000
Totals	250	34/77	.442	12/20	.600	-/42	15	13	19	8	4	80	.320

UCLA (77)   Coach: John Wooden

	Min.	Total FG/FGA	Pct.	FT/FTA	Pct.	Reb. O/T	A	TO	PF	S	Blk	TP	PPM
MEYERS, D.	42	6/9	.667	0/1	.000	-/8	1	2	4	1	0	12	.286
WILKES, J.	49	5/17	.294	5/5	1.000	-/7	0	4	5	0	0	15	.306
WALTON, B.	50	13/21	.619	3/3	1.000	-/18	4	6	2	0	0	29	.580
CURTIS, T.	45	4/8	.500	3/4	.750	-/5	2	2	5	1	0	11	.244
LEE, G.	50	4/11	.364	0/0	.000	-/4	10	5	2	2	0	8	.160
MCCARTER, A.	5	1/2	.500	0/0	.000	-/0	0	0	1	0	0	2	.400
JOHNSON, M.	9	0/3	.000	0/0	.000	-/0	0	0	0	0	0	0	.000
Totals	250	33/71	.465	11/13	.846	-/42	17	20	18	4	0	77	.308

Team Rebounds: N.C. State 2; UCLA 2. Disqualified: N.C. State—Stoddard; UCLA—Wilkes, Curtis.

	1st Half	2nd Half	1 OT	2 OT	Final
N.C. State	35	30	2	13	80
UCLA	35	30	2	10	77

Marquette (64)   Coach: Al McGuire

	Min.	Total FG/FGA	Pct.	FT/FTA	Pct.	Reb. O/T	A	TO	PF	S	Blk	TP	PPM
ELLIS, M.	39	2/9	.222	1/2	.500	-/10	0	2	3	2	1	5	.128
TATUM, E.	33	5/11	.455	4/6	.667	-/3	0	1	3	1	0	14	.424
LUCAS, M.	36	7/11	.636	4/4	1.000	-/14	2	3	2	1	4	18	.500
WALTON, L.	22	2/7	.286	3/4	.750	-/1	7	2	4	2	0	7	.318
WASHINGTON, M.	32	5/12	.417	6/11	.545	-/3	1	1	4	2	0	16	.500
DANIELS, E.	14	0/2	.000	0/0	.000	-/0	3	0	1	1	0	0	.000
CAMPBELL, R.	6	0/1	.000	0/0	.000	-/1	1	0	0	0	0	0	.000
HOMAN, J.	7	1/2	.500	0/0	.000	-/0	0	0	2	0	0	2	.286
DELSMAN, D.	9	0/1	.000	2/2	1.000	-/0	1	0	1	0	0	2	.222
VOLLMER, P.	0	0/0	.000	0/0	.000	-/0	0	0	0	0	0	0	-
JOHNSON, G.	0	0/0	.000	0/0	.000	-/0	0	0	0	0	0	0	-
BRENNAN, B.	0	0/0	.000	0/0	.000	-/0	0	0	0	0	0	0	-
BRYANT, J.	0	0/0	.000	0/0	.000	-/0	0	0	0	0	0	0	-
Totals	200	22/56	.393	20/29	.690	-/32	15	9	20	9	5	64	.320

Kansas (51)   Coach: Ted Owens

	Min.	Total FG/FGA	Pct.	FT/FTA	Pct.	Reb. O/T	A	TO	PF	S	Blk	TP	PPM
COOK, N.	35	1/3	.333	2/4	.500	-/5	1	4	5	1	0	4	.114
MORNINGSTAR, R.	40	5/13	.385	0/0	.000	-/5	2	2	4	0	0	10	.250
KNIGHT, D.	10	0/5	.000	0/0	.000	-/5	1	2	3	0	0	0	.000
KIVISTO, T.	40	2/7	.286	2/5	.400	-/2	9	5	4	1	0	6	.150
GREENLEE, D.	34	3/7	.429	0/0	.000	-/3	0	5	4	0	0	6	.176
SUTTLE, R.	28	8/13	.615	3/4	.750	-/9	1	1	2	0	4	19	.679
SMITH, T.	13	3/4	.750	0/0	.000	-/4	1	0	3	1	0	6	.462
Totals	200	22/52	.423	7/13	.538	-/33	15	19	25	3	4	51	.255

Team Rebounds: Marquette 6; Kansas 4. Disqualified: Kansas—Cook. Players who played 0 min. played less than 1 min. each.

	1st Half	2nd Half	Final
Marquette	23	41	64
Kansas	24	27	51

NATIONAL CHAMPIONSHIP

North Carolina State (76)   Coach: Norm Sloan

	Min.	Total FG / FGA	Pct.	FT / FTA	Pct.	Reb. O / T	A	TO	PF	S	Blk	TP	PPM
STODDARD, T.	26	3/ 4	.750	2/ 2	1.000	-/ 7	2	2	5	3	0	8	.308
THOMPSON, D.	40	7/12	.583	7/ 8	.875	-/ 7	2	2	3	3	1	21	.525
BURLESON, T.	36	6/ 9	.667	2/ 6	.333	-/11	0	6	4	1	7	14	.389
RIVERS, M.	40	4/ 9	.444	6/ 9	.667	-/ 2	5	4	2	3	0	14	.350
TOWE, M.	38	5/10	.500	6/ 7	.857	-/ 3	2	5	1	1	0	16	.421
SPENCE, P.	18	1/ 2	.500	1/ 2	.500	-/ 3	3	3	2	1	0	3	.167
MOELLER, M.	2	0/ 0	.000	0/ 0	.000	-/ 0	0	1	0	0	0	0	.000
Totals	200	26/46	.565	24/34	.706	-/33	14	23	17	12	8	76	.380

Marquette (64)   Coach: Al McGuire

	Min.	Total FG / FGA	Pct.	FT / FTA	Pct.	Reb. O / T	A	TO	PF	S	Blk	TP	PPM
ELLIS, M.	39	6/16	.375	0/ 0	.000	-/11	1	1	5	3	0	12	.308
TATUM, E.	20	2/ 7	.286	0/ 0	.000	-/ 3	1	3	4	0	1	4	.200
LUCAS, M.	40	7/13	.538	7/ 9	.778	-/13	0	2	4	0	1	21	.525
WALTON, L.	25	4/10	.400	0/ 0	.000	-/ 2	2	4	2	0	0	8	.320
WASHINGTON, M.	35	3/13	.231	5/ 8	.625	-/ 4	0	4	3	5	0	11	.314
DANIELS, E.	17	1/ 3	.333	1/ 2	.500	-/ 0	2	0	3	0	0	3	.176
CAMPBELL, R.	12	2/ 3	.667	0/ 0	.000	-/ 1	0	1	3	1	0	4	.333
HOMAN, J.	6	0/ 4	.000	1/ 2	.500	-/ 6	1	1	2	0	1	1	.167
DELSMAN, D.	5	0/ 0	.000	0/ 0	.000	-/ 0	0	2	2	0	0	0	.000
BRENNAN, B.	1	0/ 0	.000	0/ 0	.000	-/ 0	0	0	1	0	0	0	.000
Totals	200	25/69	.362	14/21	.667	-/40	7	18	29	9	3	64	.320

Team Rebounds: N.C. State 1; Marquette 3. Disqualified: N.C. State—Stoddard; Marquette—Ellis. Technical fouls: Marquette—Coach McGuire 2.

	1st Half	2nd Half	Final
N.C. State	39	37	76
Marquette	30	34	64

NATIONAL THIRD PLACE

UCLA (78)   Coach: John Wooden

	Min.	Total FG / FGA	Pct.	FT / FTA	Pct.	Reb. O / T	A	TO	PF	S	Blk	TP	PPM
MEYERS, D.	14	3/ 5	.600	2/ 2	1.000	-/ 1	1	0	3	0	0	8	.571
WILKES, J.	20	6/10	.600	0/ 0	.000	-/ 5	1	1	0	3	0	12	.600
WALTON, B.	20	3/ 3	1.000	0/ 3	.000	-/ 8	4	2	1	0	2	6	.300
CURTIS, T.	4	0/ 0	.000	0/ 0	.000	-/ 0	0	0	0	0	0	0	.000
LEE, G.	4	0/ 2	.000	0/ 0	.000	-/ 0	0	2	2	0	0	0	.000
TRGOVICH, P.	30	6/ 9	.667	2/ 2	1.000	-/ 2	2	3	1	0	1	14	.467
MCCARTER, A.	24	1/ 4	.250	2/ 2	1.000	-/ 4	6	4	1	1	0	4	.167
FRANKLIN, G.	13	1/ 2	.500	0/ 0	.000	-/ 3	1	0	1	0	0	2	.154
JOHNSON, M.	10	2/ 3	.667	0/ 2	.000	-/ 2	1	0	0	0	0	4	.400
DROLLINGER, R.	21	1/ 6	.167	5/ 8	.625	-/ 6	2	1	4	0	1	7	.333
WASHINGTON, R.	18	4/ 6	.667	0/ 1	.000	-/ 5	1	0	1	0	1	8	.444
WEBB, B.	11	4/ 7	.571	2/ 2	1.000	-/ 0	0	1	1	0	0	10	.909
SPILLANE, J.	6	0/ 1	.000	1/ 2	.500	-/ 1	1	1	2	1	0	1	.167
OLINDE, W.	5	1/ 1	1.000	0/ 0	.000	-/ 2	0	0	0	0	0	2	.400
Totals	200	32/59	.542	14/24	.583	-/39	20	15	17	5	5	78	.390

Kansas (61)   Coach: Ted Owens

	Min.	Total FG / FGA	Pct.	FT / FTA	Pct.	Reb. O / T	A	TO	PF	S	Blk	TP	PPM
COOK, N.	34	3/11	.273	3/ 4	.750	-/ 8	1	2	4	1	0	9	.265
MORNINGSTAR, R.	33	1/ 7	.143	1/ 2	.500	-/ 6	2	3	4	1	0	3	.091
KNIGHT, D.	26	5/10	.500	2/ 2	1.000	-/ 5	1	1	2	0	0	12	.462
KIVISTO, T.	38	2/ 5	.400	4/ 5	.800	-/ 3	5	3	3	2	0	8	.211
GREENLEE, D.	23	7/12	.583	3/ 3	1.000	-/ 3	2	1	2	1	0	17	.739
SUTTLE, R.	22	2/11	.182	0/ 0	.000	-/ 7	0	4	5	0	0	4	.182
SMITH, T.	19	3/ 7	.429	0/ 0	.000	-/ 4	0	1	4	0	0	6	.316
VON, M.	3	0/ 2	.000	0/ 0	.000	-/ 2	0	0	0	0	0	0	.000
TAYNOR, D.	2	1/ 4	.250	0/ 0	.000	-/ 0	0	0	0	0	0	2	1.000
Totals	200	24/69	.348	13/16	.813	-/38	11	15	24	5	0	61	.305

Team Rebounds: UCLA 2; Kansas 3. Disqualified: Kansas—Suttle. Technical fouls: UCLA—Drollinger.

	1st Half	2nd Half	Final
UCLA	31	47	78
Kansas	38	23	61

REGIONAL THIRD PLACE EAST

Providence (95)   Coach: Dave Gavitt

	Min.	Total FG / FGA	Pct.	FT / FTA	Pct.	Reb. O / T	A	TO	PF	S	Blk	TP	PPM
MCANDREW, M.	25	2/ 3	.667	0/ 0	.000	-/ 5	2	3	3	1	0	4	.160
COOPER, B.	28	7/10	.700	2/ 4	.500	-/ 6	0	3	3	2	0	16	.571
BARNES, M.	38	8/20	.400	2/ 2	1.000	-/21	4	3	4	2	2	18	.474
BELLO, G.	21	5/ 8	.625	0/ 0	.000	-/ 3	1	2	1	0	0	10	.476
STACOM, K.	38	8/22	.364	2/ 5	.400	-/ 7	8	2	0	2	0	18	.474
BAKER, A.	14	2/ 3	.667	3/ 4	.750	-/ 0	0	3	2	0	0	7	.500
SANTOS, E.	21	5/ 6	.833	2/ 2	1.000	-/ 2	0	1	1	0	1	12	.571
HASSETT, J.	12	4/ 7	.571	2/ 2	1.000	-/ 2	0	0	0	0	0	10	.833
DUNPHY, R.	1	0/ 0	.000	0/ 0	.000	-/ 0	0	0	0	0	0	0	.000
ALLQUIST, B.	1	0/ 1	.000	0/ 0	.000	-/ 1	0	0	0	0	0	0	.000
WALTERS, T.	1	0/ 1	.000	0/ 0	.000	-/ 0	0	0	0	0	0	0	.000
Totals	200	41/81	.506	13/19	.684	-/47	15	17	14	7	3	95	.475

Furman (83)   Coach: Joe Williams

	Min.	Total FG / FGA	Pct.	FT / FTA	Pct.	Reb. O / T	A	TO	PF	S	Blk	TP	PPM
MAYES, C.	32	9/21	.429	2/ 4	.500	-/13	2	5	3	0	0	20	.625
LYNCH, C.	29	7/10	.700	1/ 1	1.000	-/ 3	2	4	0	0	0	15	.517
LEONARD, F.	35	4/16	.250	3/ 3	1.000	-/ 9	1	1	4	0	1	11	.314
KELLEY, E.	33	5/12	.417	0/ 0	.000	-/ 6	3	4	1	0	0	10	.303
GRUMM, B.	37	8/16	.500	1/ 2	.500	-/ 2	5	2	3	2	0	17	.459
BIERLEY, B.	6	1/ 2	.500	2/ 2	1.000	-/ 2	0	0	1	1	1	4	.667
HILL, B.	7	0/ 3	.000	0/ 0	.000	-/ 1	0	3	1	0	0	0	.000
HALL, M.	18	2/11	.182	0/ 0	.000	-/ 9	0	1	3	2	1	4	.222
CLARK, G.	3	1/ 3	.333	0/ 1	.000	-/ 1	2	0	2	0	0	2	.667
Totals	200	37/94	.394	9/13	.692	-/46	15	20	18	5	3	83	.415

Team Rebounds: Providence 2; Furman 5. Disqualified: None.

	1st Half	2nd Half	Final
Providence	47	48	95
Furman	37	46	83

REGIONAL THIRD PLACE WEST

New Mexico (66)   Coach: Norm Ellenberger

	Min.	Total FG/FGA	Pct.	FT/FTA	Pct.	Reb. O/T	A	TO	PF	S	Blk	TP	PPM
HARDIN, B.	-	7/14	.500	0/ 2	.000	-/12	-	-	3	-	-	14	-
SAIERS, M.	-	4/ 7	.571	3/ 4	.750	-/ 6	-	-	1	-	-	11	-
HAGINS, B.	-	1/ 2	.500	1/ 2	.500	-/ 4	-	-	2	-	-	3	-
NAVA, G.	-	5/ 7	.714	0/ 1	.000	-/ 3	-	-	0	-	-	10	-
TAYLOR, W.	-	6/14	.429	2/ 3	.667	-/ 3	-	-	3	-	-	14	-
BATTLE, B.	-	0/ 0	.000	0/ 0	.000	-/ 2	-	-	0	-	-	0	-
POKORSKI, R.	-	2/ 3	.667	3/ 7	.429	-/ 1	-	-	3	-	-	7	-
PATTERSON, M.	-	2/ 4	.500	2/ 3	.667	-/ 6	-	-	3	-	-	6	-
KING, P.	-	0/ 3	.000	0/ 0	.000	-/ 2	-	-	0	-	-	0	-
TOPPERT, B.	-	0/ 6	.000	1/ 2	.500	-/ 2	-	-	0	-	-	1	-
DAVIS, D.	-	0/ 1	.000	0/ 0	.000	-/ 3	-	-	0	-	-	0	-
Totals	200	27/61	.443	12/24	.500	-/44	-	-	15	-	-	66	.330

Dayton (61)   Coach: Don Donoher

	Min.	Total FG/FGA	Pct.	FT/FTA	Pct.	Reb. O/T	A	TO	PF	S	Blk	TP	PPM
SYLVESTER, M.	-	4/18	.222	2/ 5	.400	-/ 6	-	-	4	-	-	10	-
ELIJAH, A.	-	6/10	.600	0/ 0	.000	-/ 9	-	-	4	-	-	12	-
VONLEHMAN, J.	-	0/ 1	.000	0/ 0	.000	-/ 4	-	-	5	-	-	0	-
SMITH, D.	-	10/20	.500	2/ 2	1.000	-/ 4	-	-	4	-	-	22	-
DAVIS, J.	-	3/10	.300	2/ 2	1.000	-/ 2	-	-	4	-	-	8	-
FISHER, J.	-	1/ 5	.200	3/ 4	.750	-/ 3	-	-	1	-	-	5	-
TESTERMAN, J.	-	0/ 0	.000	0/ 0	.000	-/ 0	-	-	1	-	-	0	-
HOLLAND, J.	-	2/ 2	1.000	0/ 0	.000	-/ 1	-	-	0	-	-	4	-
Totals	200	26/66	.394	9/13	.692	-/29	-	-	23	-	-	61	.305

Team Rebounds: New Mexico 3; Dayton 4. Disqualified: Dayton—Von Lehman.

	1st Half	2nd Half	Final
New Mexico	26	40	66
Dayton	22	39	61

REGIONAL THIRD PLACE MIDWEST

Creighton (80)   Coach: Eddie Sutton

	Min.	Total FG/FGA	Pct.	FT/FTA	Pct.	Reb. O/T	A	TO	PF	S	Blk	TP	PPM
HARMON, G.	-	7/19	.368	8/ 8	1.000	-/ 8	5	0	4	-	-	22	-
BROOKINS, D.	-	9/12	.750	1/ 1	1.000	-/ 7	0	2	2	-	-	19	-
HECK, M.	-	4/ 7	.571	0/ 0	.000	-/ 7	0	0	3	-	-	8	-
BOBIK, R.	-	2/ 7	.286	0/ 1	.000	-/ 3	8	2	4	-	-	4	-
BUTLER, C.	-	2/ 5	.400	0/ 0	.000	-/ 3	3	0	1	-	-	4	-
WEUBBEN, T.	-	5/ 6	.833	4/ 6	.667	-/ 3	0	3	2	-	-	14	-
ANDERSON, T.	-	2/ 3	.667	1/ 2	.500	-/ 2	5	1	1	-	-	5	-
SMITH, R.	-	1/ 2	.500	0/ 0	.000	-/ 2	1	0	2	-	-	2	-
PIETRO, B.	-	1/ 1	1.000	0/ 0	.000	-/ 0	0	0	0	-	-	2	-
MASSIE, J.	-	0/ 0	.000	0/ 0	.000	-/ 0	0	0	0	-	-	0	-
Totals	200	33/62	.532	14/18	.778	-/35	22	8	19	-	-	80	.400

REGIONAL THIRD PLACE MIDEAST

Notre Dame (118)   Coach: Digger Phelps

	Min.	Total FG/FGA	Pct.	FT/FTA	Pct.	Reb. O/T	A	TO	PF	S	Blk	TP	PPM
DANTLEY, A.	30	12/16	.750	5/ 5	1.000	-/10	0	3	3	1	0	29	.967
NOVAK, G.	35	8/15	.533	0/ 0	.000	-/ 6	4	4	3	2	0	16	.457
SHUMATE, J.	35	11/14	.786	8/ 8	1.000	-/ 7	1	4	4	1	2	30	.857
BROKAW, G.	33	8/12	.667	4/ 4	1.000	-/ 5	6	0	1	1	1	20	.606
CLAY, D.	28	3/ 4	.750	0/ 0	.000	-/ 3	8	1	0	0	0	6	.214
PATERNO, B.	8	3/10	.300	2/ 2	1.000	-/ 4	0	0	0	0	0	8	1.000
MARTIN, R.	12	0/ 1	.000	0/ 0	.000	-/ 3	1	1	1	1	0	0	.000
CROTTY, P.	5	0/ 3	.000	0/ 0	.000	-/ 1	0	0	1	0	0	0	.000
KUZMICZ, D.	7	0/ 2	.000	0/ 0	.000	-/ 0	0	0	1	1	0	0	.000
KNIGHT, T.	5	3/ 4	.750	0/ 0	.000	-/ 2	0	0	4	0	1	6	1.200
SCHUCKMAN, M.	2	1/ 1	1.000	1/ 2	.500	-/ 1	0	0	0	0	0	3	1.500
Totals	200	49/82	.598	20/21	.952	-/42	20	13	18	7	4	118	.590

Vanderbilt (88)   Coach: Roy Skinner

	Min.	Total FG/FGA	Pct.	FT/FTA	Pct.	Reb. O/T	A	TO	PF	S	Blk	TP	PPM
FOSNES, J.	31	9/15	.600	2/ 3	.667	-/10	1	3	3	1	1	20	.645
FORD, J.	32	4/12	.333	1/ 4	.250	-/ 2	2	0	0	1	0	9	.281
VAN, B.	31	2/ 6	.333	2/ 2	1.000	-/ 5	6	1	2	0	3	6	.194
FEHER, B.	26	1/ 7	.143	2/ 2	1.000	-/ 5	1	0	3	0	0	4	.154
COMPTON, T.	17	7/14	.500	1/ 1	1.000	-/ 1	0	1	2	1	0	15	.882
FOWLER, L.	21	6/14	.429	0/ 0	.000	-/ 5	2	2	2	0	0	12	.571
LIGON, B.	14	4/ 9	.444	0/ 0	.000	-/ 2	1	2	2	0	0	8	.571
CHESS, B.	8	0/ 3	.000	1/ 2	.500	-/ 2	2	0	0	0	0	1	.125
MOORE, M.	12	4/ 6	.667	3/ 4	.750	-/ 2	1	3	3	0	0	11	.917
NORTON, J.	4	0/ 0	.000	0/ 0	.000	-/ 0	0	0	0	0	0	0	.000
YOUNG, S.	2	0/ 1	.000	0/ 0	.000	-/ 2	0	0	0	0	0	0	.000
MCSWAIN, W.	1	0/ 0	.000	2/ 2	1.000	-/ 0	0	0	2	0	0	2	2.000
DECOURCY, N.	1	0/ 1	.000	0/ 0	.000	-/ 0	0	0	0	0	0	0	.000
Totals	200	37/88	.420	14/20	.700	-/36	16	12	19	3	4	88	.440

Team Rebounds: Notre Dame 6; Vanderbilt 4. Disqualified: None. Technical fouls: Vanderbilt—bench.

	1st Half	2nd Half	Final
Notre Dame	60	58	118
Vanderbilt	44	44	88

Louisville (71)   Coach: Denny Crum

	Min.	Total FG/FGA	Pct.	FT/FTA	Pct.	Reb. O/T	A	TO	PF	S	Blk	TP	PPM
MURPHY, A.	-	6/14	.429	1/ 2	.500	-/ 0	0	0	4	-	-	13	-
BUTLER, B.	-	2/ 8	.250	3/ 4	.750	-/ 2	1	1	2	-	-	7	-
COX, W.	-	3/ 6	.500	2/ 2	1.000	-/ 8	0	3	4	-	-	8	-
HOWARD, T.	-	3/ 4	.750	3/ 3	1.000	-/ 1	3	1	3	-	-	9	-
BRIDGEMAN, J.	-	5/13	.385	3/ 5	.600	-/ 8	6	0	1	-	-	13	-
WHITFIELD, I.	-	3/ 8	.375	1/ 2	.500	-/ 1	1	2	0	-	-	7	-
BUNTON, S.	-	0/ 1	.000	0/ 0	.000	-/ 2	0	1	4	-	-	0	-
HARMON, B.	-	0/ 0	.000	0/ 0	.000	-/ 0	0	0	1	-	-	0	-
BROWN, D.	-	5/ 6	.833	2/ 2	1.000	-/ 1	3	1	1	-	-	12	-
PROTENIC, J.	-	1/ 1	1.000	0/ 0	.000	-/ 1	0	0	1	-	-	2	-
WAYNE, J.	-	0/ 0	.000	0/ 0	.000	-/ 1	0	2	0	-	-	0	-
KINNAIRD, T.	-	0/ 1	.000	0/ 0	.000	-/ 0	0	0	0	-	-	0	-
Totals	200	28/62	.452	15/20	.750	-/25	14	11	21	-	-	71	.355

Team Rebounds: Creighton 5; Louisville 7. Disqualified: None.

	1st Half	2nd Half	Final
Creighton	38	42	80
Louisville	38	33	71

✪ ALL-STAR TEAMS ✪

ALL TOURNAMENT

TOM BURLESON	N.C. STATE
MAURICE LUCAS	MARQUETTE
MONTE TOWE	N.C. STATE
★ DAVID THOMPSON	N.C. STATE
BILL WALTON	UCLA

EAST REGIONAL

★ TOM BURLESON	N.C. STATE
BRUCE GRIMM	FURMAN
BILL KNIGHT	PITTSBURGH
★ DAVID THOMPSON	N.C. STATE
MONTE TOWE	N.C. STATE

★ Most Outstanding Player(s)

✪ INDIVIDUAL RECORDS ✪

SCORING

Most points in a single game
1	DAVID THOMPSON, N.C. STATE (vs. PROVIDENCE)	40
2	MIKE SYLVESTER, DAYTON (vs. UCLA)	36
2	CAMPY RUSSELL, MICHIGAN (vs. NOTRE DAME)	36
4	BILL KNIGHT, PITTSBURGH (vs. FURMAN)	34
4	JOHN SHUMATE, NOTRE DAME (vs. MICHIGAN)	34

Most total points in the tournament
1	DAVID THOMPSON, N.C. STATE	97
2	JOHN SHUMATE, NOTRE DAME	86
3	MAURICE LUCAS, MARQUETTE	80
4	BILL WALTON, UCLA	79
4	SAM MCCANTS, ORAL ROBERTS	79

Highest scoring average (minimum 2 games)
1	JOHN SHUMATE, NOTRE DAME (86-3)	28.67
2	CAMPY RUSSELL, MICHIGAN (57-2)	28.50
3	SAM MCCANTS, ORAL ROBERTS (79-3)	26.33
4	MIKE SYLVESTER, DAYTON (76-3)	25.33
5	DAVID THOMPSON, N.C. STATE (97-4)	24.25

FIELD GOALS

Most field goals in a single game
1	DAVID THOMPSON, N.C. STATE (vs. PROVIDENCE)	16
1	CAMPY RUSSELL, MICHIGAN (vs. NOTRE DAME)	16
3	JOHN SHUMATE, NOTRE DAME (vs. MICHIGAN)	14
4	7 tied for fourth place.	

Most total field goals in the tournament
1	DAVID THOMPSON, N.C. STATE	38
2	BILL WALTON, UCLA	36
3	JOHN SHUMATE, NOTRE DAME	35
4	MAURICE LUCAS, MARQUETTE	32
5	3 tied for fifth place.	

Most field goal attempts in a single game
1	SAM MCCANTS, ORAL ROBERTS (vs. LOUISVILLE)	33
2	CAMPY RUSSELL, MICHIGAN (vs. NOTRE DAME)	32
3	JAMES WILLIAMS, AUSTIN PEAY (vs. NOTRE DAME)	31
4	DAVID THOMPSON, N.C. STATE (vs. PROVIDENCE)	29
5	KEITH WILKES, UCLA (vs. SAN FRANCISCO)	28

Most total field goal attempts in the tournament
1	SAM MCCANTS, ORAL ROBERTS	84
2	KEITH WILKES, UCLA	70
2	DAVID THOMPSON, N.C. STATE	70
2	MAURICE LUCAS, MARQUETTE	70
5	TOM BURLESON, N.C. STATE	67

Highest field goal percentage in a single game (minimum 10 attempts)
1	JOHN SHUMATE, NOTRE DAME (vs. VANDERBILT) (11-14)	.786
2	KEVIN RESTANI, SAN FRANCISCO (vs. UCLA) (10-13)	.769
3	ADRIAN DANTLEY, NOTRE DAME (vs. VANDERBILT) (12-16)	.750
4	DOUG BROOKINS, CREIGHTON (vs. LOUISVILLE) (9-12)	.750
5	MAURICE ELLIS, MARQUETTE (vs. OHIO) (8-11)	.727

Highest field goal percentage in the tournament (minimum 20 attempts)
1	JOHN SHUMATE, NOTRE DAME (35-50)	.700
2	KEVIN RESTANI, SAN FRANCISCO (17-25)	.680
3	MARK SAIERS, NEW MEXICO (18-29)	.621
4	BOB COOPER, PROVIDENCE (21-34)	.618
5	BILL WALTON, UCLA (36-59)	.610

FREE THROWS

Most free throws in a single game
1	MIKE SYLVESTER, DAYTON (vs. UCLA)	12
1	WESLEY COX, LOUISVILLE (vs. ORAL ROBERTS)	12
3	BILL KNIGHT, PITTSBURGH (vs. FURMAN)	10
4	B. GRIMM, FURMAN (vs. PITTSBURGH)	9
5	6 tied for fifth place.	

Most total free throws in the tournament
1	MONTE TOWE, N.C. STATE	22
2	DAVID THOMPSON, N.C. STATE	21
2	SAM MCCANTS, ORAL ROBERTS	21
4	MIKE SYLVESTER, DAYTON	18
5	2 tied for fifth place.	

Most free throws attempted in a single game
1	MIKE SYLVESTER, DAYTON (vs. UCLA)	13
2	WESLEY COX, LOUISVILLE (vs. ORAL ROBERTS)	12
3	4 tied for third place.	

Most free throws attempted in the tournament
1	DAVID THOMPSON, N.C. STATE	27
1	SAM MCCANTS, ORAL ROBERTS	27
3	MARCUS WASHINGTON, MARQUETTE	26
4	TOM BURLESON, N.C. STATE	25
5	MONTE TOWE, N.C. STATE	24

Highest free throw percentage in a single game (minimum 7 attempts)
1	WESLEY COX, LOUISVILLE (vs. ORAL ROBERTS) (12-12)	1.000
2	TOM BURLESON, N.C. STATE (vs. PITTSBURGH) (8-8)	1.000
2	JOHN SHUMATE, NOTRE DAME (vs. VANDERBILT) (8-8)	1.000
2	GENE HARMON, CREIGHTON (vs. LOUISVILLE) (8-8)	1.000
5	MONTE TOWE, N.C. STATE (vs. PITTSBURGH) (7-7)	1.000

Highest free throw percentage in the tournament (minimum 15 attempts)
1	MONTE TOWE, N.C. STATE (22-24)	.917
2	JOHN SHUMATE, NOTRE DAME (16-18)	.889
3	MAURICE LUCAS, MARQUETTE (16-19)	.842
4	MIKE SYLVESTER, DAYTON (18-22)	.818
5	BILL KNIGHT, PITTSBURGH (12-15)	.800

REBOUNDS

Most rebounds in a single game
1	TOM BURLESON, N.C. STATE (vs. PROVIDENCE)	24

2	MARVIN BARNES, PROVIDENCE (vs. FURMAN)	
		21
3	BILL WALTON, UCLA (vs. DAYTON)	19
4	BILL WALTON, UCLA (vs. N.C. STATE)	18
4	CAMPY RUSSELL, MICHIGAN (vs. NOTRE DAME)	
		18

Most total rebounds in the tournament
1	TOM BURLESON, N.C. STATE	61
2	MAURICE LUCAS, MARQUETTE	60
3	BILL WALTON, UCLA	54
4	MARVIN BARNES, PROVIDENCE	51
5	MAURICE ELLIS, MARQUETTE	49

Most rebounds per game (minimum 2 games)
1	MARVIN BARNES, PROVIDENCE (51-3)	17.00

2	CAMPY RUSSELL, MICHIGAN (32-2)	16.00
3	TOM BURLESON, N.C. STATE (61-4)	15.25
4	BILL WALTON, UCLA (54-4)	13.50
5	CLYDE MAYES, FURMAN (37-3)	12.33

ASSISTS

Most assists in a single game
1	RALPH BOBIK, CREIGHTON (vs. TEXAS)	12
2	TOM KIVISTO, KANSAS (vs. ORAL ROBERTS)	10
2	GREG LEE, UCLA (vs. N.C. STATE)	10
2	SAM MCCANTS, ORAL ROBERTS (vs. LOUISVILLE)	10
2	TOM KIVISTO, KANSAS (vs. CREIGHTON)	10

Most total assists in the tournament
1	TOM KIVISTO, KANSAS	34
2	DWIGHT CLAY, NOTRE DAME	25
3	SAM MCCANTS, ORAL ROBERTS	24
4	RALPH BOBIK, CREIGHTON	20
5	3 tied for fifth place.	

Most assists per game (minimum 2 appearances)
1	TOM KIVISTO, KANSAS (34-4)	8.50
2	DWIGHT CLAY, NOTRE DAME (25-3)	8.33
3	SAM MCCANTS, ORAL ROBERTS (24-3)	8.00
4	RALPH BOBIK, CREIGHTON (20-3)	6.67
5	WAYMAN BRITT, MICHIGAN (10-2)	5.00

✪ TEAM RECORDS ✪

SCORING

Most points in a single game
1	NOTRE DAME (vs. VANDERBILT)	118
2	UCLA (vs. DAYTON)	111
3	NOTRE DAME (vs. AUSTIN PEAY)	108

Most total points in the tournament
1	MARQUETTE	354
2	UCLA	349
3	N.C. STATE	348

Highest scoring average (minimum 2 games)
1	NOTRE DAME (294-3)	98.00
2	ORAL ROBERTS (272-3)	90.67
3	UCLA (349-4)	87.25

FIELD GOALS

Most field goals in a single game
1	UCLA (vs. DAYTON)	51
2	NOTRE DAME (vs. AUSTIN PEAY)	50
3	NOTRE DAME (vs. VANDERBILT)	49

Most total field goals in the tournament
1	UCLA	154
2	MARQUETTE	144
3	N.C. STATE	129

Most field goals attempted in a single game
1	ORAL ROBERTS (vs. LOUISVILLE)	99
2	UCLA (vs. DAYTON)	97
3	FURMAN (vs. PROVIDENCE)	94

Most total field goals attempted in the tournament
1	MARQUETTE	318
2	UCLA	301
3	N.C. STATE	290

Highest field goal percentage in a single game
1	NOTRE DAME (vs. AUSTIN PEAY) (50-83)	.602
2	NOTRE DAME (vs. VANDERBILT) (49-82)	.598
3	DAYTON (vs. CAL. ST. LA) (35-60)	.583

Highest field goal percentage in the tournament (minimum 2 games)
1	NOTRE DAME (128-240)	.534
2	CREIGHTON (92-173)	.532
3	UCLA (154-301)	.512

FREE THROWS

Most free throws in a single game
1	N.C. STATE (vs. PITTSBURGH)	30
2	N.C. STATE (vs. MARQUETTE)	24
2	N.C. STATE (vs. PROVIDENCE)	24

Most total free throws in the tournament
1	N.C. STATE	90
2	MARQUETTE	66
3	DAYTON	47

Most free throws attempted in a single game
1	N.C. STATE (vs. PITTSBURGH)	37
2	N.C. STATE (vs. MARQUETTE)	34
3	N.C. STATE (vs. PROVIDENCE)	31

Most total free throws attempted in the tournament
1	N.C. STATE	122
2	MARQUETTE	93
3	UCLA	66

Highest free throw percentage in a single game
1	VANDERBILT (vs. MARQUETTE) (21-22)	.955
2	NOTRE DAME (vs. VANDERBILT) (20-21)	.952
3	MARQUETTE (vs. VANDERBILT) (13-14)	.929

Highest free throw percentage in the tournament (minimum 2 games)
1	SAN FRANCISCO (14-16)	.875
2	VANDERBILT (35-42)	.833
3	DAYTON (47-59)	.797

Fewest free throws in a single game
1	S. CAROLINA (vs. FURMAN)	3
1	TEXAS (vs. CREIGHTON)	3
3	2 tied for third place.	

Lowest free throw percentage in a single game
1	SYRACUSE (vs. ORAL ROBERTS) (6-18)	.333
2	S. CAROLINA (vs. FURMAN) (3-7)	.429
3	PITTSBURGH (vs. ST. JOSEPH'S) (6-13)	.462

Lowest free throw percentage in the tournament (minimum 2 games)
1	PITTSBURGH (27-45)	.600
2	UCLA (41-66)	.621
3	NEW MEXICO (28-43)	.651

REBOUNDS

Most rebounds in a single game
1	N.C. STATE (vs. PROVIDENCE)	52
2	UCLA (vs. DAYTON)	50
3	2 tied for third place.	

Most rebounds per game (minimum 2 games)
1	ORAL ROBERTS (139-3)	46.33
2	PROVIDENCE (133-3)	44.33
2	NOTRE DAME (133-3)	44.33

ASSISTS

Most assists in a single game
1	NOTRE DAME (vs. AUSTIN PEAY)	30
2	KANSAS (vs. ORAL ROBERTS)	28
3	PROVIDENCE (vs. PENNSYLVANIA)	24

Most assists per game (minimum 2 games)
1	NOTRE DAME (65-3)	21.67
2	KANSAS (73-4)	18.25
3	CREIGHTON (51-3)	17.00

1975

| FIRST ROUND | REGIONAL SEMIFINAL | REGIONAL FINAL | FINAL FOUR | REGIONAL FINAL | REGIONAL SEMIFINAL | FIRST ROUND |

WEST

UCLA 103 (ot)

Michigan 91

UCLA 67

Montana 69

Utah St. 63

Montana 64

UCLA 89

Arizona St. 97

Alabama 94

Arizona St. 84

UNLV 90

San Diego St. 80

UNLV 81

Arizona St. 75

UCLA 75 (ot)

UCLA 92
Kentucky 85

EAST

Syracuse 87 (ot)

La Salle 83

Syracuse 78

N. Carolina 93

New Mexico St. 69

N. Carolina 76

Syracuse 95 (ot)

Kansas St. 69

Pennsylvania 62

Kansas St. 74

Boston College 82

Furman 76

Boston College 65

Kansas St. 87

Syracuse 79

MIDWEST

Maryland 83

Creighton 79

Maryland 83

Notre Dame 77

Kansas 71

Notre Dame 71

Maryland 82

Cincinnati 87

Texas A&M 79

Cincinnati 63

Louisville 91

Rutgers 78

Louisville 78

Louisville 96

Louisville 74

Kentucky 95

MIDEAST

Indiana 78

UTEP 53

Indiana 81

Oregon St. 78

Middle Tenn. St. 67

Oregon St. 71

Indiana 90

Central Mich. 77

Georgetown 75

Central Mich. 73

Kentucky 76

Marquette 54

Kentucky 90

Kentucky 92

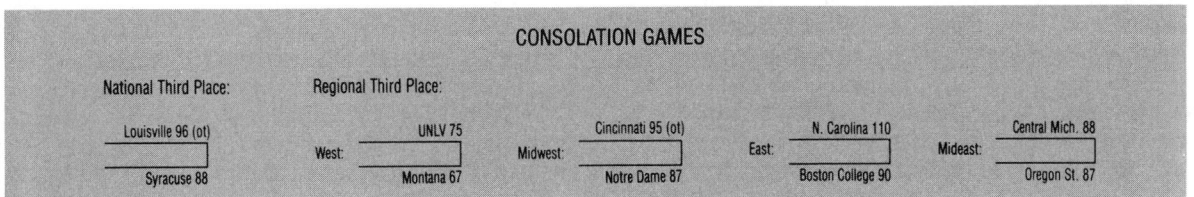

CONSOLATION GAMES

National Third Place:

Louisville 96 (ot)

Syracuse 88

Regional Third Place:

West:
UNLV 75
Montana 67

Midwest:
Cincinnati 95 (ot)
Notre Dame 87

East:
N. Carolina 110
Boston College 90

Mideast:
Central Mich. 88
Oregon St. 87

In 1975, an era ended in college basketball and another began. A group of young coaches began to make their mark on the game, and the greatest of them all said goodbye. But before John Wooden passed the torch, he worked his magic one more time. The wizard of Westwood pulled one last rabbit out of his hat.

In his third season at Georgetown, John Thompson worked a miracle by leading the Hoyas to the NCAAs for the first time in over thirty years. But it would still be some years before Thompson and his team would contend for the title.

The best team in the country was, without a doubt, 35-year-old Bob Knight's Indiana Hoosiers. They finished the regular season undefeated despite a broken arm suffered by their high scorer, Scott May, in the last weeks of the season. The Hoosiers were disciplined, motivated, known for their aggressiveness on defense and their patience on offense. But it was not to be Bob Knight's year; he would have to wait for his national championship.

In Lexington, Kentucky, Joe B. Hall, who had taken over the reins as Wildcat coach when Adolph Rupp retired in 1972, brought his team to the regional final against Indiana. Attempting to give his Hoosiers a boost, Knight penciled Scott May into the line-up. It was May's first start since he broke his arm, and the rust showed: the Indiana star was out of shape and out of the flow. Knight unintentionally upset his team's delicate balance: not only was the high-scoring forward ineffective, but John Laskowski, who had done a creditable job starting in May's place, received a signal that his coach did not have confidence in him. Despite a heroic 33 point, 23 rebound performance by Hoosier center Kent Benson, Kentucky pulled off the upset of the year and landed in the Final Four.

The Wildcats' semifinal opponent, Syracuse, also reached the Final Four in an upset, when they tied Kansas State at the buzzer and rode a 19-point overtime past the K-Staters. Against Kentucky, however, a rash of turnovers, a defense that failed to adjust to the Wildcats' running game, and Kentucky's bruisingly physical style all contributed to the Orangemen's swift demise.

Across the state from Lexington, in Louisville, John Wooden's former assistant Denny Crum had finally built a team in his own image. Unlike the Cardinals' 1972 Final Four team, which was recruited by his predecessor, this group of players was brought to Louisville by Crum himself, and they reflected his coaching philosophy. The Cardinals had a relatively easy time getting through their regional, winning three games by an average of 14 points.

Meanwhile, at UCLA, the last great stars of the Wooden dynasty—Bill Walton and Keith Wilkes—were gone. If the Bruins were to win again, it would have to be with speed, guile, emotion, and a little bit of luck.

In the opening round, UCLA barely got by unranked Michigan. With the score tied and just four seconds left,

Wolverine C. J. Kupek missed a shot that would have put his team in the regionals. In overtime, the Bruins grabbed the lead and Wooden immediately took a page from Dean Smith's coaching book; he protected his advantage with the four-corner offense. After a rough ride through a relatively weak regional, UCLA made it to the Final Four for the ninth consecutive year.

The Bruins traveled to San Diego, where they met the Louisville Cardinals in a tournament classic. Louisville surged to an early 27-18 lead, beating the Bruins downcourt and converting numerous fast-break opportunities. But UCLA came back, and by intermission the Cardinal lead had been cut to 4. The second half was tight all the way. With 1:06 left to play, Cardinal guard Phil Bond was fouled. He hit the first, raised his finger to signal that Louisville was No. 1, then hit the second. The Cardinals led by 4. UCLA's Dave Meyers drove down the lane, but Bill Bunton blocked his shot. Meyers put the ball up again, and Bunton once more turned it away. Finally Bruin Richard Washington picked up the ball and shot. With 48 seconds left, he was fouled by Bunton. After the two UCLA free throws, the lead was 2. Marques Johnson stole the inbounds pass and followed a teammate's miss, tying the score at 65. And, with time running out, Louisville's Junior Bridgeman missed the potential game-winner.

Louisville led from the first minute of overtime. With fifty seconds left and the Cardinals holding a slim 74-73 lead, Denny Crum called for a time-out. He ordered his team to go into a four-corners offense, and inserted reserve guard Terry Howard, an excellent ball handler and free-throw shooter, into the line-up. With twenty seconds left, Howard was fouled and went to the line for a one-and-one, and the chance to put the game away. Howard, who had started for the Cardinals the previous two years, was perfect at the line in 1974–75, hitting 28 straight for the season. "I thought it was in," said Howard, but instead fortune smiled on UCLA; Howard's shot bounced off the rim and Washington came down with the rebound. As the clock ran down, the pass came to Washington on the baseline. Bunton got a hand on the ball, but he tipped it over to Washington, who hit a 12-footer to win the game.

Afterward, UCLA's Dave Meyers said it was "like looking in a mirror and seeing yourself. I thought there were two UCLA teams on the court." The heartbroken Louisville players wept in their locker room, and Denny Crum said he could not have been prouder of their effort. John Wooden faced the press and announced that the championship contest against Kentucky would be his last. The man who built the UCLA dynasty was retiring.

On March 31, 1975, in the San Diego Arena, UCLA, using only six men, beat Kentucky for the title, thus bringing John Wooden one last victory in his final game. And when it was all over, 15,153 people stood and cheered for what seemed like an eternity.

FIRST ROUND WEST

UCLA (103)   Coach: John Wooden

	Min.	Total FG / FGA	Pct.	FT / FTA	Pct.	Reb. O / T	A	TO	PF	S	Blk	TP	PPM
MEYERS, D.	37	9/18	.500	8/10	.800	-/12	2	2	4	1	0	26	.703
JOHNSON, M.	43	9/20	.450	4/ 4	1.000	-/13	0	1	4	1	0	22	.512
WASHINGTON, R.	39	11/14	.786	0/ 1	.000	-/17	3	2	4	0	0	22	.564
MCCARTER, A.	39	0/ 7	.000	4/ 5	.800	-/ 2	7	3	2	2	0	4	.103
TRGOVICH, P.	43	8/16	.500	1/ 2	.500	-/ 3	2	1	4	0	0	17	.395
SPILLANE, J.	8	2/ 7	.286	0/ 0	.000	-/ 1	1	1	1	0	0	4	.500
OLINDE, W.	1	0/ 0	.000	0/ 0	.000	-/ 0	0	0	1	0	0	0	.000
TOWNSEND, R.	1	0/ 1	.000	0/ 0	.000	-/ 1	0	0	0	1	0	0	.000
DROLLINGER, R.	13	3/ 3	1.000	2/ 4	.500	-/ 3	1	0	0	0	2	8	.615
CORLISS, C.	1	0/ 0	.000	0/ 0	.000	-/ 0	0	0	0	0	0	0	.000
Totals	225	42/86	.488	19/26	.731	-/52	16	10	20	4	3	103	.458

Michigan (91)   Coach: Johnny Orr

	Min.	Total FG / FGA	Pct.	FT / FTA	Pct.	Reb. O / T	A	TO	PF	S	Blk	TP	PPM
JOHNSON, J.	45	3/12	.250	5/ 7	.714	-/ 1	6	2	4	0	0	11	.244
KUPEC, C.	45	13/25	.520	2/ 4	.500	-/ 5	1	2	3	0	1	28	.622
ROBINSON, J.	37	9/16	.563	6/ 6	1.000	-/ 7	0	1	4	1	1	24	.649
GROTE, S.	45	7/15	.467	0/ 0	.000	-/ 9	4	2	5	2	0	14	.311
BRITT, W.	38	3/ 6	.500	2/ 2	1.000	-/ 5	3	3	5	0	0	8	.211
BAXTER, D.	1	0/ 1	.000	0/ 0	.000	-/ 0	0	0	0	0	0	0	.000
WHITE, R.	14	3/ 7	.429	0/ 1	.000	-/ 6	0	0	2	0	0	6	.429
Totals	225	38/82	.463	15/20	.750	-/33	14	10	23	3	2	91	.404

Team Rebounds: UCLA 3; Michigan 6. Disqualified: Michigan—Grote, Britt. Technical fouls: None.

	1st Half	2nd Half	1st OT	Final
UCLA	46	41	16	103
Michigan	50	37	4	91

Montana (69)   Coach: Jud Heathcote

	Min.	Total FG / FGA	Pct.	FT / FTA	Pct.	Reb. O / T	A	TO	PF	S	Blk	TP	PPM
HAYS, E.	38	9/18	.500	7/ 8	.875	-/ 8	2	3	3	0	0	25	.658
SMEDLEY, L.	23	3/ 5	.600	3/ 5	.600	-/11	0	0	2	0	0	9	.391
MCKENZIE, K.	40	4/19	.211	2/ 2	1.000	-/13	3	2	4	0	2	10	.250
RICHARDSON, M.	35	4/ 6	.667	5/ 8	.625	-/ 3	2	7	2	0	0	13	.371
PECK, T.	35	5/ 8	.625	2/ 2	1.000	-/ 3	4	5	4	1	0	12	.343
DEMERS, B.	6	0/ 2	.000	0/ 0	.000	-/ 1	1	1	1	0	0	0	.000
STAMBAUGH, T.	20	0/ 1	.000	0/ 0	.000	-/ 1	2	0	5	0	0	0	.000
NORD, M.	3	0/ 1	.000	0/ 0	.000	-/ 0	0	0	0	0	0	0	.000
Totals	200	25/60	.417	19/25	.760	-/40	14	18	21	1	2	69	.345

Utah State (63)   Coach: Dutch Belnap

	Min.	Total FG / FGA	Pct.	FT / FTA	Pct.	Reb. O / T	A	TO	PF	S	Blk	TP	PPM
MOORE, J.	38	5/15	.333	0/ 3	.000	-/ 8	2	3	5	1	0	10	.263
GREGG, E.	35	5/14	.357	3/ 6	.500	-/ 7	2	1	2	0	1	13	.371
RAWS, R.	40	10/18	.556	6/ 8	.750	-/12	1	2	3	0	0	26	.650
REED, D.	27	0/10	.000	0/ 0	.000	-/ 4	2	4	3	0	0	0	.000
ROCK, M.	19	4/ 6	.667	0/ 0	.000	-/ 1	0	1	2	1	0	8	.421
MARTINEAU, B.	3	2/ 3	.667	0/ 0	.000	-/ 1	0	0	3	0	0	4	1.333
WILLIAMS, O.	35	0/ 2	.000	2/ 4	.500	-/ 1	6	5	4	2	0	2	.057
SANTOS, M.	3	0/ 1	.000	0/ 0	.000	-/ 1	0	2	1	0	1	0	.000
Totals	200	26/69	.377	11/21	.524	-/35	13	18	23	4	2	63	.315

Team Rebounds: Montana 6; Utah State 3. Disqualified: Montana—Stambaugh; Utah State—Moore. Technical fouls: None.

	1st Half	2nd Half	Final
Montana	29	40	69
Utah State	32	31	63

Arizona State (97)   Coach: Ned Wulk

	Min.	Total FG / FGA	Pct.	FT / FTA	Pct.	Reb. O / T	A	TO	PF	S	Blk	TP	PPM
MOON, M.	29	5/ 5	1.000	0/ 0	.000	-/ 2	3	2	3	1	0	10	.345
HOLLINS, L.	27	6/14	.429	5/ 6	.833	-/ 3	5	4	5	7	1	17	.630
LLOYD, S.	28	8/11	.727	2/ 3	.667	-/ 8	1	2	5	0	1	18	.643
WHITE, R.	36	5/15	.333	7/ 9	.778	-/ 3	6	9	3	3	0	17	.472
SCHRADER, J.	37	5/ 9	.556	3/ 3	1.000	-/11	3	1	4	2	0	13	.351
JACKSON, G.	8	4/ 5	.800	2/ 2	1.000	-/ 2	1	0	1	1	0	10	1.250
HOLLIMAN, J.	17	4/ 6	.667	0/ 2	.000	-/ 6	1	1	3	1	0	8	.471
DRAYTON, N.	2	1/ 1	1.000	0/ 0	.000	-/ 1	0	1	1	0	0	2	1.000
WRIGHT, K.	11	1/ 3	.333	0/ 0	.000	-/ 3	0	1	4	0	0	2	.182
WHITE, G.	2	0/ 0	.000	0/ 0	.000	-/ 0	0	0	2	0	0	0	.000
TAYLOR, R.	3	0/ 0	.000	0/ 0	.000	-/ 0	1	0	0	0	0	0	.000
Totals	200	39/69	.565	19/25	.760	-/39	21	21	31	15	2	97	.485

Alabama (94)   Coach: C.M. Newton

	Min.	Total FG / FGA	Pct.	FT / FTA	Pct.	Reb. O / T	A	TO	PF	S	Blk	TP	PPM
DUNN, T.	39	9/18	.500	3/ 5	.600	-/ 7	1	5	2	4	0	21	.538
RUSSELL, C.	22	5/13	.385	0/ 0	.000	-/ 2	3	2	5	0	0	10	.455
DOUGLAS, L.	39	12/21	.571	5/14	.357	-/21	2	6	3	1	7	29	.744
CLEVELAND, A.	38	8/19	.421	2/ 2	1.000	-/13	3	6	5	1	0	18	.474
MURRAY, A.	29	2/ 3	.667	4/ 5	.800	-/ 3	4	5	4	2	0	8	.276
BROWN, R.	21	3/ 8	.375	0/ 1	.000	-/ 3	4	0	3	1	1	6	.286
DILL, J.	12	1/ 2	.500	0/ 2	.000	-/ 1	2	0	3	0	0	2	.167
Totals	200	40/84	.476	14/29	.483	-/50	19	24	25	9	8	94	.470

Team Rebounds: Arizona St. 2; Alabama 3. Disqualified: Arizona St.—Hollins, Lloyd; Alabama—Russell, Cleveland. Technical fouls: None.

	1st Half	2nd Half	Final
Arizona St.	55	42	97
Alabama	36	58	94

UNLV (90)   Coach: Jerry Tarkanian

	Min.	Total FG / FGA	Pct.	FT / FTA	Pct.	Reb. O / T	A	TO	PF	S	Blk	TP	PPM
ROBINSON, J.	-	4/11	.364	1/ 3	.333	-/ 8	-	-	2	-	-	9	-
GONDREZICK, G.	-	4/11	.364	0/ 0	.000	-/ 4	-	-	5	-	-	8	-
BROWN, L.	-	9/14	.643	0/ 1	.000	-/12	-	-	4	-	-	18	-
OWENS, E.	-	10/15	.667	1/ 4	.250	-/ 8	-	-	2	-	-	21	-
SOBERS, R.	-	7/16	.438	7/ 8	.875	-/ 2	-	-	4	-	-	21	-
BATTS, B.	-	2/ 4	.500	2/ 3	.667	-/ 2	-	-	5	-	-	6	-
SMITH, R.	-	3/ 6	.500	1/ 2	.500	-/ 1	-	-	1	-	-	7	-
MILKE, M.	-	0/ 1	.000	0/ 0	.000	-/ 1	-	-	0	-	-	0	-
PORTER, M.	-	0/ 1	.000	0/ 1	.000	-/ 1	-	-	0	-	-	0	-
FREEMAN, J.	-	0/ 0	.000	0/ 0	.000	-/ 1	-	-	1	-	-	0	-
Totals	200	39/79	.494	12/22	.545	-/40	-	-	24	-	-	90	.450

San Diego State (80)   Coach: Tim Vezie

	Min.	Total FG / FGA	Pct.	FT / FTA	Pct.	Reb. O / T	A	TO	PF	S	Blk	TP	PPM
COPP, S.	-	5/10	.500	6/11	.545	-/17	-	-	4	-	-	16	-
KONACH, B.	-	5/11	.455	0/ 2	.000	-/ 5	-	-	3	-	-	10	-
CONNELLY, W.	-	12/22	.545	1/ 4	.250	-/12	-	-	2	-	-	25	-
BUNTING, A.	-	2/ 9	.222	0/ 0	.000	-/ 5	-	-	4	-	-	4	-
LEARY, R.	-	5/ 9	.556	0/ 0	.000	-/ 1	-	-	5	-	-	10	-
DELAMAN, M.	-	2/ 3	.667	2/ 5	.400	-/ 2	-	-	0	-	-	6	-
GREEN, B.	-	3/ 4	.750	1/ 2	.500	-/ 3	-	-	1	-	-	7	-
EARLE, G.	-	0/ 2	.000	0/ 0	.000	-/ 2	-	-	4	-	-	0	-
CONTRERAS, R.	-	1/ 1	1.000	0/ 0	.000	-/ 0	-	-	0	-	-	2	-
WELSHAUS, J.	-	0/ 0	.000	0/ 1	.000	-/ 2	-	-	1	-	-	0	-
Totals	200	35/71	.493	10/25	.400	-/49	-	-	24	-	-	80	.400

Team Rebounds: UNLV 3; San Diego St. 4. Disqualified: UNLV—Gondrezick, Batts; San Diego St.—Leary.

	1st Half	2nd Half	Final
UNLV	48	42	90
San Diego St.	43	37	80

FIRST ROUND MIDWEST

Maryland (83)   Coach: Lefty Driesell

	Min.	Total FG/FGA	Pct.	FT/FTA	Pct.	Reb. O/T	A	TO	PF	S	Blk	TP	PPM
SHEPPARD, S.	25	3/6	.500	4/5	.800	-/7	0	2	3	0	0	10	.400
LUCAS, J.	40	9/15	.600	1/2	.500	-/3	2	5	2	0	0	19	.475
HAHN, B.	5	0/0	.000	0/2	.000	-/1	0	0	0	0	0	0	.000
HOWARD, M.	32	7/11	.636	2/3	.667	-/2	1	5	5	1	0	16	.500
DAVIS, B.	31	6/9	.667	2/2	1.000	-/0	2	4	5	1	0	14	.452
BROWN, O.	40	8/11	.727	0/3	.000	-/11	2	5	3	0	1	16	.400
PATTON, C.	1	0/0	.000	2/2	1.000	-/0	0	1	0	0	0	2	2.000
ROY, T.	26	3/3	1.000	0/0	.000	-/7	1	1	5	0	2	6	.231
Totals	200	36/55	.655	11/19	.579	-/31	8	23	23	2	3	83	.415

Creighton (79)   Coach: Tom Apke

	Min.	Total FG/FGA	Pct.	FT/FTA	Pct.	Reb. O/T	A	TO	PF	S	Blk	TP	PPM
HEEKE, D.	32	6/11	.545	2/3	.667	-/2	1	2	5	1	0	14	.438
SMITH, C.	37	1/5	.200	1/4	.250	-/10	2	4	5	0	0	3	.081
BROOKINS, D.	32	9/20	.450	7/8	.875	-/5	0	1	3	1	0	25	.781
ANDERSON, T.	38	6/9	.667	1/2	.500	-/2	1	5	4	0	0	13	.342
BUTLER, C.	39	6/16	.375	6/6	1.000	-/5	2	4	2	0	0	18	.462
APKE, R.	16	1/4	.250	2/2	1.000	-/2	0	2	1	0	0	4	.250
SCRUTCHENS, B.	3	0/1	.000	0/0	.000	-/0	0	0	1	0	0	0	.000
MCCONNELL, T.	3	1/1	1.000	0/0	.000	-/0	0	0	0	0	0	2	.667
Totals	200	30/67	.448	19/25	.760	-/26	6	18	21	2	0	79	.395

Team Rebounds: Maryland 3; Creighton 4. Disqualified: Maryland—Roy, Davis, Howard; Creighton—Heeke, Smith. Technical fouls: Creighton—Anderson.

	1st Half	2nd Half	Final
Maryland	43	40	83
Creighton	31	48	79

Notre Dame (77)   Coach: Digger Phelps

	Min.	Total FG/FGA	Pct.	FT/FTA	Pct.	Reb. O/T	A	TO	PF	S	Blk	TP	PPM
PATERNO, B.	-	3/8	.375	3/4	.750	-/3	1	2	3	0	0	9	-
BATTON, D.	-	5/12	.417	8/9	.889	-/6	1	2	3	0	0	18	-
KNIGHT, T.	-	1/5	.200	4/4	1.000	-/6	0	2	4	0	0	6	-
CARPENTER, J.	-	0/0	.000	2/3	.667	-/2	0	1	3	2	0	2	-
DANTLEY, A.	-	9/15	.600	15/21	.714	-/10	1	3	2	1	0	33	-
CLAY, D.	-	2/6	.333	0/3	.000	-/3	3	1	1	0	0	4	-
CROTTY, P.	-	0/0	.000	0/0	.000	-/2	1	1	3	0	0	0	-
MARTIN, R.	-	0/2	.000	1/3	.333	-/3	1	0	0	0	0	1	-
WILLIAMS, D.	-	1/1	1.000	2/3	.667	-/0	1	0	0	0	0	4	-
KUZMICZ, D.	-	0/0	.000	0/0	.000	-/0	0	1	0	0	0	0	-
Totals	200	21/49	.429	35/50	.700	-/35	9	13	19	3	0	77	.385

Kansas (71)   Coach: Ted Owens

	Min.	Total FG/FGA	Pct.	FT/FTA	Pct.	Reb. O/T	A	TO	PF	S	Blk	TP	PPM
VONMOORE, D.	-	0/2	.000	0/0	.000	-/1	1	0	5	0	0	0	-
SUTTLE, D.	-	7/10	.700	3/5	.600	-/10	0	2	3	0	1	17	-
JOHNSON, C.	-	4/7	.571	0/0	.000	-/1	1	1	5	0	0	8	-
COOK, N.	-	3/7	.429	2/2	1.000	-/10	2	1	5	0	2	8	-
GREENLEE, D.	-	3/9	.333	0/0	.000	-/3	10	0	5	0	0	6	-
KNIGHT, D.	-	7/13	.538	1/1	1.000	-/2	0	1	2	0	0	15	-
SMITH, T.	-	2/6	.333	0/0	.000	-/2	3	0	5	0	0	4	-
MORNINGSTAR, R.	-	3/9	.333	0/1	.000	-/2	2	2	3	0	1	6	-
GIBSON, D.	-	2/3	.667	1/2	.500	-/1	6	4	5	1	0	5	-
KOENINGS, K.	-	0/0	.000	2/2	1.000	-/2	0	0	0	0	0	2	-
BARNTHOUSE, C.	-	0/1	.000	0/0	.000	-/1	0	0	1	0	0	0	-
Totals	200	31/67	.463	9/13	.692	-/35	25	11	39	1	4	71	.355

Team Rebounds: Notre Dame 0; Kansas 2. Disqualified: Kansas—Von Moore, Cook, Johnson, Greenlee, Smith, Gibson. Technical fouls: None.

	1st Half	2nd Half	Final
Notre Dame	44	33	77
Kansas	32	39	71

Cincinnati (87)   Coach: Gale Catlett

	Min.	Total FG/FGA	Pct.	FT/FTA	Pct.	Reb. O/T	A	TO	PF	S	Blk	TP	PPM
JONES, M.	24	4/8	.500	2/3	.667	-/4	1	3	5	0	0	10	.417
MILLER, R.	28	4/6	.667	5/9	.556	-/6	0	1	4	0	2	13	.464
FRANKLIN, M.	32	3/7	.429	0/0	.000	-/20	0	2	5	0	0	6	.188
KAMSTRA, G.	18	2/7	.286	3/3	1.000	-/1	0	3	1	0	0	7	.389
COLLIER, S.	35	7/16	.438	6/6	1.000	-/1	3	3	1	0	0	20	.571
WARD, H.	25	3/8	.375	2/2	1.000	-/3	2	5	2	0	0	8	.320
ARTIS, M.	4	1/4	.250	0/0	.000	-/3	0	1	0	0	0	2	.500
SHERLOCK, B.	1	0/0	.000	1/2	.500	-/0	0	0	1	0	0	1	1.000
WILLIAMS, B.	29	7/13	.538	4/4	1.000	-/10	1	2	4	0	0	18	.621
FAZEKAS, P.	4	0/0	.000	2/2	1.000	-/0	0	2	0	0	0	2	.500
Totals	200	31/69	.449	25/31	.806	-/48	7	20	25	0	2	87	.435

Texas A&M (79)   Coach: Shelby Metcalf

	Min.	Total FG/FGA	Pct.	FT/FTA	Pct.	Reb. O/T	A	TO	PF	S	Blk	TP	PPM
THORNTON, J.	25	4/12	.333	4/5	.800	-/5	1	0	3	0	0	12	.480
DAVIS, B.	33	7/24	.294	2/7	.857	-/15	0	3	1	0	0	16	.485
MERCER, J.	18	1/3	.333	0/1	.000	-/5	0	1	5	0	0	2	.111
FLOYD, M.	17	2/8	.250	2/2	1.000	-/2	1	1	3	0	0	6	.353
PARKER, S.	30	6/12	.500	2/3	.667	-/6	0	3	5	0	0	14	.467
JOSEPH, R.	15	1/2	.500	0/1	.000	-/2	1	0	1	0	1	2	.133
ROBERTS, R.	19	5/14	.357	5/6	.833	-/2	0	0	3	0	0	15	.789
WILLIAMS, W.	17	0/5	.000	0/2	.000	-/4	0	2	1	1	0	0	.000
ERWIN, G.	13	0/2	.000	0/0	.000	-/0	3	1	2	1	0	0	.000
WILLIAMS, M.	5	0/1	.000	0/0	.000	-/0	0	1	0	0	0	0	.000
TONE, C.	8	6/9	.667	0/1	.000	-/2	1	1	0	0	0	12	1.500
Totals	200	30/85	.353	19/28	.213	-/43	7	13	24	2	1	79	.395

Team Rebounds: Cincinnati 5; Texas A&M 4. Disqualified: Cincinnati—Franklin, Jones; Texas A&M—Mercer, Parker. Technical fouls: None.

	1st Half	2nd Half	Final
Cincinnati	37	50	87
Texas A&M	27	52	79

Louisville (91)   Coach: Denny Crum

	Min.	Total FG/FGA	Pct.	FT/FTA	Pct.	Reb. O/T	A	TO	PF	S	Blk	TP	PPM
MURPHY, A.	-	6/14	.429	4/5	.800	-/0	3	-	4	-	-	16	-
COX, W.	-	3/4	.750	0/0	.000	-/7	1	-	4	-	-	6	-
BUNTON, B.	-	6/11	.545	1/1	1.000	-/11	1	-	1	-	-	13	-
BRIDGEMAN, J.	-	15/18	.833	6/7	.857	-/11	5	-	3	-	-	36	-
BOND, P.	-	0/3	.000	0/0	.000	-/0	6	-	4	-	-	0	-
WHITFIELD	-	2/4	.500	0/0	.000	-/2	0	-	3	-	-	4	-
BROWN, D.	-	2/5	.400	0/0	.000	-/3	2	-	2	-	-	4	-
WILSON	-	1/6	.167	2/2	1.000	-/7	4	-	1	-	-	4	-
GALION	-	2/2	1.000	0/0	.000	-/1	1	-	1	-	-	4	-
HOWARD, T.	-	0/0	.000	4/4	1.000	-/0	0	-	0	-	-	4	-
HARMON, B.	-	0/0	.000	0/0	.000	-/0	0	-	1	-	-	0	-
BUNTON, S.	-	0/0	.000	0/0	.000	-/1	0	-	0	-	-	0	-
Totals	200	37/67	.552	17/19	.895	-/43	23	-	24	-	-	91	.455

Rutgers (78)   Coach: Tom Young

	Min.	Total FG/FGA	Pct.	FT/FTA	Pct.	Reb. O/T	A	TO	PF	S	Blk	TP	PPM
SELLERS	-	12/17	.706	5/8	.625	-/4	1	-	4	-	-	29	-
DABNEY, M.	-	4/14	.286	0/0	.000	-/5	4	-	4	-	-	8	-
PALKO, M.	-	0/1	.000	0/0	.000	-/2	2	-	0	-	-	0	-
COPELAND, H.	-	3/14	.214	3/4	.750	-/6	2	-	3	-	-	9	-
JORDAN	-	8/13	.615	3/8	.375	-/4	4	-	5	-	-	19	-
KLEINBAUM	-	2/2	1.000	0/0	.000	-/1	0	-	0	-	-	4	-
HAFELE	-	4/5	.800	1/2	.500	-/3	2	-	3	-	-	9	-
SCHERER	-	0/1	.000	0/0	.000	-/0	0	-	1	-	-	0	-
Totals	200	33/67	.493	12/22	.545	-/25	15	-	20	-	-	78	.390

Team Rebounds: Louisville 2; Rutgers 3. Disqualified: Rutgers—Jordan. Technical fouls: None.

	1st Half	2nd Half	Final
Louisville	44	47	91
Rutgers	46	32	78

FIRST ROUND EAST

Syracuse (87) Coach: Roy Danforth

	Min.	Total FG / FGA	Pct.	FT / FTA	Pct.	Reb. O/T	A	TO	PF	S	Blk	TP	PPM
HACKETT, R.	44	11/19	.579	8/10	.800	-/12	2	4	2	1	1	30	.682
SEASE, C.	35	8/11	.727	2/ 3	.667	-/ 5	1	3	5	1	0	18	.514
SEIBERT, E.	21	1/ 4	.250	0/ 0	.000	-/ 3	1	3	3	1	0	2	.095
LEE, J.	45	7/14	.500	6/ 7	.857	-/ 8	4	6	0	4	0	20	.444
WILLIAMS, J.	18	3/ 9	.333	0/ 0	.000	-/ 0	3	4	3	1	0	6	.333
KINDEL, R.	27	0/ 4	.000	3/ 4	.750	-/ 2	3	1	1	0	0	3	.111
KING, K.	25	4/ 9	.444	0/ 0	.000	-/ 6	3	2	2	1	0	8	.320
BYRNES, M.	2	0/ 1	.000	0/ 0	.000	-/ 1	0	0	1	0	0	0	.000
SHAW, S.	8	0/ 1	.000	0/ 0	.000	-/ 1	1	0	0	0	1	0	.000
Totals	225	34/72	.472	19/24	.792	-/38	18	23	17	9	2	87	.387

La Salle (83) Coach: Paul Westhead

	Min.	Total FG / FGA	Pct.	FT / FTA	Pct.	Reb. O/T	A	TO	PF	S	Blk	TP	PPM
WILBER, D.	35	3/ 8	.375	0/ 0	.000	-/10	0	4	4	0	1	6	.171
TAYLOR, B.	45	9/21	.429	2/ 4	.500	-/ 7	5	3	2	1	0	20	.444
BRYANT, J.	43	11/24	.458	3/ 6	.500	-/14	1	2	5	0	1	25	.581
WISE, C.	42	6/12	.500	2/ 2	1.000	-/ 5	4	3	3	4	0	14	.333
COLLIER, G.	40	8/14	.571	0/ 0	.000	-/ 4	5	4	2	1	1	16	.400
METZINGER, G.	6	1/ 3	.333	0/ 0	.000	-/ 1	0	0	1	0	0	2	.333
BRODZINSKI, B.	11	0/ 1	.000	0/ 0	.000	-/ 0	1	1	1	1	0	0	.000
CUTLER, V.	3	0/ 0	.000	0/ 0	.000	-/ 1	0	0	1	0	0	0	.000
Totals	225	38/83	.458	7/12	.583	-/42	16	17	19	7	3	83	.369

Team Rebounds: Syracuse 10; La Salle 3. Disqualified: Syracuse—Sease. La Salle—Bryant. Technical fouls: None.

	1st Half	2nd Half	1st OT	Final
Syracuse	36	35	16	87
La Salle	33	38	12	83

North Carolina (93) Coach: Dean Smith

	Min.	Total FG / FGA	Pct.	FT / FTA	Pct.	Reb. O/T	A	TO	PF	S	Blk	TP	PPM
FORD, P.	-	4/ 9	.444	4/ 5	.800	-/ 4	6	7	1	2	0	12	-
HOFFMAN, B.	-	7/12	.583	2/ 2	1.000	-/ 1	4	0	2	3	0	16	-
KUPCHAK, M.	-	9/11	.818	0/ 2	.000	-/ 8	1	3	4	2	2	18	-
DAVIS, W.	-	5/11	.455	1/ 2	.500	-/ 2	7	5	1	3	2	11	-
LAGARDE, T.	-	5/ 7	.714	1/ 1	1.000	-/ 4	1	1	5	2	1	11	-
STAHL, E.	-	2/ 4	.500	6/ 6	1.000	-/ 3	0	0	2	0	0	10	-
BELL, M.	-	1/ 1	1.000	3/ 4	.750	-/ 1	4	4	1	1	0	5	-
KUESTER, J.	-	1/ 2	.500	2/ 2	1.000	-/ 0	1	0	0	2	0	4	-
CHAMBERS, B.	-	1/ 1	1.000	0/ 0	.000	-/ 1	0	0	0	0	0	2	-
HANNERS, D.	-	1/ 1	1.000	0/ 0	.000	-/ 0	0	0	1	0	0	2	-
BUCKLEY, B.	-	0/ 1	.000	0/ 0	.000	-/ 0	0	1	0	0	0	0	-
ZALIAGIRIS, T.	-	1/ 1	1.000	0/ 0	.000	-/ 0	0	0	0	0	0	2	-
COLEY, W.	-	0/ 0	.000	0/ 0	.000	-/ 0	0	0	0	0	0	0	-
HARRY, E.	-	0/ 0	.000	0/ 0	.000	-/ 0	0	0	0	0	0	0	-
Totals	200	37/61	.607	19/24	.792	-/24	24	18	17	15	5	93	.465

New Mexico State (69) Coach: Lou Henson

	Min.	Total FG / FGA	Pct.	FT / FTA	Pct.	Reb. O/T	A	TO	PF	S	Blk	TP	PPM
ALLEN, B.	-	7/11	.636	0/ 0	.000	-/ 3	0	5	1	0	0	14	-
HAWKINS, D.	-	2/ 6	.333	3/ 3	1.000	-/ 0	3	9	5	2	0	7	-
BOSTIC, J.	-	11/15	.733	0/ 2	.000	-/12	1	4	4	0	1	22	-
LETZ, R.	-	4/10	.400	0/ 0	.000	-/ 8	4	3	3	0	0	8	-
ROBINSON, R.	-	5/11	.455	0/ 0	.000	-/ 4	4	3	3	0	0	10	-
GRAHAM, A.	-	0/ 4	.000	4/ 4	1.000	-/ 5	4	2	4	0	0	4	-
LOPEZ, G.	-	1/ 4	.250	0/ 1	.000	-/ 0	2	1	2	0	0	2	-
PANNELL, G.	-	0/ 1	.000	0/ 0	.000	-/ 0	0	0	1	0	0	0	-
GIBSON, R.	-	1/ 3	.333	0/ 1	.000	-/ 1	1	0	0	0	0	2	-
DOVE, J.	-	0/ 0	.000	0/ 0	.000	-/ 0	0	0	0	0	0	0	-
DIBIASE, J.	-	0/ 0	.000	0/ 0	.000	-/ 0	1	1	0	0	0	0	-
Totals	200	31/65	.477	7/ 9	.778	-/33	20	28	22	2	1	69	.345

Team Rebounds: N. Carolina 0; New Mexico St. 5. Disqualified: N. Carolina—LaGarde; New Mexico St.—Hawkins. Technical fouls: None.

	1st Half	2nd Half	Final
N. Carolina	39	54	93
New Mexico St.	37	32	69

Kansas State (69) Coach: Jack Hartman

	Min.	Total FG / FGA	Pct.	FT / FTA	Pct.	Reb. O/T	A	TO	PF	S	Blk	TP	PPM
SNIDER, D.	16	2/ 6	.333	1/ 2	.500	-/ 2	1	0	3	1	0	5	.313
DROGE, D.	40	3/10	.300	3/ 4	.750	-/ 8	0	4	4	2	0	9	.225
GERLACH, C.	40	8/13	.615	4/ 5	.800	-/16	2	3	1	1	2	20	.500
WILLIAMS, C.	40	10/22	.455	0/ 1	.000	-/ 3	1	4	1	0	0	20	.500
EVANS, M.	39	4/10	.400	5/ 5	1.000	-/ 2	7	3	1	1	0	13	.333
NOLAND, B.	24	1/ 5	.200	0/ 0	.000	-/10	0	1	4	1	1	2	.083
MOLINARI, J.	1	0/ 1	.000	0/ 0	.000	-/ 1	0	0	0	0	0	0	.000
Totals	200	28/67	.418	13/17	.765	-/42	11	15	14	6	3	69	.345

Pennsylvania (62) Coach: Chuck Daly

	Min.	Total FG / FGA	Pct.	FT / FTA	Pct.	Reb. O/T	A	TO	PF	S	Blk	TP	PPM
JOHNSON, H.	39	5/12	.417	2/ 3	.667	-/17	1	3	4	0	1	12	.308
BIGELOW, B.	39	7/16	.438	1/ 2	.500	-/ 8	2	2	2	1	0	15	.385
HAIGLER, R.	37	8/21	.381	1/ 3	.333	-/ 9	2	6	3	1	3	17	.459
LONETTO, M.	39	7/14	.500	0/ 0	.000	-/ 2	4	3	4	3	0	14	.359
BEECROFT, J.	28	1/ 4	.250	0/ 0	.000	-/ 1	0	0	4	1	0	2	.071
STEFANSKI, E.	16	1/ 1	1.000	0/ 0	.000	-/ 1	3	3	3	0	0	2	.125
JONES, B.	2	0/ 2	.000	0/ 0	.000	-/ 0	0	0	0	0	0	0	.000
Totals	200	29/70	.414	4/ 8	.500	-/38	12	17	20	6	4	62	.310

Team Rebounds: Kansas State 3; Pennsylvania 3. Disqualified: None. Technical fouls: None.

	1st Half	2nd Half	Final
Kansas State	40	29	69
Pennsylvania	28	34	62

Boston College (82) Coach: Bob Zuffelato

	Min.	Total FG / FGA	Pct.	FT / FTA	Pct.	Reb. O/T	A	TO	PF	S	Blk	TP	PPM
WELDON, M.	-	1/ 7	.143	7/ 8	.875	-/ 2	5	-	0	-	-	9	-
CARRINGTON, R.	-	8/19	.421	1/ 3	.333	-/ 8	6	-	3	-	-	17	-
MORRISON, W.	-	6/13	.462	8/10	.800	-/ 5	2	-	0	-	-	20	-
COLLINS, B.	-	7/11	.636	4/ 5	.800	-/13	2	-	3	-	-	18	-
BAILEY, J.	-	8/15	.533	0/ 0	.000	-/ 2	3	-	2	-	-	16	-
SHIREY, M.	-	1/ 1	1.000	0/ 0	.000	-/ 3	3	-	1	-	-	2	-
Totals	200	31/66	.470	20/26	.769	-/33	21	-	9	-	-	82	.410

Furman (76) Coach: Joe Williams

	Min.	Total FG / FGA	Pct.	FT / FTA	Pct.	Reb. O/T	A	TO	PF	S	Blk	TP	PPM
SMITH, R.	-	1/ 4	.250	0/ 0	.000	-/ 2	5	-	5	-	-	2	-
LEONARD, F.	-	7/15	.467	0/ 0	.000	-/14	2	-	4	-	-	14	-
MAYES, C.	-	14/31	.452	0/ 2	.000	-/19	0	-	4	-	-	28	-
LYNCH, C.	-	4/16	.250	0/ 0	.000	-/ 3	3	-	1	-	-	8	-
HALL, M.	-	7/16	.438	0/ 0	.000	-/ 5	4	-	2	-	-	14	-
GREEN, S.	-	3/ 3	1.000	0/ 0	.000	-/ 0	2	-	0	-	-	6	-
COTTINGHAM, J.	-	0/ 0	.000	0/ 0	.000	-/ 4	3	-	2	-	-	0	-
HILL, B.	-	2/ 4	.500	0/ 0	.000	-/ 3	4	-	2	-	-	4	-
Totals	200	38/89	.427	0/ 2	.000	-/50	23	-	20	-	-	76	.380

Team Rebounds: Boston College 4; Furman 6. Disqualified: Furman—Smith. Technical fouls: None.

	1st Half	2nd Half	Final
Boston College	37	45	82
Furman	34	42	76

FIRST ROUND MIDEAST

Indiana (78) Coach: Bob Knight

	Min.	Total FG / FGA	Pct.	FT / FTA	Pct.	Reb. O/T	A	TO	PF	S	Blk	TP	PPM
LASKOWSKI, J.	37	5/12	.417	5/ 6	.833	-/ 6	0	1	1	3	0	15	.405
GREEN, S.	28	5/ 7	.714	4/ 6	.667	-/ 2	2	3	4	2	1	14	.500
BENSON, K.	22	3/ 8	.375	1/ 3	.333	-/10	1	2	4	0	0	7	.318
WILKERSON, B.	37	3/ 8	.375	1/ 4	.250	-/ 5	3	0	3	2	0	7	.189
BUCKNER, Q.	35	5/15	.333	2/ 4	.500	-/ 9	0	0	3	0	0	12	.343
ABERNETHY, T.	15	4/ 7	.571	2/ 4	.500	-/ 3	0	0	2	0	0	10	.667
RADFORD, W.	11	0/ 0	.000	6/ 8	.750	-/ 2	0	0	1	1	0	6	.545
AHLFELD, S.	3	1/ 1	1.000	0/ 0	.000	-/ 0	0	0	0	0	0	2	.667
KAMSTRA, J.	1	0/ 0	.000	0/ 0	.000	-/ 0	0	0	0	0	0	0	.000
HAYMORE, M.	3	0/ 1	.000	0/ 0	.000	-/ 1	0	1	0	0	1	0	.000
WISMAN, J.	3	1/ 1	1.000	1/ 1	1.000	-/ 0	1	0	0	0	0	3	1.000
NOORT, D.	2	0/ 0	.000	0/ 0	.000	-/ 1	0	0	2	0	0	0	.000
CREWS, J.	2	1/ 1	1.000	0/ 0	.000	-/ 0	0	0	0	0	0	2	1.000
MAY, S.	1	0/ 0	.000	0/ 0	.000	-/ 1	0	0	1	0	0	0	.000
Totals	200	28/61	.459	22/36	.611	-/40	7	7	21	8	2	78	.390

UTEP (53) Coach: Don Haskins

	Min.	Total FG / FGA	Pct.	FT / FTA	Pct.	Reb. O/T	A	TO	PF	S	Blk	TP	PPM
LYNUM, E.	17	1/ 3	.333	2/ 3	.667	-/ 8	1	1	3	0	1	4	.235
SAFFLE, J.	26	1/ 3	.333	3/ 4	.750	-/ 4	0	1	4	0	1	5	.192
BREWSTER, G.	25	4/10	.400	2/ 2	1.000	-/ 2	2	6	5	0	1	10	.400
JONES, R.	30	1/ 6	.167	0/ 0	.000	-/ 1	3	6	4	0	0	2	.067
ALVAREZ, R.	20	2/ 2	1.000	0/ 0	.000	-/ 0	0	1	3	0	0	4	.200
DRAPER, C.	23	3/ 5	.600	0/ 0	.000	-/ 4	0	1	4	1	0	6	.261
POOLE, T.	18	2/ 6	.333	0/ 0	.000	-/ 0	1	0	2	0	0	4	.222
PAULING, T.	22	3/ 8	.375	0/ 0	.000	-/ 5	0	0	0	0	1	6	.273
HALE, C.	9	4/ 6	.667	2/ 2	1.000	-/ 4	0	0	0	0	0	10	1.111
WILLIAMS, T.	8	0/ 0	.000	2/ 2	1.000	-/ 0	0	0	0	0	0	2	.250
EDMONSON, J.	1	0/ 1	.000	0/ 0	.000	-/ 0	0	0	0	0	0	0	.000
RUSSELL, C.	1	0/ 1	.000	0/ 1	.000	-/ 0	0	0	0	0	0	0	.000
Totals	200	21/51	.412	11/14	.786	-/28	7	17	25	1	4	53	.265

Team Rebounds: Indiana 1; UTEP 3. Disqualified: UTEP—Brewster. Technical fouls: UTEP—Coach Haskins. UTEP credited with 1 team turnover.

	1st Half	2nd Half	Final
Indiana	31	47	78
UTEP	24	29	53

Oregon State (78) Coach: Ralph Miller

	Min.	Total FG / FGA	Pct.	FT / FTA	Pct.	Reb. O/T	A	TO	PF	S	Blk	TP	PPM
SMITH, D.	31	7/10	.700	1/ 2	.500	-/ 7	0	1	0	1	0	15	.484
SHELTON, L.	31	11/20	.550	1/ 2	.500	-/11	1	7	4	0	2	23	.742
OXSEN, D.	22	4/ 6	.667	3/ 4	.750	-/ 7	2	1	1	1	1	11	.500
NEAL, C.	36	1/ 4	.250	0/ 0	.000	-/ 1	4	1	1	7	1	2	.056
TUCKER, G.	21	1/ 4	.250	1/ 1	1.000	-/ 0	2	4	5	4	0	3	.143
MILLER, P.	23	4/ 7	.571	2/ 2	1.000	-/ 3	1	4	4	2	1	10	.435
LEE, R.	17	1/ 5	.200	0/ 1	.000	-/ 4	2	4	5	2	1	2	.118
DANIEL, R.	7	3/ 6	.500	0/ 0	.000	-/ 0	1	0	2	1	0	6	.857
JORDAN, L.	2	0/ 1	.000	2/ 2	1.000	-/ 0	0	0	2	0	0	2	1.000
BAKKE, S.	2	0/ 2	.000	0/ 0	.000	-/ 0	0	1	0	1	0	0	.000
RUNYON, C.	4	0/ 1	.000	0/ 0	.000	-/ 1	0	1	0	0	0	0	.000
HENNESSEY, T.	2	1/ 2	.500	0/ 2	.000	-/ 1	0	0	1	0	0	2	1.000
GREGG, M.	1	0/ 1	.000	0/ 0	.000	-/ 0	0	0	0	0	0	0	.000
WOOLRICH, B.	1	1/ 1	1.000	0/ 0	.000	-/ 1	0	0	0	0	0	2	2.000
Totals	200	34/70	.486	10/16	.625	-/35	13	24	25	19	6	78	.390

Middle Tennessee State (67) Coach: Jimmy Earle

	Min.	Total FG / FGA	Pct.	FT / FTA	Pct.	Reb. O/T	A	TO	PF	S	Blk	TP	PPM
SORRELL, G.	40	10/20	.500	3/ 6	.500	-/17	0	5	3	2	4	23	.575
PEELER, S.	20	2/ 5	.400	1/ 2	.500	-/ 5	2	5	3	0	0	5	.250
SISNEROS, T.	34	4/ 7	.571	2/ 5	.400	-/ 8	0	4	3	4	2	10	.294
MARTIN, J.	37	6/15	.400	6/ 9	.667	-/ 3	4	6	2	1	0	18	.486
TAYLOR, C.	19	0/ 2	.000	0/ 0	.000	-/ 1	3	3	5	1	1	0	.000
ALLEN, F.	24	0/ 6	.000	0/ 0	.000	-/ 3	0	5	1	3	0	0	.000
MALCOLM, K.	16	0/ 2	.000	0/ 0	.000	-/ 0	3	1	0	1	0	0	.000
DARCUS, D.	8	4/ 4	1.000	3/ 3	1.000	-/ 3	0	1	2	0	0	11	1.375
COLLINS, R.	1	0/ 0	.000	0/ 0	.000	-/ 0	0	0	0	0	0	0	.000
BONNER, J.	1	0/ 0	.000	0/ 0	.000	-/ 1	0	1	0	0	0	0	.000
Totals	200	26/61	.426	15/25	.600	-/41	12	31	19	12	7	67	.335

Team Rebounds: Oregon State 5; Middle Tenn. St. 3. Disqualified: Oregon State—Tucker, Lee; Middle Tenn. St.—Taylor. Technical fouls: None.

	1st Half	2nd Half	Final
Oregon State	30	48	78
Middle Tenn. St	19	48	67

Central Michigan (77) Coach: Dick Parfitt

	Min.	Total FG / FGA	Pct.	FT / FTA	Pct.	Reb. O/T	A	TO	PF	S	Blk	TP	PPM
ROUNDFIELD, D.	-	8/10	.800	3/ 8	.375	-/ 7	1	4	2	1	5	19	-
HELMINK, J.	-	7/12	.583	4/ 4	1.000	-/ 7	1	3	2	0	0	18	-
DAVIS, R.	-	3/ 9	.333	3/ 4	.750	-/ 7	2	2	1	1	1	9	-
DRAKE, L.	-	2/ 8	.250	2/ 2	1.000	-/ 2	1	6	3	2	0	6	-
MCELROY, J.	-	7/17	.412	5/ 6	.833	-/ 4	4	3	2	2	2	19	-
PARKS, D.	-	0/ 3	.000	4/ 4	1.000	-/ 3	2	0	2	0	0	4	-
CICOTTE, A.	-	0/ 0	.000	0/ 0	.000	-/ 0	0	0	0	0	0	0	-
MCCLAIN, J.	-	1/ 1	1.000	0/ 0	.000	-/ 3	0	0	0	1	0	2	-
ALEXANDER, D.	-	0/ 1	.000	0/ 0	.000	-/ 0	0	1	0	0	0	0	-
KAEDING, K.	-	0/ 0	.000	0/ 0	.000	-/ 0	0	0	0	0	0	0	-
Totals	200	28/61	.459	21/28	.750	-/33	11	19	12	7	8	77	.385

Georgetown (75) Coach: John Thompson

	Min.	Total FG / FGA	Pct.	FT / FTA	Pct.	Reb. O/T	A	TO	PF	S	Blk	TP	PPM
RILEY, M.	-	4/ 9	.444	1/ 1	1.000	-/ 1	3	3	2	0	0	9	-
THOMAS, B.	-	0/ 3	.000	0/ 0	.000	-/ 1	0	0	1	0	0	0	-
WILSON, M.	-	4/ 7	.571	0/ 0	.000	-/ 4	1	2	5	1	0	8	-
HOPKINS, E.	-	3/ 8	.375	2/ 3	.667	-/ 8	1	1	2	2	0	8	-
LONG, L.	-	4/13	.308	0/ 0	.000	-/ 5	2	3	3	3	0	8	-
SMITH, J.	-	4/ 8	.500	0/ 0	.000	-/ 3	1	1	3	0	0	8	-
LYNN, B.	-	6/17	.353	2/ 2	1.000	-/11	0	3	2	0	0	14	-
MCDERMOTT, M.	-	1/ 5	.200	0/ 0	.000	-/ 4	4	2	0	1	0	2	-
JACKSON, D.	-	9/14	.643	0/ 1	.000	-/ 6	2	1	4	1	1	18	-
ESHERICK, C.	-	0/ 0	.000	0/ 0	.000	-/ 0	0	1	0	0	0	0	-
Totals	200	35/84	.417	5/ 7	.714	-/43	14	17	22	8	1	75	.375

Team Rebounds: Central Mich. 5; Georgetown 6. Disqualified: Georgetown—Wilson. Technical fouls: Central Mich.—bench.

	1st Half	2nd Half	Final
Central Mich.	38	39	77
Georgetown	37	38	75

Kentucky (76) Coach: Joe Hall

	Min.	Total FG/FGA	Pct.	FT/FTA	Pct.	Reb. O/T	A	TO	PF	S	Blk	TP	PPM
GREVEY, K.	38	8/18	.444	3/8	.375	-/3	7	2	3	1	1	19	.500
GUYETTE, B.	35	2/8	.250	10/12	.833	-/15	1	2	1	0	0	14	.400
ROBEY, R.	17	2/4	.500	0/0	.000	-/3	0	1	5	0	1	4	.235
CONNER, J.	24	5/9	.556	3/4	.750	-/3	3	4	4	1	0	13	.542
FLYNN, M.	19	3/5	.600	2/3	.667	-/3	0	4	4	0	0	8	.421
JOHNSON, L.	27	2/5	.400	0/0	.000	-/7	1	4	2	0	0	4	.148
GIVENS, J.	3	0/0	.000	0/0	.000	-/0	0	1	0	0	1	0	.000
PHILLIPS, M.	21	5/9	.556	1/3	.333	-/6	1	2	0	0	0	11	.524
HALE, J.	9	0/0	.000	3/4	.750	-/0	1	0	0	0	0	3	.333
HALL, D.	2	0/0	.000	0/0	.000	-/0	0	0	1	0	0	0	.000
LEE, J.	2	0/0	.000	0/0	.000	-/1	0	1	0	0	0	0	.000
HASKINS, M.	1	0/0	.000	0/0	.000	-/2	0	0	0	0	0	0	.000
SMITH, G.	1	0/0	.000	0/0	.000	-/0	0	0	0	0	0	0	.000
HOLLAND, J.	1	0/0	.000	0/0	.000	-/1	0	0	1	0	0	0	.000
Totals	200	27/58	.466	22/34	.647	-/44	14	21	21	2	3	76	.380

Marquette (54) Coach: Al McGuire

	Min.	Total FG/FGA	Pct.	FT/FTA	Pct.	Reb. O/T	A	TO	PF	S	Blk	TP	PPM
ELLIS, B.	-	7/13	.538	5/8	.625	-/7	1	3	4	0	5	19	-
HOMAN, J.	-	0/8	.000	2/2	1.000	-/3	3	2	3	0	1	2	-
TATUM, E.	-	5/10	.500	0/0	.000	-/5	1	1	5	0	2	10	-
LEE, B.	-	0/3	.000	0/0	.000	-/2	3	4	2	0	0	0	-
DEISMAN, D.	-	0/2	.000	0/0	.000	-/0	0	2	0	0	0	0	-
WALTON, L.	-	5/17	.294	3/4	.750	-/3	2	9	4	1	0	13	-
CAMPBELL, R.	-	1/5	.200	0/0	.000	-/9	0	4	4	0	0	2	-
BUTRYM, C.	-	0/0	.000	0/0	.000	-/1	0	0	1	0	0	0	-
NEARY, B.	-	2/2	1.000	3/5	.600	-/4	0	0	0	1	0	7	-
ROSENBERGER, G.	-	0/2	.000	0/0	.000	-/0	1	1	2	0	0	0	-
BRENNAN, B.	-	0/0	.000	0/0	.000	-/0	0	0	0	0	0	0	-
VOLLMER, P.	-	0/0	.000	1/2	.500	-/0	1	1	1	0	0	1	-
Totals	200	20/62	.323	14/21	.667	-/34	12	27	26	2	8	54	.270

Team Rebounds: Kentucky 3; Marquette 6. Disqualified: Kentucky—Robey; Marquette—Tatum. Technical fouls: None.

	1st Half	2nd Half	Final
Kentucky	25	51	76
Marquette	28	26	54

REGIONAL SEMIFINAL WEST

UCLA (67) Coach: John Wooden

	Min.	Total FG/FGA	Pct.	FT/FTA	Pct.	Reb. O/T	A	TO	PF	S	Blk	TP	PPM
MEYERS, D.	36	6/14	.429	0/0	.000	-/5	3	1	1	0	0	12	.333
JOHNSON, M.	22	3/7	.429	1/2	.500	-/6	2	3	1	0	1	7	.318
WASHINGTON, R.	38	7/17	.412	2/2	1.000	-/11	3	0	3	0	0	16	.421
MCCARTER, A.	34	3/8	.375	0/2	.000	-/1	1	1	1	2	0	6	.176
TRGOVICH, P.	37	6/11	.545	4/6	.667	-/3	3	5	3	1	1	16	.432
SPILLANE, J.	4	0/1	.000	0/0	.000	-/0	1	0	2	0	0	0	.000
TOWNSEND, R.	2	1/1	1.000	0/0	.000	-/1	0	1	0	0	0	2	1.000
DROLLINGER, R.	24	3/5	.600	2/4	.500	-/9	0	1	3	0	1	8	.333
CORLISS, C.	2	0/1	.000	0/0	.000	-/0	0	0	1	0	0	0	.000
SMITH, G.	1	0/0	.000	0/0	.000	-/0	0	0	0	0	0	0	.000
Totals	200	29/65	.446	9/16	.563	-/36	13	12	15	3	3	67	.335

Arizona State (84) Coach: Ned Wulk

	Min.	Total FG/FGA	Pct.	FT/FTA	Pct.	Reb. O/T	A	TO	PF	S	Blk	TP	PPM
MOON, M.	29	3/10	.300	0/0	.000	-/6	6	2	2	1	0	6	.207
HOLLINS, L.	31	6/16	.375	0/3	.000	-/3	6	8	3	1	0	12	.387
LLOYD, S.	33	8/13	.615	1/1	1.000	-/3	3	3	4	0	0	17	.515
WHITE, R.	21	6/11	.545	0/0	.000	-/6	1	3	4	2	0	12	.571
SCHRADER, J.	40	5/9	.556	3/4	.750	-/15	5	6	4	0	0	13	.325
JACKSON, G.	22	8/11	.727	1/2	.500	-/6	2	0	0	1	0	17	.773
HOLLIMAN, J.	16	2/5	.400	2/3	.667	-/3	0	1	1	0	0	6	.375
WRIGHT, K.	8	0/2	.000	1/2	.500	-/0	0	0	2	0	0	1	.125
Totals	200	38/77	.494	8/15	.533	-/42	23	23	20	5	0	84	.420

Montana (64) Coach: Jud Heathcote

	Min.	Total FG/FGA	Pct.	FT/FTA	Pct.	Reb. O/T	A	TO	PF	S	Blk	TP	PPM
HAYS, E.	36	13/16	.813	6/7	.857	-/7	6	2	2	3	0	32	.889
SMEDLEY, L.	34	5/12	.417	0/0	.000	-/5	0	1	2	0	0	10	.294
MCKENZIE, T.	38	9/22	.409	2/6	.333	-/10	2	2	3	0	1	20	.526
RICHARDSON, M.	35	1/5	.200	0/0	.000	-/4	2	2	4	4	0	2	.057
PECK, L.	31	0/1	.000	0/0	.000	-/4	4	5	1	0	0	0	.000
DEMERS, B.	14	0/2	.000	0/0	.000	-/0	0	1	1	0	0	0	.000
STAMBAUGH, T.	8	0/2	.000	0/0	.000	-/2	0	0	0	0	0	0	.000
BLAINE, T.	4	0/1	.000	0/0	.000	-/0	1	1	0	0	0	0	.000
Totals	200	28/61	.459	8/13	.615	-/32	15	14	13	7	1	64	.320

Team Rebounds: UCLA 4; Montana 4. Disqualified: None. Technical fouls: None.

	1st Half	2nd Half	Final
UCLA	34	33	67
Montana	33	31	64

UNLV (81) Coach: Jerry Tarkanian

	Min.	Total FG/FGA	Pct.	FT/FTA	Pct.	Reb. O/T	A	TO	PF	S	Blk	TP	PPM
SMITH, R.	40	5/11	.455	3/3	1.000	-/1	5	3	1	3	0	13	.325
SOBERS, R.	40	6/18	.333	8/10	.800	-/3	4	7	5	2	0	20	.500
ROBINSON, J.	26	4/9	.444	0/0	.000	-/7	1	3	0	0	1	8	.308
OWENS, E.	30	8/15	.533	0/0	.000	-/6	3	3	3	0	0	16	.533
GONDREZICK, G.	19	5/8	.625	2/2	1.000	-/3	3	1	5	1	1	12	.632
MILKE, M.	1	0/0	.000	0/0	.000	-/0	0	0	0	0	0	0	.000
BROWN, L.	25	3/5	.600	0/1	.000	-/9	1	2	2	0	0	6	.240
BATTS, B.	19	2/6	.333	2/2	1.000	-/4	1	2	3	0	0	6	.316
Totals	200	33/72	.458	15/18	.833	-/33	18	21	19	6	2	81	.405

Team Rebounds: Arizona St. 5; UNLV 6. Disqualified: UNLV—Gondrezick, Sobers. Technical fouls: None.

	1st Half	2nd Half	Final
Arizona St.	42	42	84
UNLV	50	31	81

REGIONAL SEMIFINAL MIDWEST

Maryland (83)   Coach: Lefty Driesell

	Min.	Total FG / FGA	Pct.	FT / FTA	Pct.	Reb. O / T	A	TO	PF	S	Blk	TP	PPM
BOYLE, J.	1	0/ 0	.000	0/ 0	.000	-/ 0	0	0	1	0	0	0	.000
SHEPPARD, S.	20	4/ 8	.500	1/ 1	1.000	-/ 4	1	1	3	0	0	9	.450
LUCAS, J.	40	8/12	.667	8/ 8	1.000	-/ 0	3	6	3	0	0	24	.600
NEWSOME, J.	1	0/ 0	.000	0/ 1	.000	-/ 0	0	0	0	0	0	0	.000
HAHN, B.	1	0/ 0	.000	0/ 0	.000	-/ 1	0	2	0	0	0	0	.000
HOWARD, M.	27	5/ 9	.556	0/ 0	.000	-/ 4	2	2	4	1	0	10	.370
DAVIS, B.	39	4/12	.333	8/10	.800	-/ 4	9	3	0	0	1	16	.410
BROWN, O.	39	7/13	.538	4/ 5	.800	-/ 9	1	1	4	0	0	18	.462
PATTON, C.	1	0/ 0	.000	0/ 0	.000	-/ 1	0	0	0	0	0	0	.000
ROY, T.	31	3/ 4	.750	0/ 0	.000	-/ 6	2	5	4	0	0	6	.194
Totals	200	31/58	.534	21/25	.840	-/29	18	20	19	1	1	83	.415

Notre Dame (71)   Coach: Digger Phelps

	Min.	Total FG / FGA	Pct.	FT / FTA	Pct.	Reb. O / T	A	TO	PF	S	Blk	TP	PPM
PATERNO, B.	37	7/16	.438	3/ 4	.750	-/ 7	1	3	2	0	0	17	.459
BATTON, D.	25	6/ 8	.750	0/ 2	.000	-/ 1	2	0	2	0	0	12	.480
KNIGHT, T.	33	5/10	.500	1/ 2	.500	-/12	1	1	3	0	1	11	.333
CARPENTER, J.	24	1/ 3	.333	2/ 2	1.000	-/ 3	4	2	4	0	0	4	.167
DANTLEY, A.	39	10/18	.556	5/ 8	.625	-/11	2	9	5	0	0	25	.641
CLAY, D.	8	0/ 1	.000	0/ 0	.000	-/ 1	0	3	1	0	0	0	.000
MARTIN, R.	16	1/ 3	.333	0/ 0	.000	-/ 2	1	3	4	0	0	2	.125
WILLIAMS, D.	17	0/ 7	.000	0/ 1	.000	-/ 3	2	0	2	0	0	0	.000
KUZMICZ, D.	1	0/ 1	.000	0/ 0	.000	-/ 0	0	0	0	0	0	0	.000
Totals	200	30/67	.448	11/19	.579	-/40	13	21	23	0	1	71	.355

Team Rebounds: Maryland 2; Notre Dame 2. Disqualified: Notre Dame—Dantley. Technical fouls: Maryland—Roy; Notre Dame—bench.

	1st Half	2nd Half	Final
Maryland	38	45	83
Notre Dame	36	35	71

Cincinnati (63)   Coach: Gale Catlett

	Min.	Total FG / FGA	Pct.	FT / FTA	Pct.	Reb. O / T	A	TO	PF	S	Blk	TP	PPM
JONES, M.	35	9/18	.500	0/ 1	.000	-/ 6	0	3	2	0	0	18	.514
MILLER, R.	26	5/ 8	.625	1/ 2	.500	-/ 7	0	3	3	0	1	11	.423
FRANKLIN, M.	27	2/ 5	.400	0/ 0	.000	-/13	0	1	5	0	1	4	.148
KAMSTRA, G.	24	3/ 7	.429	0/ 0	.000	-/ 1	5	2	3	0	0	6	.250
COLLIER, S.	29	4/14	.286	4/ 6	.667	-/ 0	4	1	4	1	0	12	.414
WARD, H.	27	3/ 7	.429	0/ 0	.000	-/ 0	2	2	4	0	0	6	.222
ARTIS, M.	6	1/ 4	.250	0/ 0	.000	-/ 1	1	0	0	1	0	2	.333
SHERLOCK, J.	1	0/ 0	.000	0/ 0	.000	-/ 0	1	0	1	0	0	0	.000
WILLIAMS, B.	25	2/11	.182	0/ 0	.000	-/ 2	2	2	1	1	1	4	.160
Totals	200	29/74	.392	5/ 9	.556	-/30	15	14	23	3	3	63	.315

Louisville (78)   Coach: Denny Crum

	Min.	Total FG / FGA	Pct.	FT / FTA	Pct.	Reb. O / T	A	TO	PF	S	Blk	TP	PPM
BRIDGEMAN, J.	36	8/15	.533	4/ 5	.800	-/ 8	4	3	2	0	1	20	.556
GALLON, R.	17	7/11	.636	2/ 5	.400	-/ 6	0	2	1	0	1	16	.941
MURPHY, A.	25	4/ 9	.444	5/ 7	.714	-/ 6	1	4	4	2	0	13	.520
BOND, P.	31	2/ 4	.500	6/ 7	.857	-/ 7	6	2	2	0	0	10	.323
BUNTON, B.	26	1/ 1	1.000	0/ 0	.000	-/ 8	0	2	2	0	1	2	.077
WHITFIELD, I.	17	4/ 4	1.000	0/ 0	.000	-/ 4	1	0	0	1	0	8	.471
COX, W.	19	1/ 5	.200	1/ 2	.500	-/ 2	1	1	0	0	0	3	.158
WILSON, R.	13	0/ 1	.000	0/ 0	.000	-/ 1	2	5	1	0	0	0	.000
HOWARD, T.	8	0/ 1	.000	2/ 2	1.000	-/ 1	1	1	0	0	0	2	.250
BROWN, B.	6	2/ 2	1.000	0/ 0	.000	-/ 0	0	1	0	0	0	4	.667
BUNTON, S.	1	0/ 1	.000	0/ 0	.000	-/ 0	0	0	0	0	0	0	.000
HARMON, B.	1	0/ 0	.000	0/ 0	.000	-/ 0	0	0	0	0	0	0	.000
Totals	200	29/54	.537	20/28	.714	-/43	16	21	12	3	3	78	.390

Team Rebounds: Louisville 5; Cincinnati 3. Disqualified: Cincinnati—Franklin. Technical fouls: None.

	1st Half	2nd Half	Final
Cincinnati	25	38	63
Louisville	42	36	78

REGIONAL SEMIFINAL EAST

Syracuse (78)   Coach: Roy Danforth

	Min.	Total FG / FGA	Pct.	FT / FTA	Pct.	Reb. O / T	A	TO	PF	S	Blk	TP	PPM
HACKETT, R.	31	3/ 7	.429	0/ 0	.000	-/ 1	2	3	4	0	0	6	.194
SEASE, C.	37	4/ 8	.500	2/ 4	.500	-/ 6	1	3	2	0	1	10	.270
SEIBERT, E.	26	3/ 9	.333	0/ 0	.000	-/ 9	2	3	2	0	0	6	.231
LEE, J.	40	12/18	.667	0/ 0	.000	-/ 0	0	5	3	1	0	24	.600
WILLIAMS, J.	39	9/11	.818	1/ 2	.500	-/ 0	4	4	4	2	0	19	.487
KINDEL, R.	2	0/ 0	.000	0/ 0	.000	-/ 0	0	0	0	0	0	0	.000
KING, K.	23	4/ 7	.571	4/ 6	.667	-/ 2	0	3	5	1	1	12	.522
PARKER, B.	2	0/ 0	.000	1/ 2	.500	-/ 0	0	0	0	0	1	1	.500
Totals	200	35/60	.583	8/14	.571	-/18	9	21	20	4	2	78	.390

North Carolina (76)   Coach: Dean Smith

	Min.	Total FG / FGA	Pct.	FT / FTA	Pct.	Reb. O / T	A	TO	PF	S	Blk	TP	PPM
FORD, P.	37	7/10	.700	10/10	1.000	-/ 1	5	5	4	1	0	24	.649
HOFFMAN, B.	36	10/12	.833	0/ 0	.000	-/ 1	2	4	1	1	0	20	.556
KUPCHAK, M.	37	6/11	.545	0/ 0	.000	-/ 8	2	5	3	0	3	12	.324
DAVIS, W.	27	2/ 4	.500	0/ 0	.000	-/ 2	1	3	5	0	1	4	.148
LAGARDE, T.	31	5/ 6	.833	2/ 2	1.000	-/ 7	0	3	1	0	0	12	.387
STAHL, E.	7	2/ 4	.500	0/ 0	.000	-/ 1	0	0	1	0	0	4	.571
BELL, M.	8	0/ 0	.000	0/ 1	.000	-/ 1	0	1	0	0	0	0	.000
KUESTER, J.	9	0/ 1	.000	0/ 0	.000	-/ 0	1	3	1	0	0	0	.000
CHAMBERS, B.	2	0/ 1	.000	0/ 0	.000	-/ 0	0	1	1	0	0	0	.000
HANNERS, D.	2	0/ 0	.000	0/ 0	.000	-/ 0	0	0	1	0	0	0	.000
BUCKLEY, B.	3	0/ 0	.000	0/ 2	.000	-/ 0	0	0	0	0	0	0	.000
ZALIAGIRIS, T.	1	0/ 0	.000	0/ 0	.000	-/ 0	0	0	0	0	0	0	.000
Totals	200	32/49	.653	12/15	.800	-/21	11	25	18	2	4	76	.380

Team Rebounds: Syracuse 6; N.Carolina 6. Disqualified: Syracuse—King; N.Carolina—Davis. Technical fouls: None.

	1st Half	2nd Half	Final
Syracuse	41	37	78
N. Carolina	42	34	76

Kansas State (74)   Coach: Jack Hartman

	Min.	Total FG / FGA	Pct.	FT / FTA	Pct.	Reb. O / T	A	TO	PF	S	Blk	TP	PPM
SNIDER, D.	-	3/ 3	1.000	0/ 0	.000	-/ 4	6	2	3	0	1	6	-
DROGE, D.	-	3/ 9	.333	0/ 0	.000	-/ 7	3	3	3	0	0	6	-
GERLACH, C.	-	9/10	.900	2/ 4	.500	-/13	1	3	3	0	2	20	-
WILLIAMS, C.	-	15/25	.600	2/ 2	1.000	-/ 3	1	5	3	2	0	32	-
EVANS, J.	-	3/ 6	.500	1/ 2	.500	-/ 5	2	6	1	2	1	7	-
NOLAND, B.	-	1/ 1	1.000	1/ 1	1.000	-/ 0	1	3	1	0	0	3	-
Totals	200	34/54	.630	6/ 9	.667	-/32	14	22	14	4	4	74	.370

Boston College (65)   Coach: Bob Zuffelato

	Min.	Total FG / FGA	Pct.	FT / FTA	Pct.	Reb. O / T	A	TO	PF	S	Blk	TP	PPM
WELDON, M.	40	2/10	.200	2/ 2	1.000	-/ 2	2	1	4	2	0	6	.150
CARRINGTON, B.	34	5/15	.333	4/ 5	.800	-/ 4	3	4	5	2	0	14	.412
BAILEY, J.	30	5/14	.357	0/ 0	.000	-/ 3	1	4	1	0	1	10	.333
MORRISON, W.	40	7/20	.350	3/ 4	.750	-/ 9	0	0	3	0	1	17	.425
COLLINS, B.	40	8/16	.500	2/ 2	1.000	-/ 8	0	1	2	1	2	18	.450
JURGENS, J.	1	0/ 0	.000	0/ 0	.000	-/ 0	0	0	0	0	0	0	.000
SHINEY, M.	15	0/ 0	.000	0/ 0	.000	-/ 1	1	0	0	1	0	0	.000
Totals	200	27/75	.360	11/13	.846	-/27	7	10	15	6	4	65	.325

Team Rebounds: Kansas State 7; Boston College 7. Disqualified: Boston College—Carrington. Technical fouls: None.

	1st Half	2nd Half	Final
Kansas State	39	35	74
Boston College	36	29	65

REGIONAL SEMIFINAL MIDEAST

Indiana (81)   Coach: Bob Knight

	Min.	Total FG / FGA	Pct.	FT / FTA	Pct.	Reb. O/T	A	TO	PF	S	Blk	TP	PPM
LASKOWSKI, J.	38	2/ 4	.500	0/ 1	.000	-/ 6	6	1	0	0	0	4	.105
GREEN, S.	36	14/19	.737	6/ 6	1.000	-/ 2	2	3	2	0	0	34	.944
BENSON, K.	38	11/18	.611	1/ 2	.500	-/ 9	3	2	3	2	0	23	.605
WILKERSON, B.	36	4/ 8	.500	2/ 2	1.000	-/ 5	10	2	4	0	0	10	.278
BUCKNER, Q.	21	3/ 7	.429	0/ 0	.000	-/ 2	1	2	4	2	0	6	.286
ABERNETHY, T.	2	0/ 0	.000	0/ 0	.000	-/ 1	0	0	1	0	0	0	.000
RADFORD, W.	17	1/ 1	1.000	0/ 0	.000	-/ 5	1	1	1	0	0	2	.118
AHLFELD, S.	2	0/ 0	.000	0/ 0	.000	-/ 0	0	0	0	0	0	0	.000
KAMSTRA, J.	1	0/ 0	.000	0/ 1	.000	-/ 0	0	0	0	0	0	0	.000
HAYMORE, M.	2	0/ 0	.000	0/ 0	.000	-/ 0	0	0	1	0	0	0	.000
WISMAN, J.	1	0/ 0	.000	0/ 0	.000	-/ 0	0	0	0	0	0	0	.000
NOORT, D.	2	0/ 0	.000	0/ 0	.000	-/ 0	0	1	0	0	0	0	.000
CREWS, J.	1	0/ 0	.000	2/ 2	1.000	-/ 1	0	0	0	0	0	2	2.000
MAY, S.	3	0/ 2	.000	0/ 0	.000	-/ 0	0	0	1	0	0	0	.000
Totals	200	35/59	.593	11/14	.786	-/31	23	12	17	4	0	81	.405

Oregon State (71)   Coach: Ralph Miller

	Min.	Total FG / FGA	Pct.	FT / FTA	Pct.	Reb. O/T	A	TO	PF	S	Blk	TP	PPM
SMITH, D.	38	6/11	.545	2/ 3	.667	-/ 2	1	2	4	0	0	14	.368
SHELTON, L.	11	3/ 5	.600	1/ 1	1.000	-/ 6	0	1	5	0	0	7	.636
OXSEN, D.	22	2/ 4	.500	0/ 0	.000	-/ 4	3	0	0	0	0	4	.182
NEAL, C.	38	3/ 6	.500	0/ 2	.000	-/ 2	4	4	3	1	0	6	.158
TUCKER, G.	24	4/12	.333	0/ 0	.000	-/ 4	1	0	0	0	0	8	.333
MILLER, P.	32	4/10	.400	1/ 2	.500	-/ 9	5	4	4	1	0	9	.281
LEE, R.	16	4/ 7	.571	0/ 1	.000	-/ 3	0	2	0	0	1	8	.500
DANIEL, R.	10	3/ 4	.750	2/ 2	1.000	-/ 1	0	0	1	0	0	8	.800
RUNYON, C.	7	2/ 5	.400	0/ 0	.000	-/ 1	1	1	0	0	0	4	.571
HENNESSEY, T.	2	1/ 1	1.000	1/ 3	.333	-/ 1	0	0	2	0	0	3	1.500
Totals	200	32/65	.492	7/14	.500	-/33	15	14	19	2	1	71	.355

Team Rebounds: Indiana 1; Oregon State 1. Disqualified: Oregon State—Shelton. Technical fouls: None.

	1st Half	2nd Half	Final
Indiana	48	33	81
Oregon State	27	44	71

Central Michigan (73)   Coach: Dick Parfitt

	Min.	Total FG / FGA	Pct.	FT / FTA	Pct.	Reb. O/T	A	TO	PF	S	Blk	TP	PPM
DRAKE, L.	-	3/ 9	.333	3/ 5	.600	-/12	1	-	1	-	-	9	-
McELROY, J.	-	8/20	.400	1/ 3	.333	-/ 5	4	-	4	-	-	17	-
ROUNDFIELD, D.	-	6/18	.333	8/13	.615	-/11	2	-	3	-	-	20	-
DAVIS, R.	-	4/ 6	.667	2/ 2	1.000	-/ 5	0	-	5	-	-	10	-
HELMINK, J.	-	4/13	.308	2/ 2	1.000	-/ 6	3	-	3	-	-	10	-
PARKS, D.	-	1/ 1	1.000	0/ 0	.000	-/ 0	1	-	0	-	-	2	-
ALEXANDER, D.	-	2/ 4	.500	1/ 2	.500	-/ 3	0	-	1	-	-	5	-
KAEDING, K.	-	0/ 2	.000	0/ 1	.000	-/ 2	0	-	0	-	-	0	-
McCLAIN, J.	-	0/ 3	.000	0/ 0	.000	-/ 2	0	-	0	-	-	0	-
CICOTTE, A.	-	0/ 0	.000	0/ 0	.000	-/ 0	0	-	0	-	-	0	-
Totals	200	28/76	.368	17/28	.607	-/46	11	-	17	-	-	73	.365

Kentucky (90)   Coach: Joe Hall

	Min.	Total FG / FGA	Pct.	FT / FTA	Pct.	Reb. O/T	A	TO	PF	S	Blk	TP	PPM
GREVEY, K.	34	6/17	.353	5/ 6	.833	-/ 4	2	-	3	-	-	17	.500
GUYETTE, B.	21	3/ 6	.500	0/ 0	.000	-/ 7	3	-	1	-	-	6	.286
ROBEY, R.	14	5/ 9	.556	1/ 2	.500	-/ 7	0	-	4	-	-	11	.786
FLYNN, M.	26	5/ 8	.625	1/ 2	.500	-/11	4	-	3	-	-	11	.423
CONNER, J.	28	4/10	.400	0/ 0	.000	-/ 2	4	-	4	-	-	8	.286
GIVENS, J.	22	6/12	.500	0/ 0	.000	-/ 6	1	-	2	-	-	12	.545
PHILLIPS, M.	22	7/12	.583	1/ 3	.333	-/ 7	1	-	3	-	-	15	.682
JOHNSON, L.	23	2/ 5	.400	2/ 3	.667	-/ 2	4	-	3	-	-	6	.261
HALL, D.	4	0/ 1	.000	0/ 0	.000	-/ 0	0	-	1	-	-	0	.000
HALE, J.	2	1/ 2	.500	0/ 0	.000	-/ 0	0	-	0	-	-	2	1.000
LEE, J.	1	0/ 0	.000	0/ 0	.000	-/ 1	0	-	2	-	-	0	.000
SMITH, G.	1	1/ 1	1.000	0/ 0	.000	-/ 0	0	-	0	-	-	2	2.000
WARFORD, R.	1	0/ 0	.000	0/ 0	.000	-/ 0	0	-	0	-	-	0	.000
HASKINS, M.	1	0/ 0	.000	0/ 0	.000	-/ 0	0	-	0	-	-	0	.000
Totals	200	40/83	.482	10/16	.625	-/47	19	-	26	-	-	90	.450

Team Rebounds: Kentucky 3; Central Mich. 7. Disqualified: Central Mich.—Davis. Technical fouls: None.

	1st Half	2nd Half	Final
Central Mich.	37	36	73
Kentucky	44	46	90

REGIONAL FINAL WEST

UCLA (89)   Coach: John Wooden

	Min.	Total FG / FGA	Pct.	FT / FTA	Pct.	Reb. O/T	A	TO	PF	S	Blk	TP	PPM
MEYERS, D.	38	4/15	.267	3/ 4	.750	-/13	3	1	3	3	3	11	.289
JOHNSON, M.	37	14/20	.700	7/ 8	.875	-/12	3	2	1	2	1	35	.946
WASHINGTON, R.	34	8/13	.615	0/ 0	.000	-/12	2	3	5	1	3	16	.471
McCARTER, A.	40	2/ 5	.400	5/ 8	.625	-/ 5	5	5	1	0	1	9	.225
TRGOVICH, P.	40	4/14	.286	0/ 1	.000	-/ 4	5	7	3	2	0	8	.200
OLINDE, W.	2	0/ 0	.000	1/ 2	.500	-/ 1	0	0	1	0	0	1	.500
DROLLINGER, R.	9	3/ 4	.750	3/ 3	1.000	-/ 3	0	1	5	0	0	9	1.000
Totals	200	35/71	.493	19/26	.731	-/50	18	19	19	8	8	89	.445

Arizona State (75)   Coach: Ned Wulk

	Min.	Total FG / FGA	Pct.	FT / FTA	Pct.	Reb. O/T	A	TO	PF	S	Blk	TP	PPM
WHITE, R.	34	6/13	.462	3/ 4	.750	-/ 5	3	4	5	1	1	15	.441
SCHRADER, J.	27	4/12	.333	1/ 2	.500	-/12	1	2	4	2	2	9	.333
LLOYD, S.	38	8/13	.615	4/ 8	.500	-/ 9	0	1	4	0	0	20	.526
MOON, M.	18	2/ 5	.400	0/ 0	.000	-/ 0	1	0	1	0	0	4	.222
HOLLINS, L.	38	8/22	.364	0/ 1	.000	-/ 0	6	1	4	0	1	16	.421
HOLLIMAN, J.	23	1/ 5	.200	1/ 2	.500	-/ 7	1	4	3	0	0	3	.130
WRIGHT, K.	8	2/ 4	.500	0/ 1	.000	-/ 3	0	0	0	0	0	4	.500
WHITE, G.	2	0/ 0	.000	0/ 0	.000	-/ 0	0	1	0	0	0	0	.000
JACKSON, G.	12	2/ 4	.500	0/ 0	.000	-/ 2	0	2	2	0	0	4	.333
Totals	200	33/78	.423	9/18	.500	-/38	12	15	23	3	4	75	.375

Team Rebounds: UCLA 3; Arizona St. 2. Disqualified: UCLA—Washington, Drollinger; Arizona St.—R. White. Technical fouls: None.

	1st Half	2nd Half	Final
UCLA	46	43	89
Arizona St.	36	39	75

REGIONAL FINAL MIDWEST

Maryland (82)   Coach: Lefty Driesell

	Min.	Total FG / FGA	Pct.	FT / FTA	Pct.	Reb. O / T	A	TO	PF	S	Blk	TP	PPM
SHEPPARD, S.	26	2/ 6	.333	6/ 6	1.000	-/ 5	2	3	2	0	0	10	.385
LUCAS, J.	40	11/19	.579	5/ 6	.833	-/ 6	1	3	4	1	0	27	.675
HAHN, B.	1	0/ 0	.000	0/ 0	.000	-/ 0	0	0	0	0	0	0	.000
HOWARD, M.	19	1/ 6	.167	0/ 1	.000	-/ 0	0	3	5	1	0	2	.105
DAVIS, B.	33	3/ 7	.429	2/ 2	1.000	-/ 2	7	4	5	3	0	8	.242
BROWN, O.	40	8/22	.364	3/ 4	.750	-/ 7	0	3	4	0	0	19	.475
PATTON, C.	2	0/ 0	.000	0/ 0	.000	-/ 0	0	0	2	0	0	0	.000
ROY, T.	39	5/ 9	.556	6/ 6	1.000	-/20	0	1	3	2	3	16	.410
Totals	200	30/69	.435	22/25	.880	-/40	10	17	25	7	3	82	.410

Louisville (96)   Coach: Denny Crum

	Min.	Total FG / FGA	Pct.	FT / FTA	Pct.	Reb. O / T	A	TO	PF	S	Blk	TP	PPM
BRIDGEMAN, J.	29	3/11	.273	7/10	.700	-/ 3	4	3	4	4	0	13	.448
GALLON, R.	15	1/ 2	.500	0/ 1	.000	-/ 6	1	3	0	0	1	2	.133
MURPHY, A.	24	10/18	.556	0/ 0	.000	-/ 4	1	1	5	0	0	20	.833
BOND, P.	39	9/17	.529	5/ 6	.833	-/ 4	7	1	2	1	0	23	.590
BUNTON, B.	34	6/ 8	.750	1/ 3	.333	-/12	2	0	4	1	1	13	.382
WHITFIELD, I.	11	2/ 4	.500	0/ 0	.000	-/ 0	0	0	1	1	0	4	.364
COX, W.	34	6/ 9	.667	3/ 4	.750	-/ 9	2	4	2	0	1	15	.441
WILSON, R.	4	0/ 0	.000	0/ 0	.000	-/ 0	0	0	1	0	0	0	.000
HOWARD, T.	1	0/ 0	.000	2/ 2	1.000	-/ 0	0	0	0	0	0	2	2.000
BROWN, D.	7	2/ 4	.500	0/ 0	.000	-/ 0	0	0	1	0	0	4	.571
BUNTON, S.	1	0/ 0	.000	0/ 0	.000	-/ 0	0	0	0	0	0	0	.000
HARMON, B.	1	0/ 0	.000	0/ 0	.000	-/ 0	0	0	0	00	0	0	.000
Totals	200	39/73	.534	18/26	.692	-/38	17	12	20	7	3	96	.480

Team Rebounds: Louisville 2; Maryland 3. Disqualified: Louisville—Murphy; Maryland—Howard, Davis. Technical fouls: Maryland—bench.

	1st Half	2nd Half	Final
Maryland	37	45	82
Louisville	42	54	96

REGIONAL FINAL EAST

Syracuse (95)   Coach: Roy Danforth

	Min.	Total FG / FGA	Pct.	FT / FTA	Pct.	Reb. O / T	A	TO	PF	S	Blk	TP	PPM
HACKETT, R.	45	10/21	.476	8/16	.500	-/16	8	5	3	0	3	28	.622
SEASE, C.	40	5/12	.417	2/ 2	1.000	-/10	0	2	4	1	1	12	.300
SEIBERT, E.	26	1/ 4	.250	0/ 0	.000	-/ 3	2	3	3	0	0	2	.077
LEE, J.	37	10/17	.588	5/ 7	.714	-/ 3	4	2	5	2	0	25	.676
WILLIAMS, J.	35	4/ 8	.500	2/ 2	1.000	-/ 3	2	4	5	3	1	10	.286
KINDEL, R.	19	3/ 5	.600	2/ 2	1.000	-/ 4	2	4	3	2	0	8	.421
KING, K.	19	4/ 7	.571	2/ 2	1.000	-/ 4	2	2	1	1	2	10	.526
SHAW, S.	3	0/ 0	.000	0/ 1	.000	-/ 1	0	1	0	0	0	0	.000
ARRINGTON, L.	1	0/ 0	.000	0/ 0	.000	-/ 0	0	0	0	0	0	0	.000
Totals	225	37/74	.500	21/32	.656	-/44	20	23	24	9	7	95	.422

Kansas State (87)   Coach: Jack Hartman

	Min.	Total FG / FGA	Pct.	FT / FTA	Pct.	Reb. O / T	A	TO	PF	S	Blk	TP	PPM
SNIDER, D.	24	5/10	.500	1/ 3	.333	-/ 6	0	2	4	1	0	11	.458
DROGE, D.	45	5/15	.333	1/ 2	.500	-/18	1	4	4	2	0	11	.244
GERLACH, C.	28	0/ 4	.000	0/ 0	.000	-/ 4	0	3	5	0	0	0	.000
WILLIAMS, C.	45	14/27	.519	7/ 9	.778	-/ 7	4	7	2	2	0	35	.778
EVANS, M.	43	6/21	.286	8/ 8	1.000	-/ 7	5	1	5	2	1	20	.465
NOLAND, B.	26	0/ 1	.000	2/ 2	1.000	-/ 5	1	1	5	2	0	2	.077
MOLINARI, J.	2	0/ 0	.000	0/ 0	.000	-/ 0	1	1	1	0	0	0	.000
WINSTON, D.	12	4/ 6	.667	0/ 0	.000	-/ 0	1	2	2	1	0	8	.667
Totals	225	34/84	.405	19/24	.792	-/47	13	21	28	10	1	87	.387

Team Rebounds: Syracuse 5; Kansas State 7. Disqualified: Syracuse—Lee, Williams; Kansas State—Evans, Noland, Gerlach. Technical fouls: None.

	1st Half	2nd Half	1st OT	Final
Syracuse	36	40	19	95
Kansas State	38	38	11	87

REGIONAL FINAL MIDEAST

Indiana (90)   Coach: Bob Knight

	Min.	Total FG / FGA	Pct.	FT / FTA	Pct.	Reb. O / T	A	TO	PF	S	Blk	TP	PPM
LASKOWSKI, J.	33	4/13	.308	4/ 6	.667	-/ 3	3	2	3	1	0	12	.364
GREEN, S.	35	10/17	.588	1/ 1	1.000	-/ 4	1	4	4	0	2	21	.600
BENSON, K.	40	13/18	.722	7/ 9	.778	-/23	5	4	3	0	0	33	.825
WILKERSON, B.	40	6/15	.400	2/ 2	1.000	-/11	6	4	3	1	0	14	.350
BUCKNER, Q.	37	3/11	.273	2/ 2	1.000	-/ 7	4	3	5	1	1	8	.216
ABERNETHY, T.	3	0/ 1	.000	0/ 0	.000	-/ 0	0	0	0	0	0	0	.000
RADFORD, W.	4	0/ 0	.000	0/ 0	.000	-/ 0	0	0	1	0	0	0	.000
AHLFELD, S.	1	0/ 0	.000	0/ 0	.000	-/ 0	0	0	0	0	0	0	.000
MAY, S.	7	1/ 4	.250	0/ 0	.000	-/ 0	0	3	2	0	0	2	.286
Totals	200	37/79	.468	16/20	.800	-/48	19	20	21	3	3	90	.450

Kentucky (92)   Coach: Joe Hall

	Min.	Total FG / FGA	Pct.	FT / FTA	Pct.	Reb. O / T	A	TO	PF	S	Blk	TP	PPM
GREVEY, K.	34	6/19	.316	5/ 6	.833	-/ 3	5	3	4	1	0	17	.500
GUYETTE, B.	22	0/ 1	.000	2/ 4	.500	-/ 7	1	3	4	3	0	2	.091
ROBEY, R.	17	3/ 6	.500	4/ 4	1.000	-/ 4	1	1	5	1	0	10	.588
CONNER, J.	31	8/20	.400	1/ 3	.333	-/ 5	5	0	0	2	1	17	.548
FLYNN, M.	38	9/13	.692	4/ 5	.800	-/ 3	2	3	4	1	0	22	.579
JOHNSON, L.	11	3/ 5	.600	0/ 1	.000	-/ 1	1	0	0	0	0	6	.545
GIVENS, J.	29	4/ 7	.571	0/ 0	.000	-/ 6	2	0	0	1	0	8	.276
PHILLIPS, M.	13	4/ 4	1.000	2/ 2	1.000	-/ 4	0	3	5	1	0	10	.769
HALL, D.	3	0/ 0	.000	0/ 0	.000	-/ 1	0	1	0	0	0	0	.000
HASKINS, M.	2	0/ 0	.000	0/ 0	.000	-/ 0	0	0	0	0	0	0	.000
Totals	200	37/75	.493	18/25	.720	-/34	17	14	22	10	1	92	.460

Team Rebounds: Kentucky 3; Indiana 2. Disqualified: Kentucky—Robey, Phillips; Indiana—Buckner. Technical fouls: Indiana—bench, Green.

	1st Half	2nd Half	Final
Indiana	44	46	90
Kentucky	44	48	92

FINAL FOUR

UCLA (75)
Coach: John Wooden

	Min.	Total FG/FGA	Pct.	FT/FTA	Pct.	Reb. O/T	A	TO	PF	S	Blk	TP	PPM
MEYERS, D.	44	6/16	.375	4/6	.667	-/7	2	5	3	0	0	16	.364
JOHNSON, M.	36	5/10	.500	0/0	.000	-/11	1	0	2	1	0	10	.278
WASHINGTON, R.	43	11/19	.579	4/6	.667	-/8	2	2	4	1	0	26	.605
MCCARTER, A.	45	3/12	.250	0/0	.000	-/2	4	5	2	0	0	6	.133
TRGOVICH, P.	35	6/12	.500	0/0	.000	-/2	3	1	5	3	1	12	.343
SPILLANE, J.	6	1/2	.500	0/0	.000	-/1	0	0	1	0	0	2	.333
OLINDE, W.	2	0/0	.000	0/0	.000	-/0	0	0	0	0	0	0	.000
DROLLINGER, R.	14	1/2	.500	1/2	.500	-/4	1	1	5	0	1	3	.214
Totals	225	33/73	.452	9/14	.643	-/35	13	14	22	5	2	75	.333

Louisville (74)
Coach: Denny Crum

	Min.	Total FG/FGA	Pct.	FT/FTA	Pct.	Reb. O/T	A	TO	PF	S	Blk	TP	PPM
BRIDGEMAN, J.	42	4/15	.267	4/4	1.000	-/15	5	5	4	0	1	12	.286
GALLON, J.	11	0/3	.000	0/0	.000	-/2	0	0	2	0	0	0	.000
MURPHY, A.	40	14/28	.500	5/7	.714	-/2	1	4	2	1	0	33	.825
BOND, P.	39	2/6	.333	2/2	1.000	-/3	8	3	1	0	0	6	.154
BUNTON, B.	35	3/4	.750	1/2	.500	-/7	3	1	2	0	1	7	.200
WHITFIELD, I.	10	0/0	.000	0/0	.000	-/1	0	0	1	0	0	0	.000
COX, W.	38	5/8	.625	4/11	.364	-/16	4	6	2	2	1	14	.368
WILSON, R.	2	0/0	.000	0/0	.000	-/0	0	2	0	0	0	0	.000
HOWARD, T.	2	0/0	.000	0/1	.000	-/0	1	0	0	0	0	0	.000
BROWN, D.	6	1/1	1.000	0/0	.000	-/1	0	0	0	0	0	2	.333
Totals	225	29/65	.446	16/27	.593	-/47	21	22	14	3	3	74	.329

Team Rebounds: UCLA 1; Louisville 2. Disqualified: UCLA—Trgovich, Drollinger. Technical fouls: None.

	1st Half	2nd Half	1st OT	Final
UCLA	33	32	10	75
Louisville	37	28	9	74

Syracuse (79)
Coach: Roy Danforth

	Min.	Total FG/FGA	Pct.	FT/FTA	Pct.	Reb. O/T	A	TO	PF	S	Blk	TP	PPM
HACKETT, R.	26	4/6	.667	6/9	.667	-/5	3	0	5	0	2	14	.538
SEASE, C.	31	7/11	.636	4/4	1.000	-/10	1	3	4	0	1	18	.581
SEIBERT, E.	15	2/3	.667	0/2	.000	-/6	1	2	5	0	1	4	.267
LEE, J.	39	10/17	.588	3/3	1.000	-/3	3	3	4	1	1	23	.590
WILLIAMS, J.	24	2/9	.222	0/1	.000	-/2	3	7	5	0	0	4	.167
KINDEL, R.	16	1/3	.333	1/2	.500	-/1	2	2	1	1	0	3	.188
KING, K.	29	2/8	.250	1/3	.333	-/5	5	4	1	1	1	5	.172
BYRNES, M.	1	0/0	.000	0/1	.000	-/1	0	2	0	0	0	0	.000
SHAW, S.	6	0/0	.000	0/0	.000	-/2	1	1	2	1	0	0	.000
PARKER, B.	11	2/3	.667	4/7	.571	-/2	0	2	3	0	0	8	.727
KELLEY, L.	1	0/1	.000	0/0	.000	-/0	0	0	0	0	0	0	.000
MEADORS, M.	1	0/0	.000	0/0	.000	-/1	0	0	0	0	0	0	.000
Totals	200	30/61	.492	19/32	.594	-/38	20	26	30	4	6	79	.395

Kentucky (95)
Coach: Joe Hall

	Min.	Total FG/FGA	Pct.	FT/FTA	Pct.	Reb. O/T	A	TO	PF	S	Blk	TP	PPM
GREVEY, K.	29	5/13	.385	4/5	.800	-/3	3	2	5	1	0	14	.483
GUYETTE, B.	12	2/3	.667	3/4	.750	-/6	0	3	3	1	0	7	.583
ROBEY, R.	25	3/8	.375	3/7	.429	-/11	2	2	4	0	0	9	.360
CONNER, J.	35	5/9	.556	2/4	.500	-/5	3	6	4	2	1	12	.343
FLYNN, M.	30	4/9	.444	3/5	.600	-/3	7	5	4	2	0	11	.367
GIVENS, J.	28	10/20	.500	4/8	.500	-/11	2	3	2	0	0	24	.857
JOHNSON, L.	13	2/4	.500	0/0	.000	-/1	3	0	3	2	0	4	.308
PHILLIPS, M.	14	5/6	.833	0/2	.000	-/4	0	1	4	4	0	10	.714
LEE, J.	5	1/4	.250	0/1	.000	-/2	0	0	1	0	0	2	.400
HASKINS, M.	5	0/0	.000	2/2	1.000	-/1	1	1	0	0	0	2	.400
HALE, J.	1	0/1	.000	0/0	.000	-/3	0	0	0	0	0	0	.000
WARFORD, R.	1	0/0	.000	0/0	.000	-/0	0	0	0	0	0	0	.000
SMITH, G.	1	0/1	.000	0/0	.000	-/0	0	0	0	0	0	0	.000
HALL, D.	1	0/0	.000	0/0	.000	-/1	0	0	1	0	0	0	.000
Totals	200	37/78	.474	21/38	.553	-/51	21	23	31	12	2	95	.475

Team Rebounds: Kentucky 6; Syracuse 2. Disqualified: Kentucky—Grevey; Syracuse—Hackett, Seibert, Williams. Technical fouls: Syracuse—Hackett.

	1st Half	2nd Half	Final
Syracuse	32	47	79
Kentucky	44	51	95

NATIONAL CHAMPIONSHIP

UCLA (92)
Coach: John Wooden

	Min.	Total FG/FGA	Pct.	FT/FTA	Pct.	Reb. O/T	A	TO	PF	S	Blk	TP	PPM
MEYERS, D.	40	9/18	.500	6/7	.857	-/11	1	0	4	0	3	24	.600
JOHNSON, M.	24	3/9	.333	0/0	.000	-/7	1	2	2	1	3	6	.250
WASHINGTON, R.	40	12/23	.522	4/5	.800	-/12	3	5	4	0	0	28	.700
MCCARTER, A.	40	3/6	.500	2/3	.667	-/2	14	2	1	2	0	8	.200
TRGOVICH, P.	40	7/16	.438	2/4	.500	-/5	4	4	4	0	0	16	.400
DROLLINGER, R.	16	4/6	.667	2/5	.400	-/13	0	0	4	0	1	10	.625
Totals	200	38/78	.487	16/25	.640	-/50	23	13	19	3	7	92	.460

Kentucky (85)
Coach: Joe Hall

	Min.	Total FG/FGA	Pct.	FT/FTA	Pct.	Reb. O/T	A	TO	PF	S	Blk	TP	PPM
GREVEY, K.	36	13/30	.433	8/10	.800	-/5	1	2	4	1	0	34	.944
GUYETTE, B.	24	7/11	.636	2/2	1.000	-/7	3	0	3	1	0	16	.667
ROBEY, R.	14	1/3	.333	0/0	.000	-/9	1	2	5	1	0	2	.143
CONNER, J.	38	4/12	.333	1/2	.500	-/4	2	5	1	2	0	9	.237
FLYNN, M.	25	3/9	.333	4/5	.800	-/3	2	2	4	1	0	10	.400
GIVENS, J.	25	3/10	.300	2/3	.667	-/6	1	1	3	0	0	8	.320
JOHNSON, L.	17	0/3	.000	0/0	.000	-/3	1	1	3	0	0	0	.000
PHILLIPS, M.	16	1/7	.143	2/3	.667	-/6	0	2	4	0	1	4	.250
LEE, J.	2	0/0	.000	0/0	.000	-/0	1	1	1	0	0	0	.000
HALL, D.	3	1/1	1.000	0/0	.000	-/1	0	0	0	0	0	2	.667
Totals	200	33/86	.384	19/25	.760	-/45	16	13	28	6	1	85	.425

Team Rebounds: UCLA 5; Kentucky 4. Disqualified: Kentucky—Robey. Technical fouls: UCLA—Meyers.

	1st Half	2nd Half	Final
UCLA	43	49	92
Kentucky	40	45	85

NATIONAL THIRD PLACE

Louisville (96)   Coach: Denny Crum

	Min.	Total FG / FGA	Pct.	FT / FTA	Pct.	Reb. O / T	A	TO	PF	S	Blk	TP	PPM
BRIDGEMAN, J.	37	7/14	.500	7/ 8	.875	-/11	9	1	2	2	0	21	.568
GALLON, R.	21	5/ 7	.714	1/ 2	.500	-/ 7	0	4	0	0	0	11	.524
MURPHY, A.	35	9/18	.500	2/ 2	1.000	-/ 8	2	8	5	2	0	20	.571
BOND, P.	40	5/ 7	.714	2/ 3	.667	-/ 4	8	8	1	0	0	12	.300
BUNTON, B.	40	10/16	.625	4/ 5	.800	-/ 6	3	3	4	1	1	24	.600
WHITFIELD, I.	5	0/ 0	.000	0/ 0	.000	-/ 2	1	0	0	0	0	0	.000
COX, W.	18	1/ 3	.333	2/ 4	.500	-/12	4	5	3	1	1	4	.222
WILSON, R.	5	0/ 0	.000	0/ 0	.000	-/ 0	2	2	0	1	0	0	.000
HOWARD, T.	3	0/ 0	.000	0/ 0	.000	-/ 0	1	0	0	0	0	0	.000
BROWN, D.	10	2/ 5	.400	0/ 1	.000	-/ 1	1	1	2	1	0	4	.400
HARMON, B.	11	0/ 2	.000	0/ 1	.000	-/ 2	1	1	1	0	0	0	.000
Totals	225	39/72	.542	18/26	.692	-/53	32	33	18	8	2	96	.427

Syracuse (88)   Coach: Roy Danforth

	Min.	Total FG / FGA	Pct.	FT / FTA	Pct.	Reb. O / T	A	TO	PF	S	Blk	TP	PPM
HACKETT, R.	42	12/22	.545	4/ 4	1.000	-/13	3	2	5	2	2	28	.667
SEASE, C.	36	3/ 8	.375	0/ 0	.000	-/ 3	5	2	5	2	0	6	.167
SEIBERT, E.	11	0/ 1	.000	1/ 2	.500	-/ 3	2	0	1	0	0	1	.091
LEE, J.	45	12/29	.414	3/ 3	1.000	-/ 5	1	2	1	0	0	27	.600
WILLIAMS, J.	32	4/ 7	.571	2/ 3	.667	-/ 1	5	5	5	7	0	10	.313
KINDEL, R.	13	0/ 2	.000	0/ 0	.000	-/ 0	3	1	1	0	0	0	.000
KING, K.	25	3/12	.250	4/ 5	.800	-/ 5	7	4	5	2	2	10	.400
BYRNES, M.	4	0/ 0	.000	0/ 0	.000	-/ 0	0	0	2	0	0	0	.000
SHAW, S.	1	0/ 0	.000	0/ 0	.000	-/ 0	0	0	0	1	0	0	.000
PARKER, B.	15	3/ 5	.600	0/ 0	.000	-/ 3	1	1	3	0	0	6	.400
MEADORS, M.	1	0/ 0	.000	0/ 0	.000	-/ 1	0	0	0	0	0	0	.000
Totals	225	37/86	.430	14/17	.824	-/34	27	17	26	16	4	88	.391

Team Rebounds: Louisville 1; Syracuse 3. Disqualified: Louisville—Murphy; Syracuse—Hackett, Sease, Williams, King. Technical fouls: None.

	1st Half	2nd Half	1st OT	Final
Louisville	42	36	18	96
Syracuse	26	52	10	88

REGIONAL THIRD PLACE MIDWEST

Cincinnati (95)   Coach: Gale Catlett

	Min.	Total FG / FGA	Pct.	FT / FTA	Pct.	Reb. O / T	A	TO	PF	S	Blk	TP	PPM
JONES, M.	27	8/15	.533	1/ 2	.500	-/ 7	5	3	5	1	1	17	.630
MILLER, R.	43	12/17	.706	2/ 4	.500	-/10	0	1	2	0	1	26	.605
FRANKLIN, M.	33	2/10	.200	1/ 2	.500	-/16	0	3	3	0	3	5	.152
KAMSTRA, G.	34	5/11	.455	10/12	.833	-/ 0	4	2	1	0	0	20	.588
COLLIER, S.	34	0/ 9	.000	0/ 0	.000	-/ 3	5	2	2	2	1	0	.000
WARD, H.	19	2/ 4	.500	5/ 6	.833	-/ 2	1	2	5	1	0	9	.474
ARTIS, M.	9	1/ 1	1.000	0/ 1	.000	-/ 3	0	3	0	0	0	2	.222
SHERLOCK, B.	5	0/ 0	.000	0/ 0	.000	-/ 0	1	0	1	0	0	0	.000
WILLIAMS, B.	21	8/15	.533	0/ 1	.000	-/ 2	1	3	4	4	0	16	.762
Totals	225	38/82	.463	19/28	.679	-/43	17	19	23	8	6	95	.422

Notre Dame (87)   Coach: Digger Phelps

	Min.	Total FG / FGA	Pct.	FT / FTA	Pct.	Reb. O / T	A	TO	PF	S	Blk	TP	PPM
PATERNO, B.	38	10/17	.588	0/ 0	.000	-/ 7	2	2	4	0	0	20	.526
BATTON, D.	24	2/ 8	.250	0/ 1	.000	-/ 5	3	2	2	0	0	4	.167
KNIGHT, T.	39	7/19	.368	2/ 6	.333	-/15	3	3	5	2	0	16	.410
CARPENTER, J.	27	1/ 5	.200	2/ 2	1.000	-/ 5	3	5	5	1	0	4	.148
DANTLEY, A.	42	10/15	.667	14/19	.737	-/ 6	0	8	4	0	1	34	.810
CLAY, D.	10	1/ 4	.250	0/ 0	.000	-/ 2	2	2	2	0	0	2	.200
CROTTY, P.	7	0/ 1	.000	0/ 0	.000	-/ 3	1	2	1	0	0	0	.000
MARTIN, R.	16	0/ 2	.000	1/ 3	.333	-/ 2	2	2	3	1	1	1	.063
WILLIAMS, D.	12	1/ 3	.333	0/ 0	.000	-/ 1	1	1	4	0	0	2	.167
KUZMICZ, D.	10	2/ 2	1.000	0/ 0	.000	-/ 1	2	0	1	0	0	4	.400
Totals	225	34/76	.447	19/31	.613	-/47	19	27	31	4	2	87	.387

Team Rebounds: Cincinnati 7; Notre Dame 6. Disqualified: Cincinnati—Ward, Jones; Notre Dame—Carpenter, Knight. Technical fouls: Cincinnati—bench.

	1st Half	2nd Half	1st OT	Final
Cincinnati	47	29	19	95
Notre Dame	38	38	11	87

REGIONAL THIRD PLACE WEST

UNLV (75)   Coach: Jerry Tarkanian

	Min.	Total FG / FGA	Pct.	FT / FTA	Pct.	Reb. O / T	A	TO	PF	S	Blk	TP	PPM
OWENS, E.	-	3/14	.214	4/ 7	.571	-/ 7	-	-	3	-	-	10	-
GONDREZICK, G.	-	2/ 4	.500	0/ 0	.000	-/ 3	-	-	3	-	-	4	-
ROBINSON, J.	-	2/ 5	.400	2/ 4	.500	-/ 5	-	-	0	-	-	6	-
SMITH, R.	-	6/12	.500	0/ 0	.000	-/ 3	-	-	2	-	-	12	-
SOBERS, R.	-	1/11	.091	5/ 7	.714	-/ 9	-	-	4	-	-	7	-
BROWN, L.	-	9/15	.600	2/ 2	1.000	-/13	-	-	4	-	-	20	-
BATTS, B.	-	8/15	.533	0/ 0	.000	-/ 5	-	-	4	-	-	16	-
Totals	200	31/76	.408	13/20	.650	-/45	-	-	20	-	-	75	.375

Montana (67)   Coach: Jud Heathcote

	Min.	Total FG / FGA	Pct.	FT / FTA	Pct.	Reb. O / T	A	TO	PF	S	Blk	TP	PPM
HAYS, E.	-	2/ 5	.400	3/ 5	.600	-/ 4	-	-	4	-	-	7	-
SMEDLEY, L.	-	6/10	.600	3/ 4	.750	-/ 8	-	-	1	-	-	15	-
MCKENZIE, K.	-	6/11	.545	2/ 6	.333	-/11	-	-	3	-	-	14	-
RICHARDSON, M.	-	3/ 9	.333	0/ 2	.000	-/ 1	-	-	2	-	-	6	-
PECK, T.	-	4/ 7	.571	2/ 2	1.000	-/ 1	-	-	2	-	-	10	-
STAMBAUGH, T.	-	1/ 8	.125	3/ 4	.750	-/ 5	-	-	3	-	-	5	-
RICHARDSON, M.	-	3/ 6	.500	0/ 2	.000	-/ 5	-	-	0	-	-	6	-
DEMERS, B.	-	1/ 2	.500	2/ 2	1.000	-/ 1	-	-	2	-	-	4	-
Totals	200	26/58	.448	15/27	.556	-/36	-	-	17	-	-	67	.335

Team Rebounds: UNLV 5; Montana 3. Disqualified: None. Technical fouls: Montana—Coach Heathcote, McKenzie.

	1st Half	2nd Half	Final
UNLV	34	41	75
Montana	36	31	67

REGIONAL THIRD PLACE EAST
North Carolina (110)   Coach: Dean Smith

	Min.	Total FG / FGA	Pct.	FT / FTA	Pct.	Reb. O / T	A	TO	PF	S	Blk	TP	PPM
FORD, P.	34	8/16	.500	3/ 3	1.000	-/ 1	8	7	2	0	0	19	.559
HOFFMAN, B.	32	8/15	.533	0/ 0	.000	-/ 3	7	0	3	1	0	16	.500
HANNERS, D.	3	0/ 0	.000	0/ 0	.000	-/ 1	0	1	0	0	0	0	.000
KUESTER, J.	7	1/ 1	1.000	1/ 1	1.000	-/ 0	3	0	1	0	0	3	.429
KUPCHAK, M.	33	14/18	.778	8/13	.615	-/13	2	5	4	0	0	36	1.091
DAVIS, W.	29	7/12	.583	0/ 1	.000	-/ 5	6	5	5	1	0	14	.483
COLEY, W.	1	0/ 0	.000	0/ 0	.000	-/ 0	0	0	0	0	0	0	.000
BELL, M.	10	0/ 3	.000	0/ 0	.000	-/ 6	2	1	0	0	0	0	.000
VALIAGIRIS, T.	3	0/ 0	.000	2/ 2	1.000	-/ 0	0	0	0	0	0	2	.667
BUCKLEY, B.	4	0/ 0	.000	0/ 0	.000	-/ 2	0	1	1	0	0	0	.000
CHAMBERS, B.	3	0/ 1	.000	0/ 0	.000	-/ 0	0	0	0	0	0	0	.000
STAHL, E.	32	5/ 9	.556	6/ 6	1.000	-/ 9	3	2	3	0	0	16	.500
HARRY, E.	1	0/ 0	.000	0/ 0	.000	-/ 0	0	0	0	0	0	0	.000
LAGARDE, T.	8	1/ 2	.500	2/ 2	1.000	-/ 2	0	1	0	0	0	4	.500
Totals	200	44/77	.571	22/28	.786	-/42	31	23	18	2	0	110	.550

Boston College (90)   Coach: Bob Zuffelato

	Min.	Total FG / FGA	Pct.	FT / FTA	Pct.	Reb. O / T	A	TO	PF	S	Blk	TP	PPM
WELDON, M.	31	7/13	.538	0/ 0	.000	-/ 4	2	4	5	2	0	14	.452
CARRINGTON, B.	35	10/20	.500	3/ 3	1.000	-/ 2	3	4	3	4	1	23	.657
BAILEY, J.	26	2/13	.154	7/ 8	.875	-/ 1	4	3	2	1	0	11	.423
MORRISON, W.	30	5/ 8	.625	0/ 1	.000	-/ 4	1	3	4	1	0	10	.333
COLLINS, B.	33	5/ 8	.625	4/ 4	1.000	-/ 6	2	2	4	0	0	14	.424
O'BRIEN, J.	5	0/ 0	.000	0/ 0	.000	-/ 1	1	0	0	0	0	0	.000
JURGENS, J.	2	1/ 1	1.000	0/ 0	.000	-/ 0	0	0	0	0	0	2	1.000
BUONAGURO, M.	4	2/ 2	1.000	0/ 1	.000	-/ 1	0	0	1	0	0	4	1.000
TRACEY, F.	2	0/ 1	.000	0/ 0	.000	-/ 0	0	0	0	0	0	0	.000
SHIREY, M.	19	2/ 6	.333	0/ 0	.000	-/ 2	3	1	1	0	0	4	.211
SHEPARD, S.	13	3/ 6	.500	2/ 2	1.000	-/ 5	1	2	3	0	0	8	.615
Totals	200	37/78	.474	16/19	.842	-/26	17	19	23	8	1	90	.450

Team Rebounds: N. Carolina 10; Boston College 5. Disqualified: N. Carolina—Davis; Boston College—Weldon. Technical fouls: Boston College—Weldon, bench.

	1st Half	2nd Half	Final
N. Carolina	54	56	110
Boston College	37	53	90

REGIONAL THIRD PLACE MIDEAST
Central Michigan (88)   Coach: Dick Parfitt

	Min.	Total FG / FGA	Pct.	FT / FTA	Pct.	Reb. O / T	A	TO	PF	S	Blk	TP	PPM
DAVIS, R.	-	3/ 8	.375	0/ 0	.000	-/ 3	-	-	5	-	-	6	-
HELMINK, J.	-	4/10	.400	1/ 2	.500	-/ 4	-	-	0	-	-	9	-
ROUNDFIELD, D.	-	10/13	.769	5/ 9	.556	-/10	-	-	4	-	-	25	-
DRAKE, L.	-	4/ 9	.444	2/ 3	.667	-/ 8	-	-	5	-	-	10	-
McELROY, J.	-	8/16	.500	5/ 8	.625	-/ 6	-	-	1	-	-	21	-
PARKS, D.	-	0/ 0	.000	2/ 2	1.000	-/ 2	-	-	1	-	-	2	-
McCLAIN, J.	-	2/ 7	.286	0/ 0	.000	-/ 4	-	-	1	-	-	4	-
KAEDING, K.	-	1/ 1	1.000	2/ 2	1.000	-/ 2	-	-	2	-	-	4	-
ALEXANDER, D.	-	3/ 3	1.000	1/ 2	.500	-/ 3	-	-	2	-	-	7	-
CICOTTE, A.	-	0/ 0	.000	0/ 0	.000	-/ 0	-	-	0	-	-	0	-
Totals	200	35/67	.522	18/28	.643	-/42	-	-	21	-	-	88	.440

Oregon State (87)   Coach: Ralph Miller

	Min.	Total FG / FGA	Pct.	FT / FTA	Pct.	Reb. O / T	A	TO	PF	S	Blk	TP	PPM
SMITH, D.	-	9/14	.643	0/ 2	.000	-/10	-	-	0	-	-	18	-
SHELTON, L.	-	5/ 9	.556	0/ 0	.000	-/ 4	-	-	5	-	-	10	-
OXSEN, D.	-	3/ 9	.333	2/ 2	1.000	-/ 0	-	-	2	-	-	8	-
NEAL, C.	-	4/ 6	.667	2/ 2	1.000	-/ 4	-	-	4	-	-	10	-
TUCKER, G.	-	6/13	.462	1/ 2	.500	-/ 7	-	-	3	-	-	13	-
MILLER, P.	-	8/16	.500	0/ 1	.000	-/ 4	-	-	5	-	-	16	-
LEE, R.	-	4/ 6	.667	0/ 0	.000	-/ 2	-	-	2	-	-	8	-
DANIEL, R.	-	1/ 3	.333	2/ 5	.400	-/ 4	-	-	2	-	-	4	-
Totals	200	40/76	.526	7/14	.500	-/35	-	-	23	-	-	87	.435

Team Rebounds: Central Mich. 0; Oregon State 4. Disqualified: Central Mich.—Davis, Drake; Oregon State—Shelton, Miller. Technical fouls: None.

	1st Half	2nd Half	Final
Central Mich.	49	39	88
Oregon State	41	46	87

✪ ALL-STAR TEAMS ✪

ALL TOURNAMENT

KEVIN GREVEY	KENTUCKY
JIM LEE	SYRACUSE
DAVID MEYERS	UCLA
ALLEN MURPHY	LOUISVILLE
★ **RICHARD WASHINGTRON**	UCLA

★ Most Outstanding Player(s)

✪ INDIVIDUAL RECORDS ✪

SCORING

Most points in a single game
1 JUNIOR BRIDGEMAN, LOUISVILLE (vs. RUTGERS)   36
1 MITCH KUPCHAK, N. CAROLINA (vs. BOSTON COLLEGE)   36
3 CHUCKIE WILLIAMS, KANSAS STATE (vs. SYRACUSE)   35
3 MARQUES JOHNSON, UCLA (vs. ARIZONA ST.)35
5 3 tied for fifth place.

Most total points in the tournament
1 JIM LEE, SYRACUSE   119
2 RICHARD WASHINGTON, UCLA   108
3 RUDY HACKETT, SYRACUSE   106
4 ALLEN MURPHY, LOUISVILLE   102
4 JUNIOR BRIDGEMAN, LOUISVILLE   102

Highest scoring average (minimum 2 games)
1 ADRIAN DANTLEY, NOTRE DAME (92-3)   30.67
2 CHUCKIE WILLIAMS, KANSAS STATE (87-3)   29.00
3 JIM LEE, SYRACUSE (119-5)   23.80
4 JOHN LUCAS, MARYLAND (70-3)   23.33
5 STEVE GREEN, INDIANA (69-3)   23.00

FIELD GOALS

Most field goals in a single game
1　JUNIOR BRIDGEMAN, LOUISVILLE (vs. RUTGERS)　15
1　CHUCKIE WILLIAMS, KANSAS STATE (vs. BOSTON COLLEGE)　15
3　6 tied for third place.

Most total field goals in the tournament
1　JIM LEE, SYRACUSE　51
2　RICHARD WASHINGTON, UCLA　49
3　ALLEN MURPHY, LOUISVILLE　43
4　RUDY HACKETT, SYRACUSE　40
5　CHUCKIE WILLIAMS, KANSAS STATE　39

Most field goal attempts in a single game
1　CLYDE MAYES, FURMAN (vs. BOSTON COLLEGE)　31
2　KEVIN GREVY, KENTUCKY (vs. UCLA)　30
3　JIM LEE, SYRACUSE (vs. LOUISVILLE)　29
4　ALLEN MURPHY, LOUISVILLE (vs. UCLA)　28
5　CHUCKIE WILLIAMS, KANSAS STATE (vs. SYRACUSE)　27

Most total field goal attempts in the tournament
1　KEVIN GREVY, KENTUCKY　97
2　JIM LEE, SYRACUSE　95
3　ALLEN MURPHY, LOUISVILLE　87
4　RICHARD WASHINGTON, UCLA　86
5　DAVE MEYERS, UCLA　81

Highest field goal percentage in a single game (minimum 10 attempts)
1　CARL GERLACH, KANSAS STATE (vs. BOSTON COLLEGE) (9-10)　.900
2　JUNIOR BRIDGEMAN, LOUISVILLE (vs. RUTGERS) (15-18)　.833
3　BRAD HOFFMAN, N. CAROLINA (vs. SYRACUSE) (10-12)　.833
4　JIM WILLIAMS, SYRACUSE (vs. N. CAROLINA) (9-11)　.818
4　MITCH KUPCHAK, N. CAROLINA (vs. NEW MEXICO ST.) (9-11)　.818

Highest field goal percentage in the tournament (minimum 20 attempts)
1　MITCH KUPCHAK, N. CAROLINA (29-40)　.725
2　GARY JACKSON, ARIZONA ST. (14-20)　.700
2　RALPH DROLLINGER, UCLA (14-20)　.700
4　ROBERT MILLER, CINCINNATI (21-31)　.677
5　STEVE GREEN, INDIANA (29-43)　.674

FREE THROWS

Most free throws in a single game
1　ADRIAN DANTLEY, NOTRE DAME (vs. KANSAS)　15
2　ADRIAN DANTLEY, NOTRE DAME (vs. CINCINNATI)　14
3　GARRY KAMSTRA, CINCINNATI (vs. NOTRE DAME)　10
3　PHIL FORD, N. CAROLINA (vs. SYRACUSE)　10
3　BOB GUYETTE, KENTUCKY (vs. MARQUETTE)　10

Most total free throws in the tournament
1　ADRIAN DANTLEY, NOTRE DAME　34
2　JUNIOR BRIDGEMAN, LOUISVILLE　28
3　RUDY HACKETT, SYRACUSE　26
4　KEVIN GREVY, KENTUCKY　25
5　DAVE MEYERS, UCLA　21

Most free throws attempted in a single game
1　ADRIAN DANTLEY, NOTRE DAME (vs. KANSAS)　21
2　ADRIAN DANTLEY, NOTRE DAME (vs. CINCINNATI)　19
3　RUDY HACKETT, SYRACUSE (vs. KANSAS STATE)　16
4　LEON DOUGLAS, ALABAMA (vs. ARIZONA ST.)　14
5　2 tied for fifth place.

Most free throws attempted in the tournament
1　ADRIAN DANTLEY, NOTRE DAME　48
2　RUDY HACKETT, SYRACUSE　39
3　KEVIN GREVY, KENTUCKY　35
4　JUNIOR BRIDGEMAN, LOUISVILLE　34
5　DAN ROUNDFIELD, CENTRAL MICH.　30

Highest free throw percentage in a single game (minimum 7 attempts)
1　PHIL FORD, N. CAROLINA (vs. SYRACUSE) (10-10)　1.000
2　MIKE EVANS, KANSAS STATE (vs. SYRACUSE) (8-8)　1.000
2　JOHN LUCAS, MARYLAND (vs. NOTRE DAME) (8-8)　1.000
4　DAVE BATTON, NOTRE DAME (vs. KANSAS) (8-9)　.889
5　7 tied for fifth place.

Highest free throw percentage in the tournament (minimum 15 attempts)
1　PHIL FORD, N. CAROLINA (17-18)　.944
2　MIKE EVANS, KANSAS STATE (14-15)　.933
3　JOHN LUCAS, MARYLAND (14-16)　.875

4　GARRY KAMSTRA, CINCINNATI (13-15)　.867
5　JIM LEE, SYRACUSE (17-20)　.850

REBOUNDS

Most rebounds in a single game
1　KENT BENSON, INDIANA (vs. KENTUCKY)　23
2　LEON DOUGLAS, ALABAMA (vs. ARIZONA ST.)　21
3　MIKE FRANKLIN, CINCINNATI (vs. TEXAS A&M)　20
3　TOM ROY, MARYLAND (vs. LOUISVILLE)　20
5　CLYDE MAYES, FURMAN (vs. BOSTON COLLEGE)　19

Most total rebounds in the tournament
1　RICHARD WASHINGTON, UCLA　60
2　MARQUES JOHNSON, UCLA　49
2　MIKE FRANKLIN, CINCINNATI　49
4　DAVE MEYERS, UCLA　48
4　JUNIOR BRIDGEMAN, LOUISVILLE　48

Most rebounds per game (minimum 2 games)
1　MIKE FRANKLIN, CINCINNATI (49-3)　16.33
2　KENT BENSON, INDIANA (42-3)　14.00
3　JACK SCHRADER, ARIZONA ST. (38-3)　12.67
4　RICHARD WASHINGTON, UCLA (60-5)　12.00
5　KEN MCKENZIE, MONTANA (24-2)　12.00

ASSISTS

Most assists in a single game
1　ANDRE MCCARTER, UCLA (vs. KENTUCKY)　14
2　BOB WILKERSON, INDIANA (vs. OREGON STATE)　10
2　DALE GREENLEE, KANSAS (vs. NOTRE DAME)　10
4　JUNIOR BRIDGEMAN, LOUISVILLE (vs. SYRACUSE)　9
4　BRAD DAVIS, MARYLAND (vs. NOTRE DAME)　9

Most total assists in the tournament
1　PHILIP BOND, LOUISVILLE　35
2　ANDRE MCCARTER, UCLA　31
3　JUNIOR BRIDGEMAN, LOUISVILLE　27
4　JIMMY DAN CONNER, KENTUCKY　21
5　2 tied for fifth place.

Most assists per game (minimum 2 appearances)
1　PHILIP BOND, LOUISVILLE (35-5)　7.00
2　BOB WILKERSON, INDIANA (19-3)　6.33
2　PHIL FORD, N. CAROLINA (19-3)　6.33
4　ANDRE MCCARTER, UCLA (31-5)　6.20
5　BRAD DAVIS, MARYLAND (18-3)　6.00

❂ TEAM RECORDS ❂

SCORING

Most points in a single game
1　N. CAROLINA (vs. BOSTON COLLEGE)　110
2　UCLA (vs. MICHIGAN)　103
3　ARIZONA ST. (vs. ALABAMA)　97

Most total points in the tournament
1　KENTUCKY　438
2　LOUISVILLE　435
3　SYRACUSE　427

Highest scoring average (minimum 2 games)
1　N. CAROLINA (279-3)　93.00
2　KENTUCKY (438-5)　87.60
3　LOUISVILLE (435-5)　87.00

FIELD GOALS

Most field goals in a single game
1　N. CAROLINA (vs. BOSTON COLLEGE)　44
2　UCLA (vs. MICHIGAN)　42
3　OREGON STATE (vs. CENTRAL MICH.)　40
3　KENTUCKY (vs. CENTRAL MICH.)　40
3　ALABAMA (vs. ARIZONA ST.)　40

Most total field goals in the tournament
1　UCLA　177
2　KENTUCKY　174
3　2 tied for third place.

Most field goals attempted in a single game
1　FURMAN (vs. BOSTON COLLEGE)　89
2　3 tied for second place.

Most total field goals attempted in the tournament
1　KENTUCKY　380
2　UCLA　373
3　SYRACUSE　353

Highest field goal percentage in a single game
1　MARYLAND (vs. CREIGHTON) (36-55)　.655
2　N. CAROLINA (vs. SYRACUSE) (32-49)　.653
3　KANSAS STATE (vs. BOSTON COLLEGE) (34-54)　.630

Highest field goal percentage in the tournament (minimum 2 games)
1　N. CAROLINA (113-187)　.604
2　MARYLAND (97-182)　.533
3　LOUISVILLE (173-331)　.523

FREE THROWS

Most free throws in a single game
1	NOTRE DAME (vs. KANSAS)	35
2	CINCINNATI (vs. TEXAS A&M)	25
3	4 tied for third place.	

Most total free throws in the tournament
1	KENTUCKY	90
2	LOUISVILLE	89
3	SYRACUSE	81

Most free throws attempted in a single game
1	NOTRE DAME (vs. KANSAS)	50
2	KENTUCKY (vs. SYRACUSE)	38
3	INDIANA (vs. UTEP)	36

Most total free throws attempted in the tournament
1	KENTUCKY	138
2	LOUISVILLE	126
3	SYRACUSE	119

Highest free throw percentage in a single game
1	LOUISVILLE (vs. RUTGERS) (17-19)	.895
2	MARYLAND (vs. LOUISVILLE) (22-25)	.880
3	BOSTON COLLEGE (vs. KANSAS STATE) (11-13)	.846

Highest free throw percentage in the tournament (minimum 2 games)
1	BOSTON COLLEGE (47-58)	.810
2	N. CAROLINA (53-67)	.791
3	MARYLAND (54-69)	.783

Fewest free throws in a single game
1	FURMAN (vs. BOSTON COLLEGE)	0
2	PENNSYLVANIA (vs. KANSAS STATE)	4
3	2 tied for third place.	

Lowest free throw percentage in a single game
1	FURMAN (vs. BOSTON COLLEGE) (0-2)	0.000
2	SAN DIEGO ST. (vs. UNLV) (10-25)	.400
3	ALABAMA (vs. ARIZONA ST.) (14-29)	.483

Lowest free throw percentage in the tournament (minimum 2 games)
1	OREGON STATE (24-44)	.545
2	ARIZONA ST. (36-58)	.621
3	MONTANA (42-65)	.646

REBOUNDS

Most rebounds in a single game
1	LOUISVILLE (vs. SYRACUSE)	53
2	UCLA (vs. MICHIGAN)	52
3	KENTUCKY (vs. SYRACUSE)	51

Most rebounds per game (minimum 2 games)
1	LOUISVILLE (224-5)	44.80
2	UCLA (223-5)	44.60
3	KENTUCKY (221-5)	44.20

ASSISTS

Most assists in a single game
1	LOUISVILLE (vs. SYRACUSE)	32
2	N. CAROLINA (vs. BOSTON COLLEGE)	31
3	SYRACUSE (vs. LOUISVILLE)	27

Most assists per game (minimum 2 games)
1	N. CAROLINA (66-3)	22.00
2	LOUISVILLE (109-5)	21.80
3	SYRACUSE (94-5)	18.80

1976

| FIRST ROUND | REGIONAL SEMIFINAL | REGIONAL FINAL | **FINAL FOUR** | REGIONAL FINAL | REGIONAL SEMIFINAL | FIRST ROUND |

EAST

Virginia 60
DePaul 66
DePaul 69
VMI 75
VMI 81
VMI 71 (ot)
Tennessee 75
Rutgers 70
Princeton 53
Rutgers 93
Rutgers 54
Rutgers 91
Hofstra 78
U. Conn. 79
U. Conn. 80 (ot)

Indiana 65

Alabama 69
Alabama 79
N. Carolina 64
Indiana 65
Indiana 90
Indiana 74
St. John's 70

MIDEAST

Marquette 62
Western Ky. 60
Marquette 79
Marquette 56
Western Mich. 77 (ot)
Western Mich. 57
Virginia Tech 67

Indiana 86
Michigan 68

MIDWEST

Wichita St. 73
Michigan 80
Michigan 74
Michigan 95
Cincinnati 78
Notre Dame 76
Notre Dame 79
Michigan 86
Missouri 69
Missouri 86
Washington 67
Missouri 88
Texas Tech 69
Texas Tech 75
Syracuse 56

UCLA 51

Pepperdine 61
Pepperdine 87
Memphis St. 77
UCLA 82
San Diego St. 64
UCLA 70
UCLA 74

WEST

UNLV 109
Boise St. 78
UNLV 103
Arizona 66
Arizona 83
Arizona 114 (ot)
Georgetown 76

CONSOLATION GAME

National Third Place:

UCLA 106
Rutgers 92

In 1976, Bob Knight's Indiana Hoosiers were on a mission to prove they were the best. Their undefeated 1975 season had been ruined when they lost to Kentucky in the NCAA tournament, and they were not about to let it happen again.

Coach Knight drove his team hard, and they responded by sweating and putting more effort into perfecting the pressure defense and motion offense that their coach taught. They were a reflection of Knight's personality—dedicated and driven.

They refused to lose.

The team Knight assembled was one of the greatest in NCAA history. Some said the 1975 Hoosiers had stronger personnel. No matter, in 1976, college basketball's supreme squad of role players had their day. All five starters were solid team men, perfectly at home in Knight's disciplined system. Not one was a superstar, but they matched up well with the opposition at every position. The designated scorer, 6-7 forward Scott May, was an excellent outside shooter and a tenacious defender. The big man, 6-11 Kent Benson, was also a fine shooter and he was a tower of strength under the boards. The guards, 6-7 Bobby Wilkerson and 6-3 Quinn Buckner, were both strong, fast, and smart. Together they were among the best pair of defensive guards in basketball history. Buckner was also a savvy team leader, Knight's alter ego on the court. The fifth man, 6-7 Tom Abernethy, was an unselfish team player whose solid defense, strong court sense, and opportunistic scoring complemented his more celebrated teammates' contributions.

By the luck of the draw, the Hoosiers had to get through the tournament's strongest field to win the Mideast regional. After taking apart St. John's by a score of 90-70, they faced the Southeastern Conference champs, Alabama. The Crimson Tide matched up well against the Hoosiers with speed, size, and a big gun in the center in Leon Douglas. Knight knew that the Crimson Tide's strategy would be to go inside to Douglas, so he took off his defensive pressure and clogged up the middle. But Benson got into foul trouble and came out after picking up his fourth with 13:23 left; by the time he returned the lead was down to 4. With 5:11 left in the game and a 2-point Indiana lead, Douglas drove on Benson and was called for a charge. The Tide still managed to take a momentary 1-point lead, but in the end the Hoosiers made the clutch plays and Alabama lost their poise. The final was 74-69, Indiana.

The Hoosiers next came up against No. 2–ranked Marquette. This time it was Scott May who got into foul trouble, but after Butch Lee opened the second half by giving Marquette a 37-36 lead, May popped three straight jump shots. With ten minutes left, the Hoosiers were up by 10, but the Warriors clawed their way back into the game, finally closing to within 3. But Marquette Coach Al McGuire was called for his second technical of the night, and the Warriors' last fleeting hopes expired. Final score: 65-56, Indiana.

In the semis Indiana destroyed UCLA, as Tom Abernethy shut off Bruin star Richard Washington (not allowing him to score for 25 minutes), while hitting 7 of 8 from the floor himself.

Before the title contest against the Hoosiers' Big Ten rival Michigan, Knight's former teammate from the Ohio State 1960 national championship team, John Havlicek, came into the locker room to address the players. But whatever he said, it went for naught when less than three minutes into the game Bobby Wilkerson was knocked cold in a collision and had to be hospitalized with a concussion. Hoosier fans, remembering the disaster of 1975, feared the worst; in the words of the immortal Yogi Berra, it "looked like déjà vu all over again." Michigan, taking advantage of Wilkerson's absence, jumped all over the shaken Hoosiers, fast-breaking, neutralizing Benson off the boards, and taking a halftime lead of 35-29.

The Indiana players went into the dressing room fully expecting a tongue lashing from their volatile coach. Instead, May later told *The Indianapolis Star*, Knight came in quietly and said, "Hey, if you guys want to be champions, if you guys want to be No. 1 and undefeated, you've got 20 minutes to prove it." The Hoosiers came out ready. Benson and May took control of the boards, cutting off the Wolverine fast break. Wilkerson's replacements, Jim Wisman and Jim Crews, picked up ten assists between them. Buckner's all-over-the-court pressure forced turnovers and gave him five steals. And Michigan, unable to stop the Indiana big men from scoring, got into foul trouble. Playing flawless basketball, the Hoosiers dominated both ends of the court. Inevitably, inexorably, they came back. The final score wasn't even close. Indiana, 86-68.

Bob Knight had his championship. The pressure was finally off the Hoosier players. They had finished undefeated and proven to all the world that they would not be beaten.

FIRST ROUND EAST

Virginia (60)   Coach: Terry Holland

	Min.	Total FG / FGA	Pct.	FT / FTA	Pct.	Reb. O / T	A	TO	PF	S	Blk	TP	PPM
WALKER, W.	29	4/15	.267	3/ 3	1.000	-/ 7	2	0	5	0	0	11	.379
IAVARONI, M.	36	4/ 8	.500	1/ 2	.500	-/ 2	1	6	2	1	0	9	.250
FULTON, O.	32	5/ 8	.625	0/ 0	.000	-/ 8	1	4	1	1	1	10	.313
LANGLOH, B.	34	5/14	.357	4/ 4	1.000	-/ 2	2	3	5	0	0	14	.412
KOESTERS, D.	33	4/11	.364	0/ 0	.000	-/ 1	1	2	3	0	0	8	.242
CASTELLAN, S.	17	1/ 3	.333	2/ 2	1.000	-/ 3	0	0	1	0	1	4	.235
STOKES, B.	17	2/ 3	.667	0/ 0	.000	-/ 0	0	0	1	2	0	4	.235
BRISCOE, T.	2	0/ 0	.000	0/ 0	.000	-/ 0	0	0	2	0	0	0	.000
Totals	200	25/62	.403	10/11	.909	-/23	7	15	20	4	2	60	.300

DePaul (69)   Coach: Ray Meyer

	Min.	Total FG / FGA	Pct.	FT / FTA	Pct.	Reb. O / T	A	TO	PF	S	Blk	TP	PPM
NORWOOD, R.	40	11/15	.733	6/ 7	.857	-/ 2	2	5	3	0	2	28	.700
RAMSEY, R.	30	0/ 1	.000	2/ 2	1.000	-/ 1	0	1	3	0	0	2	.067
WATKINS, C.	37	3/ 4	.750	4/ 6	.667	-/ 8	1	0	2	0	1	10	.270
PANCRATZ, A.	13	3/ 5	.600	1/ 2	.500	-/ 3	0	1	1	0	2	7	.538
CORZINE, D.	33	4/10	.400	6/ 6	1.000	-/ 4	1	4	5	0	2	14	.424
PONSETTO, J.	36	3/ 9	.333	0/ 1	.000	-/12	3	4	2	1	1	6	.167
GARLAND, G.	10	1/ 2	.500	0/ 0	.000	-/ 1	0	1	0	0	0	2	.200
HOOK, R.	1	0/ 0	.000	0/ 0	.000	-/ 0	0	0	0	0	0	0	.000
Totals	200	25/46	.543	19/24	.792	-/31	7	16	16	1	8	69	.345

Team Rebounds: DePaul 3; Virginia 2. Disqualified: DePaul—Corzine; Virginia—Walker, Langloh. Technical fouls: Virginia—bench 2.

	1st Half	2nd Half	Final
Virginia	37	23	60
DePaul	31	38	69

Princeton (53)   Coach: Pete Carril

	Min.	Total FG / FGA	Pct.	FT / FTA	Pct.	Reb. O / T	A	TO	PF	S	Blk	TP	PPM
MOLLOY, P.	8	0/ 0	.000	0/ 1	.000	-/ 1	1	0	1	0	0	0	.000
OMELTCHENKO, B.	25	1/ 3	.333	0/ 0	.000	-/ 2	1	4	1	0	2	2	.080
STEURER, M.	19	1/ 2	.500	2/ 2	1.000	-/ 3	1	4	1	0	0	4	.211
HILL, A.	28	7/14	.500	0/ 1	.000	-/ 7	2	3	5	0	2	14	.500
SOWINSKI, F.	39	4/ 6	.667	3/ 3	1.000	-/ 4	0	2	4	0	1	11	.282
HAUPTFUHRER, B.	40	5/ 8	.625	2/ 2	1.000	-/ 3	3	2	1	1	1	12	.300
SLAUGHTER, B.	40	5/ 8	.625	0/ 0	.000	-/ 7	1	4	3	3	1	10	.250
RAMATI, L.	1	0/ 0	.000	0/ 0	.000	-/ 0	0	0	0	0	0	0	.000
Totals	200	23/41	.561	7/ 9	.778	-/27	9	16	19	5	5	53	.265

Rutgers (54)   Coach: Tom Young

	Min.	Total FG / FGA	Pct.	FT / FTA	Pct.	Reb. O / T	A	TO	PF	S	Blk	TP	PPM
SELLERS, P.	38	3/15	.200	7/ 9	.778	-/ 8	2	2	3	4	1	13	.342
BAILEY, J.	13	1/ 5	.200	0/ 0	.000	-/ 3	1	2	2	2	1	2	.154
JORDAN, E.	38	7/11	.636	2/ 3	.667	-/ 5	3	3	2	0	0	16	.421
DABNEY, M.	38	5/14	.357	3/ 4	.750	-/ 4	2	3	2	2	0	13	.342
COPELAND, H.	31	4/ 7	.571	0/ 0	.000	-/ 5	1	1	2	0	1	8	.258
CONLIN, M.	2	0/ 0	.000	0/ 0	.000	-/ 0	0	0	0	0	0	0	.000
HEFELE, S.	11	0/ 1	.000	0/ 0	.000	-/ 1	0	0	1	2	0	0	.000
ANDERSON, A.	29	1/ 3	.333	0/ 0	.000	-/ 2	1	0	4	0	1	2	.069
Totals	200	21/56	.375	12/16	.750	-/28	10	11	16	10	4	54	.270

Team Rebounds: Rutgers 4; Princeton 3. Disqualified: Princeton—Hill. Technical fouls: Rutgers—bench.

	1st Half	2nd Half	Final
Princeton	25	28	53
Rutgers	33	21	54

VMI (81)   Coach: Bill Blair

	Min.	Total FG / FGA	Pct.	FT / FTA	Pct.	Reb. O / T	A	TO	PF	S	Blk	TP	PPM
CARTER, R.	39	8/11	.727	3/ 6	.500	-/14	5	6	4	1	2	19	.487
REPPART, C.	39	5/ 7	.714	1/ 3	.333	-/ 1	5	5	2	1	0	11	.282
KROVIC, J.	37	6/ 9	.667	5/ 5	1.000	-/ 2	5	1	0	0	0	17	.459
BYNUM, W.	38	8/14	.571	4/ 4	1.000	-/ 4	0	2	4	1	0	20	.526
MONTGOMERY, D.	27	4/ 5	.800	2/ 4	.500	-/ 6	0	1	4	2	1	10	.370
BORGIEVICH, G.	18	2/ 4	.500	0/ 0	.000	-/ 5	0	3	3	0	0	4	.222
LOMBARD, K.	1	0/ 0	.000	0/ 0	.000	-/ 0	0	2	1	0	0	0	.000
KELLEY, P.	1	0/ 0	.000	0/ 0	.000	-/ 0	0	2	1	0	0	0	.000
Totals	200	33/50	.660	15/22	.682	-/32	15	22	19	5	3	81	.405

Tennessee (75)   Coach: Ray Mears

	Min.	Total FG / FGA	Pct.	FT / FTA	Pct.	Reb. O / T	A	TO	PF	S	Blk	TP	PPM
GRUNFELD, E.	40	13/23	.565	10/13	.769	-/ 8	0	5	3	3	0	36	.900
JACKSON, M.	39	5/13	.385	4/ 5	.800	-/ 1	0	4	5	1	0	14	.359
ASHWORTH, D.	31	3/ 6	.500	0/ 0	.000	-/ 3	2	1	2	0	0	6	.194
CLARK, A.	39	3/ 9	.333	3/ 3	1.000	-/ 8	3	0	5	1	0	9	.231
DARDEN, J.	40	4/ 8	.500	0/ 0	.000	-/ 1	6	1	2	3	0	8	.200
CROSBY, T.	10	0/ 2	.000	0/ 2	.000	-/ 1	0	1	3	1	0	0	.000
SMITHSON, M.	1	1/ 1	1.000	0/ 0	.000	-/ 1	0	0	0	0	0	2	2.000
Totals	200	29/62	.468	17/23	.739	-/23	11	12	20	12	0	75	.375

Team Rebounds: VMI 0; Tennessee 2. Disqualified: Tennessee—Jackson, Clark. Technical fouls: VMI—bench; Tennessee—bench, Darden.

	1st Half	2nd Half	Final
VMI	37	44	81
Tennessee	38	37	75

Hofstra (78)   Coach: Roger Gaeckler

	Min.	Total FG / FGA	Pct.	FT / FTA	Pct.	Reb. O / T	A	TO	PF	S	Blk	TP	PPM
KAMMERER, P.	-	3/ 5	.600	2/ 4	.500	-/ 5	1	-	4	-	-	8	-
LAUREL, R.	-	4/10	.400	3/ 3	1.000	-/ 4	3	-	5	-	-	11	-
ROOD, K.	-	8/18	.444	2/ 3	.667	-/ 0	4	-	5	-	-	18	-
TOMLIN, B.	-	7/14	.500	2/ 2	1.000	-/ 2	3	-	2	-	-	16	-
IRVING, J.	-	9/ 9	1.000	2/ 5	.400	-/13	2	-	4	-	-	20	-
JENKINS, M.	-	1/ 5	.200	0/ 0	.000	-/ 7	1	-	2	-	-	2	-
VICKERS, W.	-	1/ 2	.500	1/ 3	.333	-/ 2	1	-	2	-	-	3	-
Totals	225	33/63	.524	12/20	.600	-/33	15	17	24	-	-	78	.390

U. Conn. (80)   Coach: Dee Rowe

	Min.	Total FG / FGA	Pct.	FT / FTA	Pct.	Reb. O / T	A	TO	PF	S	Blk	TP	PPM
WHELTON, J.	-	11/22	.500	1/ 3	.333	-/ 2	5	-	2	-	-	23	-
WESTON, A.	-	6/12	.500	6/ 6	1.000	-/ 0	4	-	4	-	-	18	-
THOMAS, J.	-	1/ 3	.333	3/ 4	.750	-/11	4	-	2	-	-	5	-
HANSON, T.	-	5/10	.500	2/ 3	.667	-/ 9	2	-	5	-	-	12	-
CARR, J.	-	7/12	.583	3/ 8	.375	-/15	2	-	3	-	-	17	-
ABROMAITIS, J.	-	0/ 2	.000	0/ 0	.000	-/ 1	1	-	2	-	-	0	-
LAVIGNE, R.	-	2/ 3	.667	1/ 1	1.000	-/ 1	1	-	0	-	-	5	-
KELLY, L.	-	0/ 0	.000	0/ 1	.000	-/ 1	0	-	0	-	-	0	-
HARRIS, B.	-	0/ 0	.000	0/ 0	.000	-/ 0	1	-	1	-	-	0	-
Totals	225	32/64	.500	16/26	.615	-/40	20	11	19	-	-	80	.356

Team Rebounds: U. Conn. 4; Hofstra 3. Disqualified: U. Conn.—Hanson; Hofstra—Laurel, Rood.

	1st Half	2nd Half	1st OT	Final
Hofstra	43	32	3	78
U. Conn.	30	45	5	80

FIRST ROUND MIDWEST

Wichita State (73)   Coach: Harry Miller

	Min.	Total FG / FGA	Pct.	FT / FTA	Pct.	Reb. O / T	A	TO	PF	S	Blk	TP	PPM
JOHNSON, L.	37	5/ 9	.556	2/ 4	.500	-/ 7	2	2	3	--	--	12	.324
GRAY, R.	35	5/13	.385	0/ 0	.000	-/ 7	0	2	3	--	--	10	.286
ELMORE, B.	27	5/10	.500	8/10	.800	-/ 7	0	2	4	--	--	18	.667
BRUTON, C.	35	6/13	.462	3/ 4	.750	-/ 3	4	2	2	--	--	15	.429
TROGELE, B.	30	1/ 4	.250	3/ 4	.750	-/ 4	2	2	2	--	--	5	.167
BRENT, C.	10	3/ 5	.600	0/ 0	.000	-/ 3	0	1	1	--	--	6	.600
KALOCINSKI	9	1/ 3	.333	0/ 0	.000	-/ 3	1	0	2	--	--	2	.222
YODER, D.	14	2/ 2	1.000	1/ 2	.500	-/ 3	0	0	0	--	--	5	.357
McCULLOUGH, J.	2	0/ 0	.000	0/ 0	.000	-/ 0	0	0	0	--	--	0	.000
FORD, S.	1	0/ 0	.000	0/ 0	.000	-/ 0	0	0	0	--	--	0	.000
Totals	200	28/59	.475	17/24	.708	-/37	9	11	17	--	--	73	.365

Michigan (74)   Coach: Johnny Orr

	Min.	Total FG / FGA	Pct.	FT / FTA	Pct.	Reb. O / T	A	TO	PF	S	Blk	TP	PPM
BRITT, W.	30	2/ 8	.250	0/ 0	.000	-/ 5	3	0	2	--	--	4	.133
ROBINSON, J.	26	4/ 7	.571	2/ 2	1.000	-/ 4	1	0	3	--	--	10	.385
HUBBARD, P.	32	6/12	.500	3/ 5	.600	-/ 9	0	2	5	--	--	15	.469
GREEN, R.	31	4/17	.235	2/ 3	.667	-/ 7	1	2	3	--	--	10	.323
GROTE, S.	36	7/10	.700	3/ 4	.750	-/ 4	0	1	3	--	--	17	.472
BAXTER, D.	13	3/ 6	.500	0/ 0	.000	-/ 0	0	0	4	--	--	6	.462
HARDY, A.	10	0/ 3	.000	0/ 0	.000	-/ 3	1	1	0	--	--	0	.000
THOMPSON, J.	3	1/ 1	1.000	0/ 0	.000	-/ 1	0	0	0	--	--	2	.667
STATON, T.	11	3/ 5	.600	0/ 0	.000	-/ 0	0	1	2	--	--	6	.545
BERGEN, T.	8	2/ 5	.400	0/ 0	.000	-/ 1	0	0	4	--	--	4	.500
Totals	200	32/74	.432	10/14	.714	-/34	6	7	26	--	--	74	.370

Team Rebounds: Michigan 7; Wichita State 4. Disqualified: Michigan—Hubbard.

	1st Half	2nd Half	Final
Wichita State	41	32	73
Michigan	35	39	74

Cincinnati (78)   Coach: Gale Catlett

	Min.	Total FG / FGA	Pct.	FT / FTA	Pct.	Reb. O / T	A	TO	PF	S	Blk	TP	PPM
COLLIER, S.	20	3/ 7	.429	0/ 0	.000	-/ 2	3	2	2	1	0	6	.300
WILLIAMS, B.	34	9/19	.474	1/ 2	.500	-/ 6	0	2	2	3	1	19	.559
MILLER, R.	30	4/ 6	.667	1/ 3	.333	-/ 7	0	2	1	1	1	9	.300
JONES, M.	19	3/ 5	.600	0/ 0	.000	-/ 5	1	0	4	0	0	6	.316
CUMMINGS, P.	33	3/ 9	.429	2/ 2	1.000	-/ 4	0	1	2	1	0	8	.242
YODER, G.	24	6/ 8	.750	2/ 2	1.000	-/ 3	0	2	0	2	0	14	.583
WARD, H.	17	3/ 5	.600	6/ 6	1.000	-/ 1	0	3	1	0	0	12	.706
KAMSTRA, G.	14	1/ 2	.500	0/ 0	.000	-/ 2	1	0	0	0	0	2	.143
ARTIS, M.	9	1/ 4	.250	0/ 0	.000	-/ 0	0	0	0	0	0	2	.222
Totals	200	33/63	.524	12/15	.800	-/30	5	12	12	8	2	78	.390

Notre Dame (79)   Coach: Digger Phelps

	Min.	Total FG / FGA	Pct.	FT / FTA	Pct.	Reb. O / T	A	TO	PF	S	Blk	TP	PPM
MARTIN, R.	-	0/ 1	.000	0/ 0	.000	-/ 1	1	1	3	3	1	0	-
PATERNO, B.	-	2/ 8	.250	0/ 0	.000	-/ 4	0	0	2	0	0	4	-
BATTON, D.	-	1/ 8	.125	0/ 0	.000	-/ 6	0	0	1	0	1	2	-
FLOWERS, B.	-	4/ 5	.800	0/ 0	.000	-/ 2	1	1	3	1	0	8	-
DANTLEY, A.	-	10/18	.556	7/ 8	.875	-/ 8	1	3	3	0	0	27	-
WILLIAMS, D.	-	11/17	.647	0/ 0	.000	-/ 2	1	3	2	0	0	22	-
RENCHER, B.	-	2/ 6	.333	0/ 0	.000	-/ 4	1	0	1	0	0	4	-
KNIGHT, T.	-	6/10	.600	0/ 0	.000	-/ 6	0	3	4	0	0	12	-
Totals	200	36/73	.493	7/ 8	.875	-/33	5	11	18	5	1	79	.395

Team Rebounds: Notre Dame 5; Cincinnati 3. Disqualified: None.

	1st Half	2nd Half	Final
Cincinnati	39	39	78
Notre Dame	37	42	79

Missouri (69)   Coach: Norm Stewart

	Min.	Total FG / FGA	Pct.	FT / FTA	Pct.	Reb. O / T	A	TO	PF	S	Blk	TP	PPM
ANDERSON, K.	25	6/11	.545	0/ 3	.000	-/ 6	1	7	5	0	0	12	.480
KENNEDY, J.	30	5/11	.455	10/13	.769	-/ 4	0	1	1	2	0	20	.667
CLABON, J.	40	4/ 9	.444	0/ 1	.000	-/10	1	1	3	0	1	8	.200
CURRIE, J.	37	1/ 2	.500	1/ 2	.500	-/ 5	3	2	4	1	0	3	.081
SMITH, W.	40	7/23	.304	7/10	.700	-/ 2	7	6	3	6	0	21	.525
RAY, S.	23	2/ 3	.667	0/ 0	.000	-/ 2	0	1	2	0	0	4	.174
SIMS, S.	4	0/ 0	.000	1/ 2	.500	-/ 2	0	0	0	0	0	1	.250
ANDERSON, M.	1	0/ 0	.000	0/ 0	.000	-/ 0	0	0	0	0	0	0	.000
Totals	200	25/59	.424	19/31	.613	-/31	12	18	18	9	1	69	.345

Washington (67)   Coach: Marv Harshman

	Min.	Total FG / FGA	Pct.	FT / FTA	Pct.	Reb. O / T	A	TO	PF	S	Blk	TP	PPM
HANSEN, L.	25	6/10	.600	2/ 2	1.000	-/10	0	4	5	1	1	14	.560
STEWART, K.	34	6/ 8	.750	0/ 2	.000	-/ 6	1	5	4	1	0	12	.353
EDWARDS, J.	36	4/12	.333	4/ 4	1.000	-/10	5	2	5	1	0	12	.333
DORSEY, C.	34	3/ 4	.750	1/ 2	.500	-/ 5	7	4	5	1	0	7	.206
RAMSEY, C.	37	7/16	.438	0/ 0	.000	-/ 1	2	2	3	2	0	14	.378
LOMBARD, K.	17	1/ 4	.250	0/ 0	.000	-/ 0	0	1	5	0	0	2	.118
NEILL, M.	7	2/ 4	.500	0/ 0	.000	-/ 1	1	0	1	0	0	4	.571
PARKER	2	0/ 0	.000	0/ 0	.000	-/ 1	0	2	0	0	0	0	.000
JOCK	7	1/ 2	.500	0/ 1	.000	-/ 4	1	0	0	0	0	2	.286
SMITH	1	0/ 0	.000	0/ 0	.000	-/ 1	0	0	0	0	0	0	.000
Totals	200	30/60	.500	7/13	.538	-/39	17	20	28	6	1	67	.335

Team Rebounds: Missouri 6; Washington 6. Disqualified: Missouri—K. Anderson; Washington—Hansen, Edwards, Dorsey, Lombard.

	1st Half	2nd Half	Final
Missouri	30	39	69
Washington	36	31	67

Texas Tech (69)   Coach: Gerald Myers

	Min.	Total FG / FGA	Pct.	FT / FTA	Pct.	Reb. O / T	A	TO	PF	S	Blk	TP	PPM
NEWTON, G.	27	3/ 6	.500	0/ 0	.000	-/ 5	1	0	2	0	0	6	.222
RUSSELL, M.	39	8/13	.615	5/ 7	.714	-/12	0	3	5	0	1	21	.538
BULLOCK, R.	32	7/ 9	.778	5/ 7	.714	-/ 5	1	3	4	0	0	19	.594
KITCHENS, K.	37	3/ 6	.500	4/ 4	1.000	-/ 5	3	4	2	0	0	10	.270
DUNN, S.	37	2/ 6	.333	3/ 4	.750	-/ 2	2	6	2	3	0	7	.189
DUKES, G.	15	1/ 5	.200	0/ 0	.000	-/ 3	2	1	3	0	0	2	.133
HUSTON	5	1/ 1	1.000	0/ 0	.000	-/ 1	0	0	0	0	0	2	.400
LIGGINS, R.	5	1/ 1	1.000	0/ 0	.000	-/ 1	0	2	1	0	0	2	.400
EDWARDS, M.	1	0/ 0	.000	0/ 0	.000	-/ 0	0	0	0	0	0	0	.000
LEE, S.	1	0/ 1	.000	0/ 0	.000	-/ 0	0	0	0	0	0	0	.000
IVEY, D.	1	0/ 0	.000	0/ 0	.000	-/ 0	0	0	0	0	0	0	.000
Totals	200	26/48	.542	17/22	.773	-/34	9	19	19	3	1	69	.345

Syracuse (56)   Coach: Roy Danforth

	Min.	Total FG / FGA	Pct.	FT / FTA	Pct.	Reb. O / T	A	TO	PF	S	Blk	TP	PPM
SHACKLEFORD, D.	28	2/ 8	.250	0/ 0	.000	-/ 8	2	2	3	2	0	4	.143
SEASE, C.	29	2/ 8	.250	0/ 1	.000	-/ 2	1	0	1	1	0	4	.138
BYRNES, M.	37	4/ 7	.571	4/ 6	.667	-/ 6	0	1	3	0	1	12	.324
KINDEL, R.	20	0/ 3	.000	1/ 2	.500	-/ 2	0	0	3	3	0	1	.050
WILLIAMS	35	9/20	.450	3/ 4	.750	-/ 0	0	3	3	1	0	21	.600
SEIBERT, E.	13	0/ 2	.000	0/ 0	.000	-/ 0	1	2	1	0	1	0	.000
KELLEY, L.	24	7/ 9	.778	0/ 0	.000	-/ 1	2	0	4	1	1	14	.583
KEYS, B.	2	0/ 1	.000	0/ 2	.000	-/ 2	0	0	0	0	0	0	.000
JAMES, K.	8	0/ 1	.000	0/ 0	.000	-/ 1	1	0	0	0	0	0	.000
KING, K.	3	0/ 0	.000	0/ 0	.000	-/ 0	0	0	1	0	0	0	.000
ARRINGTON	1	0/ 2	.000	0/ 0	.000	-/ 0	0	1	1	0	0	0	.000
Totals	200	24/61	.393	8/15	.533	-/22	7	9	20	8	3	56	.280

Team Rebounds: Texas Tech 5; Syracuse 6. Disqualified: Texas Tech—Russell.

	1st Half	2nd Half	Final
Texas Tech	39	30	69
Syracuse	28	28	56

FIRST ROUND MIDEAST

Alabama (79) Coach: C.M. Newton

	Min.	Total FG/FGA	Pct.	FT/FTA	Pct.	Reb. O/T	A	TO	PF	S	Blk	TP	PPM
KING, R.	36	6/11	.545	1/2	.500	-/11	1	4	4	0	0	13	.361
BROWN, R.	38	4/12	.333	0/0	.000	-/7	3	6	3	1	0	8	.211
DOUGLAS, L.	37	16/23	.696	3/5	.600	-/17	1	5	4	0	3	35	.946
DUNN, T.	38	3/7	.429	0/0	.000	-/6	6	2	1	1	1	6	.158
MURRAY, A.	34	3/6	.500	7/12	.583	-/1	4	4	3	4	0	13	.382
MCCORD, K.	7	1/1	1.000	0/0	.000	-/0	1	0	2	0	0	2	.286
MCELVEEN, G.	10	0/2	.000	2/2	1.000	-/1	0	0	0	0	0	2	.200
Totals	200	33/62	.532	13/21	.619	-/43	16	21	17	6	4	79	.395

North Carolina (64) Coach: Dean Smith

	Min.	Total FG/FGA	Pct.	FT/FTA	Pct.	Reb. O/T	A	TO	PF	S	Blk	TP	PPM
DAVIS, W.	35	6/17	.353	4/5	.800	-/7	5	1	3	2	1	16	.457
LAGARDE, T.	29	9/16	.563	4/4	1.000	-/11	2	0	3	0	0	22	.759
KUPCHAK, M.	31	3/11	.273	2/2	1.000	-/12	1	3	2	0	1	8	.258
FORD, P.	28	1/5	.200	0/0	.000	-/2	3	5	1	3	0	2	.071
KUESTER, J.	33	3/8	.375	0/0	.000	-/1	5	4	4	2	0	6	.182
BUCKLEY, B.	10	2/4	.500	0/1	.000	-/0	0	1	0	0	0	4	.400
BRADLEY, D.	9	1/5	.200	0/0	.000	-/0	3	2	1	0	0	2	.222
SALIAGIRIS, T.	4	0/2	.000	0/0	.000	-/0	0	0	0	0	0	0	.000
HANNERS, D.	15	1/2	.500	0/0	.000	-/0	1	1	5	5	0	2	.133
COLEY, W.	2	0/1	.000	0/0	.000	-/1	0	0	0	0	0	0	.000
CHAMBERS, B.	3	1/2	.500	0/0	.000	-/0	0	0	1	0	0	2	.667
VALENTINE, K.	1	0/0	.000	0/0	.000	-/0	0	0	1	1	0	0	.000
Totals	200	27/73	.370	10/12	.833	-/34	20	17	21	13	2	64	.320

Team Rebounds: Alabama 3; N. Carolina 2. Disqualified: N. Carolina—Hanners.

	1st Half	2nd Half	Final
Alabama	40	39	79
N. Carolina	28	36	64

Indiana (90) Coach: Bob Knight

	Min.	Total FG/FGA	Pct.	FT/FTA	Pct.	Reb. O/T	A	TO	PF	S	Blk	TP	PPM
MAY, S.	38	14/23	.609	5/5	1.000	-/7	2	5	3	1	0	33	.868
ABERNETHY, T.	38	3/5	.600	1/2	.500	-/6	2	2	2	0	1	7	.184
BENSON, K.	37	8/18	.444	4/4	1.000	-/13	2	5	3	1	1	20	.541
WILKERSON, B.	24	1/5	.200	4/4	1.000	-/3	6	4	1	2	0	6	.250
BUCKNER, Q.	34	7/13	.538	1/2	.500	-/2	3	1	3	2	0	15	.441
RADFORD, W.	20	2/2	1.000	1/1	1.000	-/3	1	0	2	0	0	5	.250
WISMAN, J.	2	0/1	.000	0/0	.000	-/0	0	0	0	0	0	0	.000
CREWS, J.	1	1/1	1.000	0/0	.000	-/2	0	0	0	0	0	2	2.000
VALAVICIUS, R.	2	0/1	.000	0/0	.000	-/0	0	0	0	0	0	0	.000
BENDER, B.	1	0/0	.000	0/0	.000	-/0	0	0	0	0	0	0	.000
ROBERSON, J.	2	0/1	.000	0/0	.000	-/0	0	0	0	0	0	0	.000
HAYMORE, M.	1	1/1	1.000	0/0	.000	-/1	0	0	0	0	0	2	2.000
Totals	200	37/71	.521	16/18	.889	-/37	16	17	14	6	2	90	.450

St. John's (70) Coach: Lou Carnesecca

	Min.	Total FG/FGA	Pct.	FT/FTA	Pct.	Reb. O/T	A	TO	PF	S	Blk	TP	PPM
FARMER, J.	21	2/6	.333	0/0	.000	-/3	0	1	2	0	0	4	.190
SMITH, B.	30	2/9	.222	1/2	.500	-/8	1	6	4	2	0	5	.167
JOHNSON, G.	35	5/15	.333	0/0	.000	-/7	0	0	2	2	2	10	.286
WILLIAMS, G.	37	10/15	.667	0/1	.000	-/3	3	4	4	1	0	20	.541
ALAGIA, F.	34	7/13	.538	3/4	.750	-/6	4	4	2	3	0	17	.500
RELLFORD, C.	22	5/7	.714	0/0	.000	-/2	1	2	4	0	0	10	.455
CLARKE, B.	3	0/0	.000	0/0	.000	-/0	0	2	1	0	0	0	.000
WINFREE, K.	8	1/1	1.000	0/0	.000	-/1	0	0	1	0	0	2	.250
WEADOCK, F.	3	0/0	.000	0/0	.000	-/0	0	0	0	0	0	0	.000
MENAR, R.	1	0/0	.000	0/0	.000	-/0	0	0	0	0	0	0	.000
CALABRESE, T.	3	0/1	.000	0/0	.000	-/0	0	0	0	0	0	0	.000
ROBERTSON, H.	1	1/3	.333	0/0	.000	-/2	0	1	0	1	0	2	2.000
MCGUHINS, T.	1	0/0	.000	0/0	.000	-/0	0	0	0	0	0	0	.000
MCRAE, F.	1	0/1	.000	0/0	.000	-/1	0	0	0	0	0	0	.000
Totals	200	33/71	.465	4/7	.571	-/33	9	20	20	9	2	70	.350

Team Rebounds: Indiana 4; St. John's 3. Disqualified: None. Technical fouls: None.

	1st Half	2nd Half	Final
Indiana	44	46	90
St. John's	37	33	70

Western Kentucky (60) Coach: Jim Richards

	Min.	Total FG/FGA	Pct.	FT/FTA	Pct.	Reb. O/T	A	TO	PF	S	Blk	TP	PPM
WARNER, M.	30	1/3	.333	0/0	.000	-/4	1	1	1	0	1	2	.067
JAMES, W.	16	1/6	.167	2/3	.667	-/5	1	3	5	0	0	4	.250
JOHNSON, J.	37	3/4	.750	3/3	1.000	-/9	0	2	2	1	0	9	.243
RAWLINGS, C.	37	7/14	.500	0/0	.000	-/1	4	2	2	0	0	14	.378
BRITT, J.	37	9/17	.529	1/1	1.000	-/3	4	4	3	2	0	19	.514
SCILLIAN, B.	25	3/6	.500	0/0	.000	-/4	2	6	0	0	0	6	.240
ASHBY	14	0/0	.000	0/0	.000	-/2	1	2	0	0	0	0	.000
TERRY, L.	1	1/2	.500	2/2	1.000	-/1	0	0	2	0	1	4	4.000
GREGORY, G.	2	1/1	1.000	0/0	.000	-/0	0	0	0	0	0	2	1.000
GRIMES, D.	1	0/0	.000	0/0	.000	-/0	0	0	0	-	0	0	.000
Totals	200	26/53	.491	8/9	.889	-/27	13	20	15	3	2	60	.300

Marquette (79) Coach: Al McGuire

	Min.	Total FG/FGA	Pct.	FT/FTA	Pct.	Reb. O/T	A	TO	PF	S	Blk	TP	PPM
ELLIS, B.	40	5/14	.357	1/1	1.000	-/14	3	3	3	0	0	11	.275
TATUM, E.	38	8/14	.571	2/2	1.000	-/6	2	1	1	2	2	18	.474
WHITEHEAD, J.	33	6/9	.667	0/0	.000	-/7	0	1	3	1	0	12	.364
LEE, B.	31	10/20	.500	1/3	.333	-/5	3	1	0	0	0	21	.677
WALTON, L.	38	3/12	.250	3/4	.750	-/3	6	2	3	2	0	9	.237
TOONE, B.	5	1/1	1.000	0/0	.000	-/0	0	1	2	0	0	2	.400
NEARY, B.	2	0/1	.000	0/0	.000	-/0	0	0	0	0	0	0	.000
ROSENBERGER, G.	9	2/2	1.000	0/0	.000	-/2	2	0	0	0	0	4	.444
PAYNE, U.	2	1/1	1.000	0/0	.000	-/1	1	0	0	0	0	2	1.000
BUTRYM, C.	1	0/0	.000	0/0	.000	-/0	0	0	0	0	0	0	.000
BRENNAN, B.	1	0/0	.000	0/0	.000	-/0	1	0	0	0	0	0	.000
Totals	200	36/74	.486	7/10	.700	-/38	18	9	12	5	2	79	.395

Team Rebounds: Marquette 1; Western Ky. 1. Disqualified: Western Ky.—James. Technical fouls: None.

	1st Half	2nd Half	Final
Western Ky.	29	31	60
Marquette	36	43	79

Western Michigan (77) Coach: Eldon Miller

	Min.	Total FG/FGA	Pct.	FT/FTA	Pct.	Reb. O/T	A	TO	PF	S	Blk	TP	PPM
GRIFFIN, P.	42	5/6	.833	4/7	.571	-/15	0	2	3	1	2	14	.333
TYSON, J.	38	11/27	.407	3/5	.600	-/8	3	4	4	0	0	25	.658
CUTTER, T.	36	4/9	.444	9/11	.818	-/11	2	2	4	2	0	17	.472
KURZEN, J.	31	1/5	.200	0/0	.000	-/1	7	1	1	0	0	2	.065
HARVEY, J.	33	5/11	.455	0/0	.000	-/2	1	2	2	1	0	10	.303
MURRAY, M.	18	4/10	.400	1/3	.333	-/4	1	3	2	1	0	9	.500
DEBRUIN, D.	5	0/1	.000	0/2	.000	-/1	0	0	1	2	0	0	.000
SALES, S.	15	0/0	.000	0/2	.000	-/0	0	0	1	0	0	0	.000
REARDON, M.	5	0/3	.000	0/0	.000	-/1	0	0	0	1	0	0	.000
THROOP, M.	2	0/0	.000	0/0	.000	-/0	0	0	0	0	0	0	.000
Totals	225	30/72	.417	17/30	.567	-/43	14	14	18	8	4	77	.342

Virginia Tech (67) Coach: Don DeVoe

	Min.	Total FG/FGA	Pct.	FT/FTA	Pct.	Reb. O/T	A	TO	PF	S	Blk	TP	PPM
DAVIS, R.	40	7/18	.389	2/4	.500	-/11	1	4	4	0	1	16	.400
THIENEMAN, P.	20	2/4	.500	0/0	.000	-/1	0	1	1	0	0	4	.200
WANSLEY, E.	18	2/3	.667	0/0	.000	-/3	0	3	4	0	0	4	.222
COOKE, L.	39	5/20	.250	1/1	1.000	-/6	2	7	4	0	2	11	.282
SENSIBAUGH, D.	45	2/5	.400	0/0	.000	-/1	7	4	4	0	4	4	.089
THORPE, D.	38	7/9	.778	5/7	.714	-/9	0	3	4	0	2	19	.500
MCKEE, K.	25	4/8	.500	1/3	.333	-/10	2	1	5	1	0	9	.360
Totals	225	29/67	.433	9/15	.600	-/41	12	23	22	5	5	67	.298

Team Rebounds: Western Mich. 8; Virginia Tech 7. Disqualified: Virginia Tech—McKee. Technical fouls: None.

	1st Half	2nd Half	1st OT	Final
Western Mich.	30	35	12	77
Virginia Tech	39	26	2	67

FIRST ROUND WEST

Pepperdine (87)   Coach: Gary Colson

	Min.	Total FG / FGA	Pct.	FT / FTA	Pct.	Reb. O / T	A	TO	PF	S	Blk	TP	PPM
WILLIAMS, F.	39	6/ 9	.667	2/ 2	1.000	-/ 7	2	5	2	2	1	14	.359
JOHNSON, D.	36	3/ 9	.333	4/ 8	.500	-/ 6	5	8	4	2	0	10	.278
LEITE, M.	39	12/22	.545	10/11	.909	-/ 8	2	5	3	0	2	34	.872
SKOPHAMMER, D.	39	3/ 7	.429	2/ 3	.667	-/10	1	4	0	1	8		.205
MATSON, O.	39	7/16	.438	5/ 9	.556	-/11	4	1	3	2	1	19	.487
GOORJIAN, B.	6	0/ 1	.000	0/ 1	.000	-/ 0	1	0	0	0	0	0	.000
DALLMAR, H.	2	1/ 1	1.000	0/ 0	.000	-/ 0	0	0	1	0	0	2	1.000
Totals	200	32/65	.492	23/34	.676	-/42	15	20	17	6	5	87	.435

Memphis State (77)   Coach: Wayne Yates

	Min.	Total FG / FGA	Pct.	FT / FTA	Pct.	Reb. O / T	A	TO	PF	S	Blk	TP	PPM
WRIGHT, A.	35	2/ 6	.333	0/ 0	.000	-/ 1	4	4	3	2	0	4	.114
REED, D.	38	8/17	.471	0/ 0	.000	-/ 1	5	4	3	1	0	16	.421
COOK, B.	25	3/11	.273	7/ 8	.875	-/ 4	1	5	4	2	0	13	.520
HILLARD, M.	20	4/ 8	.500	3/ 4	.750	-/ 8	1	0	4	1	0	11	.550
WASHINGTON, J.	19	2/ 2	1.000	2/ 2	1.000	-/ 1	2	2	5	1	4	6	.316
GUNN, J.	19	5/ 8	.625	0/ 0	.000	-/ 4	0	3	2	1	0	10	.526
HANCOCK, B.	5	0/ 0	.000	3/ 4	.750	-/ 0	1	1	0	0	0	3	.600
KILZER, J.	1	0/ 0	.000	0/ 0	.000	-/ 0	0	0	0	0	0	0	.000
JONES, C.	19	3/ 6	.500	2/ 2	1.000	-/ 4	1	1	3	0	0	8	.421
WILSON, E.	19	3/ 6	.500	0/ 0	.000	-/ 9	0	0	5	0	0	6	.316
Totals	200	30/64	.469	17/20	.850	-/32	15	20	29	8	4	77	.385

Team Rebounds: Pepperdine 1; Memphis State 4. Disqualified: Memphis State—Washington, Wilson. Technical fouls: None.

	1st Half	2nd Half	Final
Pepperdine	38	49	87
Memphis State	41	36	77

San Diego State (64)   Coach: Tim Vezie

	Min.	Total FG / FGA	Pct.	FT / FTA	Pct.	Reb. O / T	A	TO	PF	S	Blk	TP	PPM
LEARY, R.	25	3/ 7	.429	0/ 0	.000	-/ 1	4	3	1	0	0	6	.240
EARLE, G.	4	0/ 2	.000	0/ 0	.000	-/ 1	0	1	1	0	0	0	.000
DELSMAN, M.	18	2/ 4	.500	0/ 0	.000	-/ 2	2	1	3	1	0	4	.222
BROWN, J.	1	0/ 0	.000	0/ 0	.000	-/ 1	0	0	0	0	0	0	.000
COPP, S.	38	8/19	.421	4/ 5	.800	-/11	0	1	3	1	1	20	.526
DODD, M.	1	0/ 0	.000	0/ 0	.000	-/ 0	0	0	0	0	0	0	.000
KOVACH, B.	34	3/11	.273	5/ 8	.625	-/ 6	1	1	3	1	0	11	.324
CONNELLY, W.	38	5/14	.357	1/ 2	.500	-/ 9	0	3	0	0	1	11	.289
KRAMER, J.	5	1/ 3	.333	0/ 0	.000	-/ 0	0	0	0	0	0	2	.400
BUNTING, A.	36	3/13	.231	4/ 4	1.000	-/ 5	2	4	3	0	1	10	.278
Totals	200	25/73	.342	14/19	.737	-/36	9	11	17	3	2	64	.320

UCLA (74)   Coach: Gene Bartow

	Min.	Total FG / FGA	Pct.	FT / FTA	Pct.	Reb. O / T	A	TO	PF	S	Blk	TP	PPM
TOWNSEND, R.	33	3/ 6	.500	0/ 0	.000	-/ 0	2	1	2	2	0	6	.182
WASHINGTON, R.	36	10/15	.667	5/ 5	1.000	-/ 8	4	5	3	0	1	25	.694
VROMAN, B.	4	0/ 0	.000	0/ 0	.000	-/ 2	0	1	2	0	0	0	.000
GREENWOOD, D.	22	1/ 3	.333	2/ 2	1.000	-/ 3	1	3	4	1	0	4	.182
DROLLINGER, R.	14	2/ 4	.500	0/ 0	.000	-/ 7	1	1	4	0	0	4	.286
SPILLANE, J.	10	1/ 2	.500	0/ 0	.000	-/ 1	1	1	2	0	0	2	.200
McCARTER, A.	38	4/ 9	.444	2/ 5	.400	-/ 5	2	1	0	2	1	10	.263
OLINDE, W.	1	0/ 0	.000	0/ 0	.000	-/ 0	0	1	0	0	0	0	.000
JOHNSON, M.	35	7/ 9	.778	5/ 6	.833	-/ 9	2	4	4	1	4	19	.543
SMITH, G.	7	2/ 7	.286	0/ 0	.000	-/ 1	1	1	1	0	0	4	.571
Totals	200	30/55	.545	14/18	.778	-/36	14	19	22	6	6	74	.370

Team Rebounds: UCLA 7; San Diego St. 3. Disqualified: None. Technical fouls: None.

	1st Half	2nd Half	Final
San Diego St.	32	32	64
UCLA	35	39	74

Boise State (78)   Coach: Bus Connor

	Min.	Total FG / FGA	Pct.	FT / FTA	Pct.	Reb. O / T	A	TO	PF	S	Blk	TP	PPM
JONES, D.	-	7/13	.538	4/ 5	.800	-/ 9	-	-	4	-	-	18	-
JOHNSON, T.	-	6/11	.545	0/ 1	.000	-/ 6	-	-	3	-	-	12	-
HOKE, P.	-	3/ 5	.600	0/ 4	.000	-/ 3	-	-	5	-	-	6	-
CONNOR, S.	-	8/16	.500	10/13	.769	-/ 1	-	-	4	-	-	26	-
MILLER, T.	-	1/ 3	.333	3/ 5	.600	-/ 1	-	-	2	-	-	5	-
MORGAN, T.	-	2/ 2	1.000	1/ 2	.500	-/ 1	-	-	1	-	-	5	-
TRUTANICH, D.	-	0/ 0	.000	0/ 0	.000	-/ 0	-	-	0	-	-	0	-
STEWART, M.	-	0/ 1	.000	2/ 2	1.000	-/ 0	-	-	0	-	-	2	-
NEWELL, K.	-	0/ 1	.000	0/ 0	.000	-/ 0	-	-	0	-	-	0	-
McKENNA, S.	-	1/ 1	1.000	2/ 2	1.000	-/ 1	-	-	2	-	-	4	-
CHRISTIANSON, M.	-	0/ 2	.000	0/ 0	.000	-/ 3	-	-	3	-	-	0	-
Totals	200	28/55	.509	22/34	.647	-/25	-	-	24	-	-	78	.390

UNLV (103)   Coach: Jerry Tarkanian

	Min.	Total FG / FGA	Pct.	FT / FTA	Pct.	Reb. O / T	A	TO	PF	S	Blk	TP	PPM
ROBINSON, J.	-	9/13	.692	2/ 3	.667	-/13	-	-	3	-	-	20	-
BATTS, B.	-	5/11	.455	1/ 1	1.000	-/ 7	-	-	4	-	-	11	-
GONDREZICK, G.	-	5/14	.357	1/ 2	.500	-/ 6	-	-	3	-	-	11	-
SMITH, R.	-	2/ 5	.400	1/ 1	1.000	-/ 0	-	-	5	-	-	5	-
OWENS, E.	-	11/18	.611	2/ 3	.667	-/ 4	-	-	5	-	-	24	-
THEUS, R.	-	2/ 3	.667	2/ 2	1.000	-/ 1	-	-	5	-	-	6	-
BROWN, L.	-	4/ 9	.444	2/ 3	.667	-/ 8	-	-	2	-	-	10	-
SMITH, S.	-	6/12	.500	4/ 6	.667	-/ 4	-	-	3	-	-	16	-
MILKE, M.	-	0/ 0	.000	0/ 0	.000	-/ 0	-	-	0	-	-	0	-
PORTER, M.	-	0/ 0	.000	0/ 0	.000	-/ 0	-	-	1	-	-	0	-
BERKOWITZ, M.	-	0/ 0	.000	0/ 0	.000	-/ 1	-	-	0	-	-	0	-
WEIMER, D.	-	0/ 1	.000	0/ 3	.000	-/ 2	-	-	0	-	-	0	-
PARAMORE, D.	-	0/ 1	.000	0/ 0	.000	-/ 3	-	-	0	-	-	0	-
Totals	200	44/87	.506	15/24	.625	-/49	-	-	31	-	-	103	.515

Team Rebounds: UNLV 8; Boise St. 9. Disqualified: UNLV—R. Smith, Owens, Theus; Boise St.—Hoke. Technical fouls: Boise St.—Connor.

	1st Half	2nd Half	Final
Boise St.	39	39	78
UNLV	48	55	103

Arizona (83)   Coach: Fred Snowden

	Min.	Total FG/FGA	Pct.	FT/FTA	Pct.	Reb. O/T	A	TO	PF	S	Blk	TP	PPM
RAPPIS, J.	34	8/13	.615	4/5	.800	-/3	3	3	4	0	0	20	.588
HARRIS, H.	34	6/12	.500	1/2	.500	-/3	8	5	3	3	0	13	.382
ELLIOTT, B.	39	5/11	.455	4/9	.444	-/8	1	7	0	1	1	14	.359
FLEMING, A.	39	3/7	.429	6/10	.600	-/12	5	4	3	2	0	12	.308
TAYLOR, P.	30	6/7	.857	3/5	.600	-/11	0	4	5	1	0	15	.500
MYLES, G.	15	1/2	.500	7/9	.778	-/5	3	5	1	1	0	9	.600
HARRISON, G.	2	0/0	.000	0/0	.000	-/0	0	0	1	0	0	0	.000
GORDY, L.	1	0/0	.000	0/0	.000	-/0	0	1	1	0	0	0	.000
MAXEY, S.	1	0/0	.000	0/0	.000	-/0	0	0	0	0	0	0	.000
ALEKSA, B.	1	0/0	.000	0/0	.000	-/0	0	0	0	0	0	0	.000
GLADNEY, J.	4	0/0	.000	0/0	.000	-/1	0	1	0	0	0	0	.000
Totals	200	29/52	.558	25/40	.625	-/43	20	30	18	8	1	83	.415

Georgetown (76)   Coach: John Thompson

	Min.	Total FG/FGA	Pct.	FT/FTA	Pct.	Reb. O/T	A	TO	PF	S	Blk	TP	PPM
RILEY, M.	9	0/0	.000	2/2	1.000	-/4	2	1	3	1	0	2	.222
JACKSON, D.	33	10/23	.435	2/3	.667	-/0	1	3	3	3	0	22	.667
WILSON, M.	19	1/4	.250	2/2	1.000	-/4	0	2	5	0	2	4	.211
YEOMAN, F.	2	0/1	.000	0/0	.000	-/2	0	0	0	0	0	0	.000
DUTCH, A.	14	2/8	.250	2/2	1.000	-/5	0	2	2	0	0	6	.429
ESHERICK, G.	2	0/2	.000	0/0	.000	-/0	0	0	0	0	0	0	.000
LYNN, B.	18	1/7	.143	0/0	.000	-/2	1	0	1	1	1	2	.111
MARTIN, S.	9	1/4	.250	0/0	.000	-/2	1	0	1	0	0	2	.222
THOMAS, B.	4	0/2	.000	0/0	.000	-/0	1	0	2	0	0	0	.000
SMITH, J.	27	9/17	.529	2/3	.667	-/4	7	2	5	2	0	20	.741
LONG, L.	26	3/8	.375	4/4	1.000	-/7	2	2	1	3	0	10	.385
WILSON, G.	8	0/0	.000	0/0	.000	-/1	0	1	4	0	0	0	.000
MCDERMOTT, M.	3	1/3	.333	0/0	.000	-/1	0	0	0	0	0	2	.667
HOPKINS, E.	26	3/3	1.000	0/0	.000	-/4	0	2	4	0	0	6	.231
Totals	200	31/82	.378	14/16	.875	-/36	15	15	31	10	3	76	.380

Team Rebounds: Arizona 7; Georgetown 4. Disqualified: Arizona—Taylor; Georgetown—M. Wilson, Smith. Technical fouls: Georgetown—Wilson, Coach Thompson 2.

	1st Half	2nd Half	Final
Arizona	41	42	83
Georgetown	32	44	76

REGIONAL SEMIFINAL EAST

DePaul (66)   Coach: Ray Meyer

	Min.	Total FG/FGA	Pct.	FT/FTA	Pct.	Reb. O/T	A	TO	PF	S	Blk	TP	PPM
NORWOOD, R.	39	9/20	.450	5/7	.714	-/3	2	0	5	1	0	23	.590
RAMSEY, R.	43	4/8	.500	0/0	.000	-/1	2	3	2	2	1	8	.186
WATKINS, C.	33	4/12	.333	2/4	.500	-/8	0	2	5	0	0	10	.303
PANCRATZ, A.	13	0/5	.000	0/0	.000	-/4	0	1	5	0	0	0	.000
CORZINE, D.	30	6/15	.400	2/4	.500	-/15	1	5	5	0	4	14	.467
PONSETTO, J.	36	2/3	.667	1/6	.167	-/3	4	6	4	1	0	5	.139
GARLAND, G.	10	1/3	.333	0/0	.000	-/4	0	1	5	0	0	2	.200
HOOK, R.	5	1/1	1.000	0/1	.000	-/0	0	0	2	1	0	2	.400
COEHLO, G.	1	0/1	.000	0/0	.000	-/0	0	0	0	0	0	0	.000
MCGOVERN, E.	10	1/6	.167	0/0	.000	-/3	0	0	2	0	0	2	.200
WYDRA, G.	5	0/0	.000	0/0	.000	-/0	0	1	0	0	0	0	.000
Totals	225	28/74	.378	10/22	.455	-/41	9	19	35	5	5	66	.293

VMI (71)   Coach: Bill Blair

	Min.	Total FG/FGA	Pct.	FT/FTA	Pct.	Reb. O/T	A	TO	PF	S	Blk	TP	PPM
CARTER, R.	45	8/14	.571	5/10	.500	-/12	1	4	4	4	2	21	.467
REPPART, C.	37	1/3	.333	3/10	.300	-/3	0	4	4	0	0	5	.135
KROVIC, J.	45	4/12	.333	0/2	.000	-/5	2	2	2	1	0	8	.178
BYNUM, W.	43	7/12	.583	8/10	.800	-/6	1	3	4	0	0	22	.512
MONTGOMERY, D.	32	4/12	.333	4/7	.571	-/14	0	2	3	2	1	12	.375
BORGIEVICH, G.	15	1/3	.333	1/3	.333	-/1	0	1	4	0	0	3	.200
LOMBARD, K.	8	0/0	.000	0/0	.000	-/0	1	0	1	0	0	0	.000
Totals	225	25/56	.446	21/42	.500	-/41	5	16	22	7	3	71	.316

Team Rebounds: VMI 5; DePaul 12. Disqualified: DePaul—Norwood, Watkins, Corzine, Garland, Pancratz. Technical fouls: DePaul—Corzine.

	1st Half	2nd Half	1 OT	Final
DePaul	33	29	4	66
VMI	31	31	9	71

Rutgers (93)   Coach: Tom Young

	Min.	Total FG/FGA	Pct.	FT/FTA	Pct.	Reb. O/T	A	TO	PF	S	Blk	TP	PPM
SELLERS, P.	-	4/13	.308	0/2	.000	-/5	3	-	3	-	-	8	-
BAILEY, J.	-	0/4	.000	0/2	.000	-/4	1	-	4	-	-	0	-
JORDAN, E.	-	6/10	.600	6/6	1.000	-/5	5	-	1	-	-	18	-
DABNEY, M.	-	8/16	.500	2/4	.500	-/6	0	-	2	-	-	18	-
COPELAND, H.	-	8/11	.727	0/0	.000	-/4	0	-	5	-	-	16	-
NANCE, S.	-	0/1	.000	0/0	.000	-/0	0	-	0	-	-	0	-
CONLIN, M.	-	0/0	.000	0/0	.000	-/1	0	-	3	-	-	0	-
KLEINBAUM, J.	-	0/2	.000	0/0	.000	-/2	0	-	0	-	-	0	-
HEFELE, S.	-	7/9	.778	0/0	.000	-/7	2	-	2	-	-	14	-
ANDERSON, A.	-	6/16	.375	7/9	.778	-/11	0	-	2	-	-	19	-
Totals	200	39/82	.476	15/23	.652	-/45	11	-	22	-	-	93	.465

U. Conn. (79)   Coach: Dee Rowe

	Min.	Total FG/FGA	Pct.	FT/FTA	Pct.	Reb. O/T	A	TO	PF	S	Blk	TP	PPM
WHELTON, J.	-	6/14	.429	2/3	.667	-/0	1	-	3	-	-	14	-
WESTON, A.	-	8/17	.471	8/8	1.000	-/5	1	-	2	-	-	24	-
THOMAS, J.	-	2/8	.250	2/4	.500	-/19	3	-	4	-	-	6	-
HANSON, T.	-	10/17	.588	3/3	1.000	-/9	0	-	4	-	-	23	-
CARR, J.	-	1/3	.333	2/2	1.000	-/1	0	-	1	-	-	4	-
LAVIGNE, R.	-	0/1	.000	0/0	.000	-/0	0	-	0	-	-	0	-
ABROMAITIS, J.	-	2/6	.333	0/0	.000	-/9	0	-	3	-	-	4	-
HARRIS, R.	-	1/4	.250	2/2	1.000	-/4	0	-	1	-	-	4	-
KELLY, L.	-	0/3	.000	0/0	.000	-/1	0	-	1	-	-	0	-
Totals	200	30/73	.411	19/22	.864	-/44	5	-	19	-	-	79	.395

Team Rebounds: Rutgers 7; U. Conn. 0. Disqualified: Rutgers—Copeland. Technical fouls: None.

	1st Half	2nd Half	Final
Rutgers	53	40	93
U. Conn.	47	32	79

REGIONAL SEMIFINAL MIDWEST

Michigan (80)　Coach: Johnny Orr

	Min.	Total FG/FGA	Pct.	FT/FTA	Pct.	Reb. O/T	A	TO	PF	S	Blk	TP	PPM
BRITT, W.	25	6/9	.667	0/0	.000	-/3	1	1	5	1	0	12	.480
ROBINSON, J.	38	5/13	.385	5/6	.833	-/8	1	2	2	1	1	15	.395
HUBBARD, P.	36	5/13	.385	1/2	.500	-/10	0	2	4	1	0	11	.306
GREEN, R.	39	8/16	.500	4/4	1.000	-/4	3	5	1	1	0	20	.513
GROTE, S.	29	4/10	.400	6/6	1.000	-/4	3	3	5	2	0	14	.483
BAXTER, D.	12	1/5	.200	0/0	.000	-/1	1	0	0	0	0	2	.167
HARDY, A.	2	0/1	.000	0/0	.000	-/1	1	0	0	0	0	0	.000
STATON, T.	15	3/6	.500	0/1	.000	-/2	0	1	3	1	0	6	.400
BERGEN, T.	4	0/0	.000	0/0	.000	-/0	0	0	0	0	0	0	.000
Totals	200	32/73	.438	16/19	.842	-/33	10	14	20	7	1	80	.400

Notre Dame (76)　Coach: Digger Phelps

	Min.	Total FG/FGA	Pct.	FT/FTA	Pct.	Reb. O/T	A	TO	PF	S	Blk	TP	PPM
MARTIN, R.	26	1/2	.500	0/1	.000	-/2	4	3	5	1	0	2	.077
PATERNO, B.	20	5/9	.556	0/0	.000	-/4	1	2	2	1	0	10	.500
BATTON, D.	34	2/8	.250	2/2	1.000	-/13	4	3	2	0	2	6	.176
FLOWERS, B.	24	3/6	.500	0/0	.000	-/9	3	1	5	1	0	6	.250
DANTLEY, A.	39	12/19	.632	7/8	.875	-/5	1	7	1	1	0	31	.795
WILLIAMS, D.	34	6/13	.462	3/4	.750	-/2	3	4	3	0	0	15	.441
RENCHER, B.	2	1/1	1.000	2/3	.667	-/0	0	0	0	0	0	4	2.000
CARPENTER, J.	1	0/0	.000	0/0	.000	-/0	0	1	0	0	0	0	.000
KNIGHT, T.	20	1/4	.250	0/0	.000	-/5	1	3	4	0	3	2	.100
Totals	200	31/62	.500	14/18	.778	-/40	17	23	23	4	5	76	.380

Team Rebounds: Michigan 3; Notre Dame 2. Disqualified: Michigan—Britt, Grote; Notre Dame—Flowers, Martin. Technical fouls: None.

	1st Half	2nd Half	Final
Michigan	40	40	80
Notre Dame	41	35	76

Missouri (86)　Coach: Norm Stewart

	Min.	Total FG/FGA	Pct.	FT/FTA	Pct.	Reb. O/T	A	TO	PF	S	Blk	TP	PPM
KENNEDY, J.	36	7/14	.500	1/3	.333	-/6	1	4	3	0	0	15	.417
ANDERSON, K.	32	7/12	.583	1/2	.500	-/11	1	0	4	1	3	15	.469
CLABON, J.	31	4/10	.400	0/0	.000	-/5	2	1	4	0	3	8	.258
CURRIE, J.	24	2/4	.500	2/3	.667	-/3	1	1	1	0	1	6	.250
SMITH, W.	39	13/21	.619	4/6	.667	-/10	7	4	2	0	0	30	.769
RAY, S.	18	4/7	.571	0/0	.000	-/6	0	2	3	0	0	8	.444
SIMS, S.	16	0/1	.000	4/4	1.000	-/3	2	0	2	0	0	4	.250
VAN, R.	2	0/0	.000	0/0	.000	-/1	0	1	0	0	0	0	.000
DROY, B.	1	0/0	.000	0/0	.000	-/0	0	0	0	0	0	0	.000
STALLMAN, D.	1	0/0	.000	0/0	.000	-/0	0	1	1	0	0	0	.000
Totals	200	37/69	.536	12/18	.667	-/45	14	14	20	1	7	86	.430

Texas Tech (75)　Coach: Gerald Myers

	Min.	Total FG/FGA	Pct.	FT/FTA	Pct.	Reb. O/T	A	TO	PF	S	Blk	TP	PPM
NEWTON, G.	29	3/6	.500	0/0	.000	-/4	2	0	3	1	0	6	.207
RUSSELL, M.	39	6/15	.400	2/4	.500	-/14	1	0	1	3	1	14	.359
BULLOCK, R.	31	8/20	.400	7/12	.583	-/14	1	3	5	0	1	23	.742
KITCHENS, K.	16	0/7	.000	0/0	.000	-/0	0	3	1	0	0	0	.000
DUNN, S.	22	2/9	.222	0/2	.000	-/2	3	0	1	0	0	4	.182
LIGGINS, R.	7	0/3	.000	0/0	.000	-/0	0	0	2	0	0	0	.000
HUSTON, G.	24	4/10	.400	2/2	1.000	-/1	3	0	2	1	0	10	.417
DUKES, G.	12	4/8	.500	0/0	.000	-/3	0	1	1	0	0	8	.667
EDWARDS, M.	18	4/8	.500	2/5	.400	-/4	0	2	4	1	0	10	.556
LEE, S.	1	0/0	.000	0/0	.000	-/0	0	0	0	0	0	0	.000
RUDOLPH, B.	1	0/1	.000	0/0	.000	-/0	0	0	0	0	0	0	.000
Totals	200	31/87	.356	13/25	.520	-/42	10	9	20	6	2	75	.375

Team Rebounds: Missouri 6; Texas Tech 4. Disqualified: Texas Tech—Bullock. Technical fouls: Missouri—bench.

	1st Half	2nd Half	Final
Missouri	45	41	86
Texas Tech	36	39	75

REGIONAL SEMIFINAL MIDEAST

Alabama (69)　Coach: C.M. Newton

	Min.	Total FG/FGA	Pct.	FT/FTA	Pct.	Reb. O/T	A	TO	PF	S	Blk	TP	PPM
KING, R.	25	2/6	.333	0/0	.000	-/6	0	3	5	0	1	4	.160
BROWN, R.	25	3/7	.429	1/2	.500	-/5	0	2	4	0	0	7	.280
DOUGLAS, L.	39	5/16	.313	2/6	.333	-/7	3	3	4	0	2	12	.308
DUNN, T.	37	7/14	.500	2/2	1.000	-/5	1	2	5	2	1	16	.432
MURRAY, A.	38	7/11	.636	1/2	.500	-/7	4	3	1	2	0	15	.395
MCCORD, K.	25	5/9	.556	1/2	.500	-/3	0	1	2	0	0	11	.440
MCELVEEN, G.	7	1/4	.250	0/0	.000	-/1	1	0	1	0	0	2	.286
BONDS, T.	4	1/2	.500	0/0	.000	-/0	0	0	1	0	0	2	.500
Totals	200	31/69	.449	7/14	.500	-/34	9	14	23	4	4	69	.345

Indiana (74)　Coach: Bob Knight

	Min.	Total FG/FGA	Pct.	FT/FTA	Pct.	Reb. O/T	A	TO	PF	S	Blk	TP	PPM
MAY, S.	40	9/22	.409	7/9	.778	-/16	0	5	2	0	0	25	.625
ABERNETHY, T.	40	2/6	.333	4/5	.800	-/6	3	1	1	0	0	8	.200
BENSON, K.	33	7/11	.636	1/2	.500	-/5	3	3	4	0	1	15	.455
WILKERSON, B.	40	6/12	.500	2/2	1.000	-/12	4	7	1	0	0	14	.350
BUCKNER, Q.	31	5/8	.625	2/5	.400	-/2	4	2	4	1	0	12	.387
RADFORD, W.	9	0/1	.000	0/0	.000	-/1	0	1	1	1	0	0	.000
WISMAN, J.	1	0/0	.000	0/0	.000	-/0	0	1	0	0	0	0	.000
VALAVICIUS, R.	6	0/0	.000	0/1	.000	-/0	0	0	0	0	0	0	.000
Totals	200	29/60	.483	16/24	.667	-/42	14	20	13	2	1	74	.370

Team Rebounds: Indiana 2; Alabama 1. Disqualified: Alabama—King, Dunn. Technical fouls: None.

	1st Half	2nd Half	Final
Alabama	29	40	69
Indiana	37	37	74

Marquette (62)　Coach: Al McGuire

	Min.	Total FG/FGA	Pct.	FT/FTA	Pct.	Reb. O/T	A	TO	PF	S	Blk	TP	PPM
ELLIS, B.	38	3/7	.429	2/2	1.000	-/7	0	-	4	1	4	8	.211
TATUM, E.	35	5/12	.417	0/0	.000	-/8	2	-	4	0	1	10	.286
WHITEHEAD, J.	35	5/10	.500	0/0	.000	-/7	0	-	1	0	1	10	.286
LEE, B.	36	8/14	.571	0/0	.000	-/0	4	-	2	1	1	16	.444
WALTON, L.	34	6/12	.500	0/0	.000	-/1	5	-	4	2	0	12	.353
TOONE, B.	7	1/1	1.000	0/0	.000	-/0	0	-	0	0	0	2	.286
NEARY, B.	3	0/0	.000	0/0	.000	-/2	0	-	0	0	0	0	.000
ROSENBERGER, G.	8	1/4	.250	2/2	1.000	-/0	0	-	0	0	0	4	.500
PAYNE, U.	4	0/1	.000	0/0	.000	-/1	0	-	0	0	0	0	.000
Totals	200	29/61	.475	4/4	1.000	-/26	11	14	15	4	7	62	.310

Western Michigan (57)　Coach: Eldon Miller

	Min.	Total FG/FGA	Pct.	FT/FTA	Pct.	Reb. O/T	A	TO	PF	S	Blk	TP	PPM
GRIFFIN, P.	31	1/2	.500	0/0	.000	-/9	6	-	3	2	0	2	.065
TYSON, J.	38	8/16	.500	2/4	.500	-/5	3	-	5	0	2	18	.474
CUTTER, T.	40	8/12	.667	5/5	1.000	-/17	1	-	1	0	1	21	.525
KURZEN, J.	30	1/2	.500	0/0	.000	-/0	2	-	2	0	0	2	.067
HARVEY, J.	28	4/13	.308	2/4	.500	-/2	1	-	0	0	0	10	.357
MURRAY, M.	24	2/9	.222	0/0	.000	-/2	1	-	2	0	0	4	.167
DEBRUIN, D.	9	0/0	.000	0/1	.000	-/3	1	-	0	0	0	0	.000
Totals	200	24/54	.444	9/14	.643	-/38	15	25	13	2	3	57	.285

Team Rebounds: Marquette 1; Western Mich. 0. Disqualified: Western Mich.—Tyson. Technical fouls: None.

	1st Half	2nd Half	Final
Marquette	28	34	62
Western Mich.	25	32	57

REGIONAL SEMIFINAL WEST

Pepperdine (61)   Coach: Gary Colson

	Min.	Total FG/FGA	Pct.	FT/FTA	Pct.	Reb. O/T	A	TO	PF	S	Blk	TP	PPM
MATSON, O.	34	4/ 9	.444	2/ 3	.667	-/ 5	3	-	5	-	-	10	.294
SKOPHAMMER, D.	39	4/11	.364	0/ 0	.000	-/ 9	2	-	4	-	-	8	.205
LEITE, M.	40	4/14	.286	8/10	.800	-/ 8	1	-	3	-	-	16	.400
WILLIAMS, F.	38	4/10	.400	2/ 2	1.000	-/ 0	2	-	3	-	-	10	.263
JOHNSON, D.	39	7/14	.500	2/ 5	.400	-/ 6	0	-	2	-	-	16	.410
DALLMAR, H.	3	0/ 0	.000	0/ 0	.000	-/ 2	0	-	1	-	-	0	.000
GOORVIAN, B.	3	0/ 0	.000	0/ 0	.000	-/ 0	0	-	0	-	-	0	.000
ELLIS, R.	4	0/ 0	.000	1/ 2	.500	-/ 2	0	-	0	-	-	1	.250
Totals	200	23/58	.397	15/22	.682	-/32	8	20	18	-	-	61	.305

UCLA (70)   Coach: Gene Bartow

	Min.	Total FG/FGA	Pct.	FT/FTA	Pct.	Reb. O/T	A	TO	PF	S	Blk	TP	PPM
TOWNSEND, R.	37	4/ 6	.667	0/ 0	.000	-/ 4	3	-	2	-	-	8	.216
WASHINGTON, R.	37	7/18	.389	2/ 5	.400	-/ 6	4	-	2	-	-	16	.432
VROMAN, B.	2	0/ 0	.000	0/ 0	.000	-/ 1	0	-	1	-	-	0	.000
GREENWOOD, D.	24	5/ 9	.556	0/ 0	.000	-/ 7	0	-	5	-	-	10	.417
DROLLINGER, R.	14	4/ 7	.571	0/ 0	.000	-/ 6	2	-	5	-	-	8	.571
SPILLANE, J.	4	0/ 0	.000	0/ 0	.000	-/ 0	0	-	0	-	-	0	.000
JOHNSON, M.	39	6/14	.429	6/ 6	1.000	-/10	2	-	3	-	-	18	.462
SMITH, G.	4	3/ 4	.750	0/ 2	.000	-/ 0	0	-	0	-	-	6	1.500
CARTER, A.	39	2/ 4	.500	0/ 0	.000	-/ 2	7	-	1	-	-	4	.103
Totals	200	31/62	.500	8/13	.615	-/36	18	17	19	-	-	70	.350

Team Rebounds: UCLA 0; Pepperdine 4. Disqualified: UCLA—Greenwood, Drollinger; Pepperdine—Matson. Technical fouls: None.

	1st Half	2nd Half	Final
Pepperdine	35	26	61
UCLA	40	30	70

UNLV (109)   Coach: Jerry Tarkanian

	Min.	Total FG/FGA	Pct.	FT/FTA	Pct.	Reb. O/T	A	TO	PF	S	Blk	TP	PPM
OWENS, E.	27	9/18	.500	3/ 3	1.000	-/ 1	1	-	5	-	-	21	.778
ROBINSON, J.	17	1/ 3	.333	0/ 1	.000	-/ 4	0	-	5	-	-	2	.118
BATTS, B.	34	4/12	.333	0/ 2	.000	-/ 9	1	-	3	-	-	8	.235
SMITH, R.	39	4/10	.400	10/10	1.000	-/ 1	4	-	4	-	-	18	.462
GONDREZIK, G.	30	4/ 9	.444	0/ 1	.000	-/ 5	2	-	5	-	-	8	.267
BROWN, L.	36	10/19	.526	4/ 5	.800	-/16	0	-	4	-	-	24	.667
SMITH, S.	28	9/20	.450	8/10	.800	-/ 5	0	-	5	-	-	26	.929
THEUS, R.	13	1/ 5	.200	0/ 1	.000	-/ 4	3	-	2	-	-	2	.154
MILKE, M.	1	0/ 0	.000	0/ 0	.000	-/ 0	0	-	1	-	-	0	.000
Totals	225	42/96	.438	25/33	.758	-/45	11	21	34	-	-	109	.484

Arizona (114)   Coach: Fred Snowden

	Min.	Total FG/FGA	Pct.	FT/FTA	Pct.	Reb. O/T	A	TO	PF	S	Blk	TP	PPM
RAPPIS, J.	32	10/14	.714	4/ 4	1.000	-/ 1	12	-	5	-	-	24	.750
HARRIS, H.	45	13/22	.591	5/10	.500	-/ 9	9	-	4	-	-	31	.689
ELLIOTT, B.	30	7/11	.636	6/ 9	.667	-/12	0	-	4	-	-	20	.667
FLEMING, A.	23	3/ 7	.429	0/ 2	.000	-/11	1	-	5	-	-	6	.261
TAYLOR, P.	36	7/15	.467	4/ 9	.444	-/15	1	-	3	-	-	18	.500
MYLES, G.	12	0/ 0	.000	3/ 4	.750	-/ 0	0	-	2	-	-	3	.250
HARRISON, G.	6	0/ 0	.000	1/ 2	.500	-/ 0	0	-	0	-	-	1	.167
GORDY, L.	30	2/ 5	.400	1/ 3	.333	-/ 6	2	-	5	-	-	5	.167
MAXEY, S.	2	0/ 0	.000	0/ 0	.000	-/ 0	0	-	1	-	-	0	.000
GLADNEY, J.	8	2/ 2	1.000	2/ 3	.667	-/ 3	0	-	0	-	-	6	.750
MARSHALL, T.	1	0/ 0	.000	0/ 0	.000	-/ 0	0	-	0	-	-	0	.000
Totals	225	44/76	.579	26/46	.565	-/57	25	31	29	-	-	114	.507

Team Rebounds: Arizona 4; UNLV 1. Disqualified: Arizona—Fleming, Rappis, Gordy; UNLV—Owens, Robinson, Gondrezik, S. Smith. Technical fouls: None.

	1st Half	2nd Half	1st OT	Final
UNLV	47	56	6	109
Arizona	51	52	11	114

REGIONAL FINAL EAST

VMI (75)   Coach: Bill Blair

	Min.	Total FG/FGA	Pct.	FT/FTA	Pct.	Reb. O/T	A	TO	PF	S	Blk	TP	PPM
CARTER, R.	34	6/12	.500	3/ 4	.750	-/ 7	2	2	4	4	0	15	.441
REPPART, C.	27	2/ 4	.500	0/ 1	.000	-/ 2	2	5	5	3	0	4	.148
KROVIC, J.	35	5/19	.263	0/ 0	.000	-/ 4	2	4	1	1	0	10	.286
BYNUM, W.	35	12/20	.600	10/12	.833	-/ 7	2	4	5	2	0	34	.971
MONTGOMERY, D.	22	2/ 3	.667	1/ 2	.500	-/ 4	0	0	5	1	0	5	.227
BORGIEVICH, G.	22	2/ 6	.333	1/ 2	.500	-/ 6	0	0	2	0	0	5	.227
LOMBARD, K.	9	0/ 0	.000	0/ 1	.000	-/ 0	0	2	5	0	0	0	.000
SLOMSKI, D.	1	1/ 2	.500	0/ 0	.000	-/ 2	0	0	0	0	2	2	2.000
SMITH, S.	9	0/ 2	.000	0/ 0	.000	-/ 3	0	2	3	0	0	0	.000
STEPHANS, D.	1	0/ 0	.000	0/ 0	.000	-/ 0	0	0	0	0	0	0	.000
NIEHAUS, H.	1	0/ 0	.000	0/ 0	.000	-/ 0	0	0	0	0	0	0	.000
KELLEY, P.	4	0/ 2	.000	0/ 0	.000	-/ 0	0	0	0	0	0	0	.000
Totals	200	30/70	.429	15/22	.682	-/35	8	19	30	11	0	75	.375

Rutgers (91)   Coach: Tom Young

	Min.	Total FG/FGA	Pct.	FT/FTA	Pct.	Reb. O/T	A	TO	PF	S	Blk	TP	PPM
SELLERS, P.	33	6/ 9	.667	4/ 5	.800	-/12	1	6	4	0	0	16	.485
BAILEY, J.	16	3/ 6	.500	0/ 0	.000	-/ 5	0	1	4	1	0	6	.375
JORDAN, E.	37	7/11	.636	9/10	.900	-/ 4	5	3	3	6	0	23	.622
DABNEY, M.	38	9/17	.529	5/ 6	.833	-/ 2	3	7	2	1	0	23	.605
COPELAND, H.	24	4/ 8	.500	0/ 0	.000	-/ 5	0	1	4	0	0	8	.333
CONLIN, M.	3	0/ 0	.000	0/ 0	.000	-/ 1	0	0	0	0	0	0	.000
HEFELE, S.	18	2/ 4	.500	0/ 3	.000	-/ 1	1	0	2	1	0	4	.222
ANDERSON, A.	26	3/ 5	.600	2/ 6	.333	-/ 9	1	3	4	0	0	8	.308
NANCE, S.	1	0/ 0	.000	0/ 0	.000	-/ 0	0	0	0	0	0	0	.000
SCHERER, B.	1	0/ 0	.000	0/ 0	.000	-/ 1	0	0	0	0	0	0	.000
KLEINBAUM, J.	2	0/ 0	.000	1/ 2	.500	-/ 0	0	0	0	0	0	1	.500
PALKO, M.	1	1/ 1	1.000	0/ 0	.000	-/ 0	0	0	0	0	0	2	2.000
Totals	200	35/61	.574	21/32	.656	-/40	11	21	23	9	0	91	.455

Team Rebounds: Rutgers 2; VMI 2. Disqualified: VMI—Reppart, Bynum, Montgomery, Lombard. Technical fouls: None.

	1st Half	2nd Half	Final
VMI	34	41	75
Rutgers	48	43	91

REGIONAL FINAL MIDWEST

Michigan (95) Coach: Johnny Orr

	Min.	Total FG/FGA	Pct.	FT/FTA	Pct.	Reb. O/T	A	TO	PF	S	Blk	TP	PPM
BRITT, W.	35	3/10	.300	1/ 2	.500	-/ 3	2	2	3	-	-	7	.200
ROBINSON, J.	39	6/12	.500	9/10	.900	-/16	4	2	2	-	-	21	.538
HUBBARD, P.	39	8/10	.800	4/ 7	.571	-/18	1	2	3	-	-	20	.513
GREEN, R.	40	9/25	.360	5/ 7	.714	-/ 2	7	4	4	-	-	23	.575
GROTE, S.	9	2/ 4	.500	0/ 0	.000	-/ 1	1	1	5	-	-	4	.444
BAXTER, D.	31	6/12	.500	6/ 8	.750	-/ 5	4	3	2	-	-	18	.581
HARDY, A.	2	0/ 0	.000	0/ 0	.000	-/ 0	0	1	2	-	-	0	.000
STATON, T.	4	1/ 2	.500	0/ 0	.000	-/ 0	1	0	0	-	-	2	.500
BERGEN, T.	1	0/ 0	.000	0/ 0	.000	-/ 0	0	0	0	-	-	0	.000
Totals	200	35/75	.467	25/34	.735	-/47	20	15	21	-	-	95	.475

Missouri (88) Coach: Norm Stewart

	Min.	Total FG/FGA	Pct.	FT/FTA	Pct.	Reb. O/T	A	TO	PF	S	Blk	TP	PPM
KENNEDY, J.	29	8/10	.800	0/ 1	.000	-/ 8	1	1	5	-	-	16	.552
ANDERSON, K.	23	2/ 6	.333	0/ 3	.000	-/ 7	2	2	5	-	-	4	.174
CLABON, J.	13	0/ 2	.000	0/ 0	.000	-/ 2	1	2	1	-	-	0	.000
CURRIE, J.	34	3/ 8	.375	1/ 3	.333	-/ 2	2	5	5	-	-	7	.206
SMITH, W.	39	18/35	.514	7/11	.636	-/ 7	3	4	4	-	-	43	1.103
RAY, S.	35	6/12	.500	1/ 2	.500	-/15	1	1	3	-	-	13	.371
SIMS, S.	6	1/ 2	.500	0/ 0	.000	-/ 2	0	0	2	-	-	2	.333
ANDERSON, M.	19	1/ 4	.250	1/ 2	.500	-/ 0	1	1	4	-	-	3	.158
VAN, R.	1	0/ 0	.000	0/ 0	.000	-/ 0	0	0	0	-	-	0	.000
STALLMAN, D.	1	0/ 0	.000	0/ 0	.000	-/ 0	0	0	0	-	-	0	.000
Totals	200	39/79	.494	10/22	.455	-/43	11	16	29	-	-	88	.440

Team Rebounds: Michigan 2; Missouri 2. Disqualified: Michigan—Grote; Missouri—Kennedy, K. Anderson, Currie. Technical fouls: None.

	1st Half	2nd Half	Final
Michigan	50	45	95
Missouri	37	51	88

REGIONAL FINAL MIDEAST

Indiana (65) Coach: Bob Knight

	Min.	Total FG/FGA	Pct.	FT/FTA	Pct.	Reb. O/T	A	TO	PF	S	Blk	TP	PPM
MAY, S.	27	7/10	.700	1/ 2	.500	-/ 3	2	4	3	0	0	15	.556
ABERNETHY, T.	40	4/ 7	.571	4/ 5	.800	-/ 5	1	3	2	0	0	12	.300
BENSON, K.	40	8/12	.667	2/ 2	1.000	-/ 9	0	4	2	0	1	18	.450
WILKERSON, B.	23	2/ 3	.667	2/ 2	1.000	-/ 3	7	0	1	0	0	6	.261
BUCKNER, Q.	40	4/ 9	.444	1/ 2	.500	-/ 8	5	6	2	0	0	9	.225
RADFORD, W.	7	1/ 4	.250	0/ 0	.000	-/ 0	0	1	0	0	0	2	.286
CREWS, J.	17	1/ 2	.500	0/ 0	.000	-/ 1	3	1	1	0	0	2	.118
VALAVICIUS, R.	6	0/ 0	.000	1/ 2	.500	-/ 2	0	0	0	0	0	1	.167
Totals	200	27/47	.574	11/15	.733	-/31	18	19	11	0	1	65	.325

Marquette (56) Coach: Al McGuire

	Min.	Total FG/FGA	Pct.	FT/FTA	Pct.	Reb. O/T	A	TO	PF	S	Blk	TP	PPM
ELLIS, B.	36	4/ 6	.667	1/ 2	.500	-/ 7	3	1	3	0	0	9	.250
TATUM, E.	36	10/15	.667	2/ 2	1.000	-/ 6	2	3	5	0	1	22	.611
WHITEHEAD, J.	35	3/10	.300	1/ 2	.500	-/ 9	0	0	4	0	1	7	.200
LEE, B.	31	4/18	.222	0/ 0	.000	-/ 2	0	3	1	0	0	8	.258
WALTON, L.	40	1/ 9	.111	0/ 0	.000	-/ 2	2	3	3	0	1	2	.050
TOONE, B.	8	2/ 5	.400	2/ 2	1.000	-/ 4	0	2	0	1	0	6	.750
NEARY, B.	6	0/ 1	.000	0/ 0	.000	-/ 2	0	0	0	0	0	0	.000
ROSENBERGER, G.	8	1/ 2	.500	0/ 1	.000	-/ 1	1	0	2	0	0	2	.250
Totals	200	25/66	.379	6/ 9	.667	-/33	8	12	18	1	3	56	.280

Team Rebounds: Indiana 2; Marquette 1. Disqualified: Marquette—Tatum. Technical fouls: Marquette—Coach McGuire 2.

	1st Half	2nd Half	Final
Indiana	36	29	65
Marquette	35	21	56

REGIONAL FINAL WEST

UCLA (82) Coach: Gene Bartow

	Min.	Total FG/FGA	Pct.	FT/FTA	Pct.	Reb. O/T	A	TO	PF	S	Blk	TP	PPM
TOWNSEND, R.	37	7/12	.583	2/ 4	.500	-/ 3	4	-	1	-	-	16	.432
WASHINGTON, R.	37	11/24	.458	0/ 0	.000	-/10	4	-	2	-	-	22	.595
VROMAN, B.	2	0/ 0	.000	0/ 1	.000	-/ 1	0	-	0	-	-	0	.000
GREENWOOD, D.	26	4/ 8	.500	2/ 2	1.000	-/ 4	1	-	2	-	-	10	.385
DROLLINGER, R.	12	1/ 5	.200	1/ 3	.333	-/ 6	0	-	3	-	-	3	.250
SPILLANE, J.	4	1/ 1	1.000	0/ 0	.000	-/ 0	0	-	1	-	-	2	.500
MCCARTER, A.	37	4/ 7	.571	1/ 2	.500	-/ 3	5	-	0	-	-	9	.243
OLINDE, W.	2	0/ 0	.000	0/ 0	.000	-/ 0	0	-	0	-	-	0	.000
JOHNSON, M.	37	7/14	.500	0/ 0	.000	-/ 7	4	-	4	-	-	14	.378
SMITH, G.	2	1/ 1	1.000	0/ 0	.000	-/ 1	0	-	0	-	-	2	1.000
HOLLAND, B.	2	2/ 2	1.000	0/ 0	.000	-/ 0	0	-	0	-	-	4	2.000
HAMILTON, R.	2	0/ 0	.000	0/ 0	.000	-/ 0	0	-	0	-	-	0	.000
Totals	200	38/74	.514	6/12	.500	-/35	18	-	13	-	-	82	.410

Arizona (66) Coach: Fred Snowden

	Min.	Total FG/FGA	Pct.	FT/FTA	Pct.	Reb. O/T	A	TO	PF	S	Blk	TP	PPM
RAPPIS, J.	34	1/ 8	.125	2/ 2	1.000	-/ 2	2	-	3	-	-	4	.118
HARRIS, H.	37	9/19	.474	0/ 0	.000	-/ 1	4	-	3	-	-	18	.486
ELLIOTT, B.	36	4/ 9	.444	2/ 3	.667	-/ 6	2	-	2	-	-	10	.278
FLEMING, A.	37	6/17	.353	2/ 3	.667	-/16	5	-	4	-	-	14	.378
TAYLOR, P.	37	7/12	.583	0/ 0	.000	-/ 7	1	-	3	-	-	14	.378
MYLES, G.	3	0/ 0	.000	0/ 0	.000	-/ 1	0	-	0	-	-	0	.000
HARRISON, G.	1	0/ 0	.000	0/ 0	.000	-/ 0	0	-	1	-	-	0	.000
GORDY, L.	3	0/ 0	.000	0/ 0	.000	-/ 0	0	-	0	-	-	0	.000
MAXEY, S.	3	0/ 1	.000	2/ 2	1.000	-/ 0	1	-	0	-	-	2	.667
ALEKSA, B.	1	0/ 0	.000	0/ 0	.000	-/ 0	0	-	0	-	-	0	.000
GLADNEY, J.	4	1/ 2	.500	0/ 0	.000	-/ 1	1	-	1	-	-	2	.500
JUNG, B.	2	0/ 0	.000	0/ 0	.000	-/ 0	0	-	0	-	-	0	.000
MARSHALL, T.	1	0/ 0	.000	0/ 0	.000	-/ 0	1	-	1	-	-	0	.000
DEMIC, L.	1	1/ 1	1.000	0/ 0	.000	-/ 1	0	-	0	-	-	2	2.000
Totals	200	29/69	.420	8/10	.800	-/35	17	-	18	-	-	66	.330

Team Rebounds: UCLA 6; Arizona 6. Disqualified: None. Technical fouls: None.

	1st Half	2nd Half	Final
UCLA	38	44	82
Arizona	35	31	66

FINAL FOUR

Rutgers (70) Coach: Tom Young

	Min.	Total FG/FGA	Pct.	FT/FTA	Pct.	Reb. O/T	A	TO	PF	S	Blk	TP	PPM
SELLERS, P.	32	5/13	.385	1/3	.333	-/8	1	-	4	-	-	11	.344
BAILEY, J.	23	1/3	.333	4/6	.667	-/6	1	-	0	-	-	6	.261
JORDAN, E.	25	6/20	.300	4/4	1.000	-/4	6	-	4	-	-	16	.640
DABNEY, M.	37	5/18	.278	0/1	.000	-/5	2	-	4	-	-	10	.270
COPELAND, H.	36	7/12	.583	1/1	1.000	-/5	2	-	3	-	-	15	.417
CONLIN, M.	16	2/2	1.000	0/0	.000	-/1	2	-	2	-	-	4	.250
HEFELE, S.	12	1/1	1.000	0/0	.000	-/1	1	-	2	-	-	2	.167
ANDERSON, A.	19	3/8	.375	0/1	.000	-/6	0	-	3	-	-	6	.316
Totals	200	30/77	.390	10/16	.625	-/36	15	-	22	-	-	70	.350

Michigan (86) Coach: Johnny Orr

	Min.	Total FG/FGA	Pct.	FT/FTA	Pct.	Reb. O/T	A	TO	PF	S	Blk	TP	PPM
BRITT, W.	34	5/9	.556	1/1	1.000	-/5	5	-	4	-	-	11	.324
ROBINSON, J.	38	8/13	.615	4/5	.800	-/16	3	-	2	-	-	20	.526
HUBBARD, P.	38	8/13	.615	0/3	.000	-/13	1	-	4	-	-	16	.421
GREEN, R.	30	7/16	.438	2/2	1.000	-/6	5	-	4	-	-	16	.533
GROTE, S.	31	4/13	.308	6/6	1.000	-/4	1	-	4	-	-	14	.452
BAXTER, D.	19	2/5	.400	1/2	.500	-/3	2	-	0	-	-	5	.263
HARDY, A.	1	0/0	.000	0/0	.000	-/0	0	-	0	-	-	0	.000
THOMPSON, J.	1	0/0	.000	0/0	.000	-/0	0	-	1	-	-	0	.000
STATON, T.	4	1/1	1.000	2/2	1.000	-/0	2	-	1	-	-	4	1.000
BERGEN, T.	1	0/0	.000	0/0	.000	-/0	0	-	0	-	-	0	.000
SCHINNERER, L.	1	0/0	.000	0/0	.000	-/0	0	-	0	-	-	0	.000
JONES, B.	1	0/0	.000	0/0	.000	-/0	0	-	0	-	-	0	.000
LILLARD, L.	1	0/0	.000	0/0	.000	-/0	0	-	0	-	-	0	.000
Totals	200	35/70	.500	16/21	.762	-/47	19	-	20	-	-	86	.430

Team Rebounds: Michigan 3; Rutgers 2. Disqualified: None. Technical fouls: None.

	1st Half	2nd Half	Final
Rutgers	29	41	70
Michigan	46	40	86

Indiana (65) Coach: Bob Knight

	Min.	Total FG/FGA	Pct.	FT/FTA	Pct.	Reb. O/T	A	TO	PF	S	Blk	TP	PPM
MAY, S.	40	5/16	.313	4/6	.667	-/4	5	3	2	2	0	14	.350
ABERNETHY, T.	33	7/8	.875	0/1	.000	-/6	2	1	3	1	0	14	.424
BENSON, K.	38	6/15	.400	4/6	.667	-/9	0	3	4	0	0	16	.421
WILKERSON, B.	38	1/5	.200	3/4	.750	-/19	7	4	3	2	1	5	.132
BUCKNER, Q.	40	6/14	.429	0/1	.000	-/3	2	5	3	1	0	12	.300
CREWS, J.	11	1/1	1.000	2/3	.667	-/3	3	0	0	1	0	4	.364
Totals	200	26/59	.441	13/21	.619	-/44	19	16	15	7	1	65	.325

UCLA (51) Coach: Gene Bartow

	Min.	Total FG/FGA	Pct.	FT/FTA	Pct.	Reb. O/T	A	TO	PF	S	Blk	TP	PPM
TOWNSEND, R.	36	2/10	.200	0/0	.000	-/3	2	2	1	2	0	4	.111
WASHINGTON, R.	38	6/15	.400	3/4	.750	-/8	3	1	3	0	0	15	.395
VROMAN, B.	3	0/0	.000	0/0	.000	-/1	0	2	0	0	0	0	.000
GREENWOOD, D.	26	2/5	.400	1/2	.500	-/10	0	2	2	0	2	5	.192
DROLLINGER, R.	8	0/3	.000	2/2	1.000	-/1	0	0	3	0	0	2	.250
SPILLANE, J.	7	0/2	.000	0/0	.000	-/1	2	0	0	0	0	0	.000
McCARTER, A.	27	2/9	.222	0/0	.000	-/4	3	3	5	0	0	4	.148
OLINDE, W.	1	0/0	.000	0/0	.000	-/0	0	0	0	0	0	0	.000
JOHNSON, M.	36	6/10	.600	0/1	.000	-/6	0	3	2	1	0	12	.333
SMITH, G.	9	3/4	.750	0/0	.000	-/0	0	0	3	1	0	6	.667
LIPPERT, C.	1	0/0	.000	2/2	1.000	-/0	0	0	0	0	0	2	2.000
HAMILTON, R.	4	0/1	.000	1/2	.500	-/0	0	0	0	0	0	1	.250
HOLLAND, B.	4	0/2	.000	0/0	.000	-/0	0	3	0	1	0	0	.000
Totals	200	21/61	.344	9/13	.692	-/34	10	14	21	5	2	51	.255

Team Rebounds: Indiana 1; UCLA 3. Disqualified: UCLA—McCarter. Technical fouls: None.

	1st Half	2nd Half	Final
Indiana	34	31	65
UCLA	26	25	51

NATIONAL CHAMPIONSHIP

Michigan (68) Coach: Johnny Orr

	Min.	Total FG/FGA	Pct.	FT/FTA	Pct.	Reb. O/T	A	TO	PF	S	Blk	TP	PPM
BRITT, W.	31	5/6	.833	1/1	1.000	-/3	2	1	5	1	0	11	.355
ROBINSON, J.	38	4/8	.500	0/1	.000	-/6	5	6	2	1	0	8	.211
HUBBARD, P.	31	4/8	.500	2/2	1.000	-/11	0	1	5	0	1	10	.323
GREEN, R.	39	7/16	.438	4/5	.800	-/6	2	4	3	1	0	18	.462
GROTE, S.	35	4/9	.444	4/6	.667	-/1	3	4	4	3	0	12	.343
BAXTER, D.	6	0/2	.000	0/0	.000	-/0	0	1	2	1	0	0	.000
HARDY, A.	4	1/2	.500	0/0	.000	-/2	0	1	0	0	2	2	.500
THOMPSON, J.	2	0/0	.000	0/0	.000	-/0	0	1	0	0	0	0	.000
STATON, T.	9	2/5	.400	3/4	.750	-/2	0	0	3	2	0	7	.778
BERGEN, T.	5	0/1	.000	0/0	.000	-/0	0	0	1	0	0	0	.000
Totals	200	27/57	.474	14/19	.737	-/31	12	19	25	9	3	68	.340

Indiana (86) Coach: Bob Knight

	Min.	Total FG/FGA	Pct.	FT/FTA	Pct.	Reb. O/T	A	TO	PF	S	Blk	TP	PPM
MAY, S.	39	10/17	.588	6/6	1.000	-/8	2	3	4	2	0	26	.667
ABERNETHY, T.	35	4/8	.500	3/3	1.000	-/4	1	3	2	1	0	11	.314
BENSON, K.	38	11/20	.550	3/5	.600	-/9	2	3	3	1	1	25	.641
WILKERSON, B.	2	0/1	.000	0/0	.000	-/0	0	0	1	0	0	0	.000
BUCKNER, Q.	39	5/10	.500	6/9	.667	-/8	4	3	4	5	1	16	.410
RADFORD, W.	7	0/1	.000	0/0	.000	-/1	0	0	0	0	0	0	.000
WISMAN, J.	21	0/1	.000	2/3	.667	-/1	6	1	4	0	0	2	.095
CREWS, J.	12	0/1	.000	2/2	1.000	-/1	4	0	1	0	0	2	.167
VALAVICIUS, R.	4	1/1	1.000	0/0	.000	-/0	0	0	0	1	0	2	.500
BENDER, B.	1	0/0	.000	0/0	.000	-/0	0	0	0	0	0	0	.000
HAYMORE, M.	1	1/1	1.000	0/0	.000	-/1	0	0	0	0	0	2	2.000
Totals	200	32/61	.525	22/28	.786	-/33	19	13	19	10	2	86	.430

Team Rebounds: Indiana 3; Michigan 1. Disqualified: Michigan—Britt, Hubbard. Technical fouls: None.

	1st Half	2nd Half	Final
Michigan	35	33	68
Indiana	29	57	86

NATIONAL THIRD PLACE

UCLA (106) Coach: Gene Bartow

	Min.	Total FG / FGA	Pct.	FT / FTA	Pct.	Reb. O / T	A	TO	PF	S	Blk	TP	PPM
TOWNSEND, R.	22	3/ 7	.429	2/ 2	1.000	-/ 2	2	1	3	3	0	8	.364
WASHINGTON, R.	22	5/ 8	.625	1/ 2	.500	-/ 0	2	3	4	0	0	11	.500
VROMAN, B.	2	0/ 0	.000	0/ 0	.000	-/ 1	0	1	1	0	0	0	.000
GREENWOOD, D.	19	2/ 4	.500	1/ 2	.500	-/ 8	0	2	5	0	0	5	.263
DROLLINGER, R.	29	6/ 8	.750	0/ 0	.000	-/16	3	4	5	0	4	12	.414
SPILLANE, J.	7	2/ 3	.667	0/ 0	.000	-/ 0	0	3	1	0	0	4	.571
MCCARTER, A.	40	11/19	.579	4/ 4	1.000	-/ 5	11	2	1	2	0	26	.650
OLINDE, W.	4	1/ 1	1.000	0/ 0	.000	-/ 1	1	1	0	0	0	2	.500
JOHNSON, M.	40	11/21	.524	8/12	.667	-/18	6	4	1	4	2	30	.750
SMITH, G.	15	3/ 9	.333	2/ 2	1.000	-/ 4	0	5	2	1	0	8	.533
Totals	200	44/80	.550	18/24	.750	-/55	25	26	23	10	6	106	.530

Rutgers (92) Coach: Tom Young

	Min.	Total FG / FGA	Pct.	FT / FTA	Pct.	Reb. O / T	A	TO	PF	S	Blk	TP	PPM
SELLERS, P.	32	8/21	.381	7/10	.700	-/12	3	3	3	0	0	23	.719
BAILEY, J.	23	3/10	.300	1/ 1	1.000	-/ 5	1	0	2	0	2	7	.304
JORDAN, E.	39	4/16	.250	0/ 2	.000	-/ 4	7	6	3	3	0	8	.205
DABNEY, M.	31	9/18	.500	3/ 5	.600	-/ 5	4	3	3	6	0	21	.677
COPELAND, H.	38	9/19	.474	0/ 2	.000	-/13	4	3	3	2	0	18	.474
CONLIN, M.	1	0/ 0	.000	0/ 0	.000	-/ 0	0	0	0	0	1	0	.000
HEFELE, S.	9	1/ 3	.333	0/ 1	.000	-/ 5	0	1	4	0	0	2	.222
ANDERSON, A.	27	4/13	.308	5/ 6	.833	-/ 4	2	3	2	1	0	13	.481
Totals	200	38/100	.380	16/27	.593	-/48	21	19	20	13	2	92	.460

Team Rebounds: UCLA 2; Rutgers 5. Disqualified: UCLA—Greenwood, Drollinger. Technical fouls: Rutgers—Dabney.

	1st Half	2nd Half	Final
UCLA	57	49	106
Rutgers	49	43	92

○ ALL-STAR TEAMS ○

ALL TOURNAMENT

TOM ABERNETHY	INDIANA
★ KENT BENSON	INDIANA
RICKEY GREEN	MICHIGAN
MARQUES JOHNSON	UCLA
SCOTT MAY	INDIANA

EAST REGIONAL

WILL BYNUM	VMI
RON CARTER	VMI
MIKE DABNEY	RUTGERS
TONY HANSON	U. CONN.
★ ED JORDAN	RUTGERS
AL WESTON	U. CONN.

MIDWEST REGIONAL

RICK BULLOCK	TEXAS TECH
ADRIAN GANTLEY	NOTRE DAME
RICKEY GREEN	MICHIGAN
PHIL HUBBARD	MICHIGAN
★ WILLIE SMITH	MISSOURI

MIDEAST REGIONAL

★ KENT BENSON	INDIANA
TOM CUTTER	WESTERN MICH.
★ SCOTT MAY	INDIANA
ANTHONY MURRAY	ALABAMA
EARL TATUM	MARQUETTE

WEST REGIONAL

AL FLEMING	ARIZONA
HERMAN HARRIS	ARIZONA
MARQUES JOHNSON	UCLA
JIM RAPPIS	ARIZONA
★ RICHARD WASHINGTON	UCLA

★ Most Outstanding Player(s)

○ INDIVIDUAL RECORDS ○

SCORING

Most points in a single game
1 WILLIE SMITH, MISSOURI (vs. MICHIGAN) 43
2 ERNIE GRUNFELD, TENNESSEE (vs. VMI) 36
3 LEON DOUGLAS, ALABAMA (vs. N. CAROLINA) 35
4 MARCOS LEITE, PEPPERDINE (vs. MEMPHIS STATE) 34
4 WILL BYNUM, VMI (vs. RUTGERS) 34

Most total points in the tournament
1 SCOTT MAY, INDIANA 113
2 WILLIE SMITH, MISSOURI 94
2 KENT BENSON, INDIANA 94
4 MARQUES JOHNSON, UCLA 93
5 RICHARD WASHINGTON, UCLA 89

Highest scoring average (minimum 2 games)
1 WILLIE SMITH, MISSOURI (94-3) 31.33
2 ADRIAN DANTLEY, NOTRE DAME (58-2) 29.00
3 RON NORWOOD, DEPAUL (51-2) 25.50
4 WILL BYNUM, VMI (76-3) 25.33
5 MARCOS LEITE, PEPPERDINE (50-2) 25.00

FIELD GOALS

Most field goals in a single game
1 WILLIE SMITH, MISSOURI (vs. MICHIGAN) 18
2 LEON DOUGLAS, ALABAMA (vs. N. CAROLINA) 16
3 SCOTT MAY, INDIANA (vs. ST. JOHN'S) 14
4 3 tied for fourth place.

Most total field goals in the tournament
1 SCOTT MAY, INDIANA 45
2 KENT BENSON, INDIANA 40
3 RICHARD WASHINGTON, UCLA 39
4 WILLIE SMITH, MISSOURI 38
5 MARQUES JOHNSON, UCLA 37

Most field goal attempts in a single game
1 WILLIE SMITH, MISSOURI (vs. MICHIGAN) 35
2 JEFF TYSON, WESTERN MICH. (vs. VIRGINIA TECH) 27
3 RICKEY GREEN, MICHIGAN (vs. MISSOURI) 25
4 RICHARD WASHINGTON, UCLA (vs. ARIZONA) 24
5 5 tied for fifth place.

Most total field goal attempts in the tournament
1 RICKEY GREEN, MICHIGAN 90
2 SCOTT MAY, INDIANA 88
3 MIKE DABNEY, RUTGERS 83
4 RICHARD WASHINGTON, UCLA 80
5 WILLIE SMITH, MISSOURI 79

Highest field goal percentage in a single game (minimum 10 attempts)
1 JIM KENNEDY, MISSOURI (vs. MICHIGAN) (8-10) .800
1 PHIL HUBBARD, MICHIGAN (vs. MISSOURI) (8-10) .800
3 RON NORWOOD, DEPAUL (vs. VIRGINIA) (11-15) .733
4 HOLLIS COPELAND, RUTGERS (vs. U. CONN.) (8-11) .727
4 RON CARTER, VMI (vs. TENNESSEE) (8-11) .727

Highest field goal percentage in the tournament (minimum 20 attempts)
1 ADRIAN DANTLEY, NOTRE DAME (22-37) .595
1 RON CARTER, VMI (22-37) .595
3 PHILIP TAYLOR, ARIZONA (20-34) .588

3	TOM ABERNETHY, INDIANA (20-34)	.588
5	WILL BYNUM, VMI (27-46)	.587

FREE THROWS

Most free throws in a single game
1   6 tied for first place.

Most total free throws in the tournament

1	SCOTT MAY, INDIANA	23
2	WILL BYNUM, VMI	22
3	ED JORDAN, RUTGERS	21
4	JOHN ROBINSON, MICHIGAN	20
5	3 tied for fifth place.	

Most free throws attempted in a single game

1	STEVE CONNOR, BOISE ST. (vs. UNLV)	13
1	JIM KENNEDY, MISSOURI (vs. WASHINGTON)	13
1	ERNIE GRUNFELD, TENNESSEE (vs. VMI)	13
4	4 tied for fourth place.	

Most free throws attempted in the tournament

1	PHIL SELLERS, RUTGERS	29
2	SCOTT MAY, INDIANA	28
3	WILLIE SMITH, MISSOURI	27
4	WILL BYNUM, VMI	26
5	2 tied for fifth place.	

Highest free throw percentage in a single game (minimum 7 attempts)

1	ROBERT SMITH, UNLV (vs. ARIZONA) (10-10)	
		1.000

2	AL WESTON, U. CONN. (vs. RUTGERS) (8-8)	
		1.000
3	MARCOS LEITE, PEPPERDINE (vs. MEMPHIS STATE) (10-11)	.909
4	ED JORDAN, RUTGERS (vs. VMI) (9-10)	.900
4	JOHN ROBINSON, MICHIGAN (vs. MISSOURI) (9-10)	.900

Highest free throw percentage in the tournament (minimum 15 attempts)

1	ADRIAN DANTLEY, NOTRE DAME (14-16)	.875
1	TOM CUTTER, WESTERN MICH. (14-16)	.875
3	STEVE GROTE, MICHIGAN (19-22)	.864
4	MARCOS LEITE, PEPPERDINE (18-21)	.857
5	WILL BYNUM, VMI (22-26)	.846

REBOUNDS

Most rebounds in a single game

1	JOHN THOMAS, U. CONN. (vs. RUTGERS)	19
1	BOB WILKERSON, INDIANA (vs. UCLA)	19
3	MARQUES JOHNSON, UCLA (vs. RUTGERS)	18
3	PHIL HUBBARD, MICHIGAN (vs. MISSOURI)	18
5	2 tied for fifth place.	

Most total rebounds in the tournament

1	PHIL HUBBARD, MICHIGAN	61
2	JOHN ROBINSON, MICHIGAN	50
2	MARQUES JOHNSON, UCLA	50
4	PHIL SELLERS, RUTGERS	45
4	KENT BENSON, INDIANA	45

Most rebounds per game (minimum 2 games)

1	JOHN THOMAS, U. CONN. (30-2)	15.00
2	TOM CUTTER, WESTERN MICH. (28-2)	14.00
3	AL FLEMING, ARIZONA (39-3)	13.00
4	MIKE RUSSELL, TEXAS TECH (26-2)	13.00
5	PHIL HUBBARD, MICHIGAN (61-5)	12.20

ASSISTS

Most assists in a single game

1	JIM RAPPIS, ARIZONA (vs. UNLV)	12
2	ANDRE MCCARTER, UCLA (vs. RUTGERS)	11
3	HERMAN HARRIS, ARIZONA (vs. UNLV)	9
4	HERMAN HARRIS, ARIZONA (vs. GEORGETOWN)	8
5	11 tied for fifth place.	

Most total assists in the tournament

1	ED JORDAN, RUTGERS	26
2	BOB WILKERSON, INDIANA	24
3	ANDRE MCCARTER, UCLA	21
3	HERMAN HARRIS, ARIZONA	21
5	2 tied for fifth place.	

Most assists per game (minimum 2 appearances)

1	HERMAN HARRIS, ARIZONA (21-3)	7.00
2	WILLIE SMITH, MISSOURI (17-3)	5.67
3	JIM RAPPIS, ARIZONA (17-3)	5.67
4	ANDRE MCCARTER, UCLA (21-4)	5.25
5	ED JORDAN, RUTGERS (26-5)	5.20

✪ TEAM RECORDS ✪

SCORING

Most points in a single game

1	ARIZONA (vs. UNLV)	114
2	UNLV (vs. ARIZONA)	109
3	UCLA (vs. RUTGERS)	106

Most total points in the tournament

1	MICHIGAN	403
2	RUTGERS	400
3	UCLA	383

Highest scoring average (minimum 2 games)

1	UNLV (212-2)	106.00
2	ARIZONA (263-3)	87.67
3	MISSOURI (243-3)	81.00

FIELD GOALS

Most field goals in a single game

1	UCLA (vs. RUTGERS)	44
1	ARIZONA (vs. UNLV)	44
1	UNLV (vs. BOISE ST.)	44

Most total field goals in the tournament

1	UCLA	164
2	RUTGERS	163
3	MICHIGAN	161

Most field goals attempted in a single game

1	RUTGERS (vs. UCLA)	100
2	UNLV (vs. ARIZONA)	96
3	2 tied for third place.	

Most total field goals attempted in the tournament

1	RUTGERS	376
2	MICHIGAN	349
3	UCLA	332

Highest field goal percentage in a single game

1	VMI (vs. TENNESSEE) (33-50)	.660
2	ARIZONA (vs. UNLV) (44-76)	.579
3	INDIANA (vs. MARQUETTE) (27-47)	.575

Highest field goal percentage in the tournament (minimum 2 games)

1	ARIZONA (102-197)	.518
2	INDIANA (151-298)	.507
3	VMI (88-176)	.500

FREE THROWS

Most free throws in a single game

1	ARIZONA (vs. UNLV)	26
2	3 tied for second place.	

Most total free throws in the tournament

1	MICHIGAN	81
2	INDIANA	78
3	RUTGERS	74

Most free throws attempted in a single game

1	ARIZONA (vs. UNLV)	46
2	VMI (vs. DEPAUL)	42
3	ARIZONA (vs. GEORGETOWN)	40

Most total free throws attempted in the tournament

1	RUTGERS	114
2	MICHIGAN	107
3	INDIANA	106

Highest free throw percentage in a single game

1	MARQUETTE (vs. WESTERN MICH.) (4-4)	1.000
2	VIRGINIA (vs. DEPAUL) (10-11)	.909
3	INDIANA (vs. ST. JOHN'S) (16-18)	.889

Highest free throw percentage in the tournament (minimum 2 games)

1	NOTRE DAME (21-26)	.808
2	MICHIGAN (81-107)	.757
3	MARQUETTE (17-23)	.739

Fewest free throws in a single game

1	ST. JOHN'S (vs. INDIANA)	4
1	MARQUETTE (vs. WESTERN MICH.)	4
3	2 tied for third place.	

Lowest free throw percentage in a single game

1	DEPAUL (vs. VMI) (10-22)	.455
1	MISSOURI (vs. MICHIGAN) (10-22)	.455
3	UCLA (vs. ARIZONA) (6-12)	.500

Lowest free throw percentage in the tournament (minimum 2 games)

1	ALABAMA (20-35)	.571
2	MISSOURI (41-71)	.578
3	WESTERN MICH. (26-44)	.591

REBOUNDS

Most rebounds in a single game

1	ARIZONA (vs. UNLV)	57
2	UCLA (vs. RUTGERS)	55
3	UNLV (vs. BOISE ST.)	49

Most rebounds per game (minimum 2 games)

1	UNLV (94-2)	47.00
2	ARIZONA (135-3)	45.00
3	U. CONN. (84-2)	42.00

ASSISTS

Most assists in a single game

1	UCLA (vs. RUTGERS)	25
2	ARIZONA (vs. UNLV)	25
3	RUTGERS (vs. UCLA)	21

Most assists per game (minimum 2 games)

1	ARIZONA (62-3)	20.67
2	INDIANA (86-5)	17.20
3	UCLA (85-5)	17.00

1977

| FIRST ROUND | REGIONAL SEMIFINAL | REGIONAL FINAL | **FINAL FOUR** | REGIONAL FINAL | REGIONAL SEMIFINAL | FIRST ROUND |

EAST

VMI 73

VMI 78

Duquesne 66

Kentucky 72

Princeton 58

Kentucky 93

Kentucky 72

N. Carolina 84

Hofstra 83

Notre Dame 77

Notre Dame 90

N. Carolina 79

N. Carolina 69

N. Carolina 79

Purdue 66

N.C.-Charlotte 49

Michigan 68

Michigan 86

Michigan 92

Holy Cross 81

Detroit 81

Middle Tenn. St. 76

Detroit 93

N.C.-Charlotte 75

N.C.-Charlotte 81

Central Mich. 86

N.C.-Charlotte 91 (ot)

Syracuse 59

Tennessee 88

Syracuse 93 (ot)

MIDEAST

Marquette 67
N. Carolina 59

WEST

UCLA 87

UCLA 75

Louisville 79

Idaho St. 90

Long Beach St. 72

Idaho St. 76

Idaho St. 83

UNLV 83

Utah 72

Utah 83

St. John's 68

UNLV 107

San Francisco 95

UNLV 88

UNLV 121

Marquette 51

Marquette 82

Marquette 67

Cincinnati 51

Marquette 66

Kansas St. 66

Kansas St. 87

Providence 80

Wake Forest 68

Wake Forest 86

Arkansas 80

Wake Forest 86

Southern Ill. 81

Southern Ill. 81

Arizona 77

MIDWEST

CONSOLATION GAME

National Third Place:

UNLV 106

N.C.-Charlotte 94

1977 saw the most wide-open tournament in more than a decade. The three top ranked teams in the nation—UCLA, Michigan, and Kentucky—were all upset in the regionals. So instead of the usual suspects there was an unexpected cast of characters as the season unfolded toward a stirring climax.

Two of the Final Four teams had never been in such rarefied atmosphere before (one, North Carolina–Charlotte, had never even been in the tournament), and none of the four semifinalists had ever—*ever*—played against any of the others. A Jerry Tarkanian team was making its first Final Four appearance. Lee Rose's hyphenated underdogs from North Carolina's largest city went farther than anyone could have imagined. Dean Smith came up short in the Final Four for the fifth time. And when all was said and done, it was Al McGuire's last hurrah.

The previous December McGuire had announced his retirement, effective at the end of the season. His team immediately went into a tailspin, barely regaining its equilibrium in time to make the tournament. From there it was far from smooth sailing for the Warriors. After breezing past Cincinnati they fell behind Kansas State, and with about eleven minutes left they still trailed by eight. When McGuire put his hand to his throat and yelled something about choking, the ref hit him with a T. McGuire protested he was just signaling his team, but his protest went unheeded—the ref was sure Al was talking about him. After Kansas State hit two free throws for a 10-point lead, it looked like history would repeat itself—McGuire's indiscretions were going to cost his team a chance at winning, just as they had in the 1974 finals and the 1976 regionals. But this time, instead of collapsing, Marquette took over, outscoring the Wildcats 17-4 in the next few minutes and finally hanging on for a one point victory.

Later, in a St. Patrick's Day tirade, McGuire told the press, "I think the NCAA brainwashes the officials in a smoke-filled room . . . prepping them so they will call technical fouls on me. . . . To call a technical foul at that time of a game," he concluded, "is a mortal sin!"

In the regional finals Marquette again trailed at the half, but this time a defensive adjustment suggested by assistant coach Rick Majerus turned the tide against Wake Forest, and the Warriors won going away.

Marquette's opponent in the semis was UNC-Charlotte, which had proven they were for real by winning the Mideast regional with upset victories over Syracuse and Michigan. Michigan's Phil Hubbard had dominated the boards with 26 rebounds in the Wolverines' second round victory over Detroit, so UNCC's coach Lee Rose designed a strategy to stop Hubbard's inside threat. Charlotte, keyed by its star center, Cedric "Cornbread" Maxwell and an aggressive defense, surged into the lead. At halftime they were beating the nation's top-ranked team by an

unbelievable 40-27. The Big Ten champs came back, using full-court pressure to outscore Charlotte 22-8 in the first eight minutes of the second half and take a one-point lead. Then the 49ers, champions of the Sun Belt Conference, showed what they were made of. A Maxwell lay-up after a time-out put them back in front, and they never looked back. After the game UNCC forward Lew Massey said, "We pressured the ball all the time. We figure it's ours if it's in the air."

In the West, UCLA lost for the first time in 11 years when Idaho State held on to beat the Bruins. Then the kids from Pocatello ran into a juggernaut. In the regional finals Jerry Tarkanian's UNLV Runnin' Rebels attacked on defense, threw up rainbows and threw down jams on offense, and blew the Bengals out 107-90 with a devastating last 22 minutes in the high altitude of Provo, Utah. Although Tarkanian complained that "the altitude makes us play like five slow white guys," his Rebels roared back from a 48-41 deficit to leave Idaho State gasping.

In the East, Dean Smith used his slowdown four corners offense for almost the entire second half as a patched-up North Carolina team held on to beat the powerful Kentucky Wildcats. Carolina's star guard, Phil Ford, had injured his elbow in a collision with two seconds left in the regional semifinal against Notre Dame. He had pulled himself off the floor to hit the two winning free throws (his 28th and 29th points of the game) in a 79-77 decision, but he was of little use against Kentucky, scoring only two. With starting center Tom LaGarde on crutches, and forward Walter Davis playing with three screws in the broken index finger of his shooting hand, Carolina's three top players were either out of action entirely or severely limited in their production. "A month ago I didn't know if we could beat a team as strong as Kentucky, even with Ford and LaGarde," said Smith. "But that's the beauty of the four corners."

The four corners was just as effective in their national semifinal against UNLV. Vegas took a 10-point lead, but when the Rebels' center, Larry Moffett, got hit in the nose and had to leave the game, the Tar Heels came back. With 15:40 to go and Carolina holding on to a slim lead, Smith called for the four corners. Time and time again, when the Runnin' Rebels came out to challenge Phil Ford, he'd hit Mike O'Koren going backdoor for an easy lay-up. The freshman finished with 31 points, and the Tar Heels sneaked into the finals, winning by a single point.

In the other semi the luck of the Irish was once again with Al McGuire. After the Warriors took a commanding early lead, UNCC scored ten straight points to make a game of it. In the second half, the 49ers led 35-30 after a Cedric Maxwell 3-point play. With 1:41 left they were still up 47-44, but then Marquette's Butch Lee hit two long jumpers. With 20 seconds left Charlotte's Lew Massey rushed a shot and the rebound kicked out onto the floor, where Gary Rosenberger picked it up for the Warriors and was fouled. Lee Rose called a time-out for UNCC to give Rosenberger time to think about his shots.

During the time-out, McGuire kept slapping Rosenberger on the arm. Finally the player hit him back and center Jerome Whitehead started yelling at his coach. McGuire later said, "Jay (Whitehead) was getting upset. He thought I was going into my psycho act and my Elmer Gantry things. The reason for hitting Rosey is that Coach Lee [Rose] called the time-out to 'ice' Rosey. The kid's being iced and you don't want him thinking and you want to keep him warm and that's why you hit him. . . . If I was wrong, I'm wrong. If I'm right, I'm right. You never know. Kids win the games; coaches don't win games."

Rosenberger hit one foul shot to put the Warriors up by a bucket, then with five seconds left, Maxwell spun and hit a six-footer to tie the game. Marquette called time out with three seconds remaining.

This time McGuire walked the length of the floor, peering up at the overhanging scoreboard-clock. "I wanted to see the height," he said. "I didn't want to hit the clock with the lob."

Butch Lee lobbed the ball the length of the floor, where Marquette's Bo Ellis and Maxwell both got their hands on it. There was contact, the ball was jarred loose, and Jerome Whitehead picked it up. He went up for a lay-up, Maxwell got a piece of the ball, but it still found the hoop just as the buzzer sounded, and Marquette was in the championship game.

It was Dean Smith against Al McGuire in the finals, two remarkably successful coaches who had never won the big one. It was the Tar Heels, four of whom had been on the victorious 1976 Olympic team, against Marquette's "back-alley scrappers." It was the ACC and Chapel Hill against the maverick Catholic independent from Milwaukee. For Marquette to have a chance, they knew they'd have to control the tempo and stop Phil Ford.

The Warriors' Jimmy Boylan refused to give Ford a step, forcing him to pull up as the big men sagged to take away his penetration. Ellis and Whitehead dominated the boards. And Marquette took a 12-point lead at the half, 39-27.

But Carolina was far from finished. Led by O'Koren, they fought back. While McGuire ranted on the sidelines, his wife, Pat, begged him to sit down—Marquette could not afford a game-turning T. The Tar Heels kept running, finally blowing by Marquette to take the lead with 13:48 left. Then they stopped.

When Dean Smith signaled four corners, McGuire's Warriors were ready. The Marquette players sagged underneath, taking away the backdoor. Carolina held the ball for three minutes, looking for a lay-up, but it never materialized. Instead Ellis blocked a Bruce Buckley shot and Marquette got the ball. Patiently, Butch Lee and the Warriors worked the ball around for a good shot. And once they regained their composure, it was just a matter of time before they took back the lead. Then it was Marquette's turn to slow it down. Where North Carolina had scored 18 points in the first 6:12 of the second half, in the next twelve minutes they scored only 4.

With Marquette up by four and less than two minutes to go, Mike O'Koren accidentally hit Bernard Toone in the eye, and Toone retaliated by throwing an elbow. A personal was called on O'Koren, a technical on Toone. The Marquette player missed, and Carolina's Walter Davis hit two free throws on the T.

Marquette was up 53-51. Jump ball.

Ellis won the jump, and Marquette controlled the ball. The Tar Heels were forced to foul, and the Warriors hit the free throws.

With six seconds left in the game, Rosenberger on the line, and the game on ice, Al McGuire came up with one more surprise. The man who once said, "Winning is only important in war and surgery," bowed his head and wept.

It was a great way to say good-bye.

FIRST ROUND EAST

VMI (73) Coach: Charlie Schmaus

	Min.	Total FG/FGA	Pct.	FT/FTA	Pct.	Reb. O/T	A	TO	PF	S	Blk	TP	PPM
CARTER, R.	36	9/18	.500	0/0	.000	-/6	3	2	2	3	0	18	.500
BYNUM, W.	38	7/17	.412	4/7	.571	-/8	1	5	1	1	0	18	.474
MONTGOMERY, D.	34	6/11	.545	5/6	.833	-/5	1	1	3	0	1	17	.500
KROVIC, J.	38	3/12	.250	2/3	.667	-/4	2	2	2	0	0	8	.211
LOMBARD, K.	31	1/1	1.000	4/4	1.000	-/4	0	1	3	0	0	6	.194
BOROJEVICH, G.	14	3/4	.750	0/0	.000	-/5	0	0	0	0	0	6	.429
KELLEY, P.	5	0/1	.000	0/0	.000	-/0	0	0	0	1	0	0	.000
SALMOND, J.	4	0/1	.000	0/0	.000	-/1	0	0	0	0	0	0	.000
Totals	200	29/65	.446	15/20	.750	-/33	7	11	11	5	1	73	.365

Duquesne (66) Coach: John Cinicola

	Min.	Total FG/FGA	Pct.	FT/FTA	Pct.	Reb. O/T	A	TO	PF	S	Blk	TP	PPM
MASER, D.	36	7/17	.412	0/0	.000	-/7	6	2	2	0	1	14	.389
COTTEN, R.	32	4/10	.400	0/0	.000	-/8	1	3	5	0	3	8	.250
GAMBRIDGE, D.	19	2/3	.667	0/0	.000	-/8	2	2	5	0	1	4	.211
NIXON, N.	36	13/24	.542	1/3	.333	-/3	3	5	5	1	0	27	.750
MCCLAIN, L.	31	3/12	.250	0/0	.000	-/3	2	0	2	0	0	6	.194
HUBBARD, L.	20	1/3	.333	1/2	.500	-/7	1	2	2	0	0	3	.150
MOORE, J.	8	0/2	.000	0/0	.000	-/0	0	0	0	0	0	0	.000
BALDWIN, J.	14	2/6	.333	0/0	.000	-/2	0	1	1	0	0	4	.286
FELIX, P.	4	0/0	.000	0/0	.000	-/0	0	0	0	0	0	0	.000
Totals	200	32/77	.416	2/5	.400	-/38	15	15	22	1	5	66	.330

Team Rebounds: VMI 5; Duquesne 7. Disqualified: Duquesne—Cotten, Gambridge, Nixon. Technical fouls: None.

	1st Half	2nd Half	Final
VMI	33	40	73
Duquesne	33	33	66

Princeton (58) Coach: Pete Carril

	Min.	Total FG/FGA	Pct.	FT/FTA	Pct.	Reb. O/T	A	TO	PF	S	Blk	TP	PPM
SOWINSKI, F.	-	4/11	.364	8/10	.800	-/3	1	6	3	2	0	16	-
SLAUGHTER, B.	-	2/6	.333	2/2	1.000	-/3	2	2	1	0	2	6	-
ROMA, R.	-	4/7	.571	0/0	.000	-/1	2	1	5	0	0	8	-
OMELTCHENKO, W.	-	2/4	.500	6/6	1.000	-/4	3	3	4	0	0	10	-
SNYDER, D.	-	3/6	.500	0/0	.000	-/3	3	1	1	0	0	6	-
KLEINERT, R.	-	0/3	.000	0/0	.000	-/2	0	0	1	2	0	0	-
RIZZUTO, R.	-	0/0	.000	0/0	.000	-/0	0	0	0	1	0	0	-
STARSIA, R.	-	0/0	.000	0/0	.000	-/0	0	0	0	0	0	0	-
LEWIS, J.	-	1/1	1.000	0/0	.000	-/1	0	0	1	0	0	2	-
OLAH, T.	-	0/0	.000	0/0	.000	-/0	1	0	1	0	0	0	-
YOUNG, T.	-	3/5	.600	4/4	1.000	-/1	0	0	2	0	0	10	-
Totals	200	19/43	.442	20/22	.909	-/18	12	13	19	5	2	58	.290

Kentucky (72) Coach: Joe Hall

	Min.	Total FG/FGA	Pct.	FT/FTA	Pct.	Reb. O/T	A	TO	PF	S	Blk	TP	PPM
GIVENS, J.	-	3/9	.333	1/3	.333	-/5	2	1	1	0	0	7	-
ROBEY, R.	-	7/9	.778	6/6	1.000	-/9	2	3	3	3	0	20	-
PHILLIPS, M.	-	1/3	.333	0/0	.000	-/3	1	3	3	1	1	2	-
JOHNSON, L.	-	3/7	.429	1/2	.500	-/2	2	0	2	1	0	7	-
SHIDLER, J.	-	3/5	.600	4/4	1.000	-/1	0	3	0	0	0	10	-
LEE, J.	-	3/4	.750	0/1	.000	-/1	1	3	4	1	1	6	-
HASKINS, M.	-	2/4	.500	0/0	.000	-/2	2	0	2	1	0	4	-
CLAYTOR, T.	-	6/8	.750	0/1	.000	-/3	2	1	0	0	0	12	-
CASEY, J.	-	0/0	.000	0/0	.000	-/1	0	0	0	0	0	0	-
WILLIAMS, L.	-	1/1	1.000	2/2	1.000	-/1	0	1	2	0	0	4	-
Totals	200	29/50	.580	14/19	.737	-/28	12	12	20	7	2	72	.360

Team Rebounds: Kentucky 2; Princeton 1. Disqualified: Princeton—Roma. Technical fouls: Princeton—Assistant Coach Dukat.

	1st Half	2nd Half	Final
Princeton	22	36	58
Kentucky	29	43	72

Hofstra (83) Coach: Roger Gaeckler

	Min.	Total FG/FGA	Pct.	FT/FTA	Pct.	Reb. O/T	A	TO	PF	S	Blk	TP	PPM
KAMMERER, P.	26	2/6	.333	0/1	.000	-/5	1	3	5	0	0	4	.154
LAUREL, R.	39	15/35	.429	5/9	.556	-/6	1	3	4	3	3	35	.897
IRVING, J.	27	7/14	.500	3/3	1.000	-/12	2	2	5	2	1	17	.630
ROOD, K.	34	7/19	.368	2/3	.667	-/6	2	2	2	1	0	16	.471
VICKERS, W.	34	1/5	.200	1/2	.500	-/4	4	1	2	1	0	3	.088
COLEMAN, A.	12	1/3	.333	2/4	.500	-/1	2	4	3	1	0	4	.333
JERKINS, M.	13	0/3	.000	0/0	.000	-/7	0	0	2	0	0	0	.000
BARRY, J.	11	0/0	.000	0/0	.000	-/3	0	1	1	0	0	0	.000
APPEL, B.	4	2/2	1.000	0/0	.000	-/1	0	0	2	0	0	4	1.000
Totals	200	35/87	.402	13/22	.481	-/45	12	16	26	8	4	83	.415

Notre Dame (90) Coach: Digger Phelps

	Min.	Total FG/FGA	Pct.	FT/FTA	Pct.	Reb. O/T	A	TO	PF	S	Blk	TP	PPM
KNIGHT, T.	35	7/15	.467	5/6	.833	-/12	1	3	5	0	1	19	.543
FLOWERS, B.	35	6/9	.667	2/5	.400	-/9	1	2	3	0	0	14	.400
BATTON, D.	20	2/4	.500	2/2	1.000	-/5	4	2	3	2	0	6	.300
BRANNING, R.	35	3/10	.300	1/3	.333	-/3	8	4	3	1	1	7	.200
WILLIAMS, D.	40	10/19	.526	5/6	.833	-/4	3	6	2	3	0	25	.625
CARPENTER, J.	5	1/1	1.000	0/0	.000	-/0	2	0	1	0	0	2	.400
HANZLIK, B.	6	1/2	.500	1/2	.500	-/2	0	0	1	0	0	3	.500
PATERNO, B.	24	5/6	.833	4/5	.800	-/2	0	2	4	1	1	14	.583
Totals	200	35/66	.530	20/29	.690	-/37	19	19	22	7	3	90	.450

Team Rebounds: Notre Dame 7; Hofstra 4. Disqualified: Notre Dame—Knight; Hofstra—Kammerer, Irving. Technical fouls: Notre Dame—Knight; Hofstra—Irving.

	1st Half	2nd Half	Final
Hofstra	37	46	83
Notre Dame	48	42	90

North Carolina (69) Coach: Dean Smith

	Min.	Total FG/FGA	Pct.	FT/FTA	Pct.	Reb. O/T	A	TO	PF	S	Blk	TP	PPM
O'KOREN, M.	33	3/8	.375	5/9	.556	-/5	1	1	3	2	1	11	.333
BUCKLEY, B.	17	0/3	.000	1/3	.333	-/3	0	3	3	0	0	1	.059
YONAKOR, R.	32	3/5	.600	0/0	.000	-/5	0	0	1	0	2	6	.188
FORD, P.	39	10/18	.556	7/7	1.000	-/1	3	3	0	0	0	27	.692
KUESTER, J.	28	1/7	.143	0/0	.000	-/2	1	3	4	0	0	2	.071
BRADLEY, D.	16	4/6	.667	0/0	.000	-/8	0	3	2	2	1	8	.500
KRAFICISIN, S.	8	2/5	.400	0/0	.000	-/5	0	0	1	0	0	4	.500
ZALIAGIRIS, T.	21	4/5	.800	0/0	.000	-/1	0	0	2	0	0	8	.381
WOLF, J.	3	1/1	1.000	0/0	.000	-/1	0	0	0	0	0	2	.667
COLEY, W.	1	0/0	.000	0/0	.000	-/0	0	0	0	0	0	0	.000
COLESCOTT, D.	1	0/0	.000	0/0	.000	-/0	0	0	1	0	0	0	.000
VIRGIL, J.	1	0/1	.000	0/0	.000	-/0	0	0	0	0	0	0	.000
Totals	200	28/59	.475	13/19	.684	-/31	5	13	17	4	4	69	.345

Purdue (66) Coach: Fred Schaus

	Min.	Total FG/FGA	Pct.	FT/FTA	Pct.	Reb. O/T	A	TO	PF	S	Blk	TP	PPM
JORDAN, W.	37	8/18	.444	0/0	.000	-/7	0	4	3	0	0	16	.432
WALLS, W.	34	5/11	.455	0/0	.000	-/6	1	0	3	2	1	10	.294
SCHEFFLER, T.	10	2/2	1.000	2/2	1.000	-/1	0	1	3	0	0	6	.600
PARKER, E.	34	5/9	.556	2/2	1.000	-/2	1	5	4	0	0	12	.353
PARKINSON, B.	29	3/4	.750	4/4	1.000	-/1	2	4	2	1	0	10	.345
CARROLL, J.	29	1/4	.250	1/1	1.000	-/8	0	1	2	0	2	3	.103
SICHTING, J.	18	1/3	.333	2/3	1.000	-/3	3	0	2	0	0	4	.222
THOMAS, G.	9	1/2	.500	3/4	.750	-/2	0	1	0	0	0	5	.556
Totals	200	26/53	.491	14/15	.933	-/28	7	16	19	3	3	66	.330

Team Rebounds: N. Carolina 2; Purdue 1. Disqualified: None. Technical fouls: Purdue—team.

	1st Half	2nd Half	Final
N. Carolina	42	27	69
Purdue	44	22	66

FIRST ROUND WEST

UCLA (87)   Coach: Gene Bartow

	Min.	Total FG/FGA	Pct.	FT/FTA	Pct.	Reb. O/T	A	TO	PF	S	Blk	TP	PPM
JOHNSON, M.	40	7/14	.500	3/4	.750	-/14	2	1	3	2	1	17	.425
GREENWOOD, D.	26	2/8	.250	4/4	1.000	-/7	2	2	3	2	1	8	.308
SIMS, G.	16	2/3	.667	0/0	.000	-/3	0	3	0	0	1	4	.250
HAMILTON, R.	17	4/6	.667	3/3	1.000	-/2	2	5	1	2	0	11	.647
SPILLANE, J.	34	4/12	.333	8/10	.800	-/4	6	0	2	3	0	16	.471
HOLLAND, B.	14	7/12	.583	2/3	.667	-/3	3	1	1	0	0	16	1.143
VROMAN, B.	12	2/3	.667	5/5	1.000	-/2	0	1	4	0	0	9	.750
OLINDE, W.	7	0/0	.000	0/0	.000	-/1	2	0	0	0	0	0	.000
VANDEWEGHE, K.	19	2/4	.500	0/1	.000	-/2	1	1	1	0	0	4	.211
TOWNSEND, R.	15	1/6	.167	0/0	.000	-/0	2	2	1	0	0	2	.133
Totals	200	31/68	.456	25/30	.833	-/38	20	16	16	9	3	87	.435

Louisville (79)   Coach: Denny Crum

	Min.	Total FG/FGA	Pct.	FT/FTA	Pct.	Reb. O/T	A	TO	PF	S	Blk	TP	PPM
COX, W.	35	8/14	.571	7/11	.636	-/12	2	5	3	1	3	23	.657
WILLIAMS, L.	32	7/13	.538	0/0	.000	-/7	2	5	5	1	0	14	.438
GALLON, R.	29	1/5	.200	2/2	1.000	-/5	1	1	1	1	0	4	.138
WILSON, R.	22	3/10	.300	0/0	.000	-/1	2	3	5	1	0	6	.273
BOND, P.	37	4/10	.400	2/2	1.000	-/5	14	3	3	0	0	10	.270
BROWN, D.	1	0/0	.000	0/0	.000	-/0	0	1	0	0	0	0	.000
BRANCH, T.	2	0/1	.000	0/0	.000	-/0	0	0	1	0	0	0	.000
TURNER, B.	24	3/5	.600	2/3	.667	-/1	1	0	1	1	0	8	.333
HARMON, B.	1	0/0	.000	0/0	.000	-/0	0	0	0	0	0	0	.000
GRIFFITH, D.	17	6/10	.600	2/6	.333	-/6	1	1	4	1	0	14	.824
Totals	200	32/68	.471	15/24	.625	-/37	23	19	22	6	3	79	.395

Team Rebounds: UCLA 7; Louisville 9. Disqualified: Louisville—Williams, Wilson. Technical fouls: None.

	1st Half	2nd Half	Final
UCLA	39	48	87
Louisville	36	43	79

Long Beach State (72)   Coach: Dwight Jones

	Min.	Total FG/FGA	Pct.	FT/FTA	Pct.	Reb. O/T	A	TO	PF	S	Blk	TP	PPM
McMILLIAN, L.	33	8/11	.727	4/5	.800	-/8	1	3	4	1	1	20	.606
WILEY, M.	37	6/15	.400	2/7	.286	-/10	2	2	2	0	1	14	.378
RUFFEN, C.	25	3/8	.375	0/0	.000	-/7	1	1	5	0	0	6	.240
JOHNSON, R.	32	3/11	.273	7/9	.778	-/6	2	1	4	1	2	13	.406
DILLON, D.	26	2/7	.286	0/0	.000	-/1	6	3	4	0	0	4	.154
AUSTIN, R.	2	0/1	.000	0/0	.000	-/0	0	0	0	0	0	0	.000
MARQUES, D.	2	1/1	1.000	0/0	.000	-/0	0	0	0	0	0	2	1.000
GERKS, G.	4	1/4	.250	0/0	.000	-/0	0	0	2	0	0	2	.500
MARTIN, D.	12	0/5	.000	0/0	.000	-/1	4	1	2	0	0	0	.000
WISE, F.	11	4/5	.800	3/4	.750	-/6	0	0	1	0	0	11	1.000
McGEE, T.	7	0/2	.000	0/2	.000	-/0	0	1	1	0	0	0	.000
DAWSON, J.	8	0/2	.000	0/2	.000	-/1	0	0	4	0	0	0	.000
STEFL, M.	1	0/0	.000	0/0	.000	-/0	0	0	1	0	0	0	.000
Totals	200	28/72	.389	16/29	.552	-/40	16	12	30	2	4	72	.360

Idaho State (83)   Coach: Jim Killingsworth

	Min.	Total FG/FGA	Pct.	FT/FTA	Pct.	Reb. O/T	A	TO	PF	S	Blk	TP	PPM
GRIFFIN, G.	39	6/19	.316	2/3	.667	-/15	3	5	2	1	0	14	.359
COOK, J.	37	5/10	.500	8/11	.727	-/16	3	3	1	1	1	18	.486
HAYES, S.	35	13/23	.565	3/7	.429	-/11	1	2	3	2	1	29	.829
THOMPSON, E.	15	1/2	.500	0/0	.000	-/2	2	2	4	0	0	2	.133
GOOLD, S.	29	1/7	.143	0/1	.000	-/3	1	0	4	0	0	2	.069
GARDNER, K.	1	0/1	.000	0/0	.000	-/0	0	0	0	0	0	0	.000
WHEELER, E.	26	4/7	.571	3/5	.600	-/3	2	0	2	0	0	11	.423
BEMIS, B.	8	1/1	1.000	0/0	.000	-/0	1	0	0	0	0	2	.250
WILSON, P.	1	0/0	.000	1/2	.500	-/1	0	1	0	0	0	1	1.000
ROBINSON, R.	7	1/2	.500	2/3	.667	-/2	1	0	2	2	0	4	.571
McQUAID, M.	1	0/1	.000	0/0	.000	-/0	0	0	2	0	0	0	.000
KLOS, S.	1	0/0	.000	0/0	.000	-/1	0	0	0	0	0	0	.000
Totals	200	32/73	.438	19/32	.594	-/54	16	13	22	6	2	83	.415

Team Rebounds: Idaho State 10; Long Beach St. 8. Disqualified: Long Beach St.—Ruffen. Technical fouls: None.

	1st Half	2nd Half	Final
Long Beach St.	30	42	72
Idaho State	33	50	83

Utah (72)   Coach: Jerry Pimm

	Min.	Total FG/FGA	Pct.	FT/FTA	Pct.	Reb. O/T	A	TO	PF	S	Blk	TP	PPM
JUDKINS, J.	-	8/17	.471	2/2	1.000	-/4	3	-	1	1	0	18	-
DEANE, G.	-	10/14	.714	5/6	.833	-/9	1	-	0	2	0	25	-
MATHENEY, B.	-	4/11	.364	0/1	.000	-/4	0	-	4	0	0	8	-
JONAS, J.	-	3/10	.300	5/6	.833	-/5	7	-	1	3	0	11	-
WILLIAMS, E.	-	1/3	.333	4/6	.667	-/3	0	-	4	2	1	6	-
RICE, D.	-	2/3	.667	0/0	.000	-/1	1	-	2	0	0	4	-
LEAVITT, C.	-	0/1	.000	0/1	.000	-/3	0	-	1	1	0	0	-
Totals	200	28/59	.475	16/22	.727	-/29	12	10	13	9	1	72	.360

St. John's (68)   Coach: Lou Carnesecca

	Min.	Total FG/FGA	Pct.	FT/FTA	Pct.	Reb. O/T	A	TO	PF	S	Blk	TP	PPM
JOHNSON, G.	-	11/20	.550	2/2	1.000	-/14	1	-	4	0	3	24	-
RELLFORD, C.	-	4/12	.333	0/2	.000	-/9	0	-	4	0	0	8	-
WRIGHT, R.	-	1/2	.500	0/0	.000	-/5	0	-	1	0	0	2	-
CALABRESE, T.	-	4/7	.571	0/0	.000	-/0	3	-	4	1	0	8	-
WILLIAMS, G.	-	7/12	.583	4/6	.667	-/5	0	-	5	0	0	18	-
WEADOCK, T.	-	0/2	.000	0/0	.000	-/2	0	-	1	0	0	0	-
WINFREE, K.	-	3/7	.429	0/2	.000	-/1	0	-	1	0	0	6	-
THOMAS, G.	-	1/1	1.000	0/0	.000	-/0	0	-	0	0	0	2	-
CLARKE, B.	-	0/0	.000	0/0	.000	-/0	0	-	1	0	0	0	-
Totals	200	31/63	.492	6/12	.500	-/36	4	17	21	1	3	68	.340

Team Rebounds: Utah 5; St. John's 4. Disqualified: St. John's—Williams. Technical fouls: None.

	1st Half	2nd Half	Final
Utah	36	36	72
St. John's	29	39	68

San Francisco (95)   Coach: Bob Gaillard

	Min.	Total FG/FGA	Pct.	FT/FTA	Pct.	Reb. O/T	A	TO	PF	S	Blk	TP	PPM
REDMOND, M.	-	11/20	.550	0/0	.000	-/13	-	-	4	-	-	22	-
HARDY, J.	-	3/9	.333	1/5	.200	-/6	-	-	5	-	-	7	-
CARTWRIGHT, B.	-	5/10	.500	5/10	.500	-/8	-	-	4	-	-	15	-
COX, J.	-	3/9	.333	3/4	.750	-/1	-	-	4	-	-	9	-
BOYNES, W.	-	10/15	.667	10/10	1.000	-/8	-	-	4	-	-	30	-
RANDELL, J.	-	3/7	.429	2/3	.667	-/8	-	-	1	-	-	8	-
WILLIAMS, R.	-	1/4	.250	0/0	.000	-/0	-	-	2	-	-	2	-
THOMPSON, A.	-	0/1	.000	0/0	.000	-/0	-	-	1	-	-	0	-
HAMILTON, R.	-	0/1	.000	0/2	.000	-/1	-	-	0	-	-	0	-
GILBERG, E.	-	0/0	.000	2/2	1.000	-/1	-	-	0	-	-	2	-
Totals	200	36/76	.474	23/36	.639	-/46	10	32	25	-	-	95	.475

UNLV (121)   Coach: Jerry Tarkanian

	Min.	Total FG/FGA	Pct.	FT/FTA	Pct.	Reb. O/T	A	TO	PF	S	Blk	TP	PPM
OWENS, E.	-	8/12	.667	6/9	.667	-/7	-	-	3	-	-	22	-
SMITH, S.	-	5/7	.714	4/4	1.000	-/2	-	-	0	-	-	14	-
MOFFETT, L.	-	2/4	.500	0/0	.000	-/4	-	-	5	-	-	4	-
SMITH, R.	-	6/12	.500	2/2	1.000	-/1	-	-	4	-	-	14	-
GONDREZICK, G.	-	8/12	.667	5/7	.714	-/5	-	-	4	-	-	21	-
THEUS, R.	-	11/18	.611	5/7	.714	-/8	-	-	3	-	-	27	-
BROWN, L.	-	5/12	.417	0/0	.000	-/7	-	-	5	-	-	10	-
SMITH, T.	-	3/7	.429	0/0	.000	-/2	-	-	1	-	-	6	-
MILKE, M.	-	0/2	.000	0/2	.000	-/1	-	-	0	-	-	0	-
PORTER, M.	-	0/0	.000	1/2	.500	-/2	-	-	0	-	-	1	-
WAGNER, G.	-	0/1	.000	0/0	.000	-/1	-	-	0	-	-	0	-
RODRIGUEZ, J.	-	1/2	.500	0/0	.000	-/2	-	-	3	-	-	2	-
Totals	200	49/89	.551	23/33	.697	-/42	19	18	28	-	-	121	.605

Team Rebounds: UNLV 8; San Francisco 7. Disqualified: UNLV—Moffett, Brown; San Francisco—Hardy. Technical Fouls: San Francisco—Thompson (ejected).

	1st Half	2nd Half	Final
San Francisco	44	51	95
UNLV	63	58	121

FIRST ROUND MIDEAST

Michigan (92)   Coach: Johnny Orr

	Min.	Total FG / FGA	Pct.	FT / FTA	Pct.	Reb. O / T	A	TO	PF	S	Blk	TP	PPM
ROBINSON, J.	37	7/13	.538	2/ 2	1.000	-/ 3	2	5	4	0	0	16	.432
STATON, T.	28	0/ 1	.000	0/ 0	.000	-/ 2	4	2	3	4	0	0	.000
HUBBARD, P.	34	6/15	.400	4/ 6	.667	-/12	1	0	4	2	1	16	.471
GROTE, S.	26	3/ 7	.429	2/ 2	1.000	-/ 3	7	6	3	3	1	8	.308
GREEN, R.	39	16/20	.800	3/ 3	1.000	-/ 4	9	2	1	3	0	35	.897
BAXTER, D.	21	6/ 8	.750	0/ 0	.000	-/ 2	6	1	0	0	0	12	.571
THOMPSON, J.	6	0/ 0	.000	1/ 2	.500	-/ 2	0	0	1	0	0	1	.167
HARDY, A.	3	1/ 1	1.000	0/ 0	.000	-/ 0	0	0	0	0	0	2	.667
BERGEN, T.	6	1/ 1	1.000	0/ 1	.000	-/ 0	0	0	2	1	0	2	.333
Totals	200	40/66	.606	12/16	.750	-/28	29	16	18	13	2	92	.460

Holy Cross (81)   Coach: George Blaney

	Min.	Total FG / FGA	Pct.	FT / FTA	Pct.	Reb. O / T	A	TO	PF	S	Blk	TP	PPM
VICENS, M.	31	11/16	.688	1/ 2	.500	-/ 8	3	6	5	1	0	23	.742
DORAN, B.	33	6/ 9	.667	2/ 3	.667	-/ 3	2	4	2	1	0	14	.424
POTTER, C.	40	9/19	.474	2/ 3	.667	-/ 7	7	1	2	3	0	20	.500
MCAULEY, K.	31	2/ 6	.333	4/ 4	1.000	-/ 5	0	7	2	2	0	8	.258
BECKENBACH, P.	32	3/ 8	.375	0/ 2	.000	-/ 2	5	1	2	1	0	6	.188
BROWNE, C.	23	3/ 9	.333	0/ 0	.000	-/ 6	2	0	3	0	3	6	.261
GASKINS, G.	10	2/ 2	1.000	0/ 0	.000	-/ 1	0	1	0	1	0	4	.400
Totals	200	36/69	.522	9/14	.643	-/32	19	20	16	9	3	81	.405

Team Rebounds: Michigan 5; Holy Cross 3. Disqualified: Holy Cross—Vicens. Technical fouls: None.

	1st Half	2nd Half	Final
Michigan	39	53	92
Holy Cross	40	41	81

Central Mich. (86)   Coach: Dick Parfitt

	Min.	Total FG / FGA	Pct.	FT / FTA	Pct.	Reb. O / T	A	TO	PF	S	Blk	TP	PPM
DRAKE, L.	-	5/12	.417	3/ 4	.750	-/ 2	4	-	5	-	-	13	-
TROPF, J.	-	7/17	.412	8/ 8	1.000	-/ 7	0	-	3	-	-	22	-
POQUETTE, B.	-	6/15	.400	3/ 4	.750	-/12	1	-	4	-	-	15	-
GRAUZER, D.	-	1/ 5	.200	0/ 0	.000	-/ 1	1	-	1	-	-	2	-
BRACEY, V.	-	7/16	.438	2/ 2	1.000	-/ 8	0	-	4	-	-	16	-
GUYDON, L.	-	7/13	.538	0/ 0	.000	-/ 7	3	-	3	-	-	14	-
JANER, K.	-	1/ 1	1.000	2/ 2	1.000	-/ 0	1	-	0	-	-	4	-
KAEDING, K.	-	0/ 0	.000	0/ 0	.000	-/ 1	0	-	0	-	-	0	-
HOSEY, T.	-	0/ 0	.000	0/ 0	.000	-/ 2	0	-	0	-	-	0	-
Totals	225	34/79	.430	18/20	.900	-/40	10	-	20	-	-	86	.382

North Carolina-Charlotte (91)   Coach: Lee Rose

	Min.	Total FG / FGA	Pct.	FT / FTA	Pct.	Reb. O / T	A	TO	PF	S	Blk	TP	PPM
MASSEY, L.	-	6/13	.462	2/ 2	1.000	-/ 4	0	-	3	-	-	14	-
KING, K.	-	4/ 7	.571	1/ 3	.333	-/ 2	2	-	4	-	-	9	-
MAXWELL, C.	-	11/15	.733	10/12	.833	-/18	1	-	4	-	-	32	-
KINCH, C.	-	6/19	.316	2/ 2	1.000	-/ 1	3	-	2	-	-	14	-
WATKINS, M.	-	5/ 8	.625	2/ 2	1.000	-/ 2	7	-	4	-	-	12	-
SCOTT, P.	-	1/ 3	.333	2/ 2	1.000	-/ 2	1	-	1	-	-	4	-
GRUBER, J.	-	2/ 3	.667	2/ 2	1.000	-/ 2	0	-	1	-	-	6	-
WHITFIELD, L.	-	0/ 0	.000	0/ 0	.000	-/ 1	0	-	1	-	-	0	-
Totals	225	35/68	.515	21/25	.840	-/32	14	-	20	-	-	91	.404

Team Rebounds: N.C.-Charlotte 6; Central Mich. 6. Disqualified: Central Mich.—Drake. Technical Fouls: Central Mich.—bench.

	1st Half	2nd Half	1 OT	Final
Central Mich.	46	35	5	86
N.C.-Charlotte	49	32	10	91

Middle Tennessee State (76)   Coach: Jimmy Earle

	Min.	Total FG / FGA	Pct.	FT / FTA	Pct.	Reb. O / T	A	TO	PF	S	Blk	TP	PPM
COLEMAN, L.	15	1/ 4	.250	0/ 0	.000	-/ 1	0	4	1	0	0	2	.133
JOYNER, G.	40	8/17	.471	7/ 8	.875	-/15	6	4	3	0	0	23	.575
MARTIN, B.	39	13/23	.565	2/ 3	.667	-/ 4	0	1	4	1	0	28	.718
MACK, L.	28	1/ 8	.125	0/ 0	.000	-/ 4	10	4	5	2	1	2	.071
TAYLOR, S.	38	4/13	.308	1/ 3	.333	-/11	2	5	6	0	0	9	.237
BROWN, J.	29	6/13	.462	0/ 0	.000	-/ 3	3	1	1	0	0	12	.414
BURREL, S.	9	0/ 1	.000	0/ 0	.000	-/ 1	3	1	1	0	0	0	.000
RENDER, D.	1	0/ 0	.000	0/ 0	.000	-/ 0	0	0	0	0	0	0	.000
THOMPSON, G.	1	0/ 0	.000	0/ 0	.000	-/ 0	0	1	1	0	0	0	.000
Totals	200	33/79	.418	10/14	.714	-/39	24	22	21	3	1	76	.380

Detroit (93)   Coach: Dick Vitale

	Min.	Total FG / FGA	Pct.	FT / FTA	Pct.	Reb. O / T	A	TO	PF	S	Blk	TP	PPM
LONG, J.	36	9/16	.563	2/ 2	1.000	-/ 3	2	6	2	2	3	20	.556
BOSTICK, R.	15	2/ 2	1.000	0/ 0	.000	-/ 4	1	1	3	0	0	4	.267
TYLER, T.	39	12/16	.750	5/ 8	.625	-/15	1	3	1	2	2	29	.744
BOYD, D.	35	6/14	.429	2/ 2	1.000	-/ 3	15	7	3	1	0	14	.400
DUEROD, T.	28	4/ 5	.800	2/ 3	.667	-/ 4	1	3	0	1	3	10	.357
MCCORMICK, W.	7	1/ 1	1.000	0/ 0	.000	-/ 0	0	0	0	0	0	2	.286
ANDERSON, T.	7	2/ 4	.500	0/ 0	.000	-/ 0	1	0	2	0	0	4	.571
ROSS, W.	4	0/ 0	.000	0/ 0	.000	-/ 0	0	1	0	0	0	0	.000
WHITLOW, J.	21	3/ 4	.750	0/ 0	.000	-/ 1	1	0	2	0	1	6	.286
JACKSON, K.	5	1/ 2	.500	0/ 0	.000	-/ 2	0	0	0	0	1	2	.400
NILES, D.	3	0/ 0	.000	2/ 3	.667	-/ 0	0	0	1	0	0	2	.667
Totals	200	40/64	.625	13/18	.722	-/32	22	20	14	6	10	93	.465

Team Rebounds: Detroit 2; Middle Tenn. St. 3. Disqualified: Middle Tenn. St.—Mack, Taylor. Technical fouls: None.

	1st Half	2nd Half	Final
Middle Tenn. St.	38	38	76
Detroit	46	47	93

Tennessee (88)   Coach: Ray Mears

	Min.	Total FG / FGA	Pct.	FT / FTA	Pct.	Reb. O / T	A	TO	PF	S	Blk	TP	PPM
GRUNFELD, E.	44	10/16	.625	6/11	.545	-/12	4	6	5	1	0	26	.591
KING, B.	38	8/19	.421	7/ 8	.875	-/12	2	9	5	0	0	23	.605
JOHNSON, R.	36	6/12	.500	5/ 5	1.000	-/10	0	1	4	0	3	17	.472
DARDEN, J.	41	3/ 8	.375	0/ 0	.000	-/ 1	12	6	2	1	0	6	.146
JACKSON, M.	30	6/13	.462	0/ 0	.000	-/ 3	5	1	5	0	0	12	.400
CROSBY, T.	15	0/ 4	.000	0/ 0	.000	-/ 3	4	3	2	0	0	0	.000
THREETHS, C.	16	0/ 0	.000	0/ 0	.000	-/ 2	0	0	1	0	0	0	.000
BERTELKAMP, B.	5	2/ 3	.667	0/ 0	.000	-/ 0	0	0	3	0	0	4	.800
Totals	225	35/75	.467	18/24	.750	-/43	27	26	27	2	3	88	.391

Syracuse (93)   Coach: Jim Boeheim

	Min.	Total FG / FGA	Pct.	FT / FTA	Pct.	Reb. O / T	A	TO	PF	S	Blk	TP	PPM
SHACKLEFORD, D.	29	3/ 4	.750	1/ 5	.200	-/ 9	4	4	4	2	0	7	.241
BYRNES, M.	41	4/ 9	.444	7/ 7	1.000	-/11	1	3	2	0	2	15	.366
BOUIE, R.	25	3/ 8	.375	2/ 2	1.000	-/ 4	0	3	5	0	2	8	.320
KELLEY, L.	37	9/15	.600	4/ 4	1.000	-/ 2	3	4	1	0	0	22	.595
WILLIAMS, J.	27	7/13	.538	2/ 2	1.000	-/ 1	7	5	2	0	0	16	.593
KINDEL, R.	26	5/ 9	.556	2/ 3	.667	-/ 2	3	3	2	2	0	12	.462
ORR, L.	28	2/ 6	.333	2/ 4	.500	-/ 9	3	3	5	0	1	6	.214
DREW, B.	10	2/ 4	.500	3/ 4	.750	-/ 2	2	0	1	0	0	7	.700
PARKER, R.	2	0/ 0	.000	0/ 0	.000	-/ 0	0	0	1	0	0	0	.000
Totals	225	35/68	.515	23/32	.719	-/40	23	25	23	4	5	93	.413

Team Rebounds: Syracuse 2; Tennessee 1. Disqualified: Syracuse—Bouie, Orr; Tennessee—Grunfeld, King, Jackson. Technical fouls: None. Syracuse credited with one team free throw attempt.

	1st Half	2nd Half	1 OT	Final
Tennessee	38	40	10	88
Syracuse	35	43	15	93

FIRST ROUND MIDWEST

Cincinnati (51)   Coach: Gale Catlett

	Min.	Total FG/FGA	Pct.	FT/FTA	Pct.	Reb. O/T	A	TO	PF	S	Blk	TP	PPM
JONES, M.	35	2/4	.500	2/2	1.000	1/4	3	3	5	1	0	6	.171
WILLIAMS, B.	32	2/6	.333	1/2	.500	0/3	2	3	4	3	0	5	.156
MILLER, R.	36	9/13	.692	2/2	1.000	4/10	0	0	4	2	0	20	.556
YODER, G.	37	3/11	.273	0/0	.000	0/2	5	3	0	0	0	6	.162
COLLIER, S.	33	3/9	.333	0/0	.000	0/1	2	3	3	0	0	6	.182
LEE, E.	21	3/3	1.000	2/3	.667	0/1	0	4	2	0	0	8	.381
HEMANS, K.	3	0/2	.000	0/0	.000	0/0	0	0	1	0	0	0	.000
SHOEMAKER, M.	1	0/0	.000	0/0	.000	0/0	0	0	0	0	0	0	.000
FAZAKAS, P.	1	0/0	.000	0/0	.000	0/0	0	0	0	0	0	0	.000
CABBEL, C.	1	0/0	.000	0/0	.000	0/0	0	0	0	0	0	0	.000
Totals	200	22/48	.458	7/9	.778	5/21	12	16	19	6	0	51	.255

Marquette (66)   Coach: Al McGuire

	Min.	Total FG/FGA	Pct.	FT/FTA	Pct.	Reb. O/T	A	TO	PF	S	Blk	TP	PPM
ELLIS, B.	40	8/13	.615	1/2	.500	1/5	1	2	3	4	2	17	.425
NEARY, B.	24	0/3	.000	2/2	1.000	2/4	0	1	1	0	0	2	.083
WHITEHEAD, J.	34	6/8	.750	3/3	1.000	4/6	1	2	3	0	0	15	.441
LEE, B.	40	6/14	.429	1/1	1.000	1/5	5	2	2	2	0	13	.325
BOYLAN, J.	21	2/5	.400	5/5	1.000	0/0	2	2	3	0	0	9	.429
TOONE, B.	20	0/2	.000	4/5	.800	0/6	1	0	2	3	0	4	.200
ROSENBERGER, G.	21	3/9	.333	0/1	.000	1/4	2	1	1	1	0	6	.286
Totals	200	25/54	.463	16/19	.842	9/30	12	10	15	10	2	66	.330

Team Rebounds: Marquette 5; Cincinnati 4. Disqualified: Cincinnati—Jones. Technical fouls: None.

	1st Half	2nd Half	Final
Cincinnati	31	20	51
Marquette	28	38	66

Kansas State (87)   Coach: Jack Hartman

	Min.	Total FG/FGA	Pct.	FT/FTA	Pct.	Reb. O/T	A	TO	PF	S	Blk	TP	PPM
REDDING, C.	-	14/18	.778	4/4	1.000	-/9	1	4	3	3	0	32	-
DASSIE, L.	-	4/11	.364	0/0	.000	-/11	1	2	2	0	3	8	-
WINSTON, D.	-	1/5	.200	4/6	.667	-/9	1	0	2	2	1	6	-
LANGTON, S.	-	9/12	.750	1/2	.500	-/3	6	2	2	1	1	19	-
EVANS, M.	-	9/19	.474	2/2	1.000	-/4	1	4	3	2	0	20	-
DROGE, D.	-	0/2	.000	0/0	.000	-/0	2	0	0	0	0	0	-
LADSON, T.	-	1/2	.500	0/0	.000	-/2	0	1	0	0	1	2	-
BLACK, J.	-	0/1	.000	0/0	.000	-/1	0	1	0	0	0	0	-
Totals	200	38/70	.543	11/14	.786	-/39	12	14	12	8	6	87	.435

Providence (80)   Coach: Dave Gavitt

	Min.	Total FG/FGA	Pct.	FT/FTA	Pct.	Reb. O/T	A	TO	PF	S	Blk	TP	PPM
EASON, B.	-	6/9	.667	0/0	.000	-/2	2	1	2	0	0	12	-
CAMPBELL, B.	-	3/8	.375	0/2	.000	-/0	0	2	4	1	0	6	-
COOPER, R.	-	5/11	.455	1/2	.500	-/8	2	1	2	0	0	11	-
HASSETT, J.	-	13/19	.684	0/0	.000	-/6	3	2	0	1	0	26	-
WILLIAMS, D.	-	4/14	.286	3/3	1.000	-/2	0	2	3	4	0	11	-
MISEVICIUS, R.	-	7/15	.467	0/0	.000	-/8	3	2	1	0	0	14	-
ORISTAGLIO, P.	-	0/1	.000	0/0	.000	-/1	0	0	1	0	0	0	-
Totals	200	38/77	.494	4/7	.571	-/27	10	10	13	8	0	80	.400

Team Rebounds: Kansas State 3; Providence 1. Disqualified: None. Technical fouls: None.

	1st Half	2nd Half	Final
Kansas State	37	50	87
Providence	40	40	80

Arkansas (80)   Coach: Eddie Sutton

	Min.	Total FG/FGA	Pct.	FT/FTA	Pct.	Reb. O/T	A	TO	PF	S	Blk	TP	PPM
COUNCE, J.	-	3/4	.750	6/6	1.000	-/3	4	10	4	0	1	12	-
DELPH, M.	-	7/14	.500	4/6	.667	-/8	2	3	2	1	0	18	-
STROUD, S.	-	3/5	.600	0/0	.000	-/3	2	1	4	0	1	6	-
BREWER, R.	-	9/11	.818	2/4	.500	-/2	3	3	3	1	1	20	-
MONCRIEF, S.	-	6/8	.750	0/0	.000	-/10	0	4	5	1	0	12	-
SCHALL, S.	-	6/7	.857	0/2	.000	-/0	1	2	3	0	0	12	-
BUCKNER, R.	-	0/1	.000	0/0	.000	-/0	0	0	2	0	0	0	-
TRUMBO, T.	-	0/0	.000	0/0	.000	-/0	1	0	1	0	0	0	-
Totals	200	34/50	.680	12/20	.600	-/26	13	23	24	3	3	80	.400

Wake Forest (86)   Coach: Carl Tacy

	Min.	Total FG/FGA	Pct.	FT/FTA	Pct.	Reb. O/T	A	TO	PF	S	Blk	TP	PPM
GRIFFIN, R.	37	10/17	.588	6/9	.667	-/10	1	1	4	1	1	26	.703
SCHELLENBERG, T.	38	6/12	.500	5/6	.833	-/3	1	1	2	6	0	17	.447
HARRISON, L.	14	0/1	.000	0/0	.000	-/5	1	1	4	1	0	0	.000
BROWN, S.	38	8/17	.471	7/8	.875	-/1	6	5	4	2	0	23	.605
JOHNSON, F.	36	4/8	.500	4/4	1.000	-/3	6	1	2	2	0	12	.333
MCDONALD, L.	17	2/6	.333	2/2	1.000	-/3	2	1	2	2	0	6	.353
PALMA, M.	1	0/0	.000	0/0	.000	-/0	0	1	0	0	0	0	.000
DALE, M.	1	0/0	.000	0/0	.000	-/1	0	1	0	0	0	0	.000
MULNIX, D.	17	1/2	.500	0/0	.000	-/1	0	1	1	0	0	2	.118
HENDLER, J.	1	0/0	.000	0/0	.000	-/1	0	0	1	0	0	0	.000
Totals	200	31/63	.492	24/29	.828	-/28	17	12	21	14	1	86	.430

Team Rebounds: Wake Forest 1; Arkansas 1. Disqualified: Arkansas—Moncrief. Technical fouls: None.

	1st Half	2nd Half	Final
Arkansas	46	34	80
Wake Forest	33	53	86

Southern Illinois (81) — Coach: Paul Lambert

	Min.	Total FG/FGA	Pct.	FT/FTA	Pct.	Reb. O/T	A	TO	PF	S	Blk	TP	PPM
FORD, R.	-	4/7	.571	0/0	.000	-/7	-	-	5	-	-	8	-
WILSON, G.	-	5/11	.455	2/5	.400	-/7	-	-	3	-	-	12	-
ABRAMS, C.	-	7/9	.778	1/2	.500	-/5	-	-	2	-	-	15	-
GLENN, M.	-	15/22	.682	5/5	1.000	-/1	-	-	0	-	-	35	-
ABRAMS, W.	-	0/4	.000	1/4	.250	-/2	-	-	3	-	-	1	-
GRANT, A.	-	1/2	.500	0/0	.000	-/1	-	-	2	-	-	2	-
SMITH, B.	-	0/0	.000	0/0	.000	-/0	-	-	0	-	-	0	-
WILLIAMS, A.	-	2/3	.667	0/0	.000	-/1	-	-	0	-	-	4	-
HUGHLETT, M.	-	2/6	.333	0/0	.000	-/2	-	-	1	-	-	4	-
Totals	200	36/64	.563	9/16	.563	-/26	-	-	16	-	-	81	.405

Arizona (77) — Coach: Fred Snowden

	Min.	Total FG/FGA	Pct.	FT/FTA	Pct.	Reb. O/T	A	TO	PF	S	Blk	TP	PPM
GORDY, L.	-	4/9	.444	2/2	1.000	-/7	-	-	3	-	-	10	-
ELLIOTT, B.	-	9/12	.750	5/6	.833	-/6	-	-	3	-	-	23	-
TAYLOR, P.	-	2/3	.667	0/0	.000	-/6	-	-	0	-	-	4	-
HARRIS, H.	-	8/20	.400	0/0	.000	-/7	-	-	3	-	-	16	-
HARRISON, G.	-	1/3	.333	0/0	.000	-/1	-	-	3	-	-	2	-
MYLES, G.	-	7/13	.538	2/2	1.000	-/1	-	-	0	-	-	16	-
MARSHALL, T.	-	0/1	.000	0/0	.000	-/4	-	-	2	-	-	0	-
DEMIC, L.	-	0/0	.000	0/0	.000	-/0	-	-	0	-	-	0	-
GLADNEY, J.	-	1/6	.167	4/6	.667	-/4	-	-	3	-	-	6	-
DAVIS, W.	-	0/0	.000	0/0	.000	-/0	-	-	0	-	-	0	-
Totals	200	32/67	.478	13/16	.813	-/36	-	-	17	-	-	77	.385

Team Rebounds: Southern Ill. 5; Arizona 6. Disqualified: Southern Ill.—Ford. Technical fouls: Arizona—Elliot.

	1st Half	2nd Half	Final
Southern Ill.	45	36	81
Arizona	40	37	77

REGIONAL SEMIFINAL EAST

VMI (78) — Coach: Charlie Schmaus

	Min.	Total FG/FGA	Pct.	FT/FTA	Pct.	Reb. O/T	A	TO	PF	S	Blk	TP	PPM
CARTER, R.	39	13/26	.500	2/4	.500	-/10	3	2	4	4	2	28	.718
BYNUM, W.	31	6/13	.462	0/0	.000	-/5	4	4	3	2	0	12	.387
MONTGOMERY, D.	30	7/12	.583	4/5	.800	-/11	0	4	0	0	0	18	.600
KROVIC, J.	37	4/16	.250	0/1	.000	-/4	2	1	0	0	0	8	.216
LOMBARD, K.	27	1/5	.200	0/0	.000	-/1	2	5	3	1	0	2	.074
BOROJEVICH, G.	17	2/4	.500	2/2	1.000	-/2	0	2	2	1	0	6	.353
KELLEY, P.	5	0/2	.000	0/0	.000	-/0	0	0	0	0	0	0	.000
SALMOND, J.	9	1/1	1.000	0/0	.000	-/3	0	3	2	0	0	2	.222
NEIHAUS, H.	3	1/2	.500	0/0	.000	-/2	0	0	0	0	0	2	.667
WAGNER, S.	1	0/0	.000	0/0	.000	-/0	0	0	0	0	0	0	.000
SLOMSKI, D.	1	0/0	.000	0/0	.000	-/0	0	0	0	0	0	0	.000
Totals	200	35/81	.432	8/12	.667	-/38	11	16	16	8	2	78	.390

Kentucky (93) — Coach: Joe Hall

	Min.	Total FG/FGA	Pct.	FT/FTA	Pct.	Reb. O/T	A	TO	PF	S	Blk	TP	PPM
GIVENS, J.	36	9/16	.563	8/9	.889	-/9	3	2	1	0	1	26	.722
ROBEY, W.	18	4/7	.571	0/1	.000	-/7	0	2	3	0	0	8	.444
PHILLIPS, M.	21	5/8	.625	0/0	.000	-/4	0	3	3	0	1	10	.476
JOHNSON, L.	22	0/4	.000	0/0	.000	-/2	6	2	3	0	0	0	.000
SHIDLER, J.	17	2/3	.667	0/0	.000	-/1	1	2	1	0	0	4	.235
LEE, J.	30	4/8	.500	4/4	1.000	-/5	0	2	3	2	0	12	.400
HASKINS, M.	11	2/2	1.000	0/0	.000	-/0	0	0	0	0	0	4	.364
CLAYTOR, T.	36	13/15	.867	3/4	.750	-/4	6	4	3	4	0	29	.806
CASEY, D.	5	0/0	.000	0/0	.000	-/2	2	0	0	0	0	0	.000
WILLIAMS, L.	4	0/2	.000	0/0	.000	-/1	0	2	1	1	0	0	.000
Totals	200	39/65	.600	15/18	.833	-/35	18	19	17	7	2	93	.465

Team Rebounds: Kentucky 3; VMI 3. Disqualified: None. Technical fouls: None.

	1st Half	2nd Half	Final
VMI	41	37	78
Kentucky	44	49	93

Notre Dame (77) — Coach: Digger Phelps

	Min.	Total FG/FGA	Pct.	FT/FTA	Pct.	Reb. O/T	A	TO	PF	S	Blk	TP	PPM
KNIGHT, T.	35	10/13	.769	2/3	.667	-/14	2	2	2	1	0	22	.629
FLOWERS, B.	27	5/5	1.000	1/3	.333	-/5	2	3	5	1	0	11	.407
BATTON, D.	23	3/5	.600	0/0	.000	-/4	2	2	3	0	0	6	.261
BRANNING, R.	40	5/7	.714	8/9	.889	-/2	1	4	2	2	0	18	.450
WILLIAMS, D.	39	6/14	.429	5/5	1.000	-/1	1	7	4	2	0	17	.436
CARPENTER, J.	1	0/0	.000	0/0	.000	-/0	0	0	0	0	0	0	.000
HANZLIK, B.	3	0/0	.000	0/0	.000	-/1	0	1	1	0	0	0	.000
PATERNO, B.	32	1/1	1.000	1/2	.500	-/3	0	2	2	0	0	3	.094
Totals	200	30/45	.667	17/22	.773	-/30	8	21	19	6	0	77	.385

North Carolina (79) — Coach: Dean Smith

	Min.	Total FG/FGA	Pct.	FT/FTA	Pct.	Reb. O/T	A	TO	PF	S	Blk	TP	PPM
O'KOREN, M.	34	6/10	.600	4/6	.667	-/5	4	0	5	0	0	16	.471
BUCKLEY, B.	9	1/1	1.000	0/0	.000	-/1	0	0	2	0	0	2	.222
YONAKOR, R.	24	1/6	.167	0/0	.000	-/4	2	1	2	0	0	2	.083
FORD, P.	39	10/22	.455	9/9	1.000	-/2	5	2	3	2	0	29	.744
KUESTER, J.	34	5/11	.455	4/4	1.000	-/1	7	1	1	1	0	14	.412
BRADLEY, D.	3	0/1	.000	0/0	.000	-/0	0	0	3	2	0	0	.000
KRAFICISIN, S.	11	1/1	1.000	0/0	.000	-/1	1	0	1	0	0	2	.083
ZALIAGIRIS, T.	14	3/6	.500	0/0	.000	-/0	0	0	2	1	0	6	.429
WOLF, J.	1	0/0	.000	0/0	.000	-/0	0	0	0	0	0	0	.000
COLESCOTT, D.	2	0/0	.000	0/0	.000	-/0	1	0	0	0	0	0	.000
DAVIS, W.	29	4/12	.333	0/0	.000	-/8	2	4	2	2	1	8	.276
Totals	200	31/70	.443	17/19	.895	-/22	22	8	21	8	1	79	.395

Team Rebounds: N. Carolina 5; Notre Dame 1. Disqualified: N. Carolina—O'Koren; Notre Dame—Flowers. Technical fouls: N. Carolina—O'Koren.

	1st Half	2nd Half	Final
Notre Dame	40	37	77
N. Carolina	30	49	79

REGIONAL SEMIFINAL WEST

UCLA (75) Coach: Gene Bartow

	Min.	Total FG / FGA	Pct.	FT / FTA	Pct.	Reb. O / T	A	TO	PF	S	Blk	TP	PPM
JOHNSON, M.	39	7/14	.500	7/ 8	.875	-/13	0	1	3	2	3	21	.538
GREENWOOD, D.	40	10/23	.435	0/ 2	.000	-/14	2	1	4	2	3	20	.500
SIMS, G.	6	0/ 1	.000	0/ 0	.000	-/ 2	0	0	1	0	0	0	.000
HAMILTON, R.	31	5/14	.357	1/ 3	.333	-/ 6	2	5	5	1	0	11	.355
SPILLANE, J.	25	2/ 8	.250	0/ 0	.000	-/ 1	4	2	5	0	0	4	.160
HOLLAND, B.	15	3/10	.300	3/ 4	.750	-/ 0	1	1	2	0	0	9	.600
VROMAN, B.	8	1/ 2	.500	0/ 0	.000	-/ 0	0	1	1	0	0	2	.250
OLINDE, W.	1	0/ 1	.000	0/ 0	.000	-/ 1	0	0	0	0	0	0	.000
VANDEWEGHE, K.	23	3/ 8	.375	0/ 0	.000	-/ 2	3	0	1	0	1	6	.261
TOWNSEND, R.	10	1/ 2	.500	0/ 0	.000	-/ 0	3	0	1	0	0	2	.200
WILKINS, J.	2	0/ 0	.000	0/ 0	.000	-/ 0	0	1	1	0	0	0	.000
Totals	200	32/83	.386	11/17	.647	-/39	15	12	24	5	7	75	.375

Idaho State (76) Coach: Jim Killingsworth

	Min.	Total FG / FGA	Pct.	FT / FTA	Pct.	Reb. O / T	A	TO	PF	S	Blk	TP	PPM
GRIFFIN, G.	33	4/14	.286	4/ 4	1.000	-/ 8	2	1	4	0	0	12	.364
COOK, J.	32	4/10	.400	0/ 0	.000	-/14	2	6	4	1	1	8	.250
HAYES, S.	38	11/20	.550	5/ 7	.714	-/12	0	1	3	0	0	27	.711
THOMPSON, E.	40	4/10	.400	6/ 8	.750	-/ 4	5	4	3	1	0	14	.350
GOOLD, S.	11	1/ 4	.250	0/ 0	.000	-/ 1	2	2	2	0	0	2	.182
WHEELER, E.	29	0/ 2	.000	4/ 4	1.000	-/ 1	5	1	2	1	0	4	.138
ROBINSON, B.	10	4/ 7	.571	0/ 0	.000	-/ 5	2	0	0	0	0	8	.800
WILSON, P.	7	0/ 2	.000	1/ 2	.500	-/ 1	0	1	1	0	1	1	.143
Totals	200	28/69	.406	20/25	.800	-/46	18	16	19	3	2	76	.380

Team Rebounds: Idaho State 9; UCLA 9. Disqualified: UCLA—Hamilton, Spillane. Technical fouls: None.

	1st Half	2nd Half	Final
UCLA	38	37	75
Idaho State	32	44	76

Utah (83) Coach: Jerry Pimm

	Min.	Total FG / FGA	Pct.	FT / FTA	Pct.	Reb. O / T	A	TO	PF	S	Blk	TP	PPM
JUDKINS, J.	e	10/18	.556	3/ 4	.750	-/ 7	3	-	2	-	-	23	-
DEANE, G.	-	4/ 7	.571	2/ 2	1.000	-/ 0	0	-	5	-	-	10	-
MATHENEY, B.	-	6/10	.600	2/ 5	.400	-/13	0	-	5	-	-	14	-
JONAS, J.	-	3/11	.273	6/ 9	.667	-/ 3	15	-	4	-	-	12	-
WILLIAMS, E.	-	6/11	.545	6/ 6	1.000	-/ 8	3	-	2	-	-	18	-
DUNN, M.	-	1/ 1	1.000	0/ 1	.000	-/ 2	1	-	1	-	-	2	-
RICE, D.	-	1/ 2	.500	0/ 0	.000	-/ 0	0	-	0	-	-	2	-
LEAVITT, C.	-	0/ 0	.000	2/ 2	1.000	-/ 2	0	-	2	-	-	2	-
Totals	200	31/60	.517	21/29	.724	-/35	22	-	21	-	-	83	.415

UNLV (88) Coach: Jerry Tarkanian

	Min.	Total FG / FGA	Pct.	FT / FTA	Pct.	Reb. O / T	A	TO	PF	S	Blk	TP	PPM
GONDREZICK, G.	-	6/12	.500	1/ 2	.500	-/ 5	1	-	5	-	-	13	-
SMITH, S.	-	4/10	.400	0/ 2	.000	-/ 2	2	-	3	-	-	8	-
MOFFETT, L.	-	1/ 7	.143	0/ 0	.000	-/17	0	-	4	-	-	2	-
SMITH, R.	-	8/14	.571	5/ 5	1.000	-/ 3	6	-	3	-	-	21	-
OWENS, E.	-	8/20	.400	0/ 0	.000	-/ 5	2	-	3	-	-	16	-
THEUS, R.	-	3/ 8	.375	8/ 9	.889	-/ 3	5	-	2	-	-	14	-
SMITH, T.	-	5/10	.500	0/ 1	.000	-/ 3	1	-	3	-	-	10	-
BROWN, L.	-	2/ 6	.333	0/ 0	.000	-/ 2	0	-	1	-	-	4	-
Totals	200	37/87	.425	14/19	.737	-/40	17	-	24	-	-	88	.440

Team Rebounds: UNLV 10; Utah 7. Disqualified: UNLV—Gondrezick; Utah—Deane, Matheney.

	1st Half	2nd Half	Final
Utah	39	44	83
UNLV	40	48	88

REGIONAL SEMIFINAL MIDEAST

Michigan (86) Coach: Johnny Orr

	Min.	Total FG / FGA	Pct.	FT / FTA	Pct.	Reb. O / T	A	TO	PF	S	Blk	TP	PPM
ROBINSON, J.	33	12/18	.667	1/ 2	.500	-/ 7	0	6	2	0	0	25	.758
STATON, T.	33	4/ 8	.500	0/ 1	.000	-/ 3	4	3	4	5	1	8	.242
HUBBARD, P.	40	8/19	.421	6/ 7	.857	-/26	2	4	3	2	1	22	.550
GROTE, S.	29	7/14	.500	2/ 3	.667	-/ 3	5	0	2	0	0	16	.552
GREEN, R.	40	4/13	.308	3/ 5	.600	-/ 5	7	5	1	2	0	11	.275
BAXTER, D.	11	0/ 2	.000	0/ 0	.000	-/ 0	0	3	1	0	0	0	.000
THOMPSON, J.	6	1/ 1	1.000	0/ 0	.000	-/ 1	1	0	0	0	0	2	.333
HARDY, A.	8	1/ 3	.333	0/ 0	.000	-/ 2	0	0	0	0	0	2	.250
Totals	200	37/78	.474	12/18	.667	-/47	19	21	13	9	2	86	.430

Detroit (81) Coach: Dick Vitale

	Min.	Total FG / FGA	Pct.	FT / FTA	Pct.	Reb. O / T	A	TO	PF	S	Blk	TP	PPM
LONG, J.	39	12/24	.500	1/ 1	1.000	-/ 7	0	2	3	1	2	25	.641
BOSTICK, R.	26	3/ 9	.333	0/ 0	.000	-/10	0	7	4	0	1	6	.231
TYLER, T.	39	8/12	.667	1/ 1	1.000	-/ 9	1	1	2	1	0	17	.436
BOYD, D.	38	8/16	.500	0/ 0	.000	-/ 1	7	4	2	5	0	16	.421
DUEROD, T.	34	5/12	.417	1/ 2	.500	-/ 0	7	2	3	2	0	11	.324
MCCORMICK, W.	2	1/ 2	.500	0/ 0	.000	-/ 1	0	0	0	0	0	2	1.000
ANDERSON, T.	6	1/ 3	.333	0/ 0	.000	-/ 0	1	0	0	0	0	2	.333
ROSS, W.	1	0/ 0	.000	0/ 0	.000	-/ 0	0	0	0	0	0	0	.000
WHITLOW, J.	15	1/ 3	.333	0/ 0	.000	-/ 2	0	1	4	0	0	2	.133
Totals	200	39/81	.481	3/ 4	.750	-/30	16	17	18	9	3	81	.405

Team Rebounds: Michigan 4; Detroit 3. Disqualified: None. Technical fouls: None.

	1st Half	2nd Half	Final
Michigan	48	38	86
Detroit	44	37	81

North Carolina-Charlotte (81)   Coach: Lee Rose

	Min.	Total FG/FGA	Pct.	FT/FTA	Pct.	Reb. O/T	A	TO	PF	S	Blk	TP	PPM
MASSEY, L.	28	7/12	.583	0/0	.000	-/6	1	2	3	2	0	14	.500
KING, K.	34	6/9	.667	1/2	.500	-/7	2	0	0	1	1	13	.382
MAXWELL, C.	38	4/6	.667	11/11	1.000	-/5	3	5	1	2	3	19	.500
KINCH, C.	31	6/8	.750	4/6	.667	-/1	5	2	0	0	0	16	.516
WATKINS, M.	33	6/8	.750	1/2	.500	-/1	7	2	2	0	1	13	.394
GRUBER, J.	10	1/4	.250	2/2	1.000	-/0	1	1	1	1	0	4	.400
CROWLEY, T.	1	0/0	.000	0/0	.000	-/0	0	0	0	0	0	0	.000
WHITFIELD, L.	6	0/0	.000	0/1	.000	-/1	1	2	0	1	0	0	.000
SCOTT, P.	13	0/3	.000	2/2	1.000	-/4	0	1	4	1	1	2	.154
ANGEL, K.	2	0/1	.000	0/0	.000	-/0	0	0	0	0	0	0	.000
HESTER, M.	4	0/2	.000	0/0	.000	-/1	0	0	1	0	0	0	.000
Totals	200	30/53	.566	21/26	.808	-/26	20	15	12	8	6	81	.405

Syracuse (59)   Coach: Jim Boeheim

	Min.	Total FG/FGA	Pct.	FT/FTA	Pct.	Reb. O/T	A	TO	PF	S	Blk	TP	PPM
SHACKLEFORD, D.	25	8/14	.571	0/0	.000	-/6	2	2	5	1	0	16	.640
BYRNES, M.	33	7/7	1.000	2/3	.667	-/3	4	3	4	1	0	16	.485
BOUIE, R.	29	6/8	.750	0/0	.000	-/5	0	3	2	3	2	12	.414
KELLEY, L.	21	0/7	.000	0/0	.000	-/2	1	1	0	1	0	0	.000
WILLIAMS, J.	25	2/8	.250	0/0	.000	-/1	3	4	3	0	0	4	.160
KINDEL, R.	16	0/3	.000	1/2	.500	-/0	1	1	1	0	0	1	.063
ORR, L.	29	1/5	.200	0/0	.000	-/1	1	0	3	2	0	2	.069
DREW, B.	18	4/13	.308	0/0	.000	-/3	3	2	3	1	0	8	.444
COHEN, H.	2	0/0	.000	0/0	.000	-/0	0	0	0	0	0	0	.000
JAMES, K.	2	0/0	.000	0/0	.000	-/0	0	1	0	0	0	0	.000
Totals	200	28/65	.431	3/5	.600	-/21	15	17	21	9	2	59	.295

Team Rebounds: N.C.-Charlotte 9; Syracuse 11. Disqualified: Syracuse—Shackleford. Technical fouls: None.

	1st Half	2nd Half	Final
N.C.-Charlotte	38	43	81
Syracuse	22	37	59

REGIONAL SEMIFINAL MIDWEST

Marquette (67)   Coach: Al McGuire

	Min.	Total FG/FGA	Pct.	FT/FTA	Pct.	Reb. O/T	A	TO	PF	S	Blk	TP	PPM
ELLIS, B.	40	5/14	.357	9/11	.818	-/3	1	2	2	0	1	19	.475
NEARY, B.	25	0/2	.000	0/0	.000	-/3	0	1	2	1	0	0	.000
WHITEHEAD, J.	23	1/9	.111	0/0	.000	-/6	1	0	2	0	0	2	.087
LEE, B.	40	12/23	.522	2/2	1.000	-/4	2	3	1	2	0	26	.650
BOYLAN, J.	22	4/4	1.000	0/0	.000	-/2	0	3	1	2	0	8	.364
TOONE, B.	19	2/4	.500	4/5	.800	-/5	0	3	4	1	0	8	.421
ROSENBERGER, G.	18	0/4	.000	0/0	.000	-/1	0	0	1	0	0	0	.000
DUDLEY, J.	13	2/3	.667	0/0	.000	-/3	1	1	3	0	0	4	.308
Totals	200	26/63	.413	15/18	.833	-/27	5	13	15	7	1	67	.335

Kansas State (66)   Coach: Jack Hartman

	Min.	Total FG/FGA	Pct.	FT/FTA	Pct.	Reb. O/T	A	TO	PF	S	Blk	TP	PPM
REDDING, C.	36	4/16	.250	4/4	1.000	-/14	4	7	5	0	1	12	.333
DASSIE, L.	36	7/12	.583	4/4	1.000	-/6	0	2	4	0	2	18	.500
WINSTON, D.	40	5/6	.833	2/4	.500	-/11	2	2	2	2	0	12	.300
LANGTON, S.	40	3/5	.600	2/2	1.000	-/5	3	6	3	0	0	8	.200
EVANS, M.	40	8/14	.571	0/0	.000	-/0	3	4	4	1	0	16	.400
DROGE, D.	6	0/1	.000	0/0	.000	-/0	0	1	1	0	0	0	.000
LADSON, T.	2	0/0	.000	0/0	.000	-/0	0	0	0	1	0	0	.000
Totals	200	27/54	.500	12/14	.857	-/36	12	22	19	4	3	66	.330

Team Rebounds: Marquette 2; Kansas State 4. Disqualified: Kansas State—Redding. Technical fouls: Marquette—Coach McGuire 1.

	1st Half	2nd Half	Final
Marquette	28	39	67
Kansas State	36	30	66

Wake Forest (86)   Coach: Carl Tacy

	Min.	Total FG/FGA	Pct.	FT/FTA	Pct.	Reb. O/T	A	TO	PF	S	Blk	TP	PPM
GRIFFIN, R.	39	8/9	.889	6/8	.750	-/5	0	2	3	0	0	22	.564
SCHELLENBERG, T.	37	9/16	.563	4/4	1.000	-/6	2	1	1	1	1	22	.595
HARRISON, L.	9	0/1	.000	0/0	.000	-/3	2	1	3	0	0	0	.000
BROWN, S.	40	7/15	.467	11/12	.917	-/2	8	2	1	3	0	25	.625
JOHNSON, F.	40	4/10	.400	0/0	.000	-/0	4	3	3	3	0	8	.200
MCDONALD, L.	28	2/3	.667	5/6	.833	-/4	0	0	2	2	2	9	.321
MULNIX, D.	3	0/0	.000	0/0	.000	-/0	0	1	1	0	0	0	.000
HENDLER, J.	4	0/1	.000	0/0	.000	-/1	0	0	1	0	0	0	.000
Totals	200	30/55	.545	26/30	.867	-/21	16	10	15	9	3	86	.430

Southern Ill. (81)   Coach: Paul Lambert

	Min.	Total FG/FGA	Pct.	FT/FTA	Pct.	Reb. O/T	A	TO	PF	S	Blk	TP	PPM
FORD, R.	36	7/10	.700	3/4	.750	-/6	3	1	5	0	1	17	.472
WILSON, G.	32	6/13	.462	0/3	.000	-/7	2	3	4	0	0	12	.375
ABRAMS, G.	34	3/4	.750	2/2	1.000	-/3	0	6	4	0	0	8	.235
GLENN, M.	40	15/23	.652	0/0	.000	-/4	3	0	3	1	0	30	.750
ABRAMS, W.	23	2/5	.400	3/4	.750	-/6	5	5	2	1	0	7	.304
GRANT, A.	10	1/7	.143	1/1	1.000	-/5	1	0	1	0	0	3	.300
SMITH, B.	8	2/2	1.000	0/1	.000	-/3	0	1	1	0	0	4	.500
HUGHLETT, M.	7	0/0	.000	0/0	.000	-/1	0	0	0	0	0	0	.000
HARRIS, T.	7	0/0	.000	0/0	.000	-/0	2	0	2	0	0	0	.000
WILLIAMS, A.	3	0/0	.000	0/0	.000	-/0	0	0	0	0	0	0	.000
Totals	200	36/64	.563	9/15	.600	-/35	16	16	22	2	1	81	.405

Team Rebounds: Wake Forest 3; Southern Ill. 4. Disqualified: Southern Ill.—Ford. Technical fouls: None.

	1st Half	2nd Half	Final
Wake Forest	34	52	86
Southern Ill.	35	46	81

REGIONAL FINAL EAST

Kentucky (72) Coach: Joe Hall

	Min.	Total FG/FGA	Pct.	FT/FTA	Pct.	Reb. O/T	A	TO	PF	S	Blk	TP	PPM
GIVENS, J.	38	10/18	.556	6/6	1.000	-/4	3	-	1	-	-	26	.684
ROBEY, R.	23	5/6	.833	5/5	1.000	-/3	0	-	5	-	-	15	.652
PHILLIPS, M.	20	6/7	.857	0/0	.000	-/3	1	-	3	-	-	12	.600
JOHNSON, L.	38	3/11	.273	3/4	.750	-/6	5	-	5	-	-	9	.237
SHIDLER, J.	13	0/4	.000	0/0	.000	-/0	1	-	2	-	-	0	.000
CLAYTOR, T.	27	2/6	.333	0/0	.000	-/2	1	-	5	-	-	4	.148
LEE, J.	23	2/9	.222	2/2	1.000	-/6	2	-	4	-	-	6	.261
HASKINS, M.	16	0/0	.000	0/1	.000	-/0	0	-	1	-	-	0	.000
CASEY, D.	2	0/0	.000	0/0	.000	-/0	0	-	0	-	-	0	.000
Totals	200	28/61	.459	16/18	.889	-/24	13	-	26	-	-	72	.360

North Carolina (79) Coach: Dean Smith

	Min.	Total FG/FGA	Pct.	FT/FTA	Pct.	Reb. O/T	A	TO	PF	S	Blk	TP	PPM
DAVIS, W.	37	7/11	.636	7/9	.778	-/6	2	-	2	-	-	21	.568
O'KOREN, M.	36	6/10	.600	2/2	1.000	-/7	1	-	2	-	-	14	.389
YONAKER, R.	24	4/7	.571	0/0	.000	-/5	0	-	5	-	-	8	.333
FORD, P.	15	1/3	.333	0/0	.000	-/0	5	-	4	-	-	2	.133
KUESTER, J.	32	3/5	.600	13/14	.929	-/3	2	-	1	-	-	19	.594
BUCKLEY, B.	4	0/0	.000	0/0	.000	-/0	0	-	2	-	-	0	.000
KRAFCISIN, S.	14	0/0	.000	8/8	1.000	-/3	1	-	2	-	-	8	.571
ZALIAGIRLS, T.	27	1/1	1.000	3/3	1.000	-/0	0	-	2	-	-	5	.185
BRADLEY, D.	3	1/1	1.000	0/0	.000	-/1	0	-	0	-	-	2	.667
WOLF, J.	2	0/0	.000	0/0	.000	-/0	0	-	1	-	-	0	.000
COLESCOTT, D.	5	0/0	.000	0/0	.000	-/0	1	-	1	-	-	0	.000
VIRGIL, J.	1	0/0	.000	0/0	.000	-/0	0	-	0	-	-	0	.000
Totals	200	23/38	.605	33/36	.917	-/25	12	-	22	-	-	79	.395

Team Rebounds: N. Carolina 1; Kentucky 3. Disqualified: N. Carolina—Yonaker; Kentucky—Robey, Johnson, Claytor.

	1st Half	2nd Half	Final
Kentucky	41	31	72
N. Carolina	53	26	79

REGIONAL FINAL WEST

Idaho State (90) Coach: Jim Killingsworth

	Min.	Total FG/FGA	Pct.	FT/FTA	Pct.	Reb. O/T	A	TO	PF	S	Blk	TP	PPM
GRIFFIN, G.	28	5/13	.385	7/7	1.000	-/7	1	2	4	0	0	17	.607
COOK, J.	33	5/10	.500	0/0	.000	-/10	2	2	1	1	1	10	.303
HAYES, S.	33	7/10	.700	2/3	.667	-/13	1	1	2	0	1	16	.485
THOMPSON, E.	38	8/16	.500	11/15	.733	-/3	4	5	3	2	1	27	.711
GOOLD, S.	18	1/4	.250	0/0	.000	-/1	1	1	3	0	0	2	.111
WHEELER, E.	20	2/5	.400	1/2	.500	-/2	2	2	1	0	0	5	.250
ROBINSON, B.	10	2/6	.333	2/2	1.000	-/1	0	3	4	0	0	6	.600
WILSON, P.	7	1/2	.500	1/2	.500	-/0	0	1	3	1	0	3	.429
BEMIS, B.	5	0/0	.000	2/2	1.000	-/0	0	0	1	0	0	2	.400
McQUAID, M.	5	1/1	1.000	0/0	.000	-/3	0	2	0	0	0	2	.400
KLES, S.	2	0/1	.000	0/0	.000	-/0	1	1	0	0	0	0	.000
GARDNER, K.	1	0/0	.000	0/0	.000	-/0	0	1	1	0	0	0	.000
Totals	200	32/68	.471	26/33	.788	-/40	12	21	23	4	3	90	.450

UNLV (107) Coach: Jerry Tarkanian

	Min.	Total FG/FGA	Pct.	FT/FTA	Pct.	Reb. O/T	A	TO	PF	S	Blk	TP	PPM
OWENS, E.	28	10/19	.526	4/5	.800	-/3	0	2	3	1	0	24	.857
GONDREZICK, G.	26	3/8	.375	1/2	.500	-/9	3	3	4	1	1	7	.269
MOFFETT, L.	29	4/8	.500	0/1	.000	-/16	1	1	5	0	3	8	.276
SMITH, R.	24	4/8	.500	2/2	1.000	-/2	2	0	4	2	0	10	.417
SMITH, S.	27	6/16	.375	4/4	1.000	-/2	2	2	3	1	0	16	.593
THEUS, R.	29	6/12	.500	4/5	.800	-/3	6	1	3	1	0	16	.552
SMITH, T.	20	7/10	.700	4/4	1.000	-/2	4	0	1	1	0	18	.900
BROWN, L.	13	4/8	.500	0/0	.000	-/4	0	1	3	0	0	8	.615
MILKE, M.	1	0/0	.000	0/0	.000	-/0	0	2	1	1	0	0	.000
PORTER, M.	1	0/0	.000	0/0	.000	-/0	0	0	0	0	0	0	.000
RODRIGUEZ, J.	1	0/0	.000	0/0	.000	-/0	0	0	0	0	0	0	.000
WAGNER, G.	1	0/1	.000	0/0	.000	-/0	0	0	0	0	0	0	.000
Totals	200	44/90	.489	19/23	.826	-/41	18	12	27	8	4	107	.535

Team Rebounds: UNLV 9; Idaho State 3. Disqualified: UNLV—Moffett. Technical fouls: None.

	1st Half	2nd Half	Final
Idaho State	52	38	90
UNLV	51	56	107

REGIONAL FINAL MIDEAST

Michigan (68) Coach: Johnny Orr

	Min.	Total FG/FGA	Pct.	FT/FTA	Pct.	Reb. O/T	A	TO	PF	S	Blk	TP	PPM
ROBINSON, J.	26	5/9	.556	1/2	.500	-/4	1	0	4	0	0	11	.423
STATON, T.	31	0/4	.000	0/0	.000	-/3	4	3	5	2	0	0	.000
HUBBARD, P.	39	5/14	.357	4/4	1.000	-/7	0	2	4	2	2	14	.359
GROTE, S.	29	3/8	.375	1/2	.500	-/3	4	2	5	2	0	7	.241
GREEN, R.	40	9/19	.474	2/6	.333	-/2	6	5	1	5	0	20	.500
BAXTER, D.	12	2/7	.286	0/0	.000	-/0	0	1	3	1	0	4	.333
THOMPSON, J.	8	3/5	.600	0/0	.000	-/1	0	0	2	0	0	6	.750
HARDY, A.	14	3/8	.375	0/0	.000	-/4	0	0	4	0	1	6	.429
BERGEN, T.	1	0/0	.000	0/0	.000	-/0	0	0	0	0	0	0	.000
Totals	200	30/74	.405	8/14	.571	-/24	15	13	28	12	3	68	.340

North Carolina-Charlotte (75) Coach: Lee Rose

	Min.	Total FG/FGA	Pct.	FT/FTA	Pct.	Reb. O/T	A	TO	PF	S	Blk	TP	PPM
MASSEY, L.	35	6/13	.462	7/9	.778	-/11	3	10	4	0	0	19	.543
KING, K.	33	2/3	.667	2/3	.667	-/3	4	2	2	3	2	6	.182
MAXWELL, C.	39	10/16	.625	5/8	.625	-/13	1	4	4	3	4	25	.641
KINCH, C.	34	3/10	.300	5/5	1.000	-/3	6	1	2	0	0	11	.324
WATKINS, M.	34	2/7	.286	2/2	1.000	-/6	3	2	2	5	0	6	.176
GRUBER, J.	13	3/3	1.000	0/0	.000	-/0	0	3	2	0	0	6	.462
SCOTT, P.	11	1/1	1.000	0/1	.000	-/1	0	1	1	0	2	2	.182
HESTER, M.	1	0/0	.000	0/0	.000	-/0	0	0	0	0	0	0	.000
Totals	200	27/53	.509	21/28	.750	-/37	17	23	17	11	8	75	.375

Team Rebounds: N.C.-Charlotte 6; Michigan 8. Disqualified: Michigan—Staton, Grote. Technical fouls: None.

	1st Half	2nd Half	Final
Michigan	27	41	68
N.C.-Charlotte	40	35	75

REGIONAL FINAL MIDWEST

Marquette (82)   Coach: Al McGuire

	Min.	Total FG/FGA	Pct.	FT/FTA	Pct.	Reb. O/T	A	TO	PF	S	Blk	TP	PPM
ELLIS, B.	40	8/14	.571	4/6	.667	-/7	1	4	3	1	1	20	.500
NEARY, B.	39	3/5	.600	1/2	.500	-/6	1	0	4	0	0	7	.179
WHITEHEAD, J.	13	1/5	.200	0/0	.000	-/5	0	0	4	0	1	2	.154
LEE, B.	40	8/15	.533	3/4	.750	-/2	1	3	2	2	0	19	.475
BOYLAN, J.	29	3/5	.600	1/2	.500	-/5	2	0	2	2	1	7	.241
TOONE, B.	24	6/11	.545	6/6	1.000	-/2	0	1	2	0	0	18	.750
ROSENBERGER, G.	12	2/4	.500	5/6	.833	-/2	0	0	1	1	0	9	.750
DUDLEY, J.	3	0/1	.000	0/0	.000	-/0	0	1	0	0	0	0	.000
Totals	200	31/60	.517	20/26	.769	-/29	5	9	18	6	3	82	.410

Wake Forest (68)   Coach: Carl Tacy

	Min.	Total FG/FGA	Pct.	FT/FTA	Pct.	Reb. O/T	A	TO	PF	S	Blk	TP	PPM
GRIFFIN, R.	37	6/10	.600	4/4	1.000	-/4	0	3	4	0	0	16	.432
SCHELLENBERG, T.	40	7/12	.583	5/8	.625	-/5	3	0	2	2	0	19	.475
HARRISON, L.	21	4/5	.800	3/4	.750	-/4	1	0	4	0	2	11	.524
BROWN, S.	40	5/12	.417	0/1	.000	-/5	6	5	4	3	0	10	.250
JOHNSON, F.	33	3/13	.231	0/0	.000	-/4	0	5	4	0	0	6	.182
MCDONALD, L.	21	0/0	.000	4/4	1.000	-/5	1	0	3	0	1	4	.190
MULNIX, D.	5	1/2	.500	0/0	.000	-/1	0	0	1	0	0	2	.400
HENDLER, J.	3	0/0	.000	0/0	.000	-/0	0	1	1	0	0	0	.000
Totals	200	26/54	.481	16/21	.762	-/28	11	14	23	5	3	68	.340

Team Rebounds: Marquette 3; Wake Forest 3. Disqualified: None. Technical fouls: None.

	1st Half	2nd Half	Final
Marquette	31	51	82
Wake Forest	35	33	68

FINAL FOUR

North Carolina (84)   Coach: Dean Smith

	Min.	Total FG/FGA	Pct.	FT/FTA	Pct.	Reb. O/T	A	TO	PF	S	Blk	TP	PPM
O'KOREN, M.	26	14/19	.737	3/5	.600	-/8	1	-	1	-	-	31	1.192
BUCKLEY, B.	14	1/5	.200	0/0	.000	-/2	0	-	3	-	-	2	.143
YONAKOR, R.	26	5/7	.714	1/4	.250	-/9	2	-	0	-	-	11	.423
FORD, P.	37	4/10	.400	4/5	.800	-/6	9	-	2	-	-	12	.324
KUESTER, J.	34	2/5	.400	5/7	.714	-/6	3	-	0	-	-	9	.265
BRADLEY, D.	6	0/1	.000	0/0	.000	-/1	0	-	0	-	-	0	.000
KRAFICISIN, S.	4	0/0	.000	0/1	.000	-/2	0	-	1	-	-	0	.000
ZALIAGIRIS, T.	4	0/1	.000	0/0	.000	-/0	0	-	0	-	-	0	.000
WOLF, J.	11	0/1	.000	0/0	.000	-/1	0	-	0	-	-	0	.000
COLESCOTT, D.	3	0/0	.000	0/0	.000	-/0	0	-	1	-	-	0	.000
DAVIS, W.	35	7/7	1.000	5/6	.833	-/5	1	-	3	-	-	19	.543
Totals	200	33/56	.589	18/28	.643	-/40	16	-	11	-	-	84	.420

UNLV (83)   Coach: Jerry Tarkanian

	Min.	Total FG/FGA	Pct.	FT/FTA	Pct.	Reb. O/T	A	TO	PF	S	Blk	TP	PPM
OWENS, E.	30	7/15	.467	0/0	.000	-/2	0	-	4	-	-	14	.467
GONDREZICK, G.	27	4/8	.500	0/0	.000	-/5	2	-	4	-	-	8	.296
MOFFETT, L.	31	6/9	.667	1/2	.500	-/9	1	-	5	-	-	13	.419
SMITH, R.	30	4/11	.364	0/1	.000	-/1	3	-	1	-	-	8	.267
SMITH, S.	37	10/18	.556	0/0	.000	-/2	0	-	1	-	-	20	.541
THEUS, R.	26	4/11	.364	0/0	.000	-/5	4	-	4	-	-	8	.308
SMITH, T.	12	6/8	.750	0/2	.000	-/1	1	-	3	-	-	12	1.000
BROWN, L.	7	0/0	.000	0/0	.000	-/1	0	-	0	-	-	0	.000
Totals	200	41/80	.513	1/5	.200	-/26	11	-	22	-	-	83	.415

Disqualified: UNLV—Moffett. Technical fouls: None.

	1st Half	2nd Half	Final
N. Carolina	43	41	84
UNLV	49	34	83

North Carolina-Charlotte (49)   Coach: Lee Rose

	Min.	Total FG/FGA	Pct.	FT/FTA	Pct.	Reb. O/T	A	TO	PF	S	Blk	TP	PPM
MASSEY, L.	38	7/13	.538	0/0	.000	-/8	0	-	1	-	-	14	.368
KING, K.	38	2/7	.286	0/0	.000	-/5	4	-	2	-	-	4	.105
MAXWELL, C.	40	5/6	.833	7/9	.778	-/12	2	-	2	-	-	17	.425
KINCH, C.	38	1/7	.143	2/2	1.000	-/4	2	-	2	-	-	4	.105
WATKINS, M.	23	2/4	.500	2/3	.667	-/0	1	-	5	-	-	6	.261
GRUBER, J.	18	2/6	.333	0/0	.000	-/0	0	-	0	-	-	4	.222
SCOTT, P.	5	0/0	.000	0/0	.000	-/0	0	-	0	-	-	0	.000
Totals	200	19/43	.442	11/14	.786	-/29	9	-	12	-	-	49	.245

Marquette (51)   Coach: Al McGuire

	Min.	Total FG/FGA	Pct.	FT/FTA	Pct.	Reb. O/T	A	TO	PF	S	Blk	TP	PPM
ELLIS, B.	40	2/8	.250	0/0	.000	-/5	0	-	4	-	-	4	.100
NEARY, B.	18	0/1	.000	0/0	.000	-/2	0	-	3	-	-	0	.000
WHITEHEAD, J.	40	10/16	.625	1/2	.500	-/16	0	-	1	-	-	21	.525
LEE, B.	40	5/18	.278	1/1	1.000	-/3	2	-	3	-	-	11	.275
BOYLAN, J.	37	4/9	.444	0/0	.000	-/3	6	-	2	-	-	8	.216
TOONE, B.	20	2/6	.333	2/2	1.000	-/1	0	-	3	-	-	6	.300
ROSENBERGER, G.	5	0/0	.000	1/2	.500	-/1	0	-	0	-	-	1	.200
Totals	200	23/58	.397	5/7	.714	-/31	8	-	16	-	-	51	.255

Disqualified: N.C.-Charlotte—Watkins, Technical fouls: None.

	1st Half	2nd Half	Final
N.C.-Charlotte	22	27	49
Marquette	25	26	51

NATIONAL CHAMPIONSHIP

North Carolina (59) — Coach: Dean Smith

	Min.	Total FG/FGA	Pct.	FT/FTA	Pct.	Reb. O/T	A	TO	PF	S	Blk	TP	PPM
DAVIS, W.	33	6/13	.462	8/10	.800	-/ 8	3	4	4	2	0	20	.606
O'KOREN, M.	31	6/10	.600	2/ 4	.500	-/11	1	1	5	1	1	14	.452
YONAKOR, R.	25	3/ 5	.600	0/ 0	.000	-/ 4	1	2	0	1	0	6	.240
FORD, P.	38	3/10	.300	0/ 0	.000	-/ 2	5	3	3	0	0	6	.158
KUESTER, J.	31	2/ 6	.333	1/ 2	.500	-/ 0	6	4	5	1	0	5	.161
KRAFCISIN, S.	10	1/ 1	1.000	0/ 0	.000	-/ 0	0	0	0	0	0	2	.200
ZALIAGIRIS, T.	10	2/ 3	.667	0/ 0	.000	-/ 0	0	0	3	1	0	4	.400
BRADLEY, D.	5	1/ 1	1.000	0/ 0	.000	-/ 0	0	0	2	0	0	2	.400
BUCKLEY, B.	10	0/ 1	.000	0/ 0	.000	-/ 0	0	0	1	0	0	0	.000
WOLF, J.	3	0/ 1	.000	0/ 0	.000	-/ 1	0	0	0	0	0	0	.000
COLESCOTT, D.	1	0/ 0	.000	0/ 0	.000	-/ 0	0	0	0	0	0	0	.000
COLEY, W.	1	0/ 0	.000	0/ 0	.000	-/ 0	0	0	0	0	0	0	.000
DOUGHTON, G.	1	0/ 0	.000	0/ 0	.000	-/ 0	0	0	0	0	0	0	.000
VIRGIL, J.	1	0/ 0	.000	0/ 0	.000	-/ 0	0	0	1	0	0	0	.000
Totals	200	24/51	.471	11/16	.688	-/26	16	14	24	6	1	59	.295

Marquette (67) — Coach: Al McGuire

	Min.	Total FG/FGA	Pct.	FT/FTA	Pct.	Reb. O/T	A	TO	PF	S	Blk	TP	PPM
ELLIS, B.	39	5/ 9	.556	4/ 5	.800	-/ 9	3	3	4	1	1	14	.359
NEARY, B.	12	0/ 2	.000	0/ 0	.000	-/ 0	0	0	1	0	0	0	.000
WHITEHEAD, J.	39	2/ 8	.250	4/ 4	1.000	-/11	2	0	2	0	2	8	.205
LEE, B.	40	6/14	.429	7/ 7	1.000	-/ 3	2	4	1	3	0	19	.475
BOYLAN, J.	33	5/ 7	.714	4/ 4	1.000	-/ 4	0	4	3	1	0	14	.424
TOONE, B.	29	3/ 6	.500	0/ 1	.000	-/ 0	0	0	1	0	0	6	.207
ROSENBERGER, G.	8	1/ 1	1.000	4/ 4	1.000	-/ 1	1	0	1	0	0	6	.750
Totals	200	22/47	.468	23/25	.920	-/28	8	11	13	5	3	67	.335

Team Rebounds: Marquette 1; N. Carolina 2. Disqualified: N. Carolina—O'Koren, Kuester. Technical fouls: Marquette—Toone.

	1st Half	2nd Half	Final
N. Carolina	27	32	59
Marquette	39	28	67

NATIONAL THIRD PLACE

UNLV (106) — Coach: Jerry Tarkanian

	Min.	Total FG/FGA	Pct.	FT/FTA	Pct.	Reb. O/T	A	TO	PF	S	Blk	TP	PPM
OWENS, E.	35	14/28	.500	6/ 8	.750	-/ 8	2	-	2	-	-	34	.971
GONDREZICK, G.	27	3/ 8	.375	1/ 2	.500	-/ 7	2	-	4	-	-	7	.259
MOFFETT, L.	26	6/ 9	.667	0/ 0	.000	-/ 6	0	-	4	-	-	12	.462
SMITH, R.	30	4/ 7	.571	2/ 2	1.000	-/ 1	3	-	1	-	-	10	.333
SMITH, S.	24	5/10	.500	0/ 0	.000	-/ 5	2	-	2	-	-	10	.417
THEUS, R.	30	11/18	.611	2/ 5	.400	-/ 5	8	-	4	-	-	24	.800
SMITH, T.	17	1/ 6	.167	0/ 0	.000	-/ 0	3	-	0	-	-	2	.118
BROWN, L.	11	3/ 9	.333	1/ 1	1.000	-/ 5	0	-	5	-	-	7	.636
Totals	200	47/95	.495	12/18	.667	-/37	20	-	22	-	-	106	.530

North Carolina-Charlotte (94) — Coach: Lee Rose

	Min.	Total FG/FGA	Pct.	FT/FTA	Pct.	Reb. O/T	A	TO	PF	S	Blk	TP	PPM
MASSEY, L.	31	11/19	.579	0/ 0	.000	-/ 7	2	-	3	-	-	22	.710
KING, K.	17	1/ 4	.250	0/ 2	.000	-/ 0	1	-	1	-	-	2	.118
MAXWELL, C.	39	9/15	.600	12/13	.923	-/16	3	-	2	-	-	30	.769
KINCH, C.	35	11/20	.550	8/ 8	1.000	-/12	3	-	5	-	-	30	.857
WATKINS, M.	29	1/ 5	.200	0/ 0	.000	-/ 4	5	-	2	-	-	2	.069
GRUBER, J.	17	1/ 1	1.000	0/ 0	.000	-/ 0	0	-	1	-	-	2	.118
CROWLEY, T.	16	0/ 0	.000	0/ 0	.000	-/ 0	1	-	0	-	-	0	.000
WHITFIELD, L.	8	0/ 0	.000	0/ 0	.000	-/ 0	1	-	0	-	-	0	.000
SCOTT, P.	7	2/ 4	.500	0/ 0	.000	-/ 6	1	-	3	-	-	4	.571
ANGEL, K.	0	0/ 1	.000	2/ 3	.667	-/ 2	1	-	1	-	-	2	-
HESTER, M.	0	0/ 1	.000	0/ 0	.000	-/ 3	0	-	0	-	-	0	-
WINSTON, J.	0	0/ 2	.000	0/ 0	.000	-/ 0	0	-	0	-	-	0	-
Totals	200	36/72	.500	22/26	.846	-/50	17	-	18	-	-	94	.470

Team Rebounds: UNLV 3; N.C.-Charlotte 1. Disqualified: UNLV—Brown; N.C.-Charlotte—Kinch. Technical fouls: None.
Players who played 0 min. played less than 1 min. each.

	1st Half	2nd Half	Final
UNLV	50	56	106
N.C.-Charlotte	55	39	94

○ ALL-STAR TEAMS ○

ALL TOURNAMENT

WALTER DAVIS	N. CAROLINA
BO ELLIS	MARQUETTE
★ BUTCH LEE	MARQUETTE
CEDRIC MAXWELL	N.C.-CHARLOTTE
MIKE O'KOREN	N. CAROLINA
JEROME WHITEHEAD	MARQUETTE

EAST REGIONAL

RON CARTER	VMI
WALTER DAVIS	N. CAROLINA
JACK GIVENS	KENTUCKY
TOBY KNIGHT	NOTRE DAME
★ JOHN KUESTER	NORTH CAROLINA

MIDEAST REGIONAL

RICKEY GREEN	MICHIGAN
PHIL HUBBARD	MICHIGAN
JOHN LONG	DETROIT
LEW MASSEY	N.C.-CHARLOTTE
★ CEDRIC MAXWELL	N.C.-CHARLOTTE

WEST REGIONAL

STEVE HAYES	IDAHO STATE
MARQUES JOHNSON	UCLA
JEFF JONAS	UTAH
★ EDDIE OWENS	UNLV
★ ROBERT SMITH	UNLV
ED THOMPSON	IDAHO STATE

MIDWEST REGIONAL

SKIP BROWN	WAKE FOREST
BO ELLIS	MARQUETTE
MIKE GLENN	SOUTHERN ILL.
★ BUTCH LEE	MARQUETTE
JERRY SCHELLENBERG	WAKE FOREST

★ Most Outstanding Player(s)

❂ INDIVIDUAL RECORDS ❂

SCORING

Most points in a single game
1 MIKE GLENN, SOUTHERN ILL. (vs. ARIZONA) 35
1 RICKEY GREEN, MICHIGAN (vs. HOLY CROSS) 35
1 RICH LAUREL, HOFSTRA (vs. NOTRE DAME) 35
4 EDDIE OWENS, UNLV (vs. N.C.-CHARLOTTE) 34
5 2 tied for fifth place.

Most total points in the tournament
1 CEDRIC MAXWELL, N.C.-CHARLOTTE   123
2 EDDIE OWENS, UNLV   110
3 REGGIE THEUS, UNLV   89
4 BUTCH LEE, MARQUETTE   88
5 MIKE O'KOREN, N. CAROLINA   86

Highest scoring average (minimum 2 games)
1 MIKE GLENN, SOUTHERN ILL. (65-2)   32.50
2 CEDRIC MAXWELL, N.C.-CHARLOTTE (123-5)
                                        24.60
3 STEVE HAYES, IDAHO STATE (72-3)   24.00
4 TERRY TYLER, DETROIT (46-2)   23.00
4 RON CARTER, VMI (46-2)   23.00

FIELD GOALS

Most field goals in a single game
1 RICKEY GREEN, MICHIGAN (vs. HOLY CROSS) 16
2 MIKE GLENN, SOUTHERN ILL. (vs. ARIZONA) 15
2 MIKE GLENN, SOUTHERN ILL. (vs. WAKE
   FOREST)   15
2 RICH LAUREL, HOFSTRA (vs. NOTRE DAME)   15
5 3 tied for fifth place.

Most total field goals in the tournament
1 EDDIE OWENS, UNLV   47
2 CEDRIC MAXWELL, N.C.-CHARLOTTE   39
3 LEW MASSEY, N.C.-CHARLOTTE   37
3 BUTCH LEE, MARQUETTE   37
5 2 tied for fifth place.

Most field goal attempts in a single game
1 RICH LAUREL, HOFSTRA (vs. NOTRE DAME) 35
2 EDDIE OWENS, UNLV (vs. N.C.-CHARLOTTE) 28
3 RON CARTER, VMI (vs. KENTUCKY)   26
4 JOHN LONG, DETROIT (vs. MICHIGAN)   24
4 NORM NIXON, DUQUESNE (vs. VMI)   24

Most total field goal attempts in the tournament
1 EDDIE OWENS, UNLV   94
2 BUTCH LEE, MARQUETTE   84
3 LEW MASSEY, N.C.-CHARLOTTE   70
4 REGGIE THEUS, UNLV   67
5 CHAD KINCH, N.C.-CHARLOTTE   64

**Highest field goal percentage in a single game
(minimum 10 attempts)**
1 TRUMAN CLAYTOR, KENTUCKY (vs. VMI) (13-
   15)   .867
2 RON BREWER, ARKANSAS (vs. WAKE FOREST)
   (9-11)   .818

3 RICKEY GREEN, MICHIGAN (vs. HOLY CROSS)
   (16-20)   .800
4 CURTIS REDDING, KANSAS STATE (vs.
   PROVIDENCE) (14-18)   .778
5 TOBY KNIGHT, NOTRE DAME (vs. N. CAROLINA)
   (10-13)   .769

**Highest field goal percentage in the tournament
(minimum 20 attempts)**
1 RICK ROBEY, KENTUCKY (16-22)   .727
2 TRUMAN CLAYTOR, KENTUCKY (21-29)   .724
3 TERRY TYLER, DETROIT (20-28)   .714
4 CEDRIC MAXWELL, N.C.-CHARLOTTE (39-58)
                                        .672
5 MIKE GLENN, SOUTHERN ILL. (30-45)   .667

FREE THROWS

Most free throws in a single game
1 JOHN KUESTER, N. CAROLINA (vs. KENTUCKY)
                                           13
2 CEDRIC MAXWELL, N.C.-CHARLOTTE (vs. UNLV)
                                           12
3 ED THOMPSON, IDAHO STATE (vs. UNLV)   11
3 SKIP BROWN, WAKE FOREST (vs. SOUTHERN
   ILL.)   11
3 CEDRIC MAXWELL, N.C.-CHARLOTTE (vs.
   SYRACUSE)   11

Most total free throws in the tournament
1 CEDRIC MAXWELL, N.C.-CHARLOTTE   45
2 JOHN KUESTER, N. CAROLINA   23
3 CHAD KINCH, N.C.-CHARLOTTE   21
4 PHIL FORD, N. CAROLINA   20
4 WALTER DAVIS, N. CAROLINA   20

Most free throws attempted in a single game
1 ED THOMPSON, IDAHO STATE (vs. UNLV)   15
2 JOHN KUESTER, N. CAROLINA (vs. KENTUCKY)
                                           14
3 CEDRIC MAXWELL, N.C.-CHARLOTTE (vs. UNLV)
                                           13
4 CEDRIC MAXWELL, N.C.-CHARLOTTE (vs.
   CENTRAL MICH.)   12
4 SKIP BROWN, WAKE FOREST (vs. SOUTHERN
   ILL.)   12

Most free throws attempted in the tournament
1 CEDRIC MAXWELL, N.C.-CHARLOTTE   53
2 JOHN KUESTER, N. CAROLINA   27
3 REGGIE THEUS, UNLV   26
3 MIKE O'KOREN, N. CAROLINA   26
5 WALTER DAVIS, N. CAROLINA   25

**Highest free throw percentage in a single game
(minimum 7 attempts)**
1 CEDRIC MAXWELL, N.C.-CHARLOTTE (vs.
   SYRACUSE) (11-11)   1.000
2 WINFORD BOYNES, SAN FRANCISCO (vs. UNLV)
   (10-10)   1.000

3 PHIL FORD, N. CAROLINA (vs. NOTRE DAME)
   (9-9)   1.000
4 3 tied for fourth place.

**Highest free throw percentage in the tournament
(minimum 15 attempts)**
1 PHIL FORD, N. CAROLINA (20-21)   .952
2 BUTCH LEE, MARQUETTE (14-15)   .933
3 CHAD KINCH, N.C.-CHARLOTTE (21-23)   .913
4 SKIP BROWN, WAKE FOREST (18-21)   .857
5 JOHN KUESTER, N. CAROLINA (23-27)   .852

REBOUNDS

Most rebounds in a single game
1 PHIL HUBBARD, MICHIGAN (vs. DETROIT)   26
2 CEDRIC MAXWELL, N.C.-CHARLOTTE (vs.
   CENTRAL MICH.)   18
3 LARRY MOFFETT, UNLV (vs. UTAH)   17
4 4 tied for fourth place.

Most total rebounds in the tournament
1 CEDRIC MAXWELL, N.C.-CHARLOTTE   64
2 LARRY MOFFETT, UNLV   52
3 PHIL HUBBARD, MICHIGAN   45
4 JEROME WHITEHEAD, MARQUETTE   44
5 JEFF COOK, IDAHO STATE   40

Most rebounds per game (minimum 2 games)
1 PHIL HUBBARD, MICHIGAN (45-3)   15.00
2 MARQUES JOHNSON, UCLA (27-2)   13.50
3 JEFF COOK, IDAHO STATE (40-3)   13.33
4 TOBY KNIGHT, NOTRE DAME (26-2)   13.00
5 CEDRIC MAXWELL, N.C.-CHARLOTTE (64-5)
                                        12.80

ASSISTS

Most assists in a single game
1 JEFF JONAS, UTAH (vs. UNLV)   15
1 DENNIS BOYD, DETROIT (vs. MIDDLE TENN.
   ST.)   15
3 PHILIP BOND, LOUISVILLE (vs. UCLA)   14
4 JOHNNY DARDEN, TENNESSEE (vs. SYRACUSE)
                                           12
5 LEWIS MACK, MIDDLE TENN. ST. (vs. DETROIT)
                                           10

Most total assists in the tournament
1 PHIL FORD, N. CAROLINA   27
2 MELVIN WATKINS, N.C.-CHARLOTTE   23
2 REGGIE THEUS, UNLV   23
4 3 tied for fourth place.

Most assists per game (minimum 2 appearances)
1 JEFF JONAS, UTAH (22-2)   11.00
1 DENNIS BOYD, DETROIT (22-2)   11.00
3 RICKEY GREEN, MICHIGAN (22-3)   7.33
4 SKIP BROWN, WAKE FOREST (20-3)   6.67
5 PHIL FORD, N. CAROLINA (27-5)   5.40

⊙ TEAM RECORDS ⊙

SCORING

Most points in a single game
1	UNLV (vs. SAN FRANCISCO)	121
2	UNLV (vs. IDAHO STATE)	107
3	UNLV (vs. N.C.-CHARLOTTE)	106

Most total points in the tournament
1	UNLV	505
2	N.C.-CHARLOTTE	390
3	N. CAROLINA	370

Highest scoring average (minimum 2 games)
1	UNLV (505-5)	101.00
2	DETROIT (174-2)	87.00
3	NOTRE DAME (167-2)	83.50

FIELD GOALS

Most field goals in a single game
1	UNLV (vs. SAN FRANCISCO)	49
2	UNLV (vs. N.C.-CHARLOTTE)	47
3	UNLV (vs. IDAHO STATE)	44

Most total field goals in the tournament
1	UNLV	218
2	N.C.-CHARLOTTE	147
3	N. CAROLINA	139

Most field goals attempted in a single game
1	UNLV (vs. N.C.-CHARLOTTE)	95
2	UNLV (vs. IDAHO STATE)	90
3	UNLV (vs. SAN FRANCISCO)	89

Most total field goals attempted in the tournament
1	UNLV	441
2	N.C.-CHARLOTTE	289
3	MARQUETTE	282

Highest field goal percentage in a single game
1	ARKANSAS (vs. WAKE FOREST) (34-50)	.680
2	NOTRE DAME (vs. N. CAROLINA) (30-45)	.667
3	DETROIT (vs. MIDDLE TENN. ST.) (40-64)	.625

Highest field goal percentage in the tournament (minimum 2 games)
1	NOTRE DAME (65-111)	.586
2	SOUTHERN ILL. (72-128)	.563
3	KENTUCKY (96-176)	.546

FREE THROWS

Most free throws in a single game
1	N. CAROLINA (vs. KENTUCKY)	33
2	WAKE FOREST (vs. SOUTHERN ILL.)	26
2	IDAHO STATE (vs. UNLV)	26

Most total free throws in the tournament
1	N.C.-CHARLOTTE	96
2	N. CAROLINA	92
3	MARQUETTE	79

Most free throws attempted in a single game
1	SAN FRANCISCO (vs. UNLV)	36
1	N. CAROLINA (vs. KENTUCKY)	36
3	2 tied for third place.	

Most total free throws attempted in the tournament
1	N.C.-CHARLOTTE	119
2	N. CAROLINA	118
3	UNLV	98

Highest free throw percentage in a single game
1	PURDUE (vs. N. CAROLINA) (14-15)	.933
2	MARQUETTE (vs. N. CAROLINA) (23-25)	.920
3	N. CAROLINA (vs. KENTUCKY) (33-36)	.917

Highest free throw percentage in the tournament (minimum 2 games)
1	MARQUETTE (79-95)	.832
2	WAKE FOREST (66-80)	.825
3	KANSAS STATE (23-28)	.821

Fewest free throws in a single game
1	UNLV (vs. N. CAROLINA)	1
2	DUQUESNE (vs. VMI)	2
3	2 tied for third place.	

Lowest free throw percentage in a single game
1	UNLV (vs. N. CAROLINA) (1-5)	.200
2	DUQUESNE (vs. VMI) (2-5)	.400
3	ST. JOHN'S (vs. UTAH) (6-12)	.500

Lowest free throw percentage in the tournament (minimum 2 games)
1	SOUTHERN ILL. (18-31)	.581
2	MICHIGAN (32-48)	.667
3	SYRACUSE (26-37)	.703

REBOUNDS

Most rebounds in a single game
1	IDAHO STATE (vs. LONG BEACH ST.)	54
2	N.C.-CHARLOTTE (vs. UNLV)	50
3	MICHIGAN (vs. DETROIT)	47

Most rebounds per game (minimum 2 games)
1	IDAHO STATE (140-3)	46.67
2	UCLA (77-2)	38.50
3	KANSAS STATE (75-2)	37.50

ASSISTS

Most assists in a single game
1	MICHIGAN (vs. HOLY CROSS)	29
2	TENNESSEE (vs. SYRACUSE)	27
3	MIDDLE TENN. ST. (vs. DETROIT)	24

Most assists per game (minimum 2 games)
1	MICHIGAN (63-3)	21.00
2	SYRACUSE (38-2)	19.00
2	DETROIT (38-2)	19.00

1978

| FIRST ROUND | REGIONAL SEMIFINAL | REGIONAL FINAL | FINAL FOUR | REGIONAL FINAL | REGIONAL SEMIFINAL | FIRST ROUND |

MIDEAST

Michigan St. 77
Michigan St. 90
Providence 63
Michigan St. 49
Western Ky. 87 (ot)
Western Ky. 69
Syracuse 86
Kentucky 64
Miami (Ohio) 84 (ot)
Miami (Ohio) 69
Marquette 81
Kentucky 52
Kentucky 85
Kentucky 91
Florida St. 76

Duke 90

Kentucky 94
Duke 88

WEST

UCLA 83
UCLA 70
Kansas 76
Arkansas 61
Weber St. 52
Arkansas 74
Arkansas 73
Arkansas 59
San Francisco 68
San Francisco 72
N. Carolina 64
Cal. St. F'lerton 58
New Mexico 85
Cal. St. F'lerton 75
Cal. St. F'lerton 90

Duke 90

Notre Dame 86

EAST

Duke 63
Duke 84
Rhode Island 62
Duke 90
Pennsylvania 92
Pennsylvania 80
St. Bonaventure 83
Furman 62
Indiana 60
Indiana 63
Villanova 72
Villanova 103
Villanova 61
La Salle 97

MIDWEST

Missouri 79
Utah 56
Utah 86 (2 ot)
Notre Dame 84
Houston 77
Notre Dame 69
Notre Dame 100
Notre Dame 86
Creighton 78
DePaul 90 (ot)
DePaul 80
DePaul 64
Louisville 76
Louisville 89
St. John's 68

CONSOLATION GAME

National Third Place:
Arkansas 71
Notre Dame 69

On December 11th, 1977, the legendary Baron of the Bluegrass, Adolph Rupp, died in Lexington, Kentucky. In the last week of March of the following year, his unsmiling successor, Joe B. Hall, led a tight-lipped squad of Kentucky Wildcats into the Final Four.

It was said at the time that the No. 1–ranked Wildcats were battling not only against their opponents on the floor, but against their reputation, the expectations of their fans, and Kentucky tradition as well. While any of the four squads that reached the Final Four had a chance to win, only Kentucky could lose.

All season long, Rupp's four championships had hung heavy on Hall's heart. "So much is expected of us," he said. "Our fans start out the first day in practice saying, 'We know you're going to win the NCAA.' " The Wildcats were a big, strong, physical, veteran team, led by a group of seniors who had played in the championship game against UCLA as freshmen, won the NIT as sophomores, and lost in the regional finals as juniors. This year would be the last chance for Jack "Goose" Givens, Rick Robey, Mike Phillips, and James Lee. They had to win.

All season long, Hall rode his players, even going so far as to call them the Folding Five when it seemed they might not have the wherewithal to go all the way. But the pressure on the Wildcats reached its peak in the NCAAs. In the regional final, they managed to come back against Michigan State and the Spartans' freshman sensation, Earvin Johnson, only because the Kentucky point guard, Purdue transfer Kyle Macy, hit 10 straight free throws down the stretch.

In the Final Four, Joe B. Hall had Jack Givens to thank for getting the monkey off his back.

Kentucky's semifinal against Arkansas was a matchup between Razorback quickness and Wildcat strength. Arkansas coach Eddie Sutton wanted to rely on a pressure man-to-man defense to force the slower Kentucky players into mistakes; instead his 6-11 center Steve Schall picked up four fouls within the first seven minutes, and his second tallest starter, 6-7 defensive specialist Jim Counce, was also whistled for his fourth before the end of the first half. Sutton, with by far the weaker bench of the two teams, had to abandon his bread and butter defense for a zone. Meanwhile Kentucky's defense was putting the clamps on the Razorbacks' main men, Ron Brewer, Sidney Moncrief, and Marvin Delph.

In the second half, Kentucky built their lead to 9 before Sutton switched back into the man-to-man. With 3:23 remaining the Razorbacks pulled to within 1, but Moncrief missed down low with a chance to put them ahead. With 1:58 left, they were still only a basket behind, but Kentucky beat their full-court press when Macy tossed the ball the length of the floor to Givens, who put in an uncontested lay-up. Givens not only put the finishing touch on Arkansas, he also outscored the four other starters on his own team, hitting on 10 of his 16 shots for 23 points. But it was nothing compared to the performance to come.

Duke had made it to the championship showdown by withstanding a furious Notre Dame rally that brought the Irish from 16 down with four minutes left to within 2 before their luck (and the clock) ran out. The young Blue Devils (two freshmen, two sophomores, and a junior) were just happy to be along for the ride, as was their coach, Bill Foster, whose teams had finished last in the ACC for four consecutive years before freshman forward Gene Banks and sophomore center Mike Gminski led them on an improbable run to a shot at the title.

Duke opened in a zone, with the Blue Devil guards pressuring their Kentucky counterparts in an attempt to prevent the ball from coming in down low to the 6-10 Rick Robey and Mike Phillips. "Hank Iba once told me never to spread your defense from baseline to midcourt because you would leave a big gap in there around the foul line," said Hall. "When we saw how open Duke was leaving the middle, we junked our game plan and just tried to get it in to Jack."

Givens found the hole in the zone and started canning line drive jumpers from the top of the key. Still, Duke stayed close on the strength of some remarkable foul shooting (they hit 20 of 21 in the first half). But inexplicably, the Blue Devils didn't adjust their defense: Givens got open again and again, and he kept on shooting. When he knocked in the last 16 Kentucky points of the half, the Wildcats left the floor with a 7-point lead.

After intermission, Givens took up where he had left off. He scored 18 second-half points to finish with 41 (only Bill Walton and Gail Goodrich ever scored more in a championship game). Despite a Duke rally that brought them to within 4 in the last minute, Givens and the Wildcats were too much for the Blue Devils to handle.

Joe B. Hall had his championship, and the ghosts of Kentucky's past were finally laid to rest.

FIRST ROUND MIDEAST

Michigan State (77)   Coach: Jud Heathcote

	Min.	Total FG/FGA	Pct.	FT/FTA	Pct.	Reb. O/T	A	TO	PF	S	Blk	TP	PPM
KELSER, G.	35	9/10	.900	5/7	.714	-/11	3	4	2	1	2	23	.657
JOHNSON, E.	37	5/9	.556	4/6	.667	-/7	7	2	3	2	1	14	.378
VINCENT, J.	26	2/3	.667	2/3	.667	-/4	1	2	1	0	1	6	.231
DONNELLY, T.	36	6/9	.667	0/0	.000	-/3	3	4	2	2	0	12	.333
CHAPMAN, J.	36	7/12	.583	0/0	.000	-/1	1	3	2	1	0	14	.389
BRKOVICH, M.	5	0/0	.000	0/0	.000	-/0	0	1	1	0	0	0	.000
CHARLES, R.	11	3/4	.750	0/2	.000	-/3	1	0	4	1	2	6	.545
FLOWERS, D.	1	0/0	.000	0/0	.000	-/0	0	1	0	0	0	0	.000
PHILLIPS, W.	1	0/1	.000	0/0	.000	-/0	1	0	0	0	0	0	.000
LONGAKER, M.	1	0/0	.000	0/0	.000	-/0	0	0	0	0	0	0	.000
WILLIAMS, L.	1	0/0	.000	0/0	.000	-/0	0	1	0	1	0	0	.000
BROWN, A.	2	0/2	.000	0/0	.000	-/1	0	1	0	0	0	0	.000
RIEWALD, D.	2	0/0	.000	0/0	.000	-/1	0	0	0	0	0	0	.000
RAYE, R.	1	0/0	.000	0/0	.000	-/0	0	0	1	0	0	0	.000
FELDREICH, S.	5	1/2	.500	0/0	.000	-/2	0	0	1	0	0	2	.400
Totals	200	33/52	.635	11/18	.611	-/33	17	19	17	8	6	77	.385

Providence (63)   Coach: Dave Gavitt

	Min.	Total FG/FGA	Pct.	FT/FTA	Pct.	Reb. O/T	A	TO	PF	S	Blk	TP	PPM
EASON, B.	30	3/10	.300	0/2	.000	-/6	2	1	4	0	0	6	.200
CAMPBELL, R.	37	9/16	.563	6/6	1.000	-/8	0	4	4	1	0	24	.649
MISEVICIUS, B.	31	6/10	.600	1/1	1.000	-/6	0	3	4	0	0	13	.419
WILLIAMS, D.	32	1/6	.167	2/4	.500	-/1	5	4	5	2	0	4	.125
ORISTAGLIO, P.	15	0/1	.000	0/0	.000	-/0	1	1	1	0	0	0	.000
SCOTT, J.	9	2/6	.333	0/1	.000	-/1	0	0	0	1	1	4	.444
FRYE, D.	4	0/1	.000	2/2	1.000	-/1	1	1	0	0	0	2	.500
NOLAN, J.	4	0/1	.000	2/2	1.000	-/0	1	1	0	1	0	2	.500
DELGATTO, E.	2	0/0	.000	0/0	.000	-/1	0	0	0	0	0	0	.000
WILLIAMS, J.	27	2/6	.333	2/4	.500	-/4	1	2	3	0	0	6	.222
HUNGER, R.	9	0/2	.000	2/2	1.000	-/1	0	0	2	1	0	2	.222
Totals	200	23/59	.390	17/24	.708	-/29	10	17	23	6	1	63	.315

Team Rebounds: Michigan St. 2; Providence 5. Disqualified: Providence—D. Williams. Technical fouls: None.

	1st Half	2nd Half	Final
Michigan St.	38	39	77
Providence	26	37	63

Western Kentucky (87)   Coach: Jim Richards

	Min.	Total FG/FGA	Pct.	FT/FTA	Pct.	Reb. O/T	A	TO	PF	S	Blk	TP	PPM
JOHNSON, J.	41	9/17	.529	3/4	.750	-/12	0	6	1	1	2	21	.512
JACKSON, G.	36	4/8	.500	3/6	.500	-/6	2	2	4	1	1	11	.306
BRYANT, A.	32	7/12	.583	2/4	.500	-/9	1	3	5	2	0	16	.500
ASHBY, S.	33	5/9	.556	2/3	.667	-/4	3	2	4	0	0	12	.364
TURNER, D.	38	5/13	.385	2/4	.500	-/4	5	5	3	3	0	12	.316
PRINCE, M.	25	4/11	.364	0/0	.000	-/2	1	3	2	1	0	8	.320
BURBACH, G.	12	0/0	.000	1/2	.500	-/2	3	1	0	0	0	1	.083
REESE, M.	8	3/4	.750	0/0	.000	-/2	1	0	0	2	0	6	.750
Totals	225	37/74	.500	13/23	.565	-/41	16	22	19	10	3	87	.387

Syracuse (86)   Coach: Jim Boeheim

	Min.	Total FG/FGA	Pct.	FT/FTA	Pct.	Reb. O/T	A	TO	PF	S	Blk	TP	PPM
BYRNES, M.	44	8/19	.421	5/9	.556	-/7	2	4	4	1	0	21	.477
ORR, L.	31	6/12	.500	2/2	1.000	-/8	2	3	4	2	1	14	.452
BOUIE, R.	37	7/14	.500	2/4	.500	-/15	0	6	1	2	8	16	.432
KINDEL, R.	20	0/1	.000	0/0	.000	-/1	0	4	0	0	0	0	.000
SHACKLEFORD, D.	15	2/4	.500	0/0	.000	-/0	0	2	5	2	0	4	.267
COHEN, H.	29	11/16	.688	1/1	1.000	-/4	3	4	5	3	0	23	.793
ROSS, E.	34	2/3	.667	0/1	1.000	-/2	4	3	1	1	2	4	.118
HEADD, M.	5	1/5	.200	0/0	.000	-/1	2	0	0	0	0	2	.400
JAMES, K.	9	1/2	.500	0/0	.000	-/1	1	1	1	0	0	2	.222
SCHAYES, D.	1	0/0	.000	0/0	.000	-/0	0	0	0	0	0	0	.000
Totals	225	38/76	.500	10/17	.588	-/39	14	27	21	11	11	86	.382

Team Rebounds: Western Ky. 4; Syracuse 5. Disqualified: Western Ky.—Bryant; Syracuse—Shackleford, Cohen. Technical fouls: None.

	1st Half	2nd Half	1 OT	Final
Western Ky.	41	35	11	87
Syracuse	41	35	10	86

Miami (Ohio) (84)   Coach: Darrell Hedric

	Min.	Total FG/FGA	Pct.	FT/FTA	Pct.	Reb. O/T	A	TO	PF	S	Blk	TP	PPM
AYERS, R.	43	7/13	.538	6/7	.857	-/10	3	-	3	0	0	20	.465
ALDRIDGE, L.	44	7/15	.467	5/6	.833	-/8	1	-	3	0	1	19	.432
LAKE, B.	14	0/2	.000	2/2	1.000	-/1	2	-	2	0	0	2	.143
GOINS, R.	40	9/13	.692	0/0	.000	-/0	4	-	3	1	0	18	.450
SHOEMAKER, J.	44	10/15	.667	0/0	.000	-/4	6	-	2	2	1	20	.455
BABCOCK, R.	2	0/0	.000	3/4	.750	-/0	0	-	0	0	0	3	1.500
JONES, T.	6	0/1	.000	0/0	.000	-/1	1	-	0	0	0	0	.000
DUNN, T.	32	1/3	.333	0/0	.000	-/4	0	-	5	0	0	2	.063
Totals	225	34/62	.548	16/19	.842	-/28	17	14	18	3	2	84	.373

Marquette (81)   Coach: Hank Raymonds

	Min.	Total FG/FGA	Pct.	FT/FTA	Pct.	Reb. O/T	A	TO	PF	S	Blk	TP	PPM
PAYNE, U.	42	5/12	.417	1/2	.500	-/4	4	-	4	2	1	11	.262
TOONE, B.	37	6/10	.600	0/1	.000	-/5	2	-	5	0	1	12	.324
WHITEHEAD, J.	36	5/8	.625	0/0	.000	-/10	2	-	3	1	1	10	.278
LEE, B.	45	10/16	.625	7/10	.700	-/3	1	-	3	3	0	27	.600
BOYLAN, J.	39	5/10	.500	5/7	.714	-/4	5	-	1	2	0	15	.385
ROSENBERGER, J.	20	2/5	.400	0/0	.000	-/2	0	-	0	1	0	4	.200
LEE, O.	6	1/1	1.000	0/0	.000	-/1	0	-	0	1	0	2	.333
Totals	225	34/62	.548	13/20	.650	-/29	14	15	16	10	3	81	.360

Disqualified: Miami (Ohio)—Dunn; Marquette—Toone. Technical fouls: Marquette—Coach Raymonds.

	1st Half	2nd Half	1st OT	Final
Miami (Ohio)	33	42	9	84
Marquette	38	37	6	81

Kentucky (85)   Coach: Joe Hall

	Min.	Total FG/FGA	Pct.	FT/FTA	Pct.	Reb. O/T	A	TO	PF	S	Blk	TP	PPM
GIVENS, J.	-	4/9	.444	3/3	1.000	-/4	0	2	5	2	2	11	-
ROBEY, R.	-	2/2	1.000	8/10	.800	-/4	1	3	5	1	0	12	-
PHILLIPS, M.	-	6/9	.667	2/2	1.000	-/6	0	1	1	2	1	14	-
MACY, K.	-	6/10	.600	2/3	.667	-/5	6	4	1	2	0	14	-
CLAYTOR, T.	-	7/13	.538	2/2	1.000	-/1	2	4	1	1	0	16	-
LEE, J.	-	2/5	.400	6/8	.750	-/3	2	2	3	1	0	10	-
SHIDLER, J.	-	1/1	1.000	0/0	.000	-/0	2	3	1	0	0	2	-
WILLIAMS, L.	-	1/2	.500	2/2	1.000	-/5	0	2	2	0	1	4	-
CASEY, D.	-	0/0	.000	0/0	.000	-/0	1	1	2	1	0	0	-
COWAN, F.	-	1/2	.500	0/0	.000	-/3	0	1	1	0	0	2	-
Totals	200	30/53	.566	25/30	.833	-/31	14	23	22	10	4	85	.425

Florida State (76)   Coach: Hugh Durham

	Min.	Total FG/FGA	Pct.	FT/FTA	Pct.	Reb. O/T	A	TO	PF	S	Blk	TP	PPM
THOMPSON, D.	37	6/14	.429	3/4	.750	-/5	2	0	3	0	1	15	.405
DAVIS, H.	30	5/10	.500	1/4	.250	-/7	2	3	3	1	1	11	.367
ANDERSON, K.	30	3/5	.600	0/0	.000	-/3	1	2	5	4	0	6	.200
JACKSON, T.	30	4/7	.571	2/2	1.000	-/5	5	8	4	2	0	10	.333
HARRIS, E.	28	4/11	.364	1/3	.333	-/3	3	3	2	2	1	9	.321
MANN, H.	2	0/0	.000	0/0	.000	-/0	0	0	0	0	0	0	.000
BOZEMAN, J.	2	0/1	.000	0/0	.000	-/0	0	0	1	0	0	0	.000
DILLARD, M.	20	8/10	.800	5/5	1.000	-/1	2	1	5	0	0	21	1.050
SMITH, J.	4	0/0	.000	0/0	.000	-/0	0	0	0	0	0	0	.000
BROWN, M.	17	2/4	.500	0/3	.000	-/3	0	3	0	0	1	4	.235
Totals	200	32/62	.516	12/21	.571	-/27	15	20	23	9	4	76	.380

Team Rebounds: Kentucky 1; Florida State 4. Disqualified: Kentucky—Givens, Robey; Florida State—Anderson, Dillard. Technical fouls: None.

	1st Half	2nd Half	Final
Kentucky	32	53	85
Florida State	39	37	76

FIRST ROUND WEST

UCLA (83) Coach: Gary Cunningham

	Min.	Total FG / FGA	Pct.	FT / FTA	Pct.	Reb. O / T	A	TO	PF	S	Blk	TP	PPM
GREENWOOD, D.	39	7/15	.467	0/ 1	.000	-/10	2	4	3	2	0	14	.359
WILKES, J.	23	0/ 3	.000	5/ 6	.833	-/ 3	2	0	0	1	1	5	.217
SIMS, G.	10	1/ 2	.500	0/ 0	.000	-/ 3	0	0	2	0	1	2	.200
HAMILTON, R.	40	6/16	.375	11/18	.611	-/ 7	10	3	3	4	0	23	.575
TOWNSEND, R.	40	8/12	.667	6/ 6	1.000	-/ 5	4	2	2	0	0	22	.550
ALLUMS, D.	30	2/ 4	.500	2/ 2	1.000	-/11	1	4	3	1	1	6	.200
VANDEWEGHE, K.	18	4/ 7	.571	3/ 6	.500	-/ 6	0	2	1	0	0	11	.611
Totals	200	28/59	.475	27/39	.692	-/45	19	15	14	8	3	83	.415

Kansas (76) Coach: Ted Owens

	Min.	Total FG / FGA	Pct.	FT / FTA	Pct.	Reb. O / T	A	TO	PF	S	Blk	TP	PPM
KOENIG, K.	26	4/ 6	.667	0/ 0	.000	-/ 6	3	5	5	0	0	8	.308
MOKESKI, P.	29	9/15	.600	0/ 2	.000	-/12	0	1	4	1	2	18	.621
DOUGLAS, J.	37	5/17	.294	4/ 6	.667	-/ 7	2	2	4	1	1	14	.378
VALENTINE, D.	29	5/14	.357	1/ 2	.500	-/ 3	6	2	5	1	0	11	.379
FOWLER, W.	9	0/ 4	.000	0/ 0	.000	-/ 0	2	0	2	0	0	0	.000
GIBSON, M.	1	0/ 0	.000	0/ 0	.000	-/ 0	0	0	0	0	0	0	.000
VON, M.	21	3/ 8	.375	2/ 4	.500	-/ 4	2	1	4	2	2	8	.381
SANDERS, B.	5	1/ 1	1.000	0/ 0	.000	-/ 0	1	0	0	0	0	2	.400
ANDERSON, S.	6	0/ 0	.000	0/ 0	.000	-/ 1	0	0	1	0	0	0	.000
JOHNSON, C.	37	7/11	.636	1/ 3	.333	-/ 1	4	1	5	3	1	15	.405
Totals	200	34/76	.447	8/17	.471	-/34	20	12	30	8	6	76	.380

Team Rebounds: UCLA 7; Kansas 8. Disqualified: Kansas—Koenig, Johnson, Valentine. Technical fouls: None.

	1st Half	2nd Half	Final
UCLA	42	41	83
Kansas	45	31	76

Weber State (52) Coach: Neil McCarthy

	Min.	Total FG / FGA	Pct.	FT / FTA	Pct.	Reb. O / T	A	TO	PF	S	Blk	TP	PPM
JOHNSON, D.	33	4/16	.250	1/ 2	.500	-/ 6	1	2	3	3	0	9	.273
MOORE, K.	25	7/10	.700	0/ 0	.000	-/ 7	2	3	2	0	0	14	.560
SMITH, R.	38	3/11	.273	2/ 2	1.000	-/ 8	0	2	4	0	0	8	.211
MATTOS, M.	34	1/ 5	.200	0/ 0	.000	-/ 2	2	3	0	0	0	2	.059
COLLINS, B.	38	5/15	.333	3/ 5	.600	-/ 5	4	2	2	1	0	13	.342
HOWLAND, B.	21	3/ 6	.500	0/ 2	.000	-/ 0	0	0	2	0	0	6	.286
MCKONE, G.	6	0/ 1	.000	0/ 0	.000	-/ 1	0	0	1	1	0	0	.000
GIBSON, J.	1	0/ 0	.000	0/ 0	.000	-/ 0	0	1	0	0	0	0	.000
BROWN, D.	4	0/ 0	.000	0/ 0	.000	-/ 0	0	0	0	0	0	0	.000
Totals	200	23/64	.359	6/11	.545	-/29	9	13	14	5	0	52	.260

Arkansas (73) Coach: Eddie Sutton

	Min.	Total FG / FGA	Pct.	FT / FTA	Pct.	Reb. O / T	A	TO	PF	S	Blk	TP	PPM
COUNCE, J.	39	2/ 3	.667	0/ 0	.000	-/ 8	5	1	2	0	0	4	.103
DELPH, M.	36	9/16	.563	2/ 2	1.000	-/ 8	0	2	1	2	1	20	.556
SCHALL, S.	22	3/ 5	.600	0/ 0	.000	-/ 4	0	0	4	0	0	6	.273
BREWER, R.	36	7/15	.467	5/ 7	.714	-/ 3	2	2	2	1	2	19	.528
MONCRIEF, S.	25	5/ 9	.556	6/ 6	1.000	-/ 5	1	4	4	0	0	16	.640
WATLEY, M.	3	0/ 2	.000	0/ 0	.000	-/ 0	0	0	0	1	0	0	.000
ZAHN, A.	15	1/ 1	1.000	0/ 0	.000	-/ 1	0	0	3	0	0	2	.133
REED, U.	20	1/ 3	.333	0/ 0	.000	-/ 0	0	0	1	1	0	2	.100
CROCKETT, J.	4	2/ 4	.500	0/ 0	.000	-/ 1	0	0	0	0	2	4	1.000
Totals	200	30/58	.517	13/15	.867	-/30	8	9	17	5	5	73	.365

Team Rebounds: Arkansas 4; Weber St. 3. Disqualified: None. Technical fouls: Weber St.—Bench.

	1st Half	2nd Half	Final
Weber St.	26	26	52
Arkansas	32	41	73

San Francisco (68) Coach: Bob Gaillard

	Min.	Total FG / FGA	Pct.	FT / FTA	Pct.	Reb. O / T	A	TO	PF	S	Blk	TP	PPM
BOYNES, W.	40	10/14	.714	0/ 0	.000	-/ 8	4	4	3	1	0	20	.500
JEMISON, D.	40	3/ 9	.333	2/ 2	1.000	-/ 5	2	0	2	0	3	8	.200
CARTWRIGHT, B.	40	9/12	.750	5/ 7	.714	-/11	6	3	3	1	2	23	.575
WILLIAMS, R.	23	1/ 4	.250	0/ 0	.000	-/ 5	5	4	2	0	0	3	.130
COX, J.	37	4/11	.364	4/ 4	1.000	-/ 5	4	3	1	1	0	12	.324
WILLIAMS, S.	20	1/ 4	.250	0/ 0	.000	-/ 2	2	5	3	1	0	2	.100
Totals	200	28/54	.519	12/15	.800	-/36	23	19	14	4	5	68	.340

North Carolina (64) Coach: Dean Smith

	Min.	Total FG / FGA	Pct.	FT / FTA	Pct.	Reb. O / T	A	TO	PF	S	Blk	TP	PPM
O'KOREN, M.	38	5/13	.385	4/ 5	.800	-/ 5	6	4	2	2	0	14	.368
BRADLEY, D.	13	2/ 3	.667	0/ 0	.000	-/ 0	0	0	2	2	0	4	.308
WOLF, J.	29	2/ 8	.250	0/ 0	.000	-/ 2	0	0	2	1	0	4	.138
ZALIAGIRIS, T.	23	3/ 5	.600	0/ 0	.000	-/ 2	0	2	1	1	1	6	.261
FORD, P.	38	7/19	.368	0/ 0	.000	-/ 1	3	1	3	4	1	14	.368
COLESCOTT, D.	4	1/ 1	1.000	0/ 0	.000	-/ 0	0	0	0	0	0	2	.500
DOUGHTON, G.	2	0/ 0	.000	0/ 0	.000	-/ 0	1	0	0	0	0	0	.000
WOOD, A.	23	3/ 9	.333	0/ 0	.000	-/ 5	1	0	2	0	1	6	.261
BUDKO, P.	2	0/ 0	.000	0/ 0	.000	-/ 0	0	0	0	0	0	0	.000
COMPTON, J.	11	2/ 5	.400	0/ 1	.000	-/ 7	2	0	3	1	1	4	.364
VIRGIL, J.	17	5/ 8	.625	0/ 0	.000	-/ 0	2	0	2	1	0	10	.588
Totals	200	30/71	.423	4/ 6	.667	-/22	15	7	17	12	4	64	.320

Team Rebounds: San Francisco 3; N. Carolina 5. Disqualified: None. Technical fouls: None.

	1st Half	2nd Half	Final
San Francisco	32	36	68
N. Carolina	32	32	64

New Mexico (85) Coach: Norm Ellenberger

	Min.	Total FG / FGA	Pct.	FT / FTA	Pct.	Reb. O / T	A	TO	PF	S	Blk	TP	PPM
JOHNSON, M.	35	7/15	.467	1/ 2	.500	-/ 1	2	-	3	-	-	15	.429
ABNEY, P.	33	7/ 9	.778	2/ 3	.667	-/ 7	2	-	4	-	-	16	.485
ALLEN, J.	19	3/ 5	.600	0/ 0	.000	-/10	0	-	2	-	-	6	.316
COOPER, M.	30	6/15	.400	0/ 1	.000	-/ 4	3	-	2	-	-	12	.400
SAUNDERS, R.	27	5/11	.455	3/ 3	1.000	-/ 2	4	-	2	-	-	13	.481
SMILEY, W.	13	3/ 5	.600	3/ 3	1.000	-/ 3	0	-	2	-	-	9	.692
HOWARD, C.	25	5/ 9	.556	0/ 1	.000	-/ 5	0	-	4	-	-	10	.400
FELIX, M.	14	1/ 3	.333	2/ 2	1.000	-/ 1	2	-	2	-	-	4	.286
STEWART, M.	4	0/ 0	.000	0/ 0	.000	-/ 0	0	-	0	-	-	0	.000
Totals	200	37/72	.514	11/15	.733	-/33	13	-	21	-	-	85	.425

California State Fullerton (90) Coach: Bob Dye

	Min.	Total FG / FGA	Pct.	FT / FTA	Pct.	Reb. O / T	A	TO	PF	S	Blk	TP	PPM
BUNCH, G.	37	8/10	.800	2/ 4	.500	-/ 5	1	-	5	-	-	18	.486
HEENEN, K.	35	10/17	.588	2/ 3	.667	-/ 5	1	-	5	-	-	22	.629
SHAW, S.	26	1/ 1	1.000	0/ 1	.000	-/ 1	1	-	2	-	-	2	.077
ANDERSON, K.	38	9/14	.643	5/ 7	.714	-/ 1	8	-	1	-	-	23	.605
LINDEN, M.	40	1/ 3	.333	4/ 4	1.000	-/ 5	12	-	2	-	-	6	.150
NILES, M.	24	7/13	.538	5/ 6	.833	-/ 6	1	-	3	-	-	19	.792
Totals	200	36/58	.621	18/25	.720	-/23	24	-	18	-	-	90	.450

Team Rebounds: Cal. St. F'lerton 1; New Mexico 2. Disqualified: Cal. St. F'lerton—Bunch, Heenen. Technical fouls: None.

	1st Half	2nd Half	Final
New Mexico	44	41	85
Cal. St. F'lerton	38	52	90

FIRST ROUND EAST

Duke (63)   Coach: Wm. E. (Bill) Foster

	Min.	Total FG/FGA	Pct.	FT/FTA	Pct.	Reb. O/T	A	TO	PF	S	Blk	TP	PPM
BANKS, E.	36	7/15	.467	0/ 1	.000	-/10	2	-	3	-	-	14	.389
DENNARD, K.	26	0/ 3	.000	0/ 1	.000	-/ 5	2	-	3	-	-	0	.000
GMINSKI, M.	35	10/18	.556	5/ 5	1.000	-/10	1	-	3	-	-	25	.714
HARRELL, J.	32	0/ 4	.000	0/ 0	.000	-/ 1	4	-	2	-	-	0	.000
SPANARKEL, J.	38	8/13	.615	2/ 5	.400	-/ 5	3	-	2	-	-	18	.474
BENDER, B.	12	0/ 3	.000	0/ 0	.000	-/ 0	1	-	3	-	-	0	.000
GOETSCH, S.	5	0/ 1	.000	0/ 0	.000	-/ 2	0	-	0	-	-	0	.000
MORRISON, H.	2	0/ 0	.000	0/ 0	.000	-/ 0	0	-	0	-	-	0	.000
GRAY, S.	2	0/ 0	.000	0/ 0	.000	-/ 0	0	-	0	-	-	0	.000
SUDDATH, J.	12	1/ 4	.250	4/ 4	1.000	-/ 4	0	-	0	-	-	6	.500
Totals	200	26/61	.426	11/16	.688	-/37	13	14	16	-	-	63	.315

Rhode Island (62)   Coach: Jack Kraft

	Min.	Total FG/FGA	Pct.	FT/FTA	Pct.	Reb. O/T	A	TO	PF	S	Blk	TP	PPM
WILLIAMS, S.	32	12/18	.667	3/ 6	.500	-/ 9	1	-	5	-	-	27	.844
WRIGHT, S.	40	4/11	.364	0/ 0	.000	-/ 3	5	-	4	-	-	8	.200
CHATMAN, I.	36	1/ 6	.167	1/ 3	.333	-/12	1	-	4	-	-	3	.083
NELSON, J.	24	3/11	.273	0/ 1	.000	-/ 4	0	-	2	-	-	6	.250
WILLIAMSON, J.	40	6/ 9	.667	0/ 0	.000	-/ 2	3	-	2	-	-	12	.300
DAVIS, P.	16	2/ 3	.667	0/ 1	.000	-/ 1	1	-	2	-	-	4	.250
WRIGHT, J.	12	1/ 7	.143	0/ 0	.000	-/ 3	0	-	2	-	-	2	.167
Totals	200	29/65	.446	4/11	.364	-/34	11	13	21	-	-	62	.310

Team Rebounds: Duke 4; Rhode Island 4. Disqualified: Rhode Island—Williams. Technical fouls: None.

	1st Half	2nd Half	Final
Duke	30	33	63
Rhode Island	31	31	62

Pennsylvania (92)   Coach: Bob Weinhauer

	Min.	Total FG/FGA	Pct.	FT/FTA	Pct.	Reb. O/T	A	TO	PF	S	Blk	TP	PPM
PRICE, T.	28	6/14	.429	4/ 4	1.000	4/12	3	1	5	2	1	16	.571
MCDONALD, K.	39	16/25	.640	5/ 6	.833	3/11	0	0	2	1	0	37	.949
WHITE, M.	12	0/ 1	.000	0/ 0	.000	0/ 2	0	3	5	1	1	0	.000
GREENE, S.	27	4/ 8	.500	0/ 0	.000	0/ 1	1	2	3	2	1	8	.296
WILLIS, B.	29	4/ 9	.444	0/ 0	.000	3/ 6	6	4	3	0	1	8	.276
CROWLEY, T.	19	3/ 4	.750	4/ 4	1.000	0/ 0	6	3	2	1	0	10	.526
SMITH, T.	31	3/ 7	.429	1/ 5	.200	2/ 2	4	3	2	0	0	7	.226
SALTERS, J.	7	1/ 2	.500	2/ 3	.667	0/ 0	1	1	0	0	0	4	.571
KUHL, E.	7	1/ 4	.250	0/ 0	.000	3/ 3	1	0	0	0	0	2	.286
BERGWALL, B.	1	0/ 1	.000	0/ 0	.000	0/ 0	0	0	1	0	0	0	.000
Totals	200	38/75	.507	16/22	.727	15/37	22	17	23	7	4	92	.460

St. Bonaventure (83)   Coach: Jim Statlin

	Min.	Total FG/FGA	Pct.	FT/FTA	Pct.	Reb. O/T	A	TO	PF	S	Blk	TP	PPM
HARROD, D.	20	6/ 9	.667	1/ 2	.500	2/ 6	1	3	5	0	1	13	.650
SANDERS, G.	39	10/24	.417	10/14	.714	9/13	1	3	4	2	0	30	.769
WATERMAN, T.	36	6/14	.429	1/ 3	.333	9/16	0	0	2	0	1	13	.361
URZETTA, N.	33	1/ 6	.167	0/ 0	.000	1/ 4	7	1	4	3	0	2	.061
HAGAN, G.	40	6/19	.316	7/ 7	1.000	0/ 1	5	7	2	2	0	19	.475
BELCHER, M.	20	1/ 2	.500	2/ 3	.667	0/ 0	0	3	2	1	0	4	.200
VIGLIANCO, D.	3	0/ 0	.000	0/ 0	.000	0/ 0	0	0	0	0	0	0	.000
SPENCER, M.	3	0/ 0	.000	0/ 0	.000	0/ 0	0	0	3	0	0	0	.000
JONES, A.	6	1/ 1	1.000	0/ 0	.000	1/ 2	0	0	2	0	0	2	.333
Totals	200	31/75	.413	21/29	.724	22/42	14	17	23	8	2	83	.415

Team Rebounds: Pennsylvania 5; St. Bonaventure 4. Disqualified: Pennsylvania—Price, White; St. Bonaventure—Harrod. Technical fouls: None.

	1st Half	2nd Half	Final
Pennsylvania	37	55	92
St. Bonaventure	42	41	83

Furman (62)   Coach: Joe Williams

	Min.	Total FG/FGA	Pct.	FT/FTA	Pct.	Reb. O/T	A	TO	PF	S	Blk	TP	PPM
ARNOLD, R.	30	5/16	.313	0/ 0	.000	-/ 0	1	1	3	0	0	10	.333
DANIEL, A.	39	9/18	.500	3/ 4	.750	-/ 7	0	1	3	1	0	21	.538
MOORE, J.	40	7/13	.538	5/ 6	.833	-/14	1	2	4	0	0	19	.475
GRIMM, B.	33	2/13	.154	2/ 3	.667	-/ 2	1	3	4	2	0	6	.182
SMITH, R.	34	1/ 1	1.000	0/ 0	.000	-/ 1	0	3	3	2	0	2	.059
CROWE, D.	9	1/ 1	1.000	0/ 0	.000	-/ 1	3	0	0	0	0	2	.222
MCKINNEY, R.	15	1/ 2	.500	0/ 0	.000	-/ 2	1	1	0	0	0	2	.133
Totals	200	26/64	.406	10/13	.769	-/27	7	11	18	5	0	62	.310

Indiana (63)   Coach: Bob Knight

	Min.	Total FG/FGA	Pct.	FT/FTA	Pct.	Reb. O/T	A	TO	PF	S	Blk	TP	PPM
RADFORD, W.	38	8/ 9	.889	4/ 4	1.000	-/ 6	5	7	5	2	0	20	.526
WOODSON, M.	40	13/24	.542	0/ 2	.000	-/ 6	0	5	3	1	1	26	.650
TOLBERT, R.	32	1/ 4	.250	0/ 0	.000	-/ 9	0	3	4	0	2	2	.063
BAKER, J.	33	2/ 3	.667	0/ 1	.000	-/ 6	2	2	2	0	0	4	.121
WISMAN, J.	38	3/ 5	.600	0/ 2	.000	-/ 2	10	3	1	0	0	6	.158
CARTER, B.	10	1/ 1	1.000	3/ 4	.750	-/ 1	1	1	2	0	0	5	.500
RISLEY, S.	9	0/ 0	.000	0/ 0	.000	-/ 1	0	0	0	0	0	0	.000
Totals	200	28/46	.609	7/13	.538	-/31	18	21	17	3	3	63	.315

Team Rebounds: Indiana 2; Furman 3. Disqualified: Indiana—Radford. Technical fouls: Furman—team.

	1st Half	2nd Half	Final
Furman	24	38	62
Indiana	34	29	63

Villanova (103)   Coach: Rollie Massimino

	Min.	Total FG/FGA	Pct.	FT/FTA	Pct.	Reb. O/T	A	TO	PF	S	Blk	TP	PPM
ROBINSON, R.	35	10/16	.625	2/ 2	1.000	4/10	4	2	5	1	0	22	.629
HERRON, K.	33	10/16	.625	4/ 7	.571	2/ 4	1	3	3	0	2	24	.727
BRADLEY, A.	39	9/18	.500	4/ 4	1.000	3/ 8	0	1	3	1	2	22	.564
SPARROW, R.	31	7/11	.636	5/ 6	.833	0/ 2	8	0	4	0	0	19	.613
RIGSBY, W.	40	5/10	.500	4/ 8	.500	1/ 7	6	3	2	3	3	14	.350
LINCOLN, S.	9	1/ 3	.333	0/ 0	.000	0/ 0	6	0	0	2	0	2	.222
UNDERMAN, J.	8	0/ 0	.000	0/ 0	.000	0/ 0	1	0	1	0	1	0	.000
SIENKIEWICZ, T.	1	0/ 1	.000	0/ 0	.000	0/ 0	0	0	0	0	0	0	.000
CARON, M.	4	0/ 1	.000	0/ 1	.000	1/ 1	0	0	1	0	0	0	.000
Totals	200	42/76	.553	19/28	.679	11/32	26	9	19	7	8	103	.515

La Salle (97)   Coach: Paul Westhead

	Min.	Total FG/FGA	Pct.	FT/FTA	Pct.	Reb. O/T	A	TO	PF	S	Blk	TP	PPM
CONNOLLY, J.	35	7/13	.538	1/ 2	.500	1/ 9	7	3	5	1	0	15	.429
WOLKIEWICZ, J.	28	8/12	.667	2/ 2	1.000	2/ 5	2	2	4	0	1	18	.643
BROOKS, M.	37	14/17	.824	7/ 9	.778	6/14	3	1	2	0	0	35	.946
GLADDEN, D.	35	6/17	.353	0/ 0	.000	0/ 3	6	7	5	1	0	12	.343
KANASKIE, K.	36	6/16	.375	3/ 4	.750	0/ 0	6	3	4	2	0	15	.417
PLAKIS, T.	18	1/ 3	.333	0/ 0	.000	1/ 4	2	1	5	0	0	2	.111
WILLIAMS, S.	4	0/ 0	.000	0/ 0	.000	0/ 1	0	0	0	0	0	0	.000
MIHALICH, J.	6	0/ 0	.000	0/ 0	.000	0/ 0	1	0	2	0	0	0	.000
DILEO, T.	1	0/ 0	.000	0/ 0	.000	0/ 0	0	0	0	0	0	0	.000
Totals	200	42/78	.538	13/17	.765	10/36	27	17	27	4	1	97	.485

Team Rebounds: Villanova 4; La Salle 6. Disqualified: Villanova—Robinson; La Salle—Connolly, Gladden, Plakis. Technical fouls: None.

	1st Half	2nd Half	Final
Villanova	46	57	103
La Salle	49	48	97

FIRST ROUND MIDWEST

Missouri (79)   Coach: Norm Stewart

	Min.	Total FG / FGA	Pct.	FT / FTA	Pct.	Reb. O / T	A	TO	PF	S	Blk	TP	PPM
JOHNSON, C.	50	13/23	.565	4/ 5	.800	-/10	1	6	4	0	0	30	.600
BERRY, C.	12	3/ 3	1.000	0/ 1	.000	-/ 0	0	0	3	0	0	6	.500
RAY, S.	46	2/ 9	.222	0/ 0	.000	-/12	5	2	2	1	0	4	.087
DREW, L.	48	7/14	.500	0/ 0	.000	-/ 1	3	8	1	3	0	14	.292
CURRIE., J.	49	7/12	.583	4/ 6	.667	-/ 7	6	5	5	2	0	18	.367
STOEHNER, K.	1	0/ 0	.000	0/ 0	.000	-/ 0	0	0	1	0	0	0	.000
FOSTER, M.	1	0/ 0	.000	0/ 0	.000	-/ 0	0	0	1	0	0	0	.000
DROY, B.	43	2/ 5	.400	3/ 4	.750	-/ 8	0	2	4	0	0	7	.163
Totals	250	34/66	.515	11/17	.647	-/38	15	23	21	6	0	79	.316

Utah (86)   Coach: Jerry Pimm

	Min.	Total FG / FGA	Pct.	FT / FTA	Pct.	Reb. O / T	A	TO	PF	S	Blk	TP	PPM
JUDKINS, J.	47	4/13	.308	3/ 5	.600	-/ 8	2	3	3	3	0	11	.234
VRANES, D.	47	7/12	.583	3/ 7	.429	-/10	6	3	4	1	1	17	.362
MATHENEY, B.	48	17/28	.607	2/ 2	1.000	-/ 8	0	4	3	0	1	36	.750
WILLIAMS, E.	37	1/ 4	.250	0/ 0	.000	-/ 7	5	4	4	5	1	2	.054
GREY, M.	50	5/10	.500	2/ 5	.400	-/ 2	9	1	3	1	0	12	.240
MARTIN, S.	3	0/ 0	.000	2/ 2	1.000	-/ 1	1	1	1	1	0	2	.667
DUNN, M.	1	1/ 1	1.000	0/ 0	.000	-/ 1	0	0	0	0	0	2	2.000
DEANE, G.	13	1/ 3	.333	0/ 0	.000	-/ 2	0	1	3	0	0	2	.154
CHAMBERS, T.	4	0/ 1	.000	2/ 2	1.000	-/ 0	0	1	1	1	0	2	.500
Totals	250	36/72	.500	14/23	.609	-/39	23	18	22	12	3	86	.344

Team Rebounds: Utah 4; Missouri 4. Disqualified: Missouri—Currie. Technical fouls: None.

	1st Half	2nd Half	1st OT	2nd OT	Final
Missouri	38	26	6	9	79
Utah	44	20	6	16	86

Houston (77)   Coach: Guy Lewis

	Min.	Total FG / FGA	Pct.	FT / FTA	Pct.	Reb. O / T	A	TO	PF	S	Blk	TP	PPM
ROSE, C.	34	4/ 9	.444	6/ 7	.857	-/ 2	3	5	3	0	0	14	.412
THOMPSON, C.	19	5/10	.500	0/ 0	.000	-/ 8	0	0	2	0	0	10	.526
SCHUTZ, M.	32	7/ 9	.778	1/ 4	.250	-/ 5	2	2	3	0	1	15	.469
CIOLLI, K.	23	0/ 1	.000	0/ 0	.000	-/ 0	1	1	3	0	0	0	.000
WILLIAMS, O.	24	7/16	.438	3/ 4	.750	-/ 2	1	7	2	0	0	17	.708
O'NEALL, C.	5	0/ 3	.000	0/ 0	.000	-/ 0	1	0	0	2	0	0	.000
TRAMMELL, M.	10	2/ 4	.500	0/ 0	.000	-/ 1	0	0	1	1	0	4	.400
GIBSON, B.	3	1/ 3	.333	0/ 0	.000	-/ 1	0	1	1	1	0	2	.667
BYRD, C.	6	0/ 2	.000	0/ 0	.000	-/ 0	0	0	1	0	0	0	.000
PORTER, W.	3	0/ 0	.000	0/ 0	.000	-/ 2	0	0	2	0	0	0	.000
WALKER, G.	20	4/ 6	.667	0/ 0	.000	-/ 4	0	0	0	0	0	8	.400
FEARS, C.	16	2/ 5	.400	3/ 4	.750	-/ 3	0	0	2	1	0	7	.438
ROPER, D.	3	0/ 0	.000	0/ 0	.000	-/ 0	0	0	2	0	0	0	.000
MITCHELL, L.	2	0/ 0	.000	0/ 0	.000	-/ 1	0	1	1	0	0	0	.000
Totals	200	32/68	.471	13/19	.684	-/29	8	17	23	5	1	77	.385

Notre Dame (100)   Coach: Digger Phelps

	Min.	Total FG / FGA	Pct.	FT / FTA	Pct.	Reb. O / T	A	TO	PF	S	Blk	TP	PPM
TRIPUCKA, K.	27	4/ 9	.444	6/ 8	.750	-/ 4	2	1	0	1	0	14	.519
BATTON, D.	23	6/ 8	.750	0/ 0	.000	-/ 6	2	0	2	1	0	12	.522
FLOWERS, B.	25	2/ 3	.667	2/ 2	1.000	-/ 2	1	1	4	0	0	6	.240
BRANNING, R.	34	7/14	.500	0/ 0	.000	-/ 0	5	4	2	1	0	14	.412
WILLIAMS, D.	35	8/14	.571	3/ 4	.750	-/ 1	1	2	1	1	0	19	.543
HEALY, T.	1	0/ 2	.000	0/ 0	.000	-/ 0	0	0	0	0	0	0	.000
HAEFNER, R.	1	0/ 1	.000	0/ 2	.000	-/ 1	0	0	0	0	0	0	.000
WILCOX, S.	10	3/ 4	.750	0/ 0	.000	-/ 1	0	1	0	0	1	6	.600
WOOLRIDGE, O.	6	1/ 2	.500	0/ 1	.000	-/ 3	0	0	2	0	0	2	.333
HANZLIK, B.	14	2/ 4	.500	0/ 0	.000	-/ 3	0	2	1	0	0	4	.286
SALINAS, B.	3	1/ 1	1.000	1/ 3	.333	-/ 2	0	0	0	0	0	3	1.000
LAIMBEER, B.	21	7/ 9	.778	6/ 6	1.000	-/ 9	2	1	4	0	0	20	.952
Totals	200	41/71	.577	18/26	.692	-/32	13	12	16	4	1	100	.500

Team Rebounds: Notre Dame 5; Houston 1. Disqualified: None. Technical fouls: None.

	1st Half	2nd Half	Final
Houston	32	45	77
Notre Dame	47	53	100

Creighton (78)   Coach: Tom Apke

	Min.	Total FG / FGA	Pct.	FT / FTA	Pct.	Reb. O / T	A	TO	PF	S	Blk	TP	PPM
MCKENNA, K.	-	8/ 9	.889	2/ 2	1.000	-/ 1	6	5	3	2	0	18	-
APKA, R.	-	7/16	.438	0/ 0	.000	-/ 4	8	3	3	1	0	14	-
WESLEY, D.	-	7/10	.700	0/ 0	.000	-/ 8	4	1	3	2	0	14	-
BECKER, R.	-	5/ 8	.625	3/ 6	.500	-/ 2	9	1	3	2	0	13	-
JOHNSON, J.	-	2/ 3	.667	1/ 2	.500	-/ 1	1	5	1	0	0	5	-
KUEHL, K.	-	5/ 7	.714	0/ 1	.000	-/ 5	2	5	2	0	0	10	-
MCCONNELL, T.	-	2/ 3	.667	0/ 0	.000	-/ 2	1	0	1	0	0	4	-
Totals	200	36/56	.643	6/11	.545	-/23	31	20	16	7	0	78	.390

DePaul (80)   Coach: Ray Meyer

	Min.	Total FG / FGA	Pct.	FT / FTA	Pct.	Reb. O / T	A	TO	PF	S	Blk	TP	PPM
PONSETTO, J.	-	4/ 9	.444	2/ 2	1.000	-/ 7	4	3	2	0	1	10	-
WATKINS, C.	-	7/10	.700	0/ 1	.000	-/ 3	2	1	5	2	0	14	-
CORZINE, D.	-	9/14	.643	1/ 2	.500	-/11	2	4	2	1	1	19	-
RAMSEY, R.	-	7/12	.583	1/ 1	1.000	-/ 3	5	0	3	3	1	15	-
CARLANI, G.	-	7/13	.538	6/ 7	.857	-/ 2	7	3	3	4	0	20	-
BRADSHAW, C.	-	0/ 2	.000	0/ 0	.000	-/ 0	0	1	2	0	0	0	-
DINE, W.	-	0/ 5	.000	2/ 4	.500	-/ 3	1	0	0	1	0	2	-
Totals	200	34/65	.523	12/17	.706	-/29	21	12	17	11	3	80	.400

Team Rebounds: DePaul 2; Creighton 7. Disqualified: DePaul—Watkins. Technical fouls: None.

	1st Half	2nd Half	Final
Creighton	48	30	78
DePaul	34	46	80

Louisville (76)   Coach: Denny Crum

	Min.	Total FG / FGA	Pct.	FT / FTA	Pct.	Reb. O / T	A	TO	PF	S	Blk	TP	PPM
TURNER, B.	33	1/ 4	.250	1/ 2	.500	-/ 2	0	4	2	0	0	3	.091
WILLIAMS, L.	35	8/13	.615	5/ 7	.714	-/12	1	2	3	0	0	21	.600
GALLON, R.	24	3/ 6	.500	2/ 2	1.000	-/ 7	0	0	3	0	1	8	.333
GRIFFITH, D.	38	9/18	.500	7/ 7	1.000	-/ 4	3	1	2	1	0	25	.658
WILSON, R.	27	4/11	.364	7/ 7	1.000	-/ 2	0	2	5	0	1	15	.556
SMITH, D.	23	0/ 1	.000	3/ 4	.750	-/ 6	1	4	0	0	1	3	.130
BRANCH, T.	20	0/ 2	.000	1/ 2	.500	-/ 0	0	4	2	0	0	1	.050
Totals	200	25/55	.455	26/31	.839	-/33	5	17	17	1	3	76	.380

St. John's (68)   Coach: Lou Carnesecca

	Min.	Total FG / FGA	Pct.	FT / FTA	Pct.	Reb. O / T	A	TO	PF	S	Blk	TP	PPM
WINFREE, K.	19	0/ 2	.000	0/ 0	.000	-/ 0	0	1	1	0	0	0	.000
JOHNSON, G.	38	10/25	.400	4/ 4	1.000	-/20	1	3	4	3	0	24	.632
MCKOY, W.	27	3/10	.300	3/ 6	.500	-/ 5	0	2	5	0	4	9	.333
CALABRESE, T.	11	1/ 3	.333	0/ 0	.000	-/ 1	0	0	3	0	0	2	.182
CARTER, R.	33	6/16	.375	2/ 2	1.000	-/ 6	2	5	5	2	0	14	.424
RENCHER, B.	29	5/15	.333	1/ 1	1.000	-/ 2	3	1	2	0	0	11	.379
PLAIR, R.	5	0/ 0	.000	0/ 0	.000	-/ 0	0	1	0	0	0	0	.000
THOMAS, G.	18	3/10	.300	1/ 3	.333	-/ 1	0	0	1	0	0	7	.389
BERZWANGER, P.	7	0/ 0	.000	0/ 0	.000	-/ 2	0	0	3	0	0	0	.000
GILROY, F.	7	0/ 1	.000	0/ 0	.000	-/ 2	0	0	0	0	0	0	.000
WRIGHT, R.	6	0/ 2	.000	1/ 2	.500	-/ 5	0	0	1	0	0	1	.167
Totals	200	28/84	.333	12/18	.667	-/44	6	10	24	9	4	68	.340

Team Rebounds: Louisville 8; St. John's 3. Disqualified: Louisville—Wilson; St. John's—McKoy, Carter. Technical fouls: None.

	1st Half	2nd Half	Final
Louisville	39	37	76
St. John's	34	34	68

REGIONAL SEMIFINAL MIDEAST

Michigan State (90)   Coach: Jud Heathcote

	Min.	Total FG/FGA	Pct.	FT/FTA	Pct.	Reb. O/T	A	TO	PF	S	Blk	TP	PPM
KELSER, G.	31	11/18	.611	1/ 2	.500	-/13	1	3	5	0	1	23	.742
JOHNSON, E.	39	3/17	.176	7/11	.636	-/ 9	14	5	2	1	0	13	.333
VINCENT, J.	27	6/ 8	.750	0/ 0	.000	-/ 6	1	1	4	0	0	12	.444
DONNELLY, T.	35	0/ 1	.000	0/ 0	.000	-/ 1	4	2	0	0	0	0	.000
CHAPMAN, R.	39	10/12	.833	3/ 6	.500	-/ 3	2	1	3	0	0	23	.590
BRKOVICH, M.	3	1/ 1	1.000	0/ 0	.000	-/ 1	1	0	1	0	0	2	.667
CHARLES, R.	21	4/ 4	1.000	5/ 6	.833	-/ 8	0	2	3	0	2	13	.619
FLOWERS, D.	1	1/ 1	1.000	0/ 0	.000	-/ 0	1	0	0	0	0	2	2.000
BROWN, A.	1	1/ 1	1.000	0/ 0	.000	-/ 1	1	0	0	0	1	2	2.000
RIEWALD, D.	1	0/ 0	.000	0/ 0	.000	-/ 0	0	0	0	0	0	0	.000
FELDREICH, S.	2	0/ 0	.000	0/ 0	.000	-/ 1	0	0	3	0	0	0	.000
Totals	200	37/63	.587	16/25	.640	-/43	25	14	21	1	4	90	.450

Western Kentucky (69)   Coach: Jim Richards

	Min.	Total FG/FGA	Pct.	FT/FTA	Pct.	Reb. O/T	A	TO	PF	S	Blk	TP	PPM
JOHNSON, J.	-	5/ 8	.625	2/ 5	.400	-/ 7	0	2	5	0	2	12	-
JACKSON, G.	-	8/12	.667	5/10	.500	-/ 6	0	2	1	1	2	21	-
BRYANT, A.	-	5/ 7	.714	2/ 2	1.000	-/ 7	0	0	5	0	1	12	-
ASHBY, S.	-	0/ 1	.000	0/ 0	.000	-/ 0	5	0	1	0	0	0	-
TURNER, D.	-	6/19	.316	0/ 0	.000	-/ 4	4	5	5	0	0	12	-
PRINCE, M.	-	2/ 7	.286	0/ 0	.000	-/ 1	3	1	0	1	0	4	-
BURBACH, G.	-	0/ 1	.000	0/ 0	.000	-/ 0	3	3	2	0	0	0	-
REESE, M.	-	3/ 6	.500	0/ 3	.000	-/ 3	2	0	2	1	0	6	-
RAHN, J.	-	1/ 4	.250	0/ 0	.000	-/ 3	0	1	0	0	2	-
THOMAS, J.	-	0/ 0	.000	0/ 0	.000	-/ 0	0	0	0	0	0	0	-
Totals	200	30/65	.462	9/20	.450	-/31	17	13	22	3	5	69	.345

Team Rebounds: Michigan St. 4; Western Ky. 3. Disqualified: Michigan St.—Kelser; Western Ky.—Johnson, Bryant, Turner. Technical fouls: None.

	1st Half	2nd Half	Final
Michigan St.	39	51	90
Western Ky.	29	40	69

Miami (Ohio) (69)   Coach: Darrell Hedric

	Min.	Total FG/FGA	Pct.	FT/FTA	Pct.	Reb. O/T	A	TO	PF	S	Blk	TP	PPM
AYERS, R.	39	9/11	.818	0/ 0	.000	-/ 8	3	2	5	0	2	18	.462
ALDRIDGE, R.	34	4/10	.400	3/ 4	.750	-/ 3	2	3	2	0	1	11	.324
LAKE, B.	12	2/ 4	.500	2/ 2	1.000	-/ 0	1	3	2	0	0	6	.500
GOINS, R.	31	6/10	.600	0/ 0	.000	-/ 2	1	4	1	0	0	12	.387
SHOEMAKER, J.	38	2/ 8	.250	6/ 6	1.000	-/ 0	4	2	1	1	0	10	.263
BABCOCK, R.	1	0/ 2	.000	0/ 0	.000	-/ 0	0	0	1	0	0	0	.000
JONES, T.	3	1/ 1	1.000	0/ 0	.000	-/ 0	0	2	2	1	0	2	.667
DUNN, T.	25	2/ 3	.667	0/ 0	.000	-/ 1	3	0	1	0	0	4	.160
BRADY, T.	8	1/ 4	.250	0/ 0	.000	-/ 4	0	1	1	0	0	2	.250
BAYS, B.	2	0/ 0	.000	0/ 1	.000	-/ 0	0	0	0	0	0	0	.000
LANTZ, R.	2	1/ 3	.333	0/ 0	.000	-/ 2	0	0	0	0	0	2	1.000
GREISINGER, P.	1	0/ 1	.000	0/ 0	.000	-/ 0	0	0	0	0	0	0	.000
HARKINS, T.	4	0/ 0	.000	2/ 3	.667	-/ 1	0	0	1	0	0	2	.500
Totals	200	28/57	.491	13/16	.813	-/21	14	17	17	2	3	69	.345

Kentucky (91)   Coach: Joe Hall

	Min.	Total FG/FGA	Pct.	FT/FTA	Pct.	Reb. O/T	A	TO	PF	S	Blk	TP	PPM
GIVENS, J.	31	6/13	.462	0/ 1	.000	-/ 9	5	1	4	0	0	12	.387
ROBEY, R.	29	6/ 8	.750	2/ 2	1.000	-/ 7	5	4	1	1	0	14	.483
PHILLIPS, M.	21	11/13	.846	2/ 3	.667	-/ 4	1	5	2	0	0	24	1.143
MACY, K.	33	1/ 3	.333	0/ 0	.000	-/ 0	2	1	1	1	0	2	.061
CLAYTOR, T.	30	6/ 7	.857	1/ 1	1.000	-/ 1	3	0	3	0	0	13	.433
LEE, J.	20	4/ 9	.444	4/ 5	.800	-/ 8	3	1	1	1	0	12	.600
SHIDLER, J.	15	0/ 1	.000	0/ 0	.000	-/ 0	4	2	2	0	0	0	.000
WILLIAMS, L.	5	1/ 1	1.000	0/ 0	.000	-/ 1	0	1	0	1	0	2	.400
COWAN, F.	8	3/ 5	.600	0/ 0	.000	-/ 1	0	3	0	0	1	6	.750
ALEKSINAS, C.	5	1/ 4	.250	0/ 0	.000	-/ 3	0	1	1	0	0	2	.400
CASEY, D.	1	1/ 1	1.000	0/ 0	.000	-/ 0	0	0	0	0	0	2	2.000
STEPHENS, T.	1	0/ 0	.000	0/ 0	.000	-/ 2	1	2	1	0	0	0	.000
COURTS, S.	1	1/ 1	1.000	0/ 0	.000	-/ 1	0	1	0	0	0	2	2.000
Totals	200	41/66	.621	9/12	.750	-/36	25	17	21	3	1	91	.455

Team Rebounds: Kentucky 1; Miami (Ohio) 2. Disqualified: Miami (Ohio)—Ayers. Technical fouls: None.

	1st Half	2nd Half	Final
Miami (Ohio)	30	39	69
Kentucky	46	45	91

REGIONAL SEMIFINAL WEST

UCLA (70)   Coach: Gary Cunningham

	Min.	Total FG/FGA	Pct.	FT/FTA	Pct.	Reb. O/T	A	TO	PF	S	Blk	TP	PPM
GREENWOOD, D.	39	8/13	.615	1/ 4	.250	-/ 4	2	2	5	1	2	17	.436
WILKES, J.	21	3/ 5	.600	0/ 0	.000	-/ 0	1	1	5	1	0	6	.286
SIMS, G.	13	0/ 1	.000	0/ 0	.000	-/ 4	1	1	2	0	1	0	.000
HAMILTON, R.	36	9/16	.563	1/ 2	.500	-/ 1	6	3	4	4	0	19	.528
TOWNSEND, R.	26	1/11	.091	0/ 0	.000	-/ 2	2	2	2	0	0	2	.077
ALLUMS, D.	27	6/ 7	.857	0/ 2	.000	-/10	0	2	4	1	0	12	.444
VANDEWEGHE, K.	17	2/ 4	.500	0/ 0	.000	-/ 4	0	1	0	0	1	4	.235
HOLLAND, B.	20	4/ 9	.444	0/ 0	.000	-/ 0	2	1	2	0	0	8	.400
THOMAS, M.	1	1/ 1	1.000	0/ 0	.000	-/ 2	0	0	0	0	0	2	2.000
Totals	200	34/67	.507	2/ 8	.250	-/27	14	13	24	7	4	70	.350

Arkansas (74)   Coach: Eddie Sutton

	Min.	Total FG/FGA	Pct.	FT/FTA	Pct.	Reb. O/T	A	TO	PF	S	Blk	TP	PPM
COUNCE, J.	39	0/ 1	.000	2/ 2	1.000	-/ 3	3	5	0	2	0	2	.051
DELPH, M.	40	11/14	.786	1/ 1	1.000	-/10	0	3	2	1	0	23	.575
SCHALL, S.	20	4/ 7	.571	0/ 0	.000	-/ 2	1	2	4	2	1	8	.400
BREWER, R.	40	5/14	.357	8/10	.800	-/ 5	5	4	0	0	0	18	.450
MONCRIEF, S.	39	7/13	.538	7/13	.538	-/11	1	1	3	0	1	21	.538
ZAHN, A.	21	1/ 1	1.000	0/ 0	.000	-/ 2	1	1	3	0	0	2	.095
REED, U.	1	0/ 0	.000	0/ 2	.000	-/ 0	0	0	0	0	0	0	.000
Totals	200	28/50	.560	18/28	.643	-/33	11	16	12	5	2	74	.370

Team Rebounds: Arkansas 3; UCLA 3. Disqualified: UCLA—Greenwood, Wilkes. Technical fouls: None.

	1st Half	2nd Half	Final
UCLA	29	41	70
Arkansas	42	32	74

San Francisco (72) Coach: Bob Gaillard

	Min.	Total FG/FGA	Pct.	FT/FTA	Pct.	Reb. O/T	A	TO	PF	S	Blk	TP	PPM
BOYNES, W.	37	8/14	.571	1/2	.500	-/2	3	-	3	-	-	17	.459
JEMISON, D.	34	5/12	.417	3/4	.750	-/11	0	-	3	-	-	13	.382
CARTWRIGHT, B.	35	9/11	.818	9/15	.600	-/9	1	-	2	-	-	27	.771
WILLIAMS, R.	29	0/3	.000	0/0	.000	-/3	3	-	4	-	-	0	.000
COX, J.	34	2/9	.222	0/0	.000	-/4	4	-	0	-	-	4	.118
WILLIAMS, S.	17	2/6	.333	0/0	.000	-/2	0	-	4	-	-	4	.235
HARDY, J.	14	3/4	.750	1/2	.500	-/4	0	-	0	-	-	7	.500
Totals	200	29/59	.492	14/23	.609	-/35	11	-	16	-	-	72	.360

California State Fullerton (75) Coach: Bob Dye

	Min.	Total FG/FGA	Pct.	FT/FTA	Pct.	Reb. O/T	A	TO	PF	S	Blk	TP	PPM
BUNCH, G.	37	11/15	.733	2/2	1.000	-/12	1	-	2	-	-	24	.649
HEENAN, K.	36	7/13	.538	1/1	1.000	-/5	2	-	1	-	-	15	.417
SHAW, S.	15	3/7	.429	0/0	.000	-/3	0	-	0	-	-	6	.400
ANDERSON, K.	37	6/15	.400	0/2	.000	-/4	8	-	3	-	-	12	.324
LINDEN, M.	40	3/9	.333	1/2	.500	-/2	5	-	3	-	-	7	.175
NILES, M.	13	3/6	.500	1/3	.333	-/3	0	-	5	-	-	7	.538
PALM, G.	22	2/4	.500	0/0	.000	-/4	1	-	4	-	-	4	.182
Totals	200	35/69	.507	5/10	.500	-/33	17	-	18	-	-	75	.375

Team Rebounds: Cal. St. F'lerton 5; San Francisco 2. Disqualified: Cal. St. F'lerton—Niles. Technical fouls: None.

	1st Half	2nd Half	Final
San Francisco	44	28	72
Cal. St. F'lerton	32	43	75

REGIONAL SEMIFINAL EAST

Duke (84) Coach: Wm. E. (Bill) Foster

	Min.	Total FG/FGA	Pct.	FT/FTA	Pct.	Reb. O/T	A	TO	PF	S	Blk	TP	PPM
BANKS, E.	-	8/17	.471	5/6	.833	-/10	2	3	4	4	0	21	-
DENNARD, K.	-	4/4	1.000	0/1	.000	-/5	2	1	4	1	0	8	-
GMINSKI, M.	-	6/14	.429	2/3	.667	-/10	0	4	1	1	7	14	-
HARRELL, J.	-	2/4	.500	2/3	.667	-/2	3	2	4	0	0	6	-
SPANARKEL, J.	-	6/14	.429	9/9	1.000	-/6	3	4	1	2	1	21	-
BENDER, B.	-	3/5	.600	2/5	.400	-/4	5	2	1	1	0	8	-
GRAY, S.	-	0/0	.000	0/0	.000	-/0	0	0	0	0	0	0	-
MORRISON, H.	-	0/1	.000	2/2	1.000	-/0	0	0	0	0	0	2	-
SUDDATH, J.	-	1/1	1.000	0/0	.000	-/1	0	0	1	0	0	2	-
GOETSCH, S.	-	1/2	.500	0/0	.000	-/4	0	0	1	0	1	2	-
Totals	200	31/62	.500	22/29	.759	-/42	15	16	17	9	9	84	.420

Pennsylvania (80) Coach: Bob Weinhauer

	Min.	Total FG/FGA	Pct.	FT/FTA	Pct.	Reb. O/T	A	TO	PF	S	Blk	TP	PPM
PRICE, T.	-	6/16	.375	5/6	.833	-/7	6	3	4	2	0	17	-
MCDONALD, K.	-	5/9	.556	0/1	.000	-/5	1	2	4	0	0	10	-
WHITE, M.	-	3/6	.500	0/2	.000	-/11	0	0	4	0	0	6	-
GREENE, S.	-	2/7	.286	2/2	1.000	-/1	2	2	5	1	0	6	-
WILLIS, B.	-	7/14	.500	2/3	.667	-/3	7	3	3	3	0	16	-
CROWLEY, T.	-	5/7	.714	2/4	.500	-/3	1	1	3	1	0	12	-
SMITH, T.	-	6/10	.600	1/2	.500	-/3	0	1	3	2	0	13	-
SALTERS, J.	-	0/0	.000	0/0	.000	-/0	1	2	3	0	0	0	-
Totals	200	34/69	.493	12/20	.600	-/33	18	13	29	9	0	80	.400

Team Rebounds: Duke 4; Pennsylvania 2. Disqualified: Pennsylvania—Greene. Technical fouls: Duke—Gminski.

	1st Half	2nd Half	Final
Duke	44	40	84
Pennsylvania	40	40	80

Indiana (60) Coach: Bob Knight

	Min.	Total FG/FGA	Pct.	FT/FTA	Pct.	Reb. O/T	A	TO	PF	S	Blk	TP	PPM
RADFORD, W.	39	8/19	.421	6/8	.750	-/6	1	6	3	0	0	22	.564
WOODSON, M.	40	11/19	.579	2/2	1.000	-/4	0	3	3	1	0	24	.600
TOLBERT, R.	18	4/8	.500	0/2	.000	-/4	1	0	5	0	1	8	.444
BAKER, T.	25	0/0	.000	0/0	.000	-/1	3	3	3	0	0	0	.000
WISMAN, J.	37	1/3	.333	4/4	1.000	-/1	10	1	0	3	0	6	.162
CARTER, B.	19	0/0	.000	0/0	.000	-/1	3	2	1	0	0	0	.000
RISLEY, S.	14	0/0	.000	0/1	.000	-/2	0	0	1	1	0	0	.000
ROBERSON, J.	8	0/0	.000	0/0	.000	-/1	0	0	1	0	1	0	.000
Totals	200	24/49	.490	12/17	.706	-/20	18	15	17	5	2	60	.300

Villanova (61) Coach: Rollie Massimino

	Min.	Total FG/FGA	Pct.	FT/FTA	Pct.	Reb. O/T	A	TO	PF	S	Blk	TP	PPM
ROBINSON, R.	35	5/13	.385	2/2	1.000	-/7	1	2	3	1	0	12	.343
HERRON, K.	37	11/16	.688	1/2	.500	-/5	2	1	2	1	0	23	.622
BRADLEY, A.	33	1/11	.091	4/4	1.000	-/12	0	3	3	1	0	6	.182
SPARROW, R.	35	5/9	.556	2/4	.500	-/2	6	2	4	2	0	12	.343
RIGSBY, W.	28	2/2	1.000	0/1	.000	-/3	3	2	4	1	0	4	.143
LINCOLN, S.	22	2/3	.667	0/0	.000	-/1	2	1	1	1	0	4	.182
UNDERMAN, J.	8	0/0	.000	0/0	.000	-/0	1	1	2	0	0	0	.000
CARON, M.	2	0/0	.000	0/0	.000	-/0	0	0	1	0	0	0	.000
Totals	200	26/54	.481	9/13	.692	-/30	15	12	20	7	0	61	.305

Team Rebounds: Villanova 7; Indiana 5. Disqualified: Indiana—Tolbert. Technical fouls: None.

	1st Half	2nd Half	Final
Indiana	43	17	60
Villanova	35	26	61

REGIONAL SEMIFINAL MIDWEST

Utah (56)   Coach: Jerry Pimm

	Min.	Total FG/FGA	Pct.	FT/FTA	Pct.	Reb. O/T	A	TO	PF	S	Blk	TP	PPM
JUDKINS, J.	40	7/17	.412	2/2	1.000	-/4	0	3	3	1	0	16	.400
VRANES, D.	40	6/10	.600	2/3	.667	-/11	1	4	4	1	0	14	.350
MATHENEY, B.	24	4/9	.444	0/0	.000	-/4	0	2	5	1	2	8	.333
WILLIAMS, E.	24	2/2	1.000	0/0	.000	-/1	3	2	1	1	0	4	.167
GREY, M.	32	1/4	.250	0/0	.000	-/1	3	3	5	0	0	2	.063
DEANE, G.	16	1/3	.333	6/7	.857	-/3	1	5	2	2	0	8	.500
CHAMBERS, T.	16	2/5	.400	0/1	.000	-/3	0	2	3	0	4	4	.250
MARTIN, S.	8	0/1	.000	0/0	.000	-/0	2	2	2	0	0	0	.000
BANKOWSKI, K.	0	0/2	.000	0/0	.000	-/0	0	0	1	0	0	0	-
JUDKINS, J.	0	0/0	.000	0/0	.000	-/0	0	0	0	0	0	0	-
LEAVITT, C.	0	0/0	.000	0/0	.000	-/0	0	0	0	0	0	0	-
Totals	200	23/53	.434	10/13	.769	-/27	10	23	26	6	2	56	.280

Notre Dame (69)   Coach: Digger Phelps

	Min.	Total FG/FGA	Pct.	FT/FTA	Pct.	Reb. O/T	A	TO	PF	S	Blk	TP	PPM
TRIPUCKA, K.	29	8/11	.727	4/5	.800	-/4	3	3	3	2	0	20	.690
BATTON, D.	37	6/12	.500	3/5	.600	-/6	3	2	3	1	15	15	.405
FLOWERS, B.	15	0/1	.000	0/1	.000	-/3	2	5	5	2	0	0	.000
BRANNING, R.	39	3/7	.429	5/7	.714	-/0	5	4	3	2	0	11	.282
WILLIAMS, D.	38	5/14	.357	0/1	.000	-/2	3	1	2	2	0	10	.263
HEALY, T.	0	0/0	.000	0/0	.000	-/0	0	0	0	0	0	0	-
HAEFNER, R.	0	0/0	.000	0/0	.000	-/0	0	0	0	0	0	0	-
WILCOX, S.	3	0/0	.000	0/0	.000	-/0	0	0	0	1	0	0	.000
WOOLRIDGE, O.	0	0/0	.000	0/0	.000	-/0	1	0	0	0	0	0	-
HANZLIK, B.	11	2/3	.667	3/3	1.000	-/2	1	2	4	0	0	7	.636
SALINAS, B.	0	0/0	.000	0/0	.000	-/1	0	0	0	0	0	0	-
LAIMBEER, B.	18	1/3	.333	2/5	.400	-/5	0	0	2	0	0	4	.222
CARPENTER, J.	0	0/0	.000	0/0	.000	-/0	0	0	0	0	0	0	-
JACKSON, T.	10	1/1	1.000	0/0	.000	-/2	0	0	0	0	0	2	.200
Totals	200	26/52	.500	17/27	.630	-/25	17	18	21	12	1	69	.345

Team Rebounds: Notre Dame 11; Utah 6. Disqualified: Notre Dame—Flowers; Utah—Matheney, Grey. Technical fouls: None. Players who played 0 min. played less than 1 min. each.

	1st Half	2nd Half	Final
Utah	26	30	56
Notre Dame	28	41	69

DePaul (90)   Coach: Ray Meyer

	Min.	Total FG/FGA	Pct.	FT/FTA	Pct.	Reb. O/T	A	TO	PF	S	Blk	TP	PPM
WATKINS, C.	47	6/10	.600	4/5	.800	-/8	2	2	2	0	1	16	.340
PONSETTO, J.	44	4/4	1.000	0/0	.000	-/4	7	5	3	1	1	8	.182
CORZINE, D.	50	18/28	.643	10/10	1.000	-/9	1	3	3	0	3	46	.920
RAMSEY, R.	45	1/3	.333	4/5	.800	-/4	4	1	4	0	0	6	.133
GARLAND, G.	47	3/11	.273	4/4	1.000	-/2	4	3	1	2	1	10	.213
BRADSHAW, C.	9	0/2	.000	0/1	.000	-/1	0	1	1	0	0	0	.000
DISE, W.	8	2/3	.667	0/0	.000	-/1	1	1	2	0	0	4	.500
WYDRA, G.	0	0/0	.000	0/0	.000	-/0	0	0	0	0	0	0	-
Totals	250	34/61	.557	22/25	.880	-/29	19	17	16	3	6	90	.360

Louisville (89)   Coach: Denny Crum

	Min.	Total FG/FGA	Pct.	FT/FTA	Pct.	Reb. O/T	A	TO	PF	S	Blk	TP	PPM
TURNER, B.	48	9/18	.500	5/5	1.000	-/8	2	1	2	1	0	23	.479
WILLIAMS, L.	44	6/12	.500	1/2	.500	-/9	1	1	4	3	0	13	.295
GALLON, R.	44	5/12	.417	2/4	.500	-/3	0	3	4	2	2	12	.273
GRIFFITH, D.	48	9/15	.600	1/3	.333	-/3	5	3	5	3	1	19	.396
WILSON, R.	42	9/20	.450	2/3	.667	-/6	1	2	3	1	0	20	.476
SMITH, D.	12	0/0	.000	0/0	.000	-/2	0	0	1	0	1	0	.000
BRANCH, T.	8	1/2	.500	0/0	.000	-/0	3	0	1	1	0	2	.250
BURKMAN, R.	4	0/0	.000	0/0	.000	-/1	1	0	3	1	0	0	.000
Totals	250	39/79	.494	11/17	.647	-/32	13	10	23	12	4	89	.356

Team Rebounds: DePaul 9; Louisville 6. Disqualified: Louisville—Griffith. Technical fouls: None. DePaul had 1 team turnover credited to team total. Player who played 0 min. played less than 1 min.

	1st Half	2nd Half	1st OT	2nd OT	Final
DePaul	36	38	8	8	90
Louisville	35	39	8	7	89

REGIONAL FINAL MIDEAST

Michigan State (49)   Coach: Jud Heathcote

	Min.	Total FG/FGA	Pct.	FT/FTA	Pct.	Reb. O/T	A	TO	PF	S	Blk	TP	PPM
KELSER, G.	40	9/12	.750	1/3	.333	-/13	1	2	3	3	2	19	.475
JOHNSON, E.	39	2/10	.200	2/2	1.000	-/4	5	6	4	2	0	6	.154
VINCENT, J.	38	4/7	.571	0/0	.000	-/1	2	1	1	0	0	8	.211
DONNELLY, T.	34	0/0	.000	2/2	1.000	-/0	5	2	5	0	1	2	.059
CHAPMAN, R.	32	5/9	.556	0/0	.000	-/1	1	1	2	5	1	0	10	.313
BRKOVICH, M.	1	0/0	.000	0/0	.000	-/0	0	0	0	0	0	0	.000
CHARLES, R.	16	2/3	.667	0/0	.000	-/0	0	1	0	0	0	4	.250
Totals	200	22/41	.537	5/7	.714	-/19	14	14	18	6	3	49	.245

Kentucky (52)   Coach: Joe Hall

	Min.	Total FG/FGA	Pct.	FT/FTA	Pct.	Reb. O/T	A	TO	PF	S	Blk	TP	PPM
GIVENS, J.	34	6/12	.500	2/3	.667	-/7	0	2	3	0	1	14	.412
ROBEY, R.	30	3/4	.750	0/0	.000	-/4	1	2	1	0	0	6	.200
PHILLIPS, M.	30	3/5	.600	4/4	1.000	-/8	1	3	1	2	0	10	.333
MACY, K.	40	4/10	.400	10/11	.909	-/1	3	0	2	1	0	18	.450
CLAYTOR, T.	30	0/5	.000	0/0	.000	-/0	3	2	2	0	0	0	.000
LEE, J.	20	1/1	1.000	0/0	.000	-/1	2	3	4	0	0	2	.100
SHIDLER, J.	10	1/2	.500	0/0	.000	-/1	0	0	2	0	0	2	.200
WILLIAMS, L.	6	0/0	.000	0/0	.000	-/1	0	2	1	0	0	0	.000
Totals	200	18/39	.462	16/18	.889	-/23	10	14	16	3	1	52	.260

Team Rebounds: Kentucky 0; Michigan St. 0. Disqualified: Michigan St.—Donnelly, Chapman. Technical fouls: None.

	1st Half	2nd Half	Final
Michigan St.	27	22	49
Kentucky	22	30	52

REGIONAL FINAL WEST

Arkansas (61) Coach: Eddie Sutton

	Min.	Total FG/FGA	Pct.	FT/FTA	Pct.	Reb. O/T	A	TO	PF	S	Blk	TP	PPM
COUNCE, J.	40	2/2	1.000	0/2	.000	-/1	7	-	4	-	-	4	.100
DELPH, M.	40	7/13	.538	0/0	.000	-/5	2	-	2	-	-	14	.350
SCHALL, S.	40	5/6	.833	0/0	.000	-/9	2	-	2	-	-	10	.250
BREWER, R.	39	11/19	.579	0/0	.000	-/3	2	-	4	-	-	22	.564
MONCRIEF, S.	39	4/7	.571	3/4	.750	-/4	1	-	4	-	-	11	.282
REED, U.	2	0/0	.000	0/0	.000	-/1	0	-	0	-	-	0	.000
Totals	200	29/47	.617	3/6	.500	-/23	14	-	16	-	-	61	.305

California State Fullerton (58) Coach: Bob Dye

	Min.	Total FG/FGA	Pct.	FT/FTA	Pct.	Reb. O/T	A	TO	PF	S	Blk	TP	PPM
BUNCH, G.	40	3/9	.333	3/4	.750	-/10	1	-	3	-	-	9	.225
HEENAN, K.	40	5/14	.357	1/2	.500	-/0	1	-	2	-	-	11	.275
SHAW, S.	16	1/4	.250	0/0	.000	-/3	1	-	1	-	-	2	.125
ANDERSON, K.	37	11/22	.500	1/1	1.000	-/9	4	-	1	-	-	23	.622
LINDEN, M.	38	1/7	.143	0/0	.000	-/3	4	-	1	-	-	2	.053
NILES, M.	26	4/6	.667	3/4	.750	-/3	0	-	4	-	-	11	.423
PALM, G.	3	0/0	.000	0/0	.000	-/0	0	-	1	-	-	.0	.000
Totals	200	25/62	.403	8/11	.727	-/28	11	-	13	-	-	58	.290

Team Rebounds: Arkansas 2; Cal. St. F'lerton 6. Disqualified: None. Technical fouls: None.

	1st Half	2nd Half	Final
Arkansas	39	22	61
Cal. St. F'lerton	24	34	58

REGIONAL FINAL EAST

Duke (90) Coach: Wm. E. (Bill) Foster

	Min.	Total FG/FGA	Pct.	FT/FTA	Pct.	Reb. O/T	A	TO	PF	S	Blk	TP	PPM
BANKS, E.	34	6/10	.600	5/6	.833	-/10	9	3	4	1	0	17	.500
DENNARD, K.	29	8/12	.667	0/0	.000	-/4	2	3	4	1	1	16	.552
GMINSKI, M.	35	10/17	.588	1/1	1.000	-/10	2	3	3	2	1	21	.600
HARRELL, J.	26	3/4	.750	2/2	1.000	-/1	2	2	1	0	0	8	.308
SPANARKEL, J.	35	9/11	.818	4/6	.667	-/5	6	4	3	2	0	22	.629
BENDER, J.	15	0/1	.000	0/0	.000	-/2	2	1	2	1	0	0	.000
GRAY, S.	3	1/1	1.000	0/0	.000	-/0	0	0	0	0	0	2	.667
MORRISON, H.	3	0/0	.000	0/0	.000	-/1	0	2	1	0	0	0	.000
SUDDATH, J.	12	2/3	.667	0/0	.000	-/0	2	0	2	0	0	4	.333
GOETSCH, S.	6	0/1	.000	0/0	.000	-/1	0	0	1	0	0	0	.000
HARDY, R.	1	0/0	.000	0/0	.000	-/1	0	0	0	0	0	0	.000
BELL, B.	1	0/0	.000	0/0	.000	-/1	1	0	0	0	0	0	.000
Totals	200	39/60	.650	12/15	.800	-/36	26	18	21	7	2	90	.450

Villanova (72) Coach: Rollie Massimino

	Min.	Total FG/FGA	Pct.	FT/FTA	Pct.	Reb. O/T	A	TO	PF	S	Blk	TP	PPM
ROBINSON, R.	29	8/17	.471	0/0	.000	-/4	0	1	0	1	3	16	.552
HERRON, R.	35	8/19	.421	4/7	.571	-/2	1	3	4	0	0	20	.571
BRADLEY, A.	32	3/7	.429	4/6	.667	-/5	0	2	2	0	0	10	.313
SPARROW, R.	33	1/4	.250	0/0	.000	-/2	8	2	4	2	0	2	.061
RIGSBY, W.	34	3/8	.375	8/10	.800	-/13	4	3	3	2	0	14	.412
LINCOLN, S.	18	2/3	.667	0/0	.000	-/1	2	0	2	0	0	4	.222
UNDERMAN, J.	6	2/3	.667	0/0	.000	-/1	1	0	1	0	0	4	.667
SIENKIEWICZ, T.	4	0/3	.000	0/0	.000	-/0	1	0	1	0	0	0	.000
CARON, M.	4	0/0	.000	0/0	.000	-/0	0	1	1	0	0	0	.000
SOCK, L.	1	1/2	.500	0/0	.000	-/0	0	0	0	0	0	2	2.000
ANDERS, B.	2	0/0	.000	0/0	.000	-/0	0	0	0	0	0	0	.000
COWAN, R.	2	0/1	.000	0/0	.000	-/0	0	0	1	1	0	0	.000
Totals	200	28/67	.418	16/23	.696	-/28	16	12	19	6	3	72	.360

Team Rebounds: Duke 4; Villanova 2. Disqualified: None. Technical fouls: Villanova—Coach Massimino.

	1st Half	2nd Half	Final
Duke	46	44	90
Villanova	32	40	72

REGIONAL FINAL MIDWEST

Notre Dame (84) Coach: Digger Phelps

	Min.	Total FG/FGA	Pct.	FT/FTA	Pct.	Reb. O/T	A	TO	PF	S	Blk	TP	PPM
TRIPUCKA, K.	34	9/22	.409	0/0	.000	-/11	0	1	2	2	0	18	.529
BATTON, D.	30	1/5	.200	5/6	.833	-/6	5	0	1	0	0	7	.233
FLOWERS, B.	12	2/2	1.000	3/3	1.000	-/1	1	1	4	0	0	7	.583
BRANNING, R.	37	6/12	.500	3/3	1.000	-/4	7	1	0	0	0	15	.405
WILLIAMS, D.	27	5/12	.417	4/4	1.000	-/3	1	1	2	0	0	14	.519
HAEFNER, R.	0	0/0	.000	0/0	.000	-/0	0	0	0	0	0	0	-
WILCOX, S.	5	0/1	.000	0/0	.000	-/1	0	0	0	0	0	0	.000
WOOLRIDGE, O.	0	0/0	.000	0/0	.000	-/0	0	0	0	0	0	0	-
HANZLIK, B.	10	2/3	.667	0/0	.000	-/3	1	3	2	2	0	4	.400
SALINAS, B.	0	0/0	.000	0/0	.000	-/0	0	0	0	0	0	0	-
LAIMBEER, B.	28	4/8	.500	4/7	.571	-/10	0	3	4	0	2	12	.429
JACKSON, T.	17	2/4	.500	1/1	1.000	-/4	2	1	1	2	1	5	.294
CARPENTER, J.	0	1/1	1.000	0/0	.000	-/0	0	0	0	0	0	2	-
Totals	200	32/70	.457	20/24	.833	-/43	17	11	16	6	3	84	.420

DePaul (64) Coach: Ray Meyer

	Min.	Total FG/FGA	Pct.	FT/FTA	Pct.	Reb. O/T	A	TO	PF	S	Blk	TP	PPM
WATKINS, C.	36	4/8	.500	0/0	.000	-/6	1	1	4	0	0	8	.222
PONSETTO, J.	30	4/12	.333	0/0	.000	-/6	3	3	5	0	0	8	.267
CORZINE, D.	39	6/11	.545	5/7	.714	-/7	1	2	2	0	2	17	.436
RAMSEY, R.	29	1/5	.200	0/0	.000	-/4	2	1	1	0	0	2	.069
GARLAND, G.	39	8/16	.500	2/2	1.000	-/6	2	3	5	2	0	18	.462
BRADSHAW, C.	15	3/8	.375	0/0	.000	-/0	1	0	2	0	0	6	.400
DISE, W.	10	2/6	.333	1/2	.500	-/3	0	3	2	1	1	5	.500
WYDRA, G.	1	0/0	.000	0/0	.000	-/0	0	0	0	0	0	0	.000
HOOK, R.	1	0/0	.000	0/0	.000	-/0	0	0	0	0	0	0	.000
Totals	200	28/66	.424	8/11	.727	-/32	10	13	21	3	3	64	.320

Team Rebounds: Notre Dame 4; DePaul 4. Disqualified: DePaul—Ponsetto, Garland. Technical fouls: None. Players who played 0 min. played less than 1 min. each.

	1st Half	2nd Half	Final
Notre Dame	37	47	84
DePaul	33	31	64

FINAL FOUR

Kentucky (64) Coach: Joe Hall

	Min.	Total FG/FGA	Pct.	FT/FTA	Pct.	Reb. O/T	A	TO	PF	S	Blk	TP	PPM
GIVENS, J.	38	10/16	.625	3/4	.750	-/9	0	1	2	1	0	23	.605
ROBEY, R.	34	3/6	.500	2/2	1.000	-/8	0	3	2	2	0	8	.235
PHILLIPS, M.	17	1/6	.167	3/4	.750	-/2	1	4	4	0	0	5	.294
MACY, K.	33	2/8	.250	3/4	.750	-/3	3	3	4	0	0	7	.212
CLAYTOR, T.	17	1/2	.500	0/1	.000	-/0	2	1	4	0	0	2	.118
LEE, J.	27	4/8	.500	5/5	1.000	-/8	0	0	4	0	0	13	.481
SHIDLER, J.	25	3/5	.600	0/0	.000	-/2	4	1	4	0	0	6	.240
WILLIAMS, L.	3	0/0	.000	0/0	.000	-/0	0	0	1	0	0	0	.000
CASEY, D.	2	0/0	.000	0/0	.000	-/0	0	1	0	0	0	0	.000
STEPHENS, T.	2	0/0	.000	0/0	.000	-/0	0	0	0	0	0	0	.000
COWAN, F.	2	0/0	.000	0/0	.000	-/0	0	0	1	0	0	0	.000
Totals	200	24/51	.471	16/20	.800	-/32	10	14	26	3	0	64	.320

Arkansas (59) Coach: Eddie Sutton

	Min.	Total FG/FGA	Pct.	FT/FTA	Pct.	Reb. O/T	A	TO	PF	S	Blk	TP	PPM
COUNCE, J.	32	2/2	1.000	2/3	.667	-/2	2	1	4	0	2	6	.188
DELPH, M.	40	5/13	.385	5/6	.833	-/8	0	3	3	0	2	15	.375
SCHALL, S.	21	3/5	.600	0/0	.000	-/3	0	2	5	1	0	6	.286
BREWER, R.	39	5/12	.417	6/8	.750	-/5	1	3	2	3	0	16	.410
MONCRIEF, S.	40	5/11	.455	3/7	.429	-/5	0	4	3	1	2	13	.325
ZAHN, A.	17	1/1	1.000	1/2	.500	-/2	1	0	3	1	0	3	.176
REED, U.	11	0/0	.000	0/0	.000	-/0	0	1	2	1	1	0	.000
Totals	200	21/44	.477	17/26	.654	-/25	4	14	22	7	7	59	.295

Team Rebounds: Kentucky 0; Arkansas 1. Disqualified: Arkansas—Schall. Technical fouls: Kentucky—Coach Hall.

	1st Half	2nd Half	Final
Kentucky	32	32	64
Arkansas	30	29	59

Duke (90) Coach: Wm. E. (Bill) Foster

	Min.	Total FG/FGA	Pct.	FT/FTA	Pct.	Reb. O/T	A	TO	PF	S	Blk	TP	PPM
BANKS, E.	39	8/15	.533	6/7	.857	-/12	3	6	1	0	0	22	.564
DENNARD, K.	34	2/3	.667	3/5	.600	-/7	0	4	5	2	0	7	.206
GMINSKI, M.	36	13/17	.765	3/4	.750	-/5	2	1	2	0	1	29	.806
HARRELL, J.	26	0/2	.000	6/6	1.000	-/2	3	3	2	1	0	6	.231
SPANARKEL, J.	37	4/11	.364	12/12	1.000	-/4	5	4	1	2	0	20	.541
BENDER, B.	19	0/1	.000	2/3	.667	-/2	5	0	2	0	0	2	.105
SUDDATH, J.	4	1/3	.333	0/0	.000	-/0	0	0	2	0	0	2	.500
GOETSCH, S.	5	1/1	1.000	0/0	.000	-/0	1	0	0	0	0	2	.400
Totals	200	29/53	.547	32/37	.865	-/32	19	18	15	5	1	90	.450

Notre Dame (86) Coach: Digger Phelps

	Min.	Total FG/FGA	Pct.	FT/FTA	Pct.	Reb. O/T	A	TO	PF	S	Blk	TP	PPM
TRIPUCKA, K.	32	5/17	.294	2/2	1.000	-/9	1	3	3	3	0	12	.375
BATTON, D.	21	3/6	.500	4/4	1.000	-/2	0	1	1	0	0	10	.476
FLOWERS, B.	17	5/8	.625	0/0	.000	-/6	2	2	3	1	0	10	.588
BRANNING, R.	37	4/10	.400	0/0	.000	-/1	5	0	3	1	0	8	.216
WILLIAMS, D.	34	8/15	.533	0/1	.000	-/6	2	2	1	2	1	16	.471
WILCOX, S.	6	2/2	1.000	0/0	.000	-/0	0	2	0	1	0	4	.667
HANZLIK, B.	17	3/8	.375	2/2	1.000	-/6	2	1	5	2	0	8	.471
LAIMBEER, B.	20	1/5	.200	5/6	.833	-/10	2	1	5	0	1	7	.350
JACKSON, T.	16	5/6	.833	1/2	.500	-/0	1	0	4	0	0	11	.688
Totals	200	36/77	.468	14/17	.824	-/36	15	11	26	9	1	86	.430

Team Rebounds: Duke 2; Notre Dame 1. Disqualified: Duke—Dennard; Notre Dame—Hanzlik, Laimbeer. Technical fouls: Notre Dame—Hanzlik.

	1st Half	2nd Half	Final
Duke	43	47	90
Notre Dame	29	57	86

NATIONAL CHAMPIONSHIP

Kentucky (94) Coach: Joe Hall

	Min.	Total FG/FGA	Pct.	FT/FTA	Pct.	Reb. O/T	A	TO	PF	S	Blk	TP	PPM
GIVENS, J.	37	18/27	.667	5/8	.625	-/8	3	2	4	-	0	41	1.108
ROBEY, R.	32	8/11	.727	4/6	.667	-/11	0	2	2	-	1	20	.625
PHILLIPS, M.	11	1/4	.250	2/2	1.000	-/2	1	0	5	-	0	4	.364
MACY, K.	38	3/3	1.000	3/4	.750	-/0	8	3	1	-	0	9	.237
CLAYTOR, T.	24	3/5	.600	2/4	.500	-/0	3	2	2	-	0	8	.333
LEE, J.	20	4/8	.500	0/0	.000	-/4	2	0	4	-	0	8	.400
SHIDLER, J.	15	1/5	.200	0/1	.000	-/1	3	1	3	-	0	2	.133
WILLIAMS, L.	11	1/3	.333	0/0	.000	-/4	0	2	2	-	0	2	.182
ALEKSINAS, C.	1	0/0	.000	0/0	.000	-/0	0	1	1	-	0	0	.000
COWAN, F.	8	0/2	.000	0/0	.000	-/2	0	0	1	-	0	0	.000
STEPHENS, T.	1	0/0	.000	0/0	.000	-/0	0	0	0	-	0	0	.000
COURTS, S.	1	0/0	.000	0/0	.000	-/0	0	0	0	-	0	0	.000
GETTELFINGER, C.	1	0/0	.000	0/0	.000	-/0	0	0	0	-	0	0	.000
CASEY, D.	0	0/0	.000	0/0	.000	-/0	0	1	0	-	0	0	-
Totals	200	39/68	.574	16/25	.640	-/32	20	14	25	9	1	94	.470

Duke (88) Coach: Wm. E. (Bill) Foster

	Min.	Total FG/FGA	Pct.	FT/FTA	Pct.	Reb. O/T	A	TO	PF	S	Blk	TP	PPM
BANKS, E.	37	6/12	.500	10/12	.833	-/8	2	3	2	0	0	22	.595
DENNARD, K.	31	5/7	.714	0/0	.000	-/9	2	5	5	1	0	10	.323
GMINSKI, M.	37	6/16	.375	8/8	1.000	-/12	2	1	3	1	1	20	.541
HARRELL, J.	24	2/2	1.000	0/0	.000	-/0	1	2	3	1	0	4	.167
SPANARKEL, J.	40	8/16	.500	5/6	.833	-/2	3	4	4	2	0	21	.525
BENDER, B.	16	1/2	.500	5/5	1.000	-/1	4	0	3	1	0	7	.438
SUDDATH, J.	9	1/3	.333	2/3	.667	-/2	0	1	1	0	0	4	.444
GOETSCH, S.	6	0/1	.000	0/0	.000	-/1	0	1	1	0	0	0	.000
Totals	200	29/59	.492	30/34	.882	-/35	14	17	22	6	1	88	.440

Team Rebounds: Kentucky 0; Duke 1. Disqualified: Kentucky—Phillips; Duke—Dennard. Technical fouls: Duke—bench. Player who played 0 min. played less than 1 min.

	1st Half	2nd Half	Final
Kentucky	45	49	94
Duke	38	50	88

NATIONAL THIRD PLACE

Arkansas (71) Coach: Eddie Sutton

	Min.	Total FG / FGA	Pct.	FT / FTA	Pct.	Reb. O/T	A	TO	PF	S	Blk	TP	PPM
COUNCE, J.	8	1/ 3	.333	0/ 0	.000	-/ 0	1	1	1	0	0	2	.250
DELPH, M.	30	7/10	.700	7/ 8	.875	-/ 5	0	2	4	0	0	21	.700
SCHALL, S.	40	3/ 9	.333	0/ 0	.000	-/11	3	4	3	1	2	6	.150
BREWER, R.	40	7/16	.438	6/ 6	1.000	-/ 6	3	2	3	0	0	20	.500
MONCRIEF, S.	38	3/ 6	.500	4/ 6	.667	-/ 4	3	5	4	1	1	10	.263
ZAHN, A.	28	4/ 6	.667	2/ 3	.667	-/ 2	1	5	2	1	0	10	.357
REED, U.	7	0/ 0	.000	0/ 0	.000	-/ 1	0	1	1	0	0	0	.000
BENNETT, C.	9	1/ 2	.500	0/ 0	.000	-/ 0	0	1	1	1	0	2	.222
Totals	200	26/52	.500	19/23	.826	-/29	11	21	19	4	3	71	.355

Notre Dame (69) Coach: Digger Phelps

	Min.	Total FG / FGA	Pct.	FT / FTA	Pct.	Reb. O/T	A	TO	PF	S	Blk	TP	PPM
TRIPUCKA, K.	28	3/ 6	.500	4/ 6	.667	-/ 5	1	2	2	0	0	10	.357
BATTON, D.	30	6/12	.500	3/ 3	1.000	-/ 7	0	1	3	0	1	15	.500
FLOWERS, B.	18	4/ 9	.444	4/ 6	.667	-/ 5	4	4	4	0	0	12	.667
BRANNING, R.	34	1/ 8	.125	1/ 2	.500	-/ 1	4	1	3	0	0	3	.088
WILLIAMS, D.	28	2/ 8	.250	1/ 2	.500	-/ 3	1	1	0	2	0	5	.179
WILCOX, S.	11	1/ 2	.500	0/ 0	.000	-/ 1	0	0	1	0	0	2	.182
WOOLRIDGE, O.	3	0/ 0	.000	1/ 2	.500	-/ 1	0	1	1	0	0	1	.333
HANZLIK, B.	14	4/ 5	.800	0/ 0	.000	-/ 2	5	3	4	3	0	8	.571
LAIMBEER, B.	13	1/ 1	1.000	0/ 0	.000	-/ 3	0	1	2	0	0	2	.154
JACKSON, T.	21	5/ 8	.625	1/ 2	.500	-/ 2	0	3	2	3	0	11	.524
Totals	200	27/59	.458	15/23	.652	-/30	15	17	22	8	1	69	.345

Team Rebounds: Arkansas 1; Notre Dame 3. Disqualified: None. Technical fouls: Arkansas—bench.

	1st Half	2nd Half	Final
Arkansas	40	31	71
Notre Dame	36	33	69

✪ ALL-STAR TEAMS ✪

ALL TOURNAMENT

RON BREWER	ARKANSAS
★ JACK GIVENS	KENTUCKY
MIKE GMINSKI	DUKE
RICK ROBEY	KENTUCKY
JIM SPANARKEL	DUKE

MIDEAST REGIONAL

JACK GIVENS	KENTUCKY
EARVIN JOHNSON	MICHIGAN STATE
GREG KELSER	MICHIGAN STATE
★ KYLE MACY	KENTUCKY
MIKE PHILLIPS	KENTUCKY

EAST REGIONAL

EUGENE BANKS	DUKE
MIKE GMINSKI	DUKE
KEITH HERRON	VILLANOVA
★ JIM SPANARKEL	DUKE
BOBBY WILLIS	PENNSYLVANIA

WEST REGIONAL

KEITH ANDERSON	CAL. ST. F'LERTON
★ RON BREWER	ARKANSAS
GREG BUNCH	CAL. ST. F'LERTON
MARVIN DELPH	ARKANSAS
SIDNEY MONCRIEF	ARKANSAS

MIDWEST REGIONAL

RICH BRANNING	NOTRE DAME
DAVE CORZINE	DEPAUL
GARY GARLAND	DEPAUL
★ KELLY TRIPUCKA	NOTRE DAME
RICK WILSON	LOUISVILLE

★ Most Outstanding Player(s)

✪ INDIVIDUAL RECORDS ✪

SCORING

Most points in a single game

1	DAVE CORZINE, DEPAUL (vs. LOUISVILLE)	46
2	JACK GIVENS, KENTUCKY (vs. DUKE)	41
3	KEVEN MCDONALD, PENNSYLVANIA (vs. ST. BONAVENTURE)	37
4	BUSTER MATHENEY, UTAH (vs. MISSOURI)	36
5	MICHAEL BROOKS, LA SALLE (vs. VILLANOVA)	35

Most total points in the tournament

1	MIKE GMINSKI, DUKE	109
2	JIM SPANARKEL, DUKE	102
3	JACK GIVENS, KENTUCKY	101
4	EUGENE BANKS, DUKE	96
5	RON BREWER, ARKANSAS	95

Highest scoring average (minimum 2 games)

1	DAVE CORZINE, DEPAUL (82-3)	27.33
2	MIKE WOODSON, INDIANA (50-2)	25.00
2	BILL CARTWRIGHT, SAN FRANCISCO (50-2)	25.00
4	KEVEN MCDONALD, PENNSYLVANIA (47-2)	23.50
5	KEITH HERRON, VILLANOVA (67-3)	22.33

FIELD GOALS

Most field goals in a single game

1	JACK GIVENS, KENTUCKY (vs. DUKE)	18
1	DAVE CORZINE, DEPAUL (vs. LOUISVILLE)	18
3	BUSTER MATHENEY, UTAH (vs. MISSOURI)	17
4	KEVEN MCDONALD, PENNSYLVANIA (vs. ST. BONAVENTURE)	16
5	MICHAEL BROOKS, LA SALLE (vs. VILLANOVA)	14

Most total field goals in the tournament

1	MIKE GMINSKI, DUKE	45
2	JACK GIVENS, KENTUCKY	44
3	MARVIN DELPH, ARKANSAS	39
4	3 tied for fourth place.	

Most field goal attempts in a single game

1	BUSTER MATHENEY, UTAH (vs. MISSOURI)	28
2	DAVE CORZINE, DEPAUL (vs. LOUISVILLE)	28
3	JACK GIVENS, KENTUCKY (vs. DUKE)	27
4	KEVEN MCDONALD, PENNSYLVANIA (vs. ST. BONAVENTURE)	25
4	GEORGE JOHNSON, ST. JOHN'S (vs. LOUISVILLE)	25

Most total field goal attempts in the tournament

1	MIKE GMINSKI, DUKE	82
2	JACK GIVENS, KENTUCKY	77
3	RON BREWER, ARKANSAS	76
4	EUGENE BANKS, DUKE	69
5	MARVIN DELPH, ARKANSAS	66

Highest field goal percentage in a single game (minimum 10 attempts)
1 GREG KELSER, MICHIGAN ST. (vs. PROVIDENCE) (9-10) .900
2 MIKE PHILLIPS, KENTUCKY (vs. MIAMI (OHIO)) (11-13) .846
3 ROBERT CHAPMAN, MICHIGAN ST. (vs. WESTERN KY.) (10-12) .833
4 MICHAEL BROOKS, LA SALLE (vs. VILLANOVA) (14-17) .824
5 3 tied for fifth place.

Highest field goal percentage in the tournament (minimum 20 attempts)
1 BILL CARTWRIGHT, SAN FRANCISCO (18-23) .783
2 GREG KELSER, MICHIGAN ST. (29-40) .725
3 RICK ROBEY, KENTUCKY (22-31) .710
4 ROBERT CHAPMAN, MICHIGAN ST. (22-33) .667
5 RANDY AYERS, MIAMI (OHIO) (16-24) .667

FREE THROWS

Most free throws in a single game
1 JIM SPANARKEL, DUKE (vs. NOTRE DAME) 12
2 ROY HAMILTON, UCLA (vs. KANSAS) 11
3 4 tied for third place.

Most total free throws in the tournament
1 JIM SPANARKEL, DUKE 32
2 EUGENE BANKS, DUKE 26
3 RON BREWER, ARKANSAS 25
4 SIDNEY MONCRIEF, ARKANSAS 23
5 MIKE GMINSKI, DUKE 19

Most free throws attempted in a single game
1 ROY HAMILTON, UCLA (vs. KANSAS) 18
2 BILL CARTWRIGHT, SAN FRANCISCO (vs. CAL. ST. F'LERTON) 15
3 GREG SANDERS, ST. BONAVENTURE (vs. PENNSYLVANIA) 14
4 SIDNEY MONCRIEF, ARKANSAS (vs. UCLA) 13
5 2 tied for fifth place.

Most free throws attempted in the tournament
1 JIM SPANARKEL, DUKE 38
2 SIDNEY MONCRIEF, ARKANSAS 36
3 EUGENE BANKS, DUKE 32
4 RON BREWER, ARKANSAS 31
5 BILL LAIMBEER, NOTRE DAME 24

Highest free throw percentage in a single game (minimum 7 attempts)
1 JIM SPANARKEL, DUKE (vs. NOTRE DAME) (12-12) 1.000
2 DAVE CORZINE, DEPAUL (vs. LOUISVILLE) (10-10) 1.000

3 JIM SPANARKEL, DUKE (vs. PENNSYLVANIA) (9-9) 1.000
4 MIKE GMINSKI, DUKE (vs. KENTUCKY) (8-8) 1.000

5 3 tied for fifth place.

Highest free throw percentage in the tournament (minimum 15 attempts)
1 MIKE GMINSKI, DUKE (19-21) .905
2 MARVIN DELPH, ARKANSAS (15-17) .882
3 MIKE PHILLIPS, KENTUCKY (13-15) .867
4 JIM SPANARKEL, DUKE (32-38) .842
5 DAVE CORZINE, DEPAUL (16-19) .842

REBOUNDS

Most rebounds in a single game
1 GEORGE JOHNSON, ST. JOHN'S (vs. LOUISVILLE) 20
2 TIM WATERMAN, ST. BONAVENTURE (vs. PENNSYLVANIA) 16
3 ROOSEVELT BOUIE, SYRACUSE (vs. WESTERN KY.) 15
4 JONATHAN MOORE, FURMAN (vs. INDIANA) 14
4 MICHAEL BROOKS, LA SALLE (vs. VILLANOVA) 14

Most total rebounds in the tournament
1 EUGENE BANKS, DUKE 50
2 MIKE GMINSKI, DUKE 47
3 BILL LAIMBEER, NOTRE DAME 37
3 GREG KELSER, MICHIGAN ST. 37
3 JACK GIVENS, KENTUCKY 37

Most rebounds per game (minimum 2 games)
1 GREG KELSER, MICHIGAN ST. (37-3) 12.33
2 LARRY WILLIAMS, LOUISVILLE (21-2) 10.50
2 DANNY VRANES, UTAH (21-2) 10.50
2 DARRELL ALLUMS, UCLA (21-2) 10.50
5 EUGENE BANKS, DUKE (50-5) 10.00

ASSISTS

Most assists in a single game
1 EARVIN JOHNSON, MICHIGAN ST. (vs. WESTERN KY.) 14
2 MIKE LINDEN, CAL. ST. F'LERTON (vs. NEW MEXICO) 12
3 JAMES WISMAN, INDIANA (vs. VILLANOVA) 10
3 JAMES WISMAN, INDIANA (vs. FURMAN) 10
3 ROY HAMILTON, UCLA (vs. KANSAS) 10

Most total assists in the tournament
1 EARVIN JOHNSON, MICHIGAN ST. 26
1 RICH BRANNING, NOTRE DAME 26
3 RORY SPARROW, VILLANOVA 22
3 KYLE MACY, KENTUCKY 22
5 MIKE LINDEN, CAL. ST. F'LERTON 21

Most assists per game (minimum 2 appearances)
1 JAMES WISMAN, INDIANA (20-2) 10.00
2 EARVIN JOHNSON, MICHIGAN ST. (26-3) 8.67
3 ROY HAMILTON, UCLA (16-2) 8.00
3 KEITH ANDERSON, CAL. ST. F'LERTON (16-2) 8.00
5 RORY SPARROW, VILLANOVA (22-3) 7.33

TURNOVERS

Most turnovers in a single game
1 LARRY DREW, MISSOURI (vs. UTAH) 8
1 TONY JACKSON, FLORIDA STATE (vs. KENTUCKY) 8
3 4 tied for third place.

Most total turnovers in the tournament
1 JIM SPANARKEL, DUKE 16
2 EUGENE BANKS, DUKE 15
3 RICK ROBEY, KENTUCKY 14
3 SIDNEY MONCRIEF, ARKANSAS 14
5 5 tied for fifth place.

SHOTS BLOCKED

Most shots blocked in a single game
1 ROOSEVELT BOUIE, SYRACUSE (vs. WESTERN KY.) 8
2 MIKE GMINSKI, DUKE (vs. PENNSYLVANIA) 7
3 WAYNE MCKOY, ST. JOHN'S (vs. LOUISVILLE) 4
4 4 tied for fourth place.

Most total shots blocked in the tournament
1 MIKE GMINSKI, DUKE 10
2 ROOSEVELT BOUIE, SYRACUSE 8
3 DAVE CORZINE, DEPAUL 6
4 GREG KELSER, MICHIGAN ST. 5
5 4 tied for fifth place.

STEALS

Most steals in a single game
1 EARL WILLIAMS, UTAH (vs. MISSOURI) 5
2 6 tied for second place.

Most total steals in the tournament
1 KELLY TRIPUCKA, NOTRE DAME 8
1 JIM SPANARKEL, DUKE 8
1 ROY HAMILTON, UCLA 8
4 BILL HANZLIK, NOTRE DAME 7
5 3 tied for fifth place.

✪ TEAM RECORDS ✪

SCORING

Most points in a single game
1	VILLANOVA (vs. LA SALLE)	103
2	NOTRE DAME (vs. HOUSTON)	100
3	LA SALLE (vs. VILLANOVA)	97

Most total points in the tournament
1	DUKE	415
2	NOTRE DAME	408
3	KENTUCKY	386

Highest scoring average (minimum 2 games)
1	PENNSYLVANIA (172-2)	86.00
2	DUKE (415-5)	83.00
3	LOUISVILLE (165-2)	82.50

FIELD GOALS

Most field goals in a single game
1	LA SALLE (vs. VILLANOVA)	42
1	VILLANOVA (vs. LA SALLE)	42
3	2 tied for third place.	

Most total field goals in the tournament
1	NOTRE DAME	162
2	DUKE	154
3	KENTUCKY	152

Most field goals attempted in a single game
1	ST. JOHN'S (vs. LOUISVILLE)	84
2	LOUISVILLE (vs. DEPAUL)	79
3	LA SALLE (vs. VILLANOVA)	78

Most total field goals attempted in the tournament
1	NOTRE DAME	329
2	DUKE	295
3	KENTUCKY	277

Highest field goal percentage in a single game
1	DUKE (vs. VILLANOVA) (39-60)	.650
2	CREIGHTON (vs. DEPAUL) (36-56)	.643
3	MICHIGAN ST. (vs. PROVIDENCE) (33-52)	.635

Highest field goal percentage in the tournament (minimum 2 games)
1	MICHIGAN ST. (92-156)	.590
2	KENTUCKY (152-277)	.549
3	INDIANA (52-95)	.547

FREE THROWS

Most free throws in a single game
1	DUKE (vs. NOTRE DAME)	32

2	DUKE (vs. KENTUCKY)	30
3	UCLA (vs. KANSAS)	27

Most total free throws in the tournament
1	DUKE	107
2	NOTRE DAME	84
3	KENTUCKY	82

Most free throws attempted in a single game
1	UCLA (vs. KANSAS)	39
2	DUKE (vs. NOTRE DAME)	37
3	DUKE (vs. KENTUCKY)	34

Most total free throws attempted in the tournament
1	DUKE	131
2	NOTRE DAME	117
3	KENTUCKY	105

Highest free throw percentage in a single game
1	KENTUCKY (vs. MICHIGAN ST.) (16-18)	.889
2	DUKE (vs. KENTUCKY) (30-34)	.882
3	DEPAUL (vs. LOUISVILLE) (22-25)	.880

Highest free throw percentage in the tournament (minimum 2 games)
1	MIAMI (OHIO) (29-35)	.829
2	DUKE (107-131)	.817
3	DEPAUL (42-53)	.793

Fewest free throws in a single game
1	UCLA (vs. ARKANSAS)	2
2	ARKANSAS (vs. CAL. ST. F'LERTON)	3
3	2 tied for third place.	

Lowest free throw percentage in a single game
1	UCLA (vs. ARKANSAS) (2-8)	.250
2	RHODE ISLAND (vs. DUKE) (4-11)	.364
3	WESTERN KY. (vs. MICHIGAN ST.) (9-20)	.450

Lowest free throw percentage in the tournament (minimum 2 games)
1	WESTERN KY. (22-43)	.512
2	UCLA (29-47)	.617
3	INDIANA (19-30)	.633

REBOUNDS

Most rebounds in a single game
1	UCLA (vs. KANSAS)	45
2	ST. JOHN'S (vs. LOUISVILLE)	44
3	2 tied for third place.	

Most rebounds per game (minimum 2 games)
1	DUKE (182-5)	36.40
2	WESTERN KY. (72-2)	36.00
2	UCLA (72-2)	36.00

ASSISTS

Most assists in a single game
1	CREIGHTON (vs. DEPAUL)	31
2	LA SALLE (vs. VILLANOVA)	27
3	2 tied for third place.	

Most assists per game (minimum 2 games)
1	PENNSYLVANIA (40-2)	20.00
2	VILLANOVA (57-3)	19.00
3	MICHIGAN ST. (56-3)	18.67

TURNOVERS

Most turnovers in a single game
1	SYRACUSE (vs. WESTERN KY.)	27
2	3 tied for second place.	

Most turnovers per game (minimum 2 games)
1	UTAH (41-2)	20.50
2	INDIANA (36-2)	18.00
3	WESTERN KY. (35-2)	17.50

SHOTS BLOCKED

Most shots blocked in a single game
1	SYRACUSE (vs. WESTERN KY.)	11
2	DUKE (vs. PENNSYLVANIA)	9
3	VILLANOVA (vs. LA SALLE)	8

Most shots blocked per game (minimum 2 games)
1	MICHIGAN ST. (13-3)	4.33
2	DEPAUL (12-3)	4.00
3	WESTERN KY. (8-2)	4.00

STEALS

Most steals in a single game
1	4 tied for first place.	

Most steals per game
1	UTAH (18-2)	9.00
2	PENNSYLVANIA (16-2)	8.00
3	NOTRE DAME (39-5)	7.80

1979

FIRST ROUND	SECOND ROUND	REGIONAL SEMIFINAL	REGIONAL FINAL	FINAL FOUR	REGIONAL FINAL	REGIONAL SEMIFINAL	SECOND ROUND	FIRST ROUND

EAST

7 Temple 70
10 St. John's 75
St. John's 80
(bye)
2 Duke 78
St. John's 67

3 Georgetown 58
(bye)
(bye)
6 Rutgers 64
Rutgers 65

St. John's 62

8 Iona 69
9 Pennsylvania 73
Pennsylvania 72
(bye)
1 N. Carolina 71
Pennsylvania 84

4 Syracuse 89
(bye)
(bye)
5 Connecticut 81
Syracuse 76
Pennsylvania 64

Pennsylvania 67

MIDEAST

7 Detroit 87
10 Lamar 95
Lamar 64
(bye)
2 Michigan St. 95
Michigan St. 87

3 Louisiana St. 71
(bye)
(bye)
6 Appalachian St. 57
Louisiana St. 71
Michigan St. 80

8 Tennessee 97
9 Eastern Ky. 81
Tennessee 67
(bye)
1 Notre Dame 73
Notre Dame 79

4 Iowa 72
(bye)
(bye)
5 Toledo 74
Toledo 71
Notre Dame 68
Michigan St. 101

Michigan St. 75
Indiana St. 64

WEST

USC 78
7 USC 86
10 Utah St. 67
DePaul 62
(bye)
2 DePaul 89

3 Marquette 73 (bye)
Marquette 56
6 Pacific 48 (bye)
DePaul 95

DePaul 74

Pepperdine 71
8 Utah 88
9 Pepperdine 92 (ot)
UCLA 99
(bye)
1 UCLA 76

4 San Francisco 86 (bye)
San Francisco 81
5 Brigham Young 63 (bye)
UCLA 91

MIDWEST

Weber St. 63
7 Weber St. 81 (ot)
10 New Mexico St. 78
Arkansas 73
(bye)
2 Arkansas 74

3 Louisville 69 (bye)
Louisville 62
6 South Alabama 66 (bye)
Arkansas 71

Indiana St. 76

Virginia Tech 69
8 Virginia Tech 70
9 Jacksonville 53
Indiana St. 93
(bye)
1 Indiana St. 86

4 Texas 76 (bye)
Oklahoma 72
5 Oklahoma 90 (bye)
Indiana St. 73

CONSOLATION GAME

National Third Place:
DePaul 96
Pennsylvania 93

Some say the game of basketball was saved in 1979. That it needed a shot in the arm, a new image, a marquee figure to raise it out of its doldrums and on to a new level of popularity. Whatever it was basketball needed, it got it—two times over—in prime time 1979.

On March 26th of that year, the two most charismatic, team-conscious players of their era—Earvin "Magic" Johnson and Larry Bird—met for the first time on the court. Magic, 6-9, was listed as a guard. Bird, also 6-9, was ostensibly a forward. Both were actually wizards of the hardwood, sleight-of-hand artists with a basketball.

In personality they couldn't have been more different. Johnson, a native of Lansing, Michigan, was exuberant, irrepressible, filled to overflowing with his love of life and of the game. Bird, a self-described hick from French Lick, Indiana, was tight-lipped, serious, and intent on the task of carrying his undefeated but unheralded team to the championship.

The two marquee figures met in the title game, but the 1979 tournament was a classic even before their final confrontation.

In the Midwest, Bird led his Indiana State team with 29 points and 5 assists in an easy victory over Big Eight champs Oklahoma. Then fortune smiled on the Sycamores in a tight battle with Arkansas and its superb guard Sidney Moncrief. After a series of defensive players had failed to stop Bird, Razorbacks' coach Eddie Sutton was finally forced to put his best defender, Moncrief, on the Indiana State star. And although he was giving up five inches in height, his tight guarding was finally keeping Bird away from the ball, thus shutting down Larry's ability to control the game. With less than two minutes left, the score was tied at 71, and Arkansas had the ball. Sutton told his Hogs to use the clock and work the ball to Moncrief for a final shot, but instead they turned it over with a little more than a minute left. Now it was the Sycamores' turn to hold for one last shot by their star. Bird finally got his hands on the ball with 11 seconds left, but Moncrief had him covered like a second skin; Bird passed to guard Steve Reed, who went up and, with nowhere to go but down, shoveled it over to reserve Bob Heaton. Heaton threw up a left-handed prayer. "I was hoping somebody would tip it in," he said. Instead it hit the rim and bounced and rolled and finally fell through the hoop with two seconds left to play.

In the Mideast regional semis, Magic and forward Greg Kelser dominated LSU and won easily. Then they hit some major-league competition in Notre Dame. Spartans' coach Jud Heathcote looked at the Irish lineup that included future pros Orlando Woolridge, Kelly Tripucka, Bill Laimbeer, Bill Hanzlik, and Tracy Jackson, and said, "Notre Dame goes at you with nine players, and we come back at you with two." It wasn't quite that bad, but Michigan State had little depth and no true center. But they had Magic.

Of the six games the Spartans had lost during the 1978–79 season, five were by two points or less and four of those five were decided in the final seconds. The one blowout was to Big Ten cellar-dweller Northwestern, and it capped a January that saw the Spartans lose four games. After the Northwestern loss, Michigan State was a team in trouble: the coaches were riding the players and the players were uptight and pressing. Nobody was having any fun. They finally had a team meeting in which, Johnson recalled, "We told the coaches to stay off our backs and we would play harder. We said we'd start diving for loose balls and everything. We'd all do it." They made good on their promise and started having a good time playing ball again. They also started winning.

Nonetheless, Notre Dame was still the region's top seed. But when Kelser controlled the tip to Johnson, who fancy-passed the ball over his head to a streaking Mike Brkovich for a lay-up, the tone of the game was set. "It was an avalanche from there," Notre Dame coach Digger Phelps said. Three times Kelser dunked off Johnson lobs, and in one first half spurt, he scored seven straight Spartan baskets, four on Johnson feeds. Michigan State coasted into the Final Four.

DePaul, like Michigan State, had little depth. At the beginning of the season, they had very little hope either. The Blue Demons had lost four starters from the previous season and they were taken apart in their season opener—by 23 points—by UCLA. And besides, their 65-year-old coach, Ray Meyer, hadn't reached the Final Four since 1943. But they had the nation's best freshman in Mark Aguirre, as well as two remarkably quick, ball-hawking guards, Clyde Bradshaw and Gary Garland. Garland also occasionally moonlighted by singing the National Anthem at home games. (He came by his musical talent naturally; his mother was Cissy Houston, his aunt Dionne Warwick, and his sister a young girl named Whitney.)

After beating USC and Marquette, the Demons played UCLA again in the West regional final. The Bruins were the best-shooting team in college basketball history with a season-long team-shooting percentage of .555, but DePaul came out aggressively, pressing and pushing the ball upcourt. They totally took the play away from UCLA and led by 17 points at halftime. But in the rarefied atmosphere of Provo, Utah, where the regional was held, the iron-man Demon five tired. UCLA came back behind David Greenwood's dunking (he finished with 37 points), but ran out of time before they could catch De Paul.

In the East, a quick Penn squad became the first Ivy League Final Four team since Bill Bradley led Princeton into the national semifinals in 1965. Led by Tony Price, the ninth-seeded Quakers held on to beat Iona and Jeff Ruland, then upset North Carolina, the nation's third-ranked team, by a point in Raleigh. After another upset, over Syracuse and its big-man tandem of Roosevelt Bouie and Louis Orr, they barely got by St. John's—the only team in the regional seeded below them—to qualify for the chance to travel to Salt Lake City and face Magic Johnson and Michigan State.

The underdog Ivy Leaguers were overmatched, overwhelmed, and hung out to dry—almost before the spectators were settled in their seats. Michigan State raced to a 38-8 lead, and went into the locker room with the largest halftime margin in Final Four history. It was, as usual, Magic to Kelser, combining on five first-half baskets. Johnson, who came out of the game for good with five-and-a-half minutes left, finished with what would soon become known as a triple double: 29 points, 10 rebounds, and 10 assists. Kelser chipped in with 28 points and 9 rebounds.

The second semi was not so easy. Indiana State moved out to an early lead, but DePaul fought back. Holding Bird in check and forcing turnovers, they overcame an 11-point second-half deficit to take a 73-71 lead with 4:59 remaining. Aguirre rebounded a Bird miss and DePaul went into a four corners stall. But this time it was DePaul that turned the ball over, and with 3:27 left, Sycamore sub Bob Heaton was once again in the right place at the right time, taking a feed from Bird for a lay-up. The game seesawed: DePaul went back up by one on a free throw, but Bird rebounded the missed second shot and Carl Nicks passed to Heaton for another lay-up and a one-point Indiana State lead. DePaul worked the ball around, looking for the high-scoring Aguirre. With time running out, Gary Garland inexplicably passed up a short jumper to try to find Aguirre, who finally got the ball in his hands 20 feet out with only four seconds to go. He couldn't bring it home. Although Bird's 11 turnovers were a major

factor in keeping the Blue Demons in the game, his all-around play was still the difference. He finished with a line that read 35 points on 16 for 19 shooting, 16 rebounds and 9 assists.

The Sycamores, a team that Bird had brought from nowhere to No. 1, needed only one more win to finish their perfect season. Bird, aware that he would soon be signing an NBA contract worth millions, minimized the importance of the game. "The Final Four means more to my teammates than it does to me," he said. "If we win or lose here, it don't make no difference to me. I'm gonna get my money anyway."

There was electricity in the air as the two great stars took the floor. But once the game began, it was no contest. Bird, who was playing with a sore thumb, was double-teamed constantly, and his teammates couldn't get him the ball. Since the Sycamores' offense was built around Bird handling the ball, popping and driving and dishing to the open man, he never was able to get his team started. He hit only a third of his 21 shots, but even worse, his passing game was cut off—he earned only two assists.

Meanwhile, on the other end, the Spartans were on a roll. Not only did Johnson connect with Kelser for the usual alley-oops, his penetration also forced Indiana State to foul. And Terry Donnelly hit five for five for 15 points.

In the end the Sycamores joined the 1961 Ohio State Buckeyes, who lost to Cincinnati, as the only two previously unbeaten teams to lose in the finals.

After the final loss, a frustrated, disheartened Bird, who had earlier spoken so nonchalantly about victory, sat on the bench, head bowed, and cried. Winning really mattered after all.

FIRST ROUND EAST

Temple (70)   Coach: Don Casey

	Min.	Total FG/FGA	Pct.	FT/FTA	Pct.	Reb. O/T	A	TO	PF	S	Blk	TP	PPM
HARROLD, B.	40	8/17	.471	2/3	.667	-/6	1	3	2	2	1	18	.450
MCCOULLOUGH, A.	26	2/7	.286	0/1	.000	-/5	0	1	2	1	0	4	.154
MONTFORD, W.	37	8/12	.667	6/10	.600	-/9	0	3	2	0	0	22	.595
PARHAM, K.	24	1/5	.200	1/2	.500	-/5	2	2	3	0	0	3	.125
REED, R.	38	7/13	.538	0/0	.000	-/0	3	2	4	2	0	14	.368
ROBINSON, N.	23	4/6	.667	1/1	1.000	-/4	2	2	4	0	0	9	.391
WISTER, R.	10	0/2	.000	0/0	.000	-/1	0	0	3	0	0	0	.000
THOMPSON, R.	2	0/0	.000	0/0	.000	-/0	0	0	0	0	0	0	.000
Totals	200	30/62	.484	10/17	.588	-/30	8	13	20	5	1	70	.350

St. John's (75)   Coach: Lou Carnesecca

	Min.	Total FG/FGA	Pct.	FT/FTA	Pct.	Reb. O/T	A	TO	PF	S	Blk	TP	PPM
PLAIR, R.	30	1/5	.200	4/4	1.000	-/10	1	3	4	1	1	6	.200
GILROY, F.	20	1/2	.500	0/0	.000	-/1	1	0	5	0	0	2	.100
MCKOY, W.	36	11/14	.786	0/4	.000	-/8	0	4	4	0	2	22	.611
RENCHER, B.	32	3/9	.333	0/0	.000	-/3	6	5	0	0	0	6	.188
CARTER, R.	37	8/14	.571	4/4	1.000	-/3	0	1	0	0	0	20	.541
WRIGHT, D.	14	2/5	.400	2/3	.667	-/5	2	1	5	1	0	6	.429
THOMAS, G.	23	5/7	.714	2/2	1.000	-/2	3	0	1	0	0	12	.522
CALABRESE, T.	7	0/0	.000	1/2	.500	-/1	1	1	0	0	0	1	.143
BOLLINGER, R.	1	0/0	.000	0/0	.000	-/0	0	0	0	0	0	0	.000
Totals	200	31/56	.554	13/19	.684	-/33	14	15	19	2	3	75	.375

Team Rebounds: St. John's 1; Temple 2. Disqualified: St. John's—Gilroy, Wright. Technical fouls: Temple—bench.

	1st Half	2nd Half	Final
Temple	37	33	70
St. John's	41	34	75

Iona (69)   Coach: Jim Valvano

	Min.	Total FG/FGA	Pct.	FT/FTA	Pct.	Reb. O/T	A	TO	PF	S	Blk	TP	PPM
BROWN, D.	4	1/3	.333	2/2	1.000	-/1	0	1	0	1	0	4	1.000
PALMA, M.	30	2/8	.250	4/4	1.000	-/2	1	3	2	0	0	8	.267
RULANO, J.	39	6/10	.600	7/9	.778	-/15	1	5	4	2	1	19	.487
VICKERS, G.	36	4/9	.444	8/8	1.000	-/1	3	3	4	1	0	16	.444
HAMILTON, K.	33	5/16	.313	2/4	.500	-/7	1	4	5	0	0	12	.364
MIDDLETON, A.	18	3/4	.750	0/0	.000	-/1	2	1	5	0	3	6	.333
GEORGE, L.	24	0/3	.000	2/2	1.000	-/2	0	2	5	1	0	2	.083
BURNS, D.	6	0/0	.000	0/0	.000	-/0	0	0	1	0	0	0	.000
VESEY, K.	5	0/1	.000	2/2	1.000	-/0	0	0	0	0	0	2	.400
IATI, T.	5	0/0	.000	0/0	.000	-/0	0	0	0	0	0	0	.000
Totals	200	21/54	.389	27/31	.871	-/29	8	19	26	5	4	69	.345

Pennsylvania (73)   Coach: Bob Weinhauer

	Min.	Total FG/FGA	Pct.	FT/FTA	Pct.	Reb. O/T	A	TO	PF	S	Blk	TP	PPM
PRICE, T.	39	11/21	.524	5/8	.625	-/12	3	2	3	2	1	27	.692
SMITH, T.	37	4/11	.364	2/3	.667	-/9	3	4	4	3	1	10	.270
WHITE, M.	11	2/3	.667	0/0	.000	-/1	0	3	5	0	1	4	.364
SALTERS, J.	35	1/6	.167	3/4	.750	-/2	0	2	2	1	0	5	.143
WILLIS, B.	27	5/9	.556	3/4	.750	-/3	6	5	5	4	0	13	.481
LEIFSEN, T.	21	1/2	.500	4/4	1.000	-/1	1	1	1	1	0	6	.286
HALL, K.	18	2/3	.667	4/4	1.000	-/1	1	1	2	0	1	8	.444
FLICK, T.	1	0/0	.000	0/0	.000	-/0	0	1	0	0	0	0	.000
ROSS, V.	11	0/2	.000	0/0	.000	-/2	0	3	1	0	0	0	.000
Totals	200	26/57	.456	21/27	.778	-/31	14	19	25	12	4	73	.365

Team Rebounds: Pennsylvania 2; Iona 3. Disqualified: Pennsylvania—White, Willis; Iona—Hamilton, Middleton, George. Technical fouls: None.

	1st Half	2nd Half	Final
Iona	29	40	69
Pennsylvania	41	32	73

FIRST ROUND MIDEAST

Detroit (87)   Coach: Dave Smokey Gaines

	Min.	Total FG/FGA	Pct.	FT/FTA	Pct.	Reb. O/T	A	TO	PF	S	Blk	TP	PPM
WHITLOW, J.	18	3/6	.500	1/2	.500	-/4	1	0	3	1	0	7	.389
DAVIS, J.	20	5/7	.714	1/3	.333	-/4	1	0	5	2	1	11	.550
CURETON, E.	23	7/11	.636	2/2	1.000	-/11	1	2	4	3	1	16	.696
MCCORMICK, W.	40	4/9	.444	4/4	1.000	-/3	3	4	3	0	0	12	.300
DUEROD, T.	29	11/26	.423	0/0	.000	-/3	3	3	1	1	0	22	.759
NILES, D.	30	7/12	.583	0/0	.000	-/5	2	1	0	0	0	14	.467
JACKSON, K.	24	1/7	.143	1/4	.250	-/5	1	2	3	1	1	3	.125
KOPICKI, J.	9	0/1	.000	0/2	.000	-/1	0	0	2	0	1	0	.000
FIELDS, G.	7	1/1	1.000	0/0	.000	-/2	0	0	0	0	0	2	.286
Totals	200	39/80	.488	9/17	.529	-/38	12	12	21	8	4	87	.435

Lamar (95)   Coach: Billy Tubbs

	Min.	Total FG/FGA	Pct.	FT/FTA	Pct.	Reb. O/T	A	TO	PF	S	Blk	TP	PPM
LEWIS, C.	29	0/4	.000	0/0	.000	-/7	1	0	3	1	0	0	.000
DAVIS, B.	30	9/19	.474	2/3	.667	-/10	1	2	5	1	1	20	.667
KEA, C.	33	11/22	.500	11/20	.550	-/19	1	1	3	0	1	33	1.000
OLLIVER, M.	40	11/24	.458	1/4	.250	-/10	5	4	2	2	0	23	.575
BELLARD, T.	40	2/4	.500	1/3	.333	-/5	3	4	4	3	0	5	.125
WILLIAMS, N.	21	5/8	.625	0/0	.000	-/5	0	2	0	0	0	10	.476
RUTTER, M.	7	2/3	.667	0/0	.000	-/0	0	1	1	0	0	4	.571
Totals	200	40/84	.476	15/30	.500	-/56	11	14	18	7	2	95	.475

Team Rebounds: Lamar 7; Detroit 7. Disqualified: Lamar—Davis; Detroit—Davis. Technical fouls: None.

	1st Half	2nd Half	Final
Detroit	41	46	87
Lamar	47	48	95

Tennessee (97)   Coach: Don Devoe

	Min.	Total FG/FGA	Pct.	FT/FTA	Pct.	Reb. O/T	A	TO	PF	S	Blk	TP	PPM
CROSBY, T.	36	7/12	.583	5/5	1.000	-/6	4	3	3	4	0	19	.528
JOHNSON, R.	27	6/14	.429	8/12	.667	-/9	2	3	4	0	0	20	.741
WOOD, H.	12	3/5	.600	1/2	.500	-/5	0	1	2	0	1	7	.583
BERTELKAMP, B.	14	1/1	1.000	0/0	.000	-/1	3	2	3	1	0	2	.143
CARTER, G.	37	7/13	.538	4/4	1.000	-/11	4	2	1	1	0	18	.486
GLENN, T.	3	1/2	.500	0/0	.000	-/1	0	0	1	0	0	2	.667
STAPLETON, M.	3	0/0	.000	0/0	.000	-/2	0	2	1	0	0	0	.000
MERIWEATHER, J.	3	1/2	.500	0/0	.000	-/1	0	0	0	0	0	2	.667
TEFFETELLER, K.	4	0/0	.000	2/2	1.000	-/0	0	1	0	0	0	2	.500
DARDEN, J.	23	3/5	.600	2/2	1.000	-/3	6	2	1	2	0	8	.348
THREETHS, C.	24	5/9	.556	1/2	.500	-/8	0	3	2	0	0	11	.458
NASH, K.	10	2/4	.500	1/2	.500	-/3	0	2	0	0	0	5	.500
RAY, S.	4	0/1	.000	1/2	.500	-/0	0	0	0	0	0	1	.250
Totals	200	36/68	.529	25/33	.758	-/50	19	21	18	8	1	97	.485

Eastern Kentucky (81)   Coach: Ed Byhre

	Min.	Total FG/FGA	Pct.	FT/FTA	Pct.	Reb. O/T	A	TO	PF	S	Blk	TP	PPM
TILLMAN, J.	40	7/17	.412	7/8	.875	-/8	0	4	3	0	0	21	.525
MERCHANT, V.	33	4/10	.400	3/5	.600	-/6	1	2	4	1	0	11	.333
BOOTCHECK, D.	10	1/2	.500	0/0	.000	-/3	0	0	5	0	1	2	.200
ELLIOTT, K.	34	5/12	.417	1/2	.500	-/2	3	2	0	0	1	11	.324
JONES, B.	33	6/19	.316	0/1	.000	-/2	9	8	2	2	0	12	.364
TIERNEY, D.	16	6/9	.667	1/2	.500	-/4	1	0	3	1	0	13	.813
MOORE, D.	3	1/2	.500	1/1	1.000	-/2	0	0	0	0	0	3	1.000
WILLIAMS, C.	7	2/4	.500	0/0	.000	-/1	1	0	1	0	0	4	.571
JENKINS, D.	24	2/5	.400	0/0	.000	-/9	1	1	5	1	0	4	.167
Totals	200	34/80	.425	13/19	.684	-/37	16	17	23	5	2	81	.405

Team Rebounds: Tennessee 3; Eastern Ky. 2. Disqualified: Eastern Ky.—Bootcheck, Jenkins. Technical fouls: None.

	1st Half	2nd Half	Final
Tennessee	44	53	97
Eastern Ky.	38	43	81

FIRST ROUND WEST

USC (86)   Coach: Bob Boyd

	Min.	Total FG/FGA	Pct.	FT/FTA	Pct.	Reb. O/T	A	TO	PF	S	Blk	TP	PPM
WILLIAMS	11	3/6	.500	0/0	.000	-/2	0	2	2	1	0	6	.545
MILLER	39	6/12	.500	4/5	.800	-/8	2	2	1	1	1	16	.410
WIDFELDT	37	4/6	.667	0/0	.000	-/14	2	2	3	1	0	8	.216
JONES	25	4/6	.667	0/0	.000	-/2	3	3	5	2	0	8	.320
CARFINO	24	5/12	.417	1/2	.500	-/2	4	4	5	1	0	11	.458
SMITH, S.	18	9/10	.900	1/1	1.000	-/3	1	4	1	0	0	19	1.056
SMITH, D.	7	1/4	.250	2/3	.667	-/3	0	0	1	0	0	4	.571
BROOKS	25	2/4	.500	3/5	.600	-/2	3	1	1	1	0	7	.280
ARNOLD	11	1/2	.500	3/4	.750	-/0	1	1	1	0	0	5	.455
RATKOVICH	2	1/1	1.000	0/0	.000	-/0	0	1	0	0	0	2	1.000
MARQUETTI	1	0/0	.000	0/0	.000	-/0	0	0	0	0	0	0	.000
Totals	200	36/63	.571	14/20	.700	-/34	18	20	20	7	1	86	.430

Utah (88)   Coach: Jerry Pimm

	Min.	Total FG/FGA	Pct.	FT/FTA	Pct.	Reb. O/T	A	TO	PF	S	Blk	TP	PPM
URANES	43	5/11	.455	9/10	.900	-/9	1	2	3	1	1	19	.442
DEANE	33	5/12	.417	2/2	1.000	-/5	1	1	4	0	0	12	.364
CHAMBERS, T.	31	13/18	.722	0/2	.000	-/12	1	5	5	0	0	26	.839
MARTIN, S.	34	3/6	.500	2/4	.500	-/3	9	5	4	1	0	8	.235
RICE	30	1/4	.250	0/0	.000	-/1	3	2	5	1	0	2	.067
JOHNSON	18	3/6	.500	2/2	1.000	-/2	0	0	2	1	0	8	.444
LEAVITT, C.	7	0/1	.000	0/0	.000	-/1	0	1	4	0	0	0	.000
CLAWSON	5	0/2	.000	2/2	1.000	-/0	0	0	1	1	0	2	.400
BAMKOWSKI	12	4/8	.500	3/6	.500	-/7	1	1	2	3	0	11	.917
JUDKINS	8	0/1	.000	0/0	.000	-/0	0	1	2	0	0	0	.000
LARSON	4	0/0	.000	0/0	.000	-/1	0	0	1	0	0	0	.000
Totals	225	34/69	.493	20/28	.714	-/40	16	18	33	8	1	88	.391

Utah State (67)   Coach: Dutch Belnap

	Min.	Total FG/FGA	Pct.	FT/FTA	Pct.	Reb. O/T	A	TO	PF	S	Blk	TP	PPM
BAILESS	25	1/2	.500	0/0	.000	-/4	1	1	5	1	1	2	.080
JACKSON	35	8/16	.500	1/2	.500	-/13	1	1	3	2	0	17	.486
HUNGER	35	4/10	.400	2/4	.500	-/7	0	2	2	0	1	10	.286
MCDONALD	34	10/18	.556	3/3	1.000	-/2	2	8	3	0	0	23	.676
PERKINS	27	3/5	.600	3/6	.500	-/0	3	1	4	1	0	9	.333
MCELRATH	15	0/1	.000	0/0	.000	-/1	2	1	3	1	0	0	.000
MILLER	3	0/0	.000	0/0	.000	-/0	0	0	1	1	0	0	.000
HOOD	20	2/8	.250	2/2	1.000	-/1	1	3	0	0	0	6	.300
CUNNINGHAM	3	0/0	.000	0/1	.000	-/0	0	1	0	0	0	0	.000
AUSTEFJORD	1	0/0	.000	0/0	.000	-/0	0	0	0	0	0	0	.000
TAYLOR	1	0/1	.000	0/0	.000	-/0	0	0	0	0	0	0	.000
PINEGAR	1	0/1	.000	0/0	.000	-/0	0	0	0	0	0	0	.000
Totals	200	28/62	.452	11/18	.611	-/28	10	18	21	5	2	67	.335

Pepperdine (92)   Coach: Gary Colson

	Min.	Total FG/FGA	Pct.	FT/FTA	Pct.	Reb. O/T	A	TO	PF	S	Blk	TP	PPM
MATSON, O.	37	6/9	.667	7/10	.700	-/7	1	3	4	1	0	19	.514
RAMSEY	38	4/11	.364	3/4	.750	-/13	4	0	2	0	1	11	.289
ELLIS	23	2/3	.667	2/3	.667	-/6	1	2	5	0	0	6	.261
BROWN	42	12/22	.545	2/4	.500	-/2	3	2	3	1	0	26	.619
FULLER	40	3/7	.429	7/12	.583	-/4	4	4	3	1	0	13	.325
GRAEBE	21	4/10	.400	0/0	.000	-/0	1	2	5	2	0	8	.381
SCOTT	19	4/7	.571	0/0	.000	-/5	0	0	3	0	0	8	.421
CAVALCANTE	4	0/1	.000	0/0	.000	-/1	0	0	3	0	0	0	.000
SOARES	1	0/0	.000	1/2	.500	-/0	0	0	0	0	1	1	1.000
Totals	225	35/70	.500	22/35	.629	-/38	14	13	28	5	1	92	.409

Team Rebounds: Pepperdine 2; Utah 1. Disqualified: Pepperdine—Ellis, Graebe, Utah—Chambers, Rice. Technical fouls; None.

	1st Half	2nd Half	1st OT	Final
Utah	38	39	11	88
Pepperdine	42	35	15	92

Team Rebounds: USC 1; Utah State 0. Disqualified: USC—Jones, Carfino; Utah State—Bailess. Technical fouls: USC—Coach Boyd.

	1st Half	2nd Half	Final
USC	35	51	86
Utah State	32	35	67

FIRST ROUND MIDWEST

Weber State (81)   Coach: Neil McCarthy

	Min.	Total FG/FGA	Pct.	FT/FTA	Pct.	Reb. O/T	A	TO	PF	S	Blk	TP	PPM
JOHNSON, D.	36	9/11	.818	1/1	1.000	-/5	5	4	3	2	0	19	.528
MOORE, K.	22	1/3	.333	0/0	.000	-/1	3	2	3	1	0	2	.091
SMITH, R.	41	5/11	.455	2/2	1.000	-/9	0	3	4	0	2	12	.293
MATTOS, M.	29	2/4	.500	1/2	.500	-/4	4	2	5	4	0	5	.172
COLLINS, B.	40	6/12	.500	3/5	.600	-/7	3	1	4	3	1	15	.375
MATTINSON, G.	8	0/1	.000	2/2	1.000	-/0	0	0	3	0	0	2	.250
HOWLAND, J.	34	6/12	.500	4/4	1.000	-/5	1	1	3	0	0	16	.471
HARPER, T.	15	5/7	.714	0/0	.000	-/0	3	1	3	0	0	10	.667
Totals	225	34/61	.557	13/16	.813	-/31	19	14	28	10	3	81	.360

New Mexico State (78)   Coach: Ken Hayes

	Min.	Total FG/FGA	Pct.	FT/FTA	Pct.	Reb. O/T	A	TO	PF	S	Blk	TP	PPM
GUNN, R.	42	9/17	.529	1/5	.200	-/11	0	4	3	0	1	19	.452
CORMIER, C.	37	3/5	.600	4/6	.667	-/4	4	2	1	2	1	10	.270
STONES, S.	41	4/12	.333	5/7	.714	-/9	1	4	2	2	0	13	.317
WEBB, G.	36	2/8	.250	5/8	.625	-/5	0	1	4	0	0	9	.250
MYERS, B.	31	2/3	.667	0/0	.000	-/3	6	5	3	0	0	4	.129
GOSLIN, C.	30	10/18	.556	3/4	.750	-/1	0	1	2	0	0	23	.767
PATE, N.	3	0/2	.000	0/0	.000	-/0	0	0	0	0	0	0	.000
CLEMENT, R.	4	0/0	.000	0/0	.000	-/0	0	2	2	0	0	0	.000
CORRIE, B.	1	0/0	.000	0/0	.000	-/0	0	0	0	0	0	0	.000
Totals	225	30/65	.462	18/30	.600	-/33	11	19	17	4	2	78	.347

Team Rebounds: Weber St. 5; New Mexico St. 8. Disqualified: Weber St.—Mattos. Technical fouls: None.

	1st Half	2nd Half	1st OT	Final
Weber St.	41	28	12	81
New Mexico St.	40	29	9	78

Virginia Tech (70)   Coach: Charles Moir

	Min.	Total FG/FGA	Pct.	FT/FTA	Pct.	Reb. O/T	A	TO	PF	S	Blk	TP	PPM
HENSON, L.	27	3/7	.429	6/8	.750	-/7	0	0	1	2	0	12	.444
ROBINSON, W.	35	1/4	.250	2/4	.500	-/9	1	3	1	1	0	4	.114
SOLOMON, D.	35	10/14	.714	4/4	1.000	-/4	0	4	2	0	0	24	.686
REID, D.	35	5/7	.714	0/0	.000	-/4	1	1	3	3	0	10	.286
ASHFORD, M.	39	7/10	.700	1/1	1.000	-/1	2	4	1	1	0	15	.385
PRICE, T.	14	0/2	.000	0/0	.000	-/3	0	0	1	1	0	0	.000
BRYAN, G.	3	0/2	.000	0/0	.000	-/1	0	1	0	0	0	0	.000
HILLENBRAND, J.	3	0/0	.000	1/3	.333	-/2	0	0	0	0	0	1	.333
SCOTT, C.	5	0/2	.000	2/3	.667	-/0	0	1	0	0	0	2	.400
BENNETT, D.	2	0/0	.000	0/0	.000	-/1	0	1	0	0	0	0	.000
SHRADER, M.	1	1/1	1.000	0/0	.000	-/0	0	0	0	0	0	2	2.000
HENSON, L.	1	0/0	.000	0/0	.000	-/0	0	0	0	0	0	0	.000
Totals	200	27/49	.551	16/23	.696	-/32	4	15	9	8	0	70	.350

Jacksonville (53)   Coach: Tates Locke

	Min.	Total FG/FGA	Pct.	FT/FTA	Pct.	Reb. O/T	A	TO	PF	S	Blk	TP	PPM
GURAM, S.	20	1/2	.500	0/0	.000	-/1	1	0	4	0	0	2	.100
TAYLOR, B.	20	3/7	.429	0/0	.000	-/2	0	2	0	0	1	6	.300
RAY, J.	31	7/14	.500	1/1	1.000	-/9	0	4	5	3	1	15	.484
WILLIAMS, C.	29	3/7	.429	0/0	.000	-/2	2	2	1	0	0	6	.207
DEVITO, P.	30	1/6	.167	0/0	.000	-/4	1	5	0	1	0	2	.067
MARTIN, J.	27	7/11	.636	0/0	.000	-/1	1	1	2	5	0	14	.519
TUTSON, S.	24	3/6	.500	0/0	.000	-/3	0	1	5	0	0	6	.250
HARRIS, G.	8	0/1	.000	0/0	.000	-/0	1	0	0	0	0	0	.000
PARISI, P.	4	0/2	.000	0/0	.000	-/0	0	0	1	0	0	0	.000
BOYLE, P.	3	0/0	.000	0/0	.000	-/1	0	0	2	0	0	0	.000
CONNEY, S.	2	0/1	.000	0/0	.000	-/0	0	0	0	0	0	0	.000
LEMMONS, F.	2	1/3	.333	0/0	.000	-/3	0	0	0	0	0	2	1.000
Totals	200	26/60	.433	1/1	1.000	-/26	6	15	20	9	2	53	.265

Team Rebounds: Virginia Tech 3; Jacksonville 2. Disqualified: Jacksonville—Ray, Tutson. Technical fouls: Jacksonville—Ray.

	1st Half	2nd Half	Final
Virginia Tech	21	49	70
Jacksonville	27	26	53

SECOND ROUND EAST

St. John's (80)   Coach: Lou Carnesecca

	Min.	Total FG/FGA	Pct.	FT/FTA	Pct.	Reb. O/T	A	TO	PF	S	Blk	TP	PPM
PLAIR, R.	35	4/8	.500	3/4	.750	-/8	3	1	4	0	0	11	.314
GILROY, F.	30	2/6	.333	0/0	.000	-/3	0	2	1	0	0	4	.133
MCKOY, W.	27	9/18	.500	0/0	.000	-/7	1	1	4	0	1	18	.667
RENCHER, B.	23	2/5	.400	2/2	1.000	-/1	2	3	1	0	0	6	.261
CARTER, R.	39	8/15	.533	5/6	.833	-/2	1	1	2	0	0	21	.538
WRIGHT, R.	20	4/5	.800	0/0	.000	-/3	0	1	4	0	0	8	.400
THOMAS, G.	26	5/7	.714	2/2	1.000	-/1	4	0	2	3	0	12	.462
Totals	200	34/64	.531	12/14	.857	-/25	11	9	18	3	1	80	.400

Duke (78)   Coach: Wm. E. (Bill) Foster

	Min.	Total FG/FGA	Pct.	FT/FTA	Pct.	Reb. O/T	A	TO	PF	S	Blk	TP	PPM
TAYLOR, V.	39	2/6	.333	2/2	1.000	-/2	1	4	5	0	0	6	.154
BANKS, E.	38	10/18	.556	4/5	.800	-/10	6	2	2	3	0	24	.632
GMINSKI, M.	31	6/14	.429	4/4	1.000	-/8	0	1	3	0	2	16	.516
HARRELL, J.	27	3/3	1.000	1/3	.333	-/0	7	1	2	0	0	7	.259
SPANARKEL, J.	38	7/11	.636	2/2	1.000	-/4	3	4	0	2	0	16	.421
SUDDATH, J.	14	3/5	.600	1/2	.500	-/2	1	0	3	0	0	7	.500
GOETSCH, S.	10	1/1	1.000	0/1	.000	-/3	0	1	0	0	0	2	.200
MORRISON, H.	2	0/0	.000	0/0	.000	-/0	0	1	1	0	0	0	.000
GRAY, S.	1	0/0	.000	0/0	.000	-/0	0	0	0	0	0	0	.000
Totals	200	32/58	.552	14/19	.737	-/29	18	13	17	5	2	78	.390

Team Rebounds: St. John's 3; Duke 0. Disqualified: Duke—Taylor. Technical fouls: None.

	1st Half	2nd Half	Final
St. John's	33	47	80
Duke	38	40	78

Georgetown (58) Coach: John Thompson

	Min.	Total FG/FGA	Pct.	FT/FTA	Pct.	Reb. O/T	A	TO	PF	S	Blk	TP	PPM
MARTIN, S.	38	3/10	.300	0/0	.000	-/5	5	1	4	0	0	6	.158
SHELTON, C.	24	5/6	.833	2/2	1.000	-/9	1	2	5	1	2	12	.500
SPRIGGS, E.	39	3/4	.750	3/4	.750	-/10	2	1	4	1	0	9	.231
FLOYD, E.	40	4/17	.235	0/0	.000	-/2	2	3	1	1	0	8	.200
DUREN, J.	40	6/15	.400	1/2	.500	-/1	3	3	4	2	0	13	.325
BULLIS, J.	14	2/2	1.000	0/0	.000	-/0	0	1	1	0	0	4	.286
SMITH, E.	5	2/2	1.000	2/3	.667	-/0	0	0	3	0	0	6	1.200
Totals	200	25/56	.446	8/11	.727	-/27	13	11	22	5	2	58	.290

Rutgers (64) Coach: Tom Young

	Min.	Total FG/FGA	Pct.	FT/FTA	Pct.	Reb. O/T	A	TO	PF	S	Blk	TP	PPM
ANDERSON, A.	21	0/1	.000	0/0	.000	-/3	3	0	5	0	0	0	.000
TROY, K.	38	5/14	.357	4/7	.571	-/8	0	1	2	0	0	14	.368
BAILEY, J.	36	7/12	.583	5/6	.833	-/14	2	4	3	1	4	19	.528
STRICKLAND, D.	37	8/14	.571	5/6	.833	-/3	2	1	1	0	1	21	.568
BROWN, T.	37	2/4	.500	2/2	1.000	-/0	7	5	2	0	0	6	.162
MADLINGER, M.	3	0/0	.000	0/0	.000	-/0	0	0	0	0	0	0	.000
GRIFFIN, D.	3	0/1	.000	0/0	.000	-/0	0	1	1	0	0	0	.000
KELLY, J.	1	0/0	.000	0/0	.000	-/0	0	0	0	0	0	0	.000
MCDANIEL, J.	19	2/2	1.000	0/1	.000	-/2	0	1	2	0	0	4	.211
MILLIGAN, T.	1	0/0	.000	0/0	.000	-/0	0	0	0	0	0	0	.000
CLARKE, B.	4	0/0	.000	0/0	.000	-/0	2	1	0	1	0	0	.000
Totals	200	24/48	.500	16/22	.727	-/30	16	14	16	2	5	64	.320

Team Rebounds: Rutgers 2; Georgetown 5. Disqualified: Rutgers—Anderson; Georgetown—Shelton. Technical fouls: Georgetown—bench.

	1st Half	2nd Half	Final
Georgetown	26	32	58
Rutgers	29	35	64

Pennsylvania (72) Coach: Bob Weinhauer

	Min.	Total FG/FGA	Pct.	FT/FTA	Pct.	Reb. O/T	A	TO	PF	S	Blk	TP	PPM
PRICE, T.	33	12/18	.667	1/1	1.000	-/9	6	3	3	1	0	25	.758
SMITH, T.	29	5/11	.455	6/6	1.000	-/7	1	2	5	2	0	16	.552
WHITE, M.	38	4/7	.571	2/2	1.000	-/8	3	4	2	0	0	10	.263
SALTERS, J.	38	6/11	.545	3/7	.429	-/1	2	5	4	4	0	15	.395
WILLIS, B.	25	1/5	.200	0/3	.000	-/1	1	1	4	2	1	2	.080
LEIFSEN, T.	1	0/0	.000	0/0	.000	-/0	0	0	0	0	0	0	.000
HALL, K.	20	0/1	.000	2/2	1.000	-/1	3	2	3	2	0	2	.100
ROSS, V.	16	1/3	.333	0/0	.000	-/0	1	0	2	1	0	2	.125
Totals	200	29/56	.518	14/21	.667	-/27	17	17	23	12	1	72	.360

North Carolina (71) Coach: Dean Smith

	Min.	Total FG/FGA	Pct.	FT/FTA	Pct.	Reb. O/T	A	TO	PF	S	Blk	TP	PPM
WOOD, A.	35	9/19	.474	2/3	.667	-/4	4	3	5	0	1	20	.571
O'KOREN, M.	38	7/12	.583	1/3	.333	-/10	1	4	4	1	0	15	.395
BUDKO, P.	10	1/2	.500	1/2	.500	-/1	0	0	2	0	0	3	.300
COLESCOTT, D.	29	6/11	.545	4/4	1.000	-/3	2	2	2	0	0	16	.552
BRADLEY, D.	33	3/9	.333	0/0	.000	-/4	2	2	3	2	0	6	.182
YONAKOR, R.	24	1/2	.500	3/4	.750	-/6	5	4	3	2	1	5	.208
DOUGHTON, G.	9	1/2	.500	0/0	.000	-/0	0	3	1	0	0	2	.222
WOLF, J.	8	0/1	.000	0/0	.000	-/1	0	0	1	0	0	0	.000
VIRGIL, J.	9	1/2	.500	2/2	1.000	-/1	0	0	1	0	0	4	.444
BLACK, J.	4	0/0	.000	0/0	.000	-/0	0	0	1	0	0	0	.000
WIEL, R.	1	0/0	.000	0/0	.000	-/0	0	0	0	0	0	0	.000
Totals	200	29/59	.492	13/18	.722	-/30	15	18	23	6	2	71	.355

Team Rebounds: Pennsylvania 1; N. Carolina 3. Disqualified: Pennsylvania—Smith; N. Carolina—Wood. Technical fouls: None.

	1st Half	2nd Half	Final
Pennsylvania	34	38	72
N. Carolina	36	35	71

Syracuse (89) Coach: Jim Boeheim

	Min.	Total FG/FGA	Pct.	FT/FTA	Pct.	Reb. O/T	A	TO	PF	S	Blk	TP	PPM
SHACKLEFORD, D.	-	6/14	.429	1/2	.500	-/9	-	-	4	-	-	13	-
ORR, L.	-	7/9	.778	4/6	.667	-/6	-	-	4	-	-	18	-
BOUIE, R.	-	9/12	.750	1/2	.500	-/6	-	-	4	-	-	19	-
COHEN, H.	-	1/4	.250	2/2	1.000	-/1	-	-	4	-	-	4	-
HEADD, M.	-	9/15	.600	0/0	.000	-/2	-	-	0	-	-	18	-
MOSS, E.	-	3/5	.600	7/10	.700	-/6	-	-	3	-	-	13	-
HARMON, R.	-	0/0	.000	0/0	.000	-/0	-	-	0	-	-	0	-
SCHAYES, D.	-	2/3	.667	0/0	.000	-/5	-	-	4	-	-	4	-
Totals	200	37/62	.597	15/22	.682	-/35	-	-	23	-	-	89	.445

U. Conn. (81) Coach: Dom Perno

	Min.	Total FG/FGA	Pct.	FT/FTA	Pct.	Reb. O/T	A	TO	PF	S	Blk	TP	PPM
MCCAY, M.	-	4/17	.235	13/14	.929	-/8	-	-	4	-	-	21	-
THOMPSON, C.	-	7/18	.389	4/4	1.000	-/12	-	-	1	-	-	18	-
CARR, J.	-	5/11	.455	7/10	.700	-/13	-	-	4	-	-	17	-
JOHNSON, C.	-	1/7	.143	0/0	.000	-/1	-	-	2	-	-	2	-
LAVIGNE, R.	-	6/15	.400	0/0	.000	-/3	-	-	1	-	-	12	-
SULLIVAN, J.	-	0/2	.000	0/0	.000	-/1	-	-	2	-	-	0	-
DULIN, R.	-	1/6	.167	3/3	1.000	-/0	-	-	4	-	-	5	-
FEARSON, J.	-	3/4	.750	0/0	.000	-/3	-	-	3	-	-	6	-
Totals	200	27/80	.338	27/31	.871	-/41	-	-	21	-	-	81	.405

Team Rebounds: Syracuse 8; U. Conn. 5. Disqualified: None. Technical fouls: None.

	1st Half	2nd Half	Final
Syracuse	52	37	89
U. Conn.	35	46	81

SECOND ROUND MIDEAST

Lamar (64)   Coach: Billy Tubbs

	Min.	Total FG/FGA	Pct.	FT/FTA	Pct.	Reb. O/T	A	TO	PF	S	Blk	TP	PPM
LEWIS, C.	30	5/15	.333	0/0	.000	-/6	2	0	1	1	0	10	.333
DAVIS, B.	30	3/12	.250	4/4	1.000	-/9	1	1	5	1	2	10	.333
KEA, C.	19	4/7	.571	3/3	1.000	-/4	3	1	5	.1	0	11	.579
OLLIVER, M.	34	3/15	.200	2/2	1.000	-/1	3	2	2	0	0	8	.235
BELLARD, N.	33	4/7	.571	2/4	.500	-/3	3	1	1	2	0	10	.303
GATHERS, E.	12	3/8	.375	0/0	.000	-/1	0	0	1	0	0	6	.500
WILLIAMS, T.	18	0/3	.000	0/0	.000	-/4	0	0	1	0	0	0	.000
JONES, C.	7	0/3	.000	0/0	.000	-/0	0	0	2	0	0	0	.000
RUTTER, M.	10	0/1	.000	1/2	.500	-/6	0	0	2	0	0	1	.100
STEPHENSON, L.	7	4/5	.800	0/0	.000	-/4	0	0	0	0	0	8	1.143
Totals	200	26/76	.342	12/15	.800	-/38	12	5	20	5	2	64	.320

Michigan State (95)   Coach: Jud Heathcote

	Min.	Total FG/FGA	Pct.	FT/FTA	Pct.	Reb. O/T	A	TO	PF	S	Blk	TP	PPM
KELSER, G.	35	12/21	.571	7/10	.700	-/14	3	7	3	1	0	31	.886
JOHNSON, E.	35	6/14	.429	1/1	1.000	-/17	10	6	1	4	0	13	.371
VINCENT, J.	13	5/10	.500	1/2	.500	-/3	1	0	2	1	0	11	.846
DONNELLY, T.	32	3/5	.600	0/0	.000	-/0	2	0	3	1	0	6	.188
BRKOVICH, M.	34	6/7	.857	0/0	.000	-/2	3	0	1	1	0	12	.353
LLOYD, G.	3	0/0	.000	0/1	.000	-/1	0	0	0	0	0	0	.000
CHARLES, R.	25	6/9	.667	0/2	.000	-/3	0	0	2	0	1	12	.480
LONGAKER, M.	5	0/1	.000	1/2	.500	-/1	0	0	0	0	0	1	.200
HUFFMAN, J.	3	1/1	1.000	0/1	.000	-/1	0	0	0	0	0	2	.667
GONZALEZ, R.	7	1/2	.500	0/0	.000	-/2	0	1	3	0	0	2	.286
KAYE, R.	4	2/2	1.000	0/0	.000	-/1	0	0	1	0	0	4	1.000
GILKIE, G.	2	0/0	.000	1/2	.500	-/1	0	0	0	0	0	1	.500
BRKOVICH, D.	2	0/0	.000	0/0	.000	-/0	0	0	0	0	0	0	.000
Totals	200	42/72	.583	11/21	.524	-/46	19	14	16	8	1	95	.475

Team Rebounds: Michigan St. 4; Lamar 5. Disqualified: Lamar—Kea, Davis. Technical fouls: Lamar—bench.

	1st Half	2nd Half	Final
Lamar	27	37	64
Michigan St.	46	49	95

Louisiana State (71)   Coach: Dale Brown

	Min.	Total FG/FGA	Pct.	FT/FTA	Pct.	Reb. O/T	A	TO	PF	S	Blk	TP	PPM
COOK	37	4/7	.571	0/0	.000	-/9	3	1	3	2	0	8	.216
HULTBERG	23	3/10	.300	0/0	.000	-/1	3	3	2	2	0	6	.261
GREEN, L.	35	4/7	.571	5/8	.625	-/16	1	1	4	0	1	13	.371
MARTIN	24	4/9	.444	0/1	.000	-/3	4	2	5	2	1	8	.333
GREEN, A.	19	4/8	.500	0/0	.000	-/3	2	2	3	0	0	8	.421
RUDOLPH, G.	11	1/1	1.000	2/3	.667	-/0	1	0	1	0	0	4	.364
BROWN	11	3/4	.750	0/1	.000	-/1	1	0	0	0	0	6	.545
SIMS, W.	15	0/4	.000	2/4	.500	-/2	1	1	2	0	0	2	.133
MATTICK	21	6/10	.600	2/5	.400	-/6	1	1	4	0	1	14	.667
BERGERON	2	0/0	.000	0/0	.000	-/0	1	0	0	0	0	0	.000
CAMPBELL	1	0/0	.000	0/0	.000	-/0	0	1	0	0	0	0	.000
DEARMOND	1	1/1	1.000	0/0	.000	-/0	0	0	0	0	0	2	2.000
Totals	200	30/61	.492	11/22	.500	-/41	18	12	24	6	3	71	.355

Appalachian State (57)   Coach: Bobby Cremins

	Min.	Total FG/FGA	Pct.	FT/FTA	Pct.	Reb. O/T	A	TO	PF	S	Blk	TP	PPM
LAWRENCE	34	7/19	.368	7/8	.875	-/6	1	2	3	1	0	21	.618
PAYTON	31	2/3	.667	2/4	.500	-/5	1	1	5	1	0	6	.194
HUBBARD	39	3/5	.600	1/3	.333	-/6	0	2	3	1	2	7	.179
ROBINSON	36	4/10	.400	1/2	.500	-/2	3	6	2	1	0	9	.250
ANDERSON	33	4/10	.400	2/5	.400	-/2	1	3	4	0	0	10	.303
FITCH	7	2/6	.333	0/0	.000	-/1	0	0	0	1	0	4	.571
JACKSON	8	0/0	.000	0/0	.000	-/1	2	0	0	0	0	0	.000
GILES	4	0/0	.000	0/0	.000	-/0	0	0	0	0	0	0	.000
KELLER	4	0/1	.000	0/0	.000	-/0	0	0	1	0	0	0	.000
LENBY	4	0/0	.000	0/0	.000	-/0	0	0	0	0	0	0	.000
Totals	200	22/54	.407	13/22	.591	-/23	8	14	18	5	2	57	.285

Team Rebounds: Louisiana St. 5; Appalachian St. 8. Disqualified: Louisiana St.—Martin; Appalachian St.—Payton. Technical fouls: Appalachian St.—Payton.

	1st Half	2nd Half	Final
Louisiana St.	31	40	71
Appalachian St.	20	37	57

Tennessee (67)   Coach: Don Devoe

	Min.	Total FG/FGA	Pct.	FT/FTA	Pct.	Reb. O/T	A	TO	PF	S	Blk	TP	PPM
CROSBY, T.	39	3/10	.300	2/2	1.000	-/5	2	0	2	1	0	8	.205
JOHNSON, R.	26	4/11	.364	5/10	.500	-/5	0	2	5	0	0	13	.500
WOOD, H.	19	4/7	.571	0/0	.000	-/7	0	3	3	0	0	8	.421
BERTELKAMP, B.	7	0/1	.000	0/0	.000	-/0	0	0	2	0	0	0	.000
CARTER, G.	38	7/16	.438	2/3	.667	-/7	0	4	5	2	0	16	.421
TEFFETELLER, K.	1	0/0	.000	0/0	.000	-/0	0	0	0	0	0	0	.000
DARDEN, J.	33	4/6	.667	2/4	.500	-/2	2	3	4	1	0	10	.303
THREETHS, C.	28	4/8	.500	2/4	.500	-/8	0	2	2	0	0	10	.357
NASH, K.	7	0/1	.000	2/2	1.000	-/0	0	2	5	1	0	2	.286
RAY, S.	2	0/0	.000	0/0	.000	-/1	0	0	1	0	0	0	.000
Totals	200	26/60	.433	15/25	.600	-/35	4	16	29	5	0	67	.335

Notre Dame (73)   Coach: Digger Phelps

	Min.	Total FG/FGA	Pct.	FT/FTA	Pct.	Reb. O/T	A	TO	PF	S	Blk	TP	PPM
TRIPUCKA, K.	-	6/7	.857	9/10	.900	-/3	0	0	2	1	0	21	-
WOOLRIDGE, O.	-	4/7	.571	0/1	.000	-/6	0	1	4	3	0	8	-
FLOWERS, B.	-	3/4	.750	0/0	.000	-/4	0	2	5	1	1	6	-
BRANNING, R.	-	3/9	.333	0/0	.000	-/1	1	2	3	0	0	6	-
HANZLIK, B.	-	6/10	.600	4/4	1.000	-/1	0	1	4	2	1	16	-
MITCHELL, M.	-	0/1	.000	0/0	.000	-/0	0	1	1	0	0	0	-
JACKSON, T.	-	1/8	.125	2/6	.333	-/2	1	0	0	0	0	4	-
LAIMBEER, B.	-	2/3	.667	8/11	.727	-/12	0	2	3	0	1	12	-
WILCOX, S.	-	0/0	.000	0/0	.000	-/0	1	1	2	0	0	0	-
Totals	200	25/49	.510	23/32	.719	-/29	2	11	24	7	3	73	.365

Team Rebounds: Notre Dame 4; Tennessee 9. Disqualified: Notre Dame—Flowers; Tennessee—Johnson, Carter, Nash. Technical fouls: None.

	1st Half	2nd Half	Final
Tennessee	32	35	67
Notre Dame	32	41	73

Iowa (72) Coach: Lute Olson

	Min.	Total FG/FGA	Pct.	FT/FTA	Pct.	Reb. O/T	A	TO	PF	S	Blk	TP	PPM
MAYFIELD, W.	28	8/11	.727	3/8	.375	-/5	1	0	4	1	1	19	.679
BOYLE	34	2/9	.222	3/6	.500	-/4	0	3	2	1	0	7	.206
WAITE	22	1/2	.500	0/0	.000	-/3	0	0	3	0	1	2	.091
LESTER, R.	38	9/13	.692	5/6	.833	-/4	6	3	4	2	1	23	.605
PETH	23	1/3	.333	1/2	.500	-/2	2	1	5	0	0	3	.130
KRAFCISIN	18	2/4	.500	2/5	.400	-/6	2	2	5	1	0	6	.333
NORMAN	17	4/8	.500	0/0	.000	-/0	1	2	5	0	0	8	.471
BROOKINS, V.	10	2/3	.667	0/0	.000	-/2	0	1	3	0	0	4	.400
ARNOLD, K.	10	0/2	.000	0/0	.000	-/1	2	0	0	0	0	0	.000
Totals	200	29/55	.527	14/27	.519	-/27	14	12	31	5	3	72	.360

Toledo (74) Coach: Bob Nichols

	Min.	Total FG/FGA	Pct.	FT/FTA	Pct.	Reb. O/T	A	TO	PF	S	Blk	TP	PPM
SWANEY	16	5/12	.417	2/2	1.000	-/4	0	2	4	0	1	12	.750
APPEL	24	2/4	.500	0/0	.000	-/3	1	0	2	0	0	4	.167
MILLER, D.	40	5/8	.625	8/17	.471	-/14	4	2	4	1	0	18	.450
JOPLIN	32	3/7	.429	9/11	.818	-/0	3	2	4	3	0	15	.469
LEHMAN, J.	35	2/4	.500	6/8	.750	-/5	3	5	2	0	0	10	.286
SELGO	23	2/4	.500	2/2	1.000	-/4	2	1	5	1	0	6	.261
KNUCKLES, H.	15	3/4	.750	1/1	1.000	-/2	0	6	2	0	0	7	.467
GARWOOD	1	0/0	.000	0/0	.000	-/0	0	1	1	0	0	0	.000
MONTAGUE, K.	14	1/2	.500	0/0	.000	-/1	0	0	0	0	0	2	.143
Totals	200	23/45	.511	28/41	.683	-/33	13	19	24	5	1	74	.370

Team Rebounds: Toledo 11; Iowa 6. Disqualified: Toledo—Selgo; Iowa—Peth, Krafcisin, Norman. Technical fouls: None.

	1st Half	2nd Half	Final
Iowa	41	31	72
Toledo	29	45	74

SECOND ROUND WEST

USC (78) Coach: Bob Boyd

	Min.	Total FG/FGA	Pct.	FT/FTA	Pct.	Reb. O/T	A	TO	PF	S	Blk	TP	PPM
WILLIAMS	22	5/10	.500	0/0	.000	-/2	3	2	5	1	0	10	.455
MILLER	39	10/13	.769	3/5	.600	-/9	1	2	3	4	0	23	.590
WIDFELDT	25	1/2	.500	1/2	.500	-/1	1	4	5	0	0	3	.120
JONES	34	2/6	.333	0/0	.000	-/0	7	4	1	1	0	4	.176
CARFINO	30	7/14	.500	6/7	.857	-/2	1	3	2	2	1	20	.667
SMITH, S.	18	7/12	.583	0/0	.000	-/2	0	1	2	0	0	14	.778
SMITH, D.	15	0/0	.000	0/0	.000	-/6	0	1	1	1	0	0	.000
BROOKS	9	0/1	.000	0/0	.000	-/2	1	2	0	0	0	0	.000
ARNOLD	1	0/0	.000	0/0	.000	-/0	1	0	0	0	0	0	.000
RATKOVICH	1	0/0	.000	0/0	.000	-/0	0	0	0	0	0	0	.000
MARQUETTI	6	1/1	1.000	0/0	.000	-/0	0	1	0	0	0	2	.333
Totals	200	33/59	.559	12/16	.750	-/24	15	20	19	9	1	78	.390

Marquette (73) Coach: Hank Raymonds

	Min.	Total FG/FGA	Pct.	FT/FTA	Pct.	Reb. O/T	A	TO	PF	S	Blk	TP	PPM
TOONE, B.	32	7/13	.538	4/4	1.000	-/5	1	4	4	0	1	18	.563
BYRD	37	2/5	.400	3/4	.750	-/6	0	2	0	2	0	7	.189
BALL	21	2/6	.333	0/0	.000	-/2	0	1	5	2	0	4	.190
WILSON	28	0/3	.000	2/3	.667	-/1	2	0	0	0	0	2	.071
WORTHEN	35	6/8	.750	6/6	1.000	-/5	6	2	2	4	0	18	.514
LEE	18	5/7	.714	0/0	.000	-/6	2	0	0	0	0	10	.556
GREEN	12	3/3	1.000	0/0	.000	-/2	1	1	3	1	1	6	.500
MARQUARDT	6	0/0	.000	0/0	.000	-/1	0	1	0	0	0	0	.000
DAVIS	5	1/1	1.000	0/0	.000	-/1	0	0	0	0	1	2	.400
HATCHETT	3	1/2	.500	2/2	1.000	-/0	0	0	1	0	0	4	1.333
SHIMON	3	0/0	.000	2/4	.500	-/0	0	0	1	1	0	2	.667
Totals	200	27/48	.563	19/23	.826	-/29	12	11	16	10	3	73	.365

DePaul (89) Coach: Ray Meyer

	Min.	Total FG/FGA	Pct.	FT/FTA	Pct.	Reb. O/T	A	TO	PF	S	Blk	TP	PPM
WATKINS, C.	40	9/14	.643	9/10	.900	-/9	0	0	2	0	0	27	.675
AGUIRRE, M.	40	10/13	.769	5/7	.714	-/7	6	3	3	1	0	25	.625
MITCHEM, J.	40	3/5	.600	2/2	1.000	-/7	1	4	2	1	0	8	.200
BRADSHAW, C.	40	5/10	.500	2/5	.400	-/4	3	2	4	2	0	12	.300
GARLAND, G.	40	7/17	.412	3/4	.750	-/1	8	3	0	10	0	17	.425
Totals	200	34/59	.576	21/28	.750	-/28	18	12	11	14	0	89	.445

Team Rebounds: DePaul 4; USC 1. Disqualified: USC—Williams, Widfeldt. Technical fouls: USC—Williams, Miller.

	1st Half	2nd Half	Final
USC	41	37	78
DePaul	44	45	89

Pacific (48) Coach: Stan Morrison

	Min.	Total FG/FGA	Pct.	FT/FTA	Pct.	Reb. O/T	A	TO	PF	S	Blk	TP	PPM
WALDRON	33	5/12	.417	0/-	-	-/7	2	0	2	1	0	10	.303
CORNELIUS	37	5/9	.556	2/2	1.000	-/6	1	2	2	0	0	12	.324
MCLAUGHLIN	28	3/4	.750	1/5	.200	-/4	1	2	4	1	0	7	.250
BRYANT	17	0/2	.000	0/1	.000	-/2	0	5	3	0	0	0	.000
CARNEY	37	5/12	.417	0/0	.000	-/1	5	2	2	2	0	10	.270
DZUBAR	14	1/3	.333	0/0	.000	-/1	1	3	3	1	0	2	.143
PAULSEN	8	0/1	.000	0/0	.000	-/2	0	0	0	1	0	0	.000
EDWARDS	9	0/2	.000	2/2	1.000	-/0	2	2	0	0	0	2	.222
BUGGS	7	1/2	.500	0/0	.000	-/1	0	0	1	0	0	2	.286
DEMSHER	3	1/1	1.000	0/0	.000	-/0	0	1	0	0	0	2	.667
HOVORKA	2	0/0	.000	0/0	.000	-/0	0	0	1	0	0	0	.000
GUNN	2	0/1	.000	1/2	.500	-/1	0	0	1	0	0	1	.500
WILL	2	0/0	.000	0/0	.000	-/0	0	1	0	0	1	0	.000
SMITH	1	0/0	.000	0/0	.000	-/0	0	0	1	0	0	0	.000
Totals	200	21/49	.429	6/12	.500	-/25	12	18	20	6	1	48	.240

Team Rebounds: Marquette 1; Pacific 0. Disqualified: Marquette—Ball. Technical fouls: None.

	1st Half	2nd Half	Final
Marquette	28	45	73
Pacific	22	26	48

Pepperdine (71)   Coach: Gary Colson

	Min.	Total FG / FGA	Pct.	FT / FTA	Pct.	Reb. O / T	A	TO	PF	S	Blk	TP	PPM
MATSON	39	6/13	.462	2/ 3	.667	-/ 9	0	2	2	1	1	14	.359
RAMSEY	33	1/ 5	.200	0/ 0	.000	-/ 3	0	1	3	3	1	2	.061
ELLIS	33	4/10	.400	2/ 4	.500	-/12	1	0	2	2	0	10	.303
BROWN	38	12/25	.480	3/ 4	.750	-/ 1	3	5	4	1	0	27	.711
FULLER	32	2/10	.200	6/ 8	.750	-/ 6	6	1	3	0	0	10	.313
GRAEBE	14	0/ 2	.000	2/ 2	1.000	-/ 1	1	1	1	0	0	2	.143
SCOTT	11	3/ 4	.750	0/ 0	.000	-/ 0	0	1	3	0	0	6	.545
Totals	200	28/69	.406	15/21	.714	-/32	11	11	18	7	2	71	.355

UCLA (76)   Coach: Gary Cunningham

	Min.	Total FG / FGA	Pct.	FT / FTA	Pct.	Reb. O / T	A	TO	PF	S	Blk	TP	PPM
GREENWOOD, D.	34	9/18	.500	0/ 0	.000	-/10	1	3	3	0	2	18	.529
VANDEWEGHE, K.	27	4/ 5	.800	0/ 0	.000	-/ 3	1	2	3	0	0	8	.296
SIMS, G.	21	4/ 6	.667	0/ 0	.000	-/ 7	0	1	2	1	1	8	.381
HOLLAND, B.	39	4/10	.400	6/ 6	1.000	-/ 2	6	3	2	0	0	14	.359
HAMILTON, R.	38	5/12	.417	4/ 8	.500	-/ 2	7	5	2	0	0	14	.368
ALLUMS, D.	14	2/ 5	.400	0/ 0	.000	-/ 7	0	0	2	0	0	4	.286
WILKES, J.	24	4/ 5	.800	0/ 0	.000	-/ 6	1	3	4	1	0	8	.333
NAULLS, T.	3	1/ 1	1.000	0/ 0	.000	-/ 0	0	0	0	0	0	2	.667
Totals	200	33/62	.532	10/14	.714	-/37	16	17	18	2	3	76	.380

Team Rebounds: UCLA 1; Pepperdine 4. Disqualified: None. Technical fouls: Pepperdine—Coach Colson.

	1st Half	2nd Half	Final
Pepperdine	38	33	71
UCLA	36	40	76

San Francisco (86)   Coach: Dan Belluomini

	Min.	Total FG / FGA	Pct.	FT / FTA	Pct.	Reb. O / T	A	TO	PF	S	Blk	TP	PPM
BOWERS	29	4/ 4	1.000	0/ 0	.000	-/ 3	4	2	2	0	0	8	.276
WILLIAMS	33	6/12	.500	0/ 3	.000	-/ 3	12	4	4	1	1	12	.364
CARTWRIGHT, B.	30	9/13	.692	6/ 7	.857	-/ 8	1	1	4	0	3	24	.800
JEMISON, D.	37	9/11	.818	0/ 2	.000	-/10	3	2	1	2	0	18	.486
REID, B.	24	4/ 7	.571	1/ 2	.500	-/ 2	4	6	2	2	1	9	.375
GILBERG	3	0/ 0	.000	0/ 0	.000	-/ 0	0	1	1	0	0	0	.000
DELOATCH, M.	7	2/ 4	.500	0/ 0	.000	-/ 1	0	1	1	0	0	4	.571
MCALISTER	2	0/ 0	.000	0/ 0	.000	-/ 0	1	1	0	0	0	0	.000
BRYANT	19	4/ 5	.800	1/ 2	.500	-/ 5	0	3	2	0	0	9	.474
CORNELIOUS, D.	16	1/ 1	1.000	0/ 0	.000	-/ 1	4	0	3	3	0	2	.125
Totals	200	39/57	.684	8/16	.500	-/33	29	21	20	8	5	86	.430

Brigham Young (63)   Coach: Frank Arnold

	Min.	Total FG / FGA	Pct.	FT / FTA	Pct.	Reb. O / T	A	TO	PF	S	Blk	TP	PPM
ROBERTS, F.	30	2/ 6	.333	2/ 4	.500	-/ 8	3	5	3	1	0	6	.200
DURRANT	27	4/ 9	.444	0/ 0	.000	-/ 1	1	1	2	0	0	8	.296
TAYLOR	33	6/17	.353	4/ 7	.571	-/ 6	0	2	2	3	0	16	.485
RUNIA	36	7/14	.500	2/ 2	1.000	-/ 4	4	3	3	0	0	16	.444
AINGE, D.	37	5/13	.385	1/ 1	1.000	-/ 2	5	5	3	1	1	11	.297
TRUMBO	13	1/ 2	.500	0/ 0	.000	-/ 3	0	1	1	0	0	2	.154
CRAIG	13	1/ 5	.200	0/ 0	.000	-/ 2	1	2	3	2	0	2	.154
RICE	5	0/ 0	.000	2/ 4	.500	-/ 1	0	1	0	0	0	2	.400
MCGUIRE	2	0/ 1	.000	0/ 0	.000	-/ 0	0	0	0	0	0	0	.000
ROBERTS, G.	2	0/ 1	.000	0/ 0	.000	-/ 1	0	0	0	0	0	0	.000
CHRISTENSEN	2	0/ 1	.000	0/ 0	.000	-/ 0	0	0	0	0	0	0	.000
Totals	200	26/69	.377	11/18	.611	-/28	14	20	17	7	1	63	.315

Team Rebounds: San Francisco 4; Brigham Young 1. Disqualified: None. Technical fouls: Brigham Young—team.

	1st Half	2nd Half	Final
San Francisco	35	51	86
Brigham Young	32	31	63

SECOND ROUND MIDWEST

Weber State (63)   Coach: Neil McCarthy

	Min.	Total FG / FGA	Pct.	FT / FTA	Pct.	Reb. O / T	A	TO	PF	S	Blk	TP	PPM
JOHNSON, D.	31	11/16	.688	1/ 1	1.000	-/ 3	3	3	4	0	1	23	.742
MOORE, K.	25	3/ 4	.750	0/ 0	.000	-/ 3	4	0	5	0	1	6	.240
SMITH, R.	38	5/11	.455	0/ 2	.000	-/ 8	1	1	3	1	0	10	.263
MATTOS, M.	15	1/ 3	.333	0/ 1	.000	-/ 2	1	2	3	1	0	2	.133
COLLINS, B.	28	1/ 5	.200	0/ 1	.000	-/ 1	0	4	0	1	1	2	.071
MATTINSON, G.	11	1/ 2	.500	0/ 0	.000	-/ 2	0	1	1	0	0	2	.182
HOWLAND, B.	25	3/ 5	.600	4/ 4	1.000	-/ 0	1	0	3	0	0	10	.400
HARPER, T.	24	3/ 7	.429	0/ 0	.000	-/ 1	2	1	3	0	0	6	.250
WILLIAMS, F.	2	1/ 1	1.000	0/ 0	.000	-/ 0	1	0	1	0	0	2	1.000
KILGORE, M.	1	0/ 0	.000	0/ 0	.000	-/ 0	0	0	0	0	0	0	.000
Totals	200	29/54	.537	5/ 9	.556	-/20	13	12	23	3	3	63	.315

Arkansas (74)   Coach: Eddie Sutton

	Min.	Total FG / FGA	Pct.	FT / FTA	Pct.	Reb. O / T	A	TO	PF	S	Blk	TP	PPM
ZAHN, A.	29	4/ 8	.500	2/ 2	1.000	-/ 5	3	1	0	2	0	10	.345
HASTINGS, S.	36	5/ 7	.714	4/ 4	1.000	-/ 4	3	0	3	0	0	14	.389
SCHALL, S.	38	9/ 9	1.000	0/ 2	.000	-/ 8	0	1	4	0	1	18	.474
REED, U.	36	3/ 9	.333	3/ 4	.750	-/ 0	0	1	4	2	0	9	.250
MONCRIEF, S.	39	5/10	.500	9/ 9	1.000	-/ 5	5	3	3	1	1	19	.487
BROWN, T.	13	1/ 2	.500	0/ 0	.000	-/ 0	1	0	0	0	0	2	.154
YOUNG, M.	3	0/ 0	.000	0/ 0	.000	-/ 1	0	1	0	0	0	0	.000
PETERSON, K.	1	0/ 0	.000	0/ 0	.000	-/ 0	0	0	1	0	0	0	.000
SCOTT, D.	1	0/ 0	.000	0/ 1	.000	-/ 0	0	0	0	0	0	0	.000
CRAFT, R.	1	0/ 0	.000	0/ 0	.000	-/ 0	0	0	0	0	0	0	.000
CROCKETT, J.	1	0/ 0	.000	0/ 0	.000	-/ 0	0	0	0	0	0	0	.000
NASH, E.	1	0/ 0	.000	0/ 0	.000	-/ 0	0	0	0	0	0	0	.000
BAILEY, A.	1	1/ 1	1.000	0/ 0	.000	-/ 1	0	0	0	0	0	2	2.000
Totals	200	28/46	.609	18/22	.818	-/24	12	7	15	5	2	74	.370

Team Rebounds: Arkansas 3; Weber St. 4. Disqualified: Weber St.—Moore. Technical fouls: None.

	1st Half	2nd Half	Final
Weber St.	27	36	63
Arkansas	40	34	74

Louisville (69)   Coach: Denny Crum

	Min.	Total FG / FGA	Pct.	FT / FTA	Pct.	Reb. O / T	A	TO	PF	S	Blk	TP	PPM
WILLIAMS, L.	40	5/ 9	.556	5/ 6	.833	-/ 9	1	-	3	-	-	15	.375
TURNER, J.	16	1/ 4	.250	2/ 2	1.000	-/ 2	0	-	2	-	-	4	.250
MCCRAY, S.	40	9/13	.692	3/ 3	1.000	-/ 6	3	-	4	-	-	21	.525
GRIFFITH, D.	37	6/14	.429	5/ 5	1.000	-/ 5	3	-	3	-	-	17	.459
SMITH, D.	25	3/ 6	.500	2/ 3	.667	-/ 7	2	-	3	-	-	8	.320
EAVES, J.	8	1/ 4	.250	0/ 0	.000	-/ 1	1	-	0	-	-	2	.250
BROWN, W.	10	0/ 0	.000	0/ 0	.000	-/ 0	0	-	2	-	-	0	.000
BURKMAN, R.	7	0/ 2	.000	0/ 0	.000	-/ 1	0	-	1	-	-	0	.000
BRANCH, T.	17	1/ 1	1.000	0/ 0	.000	-/ 2	1	-	2	-	-	2	.118
Totals	200	26/53	.491	17/19	.895	-/33	11	25	20	-	-	69	.345

South Alabama (66)   Coach: Cliff Ellis

	Min.	Total FG / FGA	Pct.	FT / FTA	Pct.	Reb. O / T	A	TO	PF	S	Blk	TP	PPM
RAINS	38	5/12	.417	5/10	.500	-/ 6	1	-	5	-	-	15	.395
WHITE	26	5/10	.500	1/ 2	.500	-/ 8	0	-	3	-	-	11	.423
MAY	17	1/ 2	.500	2/ 4	.500	-/ 4	1	-	3	-	-	4	.235
WILLIAMS	36	4/11	.364	1/ 1	1.000	-/ 1	4	-	4	-	-	9	.250
LEGETTE	28	2/10	.200	0/ 0	.000	-/ 0	5	-	4	-	-	4	.143
STILL	37	8/11	.727	2/ 4	.500	-/ 9	0	-	3	-	-	18	.486
BENNETT	4	0/ 1	.000	0/ 0	.000	-/ 1	0	-	0	-	-	0	.000
HAMPTON	14	1/ 1	1.000	3/ 4	.750	-/ 1	3	-	0	-	-	5	.357
Totals	200	26/58	.448	14/25	.560	-/30	14	17	22	-	-	66	.330

Team Rebounds: Louisville 4; South Alabama 0. Disqualified: South Alabama—Rains. Technical fouls: None.

	1st Half	2nd Half	Final
Louisville	33	36	69
South Alabama	28	38	66

Virginia Tech (69) Coach: Charles Moir

	Min.	Total FG/FGA	Pct.	FT/FTA	Pct.	Reb. O/T	A	TO	PF	S	Blk	TP	PPM
HENSON, L.	35	8/15	.533	2/2	1.000	-/8	1	1	5	2	1	18	.514
ROBINSON, W.	28	4/10	.400	2/2	1.000	-/7	0	1	3	1	0	10	.357
SOLOMON, D.	36	6/15	.400	0/1	.000	-/6	1	2	1	1	1	12	.333
REID, D.	32	4/9	.444	0/0	.000	-/6	2	1	4	1	0	8	.250
ASHFORD, M.	40	6/15	.400	3/3	1.000	-/5	1	7	4	2	1	15	.375
PRICE, T.	14	2/5	.400	0/0	.000	-/0	2	1	5	0	0	4	.286
BRYAN, G.	3	1/3	.333	0/0	.000	-/1	0	1	0	0	0	2	.667
HILLENBRAND, J.	1	0/0	.000	0/0	.000	-/0	0	0	0	0	0	0	.000
SCOTT, C.	8	0/1	.000	0/0	.000	-/0	1	0	0	0	0	0	.000
BENNETT, D.	2	0/1	.000	0/0	.000	-/1	0	0	0	0	0	0	.000
SHRADER, M.	1	0/0	.000	0/0	.000	-/0	0	0	0	0	0	0	.000
Totals	200	31/74	.419	7/8	.875	-/34	8	13	22	7	3	69	.345

Indiana State (86) Coach: Bill Hodges

	Min.	Total FG/FGA	Pct.	FT/FTA	Pct.	Reb. O/T	A	TO	PF	S	Blk	TP	PPM
MILEY, B.	33	1/2	.500	0/3	.000	-/7	1	1	0	0	0	2	.061
GILBERT, A.	27	6/8	.750	0/2	.000	-/7	0	0	1	0	3	12	.444
BIRD, L.	37	6/14	.429	10/12	.833	-/13	7	1	2	1	2	22	.595
NICKS, C.	36	9/21	.429	4/5	.800	-/3	1	4	1	1	0	22	.611
REED, S.	33	5/7	.714	2/2	1.000	-/4	6	2	2	0	0	12	.364
HEATON, B.	13	5/5	1.000	2/4	.500	-/2	0	0	3	1	0	12	.923
STALEY, L.	13	1/4	.250	0/0	.000	-/2	0	2	1	0	0	2	.154
NEMCEK, R.	2	0/1	.000	0/0	.000	-/0	0	1	0	0	0	0	.000
CURRY, E.	2	0/0	.000	0/0	.000	-/1	0	1	2	0	0	0	.000
TURNER, S.	2	0/0	.000	0/0	.000	-/1	1	0	0	0	0	0	.000
CROWDER, T.	1	1/1	1.000	0/0	.000	-/0	0	0	0	0	0	2	2.000
BITTER, B.	1	0/0	.000	0/0	.000	-/0	0	1	0	0	0	0	.000
Totals	200	34/63	.540	18/28	.643	-/40	16	13	12	3	5	86	.430

Team Rebounds: Indiana State 5; Virginia Tech 4. Disqualified: Virginia Tech—Henson, Price. Technical fouls: None.

	1st Half	2nd Half	Final
Virginia Tech	26	43	69
Indiana State	40	46	86

Texas (76) Coach: Abe Lemons

	Min.	Total FG/FGA	Pct.	FT/FTA	Pct.	Reb. O/T	A	TO	PF	S	Blk	TP	PPM
DANKS	24	3/4	.750	2/2	1.000	-/3	0	1	2	0	0	8	.333
BRANYAN	40	8/20	.400	4/5	.800	-/10	1	2	1	0	0	20	.500
STROUD	37	5/8	.625	0/0	.000	-/12	1	7	4	0	0	10	.270
MOORE	40	7/20	.350	4/6	.667	-/7	7	2	5	3	1	18	.450
KRIVACS	40	7/19	.368	2/2	1.000	-/2	2	1	1	0	0	16	.400
BAXTER	16	1/7	.143	0/0	.000	-/5	0	0	1	1	0	2	.125
DOTSON	3	0/1	.000	2/2	1.000	-/2	0	0	0	0	0	2	.667
Totals	200	31/79	.392	14/17	.824	-/41	11	13	14	4	1	76	.380

Oklahoma (90) Coach: Dave Bliss

	Min.	Total FG/FGA	Pct.	FT/FTA	Pct.	Reb. O/T	A	TO	PF	S	Blk	TP	PPM
CURRY, A.	30	7/11	.636	0/0	.000	-/6	5	2	0	0	1	14	.467
STOTTS, T.	40	6/10	.600	0/0	.000	-/5	4	1	3	1	1	12	.300
BEAL, A.	36	5/11	.455	0/2	.000	-/9	0	2	4	0	5	10	.278
MCCULLOUGH, J.	40	8/15	.533	1/1	1.000	-/7	11	4	1	0	0	17	.425
WHITLEY, R.	28	10/12	.833	5/5	1.000	-/1	4	4	0	0	0	25	.893
CARRABINE, C.	22	4/6	.667	2/2	1.000	-/2	4	0	2	0	1	10	.455
PACE, L.	4	1/1	1.000	0/0	.000	-/1	0	0	0	0	1	2	.500
Totals	200	41/66	.621	8/10	.800	-/31	28	13	14	1	10	90	.450

Team Rebounds: Oklahoma 1; Texas 1. Disqualified: Texas—Moore. Technical fouls: Texas—Stroud.

	1st Half	2nd Half	Final
Texas	39	37	76
Oklahoma	49	41	90

REGIONAL SEMIFINAL EAST

St. John's (67) Coach: Lou Carnesecca

	Min.	Total FG/FGA	Pct.	FT/FTA	Pct.	Reb. O/T	A	TO	PF	S	Blk	TP	PPM
PLAIR, R.	25	2/7	.286	0/0	.000	-/3	0	1	5	0	0	4	.160
GILROY, F.	27	2/5	.400	0/0	.000	-/8	0	1	4	2	2	4	.148
MCKOY, W.	27	5/12	.417	0/0	.000	-/7	1	1	4	1	0	10	.370
RENCHER, B.	26	3/9	.333	1/1	1.000	-/0	4	2	3	2	0	7	.269
CARTER, R.	38	9/16	.563	4/5	.800	-/5	0	4	2	0	0	22	.579
WRIGHT, R.	21	2/4	.500	2/2	1.000	-/4	0	2	0	1	0	6	.286
THOMAS, G.	28	7/10	.700	0/1	.000	-/2	3	2	2	3	0	14	.500
BOLLINGER, R.	8	0/1	.000	0/0	.000	-/1	1	0	1	0	0	0	.000
Totals	200	30/64	.469	7/9	.778	-/30	9	13	21	9	2	67	.335

Pennsylvania (84) Coach: Bob Weinhauer

	Min.	Total FG/FGA	Pct.	FT/FTA	Pct.	Reb. O/T	A	TO	PF	S	Blk	TP	PPM
PRICE, T.	35	7/10	.700	6/7	.857	-/7	6	5	4	2	1	20	.571
SMITH, T.	35	9/17	.529	0/0	.000	-/8	3	2	2	2	0	18	.514
WHITE, M.	24	5/10	.500	1/3	.333	-/8	3	4	4	1	0	11	.458
SALTERS, J.	34	5/9	.556	4/4	1.000	-/1	2	3	3	2	0	14	.412
WILLIS, B.	30	4/13	.308	0/0	.000	-/1	5	3	1	2	0	8	.267
LEIFSEN, T.	13	1/1	1.000	0/0	.000	-/2	0	3	1	0	0	2	.154
HALL, K.	17	0/2	.000	11/12	.917	-/1	1	2	1	0	0	11	.647
ROSS, V.	12	0/1	.000	0/0	.000	-/3	0	1	3	2	0	0	.000
Totals	200	31/63	.492	22/26	.846	-/31	20	23	19	11	1	84	.420

Rutgers (65) Coach: Tom Young

	Min.	Total FG/FGA	Pct.	FT/FTA	Pct.	Reb. O/T	A	TO	PF	S	Blk	TP	PPM
ANDERSON, A.	38	5/10	.500	2/5	.400	-/7	1	1	1	2	0	12	.316
TROY, K.	38	6/10	.600	3/5	.600	-/10	2	5	2	1	1	15	.395
BAILEY, J.	38	9/15	.600	1/1	1.000	-/6	0	2	2	1	4	19	.500
STRICKLAND, D.	32	4/10	.400	3/5	.600	-/3	3	4	4	0	0	11	.344
BROWN, T.	38	2/4	.500	2/2	1.000	-/1	6	4	3	0	0	6	.158
GRIFFIN, D.	10	0/0	.000	0/0	.000	-/1	1	1	2	1	0	0	.000
MCDANIEL, J.	4	0/0	.000	2/2	1.000	-/0	0	0	0	0	0	2	.500
CLARKE, B.	2	0/0	.000	0/1	.000	-/0	1	0	0	0	0	0	.000
Totals	200	26/49	.531	13/21	.619	-/28	14	17	14	5	5	65	.325

Team Rebounds: St. John's 3; Rutgers 3. Disqualified: St. John's—Plair. Technical fouls: None.

	1st Half	2nd Half	Final
St. John's	34	33	67
Rutgers	38	27	65

Syracuse (76) Coach: Jim Boeheim

	Min.	Total FG/FGA	Pct.	FT/FTA	Pct.	Reb. O/T	A	TO	PF	S	Blk	TP	PPM
SHACKLEFORD, D.	38	7/10	.700	2/2	1.000	-/4	7	5	4	0	0	16	.421
ORR, L.	30	5/10	.500	3/8	.375	-/6	0	3	4	1	0	13	.433
BOUIE, R.	38	5/8	.625	3/6	.500	-/14	0	5	1	2	6	13	.342
COHEN, H.	13	0/1	.000	0/0	.000	-/1	3	2	1	1	0	0	.000
HEADD, M.	32	5/9	.556	3/5	.600	-/3	2	5	2	3	0	13	.406
MOSS, E.	24	5/9	.556	1/2	.500	-/3	4	2	5	0	1	11	.458
HARMON, R.	7	1/1	1.000	0/0	.000	-/0	0	0	2	0	0	2	.286
SCHAYES, D.	3	1/1	1.000	0/0	.000	-/0	0	0	0	0	0	2	.667
CUBIT, M.	15	3/6	.500	0/0	.000	-/0	3	3	5	3	0	6	.400
Totals	200	32/60	.533	12/23	.522	-/31	19	25	24	10	7	76	.380

Team Rebounds: Pennsylvania 4; Syracuse 4. Disqualified: Syracuse—Moss, Cubit. Technical fouls: None.

	1st Half	2nd Half	Final
Pennsylvania	50	34	84
Syracuse	37	39	76

REGIONAL SEMIFINAL MIDEAST

Michigan State (87)   Coach: Jud Heathcote

	Min.	Total FG/FGA	Pct.	FT/FTA	Pct.	Reb. O/T	A	TO	PF	S	Blk	TP	PPM
KELSER, G.	-	6/15	.400	3/5	.600	-/9	1	4	5	3	2	15	-
JOHNSON, E.	-	5/16	.313	14/15	.933	-/5	12	3	2	3	0	24	-
DONNELLY, T.	-	2/5	.400	0/0	.000	-/1	2	3	2	0	0	4	-
BRKOVICH, M.	-	4/7	.571	3/4	.750	-/3	3	1	0	1	0	11	-
LLOYD, G.	-	0/0	.000	0/0	.000	-/0	1	2	2	0	0	0	-
CHARLES, R.	-	6/10	.600	6/10	.600	-/14	1	1	1	1	0	18	-
LONGAKER, M.	-	1/3	.333	0/0	.000	-/0	0	0	1	0	0	2	-
GONZALEZ, R.	-	4/7	.571	1/2	.500	-/1	0	2	1	2	0	9	-
KAYE, R.	-	1/1	1.000	0/0	.000	-/1	0	0	1	0	0	2	-
GILKIE, G.	-	0/1	.000	0/0	.000	-/0	0	1	0	0	0	0	-
BRKOVICH, D.	-	1/1	1.000	0/0	.000	-/1	1	1	0	0	0	2	-
Totals	200	30/66	.455	27/36	.750	-/35	21	18	15	10	2	87	.435

Louisiana State (71)   Coach: Dale Brown

	Min.	Total FG/FGA	Pct.	FT/FTA	Pct.	Reb. O/T	A	TO	PF	S	Blk	TP	PPM
GREEN, L.	-	5/8	.625	2/2	1.000	-/15	0	5	4	1	3	12	-
COOK, G.	-	1/2	.500	0/0	.000	-/6	1	1	5	1	1	2	-
MATTICK, R.	-	3/3	1.000	1/1	1.000	-/4	0	0	3	0	1	7	-
GREEN, A.	-	4/9	.444	3/4	.750	-/3	1	6	3	2	0	11	-
MARTIN, E.	-	2/6	.333	0/0	.000	-/2	7	3	1	1	0	4	-
HULTBERG, J.	-	11/20	.550	3/4	.750	-/3	3	3	4	0	1	25	-
BROWN, E.	-	0/4	.000	0/2	.000	-/0	1	2	5	1	0	0	-
CAMPBELL, A.	-	0/0	.000	0/0	.000	-/0	0	0	1	0	0	0	-
RUDOLPH, G.	-	3/3	1.000	0/0	.000	-/4	0	3	2	1	1	6	-
SIMS, W.	-	0/3	.000	0/0	.000	-/0	0	0	0	0	0	0	-
BERGERON, J.	-	2/6	.333	0/0	.000	-/0	1	2	0	0	0	4	-
Totals	200	31/64	.484	9/13	.692	-/37	14	25	28	7	7	71	.355

Team Rebounds: Michigan St. 4; Louisiana St. 3. Disqualified: Michigan St.—Kelser; Louisiana St.—Cook, Brown. Technical fouls: Louisiana St.—bench 2.

	1st Half	2nd Half	Final
Michigan St.	36	51	87
Louisiana St.	19	52	71

Notre Dame (79)   Coach: Digger Phelps

	Min.	Total FG/FGA	Pct.	FT/FTA	Pct.	Reb. O/T	A	TO	PF	S	Blk	TP	PPM
WOOLRIDGE, O.	25	5/11	.455	1/2	.500	-/6	0	-	2	-	-	11	.440
TRIPUCKA, K.	33	8/12	.667	8/8	1.000	-/4	1	-	4	-	-	24	.727
LAIMBEER, B.	29	3/5	.600	2/2	1.000	-/5	1	-	3	-	-	8	.276
BRANNING, R.	31	4/9	.444	2/3	.667	-/2	3	-	2	-	-	10	.323
HANZLIK, B.	29	4/6	.667	6/8	.750	-/4	2	-	4	-	-	14	.483
JACKSON, T.	22	2/6	.333	0/2	.000	-/6	1	-	0	-	-	4	.182
FLOWERS, B.	11	1/1	1.000	4/4	1.000	-/3	2	-	2	-	-	6	.545
WILCOX, S.	4	0/1	.000	0/0	.000	-/0	1	-	0	-	-	0	.000
MITCHELL, M.	16	1/1	1.000	0/0	.000	-/1	4	-	0	-	-	2	.125
Totals	200	28/52	.538	23/29	.793	-/31	15	-	17	-	-	79	.395

Toledo (71)   Coach: Bob Nichols

	Min.	Total FG/FGA	Pct.	FT/FTA	Pct.	Reb. O/T	A	TO	PF	S	Blk	TP	PPM
SWANEY	35	10/14	.714	6/6	1.000	-/4	1	-	3	-	-	26	.743
APPEL	12	2/3	.667	0/0	.000	-/3	1	-	0	-	-	4	.333
MILLER, D.	39	8/15	.533	2/4	.500	-/10	5	-	4	-	-	18	.462
JOPLIN	30	0/5	.000	0/2	.000	-/3	4	-	1	-	-	0	.000
LEHMAN, J.	32	4/8	.500	0/0	.000	-/2	5	-	4	-	-	8	.250
SELGO	22	4/6	.667	0/0	.000	-/2	1	-	1	-	-	8	.364
MONTAGUE, K.	6	0/0	.000	0/0	.000	-/0	0	-	0	-	-	0	.000
KNUCKLES, H.	23	3/10	.300	1/2	.500	-/3	1	-	5	-	-	7	.304
MATHIS	1	0/0	.000	0/0	.000	-/0	0	-	2	-	-	0	.000
Totals	200	31/61	.508	9/14	.643	-/27	18	-	20	-	-	71	.355

Disqualified: Toledo—Knuckles.

	1st Half	2nd Half	Final
Notre Dame	43	36	79
Toledo	33	38	71

REGIONAL SEMIFINAL WEST

DePaul (62)   Coach: Ray Meyer

	Min.	Total FG/FGA	Pct.	FT/FTA	Pct.	Reb. O/T	A	TO	PF	S	Blk	TP	PPM
WATKINS, C.	40	6/12	.500	7/8	.875	-/7	1	-	2	1	1	19	.475
AGUIRRE, M.	40	7/17	.412	5/5	1.000	-/4	4	-	1	1	0	19	.475
MITCHEM, J.	30	1/5	.200	0/0	.000	-/3	1	-	3	0	1	2	.067
BRADSHAW, C.	40	2/7	.286	3/4	.750	-/3	6	-	4	3	0	7	.175
GARLAND, G.	40	7/14	.500	1/2	.500	-/8	3	-	2	3	0	15	.375
MADLEY	10	0/0	.000	0/1	.000	-/0	2	-	0	0	0	0	.000
Totals	200	23/55	.418	16/20	.800	-/25	17	6	12	8	2	62	.310

Marquette (56)   Coach: Hank Raymonds

	Min.	Total FG/FGA	Pct.	FT/FTA	Pct.	Reb. O/T	A	TO	PF	S	Blk	TP	PPM
TOONE, B.	40	11/21	.524	4/4	1.000	-/7	0	-	2	0	0	26	.650
BYRD	40	4/5	.800	1/1	1.000	-/11	1	-	2	1	0	9	.225
BALL	28	2/5	.400	1/2	.500	-/3	0	-	5	0	0	5	.179
WILSON	37	2/6	.333	2/2	1.000	-/1	1	-	5	1	4	6	.162
WORTHEN	40	4/10	.400	0/0	.000	-/5	5	-	5	0	1	8	.200
LEE	10	1/3	.333	0/0	.000	-/3	0	-	1	0	0	2	.200
GREEN	2	0/3	.000	0/0	.000	-/0	1	-	1	0	0	0	.000
MARQUARDT	1	0/0	.000	0/0	.000	-/0	0	-	0	0	0	0	.000
DAVIS	2	0/0	.000	0/0	.000	-/0	0	-	0	0	0	0	.000
Totals	200	24/53	.453	8/9	.889	-/30	8	17	21	2	5	56	.280

Team Rebounds: DePaul 0; Marquette 0. Disqualified: Marquette—Ball, Worthen, Wilson. Technical fouls: None.

	1st Half	2nd Half	Final
DePaul	31	31	62
Marquette	28	28	56

UCLA (99)   Coach: Gary Cunningham

	Min.	Total FG/FGA	Pct.	FT/FTA	Pct.	Reb. O/T	A	TO	PF	S	Blk	TP	PPM
GREENWOOD, D.	38	6/11	.545	7/8	.875	-/5	3	3	3	1	1	19	.500
VANDEWEGHE, K.	39	5/12	.417	1/1	1.000	-/13	1	1	2	1	0	11	.282
SIMS, G.	5	0/1	.000	0/0	.000	-/0	0	4	0	4	0	2	.000
HOLLAND, B.	39	11/18	.611	0/0	.000	-/2	6	1	1	1	0	22	.564
HAMILTON, R.	39	15/20	.750	6/9	.667	-/4	7	2	2	0	0	36	.923
ALLUMS, D.	11	0/1	.000	0/0	.000	-/3	1	1	4	0	0	0	.000
WILKES, J.	25	4/5	.800	0/1	.000	-/3	2	2	1	0	0	8	.320
NAULLS, T.	1	1/1	1.000	1/2	.500	-/1	0	0	0	0	0	3	3.000
SANDERS, M.	1	0/0	.000	0/0	.000	-/0	0	1	0	1	0	0	.000
THOMAS, M.	1	0/1	.000	0/0	.000	-/0	1	0	0	0	0	0	.000
KELLY, R.	1	0/0	.000	0/0	.000	-/0	0	0	0	0	0	0	.000
Totals	200	42/70	.600	15/21	.714	-/31	21	11	17	4	3	99	.490

San Francisco (81)   Coach: Dan Belluomini

	Min.	Total FG/FGA	Pct.	FT/FTA	Pct.	Reb. O/T	A	TO	PF	S	Blk	TP	PPM
BOWERS, B.	28	2/4	.500	0/0	.000	-/5	1	2	2	0	0	4	.143
WILLIAMS, G.	37	5/12	.417	2/6	.333	-/2	3	3	4	1	0	12	.324
CARTWRIGHT, B.	35	12/19	.632	10/12	.833	-/9	1	4	4	0	1	34	.971
JEMISON, D.	26	2/5	.400	0/0	.000	-/8	0	4	5	0	0	4	.154
REID, B.	34	5/10	.500	3/4	.750	-/2	4	0	4	1	0	13	.382
GILBERG, E.	2	1/1	1.000	0/0	.000	-/0	1	1	1	0	0	2	1.000
DELOATCH, M.	6	0/2	.000	0/0	.000	-/0	0	0	0	0	0	0	.000
MCALISTER, K.	7	1/3	.333	0/0	.000	-/1	0	0	0	0	0	2	.286
BRYANT, W.	20	5/9	.556	0/0	.000	-/4	1	1	1	0	0	10	.500
CORNELIOUS, D.	5	0/0	.000	0/0	.000	-/0	3	1	1	0	0	0	.000
Totals	200	33/65	.508	15/22	.682	-/31	14	16	22	2	1	81	.405

Team Rebounds: UCLA 6; San Francisco 5. Disqualified: San Francisco—Jemison. Technical fouls: None.

	1st Qtr.	2nd Qtr.	3rd Qtr.	4th Qtr.	Final
UCLA	18	23	29	29	99
San Francisco	23	20	21	17	81

REGIONAL SEMIFINAL MIDWEST

Arkansas (73)   Coach: Eddie Sutton

	Min.	Total FG/FGA	Pct.	FT/FTA	Pct.	Reb. O/T	A	TO	PF	S	Blk	TP	PPM
ZAHN, A.	40	3/5	.600	0/0	.000	-/3	4	-	4	-	-	6	.150
HASTINGS, S.	40	3/9	.333	4/5	.800	-/8	2	-	3	-	-	10	.250
SCHALL, S.	25	2/3	.667	4/4	1.000	-/7	0	-	5	-	-	8	.320
REED, U.	34	8/17	.471	2/5	.400	-/3	2	-	0	-	-	18	.529
MONCRIEF, S.	40	7/12	.583	13/14	.929	-/12	1	-	4	-	-	27	.675
BROWN, T.	14	0/1	.000	0/1	.000	-/1	1	-	1	-	-	0	.000
CROCKETT, J.	7	2/3	.667	0/0	.000	-/1	0	-	2	-	-	4	.571
Totals	200	25/50	.500	23/29	.793	-/35	10	-	19	-	-	73	.365

Louisville (62)   Coach: Denny Crum

	Min.	Total FG/FGA	Pct.	FT/FTA	Pct.	Reb. O/T	A	TO	PF	S	Blk	TP	PPM
WILLIAMS, L.	40	5/10	.500	1/2	.500	-/6	5	-	3	-	-	11	.275
TURNER, B.	30	3/9	.333	6/6	1.000	-/7	0	-	1	-	-	12	.400
MCCRAY, S.	40	5/12	.417	4/4	1.000	-/7	2	-	4	-	-	14	.350
GRIFFITH, D.	30	5/14	.357	2/2	1.000	-/2	1	-	5	-	-	12	.400
SMITH, D.	23	0/4	.000	3/4	.750	-/2	0	-	4	-	-	3	.130
EAVES, J.	4	0/0	.000	0/0	.000	-/0	0	-	1	-	-	0	.000
BURKMAN, R.	9	0/0	.000	0/0	.000	-/0	1	-	5	-	-	0	.000
BRANCH, T.	24	3/5	.600	4/5	.800	-/3	1	-	5	-	-	10	.417
Totals	200	21/54	.389	20/23	.870	-/27	10	-	28	-	-	62	.310

Team Rebounds: Arkansas 0; Louisville 2. Disqualified: Arkansas—Schall; Louisville—Branch, Griffith, Burkman. Technical fouls: None.

	1st Half	2nd Half	Final
Arkansas	38	35	73
Louisville	26	36	62

Indiana State (93)   Coach: Bill Hodges

	Min.	Total FG/FGA	Pct.	FT/FTA	Pct.	Reb. O/T	A	TO	PF	S	Blk	TP	PPM
MILEY, B.	-	3/3	1.000	0/0	.000	-/3	1	2	1	0	0	6	-
GILBERT, A.	-	6/7	.857	0/3	.000	-/9	0	2	2	0	1	12	-
BIRD, L.	-	11/19	.579	7/8	.875	-/15	5	8	0	1	0	29	-
NICKS, C.	-	8/16	.500	4/9	.444	-/3	5	4	2	1	0	20	-
REED, S.	-	0/3	.000	4/4	1.000	-/2	2	3	5	0	0	4	-
HEATON, B.	-	3/3	1.000	3/3	1.000	-/2	0	0	2	1	0	9	-
STALEY, L.	-	3/6	.500	3/4	.750	-/7	0	3	0	0	0	9	-
NEMCEK, R.	-	1/1	1.000	2/3	.667	-/2	0	1	0	0	0	4	-
CURRY, E.	-	0/1	.000	0/0	.000	-/1	0	1	0	0	0	0	-
TURNER, S.	-	0/0	.000	0/0	.000	-/0	0	0	0	0	0	0	-
CROWDER, T.	-	0/0	.000	0/0	.000	-/1	0	1	1	0	0	0	-
MCNELLY, R.	-	0/1	.000	0/0	.000	-/2	0	1	0	0	0	0	-
Totals	200	35/60	.583	23/34	.676	-/47	13	23	16	3	1	93	.465

Oklahoma (72)   Coach: Dave Bliss

	Min.	Total FG/FGA	Pct.	FT/FTA	Pct.	Reb. O/T	A	TO	PF	S	Blk	TP	PPM
CURRY, A.	33	5/15	.333	1/2	.500	-/4	2	1	3	4	1	11	.333
STOTTS, T.	37	2/11	.182	1/2	.500	-/2	2	1	4	1	0	5	.135
BEAL, A.	22	5/7	.714	0/0	.000	-/4	0	3	5	0	0	10	.455
MCCULLOUGH, J.	36	6/10	.600	2/2	1.000	-/7	3	1	5	3	0	14	.389
WHITLEY, R.	36	9/12	.750	6/9	.667	-/1	0	8	4	0	0	24	.667
CARRABINE, C.	19	2/7	.286	0/2	.000	-/0	1	0	0	0	0	4	.211
PACE, L.	13	2/6	.333	0/0	.000	-/1	0	0	4	0	0	4	.308
DODD, K.	1	0/0	.000	0/0	.000	-/0	0	0	1	0	0	0	.000
PURVIS, I.	2	0/1	.000	0/0	.000	-/0	0	0	0	0	0	0	.000
CALVERT, D.	1	0/1	.000	0/0	.000	-/0	0	0	1	0	0	0	.000
Totals	200	31/70	.443	10/17	.588	-/19	8	14	27	8	1	72	.360

Team Rebounds: Indiana State 3; Oklahoma 3. Disqualified: Indiana State—Reed; Oklahoma—McCullough, Beal. Technical fouls: Oklahoma—Beal.

	1st Half	2nd Half	Final
Indiana State	45	48	93
Oklahoma	37	35	72

REGIONAL FINAL EAST

St. John's (62)   Coach: Lou Carnesecca

	Min.	Total FG/FGA	Pct.	FT/FTA	Pct.	Reb. O/T	A	TO	PF	S	Blk	TP	PPM
PLAIR, R.	37	9/9	1.000	3/3	1.000	-/6	1	5	3	2	1	21	.568
GILROY, F.	34	0/4	.000	4/4	1.000	-/6	2	0	5	0	1	4	.118
MCKOY, W.	28	7/14	.500	1/4	.250	-/7	1	2	3	0	0	15	.536
RENCHER, B.	25	3/8	.375	0/0	.000	-/3	5	5	5	1	1	6	.240
CARTER, R.	28	2/9	.222	0/1	.000	-/3	1	2	5	0	0	4	.143
WRIGHT, R.	12	1/1	1.000	0/0	.000	-/3	0	1	0	1	0	2	.167
THOMAS, G.	26	3/9	.333	4/4	1.000	-/3	6	2	0	0	0	10	.385
CALABRESE, T.	10	0/1	.000	0/0	.000	-/0	1	1	1	0	0	0	.000
Totals	200	25/55	.455	12/16	.750	-/31	17	18	22	4	3	62	.310

Pennsylvania (64)   Coach: Bob Weinhauer

	Min.	Total FG/FGA	Pct.	FT/FTA	Pct.	Reb. O/T	A	TO	PF	S	Blk	TP	PPM
PRICE, T.	29	7/11	.636	7/12	.583	-/4	0	3	4	1	0	21	.724
SMITH, T.	39	7/14	.500	2/2	1.000	-/3	0	3	4	1	0	16	.410
WHITE, M.	24	0/3	.000	3/4	.750	-/9	0	3	5	0	0	3	.125
SALTERS, J.	31	2/6	.333	3/4	.750	-/0	5	2	2	2	0	7	.226
WILLIS, B.	35	3/8	.375	4/4	1.000	-/3	5	2	3	4	0	10	.286
LEIFSEN, T.	11	0/0	.000	0/0	.000	-/0	0	1	1	0	0	0	.000
HALL, K.	15	2/3	.667	1/1	1.000	-/1	0	2	0	0	0	5	.333
ROSS, V.	16	1/1	1.000	0/0	.000	-/5	0	1	2	2	0	2	.125
Totals	200	22/46	.478	20/27	.741	-/25	10	17	21	10	0	64	.320

Team Rebounds: Pennsylvania 3; St. John's 6. Disqualified: Pennsylvania—White; St. John's—Rencher, Carter, Gilroy. Technical fouls: None.

	1st Half	2nd Half	Final
St. John's	26	36	62
Pennsylvania	29	35	64

REGIONAL FINAL MIDEAST

Michigan State (80)   Coach: Jud Heathcote

	Min.	Total FG/FGA	Pct.	FT/FTA	Pct.	Reb. O/T	A	TO	PF	S	Blk	TP	PPM
KELSER, G.	39	15/25	.600	4/8	.500	-/13	1	3	4	1	2	34	.872
JOHNSON, E.	40	6/10	.600	7/8	.875	-/5	13	3	2	2	0	19	.475
VINCENT, J.	3	1/2	.500	0/0	.000	-/0	0	0	0	0	0	2	.667
DONNELLY, T.	36	1/1	1.000	2/2	1.000	-/2	0	1	3	1	1	4	.111
BRKOVICH, M.	38	5/10	.500	3/4	.750	-/3	1	2	1	0	0	13	.342
CHARLES, R.	32	2/4	.500	2/2	1.000	-/4	0	0	4	0	0	6	.188
LONGAKER, M.	1	0/0	.000	0/0	.000	-/0	0	0	0	0	0	0	.000
GONZALEZ, R.	11	1/2	.500	0/0	.000	-/3	0	1	2	0	0	2	.182
Totals	200	31/54	.574	18/24	.750	-/30	15	10	16	4	3	80	.400

Notre Dame (68)   Coach: Digger Phelps

	Min.	Total FG/FGA	Pct.	FT/FTA	Pct.	Reb. O/T	A	TO	PF	S	Blk	TP	PPM
TRIPUCKA, K.	34	4/11	.364	0/0	.000	-/4	1	1	4	2	1	8	.235
WOOLRIDGE, O.	18	1/6	.167	1/2	.500	-/3	0	0	1	0	0	3	.167
FLOWERS, B.	16	0/1	.000	0/0	.000	-/6	1	4	3	2	1	0	.000
BRANNING, R.	33	4/14	.286	0/0	.000	-/3	4	2	4	1	0	8	.242
HANZLIK, B.	30	7/12	.583	5/5	1.000	-/5	4	0	5	1	0	19	.633
MITCHELL, M.	4	0/0	.000	0/0	.000	-/0	0	0	0	0	0	0	.000
JACKSON, T.	31	9/13	.692	1/4	.250	-/6	1	2	4	0	0	19	.613
LAIMBEER, B.	20	3/5	.600	1/2	.500	-/4	1	3	3	1	2	7	.350
WILCOX, S.	14	2/4	.500	0/0	.000	-/1	2	0	0	0	0	4	.286
Totals	200	30/66	.455	8/13	.615	-/32	14	12	24	7	4	68	.340

Team Rebounds: Michigan St. 3; Notre Dame 3. Disqualified: Notre Dame—Hanzlik. Technical fouls: None.

	1st Half	2nd Half	Final
Michigan St.	34	46	80
Notre Dame	23	45	68

REGIONAL FINAL WEST

DePaul (95)   Coach: Ray Meyer

	Min.	Total FG/FGA	Pct.	FT/FTA	Pct.	Reb. O/T	A	TO	PF	S	Blk	TP	PPM
WATKINS, C.	38	9/10	.900	6/6	1.000	-/8	3	3	4	1	1	24	.632
AGUIRRE, M.	40	9/16	.563	2/3	.667	-/3	2	2	3	1	0	20	.500
MITCHEM, J.	40	6/10	.600	2/5	.400	-/9	1	1	2	0	1	14	.350
BRADSHAW, C.	40	3/8	.375	7/11	.636	-/5	7	1	4	1	0	13	.325
GARLAND, G.	40	10/20	.500	4/4	1.000	-/8	8	11	3	2	0	24	.600
NIKITAS, C.	1	0/0	.000	0/0	.000	-/0	1	0	0	0	0	0	.000
MADEY, W.	1	0/0	.000	0/0	.000	-/0	0	0	0	0	0	0	.000
Totals	200	37/64	.578	21/29	.724	-/33	22	18	16	5	2	95	.475

UCLA (91)   Coach: Gary Cunningham

	Min.	Total FG/FGA	Pct.	FT/FTA	Pct.	Reb. O/T	A	TO	PF	S	Blk	TP	PPM
GREENWOOD, D.	-	17/24	.708	3/4	.750	-/10	2	4	4	0	2	37	-
VANDEWEGHE, K.	-	7/17	.412	3/3	1.000	-/9	1	2	2	2	1	17	-
SIMS, G.	-	0/0	.000	0/0	.000	-/2	0	1	0	0	1	0	-
HOLLAND, B.	-	6/15	.400	7/8	.875	-/2	2	4	4	1	0	19	-
HAMILTON, R.	-	8/12	.667	0/2	.000	-/2	10	5	4	2	0	16	-
ALLUMS, D.	-	0/0	.000	0/0	.000	-/1	1	0	4	0	1	0	-
WILKES, J.	-	1/3	.333	0/0	.000	-/2	1	0	5	1	0	2	-
NAULLS, T.	-	0/0	.000	0/0	.000	-/0	0	1	1	0	0	0	-
SANDERS, M.	-	0/0	.000	0/0	.000	-/1	0	0	1	1	0	0	-
THOMAS, M.	-	0/2	.000	0/0	.000	-/1	0	0	2	0	0	0	-
Totals	200	39/73	.534	13/17	.765	-/29	17	18	27	6	5	91	.455

Team Rebounds: DePaul 5; UCLA 6. Disqualified: UCLA—Wilkes. Technical fouls: None.

	1st Half	2nd Half	Final
DePaul	51	44	95
UCLA	34	57	91

REGIONAL FINAL MIDWEST

Arkansas (71) Coach: Eddie Sutton

	Min.	Total FG/FGA	Pct.	FT/FTA	Pct.	Reb. O/T	A	TO	PF	S	Blk	TP	PPM
ZAHN, A.	-	5/7	.714	0/0	.000	-/3	3	-	3	-	-	10	-
HASTINGS, S.	-	3/7	.429	4/4	1.000	-/3	3	-	2	-	-	10	-
SCHALL, S.	-	6/7	.857	0/2	.000	-/4	2	-	4	-	-	12	-
REED, U.	-	4/8	.500	3/3	1.000	-/4	2	-	5	-	-	11	-
MONCRIEF, S.	-	10/16	.625	4/4	1.000	-/8	2	-	2	-	-	24	-
BROWN, T.	-	0/0	.000	0/0	.000	-/0	1	-	0	-	-	0	-
YOUNG, M.	-	2/2	1.000	0/0	.000	-/1	1	-	1	-	-	4	-
Totals	200	30/47	.638	11/13	.846	-/23	14	10	17	0	0	71	.355

Indiana State (73) Coach: Bill Hodges

	Min.	Total FG/FGA	Pct.	FT/FTA	Pct.	Reb. O/T	A	TO	PF	S	Blk	TP	PPM
GILBERT, A.	22	6/9	.667	0/0	.000	-/2	0	-	3	-	-	12	.545
MILLEY, B.	35	3/3	1.000	0/0	.000	-/4	3	-	2	-	-	6	.171
BIRD, L.	40	12/22	.545	7/8	.875	-/10	3	-	3	-	-	31	.775
REED, S.	32	0/1	.000	0/0	.000	-/0	5	-	3	-	-	0	.000
NICKS, C.	33	5/11	.455	3/4	.750	-/0	3	-	4	-	-	13	.394
HEATON, B.	16	4/5	.800	0/0	.000	-/1	0	-	0	-	-	8	.500
STALEY, L.	22	1/4	.250	1/3	.333	-/3	0	-	1	-	-	3	.136
Totals	200	31/55	.564	11/15	.733	-/20	14	7	16	2	2	73	.365

Team Rebounds: Indiana State 0; Arkansas 2. Disqualified: Arkansas—Reed. Techincal fouls: None.

	1st Half	2nd Half	Final
Arkansas	39	32	71
Indiana State	37	36	73

FINAL FOUR

Pennsylvania (67) Coach: Bob Weinhauer

	Min.	Total FG/FGA	Pct.	FT/FTA	Pct.	Reb. O/T	A	TO	PF	S	Blk	TP	PPM
PRICE, T.	-	7/18	.389	4/4	1.000	-/7	0	2	5	1	0	18	-
SMITH, T.	-	0/6	.000	0/0	.000	-/0	0	2	5	0	0	0	-
WHITE, M.	-	5/12	.417	3/4	.750	-/11	1	1	4	1	0	13	-
SALTERS, J.	-	1/5	.200	0/0	.000	-/1	3	2	2	0	0	2	-
WILLIS, B.	-	4/13	.308	1/3	.333	-/6	6	5	2	3	1	9	-
LEIFSEN, T.	-	0/1	.000	1/2	.500	-/4	0	2	1	0	0	1	-
HALL, K.	-	3/8	.375	0/1	.000	-/2	1	3	1	2	0	6	-
FLICK, T.	-	0/6	.000	6/6	1.000	-/2	1	1	3	1	0	6	-
ROSS, V.	-	2/6	.333	0/0	.000	-/6	0	2	3	0	1	4	-
REYNOLDS, A.	-	1/3	.333	0/0	.000	-/0	0	0	3	0	0	2	-
JACKSON, D.	-	1/2	.500	4/4	1.000	-/1	0	3	0	0	0	6	-
KUHL, E.	-	0/2	.000	0/0	.000	-/0	0	1	0	0	0	0	-
CONDON, T.	-	0/0	.000	0/0	.000	-/2	0	0	2	0	0	0	-
Totals	200	24/82	.293	19/24	.792	-/42	12	24	31	8	2	67	.335

Michigan State (101) Coach: Jud Heathcote

	Min.	Total FG/FGA	Pct.	FT/FTA	Pct.	Reb. O/T	A	TO	PF	S	Blk	TP	PPM
KELSER, G.	34	12/19	.632	4/6	.667	-/9	3	3	2	1	4	28	.824
JOHNSON, E.	35	9/10	.900	11/12	.917	-/10	10	4	2	3	0	29	.829
VINCENT, J.	9	0/1	.000	3/4	.750	-/1	0	1	2	0	0	3	.333
DONNELLY, T.	23	3/5	.600	0/0	.000	-/3	3	0	0	0	0	6	.261
BRKOVICH, M.	24	6/10	.600	0/0	.000	-/1	3	1	4	1	0	12	.500
LLOYD, G.	7	0/2	.000	6/7	.857	-/0	1	0	2	1	2	6	.857
CHARLES, R.	19	2/2	1.000	0/0	.000	-/6	0	2	4	0	2	4	.211
LONGAKER, M.	9	2/2	1.000	0/0	.000	-/2	1	1	0	2	0	4	.444
RUFFMAN, J.	5	0/0	.000	0/1	.000	-/2	1	1	2	0	0	0	.000
GONZALEZ, R.	22	1/5	.200	0/0	.000	-/3	1	3	2	1	0	2	.091
KAYE, R.	7	2/2	1.000	1/3	.333	-/2	1	1	1	0	0	5	.714
GILKIE, G.	3	0/1	.000	0/0	.000	-/1	0	0	1	0	0	0	.000
BRKOVICH, D.	3	1/1	1.000	0/1	.000	-/1	0	0	1	0	0	2	.667
Totals	200	38/60	.633	25/34	.735	-/41	24	19	22	10	6	101	.505

Team Rebounds: Michigan St. 3; Pennsylvania 2. Disqualified: Pennsylvania—Price, Smith. Technical fouls: None.

	1st Half	2nd Half	Final
Pennsylvania	17	50	67
Michigan St.	50	51	101

DePaul (74) Coach: Ray Meyer

	Min.	Total FG/FGA	Pct.	FT/FTA	Pct.	Reb. O/T	A	TO	PF	S	Blk	TP	PPM
WATKINS, C.	40	8/11	.727	0/0	.000	-/2	2	1	4	1	0	16	.400
AGUIRRE, M.	40	9/18	.500	1/2	.500	-/5	2	3	3	2	0	19	.475
MITCHEM, J.	40	6/11	.545	0/0	.000	-/5	0	1	4	1	1	12	.300
BRADSHAW, C.	40	4/8	.500	0/0	.000	-/3	4	2	1	3	0	8	.200
GARLAND, G.	40	9/18	.500	1/3	.333	-/4	8	1	2	4	0	19	.475
Totals	200	36/66	.643	2/5	.400	-/19	16	8	14	11	1	74	.370

Indiana State (76) Coach: Bill Hodges

	Min.	Total FG/FGA	Pct.	FT/FTA	Pct.	Reb. O/T	A	TO	PF	S	Blk	TP	PPM
MILEY, B.	-	2/2	1.000	0/0	.000	-/3	3	0	1	2	0	4	-
GILBERT, A.	-	6/7	.857	0/1	.000	-/5	0	1	2	0	2	12	-
BIRD, L.	-	16/19	.842	3/4	.750	-/16	9	11	3	1	0	35	-
NICKS, C.	-	4/13	.308	2/2	1.000	-/1	5	5	3	1	0	10	-
REED, S.	-	3/5	.600	0/0	.000	-/2	2	3	0	0	0	6	-
HEATON, B.	-	3/6	.500	0/0	.000	-/3	0	1	2	0	0	6	-
STALEY, L.	-	1/4	.250	1/2	.500	-/2	0	1	3	0	0	3	-
Totals	200	35/56	.625	6/9	.667	-/32	19	22	14	4	2	76	.380

Team Rebounds: Indiana State 2; DePaul 2. Disqualified: None. Technical fouls: None.

	1st Half	2nd Half	Final
DePaul	42	32	74
Indiana State	45	31	76

NATIONAL CHAMPIONSHIP

Michigan State (75)   Coach: Jud Heathcote

	Min.	Total FG/FGA	Pct.	FT/FTA	Pct.	Reb. O/T	A	TO	PF	S	Blk	TP	PPM
KELSER, G.	32	7/13	.538	5/6	.833	-/8	9	1	4	2	2	19	.594
JOHNSON, E.	35	8/15	.533	8/10	.800	-/7	5	6	3	1	0	24	.686
VINCENT, J.	19	2/5	.400	1/2	.500	-/2	0	1	4	1	0	5	.263
DONNELLY, T.	39	5/5	1.000	5/6	.833	-/4	0	2	2	1	0	15	.385
BRKOVICH, M.	39	1/2	.500	3/7	.429	-/4	1	5	1	0	0	5	.128
CHARLES, R.	31	3/3	1.000	1/2	.500	-/7	0	1	5	1	0	7	.226
LONGAKER, M.	2	0/0	.000	0/0	.000	-/0	0	0	0	0	0	0	.000
GONZALEZ, R.	3	0/0	.000	0/0	.000	-/0	0	0	0	0	0	0	.000
Totals	200	26/43	.605	23/33	.697	-/32	15	16	19	6	2	75	.375

Indiana State (64)   Coach: Bill Hodges

	Min.	Total FG/FGA	Pct.	FT/FTA	Pct.	Reb. O/T	A	TO	PF	S	Blk	TP	PPM
MILEY, B.	-	0/0	.000	0/1	.000	-/3	0	1	0	0	0	0	-
GILBERT, A.	-	2/3	.667	0/4	.000	-/4	0	1	4	0	1	4	-
BIRD, L.	-	7/21	.333	5/8	.625	-/13	2	6	3	5	1	19	-
NICKS, C.	-	7/14	.500	3/6	.500	-/2	4	2	5	1	0	17	-
REED, S.	-	4/9	.444	0/0	.000	-/0	9	0	4	0	0	8	-
HEATON, B.	-	4/14	.286	2/2	1.000	-/6	2	0	2	0	0	10	-
STALEY, L.	-	2/2	1.000	0/1	.000	-/3	0	0	2	0	0	4	-
NEMCEK, R.	-	1/1	1.000	0/0	.000	-/0	1	1	3	0	0	2	-
Totals	200	27/64	.422	10/22	.455	-/31	18	10	24	6	2	64	.320

Team Rebounds: Michigan St. 2; Indiana State 3. Disqualified: Michigan St.—Charles; Indiana State—Nicks. Technical fouls: Indiana State—Bird.

	1st Half	2nd Half	Final
Michigan St.	37	38	75
Indiana State	28	36	64

NATIONAL THIRD PLACE

DePaul (96)   Coach: Ray Meyer

	Min.	Total FG/FGA	Pct.	FT/FTA	Pct.	Reb. O/T	A	TO	PF	S	Blk	TP	PPM
WATKINS, C.	31	7/9	.778	4/5	.800	-/11	2	2	5	1	3	18	.581
AGUIRRE, M.	45	10/23	.435	14/15	.933	-/14	2	5	3	1	0	34	.756
MITCHEM, J.	45	3/11	.273	5/6	.833	-/5	2	2	4	1	2	11	.244
BRADSHAW, C.	43	2/6	.333	4/5	.800	-/2	7	2	3	3	0	8	.186
GARLAND, G.	36	9/18	.500	4/4	1.000	-/12	5	9	5	3	0	22	.611
MCGUIRE, D.	2	0/0	.000	0/0	.000	-/0	0	1	0	0	0	0	.000
NIKITAS, C.	11	0/0	.000	2/2	1.000	-/1	1	3	0	0	1	2	.182
MADEY, W.	12	0/1	.000	1/2	.500	-/3	0	0	1	0	1	1	.083
Totals	225	31/68	.456	34/39	.872	-/48	19	23	22	9	6	96	.427

Pennsylvania (93)   Coach: Bob Weinhauer

	Min.	Total FG/FGA	Pct.	FT/FTA	Pct.	Reb. O/T	A	TO	PF	S	Blk	TP	PPM
PRICE, T.	43	14/27	.519	3/4	.750	-/14	2	1	5	3	3	31	.721
SMITH, T.	27	8/16	.500	0/3	.000	-/3	2	3	5	1	1	16	.593
WHITE, M.	17	2/7	.286	0/0	.000	-/7	1	2	5	0	0	4	.235
SALTERS, J.	37	4/11	.364	0/0	.000	-/1	2	1	3	2	0	8	.216
WILLIS, B.	36	5/13	.385	4/5	.800	-/5	9	7	3	1	0	14	.389
LEIFSEN, T.	4	2/3	.667	0/0	.000	-/2	0	0	0	0	0	4	1.000
HALL, K.	27	3/7	.429	1/1	1.000	-/1	4	1	1	3	0	7	.259
FLICK, T.	11	1/6	.167	0/0	.000	-/3	0	0	3	0	0	2	.182
ROSS, V.	19	2/3	.667	3/6	.500	-/10	0	0	5	1	0	7	.368
CONDON, T.	3	0/1	.000	0/0	.000	-/1	0	0	1	0	0	0	.000
JACKSON, D.	1	0/0	.000	0/0	.000	-/0	0	0	0	0	0	0	.000
Totals	225	41/94	.436	11/19	.579	-/47	20	15	31	11	4	93	.413

Team Rebounds: DePaul 3; Pennsylvania 3. Disqualified: DePaul—Watkins, Garland; Pennsylvania—Price, Smith, White, Ross. Technical fouls: None.

	1st Half	2nd Half	1st OT	Final
DePaul	54	31	11	96
Pennsylvania	43	42	8	93

○ ALL-STAR TEAMS ○

ALL TOURNAMENT
MARK AGUIRRE	DEPAUL
LARRY BIRD	INDIANA STATE
GARY GARLAND	DEPAUL
★ EARVIN JOHNSON	MICHIGAN STATE
GREG KELSER	MICHIGAN STATE

EAST REGIONAL
REGGIE CARTER	ST. JOHN'S
WAYNE MCKOY	ST. JOHN'S
RON PLAIR	ST. JOHN'S
★ TONY PRICE	PENNSYLVANIA
TIM SMITH	PENNSYLVANIA

WEST REGIONAL
BILL CARTWRIGHT	SAN FRANCISCO
★ GARY GARLAND	DEPAUL
DAVID GREENWOOD	UCLA
ROY HAMILTON	UCLA
CURTIS WATKINS	DEPAUL

MIDEAST REGIONAL
BILL HANZLIK	NOTRE DAME
EARVIN JOHNSON	MICHIGAN STATE
★ GREG KELSER	MICHIGAN STATE
JIM SWANEY	TOLEDO
KELLY TRIPUCKA	NOTRE DAME

MIDWEST REGIONAL
★ LARRY BIRD	INDIANA STATE
SIDNEY MONCRIEF	ARKANSAS
CARL NICKS	INDIANA STATE
STEVE SCHALL	ARKANSAS
RAYMOND WHITLEY	OKLAHOMA

★ Most Outstanding Player(s)

☉ INDIVIDUAL RECORDS ☉

SCORING

Most points in a single game
1 DAVID GREENWOOD, UCLA (vs. DEPAUL)   37
2 ROY HAMILTON, UCLA (vs. SAN FRANCISCO) 36
3 LARRY BIRD, INDIANA STATE (vs. DEPAUL) 35
4 3 tied for fourth place.

Most total points in the tournament
1 TONY PRICE, PENNSYLVANIA   142
2 LARRY BIRD, INDIANA STATE   136
3 GREG KELSER, MICHIGAN ST.   127
4 MARK AGUIRRE, DEPAUL   117
5 EARVIN JOHNSON, MICHIGAN ST.   109

Highest scoring average (minimum 2 games)
1 BILL CARTWRIGHT, SAN FRANCISCO (58-2)
                                   29.00
2 LARRY BIRD, INDIANA STATE (136-5)   27.20
3 RICCARDO BROWN, PEPPERDINE (53-2)   26.50
4 GREG KELSER, MICHIGAN ST. (127-5)   25.40
5 DAVID GREENWOOD, UCLA (74-3)   24.67

FIELD GOALS

Most field goals in a single game
1 DAVID GREENWOOD, UCLA (vs. DEPAUL)   17
2 LARRY BIRD, INDIANA STATE (vs. DEPAUL) 16
3 GREG KELSER, MICHIGAN ST. (vs. NOTRE
   DAME)   15
3 ROY HAMILTON, UCLA (vs. SAN FRANCISCO) 15
5 TONY PRICE, PENNSYLVANIA (vs. DEPAUL)   14

Most total field goals in the tournament
1 TONY PRICE, PENNSYLVANIA   58
2 GREG KELSER, MICHIGAN ST.   52
2 LARRY BIRD, INDIANA STATE   52
4 MARK AGUIRRE, DEPAUL   45
5 GARY GARLAND, DEPAUL   42

Most field goal attempts in a single game
1 TONY PRICE, PENNSYLVANIA (vs. DEPAUL)   27
2 TERRY DUEROD, DETROIT (vs. LAMAR)   26
3 GREG KELSER, MICHIGAN ST. (vs. NOTRE
   DAME)   25
3 RICCARDO BROWN, PEPPERDINE (vs. UCLA)   25
5 2 tied for fifth place.

Most total field goal attempts in tournament
1 TONY PRICE, PENNSYLVANIA   105
2 LARRY BIRD, INDIANA STATE   95
3 GREG KELSER, MICHIGAN ST.   93
4 GARY GARLAND, DEPAUL   87
4 MARK AGUIRRE, DEPAUL   87

Highest field goal percentage in a single game
(minimum 10 attempts)
1 EARVIN JOHNSON, MICHIGAN ST. (vs.
   PENNSYLVANIA)
   (9-10)   .900
1 CURTIS WATKINS, DEPAUL (vs. UCLA)
   (9-10)   .900
1 S. SMITH, USC (vs. UTAH STATE) (9-10)   .900
4 LARRY BIRD, INDIANA STATE (vs. DEPAUL)
   (16-19)   .842
5 RAYMOND WHITLEY, OKLAHOMA (vs. TEXAS)
   (10-12)   .833

Highest field goal percentage in the tournament
(minimum 20 attempts)
1 RAYMOND WHITLEY, OKLAHOMA (19-24)   .792
2 ALEX GILBERT, INDIANA STATE (26-34)   .765
3 DAVID JOHNSON, WEBER ST. (20-27)   .741
4 S. SMITH, USC (16-22)   .727
5 ROOSEVELT BOUIE, SYRACUSE (14-20)   .700

FREE THROWS

Most free throws in a single game
1 MARK AGUIRRE, DEPAUL
   (vs. PENNSYLVANIA   14
1 EARVIN JOHNSON, MICHIGAN ST. (vs.
   LOUISIANA ST.)   14
3 SIDNEY MONCRIEF, ARKANSAS (vs.
   LOUISVILLE)   13
3 MIKE MCCAY, U. CONN. (vs. SYRACUSE)   13
5 3 tied for fifth place.

Most total free throws in the tournament
1 EARVIN JOHNSON, MICHIGAN ST.   41
2 LARRY BIRD, INDIANA STATE   32
3 MARK AGUIRRE, DEPAUL   27
4 3 tied for fourth place.

Most free throws attempted in a single game
1 CLARENCE KEA, LAMAR (vs. DETROIT)   20
2 DICK MILLER, TOLEDO (vs. IOWA)   17
3 MARK AGUIRRE, DEPAUL
   (vs. PENNSYLVANIA)   15
3 EARVIN JOHNSON, MICHIGAN ST. (vs.
   LOUISIANA ST.)   15
5 2 tied for fifth place.

Most free throws attempted in the tournament
1 EARVIN JOHNSON, MICHIGAN ST.   46
2 LARRY BIRD, INDIANA STATE   40
3 TONY PRICE, PENNSYLVANIA   36
4 GREG KELSER, MICHIGAN ST.   35
5 MARK AGUIRRE, DEPAUL   32

Highest free throw percentage in a single game
(minimum 7 attempts)
1 SIDNEY MONCRIEF, ARKANSAS
   (vs. WEBER ST.) (9-9)   1.000
2 KELLY TRIPUCKA, NOTRE DAME
   (vs. TOLEDO) (8-8)   1.000
2 GLENN VICKERS, IONA
   (vs. PENNSYLVANIA) (8-8)   1.000
4 MARK AGUIRRE, DEPAUL
   (vs. PENNSYLVANIA) (14-15)   .933
4 EARVIN JOHNSON, MICHIGAN ST.
   (vs. LOUISIANA ST.) (14-15)   .933

Highest free throw percentage in the tournament
(minimum 15 attempts)
1 SIDNEY MONCRIEF, ARKANSAS (26-27)   .963
2 KELLY TRIPUCKA, NOTRE DAME (17-18)   .944
3 KEN HALL, PENNSYLVANIA (19-21)   .905
4 CURTIS WATKINS, DEPAUL (26-29)   .897
5 EARVIN JOHNSON, MICHIGAN ST. (41-46)   .891

REBOUNDS

Most rebounds in a single game
1 CLARENCE KEA, LAMAR (vs. DETROIT)   19
2 EARVIN JOHNSON, MICHIGAN ST. (vs. LAMAR)
                                   17

3 LIONEL GREEN, LOUISIANA ST. (vs.
   APPALACHIAN ST.)   16
3 LARRY BIRD, INDIANA ST. (vs. DEPAUL)   16
5 3 tied for fifth place.

Most total rebounds in the tournament
1 LARRY BIRD, INDIANA STATE   67
2 TONY PRICE, PENNSYLVANIA   53
2 GREG KELSER, MICHIGAN ST.   53
4 MATT WHITE, PENNSYLVANIA   44
4 EARVIN JOHNSON, MICHIGAN ST.   44

Most rebounds per game (minimum 2 games)
1 LIONEL GREEN, LOUISIANA ST. (31-2)   15.50
2 LARRY BIRD, INDIANA STATE (67-5)   13.40
3 DICK MILLER, TOLEDO (24-2)   12.00
4 CLARENCE KEA, LAMAR (23-2)   11.50
5 GREG KELSER, MICHIGAN ST. (53-5)   10.60

ASSISTS

Most assists in a single game
1 EARVIN JOHNSON, MICHIGAN ST. (vs. NOTRE
   DAME)   13
2 EARVIN JOHNSON, MICHIGAN ST. (vs.
   LOUISIANA ST.)   12
2 GUY WILLIAMS, SAN FRANCISCO (vs. BRIGHAM
   YOUNG)   12
4 JOHN MCCULLOUGH, OKLAHOMA (vs. TEXAS) 11
5 3 tied for fifth place.

Most total assists in the tournament
1 EARVIN JOHNSON, MICHIGAN ST.   50
2 BOBBY WILLIS, PENNSYLVANIA   32
2 GARY GARLAND, DEPAUL   32
4 CLYDE BRADSHAW, DEPAUL   27
5 LARRY BIRD, INDIANA STATE   26

Most assists per game (minimum 2 appearances)
1 EARVIN JOHNSON, MICHIGAN ST. (50-5)   10.00
2 ROY HAMILTON, UCLA (24-3)   8.00
3 GUY WILLIAMS, SAN FRANCISCO (15-2)   7.50
4 JOHN MCCULLOUGH, OKLAHOMA (14-2)   7.00
5 TOM BROWN, RUTGERS (13-2)   6.50

TURNOVERS

Most turnovers in a single game
1 LARRY BIRD, INDIANA STATE (vs. DE PAUL)   11
1 GARY GARLAND, DEPAUL (vs. UCLA)   11
3 GARY GARLAND, DEPAUL
   (vs. PENNSYLVANIA)   9
4 4 tied for fourth place.

Most total turnovers in the tournament
1 LARRY BIRD, INDIANA STATE   26
2 GARY GARLAND, DEPAUL   24
3 BOBBY WILLIS, PENNSYLVANIA   23
4 EARVIN JOHNSON, MICHIGAN ST.   22
5 GREG KELSER, MICHIGAN ST.   18

SHOTS BLOCKED

Most shots blocked in a single game
1 ROOSEVELT BOUIE, SYRACUSE (vs.
   PENNSYLVANIA)   6
2 AL BEAL, OKLAHOMA (vs. TEXAS)   5
3 4 tied for third place.

Most total shots blocked in the tournament
1 GREG KELSER, MICHIGAN ST.   10
2 JIM BAILEY, RUTGERS   8
3 ALEX GILBERT, INDIANA STATE   7
4 ROOSEVELT BOUIE, SYRACUSE   6
5 5 tied for fifth place.

STEALS

Most steals in a single game
1 GARY GARLAND, DEPAUL (vs. USC)   10
2 LARRY BIRD, INDIANA STATE (vs. MICHIGAN ST.)   5
2 JIMMY MARTIN, JACKSONVILLE (vs. VIRGINIA TECH) 5
4 10 tied for fourth place.

Most total steals in the tournament
1 GARY GARLAND, DEPAUL   22
2 BOBBY WILLIS, PENNSYLVANIA   16
3 EARVIN JOHNSON, MICHIGAN ST.   13
4 CLYDE BRADSHAW, DEPAUL   12
5 JAMES SALTERS, PENNSYLVANIA   11

✪ TEAM RECORDS ✪

SCORING

Most points in a single game
1 MICHIGAN ST. (vs. PENNSYLVANIA)   101
2 UCLA (vs. SAN FRANCISCO)   99
3 TENNESSEE (vs. EASTERN KY.)   97

Most total points in the tournament
1 PENNSYLVANIA   453
2 MICHIGAN ST.   438
3 DEPAUL   416

Highest scoring average (minimum 2 games)
1 UCLA (266-3)   88.67
2 MICHIGAN ST. (438-5)   87.60
3 SAN FRANCISCO (167-2)   83.50

FIELD GOALS

Most field goals in a single game
1 UCLA (vs. SAN FRANCISCO)   42
1 MICHIGAN ST. (vs. LAMAR)   42
3 2 tied for third place.

Most total field goals in the tournament
1 PENNSYLVANIA   173
2 MICHIGAN ST.   167
3 INDIANA STATE   162

Most field goals attempted in a single game
1 PENNSYLVANIA (vs. DEPAUL)   94
2 LAMAR (vs. DETROIT)   84
3 PENNSYLVANIA (vs. MICHIGAN ST.)   82

Most total field goals attempted in the tournament
1 PENNSYLVANIA   398
2 DEPAUL   312
3 INDIANA STATE   298

Highest field goal percentage in a single game
1 SAN FRANCISCO (vs. BRIGHAM YOUNG) (39-57)   .684
2 ARKANSAS (vs. INDIANA STATE) (30-47)   .638
3 MICHIGAN ST. (vs. PENNSYLVANIA) (38-60)   .633

Highest field goal percentage in the tournament (minimum 2 games)
1 SAN FRANCISCO (72-122)   .590
2 ARKANSAS (83-143)   .581
3 MICHIGAN ST. (167-295)   .566

FREE THROWS

Most free throws in a single game
1 DEPAUL (vs. PENNSYLVANIA)   34
2 TOLEDO (vs. IOWA)   28
3 MICHIGAN ST. (vs. LOUISIANA ST.)   27
3 U. CONN. (vs. SYRACUSE)   27
3 IONA (vs. PENNSYLVANIA)   27

Most total free throws in the tournament
1 PENNSYLVANIA   107
2 MICHIGAN ST.   104
3 DEPAUL   94

Most free throws attempted in a single game
1 TOLEDO (vs. IOWA)   41
2 DEPAUL (vs. PENNSYLVANIA)   39
3 MICHIGAN ST. (vs. LOUISIANA ST.)   36

Most total free throws attempted in the tournament
1 MICHIGAN ST.   148
2 PENNSYLVANIA   144
3 DEPAUL   121

Highest free throw percentage in a single game
1 JACKSONVILLE (vs. VIRGINIA TECH) (1-1)   1.000
2 LOUISVILLE (vs. SOUTH ALABAMA) (17-19)   .895
3 MARQUETTE (vs. DEPAUL) (8-9)   .889

Highest free throw percentage in the tournament (minimum 2 games)
1 LOUISVILLE (37-42)   .881
2 MARQUETTE (27-32)   .844
3 ARKANSAS (52-64)   .813

Fewest free throws in a single game
1 JACKSONVILLE (vs. VIRGINIA TECH)   1
2 DEPAUL (vs. INDIANA STATE)   2
3 WEBER ST. (vs. ARKANSAS)   5

Lowest free throw percentage in a single game
1 DEPAUL (vs. INDIANA STATE) (2-5)   .400
2 INDIANA STATE (vs. MICHIGAN ST.) (10-22)   .455
3 PACIFIC (vs. MARQUETTE) (6-12)   .500

Lowest free throw percentage in the tournament (minimum 2 games)
1 LOUISIANA ST. (20-35)   .571
2 LAMAR (27-45)   .600
2 SYRACUSE (27-45)   .600

REBOUNDS

Most rebounds in a single game
1 LAMAR (vs. DETROIT)   56
2 TENNESSEE (vs. EASTERN KY.)   50
3 DEPAUL (vs. PENNSYLVANIA)   48

Most rebounds per game (minimum 2 games)
1 LAMAR (94-2)   47.00
2 TENNESSEE (85-2)   42.50
3 LOUISIANA ST. (78-2)   39.00

ASSISTS

Most assists in a single game
1 SAN FRANCISCO (vs. BRIGHAM YOUNG)   29
2 OKLAHOMA (vs. TEXAS)   28
3 MICHIGAN ST. (vs. PENNSYLVANIA)   24

Most assists per game (minimum 2 games)
1 SAN FRANCISCO (43-2)   21.50
2 MICHIGAN ST. (94-5)   18.80
3 DEPAUL (92-5)   18.40

TURNOVERS

Most turnovers in a single game
1 LOUISVILLE (vs. SOUTH ALABAMA)   25
1 LOUISIANA ST. (vs. MICHIGAN ST.)   25
1 SYRACUSE (vs. PENNSYLVANIA)   25

Most turnovers per game (minimum 2 games)
1 USC (40-2)   20.00
2 PENNSYLVANIA (115-6)   19.17
3 TENNESSEE (37-2)   18.50
3 SAN FRANCISCO (37-2)   18.50
3 LOUISIANA ST. (37-2)   18.50

SHOTS BLOCKED

Most shots blocked in a single game
1 OKLAHOMA (vs. TEXAS)   10
2 LOUISIANA ST. (vs. MICHIGAN ST.)   7
2 SYRACUSE (vs. PENNSYLVANIA)   7

Most shots blocked per game (minimum 2 games)
1 OKLAHOMA (11-2)   5.50
2 RUTGERS (10-2)   5.00
2 LOUISIANA ST. (10-2)   5.00

STEALS

Most steals in a single game
1 DEPAUL (vs. USC)   14
2 PENNSYLVANIA (vs. N. CAROLINA)   12
2 PENNSYLVANIA (vs. IONA)   12

Most steals per game
1 PENNSYLVANIA (64-6)   10.67
2 DEPAUL (47-5)   9.40
3 USC (16-2)   8.00

1980

| FIRST ROUND | SECOND ROUND | REGIONAL SEMIFINAL | REGIONAL FINAL | FINAL FOUR | REGIONAL FINAL | REGIONAL SEMIFINAL | SECOND ROUND | FIRST ROUND |

EAST

8 Villanova 77
Villanova 83
9 Marquette 59

(bye)
Syracuse 77
1 Syracuse 97

5 Iowa 86
Iowa 77
12 Va. Commonwealth 72

(bye)
Iowa 88
N.C. State 64

6 *Iona 84
*Iona 71
11 Holy Cross 78

(bye)
Georgetown 74
3 Georgetown 74

7 Tennessee 80
Tennessee 75
10 Furman 69

(bye)
Maryland 68
2 Maryland 86

Syracuse 77
Iowa 81
Iowa 88

Georgetown 74
Georgetown 80

Iowa 72

MIDWEST

8 Alcorn St. 70
Alcorn St. 88
9 South Alabama 62

(bye)
Louisiana St. 68
1 Louisiana St. 98

5 Missouri 61
Missouri 87 (ot)
12 San Jose St. 51

(bye)
Missouri 63
4 Notre Dame 84

6 Texas A&M 55
Texas A&M 78 (2 ot)
11 Bradley 53

(bye)
Texas A&M 55
3 N. Carolina 61

7 Kansas St. 71
Kansas St. 69
10 Arkansas 53

(bye)
Louisiana St. 66
Louisville 80

Louisville 86
Louisville 66 (ot)
2 Louisville 71 (ot)

Louisville 59
*UCLA 54

Purdue 62

MIDEAST

8 Florida St. 94
Florida St. 78
9 Toledo 91

(bye)
Kentucky 54
1 Kentucky 97

5 Washington St. 55
Pennsylvania 42
12 Pennsylvania 62

(bye)
Duke 55
4 Duke 52

6 Purdue 90
Purdue 87
11 La Salle 82

(bye)
Purdue 76
3 St. John's 72

7 Virginia Tech 89 (ot)
Virginia Tech 59
10 Western Ky. 85

(bye)
Indiana 69
2 Indiana 68

Duke 60
Purdue 68

WEST

8 *UCLA 87
*UCLA 77
9 Old Dominion 74

(bye)
*UCLA 72
1 DePaul 71

5 Arizona St. 99
Arizona St. 75
12 *Loyola Mymt. 71

(bye)
Ohio St. 68
4 Ohio St. 89

6 Clemson 76
Clemson 71
11 Utah St. 73

(bye)
Clemson 74
3 Brigham Young 66

7 Weber St. 86
Lamar 81
10 Lamar 87

(bye)
Lamar 66
2 *Oregon St. 77

*UCLA 85
*UCLA 67

Clemson 74

*UCLA 67

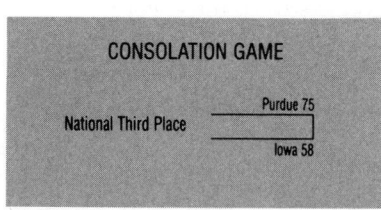

CONSOLATION GAME

National Third Place
Purdue 75
Iowa 58

*Iona's, Loyola Marymount's, Oregon State's, and UCLA's participation in 1980 tournament vacated.

It was a season of unprecedented parity in college basketball:

• The Final Four teams had a combined total of 29 losses, the second most in history.

• Only one Final Four team (Louisville) would have even qualified for the tournament the year before, but UCLA, Iowa, and Purdue were all there because, when the NCAA expanded to 48 teams in 1980, it also dropped its two-team-per-conference limit.

• In one midseason week, 9 of the Top 20–ranked teams lost (two early-season No. 1's ended the season out of the polls entirely), and of the four teams that went to Indianapolis to play for the title, only Louisville was rated higher than No. 20.

• Even top-ranked, 26-1 DePaul won 11 of their games by six points or less (they lost to UCLA in their first tournament contest).

It was indeed, as Georgetown coach John Thompson said after losing to Iowa in the regional finals, "the craziest season of basketball."

Although critics derided the expansion of the tournament, saying it meant anyone could qualify, the fact was that in 1980 virtually anyone could. "Other guys get up in the morning and go to work and nothing happens," said UNLV coach Jerry Tarkanian. "But I know every time we play a game, it's going to the wire." And Denny Crum, whose Louisville Cardinals were routed by Jimmy Valvano's unheralded Iona in February, declared, "On any given night we can beat the best 50 teams in America. On any other night they can beat us."

Even a school like Iona or Alcorn State, the nation's oldest land-grant college for blacks 90 miles from Jackson, had a chance to get into the tournament (Alcorn State lost in the second round). DePaul coach Ray Meyer attributed the change in college basketball's balance of power to recent changes in scholarship rules, which lowered maximum number of scholarships from 25 to 15. "These are rules where the rich are not going to get richer," he commented. "They have given the smaller schools a chance to compete on a national basis."

Five years after his retirement, the footprints of coach emeritus John Wooden were all over the Final Four. Even though the tournament was no longer known as "the UCLA Invitational," as it was during the Wizard's dynasty, the Bruins (with coach Larry Brown reinstituting Wooden's high post offense) were back. Wooden also had connections with the three other semifinalists: he had been an All-American player for Purdue from 1930 to 1932; his former assistant, Denny Crum, was the coach of Louisville; and after a 1942 appendectomy kept him from being shipped overseas, the Wizard of Westwood became an instructor at the Navy preflight training school on the Iowa campus during World War II.

The Iowa Hawkeyes deserved their own Purple Hearts, as star guard Ronnie Lester had knee surgery (with Lester out of the lineup Iowa went only 8-7). In addition, second high scorer Kenny Arnold played with a broken thumb, starter Vince Brookins played hurt all year, and key freshman Mark Gannon spent much of the season hobbled by a knee injury. Even with all their walking wounded, the Hawkeyes qualified for the semis by coming back from 14 down with 18:05 left against Georgetown. Iowa shot the Hoyas' lights out by hitting 71 percent from the floor and 15 straight from the line in the second half, capped by a 3-point play by Steve Waite with five seconds to go.

Louisville had an even harder time getting through the draw. Years earlier guard Darrell Griffith had promised to bring the title to Louisville, but—in Griffith's last chance (he was a senior)—they barely got through the second round. Louisville survived against Kansas State when Crum put in Tony Branch (who had started a year earlier but taken only 29 shots in 1979–80) after Griffith fouled out in overtime, and Branch hit an off-balance shot to win. In the next round, Texas A&M overcame the Cardinals' 12-2 start to force another overtime by aggressive double teaming and shot blocking. This time the extra session was decided when the Redbirds stepped up their own defensive pressure. With their zone press forcing turnovers, the Cardinals pulled away. With time running out and Louisville comfortably ahead, Branch was fouled. Crum recalled the heartbreaking 1975 semifinal loss to UCLA that turned on a previously perfect Cardinal foul shooter missing the clinching free throw. "Have you missed this year?" he asked Branch. "No," replied the player (he was 16 for 16 from the line for the season). So Crum ordered him to miss now, rather than later.

The regional final between Louisville and favored LSU was a game of streaks. Louisville pulled into an early lead but after Griffith left the game with three fouls, LSU stormed back with 16 straight to go up by 8. Then Louisville took over again, their 10-point run to finish the half just the opening salvo in a display that blew out the Tigers by 20 points. After the intermission, Louisville pulled away despite the foul trouble that limited Griffith to 18 minutes. They did it with muscle and hustle, and a ferocious 1-2-2 full-court zone press keyed by Roger Burkman, whom Al McGuire called "Instant Defense—the best sixth man in college basketball." After the game, another big contributor off the bench, Poncho Wright, shouted joyfully, "the Ville [Louisville] is going to the Nap [Indianapolis]." "There's something about this team," said Crum. "They love each other, they play hard, and they play together."

Purdue was the only Final Four team with a dominant center (7-1 Joe Barry Carroll). After winning their first two games on their home court, they beat heavily favored cross-state rival Indiana easily, even though Carroll scored just 11 and spent a good part of the game on the bench with foul trouble. Then Joe Barry scored 28 to beat Duke (which had held on to upset Kentucky in Lexington) to take the Boilermakers into the semifinal against UCLA.

The unheralded Bruins, meanwhile, had come together around midseason, when first-year coach Larry Brown put freshman guards Rod Foster and Michael Holton into the lineup, moved 6-6 sophomore Michael Sanders over to center, and reinstituted John Wooden's high post offense. A strong team effort got them to Indianapolis. Senior star Kiki Vandeweghe scored 81 points in four games, Sanders scored 67 and added 48 rebounds, and Foster scored 60 on 53 percent shooting. Meanwhile, forward James Wilkes quietly held four future NBA players to an average of 14 points and 6.7 rebounds per game.

In the semis in Naptown, UCLA's defense did it again. They sagged on Carroll, keeping him away from the ball and holding him to 17 points. Meanwhile, on the other end, Vandeweghe shot 9 of 12 for 24 points, including 4 dunks on breakaways after beating the ineffective Purdue press. Even so, the game was close until last-minute Bruin free throws put a lid on the Boilermakers' hopes.

In the game between Iowa and Louisville, Darrell Griffith hardly lived up to his name of Dr. Dunkenstein, but he did dominate, springing himself free for jumpers and hitting 14 for 21. Meanwhile, Iowa's Lester was forced to leave with a knee injury after hitting his first 4 shots, and the Cardinals' pressure defense held the Hawkeyes to a shooting percentage 15 points below their tournament average. After the game Iowa's Bob Hansen marveled, "I've guarded other players who could leap as high as Griffith. But all of them came down."

Louisville and UCLA both showed their age in the championship game by shooting poorly and playing tentatively throughout the first half. At intermission, with his team down by two, Crum told his players they were "choking." But just before the second half began, he apologized, told them he loved them, and said they should "go out and have fun."

With four minutes left in the game and a four point UCLA lead, they weren't having any fun. Vandeweghe had just stolen the ball and was driving in for what he thought would be the clincher. But Jerry Eaves was not about to concede. He raced back, forced Kiki to miss, and turned the game around. Brown grabbed the rebound, and Griffith fed Eaves for a jumper. Another Griffith-to-Eaves combination (this time for a lay-up) was followed by dunk-master Darrell popping from the top of the key. When the dust settled, Louisville had scored the last nine points of the game, Griffith had made good on his promise to bring a national title to Louisville, and Crum had finally exorcised the demon of his 1975 UCLA heartbreaker and won the big one.

FIRST ROUND EAST

Villanova (77) Coach: Rollie Massimino

	Min.	Total FG / FGA	Pct.	FT / FTA	Pct.	Reb. O / T	A	TO	PF	S	Blk	TP	PPM
HOWARD, A.	26	0/ 2	.000	2/ 2	1.000	1/ 6	1	2	4	1	2	2	.077
BRADLEY, A.	35	4/ 8	.500	4/ 6	.667	3/ 8	0	3	2	1	0	12	.343
PINONE, J.	34	7/10	.700	7/ 7	1.000	3/ 7	2	2	3	3	0	21	.618
SPARROW, R.	37	9/11	.818	6/ 7	.857	0/ 5	3	2	1	2	0	24	.649
SIENKIEWICZ, T.	16	0/ 6	.000	2/ 2	1.000	0/ 0	0	3	0	0	0	2	.125
GRANGER, S.	25	2/ 4	.500	6/ 6	1.000	0/ 1	2	6	1	2	0	10	.400
KNOEBEL, J.	1	1/ 2	.500	0/ 0	.000	0/ 0	0	0	0	0	0	2	2.000
LINCOLN, S.	3	1/ 0	.000	0/ 0	.000	0/ 0	0	1	0	1	0	2	.667
MULQUIN, M.	6	0/ 0	.000	0/ 0	.000	0/ 1	0	0	1	0	0	0	.000
BETHEA, T.	3	0/ 0	.000	0/ 0	.000	0/ 0	0	2	1	0	0	0	.000
CARON, M.	13	0/ 1	.000	2/ 2	1.000	0/ 2	0	0	3	0	0	2	.154
MCKENNA, K.	1	0/ 0	.000	0/ 0	.000	0/ 1	0	1	0	0	0	0	.000
Totals	200	24/44	.545	29/32	.906	7/31	8	22	16	9	2	77	.385

Marquette (59) Coach: Hank Raymonds

	Min.	Total FG / FGA	Pct.	FT / FTA	Pct.	Reb. O / T	A	TO	PF	S	Blk	TP	PPM
SCHLUNDT, T.	30	2/10	.200	0/ 0	.000	2/ 2	0	0	1	0	0	4	.133
BYRD, R.	39	5/ 8	.625	0/ 1	.000	7/12	2	2	2	2	0	10	.256
LEE, O.	40	5/13	.385	2/ 3	.667	2/ 4	2	4	4	4	1	12	.300
WILSON, M.	20	3/ 8	.375	1/ 2	.500	1/ 1	1	4	4	1	1	7	.350
WORTHEN, S.	38	6/15	.400	2/ 2	1.000	3/ 3	2	5	5	1	0	14	.368
DAVIS, T.	2	0/ 1	.000	0/ 0	.000	1/ 1	0	1	1	0	0	0	.000
GREEN, A.	22	3/ 8	.375	2/ 2	1.000	2/ 2	0	3	5	1	0	8	.364
HATCHETT, L.	6	1/ 2	.500	0/ 0	.000	0/ 0	0	2	2	0	0	2	.333
SHIMON, G.	1	1/ 0	.000	0/ 0	.000	0/ 0	0	2	0	1	0	2	2.000
MARQUARDT, D.	2	0/ 1	.000	0/ 0	.000	0/ 0	0	0	1	0	0	0	.000
Totals	200	26/66	.394	7/10	.700	18/25	7	19	25	10	2	59	.295

Team Rebounds: Villanova 2; Marquette 1. Disqualified: Marquette—Worthen, Green. Technical fouls: None.

	1st Half	2nd Half	Final
Villanova	32	45	77
Marquette	33	26	59

Iowa (86) Coach: Lute Olson

	Min.	Total FG / FGA	Pct.	FT / FTA	Pct.	Reb. O / T	A	TO	PF	S	Blk	TP	PPM
BOYLE, K.	39	8/14	.571	1/ 3	.333	-/ 8	4	2	3	1	0	17	.436
WAITE, S.	34	7/14	.500	3/ 4	.750	-/10	2	3	3	1	0	17	.500
KRAFCISIN, S.	32	5/ 9	.556	0/ 1	.000	-/ 9	5	4	3	1	1	10	.313
LESTER, R.	32	4/ 8	.500	9/13	.692	-/ 1	8	1	2	0	0	17	.531
ARNOLD, K.	36	8/12	.667	7/ 8	.875	-/ 4	4	0	3	2	0	23	.639
HANSEN, B.	8	0/ 0	.000	0/ 0	.000	-/ 1	1	2	1	0	0	0	.000
BROOKINS, V.	16	1/ 3	.333	0/ 0	.000	-/ 6	1	1	2	0	1	2	.125
HELLER, M.	1	0/ 0	.000	0/ 0	.000	-/ 0	0	0	0	0	0	0	.000
DARSEE, J.	1	0/ 0	.000	0/ 0	.000	-/ 0	0	0	0	0	0	0	.000
GROGAN, T.	1	0/ 0	.000	0/ 0	.000	-/ 0	0	0	0	0	0	0	.000
Totals	200	33/60	.550	20/29	.690	-/39	25	13	17	5	3	86	.430

Virginia Commonwealth (72) Coach: J. D. Barnett

	Min.	Total FG / FGA	Pct.	FT / FTA	Pct.	Reb. O / T	A	TO	PF	S	Blk	TP	PPM
KOTTAK, D.	33	4/ 9	.444	2/ 2	1.000	-/ 3	2	0	5	1	0	10	.303
MCCRAY, G.	37	9/18	.500	0/ 1	.000	-/11	1	2	4	1	2	18	.486
JONES, K.	27	2/ 5	.400	1/ 1	1.000	-/ 7	0	4	3	0	1	5	.185
KNIGHT, R.	33	6/19	.316	1/ 1	1.000	-/ 7	5	2	4	2	0	13	.394
SHEROD, E.	40	5/11	.455	4/ 7	.571	-/ 3	5	2	4	2	0	14	.350
HARRIS, T.	5	0/ 1	.000	2/ 2	1.000	-/ 0	0	0	2	0	0	2	.400
STANCELL, K.	21	5/ 7	.714	0/ 0	.000	-/ 3	1	0	2	0	0	10	.476
SHROPSHIRE, G.	2	0/ 0	.000	0/ 0	.000	-/ 0	0	0	1	0	0	0	.000
RINGO, G.	1	0/ 0	.000	0/ 0	.000	-/ 0	0	0	0	0	0	0	.000
BATES, F.	1	0/ 0	.000	0/ 0	.000	-/ 0	0	0	0	0	0	0	.000
Totals	200	31/70	.443	10/14	.714	-/34	14	10	25	6	3	72	.360

Team Rebounds: Iowa 4; Va. Commonwealth 0. Disqualified: Va. Commonwealth—Kottak. Technical fouls: None.

	1st Half	2nd Half	Final
Iowa	39	47	86
Va. Commonwealth	28	44	72

Iona (84) Coach: Jim Valvano

	Min.	Total FG / FGA	Pct.	FT / FTA	Pct.	Reb. O / T	A	TO	PF	S	Blk	TP	PPM
PALMA, M.	-	4/ -	-	4/ 5	.800	-/ -	-	-	-	-	-	12	-
MIDDLETON, A.	-	3/ -	-	3/ 5	.600	-/ -	-	-	-	-	-	9	-
RULAND, J.	-	7/ -	-	2/ 5	.400	-/ -	-	-	-	-	-	16	-
VICKERS, -	-	4/ -	-	15/17	.882	-/ -	-	-	-	-	-	23	-
HAMILTON, K.	-	8/ -	-	2/ 2	1.000	-/ -	-	-	-	-	-	18	-
IAFF	-	1/ -	-	0/ 0	.000	-/ -	-	-	-	-	-	2	-
WILLIAMS	-	2/ -	-	0/ 0	.000	-/ -	-	-	-	-	-	4	-
MCMILLAN, G.	-	0/ -	-	0/ 0	.000	-/ -	-	-	-	-	-	0	-
VESEY	-	0/ -	-	0/ 0	.000	-/ -	-	-	-	-	-	0	-
Totals	200	29/ -	-	26/34	.765	-/ -	-	-	17	-	-	84	.420

Holy Cross (78) Coach: George Blaney

	Min.	Total FG / FGA	Pct.	FT / FTA	Pct.	Reb. O / T	A	TO	PF	S	Blk	TP	PPM
WITTS	-	6/ -	-	0/ 0	.000	-/ -	-	-	-	-	-	12	-
FLOYD	-	0/ -	-	0/ 0	.000	-/ -	-	-	-	-	-	0	-
BROWNE, C.	-	5/ -	-	0/ 0	.000	-/ -	-	-	-	-	-	10	-
PERRY	-	10/ -	-	4/ 4	1.000	-/ -	-	-	-	-	-	24	-
GREANEY	-	3/ -	-	0/ 0	.000	-/ -	-	-	-	-	-	6	-
KELLY	-	3/ -	-	0/ 0	.000	-/ -	-	-	5	-	-	6	-
KANE	-	0/ -	-	0/ 0	.000	-/ -	-	-	-	-	-	0	-
MULQUIN	-	5/ -	-	3/ 8	.375	-/ -	-	-	-	-	-	13	-
LOGAN	-	1/ -	-	0/ 1	.000	-/ -	-	-	-	-	-	2	-
SEAMAN	-	2/ -	-	1/ 4	.250	-/ -	-	-	-	-	-	5	-
Totals	200	35/ -	-	8/17	.471	-/ -	-	-	23	-	-	78	.390

Disqualified: Holy Cross—Kelly.

	1st Half	2nd Half	Final
Iona	36	48	84
Holy Cross	35	43	78

Tennessee (80) Coach: Don Devoe

	Min.	Total FG / FGA	Pct.	FT / FTA	Pct.	Reb. O / T	A	TO	PF	S	Blk	TP	PPM
JOHNSON, R.	37	13/19	.684	2/ 2	1.000	-/14	3	4	2	1	3	28	.757
RAY, S.	28	0/ 3	.000	0/ 0	.000	-/ 2	1	0	5	1	1	0	.000
THREETHS, C.	10	1/ 3	.333	0/ 0	.000	-/ 5	1	2	3	0	0	2	.200
CARTER, G.	34	6/ 8	.750	1/ 2	.500	-/ 6	6	4	4	1	0	13	.382
BERTELKAMP, B.	19	1/ 3	.200	1/ 3	.333	-/ 1	8	1	5	2	0	3	.158
ELLIS, D.	14	1/ 6	.167	0/ 0	.000	-/ 3	0	0	0	0	0	2	.143
WOOD, H.	25	9/11	.818	1/ 2	.500	-/ 5	1	2	3	0	0	19	.760
NASH, J.	8	3/ 7	.429	0/ 2	.000	-/ 8	0	0	4	0	0	6	.750
PARTON, R.	19	2/ 5	.400	3/ 5	.600	-/ 1	4	3	3	1	0	7	.368
POOLE, M.	5	0/ 2	.000	0/ 0	.000	-/ 1	2	0	0	0	0	0	.000
LOVE, A.	1	0/ 0	.000	0/ 0	.000	-/ 0	0	0	0	0	0	0	.000
Totals	200	36/69	.522	8/16	.500	-/46	26	16	29	6	4	80	.400

Furman (69) Coach: Eddie Holbrook

	Min.	Total FG / FGA	Pct.	FT / FTA	Pct.	Reb. O / T	A	TO	PF	S	Blk	TP	PPM
WHITE, R.	24	3/ 7	.429	2/ 5	.400	-/ 0	0	1	0	0	1	8	.333
MCKINNEY, R.	26	3/ 6	.500	5/ 8	.625	-/ 6	0	3	1	0	0	11	.423
MOORE, J.	40	9/14	.643	4/ 8	.500	-/17	1	3	3	1	2	22	.550
DANIEL, M.	30	6/ 9	.667	3/ 5	.600	-/ 1	4	4	4	2	0	15	.500
HUNT, M.	30	2/ 6	.333	0/ 1	.000	-/ 1	1	5	3	0	0	4	.133
SMALL, R.	14	1/ 3	.333	0/ 0	.000	-/ 2	0	0	1	0	0	2	.143
CROWE, D.	13	0/ 2	.000	2/ 2	1.000	-/ 3	3	1	3	0	0	2	.154
JACKSON, T.	7	1/ 5	.200	0/ 0	.000	-/ 3	2	0	0	0	0	2	.286
BUTLER, R.	7	0/ 1	.000	0/ 0	.000	-/ 0	0	2	3	0	0	0	.000
HANKS, W.	9	1/ 3	.333	1/ 3	.333	-/ 0	0	0	0	0	0	3	.333
Totals	200	26/56	.464	17/32	.531	-/30	11	19	18	3	3	69	.345

Team Rebounds: Tennessee 1; Furman 5. Disqualified: Tennessee—Ray, Bertelkamp. Technical fouls: Tennessee—Coach Devoe.

	1st Half	2nd Half	Final
Tennessee	40	40	80
Furman	29	40	69

FIRST ROUND MIDWEST

Alcorn State (70)　Coach: Davey Whitney

	Min.	Total FG/FGA	Pct.	FT/FTA	Pct.	Reb. O/T	A	TO	PF	S	Blk	TP	PPM
SMITH, L.	-	7/13	.538	4/4	1.000	-/17	2	-	4	-	-	18	-
WYATT	-	2/7	.286	2/4	.500	-/4	2	-	1	-	-	6	-
BAKER, E.	-	9/14	.643	0/0	.000	-/4	1	-	3	-	-	18	-
JENKINS	-	0/3	.000	0/0	.000	-/2	0	-	2	-	-	0	-
BELL, E.	-	6/11	.545	4/6	.667	-/4	2	-	2	-	-	16	-
ALEXANDER	-	1/4	.250	4/6	.667	-/0	1	-	0	-	-	6	-
HOWARD	-	0/1	.000	6/7	.857	-/1	1	-	1	-	-	6	-
IRVING, A.	-	0/0	.000	0/1	.000	-/2	0	-	2	-	-	0	-
Totals	200	25/53	.472	20/28	.714	-/34	9	-	15	-	-	70	.350

South Alabama (62)　Coach: Cliff Ellis

	Min.	Total FG/FGA	Pct.	FT/FTA	Pct.	Reb. O/T	A	TO	PF	S	Blk	TP	PPM
RAINS	-	11/25	.440	-/2	-	-/9	0	-	2	-	-	22	-
HAFLEY	-	2/7	.286	0/0	.000	-/6	0	-	3	-	-	4	-
MAY	-	3/10	.300	2/2	1.000	-/9	1	-	4	-	-	8	-
ANDREW	-	4/13	.308	0/1	.000	-/3	1	-	5	-	-	8	-
WILLIAMS	-	3/8	.375	0/0	.000	-/6	4	-	5	-	-	6	-
DAVIS	-	7/14	.500	0/0	.000	-/10	2	-	4	-	-	14	-
SCOTT	-	0/0	.000	0/0	.000	-/0	0	-	0	-	-	0	-
HOGAN	-	0/0	.000	0/0	.000	-/0	0	-	1	-	-	0	-
Totals	200	30/77	.390	2/5	.400	-/43	8	-	24	-	-	62	.310

Texas A&M (55)　Coach: Shelby Metcalf

	Min.	Total FG/FGA	Pct.	FT/FTA	Pct.	Reb. O/T	A	TO	PF	S	Blk	TP	PPM
SMITH, V.	38	4/9	.444	1/2	.500	-/13	0	4	2	0	0	9	.237
WRIGHT, R.	37	6/13	.462	3/3	1.000	-/5	0	0	3	0	0	15	.405
WOODS, R.	13	0/2	.000	1/2	.500	-/3	0	0	4	0	1	1	.077
GOFF, D.	38	2/6	.333	2/2	1.000	-/5	5	5	3	1	0	6	.158
BRITTON, D.	26	4/6	.667	2/2	1.000	-/4	1	5	4	0	0	10	.385
RILEY, C.	25	4/8	.500	4/4	1.000	-/4	0	2	2	1	1	12	.480
LADSON, T.	18	0/3	.000	2/4	.500	-/1	1	2	1	2	0	2	.111
SYLESTINE, S.	5	0/1	.000	0/0	.000	-/0	0	2	0	0	0	0	.000
Totals	200	20/48	.417	15/19	.789	-/35	7	20	19	4	2	55	.275

Bradley (53)　Coach: Dick Versace

	Min.	Total FG/FGA	Pct.	FT/FTA	Pct.	Reb. O/T	A	TO	PF	S	Blk	TP	PPM
ANDERSON, M.	40	7/18	.389	3/3	1.000	-/8	1	1	2	0	2	17	.425
FORD, B.	28	3/4	.750	0/0	.000	-/1	0	1	4	2	0	6	.214
REESE, D.	30	1/6	.167	1/2	.500	-/3	0	2	2	1	0	3	.100
DUHART, E.	13	1/4	.250	1/1	1.000	-/2	1	2	1	1	0	3	.231
THIRDKILL, D.	22	2/8	.250	1/1	1.000	-/0	0	2	4	0	0	5	.227
MALNATI, R.	26	0/0	.000	0/0	.000	-/2	2	3	0	1	0	0	.000
HOUSTON, H.	28	8/10	.800	1/3	.333	-/3	0	1	1	0	0	17	.607
MCMATH, H.	13	0/2	.000	2/2	1.000	-/3	0	3	1	3	1	2	.154
Totals	200	22/52	.423	9/12	.750	-/22	4	15	15	8	3	53	.265

Team Rebounds: Alcorn St. 6; South Alabama 4. Disqualified: South Alabama—Andrew, Williams. Technical fouls: None.

Team Rebounds: Texas A&M 1; Bradley 6. Disqualified: None. Technical fouls: Texas A&M—Wright.

	1st Half	2nd Half	Final
Alcorn St.	27	43	70
South Alabama	18	44	62

	1st Half	2nd Half	Final
Texas A&M	25	30	55
Bradley	27	26	53

Missouri (61)　Coach: Norm Stewart

	Min.	Total FG/FGA	Pct.	FT/FTA	Pct.	Reb. O/T	A	TO	PF	S	Blk	TP	PPM
DRESSLER, M.	-	5/8	.625	1/1	1.000	-/8	3	-	3	-	-	11	-
FRAZIER, C.	-	9/13	.692	6/8	.750	-/3	1	-	3	-	-	24	-
STIPANOVICH	-	2/4	.500	0/0	.000	-/4	0	-	4	-	-	4	-
SUNDVOID	-	0/4	.000	2/4	.500	-/1	5	-	2	-	-	2	-
DREW, L.	-	3/10	.300	3/4	.750	-/5	5	-	1	-	-	9	-
FOSTER, M.	-	0/0	.000	0/0	.000	-/1	0	-	0	-	-	0	-
DORE	-	4/5	.800	3/6	.500	-/5	1	-	4	-	-	11	-
Totals	200	23/44	.523	15/23	.652	-/27	15	-	17	-	-	61	.305

San Jose State (51)　Coach: Bill Berry

	Min.	Total FG/FGA	Pct.	FT/FTA	Pct.	Reb. O/T	A	TO	PF	S	Blk	TP	PPM
RANK	-	6/14	.429	2/2	1.000	-/2	1	-	3	-	-	14	-
JACKSON	-	4/9	.444	3/5	.600	-/9	1	-	1	-	-	11	-
GRAHAM	-	1/9	.111	3/4	.750	-/6	1	-	1	-	-	5	-
MENDEZ	-	0/4	.000	0/0	.000	-/3	7	-	2	-	-	0	-
SULLIVAN	-	1/2	.500	0/0	.000	-/1	1	-	3	-	-	2	-
SAUNDERS	-	0/3	.000	1/2	.500	-/1	0	-	3	-	-	1	-
BYRD	-	0/2	.000	0/0	.000	-/0	1	-	0	-	-	0	-
RUSSO	-	0/0	.000	0/0	.000	-/0	0	-	2	-	-	0	-
SWARBRICK	-	2/2	1.000	0/0	.000	-/1	0	-	0	-	-	4	-
MURRAY	-	4/5	.800	0/0	.000	-/2	1	-	4	-	-	8	-
WILLIAMS	-	3/3	1.000	0/0	.000	-/4	0	-	1	-	-	6	-
Totals	200	21/53	.396	9/13	.692	-/29	13	-	20	-	-	51	.255

Team Rebounds: Missouri 2; San Jose St. 3. Disqualified: None. Technical Fouls: None.

	1st Half	2nd Half	Final
Missouri	23	38	61
San Jose St.	30	21	51

Kansas State (71)　Coach: Jack Hartman

	Min.	Total FG/FGA	Pct.	FT/FTA	Pct.	Reb. O/T	A	TO	PF	S	Blk	TP	PPM
NEALY, E.	-	3/5	.600	4/5	.800	-/8	1	2	4	3	1	10	-
WILLS, J.	-	6/10	.600	0/1	.000	-/4	1	1	1	1	0	12	-
CRAFT, L.	-	2/2	1.000	1/2	.500	-/3	4	2	4	1	0	5	-
MARSHALL, G.	-	6/10	.600	0/2	.000	-/4	1	2	0	6	1	12	-
BLACKMAN, R.	-	5/8	.625	5/8	.625	-/4	2	2	1	2	0	15	-
JANKOVICH, T.	-	0/1	.000	2/2	1.000	-/1	2	2	3	0	0	2	-
MARX	-	0/0	.000	0/0	.000	-/0	0	0	0	0	0	0	-
ADAMS, T.	-	2/4	.500	3/5	.600	-/2	2	2	2	0	1	7	-
LEWIS, B.	-	0/0	.000	0/0	.000	-/0	0	1	0	0	0	0	-
MANLEY, R.	-	1/2	.500	2/3	.667	-/4	0	1	2	1	0	4	-
DANNER, D.	-	1/1	1.000	0/0	.000	-/0	0	0	1	0	0	2	-
SALTER, E.	-	1/2	.500	0/0	.000	-/0	0	1	0	0	0	2	-
PRUDHOE, G.	-	0/0	.000	0/0	.000	-/1	0	0	1	0	0	0	-
GALVAO, E.	-	0/0	.000	0/0	.000	-/0	0	2	0	0	0	0	-
Totals	200	27/45	.600	17/28	.607	-/31	13	18	19	14	3	71	.355

Arkansas (53)　Coach: Eddie Sutton

	Min.	Total FG/FGA	Pct.	FT/FTA	Pct.	Reb. O/T	A	TO	PF	S	Blk	TP	PPM
FRIEAS, B.	-	1/3	.333	3/4	.750	-/4	1	3	3	0	0	5	-
ZAHN, A.	-	6/11	.545	1/2	.500	-/14	3	3	2	4	2	13	-
HASTINGS, S.	-	3/10	.300	2/2	1.000	-/3	4	2	5	2	1	8	-
HILLIARD, K.	-	1/3	.333	0/0	.000	-/1	3	1	1	1	2	2	-
REED, U.	-	8/18	.444	0/0	.000	-/8	1	2	3	0	0	16	-
SUTTON, L.	-	0/1	.000	0/0	.000	-/0	0	1	0	0	0	0	-
YOUNG, M.	-	1/3	.333	0/1	.000	-/0	0	1	3	0	0	2	-
BROWN, T.	-	0/4	.000	2/4	.500	-/0	3	4	4	1	0	2	-
SKULMAN, G.	-	0/0	.000	0/0	.000	-/1	0	0	2	0	0	0	-
KELLY, C.	-	1/3	.333	3/4	.750	-/0	1	0	0	0	0	5	-
Totals	200	21/56	.375	11/17	.647	-/31	15	20	23	8	4	53	.265

Team Rebounds: Kansas State 1; Arkansas 2. Disqualified: Arkansas—Hastings. Technical fouls: None.

	1st Half	2nd Half	Final
Kansas State	27	44	71
Arkansas	21	32	53

FIRST ROUND MIDEAST

Florida State (94)   Coach: Joe Williams

	Min.	Total FG/FGA	Pct.	FT/FTA	Pct.	Reb. O/T	A	TO	PF	S	Blk	TP	PPM
ARNOLD, R.	33	10/17	.588	9/10	.900	-/ 5	4	3	1	2	0	29	.879
BROWN, M.	34	12/16	.750	2/ 2	1.000	-/ 6	0	1	3	0	1	26	.765
ROLLE, E.	32	7/11	.636	1/ 2	.500	-/ 6	1	3	4	0	3	15	.469
DILLARD, M.	38	9/16	.563	4/ 5	.800	-/ 3	2	4	2	1	0	22	.579
JACKSON, T.	37	1/ 5	.200	0/ 0	.000	-/ 4	8	3	3	0	0	2	.054
TOOKES, P.	15	0/ 5	.000	0/ 0	.000	-/ 6	0	0	2	0	0	0	.000
PARKS, B.	11	0/ 1	.000	0/ 1	.000	-/ 0	3	2	3	0	0	0	.000
Totals	200	39/71	.549	16/20	.800	-/30	18	16	18	3	4	94	.470

Toledo (91)   Coach: Bob Nichols

	Min.	Total FG/FGA	Pct.	FT/FTA	Pct.	Reb. O/T	A	TO	PF	S	Blk	TP	PPM
MILLER, D.	28	9/16	.563	3/ 5	.600	-/ 8	4	4	5	0	0	21	.750
SWANEY, J.	24	10/17	.588	2/ 4	.500	-/ 8	0	0	4	0	0	22	.917
KNUCKLES, H.	39	10/14	.714	0/ 0	.000	-/ 4	2	4	3	0	2	20	.513
SELGO	39	9/14	.643	0/ 0	.000	-/ 2	4	1	4	0	0	18	.462
LEHMAN, J.	40	3/ 7	.429	4/ 4	1.000	-/ 1	6	1	1	0	0	10	.250
MONTAGUE, K.	7	0/ 1	.000	0/ 0	.000	-/ 2	0	0	0	0	0	0	.000
SEEMAN, M.	1	0/ 0	.000	0/ 0	.000	-/ 0	0	0	0	0	0	0	.000
ADAMEK, M.	18	0/ 3	.000	0/ 0	.000	-/ 6	0	0	3	0	0	0	.000
BOYLE, D.	4	0/ 1	.000	0/ 0	.000	-/ 1	0	0	0	0	0	0	.000
Totals	200	41/73	.562	9/13	.692	-/32	16	10	20	0	2	91	.455

Team Rebounds: Florida State 4; Toledo 1. Disqualified: Toledo—Miller. Technical fouls: Toledo—1 (bench).

	1st Half	2nd Half	Final
Florida State	43	51	94
Toledo	48	43	91

Washington State (55)   Coach: George Raveling

	Min.	Total FG/FGA	Pct.	FT/FTA	Pct.	Reb. O/T	A	TO	PF	S	Blk	TP	PPM
HUNTLEY, C.	3	1/ 3	.333	0/ 0	.000	-/ 0	0	0	1	1	0	2	.667
BERG, R.	1	0/ 0	.000	0/ 0	.000	-/ 0	0	0	0	0	0	0	.000
RISON, B.	38	3/ 6	.500	2/ 4	.500	-/ 2	5	5	3	2	0	8	.211
MEYERS, B.	10	0/ 1	.000	0/ 0	.000	-/ 1	1	1	2	0	0	0	.000
HILL, A.	8	0/ 0	.000	0/ 1	.000	-/ 0	0	0	1	0	0	0	.000
HASKINS, A.	2	0/ 0	.000	0/ 0	.000	-/ 0	0	0	1	0	0	0	.000
COLLINS, D.	30	9/15	.600	2/ 2	1.000	-/ 6	2	2	5	1	0	20	.667
KELLY, T.	40	5/14	.357	3/ 4	.750	-/ 1	4	2	3	0	1	13	.325
PRESTON, J.	39	3/ 4	.750	4/ 6	.667	-/ 3	0	1	3	2	0	10	.256
HOUSE, S.	29	1/ 2	.500	0/ 4	.000	-/ 2	2	6	4	1	1	2	.069
Totals	200	22/45	.489	11/21	.524	-/15	12	18	21	7	1	55	.275

Pennsylvania (62)   Coach: Bob Weinhauer

	Min.	Total FG/FGA	Pct.	FT/FTA	Pct.	Reb. O/T	A	TO	PF	S	Blk	TP	PPM
SALTERS, J.	-	5/10	.500	3/ 3	1.000	-/ 4	3	2	2	1	0	13	-
LITTLE, P.	-	2/ 7	.286	7/ 8	.875	-/ 6	2	4	3	1	0	11	-
REYNOLDS, A.	-	4/ 8	.500	0/ 0	.000	-/ 0	1	2	1	0	0	8	-
ROSS, V.	-	1/ 3	.333	0/ 0	.000	-/ 3	0	2	4	1	0	2	-
RAWLINGS, A.	-	0/ 0	.000	0/ 0	.000	-/ 2	0	1	2	1	0	0	-
HALL, A.	-	2/ 4	.500	2/ 2	1.000	-/ 5	3	0	2	3	0	6	-
LEIFSEN, T.	-	0/ 1	.000	2/ 4	.500	-/ 5	0	3	0	0	2	2	-
BROWN, M.	-	5/ 7	.714	4/ 6	.667	-/ 2	0	2	1	1	0	14	-
NOON, G.	-	2/ 4	.500	2/ 4	.500	-/ 2	0	0	4	0	1	6	-
Totals	200	21/44	.477	20/27	.741	-/29	9	16	19	8	1	62	.310

Team Rebounds: Pennsylvania 1; Washington St. 4. Disqualified: Washington St.—Collins. Technical fouls: None.

	1st Half	2nd Half	Final
Washington St.	27	28	55
Pennsylvania	27	35	62

Purdue (90)   Coach: Lee Rose

	Min.	Total FG/FGA	Pct.	FT/FTA	Pct.	Reb. O/T	A	TO	PF	S	Blk	TP	PPM
EDMONSON, K.	-	7/11	.636	4/ 4	1.000	-/ 5	1	1	3	1	1	18	-
WALKER, S.	-	1/ 1	1.000	2/ 2	1.000	-/ 1	0	0	2	1	0	4	-
WALKER, B.	-	1/ 4	.250	1/ 2	.500	-/ 2	8	3	2	1	0	3	-
ANTHROP, J.	-	0/ 0	.000	0/ 0	.000	-/ 0	0	0	1	0	0	0	-
CARROLL, J.	-	12/19	.632	9/11	.818	-/13	1	2	3	1	1	33	-
SCEARCE, M.	-	1/ 5	.200	0/ 0	.000	-/ 1	0	3	0	0	2	2	-
STALLINGS, K.	-	0/ 2	.000	0/ 1	.000	-/ 0	4	1	2	0	0	0	-
MORRIS, D.	-	8/12	.667	5/ 7	.714	-/ 2	0	1	4	3	0	21	-
BENSON, T.	-	0/ 0	.000	1/ 2	.500	-/ 1	0	1	0	0	0	1	-
KITCHEL, J.	-	0/ 0	.000	0/ 0	.000	-/ 0	0	0	0	0	0	0	-
BARNES, R.	-	0/ 1	.000	0/ 0	.000	-/ 0	0	1	0	0	0	0	-
HALLMAN, A.	-	4/10	.400	0/ 0	.000	-/ 9	0	5	4	1	1	8	-
Totals	200	34/65	.523	22/29	.759	-/34	14	14	25	8	3	90	.450

La Salle (82)   Coach: Lefty Ervin

	Min.	Total FG/FGA	Pct.	FT/FTA	Pct.	Reb. O/T	A	TO	PF	S	Blk	TP	PPM
WEBSTER, G.	12	0/ 1	.000	0/ 1	.000	-/ 1	1	0	2	0	0	0	.000
CONNOLLY, J.	31	8/11	.727	4/ 4	1.000	-/ 7	1	1	4	1	0	20	.645
KANASKIE, K.	37	5/15	.333	1/ 2	.500	-/ 2	3	6	3	2	0	11	.297
LYNAM, K.	31	7/10	.700	0/ 0	.000	-/ 1	5	4	5	0	0	14	.452
WORD, D.	15	2/ 7	.286	0/ 0	.000	-/ 4	2	3	4	0	0	4	.267
WILLIAMS, S.	32	1/ 6	.167	2/ 4	.500	-/10	2	3	4	2	0	4	.125
BROOKS, M.	39	8/16	.500	13/17	.765	-/12	1	2	4	2	0	29	.744
HARTER, P.	1	0/ 0	.000	0/ 0	.000	-/ 0	0	0	0	0	0	0	.000
GILMORE, R.	1	0/ 0	.000	0/ 0	.000	-/ 0	0	0	0	0	0	0	.000
DAVIS, D.	1	0/ 0	.000	0/ 0	.000	-/ 0	1	0	0	1	0	0	.000
Totals	200	31/66	.470	20/28	.714	-/37	15	19	26	8	0	82	.410

Team Rebounds: Purdue 2; La Salle 2. Disqualified: La Salle—Lynam. Technical fouls: None.

	1st Half	2nd Half	Final
Purdue	39	51	90
La Salle	36	46	82

Virginia Tech (89)   Coach: Charles Moir

	Min.	Total FG/FGA	Pct.	FT/FTA	Pct.	Reb. O/T	A	TO	PF	S	Blk	TP	PPM
HENSON, L.	38	4/ 9	.444	7/10	.700	-/ 3	0	4	5	2	0	15	.395
SOLOMON, D.	39	10/13	.769	2/ 2	1.000	-/11	0	3	4	0	0	22	.564
ROBINSON, W.	30	6/ 8	.750	0/ 0	.000	-/ 3	0	2	4	0	0	12	.400
REID, D.	42	4/ 8	.500	7/ 8	.875	-/ 4	4	1	3	0	0	15	.357
SCHNEIDER, J.	40	3/ 8	.375	3/ 5	.600	-/ 2	4	2	2	1	0	9	.225
SCOTT, C.	6	2/ 4	.500	2/ 3	.667	-/ 1	0	1	0	0	0	6	1.000
COOKE, M.	1	1/ 3	.333	3/ 5	.600	-/ 2	0	0	2	0	0	5	.625
HILLENBRAND, J.	16	2/ 2	1.000	0/ 0	.000	-/ 4	0	0	4	0	0	4	.250
STEPPE, R.	3	0/ 0	.000	0/ 0	.000	-/ 0	1	2	1	0	0	0	.000
BRYANT, G.	3	0/ 0	.000	1/ 2	.500	-/ 1	0	0	1	0	0	1	.333
Totals	225	32/55	.582	25/35	.714	-/31	9	15	26	3	0	89	.396

Western Kentucky (85)   Coach: Gene Keady

	Min.	Total FG/FGA	Pct.	FT/FTA	Pct.	Reb. O/T	A	TO	PF	S	Blk	TP	PPM
PRINCE, M.	11	0/ 2	.000	0/ 0	.000	-/ 1	2	3	1	0	0	0	.000
WASHINGTON, J.	38	9/12	.750	3/ 6	.500	-/11	3	3	1	0	21	21	.553
McCORMICK, C.	38	5/ 7	.714	7/ 8	.875	-/ 9	0	2	4	1	1	17	.447
BRYANT, B.	40	7/14	.500	5/ 6	.833	-/ 3	0	3	3	0	0	19	.475
TRUMBO, T.	28	0/ 0	.000	4/ 4	1.000	-/ 0	3	4	5	0	0	4	.143
REESE, M.	17	2/ 6	.333	0/ 0	.000	-/ 2	0	3	0	0	0	4	.235
WILSON, T.	27	6/10	.600	1/ 3	.333	-/ 1	1	2	4	0	0	13	.481
WRAY, R.	10	3/ 3	1.000	1/ 5	.200	-/ 3	0	0	0	0	0	7	.700
TOWNSEND, K.	8	0/ 0	.000	0/ 0	.000	-/ 1	0	1	0	0	0	0	.000
DILDY, K.	8	0/ 1	.000	0/ 0	.000	-/ 1	1	0	0	0	0	0	.000
Totals	225	32/56	.571	21/32	.656	-/29	10	18	24	2	1	85	.378

Team Rebounds: Virginia Tech 1; Western Ky. 2. Disqualified: Virginia Tech—Henson; Western Ky.—Trumbo. Technical fouls: Western Ky.—bench.

	1st Half	2nd Half	1 OT	Final
Virginia Tech	30	45	14	89
Western Ky.	48	27	10	85

FIRST ROUND WEST

UCLA (87)   Coach: Larry Brown

	Min.	Total FG/FGA	Pct.	FT/FTA	Pct.	Reb. O/T	A	TO	PF	S	Blk	TP	PPM
VANDEWEGHE, K.	39	11/20	.550	12/16	.750	-/ 9	2	6	2	0	0	34	.872
WILKES, J.	30	5/ 8	.625	5/ 6	.833	-/ 6	5	2	3	0	0	15	.500
SANDERS, M.	38	4/ 9	.444	3/ 3	1.000	-/18	7	6	3	0	2	11	.289
FOSTER, R.	29	4/ 6	.667	3/ 3	1.000	-/ 0	3	1	5	1	0	11	.379
HOLTON, M.	34	3/ 6	.500	6/ 7	.857	-/ 1	2	3	3	1	0	12	.353
DAYE, D.	16	2/ 4	.500	0/ 0	.000	-/ 1	1	3	1	2	1	4	.250
PRUITT, C.	7	0/ 2	.000	0/ 0	.000	-/ 1	0	2	1	1	0	0	.000
ANDERSON, T.	7	0/ 1	.000	0/ 0	.000	-/ 1	0	0	1	0	0	0	.000
Totals	200	29/56	.518	29/35	.829	-/37	20	23	19	5	3	87	.435

Old Dominion (74)   Coach: Paul Webb

	Min.	Total FG/FGA	Pct.	FT/FTA	Pct.	Reb. O/T	A	TO	PF	S	Blk	TP	PPM
McADOO, R.	35	11/17	.647	3/ 3	1.000	-/12	0	1	4	0	0	25	.714
VALENTINE, R.	33	5/19	.263	4/ 5	.800	-/ 2	1	4	5	4	0	14	.424
WEST, M.	19	0/ 0	.000	0/ 0	.000	-/ 5	3	1	4	0	2	0	.000
MANN, B.	31	2/10	.200	2/ 2	1.000	-/ 7	2	3	2	5	0	6	.194
ROBINSON, G.	21	0/ 5	.000	0/ 0	.000	-/ 1	2	4	1	0	0	0	.000
VAUGHAN, B.	23	6/10	.600	3/ 5	.600	-/ 3	2	1	4	2	0	15	.652
BRANCH, T.	25	4/12	.333	0/ 0	.000	-/ 2	1	4	4	1	0	8	.320
SOUTHERLAND, T.	1	0/ 0	.000	0/ 0	.000	-/ 0	0	0	0	0	0	0	.000
HAITHCOCK, B.	5	0/ 1	.000	2/ 2	1.000	-/ 2	0	1	0	0	0	2	.400
GREIKSPOOR, E.	-	0/ 0	.000	0/ 0	.000	-/ 0	0	0	0	0	0	0	-
KRAGTWIJK, B.	-	2/ 3	.667	0/ 0	.000	-/ 1	0	0	1	0	0	4	-
Totals	200	30/77	.390	14/17	.824	-/35	11	18	29	13	2	74	.370

Team Rebounds: UCLA 2; Old Dominion 4. Disqualified: UCLA—Foster; Old Dominion—Valentine. Technical fouls: Old Dominion—Branch.

	1st Half	2nd Half	Final
UCLA	36	51	87
Old Dominion	28	46	74

Arizona State (99)   Coach: Ned Wulk

	Min.	Total FG/FGA	Pct.	FT/FTA	Pct.	Reb. O/T	A	TO	PF	S	Blk	TP	PPM
WILLIAMS, S.	20	6/ 7	.857	1/ 3	.333	-/ 6	7	2	1	0	0	13	.650
NIMPHIUS, K.	21	6/ 8	.750	1/ 3	.333	-/ 7	1	0	2	0	1	13	.619
LISTER, A.	20	5/ 8	.625	2/ 3	.667	-/12	3	3	1	0	3	12	.600
SCOTT, B.	19	6/ 9	.667	0/ 0	.000	-/ 3	2	2	2	3	0	12	.632
LAFAYETTE, L.	18	3/ 6	.500	2/ 5	.400	-/ 4	2	2	2	0	0	8	.444
BRESSANT, P.	10	1/ 3	.333	3/ 6	.500	-/ 3	0	1	2	1	0	5	.500
NASH, J.	13	2/ 5	.400	0/ 0	.000	-/ 2	8	3	2	0	0	4	.308
BUTTS, J.	15	2/ 5	.400	1/ 2	.500	-/ 2	0	1	0	0	1	5	.333
KUYPER, T.	12	4/ 7	.571	0/ 0	.000	-/ 2	0	1	0	0	0	8	.667
WILLIAMS, P.	17	4/11	.364	0/ 0	.000	-/ 6	0	2	0	1	0	8	.471
THOMAS, B.	10	2/ 6	.333	0/ 2	.000	-/ 5	3	1	4	0	0	4	.400
STRAWN, M.	3	0/ 2	.000	0/ 0	.000	-/ 0	0	0	1	0	0	0	.000
WARRING, R.	3	0/ 0	.000	0/ 0	.000	-/ 1	0	0	0	0	0	0	.000
JONES, B.	16	3/ 7	.429	1/ 2	.500	-/ 5	2	0	2	0	1	7	.438
ELLISON, K.	3	0/ 2	.000	0/ 0	.000	-/ 0	0	1	0	0	0	0	.000
Totals	200	44/86	.512	11/26	.423	-/58	28	19	19	5	6	99	.495

Loyola Marymount (71)   Coach: Ron Jacobs

	Min.	Total FG/FGA	Pct.	FT/FTA	Pct.	Reb. O/T	A	TO	PF	S	Blk	TP	PPM
McCLOSKEY, J.	29	8/19	.421	8/ 8	1.000	-/ 1	4	4	3	1	0	24	.828
WORTHY, R.	29	2/ 7	.286	3/ 5	.600	-/ 4	2	2	5	0	0	7	.241
ANTOINE, M.	27	2/ 7	.286	2/ 2	1.000	-/ 6	0	1	3	1	0	6	.222
MOORE, J.	30	5/ 9	.556	0/ 0	.000	-/ 7	2	2	4	1	0	10	.333
DAVIS, D.	29	5/13	.385	1/ 2	.500	-/ 1	5	1	4	0	0	11	.379
DUNLAP, M.	5	0/ 0	.000	0/ 0	.000	-/ 2	1	1	2	1	0	0	.000
JOHNSON, C.	15	3/13	.231	0/ 0	.000	-/ 3	1	1	1	0	0	6	.400
PETERSON, M.	5	0/ 2	.000	0/ 0	.000	-/ 1	0	1	0	0	0	0	.000
PRITCHETT, S.	3	0/ 1	.000	0/ 0	.000	-/ 0	0	0	0	0	0	0	.000
YOUNG, M.	5	2/ 4	.500	0/ 0	.000	-/ 3	0	1	0	0	0	4	.800
BOKAN, P.	5	1/ 3	.333	1/ 2	.500	-/ 2	0	0	0	0	0	3	.600
CLAYBION, A.	14	0/ 3	.000	0/ 0	.000	-/ 5	0	0	1	1	0	2	.000
TODD, B.	2	0/ 0	.000	0/ 0	.000	-/ 2	0	0	1	0	0	0	.000
KOCH, K.	2	0/ 1	.000	0/ 0	.000	-/ 1	0	1	0	0	0	0	.000
Totals	200	28/82	.341	15/19	.789	-/38	15	15	23	5	2	71	.355

Team Rebounds: Arizona St. 8; Loyola-Mymt. 5. Disqualified: Loyola-Mymt.—Worthy. Technical fouls: None.

	1st Half	2nd Half	Final
Arizona St.	51	48	99
Loyola Mymt.	29	42	71

Clemson (76)   Coach: Wm. C. (Bill) Foster

	Min.	Total FG/FGA	Pct.	FT/FTA	Pct.	Reb. O/T	A	TO	PF	S	Blk	TP	PPM
NANCE, L.	23	5/10	.500	3/ 7	.429	-/ 9	3	3	4	0	0	13	.565
WYATT, H.	22	3/ 6	.500	0/ 1	.000	-/ 4	2	2	4	0	0	6	.273
CAMPBELL, J.	23	1/ 2	.500	2/ 5	.400	-/ 6	0	5	3	0	0	4	.174
CONRAD, B.	30	1/ 5	.200	1/ 2	.500	-/ 2	5	2	4	1	0	3	.100
WILLIAMS, B.	35	9/17	.529	4/ 6	.667	-/ 6	1	1	3	2	0	22	.629
DOBBS, C.	18	3/ 3	1.000	0/ 1	.000	-/ 1	4	3	2	1	0	6	.333
WIGGINS, M.	14	2/ 5	.400	0/ 0	.000	-/ 3	1	1	3	0	0	4	.286
GILLIAM, F.	28	6/ 9	.667	2/ 2	1.000	-/ 1	1	2	1	0	0	14	.500
ROSS, R.	7	2/ 2	1.000	0/ 0	.000	-/ 1	0	0	0	0	0	4	.571
Totals	200	32/59	.542	12/24	.500	-/33	17	19	22	4	0	76	.380

Utah State (73)   Coach: Rod Tueller

	Min.	Total FG/FGA	Pct.	FT/FTA	Pct.	Reb. O/T	A	TO	PF	S	Blk	TP	PPM
HUNGER, D.	38	11/21	.524	5/ 7	.714	-/13	0	4	3	0	0	27	.711
JACKSON, B.	36	3/ 8	.375	5/ 7	.714	-/ 6	2	5	4	0	1	11	.306
CUNNINGHAM, L.	23	0/ 2	.000	0/ 0	.000	-/ 6	0	1	4	0	0	0	.000
HOOD, K.	39	4/10	.400	2/ 3	.667	-/ 4	1	3	3	0	2	10	.256
McELRATH, R.	38	3/ 8	.375	5/ 7	.714	-/ 3	6	5	5	2	1	11	.289
WICKLIFFE, E.	24	5/ 9	.556	4/ 4	1.000	-/ 4	3	2	3	2	0	14	.583
BERGESON, L.	1	0/ 0	.000	0/ 0	.000	-/ 0	0	0	1	0	0	0	.000
PINEGAR, S.	1	0/ 0	.000	0/ 0	.000	-/ 0	0	0	0	0	0	0	.000
Totals	200	26/58	.448	21/28	.750	-/36	12	20	23	4	4	73	.365

Team Rebounds: Clemson—1; Utah State—2. Disqualified: Utah State—McElrath. Technical fouls: Clemson—Campbell.

	1st Half	2nd Half	Final
Clemson	40	36	76
Utah State	38	35	73

Weber State (86)   Coach: Neil McCarthy

	Min.	Total FG/FGA	Pct.	FT/FTA	Pct.	Reb. O/T	A	TO	PF	S	Blk	TP	PPM
JOHNSON, D.	36	7/16	.438	4/5	.800	-/8	3	5	4	2	0	18	.500
MARTINSON, G.	18	1/3	.333	0/0	.000	-/2	1	0	0	0	0	2	.111
SMITH, R.	29	1/3	.333	1/4	.250	-/5	1	1	0	1	0	3	.103
MATTOS, M.	28	2/3	.667	0/0	.000	-/1	4	4	3	0	0	4	.143
COLLINS, B.	40	13/26	.500	6/6	1.000	-/11	4	2	1	2	1	32	.800
HARPER, T.	24	6/11	.545	2/3	.667	-/6	0	2	5	1	0	14	.583
CONDIE, S.	2	0/0	.000	0/0	.000	-/0	0	0	0	0	0	0	.000
EDWARDS, R.	11	3/7	.429	1/3	.333	-/7	0	0	2	2	0	7	.636
WATSON, E.	4	0/3	.000	0/0	.000	-/0	0	0	1	0	0	0	.000
DOOLAN, T.	7	2/3	.667	0/1	.000	-/1	3	0	5	0	0	4	.571
PENILTON, D.	1	1/1	1.000	0/0	.000	-/1	0	0	0	0	0	2	2.000
Totals	200	36/76	.474	14/22	.636	-/42	16	14	21	8	1	86	.430

Lamar (87)   Coach: Billy Tubbs

	Min.	Total FG/FGA	Pct.	FT/FTA	Pct.	Reb. O/T	A	TO	PF	S	Blk	TP	PPM
LEWIS, C.	38	4/7	.571	1/2	.500	-/4	2	3	3	1	0	9	.237
DAVIS, B.	27	7/9	.778	6/8	.750	-/8	3	2	4	0	3	20	.741
KEA, C.	37	2/4	.500	2/4	.500	-/7	0	1	5	1	0	6	.162
OLLIVER, M.	40	17/26	.654	3/4	.750	-/5	1	3	3	0	0	37	.925
BROOKS, A.	40	2/5	.400	5/8	.625	-/1	10	6	3	3	0	9	.225
WILLIAMS, R.	18	3/5	.600	0/0	.000	-/3	0	1	2	0	0	6	.333
Totals	200	35/56	.625	17/26	.654	-/28	16	16	20	5	3	87	.435

Team Rebounds: Lamar 2; Weber St. 2. Disqualified: Lamar—Kea; Weber St.—Harper, Doolan. Technical fouls: Lamar—Kea; Weber St.—Harper.

	1st Half	2nd Half	Final
Weber St.	31	55	86
Lamar	35	52	87

SECOND ROUND EAST

Villanova (83)   Coach: Rollie Massimino

	Min.	Total FG/FGA	Pct.	FT/FTA	Pct.	Reb. O/T	A	TO	PF	S	Blk	TP	PPM
HOWARD, A.	11	0/0	.000	0/0	.000	0/0	0	1	3	0	0	0	.000
BRADLEY, A.	34	8/15	.533	3/4	.750	3/5	0	2	2	0	1	19	.559
PINONE, J.	34	3/8	.375	6/7	.857	2/5	1	2	3	0	0	12	.353
SPARROW, R.	35	5/13	.385	0/1	.000	0/0	5	6	5	2	0	10	.286
SIENKIEWICZ, T.	28	11/15	.733	0/0	.000	2/4	0	3	4	3	0	22	.786
GRANGER, S.	13	0/0	.000	0/0	.000	0/0	2	3	1	0	0	0	.000
LINCOLN, S.	15	4/4	1.000	2/2	1.000	0/0	5	4	5	3	0	10	.667
MULQUIN, M.	4	1/2	.500	2/2	1.000	0/0	0	0	0	1	0	4	1.000
BETHEA, T.	12	0/2	.000	0/0	.000	0/1	9	2	1	0	1	0	.000
CARON, M.	14	1/1	1.000	4/6	.667	0/2	1	1	2	0	0	6	.429
Totals	200	33/60	.550	17/22	.773	7/17	23	24	26	9	2	83	.415

Syracuse (97)   Coach: Jim Boeheim

	Min.	Total FG/FGA	Pct.	FT/FTA	Pct.	Reb. O/T	A	TO	PF	S	Blk	TP	PPM
SANTIFER, E.	35	13/15	.867	3/5	.600	4/6	1	2	2	1	0	29	.829
ORR, L.	37	4/8	.500	3/5	.600	3/8	1	5	4	2	0	11	.297
BOUIE, R.	10	1/2	.500	0/0	.000	1/2	0	3	5	0	2	2	.200
MOSS, E.	31	3/5	.600	8/8	1.000	1/5	5	3	1	3	0	14	.452
HEADD, M.	30	7/11	.636	0/0	.000	0/0	2	1	1	5	0	14	.467
COHEN, H.	15	1/3	.333	9/10	.900	0/3	2	1	2	1	0	11	.733
BRUIN, T.	16	2/5	.400	0/0	.000	1/2	3	3	2	0	1	4	.250
PAYTON, R.	2	0/1	.000	0/0	.000	0/1	0	2	0	0	0	0	.000
SCHAYES, D.	24	4/7	.571	4/4	1.000	1/5	2	4	5	1	1	12	.500
Totals	200	35/57	.614	27/32	.844	11/32	16	24	22	13	4	97	.485

Team Rebounds: Syracuse 1; Villanova 5. Disqualified: Syracuse—Bouie, Schayes; Villanova—Sparrow, Lincoln. Technical fouls: None.

	1st Half	2nd Half	Final
Villanova	28	55	83
Syracuse	40	57	97

Iowa (77)   Coach: Lute Olson

	Min.	Total FG/FGA	Pct.	FT/FTA	Pct.	Reb. O/T	A	TO	PF	S	Blk	TP	PPM
BOYLE, K.	33	2/4	.500	3/5	.600	-/7	3	1	3	2	0	7	.212
WAITE, S.	33	0/4	.000	3/5	.600	-/4	0	2	1	0	0	3	.091
KRAFCISIN, S.	18	1/3	.333	7/8	.875	-/4	1	1	1	0	1	9	.500
LESTER, R.	28	6/10	.600	5/6	.833	-/0	4	3	4	1	0	17	.607
ARNOLD, K.	39	6/11	.545	6/8	.750	-/4	2	0	1	0	1	18	.462
HANSEN, B.	17	2/5	.400	0/0	.000	-/2	3	1	2	1	0	4	.235
BROOKINS, V.	31	7/7	1.000	3/5	.600	-/2	0	2	2	0	2	17	.548
HELLER, M.	1	1/1	1.000	0/0	.000	-/0	0	0	0	0	0	2	2.000
Totals	200	25/45	.556	27/37	.730	-/23	13	10	14	4	4	77	.385

North Carolina State (64)   Coach: Norm Sloan

	Min.	Total FG/FGA	Pct.	FT/FTA	Pct.	Reb. O/T	A	TO	PF	S	Blk	TP	PPM
WHITNEY, H.	35	5/16	.313	0/2	.000	-/11	4	2	5	0	1	10	.286
BAILEY, T.	23	0/3	.000	2/2	1.000	-/3	0	1	3	1	0	2	.087
WATTS, C.	24	6/6	1.000	0/0	.000	-/4	1	2	2	0	2	12	.500
AUSTIN, C.	23	9/18	.500	0/0	.000	-/1	0	3	4	0	0	18	.783
LOWE, S.	33	1/3	.333	3/4	.750	-/0	10	2	3	1	0	5	.152
MATTHEWS, K.	19	3/6	.500	0/0	.000	-/0	0	1	1	0	0	6	.316
JONES, A.	28	2/4	.500	0/1	.000	-/4	2	2	3	1	0	4	.143
PARZYCH, S.	2	0/0	.000	0/0	.000	-/0	0	0	0	0	0	0	.000
WHITTENBURG, D.	7	2/4	.500	0/0	.000	-/1	0	1	0	1	0	4	.571
PERRY, M.	2	0/0	.000	0/0	.000	-/0	0	0	0	0	0	0	.000
NEVITT, C.	3	1/1	1.000	0/0	.000	-/1	0	0	3	0	1	2	.667
WEBER, P.	1	0/0	.000	1/1	1.000	-/0	2	0	0	0	0	1	1.000
Totals	200	29/61	.475	6/10	.600	-/25	19	13	25	3	4	64	.320

Team Rebounds: Iowa 7; N.C. State 4. Disqualified: N.C. State—Whitney. Technical fouls: Iowa—Hansen, Coach Olsen.

	1st Half	2nd Half	Final
Iowa	26	51	77
N.C. State	29	35	64

Iona (71)   Coach: Jim Valvano

	Min.	Total FG/FGA	Pct.	FT/FTA	Pct.	Reb. O/T	A	TO	PF	S	Blk	TP	PPM
PALMA, M.	20	2/4	.500	2/2	1.000	-/0	1	4	1	0	0	6	.300
MIDDLETON, A.	39	8/12	.667	2/2	1.000	-/13	0	2	5	1	2	18	.462
RULAND, J.	37	8/10	.800	0/2	.000	-/7	2	7	4	1	1	16	.432
VICKERS, G.	38	1/6	.167	4/4	1.000	-/3	5	4	2	0	0	6	.158
HAMILTON, K.	40	8/14	.571	1/2	.500	-/3	3	3	4	2	0	17	.425
IATI, T.	2	0/0	.000	0/1	.000	-/0	0	0	0	0	0	0	.000
VESEY, K.	4	0/0	.000	0/0	.000	-/0	0	1	0	0	0	0	.000
WILLIAMS, J.	18	2/4	.500	4/4	1.000	-/3	0	0	0	0	0	8	.444
MCMILLAN, G.	2	0/0	.000	0/0	.000	-/0	1	1	0	0	0	0	.000
Totals	200	29/50	.580	13/17	.765	-/29	12	21	17	4	3	71	.355

Georgetown (74)   Coach: John Thompson

	Min.	Total FG/FGA	Pct.	FT/FTA	Pct.	Reb. O/T	A	TO	PF	S	Blk	TP	PPM
DUTCH, A.	11	2/3	.667	0/0	.000	-/1	1	1	0	0	0	4	.364
SHELTON, C.	37	10/15	.667	7/9	.778	-/6	2	1	2	0	0	27	.730
HANCOCK, M.	1	0/0	.000	0/0	.000	-/0	0	0	1	0	1	0	.000
FLOYD, E.	32	10/19	.526	1/2	.500	-/3	3	1	4	2	0	21	.656
DUREN, J.	39	1/8	.125	0/0	.000	-/2	9	4	3	1	0	2	.051
SMITH, D.	29	3/6	.500	3/4	.750	-/2	3	3	2	0	0	9	.310
FENLON, T.	10	0/1	.000	0/0	.000	-/0	0	0	0	0	0	0	.000
BULLIS, J.	3	0/0	.000	0/0	.000	-/0	0	1	1	0	0	0	.000
SPRIGGS, E.	13	2/2	1.000	0/0	.000	-/3	0	0	4	0	1	4	.308
FRAZIER, M.	25	3/5	.600	1/1	1.000	-/3	0	1	2	0	1	7	.280
Totals	200	31/59	.525	12/16	.750	-/20	18	12	18	4	3	74	.370

Team Rebounds: Georgetown 1; Iona 0. Disqualified: Iona—Middleton. Technical fouls: None.

	1st Half	2nd Half	Final
Iona	40	31	71
Georgetown	37	37	74

Tennessee (75)   Coach: Don Devoe

	Min.	Total FG/FGA	Pct.	FT/FTA	Pct.	Reb. O/T	A	TO	PF	S	Blk	TP	PPM
JOHNSON, R.	25	10/17	.588	1/1	1.000	-/4	0	1	5	0	0	21	.840
RAY, S.	17	0/3	.000	0/0	.000	-/2	1	0	3	0	0	0	.000
THREETHS, C.	19	0/2	.000	0/0	.000	-/5	0	2	3	0	0	0	.000
CARTER, G.	40	7/12	.583	7/7	1.000	-/8	3	1	1	1	0	21	.525
BERTELKAMP, B.	39	3/8	.375	2/2	1.000	-/2	16	2	5	0	0	8	.205
ELLIS, D.	22	3/6	.500	1/2	.500	-/2	0	0	5	1	0	7	.318
WOOD, H.	25	6/13	.462	0/0	.000	-/4	0	2	0	2	1	12	.480
NASH, K.	11	2/4	.500	2/2	1.000	-/3	0	0	2	0	0	6	.545
PARTON, R.	1	0/0	.000	0/0	.000	-/0	0	1	0	0	0	0	.000
POOLE, M.	1	0/1	.000	0/0	.000	-/0	0	0	1	0	0	0	.000
Totals	200	31/66	.470	13/14	.929	-/30	20	9	25	4	1	75	.375

Maryland (86)   Coach: Lefty Driesell

	Min.	Total FG/FGA	Pct.	FT/FTA	Pct.	Reb. O/T	A	TO	PF	S	Blk	TP	PPM
KING, A.	40	10/16	.625	0/0	.000	-/6	3	6	2	1	0	20	.500
GRAHAM, E.	39	5/8	.625	4/7	.571	-/9	5	3	3	0	0	14	.359
WILLIAMS, B.	38	8/13	.615	3/6	.500	-/9	0	1	5	0	2	19	.500
MANNING, G.	39	11/15	.733	6/7	.857	-/3	3	1	0	1	0	28	.718
JACKSON, N.	35	2/4	.500	1/5	.200	-/4	10	2	2	2	0	5	.143
MORLEY, D.	7	0/1	.000	0/0	.000	-/0	0	0	0	0	0	0	.000
BALDWIN, T.	2	0/0	.000	0/0	.000	-/1	0	0	1	0	1	0	.000
Totals	200	36/57	.632	14/25	.560	-/32	21	13	13	4	3	86	.430

Team Rebounds: Maryland 4; Tennessee 0. Disqualified: Maryland —Williams; Tennessee—Johnson, Bertelkamp, Ellis. Technical fouls: Maryland—Coach Driesell; Tennessee—Coach Devoe.

	1st Half	2nd Half	Final
Tennessee	40	35	75
Maryland	32	54	86

SECOND ROUND MIDWEST

Alcorn State (88)   Coach: Dave Whitney

	Min.	Total FG/FGA	Pct.	FT/FTA	Pct.	Reb. O/T	A	TO	PF	S	Blk	TP	PPM
SMITH	23	5/11	.455	3/3	1.000	-/5	0	-	4	-	-	13	.565
WYATT	33	9/16	.563	1/1	1.000	-/12	2	-	3	-	-	19	.576
BAKER, E.	29	6/13	.462	1/2	.500	-/4	1	-	2	-	-	13	.448
JENKINS	25	3/6	.500	0/2	.000	-/2	2	-	2	-	-	6	.240
BELL, E.	31	2/10	.200	0/0	.000	-/1	2	-	4	-	-	4	.129
HOWARD	19	6/11	.545	3/4	.750	-/3	0	-	2	-	-	15	.789
ALEXANDER	24	5/10	.500	2/2	1.000	-/2	1	-	3	-	-	12	.500
IRVING, A.	16	3/5	.600	0/0	.000	-/2	0	-	1	-	-	6	.375
Totals	200	39/82	.476	10/14	.714	-/31	8	18	21	-	-	88	.440

Louisiana State (98)   Coach: Dale Brown

	Min.	Total FG/FGA	Pct.	FT/FTA	Pct.	Reb. O/T	A	TO	PF	S	Blk	TP	PPM
SCALES	13	4/5	.800	0/0	.000	-/5	0	-	4	-	-	8	.615
MACKLIN, D.	40	12/20	.600	7/7	1.000	-/19	0	-	1	-	-	31	.775
COOK, G.	37	2/4	.500	0/1	.000	-/7	2	-	5	-	-	4	.108
MARTIN, E.	38	3/14	.214	5/6	.833	-/3	2	-	2	-	-	11	.289
CARTER, H.	34	7/12	.583	0/0	.000	-/4	1	-	3	-	-	14	.412
SIMS, W.	31	13/19	.684	4/6	.667	-/5	2	-	3	-	-	30	.968
COSTELLO, J.	3	0/0	.000	0/0	.000	-/0	0	-	1	-	-	0	.000
HULTBERG, J.	4	0/0	.000	0/0	.000	-/0	0	-	0	-	-	0	.000
Totals	200	41/74	.554	16/20	.800	-/43	7	22	19	-	-	98	.490

Team Rebounds: Louisiana St. 2; Alcorn St. 7. Disqualified: Louisiana St.—Cook. Technical fouls: Louisiana St.—Sims, Scales.

	1st Half	2nd Half	Final
Alcorn St.	49	39	88
Louisiana St.	51	47	98

Missouri (87)   Coach: Norm Stewart

	Min.	Total FG/FGA	Pct.	FT/FTA	Pct.	Reb. O/T	A	TO	PF	S	Blk	TP	PPM
DRESSLER, M.	-	13/16	.813	6/8	.750	-/8	3	-	4	-	-	32	-
FRAZIER, R.	-	6/10	.600	2/2	1.000	-/8	0	-	4	-	-	14	-
STIPANOVICH	-	5/9	.556	5/8	.625	-/8	3	-	4	-	-	15	-
SUNDVOID	-	4/7	.571	2/2	1.000	-/1	1	-	3	-	-	10	-
DREW, L.	-	6/12	.500	3/3	1.000	-/5	12	-	3	-	-	15	-
FOSTER, M.	-	0/0	.000	0/0	.000	-/0	0	-	0	-	-	0	-
AMOS	-	0/0	.000	0/0	.000	-/0	0	-	0	-	-	0	-
DORE	-	0/2	.000	1/3	.333	-/3	0	-	3	-	-	1	-
Totals	225	34/56	.607	19/26	.731	-/33	19	-	21	-	-	87	.387

Notre Dame (84)   Coach: Digger Phelps

	Min.	Total FG/FGA	Pct.	FT/FTA	Pct.	Reb. O/T	A	TO	PF	S	Blk	TP	PPM
JACKSON, T.	-	13/27	.481	1/4	.250	-/19	0	-	2	-	-	27	-
TRIPUCKA	-	9/20	.450	4/6	.667	-/5	3	-	5	-	-	22	-
WOOLRIDGE, O.	-	6/9	.667	4/7	.571	-/7	0	-	2	-	-	16	-
BRANNING, R.	-	0/3	.000	0/0	.000	-/1	6	-	2	-	-	0	-
HANZLIK	-	4/9	.444	5/6	.833	-/5	1	-	5	-	-	13	-
PAXSON, J.	-	2/5	.400	2/3	.667	-/2	3	-	4	-	-	6	-
ANDREE, T.	-	0/1	.000	0/0	.000	-/0	1	-	3	-	-	0	-
SALINAS	-	0/1	.000	0/0	.000	-/0	1	-	1	-	-	0	-
Totals	225	34/75	.453	16/26	.615	-/39	15	-	24	-	-	84	.373

Team Rebounds: Missouri 2; Notre Dame 1. Disqualified: Notre Dame—Tripucka, Hanzlik. Technical Fouls: Missouri—Coach Stewart.

	1st Half	2nd Half	1st OT	Final
Missouri	36	40	11	87
Notre Dame	42	34	8	84

Texas A&M (78)   Coach: Shelby Metcalf

	Min.	Total FG/FGA	Pct.	FT/FTA	Pct.	Reb. O/T	A	TO	PF	S	Blk	TP	PPM
SMITH, V.	43	4/13	.308	3/4	.750	-/9	0	3	3	1	0	11	.256
WRIGHT, R.	47	4/11	.364	2/5	.400	-/13	1	2	5	2	1	10	.213
WOODS, R.	42	5/6	.833	4/10	.400	-/5	0	1	4	0	1	14	.333
GOFF, D.	46	1/3	.333	5/6	.833	-/1	2	1	2	2	0	7	.152
BRITTON, D.	46	8/18	.444	7/12	.583	-/6	2	4	2	1	0	23	.500
RILEY, C.	14	2/3	.667	2/2	1.000	-/6	1	1	3	0	0	6	.429
LADSON, T.	12	0/1	.000	7/9	.778	-/2	0	0	1	1	0	7	.583
Totals	250	24/55	.436	30/48	.625	-/42	6	12	20	7	2	78	.312

North Carolina (61)   Coach: Dean Smith

	Min.	Total FG/FGA	Pct.	FT/FTA	Pct.	Reb. O/T	A	TO	PF	S	Blk	TP	PPM
WOOD, A.	46	9/19	.474	8/12	.667	-/9	0	2	4	1	1	26	.565
O'KOREN, M.	45	5/13	.385	1/2	.500	-/18	1	3	5	1	0	11	.244
WOLF, J.	33	1/2	.500	0/2	.000	-/3	0	1	5	0	1	2	.061
COLESCOTT, D.	45	1/7	.143	3/3	1.000	-/1	1	1	3	1	0	5	.111
VIRGIL, J.	20	5/12	.417	1/3	.333	-/2	0	1	4	0	0	11	.550
YONAKOR, R.	16	0/3	.000	0/0	.000	-/4	0	2	5	1	0	0	.000
BLACK, J.	25	1/4	.250	2/2	1.000	-/2	1	3	5	2	0	4	.160
BRUST, C.	2	0/0	.000	0/0	.000	-/1	0	1	0	0	0	0	.000
BRADDOCK, J.	2	0/0	.000	0/0	.000	-/0	0	0	0	0	0	0	.000
BUDKO, P.	4	0/0	.000	0/0	.000	-/1	0	0	1	0	0	0	.000
PEPPER, M.	10	1/4	.250	0/0	.000	-/0	1	2	4	0	0	2	.200
KENNY, E.	2	0/0	.000	0/0	.000	-/0	0	0	0	0	0	0	.000
Totals	250	23/64	.359	15/24	.625	-/41	4	16	36	6	2	61	.244

Team Rebounds: Texas A&M 6; N. Carolina 1. Disqualified: Texas A&M—Wright; N. Carolina—O'Koren, Wolf, Yonakor, Black. Technical fouls: N. Carolina—Virgil.

	1st Half	2nd Half	1 OT	2 OT	Final
Texas A&M	30	23	0	25	78
N. Carolina	29	24	0	8	61

Kansas State (69)   Coach: Jack Hartman

	Min.	Total FG/FGA	Pct.	FT/FTA	Pct.	Reb. O/T	A	TO	PF	S	Blk	TP	PPM
NEALY, E.	45	3/12	.250	3/3	1.000	-/11	1	3	3	2	0	9	.200
WILLS, J.	33	3/5	.600	3/4	.750	-/6	2	2	3	3	0	9	.273
CRAFT, L.	24	3/4	.750	0/0	.000	-/5	1	2	2	0	0	6	.250
MARSHALL, G.	45	8/14	.571	0/0	.000	-/1	8	5	3	3	0	16	.356
BLACKMAN, R.	45	6/18	.333	7/8	.875	-/4	7	1	2	1	0	19	.422
ADAMS, T.	33	5/9	.556	0/0	.000	-/2	2	1	2	0	0	10	.303
Totals	225	28/62	.452	13/15	.867	-/29	21	14	15	9	0	69	.307

Louisville (71)   Coach: Denny Crum

	Min.	Total FG/FGA	Pct.	FT/FTA	Pct.	Reb. O/T	A	TO	PF	S	Blk	TP	PPM
MCCRAY, R.	-	4/6	.667	0/0	.000	-/5	2	7	2	1	1	8	-
SMITH, D.	-	9/14	.643	2/2	1.000	-/7	0	2	2	0	0	20	-
BROWN, W.	-	4/5	.800	1/2	.500	-/6	1	3	1	0	0	9	-
EAVES, J.	-	0/3	.000	0/0	.000	-/0	1	0	1	0	0	0	-
GRIFFITH, D.	-	8/20	.400	2/3	.667	-/6	8	4	5	0	0	18	-
BRANCH, T.	-	1/1	1.000	0/0	.000	-/0	0	0	0	0	0	2	-
BURKMAN, R.	-	1/1	1.000	2/2	1.000	-/3	3	3	3	1	1	4	-
WRIGHT, P.	-	4/6	.667	2/2	1.000	-/1	2	0	2	1	1	10	-
Totals	225	31/56	.554	9/11	.818	-/28	17	19	15	4	3	71	.316

Team Rebounds: Louisville 1; Kansas State 4. Disqualified: Louisville—Griffith. Technical fouls: None.

	1st Half	2nd Half	1 OT	Final
Kansas State	37	30	2	69
Louisville	39	28	4	71

SECOND ROUND MIDEAST

Florida State (78)   Coach: Joe Williams

	Min.	Total FG/FGA	Pct.	FT/FTA	Pct.	Reb. O/T	A	TO	PF	S	Blk	TP	PPM
ARNOLD, R.	27	2/5	.400	6/9	.667	-/1	4	3	4	0	0	10	.370
BROWN, M.	33	9/12	.750	4/12	.333	-/8	0	2	5	0	0	22	.667
ROLLE, E.	39	7/11	.636	1/4	.250	-/8	0	3	4	0	2	15	.385
DILLARD, M.	39	6/12	.500	7/11	.636	-/6	1	7	4	0	1	19	.487
JACKSON, T.	29	2/4	.500	0/0	.000	-/1	1	1	5	0	4	4	.138
PARKS, B.	12	1/1	1.000	0/0	.000	-/0	0	4	0	0	0	2	.167
TOOKES, P.	16	2/6	.333	2/3	.667	-/6	2	0	2	0	0	6	.375
COX, J.	3	0/0	.000	0/0	.000	-/0	0	0	0	0	0	0	.000
COLLINGSWORTH, G.	2	0/0	.000	0/0	.000	-/0	0	1	0	0	1	0	.000
Totals	200	29/51	.569	20/39	.513	-/30	8	22	24	0	4	78	.390

Kentucky (97)   Coach: Joe Hall

	Min.	Total FG/FGA	Pct.	FT/FTA	Pct.	Reb. O/T	A	TO	PF	S	Blk	TP	PPM
COWAN, F.	-	5/12	.417	4/4	1.000	-/7	0	2	3	2	1	14	-
WILLIAMS, L.	-	6/9	.667	2/2	1.000	-/9	0	1	5	0	0	14	-
BOWIE, S.	-	4/14	.286	5/5	1.000	-/11	1	2	4	0	3	13	-
MACY, K.	-	6/16	.375	4/4	1.000	-/6	2	2	0	2	0	16	-
MINNIEFIELD, D.	-	0/3	.000	2/2	1.000	-/4	1	0	4	0	0	2	-
HURT, C.	-	4/6	.667	0/0	.000	-/3	0	0	3	0	0	8	-
HORD, D.	-	4/7	.571	0/0	.000	-/4	0	0	5	0	0	8	-
SHIDLER, J.	-	5/12	.417	0/1	.000	-/3	2	3	3	0	0	10	-
VERDERBER, C.	-	3/3	1.000	2/3	.667	-/4	1	2	2	1	0	8	-
HEITZ, T.	-	0/0	.000	4/6	.667	-/1	2	0	1	0	0	4	-
LANTER, B.	-	0/0	.000	0/0	.000	-/0	1	2	1	0	0	0	-
GETTELFINGER, C.	-	0/0	.000	0/0	.000	-/0	0	0	1	0	0	0	-
Totals	200	37/82	.451	23/27	.852	-/52	10	14	32	5	4	97	.485

Team Rebounds: Kentucky 2; Florida State 1. Disqualified: Kentucky—Williams, Hord; Florida State—Brown, Jackson. Technical fouls: None.

	1st Half	2nd Half	Final
Florida State	27	51	78
Kentucky	49	48	97

Pennsylvania (42)   Coach: Bob Weinhauer

	Min.	Total FG/FGA	Pct.	FT/FTA	Pct.	Reb. O/T	A	TO	PF	S	Blk	TP	PPM
SALTERS, J.	37	4/13	.308	1/2	.500	-/1	4	6	4	2	0	9	.243
LITTLE, P.	22	4/8	.500	0/0	.000	-/3	1	1	4	0	0	8	.364
REYNOLDS, A.	22	3/7	.429	0/0	.000	-/0	0	0	0	1	0	6	.273
ROSS, V.	32	2/4	.500	1/2	.500	-/8	2	3	3	0	0	5	.156
RAWLINGS, A.	11	1/1	1.000	0/0	.000	-/2	0	0	0	0	0	2	.182
HALL, K.	22	1/5	.200	0/0	.000	-/1	0	0	2	0	0	2	.091
LEIFSEN, T.	27	0/1	.000	0/0	.000	-/4	1	2	5	2	0	0	.000
BROWN, M.	8	2/3	.667	2/2	1.000	-/0	0	0	0	0	0	6	.750
NOON, G.	11	0/1	.000	0/0	.000	-/1	0	4	2	0	0	0	.000
FLICK, T.	8	2/2	1.000	0/0	.000	-/0	0	1	1	0	0	4	.500
Totals	200	19/45	.422	4/6	.667	-/20	8	17	21	5	0	42	.210

Duke (52)   Coach: Wm. E. (Bill) Foster

	Min.	Total FG/FGA	Pct.	FT/FTA	Pct.	Reb. O/T	A	TO	PF	S	Blk	TP	PPM
TAYLOR, V.	32	3/4	.750	2/4	.500	-/1	2	4	3	1	1	8	.250
ENGELLAND, C.	5	2/3	.667	0/0	.000	-/0	0	0	0	0	0	4	.800
BANKS, E.	39	3/8	.375	2/5	.400	-/6	1	5	1	1	0	8	.205
BENDER, B.	32	2/2	1.000	0/0	.000	-/0	4	3	0	2	0	4	.125
EMMA, T.	11	2/3	.667	0/0	.000	-/0	0	1	2	0	0	4	.364
SUDDATH, J.	4	0/1	.000	0/0	.000	-/1	0	0	0	0	0	0	.000
TISSAW, M.	5	0/0	.000	0/0	.000	-/0	0	0	0	0	0	0	.000
DENNARD, K.	32	1/2	.500	1/3	.333	-/6	3	1	4	2	0	3	.094
WILLIAMS, A.	5	1/1	1.000	0/0	.000	-/0	1	0	0	0	0	2	.400
GMINSKI, M.	35	6/9	.667	7/8	.875	-/4	1	5	2	1	2	19	.543
Totals	200	20/33	.606	12/20	.600	-/18	12	19	12	7	3	52	.260

Team Rebounds: Duke 1; Pennsylvania 2. Disqualified: Pennsylvania—Leifsen. Technical fouls: None.

	1st Half	2nd Half	Final
Pennsylvania	23	19	42
Duke	25	27	52

Purdue (87)   Coach: Lee Rose

	Min.	Total FG/FGA	Pct.	FT/FTA	Pct.	Reb. O/T	A	TO	PF	S	Blk	TP	PPM
EDMONSON, K.	32	8/12	.667	5/5	1.000	-/9	4	2	2	0	0	21	.656
WALKER, S.	15	1/1	1.000	3/3	1.000	-/3	1	0	1	1	0	5	.333
WALKER, B.	35	0/2	.000	0/0	.000	-/4	6	4	5	5	1	0	.000
ANTHROP, J.	1	0/0	.000	0/0	.000	-/0	0	0	0	0	0	0	.000
CARROLL, J.	39	14/21	.667	8/10	.800	-/12	1	2	1	2	3	36	.923
SCEARCE, M.	1	0/0	.000	0/0	.000	-/0	0	0	0	0	0	0	.000
STALLINGS, K.	4	0/0	.000	0/0	.000	-/0	0	3	0	0	0	0	.000
MORRIS, D.	31	8/15	.533	3/8	.375	-/6	4	3	3	0	0	19	.613
BENSON, T.	1	0/0	.000	2/2	1.000	-/0	0	0	0	0	0	2	2.000
KITCHEL, J.	1	0/1	.000	0/0	.000	-/0	0	0	0	0	0	0	.000
BARNES, R.	5	0/0	.000	0/0	.000	-/0	0	1	1	0	0	0	.000
HALLMAN, A.	35	1/6	.167	2/3	.667	-/8	4	6	1	0	0	4	.114
Totals	200	32/58	.552	23/31	.742	-/42	20	21	14	8	4	87	.435

St. John's (72)   Coach: Lou Carnesecca

	Min.	Total FG/FGA	Pct.	FT/FTA	Pct.	Reb. O/T	A	TO	PF	S	Blk	TP	PPM
RENCHER, B.	37	6/10	.600	0/0	.000	-/3	6	3	4	3	0	12	.324
RUSSELL, D.	16	3/7	.429	0/2	.000	-/3	1	0	5	1	0	6	.375
WILLIAMS, K.	2	0/0	.000	0/0	.000	-/0	0	0	0	0	0	0	.000
PLAIR, R.	13	1/3	.333	0/0	.000	-/1	1	0	3	0	1	2	.154
REDDING, C.	27	7/16	.438	3/4	.750	-/6	0	3	4	0	0	17	.630
JACKSON, T.	1	0/0	.000	0/0	.000	-/0	0	0	0	0	0	0	.000
CARTER, R.	37	7/17	.412	3/5	.600	-/4	2	2	5	1	0	17	.459
GILROY, F.	28	3/10	.300	0/0	.000	-/3	0	0	2	1	0	6	.214
MCKOY, W.	39	6/15	.400	0/1	.000	-/11	1	6	4	1	2	12	.308
Totals	200	33/78	.423	6/12	.500	-/31	11	14	27	7	3	72	.360

Virginia Tech (59)   Coach: Charles Moir

	Min.	Total FG/FGA	Pct.	FT/FTA	Pct.	Reb. O/T	A	TO	PF	S	Blk	TP	PPM
HENSON, L.	36	5/12	.417	2/2	1.000	3/8	0	4	5	1	0	12	.333
SOLOMON, D.	40	3/8	.375	5/9	.556	2/6	1	5	1	0	0	11	.275
ROBINSON, W.	39	7/12	.583	2/5	.400	5/13	2	1	4	0	1	16	.410
REID, D.	32	2/7	.286	2/2	1.000	0/2	1	2	4	1	0	6	.188
SCHNEIDER, J.	31	6/8	.750	0/0	.000	0/1	1	3	2	0	0	12	.387
SCOTT, C.	17	1/3	.333	0/0	.000	0/0	0	4	1	0	2	2	.118
HILLENBRAND, J.	2	0/0	.000	0/0	.000	0/0	0	0	0	0	0	0	.000
BRYANT, G.	3	0/1	.000	0/0	.000	0/1	1	0	0	0	0	0	.000
Totals	200	24/51	.471	11/18	.611	10/31	6	15	20	3	1	59	.295

Indiana (68)   Coach: Bob Knight

	Min.	Total FG/FGA	Pct.	FT/FTA	Pct.	Reb. O/T	A	TO	PF	S	Blk	TP	PPM
RISLEY, S.	13	0/0	.000	0/0	.000	-/1	0	0	0	1	0	0	.000
WOODSON, M.	36	5/12	.417	3/4	.750	-/4	2	1	4	0	1	13	.361
TOLBERT, R.	40	5/9	.556	4/6	.667	-/4	1	4	3	0	1	14	.350
THOMAS, I.	39	7/14	.500	3/4	.750	-/2	7	2	3	0	0	17	.436
CARTER, B.	40	6/9	.667	4/5	.800	-/5	3	0	1	0	0	16	.400
TURNER, L.	13	2/3	.667	0/0	.000	-/2	0	2	4	0	0	4	.308
KITCHEL, T.	9	2/2	1.000	0/0	.000	-/4	0	2	3	0	0	4	.444
FRANZ, C.	1	0/0	.000	0/0	.000	-/0	0	0	0	0	0	0	.000
ISENBARGER, P.	9	0/1	.000	0/1	.000	-/0	0	0	3	0	0	0	.000
Totals	200	27/50	.540	14/20	.700	-/22	13	11	21	1	2	68	.340

Team Rebounds: Indiana 3; Virginia Tech 1. Disqualified: Virginia Tech—Henson. Technical fouls: None.

	1st Half	2nd Half	Final
Virginia Tech	27	32	59
Indiana	35	33	68

Team Rebounds: Purdue 2; St. John's 3. Disqualified: Purdue—Walker; St. John's—Russell, Carter. Technical fouls: St. John's—McKoy.

	1st Half	2nd Half	Final
Purdue	37	50	87
St. John's	30	42	72

SECOND ROUND WEST

UCLA (77)   Coach: Larry Brown

	Min.	Total FG/FGA	Pct.	FT/FTA	Pct.	Reb. O/T	A	TO	PF	S	Blk	TP	PPM
VANDEWEGHE, K.	40	6/11	.545	1/1	1.000	-/9	3	2	1	0	0	13	.325
WILKES, J.	29	4/6	.667	2/3	.667	-/2	0	1	5	1	1	10	.345
SANDERS, M.	31	6/12	.500	3/4	.750	-/12	1	3	3	1	0	15	.484
FOSTER, R.	39	9/17	.529	0/0	.000	-/0	1	1	1	0	0	18	.462
HOLTON, M.	39	3/5	.600	2/2	1.000	-/6	2	3	2	0	0	8	.205
DAYE, D.	3	0/0	.000	0/0	.000	-/0	0	2	1	0	0	0	.000
PRUITT, C.	12	1/3	.333	8/8	1.000	-/0	0	2	2	0	1	10	.833
ALLUMS, D.	7	1/3	.333	1/2	.500	-/2	0	0	0	0	0	3	.429
Totals	200	30/57	.526	17/20	.850	-/31	7	15	15	3	2	77	.385

DePaul (71)   Coach: Ray Meyer

	Min.	Total FG/FGA	Pct.	FT/FTA	Pct.	Reb. O/T	A	TO	PF	S	Blk	TP	PPM
AGUIRRE, M.	40	8/18	.444	3/6	.500	-/9	4	6	3	1	0	19	.475
MITCHEM, J.	20	0/4	.000	0/0	.000	-/3	2	1	2	1	0	0	.000
CUMMINGS, T.	40	9/16	.563	5/5	1.000	-/8	1	1	4	1	5	23	.575
BRADSHAW, C.	40	5/12	.417	3/6	.500	-/6	7	0	2	0	0	13	.325
DILLARD, S.	40	7/14	.500	0/0	.000	-/2	1	0	4	2	0	14	.350
GRUBBS, T.	20	1/10	.100	0/0	.000	-/3	3	1	4	0	0	2	.100
Totals	200	30/74	.405	11/17	.647	-/31	18	9	19	7	5	71	.355

Team Rebounds: UCLA 6; DePaul 7. Disqualified: UCLA—Wilkes. Technical fouls: UCLA—Coach Brown.

	1st Half	2nd Half	Final
UCLA	34	43	77
DePaul	32	39	71

Arizona State (75) Coach: Ned Wulk

	Min.	Total FG/FGA	Pct.	FT/FTA	Pct.	Reb. O/T	A	TO	PF	S	Blk	TP	PPM
WILLIAMS, S.	26	3/6	.500	1/2	.500	-/4	4	3	1	1	0	7	.269
NIMPHIUS, K.	37	3/6	.500	8/8	1.000	-/11	1	3	2	1	1	14	.378
LISTER, A.	32	7/16	.438	3/3	1.000	-/9	1	2	5	0	4	17	.531
SCOTT, B.	33	5/15	.333	2/2	1.000	-/4	5	3	5	1	0	12	.364
LAFAYETTE, L.	32	3/7	.429	3/6	.500	-/3	5	3	4	2	0	9	.281
BRESSANT, P.	3	1/1	1.000	1/4	.250	-/1	0	0	1	1	0	3	1.000
NASH, J.	24	3/7	.429	3/4	.750	-/3	6	3	1	1	1	9	.375
BUTTS, J.	1	1/1	1.000	0/0	.000	-/0	0	0	0	1	0	2	2.000
KUYPER, T.	1	0/1	.000	0/0	.000	-/2	0	0	0	0	1	0	.000
WILLIAMS, P.	11	0/2	.000	2/2	1.000	-/0	0	0	2	0	0	2	.182
Totals	200	26/62	.419	23/31	.742	-/37	22	17	21	8	7	75	.375

Ohio State (89) Coach: Eldon Miller

	Min.	Total FG/FGA	Pct.	FT/FTA	Pct.	Reb. O/T	A	TO	PF	S	Blk	TP	PPM
SMITH, J.	19	0/1	.000	1/2	.500	-/2	0	2	5	0	1	1	.053
KELLOGG, C.	27	4/10	.400	3/4	.750	-/11	1	3	5	0	0	11	.407
WILLIAMS, H.	37	8/19	.421	9/12	.750	-/9	0	2	2	1	1	25	.676
RANSEY, K.	38	11/22	.500	3/3	1.000	-/4	4	3	3	2	0	25	.658
SCOTT, C.	32	5/9	.556	6/6	1.000	-/3	1	0	2	1	0	16	.500
SIMS, N.	1	0/0	.000	0/0	.000	-/0	0	1	0	0	0	0	.000
WAITERS, B.	1	0/0	.000	0/0	.000	-/1	0	0	0	0	0	0	.000
HUGGINS, L.	8	0/2	.000	0/0	.000	-/1	0	1	2	0	0	0	.000
HALL, T.	12	1/3	.333	0/1	.000	-/5	0	2	2	2	1	2	.167
PENN, T.	1	0/1	.000	0/0	.000	-/0	0	0	0	0	0	0	.000
HAAS, M.	1	0/0	.000	0/0	.000	-/0	0	1	0	0	0	0	.000
ELLINGHAUSEN, J.	21	4/8	.500	1/2	.500	-/9	0	1	0	0	0	9	.429
KIRCHNER, C.	2	0/0	.000	0/0	.000	-/0	0	0	1	0	0	0	.000
Totals	200	33/75	.440	23/30	.767	-/45	6	16	22	6	3	89	.445

Team Rebounds: Ohio State 5; Arizona St. 2. Disqualified: Ohio State—Smith, Kellogg; Arizona St.—Lister, Scott. Technical fouls: Ohio State—Smith.

	1st Half	2nd Half	Final
Arizona St.	38	37	75
Ohio State	43	46	89

Clemson (71) Coach: Wm. C. (Bill) Foster

	Min.	Total FG/FGA	Pct.	FT/FTA	Pct.	Reb. O/T	A	TO	PF	S	Blk	TP	PPM
NANCE, L.	37	7/12	.583	2/5	.400	-/11	3	2	3	0	1	16	.432
WYATT, H.	32	2/5	.400	0/1	.000	-/4	2	2	3	1	0	4	.125
CAMPBELL, J.	23	4/6	.667	0/2	.000	-/7	0	1	5	1	1	8	.348
CONRAD, B.	14	1/2	.500	0/0	.000	-/1	1	0	5	0	0	2	.143
WILLIAMS, B.	38	10/19	.526	4/4	1.000	-/3	8	6	3	0	0	24	.632
DOBBS, C.	26	4/9	.444	3/5	.600	-/2	2	3	1	0	3	11	.423
WIGGINS, M.	5	1/1	1.000	0/0	.000	-/0	0	0	0	0	0	2	.400
GILLIAM, F.	21	2/3	.667	0/0	.000	-/6	0	0	2	0	0	4	.190
ROSS, R.	4	0/1	.000	0/0	.000	-/1	0	0	0	0	0	0	.000
Totals	200	31/58	.534	9/17	.529	-/35	16	14	22	2	5	71	.355

Brigham Young (66) Coach: Frank Arnold

	Min.	Total FG/FGA	Pct.	FT/FTA	Pct.	Reb. O/T	A	TO	PF	S	Blk	TP	PPM
ROBERTS, F.	-	4/10	.400	2/2	1.000	-/9	6	4	3	0	0	10	-
DURRANT, D.	-	2/5	.400	4/5	.800	-/3	3	2	2	0	0	8	-
TAYLOR, A.	-	10/12	.833	7/11	.636	-/12	2	1	5	1	1	27	-
AINGE, D.	-	5/12	.417	3/4	.750	-/3	0	2	5	3	0	13	-
RUNIA, S.	-	3/10	.300	2/3	.667	-/0	1	2	1	0	0	8	-
CRAIG, S.	-	0/6	.000	0/0	.000	-/2	1	1	3	0	0	0	-
TRUMBO, S.	-	0/1	.000	0/0	.000	-/3	0	3	1	0	0	0	-
KITE, G.	-	0/0	.000	0/0	.000	-/4	0	1	1	1	0	0	-
Totals	200	24/56	.429	18/25	.720	-/36	13	16	21	5	1	66	.330

Team Rebounds: Clemson 0; Brigham Young 0. Disqualified: Clemson—Campbell, Conrad; Brigham Young—Taylor, Ainge. Technical fouls: Clemson—Campbell.

	1st Half	2nd Half	Final
Clemson	38	33	71
Brigham Young	42	24	66

Lamar (81) Coach: Billy Tubbs

	Min.	Total FG/FGA	Pct.	FT/FTA	Pct.	Reb. O/T	A	TO	PF	S	Blk	TP	PPM
LEWIS, C.	38	4/8	.500	3/7	.429	-/11	2	0	2	0	0	11	.289
DAVIS, B.	32	7/18	.389	4/7	.571	-/9	1	2	3	1	2	18	.563
KEA, C.	37	5/9	.556	1/2	.500	-/7	0	2	3	0	0	11	.297
OLLIVER, M.	40	7/13	.538	4/5	.800	-/9	0	5	3	1	0	18	.450
BROOKS, A.	38	3/5	.600	9/13	.692	-/1	8	2	1	1	0	15	.395
WILLIAMS, R.	13	3/5	.600	2/2	1.000	-/5	0	1	3	0	0	8	.615
RUTTER, M.	2	0/0	.000	0/0	.000	-/1	0	0	1	0	0	0	.000
Totals	200	29/58	.500	23/36	.639	-/34	11	12	16	3	2	81	.405

Oregon State (77) Coach: Ralph Miller

	Min.	Total FG/FGA	Pct.	FT/FTA	Pct.	Reb. O/T	A	TO	PF	S	Blk	TP	PPM
HOLBROOK, R.	25	5/9	.556	0/0	.000	-/3	1	0	4	0	0	10	.400
ALLEN, D.	22	1/2	.500	0/0	.000	-/3	4	0	5	0	0	2	.091
JOHNSON, S.	32	11/18	.611	2/4	.500	-/18	2	7	5	1	1	24	.750
BLUME, R.	40	11/21	.524	0/1	.000	-/6	7	3	3	1	0	22	.550
RADFORD, M.	24	4/9	.444	1/1	1.000	-/3	3	4	5	0	0	9	.375
MARTIN, T.	16	1/5	.200	0/0	.000	-/6	1	2	2	0	0	2	.125
STOUTT, J.	10	0/4	.000	0/0	.000	-/0	0	0	0	0	0	0	.000
MCSHANE, B.	4	0/0	.000	0/0	.000	-/0	0	0	0	0	0	0	.000
BREW, W.	23	3/8	.375	2/2	1.000	-/1	1	0	1	0	0	8	.348
HINSCHEN, V.	4	0/1	.000	0/0	.000	-/1	1	1	2	0	0	0	.000
Totals	200	36/77	.468	5/8	.625	-/41	20	17	27	2	1	77	.385

Team Rebounds: Lamar 1; Oregon State 3. Disqualified: Oregon State—Johnson, Radford, Allen. Technical fouls: Oregon State—Johnson, bench.

	1st Half	2nd Half	Final
Lamar	42	39	81
Oregon State	35	42	77

REGIONAL SEMIFINAL EAST

Syracuse (77)   Coach: Jim Boeheim

	Min.	Total FG/FGA	Pct.	FT/FTA	Pct.	Reb. O/T	A	TO	PF	S	Blk	TP	PPM
SANTIFER, E.	-	5/9	.556	4/4	1.000	-/3	-	-	4	-	-	14	-
ORR, L.	-	10/17	.588	5/5	1.000	-/16	-	-	2	-	-	25	-
BOUIE, R.	-	7/8	.875	4/5	.800	-/3	-	-	5	-	-	18	-
MOSS, E.	-	4/7	.571	0/0	.000	-/1	-	-	5	-	-	8	-
HEADD, M.	-	0/7	.000	0/0	.000	-/3	-	-	2	-	-	0	-
COHEN, H.	-	0/2	.000	0/0	.000	-/1	-	-	4	-	-	0	-
BRUIN, T.	-	1/5	.200	0/0	.000	-/3	-	-	3	-	-	2	-
SCHAYES, D.	-	2/7	.286	6/9	.667	-/2	-	-	3	-	-	10	-
Totals	200	29/62	.468	19/23	.826	-/32	-	-	28	-	-	77	.385

Iowa (88)   Coach: Lute Olson

	Min.	Total FG/FGA	Pct.	FT/FTA	Pct.	Reb. O/T	A	TO	PF	S	Blk	TP	PPM
BROOKINS, V.	-	5/10	.500	11/12	.917	-/5	-	-	4	-	-	21	-
BOYLE, K.	-	8/12	.667	2/2	1.000	-/5	-	-	3	-	-	18	-
KRAFCISIN, S.	-	6/9	.667	2/2	1.000	-/3	-	-	5	-	-	14	-
LESTER, R.	-	3/10	.300	3/5	.600	-/3	-	-	1	-	-	9	-
ARNOLD, K.	-	2/7	.286	8/13	.615	-/5	-	-	1	-	-	12	-
HANSEN, B.	-	1/2	.500	2/2	1.000	-/1	-	-	4	-	-	4	-
WAITE, S.	-	4/5	.800	2/3	.667	-/5	-	-	2	-	-	10	-
Totals	200	29/55	.527	30/39	.769	-/27	-	-	20	-	-	88	.440

Team Rebounds: Iowa 4; Syracuse 5. Disqualified: Iowa—Krafcisin; Syracuse—Bouie, Moss. Technical fouls: None.

	1st Half	2nd Half	Final
Syracuse	33	44	77
Iowa	40	48	88

Georgetown (74)   Coach: John Thompson

	Min.	Total FG/FGA	Pct.	FT/FTA	Pct.	Reb. O/T	A	TO	PF	S	Blk	TP	PPM
DUTCH, A.	11	3/5	.600	1/2	.500	-/4	0	0	0	0	0	7	.636
SHELTON, C.	25	3/5	.600	1/2	.500	-/2	0	1	4	1	0	7	.280
HANCOCK, M.	15	2/4	.500	0/0	.000	-/2	1	2	1	1	0	4	.267
FLOYD, E.	35	8/17	.471	2/2	1.000	-/4	3	7	2	6	1	18	.514
DUREN, J.	37	7/15	.467	0/0	.000	-/4	7	2	3	2	0	14	.378
SMITH, E.	29	3/6	.500	7/11	.636	-/1	2	3	1	3	0	13	.448
FENLON, T.	8	0/1	.000	0/0	.000	-/0	1	0	1	0	0	0	.000
BULLIS, J.	5	0/0	.000	0/0	.000	-/0	0	2	0	0	0	0	.000
SPRIGGS, E.	22	2/3	.667	1/3	.333	-/5	0	0	0	0	0	5	.227
FRAZIER, M.	13	3/4	.750	0/0	.000	-/5	0	3	3	0	0	6	.462
Totals	200	31/60	.517	12/20	.600	-/27	14	20	15	13	1	74	.370

Maryland (68)   Coach: Lefty Driesell

	Min.	Total FG/FGA	Pct.	FT/FTA	Pct.	Reb. O/T	A	TO	PF	S	Blk	TP	PPM
KING, A.	39	6/18	.333	3/3	1.000	-/6	5	4	5	4	0	15	.385
GRAHAM, E.	38	3/8	.375	0/1	.000	-/9	4	7	3	1	0	6	.158
WILLIAMS, B.	39	8/10	.800	2/4	.500	-/15	0	3	4	2	2	18	.462
MANNING, G.	40	9/14	.643	1/1	1.000	-/1	2	3	3	1	0	19	.475
JACKSON, R.	14	2/4	.500	0/0	.000	-/1	2	5	2	1	0	4	.286
MORLEY, D.	27	3/4	.750	0/0	.000	-/1	6	4	3	3	0	6	.222
BALDWIN, T.	3	0/0	.000	0/0	.000	-/0	0	1	0	0	0	0	.000
Totals	200	31/58	.534	6/9	.667	-/33	19	27	20	12	2	68	.340

Team Rebounds: Georgetown 3; Maryland 2. Disqualified: Maryland—King. Technical fouls: None.

	1st Half	2nd Half	Final
Georgetown	38	36	74
Maryland	39	29	68

REGIONAL SEMIFINAL MIDWEST

Louisiana State (68)   Coach: Dale Brown

	Min.	Total FG/FGA	Pct.	FT/FTA	Pct.	Reb. O/T	A	TO	PF	S	Blk	TP	PPM
SCALES	35	7/17	.412	3/6	.500	-/7	0	-	4	-	-	17	.486
MACKLIN, D.	30	6/13	.462	4/5	.800	-/4	1	-	3	-	-	16	.533
COOK	36	1/3	.333	2/2	1.000	-/10	5	-	3	-	-	4	.111
MARTIN, E.	38	3/9	.333	3/3	1.000	-/0	6	-	2	-	-	9	.237
CARTER, H.	25	4/10	.400	2/2	1.000	-/0	2	-	1	-	-	10	.400
SIMS	20	3/5	.600	2/3	.667	-/2	1	-	2	-	-	8	.400
HULTBERG, J.	8	2/3	.667	0/0	.000	-/0	0	-	0	-	-	4	.500
BLACK, T.	5	0/0	.000	0/0	.000	-/0	0	-	1	-	-	0	.000
RUDOLPH	3	0/0	.000	0/0	.000	-/0	0	-	1	-	-	0	.000
Totals	200	26/60	.433	16/21	.762	-/23	15	-	17	-	-	68	.340

Missouri (63)   Coach: Norm Stewart

	Min.	Total FG/FGA	Pct.	FT/FTA	Pct.	Reb. O/T	A	TO	PF	S	Blk	TP	PPM
DRESSLER, M.	39	9/11	.818	2/4	.500	-/7	2	-	4	-	-	20	.513
FRAZIER, R.	29	6/11	.545	0/0	.000	-/8	1	-	3	-	-	12	.414
STIPANOVICH, S.	28	4/9	.444	2/2	1.000	-/5	3	-	4	-	-	10	.357
SUNDVOLD	40	1/5	.200	0/0	.000	-/4	6	-	4	-	-	2	.050
DREW, L.	39	7/10	.700	2/3	.667	-/2	4	-	2	-	-	16	.410
FOSTER, M.	5	0/0	.000	0/0	.000	-/0	0	-	1	-	-	0	.000
AMOS	1	0/0	.000	0/0	.000	-/0	0	-	0	-	-	0	.000
DORE	19	0/3	.000	3/4	.750	-/6	2	-	4	-	-	3	.158
Totals	200	27/49	.551	9/13	.692	-/32	18	-	22	-	-	63	.315

Team Rebounds: Louisiana St. 2; Missouri 0. Disqualified: None. Technical fouls: None.

	1st Half	2nd Half	Final
Louisiana St.	39	29	68
Missouri	40	23	63

Texas A&M (55)   Coach: Shelby Metcalf

	Min.	Total FG/FGA	Pct.	FT/FTA	Pct.	Reb. O/T	A	TO	PF	S	Blk	TP	PPM
SMITH, V.	40	6/13	.462	0/0	.000	3/8	0	4	4	0	1	12	.300
WRIGHT, R.	43	4/8	.500	3/4	.750	2/8	2	1	5	2	1	11	.256
WOODS, R.	24	4/7	.571	0/0	.000	4/9	0	1	4	0	3	8	.333
GOFF, D.	43	0/3	.000	2/2	1.000	1/2	6	1	2	1	0	2	.047
BRITTON, D.	44	7/15	.467	2/2	1.000	0/3	7	10	4	1	2	16	.364
LADSON, T.	5	0/0	.000	0/0	.000	0/0	0	2	1	0	0	0	.000
RILEY, C.	15	2/7	.286	0/0	.000	1/2	1	2	3	0	0	4	.267
SYLESTINE, S.	11	1/3	.333	0/0	.000	0/0	0	1	1	1	0	2	.182
Totals	225	24/56	.429	7/8	.875	11/32	16	22	24	5	7	55	.244

Louisville (66)   Coach: Denny Crum

	Min.	Total FG/FGA	Pct.	FT/FTA	Pct.	Reb. O/T	A	TO	PF	S	Blk	TP	PPM
MCCRAY, R.	35	0/4	.000	4/8	.500	3/8	3	2	2	1	1	4	.114
SMITH, D.	38	2/6	.333	2/2	1.000	3/10	5	3	4	1	1	6	.158
BROWN, W.	36	5/10	.500	5/6	.833	5/6	1	3	0	2	0	15	.417
EAVES, J.	26	4/7	.571	0/0	.000	1/3	3	2	2	1	0	8	.308
GRIFFITH, D.	43	9/24	.375	6/8	.750	5/6	2	5	2	1	0	24	.558
BRANCH, T.	4	0/0	.000	3/4	.750	0/0	1	0	0	1	0	3	.750
BURKMAN, R.	23	1/2	.500	0/1	.000	1/3	0	0	4	1	0	2	.087
WRIGHT, P.	20	2/5	.400	0/0	.000	0/0	1	1	2	0	0	4	.200
Totals	225	23/58	.397	20/29	.690	18/36	16	16	16	8	2	66	.293

Team Rebounds: Louisville 3; Texas A&M 4. Disqualified: Texas A&M—Wright. Technical fouls: None.

	1st Half	2nd Half	1st OT	Final
Texas A&M	33	20	2	55
Louisville	35	18	13	66

REGIONAL SEMIFINAL MIDEAST

Kentucky (54)　　Coach: Joe Hall

	Min.	Total FG/FGA	Pct.	FT/FTA	Pct.	Reb. O/T	A	TO	PF	S	Blk	TP	PPM
COWAN, F.	27	7/11	.636	12/14	.857	-/ 6	1	-	1	-	-	26	.963
WILLIAMS, L.	37	2/ 6	.333	2/ 2	1.000	-/ 9	1	-	3	-	-	6	.162
BOWIE, S.	9	1/ 4	.250	0/ 0	.000	-/ 3	0	-	5	-	-	2	.222
MACY, K.	35	3/ 9	.333	0/ 0	.000	-/ 0	3	-	2	-	-	6	.171
MINNIEFIELD, D.	35	2/ 4	.500	2/ 2	1.000	-/ 6	1	-	4	-	-	6	.171
SHIDLER, J.	10	1/ 3	.333	0/ 0	.000	-/ 1	1	-	1	-	-	2	.200
HORD, D.	20	2/ 5	.400	0/ 0	.000	-/ 2	3	-	3	-	-	4	.200
HEITZ, T.	4	0/ 0	.000	0/ 0	.000	-/ 1	0	-	0	-	-	0	.000
VERDERBER, C.	9	0/ 2	.000	0/ 0	.000	-/ 2	0	-	1	-	-	0	.000
HURT, C.	14	1/ 3	.333	0/ 0	.000	-/ 1	0	-	3	-	-	2	.143
Totals	200	19/47	.404	16/18	.889	-/31	10	17	23	-	-	54	.270

Duke (55)　　Coach: Wm. E. (Bill) Foster

	Min.	Total FG/FGA	Pct.	FT/FTA	Pct.	Reb. O/T	A	TO	PF	S	Blk	TP	PPM
BANKS, E.	38	3/ 6	.500	5/ 9	.556	-/ 6	5	-	2	-	-	11	.289
DENNARD, K.	35	3/ 5	.600	0/ 1	.000	-/ 5	2	-	5	-	-	6	.171
GMINSKI, M.	38	8/18	.444	1/ 3	.333	-/ 7	0	-	3	-	-	17	.447
TAYLOR, V.	37	7/ 9	.778	1/ 3	.333	-/ 1	2	-	3	-	-	15	.405
BENDER, B.	36	0/ 1	.000	4/ 7	.571	-/ 1	4	-	2	-	-	4	.111
ENGELLAND, C.	2	0/ 0	.000	0/ 0	.000	-/ 0	0	-	0	-	-	0	.000
EMMA, T.	5	0/ 0	.000	0/ 0	.000	-/ 0	0	-	1	-	-	0	.000
SUDDATH, J.	3	0/ 0	.000	0/ 0	.000	-/ 0	0	-	0	-	-	0	.000
TISSAW, M.	2	1/ 1	1.000	0/ 1	.000	-/ 0	0	-	1	-	-	2	1.000
WILLIAMS, A.	4	0/ 0	.000	0/ 0	.000	-/ 0	0	-	0	-	-	0	.000
Totals	200	22/40	.550	11/24	.458	-/20	13	16	17	-	-	55	.275

Team Rebounds: Duke 0; Kentucky 1. Disqualified: Duke—Dennard; Kentucky—Bowie. Technical fouls: None.

	1st Half	2nd Half	Final
Kentucky	23	31	54
Duke	37	18	55

Purdue (76)　　Coach: Lee Rose

	Min.	Total FG/FGA	Pct.	FT/FTA	Pct.	Reb. O/T	A	TO	PF	S	Blk	TP	PPM
EDMONSON, K.	36	5/ 9	.556	10/12	.833	-/ 4	2	1	3	1	0	20	.556
WALKER, S.	6	0/ 0	.000	0/ 0	.000	-/ 0	0	1	1	0	0	0	.000
WALKER, B.	35	2/ 5	.400	1/ 2	.500	-/ 1	5	3	3	3	0	5	.143
CARROLL, J.	27	5/11	.455	1/ 4	.250	-/ 8	0	3	3	1	1	11	.407
SCEARCE, M.	15	1/ 2	.500	9/11	.818	-/ 1	1	1	0	0	0	11	.733
STALLINGS, K.	4	0/ 0	.000	0/ 0	.000	-/ 0	0	0	1	0	0	0	.000
MORRIS, D.	38	7/14	.500	6/ 8	.750	-/ 3	1	1	4	2	0	20	.526
BENSON, T.	2	0/ 1	.000	0/ 0	.000	-/ 0	0	0	1	0	0	0	.000
KITCHEL, J.	1	0/ 0	.000	0/ 0	.000	-/ 0	0	0	0	0	0	0	.000
BARNES, T.	3	0/ 0	.000	0/ 0	.000	-/ 0	0	0	0	1	0	0	.000
HALLMAN, A.	33	2/ 4	.500	5/ 7	.714	-/ 9	2	2	5	0	0	9	.273
Totals	200	22/46	.478	32/44	.727	-/26	11	12	20	9	1	76	.380

Indiana (69)　　Coach: Bob Knight

	Min.	Total FG/FGA	Pct.	FT/FTA	Pct.	Reb. O/T	A	TO	PF	S	Blk	TP	PPM
RISLEY, S.	2	0/ 0	.000	0/ 0	.000	-/ 0	0	0	1	0	0	0	.000
WOODSON, M.	35	5/12	.417	4/ 5	.800	-/ 6	1	3	5	0	0	14	.400
TOLBERT, R.	37	3/ 7	.429	0/ 2	.000	-/11	0	1	5	0	2	6	.162
THOMAS, I.	40	13/20	.650	4/ 4	1.000	-/ 2	5	6	4	1	0	30	.750
CARTER, B.	28	2/ 6	.333	1/ 2	.500	-/ 5	6	2	4	2	0	5	.179
TURNER, L.	15	0/ 2	.000	0/ 0	.000	-/ 3	1	3	5	0	0	0	.000
KITCHEL, T.	11	1/ 2	.500	0/ 0	.000	-/ 1	0	0	1	0	0	2	.182
FRANZ, C.	2	0/ 0	.000	0/ 0	.000	-/ 0	0	0	2	0	0	0	.000
ISENBARGER, P.	12	2/ 4	.500	0/ 0	.000	-/ 2	0	3	0	0	4	.333
THOMAS, J.	4	0/ 2	.000	4/ 4	1.000	-/ 2	0	1	2	0	4	1.000
BROWN, T.	7	1/ 1	1.000	0/ 0	.000	-/ 0	1	2	0	1	0	2	.286
GRUNWALD, G.	7	1/ 2	.500	0/ 0	.000	-/ 1	0	1	2	0	0	2	.286
Totals	200	28/58	.483	13/17	.765	-/33	14	18	33	6	2	69	.345

Team Rebounds: Purdue 3; Indiana 1. Disqualified: Purdue—Hallman; Indiana—Turner, Woodson, Tolbert. Technical fouls: Indiana—Coach Knight.

	1st Half	2nd Half	Final
Purdue	37	39	76
Indiana	26	43	69

REGIONAL SEMIFINAL WEST

UCLA (72)　　Coach: Larry Brown

	Min.	Total FG/FGA	Pct.	FT/FTA	Pct.	Reb. O/T	A	TO	PF	S	Blk	TP	PPM
VANDEWEGHE, K.	35	3/13	.231	6/ 6	1.000	-/ 5	2	2	2	0	0	12	.343
WILKES, J.	31	1/ 6	.167	6/ 8	.750	-/ 9	2	3	2	4	0	8	.258
SANDERS, M.	37	7/11	.636	5/ 6	.833	-/ 8	1	1	4	1	0	19	.514
FOSTER, R.	35	6/11	.545	7/ 8	.875	-/ 4	2	2	3	2	0	19	.543
HOLTON, M.	25	0/ 2	.000	0/ 1	.000	-/ 2	0	2	0	1	0	0	.000
DAYE, D.	22	4/ 6	.667	2/ 4	.500	-/ 4	0	2	1	3	0	10	.455
PRUITT, C.	8	1/ 1	1.000	2/ 2	1.000	-/ 0	0	1	0	0	0	4	.500
ALLUMS, D.	7	0/ 2	.000	0/ 0	.000	-/ 1	0	1	2	0	0	0	.000
Totals	200	22/52	.423	28/35	.800	-/33	7	14	14	11	0	72	.360

Ohio State (68)　　Coach: Eldon Miller

	Min.	Total FG/FGA	Pct.	FT/FTA	Pct.	Reb. O/T	A	TO	PF	S	Blk	TP	PPM
SMITH, J.	19	1/ 3	.333	0/ 1	.000	-/ 4	2	0	2	0	0	2	.105
KELLOGG, C.	33	6/10	.600	0/ 0	.000	-/ 8	2	3	5	1	2	12	.364
WILLIAMS, H.	40	5/12	.417	0/ 2	.000	-/10	0	2	2	0	3	10	.250
RANSEY, K.	39	13/23	.565	3/ 3	1.000	-/ 4	2	5	5	0	0	29	.744
SCOTT, C.	28	2/ 3	.667	2/ 2	1.000	-/ 3	5	1	5	3	0	6	.214
HUGGINS, L.	6	0/ 0	.000	1/ 2	.500	-/ 0	0	1	0	0	0	1	.167
HALL, T.	11	1/ 1	1.000	0/ 0	.000	-/ 2	1	2	4	2	0	2	.182
PENN, T.	7	1/ 2	.500	0/ 0	.000	-/ 0	1	2	2	1	0	2	.286
ELLINGHAUSEN, J.	10	2/ 2	1.000	0/ 0	.000	-/ 0	0	0	1	0	0	4	.400
MILLER	7	0/ 1	.000	0/ 0	.000	-/ 0	0	2	1	0	0	0	.000
Totals	200	31/57	.544	6/10	.600	-/31	13	18	27	7	5	68	.340

Team Rebounds: UCLA 1; Ohio State 0. Disqualified: Ohio State—Kellogg, Ransey, Scott. Technical fouls: None.

	1st Half	2nd Half	Final
UCLA	35	37	72
Ohio State	31	37	68

Clemson (74) Coach: Wm. C. (Bill) Foster

	Min.	Total FG/FGA	Pct.	FT/FTA	Pct.	Reb. O/T	A	TO	PF	S	Blk	TP	PPM
NANCE, L.	35	6/14	.429	4/5	.800	8/11	2	-	2	0	2	16	.457
WYATT, H.	13	1/4	.250	1/2	.500	0/5	2	-	2	1	-	3	.231
CAMPBELL, J.	31	7/12	.583	1/3	.333	3/12	3	2	3	0	-	15	.484
CONRAD, B.	29	2/3	.667	4/5	.800	0/3	2	-	2	1	-	8	.276
WILLIAMS, B.	37	3/12	.250	6/8	.750	1/3	5	-	3	1	1	12	.324
DOBBS, C.	14	2/5	.400	0/0	.000	0/1	1	3	0	0	-	4	.286
WIGGINS, M.	18	3/4	.750	0/2	.000	1/2	0	-	2	0	-	6	.333
GILLIAM, F.	19	5/9	.556	0/0	.000	1/4	1	4	1	0	-	10	.526
ROSS, R.	1	0/0	.000	0/0	.000	0/0	0	-	0	0	-	0	.000
MCKINSTRY	1	0/0	.000	0/0	.000	0/0	0	-	0	-	-	0	.000
FUZY	1	0/0	.000	0/0	.000	0/0	0	-	0	-	-	0	.000
KEY	1	0/0	.000	0/0	.000	0/0	0	-	0	-	-	0	.000
Totals	200	29/63	.460	16/25	.640	14/41	16	23	15	3	3	74	.370

Lamar (66) Coach: Billy Tubbs

	Min.	Total FG/FGA	Pct.	FT/FTA	Pct.	Reb. O/T	A	TO	PF	S	Blk	TP	PPM
LEWIS, C.	39	4/8	.500	0/0	.000	-/6	1	-	3	-	-	8	.205
DAVIS, B.	28	6/21	.286	4/6	.667	-/7	2	-	5	-	-	16	.571
KEA, C.	30	3/8	.375	6/8	.750	-/12	0	-	5	-	-	12	.400
OLLIVER, M.	40	9/20	.450	2/2	1.000	-/1	1	-	4	-	-	20	.500
BROOKS, R.	40	2/4	.500	0/0	.000	-/5	8	-	2	-	-	4	.100
WILLIAMS, R.	23	2/5	.400	2/2	1.000	-/6	0	-	4	-	-	6	.261
Totals	200	26/66	.394	14/18	.778	-/37	12	19	23	-	-	66	.330

Team Rebounds: Clemson 2; Lamar 4. Disqualified: Lamar—Davis, Kea. Technical fouls: None.

	1st Half	2nd Half	Final
Clemson	33	41	74
Lamar	36	30	66

REGIONAL FINAL EAST

Iowa (81) Coach: Lute Olson

	Min.	Total FG/FGA	Pct.	FT/FTA	Pct.	Reb. O/T	A	TO	PF	S	Blk	TP	PPM
BROOKINS, V.	39	10/17	.588	2/2	1.000	-/4	0	1	1	1	1	22	.564
BOYLE, K.	34	7/11	.636	0/0	.000	-/3	4	1	4	1	0	14	.412
KRAFCISIN, S.	21	1/2	.500	0/1	.000	-/3	1	0	2	0	1	2	.095
LESTER, R.	39	2/7	.286	4/4	1.000	-/2	9	0	3	1	0	8	.205
ARNOLD, K.	32	5/8	.625	2/2	1.000	-/2	3	1	1	1	0	12	.375
HANSEN, B.	13	2/2	1.000	4/4	1.000	-/1	1	1	1	0	0	8	.615
WAITE, S.	22	4/4	1.000	7/7	1.000	-/4	2	2	3	0	0	15	.682
Totals	200	31/51	.608	19/20	.950	-/19	20	6	15	4	2	81	.405

Georgetown (80) Coach: John Thompson

	Min.	Total FG/FGA	Pct.	FT/FTA	Pct.	Reb. O/T	A	TO	PF	S	Blk	TP	PPM
DUTCH, A.	12	1/4	.250	0/0	.000	-/3	0	0	3	0	0	2	.167
SHELTON, C.	32	7/10	.700	2/3	.667	-/5	0	1	5	0	1	16	.500
HANCOCK, M.	12	2/3	.667	0/0	.000	-/1	0	0	1	0	0	4	.333
FLOYD, E.	36	11/14	.786	9/10	.900	-/3	2	1	0	1	0	31	.861
DUREN, J.	38	5/9	.556	0/0	.000	-/3	8	4	2	1	0	10	.263
SMITH, E.	28	2/5	.400	0/0	.000	-/0	2	1	1	0	0	4	.143
FENLON, T.	6	0/1	.000	0/0	.000	-/0	1	1	1	0	0	0	.000
BULLIS, J.	6	1/2	.500	0/0	.000	-/1	0	0	0	0	0	2	.333
SPRIGGS, E.	15	0/2	.000	2/2	1.000	-/2	0	1	2	0	1	2	.133
FRAZIER, M.	15	4/5	.800	1/1	1.000	-/3	0	1	4	1	0	9	.600
Totals	200	33/55	.600	14/16	.875	-/21	13	10	19	3	2	80	.400

Team Rebounds: Iowa 2; Georgetown 3. Disqualified: Georgetown—Shelton. Technical fouls: None.

	1st Half	2nd Half	Final
Iowa	32	49	81
Georgetown	42	38	80

REGIONAL FINAL MIDWEST

Louisiana State (66) Coach: Dale Brown

	Min.	Total FG/FGA	Pct.	FT/FTA	Pct.	Reb. O/T	A	TO	PF	S	Blk	TP	PPM
SCALES	27	5/11	.455	2/2	1.000	-/6	0	-	5	-	-	12	.444
MACKLIN, D.	34	4/7	.571	1/2	.500	-/8	1	-	4	-	-	9	.265
COOK, G.	25	2/4	.500	0/1	.000	-/7	5	-	5	-	-	4	.160
MARTIN, E.	31	1/11	.091	0/0	.000	-/2	8	-	4	-	-	2	.065
CARTER	29	5/14	.357	2/3	.667	-/7	0	-	5	-	-	12	.414
SIMS, W.	22	4/8	.500	2/2	1.000	-/1	1	-	5	-	-	10	.455
ALCORN	1	0/0	.000	0/0	.000	-/0	0	-	0	-	-	0	.000
HULFBERG	20	8/10	.800	1/3	.333	-/1	1	-	2	-	-	17	.850
BERGERON	1	0/1	.000	0/0	.000	-/0	0	-	0	-	-	0	.000
COSTELLO	6	0/1	.000	0/0	.000	-/0	0	-	0	-	-	0	.000
BLACK	1	0/0	.000	0/0	.000	-/0	0	-	0	-	-	0	.000
DEARMOND	1	0/0	.000	0/0	.000	-/0	0	-	0	-	-	0	.000
CAMPBELL	1	0/0	.000	0/0	.000	-/0	0	-	0	-	-	0	.000
RUDOLPH, G.	1	0/1	.000	0/0	.000	-/1	0	-	1	-	-	0	.000
Totals	200	29/68	.426	8/13	.615	-/33	16	17	31	-	-	66	.330

Louisville (86) Coach: Denny Crum

	Min.	Total FG/FGA	Pct.	FT/FTA	Pct.	Reb. O/T	A	TO	PF	S	Blk	TP	PPM
MCCRAY, R.	38	4/8	.500	4/6	.667	-/10	2	-	1	-	-	12	.316
SMITH, D.	33	4/9	.444	5/9	.556	-/10	3	-	4	-	-	13	.394
BROWN, W.	31	8/10	.800	0/1	.000	-/5	1	-	2	-	-	16	.516
EAVES, J.	31	3/3	1.000	3/5	.600	-/2	2	-	1	-	-	9	.290
GRIFFITH, D.	18	7/12	.583	3/4	.750	-/8	7	-	4	-	-	17	.944
BRANCH, T.	6	1/3	.333	3/4	.750	-/0	0	-	1	-	-	5	.833
BURKMAN, R.	26	2/2	1.000	4/5	.800	-/0	7	-	3	-	-	8	.308
WRIGHT, P.	13	1/5	.200	4/4	1.000	-/4	0	-	1	-	-	6	.462
DEUSER, G.	1	0/0	.000	0/0	.000	-/0	0	-	0	-	-	0	.000
PULLIAM, M.	1	0/0	.000	0/0	.000	-/0	0	-	0	-	-	0	.000
CLEVELAND, D.	1	0/0	.000	0/0	.000	-/0	0	-	0	-	-	0	.000
CLARK, S.	1	0/0	.000	0/1	.000	-/1	0	-	0	-	-	0	.000
Totals	200	30/52	.577	26/39	.667	-/40	22	16	17	-	-	86	.430

Team Rebounds: Louisville 2; Louisiana St. 2. Disqualified: Louisiana St.—Scales, Cook, Carter, Sims. Technical fouls: None.

	1st Half	2nd Half	Final
Louisiana St.	29	37	66
Louisville	31	55	86

REGIONAL FINAL MIDEAST

Duke (60)   Coach: Wm. E. (Bill) Foster

	Min.	Total FG/FGA	Pct.	FT/FTA	Pct.	Reb. O/T	A	TO	PF	S	Blk	TP	PPM
TAYLOR, V.	33	1/ 7	.143	0/ 0	.000	-/ 4	2	4	4	0	0	2	.061
ENGELLAND, C.	10	1/ 4	.250	0/ 0	.000	-/ 1	1	2	1	0	0	2	.200
BANKS, E.	35	5/ 9	.556	4/ 4	1.000	-/ 4	2	4	5	2	0	14	.400
BENDER, B.	34	3/ 7	.429	4/ 4	1.000	-/ 2	3	4	4	3	0	10	.294
EMMA, T.	11	0/ 0	.000	0/ 1	.000	-/ 0	0	1	0	0	0	0	.000
SUDDATH, J.	10	2/ 2	1.000	0/ 0	.000	-/ 0	2	2	1	0	0	4	.400
TISSAW, M.	7	0/ 0	.000	0/ 0	.000	-/ 1	0	0	1	0	0	0	.000
DENNARD, K.	22	5/ 7	.714	1/ 2	.500	-/ 4	0	4	5	0	0	11	.500
WILLIAMS, A.	5	0/ 0	.000	0/ 0	.000	-/ 0	0	0	0	0	0	0	.000
GMINSKI, M.	33	6/16	.375	5/ 6	.833	-/ 9	0	2	3	0	2	17	.515
Totals	200	23/52	.442	14/17	.824	-/25	10	22	25	5	2	60	.300

Purdue (68)   Coach: Lee Rose

	Min.	Total FG/FGA	Pct.	FT/FTA	Pct.	Reb. O/T	A	TO	PF	S	Blk	TP	PPM
EDMONSON, K.	37	4/11	.364	4/ 6	.667	-/ 5	1	4	3	0	1	12	.324
WALKER, S.	3	0/ 0	.000	0/ 0	.000	-/ 0	0	0	1	0	0	0	.000
WALKER, B.	36	2/ 4	.500	1/ 4	.250	-/ 5	6	2	3	3	0	5	.139
CARROLL, J.	35	10/16	.625	6/ 6	1.000	-/ 6	0	2	4	1	1	26	.743
SCEARCE, M.	12	1/ 4	.250	0/ 0	.000	-/ 2	0	1	0	2	0	2	.167
STALLINGS, K.	4	1/ 2	.500	0/ 0	.000	-/ 1	1	1	1	0	0	2	.500
MORRIS, D.	30	1/ 7	.143	8/ 9	.889	-/ 5	3	5	4	1	0	10	.333
BENSON, T.	5	0/ 1	.000	2/ 2	1.000	-/ 2	0	0	0	0	0	2	.400
BARNES, R.	1	0/ 0	.000	0/ 0	.000	-/ 0	0	0	0	0	0	0	.000
HALLMAN, A.	37	4/ 7	.571	1/ 2	.500	-/ 4	0	2	1	0	1	9	.243
Totals	200	23/52	.442	22/29	.759	-/30	11	17	17	7	3	68	.340

Team Rebounds: Purdue 3; Duke 3. Disqualified: Duke—Banks, Dennard. Technical fouls: None.

	1st Half	2nd Half	Final
Duke	30	30	60
Purdue	28	40	68

REGIONAL FINAL WEST

UCLA (85)   Coach: Larry Brown

	Min.	Total FG/FGA	Pct.	FT/FTA	Pct.	Reb. O/T	A	TO	PF	S	Blk	TP	PPM
VANDEWEGHE, K.	38	7/10	.700	8/11	.727	-/ 9	4	3	3	0	0	22	.579
WILKES, J.	21	0/ 4	.000	2/ 2	1.000	-/ 4	0	3	4	2	0	2	.095
SANDERS, M.	35	7/12	.583	8/ 8	1.000	-/10	4	3	4	1	0	22	.629
FOSTER, R.	35	6/13	.462	0/ 0	.000	-/ 1	3	3	4	1	0	12	.343
HOLTON, M.	28	2/ 3	.667	2/ 4	.500	-/ 2	2	2	2	0	2	6	.214
DAYE, D.	18	2/ 4	.500	3/ 4	.750	-/ 3	0	0	2	1	0	7	.389
PRUITT, C.	18	3/ 5	.600	0/ 1	.000	-/ 3	4	2	1	0	1	6	.333
ALLUMS, D.	6	2/ 2	1.000	2/ 3	.667	-/ 3	0	1	2	0	0	6	1.000
ARRILLAGA, R.	1	1/ 2	.500	0/ 0	.000	-/ 0	0	0	0	0	0	2	2.000
Totals	200	30/55	.545	25/33	.758	-/35	17	18	22	5	3	85	.425

Clemson (74)   Coach: Wm. C. (Bill) Foster

	Min.	Total FG/FGA	Pct.	FT/FTA	Pct.	Reb. O/T	A	TO	PF	S	Blk	TP	PPM
NANCE, L.	31	5/12	.417	3/ 4	.750	-/ 6	0	4	4	2	0	13	.419
WYATT, H.	22	2/ 3	.667	0/ 0	.000	-/ 5	0	0	5	0	0	4	.182
CAMPBELL, J.	16	2/ 3	.667	1/ 2	.500	-/ 3	1	1	2	0	0	5	.313
CONRAD, B.	28	2/ 6	.333	5/ 7	.714	-/ 1	7	3	5	2	0	9	.321
WILLIAMS	32	9/19	.474	0/ 0	.000	-/ 3	2	3	3	1	0	18	.563
GILLIAM	28	5/11	.455	3/ 4	.750	-/ 9	5	1	3	0	0	13	.464
WIGGINS, M.	18	2/ 7	.286	0/ 2	.000	-/ 3	0	0	3	0	0	4	.222
DODOS	24	3/ 6	.500	2/ 2	1.000	-/ 2	4	3	1	0	0	8	.333
ROSS, R.	1	0/ 0	.000	0/ 0	.000	-/ 0	0	0	0	0	0	0	.000
Totals	200	30/67	.448	14/21	.667	-/32	19	15	26	5	0	74	.370

Team Rebounds: UCLA 5; Clemson 2. Disqualified: Clemson—Wyatt, Conrad. Technical fouls: None. One UCLA team turnover included in total.

	1st Half	2nd Half	Final
UCLA	46	39	85
Clemson	35	39	74

FINAL FOUR

Iowa (72)   Coach: Lute Olson

	Min.	Total FG/FGA	Pct.	FT/FTA	Pct.	Reb. O/T	A	TO	PF	S	Blk	TP	PPM
BROOKINS, V.	33	6/18	.333	2/ 2	1.000	-/ 6	2	2	5	1	0	14	.424
BOYLE, K.	38	0/ 8	.000	0/ 0	.000	-/ 7	5	4	2	0	0	0	.000
KRAFCISIN, S.	32	4/ 5	.800	4/ 4	1.000	-/ 3	0	1	5	0	1	12	.375
LESTER, R.	12	4/ 4	1.000	2/ 2	1.000	-/ 1	1	0	2	0	0	10	.833
ARNOLD, K.	39	9/17	.529	2/ 2	1.000	-/ 3	5	1	1	1	0	20	.513
HANSEN, B.	17	2/ 8	.250	3/ 4	.750	-/ 4	4	0	2	1	0	7	.412
WAITE, S.	29	4/ 6	.667	1/ 1	1.000	-/ 2	0	3	5	2	0	9	.310
GANNON, M.	0	0/ 0	.000	0/ 0	.000	-/ 0	0	0	0	0	0	0	-
HENRY, M.	0	0/ 0	.000	0/ 0	.000	-/ 0	0	0	1	0	0	0	-
Totals	200	29/66	.439	14/15	.933	-/26	17	11	23	7	1	72	.360

Louisville (80)   Coach: Denny Crum

	Min.	Total FG/FGA	Pct.	FT/FTA	Pct.	Reb. O/T	A	TO	PF	S	Blk	TP	PPM
MCCRAY, R.	37	5/ 7	.714	4/ 4	1.000	-/ 9	3	2	2	2	2	14	.378
SMITH, D.	37	3/ 7	.429	7/ 8	.875	-/ 8	2	1	2	0	0	13	.351
BROWN, W.	29	1/ 3	.333	0/ 2	.000	-/ 5	2	4	4	0	0	2	.069
EAVES, J.	22	2/ 4	.500	4/ 5	.800	-/ 4	1	1	1	0	0	8	.364
GRIFFITH, D.	36	14/21	.667	6/ 8	.750	-/ 5	6	4	1	3	2	34	.944
BRANCH, T.	2	0/ 0	.000	0/ 0	.000	-/ 0	0	0	0	0	0	0	.000
BURKMAN, R.	22	2/ 3	.667	3/ 4	.750	-/ 2	0	5	3	1	0	7	.318
WRIGHT, P.	15	1/ 2	.500	0/ 0	.000	-/ 3	1	1	1	0	0	2	.133
DEUSER, G.	0	0/ 0	.000	0/ 0	.000	-/ 0	0	0	0	0	0	0	-
CLEVELAND, D.	0	0/ 0	.000	0/ 0	.000	-/ 0	0	0	0	0	0	0	-
PULLIAM, M.	0	0/ 0	.000	0/ 0	.000	-/ 0	0	0	0	0	0	0	-
Totals	200	28/47	.596	24/31	.774	-/36	15	18	14	6	4	80	.400

Team Rebounds: Louisville 0; Iowa 0. Disqualified: Iowa—Brookins, Krafcisin, Waite. Technical fouls: None. Players who played 0 min. played less than 1 min. each.

	1st Half	2nd Half	Final
Iowa	29	43	72
Louisville	34	46	80

Purdue (62)　Coach: Lee Rose

	Min.	Total FG / FGA	Pct.	FT / FTA	Pct.	Reb. O / T	A	TO	PF	S	Blk	TP	PPM
EDMONSON, K.	37	9/16	.563	5/ 6	.833	-/ 3	1	1	3	1	0	23	.622
WALKER, S.	12	0/ 1	.000	0/ 0	.000	-/ 1	2	1	4	0	0	0	.000
WALKER, B.	37	1/ 3	.333	4/ 5	.800	-/ 1	5	1	4	2	0	6	.162
CARROLL, J.	40	8/14	.571	1/ 4	.250	-/ 8	1	6	3	0	2	17	.425
SCEARCE, M.	5	0/ 2	.000	0/ 0	.000	-/ 3	0	1	0	1	0	0	.000
STALLINGS, K.	1	0/ 0	.000	0/ 0	.000	-/ 0	0	0	0	0	0	0	.000
MORRIS, D.	30	5/14	.357	2/ 2	1.000	-/ 6	2	3	2	0	0	12	.400
BARNES, R.	5	1/ 1	1.000	0/ 0	.000	-/ 0	0	0	1	0	0	2	.400
HALLMAN, A.	33	1/ 7	.143	0/ 0	.000	-/ 7	1	2	4	0	0	2	.061
Totals	200	25/58	.431	12/17	.706	-/29	12	15	21	3	3	62	.310

UCLA (67)　Coach: Larry Brown

	Min.	Total FG / FGA	Pct.	FT / FTA	Pct.	Reb. O / T	A	TO	PF	S	Blk	TP	PPM
VANDEWEGHE, K.	40	9/12	.750	6/ 6	1.000	-/ 5	2	0	1	0	0	24	.600
WILKES, J.	8	2/ 2	1.000	0/ 0	.000	-/ 1	0	2	5	0	0	4	.500
SANDERS, M.	38	3/ 7	.429	6/ 6	1.000	-/ 6	1	1	2	4	1	12	.316
FOSTER, R.	23	4/ 7	.571	1/ 2	.500	-/ 3	1	4	5	0	0	9	.391
HOLTON, M.	33	1/ 3	.333	2/ 2	1.000	-/ 1	2	3	1	0	0	4	.121
DAYE, D.	24	1/ 5	.200	4/ 5	.800	-/ 3	3	2	2	0	0	6	.250
PRUITT, C.	16	3/ 7	.429	2/ 2	1.000	-/ 1	0	2	1	0	0	8	.500
ALLUMS, D.	16	0/ 0	.000	0/ 2	.000	-/ 4	2	2	3	0	0	0	.000
SIMS, G.	2	0/ 3	.000	0/ 0	.000	-/ 3	0	0	1	0	1	0	.000
Totals	200	23/46	.500	21/25	.840	-/27	11	16	21	4	2	67	.335

Team Rebounds: UCLA 3; Purdue 3. Disqualified: UCLA—Wilkes, Foster. Technical fouls: None.

	1st Half	2nd Half	Final
Purdue	25	37	62
UCLA	33	34	67

NATIONAL CHAMPIONSHIP

Louisville (59)　Coach: Denny Crum

	Min.	Total FG / FGA	Pct.	FT / FTA	Pct.	Reb. O / T	A	TO	PF	S	Blk	TP	PPM
MCCRAY, R.	36	2/ 4	.500	3/ 4	.750	-/11	2	1	4	0	3	7	.194
SMITH, D.	36	3/ 9	.333	3/ 4	.750	-/ 5	1	3	2	2	0	9	.250
BROWN, W.	34	4/12	.333	0/ 2	.000	-/ 7	3	3	3	1	1	8	.235
EAVES, J.	30	4/ 7	.571	0/ 2	.000	-/ 3	3	3	3	1	0	8	.267
GRIFFITH, D.	38	9/16	.563	5/ 8	.625	-/ 2	3	4	3	1	1	23	.605
BRANCH, T.	3	0/ 0	.000	0/ 0	.000	-/ 0	0	0	0	0	0	0	.000
BURKMAN, R.	11	0/ 1	.000	0/ 0	.000	-/ 1	1	1	2	4	1	0	.000
WRIGHT, P.	12	2/ 4	.500	0/ 0	.000	-/ 4	0	1	1	2	0	4	.333
Totals	200	24/53	.453	11/20	.550	-/33	13	17	20	8	5	59	.295

UCLA (54)　Coach: Larry Brown

	Min.	Total FG / FGA	Pct.	FT / FTA	Pct.	Reb. O / T	A	TO	PF	S	Blk	TP	PPM
VANDEWEGHE, K.	37	4/ 9	.444	6/ 6	1.000	-/ 7	0	1	3	1	0	14	.378
WILKES, J.	24	1/ 4	.250	0/ 0	.000	-/ 6	0	5	3	0	1	2	.083
SANDERS, M.	34	4/10	.400	2/ 4	.500	-/ 6	0	0	4	1	0	10	.294
FOSTER, R.	38	6/15	.400	4/ 4	1.000	-/ 1	5	2	3	6	0	16	.421
HOLTON, M.	29	1/ 3	.333	2/ 2	1.000	-/ 2	3	2	2	1	0	4	.138
DAYE, D.	13	1/ 3	.333	0/ 0	.000	-/ 1	2	2	1	0	0	2	.154
PRUITT, C.	16	2/ 8	.250	2/ 2	1.000	-/ 6	1	3	2	1	2	6	.375
ANDERSON, T.	5	0/ 0	.000	0/ 0	.000	-/ 0	0	0	0	0	0	0	.000
ALLUMS, D.	4	0/ 0	.000	0/ 0	.000	-/ 2	0	1	0	0	0	0	.000
Totals	200	19/52	.365	16/18	.889	-/31	11	16	18	10	3	54	.270

Team Rebounds: Louisville 3; UCLA 3. Disqualified: None. Technical fouls: None.

	1st Half	2nd Half	Final
Louisville	26	33	59
UCLA	28	26	54

NATIONAL THIRD PLACE

Purdue (75)　Coach: Lee Rose

	Min.	Total FG / FGA	Pct.	FT / FTA	Pct.	Reb. O / T	A	TO	PF	S	Blk	TP	PPM
EDMONSON, K.	35	6/11	.545	5/ 8	.625	-/ 4	3	4	2	1	2	17	.486
WALKER, S.	25	1/ 3	.333	2/ 3	.667	-/ 4	4	0	2	1	0	4	.160
WALKER, B.	19	0/ 1	.000	0/ 0	.000	-/ 5	4	5	3	2	0	0	.000
ANTHROP, J.	2	0/ 0	.000	0/ 0	.000	-/ 0	1	0	1	0	0	0	.000
CARROLL, J.	37	14/17	.824	7/11	.636	-/12	2	7	3	0	4	35	.946
SCEARCE, M.	2	0/ 0	.000	0/ 0	.000	-/ 0	0	0	1	0	0	0	.000
STALLINGS, K.	12	1/ 3	.333	2/ 2	1.000	-/ 1	3	0	1	1	0	4	.333
MORRIS, D.	22	3/ 3	1.000	1/ 1	1.000	-/ 1	3	5	3	1	0	7	.318
BENSON, T.	3	0/ 0	.000	0/ 0	.000	-/ 0	0	0	1	0	0	0	.000
KITCHEL, J.	1	0/ 0	.000	0/ 0	.000	-/ 1	0	0	0	0	0	0	.000
BARNES, R.	8	0/ 2	.000	0/ 0	.000	-/ 1	0	0	0	0	0	0	.000
HALLMAN, A.	34	4/ 9	.444	0/ 3	.000	-/ 3	2	2	3	2	0	8	.235
Totals	200	29/49	.592	17/28	.607	-/32	22	23	20	8	6	75	.375

Iowa (58)　Coach: Lute Olson

	Min.	Total FG / FGA	Pct.	FT / FTA	Pct.	Reb. O / T	A	TO	PF	S	Blk	TP	PPM
BROOKINS, V.	20	2/ 6	.333	0/ 1	.000	-/ 6	2	2	5	0	1	4	.200
BOYLE, K.	36	3/ 8	.375	3/ 4	.750	-/ 7	2	3	4	1	0	9	.250
KRAFCISIN, S.	24	2/ 8	.250	2/ 2	1.000	-/ 6	1	3	5	1	0	6	.250
ARNOLD, K.	39	8/14	.571	3/ 5	.600	-/ 2	3	6	2	1	0	19	.487
HANSEN, B.	30	4/13	.308	2/ 2	1.000	-/ 4	3	2	4	1	0	10	.333
WAITE, S.	27	3/ 5	.600	2/ 5	.400	-/ 7	1	3	4	1	1	8	.296
GANNON, M.	15	1/ 8	.125	0/ 0	.000	-/ 3	0	0	0	0	0	2	.133
HELLER, M.	3	0/ 2	.000	0/ 0	.000	-/ 1	0	0	1	0	0	0	.000
HENRY, M.	4	0/ 1	.000	0/ 0	.000	-/ 1	0	1	1	0	1	0	.000
GROGAN, T.	1	0/ 0	.000	0/ 0	.000	-/ 0	0	0	0	0	0	0	.000
ARENS, M.	1	0/ 0	.000	0/ 0	.000	-/ 0	0	0	0	0	0	0	.000
DARSEE, J.	0	0/ 0	.000	0/ 0	.000	-/ 0	0	0	0	0	0	0	-
Totals	200	23/65	.354	12/19	.632	-/37	12	20	26	5	3	58	.290

Team Rebounds: Purdue 4; Iowa 3. Disqualified: Iowa—Brookins, Krafcisin. Technical fouls: Purdue—Edmonson.
Player who played 0 min. played less than 1 min.

	1st Half	2nd Half	Final
Purdue	32	43	75
Iowa	27	31	58

✪ ALL-STAR TEAMS ✪

ALL TOURNAMENT

JOE CARROLL	PURDUE
ROD FOSTER	UCLA
★ DARRELL GRIFFITH	LOUISVILLE
RODNEY MCCRAY	LOUISVILLE
KIKI VANDERWEGHE	UCLA

WEST REGIONAL

ROD FOSTER	UCLA
LARRY NANCE	CLEMSON
KELVIN RANSEY	OHIO STATE
★ MIKE SANDERS	UCLA
KIKI VANDERWEGHE	UCLA

EAST REGIONAL

VINCE BROOKINS	IOWA
JOHN DUREN	GEORGETOWN
★ ERIC FLOYD	GEORGETOWN
LOUIS ORR	SYRACUSE
CRAIG SHELTON	GEORGETOWN

MIDEAST REGIONAL

★ JOE CARROLL	PURDUE
FRED COWAN	KENTUCKY
MIKE GMINSKI	DUKE
DRAKE MORRIS	PURDUE
ISIAH THOMAS	INDIANA

MIDWEST REGIONAL

DAVID BRITTON	TEXAS A&M
WILEY BROWN	LOUISVILLE
MARK DRESSLER	MISSOURI
★ DARRELL GRIFFITH	LOUISVILLE
DEWAYNE SCALES	LOUISIANA ST.

★ Most Outstanding Player(s)

✪ INDIVIDUAL RECORDS ✪

SCORING

Most points in a single game
1. MIKE OLLIVER, LAMAR (vs. WEBER ST.) — 37
2. JOE BARRY CARROLL, PURDUE (vs. ST. JOHN'S) — 36
3. JOE BARRY CARROLL, PURDUE (vs. IOWA) — 35
4. DARRELL GRIFFITH, LOUISVILLE (vs. IOWA) — 34
4. KIKI VANDEWEGHE, UCLA (vs. OLD DOMINION) — 34

Most total points in the tournament
1. JOE BARRY CARROLL, PURDUE — 158
2. KIKI VANDEWEGHE, UCLA — 119
3. KEITH EDMONSON, PURDUE — 111
4. KENNY ARNOLD, IOWA — 104
5. 2 tied for fifth place.

Highest scoring average (minimum 2 games)
1. KELVIN RANSEY, OHIO STATE (54-2) — 27.00
2. JOE BARRY CARROLL, PURDUE (158-6) — 26.33
3. MIKE OLLIVER, LAMAR (75-3) — 25.00
4. REGGIE JOHNSON, TENNESSEE (49-2) — 24.50
5. MURRAY BROWN, FLORIDA STATE (48-2) — 24.00

FIELD GOALS

Most field goals in a single game
1. MIKE OLLIVER, LAMAR (vs. WEBER ST.) — 17
2. DARRELL GRIFFITH, LOUISVILLE (vs. IOWA) — 14
2. JOE BARRY CARROLL, PURDUE (vs. IOWA) — 14
2. JOE BARRY CARROLL, PURDUE (vs. ST. JOHN'S) — 14
5. 8 tied for fifth place.

Most total field goals in the tournament
1. JOE BARRY CARROLL, PURDUE — 63
2. KIKI VANDEWEGHE, UCLA — 40
3. KEITH EDMONSON, PURDUE — 39
4. KENNY ARNOLD, IOWA — 38
5. ROD FOSTER, UCLA — 35

Most field goal attempts in a single game
1. TRACY JACKSON, NOTRE DAME (vs. MISSOURI) — 27
2. BRUCE COLLINS, WEBER ST. (vs. LAMAR) — 26
2. MIKE OLLIVER, LAMAR (vs. WEBER ST.) — 26
4. RAINS, SOUTH ALABAMA (vs. ALCORN ST.) — 25
5. DARRELL GRIFFITH, LOUISVILLE (vs. TEXAS A&M) — 24

Most total field goal attempts in tournament
1. JOE BARRY CARROLL, PURDUE — 98
2. KIKI VANDEWEGHE, UCLA — 75

3. DARRELL GRIFFITH, LOUISVILLE — 72
4. KEITH EDMONSON, PURDUE — 70
5. 2 tied for fifth place.

Highest field goal percentage in a single game (minimum 10 attempts)
1. ERIC SANTIFER, SYRACUSE (vs. VILLANOVA) (13-15) — .867
2. ALAN TAYLOR, BRIGHAM YOUNG (vs. CLEMSON) (10-12) — .833
3. JOE BARRY CARROLL, PURDUE (vs. IOWA) (14-17) — .824
4. 3 tied for fourth place.

FREE THROWS

Most free throws in a single game
1. GLENN VICKERS, IONA (vs. HOLY CROSS) — 15
2. MICHAEL BROOKS, LA SALLE (vs. PURDUE) — 13
3. FRED COWAN, KENTUCKY (vs. DUKE) — 12
3. KIKI VANDEWEGHE, UCLA (vs. OLD DOMINION) — 12
5. VINCENT BROOKINS, IOWA (vs. SYRACUSE) — 11

Most total free throws in the tournament
1. KIKI VANDEWEGHE, UCLA — 39
2. KEITH EDMONSON, PURDUE — 33
3. JOE BARRY CARROLL, PURDUE — 32
4. KENNY ARNOLD, IOWA — 28
5. MIKE SANDERS, UCLA — 27

Most free throws attempted in a single game
1. GLENN VICKERS, IONA (vs. HOLY CROSS) — 17
1. MICHAEL BROOKS, LA SALLE (vs. PURDUE) — 17
3. KIKI VANDEWEGHE, UCLA (vs. OLD DOMINION) — 16
4. FRED COWAN, KENTUCKY (vs. DUKE) — 14
5. 3 tied for fifth place.

Most free throws attempted in the tournament
1. KIKI VANDEWEGHE, UCLA — 46
1. JOE BARRY CARROLL, PURDUE — 46
3. KEITH EDMONSON, PURDUE — 41
4. KENNY ARNOLD, IOWA — 38
5. DRAKE MORRIS, PURDUE — 35

Highest free throw percentage in a single game (minimum 7 attempts)
1. JIM MCCLOSKEY, LOYOLA MYMT. (vs. ARIZONA ST.) (8-8) — 1.000
1. MIKE SANDERS, UCLA (vs. CLEMSON) (8-8) — 1.000

1. KURT NIMPHIUS, ARIZONA ST. (vs. OHIO STATE) (8-8) — 1.000
1. CLIFF PRUITT, UCLA (vs. DEPAUL) (8-8) — 1.000
1. EDDIE MOSS, SYRACUSE (vs. VILLANOVA) (8-8) — 1.000

Highest free throw percentage in the tournament (minimum 15 attempts)
1. CLIFF PRUITT, UCLA (14-15) — .933
2. GLENN VICKERS, IONA (19-21) — .905
3. FRED COWAN, KENTUCKY (16-18) — .889
4. ROD FOSTER, UCLA (15-17) — .882
5. MIKE SANDERS, UCLA (27-31) — .871

REBOUNDS

Most rebounds in a single game
1. DURAND MACKLIN, LOUISIANA ST. (vs. ALCORN ST.) — 19
1. TRACY JACKSON, NOTRE DAME (vs. MISSOURI) — 19
3. MIKE O'KOREN, N. CAROLINA (vs. TEXAS A&M) — 18
3. STEVE JOHNSON, OREGON STATE (vs. LAMAR) — 18
3. MIKE SANDERS, UCLA (vs. OLD DOMINION) — 18

Most total rebounds in the tournament
1. MIKE SANDERS, UCLA — 60
2. JOE BARRY CARROLL, PURDUE — 59
3. KIKI VANDEWEGHE, UCLA — 44
4. RODNEY MCCRAY, LOUISVILLE — 43
5. 2 tied for fifth place.

Most rebounds per game (minimum 2 games)
1. CHARLES WILLIAMS, MARYLAND (24-2) — 12.00
1. LOUIS ORR, SYRACUSE (24-2) — 12.00
3. LARRY SMITH, ALCORN ST. (22-2) — 11.00
4. ALTON LISTER, ARIZONA ST. (21-2) — 10.50
5. DURAND MACKLIN, LOUISIANA ST. (31-3) — 10.33

ASSISTS

Most assists in a single game
1. BERT BERTELKAMP, TENNESSEE (vs. MARYLAND) — 16
2. LARRY DREW, MISSOURI (vs. NOTRE DAME) — 12
3. SIDNEY LOWE, N.C. STATE (vs. IOWA) — 10
3. REGGIE JACKSON, MARYLAND (vs. TENNESSEE) — 10
3. ALVIN BROOKS, LAMAR (vs. WEBER ST.) — 10

Most total assists in the tournament
1 BRIAN WALKER, PURDUE   34
2 ALVIN BROOKS, LAMAR   26
3 JOHN DUREN, GEORGETOWN   24
3 BERT BERTELKAMP, TENNESSEE   24
5 RONNIE LESTER, IOWA   22

Most assists per game (minimum 2 appearances)
1 BERT BERTELKAMP, TENNESSEE (24-2)   12.00
2 ALVIN BROOKS, LAMAR (26-3)   8.67
3 JOHN DUREN, GEORGETOWN (24-3)   8.00
4 LARRY DREW, MISSOURI (21-3)   7.00
5 JOHNNY NASH, ARIZONA ST. (14-2)   7.00

TURNOVERS

Most turnovers in a single game
1 DAVID BRITTON, TEXAS A&M (vs. LOUISVILLE)
                                           10

2 7 tied for second place.

Most total turnovers in the tournament
1 JOE BARRY CARROLL, PURDUE   22
2 ARNETTE HALLMAN, PURDUE   19
2 DAVID BRITTON, TEXAS A&M   19
4 BRIAN WALKER, PURDUE   18
4 DRAKE MORRIS, PURDUE   18

SHOTS BLOCKED

Most shots blocked in a single game
1 TERRY CUMMINGS, DE PAUL (vs. UCLA)   5
2 JOE BARRY CARROLL, PURDUE (vs. IOWA)   4
2 ALTON LISTER, ARIZONA ST. (vs. OHIO STATE) 4
4 10 tied for fourth place.

Most total shots blocked in the tournament
1 JOE BARRY CARROLL, PURDUE   12

2 RODNEY MCCRAY, LOUISVILLE   7
2 ALTON LISTER, ARIZONA ST.   7
4 5 tied for fourth place.

STEALS

Most steals in a single game
1 ROD FOSTER, UCLA (vs. LOUISVILLE)   6
1 ERIC FLOYD, GEORGETOWN (vs. MARYLAND)   6
1 GLENN MARSHALL, KANSAS STATE (vs.
   ARKANSAS)   6
4 3 tied for fourth place.

Most total steals in the tournament
1 BRIAN WALKER, PURDUE   16
2 ROD FOSTER, UCLA   11
3 GLENN MARSHALL, KANSAS STATE   9
3 ERIC FLOYD, GEORGETOWN   9
5 MIKE SANDERS, UCLA   8

✪ TEAM RECORDS ✪

SCORING

Most points in a single game
1 ARIZONA ST. (vs. LOYOLA MYMT.)   99
2 LOUISIANA ST. (vs. ALCORN ST.)   98
3 2 tied for third place.

Most total points in the tournament
1 IOWA   462
2 PURDUE   458
3 UCLA   442

Highest scoring average (minimum 2 games)
1 SYRACUSE (174-2)   87.00
1 ARIZONA ST. (174-2)   87.00
3 FLORIDA STATE (172-2)   86.00

FIELD GOALS

Most field goals in a single game
1 ARIZONA ST. (vs. LOYOLA MYMT.)   44
2 TOLEDO (vs. FLORIDA STATE)   41
2 LOUISIANA ST. (vs. ALCORN ST.)   41

Most total field goals in the tournament
1 IOWA   170
2 PURDUE   165
3 UCLA   153

Most field goals attempted in a single game
1 ARIZONA ST. (vs. LOYOLA MYMT.)   86
2 3 tied for second place.

Most total field goals attempted in the tournament
1 IOWA   342
2 PURDUE   328
3 UCLA   318

Highest field goal percentage in a single game
1 MARYLAND (vs. TENNESSEE) (36-57)   .632
2 LAMAR (vs. WEBER ST.) (35-56)   .625
3 SYRACUSE (vs. VILLANOVA) (35-57)   .614

FREE THROWS

Most free throws in a single game
1 PURDUE (vs. INDIANA)   32
2 TEXAS A&M (vs. N. CAROLINA)   30
2 IOWA (vs. SYRACUSE)   30

Most total free throws in the tournament
1 UCLA   136
2 PURDUE   128
3 IOWA   122

Most free throws attempted in a single game
1 TEXAS A&M (vs. N. CAROLINA)   48
2 PURDUE (vs. INDIANA)   44
3 FLORIDA STATE (vs. KENTUCKY)   39
3 LOUISVILLE (vs. LOUISIANA ST.)   39
3 IOWA (vs. SYRACUSE)   39

Most total free throws attempted in the tournament
1 PURDUE   178
2 UCLA   166
3 IOWA   159

Highest free throw percentage in a single game
1 IOWA (vs. GEORGETOWN) (19-20)   .950
2 IOWA (vs. LOUISVILLE) (14-15)   .933
3 TENNESSEE (vs. MARYLAND) (13-14)   .929

Highest free throw percentage in the tournament (minimum 2 games)
1 KENTUCKY (39-45)   .867
2 VILLANOVA (46-54)   .852
3 SYRACUSE (46-55)   .836

Fewest free throws in a single game
1 SOUTH ALABAMA (vs. ALCORN ST.)   2
2 PENNSYLVANIA (vs. DUKE)   4
3 OREGON STATE (vs. LAMAR)   5

Lowest free throw percentage in a single game
1 SOUTH ALABAMA (vs. ALCORN ST.) (2-5) .400
2 ARIZONA ST. (vs. LOYOLA MYMT.) (11-26) .423
3 DUKE (vs. KENTUCKY) (11-24)   .458

Lowest free throw percentage in the tournament (minimum 2 games)
1 CLEMSON (51-87)   .586
2 MARYLAND (20-34)   .588
3 ARIZONA ST. (34-57)   .597

REBOUNDS

Most rebounds in a single game
1 ARIZONA ST. (vs. LOYOLA MYMT.)   58
2 KENTUCKY (vs. FLORIDA STATE)   52
3 TENNESSEE (vs. FURMAN)   46

Most rebounds per game (minimum 2 games)
1 ARIZONA ST. (95-2)   47.50
2 KENTUCKY (83-2)   41.50
3 2 tied for third place.

ASSISTS

Most assists in a single game
1 ARIZONA ST. (vs. LOYOLA MYMT.)   28
2 TENNESSEE (vs. FURMAN)   26
3 IOWA (vs. VA COMMONWEALTH)   25

Most assists per game (minimum 2 games)
1 ARIZONA ST. (50-2)   25.00
2 TENNESSEE (46-2)   23.00
3 MARYLAND (40-2)   20.00

TURNOVERS

Most turnovers in a single game
1 MARYLAND (vs. GEORGETOWN)   27
2 SYRACUSE (vs. VILLANOVA)   24
2 VILLANOVA (vs. SYRACUSE)   24

Most turnovers per game (minimum 2 games)
1 VILLANOVA (46-2)   23.00
2 MARYLAND (40-2)   20.00
3 DUKE (57-3)   19.00

SHOTS BLOCKED

Most shots blocked in a single game
1 ARIZONA ST. (vs. OHIO STATE)   7
1 TEXAS A&M (vs. LOUISVILLE)   7
3 2 tied for third place.

Most shots blocked per game (minimum 2 games)
1 ARIZONA ST. (13-2)   6.50
2 OHIO STATE (8-2)   4.00
2 FLORIDA STATE (8-2)   4.00

STEALS

Most steals in a single game
1 KANSAS STATE (vs. ARKANSAS)   14
2 3 tied for second place.

Most steals per game
1 KANSAS STATE (23-2)   11.50
2 VILLANOVA (18-2)   9.00
3 MARYLAND (16-2)   8.00

1981

| FIRST ROUND | SECOND ROUND | REGIONAL SEMIFINAL | REGIONAL FINAL | FINAL FOUR | REGIONAL FINAL | REGIONAL SEMIFINAL | SECOND ROUND | FIRST ROUND |

MIDWEST

- 8 Lamar 71
- 9 Missouri 67
- Lamar 78
- Louisiana St. 72
- (bye)
- 1 Louisiana St. 100
- Louisiana St. 96
- 5 Arkansas 73
- 12 Mercer 67
- Arkansas 74
- Arkansas 56
- (bye)
- 4 Louisville 73
- Louisiana St. 49
- 6 Wichita St. 95
- 11 Southern-B.R. 70
- Wichita St. 60
- Wichita St. 66
- (bye)
- 3 Iowa 56
- Wichita St. 85
- 7 Kansas 69
- 10 Mississippi 66
- Kansas 88
- Kansas 65
- (bye)
- 2 Arizona St. 71

MIDEAST

- 8 Creighton 57
- 9 St. Joseph's 59
- St. Joseph's 49
- St. Joseph's 42
- (bye)
- 1 DePaul 48
- St. Joseph's 46
- 5 Boston College 93
- 12 Ball St. 90
- Boston College 67
- Boston College 41
- (bye)
- 4 Wake Forest 64
- Indiana 67
- 6 Maryland 81
- 11 Tenn.-Chatt. 69
- Maryland 64
- Indiana 87
- (bye)
- 3 Indiana 99
- Indiana 78
- 7 Ala.-Birmingham 93
- 10 Western Ky. 68
- Ala.-Birmingham 69
- Ala.-Birmingham 72
- (bye)
- 2 Kentucky 62

FINAL FOUR

- Indiana 63
- N. Carolina 50
- N. Carolina 78
- Virginia 65

WEST

- Kansas St. 57
- Kansas St. 50
- 8 Kansas St. 64
- 9 San Francisco 60
- 1 *Oregon St. 48
- (bye)
- Kansas St. 68
- Illinois 52
- Wyoming 65
- 5 Wyoming 78
- 12 Howard 43
- 4 Illinois 67
- (bye)
- N. Carolina 82
- Utah 56
- Northeastern 69
- 6 Fresno St. 53
- 11 Northeastern 55
- 3 Utah 94
- (bye)
- N. Carolina 61
- Pittsburgh 57
- 7 Idaho 69
- 10 Pittsburgh 70 (ot)
- 2 N. Carolina 74
- (bye)

EAST

- Virginia 62
- Villanova 50
- 8 Houston 72
- 9 Villanova 90
- 1 Virginia 54
- (bye)
- Virginia 74
- Tennessee 48
- Va. Commonwealth 56
- 5 Va. Commonwealth 85
- 12 LIU 69
- 4 Tennessee 58 (ot)
- (bye)
- Brigham Young 51
- Brigham Young 78
- 6 Brigham Young 60
- 11 Princeton 51
- 3 UCLA 55
- (bye)
- Brigham Young 60
- Notre Dame 50
- James Madison 45
- 7 Georgetown 55
- 10 James Madison 61
- 2 Notre Dame 54
- (bye)

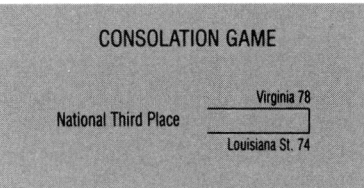

CONSOLATION GAME

National Third Place

Virginia 78
Louisiana St. 74

*Oregon State's participation in 1981 tournament vacated.

Early in the 1981 season, Isiah Lord Thomas III was unhappy being a vassal in Bob Knight's Indiana Hoosier domain. The free-spirited sophomore point guard with the engaging smile bristled at the discipline imposed by the unquestioned ruler of Hoosierdom, and as the two locked horns, the team suffered.

Bob Knight knew that Isiah Thomas was potentially the best guard in the country. He knew that a happy Isiah could turn what he called "the worst hand of cards I've ever been dealt" into a winning combination. He also knew, as the first weeks of the season passed, that Indiana—with Thomas fighting him tooth and nail—was going nowhere fast. The Hoosiers had a dispiriting 7-5 record when Knight decided that a peace offering was in order. He appointed Isiah team captain and gave him carte blanche to run the show *within the coach's system.*

Knight had yet another wild card in Landon Turner. A 6-10, 240-pound junior, Turner had great athletic ability but had never put it all together. He was too easygoing, unfocused, and in Knight's eyes, undisciplined. The coach rode Turner so hard in practice that he was often driven to tears. Finally Knight told him he would never play at Indiana. Suddenly Turner's game changed. Late in February he became a starter, and for the first time all season, the Hoosiers came together as a team.

Turner and the Hoosiers' other big man, 6-9 Ray Tolbert, formed a formidable front-court combination. With disciplined role players Ted Kitchel and Randy Wittman rounding out the starting five and 6-3 Jim Thomas (no relation) as the first man off the bench, Indiana was not exactly imposing, but they were definitely tough. And despite their nine losses, they finished the season as the Big Ten champs and came into the NCAAs with confidence in their coach and in their own ability.

There were a number of other good teams in the field in 1981, but no one was conceding the crown to anyone else. Top-ranked DePaul lost their opener when Jim Lynam's St. Joseph's Hawks lulled them to sleep with a four-corners and took the decision 49-48. The No. 1 seed in the West regional, Oregon State, also lost their first game, as did several other highly touted teams, including the defending champion Louisville Cardinals, who fell on a 50-foot, last-second shot by Arkansas' U. S. Reed.

The four teams that made it through the regionals earned their way into the Final Four. Terry Holland's defensive-minded Virginia Cavaliers, led by 7-4 Ralph Sampson and hot-shooting forward Jeff Lamp, had trouble only with Villanova on their way to the semis. North Carolina, with a brilliant front line of Al Wood, Sam Perkins, and James Worthy, threw Dean Smith's half a million defensive alignments at Utah to beat the Utes on their Salt Lake City home court (where they were previously undefeated); then they tore apart the Wildcats of Kansas State in the West regional final. Dale Brown's LSU Tigers roared through the Midwest without being tested. And in the

Mideast, Indiana was a juggernaut, winning their three games by an average of more than 27 points.

Indiana and LSU squared off in Philadelphia's Spectrum in the first semifinal, and at first the Tigers had everything their way. Point guard Ethan Martin ran the LSU attack beautifully, and even though their shots weren't falling, neither were Indiana's. The only Hoosier starter who did anything was Isiah Thomas (he shot 6 for 8), but he left the game with 3:14 to go in the half after picking up his third foul. Even though the Tigers were unable to take advantage of Thomas's absence (nobody scored again before intermission), LSU left the floor brimming with confidence and a 30-27 lead. Then the roof caved in. Indiana came out of the locker room and scored 11 straight points (7 by Landon Turner); when Isiah picked up his fourth foul with 16:33 to go, Jim Thomas came in and contributed nine rebounds, two assists, two blocked shots and a steal. Indiana poured it on, building their lead to 21 as the Tigers put only 10 points on the board in the first 17 minutes of the second half. In the end LSU lost 67-49, with Indiana holding the Tigers' explosive, 80-plus points per game offense to the their lowest point total in 17 years.

The other semi was an all-ACC affair. Twice before during the season, North Carolina had taken a commanding lead over Virginia, but each time Ralph Sampson led the Cavaliers back to win. This time, though, there would be no Virginia comeback. Al Wood was devastating, scoring 39 points, and Sampson all but vanished inside a Tar Heel zone that featured Perkins pushing him away from the basket and Worthy sloughing off to help out. North Carolina won 78-65.

In the final, the Tar Heels came out smoking. Midway through the half they led 16-8 and Sam Perkins and Al Wood were both on fire. Knight sent in Jim Thomas to play off-guard on offense and to shadow Wood on defense. Turner moved over to guard Perkins, and Randy Wittman switched from guard to forward, where he started bombing from the outside. Although Isiah shot an abysmal 1 for 7 from the floor, he fed Wittman for a shot at the buzzer that gave the Hoosiers their first lead.

As they had against LSU two nights earlier, Indiana owned the second half. Isiah opened the scoring with a steal off Jimmy Black and a breakaway lay-up. After the teams traded baskets, Thomas did it again. He hit a 14-foot jumper, and scored on a backdoor feed from Jim Thomas. While Isiah dominated offensively, the Hoosier defense shut down the Tar Heels' big three, holding the Carolina front line to 5 points and 5 rebounds in the second half. Once the game was in hand, Indiana spread out their offense and coasted to a 63-50 victory.

Knight's "worst hand of cards" had turned into a royal flush. And even if Knight was still the king, Isiah was the ace in the hole.

FIRST ROUND MIDWEST

Lamar (71)   Coach: Pat Foster

	Min.	Total FG/FGA	Pct.	FT/FTA	Pct.	Reb. O/T	A	TO	PF	S	Blk	TP	PPM
OLLIVER, M.	40	11/18	.611	3/4	.750	-/3	2	4	2	1	0	25	.625
BROOKS, A.	40	3/5	.600	0/1	.000	-/1	5	2	2	1	0	6	.150
WALLACE, M.	15	1/4	.250	0/0	.000	-/3	0	1	0	0	0	2	.133
PERKINS, K.	37	5/5	1.000	0/1	.000	-/7	5	0	3	0	0	10	.270
DAVIS, B.	23	2/7	.286	5/7	.714	-/3	2	1	4	0	1	9	.391
LONG, T.	33	7/11	.636	2/2	1.000	-/2	0	0	2	1	0	16	.485
STEPHENSON, L.	12	1/2	.500	1/1	1.000	-/3	2	0	2	0	0	3	.250
Totals	200	30/52	.577	11/16	.688	-/22	16	8	15	3	1	71	.355

Missouri (67)   Coach: Norm Stewart

	Min.	Total FG/FGA	Pct.	FT/FTA	Pct.	Reb. O/T	A	TO	PF	S	Blk	TP	PPM
BERRY, C.	32	8/10	.800	5/5	1.000	-/7	2	1	5	1	0	21	.656
TEAGUE, S.	35	6/8	.750	0/0	.000	-/1	5	3	2	2	1	12	.343
SUNDVOLD, J.	38	4/11	.364	3/3	1.000	-/3	6	1	4	2	0	11	.289
FRAZIER, R.	35	3/9	.333	1/2	.500	-/5	0	1	3	0	0	7	.200
STIPANOVICH, S.	40	6/10	.600	0/0	.000	-/2	4	2	4	0	0	12	.300
MCCRORY, M.	17	1/3	.333	2/2	1.000	-/1	1	1	0	1	0	4	.235
JONES, R.	3	0/0	.000	0/0	.000	-/1	0	0	0	0	0	0	.000
Totals	200	28/51	.549	11/12	.917	-/20	18	9	18	6	1	67	.335

Team Rebounds: Lamar 4; Missouri 4. Disqualified: Missouri—Berry. Technical fouls: None.

	1st Half	2nd Half	Final
Lamar	32	39	71
Missouri	28	39	67

Arkansas (73)   Coach: Eddie Sutton

	Min.	Total FG/FGA	Pct.	FT/FTA	Pct.	Reb. O/T	A	TO	PF	S	Blk	TP	PPM
PETERSON, K.	-	1/6	.167	3/6	.500	-/5	1	0	1	0	0	5	-
BROWN, T.	-	4/6	.667	4/5	.800	-/9	10	1	4	3	0	12	-
HASTINGS, S.	-	6/14	.429	6/10	.600	-/12	1	5	2	1	1	18	-
REED, U.	-	8/15	.533	3/6	.500	-/8	1	0	3	1	0	19	-
YOUNG, M.	-	0/2	.000	0/0	.000	-/1	0	1	0	0	0	0	-
WALKER, D.	-	8/12	.667	3/13	.231	-/5	1	1	4	2	0	19	-
KELLY, C.	-	0/1	.000	0/0	.000	-/0	1	0	1	0	0	0	-
SKULLMAN, G.	-	0/1	.000	0/0	.000	-/1	0	1	3	1	0	0	-
Totals	200	27/57	.474	19/40	.475	-/41	15	9	19	8	1	73	.365

Mercer (67)   Coach: Bill Bibb

	Min.	Total FG/FGA	Pct.	FT/FTA	Pct.	Reb. O/T	A	TO	PF	S	Blk	TP	PPM
JONES, E.	-	4/12	.333	2/3	.667	-/5	1	1	4	0	1	10	-
GATTIS, T.	-	5/11	.455	4/6	.667	-/12	4	4	5	1	0	14	-
WADE, B.	-	4/7	.571	0/1	.000	-/3	0	0	5	0	1	8	-
THOMPSON, M.	-	4/7	.571	1/3	.333	-/3	3	2	3	1	0	9	-
TALBOTT, D.	-	8/18	.444	6/7	.857	-/4	5	3	4	2	0	22	-
WALKER, R.	-	0/4	.000	0/0	.000	-/4	1	0	4	0	1	0	-
JOHNSON, T.	-	0/0	.000	0/0	.000	-/0	0	1	0	0	0	0	-
TEAGUE, T.	-	2/2	1.000	0/0	.000	-/0	0	1	2	0	0	4	-
Totals	200	27/61	.443	13/20	.650	-/31	14	11	28	4	3	67	.335

Team Rebounds: Arkansas 3; Mercer 6. Disqualified: Mercer—Gattis, Wade. Technical fouls: None.

	1st Half	2nd Half	Final
Arkansas	38	35	73
Mercer	36	31	67

Wichita State (95)   Coach: Gene Smithson

	Min.	Total FG/FGA	Pct.	FT/FTA	Pct.	Reb. O/T	A	TO	PF	S	Blk	TP	PPM
CARR, A.	38	8/11	.727	2/2	1.000	-/10	2	2	4	2	3	18	.474
JACKSON, J.	26	6/6	1.000	0/0	.000	-/1	1	3	0	1	1	12	.462
LEVINGSTON, C.	28	9/15	.600	6/9	.667	-/13	1	6	4	1	0	24	.857
MARTIN, T.	31	5/11	.455	1/2	.500	-/2	11	2	1	2	0	11	.355
SMITHSON, R.	37	6/13	.462	1/2	.500	-/4	5	2	2	1	0	13	.351
GIBBS, J.	11	0/1	.000	3/5	.600	-/0	5	1	1	1	0	3	.273
RADOVIC, Z.	1	0/0	.000	0/0	.000	-/0	0	0	0	0	0	0	.000
JONES, M.	19	5/8	.625	0/0	.000	-/6	1	1	4	1	0	10	.526
PAPKE, K.	2	1/1	1.000	2/3	.667	-/1	1	0	0	0	0	4	2.000
DENNY, M.	6	0/2	.000	0/0	.000	-/2	0	1	0	0	0	0	.000
DURISIC, Z.	1	0/0	.000	0/0	.000	-/2	0	1	0	0	0	0	.000
Totals	200	40/68	.588	15/23	.652	-/41	27	18	17	9	4	95	.475

Southern-B.R. (70)   Coach: Carl Stewart

	Min.	Total FG/FGA	Pct.	FT/FTA	Pct.	Reb. O/T	A	TO	PF	S	Blk	TP	PPM
WILKINS, M.	29	6/9	.667	0/0	.000	-/4	1	4	0	1	0	12	.414
WILLIAMS, D.	40	5/13	.385	5/6	.833	-/7	1	3	4	1	0	15	375
BRYANT, A.	40	6/13	.462	4/5	.800	-/11	1	4	3	0	0	16	.400
JACKSON, A.	32	10/25	.400	1/2	.500	-/3	4	8	4	2	1	21	.656
DAVIS, E.	30	2/7	.286	0/0	.000	-/2	4	0	4	0	0	4	133
JACKSON, J.	18	0/3	.000	0/1	.000	-/0	2	1	1	1	0	0	.000
JOHNELL, H.	4	1/2	.500	0/0	.000	-/2	0	0	0	0	0	2	.500
SCOTT, A.	7	0/1	.000	0/0	.000	-/1	0	1	3	0	0	0	.000
Totals	200	30/73	.411	10/14	.714	-/30	13	20	19	5	1	70	.350

Team Rebounds: Wichita State 3; Southern-B.R. 6. Disqualified: None. Technical fouls: None.

	1st Half	2nd Half	Final
Wichita State	45	50	95
Southern-B.R.	37	33	70

Kansas (69)   Coach: Ted Owens

	Min.	Total FG/FGA	Pct.	FT/FTA	Pct.	Reb. O/T	A	TO	PF	S	Blk	TP	PPM
MAGLEY, D.	35	4/6	.667	3/4	.750	-/7	0	2	4	2	0	11	.314
CRAWFORD, J.	40	3/5	.600	6/6	1.000	-/6	3	3	3	0	3	12	.300
HOUSEY, A.	33	4/6	.667	3/4	.750	-/6	1	3	5	0	2	11	.333
GUY, T.	40	5/10	.500	4/7	.571	-/1	2	2	2	0	0	14	.350
VALENTINE, D.	37	3/7	.429	9/10	.900	-/1	4	0	3	2	0	15	.405
NEAL, B.	9	3/6	.500	0/0	.000	-/0	0	2	1	1	0	6	.667
MITCHELL, V.	6	0/0	.000	0/1	.000	-/1	1	0	0	1	0	0	.000
Totals	200	22/40	.550	25/32	.781	-/22	11	12	18	6	5	69	.345

Mississippi (66)   Coach: Bob Weltlich

	Min.	Total FG/FGA	Pct.	FT/FTA	Pct.	Reb. O/T	A	TO	PF	S	Blk	TP	PPM
CLARK	32	3/10	.300	2/2	1.000	-/3	3	2	4	2	0	8	.250
TURNER	40	10/20	.500	2/4	.500	-/7	4	0	3	1	0	22	.550
STIEG	34	8/10	.800	1/3	.333	-/8	0	3	4	2	1	17	.500
DOWELL	21	1/5	.200	2/2	1.000	-/3	3	1	4	0	0	4	.190
TUOHY	39	1/3	.333	0/0	.000	-/2	7	2	5	1	0	2	.051
BARRETT	28	4/9	.444	2/2	1.000	-/4	0	2	2	1	0	10	.357
THOMAS	5	1/1	1.000	1/2	.500	-/1	0	0	2	0	0	3	.600
MILLER	1	0/0	.000	0/0	.000	-/0	0	0	0	0	0	0	.000
Totals	200	28/58	.483	10/15	.667	-/28	17	10	24	7	1	66	.330

Team Rebounds: Kansas 2; Mississippi 6. Disqualified: Kansas—Housey; Mississippi—Tuohy. Technical fouls: None.

	1st Half	2nd Half	Final
Kansas	32	37	69
Mississippi	29	37	66

FIRST ROUND MIDEAST

Creighton (57)   Coach: Tom Apke

	Min.	Total FG / FGA	Pct.	FT / FTA	Pct.	Reb. O / T	A	TO	PF	S	Blk	TP	PPM
STIVRINS	-	1/ 4	.250	0/ 0	.000	-/ 2	2	-	2	-	-	2	-
STOVALL	-	3/ 9	.333	0/ 0	.000	-/ 4	3	-	1	-	-	6	-
MORROW	-	4/12	.333	9/10	.900	-/14	2	-	5	-	-	17	-
PRUITT	-	4/ 9	.444	4/ 5	.750	-/ 1	3	-	2	-	-	11	-
MCKENNA	-	7/13	.538	4/ 4	1.000	-/ 4	2	-	4	-	-	18	-
ROSS	-	0/ 2	.000	1/ 2	.500	-/ 2	1	-	1	-	-	1	-
TRIESCHMAN	-	0/ 0	.000	2/ 2	1.000	-/ 0	0	-	1	-	-	2	-
Totals	200	19/49	.388	19/22	.864	-/27	13	-	16	-	-	57	.285

St. Joseph's (59)   Coach: Jim Lynam

	Min.	Total FG / FGA	Pct.	FT / FTA	Pct.	Reb. O / T	A	TO	PF	S	Blk	TP	PPM
WILLIAMS	-	2/ 5	.400	3/ 4	.750	-/ 5	1	-	4	-	-	7	-
SMITH, J.	-	8/11	.727	4/ 5	.800	-/10	3	-	4	-	-	20	-
COSTNER	-	8/10	.800	2/ 2	1.000	-/11	3	-	4	-	-	18	-
CLARK, J.	-	0/ 2	.000	2/ 2	1.000	-/ 1	3	-	2	-	-	2	-
WARRICK, B.	-	4/15	.267	0/ 3	.000	-/ 5	6	-	2	-	-	8	-
MCFARLAN, L.	-	2/ 9	.222	0/ 0	.000	-/ 2	2	-	1	-	-	4	-
MITCHELL	-	0/ 1	.000	0/ 0	.000	-/ 0	0	-	1	-	-	0	-
KEARNEY	-	0/ 0	.000	0/ 0	.000	-/ 0	0	-	1	-	-	0	-
Totals	200	24/53	.453	11/16	.688	-/34	18	-	19	-	-	59	.295

Disqualified: Creighton—Morrow. Technical fouls: None.

	1st Half	2nd Half	Final
Creighton	25	32	57
St. Joseph's	24	35	59

Boston College (93)   Coach: Tom Davis

	Min.	Total FG / FGA	Pct.	FT / FTA	Pct.	Reb. O / T	A	TO	PF	S	Blk	TP	PPM
CHANDLER, D.	29	5/15	.333	1/ 3	.333	-/ 2	4	0	2	1	0	11	.379
MURPHY, J.	22	5/ 7	.714	3/ 5	.600	-/ 6	0	2	2	0	1	13	.591
FOY, C.	11	1/ 4	.250	1/ 1	1.000	-/ 2	1	2	5	1	0	3	.273
BAGLEY, J.	33	8/19	.421	3/ 3	1.000	-/ 4	3	2	3	2	0	19	.576
CLARK, M.	19	6/10	.600	4/ 4	1.000	-/ 5	1	3	4	1	0	16	.842
O'SHEA, T.	19	0/ 0	.000	0/ 0	.000	-/ 1	1	1	1	0	0	0	.000
SHRIGLEY, R.	22	3/ 5	.600	5/ 6	.833	-/ 8	1	3	2	1	0	11	.500
ADAMS, B.	18	4/ 5	.800	0/ 0	.000	-/ 3	0	1	5	0	0	8	.444
BEAULIEU, J.	14	3/ 6	.500	4/ 4	1.000	-/11	0	1	1	0	0	10	.714
CARAHER, V.	5	1/ 2	.500	0/ 0	.000	-/ 1	0	0	1	0	0	2	.400
KRAUSE, P.	8	0/ 0	.000	0/ 0	.000	-/ 0	0	1	4	0	0	0	.000
Totals	200	36/73	.493	21/26	.808	-/43	11	16	30	6	1	93	.465

Ball State (90)   Coach: Steve Yoder

	Min.	Total FG / FGA	Pct.	FT / FTA	Pct.	Reb. O / T	A	TO	PF	S	Blk	TP	PPM
WILLIAMS, J.	33	4/ 9	.444	1/ 3	.333	-/ 4	4	3	4	3	0	9	.273
GOODEN, A.	34	5/ 7	.714	13/13	1.000	-/ 6	0	1	4	2	0	23	.676
WILLIAMS, J.	29	2/ 8	.250	10/11	.909	-/ 3	3	3	4	1	0	14	.483
MCCALLUM, R.	38	13/19	.684	0/ 0	.000	-/ 2	2	1	4	0	0	26	.684
BRADLEY, G.	16	1/ 2	.500	0/ 0	.000	-/ 2	2	1	5	1	2	2	.125
FULLOVE, C.	25	5/ 8	.625	3/ 4	.750	-/ 7	0	1	1	1	0	13	.520
ALBERTSON, B.	4	0/ 0	.000	0/ 2	.000	-/ 0	0	0	0	0	0	0	.000
PARKER, J.	8	0/ 1	.000	0/ 0	.000	-/ 1	1	0	1	0	0	0	.000
HAMPTON, R.	7	0/ 2	.000	0/ 1	.000	-/ 1	0	0	1	2	0	0	.000
MURRELL, C.	6	0/ 0	.000	3/ 4	.750	-/ 0	0	0	1	0	0	3	.500
Totals	200	30/56	.536	30/38	.789	-/26	12	10	25	10	2	90	.450

Team Rebounds: Boston College 2; Ball St. 2. Disqualified: Boston College—Foy, Adams; Ball St.—Bradley. Technical fouls: None.

	1st Half	2nd Half	Final
Boston College	44	49	93
Ball St.	44	46	90

Maryland (81)   Coach: Lefty Driesell

	Min.	Total FG / FGA	Pct.	FT / FTA	Pct.	Reb. O / T	A	TO	PF	S	Blk	TP	PPM
KING, A.	38	11/20	.550	3/ 3	1.000	-/ 5	4	2	0	0	1	25	.658
GRAHAM, E.	31	7/14	.500	4/ 7	.571	-/ 7	5	1	1	0	1	18	.581
WILLIAMS, C.	37	3/ 7	.429	7/10	.700	-/16	1	4	2	1	1	13	.351
JACKSON, R.	34	2/ 4	.500	3/ 4	.750	-/ 2	5	0	3	1	1	7	.206
MANNING, G.	36	5/ 9	.556	3/ 3	1.000	-/ 1	5	2	2	0	0	13	.361
PITTMAN, C.	15	1/ 1	1.000	1/ 2	.500	-/ 3	0	1	2	1	0	3	.200
RIVERS, S.	3	0/ 1	.000	0/ 0	.000	-/ 0	0	0	1	0	0	0	.000
MORLEY, G.	3	1/ 1	1.000	0/ 0	.000	-/ 1	1	0	1	0	0	2	.667
BALDWIN, T.	3	0/ 0	.000	0/ 0	.000	-/ 1	0	0	1	0	0	0	.000
Totals	200	30/57	.526	21/29	.724	-/36	21	10	13	3	4	81	.405

Tennessee-Chattanooga (69)   Coach: Arnold Murray

	Min.	Total FG / FGA	Pct.	FT / FTA	Pct.	Reb. O / T	A	TO	PF	S	Blk	TP	PPM
SMITH, E.	40	4/15	.267	2/ 2	1.000	-/ 4	0	3	3	0	0	10	.250
JONES, J.	34	8/17	.471	1/ 1	1.000	-/ 7	0	1	2	0	0	17	.500
LAWRENCE, N.	15	0/ 5	.000	0/ 0	.000	-/ 3	0	0	3	0	1	0	.000
MORKEN, R.	32	4/10	.400	2/ 2	1.000	-/ 4	10	3	5	1	0	10	.313
WHITE, W.	30	3/ 8	.375	4/ 4	1.000	-/ 3	4	0	3	0	0	10	.333
SCHOENE, R.	25	8/11	.727	0/ 0	.000	-/ 8	1	0	5	0	1	16	.640
CLARK, W.	18	2/ 6	.333	2/ 2	1.000	-/ 4	0	1	0	1	0	6	.333
COCHRAN, C.	6	0/ 0	.000	0/ 0	.000	-/ 1	0	2	1	0	0	0	.000
Totals	200	29/72	.403	11/11	1.000	-/34	15	10	22	2	2	69	.345

Team Rebounds: Maryland 2; Tenn.-Chatt. 2. Disqualified: Tenn.-Chatt—Morken, Schoene. Technical fouls: None.

	1st Half	2nd Half	Final
Maryland	39	42	81
Tenn.-Chatt.	41	28	69

Alabama-Birmingham (93)   Coach: Gene Bartow

	Min.	Total FG / FGA	Pct.	FT / FTA	Pct.	Reb. O / T	A	TO	PF	S	Blk	TP	PPM
GILES, C.	38	4/ 8	.500	4/ 4	1.000	-/ 7	2	1	1	0	0	12	.316
LANE, C.	31	4/ 9	.444	5/ 7	.714	-/ 7	1	6	1	4	0	13	.419
ROBINSON, O.	33	6/14	.429	4/ 4	1.000	-/ 3	3	1	4	4	0	16	.485
MARCUS, R.	35	7/ 8	.875	8/ 9	.889	-/ 2	4	0	2	3	0	22	.629
SPEER, D.	18	2/ 4	.500	0/ 0	.000	-/ 0	0	1	5	0	0	4	.222
BARTOW, M.	1	0/ 0	.000	0/ 0	.000	-/ 0	0	0	0	0	0	0	.000
MCCAMMON, B.	1	1/ 2	.500	0/ 0	.000	-/ 0	0	0	0	1	0	2	2.000
NICHOLAS, J.	11	2/ 2	1.000	9/ 9	1.000	-/ 2	1	5	1	1	0	13	1.182
FOSTER, L.	2	1/ 1	1.000	0/ 2	.000	-/ 1	0	0	0	0	0	2	1.000
SIMCIK, S.	2	0/ 1	.000	3/ 4	.750	-/ 1	1	0	0	0	0	3	1.500
ALMQUIST, T.	3	0/ 0	.000	0/ 0	.000	-/ 0	0	0	0	0	0	0	.000
MORRIS, L.	15	2/ 2	1.000	0/ 0	.000	-/ 1	0	0	2	0	1	4	.267
RICHARDS, T.	1	0/ 0	.000	2/ 2	1.000	-/ 0	0	0	0	1	0	2	2.000
ANCHRUM, N.	9	0/ 3	.000	0/ 0	.000	-/ 3	0	1	5	0	3	0	.000
Totals	200	29/54	.537	35/41	.854	-/27	12	15	21	14	4	93	.465

Western Kentucky (68)   Coach: Clem Haskins

	Min.	Total FG / FGA	Pct.	FT / FTA	Pct.	Reb. O / T	A	TO	PF	S	Blk	TP	PPM
WILSON, T.	35	6/10	.600	8/ 9	.889	-/ 9	1	2	4	1	1	20	.571
WHITE, P.	19	3/ 8	.375	1/ 3	.333	-/ 5	0	2	4	1	0	7	.368
JONES, B.	17	0/ 0	.000	0/ 0	.000	-/ 3	2	4	1	0	0	0	.000
REESE, M.	30	5/12	.417	1/ 2	.500	-/ 4	1	3	4	2	0	11	.367
MCCORMICK, C.	31	4/10	.400	0/ 2	.000	-/ 2	1	7	1	1	0	8	.258
DILDY, K.	19	0/ 1	.000	0/ 0	.000	-/ 1	1	3	1	1	0	0	.000
ELLIS, K.	14	1/ 2	.500	0/ 0	.000	-/ 1	0	2	5	0	2	2	.143
CARVER, G.	7	2/ 2	1.000	2/ 2	1.000	-/ 1	0	0	3	1	0	6	.857
HATCHER, K.	15	1/ 4	.250	0/ 0	.000	-/ 2	0	0	1	0	0	2	.133
WRAY, R.	4	1/ 2	.500	2/ 3	.667	-/ 2	0	1	0	0	0	4	1.000
TEATER, B.	6	3/ 3	1.000	0/ 0	.000	-/ 2	1	1	2	0	0	6	1.000
MOSLEY, A.	2	0/ 1	.000	0/ 0	.000	-/ 0	0	3	1	0	0	0	.000
BLANKENSHIP, S.	1	1/ 1	1.000	0/ 0	.000	-/ 0	0	1	1	0	0	2	2.000
Totals	200	27/56	.482	14/21	.667	-/32	7	25	31	7	2	68	.340

Team Rebounds: Ala.-Birmingham 3; Western Ky. 1. Disqualified: Ala.-Birmingham—Speer, Anchrum; Western Ky.— Ellis. Technical fouls: Western Ky.—McCormick.

	1st Half	2nd Half	Final
Ala.-Birmingham	39	54	93
Western Ky.	25	43	68

FIRST ROUND WEST

Kansas State (64)   Coach: Jack Hartman

	Min.	Total FG/FGA	Pct.	FT/FTA	Pct.	Reb. O/T	A	TO	PF	S	Blk	TP	PPM
ADAMS, T.	38	2/11	.182	0/1	.000	-/1	4	1	4	0	0	4	.105
REED, R.	35	11/13	.846	2/3	.667	-/5	0	0	3	0	1	24	.686
NEALY, E.	35	3/10	.300	2/3	.667	-/5	5	2	2	0	0	8	.229
JANKOVICH, T.	8	1/2	.500	0/0	.000	-/0	0	1	2	0	0	2	.250
BLACKMAN, R.	34	4/6	.667	0/0	.000	-/5	3	2	1	0	1	8	.235
BARTON, F.	10	1/4	.250	0/0	.000	-/0	2	1	0	0	0	2	.200
CRAFT, L.	22	5/6	.833	0/0	.000	-/6	2	2	0	0	0	10	.455
GALVAO, E.	17	2/3	.667	2/3	.667	-/3	3	0	2	1	0	6	.353
PRUDHOE, G.	1	0/0	.000	0/0	.000	-/0	0	0	0	0	0	0	.000
Totals	200	29/55	.527	6/10	.600	-/25	19	9	14	1	2	64	.320

San Francisco (60)   Coach: Peter Barry

	Min.	Total FG/FGA	Pct.	FT/FTA	Pct.	Reb. O/T	A	TO	PF	S	Blk	TP	PPM
HEGWOOD	30	4/8	.500	0/0	.000	-/9	1	3	4	1	0	8	.267
BOWERS	38	4/8	.500	0/0	.000	-/7	2	0	3	1	0	8	.211
BRYANT	38	7/20	.350	1/4	.250	-/6	0	0	3	1	0	15	.395
MCALISTER	37	4/4	1.000	1/2	.500	-/2	5	0	4	1	0	9	.243
DAILEY	40	8/18	.444	4/5	.800	-/4	2	3	4	1	0	20	.500
SLAYMAKER	11	0/0	.000	0/0	.000	-/2	1	0	0	0	0	0	.000
SPEIGHT	6	0/1	.000	0/0	.000	-/0	1	0	0	0	0	0	.000
Totals	200	27/59	.458	6/11	.545	-/30	12	6	18	5	0	60	.300

Team Rebounds: Kansas State 1; San Francisco 3. Disqualified: None. Technical fouls: None.

	1st Half	2nd Half	Final
Kansas State	25	39	64
San Francisco	34	26	60

Wyoming (78)   Coach: Jim Brandenburg

	Min.	Total FG/FGA	Pct.	FT/FTA	Pct.	Reb. O/T	A	TO	PF	S	Blk	TP	PPM
OLLIE, K.	29	5/8	.625	1/1	1.000	-/10	3	-	0	-	-	11	.379
GARNETT, B.	34	8/15	.533	2/2	1.000	-/8	6	-	5	-	-	18	.529
THESENVITZ	11	0/0	.000	0/0	.000	-/3	0	-	1	-	-	0	.000
BRADLEY	31	8/13	.615	4/6	.667	-/6	2	-	3	-	-	20	.645
JACKSON, M.	12	3/4	.750	0/0	.000	-/3	2	-	5	-	-	6	.500
ENGLER, C.	26	4/7	.571	1/2	.500	-/4	0	-	4	-	-	9	.346
JOHNSON, A.	22	1/2	.500	1/3	.333	-/0	3	-	0	-	-	3	.136
MCCLENDON, D.	10	0/2	.000	0/0	.000	-/1	1	-	0	-	-	0	.000
WRAPP	13	3/5	.600	3/3	1.000	-/6	2	-	1	-	-	9	.692
LADOUCEUR	4	1/3	.333	0/0	.000	-/1	1	-	1	-	-	2	.500
KOEHN	3	0/1	.000	0/0	.000	-/1	0	-	0	-	-	0	.000
ADAMS	3	0/1	.000	0/0	.000	-/0	0	-	0	-	-	0	.000
KRALY	2	0/0	.000	0/0	.000	-/2	1	-	0	-	-	0	.000
Totals	200	33/61	.541	12/17	.706	-/45	21	-	20	-	-	78	.390

Howard (43)   Coach: A. B. Williamson

	Min.	Total FG/FGA	Pct.	FT/FTA	Pct.	Reb. O/T	A	TO	PF	S	Blk	TP	PPM
SPRIGGS	25	2/7	.286	2/5	.400	-/6	0	-	5	-	-	6	.240
RATIFF	39	6/19	.316	3/4	.750	-/9	0	-	1	-	-	15	.385
TERRY	18	1/4	.250	0/0	.000	-/2	1	-	5	-	-	2	.111
WRIGHT	33	2/8	.250	0/0	.000	-/0	1	-	3	-	-	4	.121
PERRY	32	3/13	.231	0/0	.000	-/7	2	-	3	-	-	6	.188
NORFLEET	28	1/2	.500	2/5	.400	-/2	0	-	1	-	-	4	.143
WILSON	10	0/4	.000	0/0	.000	-/0	0	-	0	-	-	0	.000
BYRD	4	0/1	.000	0/0	.000	-/0	0	-	0	-	-	0	.000
PIERCE	4	0/0	.000	2/3	.667	-/0	0	-	0	-	-	2	.500
HARRIS	5	1/1	1.000	0/2	.000	-/1	0	-	2	-	-	2	.400
SCOTT	1	0/1	.000	0/1	.000	-/1	0	-	0	-	-	0	.000
WARNER	1	0/0	.000	2/2	1.000	-/0	0	-	0	-	-	2	2.000
Totals	200	16/60	.267	11/22	.500	-/28	4	-	20	-	-	43	.215

Team Rebounds: Wyoming 2; Howard 4. Disqualified: Wyoming—Garnett, Jackson; Howard—Spriggs, Terry. Technical Fouls: None.

	1st Half	2nd Half	Final
Wyoming	35	43	78
Howard	23	20	43

Fresno State (53)   Coach: Boyd Grant

	Min.	Total FG/FGA	Pct.	FT/FTA	Pct.	Reb. O/T	A	TO	PF	S	Blk	TP	PPM
HIGGINS, R.	40	10/15	.667	4/4	1.000	3/4	0	0	2	1	5	24	.600
DAVIS, B.	32	2/4	.500	1/4	.250	1/2	0	1	2	0	0	5	.156
VERHOEVEN, P.	27	4/7	.571	4/4	1.000	4/5	0	1	4	1	0	12	.444
ANDERSON, R.	40	1/1	1.000	0/0	.000	1/2	3	1	3	1	0	2	.050
MASON, J.	40	4/9	.444	0/0	.000	0/1	4	4	0	0	0	8	.200
THOMPSON, B.	11	0/0	.000	2/4	.500	0/0	0	0	1	0	0	2	.182
SEZZI, D.	7	0/0	.000	0/0	.000	1/1	0	0	1	1	0	0	.000
WEATHERSPOON, J.	3	0/0	.000	0/0	.000	0/0	0	0	1	0	0	0	.000
Totals	200	21/36	.583	11/16	.688	10/15	7	7	14	4	5	53	.265

Northeastern (55)   Coach: Jim Calhoun

	Min.	Total FG/FGA	Pct.	FT/FTA	Pct.	Reb. O/T	A	TO	PF	S	Blk	TP	PPM
LEITAO, D.	32	1/2	.500	0/0	.000	1/3	0	0	1	0	0	2	.063
RUCKER, C.	31	2/2	1.000	0/0	.000	1/1	1	0	4	0	0	4	.129
HEINECK, C.	16	0/2	.000	0/0	.000	0/0	0	0	1	0	0	0	.000
MOSS, P.	38	6/9	.667	5/8	.625	4/5	2	2	2	1	0	17	.447
HARRIS, P.	40	7/14	.500	6/7	.857	3/3	1	1	0	1	0	20	.500
BRASWALL, R.	9	1/1	1.000	0/0	.000	0/1	0	1	3	1	0	2	.222
HALSEL, M.	8	2/2	1.000	0/1	.000	0/0	0	0	0	0	0	4	.500
ROBINSON, P.	2	0/0	.000	0/0	.000	0/0	0	0	0	0	0	0	.000
JEFFERSON, E.	24	3/5	.600	0/0	.000	1/2	0	2	1	1	0	6	.250
Totals	200	22/37	.647	11/16	.688	10/15	4	6	12	4	0	55	.275

Team Rebounds: Northeastern 1; Fresno State 3. Disqualified: None. Technical fouls: None.

	1st Half	2nd Half	Final
Fresno State	36	17	53
Northeastern	30	25	55

Idaho (69)   Coach: Don Monson

	Min.	Total FG/FGA	Pct.	FT/FTA	Pct.	Reb. O/T	A	TO	PF	S	Blk	TP	PPM
FORGE, D.	40	5/10	.500	2/2	1.000	4/8	1	2	4	0	0	12	.300
HOPSON, P.	33	5/8	.625	2/4	.500	2/8	1	1	5	5	0	12	.364
MABEN, R.	45	10/14	.714	2/2	1.000	5/7	3	2	2	0	3	22	.489
KELLERMAN, B.	45	3/11	.273	1/2	.500	0/5	0	2	4	1	0	7	.156
OWENS, J.	37	4/9	.444	6/12	.500	3/4	5	7	1	4	0	14	.378
BRUDIE, J.	18	0/1	.000	0/0	.000	0/0	0	3	1	0	0	0	.000
PRIGGE, P.	7	1/1	1.000	0/0	.000	0/1	0	0	0	0	0	2	.286
WILLIAMS, A.	0	0/0	.000	0/0	.000	0/0	0	0	0	0	0	0	-
Totals	225	28/54	.519	13/22	.591	14/33	10	17	17	10	3	69	.307

Pittsburgh (70)   Coach: Roy Chipman

	Min.	Total FG/FGA	Pct.	FT/FTA	Pct.	Reb. O/T	A	TO	PF	S	Blk	TP	PPM
MCMILLEN, L.	-	3/10	.300	0/1	.000	2/9	0	3	5	1	1	6	-
CLANCY, S.	-	9/15	.600	4/7	.571	5/13	0	2	4	2	0	22	-
BROZOVICH, P.	-	0/1	.000	0/0	.000	0/0	0	1	0	0	0	0	-
NEVERSON, C.	-	3/8	.375	0/0	.000	0/2	0	2	5	1	0	6	-
WALLACE, D.	-	9/16	.563	2/2	1.000	0/2	0	5	4	3	0	20	-
BEATTY, S.	-	1/1	1.000	0/0	.000	0/1	0	0	3	0	0	2	-
VAUGHAN, C.	-	1/3	.333	0/0	.000	0/2	0	0	2	0	0	2	-
SCHNEURMANN, E.	-	0/2	.000	2/2	1.000	0/1	0	1	1	1	0	2	-
GISSENDANNER, D.	-	4/6	.667	2/2	1.000	0/0	0	1	1	1	0	10	-
Totals	225	30/62	.484	10/14	.714	7/30	0	15	25	9	1	70	.311

Team Rebounds: Pittsburgh 4; Idaho 1. Disqualified: Pittsburgh—McMillen, Neverson; Idaho—Hopson. Technical fouls: None. Player who played 0 min. played less than 1 min.

	1st Half	2nd Half	1st OT	Final
Idaho	35	26	8	69
Pittsburgh	31	30	9	70

FIRST ROUND EAST

Houston (72)   Coach: Guy Lewis

	Min.	Total FG/FGA	Pct.	FT/FTA	Pct.	Reb. O/T	A	TO	PF	S	Blk	TP	PPM
ROSE, L.	16	3/6	.500	0/0	.000	-/0	1	1	0	0	1	6	.375
WILLIAMS, R.	40	9/20	.450	3/4	.750	-/1	1	5	4	4	0	21	.525
MICHEAUX, L.	27	4/8	.500	0/1	.000	-/4	0	3	5	0	0	8	.296
DREXLER, C.	38	5/9	.556	1/2	.500	-/6	4	0	3	4	0	11	.289
YOUNG, M.	37	6/13	.462	0/2	.000	-/6	3	1	2	0	1	12	.324
ROSE, D.	1	0/1	.000	0/0	.000	-/0	0	0	0	0	0	0	.000
DAVIS, E.	15	4/6	.667	0/0	.000	-/0	3	2	2	0	0	8	.533
BROWN, D.	17	3/6	.500	0/1	.000	-/7	0	1	3	1	1	6	.353
DAVIS, A.	4	0/0	.000	0/0	.000	-/1	0	0	1	0	0	0	.000
PARKER, R.	2	0/2	.000	0/0	.000	-/0	1	0	2	0	0	0	.000
BUNCE, D.	3	0/1	.000	0/0	.000	-/0	0	0	0	0	0	0	.000
Totals	200	34/72	.472	4/10	.400	-/25	13	13	22	9	3	72	.360

Villanova (90)   Coach: Rollie Massimino

	Min.	Total FG/FGA	Pct.	FT/FTA	Pct.	Reb. O/T	A	TO	PF	S	Blk	TP	PPM
GRANGER, S.	39	2/3	.667	1/2	.500	-/2	6	2	2	0	0	5	.128
SIENKIEWICZ, T.	39	6/8	.750	4/7	.571	-/4	4	4	1	2	1	16	.410
PINONE, J.	37	7/13	.538	5/5	1.000	-/10	3	3	3	0	0	19	.514
HOWARD, A.	29	7/8	.875	1/1	1.000	-/2	1	2	2	0	1	15	.517
BRADLEY, A.	34	5/10	.500	12/15	.800	-/6	0	3	4	0	0	22	.647
MULQUIN, M.	14	5/5	1.000	0/0	.000	-/3	2	0	2	0	0	10	.714
DOBBS, F.	2	0/1	.000	1/2	.500	-/2	2	0	0	0	0	1	.500
SICES, J.	3	0/0	.000	0/0	.000	-/0	0	0	0	0	0	0	.000
KNUBEL, J.	1	1/1	1.000	0/0	.000	-/0	0	0	0	0	0	2	2.000
PAGAN, L.	1	0/0	.000	0/0	.000	-/0	0	0	0	0	0	0	.000
SHERRY, J.	1	0/0	.000	0/0	.000	-/0	0	0	0	0	0	0	.000
Totals	200	33/49	.673	24/32	.750	-/29	18	14	14	2	2	90	.450

Team Rebounds: Villanova 6, Houston 1. Disqualified: Houston—Micheaux. Technical fouls: Houston—Drexler.

	1st Half	2nd Half	Final
Houston	28	44	72
Villanova	41	49	90

Virginia Commonwealth (85)   Coach: J. D. Barnett

	Min.	Total FG/FGA	Pct.	FT/FTA	Pct.	Reb. O/T	A	TO	PF	S	Blk	TP	PPM
KNIGHT, M.	-	8/15	.533	5/7	.714	-/5	1	2	2	1	0	21	-
SHEROD, E.	-	5/8	.625	8/10	.800	-/3	7	7	2	2	0	18	-
STANCEIL, K.	-	8/10	.800	6/8	.750	-/11	0	4	3	0	0	22	-
KOTTAK, D.	-	5/8	.625	9/10	.900	-/3	6	2	2	3	0	19	-
MCCRAY, G.	-	2/7	.286	0/0	.000	-/4	1	3	4	0	2	4	-
SHROPSHIRE, G.	-	0/1	.000	1/2	.500	-/0	0	1	0	0	0	1	-
JONES, D.	-	0/1	.000	0/0	.000	-/0	0	0	1	0	0	0	-
Totals	200	28/50	.560	29/37	.784	-/26	15	19	14	6	2	85	.425

LIU (69)   Coach: Paul Lizzo

	Min.	Total FG/FGA	Pct.	FT/FTA	Pct.	Reb. O/T	A	TO	PF	S	Blk	TP	PPM
CLARIDA, R.	-	4/6	.667	0/2	.000	-/8	0	7	5	2	0	8	-
SHORT, E.	-	11/14	.786	2/2	1.000	-/6	3	1	5	0	0	24	-
MERIWETHER, J.	-	6/10	.600	1/3	.333	-/3	0	1	3	3	0	13	-
JOHNSON, R.	-	1/8	.125	2/2	1.000	-/4	6	2	4	3	0	4	-
COLE, R.	-	5/9	.556	4/6	.667	-/1	4	2	5	1	0	14	-
FULLER, E.	-	1/5	.200	0/0	.000	-/0	1	4	3	1	1	2	-
DAVIS, R.	-	2/4	.500	0/0	.000	-/2	1	1	2	0	0	4	-
BYRNES, B.	-	0/0	.000	0/0	.000	-/0	0	0	0	0	0	0	-
WILSON, R.	-	0/0	.000	0/0	.000	-/0	0	0	0	0	0	0	-
SIMS, M.	-	0/0	.000	0/0	.000	-/0	0	0	0	0	0	0	-
Totals	200	30/56	.556	9/15	.600	-/24	15	18	27	10	1	69	.345

Team Rebounds: Va. Commonwealth 3; LIU 2. Disqualified: LIU—Clarida, Short, Cole. Technical fouls: LIU—Clarida 2, Coach Lizzo.

	1st Half	2nd Half	Final
Va. Commonwealth	38	47	85
LIU	24	45	69

Brigham Young (60)   Coach: Frank Arnold

	Min.	Total FG/FGA	Pct.	FT/FTA	Pct.	Reb. O/T	A	TO	PF	S	Blk	TP	PPM
ROBERTS, F.	40	6/9	.667	7/10	.700	3/7	1	3	2	1	0	19	.475
TRUMBO, S.	33	3/5	.600	1/2	.500	2/7	0	2	1	0	0	7	.212
AINGE, D.	40	7/16	.438	7/9	.778	0/1	5	3	2	2	0	21	.525
CRAIG, S.	33	3/6	.500	0/1	.000	0/1	3	2	0	1	1	6	.182
BALLIF, G.	3	0/0	.000	0/0	.000	0/0	0	0	0	0	0	0	.000
SAARELANEN, T.	16	2/2	1.000	1/2	.500	1/1	1	0	0	0	0	5	.313
KITE, G.	35	1/3	.333	0/0	.000	1/6	0	2	5	0	0	2	.057
Totals	200	22/41	.537	16/24	.667	7/23	10	12	10	4	1	60	.300

Princeton (51)   Coach: Pete Carril

	Min.	Total FG/FGA	Pct.	FT/FTA	Pct.	Reb. O/T	A	TO	PF	S	Blk	TP	PPM
MELVILLE, R.	31	1/4	.250	0/0	.000	0/2	1	2	2	3	0	2	.065
ROBINSON, C.	19	3/6	.500	0/2	.000	0/1	1	0	5	2	0	6	.316
SIMKUS, R.	27	5/9	.556	3/3	1.000	1/4	1	1	5	1	0	13	.481
MILLS, S.	39	8/17	.471	0/1	.000	1/3	3	0	3	2	0	16	.410
RYAN, W.	40	4/8	.500	0/0	.000	1/3	3	5	0	1	0	8	.200
ENDERLE, G.	13	3/5	.600	0/1	.000	2/2	0	3	0	0	0	6	.462
BLATT, I.	1	0/0	.000	0/0	.000	0/0	0	0	1	0	0	0	.000
CHRISTEL, N.	30	0/1	.000	0/0	.000	2/3	4	2	4	1	1	0	.000
Totals	200	24/50	.480	3/7	.429	7/18	13	10	23	10	1	51	.255

Team Rebounds: Brigham Young 3; Princeton 1. Disqualified: Brigham Young—Kite; Princeton—Robinson, Simkus. Technical fouls: Brigham Young—Kite.

	1st Half	2nd Half	Final
Brigham Young	32	28	60
Princeton	28	23	51

Georgetown (55)   Coach: John Thompson

	Min.	Total FG/FGA	Pct.	FT/FTA	Pct.	Reb. O/T	A	TO	PF	S	Blk	TP	PPM
BROWN, F.	-	2/6	.333	2/4	.500	2/5	3	3	5	4	0	6	-
SMITH, E.	-	4/8	.500	0/0	.000	0/3	2	3	3	0	0	8	-
SPRIGGS, E.	-	1/1	1.000	0/0	.000	0/1	0	1	0	0	0	2	-
FLOYD, E.	-	8/17	.471	6/7	.857	0/2	1	6	3	0	0	22	-
SMITH, G.	-	1/2	.500	0/0	.000	0/0	4	2	5	2	0	2	-
KAULL, K.	-	0/0	.000	0/0	.000	0/0	0	0	0	0	0	0	-
BLAYLOCK, R.	-	0/1	.000	0/0	.000	0/0	0	0	0	0	0	0	-
HANCOCK, M.	-	4/7	.571	0/0	.000	1/2	0	1	5	0	0	8	-
BULLIS, J.	-	1/4	.250	0/0	.000	2/4	1	0	0	0	0	2	-
FRAZIER, M.	-	1/4	.250	3/8	.375	4/7	0	0	0	0	0	5	-
Totals	200	22/50	.440	11/19	.579	9/24	11	16	21	9	0	55	.275

James Madison (61)   Coach: Lou Campanelli

	Min.	Total FG/FGA	Pct.	FT/FTA	Pct.	Reb. O/T	A	TO	PF	S	Blk	TP	PPM
BLACKMON, S.	32	4/5	.800	4/4	1.000	0/3	0	1	4	0	0	12	.375
TOWNES, L.	35	7/13	.538	5/7	.714	3/5	1	4	4	0	0	19	.543
ROLAND, D.	33	6/9	.667	2/2	1.000	1/9	0	2	4	1	1	14	.350
FISHER, C.	40	5/7	.714	4/5	.800	2/3	5	1	1	0	0	14	.350
DUPONT, D.	36	1/3	.333	2/2	1.000	0/0	5	4	2	1	0	4	.111
ROSENBERG, C.	3	0/0	.000	0/0	.000	0/0	2	0	0	0	0	0	.000
SHOULDERS, T.	19	2/6	.333	0/0	.000	2/5	0	3	2	2	2	4	.211
BUONINCONTRI, J.	2	0/1	.000	0/0	.000	0/0	0	0	0	0	0	0	.000
Totals	200	22/41	.537	17/20	.850	6/24	11	19	17	5	3	61	.305

Team Rebounds: James Madison 2; Georgetown 3. Disqualified: Georgetown—Brown, G. Smith, Hancock. Technical fouls: None.

	1st Half	2nd Half	Final
Georgetown	25	30	55
James Madison	26	35	61

SECOND ROUND MIDWEST

Lamar (78)　Coach: Pat Foster

	Min.	Total FG / FGA	Pct.	FT / FTA	Pct.	Reb. O / T	A	TO	PF	S	Blk	TP	PPM
OLLIVER, M.	39	13/20	.650	3/ 5	.600	-/ 0	2	4	2	3	0	29	.744
BROOKS, A.	38	6/10	.600	1/ 3	.333	-/ 1	11	5	3	2	0	13	.342
WALLACE, M.	21	1/ 2	.500	1/ 1	1.000	-/ 4	1	1	2	0	0	3	.143
PERKINS, K.	38	5/ 7	.714	2/ 2	1.000	-/ 7	2	3	4	0	0	12	.316
DAVIS, B.	25	2/ 8	.250	4/ 6	.667	-/ 5	3	1	4	1	1	8	.320
LONG, T.	25	3/10	.300	1/ 2	.500	-/ 1	0	1	3	1	0	7	.280
STEPHENSON, L.	5	0/ 1	.000	0/ 0	.000	-/ 0	0	0	0	0	0	0	.000
GRAY, A.	6	1/ 2	.500	2/ 2	1.000	-/ 2	0	0	0	0	0	4	.667
CLAIBORNE, R.	2	0/ 1	.000	0/ 0	.000	-/ 0	0	0	0	0	0	0	.000
MARKS, P.	1	1/ 1	1.000	0/ 0	.000	-/ 0	0	0	0	0	0	2	2.000
Totals	200	32/62	.516	14/21	.667	-/20	19	15	18	7	1	78	.390

Louisiana State (100)　Coach: Dale Brown

	Min.	Total FG / FGA	Pct.	FT / FTA	Pct.	Reb. O / T	A	TO	PF	S	Blk	TP	PPM
MITCHELL, L.	32	9/13	.692	0/ 1	.000	-/ 8	2	2	0	1	0	18	.563
MACKLIN, D.	37	12/18	.667	7/ 7	1.000	-/16	2	3	4	0	1	31	.838
COOK, G.	34	4/ 7	.571	1/ 3	.333	-/ 7	5	1	3	1	1	9	.265
MARTIN, E.	25	1/ 4	.250	2/ 3	.667	-/ 0	12	2	4	1	0	4	.160
CARTER, H.	38	13/22	.591	0/ 0	.000	-/ 6	2	3	2	3	0	26	.684
SIMS, W.	14	2/ 2	1.000	0/ 0	.000	-/ 1	1	1	4	0	0	4	.286
JONES, J.	12	1/ 3	.333	0/ 0	.000	-/ 0	5	2	1	1	0	2	.167
TUDOR, J.	2	1/ 1	1.000	0/ 0	.000	-/ 0	0	0	0	0	0	2	1.000
BLACK, T.	4	1/ 3	.333	0/ 0	.000	-/ 1	0	0	0	0	0	2	.500
COSTELLO, J.	2	1/ 1	1.000	0/ 0	.000	-/ 1	0	0	0	0	0	2	1.000
Totals	200	45/74	.608	10/14	.714	-/40	29	14	18	7	2	100	.500

Team Rebounds: Louisiana St. 3; Lamar 4. Disqualified: None. Technical fouls: Louisiana St.—Mitchell.

	1st Half	2nd Half	Final
Lamar	43	35	78
Louisiana St.	55	45	100

Arkansas (74)　Coach: Eddie Sutton

	Min.	Total FG / FGA	Pct.	FT / FTA	Pct.	Reb. O / T	A	TO	PF	S	Blk	TP	PPM
BROWN, T.	13	1/ 3	.333	0/ 0	.000	-/ 2	0	2	5	1	0	2	.154
PETERSON, K.	39	2/ 4	.500	4/ 6	.667	-/ 6	0	2	3	1	0	8	.205
HASTINGS, S.	22	2/ 8	.250	8/ 8	1.000	-/ 8	0	2	4	0	0	12	.545
WALKER, D.	40	9/15	.600	5/ 7	.714	-/ 4	3	1	3	2	0	23	.575
REED, U.	40	7/14	.500	5/ 6	.833	-/ 6	6	5	3	3	1	19	.475
SKULLMAN, G.	4	0/ 0	.000	0/ 0	.000	-/ 0	1	2	0	0	0	0	.000
YOUNG, M.	25	4/ 7	.571	2/ 2	1.000	-/ 0	1	5	2	0	0	10	.400
KELLY, C.	13	0/ 1	.000	0/ 1	.000	-/ 1	0	1	3	0	0	0	.000
FRIESS, B.	4	0/ 0	.000	0/ 0	.000	-/ 0	0	0	0	0	0	0	.000
Totals	200	25/52	.481	24/30	.800	-/27	11	20	23	7	1	74	.370

Louisville (73)　Coach: Denny Crum

	Min.	Total FG / FGA	Pct.	FT / FTA	Pct.	Reb. O / T	A	TO	PF	S	Blk	TP	PPM
SMITH, D.	35	5/ 9	.556	0/ 0	.000	-/ 7	5	6	4	1	1	10	.286
MCCRAY, R.	25	4/ 4	1.000	3/ 5	.600	-/ 5	2	1	5	3	0	11	.440
JONES, C.	31	4/ 4	1.000	2/ 4	.500	-/ 3	0	1	3	0	4	10	.323
GORDON, L.	30	3/ 6	.500	2/ 3	.667	-/ 4	1	2	2	1	1	8	.267
EAVES, J.	35	3/11	.273	3/ 5	.600	-/ 4	3	8	2	1	0	9	.257
MCCRAY, S.	23	5/ 9	.556	1/ 4	.250	-/ 4	0	0	4	2	2	11	.478
BURKMAN, R.	8	0/ 0	.000	4/ 4	1.000	-/ 1	0	0	5	0	0	4	.500
WRIGHT, P.	10	2/ 5	.400	6/ 6	1.000	-/ 0	1	1	1	2	0	10	1.000
NEUSER, G.	3	0/ 1	.000	0/ 0	.000	-/ 0	1	1	0	0	0	0	.000
Totals	200	26/49	.531	21/31	.677	-/28	13	20	26	10	8	73	.365

Team Rebounds: Arkansas 7; Louisville 1. Disqualified: Arkansas—Brown; Louisville—R.McCray, Burkman. Technical fouls: None.

	1st Half	2nd Half	Final
Arkansas	37	37	74
Louisville	33	40	73

Wichita State (60)　Coach: Gene Smithson

	Min.	Total FG / FGA	Pct.	FT / FTA	Pct.	Reb. O / T	A	TO	PF	S	Blk	TP	PPM
CARR, A.	39	6/15	.400	8/10	.800	-/12	1	3	3	3	5	20	.513
JACKSON, J.	35	2/ 5	.400	0/ 0	.000	-/ 3	2	4	4	1	0	4	.114
LEVINGSTON, C.	39	10/18	.556	5/ 8	.625	-/16	1	5	2	0	0	25	.641
SMITHSON, R.	40	1/ 2	.500	4/ 6	.667	-/ 2	5	2	3	1	0	6	.150
MARTIN, T.	11	2/ 4	.500	0/ 0	.000	-/ 1	1	2	3	0	0	4	.364
GIBBS, J.	12	0/ 2	.000	0/ 0	.000	-/ 1	2	2	2	0	0	0	.000
JONES, M.	9	0/ 1	.000	1/ 2	.500	-/ 2	0	2	1	0	0	1	.111
PAPKE, K.	14	0/ 2	.000	0/ 0	.000	-/ 0	1	0	2	0	0	0	.000
DENNY, M.	1	0/ 0	.000	0/ 0	.000	-/ 0	0	0	0	0	0	0	.000
Totals	200	21/49	.429	18/26	.692	-/37	13	20	20	5	5	60	.300

Iowa (56)　Coach: Lute Olson

	Min.	Total FG / FGA	Pct.	FT / FTA	Pct.	Reb. O / T	A	TO	PF	S	Blk	TP	PPM
BROOKINS, V.	35	6/ 8	.750	4/ 6	.667	-/ 3	3	2	3	2	0	16	.457
WALTA, S.	19	2/ 4	.500	1/ 1	1.000	-/ 3	0	2	4	0	0	5	.263
KRAFCISIN, S.	24	6/13	.462	1/ 3	.333	-/ 7	0	1	5	2	0	13	.542
ARNOLD, K.	35	5/10	.500	2/ 2	1.000	-/ 1	2	3	0	1	0	12	.343
BOYLE, K.	35	2/10	.200	0/ 0	.000	-/ 1	3	3	5	4	0	4	.114
CARFINO, S.	10	0/ 1	.000	0/ 0	.000	-/ 1	0	0	1	0	0	0	.000
JOHNSON, D.	4	1/ 2	.500	0/ 0	.000	-/ 1	0	0	0	0	0	2	.500
HANSEN, B.	14	1/ 1	1.000	0/ 0	.000	-/ 2	2	3	2	0	0	2	.143
GANNON, H.	24	1/ 5	.200	0/ 0	.000	-/ 6	0	1	3	1	0	2	.083
Totals	200	24/54	.444	8/12	.667	-/25	10	15	23	10	0	56	.280

Team Rebounds: Wichita State; Iowa 1. Disqualified: Iowa—Krafcisin, Boyle. Technical fouls: Iowa—bench.

	1st Half	2nd Half	Final
Wichita State	25	35	60
Iowa	36	20	56

Kansas (88)　Coach: Ted Owens

	Min.	Total FG / FGA	Pct.	FT / FTA	Pct.	Reb. O / T	A	TO	PF	S	Blk	TP	PPM
MAGLEY, D.	28	2/ 8	.250	0/ 1	.000	-/ 8	0	4	3	0	0	4	.143
CRAWFORD, J.	35	8/12	.667	2/ 5	.400	-/ 7	3	1	1	0	1	18	.514
HOUSEY, A.	29	0/ 8	.000	0/ 0	.000	-/ 4	1	2	4	0	0	0	.000
GUY, T.	38	13/15	.867	10/12	.833	-/ 5	0	2	2	4	0	36	.947
VALENTINE, D.	39	5/10	.500	6/ 9	.667	-/ 4	7	5	3	3	0	16	.410
NEAL, B.	11	2/ 2	1.000	4/ 6	.667	-/ 3	1	2	1	0	0	8	.727
MITCHELL, V.	14	2/ 6	.333	0/ 0	.000	-/ 5	0	1	3	0	1	4	.286
SUMMERS, M.	2	1/ 1	1.000	0/ 0	.000	-/ 1	0	0	1	0	0	2	1.000
KONEK, J.	1	0/ 0	.000	0/ 0	.000	-/ 0	0	2	0	1	0	0	.000
THOMPSON, G.	1	0/ 0	.000	0/ 0	.000	-/ 1	0	0	0	0	0	0	.000
KNIGHT, M.	1	0/ 0	.000	0/ 0	.000	-/ 0	0	1	1	0	0	0	.000
WORREL, R.	1	0/ 0	.000	0/ 0	.000	-/ 0	0	0	1	0	0	0	.000
Totals	200	33/62	.532	22/33	.667	-/38	12	19	20	8	2	88	.440

Arizona State (71)　Coach: Ned Wulk

	Min.	Total FG / FGA	Pct.	FT / FTA	Pct.	Reb. O / T	A	TO	PF	S	Blk	TP	PPM
NASH, J.	30	2/ 7	.286	1/ 2	.500	-/ 4	1	3	4	1	0	5	.167
WILLIAMS, S.	34	1/10	.100	7/10	.700	-/ 7	1	4	3	1	1	9	.265
LISTER, A.	35	4/ 9	.444	4/ 6	.667	-/ 7	0	1	5	1	1	12	.343
LEVER, L.	36	4/ 9	.444	1/ 3	.333	-/ 7	6	3	3	4	0	9	.250
SCOTT, B.	40	15/22	.682	2/ 3	.667	-/ 4	1	1	2	1	0	32	.800
WILLIAMS, P.	12	0/ 4	.000	0/ 0	.000	-/ 2	1	5	2	1	0	0	.000
STONE, W.	8	2/ 2	1.000	0/ 0	.000	-/ 2	0	2	3	0	0	4	.500
EVERETT, W.	1	0/ 0	.000	0/ 0	.000	-/ 0	0	0	0	0	0	0	.000
THOMAS, B.	1	0/ 0	.000	0/ 0	.000	-/ 0	0	0	0	0	0	0	.000
BRESSANT, P.	3	0/ 0	.000	0/ 0	.000	-/ 0	0	0	2	0	0	0	.000
Totals	200	28/63	.444	15/24	.625	-/33	10	19	24	9	2	71	.355

Team Rebounds: Kansas 5; Arizona St. 3. Disqualified: Arizona St.—Lister. Technical fouls: None.

	1st Half	2nd Half	Final
Kansas	45	43	88
Arizona St.	29	42	71

SECOND ROUND MIDEAST

St. Joseph's (49)   Coach: Jim Lynam

	Min.	Total FG/FGA	Pct.	FT/FTA	Pct.	Reb. O/T	A	TO	PF	S	Blk	TP	PPM
WILLIAMS	-	3/9	.333	0/0	.000	-/4	0	-	4	-	-	6	-
SMITH, J.	-	5/9	.556	2/2	1.000	-/4	2	-	0	-	-	12	-
COSTNER	-	5/8	.625	1/2	.500	-/5	0	-	2	-	-	11	-
CLARK, J.	-	1/3	.333	0/0	.000	-/3	5	-	3	-	-	2	-
WARRICK, B.	-	6/9	.667	0/0	.000	-/2	5	-	2	-	-	12	-
MCFARLAN, L.	-	3/3	1.000	0/0	.000	-/0	3	-	0	-	-	6	-
Totals	200	23/41	.561	3/4	.750	-/18	15	7	11	4	1	49	.245

DePaul (48)   Coach: Ray Meyer

	Min.	Total FG/FGA	Pct.	FT/FTA	Pct.	Reb. O/T	A	TO	PF	S	Blk	TP	PPM
AGUIRRE, M.	-	3/6	.500	2/2	1.000	-/1	1	-	2	-	-	8	-
GRUBBS, T.	-	5/6	.833	1/1	1.000	-/10	1	-	3	-	-	11	-
CUMMINGS, T.	-	3/10	.300	0/0	.000	-/4	2	-	3	-	-	6	-
DILLARD, S.	-	5/12	.417	2/3	.667	-/6	5	-	1	-	-	12	-
BRADSHAW, C.	-	5/7	.714	1/2	.500	-/0	5	-	4	-	-	11	-
RANDOLPH, B.	-	0/0	.000	0/0	.000	-/1	1	-	0	-	-	0	-
Totals	200	21/41	.512	6/8	.750	-/22	15	7	13	3	4	48	.240

Disqualified: None. Technical fouls: None.

	1st Half	2nd Half	Final
St. Joseph's	25	24	49
DePaul	27	21	48

Boston College (67)   Coach: Tom Davis

	Min.	Total FG/FGA	Pct.	FT/FTA	Pct.	Reb. O/T	A	TO	PF	S	Blk	TP	PPM
CHANDLER, D.	32	2/3	.667	0/0	.000	-/2	1	2	2	0	0	4	.125
MURPHY, J.	23	4/6	.667	0/1	.000	-/4	1	2	3	0	0	8	.348
FOY, C.	23	0/2	.000	4/4	1.000	-/5	1	0	1	4	0	4	.174
BAGLEY, J.	32	10/16	.625	15/21	.714	-/6	2	5	3	4	0	35	1.094
CLARK, M.	25	4/8	.500	0/0	.000	-/3	1	1	2	0	0	8	.320
O'SHEA, T.	15	0/0	.000	0/0	.000	-/0	0	0	0	0	0	0	.000
SHRIGLEY, R.	19	0/3	.000	2/3	.667	-/1	1	0	3	4	0	2	.105
ADAMS, B.	18	1/4	.250	4/6	.667	-/3	0	5	4	1	3	6	.333
BEAULIEU, J.	13	0/0	.000	0/0	.000	-/0	1	1	2	0	0	0	.000
Totals	200	21/42	.500	25/35	.714	-/24	8	16	20	13	3	67	.335

Wake Forest (64)   Coach: Carl Tacy

	Min.	Total FG/FGA	Pct.	FT/FTA	Pct.	Reb. O/T	A	TO	PF	S	Blk	TP	PPM
ROGERS, A.	37	4/6	.667	0/0	.000	-/2	0	4	4	1	1	8	.216
MORGAN, G.	22	2/4	.500	4/5	.800	-/5	1	2	2	0	1	8	.364
JOHNSTONE, J.	21	3/6	.500	0/1	.000	-/4	0	2	5	0	0	6	.286
JOHNSON, F.	36	8/12	.667	4/6	.667	-/3	0	5	3	2	0	20	.556
HELMS, M.	21	3/7	.429	3/4	.750	-/3	0	3	4	0	0	9	.429
DAVIS, S.	2	0/0	.000	0/0	.000	-/0	1	0	2	1	0	0	.000
YOUNG, D.	22	5/7	.714	1/2	.500	-/2	2	1	3	0	0	11	.500
MAYERS, G.	3	0/1	.000	0/0	.000	-/1	0	0	0	0	0	0	.000
DAHMS, C.	11	0/0	.000	0/0	.000	-/1	0	3	3	0	0	0	.000
TEACHEY, A.	25	1/2	.500	0/0	.000	-/3	0	2	2	0	0	2	.080
Totals	200	26/45	.578	12/18	.667	-/24	4	22	28	4	2	64	.320

Team Rebounds: Boston College 2; Wake Forest 1. Disqualified: Wake Forest—Johnstone. Technical fouls: Boston College—Foy.

	1st Half	2nd Half	Final
Boston College	33	34	67
Wake Forest	31	33	64

Maryland (64)   Coach: Lefty Driesell

	Min.	Total FG/FGA	Pct.	FT/FTA	Pct.	Reb. O/T	A	TO	PF	S	Blk	TP	PPM
KING, A.	30	10/28	.357	2/4	.500	-/4	2	3	4	0	0	22	.733
GRAHAM, E.	30	7/18	.389	0/0	.000	-/10	3	8	4	1	0	14	.467
WILLIAMS, C.	39	7/9	.778	2/2	1.000	-/10	1	3	4	0	0	16	.410
JACKSON, R.	24	0/2	.000	0/0	.000	-/0	1	0	3	0	0	0	.000
MANNING, G.	37	3/8	.375	0/0	.000	-/0	2	1	3	0	0	6	.162
PITTMAN, C.	23	3/3	1.000	0/0	.000	-/6	0	1	0	0	0	6	.261
RIVERS, S.	8	0/0	.000	0/0	.000	-/0	1	0	0	0	0	0	.000
MORLEY, G.	9	0/1	.000	0/0	.000	-/1	4	0	2	1	0	0	.000
Totals	200	30/69	.435	4/6	.667	-/31	14	16	20	2	0	64	.320

Indiana (99)   Coach: Bob Knight

	Min.	Total FG/FGA	Pct.	FT/FTA	Pct.	Reb. O/T	A	TO	PF	S	Blk	TP	PPM
TURNER, L.	38	9/13	.692	2/2	1.000	-/7	2	5	2	2	1	20	.526
KITCHEL, T.	30	5/11	.455	3/3	1.000	-/6	2	3	3	0	0	13	.433
TOLBERT, R.	38	10/13	.769	6/6	1.000	-/8	1	0	1	1	4	26	.684
WITTMAN, R.	34	4/9	.444	2/2	1.000	-/2	4	1	0	2	0	10	.294
THOMAS, I.	35	9/11	.818	1/2	.500	-/4	14	0	2	0	1	19	.543
THOMAS, J.	6	0/0	.000	0/0	.000	-/0	1	0	0	0	0	0	.000
RISLEY, S.	8	2/3	.667	1/3	.333	-/3	0	0	1	0	0	5	.625
BROWN, T.	3	0/0	.000	2/2	1.000	-/0	0	0	0	0	0	2	.667
ISENBARGER, P.	2	2/2	1.000	0/0	.000	-/1	0	0	0	0	0	4	2.000
BOUCHIE, S.	2	0/0	.000	0/0	.000	-/1	0	0	0	0	0	0	.000
GRUNWALD, G.	1	0/0	.000	0/0	.000	-/0	1	0	0	0	0	0	.000
FRANZ, C.	2	0/1	.000	0/0	.000	-/1	0	0	0	0	0	0	.000
LAFAVE, M.	1	0/0	.000	0/0	.000	-/1	0	0	0	0	0	0	.000
Totals	200	41/63	.651	17/20	.850	-/33	25	9	9	5	6	99	.495

Team Rebounds: Indiana 0; Maryland 0. Disqualified: None. Technical fouls: Indiana—Tolbert.

	1st Half	2nd Half	Final
Maryland	34	30	64
Indiana	50	49	99

Alabama-Birmingham (69)   Coach: Gene Bartow

	Min.	Total FG/FGA	Pct.	FT/FTA	Pct.	Reb. O/T	A	TO	PF	S	Blk	TP	PPM
GILES, C.	40	5/9	.556	0/1	.000	-/10	0	-	1	-	-	10	.250
LANE, C.	13	3/4	.750	1/3	.333	-/2	0	-	4	-	-	7	.538
SPEER	34	4/12	.333	5/6	.833	-/4	0	-	3	-	-	13	.382
ROBINSON	33	5/8	.625	8/8	1.000	-/6	0	-	4	-	-	18	.545
MARCUS, G.	40	1/6	.167	12/15	.800	-/3	4	-	2	-	-	14	.350
NICHOLAS, J.	8	0/0	.000	0/0	.000	-/2	0	-	0	-	-	0	.000
MORRIS, L.	10	0/0	.000	1/3	.333	-/1	0	-	1	-	-	1	.100
ANCHRUM, N.	22	1/7	.143	4/4	1.000	-/7	0	-	5	-	-	6	.273
Totals	200	19/46	.413	31/40	.775	-/35	4	-	20	-	-	69	.345

Kentucky (62)   Coach: Joe Hall

	Min.	Total FG/FGA	Pct.	FT/FTA	Pct.	Reb. O/T	A	TO	PF	S	Blk	TP	PPM
HURT, C.	29	4/7	.571	3/5	.600	-/6	0	-	4	-	-	11	.379
VERDERBER	36	7/11	.636	2/3	.667	-/9	1	-	3	-	-	16	.444
BOWIE, S.	21	2/8	.250	4/4	1.000	-/4	2	-	5	-	-	8	.381
MINNIEFIELD, D.	39	5/13	.385	4/5	.800	-/5	3	-	4	-	-	14	.359
BEAL, D.	25	2/2	1.000	1/2	.500	-/2	3	-	3	-	-	5	.200
MASTER, J.	15	2/7	.286	0/0	.000	-/1	0	-	2	-	-	4	.267
BEARUP, B.	3	0/0	.000	0/0	.000	-/0	0	-	0	-	-	0	.000
HORD, D.	10	0/2	.000	0/0	.000	-/1	0	-	3	-	-	0	.000
COWIN	5	0/1	.000	2/2	1.000	-/0	0	-	0	-	-	2	.400
TURPIN	16	1/4	.250	0/0	.000	-/5	0	-	4	-	-	2	.125
LANTER, B.	1	0/2	.000	0/0	.000	-/0	0	-	1	-	-	0	.000
Totals	200	23/57	.404	16/21	.862	-/33	9	-	29	-	-	62	.310

Team Rebounds: Ala.-Birmingham 2; Kentucky 1. Disqualified: Ala.-Birmingham—Anchrum; Kentucky—Bowie.

	1st Half	2nd Half	Final
Ala.-Birmingham	29	40	69
Kentucky	30	32	62

SECOND ROUND WEST

Kansas State (50)   Coach: Jack Hartman

	Min.	Total FG/FGA	Pct.	FT/FTA	Pct.	Reb. O/T	A	TO	PF	S	Blk	TP	PPM
ADAMS, T.	36	4/ 5	.800	4/ 5	.800	-/ 3	1	1	4	1	0	12	.333
REED, R.	28	2/ 5	.400	1/ 2	.500	-/ 4	1	4	1	0	0	5	.179
NEALY, E.	40	2/ 3	.667	7/ 7	1.000	-/ 9	2	3	4	2	0	11	.275
JANKOVICH, T.	11	0/ 0	.000	0/ 0	.000	-/ 0	0	1	1	0	0	0	.000
BLACKMAN, R.	38	6/13	.462	2/ 2	1.000	-/ 1	2	6	3	0	0	14	.368
BARTON, F.	5	0/ 0	.000	0/ 0	.000	-/ 0	1	0	0	0	0	0	.000
CRAFT, L.	11	0/ 2	.000	0/ 0	.000	-/ 0	1	2	2	0	1	0	.000
GALVAO, E.	29	3/ 5	.600	2/ 2	1.000	-/ 3	0	3	0	0	0	8	.276
REID, S.	2	0/ 0	.000	0/ 0	.000	-/ 0	0	0	0	0	0	0	.000
Totals	200	17/33	.515	16/18	.889	-/20	8	20	15	3	1	50	.250

Oregon State (48)   Coach: Ralph Miller

	Min.	Total FG/FGA	Pct.	FT/FTA	Pct.	Reb. O/T	A	TO	PF	S	Blk	TP	PPM
CONNER	24	3/ 5	.600	0/ 0	.000	-/ 0	2	1	4	5	0	6	.250
SITTON	37	2/ 6	.333	0/ 1	.000	-/ 4	1	3	3	0	0	4	.108
JOHNSON	37	5/10	.500	6/ 8	.750	-/ 6	3	6	5	0	2	16	.432
RADFORD	40	3/ 6	.500	2/ 3	.667	-/ 1	1	0	3	2	0	8	.200
BLUME	40	5/10	.500	0/ 0	.000	-/ 4	1	3	0	1	0	10	.250
STOUTT	16	2/ 4	.500	0/ 0	.000	-/ 1	1	0	1	0	0	4	.250
HOLBROOK, R.	3	0/ 1	.000	0/ 0	.000	-/ 0	0	0	2	0	0	0	.000
MCSHANE	3	0/ 0	.000	0/ 0	.000	-/ 0	0	0	0	0	0	0	.000
Totals	200	20/42	.476	8/12	.667	-/16	9	13	18	8	2	48	.240

Team Rebounds: Kansas State 1; Oregon State 0. Disqualified: Oregon State—Johnson. Technical fouls: None.

	1st Half	2nd Half	Final
Kansas State	19	31	50
Oregon State	26	22	48

Wyoming (65)   Coach: Jim Brandenburg

	Min.	Total FG/FGA	Pct.	FT/FTA	Pct.	Reb. O/T	A	TO	PF	S	Blk	TP	PPM
OLLIE, K.	37	2/ 7	.286	1/ 2	.500	-/ 3	7	1	2	0	0	5	.135
GARNETT, B.	34	6/10	.600	3/ 3	1.000	-/ 3	2	2	4	1	0	15	.441
THESENVITZ, G.	20	1/ 2	.500	2/ 3	.667	-/ 4	0	1	1	2	0	4	.200
BRADLEY, C.	40	7/13	.538	11/13	.846	-/ 3	0	4	3	2	1	25	.625
JACKSON, M.	32	3/ 4	.667	2/ 2	1.000	-/ 1	4	5	2	0	0	10	.313
ENGLER, C.	19	1/ 2	.500	0/ 0	.000	-/ 0	0	1	4	0	1	2	.105
JOHNSON, A.	9	0/ 0	.000	0/ 0	.000	-/ 1	0	1	0	0	0	0	.000
WRAPP, M.	9	2/ 3	.667	0/ 0	.000	-/ 0	0	0	1	0	0	4	.444
Totals	200	23/43	.535	19/23	.826	-/15	13	15	17	5	2	65	.325

Illinois (67)   Coach: Lou Henson

	Min.	Total FG/FGA	Pct.	FT/FTA	Pct.	Reb. O/T	A	TO	PF	S	Blk	TP	PPM
JOHNSON, E.	38	7/17	.412	5/ 6	.833	-/ 7	3	2	3	0	0	19	.500
SMITH, M.	39	3/ 8	.375	8/ 8	1.000	-/ 8	8	7	3	1	0	14	.359
HOLCOMB, D.	25	4/ 5	.800	0/ 0	.000	-/ 1	1	3	5	2	1	8	.320
HARPER, D.	38	4/ 7	.571	0/ 0	.000	-/ 1	3	2	1	0	0	8	.211
RANGE, P.	40	5/ 9	.556	2/ 2	1.000	-/ 6	0	1	3	0	0	12	.300
TUCKER, C.	4	0/ 2	.000	0/ 0	.000	-/ 0	0	1	0	0	0	0	.000
GRIFFIN, J.	15	3/ 6	.500	0/ 1	.000	-/ 1	1	0	4	0	0	6	.400
LEONARD, B.	1	0/ 0	.000	0/ 0	.000	-/ 0	0	1	1	0	0	0	.000
Totals	200	26/54	.481	15/17	.882	-/24	16	17	20	3	1	67	.335

Team Rebounds: Illinois 2; Wyoming 2. Disqualified: Illinois—Holcomb. Technical fouls: None.

	1st Half	2nd Half	Final
Wyoming	27	38	65
Illinois	32	35	67

Northeastern (69)   Coach: Jim Calhoun

	Min.	Total FG/FGA	Pct.	FT/FTA	Pct.	Reb. O/T	A	TO	PF	S	Blk	TP	PPM
LEITAO, D.	26	0/ 1	.000	2/ 4	.500	5/ 5	0	2	4	0	1	2	.077
RUCKER, C.	22	2/ 4	.500	0/ 1	.000	0/ 1	0	1	5	0	0	4	.182
HEINECK, C.	24	0/ 2	.000	0/ 1	.000	2/ 4	1	2	4	1	0	0	.000
MOSS, P.	33	6/18	.333	8/11	.727	2/ 3	0	1	2	0	0	20	.606
HARRIS, P.	25	8/21	.381	8/10	.800	2/ 3	1	3	2	3	0	24	.960
BRASWALL, R.	11	0/ 1	.000	0/ 0	.000	3/ 3	0	1	5	0	0	0	.000
HALSEL, M.	20	1/ 4	.250	1/ 2	.500	5/ 9	0	2	5	0	0	3	.150
ROBINSON, P.	18	0/ 2	.000	0/ 0	.000	0/ 0	0	1	0	1	0	0	.000
JEFFERSON, E.	13	4/12	.333	2/ 2	1.000	2/ 2	0	0	0	0	0	10	.769
PHILLIPS, B.	2	1/ 2	.500	0/ 2	.000	2/ 4	0	0	1	0	0	2	1.000
GORDON, J.	2	0/ 1	.000	2/ 2	1.000	0/ 1	0	0	1	1	0	2	1.000
ZIEMBA, R.	2	1/ 1	1.000	0/ 0	.000	0/ 0	0	0	0	0	0	2	1.000
LEHETANN, A.	2	0/ 2	.000	0/ 0	.000	0/ 0	0	0	0	0	0	0	.000
Totals	200	23/71	.324	23/35	.657	23/35	2	13	29	6	1	69	.345

Utah (94)   Coach: Jerry Pimm

	Min.	Total FG/FGA	Pct.	FT/FTA	Pct.	Reb. O/T	A	TO	PF	S	Blk	TP	PPM
VRANES, D.	26	9/ 9	1.000	9/11	.818	9/11	0	3	3	0	0	27	1.038
BANKOWSKI, K.	25	7/11	.636	1/ 2	.500	3/ 6	1	1	2	0	0	15	.600
CHAMBERS, T.	29	6/ 9	.667	9/10	.900	11/12	0	1	1	1	1	21	.724
MANNION, P.	26	3/ 6	.500	0/ 0	.000	1/ 2	1	1	3	1	1	6	.231
MARTIN, S.	27	3/ 7	.429	0/ 2	.000	6/ 6	3	6	4	0	0	6	.222
HAMMER, C.	10	2/ 5	.400	0/ 0	.000	2/ 3	1	0	5	0	0	4	.400
ROBINSON, A.	21	2/ 4	.500	0/ 0	.000	3/ 4	1	2	2	0	0	4	.190
WILLIAMS, P.	14	1/ 3	.333	0/ 1	.000	5/ 5	0	2	1	0	0	2	.143
WINANS, C.	9	1/ 2	.500	1/ 4	.250	0/ 0	0	2	3	0	0	3	.333
MCCLAIN, S.	3	1/ 1	1.000	2/ 3	.667	0/ 0	1	1	1	0	0	4	1.333
HILL, S.	7	1/ 1	1.000	0/ 0	.000	0/ 0	0	1	1	0	0	2	.286
FOLSON, S.	3	0/ 0	.000	0/ 0	.000	1/ 1	0	0	0	0	0	0	.000
Totals	200	36/58	.621	22/33	.667	41/50	8	20	26	4	2	94	.470

Team Rebounds: Utah 2; Northeastern 3. Disqualified: Utah—Hammer; Northeastern—Rucker, Braswall, Halsel. Technical fouls: Utah—Martin, Chambers; Northeastern—Coach Calhoun.

	1st Half	2nd Half	Final
Northeastern	28	41	69
Utah	43	51	94

Pittsburgh (57)   Coach: Roy Chipman

	Min.	Total FG/FGA	Pct.	FT/FTA	Pct.	Reb. O/T	A	TO	PF	S	Blk	TP	PPM
MCMILLEN, L.	38	0/2	.000	0/0	.000	4/4	0	1	3	1	0	0	.000
CLANCY, S.	38	8/17	.471	0/0	.000	5/6	1	1	4	5	1	16	.421
BROZOVICH, P.	16	1/2	.500	0/0	.000	0/1	0	0	4	2	0	2	.125
NEVERSON, C.	35	7/14	.500	3/4	.750	1/4	0	0	4	3	0	17	.486
WALLACE, D.	21	4/14	.286	3/3	1.000	2/2	3	7	3	0	1	11	.524
BEATTY, S.	10	0/1	.000	0/0	.000	0/0	0	0	2	0	0	0	.000
VAUGHAN, C.	13	2/4	.500	5/6	.833	2/4	0	0	1	1	0	9	.692
SCHNEURMANN, E.	15	0/1	.000	0/1	.000	2/3	0	1	2	0	0	0	.000
GISSENDANNER, D.	8	0/2	.000	2/3	.667	0/0	0	1	0	0	0	2	.250
OLINGER, D.	2	0/1	.000	0/0	.000	0/0	0	0	0	0	0	0	.000
WALLACE, E.	2	0/0	.000	0/0	.000	0/0	0	0	1	0	0	0	.000
GREVEY, S.	2	0/1	.000	0/0	.000	0/0	0	0	1	0	0	0	.000
Totals	200	22/59	.373	13/17	.765	16/24	4	11	25	12	2	57	.285

North Carolina (74)   Coach: Dean Smith

	Min.	Total FG/FGA	Pct.	FT/FTA	Pct.	Reb. O/T	A	TO	PF	S	Blk	TP	PPM
WOOD, A.	24	7/12	.583	2/2	1.000	5/9	1	1	5	2	1	16	.667
WORTHY, J.	32	8/10	.800	5/9	.556	6/7	1	1	3	3	1	21	.656
PERKINS, S.	32	6/10	.600	7/10	.700	2/5	0	6	3	0	2	19	.594
PEPPER, M.	30	2/3	.667	0/0	.000	1/2	1	1	1	0	0	4	.133
BLACK, J.	36	0/1	.000	2/2	1.000	4/4	1	7	2	0	0	2	.056
BRADDOCK, J.	7	0/1	.000	2/2	1.000	0/0	0	1	2	0	0	2	.286
KENNY, E.	3	0/0	.000	0/0	.000	0/0	0	0	0	0	0	0	.000
BUDKO, P.	8	0/0	.000	0/0	.000	1/2	0	0	0	0	0	0	.000
BARLOW, J.	2	1/2	.500	1/1	1.000	0/1	0	0	0	0	0	3	1.500
DOHERTY, M.	16	3/6	.500	1/1	1.000	2/4	1	1	3	0	0	7	.438
BRUST, C.	7	0/0	.000	0/0	.000	0/0	2	0	0	0	0	0	.000
EXUM, C.	1	0/0	.000	0/0	.000	1/1	0	0	0	0	0	0	.000
SHAFFER, D.	2	0/1	.000	0/0	.000	0/0	0	0	0	0	0	0	.000
Totals	200	27/46	.587	20/27	.741	22/35	5	20	19	5	4	74	.370

Team Rebounds: N. Carolina 0; Pittsburgh 2. Disqualified: N. Carolina—Wood. Technical fouls: None.

	1st Half	2nd Half	Final
Pittsburgh	23	34	57
N. Carolina	34	40	74

SECOND ROUND EAST

Villanova (50)   Coach: Rollie Massimino

	Min.	Total FG/FGA	Pct.	FT/FTA	Pct.	Reb. O/T	A	TO	PF	S	Blk	TP	PPM
GRANGER, S.	38	8/15	.533	0/0	.000	-/2	3	2	3	0	0	16	.421
SIENKIEWICZ, T.	37	5/8	.625	1/1	1.000	-/2	3	2	2	1	0	11	.297
PINONE, J.	39	5/11	.455	1/3	.333	-/4	1	5	5	0	0	11	.282
HOWARD, A.	32	1/5	.200	1/1	1.000	-/6	0	3	4	1	0	3	.094
BRADLEY, A.	37	3/8	.375	1/2	.500	-/13	0	6	4	2	1	7	.189
MULQUIN, M.	12	1/2	.500	0/0	.000	-/1	0	1	0	2	0	2	.167
DOBBS, F.	5	0/1	.000	0/0	.000	-/0	1	0	0	0	0	0	.000
Totals	200	23/50	.460	4/7	.571	-/28	8	19	18	6	1	50	.250

Virginia (54)   Coach: Terry Holland

	Min.	Total FG/FGA	Pct.	FT/FTA	Pct.	Reb. O/T	A	TO	PF	S	Blk	TP	PPM
LAMP, J.	38	3/12	.250	4/4	1.000	-/2	1	3	2	1	0	10	.263
GATES, T.	20	1/2	.500	0/0	.000	-/3	0	0	1	0	0	2	.100
SAMPSON, R.	37	7/9	.778	3/4	.429	-/12	1	4	2	0	0	17	.459
WILSON, O.	32	1/7	.143	2/2	1.000	-/4	5	3	3	4	0	4	.125
JONES, J.	39	3/6	.500	2/2	1.000	-/0	1	3	0	1	0	8	.205
STOKES, R.	7	1/1	1.000	0/0	.000	-/0	1	0	1	0	0	2	.286
RAKER, L.	21	4/7	.571	1/2	.500	-/1	2	1	1	0	0	9	.429
LATTIMORE, C.	2	1/1	1.000	0/0	.000	-/0	0	0	0	1	0	2	1.000
ROBINSON, C.	4	0/0	.000	0/0	.000	-/1	0	0	0	0	1	0	.000
Totals	200	21/45	.467	12/17	.706	-/23	11	13	11	6	1	54	.270

Team Rebounds: Virginia 4; Villanova 2. Disqualified: Villanova—Pinone. Technical fouls: Virginia—Lamp.

	1st Half	2nd Half	Final
Villanova	27	23	50
Virginia	24	30	54

Virginia Commonwealth (56)   Coach: J. D. Barnett

	Min.	Total FG/FGA	Pct.	FT/FTA	Pct.	Reb. O/T	A	TO	PF	S	Blk	TP	PPM
KNIGHT, M.	41	5/11	.455	2/2	1.000	-/3	4	2	1	0	1	12	.293
SHEROD, E.	45	4/8	.500	2/2	1.000	-/5	3	2	1	0	0	10	.222
STANCEIL, K.	43	0/3	.000	1/3	.333	-/5	0	2	2	1	2	1	.023
KOTTAK, D.	43	5/7	.714	0/0	.000	-/2	2	4	3	1	0	10	.233
MCCRAY, G.	44	10/14	.714	3/5	.600	-/8	1	2	4	1	1	23	.523
SHROPSHIRE, G.	5	0/0	.000	0/0	.000	-/0	0	0	0	0	0	0	.000
JONES, D.	3	0/0	.000	0/0	.000	-/0	0	0	1	0	0	0	.000
DAVIS, S.	1	0/0	.000	0/0	.000	-/0	0	0	0	0	0	0	.000
Totals	225	24/43	.558	8/12	.667	-/23	10	12	12	3	4	56	.249

Tennessee (58)   Coach: Don Devoe

	Min.	Total FG/FGA	Pct.	FT/FTA	Pct.	Reb. O/T	A	TO	PF	S	Blk	TP	PPM
ELLIS, D.	45	10/13	.769	2/2	1.000	-/5	0	1	3	0	1	22	.489
RAY, S.	29	0/4	.000	0/0	.000	-/3	1	0	3	0	0	0	.000
WOOD, H.	41	7/13	.538	4/5	.800	-/4	4	2	3	0	0	18	.439
LITTLETON, E.	24	3/4	.750	0/0	.000	-/0	4	1	1	1	0	6	.250
CARTER, G.	45	5/11	.455	0/0	.000	-/5	1	3	1	3	0	10	.222
BROOKS, M.	37	0/2	.000	0/0	.000	-/1	3	2	1	0	0	0	.000
BURTON, W.	4	1/1	1.000	0/0	.000	-/0	0	0	0	0	0	2	.500
Totals	225	26/48	.542	6/7	.857	-/18	17	8	12	4	1	58	.258

Team Rebounds: Tennessee 1; Va. Commonwealth 2. Disqualified: None. Technical fouls: Tennessee—Ellis.

	1st Half	2nd Half	1 OT	Final
Va. Commonwealth	25	31	0	56
Tennessee	36	20	2	58

Brigham Young (78)   Coach: Frank Arnold

	Min.	Total FG / FGA	Pct.	FT / FTA	Pct.	Reb. O / T	A	TO	PF	S	Blk	TP	PPM
ROBERTS, F.	38	6/12	.500	5/ 5	1.000	1/ 7	2	4	4	1	1	17	.447
TRUMBO, S.	31	2/ 7	.286	0/ 0	.000	4/13	2	4	3	0	0	4	.129
AINGE, D.	39	14/22	.636	9/10	.900	1/ 4	4	2	4	3	0	37	.949
CRAIG, S.	36	4/10	.400	0/ 0	.000	0/ 1	7	3	1	1	0	8	.222
BALLIF, G.	4	0/ 1	.000	0/ 0	.000	1/ 1	0	2	1	0	0	0	.000
SAARELANEN, T.	11	0/ 4	.000	0/ 0	.000	0/ 0	0	0	2	0	0	0	.000
KITE, G.	37	4/ 7	.571	4/ 7	.571	5/11	1	2	2	1	4	12	.324
FURNISS, G.	2	0/ 1	.000	0/ 0	.000	1/ 3	0	0	0	0	0	0	.000
MCGUIRE, D.	1	0/ 1	.000	0/ 0	.000	0/ 0	0	0	0	0	0	0	.000
CHRISTENSEN, C.	1	0/ 0	.000	0/ 0	.000	0/ 0	0	0	0	0	0	0	.000
Totals	200	30/65	.462	18/22	.818	13/40	16	17	17	6	5	78	.390

UCLA (55)   Coach: Larry Brown

	Min.	Total FG / FGA	Pct.	FT / FTA	Pct.	Reb. O / T	A	TO	PF	S	Blk	TP	PPM
SANDERS, M.	30	7/12	.583	0/ 0	.000	1/ 6	2	5	4	0	1	14	.467
DAYE, D.	27	6/14	.429	0/ 1	.000	3/ 6	3	3	2	0	0	12	.444
PRUITT, C.	27	3/ 8	.375	2/ 2	1.000	1/ 6	1	4	5	1	1	8	.296
JACKSON, R.	34	0/ 5	.000	2/ 2	1.000	0/ 3	6	1	2	2	0	2	.059
HOLTON, M.	33	5/15	.333	0/ 0	.000	2/ 2	1	1	4	0	0	10	.303
FOSTER, R.	14	1/ 5	.200	0/ 0	.000	1/ 3	1	1	2	0	0	2	.143
BEARS, D.	12	0/ 0	.000	2/ 4	.500	1/ 4	0	0	0	0	0	2	.167
ANDERSON, T.	8	0/ 0	.000	1/ 2	.500	1/ 2	0	0	0	0	2	1	.125
FIELDS, K.	15	1/ 7	.143	2/ 3	.667	2/ 3	0	4	4	0	0	4	.267
Totals	200	23/66	.348	9/14	.643	12/35	14	15	23	3	4	55	.275

Team Rebounds: Brigham Young 3; UCLA 1. Disqualified: UCLA—Pruitt. Technical fouls: None.

	1st Half	2nd Half	Final
Brigham Young	31	47	78
UCLA	22	33	55

James Madison (45)   Coach: Lou Campanelli

	Min.	Total FG / FGA	Pct.	FT / FTA	Pct.	Reb. O / T	A	TO	PF	S	Blk	TP	PPM
BLACKMON, S.	-	5/10	.500	2/ 2	1.000	3/ 7	0	3	4	1	0	12	-
TOWNES, L.	-	5/12	.417	2/ 3	.667	1/ 4	1	4	4	1	0	12	-
RULAND, D.	-	4/ 6	.667	0/ 0	.000	1/ 3	1	2	3	0	1	8	-
FISHER, C.	-	2/ 7	.286	0/ 0	.000	0/ 1	3	1	2	0	0	4	-
DUPONT, D.	-	3/ 5	.600	1/ 3	.333	1/ 3	3	4	1	0	0	7	-
SHOULDERS, T.	-	1/ 4	.250	0/ 2	.000	1/ 4	1	1	3	0	0	2	-
Totals	200	20/44	.455	5/10	.500	7/22	9	15	17	2	1	45	.225

Notre Dame (54)   Coach: Digger Phelps

	Min.	Total FG / FGA	Pct.	FT / FTA	Pct.	Reb. O / T	A	TO	PF	S	Blk	TP	PPM
WOOLRIDGE, O.	39	1/ 4	.250	3/ 4	.750	1/ 2	0	1	1	1	0	5	.128
TRIPUCKA, K.	34	3/11	.273	7/ 9	.778	1/ 2	5	2	3	1	0	13	.382
ANDREE, T.	13	0/ 0	.000	0/ 0	.000	1/ 2	0	2	3	0	0	0	.000
PAXSON, J.	40	2/ 6	.333	1/ 2	.500	1/ 3	2	3	2	1	0	5	.125
JACKSON, T.	40	10/16	.625	1/ 1	1.000	4/12	2	1	2	3	0	21	.525
VARNER, B.	15	1/ 1	1.000	0/ 2	.000	0/ 0	1	0	0	0	0	2	.133
KLEINE, J.	14	3/ 6	.500	2/ 2	1.000	5/ 7	0	1	2	0	0	8	.571
SALINAS, G.	5	0/ 2	.000	0/ 0	.000	0/ 0	1	0	2	0	0	0	.000
Totals	200	20/46	.435	14/20	.700	13/28	10	11	15	6	0	54	.270

Team Rebounds: Notre Dame 0; James Madison 3. Disqualified: None. Technical fouls: None.

	1st Half	2nd Half	Final
James Madison	20	25	45
Notre Dame	23	31	54

REGIONAL SEMIFINAL MIDWEST

Louisiana State (72)   Coach: Dale Brown

	Min.	Total FG / FGA	Pct.	FT / FTA	Pct.	Reb. O / T	A	TO	PF	S	Blk	TP	PPM
MITCHELL, L.	40	4/ 8	.500	2/ 3	.667	-/ 7	2	5	4	4	2	10	.250
MACKLIN, D.	37	6/13	.462	3/ 8	.375	-/ 9	1	4	1	0	0	15	.405
COOK, G.	22	4/ 7	.571	4/ 4	1.000	-/ 7	0	3	5	1	0	12	.545
MARTIN, E.	30	5/ 8	.625	6/ 6	1.000	-/ 3	8	3	5	2	0	16	.533
CARTER, H.	40	4/13	.308	0/ 1	.000	-/ 3	2	2	2	0	0	8	.200
SIMS, W.	19	4/ 4	1.000	1/ 1	1.000	-/ 5	2	2	0	0	0	9	.474
JONES, J.	11	1/ 3	.333	0/ 1	.000	-/ 3	1	0	0	1	0	2	.182
TUDOR, J.	1	0/ 1	.000	0/ 0	.000	-/ 0	1	0	0	0	0	0	.000
Totals	200	28/57	.491	16/24	.667	-/37	17	19	17	8	2	72	.360

Arkansas (56)   Coach: Eddie Sutton

	Min.	Total FG / FGA	Pct.	FT / FTA	Pct.	Reb. O / T	A	TO	PF	S	Blk	TP	PPM
BROWN, T.	34	4/ 7	.571	0/ 0	.000	-/ 4	2	5	4	2	1	8	.235
PETERSON, K.	27	4/11	.364	1/ 2	.500	-/ 2	1	2	2	1	0	9	.333
HASTINGS, S.	27	6/12	.500	2/ 2	1.000	-/ 7	0	3	5	0	0	14	.519
WALKER, D.	31	6/14	.429	0/ 1	.000	-/ 4	4	5	4	4	0	12	.387
REED, U.	40	4/10	.400	2/ 4	.500	-/ 5	1	1	0	2	2	10	.250
FRIESS, B.	19	1/ 2	.500	0/ 0	.000	-/ 0	0	1	2	1	0	2	.105
NORTON, R.	3	0/ 0	.000	0/ 0	.000	-/ 0	3	0	1	0	0	0	.000
YOUNG, M.	7	0/ 1	.000	0/ 0	.000	-/ 0	0	3	2	0	0	0	.000
SKULMAN, G.	6	0/ 1	.000	0/ 0	.000	-/ 1	0	0	0	0	0	0	.000
KELLY, C.	6	0/ 1	.000	1/ 2	.500	-/ 1	0	1	1	1	0	1	.167
Totals	200	25/59	.424	6/11	.545	-/24	11	21	21	11	3	56	.280

Team Rebounds: Louisiana St. 4; Arkansas 7. Disqualified: Louisiana St.—Cook, Martin; Arkansas—Hastings. Technical fouls: Louisiana St.—Cook, Sims; Arkansas—Walker.

	1st Half	2nd Half	Final
Louisiana St.	34	38	72
Arkansas	18	38	56

Wichita State (66)   Coach: Gene Smithson

	Min.	Total FG / FGA	Pct.	FT / FTA	Pct.	Reb. O / T	A	TO	PF	S	Blk	TP	PPM
CARR, A.	37	6/10	.600	4/ 6	.667	-/ 9	0	2	4	1	2	16	.432
JACKSON, J.	23	1/ 7	.143	0/ 0	.000	-/ 6	1	2	3	0	0	2	.087
LEVINGSTON, C.	38	6/16	.375	6/ 8	.750	-/14	1	4	2	0	1	18	.474
PAPKE, K.	13	1/ 2	.500	0/ 0	.000	-/ 1	4	0	3	0	0	2	.154
SMITHSON, R.	40	7/14	.500	2/ 3	.667	-/ 4	7	1	3	0	0	16	.400
GIBBS, J.	2	1/ 1	1.000	0/ 0	.000	-/ 0	0	1	0	0	0	2	1.000
MARTIN, T.	25	1/ 5	.200	0/ 0	.000	-/ 2	0	4	1	0	1	2	.080
JONES, M.	21	4/ 7	.571	0/ 0	.000	-/ 1	3	1	1	1	0	8	.381
DENNY, M.	1	0/ 0	.000	0/ 0	.000	-/ 0	1	0	0	0	0	0	.000
Totals	200	27/62	.435	12/17	.706	-/37	17	15	17	2	4	66	.330

Kansas (65)   Coach: Ted Owens

	Min.	Total FG / FGA	Pct.	FT / FTA	Pct.	Reb. O / T	A	TO	PF	S	Blk	TP	PPM
MAGLEY, D.	35	4/10	.400	2/ 2	1.000	-/ 7	4	0	1	1	1	10	.286
CRAWFORD, J.	34	5/ 9	.556	1/ 3	.333	-/ 5	1	0	4	0	1	11	.324
HOUSEY, A.	35	3/ 7	.429	0/ 0	.000	-/ 6	2	2	4	1	1	6	.171
GUY, T.	36	4/12	.333	1/ 2	.500	-/ 2	0	0	1	2	0	9	.250
VALENTINE, D.	36	8/13	.615	5/ 9	.556	-/ 2	6	5	2	4	0	21	.583
NEAL, B.	12	2/ 5	.400	0/ 0	.000	-/ 1	1	1	1	1	0	4	.333
MITCHELL, V.	12	2/ 5	.400	0/ 0	.000	-/ 1	1	1	2	0	0	4	.333
Totals	200	28/61	.459	9/16	.563	-/24	15	9	15	9	3	65	.325

Team Rebounds: Wichita State 8; Kansas 8. Disqualified: None. Technical fouls: Kansas—Mitchell, Crawford.

	1st Half	2nd Half	Final
Wichita State	33	33	66
Kansas	32	33	65

REGIONAL SEMIFINAL MIDEAST

St. Joseph's (42)　Coach: Jim Lynam

	Min.	Total FG/FGA	Pct.	FT/FTA	Pct.	Reb. O/T	A	TO	PF	S	Blk	TP	PPM
WILLIAMS	24	0/7	.000	1/3	.333	-/8	0	0	4	1	1	1	.042
SMITH, J.	39	2/4	.500	0/1	.000	-/6	2	4	2	0	0	4	.103
COSTNER	32	4/7	.571	0/0	.000	-/4	0	1	4	1	1	8	.250
CLARK, J.	40	2/6	.333	1/1	1.000	-/2	1	1	1	1	0	5	.125
WARRICK, B.	40	7/11	.636	6/10	.600	-/2	1	1	2	1	0	20	.500
MCFARLAN, L.	25	2/9	.222	0/0	.000	-/6	2	0	3	2	0	4	.160
Totals	200	17/44	.386	8/15	.533	-/28	6	7	16	6	2	42	.210

Boston College (41)　Coach: Tom Davis

	Min.	Total FG/FGA	Pct.	FT/FTA	Pct.	Reb. O/T	A	TO	PF	S	Blk	TP	PPM
CLARK	31	4/8	.500	1/1	1.000	-/3	0	1	3	1	0	9	.290
FOY	22	0/0	.000	2/4	.500	-/3	1	2	3	1	0	2	.091
MURPHY	22	4/9	.444	2/2	1.000	-/7	0	1	0	0	0	10	.455
BAGLEY, J.	32	4/14	.286	3/4	.750	-/2	1	3	4	0	0	11	.344
CHANDLER	30	2/4	.500	0/0	.000	-/2	2	1	1	0	0	4	.133
ADAMS	18	1/6	.167	3/5	.600	-/5	1	0	3	0	1	5	.278
O'SHEA	19	0/0	.000	0/0	.000	-/0	0	0	0	1	0	0	.000
SHRIGLEY, R.	17	0/1	.000	0/0	.000	-/5	1	1	0	0	0	0	.000
BEAULIEU	9	0/1	.000	0/0	.000	-/1	0	0	0	1	0	0	.000
Totals	200	15/43	.349	11/16	.688	-/28	6	9	14	4	1	41	.205

Team Rebounds: St. Joseph's 3; Boston College 4. Disqualified: None. Technical fouls: None.

	1st Half	2nd Half	Final	
St. Joseph's	18	24	42	○
Boston College	22	19	41	

Indiana (87)　Coach: Bob Knight

	Min.	Total FG/FGA	Pct.	FT/FTA	Pct.	Reb. O/T	A	TO	PF	S	Blk	TP	PPM
TURNER, L.	11	0/3	.000	0/2	.000	-/1	0	0	3	0	1	0	.000
KITCHEL, T.	17	3/8	.375	3/4	.750	-/1	0	1	3	0	0	9	.529
TOLBERT, R.	39	8/12	.667	1/1	1.000	-/9	2	3	3	0	1	17	.436
WITTMAN, R.	40	7/11	.636	6/7	.857	-/4	3	1	1	1	0	20	.500
THOMAS, I.	39	7/12	.583	13/15	.867	-/4	8	2	4	3	0	27	.692
THOMAS, J.	27	3/4	.750	1/2	.500	-/6	3	0	2	0	0	7	.259
RISLEY, S.	7	0/1	.000	0/0	.000	-/2	0	0	2	0	0	0	.000
BROWN, T.	1	1/1	1.000	0/0	.000	-/0	0	0	0	0	0	2	2.000
ISENBARGER, P.	1	0/0	.000	0/0	.000	-/1	1	0	0	0	0	0	.000
BOUCHIE, S.	16	2/7	.286	1/2	.500	-/3	2	0	2	1	0	5	.313
GRUNWALD, G.	1	0/0	.000	0/0	.000	-/1	0	0	0	0	0	0	.000
FRANZ, C.	1	0/0	.000	0/0	.000	-/0	0	0	0	0	0	0	.000
Totals	200	31/59	.525	25/33	.758	-/32	19	7	20	5	2	87	.435

Alabama-Birmingham (72)　Coach: Gene Bartow

	Min.	Total FG/FGA	Pct.	FT/FTA	Pct.	Reb. O/T	A	TO	PF	S	Blk	TP	PPM
GILES, C.	-	6/11	.545	1/3	.333	-/3	1	1	3	1	0	13	-
LANE, C.	-	1/5	.200	0/2	.000	-/3	0	0	4	0	0	2	-
ROBINSON, O.	-	6/15	.400	5/5	1.000	-/2	1	1	4	0	0	17	-
MARCUS, G.	-	6/10	.600	1/1	1.000	-/1	4	2	5	1	0	13	-
SPEER, D.	-	3/8	.375	2/2	1.000	-/7	0	0	3	0	1	8	-
BARTOW, M.	-	0/0	.000	0/0	.000	-/0	0	0	0	0	0	0	-
MCCAMMON, B.	-	0/1	.000	0/0	.000	-/0	0	0	0	0	0	0	-
NICHOLAS, J.	-	0/0	.000	1/2	.500	-/1	0	1	0	0	0	1	-
FOSTER, L.	-	2/3	.667	1/1	1.000	-/1	0	0	5	1	0	5	-
SIMCIK, S.	-	0/1	.000	0/0	.000	-/0	0	0	0	0	0	0	-
ALMQUIST, T.	-	0/0	.000	0/0	.000	-/1	0	0	0	0	0	0	-
MORRIS, L.	-	1/4	.250	4/4	1.000	-/2	1	0	0	0	0	6	-
RICHARDS, T.	-	0/0	.000	0/0	.000	-/0	0	0	0	0	0	0	-
ANCHRUM, N.	-	2/5	.400	3/4	.750	-/3	0	0	5	0	2	7	-
Totals	200	27/63	.429	18/24	.750	-/24	7	5	29	3	3	72	.360

Team Rebounds: Indiana 9; Ala.-Birmingham 4. Disqualified: Ala.-Birmingham—Marcus, Anchrum, Foster. Technical fouls: None.

	1st Half	2nd Half	Final
Indiana	42	45	87
Ala.-Birmingham	37	35	72

REGIONAL SEMIFINAL WEST

Kansas State (57)　Coach: Jack Hartman

	Min.	Total FG/FGA	Pct.	FT/FTA	Pct.	Reb. O/T	A	TO	PF	S	Blk	TP	PPM
ADAMS, T.	-	5/6	.833	1/2	.500	-/2	4	1	3	0	0	11	-
REED, R.	-	3/3	1.000	1/2	.500	-/2	0	1	1	0	0	7	-
NEALY, E.	-	4/9	.444	4/4	1.000	-/14	0	0	0	3	0	12	-
JANKOVICH, T.	-	2/5	.400	4/7	.571	-/2	5	2	2	1	0	8	-
BLACKMAN, R.	-	4/9	.444	4/6	.667	-/3	1	1	0	1	0	12	-
BARTON, F.	-	1/1	1.000	0/0	.000	-/1	1	0	1	1	0	2	-
CRAFT, L.	-	0/0	.000	0/0	.000	-/1	0	2	1	1	0	0	-
GALVAO, E.	-	1/6	.167	3/4	.750	-/0	0	0	1	0	0	5	-
Totals	200	20/39	.513	17/25	.680	-/25	11	7	9	7	0	57	.285

Illinois (52)　Coach: Lou Henson

	Min.	Total FG/FGA	Pct.	FT/FTA	Pct.	Reb. O/T	A	TO	PF	S	Blk	TP	PPM
JOHNSON, E.	40	7/15	.467	1/1	1.000	-/9	0	0	4	0	1	15	.375
SMITH, M.	32	5/10	.500	0/0	.000	-/6	5	2	5	0	0	10	.313
HOLCOMB, D.	23	2/4	.500	0/0	.000	-/7	0	0	3	1	0	4	.174
HARPER, D.	33	0/7	.000	0/0	.000	-/6	7	2	0	0	2	0	.000
RANGE, P.	40	5/9	.556	0/0	.000	-/4	2	0	3	0	0	10	.250
TUCKER, C.	17	2/10	.200	1/2	.500	-/1	0	3	2	0	0	5	.294
GRIFFIN, J.	14	4/7	.571	0/0	.000	-/1	0	0	5	0	0	8	.571
RICHARDSON, Q.	1	0/0	.000	0/0	.000	-/0	0	0	0	0	0	0	.000
Totals	200	25/62	.403	2/3	.667	-/34	14	7	22	1	3	52	.260

Team Rebounds: Kansas State 2, Illinois 0. Disqualified: Illinois—Smith, Griffin. Technical fouls: None.

	1st Half	2nd Half	Final
Kansas State	30	27	57
Illinois	27	25	52

Utah (56) Coach: Jerry Pimm

	Min.	Total FG/FGA	Pct.	FT/FTA	Pct.	Reb. O/T	A	TO	PF	S	Blk	TP	PPM
VRANES, D.	40	5/14	.357	3/4	.750	-/14	1	2	1	1	1	13	.325
BANKOWSKI, K.	23	1/9	.111	0/0	.000	-/2	2	0	5	1	0	2	.087
CHAMBERS, T.	24	4/9	.444	3/4	.750	-/8	1	1	4	1	1	11	.458
MARTIN, S.	40	6/13	.462	3/3	1.000	-/1	8	4	4	3	0	15	.375
MANNION, P.	38	5/8	.625	0/0	.000	-/5	2	5	2	0	0	10	.263
WILLIAMS, P.	5	0/0	.000	0/0	.000	-/0	0	0	3	0	0	0	.000
HAMMER, C.	18	1/4	.250	0/0	.000	-/1	2	0	1	0	0	2	.111
ROBINSON, A.	1	0/0	.000	0/0	.000	-/0	0	0	0	0	0	0	.000
WINANS, C.	11	1/1	1.000	1/2	.500	-/0	1	1	1	0	0	3	.273
Totals	200	23/58	.397	10/13	.769	-/31	17	13	21	6	2	56	.280

North Carolina (61) Coach: Dean Smith

	Min.	Total FG/FGA	Pct.	FT/FTA	Pct.	Reb. O/T	A	TO	PF	S	Blk	TP	PPM
WOOD, A.	36	7/12	.583	1/3	.333	-/6	0	3	1	2	1	15	.417
PERKINS, S.	33	7/14	.500	1/2	.500	-/11	0	4	4	0	4	15	.455
WORTHY, J.	35	4/6	.667	7/10	.700	-/10	6	3	2	0	2	15	.429
PEPPER, M.	22	1/2	.500	0/0	.000	-/1	0	0	3	0	0	2	.091
BLACK, J.	35	1/3	.333	0/1	.000	-/2	8	5	4	1	0	2	.057
BRADDOCK, J.	3	0/0	.000	0/0	.000	-/0	0	0	0	0	0	0	.000
KENNY, E.	1	0/0	.000	0/0	.000	-/0	0	0	0	0	0	0	.000
BUDKO, P.	9	0/1	.000	0/0	.000	-/0	0	0	1	0	0	0	.000
DOHERTY, M.	25	3/5	.600	6/8	.750	-/2	2	3	2	0	0	12	.480
BRUST, C.	1	0/0	.000	0/0	.000	-/1	0	0	0	0	0	0	.000
Totals	200	23/43	.535	15/24	.625	-/33	16	18	17	3	7	61	.305

Team Rebounds: N. Carolina 1; Utah 1. Disqualified: Utah—Bankowski. Technical fouls: N. Carolina—Worthy.

	1st Half	2nd Half	Final
Utah	25	31	56
N. Carolina	27	34	61

REGIONAL SEMIFINAL EAST

Virginia (62) Coach: Terry Holland

	Min.	Total FG/FGA	Pct.	FT/FTA	Pct.	Reb. O/T	A	TO	PF	S	Blk	TP	PPM
LAMP, J.	36	8/11	.727	2/2	1.000	-/5	2	1	0	0	0	18	.500
GATES, T.	32	2/2	1.000	0/0	.000	-/4	1	0	1	1	0	4	.125
SAMPSON, R.	34	4/13	.308	1/2	.500	-/5	1	3	1	1	4	9	.265
WILSON, O.	34	2/3	.667	5/6	.833	-/2	2	1	1	2	0	9	.265
JONES, J.	33	3/6	.500	4/5	.800	-/3	5	2	2	4	0	10	.303
STOKES, R.	4	1/3	.333	0/0	.000	-/0	0	1	2	0	0	2	.500
RAKER, L.	17	4/5	.800	2/2	1.000	-/3	0	0	1	1	0	10	.588
LATTIMORE, L.	4	0/0	.000	0/0	.000	-/1	0	1	2	0	0	0	.000
ROBINSON, C.	4	0/0	.000	0/0	.000	-/1	0	1	0	0	0	0	.000
KLEIN, J.	1	0/0	.000	0/0	.000	-/0	0	1	0	0	0	0	.000
COLLINS, L.	1	0/0	.000	0/0	.000	-/1	0	0	0	0	0	0	.000
Totals	200	24/43	.558	14/17	.824	-/25	11	11	10	9	4	62	.310

Tennessee (48) Coach: Don Devoe

	Min.	Total FG/FGA	Pct.	FT/FTA	Pct.	Reb. O/T	A	TO	PF	S	Blk	TP	PPM
ELLIS, D.	39	6/12	.500	1/2	.500	-/9	1	5	4	0	0	13	.333
RAY, S.	33	2/4	.500	0/0	.000	-/0	1	1	1	0	0	4	.121
WOOD, H.	39	4/9	.444	0/0	.000	-/4	2	3	1	3	0	8	.205
LITTLETON, E.	13	2/3	.667	0/0	.000	-/0	2	1	3	0	0	4	.308
CARTER, G.	39	4/9	.444	1/2	.500	-/4	2	0	4	0	0	9	.231
BROOKS, M.	27	3/8	.375	0/0	.000	-/1	6	3	2	2	0	6	.222
BURTON, W.	1	0/1	.000	0/0	.000	-/0	0	0	0	0	1	0	.000
BEAMAN, T.	7	2/2	1.000	0/0	.000	-/0	2	0	3	0	0	4	.571
FEDERMANN, D.	1	0/0	.000	0/0	.000	-/0	0	0	0	0	0	0	.000
LOVE, A.	1	0/0	.000	0/0	.000	-/0	1	0	0	0	0	0	.000
Totals	200	23/48	.479	2/4	.500	-/18	17	13	18	5	1	48	.240

Team Rebounds: Virginia 2; Tennessee 1. Disqualified: None. Technical fouls: None.

	1st Half	2nd Half	Final	
Virginia	27	35	62	✎
Tennessee	26	22	48	

Brigham Young (51) Coach: Frank Arnold

	Min.	Total FG/FGA	Pct.	FT/FTA	Pct.	Reb. O/T	A	TO	PF	S	Blk	TP	PPM
ROBERTS, F.	28	5/6	.833	1/3	.333	-/5	0	2	5	0	0	11	.393
TRUMBO, S.	40	1/8	.125	0/2	.000	-/9	2	1	1	0	1	2	.050
AINGE, D.	40	4/10	.400	4/4	1.000	-/1	3	3	2	3	0	12	.300
CRAIG, S.	31	5/13	.385	0/0	.000	-/3	1	3	5	2	0	10	.323
BALLIF, G.	18	3/6	.500	4/5	.800	-/0	1	1	1	1	0	10	.556
SAARELANEN, T.	14	2/3	.667	0/0	.000	-/2	1	1	2	0	0	4	.286
KITE, G.	22	1/2	.500	0/0	.000	-/5	0	0	4	0	0	2	.091
FURNISS, G.	7	0/0	.000	0/0	.000	-/1	0	0	0	0	0	0	.000
Totals	200	21/48	.438	9/14	.643	-/26	8	11	20	6	1	51	.255

Notre Dame (50) Coach: Digger Phelps

	Min.	Total FG/FGA	Pct.	FT/FTA	Pct.	Reb. O/T	A	TO	PF	S	Blk	TP	PPM
WOOLRIDGE, O.	40	8/10	.800	1/2	.500	-/6	2	2	1	0	0	17	.425
TRIPUCKA, K.	37	7/12	.583	0/2	.000	-/2	3	5	3	1	0	14	.378
ANDREE, T.	33	1/3	.333	0/1	.000	-/2	1	1	4	1	0	2	.061
PAXSON, J.	40	1/5	.200	2/3	.667	-/4	6	2	3	0	0	4	.100
JACKSON, T.	36	3/7	.429	5/5	1.000	-/11	4	2	3	1	2	11	.306
KLEINE, J.	6	1/1	1.000	0/0	.000	-/0	0	0	0	0	0	2	.333
VARNER, B.	3	0/0	.000	0/1	.000	-/0	0	0	0	0	0	0	.000
SLUBY, T.	5	0/0	.000	0/0	.000	-/0	0	1	2	0	0	0	.000
Totals	200	21/38	.553	8/14	.571	-/25	16	13	16	3	2	50	.250

Team Rebounds: Brigham Young 2; Notre Dame 1. Disqualified: Brigham Young—Roberts, Craig. Technical fouls: None.

	1st Half	2nd Half	Final
Brigham Young	18	33	51
Notre Dame	28	22	50

REGIONAL FINAL MIDWEST

Louisiana State (96) Coach: Dale Brown

	Min.	Total FG/FGA	Pct.	FT/FTA	Pct.	Reb. O/T	A	TO	PF	S	Blk	TP	PPM
MITCHELL, L.	33	7/12	.583	3/5	.600	-/6	0	3	4	2	0	17	.515
MACKLIN, D.	28	9/11	.818	3/3	1.000	-/10	1	2	2	0	1	21	.750
COOK, G.	32	9/10	.900	1/3	.333	-/7	1	5	3	0	0	19	.594
MARTIN, E.	35	5/8	.625	3/3	1.000	-/0	10	3	3	4	0	13	.371
CARTER, H.	26	5/10	.500	1/2	.500	-/0	5	0	3	2	0	11	.423
SIMS, W.	18	2/5	.400	3/4	.750	-/1	2	3	2	0	0	7	.389
JONES, J.	8	0/1	.000	0/0	.000	-/0	0	1	0	0	0	0	.000
ENGLAND, M.	1	1/1	1.000	0/0	.000	-/0	0	0	0	0	0	2	2.000
TUDOR, J.	4	0/0	.000	0/0	.000	-/1	0	0	0	0	0	0	.000
BLACK, T.	4	1/3	.333	0/0	.000	-/1	0	0	0	0	0	2	.500
BERGERON, B.	8	0/0	.000	4/4	1.000	-/0	1	1	0	0	0	4	.500
COSTELLO, J.	1	0/0	.000	0/0	.000	-/1	0	0	0	0	0	0	.000
KISTLER, B.	1	0/0	.000	0/0	.000	-/0	0	0	0	0	0	0	.000
CAMPBELL, A.	1	0/0	.000	0/0	.000	-/0	0	0	0	0	0	0	.000
Totals	200	39/61	.639	18/24	.750	-/27	20	18	17	8	1	96	.480

Wichita State (85) Coach: Gene Smithson

	Min.	Total FG/FGA	Pct.	FT/FTA	Pct.	Reb. O/T	A	TO	PF	S	Blk	TP	PPM
CARR, A.	30	9/13	.692	4/5	.800	-/5	1	4	5	0	2	22	.733
JACKSON, J.	21	2/6	.333	0/1	.000	-/6	4	2	2	0	0	4	.190
LEVINGSTON, C.	40	8/12	.667	3/4	.750	-/10	3	3	4	3	0	19	.475
MARTIN, T.	35	5/14	.357	0/0	.000	-/3	10	2	4	1	0	10	.286
SMITHSON, R.	32	8/11	.727	2/3	.667	-/1	5	6	3	0	0	18	.563
PAPKE, K.	6	1/3	.333	0/1	.000	-/1	0	0	2	1	0	2	.333
GIBBS, J.	8	0/1	.000	0/0	.000	-/0	0	0	1	0	0	0	.000
JONES, M.	15	0/5	.000	0/1	.000	-/0	0	0	0	0	0	0	.000
DENNY, M.	11	5/10	.500	0/0	.000	-/4	1	0	2	0	0	10	.909
RADOVIC, Z.	1	0/0	.000	0/0	.000	-/0	0	0	0	0	0	0	.000
DJURICIC, Z.	1	0/0	.000	0/0	.000	-/0	0	0	0	0	0	0	.000
Totals	200	38/75	.507	9/15	.600	-/30	24	17	23	5	2	85	.425

Team Rebounds: Louisiana St. 5; Wichita State 6. Disqualified: Wichita State—Carr. Technical fouls: Louisiana St.—Mitchell.

	1st Half	2nd Half	Final
Louisiana St.	48	48	96
Wichita State	33	52	85

REGIONAL FINAL MIDEAST

St. Joseph's (46) Coach: Jim Lynam

	Min.	Total FG/FGA	Pct.	FT/FTA	Pct.	Reb. O/T	A	TO	PF	S	Blk	TP	PPM
WILLIAMS	34	2/4	.500	0/0	.000	-/4	0	0	3	0	0	4	.118
SMITH, J.	32	1/6	.167	0/0	.000	-/2	3	2	3	1	0	2	.063
COSTNER	34	3/8	.375	1/2	.500	-/4	0	1	5	1	0	7	.206
CLARK, J.	31	3/4	.750	5/6	.833	-/4	3	4	0	0	0	11	.355
WARRICK, B.	38	3/10	.300	3/3	1.000	-/0	3	4	1	1	0	9	.237
MCFARLAN, L.	20	1/7	.143	4/6	.667	-/2	2	1	0	0	0	6	.300
MITCHELL	3	0/0	.000	0/1	.000	-/0	0	0	0	0	0	0	.000
KEARNEY	3	0/0	.000	2/3	.667	-/1	0	0	1	0	0	2	.667
SPRINGMAN	3	1/3	.333	3/4	.750	-/0	0	0	0	0	0	5	1.667
DICARO	2	0/0	.000	0/0	.000	-/0	1	0	0	0	0	0	.000
Totals	200	14/42	.333	18/25	.720	-/17	9	11	17	3	0	46	.230

Indiana (78) Coach: Bob Knight

	Min.	Total FG/FGA	Pct.	FT/FTA	Pct.	Reb. O/T	A	TO	PF	S	Blk	TP	PPM
TURNER, L.	29	7/8	.875	0/0	.000	-/5	2	1	5	0	0	14	.483
KITCHEL, T.	20	1/4	.250	1/2	.500	-/3	3	1	4	1	0	3	.150
TOLBERT, R.	37	6/8	.750	2/4	.500	-/5	2	0	1	0	0	14	.378
WITTMAN, R.	13	4/4	1.000	0/0	.000	-/0	1	0	0	0	0	8	.615
THOMAS, I.	36	3/8	.375	2/3	.667	-/1	12	5	2	3	0	8	.222
THOMAS, J.	24	6/7	.857	0/0	.000	-/3	1	0	0	0	0	12	.500
RISLEY, S.	17	1/2	.500	0/1	.000	-/2	2	1	0	1	0	2	.118
BROWN, T.	4	0/1	.000	1/2	.500	-/1	2	0	2	0	0	1	.250
ISENBARGER, P.	3	3/4	.750	0/0	.000	-/0	2	0	3	0	0	6	2.000
BOUCHIE, S.	3	1/2	.500	0/0	.000	-/1	1	0	0	0	0	2	.667
GRUNWALD, G.	8	1/1	1.000	2/2	1.000	-/1	1	1	1	0	0	4	.500
FRANZ, C.	3	1/1	1.000	0/0	.000	-/0	0	0	1	0	0	2	.667
LAFAVE, M.	3	1/1	1.000	0/0	.000	-/5	0	0	0	0	0	2	.667
Totals	200	35/51	.686	8/14	.571	-/27	29	9	19	5	0	78	.390

Team Rebounds: Indiana 6; St. Joseph's 4. Disqualified: Indiana—Turner; St. Joseph's—Costner. Technical fouls: None.

	1st Half	2nd Half	Final
St. Joseph's	16	30	46
Indiana	32	46	78

REGIONAL FINAL WEST

Kansas State (68)   Coach: Jack Hartman

	Min.	Total FG / FGA	Pct.	FT / FTA	Pct.	Reb. O / T	A	TO	PF	S	Blk	TP	PPM
ADAMS, T.	27	2/ 9	.222	0/ 1	.000	-/ 7	3	2	2	0	0	4	.148
REED, R.	28	6/12	.500	7/ 7	1.000	-/ 5	0	2	4	0	1	19	.679
NEALY, E.	28	6/10	.600	0/ 0	.000	-/ 7	3	2	4	3	0	12	.429
JANKOVICH, T.	36	1/ 6	.167	2/ 4	.500	-/ 0	7	1	3	0	0	4	.111
BLACKMAN, R.	38	10/17	.588	1/ 1	1.000	-/10	2	0	1	0	0	21	.553
BARTON, F.	8	2/ 4	.500	0/ 0	.000	-/ 0	0	1	0	0	0	4	.500
CRAFT, L.	8	0/ 2	.000	0/ 0	.000	-/ 0	0	0	0	0	0	0	.000
GALVAO, E.	25	2/ 8	.250	0/ 0	.000	-/ 1	2	0	4	1	0	4	.160
REID, S.	2	0/ 1	.000	0/ 0	.000	-/ 0	0	0	1	0	0	0	.000
Totals	200	29/69	.420	10/13	.769	-/30	17	8	19	4	1	68	.340

North Carolina (82)   Coach: Dean Smith

	Min.	Total FG / FGA	Pct.	FT / FTA	Pct.	Reb. O / T	A	TO	PF	S	Blk	TP	PPM
WOOD, A.	37	10/17	.588	1/ 1	1.000	-/17	3	1	3	0	1	21	.568
WORTHY, J.	33	6/16	.375	3/ 4	.750	-/ 4	5	1	3	2	0	15	.455
PERKINS, S.	33	7/14	.500	2/ 2	1.000	-/11	4	2	3	1	1	16	.485
PEPPER, M.	14	2/ 2	1.000	0/ 0	.000	-/ 0	1	0	2	1	0	4	.286
BLACK, J.	34	1/ 3	.333	6/ 6	1.000	-/ 1	3	3	2	0	0	8	.235
BRADDOCK, J.	6	1/ 1	1.000	0/ 0	.000	-/ 0	1	1	0	0	0	2	.333
KENNY, E.	1	0/ 1	.000	0/ 0	.000	-/ 1	0	0	0	0	0	0	.000
BUDKO, P.	10	0/ 0	.000	0/ 0	.000	-/ 0	0	0	1	0	0	0	.000
BARLOW, J.	1	0/ 0	.000	0/ 0	.000	-/ 0	0	0	0	0	0	0	.000
DOHERTY, M.	28	6/ 7	.857	4/ 6	.667	-/ 5	3	0	2	2	0	16	.571
BRUST, C.	2	0/ 0	.000	0/ 0	.000	-/ 0	0	0	0	0	0	0	.000
EXUM, C.	1	0/ 0	.000	0/ 0	.000	-/ 0	0	0	0	0	0	0	.000
Totals	200	33/61	.541	16/19	.842	-/39	20	8	16	6	2	82	.410

Team Rebounds: N. Carolina 1; Kansas State 0. Disqualified: None. Technical fouls: North Carolina—Coach Smith, Worthy, Perkins.

	1st Half	2nd Half	Final
Kansas State	29	39	68
N. Carolina	42	40	82

REGIONAL FINAL EAST

Virginia (74)   Coach: Terry Holland

	Min.	Total FG / FGA	Pct.	FT / FTA	Pct.	Reb. O / T	A	TO	PF	S	Blk	TP	PPM
LAMP, J.	38	7/15	.467	4/ 5	.800	-/ 7	2	3	3	0	0	18	.474
GATES, T.	33	1/ 2	.500	0/ 1	.000	-/ 2	0	0	3	0	0	2	.061
SAMPSON, R.	36	9/16	.563	4/ 7	.571	-/12	1	1	2	0	4	22	.611
WILSON, O.	30	3/ 7	.429	4/ 4	1.000	-/ 5	5	1	4	3	1	10	.333
JONES, J.	31	2/ 4	.500	6/ 6	1.000	-/ 0	4	1	3	2	0	10	.323
STOKES, R.	4	0/ 1	.000	0/ 0	.000	-/ 0	0	1	0	1	0	0	.000
RAKER, L.	22	4/ 9	.444	4/ 4	1.000	-/ 2	1	0	2	1	0	12	.545
LATTIMORE, L.	4	0/ 0	.000	0/ 1	.000	-/ 0	0	1	1	0	0	0	.000
COLLINS, L.	1	0/ 0	.000	0/ 0	.000	-/ 0	0	0	1	0	0	0	.000
KLEIN, J.	1	0/ 0	.000	0/ 0	.000	-/ 1	0	0	0	0	0	0	.000
Totals	200	26/55	.473	22/28	.786	-/29	13	8	19	7	5	74	.370

Brigham Young (60)   Coach: Frank Arnold

	Min.	Total FG / FGA	Pct.	FT / FTA	Pct.	Reb. O / T	A	TO	PF	S	Blk	TP	PPM
ROBERTS, F.	36	6/ 8	.750	0/ 1	.000	-/ 7	5	3	5	1	1	12	.333
TRUMBO, S.	34	4/ 8	.500	3/ 4	.750	-/ 8	2	2	2	0	0	11	.324
AINGE, D.	38	4/13	.308	5/ 5	1.000	-/ 3	5	3	4	0	0	13	.342
CRAIG, S.	27	4/ 8	.500	4/ 4	1.000	-/ 1	3	1	5	1	0	12	.444
BALLIF, G.	14	2/ 4	.500	2/ 2	1.000	-/ 3	0	2	3	0	0	6	.429
SAARELANEN, T.	8	0/ 2	.000	0/ 0	.000	-/ 0	0	1	0	0	0	0	.000
KITE, G.	37	2/ 6	.333	0/ 1	.000	-/ 5	0	3	4	0	1	4	.108
FURNISS, G.	4	1/ 1	1.000	0/ 0	.000	-/ 2	0	0	0	0	0	2	.500
CHRISTENSEN, C.	1	0/ 0	.000	0/ 0	.000	-/ 0	0	0	0	0	0	0	.000
WEBB, R.	1	0/ 0	.000	0/ 0	.000	-/ 1	0	0	0	0	0	0	.000
Totals	200	23/51	.451	14/17	.824	-/30	15	14	24	2	2	60	.300

Team Rebounds: Virginia 2; Brigham Young 2. Disqualified: Brigham Young—Roberts, Craig. Technical fouls: Brigham Young—Ainge.

	1st Half	2nd Half	Final
Virginia	28	46	74
Brigham Young	31	29	60

FINAL FOUR

Louisiana State (49) Coach: Dale Brown

	Min.	Total FG/FGA	Pct.	FT/FTA	Pct.	Reb. O/T	A	TO	PF	S	Blk	TP	PPM
MITCHELL, L.	37	3/10	.300	3/4	.750	-/10	0	3	3	1	0	9	.243
MACKLIN, D.	35	2/12	.167	0/0	.000	-/8	0	4	1	0	1	4	.114
COOK, G.	34	3/5	.600	0/0	.000	-/5	0	1	5	0	0	6	.176
MARTIN, E.	31	2/8	.250	3/3	1.000	-/3	8	2	4	0	0	7	.226
CARTER, H.	32	5/10	.500	0/0	.000	-/6	1	3	3	1	1	10	.313
SIMS, W.	14	2/8	.250	1/2	.500	-/1	0	4	0	2	0	5	.357
JONES, J.	9	0/2	.000	0/1	.000	-/2	1	1	3	0	0	0	.000
TUDOR, J.	3	1/3	.333	4/4	1.000	-/2	0	0	3	0	0	6	2.000
BERGERON, B.	3	0/0	.000	0/0	.000	-/0	1	0	0	0	0	0	.000
COSTELLO, J.	1	0/0	.000	0/0	.000	-/0	0	0	0	0	0	0	.000
BLACK, T.	1	1/1	1.000	0/0	.000	-/1	0	1	0	0	0	2	2.000
Totals	200	19/59	.322	11/14	.786	-/38	11	19	22	4	2	49	.245

Indiana (67) Coach: Bob Knight

	Min.	Total FG/FGA	Pct.	FT/FTA	Pct.	Reb. O/T	A	TO	PF	S	Blk	TP	PPM
TURNER, L.	38	7/19	.368	6/7	.857	-/8	0	0	1	0	0	20	.526
KITCHEL, T.	23	3/8	.375	4/4	1.000	-/6	0	1	3	0	0	10	.435
TOLBERT, R.	36	3/7	.429	1/2	.500	-/6	5	3	3	1	0	7	.194
WITTMAN, R.	37	3/10	.300	2/2	1.000	-/2	2	2	0	0	0	8	.216
THOMAS, I.	26	6/8	.750	2/3	.667	-/2	4	3	4	0	0	14	.538
THOMAS, J.	17	0/4	.000	2/2	1.000	-/9	2	0	1	1	2	2	.118
RISLEY, S.	10	0/2	.000	1/2	.500	-/2	1	0	0	0	0	1	.100
BROWN, T.	2	0/1	.000	0/1	.000	-/0	0	0	0	0	0	0	.000
ISENBARGER, P.	2	0/1	.000	0/0	.000	-/0	0	0	0	0	0	0	.000
BOUCHIE, S.	2	0/1	.000	0/0	.000	-/2	0	0	0	0	0	0	.000
GRUNWALD, G.	3	1/2	.500	1/2	.500	-/2	0	1	0	0	0	3	1.000
FRANZ, C.	2	0/0	.000	2/2	1.000	-/0	0	1	1	0	0	2	1.000
LAFAVE, M.	2	0/0	.000	0/0	.000	-/2	0	0	1	0	0	0	.000
Totals	200	23/63	.365	21/27	.778	-/41	14	10	15	2	2	67	.335

Team Rebounds: Indiana 3; Louisiana St. 4. Disqualified: Louisiana St.—Cook. Technical fouls: Louisiana St.—Coach Brown.

	1st Half	2nd Half	Final
Louisiana St.	30	19	49
Indiana	27	40	67

North Carolina (78) Coach: Dean Smith

	Min.	Total FG/FGA	Pct.	FT/FTA	Pct.	Reb. O/T	A	TO	PF	S	Blk	TP	PPM
WOOD, A.	36	14/19	.737	11/13	.846	-/10	1	0	3	0	0	39	1.083
WORTHY, J.	40	2/8	.250	4/7	.571	-/3	1	2	2	1	2	8	.200
PERKINS, S.	40	4/7	.571	3/5	.600	-/9	1	3	4	1	1	11	.275
PEPPER, M.	11	0/4	.000	0/0	.000	-/1	0	0	2	0	0	0	.000
BLACK, J.	32	4/6	.667	2/3	.667	-/1	4	2	4	2	0	10	.313
BRADDOCK, J.	8	0/1	.000	0/0	.000	-/0	1	0	0	0	0	0	.000
KENNY, E.	1	1/1	1.000	0/0	.000	-/1	0	0	0	0	0	2	2.000
DOHERTY, M.	32	0/1	.000	8/9	.889	-/4	3	4	1	1	0	8	.250
Totals	200	25/47	.532	28/37	.757	-/29	11	11	16	5	3	78	.390

Virginia (65) Coach: Terry Holland

	Min.	Total FG/FGA	Pct.	FT/FTA	Pct.	Reb. O/T	A	TO	PF	S	Blk	TP	PPM
LAMP, J.	39	7/18	.389	4/4	1.000	-/7	4	1	5	3	0	18	.462
GATES, T.	23	1/1	1.000	0/0	.000	-/4	0	0	4	0	0	2	.087
SAMPSON, R.	36	3/10	.300	5/7	.714	-/9	1	4	3	1	3	11	.306
WILSON, O.	23	4/7	.571	0/0	.000	-/2	3	5	4	1	0	8	.348
JONES, J.	36	5/13	.385	1/1	1.000	-/3	5	3	3	1	0	11	.306
STOKES, R.	15	0/2	.000	0/0	.000	-/1	0	1	3	0	0	0	.000
RAKER, L.	26	5/9	.556	3/3	1.000	-/5	1	0	5	1	0	13	.500
LATTIMORE, L.	2	1/1	1.000	0/0	.000	-/1	0	0	0	0	0	2	1.000
Totals	200	26/61	.426	13/15	.867	-/32	14	14	27	7	3	65	.325

Team Rebounds: N. Carolina 2; Virginia 2. Disqualified: Virginia—Lamp, Raker. Technical fouls: None.

	1st Half	2nd Half	Final
N. Carolina	27	51	78
Virginia	27	38	65

NATIONAL CHAMPIONSHIP

Indiana (63) Coach: Bob Knight

	Min.	Total FG/FGA	Pct.	FT/FTA	Pct.	Reb. O/T	A	TO	PF	S	Blk	TP	PPM
TURNER, L.	34	5/8	.625	2/2	1.000	-/6	1	2	5	1	0	12	.353
KITCHEL, T.	4	0/1	.000	0/0	.000	-/0	0	3	0	0	0	0	.000
TOLBERT, R.	40	1/4	.250	3/6	.500	-/11	0	2	0	2	1	5	.125
WITTMAN, R.	40	7/13	.538	2/2	1.000	-/4	0	2	2	0	0	16	.400
THOMAS, I.	40	8/17	.471	7/8	.875	-/2	5	4	4	4	0	23	.575
THOMAS, J.	29	1/4	.250	0/0	.000	-/4	8	4	2	1	0	2	.069
RISLEY, S.	13	1/1	1.000	3/4	.750	-/4	0	1	1	0	0	5	.385
Totals	200	23/48	.479	17/22	.773	-/31	14	14	17	8	1	63	.315

North Carolina (50) Coach: Dean Smith

	Min.	Total FG/FGA	Pct.	FT/FTA	Pct.	Reb. O/T	A	TO	PF	S	Blk	TP	PPM
WOOD, A.	38	6/13	.462	6/9	.667	-/6	2	0	4	0	0	18	.474
WORTHY, J.	31	3/11	.273	1/2	.500	-/6	2	4	5	1	1	7	.226
PERKINS, S.	39	5/8	.625	1/2	.500	-/8	1	2	3	2	1	11	.275
PEPPER, M.	23	2/5	.400	2/2	1.000	-/1	0	2	1	2	0	6	.261
BLACK, J.	36	3/4	.750	0/0	.000	-/2	6	4	5	4	0	6	.167
BRADDOCK, J.	4	0/2	.000	0/0	.000	-/0	1	0	1	0	0	0	.000
KENNY, E.	1	0/1	.000	0/0	.000	-/1	0	0	0	0	0	0	.000
BUDKO, P.	1	0/1	.000	0/0	.000	-/1	0	0	0	0	0	0	.000
DOHERTY, M.	24	1/2	.500	0/1	.000	-/4	0	6	4	0	0	2	.083
BRUST, C.	3	0/0	.000	0/0	.000	-/0	0	1	0	0	0	0	.000
Totals	200	20/47	.426	10/16	.625	-/29	12	19	23	9	2	50	.250

Team Rebounds: Indiana 2; N. Carolina 0. Disqualified: Indiana—Turner; N. Carolina—Worthy, Black. Technical fouls: Indiana—Turner.

	1st Half	2nd Half	Final
Indiana	27	36	63
N. Carolina	26	24	50

NATIONAL THIRD PLACE

Virginia (78)   Coach: Terry Holland

	Min.	Total FG/FGA	Pct.	FT/FTA	Pct.	Reb. O/T	A	TO	PF	S	Blk	TP	PPM
LAMP, J.	38	7/13	.538	11/11	1.000	-/8	1	5	3	0	0	25	.658
GATES, T.	24	2/5	.400	4/5	.800	-/5	0	0	5	0	0	8	.333
SAMPSON, R.	17	3/8	.375	4/4	1.000	-/11	2	1	5	0	0	10	.588
WILSON, O.	32	1/6	.167	7/8	.875	-/1	2	2	1	1	0	9	.281
JONES, J.	26	1/2	.500	0/0	.000	-/2	2	2	0	2	0	2	.077
STOKES, R.	4	0/3	.000	0/0	.000	-/0	1	0	0	0	0	0	.000
RAKER, L.	29	7/14	.500	7/8	.875	-/5	3	5	2	0	0	21	.724
LATTIMORE, L.	18	1/4	.250	0/0	.000	-/6	1	1	3	0	0	2	.111
ROBINSON, C.	4	0/2	.000	1/2	.500	-/1	0	0	0	0	0	1	.250
KLEIN, J.	6	0/1	.000	0/0	.000	-/0	1	1	3	1	0	0	.000
COLLINS, L.	2	0/0	.000	0/0	.000	-/0	0	0	0	0	0	0	.000
Totals	200	22/58	.379	34/38	.895	-/39	13	17	22	4	0	78	.390

Louisiana State (74)   Coach: Dale Brown

	Min.	Total FG/FGA	Pct.	FT/FTA	Pct.	Reb. O/T	A	TO	PF	S	Blk	TP	PPM
MITCHELL, L.	36	7/12	.583	2/5	.400	-/12	1	1	5	2	0	16	.444
MACKLIN, D.	16	0/3	.000	0/0	.000	-/5	0	2	5	0	0	0	.000
COOK, G.	40	8/14	.571	5/8	.625	-/8	0	3	2	0	0	21	.525
MARTIN, E.	37	3/8	.375	0/1	.000	-/1	7	6	5	4	0	6	.162
CARTER, H.	24	7/14	.500	0/0	.000	-/6	1	1	5	1	0	14	.583
SIMS, W.	21	5/10	.500	3/4	.750	-/3	2	3	3	2	0	13	.619
JONES, J.	14	2/6	.333	0/0	.000	-/2	2	0	3	0	0	4	.286
TUDOR, J.	9	0/1	.000	0/0	.000	-/1	0	0	2	0	0	0	.000
BERGERON, B.	2	0/0	.000	0/0	.000	-/0	0	1	0	0	0	0	.000
BLACK, T.	1	0/1	.000	0/0	.000	-/2	0	0	0	0	0	0	.000
Totals	200	32/69	.464	10/18	.556	-/40	13	17	30	9	0	74	.370

Team Rebounds: Virginia 3; Louisiana St. 2. Disqualified: Virginia—Gates, Sampson; Louisiana St.—Martin, Mitchell, Macklin, Carter. Technical fouls: None.

	1st Half	2nd Half	Final
Virginia	37	41	78
Louisiana St.	29	45	74

✪ ALL-STAR TEAMS ✪

ALL TOURNAMENT
JEFF LAMP	VIRGINIA
LANDON TURNER	INDIANA
★ ISIAH THOMAS	INDIANA
JIM THOMAS	INDIANA
AL WOOD	N. CAROLINA

WEST REGIONAL
ROLANDO BLACKMAN	KANSAS STATE
ED NEALY	KANSAS STATE
SAM PERKINS	N. CAROLINA
★ AL WOOD	N. CAROLINA
JAMES WORTHY	N. CAROLINA

MIDEAST REGIONAL
GLENN MARCUS	ALA.-BIRMINGHAM
★ ISIAH THOMAS	INDIANA
RAY TOLBERT	INDIANA
BRIAN WARWICK	ST. JOSEPH'S
RANDY WITTMAN	INDIANA

EAST REGIONAL
DANNY AINGE	BRIGHAM YOUNG
★ JEFF LAMP	VIRGINIA
LEE RAKER	VIRGINIA
RALPH SAMPSON	VIRGINIA
ORLANDO WOOLRIDGE	NOTRE DAME

MIDWEST REGIONAL
GREG COOK	LOUISIANA ST.
CLIFF LEVINGSTON	WICHITA STATE
★ DURAND MACKLIN	LOUISIANA ST.
ETHAN MARTIN	LOUISIANA ST.
RANDY SMITHSON	WICHITA STATE

★ Most Outstanding Player(s)

✪ INDIVIDUAL RECORDS ✪

SCORING

Most points in a single game
1. AL WOOD, N. CAROLINA (vs. VIRGINIA) — 39
2. DANNY AINGE, BRIGHAM YOUNG (vs. UCLA) — 37
3. TONY GUY, KANSAS (vs. ARIZONA ST.) — 36
4. JOHN BAGLEY, BOSTON COLLEGE (vs. WAKE FOREST) — 35
5. BYRON SCOTT, ARIZONA ST. (vs. KANSAS) — 32

Most total points in the tournament
1. AL WOOD, N. CAROLINA — 109
2. ISIAH THOMAS, INDIANA — 91
3. JEFF LAMP, VIRGINIA — 89
4. CLIFF LEVINGSTON, WICHITA STATE — 86
5. DANNY AINGE, BRIGHAM YOUNG — 83

Highest scoring average (minimum 2 games)
1. MIKE OLLIVER, LAMAR (54-2) — 27.00
2. ALBERT KING, MARYLAND (47-2) — 23.50
3. P. HARRIS, NORTHEASTERN (44-2) — 22.00
4. AL WOOD, N. CAROLINA (109-5) — 21.80
5. JOHN BAGLEY, BOSTON COLLEGE (65-3) — 21.67

FIELD GOALS

Most field goals in a single game
1. BYRON SCOTT, ARIZONA ST. (vs. KANSAS) — 15
2. AL WOOD, N. CAROLINA (vs. VIRGINIA) — 14
2. DANNY AINGE, BRIGHAM YOUNG (vs. UCLA) — 14
4. 4 tied for fourth place.

Most total field goals in the tournament
1. AL WOOD, N. CAROLINA — 44
2. HOWARD CARTER, LOUISIANA ST. — 34
3. ISIAH THOMAS, INDIANA — 33
3. CLIFF LEVINGSTON, WICHITA STATE — 33
5. JEFF LAMP, VIRGINIA — 32

Most field goal attempts in a single game
1. ALBERT KING, MARYLAND (vs. INDIANA) — 28
2. ALVIN JACKSON, SOUTHERN-B.R. (vs. WICHITA STATE) — 25
3. HOWARD CARTER, LOUISIANA ST. (vs. LAMAR) — 22
3. BYRON SCOTT, ARIZONA ST. (vs. KANSAS) — 22
3. DANNY AINGE, BRIGHAM YOUNG (vs. UCLA) — 22

Most total field goal attempts in tournament
1. AL WOOD, N. CAROLINA — 73
2. JEFF LAMP, VIRGINIA — 69
2. HOWARD CARTER, LOUISIANA ST. — 69
4. CLIFF LEVINGSTON, WICHITA STATE — 61
4. DANNY AINGE, BRIGHAM YOUNG — 61

Highest field goal percentage in a single game (minimum 10 attempts)
1. GREG COOK, LOUISIANA ST. (vs. WICHITA STATE) (9-10) — .900

2 TONY GUY, KANSAS (vs. ARIZONA ST.) (13-15)
.867
3 RANDY REED, KANSAS STATE (vs. SAN FRANCISCO) (11-13) .846
4 DURAND MACKLIN, LOUISIANA ST. (vs. WICHITA STATE)
(9-11) .818
4 ISIAH THOMAS, INDIANA (vs. MARYLAND)
(9-11) .818

Highest field goal percentage in the tournament (minimum 20 attempts)

1 BYRON SCOTT, ARIZONA ST. (15-22) .682
2 RANDY REED, KANSAS STATE (22-33) .667
3 FRED ROBERTS, BRIGHAM YOUNG (23-35) .657
4 GREG COOK, LOUISIANA ST. (28-43) .651
5 DALE ELLIS, TENNESSEE (16-25) .640

FREE THROWS

Most free throws in a single game

1 JOHN BAGLEY, BOSTON COLLEGE (vs. WAKE FOREST) 15
2 AL GOODEN, BALL ST. (vs. BOSTON COLLEGE) 13
2 ISIAH THOMAS, INDIANA (vs. ALA.-BIRMINGHAM) 13
4 GLENN MARCUS, ALA.-BIRMINGHAM (vs. KENTUCKY) 12
4 ALEX BRADLEY, VILLANOVA (vs. HOUSTON) 12

Most total free throws in the tournament

1 ISIAH THOMAS, INDIANA 25
1 JEFF LAMP, VIRGINIA 25
1 DANNY AINGE, BRIGHAM YOUNG 25
4 3 tied for fourth place.

Most free throws attempted in a single game

1 JOHN BAGLEY, BOSTON COLLEGE (vs. WAKE FOREST) 21
2 GLENN MARCUS, ALA.-BIRMINGHAM (vs. KENTUCKY) 15
2 ISIAH THOMAS, INDIANA (vs. ALA.-BIRMINGHAM) 15
2 ALEX BRADLEY, VILLANOVA (vs. HOUSTON) 15
5 4 tied for fifth place.

Most free throws attempted in the tournament

1 JAMES WORTHY, N. CAROLINA 32
2 ISIAH THOMAS, INDIANA 31
3 CLIFF LEVINGSTON, WICHITA STATE 29
4 4 tied for fourth place.

Highest free throw percentage in a single game (minimum 7 attempts)

1 AL GOODEN, BALL ST. (vs. BOSTON COLLEGE)
(13-13) 1.000

2 JEFF LAMP, VIRGINIA (vs. LOUISIANA ST.)
(11-11) 1.000
3 JONATH NICHOLAS, ALA.-BIRMINGHAM (vs. WESTERN KY.)
(9-9) 1.000
4 3 tied for fourth place.

Highest free throw percentage in the tournament (minimum 15 attempts)

1 OLIVER ROBINSON, ALA.-BIRMINGHAM (17-17)
1.000
2 JEFF LAMP, VIRGINIA (25-26) .962
3 OTHELL WILSON, VIRGINIA (18-20) .900
4 LEE RAKER, VIRGINIA (17-19) .895
5 DANNY AINGE, BRIGHAM YOUNG (25-28) .893

REBOUNDS

Most rebounds in a single game

1 AL WOOD, N. CAROLINA (vs. KANSAS STATE) 17
2 CLIFF LEVINGSTON, WICHITA STATE (vs. IOWA) 16
2 DURAND MACKLIN, LOUISIANA ST. (vs. LAMAR) 16
2 CHARLES WILLIAMS, MARYLAND (vs. TENN.-CHATT.) 16
5 4 tied for fifth place.

Most total rebounds in the tournament

1 CLIFF LEVINGSTON, WICHITA STATE 53
2 RALPH SAMPSON, VIRGINIA 49
3 AL WOOD, N. CAROLINA 48
3 DURAND MACKLIN, LOUISIANA ST. 48
5 SAM PERKINS, N. CAROLINA 44

Most rebounds per game (minimum 2 games)

1 CLIFF LEVINGSTON, WICHITA STATE (53-4) 13.25
2 CHARLES WILLIAMS, MARYLAND (26-2) 13.00
3 DANNY VRANES, UTAH (25-2) 12.50
4 TRACY JACKSON, NOTRE DAME (23-2) 11.50
5 TOM CHAMBERS, UTAH (20-2) 10.00

ASSISTS

Most assists in a single game

1 ISIAH THOMAS, INDIANA (vs. MARYLAND) 14
2 ETHAN MARTIN, LOUISIANA ST. (vs. LAMAR) 12
2 ISIAH THOMAS, INDIANA (vs. ST. JOSEPH'S) 12
4 TONY MARTIN, WICHITA STATE (vs. SOUTHERN-B.R.) 11
4 ALVIN BROOKS, LAMAR (vs. LOUISIANA ST.) 11

Must total assists in the tournament

1 ETHAN MARTIN, LOUISIANA ST. 45
2 ISIAH THOMAS, INDIANA 43
3 RANDY SMITHSON, WICHITA STATE 22
3 TONY MARTIN, WICHITA STATE 22
3 JIMMY BLACK, N. CAROLINA 22

Most assists per game (minimum 2 appearances)

1 ETHAN MARTIN, LOUISIANA ST. (45-5) 9.00
2 ISIAH THOMAS, INDIANA (43-5) 8.60
3 ALVIN BROOKS, LAMAR (16-2) 8.00
4 MARK SMITH, ILLINOIS (13-2) 6.50
5 DARNELL VALENTINE, KANSAS (17-3) 5.67

TURNOVERS

Most turnovers in a single game

1 ALVIN JACKSON, SOUTHERN-B.R. (vs. WICHITA STATE) 8
1 ERNEST GRAHAM, MARYLAND (vs. INDIANA) 8
1 JERRY EAVES, LOUISVILLE (vs. ARKANSAS) 8
4 7 tied for fourth place.

Most total turnovers in the tournament

1 JIMMY BLACK, N. CAROLINA 21
2 CLIFF LEVINGSTON, WICHITA STATE 18
3 SAM PERKINS, N. CAROLINA 17
4 ETHAN MARTIN, LOUISIANA ST. 16
5 DURAND MACKLIN, LOUISIANA ST. 15

SHOTS BLOCKED

Most shots blocked in a single game

1 ANTOINE CARR, WICHITA STATE (vs. IOWA) 5
1 ROD HIGGINS, FRESNO STATE (vs. NORTHEASTERN) 5
3 6 tied for third place.

Most total shots blocked in the tournament

1 ANTOINE CARR, WICHITA STATE 12
2 RALPH SAMPSON, VIRGINIA 11
3 SAM PERKINS, N. CAROLINA 9
4 JAMES WORTHY, N. CAROLINA 6
4 RAY TOLBERT, INDIANA 6

STEALS

Most steals in a single game

1 SAM CLANCY, PITTSBURGH (vs. N. CAROLINA) 5
1 LESTER CONNER, OREGON STATE (vs. KANSAS STATE) 5
1 PHIL HOPSON, IDAHO (vs. PITTSBURGH) 5
4 At least 17 tied for fourth place.

Most total steals in the tournament

1 OTHELL WILSON, VIRGINIA 11
1 ETHAN MARTIN, LOUISIANA ST. 11
3 ISIAH THOMAS, INDIANA 10
3 LEONARD MITCHELL, LOUISIANA ST. 10
5 DARNELL VALENTINE, KANSAS 9

☺ TEAM RECORDS ☺

SCORING

Most points in a single game
1	LOUISIANA ST. (vs. LAMAR)	100
2	INDIANA (vs. MARYLAND)	99
3	LOUISIANA ST. (vs. WICHITA STATE)	96

Most total points in the tournament
1	INDIANA	394
2	LOUISIANA ST.	391
3	N. CAROLINA	345

Highest scoring average (minimum 2 games)
1	INDIANA (394-5)	78.80
2	LOUISIANA ST. (391-5)	78.20
3	ALA.-BIRMINGHAM (234-3)	78.00

FIELD GOALS

Most field goals in a single game
1	LOUISIANA ST. (vs. LAMAR)	45
2	INDIANA (vs. MARYLAND)	41
3	WICHITA STATE (vs. SOUTHERN-B.R.)	40

Most total field goals in the tournament
1	LOUISIANA ST.	163
2	INDIANA	153
3	N. CAROLINA	128

Most field goals attempted in a single game
1	WICHITA STATE (vs. LOUISIANA ST.)	75
2	LOUISIANA ST. (vs. LAMAR)	74
3	2 tied for third place.	

Most total field goals attempted in the tournament
1	LOUISIANA ST.	320
2	INDIANA	284
3	VIRGINIA	262

Highest field goal percentage in a single game
1	INDIANA (vs. ST. JOSEPH'S) (35-51)	.686
2	VILLANOVA (vs. HOUSTON) (33-49)	.674
3	INDIANA (vs. MARYLAND) (41-63)	.651

Highest field goal percentage in a tournament (minimum 2 games)
1	VILLANOVA (56-99)	.566
2	VA. COMMONWEALTH (52-93)	.559
3	LAMAR (62-114)	.544

FREE THROWS

Most free throws in a single game
1	ALA.-BIRMINGHAM (vs. WESTERN KY.)	35
2	VIRGINIA (vs. LOUISIANA ST.)	34
3	ALA.-BIRMINGHAM (vs. KENTUCKY)	31

Most total free throws in the tournament
1	VIRGINIA	95
2	N. CAROLINA	89
3	INDIANA	88

Most free throws attempted in a single game
1	ALA.-BIRMINGHAM (vs. WESTERN KY.)	41
2	ALA.-BIRMINGHAM (vs. KENTUCKY)	40
2	ARKANSAS (vs. MERCER)	40

Most total free throws attempted in the tournament
1	N. CAROLINA	123
2	INDIANA	116
3	VIRGINIA	115

Highest free throw percentage in a single game
1	TENN.-CHATT. (vs. MARYLAND) (11-11)	1.000
2	MISSOURI (vs. LAMAR) (11-12)	.917
3	VIRGINIA (vs. LOUISIANA ST.) (34-38)	.895

Highest free throw percentage in the tournament (minimum 2 games)
1	ILLINOIS (17-20)	.850
2	VIRGINIA (95-115)	.826
3	ALA.-BIRMINGHAM (84-105)	.800

Fewest free throws in a single game
1	ILLINOIS (vs. KANSAS STATE)	2
1	TENNESSEE (vs. VIRGINIA)	2
3	2 tied for third place.	

Lowest free throw percentage in a single game
1	HOUSTON (vs. VILLANOVA) (4-10)	.400
2	PRINCETON (vs. BRIGHAM YOUNG) (3-7)	.429
3	ARKANSAS (vs. MERCER) (19-40)	.475

Lowest free throw percentage in the tournament (minimum 2 games)
1	ARKANSAS (49-81)	.605
2	NOTRE DAME (22-34)	.647
3	NORTHEASTERN (34-51)	.667

REBOUNDS

Most rebounds in a single game
1	UTAH (vs. NORTHEASTERN)	50
2	WYOMING (vs. HOWARD)	45
3	BOSTON COLLEGE (vs. BALL ST.)	43

Most rebounds per game (minimum 2 games)
1	UTAH (81-2)	40.50
2	LOUISIANA ST. (182-5)	36.40
3	WICHITA STATE (145-4)	36.25

ASSISTS

Most assists in a single game
1	INDIANA (vs. ST. JOSEPH'S)	29
1	LOUISIANA ST. (vs. LAMAR)	29
3	WICHITA STATE (vs. SOUTHERN-B.R.)	27

Most assists per game (minimum 2 games)
1	WICHITA STATE (81-4)	20.25
2	INDIANA (101-5)	20.20
3	LOUISIANA ST. (90-5)	18.00

TURNOVERS

Most turnovers in a single game
1	WESTERN KY. (vs. ALA.-BIRMINGHAM)	25
2	WAKE FOREST (vs. BOSTON COLLEGE)	22
3	ARKANSAS (vs. LOUISIANA ST.)	21

Most turnovers per game (minimum 2 games)
1	WICHITA STATE (70-4)	17.50
2	LOUISIANA ST. (87-5)	17.40
3	JAMES MADISON (34-2)	17.00

SHOTS BLOCKED

Most shots blocked in a single game
1	LOUISVILLE (vs. ARKANSAS)	8
2	N. CAROLINA (vs. UTAH)	7
3	INDIANA (vs. MARYLAND)	6

Most shots blocked per game (minimum 2 games)
1	WICHITA STATE (15-4)	3.75
2	N. CAROLINA (18-5)	3.60
3	KANSAS (10-3)	3.33

STEALS

Most steals in a single game
1	ALA.-BIRMINGHAM (vs. WESTERN KY.)	14
2	BOSTON COLLEGE (vs. WAKE FOREST)	13
3	PITTSBURGH (vs. N. CAROLINA)	12

Most steals per game
1	PITTSBURGH (21-2)	10.50
2	ARKANSAS (26-3)	8.67
3	2 tied for third place.	

1982

| FIRST ROUND | SECOND ROUND | REGIONAL SEMIFINAL | REGIONAL FINAL | FINAL FOUR | REGIONAL FINAL | REGIONAL SEMIFINAL | SECOND ROUND | FIRST ROUND |

EAST

8 Ohio St. 48
James Madison 50
9 James Madison 55
N. Carolina 74
(bye)
1 N. Carolina 52
N. Carolina 70
5 St. John's 66
St. John's 68
12 Pennsylvania 56
Alabama 69
(bye)
4 Alabama 69
N. Carolina 68
6 St. Joseph's 62
Northeastern 72
11 Northeastern 63
Villanova 70
(bye)
3 Villanova 76 (3 ot)
Villanova 60
7 Wake Forest 74
Wake Forest 55
10 Old Dominion 57
*Memphis St. 66
(bye)
2 *Memphis St. 56

MIDWEST

8 Boston College 70
Boston College 82
9 San Francisco 66
Boston College 69
(bye)
1 DePaul 75
Boston College 92
5 Kansas St. 77
Kansas St. 65
12 Northern Ill. 68
Kansas St. 65
(bye)
4 Arkansas 64
Houston 63
6 Houston 94
Houston 78
11 Alcorn St. 84
Houston 79
(bye)
3 Tulsa 74
Houston 99
7 Marquette 67
Marquette 69
10 Evansville 62
Missouri 78
(bye)
2 Missouri 73

N. Carolina 63
Georgetown 62

MIDEAST

Tennessee 51
8 S.'western La. 57
Virginia 66
9 Tennessee 61
1 Virginia 54
(bye)
Ala.-Birmingham 68
Indiana 70
5 Indiana 94
Ala.-Birmingham 68
12 Robert Morris 62
4 Ala.-Birmingham 80
(bye)
Louisville 46
Middle Tenn. St. 56
6 Kentucky 44
Louisville 67
11 Middle Tenn. St. 50
3 Louisville 81
(bye)
Louisville 75
Tenn.-Chatt. 61
7 N. C. State 51
Minnesota 61
10 Tenn.-Chatt. 58
2 Minnesota 62
(bye)

WEST

Wyoming 43
8 Wyoming 61
Georgetown 58
9 USC 58
1 Georgetown 51
(bye)
Georgetown 69
West Virginia 46
5 West Virginia 102
Fresno St. 40
12 N. Carolina A&T 72
4 Fresno St. 50
(bye)
Georgetown 50
Iowa 67
6 Iowa 70
Idaho 42
11 Northeast La. 63
3 Idaho 69 (ot)
(bye)
*Oregon St. 45
Pepperdine 51
7 Pepperdine 99
*Oregon St. 60
10 Pittsburgh 88
2 *Oregon St. 70
(bye)

*Oregon State's and Memphis State's participation in 1982 tournament vacated.

In 1982, two great teams met for the national championship in front of 61,612 enthralled spectators in the New Orleans Superdome, and those who were close enough saw the game of their lives. It was Hoya Paranoia against Carolina Blue. Dean Smith, who had come up short in 1981 for the sixth time in the Final Four, against his friend and protege, John Thompson, who had built a national power in D.C. less than a decade after he was hired to salvage the wreckage known as Georgetown basketball.

North Carolina vs. Georgetown was a mutual admiration society fought down to the wire. It was two outstanding veteran teams with brilliant freshmen—Patrick Ewing for Georgetown and Michael Jordan for North Carolina. It was old friends—not just Smith and Thompson, but all-Americans James Worthy and Eric (Sleepy) Floyd as well, who had grown up together in Gastonia, North Carolina, while playing for rival high schools. Now they were once again on opposite sides of the court.

In 1982, the name of the game was defense, and nobody played it better than Georgetown. They attacked the opposition, chest to chest, and if anyone was foolish enough to slip through the vise and take it to the hoop, they had to contend with the ferociously mobile, 7-foot freshman Patrick Ewing. The Hoyas beat you by taking you out of your game and breaking your spirit; when they took the floor against the Tar Heels they had given up only 174 points in four tournament contests, an average of 43.5 points per game. (Their defense spirit continued into the Final Four, with only 342 points scored in toto in the semis and the title game; the last time so few points had been scored in the Final Four was in 1949.)

Even though the Tar Heels had struggled to get to the title contest (three of their four tournament games had been decided by 5 points or less) they had a season record of 30-2 and were considered stronger than the team that had lost in the Finals to Indiana in 1981. The terrific twosome of Sam Perkins and James Worthy were back in the front court, one year older and more experienced, and Worthy was performing without the hardware in his ankle that had caused him to play the entire previous season in pain. The third front-court man, 6-8 Matt Doherty, was a solid role player. Senior point guard Jimmy Black, the heart and soul of the team, was on a mission to bring home a title for his beloved coach. And the explosive freshman Michael Jordan, the off-guard, was the ACC Rookie of the Year.

There were other good teams in the field. Denny Crum still had four of his starters from Louisville's 1980 championship team. Houston had Akeem Olajuwon, but the soon-to-be-dominating young African center still had a lot to learn about the game. Virginia—with Ralph Sampson, Othell Wilson, and Ricky Stokes—was good. As was Gene Bartow's Alabama-Birmingham, and defensive-minded Oregon State. There were a lot of good teams. But North Carolina and Georgetown were the best.

From the beginning of the title game, Ewing was a fire-breathing dragon on defense. Every time Carolina threw up a shot, he swatted it away. Never mind that he was called for goaltending five times; the Tar Heels didn't actually put the ball through the hoop from the floor with Ewing in the game until six and a half minutes were left in the half. Still, after falling into an early 6-point hole, Carolina came back to tie the score at 18; from then on, for almost thirty minutes, neither team led by more than 4.

Smith, a master of strategy, adjusted to Ewing's presence. His team began to find the gaps in the Hoyas' zone, and James Worthy slipped in the back door. The All-American forward carried the Tar Heel offense, while Georgetown's Ewing and Floyd kept pace on the other end. Finally, just before the half ended, Georgetown took a 1-point lead on a slam dunk by Ewing off the fast break.

With Georgetown holding a 47-43 lead midway through the second half, Sleepy Floyd missed a lay-up and North Carolina took advantage of the opportunity. The Tar Heels came back, with Worthy finally putting them into the lead on two thunderous dunks. Now it was Carolina's turn to try to put the Hoyas away. But they just couldn't do it.

With 57 seconds remaining, Floyd pumped in a difficult jumper to put Georgetown back in the lead. Carolina patiently worked the ball around, and called time 25 seconds later. The play Smith called in the huddle was designed for Michael Jordan. The freshman moved across from the right side to the left side of the court, where Jimmy Black found him with the ball. Jordan floated skyward, and lifted a feathery 16-foot jumper toward the hoop. It fluttered through, touching nothing but net as it flip-flopped North Carolina into a 1-point lead. Thompson, not wanting to give Smith a chance to adjust his defense, did not call time-out to set up a last shot. Instead Georgetown took the ball out, and sophomore point guard Fred Brown dribbled downcourt. He looked for Sleepy Floyd, but Floyd was covered. Eric Smith called for the ball, and Brown picked it up off his dribble and started to pass. Smith, thinking he had found an opening in the Tar Heel defense, moved away from Brown, toward the hoop. And just as Brown started to release the ball, James Worthy moved up to cut off the passing lane. Too late, Fred Brown realized his pass would never reach his teammate, that it would end up in Worthy's hands. "If I'd had a rubber band," Brown said later, "I would've pulled it back."

When it was over, the Tar Heels had taken the first 1-point decision in a final since 1959. Dean Smith finally had his championship. Jimmy Black fell to his knees in joy and Michael Jordan lifted him up with the words "It's over." Dean Smith was hoisted skyward for the ritual cutting of the nets, and John Thompson held Fred Brown in his arms and consoled him. Life goes on.

FIRST ROUND EAST

Ohio State (48)   Coach: Eldon Miller

	Min.	Total FG/FGA	Pct.	FT/FTA	Pct.	Reb. O/T	A	TO	PF	S	Blk	TP	PPM
CAMPBELL, T.	38	4/13	.308	6/9	.667	-/6	0	4	3	1	0	14	.368
KELLOGG, C.	38	5/10	.500	4/4	1.000	-/12	0	2	1	1	0	14	.368
WAITERS, G.	25	3/4	.750	0/0	.000	-/5	1	1	2	0	0	6	.240
TAYLOR, T.	24	2/6	.333	0/0	.000	-/0	1	1	4	0	0	4	.167
HUGGINS, L.	28	1/5	.200	0/0	.000	-/1	0	2	2	0	0	2	.071
STOKES, R.	20	1/4	.250	0/0	.000	-/1	3	3	3	0	0	2	.100
JONES, D.	10	1/4	.250	0/0	.000	-/0	0	0	3	1	0	2	.200
JOHNSON, B.	4	0/0	.000	0/-	-	-/0	0	0	0	0	0	0	.000
KIRCHNER, C.	13	2/3	.667	0/0	.000	-/5	0	1	1	1	1	4	.308
Totals	200	19/49	.388	10/13	.769	-/30	5	14	19	4	1	48	.240

James Madison (55)   Coach: Lou Campanelli

	Min.	Total FG/FGA	Pct.	FT/FTA	Pct.	Reb. O/T	A	TO	PF	S	Blk	TP	PPM
JACKSON, D.	11	0/2	.000	1/2	.500	-/2	0	2	4	0	0	1	.091
TOWNES, L.	38	6/12	.500	0/1	.000	-/9	0	6	3	1	0	12	.316
RULAND, D.	37	7/11	.636	4/4	1.000	-/4	0	1	1	1	0	18	.486
FISHER, C.	34	1/5	.200	3/5	.600	-/0	1	0	2	1	0	5	.147
DUPONT, D.	34	3/6	.500	0/1	.000	-/7	4	2	1	2	0	6	.176
MASLOFF, J.	5	0/0	.000	1/4	.250	-/0	0	0	0	0	0	1	.200
STEELE, D.	11	0/1	.000	2/2	1.000	-/0	2	0	0	0	0	2	.182
BRADLEY, K.	24	3/3	1.000	2/2	1.000	-/5	2	1	1	2	1	8	.333
BOLER, W.	6	1/2	.500	0/0	.000	-/0	0	0	1	0	0	2	.333
Totals	200	21/42	.500	13/21	.619	-/27	9	12	13	7	1	55	.275

Team Rebounds: James Madison 0; Ohio State 3. Disqualified: None. Technical fouls: None.

	1st Half	2nd Half	Final
Ohio State	29	19	48
James Madison	22	33	55

St. John's (66)   Coach: Lou Carnesecca

	Min.	Total FG/FGA	Pct.	FT/FTA	Pct.	Reb. O/T	A	TO	PF	S	Blk	TP	PPM
RUSSELL, D.	37	5/11	.455	4/4	1.000	-/8	2	4	3	1	3	14	.378
GOODWIN, B.	40	9/12	.750	3/5	.600	-/5	3	1	3	1	0	21	.525
ALLEN, J.	20	0/1	.000	0/1	.000	-/5	0	0	3	0	2	0	.000
KELLY, B.	38	2/3	.667	4/6	.667	-/2	3	4	3	1	0	8	.211
MULLIN, C.	37	5/13	.385	9/12	.750	-/4	5	2	1	1	1	19	.514
WENNINGTON, B.	19	2/4	.500	0/0	.000	-/8	0	1	2	1	3	4	.211
GARRISON, G.	2	0/0	.000	0/0	.000	-/0	0	1	1	0	0	0	.000
STEWART, R.	4	0/0	.000	0/0	.000	-/1	0	0	0	0	0	0	.000
WILLIAMS, K.	3	0/0	.000	0/0	.000	-/0	0	1	1	0	0	0	.000
Totals	200	23/44	.523	20/28	.714	-/33	13	14	17	5	9	66	.330

Pennsylvania (56)   Coach: Bob Weinhauer

	Min.	Total FG/FGA	Pct.	FT/FTA	Pct.	Reb. O/T	A	TO	PF	S	Blk	TP	PPM
BROWN, M.	30	6/14	.429	5/7	.714	-/9	1	4	4	1	0	17	.567
LITTLE, P.	26	3/13	.231	0/0	.000	-/5	1	2	5	1	0	6	.231
RAWLINGS, A.	33	6/18	.333	2/3	.667	-/5	1	2	2	1	1	14	.424
OLIPHANT, W.	19	4/6	.667	0/0	.000	-/5	2	1	3	1	1	8	.421
MCCAFFERY, F.	32	1/4	.250	0/1	.000	-/0	3	0	2	2	0	2	.063
LARDNER, D.	18	2/5	.400	0/1	.000	-/1	0	0	2	0	0	4	.222
NOON, G.	15	1/4	.250	1/2	.500	-/3	2	1	5	1	0	3	.200
RACINE, K.	24	1/4	.250	0/1	.000	-/2	2	0	2	1	0	2	.083
MALONEY, R.	1	0/1	.000	0/0	.000	-/0	0	0	0	0	0	0	.000
ARNOLIE, A.	1	0/0	.000	0/0	.000	-/0	0	0	0	0	0	0	.000
WOLF, T.	1	0/0	.000	0/0	.000	-/0	0	0	0	0	0	0	.000
WARREN, K.	0	0/0	.000	0/0	.000	-/0	0	0	1	0	0	0	-
Totals	200	24/69	.348	8/15	.533	-/30	12	10	26	8	2	56	.280

Team Rebounds: St. John's 6; Pennsylvania 9. Disqualified: Pennsylvania—Little, Noon. Technical fouls: St. John's—Russell. Player who played 0 min. played less than 1 min.

	1st Half	2nd Half	Final
St. John's	31	35	66
Pennsylvania	28	28	56

St. Joseph's (62)   Coach: Jim Boyle

	Min.	Total FG/FGA	Pct.	FT/FTA	Pct.	Reb. O/T	A	TO	PF	S	Blk	TP	PPM
LOJENSKI, B.	16	0/2	.000	4/5	.800	-/0	0	3	2	0	0	4	.250
MCFARLAN, L.	34	11/17	.647	2/3	.667	-/3	2	2	1	1	0	24	.706
COSTNER, T.	39	5/6	.833	0/0	.000	-/6	0	3	5	1	1	10	.256
CLARK, J.	33	3/8	.375	0/0	.000	-/0	1	2	5	2	0	6	.182
WARRICK, B.	37	4/16	.250	2/2	1.000	-/2	10	2	3	2	0	10	.270
DEARBORN, M.	31	3/4	.750	0/0	.000	-/7	0	0	2	1	0	6	.194
MITCHELL, B.	10	1/1	1.000	0/0	.000	-/0	0	1	1	0	0	2	.200
Totals	200	27/54	.500	8/10	.800	-/18	13	13	19	7	1	62	.310

Northeastern (63)   Coach: Jim Calhoun

	Min.	Total FG/FGA	Pct.	FT/FTA	Pct.	Reb. O/T	A	TO	PF	S	Blk	TP	PPM
JEFFERSON, E.	37	8/11	.727	2/3	.667	-/3	1	5	1	1	0	18	.486
HALSEL, M.	39	3/7	.429	5/9	.556	-/13	1	3	2	2	0	11	.282
LEITAD, D.	38	4/6	.667	2/2	1.000	-/4	0	3	2	0	0	10	.263
MOSS, P.	40	9/18	.500	6/7	.857	-/2	2	4	3	3	0	24	.600
BRYANT, S.	19	0/1	.000	0/0	.000	-/1	2	5	2	0	0	0	.000
ROBINSON, P.	21	0/0	.000	0/1	.000	-/1	4	2	2	1	0	0	.000
BRASWELL, R.	2	0/0	.000	0/0	.000	-/1	0	1	1	0	0	0	.000
KING, J.	3	0/0	.000	0/0	.000	-/0	0	0	1	0	0	0	.000
HEINECK, C.	1	0/0	.000	0/0	.000	-/0	0	0	0	0	0	0	.000
Totals	200	24/43	.558	15/22	.682	-/25	10	23	14	9	0	63	.315

Team Rebounds: Northeastern 5; St. Joseph's 4. Disqualified: St. Joseph's—Costner, Clark. Technical fouls: None.

	1st Half	2nd Half	Final
St. Joseph's	36	26	62
Northeastern	35	28	63

Wake Forest (74)   Coach: Carl Tacy

	Min.	Total FG/FGA	Pct.	FT/FTA	Pct.	Reb. O/T	A	TO	PF	S	Blk	TP	PPM
TOMS, J.	19	0/3	.000	0/0	.000	-/3	0	2	3	1	0	0	.000
MORGAN, G.	31	4/5	.800	3/5	.600	-/5	0	1	5	0	0	11	.355
JOHNSTONE, J.	23	3/6	.500	0/0	.000	-/1	0	2	5	2	0	6	.261
YOUNG, D.	36	5/7	.714	3/4	.750	-/3	6	3	2	2	0	13	.361
HELMS, M.	35	7/9	.778	4/5	.800	-/0	0	1	2	1	0	18	.514
DAVIS, S.	4	0/0	.000	0/0	.000	-/0	1	1	0	0	0	0	.000
RUDD, D.	1	0/1	.000	0/0	.000	-/1	0	0	0	0	0	0	.000
KEPLEY, C.	4	0/0	.000	0/0	.000	-/0	0	0	1	0	0	0	.000
WALLACE, S.	1	0/0	.000	0/0	.000	-/0	0	0	1	0	0	0	.000
CHARLES, S.	9	0/1	.000	0/1	.000	-/0	1	0	1	0	0	0	.000
GARBER, L.	7	1/1	1.000	6/9	.667	-/0	1	0	1	0	0	8	1.143
TEACHEY, A.	30	6/11	.545	6/7	.857	-/12	1	1	0	0	1	18	.600
Totals	200	26/44	.591	22/31	.710	-/25	10	11	20	6	1	74	.370

Old Dominion (57)   Coach: Paul Webb

	Min.	Total FG/FGA	Pct.	FT/FTA	Pct.	Reb. O/T	A	TO	PF	S	Blk	TP	PPM
SOUTHERLAND, T.	20	1/3	.333	0/0	.000	-/2	0	0	3	0	0	2	.100
MCADOO, R.	32	7/12	.583	3/5	.600	-/12	0	3	4	1	0	17	.531
WEST, M.	32	3/7	.429	0/0	.000	-/4	0	3	5	0	0	6	.188
SMITH, C.	30	5/12	.417	3/4	.750	-/2	3	1	3	1	0	13	.433
MANN, B.	32	1/9	.111	2/2	1.000	-/1	4	3	3	0	0	4	.125
ROBINSON, G.	26	2/4	.500	0/0	.000	-/2	2	2	5	1	0	4	.154
DEAN, M.	1	0/0	.000	0/0	.000	-/0	0	0	0	0	0	0	.000
DAVIS, M.	4	0/2	.000	1/2	.500	-/2	0	0	3	0	0	1	.250
LAMBERT, H.	20	3/6	.500	4/5	.800	-/5	0	1	1	0	2	10	.500
FACKA, F.	1	0/0	.000	0/0	.000	-/0	0	0	0	0	0	0	.000
BUCKLAND, G.	1	0/1	.000	0/0	.000	-/0	0	0	0	0	0	0	.000
GRIEKSPOOR, E.	1	0/2	.000	0/0	.000	-/3	0	0	0	0	0	0	.000
Totals	200	22/58	.379	13/18	.722	-/33	9	13	27	3	2	57	.285

Team Rebounds: Wake Forest 3; Old Dominion 3. Disqualified: Wake Forest—Morgan, Johnstone; Old Dominion—West, Robinson. Technical fouls: Old Dominion—Griekspoor.

	1st Half	2nd Half	Final
Wake Forest	30	44	74
Old Dominion	28	29	57

FIRST ROUND MIDWEST

Boston College (70)   Coach: Tom Davis

	Min.	Total FG / FGA	Pct.	FT / FTA	Pct.	Reb. O / T	A	TO	PF	S	Blk	TP	PPM
SHRIGLEY, R.	35	4/ 9	.444	4/ 6	.667	-/ 4	3	0	2	2	0	12	.343
CLARK	31	5/ 7	.714	0/ 0	.000	-/ 3	3	6	1	0	0	10	.323
MURPHY	17	5/ 6	.833	5/ 8	.625	-/ 6	1	2	5	0	0	15	.882
CHANDLER	28	3/ 8	.375	2/ 5	.400	-/ 0	1	0	1	0	0	8	.286
BAGLEY	23	3/ 5	.600	4/ 6	.667	-/ 0	1	2	3	2	0	10	.435
ADAMS, M.	25	1/ 1	1.000	3/ 5	.600	-/ 2	6	4	1	1	0	5	.200
GARRIS	24	2/ 6	.333	0/ 0	.000	-/ 7	0	2	1	0	3	4	.167
SCHMIDT, M.	8	0/ 0	.000	2/ 2	1.000	-/ 2	2	0	1	0	0	2	.250
ADAMS, B.	8	1/ 3	.333	0/ 1	.000	-/ 3	0	0	1	0	0	2	.250
TALLEY	1	1/ 1	1.000	0/ 0	.000	-/ 1	0	0	0	0	0	2	2.000
Totals	200	25/46	.543	20/33	.606	-/29	16	16	16	5	3	70	.350

San Francisco (66)   Coach: Peter Barry

	Min.	Total FG / FGA	Pct.	FT / FTA	Pct.	Reb. O / T	A	TO	PF	S	Blk	TP	PPM
MARTENS	26	4/ 6	.667	2/ 3	.667	-/ 3	3	2	2	1	2	10	.385
HEGWOOD	21	2/ 5	.400	0/ 0	.000	-/ 8	0	2	5	0	0	4	.190
BRYANT	37	4/ 9	.444	2/ 3	.667	-/10	3	0	4	1	0	10	.270
MCALISTER	31	2/11	.182	0/ 0	.000	-/ 3	3	2	4	1	0	4	.129
DAILEY	40	13/25	.520	2/ 2	1.000	-/ 1	2	4	4	1	2	28	.700
SLAYMAKER	13	1/ 2	.500	3/ 5	.600	-/ 1	2	1	0	0	0	5	.385
BOOKER	23	2/ 4	.500	1/ 2	.500	-/ 2	5	2	4	0	0	5	.217
SPEIGHT	9	0/ 1	.000	0/ 0	.000	-/ 1	0	1	2	0	0	0	.000
Totals	200	28/63	.444	10/15	.667	-/29	18	14	25	4	4	66	.330

Team Rebounds: Boston College 5; San Francisco 4. Disqualified: Boston College—Murphy; San Francisco—Hegwood. Technical fouls: Boston College—Bench, Coach Davis, B. Adams.

	1st Half	2nd Half	Final
Boston College	40	30	70
San Francisco	28	38	66

Kansas State (77)   Coach: Jack Hartman

	Min.	Total FG / FGA	Pct.	FT / FTA	Pct.	Reb. O / T	A	TO	PF	S	Blk	TP	PPM
NEALY, E.	-	2/ 7	.286	1/ 2	.500	-/ 5	2	0	1	1	0	5	-
REED, R.	-	7/ 9	.778	1/ 4	.250	-/ 4	1	3	2	0	1	15	-
CRAFT, L.	-	5/ 7	.714	11/11	1.000	-/ 8	4	3	4	0	3	21	-
JANKOVICH, T.	-	3/ 6	.500	7/ 8	.875	-/ 1	4	3	2	0	0	13	-
ADAMS, T.	-	4/ 9	.444	2/ 2	1.000	-/ 4	2	1	2	2	0	10	-
GALVAO, E.	-	3/ 4	.750	7/ 8	.875	-/ 5	2	2	2	0	0	13	-
WATKINS, L.	-	0/ 2	.000	0/ 0	.000	-/ 2	0	2	2	0	0	0	-
WILLIAMS, K.	-	0/ 0	.000	0/ 0	.000	-/ 0	0	0	0	0	0	0	-
RORABAUGH, L.	-	0/ 0	.000	0/ 0	.000	-/ 0	0	0	0	0	0	0	-
Totals	200	24/44	.545	29/35	.829	-/29	15	14	15	3	4	77	.385

Northern Illinois (68)   Coach: John McDougall

	Min.	Total FG / FGA	Pct.	FT / FTA	Pct.	Reb. O / T	A	TO	PF	S	Blk	TP	PPM
COLLINS	-	0/ 5	.000	0/ 0	.000	-/ 2	3	1	2	0	0	0	-
DILLON	-	4/10	.400	0/ 0	.000	-/ 2	6	1	5	1	0	8	-
RAYHORN	-	6/13	.462	5/ 8	.625	-/13	0	0	5	2	2	17	-
GRAY	-	4/ 9	.444	2/ 2	1.000	-/ 1	2	3	2	0	1	10	-
HAYES	-	9/17	.529	0/ 0	.000	-/ 2	5	1	2	4	0	18	-
ARMATO	-	1/ 1	1.000	0/ 0	.000	-/ 1	2	2	1	1	0	2	-
GREEN	-	0/ 1	.000	0/ 0	.000	-/ 1	1	0	0	0	0	0	-
LINDFORS	-	4/ 7	.571	1/ 2	.500	-/ 4	2	0	4	0	0	9	-
JOHNSON	-	1/ 1	1.000	2/ 2	1.000	-/ 1	0	0	2	0	0	4	-
PADDEN	-	0/ 0	.000	0/ 0	.000	-/ 0	1	0	0	0	0	0	-
MITCHELL	-	0/ 1	.000	0/ 0	.000	-/ 0	0	1	1	0	0	0	-
PARYS	-	0/ 0	.000	0/ 0	.000	-/ 1	0	0	1	0	0	0	-
Totals	200	29/65	.446	10/14	.714	-/28	22	9	25	8	3	68	.340

Team Rebounds: Kansas State 1; Northern Ill. 5. Disqualified: Northern Ill.—Dillon, Rayhorn. Technical fouls: Northern Ill.—bench.

	1st Half	2nd Half	Final
Kansas State	31	46	77
Northern Ill.	25	43	68

Houston (94)   Coach: Guy Lewis

	Min.	Total FG / FGA	Pct.	FT / FTA	Pct.	Reb. O / T	A	TO	PF	S	Blk	TP	PPM
DREXLER, C.	31	8/11	.727	1/ 4	.250	2/ 4	3	2	2	5	3	17	.548
YOUNG, M.	31	8/10	.800	2/ 2	1.000	0/ 6	4	1	2	2	0	18	.581
MICHEAUX, L.	30	5/ 7	.714	1/ 3	.333	3/ 6	0	4	4	1	1	11	.367
ROSE, L.	24	4/ 6	.667	0/ 0	.000	0/ 1	3	2	2	1	1	8	.333
WILLIAMS, R.	31	7/14	.500	11/12	.917	1/ 3	2	5	3	1	0	25	.806
DAVIS, E.	21	0/ 0	.000	0/ 0	.000	0/ 1	3	1	2	0	0	0	.000
DICKENS, E.	3	0/ 0	.000	0/ 0	.000	0/ 1	0	0	0	0	0	0	.000
ANDERS, B.	3	0/ 0	.000	0/ 0	.000	0/ 0	1	1	0	0	0	0	.000
OLAJUWON, A.	19	5/ 8	.625	2/ 6	.333	2/ 7	0	2	3	1	1	12	.632
GETTYS, R.	3	0/ 1	.000	0/ 0	.000	0/ 0	0	1	1	0	0	0	.000
BUNCE, D.	2	0/ 0	.000	0/ 0	.000	0/ 0	0	0	0	0	0	0	.000
WILLIAMS, B.	2	1/ 1	1.000	1/ 2	.500	0/ 1	0	1	0	0	0	3	1.500
Totals	200	38/58	.655	18/29	.621	8/30	15	20	20	11	6	94	.470

Alcorn State (84)   Coach: Davey Whitney

	Min.	Total FG / FGA	Pct.	FT / FTA	Pct.	Reb. O / T	A	TO	PF	S	Blk	TP	PPM
BRANDON, A.	10	1/ 2	.500	0/ 0	.000	0/ 0	1	0	1	0	0	2	.200
IRVING, A.	31	10/13	.769	1/ 3	.333	3/ 6	2	3	2	3	0	21	.677
COLLIER, T.	34	7/14	.500	2/ 5	.400	4/ 6	0	3	3	1	1	16	.471
ARCHIE, E.	29	2/ 8	.250	4/ 4	1.000	2/ 3	6	6	4	2	0	8	.276
PHELPS, M.	27	4/ 9	.444	1/ 2	.500	1/ 2	1	2	3	0	0	9	.333
HARALSON, D.	4	0/ 1	.000	0/ 0	.000	0/ 1	0	0	3	0	0	0	.000
HORTON, R.	21	3/ 9	.333	0/ 0	.000	0/ 2	3	1	2	0	0	6	.286
BOND, W.	1	0/ 1	.000	1/ 2	.500	0/ 0	0	0	0	0	0	1	1.000
GOODIN, B.	6	2/ 3	.667	4/ 4	1.000	2/ 2	1	0	0	0	0	8	1.333
CLAYTON, D.	2	0/ 1	.000	0/ 0	.000	0/ 0	0	0	0	0	0	0	.000
MILBURN, R.	25	5/10	.500	1/ 2	.500	5/ 9	2	2	4	2	0	11	.440
WILLIAMS, D.	8	0/ 3	.000	2/ 2	1.000	0/ 3	0	0	1	0	1	2	.250
WHITE, W.	2	0/ 0	.000	0/ 0	.000	0/ 0	0	0	0	0	0	0	.000
Totals	200	34/74	.459	16/24	.667	17/34	16	17	23	8	2	84	.420

Team Rebounds: Houston 2; Alcorn St. 3. Disqualified: None. Technical fouls: None.

	1st Half	2nd Half	Final
Houston	40	54	94
Alcorn St.	35	49	84

Marquette (67)   Coach: Hank Raymonds

	Min.	Total FG / FGA	Pct.	FT / FTA	Pct.	Reb. O / T	A	TO	PF	S	Blk	TP	PPM
MAROTTA	8	0/ 2	.000	0/ 0	.000	-/ 3	2	0	0	0	0	0	.000
NYENHUIS	37	6/10	.600	2/ 6	.333	-/ 8	2	3	3	1	2	14	.378
WILSON	39	2/ 5	.400	2/ 3	.667	-/ 3	7	3	3	2	2	6	.154
RIVERS, G.	39	6/17	.353	4/ 5	.800	-/ 2	5	7	4	0	1	16	.410
JOHNSON, M.	3	0/ 0	.000	0/ 0	.000	-/ 0	0	0	0	0	0	0	.000
JOHNSON, D.	33	4/ 8	.500	2/ 3	.667	-/ 5	0	1	4	3	2	10	.303
SCHLUNDT, T.	12	0/ 2	.000	0/ 0	.000	-/ 6	1	1	1	0	0	0	.000
MARQUARDT	29	9/13	.692	3/ 4	.750	-/ 5	0	0	2	1	0	21	.724
Totals	200	27/57	.474	13/21	.619	-/32	17	15	17	7	7	67	.335

Evansville (62)   Coach: Dick Walters

	Min.	Total FG / FGA	Pct.	FT / FTA	Pct.	Reb. O / T	A	TO	PF	S	Blk	TP	PPM
BULLOCK, T.	36	6/13	.462	5/ 6	.833	-/13	3	5	5	1	0	17	.472
JOHNSON, R.	33	4/11	.364	0/ 0	.000	-/ 6	3	4	5	0	0	8	.242
TURAM, E.	19	0/ 3	.000	0/ 0	.000	-/ 4	0	2	5	2	1	0	.000
HARRIS, E.	40	4/ 7	.571	2/ 2	1.000	-/ 3	1	4	1	3	0	10	.250
LEAF, B.	35	9/25	.360	5/ 5	1.000	-/ 6	0	3	3	1	1	23	.657
EMBREY, J.	1	0/ 0	.000	0/ 0	.000	-/ 0	0	0	0	0	0	0	.000
LENDY, M.	5	0/ 1	.000	0/ 0	.000	-/ 1	0	0	0	0	0	0	.000
MCKINSTRY, R.	20	1/ 2	.500	2/ 6	.333	-/ 3	0	1	3	0	0	4	.200
PERRY, K.	11	0/ 2	.000	0/ 0	.000	-/ 1	0	0	1	0	0	0	.000
Totals	200	24/64	.375	14/19	.737	-/37	7	19	23	7	2	62	.310

Team Rebounds: Marquette 0; Evansville 5. Disqualified: Evansville—Bullock, Johnson, Turam. Technical fouls: None.

	1st Half	2nd Half	Final
Marquette	29	38	67
Evansville	20	42	62

FIRST ROUND MIDEAST

Southwestern Louisiana (57)   Coach: Bobby Paschal

	Min.	Total FG/FGA	Pct.	FT/FTA	Pct.	Reb. O/T	A	TO	PF	S	Blk	TP	PPM
BROWN, D.	38	6/10	.600	1/2	.500	-/7	0	1	3	1	0	13	.342
WARNER, G.	35	3/8	.375	0/0	.000	-/3	0	3	4	0	1	6	.171
GAY, D.	40	2/7	.286	4/4	1.000	-/4	1	2	1	1	0	8	.200
TURNER, A.	37	4/9	.444	6/9	.667	-/1	0	0	4	1	1	14	.378
COLLINS, J.	39	5/7	.714	0/0	.000	-/1	0	4	5	3	0	10	.256
ALLEN, A.	11	2/4	.500	0/0	.000	-/0	0	2	0	0	0	4	.364
Totals	200	23/46	.500	11/15	.733	-/16	1	12	17	6	2	57	.285

Tennessee (61)   Coach: Don Devoe

	Min.	Total FG/FGA	Pct.	FT/FTA	Pct.	Reb. O/T	A	TO	PF	S	Blk	TP	PPM
ELLIS, D.	40	9/15	.600	5/6	.833	-/6	2	4	3	2	0	23	.575
RAY, S.	34	2/5	.400	0/0	.000	-/4	2	0	2	2	1	4	.118
BURTON, W.	25	1/3	.333	0/0	.000	-/4	1	1	2	0	0	2	.080
BEAMAN, T.	30	4/6	.667	0/2	.000	-/2	6	2	3	2	0	8	.267
BROOKS, M.	33	5/10	.500	6/6	1.000	-/1	1	5	4	0	1	16	.485
HYATT, G.	17	0/1	.000	2/2	1.000	-/1	2	1	0	1	0	2	.118
WOODS, K.	6	1/1	1.000	0/0	.000	-/0	0	0	0	0	0	2	.333
FEDERMANN, D.	15	2/2	1.000	0/0	.000	-/3	0	1	3	0	0	4	.267
Totals	200	24/43	.558	13/16	.813	-/21	14	14	17	7	2	61	.305

Team Rebounds: Tennessee 6; S'western La. 6. Disqualified: S'western La.—Collins. Technical fouls: None. S'western La. credited with 2 points on opponent tip-in.

	1st Half	2nd Half	Final
S'western La.	29	28	57
Tennessee	29	32	61

Indiana (94)   Coach: Bob Knight

	Min.	Total FG/FGA	Pct.	FT/FTA	Pct.	Reb. O/T	A	TO	PF	S	Blk	TP	PPM
WITTMAN, R.	28	5/7	.714	6/6	1.000	-/3	1	0	0	2	0	16	.571
KITCHEL, T.	22	4/8	.500	2/2	1.000	-/3	3	1	2	0	0	10	.455
BOUCHIE, S.	24	4/7	.571	0/0	.000	-/9	0	2	3	0	1	8	.333
THOMAS, J.	28	6/9	.667	1/1	1.000	-/8	3	0	2	2	0	13	.464
DAKICH, D.	12	3/4	.750	2/2	1.000	-/2	0	1	0	0	0	8	.667
MORGAN, W.	14	1/3	.333	2/2	1.000	-/5	2	3	3	0	0	4	.286
FRANZ, C.	9	0/0	.000	2/2	1.000	-/1	0	0	3	0	0	2	.222
CAMERON, C.	8	1/2	.500	0/0	.000	-/1	1	1	1	0	0	2	.250
BLAB, U.	17	4/7	.571	5/9	.556	-/7	0	2	1	0	1	13	.765
FLOWERS, J.	13	2/9	.222	1/4	.250	-/7	0	3	3	0	0	5	.385
BROWN, T.	25	6/13	.462	1/2	.500	-/4	1	1	1	0	0	13	.520
Totals	200	36/69	.522	22/30	.733	-/50	11	14	19	4	2	94	.470

Robert Morris (62)   Coach: Matt Furjanic

	Min.	Total FG/FGA	Pct.	FT/FTA	Pct.	Reb. O/T	A	TO	PF	S	Blk	TP	PPM
COLES, P.	28	2/3	.667	4/6	.667	-/4	1	1	4	1	1	8	.286
UNDERMAN, T.	8	1/2	.500	0/0	.000	-/2	0	2	0	0	0	2	.250
JUNK, G.	26	0/1	.000	2/2	1.000	-/5	0	0	2	0	0	2	.077
HARRIS, C.	33	5/18	.278	1/2	.500	-/0	2	3	4	2	0	11	.333
CLANAGAN, B.	1	0/0	.000	0/0	.000	-/0	0	0	0	0	0	0	.000
HENSLER, T.	11	1/1	1.000	1/2	.500	-/3	0	0	2	1	0	3	.273
PARKS, T.	24	3/9	.333	1/2	.500	-/3	0	3	5	0	0	7	.292
RUSSELL, J.	13	0/4	.000	0/0	.000	-/2	1	0	3	0	0	0	.000
DOBBS, M.	17	1/2	.500	2/4	.500	-/3	0	1	1	0	0	4	.235
MCFARLAND, T.	1	0/0	.000	0/1	.000	-/0	0	0	0	0	0	0	.000
GRANT, F.	38	11/19	.579	3/5	.600	-/1	4	5	3	2	1	25	.658
Totals	200	24/59	.407	14/24	.583	-/23	8	15	24	6	2	62	.310

Team Rebounds: Indiana 2; Robert Morris 0. Disqualified: Robert Morris—Parks. Technical fouls: None.

	1st Half	2nd Half	Final
Indiana	48	46	94
Robert Morris	24	38	62

Kentucky (44)   Coach: Joe Hall

	Min.	Total FG/FGA	Pct.	FT/FTA	Pct.	Reb. O/T	A	TO	PF	S	Blk	TP	PPM
HORD, D.	39	2/16	.125	2/2	1.000	-/6	2	3	3	0	0	6	.154
VERDERBER, C.	25	1/2	.500	0/0	.000	-/5	1	0	4	0	0	2	.080
TURPIN, M.	23	4/9	.444	0/0	.000	-/5	0	2	3	1	4	8	.348
MINNIEFIELD, D.	40	4/11	.364	0/0	.000	-/3	4	0	2	0	0	8	.200
MASTER, J.	24	4/8	.500	0/0	.000	-/1	2	1	1	0	0	8	.333
BEAL, D.	16	2/2	1.000	0/0	.000	-/1	1	1	1	1	0	4	.250
HEITZ, T.	3	0/1	.000	0/0	.000	-/2	0	0	0	0	0	0	.000
MCKINLEY, T.	2	0/1	.000	0/0	.000	-/0	0	0	1	0	0	0	.000
HURT, C.	28	4/6	.667	0/0	.000	-/0	0	0	5	0	0	8	.286
Totals	200	21/56	.375	2/2	1.000	-/23	10	7	20	2	4	44	.220

Middle Tennessee State (50)   Coach: Stan Simpson

	Min.	Total FG/FGA	Pct.	FT/FTA	Pct.	Reb. O/T	A	TO	PF	S	Blk	TP	PPM
HAILEY, L.	35	1/5	.200	0/0	.000	-/6	3	1	2	0	5	2	.057
BECK, J.	40	4/7	.571	6/9	.667	-/10	0	2	1	0	0	14	.350
HARRIS, C.	35	3/6	.500	0/0	.000	-/9	1	1	2	1	1	6	.171
PERRY, E.	40	4/10	.400	1/5	.200	-/1	3	3	0	0	0	9	.225
CAMPBELL, R.	38	8/16	.500	3/3	1.000	-/7	1	3	2	1	2	19	.500
DORSEY, D.	7	0/1	.000	0/1	.000	-/1	0	0	0	0	0	0	.000
PERRY, W.	5	0/0	.000	0/0	.000	-/1	0	0	0	0	0	0	.000
Totals	200	20/45	.444	10/18	.556	-/35	8	10	7	2	8	50	.250

Team Rebounds: Middle Tenn. St. 1; Kentucky 4. Disqualified: Kentucky—Hurt. Technical fouls: None.

	1st Half	2nd Half	Final
Kentucky	30	14	44
Middle Tenn. St.	30	20	50

North Carolina State (51)   Coach: Jim Valvano

	Min.	Total FG/FGA	Pct.	FT/FTA	Pct.	Reb. O/T	A	TO	PF	S	Blk	TP	PPM
PARZYCH, S.	19	1/5	.200	1/4	.250	-/6	1	0	2	0	0	3	.158
BAILEY, T.	40	3/4	.750	4/5	.800	-/11	1	3	4	1	0	10	.250
NEVITT, C.	4	0/1	.000	0/0	.000	-/0	0	1	2	0	1	0	.000
WHITTENBURG, D.	37	4/12	.333	1/1	1.000	-/0	0	3	3	0	0	9	.243
LOWE, S.	38	9/15	.600	3/6	.500	-/8	4	2	4	3	0	21	.553
PERRY, M.	6	0/2	.000	0/0	.000	-/0	0	1	1	0	0	0	.000
PROCTOR, W.	3	0/1	.000	0/0	.000	-/1	0	0	1	0	0	0	.000
GANNON, T.	6	0/1	.000	0/0	.000	-/0	0	0	1	0	0	0	.000
THOMPSON, H.	11	0/1	.000	0/0	.000	-/2	1	0	1	0	0	0	.000
CHARLES, L.	11	1/1	1.000	2/2	1.000	-/1	0	1	4	0	0	4	.364
MCQUEEN, C.	21	1/2	.500	2/4	.500	-/0	0	2	3	0	0	4	.190
WARREN, M.	4	0/0	.000	0/0	.000	-/2	0	0	2	1	0	0	.000
Totals	200	19/45	.422	13/22	.591	-/31	7	12	25	5	1	51	.255

Tennessee-Chattanooga (58)   Coach: Arnold Murray

	Min.	Total FG/FGA	Pct.	FT/FTA	Pct.	Reb. O/T	A	TO	PF	S	Blk	TP	PPM
WHITE, W.	37	3/11	.273	6/7	.857	-/5	0	1	3	0	0	12	.324
SCHOENE, R.	31	5/7	.714	5/6	.833	-/7	0	1	4	0	0	15	.484
LAWRENCE, S.	17	1/3	.333	1/2	.500	-/3	0	1	4	0	1	3	.176
MORKEN, N.	40	5/8	.625	5/12	.417	-/6	2	2	1	4	2	15	.375
CLARK, S.	40	1/5	.200	3/4	.750	-/4	2	1	3	4	0	5	.125
COCHRAN, C.	3	0/0	.000	0/0	.000	-/0	0	0	0	0	0	0	.000
JOHNSON, J.	8	1/2	.500	0/0	.000	-/3	0	0	1	0	0	2	.250
STRICKLAND, S.	24	1/3	.333	4/4	1.000	-/1	2	3	2	1	0	6	.250
Totals	200	17/39	.436	24/35	.686	-/29	6	9	18	9	3	58	.290

Team Rebounds: Tenn.-Chatt. 4; N.C. State 4. Disqualified: None. Technical fouls: None.

	1st Half	2nd Half	Final
N.C. State	13	38	51
Tenn.-Chatt.	27	31	58

FIRST ROUND WEST

Wyoming (61) Coach: Jim Brandenburg

	Min.	Total FG/FGA	Pct.	FT/FTA	Pct.	Reb. O/T	A	TO	PF	S	Blk	TP	PPM
GARNETT, B.	40	3/12	.250	7/12	.583	-/5	2	4	4	0	1	13	.325
THESENVITZ, G.	6	0/0	.000	0/0	.000	-/1	2	0	2	0	0	0	.000
ENGLER, C.	39	7/10	.700	3/4	.750	-/9	2	3	4	0	0	17	.436
JACKSON, M.	40	5/7	.714	0/0	.000	-/4	1	5	2	2	0	10	.250
MCCLENDON, D.	39	1/3	.333	2/2	1.000	-/4	1	2	3	1	0	4	.103
WRAPP, M.	35	3/6	.500	11/13	.846	-/9	2	3	4	0	2	17	.486
GOWENS, R.	1	0/0	.000	0/0	.000	-/0	0	0	0	0	0	0	.000
Totals	200	19/38	.500	23/31	.742	-/32	10	17	19	3	3	61	.305

USC (58) Coach: Stan Morrison

	Min.	Total FG/FGA	Pct.	FT/FTA	Pct.	Reb. O/T	A	TO	PF	S	Blk	TP	PPM
HILL, J.	40	3/6	.500	4/4	1.000	-/1	2	0	0	1	0	10	.250
BAILEY, C.	10	1/2	.500	3/4	.750	-/0	0	2	4	0	0	5	.500
MCDONALD, J.	28	3/8	.375	1/2	.500	-/5	3	1	5	0	0	7	.250
JOHNSON, K.	31	4/9	.444	0/0	.000	-/6	1	1	1	2	2	8	.258
CARLANDER, W.	15	1/2	.500	0/1	.000	-/2	0	0	3	0	0	2	.133
OLIVIER, C.	6	0/1	.000	0/0	.000	-/0	0	0	4	0	0	0	.000
WILLIAMS, J.	29	1/7	.143	2/2	1.000	-/3	1	5	5	2	0	4	.138
ANDERSON, D.	38	10/21	.476	2/4	.500	-/2	0	2	2	0	0	22	.579
MENDEL, I.	3	0/0	.000	0/0	.000	-/1	0	0	2	0	0	0	.000
Totals	200	23/56	.411	12/17	.706	-/20	7	11	26	5	2	58	.290

Team Rebounds: Wyoming 3; USC 4. Disqualified: USC—Williams, McDonald. Technical fouls: Wyoming—bench.

	1st Half	2nd Half	Final
Wyoming	34	27	61
USC	32	26	58

Iowa (70) Coach: Lute Olson

	Min.	Total FG/FGA	Pct.	FT/FTA	Pct.	Reb. O/T	A	TO	PF	S	Blk	TP	PPM
BOYLE, K.	32	4/8	.500	3/3	1.000	-/6	2	0	5	0	1	11	.344
PAYNE, M.	30	0/6	.000	1/4	.250	-/14	0	4	4	0	1	1	.033
CARFINO, S.	31	4/5	.800	4/4	1.000	-/5	5	2	2	1	0	12	.387
ARNOLD, K.	39	5/9	.556	4/4	1.000	-/4	1	2	3	0	0	14	.359
ANDERSON, C.	1	0/0	.000	0/0	.000	-/0	0	0	0	0	0	0	.000
STOKES, G.	21	5/10	.500	1/2	.500	-/6	0	3	3	1	3	11	.524
GANNON, M.	15	1/5	.200	0/0	.000	-/2	2	1	1	0	0	2	.133
HANSEN, B.	31	7/14	.500	5/5	1.000	-/4	2	7	4	2	1	19	.613
Totals	200	26/57	.456	18/22	.818	-/36	12	19	22	4	6	70	.350

Northeast Louisiana (63) Coach: Mike Vining

	Min.	Total FG/FGA	Pct.	FT/FTA	Pct.	Reb. O/T	A	TO	PF	S	Blk	TP	PPM
WILSON, D.	37	6/15	.400	6/8	.750	-/10	1	2	3	1	0	18	.486
MARTIN, T.	40	6/15	.400	4/5	.800	-/11	0	4	1	0	0	16	.400
MORRIS, G.	40	5/16	.313	5/6	.833	-/7	0	4	4	1	0	15	.375
BUTLER, V.	36	5/10	.500	0/0	.000	-/2	0	2	3	0	0	10	.278
RICHARD, K.	32	2/6	.333	0/0	.000	-/0	1	3	5	0	0	4	.125
DOUGLAS, B.	5	0/2	.000	0/0	.000	-/0	1	0	0	0	0	0	.000
DEAN, M.	7	0/1	.000	0/1	.000	-/1	0	1	1	0	0	0	.000
WILLIAMS, B.	3	0/0	.000	0/0	.000	-/1	0	0	1	0	0	0	.000
Totals	200	24/65	.369	15/20	.750	-/32	3	16	18	2	0	63	.315

Team Rebounds: Iowa 5; Northeast La. 6. Disqualified: Iowa—Boyle; Northeast La.—Richard. Technical fouls: None.

	1st Half	2nd Half	Final
Iowa	28	42	70
Northeast La.	29	34	63

West Virginia (102) Coach: Gale Catlett

	Min.	Total FG/FGA	Pct.	FT/FTA	Pct.	Reb. O/T	A	TO	PF	S	Blk	TP	PPM
ROWE, L.	-	2/4	.500	3/5	.600	-/3	1	-	-	-	-	7	-
TODD, R.	-	8/11	.727	4/4	1.000	-/6	2	-	-	-	-	20	-
COLLINS, P.	-	2/4	.500	6/8	.750	-/8	0	-	-	-	-	10	-
JONES, G.	-	5/9	.556	4/6	.667	-/7	5	-	-	-	-	14	-
WASHAM, T.	-	6/9	.667	0/0	.000	-/4	3	-	-	-	-	12	-
FREEMAN, Q.	-	5/12	.417	5/7	.714	-/2	3	-	-	-	-	15	-
MOORE, N.	-	1/3	.333	0/0	.000	-/3	1	-	-	-	-	2	-
GIPSON, D.	-	4/5	.800	3/3	1.000	-/5	0	-	-	-	-	11	-
KEARNEY, T.	-	1/1	1.000	0/1	.000	-/1	0	-	-	-	-	2	-
POWELL, A.	-	0/0	.000	2/2	1.000	-/0	0	-	-	-	-	2	-
KING, M.	-	3/5	.600	1/4	.250	-/3	2	-	-	-	-	7	-
HOWE, D.	-	0/0	.000	0/0	.000	-/5	1	-	-	-	-	0	-
Totals	200	37/63	.587	28/40	.700	-/47	18	-	18	-	-	102	.510

North Carolina A&T (72) Coach: Don Corbett

	Min.	Total FG/FGA	Pct.	FT/FTA	Pct.	Reb. O/T	A	TO	PF	S	Blk	TP	PPM
HORACE, J.	-	2/9	.222	0/0	.000	-/5	0	-	-	-	-	4	-
COLLINS, A.	-	1/7	.143	0/0	.000	-/2	1	-	-	-	-	2	-
BINION, J.	-	6/14	.429	5/8	.625	-/12	1	-	-	-	-	17	-
ANDERSON, J.	-	5/15	.333	2/2	1.000	-/4	1	-	-	-	-	12	-
BOYD, E.	-	5/11	.455	3/4	.750	-/3	3	-	-	-	-	13	-
STINCHCOMB, R.	-	0/1	.000	0/0	.000	-/1	0	-	-	-	-	0	-
BOOKER, B.	-	2/3	.667	1/1	1.000	-/0	0	-	-	-	-	5	-
BATTLE, D.	-	4/8	.500	0/1	.000	-/4	0	-	-	-	-	8	-
MITCHELL, B.	-	0/1	.000	0/0	.000	-/2	0	-	-	-	-	0	-
POWELL, W.	-	4/11	.364	1/2	.500	-/1	0	-	-	-	-	9	-
LOPEZ, J.	-	1/2	.500	0/1	.000	-/1	0	-	-	-	-	2	-
Totals	200	30/82	.366	12/19	.632	-/35	6	-	30	-	-	72	.360

Team Rebounds: West Virginia 5; N. Carolina A&T 4. Disqualified: N. Carolina A&T—Horace. Technical fouls: None.

	1st Half	2nd Half	Final
West Virginia	44	58	102
N. Carolina A&T	32	40	72

Pepperdine (99) Coach: Jim Harrick

	Min.	Total FG/FGA	Pct.	FT/FTA	Pct.	Reb. O/T	A	TO	PF	S	Blk	TP	PPM
PHILLIPS, O.	35	11/14	.786	5/11	.455	-/7	1	0	4	0	0	27	.771
SADLER, B.	24	4/6	.667	5/5	1.000	-/5	2	1	5	0	1	13	.542
MCCULLUM, S.	37	2/5	.400	5/5	1.000	-/6	2	2	1	0	0	9	.243
SUTTLE, D.	34	7/12	.583	4/4	1.000	-/2	8	3	1	0	0	18	.529
BOND, B.	32	9/18	.500	6/6	1.000	-/2	3	1	2	1	0	24	.750
WILSON, M.	15	1/2	.500	0/0	.000	-/0	2	3	0	0	0	2	.133
ANGER, V.	23	2/3	.667	2/2	1.000	-/9	2	3	1	0	2	6	.261
Totals	200	36/60	.600	27/33	.818	-/31	20	13	14	1	3	99	.495

Pittsburgh (88) Coach: Roy Chipman

	Min.	Total FG/FGA	Pct.	FT/FTA	Pct.	Reb. O/T	A	TO	PF	S	Blk	TP	PPM
KIRBY, R.	24	3/8	.375	3/4	.750	-/6	0	0	3	0	0	9	.375
VAUGHAN, C.	31	8/17	.471	1/1	1.000	-/8	0	3	4	0	0	17	.548
WILLIAMS, A.	17	2/3	.667	2/2	1.000	-/3	0	1	3	0	0	6	.353
ALLEN, J.	8	1/4	.250	0/0	.000	-/0	0	1	0	0	0	2	.250
WALLACE, D.	40	8/23	.348	1/2	.500	-/1	8	1	4	0	0	17	.425
GISSENDANNER, D.	29	9/13	.692	2/3	.667	-/2	1	0	3	3	0	20	.690
BEATTY, S.	6	0/0	.000	0/0	.000	-/0	0	0	0	0	0	0	.000
WATKINS, C.	22	4/6	.667	3/6	.500	-/1	0	2	3	1	0	11	.500
JOHNSON, T.	23	3/5	.600	0/0	.000	-/4	0	0	4	1	0	6	.261
Totals	200	38/79	.481	12/18	.667	-/25	9	7	25	5	0	88	.440

Team Rebounds: Pepperdine 7; Pittsburgh 8. Disqualified: Pepperdine—Sadler. Technical fouls: None.

	1st Half	2nd Half	Final
Pepperdine	45	54	99
Pittsburgh	38	50	88

SECOND ROUND EAST

James Madison (50) Coach: Lou Campanelli

	Min.	Total FG/FGA	Pct.	FT/FTA	Pct.	Reb. O/T	A	TO	PF	S	Blk	TP	PPM
JACKSON, D.	18	2/2	1.000	1/3	.333	-/2	0	1	2	0	0	5	.278
TOWNES, L.	34	5/10	.500	2/2	1.000	-/1	3	1	4	0	0	12	.353
RULAND, D.	35	6/10	.600	0/0	.000	-/6	1	0	4	0	0	12	.343
FISHER, C.	33	5/6	.833	2/2	1.000	-/0	1	3	2	4	0	12	.364
DUPONT, D.	38	2/4	.500	0/0	.000	-/5	4	4	3	0	0	4	.105
STEELE, D.	13	0/2	.000	2/2	1.000	-/2	3	4	3	0	0	2	.154
BRADLEY, K.	27	1/3	.333	1/2	.500	-/5	0	1	4	0	0	3	.111
BOLER, W.	2	0/0	.000	0/0	.000	-/0	0	1	0	0	0	0	.000
Totals	200	21/37	.054	8/11	.727	5/21	12	15	22	4	0	50	.250

North Carolina (52) Coach: Dean Smith

	Min.	Total FG/FGA	Pct.	FT/FTA	Pct.	Reb. O/T	A	TO	PF	S	Blk	TP	PPM
DOHERTY, M.	39	2/6	.333	1/3	.333	-/2	2	3	3	1	0	5	.128
WORTHY, J.	39	4/7	.571	7/8	.875	-/4	1	3	2	1	1	15	.385
PERKINS, S.	39	7/13	.538	3/6	.500	-/10	2	4	2	1	1	17	.436
BLACK, J.	28	4/4	1.000	1/4	.250	-/0	4	0	4	2	0	9	.321
JORDAN, M.	37	3/8	.375	0/2	.000	-/1	0	2	2	0	0	6	.162
PETERSON, B.	2	0/0	.000	0/0	.000	-/0	0	0	0	0	0	0	.000
BRADDOCK, J.	13	0/0	.000	0/0	.000	-/2	1	0	2	0	0	0	.000
BARLOW, J.	1	0/0	.000	0/0	.000	-/0	0	0	0	0	0	0	.000
BRUST, C.	1	0/0	.000	0/0	.000	-/0	0	0	0	0	0	0	.000
MARTIN, W.	1	0/0	.000	0/0	.000	-/0	0	0	0	0	0	0	.000
Totals	200	20/38	.526	12/23	.522	7/19	10	12	15	5	2	52	.260

Team Rebounds: N. Carolina 1; James Madison 1. Disqualified: None. Technical fouls: None.

	1st Half	2nd Half	Final
James Madison	28	22	50
N. Carolina	31	21	52

St. John's (68) Coach: Lou Carnesecca

	Min.	Total FG/FGA	Pct.	FT/FTA	Pct.	Reb. O/T	A	TO	PF	S	Blk	TP	PPM
RUSSELL, D.	36	6/11	.545	5/5	1.000	-/7	2	6	4	0	0	17	.472
GOODWIN, B.	39	7/14	.500	4/6	.667	-/9	2	4	4	0	0	18	.462
ALLEN, J.	21	5/5	1.000	0/0	.000	-/3	0	0	4	2	1	10	.476
KELLY, B.	37	0/2	.000	2/3	.667	-/2	6	4	4	2	0	2	.054
MULLIN, C.	32	5/11	.455	4/6	.667	-/4	4	5	5	1	0	14	.438
WENNINGTON, B.	19	0/4	.000	0/0	.000	-/3	1	0	2	0	1	0	.000
GARRISON, G.	3	0/1	.000	0/0	.000	-/0	0	1	3	1	0	0	.000
STEWART, R.	4	1/1	1.000	0/1	.000	-/2	0	1	1	0	0	2	.500
WILLIAMS, K.	9	1/3	.333	3/3	1.000	-/2	0	0	2	0	0	5	.556
Totals	200	25/52	.481	18/24	.750	-/32	15	21	29	6	2	68	.340

Alabama (69) Coach: Wimp Sanderson

	Min.	Total FG/FGA	Pct.	FT/FTA	Pct.	Reb. O/T	A	TO	PF	S	Blk	TP	PPM
WINDHAM, C.	6	1/1	1.000	1/2	.500	-/2	0	1	4	0	0	3	.500
PHILLIPS, E.	37	3/10	.300	10/10	1.000	-/8	0	3	2	0	0	16	.432
HURT, B.	18	1/4	.250	6/8	.750	-/2	2	1	2	1	3	8	.444
WHATLEY, E.	36	4/9	.444	4/5	.800	-/2	5	4	1	0	0	12	.333
DAVIS, M.	39	4/8	.500	1/3	.000	-/1	0	1	4	0	0	9	.231
RICHARDSON, E.	29	2/5	.400	3/4	.750	-/1	2	1	2	2	0	7	.241
LOCKETT, P.	23	1/5	.200	4/5	.800	-/7	0	2	2	0	0	6	.261
WILLIAMS, T.	12	4/6	.667	0/0	.000	-/5	1	1	4	1	0	8	.667
Totals	200	20/48	.417	29/37	.541	-/28	10	14	21	4	3	69	.345

Team Rebounds: Alabama 3; St. John's 3. Disqualified: St. John's—Mullin. Technical fouls: St. John's—Mullin.

	1st Half	2nd Half	Final
St. John's	32	36	68
Alabama	41	28	69

Northeastern (72) Coach: Jim Calhoun

	Min.	Total FG/FGA	Pct.	FT/FTA	Pct.	Reb. O/T	A	TO	PF	S	Blk	TP	PPM
JEFFERSON, E.	53	8/17	.471	1/2	.500	-/11	2	4	5	0	0	17	.321
HALSEL, M.	43	4/9	.444	2/3	.667	-/4	0	4	2	2	0	10	.233
LEITAD, D.	54	4/12	.333	0/2	.000	-/11	0	0	5	1	0	8	.148
MOSS, P.	54	14/29	.483	3/4	.750	-/7	0	2	4	4	0	31	.574
BRYANT, S.	15	0/0	.000	0/0	.000	-/0	0	2	1	0	0	0	.000
ROBINSON, P.	43	1/3	.333	0/0	.000	-/3	1	0	4	0	0	2	.047
BRASWELL, R.	12	2/3	.667	0/0	.000	-/4	1	0	3	0	0	4	.333
KING, J.	1	0/1	.000	0/0	.000	-/0	0	1	1	1	0	0	.000
Totals	275	33/74	.446	6/11	.545	-/40	4	13	25	8	0	72	.262

Villanova (76) Coach: Rollie Massimino

	Min.	Total FG/FGA	Pct.	FT/FTA	Pct.	Reb. O/T	A	TO	PF	S	Blk	TP	PPM
PINCKNEY, E.	51	4/8	.500	4/6	.667	-/10	1	3	2	3	3	12	.235
HOWARD, A.	42	3/6	.500	2/2	1.000	-/2	2	1	4	0	0	8	.190
PINONE, J.	51	3/9	.333	6/11	.545	-/8	5	4	4	0	1	12	.235
GRANGER, S.	51	7/11	.636	2/3	.667	-/2	4	2	2	0	0	16	.314
MCCLAIN, D.	55	7/11	.636	6/8	.750	-/1	2	1	4	4	0	20	.364
MCLAIN, G.	10	2/2	1.000	0/0	.000	-/2	3	1	0	0	0	4	.400
SICES, J.	6	1/4	.250	0/0	.000	-/1	0	0	0	0	0	2	.333
DOBBS, F.	7	1/2	.500	0/0	.000	-/0	0	2	0	0	0	2	.286
MULQUIN, M.	2	0/0	.000	0/0	.000	-/1	0	0	0	0	0	0	.000
Totals	275	28/53	.528	20/30	.667	-/27	17	14	16	7	4	76	.276

Team Rebounds: Villanova 3; Northeastern 5. Disqualified: Northeastern—Jefferson, Leitad. Technical fouls: Northeastern—Moss.

	1st Half	2nd Half	1st OT	2nd OT	3rd OT	Final
Northeastern	32	24	2	7	7	72
Villanova	35	21	2	7	11	76

Wake Forest (55) Coach: Carl Tacy

	Min.	Total FG/FGA	Pct.	FT/FTA	Pct.	Reb. O/T	A	TO	PF	S	Blk	TP	PPM
TOMS, J.	14	2/2	1.000	0/0	.000	-/1	0	1	1	0	0	4	.286
MORGAN, G.	27	6/11	.545	1/2	.500	-/4	1	3	4	1	1	13	.481
JOHNSTONE, J.	27	1/3	.333	1/4	.250	-/0	2	0	3	1	0	3	.111
YOUNG, D.	38	3/7	.429	0/0	.000	-/1	4	0	3	1	0	6	.158
HELMS, M.	38	4/5	.800	1/2	.500	-/0	0	3	2	1	0	9	.237
DAVIS, S.	2	0/0	.000	0/0	.000	-/0	0	0	0	0	0	0	.000
KEPLEY, C.	2	1/1	1.000	0/0	.000	-/0	0	0	0	0	0	2	1.000
CHARLES, S.	2	1/1	1.000	0/0	.000	-/1	0	0	0	0	0	2	1.000
GARBER, L.	11	1/2	.500	0/0	.000	-/0	1	0	0	0	0	2	.182
TEACHEY, A.	39	5/8	.625	4/4	1.000	-/7	0	2	4	1	0	14	.359
Totals	200	24/40	.600	7/12	.583	-/14	8	9	17	5	1	55	.275

Memphis State (56) Coach: Dana Kirk

	Min.	Total FG/FGA	Pct.	FT/FTA	Pct.	Reb. O/T	A	TO	PF	S	Blk	TP	PPM
PARKS, B.	36	4/7	.571	4/5	.800	-/5	3	1	3	0	0	12	.333
LEE, K.	40	7/9	.778	4/5	.800	-/8	2	5	3	1	4	18	.450
PHILLIPS, D.	27	1/3	.333	2/3	.667	-/3	0	2	2	1	0	4	.148
JACKSON, O.	40	4/8	.500	1/1	1.000	-/1	5	2	1	1	0	9	.225
HAYNES, P.	40	5/7	.714	1/2	.500	-/1	2	0	1	1	0	11	.275
GIPSON, J.	11	1/3	.333	0/1	.000	-/1	0	0	1	0	0	2	.182
TAYLOR, G.	6	0/1	.000	0/0	.000	-/0	0	0	0	0	0	0	.000
Totals	200	22/38	.579	12/17	.706	-/19	12	10	11	4	4	56	.280

Team Rebounds: Memphis State 2; Wake Forest 1. Disqualified: None. Technical fouls: Memphis State—bench.

	1st Half	2nd Half	Final
Wake Forest	38	17	55
Memphis State	34	22	56

SECOND ROUND MIDWEST

Boston College (82)   Coach: Tom Davis

	Min.	Total FG/FGA	Pct.	FT/FTA	Pct.	Reb. O/T	A	TO	PF	S	Blk	TP	PPM
SHRIGLEY, R.	-	3/6	.500	6/9	.667	-/5	1	1	2	1	0	12	-
CLARK	-	3/7	.429	1/2	.500	-/8	0	1	2	0	0	7	-
MURPHY	-	2/4	.500	0/5	.000	-/3	2	1	0	0	0	4	-
CHANDLER	-	1/4	.250	1/2	.500	-/2	1	2	3	2	0	3	-
BAGLEY, J.	-	10/18	.556	6/9	.667	-/7	3	8	2	2	1	26	-
GARRIS, J.	-	4/5	.800	1/4	.250	-/8	1	1	4	4	2	9	-
ADAMS, M.	-	6/9	.667	9/11	.818	-/1	1	2	3	1	0	21	-
ADAMS, B.	-	0/1	.000	0/0	.000	-/0	0	0	0	0	0	0	-
SCHMIDT, M.	-	0/0	.000	0/0	.000	-/1	0	0	0	0	0	0	-
TALLEY	-	0/0	.000	0/0	.000	-/0	0	0	1	0	0	0	-
Totals	200	29/54	.537	24/42	.571	-/35	9	16	17	10	3	82	.410

DePaul (75)   Coach: Ray Meyer

	Min.	Total FG/FGA	Pct.	FT/FTA	Pct.	Reb. O/T	A	TO	PF	S	Blk	TP	PPM
RANDOLPH	-	7/15	.467	2/3	.667	-/6	0	1	5	3	0	16	-
CUMMINGS	-	9/16	.563	2/3	.667	-/17	2	5	4	1	2	20	-
DOWNING	-	1/1	1.000	0/0	.000	-/2	1	1	4	0	2	2	-
PATTERSON	-	3/11	.273	3/4	.750	-/2	7	5	5	2	0	9	-
DILLARD	-	7/16	.438	0/0	.000	-/0	5	1	5	1	0	14	-
CORBIN	-	3/6	.500	2/2	1.000	-/8	3	1	5	1	1	8	-
McMILLAN	-	2/5	.400	2/3	.667	-/3	1	5	5	0	0	6	-
McCOY	-	0/3	.000	0/0	.000	-/0	1	1	1	0	0	0	-
BURKHOLDER	-	0/0	.000	0/0	.000	-/0	0	0	1	0	0	0	-
ALLEN	-	0/0	.000	0/0	.000	-/0	0	0	0	0	0	0	-
Totals	200	32/73	.438	11/15	.733	-/38	20	20	35	8	5	75	.375

Team Rebounds: Boston College 5; DePaul 6. Disqualified: DePaul—Randolph, Patterson, Dillard, Corbin, McMillan. Technical fouls: None.

	1st Half	2nd Half	Final
Boston College	33	49	82
DePaul	34	41	75

Kansas State (65)   Coach: Jack Hartman

	Min.	Total FG/FGA	Pct.	FT/FTA	Pct.	Reb. O/T	A	TO	PF	S	Blk	TP	PPM
NEALY, E.	39	5/7	.714	1/4	.250	-/9	3	0	1	5	0	11	.282
REED, R.	33	4/9	.444	0/0	.000	-/9	2	4	3	1	0	8	.242
CRAFT, L.	33	6/11	.545	1/1	1.000	-/5	6	4	5	1	5	13	.394
JANKOVICH, T.	37	4/7	.571	0/0	.000	-/1	2	3	1	1	0	8	.216
ADAMS, T.	38	8/11	.727	5/6	.833	-/3	4	4	3	0	0	21	.553
GALVAO, E.	17	2/2	1.000	0/2	.000	-/2	2	1	3	0	0	4	.235
WATKINS, L.	3	0/1	.000	0/0	.000	-/0	2	1	1	0	0	0	.000
Totals	200	29/48	.604	7/13	.538	-/29	21	17	17	8	5	65	.325

Arkansas (64)   Coach: Eddie Sutton

	Min.	Total FG/FGA	Pct.	FT/FTA	Pct.	Reb. O/T	A	TO	PF	S	Blk	TP	PPM
BROWN	27	7/11	.636	1/2	.500	-/2	4	2	4	1	1	15	.556
PETERSON	39	5/7	.714	0/0	.000	-/1	2	0	1	0	0	10	.256
HASTINGS	40	8/17	.471	0/2	.000	-/8	3	4	4	1	0	16	.400
WALKER	40	5/12	.417	3/6	.500	-/10	6	1	3	4	3	13	.325
ROBERTSON, A.	24	1/4	.250	4/4	1.000	-/1	0	3	4	3	0	6	.250
FRIESS	10	0/0	.000	0/0	.000	-/1	1	1	1	0	0	0	.000
NORTON	17	1/3	.333	2/2	1.000	-/1	1	3	0	0	0	4	.235
KELLY	3	0/0	.000	0/0	.000	-/0	0	0	0	0	0	0	.000
Totals	200	27/54	.500	10/16	.625	-/24	17	14	17	9	4	64	.320

Team Rebounds: Kansas State 1; Arkansas 1. Disqualified: Kansas State—Craft. Technical fouls: None.

	1st Half	2nd Half	Final
Kansas State	31	34	65
Arkansas	32	32	64

Houston (78)   Coach: Guy Lewis

	Min.	Total FG/FGA	Pct.	FT/FTA	Pct.	Reb. O/T	A	TO	PF	S	Blk	TP	PPM
DREXLER, C.	37	7/13	.538	3/4	.750	5/9	1	4	5	3	2	17	.459
YOUNG, M.	27	2/5	.400	5/6	.833	0/4	1	5	5	2	0	9	.333
MICHEAUX, L.	36	4/7	.571	0/3	.000	3/10	0	4	4	4	0	8	.222
ROSE, L.	30	5/8	.625	2/2	1.000	0/1	3	2	3	0	1	12	.400
WILLIAMS, R.	39	10/15	.667	6/9	.667	2/4	5	7	4	2	0	26	.667
DAVIS, E.	13	1/1	1.000	0/0	.000	0/0	0	1	2	1	0	2	.154
ANDERS, B.	4	1/2	.500	0/0	.000	0/1	1	1	0	0	0	2	.500
OLAJUWON, A.	14	1/3	.333	0/3	.000	1/4	0	1	4	1	2	2	.143
Totals	200	31/54	.574	16/27	.593	11/33	11	25	27	14	5	78	.390

Tulsa (74)   Coach: Nolan Richardson

	Min.	Total FG/FGA	Pct.	FT/FTA	Pct.	Reb. O/T	A	TO	PF	S	Blk	TP	PPM
PRESSEY, P.	37	6/11	.545	4/7	.571	5/12	5	4	4	4	0	16	.432
VANLEY, B.	27	2/6	.333	3/4	.750	2/5	0	5	5	0	0	7	.259
STEWART, G.	27	6/13	.462	1/2	.500	4/10	1	3	2	0	0	13	.481
ANDERSON, M.	27	4/7	.571	3/3	1.000	0/0	3	5	5	0	0	11	.407
SRPADLING, P.	27	2/8	.250	0/1	.000	1/2	1	2	2	0	0	4	.148
HARRIS, S.	26	3/9	.333	9/9	1.000	0/1	2	1	3	1	1	15	.577
JOHNSON, H.	19	3/7	.429	2/2	1.000	2/3	0	1	1	1	0	8	.421
BALLARD, S.	3	0/1	.000	0/0	.000	0/0	0	1	1	0	0	0	.000
NILSSON, T.	1	0/0	.000	0/0	.000	0/0	0	0	0	0	0	0	.000
NORTH, C.	1	0/0	.000	0/0	.000	0/0	0	0	0	0	0	0	.000
WILLIAMS, V.	5	0/0	.000	0/0	.000	0/0	0	0	0	0	0	0	.000
Totals	200	26/62	.419	22/28	.786	14/33	12	22	23	6	1	74	.370

Team Rebounds: Houston 0; Tulsa 2. Disqualified: Houston—Drexler, Young; Tulsa—Vanley, Anderson. Technical fouls: Tulsa—Vanley, Anderson.

	1st Half	2nd Half	Final
Houston	36	42	78
Tulsa	31	43	74

Marquette (69)   Coach: Hank Raymonds

	Min.	Total FG/FGA	Pct.	FT/FTA	Pct.	Reb. O/T	A	TO	PF	S	Blk	TP	PPM
NYENHUIS	35	4/11	.364	1/2	.500	-/10	2	0	4	0	0	9	.257
WILSON	31	3/10	.300	5/8	.625	-/4	4	2	5	3	0	11	.355
RIVERS, G.	34	9/14	.643	0/0	.000	-/1	1	2	5	1	1	18	.529
JOHNSON, M.	13	2/5	.400	0/0	.000	-/1	2	1	0	2	0	4	.308
JOHNSON, D.	35	5/9	.556	0/1	.000	-/5	1	1	5	2	0	10	.286
SCHLUNDT, T.	11	1/3	.333	0/0	.000	-/3	0	1	4	0	0	2	.182
MARQUARDT	27	3/12	.250	1/2	.500	-/2	1	0	1	1	0	7	.259
REASON	6	1/3	.333	0/0	.000	-/1	0	1	0	0	0	2	.333
MAROTTA	8	1/2	.500	4/4	1.000	-/1	0	2	1	0	0	6	.750
Totals	200	29/69	.420	11/17	.647	-/28	11	10	25	9	1	69	.345

Missouri (73)   Coach: Norm Stewart

	Min.	Total FG/FGA	Pct.	FT/FTA	Pct.	Reb. O/T	A	TO	PF	S	Blk	TP	PPM
FRAZIER, R.	37	7/12	.583	6/8	.750	-/7	0	5	3	1	0	20	.541
McCRARY, M.	37	4/4	1.000	3/5	.600	-/4	2	4	2	1	0	11	.297
STIPANOVICH, S.	37	6/11	.545	7/9	.778	-/9	2	2	1	0	1	19	.514
SUNDVOLD, J.	37	2/5	.400	4/4	1.000	-/3	2	5	2	1	0	8	.216
BRIDGES, P.	30	4/4	1.000	7/8	.875	-/1	5	3	3	2	0	15	.500
DRESSLER, M.	3	0/0	.000	0/0	.000	-/0	0	2	1	0	0	0	.000
WALKER, M.	12	0/0	.000	0/0	.000	-/3	1	2	1	0	0	0	.000
CAVENER, G.	7	0/1	.000	0/0	.000	-/1	0	1	0	0	0	0	.000
Totals	200	23/37	.622	27/34	.794	-/28	12	24	13	5	1	73	.365

Team Rebounds: Missouri 3; Marquette 3. Disqualified: Marquette—Wilson, Rivers, D. Johnson. Technical fouls: None.

	1st Half	2nd Half	Final
Marquette	30	39	69
Missouri	35	38	73

SECOND ROUND MIDEAST

Tennessee (51)   Coach: Don Devoe

	Min.	Total FG/FGA	Pct.	FT/FTA	Pct.	Reb. O/T	A	TO	PF	S	Blk	TP	PPM
ELLIS, D.	37	5/10	.500	6/8	.750	-/9	0	1	5	0	0	16	.432
RAY, S.	36	2/3	.667	0/0	.000	-/3	3	2	4	0	0	4	.111
BURTON, W.	17	0/0	.000	0/0	.000	-/3	1	0	5	1	0	0	.000
BEAMAN, T.	37	0/5	.000	1/3	.333	-/0	8	2	4	2	0	1	.027
BROOKS, M.	40	11/17	.647	2/3	.667	-/2	1	0	1	1	0	24	.600
HYATT, G.	9	0/0	.000	2/2	1.000	-/0	1	0	0	0	0	2	.222
WOODS, J.	4	0/1	.000	0/0	.000	-/0	0	0	0	0	0	0	.000
FEDERMANN, D.	20	2/3	.667	0/1	.000	-/3	0	1	4	0	0	4	.200
Totals	200	20/39	.513	11/17	.647	-/20	14	6	23	4	0	51	.255

Virginia (54)   Coach: Terry Holland

	Min.	Total FG/FGA	Pct.	FT/FTA	Pct.	Reb. O/T	A	TO	PF	S	Blk	TP	PPM
MILLER, J.	17	1/2	.500	0/3	.000	-/2	0	0	3	0	0	2	.118
ROBINSON, C.	29	2/7	.286	0/0	.000	-/6	1	2	3	0	0	4	.138
SAMPSON, R.	36	9/14	.643	1/6	.167	-/9	2	0	2	0	2	19	.528
JONES, J.	38	4/6	.667	2/5	.400	-/7	3	1	2	1	1	10	.263
MULLEN, T.	24	4/6	.667	1/2	.500	-/0	0	2	2	0	0	9	.375
WILSON, O.	22	2/3	.667	1/2	.500	-/1	1	2	1	0	0	5	.227
STOKES, R.	18	0/1	.000	2/2	1.000	-/1	0	0	2	0	0	2	.111
EDELIN, K.	16	1/2	.500	1/1	1.000	-/2	0	0	4	1	0	3	.188
Totals	200	23/41	.561	8/21	.381	-/28	7	7	19	2	3	54	.270

Team Rebounds: Virginia—4; Tennessee—4. Disqualified: Tennessee—Ellis, Burton. Technical fouls: None.

	1st Half	2nd Half	Final
Tennessee	32	19	51
Virginia	25	29	54

Indiana (70)   Coach: Bob Knight

	Min.	Total FG/FGA	Pct.	FT/FTA	Pct.	Reb. O/T	A	TO	PF	S	Blk	TP	PPM
WITTMAN, R.	29	4/10	.400	0/2	.000	-/4	5	0	4	1	0	8	.276
KITCHEL, T.	37	10/27	.370	4/4	1.000	-/5	2	4	3	0	0	24	.649
BOUCHIE, S.	13	2/4	.500	0/0	.000	-/3	0	1	2	0	0	4	.308
THOMAS, J.	40	6/12	.500	0/0	.000	-/9	1	1	1	1	1	12	.300
DAKICH, D.	1	0/0	.000	0/0	.000	-/0	0	0	0	0	0	0	.000
MORGAN, W.	9	0/0	.000	0/0	.000	-/0	3	1	3	0	0	0	.000
BLAB, U.	16	3/3	1.000	1/2	.500	-/1	0	2	4	0	1	7	.438
FLOWERS, J.	23	4/6	.667	0/0	.000	-/5	1	2	1	0	0	8	.348
BROWN, T.	32	3/7	.429	1/2	.500	-/7	2	1	3	2	0	7	.219
Totals	200	32/69	.464	6/10	.600	-/34	14	12	21	4	2	70	.350

Alabama-Birmingham (80)   Coach: Gene Bartow

	Min.	Total FG/FGA	Pct.	FT/FTA	Pct.	Reb. O/T	A	TO	PF	S	Blk	TP	PPM
GILES, C.	40	6/10	.600	5/5	1.000	-/3	2	2	3	0	1	17	.425
FOSTER, L.	40	4/7	.571	5/5	1.000	-/5	0	1	0	1	0	13	.325
ANCHRUM, N.	29	4/9	.444	3/4	.750	-/7	0	1	4	0	4	11	.379
NICHOLAS, J.	19	1/2	.500	6/7	.857	-/2	1	1	2	1	0	8	.421
ROBINSON, O.	39	10/17	.588	3/4	.750	-/1	2	2	0	0	0	23	.590
LANE, C.	23	2/4	.500	2/4	.500	-/5	0	1	2	1	0	6	.261
SPEER, D.	2	0/0	.000	0/0	.000	-/1	0	2	0	0	0	0	.000
DRUM, L.	8	1/1	1.000	0/0	.000	-/1	0	2	3	0	0	2	.250
Totals	200	28/50	.560	24/29	.828	-/25	5	12	14	3	5	80	.400

Team Rebounds: Ala.-Birmingham 2; Indiana 2. Disqualified: None. Technical fouls: None.

	1st Half	2nd Half	Final
Indiana	22	48	70
Ala.-Birmingham	40	40	80

Middle Tennessee State (56)   Coach: Stan Simpson

	Min.	Total FG/FGA	Pct.	FT/FTA	Pct.	Reb. O/T	A	TO	PF	S	Blk	TP	PPM
HAILEY, L.	10	1/3	.333	0/0	.000	-/2	1	1	5	1	0	2	.200
BECK, J.	39	6/13	.462	10/11	.909	-/6	0	2	2	0	0	22	.564
HARRIS, C.	22	0/2	.000	0/0	.000	-/3	1	3	2	1	0	0	.000
PERRY, E.	25	2/4	.500	0/0	.000	-/1	1	3	0	1	0	4	.160
CAMPBELL, R.	31	6/13	.462	0/0	.000	-/1	3	8	5	0	0	12	.387
MAYFIELD, D.	8	0/0	.000	0/0	.000	-/0	2	4	3	0	0	0	.000
FROST, M.	6	0/0	.000	0/0	.000	-/2	0	0	0	0	0	0	.000
FOWLER, D.	1	0/1	.000	0/0	.000	-/0	0	0	0	0	0	0	.000
MAPES, M.	7	0/0	.000	0/0	.000	-/0	1	0	0	0	0	0	.000
DORSEY, D.	17	3/4	.750	2/2	1.000	-/3	1	2	1	1	0	8	.471
PERRY, W.	12	1/4	.250	0/0	.000	-/3	0	0	2	0	0	2	.167
BECK, K.	6	2/2	1.000	0/2	.000	-/0	0	1	2	0	0	4	.667
JOHNSON, W.	16	1/3	.333	0/0	.000	-/1	0	2	2	1	0	2	.125
Totals	200	22/49	.449	12/15	.800	-/22	10	26	24	5	0	56	.280

Louisville (81)   Coach: Denny Crum

	Min.	Total FG/FGA	Pct.	FT/FTA	Pct.	Reb. O/T	A	TO	PF	S	Blk	TP	PPM
MCCRAY, R.	34	2/3	.667	3/5	.600	-/4	2	3	1	1	0	7	.206
SMITH, D.	24	6/9	.667	5/7	.714	-/5	2	1	3	2	1	17	.708
BROWN, W.	9	1/2	.500	1/1	1.000	-/2	2	2	2	1	0	3	.333
GORDON, L.	28	2/6	.333	1/2	.500	-/1	1	2	0	1	1	5	.179
EAVES, J.	22	4/8	.500	5/5	1.000	-/0	3	4	4	4	0	13	.591
JONES, K.	2	0/0	.000	1/2	.500	-/0	0	0	1	0	0	1	.500
WAGNER, J.	21	2/5	.400	0/1	.000	-/0	0	1	0	0	0	4	.190
MCCRAY, S.	7	1/2	.500	0/0	.000	-/1	2	1	0	0	0	2	.286
JETER, J.	3	0/0	.000	0/0	.000	-/0	0	0	0	0	0	0	.000
FORREST, M.	6	2/2	1.000	0/0	.000	-/0	1	0	1	0	0	4	.667
JONES, C.	24	4/6	.667	3/3	1.000	-/5	2	1	4	2	1	11	.458
WRIGHT, P.	17	5/5	1.000	2/2	1.000	-/3	0	2	0	1	0	12	.706
MITCHELL, D.	3	1/2	.500	0/0	.000	-/1	1	0	1	0	0	2	.667
Totals	200	30/50	.600	21/29	.724	-/22	16	17	17	12	3	81	.405

Team Rebounds: Louisville 2; Middle Tenn. St. 3. Disqualified: Middle Tenn. St.—Hailey, Campbell. Technical fouls: None.

	1st Half	2nd Half	Final
Middle Tenn. St.	22	34	56
Louisville	30	51	81

Tennessee-Chattanooga (61)   Coach: Arnold Murray

	Min.	Total FG/FGA	Pct.	FT/FTA	Pct.	Reb. O/T	A	TO	PF	S	Blk	TP	PPM
WHITE, W.	40	11/13	.846	0/0	.000	-/3	2	1	4	1	0	22	.550
SCHOENE, R.	40	9/18	.500	2/2	1.000	-/12	1	3	2	0	0	20	.500
LAWRENCE, S.	19	1/3	.333	0/0	.000	-/2	0	1	5	0	0	2	.105
MORKEN, N.	40	2/4	.500	2/2	1.000	-/4	6	0	2	2	0	6	.150
CLARK, S.	40	5/10	.500	0/0	.000	-/1	3	2	3	2	0	10	.250
STRICKLAND, S.	21	0/2	.000	1/3	.333	-/3	0	1	4	0	0	1	.048
Totals	200	28/50	.560	5/7	.714	-/25	12	8	20	5	0	61	.305

Minnesota (62)   Coach: Jim Dutcher

	Min.	Total FG/FGA	Pct.	FT/FTA	Pct.	Reb. O/T	A	TO	PF	S	Blk	TP	PPM
WILEY, J.	22	0/1	.000	1/2	.500	-/5	2	0	2	0	0	1	.045
HOLMES, G.	28	2/4	.500	0/2	.000	-/2	2	2	1	1	0	4	.143
BREUER, R.	37	7/9	.778	3/6	.500	-/9	1	0	3	1	1	17	.459
MITCHELL, J.	40	7/13	.538	2/2	1.000	-/2	4	5	2	2	1	16	.400
TUCKER, T.	40	8/17	.471	4/5	.800	-/4	3	3	2	1	0	20	.500
PETERSEN, J.	10	0/0	.000	2/2	1.000	-/2	1	2	2	0	0	2	.200
DAVIS, T.	17	1/5	.200	0/0	.000	-/1	1	0	1	0	0	2	.118
HOWELL,	6	0/0	.000	0/0	.000	-/0	0	0	1	0	0	0	.000
Totals	200	25/49	.510	12/19	.632	-/25	14	12	14	5	2	62	.310

Team Rebounds: Minnesota 4; Tenn.-Chatt. 1. Disqualified: Tenn.-Chatt.—Lawrence.

	1st Half	2nd Half	Final
Tenn.-Chatt.	36	25	61
Minnesota	34	28	62

SECOND ROUND WEST

Wyoming (43) Coach: Jim Brandenburg

	Min.	Total FG/FGA	Pct.	FT/FTA	Pct.	Reb. O/T	A	TO	PF	S	Blk	TP	PPM
GARNETT, B.	-	2/5	.400	1/2	.500	-/0	0	4	4	1	0	5	-
THESENVITZ, G.	-	1/1	1.000	0/1	.000	-/3	0	0	1	0	0	2	-
ENGLER, C.	-	5/8	.625	4/4	1.000	-/5	0	2	2	0	0	14	-
JACKSON, M.	-	4/9	.444	3/3	1.000	-/3	3	7	3	3	0	11	-
McCLENDON, D.	-	1/3	.333	2/2	1.000	-/3	1	3	3	0	0	4	-
GOWENS, R.	-	0/0	.000	1/2	.500	-/0	0	2	1	0	0	1	-
IRVING, W.	-	1/1	1.000	0/0	.000	-/0	0	0	3	0	0	2	-
MARTIN, A.	-	0/0	.000	0/0	.000	-/0	0	0	0	0	0	0	-
WRAPP, M.	-	2/3	.667	0/0	.000	-/2	0	0	5	0	0	4	-
RENNER, J.	-	0/0	.000	0/0	.000	-/0	0	0	0	0	0	0	-
Totals	200	16/30	.533	11/14	.786	-/16	4	18	22	4	0	43	.215

Georgetown (51) Coach: John Thompson

	Min.	Total FG/FGA	Pct.	FT/FTA	Pct.	Reb. O/T	A	TO	PF	S	Blk	TP	PPM
SMITH, E.	-	4/8	.500	5/7	.714	-/0	5	2	2	1	0	13	-
HANCOCK, M.	-	1/3	.333	0/0	.000	-/1	0	1	3	2	0	2	-
EWING, P.	-	3/6	.500	1/3	.333	-/8	0	1	2	1	1	7	-
LLOYD, E.	-	5/8	.625	1/2	.500	-/1	3	1	4	0	0	11	-
BROWN, F.	-	2/4	.500	0/0	.000	-/2	2	2	4	2	0	4	-
JONES, A.	-	1/2	.500	0/6	.000	-/1	0	0	1	1	0	2	-
MARTIN, B.	-	0/1	.000	3/1	3.000	-/2	0	3	1	1	0	3	-
SPRIGGS, E.	-	4/7	.571	1/-	-	-/5	1	1	0	0	0	9	-
Totals	200	20/39	.513	11/19	.579	-/20	11	11	17	8	1	51	.255

Team Rebounds: Georgetown 2; Wyoming 1. Disqualified: Wyoming—Wrapp. Technical fouls: Georgetown—Floyd.

	1st Half	2nd Half	Final
Wyoming	24	19	43
Georgetown	29	22	51

West Virginia (46) Coach: Gale Catlett

	Min.	Total FG/FGA	Pct.	FT/FTA	Pct.	Reb. O/T	A	TO	PF	S	Blk	TP	PPM
ROWE, L.	37	6/6	1.000	2/2	1.000	-/5	0	3	5	0	0	14	.378
TODD, R.	32	1/3	.333	3/4	.750	-/3	0	3	3	0	0	5	.156
COLLINS, P.	29	1/2	.500	0/0	.000	-/1	3	3	3	0	0	2	.069
JONES, G.	40	6/14	.429	5/6	.833	-/1	4	1	2	3	0	17	.425
WASHAM, T.	36	1/3	.333	0/0	.000	-/0	2	4	2	0	0	2	.056
FREEMAN, Q.	4	0/1	.000	0/0	.000	-/0	0	0	0	0	0	0	.000
GIPSON, D.	8	2/2	1.000	0/0	.000	-/0	0	1	1	0	0	4	.500
KING, M.	14	0/0	.000	2/4	.500	-/2	0	3	2	0	0	2	.143
Totals	200	17/31	.548	12/16	.750	-/12	9	18	18	3	0	46	.230

Fresno State (50) Coach: Boyd Grant

	Min.	Total FG/FGA	Pct.	FT/FTA	Pct.	Reb. O/T	A	TO	PF	S	Blk	TP	PPM
HIGGINS, R.	40	6/10	.600	6/7	.857	-/4	0	2	2	1	1	18	.450
DAVIS, B.	39	3/6	.500	2/5	.400	-/4	2	1	3	0	2	8	.205
THOMPSON, B.	28	3/5	.600	1/3	.333	-/2	0	2	4	0	0	7	.250
MASON, D.	40	3/7	.429	0/0	.000	-/5	4	3	4	2	0	6	.150
BRADLEY, T.	26	4/8	.500	3/5	.600	-/0	3	0	1	3	0	11	.423
BARMORE, D.	12	0/2	.000	0/0	.000	-/1	0	0	1	0	0	0	.000
NIEVES, A.	13	0/0	.000	0/0	.000	-/0	0	2	0	0	0	0	.000
SEZZI, D.	2	0/0	.000	0/0	.000	-/0	0	2	0	0	0	0	.000
Totals	200	19/38	.500	12/20	.600	-/16	9	12	15	6	3	50	.250

Team Rebounds: Fresno State 4; West Virginia 3. Disqualified: West Virginia—Rowe. Technical fouls: Fresno State—bench; West Virginia—Gipson.

	1st Half	2nd Half	Final
West Virginia	27	19	46
Fresno State	27	23	50

Iowa (67) Coach: Lute Olson

	Min.	Total FG/FGA	Pct.	FT/FTA	Pct.	Reb. O/T	A	TO	PF	S	Blk	TP	PPM
HANSEN, B.	44	5/12	.417	1/2	.500	-/4	1	2	3	0	0	11	.250
BOYLE, K.	33	5/7	.714	0/0	.000	-/2	1	2	5	1	0	10	.303
PAYNE, M.	28	4/11	.364	1/2	.500	-/7	4	2	5	0	2	9	.321
CARFINO, S.	25	4/6	.667	0/0	.000	-/4	3	2	5	0	0	8	.320
ARNOLD, K.	45	3/8	.375	2/2	1.000	-/2	5	1	3	0	0	8	.178
BERKENPAS, T.	4	1/2	.500	0/0	.000	-/0	0	1	0	0	0	2	.500
DENNARD, J.	11	2/4	.500	2/3	.667	-/2	0	0	1	0	0	6	.545
ANDERSON, C.	22	2/4	.500	1/3	.333	-/2	1	0	0	0	0	5	.227
STOKES, G.	13	2/3	.667	4/7	.571	-/2	0	0	5	1	0	8	.615
Totals	225	28/57	.491	11/19	.579	-/25	15	10	27	2	2	67	.298

Idaho (69) Coach: Don Monson

	Min.	Total FG/FGA	Pct.	FT/FTA	Pct.	Reb. O/T	A	TO	PF	S	Blk	TP	PPM
HERBERT, G.	45	1/6	.167	2/2	1.000	-/3	1	3	3	0	0	4	.089
HOPSON, P.	45	7/12	.583	7/10	.700	-/9	1	2	3	0	1	21	.467
SMITH, K.	34	7/10	.700	2/3	.667	-/8	1	2	5	0	1	16	.471
KELLERMAN, B.	45	5/9	.556	4/6	.667	-/2	2	2	4	1	0	14	.311
OWENS, K.	45	0/5	.000	12/12	1.000	-/1	4	5	2	0	0	12	.267
PRIGGE, P.	11	0/2	.000	2/2	1.000	-/0	0	0	1	0	0	2	.182
Totals	225	20/44	.455	29/35	.829	-/23	9	14	18	1	2	69	.307

Team Rebounds: Idaho 9; Iowa 7. Disqualified: Idaho—Smith; Iowa—Boyle, Payne, Carfino, Stokes. Technical fouls: None.

	1st Half	2nd Half	1st OT	Final
Iowa	23	34	10	67
Idaho	33	24	12	69

Pepperdine (51) Coach: Jim Harrick

	Min.	Total FG/FGA	Pct.	FT/FTA	Pct.	Reb. O/T	A	TO	PF	S	Blk	TP	PPM
PHILLIPS, O.	-	8/12	.667	0/3	.000	-/12	0	1	4	0	1	16	-
SADLER, B.	-	3/5	.600	0/2	.000	-/1	1	1	5	1	0	6	-
McCOLLUM, S.	-	0/2	.000	0/0	.000	-/2	1	1	1	0	0	0	-
SUTTLE, D.	-	5/10	.500	0/0	.000	-/2	3	4	5	0	0	10	-
BOND, B.	-	3/9	.333	3/4	.750	-/2	1	1	4	1	0	9	-
WILSON, M.	-	0/2	.000	4/4	1.000	-/1	1	2	4	0	0	4	-
STEVENS, C.	-	0/0	.000	0/0	.000	-/0	0	1	2	0	0	0	-
NETHERTON, D.	-	1/1	1.000	0/0	.000	-/1	0	0	0	0	0	2	-
GONDREZICK, G.	-	0/1	.000	0/0	.000	-/0	0	0	0	0	0	0	-
ANGER, V.	-	2/2	1.000	0/0	.000	-/3	2	2	2	0	0	4	-
Totals	200	22/44	.500	7/13	.538	-/24	9	13	27	2	1	51	.255

Oregon State (70) Coach: Ralph Miller

	Min.	Total FG/FGA	Pct.	FT/FTA	Pct.	Reb. O/T	A	TO	PF	S	Blk	TP	PPM
EVANS, D.	-	7/15	.467	4/5	.800	-/4	1	0	3	0	0	18	-
GREEN, A.	-	3/7	.429	2/4	.500	-/8	1	1	2	0	0	8	-
SITTON, C.	-	4/9	.444	6/6	1.000	-/3	4	1	2	0	1	14	-
CONNER, L.	-	4/11	.364	8/9	.889	-/7	2	1	2	1	1	16	-
BREW, W.	-	3/4	.750	3/5	.600	-/2	0	3	3	4	0	9	-
TAIT, A.	-	0/0	.000	0/0	.000	-/0	0	0	1	0	0	0	-
STANGEL, J.	-	0/0	.000	0/0	.000	-/0	0	0	1	0	0	0	-
WILSON, J.	-	0/0	.000	1/2	.500	-/0	0	0	0	0	0	1	-
HOLBROOK, R.	-	2/4	.500	0/0	.000	-/2	1	0	2	0	0	4	-
Totals	200	23/50	.460	24/31	.774	-/24	12	6	17	1	2	70	.350

Team Rebounds: Oregon State 6; Pepperdine 4. Disqualified: Pepperdine—Sadler, Suttle. Technical fouls: Pepperdine—Sadler, Coach Harrick.

	1st Half	2nd Half	Final
Pepperdine	27	24	51
Oregon State	33	37	70

REGIONAL SEMIFINAL EAST

North Carolina (74)   Coach: Dean Smith

	Min.	Total FG/FGA	Pct.	FT/FTA	Pct.	Reb. O/T	A	TO	PF	S	Blk	TP	PPM
DOHERTY, M.	35	5/9	.556	6/6	1.000	-/2	3	0	2	0	0	16	.457
WORTHY, J.	35	4/11	.364	8/8	1.000	-/8	3	3	3	0	0	16	.457
PERKINS, S.	39	5/8	.625	5/7	.714	-/5	1	1	2	1	0	15	.385
BLACK, J.	39	6/7	.857	2/4	.500	-/2	6	4	1	0	0	14	.359
JORDAN, M.	33	3/6	.500	5/5	1.000	-/3	3	2	4	1	0	11	.333
PETERSON, B.	7	1/1	1.000	0/1	.000	-/1	0	0	1	1	0	2	.286
BARLOW, J.	3	0/0	.000	0/0	.000	-/1	0	0	0	0	0	0	.000
BRUST, C.	5	0/1	.000	0/0	.000	-/1	0	1	1	0	0	0	.000
BRADDOCK, J.	2	0/0	.000	0/0	.000	-/0	1	0	0	0	0	0	.000
MARTIN, W.	1	0/0	.000	0/0	.000	-/0	0	1	0	0	0	0	.000
EXUM, C.	1	0/0	.000	0/0	.000	-/0	0	0	0	0	0	0	.000
Totals	200	24/43	.558	26/31	.839	-/23	17	12	14	3	0	74	.370

Alabama (69)   Coach: Wimp Sanderson

	Min.	Total FG/FGA	Pct.	FT/FTA	Pct.	Reb. O/T	A	TO	PF	S	Blk	TP	PPM
WINDHAM, C.	9	2/4	.500	2/2	1.000	-/2	0	0	2	0	0	6	.667
PHILLIPS, E.	20	7/9	.778	2/4	.500	-/2	0	1	5	0	0	16	.800
HURT, B.	30	6/8	.750	0/0	.000	-/8	0	1	5	0	1	12	.400
WHATLEY, E.	40	4/13	.308	2/2	1.000	-/2	4	6	3	2	0	10	.250
DAVIS, M.	34	3/6	.500	1/2	.500	-/1	1	1	3	0	0	7	.206
RICHARDSON, E.	36	5/7	.714	0/0	.000	-/0	6	1	3	0	0	10	.278
LOCKETT, P.	19	1/3	.333	4/6	.667	-/3	0	0	5	0	0	6	.316
WILLIAMS, T.	12	1/3	.333	0/0	.000	-/1	0	1	1	0	1	2	.167
Totals	200	29/53	.547	11/16	.688	-/19	11	11	27	2	2	69	.345

Team Rebounds: N. Carolina 2; Alabama 2. Disqualified: Alabama—Phillips, Hurt, Lockett. Technical fouls: None.

	1st Half	2nd Half	Final
N. Carolina	41	33	74
Alabama	36	33	69

Villanova (70)   Coach: Rollie Massimino

	Min.	Total FG/FGA	Pct.	FT/FTA	Pct.	Reb. O/T	A	TO	PF	S	Blk	TP	PPM
PINCKNEY, E.	-	4/8	.500	8/12	.667	-/10	1	2	2	2	6	16	-
HOWARD, A.	-	8/10	.800	0/1	.000	-/2	0	1	4	1	0	16	-
PINONE, J.	-	8/17	.471	3/6	.500	-/12	3	0	3	2	0	19	-
GRANGER, S.	-	4/9	.444	2/2	1.000	-/2	6	6	4	2	0	10	-
MCCLAIN, D.	-	1/5	.200	0/0	.000	-/1	8	3	4	1	0	2	-
MCLAIN, G.	-	0/0	.000	0/0	.000	-/0	1	1	0	0	0	0	-
SICES, J.	-	0/0	.000	0/0	.000	-/0	0	0	1	0	0	0	-
DOBBS, F.	-	0/0	.000	0/0	.000	-/0	1	0	0	0	0	0	-
MULQUIN, M.	-	1/2	.500	5/5	1.000	-/1	0	1	0	0	0	7	-
Totals	225	26/51	.510	18/26	.692	-/28	20	14	18	8	6	70	.311

Memphis State (66)   Coach: Dana Kirk

	Min.	Total FG/FGA	Pct.	FT/FTA	Pct.	Reb. O/T	A	TO	PF	S	Blk	TP	PPM
PARKS, B.	42	4/9	.444	2/2	1.000	-/5	1	4	4	0	0	10	.238
LEE, K.	24	7/10	.700	0/1	.000	-/4	1	2	5	2	2	14	.583
PHILLIPS, D.	37	5/10	.500	2/4	.500	-/10	0	1	4	1	1	12	.324
JACKSON, O.	45	5/15	.333	3/6	.500	-/5	8	8	2	1	0	13	.289
HAYNES, P.	42	6/11	.545	1/2	.500	-/0	2	3	3	2	0	13	.310
GIPSON, J.	13	1/2	.500	0/0	.000	-/1	1	0	1	0	0	2	.154
TAYLOR, G.	22	1/2	.500	0/0	.000	-/3	1	0	1	0	0	2	.091
Totals	225	29/59	.492	8/15	.533	-/28	14	18	20	6	3	66	.293

Team Rebounds: Villanova 3; Memphis State 3. Disqualified: Memphis State—Lee. Technical fouls: None.

	1st Half	2nd Half	1st OT	Final
Villanova	35	27	8	70
Memphis State	31	31	4	66

REGIONAL SEMIFINAL MIDWEST

Boston College (69)   Coach: Tom Davis

	Min.	Total FG/FGA	Pct.	FT/FTA	Pct.	Reb. O/T	A	TO	PF	S	Blk	TP	PPM
SHRIGLEY, R.	23	0/1	.000	0/0	.000	-/2	4	2	4	0	0	0	.000
CLARK, M.	23	2/5	.400	3/3	1.000	-/6	2	1	2	0	0	7	.304
MURPHY, J.	24	2/6	.333	7/8	.875	-/7	2	1	3	1	1	11	.458
CHANDLER, D.	25	1/3	.333	0/0	.000	-/0	0	0	2	2	0	2	.080
BAGLEY, J.	38	4/12	.333	2/2	1.000	-/4	2	5	2	2	0	10	.263
ADAMS, M.	29	7/8	.875	6/8	.750	-/3	3	1	0	1	0	20	.690
GARRIS, J.	29	7/14	.500	4/5	.800	-/7	1	2	3	0	4	18	.621
SCHMIDT, M.	8	0/0	.000	0/0	.000	-/1	0	0	1	0	0	0	.000
ADAMS, B.	1	0/0	.000	1/2	.500	-/0	0	0	1	0	0	1	1.000
Totals	200	23/49	.469	23/28	.821	-/30	14	12	17	7	5	69	.345

Kansas State (65)   Coach: Jack Hartman

	Min.	Total FG/FGA	Pct.	FT/FTA	Pct.	Reb. O/T	A	TO	PF	S	Blk	TP	PPM
NEALY, E.	-	3/6	.500	0/0	.000	-/10	4	2	4	0	0	6	-
REED, R.	-	5/10	.500	6/7	.857	-/5	1	2	4	1	0	16	-
CRAFT, L.	-	2/4	.500	0/0	.000	-/4	1	1	1	0	4	4	-
JANKOVICH, T.	-	5/10	.500	0/0	.000	-/2	7	0	4	1	0	10	-
ADAMS, T.	-	8/17	.471	0/2	.000	-/5	3	3	3	0	0	16	-
GALVAO, E.	-	3/5	.600	0/0	.000	-/0	2	3	3	3	0	6	-
WATKINS, L.	-	3/6	.500	1/2	.500	-/2	2	2	2	0	0	7	-
Totals	200	29/58	.500	7/11	.636	-/28	20	13	21	5	4	65	.325

Team Rebounds: Boston College 2; Kansas State 2. Disqualified: None. Technical fouls: None.

	1st Half	2nd Half	Final
Boston College	36	33	69
Kansas State	41	24	65

Houston (79)   Coach: Guy Lewis

	Min.	Total FG/FGA	Pct.	FT/FTA	Pct.	Reb. O/T	A	TO	PF	S	Blk	TP	PPM
DREXLER, C.	37	5/9	.556	4/6	.667	5/10	3	3	4	2	1	14	.378
YOUNG, M.	34	6/11	.545	3/5	.600	2/3	2	1	5	1	1	15	.441
MICHEAUX, L.	28	5/6	.833	1/2	.500	3/9	0	3	4	0	1	11	.393
ROSE, L.	33	7/11	.636	2/2	1.000	1/2	5	3	2	0	0	16	.485
WILLIAMS, R.	32	4/15	.267	2/3	.667	1/2	0	6	3	1	0	10	.313
DAVIS, M.	11	0/0	.000	0/0	.000	0/1	0	1	1	1	0	0	.000
OLAJUWON, A.	25	5/9	.556	3/7	.429	4/11	0	1	4	3	3	13	.520
Totals	200	32/61	.525	15/25	.600	16/38	10	18	23	8	6	79	.395

Missouri (78)   Coach: Norm Stewart

	Min.	Total FG/FGA	Pct.	FT/FTA	Pct.	Reb. O/T	A	TO	PF	S	Blk	TP	PPM
FRAZIER, R.	39	11/20	.550	7/11	.636	-/8	1	5	3	3	0	29	.744
MCCRARY, M.	21	2/5	.400	0/0	.000	-/4	4	2	3	0	0	4	.190
STIPANOVICH, S.	40	7/14	.500	3/6	.500	-/12	2	8	4	1	1	17	.425
SUNDVOLD, J.	39	6/12	.500	2/2	1.000	-/3	2	1	1	0	1	14	.359
BRIDGES, P.	27	0/2	.000	3/4	.750	-/1	2	1	4	1	0	3	.111
DRESSLER, M.	9	1/1	1.000	2/2	1.000	-/2	0	0	3	0	0	4	.444
WALKER, M.	8	1/2	.500	0/0	.000	-/0	1	0	0	0	0	2	.250
CAVENER, G.	15	2/5	.400	0/4	.000	-/3	5	1	2	1	0	4	.267
JONES, R.	2	0/0	.000	1/2	.500	-/0	0	0	0	0	0	1	.500
Totals	200	30/61	.492	18/31	.581	-/33	17	18	20	6	2	78	.390

Team Rebounds: Houston 2; Missouri 3. Disqualified: Houston—Young. Technical fouls: None.

	1st Half	2nd Half	Final
Houston	38	41	79
Missouri	32	46	78

REGIONAL SEMIFINAL MIDEAST

Virginia (66)　　Coach: Terry Holland

	Min.	Total FG / FGA	Pct.	FT / FTA	Pct.	Reb. O / T	A	TO	PF	S	Blk	TP	PPM
MILLER, J.	26	3/10	.300	4/ 4	1.000	-/ 5	1	3	4	0	0	10	.385
ROBINSON, C.	21	2/ 5	.400	2/ 2	1.000	-/ 4	0	6	3	0	0	6	.286
SAMPSON, R.	37	8/18	.444	3/ 6	.500	-/21	2	1	4	0	2	19	.514
JONES, J.	33	9/ 9	1.000	0/ 0	.000	-/ 1	4	4	3	0	0	18	.545
MULLEN, T.	30	3/ 7	.429	1/ 1	1.000	-/ 3	1	2	5	0	0	7	.233
WILSON, O.	4	0/ 1	.000	0/ 0	.000	-/ 0	0	0	0	0	0	0	.000
STOKES, R.	26	1/ 3	.333	0/ 1	.000	-/ 3	2	0	2	2	0	2	.077
EDELIN, K.	23	2/ 4	.500	0/ 3	.000	-/ 7	2	2	3	2	0	4	.174
Totals	200	28/57	.491	10/17	.588	-/44	12	18	24	4	2	66	.330

Alabama-Birmingham (68)　　Coach: Gene Bartow

	Min.	Total FG / FGA	Pct.	FT / FTA	Pct.	Reb. O / T	A	TO	PF	S	Blk	TP	PPM
GILES, C.	40	2/ 7	.286	1/ 2	.500	-/ 6	2	2	3	1	0	5	.125
FOSTER, L.	37	4/ 7	.571	4/ 5	.800	-/ 3	4	0	1	2	0	12	.324
ANCHRUM, N.	27	2/10	.200	1/ 3	.333	-/ 3	0	2	3	1	2	5	.185
NICHOLAS, J.	27	4/ 6	.667	3/ 4	.750	-/ 5	0	3	2	1	1	11	.407
ROBINSON, O.	40	8/17	.471	7/ 7	1.000	-/ 5	9	5	2	1	0	23	.575
GAUSE, R.	6	0/ 1	.000	0/ 0	.000	-/ 0	0	0	1	0	0	0	.000
LANE, C.	7	0/ 0	.000	2/ 2	1.000	-/ 1	1	0	1	0	0	2	.286
SPEER, D.	16	4/ 7	.571	2/ 2	1.000	-/ 2	0	2	4	1	1	10	.625
Totals	200	24/55	.436	20/25	.800	-/25	16	11	18	8	4	68	.340

Team Rebounds: Ala.-Birmingham 3; Virginia 0. Disqualified: Virginia—Mullen. Technical fouls: Virginia—Coach Holland, bench.

	1st Half	2nd Half	Final
Virginia	37	29	66
Ala.-Birmingham	33	35	68

Louisville (67)　　Coach: Denny Crum

	Min.	Total FG / FGA	Pct.	FT / FTA	Pct.	Reb. O / T	A	TO	PF	S	Blk	TP	PPM
MCCRAY, R.	35	3/ 5	.600	2/ 2	1.000	-/ 6	2	1	3	1	1	8	.229
SMITH, D.	22	5/ 5	1.000	7/10	.700	-/ 6	4	5	4	3	0	17	.773
BROWN, W.	14	1/ 3	.333	0/ 0	.000	-/ 3	1	2	1	0	0	2	.143
GORDON, L.	39	10/14	.714	3/ 4	.750	-/ 4	0	2	3	1	0	23	.590
EAVES, J.	39	2/ 7	.286	2/ 2	1.000	-/ 2	1	2	1	1	0	6	.154
WAGNER, M.	2	1/ 1	1.000	0/ 0	.000	-/ 0	0	0	0	0	0	2	1.000
MCCRAY, S.	9	0/ 2	.000	2/ 2	1.000	-/ 0	5	0	1	1	0	2	.222
JONES, C.	30	3/ 3	1.000	0/ 1	.000	-/ 3	1	3	1	5	1	6	.200
WRIGHT, P.	10	0/ 3	.000	1/ 3	.333	-/ 2	1	2	3	0	1	1	.100
Totals	200	25/43	.581	17/24	.708	-/26	15	17	16	12	3	67	.335

Minnesota (61)　　Coach: Jim Dutcher

	Min.	Total FG / FGA	Pct.	FT / FTA	Pct.	Reb. O / T	A	TO	PF	S	Blk	TP	PPM
WILEY, J.	30	1/ 4	.250	0/ 0	.000	-/ 5	7	1	4	2	0	2	.067
HOLMES, G.	28	3/ 4	.750	1/ 2	.500	-/ 4	1	3	2	0	0	7	.250
BREUER, R.	40	9/15	.600	4/ 6	.667	-/12	1	1	2	0	3	22	.550
MITCHELL, D.	36	3/ 8	.375	0/ 0	.000	-/ 0	2	4	4	4	0	6	.167
TUCKER, T.	39	10/19	.526	2/ 2	1.000	-/ 2	3	3	4	3	0	22	.564
PETERSEN, J.	12	0/ 3	.000	0/ 0	.000	-/ 0	2	1	3	0	3	0	.000
HOWELL, Z.	6	0/ 0	.000	2/ 2	1.000	-/ 1	0	1	0	0	0	2	.333
DAVIS, T.	9	0/ 3	.000	0/ 0	.000	-/ 3	1	2	1	0	0	0	.000
Totals	200	26/56	.464	9/12	.750	-/27	17	16	20	9	6	61	.305

Team Rebounds: Louisville 0; Minnesota 1. Disqualified: None. Technical fouls: None.

	1st Half	2nd Half	Final
Louisville	32	35	67
Minnesota	31	30	61

REGIONAL SEMIFINAL WEST

Georgetown (58)　　Coach: John Thompson

	Min.	Total FG / FGA	Pct.	FT / FTA	Pct.	Reb. O / T	A	TO	PF	S	Blk	TP	PPM
SMITH, E.	36	3/ 7	.429	4/ 4	1.000	-/ 5	4	2	1	1	0	10	.278
HANCOCK, M.	14	0/ 1	.000	0/ 0	.000	-/ 1	0	0	1	0	0	0	.000
EWING, P.	31	7/ 8	.875	1/ 1	1.000	-/ 6	0	4	3	1	2	15	.484
BROWN, F.	18	1/ 1	1.000	7/ 9	.778	-/ 3	2	1	4	1	0	9	.500
FLOYD, E.	35	7/ 9	.778	2/ 2	1.000	-/ 4	1	3	3	0	0	16	.457
SMITH, G.	15	1/ 2	.500	0/ 0	.000	-/ 0	3	1	0	1	0	2	.133
SPRIGGS, E.	27	0/ 2	.000	2/ 2	1.000	-/ 2	0	0	1	0	0	2	.074
JONES, A.	10	1/ 1	1.000	0/ 0	.000	-/ 0	0	1	0	0	0	2	.200
MARTIN, B.	14	1/ 2	.500	0/ 0	.000	-/ 2	0	0	0	0	0	2	.143
Totals	200	21/33	.636	16/18	.889	-/23	10	12	13	4	2	58	.290

Fresno State (40)　　Coach: Boyd Grant

	Min.	Total FG / FGA	Pct.	FT / FTA	Pct.	Reb. O / T	A	TO	PF	S	Blk	TP	PPM
HIGGINS, R.	39	6/11	.545	0/ 0	.000	-/ 3	1	3	4	1	0	12	.308
THOMPSON, B.	27	1/ 3	.333	5/ 5	1.000	-/ 2	1	0	5	1	0	7	.259
DAVIS B.	26	2/ 5	.400	3/ 4	.750	-/ 3	3	0	1	1	0	7	.269
BRADLEY, T.	26	1/ 2	.500	0/ 0	.000	-/ 0	0	1	3	1	0	2	.077
MASON, D.	30	1/ 7	.143	0/ 0	.000	-/ 1	1	4	2	3	0	2	.067
BAREMORE, D.	26	4/ 8	.500	0/ 0	.000	-/ 2	0	1	3	0	1	8	.308
NIEVES, O.	15	0/ 0	.000	0/ 0	.000	-/ 1	1	0	1	0	0	0	.000
ARNOLD, M.	9	0/ 0	.000	0/ 0	.000	-/ 0	2	0	0	0	0	0	.000
SEZZI, D.	1	0/ 1	.000	0/ 0	.000	-/ 0	0	1	0	0	0	0	.000
WEATHERSPOON, J.	1	1/ 2	.500	0/ 0	.000	-/ 0	0	0	0	0	0	2	2.000
Totals	200	16/39	.410	8/ 9	.889	-/12	9	10	19	7	1	40	.200

Team Rebounds: Georgetown 1; Fresno State 2. Disqualified: Fresno State—Thompson. Technical fouls: None.

	1st Half	2nd Half	Final
Georgetown	25	33	58
Fresno State	20	20	40

Idaho (42)　　Coach: Don Monson

	Min.	Total FG / FGA	Pct.	FT / FTA	Pct.	Reb. O / T	A	TO	PF	S	Blk	TP	PPM
HERBERT, G.	39	4/ 9	.444	4/ 5	.800	-/ 5	4	3	3	1	0	12	.308
HOPSON, P.	39	5/ 9	.556	0/ 0	.000	-/ 5	2	1	3	0	0	10	.256
SMITH, K.	34	0/ 3	.000	1/ 2	.500	-/ 3	0	1	5	0	0	1	.029
KELLERMAN, B.	39	4/ 7	.571	2/ 2	1.000	-/ 1	2	3	2	1	0	10	.256
OWENS, K.	39	2/ 6	.333	3/ 5	.600	-/ 2	2	3	4	2	0	7	.179
PRIGGE, P.	4	1/ 2	.500	0/ 0	.000	-/ 0	0	0	1	0	0	2	.500
HASKINS, M.	1	0/ 0	.000	0/ 0	.000	-/ 0	0	0	0	0	0	0	.000
MURCHISON, A.	1	0/ 0	.000	0/ 1	.000	-/ 0	0	0	0	0	0	0	.000
ROSS, B.	1	0/ 0	.000	0/ 0	.000	-/ 0	0	0	0	0	0	0	.000
MABEN, M.	1	0/ 1	.000	0/ 0	.000	-/ 0	0	0	0	0	0	0	.000
HAATVADT, K.	1	0/ 0	.000	0/ 0	.000	-/ 0	0	0	0	0	0	0	.000
WATKINS, F.	1	0/ 1	.000	0/ 0	.000	-/ 0	0	0	1	0	0	0	.000
Totals	200	16/38	.421	10/15	.667	-/16	10	11	19	4	0	42	.210

Oregon State (60)　　Coach: Ralph Miller

	Min.	Total FG / FGA	Pct.	FT / FTA	Pct.	Reb. O / T	A	TO	PF	S	Blk	TP	PPM
EVANS, D.	36	2/ 9	.222	2/ 2	1.000	-/ 2	1	1	4	0	0	6	.167
GREEN, A.	18	4/ 6	.667	0/ 1	.000	-/ 4	0	2	3	0	0	8	.444
SITTON, C.	39	7/ 9	.778	2/ 3	.667	-/ 7	2	5	2	1	0	16	.410
CONNER, L.	39	10/14	.714	4/ 4	1.000	-/10	5	2	3	1	0	24	.615
BREW, W.	39	1/ 5	.200	0/ 1	.000	-/ 2	2	1	2	1	1	2	.051
WILTJER, G.	1	0/ 0	.000	0/ 0	.000	-/ 1	0	0	1	0	0	0	.000
WILSON, J.	1	0/ 0	.000	0/ 0	.000	-/ 1	0	0	0	0	0	0	.000
STANGEL, J.	1	0/ 0	.000	0/ 0	.000	-/ 0	0	0	0	0	0	0	.000
HOLBROOK, R.	25	1/ 3	.333	2/ 2	1.000	-/ 5	3	1	3	0	0	4	.160
TAIT, A.	1	0/ 0	.000	0/ 0	.000	-/ 0	0	0	0	0	0	0	.000
Totals	200	25/46	.543	10/13	.769	-/33	13	12	18	3	1	60	.300

Team Rebounds: Oregon State 0; Idaho 1. Disqualified: Idaho—Smith. Technical fouls: Idaho—Coach Monson.

	1st Half	2nd Half	Final
Idaho	25	17	42
Oregon State	31	29	60

REGIONAL FINAL EAST

North Carolina (70)   Coach: Dean Smith

	Min.	Total FG / FGA	Pct.	FT / FTA	Pct.	Reb. O / T	A	TO	PF	S	Blk	TP	PPM
DOHERTY, M.	37	4/ 8	.500	5/ 5	1.000	-/ 1	3	3	2	0	0	13	.351
WORTHY, J.	37	6/10	.600	2/ 3	.667	-/ 5	4	2	2	0	2	14	.378
PERKINS, S.	38	4/ 8	.500	5/ 5	1.000	-/ 7	2	1	4	1	3	13	.342
BLACK, J.	38	4/ 5	.800	3/ 4	.750	-/ 3	10	2	2	2	0	11	.289
JORDAN, M.	30	5/ 9	.556	5/ 7	.714	-/ 1	2	2	2	2	0	15	.500
PETERSON, B.	8	1/ 2	.500	0/ 0	.000	-/ 1	0	0	0	0	0	2	.250
BARLOW, J.	2	1/ 1	1.000	0/ 0	.000	-/ 0	0	0	0	0	0	2	1.000
BRUST, C.	4	0/ 0	.000	0/ 0	.000	-/ 0	0	2	0	0	0	0	.000
BRADDOCK, J.	2	0/ 0	.000	0/ 0	.000	-/ 0	0	0	0	0	0	0	.000
MARTIN, W.	1	0/ 0	.000	0/ 0	.000	-/ 0	0	0	0	0	0	0	.000
EXUM, C.	2	0/ 1	.000	0/ 0	.000	-/ 0	0	0	0	0	0	0	.000
ROBINSON, L.	1	0/ 0	.000	0/ 0	.000	-/ 0	0	1	0	0	0	0	.000
Totals	200	25/44	.568	20/24	.833	-/18	21	13	12	5	5	70	.350

Villanova (60)   Coach: Rollie Massimino

	Min.	Total FG / FGA	Pct.	FT / FTA	Pct.	Reb. O / T	A	TO	PF	S	Blk	TP	PPM
PINCKNEY, E.	39	8/13	.615	2/ 4	.500	-/10	0	3	3	2	0	18	.462
HOWARD, A.	18	3/ 5	.600	0/ 0	.000	-/ 0	0	0	5	0	0	6	.333
PINONE, J.	37	6/11	.545	2/ 3	.667	-/ 6	4	2	5	1	0	14	.378
GRANGER, S.	35	2/ 8	.250	0/ 0	.000	-/ 1	6	4	4	0	0	4	.114
MCCLAIN, D.	21	2/ 7	.286	0/ 0	.000	-/ 2	0	1	3	0	1	4	.190
MCLAIN, G.	6	2/ 2	1.000	0/ 0	.000	-/ 0	0	2	0	0	0	4	.667
SICES, J.	2	1/ 1	1.000	0/ 0	.000	-/ 0	0	0	0	0	0	2	1.000
DOBBS, F.	18	1/ 5	.200	2/ 2	1.000	-/ 1	1	0	0	0	0	4	.222
MULQUIN, M.	21	1/ 2	.500	0/ 0	.000	-/ 3	1	1	2	0	0	2	.095
SHERRY, J.	2	0/ 0	.000	0/ 0	.000	-/ 0	0	0	0	0	0	0	.000
LUTSCHAUNIG, M.	1	1/ 1	1.000	0/ 0	.000	-/ 0	0	0	0	0	0	2	2.000
Totals	200	27/55	.491	6/ 9	.667	-/23	12	13	22	3	1	60	.300

Team Rebounds: N. Carolina 2; Villanova 0. Disqualified: Villanova—Howard, Pinone. Technical fouls: None.

	1st Half	2nd Half	Final
N. Carolina	28	42	70
Villanova	22	38	60

REGIONAL FINAL MIDWEST

Boston College (92)   Coach: Tom Davis

	Min.	Total FG / FGA	Pct.	FT / FTA	Pct.	Reb. O / T	A	TO	PF	S	Blk	TP	PPM
SHRIGLEY, R.	30	5/ 6	.833	0/ 3	.000	-/ 3	3	1	4	1	0	10	.333
CLARK, M.	25	1/ 3	.333	0/ 0	.000	-/ 6	3	3	5	0	0	2	.080
MURPHY, J.	27	9/18	.500	5/ 7	.714	-/11	1	2	1	0	0	23	.852
CHANDLER, D.	23	0/ 1	.000	0/ 0	.000	-/ 2	0	1	5	2	0	0	.000
BAGLEY, J.	35	11/18	.611	4/ 6	.667	-/ 4	5	3	4	0	0	26	.743
ADAMS, M.	30	4/10	.400	0/ 0	.000	-/ 2	1	1	5	1	0	8	.267
GARRIS, J.	25	6/11	.545	7/ 9	.778	-/ 5	1	3	5	0	2	19	.760
SCHMIDT, M.	1	1/ 2	.500	0/ 0	.000	-/ 1	0	0	1	0	0	2	2.000
ADAMS, B.	4	1/ 2	.500	0/ 0	.000	-/ 2	0	0	3	1	0	2	.500
Totals	200	38/71	.535	16/25	.640	15/36	14	14	33	5	2	92	.460

Houston (99)   Coach: Guy Lewis

	Min.	Total FG / FGA	Pct.	FT / FTA	Pct.	Reb. O / T	A	TO	PF	S	Blk	TP	PPM
DREXLER, C.	35	6/ 9	.667	3/ 6	.500	4/ 9	1	3	5	2	0	15	.429
YOUNG, M.	31	3/12	.250	0/ 0	.000	2/ 7	1	1	4	1	0	6	.194
MICHEAUX, L.	35	7/11	.636	4/ 7	.571	2/ 7	0	4	2	2	3	18	.514
ROSE, L.	34	6/10	.600	3/ 5	.600	0/ 1	7	2	5	3	1	15	.441
WILLIAMS, R.	39	9/17	.529	7/10	.700	4/ 5	2	1	3	0	0	25	.641
DAVIS, E.	7	0/ 0	.000	4/ 4	1.000	1/ 3	1	0	0	0	0	4	.571
OLAJUWON, A.	11	2/ 3	.667	2/ 2	1.000	1/ 3	0	3	4	2	2	6	.545
GETTYS, R.	8	0/ 0	.000	10/10	1.000	0/ 2	0	1	0	0	0	10	1.250
Totals	200	33/62	.532	33/44	.750	14/37	12	15	23	10	6	99	.495

Team Rebounds: Houston 1; Boston College 3. Disqualified: Houston—Drexler, Rose; Boston College—Clark, Chandler, Adams, Garris. Technical fouls: None.

	1st Half	2nd Half	Final
Boston College	43	49	92
Houston	46	53	99

REGIONAL FINAL MIDEAST

Alabama-Birmingham (68)   Coach: Gene Bartow

	Min.	Total FG / FGA	Pct.	FT / FTA	Pct.	Reb. O / T	A	TO	PF	S	Blk	TP	PPM
GILES, C.	33	6/11	.545	0/ 0	.000	-/ 8	2	3	5	0	0	12	.364
FOSTER, L.	39	5/ 9	.556	3/ 4	.750	-/ 3	3	1	4	2	0	13	.333
ANCHRUM, N.	30	3/ 7	.429	3/ 4	.750	-/ 6	0	3	5	0	1	9	.300
NICHOLAS, J.	25	3/ 7	.429	2/ 2	1.000	-/ 1	4	2	3	2	0	8	.320
ROBINSON, O.	39	9/21	.429	2/ 2	1.000	-/ 6	0	5	4	1	0	20	.513
GAUSE, R.	5	0/ 0	.000	0/ 0	.000	-/ 1	0	1	1	0	0	0	.000
LANE, C.	13	1/ 3	.333	2/ 2	1.000	-/ 1	0	2	1	1	0	4	.308
SPEER, D.	14	0/ 3	.000	0/ 2	.000	-/ 0	0	0	2	0	0	0	.000
JOHNSON, M.	2	1/ 1	1.000	0/ 0	.000	-/ 1	0	0	0	0	0	2	1.000
Totals	200	28/62	.452	12/16	.750	-/27	9	17	25	6	1	68	.340

Louisville (75)   Coach: Denny Crum

	Min.	Total FG / FGA	Pct.	FT / FTA	Pct.	Reb. O / T	A	TO	PF	S	Blk	TP	PPM
MCCRAY, R.	26	3/ 4	.750	0/ 3	.000	-/11	3	3	2	0	0	6	.231
SMITH, D.	29	5/12	.417	4/ 4	1.000	-/ 6	1	4	4	0	2	14	.483
BROWN, W.	9	0/ 2	.000	0/ 0	.000	-/ 1	2	0	1	0	1	0	.000
GORDON, L.	28	4/ 7	.571	3/ 4	.750	-/ 2	5	3	3	2	0	11	.393
EAVES, J.	33	6/ 9	.667	1/ 1	1.000	-/ 3	2	6	3	0	0	13	.394
WAGNER, M.	19	2/ 2	1.000	0/ 0	.000	-/ 1	4	2	1	2	0	4	.211
MCCRAY, S.	20	3/ 3	1.000	0/ 0	.000	-/ 3	1	2	2	2	0	6	.300
JONES, C.	27	5/ 7	.714	9/13	.692	-/ 4	2	2	2	0	0	19	.704
WRIGHT, P.	9	1/ 2	.500	0/ 0	.000	-/ 1	0	0	0	0	0	2	.222
Totals	200	29/48	.604	17/25	.680	-/32	20	22	18	6	3	75	.375

Team Rebounds: Louisville 3; Ala.-Birmingham 1. Disqualified: Ala.-Birmingham—Giles, Anchrum. Technical fouls: None.

	1st Half	2nd Half	Final
Ala.-Birmingham	32	36	68
Louisville	40	35	75

REGIONAL FINAL WEST

Georgetown (69) Coach: John Thompson

	Min.	Total FG/FGA	Pct.	FT/FTA	Pct.	Reb. O/T	A	TO	PF	S	Blk	TP	PPM
SMITH, E.	-	1/ 2	.500	2/ 4	.500	-/ 1	3	0	1	1	0	4	-
HANCOCK, M.	-	1/ 2	.500	2/ 2	1.000	-/ 6	0	1	0	0	0	4	-
EWING, P.	-	6/ 9	.667	1/ 2	.500	-/ 3	0	5	5	1	1	13	-
BROWN, F.	-	4/ 4	1.000	1/ 1	1.000	-/ 7	2	3	4	1	0	9	-
FLOYD, E.	-	9/12	.750	4/ 5	.800	-/ 3	2	2	1	1	0	22	-
SPRIGGS, E.	-	4/ 5	.800	0/ 1	.000	-/ 5	0	1	2	0	1	8	-
SMITH, G.	-	0/ 0	.000	0/ 0	.000	-/ 0	1	0	0	0	0	0	-
JONES, A.	-	3/ 4	.750	1/ 2	.500	-/ 0	2	3	1	0	0	7	-
MARTIN, B.	-	0/ 0	.000	0/ 0	.000	-/ 0	0	0	0	0	0	0	-
KAULL, K.	-	1/ 1	1.000	0/ 0	.000	-/ 0	0	0	0	0	0	2	-
BLAYLOCK, R.	-	0/ 0	.000	0/ 0	.000	-/ 0	0	0	0	0	0	0	-
BLUE, D.	-	0/ 0	.000	0/ 0	.000	-/ 0	1	0	0	0	0	0	-
Totals	200	29/39	.744	11/17	.647	-/25	11	15	14	4	2	69	.345

Oregon State (45) Coach: Ralph Miller

	Min.	Total FG/FGA	Pct.	FT/FTA	Pct.	Reb. O/T	A	TO	PF	S	Blk	TP	PPM
EVANS, D.	22	4/13	.308	0/ 0	.000	-/ 2	1	1	4	0	0	8	.364
GREEN, A.	33	3/ 4	.750	4/ 8	.500	-/ 5	0	5	2	0	0	10	.303
SITTON, C.	29	6/ 9	.667	0/ 0	.000	-/ 2	1	2	5	0	1	12	.414
CONNER, L.	40	6/10	.600	1/ 2	.500	-/ 1	5	2	3	2	0	13	.325
BREW, W.	38	0/ 6	.000	0/ 0	.000	-/ 2	3	1	2	0	0	0	.000
HOLBROOK, R.	.27	1/ 7	.143	0/ 0	.000	-/ 1	2	1	4	0	0	2	.074
WILTJER, G.	4	0/ 2	.000	0/ 0	.000	-/ 2	0	0	0	0	0	0	.000
STANGEL, J.	6	0/ 1	.000	0/ 0	.000	-/ 0	0	0	0	0	0	0	.000
TAIT, A.	1	0/ 0	.000	0/ 0	.000	-/ 0	0	1	0	0	0	0	.000
Totals	200	20/52	.385	5/10	.500	-/15	12	12	20	2	1	45	.225

Team Rebounds: Georgetown 3; Oregon State 7. Disqualified: Georgetown—Ewing; Oregon State—Sitton. Technical fouls: None.

	1st Half	2nd Half	Final
Georgetown	42	27	69
Oregon State	25	20	45

FINAL FOUR

North Carolina (68) Coach: Dean Smith

	Min.	Total FG/FGA	Pct.	FT/FTA	Pct.	Reb. O/T	A	TO	PF	S	Blk	TP	PPM
DOHERTY, M.	37	2/ 7	.286	1/ 2	.500	-/ 1	5	2	1	1	0	5	.135
WORTHY, J.	39	7/10	.700	0/ 0	.000	-/ 4	3	5	3	2	2	14	.359
PERKINS, S.	39	9/11	.818	7/ 7	1.000	-/10	1	1	1	1	0	25	.641
BLACK, J.	38	1/ 2	.500	4/ 6	.667	-/ 3	4	4	4	1	0	6	.158
JORDAN, M.	39	7/14	.500	4/ 4	1.000	-/ 5	2	3	4	0	0	18	.462
PETERSON, B.	3	0/ 0	.000	0/ 0	.000	-/ 1	0	0	0	0	0	0	.000
BRUST, J.	1	0/ 0	.000	0/ 0	.000	-/ 0	0	0	1	0	0	0	.000
BRADDOCK, J.	3	0/ 0	.000	0/ 0	.000	-/ 0	0	0	0	0	0	0	.000
MARTIN, W.	1	0/ 0	.000	0/ 0	.000	-/ 0	0	0	0	0	0	0	.000
Totals	200	26/44	.591	16/19	.842	-/24	15	15	14	5	2	68	.340

Louisville (46) Coach: Denny Crum

	Min.	Total FG/FGA	Pct.	FT/FTA	Pct.	Reb. O/T	A	TO	PF	S	Blk	TP	PPM
MCCRAY, R.	30	2/ 5	.400	4/ 4	1.000	-/ 5	2	4	5	1	2	8	.267
SMITH, D.	26	4/ 8	.500	2/ 4	.500	-/ 6	1	5	4	0	2	10	.385
BROWN, W.	13	2/ 5	.400	0/ 0	.000	-/ 1	0	0	1	1	0	4	.308
GORDON, L.	29	1/ 6	.167	0/ 0	.000	-/ 1	3	2	2	2	0	2	.069
EAVES, J.	34	4/ 9	.444	0/ 0	.000	-/ 4	1	4	1	2	0	8	.235
WAGNER, M.	20	1/ 4	.250	0/ 0	.000	-/ 2	1	1	3	0	0	2	.100
MCCRAY, S.	15	0/ 1	.000	0/ 0	.000	-/ 0	1	1	1	0	2	0	.000
JONES, C.	21	4/ 7	.571	0/ 2	.000	-/ 6	0	1	0	2	0	8	.381
WRIGHT, P.	12	1/ 3	.333	2/ 2	1.000	-/ 0	0	0	1	0	0	4	.333
Totals	200	19/48	.396	8/12	.667	-/25	9	18	18	8	6	46	.230

Houston (63) Coach: Guy Lewis

	Min.	Total FG/FGA	Pct.	FT/FTA	Pct.	Reb. O/T	A	TO	PF	S	Blk	TP	PPM
DREXLER, C.	40	6/12	.500	5/ 6	.833	-/ 9	3	3	3	2	0	17	.425
YOUNG, M.	15	1/ 7	.143	0/ 1	.000	-/ 3	1	0	0	0	0	2	.133
MICHEAUX, L.	37	8/14	.571	2/ 3	.667	-/ 6	0	1	2	1	2	18	.486
ROSE, L.	36	10/15	.667	0/ 2	.000	-/ 2	3	3	2	2	0	20	.556
WILLIAMS, R.	35	0/ 8	.000	2/ 2	1.000	-/ 1	2	3	1	1	0	2	.057
DAVIS, E.	4	1/ 2	.500	0/ 0	.000	-/ 0	0	0	3	1	0	2	.500
ANDERS, B.	1	0/ 2	.000	0/ 0	.000	-/ 0	0	0	2	0	0	0	.000
OLAJUWON, A.	20	1/ 3	.333	0/ 0	.000	-/ 6	0	1	4	1	2	2	.100
WILLIAMS, B.	12	0/ 1	.000	0/ 0	.000	-/ 1	0	1	2	2	0	0	.000
Totals	200	27/64	.422	9/14	.643	-/28	9	12	19	10	4	63	.315

Team Rebounds: N. Carolina 2; Houston 5. Disqualified: None. Technical fouls: None.

	1st Half	2nd Half	Final
N. Carolina	31	37	68
Houston	29	34	63

Georgetown (50) Coach: John Thompson

	Min.	Total FG/FGA	Pct.	FT/FTA	Pct.	Reb. O/T	A	TO	PF	S	Blk	TP	PPM
SMITH, E.	36	6/10	.600	2/ 4	.500	-/ 2	1	4	2	0	1	14	.389
HANCOCK, M.	15	1/ 3	.333	0/ 0	.000	-/ 2	0	3	0	0	0	2	.133
EWING, P.	37	3/ 8	.375	2/ 2	1.000	-/10	1	4	2	2	1	8	.216
BROWN, F.	36	1/ 3	.333	2/ 3	.667	-/ 3	2	3	4	2	1	4	.111
FLOYD, E.	31	3/11	.273	7/ 8	.875	-/ 5	3	3	4	1	0	13	.419
SPRIGGS, E.	20	2/ 2	1.000	1/ 3	.333	-/ 7	0	1	2	2	1	5	.250
SMITH, G.	4	0/ 0	.000	0/ 0	.000	-/ 0	0	0	1	0	0	0	.000
JONES, A.	13	2/ 4	.500	0/ 0	.000	-/ 3	0	0	1	2	0	4	.308
MARTIN, B.	8	0/ 0	.000	0/ 0	.000	-/ 1	0	0	0	0	0	0	.000
Totals	200	18/41	.439	14/20	.700	-/33	7	18	16	9	4	50	.250

Team Rebounds: Georgetown 1; Louisville 2. Disqualified: Louisville—R. McCray. Technical fouls: None.

	1st Half	2nd Half	Final
Louisville	22	24	46
Georgetown	24	26	50

NATIONAL CHAMPIONSHIP

North Carolina (63)   Coach: Dean Smith

	Min.	Total FG / FGA	Pct.	FT / FTA	Pct.	Reb. O / T	A	TO	PF	S	Blk	TP	PPM
DOHERTY, M.	39	1/ 3	.333	2/ 3	.667	-/ 3	1	3	0	0	0	4	.103
WORTHY, J.	38	13/17	.765	2/ 7	.286	-/ 4	0	3	3	3	0	28	.737
PERKINS, S.	38	3/ 7	.429	4/ 6	.667	-/ 7	1	0	2	0	1	10	.263
BLACK, J.	38	1/ 4	.250	2/ 2	1.000	-/ 3	7	2	2	1	0	4	.105
JORDAN, M.	34	7/13	.538	2/ 2	1.000	-/ 9	2	3	2	2	0	16	.471
PETERSON, B.	7	0/ 3	.000	0/ 0	.000	-/ 1	1	2	0	1	0	0	.000
BRUST, C.	4	0/ 0	.000	1/ 2	.500	-/ 1	1	0	1	0	0	1	.250
BRADDOCK, J.	2	0/ 0	.000	0/ 0	.000	-/ 0	1	0	1	0	0	0	.000
Totals	200	25/47	.532	13/22	.591	-/28	14	13	11	7	1	63	.315

Georgetown (62)   Coach: John Thompson

	Min.	Total FG / FGA	Pct.	FT / FTA	Pct.	Reb. O / T	A	TO	PF	S	Blk	TP	PPM
SMITH, E.	35	6/ 8	.750	2/ 2	1.000	-/ 3	5	2	5	0	0	14	.400
HANCOCK, M.	8	0/ 2	.000	0/ 0	.000	-/ 0	0	1	1	0	0	0	.000
EWING, P.	37	10/15	.667	3/ 3	1.000	-/11	1	0	4	3	2	23	.622
BROWN, F.	29	1/ 2	.500	2/ 2	1.000	-/ 2	5	4	4	2	0	4	.138
FLOYD, E.	39	9/17	.529	0/ 0	.000	-/ 3	5	3	2	4	0	18	.462
SPRIGGS, E.	30	0/ 2	.000	1/ 2	.500	-/ 1	0	1	2	2	0	1	.033
SMITH, G.	7	0/ 0	.000	0/ 0	.000	-/ 0	0	0	1	0	0	0	.000
JONES, A.	10	1/ 3	.333	0/ 0	.000	-/ 0	0	0	0	0	0	2	.200
MARTIN, B.	5	0/ 2	.000	0/ 0	.000	-/ 0	0	1	1	0	0	0	.000
Totals	200	27/51	.529	8/ 9	.889	-/20	16	12	20	11	2	62	.310

Team Rebounds: N. Carolina 2; Georgetown 2. Disqualified: Georgetown—E. Smith. Technical fouls: None.

	1st Half	2nd Half	Final
N. Carolina	31	32	63
Georgetown	32	30	62

○ ALL-STAR TEAMS ○

ALL TOURNAMENT

PATRICK EWING	GEORGETOWN
ERIC FLOYD	GEORGETOWN
MICHAEL JORDAN	N. CAROLINA
SAM PERKINS	N. CAROLINA
★ JAMES WORTHY	N. CAROLINA

MIDEAST REGIONAL

LANCASTER GORDON	LOUISVILLE
CHARLES JONES	LOUISVILLE
★ OLIVER ROBINSON	ALA.-BIRMINGHAM
RALPH SAMPSON	VIRGINIA
DEREK SMITH	LOUISVILLE

EAST REGIONAL

JIMMY BLACK	N. CAROLINA
SAM PERKINS	N. CAROLINA
ED PINCKNEY	VILLANOVA
JOHN PINONE	VILLANOVA
★ JAMES WORTHY	N. CAROLINA

WEST REGIONAL

LESTER CONNER	OREGON STATE
PATRICK EWING	GEORGETOWN
★ ERIC FLOYD	GEORGETOWN
ROD HIGGINS	FRESNO STATE
CHARLIE SITTON	OREGON STATE

MIDWEST REGIONAL

JOHN BAGLEY	BOSTON COLLEGE
RICKY FRAZIER	MISSOURI
JOHN GARRIS	BOSTON COLLEGE
LARRY MICHEAUX	HOUSTON
★ ROBERT WILLIAMS	HOUSTON

★ Most Outstanding Player(s)

○ INDIVIDUAL RECORDS ○

SCORING

Most points in a single game

1	PERRY MOSS, NORTHEASTERN (vs. VILLANOVA)	31
2	RICKY FRAZIER, MISSOURI (vs. HOUSTON)	29
3	QUINTIN DAILEY, SAN FRANCISCO (vs. BOSTON COLLEGE)	28
3	JAMES WORTHY, N. CAROLINA (vs. GEORGETOWN)	28
5	ORLANDO PHILLIPS, PEPPERDINE (vs. PITTSBURGH)	27

Most total points in the tournament

1	ROBERT WILLIAMS, HOUSTON	91
2	JAMES WORTHY, N. CAROLINA	87
3	SAM PERKINS, N. CAROLINA	80
3	CLYDE DREXLER, HOUSTON	80
5	JOHN BAGLEY, BOSTON COLLEGE	72

Highest scoring average (minimum 2 games)

1	PERRY MOSS, NORTHEASTERN (55-2)	27.50
2	RICKY FRAZIER, MISSOURI (49-2)	24.50
3	OLIVER ROBINSON, ALA.-BIRMINGHAM (66-3)	22.00
4	ORLANDO PHILLIPS, PEPPERDINE (43-2)	21.50
5	TRENT TUCKER, MINNESOTA (42-2)	21.00

FIELD GOALS

Most field goals in a single game

1	PERRY MOSS, NORTHEASTERN (vs. VILLANOVA)	14
2	QUINTIN DAILEY, SAN FRANCISCO (vs. BOSTON COLLEGE)	13
2	JAMES WORTHY, N. CAROLINA (vs. GEORGETOWN)	13
4	7 tied for fourth place.	

Most total field goals in the tournament

1	JAMES WORTHY, N. CAROLINA	34
2	LYNDEN ROSE, HOUSTON	32
2	CLYDE DREXLER, HOUSTON	32
4	ROBERT WILLIAMS, HOUSTON	31
5	2 tied for fifth place.	

Most field goal attempts in a single game

1	PERRY MOSS, NORTHEASTERN (vs. VILLANOVA)	29
2	TED KITCHEL, INDIANA (vs. ALA.-BIRMINGHAM)	27
3	QUINTIN DAILEY, SAN FRANCISCO (vs. BOSTON COLLEGE)	25
3	BRAD LEAF, EVANSVILLE (vs. MARQUETTE)	25
5	DWAYNE WALLACE, PITTSBURGH (vs. PEPPERDINE)	23

Most total field goal attempts in tournament

1	ROBERT WILLIAMS, HOUSTON	71
2	JAMES WORTHY, N. CAROLINA	55
2	OLIVER ROBINSON, ALA.-BIRMINGHAM	55
4	CLYDE DREXLER, HOUSTON	54
5	JOHN BAGLEY, BOSTON COLLEGE	53

Highest field goal percentage in a single game (minimum 10 attempts)
1 WILLIE WHITE, TENN.-CHATT. (vs. MINNESOTA) (11-13) .846
2 SAM PERKINS, N. CAROLINA (vs. HOUSTON) (9-11) .818
3 AARON HOWARD, VILLANOVA (vs. MEMPHIS STATE) (8-10) .800
3 MICHAEL YOUNG, HOUSTON (vs. ALCORN ST.) (8-10) .800
5 ORLANDO PHILLIPS, PEPPERDINE (vs. PITTSBURGH) (11-14) .786

Highest field goal percentage in the tournament (minimum 20 attempts)
1 ORLANDO PHILLIPS, PEPPERDINE (19-26) .731
2 JIMMY BLACK, N. CAROLINA (16-22) .727
3 CHARLES JONES, LOUISVILLE (16-23) .696
4 RANDY BREUER, MINNESOTA (16-24) .667
5 AARON HOWARD, VILLANOVA (14-21) .667

FREE THROWS

Most free throws in a single game
1 KEN OWENS, IDAHO (vs. IOWA) 12
2 LES CRAFT, KANSAS STATE (vs. NORTHERN ILL.) 11
2 MARK WRAPP, WYOMING (vs. USC) 11
2 ROBERT WILLIAMS, HOUSTON (vs. ALCORN ST.) 11
5 3 tied for fifth place.

Most total free throws in the tournament
1 ROBERT WILLIAMS, HOUSTON 29
2 SAM PERKINS, N. CAROLINA 24
3 JAMES WORTHY, N. CAROLINA 19
4 DEREK SMITH, LOUISVILLE 18
4 MICHAEL ADAMS, BOSTON COLLEGE 18

Most free throws attempted in a single game
1 CHARLES JONES, LOUISVILLE (vs. ALA.-BIRMINGHAM) 13
1 MARK WRAPP, WYOMING (vs. USC) 13
3 6 tied for third place.

Most free throws attempted in the tournament
1 ROBERT WILLIAMS, HOUSTON 38
2 SAM PERKINS, N. CAROLINA 31
3 JAY MURPHY, BOSTON COLLEGE 28
4 JAMES WORTHY, N. CAROLINA 26
4 CLYDE DREXLER, HOUSTON 26

Highest free throw percentage in a single game (minimum 7 attempts)
1 KEN OWENS, IDAHO (vs. IOWA) (12-12) 1.000
2 LES CRAFT, KANSAS STATE (vs. NORTHERN ILL.) (11-11) 1.000

3 REID GETTYS, HOUSTON (vs. BOSTON COLLEGE) (10-10) 1.000
3 EDDIE PHILLIPS, ALABAMA (vs. ST. JOHN'S) (10-10) 1.000
5 STEVE HARRIS, TULSA (vs. HOUSTON) (9-9) 1.000

Highest free throw percentage in the tournament (minimum 15 attempts)
1 KEN OWENS, IDAHO (15-17) .882
2 ERIC FLOYD, GEORGETOWN (13-15) .867
2 LESTER CONNER, OREGON STATE (13-15) .867
4 MICHAEL JORDAN, N. CAROLINA (16-20) .800
4 JERRY BECK, MIDDLE TENN. ST. (16-20) .800

REBOUNDS

Most rebounds in a single game
1 RALPH SAMPSON, VIRGINIA (vs. ALA.-BIRMINGHAM) 21
2 TERRY CUMMINGS, DEPAUL (vs. BOSTON COLLEGE) 17
3 MICHAEL PAYNE, IOWA (vs. NORTHEAST LA.) 14
4 3 tied for fourth place.

Most total rebounds in the tournament
1 CLYDE DREXLER, HOUSTON 41
2 SAM PERKINS, N. CAROLINA 39
3 LARRY MICHEAUX, HOUSTON 38
3 PAT EWING, GEORGETOWN 38
5 AKEEM OLAJUWON, HOUSTON 31

Most rebounds per game (minimum 2 games)
1 RALPH SAMPSON, VIRGINIA (30-2) 15.00
2 STEVE STIPANOVICH, MISSOURI (21-2) 10.50
2 MICHAEL PAYNE, IOWA (21-2) 10.50
2 RANDY BREUER, MINNESOTA (21-2) 10.50
5 ED PINCKNEY, VILLANOVA (30-3) 10.00

ASSISTS

Most assists in a single game
1 BRYAN WARRICK, ST. JOSEPH'S (vs. NORTHEASTERN) 10
1 JIMMY BLACK, N. CAROLINA (vs. VILLANOVA) 10
3 OLIVER ROBINSON, ALA.-BIRMINGHAM (vs. VIRGINIA) 9
4 5 tied for fourth place.

Most total assists in the tournament
1 JIMMY BLACK, N. CAROLINA 31
2 LYNDEN ROSE, HOUSTON 21
3 ERIC SMITH, GEORGETOWN 18
4 STEWART GRANGER, VILLANOVA 16
5 2 tied for fifth place.

Most assists per game (minimum 2 appearances)
1 TYRONE BEAMAN, TENNESSEE (14-2) 7.00
2 OTIS JACKSON, MEMPHIS STATE (13-2) 6.50
3 JIMMY BLACK, N. CAROLINA (31-5) 6.20
4 M. WILSON, MARQUETTE (11-2) 5.50
4 DANE SUTTLE, PEPPERDINE (11-2) 5.50

TURNOVERS

Most turnovers in a single game
1 JOHN BAGLEY, BOSTON COLLEGE (vs. DEPAUL) 8
1 OTIS JACKSON, MEMPHIS STATE (vs. VILLANOVA) 8
1 STEVE STIPANOVICH, MISSOURI (vs. HOUSTON) 8
1 RICK CAMPBELL, MIDDLE TENN. ST. (vs. LOUISVILLE) 8
5 4 tied for fifth place.

Most total turnovers in the tournament
1 ROBERT WILLIAMS, HOUSTON 24
2 JOHN BAGLEY, BOSTON COLLEGE 18
3 JAMES WORTHY, N. CAROLINA 16
3 LARRY MICHEAUX, HOUSTON 16
3 JERRY EAVES, LOUISVILLE 16

SHOTS BLOCKED

Most shots blocked in a single game
1 ED PINCKNEY, VILLANOVA (vs. MEMPHIS STATE) 6
2 LUCIOUS HAILEY, MIDDLE TENN. ST. (vs. KENTUCKY) 5
2 LEN CRAFT, KANSAS STATE (vs. ARKANSAS) 5
4 5 tied for fourth place.

Most total shots blocked in the tournament
1 LES CRAFT, KANSAS STATE 12
2 JOHN GARRIS, BOSTON COLLEGE 11
3 AKEEM OLAJUWON, HOUSTON 10
4 ED PINCKNEY, VILLANOVA 9
5 3 tied for fifth place.

STEALS

Most steals in a single game
1 CHARLES JONES, LOUISVILLE (vs. MINNESOTA) 5
1 ED NEALY, KANSAS STATE (vs. ARKANSAS) 5
1 CLYDE DREXLER, HOUSTON (vs. ALCORN ST.) 5
4 13 tied for fourth place.

Most total steals in the tournament
1 CLYDE DREXLER, HOUSTON 14
2 CHARLES JONES, LOUISVILLE 9
3 4 tied for third place.

✪ TEAM RECORDS ✪

SCORING

Most points in a single game
1	WEST VIRGINIA (vs. N.C. A&T)	102
2	PEPPERDINE (vs. PITTSBURGH)	99
2	HOUSTON (vs. BOSTON COLLEGE)	99

Most total points in the tournament
1	HOUSTON	413
2	N. CAROLINA	327
3	BOSTON COLLEGE	313

Highest scoring average (minimum 2 games)
1	HOUSTON (413-5)	82.60
2	INDIANA (164-2)	82.00
3	BOSTON COLLEGE (313-4)	78.25

FIELD GOALS

Most field goals in a single game
1	PITTSBURGH (vs. PEPPERDINE)	38
1	BOSTON COLLEGE (vs. HOUSTON)	38
1	HOUSTON (vs. ALCORN ST.)	38

Most total field goals in the tournament
1	HOUSTON	161
2	N. CAROLINA	120
3	2 tied for third place.	

Most field goals attempted in a single game
1	N.C. A&T (vs. WEST VIRGINIA)	82
2	PITTSBURGH (vs. PEPPERDINE)	79
3	2 tied for third place.	

Most total field goals attempted in the tournament
1	HOUSTON	299
2	BOSTON COLLEGE	220
3	N. CAROLINA	216

Highest field goal percentage in a single game
1	GEORGETOWN (vs. OREGON STATE) (29-39)	.744
2	HOUSTON (vs. ALCORN ST.) (38-58)	.655
3	GEORGETOWN (vs. FRESNO STATE) (21-33)	.636

Highest field goal percentage in a tournament (minimum 2 games)
1	WAKE FOREST (50-84)	.595
2	WEST VIRGINIA (54-94)	.575
3	GEORGETOWN (115-203)	.567

FREE THROWS

Most free throws in a single game
1	HOUSTON (vs. BOSTON COLLEGE)	33
2	3 tied for second place.	

Most total free throws in the tournament
1	HOUSTON	91
2	N. CAROLINA	87
3	BOSTON COLLEGE	83

Most free throws attempted in a single game
1	HOUSTON (vs. BOSTON COLLEGE)	44
2	BOSTON COLLEGE (vs. DEPAUL)	42
3	WEST VIRGINIA (vs. N.C. A&T)	40

Most total free throws attempted in the tournament
1	HOUSTON	139
2	BOSTON COLLEGE	128
3	N. CAROLINA	119

Highest free throw percentage in a single game
1	KENTUCKY (vs. MIDDLE TENN. ST.) (2-2)	1.000
2	GEORGETOWN (vs. FRESNO STATE) (16-18)	.889
3	2 tied for third place.	

Highest free throw percentage in the tournament (minimum 2 games)
1	ALA.-BIRMINGHAM (56-70)	.800
2	IDAHO (39-50)	.780
3	WYOMING (34-45)	.756

Fewest free throws in a single game
1	KENTUCKY (vs. MIDDLE TENN. ST)	2
2	TENN.-CHATT. (vs. MINNESOTA)	5
2	OREGON STATE (vs. GEORGETOWN)	5

Lowest free throw percentage in a single game
1	VIRGINIA (vs. TENNESSEE) (8-21)	.381
2	OREGON STATE (vs. GEORGETOWN) (5-10)	.500
3	N. CAROLINA (vs. JAMES MADISON) (12-23)	.522

Lowest free throw percentage in the tournament (minimum 2 games)
1	VIRGINIA (18-38)	.474
2	MEMPHIS STATE (20-32)	.625
3	MARQUETTE (24-38)	.632

REBOUNDS

Most rebounds in a single game
1	INDIANA (vs. ROBERT MORRIS)	50
2	WEST VIRGINIA (vs. N.C. A&T)	47
3	VIRGINIA (vs. ALA.-BIRMINGHAM)	44

Most rebounds per game (minimum 2 games)
1	INDIANA (84-2)	42.00
2	VIRGINIA (72-2)	36.00
3	HOUSTON (166-5)	33.20

ASSISTS

Most assists in a single game
1	NORTHERN ILL. (vs. KANSAS STATE)	22
2	KANSAS STATE (vs. ARKANSAS)	21
2	N. CAROLINA (vs. VILLANOVA)	21

Most assists per game (minimum 2 games)
1	KANSAS STATE (56-3)	18.67
2	VILLANOVA (49-3)	16.33
3	MINNESOTA (31-2)	15.50

TURNOVERS

Most turnovers in a single game
1	MIDDLE TENN. ST. (vs. LOUISVILLE)	26
2	HOUSTON (vs. TULSA)	25
3	MISSOURI (vs. MARQUETTE)	24

Most turnovers per game (minimum 2 games)
1	MISSOURI (42-2)	21.00
2	LOUISVILLE (74-4)	18.50
3	HOUSTON (90-5)	18.00

SHOTS BLOCKED

Most shots blocked in a single game
1	ST. JOHN'S (vs. PENNSYLVANIA)	9
2	MIDDLE TENN. ST. (vs. KENTUCKY)	8
3	MARQUETTE (vs. EVANSVILLE)	7

Most shots blocked per game (minimum 2 games)
1	ST. JOHN'S (11-2)	5.50
2	HOUSTON (27-5)	5.40
3	KANSAS STATE (13-3)	4.33

STEALS

Most steals in a single game
1	HOUSTON (vs. TULSA)	14
2	LOUISVILLE (vs. MINNESOTA)	12
2	LOUISVILLE (vs. MIDDLE TENN. ST.)	12

Most steals per game
1	HOUSTON (53-5)	10.60
2	LOUISVILLE (38-4)	9.50
3	NORTHEASTERN (17-2)	8.50

1983

| FIRST ROUND | SECOND ROUND | REGIONAL SEMIFINAL | REGIONAL FINAL | FINAL FOUR | REGIONAL FINAL | REGIONAL SEMIFINAL | SECOND ROUND | FIRST ROUND |

MIDWEST

8 Maryland 52
4 Tenn.-Chatt. 51
Maryland 50
(bye)
1 Houston 60
Houston 70
5 Georgetown 68
12 Alcorn St. 63
Georgetown 57
(bye)
4 *Memphis St. 66
*Memphis St. 63
Houston 89
6 Alabama 50
11 Lamar 73
Lamar 58
(bye)
3 Villanova 60
Villanova 55
7 Iowa 64
10 Utah St. 59
Iowa 77
(bye)
2 Missouri 63
Iowa 54
Villanova 71

Houston 94

MIDEAST

8 Tennessee 57
9 Marquette 56
Tennessee 57
(bye)
1 Louisville 70
Louisville 65
5 Purdue 55
12 Robert Morris 53
Purdue 68
(bye)
4 Arkansas 78
Arkansas 63
Louisville 80 (ot)
6 Illinois St. 49
11 Ohio 51
Ohio 40
(bye)
3 Kentucky 57
Kentucky 64
7 Oklahoma 71
10 Ala.-Birmingham 63
Oklahoma 49
(bye)
2 Indiana 63
Indiana 59
Kentucky 68

Louisville 81

N.C. State 54
Houston 52

WEST

Washington St. 49
8 Washington St. 62
9 Weber St. 52
(bye)
1 Virginia 54
Virginia 95
Princeton 42
5 Oklahoma St. 53
12 Princeton 56
(bye)
4 Boston College 51
Boston College 92
Virginia 62
N. C. State 71
6 N. C. State 69 (2 ot)
11 Pepperdine 67
(bye)
3 UNLV 70
N. C. State 75
Utah 67
7 Illinois 49
10 Utah 52
(bye)
2 UCLA 61
Utah 56
N.C. State 63

N.C. State 67

EAST

Rutgers 55
8 S'western La. 53
9 Rutgers 60
(bye)
1 St. John's 66
St. John's 67
Va. Commonwealth 54
5 Va. Commonwealth 76
12 La Salle 67
(bye)
4 Georgia 56
Georgia 70
Georgia 82
Syracuse 74
6 Syracuse 74
11 Morehead St. 59
(bye)
3 Ohio St. 79
Ohio St. 51
James Madison 49
7 West Virginia 50
10 James Madison 57
(bye)
2 N. Carolina 68
N. Carolina 64
N. Carolina 77

Georgia 60

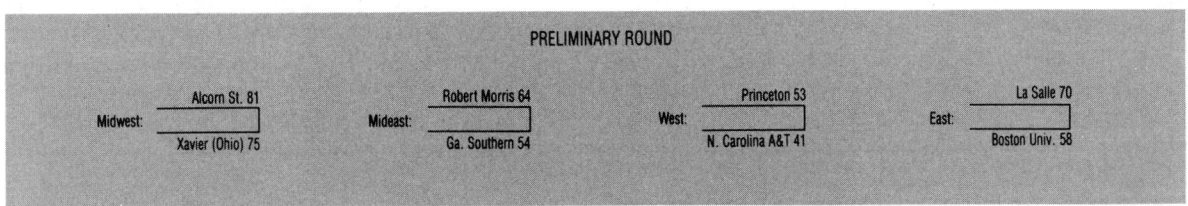
*Memphis State's participation in 1983 tournament vacated.

Maybe it was destiny. Maybe it was luck. Certainly it was utterly improbable. If the 1983 tournament were played a thousand times, it's unlikely that North Carolina State would have won more than once. But once was enough.

For one unbelievable month, Jim Valvano's Wolfpack lived on Fantasy Island. It started in the ACC tournament, which they entered with a 17-10 record. And it reached its incredible conclusion when Lorenzo Charles grabbed an off-line desperation shot and slammed it through the hoop in the final second of the NCAA tournament.

They wouldn't have even made it into the NCAAs if they hadn't beaten Wake Forest 71-70 in the first round of the ACC tourney. But once they did, they were rolling. The next night they upset North Carolina (with All-Americans Michael Jordan and Sam Perkins), and one night later they beat the nation's No. 4 team, Virginia (with All-American Ralph Sampson), to win the conference title.

In the NCAA first round (the 16 top-seeded teams didn't even have to play in the first round), they fell behind Pepperdine (ranked No. 116 by *The New York Times*) in overtime. But somehow, the Wolfpack came back from a 6-point deficit with 24 seconds remaining and Pepperdine at the foul line. North Carolina State won in the second OT.

Next, with 6-11 forward Thurl Bailey leading the charge, they came from 12 down in the last 10:46 to beat sixth-ranked UNLV. After beating Utah, they played Virginia again for the West regional championship. The Cavaliers came out in a zone, with Sampson in the middle. And the Wolfpack, as usual, fell behind. They were down by 10 with four minutes left in the first half. But they crept back, as Dereck Whittenburg lobbed high-arching mortar shots from the top of the key and beyond with pinpoint accuracy. Finally, with 3:49 left, they tied the score. Two minutes later, Sampson broke the deadlock when he slammed in his 22nd and 23rd points of the night. State came downcourt, and even the 7-4 Sampson's mammoth wingspan couldn't stop Whittenburg, who swished from downtown to tie the score at 61. Whittenburg fouled Virginia's Othell Wilson (Valvano didn't want the Cavaliers holding for a last shot). The Virginia guard hit the first, but missed the second. Bailey grabbed the rebound, passed out to Whittenburg, who found Lorenzo Charles as he moved toward the hoop. Sampson hacked him as he drove in for a lay-up. Charles hit 2, and the Wolfpack was in the Final Four.

The national title, nearly everyone believed, was sure to be decided in the semifinal between No. 1–ranked Houston and No. 2 Louisville. The survivor of that contest would have no trouble beating the winner of the game between North Carolina State and Georgia.

If State was an underdog, Georgia was too. Georgia had spent most of a quarter century in the SEC basketball cellar and had never before appeared in the NCAA tourna-ment; at Georgia, football was for Bulldogs, while basketball had always been for pussycats. But when the university hired Hugh Durham away from Florida State he began to attract real basketball players to Georgia; after Durham's dedicated Dawgs upset highly rated St. John's and North Carolina on their way to the East regional championship some folks on campus even forgot that spring football practice started the last week in March.

In the semifinal contest between the underdogs, the Wolfpack forced the speedy Bulldogs to play a half-court game, and by dominating the tempo early, State built an insurmountable lead. They won, 67-60. Only one more team stood between the Wolfpack and the title.

But that team was Akeem Olajuwon, Clyde Drexler, Larry Micheaux and the Phi Slama Jama Houston Cougars. Houston had destroyed Louisville with a 21-1 second-half dunkfest (they finished with 13 earth-shattering slams) that brought them from 8 down with 13 minutes to play to a 12-point lead with 7:39 left. And nobody was more dominating than Houston's brilliant Nigerian neophyte— although Olajuwon had picked up a basketball for the first time only four years earlier, in the second half he had 15 rebounds, 13 points, and 4 of his 8 blocked shots.

Valvano knew his North Carolina State team had to control the tempo in order to have a chance. "If the score is 100-to-something, we're not going to win the game," he said, "but if it's in the 50s . . ."

The game went according to Valvano's plan. State slowed the pace and stayed close. They got back on defense and cut off Houston's demoralizing transition game. Still, with Olajuwon dominating on both ends, the Cougars scored 17 of the first 19 points in the second half to take a 7-point lead. Then, inexplicably, Houston Coach Guy Lewis took Olajuwon out for a rest and spread his offense. Houston started turning the ball over, Whittenburg, Sidney Lowe, and Terry Gannon started hitting their long bombs, and the Cougars lost momentum. Even so, they led 52-46 after Clyde Drexler hit two foul shots with three minutes left. But Houston was a horrendous free-throw shooting team. Valvano ordered his team to foul— anyone but Drexler. Michael Young missed the front end of a one-and-one, and Whittenburg hit a jumper to bring the 'Pack to within 2. After an Olajuwon miss, it was Whittenburg again—from 24 feet—to tie. Valvano shouted at his guards to foul. And Houston's Alvin Franklin, back at the line, missed again. State set up for a last shot, but Whittenburg lost control of the ball, and when he regained the handle, he was 30 feet from the basket with time running out. He threw up a prayer. Lorenzo Charles, the 6-7 Wolfpack forward, saw that Whittenburg's shot was short. He leaped, grabbed it in midair, and jammed it home.

All season long, Guy Lewis had told his Houston team, "Most dunks wins." He was wrong. Last dunk wins.

PRELIMINARY ROUND

Alcorn State (81)   Coach: Davey Whitney

	Min.	Total FG/FGA	Pct.	FT/FTA	Pct.	Reb. O/T	A	TO	PF	S	Blk	TP	PPM
BRANDON, A.	28	6/13	.462	4/5	.800	-/4	4	3	0	1	0	16	.571
CLAYBON, D.	24	0/4	.000	1/2	.500	-/2	1	2	1	0	0	1	.042
COLLIER, T.	34	6/9	.667	3/7	.429	-/10	1	3	3	0	4	15	.441
PHELPS, M.	27	6/9	.667	6/7	.857	-/0	1	3	2	6	0	18	.667
ARCHIE, E.	32	5/11	.455	6/8	.750	-/2	4	4	4	4	0	16	.500
WHITNEY, D.	20	4/5	.800	0/1	.000	-/1	2	0	3	0	0	8	.400
BROWNER, M.	3	0/0	.000	0/0	.000	-/0	0	1	0	1	0	0	.000
WILLIAMS, D.	17	0/1	.000	3/4	.750	-/1	1	4	3	0	0	3	.176
PALMER, D.	12	1/3	.333	2/2	1.000	-/4	0	0	5	0	2	4	.333
POLLARD, T.	3	0/0	.000	0/0	.000	-/0	0	0	0	0	0	0	.000
Totals	200	28/55	.509	25/36	.694	-/24	14	20	21	12	6	81	.405

Xavier (Ohio) (75)   Coach: Bob Staak

	Min.	Total FG/FGA	Pct.	FT/FTA	Pct.	Reb. O/T	A	TO	PF	S	Blk	TP	PPM
BAILEY, D.	28	3/9	.333	4/6	.667	-/5	0	2	3	0	1	10	.357
SHIMKO, J.	17	1/1	1.000	0/0	.000	-/3	0	7	4	0	0	2	.118
JOHNSON, E.	21	3/5	.600	1/2	.500	-/11	1	2	5	2	2	7	.333
FLEMING, V.	30	8/10	.800	0/0	.000	-/2	1	5	4	0	0	16	.533
HICKS, A.	31	6/10	.600	2/4	.500	-/2	5	7	3	1	0	14	.452
JENKINS, J.	32	4/7	.571	5/7	.714	-/4	3	3	1	1	1	13	.406
WOLF, S.	16	4/6	.667	0/0	.000	-/0	2	0	1	0	0	8	.500
HARRIS, R.	7	1/1	1.000	0/0	.000	-/0	0	0	0	0	0	2	.286
LEE, R.	18	0/1	.000	3/4	.750	-/4	6	4	5	3	0	3	.167
Totals	200	30/50	.600	15/23	.652	-/31	18	30	26	7	4	75	.375

Team Rebounds: Alcorn St. 3; Xavier (Ohio) 2. Disqualified: Alcorn St.—Palmer; Xavier (Ohio)—Johnson, Lee. Technical fouls: Xavier (Ohio)—Bench.

	1st Half	2nd Half	Final
Alcorn St.	40	41	81
Xavier (Ohio)	32	43	75

Robert Morris (64)   Coach: Matt Furjanic

	Min.	Total FG/FGA	Pct.	FT/FTA	Pct.	Reb. O/T	A	TO	PF	S	Blk	TP	PPM
DUDLEY, R.	24	4/10	.400	1/1	1.000	-/5	0	1	3	0	0	9	.375
BOMBICH, E.	37	2/7	.286	4/7	.571	-/7	2	2	2	1	0	8	.216
KOSKOSKI, S.	19	0/4	.000	0/0	.000	-/3	1	1	2	1	0	0	.000
GRANT, F.	39	6/12	.500	5/6	.833	-/7	4	4	2	3	1	17	.436
HARRIS, C.	34	6/11	.545	4/6	.667	-/2	3	0	4	1	0	16	.471
PARKS, T.	28	2/7	.286	6/6	1.000	-/6	2	1	4	3	0	10	.357
COLES, P.	11	1/3	.333	1/2	.500	-/2	0	0	1	1	0	3	.273
DOBBS, M.	4	0/0	.000	1/2	.500	-/0	0	1	1	0	0	1	.250
UNDERMAN, T.	4	0/0	.000	0/1	.000	-/3	0	0	0	0	0	0	.000
Totals	200	21/54	.389	22/31	.710	-/35	12	10	19	10	1	64	.320

Georgia Southern (54)   Coach: Frank Kerns

	Min.	Total FG/FGA	Pct.	FT/FTA	Pct.	Reb. O/T	A	TO	PF	S	Blk	TP	PPM
MURPHY, D.	29	3/6	.500	2/2	1.000	-/5	1	3	1	0	0	8	.276
ADAMS, L.	28	3/5	.600	1/1	1.000	-/8	1	2	4	1	3	7	.250
WRIGHT, D.	26	0/4	.000	2/4	.500	-/11	3	0	2	0	2	2	.077
NORWOOD, E.	37	4/7	.571	0/0	.000	-/2	4	3	5	1	0	8	.216
HIGHTOWER, E.	38	5/24	.208	4/6	.667	-/5	1	1	5	0	0	14	.368
FEARS, R.	15	2/5	.400	0/0	.000	-/5	0	6	0	0	1	4	.267
RUCKER, A.	8	0/2	.000	0/1	.000	-/0	0	0	4	0	0	0	.000
McWHORTER, M.	2	0/0	.000	0/0	.000	-/0	1	0	0	0	0	0	.000
BYRD, D.	12	2/4	.500	0/0	.000	-/7	1	4	2	0	0	4	.333
FILER, T.	4	3/3	1.000	1/1	1.000	-/1	0	0	2	0	0	7	1.750
ELLIS, G.	1	0/0	.000	0/0	.000	-/0	0	0	0	0	0	0	.000
Totals	200	22/60	.367	10/15	.667	-/44	12	19	25	2	6	54	.270

Team Rebounds: Robert Morris 2; Ga. Southern 2. Disqualified: Ga. Southern—Norwood, Hightower. Technical fouls: None.

	1st Half	2nd Half	Final
Robert Morris	26	38	64
Ga. Southern	21	33	54

La Salle (70)   Coach: Lefty Ervin

	Min.	Total FG/FGA	Pct.	FT/FTA	Pct.	Reb. O/T	A	TO	PF	S	Blk	TP	PPM
LEWIS	30	5/14	.357	1/3	.333	-/9	1	2	3	0	0	11	.367
BUTTS, A.	36	6/10	.600	1/2	.500	-/12	0	4	5	1	1	13	.361
PIOTROWSKI, T.	25	4/11	.364	2/2	1.000	-/10	0	1	5	0	1	10	.400
GREENBERG	37	3/11	.273	7/8	.875	-/12	6	2	1	2	0	13	.351
BLACK	38	6/18	.333	3/3	1.000	-/4	2	6	4	0	0	15	.395
JONES	11	0/0	.000	0/2	.000	-/3	1	2	3	0	0	0	.000
PHILSON, D.	12	1/5	.200	0/0	.000	-/0	1	1	0	1	0	2	.167
KARINS	6	2/2	1.000	2/3	.667	-/1	0	0	0	0	0	6	1.000
GILMORE	1	0/0	.000	0/0	.000	-/0	0	0	0	0	0	0	.000
DAVIS	1	0/0	.000	0/0	.000	-/0	0	0	0	0	0	0	.000
CLARK	1	0/0	.000	0/0	.000	-/0	0	0	0	0	0	0	.000
BURTON	1	0/0	.000	0/0	.000	-/0	0	0	0	0	0	0	.000
TIANO	1	0/0	.000	0/1	.000	-/0	0	0	0	0	0	0	.000
Totals	200	27/71	.380	16/24	.667	-/51	11	18	21	4	2	70	.350

Boston Univ. (58)   Coach: Rick Pitino

	Min.	Total FG/FGA	Pct.	FT/FTA	Pct.	Reb. O/T	A	TO	PF	S	Blk	TP	PPM
SIMMS, T.	37	5/21	.238	6/10	.600	-/11	3	7	4	1	0	16	.432
ALEXANDER, M.	39	7/24	.292	3/5	.600	-/5	1	1	3	0	0	17	.436
IVEY, T.	12	1/2	.500	1/2	.500	-/7	0	2	3	0	0	3	.250
VINSON, D.	35	6/9	.667	0/0	.000	-/9	4	2	2	2	0	12	.343
TEAGUE, S.	34	0/5	.000	3/4	.750	-/5	2	2	4	1	0	3	.088
FIEDOR, M.	18	0/2	.000	0/0	.000	-/5	1	1	5	1	0	0	.000
BROWN, B.	13	1/4	.250	0/0	.000	-/2	1	0	2	0	0	2	.154
LEHMAN, K.	9	2/3	.667	1/1	1.000	-/2	0	1	3	0	0	5	.556
HAGAN, J.	2	0/0	.000	0/0	.000	-/0	0	0	0	0	0	0	.000
PRISCELLA, S.	1	0/0	.000	0/0	.000	-/0	0	0	0	0	0	0	.000
Totals	200	22/70	.314	14/22	.636	-/46	12	16	26	5	0	58	.290

Team Rebounds: La Salle 4; Boston Univ. 3. Disqualified: La Salle—Butts, Piotrowski; Boston Univ.—Fiedor. Technical fouls: None.

	1st Half	2nd Half	Final
La Salle	33	37	70
Boston Univ.	28	30	58

Princeton (53)   Coach: Pete Carril

	Min.	Total FG/FGA	Pct.	FT/FTA	Pct.	Reb. O/T	A	TO	PF	S	Blk	TP	PPM
ENDERLE, G.	40	6/14	.429	6/8	.750	-/8	3	2	0	0	0	18	.450
ROBINSON, C.	39	6/7	.857	3/4	.750	-/4	0	3	1	1	0	15	.385
SIMKUS, R.	39	3/4	.750	3/5	.600	-/3	4	7	4	0	0	9	.231
RYAN, W.	40	2/4	.500	0/1	.000	-/8	7	4	2	0	4	4	.100
SMYTH, J.	36	3/7	.429	1/2	.500	-/1	0	1	4	0	0	7	.194
CARTER, I.	3	0/0	.000	0/0	.000	-/0	0	0	0	0	0	0	.000
KNAPP, G.	1	0/0	.000	0/0	.000	-/1	0	0	0	0	0	0	.000
LEVY, H.	1	0/0	.000	0/0	.000	0/0	0	0	0	0	0	0	.000
MULLIN, K.	1	0/0	.000	0/0	.000	0/0	0	0	0	0	0	0	.000
Totals	200	20/36	.556	13/20	.650	-/25	14	17	11	3	0	53	.265

North Carolina A&T (41)   Coach: Don Corbett

	Min.	Total FG/FGA	Pct.	FT/FTA	Pct.	Reb. O/T	A	TO	PF	S	Blk	TP	PPM
BINION	38	6/20	.300	1/2	.500	-/9	0	3	5	3	0	13	.342
COLLINS	38	6/13	.462	0/0	.000	-/7	1	2	2	0	0	12	.316
LANAUZE	21	2/6	.333	0/0	.000	-/5	0	2	4	0	0	4	.190
BROWN	30	1/10	.100	0/0	.000	-/9	1	1	3	0	0	2	.067
BOYD	40	2/15	.133	0/0	.000	-/3	4	2	1	0	0	4	.100
BATTLE	15	0/1	.000	0/0	.000	-/4	0	0	1	2	0	0	.000
LOPEZ	4	0/0	.000	0/0	.000	-/0	0	0	0	0	0	0	.000
BOOKER	10	1/1	1.000	0/0	.000	-/1	1	0	1	2	0	2	.200
ECHOLS	4	1/4	.250	2/2	1.000	-/1	0	0	1	0	0	4	1.000
Totals	200	19/70	.271	3/4	.750	-/39	7	10	18	7	0	41	.205

Team Rebounds: Princeton 6; N.C. A&T 3. Disqualified: N.C. A&T—Binion. Technical fouls: None.

	1st Half	2nd Half	Final
Princeton	23	30	53
N. Carolina A&T	19	22	41

FIRST ROUND MIDWEST

Maryland (52)   Coach: Lefty Driesell

	Min.	Total FG/FGA	Pct.	FT/FTA	Pct.	Reb. O/T	A	TO	PF	S	Blk	TP	PPM
FARMER, E.	32	1/ 5	.200	0/ 0	.000	1/ 4	1	0	2	1	0	2	.063
BIAS, L.	29	5/ 6	.833	0/ 0	.000	1/ 7	0	2	3	2	1	10	.345
COLEMAN, B.	39	6/14	.429	2/ 3	.667	0/ 5	0	0	2	0	0	14	.359
ADKINS, J.	34	1/ 5	.200	0/ 0	.000	1/ 2	5	2	3	1	0	2	.059
BRANCH, A.	37	8/13	.615	6/10	.600	1/ 6	3	1	3	0	0	22	.595
BAXTER	6	0/ 0	.000	0/ 0	.000	0/ 6	0	2	0	0	0	0	.000
RIVERS, S.	15	0/ 2	.000	0/ 0	.000	0/ 2	2	2	2	0	1	0	.000
FOTHERGILL, M.	8	1/ 1	1.000	0/ 0	.000	0/ 3	0	2	1	0	0	2	.250
Totals	200	22/46	.478	8/13	.615	4/35	11	11	16	4	2	52	.260

Tennessee-Chattanooga (51)   Coach: Arnold Murray

	Min.	Total FG/FGA	Pct.	FT/FTA	Pct.	Reb. O/T	A	TO	PF	S	Blk	TP	PPM
WILKENS	40	5/12	.417	1/ 2	.500	2/ 6	2	2	2	1	0	11	.275
STRICKLAND	25	5/ 7	.714	1/ 2	.500	2/ 5	0	3	3	1	1	11	.440
LAWRENCE	29	1/ 3	.333	2/ 4	.500	1/ 4	2	1	3	0	0	4	.138
MCCRAY	16	0/ 1	.000	0/ 0	.000	1/ 2	2	2	1	1	0	0	.000
WHITE	40	4/15	.267	0/ 0	.000	0/ 3	3	2	1	2	0	8	.200
CLARK	24	4/11	.364	1/ 3	.333	2/ 4	1	1	2	2	0	9	.375
JOHNSON	10	0/ 2	.000	0/ 1	.000	1/ 4	0	0	1	0	1	0	.000
FERGUSON	0	0/ 0	.000	0/ 0	.000	0/ 0	0	2	0	0	0	0	-
ODEN	16	4/ 5	.800	0/ 0	.000	2/ 3	0	0	4	0	0	8	.500
Totals	200	23/56	.411	5/12	.417	11/31	10	13	16	7	2	51	.255

Team Rebounds: Maryland 2; Tenn.-Chatt. 4. Disqualified: None. Technical fouls: None. Player who played 0 min. played less than 1 min.

	1st Half	2nd Half	Final
Maryland	18	34	52
Tenn.-Chatt.	30	21	51

Georgetown (68)   Coach: John Thompson

	Min.	Total FG/FGA	Pct.	FT/FTA	Pct.	Reb. O/T	A	TO	PF	S	Blk	TP	PPM
MARTIN, B.	32	3/ 5	.600	4/ 5	.800	-/ 6	1	2	4	2	0	10	.313
WINGATE, D.	19	0/ 6	.000	5/ 7	.714	-/ 4	1	5	3	1	0	5	.263
EWING, P.	38	8/11	.727	3/ 6	.500	-/11	0	3	1	2	1	19	.500
SMITH, G.	26	1/ 3	.333	0/ 0	.000	-/ 6	4	0	4	0	0	2	.077
JACKSON, M.	27	4/ 6	.667	2/ 2	1.000	-/ 0	4	4	5	0	0	10	.370
DALTON, R.	2	1/ 1	1.000	0/ 0	.000	-/ 0	0	0	0	0	0	2	1.000
JONES, A.	24	5/ 7	.714	2/ 2	1.000	-/ 3	1	0	2	1	1	12	.500
BROADNAX, H.	15	0/ 3	.000	4/ 4	1.000	-/ 1	2	4	4	0	0	4	.267
BROWN, F.	15	1/ 2	.500	2/ 2	1.000	-/ 1	1	3	1	0	0	4	.267
DUNN, D.	2	0/ 0	.000	0/ 0	.000	-/ 0	0	0	0	0	0	0	.000
Totals	200	23/44	.523	22/28	.786	-/32	14	21	24	6	2	68	.340

Alcorn State (63)   Coach: Davey Whitney

	Min.	Total FG/FGA	Pct.	FT/FTA	Pct.	Reb. O/T	A	TO	PF	S	Blk	TP	PPM
BRANDON, A.	40	6/17	.353	0/ 0	.000	-/ 4	0	3	2	3	0	12	.300
CLAYBON, D.	22	2/ 3	.667	1/ 1	1.000	-/ 4	0	0	1	0	0	5	.227
COLLIER, T.	25	2/ 4	.500	5/ 6	.833	-/ 5	0	1	4	0	2	9	.360
ARCHIE, E.	36	2/ 8	.250	2/ 5	.400	-/ 3	7	4	4	4	1	6	.167
PHELPS, M.	36	7/15	.467	10/12	.833	-/ 5	3	1	4	4	0	24	.667
PALMER, D.	20	1/ 3	.333	2/ 2	1.000	-/ 2	0	5	5	0	0	4	.200
POLLARD, T.	8	1/ 2	.500	0/ 0	.000	-/ 2	0	0	0	0	0	2	.250
HARALSON, D.	4	0/ 1	.000	1/ 2	.500	-/ 1	0	1	1	0	0	1	.250
WHITNEY, J.	7	0/ 0	.000	0/ 0	.000	-/ 0	0	5	3	0	0	0	.000
BROWNER, M.	1	0/ 0	.000	0/ 0	.000	-/ 0	0	0	0	0	0	0	.000
WILLIAMS, D.	1	0/ 0	.000	0/ 0	.000	-/ 0	0	0	0	0	0	0	.000
Totals	200	21/53	.396	21/28	.750	-/26	10	15	24	11	3	63	.315

Team Rebounds: Georgetown 3; Alcorn St. 3. Disqualified: Georgetown—Jackson; Alcorn St.—Palmer. Technical fouls: None.

	1st Half	2nd Half	Final
Georgetown	36	32	68
Alcorn St.	34	29	63

Alabama (50)   Coach: Wimp Sanderson

	Min.	Total FG/FGA	Pct.	FT/FTA	Pct.	Reb. O/T	A	TO	PF	S	Blk	TP	PPM
JOHNSON, B.	30	3/ 6	.500	2/ 2	1.000	4/ 9	2	2	5	2	0	8	.267
WINDHAM, C.	26	2/ 5	.400	1/ 2	.500	1/ 5	0	2	5	0	0	5	.192
HURT, B.	32	6/ 8	.750	3/ 6	.500	4/12	0	2	4	1	2	15	.469
WHATLEY, E.	36	4/14	.286	2/ 2	1.000	1/ 2	6	5	4	0	0	10	.278
DAVIS, M.	30	3/14	.214	0/ 0	.000	1/ 1	2	0	3	0	0	6	.200
RICHARDSON, E.	7	0/ 3	.000	0/ 0	.000	0/ 1	1	1	0	0	0	0	.000
WHEELER, V.	6	0/ 4	.000	0/ 0	.000	1/ 1	2	1	4	0	0	0	.000
ADAMS, E.	2	1/ 1	1.000	0/ 0	.000	0/ 1	0	0	2	0	0	2	1.000
WILLIAMS, T.	28	2/ 6	.333	0/ 0	.000	0/ 3	1	2	5	0	1	4	.143
FARMER, M.	3	0/ 0	.000	0/ 0	.000	0/ 0	0	0	0	0	0	0	.000
Totals	200	21/61	.344	8/12	.667	12/35	14	15	32	3	3	50	.250

Lamar (73)   Coach: Pat Foster

	Min.	Total FG/FGA	Pct.	FT/FTA	Pct.	Reb. O/T	A	TO	PF	S	Blk	TP	PPM
KELLYBREW, B.	38	5/ 6	.833	4/ 8	.500	2/ 9	7	2	1	2	1	14	.368
PERKINS, K.	36	1/ 5	.200	3/ 4	.750	3/ 7	5	1	0	0	3	5	.139
GRAY, R.	26	2/ 9	.222	0/ 1	.000	2/ 6	0	1	3	4	1	4	.154
ROBINSON, L.	38	6/ 9	.667	8/12	.667	0/ 2	5	1	2	2	1	20	.526
SEWELL, T.	33	8/12	.667	3/ 6	.500	1/ 3	1	4	0	0	0	19	.576
WENNBERG, R.	2	0/ 0	.000	0/ 0	.000	0/ 1	0	1	0	0	0	0	.000
SNELL, N.	6	0/ 0	.000	1/ 3	.333	0/ 1	0	0	0	0	0	1	.167
MILHOUSE, G.	18	2/ 3	.667	3/ 6	.500	0/ 5	0	0	3	1	0	7	.389
MCKINNEY, W.	3	0/ 1	.000	3/ 4	.750	2/ 3	0	0	0	0	0	3	1.000
Totals	200	24/45	.533	25/44	.568	10/37	18	10	9	9	6	73	.365

Team Rebounds: Lamar 2; Alabama 1. Disqualified: Alabama—Johnson, Windham, Williams. Technical fouls: None.

	1st Half	2nd Half	Final
Alabama	28	22	50
Lamar	32	41	73

Iowa (64)   Coach: Lute Olson

	Min.	Total FG/FGA	Pct.	FT/FTA	Pct.	Reb. O/T	A	TO	PF	S	Blk	TP	PPM
PAYNE, M.	35	2/ 9	.222	2/ 2	1.000	-/10	1	3	5	1	2	6	.171
GANNON, M.	39	2/ 4	.500	5/ 8	.625	-/ 7	0	0	1	0	0	9	.231
STOKES, G.	31	7/12	.583	3/ 4	.750	-/ 9	0	3	4	1	1	17	.548
CARFINO, S.	34	1/ 5	.200	3/ 6	.500	-/ 0	3	2	3	5	0	5	.147
HANSEN, B.	38	8/20	.400	8/ 8	1.000	-/ 7	0	1	3	0	0	24	.632
BANKS, A.	9	0/ 1	.000	0/ 0	.000	-/ 1	4	0	3	0	0	0	.000
ANDERSON, C.	10	0/ 1	.000	3/ 4	.750	-/ 1	1	0	0	0	0	3	.300
DENNARD, J.	2	0/ 1	.000	0/ 0	.000	-/ 0	0	0	1	0	0	0	.000
BERKENPAS, T.	2	0/ 2	.000	0/ 0	.000	-/ 0	1	0	0	0	0	0	.000
Totals	200	20/55	.364	24/32	.750	-/35	10	9	20	7	3	64	.320

Utah State (59)   Coach: Rod Tueller

	Min.	Total FG/FGA	Pct.	FT/FTA	Pct.	Reb. O/T	A	TO	PF	S	Blk	TP	PPM
MCCULLOUGH, M.	33	4/ 8	.500	4/ 4	1.000	-/ 7	3	4	4	0	0	12	.364
ENCE, R.	35	3/ 6	.500	2/ 3	.667	-/ 5	3	1	4	1	0	8	.229
GRANT, G.	37	7/15	.467	3/ 5	.600	-/10	3	3	2	0	3	17	.459
WASHINGTON, D.	27	2/ 4	.500	0/ 0	.000	-/ 0	0	5	5	0	0	4	.148
MCMULLIN, C.	35	2/ 6	.333	0/ 2	.000	-/ 4	1	1	3	0	0	4	.114
HARRIES, S.	9	1/ 3	.333	0/ 0	.000	-/ 1	0	3	2	0	1	2	.222
PETERSON, E.	11	3/ 3	1.000	0/ 0	.000	-/ 2	0	1	2	0	0	6	.545
ROTTA, J.	13	1/ 2	.500	4/ 5	.800	-/ 1	0	0	2	0	0	6	.462
Totals	200	23/47	.489	13/19	.684	-/30	10	18	24	1	4	59	.295

Team Rebounds: Iowa 1; Utah State 2. Disqualified: Iowa—Payne; Utah State—Washington. Technical fouls: Iowa—Payne; Utah State—Harries.

	1st Half	2nd Half	Final
Iowa	30	34	64
Utah State	37	22	59

FIRST ROUND MIDEAST

Tennessee (57) Coach: Don Devoe

	Min.	Total FG / FGA	Pct.	FT / FTA	Pct.	Reb. O / T	A	TO	PF	S	Blk	TP	PPM
ELLIS, D.	40	7/ 9	.778	6/10	.600	0/ 4	0	2	3	1	0	20	.500
BURTON, W.	32	3/ 7	.429	4/ 5	.800	3/ 5	2	4	5	1	0	10	.313
FEDERMANN, D.	16	3/ 5	.600	0/ 1	.000	2/ 2	0	0	2	0	0	6	.375
BEAMON, T.	32	3/ 5	.600	0/ 0	.000	0/ 0	5	1	5	0	0	6	.188
BROOKS, M.	40	3/ 6	.500	5/ 5	1.000	1/ 4	0	2	1	0	0	11	.275
HYATT, J.	11	0/ 1	.000	0/ 1	.000	0/ 0	1	0	0	1	0	0	.000
HARPER, T.	17	2/ 3	.667	0/ 0	.000	1/ 1	1	0	0	0	0	4	.235
WOODS, K.	11	0/ 1	.000	0/ 2	.000	0/ 2	0	0	1	0	0	0	.000
JONES, R.	1	0/ 0	.000	0/ 0	.000	0/ 0	0	0	0	0	0	0	.000
Totals	200	21/37	.568	15/24	.625	7/18	9	9	17	3	0	57	.285

Marquette (56) Coach: Hank Raymonds

	Min.	Total FG / FGA	Pct.	FT / FTA	Pct.	Reb. O / T	A	TO	PF	S	Blk	TP	PPM
JOHNSON, D.	38	2/ 4	.500	3/ 4	.750	1/ 4	3	2	4	1	0	7	.184
MAROTTA, M.	39	7/12	.583	1/ 1	1.000	5/10	1	2	5	2	1	15	.385
SCHLUNDT, T.	40	6/11	.545	0/ 1	.000	1/ 6	0	2	4	0	0	12	.300
JOHNSON, M.	38	4/ 6	.667	2/ 2	1.000	0/ 0	2	0	4	3	0	10	.263
RIVERS, G.	39	4/13	.308	2/ 7	.286	4/ 5	3	4	5	1	0	10	.256
REASON, T.	3	0/ 0	.000	0/ 0	.000	0/ 0	0	0	0	0	0	0	.000
TROTTER, K.	3	1/ 1	1.000	0/ 0	.000	0/ 0	0	0	0	0	0	2	.667
Totals	200	24/47	.511	8/15	.533	11/25	9	10	22	7	1	56	.280

Team Rebounds: Tennessee 6; Marquette 5. Disqualified: Tennessee—Burton, Beamon; Marquette—Marotta, Rivers. Technical fouls: None.

	1st Half	2nd Half	Final
Tennessee	28	29	57
Marquette	28	28	56

Purdue (55) Coach: Gene Keady

	Min.	Total FG / FGA	Pct.	FT / FTA	Pct.	Reb. O / T	A	TO	PF	S	Blk	TP	PPM
BULLOCK, J.	30	1/ 2	.500	2/ 2	1.000	-/ 6	0	3	3	1	1	4	.133
ROWINSKI, J.	33	4/ 4	1.000	0/ 4	.000	-/ 8	2	5	3	2	0	8	.242
CROSS, R.	40	5/10	.500	4/ 6	.667	-/ 7	1	5	3	0	5	14	.350
CLAWSON, C.	28	2/ 8	.250	0/ 0	.000	-/ 1	3	2	3	0	0	4	.143
GADIS, M.	20	1/ 2	.500	3/ 4	.750	-/ 1	3	0	1	0	0	5	.250
PERRY, C.	1	0/ 0	.000	0/ 0	.000	-/ 0	0	0	0	0	0	0	.000
REID, S.	39	9/11	.818	2/ 4	.500	-/ 2	7	5	2	2	0	20	.513
ELBERT, G.	9	0/ 1	.000	0/ 0	.000	-/ 1	1	0	1	0	0	0	.000
Totals	200	22/38	.579	11/20	.550	-/26	17	20	16	5	6	55	.275

Robert Morris (53) Coach: Matt Furjanic

	Min.	Total FG / FGA	Pct.	FT / FTA	Pct.	Reb. O / T	A	TO	PF	S	Blk	TP	PPM
BOMBICH, E.	30	4/ 5	.800	2/ 2	1.000	-/ 2	2	1	4	2	0	10	.333
DUDLEY, R.	24	2/ 5	.400	0/ 1	.000	-/ 2	0	1	3	1	0	4	.167
KOSKOWSKI, S.	14	0/ 3	.000	0/ 0	.000	-/ 1	0	1	2	0	0	0	.000
GRANT, F.	38	4/11	.364	0/ 0	.000	-/ 3	4	2	3	1	0	8	.211
HARRIS, C.	39	7/14	.500	3/ 3	1.000	-/ 3	0	1	5	0	0	17	.436
PARKS, T.	26	6/10	.600	0/ 0	.000	-/ 3	1	7	3	1	0	12	.462
DOBBS, M.	3	0/ 0	.000	0/ 0	.000	-/ 0	0	0	0	1	0	0	.000
COLES, P.	17	0/ 2	.000	0/ 0	.000	-/ 4	0	0	4	0	0	0	.000
UNDERMAN, T.	9	1/ 2	.500	0/ 2	.000	-/ 1	2	0	0	0	0	2	.222
Totals	200	24/52	.462	5/ 8	.625	-/19	9	13	20	11	0	53	.265

Team Rebounds: Purdue 2; Robert Morris 1. Disqualified: None. Technical fouls: None.

	1st Half	2nd Half	Final
Purdue	33	22	55
Robert Morris	24	29	53

Illinois State (49) Coach: Bob Donewald

	Min.	Total FG / FGA	Pct.	FT / FTA	Pct.	Reb. O / T	A	TO	PF	S	Blk	TP	PPM
ZWART, M.	10	1/ 2	.500	0/ 1	.000	-/ 5	0	0	1	-	0	2	.200
CORNLEY	36	2/ 7	.286	0/ 2	.000	-/ 4	1	2	1	-	1	4	.111
LAMB	40	6/ 9	.667	7/ 8	.875	-/10	1	4	3	-	0	19	.475
DUNCAN	30	7/14	.500	0/ 0	.000	-/ 0	3	0	0	-	0	14	.467
MCKENNY, M.	35	1/ 4	.250	0/ 0	.000	-/ 0	4	3	1	-	0	2	.057
JOHNSON	15	1/ 1	1.000	0/ 0	.000	-/ 3	3	0	1	-	0	2	.133
STALANOVIC	4	0/ 0	.000	0/ 0	.000	-/ 0	0	0	1	-	0	0	.000
MALAINE, R.	30	3/ 6	.500	0/ 0	.000	-/ 3	2	1	4	-	0	6	.200
Totals	200	21/43	.488	7/11	.636	-/25	14	10	12	-	1	49	.245

Ohio (51) Coach: Danny Nee

	Min.	Total FG / FGA	Pct.	FT / FTA	Pct.	Reb. O / T	A	TO	PF	S	Blk	TP	PPM
HICKS	32	2/ 3	.667	0/ 0	.000	-/ 1	1	1	1	-	2	4	.125
ALEXANDER, V.	34	6/11	.545	2/ 3	.667	-/ 7	1	1	1	-	0	14	.412
DEVEREAUX, J.	29	5/13	.385	2/ 2	1.000	-/ 7	1	2	4	-	2	12	.414
THOMAS, J.	33	3/ 9	.333	2/ 2	1.000	-/ 2	6	1	0	-	0	8	.242
TALUM	33	5/ 9	.556	1/ 1	1.000	-/ 6	3	1	0	-	0	11	.333
HILTON	10	0/ 1	.000	0/ 0	.000	-/ 0	1	0	0	-	0	0	.000
BARON	4	0/ 1	.000	0/ 0	.000	-/ 1	0	1	0	-	0	0	.000
COLE, N.	19	0/ 1	.000	0/ 0	.000	-/ 0	1	2	5	-	0	0	.000
KOWALSKI, D.	6	1/ 2	.500	0/ 1	.000	-/ 2	0	1	2	-	0	2	.333
Totals	200	22/50	.440	7/ 9	.778	-/26	14	10	13	-	4	51	.255

Team Rebounds: Ohio 2; Illinois State 1. Disqualified: Ohio—Cole. Technical fouls: None.

	1st Half	2nd Half	Final
Illinois State	23	26	49
Ohio	23	28	51

Oklahoma (71) Coach: Billy Tubbs

	Min.	Total FG / FGA	Pct.	FT / FTA	Pct.	Reb. O / T	A	TO	PF	S	Blk	TP	PPM
LITTLE, D.	40	4/12	.333	2/ 2	1.000	1/ 3	2	2	2	2	0	10	.250
TISDALE, WA.	27	7/13	.538	3/ 4	.750	3/ 8	0	0	5	0	3	17	.630
JONES, C.	40	2/ 6	.333	5/ 8	.625	6/11	0	1	2	1	1	9	.225
PANNELL, J.	40	1/ 4	.250	0/ 0	.000	1/ 5	2	2	1	0	0	2	.050
BARNETT, C.	40	10/17	.588	6/ 7	.857	1/ 3	5	1	0	2	0	26	.650
PIERCE, C.	13	2/ 5	.400	3/ 3	1.000	1/ 3	0	0	1	0	0	7	.538
Totals	200	26/57	.456	19/24	.792	13/33	9	6	11	5	4	71	.355

Alabama-Birmingham (63) Coach: Gene Bartow

	Min.	Total FG / FGA	Pct.	FT / FTA	Pct.	Reb. O / T	A	TO	PF	S	Blk	TP	PPM
PRUITT, C.	35	8/16	.500	0/ 0	.000	3/ 9	0	3	4	0	0	16	.457
MINCY, J.	17	0/ 3	.000	1/ 4	.250	3/ 4	0	1	4	1	1	1	.059
DRUM, L.	14	0/ 1	.000	0/ 0	.000	0/ 4	0	0	3	0	1	0	.000
MITCHELL, S.	18	0/ 3	.000	0/ 0	.000	0/ 0	1	1	1	0	0	0	.000
GAUSE, R.	14	1/ 3	.333	0/ 0	.000	1/ 1	0	0	3	0	0	2	.143
JONES, E.	3	0/ 1	.000	0/ 0	.000	0/ 0	0	0	0	0	0	0	.000
JOHNSON, M.	18	4/ 5	.800	0/ 0	.000	4/ 7	1	1	3	0	0	8	.444
FOSTER, L.	33	8/15	.533	4/ 4	1.000	1/ 5	1	2	1	0	0	20	.606
SINGLETON, M.	32	8/19	.421	0/ 0	.000	1/ 4	2	0	3	1	0	16	.500
GORDON, A.	16	0/ 3	.000	0/ 0	.000	0/ 1	0	0	1	0	0	0	.000
Totals	200	29/69	.420	5/ 8	.625	13/35	5	8	23	2	2	63	.315

Team Rebounds: Oklahoma 6; Ala.-Birmingham 3. Disqualified: Oklahoma—Tisdale. Technical fouls: None.

	1st Half	2nd Half	Final
Oklahoma	32	39	71
Ala.-Birmingham	29	34	63

FIRST ROUND WEST

Washington State (62)   Coach: George Raveling

	Min.	Total FG/FGA	Pct.	FT/FTA	Pct.	Reb. O/T	A	TO	PF	S	Blk	TP	PPM
POLLARD, B.	29	4/7	.571	5/6	.833	-/3	1	2	3	2	0	13	.448
HARRIEL, S.	37	4/13	.308	0/0	.000	-/12	4	1	3	0	0	8	.216
BROWN, R.	29	0/3	.000	4/4	1.000	-/8	0	3	3	0	0	4	.138
EHLO, C.	34	6/10	.600	6/7	.857	-/3	4	4	2	2	0	18	.529
WINKLER, C.	17	1/6	.167	0/0	.000	-/1	0	2	4	0	0	2	.118
JENNINGS, O.	1	0/0	.000	0/0	.000	-/0	0	0	0	0	0	0	.000
RUBIN, D.	1	0/0	.000	0/0	.000	-/0	0	1	0	0	0	0	.000
RHYMES	1	0/0	.000	0/0	.000	-/0	0	0	0	0	0	0	.000
MORRISON, K.	25	1/1	1.000	2/2	1.000	-/1	2	1	0	0	0	4	.160
HASKINS, A.	25	5/7	.714	3/4	.750	-/8	1	2	4	1	0	13	.520
WURM, M.	1	0/0	.000	0/0	.000	-/0	0	0	0	0	0	0	.000
Totals	200	21/47	.447	20/23	.870	-/36	12	16	19	5	0	62	.310

Weber State (52)   Coach: Neil McCarthy

	Min.	Total FG/FGA	Pct.	FT/FTA	Pct.	Reb. O/T	A	TO	PF	S	Blk	TP	PPM
WOSTER, R.	32	3/8	.375	2/4	.500	-/4	3	2	5	0	0	8	.250
EDWARDS, R.	34	9/12	.750	1/3	.333	-/6	0	2	4	1	0	19	.559
HAYWOOD, T.	27	4/9	.444	2/2	1.000	-/3	1	2	4	1	1	10	.370
PRICE, J.	39	0/6	.000	2/3	.667	-/0	5	3	3	1	0	2	.051
ESCANDON, R.	3	0/1	.000	0/0	.000	-/0	0	0	0	0	0	0	.000
JONES, G.	30	4/11	.364	0/0	.000	-/3	0	3	1	3	0	8	.267
LARRY, T.	1	0/0	.000	0/0	.000	-/0	1	0	0	0	0	0	.000
MCDANIEL, D.	1	0/0	.000	0/0	.000	-/0	0	0	0	0	0	0	.000
HAFTERSON, H.	3	0/0	.000	0/0	.000	-/1	0	0	0	0	0	0	.000
WEBER, D.	1	1/1	1.000	0/0	.000	-/0	0	0	0	0	0	2	2.000
EILERTSON	26	1/5	.200	1/2	.500	-/2	1	0	4	0	0	3	.115
BAUM, D.	3	0/0	.000	0/0	.000	-/0	0	0	0	0	0	0	.000
Totals	200	22/53	.415	8/14	.571	-/19	11	12	21	6	1	52	.260

Team Rebounds: Washington St. 2; Weber St. 2. Disqualified: Weber St.—Woster. Technical fouls: None.

	1st Half	2nd Half	Final
Washington St.	32	30	62
Weber St.	24	28	52

Oklahoma State (53)   Coach: Paul Hansen

	Min.	Total FG/FGA	Pct.	FT/FTA	Pct.	Reb. O/T	A	TO	PF	S	Blk	TP	PPM
SELF, B.	28	3/4	.750	2/4	.500	-/4	1	0	1	0	0	8	.286
ANDREWS, L.	40	5/14	.357	3/4	.750	-/4	4	2	3	1	0	13	.325
COMBS, L.	36	6/12	.500	0/0	.000	-/8	2	5	5	0	3	12	.333
WILLIAMS, C.	12	0/1	.000	0/0	.000	-/1	0	1	2	0	0	0	.000
CLARK, M.	40	5/11	.455	5/9	.556	-/5	3	4	4	2	1	15	.375
ANDERSON, R.	10	0/1	.000	0/0	.000	-/1	0	0	2	0	0	0	.000
CRENSHAW, R.	34	2/7	.286	1/2	.500	-/7	2	1	2	0	0	5	.147
Totals	200	21/50	.420	11/19	.579	-/30	12	10	19	3	4	53	.265

Princeton (56)   Coach: Pete Carril

	Min.	Total FG/FGA	Pct.	FT/FTA	Pct.	Reb. O/T	A	TO	PF	S	Blk	TP	PPM
CARTER, I.	9	0/3	.000	2/2	1.000	-/0	0	2	2	0	0	2	.222
RYAN, B.	31	2/5	.400	0/0	.000	-/1	1	1	5	0	0	4	.129
ENDERLE, G.	40	1/4	.250	2/2	1.000	-/2	5	2	2	1	0	4	.100
SIMKUS, R.	40	7/9	.778	6/8	.750	-/7	2	4	4	2	0	20	.500
SMYTH, J.	40	3/9	.333	0/1	.000	-/2	2	2	4	2	0	6	.150
ROBINSON, C.	40	8/16	.500	4/5	.800	-/16	0	1	2	1	3	20	.500
Totals	200	21/46	.457	14/18	.778	-/28	10	12	19	6	3	56	.280

Team Rebounds: Princeton 3; Oklahoma State 1. Disqualified: Princeton—ryan; Oklahoma State—Combs. Technical fouls: Oklahoma State—team.

	1st Half	2nd Half	Final
Oklahoma State	30	23	53
Princeton	26	30	56

North Carolina State (69)   Coach: Jim Valvano

	Min.	Total FG/FGA	Pct.	FT/FTA	Pct.	Reb. O/T	A	TO	PF	S	Blk	TP	PPM
WHITTENBURG, D.	50	7/18	.389	8/11	.727	-/1	4	3	1	1	0	22	.440
LOWE, S.	44	1/5	.200	2/2	1.000	-/6	3	3	5	1	0	4	.091
BAILEY, T.	45	8/18	.444	1/3	.333	-/3	0	1	3	0	3	17	.378
CHARLES, L.	40	5/11	.455	2/6	.333	-/14	0	0	4	2	1	12	.300
MCQUEEN, C.	19	1/2	.500	0/0	.000	-/6	0	0	5	0	1	2	.105
MCCLAIN, G.	1	0/0	.000	0/0	.000	-/0	1	0	2	0	0	0	.000
THOMPSON, H.	1	0/0	.000	0/0	.000	-/0	0	0	0	0	0	0	.000
MYERS, E.	2	0/1	.000	0/0	.000	-/0	0	1	0	0	0	0	.000
BATTLE, A.	15	1/1	1.000	0/0	.000	-/0	0	1	2	2	0	2	.133
DINARDO, T.	0	0/0	.000	0/0	.000	-/0	0	0	0	0	0	0	.000
GANNON, T.	33	4/8	.500	2/3	.667	-/2	2	1	2	1	0	10	.303
Totals	250	27/64	.422	15/25	.600	-/32	10	10	24	7	5	69	.276

Pepperdine (67)   Coach: Jim Harrick

	Min.	Total FG/FGA	Pct.	FT/FTA	Pct.	Reb. O/T	A	TO	PF	S	Blk	TP	PPM
WILSON, M.	45	1/6	.167	5/6	.833	-/2	4	1	4	1	0	7	.156
SUTTLE, D.	47	5/17	.294	6/9	.667	-/2	3	3	5	0	0	16	.340
PHILLIPS, O.	38	5/10	.500	2/5	.400	-/10	0	1	4	1	2	12	.316
ANGER, V.	43	5/10	.500	1/5	.200	-/6	0	2	5	1	0	11	.256
SADLER, B.	43	7/13	.538	5/7	.714	-/10	1	6	4	3	0	19	.442
GONDREZICK, G.	25	1/2	.500	0/0	.000	-/4	0	2	2	0	0	2	.080
JOHNSON, A.	4	0/1	.000	0/0	.000	-/1	0	0	1	0	0	0	.000
STEVENS, C.	5	0/0	.000	0/0	.000	-/2	1	0	0	0	0	0	.000
Totals	250	24/59	.407	19/32	.594	-/37	9	15	25	6	2	67	.268

Team Rebounds: N.C. State 11; Pepperdine 10. Disqualified: N.C. State—Lowe, McQueen; Pepperdine—Suttle, Anger. Technial fouls: N.C. State—Whittenburg. Player who played 0 min. played less than 1 min.

	1st Half	2nd Half	1st OT	2nd OT	Final
N.C. State	27	20	12	10	69
Pepperdine	25	22	12	8	67

Illinois (49)   Coach: Lou Henson

	Min.	Total FG/FGA	Pct.	FT/FTA	Pct.	Reb. O/T	A	TO	PF	S	Blk	TP	PPM
WINTERS, E.	37	5/14	.357	1/2	.500	-/6	3	1	2	1	2	11	.297
WELCH, A.	37	5/7	.714	1/2	.500	-/6	1	5	2	1	1	11	.297
LEONARD, B.	8	0/1	.000	0/0	.000	-/2	1	0	1	1	0	0	.000
HARPER, D.	40	5/13	.385	1/1	1.000	-/4	6	1	3	3	0	11	.275
DOUGLAS, B.	30	2/6	.333	2/4	.500	-/2	2	2	3	1	0	6	.200
BOTEMPTS, K.	9	0/0	.000	0/0	.000	-/0	2	0	1	0	0	0	.000
ALTENBERGER, D.	27	3/5	.600	1/2	.500	-/3	0	0	2	0	0	7	.259
MONTGOMERY, G.	12	1/2	.500	1/1	1.000	-/1	0	2	2	0	0	3	.250
Totals	200	21/48	.438	7/12	.583	-/24	15	11	16	7	3	49	.245

Utah (52)   Coach: Jerry Pimm

	Min.	Total FG/FGA	Pct.	FT/FTA	Pct.	Reb. O/T	A	TO	PF	S	Blk	TP	PPM
WILLIAMS, P.	37	7/12	.583	-/-		-/4	0	4	3	1	1	14	.378
MANNION, P.	40	2/4	.500	1/1	1.000	-/6	5	5	1	1	0	5	.125
WINANS, C.	36	3/6	.500	1/2	.500	-/4	1	0	5	0	0	7	.194
HENDRIX, M.	35	5/11	.455	4/4	1.000	-/1	1	1	3	0	0	14	.400
ROBINSON, A.	18	3/7	.429	0/0	.000	-/2	0	1	0	1	0	6	.333
FURGIS, G.	27	1/5	.200	2/2	1.000	-/4	0	1	4	0	0	4	.148
HILL, S.	4	0/0	.000	2/2	1.000	-/0	0	0	0	0	0	2	.500
CECIL, D.	3	0/1	.000	0/0	.000	-/0	0	0	1	0	0	0	.000
Totals	200	21/46	.457	10/11	.909	-/21	7	12	17	3	1	52	.260

Team Rebounds: Utah 4; Illinois 3. Disqualified: Utah—Winans. Technical fouls: None.

	1st Half	2nd Half	Final
Illinois	23	26	49
Utah	28	24	52

FIRST ROUND EAST

Southwestern Louisiana (53)   Coach: Bobby Paschal

	Min.	Total FG/FGA	Pct.	FT/FTA	Pct.	Reb. O/T	A	TO	PF	S	Blk	TP	PPM
BROWN, D.	38	5/ 8	.625	2/ 2	1.000	-/ 8	1	-	3	-	-	12	.316
WARNER	37	7/17	.412	0/ 1	.000	-/ 9	2	-	3	-	-	14	.378
GAY	40	2/ 3	.667	2/ 2	1.000	-/ 5	0	-	3	-	-	6	.150
ALMONES	39	5/13	.385	3/ 4	.750	-/ 2	6	-	4	-	-	13	.333
COLLINS, J.	37	0/ 6	.000	0/ 0	.000	-/ 2	4	-	2	-	-	0	.000
ALLEN, A.	5	3/ 3	1.000	0/ 0	.000	-/ 0	0	-	1	-	-	6	1.200
MCGREW	3	1/ 2	.500	0/ 0	.000	-/ 0	0	-	2	-	-	2	.667
PEOPLES	1	0/ 0	.000	0/ 0	.000	-/ 0	0	-	0	-	-	0	.000
Totals	200	23/52	.442	7/ 9	.778	-/26	13	-	18	-	-	53	.265

Rutgers (60)   Coach: Tom Young

	Min.	Total FG/FGA	Pct.	FT/FTA	Pct.	Reb. O/T	A	TO	PF	S	Blk	TP	PPM
BLACK, K.	32	1/ 1	1.000	5/ 9	.556	-/ 6	1	-	2	-	-	7	.219
TILLMAN	21	4/11	.364	3/ 4	.750	-/ 5	2	-	3	-	-	11	.524
HINSON	22	3/ 7	.429	0/ 0	.000	-/ 2	0	-	4	-	-	6	.273
ELLERBE, B.	33	3/ 5	.600	3/ 4	.750	-/ 3	3	-	2	-	-	9	.273
BRUNSON, R.	33	3/ 4	.750	1/ 1	1.000	-/ 0	6	-	1	-	-	7	.212
NEBRIEN	28	2/ 2	1.000	2/ 2	1.000	-/ 1	0	-	3	-	-	6	.214
BATTLE, J.	14	4/ 6	.667	0/ 0	.000	-/ 2	1	-	0	-	-	8	.571
REMIEY	17	3/ 5	.600	0/ 0	.000	-/ 2	0	-	1	-	-	6	.353
Totals	200	23/41	.561	14/20	.700	-/21	13	-	16	-	-	60	.300

Disqualified: None.

	1st Half	2nd Half	Final
S'western La.	33	20	53
Rutgers	27	33	60

Virginia Commonwealth (76)   Coach: J. D. Barnett

	Min.	Total FG/FGA	Pct.	FT/FTA	Pct.	Reb. O/T	A	TO	PF	S	Blk	TP	PPM
BROWN, F.	30	8/13	.615	2/ 4	.500	-/ 4	2	4	4	1	0	18	.600
BROWN, M.	33	3/ 5	.600	1/ 2	.500	-/ 3	0	1	3	0	0	7	.212
SCHLEGEL, M.	38	7/ 9	.778	2/ 2	1.000	-/ 7	1	2	3	2	2	16	.421
LAMB, V.	27	0/ 0	.000	2/ 2	1.000	-/ 1	8	2	3	1	1	2	.074
DUNCAN, C.	33	5/14	.357	12/12	1.000	-/ 6	9	2	1	1	0	22	.667
DAVIS, S.	19	0/ 0	.000	1/ 2	.500	-/ 0	1	1	0	0	1	1	.053
CORKER, R.	18	3/ 6	.500	4/ 4	1.000	-/ 3	1	1	3	0	0	10	.556
MCINTOSH, G.	1	0/ 0	.000	0/ 0	.000	-/ 0	0	0	0	0	0	0	.000
SHROPSHIRE, G.	1	0/ 0	.000	0/ 0	.000	-/ 0	0	0	0	0	0	0	.000
Totals	200	26/47	.553	24/28	.857	-/24	22	13	17	5	3	76	.380

La Salle (67)   Coach: Lefty Ervin

	Min.	Total FG/FGA	Pct.	FT/FTA	Pct.	Reb. O/T	A	TO	PF	S	Blk	TP	PPM
LEWIS, R.	35	2/ 9	.222	4/ 4	1.000	-/10	0	2	5	3	1	8	.229
BUTTS, A.	40	4/ 0	.000	3/ 5	.600	-/ 8	1	0	1	0	3	11	.275
PIOTROWSKI, T.	19	1/ 4	.250	2/ 2	1.000	-/ 3	0	1	2	0	0	4	.211
GREENBERG, C.	39	2/ 7	.286	5/ 6	.833	-/ 3	5	7	3	1	0	9	.231
BLACK, S.	39	13/25	.520	5/ 6	.833	-/ 6	0	2	5	1	0	31	.795
JONES, G.	8	0/ 1	.000	0/ 0	.000	-/ 1	3	0	4	1	0	0	.000
PHILSON, D.	18	2/ 3	.667	0/ 0	.000	-/ 1	1	1	2	1	0	4	.222
GILMORE, R.	1	0/ 0	.000	0/ 0	.000	-/ 0	0	0	0	0	0	0	.000
DAVIS, D.	1	0/ 1	.000	0/ 0	.000	-/ 0	0	0	0	0	0	0	.000
Totals	200	24/50	.480	19/23	.826	-/32	10	13	22	7	4	67	.335

Team Rebounds: Va. Commonwealth 4; La Salle 2. Disqualified: La Salle—Lewis, Black. Technical fouls: La Salle—bench.

	1st Half	2nd Half	Final
Va. Commonwealth	33	43	76
La Salle	26	41	67

Syracuse (74)   Coach: Jim Boeheim

	Min.	Total FG/FGA	Pct.	FT/FTA	Pct.	Reb. O/T	A	TO	PF	S	Blk	TP	PPM
RAUTINS, L.	36	10/15	.667	1/ 1	1.000	1/ 7	5	2	2	1	0	21	.583
BRUIN, T.	21	2/ 4	.500	4/ 8	.500	0/ 4	0	0	2	0	0	8	.381
HAWKINS, A.	7	0/ 1	.000	0/ 0	.000	0/ 1	0	3	2	1	1	0	.000
WALDRON, G.	21	3/ 4	.750	1/ 1	1.000	1/ 2	6	2	3	2	0	7	.333
SANTIFER, E.	35	5/ 6	.833	9/10	.900	1/ 3	5	2	2	0	0	19	.543
ALEXIS, W.	27	5/ 8	.625	0/ 0	.000	0/ 4	0	0	3	1	1	10	.370
ADDISON, R.	22	3/ 5	.600	1/ 2	.500	0/ 3	0	0	3	2	2	7	.318
SPERA, S.	19	1/ 1	1.000	0/ 1	.000	0/ 1	4	2	1	1	0	2	.105
KERINS, S.	8	0/ 3	.000	0/ 2	.000	1/ 1	1	0	3	0	0	0	.000
LEWIS, C.	3	0/ 2	.000	0/ 0	.000	0/ 0	0	2	0	0	0	0	.000
PERRY, C.	1	0/ 0	.000	0/ 0	.000	0/ 0	0	0	0	0	0	0	.000
Totals	200	29/49	.592	16/25	.640	4/26	21	13	21	8	4	74	.370

Morehead State (59)   Coach: Wayne Martin

	Min.	Total FG/FGA	Pct.	FT/FTA	Pct.	Reb. O/T	A	TO	PF	S	Blk	TP	PPM
HARRISON, E.	30	8/10	.800	1/ 1	1.000	3/ 9	3	3	2	1	1	17	.567
TUCKER, J.	26	1/ 4	.250	0/ 4	.000	0/ 4	2	0	2	1	2	2	.077
MOORE, H.	24	3/ 5	.600	0/ 0	.000	1/ 3	0	2	4	1	0	6	.250
MINNIFIELD, G.	37	4/12	.333	4/ 5	.800	1/ 3	4	4	3	1	0	12	.324
FULTZ, J.	20	1/ 4	.250	0/ 0	.000	0/ 0	5	2	1	1	0	2	.100
ADKINS, R.	14	0/ 1	.000	0/ 0	.000	0/ 1	1	3	1	1	0	0	.000
TIPTON, J.	24	3/ 5	.600	2/ 2	1.000	0/ 3	2	2	1	0	1	8	.333
CHILDRESS, E.	11	0/ 1	.000	2/ 3	.667	0/ 1	0	0	1	0	0	2	.182
SULLIVAN, S.	10	4/ 6	.667	0/ 0	.000	1/ 2	0	2	0	0	0	8	.800
BARKER, R.	4	1/ 4	.250	0/ 0	.000	0/ 0	0	0	1	0	0	2	.500
Totals	200	25/52	.481	9/15	.600	6/26	17	16	18	6	4	59	.295

Team Rebounds: Syracuse 4; Morehead State 3. Disqualified: None. Technical fouls: None.

	1st Half	2nd Half	Final
Syracuse	37	37	74
Morehead State	27	32	59

West Virginia (50)   Coach: Gale Catlett

	Min.	Total FG/FGA	Pct.	FT/FTA	Pct.	Reb. O/T	A	TO	PF	S	Blk	TP	PPM
ROWE	37	2/ 6	.333	2/ 4	.500	-/ 7	2	2	4	-	0	6	.162
TODD	39	4/ 6	.667	3/ 5	.600	-/ 1	2	2	1	-	0	11	.282
KEARNEY	37	4/ 7	.571	2/ 2	1.000	-/ 3	2	2	4	-	3	10	.270
JONES	38	3/ 9	.333	0/ 0	.000	-/ 4	5	3	4	-	0	6	.158
BLANEY	39	6/10	.600	5/ 8	.625	-/ 2	5	5	5	-	0	17	.436
WASHAM	5	0/ 1	.000	0/ 0	.000	-/ 0	0	1	1	-	0	0	.000
KING	4	0/ 1	.000	0/ 0	.000	-/ 0	0	0	0	-	0	0	.000
CRAWL	1	0/ 1	.000	0/ 0	.000	-/ 0	0	0	0	-	0	0	.000
Totals	200	19/41	.463	12/19	.632	-/17	16	15	19	-	3	50	.250

James Madison (57)   Coach: Lou Campanelli

	Min.	Total FG/FGA	Pct.	FT/FTA	Pct.	Reb. O/T	A	TO	PF	S	Blk	TP	PPM
MOSTEN, G.	-	3/ 6	.500	0/ 1	.000	-/ 7	2	4	4	-	1	6	-
DONOHOE	-	4/ 8	.500	3/ 5	.600	-/ 4	3	2	3	-	0	11	-
RULAND, D.	-	5/13	.385	1/ 2	.500	-/10	0	3	1	-	0	11	-
FISHER	-	2/ 5	.400	9/ 9	1.000	-/ 0	3	1	2	-	0	13	-
DUPONT	-	1/ 3	.333	0/ 0	.000	-/ 5	5	2	3	-	1	2	-
JACKSON	-	0/ 1	.000	0/ 0	.000	-/ 0	0	0	1	-	0	0	-
STEELE, D.	-	3/ 3	1.000	0/ 0	.000	-/ 2	3	3	2	-	0	6	-
BRADLEY	-	4/ 4	1.000	0/ 1	.000	-/ 2	2	2	2	-	0	8	-
Totals	200	22/43	.512	13/18	.722	-/30	18	17	18	-	2	57	.285

Team Rebounds: James Madison 3; West Virginia 1. Disqualified: West Virginia—Blaney. Technical fouls: West Virginia—Rowe.

	1st Half	2nd Half	Final
West Virginia	20	30	50
James Madison	23	34	57

SECOND ROUND MIDWEST

Maryland (50) — Coach: Lefty Driesell

	Min.	Total FG/FGA	Pct.	FT/FTA	Pct.	Reb. O/T	A	TO	PF	S	Blk	TP	PPM
FARMER, E.	2	0/0	.000	1/2	.500	1/1	0	0	2	0	0	1	.500
BIAS, L.	39	7/10	.700	0/0	.000	4/7	1	2	3	0	1	14	.359
COLEMAN, B.	38	3/10	.300	2/4	.500	3/6	2	2	5	1	0	8	.211
ADKINS, J.	38	1/1	1.000	2/5	.400	0/1	2	2	5	0	0	4	.105
BRANCH, A.	40	7/16	.438	6/8	.750	1/4	1	2	4	0	0	20	.500
BAXTER, J.	4	0/0	.000	0/0	.000	0/0	0	1	1	0	0	0	.000
RIVERS, S.	3	0/0	.000	1/2	.500	0/0	0	0	2	0	0	1	.333
FOTHERGILL, M.	36	1/2	.500	0/0	.000	0/2	1	0	4	0	0	2	.056
Totals	200	19/39	.487	12/21	.571	9/21	7	9	26	1	1	50	.250

Houston (60) — Coach: Guy Lewis

	Min.	Total FG/FGA	Pct.	FT/FTA	Pct.	Reb. O/T	A	TO	PF	S	Blk	TP	PPM
DREXLER, C.	34	5/7	.714	1/2	.500	4/8	4	2	3	3	1	11	.324
MICHEAUX, L.	36	3/5	.600	1/5	.200	3/6	1	2	3	0	1	7	.194
OLAJUWON, A.	36	6/10	.600	0/4	.000	4/6	0	1	4	0	3	12	.333
FRANKLIN, A.	20	1/2	.500	5/8	.625	0/0	4	0	2	0	0	7	.350
YOUNG, M.	40	6/11	.545	4/6	.667	2/7	0	1	2	0	0	16	.400
GETTYS, R.	25	2/2	1.000	2/2	1.000	0/0	7	0	3	0	0	6	.240
ANDERS, B.	9	0/2	.000	1/2	.500	0/1	0	0	1	1	0	1	.111
Totals	200	23/39	.590	14/29	.483	13/28	16	6	18	4	5	60	.300

Team Rebounds: Houston 3; Maryland 2. Disqualified: Maryland—Coleman, Adkins. Technical fouls: None.

	1st Half	2nd Half	Final
Maryland	24	26	50
Houston	26	34	60

Georgetown (57) — Coach: John Thompson

	Min.	Total FG/FGA	Pct.	FT/FTA	Pct.	Reb. O/T	A	TO	PF	S	Blk	TP	PPM
MARTIN, B.	20	3/4	.750	0/0	.000	-/5	1	1	2	0	0	6	.300
WINGATE, D.	13	0/2	.000	0/0	.000	-/2	0	0	1	0	0	0	.000
EWING, P.	36	8/16	.500	8/8	1.000	-/9	0	1	5	1	1	24	.667
SMITH, G.	23	1/2	.500	2/3	.667	-/0	5	1	5	1	0	4	.174
JACKSON, M.	29	4/14	.286	4/7	.571	-/0	3	1	2	1	0	12	.414
DALTON, R.	8	0/1	.000	0/0	.000	-/2	0	0	2	0	0	0	.000
JONES, A.	16	1/5	.200	0/0	.000	-/0	0	1	3	1	0	2	.125
BROADNAX, H.	20	4/10	.400	0/0	.000	-/1	1	0	2	1	0	8	.400
BROWN, F.	16	0/0	.000	0/0	.000	-/1	3	1	3	3	0	0	.000
DUNN, D.	18	0/2	.000	1/2	.500	-/2	0	2	3	3	0	1	.056
BLUE, D.	1	0/0	.000	0/0	.000	-/0	0	0	0	0	0	0	.000
Totals	200	21/56	.375	15/20	.750	-/22	13	8	28	11	1	57	.285

Memphis State (66) — Coach: Dana Kirk

	Min.	Total FG/FGA	Pct.	FT/FTA	Pct.	Reb. O/T	A	TO	PF	S	Blk	TP	PPM
PARKS, B.	38	3/5	.600	3/4	.750	-/4	2	1	4	0	1	9	.237
LEE, K.	39	8/11	.727	12/16	.750	-/15	2	2	2	2	2	28	.718
PHILLIPS, D.	39	2/2	1.000	6/8	.750	-/11	0	6	2	0	0	10	.256
TURNER, A.	36	1/5	.200	2/5	.400	-/1	4	7	4	2	0	4	.111
HAYNES, P.	36	5/8	.625	3/4	.750	-/1	3	4	5	1	0	13	.361
HOLMES, B.	4	0/0	.000	0/0	.000	-/0	0	0	0	0	0	0	.000
MCCOY, R.	6	0/0	.000	2/2	1.000	-/1	0	1	0	0	0	2	.333
BATTLE, A.	1	0/0	.000	0/0	.000	-/0	0	0	0	0	0	0	.000
LUCKETT, B.	1	0/0	.000	0/0	.000	-/0	0	0	0	0	0	0	.000
Totals	200	19/31	.613	28/39	.718	-/33	11	21	17	5	3	66	.330

Team Rebounds: Memphis State 4; Georgetown 0. Disqualified: Memphis State—Haynes; Georgetown—Ewing, Smith. Technical fouls: Georgetown—Ewing.

	1st Half	2nd Half	Final
Georgetown	25	32	57
Memphis State	30	36	66

Lamar (58) — Coach: Pat Foster

	Min.	Total FG/FGA	Pct.	FT/FTA	Pct.	Reb. O/T	A	TO	PF	S	Blk	TP	PPM
KELLYBREW, B.	29	2/7	.286	1/3	.333	1/3	4	3	5	3	1	5	.172
PERKINS, K.	37	9/11	.818	1/2	.500	2/5	3	2	4	2	1	19	.514
GRAY, R.	26	2/6	.333	2/2	1.000	4/5	0	1	0	1	2	6	.231
ROBINSON, L.	38	5/11	.455	0/0	.000	1/3	7	2	4	4	0	10	.263
SEWELL, T.	38	8/18	.444	0/0	.000	0/3	1	2	3	0	2	16	.421
SNELL, N.	8	1/2	.500	0/0	.000	0/0	0	0	0	0	0	2	.250
MILHOUSE, G.	24	0/0	.000	0/0	.000	0/3	2	0	2	1	0	0	.000
Totals	200	27/55	.491	4/7	.571	8/22	17	10	18	11	6	58	.290

Villanova (60) — Coach: Rollie Massimino

	Min.	Total FG/FGA	Pct.	FT/FTA	Pct.	Reb. O/T	A	TO	PF	S	Blk	TP	PPM
MULQUIN, M.	18	2/2	1.000	0/0	.000	0/0	1	1	2	0	0	4	.222
PINCKNEY, E.	37	4/5	.800	2/4	.500	0/10	6	2	2	2	4	10	.270
PINONE, J.	40	5/8	.625	5/5	1.000	0/0	2	6	2	1	0	15	.375
GRANGER, S.	39	3/5	.600	3/5	.600	0/0	5	6	2	0	0	9	.231
MCCLAIN, D.	33	6/8	.750	2/3	.667	1/7	4	4	4	1	2	14	.424
PRESSLEY, H.	32	4/9	.444	0/0	.000	0/5	2	0	1	2	0	8	.250
MCLAIN, G.	1	0/0	.000	0/0	.000	0/0	0	0	1	0	0	0	.000
Totals	200	24/37	.649	12/17	.706	1/22	20	19	14	6	6	60	.300

Team Rebounds: Villanova 2; Lamar 0. Disqualified: Lamar—Kellybrew. Technical fouls: None.

	1st Half	2nd Half	Final
Lamar	26	32	58
Villanova	32	28	60

Iowa (77) — Coach: Lute Olson

	Min.	Total FG/FGA	Pct.	FT/FTA	Pct.	Reb. O/T	A	TO	PF	S	Blk	TP	PPM
PAYNE, M.	39	7/12	.583	5/6	.833	-/7	1	1	3	-	1	19	.487
GANNON, M.	38	4/6	.667	3/5	.600	-/9	4	1	2	-	0	11	.289
STOKES, G.	39	7/11	.636	8/10	.800	-/6	2	1	2	-	3	22	.564
CARFINO, S.	36	3/4	.750	2/3	.667	-/5	2	3	3	-	0	8	.222
HANSEN, B.	37	4/12	.333	7/8	.875	-/6	3	5	3	-	0	15	.405
BANKS, A.	7	1/1	1.000	0/1	.000	-/1	1	0	1	-	0	2	.286
ANDERSON, C.	1	0/0	.000	0/0	.000	-/0	0	0	0	-	0	0	.000
KING, W.	1	0/0	.000	0/0	.000	-/0	0	0	0	-	0	0	.000
DENNARD, J.	1	0/0	.000	0/0	.000	-/1	0	0	0	-	0	0	.000
LOHAUS, B.	1	0/0	.000	0/0	.000	-/0	0	0	0	-	0	0	.000
Totals	200	26/46	.565	25/33	.758	-/35	13	10	14	-	4	77	.385

Missouri (63) — Coach: Norm Stewart

	Min.	Total FG/FGA	Pct.	FT/FTA	Pct.	Reb. O/T	A	TO	PF	S	Blk	TP	PPM
CAVENER, G.	37	4/9	.444	1/2	.500	-/10	1	4	4	-	0	9	.243
JONES	24	2/4	.500	2/2	1.000	-/5	2	0	4	-	0	6	.250
STIPANOVICH, S.	33	3/11	.273	0/0	.000	-/6	1	2	5	-	1	6	.182
BRIDGES	35	5/7	.714	0/1	.000	-/2	2	2	4	-	0	10	.286
SUNDVOLD, J.	39	14/24	.583	1/2	.500	-/1	2	2	3	-	0	29	.744
DRESSLER	18	0/4	.000	0/0	.000	-/1	2	0	2	-	0	0	.000
WALKER	1	0/0	.000	0/0	.000	-/0	0	0	0	-	0	0	.000
MOODY	10	0/2	.000	0/2	.000	-/0	1	0	3	-	0	0	.000
ROUNDTREE	1	0/0	.000	0/0	.000	-/0	0	0	0	-	0	0	.000
LAURIG	1	1/1	1.000	1/2	.500	-/0	0	0	0	-	0	3	3.000
MUSSER	1	0/0	.000	0/0	.000	-/1	0	0	0	-	0	0	.000
Totals	200	29/62	.468	5/11	.455	-/26	11	10	25	-	1	63	.315

Team Rebounds: Iowa 1; Missouri 0. Disqualified: Missouri—Stipanovich. Technical fouls: None.

	1st Half	2nd Half	Final
Iowa	32	45	77
Missouri	20	43	63

SECOND ROUND MIDEAST

Tennessee (57) Coach: Don Devoe

	Min.	Total FG/FGA	Pct.	FT/FTA	Pct.	Reb. O/T	A	TO	PF	S	Blk	TP	PPM
ELLIS, D.	35	6/13	.462	1/3	.333	1/5	0	5	4	2	0	13	.371
BURTON, W.	36	4/10	.400	1/2	.500	4/7	2	1	0	2	2	9	.250
FEDERMANN, D.	18	1/1	1.000	1/2	.500	0/3	1	1	4	2	0	3	.167
BEAMAN, T.	33	4/7	.571	2/2	1.000	1/1	3	6	5	2	0	10	.303
BROOKS, M.	40	8/17	.471	2/2	1.000	0/1	5	4	2	2	0	18	.450
HYATT, J.	16	0/1	.000	0/0	.000	0/0	1	0	1	2	0	0	.000
HARPER, T.	8	1/4	.250	0/0	.000	2/2	0	0	1	0	0	2	.250
WOODS, K.	10	1/3	.333	0/0	.000	1/3	0	0	0	0	0	2	.200
JONES, R.	3	0/0	.000	0/0	.000	0/0	0	0	0	0	0	0	.000
CARTER, M.	1	0/0	.000	0/0	.000	0/0	0	0	0	0	0	0	.000
Totals	200	25/56	.446	7/11	.636	9/22	12	17	17	12	2	57	.285

Louisville (70) Coach: Denny Crum

	Min.	Total FG/FGA	Pct.	FT/FTA	Pct.	Reb. O/T	A	TO	PF	S	Blk	TP	PPM
MCCRAY, S.	32	5/7	.714	0/0	.000	1/5	3	3	4	2	0	10	.313
MCCRAY, R.	33	0/1	.000	1/2	.500	1/6	2	1	0	2	0	1	.030
JONES, C.	35	7/8	.875	4/7	.571	5/11	3	5	0	2	2	18	.514
GORDON, L.	36	7/15	.467	4/4	1.000	1/1	2	6	1	2	0	18	.500
WAGNER, M.	31	6/10	.600	3/4	.750	1/1	2	3	2	2	1	15	.484
VALENTINE, R.	1	0/0	.000	0/0	.000	0/0	0	0	0	0	0	0	.000
WEST, C.	1	0/0	.000	0/0	.000	0/0	0	0	0	0	0	0	.000
HALL, J.	12	0/2	.000	2/2	1.000	0/0	0	0	1	0	0	2	.167
MITCHELL, D.	1	0/0	.000	0/0	.000	0/0	0	0	0	0	0	0	.000
THOMPSON, B.	18	2/4	.500	2/4	.500	0/3	1	0	1	1	1	6	.333
Totals	200	27/47	.574	16/23	.696	9/27	13	18	8	11	6	70	.350

Ohio (40) Coach: Danny Nee

	Min.	Total FG/FGA	Pct.	FT/FTA	Pct.	Reb. O/T	A	TO	PF	S	Blk	TP	PPM
HICKS, E.	-	3/5	.600	0/0	.000	-/3	0	4	2	1	0	6	-
ALEXANDER, V.	-	3/9	.333	1/4	.250	-/2	0	1	3	1	1	7	-
DEVEREAUX, J.	-	3/12	.250	3/3	1.000	-/10	4	0	5	1	0	9	-
THOMAS, J.	-	2/10	.200	0/0	.000	-/2	3	4	0	0	1	4	-
TATUM, R.	-	2/9	.222	4/4	1.000	-/6	5	1	4	0	0	8	-
HILTON, E.	-	0/1	.000	0/0	.000	-/1	0	1	1	0	0	0	-
HARON, P.	-	0/0	.000	0/0	.000	-/0	0	2	2	0	0	0	-
COLE, N.	-	3/3	1.000	0/0	.000	-/3	1	1	3	0	0	6	-
KOWARSKI, D.	-	0/0	.000	0/0	.000	-/0	0	0	0	0	0	0	-
Totals	200	16/49	.327	8/11	.727	-/27	13	14	20	3	2	40	.200

Kentucky (57) Coach: Joe Hall

	Min.	Total FG/FGA	Pct.	FT/FTA	Pct.	Reb. O/T	A	TO	PF	S	Blk	TP	PPM
HORD, D.	20	0/2	.000	2/2	1.000	-/1	0	1	1	1	0	2	.100
HURT, C.	32	2/3	.667	5/6	.833	-/3	2	1	3	2	0	9	.281
TURPIN, M.	37	5/10	.500	4/7	.571	-/9	2	1	2	0	1	14	.378
MINNIFIELD, D.	37	5/7	.714	6/6	1.000	-/2	5	3	0	1	0	16	.432
MASTER, J.	39	4/6	.667	2/2	1.000	-/2	3	3	1	3	0	10	.256
BEAL, D.	1	0/0	.000	0/0	.000	-/0	0	0	0	0	0	0	.000
HARDIN, R.	1	1/1	1.000	0/0	.000	-/0	0	0	0	1	0	2	2.000
BEARUP, B.	10	0/1	.000	0/0	.000	-/0	3	0	2	0	1	0	.000
WALKER, K.	19	1/5	.200	2/2	1.000	-/2	0	0	1	0	0	4	.211
MCKINLEY, T.	2	0/1	.000	0/0	.000	-/1	0	0	0	0	0	0	.000
HEITZ, T.	2	0/0	.000	0/0	.000	-/0	0	0	0	0	0	0	.000
Totals	200	18/36	.500	21/25	.840	-/20	15	9	10	8	2	57	.285

Team Rebounds: Louisville 4; Tennessee 3. Disqualified: Tennessee—Beaman. Technical fouls: None.

	1st Half	2nd Half	Final
Tennessee	27	30	57
Louisville	34	36	70

Team Rebounds: Kentucky 3; Ohio 4. Disqualified: Ohio—Devereaux. Technical fouls: None.

	1st Half	2nd Half	Final
Ohio	17	23	40
Kentucky	21	36	57

Purdue (68) Coach: Gene Keady

	Min.	Total FG/FGA	Pct.	FT/FTA	Pct.	Reb. O/T	A	TO	PF	S	Blk	TP	PPM
BULLOCK, J.	-	6/10	.600	0/0	.000	-/3	0	4	2	0	1	12	-
ROWINSKI, J.	-	6/8	.750	0/1	.000	-/5	1	1	1	0	0	12	-
CROSS, R.	-	10/13	.769	2/7	.286	-/9	4	3	2	0	1	22	-
HALL, R.	-	1/3	.333	0/0	.000	-/1	3	3	2	0	0	2	-
CLAWSON, C.	-	2/4	.500	0/0	.000	-/1	0	2	1	0	0	4	-
GADIS, M.	-	0/1	.000	0/0	.000	-/1	3	3	2	0	0	0	-
PERRY, C.	-	0/0	.000	0/0	.000	-/0	0	0	0	0	0	0	-
PALOMBIZIO, D.	-	0/0	.000	0/0	.000	-/0	1	1	0	0	0	0	-
REID, S.	-	2/4	.500	8/8	1.000	-/1	9	5	5	0	0	12	-
GAMPFER, J.	-	0/0	.000	0/0	.000	-/1	0	0	0	0	0	0	-
EIFERT, G.	-	2/3	.667	0/0	.000	-/1	2	1	5	1	0	4	-
Totals	200	29/46	.630	10/16	.625	-/23	23	23	20	1	2	68	.340

Arkansas (78) Coach: Eddie Sutton

	Min.	Total FG/FGA	Pct.	FT/FTA	Pct.	Reb. O/T	A	TO	PF	S	Blk	TP	PPM
WALKER, D.	-	8/13	.615	7/14	.500	-/6	5	6	4	3	0	23	-
SUTTON	-	2/3	.667	0/0	.000	-/2	2	2	4	0	0	4	-
KLEINE, J.	-	6/7	.857	0/0	.000	-/2	0	2	3	0	0	12	-
ROBERTSON, A.	-	10/19	.526	6/7	.857	-/6	1	4	3	8	1	26	-
NORTON, R.	-	1/3	.333	3/4	.750	-/0	2	1	2	1	0	5	-
CUTTS	-	0/0	.000	0/0	.000	-/1	0	0	3	0	0	0	-
KITCHEN	-	0/0	.000	0/0	.000	-/0	0	0	0	0	0	0	-
BALENTINE, C.	-	0/0	.000	0/0	.000	-/0	0	0	0	0	0	0	-
SNIVELY	-	2/4	.500	4/4	1.000	-/1	2	0	0	0	0	8	-
BRANNON	-	0/0	.000	0/0	.000	-/0	0	0	0	0	0	0	-
KELLY, C.	-	0/0	.000	0/0	.000	-/0	1	0	0	0	0	0	-
BEDFORD, D.	-	0/1	.000	0/0	.000	-/0	0	0	0	0	0	0	-
Totals	200	29/50	.580	20/29	.690	-/18	13	15	19	12	1	78	.390

Team Rebounds: Arkansas 1; Purdue 2. Disqualified: Purdue—Reid, Eifert. Technical fouls: None.

	1st Half	2nd Half	Final
Purdue	25	43	68
Arkansas	33	45	78

Oklahoma (49) Coach: Billy Tubbs

	Min.	Total FG/FGA	Pct.	FT/FTA	Pct.	Reb. O/T	A	TO	PF	S	Blk	TP	PPM
LITTLE, D.	38	4/8	.500	1/2	.500	0/2	1	3	2	1	0	9	.237
TISDALE, WA.	38	6/12	.500	2/3	.667	0/5	1	0	3	1	3	14	.368
JONES, C.	21	2/4	.500	3/4	.750	2/5	1	1	1	0	1	7	.333
PANNELL, J.	36	1/6	.167	0/0	.000	0/3	3	2	2	0	2	2	.056
BARNETT, C.	36	3/8	.375	2/2	1.000	0/1	2	4	3	0	0	8	.222
OVERTON, B.	4	1/1	1.000	0/0	.000	0/0	1	1	2	0	0	2	.500
TISDALE, WM.	2	0/2	.000	0/0	.000	0/0	0	0	1	0	0	0	.000
CLARK, S.	4	1/5	.200	3/3	1.000	0/0	0	3	3	0	0	5	1.250
PIERCE, C.	10	0/1	.000	0/1	.000	1/2	0	1	0	0	0	0	.000
JOHNSON, J.	2	0/0	.000	0/0	.000	0/1	0	1	0	0	0	0	.000
LEE, B.	2	0/0	.000	0/1	.000	1/6	0	0	1	0	0	0	.000
GANDY, D.	7	1/2	.500	0/0	.000	0/0	0	0	1	0	0	2	.286
Totals	200	19/49	.388	11/16	.688	4/25	9	11	21	4	4	49	.245

Indiana (63) Coach: Bob Knight

	Min.	Total FG/FGA	Pct.	FT/FTA	Pct.	Reb. O/T	A	TO	PF	S	Blk	TP	PPM
WITTMAN, R.	39	10/17	.588	2/3	.667	2/4	0	1	2	0	0	22	.564
BOUCHIE, S.	26	1/5	.200	2/2	1.000	1/4	0	1	4	1	1	4	.154
BLAB, U.	21	4/8	.500	2/3	.667	2/4	0	2	3	0	2	10	.476
THOMAS, I.	39	5/6	.833	3/4	.750	3/4	1	1	3	1	0	13	.333
BROWN, T.	39	3/7	.429	0/0	.000	1/3	2	3	0	0	0	6	.154
DAKICH, D.	1	0/0	.000	0/1	.000	0/1	0	0	0	0	0	0	.000
MORGAN, W.	27	2/5	.400	1/3	.333	0/4	0	1	3	0	2	5	.185
ROBINSON, S.	1	0/0	.000	2/3	.667	0/1	0	0	0	1	0	2	2.000
CAMERON, C.	1	0/0	.000	0/0	.000	0/0	0	1	0	0	0	0	.000
GIOMI, M.	6	0/1	.000	1/2	.500	0/2	0	0	2	0	0	1	.167
Totals	200	25/49	.510	13/21	.619	9/27	3	10	17	3	5	63	.315

Team Rebounds: Indiana 7; Oklahoma 5. Disqualified: None. Technical fouls: None.

	1st Half	2nd Half	Final
Oklahoma	22	27	49
Indiana	34	29	63

SECOND ROUND WEST

Washington State (49)   Coach: George Raveling

	Min.	Total FG/FGA	Pct.	FT/FTA	Pct.	Reb. O/T	A	TO	PF	S	Blk	TP	PPM
POLLARD, B.	27	2/ 5	.400	0/ 0	.000	-/ 4	0	2	0	0	1	4	.148
HARRIEL, S.	23	2/ 6	.333	0/ 1	.000	-/ 2	2	2	5	4	0	4	.174
BROWN, R.	34	3/10	.300	3/ 4	.750	-/ 7	2	1	3	0	1	9	.265
EHLO, C.	39	5/10	.500	2/ 4	.500	-/ 6	5	7	4	1	1	12	.308
WINKLER, C.	28	2/ 4	.500	0/ 0	.000	-/ 1	4	1	5	0	0	4	.143
RUBIN, D.	6	0/ 0	.000	0/ 0	.000	-/ 1	0	2	3	0	0	0	.000
MORRISON, K.	6	0/ 0	.000	0/ 0	.000	-/ 1	1	0	2	0	0	0	.000
HASKINS, A.	33	5/10	.500	4/ 5	.800	-/ 9	0	0	2	0	0	14	.424
WURM, M.	3	0/ 0	.000	0/ 0	.000	-/ 0	0	0	1	0	0	0	.000
MORSON, C.	1	1/ 1	1.000	0/ 0	.000	-/ 0	0	0	0	0	0	2	2.000
Totals	200	20/46	.435	9/14	.643	-/31	14	15	25	5	3	49	.245

Virginia (54)   Coach: Terry Holland

	Min.	Total FG/FGA	Pct.	FT/FTA	Pct.	Reb. O/T	A	TO	PF	S	Blk	TP	PPM
MILLER, J.	28	3/ 4	.750	1/ 2	.500	-/ 0	3	2	2	0	0	7	.250
ROBINSON, C.	33	3/ 9	.333	1/ 3	.333	-/ 3	0	1	2	1	0	7	.212
SAMPSON, R.	38	6/ 8	.750	3/ 7	.429	-/12	2	0	3	2	4	15	.395
WILSON, O.	30	4/11	.364	6/10	.600	-/ 4	5	4	4	5	0	14	.467
CARLISLE, R.	36	1/ 3	.333	4/ 4	1.000	-/ 4	3	1	2	0	0	6	.167
STOKES, R.	23	2/ 3	.667	1/ 1	1.000	-/ 1	5	3	4	0	0	5	.217
EDELIN, K.	9	0/ 0	.000	0/ 0	.000	-/ 0	0	1	1	1	0	0	.000
MERRIFIELD, D.	3	0/ 0	.000	0/ 0	.000	-/ 0	0	1	1	0	0	0	.000
Totals	200	19/38	.500	16/27	.593	-/24	18	13	19	9	4	54	.270

Team Rebounds: Virginia 0; Washington St. 2. Disqualified: Washington St.—Harriel, Winkler. Technical fouls: Washington St.—Coach Raveling.

	1st Half	2nd Half	Final
Washington St.	25	24	49
Virginia	30	24	54

Princeton (42)   Coach: Pete Carril

	Min.	Total FG/FGA	Pct.	FT/FTA	Pct.	Reb. O/T	A	TO	PF	S	Blk	TP	PPM
KNAPP, G.	1	0/ 0	.000	0/ 0	.000	-/ 1	0	1	2	0	0	0	.000
CARTER, I.	7	1/ 1	1.000	0/ 0	.000	-/ 0	1	0	0	0	0	2	.286
MULLIN, K.	7	1/ 2	.500	0/ 0	.000	-/ 2	2	2	5	1	0	2	.286
RYAN, W.	40	0/ 6	.000	0/ 0	.000	-/ 3	6	2	2	0	0	0	.000
ENDERLE, G.	38	8/16	.500	1/ 2	.500	-/ 3	1	3	4	2	0	17	.447
SIMKUS, R.	34	0/ 3	.000	3/ 4	.750	-/ 8	1	2	1	1	0	3	.088
SMYTH, J.	33	3/11	.273	0/ 0	.000	-/ 2	1	4	5	1	0	6	.182
ROBINSON, C.	40	3/ 9	.333	6/ 8	.750	-/ 3	2	0	4	0	1	12	.300
Totals	200	16/48	.333	10/14	.714	-/22	14	14	24	5	1	42	.210

Boston College (51)   Coach: Gary Williams

	Min.	Total FG/FGA	Pct.	FT/FTA	Pct.	Reb. O/T	A	TO	PF	S	Blk	TP	PPM
PRESSLEY, D.	24	1/ 2	.500	4/ 5	.800	-/ 1	1	1	0	0	1	6	.250
O'SHEA, T.	3	0/ 0	.000	0/ 1	.000	-/ 1	0	0	0	0	0	0	.000
MCCREADY, R.	12	3/ 3	1.000	1/ 1	1.000	-/ 2	0	2	2	0	0	7	.583
ADAMS, M.	37	3/ 7	.429	1/ 2	.500	-/ 4	4	3	1	0	0	7	.189
TALLEY, T.	23	2/ 2	1.000	1/ 2	.500	-/ 2	4	0	2	2	0	5	.217
PRIMUS, S.	16	0/ 1	.000	0/ 0	.000	-/ 0	1	1	2	0	0	0	.000
CLARK, M.	21	1/ 2	.500	0/ 0	.000	-/ 1	1	1	1	0	0	2	.095
MURPHY, J.	34	5/ 8	.625	7/12	.583	-/10	1	3	2	0	0	17	.500
ADAMS, B.	3	0/ 0	.000	0/ 0	.000	-/ 0	0	0	0	0	0	0	.000
GARRIS, J.	27	1/ 4	.250	5/ 6	.833	-/ 6	0	4	4	0	0	7	.259
Totals	200	16/29	.552	19/29	.655	-/27	12	15	14	2	1	51	.255

Team Rebounds: Boston College 3; Princeton 4. Disqualified: Princeton—Mullin, Smyth. Technical fouls: None.

	1st Half	2nd Half	Final
Princeton	23	19	42
Boston College	24	27	51

North Carolina State (71)   Coach: Jim Valvano

	Min.	Total FG/FGA	Pct.	FT/FTA	Pct.	Reb. O/T	A	TO	PF	S	Blk	TP	PPM
MCCLAIN, G.	9	1/ 2	.500	0/ 0	.000	-/ 0	2	1	0	0	0	2	.222
GANNON, T.	18	1/ 4	.250	0/ 0	.000	-/ 1	1	0	4	0	0	2	.111
WHITTENBURG, D.	40	5/10	.500	3/ 5	.600	-/ 3	0	1	3	0	1	13	.325
MYERS, E.	4	0/ 2	.000	1/ 2	.500	-/ 0	0	0	0	0	0	1	.250
BATTLE, A.	6	0/ 1	.000	2/ 3	.667	-/ 2	0	0	0	0	1	2	.333
LOWE, S.	33	2/ 4	.500	2/ 2	1.000	-/ 6	10	3	4	0	0	6	.182
BAILEY, T.	36	12/21	.571	1/ 4	.250	-/ 9	1	0	3	1	0	25	.694
CHARLES, L.	34	7/13	.538	3/ 5	.600	-/11	0	2	3	0	0	17	.500
MCQUEEN, C.	20	1/ 3	.333	1/ 2	.500	-/ 3	1	1	4	1	0	3	.150
Totals	200	29/60	.483	13/23	.565	-/35	15	8	21	2	2	71	.355

UNLV (70)   Coach: Jerry Tarkanian

	Min.	Total FG/FGA	Pct.	FT/FTA	Pct.	Reb. O/T	A	TO	PF	S	Blk	TP	PPM
TARKANIAN, D.	38	1/ 4	.250	0/ 1	.000	-/ 3	8	0	3	0	0	2	.053
BOOKER, E.	18	1/ 1	1.000	1/ 3	.333	-/ 0	0	1	1	0	0	3	.167
GREEN, S.	39	9/16	.563	9/ 9	1.000	-/10	1	2	4	0	2	27	.692
ANDERSON, L.	37	8/22	.364	0/ 0	.000	-/ 6	1	0	3	2	1	16	.432
COLLINS, J.	25	5/ 8	.625	2/ 5	.400	-/ 1	2	1	1	1	0	12	.480
GRAHAM, G.	2	0/ 0	.000	1/ 2	.500	-/ 0	0	0	1	0	0	1	.500
HUDSON, E.	30	3/ 9	.333	1/ 3	.333	-/ 9	3	1	4	1	0	7	.233
BROZOVICH, P.	11	1/ 1	1.000	0/ 0	.000	-/ 1	0	0	4	0	0	2	.182
Totals	200	28/61	.459	14/23	.609	-/30	15	5	21	4	3	70	.350

Team Rebounds: N.C. State 7; UNLV 8. Disqualified: None. Technical fouls: None.

	1st Half	2nd Half	Final
N.C. State	27	44	71
UNLV	33	37	70

Utah (67)   Coach: Jerry Pimm

	Min.	Total FG/FGA	Pct.	FT/FTA	Pct.	Reb. O/T	A	TO	PF	S	Blk	TP	PPM
WILLIAMS, P.	40	8/16	.500	2/ 3	.667	-/ 8	3	2	3	1	0	18	.450
MANNION, P.	40	5/ 8	.625	8/ 9	.889	-/ 5	10	4	3	3	1	18	.450
WINANS, C.	29	3/ 3	1.000	1/ 4	.250	-/ 9	0	1	4	0	0	7	.241
HENDRIX, M.	37	2/ 5	.400	2/ 4	.500	-/ 3	1	1	1	0	0	6	.162
ROBINSON, A.	28	9/10	.900	0/ 0	.000	-/ 1	0	1	2	0	1	18	.643
FURGIS, G.	15	0/ 0	.000	0/ 0	.000	-/ 0	3	0	1	0	0	0	.000
MCLAUGHLIN, T.	4	0/ 0	.000	0/ 0	.000	-/ 0	0	0	1	0	0	0	.000
CECIL, D.	7	0/ 1	.000	0/ 0	.000	-/ 1	0	0	1	0	0	0	.000
Totals	200	27/43	.628	13/20	.650	-/24	19	9	16	4	2	67	.335

UCLA (61)   Coach: Larry Farmer

	Min.	Total FG/FGA	Pct.	FT/FTA	Pct.	Reb. O/T	A	TO	PF	S	Blk	TP	PPM
DAYE, D.	31	4/ 9	.444	1/ 2	.500	-/ 6	1	2	3	0	0	9	.290
FIELDS, K.	38	7/16	.438	4/ 6	.667	-/ 6	1	2	3	2	0	18	.474
WRIGHT, B.	10	1/ 1	1.000	0/ 0	.000	-/ 1	0	0	3	0	0	2	.200
JACKSON, R.	26	2/ 5	.400	0/ 0	.000	-/ 3	4	1	1	0	0	4	.154
FOSTER, R.	31	4/12	.333	6/ 6	1.000	-/ 2	3	2	3	0	1	14	.452
NOLTON, M.	24	2/ 4	.500	0/ 0	.000	-/ 0	0	1	4	0	0	4	.167
MIGUEL, N.	22	1/ 3	.333	4/ 4	1.000	-/ 3	2	0	1	1	0	6	.273
GRAY, S.	18	2/ 5	.400	0/ 0	.000	-/ 4	0	1	0	1	0	4	.222
Totals	200	23/55	.418	15/18	.833	-/25	11	9	18	4	1	61	.305

Team Rebounds: Utah 2; UCLA 3. Disqualified: None. Technical fouls: None.

	1st Half	2nd Half	Final
Utah	32	35	67
UCLA	34	27	61

SECOND ROUND EAST

Rutgers (55) Coach: Tom Young

	Min.	Total FG/FGA	Pct.	FT/FTA	Pct.	Reb. O/T	A	TO	PF	S	Blk	TP	PPM
BLACK, K.	35	4/4	1.000	3/4	.750	2/2	2	4	1	0	0	11	.314
TILLMAN, C.	25	7/11	.636	2/2	1.000	0/3	1	2	2	1	0	16	.640
HINSON, R.	34	5/12	.417	0/0	.000	0/8	1	2	4	1	3	10	.294
ELLERBE, B.	29	1/3	.333	0/0	.000	0/1	3	0	4	0	0	2	.069
BRUNSON, R.	31	0/1	.000	2/2	1.000	0/2	4	4	0	2	1	2	.065
BATTLE, J.	20	4/7	.571	2/2	1.000	1/1	3	1	3	1	1	10	.500
REMLEY, C.	16	1/2	.500	0/0	.000	1/1	1	2	1	1	0	2	.125
NIEBERLEIN, C.	10	1/1	1.000	0/0	.000	0/1	0	0	2	0	0	2	.200
Totals	200	23/41	.561	9/10	.900	4/19	15	15	17	6	5	55	.275

St. John's (66) Coach: Lou Carnesecca

	Min.	Total FG/FGA	Pct.	FT/FTA	Pct.	Reb. O/T	A	TO	PF	S	Blk	TP	PPM
RUSSELL, D.	39	2/7	.286	0/1	.000	0/4	1	2	3	1	0	4	.103
GOODWIN, B.	38	6/18	.333	2/5	.400	3/5	5	1	2	2	0	14	.368
WENNINGTON, B.	32	3/9	.333	2/4	.500	4/6	0	0	3	1	0	8	.250
KELLY, B.	16	0/1	.000	0/0	.000	1/2	4	1	1	0	0	0	.000
MULLIN, C.	40	10/13	.769	4/4	1.000	1/4	3	1	0	1	1	24	.600
WILLIAMS, K.	24	5/5	1.000	4/4	1.000	0/3	4	3	3	0	0	14	.583
STEWART, R.	3	0/0	.000	0/0	.000	0/0	0	0	0	0	0	0	.000
JACKSON, J.	8	0/0	.000	2/2	1.000	1/1	0	0	3	0	0	2	.250
Totals	200	26/53	.491	14/20	.700	10/25	17	8	15	5	1	66	.330

Team Rebounds: St. John's 2; Rutgers 5. Disqualified: None. Technical fouls: None.

	1st Half	2nd Half	Final
Rutgers	28	27	55
St. John's	29	37	66

Virginia Commonwealth (54) Coach: J. D. Barnett

	Min.	Total FG/FGA	Pct.	FT/FTA	Pct.	Reb. O/T	A	TO	PF	S	Blk	TP	PPM
BROWN, F.	36	6/10	.600	2/2	1.000	-/8	2	2	1	1	0	14	.389
BROWN, M.	28	5/7	.714	0/0	.000	-/4	2	2	4	1	0	10	.357
SCHLEGEL, M.	38	2/6	.333	0/1	.000	-/4	0	0	2	1	0	4	.105
LAMB, R.	33	3/4	.750	0/0	.000	-/4	7	6	3	0	1	6	.182
DUNCAN, D.	38	5/12	.417	3/5	.600	-/3	3	3	1	0	0	13	.342
DAVIS, S.	3	0/1	.000	0/0	.000	-/0	0	1	0	0	0	0	.000
CORKER, R.	23	2/6	.333	3/6	.500	-/2	1	0	2	0	0	7	.304
SHROPSHIRE, G.	1	0/0	.000	0/0	.000	-/0	0	0	0	0	0	0	.000
Totals	200	23/46	.500	8/14	.571	-/25	15	14	13	3	1	54	.270

Georgia (56) Coach: Hugh Durham

	Min.	Total FG/FGA	Pct.	FT/FTA	Pct.	Reb. O/T	A	TO	PF	S	Blk	TP	PPM
BANKS, J.	40	7/12	.583	0/0	.000	-/6	8	4	2	2	0	14	.350
HEARD, L.	40	1/2	.500	0/2	.000	-/9	5	2	3	3	0	2	.050
FAIR, T.	39	4/10	.400	1/2	.500	-/6	1	4	3	1	1	9	.231
CROSBY, G.	31	5/13	.385	1/2	.500	-/2	3	1	3	1	1	11	.355
FLEMING, V.	30	7/13	.538	2/3	.667	-/5	3	2	4	1	0	16	.533
HARTRY, D.	18	1/3	.333	2/2	1.000	-/3	0	0	2	0	0	4	.222
CORHEN, R.	1	0/0	.000	0/0	.000	-/0	0	0	0	0	0	0	.000
FLOYD, D.	1	0/0	.000	0/0	.000	-/0	0	0	0	0	0	0	.000
Totals	200	25/53	.472	6/11	.545	-/31	20	13	17	8	2	56	.280

Team Rebounds: Georgia 1; Va. Commonwealth 1. Disqualified: None. Technical fouls: None.

	1st Half	2nd Half	Final
Va. Commonwealth	27	27	54
Georgia	29	27	56

Syracuse (74) Coach: Jim Boeheim

	Min.	Total FG/FGA	Pct.	FT/FTA	Pct.	Reb. O/T	A	TO	PF	S	Blk	TP	PPM
RAUTINS, L.	29	7/14	.500	2/4	.500	1/4	1	1	5	0	0	16	.552
BRUIN, T.	18	2/7	.286	6/6	1.000	3/6	2	3	5	0	0	10	.556
HAWKINS, A.	18	2/2	1.000	1/2	.500	0/2	0	0	1	0	1	5	.278
WALDRON, G.	39	5/14	.357	2/2	1.000	3/11	7	4	5	3	1	12	.308
SANTIFER, E.	39	7/16	.438	10/12	.833	4/6	2	1	4	1	1	24	.615
ALEXIS, W.	29	0/3	.000	3/4	.750	0/3	0	0	4	1	0	3	.103
ADDISON, R.	24	2/9	.222	0/0	.000	5/6	1	1	5	0	0	4	.167
SPERA, S.	1	0/1	.000	0/0	.000	0/0	0	0	0	0	0	0	.000
PERRY, C.	1	0/0	.000	0/0	.000	0/0	0	0	0	0	0	0	.000
KERINS, S.	2	0/0	.000	0/0	.000	0/1	1	0	0	0	0	0	.000
Totals	200	25/66	.379	24/30	.800	16/38	14	10	29	5	3	74	.370

Ohio State (79) Coach: Eldon Miller

	Min.	Total FG/FGA	Pct.	FT/FTA	Pct.	Reb. O/T	A	TO	PF	S	Blk	TP	PPM
CAMPBELL, T.	23	7/12	.583	3/4	.750	6/9	0	2	5	1	0	17	.739
CONCHECK, J.	38	6/12	.500	0/0	.000	4/9	6	2	4	0	0	12	.316
WAITERS, G.	28	5/7	.714	2/4	.500	2/5	1	1	5	0	1	12	.429
TAYLOR, T.	35	5/11	.455	5/8	.625	1/3	5	2	2	1	0	15	.429
HUGGINS, L.	36	6/10	.600	0/2	.000	0/6	2	1	2	3	0	12	.333
STOKES, R.	14	1/3	.333	5/7	.714	0/0	1	0	3	1	0	7	.500
JONES, D.	8	1/3	.333	1/3	.333	0/0	0	0	0	0	0	3	.375
WESSON, K.	18	0/0	.000	1/4	.250	1/4	0	1	4	0	0	1	.056
Totals	200	31/58	.534	17/32	.531	14/36	15	9	25	6	1	79	.395

Team Rebounds: Ohio State 4; Syracuse 6. Disqualified: Ohio State—Campbell, Waiters; Syracuse—Rautins, Bruin, Waldron, Addison. Technical fouls: None.

	1st Half	2nd Half	Final
Syracuse	35	39	74
Ohio State	27	52	79

James Madison (49) Coach: Lou Campanelli

	Min.	Total FG/FGA	Pct.	FT/FTA	Pct.	Reb. O/T	A	TO	PF	S	Blk	TP	PPM
MOSTEN, G.	22	0/3	.000	0/0	.000	-/1	1	2	3	1	0	0	.000
DONOHOE, B.	22	3/5	.600	0/0	.000	-/3	1	1	3	0	0	6	.273
RULAND, D.	38	6/13	.462	3/3	1.000	-/3	1	3	4	3	0	15	.395
FISHER, C.	38	8/10	.800	0/0	.000	-/1	2	4	3	3	0	16	.421
DUPONT, D.	33	3/7	.429	1/2	.500	-/1	6	5	4	1	0	7	.212
JACKSON, D.	5	0/0	.000	0/0	.000	-/0	1	1	0	0	0	0	.000
STEELE, D.	21	2/8	.250	0/0	.000	-/1	5	1	1	1	0	4	.190
BRADLEY, K.	12	0/2	.000	0/0	.000	-/2	1	1	4	0	0	0	.000
MASLOFF, J.	1	0/0	.000	0/0	.000	-/1	0	1	0	0	0	0	.000
HUGHES, W.	5	0/1	.000	0/0	.000	-/1	1	0	1	0	0	0	.000
BOLER, W.	1	0/0	.000	1/3	.333	-/2	0	0	0	0	0	1	1.000
ESCH, E.	2	0/0	.000	0/0	.000	-/1	0	0	0	0	0	0	.000
Totals	200	22/49	.449	5/8	.625	-/17	19	19	23	9	0	49	.245

North Carolina (68) Coach: Dean Smith

	Min.	Total FG/FGA	Pct.	FT/FTA	Pct.	Reb. O/T	A	TO	PF	S	Blk	TP	PPM
DOHERTY, M.	38	4/6	.667	6/8	.750	-/4	4	3	2	1	0	14	.368
PERKINS, S.	38	7/11	.636	4/8	.500	-/6	2	1	0	1	3	18	.474
DAUGHERTY, B.	26	2/3	.667	1/3	.333	-/3	1	2	5	1	0	5	.192
BRADDOCK, J.	36	3/6	.500	0/0	.000	-/1	7	3	0	3	0	6	.167
JORDAN, M.	30	6/8	.750	4/4	1.000	-/3	3	2	4	0	3	16	.533
MARTIN, W.	15	1/1	1.000	2/2	1.000	-/5	1	2	1	0	0	4	.267
HALE, S.	5	0/1	.000	0/0	.000	-/0	0	0	1	0	0	0	.000
HUNTER, C.	8	2/2	1.000	0/0	.000	-/0	1	3	1	2	0	4	.500
BROWNLEE, J.	1	0/0	.000	1/3	.333	-/0	0	0	0	0	0	1	1.000
EXUM, C.	3	0/0	.000	0/0	.000	-/2	1	1	0	0	1	0	.000
Totals	200	25/38	.658	18/28	.643	-/24	20	17	13	9	7	68	.340

Team Rebounds: N. Carolina 3; James Madison 4. Disqualified: N. Carolina—Daugherty. Technical fouls: James Madison—Coach Campanelli.

	1st Half	2nd Half	Final
James Madison	17	32	49
N. Carolina	28	40	68

REGIONAL SEMIFINAL MIDWEST

Houston (70)   Coach: Guy Lewis

	Min.	Total FG/FGA	Pct.	FT/FTA	Pct.	Reb. O/T	A	TO	PF	S	Blk	TP	PPM
DREXLER, C.	32	4/8	.500	0/0	.000	3/7	4	4	5	6	1	8	.250
MICHEAUX, L.	34	2/6	.333	6/7	.857	2/7	0	0	4	1	2	10	.294
OLAJUWON, A.	33	10/14	.714	1/2	.500	5/6	0	1	3	1	2	21	.636
FRANKLIN, A.	23	0/4	.000	4/4	1.000	0/0	3	0	0	0	0	4	.174
YOUNG, M.	35	6/12	.500	5/7	.714	1/5	0	3	1	0	0	17	.486
GETTYS, R.	20	1/3	.333	0/0	.000	0/0	4	1	2	1	0	2	.100
ANDERS, B.	6	2/3	.667	0/0	.000	0/0	0	1	1	0	0	4	.667
WILLIAMS, L.	5	1/1	1.000	0/0	.000	1/1	0	0	1	0	2	2	.400
ROSE, D.	4	0/1	.000	0/0	.000	1/1	1	0	0	0	0	0	.000
GILES, D.	8	1/1	1.000	0/0	.000	0/0	0	3	0	2	0	2	.250
Totals	200	27/53	.509	16/20	.800	13/27	12	13	17	11	7	70	.350

Memphis State (63)   Coach: Dana Kirk

	Min.	Total FG/FGA	Pct.	FT/FTA	Pct.	Reb. O/T	A	TO	PF	S	Blk	TP	PPM
PARKS, B.	40	7/12	.583	3/4	.750	-/5	2	3	5	2	0	17	.425
LEE, K.	38	6/15	.400	1/2	.500	-/8	0	4	3	0	2	13	.342
PHILLIPS, D.	38	5/5	1.000	3/4	.750	-/5	1	1	1	0	0	13	.342
TURNER, A.	40	5/13	.385	0/0	.000	-/2	8	6	2	4	0	10	.250
HAYNES, P.	40	4/10	.400	2/4	.500	-/3	1	1	3	1	0	10	.250
HOLMES, B.	4	0/1	.000	0/0	.000	-/0	0	0	0	0	0	0	.000
Totals	200	27/56	.482	9/14	.643	8/23	12	15	14	7	2	63	.315

Team Rebounds: Houston 2; Memphis State 4. Disqualified: Houston—Drexler; Memphis State—Parks. Technical fouls: None.

	1st Half	2nd Half	Final
Houston	34	36	70
Memphis State	34	29	63

Villanova (55)   Coach: Rollie Massimino

	Min.	Total FG/FGA	Pct.	FT/FTA	Pct.	Reb. O/T	A	TO	PF	S	Blk	TP	PPM
MULQUIN, M.	-	2/2	1.000	0/0	.000	-/1	1	0	4	0	0	4	-
PINCKNEY, E.	-	2/6	.333	4/4	1.000	-/11	3	1	4	2	1	8	-
PINONE, J.	-	6/12	.500	6/6	1.000	-/9	1	3	4	1	1	18	-
GRANGER, S.	-	5/9	.556	1/4	.250	-/1	4	4	1	1	0	11	-
McCLAIN, D.	-	5/9	.556	0/0	.000	-/1	1	3	3	1	0	10	-
PRESSLEY, H.	-	1/5	.200	0/0	.000	-/3	3	1	0	1	1	2	-
MCLAIN, G.	-	0/1	.000	2/2	1.000	-/0	0	1	2	0	0	2	-
DOBBS, F.	-	0/0	.000	0/0	.000	-/0	0	0	0	0	0	0	-
Totals	200	21/44	.477	13/16	.813	-/26	13	13	18	6	3	55	.275

Iowa (54)   Coach: Lute Olson

	Min.	Total FG/FGA	Pct.	FT/FTA	Pct.	Reb. O/T	A	TO	PF	S	Blk	TP	PPM
PAYNE, M.	23	1/6	.167	1/2	.500	-/2	1	2	5	0	0	3	.130
GANNON, M.	30	2/5	.400	0/0	.000	-/1	0	1	3	2	0	4	.133
STOKES, G.	39	10/15	.667	2/4	.500	-/11	1	3	3	2	1	22	.564
CARFINO, S.	39	1/7	.143	0/0	.000	-/5	5	1	3	4	0	2	.051
HANSEN, B.	40	9/15	.600	3/4	.750	-/8	3	2	2	0	0	21	.525
BANKS, A.	23	1/4	.250	0/1	.000	-/2	0	1	0	1	1	2	.087
ANDERSON, C.	6	0/1	.000	0/0	.000	-/0	0	0	0	0	0	0	.000
Totals	200	24/53	.453	6/11	.545	-/29	10	10	16	9	2	54	.270

Team Rebounds: Villanova 1; Iowa 1. Disqualified: Iowa—Payne. Technical fouls: None.

	1st Half	2nd Half	Final
Villanova	24	31	55
Iowa	24	30	54

REGIONAL SEMIFINAL MIDEAST

Louisville (65)   Coach: Denny Crum

	Min.	Total FG/FGA	Pct.	FT/FTA	Pct.	Reb. O/T	A	TO	PF	S	Blk	TP	PPM
MCCRAY, S.	36	7/12	.583	3/5	.600	-/4	1	2	3	0	2	17	.472
MCCRAY, R.	33	2/5	.400	1/2	.500	-/5	2	1	4	1	0	5	.152
JONES, C.	29	3/4	.750	0/1	.000	-/2	3	2	4	3	0	6	.207
GORDON, L.	34	9/12	.750	1/2	.500	-/4	0	6	1	4	0	19	.559
WAGNER, M.	35	5/12	.417	0/0	.000	-/1	6	3	3	1	1	10	.286
HALL, J.	11	1/3	.333	0/0	.000	-/0	0	2	1	0	0	2	.182
THOMPSON, B.	22	3/6	.500	0/0	.000	-/4	1	1	3	1	1	6	.273
Totals	200	30/54	.556	5/10	.500	-/20	13	17	19	10	4	65	.325

Arkansas (63)   Coach: Eddie Sutton

	Min.	Total FG/FGA	Pct.	FT/FTA	Pct.	Reb. O/T	A	TO	PF	S	Blk	TP	PPM
BALENTINE, C.	29	3/6	.500	1/3	.333	-/3	0	2	1	1	0	7	.241
SUTTON, L.	35	5/5	1.000	2/2	1.000	-/1	0	5	3	0	1	12	.343
KLEINE, J.	38	8/13	.615	5/6	.833	-/7	0	2	4	0	0	21	.553
ROBERTSON, A.	35	2/8	.250	0/3	.000	-/3	7	6	4	5	0	4	.114
NORTON, R.	9	0/1	.000	0/0	.000	-/0	0	0	0	0	0	0	.000
SNIVELY, J.	2	0/2	.000	0/0	.000	-/0	0	0	0	0	0	0	.000
KELLEY, C.	14	2/3	.667	0/0	.000	-/7	1	1	1	0	1	4	.286
WALKER, D.	38	5/11	.455	5/7	.714	-/8	2	6	3	0	0	15	.395
Totals	200	25/49	.510	13/21	.619	-/29	10	22	16	6	2	63	.315

Team Rebounds: Louisville 4; Arkansas 2. Disqualified: None. Technical fouls: None.

	1st Half	2nd Half	Final
Louisville	27	38	65
Arkansas	37	26	63

Kentucky (64)   Coach: Joe Hall

	Min.	Total FG/FGA	Pct.	FT/FTA	Pct.	Reb. O/T	A	TO	PF	S	Blk	TP	PPM
HORD, D.	11	0/1	.000	0/0	.000	-/1	0	0	0	0	0	0	.000
HURT, C.	36	0/2	.000	2/4	.500	-/2	2	1	2	0	0	2	.056
TURPIN, M.	36	8/13	.615	0/0	.000	-/5	1	1	2	0	1	16	.444
MINNIFIELD, D.	32	5/7	.714	1/3	.333	-/5	5	5	4	1	0	11	.344
MASTER, J.	31	4/7	.571	4/4	1.000	-/3	1	2	1	1	0	12	.387
BEAL, D.	15	0/2	.000	2/2	1.000	-/0	2	1	1	1	0	2	.133
HARDIN, R.	2	0/0	.000	0/0	.000	-/0	0	0	0	0	0	0	.000
BEARUP, B.	14	4/5	.800	0/0	.000	-/1	0	0	2	0	2	8	.571
WALKER, K.	22	6/6	1.000	1/2	.500	-/3	0	1	0	1	1	13	.591
MCKINLEY, T.	1	0/0	.000	0/0	.000	-/0	0	0	0	0	0	0	.000
Totals	200	27/43	.628	10/15	.667	-/20	11	10	13	3	4	64	.320

Indiana (59)   Coach: Bob Knight

	Min.	Total FG/FGA	Pct.	FT/FTA	Pct.	Reb. O/T	A	TO	PF	S	Blk	TP	PPM
WITTMAN, R.	40	8/16	.500	2/2	1.000	-/5	1	0	1	1	0	18	.450
BOUCHIE, S.	39	4/10	.400	0/0	.000	-/4	2	1	4	1	0	8	.205
BLAB, U.	34	6/12	.500	5/9	.556	-/3	0	4	4	1	0	17	.500
THOMAS, J.	36	2/4	.500	0/0	.000	-/7	3	1	3	1	0	4	.111
BROWN, T.	40	3/6	.500	2/2	1.000	-/4	6	4	3	0	0	8	.200
MORGAN, W.	6	0/0	.000	0/0	.000	-/0	1	0	2	0	0	0	.000
GIOMI, M.	5	2/2	1.000	0/0	.000	-/0	0	0	0	0	0	4	.800
Totals	200	25/50	.500	9/13	.692	-/23	13	10	17	4	0	59	.295

Team Rebounds: Kentucky 1; Indiana 0. Disqualified: None. Technical fouls: None.

	1st Half	2nd Half	Final
Kentucky	32	32	64
Indiana	29	30	59

REGIONAL SEMIFINAL WEST

Virginia (95)   Coach: Terry Holland

	Min.	Total FG/FGA	Pct.	FT/FTA	Pct.	Reb. O/T	A	TO	PF	S	Blk	TP	PPM
MILLER, J.	28	4/12	.333	0/0	.000	-/2	1	2	5	0	0	8	.286
ROBINSON, C.	36	2/7	.286	5/9	.556	-/15	1	3	3	0	1	9	.250
SAMPSON, R.	19	9/13	.692	1/3	.333	-/11	1	0	5	1	4	19	1.000
WILSON, O.	36	8/18	.444	2/5	.400	-/3	9	4	2	0	1	18	.500
CARLISLE, R.	32	7/13	.538	8/8	1.000	-/5	1	0	3	0	0	22	.688
STOKES, R.	26	4/4	1.000	4/5	.800	-/1	5	3	4	0	0	12	.462
EDELIN, K.	18	2/3	.667	1/4	.250	-/11	0	1	5	0	0	5	.278
MERRIFIELD, D.	1	0/0	.000	0/0	.000	-/0	0	0	0	0	0	0	.000
MULLEN, T.	4	0/2	.000	2/2	1.000	-/1	1	0	0	0	0	2	.500
Totals	200	36/72	.500	23/36	.639	-/49	19	13	27	1	6	95	.475

Boston College (92)   Coach: Gary Williams

	Min.	Total FG/FGA	Pct.	FT/FTA	Pct.	Reb. O/T	A	TO	PF	S	Blk	TP	PPM
PRESSLEY, D.	27	4/8	.500	3/6	.500	-/5	3	1	4	1	1	11	.407
O'SHEA, T.	2	0/0	.000	0/0	.000	-/1	0	0	0	0	0	0	.000
MCCREADY, R.	4	1/2	.500	1/2	.500	-/0	0	1	1	0	0	3	.750
ADAMS, M.	34	7/22	.318	4/5	.800	-/5	8	3	2	1	0	18	.529
TALLEY, T.	13	3/6	.500	0/0	.000	-/3	0	2	4	0	0	6	.462
PRIMUS, S.	19	1/5	.200	0/0	.000	-/3	0	2	5	0	0	2	.105
CLARK, M.	26	1/4	.250	2/3	.667	-/3	3	1	4	0	0	4	.154
MURPHY, J.	31	9/15	.600	5/8	.625	-/12	0	2	2	0	1	23	.742
ADAMS, B.	8	0/1	.000	0/0	.000	-/1	0	0	5	0	0	0	.000
GARRIS, J.	36	8/15	.533	9/10	.900	-/12	1	1	2	0	4	25	.694
Totals	200	34/78	.436	24/34	.706	-/45	15	13	29	2	6	92	.460

Team Rebounds: Virginia 1; Boston College 2. Disqualified: Virginia—Miller, Sampson, Edelin; Boston College—Primus, B. Adams. Technical fouls: None.

	1st Half	2nd Half	Final
Virginia	45	50	95
Boston College	44	48	92

North Carolina State (75)   Coach: Jim Valvano

	Min.	Total FG/FGA	Pct.	FT/FTA	Pct.	Reb. O/T	A	TO	PF	S	Blk	TP	PPM
MCCLAIN, G.	10	1/1	1.000	0/0	.000	-/1	1	1	0	0	0	2	.200
GANNON, T.	18	4/5	.800	2/2	1.000	-/1	2	1	1	1	0	10	.556
WHITTENBURG, D.	38	10/13	.769	7/7	1.000	-/2	3	5	3	0	0	27	.711
MYERS, E.	2	0/1	.000	2/2	1.000	-/0	0	0	0	0	0	2	1.000
BATTLE, A.	4	0/0	.000	0/0	.000	-/0	0	0	0	0	0	0	.000
LOWE, S.	39	2/2	1.000	0/0	.000	-/4	5	3	1	2	1	4	.103
BAILEY, T.	37	4/10	.400	2/2	1.000	-/9	1	1	0	0	4	10	.270
CHARLES, L.	35	7/9	.778	4/4	1.000	-/3	0	0	1	0	0	18	.514
MCQUEEN, C.	13	0/0	.000	1/2	.500	-/2	0	2	1	0	0	1	.077
THOMPSON, H.	1	0/0	.000	0/0	.000	-/0	0	0	1	0	0	0	.000
WARREN, D.	1	0/0	.000	1/2	.500	-/0	0	0	0	0	0	1	1.000
LEONARD, Q.	1	0/0	.000	0/0	.000	-/0	0	0	0	0	0	0	.000
DENSMORE, W.	1	0/0	.000	0/1	.000	-/1	0	0	0	0	0	0	.000
Totals	200	28/41	.683	19/22	.864	-/23	12	13	8	3	5	75	.375

Utah (56)   Coach: Jerry Pimm

	Min.	Total FG/FGA	Pct.	FT/FTA	Pct.	Reb. O/T	A	TO	PF	S	Blk	TP	PPM
WILLIAMS, P.	38	7/15	.467	1/1	1.000	-/6	1	1	2	1	0	15	.395
MANION, P.	38	6/10	.600	1/4	.250	-/4	4	2	4	2	0	13	.342
WINANS, C.	31	3/4	.750	0/0	.000	-/8	4	2	3	1	0	6	.194
HENDRIX, M.	29	2/6	.333	0/0	.000	-/0	1	4	1	0	1	4	.138
ROBINSON, A.	31	4/12	.333	0/0	.000	-/1	1	2	2	0	0	8	.258
CECIL, D.	8	1/1	1.000	0/0	.000	-/0	0	0	1	0	0	2	.250
FURGIS, G.	17	1/3	.333	0/0	.000	-/1	0	1	2	1	0	2	.118
HILL, S.	1	0/2	.000	0/0	.000	-/0	1	1	1	0	0	0	.000
HILL, M.	1	0/0	.000	0/0	.000	-/1	0	0	0	0	0	0	.000
WHITE, J.	2	1/2	.500	0/0	.000	-/2	0	0	0	0	0	2	1.000
RIVERS, C.	2	1/3	.333	0/0	.000	-/0	0	0	1	0	0	2	1.000
BOZNER, M.	2	1/2	.500	0/0	.000	-/3	1	0	1	0	0	2	1.000
Totals	200	27/60	.450	2/5	.400	-/26	13	13	18	5	1	56	.280

Team Rebounds: N.C. State 1; Utah 2. Disqualified: None. Technical fouls: None.

	1st Half	2nd Half	Final
N. C. State	30	45	75
Utah	26	30	56

REGIONAL SEMIFINAL EAST

St. John's (67)   Coach: Lou Carnesecca

	Min.	Total FG/FGA	Pct.	FT/FTA	Pct.	Reb. O/T	A	TO	PF	S	Blk	TP	PPM
RUSSELL, D.	40	4/8	.500	6/7	.857	5/12	1	3	3	1	0	14	.350
GOODWIN, B.	33	6/12	.500	0/2	.000	1/6	4	3	4	0	0	12	.364
WENNINGTON, B.	33	5/8	.625	0/0	.000	3/10	2	1	3	0	3	10	.303
KELLY, B.	20	0/2	.000	0/0	.000	1/1	3	2	3	1	0	0	.000
MULLIN, C.	40	6/11	.545	7/8	.875	2/3	4	6	2	0	0	19	.475
WILLIAMS, K.	20	4/7	.571	4/4	1.000	1/2	1	3	5	0	0	12	.600
STEWART, R.	7	0/2	.000	0/0	.000	0/1	1	0	2	0	0	0	.000
JACKSON, T.	7	0/0	.000	0/0	.000	1/1	0	0	1	1	1	0	.000
Totals	200	25/50	.500	17/21	.810	14/36	16	18	23	3	4	67	.335

Georgia (70)   Coach: Hugh Durham

	Min.	Total FG/FGA	Pct.	FT/FTA	Pct.	Reb. O/T	A	TO	PF	S	Blk	TP	PPM
BANKS, J.	40	4/8	.500	2/3	.667	2/3	2	2	3	0	1	10	.250
HEARD, L.	33	3/5	.600	5/6	.833	3/5	2	1	4	1	0	11	.333
FAIR, T.	40	11/21	.524	5/8	.625	6/9	3	1	2	5	3	27	.675
CROSBY, G.	26	3/9	.333	2/2	1.000	1/1	0	1	4	2	0	8	.308
FLEMING, V.	35	5/11	.455	0/0	.000	1/4	2	3	5	0	0	10	.286
HARTRY, D.	18	1/3	.333	2/2	1.000	0/0	2	0	1	1	0	4	.222
CORHEN, R.	7	0/2	.000	0/1	.000	2/3	1	0	0	0	0	0	.000
HITCHCOCK, T.	1	0/0	.000	0/0	.000	0/0	0	0	0	1	0	0	.000
Totals	200	27/59	.458	16/22	.727	15/25	12	8	19	10	4	70	.350

Team Rebounds: Georgia 2; St. John's 2. Disqualified: Georgia—Fleming; St. John's—Williams. Technical fouls: None.

	1st Half	2nd Half	Final
St. John's	29	38	67
Georgia	27	43	70

Ohio State (51) Coach: Eldon Miller

	Min.	Total FG/FGA	Pct.	FT/FTA	Pct.	Reb. O/T	A	TO	PF	S	Blk	TP	PPM
CAMPBELL, T.	38	6/12	.500	1/2	.500	3/6	0	1	2	0	0	13	.342
CONCHECK, J.	27	5/9	.556	4/5	.800	1/5	1	0	3	0	0	14	.519
WAITERS, G.	35	2/5	.400	1/3	.333	2/5	0	1	4	1	2	5	.143
TAYLOR, T.	33	3/9	.333	4/5	.800	1/2	4	4	4	3	0	10	.303
HUGGINS, L.	26	2/5	.400	0/0	.000	0/3	0	3	1	0	0	4	.154
STOKES, R.	19	1/2	.500	0/0	.000	0/0	4	3	4	0	0	2	.105
JONES, D.	8	0/2	.000	0/0	.000	1/2	0	0	2	1	0	0	.000
WESSON, K.	8	1/1	1.000	0/0	.000	1/2	0	2	2	0	0	2	.250
KORTOKRAX, A.	2	0/0	.000	0/0	.000	0/0	0	0	0	0	0	0	.000
HAAS, M.	1	0/0	.000	0/0	.000	0/0	0	0	1	0	0	0	.000
GRACE, H.	1	0/0	.000	0/0	.000	0/0	0	1	0	0	0	0	.000
SMITH, C.	1	0/0	.000	1/2	.500	0/0	0	0	1	0	0	1	1.000
POLK, D.	1	0/0	.000	0/0	.000	0/0	0	0	0	0	0	0	.000
Totals	200	20/45	.444	11/17	.647	9/25	9	15	23	6	2	51	.255

North Carolina (64) Coach: Dean Smith

	Min.	Total FG/FGA	Pct.	FT/FTA	Pct.	Reb. O/T	A	TO	PF	S	Blk	TP	PPM
DAUGHERTY, B.	28	4/6	.667	0/0	.000	2/6	1	3	4	0	0	8	.286
DOHERTY, M.	39	2/5	.400	4/4	1.000	1/2	3	2	1	0	0	8	.205
PERKINS, S.	23	5/12	.417	5/6	.833	1/6	0	1	4	2	0	15	.652
JORDAN, M.	36	5/15	.333	7/9	.778	2/7	0	1	3	0	1	17	.472
BRADDOCK, J.	38	2/3	.667	6/6	1.000	0/2	3	2	1	0	0	10	.263
HUNTER, C.	10	1/1	1.000	0/0	.000	0/1	2	0	2	0	0	2	.200
MARTIN, W.	17	2/3	.667	0/0	.000	1/1	1	0	0	0	1	4	.235
HALE, S.	2	0/0	.000	0/0	.000	0/0	1	0	1	0	0	0	.000
BROWNLEE, J.	5	0/0	.000	0/0	.000	0/0	0	1	0	1	0	0	.000
EXUM, C.	1	0/0	.000	0/0	.000	0/0	0	0	1	0	0	0	.000
MAKKONEN, T.	1	0/0	.000	0/0	.000	0/0	0	0	0	0	0	0	.000
Totals	200	21/45	.467	22/25	.880	7/25	11	10	17	3	2	64	.320

Team Rebounds: N. Carolina 1; Ohio State 3. Disqualified: None. Technical fouls: None.

	1st Half	2nd Half	Final
Ohio State	30	21	51
N. Carolina	29	35	64

REGIONAL FINAL MIDWEST

Houston (89) Coach: Guy Lewis

	Min.	Total FG/FGA	Pct.	FT/FTA	Pct.	Reb. O/T	A	TO	PF	S	Blk	TP	PPM
DREXLER, C.	36	6/12	.500	0/1	.000	-/5	3	3	5	1	0	12	.333
MICHEAUX, L.	35	11/17	.647	8/10	.800	-/12	2	3	2	1	4	30	.857
OLAJUWON, A.	31	10/11	.909	0/1	.000	-/13	1	0	4	2	8	20	.645
FRANKLIN, A.	24	2/5	.400	0/0	.000	-/2	2	1	1	0	0	4	.167
YOUNG, M.	37	9/16	.563	2/2	1.000	-/6	3	2	2	1	0	20	.541
GETTYS, R.	21	0/1	.000	0/2	.000	-/4	3	2	3	0	0	0	.000
ANDERS, B.	5	0/3	.000	0/0	.000	-/0	0	1	2	0	0	0	.000
WILLIAMS, B.	2	0/0	.000	0/0	.000	-/1	0	1	0	1	0	0	.000
ROSE, D.	1	1/1	1.000	1/2	.500	-/0	0	0	0	0	0	3	3.000
BUNCE, D.	2	0/0	.000	0/0	.000	-/0	0	0	0	0	0	0	.000
DICKENS, E.	2	0/1	.000	0/0	.000	-/0	0	1	0	0	0	0	.000
ORSAK, G.	2	0/0	.000	0/1	.000	-/0	0	0	0	0	0	0	.000
THOMAS, R.	1	0/0	.000	0/0	.000	-/0	0	1	0	0	0	0	.000
GILES, D.	1	0/0	.000	0/0	.000	-/0	0	0	0	0	0	0	.000
Totals	200	39/67	.582	11/19	.579	-/43	14	15	21	5	13	89	.445

Villanova (71) Coach: Rollie Massimino

	Min.	Total FG/FGA	Pct.	FT/FTA	Pct.	Reb. O/T	A	TO	PF	S	Blk	TP	PPM
MULQUIN, M.	11	1/3	.333	1/1	1.000	-/1	0	0	4	0	0	3	.273
PINCKNEY, E.	36	6/11	.545	6/9	.667	-/12	5	3	4	2	1	18	.500
PINONE, J.	34	7/17	.412	4/4	1.000	-/9	1	0	4	1	0	18	.529
GRANGER, S.	33	3/15	.200	2/2	1.000	-/1	3	7	4	1	0	8	.242
MCCLAIN, D.	29	8/14	.571	1/1	1.000	-/7	0	1	2	1	0	17	.586
PRESSLEY, H.	26	0/9	.000	1/2	.500	-/3	1	1	1	0	0	1	.038
MCLAIN, G.	15	0/3	.000	0/0	.000	-/2	3	1	2	0	0	0	.000
MAKER, W.	5	1/1	1.000	0/1	.000	-/2	0	0	1	0	0	2	.400
DOBBS, F.	3	0/0	.000	0/0	.000	-/0	0	0	1	0	0	0	.000
LUTSCHANNIG, M.	2	0/4	.000	0/0	.000	-/1	0	0	0	0	0	0	.000
WILBER, D.	2	1/4	.250	0/0	.000	-/2	1	0	1	0	0	2	1.000
MASSIMINO, R.	2	0/0	.000	0/0	.000	-/0	0	0	0	0	0	0	.000
EVERSON, C.	2	1/1	1.000	0/0	.000	-/1	0	0	0	0	0	2	1.000
Totals	200	28/82	.341	15/20	.750	-/41	14	13	24	5	1	71	.355

Team Rebounds: Houston 4; Villanova 2. Disqualified: Houston—Drexler. Technical fouls: None.

	1st Half	2nd Half	Final
Houston	37	52	89
Villanova	27	44	71

REGIONAL FINAL MIDEAST

Louisville (80) Coach: Denny Crum

	Min.	Total FG/FGA	Pct.	FT/FTA	Pct.	Reb. O/T	A	TO	PF	S	Blk	TP	PPM
MCCRAY, S.	40	3/6	.500	1/1	1.000	-/7	4	2	3	3	1	7	.175
MCCRAY, R.	42	7/7	1.000	1/2	.500	-/8	2	1	3	1	2	15	.357
JONES, C.	38	4/9	.444	4/6	.667	-/7	2	2	1	0	2	12	.316
GORDON, L.	42	11/21	.524	2/3	.667	-/1	2	2	1	4	0	24	.571
WAGNER, M.	39	7/10	.700	4/4	1.000	-/2	4	3	2	2	0	18	.462
VALENTINE, R.	1	0/0	.000	0/0	.000	-/0	0	0	0	0	0	0	.000
WEST, C.	1	0/0	.000	0/0	.000	-/0	0	0	0	0	0	0	.000
HALL, J.	9	0/0	.000	0/0	.000	-/0	0	0	1	1	0	0	.000
THOMPSON, B.	13	2/4	.500	0/1	.000	-/2	1	1	1	0	0	4	.308
Totals	225	34/57	.596	12/17	.706	-/27	15	11	12	11	5	80	.356

Kentucky (68) Coach: Joe Hall

	Min.	Total FG/FGA	Pct.	FT/FTA	Pct.	Reb. O/T	A	TO	PF	S	Blk	TP	PPM
HORD, D.	30	4/9	.444	1/2	.500	-/2	0	0	1	0	0	9	.300
HURT, C.	31	3/5	.600	1/2	.500	-/6	1	3	3	0	0	7	.226
TURPIN, M.	36	8/13	.615	2/2	1.000	-/9	1	3	4	3	1	18	.500
MINNIFIELD, D.	37	6/13	.462	0/0	.000	-/3	5	6	4	3	0	12	.324
MASTER, J.	40	9/13	.692	0/0	.000	-/2	2	2	4	0	0	18	.450
BEAL, D.	15	0/0	.000	0/0	.000	-/0	4	2	3	0	0	0	.000
HARDIN, R.	1	0/0	.000	0/0	.000	-/0	0	1	0	0	0	0	.000
BEARUP, B.	9	1/1	1.000	0/2	.000	-/3	0	0	0	0	0	2	.222
WALKER, K.	26	1/3	.333	0/0	.000	-/1	0	1	1	0	0	2	.077
Totals	225	32/57	.561	4/8	.500	-/26	13	18	20	6	1	68	.302

Team Rebounds: Louisville 1; Kentucky 1. Disqualified: None. Technical fouls: None.

	1st Half	2nd Half	1st OT	Final
Louisville	30	32	18	80
Kentucky	37	25	6	68

REGIONAL FINAL WEST

Virginia (62)   Coach: Terry Holland

	Min.	Total FG/FGA	Pct.	FT/FTA	Pct.	Reb. O/T	A	TO	PF	S	Blk	TP	PPM
MILLER, J.	15	3/ 5	.600	0/ 0	.000	-/ 0	0	0	0	0	0	6	.400
ROBINSON, C.	34	4/ 9	.444	0/ 0	.000	-/ 5	1	4	4	0	0	8	.235
SAMPSON, R.	33	8/10	.800	7/11	.636	-/11	2	3	4	1	4	23	.697
WILSON, O.	35	3/ 5	.600	1/ 2	.500	-/ 2	9	3	3	0	0	7	.200
CARLISLE, R.	37	4/ 7	.571	0/ 1	.000	-/ 4	4	3	1	0	0	8	.216
STOKES, R.	21	3/ 3	1.000	2/ 3	.667	-/ 1	2	2	2	0	1	8	.381
EDELIN, K.	19	1/ 1	1.000	0/ 2	.000	-/ 4	1	0	3	0	0	2	.105
MULLEN, T.	6	0/ 1	.000	0/ 0	.000	-/ 0	0	0	0	0	0	0	.000
Totals	200	26/41	.634	10/19	.526	-/27	19	15	17	1	5	62	.310

North Carolina State (63)   Coach: Jim Valvano

	Min.	Total FG/FGA	Pct.	FT/FTA	Pct.	Reb. O/T	A	TO	PF	S	Blk	TP	PPM
MCCLAIN, G.	2	0/ 1	.000	1/ 2	.500	-/ 0	0	0	0	0	0	1	.500
GANNON, T.	10	0/ 1	.000	0/ 0	.000	-/ 0	0	0	1	0	0	0	.000
WHITTENBURG, D.	39	11/16	.688	2/ 2	1.000	-/ 3	4	1	4	1	0	24	.615
MYERS, E.	6	2/ 3	.667	0/ 0	.000	-/ 0	0	0	0	0	0	4	.667
BATTLE, A.	7	0/ 1	.000	1/ 2	.500	-/ 2	0	2	0	0	0	1	.143
LOWE, S.	40	2/ 8	.250	4/ 4	1.000	-/ 0	8	1	1	0	0	8	.200
BAILEY, T.	38	7/17	.412	0/ 0	.000	-/ 6	0	1	4	1	0	14	.368
CHARLES, L.	35	4/ 5	.800	3/ 4	.750	-/10	1	0	2	0	0	11	.314
MCQUEEN, C.	23	0/ 3	.000	0/ 0	.000	-/ 6	1	1	4	4	1	0	.000
Totals	200	26/55	.473	11/14	.786	-/27	14	6	16	6	1	63	.315

Team Rebounds: N.C. State 0; Virginia 1. Disqualified: None. Technical fouls: None.

	1st Half	2nd Half	Final
Virginia	33	29	62
N.C. State	28	35	63

REGIONAL FINAL EAST

Georgia (82)   Coach: Hugh Durham

	Min.	Total FG/FGA	Pct.	FT/FTA	Pct.	Reb. O/T	A	TO	PF	S	Blk	TP	PPM
BANKS, J.	37	7/10	.700	6/ 6	1.000	-/ 5	3	2	3	-	0	20	.541
HEARD, L.	40	4/ 6	.667	0/ 0	.000	-/ 9	2	0	1	-	0	8	.200
FAIR, T.	22	5/ 6	.833	1/ 2	.500	-/ 6	1	0	4	-	0	11	.500
CROSBY, G.	33	6/12	.500	5/ 8	.625	-/ 3	2	5	3	-	0	17	.515
FLEMING, V.	39	6/16	.375	5/ 8	.625	-/ 8	5	2	3	-	0	17	.436
HARTRY, D.	8	1/ 1	1.000	0/ 0	.000	-/ 0	1	0	0	-	0	2	.250
FLOYD, D.	3	0/ 0	.000	0/ 0	.000	-/ 0	1	0	0	-	0	0	.000
CORHEN, R.	18	3/ 6	.500	1/ 4	.250	-/ 3	1	1	3	-	2	7	.389
Totals	200	32/57	.561	18/28	.643	-/34	16	10	17	-	2	82	.410

North Carolina (77)   Coach: Dean Smith

	Min.	Total FG/FGA	Pct.	FT/FTA	Pct.	Reb. O/T	A	TO	PF	S	Blk	TP	PPM
DAUGHERTY, B.	29	6/10	.600	3/ 3	1.000	-/ 9	0	0	4	-	1	15	.517
DOHERTY, M.	38	3/ 8	.375	4/ 4	1.000	-/ 2	4	1	3	-	0	10	.263
PERKINS, S.	38	5/ 9	.556	4/ 4	1.000	-/11	2	3	3	-	3	14	.368
JORDAN, M.	34	11/23	.478	4/ 5	.800	-/ 6	0	2	5	-	1	26	.765
BRADDOCK, J.	36	5/ 9	.556	0/ 1	.000	-/ 2	7	4	2	-	0	10	.278
HUNTER, C.	13	1/ 3	.333	0/ 0	.000	-/ 0	0	0	5	-	0	2	.154
MARTIN, W.	5	0/ 0	.000	0/ 0	.000	-/ 2	0	0	0	-	0	0	.000
HALE, S.	7	0/ 1	.000	0/ 0	.000	-/ 0	0	0	4	-	0	0	.000
Totals	200	31/63	.492	15/17	.882	-/32	13	10	26	-	5	77	.385

Team Rebounds: Georgia 3; N. Carolina 0. Disqualified: N. Carolina—Jordan, Hunter. Technical fouls: None.

	1st Half	2nd Half	Final
Georgia	37	45	82
N. Carolina	35	42	77

FINAL FOUR

Houston (94)   Coach: Guy Lewis

	Min.	Total FG/FGA	Pct.	FT/FTA	Pct.	Reb. O/T	A	TO	PF	S	Blk	TP	PPM
DREXLER, C.	37	10/15	.667	1/ 2	.500	-/ 7	6	1	2	1	0	21	.568
MICHEAUX, L.	23	4/ 7	.571	0/ 1	.000	-/ 3	1	4	5	0	0	8	.348
OLAJUWON, A.	36	9/14	.643	3/ 7	.429	-/22	0	2	4	1	8	21	.583
FRANKLIN, A.	29	5/ 8	.625	3/ 4	.750	-/ 1	3	1	0	5	0	13	.448
YOUNG, M.	35	7/18	.389	2/ 3	.667	-/ 4	3	1	2	2	1	16	.457
GETTYS, R.	13	0/ 0	.000	0/ 0	.000	-/ 1	4	3	2	0	0	0	.000
ANDERS, B.	19	5/ 9	.556	3/ 5	.600	-/ 6	2	0	4	2	1	13	.684
WILLIAMS, B.	1	1/ 1	1.000	0/ 0	.000	-/ 0	0	0	0	0	0	2	2.000
ROSE, D.	6	0/ 2	.000	0/ 0	.000	-/ 0	0	0	3	0	0	0	.000
GILES, D.	1	0/ 0	.000	0/ 1	.000	-/ 0	0	0	0	0	0	0	.000
Totals	200	41/74	.554	12/23	.522	-/44	19	12	22	11	10	94	.470

Louisville (81)   Coach: Denny Crum

	Min.	Total FG/FGA	Pct.	FT/FTA	Pct.	Reb. O/T	A	TO	PF	S	Blk	TP	PPM
MCCRAY, S.	35	5/ 8	.625	0/ 0	.000	-/ 6	4	4	4	2	2	10	.286
MCCRAY, R.	35	3/ 6	.500	2/ 8	.250	-/ 5	5	2	4	1	0	8	.229
JONES, C.	33	3/10	.300	6/ 8	.750	-/11	1	3	3	1	2	12	.364
GORDON, L.	36	6/15	.400	5/ 6	.833	-/ 6	2	2	3	1	0	17	.472
WAGNER, M.	36	12/23	.522	0/ 0	.000	-/ 2	4	1	4	1	0	24	.667
THOMPSON, B.	15	1/ 4	.250	4/ 5	.800	-/ 5	1	3	4	2	1	6	.400
HALL, J.	8	2/ 4	.500	0/ 0	.000	-/ 1	0	1	0	0	0	4	.500
WEST, C.	1	0/ 0	.000	0/ 0	.000	-/ 0	0	0	1	0	0	0	.000
VALENTINE, R.	1	0/ 0	.000	0/ 0	.000	-/ 0	0	0	0	0	0	0	.000
Totals	200	32/70	.457	17/27	.630	-/36	17	16	23	8	6	81	.405

Team Rebounds: Houston 1; Louisville 4. Disqualified: Houston—Micheaux. Technical fouls: Houston—bench.

	1st Half	2nd Half	Final
Houston	36	58	94
Louisville	41	40	81

North Carolina State (67)   Coach: Jim Valvano

	Min.	Total FG/FGA	Pct.	FT/FTA	Pct.	Reb. O/T	A	TO	PF	S	Blk	TP	PPM
GANNON, T.	12	1/ 4	.250	2/ 2	1.000	-/ 1	0	0	0	1	0	4	.333
WHITTENBURG, D.	39	8/18	.444	4/ 4	1.000	-/ 0	6	3	1	0	0	20	.513
BATTLE, A.	7	0/ 0	.000	0/ 0	.000	-/ 2	0	1	0	0	1	0	.000
LOWE, S.	37	4/ 6	.667	2/ 2	1.000	-/ 5	11	8	3	1	0	10	.270
BAILEY, T.	38	9/17	.529	2/ 5	.400	-/10	1	0	3	0	2	20	.526
CHARLES, L.	29	2/ 2	1.000	1/ 2	.500	-/ 6	0	1	1	0	0	5	.172
MCQUEEN, C.	38	4/ 5	.800	0/ 0	.000	-/13	1	3	5	1	4	8	.211
Totals	200	28/52	.538	11/15	.733	-/37	19	16	13	3	7	67	.335

Georgia (60)   Coach: Hugh Durham

	Min.	Total FG/FGA	Pct.	FT/FTA	Pct.	Reb. O/T	A	TO	PF	S	Blk	TP	PPM
BANKS, J.	35	5/19	.263	3/ 5	.600	-/ 2	0	2	3	0	0	13	.371
HEARD, L.	35	3/ 5	.600	2/ 3	.667	-/10	1	0	2	3	0	8	.229
FAIR, T.	32	2/ 9	.222	1/ 2	.500	-/ 6	0	4	3	6	0	5	.156
CROSBY, G.	35	5/15	.333	2/ 2	1.000	-/ 1	2	1	3	3	0	12	.343
FLEMING, V.	31	7/17	.412	0/ 0	.000	-/11	2	3	4	0	0	14	.452
CORHEN, R.	16	3/ 6	.500	0/ 1	.000	-/ 7	1	0	2	0	0	6	.375
HARTRY, D.	14	1/ 3	.333	0/ 0	.000	-/ 0	1	0	3	0	0	2	.143
FLOYD, D.	2	0/ 0	.000	0/ 0	.000	-/ 0	0	0	0	0	0	0	.000
Totals	200	26/74	.351	8/13	.615	-/37	7	10	20	12	0	60	.300

Team Rebounds: N.C. State 0; Georgia 2. Disqualified: N.C. State—McQueen. Technical fouls: None.

	1st Half	2nd Half	Final
N.C. State	33	34	67
Georgia	22	38	60

NATIONAL CHAMPIONSHIP

Houston (52)   Coach: Guy Lewis

	Min.	Total FG/FGA	Pct.	FT/FTA	Pct.	Reb. O/T	A	TO	PF	S	Blk	TP	PPM
DREXLER, C.	25	1/ 5	.200	2/ 2	1.000	-/ 2	0	1	4	0	0	4	.160
MICHEAUX, L.	18	2/ 6	.333	0/ 0	.000	-/ 6	0	3	1	0	0	4	.222
OLAJUWON, A.	38	7/15	.467	6/ 7	.857	-/18	1	2	1	0	7	20	.526
FRANKLIN, A.	35	2/ 6	.333	0/ 1	.000	-/ 0	3	3	0	0	0	4	.114
YOUNG, M.	30	3/10	.300	0/ 4	.000	-/ 8	1	0	0	0	1	6	.200
GETTYS, R.	20	2/ 2	1.000	0/ 0	.000	-/ 2	2	0	3	0	0	4	.200
ANDERS, B.	17	4/ 9	.444	2/ 5	.400	-/ 2	1	4	2	0	0	10	.588
WILLIAMS, B.	10	0/ 1	.000	0/ 0	.000	-/ 4	1	0	3	0	0	0	.000
ROSE, D.	7	0/ 1	.000	0/ 0	.000	-/ 1	0	0	2	0	0	0	.000
Totals	200	21/55	.382	10/19	.526	-/43	9	13	16	0	8	52	.260

North Carolina State (54)   Coach: Jim Valvano

	Min.	Total FG/FGA	Pct.	FT/FTA	Pct.	Reb. O/T	A	TO	PF	S	Blk	TP	PPM
GANNON, T.	18	3/ 4	.750	1/ 2	.500	-/ 1	2	0	3	1	0	7	.389
WHITTENBURG, D.	39	6/17	.353	2/ 2	1.000	-/ 5	1	2	3	0	0	14	.359
MYERS, E.	1	0/ 0	.000	0/ 0	.000	-/ 1	0	0	0	0	0	0	.000
BATTLE, A.	4	0/ 1	.000	2/ 2	1.000	-/ 1	1	1	1	0	0	2	.500
LOWE, S.	40	4/ 9	.444	0/ 1	.000	-/ 0	8	0	2	5	0	8	.200
BAILEY, T.	39	7/16	.438	1/ 2	.500	-/ 5	0	1	1	0	0	15	.385
CHARLES, L.	25	2/ 7	.286	0/ 2	.000	-/ 7	0	0	2	0	1	4	.160
MCQUEEN, C.	34	1/ 5	.200	2/ 2	1.000	-/12	1	2	4	1	1	4	.118
Totals	200	23/59	.390	8/11	.727	-/32	13	6	16	7	2	54	.270

Team Rebounds: N.C. State 2; Houston 1. Disqualified: None. Technical fouls: None.

	1st Half	2nd Half	Final
Houston	25	27	52
N.C. State	33	21	54

✪ ALL-STAR TEAMS ✪

ALL TOURNAMENT

THURL BAILEY	N.C. STATE
SIDNEY LOWE	N.C. STATE
★ AKEEM OLAJUWON	HOUSTON
MILT WAGNER	LOUISVILLE
DERECK WHITTENBURG	N.C. STATE

MIDWEST REGIONAL

LARRY MICHEAUX	HOUSTON
★ AKEEM OLAJUWON	HOUSTON
JOHN PINONE	VILLANOVA
GREG STOKES	IOWA
MICHAEL YOUNG	HOUSTON

WEST REGIONAL

THURL BAILEY	N.C. STATE
LORENZO CHARLES	N.C. STATE
JOHN GARRIS	BOSTON COLLEGE
RALPH SAMPSON	VIRGINIA
★ DERECK WHITTENBURG	N.C. STATE

MIDEAST REGIONAL

★ LANCASTER GORDON	LOUISVILLE
JIM MASTER	KENTUCKY
SCOOTER MCCRAY	LOUISVILLE
MELVIN TURPIN	KENTUCKY
DARRELL WALKER	ARKANSAS

EAST REGIONAL

★ JAMES BANKS	GEORGIA
TERRY FAIR	GEORGIA
VERN FLEMING	GEORGIA
MICHAEL JORDON	N. CAROLINA
CHRIS MULLIN	ST. JOHN'S

★ Most Outstanding Player(s)

✪ INDIVIDUAL RECORDS ✪

SCORING

Most points in a single game
1. STEVE BLACK, LA SALLE (vs. VA. COMMONWEALTH) — 31
2. LARRY MICHEAUX, HOUSTON (vs. VILLANOVA) — 30
3. JON SUNDVOLD, MISSOURI (vs. IOWA) — 29
4. KEITH LEE, MEMPHIS STATE (vs. GEORGETOWN) — 28
5. 3 tied for fifth place.

Most total points in the tournament
1. DERECK WHITTENBURG, N.C. STATE — 120
2. THURL BAILEY, N.C. STATE — 101
3. AKEEM OLAJUWON, HOUSTON — 94
4. LANCASTER GORDON, LOUISVILLE — 78
5. MICHAEL YOUNG, HOUSTON — 75

Highest scoring average (minimum 2 games)
1. STEVE BLACK, LA SALLE (46-2) — 23.00
2. ERIC SANTIFER, SYRACUSE (43-2) — 21.50
2. CHRIS MULLIN, ST. JOHN'S (43-2) — 21.50
2. PAT EWING, GEORGETOWN (43-2) — 21.50
5. 2 tied for fifth place.

FIELD GOALS

Most field goals in a single game
1. JON SUNDVOLD, MISSOURI (vs. IOWA) — 14
2. STEVE BLACK, LA SALLE (vs. VA. COMMONWEALTH) — 13
3. MILT WAGNER, LOUISVILLE (vs. HOUSTON) — 12
3. THURL BAILEY, N.C. STATE (vs. UNLV) — 12
5. 5 tied for fifth place.

Most total field goals in the tournament
1. DERECK WHITTENBURG, N.C. STATE — 47
1. THURL BAILEY, N.C. STATE — 47
3. AKEEM OLAJUWON, HOUSTON — 42
4. LANCASTER GORDON, LOUISVILLE — 33
5. MICHAEL YOUNG, HOUSTON — 31

Most field goal attempts in a single game
1. STEVE BLACK, LA SALLE (vs. VA. COMMONWEALTH) — 25
2. ERIC HIGHTOWER, GA. SOUTHERN (vs. ROBERT MORRIS) — 24

2. MIKE ALEXANDER, BOSTON UNIV. (vs. LA SALLE) — 24
2. JON SUNDVOLD, MISSOURI (vs. IOWA) — 24
5. 2 tied for fifth place.

Most total field goal attempts in tournament
1. THURL BAILEY, N.C. STATE — 99
2. DERECK WHITTENBURG, N.C. STATE — 92
3. MICHAEL YOUNG, HOUSTON — 67
4. AKEEM OLAJUWON, HOUSTON — 64
5. LANCASTER GORDON, LOUISVILLE — 63

Highest field goal percentage in a single game (minimum 10 attempts)
1. AKEEM OLAJUWON, HOUSTON (vs. VILLANOVA) (10-11) — .909
2. ANGELO ROBINSON, UTAH (vs. UCLA) (9-10) — .900
3. KENNETH PERKINS, LAMAR (vs. VILLANOVA) (9-11) — .818
3. STEVE REID, PURDUE (vs. ROBERT MORRIS) (9-11) — .818
5. 4 tied for fifth place.

Highest field goal percentage in the tournament (minimum 20 attempts)
1. RALPH SAMPSON, VIRGINIA (23-31) — .742
2. JOE KLEINE, ARKANSAS (14-20) — .700
3. CHRIS MULLIN, ST. JOHN'S (16-24) — .667
4. AKEEM OLAJUWON, HOUSTON (42-64) — .656
5. JIM MASTER, KENTUCKY (17-26) — .654

FREE THROWS

Most free throws in a single game
1. KEITH LEE, MEMPHIS STATE (vs. GEORGETOWN) — 12
1. CALVIN DUNCAN, VA. COMMONWEALTH (vs. LA SALLE) — 12
3. MICHAEL PHELPS, ALCORN ST. (vs. GEORGETOWN) — 10
3. ERIC SANTIFER, SYRACUSE (vs. OHIO STATE) — 10
5. 4 tied for fifth place.

Most total free throws in the tournament
1. DERECK WHITTENBURG, N.C. STATE — 26
2. ERIC SANTIFER, SYRACUSE — 19
3. BOB HANSEN, IOWA — 18

4. MICHAEL PHELPS, ALCORN ST. — 16
5. 4 tied for fifth place.

Most free throws attempted in a single game
1. KEITH LEE, MEMPHIS STATE (vs. GEORGETOWN) — 16
2. DARYL WALKER, ARKANSAS (vs. PURDUE) — 14
3. 5 tied for third place.

Most free throws attempted in the tournament
1. DERECK WHITTENBURG, N.C. STATE — 31
2. LARRY MICHEAUX, HOUSTON — 23
3. MICHAEL YOUNG, HOUSTON — 22
3. ERIC SANTIFER, SYRACUSE — 22
3. CHARLES JONES, LOUISVILLE — 22

Highest free throw percentage in a single game (minimum 7 attempts)
1. CALVIN DUNCAN, VA. COMMONWEALTH (vs. LA SALLE) (12-12) — 1.000
2. SIDNEY GREEN, UNLV (vs. N.C. STATE) (9-9) — 1.000
2. CHARLES FISHER, JAMES MADISON (vs. WEST VIRGINIA) (9-9) — 1.000
4. 4 tied for fourth place.

Highest free throw percentage in the tournament (minimum 15 attempts)
1. JOHN PINONE, VILLANOVA (15-15) — 1.000
2. BOB HANSEN, IOWA (18-20) — .900
3. CALVIN DUNCAN, VA. COMMONWEALTH (15-17) — .882
4. JOHN GARRIS, BOSTON COLLEGE (14-16) — .875
4. MATT DOHERTY, N. CAROLINA (14-16) — .875

REBOUNDS

Most rebounds in a single game
1. AKEEM OLAJUWON, HOUSTON (vs. LOUISVILLE) — 22
2. AKEEM OLAJUWON, HOUSTON (vs. N.C. STATE) — 18
3. CRAIG ROBINSON, PRINCETON (vs. OKLAHOMA STATE) — 16
4. KEITH LEE, MEMPHIS STATE (vs. GEORGETOWN) — 15

4 CRAIG ROBINSON, VIRGINIA (vs. BOSTON COLLEGE) 15

Most total rebounds in the tournament
1 AKEEM OLAJUWON, HOUSTON 65
2 LORENZO CHARLES, N.C. STATE 51
3 COZELL MCQUEEN, N.C. STATE 42
3 THURL BAILEY, N.C. STATE 42
5 2 tied for fifth place.

Most rebounds per game (minimum 2 games)
1 AKEEM OLAJUWON, HOUSTON (65-5) 13.00
2 KEITH LEE, MEMPHIS STATE (23-2) 11.50
3 RALPH SAMPSON, VIRGINIA (34-3) 11.33
4 ED PINCKNEY, VILLANOVA (33-3) 11.00
5 JAY MURPHY, BOSTON COLLEGE (22-2) 11.00

ASSISTS

Most assists in a single game
1 SIDNEY LOWE, N.C. STATE (vs. GEORGIA) 11
2 PACE MANNION, UTAH (vs. UCLA) 10
2 SIDNEY LOWE, N.C. STATE (vs. UNLV) 10
4 4 tied for fourth place.

Most total assists in the tournament
1 SIDNEY LOWE, N.C. STATE 45
2 OTHELL WILSON, VIRGINIA 23
3 REID GETTYS, HOUSTON 20
4 DERECK WHITTENBURG, N.C. STATE 18
5 2 tied for fifth place.

Most assists per game (minimum 2 appearances)
1 STEVE REID, PURDUE (16-2) 8.00
2 OTHELL WILSON, VIRGINIA (23-3) 7.67
3 SIDNEY LOWE, N.C. STATE (45-6) 7.50
4 PACE MANNION, UTAH (15-2) 7.50
4 ROLANDO LAMB, VA. COMMONWEALTH (15-2) 7.50

TURNOVERS

Most turnovers in a single game
1 SIDNEY LOWE, N.C. STATE (vs. GEORGIA) 8
2 9 tied for second place.

Most total turnovers in the tournament
1 SIDNEY LOWE, N.C. STATE 18
2 STEWART GRANGER, VILLANOVA 17
3 LANCASTER GORDON, LOUISVILLE 16
4 DERECK WHITTENBURG, N.C. STATE 15
5 DIRK MINNIEFIELD, KENTUCKY 14

SHOTS BLOCKED

Most shots blocked in a single game
1 AKEEM OLAJUWON, HOUSTON (vs. LOUISVILLE) 8
1 AKEEM OLAJUWON, HOUSTON (vs. VILLANOVA) 8
3 AKEEM OLAJUWON, HOUSTON (vs. N.C. STATE) 7

4 RUSSELL CROSS, PURDUE (vs. ROBERT MORRIS) 5
5 9 tied for fifth place.

Most total shots blocked in the tournament
1 AKEEM OLAJUWON, HOUSTON 28
2 RALPH SAMPSON, VIRGINIA 12
3 THURL BAILEY, N.C. STATE 9
4 3 tied for fourth place.

STEALS

Most steals in a single game
1 ALVIN ROBERTSON, ARKANSAS (vs. PURDUE) 8
2 MICHAEL PHELPS, ALCORN ST. (vs. XAVIER [OHIO]) 6
2 TERRY FAIR, GEORGIA (vs. N.C. STATE) 6
2 CLYDE DREXLER, HOUSTON (vs. MEMPHIS STATE) 6
5 7 tied for fifth place.

Most total steals in the tournament
1 ALVIN ROBERTSON, ARKANSAS 13
2 TERRY FAIR, GEORGIA 12
3 LANCASTER GORDON, LOUISVILLE 11
3 CLYDE DREXLER, HOUSTON 11
5 MICHAEL PHELPS, ALCORN ST. 10

✪ TEAM RECORDS ✪

SCORING

Most points in a single game
1 VIRGINIA (vs. BOSTON COLLEGE) 95
2 HOUSTON (vs. LOUISVILLE) 94
3 BOSTON COLLEGE (vs. VIRGINIA) 92

Most total points in the tournament
1 N.C. STATE 399
2 HOUSTON 365
3 LOUISVILLE 296

Highest scoring average (minimum 2 games)
1 LOUISVILLE (296-4) 74.00
2 SYRACUSE (148-2) 74.00
3 HOUSTON (365-5) 73.00

FIELD GOALS

Most field goals in a single game
1 HOUSTON (vs. LOUISVILLE) 41
2 HOUSTON (vs. VILLANOVA) 39
3 VIRGINIA (vs. BOSTON COLLEGE) 36

Most total field goals in the tournament
1 N.C. STATE 161
2 HOUSTON 151
3 LOUISVILLE 123

Most field goals attempted in a single game
1 VILLANOVA (vs. HOUSTON) 82
2 BOSTON COLLEGE (vs. VIRGINIA) 78
3 2 tied for third place.

Most total field goals attempted in the tournament
1 N.C. STATE 331
2 HOUSTON 288
3 GEORGIA 243

Highest field goal percentage in a single game
1 N.C. STATE (vs. UTAH) (28-41) .683
2 N. CAROLINA (vs. JAMES MADISON) (25-38) .658
3 VILLANOVA (vs. LAMAR) (24-37) .649

Highest field goal percentage in a tournament (minimum 2 games)
1 PURDUE (51-84) .607
2 KENTUCKY (77-136) .566
3 RUTGERS (46-82) .561

FREE THROWS

Most free throws in a single game
1 MEMPHIS STATE (vs. GEORGETOWN) 28
2 3 tied for second place.

Most total free throws in the tournament
1 N.C. STATE 77
2 HOUSTON 63
3 2 tied for third place.

Most free throws attempted in a single game
1 LAMAR (vs. ALABAMA) 44
2 MEMPHIS STATE (vs. GEORGETOWN) 39
3 2 tied for third place.

Most total free throws attempted in the tournament
1 N.C. STATE 110
1 HOUSTON 110
3 VIRGINIA 82

Highest free throw percentage in a single game
1 UTAH (vs. ILLINOIS) (10-11) .909
2 RUTGERS (vs. ST. JOHN'S) (9-10) .900
3 N. CAROLINA (vs. GEORGIA) (15-17) .882

Highest free throw percentage in the tournament (minimum 2 games)
1 N. CAROLINA (55-70) .786
2 WASHINGTON ST. (29-37) .784
3 GEORGETOWN (37-48) .771

Fewest free throws in a single game
1 UTAH (vs. N.C. STATE) 2
2 N.C. A&T (vs. PRINCETON) 3
3 2 tied for third place.

Lowest free throw percentage in a single game
1 UTAH (vs. N.C. STATE) (2-5) .400
2 TENN.-CHATT. (vs. MARYLAND) (5-12) .417
3 MISSOURI (vs. IOWA) (5-11) .455

Lowest free throw percentage in the tournament (minimum 2 games)
1 LAMAR (29-51) .569
2 OHIO STATE (28-49) .571
3 HOUSTON (63-110) .573

REBOUNDS

Most rebounds in a single game
1 LA SALLE (vs. BOSTON UNIV.) 51
2 VIRGINIA (vs. BOSTON COLLEGE) 49
3 BOSTON UNIV. (vs. LA SALLE) 46

Most rebounds per game (minimum 2 games)
1 LA SALLE (83-2) 41.50
2 HOUSTON (185-5) 37.00
3 BOSTON COLLEGE (72-2) 36.00

ASSISTS

Most assists in a single game
1 PURDUE (vs. ARKANSAS) 23
2 VA. COMMONWEALTH (vs. LA SALLE) 22
3 SYRACUSE (vs. MOREHEAD STATE) 21

Most assists per game (minimum 2 games)
1 PURDUE (40-2) 20.00
2 VIRGINIA (56-3) 18.67
3 2 tied for third place.

TURNOVERS

Most turnovers in a single game
1 XAVIER (OHIO) (vs. ALCORN ST.) 30

2 PURDUE (vs. ARKANSAS) 23
3 ARKANSAS (vs. LOUISVILLE) 22

Most turnovers per game (minimum 2 games)
1 PURDUE (43-2) 21.50
2 ARKANSAS (37-2) 18.50
3 2 tied for third place.

SHOTS BLOCKED

Most shots blocked in a single game
1 HOUSTON (vs. VILLANOVA) 13
2 HOUSTON (vs. LOUISVILLE) 10
3 HOUSTON (vs. N.C. STATE) 8

Most shots blocked per game (minimum 2 games)
1 HOUSTON (43-5) 8.60
2 LAMAR (12-2) 6.00
3 LOUISVILLE (21-4) 5.25

STEALS

Most steals in a single game
1 4 tied for first place.

Most steals per game
1 ALCORN ST. (23-2) 11.50
2 ROBERT MORRIS (21-2) 10.50
3 LOUISVILLE (40-4) 10.00

1984

FIRST ROUND	SECOND ROUND	REGIONAL SEMIFINAL	REGIONAL FINAL	FINAL FOUR	REGIONAL FINAL	REGIONAL SEMIFINAL	SECOND ROUND	FIRST ROUND

MIDEAST

8 Brigham Young 84
9 Ala.-Birmingham 68
Brigham Young 68
Kentucky 72
(bye)
1 Kentucky 93
Kentucky 54

5 Louisville 72
12 Morehead St. 59
Louisville 69
Louisville 67
(bye)
4 Tulsa 67

Kentucky 40

6 Oregon St. 62
11 West Virginia 64
West Virginia 77
Maryland 70
(bye)
3 Maryland 102
Illinois 51

7 Villanova 84
10 Marshall 72
Villanova 56
Illinois 72
(bye)
2 Illinois 64

WEST

8 Miami (Ohio) 69
9 SMU 83
SMU 36
Georgetown 62
(bye)
1 Georgetown 37
Georgetown 61

5 UNLV 68
12 Princeton 56
UNLV 73
UNLV 48
(bye)
4 UTEP 60

Georgetown 53

6 Washington 64
11 Nevada-Reno 54
Washington 80
Washington 58
(bye)
3 Duke 78
Dayton 49

7 Louisiana St. 66
10 Dayton 74
Dayton 89
Dayton 64
(bye)
2 Oklahoma 85

FINAL FOUR

Georgetown 84
Houston 75

EAST

Temple 66
N. Carolina 68
8 Temple 65
9 St. John's 63
(bye)
1 N. Carolina 77

Indiana 48
Richmond 67
Indiana 72
5 Auburn 71
12 Richmond 72
(bye)
4 Indiana 75

Virginia 47

Va. Commonwealth 63
Syracuse 55
6 Va. Commonwealth 70
11 Northeastern 69
(bye)
3 Syracuse 78

Virginia 50

Virginia 53 (ot)
Virginia 63
7 Virginia 58
10 Iona 57
(bye)
2 Arkansas 51

MIDWEST

Illinois St. 61
DePaul 71
8 Illinois St. 49
9 Alabama 48
(bye)
1 DePaul 75

Wake Forest 63

Kansas 59
Wake Forest 73 (ot)
5 Kansas 57
12 Alcorn St. 56
(bye)
4 Wake Forest 69

Houston 49 (ot)

*Memphis St. 66
*Memphis St. 71
6 *Memphis St. 92
11 Oral Roberts 83
(bye)
3 Purdue 48

Houston 68

Louisiana Tech. 69
Houston 78
7 Fresno St. 56
10 Louisiana Tech 66
(bye)
2 Houston 77

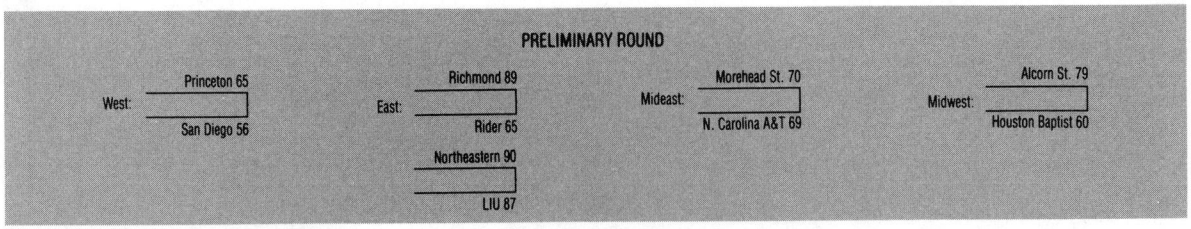

PRELIMINARY ROUND

West:
Princeton 65
San Diego 56

East:
Richmond 89
Rider 65

Northeastern 90
LIU 87

Mideast:
Morehead St. 70
N. Carolina A&T 69

Midwest:
Alcorn St. 79
Houston Baptist 60

*Memphis State's participation in 1984 tournament vacated.

In 1984 Jim Valvano's North Carolina State Wolfpack did not get a chance to defend either title; they were passed over by the selection committee after compiling a 19-13 record.

Larry Brown returned to the college coaching ranks and brought Kansas, with its proud basketball tradition, a Big Eight title and a tournament slot. He also fueled controversy when a professor accused him of trying to influence a player's grade, as well as for hiring Ed Manning as his assistant coach (many skeptics felt nine-year pro player Manning's chief qualification for the job was his son, a super prospect named Danny, who indeed did agree to attend Kansas the following fall).

St. John's ended its "jinxed" season of last minute or overtime losses when—with a ninth close game on the line—Chris Mullin, a 91 percent foul shooter, missed the front end of a one-and-one that would have given the Redmen a lead over Temple, and the Owls' Terence Stansbury canned a 25-footer, all in the last eight seconds.

The grand old man of the coaching profession, Ray Meyer of DePaul, was forced into early retirement when his team lost an eight-point lead in the last three minutes and was eliminated in overtime by Wake Forest, which then lost to Houston.

Under the floor leadership of a clean-cut freshman guard named Steve Alford, unheralded Indiana missed the Final Four by a bucket. Little more than an hour before the Hoosiers' game against No. 1–ranked North Carolina, Bob Knight told sometime starter Dan Dakich that he would be guarding Michael Jordan. "I went right back to my room and threw up," said Dakich, who then helped hold Jordan to six points in the first 35 minutes as Indiana upset the Tar Heels. But Dakich went from hero to goat as Virginia walk-on and future law student Kenton Edelin (who had been a perfect 10 for 10 in his first three tournament games) stole the ball from the Indiana guard and drove in for a lay-up that put his team ahead for good with 1:27 left in the East Regional finals.

Virginia, starting over without Ralph Sampson, had been fortunate to get a tourney bid after finishing fifth in the ACC. The Cavaliers' luck continued as they survived a series of squeakers to make it into the Final Four. First they beat Iona by a point after the Gaels' Rory Grimes missed a foul shot that would have tied the score with two seconds left; then they beat Arkansas in overtime when an Alvin Robertson block fell into the hands of Rick Carlisle, who canned the clincher with four seconds left; then, after a sloppy victory over Syracuse, they survived Indiana. But there was still one more squeaker to go.

It was a game that, by every odds maker's estimation, should have taken place the year before, when Ralph Sampson and the top-seeded Cavaliers got derailed by N.C. State by a point in the semis. Houston was arguably not as strong, either, because this time the Cougars (who were making their third straight Final Four appearance) would have to go without Clyde Drexler and Larry Micheaux, both of whom had gone on to the NBA. (Wake Forest coach Carl Tacy disagreed; after losing to the Cougars, he said he thought Houston was "much improved," because it had more poise and was "more of a together group.")

Virginia's luck finally ran out in their semifinal with Houston. After falling behind early in the first half, they fought back, using a diamond and one defense to neutralize Olajuwon and the Cougars' top scorer, Michael Young. Finally, with 29 seconds left, Virginia's Othell Wilson stole the ball and scored for a tie, and after a Houston turnover, Virginia had a chance to win. But Olajuwon knocked away a Wilson pass, and the game went into overtime.

Houston took a lead in the extra period, but when Young missed the front end of a one-and-one with 15 seconds left, Virginia had the ball needing only a two-pointer to tie. But Olajuwon again tipped away a Wilson pass, and Houston was in the finals.

After the game the real world intruded on Michael Young. He learned his brother had been shot in the head by a former mental patient the previous day. Luckily his brother received only superficial injuries, but the news put his own disappointing performance into a different perspective.

On the other side of the draw the University of Kentucky won Bluegrass bragging rights by beating Louisville (in front of a hometown crowd in Lexington) in the Mideast regional semifinals. Then the Wildcats, with their monster front line of 7-1 Sam Bowie, 6-11 Melvin Turpin, and 6-8 Kenny Walker, advanced to the Final Four when, with only seconds left in the game, guard Dicky Beal (who was named the region's Most Outstanding Player) careened into Illinois's Bruce Douglas just across midcourt—and the call went against Douglas. "I am not going to cry about the officiating," said Illinois coach Jim Henson, "but we cannot come to Kentucky and have the fouls go against us 11-2 with about a minute left and win the ball game."

The Wildcats were paired against Georgetown, which had lost by a point in the finals two years earlier. This time 7-footer Jon Koncak played Patrick Ewing to a standstill in Georgetown's first tournament game, but Ewing tipped in a missed Gene Smith free throw with 51 seconds left to help the Hoyas escape with a 37-36 victory over SMU. "I hope that's the bad game we have to get out of our system," said coach John Thompson. It was.

Georgetown dominated UNLV, then overwhelmed the tenth-seeded Dayton Flyers. Dayton, making its first tournament appearance since 1974, had begun to call the season their "Year of Dreams," but they woke up to what their top scorer, Roosevelt Chapman, described as a nightmare. "It's frightening," said Chapman. "Ewing is very mammoth. He's like an octopus with hands all over the place." And it wasn't just Ewing; Bill Martin swept the boards with 10 rebounds, the intimidating freshman Michael Graham shook the arena with his dunks, and the Hoyas were unrelenting in their physical, full-court pressure.

The Georgetown pressure game reached its apex in the second half of their semifinal against Kentucky. With 3:04 left in the first half the Wildcats led 27-15 and Ewing had three fouls. Then the Hoyas turned the screws. Kentucky scored only one more bucket before the intermission, and they didn't score a point in the second half until ten minutes had elapsed. By then Georgetown was in control. The game ended at 53-40. Georgetown had put Kentucky away with a 31-11 second half, holding them to an unbelievable 3 of 33 from the floor. "We play pretty good defense," said Georgetown guard Michael Jackson after the game, thus proving himself to be a master of understatement.

Finally it was Houston and Georgetown—the matchup everyone was waiting for. Like Russell and Chamberlain, or Alcindor and Hayes, the meeting between Ewing and Olajuwon was supposed to be a classic confrontation between dominant centers. Each of the big men was in his second championship contest. For each, the first had ended in disappointment in the last seconds.

The game began with Georgetown guard Gene Smith, one of the Hoyas' top defensive catalysts, out with an injury. Like Kentucky, the Cougars' Phi Slama Jama fraternity of deadly slam dunkers took a commanding early lead. They hit their first seven shots, but they were mostly bombs from the outside, not earth-shattering slams. Then John Thompson sent in freshman Michael Graham, whose shaved head made him appear even more menacing than his overt aggressiveness already made him. And the tide turned.

The battle of the big men never did take place. With both Ewing and Olajuwon limited by foul trouble, the great confrontation between the two was put on hold until both became NBA all-pros.

Instead, five Georgetown players, led by smooth-shooting freshman Reggie Williams scored in double figures. The Hoyas got 33 from their bench. And while Thompson molded his players into a single dedicated unit, Houston dissolved into finger pointing. "We blew it," said Olajuwon. "We didn't play as a team. We were selfish." "Akeem just doesn't understand the game yet," was coach Guy Lewis's response. Houston's talented sub Benny Anders, whose two baskets and a steal helped keep the Cougars in the contest in the first half (and who didn't get back in until the game was all but over), criticized his lack of playing time.

The Cougars' great individual talent could only take them so far; it couldn't take them over the top to the championship. "We've been playing like this all year long," said Olajuwon. "But you can't do it against a real good team." "We never ran into any Georgetowns," explained Anders.

In the end Georgetown provided an exclamation point to what the best coaches have stressed throughout the game's history. Basketball is not just a game of athletic ability and individual heroics. The better TEAM wins.

PRELIMINARY ROUND

Princeton (65)   Coach: Pete Carril

	Min.	Total FG/FGA	Pct.	FT/FTA	Pct.	Reb. O/T	A	TO	PF	S	Blk	TP	PPM
MULLIN, K.	40	12/15	.800	14/16	.875	-/7	1	-	1	-	-	38	.950
SMYTH	40	5/10	.500	3/4	.750	-/4	1	-	3	-	-	13	.325
LEVY, H.	36	1/5	.200	4/5	.800	-/4	2	-	3	-	-	6	.167
CARTER, I.	40	0/1	.000	4/4	1.000	-/3	1	-	1	-	-	4	.100
RYAN	28	0/3	.000	2/2	1.000	-/2	6	-	4	-	-	2	.071
SCOTT	12	1/1	1.000	0/0	.000	-/2	0	-	3	-	-	2	.167
WILLIAMS	4	0/0	.000	0/0	.000	-/1	0	-	0	-	-	0	.000
Totals	200	19/35	.543	27/31	.871	-/23	11	13	15	-	-	65	.325

San Diego (56)   Coach: Jim Brovelli

	Min.	Total FG/FGA	Pct.	FT/FTA	Pct.	Reb. O/T	A	TO	PF	S	Blk	TP	PPM
WHITMARSH	-	6/10	.600	5/8	.625	-/5	2	-	4	-	-	17	-
REUSS	-	3/4	.750	1/3	.333	-/2	3	-	3	-	-	7	-
THOMPSON	-	2/3	.667	0/0	.000	-/8	0	-	3	-	-	4	-
CARR	-	2/4	.500	2/2	1.000	-/1	1	-	4	-	-	6	-
BOSTIC	-	2/5	.400	0/0	.000	-/6	0	-	4	-	-	4	-
PRUNTY	-	5/12	.417	0/0	.000	-/0	2	-	3	-	-	10	-
MOSCATEL, A.	-	3/11	.273	0/0	.000	-/2	3	-	4	-	-	6	-
PRALLMAN	-	0/0	.000	0/0	.000	-/0	0	-	1	-	-	0	-
MUSSELMAN, E.	-	0/2	.000	0/0	.000	-/0	1	-	0	-	-	0	-
McIVER, D.	-	1/1	1.000	0/0	.000	-/1	0	-	0	-	-	2	-
BRICKLEY	-	0/1	.000	0/0	.000	-/0	0	-	0	-	-	0	-
PENFOLD	-	0/0	.000	0/0	.000	-/0	0	-	0	-	-	0	-
Totals	200	24/53	.453	8/13	.615	-/25	12	11	26	-	-	56	.280

Team Rebounds: Princeton 1; San Diego 2. Disqualified: None. Technical fouls: None.

	1st Half	2nd Half	Final
Princeton	33	32	65
San Diego	24	32	56

Northeastern (90)   Coach: Jim Calhoun

	Min.	Total FG/FGA	Pct.	FT/FTA	Pct.	Reb. O/T	A	TO	PF	S	Blk	TP	PPM
HALSEL	40	4/8	.500	2/2	1.000	-/14	5	-	4	-	-	10	.250
LEWIS, R.	26	8/13	.615	5/7	.714	-/5	2	-	2	-	-	21	.808
FULLER, W.	39	9/13	.692	4/6	.667	-/8	2	-	3	-	-	22	.564
LAFLEUR, A.	35	4/7	.571	6/8	.750	-/4	3	-	2	-	-	14	.400
MILLER, G.	40	4/6	.667	7/9	.778	-/5	6	-	2	-	-	15	.375
DALE	17	2/6	.333	4/4	1.000	-/4	0	-	1	-	-	8	.471
ROBINSON	3	0/1	.000	0/0	.000	-/0	0	-	1	-	-	0	.000
Totals	200	31/54	.574	28/36	.778	-/40	18	22	15	-	-	90	.450

LIU (87)   Coach: Paul Lizzo

	Min.	Total FG/FGA	Pct.	FT/FTA	Pct.	Reb. O/T	A	TO	PF	S	Blk	TP	PPM
MERIWETHER, J.	37	7/19	.368	1/2	.500	-/7	1	-	5	-	-	15	.405
SCURRY	31	7/14	.500	0/0	.000	-/9	0	-	5	-	-	14	.452
WIGGINS	17	1/4	.250	0/0	.000	-/3	0	-	1	-	-	2	.118
BROWN	40	13/25	.520	1/2	.500	-/4	4	-	2	-	-	27	.675
JAMES	39	6/12	.500	3/3	1.000	-/5	7	-	5	-	-	15	.385
JORDON	17	5/12	.417	0/0	.000	-/5	7	-	5	-	-	10	.588
WHITEHEAD	16	0/1	.000	4/4	1.000	-/3	1	-	2	-	-	4	.250
VILLANUOVA	1	0/0	.000	0/0	.000	-/0	0	-	0	-	-	0	.000
POWELL	1	0/0	.000	0/0	.000	-/0	0	-	0	-	-	0	.000
TOWNES	1	0/0	.000	0/0	.000	-/0	0	-	0	-	-	0	.000
Totals	200	39/87	.448	9/11	.818	-/36	20	13	25	-	-	87	.435

Team Rebounds: Northeastern 1; LIU 2. Disqualified: LIU—Meriwether, Scurry, James, Jordon. Technical fouls: Northeastern—Halsel.

	1st Half	2nd Half	Final
Northeastern	48	42	90
LIU	34	53	87

Richmond (89)   Coach: Dick Tarrant

	Min.	Total FG/FGA	Pct.	FT/FTA	Pct.	Reb. O/T	A	TO	PF	S	Blk	TP	PPM
NEWMAN, J.	37	11/19	.579	3/4	.750	-/8	1	-	1	-	-	25	.676
DAVIS, J.	36	1/4	.250	1/5	.200	-/10	6	-	3	-	-	3	.083
SLAYE	31	8/11	.727	3/5	.600	-/4	4	-	4	-	-	19	.613
BECKWITH, G.	34	3/4	.750	2/3	.667	-/4	9	-	2	-	-	8	.235
JOHNSON, K.	37	11/14	.786	0/1	.000	-/3	5	-	1	-	-	22	.595
HARDIN, T.	9	0/2	.000	0/2	.000	-/5	0	-	2	-	-	0	.000
GROSS	3	0/0	.000	0/0	.000	-/1	0	-	1	-	-	0	.000
RUNK	4	0/0	.000	4/5	.800	-/0	1	-	0	-	-	4	1.000
FELLS	2	0/0	.000	0/2	.000	-/2	0	-	0	-	-	0	.000
TUCKER	3	1/3	.333	4/6	.667	-/3	0	-	1	-	-	6	2.000
SIMMONS	2	1/2	.500	0/0	.000	-/3	0	-	1	-	-	2	1.000
JOHNSON, M.	1	0/0	.000	0/1	.000	-/0	1	-	0	-	-	0	.000
PHILLIPS	1	0/1	.000	0/0	.000	-/2	0	-	1	-	-	0	.000
Totals	200	36/60	.600	17/34	.500	-/45	27	16	17	-	-	89	.445

Rider (65)   Coach: John Carpenter

	Min.	Total FG/FGA	Pct.	FT/FTA	Pct.	Reb. O/T	A	TO	PF	S	Blk	TP	PPM
LAMAR	-	5/10	.500	0/0	.000	-/4	2	-	2	-	-	10	-
BOLGER	-	5/9	.556	6/8	.750	-/7	2	-	4	-	-	16	-
THOMAS	-	4/10	.400	0/0	.000	-/10	0	-	4	-	-	8	-
LEE	-	3/15	.200	0/0	.000	-/2	8	-	4	-	-	6	-
BURKE	-	5/18	.278	0/0	.000	-/6	2	-	4	-	-	10	-
BENNOF	-	0/0	.000	0/0	.000	-/1	0	-	1	-	-	0	-
GRANT	-	0/0	.000	0/0	.000	-/0	0	-	0	-	-	0	-
NICHOLSON	-	0/0	.000	1/2	.500	-/3	0	-	2	-	-	1	-
MORALES	-	2/4	.500	0/0	.000	-/1	3	-	5	-	-	4	-
CARTER	-	1/1	1.000	0/0	.000	-/2	0	-	1	-	-	2	-
HAMMER	-	3/4	.750	0/0	.000	-/1	0	-	3	-	-	6	-
RICE	-	1/2	.500	0/2	.000	-/0	0	-	3	-	-	2	-
KOUAC	-	0/2	.000	0/2	.000	-/1	0	-	0	-	-	0	-
Totals	200	29/75	.387	7/14	.500	-/38	17	20	33	-	-	65	.325

Team Rebounds: Richmond 2; Rider 4. Disqualified: Rider—Morales. Technical fouls: None.

	1st Half	2nd Half	Final
Richmond	40	49	89
Rider	27	38	65

Morehead State (70)   Coach: Wayne Marvin

	Min.	Total FG/FGA	Pct.	FT/FTA	Pct.	Reb. O/T	A	TO	PF	S	Blk	TP	PPM
CHILDRESS, E.	33	10/12	.833	0/0	.000	-/5	2	-	2	-	-	20	.606
HARRISON, E.	28	4/7	.571	3/4	.750	-/7	0	-	2	-	-	11	.393
TIPTON	33	6/9	.667	4/4	1.000	-/5	3	-	2	-	-	16	.485
FULTZ, J.	32	3/5	.600	0/1	.000	-/2	8	-	2	-	-	6	.188
MINNIFIELD, G.	24	1/4	.250	0/1	.000	-/1	2	-	2	-	-	2	.083
SULLIVAN	26	4/7	.571	4/6	.667	-/1	2	-	1	-	-	12	.462
TUCKER	24	1/5	.200	1/2	.500	-/2	1	-	1	-	-	3	.125
Totals	200	29/49	.592	12/18	.667	-/23	18	11	12	-	-	70	.350

North Carolina A&T (69)   Coach: Don Corbett

	Min.	Total FG/FGA	Pct.	FT/FTA	Pct.	Reb. O/T	A	TO	PF	S	Blk	TP	PPM
BOYD, E.	39	10/19	.526	3/4	.750	-/2	4	-	1	-	-	23	.590
HORACE, J.	30	3/4	.750	2/4	.500	-/5	1	-	3	-	-	8	.267
BINION, J.	33	5/10	.500	0/0	.000	-/13	4	-	5	-	-	10	.303
BROWN, J.	34	8/11	.727	0/0	.000	-/2	2	-	1	-	-	16	.471
BOOKER	40	4/5	.800	0/2	.000	-/1	2	-	2	-	-	8	.200
BRASWELL, M.	8	1/1	1.000	0/0	.000	-/0	0	-	2	-	-	2	.250
BATTLE, D.	16	1/2	.500	0/0	.000	-/1	0	-	2	-	-	2	.125
Totals	200	32/52	.615	5/10	.500	-/22	13	11	16	-	-	69	.345

Team Rebounds: Morehead St. 1; N. Carolina A&T 0. Disqualified: N. Carolina A&T—Binion. Technical fouls: None.

	1st Half	2nd Half	Final
Morehead St.	35	35	70
N. Carolina A&T	38	31	69

Alcorn State (79) Coach: Davey Whitney

	Min.	Total FG/FGA	Pct.	FT/FTA	Pct.	Reb. O/T	A	TO	PF	S	Blk	TP	PPM
GANBON	28	7/10	.700	1/2	.500	-/7	2	-	3	-	-	15	.536
CHYBON	30	2/6	.333	6/10	.600	-/5	2	-	0	-	-	10	.333
COLLIER, T.	16	2/5	.400	2/2	1.000	-/8	0	-	3	-	-	6	.375
GOCHIE	29	2/6	.333	8/10	.800	-/2	3	-	1	-	-	12	.414
PHELPS, M.	31	8/15	.533	5/5	1.000	-/5	3	-	2	-	-	21	.677
WILMA	23	1/2	.500	2/2	1.000	-/3	0	-	4	-	-	4	.174
WHITNEY	18	1/2	.500	1/2	.500	-/2	1	-	3	-	-	3	.167
HECKER	21	4/9	.444	0/1	.000	-/2	2	-	0	-	-	8	.381
BALLARD	1	0/1	.000	0/0	.000	-/0	0	-	0	-	-	0	.000
ANDREW	1	0/0	.000	0/0	.000	-/0	0	-	0	-	-	0	.000
JAMES, T.	1	0/1	.000	0/0	.000	-/0	0	-	0	-	-	0	.000
HARALSON, D.	1	0/0	.000	0/0	.000	-/0	0	-	0	-	-	0	.000
Totals	200	27/57	.474	25/34	.735	-/34	13	13	16	-	-	79	.395

Houston Baptist (60) Coach: Gene Iba

	Min.	Total FG/FGA	Pct.	FT/FTA	Pct.	Reb. O/T	A	TO	PF	S	Blk	TP	PPM
HAIRSTON	28	6/10	.600	0/2	.000	-/2	2	-	3	-	-	12	.429
HOLLINS	37	3/7	.429	2/2	1.000	-/6	3	-	3	-	-	8	.216
LAVODRAME	31	4/10	.400	6/12	.500	-/7	1	-	5	-	-	14	.452
ENGLAND	29	4/7	.571	1/2	.500	-/2	2	-	3	-	-	9	.310
JONES	31	2/4	.500	2/2	1.000	-/4	7	-	4	-	-	6	.194
ALMANZO	15	0/0	.000	0/0	.000	-/0	0	-	1	-	-	0	.000
RIGOTT	19	2/3	.667	2/2	1.000	-/0	1	-	3	-	-	6	.316
LEWIS	5	2/2	1.000	1/1	1.000	-/1	0	-	1	-	-	5	1.000
KONPAWAIN	4	0/1	.000	0/0	.000	-/2	0	-	4	-	-	0	.000
GAGORA	1	0/0	.000	0/0	.000	-/0	0	-	0	-	-	0	.000
Totals	200	23/44	.523	14/23	.609	-/24	16	19	27	-	-	60	.300

Team Rebounds: Alcorn St. 2; Houston Baptist 1. Disqualified: Houston Baptist—Lavodrame. Technical fouls: None.

	1st Half	2nd Half	Final
Alcorn St.	29	50	79
Houston Baptist	27	33	60

FIRST ROUND MIDEAST

Brigham Young (84) Coach: Ladell Anderson

	Min.	Total FG/FGA	Pct.	FT/FTA	Pct.	Reb. O/T	A	TO	PF	S	Blk	TP	PPM
DURRANT, D.	39	8/16	.500	7/8	.875	-/10	2	6	3	-	3	23	.590
APPLEGATE, B.	38	5/9	.556	3/4	.750	-/13	3	6	3	-	2	13	.342
USEVITCH, J.	33	6/7	.857	5/7	.714	-/10	2	2	2	-	2	17	.515
SINEK, S.	39	3/8	.375	0/0	.000	-/1	4	2	1	-	0	6	.154
NIKCHEVICH, C.	16	3/4	.750	1/2	.500	-/1	1	1	4	-	1	7	.438
PERRY, M.	26	0/1	.000	6/6	1.000	-/1	1	3	2	-	0	6	.231
TAYLOR, B.	2	0/0	.000	3/4	.750	-/0	0	0	0	-	0	3	1.500
WEBB, R.	1	0/0	.000	2/2	1.000	-/0	0	0	0	-	2	2	2.000
SMITH, M.	5	3/3	1.000	1/2	.500	-/4	0	0	1	-	0	7	1.400
POLLARD, C.	1	0/0	.000	0/0	.000	-/1	0	0	0	-	0	0	.000
Totals	200	28/48	.583	28/35	.800	-/41	13	20	16	-	7	84	.420

Louisville (72) Coach: Denny Crum

	Min.	Total FG/FGA	Pct.	FT/FTA	Pct.	Reb. O/T	A	TO	PF	S	Blk	TP	PPM
FORREST, M.	25	3/3	1.000	2/2	1.000	-/2	1	1	4	2	0	8	.320
THOMPSON, B.	26	1/4	.250	0/0	.000	-/0	4	5	4	0	0	2	.077
JONES, C.	34	7/12	.583	2/2	1.000	-/7	2	4	1	3	2	16	.471
GORDON, L.	34	7/14	.500	3/4	.750	-/4	3	2	1	0	0	17	.500
WAGNER, M.	35	6/8	.750	5/6	.833	-/4	6	4	0	1	0	17	.486
SUMPTER, B.	12	2/3	.667	0/0	.000	-/5	2	1	1	1	0	4	.333
HALL, J.	14	1/3	.333	0/1	.000	-/1	0	0	0	1	0	2	.143
MCSWAIN, M.	17	1/3	.333	1/1	1.000	-/5	0	2	0	0	3	3	.176
JETER, J.	2	0/0	.000	3/5	.600	-/0	0	0	1	0	0	3	1.500
MITCHELL, D.	1	0/0	.000	0/0	.000	-/0	0	0	0	0	0	0	.000
Totals	200	28/50	.560	16/21	.762	-/28	18	17	14	8	2	72	.360

Alabama-Birmingham (68) Coach: Gene Bartow

	Min.	Total FG/FGA	Pct.	FT/FTA	Pct.	Reb. O/T	A	TO	PF	S	Blk	TP	PPM
SINGLETON, M.	38	14/23	.609	6/8	.750	-/5	2	1	3	-	0	34	.895
MINCY, J.	22	2/7	.286	0/0	.000	-/5	0	1	4	-	1	4	.182
GORDON, A.	28	1/6	.167	2/2	1.000	-/8	1	2	2	-	1	4	.143
MITCHELL, S.	36	4/14	.286	0/0	.000	-/4	7	4	3	-	0	8	.222
FOSTER	31	2/10	.200	1/3	.333	-/1	2	1	4	-	0	5	.161
JONES, E.	3	0/0	.000	0/0	.000	-/0	0	0	0	-	0	0	.000
MATTA, G.	2	0/3	.000	0/0	.000	-/1	0	0	2	-	0	0	.000
BARTOW, M.	2	0/2	.000	0/0	.000	-/1	0	0	0	-	0	0	.000
JOHNSON, M.	19	3/4	.750	0/0	.000	-/6	0	3	3	-	0	6	.316
PONDER, J.	9	1/4	.250	0/1	.000	-/1	3	3	2	-	0	2	.222
MARRERO, P.	2	1/1	1.000	1/1	1.000	-/0	0	0	1	-	0	3	1.500
TATUM, B.	2	0/1	.000	0/0	.000	-/0	0	0	2	-	0	0	.000
JOHNSON, A.	6	1/1	1.000	0/1	.000	-/2	0	0	0	-	0	2	.333
Totals	200	29/76	.382	10/16	.625	-/34	15	15	26	-	2	68	.340

Morehead State (59) Coach: Wayne Martin

	Min.	Total FG/FGA	Pct.	FT/FTA	Pct.	Reb. O/T	A	TO	PF	S	Blk	TP	PPM
CHILDRESS, E.	28	5/10	.500	0/0	.000	-/1	4	3	0	2	0	10	.357
HARRISON, E.	27	6/12	.500	2/2	1.000	-/5	0	3	3	3	0	14	.519
TIPTON, J.	32	5/9	.556	6/7	.857	-/5	1	4	2	2	1	16	.500
FULTZ, J.	30	0/0	.000	0/0	.000	-/1	4	4	3	0	0	0	.000
MINNIFIELD, G.	28	1/5	.200	0/0	.000	-/3	6	0	5	0	0	2	.071
SULLIVAN, A.	22	4/10	.400	0/0	.000	-/1	2	1	3	1	0	8	.364
TUCKER, J.	27	3/7	.429	0/0	.000	-/5	0	2	4	0	1	6	.222
BARKER, R.	1	0/1	.000	0/0	.000	-/0	0	0	0	0	0	0	.000
CLEMENTS, P.	1	1/1	1.000	1/1	1.000	-/1	0	0	0	0	0	3	3.000
EVERETT, M.	1	0/0	.000	0/0	.000	-/0	0	0	0	0	0	0	.000
KELLY, B.	1	0/0	.000	0/0	.000	-/0	0	0	0	0	0	0	.000
VANCE, T.	1	0/0	.000	0/0	.000	-/0	0	0	0	0	0	0	.000
BROOKS, S.	1	0/0	.000	0/0	.000	-/0	0	0	0	0	0	0	.000
Totals	200	25/55	.455	9/10	.900	-/22	17	17	20	8	2	59	.295

Team Rebounds: Brigham Young 1; Ala.-Birmingham 1. Disqualified: None. Technical fouls: None.

	1st Half	2nd Half	Final
Brigham Young	40	44	84
Ala.-Birmingham	32	36	68

Team Rebounds: Louisville 1; Morehead State 2. Disqualified: Morehead State—Minnifield. Technical fouls: Morehead State—Coach Martin.

	1st Half	2nd Half	Final
Louisville	29	43	72
Morehead State	20	39	59

Oregon State (62) Coach: Ralph Miller

	Min.	Total FG/FGA	Pct.	FT/FTA	Pct.	Reb. O/T	A	TO	PF	S	Blk	TP	PPM
GREEN, A.	40	5/5	1.000	8/10	.800	-/10	1	4	1	1	0	18	.450
SITTON, C.	40	6/11	.545	3/5	.600	-/1	3	6	3	1	0	15	.375
WOODSIDE, S.	33	4/8	.500	4/5	.800	-/6	3	4	3	1	1	12	.364
FLOWERS, D.	33	1/5	.200	0/0	.000	-/4	3	2	2	0	0	2	.061
TAIT, A.	37	3/6	.500	4/6	.667	-/2	1	1	4	2	0	10	.270
HOUSTON, D.	10	2/7	.286	0/0	.000	-/1	2	0	2	1	0	4	.400
STANGEL, J.	1	0/0	.000	0/0	.000	-/1	0	0	0	0	0	0	.000
MILLER, T.	6	0/0	.000	1/2	.500	-/3	1	1	0	0	0	1	.167
Totals	200	21/42	.500	20/28	.714	-/28	14	18	15	6	1	62	.310

West Virginia (64) Coach: Gale Catlett

	Min.	Total FG/FGA	Pct.	FT/FTA	Pct.	Reb. O/T	A	TO	PF	S	Blk	TP	PPM
ROWE, L.	23	5/11	.455	1/1	1.000	-/6	1	4	5	0	0	11	.478
KING, M.	35	4/9	.444	0/0	.000	-/5	3	2	4	0	0	8	.229
KEARNEY, T.	40	4/5	.800	0/0	.000	-/6	2	2	3	1	0	8	.200
ODOM, V.	33	5/12	.417	5/6	.833	-/3	3	3	3	2	0	15	.455
BLANEY, D.	36	2/4	.500	6/6	1.000	-/0	3	3	2	2	0	10	.278
CRAWL, J.	16	2/4	.500	0/1	.000	-/0	1	1	2	2	0	4	.250
PICKNEY, D.	1	0/0	.000	0/0	.000	-/0	0	0	0	0	0	0	.000
BROWN, R.	16	4/5	.800	0/0	.000	-/1	0	0	5	1	1	8	.500
Totals	200	26/50	.520	12/14	.857	-/21	13	15	24	8	2	64	.320

Team Rebounds: West Virginia 1; Oregon State 2. Disqualified: West Virginia—Rowe, Brown. Technical fouls: Oregon State—Bench.

	1st Half	2nd Half	Final
Oregon State	31	31	62
West Virginia	28	36	64

Villanova (84) Coach: Rollie Massimino

	Min.	Total FG/FGA	Pct.	FT/FTA	Pct.	Reb. O/T	A	TO	PF	S	Blk	TP	PPM
MCCLAIN, D.	35	10/11	.909	4/4	1.000	-/3	4	4	5	0	0	24	.686
PRESSLEY, H.	38	6/8	.750	3/5	.600	-/7	4	6	3	2	3	15	.395
PINCKNEY, E.	37	7/9	.778	8/10	.800	-/10	2	0	4	2	1	22	.595
DOBBS, F.	36	3/6	.500	6/7	.857	-/4	2	3	0	1	0	12	.333
MCLAIN, G.	25	1/2	.500	3/4	.750	-/0	3	5	4	0	0	5	.200
WILBUR, D.	20	3/6	.500	0/0	.000	-/1	1	2	2	0	0	6	.300
EVERSON, C.	2	0/0	.000	0/0	.000	-/1	0	2	0	0	0	0	.000
JENSEN, H.	2	0/0	.000	0/0	.000	-/0	0	0	0	0	0	0	.000
MASSIMINO, R.	1	0/0	.000	0/0	.000	-/0	0	0	0	0	0	0	.000
HARRINGTON, B.	1	0/0	.000	0/0	.000	-/0	0	0	0	0	0	0	.000
BROWN, C.	1	0/0	.000	0/0	.000	-/0	0	0	0	0	0	0	.000
PINONE, S.	1	0/0	.000	0/0	.000	-/0	0	0	0	0	0	0	.000
ENRIGHT, M.	1	0/0	.000	0/0	.000	-/0	0	0	0	0	0	0	.000
Totals	200	30/42	.714	24/30	.800	-/26	16	22	18	5	4	84	.420

Marshall (72) Coach: Ricky Huckabay

	Min.	Total FG/FGA	Pct.	FT/FTA	Pct.	Reb. O/T	A	TO	PF	S	Blk	TP	PPM
ERVIN, S.	9	1/1	1.000	0/0	.000	-/2	0	1	2	0	0	2	.222
WADE, D.	32	4/10	.400	0/2	.000	-/2	2	2	5	3	0	8	.250
EPPES, R.	24	2/3	.667	0/0	.000	-/3	0	2	4	1	0	4	.167
HENRY, S.	18	0/2	.000	1/2	.500	-/1	2	1	1	0	0	1	.056
WINLEY, S.	16	4/11	.364	1/3	.333	-/6	1	0	2	0	0	9	.563
TURNEY, D.	25	6/11	.545	0/0	.000	-/0	0	0	2	1	0	12	.480
BATTLE, J.	22	5/9	.556	0/2	.000	-/2	4	3	1	2	0	10	.455
NELSON, R.	8	2/5	.400	0/0	.000	-/0	2	0	4	0	0	4	.500
RICHARDSON, J.	4	0/0	.000	0/0	.000	-/0	0	0	0	0	0	0	.000
DOBSON, M.	5	0/0	.000	0/0	.000	-/0	2	0	0	0	0	0	.000
MORRIS, B.	1	0/0	.000	0/0	.000	-/0	0	0	0	0	0	0	.000
AMENDOLA, J.	1	0/1	.000	0/0	.000	-/1	1	0	0	0	0	0	.000
ROBERTS, J.	1	0/0	.000	0/0	.000	-/0	0	0	0	0	0	0	.000
EVANS, L.	34	9/15	.600	4/5	.800	-/3	2	2	2	2	0	22	.647
Totals	200	33/68	.485	6/14	.429	-/20	14	13	23	9	0	72	.360

Team Rebounds: Villanova 2; Marshall 3. Disqualified: Villanova—McClain; Marshall—Wade. Technical fouls: None.

	1st Half	2nd Half	Final
Villanova	33	51	84
Marshall	40	32	72

FIRST ROUND WEST

Miami (Ohio) (69) Coach: Darrell Hedric

	Min.	Total FG/FGA	Pct.	FT/FTA	Pct.	Reb. O/T	A	TO	PF	S	Blk	TP	PPM
HARPER, R.	37	7/18	.389	6/6	1.000	7/10	4	4	4	1	0	20	.541
DAHN, C.	34	1/4	.250	0/0	.000	2/7	5	1	3	0	0	2	.059
MARX, J.	24	4/9	.444	2/3	.667	1/2	0	0	4	0	1	10	.417
WILLOUGHBY, J.	32	3/7	.429	4/4	1.000	0/4	1	3	5	0	0	10	.313
STAHL, C.	33	4/10	.400	0/0	.000	0/1	6	1	4	1	0	8	.242
NEWSOME, E.	14	5/12	.417	0/0	.000	3/5	0	1	4	0	0	10	.714
HUNTER, R.	2	1/3	.333	0/0	.000	0/0	1	0	2	0	0	2	1.000
SUDDUTH, S.	7	1/3	.333	0/0	.000	1/1	1	1	2	0	0	2	.286
LEHMAN, T.	15	2/4	.500	0/0	.000	0/1	0	0	2	0	1	4	.267
DOYLE, R.	1	0/0	.000	0/0	.000	0/0	0	0	1	0	0	0	.000
HALL, M.	1	0/0	.000	1/2	.500	1/1	0	0	0	0	0	1	1.000
Totals	200	28/70	.400	13/15	.867	15/32	18	11	31	2	2	69	.345

SMU (83) Coach: Dave Bliss

	Min.	Total FG/FGA	Pct.	FT/FTA	Pct.	Reb. O/T	A	TO	PF	S	Blk	TP	PPM
LEWIS, K.	12	0/1	.000	0/0	.000	1/3	0	2	2	0	0	0	.000
DAVIS, L.	38	5/10	.500	0/4	.000	3/8	0	2	4	0	0	10	.263
KONCAK, J.	38	12/17	.706	8/9	.889	2/8	4	2	3	0	7	32	.842
MOORE, B.	31	5/6	.833	6/7	.857	0/1	2	1	1	2	0	16	.516
WRIGHT, C.	35	3/7	.429	4/10	.400	2/4	14	3	2	4	1	10	.286
GADIS, D.	9	2/3	.667	1/1	1.000	0/1	0	1	0	0	0	5	.556
FULLER, J.	0	0/0	.000	0/0	.000	0/1	1	0	0	0	0	0	-
ANDERSON, C.	24	2/2	1.000	2/3	.667	1/3	1	1	2	0	0	6	.250
PINK, R.	0	1/1	1.000	0/1	.000	0/0	0	0	0	0	0	2	-
JOHNSON, S.	9	0/1	.000	0/1	.000	0/2	1	0	1	0	0	0	.000
BRIGGS, J.	0	0/0	.000	0/0	.000	0/1	0	0	0	0	0	0	-
WILLIAMS, T.	4	0/0	.000	0/1	.000	0/1	1	0	0	0	0	0	.000
LUNDBLADE, K.	0	0/0	.000	0/0	.000	0/0	0	0	0	0	0	0	-
Totals	200	30/48	.625	21/37	.568	9/33	24	12	15	6	8	83	.415

Team Rebounds: SMU 8; Miami (Ohio) 5. Disqualified: Miami (Ohio)—Willoughby. Technical fouls: None. Players who played 0 min. played less than 1 min. each. SMU given 2 pts. for opponent tip-in (not included in FG totals).

	1st Half	2nd Half	Final
Miami (Ohio)	30	39	69
SMU	39	44	83

UNLV (68) Coach: Jerry Tarkanian

	Min.	Total FG/FGA	Pct.	FT/FTA	Pct.	Reb. O/T	A	TO	PF	S	Blk	TP	PPM
CATCHINGS, E.	33	7/9	.778	4/5	.800	-/4	1	2	2	0	0	18	.545
JAMES, F.	32	6/7	.857	2/3	.667	-/5	5	2	1	0	2	14	.438
ADAMS, R.	20	4/4	1.000	2/2	1.000	-/2	0	2	5	0	1	10	.500
TARKANIAN, D.	40	1/6	.167	1/2	.500	-/1	8	1	2	3	0	3	.075
COLLINS, J.	6	0/0	.000	0/0	.000	-/0	2	0	1	0	0	0	.000
BOOKER, E.	36	7/11	.636	4/5	.800	-/5	3	1	1	0	0	18	.500
BROZOVICH, P.	9	0/0	.000	0/0	.000	-/3	1	0	0	0	0	0	.000
FLOWERS, J.	20	1/4	.250	0/0	.000	-/4	0	2	1	0	0	2	.100
BANKS, F.	4	0/0	.000	3/4	.750	-/0	0	0	3	1	0	3	.750
Totals	200	26/41	.634	16/21	.762	-/24	20	10	16	4	3	68	.340

Princeton (56) Coach: Pete Carril

	Min.	Total FG/FGA	Pct.	FT/FTA	Pct.	Reb. O/T	A	TO	PF	S	Blk	TP	PPM
MULLIN, K.	40	7/12	.583	4/4	1.000	-/3	2	4	2	0	0	18	.450
SMYTH, J.	40	2/7	.286	0/0	.000	-/3	3	0	4	1	0	4	.100
CARTER, I.	28	1/3	.333	0/0	.000	-/1	3	0	2	0	0	2	.071
RYAN, W.	40	1/3	.333	4/4	1.000	-/3	7	2	5	1	0	6	.150
SCOTT, J.	11	1/2	.500	0/0	.000	-/0	0	0	5	0	0	2	.182
PAGANO, J.	1	0/0	.000	0/0	.000	-/0	0	0	0	0	0	0	.000
LEVY, H.	40	10/13	.769	4/7	.571	-/5	3	2	2	0	0	24	.600
Totals	200	22/40	.550	12/15	.800	-/15	18	8	20	2	0	56	.280

Team Rebounds: UNLV 1; Princeton 1. Disqualified: UNLV—Adams; Princeton—Ryan, Scott. Technical fouls: None.

	1st Half	2nd Half	Final
UNLV	28	40	68
Princeton	25	31	56

Washington (64) Coach: Marv Harshman

	Min.	Total FG/FGA	Pct.	FT/FTA	Pct.	Reb. O/T	A	TO	PF	S	Blk	TP	PPM
SCHREMPF	40	9/15	.600	5/8	.625	-/13	3	-	3	-	-	23	.575
FORTIER, P.	34	2/6	.333	0/0	.000	-/4	2	-	3	-	-	4	.118
WELP	30	5/7	.714	6/8	.750	-/10	2	-	2	-	-	16	.533
VAUGHN	37	2/2	1.000	2/4	.500	-/2	3	-	2	-	-	6	.162
WILLIAMS	20	2/8	.250	0/0	.000	-/3	2	-	2	-	-	4	.200
DAMON, C.	17	4/7	.571	0/1	.000	-/0	4	-	1	-	-	8	.471
KOEHLER	3	0/1	.000	0/0	.000	-/1	0	-	0	-	-	0	.000
GARDNER	1	0/0	.000	0/0	.000	-/0	0	-	0	-	-	0	.000
VIDATO	1	0/0	.000	0/0	.000	-/0	0	-	0	-	-	0	.000
KUYPER	5	0/2	.000	0/0	.000	-/1	0	-	0	-	-	0	.000
ROGERS	10	0/5	.000	2/4	.500	-/2	0	-	2	-	-	2	.200
SIGURDSSON	1	0/0	.000	0/0	.000	-/1	0	-	1	-	-	0	.000
SHIMER	1	0/0	.000	1/2	.500	-/1	0	-	0	-	-	1	1.000
Totals	200	24/53	.453	16/27	.593	-/38	16	18	16	-	-	64	.320

Nevada-Reno (54) Coach: Sonny Allen

	Min.	Total FG/FGA	Pct.	FT/FTA	Pct.	Reb. O/T	A	TO	PF	S	Blk	TP	PPM
PORTER, E.	13	1/4	.250	0/0	.000	-/3	1	-	2	-	-	2	.154
SOMMERS	32	5/8	.625	2/3	.667	-/2	0	-	4	-	-	12	.375
STEPHENS	14	1/2	.500	0/0	.000	-/2	0	-	4	-	-	2	.143
JONES	37	1/10	.100	3/4	.750	-/11	4	-	1	-	-	5	.135
HIGH, C.	37	9/23	.391	3/4	.750	-/3	3	-	4	-	-	21	.568
RONZONE	8	0/3	.000	0/0	.000	-/3	0	-	0	-	-	0	.000
WELCH	4	0/1	.000	0/0	.000	-/0	0	-	1	-	-	0	.000
GOSSE	27	3/7	.429	0/1	.000	-/3	2	-	2	-	-	6	.222
REED	1	0/0	.000	0/0	.000	-/0	0	-	0	-	-	0	.000
PARILLO, M.	27	1/6	.167	4/4	1.000	-/3	0	-	1	-	-	6	.222
Totals	200	21/64	.328	12/16	.750	-/29	10	11	19	-	-	54	.270

Disqualified: None. Technical foul: Nevada-Reno—Coach Allen.

	1st Half	2nd Half	Final
Washington	32	32	64
Nevada-Reno	24	30	54

Louisiana State (66) Coach: Dale Brown

	Min.	Total FG/FGA	Pct.	FT/FTA	Pct.	Reb. O/T	A	TO	PF	S	Blk	TP	PPM
REYNOLDS, J.	35	6/9	.667	3/6	.500	-/13	4	2	4	2	0	15	.429
REDDEN, D.	29	5/14	.357	0/0	.000	-/3	2	1	3	0	0	10	.345
WILSON, N.	29	4/9	.444	3/4	.750	-/9	2	2	2	1	1	11	.379
TAYLOR, D.	31	4/10	.400	4/4	1.000	-/2	4	1	3	1	0	12	.387
TUDOR, D.	13	2/4	.500	2/2	1.000	-/0	2	1	5	0	0	6	.462
WILSON, A.	2	0/0	.000	0/0	.000	-/0	0	0	0	0	0	0	.000
JONES, J.	25	2/8	.250	1/2	.500	-/0	2	2	4	1	0	5	.200
JOHNSON, J.	1	0/0	.000	0/0	.000	-/0	0	0	0	0	0	0	.000
BROWN, D.	7	0/1	.000	1/2	.500	-/0	1	0	1	0	1	1	.143
MITCHELL., L.	16	2/5	.400	0/0	.000	-/3	1	1	5	0	1	4	.250
BROWN, O.	9	0/0	.000	0/0	.000	-/3	0	0	0	0	0	0	.000
VANCE, D.	3	1/2	.500	0/0	.000	-/1	1	0	1	0	0	2	.667
Totals	200	26/62	.419	14/20	.700	-/34	18	11	27	5	3	66	.330

Dayton (74) Coach: Don Donoher

	Min.	Total FG/FGA	Pct.	FT/FTA	Pct.	Reb. O/T	A	TO	PF	S	Blk	TP	PPM
CHAPMAN, R.	40	10/15	.667	9/9	1.000	-/8	2	8	3	1	0	29	.725
YOUNG, E.	18	1/3	.333	0/0	.000	-/2	0	0	4	0	0	2	.111
GOODWIN, D.	40	4/10	.400	8/8	1.000	-/9	4	1	1	1	0	16	.400
TONEY, S.	31	5/14	.357	2/5	.400	-/3	4	1	3	0	0	12	.387
SCHELLENBERG, L.	40	3/4	.750	3/6	.500	-/8	4	1	2	1	0	9	.225
CHRISTIE, D.	9	0/1	.000	0/1	.000	-/0	2	2	2	0	0	0	.000
HUGHES, D.	2	0/1	.000	0/0	.000	-/0	0	0	0	0	0	0	.000
ZERN, J.	20	2/3	.667	2/3	.667	-/8	0	1	2	0	0	6	.300
Totals	200	25/51	.490	24/32	.750	-/38	16	14	17	3	0	74	.370

Team Rebounds: Dayton 1; Louisiana St. 0. Disqualified: Louisiana St.—Tudor, Mitchell. Technical fouls: None.

	1st Half	2nd Half	Final
Louisiana St.	32	34	66
Dayton	32	42	74

FIRST ROUND EAST

Temple (65)   Coach: John Chaney

	Min.	Total FG/FGA	Pct.	FT/FTA	Pct.	Reb. O/T	A	TO	PF	S	Blk	TP	PPM
HALL, G.	32	6/12	.500	8/10	.800	-/ 6	0	1	3	2	0	20	.625
STANSBURY, T.	40	7/14	.500	0/ 0	.000	-/ 4	4	3	1	0	0	14	.350
MCNISH, C.	29	2/ 2	1.000	0/ 0	.000	-/ 4	0	1	2	2	0	4	.138
COE, E.	33	4/ 6	.667	0/ 0	.000	-/ 0	3	2	2	2	0	8	.242
MCLOUGHLIN, J.	27	7/11	.636	0/ 0	.000	-/ 2	3	1	5	1	0	14	.519
RAYNE, C.	19	2/ 2	1.000	0/ 0	.000	-/ 4	1	1	3	0	0	4	.211
BLACKWELL, N.	19	0/ 3	.000	1/ 2	.500	-/ 2	0	0	1	0	0	1	.053
CLIFTON, K.	1	0/ 0	.000	0/ 0	.000	-/ 0	0	0	0	0	0	0	.000
Totals	200	28/50	.560	9/12	.750	-/22	11	9	17	7	0	65	.325

St. John's (63)   Coach: Lou Carnesecca

	Min.	Total FG/FGA	Pct.	FT/FTA	Pct.	Reb. O/T	A	TO	PF	S	Blk	TP	PPM
MULLIN, C.	40	8/18	.444	5/ 7	.714	-/ 4	4	5	3	1	0	21	.525
ALLEN, J.	23	2/ 2	1.000	1/ 2	.500	-/ 4	0	0	4	0	0	5	.217
WENNINGTON, B.	36	8/12	.667	1/ 4	.250	-/10	2	1	3	1	0	17	.472
JACKSON, M.	40	5/ 8	.625	1/ 2	.500	-/ 4	5	3	1	0	0	11	.275
MOSES, M.	40	2/ 7	.286	1/ 1	1.000	-/ 1	3	1	1	1	0	5	.125
STEWART, R.	7	0/ 0	.000	0/ 0	.000	-/ 0	0	0	0	0	0	0	.000
GLASS, W.	14	2/ 2	1.000	0/ 0	.000	-/ 2	0	1	1	0	0	4	.286
Totals	200	27/49	.551	9/16	.563	-/25	14	11	13	3	0	63	.315

Team Rebounds: Temple 2; St. John's 2. Disqualified: Temple—McLoughlin. Technical fouls: None.

	1st Half	2nd Half	Final
Temple	37	28	65
St. John's	36	27	63

Auburn (71)   Coach: Sonny Smith

	Min.	Total FG/FGA	Pct.	FT/FTA	Pct.	Reb. O/T	A	TO	PF	S	Blk	TP	PPM
TURNER, G.	32	4/ 9	.444	4/ 6	.667	-/ 3	1	3	2	0	1	12	.375
PERSON, C.	34	5/16	.313	0/ 1	.000	-/ 9	1	2	5	1	0	10	.294
BARKLEY, C.	32	8/10	.800	7/ 9	.778	-/17	4	4	4	2	2	23	.719
WHITE, G.	33	4/10	.400	1/ 1	1.000	-/ 0	3	3	4	0	0	9	.273
FORD, F.	22	0/ 1	.000	0/ 0	.000	-/ 2	2	1	0	0	0	0	.000
DANIELS, P.	25	2/ 3	.667	0/ 0	.000	-/ 1	2	1	3	0	1	4	.160
STRICKLAND, V.	21	5/10	.500	1/ 2	.500	-/ 1	1	1	3	2	0	11	.524
HOLLAND, C.	1	1/ 1	1.000	0/ 0	.000	-/ 0	0	0	0	0	0	2	2.000
Totals	200	29/60	.483	13/19	.684	-/33	14	15	21	5	4	71	.355

Richmond (72)   Coach: Dick Tarrant

	Min.	Total FG/FGA	Pct.	FT/FTA	Pct.	Reb. O/T	A	TO	PF	S	Blk	TP	PPM
NEWMAN, J.	39	11/22	.500	4/ 5	.800	-/ 1	0	3	3	1	2	26	.667
DAVIS, J.	36	3/ 5	.600	0/ 1	.000	-/12	4	2	4	2	0	6	.167
FLYE, B.	38	8/14	.571	3/ 4	.750	-/ 5	0	4	5	2	0	19	.500
BECKWITH, G.	40	1/ 3	.333	3/ 4	.750	-/ 7	9	1	1	4	0	5	.125
JOHNSON, K.	40	6/10	.600	4/ 5	.800	-/ 2	2	3	3	0	0	16	.400
HARDIN, T.	5	0/ 1	.000	0/ 0	.000	-/ 1	0	0	2	0	0	0	.000
GOSS, L.	2	0/ 0	.000	0/ 1	.000	-/ 0	0	0	0	0	0	0	.000
Totals	200	29/55	.527	14/20	.700	-/28	15	13	18	9	2	72	.360

Team Rebounds: Richmond 1; Auburn 3. Disqualified: Richmond—Flye; Auburn—Person. Technical fouls: None.

	1st Half	2nd Half	Final
Auburn	22	49	71
Richmond	39	33	72

Virginia Commonwealth (70)   Coach: J. D. Barnett

	Min.	Total FG/FGA	Pct.	FT/FTA	Pct.	Reb. O/T	A	TO	PF	S	Blk	TP	PPM
BROWN, M.	38	8/12	.667	0/ 1	.000	-/ 4	1	0	1	1	0	16	.421
FRANCO, D.	28	4/ 7	.571	2/ 3	.667	-/ 1	1	0	2	0	0	10	.357
SCHLEGEL, M.	40	8/10	.800	0/ 0	.000	-/ 3	0	1	2	0	0	16	.400
DUNCAN, C.	40	7/15	.467	0/ 2	.000	-/ 5	8	1	2	1	0	14	.350
JONES, N.	12	1/ 1	1.000	0/ 0	.000	-/ 1	3	2	1	0	0	2	.167
LAMB, R.	28	4/ 6	.667	2/ 2	1.000	-/ 2	9	0	1	3	1	10	.357
DICKERSON, R.	9	1/ 2	.500	0/ 0	.000	-/ 0	0	1	1	1	0	2	.222
WAKE, N.	5	0/ 0	.000	0/ 0	.000	-/ 0	0	1	1	1	0	0	.000
Totals	200	33/53	.623	4/ 8	.500	-/16	22	6	11	7	1	70	.350

Northeastern (69)   Coach: Jim Calhoun

	Min.	Total FG/FGA	Pct.	FT/FTA	Pct.	Reb. O/T	A	TO	PF	S	Blk	TP	PPM
HALSEL, M.	39	9/12	.750	1/ 3	.333	-/ 4	4	1	0	1	0	19	.487
LEWIS, R.	37	15/17	.882	1/ 4	.250	-/ 5	1	4	0	1	0	31	.838
FULLER, W.	36	3/ 5	.600	0/ 0	.000	-/ 3	6	3	4	0	1	6	.167
LAFLEUR, J.	37	1/ 1	1.000	0/ 0	.000	-/ 3	8	1	2	0	0	2	.054
MILLER, G.	36	2/ 5	.400	1/ 2	.500	-/ 0	0	5	3	1	0	5	.139
DALE, Q.	12	3/ 3	1.000	0/ 0	.000	-/ 5	0	2	1	0	0	6	.500
ROBINSON, P.	3	0/ 1	.000	0/ 0	.000	-/ 0	0	0	0	0	0	0	.000
Totals	200	33/44	.750	3/ 9	.333	-/20	19	16	10	3	1	69	.345

Team Rebounds: VA Commonwealth 2; Northeastern 3. Disqualified: None. Technical fouls: None.

	1st Half	2nd Half	Final
Va. Commonwealth	34	36	70
Northeastern	36	33	69

Virginia (58)   Coach: Terry Holland

	Min.	Total FG/FGA	Pct.	FT/FTA	Pct.	Reb. O/T	A	TO	PF	S	Blk	TP	PPM
MILLER, J.	31	4/12	.333	0/ 1	.000	-/ 3	0	2	3	1	0	8	.258
EDELIN, K.	26	2/ 2	1.000	1/ 3	.333	-/ 9	1	0	4	1	0	5	.192
POLYNICE, O.	37	5/ 9	.556	4/ 9	.444	-/10	1	6	3	0	1	14	.378
WILSON, O.	39	8/ 9	.889	1/ 3	.333	-/ 4	3	1	2	2	1	17	.436
CARLISLE, R.	31	4/ 7	.571	0/ 1	.000	-/ 2	3	2	4	0	0	8	.258
STOKES, R.	19	2/ 3	.667	2/ 3	.667	-/ 2	2	1	1	0	0	6	.316
SHEEHEY, T.	11	0/ 2	.000	0/ 0	.000	-/ 1	0	0	1	1	0	0	.000
MULLEN, T.	2	0/ 0	.000	0/ 0	.000	-/ 0	0	0	0	0	0	0	.000
MERRIFIELD, D.	4	0/ 0	.000	0/ 0	.000	-/ 0	0	0	1	0	0	0	.000
Totals	200	25/44	.568	8/20	.400	-/31	10	12	19	5	2	58	.290

Iona (57)   Coach: Pat Kennedy

	Min.	Total FG/FGA	Pct.	FT/FTA	Pct.	Reb. O/T	A	TO	PF	S	Blk	TP	PPM
HARGRAVES, T.	37	3/ 9	.333	0/ 2	.000	-/ 3	7	1	4	0	1	6	.162
SPRINGER, G.	35	4/10	.400	0/ 0	.000	-/ 8	1	0	4	1	0	8	.229
TRUESDALE, T.	31	4/ 5	.800	0/ 3	.000	-/14	0	3	4	0	3	8	.258
GRIMES, R.	34	0/12	.000	1/ 4	.250	-/ 3	4	1	3	6	0	1	.029
BURTT, S.	32	13/19	.684	2/ 2	1.000	-/ 4	0	1	4	0	2	28	.875
WALTERS, W.	8	0/ 0	.000	2/ 2	1.000	-/ 1	0	0	2	0	0	2	.250
GREEN, C.	9	0/ 0	.000	2/ 2	1.000	-/ 1	0	0	1	0	0	2	.222
RUSSELL, A.	14	0/ 1	.000	2/ 2	1.000	-/ 1	0	1	0	1	1	2	.143
Totals	200	24/56	.429	9/17	.529	-/35	12	7	22	8	7	57	.285

Team Rebounds: Virginia 3; Iona 0. Disqualified: None. Technical fouls: None.

	1st Half	2nd Half	Final
Virginia	34	24	58
Iona	29	28	57

FIRST ROUND MIDWEST

Illinois State (49)   Coach: Bob Donewald

	Min.	Total FG/FGA	Pct.	FT/FTA	Pct.	Reb. O/T	A	TO	PF	S	Blk	TP	PPM
STEFANOVIC, L.	28	4/11	.364	0/0	.000	-/2	0	1	2	2	0	8	.286
CORNLEY, H.	40	5/13	.385	0/0	.000	-/6	1	3	2	0	0	10	.250
ZWART, M.	34	3/5	.600	0/0	.000	-/11	2	3	3	0	0	6	.176
MCKENNEY, M.	36	5/11	.455	0/0	.000	-/2	5	2	2	1	1	10	.278
JOHNSON, R.	40	3/8	.375	1/2	.500	-/3	4	0	1	3	0	7	.175
DUNCAN, B.	21	4/6	.667	0/0	.000	-/0	1	0	1	0	0	8	.381
BRAKSICK, B.	1	0/0	.000	0/0	.000	-/0	0	0	0	0	0	0	.000
Totals	200	24/54	.444	1/2	.500	-/24	13	9	11	6	1	49	.245

Alabama (48)   Coach: Wimp Sanderson

	Min.	Total FG/FGA	Pct.	FT/FTA	Pct.	Reb. O/T	A	TO	PF	S	Blk	TP	PPM
JOHNSON, B.	36	4/10	.400	0/0	.000	-/6	1	5	5	0	1	8	.222
WILLIAMS, T.	40	8/11	.727	0/0	.000	-/4	4	1	1	0	0	16	.400
HIRT, B.	39	7/10	.700	2/2	1.000	-/10	2	1	2	0	0	16	.410
RICHARDSON, E.	40	3/10	.300	0/0	.000	-/2	3	3	1	2	0	6	.150
CONER, T.	15	0/1	.000	0/0	.000	-/2	2	2	0	0	0	0	.000
NEAL, D.	28	1/7	.143	0/0	.000	-/1	2	0	2	0	0	2	.071
FARMER, M.	2	0/0	.000	0/0	.000	-/0	0	0	1	0	0	0	.000
Totals	200	23/49	.469	2/2	1.000	-/25	14	12	12	2	1	48	.240

Team Rebounds: Illinois State 2; Alabama 4. Disqualified: Alabama—Johnson. Technical fouls: None.

	1st Half	2nd Half	Final
Illinois State	26	23	49
Alabama	30	18	48

Kansas (57)   Coach: Larry Brown

	Min.	Total FG/FGA	Pct.	FT/FTA	Pct.	Reb. O/T	A	TO	PF	S	Blk	TP	PPM
KNIGHT, K.	39	2/5	.400	0/1	.000	-/8	1	3	3	1	1	4	.103
THOMPSON, C.	31	9/13	.692	2/3	.667	-/2	0	2	3	0	1	20	.645
DREILING, G.	19	3/5	.600	2/5	.400	-/3	0	0	2	0	3	8	.421
TURGEON, M.	31	0/1	.000	0/0	.000	-/1	8	3	3	0	0	0	.000
HENRY, C.	40	6/15	.400	1/4	.250	-/8	2	1	1	1	0	13	.325
BANKS, T.	3	0/0	.000	0/0	.000	-/0	2	0	2	1	0	0	.000
BOYLE, T.	11	0/0	.000	0/0	.000	-/1	0	0	0	0	0	0	.000
KELLOGG, R.	25	4/9	.444	4/4	1.000	-/4	1	2	0	0	0	12	.480
MARTIN, B.	1	0/0	.000	0/0	.000	-/0	0	0	0	0	0	0	.000
Totals	200	24/48	.500	9/17	.529	-/27	14	11	14	3	5	57	.285

Alcorn State (56)   Coach: Davey Whitney

	Min.	Total FG/FGA	Pct.	FT/FTA	Pct.	Reb. O/T	A	TO	PF	S	Blk	TP	PPM
BRANDON, A.	35	9/14	.643	0/0	.000	-/5	1	2	4	1	0	18	.514
CLAYBON, B.	31	3/7	.429	0/1	.000	-/5	1	1	2	0	0	6	.194
COLLIER, T.	30	2/5	.400	0/0	.000	-/7	0	2	4	0	0	4	.133
ARCHIE, E.	37	2/5	.400	0/0	.000	-/2	7	6	3	5	0	4	.108
PHELPS, M.	33	5/8	.625	6/12	.500	-/4	0	3	3	2	0	16	.485
WHITNEY, D.	9	1/3	.333	0/0	.000	-/2	1	1	0	1	0	2	.222
JAMES, T.	1	0/0	.000	0/0	.000	-/0	0	0	0	0	0	0	.000
PARKER, T.	10	1/2	.500	0/0	.000	-/1	0	1	2	0	0	2	.200
PALMER, D.	14	2/3	.667	0/0	.000	-/3	0	0	2	0	0	4	.286
Totals	200	25/47	.532	6/13	.462	-/29	10	16	20	9	0	56	.280

Team Rebounds: Kansas 0; Alcorn St. 2. Disqualified: None. Technical fouls: None.

	1st Half	2nd Half	Final
Kansas	19	38	57
Alcorn St.	30	26	56

Memphis State (92)   Coach: Dana Kirk

	Min.	Total FG/FGA	Pct.	FT/FTA	Pct.	Reb. O/T	A	TO	PF	S	Blk	TP	PPM
HOLMES, B.	31	6/8	.750	6/8	.750	-/11	6	0	1	-	0	18	.581
LEE, K.	33	12/18	.667	2/4	.500	-/11	3	4	4	-	2	26	.788
BEDFORD, W.	37	9/15	.600	2/3	.667	-/8	2	1	3	-	5	20	.541
HAYNES, P.	33	2/13	.154	4/4	1.000	-/2	5	2	1	-	0	8	.242
TURNER, A.	35	5/6	.833	2/5	.400	-/1	4	6	3	-	0	12	.343
PHILLIPS, D.	8	1/3	.333	0/0	.000	-/4	1	1	0	-	0	2	.250
BECTON, W.	9	0/1	.000	0/2	.000	-/3	0	1	1	-	0	0	.000
MCCOY, R.	5	0/0	.000	0/0	.000	-/0	0	0	0	-	0	0	.000
BUSH, L.	2	0/0	.000	0/0	.000	-/0	0	0	0	-	0	0	.000
ALBRIGHT, J.	7	1/1	1.000	4/4	1.000	-/0	0	1	1	-	0	6	.857
Totals	200	36/65	.554	20/30	.667	-/40	21	15	13	-	7	92	.460

Oral Roberts (83)   Coach: Dick Acres

	Min.	Total FG/FGA	Pct.	FT/FTA	Pct.	Reb. O/T	A	TO	PF	S	Blk	TP	PPM
POTTER	33	4/17	.235	1/1	1.000	-/3	5	2	3	-	0	9	.273
ACRES, J.	25	7/19	.368	2/2	1.000	-/10	0	1	5	-	0	16	.640
ACRES, M.	39	11/25	.440	6/6	1.000	-/18	2	2	4	-	0	28	.718
MCGEE	25	3/6	.500	0/0	.000	-/4	1	1	1	-	0	6	.240
DORSEY	39	9/12	.750	0/2	.000	-/4	8	2	4	-	0	18	.462
MILES	20	1/4	.250	0/0	.000	-/1	0	0	2	-	0	2	.100
BERRY	14	1/2	.500	0/0	.000	-/1	3	1	3	-	0	2	.143
BROWN	1	1/1	1.000	0/0	.000	-/0	0	1	0	-	0	2	2.000
WILSON	1	0/0	.000	0/0	.000	-/0	0	0	0	-	0	0	.000
A-OTIKO	1	0/0	.000	0/0	.000	-/0	0	0	0	-	0	0	.000
GIVENS	1	0/0	.000	0/0	.000	-/0	0	0	0	-	0	0	.000
HARPER	1	0/0	.000	0/0	.000	-/0	0	0	0	-	0	0	.000
Totals	200	37/86	.430	9/11	.818	-/41	19	10	22	-	0	83	.415

Team Rebounds: Memphis State 2; Oral Roberts 3. Disqualified: Oral Roberts—J. Acres. Technical fouls: None.

	1st Half	2nd Half	Final
Memphis State	46	46	92
Oral Roberts	34	49	83

Fresno State (56)   Coach: Boyd Grant

	Min.	Total FG/FGA	Pct.	FT/FTA	Pct.	Reb. O/T	A	TO	PF	S	Blk	TP	PPM
THOMPSON	39	4/11	.364	2/2	1.000	-/4	0	3	5	-	0	10	.256
ANDERSON, R.	39	9/17	.529	0/0	.000	-/2	2	0	2	-	0	18	.462
BARNES	35	6/8	.750	4/6	.667	-/10	2	2	5	-	1	16	.457
STRAIN	28	0/2	.000	1/4	.250	-/5	4	2	4	-	0	1	.036
ARNOLD	39	4/9	.444	1/2	.500	-/6	3	2	2	-	0	9	.231
LEWIS	2	0/0	.000	0/0	.000	-/0	0	0	0	-	0	0	.000
CARTER	11	1/4	.250	0/0	.000	-/0	1	3	1	-	0	2	.182
MOSBAR	7	0/0	.000	0/0	.000	-/1	1	0	1	-	0	0	.000
Totals	200	24/51	.471	8/14	.571	-/28	13	12	20	-	1	56	.280

Louisiana Tech (66)   Coach: Andy Russo

	Min.	Total FG/FGA	Pct.	FT/FTA	Pct.	Reb. O/T	A	TO	PF	S	Blk	TP	PPM
BAILEY, R.	40	4/6	.667	6/6	1.000	-/4	4	2	1	-	0	14	.350
MALONE, K.	40	9/13	.692	6/7	.857	-/12	3	4	4	-	2	24	.600
SIMMONS, W.	24	1/4	.250	0/0	.000	-/5	0	1	5	-	2	2	.083
DAVIS, A.	29	1/5	.200	2/6	.333	-/1	5	2	4	-	0	4	.138
SMITH, W.	39	8/13	.615	0/0	.000	-/4	3	2	1	-	0	16	.410
GODBOLT, R.	21	1/2	.500	0/0	.000	-/1	0	0	0	-	0	2	.095
FRANK, A.	1	0/0	.000	2/2	1.000	-/0	0	1	0	-	0	2	2.000
ROBERSON, K.	6	1/1	1.000	0/2	.000	-/1	0	1	0	-	0	2	.333
Totals	200	25/44	.568	16/23	.696	-/28	15	13	15	-	4	66	.330

Team Rebounds: Louisiana Tech 0; Fresno State 2. Disqualified: Louisiana Tech—Simmons; Fresno State—Thompson, Barnes. Technical fouls: None.

	1st Half	2nd Half	Final
Fresno State	25	31	56
Louisiana Tech	27	39	66

SECOND ROUND MIDEAST

Brigham Young (68) Coach: Ladell Anderson

	Min.	Total FG/FGA	Pct.	FT/FTA	Pct.	Reb. O/T	A	TO	PF	S	Blk	TP	PPM
DURRANT, D.	38	11/19	.579	6/8	.750	-/3	3	3	4	1	0	28	.737
APPLEGATE, B.	29	1/8	.125	4/4	1.000	-/10	1	3	3	1	0	6	.207
USEVITCH, J.	26	4/6	.667	2/2	1.000	-/7	0	4	2	0	1	10	.385
SINEK, S.	23	2/6	.333	0/0	.000	-/4	2	4	4	0	0	4	.174
NIKCHEVICH, C.	15	1/5	.200	0/0	.000	-/0	2	2	4	3	0	2	.133
PERRY, M.	17	1/1	1.000	0/1	.000	-/1	2	1	1	0	0	2	.118
TAYLOR, B.	17	0/1	.000	1/2	.500	-/0	5	3	2	0	0	1	.059
WEBB, R.	5	2/3	.667	0/0	.000	-/0	0	0	0	0	1	4	.800
DRECKSEL, P.	2	1/2	.500	0/0	.000	-/0	1	0	1	0	0	2	1.000
ASTLE, A.	2	0/0	.000	0/0	.000	-/0	0	0	0	0	0	0	.000
SMITH, M.	10	3/4	.750	1/1	1.000	-/2	2	0	1	0	0	7	.700
NIELSEN, K.	5	0/1	.000	0/0	.000	-/1	0	1	0	0	0	0	.000
POLLARD, C.	11	1/4	.250	0/0	.000	-/3	0	1	3	0	1	2	.182
Totals	200	27/60	.450	14/18	.778	-/31	18	22	25	5	3	68	.340

Kentucky (93) Coach: Joe Hall

	Min.	Total FG/FGA	Pct.	FT/FTA	Pct.	Reb. O/T	A	TO	PF	S	Blk	TP	PPM
BOWIE, S.	20	6/8	.750	4/4	1.000	-/6	0	5	4	1	1	16	.800
WALKER, K.	34	6/12	.500	7/8	.875	-/8	3	1	4	2	0	19	.559
TURPIN, M.	26	6/15	.400	3/4	.750	-/5	0	1	3	2	2	15	.577
BEAL, D.	33	4/8	.500	0/0	.000	-/2	14	3	1	2	0	8	.242
MASTER, J.	28	6/11	.545	1/2	.500	-/4	1	1	1	0	0	13	.464
BLACKMON, J.	9	2/2	1.000	0/1	.000	-/0	0	1	2	0	0	4	.444
BYRD, L.	1	0/1	.000	0/0	.000	-/0	0	0	0	0	0	0	.000
ANDREWS, P.	2	0/0	.000	1/2	.500	-/2	0	0	0	0	0	1	.500
HARDEN, R.	7	1/1	1.000	0/0	.000	-/3	1	0	0	1	0	2	.286
BEARUP, B.	13	1/2	.500	2/2	1.000	-/2	1	0	2	0	0	4	.308
BENNETT, W.	24	3/6	.500	5/7	.714	-/6	0	1	1	0	0	11	.458
HEITZ, T.	2	0/0	.000	0/0	.000	-/0	0	1	2	0	0	0	.000
MCKINLEY, T.	1	0/0	.000	0/0	.000	-/0	0	0	0	0	0	0	.000
Totals	200	35/66	.530	23/30	.767	-/38	20	13	20	8	3	93	.465

Team Rebounds: Kentucky 0; Brigham Young 3. Disqualified: None. Technical fouls: Brigham Young—Bench.

	1st Half	2nd Half	Final
Brigham Young	29	39	68
Kentucky	42	51	93

Louisville (69) Coach: Denny Crum

	Min.	Total FG/FGA	Pct.	FT/FTA	Pct.	Reb. O/T	A	TO	PF	S	Blk	TP	PPM
FORREST, M.	24	1/4	.250	4/5	.800	-/3	2	2	4	0	0	6	.250
THOMPSON, B.	28	2/3	.667	2/2	1.000	-/4	2	3	3	0	0	6	.214
JONES, C.	39	6/7	.857	3/7	.429	-/11	1	3	2	3	2	15	.385
GORDON, L.	29	4/12	.333	9/10	.900	-/6	4	3	5	0	3	17	.586
WAGNER, M.	37	6/12	.500	3/5	.600	-/4	3	4	2	1	2	15	.405
HALL, J.	16	2/4	.500	2/2	1.000	-/1	2	2	3	1	0	6	.375
MCSWAIN, M.	16	2/2	1.000	0/0	.000	-/1	0	3	3	1	0	4	.250
SUMPTER, B.	10	0/1	.000	0/0	.000	-/3	0	2	0	0	1	0	.000
JETER, J.	1	0/0	.000	0/0	.000	-/0	0	0	0	0	0	0	.000
Totals	200	23/45	.511	23/31	.742	-/33	14	22	22	6	8	69	.345

Tulsa (67) Coach: Nolan Richardson

	Min.	Total FG/FGA	Pct.	FT/FTA	Pct.	Reb. O/T	A	TO	PF	S	Blk	TP	PPM
JOHNSON, H.	36	0/5	.000	4/8	.500	-/10	3	1	4	1	1	4	.111
WILLIAMS, V.	23	0/0	.000	0/0	.000	-/3	2	3	4	0	0	0	.000
FOBBS, A.	7	0/1	.000	1/2	.500	-/1	0	1	3	1	0	1	.143
HARRIS, S.	35	9/20	.450	3/5	.600	-/0	1	3	3	4	0	21	.600
ROSS, R.	39	11/21	.524	6/9	.667	-/3	2	0	2	2	1	28	.718
SHEPHERD, W.	3	0/1	.000	0/0	.000	-/0	0	0	0	0	1	0	.000
MOSS, D.	29	1/8	.125	3/3	1.000	-/6	0	2	4	4	0	5	.172
MCKINNEY, C.	16	3/4	.750	0/0	.000	-/3	0	1	2	0	0	6	.375
SUGGS, H.	5	1/2	.500	0/0	.000	-/0	0	2	4	0	0	2	.400
BOUDREAUX, B.	1	0/0	.000	0/0	.000	-/0	0	0	0	0	0	0	.000
VANLEY, B.	6	0/1	.000	0/0	.000	-/0	0	0	0	0	0	0	.000
Totals	200	25/63	.397	17/27	.630	-/26	8	13	26	12	3	67	.335

Team Rebounds: Louisville 5; Tulsa 5. Disqualified: Louisville—Gordon. Technical fouls: None.

	1st Half	2nd Half	Final
Louisville	41	28	69
Tulsa	28	39	67

West Virginia (77) Coach: Gale Catlett

	Min.	Total FG/FGA	Pct.	FT/FTA	Pct.	Reb. O/T	A	TO	PF	S	Blk	TP	PPM
ROWE, L.	29	8/17	.471	2/4	.500	-/5	2	3	4	1	0	18	.621
KING, M.	11	1/4	.250	2/2	1.000	-/2	0	0	2	1	0	4	.364
KEARNEY, T.	31	5/8	.625	0/0	.000	-/4	0	3	3	1	0	10	.323
ODOM, V.	26	6/12	.500	2/2	1.000	-/3	2	2	5	0	0	14	.538
BLANEY, D.	31	4/9	.444	1/2	.500	-/1	5	0	3	1	0	9	.290
CRAWL, J.	22	3/10	.300	3/4	.750	-/1	2	1	1	0	0	9	.409
PICKNEY, D.	9	3/3	1.000	1/1	1.000	-/7	0	3	1	0	1	7	.778
BROWN, R.	27	2/9	.222	0/0	.000	-/6	2	2	5	1	0	4	.148
SEMISCH, E.	12	1/2	.500	0/0	.000	-/1	0	0	2	0	0	2	.167
WEARY, L.	1	0/0	.000	0/0	.000	-/0	0	0	0	1	0	0	.000
SORINE, A.	1	0/0	.000	0/0	.000	-/0	0	0	0	0	0	0	.000
Totals	200	33/74	.446	11/15	.733	-/30	13	14	26	6	1	77	.385

Maryland (102) Coach: Lefty Driesell

	Min.	Total FG/FGA	Pct.	FT/FTA	Pct.	Reb. O/T	A	TO	PF	S	Blk	TP	PPM
VEAL, H.	26	6/6	1.000	6/7	.857	-/11	1	1	2	0	1	18	.692
BIAS, L.	29	6/9	.667	6/6	1.000	-/3	2	2	3	1	2	18	.621
COLEMAN, B.	30	8/9	.889	3/4	.750	-/6	3	2	2	0	2	19	.633
ADKINS, J.	22	2/3	.667	0/0	.000	-/0	4	0	1	0	0	4	.182
BRANCH, A.	24	2/5	.400	8/9	.889	-/2	3	3	2	1	0	12	.500
GATLIN, K.	23	5/8	.625	0/0	.000	-/2	7	1	3	2	0	10	.435
BAXTER, J.	10	3/4	.750	3/3	1.000	-/0	1	0	0	1	0	9	.900
FOTHERGILL, M.	9	0/0	.000	2/2	1.000	-/1	0	0	3	0	0	2	.222
LONG, T.	14	1/3	.333	0/0	.000	-/2	0	0	2	0	1	2	.143
DRIESELL, C.	7	3/3	1.000	2/5	.400	-/2	1	1	0	0	0	8	1.143
HOLBERT, P.	6	0/4	.000	0/0	.000	-/3	0	0	0	0	0	0	.000
Totals	200	36/54	.667	30/36	.833	-/32	22	10	18	5	7	102	.510

Team Rebounds: Maryland 2; West Virginia 2. Disqualified: West Virginia—Odom, Brown. Technical fouls: Maryland—Bias.

	1st Half	2nd Half	Final
West Virginia	39	38	77
Maryland	55	47	102

Villanova (56)　Coach: Rollie Massimino

	Min.	Total FG/FGA	Pct.	FT/FTA	Pct.	Reb. O/T	A	TO	PF	S	Blk	TP	PPM
MCCLAIN, D.	39	6/12	.500	3/4	.750	-/4	1	2	4	1	0	15	.385
PRESSLEY, H.	36	4/13	.308	1/2	.500	-/10	3	4	5	3	0	9	.250
PINCKNEY, E.	39	7/13	.538	10/13	.769	-/14	2	5	4	2	0	24	.615
DOBBS, F.	36	1/7	.143	0/0	.000	-/2	4	4	4	2	0	2	.056
MCLAIN, G.	28	0/3	.000	0/0	.000	-/3	3	3	4	2	0	0	.000
WILBUR, D.	18	3/5	.600	0/0	.000	-/0	1	0	1	0	0	6	.333
EVERSON, C.	1	0/0	.000	0/0	.000	-/0	0	0	0	0	0	0	.000
JENSEN, H.	3	0/2	.000	0/0	.000	-/0	1	0	0	1	0	0	.000
Totals	200	21/55	.382	14/19	.737	-/33	15	18	22	11	0	56	.280

Illinois (64)　Coach: Lou Henson

	Min.	Total FG/FGA	Pct.	FT/FTA	Pct.	Reb. O/T	A	TO	PF	S	Blk	TP	PPM
ALTENBERGER, D.	39	6/9	.667	0/1	.000	-/2	1	0	2	3	0	12	.308
WINTERS, E.	32	5/9	.556	2/2	1.000	-/14	1	3	4	0	0	12	.375
MONTGOMERY, G.	32	4/10	.400	0/2	.000	-/5	2	2	5	1	0	8	.250
DOUGLAS, B.	39	3/12	.250	7/8	.875	-/5	8	8	1	3	0	13	.333
RICHARDSON, Q.	35	4/8	.500	3/4	.750	-/0	2	0	3	2	0	11	.314
MEENTS, S.	15	1/5	.200	1/2	.500	-/5	0	1	3	0	2	3	.200
SCHAFER, T.	5	1/1	1.000	1/1	1.000	-/0	0	0	1	0	0	3	.600
KLUSENDORF, D.	1	0/0	.000	2/2	1.000	-/1	0	0	0	0	0	2	2.000
WOODWARD, R.	1	0/0	.000	0/0	.000	-/0	0	0	0	0	0	0	.000
WYSINGER, T.	1	0/0	.000	0/0	.000	-/0	0	0	0	0	0	0	.000
Totals	200	24/54	.444	16/22	.727	-/32	14	14	19	9	2	64	.320

Team Rebounds: Illinois 5; Villanova 1. Disqualified: Illinois—Montgomery; Villanova—Pressley. Technical fouls: None.

	1st Half	2nd Half	Final
Villanova	20	36	56
Illinois	24	40	64

SECOND ROUND WEST

SMU (36)　Coach: Dave Bliss

	Min.	Total FG/FGA	Pct.	FT/FTA	Pct.	Reb. O/T	A	TO	PF	S	Blk	TP	PPM
DAVIS, L.	40	5/10	.500	2/2	1.000	3/9	0	3	1	2	0	12	.300
LEWIS, K.	14	1/4	.250	0/0	.000	1/2	0	1	0	0	0	2	.143
KONCAK, J.	40	6/11	.545	1/1	1.000	2/7	0	1	3	0	1	13	.325
MOORE, B.	26	0/1	.000	0/0	.000	1/2	0	1	0	1	0	0	.000
WRIGHT, C.	38	4/13	.308	1/3	.333	2/9	5	4	3	2	0	9	.237
GADIS, D.	5	0/0	.000	0/0	.000	0/0	0	2	1	0	0	0	.000
FULLER, J.	4	0/1	.000	0/0	.000	0/0	0	0	2	0	0	0	.000
ANDERSON, C.	20	0/1	.000	0/0	.000	0/1	1	0	5	0	0	0	.000
PINK, R.	7	0/1	.000	0/0	.000	0/0	1	1	0	1	0	0	.000
JOHNSON, S.	6	0/0	.000	0/0	.000	0/0	0	0	0	0	0	0	.000
Totals	200	16/42	.381	4/6	.667	9/30	7	13	15	6	1	36	.180

Georgetown (37)　Coach: John Thompson

	Min.	Total FG/FGA	Pct.	FT/FTA	Pct.	Reb. O/T	A	TO	PF	S	Blk	TP	PPM
DALTON, R.	3	0/0	.000	0/0	.000	0/0	0	1	3	0	0	0	.000
WINGATE, D.	20	3/8	.375	0/1	.000	0/0	0	1	1	0	0	6	.300
EWING, P.	36	5/7	.714	0/2	.000	3/7	0	2	1	1	2	10	.278
BROWN, F.	8	0/0	.000	0/0	.000	0/0	0	1	0	0	0	0	.000
JACKSON, M.	34	3/11	.273	1/2	.500	1/4	2	2	4	0	0	7	.206
SMITH, G.	29	0/0	.000	0/1	.000	0/0	3	1	1	1	0	0	.000
MARTIN, B.	10	1/2	.500	0/0	.000	0/0	0	1	0	0	0	2	.200
BROADNAX, H.	5	0/1	.000	0/0	.000	0/0	3	0	0	0	0	0	.000
WILLIAMS, R.	24	3/7	.429	0/0	.000	1/1	1	2	2	1	0	6	.250
GRAHAM, M.	31	2/3	.667	2/3	.667	0/8	2	2	1	0	1	6	.194
Totals	200	17/39	.436	3/9	.333	5/20	11	12	14	3	3	37	.185

Team Rebounds: Georgetown 4; SMU 2. Disqualified: SMU—Anderson. Technical fouls: None.

	1st Half	2nd Half	Final
SMU	24	12	36
Georgetown	16	21	37

UNLV (73)　Coach: Jerry Tarkanian

	Min.	Total FG/FGA	Pct.	FT/FTA	Pct.	Reb. O/T	A	TO	PF	S	Blk	TP	PPM
CATCHINGS, E.	18	5/9	.556	4/5	.800	-/8	0	0	0	0	0	14	.778
JAMES, F.	33	5/10	.500	0/0	.000	-/1	5	3	4	0	0	10	.303
ADAMS, R.	37	5/11	.455	3/6	.500	-/14	0	0	2	2	1	13	.351
TARKANIAN, D.	36	2/5	.400	9/11	.818	-/5	4	3	4	0	0	13	.361
COLLINS, J.	9	1/2	.500	0/0	.000	-/1	1	1	1	0	0	2	.222
BOOKER, E.	32	1/4	.250	2/3	.667	-/2	4	4	4	0	0	4	.125
BROZOVICH, P.	1	0/0	.000	1/2	.500	-/1	0	1	0	0	0	1	1.000
FLOWERS, J.	22	2/3	.667	6/6	1.000	-/3	0	0	3	1	0	10	.455
BANKS, F.	9	2/3	.667	2/2	1.000	-/1	0	0	1	0	0	6	.667
ROBERTS, T.	1	0/0	.000	0/0	.000	-/0	0	0	0	0	0	0	.000
POSTI, G.	1	0/0	.000	0/0	.000	-/0	0	0	0	0	0	0	.000
COLLIER, R.	1	0/1	.000	0/0	.000	-/0	0	0	1	0	0	0	.000
Totals	200	23/48	.479	27/35	.771	-/36	14	12	20	3	1	73	.365

UTEP (60)　Coach: Don Haskins

	Min.	Total FG/FGA	Pct.	FT/FTA	Pct.	Reb. O/T	A	TO	PF	S	Blk	TP	PPM
REYNOLDS, F.	30	6/10	.600	3/4	.750	-/1	2	3	5	0	0	15	.500
CUNNINGHAM, P.	17	0/1	.000	0/0	.000	-/2	0	0	4	0	0	0	.000
SMITH, J.	31	0/6	.000	3/4	.750	-/7	1	5	3	4	1	3	.097
GOODWIN, L.	33	7/13	.538	2/2	1.000	-/3	2	3	5	0	0	16	.485
LOCKHART, K.	34	5/11	.455	3/3	1.000	-/3	4	2	4	1	0	13	.382
HAMILTON, K.	23	0/1	.000	0/0	.000	-/3	0	1	1	0	0	0	.000
ALLEN, D.	9	1/3	.333	1/1	1.000	-/2	0	1	1	0	0	3	.333
JACKSON, J.	8	2/2	1.000	1/2	.500	-/0	1	0	0	0	0	5	.625
GATES, Q.	6	0/0	.000	1/2	.500	-/1	2	0	0	0	0	1	.167
FEITL, D.	5	0/1	.000	2/2	1.000	-/0	0	1	3	0	0	2	.400
CLANTON, L.	1	0/0	.000	0/0	.000	-/0	0	0	0	0	0	0	.000
BAILEY, A.	3	1/2	.500	0/0	.000	-/0	1	0	2	0	0	2	.667
Totals	200	22/50	.440	16/20	.800	-/22	13	16	28	5	1	60	.300

Team Rebounds: UNLV 1; UTEP 2. Disqualified: UTEP—Reynolds, Goodwin. Technical fouls: None.

	1st Half	2nd Half	Final
UNLV	29	44	73
UTEP	26	34	60

Washington (80)   Coach: Marv Harshman

	Min.	Total FG/FGA	Pct.	FT/FTA	Pct.	Reb. O/T	A	TO	PF	S	Blk	TP	PPM
FORTIER	33	4/ 6	.667	5/ 5	1.000	-/ 2	0	6	5	-	1	13	.394
SCHREMPF, D.	40	11/14	.786	8/12	.667	-/ 2	3	1	4	-	1	30	.750
WELP	20	3/ 3	1.000	2/ 2	1.000	-/ 5	0	1	4	-	0	8	.400
WILLIAMS	24	7/ 9	.778	0/ 0	.000	-/ 3	1	1	2	-	1	14	.583
VAUGHN	37	2/ 7	.286	1/ 3	.333	-/ 1	12	3	2	-	0	5	.135
KOEHLER	3	0/ 0	.000	0/ 0	.000	-/ 0	0	2	2	-	0	0	.000
ROGERS	23	4/ 5	.800	2/ 5	.400	-/ 4	1	4	3	-	0	10	.435
DAMON	16	0/ 0	.000	0/ 0	.000	-/ 0	1	2	2	-	0	0	.000
KUYPER	4	0/ 0	.000	0/ 0	.000	-/ 0	0	0	2	-	0	0	.000
Totals	200	31/44	.705	18/27	.667	-/17	18	20	26	-	3	80	.400

Duke (78)   Coach: Mike Krzyzewski

	Min.	Total FG/FGA	Pct.	FT/FTA	Pct.	Reb. O/T	A	TO	PF	S	Blk	TP	PPM
MEAGHER, D.	29	2/ 2	1.000	0/ 2	.000	-/ 1	1	1	3	-	0	4	.138
ALARIE, M.	33	7/11	.636	6/ 7	.857	-/ 7	0	2	4	-	0	20	.606
BILAS, J.	19	2/ 3	.667	6/ 6	1.000	-/ 3	0	3	5	-	0	10	.526
DAWKINS, J.	39	6/11	.545	10/13	.769	-/ 3	4	8	4	-	0	22	.564
AMAKER, T.	38	3/ 8	.375	2/ 2	1.000	-/ 4	9	2	2	-	0	8	.211
MCNEELY, D.	11	0/ 1	.000	0/ 0	.000	-/ 2	0	0	3	-	0	0	.000
HENDERSON, D.	30	6/10	.600	2/ 4	.500	-/ 2	5	4	5	-	0	14	.467
ANDERSON, T.	1	0/ 0	.000	0/ 0	.000	-/ 0	0	0	1	-	0	0	.000
Totals	200	26/46	.565	26/34	.765	-/22	19	20	27	-	0	78	.390

Team Rebounds: Washington 4; Duke 4. Disqualified: Washington—Fortier; Duke—Bilas, Henderson. Technical fouls: None.

	1st Half	2nd Half	Final
Washington	35	45	80
Duke	43	35	78

Dayton (89)   Coach: Don Donoher

	Min.	Total FG/FGA	Pct.	FT/FTA	Pct.	Reb. O/T	A	TO	PF	S	Blk	TP	PPM
CHAPMAN, R.	40	13/22	.591	15/19	.789	-/ 8	1	5	4	0	1	41	1.025
YOUNG, E.	25	1/ 4	.250	1/ 2	.500	-/ 5	1	0	4	0	0	3	.120
GOODWIN, D.	35	7/11	.636	0/ 0	.000	-/ 6	1	2	3	0	0	14	.400
TONEY, S.	40	7/14	.500	2/ 6	.333	-/ 7	6	2	4	2	0	16	.400
SCHELLENBERG, L.	40	4/ 7	.571	1/ 2	.500	-/ 2	8	1	1	1	0	9	.225
CHRISTIE, D.	5	0/ 0	.000	2/ 2	1.000	-/ 0	1	0	1	0	0	2	.400
HUGHES, D.	1	0/ 0	.000	0/ 0	.000	-/ 0	0	0	1	0	0	0	.000
ZERN, J.	14	2/ 2	1.000	0/ 0	.000	-/ 2	0	0	5	2	0	4	.286
Totals	200	34/60	.567	21/31	.677	-/30	18	10	23	5	1	89	.445

Oklahoma (85)   Coach: Billy Tubbs

	Min.	Total FG/FGA	Pct.	FT/FTA	Pct.	Reb. O/T	A	TO	PF	S	Blk	TP	PPM
KENNEDY, D.	16	1/ 6	.167	0/ 0	.000	-/ 6	0	1	2	0	0	2	.125
PIERCE, C.	33	7/10	.700	1/ 2	.500	-/ 9	1	4	5	0	0	15	.455
TISDALE, WA.	34	12/25	.480	12/12	1.000	-/11	1	3	4	0	0	36	1.059
PANNALL, J.	39	7/11	.636	4/ 6	.667	-/ 8	4	2	5	0	0	18	.462
MCCALISTER, T.	35	3/10	.300	0/ 1	.000	-/ 3	9	1	4	0	0	6	.171
TISDALE, WM.	1	0/ 0	.000	0/ 0	.000	-/ 0	0	0	1	0	0	0	.000
CLACK	27	2/ 5	.400	0/ 0	.000	-/ 4	3	0	3	0	0	4	.148
GANDY, D.	7	1/ 2	.500	0/ 0	.000	-/ 3	0	0	2	0	0	2	.286
JOHNSON, D.	8	1/ 4	.250	0/ 0	.000	-/ 1	0	1	0	0	0	2	.250
Totals	200	34/73	.466	17/21	.810	-/45	18	12	26	0	0	85	.425

Team Rebounds:Dayton 1; Oklahoma 1. Disqualified: Dayton—Zern; Oklahoma—Pierce, Pannall. Technical fouls: None.

	1st Half	2nd Half	Final
Dayton	43	46	89
Oklahoma	39	46	85

SECOND ROUND EAST

Temple (66)   Coach: John Chaney

	Min.	Total FG/FGA	Pct.	FT/FTA	Pct.	Reb. O/T	A	TO	PF	S	Blk	TP	PPM
STANSBURY, T.	39	12/24	.500	2/ 3	.667	-/ 4	0	1	5	1	0	26	.667
HALL, G.	33	6/15	.400	1/ 3	.333	-/12	0	4	3	3	0	13	.394
MCNISH, C.	17	0/ 2	.000	0/ 0	.000	-/ 2	0	0	3	0	0	0	.000
COE, E.	24	2/ 8	.250	0/ 0	.000	-/ 2	2	3	5	1	0	4	.167
MCLOUGHLIN, J.	39	5/13	.385	0/ 2	.000	-/ 3	6	1	4	3	0	10	.256
RAYNE, C.	28	4/ 7	.571	1/ 1	1.000	-/ 6	0	2	3	0	0	9	.321
BLACKWELL, N.	16	2/ 5	.400	0/ 0	.000	-/ 2	1	0	2	0	4	4	.250
CLIFTON, K.	1	0/ 0	.000	0/ 0	.000	-/ 1	0	0	0	0	0	0	.000
BAGGOT, S.	1	0/ 1	.000	0/ 0	.000	-/ 1	0	0	0	0	0	0	.000
POPALAWSKI, M.	1	0/ 1	.000	0/ 2	.000	-/ 2	0	0	0	0	0	0	.000
AGUILAR, P.	1	0/ 0	.000	0/ 0	.000	-/ 0	0	0	0	0	0	0	.000
Totals	200	31/76	.408	4/11	.364	-/35	9	11	23	10	0	66	.330

North Carolina (77)   Coach: Dean Smith

	Min.	Total FG/FGA	Pct.	FT/FTA	Pct.	Reb. O/T	A	TO	PF	S	Blk	TP	PPM
DOHERTY, M.	35	4/ 9	.444	0/ 0	.000	-/ 6	5	2	1	3	3	8	.229
PERKINS, S.	35	4/ 8	.500	4/ 4	1.000	-/14	1	2	3	0	4	12	.343
DAUGHERTY, B.	35	4/ 5	.800	2/ 4	.500	-/ 7	2	3	4	0	1	10	.286
SMITH, K.	35	3/ 8	.375	5/ 7	.714	-/ 4	6	6	0	1	0	11	.314
JORDAN, M.	33	11/15	.733	5/ 7	.714	-/ 6	0	1	2	0	2	27	.818
HALE, S.	14	3/ 6	.500	1/ 2	.500	-/ 0	1	3	2	0	0	7	.500
WOLF, J.	8	1/ 3	.333	0/ 0	.000	-/ 4	0	1	1	0	0	2	.250
POPSON, D.	2	0/ 0	.000	0/ 0	.000	-/ 0	0	0	1	0	0	0	.000
PETERSON, B.	1	0/ 0	.000	0/ 0	.000	-/ 0	0	1	0	0	0	0	.000
EXUM, C.	2	0/ 0	.000	0/ 0	.000	-/ 1	0	0	2	0	0	0	.000
Totals	200	30/54	.556	17/24	.708	-/42	15	19	16	4	10	77	.385

Team Rebounds: N. Carolina 1; Temple 3. Disqualified: Temple—Stansbury, Coe. Technical fouls: None.

	1st Half	2nd Half	Final
Temple	29	37	66
N. Carolina	32	45	77

Richmond (67)   Coach: Dick Tarrant

	Min.	Total FG/FGA	Pct.	FT/FTA	Pct.	Reb. O/T	A	TO	PF	S	Blk	TP	PPM
NEWMAN, J.	33	9/17	.529	2/ 3	.667	-/ 8	0	3	3	1	0	20	.606
DAVIS, J.	38	1/ 3	.333	4/ 5	.800	-/11	5	1	5	0	0	6	.158
FLYE, B.	39	4/14	.286	2/ 2	1.000	-/ 5	1	3	3	0	0	10	.256
BECKWITH, G.	39	1/ 3	.333	0/ 0	.000	-/ 2	8	1	5	1	0	2	.051
JOHNSON, K.	36	12/14	.857	3/ 4	.750	-/ 2	2	3	4	1	0	27	.750
HARDIN, T.	6	0/ 2	.000	0/ 0	.000	-/ 0	0	0	1	0	0	0	.000
GOSS, L.	1	0/ 0	.000	0/ 0	.000	-/ 0	0	0	0	0	0	0	.000
FELLS, L.	4	1/ 1	1.000	0/ 0	.000	-/ 0	0	0	1	0	0	2	.500
RUNK, J.	1	0/ 0	.000	0/ 0	.000	-/ 0	0	0	0	0	0	0	.000
TUCKER, R.	1	0/ 1	.000	0/ 0	.000	-/ 0	0	0	1	0	0	0	.000
JOHNSON, M.	1	0/ 0	.000	0/ 0	.000	-/ 0	0	0	0	0	0	0	.000
SIMMONS, B.	1	0/ 0	.000	0/ 0	.000	-/ 0	0	0	0	0	0	0	.000
Totals	200	28/55	.509	11/14	.786	-/28	16	11	22	3	0	67	.335

Indiana (75)   Coach: Bob Knight

	Min.	Total FG/FGA	Pct.	FT/FTA	Pct.	Reb. O/T	A	TO	PF	S	Blk	TP	PPM
GIOMI, M.	25	4/ 8	.500	0/ 0	.000	-/ 3	0	0	1	0	0	8	.320
SIMMONS, M.	23	1/ 3	.333	0/ 0	.000	-/ 2	3	0	4	1	0	2	.087
BLAB, U.	21	7/11	.636	0/ 0	.000	-/ 7	0	1	5	0	1	14	.667
DAKICH, D.	18	2/ 2	1.000	3/ 5	.600	-/ 3	5	0	2	0	0	7	.389
ALFORD, S.	40	6/12	.500	10/10	1.000	-/ 3	4	3	1	1	0	22	.550
ROBINSON, S.	18	4/ 7	.571	0/ 0	.000	-/ 2	3	1	1	1	0	8	.444
MEIER, T.	25	3/ 6	.500	0/ 2	.000	-/ 2	1	2	2	1	0	6	.240
FRANZ, C.	22	1/ 3	.333	0/ 0	.000	-/ 0	1	0	1	0	0	2	.091
WITTE, C.	7	1/ 1	1.000	4/ 6	.667	-/ 3	0	0	0	0	0	6	.857
THOMAS, J.	1	0/ 0	.000	0/ 0	.000	-/ 0	0	0	0	0	0	0	.000
Totals	200	29/53	.547	17/23	.739	-/25	17	7	17	4	1	75	.375

Team Rebounds: Indiana 4; Richmond 1. Disqualified: Indiana—Blab; Richmond—Davis, Beckwith. Technical fouls: None.

	1st Half	2nd Half	Final
Richmond	34	33	67
Indiana	36	39	75

Virginia Commonwealth (63)   Coach: J. D. Barnett

	Min.	Total FG / FGA	Pct.	FT / FTA	Pct.	Reb. O / T	A	TO	PF	S	Blk	TP	PPM
BROWN, M.	20	5/ 5	1.000	0/ 0	.000	-/ 1	2	0	5	3	0	10	.500
FRANCO, D.	29	2/ 5	.400	0/ 0	.000	-/ 2	0	5	3	0	0	4	.138
SCHLEGEL, M.	38	6/15	.400	4/ 5	.800	-/14	0	1	4	1	0	16	.421
DUNCAN, C.	39	6/15	.400	2/ 4	.500	-/ 5	6	2	2	0	1	14	.359
JONES, M.	24	2/ 6	.333	1/ 2	.500	-/ 2	3	2	4	0	0	5	.208
LAMB, R.	19	3/ 7	.429	0/ 0	.000	-/ 2	6	2	4	1	0	6	.316
ALLEN, B.	2	1/ 3	.333	0/ 0	.000	-/ 0	0	0	3	1	0	2	1.000
DAVIS, S.	3	0/ 1	.000	0/ 0	.000	-/ 0	0	0	1	0	0	0	.000
DICKERSON, R.	23	2/ 7	.286	2/ 2	1.000	-/ 3	0	0	2	0	1	6	.261
WAKE, N.	3	0/ 0	.000	0/ 0	.000	-/ 0	0	0	0	0	0	0	.000
Totals	200	27/64	.422	9/13	.692	-/29	17	12	28	6	2	63	.315

Syracuse (78)   Coach: Jim Boeheim

	Min.	Total FG / FGA	Pct.	FT / FTA	Pct.	Reb. O / T	A	TO	PF	S	Blk	TP	PPM
ADDISON, R.	39	9/13	.692	6/ 6	1.000	-/ 9	1	4	0	3	0	24	.615
KERINS, S.	33	6/14	.429	4/ 4	1.000	-/ 4	1	0	1	0	0	16	.485
HAWKINS, A.	32	4/ 7	.571	6/ 8	.750	-/ 7	1	3	2	3	2	14	.438
WASHINGTON, D.	36	5/ 9	.556	8/10	.800	-/ 0	4	2	1	3	0	18	.500
WALDRON, G.	18	0/ 0	.000	2/ 3	.667	-/ 3	3	1	4	1	0	2	.111
MONROE, G.	21	0/ 2	.000	2/ 2	1.000	-/ 3	4	0	0	0	0	2	.095
SPERA, S.	1	0/ 1	.000	2/ 2	1.000	-/ 1	0	1	0	0	0	2	2.000
TRICHE, H.	1	0/ 0	.000	0/ 0	.000	-/ 0	0	0	1	0	0	0	.000
PAPADAKOS, G.	2	0/ 0	.000	0/ 0	.000	-/ 0	0	0	0	0	0	0	.000
KARPIS, J.	1	0/ 0	.000	0/ 0	.000	-/ 1	0	0	0	0	0	0	.000
ALEXIS, W.	16	0/ 1	.000	0/ 1	.000	-/ 5	1	1	3	0	0	0	.000
Totals	200	24/47	.511	30/36	.833	-/33	15	12	12	10	2	78	.390

Team Rebounds: Syracuse 3; Va. Commonwealth 3. Disqualified: Va. Commonwealth—Brown. Technical fouls: None.

	1st Half	2nd Half	Final
Va. Commonwealth	36	27	63
Syracuse	37	41	78

Virginia (53)   Coach: Terry Holland

	Min.	Total FG / FGA	Pct.	FT / FTA	Pct.	Reb. O / T	A	TO	PF	S	Blk	TP	PPM
MILLER, J.	29	4/ 5	.800	1/ 2	.500	-/ 0	0	2	4	0	0	9	.310
EDELIN, K.	41	4/ 4	1.000	0/ 0	.000	-/ 6	1	1	1	2	2	8	.195
POLYNICE, O.	38	2/ 4	.500	1/ 2	.500	-/ 4	0	2	4	0	0	5	.132
WILSON, O.	43	6/14	.429	1/ 2	.500	-/ 2	3	3	2	4	1	13	.302
CARLISLE, R.	36	6/10	.600	0/ 0	.000	-/ 6	7	6	0	0	0	12	.333
STOKES, R.	24	2/ 4	.500	0/ 0	.000	-/ 0	2	0	3	1	0	4	.167
SHEEHEY, T.	6	1/ 1	1.000	0/ 0	.000	-/ 0	0	2	1	1	0	2	.333
MERRIFIELD, D.	8	0/ 0	.000	0/ 0	.000	-/ 0	0	1	0	0	0	0	.000
Totals	225	25/42	.595	3/ 6	.500	-/18	13	17	15	8	3	53	.236

Arkansas (51)   Coach: Eddie Sutton

	Min.	Total FG / FGA	Pct.	FT / FTA	Pct.	Reb. O / T	A	TO	PF	S	Blk	TP	PPM
BALENTINE, C.	43	3/ 7	.429	2/ 2	1.000	-/ 1	2	1	1	1	0	8	.186
SUTTON, L.	42	0/ 2	.000	3/ 4	.750	-/ 2	0	3	2	1	1	3	.071
KLEINE, J.	45	6/10	.600	3/ 4	.750	-/ 7	0	6	2	3	1	15	.333
NORTON, R.	43	5/10	.500	1/ 2	.500	-/ 1	2	2	4	0	1	11	.256
ROBERTSON, A.	45	6/12	.500	2/ 4	.500	-/ 4	7	4	4	8	3	14	.311
ROSE, S.	2	0/ 1	.000	0/ 0	.000	-/ 0	0	0	0	0	0	0	.000
RATLIFF, M.	2	0/ 0	.000	0/ 0	.000	-/ 0	0	0	0	0	0	0	.000
BEDFORD, D.	3	0/ 0	.000	0/ 0	.000	-/ 1	1	0	1	0	0	0	.000
Totals	225	20/42	.476	11/16	.688	-/16	12	16	14	13	6	51	.227

Team Rebounds: Virginia 3; Arkansas 6. Disqualified: None. Technical fouls: None.

	1st Half	2nd Half	1st OT	Final
Virginia	21	28	4	53
Arkansas	21	28	2	51

SECOND ROUND MIDWEST

Illinois State (61)   Coach: Bob Donewald

	Min.	Total FG / FGA	Pct.	FT / FTA	Pct.	Reb. O / T	A	TO	PF	S	Blk	TP	PPM
STEFANOVIC, L.	-	2/ 8	.250	0/ 0	.000	-/ 2	2	0	4	-	0	4	-
CORNLEY, H.	-	2/11	.182	2/ 2	1.000	-/ 6	2	2	4	-	0	6	-
ZWART, M.	-	3/ 9	.333	3/ 4	.750	-/ 6	1	2	3	-	0	9	-
MCKENNEY, M.	-	5/ 9	.556	0/ 0	.000	-/ 3	2	4	1	-	0	10	-
JOHNSON, R.	-	5/ 8	.625	4/ 6	.667	-/ 4	1	1	3	-	0	14	-
DUNCAN, B.	-	5/11	.455	0/ 0	.000	-/ 1	3	3	4	-	0	10	-
BRAKSICK, B.	-	2/ 3	.667	0/ 0	.000	-/ 2	0	0	3	-	1	4	-
ANDERSON	-	0/ 0	.000	0/ 0	.000	-/ 0	0	0	0	-	0	0	-
CORNLEY, H.	-	0/ 1	.000	0/ 0	.000	-/ 0	0	0	0	-	0	0	-
SANDERS	-	2/ 4	.500	0/ 0	.000	-/ 2	0	1	2	-	0	4	-
Totals	200	26/64	.406	9/12	.750	-/26	11	13	24	-	1	61	.305

DePaul (75)   Coach: Ray Meyer

	Min.	Total FG / FGA	Pct.	FT / FTA	Pct.	Reb. O / T	A	TO	PF	S	Blk	TP	PPM
CORBIN, T.	-	6/ 9	.667	8/ 8	1.000	-/ 9	4	3	2	-	1	20	-
HOLMES, K.	-	3/ 7	.429	1/ 2	.500	-/ 6	1	3	3	-	1	7	-
EMBRY, M.	-	3/ 4	.750	3/ 4	.750	-/ 5	0	1	4	-	0	9	-
PATTERSON, K.	-	6/ 9	.667	2/ 6	.333	-/ 2	4	2	2	-	0	14	-
MCMILLAN, J.	-	1/ 3	.333	1/ 3	.333	-/ 2	5	1	1	-	1	3	-
COMEGYS, D.	-	5/10	.500	4/ 5	.800	-/ 8	1	3	3	-	1	14	-
JACKSON, T.	-	3/ 9	.333	2/ 5	.400	-/ 1	1	1	2	-	0	8	-
MCCOY	-	0/ 0	.000	0/ 1	.000	-/ 0	0	0	0	-	0	0	-
LAMPLEY, L.	-	0/ 0	.000	0/ 0	.000	-/ 0	0	0	0	-	0	0	-
WEST, L.	-	0/ 0	.000	0/ 0	.000	-/ 0	0	0	0	-	0	0	-
LATTNER	-	0/ 0	.000	0/ 0	.000	-/ 0	0	0	0	-	0	0	-
Totals	200	27/51	.529	21/31	.677	-/33	16	14	17	-	4	75	.375

Team Rebounds: DePaul 4; Illinois State 5. Disqualified: None. Technical fouls: None.

	1st Half	2nd Half	Final
Illinois State	28	33	61
DePaul	37	38	75

Kansas (59)   Coach: Larry Brown

	Min.	Total FG / FGA	Pct.	FT / FTA	Pct.	Reb. O / T	A	TO	PF	S	Blk	TP	PPM
KNIGHT, K.	37	6/14	.429	0/ 0	.000	-/ 8	2	4	3	2	0	12	.324
THOMPSON, C.	30	5/ 8	.625	1/ 2	.500	-/ 3	5	3	4	1	0	11	.367
DREILING, G.	24	5/ 7	.714	0/ 0	.000	-/ 2	0	2	2	0	0	10	.417
TURGEON, M.	24	0/ 0	.000	0/ 0	.000	-/ 0	9	1	1	1	0	0	.000
HENRY, C.	39	5/11	.455	0/ 0	.000	-/ 5	2	3	1	0	0	10	.256
BANKS, T.	16	2/ 2	1.000	0/ 0	.000	-/ 1	2	1	2	0	0	4	.250
BOYLE, T.	1	0/ 1	.000	0/ 0	.000	-/ 0	0	0	0	0	0	0	.000
KELLOGG, R.	24	4/ 8	.500	0/ 0	.000	-/ 4	3	0	3	3	0	8	.333
MARTIN, B.	5	2/ 3	.667	0/ 0	.000	-/ 3	0	0	1	0	0	4	.800
Totals	200	29/54	.537	1/ 2	.500	-/26	23	14	17	7	0	59	.295

Wake Forest (69)   Coach: Carl Tacy

	Min.	Total FG / FGA	Pct.	FT / FTA	Pct.	Reb. O / T	A	TO	PF	S	Blk	TP	PPM
TOMS, J.	2	0/ 1	.000	0/ 0	.000	-/ 1	1	0	0	0	0	0	.000
GREEN, K.	39	10/16	.625	0/ 1	.000	-/ 5	2	0	0	1	0	20	.513
TEACHEY, A.	40	4/ 8	.500	5/ 7	.714	-/15	4	1	2	0	0	13	.325
RUDD, D.	37	2/10	.200	2/ 2	1.000	-/ 1	3	3	2	2	0	6	.162
YOUNG, D.	31	4/10	.400	0/ 0	.000	-/ 2	2	0	3	0	0	8	.258
BOGUES, T.	11	0/ 1	.000	0/ 0	.000	-/ 1	2	0	1	0	0	0	.000
KEPLEY, C.	1	0/ 0	.000	0/ 0	.000	-/ 0	0	0	0	0	0	0	.000
GARBER, L.	24	5/ 6	.833	3/ 5	.600	-/ 3	3	3	1	1	0	13	.542
CLINE, M.	15	3/ 6	.500	3/ 4	.750	-/ 3	1	0	1	0	0	9	.600
Totals	200	28/58	.483	13/19	.684	-/31	18	9	7	7	0	69	.345

Team Rebounds: Wake Forest 3; Kansas 1. Disqualified: None. Technical fouls: None.

	1st Half	2nd Half	Final
Kansas	32	27	59
Wake Forest	31	38	69

Memphis State (66)   Coach: Dana Kirk

	Min.	Total FG / FGA	Pct.	FT / FTA	Pct.	Reb. O / T	A	TO	PF	S	Blk	TP	PPM
HOLMES, B.	33	4/ 9	.444	0/ 3	.000	-/ 6	1	2	0	0	0	8	.242
LEE, K.	37	11/17	.647	7/ 7	1.000	-/16	3	2	4	1	2	29	.784
BEDFORD, W.	25	3/ 5	.600	0/ 0	.000	-/ 8	1	1	3	0	1	6	.240
HAYNES, P.	36	3/ 9	.333	1/ 1	1.000	-/ 5	2	1	0	1	0	7	.194
TURNER, A.	34	3/ 4	.750	4/ 5	.800	-/ 3	7	8	3	1	0	10	.294
PHILLIPS, D.	15	1/ 2	.500	0/ 0	.000	-/ 6	1	1	1	0	0	2	.133
BECTON, W.	3	0/ 0	.000	0/ 0	.000	-/ 0	0	1	0	0	0	0	.000
MCCOY, R.	4	0/ 0	.000	0/ 1	.000	-/ 1	0	0	0	0	0	0	.000
BUSH, L.	6	1/ 2	.500	2/ 4	.500	-/ 3	0	1	0	0	0	4	.667
ALBRIGHT, J.	6	0/ 0	.000	0/ 0	.000	-/ 0	0	1	1	0	0	0	.000
WILFONG, J.	1	0/ 0	.000	0/ 0	.000	-/ 0	0	0	0	0	0	0	.000
Totals	200	26/48	.542	14/21	.667	-/48	15	18	12	3	3	66	.330

Purdue (48)   Coach: Gene Keady

	Min.	Total FG / FGA	Pct.	FT / FTA	Pct.	Reb. O / T	A	TO	PF	S	Blk	TP	PPM
ATKINSON, M.	34	1/ 9	.111	0/ 2	.000	-/ 5	1	1	4	0	2	2	.059
EIFERT, G.	9	0/ 3	.000	0/ 0	.000	-/ 4	0	0	3	0	0	0	.000
ROWINSKI, J.	38	5/11	.455	4/ 6	.667	-/ 4	0	2	1	0	0	14	.368
HALL, R.	30	3/11	.273	2/ 2	1.000	-/ 4	3	1	4	2	0	8	.267
REID, S.	34	4/14	.286	4/ 4	1.000	-/ 2	2	3	2	1	0	12	.353
BULLOCK, J.	28	1/ 2	.500	0/ 4	.000	-/ 7	0	4	1	0	2	2	.071
CLAWSON, C.	18	3/13	.231	0/ 0	.000	-/ 1	1	1	2	0	0	6	.333
ROBINSON, H.	2	0/ 2	.000	0/ 0	.000	-/ 0	0	0	0	0	0	0	.000
GADIS, M.	7	2/ 3	.667	0/ 0	.000	-/ 1	0	0	3	0	0	4	.571
Totals	200	19/68	.279	10/18	.556	-/28	7	9	23	4	2	48	.240

Team Rebounds: Memphis State 1; Purdue 4. Disqualified: None. Technical fouls: Memphis State—Bench; Purdue—Coach Keady.

	1st Half	2nd Half	Final
Memphis State	35	31	66
Purdue	22	26	48

Louisiana Tech (69)   Coach: Andy Russo

	Min.	Total FG / FGA	Pct.	FT / FTA	Pct.	Reb. O / T	A	TO	PF	S	Blk	TP	PPM
BAILEY, R.	34	8/13	.615	2/ 4	.500	-/ 4	3	2	5	3	0	18	.529
MALONE, K.	37	5/12	.417	8/ 9	.889	-/ 8	0	1	4	0	1	18	.486
SIMMONS, W.	35	5/13	.385	2/ 2	1.000	-/ 5	1	0	2	0	3	12	.343
DAVIS, A.	23	2/ 6	.333	0/ 0	.000	-/ 1	2	3	3	1	0	4	.174
SMITH, W.	35	2/ 6	.333	0/ 0	.000	-/ 2	9	3	5	1	0	4	.114
GODBOLT, R.	20	2/ 4	.500	0/ 0	.000	-/ 1	0	0	3	1	0	4	.200
FRANK, A.	6	0/ 2	.000	3/ 5	.600	-/ 0	0	0	1	0	0	3	.500
DAWSON, T.	4	1/ 2	.500	0/ 0	.000	-/ 1	1	0	3	1	0	2	.500
ROBERSON, K.	3	1/ 3	.333	2/ 2	1.000	-/ 3	0	0	0	0	0	4	1.333
HARRIS, H.	2	0/ 1	.000	0/ 0	.000	-/ 1	0	0	0	0	0	0	.000
HANNIBAL, R.	1	0/ 0	.000	0/ 0	.000	-/ 0	0	0	0	0	0	0	.000
Totals	200	26/62	.419	17/22	.773	-/26	16	9	26	7	4	69	.345

Houston (77)   Coach: Guy Lewis

	Min.	Total FG / FGA	Pct.	FT / FTA	Pct.	Reb. O / T	A	TO	PF	S	Blk	TP	PPM
WINSLOW, R.	35	4/ 6	.667	6/ 7	.857	-/10	1	1	3	1	2	14	.400
YOUNG, M.	40	6/12	.500	4/ 4	1.000	-/ 6	3	1	2	1	0	16	.400
OLAJUWON, A.	34	6/ 9	.667	4/ 6	.667	-/12	1	4	5	2	4	16	.471
FRANKLIN, A.	37	5/ 9	.556	11/12	.917	-/ 4	4	3	4	0	0	21	.568
GETTYS, R.	34	2/ 4	.500	2/ 2	1.000	-/ 0	4	4	3	1	0	6	.176
GILES, D.	5	1/ 3	.333	0/ 2	.000	-/ 1	1	1	0	0	0	2	.400
ANDERS, R.	9	1/ 4	.250	0/ 1	.000	-/ 1	0	0	3	0	1	2	.222
ANDERSON, G.	5	0/ 0	.000	0/ 0	.000	-/ 1	0	1	2	0	0	0	.000
CLARK, B.	1	0/ 0	.000	0/ 0	.000	-/ 0	0	0	0	0	0	0	.000
Totals	200	25/47	.532	27/34	.794	-/35	14	15	22	5	7	77	.385

Team Rebounds: Houston 2; Louisiana Tech 2. Disqualified: Houston—Olajuwon; Louisiana Tech—Bailey, Smith. Technical fouls: None.

	1st Half	2nd Half	Final
Louisiana Tech	27	42	69
Houston	34	43	77

REGIONAL SEMIFINAL MIDEAST

Kentucky (72)   Coach: Joe Hall

	Min.	Total FG / FGA	Pct.	FT / FTA	Pct.	Reb. O / T	A	TO	PF	S	Blk	TP	PPM
BOWIE, S.	38	3/ 9	.333	2/ 2	1.000	-/12	2	5	3	1	3	8	.211
WALKER, K.	35	2/ 7	.286	4/ 4	1.000	-/ 6	3	0	3	2	1	8	.229
TURPIN, M.	32	6/10	.600	2/ 2	1.000	-/ 5	2	5	3	0	2	14	.438
BEAL, D.	39	6/ 9	.667	3/ 4	.750	-/ 2	9	6	3	6	0	15	.385
MASTER, J.	30	6/10	.600	3/ 4	.750	-/ 4	0	2	3	0	0	15	.500
BLACKMON, J.	10	1/ 1	1.000	0/ 0	.000	-/ 1	0	1	0	0	0	2	.200
HARDEN, R.	1	0/ 0	.000	0/ 0	.000	-/ 0	0	0	1	0	0	0	.000
BENNETT, W.	15	4/ 9	.444	2/ 4	.500	-/ 5	0	1	3	0	0	10	.667
Totals	200	28/55	.509	16/20	.800	-/35	16	20	19	9	6	72	.360

Louisville (67)   Coach: Denny Crum

	Min.	Total FG / FGA	Pct.	FT / FTA	Pct.	Reb. O / T	A	TO	PF	S	Blk	TP	PPM
FORREST, M.	35	3/ 4	.750	0/ 1	.000	-/ 4	2	1	5	2	1	6	.171
THOMPSON, B.	26	2/ 8	.250	0/ 3	.000	-/ 5	1	4	4	0	0	4	.154
JONES, C.	37	2/ 9	.222	4/ 4	1.000	-/ 9	0	0	1	3	0	8	.216
GORDON, L.	34	10/18	.556	5/ 6	.833	-/ 3	2	6	2	1	0	25	.735
WAGNER, M.	36	10/17	.588	2/ 2	1.000	-/ 2	5	4	2	1	0	22	.611
SUMPTER, B.	5	0/ 0	.000	0/ 0	.000	-/ 0	0	1	2	0	0	0	.000
HALL, J.	11	1/ 4	.250	0/ 0	.000	-/ 0	0	0	3	1	0	2	.182
MCSWAIN, M.	15	0/ 1	.000	0/ 0	.000	-/ 0	1	0	1	0	0	0	.000
JETER, J.	1	0/ 0	.000	0/ 0	.000	-/ 0	0	0	0	0	0	0	.000
Totals	200	28/61	.459	11/16	.688	-/23	11	16	20	8	1	67	.335

Team Rebounds: Kentucky 1; Louisville 6. Disqualified: Louisville—Forrest. Technical fouls: None.

	1st Half	2nd Half	Final
Kentucky	32	40	72
Louisville	36	31	67

Maryland (70)   Coach: Lefty Driesell

	Min.	Total FG / FGA	Pct.	FT / FTA	Pct.	Reb. O / T	A	TO	PF	S	Blk	TP	PPM
VEAL, H.	34	5/ 7	.714	0/ 1	.000	-/ 9	0	1	4	0	0	10	.294
BIAS, L.	38	8/17	.471	0/ 0	.000	-/ 8	2	1	2	0	2	16	.421
COLEMAN, B.	37	5/13	.385	2/ 3	.667	-/ 9	0	3	4	0	1	12	.324
ADKINS, J.	12	1/ 3	.333	0/ 1	.000	-/ 1	3	0	3	0	0	2	.167
BRANCH, A.	37	6/11	.545	7/ 9	.778	-/ 3	3	2	4	2	0	19	.514
GATLIN, K.	32	3/ 7	.429	1/ 1	1.000	-/ 3	10	3	4	0	0	7	.219
BAXTER, J.	3	1/ 2	.500	0/ 0	.000	-/ 0	0	0	1	0	0	2	.667
FOTHERGILL, M.	3	0/ 1	.000	0/ 0	.000	-/ 1	0	0	2	0	0	0	.000
LONG, T.	4	1/ 1	1.000	0/ 0	.000	-/ 0	0	0	0	0	0	2	.500
Totals	200	30/62	.484	10/15	.667	-/34	18	10	24	2	3	70	.350

Illinois (72)   Coach: Lou Henson

	Min.	Total FG / FGA	Pct.	FT / FTA	Pct.	Reb. O / T	A	TO	PF	S	Blk	TP	PPM
WINTERS, E.	33	5/12	.417	1/ 2	.500	-/ 6	2	2	2	0	0	11	.333
ALTENBERGER, D.	39	4/ 9	.444	4/ 7	.571	-/ 2	2	0	5	2	0	12	.308
MONTGOMERY, G.	33	5/ 5	1.000	5/ 8	.625	-/ 7	1	0	4	0	0	15	.455
DOUGLAS, B.	38	4/10	.400	3/ 5	.600	-/ 6	8	1	3	1	0	11	.289
RICHARDSON, Q.	37	4/ 4	1.000	4/ 4	1.000	-/ 1	6	1	2	1	0	12	.324
SCHAEFER, T.	7	2/ 2	1.000	0/ 1	.000	-/ 0	0	0	0	0	0	4	.571
MEENTS, S.	12	3/ 4	.750	1/ 2	.500	-/ 2	1	2	5	1	0	7	.583
WYSINGER, T.	1	0/ 0	.000	0/ 1	.000	-/ 1	0	0	0	0	0	0	.000
Totals	200	27/46	.587	18/30	.600	-/25	20	6	21	5	0	72	.360

Team Rebounds: Illinois 1; Maryland 3. Disqualified: Illinois—Altenberger, Meents. Technical fouls: None.

	1st Half	2nd Half	Final
Maryland	32	38	70
Illinois	30	42	72

REGIONAL SEMIFINAL WEST

Georgetown (62)   Coach: John Thompson

	Min.	Total FG / FGA	Pct.	FT / FTA	Pct.	Reb. O / T	A	TO	PF	S	Blk	TP	PPM
DALTON, R.	3	0/ 0	.000	0/ 0	.000	-/ 0	0	2	0	0	0	0	.000
WINGATE, D.	22	3/ 6	.500	0/ 0	.000	-/ 3	0	2	2	1	0	6	.273
EWING, P.	33	5/10	.500	6/ 7	.857	-/15	1	0	2	0	6	16	.485
BROWN, F.	6	1/ 2	.500	0/ 1	.000	-/ 3	1	0	1	1	0	2	.333
JACKSON, M.	32	2/ 8	.250	12/12	1.000	-/ 2	4	6	2	1	0	16	.500
SMITH, G.	17	0/ 2	.000	0/ 3	.000	-/ 3	1	0	2	0	0	0	.000
MARTIN, B.	30	3/ 6	.500	0/ 2	.000	-/ 6	0	2	2	1	0	6	.200
BROADNAX, H.	24	3/ 5	.600	3/ 5	.600	-/ 4	2	3	0	0	0	9	.375
WILLIAMS, R.	20	2/ 4	.500	3/ 4	.750	-/ 2	3	2	2	0	0	7	.350
GRAHAM, M.	13	0/ 0	.000	0/ 1	.000	-/ 5	0	1	2	1	0	0	.000
Totals	200	19/43	.442	24/35	.686	-/43	12	18	15	5	6	62	.310

UNLV (48)   Coach: Jerry Tarkanian

	Min.	Total FG / FGA	Pct.	FT / FTA	Pct.	Reb. O / T	A	TO	PF	S	Blk	TP	PPM
CATCHINGS, E.	15	0/ 2	.000	2/ 2	1.000	-/ 6	0	1	0	0	0	2	.133
JAMES, F.	28	2/ 8	.250	0/ 2	.000	-/ 2	1	1	4	0	0	4	.143
ADAMS, R.	31	2/ 8	.250	2/ 4	.500	-/ 7	0	1	5	3	2	6	.194
TARKANIAN, D.	34	3/ 9	.333	2/ 3	.667	-/ 2	3	3	5	1	0	8	.235
COLLINS, J.	17	1/ 4	.250	0/ 0	.000	-/ 3	0	1	4	0	0	2	.118
BOOKER, E.	24	3/ 7	.429	2/ 4	.500	-/ 3	0	2	1	2	0	8	.333
BROZOVICH, P.	2	0/ 0	.000	0/ 0	.000	-/ 1	0	0	0	0	0	0	.000
FLOWERS, J.	31	3/ 9	.333	4/ 6	.667	-/ 2	1	1	3	2	0	10	.323
BANKS, F.	18	4/11	.364	0/ 0	.000	-/ 2	0	0	4	1	0	8	.444
Totals	200	18/58	.310	12/21	.571	-/28	5	10	26	9	2	48	.240

Team Rebounds: Georgetown 2; UNLV 3. Disqualified: UNLV—Adams, Tarkanian. Technical fouls: UNLV—Booker.

	1st Half	2nd Half	Final
Georgetown	22	40	62
UNLV	21	27	48

Washington (58)   Coach: Marv Harshman

	Min.	Total FG / FGA	Pct.	FT / FTA	Pct.	Reb. O / T	A	TO	PF	S	Blk	TP	PPM
FORTIER	33	4/ 8	.500	0/ 0	.000	-/ 7	2	2	4	4	1	8	.242
SCHREMPF, D.	40	8/19	.421	2/ 4	.500	-/11	1	3	5	0	0	18	.450
WELP	28	3/ 8	.375	1/ 2	.500	-/ 8	1	3	4	1	0	7	.250
WILLIAMS	21	3/ 6	.500	0/ 2	.000	-/ 5	1	5	1	0	1	6	.286
VAUGHN	22	3/11	.273	1/ 2	.500	-/ 1	2	2	4	2	0	7	.318
KOEHLER	18	0/ 1	.000	0/ 0	.000	-/ 0	4	1	2	2	0	0	.000
ROGERS	12	3/ 4	.750	0/ 3	.000	-/ 4	0	0	1	0	1	6	.500
DAMON	13	1/ 6	.167	0/ 0	.000	-/ 1	0	0	1	0	0	2	.154
KUYPER	6	1/ 1	1.000	0/ 0	.000	-/ 0	0	0	0	0	0	2	.333
GARDNER	6	1/ 3	.333	0/ 0	.000	-/ 0	0	0	4	0	0	2	.333
SHIMER	1	0/ 0	.000	0/ 0	.000	-/ 0	0	0	1	0	0	0	.000
Totals	200	27/67	.403	4/13	.308	-/37	11	16	27	9	3	58	.290

Dayton (64)   Coach: Don Donoher

	Min.	Total FG / FGA	Pct.	FT / FTA	Pct.	Reb. O / T	A	TO	PF	S	Blk	TP	PPM
CHAPMAN, R.	39	7/12	.583	8/13	.615	-/ 9	3	7	3	4	2	22	.564
YOUNG, E.	37	3/ 8	.375	0/ 2	.000	-/ 7	0	1	2	0	0	6	.162
GOODWIN, D.	39	2/ 8	.250	4/ 5	.800	-/ 5	0	1	0	0	0	8	.205
TONEY, S.	30	6/ 8	.750	2/ 3	.667	-/ 2	2	5	3	1	0	14	.467
SCHELLENBERG, L.	33	2/ 4	.500	4/ 6	.667	-/ 7	3	2	1	1	1	8	.242
CHRISTIE, D.	15	0/ 0	.000	6/ 6	1.000	-/ 3	0	2	3	0	0	6	.400
ZERN, J.	2	0/ 1	.000	0/ 0	.000	-/ 0	0	0	0	0	0	0	.000
HARRIS, T.	1	0/ 0	.000	0/ 0	.000	-/ 0	0	0	0	0	0	0	.000
TRESSLER, J.	1	0/ 0	.000	0/ 0	.000	-/ 0	0	0	0	0	0	0	.000
DAHLINGHAUS, R.	1	0/ 0	.000	0/ 0	.000	-/ 0	0	0	0	0	0	0	.000
GRANT, A.	1	0/ 0	.000	0/ 0	.000	-/ 0	0	0	0	0	0	0	.000
SHIELDS, J.	1	0/ 0	.000	0/ 0	.000	-/ 0	0	0	0	0	0	0	.000
Totals	200	20/41	.488	24/35	.686	-/33	8	18	12	6	3	64	.320

Team Rebounds: Dayton 1; Washington 1. Disqualified: Washington—Schrempf. Technical fouls: None.

	1st Half	2nd Half	Final
Washington	22	36	58
Dayton	21	43	64

REGIONAL SEMIFINAL EAST

North Carolina (68)   Coach: Dean Smith

	Min.	Total FG / FGA	Pct.	FT / FTA	Pct.	Reb. O / T	A	TO	PF	S	Blk	TP	PPM
PERKINS, S.	35	8/17	.471	10/12	.833	-/ 9	2	2	3	0	0	26	.743
DOHERTY, M.	37	3/ 8	.375	1/ 2	.500	-/ 7	4	1	5	1	1	7	.189
DAUGHERTY, B.	23	1/ 3	.333	1/ 2	.500	-/ 4	0	2	2	1	1	3	.130
JORDAN, M.	26	6/14	.429	1/ 2	.500	-/ 1	1	4	5	1	0	13	.500
SMITH, K.	32	3/ 8	.375	2/ 2	1.000	-/ 0	5	2	2	0	0	8	.250
WOLF, J.	16	2/ 4	.500	1/ 2	.500	-/10	1	1	3	0	0	5	.313
HALE, S.	23	2/ 4	.500	0/ 1	.000	-/ 3	2	0	5	2	0	4	.174
POPSON, D.	3	0/ 0	.000	0/ 0	.000	-/ 0	0	1	0	0	0	0	.000
PETERSON, B.	4	1/ 4	.250	0/ 0	.000	-/ 0	0	0	1	0	0	2	.500
EXUM, C.	1	0/ 0	.000	0/ 0	.000	-/ 0	0	0	1	0	0	0	.000
Totals	200	26/62	.419	16/23	.696	-/34	15	13	27	5	2	68	.340

Indiana (72)   Coach: Bob Knight

	Min.	Total FG / FGA	Pct.	FT / FTA	Pct.	Reb. O / T	A	TO	PF	S	Blk	TP	PPM
GIOMI, M.	27	2/ 4	.500	3/ 4	.750	-/ 6	2	3	4	0	0	7	.259
SIMMONS, M.	18	1/ 1	1.000	2/ 5	.400	-/ 2	2	2	2	0	0	4	.222
BLAB, U.	36	5/ 7	.714	6/ 8	.750	-/ 3	0	4	3	1	1	16	.444
DAKICH, D.	33	2/ 3	.667	0/ 0	.000	-/ 3	3	1	5	0	0	4	.121
ALFORD, S.	40	9/13	.692	9/10	.900	-/ 6	3	3	2	2	0	27	.675
ROBINSON, S.	34	5/ 8	.625	4/ 7	.571	-/ 4	3	3	2	3	0	14	.412
MEIER, T.	7	0/ 1	.000	0/ 0	.000	-/ 2	0	0	1	0	0	0	.000
FRANZ, C.	4	0/ 0	.000	0/ 1	.000	-/ 0	0	1	0	0	0	0	.000
WITTE, C.	1	0/ 0	.000	0/ 0	.000	-/ 0	0	0	0	0	0	0	.000
Totals	200	24/37	.649	24/35	.686	-/26	13	17	19	6	1	72	.360

Team Rebounds: Indiana 2; N. Carolina 3. Disqualified: Indiana—Dakich; N. Carolina—Doherty, Jordan, Hale. Technical fouls: None.

	1st Half	2nd Half	Final
N. Carolina	28	40	68
Indiana	32	40	72

Syracuse (55) Coach: Jim Boeheim

	Min.	Total FG/FGA	Pct.	FT/FTA	Pct.	Reb. O/T	A	TO	PF	S	Blk	TP	PPM
ADDISON, R.	38	7/18	.389	4/5	.800	2/4	0	3	5	1	1	18	.474
KERINS, S.	35	5/14	.357	0/0	.000	2/12	3	1	3	2	0	10	.286
HAWKINS, A.	19	0/0	.000	0/0	.000	1/3	0	1	5	0	0	0	.000
WASHINGTON, D.	32	3/10	.300	2/2	1.000	0/0	3	3	5	1	0	8	.250
WALDRON, G.	31	4/8	.500	0/0	.000	0/1	6	3	5	1	0	8	.258
MONROE, G.	16	1/4	.250	0/1	.000	1/2	5	2	2	0	0	2	.125
SPERA, S.	2	1/1	1.000	0/0	.000	1/1	0	1	1	0	0	2	1.000
TRICHE, H.	2	0/0	.000	1/2	.500	1/2	0	1	3	0	0	1	.500
PAPADAKOS, G.	1	0/0	.000	0/0	.000	1/2	0	0	0	0	0	0	.000
ALEXIS, W.	24	2/6	.333	2/2	1.000	2/8	3	2	5	3	1	6	.250
Totals	200	23/61	.377	9/12	.750	11/35	20	17	34	8	2	55	.275

Virginia (63) Coach: Terry Holland

	Min.	Total FG/FGA	Pct.	FT/FTA	Pct.	Reb. O/T	A	TO	PF	S	Blk	TP	PPM
MILLER, J.	25	2/9	.222	1/2	.500	0/2	0	0	5	0	0	5	.200
EDELIN, K.	34	4/4	1.000	2/4	.500	2/14	1	2	2	2	0	10	.294
POLYNICE, O.	31	4/8	.500	4/7	.571	2/5	0	2	2	0	1	12	.387
WILSON, O.	37	4/8	.500	9/11	.818	1/6	3	5	5	3	0	17	.459
CARLISLE, R.	33	3/7	.429	2/5	.400	1/5	7	3	1	0	0	8	.242
STOKES, R.	21	4/7	.571	0/3	.000	0/2	3	1	3	2	0	8	.381
SHEEHEY, T.	11	1/2	.500	0/0	.000	0/1	1	1	1	1	0	2	.182
MULLEN, T.	1	0/0	.000	0/1	.000	0/0	0	0	0	0	0	0	.000
MERRIFIELD, D.	5	0/0	.000	1/3	.333	1/1	1	1	0	0	0	1	.200
SOLOMON, A.	1	0/0	.000	0/0	.000	0/0	0	0	0	0	0	0	.000
JOHNSON, K.	1	0/0	.000	0/0	.000	0/0	0	0	0	0	0	0	.000
Totals	200	22/45	.489	19/36	.528	7/36	16	15	19	8	1	63	.315

Team Rebounds: Virginia 5; Syracuse 4. Disqualified: Virginia—Miller, Wilson; Syracuse—Addison, Hawkins, Washington, Waldron, Alexis. Technical fouls: None.

	1st Half	2nd Half	Final
Syracuse	16	39	55
Virginia	26	37	63

REGIONAL SEMIFINAL MIDWEST
DePaul (71) Coach: Ray Meyer

	Min.	Total FG/FGA	Pct.	FT/FTA	Pct.	Reb. O/T	A	TO	PF	S	Blk	TP	PPM
CORBIN, T.	44	5/11	.455	3/3	1.000	-/5	4	4	4	2	0	13	.295
HOLMES, K.	16	4/5	.800	0/0	.000	-/2	1	4	4	1	0	8	.500
EMBRY, M.	31	3/5	.600	2/4	.500	-/9	4	2	4	0	3	8	.258
PATTERSON, K.	42	3/12	.250	2/4	.500	-/3	9	4	3	4	0	8	.190
MCMILLAN, J.	37	7/11	.636	0/0	.000	-/5	0	0	3	2	0	14	.378
COMEGYS, D.	37	8/15	.533	1/2	.500	-/13	0	3	4	0	1	17	.459
JACKSON, T.	18	1/7	.143	1/2	.500	-/3	0	1	1	2	0	3	.167
Totals	225	31/66	.470	9/15	.600	-/40	18	18	23	11	4	71	.316

Wake Forest (73) Coach: Carl Tacy

	Min.	Total FG/FGA	Pct.	FT/FTA	Pct.	Reb. O/T	A	TO	PF	S	Blk	TP	PPM
GREEN, K.	38	11/19	.579	3/4	.750	-/13	0	4	4	2	0	25	.658
GARBER, L.	15	1/4	.250	1/1	1.000	-/1	2	1	2	0	1	3	.200
TEACHEY, A.	45	4/11	.364	9/14	.643	-/6	3	1	3	4	2	17	.378
RUDD, T.	42	4/7	.571	4/5	.800	-/2	1	5	2	0	0	12	.286
YOUNG, D.	41	4/8	.500	0/0	.000	-/5	9	1	2	2	0	8	.195
TOMS, J.	5	0/3	.000	0/0	.000	-/2	0	3	0	0	0	0	.000
BOGUES, T.	6	0/1	.000	0/0	.000	-/0	0	0	1	1	0	0	.000
CLINE, M.	32	3/9	.333	2/4	.500	-/9	1	0	0	0	0	8	.250
KEPLEY, C.	1	0/0	.000	0/0	.000	-/0	0	0	1	0	0	0	.000
Totals	225	27/62	.435	19/28	.679	-/38	16	15	15	9	3	73	.324

Team Rebounds: Wake Forest 1; DePaul 3. Disqualified: None. Technical fouls: None.

	1st Half	2nd Half	1st OT	Final
DePaul	39	28	4	71
Wake Forest	35	32	6	73

Memphis State (71) Coach: Dana Kirk

	Min.	Total FG/FGA	Pct.	FT/FTA	Pct.	Reb. O/T	A	TO	PF	S	Blk	TP	PPM
HOLMES, B.	22	4/8	.500	0/0	.000	-/4	4	1	5	0	0	8	.364
LEE, K.	39	6/13	.462	3/6	.500	-/10	3	4	5	1	6	15	.385
BEDFORD, W.	31	10/12	.833	1/2	.500	-/4	0	0	5	0	3	21	.677
HAYNES, P.	40	7/14	.500	1/1	1.000	-/5	1	1	0	0	0	15	.375
TURNER, A.	38	5/8	.625	0/0	.000	-/3	7	4	4	2	0	10	.263
PHILLIPS, D.	11	1/3	.333	0/0	.000	-/1	0	1	0	0	0	2	.182
BECTON, W.	8	0/2	.000	0/0	.000	-/2	0	0	2	0	0	0	.000
MCCOY, R.	7	0/1	.000	0/0	.000	-/2	0	0	1	0	1	0	.000
BUSH, L.	1	0/0	.000	0/0	.000	-/1	0	0	1	0	0	0	.000
ALBRIGHT, J.	3	0/0	.000	0/0	.000	-/0	0	0	2	0	0	0	.000
Totals	200	33/61	.541	5/9	.556	-/32	15	11	25	3	10	71	.355

Houston (78) Coach: Guy Lewis

	Min.	Total FG/FGA	Pct.	FT/FTA	Pct.	Reb. O/T	A	TO	PF	S	Blk	TP	PPM
WINSLOW, R.	36	5/7	.714	2/4	.500	-/12	1	1	0	2	0	12	.333
YOUNG, M.	38	5/22	.227	3/5	.600	-/9	2	5	1	1	0	13	.342
OLAJUWON, A.	40	9/17	.529	7/15	.467	-/13	3	1	4	1	4	25	.625
FRANKLIN, A.	38	7/13	.538	10/12	.833	-/2	2	1	2	1	0	24	.632
GETTYS, R.	39	2/5	.400	0/0	.000	-/3	9	1	3	1	0	4	.103
ANDERS, B.	5	0/2	.000	0/0	.000	-/0	0	0	1	0	0	0	.000
ANDERSON, G.	4	0/0	.000	0/0	.000	-/1	0	0	0	0	0	0	.000
Totals	200	28/66	.424	22/36	.611	-/40	17	9	11	6	4	78	.390

Team Rebounds: Houston 4; Memphis State 1. Disqualified: Memphis State—Lee, Holmes, Bedford. Technical fouls: None.

	1st Half	2nd Half	Final
Memphis State	40	31	71
Houston	41	37	78

REGIONAL FINAL MIDEAST
Kentucky (54) Coach: Joe Hall

	Min.	Total FG/FGA	Pct.	FT/FTA	Pct.	Reb. O/T	A	TO	PF	S	Blk	TP	PPM
BOWIE, S.	37	3/6	.500	5/7	.714	-/14	1	3	2	1	1	11	.297
WALKER, K.	26	3/4	.750	0/0	.000	-/2	3	0	0	0	0	6	.231
TURPIN, M.	39	6/12	.500	1/2	.500	-/6	2	4	2	0	0	13	.333
BEAL, D.	39	3/6	.500	3/4	.750	-/3	6	5	2	2	0	9	.231
MASTER, J.	34	3/6	.500	0/0	.000	-/1	1	0	3	0	0	6	.176
BLACKMON, J.	7	0/0	.000	0/0	.000	-/0	0	1	0	0	0	0	.000
BEARUP, B.	3	0/0	.000	1/2	.500	-/0	0	0	0	0	0	1	.333
BENNETT, W.	15	3/4	.750	2/2	1.000	-/0	0	1	4	0	0	8	.533
Totals	200	21/38	.553	12/17	.706	-/26	13	13	14	3	1	54	.270

Illinois (51) Coach: Lou Henson

	Min.	Total FG/FGA	Pct.	FT/FTA	Pct.	Reb. O/T	A	TO	PF	S	Blk	TP	PPM
ALTENBERGER, D.	40	5/11	.455	3/4	.750	-/3	3	0	2	0	0	13	.325
WINTERS, E.	37	3/9	.333	1/3	.333	-/4	0	0	1	0	0	7	.189
MONTGOMERY, G.	28	2/4	.500	0/0	.000	-/2	0	1	3	0	0	4	.143
DOUGLAS, B.	40	3/9	.333	1/2	.500	-/5	11	4	3	3	0	7	.175
RICHARDSON, Q.	35	8/11	.727	0/0	.000	-/3	3	1	3	0	0	16	.457
MEENTS, S.	19	2/6	.333	0/0	.000	-/3	0	1	3	0	2	4	.211
WYSINGER, T.	1	0/0	.000	0/0	.000	-/0	0	0	0	0	0	0	.000
Totals	200	23/50	.460	5/9	.556	-/20	17	7	15	3	2	51	.255

Team Rebounds: Kentucky 0; Illinois 1. Disqualified: None. Technical fouls: None.

	1st Half	2nd Half	Final
Kentucky	24	30	54
Illinois	22	29	51

REGIONAL FINAL WEST

Georgetown (61)   Coach: John Thompson

	Min.	Total FG/FGA	Pct.	FT/FTA	Pct.	Reb. O/T	A	TO	PF	S	Blk	TP	PPM
DALTON, R.	10	1/2	.500	0/0	.000	-/3	0	0	1	0	0	2	.200
WINGATE, D.	24	2/6	.333	2/2	1.000	-/4	0	0	0	2	0	6	.250
EWING, P.	35	6/10	.600	3/3	1.000	-/7	3	1	1	2	3	15	.429
BROWN, F.	9	1/1	1.000	0/0	.000	-/0	0	0	1	0	0	2	.222
JACKSON, M.	38	6/17	.353	2/3	.667	-/0	4	2	3	2	0	14	.368
SMITH, G.	26	0/0	.000	0/1	.000	-/2	1	3	1	0	0	0	.000
MARTIN, B.	22	2/4	.500	2/4	.500	-/10	0	0	3	0	0	6	.273
BROADNAX, H.	6	0/2	.000	0/0	.000	-/0	1	2	1	0	0	0	.000
WILLIAMS, R.	17	3/3	1.000	2/2	1.000	-/2	0	2	2	1	0	8	.471
GRAHAM, M.	13	4/7	.571	0/0	.000	-/5	0	0	1	0	0	8	.615
Totals	200	25/52	.481	11/15	.733	-/33	9	10	14	7	3	61	.305

Dayton (49)   Coach: Don Donoher

	Min.	Total FG/FGA	Pct.	FT/FTA	Pct.	Reb. O/T	A	TO	PF	S	Blk	TP	PPM
CHAPMAN, R.	40	5/10	.500	3/4	.750	-/5	2	2	2	2	2	13	.325
YOUNG, E.	40	6/9	.667	2/2	1.000	-/5	0	1	4	1	1	14	.350
GOODWIN, D.	35	2/7	.286	0/0	.000	-/2	1	0	3	0	0	4	.114
TONEY, S.	34	3/13	.231	0/0	.000	-/4	0	1	2	1	0	6	.176
SCHELLENBERG, L.	29	2/2	1.000	0/0	.000	-/3	3	4	1	1	0	4	.138
CHRISTIE, D.	17	2/7	.286	2/2	1.000	-/1	0	0	4	0	0	6	.353
HARRIS, T.	5	1/3	.333	0/0	.000	-/0	0	1	2	0	0	2	.400
Totals	200	21/51	.412	7/8	.875	-/20	6	9	18	5	3	49	.245

Team Rebounds: Georgetown 2; Dayton 0. Disqualified: None. Technical fouls: None.

	1st Half	2nd Half	Final
Georgetown	30	31	61
Dayton	24	25	49

REGIONAL FINAL EAST

Indiana (48)   Coach: Bob Knight

	Min.	Total FG/FGA	Pct.	FT/FTA	Pct.	Reb. O/T	A	TO	PF	S	Blk	TP	PPM
GIOMI, M.	39	5/9	.556	2/2	1.000	1/7	0	2	4	1	0	12	.308
SIMMONS, M.	16	1/2	.500	0/0	.000	0/1	4	0	1	0	0	2	.125
BLAB, U.	39	5/14	.357	2/2	1.000	1/8	1	0	4	1	1	12	.308
DAKICH, D.	23	2/3	.667	0/0	.000	0/1	3	4	4	0	0	4	.174
ALFORD, S.	38	2/7	.286	2/2	1.000	1/1	2	4	2	1	0	6	.158
ROBINSON, S.	32	4/8	.500	0/0	.000	0/1	6	1	2	1	0	8	.250
MEIER, T.	9	2/2	1.000	0/0	.000	0/0	0	0	1	0	0	4	.444
THOMAS, D.	1	0/0	.000	0/0	.000	0/0	0	0	0	0	0	0	.000
FRANZ, C.	3	0/0	.000	0/0	.000	0/0	0	0	0	0	0	0	.000
Totals	200	21/45	.467	6/6	1.000	3/19	16	11	18	4	1	48	.240

Virginia (50)   Coach: Terry Holland

	Min.	Total FG/FGA	Pct.	FT/FTA	Pct.	Reb. O/T	A	TO	PF	S	Blk	TP	PPM
MILLER, J.	29	8/11	.727	3/3	1.000	0/3	1	0	1	1	0	19	.655
EDELIN, K.	38	1/2	.500	3/4	.750	1/7	1	1	2	2	0	5	.132
POLYNICE, O.	38	4/7	.571	4/6	.667	2/6	0	1	2	1	0	12	.316
WILSON, O.	34	2/9	.222	0/0	.000	0/1	3	6	5	0	0	4	.118
CARLISLE, R.	32	2/5	.400	4/5	.800	0/3	4	3	0	0	0	8	.250
STOKES, R.	25	1/5	.200	0/0	.000	1/2	1	1	2	1	0	2	.080
SHEEHEY, T.	4	0/0	.000	0/0	.000	0/1	1	0	0	0	0	0	.000
Totals	200	18/39	.462	14/18	.778	4/23	11	12	12	5	0	50	.250

Team Rebounds: Virginia 3; Indiana 2. Disqualified: Virginia—Wilson. Technical fouls: None.

	1st Half	2nd Half	Final
Indiana	26	22	48
Virginia	23	27	50

REGIONAL FINAL MIDWEST

Wake Forest (63)   Coach: Carl Tacy

	Min.	Total FG/FGA	Pct.	FT/FTA	Pct.	Reb. O/T	A	TO	PF	S	Blk	TP	PPM
GREEN, K.	40	8/14	.571	2/2	1.000	-/16	2	2	2	0	0	18	.450
TEACHEY, A.	40	5/8	.625	3/3	1.000	-/7	2	1	4	3	2	13	.325
RUDD, D.	40	6/13	.462	0/0	.000	-/1	5	2	4	0	0	12	.300
YOUNG, D.	38	4/8	.500	0/0	.000	-/1	7	2	3	1	1	8	.211
BOGUES, T.	2	0/0	.000	0/0	.000	-/0	0	0	1	0	0	0	.000
GARBER, L.	12	0/4	.000	2/3	.667	-/1	1	1	2	0	0	2	.167
CLINE, M.	26	5/10	.500	0/0	.000	-/3	1	0	2	0	0	10	.385
TOMS, J.	2	0/0	.000	0/0	.000	-/0	0	0	2	0	0	0	.000
Totals	200	28/57	.491	7/8	.875	-/29	18	8	20	4	3	63	.315

Houston (68)   Coach: Guy Lewis

	Min.	Total FG/FGA	Pct.	FT/FTA	Pct.	Reb. O/T	A	TO	PF	S	Blk	TP	PPM
WINSLOW, R.	36	4/9	.444	2/2	1.000	-/6	0	1	3	2	0	10	.278
YOUNG, M.	40	7/18	.389	1/6	.167	-/8	1	0	0	2	1	15	.375
OLAJUWON, A.	40	14/16	.875	1/5	.200	-/12	2	3	3	2	3	29	.725
FRANKLIN, A.	35	2/5	.400	5/6	.833	-/2	3	1	0	1	0	9	.257
GETTYS, R.	37	1/4	.250	0/0	.000	-/3	10	2	2	0	0	2	.054
GILES, D.	1	0/1	.000	1/2	.500	-/2	0	0	1	0	0	1	1.000
ANDERS, B.	4	1/3	.333	0/0	.000	-/0	1	0	1	0	0	2	.500
THOMAS, R.	3	0/0	.000	0/0	.000	-/0	0	0	0	0	0	0	.000
DICKENS, E.	4	0/0	.000	0/0	.000	-/0	1	0	1	0	0	0	.000
Totals	200	29/56	.518	10/21	.476	-/33	18	7	11	7	4	68	.340

Team Rebounds: Houston 2; Wake Forest 2. Disqualified: None. Technical fouls: None.

	1st Half	2nd Half	Final
Wake Forest	31	32	63
Houston	34	34	68

FINAL FOUR

Kentucky (40)   Coach: Joe Hall

	Min.	Total FG/FGA	Pct.	FT/FTA	Pct.	Reb. O/T	A	TO	PF	S	Blk	TP	PPM
BOWIE, S.	34	3/10	.300	4/4	1.000	-/11	1	2	3	0	2	10	.294
WALKER, K.	29	1/3	.333	2/2	1.000	-/3	1	1	3	1	0	4	.138
TURPIN, M.	27	2/11	.182	1/2	.500	-/5	1	0	2	1	1	5	.185
BEAL, D.	35	2/8	.250	2/2	1.000	-/1	4	6	4	2	0	6	.171
MASTER, J.	23	2/7	.286	2/2	1.000	-/1	0	1	1	0	0	6	.261
BLACKMON, J.	22	2/5	.400	1/2	.500	-/1	2	1	3	3	0	5	.227
HARDEN, R.	2	0/1	.000	0/0	.000	-/2	0	1	1	0	0	0	.000
BEARUP, B.	4	0/0	.000	2/2	1.000	-/0	0	0	0	0	0	2	.500
BENNETT, W.	24	1/8	.125	0/0	.000	-/7	0	3	5	0	0	2	.083
Totals	200	13/53	.245	14/16	.875	-/31	9	15	22	7	3	40	.200

Georgetown (53)   Coach: John Thompson

	Min.	Total FG/FGA	Pct.	FT/FTA	Pct.	Reb. O/T	A	TO	PF	S	Blk	TP	PPM
DALTON, R.	17	0/1	.000	0/0	.000	-/4	0	0	1	0	0	0	.000
WINGATE, D.	25	5/8	.625	1/2	.500	-/3	2	3	0	1	0	11	.440
EWING, P.	29	4/6	.667	0/0	.000	-/9	1	2	3	0	0	8	.276
BROWN, F.	11	0/1	.000	0/1	.000	-/2	1	0	4	0	0	0	.000
JACKSON, M.	33	4/9	.444	4/6	.667	-/10	3	5	2	0	0	12	.364
SMITH, G.	17	2/4	.500	1/2	.500	-/2	1	0	2	0	0	5	.294
MARTIN, B.	5	1/4	.250	0/0	.000	-/1	0	2	1	0	0	2	.400
BROADNAX, H.	12	2/4	.500	1/2	.500	-/1	0	0	0	0	0	5	.417
WILLIAMS, R.	18	1/7	.143	0/0	.000	-/3	2	4	3	0	0	2	.111
GRAHAM, M.	33	4/6	.667	0/2	.000	-/6	1	3	3	0	3	8	.242
Totals	200	23/50	.460	7/15	.467	-/41	11	19	19	1	3	53	.265

Team Rebounds: Georgetown 2; Kentucky 2. Disqualified: Kentucky—Bennett. Technical fouls: None.

	1st Half	2nd Half	Final
Kentucky	29	11	40
Georgetown	22	31	53

Virginia (47)   Coach: Terry Holland

	Min.	Total FG/FGA	Pct.	FT/FTA	Pct.	Reb. O/T	A	TO	PF	S	Blk	TP	PPM
MILLER, J.	37	6/15	.400	0/0	.000	-/4	1	3	2	0	0	12	.324
EDELIN, K.	39	1/2	.500	0/0	.000	-/3	2	1	3	0	1	2	.051
POLYNICE, O.	43	4/7	.571	1/1	1.000	-/7	0	1	1	1	0	9	.209
WILSON, O.	45	5/12	.417	2/2	1.000	-/3	5	4	2	2	1	12	.267
CARLISLE, R.	29	3/14	.214	2/2	1.000	-/6	0	0	2	0	0	8	.276
STOKES, R.	24	1/1	1.000	0/2	.000	-/2	3	0	4	2	0	2	.083
SHEEHEY, T.	8	1/3	.333	0/0	.000	-/1	1	0	0	0	0	2	.250
Totals	225	21/54	.389	5/7	.714	-/26	12	9	14	5	2	47	.209

Houston (49)   Coach: Guy Lewis

	Min.	Total FG/FGA	Pct.	FT/FTA	Pct.	Reb. O/T	A	TO	PF	S	Blk	TP	PPM
WINSLOW, R.	44	4/7	.571	0/0	.000	-/7	0	1	2	2	1	8	.182
YOUNG, M.	45	8/16	.500	1/4	.250	-/7	1	2	1	0	0	17	.378
OLAJUWON, A.	45	4/5	.800	4/6	.667	-/11	1	8	3	2	5	12	.267
FRANKLIN, A.	45	2/7	.286	2/2	1.000	-/4	7	1	1	1	0	6	.133
GETTYS, R.	45	3/7	.429	0/0	.000	-/3	6	3	3	0	0	6	.133
DICKENS, E.	0	0/0	.000	0/0	.000	-/0	0	0	0	0	0	0	-
ALEXANDER, M.	0	0/0	.000	0/0	.000	-/0	0	0	0	0	0	0	-
Totals	225	21/42	.500	7/12	.583	-/32	15	15	10	5	6	49	.218

Team Rebounds: Houston 0; Virginia 2. Disqualified: None. Players who played 0 min. played less than 1 min. each.

	1st Half	2nd Half	1 OT	Final
Virginia	23	20	4	47
Houston	25	18	6	49

NATIONAL CHAMPIONSHIP

Georgetown (84)   Coach: John Thompson

	Min.	Total FG/FGA	Pct.	FT/FTA	Pct.	Reb. O/T	A	TO	PF	S	Blk	TP	PPM
DALTON, R.	13	0/0	.000	0/0	.000	-/2	0	1	1	0	1	0	.000
WINGATE, D.	32	5/10	.500	6/9	.667	-/1	3	2	4	0	0	16	.500
EWING, P.	30	4/8	.500	2/2	1.000	-/9	3	1	4	0	4	10	.333
BROWN, F.	15	1/2	.500	2/2	1.000	-/4	4	0	4	0	0	4	.267
JACKSON, M.	35	3/4	.750	5/5	1.000	-/0	6	2	4	0	0	11	.314
MARTIN, B.	16	3/6	.500	0/0	.000	-/2	0	0	0	0	0	6	.375
BROADNAX, H.	8	2/3	.667	0/0	.000	-/0	0	0	2	0	0	4	.400
WILLIAMS, R.	26	9/18	.500	1/2	.500	-/7	3	1	2	0	0	19	.731
GRAHAM, M.	24	7/9	.778	0/2	.000	-/5	0	2	4	0	1	14	.583
MORRIS, V.	1	0/0	.000	0/0	.000	-/0	0	0	0	0	0	0	.000
Totals	200	34/60	.567	16/22	.727	-/30	19	9	25	0	6	84	.420

Houston (75)   Coach: Guy Lewis

	Min.	Total FG/FGA	Pct.	FT/FTA	Pct.	Reb. O/T	A	TO	PF	S	Blk	TP	PPM
WINSLOW, R.	33	0/1	.000	2/2	1.000	-/6	3	3	4	0	1	2	.061
YOUNG, M.	37	8/21	.381	2/3	.667	-/5	1	1	3	2	1	18	.486
OLAJUWON, A.	32	6/9	.667	3/7	.429	-/9	0	2	4	0	2	15	.469
FRANKLIN, A.	38	8/15	.533	5/6	.833	-/2	9	3	3	0	0	21	.553
GETTYS, R.	29	3/3	1.000	0/0	.000	-/1	7	1	2	0	0	6	.207
GILES, D.	2	0/0	.000	0/0	.000	-/0	0	0	0	0	0	0	.000
ANDERS, R.	10	2/2	1.000	0/2	.000	-/0	0	1	0	1	0	4	.400
ANDERSON, G.	6	1/1	1.000	0/0	.000	-/2	0	0	0	0	0	2	.333
CLARK, B.	1	0/0	.000	0/0	.000	-/0	0	0	0	0	0	0	.000
DICKENS, E.	6	2/3	.667	1/2	.500	-/0	1	5	0	0	5	.833
THOMAS, R.	2	0/0	.000	0/0	.000	-/0	0	1	0	0	0	0	.000
WEAVER, J.	1	0/0	.000	0/0	.000	-/0	0	0	0	0	0	0	.000
ORSAK, G.	1	1/1	1.000	0/0	.000	-/0	0	0	0	0	0	2	2.000
ALEXANDER, M.	1	0/0	.000	0/0	.000	-/1	0	0	0	0	0	0	.000
BELCHER, S.	1	0/0	.000	0/0	.000	-/0	0	0	0	0	0	0	.000
Totals	200	31/56	.554	13/22	.591	-/26	20	13	21	3	4	75	.375

Team Rebounds: Houston 0; Virginia 2. Disqualified: None. Players who played 0 min. played less than 1 min. each. Technical fouls: None.

	1st Half	2nd Half	Final
Georgetown	40	44	84
Houston	30	45	75

✪ ALL-STAR TEAMS ✪

ALL TOURNAMENT

★ PATRICK EWING	GEORGETOWN
ALVIN FRANKLIN	HOUSTON
MICHAEL GRAHAM	GEORGETOWN
AKEEM OLAJUWON	HOUSTON
MICHAEL YOUNG	HOUSTON

MIDWEST REGIONAL

WILLIAM BEDFORD	MEMPHIS STATE
KENNY GREEN	WAKE FOREST
★ AKEEM OLAJUWON	HOUSTON
DELANEY RUDD	WAKE FOREST
MICHAEL YOUNG	HOUSTON

EAST REGIONAL

STEVE ALFORD	INDIANA
UWE BLAB	INDIANA
★ JIM MILLER	VIRGINIA
SAM PERKINS	N. CAROLINA
OLDEN POLYNICE	VIRGINIA

MIDEAST REGIONAL

★ DICKY BEAL	KENTUCKY
SAM BOWIE	KENTUCKY
BRUCE DOUGLAS	ILLINOIS
LANCASTER GORDON	LOUISVILLE
MELVIN TURPIN	KENTUCKY

WEST REGIONAL

ROOSEVELT CHAPMAN	DAYTON
★ PATRICK EWING	GEORGETOWN
MICHAEL JACKSON	GEORGETOWN
DETLEF SCHREMPF	WASHINGTON
ED YOUNG	DAYTON

★ Most Outstanding Player(s)

✪ INDIVIDUAL RECORDS ✪

SCORING

Most points in a single game
1. ROOSEVELT CHAPMAN, DAYTON (vs. OKLAHOMA) — 41
2. KEVIN MULLIN, PRINCETON (vs. SAN DIEGO) — 38
3. WAYMON TISDALE, OKLAHOMA (vs. DAYTON) — 36
4. MCKINLEY SINGLETON, ALA.-BIRMINGHAM (vs. BRIGHAM YOUNG) — 34
5. JON KONCAK, SMU (vs. MIAMI [OHIO]) — 32

Most total points in the tournament
1. ROOSEVELT CHAPMAN, DAYTON — 105
2. AKEEM OLAJUWON, HOUSTON — 97
3. ALVIN FRANKLIN, HOUSTON — 81
4. MICHAEL YOUNG, HOUSTON — 79
5. 2 tied for fifth place.

Highest scoring average (minimum 2 games)
1. KEVIN MULLIN, PRINCETON (56-2) — 28.00
2. ROOSEVELT CHAPMAN, DAYTON (105-4) — 26.25
3. REGGIE LEWIS, NORTHEASTERN (52-2) — 26.00
4. DEVIN DURRANT, BRIGHAM YOUNG (51-2) 25.50
5. 2 tied for fifth place.

FIELD GOALS

Most field goals in a single game
1. REGGIE LEWIS, NORTHEASTERN (vs. VA. COMMONWEALTH) — 15
2. MCKINLEY SINGLETON, ALA.-BIRMINGHAM (vs. BRIGHAM YOUNG) — 14
2. AKEEM OLAJUWON, HOUSTON (vs. WAKE FOREST) — 14
4. 3 tied for fourth place.

Most total field goals in the tournament
1. AKEEM OLAJUWON, HOUSTON — 39
2. ROOSEVELT CHAPMAN, DAYTON — 35
3. MICHAEL YOUNG, HOUSTON — 34
4. JOHN NEWMAN, RICHMOND — 31
5. 3 tied for fifth place.

Most field goal attempts in a single game
1. BROWN, LIU (vs. NORTHEASTERN) — 25
1. MARK ACRES, ORAL ROBERTS (vs. MEMPHIS STATE) — 25
1. WAYMON TISDALE, OKLAHOMA (vs. DAYTON) 25

4. TERENCE STANSBURY, TEMPLE (vs. N. CAROLINA) — 24
5. 2 tied for fifth place.

Most total field goal attempts in tournament
1. MICHAEL YOUNG, HOUSTON — 89
2. ROOSEVELT CHAPMAN, DAYTON — 59
3. JOHN NEWMAN, RICHMOND — 58
4. AKEEM OLAJUWON, HOUSTON — 56
5. 2 tied for fifth place.

Highest field goal percentage in a single game (minimum 10 attempts)
1. DWAYNE MCCLAIN, VILLANOVA (vs. MARSHALL) (10-11) — .909
2. REGGIE LEWIS, NORTHEASTERN (vs. VA. COMMONWEALTH) (15-17) — .882
3. AKEEM OLAJUWON, HOUSTON (vs. WAKE FOREST) (14-16) — .875
4. KELVIN JOHNSON, RICHMOND (vs. INDIANA) (12-14) — .857
5. 2 tied for fifth place.

Highest field goal percentage in the tournament (minimum 20 attempts)
1. REGGIE LEWIS, NORTHEASTERN (23-30) — .767
2. KELVIN JOHNSON, RICHMOND (29-38) — .763
3. KEVIN MULLIN, PRINCETON (19-27) — .704
4. AKEEM OLAJUWON, HOUSTON (39-56) — .696
5. 2 tied for fifth place.

FREE THROWS

Most free throws in a single game
1. ROOSEVELT CHAPMAN, DAYTON (vs. OKLAHOMA) — 15
2. KEVIN MULLIN, PRINCETON (vs. SAN DIEGO) 14
3. MICHAEL JACKSON, GEORGETOWN (vs. UNLV) — 12
3. WAYMON TISDALE, OKLAHOMA (vs. DAYTON) 12
5. ALVIN FRANKLIN, HOUSTON (vs. LOUISIANA TECH) — 11

Most total free throws in the tournament
1. ROOSEVELT CHAPMAN, DAYTON — 35
2. ALVIN FRANKLIN, HOUSTON — 33
3. MICHAEL JACKSON, GEORGETOWN — 24

4. STEVE ALFORD, INDIANA — 21
5. AKEEM OLAJUWON, HOUSTON — 19

Most free throws attempted in a single game
1. ROOSEVELT CHAPMAN, DAYTON (vs. OKLAHOMA) — 19
2. KEVIN MULLIN, PRINCETON (vs. SAN DIEGO) 16
3. AKEEM OLAJUWON, HOUSTON (vs. MEMPHIS STATE) — 15
4. ANTHONY TEACHEY, WAKE FOREST (vs. DEPAUL) — 14
5. 3 tied for fifth place.

Most free throws attempted in the tournament
1. ROOSEVELT CHAPMAN, DAYTON — 45
2. AKEEM OLAJUWON, HOUSTON — 39
3. ALVIN FRANKLIN, HOUSTON — 38
4. MICHAEL JACKSON, GEORGETOWN — 28
5. OLDEN POLYNICE, VIRGINIA — 25

Highest free throw percentage in a single game (minimum 7 attempts)
1. MICHAEL JACKSON, GEORGETOWN (vs. UNLV) (12-12) — 1.000
1. WAYMON TISDALE, OKLAHOMA (vs. DAYTON) (12-12) — 1.000
3. STEVE ALFORD, INDIANA (vs. RICHMOND) (10-10) — 1.000
4. ROOSEVELT CHAPMAN, DAYTON (vs. LOUISIANA ST.) (9-9) — 1.000
5. 2 tied for fifth place.

Highest free throw percentage in the tournament (minimum 15 attempts)
1. STEVE ALFORD, INDIANA (21-22) — .955
2. KEVIN MULLIN, PRINCETON (18-20) — .900
3. SAM BOWIE, KENTUCKY (15-17) — .882
4. SAM PERKINS, N. CAROLINA (14-16) — .875
4. KARL MALONE, LOUISIANA TECH (14-16) — .875

REBOUNDS

Most rebounds in a single game
1. MARK ACRES, ORAL ROBERTS (vs. MEMPHIS STATE) — 18
2. CHARLES BARKLEY, AUBURN (vs. RICHMOND) — 17
3. KENNY GREEN, WAKE FOREST (vs. HOUSTON) 16

| 3 | KEITH LEE, MEMPHIS STATE (vs. PURDUE) | 16 |
| 5 | 2 tied for fifth place. | |

Most total rebounds in the tournament

1	AKEEM OLAJUWON, HOUSTON	57
2	PAT EWING, GEORGETOWN	47
3	SAM BOWIE, KENTUCKY	43
4	RICKY WINSLOW, HOUSTON	41
5	KENTON EDELIN, VIRGINIA	39

Most rebounds per game (minimum 2 games)

1	KEITH LEE, MEMPHIS STATE (37-3)	12.33
2	ED PINCKNEY, VILLANOVA (24-2)	12.00
3	SAM PERKINS, N. CAROLINA (23-2)	11.50
3	BRETT APPLEGATE, BRIGHAM YOUNG (23-2)	11.50
5	AKEEM OLAJUWON, HOUSTON (57-5)	11.40

ASSISTS

Most assists in a single game

1	DICKEY BEAL, KENTUCKY (vs. BRIGHAM YOUNG)	14
1	CARL WRIGHT, SMU (vs. MIAMI [OHIO])	14
3	VAUGHN, WASHINGTON (vs. DUKE)	12
4	BRUCE DOUGLAS, ILLINOIS (vs. KENTUCKY)	11
5	2 tied for fifth place.	

Most total assists in the tournament

| 1 | REID GETTYS, HOUSTON | 36 |
| 2 | DICKEY BEAL, KENTUCKY | 33 |

3	BRUCE DOUGLAS, ILLINOIS	27
4	GREG BECKWITH, RICHMOND	26
5	ALVIN FRANKLIN, HOUSTON	25

Most assists per game (minimum 2 appearances)

1	CARL WRIGHT, SMU (19-2)	9.50
2	BRUCE DOUGLAS, ILLINOIS (27-3)	9.00
3	GREG BECKWITH, RICHMOND (26-3)	8.67
4	MARK TURGEON, KANSAS (17-2)	8.50
4	KEITH GATLIN, MARYLAND (17-2)	8.50

TURNOVERS

Most turnovers in a single game

1	JOHNNY DAWKINS, DUKE (vs. WASHINGTON)	8
1	AKEEM OLAJUWON, HOUSTON (vs. VIRGINIA)	8
1	ANDRE TURNER, MEMPHIS STATE (vs. PURDUE)	8
1	BRUCE DOUGLAS, ILLINOIS (vs. VILLANOVA)	8
1	ROOSEVELT CHAPMAN, DAYTON (vs. LOUISIANA ST.)	8

Most total turnovers in the tournament

1	ROOSEVELT CHAPMAN, DAYTON	22
2	DICKEY BEAL, KENTUCKY	20
3	OTHELL WILSON, VIRGINIA	19
4	ANDRE TURNER, MEMPHIS STATE	18
4	AKEEM OLAJUWON, HOUSTON	18

SHOTS BLOCKED

Most shots blocked in a single game

1	JON KONCAK, SMU (vs. MIAMI [OHIO])	7
2	PAT EWING, GEORGETOWN (vs. UNLV)	6
2	KEITH LEE, MEMPHIS STATE (vs. HOUSTON)	6
4	WILLIAM BEDFORD, MEMPHIS STATE (vs. ORAL ROBERTS)	5
4	AKEEM OLAJUWON, HOUSTON (vs. VIRGINIA)	5

Most total shots blocked in the tournament

1	AKEEM OLAJUWON, HOUSTON	18
2	PAT EWING, GEORGETOWN	15
3	KEITH LEE, MEMPHIS STATE	10
4	WILLIAM BEDFORD, MEMPHIS STATE	9
5	JON KONCAK, SMU	8

STEALS

Most steals in a single game

1	ALVIN ROBERTSON, ARKANSAS (vs. VIRGINIA)	8
2	DICKEY BEAL, KENTUCKY (vs. LOUISVILLE)	6
2	RORY GRIMES, IONA (vs. VIRGINIA)	6
4	EDDIE ARCHIE, ALCORN ST. (vs. KANSAS)	5
5	10 tied for fifth place.	

Most total steals in the tournament

1	DICKEY BEAL, KENTUCKY	12
2	OTHELL WILSON, VIRGINIA	11
3	CHARLES JONES, LOUISVILLE	9
4	ALVIN ROBERTSON, ARKANSAS	8
5	6 tied for fifth place.	

✪ TEAM RECORDS ✪

SCORING

Most points in a single game

1	MARYLAND (vs. WEST VIRGINIA)	102
2	KENTUCKY (vs. BRIGHAM YOUNG)	93
3	MEMPHIS STATE (vs. ORAL ROBERTS)	92

Most total points in the tournament

1	HOUSTON	347
2	GEORGETOWN	297
3	DAYTON	276

Highest scoring average (minimum 2 games)

1	MARYLAND (172-2)	86.00
2	NORTHEASTERN (159-2)	79.50
3	MEMPHIS STATE (229-3)	76.33

FIELD GOALS

Most field goals in a single game

1	LIU (vs. NORTHEASTERN)	39
2	ORAL ROBERTS (vs. MEMPHIS STATE)	37
3	RICHMOND (vs. RIDER)	36
3	MEMPHIS STATE (vs. ORAL ROBERTS)	36
3	MARYLAND (vs. WEST VIRGINIA)	36

Most total field goals in the tournament

1	HOUSTON	134
2	GEORGETOWN	118
3	VIRGINIA	111

Most field goals attempted in a single game

1	LIU (vs. NORTHEASTERN)	87
2	ORAL ROBERTS (vs. MEMPHIS STATE)	86
3	2 tied for third place.	

Most total field goals attempted in the tournament

1	HOUSTON	267
2	GEORGETOWN	244
3	VIRGINIA	224

Highest field goal percentage in a single game

1	NORTHEASTERN (vs. VA COMMONWEALTH) (33-44)	.750
2	VILLANOVA (vs. MARSHALL) (30-42)	.714
3	WASHINGTON (vs. DUKE) (31-44)	.705

Highest field goal percentage in a tournament (minimum 2 games)

1	NORTHEASTERN (64-98)	.653
2	MARYLAND (66-116)	.569
3	INDIANA (74-135)	.548

FREE THROWS

Most free throws in a single game

1	SYRACUSE (vs. VA. COMMONWEALTH)	30
1	MARYLAND (vs. WEST VIRGINIA)	30
3	2 tied for third place.	

Most total free throws in the tournament

1	HOUSTON	79
2	DAYTON	76
3	KENTUCKY	65

Most free throws attempted in a single game

| 1 | SMU (vs. MIAMI [OHIO]) | 37 |
| 2 | 5 tied for second place. | |

Most total free throws attempted in the tournament

1	HOUSTON	125
2	DAYTON	106
3	GEORGETOWN	96

Highest free throw percentage in a single game

1	INDIANA (vs. VIRGINIA) (6-6)	1.000
2	ALABAMA (vs. ILLINOIS STATE) (2-2)	1.000
3	MOREHEAD STATE (vs. LOUISVILLE) (9-10)	.900

Highest free throw percentage in the tournament (minimum 2 games)

1	PRINCETON (39-46)	.848
2	SYRACUSE (39-48)	.813
3	WEST VIRGINIA (23-29)	.793

Fewest free throws in a single game

1	ILLINOIS STATE (vs. ALABAMA)	1
1	KANSAS (vs. WAKE FOREST)	1
3	ALABAMA (vs. ILLINOIS STATE)	2

Lowest free throw percentage in a single game

1	WASHINGTON (vs. DAYTON) (4-13)	.308
2	GEORGETOWN (vs. SMU) (3-9)	.333
2	NORTHEASTERN (vs. VA. COMMONWEALTH) (3-9)	.333

Lowest free throw percentage in the tournament (minimum 2 games)

1	KANSAS (10-19)	.526
2	VIRGINIA (49-87)	.563
3	TEMPLE (13-23)	.565

REBOUNDS

Most rebounds in a single game

1	MEMPHIS STATE (vs. PURDUE)	48
2	RICHMOND (vs. RIDER)	45
2	OKLAHOMA (vs. DAYTON)	45

Most rebounds per game (minimum 2 games)
1	MEMPHIS STATE(120-3)	40.00
2	N. CAROLINA (76-2)	38.00
3	DEPAUL (73-2)	36.50

ASSISTS

Most assists in a single game
1	RICHMOND (vs. RIDER)	27
2	SMU (vs. MIAMI [OHIO])	24
3	KANSAS (vs. WAKE FOREST)	23

Most assists per game (minimum 2 games)
1	MARYLAND (40-2)	20.00
2	VA. COMMONWEALTH (39-2)	19.50
3	RICHMOND (58-3)	19.33

TURNOVERS

Most turnovers in a single game
1	4 tied for first place.

Most turnovers per game (minimum 2 games)
1	BRIGHAM YOUNG (42-2)	21.00
2	VILLANOVA (40-2)	20.00
3	NORTHEASTERN (38-2)	19.00

SHOTS BLOCKED

Most shots blocked in a single game
1	MEMPHIS STATE (vs. HOUSTON)	10
1	N. CAROLINA (vs. TEMPLE)	10
3	2 tied for third place.	

Most shots blocked per game (minimum 2 games)
1	MEMPHIS STATE (20-3)	6.67
2	N. CAROLINA (12-2)	6.00
3	HOUSTON (25-5)	5.00

STEALS

Most steals in a single game
1	ARKANSAS (vs. VIRGINIA)	13
2	TULSA (vs. LOUISVILLE)	12
3	2 tied for third place.	

Most steals per game
1	SYRACUSE (18-2)	9.00
2	TEMPLE (17-2)	8.50
3	VILLANOVA (16-2)	8.00

1985

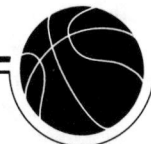

WEST

FIRST ROUND
- 1 St. John's 83 — 16 Southern-B.R. 59
- 8 Iowa 54 — 9 Arkansas 63
- 5 Washington 58 — 12 Kentucky 66
- 4 UNLV 85 — 13 San Diego St. 80
- 6 Tulsa 75 — 11 UTEP 79
- 3 N.C. State 65 — 14 Nevada-Reno 56
- 7 Alabama 50 — 10 Arizona 41
- 2 Va. Commonwealth 81 — 15 Marshall 65

SECOND ROUND
- St. John's 68 — Arkansas 65
- Kentucky 64 — UNLV 61
- UTEP 73 — N.C. State 86
- Alabama 63 — Va. Commonwealth 59

REGIONAL SEMIFINAL
- St. John's 86 — Kentucky 70
- N.C. State 61 — Alabama 55

REGIONAL FINAL
- St. John's 69 — N.C. State 60

EAST

FIRST ROUND
- 1 Georgetown 68 — 16 Lehigh 43
- 8 Temple 60 — 9 Virginia Tech 57
- 5 SMU 85 — 12 Old Dominion 68
- 4 Loyola-Chicago 59 — 16 Iona 58
- 6 *Georgia 67 — 11 Wichita St. 59
- 3 Illinois 76 — 14 Northeastern 57
- 7 Syracuse 70 — 10 DePaul 65
- 2 Georgia Tech 65 — 15 Mercer 58

SECOND ROUND
- Georgetown 63 — Temple 46
- SMU 57 — Loyola-Chicago 70
- *Georgia 58 — Illinois 74
- Syracuse 53 — Georgia Tech 70

REGIONAL SEMIFINAL
- Georgetown 65 — Loyola-Chicago 53
- Illinois 53 — Georgia Tech 61

REGIONAL FINAL
- Georgetown 60 — Georgia Tech 54

FINAL FOUR
- St. John's 59 — Georgetown 77
- *Memphis St. 45 — Villanova 52
- Villanova 66 — Georgetown 64

MIDWEST

FIRST ROUND
- 1 Oklahoma 96 — 16 N.C. A&T 83
- 8 USC 55 — 9 Illinois St. 58
- 5 Louisiana Tech 78 — 12 Pittsburgh 54
- 4 Ohio St. 75 — 12 Iowa St. 64
- 6 Texas Tech 53 — 11 Boston College 55
- 3 Duke 75 — 14 Pepperdine 62
- 7 Ala.-Birmingham 70 — 10 Michigan St. 68
- 2 *Memphis St. 67 — 15 Pennsylvania 55

SECOND ROUND
- Oklahoma 75 — Illinois St. 69
- Louisiana Tech 79 — Ohio St. 67
- Boston College 74 — Duke 73
- Ala.-Birmingham 66 — *Memphis St. 67 (2 ot)

REGIONAL SEMIFINAL
- Oklahoma 86 (ot) — Louisiana Tech 84
- Boston College 57 — *Memphis St. 59

REGIONAL FINAL
- Oklahoma 61 — *Memphis St. 63

SOUTHEAST

FIRST ROUND
- 1 Michigan 59 — 16 F. Dickinson 55
- 8 Villanova 51 — 9 Dayton 49
- 6 Maryland 69 (ot) — 12 Miami (Ohio) 68
- 4 Louisiana St. 55 — 13 Navy 78
- 6 Purdue 58 — 11 Auburn 59
- 3 Kansas 49 — 14 Ohio 38
- 7 Notre Dame 79 — 10 Oregon St. 70
- 2 N. Carolina 76 — 15 Middle Tenn. St. 57

SECOND ROUND
- Michigan 55 — Villanova 59
- Maryland 64 — Navy 59
- Auburn 66 — Kansas 64
- Notre Dame 58 — N. Carolina 60

REGIONAL SEMIFINAL
- Villanova 46 — Maryland 43
- Auburn 56 — N. Carolina 62

REGIONAL FINAL
- Villanova 56 — N. Carolina 44

*Georgia's and Memphis State's participation in 1985 tournament vacated.

1985 was the year the tournament expanded to 64 teams, evening the brackets and giving small, underdog schools—like Marist, Montana State, Lehigh, Mississippi Valley, and Fairleigh Dickinson—a chance to get into the game. And although every fifteenth and sixteenth seed lost, and some even got blown out, the little guys proved that they put on their sneakers the same way that the big boys did. In fact Michigan, the nation's second-ranked team, barely survived Fairleigh Dickinson when four of the Jersey school's starters fouled out.

The bigger field also opened up the tourney to more major conference also-rans, like the SEC's 16-12 Kentucky and a total of six Big East, six Big Ten, and five ACC schools. Some of them proved they belonged too.

Early in the week of the Final Four a new scandal hit college basketball, as the New Orleans district attorney accused three Tulane players of shaving points. (Tulane would subsequently suspend its basketball program until the 1989–1990 campaign.)

It was the last year the tournament would be held without the 45-second shot clock.

And it was the year of THE GAME.

It all led up to this: On the one side, Mighty Georgetown. Under coach John Thompson the Hoyas had become a perennial national power (this was their fourth final-eight finish in six years). They were the 1984 national champs, the 1982 runners-up. Led by the awesome Patrick Ewing, they were one year older, one year more experienced, and, most everybody believed, one year better than the previous year's championship team.

Georgetown led the nation in holding their opponents to 39.9 percent field goal shooting, and in rebounding with a 9.2 per-game edge over their opponents. They lost only two games all year and, holding Chris Mullin to single digits for the first time in 101 games, dismantled a strong St. John's team 77-59 in the semis. The expert consensus was that they were one of the best college teams ever. St. John's coach Lou Carnesecca put them up with "the great San Francisco teams with Bill Russell and K. C. Jones, the overall physical strength of that great Kentucky team of Robey and Phillips and Macy, the structured play of the Indiana teams, and the great UCLA teams with Jabbar and Walton." Besides Ewing, NBA director of scouting Marty Blake felt the Hoyas had four other sure blue-chip players (first- or early second-round NBA draft picks): forward Billy Martin, point guard Michael Jackson, and swingmen David Wingate and Reggie Williams. And besides, they had defeated Villanova twice during the regular season.

On the other side were the Wildcats of Villanova. They went into the tournament with a 19-10 record (nine and seven in Big East competition) and were seeded eighth in the Southeast regional. They had only one likely NBA first-round draft, 6-9 center Ed Pinckney. And Villanova coach Rollie Massimino had never before led a team past the round of eight.

A mismatch. Except nobody told Villanova. Led by Pinckney and his fellow seniors Gary McLain and forward Dwayne McClain, Villanova's matchup zone defense had confused and demoralized opponents throughout the competition; no one had scored more than 55 points against them in the five rounds leading up to the final. And they were patient; although the 45-second clock had been instituted for regular-season play during the 1984–1985 campaign, it was not in use during the tournament, and the Wildcats worked the ball around endlessly, or at least until they could get a good shot opportunity (they averaged only about 40 shots per game, far fewer than most teams). The Memphis State crowd in the semis had chanted "Boring! Boring!" but their players were lulled into mistakes that brought Villanova still another upset of a highly rated team. (The Wildcats hadn't been ranked in the top twenty all year, but along the way to the title game they beat three of the top seven ranked teams in the country.)

The Villanova strategy against No. 1 Georgetown was much the same as it had been all tournament: Take the air out of the ball, work it around the perimeter and wait for an opening, and play tough defense. "We're in the final game," said Gary McLain. "We're ready to play our hearts out."

The Hoyas, with their pressure defense keying an explosive offense, had broken the hearts of most of their opponents all season. And when Reggie Williams hit three straight halfway through the first half, Georgetown, with an 18-12 lead, threatened to break the game wide open. But the Wildcats fought back, remaining patient, and finally tied the score at 20. In the last minutes of the half, Ewing, who had been unable to shake himself free from Villanova's sagging defense, slammed home a monster dunk and two alley-oops. Georgetown turned up the pressure, trapping all over the court. But the Wildcats never lost their composure; McLain slowed the pace, and his team answered each of Ewing's dunks with two points of their own. The half ended with the score 29-28 Villanova.

The lead changed hands nine times in the second half. Pinckney scored six in an 8-2 Wildcat surge to give them a 53-48 lead with 6:02 left. But when David Wingate hit a jumper a minute and a quarter later, the Hoyas were back in the lead.

Villanova dug a little bit deeper. They refused to lose their composure. After a Pinckney turnover and a Georgetown error, substitute guard Harold Jensen hit an 18-footer, redeeming himself from two turnovers he had committed during Georgetown's last spurt. Pinckney stole the ball for two more, and when David Wingate rushed a shot from the corner, Villanova got the ball again. They spread the floor, forcing Georgetown to come out and get the ball. But the ball, the lead, and the national championship all evaded the Hoyas.

Villanova had played the perfect game and pulled off one of the greatest upsets in basketball history. Against the most ferocious team defense in the country, they shot 22 of 28 from the floor—almost 79 percent—including an incredible 9 of 10 in the second half. It was a fiercely competitive game and one that reflected the best in college basketball, from the family feeling and togetherness of Rollie Massimino's team to the dignity and decorum of Georgetown's disappointed warriors.

As the Villanova players walked to the podium to be honored as national champions, the Hoyas stood and applauded. Big East Commissioner Dave Gavitt, who had seen three of his conference teams in the Final Four, was moved to say of John Thompson and his players: "They taught college basketball how to win this season. Tonight they taught college basketball how to lose."

FIRST ROUND WEST

St. John's (83)   Coach: Lou Carnesecca

	Min.	Total FG/FGA	Pct.	FT/FTA	Pct.	Reb. O/T	A	TO	PF	S	Blk	TP	PPM
BERRY, W.	34	9/17	.529	6/7	.857	-/13	1	3	2	0	0	24	.706
GLASS, W.	27	1/2	.500	2/2	1.000	-/6	2	0	1	0	1	4	.148
WENNINGTON, B.	36	10/12	.833	3/5	.600	-/8	5	0	3	1	1	23	.639
MULLIN, C.	36	7/12	.583	7/10	.700	-/4	6	7	2	3	0	21	.583
MOSES, M.	23	0/2	.000	3/5	.600	-/0	3	3	3	2	1	3	.130
BROSS, T.	1	1/1	1.000	0/0	.000	-/0	0	0	1	0	0	2	2.000
ROWAN, R.	3	0/0	.000	0/0	.000	-/0	0	0	0	0	0	0	.000
JACKSON, M.	17	1/4	.250	2/2	1.000	-/3	2	1	2	2	0	4	.235
JONES, S.	7	1/1	1.000	0/0	.000	-/3	0	2	2	0	0	2	.286
STEWART, R.	15	0/0	.000	0/1	.000	-/0	0	1	2	1	0	0	.000
SHURINA, S.	1	0/0	.000	0/0	.000	-/0	0	0	0	0	0	0	.000
Totals	200	30/51	.588	23/32	.719	-/37	19	17	18	9	3	83	.415

Southern-B.R. (59)   Coach: Robert Hopkins

	Min.	Total FG/FGA	Pct.	FT/FTA	Pct.	Reb. O/T	A	TO	PF	S	Blk	TP	PPM
STAVES	13	0/2	.000	0/0	.000	-/3	0	1	5	0	0	0	.000
LEE	32	5/14	.357	0/0	.000	-/5	0	2	4	2	0	10	.313
HOSKINS	39	6/12	.500	5/6	.833	-/5	0	2	4	1	0	17	.436
GABRIEL	39	5/13	.385	3/3	1.000	-/2	4	2	3	2	0	13	.333
DEDMON	39	4/10	.400	4/5	.800	-/5	5	5	2	2	1	12	.308
FAULKNER, J.	21	2/4	.500	1/4	.250	-/2	1	2	3	0	0	5	.238
PONTON	6	0/0	.000	0/3	.000	-/0	0	0	0	1	0	0	.000
KELLY	1	0/1	.000	0/0	.000	-/0	0	0	0	0	0	0	.000
LEGARD	1	1/1	1.000	0/0	.000	-/1	0	0	0	1	0	2	2.000
JOHNSON	1	0/0	.000	0/0	.000	-/0	0	0	0	0	0	0	.000
FAULKNER, J.	1	0/1	.000	0/0	.000	-/0	0	0	1	0	0	0	.000
BRIDGES	7	0/2	.000	0/0	.000	-/0	0	1	1	0	0	0	.000
Totals	200	23/60	.383	13/21	.619	-/23	10	14	22	9	1	59	.295

Team Rebounds: St. John's 2; Southern-B.R. 4. Disqualified: Southern-B.R.—Staves. Technical fouls: None.

	1st Half	2nd Half	Final
St. John's	34	49	83
Southern-B.R.	18	41	59

Iowa (54)   Coach: George Raveling

	Min.	Total FG/FGA	Pct.	FT/FTA	Pct.	Reb. O/T	A	TO	PF	S	Blk	TP	PPM
PAYNE, M.	33	1/4	.250	0/0	.000	-/4	1	-	2	-	-	2	.061
LORENZEN, A.	21	1/3	.333	0/2	.000	-/3	0	-	3	-	-	2	.095
STOKES	32	6/12	.500	2/2	1.000	-/8	2	-	5	-	-	14	.438
BABKS	35	3/8	.375	0/1	.000	-/5	6	-	3	-	-	6	.171
BERKENPAS, T.	31	8/17	.471	0/1	.000	-/2	2	-	3	-	-	16	.516
WRIGHT	25	5/7	.714	4/7	.571	-/5	2	-	3	-	-	14	.560
REAVES, M.	8	0/2	.000	0/0	.000	-/0	1	-	1	-	-	0	.000
JONES, B.	3	0/1	.000	0/2	.000	-/1	1	-	2	-	-	0	.000
MOE	7	0/2	.000	0/0	.000	-/0	2	-	0	-	-	0	.000
MORGAN, M.	1	0/1	.000	0/0	.000	-/0	0	-	0	-	-	0	.000
SNEDEKER	3	0/0	.000	0/0	.000	-/1	0	-	1	-	-	0	.000
HILL, K.	1	0/0	.000	0/0	.000	-/0	1	-	1	-	-	0	.000
Totals	200	24/57	.421	6/15	.400	-/29	18	16	24	-	-	54	.270

Arkansas (63)   Coach: Eddie Sutton

	Min.	Total FG/FGA	Pct.	FT/FTA	Pct.	Reb. O/T	A	TO	PF	S	Blk	TP	PPM
MILLS, W.	27	2/6	.333	6/8	.750	-/3	5	-	4	-	-	10	.370
BALENTINE, C.	39	6/7	.857	2/2	1.000	-/8	3	-	4	-	-	14	.359
KLEINE, J.	38	10/17	.588	5/8	.625	-/14	0	-	3	-	-	25	.658
HUTCHINSON, K.	30	0/3	.000	4/7	.571	-/3	5	-	3	-	-	4	.133
FREEMAN	28	3/5	.600	0/0	.000	1/4	2	-	0	-	-	6	.214
REHL	6	1/2	.500	0/0	.000	-/0	1	-	2	-	-	2	.333
IRVIN, B.	14	1/6	.167	0/0	.000	-/1	0	-	0	-	-	2	.143
MOORE	9	0/0	.000	0/0	.000	-/1	0	-	0	-	-	0	.000
LANG	8	0/0	.000	0/2	.000	-/0	0	-	2	-	-	0	.000
POERSCHKE, E.	1	0/0	.000	0/0	.000	-/0	0	-	0	-	-	0	.000
Totals	200	23/46	.500	17/27	.630	-/34	16	17	18	-	-	63	.315

Disqualified: Iowa—Stokes. Technical fouls: None.

	1st Half	2nd Half	Final
Iowa	33	21	54
Arkansas	26	37	63

Washington (58)   Coach: Marv Harshman

	Min.	Total FG/FGA	Pct.	FT/FTA	Pct.	Reb. O/T	A	TO	PF	S	Blk	TP	PPM
SCHREMPF, D.	40	7/11	.636	2/5	.400	-/7	5	8	4	0	1	16	.400
FORTIER, P.	36	7/14	.500	2/8	.250	-/6	4	0	4	1	0	16	.444
WELP, C.	34	4/11	.364	2/2	1.000	-/9	0	0	4	0	3	10	.294
DAMON, C.	24	2/5	.400	0/0	.000	-/2	4	2	5	0	0	4	.167
WILLIAMS, S.	35	4/8	.500	0/0	.000	-/7	0	3	3	1	0	8	.229
WILSON, D.	1	0/0	.000	0/0	.000	-/0	0	0	0	0	0	0	.000
VIDATO, K.	7	1/2	.500	0/0	.000	-/1	1	0	1	0	0	2	.286
MORRELL, T.	17	0/2	.000	0/1	.000	-/1	1	2	4	2	1	0	.000
ROGERS, R.	5	1/2	.500	0/0	.000	-/0	0	0	2	1	1	2	.400
TAYLOR, J.	1	0/0	.000	0/0	.000	-/0	0	0	1	0	0	0	.000
Totals	200	26/55	.473	6/16	.375	-/33	15	15	28	5	6	58	.290

Kentucky (66)   Coach: Joe Hall

	Min.	Total FG/FGA	Pct.	FT/FTA	Pct.	Reb. O/T	A	TO	PF	S	Blk	TP	PPM
BENNETT, W.	-	1/5	.200	1/2	.500	-/2	2	2	2	0	0	3	-
WALKER, K.	-	8/15	.533	13/15	.867	-/10	1	1	3	0	0	29	-
BEARUP, B.	-	1/5	.200	5/6	.833	-/6	2	1	5	0	0	7	-
DAVENDER, E.	-	2/8	.250	5/7	.714	-/4	3	3	1	3	0	9	-
HARDEN, R.	-	1/5	.200	2/4	.500	-/3	4	2	2	4	0	4	-
BLACKMON, J.	-	1/3	.333	0/2	.000	-/3	0	1	3	0	0	2	-
MADISON, R.	-	3/3	1.000	4/4	1.000	-/3	0	1	1	0	1	10	-
LOCK, R.	-	0/0	.000	0/0	.000	-/3	0	1	0	0	1	0	-
JENKINS, C.	-	0/2	.000	0/0	.000	-/2	0	0	2	0	0	0	-
MCKINLEY, T.	-	1/1	1.000	0/0	.000	-/0	0	0	0	0	0	2	-
Totals	200	18/47	.383	30/40	.750	-/36	12	11	17	10	2	66	.330

Team Rebounds: Kentucky 1; Washington 2. Disqualified: Kentucky—Bearup; Washington—Damon. Technical fouls: None.

	1st Half	2nd Half	Final
Washington	24	34	58
Kentucky	27	39	66

UNLV (85) — Coach: Jerry Tarkanian

	Min.	Total FG/FGA	Pct.	FT/FTA	Pct.	Reb. O/T	A	TO	PF	S	Blk	TP	PPM
JAMES, F.	27	3/8	.375	4/4	1.000	-/2	4	3	3	1	0	10	.370
GILLIAM, A.	31	7/12	.583	7/12	.583	-/10	2	2	2	2	1	21	.677
ADAMS, R.	23	4/11	.364	2/2	1.000	-/4	0	0	4	2	0	10	.435
JONES, A.	34	9/13	.692	0/1	.000	-/4	4	2	3	1	1	18	.529
BANKS, F.	31	2/7	.286	4/5	.800	-/5	8	4	1	3	0	8	.258
ROBINSON, R.	20	3/7	.429	0/0	.000	-/2	0	1	5	0	1	6	.300
CATCHINGS, E.	15	2/4	.500	4/4	1.000	-/3	1	1	2	0	0	8	.533
GRAHAM, G.	13	1/3	.333	0/0	.000	-/0	3	0	2	0	0	2	.154
HUDSON, E.	6	1/2	.500	0/0	.000	-/1	1	0	2	0	0	2	.333
Totals	200	32/67	.478	21/28	.750	-/31	23	13	24	9	3	85	.425

San Diego State (80) — Coach: Dave Smokey Gaines

	Min.	Total FG/FGA	Pct.	FT/FTA	Pct.	Reb. O/T	A	TO	PF	S	Blk	TP	PPM
KENNEDY	29	5/8	.625	1/3	.333	-/8	0	1	3	0	1	11	.379
MARTENS	28	4/8	.500	3/4	.750	-/2	0	4	4	0	0	11	.393
ALLEN	36	8/10	.800	7/10	.700	-/9	0	0	4	3	4	23	.639
WATSON	33	6/13	.600	1/4	.250	-/3	6	4	5	2	0	19	.576
DORSEY	31	0/3	.000	2/4	.500	-/6	8	4	3	0	0	2	.065
KONEK	20	1/5	.200	3/4	.750	-/3	7	3	4	0	0	5	.250
OWENS	8	2/3	.667	0/0	.000	-/0	0	1	0	1	0	4	.500
ROSS	8	2/4	.500	1/1	1.000	-/3	0	1	1	0	1	5	.625
MURRAY	7	0/0	.000	0/0	.000	-/0	0	0	1	0	0	0	.000
Totals	200	31/56	.554	18/30	.600	-/34	21	18	25	6	6	80	.400

Team Rebounds: UNLV 3; San Diego St. 5. Disqualified: UNLV—Robinson; San Diego St.—Watson. Technical fouls: None.

	1st Half	2nd Half	Final
UNLV	43	42	85
San Diego St.	33	47	80

North Carolina State (65) — Coach: Jim Valvano

	Min.	Total FG/FGA	Pct.	FT/FTA	Pct.	Reb. O/T	A	TO	PF	S	Blk	TP	PPM
MCMILLAN, N.	29	3/5	.600	1/3	.333	-/3	2	4	4	2	1	7	.241
CHARLES, L.	34	8/14	.571	6/7	.857	-/12	0	1	1	1	0	22	.647
MCQUEEN, C.	29	2/3	.667	0/0	.000	-/4	1	2	4	0	1	4	.138
WEBB, A.	39	4/8	.500	3/4	.750	-/0	4	4	3	1	0	11	.282
MYERS, E.	12	2/6	.333	1/1	1.000	-/6	1	2	2	0	0	5	.417
BOLTON, B.	11	3/4	.750	0/0	.000	-/5	0	1	1	0	0	6	.545
CANNON, T.	29	2/11	.182	4/4	1.000	-/1	5	1	0	1	0	8	.276
PIERCE, R.	16	1/4	.250	0/0	.000	-/3	0	2	1	0	2	2	.125
JACKSON, Q.	1	0/1	.000	0/0	.000	-/0	0	0	0	0	0	0	.000
Totals	200	25/56	.446	15/19	.789	-/34	13	17	16	5	4	65	.325

Nevada-Reno (56) — Coach: Sonny Allen

	Min.	Total FG/FGA	Pct.	FT/FTA	Pct.	Reb. O/T	A	TO	PF	S	Blk	TP	PPM
RANDALL, D.	36	6/13	.462	2/2	1.000	-/9	0	2	3	4	0	14	.389
SOMMERS, T.	32	6/10	.600	1/3	.333	-/6	1	2	4	2	0	13	.406
STEPHENS, Q.	20	0/1	.000	0/4	.000	-/3	0	0	2	0	1	0	.000
HARDEN, R.	36	6/12	.500	0/0	.000	-/1	4	4	3	0	0	12	.333
HIGH, C.	34	6/12	.500	2/2	1.000	-/3	1	4	5	3	0	14	.412
PORTER, E.	21	0/1	.000	1/2	.500	-/3	0	0	0	0	0	1	.048
RONZONE, T.	9	0/1	.000	0/0	.000	-/1	0	3	1	0	0	0	.000
JUBY, M.	1	0/0	.000	0/0	.000	-/0	0	0	0	0	0	0	.000
PARILLO, M.	11	1/5	.200	0/0	.000	-/1	0	1	1	0	0	2	.182
Totals	200	25/55	.455	6/13	.462	-/27	6	16	19	9	1	56	.280

Team Rebounds: N.C. State 2; Nevada-Reno 7. Disqualified: Nevada-Reno—High. Technical fouls: None.

	1st Half	2nd Half	Final
N.C. State	38	27	65
Nevada-Reno	29	27	56

Tulsa (75) — Coach: Nolan Richardson

	Min.	Total FG/FGA	Pct.	FT/FTA	Pct.	Reb. O/T	A	TO	PF	S	Blk	TP	PPM
WILLIAMS, V.	22	3/3	1.000	2/3	.667	-/2	0	1	5	0	0	8	.364
JOHNSON, H.	39	4/12	.333	2/3	.667	-/8	2	2	3	0	0	10	.256
FOBBS, A.	12	0/0	.000	0/1	.000	-/2	0	0	4	0	0	0	.000
HARRIS, S.	39	12/22	.545	7/8	.875	-/5	2	4	5	2	0	31	.795
BOUDREAUX, B.	22	2/5	.400	0/0	.000	-/0	2	1	3	0	0	4	.182
SUGGE, H.	2	0/0	.000	0/0	.000	-/0	0	0	2	1	0	0	.000
MOSS, D.	31	5/9	.556	2/2	1.000	-/6	0	0	4	1	0	12	.387
RAHILLY, J.	3	0/1	.000	0/0	.000	-/0	1	0	0	0	0	0	.000
MCKINNEY, C.	7	0/1	.000	0/0	.000	-/0	0	1	1	0	0	0	.000
MOORE, T.	19	3/6	.500	4/4	1.000	-/1	1	4	4	0	0	10	.526
LANGFORD, C.	4	0/0	.000	0/0	.000	-/1	0	1	3	0	0	0	.000
Totals	200	29/59	.492	17/21	.810	-/25	8	14	34	4	0	75	.375

UTEP (79) — Coach: Don Haskins

	Min.	Total FG/FGA	Pct.	FT/FTA	Pct.	Reb. O/T	A	TO	PF	S	Blk	TP	PPM
SMITH, J.	30	4/6	.667	5/6	.833	-/3	2	4	5	0	0	13	.433
HAMILTON, K.	27	0/1	.000	2/5	.400	-/6	1	1	3	0	0	2	.074
FEITL, D.	30	4/11	.364	9/12	.750	-/9	0	2	2	3	0	17	.567
GOODWIN, L.	39	7/13	.538	9/10	.900	-/5	0	1	3	0	0	23	.590
LOCKHART, K.	33	4/8	.500	8/10	.800	-/2	3	5	5	2	0	16	.485
GATES, Q.	16	1/1	1.000	1/2	.500	-/1	0	1	4	0	0	3	.188
JACKSON, J.	12	0/1	.000	5/8	.625	-/1	1	1	1	0	0	5	.417
ALLEN, D.	13	0/1	.000	0/2	.000	-/3	0	0	1	0	0	0	.000
Totals	200	20/42	.476	39/55	.709	-/30	7	15	24	5	0	79	.395

Team Rebounds: UTEP 4; Tulsa 6. Disqualified: UTEP—Smith, Lockhart; Tulsa—Williams, Harris. Technical fouls: None.

	1st Half	2nd Half	Final
Tulsa	32	43	75
UTEP	30	49	79

Alabama (50) — Coach: Wimp Sanderson

	Min.	Total FG/FGA	Pct.	FT/FTA	Pct.	Reb. O/T	A	TO	PF	S	Blk	TP	PPM
JOHNSON, B.	36	5/6	.833	2/4	.500	-/5	2	3	4	0	0	12	.333
MCKEY, D.	27	0/2	.000	0/0	.000	-/3	2	5	1	2	0	0	.000
HURT, B.	38	5/7	.714	4/9	.444	-/6	0	2	4	2	2	14	.368
GOTTFRIED, M.	22	1/3	.333	2/2	1.000	-/2	0	1	1	0	0	4	.182
CONER, T.	38	2/7	.286	6/6	1.000	-/4	5	4	2	0	0	10	.263
FARMER, J.	23	4/7	.571	0/0	.000	-/4	0	2	0	0	0	8	.348
NEAL, D.	16	1/4	.250	0/0	.000	-/3	0	1	2	0	0	2	.125
Totals	200	18/36	.500	14/21	.667	-/27	9	15	18	4	4	50	.250

Arizona (41) — Coach: Lute Olson

	Min.	Total FG/FGA	Pct.	FT/FTA	Pct.	Reb. O/T	A	TO	PF	S	Blk	TP	PPM
SMITH, E.	38	2/11	.182	5/6	.833	-/6	2	2	4	1	1	9	.237
TAYLOR, M.	26	0/5	.000	4/6	.667	-/6	1	5	0	0	0	4	.154
WILLIAMS, P.	40	3/11	.273	4/5	.800	-/7	1	3	4	1	0	10	.250
BRUNKHORST, B.	31	1/7	.143	0/0	.000	-/2	3	2	1	1	0	2	.065
KERR, S.	40	4/8	.500	0/0	.000	-/5	0	2	0	0	0	8	.200
MCMILLAN, C.	25	4/6	.667	0/2	.000	-/1	1	2	4	1	0	8	.320
Totals	200	14/48	.292	13/19	.684	-/27	7	12	18	6	2	41	.205

Team Rebounds: Alabama 5; Arizona 2. Disqualified: Alabama—McKey; Arizona—Taylor. Technical fouls: None.

	1st Half	2nd Half	Final
Alabama	19	31	50
Arizona	17	24	41

Virginia Commonwealth (81)　Coach: J. D. Barnett

	Min.	Total FG/FGA	Pct.	FT/FTA	Pct.	Reb. O/T	A	TO	PF	S	Blk	TP	PPM
BROWN, M.	39	3/ 6	.500	0/ 1	.000	-/ 3	4	0	4	2	0	6	.154
WAKE, N.	15	2/ 3	.667	3/ 4	.750	-/ 3	1	0	4	0	0	7	.467
SCHLEGEL, M.	38	5/10	.500	4/ 7	.571	-/ 6	3	3	3	0	1	14	.368
DUNCAN, C.	36	6/13	.462	7/ 9	.778	-/ 4	5	6	0	2	0	19	.528
LAMB, R.	36	12/17	.706	6/ 7	.857	-/ 4	4	4	3	6	1	30	.833
ALLEN, B.	1	0/ 0	.000	1/ 3	.333	-/ 0	0	0	0	1	0	1	1.000
DICKERSON, R.	20	1/ 3	.333	0/ 0	.000	-/ 3	0	0	2	0	0	2	.100
STINNIE, P.	3	0/ 0	.000	0/ 0	.000	-/ 1	0	1	0	0	0	0	.000
ROBINSON, A.	10	0/ 0	.000	0/ 0	.000	-/ 2	0	2	4	0	1	0	.000
FRANCO, D.	2	0/ 0	.000	2/ 2	1.000	-/ 2	0	0	0	0	0	2	1.000
Totals	200	29/52	.558	23/33	.697	-/28	17	16	20	11	3	81	.405

Marshall (65)　Coach: Ricky Huckabay

	Min.	Total FG/FGA	Pct.	FT/FTA	Pct.	Reb. O/T	A	TO	PF	S	Blk	TP	PPM
GUTHRIE, J.	37	2/ 6	.333	2/ 2	1.000	-/ 5	1	1	4	1	0	6	.162
EPPES, R.	15	4/ 5	.800	2/ 2	1.000	-/ 3	0	1	1	0	0	10	.667
RICHARDSON, J.	25	3/ 8	.375	1/ 2	.500	-/ 4	0	2	4	1	0	7	.280
HENDERSON, S.	33	8/15	.533	3/ 4	.750	-/ 4	3	3	3	1	0	19	.576
MORRIS, B.	10	0/ 2	.000	0/ 0	.000	-/ 1	0	4	0	1	0	0	.000
HULDEN, R.	17	3/ 3	1.000	0/ 2	.000	-/ 6	0	0	2	0	0	6	.353
TAYLOR, K.	7	1/ 4	.250	0/ 0	.000	-/ 1	1	2	1	0	0	2	.286
BATTLE, J.	28	4/12	.333	2/ 2	1.000	-/ 4	4	5	4	2	0	10	.357
AMENDOLA, J.	2	0/ 2	.000	0/ 0	.000	-/ 1	0	0	0	1	0	0	.000
SMITH, M.	2	0/ 0	.000	0/ 0	.000	-/ 0	0	0	0	0	0	0	.000
ROBERTS, J.	8	0/ 0	.000	0/ 0	.000	-/ 1	0	1	2	1	0	0	.000
BRYSON, M.	2	0/ 1	.000	1/ 2	.500	-/ 2	0	1	1	0	0	1	.500
CURRY, T.	14	1/ 4	.250	2/ 3	.667	-/ 1	0	0	4	0	2	4	.286
Totals	200	26/62	.419	13/19	.684	-/33	9	20	26	8	2	65	.325

Team Rebounds: Va. Commonwealth 6; Marshall 5. Disqualified: None. Technical fouls: Marshall—Curry.

	1st Half	2nd Half	Final
Va. Commonwealth	32	49	81
Marshall	23	42	65

FIRST ROUND EAST

Georgetown (68)　Coach: John Thompson

	Min.	Total FG/FGA	Pct.	FT/FTA	Pct.	Reb. O/T	A	TO	PF	S	Blk	TP	PPM
MARTIN, B.	31	3/11	.273	4/ 4	1.000	1/ 7	0	3	1	0	0	10	.323
WILLIAMS, R.	32	7/11	.636	0/ 0	.000	1/ 6	4	0	0	3	1	14	.438
EWING, P.	28	3/ 9	.333	5/ 6	.833	2/ 4	0	4	2	3	6	11	.393
JACKSON, M.	21	4/ 6	.667	2/ 2	1.000	0/ 1	3	4	4	2	0	10	.476
WINGATE, D.	32	6/12	.500	2/ 6	.333	6/ 7	4	1	2	1	1	14	.438
MCDONALD, P.	15	2/ 4	.500	1/ 3	.333	0/ 4	0	2	1	0	0	5	.333
BROADNAX, H.	19	0/ 2	.000	0/ 0	.000	0/ 5	4	0	4	0	0	0	.000
DALTON, R.	8	1/ 2	.500	0/ 0	.000	0/ 2	0	0	1	0	0	2	.250
MATEEN, G.	6	0/ 0	.000	0/ 0	.000	0/ 1	0	0	2	0	0	0	.000
FLOYD, K.	4	0/ 0	.000	0/ 0	.000	0/ 1	1	1	0	0	0	0	.000
HIGHSMITH, R.	3	0/ 0	.000	2/ 4	.500	0/ 0	0	0	0	1	1	2	.667
LOCKHART, T.	1	0/ 0	.000	0/ 0	.000	0/ 0	0	0	0	0	0	0	.000
Totals	200	26/57	.456	16/25	.640	10/38	16	15	17	10	9	68	.340

Lehigh (43)　Coach: Tom Schneider

	Min.	Total FG/FGA	Pct.	FT/FTA	Pct.	Reb. O/T	A	TO	PF	S	Blk	TP	PPM
QUEENAN, D.	35	2/12	.167	9/10	.900	4/ 7	2	0	2	2	0	13	.371
WICKMAN, P.	10	0/ 1	.000	0/ 0	.000	0/ 2	0	5	0	0	0	0	.000
HENDERSON, D.	24	2/ 6	.333	0/ 0	.000	1/ 1	1	3	4	0	0	4	.167
ANDROLEWICZ, M.	20	1/ 6	.167	0/ 0	.000	1/ 2	3	3	0	0	0	2	.100
POLAHA, M.	39	9/17	.529	2/ 2	1.000	0/ 1	1	4	1	0	0	20	.513
RUSSELL, T.	26	0/ 2	.000	0/ 0	.000	0/ 4	1	1	2	0	0	0	.000
GREENE, K.	6	0/ 0	.000	0/ 0	.000	0/ 1	0	3	2	0	0	0	.000
DOWLING, S.	9	0/ 0	.000	0/ 0	.000	0/ 1	1	2	0	0	0	0	.000
DOSWELL, V.	4	0/ 1	.000	0/ 0	.000	0/ 0	0	0	0	0	0	0	.000
CHESLOCK, B.	7	0/ 1	.000	2/ 2	1.000	0/ 1	0	0	0	0	0	2	.286
GREGORY, R.	12	0/ 3	.000	0/ 0	.000	0/ 0	0	1	1	1	0	0	.000
MARTIN, G.	4	0/ 1	.000	2/ 2	1.000	0/ 0	0	0	2	1	0	2	.500
BRONNER, E.	2	0/ 0	.000	0/ 0	.000	0/ 0	0	2	0	0	0	0	.000
MCKAY, V.	1	0/ 0	.000	0/ 0	.000	0/ 0	0	0	1	0	0	0	.000
MCGARVEY, J.	1	0/ 0	.000	0/ 0	.000	0/ 0	0	0	0	0	0	0	.000
Totals	200	14/50	.280	15/16	.938	6/20	8	18	22	4	0	43	.215

Team Rebounds: Georgetown 6; Lehigh 7. Disqualified: Lehigh—Wickman. Technical fouls: None.

	1st Half	2nd Half	Final
Georgetown	39	29	68
Lehigh	11	32	43

Temple (60)　Coach: John Chaney

	Min.	Total FG/FGA	Pct.	FT/FTA	Pct.	Reb. O/T	A	TO	PF	S	Blk	TP	PPM
HALL, G.	38	8/14	.571	6/12	.500	4/13	1	2	4	1	2	22	.579
RAYNE, C.	40	3/ 9	.333	6/ 8	.750	4/10	3	4	2	1	0	12	.300
PERRY, T.	11	0/ 0	.000	0/ 0	.000	1/ 1	0	0	2	1	2	0	.000
BLACKWELL, N.	40	3/ 5	.600	7/ 8	.875	4/ 5	5	4	3	1	0	13	.325
COE, E.	35	3/ 8	.375	4/ 8	.500	1/ 6	2	2	2	0	1	10	.286
BRANTLEY, D.	7	0/ 0	.000	0/ 0	.000	0/ 0	0	0	1	0	0	0	.000
EVANS, H.	29	1/ 4	.250	1/ 3	.333	1/ 2	2	1	2	0	1	3	.103
Totals	200	18/40	.450	24/39	.615	15/37	13	13	16	4	6	60	.300

Virginia Tech (57)　Coach: Charles Moir

	Min.	Total FG/FGA	Pct.	FT/FTA	Pct.	Reb. O/T	A	TO	PF	S	Blk	TP	PPM
COLBERT, K.	36	3/ 8	.375	5/ 8	.625	3/10	3	5	5	1	0	11	.306
WILLIAMS, P.	16	1/ 1	1.000	0/ 0	.000	1/ 3	1	1	1	0	0	2	.125
BEECHER, B.	16	4/ 5	.800	0/ 1	.000	2/ 2	0	0	5	0	0	8	.500
CURRY, D.	37	6/14	.429	1/ 1	1.000	1/ 3	5	3	5	2	0	13	.351
EVERHART, R.	18	2/ 4	.500	0/ 0	.000	1/ 2	0	1	0	0	0	4	.222
BURGESS, D.	22	1/ 2	.500	1/ 1	1.000	0/ 2	0	0	3	0	0	3	.136
YOUNG, T.	29	4/14	.286	2/ 5	.400	3/ 5	1	0	4	1	0	10	.345
LEWIS, T.	26	3/10	.300	0/ 1	.000	1/ 1	1	1	2	3	0	6	.231
Totals	200	24/58	.414	9/17	.529	12/28	11	11	25	7	0	57	.285

Team Rebounds: Temple 3; Virginia Tech 3. Disqualified: Virginia Tech—Colbert, Beecher, Curry. Technical fouls: None.

	1st Half	2nd Half	Final
Temple	25	35	60
Virginia Tech	19	38	57

SMU (85) Coach: Dave Bliss

	Min.	Total FG/FGA	Pct.	FT/FTA	Pct.	Reb. O/T	A	TO	PF	S	Blk	TP	PPM
PINK, R.	4	0/0	.000	0/0	.000	0/2	0	0	1	0	0	0	.000
DAVIS, L.	37	8/14	.571	1/1	1.000	5/15	2	1	1	2	0	17	.459
KONCAK, J.	27	8/14	.571	1/6	.167	6/11	1	2	4	0	3	17	.630
MOORE, B.	34	6/8	.750	2/4	.500	0/2	10	3	2	0	0	14	.412
WRIGHT, C.	34	8/16	.500	2/2	1.000	0/3	7	4	1	2	0	18	.529
LEWIS, K.	21	1/3	.333	0/0	.000	0/2	1	5	2	0	0	2	.095
FULLER, J.	3	0/0	.000	0/0	.000	0/0	0	0	0	0	0	0	.000
WILLIAMS, T.	14	7/7	1.000	1/2	.500	1/6	0	2	1	0	0	15	1.071
JOHNSON, S.	21	0/2	.000	2/2	1.000	0/1	0	1	0	1	0	2	.095
BRIGGS, J.	1	0/0	.000	0/0	.000	0/1	0	1	0	0	0	0	.000
THOMAS, T.	1	0/0	.000	0/0	.000	0/0	0	0	0	0	0	0	.000
WINBORN, C.	1	0/0	.000	0/0	.000	0/0	0	0	0	0	0	0	.000
COZART, A.	1	0/0	.000	0/0	.000	0/0	0	0	0	0	0	0	.000
PUDDY, G.	1	0/0	.000	0/0	.000	0/0	0	0	0	0	0	0	.000
Totals	200	38/64	.594	9/17	.529	12/42	22	18	13	5	3	85	.425

Old Dominion (68) Coach: Paul Webb

	Min.	Total FG/FGA	Pct.	FT/FTA	Pct.	Reb. O/T	A	TO	PF	S	Blk	TP	PPM
DAVIS, M.	35	14/22	.636	4/4	1.000	5/10	3	1	4	2	0	32	.914
GATTISON, K.	32	5/15	.333	1/2	.500	5/10	2	1	4	0	0	11	.344
HANLEY, C.	21	2/6	.333	1/2	.500	1/3	1	0	4	0	0	5	.238
SMITH, F.	37	1/5	.200	1/2	.500	0/1	8	1	1	1	0	3	.081
THOMAS, K.	24	2/13	.154	0/0	.000	4/5	1	2	2	1	0	4	.167
SMITH, C.	17	4/9	.444	1/2	.500	0/2	2	1	0	1	0	9	.529
CHARLES, S.	20	2/5	.400	0/0	.000	1/2	1	0	0	1	0	4	.200
WADE, R.	4	0/0	.000	0/1	.000	0/0	0	0	1	0	0	0	.000
LAMBERT, H.	6	0/1	.000	0/0	.000	0/1	2	0	2	0	0	0	.000
WHITE, M.	1	0/0	.000	0/0	.000	0/0	0	0	0	0	0	0	.000
TRAX, S.	1	0/1	.000	0/0	.000	0/0	0	0	0	0	0	0	.000
FACKA, F.	1	0/0	.000	0/0	.000	0/0	0	0	0	0	0	0	.000
TOLSON, D.	1	0/0	.000	0/0	.000	0/0	0	0	0	0	0	0	.000
Totals	200	30/77	.390	8/13	.615	16/34	20	6	18	6	0	68	.340

Team Rebounds: SMU 2; Old Dominion 4. Disqualified: None. Technical fouls: None.

	1st Half	2nd Half	Final
SMU	36	49	85
Old Dominion	28	40	68

Loyola-Chicago (59) Coach: Gene Sullivan

	Min.	Total FG/FGA	Pct.	FT/FTA	Pct.	Reb. O/T	A	TO	PF	S	Blk	TP	PPM
HUGHES, A.	-	10/23	.435	4/7	.571	-/11	1	-	3	-	-	24	-
BATTLE, A.	-	7/18	.389	1/2	.500	-/6	2	-	3	-	-	15	-
MOORE, A.	-	4/6	.667	0/0	.000	-/5	0	-	5	-	-	8	-
WILLIAMS, G.	-	1/2	.500	2/2	1.000	-/6	2	-	3	-	-	4	-
GOLSTON, C.	-	3/8	.375	2/3	.667	-/0	12	-	2	-	-	8	-
CENAR, M.	-	0/1	.000	0/0	.000	-/1	0	-	1	-	-	0	-
YOUNG, I.	-	0/0	.000	0/1	.000	-/1	0	-	3	-	-	0	-
Totals	200	25/58	.431	9/15	.600	-/30	17	5	20	4	1	59	.295

Iona (58) Coach: Pat Kennedy

	Min.	Total FG/FGA	Pct.	FT/FTA	Pct.	Reb. O/T	A	TO	PF	S	Blk	TP	PPM
TRUESDALE	-	1/2	.500	4/5	.800	-/8	2	-	4	-	-	6	-
HARGRAVES, T.	-	9/16	.563	1/7	.143	-/7	0	-	3	-	-	19	-
COLEMAN	-	6/11	.545	2/3	.667	-/16	0	-	2	-	-	14	-
GNMES	-	5/13	.385	0/1	.000	-/1	7	-	4	-	-	10	-
SIMMONDS	-	0/3	.000	1/2	.500	-/0	1	-	0	-	-	1	-
KIPNEK	-	2/3	.667	4/4	1.000	-/3	1	-	2	-	-	8	-
RUSSELL	-	0/3	.000	0/0	.000	-/1	0	-	2	-	-	0	-
WALTERS	-	0/0	.000	0/0	.000	-/1	0	-	0	-	-	0	-
Totals	200	23/51	.451	12/22	.545	-/37	11	11	17	1	1	58	.290

Team Rebounds: Loyola-Chicago 3; Iona 4. Disqualified: Loyola-Chicago—Moore. Technical fouls: None.

	1st Half	2nd Half	Final
Loyola-Chicago	30	29	59
Iona	32	26	58

Georgia (67) Coach: Hugh Durham

	Min.	Total FG/FGA	Pct.	FT/FTA	Pct.	Reb. O/T	A	TO	PF	S	Blk	TP	PPM
CORHEN, R.	24	2/5	.400	3/4	.750	-/6	1	2	1	0	0	7	.292
WARD, J.	23	5/10	.500	0/0	.000	-/5	1	1	2	1	0	10	.435
HENDERSON, C.	24	10/18	.556	0/2	.000	-/6	2	0	4	2	1	20	.833
CROSBY, G.	31	5/8	.625	3/4	.750	-/2	5	1	1	2	0	13	.419
HARTRY, D.	34	2/7	.286	0/0	.000	-/4	3	0	0	1	0	4	.118
MCMILLAN, H.	24	3/3	1.000	0/0	.000	-/2	3	3	2	0	0	6	.250
DUNN, D.	16	0/3	.000	0/0	.000	-/6	0	2	0	1	1	0	.000
HOWARD, M.	15	2/3	.667	2/4	.500	-/1	1	1	0	0	0	6	.400
KESSLER, C.	9	0/0	.000	1/3	.333	-/1	0	0	0	0	0	1	.111
Totals	200	29/57	.509	9/17	.529	-/33	16	10	10	7	2	67	.335

Wichita State (59) Coach: Gene Smithson

	Min.	Total FG/FGA	Pct.	FT/FTA	Pct.	Reb. O/T	A	TO	PF	S	Blk	TP	PPM
COLEMAN, C.	32	2/3	.667	0/2	.000	-/8	2	0	1	2	0	4	.125
MCDANIEL, X.	37	11/18	.611	0/0	.000	-/11	0	3	5	1	0	22	.595
CARR, H.	26	1/3	.333	0/0	.000	-/4	0	3	3	0	1	2	.077
ARLINE, M.	31	1/7	.143	1/2	.500	-/0	3	2	1	2	0	3	.097
SHERROD, A.	40	8/16	.500	1/1	1.000	-/3	1	3	4	0	0	17	.425
PAPKE, K.	22	5/10	.500	1/1	1.000	-/5	2	3	4	0	0	11	.500
NORMOORE, C.	9	0/1	.000	0/0	.000	-/0	0	1	0	0	0	0	.000
KOSCH, T.	1	0/0	.000	0/0	.000	-/0	0	0	1	0	0	0	.000
BAILEY, C.	2	0/0	.000	0/0	.000	-/1	0	0	1	0	0	0	.000
Totals	200	28/58	.483	3/6	.500	-/32	8	15	19	5	1	59	.295

Team Rebounds: Georgia 1; Wichita State 0. Disqualified: Wichita State—McDaniel. Technical fouls: Georgia—Dunn.

	1st Half	2nd Half	Final
Georgia	27	40	67
Wichita State	27	32	59

Illinois (76) Coach: Lou Henson

	Min.	Total FG/FGA	Pct.	FT/FTA	Pct.	Reb. O/T	A	TO	PF	S	Blk	TP	PPM
NORMAN, K.	33	8/11	.727	7/7	1.000	-/9	4	4	1	1	0	23	.697
WELCH, A.	25	6/11	.545	1/2	.500	-/2	2	0	2	1	0	13	.520
WINTERS, E.	31	4/5	.800	3/4	.750	-/7	4	0	1	1	1	11	.355
ALTENBERGER, D.	30	6/10	.600	1/2	.500	-/3	2	0	2	0	0	13	.433
DOUGLAS, B.	32	1/5	.200	1/2	.500	-/4	5	2	2	0	0	3	.094
MEENTS, S.	16	2/3	.667	0/1	.000	-/1	2	2	1	1	0	4	.250
WYSINGER, T.	23	2/4	.500	2/2	1.000	-/3	2	3	2	1	0	6	.261
HAFTNER, S.	6	0/2	.000	1/2	.500	-/3	0	1	0	0	1	1	.167
WOODWARD, R.	4	1/1	1.000	0/0	.000	-/0	1	1	2	0	0	2	.500
Totals	200	30/52	.577	16/22	.727	-/32	21	16	13	8	1	76	.380

Northeastern (57) Coach: Jim Calhoun

	Min.	Total FG/FGA	Pct.	FT/FTA	Pct.	Reb. O/T	A	TO	PF	S	Blk	TP	PPM
DALE, Q.	33	4/10	.400	2/2	1.000	-/7	0	0	4	0	0	10	.303
LEWIS, R.	34	11/28	.393	0/0	.000	-/5	1	3	3	0	0	22	.647
MCDUFFIE, K.	29	2/3	.667	2/4	.500	-/5	0	4	2	1	0	6	.207
LAFLEUR, A.	38	3/6	.500	0/0	.000	-/1	7	4	2	1	1	6	.158
WILLIAMS, J.	24	4/6	.667	1/4	.250	-/3	3	5	2	0	0	9	.375
FULLER, W.	25	0/0	.000	0/0	.000	-/4	0	3	1	2	0	0	.000
MCDONALD, E.	8	1/2	.500	0/0	.000	-/0	0	3	1	0	0	2	.250
CORCORAN, G.	5	1/1	1.000	0/0	.000	-/2	0	0	1	1	0	2	.400
EVANS, S.	4	0/2	.000	0/0	.000	-/0	0	0	0	0	0	0	.000
Totals	200	26/58	.448	5/10	.500	-/25	11	20	19	7	1	57	.285

Team Rebounds: Illinois 1; Northeastern 1. Disqualified: Northeastern—Williams. Technical fouls: None.

	1st Half	2nd Half	Final
Illinois	35	41	76
Northeastern	23	34	57

Syracuse (70)   Coach: Jim Boeheim

	Min.	Total FG/FGA	Pct.	FT/FTA	Pct.	Reb. O/T	A	TO	PF	S	Blk	TP	PPM
ADDISON, R.	40	2/13	.154	4/4	1.000	-/9	3	5	4	0	3	8	.200
HAWKINS, A.	17	0/2	.000	1/3	.333	-/4	0	1	1	0	0	1	.059
SEIKALY, R.	29	7/9	.778	3/4	.750	-/9	0	0	4	0	3	17	.586
WASHINGTON, D.	40	4/8	.500	15/16	.938	-/3	4	5	1	1	0	23	.575
BROWN, M.	11	1/2	.500	0/0	.000	-/0	0	1	2	1	0	2	.182
ALEXIS, W.	27	3/3	1.000	3/4	.750	-/5	4	1	4	0	0	9	.333
MONROE, G.	28	4/6	.667	0/1	.000	-/2	2	1	0	1	0	8	.286
HARRIED, H.	8	1/3	.333	0/0	.000	-/2	0	0	1	0	0	2	.250
Totals	200	22/46	.478	26/32	.813	-/34	13	14	17	3	6	70	.350

DePaul (65)   Coach: Joey Meyer

	Min.	Total FG/FGA	Pct.	FT/FTA	Pct.	Reb. O/T	A	TO	PF	S	Blk	TP	PPM
CORBIN, T.	40	7/14	.500	3/6	.500	-/8	1	2	4	3	0	17	.425
COMEGYS, D.	35	5/15	.333	5/7	.714	-/10	1	1	1	0	2	15	.429
EMBRY, M.	23	5/6	.833	2/2	1.000	-/2	0	1	5	0	0	12	.522
PATTERSON, K.	40	5/13	.385	1/1	1.000	-/4	15	2	4	4	0	11	.275
JACKSON, T.	9	0/2	.000	1/2	.500	-/1	0	1	2	0	0	1	.111
WEST, L.	31	4/11	.364	1/2	.500	-/3	3	3	5	0	0	9	.290
HOLMES, K.	15	0/0	.000	0/0	.000	-/2	0	3	3	1	0	0	.000
LAMPLEY, L.	6	0/0	.000	0/0	.000	-/0	0	1	0	0	0	0	.000
PETTUS, R.	1	0/0	.000	0/0	.000	-/0	0	0	0	0	0	0	.000
Totals	200	26/61	.426	13/20	.650	-/30	20	11	24	8	2	65	.325

Team Rebounds: Syracuse 0; DePaul 3. Disqualified: DePaul—Embry, West. Technical fouls: None.

	1st Half	2nd Half	Final
Syracuse	36	34	70
DePaul	27	38	65

Georgia Tech (65)   Coach: Bobby Cremins

	Min.	Total FG/FGA	Pct.	FT/FTA	Pct.	Reb. O/T	A	TO	PF	S	Blk	TP	PPM
SALLEY, J.	28	2/4	.500	4/8	.500	-/7	2	5	3	1	4	8	.286
PETWAY, S.	40	3/5	.600	1/3	.333	-/3	4	2	4	0	0	7	.175
JOSEPH, Y.	36	8/13	.615	3/4	.750	-/9	0	2	3	0	0	19	.528
PRICE, M.	40	5/13	.385	4/8	.500	-/2	4	5	2	3	0	14	.350
DALRYMPLE, B.	37	3/11	.273	7/8	.875	-/11	4	2	4	1	0	13	.351
FORD, A.	10	2/4	.500	0/0	.000	-/3	1	1	2	2	2	4	.400
MANSELL, J.	6	0/0	.000	0/0	.000	-/2	0	1	0	0	0	0	.000
MARTINSON, J.	3	0/0	.000	0/0	.000	-/0	1	1	0	0	0	0	.000
Totals	200	23/50	.460	19/31	.613	-/37	16	19	18	7	6	65	.325

Mercer (58)   Coach: Bill Bibb

	Min.	Total FG/FGA	Pct.	FT/FTA	Pct.	Reb. O/T	A	TO	PF	S	Blk	TP	PPM
MITCHELL, S.	40	5/16	.313	7/8	.875	-/6	0	1	4	3	1	17	.425
WALKER, E.	39	8/20	.400	1/2	.500	-/14	2	3	2	2	0	17	.436
MOORE, C.	23	1/6	.167	1/3	.333	-/6	0	0	5	1	1	3	.130
CZAPLA, K.	23	0/2	.000	0/1	.000	-/3	4	5	4	3	0	0	.000
RANDALL, M.	30	8/11	.727	1/1	1.000	-/2	2	4	3	2	0	17	.567
HARRIS, E.	18	0/0	.000	0/0	.000	-/0	4	2	4	0	0	0	.000
GETER, P.	14	0/3	.000	0/0	.000	-/2	1	4	2	0	0	0	.000
GUTHRIE, D.	12	1/2	.500	2/2	1.000	-/3	0	0	3	0	0	4	.333
CHAMBERS, E.	1	0/0	.000	0/0	.000	-/0	0	0	0	0	0	0	.000
Totals	200	23/60	.383	12/17	.706	-/36	13	19	27	11	2	58	.290

Team Rebounds: Georgia Tech 1; Mercer 2. Disqualified: Mercer—Moore. Technical fouls: Mercer—Coach Bibb.

	1st Half	2nd Half	Final
Georgia Tech	41	24	65
Mercer	25	33	58

FIRST ROUND MIDWEST

Oklahoma (96)   Coach: Billy Tubbs

	Min.	Total FG/FGA	Pct.	FT/FTA	Pct.	Reb. O/T	A	TO	PF	S	Blk	TP	PPM
BOWIE, A.	34	5/12	.417	3/3	1.000	2/7	6	1	2	1	0	13	.382
KENNEDY, D.	33	8/15	.533	1/1	1.000	4/10	1	0	4	1	1	17	.515
TISDALE, WA.	38	12/16	.750	4/4	1.000	5/12	0	2	3	0	1	28	.737
MCCALISTER, T.	38	9/17	.529	5/6	.833	1/1	5	6	1	1	2	23	.605
DAVIS, L.	22	0/3	.000	0/0	.000	0/1	8	2	0	0	0	0	.000
CLARK, S.	26	3/7	.429	4/4	1.000	1/3	3	2	1	3	0	10	.385
JOHNSON, D.	9	2/4	.500	1/2	.500	1/1	1	0	2	1	0	5	.556
Totals	200	39/74	.527	18/20	.900	14/35	24	13	13	7	4	96	.480

North Carolina A&T (83)   Coach: Don Corbett

	Min.	Total FG/FGA	Pct.	FT/FTA	Pct.	Reb. O/T	A	TO	PF	S	Blk	TP	PPM
BROWN, J.	39	8/17	.471	4/8	.500	4/8	2	4	4	1	0	20	.513
CALE, G.	38	10/14	.714	0/0	.000	3/5	2	3	3	1	0	20	.526
WILLIAMS, C.	25	3/9	.333	2/4	.500	3/8	3	1	5	2	1	8	.320
GRIFFIS, T.	36	4/5	.800	0/0	.000	1/4	4	0	1	2	0	8	.222
BOYD, E.	38	6/15	.400	6/6	1.000	0/2	2	1	3	3	0	18	.474
BRASWELL, M.	15	3/7	.429	0/0	.000	1/3	0	0	3	0	0	7	.467
ROBINSON, L.	8	1/2	.500	0/0	.000	0/0	0	1	0	0	0	2	.250
GAITHER, M.	1	0/1	.000	0/0	.000	0/0	0	0	0	0	0	0	.000
Totals	200	35/70	.500	13/20	.650	12/30	13	10	19	9	1	83	.415

Team Rebounds: Oklahoma 5; N.C. A&T 1. Disqualified: N.C. A&T—Williams. Technical fouls: None.

	1st Half	2nd Half	Final
Oklahoma	49	47	96
N. Carolina A&T	35	48	83

USC (55)   Coach: Stan Morrison

	Min.	Total FG/FGA	Pct.	FT/FTA	Pct.	Reb. O/T	A	TO	PF	S	Blk	TP	PPM
DOWELL, D.	30	2/7	.286	0/0	.000	1/3	3	1	1	1	0	4	.133
CARLANDER, W.	39	2/8	.250	6/6	1.000	2/8	1	2	3	0	0	10	.256
OLIVIER, C.	28	2/5	.400	3/4	.750	1/5	0	2	2	1	0	7	.250
FRIEND, L.	37	1/5	.200	2/2	1.000	0/1	4	0	3	0	0	4	.108
HOLMES, R.	26	4/6	.667	2/2	1.000	1/3	1	2	3	0	0	10	.385
SMITH, G.	30	7/15	.467	1/1	1.000	1/1	0	0	3	1	0	15	.500
SIMPSON, C.	10	2/3	.667	1/2	.500	0/0	0	1	4	1	0	5	.500
Totals	200	20/49	.408	15/17	.882	6/21	9	8	19	4	0	55	.275

Illinois State (58)   Coach: Bob Donewald

	Min.	Total FG/FGA	Pct.	FT/FTA	Pct.	Reb. O/T	A	TO	PF	S	Blk	TP	PPM
SANDERS, D.	17	3/6	.500	0/0	.000	1/2	1	0	4	1	0	6	.353
STEFANOVIC, L.	35	7/13	.538	1/2	.500	1/4	1	3	1	2	0	15	.429
BRAKSICK, B.	40	2/4	.500	7/9	.778	2/4	1	1	3	0	1	11	.275
MCKENNY, M.	40	2/7	.286	6/6	1.000	1/5	8	0	1	2	0	10	.250
JOHNSON, R.	36	4/8	.500	4/6	.667	1/10	1	4	3	0	1	12	.333
DUNCAN, B.	20	2/3	.667	0/0	.000	1/2	1	0	1	0	0	4	.200
TAPHORN, M.	2	0/0	.000	0/0	.000	0/0	0	0	0	0	0	0	.000
HOLIFIELD, T.	10	0/0	.000	0/0	.000	0/0	0	0	2	0	1	0	.000
Totals	200	20/41	.488	18/23	.783	7/27	13	8	15	5	3	58	.290

Team Rebounds: Illinois State 0; USC 7. Disqualified: None. Technical fouls: None.

	1st Half	2nd Half	Final
USC	30	25	55
Illinois State	26	32	58

Louisiana Tech (78)   Coach: Andy Russo

	Min.	Total FG / FGA	Pct.	FT / FTA	Pct.	Reb. O / T	A	TO	PF	S	Blk	TP	PPM
SIMMONS, W.	27	5/10	.500	3/ 6	.500	5/10	0	1	4	0	3	13	.481
GODBOLT, R.	26	4/ 6	.667	9/10	.900	5/ 8	0	0	0	0	0	17	.654
MALONE, K.	25	4/10	.400	1/ 2	.500	6/10	2	1	3	2	2	9	.360
DAVIS, A.	31	1/ 5	.200	2/ 2	1.000	1/ 4	5	3	3	1	0	4	.129
SMITH, W.	26	2/ 8	.250	0/ 0	.000	0/ 6	7	1	0	1	0	4	.154
BLAND, W.	21	7/10	.700	2/ 4	.500	4/ 4	1	2	2	1	0	16	.762
TROUTMAN, K.	4	0/ 0	.000	0/ 0	.000	0/ 0	0	1	1	0	0	0	.000
EMERSON, D.	7	1/ 1	1.000	0/ 0	.000	0/ 1	0	1	0	0	0	2	.286
HANNIBAL, R.	5	0/ 4	.000	0/ 0	.000	2/ 3	1	1	0	1	0	0	.000
LEWIS, J.	5	0/ 1	.000	0/ 0	.000	0/ 1	0	2	1	0	0	0	.000
FRANK, A.	14	4/ 5	.800	3/ 4	.750	0/ 3	1	3	0	0	0	11	.786
JORDAN, D.	9	1/ 3	.333	0/ 0	.000	1/ 1	0	1	2	0	0	2	.222
Totals	200	29/63	.460	20/28	.714	24/51	17	17	16	6	5	78	.390

Pittsburgh (54)   Coach: Roy Chipman

	Min.	Total FG / FGA	Pct.	FT / FTA	Pct.	Reb. O / T	A	TO	PF	S	Blk	TP	PPM
SHEPHERD, D.	32	9/18	.500	0/ 0	.000	2/ 7	1	3	2	5	0	18	.563
WILLIAMS, A.	8	0/ 1	.000	0/ 0	.000	1/ 2	0	1	5	0	0	0	.000
SMITH, C.	35	3/ 8	.375	3/ 5	.600	0/ 2	1	3	2	0	4	9	.257
DAVID, J.	18	2/ 4	.500	0/ 0	.000	0/ 1	0	0	0	0	0	4	.222
GORE, D.	30	4/12	.333	0/ 0	.000	1/ 2	0	3	3	0	0	8	.267
AIKEN, C.	15	0/ 1	.000	0/ 0	.000	0/ 2	3	1	1	1	0	0	.000
FERGUSON, M.	7	2/ 3	.667	2/ 2	1.000	2/ 3	0	1	0	0	0	6	.857
BLANTON, J.	1	0/ 0	.000	0/ 0	.000	0/ 0	1	0	0	0	0	0	.000
THOMPSON, C.	9	0/ 2	.000	0/ 0	.000	0/ 0	3	2	2	0	0	0	.000
LEWIS, J.	8	1/ 3	.333	4/ 4	1.000	0/ 0	1	0	1	0	0	6	.750
WATKINS, C.	8	1/ 3	.333	0/ 0	.000	0/ 0	0	0	3	0	0	2	.250
MIKLASEVICH, M.	14	0/ 4	.000	0/ 0	.000	1/ 2	1	0	1	1	0	0	.000
ARMSTRONG, K.	15	0/ 3	.000	1/ 2	.500	3/ 3	1	3	1	1	1	1	.067
Totals	200	22/62	.355	10/15	.667	10/24	12	17	21	8	7	54	.270

Team Rebounds: Louisiana Tech 5; Pittsburgh 2. Disqualified: Pittsburgh—Williams. Technical fouls: None.

	1st Half	2nd Half	Final
Louisiana Tech	37	41	78
Pittsburgh	20	34	54

Ohio State (75)   Coach: Eldon Miller

	Min.	Total FG / FGA	Pct.	FT / FTA	Pct.	Reb. O / T	A	TO	PF	S	Blk	TP	PPM
HOPSON, D.	34	7/ 9	.778	5/ 6	.833	-/ 9	0	1	1	0	0	19	.559
CONCHECK, J.	20	0/ 1	.000	0/ 0	.000	-/ 2	2	1	3	0	0	0	.000
SELLERS, B.	36	5/13	.385	4/ 5	.800	-/10	0	0	2	1	4	14	.389
STOKES, R.	39	7/10	.700	7/ 7	1.000	-/ 1	2	4	4	1	0	21	.538
TAYLOR, T.	39	8/12	.667	1/ 6	.167	-/ 3	5	5	2	0	0	17	.436
JONES, J.	30	2/ 5	.400	0/ 0	.000	-/ 2	3	1	4	2	0	4	.133
HONINGFORD, J.	1	0/ 0	.000	0/ 0	.000	-/ 0	0	0	0	0	0	0	.000
ANDERSON, S.	1	0/ 0	.000	0/ 0	.000	-/ 0	0	0	0	0	0	0	.000
Totals	200	29/50	.580	17/24	.708	-/27	12	12	16	4	4	75	.375

Iowa State (64)   Coach: Johnny Orr

	Min.	Total FG / FGA	Pct.	FT / FTA	Pct.	Reb. O / T	A	TO	PF	S	Blk	TP	PPM
PETERSON, T.	28	1/ 1	1.000	0/ 0	.000	-/ 1	1	0	2	0	0	2	.071
GRAYER, J.	39	8/14	.571	5/ 6	.833	-/ 9	3	3	3	2	0	21	.538
HILL, S.	22	2/ 4	.500	0/ 0	.000	-/ 5	0	2	2	0	0	4	.182
STEVENS, B.	38	12/24	.500	0/ 1	.000	-/ 4	2	1	4	0	0	24	.632
HORNACEK, J.	38	2/ 9	.222	1/ 2	.500	-/ 3	7	2	4	2	0	5	.132
THOMPKINS, G.	16	2/ 3	.667	0/ 0	.000	-/ 0	1	0	3	1	0	4	.250
RHODES, L.	1	1/ 1	1.000	0/ 0	.000	-/ 0	0	1	1	0	0	2	2.000
VIRGIL, R.	3	0/ 1	.000	0/ 0	.000	-/ 1	0	1	0	0	0	0	.000
PARKER, E.	1	1/ 1	1.000	0/ 0	.000	-/ 1	0	0	0	0	0	2	2.000
HARRIS, R.	1	0/ 0	.000	0/ 0	.000	-/ 0	0	0	0	0	0	0	.000
WALLACE, W.	1	0/ 0	.000	0/ 1	.000	-/ 0	1	0	0	0	0	0	.000
MOSS, D.	12	0/ 1	.000	0/ 0	.000	-/ 1	1	0	0	0	0	0	.000
Totals	200	29/60	.483	6/10	.600	-/25	15	15	18	5	0	64	.320

Team Rebounds: Ohio State 1; Iowa State 5. Disqualified: None. Technical fouls: None.

	1st Half	2nd Half	Final
Ohio State	39	36	75
Iowa State	37	27	64

Texas Tech (53)   Coach: Gerald Myers

	Min.	FG / FGA	Pct.	FT / FTA	Pct.	Reb. O / T	A	TO	PF	S	Blk	TP	PPM
ANDERSON	-	1/ 5	.200	4/ 4	1.000	-/ 5	0	-	1	-	-	6	-
TAYLOR	-	6/ 9	.667	0/ 0	.000	-/12	1	-	3	-	-	12	-
IRVIN, R.	-	3/ 6	.500	1/ 2	.500	-/ 8	0	-	3	-	-	7	-
JENNINGS	-	8/17	.471	0/ 0	.000	-/ 1	2	-	3	-	-	16	-
WALLACE	-	1/ 6	.167	0/ 2	.000	-/ 2	7	-	3	-	-	2	-
DODE	-	1/ 3	.333	2/ 3	.667	-/ 0	1	-	0	-	-	4	-
PHILLIPS	-	0/ 1	.000	0/ 0	.000	-/ 1	0	-	1	-	-	0	-
BENFORD, T.	-	3/ 8	.375	0/ 0	.000	-/ 0	4	-	3	-	-	6	-
Totals	200	23/55	.418	7/11	.636	-/29	15	15	17	-	-	53	.265

Boston College (55)   Coach: Gary Williams

	Min.	Total FG / FGA	Pct.	FT / FTA	Pct.	Reb. O / T	A	TO	PF	S	Blk	TP	PPM
MCCREADY, R.	-	7/ 9	.778	1/ 4	.250	-/ 8	0	-	3	-	-	15	-
TALLEY	-	2/ 3	.667	4/ 4	1.000	-/ 5	6	-	2	-	-	8	-
GORDON	-	0/ 3	.000	2/ 6	.333	-/ 6	0	-	2	-	-	2	-
ADAMS, M.	-	7/16	.438	3/ 3	1.000	-/ 5	0	-	1	-	-	17	-
PRESSLEY, D.	-	1/ 3	.333	1/ 2	.500	-/ 1	1	-	4	-	-	3	-
SCHMIDT	-	0/ 0	.000	0/ 0	.000	-/ 0	0	-	0	-	-	0	-
PRIMUS, S.	-	2/ 4	.500	3/ 4	.750	-/ 2	1	-	2	-	-	7	-
BARRY	-	0/ 1	.000	0/ 0	.000	-/ 0	0	-	1	-	-	0	-
BOWERS	-	1/ 2	.500	1/ 2	.500	-/ 0	0	-	2	-	-	3	-
Totals	200	20/41	.488	15/25	.600	-/27	8	17	17	-	-	55	.275

Team Rebounds: Boston College 2; Texas Tech 2. Disqualified: None. Technical fouls: None.

	1st Half	2nd Half	Final
Texas Tech	28	25	53
Boston College	33	22	55

Duke (75)   Coach: Mike Krzyzewski

	Min.	Total FG / FGA	Pct.	FT / FTA	Pct.	Reb. O / T	A	TO	PF	S	Blk	TP	PPM
ALARIE, M.	31	7/11	.636	2/ 2	1.000	1/ 9	1	0	1	0	0	16	.516
MEAGHER, D.	29	3/ 6	.500	0/ 0	.000	1/ 8	3	1	2	2	0	6	.207
BILAS, J.	20	3/ 6	.500	1/ 3	.333	1/ 3	1	3	4	2	0	7	.350
AMAKER, T.	37	1/ 3	.333	0/ 0	.000	0/ 1	5	1	2	1	2	2	.054
DAWKINS, J.	39	8/13	.615	5/ 9	.556	2/ 4	4	4	1	1	0	21	.538
HENDERSON, D.	28	7/12	.583	8/14	.571	1/ 3	2	3	2	0	0	22	.786
STRICKLAND, K.	6	0/ 1	.000	0/ 0	.000	1/ 1	1	1	1	0	0	0	.000
BRYAN, J.	1	0/ 0	.000	1/ 2	.500	0/ 1	0	1	0	0	0	1	1.000
WILLIAMS, W.	2	0/ 0	.000	0/ 0	.000	0/ 0	0	1	0	0	0	0	.000
ANDERSON, T.	1	0/ 0	.000	0/ 0	.000	0/ 0	0	0	1	0	0	0	.000
NESSLEY, M.	2	0/ 0	.000	0/ 0	.000	0/ 0	0	0	1	0	0	0	.000
KING, B.	4	0/ 0	.000	0/ 0	.000	0/ 1	0	0	0	0	0	0	.000
Totals	200	29/52	.558	17/30	.567	7/31	17	15	16	7	2	75	.375

Pepperdine (62)   Coach: Jim Harrick

	Min.	Total FG / FGA	Pct.	FT / FTA	Pct.	Reb. O / T	A	TO	PF	S	Blk	TP	PPM
WHITE, E.	37	12/17	.706	2/ 5	.400	6/13	2	1	2	0	1	26	.703
FREDERICK, A.	28	2/ 9	.222	0/ 0	.000	3/ 9	1	6	5	2	3	4	.143
MIDDLEBROOKS, L.	33	5/11	.455	1/ 2	.500	2/ 4	0	0	2	0	0	11	.333
KORFAS, J.	32	4/ 7	.571	3/ 4	.750	0/ 1	8	6	2	0	0	11	.344
POLEE, D.	32	2/11	.182	1/ 2	.500	2/ 2	2	3	5	1	0	5	.156
WILSON, M.	14	1/ 3	.333	1/ 2	.500	1/ 2	1	1	0	0	0	3	.214
ASBERRY, J.	1	0/ 0	.000	0/ 0	.000	0/ 0	0	0	0	0	0	0	.000
JONES, A.	1	0/ 0	.000	0/ 0	.000	0/ 0	0	0	0	0	0	0	.000
MOUNTS, M.	1	0/ 0	.000	0/ 0	.000	0/ 0	0	0	1	1	0	0	.000
CONAWAY, P.	1	0/ 0	.000	0/ 0	.000	0/ 0	0	0	0	0	0	0	.000
BRITTAIN, T.	20	1/ 3	.333	0/ 1	.000	0/ 3	1	0	3	0	0	2	.100
Totals	200	27/61	.443	8/16	.500	14/34	15	17	20	4	4	62	.310

Team Rebounds: Duke 3; Pepperdine 4. Disqualified: Pepperdine—Fredrick, Polee. Technical fouls: Pepperdine—Coach Harrick.

	1st Half	2nd Half	Final
Duke	34	41	75
Pepperdine	32	30	62

Alabama-Birmingham (70)   Coach: Gene Bartow

	Min.	Total FG/FGA	Pct.	FT/FTA	Pct.	Reb. O/T	A	TO	PF	S	Blk	TP	PPM
JOHNSON, M.	9	0/0	.000	0/0	.000	0/0	2	0	0	1	0	0	.000
MINCY, J.	37	6/15	.400	6/13	.462	4/7	0	2	2	1	2	18	.486
GORDON, A.	7	0/0	.000	0/1	.000	0/0	0	1	2	0	0	0	.000
MITCHELL, S.	38	8/12	.667	2/2	1.000	0/0	5	3	3	0	0	18	.474
PONDER, J.	37	3/9	.333	9/10	.900	1/2	1	1	1	1	0	15	.405
FOSTER, T.	10	1/2	.500	0/0	.000	0/0	1	2	0	0	0	2	.200
BARTOW, M.	6	0/0	.000	0/0	.000	0/1	0	0	0	0	0	0	.000
CHARLES, M.	21	2/4	.500	3/4	.750	1/5	2	0	3	1	0	7	.333
JOHNSON, A.	35	4/6	.667	2/4	.500	6/10	1	2	1	0	0	10	.286
Totals	200	24/48	.500	22/34	.647	12/26	12	11	12	4	2	70	.350

Michigan State (68)   Coach: Jud Heathcote

	Min.	Total FG/FGA	Pct.	FT/FTA	Pct.	Reb. O/T	A	TO	PF	S	Blk	TP	PPM
MUDD, R.	23	1/4	.250	0/0	.000	4/8	0	3	5	1	1	2	.087
POLEC, L.	35	4/7	.571	0/0	.000	1/3	0	1	5	0	0	8	.229
JOHNSON, K.	37	4/8	.500	1/1	1.000	5/11	1	3	4	0	0	9	.243
SKILES, J.	39	6/13	.462	3/4	.750	1/4	8	3	4	2	0	15	.385
VINCENT, S.	39	13/23	.565	6/6	1.000	4/6	2	2	3	1	0	32	.821
JOHNSON, D.	24	1/5	.200	0/0	.000	1/1	4	1	2	1	0	2	.083
WALKER, R.	2	0/0	.000	0/0	.000	0/0	0	0	2	0	0	0	.000
PEDRO, G.	1	0/0	.000	0/0	.000	0/0	0	0	0	0	0	0	.000
Totals	200	29/60	.483	10/11	.909	16/33	15	13	25	5	1	68	.340

Team Rebounds: Ala.-Birmingham 3; Michigan St. 2. Disqualified: Michigan St.—Mudd, Polec. Technical fouls: None.

	1st Half	2nd Half	Final
Ala.-Birmingham	32	38	70
Michigan St.	35	33	68

Memphis State (67)   Coach: Dana Kirk

	Min.	Total FG/FGA	Pct.	FT/FTA	Pct.	Reb. O/T	A	TO	PF	S	Blk	TP	PPM
LEE, K.	20	4/8	.500	0/2	.000	1/3	0	1	4	1	1	8	.400
HOLMES, B.	36	3/6	.500	2/3	.667	3/7	1	0	2	0	0	8	.222
BEDFORD, W.	29	5/5	1.000	1/4	.250	3/8	0	0	3	0	3	11	.379
TURNER, A.	36	8/14	.571	0/0	.000	2/3	8	5	4	2	0	16	.444
ASKEW, V.	32	6/10	.600	0/0	.000	3/5	3	1	0	3	0	12	.375
MCCOY, R.	4	0/0	.000	3/4	.750	0/2	0	0	0	0	0	3	.750
WILFONG, J.	5	0/1	.000	1/2	.500	0/0	0	1	0	1	0	1	.200
BOYD, D.	19	2/6	.333	0/0	.000	2/3	5	0	1	0	1	4	.211
BAILEY, D.	4	0/0	.000	2/2	1.000	0/1	0	2	1	0	1	2	.500
JENSEN, D.	2	0/1	.000	0/0	.000	0/0	0	0	0	0	0	0	.000
BECTON, W.	13	1/2	.500	0/0	.000	0/0	2	2	1	0	0	2	.154
Totals	200	29/53	.547	9/17	.529	14/32	19	12	16	7	6	67	.335

Pennsylvania (55)   Coach: Craig Littlepage

	Min.	Total FG/FGA	Pct.	FT/FTA	Pct.	Reb. O/T	A	TO	PF	S	Blk	TP	PPM
PITTS, P.	32	5/7	.714	2/2	1.000	1/3	0	1	4	3	0	12	.375
LEFKOWITZ, B.	27	2/6	.333	3/4	.750	3/8	3	3	2	1	1	7	.259
BERNSTEIN, N.	28	0/0	.000	0/1	.000	0/2	0	1	4	0	0	0	.000
BROMWELL, P.	36	6/11	.545	4/4	1.000	0/2	1	1	1	3	1	16	.444
RACINE, K.	32	4/5	.800	0/1	.000	0/1	6	5	1	1	0	8	.250
WILSON, J.	2	0/0	.000	0/0	.000	0/0	0	0	2	0	0	0	.000
ELZEY, C.	21	2/7	.286	0/0	.000	1/2	2	0	2	0	0	4	.190
MALONEY, R.	9	1/1	1.000	0/0	.000	0/1	2	3	1	2	1	2	.222
MASCIOLI, S.	1	3/3	1.000	0/0	.000	1/2	0	0	1	0	0	6	6.000
ARNOLIE, A.	9	0/1	.000	0/0	.000	0/0	0	0	1	0	0	0	.000
COHAN, R.	1	0/1	.000	0/0	.000	1/2	0	0	0	1	0	0	.000
BORRILLO, C.	1	0/0	.000	0/0	.000	0/0	0	0	1	0	0	0	.000
WIDMER, K.	1	0/0	.000	0/0	.000	0/1	1	0	0	0	0	0	.000
Totals	200	23/42	.548	9/13	.692	9/26	13	14	20	8	3	55	.275

Team Rebounds: Memphis State 0; Pennsylvania 1. Disqualified: None. Technical fouls: None.

	1st Half	2nd Half	Final
Memphis State	26	41	67
Pennsylvania	25	30	55

FIRST ROUND SOUTHEAST

Michigan (59)   Coach: Bill Freider

	Min.	Total FG/FGA	Pct.	FT/FTA	Pct.	Reb. O/T	A	TO	PF	S	Blk	TP	PPM
RELLFORD	25	4/8	.500	2/2	1.000	-/4	2	-	2	-	-	10	.400
WADE	26	1/2	.500	1/3	.333	-/5	0	-	4	-	-	3	.115
TARPLEY	31	6/14	.429	3/4	.750	-/13	0	-	4	-	-	15	.484
JOUBERT, A.	27	1/9	.111	1/1	1.000	-/3	5	-	4	-	-	3	.111
GRANT, G.	34	3/8	.375	0/0	.000	-/3	6	-	2	-	-	6	.176
ROCKYMORE	19	3/6	.500	4/7	.571	-/1	3	-	1	-	-	10	.526
THOMPSON	12	0/2	.000	2/2	1.000	-/2	0	-	3	-	-	2	.167
HENDERSON	25	4/5	.800	2/3	.667	-/4	1	-	1	-	-	10	.400
STOYKO	1	0/0	.000	0/0	.000	-/0	0	-	0	-	-	0	.000
Totals	200	22/54	.407	15/22	.682	-/35	17	-	21	-	-	59	.295

Fairleigh Dickinson (55)   Coach: Tom Green

	Min.	Total FG/FGA	Pct.	FT/FTA	Pct.	Reb. O/T	A	TO	PF	S	Blk	TP	PPM
RIDDICK	24	3/5	.600	0/2	.000	-/1	1	-	5	-	-	6	.250
HAMPTON	35	4/9	.444	2/4	.500	-/6	1	-	5	-	-	10	.286
WILSON	34	2/2	1.000	8/8	1.000	-/5	0	-	5	-	-	12	.353
COLLINS	38	2/6	.333	2/4	.500	-/3	4	-	5	-	-	6	.158
DUNCAN	15	1/4	.250	3/3	1.000	-/3	0	-	2	-	-	5	.333
LATNEY	18	4/8	.500	0/0	.000	-/5	1	-	1	-	-	8	.444
JACKSON	30	3/3	1.000	2/3	.667	-/1	4	-	3	-	-	8	.267
MALLOY	3	0/0	.000	0/0	.000	-/1	0	-	0	-	-	0	.000
THOMAS	2	0/1	.000	0/0	.000	-/0	0	-	0	-	-	0	.000
SHOKAI	1	0/0	.000	0/0	.000	-/0	0	-	0	-	-	0	.000
Totals	200	19/38	.500	17/24	.708	-/25	11	-	26	-	-	55	.275

Team Rebounds: Michigan 0; F. Dickinson 2. Disqualified: F. Dickinson—Riddick, Hampton, Wilson, Collins.

	1st Half	2nd Half	Final
Michigan	20	39	59
F. Dickinson	26	29	55

Villanova (51)   Coach: Rollie Massimino

	Min.	Total FG/FGA	Pct.	FT/FTA	Pct.	Reb. O/T	A	TO	PF	S	Blk	TP	PPM
PRESSLEY, H.	38	4/9	.444	0/1	.000	-/5	1	1	3	4	2	8	.211
MCCLAIN, D.	36	5/9	.556	1/1	1.000	-/5	3	3	4	1	1	11	.306
PINCKNEY, E.	40	6/10	.600	8/13	.615	-/6	1	2	3	2	4	20	.500
WILBUR, D.	23	1/5	.200	0/0	.000	-/1	1	2	2	1	0	2	.087
MCLAIN, G.	37	1/4	.250	0/0	.000	-/2	1	3	3	0	0	2	.054
JENSEN, H.	24	3/5	.600	2/2	1.000	-/0	1	1	1	0	0	8	.333
PLANSKY, M.	1	0/0	.000	0/0	.000	-/1	0	0	1	0	0	0	.000
EVERSON, C.	1	0/0	.000	0/0	.000	-/0	0	0	0	0	0	0	.000
Totals	200	20/42	.476	11/17	.647	-/20	8	12	17	8	7	51	.255

Dayton (49)   Coach: Don Donoher

	Min.	Total FG/FGA	Pct.	FT/FTA	Pct.	Reb. O/T	A	TO	PF	S	Blk	TP	PPM
GRANT, A.	21	1/5	.200	0/0	.000	-/8	0	3	2	0	1	2	.095
GOODWIN, D.	38	4/8	.500	8/8	1.000	-/9	2	2	3	1	0	16	.421
COLBERT, D.	39	2/5	.400	1/1	1.000	-/6	1	3	3	1	0	5	.128
SCHELLENBERG, L.	40	3/6	.500	6/6	1.000	-/4	3	4	3	2	1	12	.300
TONEY, S.	37	5/16	.313	2/2	1.000	-/0	4	1	0	1	0	12	.324
ZERN, J.	17	1/2	.500	0/0	.000	-/1	0	3	5	0	1	2	.118
CHRISTIE, D.	7	0/1	.000	0/0	.000	-/1	1	1	1	1	0	0	.000
HARRIS, T.	1	0/0	.000	0/0	.000	-/0	0	0	0	0	0	0	.000
Totals	200	16/43	.372	17/17	1.000	-/30	12	16	16	5	2	49	.245

Team Rebounds: Villanova 1; Dayton 2. Disqualified: Dayton—Zern. Technical fouls: None.

	1st Half	2nd Half	Final
Villanova	21	30	51
Dayton	23	26	49

Maryland (69) Coach: Lefty Driesell

	Min.	Total FG / FGA	Pct.	FT / FTA	Pct.	Reb. O / T	A	TO	PF	S	Blk	TP	PPM
BIAS, L.	42	10/17	.588	5/ 6	.833	-/ 9	1	4	5	1	1	25	.595
BRANCH, A.	45	9/20	.450	6/ 6	1.000	-/ 5	0	4	3	2	3	24	.533
LEWIS, D.	25	1/ 1	1.000	0/ 0	.000	-/ 6	1	3	5	1	4	2	.080
GATLIN, K.	44	1/ 6	.167	0/ 0	.000	-/ 3	10	4	2	0	0	2	.045
ADKINS, J.	45	6/ 9	.667	0/ 0	.000	-/ 2	3	0	2	3	0	12	.267
LONG, T.	7	0/ 0	.000	0/ 0	.000	-/ 0	0	0	1	0	0	0	.000
JONES, T.	15	2/ 2	1.000	0/ 0	.000	-/ 0	0	0	1	0	0	4	.267
BAXTER, J.	2	0/ 0	.000	0/ 0	.000	-/ 0	0	0	0	0	0	0	.000
Totals	225	29/55	.527	11/12	.917	-/25	15	15	19	7	8	69	.307

Miami (Ohio) (68) Coach: Jerry Irson

	Min.	Total FG / FGA	Pct.	FT / FTA	Pct.	Reb. O / T	A	TO	PF	S	Blk	TP	PPM
HARPER, R.	44	9/14	.643	8/11	.727	-/ 8	3	4	3	3	0	26	.591
HUNTER, R.	22	3/ 9	.333	1/ 2	.500	-/ 3	0	3	2	0	0	7	.318
LAMPE, T.	18	1/ 4	.250	0/ 0	.000	-/ 2	0	3	0	0	2	2	.111
SCHILLING, E.	30	2/ 6	.333	0/ 0	.000	-/ 4	6	4	2	1	0	4	.133
NEWSOME, E.	41	4/10	.400	7/ 9	.778	-/ 2	2	2	3	2	0	15	.366
HALL, M.	12	0/ 2	.000	0/ 0	.000	-/ 2	0	1	1	0	0	0	.000
STAKER, T.	32	3/ 8	.375	0/ 0	.000	-/ 3	1	0	2	1	1	6	.188
HANNA, L.	26	4/ 6	.667	0/ 0	.000	-/ 8	0	0	1	0	0	8	.308
Totals	225	26/59	.441	16/22	.727	-/32	12	17	14	7	1	68	.302

Team Rebounds: Maryland 3; Miami (Ohio) 4. Disqualified: Maryland—Bias, Lewis. Technical fouls: Maryland—Adkins.

	1st Half	2nd Half	1st OT	Final
Maryland	36	23	10	69
Miami (Ohio)	29	30	9	68

Louisiana State (55) Coach: Dale Brown

	Min.	Total FG / FGA	Pct.	FT / FTA	Pct.	Reb. O / T	A	TO	PF	S	Blk	TP	PPM
WILLIAMS, J.	-	6/ 8	.750	0/ 0	.000	-/ 5	1	1	4	0	0	12	-
REYNOLDS, J.	-	1/ 8	.125	2/ 2	1.000	-/ 4	2	2	3	1	2	4	-
WILSON, N.	-	4/ 8	.500	1/ 2	.500	-/ 5	0	3	5	3	0	9	-
TAYLOR, D.	-	2/13	.154	0/ 0	.000	-/ 1	3	4	4	1	0	4	-
REDDEN, D.	-	1/ 5	.200	0/ 0	.000	-/ 3	2	2	2	1	0	2	-
BLANTON, R.	-	1/ 1	1.000	2/ 4	.500	-/ 3	1	1	3	1	0	4	-
BROWN, D.	-	4/10	.400	0/ 0	.000	-/ 2	2	0	3	0	0	8	-
BROWN, O.	-	1/ 3	.333	2/ 2	1.000	-/ 5	1	0	2	2	1	4	-
VARGAS, J.	-	1/ 2	.500	0/ 0	.000	-/ 0	0	0	3	0	0	2	-
JOVANOVICH, Z.	-	0/ 1	.000	0/ 0	.000	-/ 2	0	0*	1	0	0	0	-
WILSON, A.	-	1/ 6	.167	0/ 0	.000	-/ 1	0	1	0	0	0	2	-
CONLEY, O.	-	1/ 3	.333	2/ 3	.667	-/ 2	0	0	0	0	0	4	-
BUKUMIROVICH, N.	-	0/ 0	.000	0/ 0	.000	-/ 0	2	0	1	0	0	0	-
Totals	200	23/68	.338	9/13	.692	-/33	14	13	32	9	3	55	.275

Navy (78) Coach: Paul Evans

	Min.	Total FG / FGA	Pct.	FT / FTA	Pct.	Reb. O / T	A	TO	PF	S	Blk	TP	PPM
BUTLER, V.	37	5/11	.455	10/10	1.000	-/ 9	2	2	4	0	0	20	.541
WHITAKER, K.	38	2/ 7	.286	9/10	.900	-/ 4	2	3	2	1	0	13	.342
ROBINSON, D.	38	8/14	.571	2/ 7	.286	-/18	0	3	2	1	3	18	.474
REES, C.	27	1/ 3	.333	2/ 2	1.000	-/ 1	2	3	1	2	1	4	.148
WOJCIK, D.	36	5/ 7	.714	8/ 8	1.000	-/ 3	8	3	2	0	0	18	.500
LIEBERT, C.	7	0/ 1	.000	0/ 2	.000	-/ 1	0	1	1	0	0	0	.000
WELLS, T.	7	0/ 1	.000	0/ 0	.000	-/ 1	0	0	2	0	0	0	.000
COYNE, K.	2	0/ 0	.000	1/ 2	.500	-/ 0	0	0	0	0	0	1	.500
MATA, S.	2	0/ 0	.000	2/ 2	1.000	-/ 0	0	0	0	0	0	2	1.000
MANHERTZ, C.	2	0/ 0	.000	0/ 0	.000	-/ 1	0	0	2	0	0	0	.000
KLOOSTER, M.	2	0/ 0	.000	0/ 0	.000	-/ 0	0	0	0	0	0	0	.000
REED, J.	1	0/ 0	.000	0/ 0	.000	-/ 0	0	0	0	0	0	0	.000
KURKA, M.	1	1/ 1	1.000	0/ 0	.000	-/ 0	0	0	0	0	0	2	2.000
Totals	200	22/45	.489	34/43	.791	-/38	14	15	16	4	4	78	.390

Team Rebounds: Navy 3; Louisiana St. 2. Disqualified: Louisiana St.—Wilson. Technical fouls: None.

	1st Half	2nd Half	Final
Louisiana St.	24	31	55
Navy	28	50	78

Purdue (58) Coach: Gene Keady

	Min.	Total FG / FGA	Pct.	FT / FTA	Pct.	Reb. O / T	A	TO	PF	S	Blk	TP	PPM
ATKINSON, M.	36	0/ 2	.000	0/ 0	.000	-/ 3	2	0	4	1	1	0	.000
MITCHELL, T.	11	0/ 2	.000	0/ 0	.000	-/ 2	0	0	2	2	0	0	.000
BULLOCK, J.	40	6/15	.400	1/ 3	.333	-/10	0	3	4	0	0	13	.325
LEWIS, T.	30	9/17	.529	1/ 2	.500	-/ 2	1	0	1	1	0	19	.633
REID, S.	39	9/17	.529	0/ 2	.000	-/ 3	6	1	4	2	1	18	.462
GADIS, M.	10	0/ 1	.000	0/ 0	.000	-/ 0	1	0	1	0	0	0	.000
ROBINSON, H.	5	0/ 0	.000	0/ 0	.000	-/ 0	0	0	0	0	0	0	.000
LITTLEJOHN, R.	29	3/ 5	.600	2/ 2	1.000	-/ 9	0	2	0	1	0	8	.276
Totals	200	27/59	.458	4/ 9	.444	-/29	9	7	15	7	2	58	.290

Auburn (59) Coach: Sonny Smith

	Min.	Total FG / FGA	Pct.	FT / FTA	Pct.	Reb. O / T	A	TO	PF	S	Blk	TP	PPM
MORRIS, C.	37	9/14	.643	1/ 2	.500	-/ 3	0	2	1	0	2	19	.514
PERSON, C.	39	9/17	.529	2/ 2	1.000	-/ 8	0	2	3	2	1	20	.513
MOORE, J.	28	1/ 5	.200	0/ 0	.000	-/ 7	1	1	3	0	1	2	.071
WHITE, G.	37	3/ 5	.600	1/ 4	.250	-/ 5	4	3	1	0	0	7	.189
FORD, F.	39	4/ 7	.571	1/ 1	1.000	-/ 6	3	3	2	3	0	9	.231
LYNN, J.	7	0/ 2	.000	0/ 0	.000	-/ 0	0	0	0	0	0	0	.000
GUEST, D.	3	0/ 1	.000	0/ 0	.000	-/ 0	0	0	0	0	0	0	.000
HOLLAND, C.	10	1/ 1	1.000	0/ 0	.000	-/ 0	0	0	1	0	0	2	.200
Totals	200	27/52	.519	5/ 9	.556	-/30	8	11	11	5	4	59	.295

Team Rebounds: Auburn 5; Purdue 0. Disqualified: None. Technical fouls: None.

	1st Half	2nd Half	Final
Purdue	25	33	58
Auburn	31	28	59

Kansas (49) Coach: Larry Brown

	Min.	Total FG / FGA	Pct.	FT / FTA	Pct.	Reb. O / T	A	TO	PF	S	Blk	TP	PPM
MANNING, D.	38	4/ 5	.800	1/ 2	.500	-/ 6	1	4	4	2	1	9	.237
KELLOGG, R.	38	4/ 9	.444	2/ 3	.667	-/ 1	0	1	3	0	0	10	.263
DREILING, G.	36	3/ 4	.750	4/ 4	1.000	-/ 8	0	0	3	0	4	10	.278
HUNTER, C.	37	2/ 3	.667	0/ 2	.000	-/ 3	4	1	1	2	0	4	.108
THOMPSON, C.	34	3/ 7	.429	6/ 8	.750	-/ 2	1	0	4	2	0	12	.353
TURGEON, M.	2	0/ 0	.000	0/ 0	.000	-/ 0	2	0	1	1	0	0	.000
CAMPBELL, A.	2	0/ 0	.000	0/ 2	.000	-/ 0	0	1	0	0	0	0	.000
HULL, R.	2	0/ 0	.000	0/ 0	.000	-/ 0	0	0	0	0	0	0	.000
NEWTON, M.	6	0/ 0	.000	1/ 2	.500	-/ 1	0	0	0	0	0	1	.167
PIPER, C.	2	0/ 0	.000	0/ 0	.000	-/ 0	0	0	1	0	0	0	.000
BOYLE, T.	1	0/ 0	.000	3/ 4	.750	-/ 0	0	0	0	0	0	3	3.000
PELLOCK, M.	1	0/ 0	.000	0/ 1	.000	-/ 0	2	0	0	0	0	0	.000
JOHNSON, J.	1	0/ 0	.000	0/ 0	.000	-/ 0	0	0	0	0	0	0	.000
Totals	200	16/28	.571	17/28	.607	-/21	8	8	17	7	6	49	.245

Ohio (38) Coach: Danny Nee

	Min.	Total FG / FGA	Pct.	FT / FTA	Pct.	Reb. O / T	A	TO	PF	S	Blk	TP	PPM
SCARBERRY, R.	27	2/ 7	.286	0/ 0	.000	-/ 1	1	1	1	1	0	4	.148
HICKS, E.	37	0/ 3	.000	3/ 4	.750	-/ 7	0	0	3	0	0	3	.081
STANFEL, R.	6	0/ 0	.000	0/ 0	.000	-/ 0	0	0	0	0	0	0	.000
TATUM, R.	37	1/ 8	.125	0/ 0	.000	-/ 0	2	1	5	1	0	2	.054
BARON, P.	34	1/ 3	.333	2/ 5	.400	-/ 6	2	3	4	1	0	4	.118
SMITH, R.	2	0/ 0	.000	2/ 2	1.000	-/ 1	0	1	0	0	0	2	1.000
WASHINGTON, E.	3	0/ 3	.000	0/ 0	.000	-/ 0	0	1	1	1	0	0	.000
LEHMANN, M.	2	1/ 1	1.000	0/ 0	.000	-/ 0	0	1	0	0	0	2	1.000
SMITH, H.	17	2/ 7	.286	0/ 1	.000	-/ 5	0	2	1	0	0	4	.235
BROCK, J.	1	1/ 1	1.000	0/ 0	.000	-/ 0	1	0	1	0	0	2	2.000
RHODES, J.	2	0/ 0	.000	0/ 0	.000	-/ 3	0	0	2	0	0	0	.000
ALEXANDER, V.	32	6/ 9	.667	3/ 3	1.000	-/ 3	0	2	3	1	0	15	.469
Totals	200	14/42	.333	10/15	.667	-/26	5	11	22	6	0	38	.190

Team Rebounds: Kansas 0; Ohio 5. Disqualified: Ohio—Tatum. Technical fouls: None.

	1st Half	2nd Half	Final
Kansas	18	31	49
Ohio	15	23	38

Notre Dame (79)   Coach: Digger Phelps

	Min.	Total FG/FGA	Pct.	FT/FTA	Pct.	Reb. O/T	A	TO	PF	S	Blk	TP	PPM
ROYAL, D.	29	4/ 7	.571	4/ 4	1.000	-/ 4	0	3	5	0	0	12	.414
PRICE, J.	34	7/ 9	.778	2/ 2	1.000	-/ 3	2	3	4	0	0	16	.471
KEMPTON, T.	27	3/ 5	.600	3/ 4	.750	-/ 5	0	2	3	0	1	9	.333
RIVERS, D.	36	8/12	.667	5/ 6	.833	-/ 1	3	4	1	0	0	21	.583
HICKS, S.	35	5/ 8	.625	4/ 4	1.000	-/ 5	0	1	2	0	0	14	.400
DUFF, D.	4	0/ 0	.000	0/ 0	.000	-/ 1	0	1	0	0	0	0	.000
DOLAN, J.	19	3/ 3	1.000	1/ 1	1.000	-/ 6	0	2	2	0	1	7	.368
BARLOW, K.	15	0/ 3	.000	0/ 0	.000	-/ 1	1	0	2	0	0	0	.000
VOCE, G.	1	0/ 0	.000	0/ 0	.000	-/ 0	0	0	0	0	0	0	.000
Totals	200	30/47	.638	19/21	.905	-/26	6	16	19	0	2	79	.395

North Carolina (76)   Coach: Dean Smith

	Min.	Total FG/FGA	Pct.	FT/FTA	Pct.	Reb. O/T	A	TO	PF	S	Blk	TP	PPM
WOLF, J.	34	6/ 9	.667	6/ 7	.857	-/11	0	4	2	0	1	18	.529
POPSON, D.	9	1/ 4	.250	0/ 0	.000	-/ 1	0	1	1	0	1	2	.222
DAUGHERTY, B.	35	11/15	.733	3/ 4	.750	-/11	1	3	3	0	2	25	.714
PETERSON, B.	18	1/ 2	.500	4/ 4	1.000	-/ 2	1	0	0	0	0	6	.333
SMITH, K.	39	1/ 6	.167	4/ 4	1.000	-/ 4	7	5	1	1	0	6	.154
SMITH, R.	3	0/ 1	.000	0/ 0	.000	-/ 1	0	0	0	0	0	0	.000
HUNTER, C.	7	1/ 4	.250	1/ 3	.333	-/ 0	0	0	0	1	0	3	.429
MARTIN, W.	23	6/ 8	.750	2/ 5	.400	-/ 7	0	4	0	0	6	14	.609
HALE, S.	32	1/ 4	.250	0/ 0	.000	-/ 4	2	3	1	1	0	2	.063
Totals	200	28/53	.528	20/27	.741	-/41	11	16	12	3	10	76	.380

Oregon State (70)   Coach: Ralph Miller

	Min.	Total FG/FGA	Pct.	FT/FTA	Pct.	Reb. O/T	A	TO	PF	S	Blk	TP	PPM
MILLER, T.	31	3/ 4	.750	4/ 4	1.000	-/ 3	1	0	5	1	1	10	.323
GREEN, A.	40	10/14	.714	6/ 9	.667	-/12	1	6	1	0	1	26	.650
WOODSIDE, S.	39	2/ 8	.250	1/ 2	.500	-/ 4	0	2	2	0	0	5	.128
KNOX, E.	19	2/ 5	.400	0/ 0	.000	-/ 1	0	2	3	1	0	4	.211
FLOWERS, D.	37	6/12	.500	1/ 1	1.000	-/ 1	3	5	4	1	0	13	.351
GUISTI, P.	1	0/ 0	.000	0/ 0	.000	-/ 0	0	0	0	0	0	0	.000
DERRAH, D.	4	0/ 0	.000	0/ 0	.000	-/ 0	0	0	1	0	0	0	.000
HOUSTON, D.	26	6/13	.462	0/ 1	.000	-/ 1	0	2	1	4	0	12	.462
KASKA, M.	3	0/ 0	.000	0/ 0	.000	-/ 0	0	1	1	0	0	0	.000
Totals	200	29/56	.518	12/17	.706	-/22	5	18	18	7	2	70	.350

Team Rebounds: Notre Dame 0; Oregon State 3. Disqualified: Notre Dame—Royal; Oregon State—Miller. Technical fouls: None.

	1st Half	2nd Half	Final
Notre Dame	35	44	79
Oregon State	26	44	70

Middle Tennessee State (57)   Coach: Bruce Stewart

	Min.	Total FG/FGA	Pct.	FT/FTA	Pct.	Reb. O/T	A	TO	PF	S	Blk	TP	PPM
THOMPSON, L.	37	10/17	.588	0/ 0	.000	-/ 8	3	1	4	1	0	20	.541
HAMMONDS, K.	40	3/18	.167	3/ 4	.750	-/ 7	0	5	4	1	0	9	.225
MILLER, B.	24	1/ 2	.500	0/ 0	.000	-/ 2	0	1	3	0	2	2	.083
COOKSEY, K.	38	7/22	.318	0/ 1	.000	-/ 5	2	1	3	1	0	14	.368
JOHNSON, J.	26	4/ 6	.667	0/ 2	.000	-/ 6	0	2	5	4	0	8	.308
MURRAY, N.	14	0/ 0	.000	0/ 0	.000	-/ 1	1	1	0	1	0	0	.000
STEVENSON, G.	5	2/ 3	.667	0/ 0	.000	-/ 1	1	1	0	0	0	4	.800
SMITH, R.	16	0/ 2	.000	0/ 0	.000	-/ 1	0	0	2	0	0	0	.000
Totals	200	27/70	.386	3/ 7	.429	-/31	7	12	21	8	2	57	.285

Team Rebounds: N. Carolina 0; Middle Tenn. St. 1. Disqualified: Middle Tenn. St.—Johnson. Technical fouls: None.

	1st Half	2nd Half	Final
N. Carolina	31	45	76
Middle Tenn. St.	31	26	57

SECOND ROUND WEST

St. John's (68)   Coach: Lou Carnesecca

	Min.	Total FG/FGA	Pct.	FT/FTA	Pct.	Reb. O/T	A	TO	PF	S	Blk	TP	PPM
BERRY, W.	40	6/11	.545	4/ 5	.800	-/ 6	0	4	3	0	2	16	.400
GLASS, W.	32	4/ 5	.800	1/ 2	.500	-/ 4	2	2	2	0	0	9	.281
WENNINGTON, B.	33	3/ 4	.750	1/ 2	.500	-/ 9	0	3	3	1	1	7	.212
MULLIN, C.	40	8/15	.533	10/10	1.000	-/ 5	4	6	4	3	0	26	.650
MOSES, M.	32	2/ 4	.500	4/ 5	.800	-/ 2	5	3	1	1	0	8	.250
JACKSON, M.	8	0/ 0	.000	2/ 4	.500	-/ 0	1	0	0	0	0	2	.250
JONES, S.	8	0/ 0	.000	0/ 0	.000	-/ 1	1	0	1	0	0	0	.000
STEWART, R.	7	0/ 0	.000	0/ 0	.000	-/ 0	0	0	1	0	0	0	.000
Totals	200	23/39	.590	22/28	.786	-/27	13	18	15	5	3	68	.340

Kentucky (64)   Coach: Joe Hall

	Min.	Total FG/FGA	Pct.	FT/FTA	Pct.	Reb. O/T	A	TO	PF	S	Blk	TP	PPM
BENNETT, W.	-	1/ 2	.500	2/ 2	1.000	-/ 4	2	1	3	0	0	4	-
WALKER, K.	-	10/14	.714	3/ 5	.600	-/ 6	1	0	1	0	2	23	-
BEARUP, B.	-	0/ 2	.000	2/ 2	1.000	-/ 1	3	3	1	0	0	2	-
DAVENDER, E.	-	6/10	.600	1/ 2	.500	-/ 4	1	3	0	1	0	13	-
HARDEN, R.	-	4/ 6	.667	0/ 0	.000	-/ 1	6	5	3	1	0	8	-
BLACKMON, J.	-	2/ 6	.333	0/ 0	.000	-/ 2	2	1	0	0	0	4	-
MADISON, R.	-	2/ 4	.500	3/ 3	1.000	-/ 3	0	1	0	0	0	7	-
LOCK, R.	-	0/ 1	.000	1/ 2	.500	-/ 1	0	0	1	0	0	1	-
JENKINS, C.	-	1/ 2	.500	0/ 0	.000	-/ 2	0	0	1	0	0	2	-
Totals	200	26/47	.553	12/16	.750	-/24	15	14	10	2	2	64	.320

Arkansas (65)   Coach: Eddie Sutton

	Min.	Total FG/FGA	Pct.	FT/FTA	Pct.	Reb. O/T	A	TO	PF	S	Blk	TP	PPM
MILLS, W.	30	6/15	.400	0/ 0	.000	-/ 0	4	3	3	3	0	12	.400
BALENTINE, C.	40	4/ 8	.500	0/ 1	.000	-/ 5	4	3	3	1	0	8	.200
KLEINE, J.	40	7/15	.467	9/10	.900	-/11	1	2	4	0	0	23	.575
HUTCHINSON, K.	25	2/ 3	.667	0/ 0	.000	-/ 3	3	2	5	2	0	4	.160
FREEMAN, A.	34	5/ 7	.714	1/ 2	.500	-/ 1	0	1	5	1	0	11	.324
ROSE, S.	2	0/ 0	.000	0/ 0	.000	-/ 0	1	0	1	0	0	0	.000
REHL, K.	1	1/ 1	1.000	0/ 0	.000	-/ 0	0	1	0	0	0	2	2.000
IRVIN, B.	18	2/ 6	.333	1/ 2	.500	-/ 3	4	1	2	1	0	5	.278
LANG, A.	6	0/ 0	.000	0/ 0	.000	-/ 1	0	0	1	0	0	0	.000
POERSCHKE, E.	4	0/ 1	.000	0/ 0	.000	-/ 1	0	0	0	0	0	0	.000
Totals	200	27/56	.482	11/15	.733	-/25	17	12	24	8	0	65	.325

UNLV (61)   Coach: Jerry Tarkanian

	Min.	Total FG/FGA	Pct.	FT/FTA	Pct.	Reb. O/T	A	TO	PF	S	Blk	TP	PPM
JAMES, F.	28	5/ 8	.625	0/ 0	.000	-/ 1	5	1	0	0	0	10	.357
GILLIAM, A.	21	3/ 3	1.000	0/ 0	.000	-/ 1	0	0	3	0	0	6	.286
ADAMS, R.	34	6/14	.429	2/ 2	1.000	-/13	1	3	4	4	0	14	.412
JONES, A.	35	6/14	.429	1/ 1	1.000	-/ 4	4	0	1	0	0	13	.371
BANKS, F.	27	4/ 8	.500	0/ 0	.000	-/ 1	2	3	5	0	0	8	.296
ROBINSON, R.	17	0/ 3	.000	2/ 2	1.000	-/ 2	0	0	2	0	2	2	.118
CATCHINGS, E.	20	4/ 6	.667	0/ 1	.000	-/ 2	3	1	2	0	0	8	.400
GRAHAM, G.	13	0/ 1	.000	0/ 0	.000	-/ 0	2	1	1	1	0	0	.000
HUDSON, E.	5	0/ 1	.000	0/ 0	.000	-/ 0	0	0	1	0	0	0	.000
Totals	200	28/58	.483	5/ 6	.833	-/24	17	9	18	5	2	61	.305

Team Rebounds: St. John's 1; Arkansas 0. Disqualified: Arkansas—Hutchinson, Freeman. Technical fouls: Arkansas—Coach Sutton.

	1st Half	2nd Half	Final
St. John's	32	36	68
Arkansas	26	39	65

Team Rebounds: Kentucky 4; UNLV 3. Disqualified: UNLV—Banks. Technical fouls: UNLV—Jones.

	1st Half	2nd Half	Final
Kentucky	30	34	64
UNLV	30	31	61

UTEP (73)   Coach: Don Haskins

	Min.	Total FG/FGA	Pct.	FT/FTA	Pct.	Reb. O/T	A	TO	PF	S	Blk	TP	PPM
SMITH, J.	38	3/12	.250	4/6	.667	-/5	1	3	4	1	0	10	.263
HAMILTON, K.	20	0/1	.000	0/0	.000	-/0	0	0	1	0	0	0	.000
FEITL, D.	26	5/9	.556	2/3	.667	-/7	2	3	4	0	1	12	.462
GOODWIN, L.	38	9/15	.600	4/4	1.000	-/0	2	0	5	0	0	22	.579
LOCKHART, K.	32	4/11	.364	2/2	1.000	-/2	1	1	5	3	0	10	.313
GATES, Q.	15	2/4	.500	1/1	1.000	-/2	0	0	1	1	1	5	.333
JACKSON, J.	10	3/5	.600	0/0	.000	-/2	3	1	4	1	0	6	.600
ALLEN, D.	18	2/3	.667	4/4	1.000	-/0	0	0	2	0	0	8	.444
CLANTON, L.	2	0/1	.000	0/0	.000	-/0	0	0	0	0	0	0	.000
WASHINGTON, M.	1	0/0	.000	0/0	.000	-/0	0	1	1	0	0	0	.000
Totals	200	28/61	.459	17/20	.850	-/18	9	9	29	6	2	73	.365

North Carolina State (86)   Coach: Jim Valvano

	Min.	Total FG/FGA	Pct.	FT/FTA	Pct.	Reb. O/T	A	TO	PF	S	Blk	TP	PPM
PIERRE, R.	17	2/4	.500	3/6	.500	-/9	0	4	3	0	0	7	.412
CHARLES, L.	38	12/15	.800	6/10	.600	-/10	0	4	3	2	2	30	.789
MCQUEEN, C.	40	2/3	.667	0/0	.000	-/3	0	3	2	0	2	4	.100
WEBB, A.	37	8/9	.889	13/17	.765	-/2	7	2	3	1	0	29	.784
MCMILLAN, N.	31	3/3	1.000	3/5	.600	-/3	5	0	4	0	1	9	.290
BOLTON, B.	19	2/3	.667	1/2	.500	-/2	0	3	2	0	0	5	.263
GANNON, T.	7	0/1	.000	0/0	.000	-/1	1	1	1	0	0	0	.000
MYERS, E.	9	1/3	.333	0/0	.000	-/2	1	1	1	0	0	2	.222
JACKSON, Q.	1	0/0	.000	0/0	.000	-/0	0	1	0	0	0	0	.000
WARREN, M.	1	0/0	.000	0/0	.000	-/0	0	0	0	0	0	0	.000
Totals	200	30/41	.732	26/40	.650	-/32	14	19	19	3	5	86	.430

Team Rebounds: N.C. State 4; UTEP 5. Disqualified: UTEP—Goodwin, Lockhart. Technical fouls: None.

	1st Half	2nd Half	Final
UTEP	28	45	73
N.C. State	31	55	86

Alabama (63)   Coach: Wimp Sanderson

	Min.	Total FG/FGA	Pct.	FT/FTA	Pct.	Reb. O/T	A	TO	PF	S	Blk	TP	PPM
JOHNSON, B.	35	1/5	.200	4/5	.800	-/10	2	1	3	2	1	6	.171
MCKEY, D.	35	3/7	.429	0/1	.000	-/3	3	3	2	1	3	6	.171
HURT, B.	40	8/10	.800	3/4	.750	-/13	0	1	2	0	1	19	.475
GOTTFRIED, M.	20	3/8	.375	4/4	1.000	-/2	0	4	2	0	1	10	.500
CONER, T.	37	5/7	.714	4/6	.667	-/1	5	3	3	1	0	14	.378
FARMER, J.	24	4/10	.400	0/2	.000	-/2	0	1	1	0	1	8	.333
NEAL, D.	9	0/1	.000	0/0	.000	-/2	0	0	3	0	0	0	.000
Totals	200	24/48	.500	15/22	.682	-/33	10	13	16	4	7	63	.315

Virginia Commonwealth (59)   Coach: J. D. Barnett

	Min.	Total FG/FGA	Pct.	FT/FTA	Pct.	Reb. O/T	A	TO	PF	S	Blk	TP	PPM
BROWN, M.	40	2/9	.222	1/2	.500	-/4	1	2	3	0	0	5	.125
WAKE, N.	22	0/1	.000	1/3	.333	-/7	0	0	2	0	1	1	.045
SCHLEGEL, M.	40	7/12	.583	1/3	.333	-/8	2	4*	4	0	0	15	.375
DUNCAN, C.	37	5/16	.313	1/3	.333	-/8	1	1	5	0	0	11	.297
LAMB, R.	39	12/23	.522	1/2	.500	-/7	3	2	5	3	0	25	.641
ALLEN, B.	1	0/0	.000	0/0	.000	-/0	0	0	0	0	0	0	.000
DICKERSON, R.	14	1/2	.500	0/0	.000	-/0	0	0	5	1	0	2	.143
STINNIE, P.	2	0/0	.000	0/0	.000	-/0	0	0	0	0	0	0	.000
ROBINSON, A.	5	0/0	.000	0/0	.000	-/0	0	0	1	0	0	0	.000
Totals	200	27/63	.429	5/13	.385	-/34	7	9	25	4	0	59	.295

Team Rebounds: Alabama 3; Va. Commonwealth 0. Disqualified: Va. Commonwealth—Duncan, Lamb, Dickerson. Technical fouls: None.

	1st Half	2nd Half	Final
Alabama	27	36	63
Va. Commonwealth	19	40	59

SECOND ROUND EAST

Georgetown (63)   Coach: John Thompson

	Min.	Total FG/FGA	Pct.	FT/FTA	Pct.	Reb. O/T	A	TO	PF	S	Blk	TP	PPM
MARTIN, B.	36	2/9	.222	2/5	.400	2/3	0	2	2	3	0	6	.167
WILLIAMS, R.	35	3/7	.429	7/8	.875	3/6	5	2	4	2	0	13	.371
EWING, P.	36	4/6	.667	4/7	.571	1/7	1	1	4	0	0	12	.333
JACKSON, M.	33	6/7	.857	2/3	.667	0/1	5	1	3	1	0	14	.424
WINGATE, D.	32	3/5	.600	6/8	.750	2/3	2	2	4	1	0	12	.375
MCDONALD, P.	4	0/0	.000	0/0	.000	0/0	0	0	0	0	0	0	.000
BROADNAX, H.	11	0/0	.000	0/1	.000	0/1	1	3	0	0	0	0	.000
DALTON, R.	11	3/4	.750	0/1	.000	0/1	0	0	1	0	0	6	.545
MATEEN, G.	1	0/0	.000	0/0	.000	1/2	0	0	1	0	0	0	.000
LOCKHART, T.	1	0/0	.000	0/0	.000	0/0	0	0	0	0	0	0	.000
Totals	200	21/38	.553	21/33	.636	9/24	14	11	19	7	0	63	.315

Temple (46)   Coach: John Chaney

	Min.	Total FG/FGA	Pct.	FT/FTA	Pct.	Reb. O/T	A	TO	PF	S	Blk	TP	PPM
HALL, G.	21	2/4	.500	3/5	.600	0/3	1	2	4	1	0	7	.333
RAYNE, C.	39	2/9	.222	2/2	1.000	3/7	1	2	5	0	0	6	.154
PERRY, T.	31	0/1	.000	0/1	.000	2/2	0	0	2	0	2	0	.000
BLACKWELL, N.	39	5/12	.417	5/5	1.000	2/2	3	5	5	0	0	15	.385
COE, E.	24	4/7	.571	2/3	.667	0/2	1	1	4	1	1	10	.417
BRANTLEY, D.	12	1/2	.500	0/1	.000	2/3	0	0	3	0	0	2	.167
EVANS, H.	30	3/9	.333	0/0	.000	1/1	6	3	3	1	0	6	.200
CLIFTON, K.	1	0/0	.000	0/0	.000	0/0	0	1	0	0	0	0	.000
POPLAWSKI, M.	1	0/0	.000	0/0	.000	0/0	0	0	1	0	0	0	.000
JOHNSON, S.	1	0/0	.000	0/0	.000	0/0	0	0	0	0	0	0	.000
FORRESTER, D.	1	0/0	.000	0/0	.000	0/0	0	0	0	0	0	0	.000
Totals	200	17/44	.386	12/17	.706	10/20	12	13	27	3	3	46	.230

Team Rebounds: Georgetown—7; Temple—5. Disqualified: Temple—Rayne, Blackwell. Technical fouls: Georgetown—Dalton.

	1st Half	2nd Half	Final
Georgetown	31	32	63
Temple	23	23	46

SMU (57)   Coach: Dave Bliss

	Min.	Total FG/FGA	Pct.	FT/FTA	Pct.	Reb. O/T	A	TO	PF	S	Blk	TP	PPM
PINK, R.	13	0/2	.000	0/0	.000	0/1	0	1	0	0	0	0	.000
DAVIS, L.	31	7/13	.538	0/0	.000	4/9	0	1	2	0	2	14	.452
KONCAK, J.	32	8/12	.667	3/4	.750	2/10	2	3	3	0	1	19	.594
MOORE, B.	30	1/4	.250	0/0	.000	2/6	9	3	5	0	0	2	.067
WRIGHT, C.	36	6/16	.375	1/2	.500	2/4	5	5	3	2	0	13	.361
LEWIS, K.	18	1/2	.500	0/0	.000	1/4	1	1	2	0	0	2	.111
FULLER, J.	11	1/1	1.000	0/0	.000	0/2	2	3	0	0	0	2	.182
WILLIAMS, J.	17	2/8	.250	1/2	.500	3/7	1	0	1	1	0	5	.294
JOHNSON, S.	12	0/1	.000	0/0	.000	0/1	1	0	0	0	0	0	.000
Totals	200	26/59	.441	5/8	.625	14/42	21	16	19	3	3	57	.285

Loyola-Chicago (70)   Coach: Gene Sullivan

	Min.	Total FG/FGA	Pct.	FT/FTA	Pct.	Reb. O/T	A	TO	PF	S	Blk	TP	PPM
HUGHES, A.	39	7/19	.368	0/0	.000	2/6	1	1	3	2	1	14	.359
BATTLE, A.	31	5/13	.385	2/3	.667	1/3	2	0	3	0	0	12	.387
MOORE, A.	39	3/9	.333	2/3	.667	6/10	0	0	3	0	2	8	.205
WILLIAMS, G.	39	4/7	.571	2/2	1.000	2/4	7	0	2	1	0	10	.256
GOLSTON, C.	39	6/14	.429	8/10	.800	0/4	5	2	1	0	0	20	.513
CENAR, M.	9	2/4	.500	0/0	.000	2/3	0	1	0	1	0	4	.444
CLARK, J.	1	0/0	.000	0/0	.000	0/0	1	1	0	0	0	0	.000
YOUNG, I.	1	0/1	.000	0/0	.000	1/1	0	0	1	0	0	0	.000
KLUSENDORF, D.	1	1/1	1.000	0/0	.000	0/0	0	0	0	0	0	2	2.000
BROOKS, N.	1	0/0	.000	0/0	.000	0/1	0	1	0	0	0	0	.000
Totals	200	28/68	.412	14/18	.778	13/31	16	5	13	7	3	70	.350

Team Rebounds: Loyola-Chicago—5; SMU—1. Disqualified: SMU—Moore. Technical fouls: None.

	1st Half	2nd Half	Final
SMU	30	27	57
Loyola-Chicago	31	39	70

Georgia (58)   Coach: Hugh Durham

	Min.	Total FG / FGA	Pct.	FT / FTA	Pct.	Reb. O / T	A	TO	PF	S	Blk	TP	PPM
CORHEN, R.	18	1/ 2	.500	0/ 0	.000	-/ 2	0	2	4	2	1	2	.111
WARD, J.	24	7/15	.467	3/ 3	1.000	-/ 3	3	1	2	1	0	17	.708
HENDERSON, D.	33	5/14	.357	3/ 4	.750	-/ 5	0	1	4	3	1	13	.394
CROSBY, G.	37	4/ 9	.444	0/ 0	.000	-/ 2	6	3	1	1	0	8	.216
HARTRY, D.	19	0/ 2	.000	0/ 0	.000	-/ 1	4	1	0	0	0	0	.000
HOWARD, M.	21	1/ 3	.333	1/ 2	.500	-/ 1	2	4	3	0	0	3	.143
KESSLER, C.	11	2/ 3	.667	0/ 0	.000	-/ 2	0	2	0	0	0	4	.364
MCMILLAN, H.	16	1/ 4	.250	0/ 3	.000	-/ 3	0	1	1	0	0	2	.125
DUNN, D.	18	3/ 3	1.000	1/ 1	1.000	-/ 7	0	2	3	2	0	7	.389
WILLIAMS, D.	3	1/ 1	1.000	0/ 0	.000	-/ 0	0	0	1	0	0	2	.667
Totals	200	25/56	.446	8/13	.615	-/26	15	17	18	10	2	58	.290

Illinois (74)   Coach: Lou Henson

	Min.	Total FG / FGA	Pct.	FT / FTA	Pct.	Reb. O / T	A	TO	PF	S	Blk	TP	PPM
NORMAN, K.	37	7/11	.636	1/ 2	.500	-/ 9	0	2	0	0	1	15	.405
WELCH, A.	34	4/ 8	.500	0/ 0	.000	-/ 3	3	1	0	0	0	8	.235
WINTERS, E.	25	6/ 9	.667	7/ 7	1.000	-/ 5	0	3	5	3	1	19	.760
ALTENBERGER, D.	35	7/10	.700	2/ 2	1.000	-/ 4	1	3	2	1	1	16	.457
DOUGLAS, B.	39	2/ 9	.222	1/ 2	.500	-/ 9	11	3	2	6	0	5	.128
MEENTS, S.	10	1/ 3	.333	0/ 0	.000	-/ 1	2	1	3	0	0	2	.200
WYSINGER, T.	16	2/ 3	.667	3/ 4	.750	-/ 1	1	2	3	0	0	7	.438
HAFTNER, S.	2	1/ 2	.500	0/ 0	.000	-/ 0	0	0	0	0	0	2	1.000
WOODWARD, R.	2	0/ 0	.000	0/ 0	.000	-/ 0	1	2	0	0	0	0	.000
Totals	200	30/55	.545	14/17	.824	-/32	19	17	15	10	3	74	.370

Team Rebounds: Illinois 2; Georgia 0. Disqualified: Illinois—Winters. Technical fouls: Illinois—Coach Henson.

	1st Half	2nd Half	Final
Georgia	19	39	58
Illinois	34	40	74

Syracuse (53)   Coach: Jim Boeheim

	Min.	Total FG / FGA	Pct.	FT / FTA	Pct.	Reb. O / T	A	TO	PF	S	Blk	TP	PPM
ADDISON, R.	40	6/13	.462	5/ 6	.833	-/ 5	1	2	4	1	0	17	.425
HAWKINS, A.	11	1/ 4	.250	0/ 0	.000	-/ 2	0	0	2	0	0	2	.182
SEIKALY, R.	32	3/ 8	.375	2/ 4	.500	-/ 5	0	1	3	2	2	8	.250
WASHINGTON, D.	38	2/ 9	.222	3/ 4	.750	-/ 2	11	6	4	1	0	7	.184
BROWN, M.	30	4/ 9	.444	0/ 0	.000	-/ 3	1	0	4	1	0	8	.267
ALEXIS, W.	33	5/ 8	.625	1/ 2	.500	-/ 4	0	2	5	0	1	11	.333
MONROE, G.	13	0/ 1	.000	0/ 0	.000	-/ 1	1	0	1	0	0	0	.000
HARRIED, H.	3	0/ 1	.000	0/ 1	.000	-/ 1	0	0	1	0	0	0	.000
Totals	200	21/53	.396	11/17	.647	-/23	14	11	24	5	3	53	.265

Georgia Tech (70)   Coach: Bobby Cremins

	Min.	Total FG / FGA	Pct.	FT / FTA	Pct.	Reb. O / T	A	TO	PF	S	Blk	TP	PPM
SALLEY, J.	40	5/ 8	.625	3/ 6	.500	-/ 9	2	4	3	2	3	13	.325
PETWAY, S.	36	2/ 5	.400	4/ 4	1.000	-/ 7	2	1	4	2	0	8	.222
JOSEPH, Y.	36	4/ 8	.500	9/10	.900	-/ 5	3	1	2	0	1	17	.472
PRICE, M.	40	6/14	.429	6/ 6	1.000	-/ 3	2	5	2	0	0	18	.450
DALRYMPLE, B.	36	3/ 7	.429	4/ 5	.800	-/10	6	3	5	0	1	10	.278
FORD, A.	4	0/ 1	.000	0/ 0	.000	-/ 0	0	1	0	0	0	0	.000
FERRELL, D.	7	1/ 2	.500	0/ 0	.000	-/ 1	2	0	0	1	0	2	.286
MANSELL, J.	1	0/ 0	.000	2/ 2	1.000	-/ 2	0	0	0	0	0	2	2.000
Totals	200	21/45	.467	28/33	.848	-/37	17	15	16	5	5	70	.350

Team Rebounds: Georgia Tech 1; Syracuse 1. Disqualified: Georgia Tech—Dalrymple; Syracuse—Alexis. Technical fouls: None.

	1st Half	2nd Half	Final
Syracuse	27	26	53
Georgia Tech	28	42	70

SECOND ROUND MIDWEST

Oklahoma (75)   Coach: Billy Tubbs

	Min.	Total FG / FGA	Pct.	FT / FTA	Pct.	Reb. O / T	A	TO	PF	S	Blk	TP	PPM
BOWIE, A.	40	5/ 9	.556	2/ 2	1.000	1/ 5	7	2	3	1	0	12	.300
KENNEDY, D.	37	7/10	.700	2/ 2	1.000	2/ 8	7	4	2	1	0	16	.432
TISDALE, WA.	40	14/16	.875	1/ 4	.250	1/ 8	0	2	3	0	2	29	.725
MCCALISTER, T.	40	6/12	.500	0/ 1	.000	0/ 2	7	3	2	3	2	12	.300
DAVIS, L.	30	1/ 2	.500	0/ 0	.000	1/ 4	2	2	1	1	0	2	.067
CLARK, S.	10	2/ 4	.500	0/ 0	.000	0/ 0	1	2	1	1	0	4	.400
JOHNSON, D.	3	0/ 0	.000	0/ 0	.000	0/ 0	0	1	2	0	0	0	.000
Totals	200	35/53	.660	5/11	.455	5/27	24	16	14	6	2	75	.375

Illinois State (69)   Coach: Bob Donewald

	Min.	Total FG / FGA	Pct.	FT / FTA	Pct.	Reb. O / T	A	TO	PF	S	Blk	TP	PPM
SANDERS, D.	18	2/ 5	.400	0/ 0	.000	2/ 3	0	2	2	0	0	4	.222
STEFANOVIC, L.	40	10/19	.526	1/ 1	1.000	0/ 4	3	0	3	2	0	21	.525
BRAKSICK, B.	27	3/ 7	.429	1/ 2	.500	1/ 3	2	3	4	0	0	7	.259
MCKENNY, M.	38	5/ 6	.833	0/ 0	.000	2/ 5	3	1	3	2	0	10	.263
JOHNSON, R.	32	6/10	.600	2/ 3	.667	0/ 2	4	3	2	3	0	14	.438
ANDERSON, W.	3	0/ 0	.000	0/ 0	.000	1/ 1	1	0	1	0	0	0	.000
DUNCAN, B.	28	5/12	.417	1/ 1	1.000	0/ 1	0	2	1	0	0	11	.393
TAPHORN, M.	11	1/ 2	.500	0/ 0	.000	0/ 1	2	0	0	0	0	2	.182
HOLIFIELD, T.	3	0/ 0	.000	0/ 0	.000	0/ 0	0	1	0	0	0	0	.000
Totals	200	32/61	.525	5/ 7	.714	6/20	15	12	16	7	0	69	.345

Team Rebounds: Oklahoma 3; Illinois State 2. Disqualified: None. Technical fouls: None.

	1st Half	2nd Half	Final
Oklahoma	35	40	75
Illinois State	31	38	69

Louisiana Tech (79)   Coach: Andy Russo

	Min.	Total FG / FGA	Pct.	FT / FTA	Pct.	Reb. O / T	A	TO	PF	S	Blk	TP	PPM
SIMMONS, W.	28	5/12	.417	0/ 0	.000	-/ 6	0	1	2	0	3	10	.357
GODBOLT, R.	34	3/ 7	.429	0/ 0	.000	-/ 6	2	2	1	0	0	6	.176
MALONE, K.	30	11/22	.500	5/10	.500	-/14	3	3	4	1	0	27	.900
DAVIS, A.	21	3/ 3	1.000	0/ 0	.000	-/ 0	1	1	5	0	0	6	.286
SMITH, W.	37	4/ 6	.667	3/ 4	.750	-/ 6	11	6	2	1	0	11	.297
BLAND, W.	25	3/ 5	.600	2/ 4	.500	-/ 4	1	2	0	1	1	8	.320
TROUTMAN, K.	1	0/ 0	.000	0/ 0	.000	-/ 0	0	0	0	0	0	0	.000
EMERSON, D.	1	0/ 0	.000	0/ 0	.000	-/ 0	0	0	0	0	0	0	.000
HANNIBAL, R.	1	0/ 0	.000	0/ 0	.000	-/ 0	0	0	0	0	0	0	.000
LEWIS, K.	2	1/ 1	1.000	0/ 1	.000	-/ 0	0	0	0	0	0	2	1.000
FRANK, A.	19	3/ 5	.600	3/ 3	1.000	-/ 2	4	0	1	3	0	9	.474
JORDAN, D.	1	0/ 0	.000	0/ 0	.000	-/ 0	0	0	0	0	0	0	.000
Totals	200	33/61	.541	13/22	.591	-/38	22	15	15	6	4	79	.395

Ohio State (67)   Coach: Eldon Miller

	Min.	Total FG / FGA	Pct.	FT / FTA	Pct.	Reb. O / T	A	TO	PF	S	Blk	TP	PPM
HOPSON, D.	39	9/17	.529	2/ 3	.667	-/ 9	1	2	5	1	0	20	.513
CONCHECK, J.	30	2/ 6	.333	0/ 0	.000	-/ 6	2	1	3	2	0	4	.133
SELLERS, B.	30	3/ 8	.375	0/ 0	.000	-/ 6	0	2	5	0	4	6	.200
STOKES, R.	39	3/ 9	.333	5/ 6	.833	-/ 3	5	2	4	2	0	11	.282
TAYLOR, T.	35	9/18	.500	0/ 1	.000	-/ 3	7	6	4	2	0	18	.514
JONES, D.	21	4/ 6	.667	0/ 0	.000	-/ 2	1	0	0	1	0	8	.381
HONINGFORD, J.	1	0/ 0	.000	0/ 0	.000	-/ 0	0	1	0	0	0	0	.000
ANDERSON, S.	1	0/ 0	.000	0/ 0	.000	-/ 1	0	0	0	0	0	0	.000
ANDERSON, J.	3	0/ 0	.000	0/ 0	.000	-/ 0	0	0	1	0	0	0	.000
MCGEE, C.	1	0/ 0	.000	0/ 0	.000	-/ 1	0	0	0	0	0	0	.000
Totals	200	30/64	.469	7/10	.700	-/31	16	13	22	8	4	67	.335

Team Rebounds: Louisiana Tech 4; Ohio State 1. Disqualified: Louisiana Tech—Davis; Ohio State—Hopson, Sellers. Technical fouls: None.

	1st Half	2nd Half	Final
Louisiana Tech	37	42	79
Ohio State	28	39	67

Boston College (74)   Coach: Gary Williams

	Min.	Total FG / FGA	Pct.	FT / FTA	Pct.	Reb. O / T	A	TO	PF	S	Blk	TP	PPM
MCCREADY, R.	34	6/13	.462	8/10	.800	-/ 7	1	-	1	-	-	20	.588
TALLEY	21	0/ 0	.000	2/ 3	.667	-/ 2	0	-	4	-	-	2	.095
GORDON	9	0/ 0	.000	0/ 2	.000	-/ 0	0	-	2	-	-	0	.000
ADAMS, M.	34	9/15	.600	1/ 2	.500	-/ 4	4	-	4	-	-	19	.559
PRESSLEY, D.	25	3/ 7	.429	1/ 2	.500	-/ 6	2	-	3	-	-	7	.280
SCHMIDT	11	0/ 1	.000	0/ 0	.000	-/ 1	2	-	3	-	-	0	.000
PRIMUS, S.	25	3/ 6	.500	2/ 2	1.000	-/ 3	3	-	3	-	-	8	.320
BARRY	12	2/ 6	.333	0/ 0	.000	-/ 4	0	-	1	-	-	4	.333
SCOTT	15	2/ 2	1.000	2/ 4	.500	-/ 4	0	-	4	-	-	6	.400
BOWERS	14	3/ 4	.750	2/ 2	1.000	-/ 2	0	-	3	-	-	8	.571
Totals	200	28/54	.519	18/27	.667	-/33	12	18	28	-	-	74	.370

Duke (73)   Coach: Mike Krzyzewski

	Min.	Total FG / FGA	Pct.	FT / FTA	Pct.	Reb. O / T	A	TO	PF	S	Blk	TP	PPM
ALARIE, M.	30	5/12	.417	2/ 2	1.000	-/ 6	1	-	5	-	-	12	.400
MEAGHER, D.	34	1/ 3	.333	1/ 3	.333	-/ 7	4	-	4	-	-	3	.088
BILAS, J.	37	4/ 7	.571	7/10	.700	-/13	4	-	3	-	-	15	.405
AMAKER, T.	36	5/13	.385	9/10	.900	-/ 1	5	-	2	-	-	19	.528
DAWKINS, J.	40	6/21	.286	6/ 8	.750	-/10	5	-	2	-	-	18	.450
HENDERSON, J.	11	1/ 4	.250	0/ 0	.000	-/ 2	0	-	1	-	-	2	.182
STRICKLAND, K.	2	0/ 0	.000	0/ 0	.000	-/ 1	0	-	1	-	-	0	.000
WILLIAMS, W.	4	1/ 2	.500	0/ 0	.000	-/ 0	0	-	0	-	-	2	.500
KING, B.	6	0/ 0	.000	2/ 4	.500	-/ 2	0	-	3	-	-	2	.333
Totals	200	23/62	.371	27/37	.730	-/42	19	5	21	-	-	73	.365

Team Rebounds: Boston College 4; Duke 3. Disqualified: Duke—Alarie. Technical fouls: None.

	1st Half	2nd Half	Final
Boston College	32	42	74
Duke	37	36	73

Alabama-Birmingham (66)   Coach: Gene Bartow

	Min.	Total FG / FGA	Pct.	FT / FTA	Pct.	Reb. O / T	A	TO	PF	S	Blk	TP	PPM
JOHNSON, M.	5	0/ 0	.000	1/ 2	.500	0/ 1	0	1	0	0	0	1	.200
MINCY, J.	29	0/ 8	.000	7/11	.636	5/ 9	0	2	4	0	0	7	.241
GORDON, A.	41	6/13	.462	2/ 2	1.000	10/15	1	0	2	2	0	14	.341
MITCHELL, S.	41	6/15	.400	1/ 2	.500	0/ 2	1	1	3	0	0	13	.317
PONDER, J.	44	5/13	.385	8/ 9	.889	1/ 4	1	2	2	0	0	18	.409
FOSTER, T.	2	0/ 0	.000	0/ 0	.000	0/ 0	0	1	0	0	0	0	.000
BARTOW, M.	3	0/ 0	.000	0/ 0	.000	0/ 0	1	0	0	0	0	0	.000
CHARLES, M.	40	3/ 4	.750	3/ 4	.750	1/ 3	4	1	2	2	0	9	.225
COLLINS, E.	7	0/ 1	.000	0/ 0	.000	0/ 0	0	0	1	0	1	0	.000
JOHNSON, A.	13	2/ 3	.667	0/ 0	.000	3/ 4	0	1	2	0	1	4	.308
Totals	225	22/57	.386	22/30	.733	20/38	7	10	16	4	2	66	.293

Memphis State (67)   Coach: Dana Kirk

	Min.	Total FG / FGA	Pct.	FT / FTA	Pct.	Reb. O / T	A	TO	PF	S	Blk	TP	PPM
LEE, K.	36	12/17	.706	4/ 6	.667	4/ 6	0	1	5	0	0	28	.778
HOLMES, B.	39	2/ 7	.286	4/ 4	1.000	2/ 8	2	1	3	0	0	8	.205
BEDFORD, W.	37	3/12	.250	0/ 1	.000	3/ 6	0	5	3	1	3	6	.162
TURNER, A.	45	11/17	.647	1/ 2	.500	0/ 0	8	0	4	2	0	23	.511
ASKEW, V.	41	1/ 3	.333	0/ 0	.000	0/ 5	7	2	3	2	1	2	.049
WILFONG, J.	6	0/ 1	.000	0/ 0	.000	1/ 1	1	0	1	0	0	0	.000
BOYD, D.	9	0/ 2	.000	0/ 0	.000	2/ 3	0	2	1	0	0	0	.000
BECTON, W.	12	0/ 0	.000	0/ 0	.000	0/ 0	0	1	3	0	0	0	.000
Totals	225	29/59	.492	9/13	.692	12/29	18	10	24	6	4	67	.298

Team Rebounds: Memphis State 2; Ala.-Birmingham 2. Disqualified: Memphis State—Lee. Technical fouls: None.

	1st Half	2nd Half	1st OT	Final
Ala.-Birmingham	32	29	5	66
Memphis State	27	34	6	67

SECOND ROUND SOUTHEAST

Michigan (55)   Coach: Bill Freider

	Min.	Total FG / FGA	Pct.	FT / FTA	Pct.	Reb. O / T	A	TO	PF	S	Blk	TP	PPM
RELLFORD, R.	28	5/ 7	.714	1/ 2	.500	-/ 2	0	3	4	0	0	11	.393
WADE, B.	25	0/ 1	.000	0/ 0	.000	-/ 8	3	1	3	2	0	0	.000
TARPLEY, R.	40	7/14	.500	0/ 0	.000	-/13	1	2	1	1	0	14	.350
JOUBERT, A.	30	6/13	.462	0/ 0	.000	-/ 1	3	3	5	1	0	12	.400
GRANT, G.	33	0/ 4	.000	0/ 0	.000	-/ 0	1	3	5	0	0	0	.000
THOMPSON, G.	18	3/ 5	.600	2/ 3	.667	-/ 1	2	0	2	3	0	8	.444
HENDERSON, R.	15	2/ 3	.667	0/ 0	.000	-/ 2	1	1	1	0	0	4	.267
ROCKYMORE, L.	11	3/ 4	.750	0/ 0	.000	-/ 1	1	0	2	1	0	6	.545
Totals	200	26/51	.510	3/ 5	.600	-/28	12	13	23	8	0	55	.275

Villanova (59)   Coach: Rollie Massimino

	Min.	Total FG / FGA	Pct.	FT / FTA	Pct.	Reb. O / T	A	TO	PF	S	Blk	TP	PPM
PRESSLEY, H.	34	3/10	.300	3/ 5	.600	-/ 7	2	1	3	5	0	9	.265
MCCLAIN, D.	36	8/12	.667	4/ 4	1.000	-/ 4	1	2	2	0	0	20	.556
PINCKNEY, E.	40	2/ 4	.500	10/11	.909	-/ 7	1	2	2	0	0	14	.350
WILBUR, D.	15	0/ 1	.000	0/ 0	.000	-/ 0	1	1	1	0	0	0	.000
MCLAIN, G.	37	3/ 5	.600	3/ 5	.600	-/ 0	3	1	2	2	0	9	.243
JENSEN, H.	27	0/ 1	.000	3/ 4	.750	-/ 2	1	3	0	0	0	3	.111
PLANSKY, M.	9	1/ 1	1.000	2/ 2	1.000	-/ 1	1	0	1	0	0	4	.444
EVERSON, C.	2	0/ 0	.000	0/ 0	.000	-/ 0	0	0	0	0	0	0	.000
Totals	200	17/35	.486	25/31	.806	-/21	10	10	11	7	0	59	.295

Team Rebounds: Villanova 0; Michigan 0. Disqualified: Michigan—Joubert, Grant. Technical fouls: Michigan—Wade.

	1st Half	2nd Half	Final
Michigan	26	29	55
Villanova	30	29	59

Maryland (64)   Coach: Lefty Driesell

	Min.	Total FG / FGA	Pct.	FT / FTA	Pct.	Reb. O / T	A	TO	PF	S	Blk	TP	PPM
BIAS, L.	40	7/11	.636	6/ 9	.667	-/ 8	1	4	3	0	1	20	.500
BRANCH, A.	29	5/13	.385	1/ 1	1.000	-/ 2	1	3	4	0	0	11	.379
LEWIS, D.	16	1/ 2	.500	0/ 0	.000	-/ 7	0	0	3	1	0	2	.125
GATLIN, K.	40	4/ 8	.500	2/ 2	1.000	-/ 1	12	1	1	1	0	10	.250
ADKINS, J.	37	5/12	.417	3/ 3	1.000	-/ 2	4	0	2	0	3	13	.351
LONG, T.	15	1/ 1	1.000	0/ 0	.000	-/ 2	0	0	2	0	0	2	.133
JONES, T.	22	3/ 4	.750	0/ 0	.000	-/ 1	0	0	3	0	0	6	.273
BAXTER, J.	1	0/ 0	.000	0/ 0	.000	-/ 0	0	0	0	0	0	0	.000
Totals	200	26/51	.510	12/15	.800	-/23	18	8	16	4	1	64	.320

Navy (59)   Coach: Paul Evans

	Min.	Total FG / FGA	Pct.	FT / FTA	Pct.	Reb. O / T	A	TO	PF	S	Blk	TP	PPM
BUTLER, V.	40	4/ 8	.500	4/ 5	.800	-/ 8	3	3	1	1	0	12	.300
WHITAKER, K.	40	5/10	.500	0/ 0	.000	-/ 1	5	2	2	0	0	10	.250
ROBINSON, D.	38	11/18	.611	0/ 3	.000	-/ 8	0	2	2	1	2	22	.579
REES, C.	27	3/ 6	.500	0/ 0	.000	-/ 1	3	0	2	0	0	6	.222
WOJCIK, D.	40	0/ 1	.000	0/ 0	.000	-/ 2	7	4	4	0	0	0	.000
LIEBERT, C.	13	3/ 4	.750	3/ 4	.750	-/ 2	0	1	1	0	0	9	.692
WELLS, T.	2	0/ 0	.000	0/ 0	.000	-/ 0	0	1	0	0	0	0	.000
Totals	200	26/47	.553	7/12	.583	-/23	18	13	12	2	2	59	.295

Team Rebounds: Maryland 0; Navy 3. Disqualified: None. Technical fouls: None.

	1st Half	2nd Half	Final
Maryland	32	32	64
Navy	37	22	59

Auburn (66)   Coach: Sonny Smith

	Min.	Total FG / FGA	Pct.	FT / FTA	Pct.	Reb. O / T	A	TO	PF	S	Blk	TP	PPM
MORRIS, C.	40	4/ 9	.444	0/ 1	.000	-/ 4	1	0	1	0	1	8	.200
PERSON, C.	31	10/19	.526	1/ 2	.500	-/ 5	2	0	4	0	0	21	.677
MOORE, J.	25	2/ 7	.286	1/ 1	1.000	-/ 5	0	1	1	0	1	5	.200
WHITE, G.	38	1/ 2	.500	7/ 8	.875	-/ 2	5	4	3	0	0	9	.237
FORD, F.	37	9/ 9	1.000	5/ 6	.833	-/ 7	1	4	3	0	0	23	.622
LYNN, J.	5	0/ 0	.000	0/ 0	.000	-/ 0	0	0	0	0	0	0	.000
GUEST, D.	4	0/ 3	.000	0/ 0	.000	-/ 5	0	1	0	1	1	0	.000
HOLLAND, C.	20	0/ 0	.000	0/ 0	.000	-/ 3	0	1	2	0	0	0	.000
Totals	200	26/49	.531	14/18	.778	-/31	9	11	14	1	3	66	.330

Kansas (64)   Coach: Larry Brown

	Min.	Total FG / FGA	Pct.	FT / FTA	Pct.	Reb. O / T	A	TO	PF	S	Blk	TP	PPM
MANNING, D.	22	3/12	.250	1/ 2	.500	-/ 8	1	0	4	1	0	7	.318
KELLOGG, R.	38	8/16	.500	1/ 1	1.000	-/ 5	1	0	2	1	0	17	.447
DREILING, G.	29	1/ 4	.250	0/ 0	.000	-/ 6	0	3	4	0	0	2	.069
HUNTER, C.	33	4/ 9	.444	1/ 2	.500	-/ 3	4	0	2	2	0	9	.273
THOMPSON, C.	37	10/16	.625	1/ 2	.500	-/ 1	2	1	3	0	0	21	.568
TURGEON, M.	7	1/ 2	.500	0/ 0	.000	-/ 1	0	1	0	0	0	2	.286
NEWTON, M.	4	0/ 1	.000	0/ 0	.000	-/ 1	0	0	0	0	0	0	.000
PIPER, C.	20	3/ 4	.750	0/ 0	.000	-/ 1	1	0	3	2	1	6	.300
BOYLE, T.	2	0/ 0	.000	0/ 0	.000	-/ 0	0	0	0	0	0	0	.000
PELLOCK, M.	8	0/ 0	.000	0/ 0	.000	-/ 1	0	0	0	1	0	0	.000
Totals	200	30/64	.469	4/ 7	.571	-/27	9	5	18	7	1	64	.320

Team Rebounds: Auburn 2; Kansas 3. Disqualified: None. Technical fouls: None.

	1st Half	2nd Half	Final
Auburn	28	38	66
Kansas	30	34	64

Notre Dame (58)   Coach: Digger Phelps

	Min.	Total FG / FGA	Pct.	FT / FTA	Pct.	Reb. O / T	A	TO	PF	S	Blk	TP	PPM
ROYAL, D.	38	1/ 3	.333	6/10	.600	-/ 5	2	4	0	1	0	8	.211
PRICE, J.	25	3/ 5	.600	3/ 4	.750	-/ 2	1	0	3	2	2	9	.360
KEMPTON, T.	20	1/ 3	.333	2/ 2	1.000	-/ 4	0	1	3	2	0	4	.200
RIVERS, D.	37	8/14	.571	1/ 4	.250	-/ 0	3	3	4	0	0	17	.459
HICKS, S.	30	3/ 9	.333	2/ 2	1.000	-/ 0	4	1	1	1	0	8	.267
DUFF, D.	3	0/ 0	.000	0/ 0	.000	-/ 0	0	0	0	0	0	0	.000
DOLAN, J.	20	2/ 2	1.000	0/ 2	.000	-/ 6	0	0	4	1	0	4	.200
BARLOW, K.	27	4/ 9	.444	0/ 2	.000	-/ 3	0	0	3	1	1	8	.296
Totals	200	22/45	.489	14/26	.538	-/20	10	9	18	8	3	58	.290

North Carolina (60)   Coach: Dean Smith

	Min.	Total FG / FGA	Pct.	FT / FTA	Pct.	Reb. O / T	A	TO	PF	S	Blk	TP	PPM
WOLF, J.	38	3/ 7	.429	0/ 0	.000	-/ 6	0	3	4	0	0	6	.158
POPSON, D.	17	4/ 6	.667	0/ 0	.000	-/ 2	0	2	1	0	2	8	.471
DAUGHERTY, B.	31	6/ 8	.750	6/ 6	1.000	-/12	2	3	4	0	1	18	.581
PETERSON, B.	36	3/ 5	.600	1/ 3	.333	-/ 2	2	0	1	1	0	7	.194
SMITH, K.	40	6/11	.545	0/ 2	.000	-/ 2	5	1	3	3	0	12	.300
SMITH, R.	4	0/ 2	.000	0/ 0	.000	-/ 0	0	1	0	0	0	0	.000
HUNTER, C.	8	1/ 3	.333	0/ 0	.000	-/ 1	0	0	0	0	0	2	.250
MARTIN, W.	26	3/ 5	.600	1/ 1	1.000	-/ 5	2	4	5	0	0	7	.269
Totals	200	26/47	.553	8/12	.667	-/30	11	14	18	4	3	60	.300

Team Rebounds: N. Carolina 0; Notre Dame 3. Disqualified: N. Carolina—Martin. Technical fouls: None.

	1st Half	2nd Half	Final
Notre Dame	35	23	58
N. Carolina	35	25	60

REGIONAL SEMIFINAL WEST

St. John's (86)   Coach: Lou Carnesecca

	Min.	Total FG / FGA	Pct.	FT / FTA	Pct.	Reb. O / T	A	TO	PF	S	Blk	TP	PPM
BERRY, W.	36	7/13	.538	8/11	.727	-/12	2	2	4	0	3	22	.611
GLASS, W.	38	4/ 5	.800	2/ 2	1.000	-/ 9	3	0	1	0	0	10	.263
WENNINGTON, B.	24	4/ 7	.571	2/ 2	1.000	-/ 3	2	0	4	0	0	10	.417
MULLIN, C.	40	11/23	.478	8/10	.800	-/ 5	7	1	0	2	0	30	.750
MOSES, M.	21	0/ 3	.000	0/ 0	.000	-/ 0	1	1	2	0	0	0	.000
JACKSON, M.	19	3/ 4	.750	6/ 8	.750	-/ 2	4	1	2	2	0	12	.632
JONES, S.	6	0/ 0	.000	0/ 0	.000	-/ 0	0	0	0	0	0	0	.000
STEWART, R.	16	1/ 1	1.000	0/ 0	.000	-/ 2	0	0	1	0	0	2	.125
Totals	200	30/56	.536	26/33	.788	-/33	19	5	14	4	3	86	.430

Kentucky (70)   Coach: Joe Hall

	Min.	Total FG / FGA	Pct.	FT / FTA	Pct.	Reb. O / T	A	TO	PF	S	Blk	TP	PPM
BENNETT, W.	24	2/ 2	1.000	2/ 2	1.000	-/ 3	0	1	5	0	0	6	.250
WALKER, K.	36	10/14	.714	3/ 3	1.000	-/ 8	4	0	5	1	1	23	.639
BEARUP, B.	19	1/ 3	.333	0/ 0	.000	-/ 3	2	1	5	0	0	2	.105
DAVENDER, E.	25	5/10	.500	1/ 2	.500	-/ 3	3	0	2	1	0	11	.440
HARDEN, R.	28	6/10	.600	1/ 1	1.000	-/ 2	7	3	3	0	0	13	.464
BYRD, L.	1	0/ 0	.000	0/ 0	.000	-/ 0	0	0	0	0	0	0	.000
BLACKMON, J.	13	0/ 4	.000	0/ 0	.000	-/ 1	1	0	1	1	1	0	.000
ANDREWS, P.	2	0/ 0	.000	0/ 0	.000	-/ 0	0	0	0	0	0	0	.000
ZIEGLER, T.	1	0/ 0	.000	0/ 0	.000	-/ 0	0	0	0	0	0	0	.000
MCKINLEY, T.	16	4/ 6	.667	0/ 0	.000	-/ 2	1	1	1	1	0	8	.500
MADISON, R.	29	2/ 9	.222	1/ 3	.333	-/ 4	1	2	1	0	0	5	.172
LOCK, R.	3	0/ 0	.000	0/ 0	.000	-/ 0	0	0	1	0	0	0	.000
JENKINS, C.	3	1/ 1	1.000	0/ 0	.000	-/ 1	0	1	0	0	0	2	.667
Totals	200	31/59	.525	8/11	.727	-/27	19	9	24	4	2	70	.350

Team Rebounds: St. John's 3; Kentucky 0. Disqualified: Kentucky—Bennett, Walker, Bearup. Technical fouls: St. John's—Mullin.

	1st Half	2nd Half	Final
St. John's	39	47	86
Kentucky	38	32	70

North Carolina State (61)   Coach: Jim Valvano

	Min.	Total FG / FGA	Pct.	FT / FTA	Pct.	Reb. O / T	A	TO	PF	S	Blk	TP	PPM
PIERRE, R.	29	2/ 4	.500	4/ 5	.800	-/ 6	0	1	2	1	0	8	.276
CHARLES, L.	35	5/11	.455	4/ 6	.667	-/ 6	3	0	0	0	0	14	.400
MCQUEEN, C.	25	2/ 5	.400	0/ 0	.000	-/ 4	0	1	5	1	0	4	.160
WEBB, A.	38	5/12	.417	4/ 6	.667	-/ 4	5	2	4	1	0	14	.368
MCMILLAN, N.	22	0/ 2	.000	2/ 6	.333	-/ 5	4	3	3	1	0	2	.091
BOLTON, B.	30	4/ 8	.500	3/ 4	.750	-/ 1	1	2	2	1	1	11	.367
GANNON, T.	14	4/ 4	1.000	0/ 0	.000	-/ 0	2	1	1	0	0	8	.571
MYERS, E.	6	0/ 1	.000	0/ 0	.000	-/ 0	0	0	2	0	0	0	.000
THOMPSON, J.	1	0/ 0	.000	0/ 0	.000	-/ 0	0	0	0	0	0	0	.000
Totals	200	22/47	.468	17/27	.630	-/26	15	10	19	5	1	61	.305

Alabama (55)   Coach: Wimp Sanderson

	Min.	Total FG / FGA	Pct.	FT / FTA	Pct.	Reb. O / T	A	TO	PF	S	Blk	TP	PPM
JOHNSON, B.	38	7/11	.636	2/ 5	.400	-/14	2	2	5	0	1	16	.421
MCKEY, D.	32	3/ 8	.375	0/ 0	.000	-/ 4	1	0	5	0	1	6	.188
HURT, B.	39	4/ 9	.444	1/ 3	.333	-/ 5	0	0	2	0	1	9	.231
GOTTFRIED, M.	23	1/ 6	.167	0/ 0	.000	-/ 0	2	0	2	0	0	2	.087
CONER, T.	33	6/10	.600	6/10	.600	-/ 4	4	5	4	2	0	18	.545
FARMER, J.	25	2/ 4	.500	0/ 0	.000	-/ 1	3	3	3	1	0	4	.160
NEAL, D.	9	0/ 2	.000	0/ 0	.000	-/ 2	0	1	0	0	0	0	.000
FARMER, M.	1	0/ 0	.000	0/ 0	.000	-/ 0	0	0	0	0	0	0	.000
Totals	200	23/50	.460	9/18	.500	-/30	12	11	21	3	3	55	.275

Team Rebounds: N.C. State 5; Alabama 7. Disqualified: N.C. State—McQueen; Alabama—Johnson, McKey. Technical fouls: None.

	1st Half	2nd Half	Final
N.C. State	28	33	61
Alabama	27	28	55

REGIONAL SEMIFINAL EAST

Georgetown (65)   Coach: John Thompson

	Min.	Total FG/FGA	Pct.	FT/FTA	Pct.	Reb. O/T	A	TO	PF	S	Blk	TP	PPM
MARTIN, B.	37	4/7	.571	0/3	.000	1/3	1	1	2	0	0	8	.216
WILLIAMS, R.	24	2/7	.286	4/4	1.000	2/5	1	3	3	0	3	8	.333
EWING, P.	36	9/15	.600	3/4	.750	5/14	2	2	1	1	5	21	.583
JACKSON, M.	35	3/8	.375	2/3	.667	3/7	12	2	2	0	0	8	.229
WINGATE, D.	34	7/14	.500	0/1	.000	2/3	1	4	0	1	0	14	.412
McDONALD, P.	12	0/0	.000	1/2	.500	0/2	0	2	0	1	0	1	.083
BROADNAX, H.	11	0/2	.000	2/2	1.000	0/1	0	1	1	0	0	2	.182
DALTON, R.	9	1/1	1.000	1/2	.500	2/4	0	0	0	0	0	3	.333
HIGHSMITH, R.	1	0/0	.000	0/0	.000	0/0	0	0	0	0	0	0	.000
LOCKHART, T.	1	0/0	.000	0/0	.000	0/0	0	0	0	0	0	0	.000
Totals	200	26/54	.481	13/21	.619	15/39	17	15	9	3	8	65	.325

Loyola-Chicago (53)   Coach: Gene Sullivan

	Min.	Total FG/FGA	Pct.	FT/FTA	Pct.	Reb. O/T	A	TO	PF	S	Blk	TP	PPM
HUGHES, A.	29	4/13	.308	0/1	.000	1/5	0	4	3	1	0	8	.276
BATTLE, A.	39	5/13	.385	0/0	.000	1/3	0	3	4	3	0	10	.256
MOORE, A.	39	8/13	.615	3/3	1.000	5/8	1	1	3	0	1	19	.487
WILLIAMS, G.	27	2/4	.500	0/0	.000	1/3	3	1	5	1	1	4	.148
GOLSTON, C.	39	3/12	.250	0/0	.000	1/3	7	2	2	4	1	6	.154
CENAR, M.	7	1/2	.500	0/0	.000	0/0	0	0	2	0	0	2	.286
CLARK, B.	1	1/2	.500	0/0	.000	1/2	0	0	0	0	0	2	2.000
YOUNG, I.	17	1/5	.200	0/0	.000	1/3	0	1	0	0	0	2	.118
KLUSENDORF, D.	1	0/1	.000	0/0	.000	0/0	0	0	0	0	0	0	.000
BROOKS, N.	1	0/0	.000	0/0	.000	0/0	0	0	1	0	0	0	.000
Totals	200	25/65	.385	3/4	.750	11/27	11	12	20	9	3	53	.265

Team Rebounds: Georgetown 5; Loyola-Chicago 4. Disqualified: Loyola-Chicago—Williams. Technical fouls: None.

	1st Half	2nd Half	Final
Georgetown	26	39	65
Loyola-Chicago	28	25	53

Illinois (53)   Coach: Lou Henson

	Min.	Total FG/FGA	Pct.	FT/FTA	Pct.	Reb. O/T	A	TO	PF	S	Blk	TP	PPM
NORMAN, K.	38	3/3	1.000	3/3	1.000	1/7	7	2	3	3	1	9	.237
WELCH, A.	37	5/10	.500	0/0	.000	2/5	2	3	0	2	0	10	.270
WINTERS, E.	36	2/5	.400	0/2	.000	2/4	1	2	3	1	0	4	.111
ALTENBERGER, D.	38	11/17	.647	2/3	.667	1/3	1	2	5	2	0	24	.632
DOUGLAS, B.	33	1/6	.167	2/2	1.000	1/2	1	9	2	0	0	4	.121
MEENTS, S.	6	1/2	.500	0/0	.000	0/0	1	0	4	0	0	2	.333
WYSINGER, T.	12	0/4	.000	0/0	.000	0/1	2	1	3	0	0	0	.000
Totals	200	23/47	.489	7/10	.700	7/22	15	19	20	8	1	53	.265

Georgia Tech (61)   Coach: Bobby Cremins

	Min.	Total FG/FGA	Pct.	FT/FTA	Pct.	Reb. O/T	A	TO	PF	S	Blk	TP	PPM
SALLEY, J.	36	5/12	.417	4/5	.800	1/4	3	3	3	0	1	14	.389
PETWAY, S.	28	0/2	.000	2/2	1.000	1/2	2	2	2	3	0	2	.071
JOSEPH, Y.	35	4/6	.667	6/8	.750	1/3	1	4	4	2	0	14	.400
PRICE, M.	38	9/12	.750	2/3	.667	0/2	2	3	0	0	0	20	.526
DALRYMPLE, B.	36	3/4	.750	2/4	.500	0/4	3	1	2	2	0	8	.222
FORD, A.	7	0/0	.000	0/0	.000	0/1	0	0	1	0	0	0	.000
FERRELL, D.	16	1/3	.333	1/2	.500	1/1	2	0	0	1	0	3	.188
MANSELL, J.	2	0/0	.000	0/0	.000	0/0	0	1	0	0	0	0	.000
MARTINSON, J.	2	0/0	.000	0/0	.000	0/0	0	0	0	0	0	0	.000
Totals	200	22/39	.564	17/24	.708	4/17	13	14	12	11	1	61	.305

Team Rebounds: Georgia Tech 4; Illinois 5. Disqualified: Illinois—Altenberger. Technical fouls: None.

	1st Half	2nd Half	Final
Illinois	29	24	53
Georgia Tech	29	32	61

REGIONAL SEMIFINAL MIDWEST

Oklahoma (86)   Coach: Billy Tubbs

	Min.	Total FG/FGA	Pct.	FT/FTA	Pct.	Reb. O/T	A	TO	PF	S	Blk	TP	PPM
BOWIE, A.	45	8/11	.727	0/1	.000	2/10	7	4	1	2	0	16	.356
KENNEDY, D.	43	8/11	.727	5/7	.714	3/11	3	3	5	0	1	21	.488
TISDALE, WA.	40	10/17	.588	3/7	.429	5/11	1	2	4	1	3	23	.575
McCALISTER, T.	45	5/18	.278	0/0	.000	0/3	3	3	3	0	0	10	.222
DAVIS, L.	19	2/5	.400	2/2	1.000	1/1	1	1	2	0	0	6	.316
CLARK, S.	1	0/0	.000	0/0	.000	0/0	0	0	0	0	0	0	.000
JOHNSON, D.	31	4/5	.800	2/3	.667	1/4	3	4	5	1	0	10	.323
WATSON, C.	1	0/0	.000	0/0	.000	0/0	0	0	0	0	0	0	.000
Totals	225	37/67	.552	12/20	.600	12/40	18	17	20	4	4	86	.382

Louisiana Tech (84)   Coach: Andy Russo

	Min.	Total FG/FGA	Pct.	FT/FTA	Pct.	Reb. O/T	A	TO	PF	S	Blk	TP	PPM
SIMMONS, W.	24	3/11	.273	4/4	1.000	2/2	1	0	4	0	1	10	.417
GODBOLT, R.	37	4/15	.267	2/3	.667	3/5	2	3	3	0	0	10	.270
MALONE, K.	45	9/19	.474	2/4	.500	6/16	3	2	4	0	0	20	.444
DAVIS, A.	40	9/15	.600	0/0	.000	2/6	8	1	3	4	0	18	.450
SMITH, W.	42	2/11	.182	2/2	1.000	2/5	8	2	1	2	0	6	.143
BLAND, W.	29	7/11	.636	4/6	.667	6/6	1	2	2	5	0	18	.621
FRANK, A.	8	0/2	.000	2/2	1.000	0/1	3	0	0	0	0	2	.250
Totals	225	34/84	.405	16/21	.762	21/41	26	10	17	11	1	84	.373

Team Rebounds: Oklahoma 3; Louisiana Tech 5. Disqualified: Oklahoma—Kennedy, Johnson. Technical fouls: None.

	1st Half	2nd Half	1st OT	Final
Oklahoma	32	42	12	86
Louisiana Tech	28	46	10	84

Boston College (57)   Coach: Gary Williams

	Min.	Total FG/FGA	Pct.	FT/FTA	Pct.	Reb. O/T	A	TO	PF	S	Blk	TP	PPM
McCREADY, R.	-	2/7	.286	5/6	.833	-/3	0	-	1	-	-	9	-
TALLEY	-	5/8	.625	1/2	.500	-/4	1	-	4	-	-	11	-
GORDON	-	3/3	1.000	3/5	.600	-/6	0	-	4	-	-	9	-
ADAMS, M.	-	6/14	.429	0/0	.000	-/2	4	-	2	-	-	12	-
PRESSLEY, D.	-	1/2	.500	0/0	.000	-/1	1	-	0	-	-	2	-
PRIMUS, S.	-	7/13	.538	0/0	.000	-/3	1	-	2	-	-	14	-
BOWERS	-	0/2	.000	0/0	.000	-/2	0	-	3	-	-	0	-
BARRY	-	0/5	.000	0/0	.000	-/4	1	-	0	-	-	0	-
SCHMIDT	-	0/1	.000	0/0	.000	-/0	1	-	0	-	-	0	-
SCOTT	-	0/0	.000	0/0	.000	-/0	0	-	0	-	-	0	-
Totals	200	24/55	.436	9/13	.692	-/25	9	-	16	-	-	57	.285

Memphis State (59)   Coach: Dana Kirk

	Min.	Total FG/FGA	Pct.	FT/FTA	Pct.	Reb. O/T	A	TO	PF	S	Blk	TP	PPM
LEE, K.	-	3/12	.250	2/3	.667	-/8	4	-	4	-	-	8	-
HOLMES, B.	-	2/7	.286	0/0	.000	-/3	1	-	2	-	-	4	-
BEDFORD, W.	-	10/13	.769	3/4	.750	-/8	0	-	3	-	-	23	-
TURNER, A.	-	6/12	.500	0/0	.000	-/2	7	-	1	-	-	12	-
ASKEW, V.	-	1/3	.333	0/0	.000	-/4	9	-	0	-	-	2	-
BECTON, W.	-	4/10	.400	0/0	.000	-/5	0	-	2	-	-	8	-
BOYD, D.	-	1/1	1.000	0/1	.000	-/0	0	-	0	-	-	2	-
Totals	200	27/58	.466	5/8	.625	-/30	21	-	12	-	-	59	.295

Team Rebounds: Memphis State 5; Boston College 5. Disqualified: None.

	1st Half	2nd Half	Final
Boston College	31	26	57
Memphis State	31	28	59

REGIONAL SEMIFINAL SOUTHEAST

Villanova (46)   Coach: Rollie Massimino

	Min.	Total FG/FGA	Pct.	FT/FTA	Pct.	Reb. O/T	A	TO	PF	S	Blk	TP	PPM
PRESSLEY, H.	35	3/12	.250	1/4	.250	-/10	1	2	2	0	1	7	.200
MCCLAIN, D.	40	5/9	.556	2/2	1.000	-/4	2	3	3	0	0	12	.300
PINCKNEY, E.	36	5/7	.714	6/7	.857	-/13	1	3	4	0	1	16	.444
WILBUR, D.	25	1/5	.200	2/2	1.000	-/4	3	1	0	0	0	4	.160
MCLAIN, G.	36	1/5	.200	1/2	.500	-/2	1	2	0	1	0	3	.083
JENSEN, H.	11	0/5	.000	0/1	.000	-/0	1	0	1	0	0	0	.000
PLANSKY, M.	13	2/3	.667	0/0	.000	-/4	2	1	0	0	0	4	.308
EVERSON, C.	4	0/0	.000	0/0	.000	-/0	0	0	0	0	0	0	.000
Totals	200	17/46	.370	12/18	.667	-/37	11	12	10	1	2	46	.230

Auburn (56)   Coach: Sonny Smith

	Min.	Total FG/FGA	Pct.	FT/FTA	Pct.	Reb. O/T	A	TO	PF	S	Blk	TP	PPM
MORRIS, C.	38	3/10	.300	1/2	.500	-/9	0	0	2	2	0	7	.184
PERSON, C.	39	8/25	.320	0/0	.000	-/12	3	3	4	2	1	16	.410
MOORE, J.	17	2/3	.667	0/0	.000	-/2	1	0	3	0	0	4	.235
WHITE, G.	37	2/5	.400	0/0	.000	-/1	2	0	4	0	0	4	.108
FORD, F.	37	8/14	.571	1/2	.500	-/4	3	2	2	0	0	17	.459
LYNN, J.	5	0/0	.000	0/0	.000	-/0	0	0	1	0	0	0	.000
GUEST, D.	5	0/0	.000	0/0	.000	-/1	0	0	0	0	0	0	.000
HOLLAND, C.	22	2/2	1.000	4/8	.500	-/1	0	0	2	0	1	8	.364
Totals	200	25/59	.424	6/12	.500	-/30	9	5	18	4	2	56	.280

Maryland (43)   Coach: Lefty Driesell

	Min.	Total FG/FGA	Pct.	FT/FTA	Pct.	Reb. O/T	A	TO	PF	S	Blk	TP	PPM
BIAS, L.	38	4/13	.308	0/0	.000	-/5	1	0	4	0	0	8	.200
BRANCH, A.	39	9/19	.474	3/5	.600	-/5	2	1	3	1	0	21	.538
LEWIS, D.	24	0/2	.000	0/0	.000	-/5	0	1	4	0	2	0	.000
GATLIN, K.	30	2/7	.286	0/0	.000	-/4	2	3	1	1	0	4	.133
ADKINS, J.	29	2/7	.286	0/0	.000	-/4	4	0	2	1	0	4	.138
LONG, T.	16	0/1	.000	2/2	1.000	-/4	0	0	1	2	1	2	.125
JONES, T.	12	0/2	.000	0/0	.000	-/2	1	1	3	0	0	0	.000
BAXTER, J.	10	2/2	1.000	0/0	.000	-/0	0	0	2	0	0	4	.400
Totals	200	19/53	.358	5/7	.714	-/29	10	6	20	5	3	43	.215

North Carolina (62)   Coach: Dean Smith

	Min.	Total FG/FGA	Pct.	FT/FTA	Pct.	Reb. O/T	A	TO	PF	S	Blk	TP	PPM
WOLF, J.	35	4/6	.667	2/2	1.000	-/7	3	1	3	0	0	10	.286
POPSON, D.	14	2/4	.500	0/0	.000	-/4	0	0	1	0	0	4	.286
DAUGHERTY, B.	39	5/8	.625	0/2	.000	-/8	3	2	2	0	2	10	.256
PETERSON, B.	29	0/5	.000	0/0	.000	-/2	2	4	2	0	0	0	.000
SMITH, K.	38	9/12	.750	4/5	.800	-/3	6	0	1	2	0	22	.579
SMITH, R.	14	1/5	.200	2/2	1.000	-/2	1	0	0	0	0	4	.286
HUNTER, C.	5	0/1	.000	0/2	.000	-/1	0	0	0	0	0	0	.000
MARTIN, W.	26	4/8	.500	4/5	.800	-/5	1	1	3	0	1	12	.462
Totals	200	25/49	.510	12/18	.667	-/32	16	8	12	2	3	62	.310

Team Rebounds: Villanova 3; Maryland 0. Disqualified: None. Technical fouls: None.
Team Rebounds: N. Carolina 0; Auburn 3. Disqualified: None. Technical fouls: None.

	1st Half	2nd Half	Final
Villanova	19	27	46
Maryland	20	23	43

	1st Half	2nd Half	Final
Auburn	23	33	56
N. Carolina	33	29	62

REGIONAL FINAL WEST

St. John's (69)   Coach: Lou Carnesecca

	Min.	Total FG/FGA	Pct.	FT/FTA	Pct.	Reb. O/T	A	TO	PF	S	Blk	TP	PPM
BERRY, W.	40	8/12	.667	3/4	.750	-/5	0	1	2	1	1	19	.475
GLASS, W.	24	0/5	.000	0/0	.000	-/3	2	1	4	1	0	0	.000
WENNINGTON, B.	36	3/5	.600	8/9	.889	-/10	0	2	2	1	0	14	.389
MULLIN, C.	40	9/19	.474	7/7	1.000	-/5	1	2	4	3	1	25	.625
MOSES, J.	22	1/4	.250	2/3	.667	-/2	5	0	2	1	0	4	.182
JACKSON, M.	19	0/1	.000	0/1	.000	-/3	5	2	4	1	1	0	.000
STEWART, R.	19	1/3	.333	5/7	.714	-/3	1	0	0	0	0	7	.368
Totals	200	22/49	.449	25/31	.806	-/31	14	8	18	8	3	69	.345

North Carolina State (60)   Coach: Jim Valvano

	Min.	Total FG/FGA	Pct.	FT/FTA	Pct.	Reb. O/T	A	TO	PF	S	Blk	TP	PPM
PIERRE, R.	25	3/6	.500	0/0	.000	-/3	0	1	5	1	1	6	.240
CHARLES, L.	39	4/9	.444	7/9	.778	-/11	1	2	1	0	1	15	.385
MCQUEEN, C.	40	2/4	.500	4/6	.667	-/11	1	3	4	0	0	8	.200
WEBB, A.	39	5/14	.357	4/5	.800	-/1	9	5	3	0	0	14	.359
MCMILLAN, N.	11	0/3	.000	2/2	1.000	-/3	1	2	5	0	1	2	.182
BOLTON, B.	27	4/10	.400	1/1	1.000	-/0	0	1	3	1	0	9	.333
GANNON, T.	18	3/7	.429	0/0	.000	-/1	0	0	4	0	0	6	.333
MYERS, E.	1	0/0	.000	0/0	.000	-/0	0	0	1	0	0	0	.000
Totals	200	21/53	.396	18/23	.783	-/30	12	12	27	2	3	60	.300

Team Rebounds: St. John's 4; N.C. State 3. Disqualified: N.C. State—Pierre, McMillan. Technical fouls: None.

	1st Half	2nd Half	Final
St. John's	30	39	69
N.C. State	29	31	60

REGIONAL FINAL EAST

Georgetown (60)   Coach: John Thompson

	Min.	Total FG/FGA	Pct.	FT/FTA	Pct.	Reb. O/T	A	TO	PF	S	Blk	TP	PPM
MARTIN, B.	32	5/10	.500	2/3	.667	1/2	0	0	4	4	0	12	.375
WILLIAMS, R.	33	4/6	.667	4/4	1.000	4/5	2	2	3	1	0	12	.364
EWING, P.	25	5/9	.556	4/9	.444	2/4	1	0	4	1	0	14	.560
JACKSON, M.	28	0/6	.000	0/0	.000	1/1	5	2	4	2	0	0	.000
WINGATE, D.	34	3/8	.375	1/2	.500	1/1	1	3	3	0	0	7	.206
MCDONALD, P.	2	0/1	.000	0/0	.000	1/2	0	1	0	0	0	0	.000
BROADNAX, H.	18	3/4	.750	3/4	.750	0/3	1	0	0	0	0	9	.500
DALTON, R.	25	1/2	.500	4/4	1.000	2/6	0	2	4	0	1	6	.240
MATEEN, G.	3	0/0	.000	0/0	.000	1/1	0	0	0	0	0	0	.000
Totals	200	21/46	.457	18/26	.692	13/25	10	10	22	8	1	60	.300

Georgia Tech (54)   Coach: Bobby Cremins

	Min.	Total FG/FGA	Pct.	FT/FTA	Pct.	Reb. O/T	A	TO	PF	S	Blk	TP	PPM
SALLEY, J.	29	5/8	.625	5/5	1.000	1/5	2	3	5	0	0	15	.517
PETWAY, S.	24	1/2	.500	0/0	.000	0/0	4	0	3	1	0	2	.083
JOSEPH, Y.	38	1/4	.250	1/2	.500	2/4	2	2	4	0	0	3	.079
PRICE, M.	40	3/16	.188	7/8	.875	1/1	1	1	1	0	0	13	.325
DALRYMPLE, B.	38	3/5	.600	7/7	1.000	4/4	0	3	4	0	0	13	.342
FORD, A.	12	2/2	1.000	2/2	1.000	0/1	1	2	2	0	0	6	.500
FERRELL, D.	18	1/3	.333	0/0	.000	3/4	0	1	3	0	0	2	.111
MANSELL, J.	1	0/0	.000	0/0	.000	0/0	0	0	0	0	0	0	.000
Totals	200	16/40	.400	22/24	.917	11/19	10	12	22	1	0	54	.270

Team Rebounds: Georgetown 7; Georgia Tech 4. Disqualified: Georgia Tech—Salley. Technical fouls: None.

	1st Half	2nd Half	Final
Georgetown	29	31	60
Georgia Tech	29	25	54

REGIONAL FINAL MIDWEST

Oklahoma (61) Coach: Billy Tubbs

	Min.	Total FG / FGA	Pct.	FT / FTA	Pct.	Reb. O / T	A	TO	PF	S	Blk	TP	PPM
BOWIE, A.	40	5/12	.417	0/ 2	.000	1/ 2	5	7	2	1	0	10	.250
KENNEDY, D.	38	7/15	.467	2/ 2	1.000	2/ 5	3	3	3	2	0	16	.421
TISDALE, WA.	40	5/10	.500	1/ 1	1.000	1/12	4	0	3	0	0	11	.275
McCALISTER, T.	39	6/12	.500	2/ 2	1.000	0/ 0	5	0	5	3	1	14	.359
DAVIS, L.	4	0/ 0	.000	0/ 0	.000	0/ 0	1	1	3	0	0	0	.000
CLARK, S.	3	0/ 1	.000	0/ 0	.000	0/ 0	0	0	0	1	0	0	.000
JOHNSON, D.	36	3/ 6	.500	4/ 6	.667	4/ 7	2	2	3	2	0	10	.278
Totals	200	26/56	.464	9/13	.692	8/26	20	13	19	9	1	61	.305

Memphis State (63) Coach: Dana Kirk

	Min.	Total FG / FGA	Pct.	FT / FTA	Pct.	Reb. O / T	A	TO	PF	S	Blk	TP	PPM
LEE, K.	27	9/22	.409	5/ 5	1.000	3/11	0	4	4	1	1	23	.852
HOLMES, B.	21	2/ 4	.500	0/ 0	.000	2/ 4	0	4	1	2	0	4	.190
BEDFORD, W.	24	4/ 5	.800	4/ 4	1.000	2/ 4	2	2	4	0	2	12	.500
TURNER, A.	40	5/ 9	.556	2/ 5	.400	0/ 3	12	1	3	2	0	12	.300
ASKEW, V.	37	0/ 1	.000	1/ 2	.500	0/ 1	1	4	1	1	0	1	.027
BOYD, D.	11	1/ 2	.500	0/ 0	.000	0/ 0	2	1	0	0	1	2	.182
BAILEY, D.	21	1/ 2	.500	0/ 0	.000	1/ 5	0	2	1	2	1	2	.095
BECTON, W.	19	3/ 4	.750	1/ 2	.500	0/ 2	2	0	2	2	0	7	.368
Totals	200	25/49	.510	13/18	.722	8/30	19	18	16	10	5	63	.315

Team Rebounds: Memphis State 2; Oklahoma 1. Disqualified: Oklahoma—McCalister. Technical fouls: None.

	1st Half	2nd Half	Final
Oklahoma	33	28	61
Memphis State	33	30	63

REGIONAL FINAL SOUTHEAST

Villanova (56) Coach: Rollie Massimino

	Min.	Total FG / FGA	Pct.	FT / FTA	Pct.	Reb. O / T	A	TO	PF	S	Blk	TP	PPM
PRESSLEY, H.	38	7/13	.538	1/ 2	.500	-/ 3	1	2	1	2	0	15	.395
McCLAIN, D.	36	4/11	.364	3/ 3	1.000	-/ 5	2	4	3	3	0	11	.306
PINCKNEY, E.	38	3/ 6	.500	3/ 6	.500	-/ 7	3	0	3	3	2	9	.237
WILBUR, D.	9	0/ 3	.000	0/ 0	.000	-/ 2	1	1	0	1	0	0	.000
McLAIN, G.	39	3/ 5	.600	5/ 6	.833	-/ 2	2	1	2	1	0	11	.282
JENSEN, H.	31	5/ 7	.714	0/ 0	.000	-/ 3	3	2	1	3	0	10	.323
PLANSKY, M.	7	0/ 1	.000	0/ 0	.000	-/ 1	1	0	0	0	0	0	.000
EVERSON, C.	2	0/ 1	.000	0/ 0	.000	-/ 0	0	0	1	0	0	0	.000
Totals	200	22/47	.468	12/17	.706	-/23	13	10	11	13	2	56	.280

North Carolina (44) Coach: Dean Smith

	Min.	Total FG / FGA	Pct.	FT / FTA	Pct.	Reb. O / T	A	TO	PF	S	Blk	TP	PPM
WOLF, J.	34	2/ 6	.333	0/ 0	.000	-/ 4	5	3	3	0	0	4	.118
POPSON, D.	14	2/ 3	.667	1/ 1	1.000	-/ 2	0	1	0	0	0	5	.357
DAUGHERTY, B.	38	7/ 9	.778	3/ 6	.500	-/12	0	2	3	0	0	17	.447
PETERSON, B.	20	0/ 3	.000	0/ 0	.000	-/ 0	0	1	1	0	0	0	.000
SMITH, K.	40	2/ 7	.286	0/ 0	.000	-/ 3	5	3	3	1	0	4	.100
SMITH, R.	20	3/10	.300	0/ 0	.000	-/ 4	0	3	2	1	0	6	.300
HUNTER, C.	16	3/ 4	.750	0/ 0	.000	-/ 2	0	4	2	1	0	6	.375
MARTIN, W.	16	1/ 2	.500	0/ 0	.000	-/ 1	1	2	2	0	2	2	.125
MORRIS, C.	2	0/ 0	.000	0/ 0	.000	-/ 0	0	0	0	0	0	0	.000
Totals	200	20/44	.455	4/ 7	.571	-/28	11	19	16	3	2	44	.220

Team Rebounds: Villanova 3; N. Carolina 1. Disqualified: None. Technical fouls: None.

	1st Half	2nd Half	Final
Villanova	17	39	56
N. Carolina	22	22	44

FINAL FOUR

St. John's (59) Coach: Lou Carnesecca

	Min.	Total FG / FGA	Pct.	FT / FTA	Pct.	Reb. O / T	A	TO	PF	S	Blk	TP	PPM
BERRY, W.	37	4/ 8	.500	4/ 5	.800	2/ 6	3	2	4	1	2	12	.324
GLASS, W.	25	4/ 4	1.000	5/ 7	.714	2/ 2	0	2	4	1	0	13	.520
WENNINGTON, B.	38	4/ 7	.571	4/ 5	.800	2/ 5	0	4	2	0	3	12	.316
MULLIN, C.	39	4/ 8	.500	0/ 0	.000	1/ 5	1	4	2	0	0	8	.205
MOSES, M.	17	3/ 7	.429	0/ 0	.000	0/ 1	2	3	3	1	0	6	.353
BROSS, T.	1	0/ 0	.000	0/ 0	.000	0/ 0	0	0	1	0	0	0	.000
JACKSON, M.	22	3/ 4	.750	0/ 2	.000	1/ 2	5	2	1	1	0	6	.273
JONES, S.	12	1/ 4	.250	0/ 0	.000	1/ 2	1	0	1	0	0	2	.167
STEWART, R.	6	0/ 0	.000	0/ 0	.000	0/ 0	0	0	2	0	1	0	.000
SHURINA, S.	2	0/ 0	.000	0/ 0	.000	0/ 0	0	0	0	0	0	0	.000
CORNEGY, R.	1	0/ 0	.000	0/ 0	.000	0/ 1	0	1	0	0	0	0	.000
Totals	200	23/42	.548	13/19	.684	9/24	12	18	20	4	6	59	.295

Georgetown (77) Coach: John Thompson

	Min.	Total FG / FGA	Pct.	FT / FTA	Pct.	Reb. O / T	A	TO	PF	S	Blk	TP	PPM
MARTIN, B.	29	4/ 8	.500	4/ 4	1.000	4/ 7	0	2	4	0	0	12	.414
WILLIAMS, R.	33	8/15	.533	4/ 4	1.000	4/ 4	2	0	1	1	0	20	.606
EWING, P.	32	7/12	.583	2/ 4	.500	1/ 5	2	2	4	1	0	16	.500
JACKSON, M.	24	2/ 5	.400	0/ 0	.000	0/ 0	11	1	4	1	0	4	.167
WINGATE, D.	36	3/ 8	.375	6/ 8	.750	3/ 6	2	1	2	1	0	12	.333
McDONALD, P.	3	0/ 1	.000	0/ 0	.000	0/ 1	0	0	0	1	0	0	.000
BROADNAX, H.	20	3/ 4	.750	3/ 4	.750	2/ 3	1	1	0	2	0	9	.450
DALTON, R.	17	2/ 2	1.000	0/ 0	.000	0/ 1	0	0	3	0	0	4	.235
MATEEN, G.	3	0/ 1	.000	0/ 0	.000	0/ 0	0	0	0	0	0	0	.000
FLOYD, K.	1	0/ 0	.000	0/ 0	.000	1/ 1	0	0	0	0	0	0	.000
HIGHSMITH, R.	1	0/ 0	.000	0/ 0	.000	1/ 1	0	0	0	0	0	0	.000
LOCKHART, T.	1	0/ 0	.000	0/ 0	.000	0/ 0	0	0	0	0	0	0	.000
Totals	200	29/57	.509	19/24	.792	16/29	18	7	18	6	1	77	.385

Team Rebounds: Georgetown 0; St. John's 0. Disqualified: None. Technical fouls: None.

	1st Half	2nd Half	Final
St. John's	28	31	59
Georgetown	32	45	77

Memphis State (45) Coach: Dana Kirk

	Min.	Total FG/FGA	Pct.	FT/FTA	Pct.	Reb. O/T	A	TO	PF	S	Blk	TP	PPM
LEE, K.	23	3/9	.333	4/4	1.000	0/7	1	2	5	0	1	10	.435
HOLMES, B.	31	4/8	.500	0/0	.000	2/2	0	1	5	0	0	8	.258
BEDFORD, W.	32	4/9	.444	0/0	.000	3/7	0	2	4	1	1	8	.250
TURNER, A.	40	5/13	.385	1/2	.500	0/4	3	2	3	2	0	11	.275
ASKEW, V.	40	1/3	.333	0/1	.000	6/7	7	2	2	0	0	2	.050
WILFONG, J.	1	0/1	.000	0/0	.000	1/1	0	0	1	0	0	0	.000
BOYD, D.	3	0/2	.000	0/0	.000	0/0	0	1	0	0	0	0	.000
BAILEY, D.	8	1/1	1.000	0/0	.000	0/0	0	1	2	0	0	2	.250
BECTON, W.	22	1/4	.250	2/2	1.000	1/5	1	0	1	1	0	4	.182
Totals	200	19/50	.380	7/9	.778	13/33	12	11	23	4	2	45	.225

Villanova (52) Coach: Rollie Massimino

	Min.	Total FG/FGA	Pct.	FT/FTA	Pct.	Reb. O/T	A	TO	PF	S	Blk	TP	PPM
PRESSLEY, H.	-	1/8	.125	1/2	.500	4/6	1	1	3	1	0	3	-
MCCLAIN, D.	-	6/9	.667	7/7	1.000	0/4	2	2	4	1	0	19	-
PINCKNEY, E.	-	3/7	.429	6/9	.667	3/9	1	1	3	0	3	12	-
WILBUR, D.	-	0/2	.000	0/0	.000	1/1	0	0	1	1	0	0	-
MCLAIN, G.	-	2/5	.400	5/5	1.000	0/2	2	4	1	1	1	9	-
JENSEN, H.	-	3/6	.500	0/0	.000	0/4	1	2	0	1	0	6	-
PLANSKY, M.	-	1/1	1.000	1/3	.333	0/0	2	1	1	0	0	3	-
EVERSON, C.	-	0/0	.000	0/0	.000	0/0	0	0	0	0	0	0	-
Totals	200	16/38	.421	20/26	.769	8/26	9	11	13	5	4	52	.260

Team Rebounds: Villanova 1; Memphis State 0. Disqualified: Memphis State—Lee, Holmes. Technical fouls: Memphis State—Bedford.

	1st Half	2nd Half	Final
Memphis State	23	22	45
Villanova	23	29	52

NATIONAL CHAMPIONSHIP

Georgetown (64) Coach: John Thompson

	Min.	Total FG/FGA	Pct.	FT/FTA	Pct.	Reb. O/T	A	TO	PF	S	Blk	TP	PPM
MARTIN, B.	37	4/6	.667	2/2	1.000	3/5	1	1	2	0	0	10	.270
WILLIAMS, R.	29	5/9	.556	0/2	.000	4/4	2	3	3	1	0	10	.345
EWING, P.	39	7/13	.538	0/0	.000	2/5	2	1	4	2	1	14	.359
JACKSON, M.	37	4/7	.571	0/0	.000	0/0	9	0	4	1	0	8	.216
WINGATE, D.	39	8/14	.571	0/0	.000	1/2	2	4	4	1	0	16	.410
MCDONALD, P.	2	0/1	.000	0/0	.000	0/0	0	1	0	0	0	0	.000
BROADNAX, H.	13	1/2	.500	2/2	1.000	0/1	2	1	4	1	0	4	.308
DALTON, R.	4	0/1	.000	2/2	1.000	0/0	0	0	1	0	0	2	.500
Totals	200	29/53	.547	6/8	.750	10/17	18	11	22	6	1	64	.320

Villanova (66) Coach: Rollie Massimino

	Min.	Total FG/FGA	Pct.	FT/FTA	Pct.	Reb. O/T	A	TO	PF	S	Blk	TP	PPM
PRESSLEY, H.	40	4/6	.667	3/4	.750	1/4	1	1	1	3	1	11	.275
MCCLAIN, D.	40	5/7	.714	7/8	.875	0/1	3	5	3	2	0	17	.425
PINCKNEY, E.	37	5/7	.714	6/7	.857	1/6	5	3	3	2	0	16	.432
WILBUR, D.	5	0/0	.000	0/0	.000	0/0	1	0	0	0	0	0	.000
MCLAIN, G.	40	3/3	1.000	2/2	1.000	0/2	2	2	2	0	0	8	.200
JENSEN, H.	34	5/5	1.000	4/5	.800	0/1	2	6	2	1	0	14	.412
PLANSKY, M.	1	0/0	.000	0/1	.000	0/0	0	0	1	0	0	0	.000
EVERSON, C.	3	0/0	.000	0/0	.000	0/0	0	0	0	0	0	0	.000
Totals	200	22/28	.786	22/27	.815	2/14	14	17	12	8	1	66	.330

Team Rebounds: Villanova 3; Georgetown 0. Disqualified: None. Technical fouls: None.

	1st Half	2nd Half	Final
Georgetown	28	36	64
Villanova	29	37	66

○ ALL-STAR TEAMS ○

ALL TOURNAMENT

PATRICK EWING	GEORGETOWN
HAROLD JENSEN	VILLANOVA
DWAYNE MCCLAIN	VILLANOVA
GARY MCLAIN	VILLANOVA
★ ED PINCKNEY	VILLANOVA

EAST REGIONAL

DOUG ALTENBERGER	ILLINOIS
BRUCE DALRYMPLE	GEORGIA TECH
★ PATRICK EWING	GEORGETOWN
MARK PRICE	GEORGIA TECH
JOHN SALLEY	GEORGIA TECH
DAVID WINGATE	GEORGETOWN

SOUTHEAST REGIONAL

ADRIAN BRANCH	MARYLAND
BRAD DAUGHERTY	N. CAROLINA
★ ED PINCKNEY	VILLANOVA
HAROLD PRESSLEY	VILLANOVA
KENNY SMITH	N. CAROLINA

WEST REGIONAL

WALTER BERRY	ST. JOHN'S
LORENZO CHARLES	N.C. STATE
★ CHRIS MULLIN	ST. JOHN'S
KENNY WALKER	KENTUCKY
ANTHONY WEBB	N.C. STATE

MIDWEST REGIONAL

WILLIAM BEDFORD	MEMPHIS STATE
DARRYL KENNEDY	OKLAHOMA
KEITH LEE	MEMPHIS STATE
KARL MALONE	LOUISANA TECH
WAYMAN TISDALE	OKLAHOMA
★ ANDRE TURNER	MEMPHIS STATE

★ Most Outstanding Player(s)

✪ INDIVIDUAL RECORDS ✪

SCORING

Most points in a single game
1 SAM VINCENT, MICHIGAN ST. (vs. ALA.-BIRMINGHAM) 32
1 MARK DAVIS, OLD DOMINION (vs. SMU) 32
3 STEVE HARRIS, TULSA (vs. UTEP) 31
4 3 tied for fourth place.

Most total points in the tournament
1 CHRIS MULLIN, ST. JOHN'S 110
2 LORENZO CHARLES, N.C. STATE 103
3 WALTER BERRY, ST. JOHN'S 93
4 WAYMON TISDALE, OKLAHOMA 91
5 DWAYNE MCCLAIN, VILLANOVA 90

Highest scoring average (minimum 2 games)
1 ROLANDO LAMB, VA COMMONWEALTH (55-2) 27.50
2 KENNY WALKER, KENTUCKY (75-3) 25.00
3 JOE KLEINE, ARKANSAS (48-2) 24.00
4 WAYMON TISDALE, OKLAHOMA (91-4) 22.75
5 LUSTER GOODWIN, UTEP (45-2) 22.50

FIELD GOALS

Most field goals in a single game
1 WAYMON TISDALE, OKLAHOMA (vs. ILLINOIS STATE) 14
1 MARK DAVIS, OLD DOMINION (vs. SMU) 14
3 SAM VINCENT, MICHIGAN ST. (vs. ALA.-BIRMINGHAM) 13
4 8 tied for fourth place.

Most total field goals in the tournament
1 WAYMON TISDALE, OKLAHOMA 41
2 CHRIS MULLIN, ST. JOHN'S 39
3 LORENZO CHARLES, N.C. STATE 37
4 ANDRE TURNER, MEMPHIS STATE 35
4 PAT EWING, GEORGETOWN 35

Most field goal attempts in a single game
1 REGGIE LEWIS, NORTHEASTERN (vs. ILLINOIS) 28
2 CHUCK PERSON, AUBURN (vs. N. CAROLINA) 25
3 BARRY STEVENS, IOWA STATE (vs. OHIO STATE) 24
4 4 tied for fourth place.

Most total field goal attempts in tournament
1 CHRIS MULLIN, ST. JOHN'S 77
2 KEITH LEE, MEMPHIS STATE 68
3 ANDRE TURNER, MEMPHIS STATE 65
4 PAT EWING, GEORGETOWN 64
5 LORENZO CHARLES, N.C. STATE 63

Highest field goal percentage in a single game (minimum 10 attempts)
1 WAYMON TISDALE, OKLAHOMA (vs. ILLINOIS STATE) (14-16) .875
2 BILL WENNINGTON, ST. JOHN'S (vs. SOUTHERN-B.R.) (10-12) .833
3 LORENZO CHARLES, N.C. STATE (vs. UTEP) (12-15) .800
4 ALLEN, SAN DIEGO ST. (vs. UNLV) (8-10) .800
4 BOBBY LEE HURT, ALABAMA (vs. VA COMMONWEALTH) (8-10) .800

Highest field goal percentage in the tournament (minimum 20 attempts)
1 BRAD DAUGHERTY, N. CAROLINA (29-40) .725
2 KEN NORMAN, ILLINOIS (18-25) .720
3 FRANK FORD, AUBURN (21-30) .700
4 WAYMON TISDALE, OKLAHOMA (41-59) .695
5 BILL WENNINGTON, ST. JOHN'S (24-35) .686

FREE THROWS

Most free throws in a single game
1 DWAYNE WASHINGTON, SYRACUSE (vs. DEPAUL) 15
2 SPUD WEBB, N.C. STATE (vs. UTEP) 13
2 KENNY WALKER, KENTUCKY (vs. WASHINGTON) 13
4 3 tied for fourth place.

Most total free throws in the tournament
1 ED PINCKNEY, VILLANOVA 39
2 CHRIS MULLIN, ST. JOHN'S 32
3 LORENZO CHARLES, N.C. STATE 29
4 SPUD WEBB, N.C. STATE 27
5 WALTER BERRY, ST. JOHN'S 25

Most free throws attempted in a single game
1 SPUD WEBB, N.C. STATE (vs. UTEP) 17
2 DWAYNE WASHINGTON, SYRACUSE (vs. DEPAUL) 16
3 KENNY WALKER, KENTUCKY (vs. WASHINGTON) 15
4 DAVID HENDERSON, DUKE (vs. PEPPERDINE) 14
5 2 tied for fifth place.

Most free throws attempted in the tournament
1 ED PINCKNEY, VILLANOVA 53
2 LORENZO CHARLES, N.C. STATE 39
3 CHRIS MULLIN, ST. JOHN'S 37
4 SPUD WEBB, N.C. STATE 36
5 WALTER BERRY, ST. JOHN'S 32

Highest free throw percentage in a single game (minimum 7 attempts)
1 CHRIS MULLIN, ST. JOHN'S (vs. ARKANSAS) (10-10) 1.000
1 VERNON BUTLER, NAVY (vs. LOUISIANA ST.) (10-10) 1.000
3 GARY WILSON, F. DICKINSON (vs. MICHIGAN) (8-8) 1.000
3 DAMON GOODWIN, DAYTON (vs. VILLANOVA) (8-8) 1.000
3 DOUG WOJCIK, NAVY (vs. LOUISIANA ST.) (8-8) 1.000

Highest free throw percentage in the tournament (minimum 15 attempts)
1 DWAYNE MCCLAIN, VILLANOVA (24-25) .960
2 VERNON BUTLER, NAVY (14-15) .933
3 DWAYNE WASHINGTON, SYRACUSE (18-20) .900
4 JAMES PONDER, ALA.-BIRMINGHAM (17-19) .895
5 CHRIS MULLIN, ST. JOHN'S (32-37) .865

REBOUNDS

Most rebounds in a single game
1 DAVID ROBINSON, NAVY (vs. LOUISIANA ST.) 18
2 COLEMAN, IONA (vs. LOYOLA-CHICAGO) 16
2 KARL MALONE, LOUISIANA TECH (vs. OKLAHOMA) 16

4 ANTHONY GORDON, ALA.-BIRMINGHAM (vs. MEMPHIS STATE) 15
4 LARRY DAVIS, SMU (vs. OLD DOMINION) 15

Most total rebounds in the tournament
1 LORENZO CHARLES, N.C. STATE 51
2 ED PINCKNEY, VILLANOVA 48
3 WAYMON TISDALE, OKLAHOMA 43
3 BRAD DAUGHERTY, N. CAROLINA 43
5 WALTER BERRY, ST. JOHN'S 42

Most rebounds per game (minimum 2 games)
1 KARL MALONE, LOUISIANA TECH (40-3) 13.33
2 ROY TARPLEY, MICHIGAN (26-2) 13.00
3 DAVID ROBINSON, NAVY (26-2) 13.00
4 JOE KLEINE, ARKANSAS (25-2) 12.50
5 LARRY DAVIS, SMU (24-2) 12.00

ASSISTS

Most assists in a single game
1 KENNY PATTERSON, DEPAUL (vs. SYRACUSE) 15
2 CARL GOLSTON, LOYOLA-CHICAGO (vs. IONA) 12
2 ANDRE TURNER, MEMPHIS STATE (vs. OKLAHOMA) 12
2 MICHAEL JACKSON, GEORGETOWN (vs. LOYOLA-CHICAGO) 12
2 KEITH GATLIN, MARYLAND (vs. NAVY) 12

Most total assists in the tournament
1 MICHAEL JACKSON, GEORGETOWN 45
2 ANDRE TURNER, MEMPHIS STATE 38
3 SPUD WEBB, N.C. STATE 29
4 VINCENT ASKEW, MEMPHIS STATE 27
5 WAYNE SMITH, LOUISIANA TECH 26

Most assists per game (minimum 2 appearances)
1 BUTCH MOORE, SMU (19-2) 9.50
2 WAYNE SMITH, LOUISIANA TECH (26-3) 8.67
3 CARL GOLSTON, LOYOLA-CHICAGO (24-3) 8.00
3 KEITH GATLIN, MARYLAND (24-3) 8.00
5 ANDRE TURNER, MEMPHIS STATE (38-5) 7.60

TURNOVERS

Most turnovers in a single game
1 BRUCE DOUGLAS, ILLINOIS (vs. GEORGIA TECH) 9
2 DETLEF SCHREMPF, WASHINGTON (vs. KENTUCKY) 8
3 ANTHONY BOWIE, OKLAHOMA (vs. MEMPHIS STATE) 7
3 BARRY STEVENS, IOWA STATE (vs. OHIO STATE) 7
3 CHRIS MULLIN, ST. JOHN'S (vs. SOUTHERN-B.R.) 7

Most total turnovers in the tournament
1 CHRIS MULLIN, ST. JOHN'S 20
2 DWAYNE MCCLAIN, VILLANOVA 19
3 SPUD WEBB, N.C. STATE 17
3 BRUCE DOUGLAS, ILLINOIS 17
5 2 tied for fifth place.

SHOTS BLOCKED

Most shots blocked in a single game
1 WARREN MARTIN, N. CAROLINA (vs. MIDDLE TENN. ST.) 6
1 PAT EWING, GEORGETOWN (vs. LEHIGH) 6

3 PAT EWING, GEORGETOWN (vs. LOYOLA-
   CHICAGO)   5
4 8 tied for fourth place.

Most total shots blocked in the tournament
1 PAT EWING, GEORGETOWN   13
2 ED PINCKNEY, VILLANOVA   10
3 WARREN MARTIN, N. CAROLINA   9
3 WILLIAM BEDFORD, MEMPHIS STATE   9
5 3 tied for fifth place.

STEALS

Most steals in a single game
1 ROLANDO LAMB, VA. COMMONWEALTH (vs.
   MARSHALL)   6
1 BRUCE DOUGLAS, ILLINOIS (vs. GEORGIA)   6
3 WILLIE BLAND, LOUISIANA TECH (vs.
   OKLAHOMA)   5
3 DARYL SHEPHERD, PITTSBURGH (vs.
   LOUISIANA TECH)   5

3 HAROLD PRESSLEY, VILLANOVA (vs. MICHIGAN)
                                                    5

Most total steals in the tournament
1 HAROLD PRESSLEY, VILLANOVA   15
2 CHRIS MULLIN, ST. JOHN'S   11
3 ROLANDO LAMB, VA. COMMONWEALTH   9
4 3 tied for fourth place.

✪ TEAM RECORDS ✪

SCORING

Most points in a single game
1 OKLAHOMA (vs. N.C. A&T)   96
2 3 tied for second place.

Most total points in the tournament
1 GEORGETOWN   397
2 ST. JOHN'S   365
3 VILLANOVA   330

Highest scoring average (minimum 2 games)
1 LOUISIANA TECH (241-3)   80.33
2 OKLAHOMA (318-4)   79.50
3 UTEP (152-2)   76.00

FIELD GOALS

Most field goals in a single game
1 OKLAHOMA (vs. N.C. A&T)   39
2 SMU (vs. OLD DOMINION)   38
3 OKLAHOMA (vs. LOUISIANA TECH)   37

Most total field goals in the tournament
1 GEORGETOWN   152
2 OKLAHOMA   137
3 MEMPHIS STATE   129

Most field goals attempted in a single game
1 LOUISIANA TECH (vs. OKLAHOMA)   84
2 OLD DOMINION (vs. SMU)   77
3 OKLAHOMA (vs. N.C. A&T)   74

Most total field goals attempted in the tournament
1 GEORGETOWN   305
2 MEMPHIS STATE   269
3 OKLAHOMA   250

Highest field goal percentage in a single game
1 VILLANOVA (vs. GEORGETOWN) (22-28)   .786
2 N.C. STATE (vs. UTEP) (30-41)   .732
3 OKLAHOMA (vs. ILLINOIS STATE) (35-53)   .660

Highest field goal percentage in a tournament (minimum 2 games)
1 NOTRE DAME (52-92)   .565
2 SAN DIEGO ST. (31-56)   .554
3 OKLAHOMA (137-250)   .548

FREE THROWS

Most free throws in a single game
1 UTEP (vs. TULSA)   39
2 NAVY (vs. LOUISIANA ST.)   34
3 KENTUCKY (vs. WASHINGTON)   30

Most total free throws in the tournament
1 ST. JOHN'S   109
2 VILLANOVA   102
3 GEORGETOWN   93

Most free throws attempted in a single game
1 UTEP (vs. TULSA)   55
2 NAVY (vs. LOUISIANA ST.)   43
3 2 tied for third place.

Most total free throws attempted in the tournament
1 ST. JOHN'S   143
2 GEORGETOWN   137
3 VILLANOVA   136

Highest free throw percentage in a single game
1 DAYTON (vs. VILLANOVA) (17-17)   1.000
2 LEHIGH (vs. GEORGETOWN) (15-16)   .938
3 GEORGIA TECH (vs. GEORGETOWN) (22-24)   .917

Highest free throw percentage in the tournament (minimum 2 games)
1 MARYLAND (28-34)   .824
2 GEORGIA TECH (86-112)   .768
3 ILLINOIS STATE (23-30)   .767

Fewest free throws in a single game
1 4 tied for first place.

Lowest free throw percentage in a single game
1 WASHINGTON (vs. KENTUCKY) (6-16)   .375
2 VA. COMMONWEALTH (vs. ALABAMA) (5-13)
                                                 .385
3 IOWA (vs. ARKANSAS) (6-15)   .400

Lowest free throw percentage in the tournament (minimum 2 games)
1 SMU (14-25)   .560
2 GEORGIA (17-30)   .567
3 KANSAS (21-35)   .600

REBOUNDS

Most rebounds in a single game
1 LOUISIANA TECH (vs. PITTSBURGH)   51
2 3 tied for second place.

Most rebounds per game (minimum 2 games)
1 LOUISIANA TECH (130-3)   43.33
2 SMU (84-2)   42.00
3 DUKE (73-2)   36.50

ASSISTS

Most assists in a single game
1 LOUISIANA TECH (vs. OKLAHOMA)   26
2 OKLAHOMA (vs. ILLINOIS STATE)   24
2 OKLAHOMA (vs. N.C. A&T)   24

Most assists per game (minimum 2 games)
1 LOUISIANA TECH (65-3)   21.67
2 OKLAHOMA (86-4)   21.50
3 SMU (43-2)   21.50

TURNOVERS

Most turnovers in a single game
1 NORTHEASTERN (vs. ILLINOIS)   20
1 MARSHALL (vs. VA. COMMONWEALTH)   20
3 5 tied for third place.

Most turnovers per game (minimum 2 games)
1 ILLINOIS (52-3)   17.33
2 SMU (34-2)   17.00
3 GEORGIA TECH (60-4)   15.00

SHOTS BLOCKED

Most shots blocked in a single game
1 N. CAROLINA (vs. MIDDLE TENN. ST.)   10
2 GEORGETOWN (vs. LEHIGH)   9
3 2 tied for third place.

Most shots blocked per game (minimum 2 games)
1 ALABAMA (14-3)   4.67
2 N. CAROLINA (18-4)   4.50
3 2 tied for third place.

STEALS

Most steals in a single game
1 VILLANOVA (vs. N. CAROLINA)   13
2 LOUISIANA TECH (vs. OKLAHOMA)   11
2 GEORGIA TECH (vs. ILLINOIS)   11
2 MERCER (vs. GEORGIA TECH)   11
2 VA. COMMONWEALTH (vs. MARSHALL)   11

Most steals per game
1 ILLINOIS (26-3)   8.67
2 GEORGIA (17-2)   8.50
3 LOUISIANA TECH (23-3)   7.67

1986

| FIRST ROUND | SECOND ROUND | REGIONAL SEMIFINAL | REGIONAL FINAL | FINAL FOUR | REGIONAL FINAL | REGIONAL SEMIFINAL | SECOND ROUND | FIRST ROUND |

SOUTHEAST

1 Kentucky 75
16 Davidson 55
  Kentucky 71
8 Western Ky. 67
9 Nebraska 59
  Western Ky. 64
    Kentucky 68
5 Alabama 97
12 Xavier 80
  Alabama 58
4 Illinois 75
13 Fairfield 51
  Illinois 56
    Alabama 63
      Kentucky 57
6 Purdue 87
11 Louisiana St. 94 (2 ot)
  Louisiana St. 83
3 *Memphis St. 95
14 Ball St. 63
  *Memphis St. 81
    Louisiana St. 70
7 Virginia Tech 62
10 Villanova 71
  Villanova 61
2 Georgia Tech 68
15 Marist 53
  Georgia Tech 66
    Georgia Tech 64
        Louisiana St. 59

          Louisiana 77

WEST

1 St. John's 83
16 Montana St. 74
  St. John's 65
8 Auburn 73
9 Arizona 63
  Auburn 81
    Auburn 70
5 Maryland 69
12 Pepperdine 64
  Maryland 64
4 UNLV 74
13 Northeast La. 51
  UNLV 70
    UNLV 63
      Auburn 76
6 Ala.-Birmingham 66
11 Missouri 64
  Ala.-Birmingham 59
3 N. Carolina 84
14 Utah 72
  N. Carolina 77
    N. Carolina 79
7 Bradley 83
10 UTEP 65
  Bradley 68
2 Louisville 93
15 Drexel 73
  Louisville 82
    Louisville 94
      Louisville 84

          Louisville 88

FINAL FOUR

Louisville 72
Duke 69

EAST

1 Duke 85
16 Miss. Valley 78
  Duke 89
8 Old Dominion 72
9 West Virginia 64
  Old Dominion 61
    Duke 74
5 Virginia 68
12 DePaul 72
  DePaul 74
4 Oklahoma 80
13 Northeastern 74
  Oklahoma 69
    DePaul 67
      Duke 71
6 St. Joseph's 60
11 Richmond 59
  St. Joseph's 69
3 Indiana 79
14 Cleveland St. 83
  Cleveland St. 75
    Cleveland St. 70
7 Navy 87
10 Tulsa 68
  Navy 97
2 Syracuse 101
15 Brown 52
  Syracuse 85
    Navy 71
        Navy 50

          Duke 71

MIDWEST

1 Kansas 71
16 N. Carolina A&T 46
  Kansas 65
8 Jacksonville 50
9 Temple 61 (ot)
  Temple 43
    Kansas 96 (ot)
5 Michigan St. 72
12 Washington 70
  Michigan St. 80
4 Georgetown 70
13 Texas Tech 64
  Georgetown 68
    Michigan St. 86
      Kansas 75
6 N.C. State 66
11 Iowa 64
  N.C. State 80 (2 ot)
3 Notre Dame 83
14 Ark.-Little Rock 90
  Ark.-Little Rock 66
    N.C. State 70
7 Iowa St. 81 (ot)
10 Miami (Ohio) 29
  Iowa 72
2 Michigan 70
15 Akron 64
  Michigan 69
    Iowa St. 66
        N.C. State 67

          Kansas 67

*Memphis State's participation in 1986 tournament vacated.

It was a tournament of controversy, of underdogs, of tight-fought games and new faces. And finally, another championship for Denny Crum.

The most intriguing regional was probably the East, with the powerful Blue Devils of Duke, Navy's brilliant David Robinson, and Cleveland State.

Cleveland State? Coach Calvin Mackey described his players as "off-Broadway guys; players who watch every game on the tubes and eat their hearts out waiting for their chance." They had qualified for an at-large bid by winning the Mid-America conference title with players like center Eric Mudd, who joined the team after a relative talked Mackey into giving him a chance, freshman guard Kenny "The Mouse" McFadden (who didn't even play high school ball), and forward Clinton Ransey, whose choice of Cleveland State was dictated by a lack of other interested parties. No Viking player had averaged more than 26 minutes a game; their relentless full-court pressure on defense and a "run-and-stun" offense that was second in the nation in scoring was too much for Bob Knight's Big Ten powerhouse Indiana Hoosiers to handle. After wearing down St. Joseph's, the Vikings proceeded to a game Mackey called "the U.S. Navy Department of Defense against the U.S. Stun and Gun, Streetfighters, Inc."

Navy sailed into the regional finals behind their tall ship, 6-11 Midshipman David Robinson. After an easy first round victory, the Middies loosed their big gun to sink Syracuse, the No. 9–ranked team in the nation, on its home court. Robinson finished with 35 points, 11 rebounds, 7 blocked shots, and countless intimidations, and sent the Orangemen back to their dorms in dejection.

The Middies took an early lead in their showdown against the Vikings. But eventually Cleveland State's physical pressure began to take its toll. The Vikings caught Navy with nine minutes to play, and Robinson was hardly getting his hands on the ball. Then the big man got more aggressive, taking control and scoring 13 of Navy's last 17 points, including the game winner with six seconds left.

Navy was finally torpedoed by the Blue Devils of Duke.

Duke had entered the tournament the No. 1–ranked team in the country. But the Blue Devils were bedeviled in the first round by the Delta Devils of Mississippi Valley State. The 16-point underdogs from Itta Bena were the proud representatives of the smallest school in the Mississippi state system. In January the state legislature had recommended closing the college as a cost-cutting measure, but the $167,060 Valley State received for its tourney appearance helped the 2,200-student campus remain open. The Delta Devils weren't satisfied with just making an appearance, however; they came to play and they scared Duke half to death. With fourteen and a half minutes left they led 54-49, but with four of their starters sitting with four fouls each, they finally succumbed to

Duke's depth. Then, after Duke scored an easy second round victory over Old Dominion, the Blue Devils met the Blue Demons of DePaul. The Chicagoans had already gone farther than anyone expected after finishing the regular season at 16-12, but they, too, refused to give up without a fight. Duke took nothing for granted, and despite a horrendous shooting night, they hit the boards, hustled for loose balls, and won 74-67. After the game, in which Duke outrebounded DePaul 45-28, the Blue Demons' center, Marty Embry, said, "They were sending eight guys to the boards."

That's just what it felt like to Navy too. The small and slow Duke front line (6-8 center Jay Bilas said, "What I lack in size, I make up for in lack of quickness") crashed the boards in waves and outrebounded Robinson and the Middies 49-29. Midway through the first half, Navy led 20-16, but an 18-2 Duke onslaught paced by All-American guard Johnny Dawkins gave the Blue Devils a 12-point lead at the half and sent the Midshipmen into dry dock.

The one true underdog in the Final Four was LSU. They lost their top player, Nikita Wilson, at midseason for academic reasons. They finished fifth in the SEC and lost to Kentucky for the third time during the conference tourney. But they played the first two rounds at home in Baton Rouge. And though they were the underdog in every round, somehow the Tigers found a way to win four straight. First they outlasted Purdue in double overtime. Neither team could take control in regulation or in the first extra period, but the Tigers scored the first 10 points of the second OT as Purdue turned the ball over three times and missed four straight shots. But the lead evaporated and was down to 2 with 18 seconds left before Anthony Wilson made 7 of 8 from the line to seal the victory.

The second round was more of the same. This time LSU came from 12 back in the second half and won on a last-second shot. In the regional semis the Tigers overcame a four-point Georgia Tech lead with 6:19 left and finished with a six-point triumph, their biggest edge of the night. The Tigers followed the same script in defeating Kentucky to advance to the Final Four. At no point in the game did either team lead by more than five. With 5:52 left the Wildcats led by four. But LSU came back and held on to pull one more upset.

Unlike LSU, Louisville dominated in the early rounds, winning each of its first three games by at least 14 points. They outran, outjumped and outshot their opponents, and their balanced attack, led by seniors Billy Thompson and Milt Wagner and freshman Pervis Ellison, was devastating. Then they came up against a red-hot Auburn squad, who used their bruising strength to run over their opponents.

The game was a classic, with brilliant individual play on both sides. With about 10 minutes left and Auburn nursing a three-point lead, Louisville coach Denny Crum signaled for a defensive switch into a 1-3-1 zone. The zone upset Auburn's tempo, forcing them to take outside shots. Before they were able to adjust, Louisville took the lead. In what may have been the key play of the game, "Never Nervous" Pervis Ellison, who had just tipped in a miss for a three-point advantage, raced back on defense to reject a shot by Auburn center Jeff Moore. "I just didn't see him until I released the ball," said Moore. Jeff Hall, who had taken off downcourt when he realized Ellison was going to block the shot, picked up the loose ball near midcourt and drove in for the dunk that ended Auburn's hopes.

In the Midwest regional, Kansas survived with only one serious controversy. After breezing through their first two games, a malfunctioning clock played a critical role in the Jayhawks' bizarre overtime victory over Michigan State.

With 2:21 left in the game Michigan State was up by four. About 15 seconds later, when Kansas's Ron Kellogg converted an offensive rebound, the lead was 2 . . . and the clock read 2:20 left. The Spartans, obviously rattled, proceeded to miss three critical foul shots in the last two minutes, and lost in OT.

The difference in Duke's semifinal victory over Kansas was Mark Alarie. The Blue Devils' senior forward was assigned to guard Danny Manning and held the Jayhawks' star to a season low of 4 points.

Even so, Kansas had a great chance to win. Behind Ron Kellogg's 22 points, they were up 65-61 when they missed a lay-up that gave Duke a chance to stay in the game. The Blue Devils tied the score, and with 23 seconds left Dawkins kept the ball alive and freshman reserve Danny Ferry laid it in for the lead. With 11 seconds left, Ferry planted himself in front of a driving Kellogg, who was called for the charge. Duke held on for the victory.

In the other semifinal, Louisville ended LSU's Cinderella tournament when they turned up the juice in the second half and streaked past the Tigers into the title game. The Cardinals were simply stupendous in every area, stepping up the defensive pressure, shooting 63 percent, and outscoring LSU 52-33 for the half. Senior forward Billy Thompson couldn't miss (he hit 10 of 11 for

the game), and he stopped LSU star John Williams cold. Guard Milt Wagner added 14 second-half points, and Ellison swept the boards for a game-high 13 rebounds. LSU coach Dale Brown, all but conceding that his squad had lost to the better team, praised his players' determination and accomplishments. "They played their hearts out," he said, "and I'm proud of them."

Louisville against Duke: The Cardinals, winners of 16 straight games, had blinding speed and superb balance; coach Mike Krzyzweski's Blue Devils, the nation's top-ranked team, had a 21-game winning streak and were extraordinarily disciplined, fundamentally sound, and led by star guard Johnny Dawkins. Both teams were determined to take away the other's advantage.

For the first 33 minutes of the title contest, it looked like Duke would have its way. Their defense smothered Louisville's fast break, and Dawkins started out on fire. He scored 11 points before either of Louisville's senior stars even attempted a shot. With a little over seven minutes left Duke led by 6, and both Thompson and Wagner—the team's top two scorers—had drawn their fourth personal fouls. But the Cardinals came back. They denied Dawkins the ball and began to bull their way to the basket. When Wagner followed Ellison's lay-up with a three-point play, the lead was down to one.

Dawkins, who scored 13 of Duke's first 25 points and finished with 24 for the game, was held to just two foul shots in the last 15:28. Wagner, meanwhile, who had started so poorly, responded to coach Crum's encouragement ("I just kept telling Milt how much I loved him," Crum said. "I just told him to play a little bit harder and everything will be fine") and scored 7 of his 9 points in the last six minutes. And Never Nervous Pervis came up with the game of his life, rebounding and hitting five of six in the second half to become the second freshman ever to win the tournament Most Outstanding Player award.

"The thing about this team all year," said Crum, "is it didn't matter who we played. When we got down the stretch, we responded and found a way to win."

FIRST ROUND SOUTHEAST

Kentucky (75)   Coach: Eddie Sutton

	Min.	Total FG/FGA	Pct.	FT/FTA	Pct.	Reb. O/T	A	TO	PF	S	Blk	TP	PPM
BENNETT, W.	24	3/6	.500	8/12	.667	-/6	1	-	3	-	-	14	.583
WALKER, K.	33	7/9	.778	6/9	.667	-/10	1	-	2	-	-	20	.606
BLACKMON, J.	29	4/7	.571	1/2	.500	-/11	1	-	2	-	-	9	.310
DAVENDER, E.	28	5/12	.417	1/2	.500	-/1	2	-	0	-	-	11	.393
HARDEN, R.	29	2/5	.400	0/0	.000	-/0	3	-	0	-	-	4	.138
JENKINS, C.	20	2/3	.667	2/3	.667	-/4	0	-	0	-	-	6	.300
BYRD, L.	7	0/0	.000	3/4	.750	-/0	2	-	0	-	-	3	.429
ANDREWS, P.	11	2/3	.667	0/0	.000	-/1	0	-	1	-	-	4	.364
THOMAS, I.	6	1/1	1.000	0/0	.000	-/1	0	-	1	-	-	2	.333
ZIEGLER, T.	2	1/1	1.000	0/0	.000	-/0	0	-	2	-	-	2	1.000
LOCK, R.	11	0/2	.000	0/0	.000	-/3	0	-	3	-	-	0	.000
Totals	200	27/49	.551	21/32	.656	-/37	10	14	16	-	-	75	.375

Davidson (55)   Coach: Bobby Hussey

	Min.	Total FG/FGA	Pct.	FT/FTA	Pct.	Reb. O/T	A	TO	PF	S	Blk	TP	PPM
BORN, G.	26	6/8	.750	1/1	1.000	-/3	0	-	4	-	-	13	.500
TANNER, A.	33	0/5	.000	0/0	.000	-/2	3	-	4	-	-	0	.000
MCCONKEY, J.	23	1/4	.250	2/2	1.000	-/2	0	-	4	-	-	4	.174
HEINEMAN, C.	30	2/6	.333	0/0	.000	-/0	1	-	4	-	-	4	.133
RUCKER, D.	34	5/13	.385	0/0	.000	-/2	3	-	1	-	-	10	.294
BEGO, P.	14	1/2	.500	2/2	1.000	-/4	2	-	1	-	-	4	.286
RIAZZI, P.	1	0/0	.000	0/0	.000	-/0	0	-	1	-	-	0	.000
KEENER, D.	1	0/0	.000	0/0	.000	-/0	0	-	0	-	-	0	.000
FITZGERALD, D.	1	0/0	.000	0/0	.000	-/0	0	-	0	-	-	0	.000
HIMES, J.	13	6/8	.750	1/2	.500	-/1	2	-	5	-	-	13	1.000
GYNN, M.	1	0/0	.000	0/0	.000	-/0	0	-	0	-	-	0	.000
WOLFE, T.	2	0/1	.000	0/0	.000	-/0	0	-	0	-	-	0	.000
NEIBUHR, K.	13	1/3	.333	0/0	.000	-/2	0	-	0	-	-	2	.154
SELLERS, B.	1	0/0	.000	0/0	.000	-/0	0	-	0	-	-	0	.000
SCOTT, T.	7	2/3	.667	1/1	1.000	-/2	0	-	0	-	-	5	.714
Totals	200	24/53	.453	7/8	.875	-/18	11	14	24	-	-	55	.275

Team Rebounds: Kentucky 0; Davidson 1. Disqualified: Davidson—Himes. Technical fouls: None.

	1st Half	2nd Half	Final
Kentucky	38	37	75
Davidson	26	29	55

Western Kentucky (67)   Coach: Clem Haskins

	Min.	Total FG/FGA	Pct.	FT/FTA	Pct.	Reb. O/T	A	TO	PF	S	Blk	TP	PPM
JOHNSON, K.	24	4/11	.364	2/2	1.000	3/7	0	0	4	0	0	10	.417
SWOGGER, R.	35	8/15	.533	0/0	.000	4/6	1	0	1	0	0	16	.457
MARTIN, C.	33	5/8	.625	1/3	.333	6/12	0	1	3	0	0	11	.333
MCNARY, J.	32	0/8	.000	8/8	1.000	0/4	7	1	2	0	0	8	.250
GORDON, B.	35	6/16	.375	0/0	.000	0/1	2	0	2	1	0	12	.343
LEE, K.	7	0/0	.000	0/0	.000	0/0	1	0	1	0	0	0	.000
MCNEIL, B.	7	2/4	.500	0/0	.000	0/0	0	0	0	0	0	4	.571
TISDALE, F.	3	0/0	.000	0/0	.000	0/0	0	1	1	0	0	0	.000
FRANK, T.	24	3/6	.500	0/0	.000	1/4	0	1	4	0	0	6	.250
Totals	200	28/68	.412	11/13	.846	14/34	11	4	18	1	0	67	.335

Nebraska (59)   Coach: Moe Iba

	Min.	Total FG/FGA	Pct.	FT/FTA	Pct.	Reb. O/T	A	TO	PF	S	Blk	TP	PPM
DAY, B.	40	8/14	.571	2/4	.500	0/9	2	2	3	0	0	18	.450
MATZKE, J.	22	0/1	.000	0/0	.000	1/2	0	1	3	0	0	0	.000
LOGAN, C.	40	3/5	.600	4/8	.500	6/12	0	3	3	1	0	10	.250
MARSHALL, H.	30	4/9	.444	3/3	1.000	1/4	0	1	0	1	0	11	.367
CARR, B.	38	4/12	.333	2/2	1.000	0/0	5	4	4	0	0	10	.263
BROWN, D.	5	0/0	.000	0/0	.000	0/1	1	0	0	0	0	0	.000
BAILOUS, A.	25	4/6	.667	2/2	1.000	1/3	0	2	1	0	0	10	.400
Totals	200	23/47	.489	13/19	.684	9/31	8	13	14	2	0	59	.295

Team Rebounds: Western Ky. 1, Nebraska 4. Disqualified: None. Technical fouls: None.

	1st Half	2nd Half	Final
Western Ky.	33	34	67
Nebraska	26	33	59

Alabama (97)   Coach: Wimp Sanderson

	Min.	Total FG/FGA	Pct.	FT/FTA	Pct.	Reb. O/T	A	TO	PF	S	Blk	TP	PPM
FARMER, J.	39	10/15	.667	4/5	.800	2/7	1	2	3	0	0	24	.615
JOHNSON, B.	32	11/16	.688	0/2	.000	1/7	2	5	4	1	1	22	.688
MCKEY, D.	25	7/8	.875	2/2	1.000	0/3	4	1	3	0	3	16	.640
GOTTFRIED, M.	20	3/6	.500	0/0	.000	0/0	2	1	1	1	0	6	.300
CONER, T.	37	5/8	.625	4/4	1.000	0/1	9	2	1	1	2	14	.378
JACKSON, J.	11	1/2	.500	1/2	.500	0/0	1	1	0	2	0	3	.273
ANSLEY, M.	29	5/8	.625	0/0	.000	1/9	0	2	3	0	0	10	.345
WHITE, G.	1	0/0	.000	0/0	.000	0/0	0	0	0	0	0	0	.000
DUDLEY, C.	6	1/1	1.000	0/0	.000	0/0	0	0	0	0	0	2	.333
Totals	200	43/64	.672	11/15	.733	4/27	19	14	15	5	6	97	.485

Xavier (Ohio) (80)   Coach: Pete Gillen

	Min.	Total FG/FGA	Pct.	FT/FTA	Pct.	Reb. O/T	A	TO	PF	S	Blk	TP	PPM
HARRIS, R.	35	11/19	.579	2/3	.667	4/11	0	0	2	2	0	24	.686
MCBRIDE, W.	36	4/8	.500	0/0	.000	2/4	1	3	1	1	0	8	.222
JOHNSON, E.	35	7/12	.583	1/3	.333	5/9	0	1	3	1	0	15	.429
LEE, R.	37	0/4	.000	2/2	1.000	3/4	9	5	4	0	0	2	.054
LARKIN, B.	36	10/26	.385	3/5	.600	1/2	1	2	2	1	0	23	.639
BOWMAN, J.	1	0/0	.000	0/0	.000	0/0	1	0	0	0	0	0	.000
WILLIAMSON, K.	2	1/1	1.000	0/0	.000	0/1	0	0	0	0	0	2	1.000
GREENIDGE, L.	8	1/4	.250	0/0	.000	0/0	1	0	1	0	0	2	.250
RAMEY, M.	1	1/1	1.000	0/0	.000	0/0	1	0	0	0	0	2	2.000
KELLEY, J.	1	0/0	.000	0/0	.000	0/0	0	0	1	0	0	0	.000
CAMPBELL, D.	1	0/0	.000	0/0	.000	0/1	1	1	2	0	0	0	.000
DONNELLEY, A.	7	1/2	.500	0/0	.000	3/3	0	1	1	0	1	2	.286
Totals	200	36/77	.468	8/13	.615	18/34	15	14	15	8	1	80	.400

Team Rebounds: Alabama 5; Xavier (Ohio) 2. Disqualified: None. Technical fouls: None.

	1st Half	2nd Half	Final
Alabama	39	58	97
Xavier (Ohio)	33	47	80

Illinois (75)   Coach: Lou Henson

	Min.	Total FG/FGA	Pct.	FT/FTA	Pct.	Reb. O/T	A	TO	PF	S	Blk	TP	PPM
WINTERS, E.	31	2/8	.250	1/2	.500	1/5	0	0	3	0	0	5	.161
WELCH, A.	25	11/16	.688	0/0	.000	3/5	0	1	1	1	0	22	.880
NORMAN, K.	29	6/11	.545	1/1	1.000	3/7	0	2	3	0	0	13	.448
BLACKWELL, G.	22	1/6	.167	0/0	.000	0/1	4	0	0	0	0	2	.091
DOUGLAS, B.	37	2/4	.500	3/4	.750	0/3	5	0	0	3	0	7	.189
WYSINGER, T.	29	6/8	.750	0/0	.000	0/1	6	1	3	1	0	12	.414
MEENTS, S.	16	5/6	.833	0/0	.000	0/1	1	0	4	1	0	10	.625
HAMILTON, L.	3	2/2	1.000	0/1	.000	1/1	0	0	0	0	0	4	1.333
KELLER, C.	1	0/1	.000	0/0	.000	0/0	0	0	0	0	0	0	.000
TAYLOR, C.	3	0/1	.000	0/0	.000	0/2	1	0	0	0	0	0	.000
KUJAWA	3	0/0	.000	0/0	.000	0/1	0	0	0	0	0	0	.000
BLAB	1	0/0	.000	0/0	.000	0/1	0	0	0	0	1	0	.000
Totals	200	35/63	.556	5/8	.625	8/28	16	4	14	6	2	75	.375

Fairfield (51)   Coach: Mitch Buonaguro

	Min.	Total FG/FGA	Pct.	FT/FTA	Pct.	Reb. O/T	A	TO	PF	S	Blk	TP	PPM
GEORGE, T.	40	5/13	.385	0/0	.000	0/6	3	2	2	0	0	10	.250
YERINA, P.	27	5/7	.714	3/3	1.000	1/4	1	3	5	0	0	13	.481
GROMOS, J.	40	5/10	.500	6/7	.857	0/6	0	1	1	0	0	16	.400
WYNDER, R.	40	4/6	.667	4/4	1.000	0/0	1	2	1	0	0	12	.300
GOLDEN, E.	37	0/2	.000	0/0	.000	0/2	3	1	0	0	0	0	.000
BRADFORD, T.	3	0/1	.000	0/0	.000	0/0	2	0	0	0	0	0	.000
BARRY, R.	1	0/2	.000	0/0	.000	0/0	0	0	0	1	0	0	.000
SQUERI, T.	10	0/2	.000	0/0	.000	0/2	0	1	2	0	1	0	.000
SIMENZ, C.	1	0/1	.000	0/0	.000	1/1	0	0	1	0	0	0	.000
MCLEOD, K.	1	0/0	.000	0/0	.000	0/0	0	0	0	0	0	0	.000
Totals	200	19/44	.432	13/14	.929	2/21	8	12	11	0	2	51	.255

Team Rebounds: Illinois 2; Fairfield 4. Disqualified: Fairfield—Yerina. Technical fouls: None.

	1st Half	2nd Half	Final
Illinois	34	41	75
Fairfield	22	29	51

Purdue (87)　Coach: Gene Keady

	Min.	Total FG / FGA	Pct.	FT / FTA	Pct.	Reb. O / T	A	TO	PF	S	Blk	TP	PPM
MITCHELL, T.	48	11/13	.846	9/12	.750	5/ 8	0	3	4	1	1	31	.646
LEE, D.	48	10/23	.435	0/ 1	.000	5/11	1	3	4	0	0	20	.417
MCCANTS, M.	15	1/ 2	.500	0/ 0	.000	4/ 6	0	2	1	0	0	2	.133
GADIS, M.	21	0/ 4	.000	0/ 0	.000	0/ 2	6	0	1	0	0	0	.000
LEWIS, T.	46	8/20	.400	4/ 4	1.000	5/ 7	2	4	3	1	0	20	.435
STEPHENS, E.	33	2/10	.200	0/ 0	.000	0/ 1	8	7	4	4	0	4	.121
JONES, K.	1	0/ 0	.000	0/ 0	.000	0/ 0	0	0	0	0	0	0	.000
ROBINSON, H.	6	1/ 1	1.000	0/ 0	.000	1/ 4	0	1	3	2	0	2	.333
ARNOLD, J.	32	4/ 4	1.000	0/ 0	.000	1/ 3	0	0	1	0	0	8	.250
Totals	250	37/77	.481	13/17	.765	21/42	17	20	21	8	1	87	.348

Louisiana State (94)　Coach: Dale Brown

	Min.	Total FG / FGA	Pct.	FT / FTA	Pct.	Reb. O / T	A	TO	PF	S	Blk	TP	PPM
WILLIAMS, J.	44	8/22	.364	0/01	.000	7/12	8	4	5	3	1	16	.364
REDDEN, D.	44	8/18	.444	5/ 5	1.000	4/ 8	2	4	2	3	0	21	.477
BLANTON, R.	47	5/ 6	.833	0/ 0	.000	6/11	2	0	1	0	0	10	.213
TAYLOR, D.	44	7/15	.467	6/ 7	.857	1/ 2	5	4	5	5	0	20	.455
WILSON, A.	50	9/14	.643	7/ 8	.875	0/ 6	3	4	2	1	0	25	.500
BUKUMIROVICH, N.	6	0/ 0	.000	0/ 0	.000	0/ 0	2	0	0	0	0	0	.000
WOODSIDE, B.	5	0/ 0	.000	0/ 1	.000	1/ 1	0	0	0	0	0	0	.000
BROWN, O.	7	1/ 2	.500	0/ 0	.000	1/ 1	0	1	0	0	0	2	.286
VARGAS, J.	3	0/ 1	.000	0/ 0	.000	1/ 1	0	0	3	0	0	0	.000
Totals	250	38/78	.487	18/22	.818	21/42	22	17	18	12	1	94	.376

Team Rebounds: Louisiana St. 3; Purdue 0. Disqualified: Louisiana St.—Williams, Taylor. Technical fouls: Purdue—Bench.

	1st Half	2nd Half	1st OT	2nd OT	Final
Purdue	35	34	4	14	87
Louisiana St.	39	30	4	21	94

Memphis State (95)　Coach: Dana Kirk

	Min.	Total FG / FGA	Pct.	FT / FTA	Pct.	Reb. O / T	A	TO	PF	S	Blk	TP	PPM
HOLMES, B.	15	7/ 9	.778	0/ 0	.000	2/ 4	0	0	4	0	0	14	.933
ASKEW, V.	32	11/17	.647	5/ 4	.500	2/ 8	4	1	0	3	0	23	.719
BEDFORD, W.	25	7/13	.538	2/ 4	.500	2/ 8	1	1	4	0	4	16	.640
BOYD, D.	22	5/10	.500	2/ 2	1.000	0/ 0	1	2	2	1	1	12	.545
TURNER, A.	32	1/ 9	.111	0/ 0	.000	0/ 2	9	1	2	3	0	2	.063
WILFONG, I.	16	1/ 3	.333	2/ 2	1.000	1/ 4	0	0	1	1	0	4	.250
ROBINSON, V.	4	1/ 2	.500	0/ 0	.000	1/ 3	0	0	1	1	0	2	.500
MODDY, K.	12	1/ 3	.333	0/ 0	.000	0/ 3	2	0	0	0	0	2	.167
DOUGLAS, R.	4	0/ 2	.000	0/ 0	.000	0/ 0	0	0	2	0	1	0	.000
BAILEY, D.	25	0/ 4	.000	10/12	.833	1/ 7	0	0	3	0	1	10	.400
JENSEN, D.	4	0/ 3	.000	0/ 0	.000	0/ 4	0	0	2	0	0	0	.000
ALEXANDER, M.	9	3/ 3	1.000	4/ 4	1.000	1/ 2	0	0	1	0	0	10	1.111
Totals	200	37/78	.474	21/26	.808	10/45	17	5	22	9	7	95	.475

Ball State (63)　Coach: Al Brown

	Min.	Total FG / FGA	Pct.	FT / FTA	Pct.	Reb. O / T	A	TO	PF	S	Blk	TP	PPM
PALOMBIZIO, E.	37	5/22	.227	7/ 8	.875	6/14	1	1	4	0	0	17	.459
WESLEY, D.	24	1/ 5	.200	1/ 2	.500	1/ 6	2	2	4	0	0	3	.125
REED, L.	24	5/ 9	.556	2/ 3	.667	1/ 2	1	5	2	0	0	12	.500
SHELTON, C.	18	5/14	.357	1/ 1	1.000	1/ 6	3	4	5	1	0	11	.611
SMITH, C.	30	2/ 4	.500	1/ 2	.500	1/ 2	1	2	1	0	0	5	.167
EHA, D.	16	0/ 1	.000	0/ 0	.000	0/ 1	0	2	0	0	0	0	.000
KAMIAK, R.	3	1/ 4	.250	0/ 2	.000	1/ 3	0	0	1	0	0	2	.667
LUEDKE, J.	16	2/ 4	.500	0/ 0	.000	3/ 4	2	2	2	0	0	4	.250
HALL, R.	2	0/ 2	.000	1/ 2	.500	1/ 4	0	0	0	0	0	1	.500
FAULKNER, D.	3	0/ 0	.000	0/ 0	.000	0/ 0	0	0	0	0	0	0	.000
WHITTINGTON, J.	12	3/ 4	.750	0/ 2	.000	2/ 2	0	0	0	0	0	6	.500
DZIATCZAK, S.	15	1/ 5	.200	0/ 0	.000	1/ 2	0	2	3	0	0	2	.133
Totals	200	25/74	.338	13/22	.591	18/46	10	20	22	1	0	63	.315

Team Rebounds: Memphis State 4; Ball St. 6. Disqualified: Ball St.—Shelton. Technical fouls: None.

	1st Half	2nd Half	Final
Memphis State	40	55	95
Ball St.	34	29	63

Virginia Tech (62)　Coach: Charles Moir

	Min.	Total FG / FGA	Pct.	FT / FTA	Pct.	Reb. O / T	A	TO	PF	S	Blk	TP	PPM
COLBERT, K.	40	10/19	.526	1/ 1	1.000	2/ 4	3	5	5	1	0	21	.525
BEECHER, B.	39	6/14	.429	3/ 4	.750	5/12	1	4	3	2	0	15	.385
BURGESS, D.	18	1/ 1	1.000	0/ 0	.000	0/ 1	1	0	2	0	0	2	.111
FORT, J.	23	0/ 0	.000	0/ 0	.000	0/ 0	2	4	0	0	0	0	.000
CURRY, D.	28	4/12	.333	4/ 4	1.000	2/ 4	0	2	4	2	0	12	.429
CAESAR, G.	29	3/ 7	.429	1/ 1	1.000	2/ 3	1	0	4	0	0	7	.241
ANDERSON, T.	18	2/ 2	1.000	1/ 3	.333	2/ 5	0	4	1	0	0	5	.278
WILLIAMS, P.	4	0/ 1	.000	0/ 0	.000	0/ 1	0	1	0	0	0	0	.000
BROW, R.	1	0/ 0	.000	0/ 0	.000	0/ 0	0	0	0	0	0	0	.000
Totals	200	26/56	.464	10/13	.769	13/30	6	18	23	5	0	62	.310

Villanova (71)　Coach: Rollie Massimino

	Min.	Total FG / FGA	Pct.	FT / FTA	Pct.	Reb. O / T	A	TO	PF	S	Blk	TP	PPM
PRESSLEY, H.	28	6/10	.600	5/ 6	.833	6/10	0	2	4	1	1	17	.607
PLANSKY, M.	38	4/ 7	.571	2/ 5	.400	2/ 8	2	4	4	4	0	10	.263
WEST, D.	28	5/11	.455	1/ 2	.500	1/ 3	0	3	4	1	1	11	.393
WILSON, K.	38	4/ 9	.444	3/ 5	.600	1/ 4	9	2	1	3	0	11	.289
JENSEN, H.	39	10/17	.588	0/ 0	.000	0/ 2	3	2	1	0	0	20	.513
ENRIGHT, P.	1	0/ 0	.000	0/ 0	.000	0/ 0	0	0	0	0	0	0	.000
MASSIMINO, R.	1	0/ 0	.000	0/ 0	.000	0/ 0	0	0	0	0	0	0	.000
MASSEY, G.	15	0/ 0	.000	2/ 3	.667	0/ 3	0	1	0	1	2	2	.133
PINONE, S.	1	0/ 1	.000	0/ 0	.000	1/ 1	0	0	0	0	0	0	.000
EVERSON, C.	1	0/ 0	.000	0/ 0	.000	0/ 0	0	0	0	0	0	0	.000
MAKER, W.	7	0/ 0	.000	0/ 0	.000	0/ 0	2	3	2	0	0	0	.000
BROWN, C.	3	0/ 0	.000	0/ 0	.000	0/ 0	0	0	1	0	0	0	.000
Totals	200	29/55	.527	13/21	.619	11/31	16	17	17	10	4	71	.355

Team Rebounds: Villanova 3; Virginia Tech 0. Disqualified: Virginia Tech—Colbert. Technical fouls: None.

	1st Half	2nd Half	Final
Virginia Tech	22	40	62
Villanova	34	37	71

Georgia Tech (68)　Coach: Bobby Cremins

	Min.	Total FG / FGA	Pct.	FT / FTA	Pct.	Reb. O / T	A	TO	PF	S	Blk	TP	PPM
HAMMONDS, T.	32	4/ 7	.571	2/ 5	.400	1/ 5	2	3	1	0	0	10	.313
FERRELL, D.	31	5/ 7	.714	0/ 0	.000	3/ 7	4	3	3	0	0	10	.323
SALLEY, J.	37	6/ 9	.667	1/ 2	.500	2/ 5	4	5	1	1	2	13	.351
PRICE, M.	35	10/17	.588	0/ 0	.000	1/ 4	3	2	2	0	0	20	.571
DALRYMPLE, B.	35	2/ 6	.333	2/ 2	1.000	0/ 7	3	3	2	0	0	6	.171
NEAL, C.	16	1/ 1	1.000	1/ 3	.333	0/ 2	1	3	2	1	0	3	.188
FORD, A.	10	2/ 3	.667	0/ 0	.000	1/ 2	0	0	3	0	1	4	.400
MANSELL, J.	1	0/ 0	.000	0/ 0	.000	0/ 0	0	0	0	0	0	0	.000
SHERROD, A.	3	1/ 2	.500	0/ 0	.000	0/ 0	0	1	0	1	0	2	.667
Totals	200	31/52	.596	6/12	.500	8/32	17	20	14	3	3	68	.340

Marist (53)　Coach: Matt Furjanic

	Min.	Total FG / FGA	Pct.	FT / FTA	Pct.	Reb. O / T	A	TO	PF	S	Blk	TP	PPM
BECKWITH, T.	31	2/ 5	.400	2/ 2	1.000	3/ 3	1	3	3	1	0	6	.194
SHAMLEY, M.	25	1/ 8	.125	0/ 0	.000	0/ 2	0	3	3	0	0	2	.080
SMITS, R.	27	9/14	.643	4/ 4	1.000	3/ 4	1	0	5	1	0	22	.815
DRAFTON, D.	36	5/ 8	.625	2/ 2	1.000	1/ 7	5	8	2	4	0	12	.333
MCCANTS, R.	40	2/ 6	.333	3/ 6	.500	1/ 3	3	4	1	2	0	7	.175
WADE, C.	8	0/ 2	.000	0/ 0	.000	0/ 2	0	1	0	1	0	0	.000
PECARSKI, M.	24	2/ 6	.333	0/ 0	.000	0/ 2	0	0	2	1	0	4	.167
BOURGAREL, R.	9	0/ 4	.000	0/ 0	.000	0/ 1	1	0	1	0	0	0	.000
Totals	200	21/53	.396	11/14	.786	8/24	10	19	17	10	0	53	.265

Team Rebounds: Georgia Tech 3; Marist 2. Disqualified: Marist—Smits. Technical fouls: None.

	1st Half	2nd Half	Final
Georgia Tech	31	37	68
Marist	26	27	53

FIRST ROUND WEST

St. John's (83)   Coach: Lou Carnesecca

	Min.	Total FG / FGA	Pct.	FT / FTA	Pct.	Reb. O / T	A	TO	PF	S	Blk	TP	PPM
GLASS	30	5/10	.500	2/ 2	1.000	-/ 6	1	-	4	-	-	12	.400
JONES, S.	27	2/ 4	.500	0/ 0	.000	-/ 5	3	-	3	-	-	4	.148
BERRY, W.	38	10/16	.625	11/13	.846	-/11	1	-	2	-	-	31	.816
ROWAN	39	2/ 8	.250	3/ 5	.600	-/ 5	5	-	2	-	-	7	.179
JACKSON, M.	40	5/ 8	.625	4/ 7	.571	-/ 4	5	-	1	-	-	14	.350
BROSS, T.	9	1/ 1	1.000	0/ 0	.000	-/ 1	0	-	2	-	-	2	.222
HEMPEL	16	6/ 7	.857	1/ 1	1.000	-/ 5	0	-	2	-	-	13	.813
SHURINA	1	0/ 0	.000	0/ 0	.000	-/ 0	0	-	0	-	-	0	.000
Totals	200	31/54	.574	21/28	.750	-/37	15	15	16	-	-	83	.415

Montana State (74)   Coach: Stu Starner

	Min.	Total FG / FGA	Pct.	FT / FTA	Pct.	Reb. O / T	A	TO	PF	S	Blk	TP	PPM
FERCH, K.	39	7/13	.538	6/ 7	.857	-/ 5	1	-	5	-	-	20	.513
DOMAKO	36	8/15	.533	0/ 0	.000	-/ 3	2	-	3	-	-	16	.444
WALTERS	31	1/ 7	.143	1/ 2	.500	-/ 6	2	-	5	-	-	3	.097
WILLIS	23	1/ 5	.200	0/ 0	.000	-/ 1	5	-	1	-	-	2	.087
HAMPTON	40	9/16	.563	3/ 3	1.000	-/ 8	6	-	1	-	-	21	.525
FERCH, S.	17	3/ 8	.375	2/ 2	1.000	-/ 2	2	-	5	-	-	8	.471
FELLOWS	13	2/ 6	.333	0/ 0	.000	-/ 3	0	-	3	-	-	4	.308
LIGONS	1	0/ 1	.000	0/ 0	.000	-/ 0	0	-	0	-	-	0	.000
Totals	200	31/71	.437	12/14	.857	-/28	18	7	23	-	-	74	.370

Team Rebounds: St. John's 3; Montana St. 3. Disqualified: Montana St.—K. Ferch, Walters, S. Ferch. Technical fouls: None.

	1st Half	2nd Half	Final
St. John's	40	43	83
Montana St.	33	41	74

Auburn (73)   Coach: Sonny Smith

	Min.	Total FG / FGA	Pct.	FT / FTA	Pct.	Reb. O / T	A	TO	PF	S	Blk	TP	PPM
MORRIS, C.	31	5/ 7	.714	0/ 1	.000	2/ 4	2	0	1	0	1	10	.323
PERSON, C.	37	9/22	.409	2/ 2	1.000	1/ 8	0	4	3	0	0	20	.541
MOORE, J.	28	4/ 8	.500	3/ 5	1.000	5/12	3	4	3	1	0	11	.393
WHITE, G.	32	4/ 5	.800	4/ 5	.800	3/ 6	6	1	1	1	0	12	.375
FORD, F.	39	3/ 6	.500	2/ 3	.667	1/ 2	2	0	1	1	1	8	.205
JONES, M.	21	5/ 6	.833	2/ 2	1.000	1/ 3	0	3	3	0	1	12	.571
HOWARD, T.	8	0/ 2	.000	0/ 0	.000	0/ 0	2	0	0	0	0	0	.000
HARALSON, M.	1	0/ 0	.000	0/ 0	.000	0/ 0	0	0	0	0	0	0	.000
LYNN, J.	1	0/ 1	.000	0/ 1	.000	0/ 0	0	0	0	0	0	0	.000
JONES, R.	1	0/ 0	.000	0/ 0	.000	0/ 1	0	0	0	1	0	0	.000
GODFREY, G.	1	0/ 0	.000	0/ 0	.000	0/ 0	0	0	0	0	0	0	.000
Totals	200	30/57	.526	13/17	.765	13/36	15	12	12	4	3	73	.365

Arizona (63)   Coach: Lute Olson

	Min.	Total FG / FGA	Pct.	FT / FTA	Pct.	Reb. O / T	A	TO	PF	S	Blk	TP	PPM
COOK, A.	35	4/ 6	.667	0/ 0	.000	1/ 6	0	2	2	0	1	8	.229
ELLIOTT, S.	38	10/17	.588	0/ 0	.000	2/ 6	6	1	2	0	0	20	.526
EDGAR, J.	35	7/11	.636	1/ 3	.333	1/ 2	3	3	0	0	1	15	.429
MCMILLAN, C.	40	3/12	.250	2/ 4	.500	0/ 0	6	3	4	3	0	8	.200
KERR, S.	37	5/12	.417	0/ 0	.000	0/ 3	3	0	4	2	0	10	.270
TURNER, J.	8	1/ 2	.500	0/ 0	.000	2/ 3	1	0	0	0	0	2	.250
LOFTON, K.	2	0/ 0	.000	0/ 0	.000	0/ 0	1	0	3	0	0	0	.000
JACOBS, R.	1	0/ 0	.000	0/ 0	.000	0/ 0	0	0	1	0	0	0	.000
COOPER, E.	1	0/ 0	.000	0/ 0	.000	0/ 0	0	1	1	0	0	0	.000
FRASER, B.	1	0/ 0	.000	0/ 0	.000	0/ 0	0	0	0	0	0	0	.000
HASKIN, D.	1	0/ 0	.000	0/ 0	.000	0/ 1	0	0	0	0	0	0	.000
WHEATLEY, B.	1	0/ 0	.000	0/ 0	.000	0/ 0	0	0	0	0	0	0	.000
Totals	200	30/60	.500	3/ 7	.429	6/21	20	10	17	5	2	63	.315

Team Rebounds: Auburn 1; Arizona 2. Disqualified: None. Technical fouls: None.

	1st Half	2nd Half	Final
Auburn	32	41	73
Arizona	34	29	63

Maryland (69)   Coach: Lefty Driesell

	Min.	Total FG / FGA	Pct.	FT / FTA	Pct.	Reb. O / T	A	TO	PF	S	Blk	TP	PPM
LEWIS, D.	34	4/ 7	.571	5/10	.500	3/11	1	1	3	2	2	13	.382
BIAS, L.	40	7/14	.500	12/14	.857	3/ 8	0	3	2	1	0	26	.650
LONG, T.	12	0/ 2	.000	0/ 0	.000	1/ 3	0	0	2	0	0	0	.000
GATLIN, K.	40	4/ 8	.500	2/ 3	.667	1/ 7	9	6	1	0	0	10	.250
BAXTER, J.	40	3/10	.300	2/ 2	1.000	0/ 2	1	3	3	0	0	8	.200
JONES, T.	34	6/ 9	.667	0/ 0	.000	2/ 4	3	1	2	0	0	12	.353
Totals	200	24/50	.480	21/29	1.105	10/35	14	14	13	3	2	69	.345

Pepperdine (64)   Coach: Jim Harrick

	Min.	Total FG / FGA	Pct.	FT / FTA	Pct.	Reb. O / T	A	TO	PF	S	Blk	TP	PPM
WHITE, E.	34	8/13	.615	1/ 2	.500	3/ 5	0	2	5	1	0	17	.500
FREDERICK, A.	38	2/ 9	.222	0/ 0	.000	5/12	2	3	5	1	1	4	.105
MIDDLEBROOKS, L.	32	3/ 6	.500	0/ 0	.000	1/ 4	0	2	2	0	0	6	.188
KORFAS, J.	30	3/ 7	.429	2/ 2	1.000	0/ 2	1	1	2	0	0	8	.267
POLEE, D.	38	4/13	.308	4/ 4	1.000	1/ 7	3	0	2	4	1	12	.316
GONDREZICK, G.	27	5/11	.455	7/10	.700	2/ 2	4	1	3	1	0	17	.630
MOUNTS, M.	1	0/ 0	.000	0/ 0	.000	0/ 0	0	0	0	0	0	0	.000
Totals	200	25/59	.424	14/18	.778	12/32	10	9	19	7	2	64	.320

Team Rebounds: Maryland 0; Pepperdine 2. Disqualified: Pepperdine—White, Frederick. Technical fouls: Maryland—Bias; Pepperdine—Polee, Korfas.

	1st Half	2nd Half	Final
Maryland	31	38	69
Pepperdine	31	33	64

UNLV (74)   Coach: Jerry Tarkanian

	Min.	Total FG / FGA	Pct.	FT / FTA	Pct.	Reb. O / T	A	TO	PF	S	Blk	TP	PPM
JONES, A.	34	9/16	.563	0/ 0	.000	-/ 6	1	1	3	3	1	18	.529
GILLIAM, A.	28	7/18	.389	2/ 2	1.000	-/13	0	1	3	1	1	16	.571
FLOWERS, J.	18	2/ 5	.400	0/ 0	.000	-/ 3	2	0	2	0	0	4	.222
WADE, M.	33	0/ 1	.000	0/ 0	.000	-/ 1	8	2	4	2	0	0	.000
BANKS, F.	31	2/10	.200	2/ 3	.667	-/ 5	0	2	1	1	0	6	.194
HUDSON, E.	19	4/12	.333	0/ 1	.000	-/ 9	2	1	2	1	1	8	.421
GRAHAM, G.	7	1/ 3	.333	0/ 0	.000	-/ 2	2	1	0	0	0	2	.286
BASNIGHT, J.	15	3/ 5	.600	2/ 3	.667	-/ 3	0	3	3	0	0	8	.533
COLLIER, R.	5	3/ 4	.750	0/ 2	.000	-/ 1	1	0	2	0	0	6	1.200
WELCH, J.	7	2/ 2	1.000	2/ 2	1.000	-/ 0	1	2	1	0	0	6	.857
STAALESON, B.	3	0/ 1	.000	0/ 0	.000	-/ 0	0	0	0	0	0	0	.000
Totals	200	33/77	.429	8/13	.615	-/43	17	13	23	8	3	74	.370

Northeast Louisiana (51)   Coach: Mike Vining

	Min.	Total FG / FGA	Pct.	FT / FTA	Pct.	Reb. O / T	A	TO	PF	S	Blk	TP	PPM
PAULFREY, S.	34	2/ 4	.500	3/ 7	.429	-/ 2	0	4	2	0	1	7	.206
JENKINS, B.	35	4/16	.250	5/13	.385	-/10	1	6	4	1	0	13	.371
PHILLIPS, G.	26	0/ 3	.000	0/ 0	.000	-/ 4	2	2	3	0	0	0	.000
HAYES, A.	36	3/12	.250	5/ 5	1.000	-/ 8	2	4	3	2	0	11	.306
JAMES, E.	36	5/12	.417	2/ 2	1.000	-/ 2	2	2	0	1	1	12	.333
VINING, R.	2	0/ 0	.000	0/ 0	.000	-/ 1	0	0	1	0	0	0	.000
SPENCER, B.	6	0/ 0	.000	2/ 2	1.000	-/ 0	2	2	0	1	0	2	.333
ROBBS, B.	10	0/ 1	.000	0/ 0	.000	-/ 1	0	0	1	0	0	0	.000
SPENCER, M.	15	3/ 4	.750	0/ 0	.000	-/ 2	1	0	2	0	0	6	.400
Totals	200	17/52	.327	17/29	.586	-/30	10	20	16	5	2	51	.255

Team Rebounds: UNLV 10; Northeast La. 5. Disqualified: None. Technical fouls: Northeast La.—Jenkins; UNLV—Flowers.

	1st Half	2nd Half	Final
UNLV	31	43	74
Northeast La.	21	30	51

Alabama-Birmingham (66)   Coach: Gene Bartow

	Min.	Total FG/FGA	Pct.	FT/FTA	Pct.	Reb. O/T	A	TO	PF	S	Blk	TP	PPM
JOHNSON, A.	26	2/4	.500	2/2	1.000	1/4	0	2	2	0	1	6	.231
CHARLES, M.	21	3/3	1.000	0/0	.000	0/0	3	1	2	0	0	6	.286
MINCY, J.	34	5/9	.556	4/9	.444	3/11	0	2	3	2	0	14	.412
PONDER, J.	29	3/8	.375	3/4	.750	0/2	1	2	2	1	0	9	.310
MITCHELL, S.	36	9/20	.450	3/4	.750	1/5	4	1	1	1	0	21	.583
FOSTER, T.	13	3/6	.500	0/0	.000	1/2	0	0	2	0	0	6	.462
COLLINS, E.	11	1/4	.250	0/0	.000	0/0	0	0	3	0	0	2	.182
TURNER, R.	0	0/0	.000	0/0	.000	0/0	0	0	0	0	0	0	-
HOWARD, D.	0	0/0	.000	0/0	.000	0/0	0	1	1	0	0	0	-
GORDON, A.	28	1/1	1.000	0/0	.000	0/2	3	1	3	1	1	2	.071
EVANS, C.	2	0/0	.000	0/0	.000	0/0	0	0	0	0	0	0	.000
Totals	200	27/55	.491	12/19	.632	6/26	11	10	19	5	2	66	.330

Missouri (64)   Coach: Norm Stewart

	Min.	Total FG/FGA	Pct.	FT/FTA	Pct.	Reb. O/T	A	TO	PF	S	Blk	TP	PPM
CHIEVOUS, D.	39	7/13	.538	7/7	1.000	0/6	0	3	1	0	0	21	.538
BINGENHEIMER, D.	23	2/4	.500	6/8	.750	1/5	0	4	5	0	0	10	.435
LEONARD, G.	27	4/6	.667	2/2	1.000	2/8	0	1	0	1	0	10	.370
STRONG, J.	39	9/19	.474	1/4	.250	2/5	2	4	4	0	0	19	.487
HARDY, L.	34	1/4	.250	0/0	.000	0/2	4	2	4	0	0	2	.059
ROUNDTREE, B.	7	0/1	.000	0/0	.000	0/0	1	0	0	1	1	0	.000
BROCKMAN, K.	1	0/0	.000	0/0	.000	0/0	0	0	0	0	0	0	.000
CHURCH, G.	4	0/1	.000	0/0	.000	1/2	0	0	0	0	0	0	.000
SUTTON, B.	0	0/0	.000	0/0	.000	0/0	0	0	0	0	0	0	-
MUSSER, S.	0	0/0	.000	0/0	.000	0/0	0	0	0	0	0	0	-
SANDBOTHE, M.	26	1/1	1.000	0/0	.000	1/4	3	3	2	1	0	2	.077
Totals	200	24/49	.490	16/21	.762	7/32	10	16	17	2	2	64	.320

Team Rebounds: Ala.-Birmingham 2; Missouri 1. Disqualified: Missouri—Bingenheimer. Technical fouls: None. Players who played 0 min. played less than 1 min. each.

	1st Half	2nd Half	Final
Ala.-Birmingham	31	35	66
Missouri	34	30	64

North Carolina (84)   Coach: Dean Smith

	Min.	Total FG/FGA	Pct.	FT/FTA	Pct.	Reb. O/T	A	TO	PF	S	Blk	TP	PPM
WOLF, J.	25	4/8	.500	1/4	.250	2/7	2	3	0	1	4	9	.360
HALE, S.	36	5/10	.500	4/4	1.000	0/6	5	3	2	0	0	14	.389
DAUGHERTY, B.	38	12/14	.857	3/5	.600	1/5	2	0	3	0	1	27	.711
SMITH, K.	36	7/10	.700	2/2	1.000	1/2	4	1	1	0	0	16	.444
LEBO, J.	32	1/6	.167	5/6	.833	1/7	7	1	1	2	0	7	.219
BUCKNELL, S.	2	0/0	.000	0/0	.000	0/0	0	1	0	0	0	0	.000
MADDEN, K.	1	0/0	.000	0/0	.000	0/0	0	0	0	0	0	0	.000
SMITH, R.	1	0/0	.000	0/0	.000	0/0	0	0	1	0	0	0	.000
POPSON, D.	4	0/0	.000	0/0	.000	0/0	0	1	0	0	0	0	.000
HUNTER, C.	10	1/3	.333	3/4	.750	1/2	0	0	2	1	0	5	.500
MARTIN, W.	15	1/3	.333	4/4	1.000	0/0	0	2	4	0	2	6	.400
Totals	200	31/54	.574	22/29	.759	6/29	21	11	14	4	7	84	.420

Utah (72)   Coach: Lynn Archibald

	Min.	Total FG/FGA	Pct.	FT/FTA	Pct.	Reb. O/T	A	TO	PF	S	Blk	TP	PPM
STROMAN, J.	33	7/16	.438	4/5	.800	2/5	1	0	2	2	0	18	.545
SPRINGS, A.	27	2/5	.400	0/1	.000	3/9	3	3	3	1	2	4	.148
SMITH, M.	27	3/6	.500	0/0	.000	1/2	3	1	5	2	1	6	.222
HENDRIX, J.	35	7/18	.389	0/0	.000	0/3	1	3	3	1	0	14	.400
UPSHAW, K.	38	8/13	.615	2/2	1.000	1/6	5	5	4	2	0	18	.474
GONDREZICK, G.	5	3/4	.750	0/0	.000	1/1	0	0	1	0	0	6	1.200
DORRON, T.	2	1/1	1.000	0/0	.000	0/0	0	0	0	0	0	2	1.000
MOORE, S.	4	0/0	.000	2/2	1.000	1/1	0	1	2	0	0	2	.500
MADISON, J.	11	1/2	.500	0/0	.000	2/2	0	5	0	1	2	2	.182
ADAIR, B.	17	0/2	.000	0/0	.000	0/2	1	3	2	0	1	0	.000
MONSON, R.	1	0/0	.000	0/0	.000	0/0	0	0	0	0	0	0	.000
Totals	200	32/67	.478	8/10	.800	11/31	15	15	26	8	5	72	.360

Team Rebounds: N. Carolina 0; Utah 3. Disqualified: Utah—Smith, Madison. Technical fouls: N. Carolina—K. Smith

	1st Half	2nd Half	Final
N. Carolina	39	45	84
Utah	38	34	72

Bradley (83)   Coach: Dick Versace

	Min.	Total FG/FGA	Pct.	FT/FTA	Pct.	Reb. O/T	A	TO	PF	S	Blk	TP	PPM
TRIMPE	27	2/4	.500	0/0	.000	-/2	4	-	2	-	-	4	.148
POWELL, D.	20	2/3	.667	1/2	.500	-/3	2	-	5	-	-	5	.250
WILLIAMS	31	7/9	.778	4/6	.667	-/9	0	-	4	-	-	18	.581
HAWKINS	40	8/17	.471	5/7	.714	-/5	4	-	3	-	-	21	.525
LES	39	4/7	.571	14/17	.824	-/5	12	-	3	-	-	22	.564
MANUEL, A.	1	0/0	.000	0/0	.000	-/0	0	-	0	-	-	0	.000
THOMAS	29	5/7	.714	1/1	1.000	-/3	0	-	3	-	-	11	.379
JONES	1	0/0	.000	0/0	.000	-/0	0	-	0	-	-	0	.000
BERTOLINI	12	1/4	.250	0/0	.000	-/0	0	-	0	-	-	2	.167
Totals	200	29/51	.569	25/33	.758	-/27	22	6	20	-	-	83	.415

UTEP (65)   Coach: Don Haskins

	Min.	Total FG/FGA	Pct.	FT/FTA	Pct.	Reb. O/T	A	TO	PF	S	Blk	TP	PPM
GATES, Q.	30	2/6	.333	2/2	1.000	-/5	4	-	1	-	-	6	.200
CAMPBELL, W.	13	1/5	.200	2/2	1.000	-/5	0	-	0	-	-	4	.308
FEITL, D.	35	9/15	.600	9/12	.750	-/11	1	-	4	-	-	27	.771
JACKSON, J.	30	1/5	.200	1/1	1.000	-/2	4	-	5	-	-	3	.100
SMITH	26	3/7	.429	1/1	1.000	-/2	2	-	5	-	-	7	.269
HARDAWAY, T.	10	0/1	.000	0/0	.000	-/1	2	-	4	-	-	0	.000
STALLWORTH	23	2/3	.667	0/0	.000	-/0	1	-	1	-	-	4	.174
HAMILTON, K.	4	0/0	.000	0/0	.000	-/0	1	-	2	-	-	0	.000
RICHMOND	29	5/9	.556	4/4	1.000	-/6	0	-	2	-	-	14	.483
Totals	200	23/51	.451	19/22	.864	-/32	15	17	24	-	-	65	.325

Team Rebounds: Bradley 1; UTEP 0. Disqualified: Bradley—Powell; UTEP—Jackson, Smith. Technical fouls: None.

	1st Half	2nd Half	Final
Bradley	39	44	83
UTEP	37	28	65

Louisville (93)   Coach: Denny Crum

	Min.	Total FG/FGA	Pct.	FT/FTA	Pct.	Reb. O/T	A	TO	PF	S	Blk	TP	PPM
VALENTINE, R.	2	0/0	.000	0/0	.000	0/1	1	1	0	0	0	0	.000
PAYNE, K.	6	1/3	.333	0/0	.000	0/1	0	2	0	0	0	2	.333
ABRAM, M.	5	0/1	.000	0/0	.000	0/2	2	1	0	0	0	0	.000
CROOK, H.	18	3/5	.600	1/2	.500	2/3	1	2	3	0	0	7	.389
THOMPSON, B.	35	9/12	.750	6/6	1.000	2/10	3	4	2	2	3	24	.686
ELLISON, P.	26	5/7	.714	1/2	.500	0/9	1	3	3	1	2	11	.423
WAGNER, M.	25	4/11	.364	6/7	.857	0/1	6	2	2	1	0	14	.560
HALL, J.	30	4/9	.444	0/0	.000	1/1	3	1	3	0	0	8	.267
McSWAIN, M.	19	5/6	.833	5/5	1.000	2/8	0	2	0	1	0	15	.789
WALLS, K.	15	3/5	.600	0/0	.000	1/1	1	2	1	0	0	6	.400
KIMBRO, T.	17	3/3	1.000	0/0	.000	0/3	1	0	2	0	0	6	.353
WEST, C.	1	0/0	.000	0/0	.000	0/0	0	0	0	0	0	0	.000
OLLIGES, W.	1	0/0	.000	0/0	.000	0/0	0	0	0	0	0	0	.000
Totals	200	37/62	.597	19/22	.864	8/40	19	20	18	4	7	93	.465

Drexel (73)   Coach: Eddie Burke

	Min.	Total FG/FGA	Pct.	FT/FTA	Pct.	Reb. O/T	A	TO	PF	S	Blk	TP	PPM
COOPER, C.	31	7/11	.636	1/4	.250	1/6	0	5	5	1	0	15	.484
RAFFERTY, P.	25	2/5	.400	0/0	.000	0/3	4	2	2	0	0	4	.160
RANKIN, J.	34	9/14	.643	1/2	.500	1/6	1	1	4	3	1	19	.559
ANDERSON, C.	36	8/16	.500	2/7	.286	2/4	8	7	4	5	0	18	.500
O'BRIEN, C.	33	4/11	.364	0/1	.000	0/1	1	2	3	0	0	8	.242
STRIBLING, T.	8	0/3	.000	0/0	.000	1/1	1	1	0	0	0	0	.000
PAPES, R.	5	0/0	.000	0/0	.000	0/0	0	1	0	0	0	0	.000
FULLER, W.	25	4/6	.667	1/1	1.000	1/2	2	1	5	1	0	9	.360
STRAVESKI, M.	1	0/0	.000	0/0	.000	0/0	0	0	0	0	0	0	.000
PARKER, C.	1	0/0	.000	0/0	.000	0/0	0	0	0	0	0	0	.000
ARIZIN, C.	1	0/0	.000	0/0	.000	0/0	0	0	0	0	0	0	.000
Totals	200	34/66	.515	5/15	.333	6/23	17	19	23	11	1	73	.365

Team Rebounds: Louisville 2; Drexel 3. Disqualified: Drexel—Cooper, Fuller. Technical fouls: None.

	1st Half	2nd Half	Final
Louisville	48	45	93
Drexel	42	31	73

FIRST ROUND EAST

Duke (85) Coach: Mike Krzyzewski

	Min.	Total FG / FGA	Pct.	FT / FTA	Pct.	Reb. O / T	A	TO	PF	S	Blk	TP	PPM
HENDERSON, D.	35	5/10	.500	2/ 2	1.000	-/ 6	1	2	0	0	0	12	.343
ALARIE, M.	30	7/12	.583	5/ 7	.714	-/ 9	2	3	5	1	1	19	.633
BILAS, J.	19	1/ 1	1.000	7/ 8	.875	-/ 6	0	2	3	0	0	9	.474
AMAKER, T.	28	2/ 2	1.000	0/ 2	.000	-/ 3	1	6	3	0	0	4	.143
DAWKINS, J.	38	11/17	.647	5/ 7	.714	-/ 5	1	2	1	0	0	27	.711
FERRY, D.	28	4/ 7	.571	5/ 6	.833	-/11	1	4	1	0	0	13	.464
KING, B.	8	0/ 1	.000	1/ 3	.333	-/ 2	2	2	4	1	0	1	.125
STRICKLAND, K.	2	0/ 0	.000	0/ 2	.000	-/ 0	0	1	1	0	0	0	.000
WILLIAMS, W.	1	0/ 0	.000	0/ 0	.000	-/ 0	0	0	0	0	0	0	.000
SNYDER, Q.	11	0/ 1	.000	0/ 0	.000	-/ 1	4	1	1	1	0	0	.000
Totals	200	30/51	.588	25/37	.676	-/43	12	23	19	3	1	85	.425

Mississippi Valley State (78) Coach: Lafayette Stribling

	Min.	Total FG / FGA	Pct.	FT / FTA	Pct.	Reb. O / T	A	TO	PF	S	Blk	TP	PPM
CURRY, C.	27	2/ 4	.500	0/ 0	.000	-/ 2	0	2	5	0	2	4	.148
IVORY, G.	39	4/10	.400	6/ 8	.750	-/ 1	7	1	1	2	0	14	.359
FERGUSON, M.	26	9/12	.750	0/ 0	.000	-/ 5	1	2	5	1	0	18	.692
KILBERT, N.	23	3/ 4	.750	0/ 2	.000	-/ 0	1	1	4	1	0	6	.261
JONES, C.	5	1/ 1	1.000	0/ 0	.000	-/ 0	0	0	0	0	0	2	.400
COLEMAN, R.	2	0/ 0	.000	0/ 0	.000	-/ 0	0	1	0	0	0	0	.000
BINDER, C.	13	1/ 3	.333	0/ 2	.000	-/ 5	0	0	3	1	0	2	.154
MCKINLEY, J.	10	2/ 3	.667	0/ 0	.000	-/ 0	0	1	2	0	1	4	.400
COLEMAN, M.	32	10/22	.455	4/ 8	.500	-/ 6	4	2	5	2	2	24	.750
BLOODSAW, T.	23	2/ 6	.333	0/ 0	.000	-/ 3	1	0	5	5	0	4	.174
Totals	200	34/65	.523	10/20	.500	-/22	14	10	30	12	5	78	.390

Team Rebounds: Duke 1; Miss. Valley St. 1. Disqualified: Duke—Alarie; Miss. Valley St.—Coleman, Bloodsaw, Curry, Ferguson. Technical fouls: None.

	1st Half	2nd Half	Final
Duke	37	48	85
Miss. Valley St.	40	38	78

Old Dominion (72) Coach: Tom Young

	Min.	Total FG / FGA	Pct.	FT / FTA	Pct.	Reb. O / T	A	TO	PF	S	Blk	TP	PPM
GATTISON, K.	35	9/12	.750	9/11	.818	-/ 9	1	3	4	0	1	27	.771
WADE, R.	34	5/ 7	.714	2/ 7	.286	-/ 6	2	0	3	1	1	12	.353
HANLEY, C.	13	1/ 4	.250	0/ 0	.000	-/ 3	1	2	0	0	1	2	.154
SMITH, F.	39	3/11	.273	2/ 3	.667	-/ 1	7	3	2	0	0	8	.205
THOMAS, K.	38	6/12	.500	7/ 8	.875	-/ 2	1	2	2	3	0	19	.500
CHARLES, S.	21	1/ 1	1.000	0/ 1	.000	-/ 3	0	1	1	1	0	2	.095
ROYSTER, B.	4	0/ 2	.000	0/ 0	.000	-/ 1	0	0	1	0	0	0	.000
TOLSON, D.	3	0/ 0	.000	0/ 0	.000	-/ 1	0	0	0	0	0	0	.000
DAVIS, G.	13	0/ 0	.000	2/ 2	1.000	-/ 2	1	1	1	0	1	2	.154
Totals	200	25/49	.510	22/32	.688	-/28	13	12	14	5	4	72	.360

West Virginia (64) Coach: Gale Catlett

	Min.	Total FG / FGA	Pct.	FT / FTA	Pct.	Reb. O / T	A	TO	PF	S	Blk	TP	PPM
YEARWOOD, W.	30	6/10	.600	0/ 0	.000	-/ 8	0	2	5	2	0	12	.400
BROWN, R.	25	2/ 7	.286	0/ 0	.000	-/ 6	0	0	2	0	0	4	.160
PINCKNEY, D.	25	3/ 4	.750	0/ 0	.000	-/ 4	1	5	5	0	0	6	.240
HARLEY, H.	35	5/18	.278	1/ 2	.500	-/ 3	5	4	4	3	0	11	.314
BLANEY, D.	32	6/13	.462	5/ 7	.714	-/ 3	2	1	3	1	1	17	.531
ODOM, V.	22	3/ 9	.333	2/ 2	1.000	-/ 5	1	2	5	0	0	8	.364
PRUE, D.	20	2/ 3	.667	0/ 0	.000	-/ 5	0	1	3	0	0	4	.200
BROOKS, H.	1	0/ 0	.000	0/ 0	.000	-/ 0	0	1	0	0	0	0	.000
SERNISCH, E.	10	1/ 3	.333	0/ 0	.000	-/ 3	0	1	1	0	0	2	.200
Totals	200	28/67	.418	8/11	.727	-/37	9	16	29	6	1	64	.320

Team Rebounds: Old Dominion 2; West Virginia 3. Disqualified: West Virginia—Yearwood, Pinckney, Odom. Technical fouls: None. Team Turnovers: West Virginia.

	1st Half	2nd Half	Final
Old Dominion	34	38	72
West Virginia	31	33	64

Virginia (68) Coach: Terry Holland

	Min.	Total FG / FGA	Pct.	FT / FTA	Pct.	Reb. O / T	A	TO	PF	S	Blk	TP	PPM
SHEEHEY, T.	36	4/ 7	.571	2/ 2	1.000	-/ 3	2	1	4	1	0	10	.278
KENNEDY, A.	30	8/12	.667	2/ 5	.400	-/ 9	1	2	4	1	0	18	.600
POLYNICE, O.	37	4/ 9	.444	5/11	.455	-/ 9	0	2	4	0	1	13	.351
KENNEDY, M.	37	3/ 9	.333	1/ 3	.333	-/ 6	2	1	5	0	0	7	.189
CALLOWAY, T.	23	5/ 7	.714	2/ 2	1.000	-/ 1	4	2	5	2	0	12	.522
JOHNSON, J.	23	2/ 7	.286	0/ 0	.000	-/ 1	1	0	1	1	0	4	.174
MORGAN, R.	8	1/ 4	.250	0/ 0	.000	-/ 1	0	1	1	0	0	2	.250
SOLOMAN, A.	1	1/ 1	1.000	0/ 0	.000	-/ 0	0	0	0	0	0	2	2.000
DANIEL, J.	5	0/ 1	.000	0/ 0	.000	-/ 1	0	0	2	0	0	0	.000
Totals	200	28/57	.491	12/23	.522	-/31	10	9	26	5	1	68	.340

DePaul (72) Coach: Joey Meyer

	Min.	Total FG / FGA	Pct.	FT / FTA	Pct.	Reb. O / T	A	TO	PF	S	Blk	TP	PPM
HOLMES, K.	16	5/ 8	.625	2/ 3	.667	-/ 3	1	0	4	0	0	12	.750
LAMPLEY, L.	29	5/ 9	.556	5/ 6	.833	-/ 7	1	1	1	1	2	15	.517
EMBRY, M.	40	2/ 6	.333	1/ 2	.500	-/11	1	2	3	0	0	5	.125
STRICKLAND, R.	39	6/11	.545	0/ 2	.000	-/ 1	3	1	4	1	0	12	.308
JACKSON, T.	35	3/ 8	.375	3/ 5	.600	-/ 3	7	3	3	2	0	9	.257
GREENE, T.	12	1/ 1	1.000	5/ 6	.833	-/ 0	1	3	2	0	0	7	.583
LAUX, A.	5	0/ 2	.000	0/ 0	.000	-/ 0	0	0	0	0	0	0	.000
BRUNDY, S.	1	0/ 1	.000	0/ 0	.000	-/ 1	0	0	0	0	0	0	.000
COMEGYS, D.	23	4/ 8	.500	4/ 5	.800	-/ 5	0	2	5	0	1	12	.522
Totals	200	26/54	.481	20/29	.690	-/31	14	12	22	4	3	72	.360

Team Rebounds: DePaul 4; Virginia 1. Disqualified: DePaul—Comegys; Virginia—Kennedy, Calloway. Technical fouls: None.

	1st Half	2nd Half	Final
Virginia	26	42	68
DePaul	34	38	72

Oklahoma (80) Coach: Billy Tubbs

	Min.	Total FG / FGA	Pct.	FT / FTA	Pct.	Reb. O / T	A	TO	PF	S	Blk	TP	PPM
KENNEDY, D.	40	9/18	.500	3/ 5	.600	-/ 9	3	1	4	1	0	21	.525
WATSON, C.	12	1/ 1	1.000	0/ 1	.000	-/ 1	0	0	4	0	0	2	.167
JOHNSON, D.	34	7/14	.500	10/14	.714	-/14	0	0	2	0	2	24	.706
DAVIS, L.	35	0/ 5	.000	1/ 2	.500	-/ 3	9	2	3	1	0	1	.029
BOWIE, A.	40	9/17	.529	2/ 3	.667	-/ 3	5	3	1	1	0	20	.500
PHIPPS, C.	5	1/ 5	.200	0/ 0	.000	-/ 1	0	0	0	0	0	2	.400
ROBERTS, R.	30	3/ 5	.600	4/ 5	.800	-/ 8	0	2	5	0	0	10	.333
SIEGER, D.	4	0/ 0	.000	0/ 0	.000	-/ 0	1	0	0	0	0	0	.000
Totals	200	30/65	.462	20/30	.667	-/39	18	8	19	3	2	80	.400

Northeastern (74) Coach: Jim Calhoun

	Min.	Total FG / FGA	Pct.	FT / FTA	Pct.	Reb. O / T	A	TO	PF	S	Blk	TP	PPM
LEWIS, R.	36	12/34	.353	11/13	.846	-/15	3	2	4	1	0	35	.972
FULLER, W.	37	4/ 8	.500	3/ 3	1.000	-/ 7	1	2	4	2	0	11	.297
MCDUFFIE, K.	22	2/ 5	.400	0/ 0	.000	-/ 7	0	2	5	0	1	4	.182
LAFLEUR, A.	38	2/ 6	.333	4/ 6	.667	-/ 2	6	3	4	3	0	8	.211
WILLIAMS, J.	26	3/11	.273	2/ 2	1.000	-/ 1	0	4	5	1	0	8	.308
SKEEN, E.	16	1/ 4	.250	0/ 0	.000	-/ 2	0	0	1	0	0	2	.125
HENRIQUEZ, S.	1	0/ 1	.000	0/ 0	.000	-/ 1	0	0	0	0	0	0	.000
CORCORAN, G.	22	3/ 5	.600	0/ 0	.000	-/ 6	1	0	5	0	0	6	.273
HALL, E.	2	0/ 0	.000	0/ 0	.000	-/ 2	0	1	1	0	0	0	.000
Totals	200	27/74	.365	20/24	.833	-/43	11	14	29	7	1	74	.370

Team Rebounds: Oklahoma 2; Northeastern 3. Disqualified: Oklahoma—Roberts; Northeastern—McDuffie, Williams, Corcoran. Technical fouls: None.

	1st Half	2nd Half	Final
Oklahoma	32	48	80
Northeastern	31	43	74

St. Joseph's (60) Coach: Jim Boyle

	Min.	Total FG/FGA	Pct.	FT/FTA	Pct.	Reb. O/T	A	TO	PF	S	Blk	TP	PPM
MULLEE	37	5/8	.625	0/0	.000	2/9	1	1	1	0	1	10	.270
SLATTERY	8	0/1	.000	0/0	.000	1/1	1	0	1	0	0	0	.000
BLAKE	39	4/6	.667	5/5	1.000	1/4	0	5	2	1	4	13	.333
MARTIN	38	6/14	.429	9/10	.900	2/5	2	4	3	2	0	21	.553
ARNOLD	36	1/8	.125	0/2	.000	2/4	10	1	2	1	0	2	.056
FLINT	5	0/1	.000	0/0	.000	1/1	1	2	1	0	0	0	.000
WILLIAMS	36	5/6	.833	4/5	.800	1/3	0	0	1	0	0	14	.389
LEAHY	1	0/1	.000	0/0	.000	0/0	0	0	0	0	0	0	.000
Totals	200	21/45	.467	18/22	.818	10/27	15	13	11	4	5	60	.300

Richmond (59) Coach: Dick Tarrant

	Min.	Total FG/FGA	Pct.	FT/FTA	Pct.	Reb. O/T	A	TO	PF	S	Blk	TP	PPM
NEWMAN, J.	39	10/19	.526	5/5	1.000	2/7	2	2	4	0	1	25	.641
WOOLFOLK, P.	38	5/19	.263	0/2	.000	5/8	1	1	3	1	0	10	.263
KRATZER, S.	37	3/11	.273	0/0	.000	7/9	1	3	3	2	0	6	.162
BECKWITH, G.	39	1/1	1.000	0/1	.000	0/3	12	2	5	2	0	2	.051
RICE, R.	40	7/13	.538	0/0	.000	2/3	3	0	3	1	0	14	.350
WINIECKI, M.	5	0/0	.000	0/0	.000	0/0	1	0	1	0	0	0	.000
ENGLISH, E.	1	0/0	.000	0/0	.000	0/0	0	0	0	0	0	0	.000
RUNK, J.	1	1/1	1.000	0/0	.000	0/0	0	0	0	0	0	2	2.000
Totals	200	27/64	.422	5/8	.625	16/30	20	8	19	6	1	59	.295

Team Rebounds: St. Joseph's 4; Richmond 5. Disqualified: Richmond—Beckwith. Technical fouls: None.

	1st Half	2nd Half	Final
St. Joseph's	28	32	60
Richmond	30	29	59

Indiana (79) Coach: Bob Knight

	Min.	Total FG/FGA	Pct.	FT/FTA	Pct.	Reb. O/T	A	TO	PF	S	Blk	TP	PPM
CALLOWAY, R.	28	4/8	.500	2/4	.500	1/7	0	2	2	0	0	10	.357
HARRIS, A.	35	8/10	.800	0/2	.000	5/10	1	1	3	0	2	16	.457
THOMAS, D.	23	4/6	.667	3/4	.750	2/4	1	3	4	0	0	11	.478
ALFORD, S.	40	10/20	.500	4/4	1.000	1/2	7	1	1	1	0	24	.600
MORGAN, W.	16	1/1	1.000	0/0	.000	1/2	5	5	2	0	0	2	.125
ROBINSON, S.	39	3/9	.333	4/5	.800	0/1	4	2	2	1	0	10	.256
MEIER, T.	5	1/2	.500	0/0	.000	0/2	0	0	2	0	0	2	.400
JADLOW, T.	6	0/1	.000	2/2	1.000	0/0	0	1	3	0	0	2	.333
EYL, S.	8	1/2	.500	0/0	.000	0/0	0	0	2	0	0	2	.250
Totals	200	32/59	.542	15/21	.714	10/28	18	15	21	2	2	79	.395

Cleveland State (83) Coach: Kevin MacKey

	Min.	Total FG/FGA	Pct.	FT/FTA	Pct.	Reb. O/T	A	TO	PF	S	Blk	TP	PPM
SMITH, C.	23	5/10	.500	2/2	1.000	1/2	3	2	4	2	0	12	.522
RANSEY, C.	33	9/15	.600	9/13	.692	1/5	1	4	3	2	0	27	.818
MUDD, E.	31	6/7	.857	4/5	.800	2/10	1	1	3	1	0	16	.516
BRYANT, E.	28	1/4	.250	0/0	.000	1/1	4	0	3	0	0	2	.071
McFADDEN, K.	30	4/8	.500	1/1	1.000	0/1	2	3	3	1	0	9	.300
STEWART, P.	17	3/4	.750	0/0	.000	1/3	0	0	3	0	0	6	.353
CRAWFORD, B.	9	2/3	.667	0/0	.000	0/3	0	0	2	0	0	4	.444
HOOD, S.	12	1/2	.500	0/0	.000	1/1	4	0	0	0	0	2	.167
SALTERS, R.	7	0/0	.000	1/2	.500	1/1	0	2	0	0	0	1	.143
CORBIN, S.	10	2/3	.667	0/0	.000	1/2	0	1	1	0	0	4	.400
Totals	200	33/56	.589	17/23	.739	9/29	15	13	22	6	0	83	.415

Team Rebounds: Cleveland St. 3; Indiana 2. Disqualified: None. Technical fouls: None. Team Turnovers: Cleveland St. 1.

	1st Half	2nd Half	Final
Indiana	41	38	79
Cleveland St.	45	38	83

Navy (87) Coach: Paul Evans

	Min.	Total FG/FGA	Pct.	FT/FTA	Pct.	Reb. O/T	A	TO	PF	S	Blk	TP	PPM
LIEBERT, C.	25	3/3	1.000	3/4	.750	0/1	2	0	1	3	0	9	.360
BUTLER, V.	39	9/14	.643	7/11	.636	5/11	2	3	2	0	0	25	.641
ROBINSON, D.	36	11/16	.688	8/14	.571	5/12	2	2	3	0	5	30	.833
WHITAKOR, K.	38	5/10	.500	5/5	1.000	0/1	11	1	0	0	0	15	.395
WOJCIK, D.	37	2/4	.500	0/0	.000	1/1	8	2	0	2	0	4	.108
BAILEY, N.	10	0/0	.000	0/2	.000	0/1	0	1	1	0	0	0	.000
REES, C.	8	0/0	.000	0/0	.000	0/1	0	0	0	0	0	0	.000
TURNER, D.	3	1/2	.500	0/0	.000	0/1	0	0	3	0	0	2	.667
FENTON, N.	1	0/0	.000	0/0	.000	0/0	1	0	0	0	0	0	.000
WELLS, T.	1	0/0	.000	0/0	.000	0/0	0	0	0	0	0	0	.000
JONES, B.	1	1/1	1.000	0/0	.000	0/0	0	0	0	0	0	2	2.000
MANHERTZ, C.	1	0/0	.000	0/0	.000	0/1	0	0	0	0	0	0	.000
Totals	200	32/50	.640	23/36	.639	11/30	26	9	10	5	5	87	.435

Tulsa (68) Coach: J. D. Barnett

	Min.	Total FG/FGA	Pct.	FT/FTA	Pct.	Reb. O/T	A	TO	PF	S	Blk	TP	PPM
MOSS, D.	29	4/7	.571	2/2	1.000	2/4	2	2	5	2	0	10	.345
RAHILLY, B.	40	8/15	.533	0/0	.000	4/6	2	2	4	0	0	16	.400
FOBBS, A.	6	1/3	.333	0/0	.000	1/2	0	1	5	0	0	2	.333
BOUDREAUX, B.	40	4/9	.444	2/2	1.000	1/2	8	2	2	1	0	10	.250
MOORE, T.	40	8/20	.400	0/0	.000	1/3	1	1	3	1	1	16	.400
RAHILLY, J.	16	4/7	.571	0/0	.000	3/6	0	0	5	0	1	8	.500
DECKARD, D.	23	3/6	.500	0/0	.000	0/1	2	1	0	1	1	6	.261
CELESTINE, C.	5	0/0	.000	0/1	.000	1/3	0	0	2	0	0	0	.000
OTTO, D.	1	0/0	.000	0/0	.000	0/0	0	0	0	0	0	0	.000
Totals	200	32/67	.478	4/5	.800	13/27	15	9	26	5	3	68	.340

Team Rebounds: Navy 3; Tulsa 5. Disqualified: Tulsa—Moss, Fobbs, Rahilly. Technical fouls: Tulsa—Bench.

	1st Half	2nd Half	Final
Navy	41	46	87
Tulsa	38	30	68

Syracuse (101) Coach: Jim Boeheim

	Min.	Total FG/FGA	Pct.	FT/FTA	Pct.	Reb. O/T	A	TO	PF	S	Blk	TP	PPM
TRICHE, H.	23	2/8	.250	0/0	.000	1/7	2	0	2	1	0	4	.174
ALEXIS, W.	18	2/4	.500	2/2	1.000	2/9	2	3	0	0	1	6	.333
SEIKALY, R.	17	5/8	.625	2/5	.400	4/7	0	1	2	1	5	12	.706
ADDISON, R.	24	7/12	.583	3/3	1.000	2/7	5	1	2	0	0	17	.708
WASHINGTON, D.	18	9/11	.818	3/3	1.000	0/1	7	0	2	3	0	21	1.167
MONROE, R.	16	2/5	.400	0/0	.000	0/0	4	0	1	2	0	4	.250
WALKER, R.	22	5/10	.500	5/9	.556	3/9	1	1	4	1	0	15	.682
DOUGLAS, S.	26	4/9	.444	0/0	.000	1/4	5	2	0	1	0	8	.308
KATZ, J.	11	0/2	.000	3/4	.750	1/3	3	1	2	0	0	3	.273
KOHM, J.	11	0/3	.000	1/2	.500	0/3	0	0	0	0	1	1	.091
BROWN, M.	7	2/3	.667	2/2	1.000	0/5	1	0	0	0	0	6	.857
BARNES, R.	7	2/3	.667	0/0	.000	1/1	1	1	2	0	0	4	.571
Totals	200	40/78	.513	21/31	.677	15/56	31	10	17	9	6	101	.505

Brown (52) Coach: Mike Cingiser

	Min.	Total FG/FGA	Pct.	FT/FTA	Pct.	Reb. O/T	A	TO	PF	S	Blk	TP	PPM
LYNCH, P.	16	2/9	.222	3/4	.750	2/2	0	2	1	0	0	7	.438
MURRAY, J.	27	3/7	.429	1/2	.500	2/6	1	4	3	0	0	7	.259
TURNER, J.	27	3/11	.273	7/7	1.000	2/5	1	1	2	1	0	13	.481
BRADY, D.	18	1/5	.200	0/0	.000	0/3	4	1	3	1	0	2	.111
WAITKUS, M.	30	2/12	.167	0/0	.000	0/2	2	5	1	2	0	4	.133
VISSCHER, D.	18	0/2	.000	1/2	.500	2/3	0	2	1	3	0	1	.056
THOMPSON, M.	18	2/11	.182	0/2	.000	2/3	1	0	2	0	1	4	.222
KATSAROS, A.	9	1/2	.500	0/0	.000	1/5	0	1	2	0	0	2	.222
TODD, B.	7	0/1	.000	0/0	.000	0/2	0	2	0	0	0	0	.000
TAYLOR, D.	9	1/3	.333	0/0	.000	0/3	1	0	2	0	0	2	.222
CHANEY, T.	7	0/3	.000	1/4	.250	0/1	1	0	1	0	0	1	.143
MORAN, S.	4	3/4	.750	1/1	1.000	0/0	1	0	2	0	0	7	1.750
GORE, G.	4	0/3	.000	0/0	.000	0/0	1	0	0	0	0	0	.000
SMITH, T.	4	1/2	.500	0/0	.000	1/1	0	0	0	0	0	2	.500
KEY, T.	2	0/0	.000	0/0	.000	0/0	0	0	0	0	0	0	.000
Totals	200	19/75	.253	14/22	.636	12/35	11	18	21	7	1	52	.260

Team Rebounds: Syracuse 7; Brown 4. Disqualified: None. Technical fouls: Brown—Bench

	1st Half	2nd Half	Final
Syracuse	51	50	101
Brown	23	29	52

FIRST ROUND MIDWEST

Kansas (71)　Coach: Larry Brown

	Min.	Total FG/FGA	Pct.	FT/FTA	Pct.	Reb. O/T	A	TO	PF	S	Blk	TP	PPM
MANNING, D.	28	7/9	.778	1/1	1.000	1/4	3	3	2	2	0	15	.536
KELLOGG, R.	8	1/3	.333	0/0	.000	1/1	0	0	0	0	0	2	.250
DREILING, G.	27	3/6	.500	6/6	1.000	4/6	0	0	3	0	0	12	.444
HUNTER, C.	24	3/7	.429	2/3	.667	1/2	11	3	1	0	0	8	.333
THOMPSON, C.	27	7/7	1.000	0/0	.000	0/3	3	0	0	4	0	14	.519
TURGEON, M.	15	1/4	.250	1/2	.500	0/1	2	1	1	0	0	3	.200
MARSHALL, A.	26	5/11	.455	0/0	.000	4/10	4	2	2	2	1	10	.385
PIPER, C.	22	1/6	.167	0/0	.000	1/6	0	1	3	0	0	2	.091
HULL, R.	9	0/3	.000	2/2	1.000	1/1	0	1	1	1	0	2	.222
BARRY, R.	4	1/2	.500	1/1	1.000	0/0	0	1	1	0	0	3	.750
JOHNSON, J.	5	0/1	.000	0/0	.000	1/1	1	0	0	0	0	0	.000
CAMPBELL, A.	5	0/0	.000	0/0	.000	0/1	1	1	2	0	0	0	.000
Totals	200	29/59	.492	13/15	.867	14/36	25	13	16	9	1	71	.355

North Carolina A&T (46)　Coach: Don Corbett

	Min.	Total FG/FGA	Pct.	FT/FTA	Pct.	Reb. O/T	A	TO	PF	S	Blk	TP	PPM
ROBINSON, L.	40	4/6	.667	2/2	1.000	0/4	0	1	3	1	0	10	.250
BECTON, C.	24	3/4	.750	0/0	.000	2/2	2	2	5	1	0	6	.250
WILLIAMS, C.	36	5/9	.556	3/6	.500	3/7	3	8	3	2	1	13	.361
CALE, G.	35	3/12	.250	3/4	.750	0/1	1	3	3	3	0	9	.257
GRIFFIS, T.	40	1/8	.125	2/2	1.000	0/4	1	2	2	1	0	4	.100
COX, K.	20	1/3	.333	2/4	.500	1/5	3	3	0	0	2	4	.200
DAVIS, C.	5	0/1	.000	0/0	.000	0/0	0	0	0	0	0	0	.000
Totals	200	17/43	.395	12/18	.667	6/23	10	19	16	8	3	46	.230

Team Rebounds: Kansas 2; N.C. A&T 1. Disqualified: N.C. A&T—Becton. Technical fouls: None.

	1st Half	2nd Half	Final
Kansas	32	39	71
N. Carolina A&T	19	27	46

Jacksonville (50)　Coach: Bob Wenzel

	Min.	Total FG/FGA	Pct.	FT/FTA	Pct.	Reb. O/T	A	TO	PF	S	Blk	TP	PPM
SMITH	42	3/11	.273	5/7	.714	-/8	-	-	2	-	-	11	.262
MURPHY	43	9/21	.429	4/5	.800	-/7	-	-	3	-	-	22	.512
MCDUFFIE	9	1/2	.500	0/0	.000	-/2	-	-	1	-	-	2	.222
PEARSON	41	3/8	.375	1/2	.500	-/3	-	-	4	-	-	7	.171
LAGUERRE	27	0/0	.000	0/0	.000	-/2	-	-	0	-	-	0	.000
KITTLES	29	1/1	1.000	0/0	.000	-/2	-	-	5	-	-	2	.069
WILLIAMS	26	2/8	.250	0/0	.000	-/5	-	-	1	-	-	4	.154
TERRELL	7	0/0	.000	2/2	1.000	-/1	-	-	2	-	-	2	.286
WORSOWICZ	1	0/0	.000	0/0	.000	-/0	-	-	0	-	-	0	.000
Totals	225	19/51	.373	12/16	.750	-/30	12	14	18	2	4	50	.222

Temple (61)　Coach: John Chaney

	Min.	Total FG/FGA	Pct.	FT/FTA	Pct.	Reb. O/T	A	TO	PF	S	Blk	TP	PPM
PERRY, T.	45	4/8	.500	3/10	.300	-/18	-	-	2	-	-	11	.244
COE, E.	45	8/18	.444	0/0	.000	-/8	-	-	4	-	-	16	.356
RIVAS, R.	11	1/2	.500	1/2	.500	-/1	-	-	4	-	-	3	.273
EVANS, H.	45	4/14	.286	5/5	1.000	-/0	-	-	3	-	-	13	.289
BLACKWELL, N.	38	4/11	.364	0/0	.000	-/1	-	-	0	-	-	8	.211
CLIFTON, K.	7	0/0	.000	6/6	1.000	-/4	-	-	1	-	-	6	.857
BRANTLEY, D.	34	1/6	.167	2/2	1.000	-/7	-	-	1	-	-	4	.118
Totals	225	22/59	.373	17/25	.680	-/39	13	9	15	6	2	61	.271

Team Rebounds: Temple 5; Jacksonville 3. Disqualified: Jacksonville—Kittles. Technical fouls: None.

	1st Half	2nd Half	1st OT	Final
Jacksonville	24	19	7	50
Temple	23	20	18	61

Michigan State (72)　Coach: Jud Heathcote

	Min.	Total FG/FGA	Pct.	FT/FTA	Pct.	Reb. O/T	A	TO	PF	S	Blk	TP	PPM
POLEC, L.	29	2/5	.400	0/0	.000	1/3	0	2	4	0	0	4	.138
CARR, V.	36	6/10	.600	3/5	.600	2/5	2	3	2	0	0	15	.417
FORDHAM, B.	37	0/2	.000	0/0	.000	3/5	0	1	2	1	1	0	.000
JOHNSON, D.	37	11/13	.846	0/0	.000	1/4	3	1	3	1	0	22	.595
SKILES, S.	40	12/21	.571	7/7	1.000	0/0	7	3	2	3	0	31	.775
WALKER, R.	15	0/0	.000	0/0	.000	1/5	0	2	4	0	0	0	.000
VALENTINE, C.	4	0/1	.000	0/0	.000	0/1	0	0	0	0	0	0	.000
IZZO, M.	2	0/0	.000	0/0	.000	1/1	0	0	0	0	0	0	.000
Totals	200	31/52	.596	10/12	.833	9/24	12	12	17	5	1	72	.360

Washington (70)　Coach: Andy Russo

	Min.	Total FG/FGA	Pct.	FT/FTA	Pct.	Reb. O/T	A	TO	PF	S	Blk	TP	PPM
WILLIAMS, S.	35	8/10	.800	0/0	.000	6/7	5	2	4	0	0	16	.457
FORTIER, P.	38	1/7	.143	6/8	.750	4/7	2	1	1	0	0	8	.211
WELP, C.	38	10/21	.476	2/5	.400	4/9	1	3	2	0	0	22	.579
DAMON, C.	26	4/7	.571	2/2	1.000	1/2	5	0	1	0	0	10	.385
HILL, G.	40	7/11	.636	0/0	.000	0/2	4	2	2	1	0	14	.350
MOSCATEL, A.	14	0/3	.000	0/0	.000	0/1	2	0	4	0	0	0	.000
ZEVENBERGEN, P.	9	0/1	.000	0/0	.000	1/2	0	2	0	0	0	0	.000
Totals	200	30/60	.500	10/15	.667	16/30	19	10	14	1	0	70	.350

Team Rebounds: Michigan St. 1; Washington 1. Disqualified: None. Technical fouls: None.

	1st Half	2nd Half	Final
Michigan St.	26	46	72
Washington	36	34	70

Georgetown (70)　Coach: John Thompson

	Min.	Total FG/FGA	Pct.	FT/FTA	Pct.	Reb. O/T	A	TO	PF	S	Blk	TP	PPM
WILLIAMS, R.	36	9/19	.474	4/6	.667	5/7	2	3	3	1	0	22	.611
HIGHSMITH, R.	24	3/6	.500	1/2	.500	2/6	0	1	4	0	1	7	.292
DALTON, R.	24	3/6	.500	2/3	.667	3/5	1	1	3	0	0	8	.333
WINGATE, D.	32	2/12	.167	5/6	.833	2/7	3	1	1	1	0	9	.281
JACKSON, M.	28	5/7	.714	2/2	1.000	0/0	4	1	4	0	0	12	.429
EDWARDS, J.	23	2/2	1.000	2/2	1.000	3/6	1	0	3	0	0	6	.261
JACKSON, J.	5	0/1	.000	0/0	.000	0/1	0	0	0	0	0	0	.000
BROADNAX, H.	11	1/3	.333	0/0	.000	1/1	0	2	0	0	0	2	.182
MCDONALD, P.	10	1/1	1.000	2/4	.500	1/3	1	1	2	0	0	4	.400
SMITH, C.	7	0/2	.000	0/0	.000	0/0	1	0	1	1	0	0	.000
Totals	200	26/59	.441	18/25	.720	17/36	13	10	21	3	1	70	.350

Texas Tech (64)　Coach: Gerald Myers

	Min.	Total FG/FGA	Pct.	FT/FTA	Pct.	Reb. O/T	A	TO	PF	S	Blk	TP	PPM
DODA, T.	39	2/6	.333	0/0	.000	1/4	5	2	2	1	1	4	.103
CROWE, G.	19	1/4	.250	0/3	.000	3/8	0	3	2	0	1	2	.105
IRVIN, R.	16	0/1	.000	0/0	.000	0/4	2	1	2	0	0	0	.000
GAY, S.	23	4/8	.500	1/1	1.000	1/1	1	1	1	0	0	9	.391
BENFORD, T.	37	8/11	.727	1/3	.333	0/4	3	1	5	1	0	17	.459
CHISM, D.	35	4/6	.667	2/5	.400	2/4	2	2	1	1	1	10	.286
NELSON, M.	3	0/2	.000	0/0	.000	0/0	0	0	1	0	0	0	.000
WOJCIECHOSKI, K.	3	0/0	.000	0/0	.000	0/0	0	0	2	0	0	0	.000
OWENS, W.	25	7/9	.778	8/10	.800	1/1	4	2	2	3	0	22	.880
Totals	200	26/47	.553	12/22	.545	8/26	17	12	18	6	3	64	.320

Team Rebounds: Georgetown 4; Texas Tech 3. Disqualified: Texas Tech—Benford. Technical fouls: None.

	1st Half	2nd Half	Final
Georgetown	38	32	70
Texas Tech	32	32	64

North Carolina State (66) Coach: Jim Valvano

	Min.	Total FG/FGA	Pct.	FT/FTA	Pct.	Reb. O/T	A	TO	PF	S	Blk	TP	PPM
BOLTON, B.	33	5/7	.714	3/4	.750	-/6	2	0	5	0	0	13	.394
SHACKLEFORD, C.	35	5/10	.500	0/3	.000	-/8	0	0	3	1	0	10	.286
WASHBURN, C.	34	8/20	.400	2/7	.286	-/9	2	2	2	1	0	18	.529
MCMILLAN, N.	40	5/10	.500	5/6	.833	-/6	3	4	4	1	0	15	.375
MEYERS, E.	36	2/8	.250	0/0	.000	-/2	0	2	3	1	0	4	.111
BROWN, C.	10	1/2	.500	0/0	.000	-/2	0	0	0	0	0	2	.200
WEEMS, K.	4	0/1	.000	0/0	.000	-/0	0	0	1	0	0	0	.000
JACKSON, Q.	1	0/0	.000	0/0	.000	-/0	0	0	1	0	0	0	.000
BINNS, T.	7	2/3	.667	0/1	.000	-/2	1	0	0	1	0	4	.571
Totals	200	28/61	.459	10/21	.476	-/35	8	8	19	5	0	66	.330

Iowa (64) Coach: George Raveling

	Min.	Total FG/FGA	Pct.	FT/FTA	Pct.	Reb. O/T	A	TO	PF	S	Blk	TP	PPM
WRIGHT, J.	33	5/8	.625	5/5	1.000	-/7	1	2	5	1	0	15	.455
MARBLE, R.	36	5/11	.455	5/12	.417	-/5	1	1	3	1	1	15	.417
LORENZEN, A.	25	3/5	.600	2/4	.500	-/5	0	0	5	0	0	8	.320
JONES, B.	30	3/7	.429	2/2	1.000	-/1	1	1	1	1	0	8	.267
BANKS, A.	40	8/13	.615	0/0	.000	-/4	0	1	2	2	0	16	.400
GAMBLE, K.	1	0/0	.000	0/0	.000	-/0	0	0	0	0	0	0	.000
MOE, J.	13	1/3	.333	0/1	.000	-/0	1	1	1	0	0	2	.154
HORTON, E.	10	0/0	.000	0/2	.000	-/1	0	0	4	1	0	0	.000
LOHAUS, B.	11	0/1	.000	0/0	.000	-/1	0	1	0	0	0	0	.000
REAVES, M.	1	0/0	.000	0/0	.000	-/0	0	0	0	0	0	0	.000
Totals	200	25/48	.521	14/26	.538	-/24	4	7	21	6	1	64	.320

Team Rebounds: N.C. State 7; Iowa 7. Disqualified: N.C. State—Bolton; Iowa—Wright, Lorenzen. Technical fouls: None.

	1st Half	2nd Half	Final
N.C. State	36	30	66
Iowa	39	25	64

Notre Dame (83) Coach: Digger Phelps

	Min.	Total FG/FGA	Pct.	FT/FTA	Pct.	Reb. O/T	A	TO	PF	S	Blk	TP	PPM
BARLOW, K.	23	5/10	.500	0/0	.000	-/2	2	2	5	0	0	10	.435
ROYAL, D.	30	4/7	.571	4/6	.667	-/8	0	0	4	0	0	12	.400
KEMPTON, T.	30	4/8	.500	0/0	.000	-/7	0	0	2	1	0	8	.267
RIVERS, D.	35	9/19	.474	7/8	.875	-/0	6	7	4	1	0	25	.714
STEVENSON, M.	21	4/9	.444	0/0	.000	-/1	0	3	5	0	0	8	.381
PRICE, J.	16	2/5	.400	0/0	.000	-/3	0	0	1	1	0	4	.250
DOLAN, J.	16	2/2	1.000	2/2	1.000	-/4	0	0	5	2	0	6	.375
VOCE, G.	2	0/0	.000	0/0	.000	-/1	0	0	0	0	0	0	.000
CONNOR, S.	2	0/0	.000	0/0	.000	-/0	0	0	0	0	0	0	.000
SMITH, M.	1	0/0	.000	0/0	.000	-/0	0	0	0	0	0	0	.000
HICKS, S.	24	5/7	.714	0/0	.000	-/2	2	0	2	1	0	10	.417
Totals	200	35/67	.522	13/16	.813	-/28	10	12	28	6	0	83	.415

Arkansas-Little Rock (90) Coach: Mike Newell

	Min.	Total FG/FGA	Pct.	FT/FTA	Pct.	Reb. O/T	A	TO	PF	S	Blk	TP	PPM
CLARKE, M.	40	8/13	.615	11/14	.786	-/9	1	2	2	0	0	27	.675
MEYERS, P.	29	10/14	.714	9/12	.750	-/7	5	4	3	1	0	29	1.000
MCCURDY, P.	6	0/0	.000	0/0	.000	-/0	0	0	1	1	0	0	.000
SPRINGER, P.	40	3/5	.600	4/5	.800	-/0	2	3	2	2	1	10	.250
JACKSON, M.	40	11/18	.611	0/1	.000	-/5	1	2	3	0	0	22	.550
WORTHY, K.	29	0/1	.000	0/0	.000	-/5	4	3	2	1	0	0	.000
SMITH, R.	14	1/2	.500	0/0	.000	0/1	0	0	3	0	0	2	.143
KIDD, C.	2	0/0	.000	0/0	.000	-/0	0	0	2	0	0	0	.000
Totals	200	33/53	.623	24/32	.750	-/27	13	14	18	5	1	90	.450

Team Rebounds: Ark.-Little Rock 4; Notre Dame 3. Disqualified: Notre Dame—Barlow, Stevenson, Dolan. Technical fouls: None.

	1st Half	2nd Half	Final
Notre Dame	39	44	83
Ark.-Little Rock	40	50	90

Iowa State (81) Coach: Johnny Orr

	Min.	Total FG/FGA	Pct.	FT/FTA	Pct.	Reb. O/T	A	TO	PF	S	Blk	TP	PPM
GRAYER, J.	45	8/10	.800	3/8	.375	-/11	2	2	3	2	0	19	.422
VIRGIL, R.	33	7/12	.583	0/0	.000	-/2	1	0	4	2	0	14	.424
HILL, S.	39	4/7	.571	0/1	.000	-/4	0	0	4	1	1	8	.205
THOMPKINS, G.	31	4/9	.444	2/2	1.000	-/2	4	6	1	0	0	10	.323
HORNACEK, J.	42	7/11	.636	1/3	.333	-/3	3	2	4	3	0	15	.357
ROBINSON, E.	24	5/9	.556	3/5	.600	-/4	3	2	2	0	0	13	.542
MOSS, D.	5	1/2	.500	0/0	.000	-/0	0	0	2	0	0	2	.400
SCHAFER, T.	6	0/1	.000	0/0	.000	-/0	0	0	0	0	0	0	.000
Totals	225	36/61	.590	9/19	.474	-/26	13	12	20	8	1	81	.360

Miami (Ohio) (79) Coach: Jerry Irson

	Min.	Total FG/FGA	Pct.	FT/FTA	Pct.	Reb. O/T	A	TO	PF	S	Blk	TP	PPM
CLAYBORNE, K.	32	3/3	1.000	2/2	1.000	-/6	0	0	1	0	0	8	.250
HARPER, R.	45	7/22	.318	3/4	.750	-/13	3	3	4	3	1	17	.378
HANNA, L.	32	7/12	.583	3/6	.500	-/7	2	2	5	0	0	17	.531
STAKER, T.	29	3/6	.500	0/0	.000	-/3	2	3	3	2	0	6	.207
NEWSOME, S.	39	6/15	.400	4/4	1.000	-/5	2	4	2	0	0	16	.410
FUERST, J.	3	0/1	.000	0/0	.000	-/1	0	0	0	0	0	0	.000
SCHILLING, E.	23	0/7	.000	1/2	.500	-/0	0	3	2	3	0	1	.043
HUNTER, R.	19	6/6	1.000	0/0	.000	-/3	0	1	3	0	0	12	.632
LAMPE, T.	3	0/0	.000	2/2	1.000	-/1	0	0	0	0	0	2	.667
Totals	225	32/72	.444	15/20	.750	-/39	9	16	20	8	1	79	.351

Team Rebounds: Iowa State 5; Miami (Ohio) 7. Disqualified: Miami (Ohio)—Hanna. Technical fouls: None.

	1st Half	2nd Half	1 OT	Final
Iowa State	30	35	16	81
Miami (Ohio)	31	34	14	79

Michigan (70) Coach: Bill Freider

	Min.	Total FG/FGA	Pct.	FT/FTA	Pct.	Reb. O/T	A	TO	PF	S	Blk	TP	PPM
REILFORD, R.	25	2/3	.667	3/4	.750	-/3	1	0	4	0	0	7	.280
WADE, B.	26	2/4	.500	0/3	.000	-/3	0	0	3	1	1	4	.154
TARPLEY, R.	29	4/11	.364	5/5	1.000	-/9	1	3	3	0	1	13	.448
JOUBERT, A.	33	5/12	.417	2/2	1.000	-/2	1	3	0	0	0	12	.364
GRANT, G.	31	3/5	.600	0/0	.000	-/1	7	3	2	0	0	6	.194
HENDERSON, R.	19	2/4	.500	2/3	.667	-/4	0	1	0	0	1	6	.316
RICE, G.	21	6/9	.667	2/2	1.000	-/2	1	0	2	0	0	14	.667
THOMPSON, G.	16	3/3	1.000	2/2	1.000	-/0	0	1	0	0	0	8	.500
Totals	200	27/51	.529	16/21	.762	-/24	11	11	14	1	3	70	.350

Akron (64) Coach: Bob Huggins

	Min.	Total FG/FGA	Pct.	FT/FTA	Pct.	Reb. O/T	A	TO	PF	S	Blk	TP	PPM
HOLMES, R.	27	2/9	.222	2/2	1.000	-/6	1	6	4	0	0	6	.222
ROBERTS, S.	23	1/6	.167	0/0	.000	-/3	1	1	2	0	0	2	.087
BOYCE, M.	31	8/16	.500	1/3	.333	-/8	0	2	4	0	1	17	.548
DOWDELL, M.	32	4/8	.500	3/4	.750	-/2	2	0	2	2	0	11	.344
LOYER, J.	25	2/2	1.000	1/2	.500	-/3	0	0	1	0	0	5	.200
SCHULZ, D.	26	2/6	.333	2/2	1.000	-/4	1	0	1	0	0	6	.231
TAYLOR, R.	5	0/0	.000	1/2	.500	-/0	0	0	2	0	0	1	.200
MCLAUGHLIN, E.	30	7/11	.636	0/0	.000	-/2	1	4	2	0	0	14	.467
MCLENDON, M.	1	1/2	.500	0/0	.000	-/0	0	0	1	1	0	2	2.000
Totals	200	27/60	.450	10/15	.667	-/28	6	13	19	3	1	64	.320

Team Rebounds: Michigan 4; Akron 6. Disqualified: None. Technical fouls: None.

	1st Half	2nd Half	Final
Michigan	30	40	70
Akron	32	32	64

SECOND ROUND SOUTHEAST

Kentucky (71)   Coach: Eddie Sutton

	Min.	Total FG/FGA	Pct.	FT/FTA	Pct.	Reb. O/T	A	TO	PF	S	Blk	TP	PPM
BENNETT, W.	40	5/11	.455	3/5	.600	2/6	3	3	2	1	0	13	.325
WALKER, K.	40	11/11	1.000	10/13	.769	0/8	2	3	3	0	1	32	.800
BLACKMON, J.	22	1/5	.200	0/0	.000	1/2	1	2	2	0	2	2	.091
DAVENDER, E.	30	2/7	.286	5/6	.833	1/5	2	0	2	1	0	9	.300
HARDEN, R.	35	1/6	.167	0/0	.000	0/3	5	4	2	1	0	2	.057
BYRD, L.	1	0/1	.000	0/0	.000	0/0	0	0	0	0	0	0	.000
ANDREWS, P.	1	0/0	.000	0/0	.000	0/0	0	0	0	0	0	0	.000
THOMAS, I.	2	0/0	.000	0/0	.000	1/1	0	0	0	0	0	0	.000
MADISON, R.	4	0/0	.000	2/2	1.000	0/0	0	0	0	0	0	2	.500
LOCK, R.	4	1/2	.500	0/0	.000	1/1	0	0	2	0	0	2	.500
JENKINS, C.	21	3/3	1.000	3/4	.750	0/2	0	0	3	0	0	9	.429
Totals	200	24/46	.522	23/30	.767	6/28	13	12	16	3	3	71	.355

Western Kentucky (64)   Coach: Clem Haskins

	Min.	Total FG/FGA	Pct.	FT/FTA	Pct.	Reb. O/T	A	TO	PF	S	Blk	TP	PPM
JOHNSON, K.	36	7/16	.438	6/8	.750	2/6	1	0	3	1	0	20	.556
SWOGGER, R.	20	2/8	.250	1/1	1.000	1/4	1	2	3	3	1	5	.250
MARTIN, C.	26	0/0	.000	1/2	.500	0/7	1	1	4	0	0	1	.038
MCNARY, J.	11	1/3	.333	0/0	.000	1/1	5	1	1	0	0	2	.182
GORDON, B.	27	7/16	.438	0/0	.000	2/4	2	1	3	0	1	14	.519
LICKLITER, K.	2	1/1	1.000	0/0	.000	0/0	0	0	0	0	0	2	1.000
LEE, K.	26	3/4	.750	0/1	.000	1/1	1	0	4	0	0	6	.231
MCNEIL, B.	4	0/2	.000	0/0	.000	0/0	0	0	0	0	0	0	.000
MILLER, S.	9	0/1	.000	0/0	.000	0/2	0	0	0	0	0	0	.000
TISDALE, F.	10	1/3	.333	1/2	.500	1/3	0	1	1	0	0	3	.300
TAYLOR, C.	1	1/1	1.000	0/0	.000	1/1	0	0	0	0	0	2	2.000
FRANK, T.	21	4/8	.500	1/1	1.000	2/2	0	1	5	0	0	9	.429
ASBERRY, B.	7	0/2	.000	0/0	.000	0/1	0	0	0	0	0	0	.000
Totals	200	27/65	.415	10/15	.667	11/32	11	7	24	4	2	64	.320

Team Rebounds: Kentucky 6; Western Ky. 4. Disqualified: Western Ky.—Frank. Technical fouls: None.

	1st Half	2nd Half	Final
Kentucky	36	35	71
Western Ky.	24	40	64

Alabama (58)   Coach: Wimp Sanderson

	Min.	Total FG/FGA	Pct.	FT/FTA	Pct.	Reb. O/T	A	TO	PF	S	Blk	TP	PPM
FARMER, J.	40	6/11	.545	1/3	.333	2/5	0	2	3	0	0	13	.325
JOHNSON, B.	40	6/13	.462	0/0	.000	2/7	2	3	1	1	1	12	.300
MCKEY, D.	25	2/5	.400	3/4	.750	2/4	0	0	4	0	1	7	.280
GOTTFRIED, M.	27	4/7	.571	0/0	.000	1/3	1	1	0	0	0	8	.296
CONER, T.	40	5/14	.357	2/2	1.000	0/5	10	3	2	0	1	12	.300
JACKSON, J.	14	2/2	1.000	0/0	.000	0/0	1	0	0	1	0	4	.286
ANSLEY, M.	14	1/1	1.000	0/0	.000	0/1	0	0	1	1	0	2	.143
Totals	200	26/53	.491	6/9	.667	7/25	14	9	11	3	3	58	.290

Illinois (56)   Coach: Lou Henson

	Min.	Total FG/FGA	Pct.	FT/FTA	Pct.	Reb. O/T	A	TO	PF	S	Blk	TP	PPM
WINTERS, E.	32	0/5	.000	0/0	.000	2/7	5	1	2	1	1	0	.000
WELCH, A.	31	7/14	.500	0/0	.000	4/8	0	0	3	0	0	14	.452
NORMAN, K.	30	5/7	.714	0/0	.000	2/2	0	1	4	0	1	10	.333
BLACKWELL, G.	22	2/6	.333	0/0	.000	2/3	2	2	0	3	0	4	.182
DOUGLAS, B.	33	3/7	.429	0/0	.000	0/2	7	1	1	0	0	6	.182
WYSINGER, T.	34	9/14	.643	0/0	.000	0/3	4	0	2	2	0	18	.529
MEENTS, S.	17	2/7	.286	0/0	.000	0/3	0	1	1	1	0	4	.235
HAMILTON, L.	1	0/0	.000	0/0	.000	0/0	0	0	0	0	-0	0	.000
Totals	200	28/60	.467	0/0		10/28	18	6	13	7	2	56	.280

Team Rebounds: Alabama 4; Illinois 3. Disqualified: None. Technical fouls: None.

	1st Half	2nd Half	Final
Alabama	33	25	58
Illinois	24	32	56

Louisiana State (83)   Coach: Dale Brown

	Min.	Total FG/FGA	Pct.	FT/FTA	Pct.	Reb. O/T	A	TO	PF	S	Blk	TP	PPM
BLANTON, R.	37	4/8	.500	3/3	1.000	6/11	1	1	1	1	0	11	.297
REDDEN, D.	33	8/14	.571	7/11	.636	2/3	1	5	3	0	0	23	.697
WILLIAM, J.	32	6/13	.462	7/8	.875	5/13	2	1	4	1	1	19	.594
TAYLOR, D.	37	9/18	.500	0/0	.000	0/1	5	0	3	2	0	18	.486
WILSON, A.	31	3/10	.300	0/0	.000	3/3	1	0	0	2	0	6	.194
BUKUMIROVICH, N.	3	0/1	.000	2/2	1.000	0/0	1	0	1	0	0	2	.667
WOODSIDE, B.	6	0/0	.000	0/0	.000	0/0	0	1	2	0	0	0	.000
BROWN, O.	18	1/1	1.000	2/4	.500	2/3	3	1	1	1	0	4	.222
VARGAS, J.	3	0/0	.000	0/0	.000	0/0	0	0	1	0	0	0	.000
Totals	200	31/65	.477	21/28	.750	18/34	14	9	16	7	1	83	.415

Memphis State (81)   Coach: Dana Kirk

	Min.	Total FG/FGA	Pct.	FT/FTA	Pct.	Reb. O/T	A	TO	PF	S	Blk	TP	PPM
ASKEW, V.	26	5/11	.455	0/0	.000	0/4	0	0	3	1	1	10	.385
HOLMES, B.	40	9/17	.529	2/3	.667	4/9	0	2	3	0	1	20	.500
BEDFORD, W.	29	7/10	.700	1/3	.333	1/6	0	1	4	0	1	15	.517
TURNER, A.	34	6/11	.545	0/0	.000	1/3	10	5	2	2	0	12	.353
BOYD, D.	28	5/8	.625	2/2	1.000	1/2	1	2	4	1	2	12	.429
WILFONG, J.	7	2/2	1.000	2/2	1.000	0/1	0	1	1	0	0	6	.857
BAILEY, D.	20	1/1	1.000	2/2	1.000	2/4	0	2	0	0	0	4	.200
ALEXANDER, M.	16	1/2	.500	0/2	.000	2/3	0	1	4	0	0	2	.125
Totals	200	36/62	.581	9/14	.643	11/32	11	14	21	4	5	81	.405

Team Rebounds: Louisiana St. 0; Memphis State 1. Disqualified: None. Technical fouls: None.

	1st Half	2nd Half	Final
Louisiana St.	41	42	83
Memphis State	47	34	81

Villanova (61)   Coach: Rollie Massimino

	Min.	Total FG/FGA	Pct.	FT/FTA	Pct.	Reb. O/T	A	TO	PF	S	Blk	TP	PPM
PRESSLEY, H.	40	8/17	.471	3/3	1.000	5/10	1	2	4	2	1	19	.475
PLANSKY, M.	28	1/3	.333	0/0	.000	1/5	0	1	5	3	1	2	.071
WEST, D.	35	10/18	.556	0/0	.000	2/5	0	2	4	1	0	20	.571
WILSON, K.	38	4/13	.308	6/6	1.000	1/3	4	2	4	1	0	14	.368
JENSEN, H.	32	2/9	.222	0/0	.000	1/1	0	4	1	0	4	4	.125
MASSEY, G.	19	0/0	.000	2/2	1.000	0/0	0	2	0	0	0	2	.105
MAKER, W.	1	0/1	.000	0/0	.000	1/1	0	1	0	0	0	0	.000
BROWN, C.	2	0/1	.000	0/0	.000	1/1	0	1	0	0	0	0	.000
WILBUR, D.	5	0/1	.000	0/0	.000	0/0	0	1	0	0	0	0	.000
Totals	200	25/63	.397	11/11	1.000	12/26	5	9	24	8	2	61	.305

Georgia Tech (66)   Coach: Bobby Cremins

	Min.	Total FG/FGA	Pct.	FT/FTA	Pct.	Reb. O/T	A	TO	PF	S	Blk	TP	PPM
HAMMONDS, T.	33	2/8	.250	2/2	1.000	6/10	0	3	0	0	0	6	.182
FERRELL, D.	38	6/11	.545	2/2	1.000	5/8	2	2	2	3	0	14	.368
SALLEY, J.	36	4/9	.444	2/3	.667	4/11	2	5	3	0	1	10	.278
PRICE, M.	37	5/12	.417	10/12	.833	1/2	4	0	2	1	0	20	.541
DALRYMPLE, B.	32	2/4	.500	5/8	.625	2/9	1	5	2	0	0	9	.281
NEAL, C.	10	0/3	.000	4/4	1.000	0/0	2	0	1	1	1	4	.400
FORD, A.	14	1/1	1.000	1/2	.500	1/2	0	3	0	0	0	3	.214
Totals	200	20/48	.417	26/33	.788	19/42	8	19	11	6	3	66	.330

Team Rebounds: Georgia Tech 0; Villanova 1. Disqualified: Villanova—Plansky. Technical fouls: Villanova—Bench.

	1st Half	2nd Half	Final
Villanova	30	31	61
Georgia Tech	40	26	66

SECOND ROUND WEST

St. John's (65)   Coach: Lou Carnesecca

	Min.	Total FG/FGA	Pct.	FT/FTA	Pct.	Reb. O/T	A	TO	PF	S	Blk	TP	PPM
GLASS, W.	32	5/9	.556	2/2	1.000	-/1	1	3	0	3	0	12	.375
JONES, S.	29	3/4	.750	0/0	.000	-/4	0	2	1	1	0	6	.207
BERRY, W.	39	9/14	.643	2/2	1.000	-/7	0	3	3	1	1	20	.513
ROWAN, R.	36	6/16	.375	2/2	1.000	-/2	2	3	4	2	0	14	.389
JACKSON, M.	38	1/8	.125	1/2	.500	-/4	12	3	4	1	0	3	.079
HEMPEL, J.	16	4/6	.667	0/0	.000	-/1	0	1	2	1	0	8	.500
BROSS, T.	8	1/2	.500	0/0	.000	-/1	0	1	1	0	0	2	.250
SHURINA, S.	2	0/0	.000	0/0	.000	-/0	0	0	1	0	0	0	.000
Totals	200	29/59	.492	7/8	.875	-/20	15	16	16	9	1	65	.325

Auburn (81)   Coach: Sonny Smith

	Min.	Total FG/FGA	Pct.	FT/FTA	Pct.	Reb. O/T	A	TO	PF	S	Blk	TP	PPM
MORRIS, C.	36	4/8	.500	1/1	1.000	-/5	2	4	0	1	0	9	.250
PERSON, C.	37	12/22	.545	3/3	1.000	-/15	1	1	1	2	0	27	.730
MOORE, J.	26	7/14	.500	1/1	1.000	-/5	0	1	3	0	0	15	.577
WHITE, G.	30	3/5	.600	4/5	.800	-/3	9	5	2	4	0	10	.333
FORD, F.	37	4/9	.444	0/0	.000	-/5	2	2	1	0	0	8	.216
HOWARD, T.	14	3/4	.750	0/0	.000	-/2	2	0	2	0	0	6	.429
JONES, M.	20	2/4	.500	2/3	.667	-/2	0	2	2	0	1	6	.300
Totals	200	35/66	.530	11/13	.846	-/37	16	15	11	7	1	81	.405

Team Rebounds: Auburn 1; St. John's 2. Disqualified: None. Technical fouls: None.

	1st Half	2nd Half	Final
St. John's	32	33	65
Auburn	44	37	81

Maryland (64)   Coach: Lefty Driesell

	Min.	Total FG/FGA	Pct.	FT/FTA	Pct.	Reb. O/T	A	TO	PF	S	Blk	TP	PPM
LEWIS, D.	29	1/3	.333	3/4	.750	-/2	0	3	5	0	4	5	.172
BIAS, L.	39	11/23	.478	9/9	1.000	-/12	0	2	5	0	0	31	.795
LONG, T.	18	0/0	.000	0/0	.000	-/5	0	2	4	1	0	0	.000
GATLIN, K.	40	6/10	.600	0/0	.000	-/4	6	1	0	1	0	12	.300
BAXTER, J.	26	1/4	.250	0/0	.000	-/1	6	2	3	0	0	2	.077
JONES, T.	34	4/7	.571	0/2	.000	-/7	1	0	2	0	1	8	.235
JOHNSON, J.	12	3/4	.750	0/3	.000	-/1	0	1	2	0	0	6	.500
DICKERSON, D.	2	0/0	.000	0/0	.000	-/0	0	0	1	0	0	0	.000
Totals	200	26/51	.510	12/18	.667	-/32	13	11	22	2	5	64	.320

UNLV (70)   Coach: Jerry Tarkanian

	Min.	Total FG/FGA	Pct.	FT/FTA	Pct.	Reb. O/T	A	TO	PF	S	Blk	TP	PPM
JONES, A.	38	9/20	.450	7/8	.875	-/10	0	0	2	0	0	25	.658
GILLIAM, A.	37	6/20	.300	6/7	.857	-/14	0	1	4	2	1	18	.486
FLOWERS, J.	24	3/4	.750	0/1	.000	-/7	1	1	1	0	0	6	.250
WADE, M.	37	2/5	.400	1/3	.333	-/2	12	1	4	2	0	5	.135
BANKS, F.	33	5/14	.357	0/0	.000	-/2	2	0	4	2	0	10	.303
HUDSON, E.	13	2/4	.500	0/1	.000	-/0	0	0	4	1	0	4	.308
GRAHAM, G.	10	1/1	1.000	0/0	.000	-/2	2	0	2	0	0	2	.200
BASNIGHT, J.	8	0/0	.000	0/0	.000	-/1	0	1	2	0	0	0	.000
Totals	200	28/68	.412	14/20	.700	-/38	17	4	23	7	1	70	.350

Team Rebounds: UNLV 2; Maryland 4. Disqualified: Maryland—Lewis, Bias. Technical fouls: None.

	1st Half	2nd Half	Final
Maryland	27	37	64
UNLV	33	37	70

Alabama-Birmingham (59)   Coach: Gene Bartow

	Min.	Total FG/FGA	Pct.	FT/FTA	Pct.	Reb. O/T	A	TO	PF	S	Blk	TP	PPM
MINCY, J.	27	4/13	.308	1/2	.500	0/5	0	0	4	2	0	9	.333
GORDON, A.	19	4/9	.444	2/6	.333	4/11	0	0	4	0	0	10	.526
JOHNSON, A.	25	1/5	.200	4/4	1.000	4/5	1	1	5	0	0	6	.240
MITCHELL, S.	33	3/21	.143	1/6	.167	1/5	4	0	0	0	0	7	.212
PONDER, J.	26	2/8	.250	3/4	.750	0/2	0	0	3	2	0	7	.269
FOSTER, T.	19	4/9	.444	2/2	1.000	0/0	0	2	2	0	0	10	.526
CHARLES, M.	31	2/3	.667	2/3	.667	4/11	8	4	4	1	0	6	.194
COLLINS, E.	5	0/0	.000	0/0	.000	0/1	0	1	1	0	0	0	.000
TURNER, R.	3	1/2	.500	0/0	.000	1/1	0	0	0	0	0	2	.667
HOWARD, D.	2	1/3	.333	0/0	.000	0/0	0	0	0	0	0	2	1.000
EVANS, C.	10	0/0	.000	0/0	.000	0/2	1	1	3	0	3	0	.000
Totals	200	22/73	.301	15/27	.556	14/43	14	9	26	5	3	59	.295

North Carolina (77)   Coach: Dean Smith

	Min.	Total FG/FGA	Pct.	FT/FTA	Pct.	Reb. O/T	A	TO	PF	S	Blk	TP	PPM
WOLF, J.	34	2/8	.250	6/7	.857	3/16	4	0	1	1	1	10	.294
HALE, S.	33	5/10	.500	6/7	.857	1/5	3	2	4	0	0	16	.485
DAUGHERTY, B.	25	4/8	.500	5/8	.625	1/13	3	5	4	0	1	13	.520
LEBO, J.	32	4/11	.364	0/0	.000	1/5	3	3	4	0	0	8	.250
SMITH, K.	35	7/12	.583	3/5	.600	0/2	4	4	4	1	0	17	.486
DAYE, J.	1	0/0	.000	0/0	.000	0/0	0	0	0	0	0	0	.000
BUCKNALL, S.	1	0/0	.000	0/0	.000	0/1	1	0	0	0	0	0	.000
MADDEN, K.	2	0/0	.000	0/0	.000	0/0	0	1	0	0	0	0	.000
SMITH, R.	3	0/0	.000	0/0	.000	0/0	0	0	1	0	0	0	.000
POPSON, D.	8	0/1	.000	2/2	1.000	0/1	0	2	0	2	2	2	.250
HUNTER, C.	14	3/5	.600	0/0	.000	0/4	1	1	1	0	0	6	.429
MARTIN, W.	12	1/2	.500	3/5	.600	1/5	0	0	5	0	0	5	.417
Totals	200	26/57	.456	25/34	.735	7/52	18	16	25	2	4	77	.385

Team Rebounds: N. Carolina 1; Ala.-Birmingham 2. Disqualified: Ala.-Birmingham—Johnson; N. Carolina—Martin. Technical fouls: Ala.-Birmingham—Mincy.

	1st Half	2nd Half	Final
Ala.-Birmingham	27	32	59
N. Carolina	34	43	77

Bradley (68)   Coach: Dick Versace

	Min.	Total FG/FGA	Pct.	FT/FTA	Pct.	Reb. O/T	A	TO	PF	S	Blk	TP	PPM
TRIMPE, T.	39	2/7	.286	0/0	.000	0/4	7	3	3	0	0	4	.103
POWELL, D.	23	3/4	.750	2/6	.333	3/8	1	5	1	0	0	8	.348
WILLIAMS, M.	38	7/15	.467	3/5	.600	3/8	1	0	4	0	0	17	.447
HAWKINS, H.	40	11/22	.500	0/1	.000	5/7	3	2	3	0	0	22	.550
LESS, J.	40	6/12	.500	3/4	.750	2/4	6	3	4	2	0	15	.375
THOMAS, J.	18	1/4	.250	0/1	.000	3/5	1	0	3	0	0	2	.111
MANUEL, A.	2	0/0	.000	0/0	.000	0/0	1	0	0	0	0	0	.000
Totals	200	30/64	.469	8/17	.471	16/36	20	13	18	2	0	68	.340

Louisville (82)   Coach: Denny Crum

	Min.	Total FG/FGA	Pct.	FT/FTA	Pct.	Reb. O/T	A	TO	PF	S	Blk	TP	PPM
VALENTINE, R.	1	1/1	1.000	1/2	.500	0/2	0	0	0	0	0	3	3.000
PAYNE, K.	1	0/0	.000	0/0	.000	0/0	0	0	1	0	0	0	.000
ABRAM, M.	1	0/1	.000	0/0	.000	0/1	0	0	0	0	0	0	.000
CROOK, H.	22	3/9	.333	3/4	.750	1/5	3	1	1	0	0	9	.409
THOMPSON, M.	31	5/8	.625	4/4	1.000	3/7	6	2	4	0	1	14	.452
ELLISON, P.	35	7/10	.700	2/3	.667	2/8	0	2	5	1	1	16	.457
WAGNER, M.	35	6/13	.462	4/6	.667	1/3	1	3	1	2	1	16	.457
HALL, J.	25	5/9	.556	1/2	.500	0/2	1	1	2	1	0	11	.440
MCSWAIN, M.	20	2/2	1.000	1/2	.500	1/5	1	0	1	0	1	5	.250
WALLS, K.	4	0/0	.000	0/0	.000	0/0	1	0	1	0	0	0	.000
KIMBRO, T.	23	3/5	.600	2/2	1.000	0/1	4	0	2	0	0	8	.348
WEST, C.	1	0/0	.000	0/0	.000	0/0	0	0	0	0	0	0	.000
OLLIGES, W.	1	0/0	.000	0/0	.000	0/1	1	0	0	0	0	0	.000
Totals	200	32/58	.552	18/25	.720	8/34	17	9	17	4	4	82	.410

Disqualified: Louisville—Ellison. Technical fouls: Louisville—Ellison.

	1st Half	2nd Half	Final
Bradley	31	37	68
Louisville	35	47	82

SECOND ROUND EAST

Duke (89)   Coach: Mike Krzyzewski

	Min.	Total FG / FGA	Pct.	FT / FTA	Pct.	Reb. O / T	A	TO	PF	S	Blk	TP	PPM
HENDERSON, D.	27	1/ 4	.250	6/ 6	1.000	-/ 3	1	-	2	-	-	8	.296
ALARIE, M.	30	5/12	.417	3/ 4	.750	-/14	0	-	1	-	-	13	.433
BILAS, J.	18	3/ 4	.750	4/ 8	.500	-/ 1	0	-	3	-	-	10	.556
AMAKER, T.	30	4/ 7	.571	2/ 5	.400	-/ 1	7	-	1	-	-	10	.333
DAWKINS, J.	26	10/12	.833	5/ 5	1.000	-/ 2	4	-	3	-	-	25	.962
SNYDER, Q.	13	0/ 1	.000	0/ 0	.000	-/ 1	0	-	4	-	-	0	.000
STRICKLAND, K.	7	2/ 2	1.000	0/ 0	.000	-/ 0	0	-	0	-	-	4	.571
JOHNSMITH	4	0/ 1	.000	0/ 0	.000	-/ 1	0	-	0	-	-	0	.000
FERRY, D.	19	5/ 7	.714	0/ 0	.000	-/ 3	1	-	4	-	-	10	.526
WILLIAMS, W.	4	0/ 1	.000	2/ 2	1.000	-/ 1	0	-	1	-	-	2	.500
NESSLEY, M.	6	2/ 4	.500	1/ 2	.500	-/ 2	0	-	4	-	-	5	.833
KING, B.	16	1/ 3	.333	0/ 0	.000	-/ 4	0	-	3	-	-	2	.125
Totals	200	33/58	.569	23/32	.719	-/33	13	17	26	-	-	89	.445

Old Dominion (61)   Coach: Tom Young

	Min.	Total FG / FGA	Pct.	FT / FTA	Pct.	Reb. O / T	A	TO	PF	S	Blk	TP	PPM
WADE	27	3/ 5	.600	4/ 6	.667	-/ 2	0	-	2	-	-	10	.370
GATTISON	37	7/17	.412	3/ 7	.429	-/ 5	0	-	3	-	-	17	.459
HANELEY	4	0/ 2	.000	0/ 0	.000	-/ 0	0	-	1	-	-	0	.000
SMITH	33	1/ 4	.250	1/ 2	.500	-/ 1	7	-	3	-	-	3	.091
THOMAS	31	5/13	.385	3/ 4	.750	-/ 0	0	-	4	-	-	13	.419
CHARLES	18	1/ 3	.333	1/ 2	.500	-/ 4	1	-	3	-	-	3	.167
JONES	2	0/ 0	.000	0/ 0	.000	-/ 1	0	-	0	-	-	0	.000
CARLISLE	3	1/ 2	.500	1/ 2	.500	-/ 1	0	-	0	-	-	3	1.000
TROTT	4	1/ 2	.500	0/ 0	.000	-/ 0	0	-	1	-	-	2	.500
ROISTER	11	0/ 1	.000	0/ 2	.000	-/ 1	0	-	2	-	-	0	.000
TOLSON	12	4/ 6	.667	1/ 2	.500	-/ 1	0	-	1	-	-	9	.750
DAVIS, G.	18	0/ 1	.000	1/ 2	.500	-/ 7	2	-	4	-	-	1	.056
Totals	200	23/56	.411	15/29	.517	-/23	10	22	24	-	-	61	.305

Team Rebounds: Duke 4; Old Dominion 6. Disqualified: None. Technical fouls: None.

	1st Half	2nd Half	Final
Duke	43	46	89
Old Dominion	31	30	61

DePaul (74)   Coach: Joey Meyer

	Min.	Total FG / FGA	Pct.	FT / FTA	Pct.	Reb. O / T	A	TO	PF	S	Blk	TP	PPM
HOLMES, K.	34	5/10	.500	0/ 2	.000	-/ 6	2	3	2	1	0	10	.294
LAMPLEY, L.	22	5/ 7	.714	0/ 2	.000	-/ 0	1	1	3	0	0	10	.455
EMBRY, M.	34	8/11	.727	3/ 3	1.000	-/11	0	0	2	0	0	19	.559
STRICKLAND, R.	38	6/12	.500	3/ 3	1.000	-/ 4	7	4	2	1	0	15	.395
JACKSON, T.	33	3/ 6	.500	2/ 6	.333	-/ 7	1	0	4	0	1	8	.242
GREENE, T.	12	1/ 1	1.000	2/ 3	.667	-/ 2	2	0	0	1	0	4	.333
LAUX, J.	4	0/ 0	.000	0/ 0	.000	-/ 0	1	0	1	0	0	0	.000
COMEGYS, D.	23	4/ 8	.500	0/ 2	.000	-/ 3	5	2	1	0	1	8	.348
Totals	200	32/55	.582	10/21	.476	-/33	19	10	15	3	2	74	.370

Oklahoma (69)   Coach: Billy Tubbs

	Min.	Total FG / FGA	Pct.	FT / FTA	Pct.	Reb. O / T	A	TO	PF	S	Blk	TP	PPM
KENNEDY, D.	37	10/13	.769	1/ 3	.333	-/ 9	3	2	4	0	0	21	.568
WATSON, C.	2	0/ 1	.000	0/ 0	.000	-/ 2	0	0	0	0	0	0	.000
JOHNSON, D.	22	4/11	.364	2/ 6	.333	-/ 6	0	1	4	0	0	10	.455
DAVIS, L.	35	3/ 9	.333	0/ 0	.000	-/ 3	4	2	4	1	0	6	.171
BOWIE, A.	40	5/14	.357	0/ 0	.000	-/ 4	5	2	1	2	0	10	.250
ROBERTS, R.	23	1/ 2	.500	2/ 2	1.000	-/ 4	0	1	4	0	1	4	.174
SIEGER, D.	1	0/ 0	.000	0/ 0	.000	-/ 1	0	0	1	0	0	0	.000
MCCALISTER, T.	40	9/17	.529	0/ 0	.000	-/ 3	7	2	4	0	0	18	.450
Totals	200	32/67	.478	5/11	.455	-/32	19	10	22	3	1	69	.345

Team Rebounds: DePaul 0; Oklahoma 5. Disqualified: None. Technical fouls: None.

	1st Half	2nd Half	Final
DePaul	38	36	74
Oklahoma	33	36	69

St. Joseph's (69)   Coach: Jim Boyle

	Min.	Total FG / FGA	Pct.	FT / FTA	Pct.	Reb. O / T	A	TO	PF	S	Blk	TP	PPM
MULLEE	37	2/ 5	.400	0/ 0	.000	-/ 4	2	5	4	0	0	4	.108
SLATTERY	11	0/ 1	.000	0/ 0	.000	-/ 3	0	0	2	0	0	0	.000
BLAKE	37	5/10	.500	5/ 7	.714	-/ 8	2	2	3	0	5	15	.405
MARTIN	24	6/11	.545	3/ 4	.750	-/ 9	2	5	4	1	0	15	.625
ARNOLD	29	4/ 9	.444	0/ 0	.000	-/ 5	1	3	3	1	0	8	.276
FLINT	27	1/ 3	.333	0/ 0	.000	-/ 0	7	0	2	1	0	2	.074
WILLIAMS	35	11/20	.550	3/ 5	.600	-/ 4	2	3	4	2	0	25	.714
Totals	200	29/59	.492	11/16	.688	-/33	16	18	22	5	5	69	.345

Cleveland State (75)   Coach: Kevin MacKey

	Min.	Total FG / FGA	Pct.	FT / FTA	Pct.	Reb. O / T	A	TO	PF	S	Blk	TP	PPM
SMITH, C.	34	8/16	.500	0/ 1	.000	-/15	2	2	1	1	0	16	.471
RANSEY, C.	31	5/15	.333	7/10	.700	-/ 8	1	2	2	1	0	17	.548
MUDD, E.	22	2/ 7	.286	0/ 1	.000	-/ 6	0	1	2	1	0	4	.182
BRYANT, E.	18	1/ 3	.333	6/ 6	1.000	-/ 2	2	1	1	2	0	8	.444
MCFADDEN, K.	30	10/15	.667	3/ 4	.750	-/ 2	3	3	1	2	0	23	.767
STEWART, P.	10	1/ 2	.500	0/ 0	.000	-/ 1	0	2	3	2	0	2	.200
CRAWFORD, B.	20	1/ 4	.250	0/ 0	.000	-/ 3	0	1	3	0	1	2	.100
HOOD, S.	22	1/ 1	1.000	1/ 5	.200	-/ 1	3	1	1	1	0	3	.136
SALTERS, R.	3	0/ 0	.000	0/ 0	.000	-/ 0	0	0	0	0	0	0	.000
CORBIN, S.	10	0/ 3	.000	0/ 2	.000	-/ 1	1	0	2	1	0	0	.000
Totals	200	29/66	.439	17/29	.586	-/39	12	13	17	11	1	75	.375

Team Rebounds: Cleveland St. 5; St. Joseph's 1. Disqualified: None. Technical fouls: None.

	1st Half	2nd Half	Final
St. Joseph's	26	43	69
Cleveland St.	26	49	75

Navy (97)   Coach: Paul Evans

	Min.	Total FG / FGA	Pct.	FT / FTA	Pct.	Reb. O / T	A	TO	PF	S	Blk	TP	PPM
LIEBERT, C.	9	0/ 0	.000	0/ 0	.000	0/ 2	1	0	1	0	0	0	.000
BUTLER, V.	39	11/15	.733	1/ 4	.250	0/ 9	1	3	3	0	0	23	.590
ROBINSON, D.	35	7/13	.538	21/27	.778	5/11	0	5	5	3	7	35	1.000
WHITAKOR, K.	32	3/11	.273	2/ 4	.500	2/ 3	7	5	2	0	0	8	.250
WOJCIK, D.	38	1/ 2	.500	6/ 6	1.000	0/ 3	5	4	3	1	0	8	.211
BAILEY, N.	23	3/ 4	.750	1/ 1	1.000	3/ 4	0	2	4	0	0	7	.304
REES, C.	18	2/ 4	.500	10/10	1.000	0/ 1	3	1	0	0	0	14	.778
TURNER, D.	2	1/ 1	1.000	0/ 0	.000	0/ 0	0	0	1	0	0	2	1.000
FENTON, N.	1	0/ 0	.000	0/ 0	.000	0/ 0	0	0	0	0	0	0	.000
WELLS, T.	1	0/ 0	.000	0/ 0	.000	0/ 0	0	0	0	0	0	0	.000
BRENNAN, R.	1	0/ 0	.000	0/ 0	.000	0/ 0	0	0	0	0	0	0	.000
JONES, B.	1	0/ 0	.000	0/ 0	.000	0/ 0	0	0	0	0	0	0	.000
Totals	200	28/50	.560	41/52	.788	10/33	17	20	19	4	7	97	.485

Syracuse (85)   Coach: Jim Boeheim

	Min.	Total FG / FGA	Pct.	FT / FTA	Pct.	Reb. O / T	A	TO	PF	S	Blk	TP	PPM
TRICHE, H.	23	3/ 7	.429	0/ 0	.000	3/ 3	0	1	5	2	0	6	.261
ALEXIS, W.	36	8/16	.500	3/ 4	.750	6/13	0	2	4	3	2	19	.528
SEIKALY, R.	27	2/ 8	.250	0/ 0	.000	0/ 4	0	2	5	2	3	4	.148
ADDISON, R.	39	4/11	.364	3/ 4	.750	3/ 3	3	1	4	2	0	11	.282
WASHINGTON, D.	39	11/22	.500	6/ 7	.857	2/ 5	8	3	5	1	0	28	.718
MONROE, G.	17	7/ 9	.778	1/ 2	.500	0/ 1	2	1	2	0	0	15	.882
WALKER, R.	9	0/ 1	.000	0/ 0	.000	0/ 1	1	1	5	0	0	0	.000
DOUGLAS, S.	7	1/ 3	.333	0/ 0	.000	0/ 1	0	1	4	1	0	2	.286
KATZ, J.	1	0/ 0	.000	0/ 0	.000	0/ 0	0	0	0	0	0	0	.000
KOHM, J.	1	0/ 0	.000	0/ 0	.000	0/ 0	0	0	0	0	0	0	.000
BARNES, R.	1	0/ 0	.000	0/ 0	.000	0/ 0	0	0	0	0	0	0	.000
Totals	200	36/77	.468	13/20	.650	14/31	14	12	34	11	5	85	.425

Team Rebounds: Navy 7; Syracuse 7. Disqualified: Navy—Robinson; Syracuse—Triche, Seikaly, Washington, Walker. Technical fouls: None.

	1st Half	2nd Half	Final
Navy	32	65	97
Syracuse	31	54	85

SECOND ROUND MIDWEST

Kansas (65)   Coach: Larry Brown

	Min.	Total FG/FGA	Pct.	FT/FTA	Pct.	Reb. O/T	A	TO	PF	S	Blk	TP	PPM
MANNING, D.	33	6/13	.462	2/ 4	.500	1/ 6	2	1	2	3	2	14	.424
KELLOGG, R.	31	6/ 7	.857	2/ 2	1.000	1/ 2	1	1	1	0	0	14	.452
DREILING, G.	19	1/ 5	.200	0/ 0	.000	3/ 4	0	3	4	0	0	2	.105
HUNTER, C.	34	3/ 7	.429	3/ 3	1.000	2/ 3	9	1	0	3	0	9	.265
THOMPSON, C.	33	5/11	.455	4/ 6	.667	0/ 7	3	3	3	0	1	14	.424
TURGEON, M.	6	1/ 2	.500	0/ 0	.000	0/ 1	1	0	1	0	0	2	.333
MARSHALL, A.	16	1/ 2	.500	2/ 2	1.000	1/ 3	1	2	3	0	0	4	.250
PIPER, C.	20	0/ 0	.000	0/ 0	.000	1/ 3	0	1	2	1	0	0	.000
CAMPBELL, A.	2	0/ 1	.000	2/ 2	1.000	1/ 1	1	0	0	0	0	2	1.000
HULL, R.	2	0/ 0	.000	0/ 0	.000	0/ 0	0	0	0	0	1	0	.000
BARRY, R.	2	0/ 0	.000	2/ 2	1.000	0/ 2	0	0	0	0	0	2	1.000
JOHNSON, J.	2	0/ 0	.000	2/ 4	.500	0/ 0	0	0	0	0	0	2	1.000
Totals	200	23/48	.479	19/25	.760	10/32	18	12	16	7	4	65	.325

Temple (43)   Coach: John Chaney

	Min.	Total FG/FGA	Pct.	FT/FTA	Pct.	Reb. O/T	A	TO	PF	S	Blk	TP	PPM
PERRY, T.	38	3/ 4	.750	1/ 2	.500	1/ 8	0	2	4	1	2	7	.184
COE, E.	34	2/10	.200	2/ 2	1.000	0/ 3	6	5	2	0	1	6	.176
RIVAS, R.	27	1/ 2	.500	1/ 2	.500	1/ 2	0	2	3	0	0	3	.111
BLACKWELL, N.	40	7/13	.538	0/ 0	.000	0/ 1	1	0	2	1	0	14	.350
EVANS, H.	39	2/ 8	.250	2/ 2	1.000	0/ 2	6	2	5	3	1	6	.154
CLIFTON, K.	8	0/ 0	.000	4/ 4	1.000	0/ 0	0	0	0	0	0	4	.500
VREESWYK, M.	5	1/ 5	.200	1/ 2	.500	0/ 2	0	0	1	0	1	3	.600
DOWDELL, J.	2	0/ 0	.000	0/ 0	.000	0/ 0	0	0	2	0	0	0	.000
PEARSALL, D.	2	0/ 2	.000	0/ 0	.000	2/ 3	0	0	0	0	0	0	.000
BRANTLEY, D.	5	0/ 1	.000	0/ 0	.000	0/ 0	1	2	0	0	0	0	.000
Totals	200	16/45	.356	11/14	.786	5/23	13	12	21	5	5	43	.215

Team Rebounds: Kansas 2; Temple 0. Disqualified: Temple—Evans. Technical fouls: Temple—Bench

	1st Half	2nd Half	Final
Kansas	26	39	65
Temple	21	22	43

Michigan State (80)   Coach: Jud Heathcote

	Min.	Total FG/FGA	Pct.	FT/FTA	Pct.	Reb. O/T	A	TO	PF	S	Blk	TP	PPM
POLEC, L.	32	4/ 7	.571	8/ 8	1.000	3/10	0	1	4	0	0	16	.500
CARR, V.	30	3/ 6	.500	7/ 8	.875	2/ 6	1	0	2	0	0	13	.433
FORDHAM, B.	37	4/ 6	.667	0/ 2	.000	1/ 4	0	1	2	0	0	8	.216
JOHNSON, D.	40	6/12	.500	0/ 0	.000	1/ 2	6	0	2	2	0	12	.300
SKILES, S.	40	7/14	.500	10/11	.909	0/ 2	5	6	2	1	0	24	.600
WALKER, R.	12	0/ 0	.000	2/ 2	1.000	0/ 3	0	0	1	1	0	2	.167
VALENTINE, C.	9	2/ 3	.667	1/ 2	.500	2/ 4	1	1	0	0	0	5	.556
Totals	200	26/48	.542	28/33	.848	9/31	13	9	13	4	0	80	.400

Georgetown (68)   Coach: John Thompson

	Min.	Total FG/FGA	Pct.	FT/FTA	Pct.	Reb. O/T	A	TO	PF	S	Blk	TP	PPM
WILLIAMS, R.	30	7/13	.538	1/ 2	.500	0/ 4	1	1	5	1	0	15	.500
HIGHSMITH, R.	21	3/ 3	1.000	0/ 0	.000	3/ 3	0	0	5	0	0	6	.286
DALTON, R.	33	3/ 9	.333	3/ 4	.750	5/10	0	3	3	0	1	9	.273
WINGATE, D.	30	5/12	.417	7/ 8	.875	1/ 3	3	1	3	2	0	17	.567
JACKSON, M.	29	1/ 7	.143	1/ 2	.500	0/ 3	9	2	2	1	0	3	.103
EDWARDS, J.	14	2/ 3	.667	0/ 0	.000	0/ 2	0	0	0	0	1	4	.286
JACKSON, J.	14	1/ 4	.250	0/ 0	.000	0/ 3	0	3	3	0	0	2	.143
BROADNAX, H.	14	3/ 7	.429	0/ 0	.000	1/ 1	1	0	2	1	0	6	.429
MCDONALD, P.	10	3/ 3	1.000	0/ 1	.000	2/ 2	0	0	1	0	0	6	.600
WINSTON, B.	2	0/ 0	.000	0/ 0	.000	0/ 0	0	0	0	0	0	0	.000
SMITH, C.	3	0/ 0	.000	0/ 0	.000	0/ 0	0	1	0	0	0	0	.000
Totals	200	28/61	.459	12/17	.706	12/26	17	7	25	5	2	68	.340

Team Rebounds: Michigan St. 3; Georgetown 3. Disqualified: Georgetown—Williams, Highsmith. Technical fouls: None.

	1st Half	2nd Half	Final
Michigan St.	32	48	80
Georgetown	30	38	68

North Carolina State (80)   Coach: Jim Valvano

	Min.	Total FG/FGA	Pct.	FT/FTA	Pct.	Reb. O/T	A	TO	PF	S	Blk	TP	PPM
BOLTON, B.	42	6/14	.429	12/15	.800	-/ 6	1	2	4	0	1	24	.571
SHACKLEFORD, C.	44	7/15	.467	1/ 2	.500	-/11	0	1	3	1	2	15	.341
WASHBURN, C.	49	8/13	.615	6/ 7	.857	-/ 7	0	1	2	2	2	22	.449
MCMILLAN, N.	38	2/ 4	.500	1/ 3	.333	-/ 5	4	3	5	1	0	5	.132
MEYERS, E.	31	2/ 6	.333	2/ 3	.667	-/ 7	0	6	2	1	1	6	.194
DEL, N.	22	1/ 4	.250	0/ 0	.000	-/ 2	1	1	1	2	0	2	.091
BROWN, C.	5	1/ 2	.500	0/ 0	.000	-/ 2	0	1	0	0	0	2	.400
LAMBIOTTE, W.	16	2/ 5	.400	0/ 1	.000	-/ 0	1	0	0	0	0	4	.250
WEEMS, K.	2	0/ 0	.000	0/ 0	.000	-/ 0	0	0	1	0	0	0	.000
JACKSON, Q.	1	0/ 0	.000	0/ 0	.000	-/ 0	0	1	0	0	0	0	.000
Totals	250	29/63	.460	22/31	.710	-/40	7	16	18	7	6	80	.320

Arkansas-Little Rock (66)   Coach: Mike Newell

	Min.	Total FG/FGA	Pct.	FT/FTA	Pct.	Reb. O/T	A	TO	PF	S	Blk	TP	PPM
CLARKE, M.	23	4/ 5	.800	2/ 4	.500	-/ 6	0	2	5	0	0	10	.435
MEYERS, P.	46	5/20	.250	6/ 6	1.000	-/11	1	3	3	1	0	16	.348
MCCURDY, P.	23	4/ 6	.667	0/ 0	.000	-/ 5	0	1	5	0	1	8	.348
SPRINGER, P.	35	0/ 4	.000	0/ 0	.000	-/ 3	5	2	1	0	0	0	.000
JACKSON, M.	49	10/29	.345	3/ 5	.600	-/ 2	1	3	5	2	0	23	.469
WORTHY, K.	34	2/ 4	.500	1/ 2	.500	-/ 4	1	4	4	0	0	5	.147
SMITH, R.	5	1/ 1	1.000	0/ 0	.000	-/ 1	0	0	0	0	0	2	.400
CAMPBELL, K.	17	1/ 4	.250	0/ 0	.000	-/ 2	0	4	2	1	0	2	.118
KIDD, C.	18	0/ 1	.000	0/ 0	.000	-/ 3	0	1	4	2	0	0	.000
Totals	250	27/74	.365	12/17	.706	-/37	8	20	29	6	1	66	.264

Team Rebounds: N.C. State—7; Ark.-Little Rock 7. Disqualified: N.C. State—McMillan; Ark.-Little Rock—Clarke, McCurdy, Jackson. Technical fouls: None.

	1st Half	2nd Half	1st OT	2nd OT	Final
N.C. State	37	19	8	16	80
Ark.-Little Rock	33	23	8	2	66

Iowa State (72)   Coach: Johnny Orr

	Min.	Total FG/FGA	Pct.	FT/FTA	Pct.	Reb. O/T	A	TO	PF	S	Blk	TP	PPM
GRAYER, J.	37	5/12	.417	6/ 7	.857	-/ 5	0	-	0	-	-	16	.432
VIRGIL, R.	34	7/ 8	.875	0/ 0	.000	-/ 3	4	-	2	-	-	14	.412
HILL, S.	26	3/ 6	.500	5/ 8	.625	-/ 4	0	-	4	-	-	11	.423
THOMPKINS, G.	29	4/ 5	.800	0/ 0	.000	-/ 0	3	-	3	-	-	8	.276
HORNACEK, J.	35	3/ 6	.500	1/ 2	.500	-/ 2	6	-	4	-	-	7	.200
ROBINSON, E.	15	2/ 3	.667	5/ 7	.714	-/ 2	0	-	2	-	-	9	.600
MOSS, D.	15	2/ 2	1.000	2/ 2	1.000	-/ 0	0	-	3	-	-	6	.400
SCHAFER, T.	9	0/ 1	.000	1/ 2	.500	-/ 1	0	-	1	-	-	1	.111
Totals	200	26/43	.605	20/28	.714	-/17	13	-	19	-	-	72	.360

Michigan (69)   Coach: Bill Freider

	Min.	Total FG/FGA	Pct.	FT/FTA	Pct.	Reb. O/T	A	TO	PF	S	Blk	TP	PPM
REILFORD, R.	30	5/ 8	.625	3/ 4	.750	-/ 4	0	1	2	0	0	13	.433
WADE, B.	18	2/ 3	.667	0/ 0	.000	-/ 1	0	1	4	0	0	4	.222
TARPLEY, R.	38	9/18	.500	7/ 9	.778	-/14	1	3	5	3	0	25	.658
JOUBERT, J.	31	5/ 8	.625	1/ 2	.500	-/ 1	1	4	5	1	0	11	.355
GRANT, G.	36	1/ 9	.111	2/ 3	.667	-/ 2	5	4	5	1	1	4	.111
HENDERSON, R.	26	3/ 4	.750	2/ 3	.667	-/ 5	0	0	2	0	1	8	.308
RICE, G.	7	1/ 3	.333	0/ 0	.000	-/ 4	0	1	0	0	0	2	.286
THOMPSON, G.	14	0/ 4	.000	2/ 2	1.000	-/ 2	1	1	0	0	0	2	.143
Totals	200	26/57	.456	17/23	.739	-/33	8	15	26	5	2	69	.345

Team Rebounds: Iowa State 4; Michigan 4. Disqualified: Michigan—Tarpley, Joubert, Grant. Technical fouls: None.

	1st Half	2nd Half	Final
Iowa State	40	32	72
Michigan	31	38	69

REGIONAL SEMIFINAL SOUTHEAST

Kentucky (68)   Coach: Eddie Sutton

	Min.	Total FG/FGA	Pct.	FT/FTA	Pct.	Reb. O/T	A	TO	PF	S	Blk	TP	PPM
BENNETT, W.	39	6/11	.545	2/4	.500	-/12	1	2	3	0	0	14	.359
WALKER, K.	40	9/19	.474	4/4	1.000	-/7	1	4	4	2	3	22	.550
BLACKMON, J.	35	5/7	.714	1/4	.250	-/3	0	0	1	0	0	11	.314
DAVENDER, E.	24	4/8	.500	5/6	.833	-/3	2	2	3	2	0	13	.542
HARDEN, R.	37	1/4	.250	0/1	.000	-/1	9	2	1	1	0	2	.054
JENKINS, C.	23	2/3	.667	2/2	1.000	-/4	1	0	5	0	0	6	.261
MADISON, R.	2	0/0	.000	0/0	.000	-/0	0	1	1	0	0	0	.000
Totals	200	27/52	.519	14/21	.667	-/30	14	11	18	5	3	68	.340

Alabama (63)   Coach: Wimp Sanderson

	Min.	Total FG/FGA	Pct.	FT/FTA	Pct.	Reb. O/T	A	TO	PF	S	Blk	TP	PPM
FARMER, J.	36	3/9	.333	1/2	.500	-/4	0	1	3	1	0	7	.194
JOHNSON, B.	40	6/14	.429	4/4	1.000	-/9	0	5	4	2	0	16	.400
MCKEY, D.	40	4/8	.500	4/4	1.000	-/12	1	0	3	0	1	12	.300
GOTTFRIED, M.	18	1/3	.333	0/0	.000	-/2	0	1	0	0	0	2	.111
CONER, T.	38	7/12	.583	6/7	.857	-/4	4	2	3	2	0	20	.526
JACKSON, J.	16	1/4	.250	1/2	.500	-/1	0	2	2	0	1	3	.188
ANSLEY, M.	11	1/3	.333	1/2	.500	-/1	0	0	2	1	1	3	.273
DUDLEY, C.	1	0/1	.000	0/0	.000	-/0	0	0	2	0	0	0	.000
Totals	200	23/54	.426	17/21	.810	-/33	5	11	19	6	3	63	.315

Team Rebounds: Kentucky 0; Alabama 1. Disqualified: Kentucky—Jenkins. Technical fouls: None.

	1st Half	2nd Half	Final
Kentucky	32	36	68
Alabama	28	35	63

Louisiana State (70)   Coach: Dale Brown

	Min.	Total FG/FGA	Pct.	FT/FTA	Pct.	Reb. O/T	A	TO	PF	S	Blk	TP	PPM
WILLIAMS, J.	30	2/15	.133	1/2	.500	-/7	3	0	2	0	0	5	.167
REDDEN, D.	39	10/16	.625	7/10	.700	-/6	1	3	2	1	0	27	.692
TAYLOR, D.	40	9/18	.500	5/6	.833	-/3	2	1	1	5	0	23	.575
WILSON, A.	34	4/14	.286	0/0	.000	-/10	0	0	3	2	0	8	.235
BLANTON, R.	34	2/3	.667	0/0	.000	-/4	2	1	0	2	0	4	.118
VARGAS, J.	6	0/1	.000	0/0	.000	-/0	0	0	0	0	0	0	.000
BROWN, O.	16	1/1	1.000	1/1	1.000	-/2	3	0	3	0	0	3	.188
WOODSIDE, B.	1	0/0	.000	0/0	.000	-/0	0	0	0	0	0	0	.000
Totals	200	28/68	.412	14/19	.737	-/32	11	5	11	10	0	70	.350

Georgia Tech (64)   Coach: Bobby Cremins

	Min.	Total FG/FGA	Pct.	FT/FTA	Pct.	Reb. O/T	A	TO	PF	S	Blk	TP	PPM
HAMMONDS, T.	33	7/9	.778	2/2	1.000	-/8	0	2	1	0	0	16	.485
FERRELL, D.	38	3/6	.500	0/0	.000	-/4	4	6	3	1	1	6	.158
SALLEY, J.	38	5/6	.833	1/3	.333	-/10	2	3	4	0	1	11	.289
PRICE, M.	38	8/16	.500	4/4	1.000	-/5	4	1	4	0	1	20	.526
DALRYMPLE, B.	31	3/7	.429	0/2	.000	-/3	4	4	5	0	0	6	.194
NEAL, C.	13	2/4	.500	0/0	.000	-/2	4	1	1	2	0	4	.308
FORD, A.	6	0/0	.000	1/2	.500	-/1	0	0	0	0	0	1	.167
MANSELL, J.	1	0/0	.000	0/0	.000	-/0	0	0	0	0	0	0	.000
REESE, W.	1	0/0	.000	0/0	.000	-/0	0	0	0	0	0	0	.000
MARTINSON, J.	1	0/0	.000	0/0	.000	-/0	0	0	0	0	0	0	.000
Totals	200	28/48	.583	8/13	.615	-/33	18	17	18	3	3	64	.320

Team Rebounds: Louisiana St. 0; Georgia Tech 1. Disqualified: Georgia Tech—Dalrymple. Technical fouls: None.

	1st Half	2nd Half	Final
Louisiana St.	36	34	70
Georgia Tech	30	34	64

REGIONAL SEMIFINAL WEST

Auburn (70)   Coach: Sonny Smith

	Min.	Total FG/FGA	Pct.	FT/FTA	Pct.	Reb. O/T	A	TO	PF	S	Blk	TP	PPM
MORRIS, C.	39	3/8	.375	3/3	1.000	-/8	0	2	4	1	1	9	.231
PERSON, C.	37	12/22	.545	1/2	.500	-/11	0	1	1	2	0	25	.676
MOORE, J.	32	5/10	.500	1/2	.500	-/9	4	5	2	1	0	11	.344
WHITE, G.	33	3/4	.750	6/7	.857	-/1	10	3	2	1	0	12	.364
FORD, F.	39	3/8	.375	3/4	.750	-/6	1	5	0	5	0	9	.231
HOWARD, T.	8	0/1	.000	0/0	.000	-/0	0	1	1	0	0	0	.000
JONES, M.	12	2/5	.400	0/0	.000	-/1	2	3	2	0	1	4	.333
Totals	200	28/58	.483	14/18	.778	-/36	17	20	12	10	2	70	.350

UNLV (63)   Coach: Jerry Tarkanian

	Min.	Total FG/FGA	Pct.	FT/FTA	Pct.	Reb. O/T	A	TO	PF	S	Blk	TP	PPM
JONES, A.	39	8/19	.421	0/3	.000	-/4	4	1	1	1	0	16	.410
GILLIAM, A.	37	9/13	.692	3/4	.750	-/3	0	1	1	0	0	21	.568
FLOWERS, J.	20	1/1	1.000	0/0	.000	-/0	0	1	2	0	0	2	.100
WADE, M.	36	0/0	.000	0/1	.000	-/3	12	6	5	2	0	0	.000
BANKS, F.	35	9/21	.429	2/2	1.000	-/1	6	1	2	1	0	20	.571
HUDSON, E.	24	2/5	.400	0/0	.000	-/9	2	1	4	2	0	4	.167
GRAHAM, G.	9	0/2	.000	0/0	.000	-/2	1	1	4	0	0	0	.000
Totals	200	29/61	.475	5/10	.500	-/22	25	12	19	6	0	63	.315

Team Rebounds: Auburn 5; UNLV 6. Disqualified: UNLV—Wade. Technical fouls: None.

	1st Half	2nd Half	Final
Auburn	25	45	70
UNLV	34	29	63

North Carolina (79)   Coach: Dean Smith

	Min.	Total FG/FGA	Pct.	FT/FTA	Pct.	Reb. O/T	A	TO	PF	S	Blk	TP	PPM
WOLF, J.	34	9/15	.600	2/3	.667	2/4	2	2	4	0	0	20	.588
DAUGHERTY, B.	39	8/14	.571	3/7	.429	6/15	6	2	4	0	1	19	.487
LEBO, J.	35	8/13	.615	2/4	.500	1/4	4	1	2	1	0	18	.514
HALE, S.	31	2/10	.200	0/0	.000	4/6	5	4	5	0	0	4	.129
SMITH, K.	37	4/12	.333	4/4	1.000	1/4	8	5	5	1	0	12	.324
DAYE, J.	1	0/0	.000	0/0	.000	0/0	0	0	0	0	0	0	.000
BUCKNALL, S.	1	0/0	.000	0/0	.000	0/0	0	0	0	0	0	0	.000
SMITH, R.	1	0/2	.000	0/0	.000	0/0	0	0	1	0	0	0	.000
POPSON, D.	7	0/0	.000	0/0	.000	0/1	0	2	0	0	0	0	.000
HUNTER, C.	7	2/2	1.000	0/0	.000	0/1	0	2	2	0	0	4	.571
MARTIN, W.	6	1/1	1.000	0/0	.000	1/3	0	3	0	0	0	2	.333
MADDEN, K.	1	0/0	.000	0/0	.000	0/0	0	0	0	0	0	0	.000
Totals	200	34/69	.493	11/18	.611	15/38	25	18	26	2	1	79	.395

Louisville (94)   Coach: Denny Crum

	Min.	Total FG/FGA	Pct.	FT/FTA	Pct.	Reb. O/T	A	TO	PF	S	Blk	TP	PPM
CROOK, H.	34	5/9	.556	10/10	1.000	3/9	2	3	4	1	0	20	.588
THOMPSON, B.	33	10/16	.625	4/5	.800	2/9	5	1	4	1	2	24	.727
ELLISON, P.	37	6/12	.500	3/4	.750	2/6	3	3	3	2	3	15	.405
WAGNER, M.	36	5/12	.417	4/4	1.000	0/1	5	2	2	1	0	14	.389
HALL, J.	37	5/11	.455	2/2	1.000	0/3	5	1	1	1	0	12	.324
MCSWAIN, M.	9	1/3	.333	2/4	.500	1/1	1	2	1	0	0	4	.444
WALLS, K.	5	1/1	1.000	2/2	1.000	0/0	0	0	0	0	0	4	.800
KIMBRO, T.	6	0/1	.000	1/2	.500	1/1	0	2	0	0	1	1	.167
VALENTINE, R.	1	0/0	.000	0/0	.000	0/0	0	0	0	0	0	0	.000
PAYNE, K.	1	0/0	.000	0/0	.000	0/0	0	0	0	0	0	0	.000
ABRAM, M.	1	0/0	.000	0/0	.000	0/1	1	0	0	0	0	0	.000
Totals	200	33/65	.508	28/33	.848	9/31	22	12	17	6	5	94	.470

Team Rebounds: Louisville 2; N. Carolina 2. Disqualified: N. Carolina—K. Smith, Hale; Louisville—None. Technical fouls: None.

	1st Half	2nd Half	Final
N. Carolina	43	36	79
Louisville	43	51	94

REGIONAL SEMIFINAL EAST

Duke (74)   Coach: Mike Krzyzewski

	Min.	Total FG / FGA	Pct.	FT / FTA	Pct.	Reb. O / T	A	TO	PF	S	Blk	TP	PPM
HENDERSON, D.	33	5/14	.357	1/ 6	.167	-/ 4	1	3	3	2	0	11	.333
ALARIE, M.	37	6/17	.353	9/ 9	1.000	-/ 8	1	1	2	2	0	21	.568
BILAS, J.	19	2/ 3	.667	2/ 2	1.000	-/ 4	0	0	4	1	1	6	.316
AMAKER, T.	33	0/ 5	.000	4/ 6	.667	-/ 2	6	0	2	1	0	4	.121
DAWKINS, J.	39	11/20	.550	3/ 4	.750	-/10	1	5	0	2	1	25	.641
SNYDER, Q.	4	1/ 1	1.000	0/ 1	.000	-/ 1	1	2	2	1	0	2	.500
STRICKLAND, K.	1	0/ 0	.000	0/ 0	.000	-/ 0	0	0	0	0	0	0	.000
FERRY, D.	23	2/ 6	.333	0/ 1	.000	-/ 4	2	3	1	0	0	4	.174
WILLIAMS, W.	1	0/ 0	.000	0/ 0	.000	-/ 0	0	1	0	0	0	0	.000
KING, B.	10	0/ 0	.000	1/ 4	.250	-/ 2	1	0	1	0	0	1	.100
Totals	200	27/66	.409	20/33	.606	-/35	13	15	15	9	2	74	.370

DePaul (67)   Coach: Joey Meyer

	Min.	Total FG / FGA	Pct.	FT / FTA	Pct.	Reb. O / T	A	TO	PF	S	Blk	TP	PPM
LAMPLEY, L.	25	3/ 5	.600	0/ 0	.000	-/ 1	1	1	2	0	2	6	.240
HOLMES, K.	20	5/ 8	.625	0/ 1	.000	-/ 3	0	3	5	2	2	10	.500
EMBRY, M.	36	5/ 7	.714	2/ 2	1.000	-/ 6	1	3	4	2	0	12	.333
STRICKLAND, R.	37	7/11	.636	1/ 4	.250	-/ 3	3	3	3	2	1	15	.405
JACKSON, T.	31	2/ 6	.333	2/ 2	1.000	-/ 4	2	4	5	0	0	6	.194
GREENE, T.	20	4/ 7	.571	0/ 0	.000	-/ 2	1	1	4	0	0	8	.400
LAUX, A.	3	0/ 1	.000	0/ 0	.000	-/ 0	0	0	1	0	0	0	.000
COMEGYS, D.	28	4/ 6	.667	2/ 4	.500	-/ 3	2	5	4	0	2	10	.357
Totals	200	30/51	.588	7/13	.538	-/22	10	20	28	6	7	67	.335

Cleveland State (70)   Coach: Kevin MacKey

	Min.	Total FG / FGA	Pct.	FT / FTA	Pct.	Reb. O / T	A	TO	PF	S	Blk	TP	PPM
SMITH, C.	31	8/15	.533	0/ 0	.000	-/ 7	0	2	2	4	1	16	.516
RANSEY, C.	31	3/11	.273	2/ 2	1.000	-/ 5	1	4	5	1	0	8	.258
MUDD, E.	29	5/13	.385	1/ 2	.500	-/11	0	1	4	0	0	11	.379
BRYANT, E.	24	3/ 5	.600	0/ 0	.000	-/ 1	3	2	2	0	1	6	.250
MCFADDEN, K.	35	8/15	.533	0/ 1	.000	-/ 4	0	1	1	1	0	16	.457
STEWART, P.	12	3/ 5	.600	1/ 4	.250	-/ 3	0	1	2	0	0	7	.583
CRAWFORD, B.	11	0/ 3	.000	1/ 2	.500	-/ 1	0	0	2	0	2	1	.091
HOOD, S.	15	1/ 2	.500	1/ 1	1.000	-/ 1	1	1	0	1	0	3	.200
SALTERS, R.	6	1/ 4	.250	0/ 0	.000	-/ 4	2	0	2	0	0	2	.333
CORBIN, S.	6	0/ 2	.000	0/ 0	.000	-/ 2	0	0	2	1	0	0	.000
Totals	200	32/75	.427	6/12	.500	-/39	7	12	22	8	4	70	.350

Navy (71)   Coach: Paul Evans

	Min.	Total FG / FGA	Pct.	FT / FTA	Pct.	Reb. O / T	A	TO	PF	S	Blk	TP	PPM
LIEBERT, C.	9	0/ 0	.000	0/ 0	.000	-/ 1	0	1	2	0	0	0	.000
BUTLER, V.	40	7/15	.467	2/ 3	.667	-/ 3	2	1	3	1	0	16	.400
ROBINSON, J.	34	7/11	.636	8/10	.800	-/14	1	3	3	1	9	22	.647
WHITAKOR, K.	40	10/15	.667	3/ 3	1.000	-/ 1	10	4	2	1	0	23	.575
WOJCIK, D.	40	1/ 5	.200	2/ 3	.667	-/ 5	7	2	0	1	0	4	.100
BAILEY, N.	20	1/ 5	.200	0/ 2	.000	-/ 2	0	2	1	0	0	2	.100
REES, C.	11	2/ 2	1.000	0/ 0	.000	-/ 0	1	1	1	0	0	4	.364
TURNER, D.	6	0/ 1	.000	0/ 0	.000	-/ 3	0	1	2	0	0	0	.000
Totals	200	28/54	.519	15/21	.714	-/29	21	16	13	4	9	71	.355

Team Rebounds: Duke 10; DePaul 5. Disqualified: DePaul—Holmes, Jackson. Technical fouls: None.

	1st Half	2nd Half	Final
Duke	37	37	74
DePaul	32	35	67

Team Rebounds: Navy 7; Cleveland St. 5. Disqualified: Cleveland St.—Ransey. Technical fouls: None.

	1st Half	2nd Half	Final
Cleveland St.	30	40	70
Navy	39	32	71

REGIONAL SEMIFINAL MIDWEST

Kansas (96)   Coach: Larry Brown

	Min.	Total FG / FGA	Pct.	FT / FTA	Pct.	Reb. O / T	A	TO	PF	S	Blk	TP	PPM
MANNING, D.	25	7/12	.583	3/ 3	1.000	2/ 3	0	2	5	1	1	17	.680
KELLOGG, R.	24	7/12	.583	0/ 0	.000	4/ 5	2	1	5	0	0	14	.583
DREILING, G.	32	3/10	.300	4/ 7	.571	0/ 7	1	2	0	0	1	10	.313
HUNTER, C.	43	4/ 9	.444	3/ 4	.750	3/ 4	10	0	3	3	0	11	.256
THOMPSON, C.	43	10/19	.526	6/ 9	.667	2/ 4	4	0	2	0	1	26	.605
TURGEON, M.	7	0/ 1	.000	0/ 0	.000	0/ 0	1	1	2	1	0	0	.000
MARSHALL, A.	31	7/12	.583	2/ 2	1.000	7/13	1	1	2	0	0	16	.516
PIPER, C.	20	1/ 2	.500	0/ 0	.000	0/ 2	1	0	2	1	0	2	.100
Totals	225	39/77	.506	18/25	.720	18/38	20	7	21	6	3	96	.427

Michigan State (86)   Coach: Jud Heathcote

	Min.	Total FG / FGA	Pct.	FT / FTA	Pct.	Reb. O / T	A	TO	PF	S	Blk	TP	PPM
POLEC, L.	39	6/ 7	.857	4/ 5	.800	5/11	2	3	5	2	0	16	.410
CARR, V.	42	7/13	.538	3/ 6	.500	2/ 4	3	2	3	0	0	17	.405
FORDHAM, B.	45	7/ 9	.778	1/ 3	.333	2/ 5	0	0	3	0	0	15	.333
JOHNSON, D.	37	4/11	.364	2/ 2	1.000	1/ 4	9	2	4	1	0	10	.270
SKILES, S.	38	6/14	.429	8/10	.800	0/ 2	7	4	3	1	0	20	.526
WALKER, R.	11	0/ 1	.000	2/ 2	1.000	1/ 3	0	0	1	0	0	2	.182
VALENTINE, C.	6	2/ 4	.500	0/ 0	.000	0/ 1	0	2	0	0	0	4	.667
BROWN, M.	7	1/ 2	.500	0/ 1	.000	1/ 1	0	0	1	0	0	2	.286
Totals	225	33/61	.541	20/29	.690	12/31	21	13	20	4	0	86	.382

North Carolina State (70)   Coach: Jim Valvano

	Min.	Total FG / FGA	Pct.	FT / FTA	Pct.	Reb. O / T	A	TO	PF	S	Blk	TP	PPM
BOLTON, B.	28	3/ 7	.429	1/ 2	.500	1/ 8	2	2	5	0	0	7	.250
SHACKLEFORD, C.	40	9/15	.600	4/ 6	.667	3/ 7	0	6	3	1	0	22	.550
WASHBURN, C.	40	10/16	.625	0/ 0	.000	3/ 6	1	1	2	0	2	20	.500
MCMILLAN, N.	40	1/ 4	.250	3/ 7	.429	1/ 4	9	1	2	3	1	5	.125
MEYERS, E.	37	7/11	.636	2/ 3	.667	1/ 1	2	2	2	1	0	16	.432
DEL, N.	9	0/ 1	.000	0/ 1	.000	0/ 1	0	0	2	0	0	0	.000
BROWN, C.	6	0/ 0	.000	0/ 0	.000	0/ 0	1	0	1	0	0	0	.000
Totals	200	30/54	.556	10/19	.526	9/27	15	12	17	5	3	70	.350

Iowa State (66)   Coach: Johnny Orr

	Min.	Total FG / FGA	Pct.	FT / FTA	Pct.	Reb. O / T	A	TO	PF	S	Blk	TP	PPM
GRAYER, J.	40	6/16	.375	9/10	.900	4/ 8	2	1	2	0	0	21	.525
VIRGIL, R.	29	3/ 9	.333	0/ 0	.000	1/ 3	5	1	4	1	0	6	.207
HILL, S.	33	8/13	.615	5/ 6	.833	2/ 9	0	3	3	2	1	21	.636
THOMPKINS, G.	31	3/ 6	.500	0/ 0	.000	1/ 3	4	4	4	0	0	6	.194
HORNACEK, J.	38	3/ 9	.333	0/ 0	.000	2/ 4	8	2	2	3	0	6	.158
ROBINSON, E.	16	2/ 6	.333	0/ 0	.000	4/ 8	0	2	4	0	0	4	.250
MOSS, D.	7	0/ 3	.000	0/ 0	.000	2/ 3	0	0	0	0	0	0	.000
SCHAFER, T.	6	1/ 2	.500	0/ 0	.000	1/ 1	0	1	0	0	0	2	.333
Totals	200	26/64	.406	14/16	.875	17/39	19	14	19	6	1	66	.330

Team Rebounds: Kansas 2; Michigan St. 5. Disqualified: Kansas—Manning, Kellogg; Michigan St.—Polec. Technical fouls: Kansas—Coach Brown.

	1st Half	2nd Half	1st OT	Final
Kansas	46	34	16	96
Michigan St.	37	43	6	86

Team Rebounds: N.C. State 3; Iowa State 3. Disqualified: N.C. State—Bolton. Technical fouls: None.

	1st Half	2nd Half	Final
N.C. State	40	30	70
Iowa State	29	37	66

REGIONAL FINAL SOUTHEAST

Kentucky (57) Coach: Eddie Sutton

	Min.	Total FG/FGA	Pct.	FT/FTA	Pct.	Reb. O/T	A	TO	PF	S	Blk	TP	PPM
BENNETT, W.	36	3/13	.231	2/ 4	.500	-/12	1	-	4	-	-	8	.222
WALKER, K.	38	8/11	.727	4/ 6	.667	-/ 7	3	-	2	-	-	20	.526
BLACKMON, J.	31	5/12	.417	0/ 1	.000	-/ 2	0	-	2	-	-	10	.323
DAVENDER, E.	35	1/ 6	.167	3/ 4	.750	-/ 4	2	-	4	-	-	5	.143
HARDEN, R.	38	6/ 8	.750	0/ 0	.000	-/ 5	5	-	1	-	-	12	.316
LOCK, R.	3	0/ 0	.000	0/ 0	.000	-/ 0	0	-	1	-	-	0	.000
JENKINS, C.	19	1/ 2	.500	0/ 1	.000	-/ 3	1	-	3	-	-	2	.105
Totals	200	24/52	.462	9/16	.563	-/33	12	12	17	-	-	57	.285

Louisiana State (59) Coach: Dale Brown

	Min.	Total FG/FGA	Pct.	FT/FTA	Pct.	Reb. O/T	A	TO	PF	S	Blk	TP	PPM
WILLIAMS, J.	39	7/15	.467	2/ 4	.500	-/ 4	1	-	2	-	-	16	.410
REDDEN, D.	34	6/13	.462	3/ 4	.750	-/ 8	3	-	3	-	-	15	.441
TAYLOR, D.	34	0/ 9	.000	4/ 4	1.000	-/ 1	3	-	3	-	-	4	.118
WILSON, A.	35	6/ 9	.667	0/ 0	.000	-/ 2	0	-	2	-	-	12	.343
BLANTON, R.	28	5/ 5	1.000	2/ 2	1.000	-/ 8	3	-	4	-	-	12	.429
VARGAS, J.	1	0/ 0	.000	0/ 0	.000	-/ 0	0	-	1	-	-	0	.000
BROWN, O.	18	0/ 2	.000	0/ 0	.000	-/ 3	1	-	2	-	-	0	.000
WOODSIDE, B.	5	0/ 0	.000	0/ 0	.000	-/ 0	1	-	0	-	-	0	.000
BUKUMIROVICH, N.	6	0/ 0	.000	0/ 0	.000	-/ 0	0	-	0	-	-	0	.000
Totals	200	24/53	.453	11/14	.786	-/26	12	9	17	-	-	59	.295

Team Rebounds: Louisiana St. 6; Kentucky 1. Disqualified: None. Technical fouls: None.

	1st Half	2nd Half	Final
Kentucky	34	23	57
Louisiana St.	33	26	59

REGIONAL FINAL WEST

Auburn (76) Coach: Sonny Smith

	Min.	Total FG/FGA	Pct.	FT/FTA	Pct.	Reb. O/T	A	TO	PF	S	Blk	TP	PPM
MORRIS, C.	34	7/10	.700	3/ 3	1.000	6/ 9	1	4	4	4	1	17	.500
PERSON, C.	38	11/24	.458	1/ 2	.500	0/ 4	1	2	3	0	0	23	.605
MOORE, J.	31	4/ 8	.500	3/ 5	.600	2/ 6	2	0	2	0	0	11	.355
WHITE, G.	34	3/ 6	.500	2/ 2	1.000	0/ 2	9	4	2	1	0	8	.235
FORD, F.	34	6/10	.600	1/ 2	.500	2/ 3	5	0	4	1	0	13	.382
HOWARD, T.	12	1/ 1	1.000	0/ 0	.000	0/ 0	2	0	3	0	0	2	.167
JONES, M.	17	1/ 3	.333	0/ 0	.000	0/ 1	0	0	3	0	1	2	.118
Totals	200	33/62	.532	10/14	.714	10/25	20	10	21	6	2	76	.380

Louisville (84) Coach: Denny Crum

	Min.	Total FG/FGA	Pct.	FT/FTA	Pct.	Reb. O/T	A	TO	PF	S	Blk	TP	PPM
CROOK, H.	39	8/12	.667	4/ 5	.800	5/11	3	1	3	1	0	20	.513
THOMPSON, B.	26	5/10	.500	3/ 4	.750	2/ 7	4	4	4	1	0	13	.500
ELLISON, P.	35	7/14	.500	1/ 3	.333	3/10	0	2	2	3	2	15	.429
WAGNER, M.	40	4/ 9	.444	8/ 8	1.000	1/ 2	9	2	2	0	0	16	.400
HALL, J.	36	7/12	.583	0/ 0	.000	0/ 0	2	1	1	0	0	14	.389
MCSWAIN, M.	15	2/ 3	.667	0/ 0	.000	2/ 4	2	1	2	0	0	4	.267
WALLS, K.	4	1/ 2	.500	0/ 0	.000	0/ 0	0	0	1	0	0	2	.500
KIMBRO, T.	5	0/ 1	.000	0/ 0	.000	0/ 1	0	1	0	0	0	0	.000
Totals	200	34/63	.540	16/20	.800	13/35	20	12	15	5	2	84	.420

Team Rebounds: Louisville 2; Auburn 2. Disqualified: None. Technical fouls: None.

	1st Half	2nd Half	Final
Auburn	43	33	76
Louisville	44	40	84

REGIONAL FINAL EAST

Duke (71) Coach: Mike Krzyzewski

	Min.	Total FG/FGA	Pct.	FT/FTA	Pct.	Reb. O/T	A	TO	PF	S	Blk	TP	PPM
HENDERSON, D.	26	4/10	.400	0/ 0	.000	-/ 4	2	2	3	1	0	8	.308
ALARIE, M.	31	8/20	.400	2/ 2	1.000	-/ 8	0	1	2	4	0	18	.581
BILAS, J.	26	1/ 4	.250	2/ 4	.500	-/10	0	0	2	0	0	4	.154
AMAKER, J.	37	1/ 6	.167	2/ 2	1.000	-/ 5	5	4	3	0	0	4	.108
DAWKINS, J.	39	13/25	.520	2/ 2	1.000	-/ 7	3	3	1	1	0	28	.718
FERRY, D.	21	1/ 2	.500	0/ 0	.000	-/ 5	1	0	4	1	0	2	.095
NESSLEY, M.	3	0/ 0	.000	0/ 1	.000	-/ 2	0	0	0	0	0	0	.000
KING, B.	12	2/ 2	1.000	1/ 2	.500	-/ 3	0	0	4	0	1	5	.417
STRICKLAND, K.	2	1/ 2	.500	0/ 0	.000	-/ 0	0	0	0	0	0	2	1.000
SMITH, J.	1	0/ 0	.000	0/ 0	.000	-/ 0	1	1	0	0	0	0	.000
WILLIAMS, W.	2	0/ 0	.000	0/ 0	.000	-/ 1	0	0	1	0	1	0	.000
Totals	200	31/71	.437	9/13	.692	-/45	12	11	20	7	2	71	.355

Navy (50) Coach: Paul Evans

	Min.	Total FG/FGA	Pct.	FT/FTA	Pct.	Reb. O/T	A	TO	PF	S	Blk	TP	PPM
LIEBERT, C.	9	1/ 2	.500	0/ 0	.000	-/ 0	0	2	3	1	0	2	.222
BUTLER, V.	32	1/ 5	.200	6/ 8	.750	-/ 6	1	2	3	0	0	8	.250
ROBINSON, D.	39	10/17	.588	3/ 4	.750	-/10	0	2	3	3	2	23	.590
WHITAKER, K.	29	5/12	.417	0/ 0	.000	-/ 3	7	2	2	0	0	10	.345
WOJCIK, D.	29	1/ 3	.333	0/ 1	.000	-/ 0	5	4	3	1	0	2	.069
TURNER, D.	20	1/ 1	1.000	1/ 3	.333	-/ 1	0	1	2	0	1	3	.150
BAILEY, N.	13	0/ 0	.000	0/ 1	.000	-/ 2	1	2	1	1	0	0	.000
REES, C.	10	0/ 5	.000	0/ 0	.000	-/ 0	0	0	1	0	0	0	.000
FENTON, N.	9	0/ 0	.000	0/ 0	.000	-/ 1	1	0	0	0	0	0	.000
JONES, B.	1	0/ 1	.000	2/ 2	1.000	-/ 0	0	0	1	0	0	2	2.000
PRATHER, C.	3	0/ 0	.000	0/ 0	.000	-/ 1	0	0	0	0	0	0	.000
WELLS, T.	2	0/ 1	.000	0/ 0	.000	-/ 1	0	1	1	0	0	0	.000
GREGORY, B.	2	0/ 1	.000	0/ 0	.000	-/ 0	0	1	0	0	0	0	.000
MANHERTZ, C.	1	0/ 0	.000	0/ 0	.000	-/ 1	0	0	0	0	0	0	.000
BRENNAN, R.	1	0/ 0	.000	0/ 0	.000	-/ 0	0	0	0	0	0	0	.000
Totals	200	19/48	.396	12/19	.632	-/26	15	17	20	6	3	50	.250

Team Rebounds: Duke 4; Navy 3. Disqualified: None. Technical fouls: None.

	1st Half	2nd Half	Final
Duke	34	37	71
Navy	22	28	50

REGIONAL FINAL MIDWEST
Kansas (75) Coach: Larry Brown

	Min.	Total FG/FGA	Pct.	FT/FTA	Pct.	Reb. O/T	A	TO	PF	S	Blk	TP	PPM
MANNING, D.	32	11/17	.647	0/ 0	.000	5/ 6	1	4	4	2	1	22	.688
KELLOGG, R.	35	5/ 9	.556	2/ 4	.500	1/ 3	2	0	2	0	0	12	.343
DREILING, G.	33	7/11	.636	5/ 6	.833	3/12	2	2	4	0	0	19	.576
HUNTER, C.	40	2/ 4	.500	1/ 3	.333	0/ 0	9	3	4	2	0	5	.125
THOMPSON, C.	38	3/ 7	.429	3/ 4	.750	0/ 4	1	1	2	1	0	9	.237
TURGEON, M.	1	0/ 0	.000	2/ 2	1.000	0/ 0	0	0	0	0	0	2	2.000
MARSHALL, A.	12	2/ 4	.500	0/ 0	.000	0/ 1	1	1	3	0	0	4	.333
PIPER, C.	9	0/ 0	.000	2/ 2	1.000	0/ 0	0	2	1	0	0	2	.222
Totals	200	30/52	.577	15/21	.714	9/26	16	13	20	5	1	75	.375

North Carolina State (67) Coach: Jim Valvano

	Min.	Total FG/FGA	Pct.	FT/FTA	Pct.	Reb. O/T	A	TO	PF	S	Blk	TP	PPM
BOLTON, B.	39	6/12	.500	0/ 0	.000	0/ 3	2	2	3	0	0	12	.308
SHACKELFORD, C.	40	8/13	.615	4/ 5	.800	2/ 6	1	2	4	0	0	20	.500
WASHBURN, C.	40	5/11	.455	7/10	.700	3/ 5	2	3	2	1	0	17	.425
MCMILLAN, N.	40	4/ 6	.667	3/ 4	.750	2/ 5	7	3	4	2	2	11	.275
MEYERS, E.	33	2/ 7	.286	2/ 4	.500	2/ 3	4	3	5	0	0	6	.182
DEL, N.	7	0/ 1	.000	0/ 0	.000	0/ 1	0	1	1	0	0	0	.000
BROWN, C.	1	0/ 0	.000	1/ 2	.500	0/ 0	0	0	0	0	0	1	1.000
Totals	200	25/50	.500	17/25	.680	9/23	16	14	19	3	2	67	.335

Team Rebounds: Kansas 4; N.C. State 3. Disqualified: N.C. State—Meyers. Technical fouls: None.

	1st Half	2nd Half	Final
Kansas	35	40	75
N.C. State	33	34	67

FINAL FOUR
Louisiana State (77) Coach: Dale Brown

	Min.	Total FG/FGA	Pct.	FT/FTA	Pct.	Reb. O/T	A	TO	PF	S	Blk	TP	PPM
WILLIAMS, J.	35	7/17	.412	0/ 1	.000	4/ 9	6	4	4	0	0	14	.400
REDDEN, D.	28	10/20	.500	2/ 3	.667	5/ 6	1	2	3	0	0	22	.786
BLANTON, R.	38	3/ 5	.600	3/ 6	.500	5/12	2	0	4	1	1	9	.237
TAYLOR, D.	39	7/17	.412	2/ 2	1.000	1/ 1	4	1	2	3	0	16	.410
WILSON, A.	39	7/15	.467	1/ 1	1.000	3/ 3	0	0	3	1	0	15	.385
WOODSIDE, B.	2	0/ 0	.000	0/ 0	.000	0/ 0	0	0	0	0	0	0	.000
BROWN, O.	13	0/ 1	.000	1/ 2	.500	0/ 3	0	1	0	0	0	1	.077
VARGAS, J.	6	0/ 0	.000	0/ 0	.000	0/ 0	0	0	0	0	0	0	.000
Totals	200	34/75	.453	9/15	.600	18/34	13	8	16	5	1	77	.385

Duke (71) Coach: Mike Krzyzewski

	Min.	Total FG/FGA	Pct.	FT/FTA	Pct.	Reb. O/T	A	TO	PF	S	Blk	TP	PPM
HENDERSON, D.	33	3/12	.250	7/ 8	.875	2/ 4	3	6	1	2	0	13	.394
ALARIE, M.	35	4/13	.308	4/ 6	.667	3/ 8	1	3	3	4	1	12	.343
BILAS, J.	29	1/ 2	.500	5/ 7	.714	2/ 5	1	1	2	1	0	7	.241
AMAKER, T.	37	2/ 5	.400	3/ 4	.750	0/ 2	6	3	1	3	0	7	.189
DAWKINS, J.	38	11/17	.647	2/ 4	.500	2/ 3	0	1	3	0	0	24	.632
FERRY, D.	15	4/ 5	.800	0/ 1	.000	2/ 3	0	1	1	0	0	8	.533
KING, B.	9	0/ 0	.000	0/ 0	.000	1/ 3	1	3	0	0	0	0	.000
STRICKLAND, K.	4	0/ 1	.000	0/ 0	.000	0/ 0	0	2	0	0	0	0	.000
Totals	200	25/55	.455	21/30	.700	12/28	12	17	14	10	1	71	.355

Louisville (88) Coach: Denny Crum

	Min.	Total FG/FGA	Pct.	FT/FTA	Pct.	Reb. O/T	A	TO	PF	S	Blk	TP	PPM
CROOK, H.	32	8/13	.615	0/ 1	.000	6/ 9	3	2	3	0	0	16	.500
THOMPSON, B.	36	10/11	.909	2/ 5	.400	2/10	4	3	4	1	1	22	.611
ELLISON, P.	34	5/11	.455	1/ 2	.500	5/13	1	1	3	0	1	11	.324
WAGNER, M.	36	8/16	.500	6/ 6	1.000	0/ 4	11	4	1	1	0	22	.611
HALL, J.	32	6/11	.545	2/ 2	1.000	0/ 1	2	2	1	0	0	14	.438
MCSWAIN, M.	14	1/ 2	.500	1/ 1	1.000	2/ 4	0	0	2	0	1	3	.214
WALLS, K.	8	0/ 2	.000	0/ 0	.000	0/ 0	4	0	0	0	0	0	.000
KIMBRO, T.	8	0/ 2	.000	0/ 0	.000	0/ 0	1	2	1	1	0	0	.000
Totals	200	38/68	.559	12/17	.706	15/41	26	14	15	3	3	88	.440

Team Rebounds: Louisville 6; Louisiana St. 2. Disqualified: None. Technical fouls: None.

	1st Half	2nd Half	Final
Louisiana St.	44	33	77
Louisville	36	52	88

Kansas (67) Coach: Larry Brown

	Min.	Total FG/FGA	Pct.	FT/FTA	Pct.	Reb. O/T	A	TO	PF	S	Blk	TP	PPM
MANNING, D.	23	2/ 9	.222	0/ 0	.000	1/ 5	1	1	5	1	1	4	.174
KELLOGG, R.	33	11/15	.733	0/ 0	.000	2/ 3	3	3	4	2	0	22	.667
DREILING, G.	30	1/ 7	.143	4/ 4	1.000	1/ 6	2	3	5	0	3	6	.200
HUNTER, C.	22	2/ 5	.400	1/ 4	.250	2/ 8	3	4	5	0	0	5	.227
THOMPSON, C.	39	5/12	.417	3/ 3	1.000	1/ 5	3	3	1	1	0	13	.333
TURGEON, M.	19	1/ 1	1.000	0/ 0	.000	0/ 0	5	4	3	0	0	2	.105
MARSHALL, A.	19	6/10	.600	1/ 1	1.000	2/ 2	0	2	3	0	0	13	.684
PIPER, C.	13	1/ 1	1.000	0/ 0	.000	1/ 1	0	0	0	0	0	2	.154
CAMPBELL, A.	1	0/ 0	.000	0/ 0	.000	0/ 0	1	1	0	0	0	0	.000
HULL, R.	1	0/ 0	.000	0/ 0	.000	0/ 0	0	0	0	0	0	0	.000
Totals	200	29/60	.483	9/12	.750	10/30	18	21	26	4	4	67	.335

Team Rebounds: Duke 7; Kansas 4. Disqualified: Kansas—Manning, Dreiling, Hunter. Technical fouls: Duke—Bilas.

	1st Half	2nd Half	Final
Duke	36	35	71
Kansas	33	34	67

NATIONAL CHAMPIONSHIP

Louisville (72) Coach: Denny Crum

	Min.	Total FG/FGA	Pct.	FT/FTA	Pct.	Reb. O/T	A	TO	PF	S	Blk	TP	PPM
CROOK, H.	32	5/9	.556	0/3	.000	2/12	5	9	2	0	0	10	.313
THOMPSON, B.	31	6/8	.750	1/3	.333	1/4	2	2	4	0	2	13	.419
ELLISON, P.	35	10/14	.714	5/6	.833	5/11	1	0	4	1	2	25	.714
WAGNER, M.	30	2/6	.333	5/5	1.000	0/3	2	5	4	1	1	9	.300
HALL, J.	33	2/4	.500	0/0	.000	2/2	2	3	2	2	0	4	.121
McSWAIN, M.	17	2/4	.500	1/2	.500	1/3	2	1	1	1	0	5	.294
WALLS, K.	8	0/1	.000	0/0	.000	0/1	0	4	2	0	0	0	.000
KIMBRO, T.	14	2/4	.500	2/2	1.000	0/2	2	0	1	0	2	6	.429
Totals	200	29/50	.580	14/21	.667	11/38	16	24	20	5	7	72	.360

Duke (69) Coach: Mike Krzyzewski

	Min.	Total FG/FGA	Pct.	FT/FTA	Pct.	Reb. O/T	A	TO	PF	S	Blk	TP	PPM
HENDERSON, D.	28	5/15	.333	4/4	1.000	3/4	4	5	5	3	0	14	.500
ALARIE, M.	33	4/11	.364	4/4	1.000	2/6	0	1	5	1	0	12	.364
BILAS, J.	26	2/3	.667	0/0	.000	1/3	0	1	4	0	0	4	.154
AMAKER, T.	38	3/10	.300	5/6	.833	1/2	7	3	3	7	0	11	.289
DAWKINS, J.	40	10/19	.526	4/4	1.000	2/4	0	3	1	2	0	24	.600
FERRY, D.	20	1/2	.500	2/2	1.000	2/4	0	1	2	0	0	4	.200
KING, B.	13	0/1	.000	0/1	.000	0/0	1	0	2	0	0	0	.000
WILLIAMS, W.	2	0/1	.000	0/0	.000	0/0	0	0	0	0	0	0	.000
Totals	200	25/62	.403	19/21	.905	11/23	12	14	22	13	0	69	.345

Team Rebounds: Louisville 1; Duke 4. Disqualified: Duke—Henderson, Alarie. Technical fouls: None.

	1st Half	2nd Half	Final
Louisville	34	38	72
Duke	37	32	69

○ ALL-STAR TEAMS ○

ALL TOURNAMENT
MARK ALARIE	DUKE
TOMMY AMAKER	DUKE
JOHNNY DAWKINS	DUKE
★ PERVIS ELLISON	LOUISVILLE
BILLY THOMPSON	LOUISVILLE

EAST REGIONAL
MARK ALARIE	DUKE
★ JOHNNY DAWKINS	DUKE
KEN McFADDEN	CLEVELAND ST.
DAVID ROBINSON	NAVY
KYLOR WHITAKER	NAVY

SOUTHEAST REGIONAL
WINSTON BENNETT	KENTUCKY
RICKY BLANTON	LOUISIANA ST.
MARK PRICE	GEORGIA TECH
★ DON REDDEN	LOUISIANA ST.
KENNY WALKER	KENTUCKY

WEST REGIONAL
HERBERT CROOK	LOUISVILLE
BRAD DAUGHERTY	N. CAROLINA
PERVIS ELLISON	LOUISVILLE
★ CHUCK PERSON	AUBURN
BILLY THOMPSON	LOUISVILLE

MIDWEST REGIONAL
★ DANNY MANNING	KANSAS
CHARLES SHACKLEFORD	N.C. STATE
SCOTT SKILES	MICH. ST.
CALVIN THOMPSON	KANSAS
CHRIS WASHBURN	N.C. STATE

★ Most Outstanding Player(s)

○ INDIVIDUAL RECORDS ○

SCORING

Most points in a single game
1	REGGIE LEWIS, NORTHEASTERN (vs. OKLAHOMA)	35
1	DAVID ROBINSON, NAVY (vs. SYRACUSE)	35
3	KENNY WALKER, KENTUCKY (vs. WESTERN KY.)	32
4	4 tied for fourth place.	

Most total points in the tournament
1	JOHNNY DAWKINS, DUKE	153
2	BILLY THOMPSON, LOUISVILLE	110
2	DAVID ROBINSON, NAVY	110
4	DON REDDEN, LOUISIANA ST.	108
5	2 tied for fifth place.	

Highest scoring average (minimum 2 games)
1	LEN BIAS, MARYLAND (57-2)	28.50
2	DAVID ROBINSON, NAVY (110-4)	27.50
3	JOHNNY DAWKINS, DUKE (153-6)	25.50
4	WALTER BERRY, ST. JOHN'S (51-2)	25.50
5	SCOTT SKILES, MICHIGAN ST. (75-3)	25.00

FIELD GOALS

Most field goals in a single game
1	JOHNNY DAWKINS, DUKE (vs. NAVY)	13
2	5 tied for second place.	

Most total field goals in the tournament
1	JOHNNY DAWKINS, DUKE	66
2	BILLY THOMPSON, LOUISVILLE	45
3	CHUCK PERSON, AUBURN	44
4	DON REDDEN, LOUISIANA ST.	42
5	PERVIS ELLISON, LOUISVILLE	40

Most field goal attempts in a single game
1	REGGIE LEWIS, NORTHEASTERN (vs. OKLAHOMA)	34
2	MYRON JACKSON, ARK.-LITTLE ROCK (vs. N.C. STATE)	29
3	BYRON LARKIN, XAVIER (OHIO) (vs. ALABAMA)	26
4	JOHNNY DAWKINS, DUKE (vs. NAVY)	25
5	CHUCK PERSON, AUBURN (vs. LOUISVILLE)	24

Most total field goal attempts in tournament
1	JOHNNY DAWKINS, DUKE	110
2	CHUCK PERSON, AUBURN	90
3	MARK ALARIE, DUKE	85
4	DON REDDEN, LOUISIANA ST.	81
5	DERRICK TAYLOR, LOUISIANA ST.	77

Highest field goal percentage in a single game (minimum 10 attempts)
1	KENNY WALKER, KENTUCKY (vs. WESTERN KY.) (11-11)	1.000
2	BILLY THOMPSON, LOUISVILLE (vs. LOUISIANA ST.) (10-11)	.909
3	BRAD DAUGHERTY, N. CAROLINA (vs. UTAH) (12-14)	.857
4	DARRYL JOHNSON, MICHIGAN ST. (vs. WASHINGTON) (11-13)	.846
4	TODD MITCHELL, PURDUE (vs. LOUISIANA ST.) (11-13)	.846

Highest field goal percentage in the tournament (minimum 20 attempts)

1	RICKY BLANTON, LOUISIANA ST. (19-27)	.704
2	KENNY WALKER, KENTUCKY (35-50)	.700
3	BILLY THOMPSON, LOUISVILLE (45-65)	.692
4	TONY WYSINGER, ILLINOIS (15-22)	.682
5	BRAD DAUGHERTY, N. CAROLINA (24-36)	.667

FREE THROWS

Most free throws in a single game

1	DAVID ROBINSON, NAVY (vs. SYRACUSE)	21
2	JIM LES, BRADLEY (vs. UTEP)	14
3	LEN BIAS, MARYLAND (vs. PEPPERDINE)	12
3	BENNIE BOLTON, N.C. STATE (vs. ARK.-LITTLE ROCK)	12
5	3 tied for fifth place.	

Most total free throws in the tournament

1	DAVID ROBINSON, NAVY	40
2	MILT WAGNER, LOUISVILLE	33
3	MARK ALARIE, DUKE	27
4	SCOTT SKILES, MICHIGAN ST.	25
5	2 tied for fifth place.	

Most free throws attempted in a single game

1	DAVID ROBINSON, NAVY (vs. SYRACUSE)	27
2	JIM LES, BRADLEY (vs. UTEP)	17
3	BENNIE BOLTON, N.C. STATE (vs. ARK.-LITTLE ROCK)	15
4	4 tied for fourth place.	

Most free throws attempted in the tournament

1	DAVID ROBINSON, NAVY	55
2	MILT WAGNER, LOUISVILLE	36
3	DON REDDEN, LOUISIANA ST.	33
4	KENNY WALKER, KENTUCKY	32
4	MARK ALARIE, DUKE	32

Highest free throw percentage in a single game (minimum 7 attempts)

1	HERBERT CROOK, LOUISVILLE (vs. N. CAROLINA) (10-10)	1.000
1	CLIFF REES, NAVY (vs. SYRACUSE) (10-10)	1.000
3	MARK ALARIE, DUKE (vs. DEPAUL) (9-9)	1.000
3	LEN BIAS, MARYLAND (vs. UNLV) (9-9)	1.000
5	3 tied for fifth place.	

Highest free throw percentage in the tournament (minimum 15 attempts)

1	MILT WAGNER, LOUISVILLE (33-36)	.917
2	LEN BIAS, MARYLAND (21-23)	.913
3	DERRICK TAYLOR, LOUISIANA ST. (17-19)	.895
4	SCOTT SKILES, MICHIGAN ST. (25-28)	.893
5	MARK PRICE, GEORGIA TECH (14-16)	.875

REBOUNDS

Most rebounds in a single game

1	TIM PERRY, TEMPLE (vs. JACKSONVILLE)	18
2	JOE WOLF, N. CAROLINA (vs. ALA.-BIRMINGHAM)	16
3	4 tied for third place.	

Most total rebounds in the tournament

1	PERVIS ELLISON, LOUISVILLE	57
2	MARK ALARIE, DUKE	53
3	HERBERT CROOK, LOUISVILLE	49
4	BILLY THOMPSON, LOUISVILLE	47
4	DAVID ROBINSON, NAVY	47

Most rebounds per game (minimum 2 games)

1	TIM PERRY, TEMPLE (26-2)	13.00
2	DAVID ROBINSON, NAVY (47-4)	11.75
3	ROY TARPLEY, MICHIGAN (23-2)	11.50
4	BRAD DAUGHERTY, N. CAROLINA (33-3)	11.00
5	WENDELL ALEXIS, SYRACUSE (22-2)	11.00

ASSISTS

Most assists in a single game

1	JIM LES, BRADLEY (vs. UTEP)	12
1	GREG BECKWITH, RICHMOND (vs. ST. JOSEPH'S)	12
1	MARK WADE, UNLV (vs. AUBURN)	12
1	MARK WADE, UNLV (vs. MARYLAND)	12
1	MARK JACKSON, ST. JOHN'S (vs. AUBURN)	12

Most total assists in the tournament

1	CEDRIC HUNTER, KANSAS	42
2	GERLAD WHITE, AUBURN	34
2	MILT WAGNER, LOUISVILLE	34
4	MARK WADE, UNLV	32
4	TOMMY AMAKER, DUKE	32

Most assists per game (minimum 2 appearances)

1	MARK WADE, UNLV (32-3)	10.67

2	ANDRE TURNER, MEMPHIS STATE (19-2)	9.50
3	KYLOR WHITAKOR, NAVY (28-3)	9.33
4	GERLAD WHITE, AUBURN (34-4)	8.50
5	MARK JACKSON, ST. JOHN'S (17-2)	8.50

TURNOVERS

Most turnovers in a single game

1	HERBERT CROOK, LOUISVILLE (vs. DUKE)	9
2	DAVIS DRAFTON, MARIST (vs. GEORGIA TECH)	8
2	CLAUDE WILLIAMS, N.C. A&T (vs. KANSAS)	8
4	3 tied for fourth place.	

Most total turnovers in the tournament

1	MILT WAGNER, LOUISVILLE	18
1	DAVID HENDERSON, DUKE	18
1	HERBERT CROOK, LOUISVILLE	18
4	BILLY THOMPSON, LOUISVILLE	16
4	TOMMY AMAKER, DUKE	16

SHOTS BLOCKED

Most shots blocked in a single game

1	DAVID ROBINSON, NAVY (vs. CLEVELAND ST.)	9
2	DAVID ROBINSON, NAVY (vs. SYRACUSE)	7
3	DAVID ROBINSON, NAVY (vs. TULSA)	5
3	RODNEY BLAKE, ST. JOSEPH'S (vs. CLEVELAND ST.)	5
3	RONY SEIKALY, SYRACUSE (vs. BROWN)	5

Most total shots blocked in the tournament

1	DAVID ROBINSON, NAVY	23
2	PERVIS ELLISON, LOUISVILLE	11
3	BILLY THOMPSON, LOUISVILLE	9
3	RODNEY BLAKE, ST. JOSEPH'S	9
5	RONY SEIKALY, SYRACUSE	8

STEALS

Most steals in a single game

1	TOMMY AMAKER, DUKE (vs. LOUISVILLE)	7
2	6 tied for second place.	

Most total steals in the tournament

1	DERRICK TAYLOR, LOUISIANA ST.	15
2	MARK ALARIE, DUKE	12
3	TOMMY AMAKER, DUKE	11
4	TEDDY BLOODSAW, MISS. VALLEY ST.	10
5	DANNY MANNING, KANSAS	9

✪ TEAM RECORDS ✪

SCORING

Most points in a single game

1	SYRACUSE (vs. BROWN)	101
2	NAVY (vs. SYRACUSE)	97
2	ALABAMA (vs. XAVIER [OHIO])	97

Most total points in the tournament

1	LOUISVILLE	513
2	DUKE	459
3	LOUISIANA ST.	383

Highest scoring average (minimum 2 games)

1	SYRACUSE (186-2)	93.00
2	MEMPHIS STATE (176-2)	88.00
3	LOUISVILLE (513-6)	85.50

FIELD GOALS

Most field goals in a single game

1	ALABAMA (vs. XAVIER [OHIO])	43
2	SYRACUSE (vs. BROWN)	40
3	KANSAS (vs. MICHIGAN ST.)	39

Most total field goals in the tournament

1	LOUISVILLE	203
2	DUKE	171
3	LOUISIANA ST.	155

Most field goals attempted in a single game

1	SYRACUSE (vs. BROWN)	78
1	MEMPHIS STATE (vs. BALL ST.)	78
1	LOUISIANA ST. (vs. PURDUE)	78

Most total field goals attempted in the tournament

1	LOUISVILLE	366
2	DUKE	363
3	LOUISIANA ST.	339

Highest field goal percentage in a single game

1	ALABAMA (vs. XAVIER [OHIO]) (43-64)	.672
2	NAVY (vs. TULSA) (32-50)	.640
3	ARK.-LITTLE ROCK (vs. NOTRE DAME) (33-53)	.623

Highest field goal percentage in a tournament (minimum 2 games)

1	MICHIGAN ST. (90-161)	.559
2	LOUISVILLE (203-366)	.555
3	DEPAUL (88-160)	.550

FREE THROWS

Most free throws in a single game
1	NAVY (vs. SYRACUSE)	41
2	MICHIGAN ST. (vs. GEORGETOWN)	28
2	LOUISVILLE (vs. N. CAROLINA)	28

Most total free throws in the tournament
1	DUKE	117
2	LOUISVILLE	107
3	NAVY	91

Most free throws attempted in a single game
1	NAVY (vs. SYRACUSE)	52
2	DUKE (vs. MISS. VALLEY ST.)	37
3	NAVY (vs. TULSA)	36

Most total free throws attempted in the tournament
1	DUKE	166
2	LOUISVILLE	138
3	NAVY	128

Highest free throw percentage in a single game
1	VILLANOVA (vs. GEORGIA TECH) (11-11)	1.000
2	FAIRFIELD (vs. ILLINOIS) (13-14)	.929
3	DUKE (vs. LOUISVILLE) (19-21)	.905

Highest free throw percentage in the tournament (minimum 2 games)
1	MICHIGAN ST. (58-74)	.784
2	ST. JOHN'S (28-36)	.778
3	LOUISVILLE (107-138)	.776

Fewest free throws in a single game
1	ILLINOIS (vs. ALABAMA)	0
2	ARIZONA (vs. AUBURN)	3
3	TULSA (vs. NAVY)	4

Lowest free throw percentage in a single game
1	DREXEL (vs. LOUISVILLE) (5-15)	.333
2	ARIZONA (vs. AUBURN) (3-7)	.429
3	OKLAHOMA (vs. DEPAUL) (5-11)	.455

Lowest free throw percentage in the tournament (minimum 2 games)
1	ALA.-BIRMINGHAM (27-46)	.587
2	DEPAUL (37-63)	.587
3	OLD DOMINION (37-61)	.607

REBOUNDS

Most rebounds in a single game
1	SYRACUSE (vs. BROWN)	56
2	N. CAROLINA (vs. ALA.-BIRMINGHAM)	52
3	BALL ST. (vs. MEMPHIS STATE)	46

Most rebounds per game (minimum 2 games)
1	SYRACUSE (87-2)	43.50
2	N. CAROLINA (119-3)	39.67
3	MEMPHIS STATE (77-2)	38.50

ASSISTS

Most assists in a single game
1	SYRACUSE (vs. BROWN)	31
2	LOUISVILLE (vs. LOUISIANA ST.)	26
2	NAVY (vs. TULSA)	26

Most assists per game (minimum 2 games)
1	SYRACUSE (45-2)	22.50
2	N. CAROLINA (64-3)	21.33
3	BRADLEY (42-2)	21.00

TURNOVERS

Most turnovers in a single game
1	LOUISVILLE (vs. DUKE)	24
2	DUKE (vs. MISS. VALLEY ST.)	23
3	OLD DOMINION (vs. DUKE)	22

Most turnovers per game (minimum 2 games)
1	GEORGIA TECH (56-3)	18.67
2	OLD DOMINION (34-2)	17.00
2	ARK.-LITTLE ROCK (34-2)	17.00

SHOTS BLOCKED

Most shots blocked in a single game
1	NAVY (vs. CLEVELAND ST.)	9
2	6 tied for second place.	

Most shots blocked per game (minimum 2 games)
1	NAVY (24-4)	6.00
2	MEMPHIS STATE (12-2)	6.00
3	SYRACUSE (11-2)	5.50

STEALS

Most steals in a single game
1	DUKE (vs. LOUISVILLE)	13
2	MISS. VALLEY ST. (vs. DUKE)	12
2	LOUISIANA ST. (vs. PURDUE)	12

Most steals per game
1	SYRACUSE (20-2)	10.00
2	VILLANOVA (18-2)	9.00
3	CLEVELAND ST. (25-3)	8.33

1987

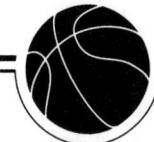

FIRST ROUND | SECOND ROUND | REGIONAL SEMIFINAL | REGIONAL FINAL | FINAL FOUR | REGIONAL FINAL | REGIONAL SEMIFINAL | SECOND ROUND | FIRST ROUND

WEST

First Round
- 1 UNLV 95
- 16 Idaho State 70
- 8 Georgia 79
- 9 Kansas St. 82 (ot)
- 5 Virginia 60
- 12 Wyoming 64
- 4 UCLA 92
- 13 Central Mich. 73
- 6 Oklahoma 74
- 11 Tulsa 69
- 8 Pittsburgh 93
- 14 Marist 68
- 7 UTEP 98 (ot)
- 10 Arizona 91
- 2 Iowa 99
- 18 Santa Clara 76

Second Round
- UNLV 80
- Kansas St. 61
- Wyoming 78
- UCLA 68
- Oklahoma 96
- Pittsburgh 93
- UTEP 82
- Iowa 84

Regional Semifinal
- UNLV 92
- Wyoming 78
- Oklahoma 91
- Iowa 93 (ot)

Regional Final
- UNLV 84
- Iowa 81

Final Four
- UNLV 93

MIDWEST

First Round
- 1 Indiana 92
- 16 Fairfield 58
- 8 Auburn 62
- 9 San Diego 61
- 5 Duke 58
- 12 Texas A&M 51
- 4 Missouri 69
- 13 Xavier (Ohio) 70
- 6 St. John's 57
- 11 Wichita St. 55
- 3 DePaul 76
- 14 Louisiana Tech 62
- 7 Georgia Tech 79
- 10 Louisiana St. 85
- 2 Temple 75
- 15 Southern-B.R. 56

Second Round
- Indiana 107
- Auburn 90
- Duke 65
- Xavier (Ohio) 60
- St. John's 75
- DePaul 83 (ot)
- Louisiana St. 72
- Temple 62

Regional Semifinal
- Indiana 88
- Duke 82
- DePaul 58
- Louisiana St. 63

Regional Final
- Indiana 77
- Louisiana St. 76

Final Four
- Indiana 97

FINAL FOUR

- Indiana 74
- Syracuse 73

SOUTHEAST

First Round
- 1 Georgetown 75
- 16 Bucknell 53
- 8 Kentucky 77
- 9 Ohio St. 91
- 5 Kansas 66
- 12 Houston 55
- 4 Clemson 60
- 13 SW Missouri St. 65
- 6 Providence 90
- 11 Ala.-Birmingham 68
- 3 Illinois 67
- 14 Austin Peay 68
- 7 New Orleans 83
- 10 Brigham Young 79
- 2 *Alabama 88
- 15 N. Carolina A&T 71

Second Round
- Georgetown 82
- Ohio St. 79
- Kansas 67
- SW Missouri St. 63
- Providence 90 (ot)
- Austin Peay 87
- New Orleans 76
- *Alabama 101

Regional Semifinal
- Georgetown 70
- Kansas 57
- Providence 103
- *Alabama 82

Regional Final
- Georgetown 73
- Providence 88

Final Four
- Providence 63

EAST

First Round
- 1 N. Carolina 113
- 16 Pennsylvania 82
- 8 Navy 82
- 9 Michigan 97
- 5 Notre Dame 84
- 12 Middle Tenn. St. 71
- 4 TCU 76
- 13 Marshall 60
- 6 Florida 82
- 11 N.C. State 70
- 3 Purdue 104
- 14 Northeastern 95
- 7 West Virginia 62
- 10 Western Ky. 64
- 2 Syracuse 79
- 15 Ga. Southern 73

Second Round
- N. Carolina 109
- Michigan 97
- Notre Dame 58
- TCU 57
- Florida 85
- Purdue 66
- Western Ky. 86
- Syracuse 104

Regional Semifinal
- N. Carolina 74
- Notre Dame 68
- Florida 81
- Syracuse 87

Regional Final
- N. Carolina 75
- Syracuse 79

Final Four
- Syracuse 77

*Alabama's participation in 1987 tournament vacated.

Somewhere in Indiana on March 31st, 1987, a banner headline may have proclaimed: *Hoosier Homeboys Hometown Heroes!* The previous night, the Indiana coach, old reliable Bob Knight, proved to all Hoosierdom that he not only could draw the most from the least, but that he was also a master of the unexpected, as his bombing, freelancing, unlikely champions from Indiana, Ohio, and Louisiana finished their tightrope walk to the NCAA title.

That season, Knight himself was coming through a period of personal and professional turmoil. After he coached the 1984 Olympic team, some observers thought he was burned out. His personal life was in a shambles, the Hoosiers, at 19-14, had their worst record in his tenure as coach, and, for a time, his whole strict system seemed to be falling apart.

In addition, new rules changes made his traditional style of play obsolete. In 1984–85 the NCAA instituted a 45-second time clock on offense during the regular season, and the following year the change was extended to the postseason tournament. In 1986–87, the rules committee made another important change, altering a field goal to a 3-point shot at distances beyond 19 feet, 9 inches from the hoop.

Also, by 1985, Indiana high school hot shots were no longer shoo-ins to be Hoosiers. Recruiting was increasingly national, as the top teams signed up talented players from everywhere. Things looked bleak indeed for Knight's future at Indiana.

For a time the Hoosier coach didn't seem to care. He neglected his recruiting, leaving the task of finding new student-athletes to his assistants. He didn't come to practices. He stopped doing what he did best—teaching—and he stopped preparing his teams for their opponents.

Then Bob Knight adjusted. In Bloomington, where his ball-control offense and in-your-face man-to-man defense had become gospel, he suddenly did things he promised he would never do. He had long sworn that he would never recruit jucos, but in 1987, two of his key players were junior college transfers. He had always proclaimed that he would never use a zone, but he started mixing up his defenses and switching between a man and a zone in 1987. He had always taught a methodical, set-up offense—but in 1987 his players suddenly started pushing the ball downcourt, jogging old-timers' memories of Branch McCracken and the Hurryin' Hoosiers. And Knight, while declaring his unalterable opposition to the 3-point shot, ordered eagle-eye Steve Alford to set up around the perimeter and let fly with a steady barrage of long-range bombs.

The 3-pointer did, in fact, significantly change the face of college basketball. The little man became a bigger part of the game. And it became increasingly difficult to defend a lead against a team with sharpshooters. Some coaches, like Rick Pitino of Providence and Jerry Tarkanian of UNLV, instituted new-style offenses based on running downcourt and throwing up 20-footers to finish off three-on-one fast breaks. Pitino even made outside shooting a key part of his practices, and it paid off as gunners Billy Donovan and Delray Brooks hit enough treys (3-pointers) to carry the Friars into the Final Four. Scores, which had shot up with the institution of the shot clock, went through the roof; a 1986–87 midseason review showed an increase of 6.6 points per game above the previous year. For the season, one in every seven shots attempted was from behind the 19-foot 9-inch line.

Blustery Bob Knight made sure that Indiana was in the center of the action. Although he publicly doubted his squad's ability in the weeks before the NCAAs, the Hoosiers still entered the fracas as the Midwest region's No. 1 seed.

After a first-round romp over overmatched Fairfield, Indiana fell behind Auburn by 14 points, but native son Steve Alford led his team back with 31 points (including 7 of 11 3-pointers) in front of 34,000 Hoosier fanatics at the Hoosier Dome in Indianapolis. In the regionals in Cincinnati, Rick Calloway returned to his hometown and scored a season high 21 to lead Indiana to a comeback victory over Duke. In the regional final against LSU, Calloway went down with an aggravated knee injury with the score 59-51 LSU. It was up to 63-51 before he returned. With the help of a momentum-breaking, technical-drawing, telephone-trashing tantrum by Knight (that later cost the university a fine and the coach an NCAA slap on the wrist), Indiana clawed their way back. (LSU coach Dale Brown nearly busted a gut at Knight's antics, asking, "When is somebody going to say, 'Sit your butt down, pal, or you're out'?") It would be fair to point out that the Indiana intimidator convinced officials all tournament long that his team was as clean as a baby's bottom; his players were whistled for far fewer infractions than the opposition. It would also be fair to say that the underdog Tigers lost because Coach Brown went into a delay game when his team recovered the ball after Rick Calloway missed a dunk with 4:38 left; as their 9-point lead disappeared, LSU took only one more shot from the floor.

LSU still led 76-75 in the last minute when they missed the front end of a one-and-one and Indiana grabbed the rebound. With less than ten seconds left to play, Daryl Thomas put up an air ball. Calloway grabbed it and laid it in for the victory.

In the Final Four, Indiana played UNLV, and Syracuse squared off against their Big East rival Providence. The Friars were the big surprise. After finishing far back in the Big East pack, they were seeded sixth in the Southeast region. But they arrived in the semis on the strength of a long-range attack that produced an impressive 92 points a game through the first four rounds. Providence, with the backcourt tandem of Billy Donovan and Indiana transfer Delray Brooks leading the way, hit 14 of 22 from 3-point range to upset Alabama, then shocked the Big East champion Hoyas of Georgetown in the regional final. But the Syracuse defense stopped Providence's divine run by containing Donovan (who scored only 8 after averaging 26.5 per game for the tournament) and holding the Friars to a measly 63 points.

As for the other semi, Baltimore sportswriter Mike Littwin wrote that the matchup between Jerry Tarkanian's UNLV Runnin' Rebels and Bob Knight's Hoosiers was one of "good vs. evil. But which is which?" Tark's No. 1–ranked Rebs were led by the inside-outside tandem of Armon Gilliam and Freddie Banks. They were known for their running and gunning, and it was assumed that Knight would slow down the action to stop UNLV. But instead he decided to beat UNLV at their own game. The Hoosiers didn't stop Gilliam and Banks—Armon banged away for 32, and Fearless Freddie scored 38 on 10 for 19 three-pointers, mostly on feeds from Mark Wade, who finished with 18 assists. But Alford almost matched Banks with 33 points, and the Hoosiers as a whole shot over 60 percent from the floor. And with Indiana—and Alford—in the midst of a second-half run, two crucial UNLV offensive fouls were called away from the ball. After the game Banks said, "My shooting was tremendous," but he must have forgotten about the treys he missed with 49 and 28 seconds left, along with the pair of free throws and the lay-up he could not convert in the crunch. Indiana won 97-93.

The championship game was played before 64,959 fans in the New Orleans Superdome, and for most of the spectators the players must have looked like small spots scurrying around in the distance. It was, again, the same Hoosier script: Indiana falls behind . . . opponents make mistakes . . . hometown boy comes through.

The hometown boy this time was Keith Smart. He was actually a native of Baton Rouge, just a hop, skip, and a jump upriver from the Crescent City. Smart, the short half of Indiana's juco transfer team (the tall one was center Dean Garrett), attracted no Division I interest while in high school, even though he did grow from a 5-3 junior all the way up to 5-9 before graduation. After flipping burgers for a year at McDonald's, Keith was up to 6 feet; he then went to Garden City (Kansas) Junior College, where his quickness attracted Knight's interest.

Knight yanked Smart after an errant pass with 16:41 left and Indiana up by 1. Syracuse proceeded to go on a 14-3 tear, and almost put the game on ice. But Greg Monroe missed a 3-pointer, Knight put Smart back in the game and the Hoosiers scored 10 straight.

The Orangemen still dominated the boards, as they had against North Carolina in the regional finals and against Providence in the semis. Freshman Derrick Coleman pulled down 19 rebounds and along with Beirut-born Rony Seikaly (who never played organized ball until he walked into the Syracuse gym and asked for a chance to play) outrebounded the Hoosiers. On the strength of their big men and a defense that suffocated Alford in the second half, Syracuse led 61–56 with 7:22 left. Then Keith Smart took over. The homeboy was on fire on the bayou, penetrating for three lay-ups and another shot in the lane. Still, Syracuse led 73-70 with just over half a minute to go. But when the Orange's Howard Triche missed the second of two free throws, Smart raced downcourt for a transition basket, pulling up for a short jumper in front of the retreating Syracuse defenders. After Syracuse inbounded, Smart immediately fouled Derrick Coleman. When the freshman went to the line for a one-and-one with 28 seconds left, Syracuse Coach Jim Boeheim, trying to prevent another quick transition basket by Indiana, didn't contest the rebound. Coleman shot with all his teammates downcourt. Coleman missed the first free throw, and Smart brought it across for Indiana. The first option was to Alford, but he was covered. The ball went down low to Daryl Thomas, who kicked it back out to Smart. Five seconds before the buzzer, Smart's 15-footer found twine. Before a stunned Syracuse could call time out, the clock had run down to the last second.

In the final minutes, Keith Smart was the entire Hoosier offense, scoring 12 of the last 15 Indiana points. And Bob Knight was once again on top of the heap.

FIRST ROUND WEST

UNLV (95)　Coach: Jerry Tarkanian

	Min.	Total FG/FGA	Pct.	3-Pt. FG/FGA	Pct.	FT/FTA	Pct.	Reb. O/T	A	TO	PF	S	Blk	TP	PPM
WADE, M.	28	1/1	1.000	0/0	.000	0/0	.000	1/6	9	4	2	5	0	2	.071
BANKS, F.	21	7/16	.438	7/13	.538	2/2	1.000	0/1	0	0	2	0	0	23	1.095
PADDIO, G.	29	3/9	.333	1/3	.333	4/5	.800	0/3	2	3	2	0	0	11	.379
GILLIAM, A.	26	4/8	.500	0/0	.000	4/5	.800	1/8	0	4	2	0	0	12	.462
BASNIGHT, J.	16	4/5	.800	0/0	.000	0/0	.000	0/2	1	0	0	1	2	8	.500
ROBINSON, R.	12	0/0	.000	0/0	.000	0/0	.000	0/0	0	0	1	0	0	0	.000
WEST, L.	8	1/5	.200	0/0	.000	0/0	.000	2/2	1	1	0	0	0	2	.250
SYMANSKI, L.	2	0/0	.000	0/0	.000	0/0	.000	0/1	1	0	1	0	0	0	.000
CVIJANOVICH, S.	8	0/2	.000	0/0	.000	3/6	.500	2/3	2	0	2	0	0	3	.375
GRAHAM, G.	14	6/7	.857	1/1	1.000	5/6	.833	0/0	0	2	1	1	0	18	1.286
HUDSON, E.	18	1/6	.167	0/1	.000	1/3	.333	4/10	1	1	1	2	0	3	.167
WILLARD, D.	18	3/4	.750	0/0	.000	7/8	.875	1/3	0	1	1	1	0	13	.722
Totals	200	30/63	.476	9/19	.474	26/35	.743	11/39	17	16	15	10	2	95	.475

Idaho State (70)　Coach: Jim Boutin

	Min.	Total FG/FGA	Pct.	3-Pt. FG/FGA	Pct.	FT/FTA	Pct.	Reb. O/T	A	TO	PF	S	Blk	TP	PPM
MILES, T.	30	2/7	.286	2/5	.400	0/0	.000	0/1	3	3	5	0	0	6	.200
RHODE, J.	28	6/16	.375	2/5	.400	0/0	.000	4/9	3	3	5	3	1	14	.500
HOLSTON, D.	31	9/19	.474	2/4	.500	0/1	.000	0/4	1	0	5	0	0	20	.645
DAVIS, G.	31	5/11	.455	0/1	.000	2/4	.500	3/4	1	5	2	0	0	12	.387
YETENEKIAN, T.	29	3/5	.600	0/1	.000	2/2	1.000	3/9	4	4	4	2	0	8	.276
CHATTERTON, M.	10	1/2	.500	0/1	.000	0/0	.000	1/1	2	3	1	0	0	2	.200
PURVIS, R.	13	1/7	.143	0/0	.000	0/0	.000	2/3	0	1	3	0	0	2	.154
SULLIVAN, J.	2	0/0	.000	0/0	.000	2/2	1.000	0/2	0	1	1	0	0	2	1.000
HARRIS, R.	10	1/1	1.000	0/0	.000	0/0	.000	0/3	0	0	1	0	0	2	.200
DEAN, G.	10	0/2	.000	0/1	.000	0/0	.000	0/4	0	2	1	0	0	0	.000
ALLEMAN, D.	6	1/1	1.000	0/0	.000	0/0	.000	0/1	0	1	1	0	0	2	.333
Totals	200	29/71	.408	6/19	.316	6/9	.667	13/41	14	23	29	5	1	70	.350

Team Rebounds: UNLV 2; Idaho State 3. Disqualified: Idaho State—Miles, Rhode, Holston. Technical fouls: None.

	1st Half	2nd Half	Final
UNLV	46	49	95
Idaho State	27	43	70

Georgia (79)　Coach: Hugh Durham

	Min.	Total FG/FGA	Pct.	3-Pt. FG/FGA	Pct.	FT/FTA	Pct.	Reb. O/T	A	TO	PF	S	Blk	TP	PPM
KESSLER, C.	44	7/11	.636	0/0	.000	2/4	.500	2/6	1	1	2	1	0	16	.364
KIRCE	34	1/2	.500	0/0	.000	0/0	.000	1/3	5	3	4	1	0	2	.059
BURDETTE	22	3/5	.600	0/0	.000	2/2	1.000	2/5	0	3	4	1	0	8	.364
WILLIAMS	34	3/12	.250	0/0	.000	0/0	.000	2/5	5	2	4	1	0	6	.176
ANDERSON	44	13/20	.650	3/5	.600	6/6	1.000	1/3	5	6	3	2	0	35	.795
BLAKLEY	11	1/4	.250	0/2	.000	0/0	.000	0/1	2	0	1	1	0	2	.182
HARRON	7	0/0	.000	0/0	.000	1/2	.500	0/0	0	1	1	0	0	1	.143
KESSLER, A.	29	4/5	.800	0/0	.000	1/2	.500	3/6	0	1	2	1	0	9	.310
Totals	225	32/59	.542	3/7	.429	12/16	.750	11/29	18	17	21	8	0	79	.351

Kansas State (82)　Coach: Lon Kruger

	Min.	Total FG/FGA	Pct.	3-Pt. FG/FGA	Pct.	FT/FTA	Pct.	Reb. O/T	A	TO	PF	S	Blk	TP	PPM
BLEDSOE, C.	40	6/12	.500	0/0	.000	1/4	.250	2/5	1	4	3	1	2	13	.325
SIMMONS, L.	14	0/1	.000	0/0	.000	0/0	.000	0/0	0	2	3	0	0	0	.000
RICHMOND, M.	40	10/19	.526	5/5	1.000	9/12	.750	5/11	5	3	2	1	0	34	.850
SMITH, L.	21	0/0	.000	0/0	.000	0/0	.000	0/0	4	1	2	0	0	0	.000
HENSON, S.	41	1/3	.333	0/0	.000	2/2	1.000	0/0	5	1	4	2	0	4	.098
SCOTT, W.	26	5/8	.625	3/4	.750	4/4	1.000	1/2	2	2	2	2	0	17	.654
DOBBINS, R.	4	0/0	.000	0/0	.000	0/0	.000	0/0	0	1	0	0	0	0	.000
COLEMAN, N.	36	6/12	.500	0/0	.000	2/4	.500	5/11	0	2	0	0	0	14	.389
MEYER, R.	3	0/0	.000	0/0	.000	2/0	.000	1/1	0	1	0	0	0	0	.000
Totals	225	28/55	.509	8/9	.889	18/26	.692	14/30	17	17	16	6	2	82	.364

Team Rebounds: Kansas State 2; Georgia 2. Disqualified: None. Technical fouls: None.

	1st Half	2nd Half	1st OT	Final
Georgia	29	43	7	79
Kansas State	31	41	10	82

Virginia (60)　Coach: Terry Holland

	Min.	Total FG/FGA	Pct.	3-Pt. FG/FGA	Pct.	FT/FTA	Pct.	Reb. O/T	A	TO	PF	S	Blk	TP	PPM
JOHNSON, J.	40	5/10	.500	0/0	.000	2/2	1.000	0/0	8	3	2	2	0	12	.300
MORGAN, R.	24	2/7	.286	0/1	.000	0/0	.000	1/4	1	3	0	1	0	4	.167
KENNEDY, M.	29	4/8	.500	1/1	1.000	2/2	1.000	1/3	2	3	4	0	1	11	.379
SHEEHEY, T.	20	4/4	1.000	0/0	.000	0/0	.000	1/5	0	1	5	0	1	8	.400
KENNEDY, A.	40	5/14	.357	0/0	.000	4/5	.800	4/9	1	1	2	1	0	14	.350
SIMMS, D.	16	3/3	1.000	2/2	1.000	0/0	.000	0/0	0	0	1	0	0	8	.500
COOKE, M.	8	0/1	.000	0/0	.000	0/0	.000	0/0	0	0	0	0	0	0	.000
BATTS, B.	13	1/1	1.000	0/0	.000	0/0	.000	1/6	1	0	1	0	1	2	.154
MARTIN, T.	10	0/2	.000	0/0	.000	1/2	.500	0/1	1	3	2	1	0	1	.100
Totals	200	24/50	.480	3/4	.750	9/11	.818	8/28	14	14	17	5	3	60	.300

Wyoming (64)　Coach: Jim Brandenburg

	Min.	Total FG/FGA	Pct.	3-Pt. FG/FGA	Pct.	FT/FTA	Pct.	Reb. O/T	A	TO	PF	S	Blk	TP	PPM
DENT, S.	38	4/7	.571	0/0	.000	2/2	1.000	0/0	9	4	4	3	0	10	.263
FOX, R.	37	3/7	.429	1/2	.500	1/2	.500	0/1	2	1	0	0	0	8	.296
DEMBO, F.	39	6/16	.375	2/7	.286	2/3	.667	4/9	3	1	2	0	0	16	.410
LECKNER, E.	39	10/13	.769	0/0	.000	2/5	.400	1/6	1	1	3	1	1	22	.564
SOMMERS, J.	15	0/2	.000	0/0	.000	0/0	.000	2/5	0	3	0	0	0	0	.000
BOYD, T.	15	2/3	.667	0/0	.000	0/0	.000	0/0	0	2	0	3	0	4	.267
JONES, W.	26	1/3	.333	0/0	.000	2/2	1.000	0/3	5	3	2	0	1	4	.154
LODGINS, D.	1	0/0	.000	0/0	.000	0/0	.000	0/0	0	0	0	0	0	0	.000
Totals	200	26/51	.510	3/9	.333	9/14	.643	7/24	20	12	14	7	2	64	.320

Team Rebounds: Wyoming 1; Virginia 1. Disqualified: Virginia—Sheehey. Technical fouls: None.

	1st Half	2nd Half	Final
Virginia	30	30	60
Wyoming	29	35	64

UCLA (92)　Coach: Walt Hazzard

	Min.	Total FG/FGA	Pct.	3-Pt. FG/FGA	Pct.	FT/FTA	Pct.	Reb. O/T	A	TO	PF	S	Blk	TP	PPM
HALEY, J.	22	1/6	.167	0/0	.000	1/4	.250	2/7	0	0	2	1	2	3	.136
RICHARDSON	33	4/8	.500	0/0	.000	5/7	.714	0/8	6	7	3	0	0	13	.394
IMMEL	29	4/5	.800	1/1	1.000	2/3	.667	1/3	4	1	2	2	0	11	.379
MILLER, R.	34	10/13	.769	3/4	.750	9/12	.750	1/13	2	5	2	2	0	32	.941
ROCHELIN, C.	25	4/5	.800	0/0	.000	1/2	.500	1/6	1	1	1	0	1	9	.360
WILSON, T.	15	4/6	.667	0/0	.000	0/0	.000	3/5	0	1	1	0	0	8	.533
HATCHER	19	4/6	.667	0/0	.000	0/0	.000	0/1	2	2	1	1	0	8	.421
FOSTER	16	2/3	.667	0/0	.000	2/3	.667	0/3	2	2	2	1	0	6	.375
WALKER, K.	3	0/0	.000	0/0	.000	0/0	.000	0/0	0	1	1	0	0	0	.000
JACKSON	4	1/2	.500	0/0	.000	0/0	.000	0/0	0	2	0	0	0	2	.500
Totals	200	34/54	.630	4/5	.800	20/31	.645	8/46	17	22	15	7	3	92	.460

Central Michigan (73)　Coach: Charles Coles

	Min.	Total FG/FGA	Pct.	3-Pt. FG/FGA	Pct.	FT/FTA	Pct.	Reb. O/T	A	TO	PF	S	Blk	TP	PPM
MURRAY	31	6/13	.462	0/1	.000	1/2	.500	2/3	1	0	1	1	0	13	.419
LEAVY	28	6/16	.375	2/3	.667	0/0	.000	0/1	3	2	4	0	0	14	.500
JOHNSON	31	6/15	.400	4/8	.500	2/2	1.000	0/0	2	4	3	4	0	18	.581
MILLER, D.	26	1/5	.200	0/0	.000	0/0	.000	3/7	0	3	3	2	0	2	.077
MAJERLE	37	8/20	.400	1/2	.500	0/3	.000	6/13	1	2	4	1	0	17	.459
RICHMOND	15	1/2	.500	1/2	.500	0/0	.000	0/0	4	2	2	2	0	3	.200
SCOTT	14	1/3	.333	0/0	.000	0/0	.000	0/1	1	0	2	0	0	2	.143
WILCOX	4	0/2	.000	0/0	.000	0/0	.000	1/1	0	0	1	0	0	0	.000
MCGUIRE	14	2/3	.667	0/0	.000	0/1	.000	3/4	0	0	1	0	0	4	.286
Totals	200	31/79	.392	8/16	.500	3/8	.375	15/30	12	13	21	10	0	73	.365

Team Rebounds: UCLA 1; Central Mich. 0. Disqualified: None. Technical fouls: Central Mich.—Scott.

	1st Half	2nd Half	Final
UCLA	53	39	92
Central Mich.	21	52	73

Oklahoma (74)   Coach: Billy Tubbs

	Min.	Total FG/FGA	Pct.	3-Pt. FG/FGA	Pct.	FT/FTA	Pct.	Reb. O/T	A	TO	PF	S	Blk	TP	PPM
SIEGER, D.	30	3/5	.600	1/3	.333	0/0	.000	1/2	0	1	2	1	0	7	.233
GRANT, H.	39	9/16	.563	0/0	.000	3/4	.750	8/17	3	3	3	0	1	21	.538
JOHNSON, D.	19	5/8	.625	0/0	.000	1/3	.333	0/0	1	1	1	0	0	11	.579
MCCALLISTER, T.	40	4/10	.400	2/3	.667	6/8	.750	1/4	5	1	2	1	0	16	.400
GRACE, R.	21	3/4	.750	1/2	:500	7/8	.875	1/1	2	3	2	3	0	14	.667
KING, S.	11	1/1	1.000	0/0	.000	0/0	.000	0/0	0	0	1	1	0	2	.182
KENNEDY, J.	36	1/10	.100	0/0	.000	1/2	.500	4/8	3	1	3	1	0	3	.083
WATSON, C.	4	0/0	.000	0/0	.000	0/0	.000	0/0	0	1	1	0	0	0	.000
Totals	200	26/54	.481	4/8	.500	18/25	.720	15/32	14	12	15	6	1	74	.370

Tulsa (69)   Coach: J. D. Barnett

	Min.	Total FG/FGA	Pct.	3-Pt. FG/FGA	Pct.	FT/FTA	Pct.	Reb. O/T	A	TO	PF	S	Blk	TP	PPM
MOSS, D.	39	9/19	.474	6/10	.600	0/1	.000	0/2	3	1	3	2	0	24	.615
RAHILLY, B.	33	3/6	.500	1/2	.500	1/2	.500	4/9	3	3	2	2	0	8	.242
RAHILLY, J.	23	2/2	1.000	0/0	.000	0/0	.000	0/1	1	0	1	0	0	4	.174
BOUDREAUX, B.	40	1/6	.167	0/5	.000	0/0	.000	1/2	5	2	4	0	2	2	.050
MOORE, T.	31	4/15	.267	1/1	1.000	2/2	1.000	2/5	1	2	5	0	0	11	.355
ROYSTER, D.	31	8/9	.889	0/0	.000	4/6	.667	4/5	2	1	2	0	4	20	.645
BUCKWALTER, J.	2	0/1	.000	0/0	.000	0/0	.000	0/0	0	0	0	0	0	0	.000
LOYD, B.	1	0/0	.000	0/0	.000	0/0	.000	0/0	0	0	0	0	0	0	.000
Totals	200	27/58	.466	8/18	.444	7/11	.636	11/24	15	9	17	4	4	69	.345

Team Rebounds: Oklahoma 5; Tulsa 2. Disqualified: Tulsa—Moore. Technical fouls: None.

	1st Half	2nd Half	Final
Oklahoma	29	45	74
Tulsa	28	41	69

Pittsburgh (93)   Coach: Paul Evans

	Min.	Total FG/FGA	Pct.	3-Pt. FG/FGA	Pct.	FT/FTA	Pct.	Reb. O/T	A	TO	PF	S	Blk	TP	PPM
LANE, J.	28	5/9	.556	0/0	.000	1/3	.333	5/7	3	1	4	1	0	11	.393
GORE, D.	29	8/16	.500	0/3	.000	6/6	1.000	1/2	1	1	2	4	0	22	.759
SMITH, C.	31	7/11	.636	0/1	.000	8/10	.800	1/7	0	3	4	1	0	22	.710
AIKEN	19	1/5	.200	0/0	.000	1/1	1.000	0/0	4	0	0	1	0	3	.158
GOODSON	26	3/5	.600	1/2	.500	2/3	.667	0/1	1	1	2	0	0	9	.346
CAVANAUGH, P.	21	2/3	.667	0/0	.000	0/0	.000	0/2	5	2	0	1	0	4	.190
BROOKIN, R.	20	7/10	.700	0/2	.000	0/1	.000	2/4	1	4	0	1	0	14	.700
COOPER	19	3/4	.750	0/0	.000	2/2	1.000	5/7	2	1	1	1	0	8	.421
FERGUSON	3	0/1	.000	0/0	.000	0/2	.000	1/1	0	0	0	0	0	0	.000
RASP	1	0/0	.000	0/0	.000	0/0	.000	0/1	0	0	0	0	0	0	.000
COLOMBO	1	0/0	.000	0/0	.000	0/0	.000	0/1	0	0	0	0	0	0	.000
LUTHER	1	0/0	.000	0/0	.000	0/0	.000	0/0	0	0	0	0	0	0	.000
MASLER	1	0/0	.000	0/0	.000	0/0	.000	0/0	0	0	0	0	0	0	.000
Totals	200	36/65	.554	1/8	.125	20/29	.690	15/32	17	13	13	10	0	93	.465

Marist (68)   Coach: Dave Magarity

	Min.	Total FG/FGA	Pct.	3-Pt. FG/FGA	Pct.	FT/FTA	Pct.	Reb. O/T	A	TO	PF	S	Blk	TP	PPM
MCCANTS, R.	30	2/6	.333	1/2	.500	0/0	.000	0/3	5	2	1	1	0	5	.167
KRASOVEC, P.	27	3/6	.500	3/6	.500	0/0	.000	0/0	4	2	0	0	9	.333
SMITS, R.	24	8/9	.889	0/0	.000	0/2	.000	0/2	1	4	4	0	1	16	.667
DAVIS, D.	39	6/13	.462	0/2	.000	2/3	.667	1/5	11	2	4	4	0	14	.359
PECARSKI, M.	34	9/13	.692	0/0	.000	0/0	.000	2/5	0	1	2	0	0	18	.529
BOURGAREL, R.	13	0/4	.000	0/0	.000	1/2	.500	2/3	0	2	4	0	1	1	.077
SHAMLEY, M.	14	0/2	.000	0/0	.000	0/0	.000	0/1	0	4	0	0	0	0	.000
SHARPENTER, T.	3	0/0	.000	0/0	.000	0/0	.000	0/0	0	0	0	0	0	0	.000
MCCLUNG, D.	10	2/2	1.000	1/1	1.000	0/0	.000	0/0	1	1	1	1	0	5	.500
GREEN, C.	2	0/0	.000	0/0	.000	0/0	.000	0/0	1	0	1	0	0	0	.000
MURPHY, T.	2	0/2	.000	0/1	.000	0/0	.000	0/0	0	0	2	0	0	0	.000
MCDONOUGH, J.	1	0/1	.000	0/0	.000	0/0	.000	0/0	0	0	0	0	0	0	.000
SCHOENFELD, M.	1	0/0	.000	0/0	.000	0/0	.000	0/0	0	0	0	0	0	0	.000
Totals	200	30/58	.517	5/12	.417	3/7	.429	5/19	17	20	22	6	2	68	.340

Team Rebounds: Pittsburgh 3; Marist 4. Disqualified: None. Technical fouls: Marist—Pecarski.

	1st Half	2nd Half	Final
Pittsburgh	39	54	93
Marist	21	47	68

UTEP (98)   Coach: Don Haskins

	Min.	Total FG/FGA	Pct.	3-Pt. FG/FGA	Pct.	FT/FTA	Pct.	Reb. O/T	A	TO	PF	S	Blk	TP	PPM
SANDLE, C.	31	4/11	.364	0/0	.000	1/2	.500	2/5	5	2	5	1	1	9	.290
GATES, Q.	32	10/15	.667	4/6	.667	2/3	.667	4/8	1	4	5	0	0	26	.813
RICHMOND, M.	35	7/12	.583	0/0	.000	4/4	1.000	2/11	0	1	4	1	0	18	.514
HARDAWAY, T.	30	1/5	.200	0/0	.000	0/0	.000	1/2	6	3	5	1	0	2	.067
JACKSON, J.	34	7/15	.467	4/7	.571	5/5	1.000	0/5	3	4	4	3	0	23	.676
BLOCKER, C.	25	2/8	.250	0/0	.000	8/12	.667	0/1	3	3	3	0	0	12	.480
CAMPBELL, W.	23	2/4	.500	0/0	.000	1/1	1.000	2/4	0	2	5	1	0	5	.217
STALLWORTH, T.	8	1/2	.500	0/1	.000	1/2	.500	0/0	2	0	2	0	0	3	.375
DAVIS, A.	7	0/0	.000	0/0	.000	0/0	.000	0/0	0	1	1	1	0	0	.000
Totals	225	34/72	.472	8/14	.571	22/29	.759	11/36	20	20	34	8	2	98	.436

Arizona (91)   Coach: Lute Olson

	Min.	Total FG/FGA	Pct.	3-Pt. FG/FGA	Pct.	FT/FTA	Pct.	Reb. O/T	A	TO	PF	S	Blk	TP	PPM
COOK, A.	41	4/10	.400	0/0	.000	5/9	.556	5/11	1	3	3	2	7	13	.317
ELLIOTT, S.	43	9/16	.563	3/3	1.000	5/8	.625	3/6	4	6	5	1	0	26	.605
TURNER, J.	32	2/4	.500	0/0	.000	6/8	.750	3/7	0	1	1	2	3	10	.313
LOFTON, K.	35	2/9	.222	1/6	.167	7/9	.778	0/1	2	3	5	2	0	12	.343
MCMILLAN, C.	44	6/13	.462	1/7	.143	2/4	.500	1/5	7	1	3	0	1	15	.341
TOLBERT, T.	16	5/10	.500	0/1	.000	5/5	1.000	3/3	1	1	5	0	0	15	.938
BUECHLER, J.	7	0/0	.000	0/0	.000	0/0	.000	0/2	0	1	0	0	0	0	.000
MASON, H.	5	0/1	.000	0/1	.000	0/0	.000	0/1	1	0	0	0	0	0	.000
DAVID, B.	1	0/0	.000	0/0	.000	0/0	.000	0/0	0	0	0	0	0	0	.000
FRASER, B.	1	0/0	.000	0/0	.000	0/0	.000	0/0	0	0	0	0	0	0	.000
Totals	225	28/63	.444	5/18	.278	30/43	.698	15/36	16	17	22	7	11	91	.404

Team Rebounds: UTEP 5; Arizona 3. Disqualified: UTEP—Gates, Sandle, Hardaway, Campbell; Arizona—Elliott, Lofton, Tolbert. Technical fouls: UTEP—Gates.

	1st Half	2nd Half	1st OT	Final
UTEP	41	38	19	98
Arizona	39	40	12	91

Iowa (99)   Coach: Tom Davis

	Min.	Total FG/FGA	Pct.	3-Pt. FG/FGA	Pct.	FT/FTA	Pct.	Reb. O/T	A	TO	PF	S	Blk	TP	PPM
MARBLE, R.	22	8/10	.800	0/2	.000	0/0	.000	4/7	2	2	1	2	1	16	.727
GAMBLE, K.	18	8/8	1.000	0/0	.000	2/2	1.000	0/1	1	0	2	2	0	18	1.000
LOHAUS, B.	18	2/4	.500	0/1	.000	2/2	1.000	0/1	1	1	0	0	6	.333
ARMSTRONG, B.	18	1/3	.333	0/1	.000	0/0	.000	0/1	4	1	1	2	0	2	.111
WRIGHT, G.	18	1/4	.250	0/0	.000	2/4	.500	1/3	0	2	3	1	0	4	.222
JONES, B.	15	0/4	.000	0/0	.000	4/6	.667	4/5	1	1	2	2	0	4	.267
MOE, J.	17	3/5	.600	2/3	.667	4/4	1.000	2/4	1	2	3	0	0	12	.706
HORTON, E.	14	4/7	.571	0/0	.000	3/4	.750	0/2	1	1	2	1	0	11	.786
LORENZEN, A.	16	4/6	.667	0/1	.000	0/0	.000	1/4	1	1	3	1	0	8	.500
REAVES, M.	14	2/2	1.000	0/0	.000	5/6	.833	1/3	0	4	1	1	0	9	.643
HILL, K.	9	0/2	.000	0/0	.000	1/2	.500	3/4	1	2	1	0	1	1	.111
MORGAN, M.	11	2/4	.500	0/0	.000	0/0	.000	1/3	0	2	2	1	0	4	.364
JEPSEN, L.	5	1/2	.500	0/0	.000	0/1	.000	1/3	0	1	3	0	0	2	.400
JEWELL, M.	5	1/2	.500	0/0	.000	0/0	.000	0/1	1	0	0	0	0	2	.400
Totals	200	37/63	.587	2/8	.250	23/31	.742	18/41	14	20	24	13	1	99	.495

Santa Clara (76)   Coach: Carroll Williams

	Min.	Total FG/FGA	Pct.	3-Pt. FG/FGA	Pct.	FT/FTA	Pct.	Reb. O/T	A	TO	PF	S	Blk	TP	PPM
GORDON	37	9/14	.643	0/0	.000	6/6	1.000	3/6	0	3	3	0	0	24	.649
MOODY	17	0/5	.000	0/2	.000	1/2	.500	2/2	1	3	4	0	1	1	.059
WEISS	28	2/4	.500	0/0	.000	5/7	.714	1/2	1	1	2	0	0	9	.321
APPIAH	24	1/6	.167	0/0	.000	2/3	.667	1/2	2	2	4	0	0	4	.167
LANE	33	6/11	.545	2/2	1.000	4/4	1.000	0/1	3	3	4	4	0	18	.545
HORVATH	17	1/1	1.000	0/0	.000	0/0	.000	1/1	0	3	1	1	0	2	.118
BURLEY	20	4/12	.333	3/9	.333	0/0	.000	2/4	3	0	4	0	0	11	.550
AARON	3	0/0	.000	0/0	.000	2/2	1.000	0/1	0	1	0	0	0	2	.667
MCPHERSON	13	0/2	.000	0/0	.000	0/0	.000	1/3	0	1	1	0	0	0	.000
LARSEN	4	0/0	.000	0/0	.000	0/0	.000	0/0	0	0	0	0	0	0	.000
UNDERWOOD	1	1/1	1.000	0/0	.000	0/1	.000	0/1	0	0	0	0	0	2	2.000
TURNER	1	0/0	.000	0/0	.000	0/1	.000	0/1	0	0	0	0	0	0	.000
RASK	3	1/1	1.000	1/1	1.000	0/0	.000	0/0	0	0	0	0	0	3	1.000
Totals	200	25/57	.439	6/14	.429	20/26	.769	9/20	9	21	23	5	1	76	.380

Team Rebounds: Iowa 2; Santa Clara 3. Disqualified: None. Technical fouls: Iowa—Horton.

	1st Half	2nd Half	Final
Iowa	51	48	99
Santa Clara	22	54	76

FIRST ROUND MIDWEST

Indiana (92)   Coach: Bob Knight

	Min.	Total FG/FGA	Pct.	3-Pt. FG/FGA	Pct.	FT/FTA	Pct.	Reb. O/T	A	TO	PF	S	Blk	TP	PPM
CALLOWAY, R.	27	6/11	.545	0/0	.000	5/5	1.000	1/8	3	2	2	2	1	17	.630
THOMAS, D.	21	6/8	.750	0/0	.000	2/2	1.000	0/2	0	2	2	1	1	14	.667
GARRETT, D.	32	7/11	.636	0/0	.000	6/8	.750	1/7	0	3	2	2	2	20	.625
ALFORD, S.	25	4/5	.800	2/2	1.000	3/3	1.000	0/2	3	2	3	3	0	13	.520
SMART, K.	16	1/7	.143	0/1	.000	2/2	1.000	0/2	2	0	3	1	0	4	.250
SMITH, K.	5	1/1	1.000	0/0	.000	0/0	.000	1/1	1	0	0	0	0	2	.400
EYL, S.	13	2/4	.500	0/0	.000	0/0	.000	2/4	3	0	0	1	1	4	.308
HILLMAN, J.	13	1/1	1.000	0/0	.000	0/2	.000	0/1	3	0	1	0	1	2	.154
FREEMAN, T.	17	1/1	1.000	0/0	.000	2/2	1.000	0/1	1	1	2	0	0	4	.235
MEIER, T.	4	0/0	.000	0/0	.000	0/0	.000	0/2	0	1	2	0	0	0	.000
PELKOWSKI, M.	8	1/4	.250	0/0	.000	0/0	.000	0/3	1	2	2	0	0	2	.250
SLOAN, B.	7	1/3	.333	0/0	.000	4/4	1.000	2/3	0	1	0	0	0	6	.857
MINOR, D.	7	0/1	.000	0/0	.000	2/2	1.000	1/1	0	0	1	0	0	2	.286
OLIPHANT, J.	5	0/0	.000	0/0	.000	2/3	.667	1/3	1	0	1	0	0	2	.400
Totals	200	31/57	.544	2/3	.667	28/33	.848	9/40	18	14	21	10	6	92	.460

Fairfield (58)   Coach: Mitch Buonaguro

	Min.	Total FG/FGA	Pct.	3-Pt. FG/FGA	Pct.	FT/FTA	Pct.	Reb. O/T	A	TO	PF	S	Blk	TP	PPM
O'TOOLE, T.	24	2/7	.286	0/0	.000	3/5	.600	1/3	0	1	5	2	0	7	.292
DUNCAN, E.	25	1/3	.333	0/0	.000	0/0	.000	1/1	1	2	2	0	0	2	.080
GROMOS, J.	39	8/19	.421	0/0	.000	5/8	.625	4/11	2	3	3	1	0	21	.538
WYNDER, A.	34	4/12	.333	0/2	.000	7/9	.778	1/5	3	6	4	2	0	15	.441
GOLDEN, E.	33	5/7	.714	0/0	.000	1/1	1.000	1/5	3	5	3	0	0	11	.333
BRADFORD, J.	19	0/6	.000	0/2	.000	0/0	.000	0/0	0	1	2	0	0	0	.000
WOODTLI, A.	14	0/1	.000	0/0	.000	0/0	.000	0/1	0	0	5	0	0	0	.000
COOK, T.	3	0/0	.000	0/0	.000	0/0	.000	0/1	0	0	1	0	0	0	.000
WALTERS, M.	5	0/1	.000	0/0	.000	2/2	1.000	0/0	0	2	0	0	0	2	.400
BARRY, R.	4	0/0	.000	0/0	.000	0/0	.000	0/0	0	0	2	0	0	0	.000
Totals	200	20/56	.357	0/4	.000	18/25	.720	8/27	9	20	27	5	0	58	.290

Team Rebounds: Indiana 1; Fairfield 2. Disqualified: Fairfield—O'Toole, Woodtli. Technical fouls: None.

	1st Half	2nd Half	Final
Indiana	46	46	92
Fairfield	21	37	58

Auburn (62)   Coach: Sonny Smith

	Min.	Total FG/FGA	Pct.	3-Pt. FG/FGA	Pct.	FT/FTA	Pct.	Reb. O/T	A	TO	PF	S	Blk	TP	PPM
JONES, M.	32	11/16	.688	0/0	.000	2/4	.500	-/7	2	1	3	0	2	24	.750
MORRIS, C.	38	6/12	.500	1/2	.500	1/1	1.000	-/11	2	2	3	0	2	14	.368
MOORE, J.	33	4/13	.308	0/0	.000	6/7	.857	-/14	0	0	3	0	0	14	.424
WHITE, G.	34	2/6	.333	0/4	.000	0/0	.000	-/3	5	1	2	2	0	4	.118
FORD, F.	40	2/9	.222	0/2	.000	2/4	.500	-/5	3	4	2	3	0	6	.150
HOWARD, T.	17	0/1	.000	0/1	.000	0/0	.000	-/0	0	1	1	0	0	0	.000
LYNN, J.	5	0/2	.000	0/0	.000	0/0	.000	-/0	0	0	0	0	0	0	.000
CAYLOR, J.	1	0/0	.000	0/0	.000	0/0	.000	-/0	0	0	0	0	0	0	.000
Totals	200	25/59	.424	1/9	.111	11/16	.688	-/40	12	9	14	5	4	62	.310

San Diego (61)   Coach: Hank Egan

	Min.	Total FG/FGA	Pct.	3-Pt. FG/FGA	Pct.	FT/FTA	Pct.	Reb. O/T	A	TO	PF	S	Blk	TP	PPM
MANOR, M.	31	5/10	.500	1/2	.500	0/0	.000	-/5	3	1	2	0	0	11	.355
MADDEN, M.	34	3/8	.375	0/0	.000	1/3	.333	-/11	3	2	1	1	2	7	.206
THOMPSON, M.	25	5/11	.455	0/1	.000	4/4	1.000	-/4	1	2	4	0	1	14	.560
LEONARD, P.	38	3/7	.429	0/2	.000	0/0	.000	-/2	5	3	1	1	0	6	.158
MEANS, D.	30	7/12	.583	2/5	.400	2/3	.667	-/4	2	0	1	3	0	18	.600
KRALLMAN, D.	20	1/2	.500	0/0	.000	0/2	.000	-/2	0	1	2	1	0	2	.100
MUNN, M.	11	0/2	.000	0/2	.000	0/0	.000	-/0	0	0	2	0	0	0	.000
MUSSELMAN, E.	2	1/2	.500	1/2	.500	0/0	.000	-/0	0	0	1	0	0	3	1.500
HAUPT, M.	9	0/0	.000	0/0	.000	0/0	.000	-/1	1	1	1	1	0	0	.000
Totals	200	25/54	.463	4/14	.286	7/12	.583	-/29	15	10	15	7	3	61	.305

Team Rebounds: Auburn 2; San Diego 1. Disqualified: None. Technical fouls: None.

	1st Half	2nd Half	Final
Auburn	28	34	62
San Diego	33	28	61

Duke (58)   Coach: Mike Krzyzewski

	Min.	Total FG/FGA	Pct.	3-Pt. FG/FGA	Pct.	FT/FTA	Pct.	Reb. O/T	A	TO	PF	S	Blk	TP	PPM
FERRY, D.	23	0/1	.000	0/0	.000	0/0	.000	1/5	4	6	0	0	1	0	.000
KING, B.	31	1/3	.333	0/0	.000	3/4	.750	0/0	1	3	4	0	0	5	.161
SMITH, J.	27	2/2	1.000	0/0	.000	2/2	1.000	0/4	1	1	4	1	0	6	.222
AMAKER, T.	40	5/7	.714	1/1	1.000	0/0	.000	1/4	3	5	1	5	0	11	.275
STRICKLAND, K.	31	6/12	.500	3/6	.500	5/8	.625	1/3	1	6	3	2	2	20	.645
SNYDER, Q.	7	0/2	.000	0/0	.000	0/0	.000	0/0	1	0	4	1	0	0	.000
BRICKEY, R.	29	5/6	.833	0/0	.000	2/6	.333	2/5	1	0	1	1	0	12	.414
ABDELNABY, A.	5	1/2	.500	0/0	.000	2/2	1.000	0/0	0	1	0	0	0	4	.800
NESSLEY, M.	7	0/1	.000	0/0	.000	0/0	.000	0/2	0	1	1	0	0	0	.000
Totals	200	20/36	.556	4/7	.571	14/22	.636	5/23	12	23	18	10	3	58	.290

Texas A&M (51)   Coach: Shelby Metcalf

	Min.	Total FG/FGA	Pct.	3-Pt. FG/FGA	Pct.	FT/FTA	Pct.	Reb. O/T	A	TO	PF	S	Blk	TP	PPM
CRITTE	36	6/9	.667	0/0	.000	1/4	.250	1/1	1	2	3	2	1	13	.361
TREZVANT	30	4/11	.364	0/0	.000	2/4	.500	3/7	2	2	4	2	1	10	.333
CLIFFORD	32	2/4	.500	0/0	.000	0/0	.000	1/5	0	3	4	4	0	4	.125
MCDONALD	37	3/8	.375	0/0	.000	5/6	.833	2/6	5	5	3	3	1	11	.297
HOLLOWAY	40	2/9	.222	0/1	.000	4/4	1.000	1/5	0	5	1	1	0	8	.200
GRAVES	9	1/3	.333	1/1	1.000	0/0	.000	0/0	0	3	2	0	0	3	.333
THOMAS	12	1/1	1.000	0/0	.000	0/0	.000	0/0	0	2	0	0	0	2	.167
CRAWFORD, P.	4	0/2	.000	0/0	.000	0/0	.000	1/1	0	0	0	0	0	0	.000
Totals	200	19/47	.404	1/2	.500	12/18	.667	9/25	8	22	17	12	3	51	.255

Team Rebounds: Duke 5; Texas A&M 4. Disqualified: None. Technical fouls: None.

	1st Half	2nd Half	Final
Duke	30	28	58
Texas A&M	22	29	51

Missouri (69)   Coach: Norm Stewart

	Min.	Total FG/FGA	Pct.	3-Pt. FG/FGA	Pct.	FT/FTA	Pct.	Reb. O/T	A	TO	PF	S	Blk	TP	PPM
CHIEVOUS, D.	38	6/11	.545	0/0	.000	4/6	.667	4/9	2	3	4	0	0	16	.421
SANDBOTHE, M.	36	3/6	.500	0/0	.000	2/3	.667	1/2	5	2	5	2	0	8	.222
LEONARD, G.	8	1/2	.500	0/0	.000	0/0	.000	1/2	0	0	1	0	0	2	.250
COWARD, L.	32	2/8	.250	0/4	.000	2/2	1.000	0/1	1	3	2	5	0	6	.188
HARDY, L.	29	9/22	.409	3/10	.300	0/0	.000	1/2	1	1	1	4	1	21	.724
CHURCH, G.	26	3/3	1.000	0/0	.000	2/3	.667	1/6	2	0	5	2	0	8	.308
BUNTIN, N.	24	4/7	.571	0/0	.000	0/0	.000	0/3	1	4	0	0	1	8	.333
SUTTON, B.	3	0/0	.000	0/0	.000	0/0	.000	0/0	0	0	0	0	0	0	.000
ROLF, D.	3	0/0	.000	0/0	.000	0/0	.000	0/0	0	0	0	0	0	0	.000
INGRAM, M.	1	0/0	.000	0/0	.000	0/0	.000	0/0	0	0	0	0	0	0	.000
Totals	200	28/59	.475	3/14	.214	10/14	.714	8/25	14	12	24	5	1	69	.345

Xavier (Ohio) (70)   Coach: Pete Gillen

	Min.	Total FG/FGA	Pct.	3-Pt. FG/FGA	Pct.	FT/FTA	Pct.	Reb. O/T	A	TO	PF	S	Blk	TP	PPM
TAYLOR, K.	16	1/3	.333	0/2	.000	1/2	.500	0/1	1	3	0	0	0	3	.188
CAMPBELL, D.	35	3/4	.750	0/0	.000	7/8	.875	2/6	0	1	3	0	0	13	.371
HILL, T.	39	3/6	.500	0/0	.000	0/0	.000	9/13	0	3	2	1	0	6	.154
KIMBROUGH, D.	38	6/14	.429	1/4	.250	1/3	.333	3/6	2	2	4	1	0	14	.368
LARKIN, B.	38	6/20	.300	1/3	.333	16/20	.800	2/10	4	4	4	1	1	29	.763
BARNETT, J.	30	2/7	.286	0/0	.000	1/2	.500	4/7	3	1	3	2	0	5	.167
KOESTER, B.	4	0/0	.000	0/0	.000	0/0	.000	0/0	0	0	0	0	0	0	.000
Totals	200	21/54	.389	2/9	.222	26/35	.743	20/43	10	14	16	5	1	70	.350

Team Rebounds: Xavier (Ohio) 0; Missouri 4. Disqualified: Missouri—Sandbothe, Coward, Church. Technical fouls: None.

	1st Half	2nd Half	Final
Missouri	32	37	69
Xavier (Ohio)	36	34	70

St. John's (57)   Coach: Lou Carnesecca

	Min.	Total FG/FGA	Pct.	3–Pt. FG/FGA	Pct.	FT/FTA	Pct.	Reb. O/T	A	TO	PF	S	Blk	TP	PPM
GLASS, W.	40	9/15	.600	0/0	.000	0/0	.000	1/4	1	1	1	1	1	18	.450
JONES, S.	30	1/7	.143	0/0	.000	1/2	.500	0/5	2	0	4	0	0	3	.100
BROSS, T.	11	1/2	.500	0/0	.000	0/0	.000	0/0	1	0	3	0	1	2	.182
BRUST, M.	36	3/3	1.000	0/0	.000	0/0	.000	2/5	3	0	3	1	0	6	.167
JACKSON, M.	40	6/18	.333	0/4	.000	3/3	1.000	1/3	3	1	2	1	0	15	.375
BALDI, M.	29	5/5	1.000	0/0	.000	1/1	1.000	1/3	1	0	2	0	0	11	.379
HEMPEL, J.	10	1/2	.500	0/0	.000	0/0	.000	0/1	0	1	0	0	0	2	.200
LEWIS, E.	4	0/0	.000	0/0	.000	0/0	.000	0/0	0	0	1	0	0	0	.000
Totals	200	26/52	.500	0/4		5/6	.833	5/21	11	2	17	3	2	57	.285

Wichita State (55)   Coach: Eddie Fogler

	Min.	Total FG/FGA	Pct.	3–Pt. FG/FGA	Pct.	FT/FTA	Pct.	Reb. O/T	A	TO	PF	S	Blk	TP	PPM
GRAYER, S.	30	3/5	.600	0/0	.000	0/0	.000	3/9	1	2	1	0	0	6	.200
RADUNOVICH, S.	31	6/12	.500	0/1	.000	6/7	.857	2/4	1	0	1	0	0	18	.581
CARR	22	1/3	.333	0/0	.000	1/4	.250	2/4	1	2	3	0	0	3	.136
CUNDIFF	27	0/2	.000	0/1	.000	0/0	.000	1/1	1	1	0	0	0	0	.000
GRIFFIN	24	2/4	.500	2/4	.500	0/0	.000	1/2	3	3	1	0	0	6	.250
SANTOS	27	3/11	.273	0/1	.000	0/1	.000	3/6	2	1	1	0	0	6	.222
PRAYLOW, DWI.	22	6/12	.500	2/3	.667	2/2	1.000	1/4	1	0	2	0	0	16	.727
PRAYLOW, DWA.	17	0/1	.000	0/0	.000	0/0	.000	2/2	1	0	0	0	0	0	.000
Totals	200	21/50	.420	4/10	.400	9/14	.643	15/32	11	9	9	0	0	55	.275

Team Rebounds: St. John's 2; Wichita State 3. Disqualified: None. Technical fouls: None.

	1st Half	2nd Half	Final
St. John's	28	29	57
Wichita State	25	30	55

DePaul (76)   Coach: Joey Meyer

	Min.	Total FG/FGA	Pct.	3–Pt. FG/FGA	Pct.	FT/FTA	Pct.	Reb. O/T	A	TO	PF	S	Blk	TP	PPM
GOLDEN, K.	21	0/3	.000	0/0	.000	3/4	.750	0/1	0	1	3	0	1	3	.143
GREENE, T.	24	0/3	.000	0/1	.000	3/4	.750	0/4	6	4	2	1	0	3	.125
COMEGYS, D.	38	12/14	.857	0/0	.000	5/12	.417	4/8	1	5	2	1	2	29	.763
EDWARDS, K.	31	6/10	.600	0/1	.000	0/0	.000	1/8	2	3	1	1	0	12	.387
STRICKLAND, R.	37	9/11	.818	1/1	1.000	6/6	1.000	0/0	8	3	1	5	0	25	.676
LAUX, A.	25	0/0	.000	0/0	.000	0/0	.000	0/0	3	1	2	0	0	0	.000
BRUNDY, S.	20	2/4	.500	0/0	.000	0/0	.000	0/3	1	0	2	0	0	4	.200
HOLLAND, K.	1	0/2	.000	0/0	.000	0/0	.000	2/2	0	0	1	0	0	0	.000
SOWELL, C.	1	0/0	.000	0/0	.000	0/0	.000	0/0	0	0	0	0	0	0	.000
O'SHAUGHNESSY	1	0/1	.000	0/1	.000	0/0	.000	0/0	0	0	0	0	0	0	.000
TUNE, J.	1	0/0	.000	0/0	.000	0/0	.000	0/0	0	0	0	0	0	0	.000
Totals	200	29/48	.604	1/4	.250	17/26	.654	7/26	21	17	14	8	3	76	.380

Louisiana Tech (62)   Coach: Tommy Eagles

	Min.	Total FG/FGA	Pct.	3–Pt. FG/FGA	Pct.	FT/FTA	Pct.	Reb. O/T	A	TO	PF	S	Blk	TP	PPM
COOK	27	2/11	.182	0/0	.000	0/0	.000	2/7	1	3	3	1	0	4	.148
GODBOLT	37	9/13	.692	1/1	1.000	2/3	.667	6/11	3	4	2	4	0	21	.568
WHITE	20	2/7	.286	0/0	.000	6/8	.750	2/3	0	0	5	0	0	10	.500
LEWIS	40	3/5	.600	0/0	.000	1/2	.500	1/4	4	1	4	1	1	7	.175
NEWTON	28	0/3	.000	0/0	.000	0/1	.000	0/2	2	4	1	3	0	0	.000
JACKSON	33	6/13	.462	4/6	.667	0/0	.000	1/1	0	1	2	0	0	16	.485
GUILLORY	10	1/2	.500	0/1	.000	0/0	.000	0/0	1	2	0	0	0	2	.200
BOWMAN	3	0/0	.000	0/0	.000	2/2	1.000	0/0	1	0	2	0	0	2	.667
HANNIBAL	2	0/1	.000	0/0	.000	0/0	.000	0/1	0	0	0	0	0	0	.000
Totals	200	23/55	.418	5/8	.625	11/16	.688	12/29	11	19	19	9	1	62	.310

Team Rebounds: DePaul 2; Louisiana Tech 3. Disqualified: Louisiana Tech—White. Technical fouls: None.

	1st Half	2nd Half	Final
DePaul	37	39	76
Louisiana Tech	28	34	62

Georgia Tech (79)   Coach: Bobby Cremins

	Min.	Total FG/FGA	Pct.	3–Pt. FG/FGA	Pct.	FT/FTA	Pct.	Reb. O/T	A	TO	PF	S	Blk	TP	PPM
FERRELL, D.	39	6/13	.462	0/1	.000	5/6	.833	5/9	4	3	3	1	0	17	.436
HAMMONDS, T.	40	11/15	.733	0/0	.000	2/2	1.000	2/9	0	4	1	0	1	24	.600
FORD, A.	32	1/5	.200	0/0	.000	3/4	.750	2/4	0	0	3	1	1	5	.156
DALRYMPLE, B.	32	3/9	.333	2/4	.500	3/4	.750	2/4	2	4	3	1	0	11	.344
OLIVER, B.	27	2/5	.400	1/2	.500	5/6	.833	1/3	4	2	4	1	0	10	.370
NEAL, C.	28	3/8	.375	2/7	.286	2/2	1.000	2/2	9	3	3	3	0	10	.357
MUNLYN, J.	2	0/0	.000	0/0	.000	2/2	1.000	0/0	0	0	0	0	0	2	1.000
Totals	200	26/55	.473	5/14	.357	22/26	.846	14/31	19	16	17	7	2	79	.395

Louisiana State (85)   Coach: Dale Brown

	Min.	Total FG/FGA	Pct.	3–Pt. FG/FGA	Pct.	FT/FTA	Pct.	Reb. O/T	A	TO	PF	S	Blk	TP	PPM
WOODSIDE, S.	27	3/7	.429	0/1	.000	0/0	.000	2/2	4	1	3	1	0	6	.222
BROWN	39	1/1	1.000	0/0	.000	1/4	.250	1/8	9	1	3	3	1	3	.077
WILSON, N.	38	9/19	.474	0/0	.000	0/0	.000	1/5	5	2	3	0	0	18	.474
WILSON, A.	40	8/16	.500	2/7	.286	2/2	1.000	5/5	1	4	3	2	0	20	.500
JOE, D.	35	8/12	.667	7/9	.778	5/6	.833	0/3	3	3	4	3	0	28	.800
IRVIN, F.	3	0/0	.000	0/0	.000	0/0	.000	0/0	1	0	0	0	0	0	.000
VARGAS, J.	18	4/6	.667	0/0	.000	2/5	.400	4/5	1	0	3	0	1	10	.556
Totals	200	33/61	.541	9/17	.529	10/17	.588	13/28	23	12	19	9	2	85	.425

Team Rebounds: Louisiana St. 2; Georgia Tech 4. Disqualified: None. Technical fouls: None.

	1st Half	2nd Half	Final
Georgia Tech	37	42	79
Louisiana St.	40	45	85

Temple (75)   Coach: John Chaney

	Min.	Total FG/FGA	Pct.	3–Pt. FG/FGA	Pct.	FT/FTA	Pct.	Reb. O/T	A	TO	PF	S	Blk	TP	PPM
PERRY, T.	40	7/12	.583	0/0	.000	7/8	.875	-/17	0	-	1	-	7	21	.525
VREESWYK, M.	33	3/9	.333	2/5	.400	2/2	1.000	-/6	2	-	5	-	-	10	.303
RIVAS, R.	25	1/2	.500	0/0	.000	3/4	.750	-/7	1	-	3	2	-	5	.200
BLACKWELL, N.	40	7/17	.412	2/6	.333	8/8	1.000	-/4	5	-	3	3	-	24	.600
EVANS, H.	40	3/9	.333	1/3	.333	4/4	1.000	-/7	7	-	2	-	-	11	.275
BRANTLEY, J.	12	1/2	.500	0/0	.000	0/0	.000	-/2	2	-	2	-	-	2	.167
JOHNSON, S.	1	0/0	.000	0/0	.000	0/0	.000	-/1	0	-	0	-	-	0	.000
PEARSALL, D.	8	1/3	.333	0/0	.000	0/0	.000	-/2	0	-	1	-	-	2	.250
DOWDELL, J.	1	0/0	.000	0/0	.000	0/0	.000	-/1	0	-	1	-	-	0	.000
Totals	200	23/54	.426	5/14	.357	24/26	.923	-/47	17	18	18	7	8	75	.375

Southern-B.R. (56)   Coach: Ben Jobe

	Min.	Total FG/FGA	Pct.	3–Pt. FG/FGA	Pct.	FT/FTA	Pct.	Reb. O/T	A	TO	PF	S	Blk	TP	PPM
FAULKNER	-	6/20	.300	0/1	.000	3/4	.750	-/9	0	-	4	-	-	15	-
FLORENT	-	7/16	.438	1/2	.500	4/6	.667	-/9	0	-	5	3	-	19	-
POLLARD	-	2/10	.200	0/0	.000	2/2	1.000	-/5	0	-	4	-	-	6	-
JOHNSON, A.	-	1/8	.125	1/3	.333	2/2	1.000	-/2	8	-	4	4	-	5	-
JOHNSON, D.	-	2/14	.143	1/5	.200	0/0	.000	-/5	2	-	2	-	-	5	-
WASHINGTON	-	2/2	1.000	0/0	.000	2/3	.667	-/6	0	-	2	-	-	6	-
GARNER	-	0/2	.000	0/0	.000	0/0	.000	-/1	0	-	0	-	-	0	-
WILLIAMS	-	0/1	.000	0/0	.000	0/0	.000	-/1	0	-	0	-	-	0	-
Totals	200	20/73	.274	3/11	.273	13/17	.765	-/38	10	11	21	10	1	56	.280

Team Rebounds: Temple 1; Southern-B.R. 3. Disqualified: Temple—Vreeswyk; Southern-B.R.—Florent. Technical fouls: None.

	1st Half	2nd Half	Final
Temple	35	40	75
Southern-B.R.	29	27	56

FIRST ROUND SOUTHEAST

Georgetown (75) Coach: John Thompson

	Min.	Total FG/FGA	Pct.	3-Pt. FG/FGA	Pct.	FT/FTA	Pct.	Reb. O/T	A	TO	PF	S	Blk	TP	PPM
MCDONALD, P.	31	5/9	.556	0/0	.000	1/1	1.000	-/6	1	-	3	-	-	11	.355
WILLIAMS, R.	32	9/19	.474	3/9	.333	0/0	.000	-/10	3	-	1	-	-	21	.656
GILLERY, B.	3	1/1	1.000	0/0	.000	0/0	.000	-/3	0	-	1	-	-	2	.667
BRYANT	22	2/2	1.000	1/1	1.000	0/0	.000	-/1	5	-	2	-	-	5	.227
TILLMON, M.	20	5/10	.500	1/3	.333	3/4	.750	-/3	1	-	1	-	-	14	.700
HIGHSMITH	19	1/1	1.000	0/0	.000	0/0	.000	-/1	0	-	0	-	-	2	.105
WINSTON, B.	17	1/1	1.000	0/0	.000	0/2	.000	-/3	7	-	2	-	-	2	.118
SMITH, C.	19	1/5	.200	0/1	.000	3/4	.750	-/1	0	-	1	-	-	5	.263
EDWARDS	3	0/0	.000	0/0	.000	0/0	.000	-/0	0	-	1	-	-	0	.000
JACKSON, J.	10	3/3	1.000	0/0	.000	0/0	.000	-/3	0	-	1	-	-	6	.600
ALLEN	16	2/6	.333	0/0	.000	0/0	.000	-/3	0	-	1	-	-	4	.250
LANG	1	0/0	.000	0/0	.000	1/2	.500	-/0	0	-	0	-	-	1	1.000
JEFFERSON, S.	7	1/1	1.000	0/0	.000	0/0	.000	-/1	1	-	0	-	-	2	.286
Totals	200	31/58	.534	5/14	.357	8/13	.615	-/35	18	-	14	-	-	75	.375

Bucknell (53) Coach: Charles Woollum

	Min.	Total FG/FGA	Pct.	3-Pt. FG/FGA	Pct.	FT/FTA	Pct.	Reb. O/T	A	TO	PF	S	Blk	TP	PPM
ATKINSON	34	3/5	.600	0/0	.000	5/6	.833	-/4	2	-	0	-	-	11	.324
SCHRAEDER	23	4/8	.500	2/4	.500	0/0	.000	-/2	1	-	5	-	-	10	.435
HEIDEN	17	5/6	.833	0/0	.000	0/0	.000	-/2	0	-	1	-	-	10	.588
SENECA	39	3/7	.429	2/3	.667	0/0	.000	-/2	9	-	2	-	-	8	.205
ALLSTEAD	30	2/9	.222	1/2	.500	0/0	.000	-/3	3	-	3	-	-	5	.167
BUTTS	23	1/4	.250	0/0	.000	3/4	.750	-/1	0	-	1	-	-	5	.217
BEECY	19	1/2	.500	0/1	.000	0/0	.000	-/0	0	-	1	-	-	2	.105
ACETO	8	0/3	.000	0/1	.000	2/2	1.000	-/0	0	-	0	-	-	2	.250
JOSEPH, M.	1	0/1	.000	0/0	.000	0/0	.000	-/0	0	-	1	-	-	0	.000
WATSON	1	0/0	.000	0/0	.000	0/0	.000	-/0	0	-	0	-	-	0	.000
WOOLLUM	1	0/0	.000	0/0	.000	0/0	.000	-/0	0	-	0	-	-	0	.000
MOYLAN	1	0/0	.000	0/0	.000	0/0	.000	-/1	0	-	0	-	-	0	.000
ALLEN	1	0/0	.000	0/0	.000	0/0	.000	-/0	0	-	1	-	-	0	.000
LEGGETT, G.	1	0/1	.000	0/0	.000	0/0	.000	-/0	0	-	0	-	-	0	.000
ALBEE	1	0/0	.000	0/0	.000	0/0	.000	-/0	0	-	0	-	-	0	.000
Totals	200	19/46	.413	5/11	.455	10/12	.833	-/15	15	-	15	-	-	53	.265

Disqualified: Bucknell—Schraeder. Technical fouls: None.

	1st Half	2nd Half	Final
Georgetown	37	38	75
Bucknell	29	24	53

Kentucky (77) Coach: Eddie Sutton

	Min.	Total FG/FGA	Pct.	3-Pt. FG/FGA	Pct.	FT/FTA	Pct.	Reb. O/T	A	TO	PF	S	Blk	TP	PPM
CHAPMAN, R.	33	4/16	.250	2/9	.222	3/3	1.000	1/4	2	3	5	1	0	13	.394
MADISON, R.	34	4/7	.571	0/0	.000	1/3	.333	1/4	1	2	3	0	0	9	.265
LOCK, R.	27	6/8	.750	0/0	.000	2/3	.667	4/5	0	2	4	0	1	14	.519
BLACKMAN, J.	26	2/6	.333	2/6	.333	0/0	.000	2/3	3	1	1	3	0	6	.231
DAVENDER, E.	35	7/13	.538	2/4	.500	7/8	.875	0/1	5	2	3	3	0	23	.657
ANDREWS, P.	20	3/5	.600	0/1	.000	0/0	.000	1/1	1	1	4	2	0	6	.300
THOMAS, I.	9	0/0	.000	0/0	.000	0/0	.000	0/0	2	1	3	2	0	0	.000
JENKINS, C.	10	0/0	.000	0/0	.000	0/0	.000	0/2	1	0	0	0	0	0	.000
MILLER, D.	5	2/3	.667	2/3	.667	0/0	.000	0/0	0	0	1	0	0	6	1.200
SCOTT, M.	1	0/0	.000	0/0	.000	0/1	.000	0/1	0	0	0	0	0	0	.000
Totals	200	28/58	.483	8/23	.348	13/17	.765	9/21	15	12	24	11	1	77	.385

Ohio State (91) Coach: Gary Williams

	Min.	Total FG/FGA	Pct.	3-Pt. FG/FGA	Pct.	FT/FTA	Pct.	Reb. O/T	A	TO	PF	S	Blk	TP	PPM
HOPSON, D.	36	12/19	.632	1/2	.500	7/8	.875	2/6	5	1	3	1	0	32	.889
FRANCIS, J.	31	3/5	.600	0/0	.000	9/11	.818	1/5	0	1	2	3	0	15	.484
ANDERSON, J.	30	4/5	.800	0/0	.000	2/2	1.000	2/4	0	1	2	0	0	10	.333
WILSON, J.	32	7/10	.700	1/1	1.000	4/4	1.000	0/4	6	8	2	2	0	19	.594
BURSON, J.	34	5/9	.556	0/0	.000	1/3	.333	1/4	6	2	2	1	0	11	.324
WHITE, T.	12	1/1	1.000	0/0	.000	0/1	.000	1/4	0	1	0	0	0	2	.167
WESSON, K.	10	0/0	.000	0/0	.000	0/0	.000	0/0	0	1	1	0	0	0	.000
LOMAX, K.	15	1/1	1.000	0/0	.000	0/1	.000	0/2	1	0	4	0	0	2	.133
Totals	200	33/50	.660	2/3	.667	23/30	.767	7/29	18	15	16	7	0	91	.455

Team Rebounds: Ohio State 3; Kentucky 2. Disqualified: Kentucky—Chapman. Technical fouls: None.

	1st Half	2nd Half	Final
Kentucky	40	37	77
Ohio State	42	49	91

Kansas (66) Coach: Larry Brown

	Min.	Total FG/FGA	Pct.	3-Pt. FG/FGA	Pct.	FT/FTA	Pct.	Reb. O/T	A	TO	PF	S	Blk	TP	PPM
PIPER, C.	32	4/8	.500	0/0	.000	2/2	1.000	1/5	3	0	0	1	0	10	.313
MANNING, D.	39	6/13	.462	0/0	.000	0/0	.000	1/7	1	2	2	1	0	12	.308
PELLOCK, M.	21	1/4	.250	0/0	.000	1/2	.500	2/4	1	1	3	0	0	3	.143
PRITCHARD, K.	30	7/11	.636	1/2	.500	2/2	1.000	0/2	3	0	4	1	0	17	.567
HUNTER, C.	32	6/12	.500	0/1	.000	0/1	.000	2/4	8	2	0	4	0	12	.375
TURGEON, D.	16	2/3	.667	0/0	.000	0/0	.000	0/1	2	2	1	2	0	4	.250
RANDALL, M.	5	0/2	.000	0/0	.000	0/0	.000	1/1	0	1	0	1	0	0	.000
HARRIS, K.	15	1/3	.333	0/0	.000	0/0	.000	1/1	2	3	1	2	0	2	.133
NEWTON, M.	7	3/6	.500	0/0	.000	0/0	.000	1/2	0	0	1	0	0	6	.857
BARRY, R.	3	0/0	.000	0/0	.000	0/0	.000	0/0	1	0	0	0	0	0	.000
Totals	200	30/62	.484	1/3	.333	5/7	.714	9/27	21	11	12	12	1	66	.330

Houston (55) Coach: Pat Foster

	Min.	Total FG/FGA	Pct.	3-Pt. FG/FGA	Pct.	FT/FTA	Pct.	Reb. O/T	A	TO	PF	S	Blk	TP	PPM
WINSLOW, R.	37	9/11	.818	1/1	1.000	2/2	1.000	3/8	4	0	4	1	1	21	.568
ANDERSON, G.	33	8/11	.727	0/0	.000	2/5	.400	1/6	0	5	2	1	2	18	.545
FERREIRA, R.	34	3/8	.375	0/0	.000	0/0	.000	1/8	1	1	1	0	1	6	.176
BROWN, R.	25	0/0	.000	0/0	.000	0/0	.000	0/3	5	5	1	1	0	0	.000
HOBBY, T.	18	0/5	.000	0/1	.000	2/2	1.000	0/3	3	0	1	0	0	2	.111
MCARTHUR, D.	20	1/4	.250	0/0	.000	0/0	.000	0/3	4	5	0	0	0	2	.100
BREWER	9	0/2	.000	0/1	.000	0/0	.000	0/0	0	2	1	0	0	0	.000
JACKSON, R.	18	2/7	.286	2/4	.500	0/0	.000	1/1	0	1	1	0	1	6	.333
GRANT, T.	1	0/0	.000	0/0	.000	0/0	.000	0/0	0	1	0	0	0	0	.000
BELCHER, S.	5	0/0	.000	0/0	.000	0/0	.000	0/0	0	0	0	0	0	0	.000
Totals	200	23/48	.479	3/7	.429	6/9	.667	6/29	17	20	11	3	5	55	.275

Team Rebounds: Kansas 3; Houston 1. Disqualified: None. Technical fouls: None.

	1st Half	2nd Half	Final
Kansas	34	32	66
Houston	21	34	55

Clemson (60) Coach: Cliff Ellis

	Min.	Total FG/FGA	Pct.	3-Pt. FG/FGA	Pct.	FT/FTA	Pct.	Reb. O/T	A	TO	PF	S	Blk	TP	PPM
PRYOR, J.	24	2/6	.333	0/0	.000	0/0	.000	0/1	2	1	1	0	0	4	.167
JENKINS, A.	10	0/0	.000	0/1	.000	0/0	.000	1/2	2	1	0	1	0	0	.000
GRANT, H.	40	7/11	.636	0/0	.000	2/3	.667	0/7	2	6	3	3	0	16	.400
TAIT, M.	26	2/6	.333	2/4	.500	0/0	.000	2/3	2	1	3	0	0	6	.231
MARSHALL, G.	37	1/2	.500	1/1	1.000	0/0	.000	0/2	5	4	2	0	0	3	.081
MIDDLETON, L.	27	4/8	.500	0/0	.000	3/3	1.000	3/3	4	1	5	1	0	11	.407
CAMPBELL, E.	15	3/4	.750	0/0	.000	0/0	.000	0/1	0	1	4	0	2	6	.400
BROWN, M.	20	6/7	.857	2/3	.667	0/0	.000	1/1	1	0	3	0	2	14	.700
HOLSTEIN, J.	1	0/0	.000	0/0	.000	0/0	.000	0/0	0	0	0	0	0	0	.000
Totals	200	25/46	.543	5/9	.556	5/6	.833	7/20	18	15	21	5	4	60	.300

South Western Missouri State (65) Coach: Charles Spoonhour

	Min.	Total FG/FGA	Pct.	3-Pt. FG/FGA	Pct.	FT/FTA	Pct.	Reb. O/T	A	TO	PF	S	Blk	TP	PPM
WORTHY, S.	17	3/6	.500	0/0	.000	0/0	.000	0/3	2	1	2	1	0	6	.353
BELL, G.	40	1/4	.250	0/0	.000	5/8	.625	3/3	0	1	2	2	0	7	.175
STUCKEY, K.	28	2/4	.500	0/0	.000	2/3	.667	3/4	0	1	4	0	0	6	.214
ROBINSON, B.	37	5/7	.714	1/2	.500	2/2	1.000	0/2	6	2	3	1	0	13	.351
GARLAND, W.	40	8/16	.500	2/2	1.000	6/8	.750	2/6	3	8	0	2	0	24	.600
KICKOX, S.	15	0/1	.000	0/0	.000	0/0	.000	1/3	0	1	0	0	0	0	.000
HOLT, C.	23	3/8	.375	1/4	.250	2/2	1.000	0/1	2	0	2	1	0	9	.391
Totals	200	22/46	.478	4/8	.500	17/23	.739	9/22	13	13	14	7	0	65	.325

Team Rebounds: SW Missouri St. 7; Clemson 2. Disqualified: Clemson—Middleton. Technical fouls: None.

	1st Half	2nd Half	Final
Clemson	28	32	60
SW Missouri St.	28	37	65

Providence (90) — Coach: Rick Pitino

	Min.	Total FG/FGA	Pct.	3-Pt. FG/FGA	Pct.	FT/FTA	Pct.	Reb. O/T	A	TO	PF	S	Blk	TP	PPM
KIPFER, D.	28	4/11	.364	0/0	.000	2/2	1.000	2/5	0	1	3	2	0	10	.357
LEWIS, E.	26	2/8	.250	1/6	.167	0/0	.000	0/3	2	0	3	2	0	5	.192
DUDA, J.	15	1/3	.333	0/0	.000	0/0	.000	3/6	0	1	4	0	0	2	.133
BROOKS, D.	37	6/11	.545	3/5	.600	1/2	.500	1/9	3	3	1	2	0	16	.432
DONOVAN, B.	36	12/17	.706	6/9	.667	5/7	.714	1/4	12	6	3	3	0	35	.972
FORD, R.	6	0/2	.000	0/1	.000	0/0	.000	0/0	0	0	0	0	0	0	.000
SHAMSID-DEEN, A.	19	5/7	.714	0/0	.000	2/4	.500	3/5	0	2	3	1	1	12	.632
CONLON, M.	9	1/1	1.000	0/0	.000	0/0	.000	0/0	0	0	3	0	0	2	.222
SMEDEKER, D.	3	0/0	.000	0/0	.000	0/0	.000	0/0	0	0	0	0	0	0	.000
WRIGHT, D.	15	4/7	.571	0/1	.000	0/0	.000	0/3	0	0	2	1	0	8	.533
BENHAM, B.	1	0/0	.000	0/0	.000	0/0	.000	0/1	0	0	0	0	0	0	.000
WRIGHT, S.	5	0/1	.000	0/0	.000	0/0	.000	0/0	0	0	5	0	0	0	.000
Totals	200	35/68	.515	10/22	.455	10/15	.667	10/36	17	13	27	11	1	90	.450

Alabama-Birmingham (68) — Coach: Gene Bartow

	Min.	Total FG/FGA	Pct.	3-Pt. FG/FGA	Pct.	FT/FTA	Pct.	Reb. O/T	A	TO	PF	S	Blk	TP	PPM
TURNER	27	1/4	.250	0/1	.000	2/4	.500	6/8	3	3	5	0	0	4	.148
REMBERT, L.	7	0/3	.000	0/0	.000	0/0	.000	0/1	0	2	1	0	1	0	.000
COLLINS	23	5/11	.455	0/0	.000	7/8	.875	2/10	0	1	0	0	0	17	.739
FOSTER	28	2/8	.250	1/4	.250	4/4	1.000	2/2	1	1	3	2	0	9	.321
PONDER	28	4/13	.308	1/6	.167	3/4	.750	3/5	1	4	4	0	0	12	.429
BEARDEN	10	1/2	.500	0/1	.000	0/1	.000	0/2	1	1	1	0	0	2	.200
WICKSELL	1	0/0	.000	0/0	.000	0/1	.000	0/1	0	1	0	0	0	0	.000
CHARLES	19	0/5	.000	0/0	.000	0/0	.000	1/4	3	6	1	0	0	0	.000
THOMAS	3	0/1	.000	0/1	.000	0/0	.000	0/0	0	0	0	0	0	0	.000
HOWARD	32	3/6	.500	0/0	.000	7/8	.875	3/5	3	1	2	1	1	13	.406
EVANS	3	1/1	1.000	0/0	.000	0/0	.000	1/1	0	0	0	0	0	2	.667
OGG	19	4/6	.667	0/0	.000	1/3	.333	2/6	0	0	3	1	1	9	.474
Totals	200	21/60	.350	2/13	.154	24/33	.727	20/45	12	20	20	4	3	68	.340

Team Rebounds: Providence 3; Ala.-Birmingham 1. Disqualified: Providence—S. Wright; Ala.-Birmingham—Turner. Technical fouls: None.

	1st Half	2nd Half	Final
Providence	49	41	90
Ala.-Birmingham	37	31	68

Illinois (67) — Coach: Lou Henson

	Min.	Total FG/FGA	Pct.	3-Pt. FG/FGA	Pct.	FT/FTA	Pct.	Reb. O/T	A	TO	PF	S	Blk	TP	PPM
ALTENBERGER, D.	36	4/10	.400	0/5	.000	4/5	.800	3/6	4	1	4	0	0	12	.333
NORMAN, K.	40	7/14	.500	0/0	.000	3/5	.600	5/12	1	3	3	0	0	17	.425
KUJAWA, J.	15	1/5	.200	0/0	.000	0/0	.000	1/4	0	0	3	0	0	2	.133
WYSINGER, T.	36	7/12	.583	0/2	.000	2/2	1.000	0/2	5	1	2	2	0	16	.444
BARDO, S.	30	3/9	.333	0/0	.000	0/1	.000	2/3	4	7	3	2	1	6	.200
GILL, K.	3	0/0	.000	0/0	.000	0/0	.000	0/0	0	0	0	0	1	0	.000
BLACKWELL, G.	15	1/3	.333	0/0	.000	0/1	.000	2/4	1	2	1	0	1	2	.133
HAMILTON, L.	25	6/8	.750	0/0	.000	0/0	.000	2/7	0	0	4	0	3	12	.480
Totals	200	29/61	.475	0/7	.000	9/14	.643	15/38	15	14	20	5	5	67	.335

Austin Peay (68) — Coach: Lake Kelly

	Min.	Total FG/FGA	Pct.	3-Pt. FG/FGA	Pct.	FT/FTA	Pct.	Reb. O/T	A	TO	PF	S	Blk	TP	PPM
RAYE, T.	33	0/0	.000	0/0	.000	6/9	.667	2/5	2	1	4	1	0	6	.182
MITCHELL, L.	37	7/19	.368	1/3	.333	7/11	.636	3/7	2	1	4	0	0	22	.595
BEDFORD, D.	35	9/20	.450	5/13	.385	1/2	.500	0/6	1	4	4	1	1	24	.686
ARMSTRONG, R.	40	4/7	.571	0/0	.000	0/0	.000	2/5	4	4	4	0	0	8	.200
HICKS, M.	40	4/8	.500	0/0	.000	0/2	.000	3/4	3	1	2	2	0	8	.200
ORR, E.	11	0/2	.000	0/0	.000	0/0	.000	0/1	0	1	1	1	0	0	.000
THOMAS, B.	4	0/1	.000	0/0	.000	0/0	.000	1/1	1	0	0	0	0	0	.000
Totals	200	24/57	.421	6/16	.375	14/24	.583	11/29	13	12	19	5	1	68	.340

Team Rebounds: Austin Peay 5; Illinois 3. Disqualified: None. Technical fouls: None.

	1st Half	2nd Half	Final
Illinois	32	35	67
Austin Peay	32	36	68

New Orleans (83) — Coach: Benny Dees

	Min.	Total FG/FGA	Pct.	3-Pt. FG/FGA	Pct.	FT/FTA	Pct.	Reb. O/T	A	TO	PF	S	Blk	TP	PPM
JONES, S.	27	3/7	.429	1/3	.333	0/0	.000	1/3	0	3	0	0	0	7	.259
GRANDISON, R.	29	5/7	.714	0/0	.000	5/7	.714	4/11	0	1	4	3	0	15	.517
SMITH, M.	20	1/2	.500	0/0	.000	2/4	.500	2/4	1	0	3	0	0	4	.200
CORCHIANI, G.	31	2/6	.333	2/3	.667	3/4	.750	0/2	7	3	1	0	0	9	.290
EACKLES, L.	35	9/19	.474	4/6	.667	3/5	.600	1/3	0	1	1	0	0	25	.714
RICHARDSON, W.	10	0/2	.000	0/0	.000	0/0	.000	0/1	2	1	2	0	0	0	.000
PERKINS, W.	12	1/5	.200	0/1	.000	0/0	.000	0/0	1	1	0	0	0	2	.167
IRVING, E.	13	2/4	.500	1/1	1.000	1/1	1.000	0/0	0	0	4	0	0	6	.462
BELLOCK, T.	20	6/8	.750	0/0	.000	3/4	.750	3/3	1	2	3	1	0	15	.750
VANCE, D.	3	0/0	.000	0/0	.000	0/0	.000	0/0	0	0	1	0	0	0	.000
Totals	200	29/60	.483	8/14	.571	17/25	.680	11/27	12	12	19	4	0	83	.415

Brigham Young (79) — Coach: Ladell Anderson

	Min.	Total FG/FGA	Pct.	3-Pt. FG/FGA	Pct.	FT/FTA	Pct.	Reb. O/T	A	TO	PF	S	Blk	TP	PPM
CHATMAN, J.	31	11/17	.647	0/0	.000	3/4	.750	4/10	0	3	5	0	0	25	.806
SMITH, M.	35	9/25	.360	0/3	.000	5/5	1.000	7/15	3	3	2	0	0	23	.657
GNEITING, T.	23	1/5	.200	0/0	.000	0/1	.000	4/10	2	1	4	0	0	2	.087
CALL, N.	19	1/2	.500	0/0	.000	0/0	.000	1/2	3	2	1	0	0	2	.105
CAPENER, B.	26	2/6	.333	0/1	.000	0/0	.000	0/2	2	0	1	0	0	4	.154
TAYLOR, B.	14	2/2	1.000	1/1	1.000	1/1	1.000	1/2	3	2	2	0	0	6	.429
HAWS, M.	21	2/4	.500	0/0	.000	1/2	.500	0/1	1	4	1	1	0	5	.238
STEPHENSON, B.	14	1/2	.500	0/0	.000	2/4	.500	1/2	0	2	1	0	0	4	.286
USEVITCH, J.	17	3/3	1.000	0/0	.000	2/4	.500	1/5	0	1	5	1	1	8	.471
Totals	200	32/66	.485	1/5	.200	14/21	.667	19/47	14	20	22	4	1	79	.395

Team Rebounds: New Orleans 2; Brigham Young 3. Disqualified: Brigham Young—Chatman, Usevitch. Technical fouls: Brigham Young—Smith.

	1st Half	2nd Half	Final
New Orleans	40	43	83
Brigham Young	29	50	79

Alabama (88) — Coach: Wimp Sanderson

	Min.	Total FG/FGA	Pct.	3-Pt. FG/FGA	Pct.	FT/FTA	Pct.	Reb. O/T	A	TO	PF	S	Blk	TP	PPM
FARMER, J.	37	12/17	.706	4/5	.800	1/1	1.000	1/1	2	4	2	0	0	29	.784
ANSLEY, M.	31	2/5	.400	0/0	.000	2/3	.667	0/5	2	1	4	0	0	6	.194
MCKEY, D.	37	8/14	.571	1/1	1.000	8/8	1.000	5/14	2	4	3	0	2	25	.676
GOTTFRIED, M.	28	3/5	.600	2/3	.667	0/0	.000	1/2	3	1	2	5	0	8	.286
CONER, T.	30	1/3	.333	0/0	.000	0/0	.000	0/4	4	5	1	2	0	2	.067
JACKSON, J.	20	3/4	.750	2/2	1.000	2/2	1.000	0/1	2	2	0	3	0	10	.500
ASKINS, K.	12	2/5	.400	0/0	.000	2/2	1.000	2/2	1	2	2	0	0	6	.500
DEVAUGHN, K.	4	1/2	.500	0/0	.000	0/0	.000	1/1	0	0	1	0	1	2	.500
COMEGY	1	0/0	.000	0/0	.000	0/0	.000	0/0	0	0	1	0	0	0	.000
Totals	200	32/55	.582	9/11	.818	15/16	.938	10/30	16	19	16	10	3	88	.440

North Carolina A&T (71) — Coach: Don Corbett

	Min.	Total FG/FGA	Pct.	3-Pt. FG/FGA	Pct.	FT/FTA	Pct.	Reb. O/T	A	TO	PF	S	Blk	TP	PPM
WILLIAMS, C.	38	10/14	.714	0/0	.000	5/8	.625	5/7	3	2	4	2	1	25	.658
BECTON, C.	11	0/2	.000	0/1	.000	0/0	.000	0/2	0	4	1	0	0	0	.000
ROBINSON, L.	30	2/5	.400	0/0	.000	1/2	.500	1/4	2	0	2	1	0	5	.167
GRIFFIS, T.	40	4/15	.267	2/6	.333	3/3	1.000	2/3	6	3	2	0	0	13	.325
CALE, G.	37	8/13	.615	0/0	.000	0/0	.000	2/4	3	2	4	2	0	16	.432
DAVIS	28	3/13	.231	0/5	.000	2/2	1.000	3/4	1	4	0	0	0	8	.286
COX, K.	13	1/5	.200	0/0	.000	2/4	.500	3/5	1	0	2	1	1	4	.308
MCRAE	3	0/0	.000	0/0	.000	0/0	.000	0/0	0	0	1	0	0	0	.000
Totals	200	28/67	.418	2/12	.167	13/19	.684	16/29	16	15	16	9	2	71	.355

Team Rebounds: Alabama 2; N. Carolina A&T 5. Disqualified: None. Technical fouls: Alabama—DeVaughn.

	1st Half	2nd Half	Final
Alabama	37	51	88
N. Carolina A&T	27	44	71

FIRST ROUND EAST

North Carolina (113)   Coach: Dean Smith

	Min.	Total FG/FGA	Pct.	3-Pt. FG/FGA	Pct.	FT/FTA	Pct.	Reb. O/T	A	TO	PF	S	Blk	TP	PPM
WOLF, J.	28	9/14	.643	0/1	.000	7/10	.700	2/4	2	1	3	1	0	25	.893
POPSON, D.	16	5/9	.556	0/0	.000	1/1	1.000	2/5	1	1	4	1	1	11	.688
REID, J.	26	2/5	.400	0/0	.000	7/10	.700	2/7	1	0	5	1	0	11	.423
LEBO, J.	29	6/9	.667	4/7	.571	2/2	1.000	0/2	6	2	3	0	0	18	.621
SMITH, K.	28	4/10	.400	3/7	.429	4/4	1.000	2/4	11	3	0	2	0	15	.536
BUCKNALL, S.	21	4/5	.800	0/1	.000	2/4	.500	3/4	4	2	0	0	0	10	.476
SMITH, R.	14	2/4	.500	1/1	1.000	4/4	1.000	2/3	2	0	0	0	0	9	.643
WILLIAMS, S.	13	1/2	.500	0/0	.000	4/6	.667	1/5	0	4	0	3	6	.462
O'KOREN, M.	5	0/0	.000	0/0	.000	1/2	.500	0/0	0	1	1	1	0	1	.200
HUNTER, C.	8	2/5	.400	0/2	.000	0/0	.000	1/1	1	0	0	0	0	4	.500
HENSLEY, M.	4	1/1	1.000	0/0	.000	1/2	.500	2/3	0	0	0	0	0	3	.750
DENNY, J.	4	0/1	.000	0/1	.000	0/0	.000	0/0	0	0	0	0	0	0	.000
HYATT, R.	4	0/0	.000	0/0	.000	0/0	.000	0/0	2	0	1	0	0	0	.000
Totals	200	36/65	.554	8/20	.400	33/45	.733	17/38	30	10	21	6	4	113	.565

Pennsylvania (82)   Coach: Tom Schneider

	Min.	Total FG/FGA	Pct.	3-Pt. FG/FGA	Pct.	FT/FTA	Pct.	Reb. O/T	A	TO	PF	S	Blk	TP	PPM
PITTS, T.	27	4/14	.286	0/0	.000	4/6	.667	2/4	1	3	3	1	0	12	.444
STOVALL, J.	36	6/11	.545	0/0	.000	1/2	.500	2/5	1	3	5	0	1	13	.361
LEFKOWITZ, B.	32	6/12	.500	0/0	.000	8/12	.667	4/8	0	1	5	1	0	20	.625
BROMWELL, P.	33	8/15	.533	3/4	.750	0/0	.000	0/1	0	7	3	1	0	19	.576
WILSON, J.	22	1/1	1.000	0/0	.000	0/0	.000	0/0	6	2	3	2	0	2	.091
FRAZIER, W.	4	2/3	.667	0/0	.000	0/0	.000	0/0	0	0	0	0	0	4	1.000
FIKES, K.	6	3/6	.500	0/0	.000	0/0	.000	1/1	0	1	1	0	0	6	1.000
ELZEY, C.	11	0/0	.000	0/0	.000	0/0	.000	0/0	2	0	1	0	0	0	.000
TAVAREZ, J.	1	0/0	.000	0/0	.000	0/0	.000	0/0	0	0	1	0	0	0	.000
BENTIVEGNA, P.	2	0/0	.000	0/0	.000	0/0	.000	0/0	0	0	0	0	0	0	.000
SIMON, J.	15	0/0	.000	0/0	.000	0/0	.000	0/0	3	3	0	0	0	0	.000
OKORODUDO, A.	7	0/0	.000	0/0	.000	0/2	.000	0/1	0	1	3	0	0	0	.000
MILHOLLAND, K.	4	2/2	1.000	0/0	.000	2/3	.667	0/0	0	0	1	0	0	6	1.500
Totals	200	32/64	.500	3/4	.750	15/25	.600	9/20	10	21	29	5	1	82	.410

Team Rebounds: N. Carolina 5; Pennsylvania 12. Disqualified: N. Carolina—Reid; Pennsylvania—Stovall, Lefkowitz. Technical fouls: None.

	1st Half	2nd Half	Final
N. Carolina	55	58	113
Pennsylvania	53	29	82

Navy (82)   Coach: Pete Hermann

	Min.	Total FG/FGA	Pct.	3-Pt. FG/FGA	Pct.	FT/FTA	Pct.	Reb. O/T	A	TO	PF	S	Blk	TP	PPM
TURNER, D.	32	2/6	.333	0/0	.000	0/0	.000	5/6	2	1	4	0	0	4	.125
LIEBERT, C.	33	5/10	.500	0/0	.000	2/3	.667	4/8	5	3	3	0	0	12	.364
ROBINSON, D.	40	22/37	.595	0/0	.000	6/12	.500	5/13	0	1	2	3	2	50	1.250
WOJCIK, J.	38	0/6	.000	0/0	.000	1/2	.500	3/4	6	3	5	1	0	1	.026
REES, C.	40	5/12	.417	2/4	.500	0/0	.000	1/2	3	2	2	1	0	12	.300
FENTON, N.	7	1/4	.250	1/4	.250	0/1	.000	1/1	2	0	3	0	0	3	.429
PRATHER, C.	3	0/0	.000	0/0	.000	0/0	.000	0/0	1	2	1	1	0	0	.000
MANHERTZ, J.	3	0/0	.000	0/0	.000	0/0	.000	0/1	0	0	0	0	0	0	.000
HOPKINS, B.	4	0/0	.000	0/0	.000	0/0	.000	0/0	0	0	0	0	0	0	.000
Totals	200	35/75	.467	3/14	.214	9/18	.500	19/35	19	12	20	6	2	82	.410

Michigan (97)   Coach: Bill Freider

	Min.	Total FG/FGA	Pct.	3-Pt. FG/FGA	Pct.	FT/FTA	Pct.	Reb. O/T	A	TO	PF	S	Blk	TP	PPM
JOUBERT, A.	36	1/5	.200	1/4	.250	3/4	.750	0/1	3	2	2	1	0	6	.167
RICE, G.	39	10/17	.588	0/0	.000	1/2	.500	4/12	3	1	2	3	0	21	.538
HUGHES, M.	23	0/2	.000	0/0	.000	0/0	.000	3/6	2	0	4	0	1	0	.000
GRANT, G.	39	9/17	.529	2/4	.500	6/8	.750	2/4	6	3	2	0	1	26	.667
THOMPSON, G.	39	11/14	.786	9/12	.750	2/3	.667	0/1	6	3	3	2	0	33	.846
GIBAS, R.	1	0/0	.000	0/0	.000	0/0	.000	0/0	0	0	0	0	0	0	.000
KRAMER, J.	2	0/0	.000	0/0	.000	3/4	.750	0/0	0	0	1	0	0	3	1.500
VAUGHT, L.	16	3/3	1.000	0/0	.000	0/0	.000	2/7	0	2	3	0	1	6	.375
OOSTERBAAN, J.	5	1/2	.500	0/0	.000	0/0	.000	0/0	0	0	3	0	0	2	.400
Totals	200	35/60	.583	12/20	.600	15/21	.714	11/31	20	11	20	6	3	97	.485

Team Rebounds: Michigan 2; Navy 7. Disqualified: Navy—Wojcik. Technical fouls: None.

	1st Half	2nd Half	Final
Navy	44	38	82
Michigan	49	48	97

Notre Dame (84)   Coach: Digger Phelps

	Min.	Total FG/FGA	Pct.	3-Pt. FG/FGA	Pct.	FT/FTA	Pct.	Reb. O/T	A	TO	PF	S	Blk	TP	PPM
ROYAL, D.	40	8/15	.533	0/0	.000	8/10	.800	3/7	3	1	3	1	0	24	.600
STEVENSON, M.	38	5/11	.455	0/0	.000	7/9	.778	3/6	2	3	3	0	1	17	.447
VOCE, G.	35	1/1	1.000	0/0	.000	0/0	.000	0/3	1	1	4	0	0	2	.057
RIVERS, D.	40	8/15	.533	1/2	.500	10/11	.909	0/7	6	1	2	2	0	27	.675
HICKS, S.	31	6/10	.600	0/0	.000	2/2	1.000	0/3	0	0	3	1	0	14	.452
CONNOR, S.	3	0/0	.000	0/0	.000	0/0	.000	0/0	0	0	0	0	0	0	.000
JACKSON, J.	8	0/1	.000	0/0	.000	0/0	.000	1/2	0	0	0	0	0	0	.000
PADDOCK, S.	5	0/0	.000	0/0	.000	0/0	.000	0/0	0	0	1	0	0	0	.000
Totals	200	28/53	.528	1/2	.500	27/32	.844	7/28	12	6	16	4	1	84	.420

Middle Tennessee State (71)   Coach: Bruce Stewart

	Min.	Total FG/FGA	Pct.	3-Pt. FG/FGA	Pct.	FT/FTA	Pct.	Reb. O/T	A	TO	PF	S	Blk	TP	PPM
TURNSTILL, A.	35	2/4	.500	0/0	.000	2/3	.667	2/4	5	1	4	1	0	6	.171
HENRY, R.	21	6/11	.545	0/0	.000	1/2	.500	3/3	0	2	3	0	0	13	.619
RAINEY, D.	36	8/19	.421	0/0	.000	6/7	.857	4/6	1	2	5	0	0	22	.611
WASHINGTON, D.	39	1/9	.111	0/1	.000	0/0	.000	1/9	7	2	4	1	0	2	.051
RAINEY, C.	23	4/7	.571	2/3	.667	0/0	.000	0/0	0	1	2	0	0	10	.435
BAYNHAM, T.	20	2/4	.500	0/0	.000	3/4	.750	2/3	2	1	4	0	0	7	.350
SNELL, P.	1	0/1	.000	0/1	.000	0/0	.000	0/0	0	0	0	0	0	0	.000
HARRIS, G.	1	0/1	.000	0/-	.000	0/0	.000	0/0	0	0	0	0	0	0	.000
COOK, T.	1	0/0	.000	0/0	.000	0/0	.000	1/1	0	0	0	0	0	0	.000
MILLER, B.	1	0/0	.000	0/0	.000	0/0	.000	0/0	0	0	0	0	0	0	.000
HAMMONDS, K.	21	4/7	.571	0/0	.000	3/3	1.000	1/4	1	1	2	0	1	11	.524
MCGILL, J.	1	0/0	.000	0/0	.000	0/0	.000	0/0	0	0	0	0	0	0	.000
Totals	200	27/63	.429	2/5	.400	15/19	.789	14/30	16	10	24	2	1	71	.355

Team Rebounds: Notre Dame 5; Middle Tenn. St. 5. Disqualified: Middle Tenn. St.—Rainey. Technical fouls: None.

	1st Half	2nd Half	Final
Notre Dame	37	47	84
Middle Tenn. St.	31	40	71

TCU (76)   Coach: Jim Killingsworth

	Min.	Total FG/FGA	Pct.	3-Pt. FG/FGA	Pct.	FT/FTA	Pct.	Reb. O/T	A	TO	PF	S	Blk	TP	PPM
RICHARD, L.	25	1/4	.250	0/0	.000	5/6	.833	5/5	0	3	4	0	0	7	.280
ANDERSON, N.	31	3/7	.429	0/0	.000	2/2	1.000	1/4	7	3	3	2	0	8	.258
PAPPA, T.	20	2/2	1.000	0/0	.000	2/2	1.000	1/2	1	0	3	2	0	6	.300
DIXON, J.	40	2/6	.333	1/2	.500	6/7	.857	0/4	4	2	2	1	0	11	.275
HOLCOMBE, C.	40	14/17	.824	0/0	.000	2/3	.667	1/3	5	3	1	0	2	30	.750
LOTT, C.	36	7/9	.778	0/0	.000	0/3	.000	1/4	1	0	0	1	0	14	.389
MINNIS, M.	6	0/0	.000	0/0	.000	0/0	.000	0/0	0	0	1	1	0	0	.000
MORTIMER, T.	2	0/0	.000	0/0	.000	0/0	.000	0/0	2	0	0	0	0	0	.000
Totals	200	29/45	.644	1/2	.500	17/23	.739	9/22	20	11	14	7	2	76	.380

Marshall (60)   Coach: Ricky Huckabay

	Min.	Total FG/FGA	Pct.	3-Pt. FG/FGA	Pct.	FT/FTA	Pct.	Reb. O/T	A	TO	PF	S	Blk	TP	PPM
HOLDEN, R.	34	2/4	.500	0/0	.000	3/6	.500	4/4	0	0	1	0	0	7	.206
LEWIS, D.	39	5/14	.357	1/2	.500	6/6	1.000	2/5	3	5	4	2	0	17	.436
CURRY, T.	26	2/2	1.000	0/0	.000	6/7	.857	2/3	4	1	4	0	1	10	.385
HENDERSON, S.	40	5/13	.385	4/8	.500	0/0	.000	0/1	1	2	1	1	0	14	.350
HUMPHREY, J.	33	4/8	.500	0/0	.000	2/2	1.000	0/3	1	5	4	0	0	10	.303
BROWN, P.	1	0/0	.000	0/0	.000	0/0	.000	0/0	0	0	0	0	0	0	.000
FISH, B.	7	0/1	.000	0/0	.000	0/0	.000	0/0	0	0	0	0	0	0	.000
BRYSON, M.	20	1/3	.333	0/0	.000	0/0	.000	0/0	0	2	3	1	1	2	.100
Totals	200	19/45	.422	5/10	.500	17/21	.810	8/16	5	15	19	4	2	60	.300

Team Rebounds: TCU 4; Marshall 4. Disqualified: None. Technical fouls: None.

	1st Half	2nd Half	Final
TCU	38	38	76
Marshall	27	33	60

Florida (82)   Coach: Norm Sloan

	Min.	Total FG / FGA	Pct.	3-Pt. FG / FGA	Pct.	FT / FTA	Pct.	Reb. O / T	A	TO	PF	S	Blk	TP	PPM
LAWRENCE, J.	32	3/ 5	.600	2/ 4	.500	0/ 0	.000	0/ 1	2	1	3	0	0	8	.250
LAWRENCE, P.	17	2/ 3	.667	1/ 2	.500	0/ 0	.000	1/ 4	1	0	4	0	0	5	.294
SCHINTZIUS, D.	32	4/12	.333	0/ 0	.000	1/ 1	1.000	0/ 4	4	4	2	0	3	9	.281
MAXWELL, V.	37	6/16	.375	2/ 4	.500	14/21	.667	3/ 7	1	1	2	2	0	28	.757
MOTEN, A.	32	5/ 8	.625	2/ 3	.667	7/ 7	1.000	1/ 7	3	2	0	0	0	19	.594
MONTGOMERY, R.	10	0/ 2	.000	0/ 1	.000	0/ 0	.000	0/ 1	0	0	0	0	0	0	.000
LETT, C.	11	0/ 1	.000	0/ 0	.000	1/ 2	.500	2/ 4	0	0	2	1	0	1	.091
CAPERS, C.	20	1/ 2	.500	0/ 0	.000	2/ 2	1.000	0/ 3	1	0	2	1	1	4	.200
MCCLARY, K.	9	4/ 5	.800	0/ 0	.000	0/ 1	.000	1/ 3	1	0	3	0	0	8	.889
Totals	200	25/54	.463	7/14	.500	25/34	.735	8/34	13	8	18	4	4	82	.410

North Carolina State (70)   Coach: Jim Valvano

	Min.	Total FG / FGA	Pct.	3-Pt. FG / FGA	Pct.	FT / FTA	Pct.	Reb. O / T	A	TO	PF	S	Blk	TP	PPM
BROWN, C.	29	3/ 5	.600	0/ 0	.000	3/ 4	.750	1/ 5	0	1	1	0	0	9	.310
BOLTON, B.	37	7/14	.500	4/ 7	.571	2/ 3	.667	0/ 4	2	3	3	1	0	20	.541
SHAKLEFORD, C.	32	6/10	.600	0/ 0	.000	0/ 2	.000	1/ 8	3	3	1	2	1	12	.375
JACKSON, Q.	34	4/ 8	.500	1/ 3	.333	2/ 2	1.000	1/ 5	5	1	2	1	0	9	.265
DEL NEGRO, V.	36	6/14	.429	0/ 3	.000	0/ 0	.000	1/ 4	4	1	5	0	0	12	.333
GIOMO, M.	12	0/ 3	.000	0/ 0	.000	0/ 0	.000	2/ 5	1	0	1	1	0	0	.000
LESTER, A.	3	0/ 0	.000	0/ 0	.000	0/ 0	.000	0/ 0	0	0	3	0	0	0	.000
WEEMS, K.	7	1/ 2	.500	0/ 0	.000	0/ 0	.000	0/ 1	0	0	2	1	0	2	.286
LAMBIOTTE, W.	6	1/ 2	.500	0/ 1	.000	0/ 0	.000	0/ 0	0	0	2	0	0	2	.333
HOWARD, B.	4	1/ 2	.500	0/ 0	.000	0/ 0	.000	0/ 0	0	1	2	0	0	2	.500
KENNEDY, A.	0	1/ 1	1.000	0/ 0	.000	0/ 0	.000	0/ 0	0	0	0	0	0	2	-
Totals	200	29/59	.492	5/14	.357	7/11	.636	6/32	15	10	22	6	1	70	.350

Team Rebounds: Florida 3; N.C. State 2. Disqualified: N.C. State—Del Negro. Technical fouls: None. Player who played 0 min. played less than 1 min.

	1st Half	2nd Half	Final
Florida	33	49	82
N.C. State	30	40	70

Purdue (104)   Coach: Gene Keady

	Min.	Total FG / FGA	Pct.	3-Pt. FG / FGA	Pct.	FT / FTA	Pct.	Reb. O / T	A	TO	PF	S	Blk	TP	PPM
MITCHELL, T.	30	3/ 9	.333	0/ 0	.000	4/ 6	.667	0/ 5	0	4	5	0	0	10	.333
LEE, D.	35	10/14	.714	6/ 8	.750	3/ 5	.600	6/13	3	5	2	2	0	29	.829
MCCANTS, M.	25	5/ 9	.556	0/ 0	.000	7/11	.636	3/ 7	0	0	3	0	0	17	.680
LEWIS, T.	38	6/14	.429	1/ 4	.250	7/10	.700	0/ 1	10	3	2	2	0	20	.526
STEPHENS, E.	32	6/ 7	.857	2/ 2	1.000	4/ 4	1.000	1/ 2	4	2	5	1	0	18	.563
JONES, T.	10	0/ 0	.000	0/ 0	.000	4/ 6	.667	0/ 2	4	2	3	1	0	4	.400
JONES, K.	11	1/ 1	1.000	0/ 0	.000	0/ 0	.000	0/ 0	0	0	2	0	0	2	.182
ARNOLD, J.	16	1/ 3	.333	0/ 0	.000	0/ 1	.000	1/ 5	1	0	3	1	0	2	.125
FISHER, T.	2	0/ 0	.000	0/ 0	.000	2/ 2	1.000	0/ 1	0	0	0	0	0	2	1.000
STACK, D.	1	0/ 0	.000	0/ 0	.000	0/ 0	.000	0/ 0	0	0	0	0	0	0	.000
Totals	200	32/57	.561	9/14	.643	31/45	.689	11/36	22	16	25	7	0	104	.520

Northeastern (95)   Coach: Karl Fogel

	Min.	Total FG / FGA	Pct.	3-Pt. FG / FGA	Pct.	FT / FTA	Pct.	Reb. O / T	A	TO	PF	S	Blk	TP	PPM
LEWIS, R.	37	5/12	.417	1/ 4	.250	12/16	.750	2/ 3	1	3	5	2	1	23	.622
FULLER, W.	31	4/10	.400	0/ 0	.000	1/ 2	.500	2/ 6	1	1	5	2	0	9	.290
MCDUFFIE, K.	34	3/10	.300	0/ 0	.000	3/ 5	.600	3/12	2	0	4	2	0	9	.265
WILLIAMS, J.	18	4/11	.364	2/ 7	.286	0/ 0	.000	1/ 3	2	0	2	1	0	10	.556
LAFLEUR, A.	40	8/13	.615	0/ 5	.000	6/ 7	.857	2/ 3	3	3	4	1	0	22	.550
LEWIS, D.	24	6/13	.462	3/ 3	1.000	4/ 4	1.000	1/ 4	0	2	5	0	0	19	.792
CORCORAN, G.	14	0/ 3	.000	0/ 0	.000	2/ 2	1.000	2/ 2	0	0	5	0	0	2	.143
HALL, E.	1	0/ 0	.000	0/ 0	.000	1/ 2	.500	1/ 2	0	0	4	0	0	1	1.000
SKEEN, E.	1	0/ 0	.000	0/ 0	.000	0/ 0	.000	0/ 0	0	0	0	0	0	0	.000
Totals	200	30/72	.417	6/21	.286	29/38	.763	14/35	9	9	34	8	1	95	.475

Team Rebounds: Purdue 6; Northeastern 5. Disqualified: Purdue—Mitchell, Stephens; Northeastern—R. Lewis, Fuller, D. Lewis, Corcoran. Technical fouls: Purdue—McCants (ejected, flagrant foul); Northeastern—Bench (2), Williams.

	1st Half	2nd Half	Final
Purdue	44	60	104
Northeastern	41	54	95

West Virginia (62)   Coach: Gale Catlett

	Min.	Total FG / FGA	Pct.	3-Pt. FG / FGA	Pct.	FT / FTA	Pct.	Reb. O / T	A	TO	PF	S	Blk	TP	PPM
SHAW, T.	34	6/10	.600	0/ 0	.000	6/ 8	.750	3/ 9	1	3	3	1	0	18	.529
YEARWOOD, D.	29	3/11	.273	0/ 1	.000	4/ 5	.800	0/ 4	3	3	1	1	0	10	.345
PRUE, D.	28	9/14	.643	0/ 0	.000	0/ 3	.000	0/ 5	1	2	3	1	1	18	.643
CRAWL, J.	35	1/ 5	.200	0/ 1	.000	2/ 2	1.000	1/ 4	5	1	1	1	0	4	.114
BROOKS, H.	15	3/ 6	.500	0/ 0	.000	0/ 0	.000	4/ 4	2	0	0	1	0	6	.400
BERGER, S.	16	0/ 1	.000	0/ 0	.000	0/ 0	.000	0/ 2	1	0	2	0	0	0	.000
SEMISCH, E.	8	0/ 1	.000	0/ 0	.000	0/ 0	.000	1/ 1	0	1	1	0	0	0	.000
PINCKNEY, D.	35	2/ 9	.222	0/ 0	.000	2/ 4	.500	7/10	1	0	4	0	2	6	.171
Totals	200	24/57	.421	0/ 2	.000	14/22	.636	16/39	14	10	15	5	3	62	.310

Western Kentucky (64)   Coach: Murray Arnold

	Min.	Total FG / FGA	Pct.	3-Pt. FG / FGA	Pct.	FT / FTA	Pct.	Reb. O / T	A	TO	PF	S	Blk	TP	PPM
JOHNSON, K.	35	6/12	.500	0/ 0	.000	3/ 3	1.000	0/ 3	3	1	4	1	1	15	.429
MARTIN, C.	8	2/ 2	1.000	0/ 0	.000	0/ 0	.000	0/ 3	0	0	5	1	0	4	.500
MCNEAL, B.	33	6/12	.500	0/ 1	.000	0/ 0	.000	1/ 6	1	1	0	1	0	12	.364
LEE, K.	28	0/ 3	.000	0/ 2	.000	0/ 0	.000	1/ 3	9	2	2	1	0	0	.000
ASBERRY, B.	32	4/ 6	.667	0/ 0	.000	8/11	.727	2/ 6	0	4	0	1	0	16	.500
MCNARY, J.	17	0/ 2	.000	0/ 0	.000	0/ 0	.000	1/ 2	5	2	4	1	0	0	.000
SWOGGER, R.	10	0/ 3	.000	0/ 0	.000	0/ 0	.000	1/ 1	0	1	0	1	0	0	.000
SHELTON, R.	2	0/ 0	.000	0/ 0	.000	0/ 0	.000	0/ 0	1	0	1	0	0	0	.000
TELLIS, F.	35	8/17	.471	0/ 0	.000	1/ 1	1.000	1/ 4	1	3	3	0	1	17	.486
Totals	200	26/57	.456	0/ 3	.000	12/15	.800	7/28	19	11	22	6	3	64	.320

Team Rebounds: Western Ky. 2; West Virginia 3. Disqualified: Western Ky.—Martin. Technical fouls: None.

	1st Half	2nd Half	Final
West Virginia	35	27	62
Western Ky.	32	32	64

Syracuse (79)   Coach: Jim Boeheim

	Min.	Total FG / FGA	Pct.	3-Pt. FG / FGA	Pct.	FT / FTA	Pct.	Reb. O / T	A	TO	PF	S	Blk	TP	PPM
COLEMAN, D.	39	5/10	.500	0/ 0	.000	6/ 6	1.000	6/10	0	1	3	0	3	16	.410
TRICHE, H.	25	1/ 2	.500	0/ 0	.000	2/ 4	.500	0/ 3	5	1	4	1	0	4	.160
SEIKALY, R.	34	9/15	.600	0/ 0	.000	4/10	.400	6/ 7	1	1	2	2	1	22	.647
DOUGLAS, S.	40	7/14	.500	1/ 2	.500	2/ 3	.667	0/ 9	9	3	1	1	0	17	.425
MONROE, G.	31	6/10	.600	4/ 8	.500	0/ 1	.000	0/ 1	4	1	2	2	1	16	.516
BROWER, D.	7	0/ 1	.000	0/ 0	.000	2/ 2	1.000	1/ 2	0	1	3	2	1	2	.286
THOMPSON, S.	13	0/ 1	.000	0/ 0	.000	0/ 0	.000	0/ 2	0	1	0	0	0	0	.000
HARRIED, H.	10	1/ 2	.500	0/ 0	.000	0/ 0	.000	1/ 2	0	0	2	0	0	2	.200
HUGHES, K.	1	0/ 0	.000	0/ 0	.000	0/ 0	.000	0/ 0	0	0	0	0	0	0	.000
Totals	200	29/55	.527	5/10	.500	16/26	.615	14/27	19	9	17	8	6	79	.395

Georgia Southern (73)   Coach: Frank Kerns

	Min.	Total FG / FGA	Pct.	3-Pt. FG / FGA	Pct.	FT / FTA	Pct.	Reb. O / T	A	TO	PF	S	Blk	TP	PPM
NEWTON, B.	40	8/13	.615	0/ 0	.000	2/ 4	.500	1/ 1	0	1	0	1	0	18	.450
JONES, F.	22	1/ 6	.167	0/ 0	.000	4/ 4	1.000	0/ 5	0	4	2	1	6	6	.273
SANDERS, J.	20	1/ 3	.333	0/ 0	.000	2/ 2	1.000	1/ 3	3	3	5	0	0	4	.200
FORREST, A.	38	8/11	.727	0/ 0	.000	0/ 0	.000	3/ 5	6	5	5	2	0	16	.421
STOKES, M.	40	5/ 6	.833	4/ 4	1.000	2/ 2	1.000	0/ 1	8	4	0	0	0	16	.400
HOLLIDAY, W.	13	2/ 4	.500	2/ 2	1.000	1/ 2	.500	0/ 1	0	1	1	0	0	7	.538
CURRY, M.	4	0/ 1	.000	0/ 0	.000	0/ 0	.000	0/ 1	0	0	2	0	0	0	.000
MILLER, T.	20	2/ 5	.400	0/ 0	.000	2/ 2	1.000	3/ 5	1	1	3	0	0	6	.300
DIXON, K.	1	0/ 0	.000	0/ 0	.000	0/ 0	.000	0/ 1	0	1	0	0	0	0	.000
MACK, B.	1	0/ 0	.000	0/ 0	.000	0/ 0	.000	0/ 0	0	0	0	0	0	0	.000
VOITIK, M.	1	0/ 0	.000	0/ 0	.000	0/ 0	.000	0/ 0	0	0	0	0	0	0	.000
Totals	200	27/49	.551	6/ 6	1.000	13/16	.813	8/23	18	15	20	5	1	73	.365

Team Rebounds: Syracuse 2; Ga. Southern 5. Disqualified: Ga. Southern—Sanders, Forrest. Technical fouls: None.

	1st Half	2nd Half	Final
Syracuse	39	40	79
Ga. Southern	40	33	73

SECOND ROUND WEST

UNLV (80)   Coach: Jerry Tarkanian

	Min.	Total FG / FGA	Pct.	3-Pt. FG / FGA	Pct.	FT / FTA	Pct.	Reb. O / T	A	TO	PF	S	Blk	TP	PPM
WADE, M.	33	1/ 5	.200	0/ 2	.000	0/ 1	.000	2/ 5	13	2	3	2	0	2	.061
BANKS, F.	36	5/13	.385	3/10	.300	2/ 2	1.000	1/ 2	1	4	1	1	2	15	.417
PADDIO, G.	24	4/15	.267	2/10	.200	0/ 0	.000	2/ 2	0	1	0	0	10	.417
GILLIAM, A.	35	9/17	.529	0/ 0	.000	6/ 6	1.000	3/11	1	1	2	1	0	24	.686
BASNIGHT, J.	28	4/ 4	1.000	0/ 0	.000	6/ 6	1.000	5/10	0	3	4	0	1	14	.500
ROBINSON, R.	2	0/ 0	.000	0/ 0	.000	0/ 0	.000	0/ 0	0	0	0	0	0	0	.000
WEST, L.	2	0/ 0	.000	0/ 0	.000	0/ 0	.000	0/ 0	0	0	0	0	0	0	.000
CVIJANOVICH, S.	2	0/ 0	.000	0/ 0	.000	2/ 2	1.000	0/ 0	1	0	0	1	0	2	1.000
GRAHAM, G.	17	3/ 5	.600	1/ 3	.333	2/ 2	1.000	0/ 0	1	3	5	1	0	9	.529
HUDSON, E.	11	1/ 1	1.000	0/ 0	.000	0/ 0	.000	0/ 1	0	1	2	2	0	2	.182
WILLARD, D.	10	1/ 4	.250	0/ 0	.000	0/ 0	.000	1/ 4	1	2	2	0	2	2	.200
Totals	200	28/64	.438	6/25	.240	18/19	.947	14/35	18	16	20	8	5	80	.400

Kansas State (61)   Coach: Lon Kruger

	Min.	Total FG / FGA	Pct.	3-Pt. FG / FGA	Pct.	FT / FTA	Pct.	Reb. O / T	A	TO	PF	S	Blk	TP	PPM
BLEDSOE, C.	29	3/ 4	.750	0/ 0	.000	1/ 2	.500	2/ 4	1	6	3	2	1	7	.241
SIMMONS, L.	12	0/ 2	.000	0/ 0	.000	0/ 1	.000	2/ 2	0	1	0	0	0	0	.000
RICHMOND, M.	35	8/18	.444	0/ 1	.000	3/ 6	.500	4/14	4	4	2	1	1	19	.543
SMITH, L.	26	0/ 2	.000	0/ 0	.000	0/ 0	.000	0/ 1	1	4	5	1	0	0	.000
HENSON, S.	37	3/ 9	.333	0/ 2	.000	0/ 0	.000	0/ 3	4	6	3	0	0	6	.162
SCOTT, W.	17	4/ 7	.571	2/ 2	1.000	3/ 5	.600	0/ 1	1	1	1	0	0	13	.765
DOBBINS, M.	3	0/ 0	.000	0/ 0	.000	0/ 0	.000	0/ 0	0	0	0	0	0	0	.000
COLEMAN, N.	28	6/ 9	.667	0/ 0	.000	2/ 3	.667	1/ 5	0	1	3	1	2	14	.500
MEYER, R.	12	1/ 1	1.000	0/ 0	.000	0/ 0	.000	1/ 2	0	0	1	0	0	2	.167
EDDIE, P.	1	0/ 0	.000	0/ 0	.000	0/ 0	.000	0/ 0	0	0	0	0	0	0	.000
Totals	200	25/52	.481	2/ 5	.400	9/17	.529	10/32	11	23	18	5	4	61	.305

Team Rebounds: UNLV 0; Kansas State 1. Disqualified: UNLV—Graham; Kansas State—Smith. Technical fouls: None.

	1st Half	2nd Half	Final
UNLV	36	44	80
Kansas State	27	34	61

Wyoming (78)   Coach: Jim Brandenburg

	Min.	Total FG / FGA	Pct.	3-Pt. FG / FGA	Pct.	FT / FTA	Pct.	Reb. O / T	A	TO	PF	S	Blk	TP	PPM
DENT, S.	34	0/ 1	.000	0/ 0	.000	2/ 3	.667	2/ 4	6	5	4	2	0	2	.059
FOX, R.	22	0/ 3	.000	0/ 1	.000	1/ 2	.500	0/ 0	2	3	3	0	0	1	.045
DEMBO, F.	39	9/14	.643	7/10	.700	16/16	1.000	0/ 9	6	4	2	0	1	41	1.051
LECKNER, E.	38	7/15	.467	0/ 0	.000	6/ 8	.750	3/14	0	1	3	0	2	20	.526
SOMMERS, J.	31	2/ 5	.400	0/ 0	.000	2/ 2	1.000	4/ 8	4	4	3	0	0	6	.194
BOYD, T.	23	3/ 5	.600	0/ 0	.000	0/ 1	.000	0/ 1	1	3	1	1	0	6	.261
JONES, W.	10	1/ 1	1.000	0/ 0	.000	0/ 0	.000	0/ 0	0	1	4	1	0	2	.200
LODGINS, D.	2	0/ 0	.000	0/ 0	.000	0/ 0	.000	0/ 0	0	0	0	0	0	0	.000
HUNT, T.	1	0/ 0	.000	0/ 0	.000	0/ 0	.000	0/ 1	0	0	0	0	0	0	.000
Totals	200	22/44	.500	7/11	.636	27/32	.844	9/37	19	21	20	4	3	78	.390

UCLA (68)   Coach: Walt Hazzard

	Min.	Total FG / FGA	Pct.	3-Pt. FG / FGA	Pct.	FT / FTA	Pct.	Reb. O / T	A	TO	PF	S	Blk	TP	PPM
HALEY, J.	28	1/ 6	.167	0/ 0	.000	3/ 4	.750	2/ 2	0	0	2	0	0	5	.179
RICHARDSON	32	2/ 7	.286	0/ 1	.000	4/ 4	1.000	2/ 5	6	2	3	1	0	8	.250
IMMEL	25	4/12	.333	0/ 6	.000	2/ 2	1.000	0/ 2	1	1	4	3	1	10	.400
MILLER, R.	38	8/17	.471	2/ 4	.500	6/ 7	.857	6/ 9	1	3	5	7	0	24	.632
ROCHELIN, C.	24	1/ 6	.167	0/ 2	.000	3/ 4	.750	0/ 5	1	1	4	0	0	5	.208
WILSON	9	0/ 0	.000	0/ 0	.000	2/ 2	1.000	0/ 2	0	2	3	1	0	2	.222
HAZZARD, W.	18	4/12	.333	2/ 5	.400	0/ 0	.000	2/ 2	1	1	2	0	0	10	.556
FOSTER	12	0/ 1	.000	0/ 0	.000	0/ 0	.000	0/ 0	1	2	2	1	1	0	.000
PALMER	1	0/ 0	.000	0/ 0	.000	0/ 0	.000	0/ 0	0	0	0	0	0	0	.000
JACKSON	13	2/ 3	.667	0/ 0	.000	0/ 0	.000	1/ 1	0	2	2	0	0	4	.308
Totals	200	22/64	.344	4/18	.222	20/23	.870	11/28	11	14	27	13	2	68	.340

Team Rebounds: Wyoming 3; UCLA 2. Disqualified: UCLA—Miller. Technical fouls: None.

	1st Half	2nd Half	Final
Wyoming	38	40	78
UCLA	44	24	68

Oklahoma (96)   Coach: Billy Tubbs

	Min.	Total FG / FGA	Pct.	3-Pt. FG / FGA	Pct.	FT / FTA	Pct.	Reb. O / T	A	TO	PF	S	Blk	TP	PPM
SIEGER, D.	18	0/ 4	.000	0/ 2	.000	1/ 2	.500	2/ 3	2	3	5	4	0	1	.056
GRANT, H.	29	6/11	.545	0/ 0	.000	6/10	.600	5/ 8	2	0	4	1	2	18	.621
JOHNSON, D.	26	4/13	.308	0/ 0	.000	0/ 2	.000	7/10	0	3	0	0	8	8	.308
McCALISTER, T.	40	10/22	.455	4/ 8	.500	4/ 4	1.000	1/ 3	6	3	4	2	0	28	.700
GRACE, R.	39	6/ 8	.750	3/ 4	.750	0/ 1	.000	1/ 5	6	5	4	4	1	15	.385
KING, S.	23	8/15	.533	0/ 0	.000	3/ 3	1.000	4/ 8	1	0	3	2	0	19	.826
KENNEDY, D.	25	2/ 9	.222	0/ 0	.000	3/ 4	.750	1/ 4	1	2	3	0	0	7	.280
Totals	200	36/82	.439	7/14	.500	17/26	.654	21/41	18	13	26	13	3	96	.480

Pittsburgh (93)   Coach: Paul Evans

	Min.	Total FG / FGA	Pct.	3-Pt. FG / FGA	Pct.	FT / FTA	Pct.	Reb. O / T	A	TO	PF	S	Blk	TP	PPM
LANE, J.	30	6/10	.600	0/ 1	.000	2/ 6	.333	5/13	7	5	4	1	0	14	.467
GORE, D.	23	7/ 9	.778	1/ 2	.500	2/ 2	1.000	0/ 2	0	3	4	0	0	17	.739
SMITH, C.	39	10/13	.769	0/ 0	.000	3/ 7	.429	3/ 8	3	3	5	1	2	23	.590
AIKEN	30	0/ 4	.000	0/ 2	.000	2/ 4	.500	0/ 0	4	0	3	2	0	2	.067
GOODSON	27	4/11	.364	2/ 8	.250	0/ 0	.000	3/ 4	3	4	2	0	0	10	.370
CAVANAUGH, P.	13	1/ 2	.500	0/ 0	.000	0/ 0	.000	0/ 1	2	3	1	1	0	2	.154
BROOKIN, R.	27	10/18	.556	2/ 6	.333	1/ 5	.200	1/ 5	4	4	1	1	0	23	.852
COOPER	10	0/ 0	.000	0/ 0	.000	2/ 3	.667	0/ 8	0	0	4	0	0	2	.200
FERGUSON	1	0/ 1	.000	0/ 0	.000	0/ 0	.000	0/ 0	0	0	0	0	0	0	.000
Totals	200	38/68	.559	5/19	.263	12/27	.444	12/41	23	22	24	6	2	93	.465

Team Rebounds: Oklahoma 4; Pittsburgh 4. Disqualified: Oklahoma—Sieger; Pittsburgh—Smith. Technical fouls: None.

	1st Half	2nd Half	Final
Oklahoma	51	45	96
Pittsburgh	41	52	93

UTEP (82)   Coach: Don Haskins

	Min.	Total FG / FGA	Pct.	3-Pt. FG / FGA	Pct.	FT / FTA	Pct.	Reb. O / T	A	TO	PF	S	Blk	TP	PPM
SANDLE, C.	24	4/ 6	.667	0/ 1	.000	0/ 0	.000	0/ 4	1	0	5	1	0	8	.333
GATES, Q.	31	4/13	.308	1/ 4	.250	1/ 2	.500	1/ 3	1	1	4	1	0	10	.323
RICHMOND, M.	29	6/11	.545	0/ 0	.000	6/ 7	.857	4/ 5	0	1	2	2	1	18	.621
HARDAWAY, T.	29	5/ 7	.714	1/ 1	1.000	0/ 0	.000	0/ 2	6	0	3	2	1	11	.379
JACKSON, D.	30	7/17	.412	2/ 5	.400	0/ 1	.000	0/ 1	3	2	2	5	0	16	.533
BLOCKER, C.	23	4/12	.333	1/ 2	.500	0/ 2	.000	1/ 2	4	2	3	1	0	9	.391
CAMPBELL, W.	25	5/ 9	.556	0/ 0	.000	0/ 0	.000	3/ 5	1	3	2	0	0	10	.400
STALLWORTH, T.	7	0/ 0	.000	0/ 0	.000	0/ 0	.000	0/ 0	0	1	2	1	0	0	.000
DAVIS, A.	2	0/ 1	.000	0/ 0	.000	0/ 0	.000	0/ 1	0	1	0	0	0	0	.000
Totals	200	35/76	.461	5/13	.385	7/12	.583	9/23	16	11	23	13	2	82	.410

Iowa (84)   Coach: Tom Davis

	Min.	Total FG / FGA	Pct.	3-Pt. FG / FGA	Pct.	FT / FTA	Pct.	Reb. O / T	A	TO	PF	S	Blk	TP	PPM
MARBLE, R.	36	9/14	.643	0/ 1	.000	10/11	.909	4/ 7	3	4	1	1	1	28	.778
GAMBLE, K.	32	6/ 9	.667	0/ 1	.000	2/ 3	.667	0/ 4	2	3	3	1	0	14	.438
LOHAUS, B.	30	2/ 7	.286	2/ 4	.500	1/ 2	.500	0/ 5	2	2	0	1	1	7	.233
ARMSTRONG, B.	29	5/ 8	.625	3/ 4	.750	3/ 4	.750	0/ 2	1	3	0	0	0	16	.552
WRIGHT, G.	20	2/ 3	.667	0/ 0	.000	3/ 5	.600	0/ 4	1	4	1	0	1	7	.350
JONES, B.	7	0/ 0	.000	0/ 0	.000	0/ 0	.000	0/ 3	0	2	0	0	0	0	.000
MOE, J.	12	2/ 4	.500	1/ 3	.333	0/ 0	.000	0/ 0	1	1	1	0	0	5	.417
HORTON, E.	20	1/ 4	.250	0/ 0	.000	1/ 2	.500	3/ 6	1	1	5	0	0	3	.150
LORENZEN, A.	10	2/ 2	1.000	0/ 0	.000	0/ 2	.000	0/ 2	3	0	1	0	0	4	.400
REAVES, M.	4	0/ 0	.000	0/ 0	.000	0/ 0	.000	0/ 0	1	0	0	0	0	0	.000
Totals	200	29/51	.569	6/13	.462	20/29	.690	7/33	15	20	12	3	3	84	.420

Team Rebounds: Iowa 4; UTEP 5. Disqualified: Iowa—Horton; UTEP—Sandle. Technical fouls: None.

	1st Half	2nd Half	Final
UTEP	42	40	82
Iowa	38	46	84

SECOND ROUND MIDWEST

Indiana (107) Coach: Bob Knight

	Min.	Total FG/FGA	Pct.	3–Pt. FG/FGA	Pct.	FT/FTA	Pct.	Reb. O/T	A	TO	PF	S	Blk	TP	PPM
CALLOWAY, R.	39	7/12	.583	0/ 0	.000	4/ 4	1.000	2/13	1	5	0	1	0	18	.462
THOMAS, D.	36	9/14	.643	0/ 0	.000	9/10	.900	2/ 8	0	4	1	3	0	27	.750
GARRETT, D.	16	4/ 6	.667	0/ 0	.000	1/ 2	.500	1/ 3	0	1	4	0	2	9	.563
ALFORD, S.	38	10/17	.588	7/11	.636	4/ 5	.800	0/ 3	5	2	2	0	0	31	.816
SMART, K.	39	7/12	.583	0/ 2	.000	6/ 7	.857	2/ 9	15	5	3	1	0	20	.513
SMITH, K.	2	0/ 0	.000	0/ 0	.000	0/ 0	.000	0/ 0	0	0	0	0	0	0	.000
EYL, S.	16	0/ 0	.000	0/ 0	.000	0/ 0	.000	2/ 5	2	1	3	0	0	0	.000
HILLMAN, J.	2	1/ 2	.500	0/ 0	.000	0/ 0	.000	0/ 0	0	0	0	0	0	2	1.000
FREEMAN, T.	1	0/ 0	.000	0/ 0	.000	0/ 0	.000	0/ 0	0	0	0	0	0	0	.000
MEIER, T.	9	0/ 0	.000	0/ 0	.000	0/ 0	.000	1/ 2	0	1	0	0	0	0	.000
SLOAN, B.	3	0/ 0	.000	0/ 0	.000	0/ 0	.000	0/ 1	0	0	0	0	0	0	.000
MINOR, D.	1	0/ 0	.000	0/ 0	.000	0/ 0	.000	1/ 1	0	0	0	0	0	0	.000
Totals	200	38/63	.603	7/13	.538	24/28	.857	11/44	24	18	14	5	2	107	.535

Auburn (90) Coach: Sonny Smith

	Min.	Total FG/FGA	Pct.	3–Pt. FG/FGA	Pct.	FT/FTA	Pct.	Reb. O/T	A	TO	PF	S	Blk	TP	PPM
JONES, M.	36	10/22	.455	1/ 2	.500	9/ 9	1.000	2/ 9	1	2	1	1	0	30	.833
MORRIS, C.	22	5/11	.455	0/ 0	.000	0/ 1	.000	4/ 4	2	0	5	0	0	10	.455
MOORE, J.	33	11/20	.550	0/ 0	.000	2/ 2	1.000	5/10	1	0	4	1	0	24	.727
WHITE, G.	37	6/13	.462	4/ 9	.444	1/ 1	1.000	0/ 1	10	4	2	1	1	17	.459
FORD, F.	28	4/11	.364	1/ 2	.500	0/ 0	.000	1/ 3	0	5	0	0	9	.321
HOWARD, J.	19	0/ 4	.000	0/ 0	.000	0/ 0	.000	3/ 4	1	2	4	0	0	0	.000
LYNN, J.	13	0/ 4	.000	0/ 1	.000	0/ 0	.000	1/ 2	0	2	2	1	0	0	.000
CAYLOR, J.	10	0/ 0	.000	0/ 0	.000	0/ 0	.000	0/ 0	1	2	2	0	0	0	.000
DENNISON, D.	2	0/ 1	.000	0/ 0	.000	0/ 0	.000	0/ 0	0	0	0	0	0	0	.000
Totals	200	36/86	.419	6/14	.429	12/13	.923	16/33	15	11	25	6	1	90	.450

Team Rebounds: Indiana 1; Auburn 1. Disqualified: Auburn—Morris, Ford. Technical fouls: None.

	1st Half	2nd Half	Final
Indiana	53	54	107
Auburn	48	42	90

Duke (65) Coach: Mike Krzyzewski

	Min.	Total FG/FGA	Pct.	3–Pt. FG/FGA	Pct.	FT/FTA	Pct.	Reb. O/T	A	TO	PF	S	Blk	TP	PPM
FERRY, D.	21	4/ 7	.571	0/ 1	.000	0/ 0	.000	3/ 5	1	2	4	1	0	8	.381
KING, B.	29	1/ 3	.333	0/ 0	.000	3/ 7	.429	1/ 2	4	3	4	2	2	5	.172
SMITH, J.	28	3/ 5	.600	0/ 0	.000	0/ 0	.000	1/ 2	0	0	1	0	6	.214
AMAKER, T.	40	8/12	.667	2/ 4	.500	2/ 2	1.000	1/ 2	0	2	3	2	1	20	.500
STRICKLAND, K.	37	2/13	.154	2/ 9	.222	6/ 7	.857	5/ 9	9	0	2	1	1	12	.324
SNYDER, Q.	9	0/ 0	.000	0/ 0	.000	0/ 0	.000	0/ 0	0	0	0	0	0	0	.000
BRICKEY, R.	28	6/ 8	.750	0/ 0	.000	0/ 0	.000	1/ 1	0	3	1	0	0	12	.429
ABDELNABY, A.	7	1/ 2	.500	0/ 0	.000	0/ 0	.000	0/ 1	0	0	0	0	0	2	.286
NESSLEY, M.	7	0/ 0	.000	0/ 0	.000	0/ 0	.000	0/ 0	1	0	1	0	0	0	.000
Totals	200	25/50	.500	4/14	.286	11/16	.688	12/22	15	10	16	6	4	65	.325

Xavier (Ohio) (60) Coach: Pete Gillen

	Min.	Total FG/FGA	Pct.	3–Pt. FG/FGA	Pct.	FT/FTA	Pct.	Reb. O/T	A	TO	PF	S	Blk	TP	PPM
TAYLOR, K.	35	3/ 6	.500	2/ 4	.500	0/ 1	.000	0/ 2	6	1	0	1	0	8	.229
CAMPBELL, D.	30	4/ 6	.667	0/ 0	.000	2/ 2	1.000	2/ 6	0	2	4	2	0	10	.333
HILL, T.	39	2/ 5	.400	0/ 0	.000	3/ 4	.750	2/ 6	0	1	4	1	0	9	.243
KIMBROUGH, S.	39	5/12	.417	1/ 2	.500	2/ 2	1.000	2/ 5	3	8	5	1	0	13	.333
LARKIN, B.	38	7/12	.583	2/ 2	1.000	2/ 2	1.000	0/ 2	3	5	3	1	0	18	.474
BARNETT, J.	16	1/ 4	.250	0/ 0	.000	0/ 0	.000	1/ 1	0	0	3	0	0	2	.125
KOESTER, B.	5	0/ 0	.000	0/ 0	.000	0/ 0	.000	0/ 0	0	0	0	0	0	0	.000
Totals	200	23/45	.511	5/ 8	.625	9/11	.818	7/22	12	17	19	6	0	60	.300

Team Rebounds: Duke 3; Xavier (Ohio) 4. Disqualified: Xavier (Ohio)—Kimbrough. Technical fouls: None.

	1st Half	2nd Half	Final
Duke	36	29	65
Xavier (Ohio)	32	28	60

St. John's (75) Coach: Lou Carnesecca

	Min.	Total FG/FGA	Pct.	3–Pt. FG/FGA	Pct.	FT/FTA	Pct.	Reb. O/T	A	TO	PF	S	Blk	TP	PPM
GLASS, W.	44	9/13	.692	0/ 0	.000	1/ 3	.333	1/ 2	2	0	2	1	1	19	.432
JONES, S.	45	6/13	.462	0/ 0	.000	3/ 5	.600	5/11	3	3	2	1	2	15	.333
BROSS, T.	16	0/ 1	.000	0/ 0	.000	0/ 1	.000	2/ 4	0	3	0	0	0	0	.000
BRUST, M.	25	2/ 4	.500	0/ 0	.000	1/ 1	1.000	1/ 5	3	3	5	1	0	5	.200
JACKSON, M.	45	8/23	.348	3/ 8	.375	4/ 4	1.000	0/ 2	7	2	4	1	0	23	.511
BROADNAX,	13	0/ 1	.000	0/ 0	.000	0/ 0	.000	0/ 1	0	3	1	0	0	0	.000
BALDI, M.	24	5/ 6	.833	0/ 0	.000	0/ 0	.000	2/ 3	0	3	5	0	0	10	.417
HEMPEL, J.	9	1/ 2	.500	1/ 1	1.000	0/ 0	.000	0/ 0	1	0	1	0	0	3	.333
LEWIS, E.	4	0/ 0	.000	0/ 0	.000	0/ 0	.000	0/ 0	0	0	1	0	0	0	.000
Totals	225	31/63	.492	4/ 9	.444	9/14	.643	11/28	16	11	26	5	3	75	.333

DePaul (83) Coach: Joey Meyer

	Min.	Total FG/FGA	Pct.	3–Pt. FG/FGA	Pct.	FT/FTA	Pct.	Reb. O/T	A	TO	PF	S	Blk	TP	PPM
GOLDEN, K.	23	1/ 1	1.000	0/ 0	.000	2/ 2	1.000	2/ 4	0	2	0	0	4	.174
GREENE, T.	33	5/ 8	.625	0/ 0	.000	0/ 0	.000	1/ 4	3	5	5	0	0	10	.303
COMEGYS, D.	42	6/14	.429	0/ 0	.000	3/ 5	.600	2/10	2	3	2	1	1	15	.357
EDWARDS, K.	44	9/15	.600	1/ 3	.333	7/ 7	1.000	3/ 5	4	0	1	0	0	26	.591
STRICKLAND, R.	41	6/15	.400	0/ 1	.000	4/ 6	.667	1/ 3	5	0	2	3	0	16	.390
LAUX, A.	17	1/ 1	1.000	1/ 1	1.000	4/ 4	1.000	1/ 2	1	0	1	0	0	7	.412
BRUNDY, S.	25	2/ 2	1.000	0/ 0	.000	1/ 1	1.000	1/ 4	1	1	2	1	5	.200
Totals	225	30/56	.536	2/ 5	.400	21/25	.840	11/32	16	9	14	6	2	83	.369

Team Rebounds: DePaul 0; St. John's 4. Disqualified: DePaul—Greene; St. John's—Brust, Baldi. Technical fouls: None.

	1st Half	2nd Half	1 OT	Final
St. John's	30	39	6	75
DePaul	42	27	14	83

Louisiana State (72) Coach: Dale Brown

	Min.	Total FG/FGA	Pct.	3–Pt. FG/FGA	Pct.	FT/FTA	Pct.	Reb. O/T	A	TO	PF	S	Blk	TP	PPM
WOODSIDE, B.	31	0/ 3	.000	0/ 2	.000	3/ 4	.750	1/ 7	0	1	2	0	0	3	.097
BROWN, O.	30	1/ 3	.333	0/ 0	.000	2/ 5	.400	0/ 4	3	1	3	1	0	4	.133
WILSON, N.	40	8/10	.800	0/ 0	.000	0/ 0	.000	3/11	2	0	2	0	1	16	.400
WILSON, A.	36	6/13	.462	3/ 5	.600	6/ 8	.750	1/ 4	4	3	3	1	0	21	.583
JOE, D.	33	5/ 7	.714	2/ 3	.667	7/ 8	.875	0/ 6	4	1	3	1	0	19	.576
IRVIN, F.	13	1/ 1	1.000	0/ 0	.000	0/ 0	.000	0/ 0	1	0	0	0	2	.154
VARGAS, J.	17	3/ 7	.429	0/ 0	.000	1/ 2	.500	1/ 3	0	3	1	0	1	7	.412
Totals	200	24/44	.545	5/10	.500	19/27	.704	6/35	14	9	14	3	2	72	.360

Temple (62) Coach: John Chaney

	Min.	Total FG/FGA	Pct.	3–Pt. FG/FGA	Pct.	FT/FTA	Pct.	Reb. O/T	A	TO	PF	S	Blk	TP	PPM
VREESWYK, M.	40	9/19	.474	6/ 9	.667	2/ 2	1.000	2/ 8	2	0	4	2	0	26	.650
PERRY	38	3/ 7	.429	0/ 0	.000	1/ 2	.500	3/11	0	0	5	0	1	7	.184
RIVAS, R.	34	3/ 5	.600	0/ 0	.000	0/ 0	.000	3/ 7	0	0	4	0	6	.176
BLACKWELL	40	6/19	.316	1/ 6	.167	3/ 4	.750	1/ 3	3	1	3	0	0	16	.400
EVANS	40	2/11	.182	1/ 4	.250	2/ 2	1.000	1/ 1	8	3	3	3	0	7	.175
PEARSALL, D.	7	0/ 0	.000	0/ 0	.000	0/ 0	.000	0/ 0	0	1	2	0	0	0	.000
BRANTLEY	1	0/ 2	.000	0/ 0	.000	0/ 0	.000	0/ 0	0	0	0	0	0	0	.000
Totals	200	23/63	.365	8/19	.421	8/10	.800	10/30	13	5	21	5	1	62	.310

Team Rebounds: Louisiana St. 1; Temple 2. Disqualified: Temple—Perry. Technical fouls: None.

	1st Half	2nd Half	Final
Louisiana St.	37	35	72
Temple	33	29	62

SECOND ROUND SOUTHEAST

Georgetown (82)   Coach: John Thompson

	Min.	Total FG/FGA	Pct.	3-Pt. FG/FGA	Pct.	FT/FTA	Pct.	Reb. O/T	A	TO	PF	S	Blk	TP	PPM
MCDONALD, P.	37	8/9	.889	0/0	.000	0/1	.000	1/3	3	3	1	2	0	16	.432
WILLIAMS, R.	33	7/14	.500	4/8	.500	6/6	1.000	1/5	6	3	3	2	2	24	.727
GILLERY, B.	2	1/2	.500	0/0	.000	0/0	.000	1/1	0	0	0	0	0	2	1.000
BRYANT, D.	16	1/1	1.000	0/0	.000	0/1	.000	0/0	4	2	4	0	0	2	.125
TILLMON, M.	16	1/8	.125	0/2	.000	1/1	1.000	0/0	2	3	1	1	0	3	.188
HIGHSMITH, R.	8	1/1	1.000	0/0	.000	0/0	.000	1/1	0	0	1	0	0	2	.250
WINSTON, B.	25	0/2	.000	0/0	.000	1/2	.500	1/2	3	2	3	2	0	1	.040
ALLEN, A.	24	1/1	1.000	0/0	.000	4/4	1.000	0/2	0	2	3	1	2	6	.250
SMITH, C.	24	8/13	.615	5/7	.714	1/1	1.000	1/1	1	0	1	2	0	22	.917
EDWARDS, J.	5	1/1	1.000	0/0	.000	0/0	.000	1/2	0	0	2	0	1	2	.400
JACKSON, J.	8	0/2	.000	0/0	.000	2/2	1.000	1/2	1	0	1	1	0	2	.250
JEFFERSON, S.	2	0/0	.000	0/0	.000	0/0	.000	0/0	0	1	0	0	0	0	.000
Totals	200	29/54	.537	9/17	.529	15/18	.833	8/19	20	16	20	11	5	82	.410

Ohio State (79)   Coach: Gary Williams

	Min.	Total FG/FGA	Pct.	3-Pt. FG/FGA	Pct.	FT/FTA	Pct.	Reb. O/T	A	TO	PF	S	Blk	TP	PPM
HOPSON, D.	31	8/16	.500	2/5	.400	2/2	1.000	4/6	8	3	4	0	0	20	.645
FRANCIS, J.	34	5/10	.500	0/1	.000	8/10	.800	1/3	0	1	3	0	0	18	.529
ANDERSON, J.	34	5/8	.625	0/0	.000	0/0	.000	1/5	3	4	4	1	1	10	.294
WILSON, C.	27	4/9	.444	1/1	1.000	1/2	.500	0/2	3	6	1	3	0	10	.370
BURSON, J.	37	7/11	.636	0/1	.000	2/2	1.000	5/8	4	4	2	2	0	16	.432
WHITE, T.	14	1/3	.333	0/0	.000	2/2	1.000	1/1	2	1	4	0	0	4	.286
WESSON, K.	5	0/2	.000	0/0	.000	0/0	.000	1/1	0	0	0	0	0	0	.000
LOMAX, K.	17	0/0	.000	0/0	.000	1/2	.500	0/1	1	1	2	1	0	1	.059
ANDERSON, S.	1	0/0	.000	0/0	.000	0/0	.000	0/0	0	0	0	0	0	0	.000
Totals	200	30/59	.508	3/8	.375	16/20	.800	13/27	21	20	20	7	1	79	.395

Team Rebounds: Georgetown 5; Ohio State 10. Disqualified: None. Technical fouls: None.

	1st Half	2nd Half	Final
Georgetown	29	53	82
Ohio State	39	40	79

Kansas (67)   Coach: Larry Brown

	Min.	Total FG/FGA	Pct.	3-Pt. FG/FGA	Pct.	FT/FTA	Pct.	Reb. O/T	A	TO	PF	S	Blk	TP	PPM
PIPER, C.	14	0/0	.000	0/0	.000	2/2	1.000	0/2	0	1	4	0	0	2	.143
MANNING, D.	40	16/26	.615	0/0	.000	10/12	.833	0/4	2	5	2	0	0	42	1.050
PELLOCK, M.	9	0/1	.000	0/0	.000	0/0	.000	1/1	0	0	2	0	0	0	.000
PRITCHARD, K.	26	2/4	.500	0/0	.000	0/0	.000	0/0	1	2	4	0	1	4	.154
HUNTER, C.	28	3/5	.600	0/0	.000	0/0	.000	1/3	10	1	4	2	0	6	.214
TURGEON, M.	24	2/2	1.000	0/0	.000	0/0	.000	1/2	5	0	2	0	0	4	.167
RANDALL, M.	7	0/0	.000	0/0	.000	0/0	.000	0/1	0	1	0	1	0	0	.000
HARRIS, K.	17	0/0	.000	0/0	.000	0/0	.000	0/2	0	1	0	0	0	0	.000
NEWTON, M.	13	2/4	.500	0/0	.000	0/0	.000	1/4	1	0	0	1	0	4	.308
BARRY, R.	4	0/0	.000	0/0	.000	0/0	.000	0/0	2	0	0	1	0	0	.000
GUELDNER, J.	18	2/3	.667	1/1	1.000	0/0	.000	0/1	2	0	0	1	0	5	.278
Totals	200	27/45	.600	1/1	1.000	12/14	.857	5/20	23	10	19	4	2	67	.335

SW Missouri State (63)   Coach: Charles Spoonhour

	Min.	Total FG/FGA	Pct.	3-Pt. FG/FGA	Pct.	FT/FTA	Pct.	Reb. O/T	A	TO	PF	S	Blk	TP	PPM
WORTHY, S.	26	2/3	.667	0/0	.000	0/1	.000	3/4	4	2	1	2	1	4	.154
BELL, G.	36	1/3	.333	0/0	.000	2/2	1.000	1/4	1	4	4	3	0	4	.111
STUCKEY, K.	35	2/3	.667	0/0	.000	4/5	.800	4/5	1	1	3	1	2	8	.229
ROBINSON, J.	39	6/9	.667	0/1	.000	6/6	1.000	0/2	2	3	4	0	0	18	.462
GARLAND, W.	40	10/23	.435	2/5	.400	2/3	.667	1/2	5	0	3	1	0	24	.600
KICKOX, S.	9	0/0	.000	0/0	.000	0/0	.000	0/1	0	0	0	0	0	0	.000
HOLT, C.	15	2/7	.286	1/5	.000	2/0	.000	1/1	1	0	1	0	0	5	.333
Totals	200	23/48	.479	3/11	.273	14/17	.824	10/19	14	10	16	7	3	63	.315

Team Rebounds: Kansas 4; SW Missouri St. 4. Disqualified: None. Technical fouls: None.

	1st Half	2nd Half	Final
Kansas	31	36	67
SW Missouri St.	33	30	63

Providence (90)   Coach: Rick Pitino

	Min.	Total FG/FGA	Pct.	3-Pt. FG/FGA	Pct.	FT/FTA	Pct.	Reb. O/T	A	TO	PF	S	Blk	TP	PPM
KIPFER, D.	20	2/4	.500	0/0	.000	3/3	1.000	0/7	1	4	5	1	1	7	.350
LEWIS, E.	40	9/21	.429	6/14	.429	2/3	.667	1/4	0	0	4	1	0	26	.650
DUDA, J.	22	1/4	.250	0/0	.000	2/6	.333	1/5	0	4	3	1	0	4	.182
BROOKS, D.	40	3/13	.231	2/7	.286	0/0	.000	3/4	8	3	5	7	1	8	.200
DONOVAN, B.	40	9/17	.529	2/3	.667	5/7	.714	1/3	7	5	2	5	0	25	.625
SHAMSID-DEEN, A.	1	0/0	.000	0/0	.000	0/0	.000	0/0	0	0	1	0	0	0	.000
CONLON, M.	21	1/1	1.000	0/0	.000	0/0	.000	3/6	1	2	3	1	0	2	.095
SMEDEKER, D.	3	0/0	.000	0/0	.000	0/0	.000	0/0	0	0	0	0	0	0	.000
WRIGHT, D.	9	1/3	.333	1/1	1.000	3/5	.600	0/1	0	0	1	0	1	6	.667
WRIGHT, S.	22	6/8	.750	0/0	.000	0/1	.000	4/8	6	5	3	3	3	12	.545
SCREEN, C.	7	0/1	.000	-/-	-	0/0	.000	0/0	1	1	0	0	0	0	.000
Totals	225	32/72	.444	11/25	.440	15/25	.600	13/38	18	21	29	19	6	90	.400

Austin Peay (87)   Coach: Lake Kelly

	Min.	Total FG/FGA	Pct.	3-Pt. FG/FGA	Pct.	FT/FTA	Pct.	Reb. O/T	A	TO	PF	S	Blk	TP	PPM
RAYE, T.	31	2/4	.500	0/0	.000	2/2	1.000	5/11	1	2	5	0	0	6	.194
MITCHELL, L.	45	8/23	.348	1/2	.500	10/13	.769	6/6	1	5	3	0	0	27	.600
BEDFORD, T.	32	6/12	.500	3/5	.600	4/4	1.000	3/9	6	4	5	2	0	19	.594
ARMSTRONG, R.	21	3/7	.429	0/2	.000	2/3	.667	1/5	2	3	5	1	0	8	.381
HICKS, M.	38	5/13	.385	0/1	.000	0/0	.000	5/6	2	5	4	3	0	10	.263
ORR, E.	9	0/0	.000	0/0	.000	0/0	.000	0/4	0	0	1	0	0	0	.000
THOMAS, B.	18	1/1	1.000	0/0	.000	2/2	.286	2/9	0	2	3	0	0	4	.222
BROOKS, V.	31	5/14	.357	2/8	.250	1/2	.500	1/5	5	3	0	1	0	13	.419
Totals	225	30/74	.405	6/18	.333	21/31	.677	23/55	17	24	26	7	0	87	.387

Team Rebounds: Providence 6; Austin Peay 3. Disqualified: Providence—Kipfer, Brooks, S. Wright; Austin Peay—Raye, Bedford, Armstrong. Technical fouls: Providence—Kipfer.

	1st Half	2nd Half	1 OT	Final
Providence	38	44	8	90
Austin Peay	46	36	5	87

New Orleans (76)   Coach: Benny Dees

	Min.	Total FG/FGA	Pct.	3-Pt. FG/FGA	Pct.	FT/FTA	Pct.	Reb. O/T	A	TO	PF	S	Blk	TP	PPM
JONES, S.	18	2/4	.500	0/1	.000	0/0	.000	1/2	0	1	2	1	0	4	.222
GRANDISON, R.	36	6/13	.462	0/0	.000	6/7	.857	5/6	0	2	3	4	0	18	.500
SMITH, M.	10	0/3	.000	0/0	.000	0/0	.000	1/3	0	1	2	0	2	0	.000
CORCHIANI, G.	20	4/6	.667	2/3	.667	1/1	1.000	1/3	5	3	3	1	0	11	.550
EACKLES, L.	36	5/13	.385	3/7	.429	3/6	.500	0/1	1	1	0	0	0	16	.444
RICHARDSON, W.	18	3/4	.750	0/0	.000	0/0	.000	0/1	2	0	3	1	0	6	.333
PERKINS, W.	8	0/1	.000	0/0	.000	0/0	.000	0/0	0	0	1	0	0	0	.000
IRVING, E.	11	1/2	.500	0/1	.000	1/2	.500	1/1	0	2	1	0	0	3	.273
BELLOCK, T.	18	2/4	.500	0/0	.000	4/6	.667	1/2	2	0	4	2	0	8	.444
VANCE, D.	6	1/2	.500	0/0	.000	1/2	.500	0/2	0	1	0	0	0	3	.500
COLEMAN, E.	9	1/3	.333	0/1	.000	1/2	.500	0/0	1	0	0	0	0	3	.333
HODO, D.	6	0/1	.000	0/1	.000	4/4	1.000	1/1	0	1	1	0	0	4	.667
COJOE, T.	4	0/0	.000	0/0	.000	0/0	.000	0/0	0	0	0	0	0	0	.000
Totals	200	25/56	.446	5/14	.357	21/30	.700	11/22	10	12	21	9	2	76	.380

Alabama (101)   Coach: Wimp Sanderson

	Min.	Total FG/FGA	Pct.	3-Pt. FG/FGA	Pct.	FT/FTA	Pct.	Reb. O/T	A	TO	PF	S	Blk	TP	PPM
FARMER, J.	36	6/13	.462	2/3	.667	5/5	1.000	2/6	2	2	1	1	0	19	.528
ANSLEY, M.	16	2/3	.667	0/0	.000	0/0	.000	2/5	0	2	4	0	0	4	.250
MCKEY, D.	35	10/12	.833	0/0	.000	6/6	1.000	0/4	4	2	2	2	5	26	.743
GOTTFRIED, M.	33	7/9	.778	4/6	.667	2/2	1.000	0/1	1	0	6	2	1	20	.606
CONER, T.	30	8/10	.800	4/6	.667	1/2	.500	1/1	7	2	2	0	0	17	.567
JACKSON, J.	17	4/5	.800	1/1	1.000	0/1	.000	1/3	0	0	1	1	0	9	.529
ASKINS, K.	23	3/3	1.000	0/0	.000	0/1	.000	2/6	1	1	3	0	0	6	.261
DEVAUGHN, W.	5	0/0	.000	0/0	.000	0/0	.000	0/1	0	2	0	0	0	0	.000
KORNEGY, R.	5	0/0	.000	0/0	.000	0/2	.000	0/0	3	0	1	0	0	0	.000
Totals	200	40/55	.727	7/11	.636	14/19	.737	8/26	15	15	20	5	6	101	.505

Team Rebounds: Alabama 1; New Orleans 3. Disqualified: None. Technical fouls: None.

	1st Half	2nd Half	Final
New Orleans	39	37	76
Alabama	58	43	101

SECOND ROUND EAST
North Carolina (109)   Coach: Dean Smith

	Min.	Total FG/FGA	Pct.	3-Pt. FG/FGA	Pct.	FT/FTA	Pct.	Reb. O/T	A	TO	PF	S	Blk	TP	PPM
WOLF, J.	20	3/5	.600	1/1	1.000	2/3	.667	2/7	1	0	1	0	0	9	.450
POPSON, D.	19	3/7	.429	0/0	.000	0/0	.000	3/6	1	2	4	0	0	6	.316
REID, J.	38	9/16	.563	0/0	.000	9/11	.818	1/10	2	0	1	1	0	27	.711
LEBO, J.	32	5/10	.500	2/6	.333	4/4	1.000	0/0	4	0	2	1	0	16	.500
SMITH, K.	31	6/10	.600	5/8	.625	5/6	.833	2/2	6	5	2	2	0	22	.710
DENNY, J.	1	0/0	.000	0/0	.000	0/0	.000	0/0	0	0	0	0	0	0	.000
HYATT, R.	1	0/0	.000	0/0	.000	0/0	.000	0/0	0	1	0	0	0	0	.000
BUCKNALL, S.	25	3/5	.600	0/0	.000	4/5	.800	1/3	2	0	2	0	0	10	.400
NORWOOD, M.	1	0/0	.000	0/0	.000	0/0	.000	0/0	0	0	0	0	0	0	.000
SMITH, R.	14	3/4	.750	2/2	1.000	0/1	.000	0/3	0	0	1	0	0	8	.571
WILLIAMS, S.	15	4/8	.500	0/0	.000	3/6	.500	5/6	2	3	3	2	0	11	.733
HENSLEY, M.	3	0/0	.000	0/0	.000	0/0	.000	0/0	0	0	0	0	0	0	.000
Totals	200	36/65	.554	10/17	.588	27/36	.750	14/37	18	11	16	6	0	109	.545

Michigan (97)   Coach: Bill Frieder

	Min.	Total FG/FGA	Pct.	3-Pt. FG/FGA	Pct.	FT/FTA	Pct.	Reb. O/T	A	TO	PF	S	Blk	TP	PPM
JOUBERT, A.	36	7/18	.389	2/7	.286	4/5	.800	3/6	3	2	3	1	0	20	.556
RICE, G.	37	10/17	.588	1/2	.500	1/1	1.000	2/10	1	2	4	0	1	22	.595
HUGHES, M.	25	3/4	.750	0/0	.000	0/0	.000	1/3	0	0	5	0	0	6	.240
GRANT, G.	39	11/23	.478	0/1	.000	2/2	1.000	7/10	10	2	5	1	0	24	.615
THOMPSON, G.	38	5/9	.556	3/4	.750	3/3	1.000	0/1	6	5	4	1	0	16	.421
GRIFFIN, M.	7	0/2	.000	0/0	.000	0/0	.000	0/0	0	1	0	0	0	0	.000
KRAMER, J.	2	0/0	.000	0/0	.000	1/3	.333	1/1	0	0	1	0	0	1	.500
VAUGHT, L.	13	3/8	.375	0/0	.000	0/0	.000	0/4	0	0	4	0	0	6	.462
OOSTERBAAN, J.	3	1/2	.500	0/0	.000	0/0	.000	2/2	0	0	2	0	0	2	.667
Totals	200	40/83	.482	6/14	.429	11/14	.786	16/37	21	11	29	3	1	97	.485

Team Rebounds: N. Carolina 5; Michigan 2. Disqualified: Michigan—Hughes, Grant. Technical fouls: None.

	1st Half	2nd Half	Final
N. Carolina	60	49	109
Michigan	43	54	97

Notre Dame (58)   Coach: Digger Phelps

	Min.	Total FG/FGA	Pct.	3-Pt. FG/FGA	Pct.	FT/FTA	Pct.	Reb. O/T	A	TO	PF	S	Blk	TP	PPM
ROYAL, D.	40	2/6	.333	0/0	.000	5/5	1.000	1/4	0	1	3	2	0	9	.225
STEVENSON, M.	39	4/8	.500	0/0	.000	0/0	.000	1/5	2	4	1	0	1	8	.205
VOCE, G.	34	2/2	1.000	0/0	.000	2/2	1.000	1/4	1	1	2	2	1	6	.176
RIVERS, D.	40	9/15	.600	5/11	.455	1/2	.500	0/1	2	1	2	0	0	24	.600
HICKS, S.	31	4/6	.667	2/2	1.000	1/1	1.000	0/0	3	1	3	1	0	11	.355
CONNOR, S.	7	0/3	.000	0/0	.000	0/0	.000	0/0	2	0	2	0	0	0	.000
JACKSON, J.	3	0/0	.000	0/0	.000	0/0	.000	0/0	0	1	0	0	0	0	.000
PADDOCK, S.	6	0/0	.000	0/0	.000	0/0	.000	0/2	0	0	0	0	0	0	.000
Totals	200	21/40	.525	7/13	.538	9/10	.900	3/16	10	9	13	5	2	58	.290

TCU (57)   Coach: Jim Killingsworth

	Min.	Total FG/FGA	Pct.	3-Pt. FG/FGA	Pct.	FT/FTA	Pct.	Reb. O/T	A	TO	PF	S	Blk	TP	PPM
RICHARD, L.	40	4/9	.444	0/0	.000	4/4	1.000	3/10	1	1	2	1	1	12	.300
ANDERSON, N.	28	4/5	.800	0/0	.000	0/0	.000	2/2	4	3	2	0	0	8	.286
PAPPA, T.	21	0/1	.000	0/0	.000	0/0	.000	0/1	0	0	1	0	0	0	.000
DIXON, J.	38	2/7	.286	1/1	1.000	5/5	1.000	0/1	6	2	3	0	0	10	.263
HOLCOMBE, C.	40	7/13	.538	0/0	.000	3/3	1.000	2/6	1	0	3	0	0	17	.425
LOTT, C.	27	5/11	.455	0/1	.000	0/0	.000	0/1	0	1	0	0	0	10	.370
MINNIS, M.	6	0/0	.000	0/0	.000	0/0	.000	1/1	0	0	2	0	0	0	.000
Totals	200	22/46	.478	1/2	.500	12/12	1.000	8/22	12	7	13	1	1	57	.285

Team Rebounds: Notre Dame 2; TCU 4. Disqualified: None. Technical fouls: None.

	1st Half	2nd Half	Final
Notre Dame	29	29	58
TCU	25	32	57

Florida (85)   Coach: Norm Sloan

	Min.	Total FG/FGA	Pct.	3-Pt. FG/FGA	Pct.	FT/FTA	Pct.	Reb. O/T	A	TO	PF	S	Blk	TP	PPM
LAWRENCE, J.	24	3/6	.500	1/4	.250	0/0	.000	1/4	3	0	1	0	0	7	.292
SCHINTZIUS, D.	29	7/10	.700	0/0	.000	7/8	.875	0/4	6	0	2	0	1	21	.724
MAXWELL, V.	37	9/20	.450	3/4	.750	3/5	.600	0/5	4	3	4	1	0	24	.649
MOTEN, A.	24	1/7	.143	1/4	.250	2/2	1.000	0/3	5	2	0	2	0	5	.208
MONTGOMERY, R.	18	2/2	1.000	0/0	.000	0/1	.000	0/1	4	2	2	1	0	4	.222
LETT, C.	8	0/2	.000	0/1	.000	0/0	.000	0/0	0	0	0	0	0	0	.000
CAPERS, C.	16	1/2	.500	0/0	.000	2/2	1.000	2/2	1	1	3	0	0	4	.250
MCCLARY, K.	11	1/2	.500	0/0	.000	0/0	.000	1/4	2	3	2	0	0	2	.182
JONES, M.	24	6/6	1.000	0/0	.000	1/2	.500	2/6	0	0	2	0	0	13	.542
LAWRENCE, P.	9	2/3	.667	1/2	.500	0/0	.000	0/0	1	0	1	0	0	5	.556
Totals	200	32/60	.533	6/15	.400	15/19	.789	6/29	26	11	15	6	1	85	.425

Purdue (66)   Coach: Gene Keady

	Min.	Total FG/FGA	Pct.	3-Pt. FG/FGA	Pct.	FT/FTA	Pct.	Reb. O/T	A	TO	PF	S	Blk	TP	PPM
MITCHELL, T.	31	7/13	.538	0/1	.000	0/0	.000	5/7	1	2	5	0	0	14	.452
LEE, D.	39	2/9	.222	0/4	.000	0/1	.000	1/4	4	2	4	1	0	4	.103
MCCANTS, M.	25	4/6	.667	0/0	.000	0/0	.000	0/1	0	2	5	0	2	8	.320
LEWIS, T.	40	7/18	.389	1/7	.143	0/0	.000	3/5	3	3	2	3	0	15	.375
STEPHENS, E.	31	5/11	.455	4/9	.444	1/2	.500	0/2	10	3	2	3	1	15	.484
JONES, K.	10	1/1	1.000	0/0	.000	0/2	.000	0/2	1	0	2	0	0	2	.200
JONES, T.	6	0/0	.000	0/0	.000	0/0	.000	0/0	1	0	0	0	0	0	.000
ARNOLD, J.	11	1/1	1.000	0/0	.000	4/6	.667	0/2	0	0	1	0	0	6	.545
FISHER, T.	3	0/0	.000	0/0	.000	0/0	.000	0/1	0	0	0	0	0	0	.000
SCHEFFLER, S.	4	1/1	1.000	0/0	.000	0/0	.000	0/1	0	0	0	0	0	2	.500
Totals	200	28/60	.467	5/21	.238	5/11	.455	9/24	19	13	21	7	3	66	.330

Team Rebounds: Florida 8; Purdue 7. Disqualified: Purdue—Mitchell, McCants. Technical fouls: None.

	1st Half	2nd Half	Final
Florida	31	54	85
Purdue	29	37	66

Western Kentucky (86)   Coach: Murray Arnold

	Min.	Total FG/FGA	Pct.	3-Pt. FG/FGA	Pct.	FT/FTA	Pct.	Reb. O/T	A	TO	PF	S	Blk	TP	PPM
JOHNSON, K.	27	2/7	.286	0/0	.000	4/6	.667	4/5	1	4	0	2	0	8	.296
MARTIN, C.	18	3/4	.750	0/0	.000	2/3	.667	0/2	0	1	4	0	1	8	.444
MCNEAL, B.	39	10/12	.833	0/1	.000	0/0	.000	0/4	4	4	3	0	0	20	.513
LEE, K.	24	4/10	.400	3/5	.600	0/0	.000	3/6	4	1	4	0	0	11	.458
ASBERRY, B.	28	11/17	.647	0/0	.000	0/1	.000	5/8	0	0	1	0	0	22	.786
MCNARY, J.	16	0/2	.000	0/0	.000	0/2	.000	0/0	2	3	3	2	0	0	.000
SWAGGER, R.	3	1/1	1.000	0/0	.000	0/1	.000	1/1	0	0	1	0	0	2	.667
TISDALE, F.	3	1/2	.500	0/1	.000	0/0	.000	0/0	0	0	0	0	0	2	.667
SHELTON, T.	2	0/0	.000	0/0	.000	0/0	.000	0/0	1	0	5	0	0	0	.000
GARMON, D.	1	0/0	.000	0/0	.000	1/2	.500	0/0	0	0	0	0	0	1	1.000
TELLIS, F.	39	5/15	.333	0/0	.000	2/2	1.000	0/4	2	1	5	1	0	12	.308
Totals	200	37/70	.529	3/7	.429	9/17	.529	13/30	14	14	26	5	1	86	.430

Syracuse (104)   Coach: Jim Boeheim

	Min.	Total FG/FGA	Pct.	3-Pt. FG/FGA	Pct.	FT/FTA	Pct.	Reb. O/T	A	TO	PF	S	Blk	TP	PPM
COLEMAN, D.	36	2/6	.333	0/0	.000	0/0	.000	5/9	2	3	3	0	4	4	.111
TRICHE, H.	35	8/13	.615	0/0	.000	5/6	.833	1/6	4	1	2	4	0	21	.600
SEIKALY, R.	34	8/13	.615	0/0	.000	7/11	.636	4/10	0	3	4	1	1	23	.676
DOUGLAS, S.	37	10/14	.714	0/1	.000	7/8	.875	0/4	8	4	1	2	0	27	.730
MONROE, G.	37	8/11	.727	2/3	.667	2/2	1.000	0/1	3	0	3	0	0	20	.541
BROWER, D.	8	0/0	.000	0/0	.000	0/6	.000	1/2	0	0	6	0	0	0	.000
THOMPSON, S.	9	4/5	.800	0/0	.000	1/3	.333	1/4	0	0	1	0	0	9	1.000
MATT, R.	2	0/0	.000	0/0	.000	0/0	.000	0/0	0	0	1	0	0	0	.000
KATZ, J.	1	0/0	.000	0/0	.000	0/0	.000	0/0	0	0	0	0	0	0	.000
KOHM, J.	1	0/0	.000	0/0	.000	0/0	.000	0/0	1	0	1	0	0	0	.000
Totals	200	40/62	.645	2/4	.500	22/36	.611	11/35	20	11	17	7	5	104	.520

Team Rebounds: Syracuse 4; Western Ky. 3. Disqualified: Western Ky.—Tellis, Shelton. Technical fouls: Western Ky.—Shelton.

	1st Half	2nd Half	Final
Western Ky.	40	46	86
Syracuse	42	62	104

REGIONAL SEMIFINAL WEST

UNLV (92)   Coach: Jerry Tarkanian

	Min.	Total FG/FGA	Pct.	3-Pt. FG/FGA	Pct.	FT/FTA	Pct.	Reb. O/T	A	TO	PF	S	Blk	TP	PPM
WADE, M.	37	1/2	.500	0/1	.000	0/1	.000	0/4	9	4	2	5	0	2	.054
BANKS, F.	34	5/16	.313	2/10	.200	2/2	1.000	1/3	2	0	1	1	0	14	.412
PADDIO, G.	15	2/9	.222	1/7	.143	0/0	.000	4/4	2	2	2	1	1	5	.333
GILLIAM, A.	39	17/24	.708	0/0	.000	4/7	.571	7/13	4	3	3	1	1	38	.974
BASNIGHT, J.	26	4/7	.571	0/0	.000	0/1	.000	2/5	0	3	3	0	0	8	.308
ROBINSON, R.	3	0/0	.000	0/0	.000	0/0	.000	0/1	0	0	0	0	0	0	.000
GRAHAM, G.	26	2/8	.250	1/5	.200	8/8	1.000	0/0	1	1	4	1	0	13	.500
HUDSON, E.	14	3/5	.600	0/0	.000	0/0	.000	2/2	0	0	1	1	0	6	.429
WILLARD, D.	6	2/2	1.000	0/0	.000	2/2	1.000	2/3	0	1	5	0	0	6	1.000
Totals	200	36/73	.493	4/23	.174	16/22	.727	18/35	18	14	21	10	2	92	.460

Wyoming (78)   Coach: Jim Brandenburg

	Min.	Total FG/FGA	Pct.	3-Pt. FG/FGA	Pct.	FT/FTA	Pct.	Reb. O/T	A	TO	PF	S	Blk	TP	PPM
DENT, S.	35	3/6	.500	0/0	.000	0/0	.000	0/1	6	4	5	1	1	6	.171
FOX, R.	11	0/3	.000	0/2	.000	0/0	.000	0/2	1	3	3	1	1	0	.000
DEMBO, F.	39	10/15	.667	2/4	.500	5/9	.556	2/9	4	2	4	2	0	27	.692
LECKNER, E.	34	7/17	.412	0/0	.000	4/6	.667	2/7	0	3	4	1	0	18	.529
SOMMERS, J.	11	0/1	.000	0/0	.000	0/0	.000	1/2	1	1	0	0	0	0	.000
BOYD, T.	34	5/6	.833	0/1	.000	4/4	1.000	0/2	2	7	3	1	0	14	.412
JONES, W.	29	3/6	.500	1/1	1.000	3/4	.750	0/6	5	2	3	2	2	10	.345
LODGINS, D.	5	0/1	.000	0/0	.000	0/0	.000	2/2	0	0	2	0	0	0	.000
HUNT, T.	1	1/1	1.000	1/1	1.000	0/0	.000	0/0	1	0	0	0	0	3	3.000
WORTH, Q.	1	0/0	.000	0/0	.000	0/0	.000	0/0	0	0	0	0	0	0	.000
Totals	200	29/56	.518	4/9	.444	16/24	.667	7/31	20	22	24	8	4	78	.390

Team Rebounds: UNLV 1; Wyoming 3. Disqualified: UNLV—Willard; Wyoming—Dent. Technical fouls: UNLV—Hudson, Banks.

	1st Half	2nd Half	Final
UNLV	38	54	92
Wyoming	39	39	78

Oklahoma (91)   Coach: Billy Tubbs

	Min.	Total FG/FGA	Pct.	3-Pt. FG/FGA	Pct.	FT/FTA	Pct.	Reb. O/T	A	TO	PF	S	Blk	TP	PPM
SIEGER, D.	25	2/6	.333	0/1	.000	2/4	.500	2/3	5	1	1	0	0	6	.240
GRANT, H.	36	6/12	.500	0/0	.000	3/3	1.000	3/7	1	2	4	0	3	15	.417
JOHNSON, D.	36	8/12	.667	0/0	.000	4/8	.500	8/12	0	4	3	1	0	20	.556
MCCALISTER, T.	45	9/18	.500	7/11	.636	1/5	.200	2/6	3	3	2	4	0	26	.578
GRACE, R.	26	2/4	.500	0/2	.000	2/2	1.000	0/0	8	1	4	7	0	6	.231
KING, S.	13	1/4	.250	0/0	.000	0/1	.000	1/2	0	2	1	2	2	2	.154
KENNEDY, D.	40	8/16	.500	0/0	.000	0/1	.000	3/3	4	2	4	1	0	16	.400
WATSON, C.	4	0/0	.000	0/0	.000	0/0	.000	0/0	0	0	1	0	0	0	.000
Totals	225	36/72	.500	7/14	.500	12/24	.500	19/33	21	13	21	14	5	91	.404

Iowa (93)   Coach: Tom Davis

	Min.	Total FG/FGA	Pct.	3-Pt. FG/FGA	Pct.	FT/FTA	Pct.	Reb. O/T	A	TO	PF	S	Blk	TP	PPM
MARBLE, R.	43	4/13	.308	0/0	.000	3/5	.600	3/7	2	5	2	0	0	11	.256
GAMBLE, K.	31	11/13	.846	2/2	1.000	2/6	.333	2/3	4	1	1	2	1	26	.839
LOHAUS, B.	33	4/8	.500	1/2	.500	0/0	.000	2/5	3	1	2	1	1	9	.273
ARMSTRONG, B.	38	4/8	.500	2/4	.500	6/6	1.000	0/3	10	2	1	1	0	16	.421
WRIGHT, D.	26	4/9	.444	0/0	.000	2/2	1.000	3/5	1	0	5	0	1	10	.385
JONES, B.	1	0/0	.000	0/0	.000	0/0	.000	0/0	0	0	1	0	0	0	.000
MOE, J.	18	2/8	.250	0/3	.000	1/2	.500	3/3	0	1	1	0	0	5	.278
HORTON, E.	19	2/5	.400	0/0	.000	2/2	1.000	1/4	1	3	4	2	0	6	.316
LORENZEN, A.	10	3/5	.600	0/0	.000	4/4	1.000	4/5	0	2	3	0	0	10	1.000
REAVES, M.	6	0/0	.000	0/0	.000	0/0	.000	0/1	0	0	0	0	0	0	.000
Totals	225	34/69	.493	5/11	.455	20/27	.741	18/36	21	15	20	6	3	93	.413

Team Rebounds: Iowa 6; Oklahoma 7. Disqualified: Iowa—Wright. Technical fouls: None.

	1st Half	2nd Half	1 OT	Final
Oklahoma	41	44	6	91
Iowa	40	45	8	93

REGIONAL SEMIFINAL MIDWEST

Indiana (88)   Coach: Bob Knight

	Min.	Total FG/FGA	Pct.	3-Pt. FG/FGA	Pct.	FT/FTA	Pct.	Reb. O/T	A	TO	PF	S	Blk	TP	PPM
CALLOWAY, R.	39	8/13	.615	0/0	.000	5/6	.833	3/8	2	3	2	0	0	21	.538
THOMAS, D.	22	6/10	.600	0/0	.000	3/3	1.000	1/3	0	5	4	2	1	15	.682
GARRETT, D.	39	4/7	.571	0/0	.000	3/5	.600	1/9	0	0	2	0	3	11	.282
ALFORD, S.	38	6/16	.375	1/3	.333	5/7	.714	0/2	5	2	2	0	0	18	.474
SMART, K.	30	8/11	.727	0/0	.000	5/6	.833	2/7	3	3	3	1	0	21	.700
MEIER, J.	4	0/0	.000	0/0	.000	0/0	.000	0/0	0	0	1	0	0	0	.000
MINOR, D.	1	0/0	.000	0/0	.000	0/0	.000	0/0	0	0	0	0	0	0	.000
EYL, S.	14	0/0	.000	0/0	.000	2/4	.500	2/5	3	0	1	1	0	2	.143
SMITH, K.	1	0/0	.000	0/0	.000	0/0	.000	0/0	0	0	0	0	0	0	.000
HILLMAN, J.	12	0/0	.000	0/0	.000	0/0	.000	0/2	3	1	1	0	0	0	.000
Totals	200	32/57	.561	1/3	.333	23/31	.742	9/36	16	14	16	4	4	88	.440

Duke (82)   Coach: Mike Krzyzewski

	Min.	Total FG/FGA	Pct.	3-Pt. FG/FGA	Pct.	FT/FTA	Pct.	Reb. O/T	A	TO	PF	S	Blk	TP	PPM
FERRY, D.	37	7/13	.538	4/4	1.000	2/3	.667	1/7	4	4	3	0	0	20	.541
KING, B.	28	3/5	.600	0/0	.000	0/0	.000	1/4	1	1	3	2	0	6	.214
SMITH, J.	18	4/6	.667	0/0	.000	3/4	.750	0/0	1	4	5	0	0	11	.611
AMAKER, T.	40	8/17	.471	3/3	1.000	4/4	1.000	1/2	3	2	1	1	0	23	.575
STRICKLAND, K.	32	5/15	.333	1/4	.250	0/0	.000	1/6	1	2	5	1	1	11	.344
SNYDER, Q.	15	0/0	.000	0/0	.000	0/0	.000	0/0	2	0	3	0	0	0	.000
BRICKEY, R.	20	3/8	.375	0/0	.000	1/2	.500	3/5	0	3	1	1	7	.350	
ABDELNABY, A.	7	2/3	.667	0/0	.000	0/0	.000	0/0	0	0	1	0	0	4	.571
NESSLEY, M.	3	0/0	.000	0/0	.000	0/0	.000	0/1	0	0	1	0	0	0	.000
Totals	200	32/67	.478	8/11	.727	10/13	.769	7/25	12	13	25	5	3	82	.410

Team Rebounds: Indiana 2; Duke 3. Disqualified: Duke—Smith, Strickland. Technical fouls: None.

	1st Half	2nd Half	Final
Indiana	49	39	88
Duke	39	43	82

DePaul (58)   Coach: Joey Meyer

	Min.	Total FG/FGA	Pct.	3-Pt. FG/FGA	Pct.	FT/FTA	Pct.	Reb. O/T	A	TO	PF	S	Blk	TP	PPM
GOLDEN, K.	17	2/4	.500	0/0	.000	2/2	1.000	0/1	0	1	2	0	0	6	.353
COMEGYS, D.	37	7/13	.538	0/0	.000	0/0	.000	2/8	1	4	3	1	3	14	.378
GREENE, T.	28	4/11	.364	1/2	.500	1/2	.500	1/5	1	5	2	0	0	10	.357
EDWARDS, K.	37	4/7	.571	1/3	.333	3/4	.750	0/1	1	1	2	0	0	12	.324
STRICKLAND, R.	36	4/9	.444	1/2	.500	0/2	.000	0/2	4	4	1	1	0	9	.250
LAUX, A.	19	0/0	.000	0/0	.000	1/2	.500	1/2	0	2	2	0	0	1	.053
BRUNDY, S.	26	3/3	1.000	0/0	.000	0/0	.000	2/5	1	0	4	3	0	6	.231
Totals	200	24/47	.511	3/7	.429	7/12	.583	6/24	8	17	16	5	3	58	.290

Louisiana State (63)   Coach: Dale Brown

	Min.	Total FG/FGA	Pct.	3-Pt. FG/FGA	Pct.	FT/FTA	Pct.	Reb. O/T	A	TO	PF	S	Blk	TP	PPM
WOODSIDE, B.	33	5/8	.625	0/0	.000	1/1	1.000	6/7	4	2	3	1	0	11	.333
BROWN, O.	31	1/5	.200	0/0	.000	0/2	.000	2/9	4	4	3	3	0	2	.065
WILSON, N.	40	12/19	.632	0/0	.000	0/0	.000	3/6	0	2	2	0	0	24	.600
WILSON, A.	40	7/20	.350	3/9	.333	0/0	.000	3/5	3	1	1	0	0	17	.425
JOE, D.	32	0/6	.000	0/4	.000	0/0	.000	1/2	8	3	4	5	0	0	.000
IRVIN, F.	8	0/0	.000	0/0	.000	0/0	.000	0/1	1	1	0	0	0	0	.000
VARGAS, J.	16	4/6	.667	0/0	.000	1/4	.250	0/1	1	1	3	0	0	9	.563
Totals	200	29/64	.453	3/13	.231	2/7	.286	15/31	21	14	16	9	0	63	.315

Team Rebounds: Louisiana St. 2; DePaul 3. Disqualified: None. Technical fouls: None.

	1st Half	2nd Half	Final
DePaul	34	24	58
Louisiana St.	38	25	63

REGIONAL SEMIFINAL SOUTHEAST

Georgetown (70)   Coach: John Thompson

	Min.	Total FG/FGA	Pct.	3-Pt. FG/FGA	Pct.	FT/FTA	Pct.	Reb. O/T	A	TO	PF	S	Blk	TP	PPM
MCDONALD, P.	34	2/ 3	.667	0/ 0	.000	6/11	.545	3/ 7	0	0	0	0	1	10	.294
WILLIAMS, R.	39	8/21	.381	2/ 7	.286	16/18	.889	4/ 9	1	2	2	4	1	34	.872
GILLERY, B.	2	0/ 0	.000	0/ 0	.000	0/ 0	.000	0/ 1	0	0	0	0	0	0	.000
BRYANT, D.	16	0/ 1	.000	0/ 0	.000	0/ 0	.000	0/ 2	1	2	0	0	0	0	.000
TILLMON, M.	23	3/ 5	.600	0/ 0	.000	1/ 1	1.000	2/ 3	0	2	3	1	0	7	.304
HIGHSMITH, R.	14	1/ 2	.500	0/ 0	.000	0/ 1	.000	0/ 4	0	1	4	0	0	2	.143
WINSTON, B.	25	0/ 1	.000	0/ 0	.000	1/ 2	.500	2/ 4	5	1	0	0	1	1	.040
ALLEN, A.	20	1/ 1	1.000	0/ 0	.000	1/ 2	.500	3/ 5	0	2	2	0	1	3	.150
SMITH, C.	17	5/ 9	.556	1/ 2	.500	2/ 2	1.000	0/ 2	0	1	2	1	1	13	.765
EDWARDS, J.	3	0/ 0	.000	0/ 0	.000	0/ 0	.000	0/ 1	0	1	1	0	0	0	.000
JACKSON, J.	6	0/ 0	.000	0/ 0	.000	0/ 0	.000	0/ 1	0	2	1	1	0	0	.000
JEFFERSON, S.	1	0/ 0	.000	0/ 0	.000	0/ 0	.000	0/ 0	0	0	0	0	0	0	.000
Totals	200	20/43	.465	3/ 9	.333	27/37	.730	14/37	6	18	16	7	4	70	.350

Kansas (57)   Coach: Larry Brown

	Min.	Total FG/FGA	Pct.	3-Pt. FG/FGA	Pct.	FT/FTA	Pct.	Reb. O/T	A	TO	PF	S	Blk	TP	PPM
PIPER, C.	34	3/ 7	.429	0/ 0	.000	0/ 0	.000	0/ 3	2	2	5	1	2	6	.176
MANNING, D.	40	9/16	.563	0/ 0	.000	5/ 9	.556	4/12	0	5	4	0	0	23	.575
PELLOCK, M.	11	0/ 1	.000	0/ 0	.000	0/ 0	.000	1/ 1	1	1	2	1	0	0	.000
PRITCHARD, K.	20	2/ 4	.500	0/ 1	.000	0/ 0	.000	0/ 1	2	1	4	0	0	4	.200
HUNTER, C.	34	4/12	.333	0/ 0	.000	1/ 2	.500	2/ 4	1	4	1	1	0	9	.265
TURGEON, M.	27	2/ 5	.400	2/ 4	.500	0/ 0	.000	1/ 2	4	1	2	0	0	6	.222
HARRIS, K.	19	2/ 3	.667	0/ 0	.000	1/ 2	.500	2/ 3	2	0	2	2	0	5	.263
NEWTON, M.	8	0/ 4	.000	0/ 0	.000	0/ 0	.000	0/ 0	0	0	2	0	0	0	.000
BARRY, R.	2	0/ 0	.000	0/ 0	.000	1/ 3	.333	2/ 2	1	0	1	0	0	1	.500
GUELDNER, J.	5	1/ 2	.500	1/ 2	.500	0/ 0	.000	0/ 0	1	0	2	0	0	3	.600
Totals	200	23/54	.426	3/ 7	.429	8/16	.500	11/28	14	14	25	5	2	57	.285

Team Rebounds: Georgetown 3; Kansas 0. Disqualified: Kansas—Piper. Technical fouls: Kansas—Bench.

	1st Half	2nd Half	Final
Georgetown	34	36	70
Kansas	29	28	57

Providence (103)   Coach: Rick Pitino

	Min.	Total FG/FGA	Pct.	3-Pt. FG/FGA	Pct.	FT/FTA	Pct.	Reb. O/T	A	TO	PF	S	Blk	TP	PPM
KIPFER, D.	25	3/ 5	.600	0/ 0	.000	3/ 5	.600	0/ 1	1	1	5	0	0	9	.360
LEWIS, E.	28	3/ 6	.500	3/ 6	.500	0/ 0	.000	1/ 3	3	2	5	0	0	9	.321
DUDA, J.	16	0/ 1	.000	0/ 0	.000	0/ 0	.000	1/ 3	0	1	1	0	0	0	.000
BROOKS, D.	36	7/11	.636	5/ 6	.833	4/ 5	.800	2/ 7	4	2	2	2	0	23	.639
DONOVAN, B.	30	6/ 7	.857	5/ 6	.833	9/10	.900	0/ 3	10	3	5	1	0	26	.867
CONLON, M.	14	1/ 1	1.000	0/ 0	.000	4/ 4	1.000	3/ 4	2	0	1	0	0	6	.429
SMEDEKER, D.	1	0/ 0	.000	0/ 0	.000	0/ 0	.000	0/ 1	0	0	0	0	0	0	.000
WRIGHT, D.	12	5/ 6	.833	1/ 2	.500	2/ 4	.500	1/ 2	0	1	0	0	0	13	1.083
WRIGHT, S.	24	7/ 9	.778	0/ 0	.000	1/ 1	1.000	0/ 5	0	2	3	0	1	15	.625
SCREEN, C.	14	1/ 2	.500	0/ 0	.000	0/ 1	.000	0/ 0	4	2	1	0	0	2	.143
Totals	200	33/48	.688	14/20	.700	23/30	.767	8/29	24	13	24	3	1	103	.515

Alabama (82)   Coach: Wimp Sanderson

	Min.	Total FG/FGA	Pct.	3-Pt. FG/FGA	Pct.	FT/FTA	Pct.	Reb. O/T	A	TO	PF	S	Blk	TP	PPM
FARMER, J.	36	7/19	.368	2/ 9	.222	8/ 8	1.000	1/ 1	3	1	4	2	0	24	.667
ANSLEY, M.	31	6/ 9	.667	0/ 0	.000	2/ 2	1.000	2/ 6	0	1	2	0	0	14	.452
MCKEY, D.	37	3/ 6	.500	0/ 1	.000	5/ 5	1.000	2/ 4	2	0	5	1	1	11	.297
GOTTFRIED, M.	27	5/10	.500	4/ 9	.444	0/ 2	.000	2/ 3	4	4	5	0	0	14	.519
CONER, T.	33	5/ 7	.714	0/ 0	.000	2/ 3	.667	0/ 2	4	5	3	0	0	12	.364
JACKSON, J.	22	1/ 5	.200	1/ 2	.500	4/ 4	1.000	1/ 2	0	0	4	1	0	7	.318
ASKINS, K.	14	0/ 3	.000	0/ 2	.000	0/ 0	.000	1/ 3	0	0	3	2	0	0	.000
Totals	200	27/59	.458	7/23	.304	21/24	.875	9/21	13	11	26	6	1	82	.410

Team Rebounds: Providence 4; Alabama 2. Disqualified: Providence—Kipfer, Lewis, Donovan; Alabama—McKey, Gottfried. Technical fouls: None.

	1st Half	2nd Half	Final
Providence	49	54	103
Alabama	41	41	82

REGIONAL SEMIFINAL EAST

North Carolina (74)   Coach: Dean Smith

	Min.	Total FG/FGA	Pct.	3-Pt. FG/FGA	Pct.	FT/FTA	Pct.	Reb. O/T	A	TO	PF	S	Blk	TP	PPM
WOLF, J.	33	6/ 7	.857	1/ 1	1.000	0/ 1	.000	2/ 7	3	1	1	1	0	13	.394
POPSON, D.	23	5/ 7	.714	0/ 0	.000	1/ 1	1.000	0/ 1	0	4	1	0	1	11	.478
REID, J.	35	15/18	.833	0/ 0	.000	1/ 3	.333	2/ 5	0	1	1	3	1	31	.886
LEBO, J.	38	2/ 5	.400	0/ 2	.000	3/ 4	.750	0/ 2	0	2	1	0	1	7	.184
SMITH, K.	34	2/ 8	.250	0/ 4	.000	0/ 0	.000	0/ 0	12	4	3	0	0	4	.118
BUCKNALL, S.	14	2/ 3	.667	0/ 0	.000	0/ 0	.000	1/ 1	1	1	3	0	0	4	.286
SMITH, R.	8	0/ 1	.000	0/ 0	.000	0/ 0	.000	0/ 0	0	0	0	0	0	0	.000
WILLIAMS, S.	15	2/ 3	.667	0/ 0	.000	0/ 0	.000	1/ 2	0	1	2	0	1	4	.267
Totals	200	34/52	.654	1/ 7	.143	5/ 9	.556	6/18	17	10	15	5	3	74	.370

Notre Dame (68)   Coach: Digger Phelps

	Min.	Total FG/FGA	Pct.	3-Pt. FG/FGA	Pct.	FT/FTA	Pct.	Reb. O/T	A	TO	PF	S	Blk	TP	PPM
ROYAL, D.	36	7/12	.583	0/ 0	.000	5/ 7	.714	5/10	1	3	4	0	0	19	.528
STEVENSON, M.	34	7/14	.500	0/ 0	.000	0/ 0	.000	2/ 4	0	4	1	2	0	14	.412
VOCE, G.	36	3/ 5	.600	0/ 0	.000	2/ 2	1.000	2/ 6	1	1	3	1	1	8	.222
RIVERS, D.	40	8/16	.500	3/ 6	.500	4/ 4	1.000	0/ 0	2	3	3	1	0	23	.575
HICKS, S.	38	2/ 9	.222	0/ 1	.000	0/ 0	.000	2/ 5	3	0	2	1	0	4	.105
CONNOR, J.	9	0/ 0	.000	0/ 0	.000	0/ 0	.000	0/ 2	0	1	0	0	0	0	.000
JACKSON, J.	3	0/ 0	.000	0/ 0	.000	0/ 0	.000	0/ 0	0	0	0	0	0	0	.000
PADDOCK, S.	3	0/ 0	.000	0/ 0	.000	0/ 0	.000	0/ 1	0	0	0	0	0	0	.000
SMITH, M.	1	0/ 0	.000	0/ 0	.000	0/ 0	.000	0/ 0	0	0	0	0	0	0	.000
Totals	200	27/56	.482	3/ 7	.429	11/13	.846	11/26	9	11	14	5	1	68	.340

Team Rebounds: N. Carolina 3; Notre Dame 3. Disqualified: None. Technical fouls: None.

	1st Half	2nd Half	Final
N. Carolina	36	38	74
Notre Dame	26	42	68

Florida (81)   Coach: Norm Sloan

	Min.	Total FG/FGA	Pct.	3-Pt. FG/FGA	Pct.	FT/FTA	Pct.	Reb. O/T	A	TO	PF	S	Blk	TP	PPM
LAWRENCE, J.	14	1/ 2	.500	1/ 2	.500	0/ 0	.000	0/ 0	0	0	0	0	0	3	.214
SCHINTZIUS, D.	29	3/10	.300	0/ 0	.000	0/ 0	.000	2/11	3	2	5	1	3	6	.207
MAXWELL, V.	35	11/23	.478	3/ 6	.500	0/ 0	.000	3/ 4	0	4	1	1	0	25	.714
MOTEN, A.	35	7/18	.389	1/ 7	.143	3/ 4	.750	2/ 2	2	1	3	4	0	18	.514
MONTGOMERY, R.	10	0/ 0	.000	0/ 0	.000	0/ 0	.000	0/ 2	0	0	0	1	0	0	.000
LETT, C.	9	2/ 2	1.000	1/ 1	1.000	1/ 2	.500	1/ 1	0	0	2	0	0	6	.667
MCCLARY, K.	22	2/ 6	.333	0/ 0	.000	3/ 4	.750	2/ 6	1	3	4	0	2	7	.318
CAPERS, C.	6	1/ 1	1.000	0/ 0	.000	0/ 0	.000	1/ 1	0	1	0	1	0	2	.333
JONES, M.	15	0/ 3	.000	0/ 0	.000	0/ 0	.000	1/ 2	2	0	1	1	0	0	.000
LAWRENCE, P.	25	5/ 9	.556	4/ 6	.667	0/ 0	.000	4/ 4	3	0	3	1	0	14	.560
Totals	200	32/74	.432	10/22	.455	7/10	.700	16/31	13	11	19	9	6	81	.405

Syracuse (87)   Coach: Jim Boeheim

	Min.	Total FG/FGA	Pct.	3-Pt. FG/FGA	Pct.	FT/FTA	Pct.	Reb. O/T	A	TO	PF	S	Blk	TP	PPM
COLEMAN, D.	38	4/ 9	.444	0/ 0	.000	7/ 8	.875	1/ 9	2	2	2	1	1	15	.395
TRICHE, H.	39	8/12	.667	0/ 0	.000	1/ 1	1.000	1/ 4	5	1	2	0	0	17	.436
SEIKALY, R.	38	14/20	.700	0/ 0	.000	5/ 6	.833	5/ 9	0	3	3	0	2	33	.868
DOUGLAS, S.	36	4/12	.333	0/ 2	.000	2/ 3	.667	2/ 4	10	5	3	0	0	10	.278
MONROE, G.	38	5/ 8	.625	0/ 2	.000	2/ 2	1.000	0/ 3	2	3	0	1	0	12	.316
BROWER, D.	4	0/ 0	.000	0/ 0	.000	0/ 0	.000	0/ 1	1	0	1	0	0	0	.000
THOMPSON, S.	7	0/ 0	.000	0/ 0	.000	0/ 0	.000	0/ 0	0	1	0	0	0	0	.000
Totals	200	35/61	.574	0/ 4	.000	17/20	.850	9/30	20	15	11	2	3	87	.435

Team Rebounds: Syracuse 6; Florida 3. Disqualified: Florida—Schintzius. Technical fouls: None.

	1st Half	2nd Half	Final
Florida	33	48	81
Syracuse	40	47	87

REGIONAL FINAL WEST

UNLV (84) Coach: Jerry Tarkanian

	Min.	Total FG/FGA	Pct.	3-Pt. FG/FGA	Pct.	FT/FTA	Pct.	Reb. O/T	A	TO	PF	S	Blk	TP	PPM
WADE, M.	35	1/2	.500	1/1	1.000	0/0	.000	2/4	12	4	4	2	0	3	.086
BANKS, F.	37	5/20	.250	4/13	.308	3/5	.600	3/3	5	1	1	0	0	17	.459
PADDIO, G.	29	7/16	.438	4/11	.364	2/2	1.000	2/4	2	2	3	0	0	20	.690
GILLIAM, A.	38	11/16	.688	0/0	.000	5/6	.833	5/10	0	2	4	2	2	27	.711
BASNIGHT, J.	25	3/3	1.000	0/0	.000	1/2	.500	1/2	0	1	4	1	0	7	.280
ROBINSON, R.	4	0/0	.000	0/0	.000	0/0	.000	0/0	0	0	0	1	1	0	.000
WEST, L.	1	0/0	.000	0/0	.000	0/0	.000	0/0	0	0	1	0	0	0	.000
GRAHAM, G.	14	3/10	.300	2/5	.400	2/2	1.000	0/1	2	2	4	0	0	10	.714
HUDSON, E.	15	0/1	.000	0/0	.000	0/0	.000	3/6	1	1	3	0	0	0	.000
WILLARD, D.	2	0/0	.000	0/0	.000	0/0	.000	0/1	0	1	2	0	0	0	.000
Totals	200	30/68	.441	11/30	.367	13/17	.765	16/31	22	14	26	6	3	84	.420

Iowa (81) Coach: Tom Davis

	Min.	Total FG/FGA	Pct.	3-Pt. FG/FGA	Pct.	FT/FTA	Pct.	Reb. O/T	A	TO	PF	S	Blk	TP	PPM
MARBLE, R.	35	3/11	.273	0/1	.000	3/7	.429	1/6	5	4	3	1	0	9	.257
GAMBLE, K.	27	7/11	.636	1/2	.500	3/3	1.000	0/3	2	4	4	1	0	18	.667
LOHAUS, B.	29	4/6	.667	0/1	.000	4/5	.800	5/7	1	2	2	1	0	12	.414
ARMSTRONG, B.	32	6/12	.500	0/1	.000	6/7	.857	0/2	2	1	1	1	0	18	.563
WRIGHT, G.	26	3/5	.600	0/0	.000	2/4	.500	0/3	4	2	3	2	0	8	.308
JONES, B.	2	0/0	.000	0/0	.000	0/0	.000	0/0	0	0	0	0	0	0	.000
MOE, J.	16	1/2	.500	1/1	1.000	1/2	.500	0/1	0	1	3	0	0	4	.250
HORTON, E.	14	4/5	.800	0/0	.000	0/1	.000	0/4	1	1	2	0	0	8	.571
LORENZEN, A.	11	0/0	.000	0/0	.000	0/0	.000	0/1	2	1	3	0	0	0	.000
REAVES, M.	8	2/2	1.000	0/0	.000	0/0	.000	1/1	1	2	1	1	0	4	.500
Totals	200	30/54	.556	2/6	.333	19/29	.655	7/28	18	18	22	7	0	81	.405

Team Rebounds: UNLV 2; Iowa 5. Disqualified: None. Technical fouls: None.

	1st Half	2nd Half	Final
UNLV	42	42	84
Iowa	58	23	81

REGIONAL FINAL MIDWEST

Indiana (77) Coach: Bob Knight

	Min.	Total FG/FGA	Pct.	3-Pt. FG/FGA	Pct.	FT/FTA	Pct.	Reb. O/T	A	TO	PF	S	Blk	TP	PPM
CALLOWAY, R.	37	5/10	.500	0/0	.000	1/2	.500	1/5	5	2	4	1	0	11	.297
THOMAS, D.	39	5/11	.455	0/0	.000	6/6	1.000	2/7	0	3	3	1	0	16	.410
GARRETT, D.	38	8/10	.800	0/0	.000	1/3	.333	3/15	1	3	3	0	3	17	.447
ALFORD, S.	40	4/9	.444	2/4	.500	10/10	1.000	0/0	7	0	1	0	0	20	.500
SMART, K.	39	4/10	.400	0/1	.000	2/2	1.000	2/2	1	3	2	1	0	10	.256
SMITH, K.	1	0/1	.000	0/1	.000	0/0	.000	1/1	0	0	0	0	0	0	.000
EYL, S.	5	0/1	.000	0/0	.000	0/0	.000	1/3	0	1	0	1	0	0	.000
HILLMAN, J.	1	1/1	1.000	0/0	.000	1/1	1.000	0/0	0	0	0	0	0	3	3.000
Totals	200	27/53	.509	2/6	.333	21/24	.875	10/33	14	12	13	4	3	77	.385

Louisiana State (76) Coach: Dale Brown

	Min.	Total FG/FGA	Pct.	3-Pt. FG/FGA	Pct.	FT/FTA	Pct.	Reb. O/T	A	TO	PF	S	Blk	TP	PPM
WOODSIDE, B.	26	6/10	.600	1/1	1.000	0/1	.000	6/7	1	1	5	1	0	13	.500
OLIVER, B.	34	3/6	.500	0/0	.000	0/2	.000	3/7	8	0	2	3	0	6	.176
WILSON, N.	40	9/16	.563	0/0	.000	2/2	1.000	1/6	0	2	3	0	0	20	.500
WILSON, A.	40	6/15	.400	2/9	.222	1/2	.500	1/4	1	1	2	0	0	15	.375
DARRYL, J.	21	1/7	.143	1/4	.250	1/2	.500	0/2	2	3	3	1	0	4	.190
IRVIN, F.	22	6/7	.857	2/3	.667	0/1	.000	0/0	3	2	1	0	0	14	.636
VARGAS, J.	17	2/4	.500	0/0	.000	0/0	.000	0/1	2	2	3	1	1	4	.235
Totals	200	33/65	.508	6/17	.353	4/10	.400	11/27	17	11	19	6	1	76	.380

Team Rebounds: Indiana 0; Louisiana St. 4. Disqualified: Louisiana St.—Woodside. Technical fouls: Indiana—Bench.

	1st Half	2nd Half	Final
Indiana	47	30	77
Louisiana St.	46	30	76

REGIONAL FINAL SOUTHEAST

Georgetown (73) Coach: John Thompson

	Min.	Total FG/FGA	Pct.	3-Pt. FG/FGA	Pct.	FT/FTA	Pct.	Reb. O/T	A	TO	PF	S	Blk	TP	PPM
MCDONALD, P.	28	3/11	.273	0/0	.000	2/5	.400	6/10	0	1	2	0	0	8	.286
WILLIAMS, R.	29	9/23	.391	2/8	.250	5/6	.833	3/9	1	1	4	1	0	25	.862
GILLERY, B.	1	0/0	.000	0/0	.000	0/0	.000	0/0	0	0	1	0	0	0	.000
BRYANT, D.	20	2/6	.333	0/2	.000	4/4	1.000	3/3	2	2	3	1	0	8	.400
TILLMON, M.	26	4/13	.308	1/4	.250	1/2	.500	2/2	0	2	3	1	0	10	.385
HIGHSMITH, R.	9	1/1	1.000	0/0	.000	0/0	.000	1/5	0	1	5	0	0	2	.222
WINSTON, B.	20	0/0	.000	0/0	.000	0/2	.000	0/1	4	3	3	2	0	0	.000
ALLEN, A.	23	1/2	.500	0/0	.000	5/6	.833	3/4	0	0	3	1	3	7	.304
SMITH, C.	27	4/14	.286	1/6	.167	0/0	.000	4/5	1	1	5	0	1	9	.333
EDWARDS, J.	7	1/2	.500	0/0	.000	2/2	1.000	2/2	0	1	2	0	0	2	.286
JACKSON, J.	8	1/4	.250	0/1	.000	0/0	.000	0/1	1	2	0	0	0	2	.250
JEFFERSON, S.	1	0/0	.000	0/0	.000	0/0	.000	0/0	0	0	0	0	0	0	.000
LANG, T.	1	0/0	.000	0/0	.000	0/0	.000	0/0	0	0	0	0	0	0	.000
Totals	200	26/76	.342	4/21	.190	17/25	.680	24/41	9	15	27	6	4	73	.365

Providence (88) Coach: Rick Pitino

	Min.	Total FG/FGA	Pct.	3-Pt. FG/FGA	Pct.	FT/FTA	Pct.	Reb. O/T	A	TO	PF	S	Blk	TP	PPM
KIPFER, D.	25	4/7	.571	0/0	.000	3/3	1.000	0/5	1	3	3	1	0	11	.440
LEWIS, E.	17	3/7	.429	1/3	.333	0/0	.000	0/4	2	0	5	0	0	7	.412
DUDA, J.	7	0/0	.000	0/0	.000	0/0	.000	0/2	0	1	1	0	0	0	.000
BROOKS, D.	27	0/2	.000	0/1	.000	0/0	.000	2/3	2	3	3	2	0	0	.000
DONOVAN, B.	37	2/5	.400	0/1	.000	16/18	.889	1/4	6	4	3	1	0	20	.541
SCREEN, C.	16	2/3	.667	0/0	.000	5/7	.714	2/4	2	2	0	1	0	9	.563
SHAMSID-DEEN, A.	6	0/0	.000	0/0	.000	2/2	1.000	1/1	0	0	0	0	2	2	.333
CONLON, M.	15	3/5	.600	0/0	.000	1/1	1.000	0/3	1	2	1	0	0	7	.467
WRIGHT, D.	22	6/6	1.000	4/4	1.000	4/5	.800	0/2	0	1	3	0	0	20	.909
WRIGHT, S.	27	5/11	.455	0/0	.000	2/2	1.000	0/3	0	0	3	1	7	12	.444
BENHAM, B.	1	0/0	.000	0/0	.000	0/0	.000	0/0	0	0	0	0	0	0	.000
Totals	200	25/46	.543	5/9	.556	33/38	.868	6/31	14	16	22	6	10	88	.440

Team Rebounds: Providence 0; Georgetown 5. Disqualified: Providence—Lewis; Georgetown—Smith. Technical fouls: Providence—Donovan; Georgetown—Smith.

	1st Half	2nd Half	Final
Georgetown	37	36	73
Providence	54	34	88

REGIONAL FINAL EAST

North Carolina (75) Coach: Dean Smith

	Min.	Total FG/FGA	Pct.	3-Pt. FG/FGA	Pct.	FT/FTA	Pct.	Reb. O/T	A	TO	PF	S	Blk	TP	PPM
WOLF, J.	37	5/7	.714	1/1	1.000	1/2	.500	2/10	4	4	4	0	0	12	.324
POPSON, D.	20	5/9	.556	0/0	.000	0/0	.000	2/4	0	1	4	1	0	10	.500
REID, J.	38	7/14	.500	0/0	.000	1/2	.500	0/6	1	1	4	0	3	15	.395
LEBO, J.	28	0/5	.000	0/5	.000	2/2	1.000	2/3	4	2	3	0	0	2	.071
SMITH, K.	38	10/19	.526	4/11	.364	1/1	1.000	0/2	7	6	3	2	0	25	.658
BUCKNALL, S.	10	0/1	.000	0/0	.000	0/0	.000	0/0	0	0	3	0	0	0	.000
SMITH, R.	17	4/5	.800	3/3	1.000	0/0	.000	1/1	2	0	1	0	1	11	.647
WILLIAMS, S.	12	0/4	.000	0/0	.000	0/1	.000	0/0	0	0	2	0	0	0	.000
Totals	200	31/64	.484	8/20	.400	5/8	.625	7/26	18	14	23	4	3	75	.375

Syracuse (79) Coach: Jim Boeheim

	Min.	Total FG/FGA	Pct.	3-Pt. FG/FGA	Pct.	FT/FTA	Pct.	Reb. O/T	A	TO	PF	S	Blk	TP	PPM
COLEMAN, D.	38	2/10	.200	0/0	.000	4/6	.667	7/14	3	1	2	2	3	8	.211
TRICHE, H.	37	5/9	.556	0/0	.000	0/1	.000	0/6	3	1	2	2	0	10	.270
SEIKALY, R.	37	11/15	.733	0/0	.000	4/7	.571	4/11	0	3	2	1	2	26	.703
DOUGLAS, S.	38	6/13	.462	0/1	.000	2/5	.400	2/3	9	5	3	2	0	14	.368
MONROE, G.	29	3/8	.375	2/5	.400	4/4	1.000	1/1	2	2	4	0	0	12	.414
BROWER, D.	6	1/2	.500	0/0	.000	0/0	.000	1/1	0	0	2	0	0	2	.333
THOMPSON, S.	13	3/3	1.000	0/0	.000	1/5	.200	2/2	0	1	1	0	0	7	.538
HARRIED, H.	2	0/0	.000	0/0	.000	0/0	.000	0/0	0	0	0	0	0	0	.000
Totals	200	31/60	.517	2/6	.333	15/29	.517	17/38	17	13	16	7	5	79	.395

Team Rebounds: Syracuse 4; N. Carolina 6. Disqualified: None. Technical fouls: None.

	1st Half	2nd Half	Final
N. Carolina	30	45	75
Syracuse	41	38	79

FINAL FOUR

UNLV (93) Coach: Jerry Tarkanian

	Min.	Total FG/FGA	Pct.	3-Pt. FG/FGA	Pct.	FT/FTA	Pct.	Reb. O/T	A	TO	PF	S	Blk	TP	PPM
PADDIO, G.	22	2/13	.154	2/8	.250	0/0	.000	2/6	1	2	1	0	0	6	.273
GILLIAM, A.	39	14/26	.538	0/0	.000	4/6	.667	7/10	1	3	0	3	3	32	.821
BASNIGHT, J.	22	3/4	.750	0/0	.000	0/1	.000	2/2	1	0	5	0	0	6	.273
WADE, M.	35	1/6	.167	1/6	.167	1/2	.500	2/4	18	0	4	4	0	4	.114
BANKS, F.	35	12/23	.522	10/19	.526	4/6	.667	4/8	1	3	4	0	0	38	1.086
ROBINSON, R.	5	0/0	.000	0/0	.000	0/0	.000	0/1	0	1	0	0	0	0	.000
GRAHAM, G.	25	0/5	.000	0/2	.000	1/4	.250	0/2	0	2	4	0	0	1	.040
HUDSON, E.	13	3/4	.750	0/0	.000	0/0	.000	4/5	1	0	2	1	0	6	.462
WILLARD, D.	4	0/1	.000	0/0	.000	0/0	.000	0/0	0	1	2	0	0	0	.000
Totals	200	35/82	.427	13/35	.371	10/19	.526	21/38	23	9	26	5	3	93	.465

Indiana (97) Coach: Bob Knight

	Min.	Total FG/FGA	Pct.	3-Pt. FG/FGA	Pct.	FT/FTA	Pct.	Reb. O/T	A	TO	PF	S	Blk	TP	PPM
CALLOWAY, R.	40	6/10	.600	0/0	.000	0/0	.000	1/6	6	3	3	1	0	12	.300
THOMAS, D.	18	3/5	.600	0/0	.000	0/0	.000	1/4	1	2	3	0	0	6	.333
GARRETT, D.	40	7/10	.700	0/0	.000	4/5	.800	4/11	1	2	2	0	2	18	.450
ALFORD, S.	37	10/19	.526	2/4	.500	11/13	.846	0/4	2	2	4	0	0	33	.892
SMART, K.	23	5/7	.714	0/0	.000	4/5	.800	0/2	1	2	5	0	0	14	.609
SMITH, K.	2	0/2	.000	0/0	.000	0/0	.000	1/1	0	0	0	0	0	0	.000
EYL, S.	20	3/3	1.000	0/0	.000	1/2	.500	1/5	2	1	4	0	0	7	.350
HILLMAN, J.	17	3/4	.750	0/0	.000	1/3	.333	2/3	3	2	2	0	0	7	.412
MEIER, T.	3	0/0	.000	0/0	.000	0/0	.000	0/3	0	0	0	0	0	0	.000
Totals	200	37/60	.617	2/4	.500	21/28	.750	10/39	16	14	23	1	2	97	.485

Team Rebounds: Indiana 3; UNLV 2. Disqualified: Indiana—Smart; UNLV—Basnight. Technical fouls: None.

	1st Half	2nd Half	Final
UNLV	47	46	93
Indiana	53	44	97

Providence (63) Coach: Rick Pitino

	Min.	Total FG/FGA	Pct.	3-Pt. FG/FGA	Pct.	FT/FTA	Pct.	Reb. O/T	A	TO	PF	S	Blk	TP	PPM
KIPFER, D.	29	4/10	.400	0/0	.000	0/1	.000	1/5	0	1	4	2	0	8	.276
LEWIS, E.	32	2/12	.167	1/8	.125	2/2	1.000	1/5	1	0	3	4	0	7	.219
DUDA, J.	24	2/7	.286	0/0	.000	0/1	.000	3/7	0	0	4	1	0	4	.167
BROOKS, D.	24	4/9	.444	1/5	.200	0/0	.000	2/3	2	2	4	0	0	9	.375
DONOVAN, B.	36	3/12	.250	1/3	.333	1/1	1.000	0/1	7	3	3	2	0	8	.222
SCREEN, C.	22	5/6	.833	1/1	1.000	7/10	.700	1/2	0	0	2	1	0	18	.818
SHAMSID-DEEN, A.	4	1/2	.500	0/0	.000	0/0	.000	1/2	0	1	1	0	1	2	.500
CONLON, M.	10	1/1	1.000	0/0	.000	0/0	.000	2/3	1	3	4	0	1	2	.200
WRIGHT, D.	8	1/4	.250	1/2	.500	0/0	.000	0/0	1	1	2	0	0	3	.375
WRIGHT, S.	9	1/3	.333	0/0	.000	0/0	.000	1/4	0	2	5	1	1	2	.222
SMEDEKER, D.	2	0/0	.000	0/0	.000	0/0	.000	0/0	0	0	1	0	0	0	.000
Totals	200	24/66	.364	5/19	.263	10/15	.667	12/32	12	13	33	11	3	63	.315

Syracuse (77) Coach: Jim Boeheim

	Min.	Total FG/FGA	Pct.	3-Pt. FG/FGA	Pct.	FT/FTA	Pct.	Reb. O/T	A	TO	PF	S	Blk	TP	PPM
COLEMAN, D.	34	4/6	.667	0/0	.000	4/7	.571	3/12	0	4	3	2	2	12	.353
TRICHE, H.	37	4/10	.400	0/0	.000	4/5	.800	4/11	1	3	3	0	0	12	.324
SEIKALY, R.	31	4/11	.364	0/0	.000	8/11	.727	2/6	2	3	3	0	2	16	.516
DOUGLAS, S.	35	5/11	.455	0/1	.000	2/6	.333	5/11	6	4	3	2	0	12	.343
MONROE, G.	32	4/9	.444	3/7	.429	6/10	.600	0/4	3	4	2	1	0	17	.531
BROWER, D.	14	0/1	.000	0/0	.000	0/0	.000	4/4	1	1	2	2	0	0	.000
THOMPSON, S.	15	3/5	.600	0/0	.000	1/3	.333	3/5	0	1	1	0	0	7	.467
HARRIED, H.	2	0/0	.000	0/0	.000	1/2	.500	0/0	0	0	0	0	0	1	.500
Totals	200	24/53	.453	3/8	.375	26/44	.591	21/53	13	20	17	7	4	77	.385

Team Rebounds: Syracuse 0; Providence 3. Disqualified: Providence—S. Wright. Technical fouls: Syracuse—Coleman.

	1st Half	2nd Half	Final
Providence	26	37	63
Syracuse	36	41	77

NATIONAL CHAMPIONSHIP

Indiana (74) Coach: Bob Knight

	Min.	Total FG/FGA	Pct.	3–Pt. FG/FGA	Pct.	FT/FTA	Pct.	Reb. O/T	A	TO	PF	S	Blk	TP	PPM
CALLOWAY, R.	14	0/3	.000	0/0	.000	0/0	.000	0/2	1	2	3	0	0	0	.000
THOMAS, D.	40	8/18	.444	0/0	.000	4/7	.571	1/7	1	3	1	0	0	20	.500
GARRETT, D.	33	5/10	.500	0/0	.000	0/0	.000	3/10	0	0	4	0	3	10	.303
ALFORD, S.	40	8/15	.533	7/10	.700	0/0	.000	1/3	5	3	2	2	0	23	.575
SMART, K.	35	9/15	.600	0/1	.000	3/4	.750	0/5	6	2	2	2	0	21	.600
SMITH, K.	1	0/0	.000	0/0	.000	0/0	.000	0/0	0	0	1	0	0	0	.000
EYL, S.	13	0/0	.000	0/0	.000	0/0	.000	0/1	1	1	2	0	0	0	.000
HILLMAN, J.	20	0/1	.000	0/0	.000	0/0	.000	1/2	6	2	3	0	0	0	.000
MEIER, T.	4	0/0	.000	0/0	.000	0/1	.000	0/1	0	0	0	0	0	0	.000
Totals	200	30/62	.484	7/11	.636	7/12	.583	6/31	20	11	17	7	3	74	.370

Syracuse (73) Coach: Jim Boeheim

	Min.	Total FG/FGA	Pct.	3–Pt. FG/FGA	Pct.	FT/FTA	Pct.	Reb. O/T	A	TO	PF	S	Blk	TP	PPM
COLEMAN, D.	37	3/7	.429	0/0	.000	2/4	.500	3/19	1	2	2	1	3	8	.216
TRICHE, H.	32	3/9	.333	0/0	.000	2/4	.500	0/1	1	0	4	0	0	8	.250
SEIKALY, R.	34	7/13	.538	0/0	.000	4/6	.667	6/10	1	3	3	1	3	18	.529
DOUGLAS, S.	39	8/15	.533	2/2	1.000	2/2	1.000	1/2	7	4	3	1	0	20	.513
MONROE, G.	32	5/11	.455	2/8	.250	0/1	.000	0/2	3	2	1	2	0	12	.375
BROWER, D.	9	3/3	1.000	0/0	.000	1/3	.333	1/1	0	0	3	0	0	7	.778
THOMPSON, S.	17	0/2	.000	0/0	.000	0/0	.000	1/3	1	3	0	0	1	0	.000
Totals	200	29/60	.483	4/10	.400	11/20	.550	12/38	14	14	16	5	7	73	.365

Team Rebounds: Indiana 4; Syracuse 0. Disqualified: None. Technical fouls: None.

	1st Half	2nd Half	Final
Indiana	34	40	74
Syracuse	33	40	73

⊙ ALL-STAR TEAMS ⊙

ALL TOURNAMENT
STEVE ALFORD	INDIANA
DERRICK COLEMAN	SYRACUSE
SHERMAN DOUGLAS	SYRACUSE
ARMON GILLIAM	UNLV
★ KEITH SMART	INDIANA

EAST REGIONAL
DERRICK COLEMAN	SYRACUSE
SHERMAN DOUGLAS	SYRACUSE
J. R. REID	N. CAROLINA
DAVID RIVERS	NOTRE DAME
★ RONY SEIKALY	SYRACUSE

SOUTHEAST REGIONAL
★ BILLY DONOVAN	PROVIDENCE
DANNY MANNING	KANSAS
REGGIE WILLIAMS	GEORGETOWN
DARRYL WRIGHT	PROVIDENCE
STEVE WRIGHT	PROVIDENCE

WEST REGIONAL
B. J. ARMSTRONG	IOWA
FENNIS DEMBO	WYOMING
KEVIN GAMBLE	IOWA
★ ARMON GILLIAM	UNLV
TIM McCALISTER	OKLAHOMA

MIDWEST REGIONAL
STEVE ALFORD	INDIANA
TOMMY AMAKER	DUKE
RICK CALLOWAY	INDIANA
ANTHONY WILSON	LOUISANA ST.
★ NIKITA WILSON	LOUISANA ST.

★ Most Outstanding Player(s)

⊙ INDIVIDUAL RECORDS ⊙

SCORING

Most points in a single game
1. DAVID ROBINSON, NAVY (vs. MICHIGAN) — 50
2. DANNY MANNING, KANSAS (vs. SW MISSOURI ST.) — 42
3. FENNIS DEMBO, WYOMING (vs. UCLA) — 41
4. ARMON GILLIAM, UNLV (vs. WYOMING) — 38
4. FREDDIE BANKS, UNLV (vs. INDIANA) — 38

Most total points in the tournament
1. RONY SEIKALY, SYRACUSE — 138
1. STEVE ALFORD, INDIANA — 138
3. ARMON GILLIAM, UNLV — 133
4. BILLY DONOVAN, PROVIDENCE — 114
5. FREDDIE BANKS, UNLV — 107

Highest scoring average (minimum 2 games)
1. FENNIS DEMBO, WYOMING (84-3) — 28.00
2. REGGIE MILLER, UCLA (56-2) — 28.00
3. MIKE JONES, AUBURN (54-2) — 27.00
4. ARMON GILLIAM, UNLV (133-5) — 26.60
5. MITCH RICHMOND, KANSAS STATE (53-2) — 26.50

FIELD GOALS

Most field goals in a single game
1. DAVID ROBINSON, NAVY (vs. MICHIGAN) — 22
2. ARMON GILLIAM, UNLV (vs. WYOMING) — 17
3. DANNY MANNING, KANSAS (vs. SW MISSOURI ST.) — 16
4. J.R. REID, N. CAROLINA (vs. NOTRE DAME) — 15
5. 3 tied for fifth place.

Most total field goals in the tournament
1. ARMON GILLIAM, UNLV — 55
2. RONY SEIKALY, SYRACUSE — 53
3. STEVE ALFORD, INDIANA — 42
4. SHERMAN DOUGLAS, SYRACUSE — 40
5. NIKITA WILSON, LOUISIANA ST. — 38

Most field goal attempts in a single game
1. DAVID ROBINSON, NAVY (vs. MICHIGAN) — 37
2. ARMON GILLIAM, UNLV (vs. INDIANA) — 26
2. DANNY MANNING, KANSAS (vs. SW MISSOURI ST.) — 26
4. MICHAEL SMITH, BRIGHAM YOUNG (vs. NEW ORLEANS) — 25

5. ARMON GILLIAM, UNLV (vs. WYOMING) — 24

Most total field goal attempts in tournament
1. ARMON GILLIAM, UNLV — 91
2. FREDDIE BANKS, UNLV — 88
3. RONY SEIKALY, SYRACUSE — 87
4. STEVE ALFORD, INDIANA — 81
5. SHERMAN DOUGLAS, SYRACUSE — 79

Highest field goal percentage in a single game (minimum 10 attempts)
1. DALLAS COMEGYS, DEPAUL (vs. LOUISIANA TECH) (12-14) — .857
2. KEVIN GAMBLE, IOWA (vs. OKLAHOMA) (11-13) — .846
3. J.R. REID, N. CAROLINA (vs. NOTRE DAME) (15-18) — .833
4. DERRICK McKEY, ALABAMA (vs. NEW ORLEANS) (10-12) — .833
4. BRETT McNEAL, WESTERN KY. (vs. SYRACUSE) (10-12) — .833

Highest field goal percentage in the tournament (minimum 20 attempts)

1	JARVIS BASNIGHT, UNLV (18-23)	.783
2	KEVIN GAMBLE, IOWA (32-41)	.781
3	CARVEN HOLCOMBE, TCU (21-30)	.700
4	TERRY CONER, ALABAMA (14-20)	.700
5	JOE WOLF, N. CAROLINA (23-33)	.697

3-PT. FIELD GOALS

Most 3-pt. field goals in a single game

1	FREDDIE BANKS, UNLV (vs. INDIANA)	10
2	GARDE THOMPSON, MICHIGAN (vs. NAVY)	9
3	6 tied for third place.	

Most total 3-pt. field goals in the tournament

1	FREDDIE BANKS, UNLV	26
2	STEVE ALFORD, INDIANA	21
3	BILLY DONOVAN, PROVIDENCE	14
4	GREG MONROE, SYRACUSE	13
4	TIM MCCALISTER, OKLAHOMA	13

Most 3-pt. field goals attempted in a single game

1	FREDDIE BANKS, UNLV (vs. INDIANA)	19
2	ERNIE LEWIS, PROVIDENCE (vs. AUSTIN PEAY)	14
3	FREDDIE BANKS, UNLV (vs. IOWA)	13
3	FREDDIE BANKS, UNLV (vs. IDAHO STATE)	13
3	DARRYL BEDFORD, AUSTIN PEAY (vs. ILLINOIS)	13

Most total 3-pt. field goals attempted in the tournament

1	FREDDIE BANKS, UNLV	65
2	GERALD PADDIO, UNLV	39
3	ERNIE LEWIS, PROVIDENCE	37
4	STEVE ALFORD, INDIANA	34
5	GREG MONROE, SYRACUSE	33

Highest 3-pt. field goal percentage in a single game (minimum 4 attempts)

1	MITCH RICHMOND, KANSAS STATE (vs. GEORGIA) (5-5)	1.000
2	DARRYL WRIGHT, PROVIDENCE (vs. GEORGETOWN) (4-4)	1.000
2	DANNY FERRY, DUKE (vs. INDIANA) (4-4)	1.000
2	MICHAEL STOKES, GA. SOUTHERN (vs. SYRACUSE) (4-4)	1.000
5	2 tied for fifth place.	

Highest 3-pt. field goal percentage in the tournament (minimum 8 attempts)

1	GARDE THOMPSON, MICHIGAN (12-16)	.750
2	TOMMY AMAKER, DUKE (6-8)	.750
3	DARRYL WRIGHT, PROVIDENCE (7-10)	.700
4	BILLY DONOVAN, PROVIDENCE (14-22)	.636
5	REGGIE MILLER, UCLA (5-8)	.625

FREE THROWS

Most free throws in a single game

1	FENNIS DEMBO, WYOMING (vs. UCLA)	16
1	BYRON LARKIN, XAVIER (OHIO) (vs. MISSOURI)	16
1	BILLY DONOVAN, PROVIDENCE (vs. GEORGETOWN)	16
1	REGGIE WILLIAMS, GEORGETOWN (vs. KANSAS)	16
5	VERNON MAXWELL, FLORIDA (vs. N.C. STATE)	14

Most total free throws in the tournament

1	BILLY DONOVAN, PROVIDENCE	36
2	STEVE ALFORD, INDIANA	33
3	RONY SEIKALY, SYRACUSE	32
4	REGGIE WILLIAMS, GEORGETOWN	27
5	DARYL THOMAS, INDIANA	24

Most free throws attempted in a single game

1	VERNON MAXWELL, FLORIDA (vs. N.C. STATE)	21
2	BYRON LARKIN, XAVIER (OHIO) (vs. MISSOURI)	20
3	BILLY DONOVAN, PROVIDENCE (vs. GEORGETOWN)	18
3	REGGIE WILLIAMS, GEORGETOWN (vs. KANSAS)	18
5	2 tied for fifth place.	

Most free throws attempted in the tournament

1	RONY SEIKALY, SYRACUSE	51
2	BILLY DONOVAN, PROVIDENCE	43
3	STEVE ALFORD, INDIANA	38
4	DERRICK COLEMAN, SYRACUSE	31
5	2 tied for fifth place.	

Highest free throw percentage in a single game (minimum 7 attempts)

1	FENNIS DEMBO, WYOMING (vs. UCLA) (16-16)	1.000
2	STEVE ALFORD, INDIANA (vs. LOUISIANA ST.) (10-10)	1.000
3	MIKE JONES, AUBURN (vs. INDIANA) (9-9)	1.000
4	4 tied for fourth place.	

Highest free throw percentage in the tournament (minimum 15 attempts)

1	DERRICK MCKEY, ALABAMA (19-19)	1.000
2	REGGIE WILLIAMS, GEORGETOWN (27-30)	.900
3	DAVID RIVERS, NOTRE DAME (15-17)	.882
3	RICK CALLOWAY, INDIANA (15-17)	.882
3	B.J. ARMSTRONG, IOWA (15-17)	.882

REBOUNDS

Most rebounds in a single game

1	DERRICK COLEMAN, SYRACUSE (vs. INDIANA)	19
2	TIM PERRY, TEMPLE (vs. SOUTHERN-B.R.)	17
2	HARVEY GRANT, OKLAHOMA (vs. TULSA)	17
4	DEAN GARRETT, INDIANA (vs. LOUISIANA ST.)	15
4	MICHAEL SMITH, BRIGHAM YOUNG (vs. NEW ORLEANS)	15

Most total rebounds in the tournament

1	DERRICK COLEMAN, SYRACUSE	73
2	DEAN GARRETT, INDIANA	55
3	RONY SEIKALY, SYRACUSE	53
4	ARMON GILLIAM, UNLV	52
5	RICK CALLOWAY, INDIANA	42

Most rebounds per game (minimum 2 games)

1	TIM PERRY, TEMPLE (28-2)	14.00
2	MITCH RICHMOND, KANSAS STATE (25-2)	12.50
3	DERRICK COLEMAN, SYRACUSE (73-6)	12.17
4	JEFF MOORE, AUBURN (24-2)	12.00
5	2 tied for fifth place.	

ASSISTS

Most assists in a single game

1	MARK WADE, UNLV (vs. INDIANA)	18
2	KEITH SMART, INDIANA (vs. AUBURN)	15
3	MARK WADE, UNLV (vs. KANSAS STATE)	13
4	3 tied for fourth place.	

Most total assists in the tournament

1	MARK WADE, UNLV	61
2	SHERMAN DOUGLAS, SYRACUSE	49
3	BILLY DONOVAN, PROVIDENCE	42
4	KENNY SMITH, N. CAROLINA	36
5	KEITH SMART, INDIANA	28

Most assists per game (minimum 2 appearances)

1	MARK WADE, UNLV (61-5)	12.20
2	KENNY SMITH, N. CAROLINA (36-4)	9.00
3	BILLY DONOVAN, PROVIDENCE (42-5)	8.40
4	SHERMAN DOUGLAS, SYRACUSE (49-6)	8.17
5	GARY GRANT, MICHIGAN (16-2)	8.00

TURNOVERS

Most turnovers in a single game

1	WINSTON GARLAND, SW MISSOURI ST. (vs. CLEMSON)	8
1	STAN KIMBROUGH, XAVIER (OHIO) (vs. DUKE)	8
1	CURTIS WILSON, OHIO STATE (vs. KENTUCKY)	8
4	4 tied for fourth place.	

Most total turnovers in the tournament

1	SHERMAN DOUGLAS, SYRACUSE	25
2	BILLY DONOVAN, PROVIDENCE	21
3	DARYL THOMAS, INDIANA	19
4	KENNY SMITH, N. CAROLINA	18
5	RICK CALLOWAY, INDIANA	17

SHOTS BLOCKED

Most shots blocked in a single game

1	TIM PERRY, TEMPLE (vs. SOUTHERN-B.R.)	7
1	ANTHONY COOK, ARIZONA (vs. UTEP)	7
1	STEVE WRIGHT, PROVIDENCE (vs. GEORGETOWN)	7
4	DERRICK MCKEY, ALABAMA (vs. NEW ORLEANS)	5
5	2 tied for fifth place.	

Most total shots blocked in the tournament

1	DERRICK COLEMAN, SYRACUSE	16
2	DEAN GARRETT, INDIANA	15
3	STEVE WRIGHT, PROVIDENCE	12
4	RONY SEIKALY, SYRACUSE	11
5	2 tied for fifth place.	

STEALS

Most steals in a single game

1	DELRAY BROOKS, PROVIDENCE (vs. AUSTIN PEAY)	7
1	RICKY GRACE, OKLAHOMA (vs. IOWA)	7
1	REGGIE MILLER, UCLA (vs. WYOMING)	7
4	8 tied for fourth place.	

Most total steals in the tournament

1	MARK WADE, UNLV	18
2	RICKY GRACE, OKLAHOMA	14
3	JAMERE JACKSON, NOTRE DAME	13
3	DELRAY BROOKS, PROVIDENCE	13
5	BILLY DONOVAN, PROVIDENCE	12

✪ TEAM RECORDS ✪

SCORING

Most points in a single game
1	N. CAROLINA (vs. PENNSYLVANIA)	113
2	N. CAROLINA (vs. MICHIGAN)	109
3	INDIANA (vs. AUBURN)	107

Most total points in the tournament
1	INDIANA	535
2	SYRACUSE	499
3	UNLV	444

Highest scoring average (minimum 2 games)
1	MICHIGAN (194-2)	97.00
2	PITTSBURGH (186-2)	93.00
3	N. CAROLINA (371-4)	92.75

FIELD GOALS

Most field goals in a single game
1	SYRACUSE (vs. WESTERN KY.)	40
1	MICHIGAN (vs. N. CAROLINA)	40
1	ALABAMA (vs. NEW ORLEANS)	40

Most total field goals in the tournament
1	INDIANA	195
2	SYRACUSE	188
3	UNLV	159

Most field goals attempted in a single game
1	AUBURN (vs. INDIANA)	86
2	MICHIGAN (vs. N. CAROLINA)	83
3	2 tied for third place.	

Most total field goals attempted in the tournament
1	INDIANA	352
2	SYRACUSE	351
3	UNLV	350

Highest field goal percentage in a single game
1	ALABAMA (vs. NEW ORLEANS) (40-55)	.727
2	PROVIDENCE (vs. ALABAMA) (33-48)	.688
3	OHIO STATE (vs. KENTUCKY) (33-50)	.660

Highest field goal percentage in a tournament (minimum 2 games)
1	ALABAMA (99-169)	.586
2	OHIO STATE (63-109)	.578
3	TCU (51-91)	.561

3-PT. FIELD GOALS

Most 3-pt. field goals in a single game
1	PROVIDENCE (vs. ALABAMA)	14
2	UNLV (vs. INDIANA)	13
3	MICHIGAN (vs. NAVY)	12

Most total 3-pt. field goals in the tournament
1	PROVIDENCE	45
2	UNLV	43
3	N. CAROLINA	27

Most 3-pt. field goals attempted in a single game
1	UNLV (vs. INDIANA)	35

2	UNLV (vs. IOWA)	30
3	2 tied for third place.	

Most total 3-pt. field goals attempted in the tournament
1	UNLV	132
2	PROVIDENCE	95
3	N. CAROLINA	64

Highest 3-pt. field goal percentage in a single game (minimum 10 attempts)
1	ALABAMA (vs. N.C. A&T) (9-11)	.818
2	DUKE (vs. INDIANA) (8-11)	.727
3	PROVIDENCE (vs. ALABAMA) (14-20)	.700

Highest 3-pt. field goal percentage in the tournament (minimum 20 attempts)
1	MICHIGAN (18-34)	.529
2	INDIANA (21-40)	.525
3	ALABAMA (23-45)	.511

FREE THROWS

Most free throws in a single game
1	N. CAROLINA (vs. PENNSYLVANIA)	33
1	PROVIDENCE (vs. GEORGETOWN)	33
3	PURDUE (vs. NORTHEASTERN)	31

Most total free throws in the tournament
1	INDIANA	124
2	SYRACUSE	107
3	PROVIDENCE	91

Most free throws attempted in a single game
1	PURDUE (vs. NORTHEASTERN)	45
1	N. CAROLINA (vs. PENNSYLVANIA)	45
3	SYRACUSE (vs. PROVIDENCE)	44

Most total free throws attempted in the tournament
1	SYRACUSE	175
2	INDIANA	156
3	PROVIDENCE	123

Highest free throw percentage in a single game
1	TCU (vs. NOTRE DAME) (12-12)	1.000
2	UNLV (vs. KANSAS STATE) (18-19)	.947
3	ALABAMA (vs. N.C. A&T) (15-16)	.938

Highest free throw percentage in the tournament (minimum 2 games)
1	TEMPLE (32-36)	.889
2	NOTRE DAME (47-55)	.855
3	ALABAMA (50-59)	.848

Fewest free throws in a single game
1	LOUISIANA ST. (vs. DEPAUL)	2
2	CENTRAL MICH. (vs. UCLA)	3
2	MARIST (vs. PITTSBURGH)	3

Lowest free throw percentage in a single game
1	LOUISIANA ST. (vs. DEPAUL) (2-7)	.286
2	CENTRAL MICH. (vs. UCLA) (3-8)	.375
3	LOUISIANA ST. (vs. INDIANA) (4-10)	.400

Lowest free throw percentage in the tournament (minimum 2 games)
1	PITTSBURGH (32-56)	.571
2	LOUISIANA ST. (35-61)	.574
3	SYRACUSE (107-175)	.612

REBOUNDS

Most rebounds in a single game
1	AUSTIN PEAY (vs. PROVIDENCE)	55
2	SYRACUSE (vs. PROVIDENCE)	53
3	2 tied for third place.	

Most rebounds per game (minimum 2 games)
1	AUSTIN PEAY (84-2)	42.00
2	TEMPLE (77-2)	38.50
3	INDIANA (223-6)	37.17

ASSISTS

Most assists in a single game
1	N. CAROLINA (vs. PENNSYLVANIA)	30
2	FLORIDA (vs. PURDUE)	26
3	2 tied for third place.	

Most assists per game (minimum 2 games)
1	N. CAROLINA (83-4)	20.75
2	PURDUE (41-2)	20.50
2	MICHIGAN (41-2)	20.50

TURNOVERS

Most turnovers in a single game
1	AUSTIN PEAY (vs. PROVIDENCE)	24
2	3 tied for second place.	

Most turnovers per game (minimum 2 games)
1	KANSAS STATE (40-2)	20.00
2	WYOMING (55-3)	18.33
3	IOWA (73-4)	18.25

SHOTS BLOCKED

Most shots blocked in a single game
1	ARIZONA (vs. UTEP)	11
2	PROVIDENCE (vs. GEORGETOWN)	10
3	TEMPLE (vs. SOUTHERN-B.R.)	8

Most shots blocked per game (minimum 2 games)
1	SYRACUSE (30-6)	5.00
2	TEMPLE (9-2)	4.50
3	PROVIDENCE (21-5)	4.20

STEALS

Most steals in a single game
1	PROVIDENCE (vs. AUSTIN PEAY)	19
2	OKLAHOMA (vs. IOWA)	14
3	4 tied for third place.	

Most steals per game (minimum 2 games)
1	OKLAHOMA (33-3)	11.00
2	UTEP (21-2)	10.50
3	PROVIDENCE (50-5)	10.00

1988

FIRST ROUND	SECOND ROUND	REGIONAL SEMIFINAL	REGIONAL FINAL	FINAL FOUR	REGIONAL FINAL	REGIONAL SEMIFINAL	SECOND ROUND	FIRST ROUND

MIDWEST

- **1** Purdue 94
- **16** F. Dickinson 79
  - Purdue 100
- **8** Baylor 60
- **9** Memphis St. 75
  - Memphis St. 73
    - Purdue 70
- **5** DePaul 83
- **12** Wichita St. 62
  - DePaul 58
- **4** Kansas St. 66
- **13** La Salle 53
  - Kansas St. 66
    - Kansas St. 73
      - Kansas St. 58
- **6** Kansas 85
- **11** Xavier (Ohio) 72
  - Kansas 61
- **3** N.C. State 75
- **14** Murray St. 78
  - Murray St. 58
    - Kansas 77
- **7** Vanderbilt 80
- **10** Utah St. 77
  - Vanderbilt 80 (ot)
- **2** Pittsburgh 108
- **15** Eastern Mich. 90
  - Pittsburgh 74
    - Vanderbilt 64
      - Kansas 71
        - Kansas 66

EAST

- **1** Temple 87
- **16** Lehigh 73
  - Temple 74
- **8** Georgetown 66
- **9** Louisiana St. 63
  - Georgetown 53
    - Temple 69
- **5** Georgia Tech 90
- **12** Iowa St. 78
  - Georgia Tech 55
- **4** Indiana 69
- **13** Richmond 72
  - Richmond 59
    - Richmond 47
      - Temple 53
- **6** Missouri 80
- **11** Rhode Island 87
  - Rhode Island 97
- **3** Syracuse 69
- **14** N. Carolina A&T 55
  - Syracuse 94
    - Rhode Island 72
- **7** SMU 83
- **18** Notre Dame 75
  - SMU 79
- **2** Duke 85
- **15** Boston Univ. 69
  - Duke 94
    - Duke 73
      - Duke 63
        - Duke 59

FINAL FOUR

- Kansas 83
- Oklahoma 79

WEST

- **1** Arizona 90
- **16** Cornell 50
  - Arizona 84
- **8** Seton Hall 80
- **9** UTEP 64
  - Seton Hall 55
    - Arizona 99
- **5** Iowa 102
- **12** Florida St. 98
  - Iowa 104
- **4** UNLV 54
- **13** SW Missouri St. 50
  - UNLV 86
    - Iowa 79
      - Arizona 70
- **6** Florida 62
- **11** St. John's 59
  - Florida 85
- **3** Michigan 63
- **14** Boise St. 58
  - Michigan 108
    - Michigan 69
- **7** Wyoming 115
- **10** Loyola Mymt. 119
  - Loyola Mymt. 97
- **2** N. Carolina 83
- **15** North Texas 65
  - N. Carolina 123
    - N. Carolina 78
      - N. Carolina 52
        - Arizona 78

SOUTHWEST

- **1** Oklahoma 94
- **16** Tenn.-Chatt. 66
  - Oklahoma 107
- **8** Auburn 90
- **9** Bradley 86
  - Auburn 87
    - Oklahoma 108
- **5** Louisville 70
- **12** Oregon St. 61
  - Louisville 97
- **4** Brigham Young 98 (ot)
- **12** N. C.-Charlotte 92
  - Brigham Young 76
    - Louisville 98
      - Oklahoma 78
- **6** Villanova 82
- **11** Arkansas 74
  - Villanova 66
- **3** Illinois 81
- **14** Texas-San Ant. 72
  - Illinois 63
    - Villanova 80
- **7** Maryland 92
- **10** UC Santa Barb. 82
  - Maryland 81
- ***2** Kentucky 99
- **15** Southern-B.R. 84
  - *Kentucky 90
    - *Kentucky 74
      - Villanova 59
        - Oklahoma 86

*Kentucky's participation in 1988 tournament vacated.

In 1988, for the third time in six years, the team that had the horses lost the race. Oklahoma had a superb stable of athletes—Mookie Blaylock, Stacey King, Harvey Grant, and Ricky Grace were all pro prospects—and Arizona and Duke also appeared to have great overall depth. Only Kansas seemed to have no business being in the Final Four. Of course the Jayhawks, unlike longshots North Carolina State in 1983 and Villanova in 1985, did have one important factor in their favor: They were paced by a certifiable thoroughbred. Danny Manning was, by general consensus, the nation's best college basketball player. Even with Manning, though, by February Kansas had a mediocre 12-8 record, and it wasn't until March that they were certain of an invitation to the 64-guest NCAA party. For the unranked Jayhawks, a trip to the Final Four seemed almost as unlikely as a trip to Oz.

Kansas barely made it past Murray State in the second round, surviving only because Manning hit a 2-pointer, rebounded a missed 12-footer, and clinched the game with a pair of free throws, all in the last 37 seconds. He then single-handedly destroyed Vanderbilt, scoring 38 points to pace a 77-64 rout. In the regional final, Kansas played Kansas State, whose Wildcats had just eliminated No. 1–ranked Purdue. The Jayhawks needed more than Manning to win this one. Down by a basket at the half, they received major contributions from forward Milt Newton, who outplayed Kansas State star Mitch Richmond, and reserve guard Scooter Barry, who put the brakes on William Scott, the Wildcats' best outside threat, while throwing in a career-high 15 points of his own on near flawless shooting. (Barry, like Manning, was the son of a former pro basketball player. But unlike Danny, whose star far outshone that of his father Ed, Scooter lived in the shadow of one of the game's legendary gunners, Rick Barry.)

Surprisingly, considering their reputations, the other three qualifiers—Oklahoma, Arizona, and Duke—also had to come from behind after intermission to get through their regionals. In the West, seventh-ranked North Carolina led five and a half minutes into the second half 42-40 when Arizona center Tom Tolbert threw the ball wildly toward the hoop as the Tar Heels' J. R. Reid crashed into him. The shot went in, and Arizona—the Wildcats of the West—took off down the interstate like a runaway truck. Sean Elliott, the man of a thousand moves, juked up a couple of 2-pointers, long-range bomber Steve Kerr banged one in from downtown, and Tolbert crashed his way inside for a couple more buckets of his own. And Carolina scored only 10 points the rest of the way. The final was 70-52 Arizona.

It was much the same story in the Southeast, as third-ranked Oklahoma erupted in the last five minutes to destroy Villanova's hopes for a second miracle champion-

ship in four years. Villanova led 48-40 with fourteen minutes remaining, but the badly outmanned Wildcats of Philadelphia couldn't hold on. The Sooners' defensive pressure keyed a 32-7 run, and Oklahoma coasted in with a 78-59 victory.

In the East the story was the Duke defense. Top-ranked Temple's fabulous freshman, Mark Macon, was straitjacketed by the Blue Devils' Billy King. Despite the coverage, Macon assumed he'd eventually start hitting—he always did—so he kept firing up shots. Only this time, Macon shot 6 for 29 (20.7 percent), while Duke's Danny Ferry (yet another son of a former pro star) scored 7 more points on 18 fewer shots.

After their victory over Temple, Duke was expected to have little trouble with Kansas. The two teams had met before, in the 1986 semis, and on that occasion the Blue Devils had made Danny Manning's life miserable, holding him to 4 points. Kansas lost to Duke again just weeks before the 1988 tournament began, at home in Lawrence on February 20th, when the Blue Devils stormed back from an early deficit to eke out an overtime decision. So this time the Jayhawks' Milt Newton came out and hit a couple of early treys and Kansas stole the ball three times in Duke's first four possessions. After five minutes the lid was still on the Duke basket and the score was 14-0. Four minutes later it was 24-6. Duke fought back, closing to within 3 late in the second half, but they were finally finished off by too much Manning. The Player of the Year finished with 25 points, 10 rebounds, 4 steals, and 6 blocks. And Kansas won, 66-59.

In the other semi, Oklahoma's unrelenting full-court pressure and inside firepower proved to be too much for Arizona. Sean Elliott was his usual spectacular self, scoring 31, but Steve Kerr couldn't shake Mookie Blaylock and shot a pitiful 2 for 13. Oklahoma's two big men, Harvey Grant and Stacey King, each scored 21. And a 12-3 second-half run clinched the Sooners' 86-78 victory.

Thus, two Big Eight teams (the first two in the eighties) met to decide the national championship. It was expected to be no contest. Oklahoma was too big, too strong, too fast, and too deep. Oklahoma had won each of their two regular season contests by 8 points, with Manning at his best. But Kansas was not intimidated.

As usual in big games, Manning was brilliant. But this time it was not a one-man show—the entire Kansas team raised their game a notch. They broke the fearsome Oklahoma full-court press and got the Sooners' guards, Mookie Blaylock and Ricky Grace, into foul trouble. At the half, the score was tied 50-50; the Jayhawks had blistered the nets at a 71 percent rate while Oklahoma's Dave Sieger countered with 6 of 8 3-point bombs.

In the second half, Kansas coach Larry Brown wanted his team to stay close, to prevent an Oklahoma explosion like the ones that had destroyed both Villanova and Arizona. If the game was close, he reasoned, anything could happen at the end. Brown ordered tighter defensive pressure on Sieger, and urged his inside players to be more aggressive with the Oklahoma strongmen. He told his Jayhawks to slow the tempo, to use the clock. "Get them to the last five minutes," he exhorted his team. And Oklahoma coach Billy Tubbs, not wanting to risk fouling out his guards, unknowingly cooperated with Brown's second-half game plan by calling off the Sooners' full-court pressure.

When play resumed, the Jayhawks' defense held. Sieger stopped getting open shots, and in the last twelve minutes, Oklahoma's inside power pair, Grant and King, were stopped cold. Kansas stayed close, *and* they had the best player on the floor. With five seconds left, Manning already had 29 points, 18 rebounds, five steals, two blocks, two assists—and he was going to the line for two free throws with the Jayhawks holding a 2-point lead. "It's over," he said, and calmly sank two to salt the game away.

FIRST ROUND MIDWEST

Purdue (94)   Coach: Gene Keady

	Min.	Total FG/FGA	Pct.	3-Pt. FG/FGA	Pct.	FT/FTA	Pct.	Reb. O/T	A	TO	PF	S	Blk	TP	PPM
JONES, K.	18	3/7	.429	0/0	.000	0/1	.000	5/9	0	4	0	0	0	6	.333
MITCHELL, T.	28	5/10	.500	0/0	.000	6/9	.667	3/8	3	2	3	0	0	16	.571
MCCANTS, M.	30	11/15	.733	0/0	.000	4/4	1.000	1/5	2	1	1	1	0	26	.867
STEPHENS, E.	28	1/5	.200	0/1	.000	2/3	.667	2/7	8	3	1	0	0	4	.143
LEWIS, T.	30	8/16	.500	3/5	.600	0/0	.000	0/5	5	4	3	1	0	19	.633
REID, B.	2	0/2	.000	0/1	.000	0/0	.000	1/1	1	0	1	0	0	0	.000
BERNING, R.	15	2/5	.400	1/2	.500	1/2	.500	0/1	3	0	0	0	1	6	.400
BARRETT, D.	1	0/0	.000	0/0	.000	0/0	.000	0/0	0	0	0	0	0	0	.000
JONES, T.	23	3/4	.750	0/0	.000	0/0	.000	0/3	2	0	1	3	1	6	.261
EWER, E.	2	1/1	1.000	0/0	.000	0/0	.000	0/0	0	0	0	0	0	2	1.000
BRUGOS, J.	6	0/0	.000	0/0	.000	0/1	.000	0/2	0	0	2	0	0	0	.000
SCHEFFLER, S.	17	3/4	.750	0/0	.000	3/4	.750	3/4	0	0	2	0	1	9	.529
Totals	200	37/69	.536	4/9	.444	16/24	.667	15/45	24	14	14	5	3	94	.470

Fairleigh Dickinson (79)   Coach: Tom Green

	Min.	Total FG/FGA	Pct.	3-Pt. FG/FGA	Pct.	FT/FTA	Pct.	Reb. O/T	A	TO	PF	S	Blk	TP	PPM
LATNEY, J.	23	5/10	.500	0/0	.000	2/6	.333	2/5	1	2	4	2	0	12	.522
BOZEMAN, M.	29	3/8	.375	2/5	.400	1/2	.500	1/3	6	0	2	1	0	9	.310
RIDDICK, D.	35	11/23	.478	0/0	.000	3/4	.750	1/3	0	2	5	0	1	25	.714
ROBERTS, C.	40	6/13	.462	2/7	.286	0/0	.000	1/3	6	2	1	1	0	14	.350
MOORE, R.	29	3/6	.500	1/2	.500	1/2	.500	0/4	2	2	2	2	0	8	.276
BIGELOW, K.	16	1/3	.333	1/1	1.000	0/0	.000	0/1	1	0	0	0	0	3	.188
ODOM, E.	20	3/4	.750	0/0	.000	2/2	1.000	3/5	1	0	3	0	0	8	.400
TRUDELL, M.	2	0/0	.000	0/0	.000	0/0	.000	0/0	0	0	0	0	0	0	.000
STEIN, T.	6	0/0	.000	0/0	.000	0/0	.000	0/1	0	1	3	0	0	0	.000
Totals	200	32/67	.478	6/15	.400	9/16	.563	8/25	17	9	20	6	1	79	.395

Team Rebounds: Purdue 2; Fairleigh Dickinson 4. Disqualified: Fairleigh Dickinson—Riddick. Technical fouls: None.

	1st Half	2nd Half	Final
Purdue	41	53	94
F. Dickinson	28	51	79

Baylor (60)   Coach: Gene Iba

	Min.	Total FG/FGA	Pct.	3-Pt. FG/FGA	Pct.	FT/FTA	Pct.	Reb. O/T	A	TO	PF	S	Blk	TP	PPM
WILLIAMS, F.	18	2/3	.667	0/0	.000	0/0	.000	0/1	1	2	1	1	1	4	.222
MCLEMORE, R.	14	0/1	.000	0/0	.000	0/0	.000	1/1	0	1	2	1	0	0	.000
MIDDLETON, D.	39	10/14	.714	0/0	.000	2/5	.400	2/8	2	4	2	1	0	22	.564
HOBBS, M.	29	4/9	.444	0/1	.000	2/2	1.000	1/1	3	4	1	0	0	10	.345
WILLIAMS, M.	38	4/11	.364	1/4	.250	4/6	.667	0/3	3	5	3	2	0	13	.342
BROWN, B.	14	0/0	.000	0/0	.000	0/0	.000	0/2	1	2	0	0	0	0	.000
LINDSEY, D.	10	1/1	1.000	1/1	1.000	2/2	1.000	0/0	0	2	5	0	0	5	.500
JONES, I.	16	1/3	.333	0/0	.000	0/0	.000	1/3	0	2	3	1	0	2	.125
HUNT, M.	6	0/1	.000	0/0	.000	0/0	.000	0/0	2	0	2	1	0	0	.000
FRANCIS, J.	16	2/4	.500	0/0	.000	0/0	.000	1/1	0	1	2	2	0	4	.250
Totals	200	24/47	.511	2/6	.333	10/15	.667	6/20	12	23	21	9	1	60	.300

Memphis State (75)   Coach: Larry Finch

	Min.	Total FG/FGA	Pct.	3-Pt. FG/FGA	Pct.	FT/FTA	Pct.	Reb. O/T	A	TO	PF	S	Blk	TP	PPM
DOUGLAS, R.	26	10/17	.588	0/0	.000	2/2	1.000	5/7	2	4	2	6	0	22	.846
BALLARD, S.	21	1/4	.250	0/0	.000	0/0	.000	4/5	1	3	4	1	0	2	.095
BAILEY, D.	30	4/6	.667	0/0	.000	5/6	.833	0/4	1	1	4	0	0	13	.433
BOYD, D.	29	7/17	.412	0/0	.000	6/7	.857	1/1	2	4	3	0	0	20	.690
PERRY, E.	35	4/9	.444	0/1	.000	0/0	.000	1/4	4	1	2	2	0	8	.229
WILLIAMS, J.	1	0/0	.000	0/0	.000	0/0	.000	0/0	0	0	0	0	0	0	.000
GIBSON, C.	8	1/2	.500	0/0	.000	4/4	1.000	0/0	1	1	0	1	1	6	.750
MCLAUGLIN, J.	18	0/2	.000	0/0	.000	0/0	.000	1/2	3	2	4	0	0	0	.000
MCCLAIN, R.	1	0/0	.000	0/0	.000	0/0	.000	0/0	0	0	0	0	0	0	.000
YOUNG, R.	17	0/1	.000	0/0	.000	0/2	.000	1/1	1	1	1	0	0	0	.000
MUNDT, B.	14	2/3	.667	0/0	.000	0/0	.000	1/5	0	0	1	0	0	4	.286
Totals	200	29/61	.475	0/1	.000	17/19	.895	13/30	16	17	21	12	1	75	.375

Team Rebounds: Memphis State 7; Baylor 1. Disqualified: Baylor—Lindsey. Technical fouls: Baylor—Bench.

	1st Half	2nd Half	Final
Baylor	30	30	60
Memphis State	33	42	75

DePaul (83)   Coach: Joey Meyer

	Min.	Total FG/FGA	Pct.	3-Pt. FG/FGA	Pct.	FT/FTA	Pct.	Reb. O/T	A	TO	PF	S	Blk	TP	PPM
LAUX, A.	29	1/1	1.000	1/1	1.000	0/0	.000	0/3	0	1	0	2	0	3	.103
HOLLAND, K.	25	2/3	.667	0/0	.000	0/0	.000	0/3	1	2	2	1	1	4	.160
BRUNDY, S.	32	12/16	.750	0/0	.000	2/4	.500	3/9	2	0	2	3	1	26	.813
STRICKLAND, R.	28	9/15	.600	0/0	.000	1/1	1.000	1/1	13	3	3	3	0	19	.679
EDWARDS, K.	33	9/13	.692	0/1	.000	3/3	1.000	1/6	4	3	3	4	1	21	.636
TUNE, J.	2	0/0	.000	0/0	.000	0/0	.000	0/0	0	0	0	0	0	0	.000
GREENE, T.	22	2/4	.500	1/2	.500	1/4	.250	0/3	1	4	2	1	0	6	.273
NIEMANN, B.	5	0/1	.000	0/0	.000	0/0	.000	0/1	0	1	2	0	0	0	.000
HENDERSON, C.	1	0/0	.000	0/0	.000	0/0	.000	0/0	0	0	0	0	0	0	.000
HEPPNER, B.	3	1/1	1.000	0/0	.000	0/0	.000	0/0	0	0	0	0	0	2	.667
HAMBY, J.	11	0/0	.000	0/0	.000	0/0	.000	0/0	0	0	4	0	0	0	.000
JACKSON, C.	2	0/1	.000	0/0	.000	0/0	.000	0/1	0	0	0	0	0	0	.000
GOLDEN, K.	7	0/1	.000	0/0	.000	2/2	1.000	0/0	0	0	0	0	0	2	.286
Totals	200	36/56	.643	2/4	.500	9/14	.643	5/26	22	14	18	14	3	83	.415

Wichita State (62)   Coach: Eddie Fogler

	Min.	Total FG/FGA	Pct.	3-Pt. FG/FGA	Pct.	FT/FTA	Pct.	Reb. O/T	A	TO	PF	S	Blk	TP	PPM
HILL, L.	25	1/8	.125	0/3	.000	5/6	.833	0/2	4	2	3	2	0	7	.280
PRAYLOW, D.	30	4/8	.500	0/0	.000	0/0	.000	1/2	1	3	0	2	0	8	.267
RADUNOVICH, S.	25	4/7	.571	0/1	.000	10/10	1.000	0/3	1	4	2	0	0	18	.720
GRIFFIN, J.	28	0/1	.000	0/1	.000	0/0	.000	0/1	4	3	2	1	0	0	.000
PRAYLOW, D.	21	4/7	.571	1/2	.500	0/0	.000	0/1	1	3	2	3	0	9	.429
BASS, B.	2	0/0	.000	0/0	.000	0/0	.000	0/0	0	0	0	0	0	0	.000
COLEMAN, C.	11	0/1	.000	0/0	.000	0/0	.000	1/2	3	0	0	1	1	0	.000
COOPER, J.	15	1/5	.200	1/4	.250	0/0	.000	0/2	1	2	2	1	0	3	.200
GUFFROVICH, P.	18	1/5	.200	1/4	.250	0/0	.000	0/0	1	1	1	0	0	3	.167
GRAYER, S.	20	2/4	.500	0/0	.000	4/5	.800	2/5	1	2	3	0	0	8	.400
KOSICH, T.	3	1/2	.500	0/0	.000	0/0	.000	1/4	0	1	0	0	0	2	.667
DAVIS, A.	2	2/3	.667	0/0	.000	0/0	.000	1/2	0	0	1	0	0	4	2.000
Totals	200	20/51	.392	3/15	.200	19/21	.905	6/24	17	21	16	10	1	62	.310

Team Rebounds: DePaul 2; Wichita State 4. Disqualified: None. Technical fouls: None.

	1st Half	2nd Half	Final
DePaul	39	44	83
Wichita State	25	37	62

Kansas State (66)   Coach: Lon Kruger

	Min.	Total FG/FGA	Pct.	3-Pt. FG/FGA	Pct.	FT/FTA	Pct.	Reb. O/T	A	TO	PF	S	Blk	TP	PPM
RICHMOND, M.	36	9/17	.529	2/5	.400	10/10	1.000	2/7	9	3	2	1	1	30	.833
BLEDSOE, C.	26	3/4	.750	0/0	.000	1/2	.500	2/8	2	2	3	0	0	7	.269
MEYER, R.	28	3/3	1.000	0/0	.000	1/1	1.000	2/2	0	2	2	0	1	7	.250
HENSON, C.	40	1/6	.167	1/4	.250	0/0	.000	0/2	3	2	0	1	0	3	.075
SCOTT, W.	30	6/12	.500	5/11	.455	0/0	.000	0/3	3	2	0	0	0	17	.567
GLOVER, B.	9	1/2	.500	0/0	.000	0/0	.000	0/2	3	0	0	0	0	2	.222
DIGGINS, C.	4	0/0	.000	0/0	.000	0/0	.000	0/0	0	1	0	0	0	0	.000
DE, A.	1	0/0	.000	0/0	.000	0/0	.000	0/0	0	0	0	0	0	0	.000
DOBBINS, M.	22	0/0	.000	0/0	.000	0/0	.000	0/5	0	0	1	0	0	0	.000
MCCOY, F.	4	0/1	.000	0/0	.000	0/0	.000	0/1	0	0	0	0	0	0	.000
Totals	200	23/45	.511	8/20	.400	12/13	.923	6/30	20	13	8	2	2	66	.330

La Salle (53)   Coach: Bill Morris

	Min.	Total FG/FGA	Pct.	3-Pt. FG/FGA	Pct.	FT/FTA	Pct.	Reb. O/T	A	TO	PF	S	Blk	TP	PPM
SIMMONS, L.	40	7/14	.500	0/0	.000	6/12	.500	5/10	2	4	4	1	1	20	.500
LEGLER, B.	40	4/9	.444	2/6	.333	0/0	.000	0/0	3	1	3	0	1	10	.250
CONLIN, C.	31	3/6	.500	0/0	.000	0/0	.000	2/3	1	2	2	0	0	6	.194
OVERTON, D.	33	4/10	.400	1/4	.250	0/0	.000	0/3	1	0	1	2	0	9	.273
TARR, R.	40	1/11	.091	1/7	.143	0/0	.000	0/3	2	1	2	1	0	3	.075
RINES, L.	1	1/2	.500	1/1	1.000	0/0	.000	0/0	0	0	0	0	0	3	3.000
JOHNSON, B.	7	1/4	.250	0/0	.000	0/0	.000	1/2	0	0	1	1	0	2	.286
FLOWERS, R.	1	0/1	.000	0/0	.000	0/0	.000	0/0	0	1	0	0	0	0	.000
LEE, E.	1	0/0	.000	0/0	.000	0/0	.000	0/0	0	0	0	0	0	0	.000
PALCZEWSKI, K.	6	0/0	.000	0/0	.000	0/0	.000	0/0	0	0	0	0	0	0	.000
Totals	200	21/57	.368	5/19	.263	6/12	.500	10/21	9	6	13	6	2	53	.265

Team Rebounds: Kansas State 6; La Salle 2. Disqualified: None. Technical fouls: None.

	1st Half	2nd Half	Final
Kansas State	34	32	66
La Salle	23	30	53

Xavier (Ohio) (72)   Coach: Pete Gillen

	Min.	Total FG/FGA	Pct.	3–Pt. FG/FGA	Pct.	FT/FTA	Pct.	Reb. O/T	A	TO	PF	S	Blk	TP	PPM
BARNETT, J.	29	2/6	.333	1/3	.333	0/0	.000	1/3	2	2	4	3	0	5	.172
HILL, T.	24	1/5	.200	0/0	.000	2/4	.500	2/4	0	3	5	0	0	4	.167
STRONG, T.	27	4/5	.800	0/0	.000	6/6	1.000	2/10	0	0	4	3	0	14	.519
LARKIN, B.	37	6/18	.333	0/3	.000	4/10	.400	0/1	3	2	5	3	0	16	.432
KIMBROUGH, S.	37	5/13	.385	2/6	.333	6/7	.857	0/2	4	2	4	4	0	18	.486
WALKER, J.	20	3/10	.300	0/2	.000	1/2	.500	1/1	3	3	5	3	0	7	.350
KENNEDY, J.	1	0/1	.000	0/0	.000	0/0	.000	0/0	1	0	0	0	0	0	.000
DAVENPORT, M.	2	0/0	.000	0/0	.000	0/0	.000	0/0	0	1	2	0	0	0	.000
BUTLER, J.	1	1/2	.500	0/0	.000	0/0	.000	1/1	0	0	0	0	0	2	2.000
RAMEY, M.	1	0/0	.000	0/0	.000	0/0	.000	1/1	0	0	0	0	0	0	.000
PARKER, C.	1	0/2	.000	0/0	.000	0/0	.000	1/2	0	0	0	0	0	0	.000
CAMPBELL, D.	19	2/2	1.000	0/0	.000	2/3	.667	0/2	0	2	3	1	2	6	.316
KOESTER, B.	1	0/0	.000	0/0	.000	0/0	.000	0/0	0	0	0	0	0	0	.000
Totals	200	24/64	.375	3/14	.214	21/32	.656	9/27	13	15	32	17	2	72	.360

Kansas (85)   Coach: Larry Brown

	Min.	Total FG/FGA	Pct.	3–Pt. FG/FGA	Pct.	FT/FTA	Pct.	Reb. O/T	A	TO	PF	S	Blk	TP	PPM
PIPER, C.	29	2/3	.667	0/0	.000	5/7	.714	2/9	7	8	3	1	0	9	.310
GUELDNER, J.	18	3/4	.750	1/1	1.000	1/2	.500	0/5	1	4	2	0	0	8	.444
MANNING, D.	37	8/14	.571	0/0	.000	8/9	.889	3/12	3	5	4	1	3	24	.649
PRITCHARD, K.	33	2/5	.400	0/0	.000	4/5	.800	1/4	3	3	3	1	1	8	.242
NEWTON, M.	34	9/14	.643	0/2	.000	3/4	.750	4/12	3	4	2	0	0	21	.618
BARRY, R.	21	1/2	.500	0/0	.000	3/4	.750	1/2	5	0	3	0	0	5	.238
MADDOX, M.	5	2/4	.500	0/0	.000	0/0	.000	1/2	0	0	1	0	0	4	.800
HARRIS, K.	8	2/3	.667	0/0	.000	2/2	1.000	0/0	0	1	3	0	0	6	.750
NORMORE, C.	8	0/3	.000	0/2	.000	0/1	.000	0/1	0	3	2	0	0	0	.000
MINOR, L.	6	0/1	.000	0/0	.000	0/0	.000	0/0	0	0	2	0	0	0	.000
MATTOX, M.	1	0/0	.000	0/0	.000	0/0	.000	0/0	0	0	0	0	0	0	.000
Totals	200	29/53	.547	1/5	.200	26/34	.765	12/47	22	30	23	3	4	85	.425

Team Rebounds: Kansas 3; Xavier (Ohio) 3. Disqualified: Xavier (Ohio)—Hill, Larkin, Walker. Technical fouls: None.

	1st Half	2nd Half	Final
Xavier (Ohio)	29	43	72
Kansas	48	37	85

North Carolina State (75)   Coach: Jim Valvano

	Min.	Total FG/FGA	Pct.	3–Pt. FG/FGA	Pct.	FT/FTA	Pct.	Reb. O/T	A	TO	PF	S	Blk	TP	PPM
BROWN, C.	36	7/14	.500	0/0	.000	1/3	.333	4/8	0	2	3	0	0	15	.417
HOWARD, B.	21	3/7	.429	0/0	.000	2/3	.667	1/3	5	2	3	0	0	8	.381
SHACKLEFORD, C.	35	7/17	.412	0/0	.000	1/3	.333	7/12	2	1	3	0	0	15	.429
CORCHIANI, C.	29	2/7	.286	2/3	.667	1/2	.500	2/4	5	1	1	1	0	7	.241
DEL, N.	39	6/12	.500	2/5	.400	2/2	1.000	3/9	5	1	3	1	0	16	.410
WEEMS, K.	11	1/1	1.000	0/0	.000	0/0	.000	0/1	3	0	0	1	0	2	.182
MONROE, R.	24	5/15	.333	2/6	.333	0/0	.000	1/4	1	0	1	0	0	12	.500
LESTER, A.	5	0/0	.000	0/0	.000	0/0	.000	0/1	0	0	1	0	0	0	.000
Totals	200	31/73	.425	6/14	.429	7/13	.538	18/42	21	7	15	3	0	75	.375

Murray State (78)   Coach: Steve Newton

	Min.	Total FG/FGA	Pct.	3–Pt. FG/FGA	Pct.	FT/FTA	Pct.	Reb. O/T	A	TO	PF	S	Blk	TP	PPM
OGDEN, C.	31	6/7	.857	0/0	.000	0/1	.000	5/11	1	1	3	0	0	12	.387
MARTIN, J.	34	7/11	.636	0/1	.000	9/10	.900	0/5	2	1	3	0	0	23	.676
SIAS, C.	33	4/13	.308	0/0	.000	1/2	.500	1/7	2	2	2	0	0	9	.273
MANN, D.	40	5/14	.357	4/9	.444	2/4	.500	0/6	8	1	2	1	0	16	.400
KING, P.	38	3/7	.429	2/4	.500	1/2	.500	0/2	2	2	2	1	1	9	.237
BROOKS, T.	8	0/1	.000	0/0	.000	0/0	.000	0/1	0	1	0	0	0	0	.000
MCCLATCHEY, R.	7	3/3	1.000	0/0	.000	0/0	.000	0/1	0	0	1	0	0	6	.857
FOSTER, L.	9	1/2	.500	0/0	.000	1/3	.333	3/3	0	0	2	0	0	3	.333
Totals	200	29/58	.500	6/14	.429	14/22	.636	9/36	15	8	15	2	1	78	.390

Team Rebounds: Murray State 1; N.C. State 1. Disqualified: None. Technical fouls: None. Team Turnovers: Murray State 1.

	1st Half	2nd Half	Final
N.C. State	36	39	75
Murray State	41	37	78

Vanderbilt (80)   Coach: C.M. Newton

	Min.	Total FG/FGA	Pct.	3–Pt. FG/FGA	Pct.	FT/FTA	Pct.	Reb. O/T	A	TO	PF	S	Blk	TP	PPM
KORNET, F.	35	10/13	.769	0/0	.000	0/0	.000	4/10	3	1	2	1	0	20	.571
REID, E.	23	1/6	.167	0/0	.000	2/2	1.000	1/8	1	3	2	0	0	4	.174
PERDUE, W.	38	9/18	.500	0/1	.000	2/2	1.000	2/11	5	3	5	0	0	20	.526
BOOKER, B.	30	3/11	.273	2/8	.250	0/0	.000	0/5	2	2	3	2	0	8	.267
GOHEEN, B.	28	5/6	.833	1/1	1.000	3/3	1.000	1/3	8	3	0	0	1	14	.500
MAYES, C.	12	0/1	.000	0/1	.000	2/2	1.000	3/6	1	2	1	0	0	2	.167
GRANT, S.	4	0/0	.000	0/0	.000	0/0	.000	0/1	0	1	0	0	0	0	.000
WILCOX, C.	10	1/2	.500	0/0	.000	2/4	.500	0/0	2	1	2	0	0	4	.400
DRAUD, S.	20	3/8	.375	2/4	.500	0/0	.000	0/2	0	2	0	0	0	8	.400
Totals	200	32/65	.492	5/15	.333	11/13	.846	11/44	24	16	19	3	1	80	.400

Utah State (77)   Coach: Rod Tueller

	Min.	Total FG/FGA	Pct.	3–Pt. FG/FGA	Pct.	FT/FTA	Pct.	Reb. O/T	A	TO	PF	S	Blk	TP	PPM
CONWAY, D.	36	5/11	.455	0/0	.000	4/9	.444	4/12	1	4	3	0	0	14	.389
PETE, G.	25	3/6	.500	0/0	.000	2/2	1.000	1/3	0	0	2	0	2	8	.320
HOUSKEERPER, G.	29	4/5	.800	0/0	.000	3/5	.600	1/4	0	0	2	0	0	11	.379
NIXON, A.	40	6/13	.462	1/2	.500	2/4	.500	1/6	7	1	1	4	0	15	.375
NEWEY, R.	34	3/15	.200	3/12	.250	0/0	.000	0/3	0	3	2	3	0	9	.265
ANDERSON, J.	27	6/13	.462	2/7	.286	4/6	.667	1/3	6	1	2	1	0	18	.667
JUDKINS, J.	9	1/2	.500	0/1	.000	0/0	.000	2/3	2	1	1	0	0	2	.222
Totals	200	28/65	.431	6/22	.273	15/26	.577	10/31	19	9	14	5	2	77	.385

Team Rebounds: Vanderbilt 3; Utah State 3. Disqualified: Vanderbilt—Perdue. Technical fouls: None.

	1st Half	2nd Half	Final
Vanderbilt	38	42	80
Utah State	28	49	77

Pittsburgh (108)   Coach: Paul Evans

	Min.	Total FG/FGA	Pct.	3–Pt. FG/FGA	Pct.	FT/FTA	Pct.	Reb. O/T	A	TO	PF	S	Blk	TP	PPM
GORE, D.	24	10/17	.588	0/0	.000	4/4	1.000	2/3	1	2	3	0	0	24	1.000
LANE, J.	35	10/12	.833	0/0	.000	2/3	.667	4/17	8	4	4	0	0	22	.629
SMITH, C.	40	13/20	.650	0/1	.000	5/7	.714	2/12	0	2	4	1	2	31	.775
MILLER, S.	27	1/5	.200	1/2	.500	0/0	.000	0/2	9	1	3	1	0	3	.111
PORTER, D.	27	2/4	.500	0/0	.000	4/6	.667	1/4	10	1	0	1	0	8	.296
MATTHEWS, J.	14	5/7	.714	0/0	.000	0/1	.000	1/3	0	1	5	0	1	10	.714
MARTIN, B.	17	1/2	.500	0/1	.000	4/4	1.000	1/2	0	1	2	0	1	6	.353
BAILEY, N.	3	0/0	.000	0/0	.000	0/0	.000	0/0	0	0	1	0	0	0	.000
CAVANAUGH, P.	13	1/2	.500	0/0	.000	2/2	1.000	0/0	1	1	0	1	0	4	.308
Totals	200	43/69	.623	1/4	.250	21/27	.778	11/43	29	13	22	3	4	108	.540

Eastern Michigan (90)   Coach: Ben Braun

	Min.	Total FG/FGA	Pct.	3–Pt. FG/FGA	Pct.	FT/FTA	Pct.	Reb. O/T	A	TO	PF	S	Blk	TP	PPM
HENDERSON, I.	30	5/6	.833	0/0	.000	0/0	.000	0/4	0	2	4	1	0	10	.333
SOUCIE, B.	27	8/16	.500	8/14	.571	2/3	.667	1/3	0	2	1	0	0	26	.963
LONG, G.	31	5/8	.625	0/0	.000	5/8	.625	0/5	2	1	3	1	0	15	.484
CHAMBERS, H.	31	1/7	.143	0/1	.000	1/2	.500	1/1	1	1	1	0	0	3	.097
NEELY, L.	37	7/16	.438	0/0	.000	4/5	.800	0/1	9	2	2	3	0	18	.486
GOHEEN, D.	8	1/3	.333	1/2	.500	0/0	.000	0/0	1	3	2	0	0	3	.375
NOLAN, B.	7	1/1	1.000	0/0	.000	0/0	.000	0/2	0	0	4	1	0	2	.286
THOMAS, C.	19	4/9	.444	3/5	.600	1/2	.500	0/0	1	2	1	0	0	12	.632
CLUM, D.	6	0/0	.000	0/0	.000	0/0	.000	0/0	0	1	1	0	0	0	.000
SMITH, H.	4	0/0	.000	0/0	.000	1/2	.500	0/2	0	0	1	0	0	1	.250
Totals	200	32/66	.485	12/22	.545	14/22	.636	3/20	15	12	21	7	0	90	.450

Team Rebounds: Pittsburgh 3; Eastern Mich. 4. Disqualified: Pittsburgh—Matthews. Technical fouls: None.

	1st Half	2nd Half	Final
Pittsburgh	52	56	108
Eastern Mich.	49	41	90

FIRST ROUND EAST

Temple (87)   Coach: John Chaney

	Min.	FG/FGA	Pct.	3-Pt. FG/FGA	Pct.	FT/FTA	Pct.	Reb. O/T	A	TO	PF	S	Blk	TP	PPM
VREESWYK, M.	38	3/11	.273	1/6	.167	8/8	1.000	1/2	1	0	4	1	0	15	.395
PERRY, T.	28	10/14	.714	0/0	.000	7/9	.778	2/12	0	1	2	1	8	27	.964
RIVAS, R.	32	1/4	.250	0/0	.000	0/0	.000	0/1	1	1	3	0	0	2	.063
MACON, M.	31	10/18	.556	2/4	.500	2/2	1.000	3/9	2	1	5	2	1	24	.774
EVANS, H.	40	2/4	.500	1/3	.333	3/3	1.000	1/7	7	3	4	2	0	8	.200
DOWDELL, J.	8	0/1	.000	0/1	.000	7/9	.778	0/0	1	0	3	0	0	7	.875
CAUSWELL, D.	16	1/3	.333	0/0	.000	1/2	.500	1/2	0	0	2	0	0	3	.188
BRANTLEY, D.	4	0/0	.000	0/0	.000	1/2	.500	0/1	0	0	1	0	0	1	.250
PEARSALL, D.	3	0/0	.000	0/0	.000	0/0	.000	0/0	0	0	1	0	0	0	.000
Totals	200	27/55	.491	4/14	.286	29/35	.829	8/34	12	6	25	6	9	87	.435

Lehigh (73)   Coach: Fran McCaffery

	Min.	FG/FGA	Pct.	3-Pt. FG/FGA	Pct.	FT/FTA	Pct.	Reb. O/T	A	TO	PF	S	Blk	TP	PPM
QUEENAN, D.	39	8/23	.348	1/4	.250	4/7	.571	0/7	1	4	4	0	1	21	.538
RUSSELL, T.	22	1/4	.250	0/0	.000	1/2	.500	2/5	0	0	4	0	0	3	.136
CHESLOCK, B.	29	3/5	.600	0/0	.000	2/4	.500	4/8	1	1	5	0	0	8	.276
LAYER, S.	40	4/11	.364	4/7	.571	0/0	.000	2/5	5	2	3	1	0	12	.300
POLAHA, M.	39	8/15	.533	5/9	.556	6/10	.600	4/8	4	4	4	0	0	27	.692
MARTIN, T.	6	0/0	.000	0/0	.000	0/0	.000	0/0	0	1	0	0	0	0	.000
BLOCK, C.	12	0/1	.000	0/0	.000	0/0	.000	0/1	1	0	2	0	0	0	.000
BERLINER, G.	9	1/3	.333	0/0	.000	0/0	.000	1/2	0	0	3	0	0	2	.222
RUDMAN, P.	1	0/1	.000	0/1	.000	0/0	.000	0/0	0	0	0	0	0	0	.000
O'HARA, M.	1	0/2	.000	0/1	.000	0/0	.000	0/0	0	1	0	0	0	0	.000
BREDER, B.	1	0/0	.000	0/0	.000	0/0	.000	0/0	0	0	1	0	0	0	.000
ROGERS, D.	1	0/0	.000	0/0	.000	0/0	.000	0/0	0	0	0	0	0	0	.000
Totals	200	25/65	.385	10/22	.455	13/23	.565	13/36	12	11	27	1	1	73	.365

Team Rebounds: Temple 6; Lehigh 3. Disqualified: Temple—Macon; Lehigh—Cheslock. Technical fouls: Lehigh—Block.

	1st Half	2nd Half	Final
Temple	38	49	87
Lehigh	35	38	73

Georgetown (66)   Coach: John Thompson

	Min.	FG/FGA	Pct.	3-Pt. FG/FGA	Pct.	FT/FTA	Pct.	Reb. O/T	A	TO	PF	S	Blk	TP	PPM
MCDONALD, P.	32	4/7	.571	0/0	.000	1/2	.500	5/9	1	3	2	1	0	9	.281
HIGHSMITH, R.	30	2/4	.500	0/0	.000	0/0	.000	3/9	0	3	4	0	0	4	.133
GILLERY, B.	2	0/0	.000	0/0	.000	0/0	.000	0/0	0	0	0	0	0	0	.000
SMITH, C.	31	4/13	.308	2/5	.400	0/0	.000	2/5	2	0	4	1	0	10	.323
TILLMON, M.	32	5/15	.333	3/8	.375	2/4	.500	1/6	2	1	3	4	0	15	.469
JACKSON, J.	38	8/17	.471	4/8	.500	0/1	.000	2/3	1	3	1	2	0	20	.606
WINSTON, B.	7	0/0	.000	0/0	.000	0/0	.000	0/1	3	0	1	0	0	0	.000
BRYANT, D.	19	3/6	.500	0/0	.000	0/0	.000	0/0	4	0	1	0	0	6	.316
EDWARDS, J.	7	0/1	.000	0/0	.000	0/0	.000	1/2	0	1	4	1	0	0	.000
ALLEN, A.	6	1/2	.500	0/0	.000	0/0	.000	1/1	0	0	3	0	0	2	.333
TUCKER, A.	1	0/0	.000	0/0	.000	0/0	.000	0/0	0	0	0	0	0	0	.000
Totals	200	27/65	.415	9/21	.429	3/7	.429	15/36	13	11	23	9	0	66	.330

Louisiana State (63)   Coach: Dale Brown

	Min.	FG/FGA	Pct.	3-Pt. FG/FGA	Pct.	FT/FTA	Pct.	Reb. O/T	A	TO	PF	S	Blk	TP	PPM
BLANTON, R.	40	4/7	.571	1/1	1.000	4/4	1.000	3/9	4	0	2	1	0	13	.325
SIMS, W.	39	6/11	.545	0/0	.000	4/4	1.000	1/5	1	2	2	0	1	16	.410
VARGAS, J.	37	4/9	.444	0/0	.000	5/9	.556	0/5	2	4	1	0	0	13	.351
JOE, D.	37	4/13	.308	2/6	.333	4/6	.667	1/3	1	3	4	0	0	14	.378
WOODSIDE, B.	26	1/5	.200	0/1	.000	1/2	.500	6/8	3	2	1	0	0	3	.115
MOUTON, L.	18	1/7	.143	1/4	.250	1/2	.500	2/7	1	1	1	2	0	4	.222
IRVIN, F.	3	0/0	.000	0/0	.000	0/0	.000	0/0	0	0	1	0	0	0	.000
Totals	200	20/52	.385	4/12	.333	19/27	.704	13/37	12	13	13	3	1	63	.315

Team Rebounds: Georgetown 3; Louisiana State 5. Disqualified: None. Technical fouls: None.

	1st Half	2nd Half	Final
Georgetown	35	31	66
Louisiana St.	37	26	63

Georgia Tech (90)   Coach: Bobby Cremins

	Min.	FG/FGA	Pct.	3-Pt. FG/FGA	Pct.	FT/FTA	Pct.	Reb. O/T	A	TO	PF	S	Blk	TP	PPM
SCOTT, D.	39	7/12	.583	5/6	.833	4/4	1.000	0/4	6	3	4	2	1	23	.590
FERRELL, D.	30	3/9	.333	0/0	.000	2/3	.667	1/7	0	6	2	1	2	8	.267
HAMMONDS, T.	31	7/10	.700	0/0	.000	19/21	.905	2/9	1	4	3	0	0	33	1.065
NEAL, C.	37	2/4	.500	0/2	.000	5/8	.625	0/2	3	4	1	2	0	9	.243
OLIVER, B.	38	1/5	.200	1/2	.500	4/4	1.000	0/1	5	2	4	0	0	7	.184
MUNLYN, J.	15	2/4	.500	0/0	.000	0/0	.000	2/5	0	3	1	1	0	4	.267
SHERROD, A.	10	2/4	.500	0/0	.000	2/2	1.000	1/2	0	0	1	0	0	6	.600
Totals	200	24/48	.500	6/10	.600	36/42	.857	6/30	15	22	16	6	3	90	.450

Iowa State (78)   Coach: Johnny Orr

	Min.	FG/FGA	Pct.	3-Pt. FG/FGA	Pct.	FT/FTA	Pct.	Reb. O/T	A	TO	PF	S	Blk	TP	PPM
ROBINSON, E.	32	2/9	.222	1/5	.200	3/4	.750	1/3	3	1	4	1	2	8	.250
GRAYER, J.	36	13/23	.565	0/1	.000	3/4	.750	2/8	4	4	4	1	0	29	.806
RHODES, L.	38	14/32	.438	2/4	.500	4/4	1.000	6/9	1	5	5	2	0	34	.895
THOMPKINS, G.	22	0/2	.000	0/0	.000	0/0	.000	0/2	6	3	5	1	0	0	.000
BREITBACH, D.	26	0/1	.000	0/0	.000	1/2	.500	0/1	4	1	4	1	0	1	.038
DOERRFELD, P.	7	0/1	.000	0/0	.000	0/0	.000	0/4	0	0	3	1	0	0	.000
BORN, M.	25	3/8	.375	0/4	.000	0/0	.000	3/5	2	2	5	2	0	6	.240
WOODS, T.	6	0/0	.000	0/0	.000	0/0	.000	0/0	1	1	1	0	0	0	.000
BAUGH, M.	6	0/1	.000	0/1	.000	0/0	.000	0/0	1	0	0	0	0	0	.000
ALEXANDER, V.	1	0/0	.000	0/0	.000	0/0	.000	0/0	0	0	0	0	0	0	.000
URQUHART, M.	1	0/0	.000	0/0	.000	0/0	.000	0/0	0	0	0	0	0	0	.000
Totals	200	32/77	.416	3/15	.200	11/14	.786	12/32	22	17	31	9	2	78	.390

Team Rebounds: Georgia Tech 7; Iowa State 8. Disqualified: Iowa State—Rhodes, Thompkins, Born. Technical fouls: None.

	1st Half	2nd Half	Final
Georgia Tech	38	52	90
Iowa State	41	37	78

Indiana (69)   Coach: Bob Knight

	Min.	FG/FGA	Pct.	3-Pt. FG/FGA	Pct.	FT/FTA	Pct.	Reb. O/T	A	TO	PF	S	Blk	TP	PPM
EDWARDS, J.	34	6/10	.600	4/6	.667	0/0	.000	0/0	5	0	2	0	1	16	.471
EYL, S.	16	1/1	1.000	0/0	.000	0/0	.000	1/2	0	1	1	0	0	2	.125
GARRETT, D.	38	4/16	.250	0/0	.000	1/3	.333	4/10	0	2	4	3	4	9	.237
JONES, L.	32	3/7	.429	0/0	.000	2/2	1.000	0/2	8	2	2	0	0	8	.250
SMART, K.	40	10/18	.556	0/0	.000	3/3	1.000	1/4	2	3	3	2	1	23	.575
JADLOW, T.	25	4/5	.800	0/0	.000	3/4	.750	2/2	1	0	3	0	1	11	.440
HILLMAN, J.	15	0/4	.000	0/1	.000	0/0	.000	1/2	1	0	0	0	0	0	.000
Totals	200	28/61	.459	4/7	.571	9/12	.750	9/22	17	8	15	5	7	69	.345

Richmond (72)   Coach: Dick Tarrant

	Min.	FG/FGA	Pct.	3-Pt. FG/FGA	Pct.	FT/FTA	Pct.	Reb. O/T	A	TO	PF	S	Blk	TP	PPM
STAPLETON, S.	25	0/4	.000	0/0	.000	1/2	.500	0/2	2	3	3	1	0	1	.040
WOOLFOLK, P.	30	6/12	.500	0/0	.000	4/5	.800	1/5	0	0	3	1	0	16	.533
KRATZER, S.	36	6/12	.500	0/0	.000	0/1	.000	8/12	2	1	2	1	3	12	.333
ATKINSON, K.	33	5/6	.833	0/0	.000	4/6	.667	1/4	3	1	1	1	0	14	.424
RICE, R.	40	9/17	.529	3/7	.429	0/0	.000	0/1	2	1	3	1	0	21	.525
ENGLISH, E.	15	1/2	.500	0/0	.000	2/2	1.000	0/1	0	4	1	0	0	4	.267
WINECKI, M.	13	2/2	1.000	0/0	.000	0/0	.000	0/1	3	1	2	0	2	4	.308
TAYLOR, J.	7	0/0	.000	0/0	.000	0/0	.000	0/0	3	0	0	0	0	0	.000
DUDEK, H.	1	0/0	.000	0/0	.000	0/0	.000	0/0	0	0	0	0	0	0	.000
Totals	200	29/55	.527	3/7	.429	11/16	.688	10/26	15	11	15	5	5	72	.360

Team Rebounds: Richmond 10; Indiana 6. Disqualified: None. Technical fouls: None.

	1st Half	2nd Half	Final
Indiana	38	31	69
Richmond	44	28	72

Missouri (80)   Coach: Norm Stewart

	Min.	Total FG/FGA	Pct.	3-Pt. FG/FGA	Pct.	FT/FTA	Pct.	Reb. O/T	A	TO	PF	S	Blk	TP	PPM
CHIEVOUS, D.	40	16/25	.640	0/1	.000	3/6	.500	1/8	2	1	4	1	0	35	.875
SANDBOTHE, M.	26	2/3	.667	0/1	.000	2/4	.500	1/4	2	3	3	0	0	6	.231
CHURCH, G.	22	5/6	.833	0/0	.000	1/1	1.000	1/3	0	2	3	1	0	11	.500
COWARD, L.	17	2/7	.286	2/3	.667	0/0	.000	1/3	2	2	3	1	0	6	.353
IRVIN, B.	40	4/11	.364	0/3	.000	2/2	1.000	0/2	3	3	4	0	1	10	.250
SMITH, D.	18	3/3	1.000	0/0	.000	0/0	.000	1/3	1	3	5	0	1	6	.333
BUNTIN, N.	3	0/2	.000	0/0	.000	0/0	.000	0/0	0	1	0	0	0	0	.000
HARDY, L.	23	0/2	.000	0/1	.000	0/0	.000	0/3	5	1	3	1	0	0	.000
LEONARD, G.	11	2/2	1.000	0/0	.000	2/2	1.000	1/2	1	2	1	0	0	6	.545
Totals	200	34/61	.557	2/9	.222	10/15	.667	6/28	16	18	26	4	2	80	.400

Rhode Island (87)   Coach: Tom Penders

	Min.	Total FG/FGA	Pct.	3-Pt. FG/FGA	Pct.	FT/FTA	Pct.	Reb. O/T	A	TO	PF	S	Blk	TP	PPM
EVANS, J.	40	3/7	.429	0/0	.000	5/6	.833	2/10	1	0	2	0	0	11	.275
SINA, M.	38	2/8	.250	0/2	.000	2/2	1.000	1/2	3	2	4	0	0	6	.158
COLSON, B.	8	1/2	.500	0/0	.000	0/0	.000	0/0	0	4	0	0	2	.250
OWENS, C.	40	7/16	.438	2/5	.400	9/10	.900	1/1	4	5	1	1	0	25	.625
GARRICK, T.	40	10/23	.435	0/0	.000	9/12	.750	7/12	2	2	5	1	29	.725
GREEN, K.	34	6/10	.600	0/0	.000	2/4	.500	2/7	0	3	2	2	1	14	.412
Totals	220	29/66	.439	2/7	.286	27/34	.794	13/32	10	12	15	8	2	87	.435

Team Rebounds: Rhode Island 3; Missouri 4. Disqualified: Missouri—Smith. Technical fouls: None.

	1st Half	2nd Half	Final
Missouri	40	40	80
Rhode Island	38	49	87

Syracuse (69)   Coach: Jim Boeheim

	Min.	Total FG/FGA	Pct.	3-Pt. FG/FGA	Pct.	FT/FTA	Pct.	Reb. O/T	A	TO	PF	S	Blk	TP	PPM
THOMPSON, S.	40	9/10	.900	0/0	.000	3/4	.750	2/7	2	3	1	2	1	21	.525
COLEMAN, D.	27	2/9	.222	0/0	.000	0/0	.000	4/11	1	2	4	0	1	4	.148
SEIKALY, R.	36	9/19	.474	0/0	.000	2/6	.333	6/16	0	1	4	0	7	20	.556
ROE, M.	29	3/9	.333	2/6	.333	0/0	.000	2/6	1	1	3	0	0	8	.276
DOUGLAS, S.	35	4/8	.500	0/0	.000	3/7	.429	1/2	8	5	1	0	0	11	.314
BROWER, D.	15	0/1	.000	0/0	.000	0/1	.000	0/3	2	1	3	1	0	0	.000
DUNCAN, E.	18	2/5	.400	1/2	.500	0/0	.000	0/0	2	3	2	0	0	5	.278
Totals	200	29/61	.475	3/8	.375	8/18	.444	15/45	16	16	18	3	9	69	.345

North Carolina A&T (55)   Coach: Don Corbett

	Min.	Total FG/FGA	Pct.	3-Pt. FG/FGA	Pct.	FT/FTA	Pct.	Reb. O/T	A	TO	PF	S	Blk	TP	PPM
WILLIAMS, C.	36	6/11	.545	0/1	.000	5/9	.556	6/10	1	3	2	3	1	17	.472
BECTON, C.	30	4/12	.333	3/6	.500	0/0	.000	0/1	0	2	3	1	0	11	.367
COX, K.	37	4/15	.267	0/0	.000	2/5	.400	5/9	1	2	5	0	0	10	.270
DAVIS, C.	23	1/5	.200	1/3	.333	0/0	.000	0/1	2	1	5	1	0	3	.130
GRIFFIS, T.	40	5/14	.357	1/2	.500	1/1	1.000	0/4	3	3	4	3	0	12	.300
HOWARD, C.	10	0/0	.000	0/0	.000	0/0	.000	0/4	0	0	0	0	0	0	.000
TAGGART, G.	17	0/4	.000	0/3	.000	0/0	.000	0/0	0	1	2	0	0	0	.000
ROBINSON, L.	6	0/1	.000	0/0	.000	2/3	.667	0/0	0	1	1	0	0	2	.333
BROWN, T.	1	0/1	.000	0/0	.000	0/0	.000	1/1	0	0	0	0	0	0	.000
Totals	200	20/63	.317	5/15	.333	10/18	.556	12/30	7	13	22	8	1	55	.275

Team Rebounds: Syracuse 2; N.C. A&T 4. Disqualified: N.C. A&T—Cox, Davis. Technical fouls: None.

	1st Half	2nd Half	Final
Syracuse	31	38	69
N. Carolina A&T	31	24	55

SMU (83)   Coach: Dave Bliss

	Min.	Total FG/FGA	Pct.	3-Pt. FG/FGA	Pct.	FT/FTA	Pct.	Reb. O/T	A	TO	PF	S	Blk	TP	PPM
THOMAS, T.	40	6/8	.750	0/0	.000	5/6	.833	6/8	1	0	3	0	1	17	.425
MCKINNEY, C.	31	6/11	.545	1/1	1.000	0/0	.000	2/3	3	1	4	1	0	13	.419
PUDDY, G.	13	0/2	.000	0/0	.000	0/0	.000	1/4	0	2	4	0	0	0	.000
ARMSTRONG, K.	37	13/22	.591	0/0	.000	3/4	.750	0/2	2	1	2	1	0	29	.784
LONGINO, E.	20	2/7	.286	0/1	.000	0/0	.000	0/2	1	1	1	2	0	4	.200
ALEXANDER, T.	32	4/13	.308	1/4	.250	2/2	1.000	2/3	5	2	4	3	0	11	.344
PERDUE, V.	27	4/4	1.000	0/0	.000	1/2	.500	0/5	2	0	2	0	0	9	.333
Totals	200	35/67	.522	2/6	.333	11/14	.786	11/27	14	7	20	7	1	83	.415

Notre Dame (75)   Coach: Digger Phelps

	Min.	Total FG/FGA	Pct.	3-Pt. FG/FGA	Pct.	FT/FTA	Pct.	Reb. O/T	A	TO	PF	S	Blk	TP	PPM
ROBINSON, K.	28	4/9	.444	0/0	.000	1/2	.500	4/8	0	0	5	0	0	9	.321
JACKSON, J.	38	8/10	.800	0/0	.000	4/6	.667	2/2	0	1	4	1	0	20	.526
VOCE, G.	38	9/13	.692	0/0	.000	6/8	.750	2/11	0	5	4	1	2	24	.632
FREDRICK, J.	21	0/2	.000	0/1	.000	0/0	.000	0/0	5	1	1	0	0	0	.000
RIVERS, D.	36	5/15	.333	0/3	.000	2/3	.667	1/9	5	4	3	1	1	12	.333
STEVENSON, M.	23	4/8	.500	0/0	.000	2/3	.667	0/2	2	1	0	1	0	10	.435
PADDOCK, S.	5	0/0	.000	0/0	.000	0/0	.000	0/0	0	1	1	0	0	0	.000
SINGLETON, T.	4	0/0	.000	0/0	.000	0/0	.000	0/0	1	1	0	0	0	0	.000
JACKSON, T.	7	0/0	.000	0/0	.000	1/3	.667	1/1	1	1	0	0	1	0	.000
Totals	200	30/57	.526	0/4	.000	15/22	.682	10/31	18	15	18	4	4	75	.375

Team Rebounds: SMU 2; Notre Dame 2. Disqualified: Notre Dame—Robinson. Technical fouls: None.

	1st Half	2nd Half	Final
SMU	37	46	83
Notre Dame	36	39	75

Duke (85)   Coach: Mike Krzyzewski

	Min.	Total FG/FGA	Pct.	3-Pt. FG/FGA	Pct.	FT/FTA	Pct.	Reb. O/T	A	TO	PF	S	Blk	TP	PPM
FERRY, D.	32	7/19	.368	0/0	.000	7/8	.875	3/8	3	4	3	0	2	21	.656
KING, B.	29	4/6	.667	0/0	.000	0/1	.000	2/4	3	0	1	1	0	8	.276
BRICKEY, R.	23	5/5	1.000	0/0	.000	2/3	.667	2/4	0	0	2	1	1	12	.522
SNYDER, Q.	23	2/4	.500	2/3	.667	1/2	.500	0/3	3	4	3	2	0	7	.304
STRICKLAND, K.	26	7/10	.700	1/2	.500	2/2	1.000	4/5	2	3	2	1	0	17	.654
KOUBEK, G.	8	0/0	.000	0/0	.000	0/1	.000	1/1	2	0	1	0	0	0	.000
ABDELNABY, A.	8	2/3	.667	0/0	.000	0/0	.000	0/4	0	1	2	0	0	4	.500
SMITH, J.	16	3/3	1.000	0/0	.000	1/2	.500	0/3	1	1	1	0	0	7	.438
HENDERSON, P.	24	3/8	.375	0/3	.000	0/0	.000	1/1	3	5	1	0	0	6	.250
COOK, J.	10	0/4	.000	0/0	.000	1/2	.500	1/2	2	1	1	2	0	1	.100
BUCKLEY, C.	1	1/1	1.000	0/0	.000	0/0	.000	0/0	0	0	0	0	0	2	2.000
Totals	200	34/63	.540	3/8	.375	14/21	.667	14/35	19	19	17	7	3	85	.425

Boston University (69)   Coach: Mike Jarvis

	Min.	Total FG/FGA	Pct.	3-Pt. FG/FGA	Pct.	FT/FTA	Pct.	Reb. O/T	A	TO	PF	S	Blk	TP	PPM
IRVING, D.	28	5/11	.455	1/3	.333	3/4	.750	0/1	2	1	3	0	0	14	.500
JONES, L.	36	6/14	.429	0/0	.000	2/2	1.000	5/10	0	2	4	1	0	14	.389
MOSES, R.	12	0/2	.000	0/0	.000	0/0	.000	1/1	0	0	2	0	0	0	.000
DACOSTA, T.	32	1/4	.250	0/0	.000	4/4	1.000	1/3	2	3	2	1	0	6	.188
TIMBERLAKE, J.	32	7/13	.538	1/2	.500	3/4	.750	1/4	6	5	3	2	0	18	.563
WHITE, S.	15	3/4	.750	0/0	.000	1/3	.333	1/1	0	1	1	0	0	7	.467
KEY, S.	20	3/8	.375	0/0	.000	0/0	.000	1/3	0	3	3	1	0	6	.300
JARVIS, R.	16	1/4	.250	0/0	.000	0/0	.000	0/4	0	0	3	0	0	2	.125
DAVY, F.	4	0/1	.000	0/0	.000	0/0	.000	0/0	0	0	0	2	0	0	.000
STEWART, R.	3	1/1	1.000	0/0	.000	0/0	.000	0/0	1	1	0	0	0	2	.667
KODSI, I.	1	0/0	.000	0/0	.000	0/0	.000	0/0	0	0	0	0	0	0	.000
KALITSI, F.	1	0/0	.000	0/0	.000	0/1	.000	0/0	0	0	0	0	0	0	.000
Totals	200	27/62	.435	2/5	.400	13/17	.765	10/28	11	16	21	7	0	69	.345

Team Rebounds: Duke 3; Boston Univ. 4. Disqualified: None. Technical fouls: Boston Univ.—Bench.

	1st Half	2nd Half	Final
Duke	43	42	85
Boston Univ.	32	37	69

FIRST ROUND WEST

Arizona (90)   Coach: Lute Olson

	Min.	Total FG/FGA	Pct.	3–Pt. FG/FGA	Pct.	FT/FTA	Pct.	Reb. O/T	A	TO	PF	S	Blk	TP	PPM
COOK, A.	-	8/12	.667	0/0	.000	8/9	.889	2/5	0	0	1	4	0	24	-
ELLIOTT, S.	-	6/10	.600	3/4	.750	2/2	1.000	0/5	3	2	2	1	2	17	-
TOLBERT, T.	-	5/7	.714	0/0	.000	0/0	.000	0/1	1	0	0	0	0	10	-
MCMILLAN, C.	-	2/3	.667	0/1	.000	1/1	1.000	0/2	5	2	2	0	0	5	-
KERR, S.	-	2/5	.400	1/2	.500	0/0	.000	2/3	3	1	0	1	0	5	-
TURNER, J.	-	2/4	.500	0/0	.000	2/2	1.000	2/3	0	1	2	3	1	6	-
MASON, H.	-	2/3	.667	0/0	.000	5/6	.833	2/2	2	1	0	1	0	9	-
BUECHLER, J.	-	3/6	.500	0/1	.000	4/4	1.000	0/4	1	2	3	0	0	10	-
LOFTON, K.	-	2/5	.400	0/1	.000	0/0	.000	1/2	1	3	3	0	0	4	-
MUEHLEBACH, M.	-	0/1	.000	0/1	.000	0/0	.000	0/0	0	1	0	0	0	0	-
BERGMAN, C.	-	0/2	.000	0/1	.000	0/0	.000	0/0	0	0	2	0	0	0	-
Totals	200	32/58	.552	4/11	.364	22/24	.917	9/27	16	13	15	10	3	90	.450

Cornell (50)   Coach: Mike Dement

	Min.	Total FG/FGA	Pct.	3–Pt. FG/FGA	Pct.	FT/FTA	Pct.	Reb. O/T	A	TO	PF	S	Blk	TP	PPM
FLORIN	16	0/4	.000	0/0	.000	0/0	.000	0/1	0	2	2	0	0	0	.000
KARTSONAS	24	0/2	.000	0/0	.000	0/0	.000	0/2	1	0	0	0	0	0	.000
PAUL	16	2/5	.400	0/0	.000	2/2	1.000	0/0	0	3	4	0	0	6	.375
WEXLER	27	2/7	.286	0/2	.000	0/0	.000	0/3	3	3	0	0	0	4	.148
JACOBS	24	4/7	.571	2/5	.400	0/0	.000	0/1	1	6	2	2	0	10	.417
MILLANE	16	4/5	.800	0/0	.000	0/0	.000	0/1	0	2	2	0	0	8	.500
GILDA	18	3/6	.500	0/0	.000	0/0	.000	2/5	0	2	4	0	1	6	.333
BOYKIN	8	0/0	.000	0/0	.000	0/0	.000	0/1	1	0	0	0	0	0	.000
PASCAL	13	0/1	.000	0/0	.000	0/0	.000	1/2	1	2	2	0	0	0	.000
GRANT	16	0/3	.000	0/0	.000	7/9	.778	1/4	0	1	3	0	0	7	.438
JOHNSON	5	0/1	.000	0/0	.000	0/0	.000	0/1	0	2	0	1	0	0	.000
BRASLOW	4	0/0	.000	0/0	.000	0/0	.000	0/0	1	1	0	0	0	0	.000
JACKSON	6	3/7	.429	0/0	.000	0/2	.000	6/7	0	0	0	0	0	6	1.000
HOMER	5	0/0	.000	0/0	.000	1/2	.500	0/0	0	1	0	0	0	1	.200
HALPERN	2	0/1	.000	0/0	.000	2/2	1.000	0/1	0	1	0	0	0	2	1.000
Totals	200	18/49	.367	2/7	.286	12/17	.706	10/26	8	26	19	3	1	50	.250

Team Rebounds: Arizona 1; Cornell 4. Disqualified: None. Technical fouls: None. Team Turnovers: Cornell 1.

	1st Half	2nd Half	Final
Arizona	36	54	90
Cornell	19	31	50

Seton Hall (80)   Coach: P. J. Carlesimo

	Min.	Total FG/FGA	Pct.	3–Pt. FG/FGA	Pct.	FT/FTA	Pct.	Reb. O/T	A	TO	PF	S	Blk	TP	PPM
SALLEY, M.	21	1/4	.250	0/0	.000	1/2	.500	2/5	2	2	1	1	0	3	.143
BRYANT, M.	30	13/18	.722	0/0	.000	4/5	.800	6/12	0	5	2	0	0	30	1.000
RAMOS, R.	34	2/4	.500	0/0	.000	1/1	1.000	0/1	0	0	3	0	0	5	.147
MORTON, J.	27	3/4	.750	0/0	.000	12/12	1.000	0/0	7	4	2	3	0	18	.667
GREENE, G.	20	3/4	.750	0/0	.000	2/3	.667	0/6	3	2	4	0	0	8	.400
MAJOR, J.	23	3/8	.375	1/1	1.000	0/0	.000	1/2	1	2	3	1	1	7	.304
COOPER, M.	20	3/5	.600	0/0	.000	1/2	.500	1/2	1	0	3	0	0	7	.350
WIGINGTON, P.	8	0/2	.000	0/0	.000	0/0	.000	0/0	0	1	0	0	0	0	.000
WALKER, D.	11	1/6	.167	0/0	.000	0/0	.000	2/6	0	1	2	0	0	2	.182
KATSIKIS, N.	3	0/0	.000	0/0	.000	0/0	.000	0/0	0	0	0	0	0	0	.000
VOLCY, F.	1	0/1	.000	0/0	.000	0/2	.000	1/1	0	0	0	0	0	0	.000
LONG, K.	1	0/0	.000	0/0	.000	0/0	.000	1/2	0	0	0	0	0	0	.000
REBIMBAS, J.	1	0/2	.000	0/2	.000	0/0	.000	0/0	0	0	0	0	0	0	.000
Totals	200	29/58	.500	1/3	.333	21/27	.778	14/37	15	16	20	5	1	80	.400

UTEP (64)   Coach: Don Haskins

	Min.	Total FG/FGA	Pct.	3–Pt. FG/FGA	Pct.	FT/FTA	Pct.	Reb. O/T	A	TO	PF	S	Blk	TP	PPM
SANDLE, C.	37	8/15	.533	1/2	.500	11/13	.846	0/6	2	5	4	0	1	28	.757
STALLWORTH, T.	34	1/8	.125	1/3	.333	0/0	.000	0/1	1	3	5	1	0	3	.088
CAMPBELL, W.	38	4/7	.571	0/0	.000	1/2	.500	3/8	1	4	5	2	0	9	.237
STEWART, P.	28	2/4	.500	1/2	.500	0/0	.000	1/1	0	0	4	1	0	5	.179
HARDAWAY, T.	39	6/13	.462	0/1	.000	0/1	.000	1/3	4	4	4	1	0	12	.308
WILLIAMS	12	2/2	1.000	1/1	1.000	2/2	1.000	0/0	1	0	1	1	0	7	.583
MCCALL, M.	9	0/0	.000	0/0	.000	0/1	.000	0/0	0	1	1	1	1	0	.000
BOYKIN	3	0/0	.000	0/0	.000	0/0	.000	0/0	0	0	0	0	0	0	.000
Totals	200	23/49	.469	4/9	.444	14/19	.737	5/19	9	16	24	7	2	64	.320

Team Rebounds: Seton Hall 2; UTEP 4. Disqualified: UTEP—Stallworth, Campbell. Technical fouls: None.

	1st Half	2nd Half	Final
Seton Hall	29	51	80
UTEP	25	39	64

Iowa (102)   Coach: Tom Davis

	Min.	Total FG/FGA	Pct.	3–Pt. FG/FGA	Pct.	FT/FTA	Pct.	Reb. O/T	A	TO	PF	S	Blk	TP	PPM
HILL, K.	26	4/5	.800	0/0	.000	2/3	.667	4/8	2	2	2	0	0	10	.385
MARBLE, R.	27	3/6	.500	0/0	.000	8/10	.800	4/7	1	1	4	0	0	14	.519
HORTON, E.	32	6/7	.857	0/0	.000	2/4	.500	2/6	2	2	4	0	0	14	.438
ARMSTRONG, B.	33	8/14	.571	3/6	.500	16/20	.800	0/0	3	2	1	1	0	35	1.061
MOE, J.	27	4/7	.571	2/5	.400	3/4	.750	0/2	0	1	-1	1	0	13	.481
REAVES, M.	20	2/5	.400	1/3	.333	0/0	.000	0/0	1	0	0	0	0	5	.250
JONES, B.	22	5/8	.625	0/0	.000	1/2	.500	1/3	2	1	2	2	0	11	.500
MORGAN, M.	13	0/1	.000	0/0	.000	0/0	.000	0/3	0	0	0	0	0	0	.000
Totals	200	32/53	.604	6/14	.429	32/43	.744	11/26	14	9	14	4	0	102	.510

Florida State (98)   Coach: Pat Kennedy

	Min.	Total FG/FGA	Pct.	3–Pt. FG/FGA	Pct.	FT/FTA	Pct.	Reb. O/T	A	TO	PF	S	Blk	TP	PPM
JOHNSON, B.	26	4/5	.800	3/3	1.000	1/1	1.000	0/0	3	0	3	1	0	12	.462
DAWSON, T.	35	13/21	.691	0/0	.000	4/5	.800	3/4	1	2	5	2	0	30	.857
HUNTER, T.	25	2/6	.333	0/0	.000	0/0	.000	5/9	1	1	3	0	0	4	.160
MAYES, T.	30	7/14	.500	2/7	.286	1/2	.500	1/3	2	1	5	0	0	17	.567
MCCLOUD, G.	35	8/19	.421	5/13	.385	0/1	.000	1/3	0	2	5	0	0	21	.600
POLITE, M.	16	1/3	.333	0/0	.000	2/2	1.000	2/4	0	2	1	0	0	4	.250
FITCHETT	10	1/2	.500	0/0	.000	1/2	.500	0/0	1	3	1	1	0	3	.300
BOYD, A.	11	3/4	.750	1/1	1.000	0/0	.000	1/2	2	1	4	0	0	7	.636
MITCHELL, D.	10	0/1	.000	0/0	.000	1/1	1.000	1/1	0	3	5	0	0	0	.000
WHITE, D.	2	0/0	.000	0/0	.000	0/0	.000	0/0	0	0	0	0	0	0	.000
Totals	200	39/75	.520	12/26	.462	8/11	.727	15/29	10	13	32	3	0	98	.000

Team Rebounds: Iowa 1; Florida State 7. Disqualified: Florida State—Dawson, Mayes McCloud, Mitchell. Technical fouls: Iowa—Jones.

	1st Half	2nd Half	Final
Iowa	51	51	102
Florida State	46	52	98

UNLV (54)　Coach: Jerry Tarkanian

	Min.	Total FG/FGA	Pct.	3–Pt. FG/FGA	Pct.	FT/FTA	Pct.	Reb. O/T	A	TO	PF	S	Blk	TP	PPM
BASNIGHT, J.	36	8/13	.615	0/0	.000	1/2	.500	1/9	1	6	4	1	2	17	.472
PADDIO, G.	37	3/13	.231	2/6	.333	2/4	.500	0/2	1	2	2	2	0	10	.270
TODD, A.	17	0/1	.000	0/0	.000	3/4	.750	0/3	0	1	3	0	0	3	.176
AUGMON, S.	24	1/2	.500	0/0	.000	1/2	.500	2/3	1	1	4	2	1	3	.125
JAMES, K.	38	4/9	.444	0/1	.000	0/0	.000	0/0	3	4	2	2	0	8	.211
ROBINSON, R.	20	5/8	.625	0/0	.000	0/0	.000	3/5	0	2	5	0	0	10	.500
ROSSUM, C.	23	0/1	.000	0/0	.000	1/2	.500	0/1	2	0	3	0	0	1	.043
CVIJANOVICH, S.	5	1/2	.500	0/0	.000	0/0	.000	0/0	0	1	1	0	0	2	.400
Totals	200	22/49	.449	2/7	.286	8/14	.571	6/23	8	17	24	7	3	54	.270

Southwest Missouri State (50)　Coach: Charles Spoonhour

	Min.	Total FG/FGA	Pct.	3–Pt. FG/FGA	Pct.	FT/FTA	Pct.	Reb. O/T	A	TO	PF	S	Blk	TP	PPM
HOLT, C.	33	4/9	.444	1/5	.200	0/0	.000	1/3	3	4	3	1	0	9	.273
WORTHY, S.	40	2/5	.400	0/1	.000	2/2	1.000	0/4	2	3	3	2	0	6	.150
STUCKEY, K.	38	8/10	.800	0/0	.000	2/5	.400	3/8	1	4	2	1	0	18	.474
LEWIS, D.	37	1/4	.250	0/2	.000	0/0	.000	0/3	1	7	4	0	0	2	.054
JACKSON, K.	39	0/7	.000	0/4	.000	2/4	.500	1/3	1	2	2	1	0	2	.051
DAVIS, C.	9	1/3	.333	0/0	.000	10/12	.833	3/3	0	0	2	0	0	12	1.333
BROWN, B.	4	0/0	.000	0/0	.000	1/2	.500	0/1	0	0	0	0	0	1	.250
Totals	200	16/38	.421	1/12	.083	17/25	.680	8/25	8	20	16	5	0	50	.250

Team Rebounds: UNLV 1; SW Missouri St. 1. Disqualified: UNLV—Robinson. Technical fouls: None.

	1st Half	2nd Half	Final
UNLV	31	23	54
SW Missouri St.	34	16	50

Florida (62)　Coach: Norm Sloan

	Min.	Total FG/FGA	Pct.	3–Pt. FG/FGA	Pct.	FT/FTA	Pct.	Reb. O/T	A	TO	PF	S	Blk	TP	PPM
LAWRENCE, P.	31	4/8	.500	1/4	.250	0/0	.000	1/6	0	0	1	0	1	9	.290
CHATMAN, L.	35	5/13	.385	0/0	.000	1/2	.500	3/6	2	2	2	2	0	11	.314
SCHINTZIUS, D.	25	3/7	.429	0/0	.000	2/3	.667	1/5	1	1	2	0	8	.320
MAXWELL, V.	37	5/15	.333	2/4	.500	6/8	.750	2/7	6	5	1	2	0	18	.486
LETT, C.	33	1/3	.333	0/1	.000	1/2	.500	1/1	3	4	1	2	0	3	.091
JENKINS, W.	10	0/2	.000	0/0	.000	0/0	.000	0/0	2	0	0	0	0	0	.000
DAVIS, D.	29	6/8	.750	0/0	.000	1/2	.500	2/5	1	0	2	0	1	13	.448
Totals	200	24/56	.429	3/9	.333	11/17	.647	10/30	15	12	9	6	2	62	.310

St. John's (59)　Coach: Lou Carnesecca

	Min.	Total FG/FGA	Pct.	3–Pt. FG/FGA	Pct.	FT/FTA	Pct.	Reb. O/T	A	TO	PF	S	Blk	TP	PPM
BRUST, M.	40	6/11	.545	0/0	.000	0/0	.000	2/4	3	1	2	0	0	12	.300
JONES, S.	40	8/16	.500	0/0	.000	1/2	.500	0/9	1	2	4	3	1	17	.425
BALDI, M.	27	3/4	.750	0/0	.000	0/0	.000	1/3	0	2	2	1	0	6	.222
HARVEY, B.	38	7/12	.583	0/1	.000	0/0	.000	0/2	6	2	2	1	0	14	.368
PORTER, M.	33	2/6	.333	0/2	.000	0/0	.000	0/4	6	1	4	2	1	4	.121
WILLIAMS, J.	15	1/2	.500	0/0	.000	4/6	.667	1/4	0	3	4	0	0	6	.400
LEWIS, E.	7	0/2	.000	0/0	.000	0/0	.000	0/0	0	0	1	0	0	0	.000
Totals	200	27/53	.509	0/3	.000	5/8	.625	4/26	16	11	17	8	4	59	.295

Team Rebounds: Florida 1; St. John's 0. Disqualified: None. Technical fouls: None.

	1st Half	2nd Half	Final
Florida	33	29	62
St. John's	23	36	59

Michigan (63)　Coach: Bill Freider

	Min.	Total FG/FGA	Pct.	3–Pt. FG/FGA	Pct.	FT/FTA	Pct.	Reb. O/T	A	TO	PF	S	Blk	TP	PPM
RICE, G.	36	3/7	.429	0/0	.000	2/4	.500	-/3	1	-	3	-	-	8	.222
MILLS, T.	27	6/7	.857	0/0	.000	0/1	.000	-/5	1	-	3	-	-	12	.444
VAUGHT, L.	27	6/9	.667	0/0	.000	1/2	.500	-/6	0	-	1	-	-	13	.481
ROBINSON, R.	29	1/2	.500	0/0	.000	7/8	.875	-/3	8	-	1	-	-	9	.310
GRANT, G.	36	4/7	.571	1/1	1.000	0/2	.000	-/0	5	-	2	-	-	9	.250
GRIFFIN, M.	18	1/2	.500	0/0	.000	2/3	.667	-/4	0	-	2	-	-	4	.222
HUGHES, M.	27	4/4	1.000	0/0	.000	0/0	.000	-/5	1	-	2	-	-	8	.296
Totals	200	25/38	.658	1/1	1.000	12/20	.600	-/26	16	-	14	-	-	63	.315

Boise State (58)　Coach: Bob Dye

	Min.	Total FG/FGA	Pct.	3–Pt. FG/FGA	Pct.	FT/FTA	Pct.	Reb. O/T	A	TO	PF	S	Blk	TP	PPM
FOSTER	28	4/11	.364	1/5	.200	2/2	1.000	-/3	0	-	5	-	-	11	.393
JONES	34	5/11	.455	0/0	.000	3/4	.750	-/7	2	-	3	-	-	13	.382
DODD	36	4/8	.500	0/0	.000	0/0	.000	-/10	0	-	3	-	-	8	.222
CHILDS	36	3/9	.333	1/4	.250	4/4	1.000	-/0	3	-	5	-	-	11	.306
USITELO	23	1/4	.250	0/0	.000	2/2	1.000	-/3	4	-	2	-	-	4	.174
KING	21	3/9	.333	3/6	.500	0/0	.000	-/1	2	-	1	-	-	9	.429
SANOR	14	0/1	.000	0/0	.000	2/2	1.000	-/2	1	-	2	-	-	2	.143
SPERRY	8	0/0	.000	0/0	.000	0/0	/000	-/0	0	-	0	-	-	0	.000
Totals	200	20/53	.377	5/15	.333	13/14	.929	-/26	12	-	21	-	-	58	.290

Disqualified: Boise St.—Foster, Childs. Technical fouls: None.

	1st Half	2nd Half	Final
Michigan	36	27	63
Boise St.	20	38	58

Wyoming (115)　Coach: Benny Dees

	Min.	Total FG/FGA	Pct.	3–Pt. FG/FGA	Pct.	FT/FTA	Pct.	Reb. O/T	A	TO	PF	S	Blk	TP	PPM
DEMBO, F.	30	5/11	.455	0/3	.000	4/6	.667	1/7	8	2	5	1	2	14	.467
SOMMERS, J.	10	2/2	1.000	0/0	.000	0/0	.000	0/0	1	1	0	0	4	4	.400
LECKNER, E.	30	10/17	.588	0/0	.000	3/4	.750	3/8	2	4	5	0	1	23	.767
DAVIS, R.	29	9/15	.600	1/2	.500	0/0	.000	3/6	1	4	2	1	0	19	.655
FOX, R.	14	7/9	.778	2/4	.500	0/0	.000	1/2	3	1	5	1	0	16	1.143
DENT, S.	21	2/3	.667	0/0	.000	0/0	.000	0/2	6	2	5	1	0	4	.190
SAMUELS, K.	1	0/0	.000	0/0	.000	0/0	.000	0/0	0	0	0	0	0	0	.000
BOYD, T.	25	4/11	.364	0/3	.000	1/1	1.000	2/5	3	4	5	2	0	9	.360
JONES, W.	25	4/7	.571	0/0	.000	4/6	.667	5/10	5	4	4	1	0	12	.480
WILLIAMS, C.	12	3/4	.750	2/2	1.000	3/4	.750	2/3	0	1	2	1	0	11	.917
TYSON, R.	1	1/2	.500	1/2	.500	0/0	.000	1/1	0	0	0	0	0	3	3.000
LODGINS, D.	2	0/1	.000	0/0	.000	0/0	.000	0/0	0	0	0	0	0	0	.000
Totals	200	47/82	.573	6/16	.375	15/21	.714	18/44	29	23	33	8	3	115	.575

Loyola Marymount (119)　Coach: Paul Westhead

	Min.	Total FG/FGA	Pct.	3–Pt. FG/FGA	Pct.	FT/FTA	Pct.	Reb. O/T	A	TO	PF	S	Blk	TP	PPM
ARMSTRONG, M.	29	6/8	.750	0/0	.000	3/5	.600	4/8	2	2	4	1	0	15	.517
YOEST, M.	34	5/9	.556	0/0	.000	15/17	.882	6/9	2	2	4	1	0	25	.735
GATHERS, H.	34	9/16	.563	0/0	.000	1/4	.250	6/22	2	3	2	4	2	19	.559
KIMBLE, B.	30	12/22	.545	4/9	.444	1/3	.333	1/2	3	2	4	3	0	29	.967
FRYER, J.	21	5/11	.455	3/6	.500	4/4	1.000	2/3	1	0	3	3	0	17	.810
GAINES, C.	28	3/9	.333	0/2	.000	3/4	.750	1/2	10	3	4	1	0	9	.321
SIMMONS, E.	20	2/8	.250	1/3	.333	0/0	.000	2/4	3	0	3	0	5	5	.250
VEARGASON, J.	4	0/0	.000	0/0	.000	0/0	.000	0/0	0	1	1	0	0	0	.000
Totals	200	42/82	.512	8/20	.400	27/37	.730	21/40	23	13	22	16	2	119	.595

Team Rebounds: Loyola Mymt. 2; Wyoming 2. Disqualified: Wyoming—Dembo, Leckner, Fox, Dent, Boyd. Technical fouls: None.

	1st Half	2nd Half	Final
Wyoming	52	63	115
Loyola Mymt.	63	56	119

North Carolina (83)   Coach: Dean Smith

	Min.	Total FG/FGA	Pct.	3-Pt. FG/FGA	Pct.	FT/FTA	Pct.	Reb. O/T	A	TO	PF	S	Blk	TP	PPM
BUCKNALL, S.	28	2/4	.500	1/2	.500	2/2	1.000	0/2	3	2	1	1	0	7	.250
REID, J.	31	10/16	.625	0/0	.000	9/10	.900	4/9	1	2	4	0	0	29	.935
WILLIAMS, S.	23	5/9	.556	0/1	.000	0/1	.000	0/11	0	3	4	2	1	10	.435
LEBO, J.	31	2/5	.400	1/3	.333	2/2	1.000	0/1	9	3	2	2	0	7	.226
MADDEN, K.	17	3/5	.600	0/0	.000	0/1	.000	1/5	1	2	0	0	0	6	.353
DENNY, J.	3	1/1	1.000	0/0	.000	0/0	.000	0/1	0	0	0	0	0	2	.667
HYATT, R.	2	0/1	.000	0/0	.000	0/1	.000	0/0	1	0	0	0	0	0	.000
RICE, K.	16	1/2	.500	1/1	1.000	0/0	.000	0/3	2	2	2	1	0	3	.188
ELSTUN, D.	1	0/0	.000	0/0	.000	0/0	.000	0/0	0	0	0	0	0	0	.000
MAY, D.	1	0/0	.000	0/0	.000	0/0	.000	0/0	0	0	0	0	0	0	.000
CHILCUTT, P.	12	0/3	.000	0/0	.000	0/0	.000	2/3	0	0	1	0	0	0	.000
SMITH, R.	22	4/6	.667	2/4	.500	5/6	.833	2/2	2	1	0	1	0	15	.682
JENKINS, J.	2	1/1	1.000	0/0	.000	0/0	.000	1/1	0	0	0	1	0	2	1.000
FOX, R.	11	1/4	.250	0/0	.000	0/0	.000	0/2	1	2	1	3	0	2	.182
Totals	200	30/57	.526	5/11	.455	18/23	.783	10/40	20	17	15	11	1	83	.415

North Texas (65)   Coach: Jimmy Gales

	Min.	Total FG/FGA	Pct.	3-Pt. FG/FGA	Pct.	FT/FTA	Pct.	Reb. O/T	A	TO	PF	S	Blk	TP	PPM
WORRELL, T.	37	6/17	.353	2/7	.286	1/2	.500	3/7	2	4	4	1	0	15	.405
MORGAN, R.	36	3/9	.333	0/0	.000	1/4	.250	7/19	0	0	3	2	0	7	.194
WILLIAMS, W.	19	3/4	.750	0/0	.000	0/0	.000	0/1	0	1	5	0	0	6	.316
ROBERTSON, R.	26	2/8	.250	0/3	.000	5/6	.833	2/2	0	3	2	2	0	9	.346
HUNTER, D.	26	6/17	.353	3/7	.429	0/0	.000	0/1	2	1	1	2	0	15	.577
GULLEY, K.	25	0/2	.000	0/0	.000	2/2	1.000	0/0	1	2	2	1	0	2	.080
GREENE, R.	1	0/0	.000	0/0	.000	0/0	.000	0/0	0	0	0	0	0	0	.000
DURYEA, T.	6	0/1	.000	0/1	.000	0/0	.000	1/1	3	2	0	1	0	0	.000
CHOPLICK, A.	4	0/3	.000	0/0	.000	0/0	.000	1/1	0	0	0	1	0	0	.000
SMITH, W.	10	2/4	.500	1/1	1.000	4/4	1.000	2/2	1	2	2	0	0	9	.900
WHITTINGTON, D.	10	0/1	.000	0/0	.000	2/2	1.000	2/5	0	0	1	1	0	2	.200
Totals	200	22/66	.333	6/19	.316	15/20	.750	18/39	9	15	20	11	0	65	.325

Team Rebounds: N. Carolina 3; North Texas 0. Disqualified: North Texas—Williams. Technical fouls: None.

	1st Half	2nd Half	Final
N. Carolina	40	43	83
North Texas	24	41	65

FIRST ROUND SOUTHWEST

Oklahoma (94)   Coach: Billy Tubbs

	Min.	Total FG/FGA	Pct.	3-Pt. FG/FGA	Pct.	FT/FTA	Pct.	Reb. O/T	A	TO	PF	S	Blk	TP	PPM
GRANT, H.	29	9/12	.750	0/0	.000	7/9	.778	1/6	0	3	5	0	0	25	.862
SIEGER, D.	36	2/6	.333	1/5	.200	0/0	.000	2/5	8	3	2	1	0	5	.139
KING, S.	29	12/19	.632	0/0	.000	1/4	.250	2/7	1	2	3	2	3	25	.862
BLAYLOCK, M.	32	2/5	.400	0/1	.000	0/0	.000	0/3	9	3	3	4	0	4	.125
GRACE, R.	37	5/10	.500	2/6	.333	1/3	.333	1/2	5	2	4	4	0	13	.351
POLLARD, A.	2	1/2	.500	0/0	.000	0/0	.000	0/0	0	0	0	0	0	2	1.000
BELL, M.	2	2/2	1.000	0/0	.000	0/0	.000	0/1	0	0	1	0	1	4	2.000
MULLINS, T.	8	0/1	.000	0/1	.000	0/2	.000	0/0	2	0	4	1	0	0	.000
WILEY, A.	15	5/9	.556	0/0	.000	6/6	1.000	4/9	0	1	1	0	0	16	1.067
MARTIN, A.	8	0/0	.000	0/0	.000	0/0	.000	0/1	0	1	1	0	1	0	.000
JONES	1	0/0	.000	0/0	.000	0/0	.000	0/0	0	0	1	0	0	0	.000
SKURCENSKI, J.	1	0/0	.000	0/0	.000	0/0	.000	0/0	0	1	0	0	0	0	.000
Totals	200	38/66	.576	3/13	.231	15/24	.625	10/34	25	16	25	12	5	94	.470

Tennessee-Chattanooga (66)   Coach: Mack McCarthy

	Min.	Total FG/FGA	Pct.	3-Pt. FG/FGA	Pct.	FT/FTA	Pct.	Reb. O/T	A	TO	PF	S	Blk	TP	PPM
CHANDLER, D.	32	4/12	.333	0/3	.000	2/2	1.000	2/4	2	4	4	1	0	10	.313
MOON	21	3/4	.750	0/0	.000	1/2	.500	3/5	2	1	2	1	0	7	.333
FULSE	34	3/7	.429	0/1	.000	6/7	.857	3/6	1	0	4	0	0	12	.353
LYONS	35	4/9	.444	0/2	.000	1/3	.333	1/4	4	10	2	5	0	9	.257
GREEN	32	7/17	.412	2/10	.200	2/3	.667	0/4	2	5	3	1	0	18	.563
ROBINSON	20	1/5	.200	0/1	.000	1/4	.250	4/11	0	3	4	0	0	3	.150
BEHRENDS	12	1/3	.333	0/0	.000	1/1	1.000	3/4	0	1	2	0	0	3	.250
COLLINS	6	0/0	.000	0/0	.000	2/2	1.000	0/0	0	2	0	0	0	2	.333
SHEPPHARD	7	1/4	.250	0/1	.000	0/0	.000	0/1	0	0	1	0	0	2	.286
SPUNAR	1	0/0	.000	0/0	.000	0/0	.000	0/0	0	0	0	0	0	0	.000
Totals	200	24/61	.393	2/18	.111	16/24	.667	16/39	11	26	22	8	0	66	.330

Team Rebounds: Oklahoma 3; Tenn.-Chatt. 3. Disqualified: Oklahoma—Grant. Technical fouls: None.

	1st Half	2nd Half	Final
Oklahoma	34	60	94
Tenn.-Chatt.	29	37	66

Auburn (90)   Coach: Sonny Smith

	Min.	Total FG/FGA	Pct.	3-Pt. FG/FGA	Pct.	FT/FTA	Pct.	Reb. O/T	A	TO	PF	S	Blk	TP	PPM
CAYLOR, J.	38	5/8	.625	3/6	.500	5/6	.833	-/5	2	3	2	2	0	18	.474
MORRIS, C.	37	11/23	.478	2/5	.400	12/13	.923	-/12	4	3	3	2	3	36	.973
MOORE, J.	36	6/16	.375	0/0	.000	1/1	1.000	-/13	1	2	2	1	1	13	.361
HOWARD, T.	24	2/4	.500	0/1	.000	0/0	.000	-/5	5	1	1	1	0	4	.167
DENNISON, D.	17	1/6	.167	1/2	.500	2/2	1.000	-/1	3	0	3	1	0	5	.294
LYNN, J.	21	1/4	.250	0/1	.333	0/0	.000	-/0	7	1	0	1	0	3	.143
GEIGER, M.	7	1/3	.333	0/0	.000	1/3	.333	-/3	1	2	3	0	0	3	.429
CARPENTER, K.	20	3/8	.375	0/1	.000	2/2	1.000	-/2	0	0	3	1	0	8	.400
Totals	200	30/72	.417	7/18	.389	23/27	.852	-/41	23	12	17	9	4	90	.450

Bradley (86)   Coach: Stan Albeck

	Min.	Total FG/FGA	Pct.	3-Pt. FG/FGA	Pct.	FT/FTA	Pct.	Reb. O/T	A	TO	PF	S	Blk	TP	PPM
POWELL, D.	37	4/9	.444	0/0	.000	2/5	.400	-/7	1	0	5	3	0	10	.270
TRIMPE, T.	11	1/4	.250	1/4	.250	0/0	.000	-/1	2	0	1	0	0	3	.273
JACKSON, L.	34	7/10	.700	0/1	.000	0/3	.000	-/5	2	3	2	0	0	14	.412
MANUEL, A.	40	0/3	.000	0/0	.000	0/0	.000	-/4	10	6	4	0	0	0	.000
HAWKINS, H.	40	15/25	.600	6/8	.750	8/11	.727	-/10	6	4	3	3	2	44	1.100
THOMAS, J.	25	4/9	.444	0/1	.000	0/0	.000	-/1	3	0	5	0	0	8	.320
WILSON, P.	13	3/6	.500	1/3	.333	0/2	.000	-/5	1	2	3	1	0	7	.538
Totals	200	34/66	.515	8/17	.471	10/21	.476	-/33	25	15	23	7	2	86	.430

Team Rebounds: Auburn 3; Bradley 5. Disqualified: Bradley—Powell, Thomas. Technical fouls: Auburn—Morris.

	1st Half	2nd Half	Final
Auburn	45	45	90
Bradley	53	33	86

Louisville (70)   Coach: Denny Crum

	Min.	Total FG/FGA	Pct.	3-Pt. FG/FGA	Pct.	FT/FTA	Pct.	Reb. O/T	A	TO	PF	S	Blk	TP	PPM
PAYNE, K.	26	2/8	.250	1/3	.333	0/0	.000	0/4	3	1	2	0	0	5	.192
CROOK, H.	39	11/17	.647	0/0	.000	0/0	.000	2/11	3	1	3	0	1	22	.564
ELLISON, P.	33	9/14	.643	0/0	.000	5/9	.556	3/11	4	3	4	0	1	23	.697
WILLIAMS, K.	32	3/5	.600	0/1	.000	0/2	.000	2/4	6	2	1	1	0	6	.188
SMITH, L.	33	1/3	.333	0/2	.000	8/8	1.000	2/3	4	6	2	2	1	10	.303
ABRAM, M.	24	0/3	.000	0/1	.000	0/1	.000	1/2	3	4	2	0	0	0	.000
SPENCER, F.	13	2/3	.667	0/0	.000	0/2	.000	2/3	0	3	1	1	1	4	.308
Totals	200	28/53	.528	1/7	.143	13/22	.591	12/38	23	20	15	4	4	70	.350

Oregon State (61)   Coach: Ralph Miller

	Min.	Total FG/FGA	Pct.	3-Pt. FG/FGA	Pct.	FT/FTA	Pct.	Reb. O/T	A	TO	PF	S	Blk	TP	PPM
MARTIN	40	7/15	.467	0/1	.000	6/7	.857	3/6	3	2	2	3	0	20	.500
BRANTLEY	37	4/6	.667	0/0	.000	0/2	.000	0/4	2	1	4	3	0	8	.216
SHERWOOD	33	6/13	.462	2/6	.333	3/4	.750	4/5	0	3	5	1	0	17	.515
KNOX	31	1/9	.111	0/2	.000	2/2	1.000	0/3	2	2	5	2	0	4	.129
PAYTON, G.	40	5/11	.455	1/3	.333	1/1	1.000	0/4	8	4	4	1	0	12	.300
CAVELL	5	0/2	.000	0/0	.000	0/0	.000	0/1	0	0	0	0	0	0	.000
FREEMAN	5	0/1	.000	0/0	.000	0/0	.000	0/0	0	1	0	1	0	0	.000
HARGE	4	0/0	.000	0/0	.000	0/0	.000	0/0	1	0	0	0	0	0	.000
CELESTINE	5	0/0	.000	0/0	.000	0/0	.000	0/0	0	1	2	0	0	0	.000
Totals	200	23/57	.404	3/12	.250	12/16	.750	7/23	16	14	22	11	0	61	.305

Team Rebounds: Louisville 4; Oregon State 4. Disqualified: Oregon State—Sherwood, Knox. Technical fouls: None.

	1st Half	2nd Half	Final
Louisville	28	42	70
Oregon State	28	33	61

Brigham Young (98)   Coach: Ladell Anderson

	Min.	Total FG/FGA	Pct.	3-Pt. FG/FGA	Pct.	FT/FTA	Pct.	Reb. O/T	A	TO	PF	S	Blk	TP	PPM
SMITH	42	11/17	.647	1/2	.500	6/6	1.000	-/13	2	7	4	0	0	29	.690
CHATMAN, J.	37	7/12	.583	0/0	.000	3/4	.750	-/8	1	4	2	2	0	17	.459
USEVITCH	40	7/12	.583	0/0	.000	1/3	.333	-/6	1	3	4	1	1	15	.375
HAWS, M.	38	4/9	.444	0/0	.000	8/9	.889	-/1	3	2	2	2	0	16	.421
TOOLSON	17	1/4	.250	0/2	.000	1/2	.500	-/3	3	1	0	1	0	3	.176
CALL	16	3/3	1.000	2/2	1.000	0/0	.000	-/3	2	1	1	1	0	8	.500
TAYLOR	34	4/6	.667	0/0	.000	2/2	1.000	-/5	6	5	3	0	0	10	.294
ASTLE, D.	1	0/0	.000	0/0	.000	0/0	.000	-/0	0	0	1	0	0	0	.000
Totals	225	37/63	.587	3/6	.500	21/26	.808	-/39	18	23	17	7	1	98	.436

North Carolina-Charlotte (92)   Coach: Jeff Mullins

	Min.	Total FG/FGA	Pct.	3-Pt. FG/FGA	Pct.	FT/FTA	Pct.	Reb. O/T	A	TO	PF	S	Blk	TP	PPM
PERSLEY, F.	39	5/16	.313	1/7	.143	0/2	.000	-/6	0	1	3	1	0	11	.282
BALL, C.	31	6/11	.545	0/0	.000	4/5	.800	-/8	0	2	2	2	0	16	.516
PLONDKE	38	4/11	.364	1/1	1.000	0/2	.000	-/4	2	2	4	0	0	9	.237
DINKINS	32	8/19	.421	3/4	.750	2/4	.500	-/3	9	4	5	6	0	21	.656
WEST	38	5/9	.556	4/7	.571	6/8	.750	-/3	5	3	2	1	0	20	.526
BARNES	19	2/3	.667	1/1	1.000	0/0	.000	-/0	1	1	3	2	0	5	.263
BELLAMY	4	0/0	.000	0/0	.000	0/0	.000	-/1	0	0	1	0	0	0	.000
WASHINGTON	17	4/8	.500	0/0	.000	0/0	.000	-/5	0	1	2	0	0	8	.471
BANISTER	4	1/1	1.000	0/0	.000	0/0	.000	-/0	0	1	1	0	0	2	.500
PULLEY	2	0/0	.000	0/0	.000	0/0	.000	-/0	1	0	1	0	0	0	.000
BENNETT	1	0/0	.000	0/0	.000	0/0	.000	-/0	0	0	0	0	0	0	.000
Totals	225	35/78	.449	10/20	.500	12/21	.571	-/30	18	15	24	12	0	92	.409

Team Rebounds: Brigham Young 5; N.C.-Charlotte 3. Disqualified: N.C.-Charlotte—Dinkins. Technical fouls: Brigham Young—bench.

	1st Half	2nd Half	1 OT	Final
Brigham Young	43	39	16	98
N.C.-Charlotte	45	37	10	92

Villanova (82)   Coach: Rollie Massimino

	Min.	Total FG/FGA	Pct.	3-Pt. FG/FGA	Pct.	FT/FTA	Pct.	Reb. O/T	A	TO	PF	S	Blk	TP	PPM
PLANSKY, M.	22	3/5	.600	1/2	.500	5/6	.833	0/2	0	3	5	0	0	12	.545
TAYLOR, R.	32	5/9	.556	0/0	.000	2/4	.500	2/9	1	3	3	0	1	12	.375
GREIS, T.	38	5/7	.714	0/0	.000	5/5	1.000	2/8	0	3	3	0	2	15	.395
WILSON, D.	39	4/9	.444	1/4	.250	8/8	1.000	0/5	6	5	3	0	0	17	.436
WEST, D.	35	8/14	.571	3/6	.500	3/5	.600	0/5	1	2	2	2	0	22	.629
MASSEY, G.	27	1/2	.500	0/0	.000	0/1	.000	0/2	2	3	1	0	0	2	.074
ENRIGHT, P.	4	0/0	.000	0/0	.000	2/2	1.000	0/1	0	0	1	0	0	2	.500
BEKKEDAM, B.	3	0/0	.000	0/0	.000	0/0	.000	0/1	0	0	0	0	0	0	.000
Totals	200	26/46	.565	5/12	.417	25/31	.806	4/33	10	19	18	2	3	82	.410

Arkansas (74)   Coach: Nolan Richardson

	Min.	Total FG/FGA	Pct.	3-Pt. FG/FGA	Pct.	FT/FTA	Pct.	Reb. O/T	A	TO	PF	S	Blk	TP	PPM
HUERY, R.	37	7/16	.438	5/11	.455	2/4	.500	0/5	0	2	1	1	1	21	.568
CREDIT, M.	32	4/7	.571	0/0	.000	5/6	.833	3/9	0	5	3	1	1	13	.406
LANG, A.	22	5/9	.556	0/0	.000	0/0	.000	5/8	0	0	4	0	2	10	.455
FREEMAN, A.	34	3/7	.429	0/3	.000	0/0	.000	0/0	2	2	3	1	0	6	.176
WILSON, K.	33	3/11	.273	1/4	.250	0/0	.000	1/4	1	0	3	0	0	7	.212
SCOTT, T.	20	3/9	.333	1/5	.200	3/5	.600	1/1	0	1	5	1	0	10	.500
MARKS, L.	18	2/7	.286	0/0	.000	0/0	.000	1/2	0	3	2	0	1	4	.222
WHITBY, C.	4	1/3	.333	0/1	.000	1/2	.500	0/0	0	0	4	0	0	3	.750
Totals	200	28/69	.406	7/24	.292	11/17	.647	11/29	3	13	25	4	5	74	.370

Team Rebounds: Villanova 1; Arkansas 2. Disqualified: Villanova—Plansky; Arkansas—Scott. Technical fouls: None.

	1st Half	2nd Half	Final
Villanova	40	42	82
Arkansas	33	41	74

Illinois (81)   Coach: Lou Henson

	Min.	Total FG/FGA	Pct.	3-Pt. FG/FGA	Pct.	FT/FTA	Pct.	Reb. O/T	A	TO	PF	S	Blk	TP	PPM
ANDERSON, N.	20	4/7	.571	0/0	.000	1/1	1.000	0/3	0	4	4	0	1	9	.450
BATTLE, K.	25	4/6	.667	0/0	.000	0/0	.000	0/7	0	1	2	0	1	8	.320
KAJAWA, J.	29	4/6	.667	0/0	.000	2/4	.500	3/7	0	0	4	0	0	10	.345
BLACKWELL, G.	32	6/13	.462	0/1	.000	7/8	.875	1/5	4	3	2	1	0	19	.594
BARDO, S.	40	1/3	.333	0/0	.000	6/6	1.000	0/4	5	2	4	1	0	8	.200
GILL, K.	28	3/9	.333	0/0	.000	0/0	.000	0/3	5	1	1	0	0	6	.214
HAMILTON, D.	23	10/12	.833	0/0	.000	1/2	.500	2/7	2	1	2	2	0	21	.913
KUNZ, P.	2	0/0	.000	0/0	.000	0/0	.000	0/0	0	0	0	0	0	0	.000
SMALL, E.	1	0/0	.000	0/0	.000	0/0	.000	0/0	0	0	0	0	0	0	.000
Totals	200	32/56	.571	0/1	.000	17/21	.810	6/36	16	12	19	4	2	81	.405

Texas-San Antonio (72)   Coach: Ken Burmeister

	Min.	Total FG/FGA	Pct.	3-Pt. FG/FGA	Pct.	FT/FTA	Pct.	Reb. O/T	A	TO	PF	S	Blk	TP	PPM
HAMPTON, F.	37	6/15	.400	0/0	.000	5/6	.833	0/3	0	1	3	0	0	17	.459
MCGEE, C.	26	4/9	.444	0/0	.000	1/3	.333	3/5	0	1	2	0	0	9	.346
WHEATLEY, B.	23	2/6	.333	0/0	.000	3/3	1.000	2/4	0	1	2	0	0	7	.304
BARNES, T.	22	0/3	.000	0/2	.000	0/0	.000	0/2	1	1	0	0	0	0	.000
COOPER, E.	32	6/15	.400	3/8	.375	2/2	1.000	0/2	4	2	4	2	0	17	.531
MOORE, L.	25	2/7	.286	0/2	.000	2/2	1.000	2/5	1	2	2	0	1	6	.240
SMITH, S.	17	4/7	.571	2/4	.500	3/4	.750	1/2	1	1	1	2	1	13	.765
PETTUS, D.	12	1/2	.500	0/0	.000	0/0	.000	0/0	0	1	1	0	0	2	.167
MARTIN, G.	6	0/0	.000	0/0	.000	1/2	.500	0/2	0	0	1	0	0	1	.167
Totals	200	25/64	.391	5/16	.313	17/23	.739	8/23	6	10	18	4	1	72	.360

Team Rebounds: Illinois 0; Texas-San Ant. 5. Disqualified: None. Technical fouls: None.

	1st Half	2nd Half	Final
Illinois	38	43	81
Texas-San Ant.	31	41	72

Maryland (92) Coach: Bob Wade

	Min.	Total FG/FGA	Pct.	3-Pt. FG/FGA	Pct.	FT/FTA	Pct.	Reb. O/T	A	TO	PF	S	Blk	TP	PPM
MASSENBURG, T.	36	4/4	1.000	0/0	.000	3/4	.750	2/7	0	1	4	0	1	11	.306
LEWIS, D.	37	11/15	.733	1/1	1.000	2/6	.333	2/8	2	2	4	5	1	25	.676
WILLIAMS, B.	23	3/6	.500	0/0	.000	5/6	.833	1/2	1	1	4	1	1	11	.478
GATLIN, K.	40	8/13	.615	5/8	.625	2/2	1.000	2/7	6	2	2	0	0	23	.575
ARCHER, R.	33	3/6	.500	1/2	.500	11/12	.917	0/1	4	4	1	1	0	18	.545
DICKERSON, D.	4	0/0	.000	0/0	.000	0/0	.000	0/0	1	0	0	0	0	0	.000
HOOD, S.	16	0/3	.000	0/3	.000	2/2	1.000	0/0	2	1	0	0	0	2	.125
MCCOY, T.	11	1/3	.333	0/2	.000	0/0	.000	0/1	1	1	3	0	0	2	.182
Totals	200	30/50	.600	7/16	.438	25/32	.781	7/26	17	12	18	7	3	92	.460

UC Santa Barbara (82) Coach: Jerry Pimm

	Min.	Total FG/FGA	Pct.	3-Pt. FG/FGA	Pct.	FT/FTA	Pct.	Reb. O/T	A	TO	PF	S	Blk	TP	PPM
DEHART, C.	27	6/10	.600	4/8	.500	2/2	1.000	1/1	2	3	4	0	0	18	.667
GRAY, G.	14	0/2	.000	0/0	.000	0/0	.000	1/2	0	0	1	0	0	0	.000
MCARTHUR, E.	26	3/5	.600	0/0	.000	3/4	.750	3/8	0	5	4	2	0	9	.346
JOHNSON, B.	32	5/10	.500	4/6	.667	0/0	.000	0/0	4	1	3	0	0	14	.438
SHAW, B.	40	5/13	.385	3/5	.600	1/1	1.000	2/6	5	4	3	0	0	14	.350
WESTBELD	8	0/0	.000	0/0	.000	1/2	.500	0/0	0	0	2	0	0	1	.125
DOYLE, M.	30	8/14	.571	0/1	.000	4/6	.667	5/7	1	0	4	1	0	20	.667
DAVENPORT, C.	22	1/4	.250	0/0	.000	2/3	.667	2/3	6	2	0	0	0	4	.182
ELLIOT, M.	1	0/0	.000	0/0	.000	2/2	1.000	0/0	0	0	1	0	0	2	2.000
Totals	200	28/58	.483	11/20	.550	15/20	.750	14/27	18	15	22	3	0	82	.410

Team Rebounds: Maryland 1; UC Santa Barb. 0. Disqualified: None. Technical fouls: None.

	1st Half	2nd Half	Final
Maryland	39	53	92
UC Santa Barb.	44	38	82

Kentucky (99) Coach: Eddie Sutton

	Min.	Total FG/FGA	Pct.	3-Pt. FG/FGA	Pct.	FT/FTA	Pct.	Reb. O/T	A	TO	PF	S	Blk	TP	PPM
MANUEL, E.	34	5/10	.500	0/0	.000	3/4	.750	-/10	5	-	0	-	-	13	.382
BENNETT, W.	28	5/5	1.000	0/0	.000	2/3	.667	-/7	3	-	4	-	-	12	.429
LOCK, R.	29	2/8	.250	0/0	.000	8/11	.727	-/6	2	-	3	-	-	12	.414
CHAPMAN, R.	38	10/13	.769	2/3	.667	1/1	1.000	-/6	5	-	2	-	-	23	.605
DAVENDER, E.	36	12/16	.750	2/4	.500	4/4	1.000	-/4	1	-	1	-	-	30	.833
ELLIS, L.	12	2/2	1.000	0/0	.000	0/0	.000	-/3	0	-	3	-	-	4	.333
MADISON, R.	11	1/2	.500	0/0	.000	0/0	.000	-/3	1	-	0	-	-	2	.182
JENKINS, C.	8	1/1	1.000	0/0	.000	1/1	1.000	-/1	0	-	0	-	-	3	.375
SCOTT, M.	1	0/0	.000	0/0	.000	0/0	.000	-/0	0	-	0	-	-	0	.000
SUTTON	2	0/0	.000	0/0	.000	0/0	.000	-/0	0	-	0	-	-	0	.000
HANSON	1	0/0	.000	0/0	.000	0/0	.000	-/0	0	-	0	-	-	0	.000
Totals	200	38/57	.667	4/7	.571	19/24	.792	-/40	17	-	13	-	-	99	.495

Southern-B.R. (84) Coach: Ben Jobe

	Min.	Total FG/FGA	Pct.	3-Pt. FG/FGA	Pct.	FT/FTA	Pct.	Reb. O/T	A	TO	PF	S	Blk	TP	PPM
FLORENT	26	10/16	.625	3/6	.500	2/4	.500	-/4	0	-	4	-	-	25	.962
BATTLES, D.	39	9/14	.643	0/0	.000	2/3	.667	-/10	0	-	4	-	-	20	.513
WASHINGTON	39	4/9	.444	0/0	.000	6/6	1.000	-/5	1	-	3	-	-	14	.359
JOHNSON, A.	40	1/6	.167	0/1	.000	0/0	.000	-/3	9	-	3	-	-	2	.050
JOHNSON, D.	17	2/12	.167	1/5	.200	0/0	.000	-/1	0	-	3	-	-	5	.294
GARNER	27	3/17	.176	2/5	.400	0/0	.000	-/1	0	-	1	-	-	8	.296
SAMPLE, C.	10	3/7	.429	0/2	.000	2/4	.500	-/2	0	-	0	-	-	2	.800
PHILLS, B.	1	1/1	1.000	0/0	.000	0/0	.000	-/0	0	-	0	-	-	2	2.000
JONES, R.	0	0/0	.000	0/0	.000	0/0	.000	-/1	1	-	1	-	-	0	.000
Totals	200	33/82	.402	6/19	.316	12/17	.706	-/27	11	-	19	-	-	84	.420

Disqualified: None.

	1st Half	2nd Half	Final
Kentucky	48	51	99
Southern-B.R.	40	44	84

SECOND ROUND MIDWEST

Purdue (100) Coach: Gene Keady

	Min.	Total FG/FGA	Pct.	3-Pt. FG/FGA	Pct.	FT/FTA	Pct.	Reb. O/T	A	TO	PF	S	Blk	TP	PPM
JONES, K.	24	2/4	.500	0/0	.000	2/6	.333	3/8	4	3	0	2	0	6	.250
MITCHELL, T.	33	4/9	.444	0/0	.000	7/8	.875	1/5	3	2	2	2	0	15	.455
MCCANTS, M.	29	7/13	.538	0/0	.000	6/9	.667	0/7	2	2	4	0	1	20	.690
STEPHENS, E.	28	4/9	.444	1/5	.200	0/0	.000	2/4	3	2	4	0	0	9	.321
LEWIS, T.	28	8/13	.615	4/8	.500	2/3	.667	1/5	7	2	4	1	0	22	.786
REID, B.	4	0/1	.000	0/1	.000	0/0	.000	0/0	3	1	0	0	0	0	.000
BERNING, R.	6	1/3	.333	0/0	.000	1/1	1.000	0/3	1	0	2	0	0	3	.500
BARRETT, D.	2	0/0	.000	0/0	.000	0/0	.000	0/0	0	1	0	0	0	0	.000
JONES, T.	24	4/6	.667	0/0	.000	2/2	1.000	2/4	6	1	0	3	0	10	.417
EWER, E.	1	0/0	.000	0/0	.000	0/0	.000	0/0	0	0	0	0	0	0	.000
BRUGOS, J.	3	1/1	1.000	0/0	.000	0/0	.000	0/0	0	0	0	0	0	2	.667
SCHEFFLER, S.	17	4/6	.667	0/0	.000	5/5	1.000	5/6	1	2	1	1	1	13	.765
REA, M.	1	0/0	.000	0/0	.000	0/0	.000	0/0	0	0	0	0	0	0	.000
Totals	200	35/65	.538	5/14	.357	25/34	.806	14/42	30	16	17	9	2	100	.500

Memphis State (73) Coach: Larry Finch

	Min.	Total FG/FGA	Pct.	3-Pt. FG/FGA	Pct.	FT/FTA	Pct.	Reb. O/T	A	TO	PF	S	Blk	TP	PPM
DOUGLAS, R.	28	2/5	.400	0/1	.000	2/3	.667	5/7	6	2	2	2	1	6	.214
BALLARD, S.	20	1/1	1.000	0/0	.000	0/0	.000	0/1	0	0	5	0	0	2	.100
BAILEY, D.	16	1/6	.167	0/0	.000	0/0	.000	0/3	3	0	4	0	0	2	.125
BOYD, D.	30	6/12	.500	0/1	.000	6/7	.857	1/3	3	2	2	1	0	18	.600
PERRY, E.	25	2/8	.250	0/4	.000	0/0	.000	0/1	1	2	1	1	0	4	.160
WILLIAMS, J.	2	0/0	.000	0/0	.000	0/0	.000	0/0	0	0	1	0	0	0	.000
GIBSON, C.	14	2/10	.200	2/6	.333	1/2	.500	3/4	1	1	1	2	0	7	.500
MCLAUGHLIN, J.	21	4/10	.400	4/8	.500	2/2	1.000	0/2	3	2	2	2	0	14	.667
MCCLAIN, R.	8	3/5	.600	1/2	.500	0/0	.000	1/2	1	1	3	0	0	7	.875
YOUNG, R.	10	0/2	.000	0/0	.000	0/0	.000	0/3	1	1	2	0	0	0	.000
MUNDT, B.	26	6/12	.500	0/0	.000	1/1	1.000	1/3	0	3	4	0	0	13	.500
Totals	200	27/71	.380	7/22	.318	12/15	.800	11/29	19	14	26	8	1	73	.365

Team Rebounds: Purdue 5; Memphis State 4. Disqualified: Memphis State—Ballard. Technical fouls: Memphis State—Bench.

	1st Half	2nd Half	Final
Purdue	38	62	100
Memphis State	33	40	73

DePaul (58) Coach: Joey Meyer

	Min.	Total FG/FGA	Pct.	3-Pt. FG/FGA	Pct.	FT/FTA	Pct.	Reb. O/T	A	TO	PF	S	Blk	TP	PPM
LAUX, A.	21	2/5	.400	2/5	.400	0/0	.000	0/0	2	0	2	0	0	6	.286
HOLLAND, K.	35	4/5	.800	0/0	.000	0/0	.000	7/9	0	0	3	2	0	8	.229
BRUNDY, S.	34	2/5	.400	0/0	.000	4/6	.667	3/11	0	0	2	2	1	8	.235
STRICKLAND, R.	37	7/19	.368	3/8	.375	2/4	.500	1/4	8	0	4	1	0	19	.514
EDWARDS, K.	34	3/14	.214	0/1	.000	0/0	.000	0/1	4	3	3	3	0	6	.176
GREENE, T.	28	3/10	.300	3/7	.429	0/2	.000	3/6	3	2	3	0	0	9	.321
HAMBY, J.	5	0/0	.000	0/0	.000	0/0	.000	0/0	0	1	1	0	1	0	.000
GOLDEN, K.	6	1/1	1.000	0/0	.000	0/0	.000	1/1	0	0	0	0	0	2	.333
Totals	200	22/59	.373	8/21	.381	6/12	.500	15/32	17	6	18	8	2	58	.290

Kansas State (66) Coach: Lon Kruger

	Min.	Total FG/FGA	Pct.	3-Pt. FG/FGA	Pct.	FT/FTA	Pct.	Reb. O/T	A	TO	PF	S	Blk	TP	PPM
RICHMOND, M.	38	6/14	.429	1/2	.500	6/7	.857	1/8	3	4	2	0	0	19	.500
BLEDSOE, C.	33	2/7	.286	0/0	.000	0/3	.000	1/10	2	1	2	0	0	4	.121
MEYER, R.	33	4/4	1.000	0/0	.000	1/2	.500	0/0	0	1	2	1	0	9	.273
HENSON, S.	38	3/7	.429	2/3	.667	2/4	.500	0/1	4	0	2	1	0	10	.263
SCOTT, W.	34	7/10	.700	7/8	.875	2/2	1.000	1/4	4	4	1	1	0	23	.676
GLOVER, B.	6	0/0	.000	0/0	.000	0/0	.000	0/0	0	0	0	0	0	0	.000
DOBBINS, M.	12	0/0	.000	0/0	.000	0/0	.000	1/3	2	0	0	0	0	0	.000
MCCOY, F.	4	0/1	.000	0/0	.000	1/1	1.000	1/1	0	1	0	0	0	1	.250
NELSON, M.	2	0/0	.000	0/0	.000	0/0	.000	0/0	0	0	0	0	0	0	.000
Totals	200	22/43	.512	10/13	.769	12/19	.632	5/27	15	11	9	3	0	66	.330

Team Rebounds: Kansas State 1; DePaul 4. Disqualified: None. Technical fouls: None.

	1st Half	2nd Half	Final
DePaul	29	29	58
Kansas State	30	36	66

Kansas (61) Coach: Larry Brown

	Min.	Total FG/FGA	Pct.	3-Pt. FG/FGA	Pct.	FT/FTA	Pct.	Reb. O/T	A	TO	PF	S	Blk	TP	PPM
NEWTON, M.	29	5/10	.500	0/2	.000	1/2	.500	2/3	2	2	3	1	1	11	.379
PIPER, C.	21	1/3	.333	0/0	.000	0/2	.000	1/5	3	3	5	1	1	2	.095
MANNING, D.	35	10/19	.526	0/1	.000	5/7	.714	3/5	1	3	2	1	1	25	.714
PRITCHARD, K.	38	4/9	.444	4/6	.667	4/4	1.000	0/4	2	0	1	0	0	16	.421
GUELDNER, J.	23	1/4	.250	1/2	.500	0/0	.000	1/4	2	2	0	2	0	3	.130
BARRY, S.	17	0/0	.000	0/0	.000	0/0	.000	0/0	4	0	2	2	0	0	.000
MADDOX, M.	12	0/1	.000	0/0	.000	0/0	.000	1/3	0	2	0	1	0	0	.000
HARRIS, K.	22	2/3	.667	0/0	.000	0/0	.000	1/8	3	3	1	3	0	4	.182
NORMORE, C.	2	0/0	.000	0/0	.000	0/0	.000	0/0	0	0	1	0	0	0	.000
MINOR, L.	1	0/0	.000	0/0	.000	0/0	.000	0/0	0	0	0	0	0	0	.000
Totals	200	23/49	.469	5/11	.455	10/15	.667	9/32	17	15	16	12	3	61	.305

Murray State (58) Coach: Steve Newton

	Min.	Total FG/FGA	Pct.	3-Pt. FG/FGA	Pct.	FT/FTA	Pct.	Reb. O/T	A	TO	PF	S	Blk	TP	PPM
MARTIN, J.	40	7/16	.438	1/2	.500	7/7	1.000	2/7	3	2	2	0	0	22	.550
OGDEN, C.	31	1/4	.250	0/0	.000	0/0	.000	2/4	1	2	1	1	0	2	.065
SIAS, C.	26	1/3	.333	0/0	.000	0/0	.000	1/4	0	1	5	0	0	2	.065
MANN, D.	39	4/15	.267	2/9	.222	6/7	.857	0/4	6	2	1	3	0	16	.410
KING, P.	32	3/7	.429	3/6	.500	0/0	.000	0/1	0	1	1	0	0	9	.281
MCCLATCHEY, R.	14	1/1	1.000	0/0	.000	0/2	.000	0/0	0	2	1	0	1	2	.143
FOSTER, L.	9	0/0	.000	0/0	.000	0/0	.000	0/3	0	2	1	0	0	0	.000
BROOKS, T.	9	2/5	.400	1/1	1.000	0/0	.000	0/0	0	1	0	1	0	5	.556
Totals	200	19/51	.373	7/18	.389	13/16	.813	5/12	10	13	12	5	1	58	.290

Team Rebounds: Kansas 2; Murray State 5. Disqualified: Kansas—Piper; Murray State—Sias. Technical fouls: None.

	1st Half	2nd Half	Final
Kansas	28	33	61
Murray State	23	35	58

Vanderbilt (80) Coach: C.M. Newton

	Min.	Total FG/FGA	Pct.	3-Pt. FG/FGA	Pct.	FT/FTA	Pct.	Reb. O/T	A	TO	PF	S	Blk	TP	PPM
KORNET, F.	40	2/7	.286	0/0	.000	0/1	.000	0/2	2	0	4	2	0	4	.100
REID, E.	37	5/11	.455	0/0	.000	2/2	1.000	2/4	1	0	0	0	0	12	.324
PERDUE, W.	36	6/11	.545	0/0	.000	3/5	.600	3/5	4	1	5	0	1	15	.417
BOOKER, B.	37	6/9	.667	3/6	.500	1/2	.500	2/5	1	2	1	0	0	16	.432
GOHEEN, B.	33	6/13	.462	2/3	.667	8/9	.889	0/5	3	1	2	2	0	22	.667
MAYES, C.	17	2/3	.667	2/2	1.000	0/0	.000	0/2	1	0	1	0	0	6	.353
GRANT, S.	4	0/1	.000	0/0	.000	0/0	.000	0/0	0	1	1	0	0	0	.000
WILCOX, D.	5	0/1	.000	0/1	.000	0/0	.000	0/1	1	0	0	1	0	0	.000
DRAUD, S.	16	1/3	.333	1/3	.333	2/2	1.000	0/0	4	1	0	0	0	5	.313
Totals	225	28/59	.475	8/15	.533	16/21	.762	7/24	17	6	14	5	1	80	.356

Pittsburgh (74) Coach: Paul Evans

	Min.	Total FG/FGA	Pct.	3-Pt. FG/FGA	Pct.	FT/FTA	Pct.	Reb. O/T	A	TO	PF	S	Blk	TP	PPM
GORE, D.	34	6/14	.429	1/2	.500	1/1	1.000	1/4	3	6	4	2	0	14	.412
LANE, J.	44	3/5	.600	0/1	.000	2/4	.500	7/20	5	6	3	1	0	8	.182
SMITH, C.	38	7/18	.389	0/1	.000	7/8	.875	4/10	1	2	5	0	1	21	.553
MILLER, S.	45	2/7	.286	1/4	.250	2/2	1.000	0/0	7	1	3	0	0	7	.156
PORTER, D.	26	6/10	.600	2/4	.500	0/0	.000	1/2	1	0	1	1	0	14	.538
MATTHEWS, J.	15	2/3	.667	2/3	.667	2/2	1.000	0/1	1	0	2	0	0	8	.533
MARTIN, B.	20	0/1	.000	0/0	.000	2/2	1.000	1/5	0	0	3	0	0	2	.100
BAILEY, N.	3	0/0	.000	0/0	.000	0/0	.000	0/0	0	0	0	0	0	0	.000
Totals	225	26/58	.448	6/15	.400	16/19	.842	14/42	18	15	21	4	1	74	.329

Team Rebounds: Vanderbilt 3; Pittsburgh 0. Disqualified: Vanderbilt—Perdue; Pittsburgh—Smith. Technical fouls: Pittsburgh—Smith.

	1st Half	2nd Half	1st OT	Final
Vanderbilt	34	35	11	80
Pittsburgh	34	35	5	74

SECOND ROUND EAST

Temple (74) Coach: John Chaney

	Min.	Total FG/FGA	Pct.	3-Pt. FG/FGA	Pct.	FT/FTA	Pct.	Reb. O/T	A	TO	PF	S	Blk	TP	PPM
VREESWYK, M.	40	6/13	.462	2/6	.333	7/7	1.000	3/8	0	6	2	3	0	21	.525
PERRY, T.	34	5/6	.833	0/0	.000	2/2	1.000	1/5	0	2	3	2	2	12	.353
RIVAS, R.	39	3/3	1.000	0/0	.000	7/8	.875	1/12	1	0	2	2	0	13	.333
MACON, M.	35	5/15	.333	1/2	.500	10/11	.909	3/4	1	4	2	0	0	21	.600
EVANS, H.	39	2/4	.500	0/2	.000	2/2	1.000	0/0	5	3	2	2	0	6	.154
CAUSWELL, D.	7	0/0	.000	0/0	.000	0/0	.000	0/1	0	0	0	0	0	0	.000
DOWDELL, J.	6	0/0	.000	0/0	.000	1/2	.500	0/3	0	1	0	0	0	1	.167
Totals	200	21/41	.512	3/10	.300	29/32	.906	8/33	7	16	11	9	2	74	.370

Georgetown (53) Coach: John Thompson

	Min.	Total FG/FGA	Pct.	3-Pt. FG/FGA	Pct.	FT/FTA	Pct.	Reb. O/T	A	TO	PF	S	Blk	TP	PPM
MCDONALD, P.	26	2/12	.167	0/0	.000	1/2	.500	7/9	0	1	2	0	0	5	.192
HIGHSMITH, R.	24	3/4	.750	0/0	.000	0/0	.000	3/5	0	1	3	0	0	6	.250
GILLERY, B.	1	0/0	.000	0/0	.000	0/0	.000	0/0	0	0	0	0	0	0	.000
SMITH, C.	30	5/14	.357	0/4	.000	3/3	1.000	0/1	2	1	4	1	0	13	.433
TILLMON, M.	28	5/11	.455	3/8	.375	0/2	.000	0/0	4	4	4	0	2	13	.464
JACKSON, J.	31	3/15	.200	2/7	.286	5/6	.833	1/3	0	3	3	3	1	13	.419
WINSTON, B.	3	0/0	.000	0/0	.000	0/0	.000	0/0	1	1	0	1	0	0	.000
BRYANT, D.	23	1/5	.200	0/0	.000	1/2	.500	3/5	0	4	3	0	0	3	.130
EDWARDS, J.	12	0/1	.000	0/0	.000	0/0	.000	2/4	0	0	2	0	0	0	.000
ALLEN, A.	2	0/0	.000	0/0	.000	0/0	.000	0/0	0	0	1	0	0	0	.000
TUCKER, A.	5	0/0	.000	0/0	.000	0/0	.000	0/0	0	0	0	0	0	0	.000
JEFFERSON, S.	12	0/0	.000	0/0	.000	0/0	.000	0/0	0	0	5	0	0	0	.000
LANG, T.	2	0/1	.000	0/0	.000	0/0	.000	0/0	0	0	0	0	0	0	.000
JONES, J.	1	0/0	.000	0/0	.000	0/0	.000	0/0	0	0	0	0	0	0	.000
Totals	200	19/63	.302	5/19	.263	10/15	.667	16/27	7	15	27	5	3	53	.265

Team Rebounds: Temple 4; Georgetown 5. Disqualified: Georgetown—Jefferson. Technical fouls: Temple—Bench, Vreeswyk.

	1st Half	2nd Half	Final
Temple	30	44	74
Georgetown	26	27	53

Georgia Tech (55) Coach: Bobby Cremins

	Min.	Total FG/FGA	Pct.	3-Pt. FG/FGA	Pct.	FT/FTA	Pct.	Reb. O/T	A	TO	PF	S	Blk	TP	PPM
SCOTT, D.	38	6/19	.316	3/13	.231	0/2	.000	2/8	3	1	5	1	2	15	.395
FERRELL, D.	37	2/10	.200	0/2	.000	5/7	.714	3/8	1	1	3	1	1	9	.243
HAMMONDS, T.	34	4/8	.500	0/0	.000	0/0	.000	2/5	0	4	4	0	1	8	.235
NEAL, C.	34	1/4	.250	1/3	.333	1/4	.250	0/2	8	2	3	1	0	4	.118
OLIVER, B.	34	5/13	.385	1/4	.250	4/4	1.000	2/5	1	1	4	0	0	15	.441
MUNLYN, J.	10	0/0	.000	0/0	.000	0/0	.000	0/1	0	1	0	0	1	0	.000
SHERROD, A.	13	1/3	.333	0/0	.000	2/2	1.000	2/3	0	1	3	0	0	4	.308
Totals	200	19/57	.333	5/22	.227	12/19	.632	11/32	13	11	22	3	5	55	.275

Richmond (59) Coach: Dick Tarrant

	Min.	Total FG/FGA	Pct.	3-Pt. FG/FGA	Pct.	FT/FTA	Pct.	Reb. O/T	A	TO	PF	S	Blk	TP	PPM
STAPLETON, S.	29	3/6	.500	0/0	.000	2/2	1.000	2/6	4	2	3	4	0	8	.276
WOOLFOLK, P.	36	11/21	.524	0/0	.000	5/12	.417	2/9	2	3	3	1	0	27	.750
KRATZER, S.	29	1/4	.250	0/0	.000	2/5	.400	3/12	0	0	4	1	0	4	.138
ATKINSON, K.	39	1/6	.167	0/2	.000	4/5	.800	0/0	2	2	3	0	0	6	.154
RICE, R.	40	2/7	.286	1/6	.167	0/0	.000	0/4	5	2	1	0	0	5	.125
ENGLISH, E.	10	0/1	.000	0/0	.000	0/0	.000	1/2	1	2	1	0	0	0	.000
WINECKI, M.	15	3/4	.750	0/0	.000	1/2	.500	0/4	1	0	3	0	0	7	.467
TAYLOR, B.	2	0/0	.000	0/0	.000	2/3	.667	0/1	0	0	0	0	0	2	1.000
Totals	200	21/49	.429	1/8	.125	16/29	.552	8/38	16	10	19	7	0	59	.295

Team Rebounds: Richmond 6; Georgia Tech 5. Disqualified: Georgia Tech—Scott. Technical fouls: None.

	1st Half	2nd Half	Final
Georgia Tech	18	37	55
Richmond	29	30	59

Rhode Island (97) Coach: Tom Penders

	Min.	Total FG/FGA	Pct.	3-Pt. FG/FGA	Pct.	FT/FTA	Pct.	Reb. O/T	A	TO	PF	S	Blk	TP	PPM
SINA, M.	33	2/4	.500	1/1	1.000	1/2	.500	2/5	2	0	4	1	0	6	.182
EVANS, J.	34	4/7	.571	0/0	.000	6/8	.750	3/4	2	0	2	1	0	14	.412
COLSON, B.	23	4/6	.667	0/0	.000	0/0	.000	2/3	0	2	4	0	0	8	.348
GARRICK, T.	39	10/14	.714	2/3	.667	6/9	.667	2/4	6	1	2	2	0	28	.718
OWENS, C.	40	5/14	.357	4/6	.667	4/5	.800	1/2	7	0	1	0	0	18	.450
GREEN, K.	30	8/15	.533	0/0	.000	7/12	.583	5/6	1	1	3	1	2	23	.767
TABISZ, D.	1	0/0	.000	0/0	.000	0/0	.000	0/1	0	0	0	0	0	0	.000
Totals	200	33/60	.550	7/10	.700	24/36	.667	15/25	18	4	16	5	2	97	.485

Syracuse (94) Coach: Jim Boeheim

	Min.	Total FG/FGA	Pct.	3-Pt. FG/FGA	Pct.	FT/FTA	Pct.	Reb. O/T	A	TO	PF	S	Blk	TP	PPM
THOMPSON, S.	31	7/10	.700	0/0	.000	4/6	.667	3/5	3	1	5	0	0	18	.581
COLEMAN, D.	29	7/8	.875	0/0	.000	2/2	1.000	3/9	2	2	5	0	2	16	.552
SEIKALY, R.	34	12/17	.706	0/0	.000	3/4	.750	2/10	1	2	4	0	2	27	.794
ROE, M.	25	3/6	.500	3/5	.600	0/0	.000	0/2	2	0	2	0	0	9	.360
DOUGLAS, S.	38	4/11	.364	0/2	.000	0/1	.000	0/0	12	3	3	1	0	8	.211
BROWER, D.	14	2/4	.500	0/0	.000	2/4	.500	3/5	0	0	4	0	0	6	.429
DUNCAN, E.	26	4/10	.400	2/6	.333	0/0	.000	1/3	3	2	3	0	0	10	.385
HARRIED, H.	3	0/0	.000	0/0	.000	0/0	.000	1/2	1	0	0	0	0	0	.000
Totals	200	39/66	.591	5/13	.385	11/17	.647	13/36	24	10	26	1	4	94	.470

Team Rebounds: Rhode Island 2; Syracuse 1. Disqualified: Syracuse—Coleman, Thompson. Technical fouls: None.

	1st Half	2nd Half	Final
Rhode Island	56	41	97
Syracuse	49	45	94

SMU (79) Coach: Dave Bliss

	Min.	Total FG/FGA	Pct.	3-Pt. FG/FGA	Pct.	FT/FTA	Pct.	Reb. O/T	A	TO	PF	S	Blk	TP	PPM
THOMAS, T.	31	2/5	.400	0/0	.000	5/9	.556	2/4	1	2	4	3	0	9	.290
MCKINNEY, C.	28	8/10	.800	0/2	.500	0/0	.000	0/4	1	5	5	1	0	17	.607
PUDDY, G.	21	3/5	.600	0/0	.000	0/0	.000	2/11	2	2	4	0	0	6	.286
ARMSTRONG, K.	35	6/22	.273	1/4	.250	3/3	1.000	0/2	6	4	1	0	0	16	.457
LONGINO, E.	27	3/7	.429	0/1	.000	0/0	.000	1/3	2	1	1	0	0	6	.222
ALEXANDER, T.	31	5/10	.500	3/7	.429	4/4	1.000	0/1	2	0	4	0	0	17	.548
PERDUE, V.	23	2/2	1.000	0/0	.000	0/2	.000	3/3	0	1	1	1	0	4	.174
GREEN, J.	2	1/2	.500	0/0	.000	0/0	.000	0/0	0	1	0	1	0	2	1.000
LUCAS, M.	1	0/0	.000	0/0	.000	0/0	.000	0/0	0	0	0	0	0	0	.000
MUHAMMAD, R.	1	1/1	1.000	0/0	.000	0/0	.000	1/1	0	0	1	0	0	2	2.000
Totals	200	31/64	.484	5/14	.357	12/18	.667	9/29	14	16	21	6	0	79	.395

Duke (94) Coach: Mike Krzyzewski

	Min.	Total FG/FGA	Pct.	3-Pt. FG/FGA	Pct.	FT/FTA	Pct.	Reb. O/T	A	TO	PF	S	Blk	TP	PPM
FERRY, D.	32	5/14	.357	0/3	.000	2/3	.667	1/9	3	3	2	0	1	12	.375
KING, B.	31	4/4	1.000	0/0	.000	4/4	1.000	1/6	4	1	3	4	1	12	.387
BRICKEY, R.	27	6/8	.750	0/0	.000	5/7	.714	3/6	1	2	3	1	0	17	.630
SNYDER, Q.	34	0/2	.000	0/2	.000	1/2	.500	0/3	12	2	1	1	0	1	.029
STRICKLAND, K.	31	11/18	.611	2/8	.250	7/7	1.000	2/4	1	1	2	1	0	31	1.000
KOUBEK, G.	2	0/0	.000	0/0	.000	2/2	1.000	0/1	0	1	0	0	0	2	1.000
ABDELNABY, A.	14	6/6	1.000	0/0	.000	1/2	.500	1/4	0	1	2	0	0	13	.929
SMITH, J.	8	0/4	.000	0/0	.000	0/0	.000	0/1	2	2	0	0	0	0	.000
HENDERSON, P.	17	3/6	.333	1/2	.500	1/2	.500	0/1	0	0	2	1	0	6	.353
COOK, J.	2	0/0	.000	0/0	.000	0/0	.000	0/0	2	0	0	0	0	0	.000
BUCKLEY, C.	2	0/0	.000	0/0	.000	0/0	.000	0/0	0	0	0	0	0	0	.000
Totals	200	34/62	.548	3/15	.200	23/29	.793	8/35	21	13	17	8	2	94	.470

Team Rebounds: Duke 2; SMU 2. Disqualified: SMU—McKinney. Technical fouls: None.

	1st Half	2nd Half	Final
SMU	35	44	79
Duke	52	42	94

SECOND ROUND WEST

Arizona (84)   Coach: Lute Olson

	Min.	Total FG/FGA	Pct.	3–Pt. FG/FGA	Pct.	FT/FTA	Pct.	Reb. O/T	A	TO	PF	S	Blk	TP	PPM
COOK, A.	33	6/9	.667	0/0	.000	8/11	.727	4/6	0	1	0	0	0	20	.606
ELLIOTT, S.	34	7/14	.500	2/3	.667	3/3	1.000	0/5	3	1	1	0	0	19	.559
TOLBERT, T.	30	5/12	.417	0/0	.000	3/3	1.000	4/5	0	3	2	0	0	13	.433
MCMILLAN, C.	21	1/3	.333	0/1	.000	0/1	.000	0/3	3	2	1	2	1	2	.095
KERR, S.	38	3/9	.333	1/4	.250	6/7	.857	0/4	3	1	1	3	1	13	.342
TURNER, J.	9	2/3	.667	0/0	.000	0/0	.000	1/1	0	0	0	0	0	4	.444
MASON, H.	17	1/2	.500	0/0	.000	1/2	.500	1/2	1	1	2	0	1	3	.176
BUECHLER, J.	12	2/2	1.000	0/0	.000	0/0	.000	1/1	3	0	0	0	0	4	.333
LOFTON, K.	2	2/2	1.000	0/0	.000	0/1	.000	0/1	0	0	0	1	0	4	2.000
MUEHLEBACH, M.	2	0/1	.000	0/0	.000	0/0	.000	0/1	1	0	0	0	0	0	.000
BERGMAN, C.	2	1/1	1.000	0/0	.000	0/0	.000	1/1	0	0	0	0	0	2	1.000
Totals	200	30/58	.517	3/8	.375	21/28	.750	12/30	14	9	7	6	3	84	.420

Seton Hall (55)   Coach: P. J. Carlesimo

	Min.	Total FG/FGA	Pct.	3–Pt. FG/FGA	Pct.	FT/FTA	Pct.	Reb. O/T	A	TO	PF	S	Blk	TP	PPM
SALLEY, M.	25	6/7	.857	0/0	.000	0/1	.000	5/5	0	1	4	0	0	12	.480
BRYANT, M.	26	4/11	.364	0/0	.000	3/3	1.000	0/7	0	3	4	0	0	11	.423
RAMOS, R.	29	0/2	.000	0/0	.000	0/0	.000	0/7	0	0	1	1	2	0	.000
MORTON, J.	30	7/14	.500	0/2	.000	2/2	1.000	0/0	2	6	2	1	1	16	.533
GREENE, G.	21	1/3	.333	0/1	.000	0/0	.000	0/1	2	0	1	0	0	2	.095
MAJOR, J.	17	3/10	.300	1/6	.167	0/0	.000	0/2	0	1	0	0	0	7	.412
COOPER, M.	18	1/1	1.000	0/0	.000	0/0	.000	1/1	1	1	3	1	0	2	.111
WIGINGTON, P.	6	0/0	.000	0/0	.000	0/0	.000	0/0	2	3	2	0	0	0	.000
KATSIKIS, N.	11	0/2	.000	0/2	.000	0/0	.000	0/0	0	1	1	0	0	0	.000
VOLCY, C.	6	1/2	.500	0/0	.000	1/1	1.000	1/1	0	0	0	0	0	3	.500
LONG, K.	1	0/1	.000	0/0	.000	0/0	.000	0/0	0	0	0	0	0	0	.000
REBIMBAS, J.	1	0/0	.000	0/0	.000	0/0	.000	0/0	0	0	1	0	0	0	.000
WALKER, D.	9	1/1	1.000	0/0	.000	0/0	.000	0/0	0	2	2	0	0	2	.222
Totals	200	24/54	.444	1/11	.091	6/7	.857	7/24	7	18	21	3	3	55	.275

Team Rebounds: Arizona 3; Seton Hall 1. Disqualified: None. Technical fouls: Seton Hall—Bryant.

	1st Half	2nd Half	Final
Arizona	45	39	84
Seton Hall	25	30	55

Iowa (104)   Coach: Tom Davis

	Min.	Total FG/FGA	Pct.	3–Pt. FG/FGA	Pct.	FT/FTA	Pct.	Reb. O/T	A	TO	PF	S	Blk	TP	PPM
JONES, B.	28	5/10	.500	0/0	.000	2/2	1.000	-/6	2	2	2	3	0	12	.429
MARBLE, R.	30	7/12	.583	0/0	.000	8/10	.800	-/5	3	1	0	3	0	22	.733
HORTON, E.	32	10/16	.625	0/0	.000	4/11	.364	-/9	0	2	3	0	2	24	.750
MOE, J.	25	7/10	.700	3/6	.500	7/9	.778	-/1	5	1	1	1	0	24	.960
ARMSTRONG, B.	33	2/7	.286	0/3	.000	5/6	.833	-/2	7	3	2	2	0	9	.273
REAVES, M.	20	0/1	.000	0/1	.000	2/4	.500	-/5	2	4	1	1	0	2	.100
HILL, K.	15	3/	.000	0/0	.000	2/2	1.000	-/3	0	2	3	1	0	8	.533
MORGAN, M.	10	1/3	.333	0/0	.000	1/2	.500	-/1	0	1	0	0	0	3	.300
JEPSEN, L.	2	0/0	.000	0/0	.000	0/0	.000	-/0	0	0	0	0	1	0	.000
JEWELL, M.	3	0/0	.000	0/0	.000	0/0	.000	-/0	0	0	1	0	0	0	.000
WESTEN, K.	2	0/0	.000	0/0	.000	0/0	.000	-/0	0	0	0	0	0	0	.000
Totals	200	35/62	.565	3/10	.300	31/46	.674	-/32	19	16	13	11	3	104	.520

UNLV (86)   Coach: Jerry Tarkanian

	Min.	Total FG/FGA	Pct.	3–Pt. FG/FGA	Pct.	FT/FTA	Pct.	Reb. O/T	A	TO	PF	S	Blk	TP	PPM
BASNIGHT, J.	15	1/1	1.000	0/0	.000	0/0	.000	-/6	0	4	5	0	0	2	.133
PADDIO, G.	38	12/26	.462	8/19	.421	2/2	1.000	-/6	2	0	3	1	0	34	.895
TODD, A.	14	0/1	.000	0/0	.000	0/0	.000	-/3	0	3	2	0	0	0	.000
AUGMON, S.	37	5/6	.833	0/0	.000	0/1	.000	-/10	4	5	4	2	0	10	.270
JAMES, K.	31	8/19	.421	1/5	.200	4/4	1.000	-/2	4	6	4	2	0	21	.677
ROBINSON, R.	24	2/4	.500	0/0	.000	0/0	.000	-/4	0	2	5	0	1	4	.167
ROSSUM, C.	24	4/10	.400	1/3	.333	2/2	1.000	-/2	1	0	2	0	0	11	.458
CVIJANOVICH, S.	14	2/4	.500	0/2	.000	0/1	.000	-/1	0	1	3	1	0	4	.286
WILLARD, D.	3	0/6	.000	0/0	.000	0/0	.000	-/3	0	0	0	0	0	0	.000
Totals	200	34/77	.507	10/29	.345	8/10	.800	-/37	11	21	28	6	1	86	.430

Team Rebounds: Iowa 2; UNLV 4. Disqualified: UNLV—Basnight, Robinson. Technical fouls: None.

	1st Half	2nd Half	Final
Iowa	51	53	104
UNLV	39	47	86

Florida (85)   Coach: Norm Sloan

	Min.	Total FG/FGA	Pct.	3–Pt. FG/FGA	Pct.	FT/FTA	Pct.	Reb. O/T	A	TO	PF	S	Blk	TP	PPM
LAWRENCE, P.	20	2/3	.667	0/0	.000	0/1	.000	0/0	2	0	0	0	0	4	.200
CHATMAN, L.	34	3/10	.300	0/1	.000	1/2	.500	0/3	2	3	2	1	0	7	.206
SCHINTZIUS, D.	36	8/18	.444	0/1	.000	1/2	.500	4/9	2	1	3	0	1	17	.472
MAXWELL, V.	38	8/16	.500	3/6	.500	4/7	.571	0/0	10	1	2	0	0	23	.605
LETT, C.	20	3/6	.500	0/2	.000	5/8	.625	2/2	1	1	3	1	1	11	.550
JENKINS, W.	5	0/1	.000	0/0	.000	0/1	.000	0/1	0	1	1	0	0	0	.000
DAVIS, D.	26	8/10	.800	0/0	.000	5/8	.625	2/7	1	0	2	0	2	21	.808
GURLEY, B.	1	0/1	.000	0/0	.000	0/0	.000	0/0	0	0	0	0	0	0	.000
MONTGOMERY, R.	20	1/2	.500	0/1	.000	0/1	.000	1/4	6	3	3	0	0	2	.100
Totals	200	33/67	.493	3/11	.273	16/29	.552	9/25	25	9	15	4	4	85	.425

Michigan (108)   Coach: Bill Freider

	Min.	Total FG/FGA	Pct.	3–Pt. FG/FGA	Pct.	FT/FTA	Pct.	Reb. O/T	A	TO	PF	S	Blk	TP	PPM
RICE, G.	36	16/24	.667	3/3	1.000	4/4	1.000	1/5	5	0	3	2	1	39	1.083
MILLS, T.	29	7/11	.636	0/0	.000	2/2	1.000	2/9	2	0	1	0	1	16	.552
VAUGHT, L.	28	9/11	.818	0/0	.000	4/4	1.000	5/15	1	2	3	0	0	22	.786
ROBINSON, R.	24	3/4	.750	0/0	.000	2/4	.500	0/1	7	3	5	2	0	8	.333
GRANT, G.	34	7/11	.636	2/3	.667	3/5	.600	0/3	11	3	3	1	0	19	.559
GRIFFIN, M.	19	0/1	.000	0/0	.000	0/0	.000	2/4	2	2	3	0	0	0	.000
TAYLOR, K.	3	0/1	.000	0/0	.000	0/0	.000	1/2	1	0	1	0	0	0	.000
STOYKO, S.	3	0/0	.000	0/0	.000	0/0	.000	0/0	0	0	0	0	0	0	.000
OOSTERBAAN, J.	6	0/0	.000	0/0	.000	0/0	.000	0/1	1	0	2	0	0	0	.000
HUGHES, M.	18	2/5	.400	0/0	.000	0/0	.000	0/1	0	1	3	0	0	4	.222
Totals	200	44/68	.647	5/6	.833	15/19	.789	11/41	30	11	24	5	2	108	.540

Team Rebounds: Michigan 1; Florida 1. Disqualified: Michigan—Robinson. Technical fouls: None.

	1st Half	2nd Half	Final
Florida	35	50	85
Michigan	54	54	108

Loyola Marymount (97)   Coach: Paul Westhead

	Min.	Total FG/FGA	Pct.	3-Pt. FG/FGA	Pct.	FT/FTA	Pct.	Reb. O/T	A	TO	PF	S	Blk	TP	PPM
ARMSTRONG, M.	30	3/7	.429	0/0	.000	1/2	.500	1/3	1	1	5	0	0	7	.233
YOEST, M.	32	2/10	.200	0/1	.000	6/10	.600	8/12	2	0	4	3	0	10	.313
GATHERS, H.	28	7/17	.412	0/0	.000	3/10	.300	9/12	0	3	4	1	0	17	.607
GAINES, C.	32	5/20	.250	1/5	.200	5/6	.833	1/1	10	1	3	2	0	16	.500
KIMBLE, B.	32	3/21	.143	1/9	.111	1/2	.500	3/3	1	0	4	1	0	8	.250
LEE, M.	0	0/0	.000	0/0	.000	0/0	.000	0/0	0	0	0	0	0	0	-
FRYER, J.	18	9/16	.563	7/14	.500	2/2	1.000	2/2	1	1	4	1	0	27	1.500
MEYER, P.	1	0/0	.000	0/0	.000	0/0	.000	0/0	0	0	0	0	0	0	.000
ROSCOE, J.	0	0/0	.000	0/0	.000	0/0	.000	0/0	0	0	0	0	0	0	-
SIMMONS, E.	21	4/11	.364	4/9	.444	0/0	.000	2/4	2	0	3	0	12	.571
VEARGASON, J.	5	0/0	.000	0/0	.000	0/0	.000	1/2	0	0	0	1	0	.000
SLATER, M.	1	0/1	.000	0/1	.000	0/0	.000	0/0	0	0	0	0	0	0	.000
Totals	200	33/103	.320	13/39	.333	18/32	.563	27/39	17	6	24	11	1	97	.485

North Carolina (123)   Coach: Dean Smith

	Min.	Total FG/FGA	Pct.	3-Pt. FG/FGA	Pct.	FT/FTA	Pct.	Reb. O/T	A	TO	PF	S	Blk	TP	PPM
BUCKNALL, S.	20	5/7	.714	0/0	.000	3/5	.600	0/5	3	0	3	0	0	13	.650
REID, J.	30	8/10	.800	0/0	.000	3/6	.500	4/15	5	6	3	1	1	19	.633
WILLIAMS, S.	25	3/3	1.000	0/0	.000	2/2	1.000	1/8	3	2	5	0	1	8	.320
LEBO, J.	33	6/9	.667	3/4	.750	4/4	1.000	1/5	7	5	3	0	0	19	.576
MADDEN, K.	27	7/9	.778	0/0	.000	2/2	1.000	0/4	9	1	1	0	1	16	.593
DENNY, J.	2	0/0	.000	0/0	.000	0/0	.000	1/1	0	0	1	0	0	0	.000
HYATT, R.	1	1/1	1.000	0/0	.000	0/0	.000	0/0	0	0	0	0	0	2	2.000
RICE, K.	7	1/1	1.000	0/0	.000	2/2	1.000	0/1	2	4	2	0	0	4	.571
ELSTUN, D.	1	0/0	.000	0/0	.000	0/0	.000	0/0	0	0	0	0	0	0	.000
MAY, D.	1	0/0	.000	0/0	.000	0/0	.000	0/0	0	0	0	0	0	0	.000
CHILCUTT, P.	13	2/2	1.000	0/0	.000	1/3	.333	0/6	2	1	0	0	1	5	.385
SMITH, R.	18	11/14	.786	3/5	.600	2/3	.667	1/4	0	2	1	0	0	27	1.500
JENKINS, J.	3	1/2	.500	0/0	.000	0/0	.000	0/1	1	2	0	0	0	2	.667
FOX, R.	19	4/4	1.000	0/0	.000	0/0	.000	0/4	4	3	4	0	0	8	.421
Totals	200	49/62	.790	6/9	.667	19/27	.704	8/54	36	26	23	1	4	123	.615

Team Rebounds: N. Carolina 2; Loyola Mymt. 2. Disqualified: N. Carolina—Williams; Loyola Mymt.—Armstrong. Technical fouls: N. Carolina—Madden, Reid. Players who played 0 min. played less than 1 min. each.

	1st Half	2nd Half	Final
Loyola Mymt.	40	57	97
N. Carolina	65	58	123

SECOND ROUND SOUTHWEST

Oklahoma (107)   Coach: Billy Tubbs

	Min.	Total FG/FGA	Pct.	3-Pt. FG/FGA	Pct.	FT/FTA	Pct.	Reb. O/T	A	TO	PF	S	Blk	TP	PPM
GRANT, H.	19	4/10	.400	0/0	.000	0/1	.000	1/2	1	2	4	1	1	8	.421
SIEGER, D.	28	5/9	.556	5/9	.556	0/0	.000	0/1	6	0	4	4	0	15	.536
KING, S.	40	14/22	.636	0/0	.000	9/12	.750	2/9	3	3	2	1	2	37	.925
BLAYLOCK, M.	39	8/14	.571	2/4	.500	3/3	1.000	1/4	9	1	1	4	0	21	.538
GRACE, R.	37	5/9	.556	1/3	.333	4/4	1.000	1/6	8	2	3	2	0	15	.405
POLLARD, A.	1	0/0	.000	0/0	.000	0/0	.000	0/0	0	1	0	0	0	0	.000
BELL, M.	2	0/0	.000	0/0	.000	0/0	.000	0/1	0	1	0	0	1	0	.000
MULLINS, T.	12	4/6	.667	1/1	1.000	0/1	.000	2/4	2	0	2	1	0	9	.750
WILEY, A.	9	0/0	.000	0/0	.000	0/2	.000	0/1	1	2	5	1	0	0	.000
MARTIN, A.	13	1/6	.167	0/0	.000	0/0	.000	1/3	1	1	2	2	0	2	.154
Totals	200	41/76	.539	9/17	.529	16/23	.696	8/31	31	13	23	16	4	107	.535

Auburn (87)   Coach: Sonny Smith

	Min.	Total FG/FGA	Pct.	3-Pt. FG/FGA	Pct.	FT/FTA	Pct.	Reb. O/T	A	TO	PF	S	Blk	TP	PPM
CAYLOR, J.	25	6/12	.500	2/5	.400	0/0	.000	5/9	2	4	5	0	0	14	.560
MORRIS, C.	23	6/13	.462	1/4	.250	4/4	1.000	4/5	2	3	5	0	3	17	.739
MOORE, J.	34	5/18	.278	0/0	.000	12/13	.923	5/11	2	1	4	1	1	22	.647
HOWARD, T.	34	3/13	.231	1/6	.167	0/0	.000	2/4	8	8	2	1	0	7	.206
DENNISON, D.	23	3/9	.333	1/1	1.000	0/1	.000	3/7	0	5	2	1	0	7	.304
LYNN, J.	23	4/5	.800	3/4	.750	3/3	1.000	1/3	3	4	2	1	0	14	.609
GEIGER, M.	15	0/1	.000	0/0	.000	2/2	1.000	0/3	1	0	3	1	0	2	.133
CARPENTER, K.	20	2/10	.200	0/4	.000	0/0	.000	1/2	0	0	1	0	0	4	.200
MCBEE, P.	1	0/0	.000	0/0	.000	0/0	.000	0/0	0	0	0	0	0	0	.000
WALKER, J.	1	0/3	.000	0/0	.000	0/0	.000	1/1	0	0	0	0	0	0	.000
HESTER, D.	1	0/0	.000	0/0	.000	0/0	.000	0/0	0	0	0	0	0	0	.000
Totals	200	29/84	.345	8/24	.333	21/23	.913	22/45	18	25	24	5	4	87	.435

Team Rebounds: Oklahoma 8; Auburn 12. Disqualified: Oklahoma—Wiley; Auburn—Caylor, Morris. Technical fouls: None.

	1st Half	2nd Half	Final
Oklahoma	51	56	107
Auburn	37	50	87

Louisville (97)   Coach: Denny Crum

	Min.	Total FG/FGA	Pct.	3-Pt. FG/FGA	Pct.	FT/FTA	Pct.	Reb. O/T	A	TO	PF	S	Blk	TP	PPM
PAYNE, K.	32	6/11	.545	4/5	.800	0/0	.000	3/6	0	0	3	0	0	16	.500
CROOK, H.	34	6/14	.429	0/0	.000	0/0	.000	1/5	7	0	3	1	0	12	.353
ELLISON, P.	30	10/15	.667	0/0	.000	4/7	.571	3/8	3	0	2	1	3	24	.800
WILLIAMS, K.	35	2/4	.500	0/0	.000	7/8	.875	0/4	12	2	0	2	0	11	.314
SMITH, L.	31	4/11	.364	0/3	.000	4/4	1.000	0/4	2	4	3	2	2	12	.387
ABRAM, M.	20	3/6	.500	0/0	.000	0/0	.000	1/3	0	2	1	0	6	.300
SPENCER, F.	13	6/10	.600	0/0	.000	4/5	.800	3/6	0	0	3	0	1	16	1.231
HAWLEY, C.	1	0/0	.000	0/0	.000	0/0	.000	0/0	0	0	0	0	0	0	.000
FRALEY, S.	1	0/1	.000	0/1	.000	0/0	.000	0/0	0	0	0	0	0	0	.000
OLLIGES, W.	1	0/0	.000	0/0	.000	0/0	.000	0/0	0	0	1	0	0	0	.000
ROBINSON, D.	1	0/0	.000	0/0	.000	0/0	.000	1/1	0	1	0	0	0	0	.000
HUGHES, M.	1	0/1	.000	0/0	.000	0/0	.000	1/1	0	0	1	0	0	0	.000
Totals	200	37/73	.507	4/9	.444	19/24	.792	13/34	29	6	17	7	4	97	.485

Brigham Young (76)   Coach: Ladell Anderson

	Min.	Total FG/FGA	Pct.	3-Pt. FG/FGA	Pct.	FT/FTA	Pct.	Reb. O/T	A	TO	PF	S	Blk	TP	PPM
SMITH	31	8/20	.400	4/9	.444	1/2	.500	0/11	4	3	4	0	0	21	.677
CHATMAN	33	7/11	.636	0/0	.000	5/6	.833	2/5	3	2	3	0	2	19	.576
USEVITCH	33	2/4	.500	0/0	.000	9/10	.900	3/6	1	0	4	0	0	13	.394
HAWS, M.	30	2/5	.400	1/2	.500	0/0	.000	0/3	5	5	4	0	0	5	.167
TOOLSON	27	3/7	.429	3/5	.600	0/0	.000	1/4	1	1	4	0	0	9	.333
TAYLOR	27	2/4	.500	0/1	.000	0/0	.000	1/2	2	4	3	0	0	4	.148
CALL	10	0/0	.000	0/1	.000	0/0	.000	0/2	2	1	1	0	0	0	.000
ASTLE	1	0/0	.000	0/0	.000	0/0	.000	0/0	0	1	0	1	0	0	.000
HERRING	1	0/0	.000	0/0	.000	0/0	.000	0/0	0	0	1	0	0	0	.000
BRYAN	1	0/0	.000	0/0	.000	2/2	1.000	1/1	0	0	0	0	0	2	2.000
TROST	5	1/2	.500	0/1	.000	1/2	.500	0/1	0	0	0	0	0	3	.600
WOLFE	1	0/0	.000	0/0	.000	0/0	.000	0/2	0	0	0	0	0	0	.000
Totals	200	25/54	.463	8/18	.444	18/22	.818	8/33	19	16	24	1	2	76	.380

Team Rebounds: Louisville 2; BYU 3. Disqualified: None. Technical fouls: None.

	1st Half	2nd Half	Final
Louisville	51	46	97
Brigham Young	42	34	76

Villanova (66)   Coach: Rollie Massimino

	Min.	Total FG/FGA	Pct.	3-Pt. FG/FGA	Pct.	FT/FTA	Pct.	Reb. O/T	A	TO	PF	S	Blk	TP	PPM
PLANSKY, M.	37	4/10	.400	3/7	.429	5/7	.714	0/3	7	3	2	1	0	16	.432
TAYLOR, R.	30	3/4	.750	0/0	.000	4/4	1.000	1/8	1	4	3	1	0	10	.333
GREIS, T.	34	5/8	.625	0/0	.000	6/6	1.000	2/13	0	3	5	0	2	16	.471
WILSON, K.	36	3/11	.273	3/6	.500	0/0	.000	0/2	3	2	2	0	0	9	.250
WEST, D.	31	2/8	.250	0/1	.000	3/6	.500	1/3	1	3	2	1	0	7	.226
MASSEY, G.	23	2/2	1.000	0/0	.000	1/4	.250	2/3	0	2	5	1	0	5	.217
ENRIGHT, P.	6	1/2	.500	1/1	1.000	0/0	.000	0/0	0	0	2	0	0	3	.500
BEKKEDAM, B.	3	0/0	.000	0/0	.000	0/0	.000	0/1	0	0	2	0	0	0	.000
Totals	200	20/45	.444	7/15	.467	19/27	.704	6/33	12	17	23	4	2	66	.330

Illinois (63)   Coach: Lou Henson

	Min.	Total FG/FGA	Pct.	3-Pt. FG/FGA	Pct.	FT/FTA	Pct.	Reb. O/T	A	TO	PF	S	Blk	TP	PPM
ANDERSON, N.	31	6/19	.316	0/0	.000	1/2	.500	5/6	0	0	4	0	0	13	.419
BATTLE, K.	32	6/9	.667	0/0	.000	3/7	.429	2/6	1	3	5	0	1	15	.469
KAJAWA, J.	36	2/7	.286	0/0	.000	1/3	.333	3/12	3	3	2	0	0	5	.139
BLACKWELL, G.	21	1/2	.500	0/0	.000	1/2	.500	0/1	0	1	3	2	0	3	.143
BARDO, S.	36	5/7	.714	0/0	.000	3/6	.500	0/2	1	2	4	1	0	13	.361
GILL, K.	25	4/7	.571	1/2	.500	1/1	1.000	0/1	3	1	2	2	1	10	.400
HAMILTON, L.	18	2/5	.400	0/0	.000	0/2	.000	2/5	0	2	2	0	0	4	.222
SMITH, L.	1	0/0	.000	0/0	.000	0/0	.000	0/0	0	0	0	0	0	0	.000
Totals	200	26/56	.464	1/2	.500	10/23	.435	12/33	8	12	22	5	2	63	.315

Maryland (81)   Coach: Bob Wade

	Min.	Total FG/FGA	Pct.	3-Pt. FG/FGA	Pct.	FT/FTA	Pct.	Reb. O/T	A	TO	PF	S	Blk	TP	PPM
MASSENBURG, T.	18	2/4	.500	0/0	.000	0/0	.000	2/6	0	1	2	0	1	4	.222
LEWIS, D.	34	4/10	.400	0/1	.000	2/2	1.000	0/6	3	2	4	0	1	10	.294
WILLIAMS, B.	34	8/11	.727	0/0	.000	4/6	.667	1/4	0	3	2	1	1	20	.588
GATLIN, K.	40	6/12	.500	4/8	.500	2/2	1.000	0/1	7	0	4	1	0	18	.450
ARCHER, R.	31	5/13	.385	2/7	.286	2/2	1.000	0/0	2	3	4	0	0	14	.452
DICKERSON, D.	10	1/1	1.000	0/0	.000	0/0	.000	0/0	1	0	2	0	0	2	.200
WALKER, R.	2	0/0	.000	0/0	.000	0/0	.000	0/1	0	0	0	0	0	0	.000
HOOD, S.	9	0/4	.000	0/0	.000	2/2	1.000	0/2	0	0	2	0	0	2	.222
MCCOY, T.	22	3/5	.600	3/5	.600	0/0	.000	1/2	2	0	3	0	0	11	.500
Totals	200	29/60	.483	9/23	.391	14/16	.875	4/20	15	9	23	2	3	81	.405

Kentucky (90)   Coach: Eddie Sutton

	Min.	Total FG/FGA	Pct.	3-Pt. FG/FGA	Pct.	FT/FTA	Pct.	Reb. O/T	A	TO	PF	S	Blk	TP	PPM
BENNETT, W.	35	7/9	.778	0/0	.000	3/4	.750	1/12	0	1	3	1	0	17	.486
MANUEL, E.	40	4/7	.571	1/2	.500	4/4	1.000	1/4	5	2	1	0	0	13	.325
LOCK, R.	24	5/7	.714	0/0	.000	0/0	.000	3/4	0	2	3	0	0	10	.417
CHAPMAN, R.	40	9/18	.500	3/7	.429	2/7	.286	0/1	1	2	0	1	0	23	.575
DAVENDER, E.	40	9/16	.556	0/0	.000	13/14	.929	3/8	5	3	2	2	0	23	.575
ELLIS, L.	15	2/6	.333	0/0	.000	0/0	.000	2/4	0	0	3	1	3	4	.267
MADISON, R.	5	0/0	.000	0/0	.000	0/0	.000	0/0	0	0	1	0	0	0	.000
JENKINS, C.	1	0/0	.000	0/0	.000	0/0	.000	0/0	0	0	0	0	0	0	.000
Totals	200	32/56	.571	4/9	.444	22/29	.759	10/33	11	10	13	5	3	90	.450

Team Rebounds: Villanova 2; Illinois 0. Disqualified: Villanova—Greis, Massey; Illinois—Battle. Technical fouls: None.

Team Rebounds: Kentucky 1; Maryland 3. Disqualified: None. Technical fouls: None.

	1st Half	2nd Half	Final
Villanova	20	46	66
Illinois	30	33	63

	1st Half	2nd Half	Final
Maryland	41	40	81
Kentucky	42	48	90

REGIONAL SEMIFINAL MIDWEST

Purdue (70)   Coach: Gene Keady

	Min.	Total FG/FGA	Pct.	3-Pt. FG/FGA	Pct.	FT/FTA	Pct.	Reb. O/T	A	TO	PF	S	Blk	TP	PPM
JONES, K.	21	0/0	.000	0/0	.000	0/0	.000	3/6	1	0	1	0	0	0	.000
MITCHELL, T.	30	6/15	.400	0/1	.000	1/4	.250	5/9	0	1	4	1	1	13	.433
MCCANTS, M.	33	5/12	.417	0/0	.000	3/4	.750	0/2	0	3	3	0	2	13	.394
STEPHENS, E.	35	7/11	.636	5/7	.714	1/1	1.000	0/5	9	6	2	0	2	20	.571
LEWIS, T.	38	5/11	.455	4/8	.500	5/6	.833	1/5	2	2	2	1	0	19	.500
BERNING, R.	3	1/1	1.000	0/0	.000	0/0	.000	0/0	0	0	0	0	0	2	.667
JONES, T.	30	1/3	.333	0/0	.000	0/0	.000	1/4	6	0	4	2	0	2	.067
SCHEFFLER, S.	10	0/0	.000	0/0	.000	1/2	.500	0/1	0	0	2	0	0	1	.100
Totals	200	25/53	.472	9/16	.563	11/17	.647	10/32	18	12	18	4	5	70	.350

Kansas (77)   Coach: Larry Brown

	Min.	Total FG/FGA	Pct.	3-Pt. FG/FGA	Pct.	FT/FTA	Pct.	Reb. O/T	A	TO	PF	S	Blk	TP	PPM
PIPER, C.	33	3/5	.600	0/0	.000	2/2	1.000	2/10	2	2	2	1	0	8	.242
GUELDNER, J.	22	1/2	.500	0/0	.000	0/0	.000	0/2	7	1	2	1	0	2	.091
MANNING, D.	29	16/29	.552	2/3	.667	4/7	.571	2/5	1	5	2	1	1	38	1.310
PRITCHARD, K.	33	5/6	.833	1/1	1.000	0/2	.000	0/1	5	2	3	1	1	11	.333
NEWTON, M.	23	2/7	.286	0/0	.000	0/0	.000	1/7	1	1	2	0	1	4	.174
BARRY, R.	26	2/4	.500	0/1	.000	4/6	.667	0/3	3	0	0	0	0	8	.308
MADDOX, M.	7	0/0	.000	0/0	.000	4/4	1.000	0/0	1	1	2	0	0	4	.571
HARRIS, K.	22	0/3	.000	0/0	.000	0/0	.000	4/6	1	0	0	1	0	0	.000
NORMORE, C.	3	0/0	.000	0/0	.000	0/0	.000	0/1	0	0	0	0	0	0	.000
MINOR, L.	1	0/0	.000	0/0	.000	0/0	.000	0/0	0	0	1	0	0	0	.000
MATTOX, M.	1	1/1	1.000	0/0	.000	0/0	.000	0/0	0	0	0	1	0	2	2.000
Totals	200	30/57	.526	3/5	.600	14/21	.667	9/35	21	12	14	6	3	77	.385

Kansas State (73)   Coach: Lon Kruger

	Min.	Total FG/FGA	Pct.	3-Pt. FG/FGA	Pct.	FT/FTA	Pct.	Reb. O/T	A	TO	PF	S	Blk	TP	PPM
RICHMOND, M.	40	10/20	.500	2/4	.500	5/8	.625	3/11	3	2	2	0	0	27	.675
BLEDSOE, C.	17	2/6	.333	0/0	.000	1/3	.333	3/4	0	2	3	2	1	5	.294
MEYER, R.	27	2/8	.250	0/0	.000	1/2	.500	2/2	3	1	3	0	2	5	.185
HENSON, S.	39	1/3	.333	1/1	1.000	2/2	1.000	0/1	12	1	4	2	0	5	.128
SCOTT, W.	33	6/11	.545	5/5	1.000	0/0	.000	1/3	0	0	3	0	0	17	.515
GLOVER, B.	8	1/1	1.000	0/0	.000	0/0	.000	0/0	0	0	2	0	0	2	.250
DOBBINS, M.	23	2/4	.500	0/0	.000	0/0	.000	1/3	0	0	1	0	0	4	.174
MCCOY, F.	13	4/8	.500	0/0	.000	0/1	.000	3/6	0	1	2	0	0	8	.615
Totals	200	28/61	.459	8/10	.800	9/16	.563	13/30	18	7	20	4	3	73	.365

Vanderbilt (64)   Coach: C.M. Newton

	Min.	Total FG/FGA	Pct.	3-Pt. FG/FGA	Pct.	FT/FTA	Pct.	Reb. O/T	A	TO	PF	S	Blk	TP	PPM
KORNET, F.	29	2/5	.400	0/0	.000	0/0	.000	3/7	4	5	2	2	0	4	.138
REID, E.	23	1/5	.200	0/0	.000	0/0	.000	3/5	1	0	0	0	2	2	.087
PERDUE, W.	36	7/13	.538	0/0	.000	2/3	.667	1/8	1	1	5	0	2	16	.444
BOOKER, B.	33	8/16	.500	6/13	.462	0/0	.000	0/3	3	2	1	0	1	22	.667
GOHEEN, B.	31	1/7	.143	0/2	.000	1/2	.500	0/4	4	2	3	1	0	3	.097
MAYES, C.	9	0/1	.000	0/1	.000	0/0	.000	0/2	0	0	0	0	0	0	.000
GRANT, S.	14	1/2	.500	0/0	.000	2/2	1.000	0/0	0	1	1	0	0	4	.286
WILCOX, D.	11	3/4	.750	1/1	1.000	0/0	.000	1/2	0	3	2	2	0	7	.636
DRAUD, S.	13	1/3	.333	1/3	.333	1/2	.500	0/0	2	1	4	1	0	4	.308
BENJAMIN, F.	1	1/1	1.000	0/0	.000	0/0	.000	0/1	0	0	0	0	0	2	2.000
Totals	200	25/57	.439	8/20	.400	6/9	.667	8/26	17	15	18	6	3	64	.320

Team Rebounds: Kansas State 3; Purdue 3. Disqualified: None. Technical fouls: None.

Team Rebounds: Kansas 1; Vanderbilt 0. Disqualified: Vanderbilt—Perdue. Technical fouls: Vanderbilt—Bench.

	1st Half	2nd Half	Final
Purdue	43	27	70
Kansas State	34	39	73

	1st Half	2nd Half	Final
Kansas	41	36	77
Vanderbilt	29	35	64

REGIONAL SEMIFINAL EAST

Temple (69)   Coach: John Chaney

	Min.	Total FG/FGA	Pct.	3-Pt. FG/FGA	Pct.	FT/FTA	Pct.	Reb. O/T	A	TO	PF	S	Blk	TP	PPM
VREESWYK, M.	40	6/13	.462	5/9	.556	2/2	1.000	1/4	2	1	2	1	0	19	.475
PERRY, T.	40	5/7	.714	0/0	.000	1/3	.333	5/13	1	0	1	1	4	11	.275
RIVAS, R.	9	1/1	1.000	0/0	.000	0/0	.000	1/1	0	1	4	0	0	2	.222
MACON, M.	40	11/23	.478	0/6	.000	2/4	.500	1/2	3	2	1	2	0	24	.600
EVANS, H.	40	4/6	.667	3/5	.600	0/0	.000	0/1	11	1	1	0	0	11	.275
CAUSWELL, D.	16	0/1	.000	0/0	.000	0/0	.000	0/2	0	0	3	0	0	0	.000
BRANTLEY	14	1/3	.333	0/0	.000	0/0	.000	2/4	0	0	1	2	0	2	.143
JOHNSON	1	0/0	.000	0/0	.000	0/0	.000	0/0	0	0	0	0	0	0	.000
Totals	200	28/54	.519	8/20	.400	5/9	.556	10/27	17	5	13	6	4	69	.345

Richmond (47)   Coach: Dick Tarrant

	Min.	Total FG/FGA	Pct.	3-Pt. FG/FGA	Pct.	FT/FTA	Pct.	Reb. O/T	A	TO	PF	S	Blk	TP	PPM
STAPLETON, S.	30	1/4	.250	0/0	.000	0/0	.000	2/5	6	4	0	0	0	2	.067
WOOLFOLK, P.	38	6/13	.462	0/0	.000	0/1	.000	6/10	0	2	1	0	0	12	.316
KRATZER, S.	33	1/3	.333	0/0	.000	2/6	.333	3/4	0	2	3	1	0	4	.121
ATKINSON, K.	38	5/9	.556	5/7	.714	0/1	.000	1/3	2	2	0	0	0	15	.395
RICE, A.	38	4/14	.286	3/12	.250	0/0	.000	0/4	1	0	4	0	0	11	.289
ENGLISH, E.	5	0/0	.000	0/0	.000	0/0	.000	0/0	2	1	0	0	0	0	.000
WINECKI, M.	9	1/1	1.000	0/0	.000	1/2	.500	0/1	1	0	3	0	0	3	.333
TAYLOR, B.	8	0/3	.000	0/3	.000	0/0	.000	0/0	1	2	0	0	0	0	.000
FLOYD, S.	1	0/1	.000	0/1	.000	0/0	.000	0/0	0	0	0	0	0	0	.000
Totals	200	18/48	.375	8/23	.348	3/10	.300	12/27	13	13	11	1	0	47	.235

Team Rebounds: Temple 3; Richmond 6. Disqualified: None. Technical fouls: None.

	1st Half	2nd Half	Final
Temple	32	37	69
Richmond	26	21	47

Rhode Island (72)   Coach: Tom Penders

	Min.	Total FG/FGA	Pct.	3-Pt. FG/FGA	Pct.	FT/FTA	Pct.	Reb. O/T	A	TO	PF	S	Blk	TP	PPM
SINA, M.	38	6/8	.750	0/0	.000	2/3	.667	-/8	4	1	1	0	0	14	.368
EVANS, J.	38	4/9	.444	0/0	.000	6/8	.750	-/7	3	1	1	6	0	14	.368
COLSON, B.	15	0/0	.000	0/0	.000	0/0	.000	-/1	2	0	0	1	4	0	.000
GARRICK, T.	39	7/19	.368	0/0	.000	0/0	.000	-/2	4	3	2	0	0	14	.359
OWENS, C.	39	5/13	.385	1/2	.500	8/8	1.000	-/3	4	5	4	1	0	19	.487
GREEN, K.	29	3/9	.333	0/0	.000	5/8	.625	-/8	3	1	0	2	2	11	.379
LANE	1	0/0	.000	0/0	.000	0/0	.000	-/1	0	1	0	0	0	0	.000
OPPENHEIMER	1	0/1	.000	0/1	.000	0/0	.000	-/0	0	0	0	0	0	0	.000
Totals	200	25/59	.424	1/3	.333	21/27	.778	-/30	20	12	8	10	6	72	.360

Duke (73)   Coach: Mike Krzyzewski

	Min.	Total FG/FGA	Pct.	3-Pt. FG/FGA	Pct.	FT/FTA	Pct.	Reb. O/T	A	TO	PF	S	Blk	TP	PPM
FERRY, D.	34	8/15	.533	0/0	.000	1/2	.500	-/12	4	3	3	1	1	17	.500
KING, B.	34	1/7	.143	0/0	.000	1/2	.500	-/5	4	3	2	1	0	3	.088
BRICKEY, R.	21	4/6	.667	0/0	.000	7/9	.778	-/7	4	4	0	2	1	15	.714
SNYDER, Q.	33	2/4	.500	0/0	.000	0/1	.000	-/5	6	2	3	2	3	4	.121
STRICKLAND, K.	30	5/10	.500	1/4	.250	3/5	.600	-/3	4	2	1	0	1	14	.467
KOUBEK, G.	8	2/5	.400	0/1	.000	0/0	.000	-/1	1	1	0	0	0	4	.500
ABDELNABY, A.	7	0/2	.000	0/0	.000	2/2	1.000	-/1	2	1	0	0	0	2	.286
SMITH, J.	14	6/8	.750	0/0	.000	0/0	.000	-/4	0	0	1	0	0	12	.857
HENDERSON, P.	19	1/7	.143	0/2	.000	0/1	.000	-/2	1	1	0	2	0	2	.105
Totals	200	29/64	.453	1/7	.143	14/24	.583	-/40	26	17	10	8	6	73	.365

Team Rebounds: Duke 7; Rhode Island 3. Disqualified: None. Technical fouls: None.

	1st Half	2nd Half	Final
Rhode Island	37	35	72
Duke	38	35	73

REGIONAL SEMIFINAL WEST

Arizona (99)   Coach: Lute Olson

	Min.	Total FG/FGA	Pct.	3-Pt. FG/FGA	Pct.	FT/FTA	Pct.	Reb. O/T	A	TO	PF	S	Blk	TP	PPM
COOK, A.	31	8/12	.667	0/0	.000	3/3	1.000	1/6	0	1	2	0	1	19	.613
ELLIOTT, S.	39	11/18	.611	1/5	.200	2/2	1.000	2/3	8	4	3	2	0	25	.641
TOLBERT, T.	36	7/13	.538	0/0	.000	3/4	.750	4/9	1	4	2	3	0	17	.472
McMILLAN, C.	22	2/6	.333	2/5	.400	2/2	1.000	0/2	4	0	3	1	0	8	.364
KERR, S.	39	5/11	.455	5/10	.500	2/3	.667	1/4	8	0	2	1	0	17	.436
TURNER, J.	7	0/0	.000	0/0	.000	1/2	.500	1/1	0	0	3	0	0	1	.143
MASON, H.	8	2/3	.667	2/2	1.000	0/1	.000	1/1	0	1	0	0	0	6	.750
BUECHLER, J.	5	0/0	.000	0/0	.000	0/0	.000	0/1	0	2	0	2	0	0	.000
LOFTON, K.	11	2/3	.667	1/2	.500	1/2	.500	0/0	1	1	1	3	0	6	.545
MUEHLEBACH, M.	1	0/0	.000	0/0	.000	0/0	.000	0/0	0	0	0	0	0	0	.000
BERGMAN, C.	1	0/0	.000	0/0	.000	0/0	.000	0/0	0	0	0	0	0	0	.000
Totals	200	37/66	.561	11/24	.458	14/19	.737	10/27	22	13	16	12	1	99	.495

Iowa (79)   Coach: Tom Davis

	Min.	Total FG/FGA	Pct.	3-Pt. FG/FGA	Pct.	FT/FTA	Pct.	Reb. O/T	A	TO	PF	S	Blk	TP	PPM
JONES, B.	31	4/6	.667	0/1	.000	4/6	.667	3/6	3	0	3	1	0	12	.387
MARBLE, R.	36	6/15	.400	0/1	.000	2/3	.667	5/5	2	1	3	1	0	14	.389
HORTON, E.	22	2/5	.400	0/0	.000	0/0	.000	1/3	0	2	5	1	0	4	.182
MOE, J.	26	4/9	.444	3/8	.375	0/0	.000	0/1	1	4	3	1	0	11	.423
ARMSTRONG, B.	34	11/21	.524	3/7	.429	2/3	.667	0/1	7	5	1	3	0	27	.794
REAVES, M.	20	1/6	.167	0/3	.000	0/0	.000	2/3	1	2	1	1	0	2	.100
HILL, K.	23	4/5	.800	0/0	.000	1/2	.500	3/7	0	3	5	0	0	9	.391
MORGAN, M.	4	0/0	.000	0/0	.000	0/0	.000	0/1	0	0	1	0	0	0	.000
JEPSEN, J.	2	0/0	.000	0/0	.000	0/0	.000	0/0	0	0	0	0	0	0	.000
JEWELL, M.	2	0/0	.000	0/0	.000	0/0	.000	0/2	0	0	1	0	0	0	.000
WESTEN, K.	-	-/-	-	-/-	-	-/-	-	-/-	-	-	-	-	-	-	-
Totals	200	32/67	.478	6/20	.300	9/14	.643	14/28	14	17	23	8	0	79	.395

Team Rebounds: Arizona 5; Iowa 2. Disqualified: Iowa—Horton, Hill. Technical fouls: None.

	1st Half	2nd Half	Final
Arizona	38	61	99
Iowa	34	45	79

Michigan (69)   Coach: Bill Freider

	Min.	Total FG/FGA	Pct.	3-Pt. FG/FGA	Pct.	FT/FTA	Pct.	Reb. O/T	A	TO	PF	S	Blk	TP	PPM
RICE, G.	39	7/16	.438	4/8	.500	0/0	.000	2/7	3	1	2	0	2	18	.462
MILLS, T.	30	6/12	.500	0/0	.000	0/0	.000	1/4	1	1	3	0	2	12	.400
VAUGHT, L.	26	1/3	.333	0/0	.000	0/0	.000	0/5	0	3	3	0	0	2	.077
ROBINSON, R.	39	10/14	.714	1/3	.333	8/11	.727	5/13	6	3	3	2	0	29	.744
GRANT, G.	29	3/10	.300	1/5	.200	0/0	.000	1/3	4	5	5	1	0	7	.241
HUGHES, M.	17	0/0	.000	0/0	.000	1/2	.500	1/2	1	0	5	0	0	1	.059
OOSTERBAAN, J.	1	0/0	.000	0/0	.000	0/0	.000	0/1	0	0	0	0	0	0	.000
GRIFFIN, M.	19	0/0	.000	0/0	.000	0/0	.000	0/3	0	0	3	0	0	0	.000
Totals	200	27/55	.491	6/16	.375	9/13	.692	7/30	15	13	24	3	4	69	.345

North Carolina (78)   Coach: Dean Smith

	Min.	Total FG/FGA	Pct.	3-Pt. FG/FGA	Pct.	FT/FTA	Pct.	Reb. O/T	A	TO	PF	S	Blk	TP	PPM
REID, J.	32	7/14	.500	0/0	.000	4/7	.571	3/8	1	2	3	1	0	18	.563
BUCKNALL, S.	31	2/6	.333	1/2	.500	2/2	1.000	0/2	1	0	2	1	0	7	.226
WILLIAMS, S.	28	5/9	.556	0/0	.000	9/13	.692	1/7	1	5	3	0	2	19	.679
LEBO, J.	33	2/5	.400	1/3	.333	4/4	1.000	1/2	2	2	1	1	0	9	.273
MADDEN, K.	18	2/4	.500	0/1	.000	2/2	1.000	3/6	3	0	1	1	0	6	.333
SMITH, R.	20	3/6	.500	2/5	.400	0/1	.000	0/3	3	0	0	1	0	8	.400
FOX, R.	12	3/5	.600	1/3	.333	0/0	.000	0/1	3	0	2	0	0	7	.583
RICE, K.	15	1/2	.500	0/1	.000	0/0	.000	0/0	1	0	1	0	0	2	.133
CHILCUTT, P.	11	1/1	1.000	0/0	.000	0/0	.000	0/0	1	0	1	0	0	2	.182
Totals	200	26/52	.500	5/15	.333	21/30	.700	8/27	17	11	14	6	2	78	.390

Team Rebounds: N. Carolina 4; Michigan 1. Disqualified: Michigan—Grant, Hughes. Technical fouls: None.

	1st Half	2nd Half	Final
Michigan	30	39	69
N. Carolina	31	47	78

REGIONAL SEMIFINAL SOUTHWEST

Oklahoma (108)   Coach: Billy Tubbs

	Min.	Total FG/FGA	Pct.	3-Pt. FG/FGA	Pct.	FT/FTA	Pct.	Reb. O/T	A	TO	PF	S	Blk	TP	PPM
GRANT, H.	38	14/21	.667	0/0	.000	6/10	.600	2/7	1	4	3	4	0	34	.895
SIEGER, D.	35	4/7	.571	3/5	.600	0/0	.000	1/2	7	0	3	3	0	11	.314
KING, S.	36	9/20	.450	0/0	.000	6/13	.462	4/12	1	4	4	1	2	24	.667
BLAYLOCK, M.	40	7/13	.538	3/5	.600	1/3	.333	4/6	7	4	2	2	0	18	.450
GRACE, R.	40	3/11	.273	3/8	.375	6/8	.750	1/3	8	4	2	3	0	15	.375
MULLINS, T.	5	1/1	1.000	1/1	1.000	0/0	.000	0/0	0	0	1	0	0	3	.600
WILEY, A.	6	1/1	1.000	0/0	.000	1/2	.500	2/2	1	0	1	0	0	3	.500
Totals	200	39/74	.527	10/19	.526	20/36	.556	14/32	25	16	16	13	2	108	.540

Louisville (98)   Coach: Denny Crum

	Min.	Total FG/FGA	Pct.	3-Pt. FG/FGA	Pct.	FT/FTA	Pct.	Reb. O/T	A	TO	PF	S	Blk	TP	PPM
PAYNE, K.	31	6/12	.500	4/8	.500	2/2	1.000	1/5	2	1	2	1	0	18	.581
CROOK, H.	27	7/10	.700	0/0	.000	2/2	1.000	1/2	2	7	3	3	0	16	.593
ELLISON, P.	38	11/16	.688	0/1	.000	1/1	1.000	6/14	2	4	3	0	4	23	.605
WILLIAMS, K.	32	4/10	.400	0/0	.000	2/3	.667	2/2	2	4	4	2	0	10	.313
SMITH, L.	22	3/8	.375	1/2	.500	3/3	1.000	0/0	5	2	5	1	0	10	.455
ABRAM, M.	22	2/3	.667	0/0	.000	0/0	.000	0/2	2	2	4	1	0	4	.182
SPENCER, F.	24	6/9	.667	0/0	.000	3/5	.600	3/7	1	1	4	0	0	15	.625
HAWLEY, C.	4	1/1	1.000	0/0	.000	0/0	.000	0/0	0	1	0	0	0	2	.500
Totals	200	40/69	.580	5/11	.455	13/16	.813	13/32	16	22	25	8	4	98	.490

Team Rebounds: Oklahoma 6; Louisville 6. Disqualified: Louisville—Smith. Technical fouls: None.

	1st Half	2nd Half	Final
Oklahoma	55	53	108
Louisville	51	47	98

Villanova (80)   Coach: Rollie Massimino

	Min.	Total FG/FGA	Pct.	3-Pt. FG/FGA	Pct.	FT/FTA	Pct.	Reb. O/T	A	TO	PF	S	Blk	TP	PPM
PLANSKY, M.	40	5/12	.417	2/5	.400	4/4	1.000	2/8	3	2	2	0	0	16	.400
TAYLOR, R.	29	3/5	.600	0/0	.000	5/5	1.000	3/8	1	2	3	0	0	11	.379
GREIS, T.	22	5/5	1.000	0/0	.000	0/0	.000	1/3	3	1	5	0	0	10	.455
WILSON, K.	40	4/10	.400	1/3	.333	6/6	1.000	1/2	6	1	0	0	0	15	.375
WEST, D.	38	9/16	.563	2/5	.400	0/0	.000	2/3	1	1	2	0	0	20	.526
MASSEY, G.	30	3/3	1.000	0/0	.000	2/2	1.000	0/2	0	2	2	3	0	8	.267
ENRIGHT, P.	1	0/0	.000	0/0	.000	0/0	.000	0/0	0	0	0	0	0	0	.000
Totals	200	29/51	.569	5/13	.385	17/17	1.000	9/26	14	9	14	3	0	80	.400

Kentucky (74)   Coach: Eddie Sutton

	Min.	Total FG/FGA	Pct.	3-Pt. FG/FGA	Pct.	FT/FTA	Pct.	Reb. O/T	A	TO	PF	S	Blk	TP	PPM
BENNETT, W.	22	6/9	.667	0/0	.000	4/4	1.000	5/7	0	0	4	0	0	16	.727
MANUEL, E.	38	3/10	.300	3/5	.600	0/0	.000	5/8	6	5	0	1	0	9	.237
LOCK, R.	22	5/6	.833	0/0	.000	1/4	.250	3/3	0	2	4	1	0	11	.500
CHAPMAN, R.	39	11/19	.579	5/9	.556	3/3	1.000	0/1	5	1	3	2	0	30	.769
DAVENDER, E.	40	2/12	.167	0/2	.000	2/2	1.000	0/2	3	1	3	0	0	6	.150
ELLIS, L.	28	0/2	.000	0/0	.000	2/4	.500	4/7	1	1	2	0	2	2	.071
MADISON, R.	11	0/1	.000	0/0	.000	0/0	.000	0/1	0	1	1	0	0	0	.000
Totals	200	27/59	.458	8/16	.500	12/17	.706	17/29	15	11	17	4	0	74	.370

Team Rebounds: Villanova 2; Kentucky 1. Disqualified: Villanova—Greis. Technical fouls: None.

	1st Half	2nd Half	Final
Villanova	43	37	80
Kentucky	32	42	74

REGIONAL FINAL MIDWEST

Kansas State (58)   Coach: Lon Kruger

	Min.	Total FG/FGA	Pct.	3-Pt. FG/FGA	Pct.	FT/FTA	Pct.	Reb. O/T	A	TO	PF	S	Blk	TP	PPM
RICHMOND, M.	37	4/14	.286	1/5	.200	2/4	.500	2/4	5	6	3	0	0	11	.297
BLEDSOE, C.	33	5/6	.833	0/0	.000	0/4	.000	4/9	1	4	4	0	1	10	.303
MEYER, R.	26	1/3	.333	0/0	.000	0/0	.000	1/2	2	0	0	1	0	2	.077
HENSON, S.	40	2/8	.250	2/6	.333	0/0	.000	1/3	5	2	4	1	1	6	.150
SCOTT, W.	30	6/15	.400	4/10	.400	2/2	1.000	0/0	1	0	0	2	1	18	.600
GLOVER, B.	9	1/3	.333	0/1	.000	0/0	.000	0/1	1	0	0	0	0	2	.222
DIGGINS, C.	3	0/0	.000	0/0	.000	0/0	.000	0/0	0	0	1	0	0	0	.000
DOBBINS, M.	3	0/0	.000	0/0	.000	0/0	.000	0/1	0	0	0	0	0	0	.000
MCCOY, E.	18	3/5	.600	0/0	.000	3/4	.750	3/5	0	0	2	0	0	9	.500
STANFIELD, T.	1	0/0	.000	0/0	.000	0/0	.000	0/1	0	0	0	0	0	0	.000
Totals	200	22/54	.407	7/22	.318	7/14	.500	11/26	15	12	14	4	3	58	.290

Kansas (71)   Coach: Larry Brown

	Min.	Total FG/FGA	Pct.	3-Pt. FG/FGA	Pct.	FT/FTA	Pct.	Reb. O/T	A	TO	PF	S	Blk	TP	PPM
PIPER, C.	36	3/6	.500	0/1	.000	0/2	.000	2/4	1	1	2	0	0	6	.167
GUELDNER, J.	11	0/3	.000	0/1	.000	0/0	.000	0/0	2	1	1	0	0	0	.000
MANNING, D.	39	10/18	.556	0/1	.000	0/1	.000	2/6	1	0	3	0	1	20	.513
PRITCHARD, K.	38	2/7	.286	1/4	.250	3/4	.750	0/3	7	2	3	2	0	8	.211
NEWTON, M.	29	7/10	.700	2/3	.667	2/2	1.000	4/9	7	2	3	1	0	18	.621
BARRY, R.	25	5/6	.833	1/1	1.000	4/4	1.000	0/5	3	3	1	1	0	15	.600
MADDOX, M.	1	0/0	.000	0/0	.000	0/0	.000	0/0	0	0	0	0	0	0	.000
HARRIS, K.	15	2/3	.667	0/0	.000	0/0	.000	0/1	0	0	2	0	4	.267
NORMORE, C.	1	0/0	.000	0/0	.000	0/0	.000	0/0	0	0	0	0	0	0	.000
MINOR, L.	4	0/1	.000	0/0	.000	0/0	.000	0/0	1	1	0	0	0	0	.000
MATTOX, M.	1	0/0	.000	0/0	.000	0/1	.000	0/0	0	0	0	0	0	0	.000
Totals	200	29/54	.537	4/11	.364	9/14	.643	8/28	22	10	13	6	1	71	.355

Team Rebounds: Kansas 4; Kansas State 3. Disqualified: None. Technical fouls: None.

	1st Half	2nd Half	Final
Kansas State	29	29	58
Kansas	27	44	71

REGIONAL FINAL EAST

Temple (53) Coach: John Chaney

	Min.	Total FG/FGA	Pct.	3-Pt. FG/FGA	Pct.	FT/FTA	Pct.	Reb. O/T	A	TO	PF	S	Blk	TP	PPM
VREESWYK, M.	39	2/12	.167	1/6	.167	1/1	1.000	2/7	0	1	3	0	0	6	.154
PERRY, T.	34	6/9	.667	0/0	.000	1/1	1.000	5/7	0	1	4	1	6	13	.382
RIVAS, R.	32	0/2	.000	0/0	.000	4/4	1.000	5/6	0	3	4	0	0	4	.125
MACON, M.	40	6/29	.207	1/8	.125	0/0	.000	0/7	2	0	2	0	0	13	.325
EVANS, H.	40	2/8	.250	1/3	.333	7/8	.875	2/6	3	4	4	1	0	12	.300
DOWDELL, J.	2	1/1	1.000	1/1	1.000	0/0	.000	0/0	0	0	0	0	0	3	1.500
BRANTLEY, D.	4	1/1	1.000	0/0	.000	0/0	.000	1/1	0	1	2	0	0	2	.500
CAUSWELL, D.	9	0/1	.000	0/0	.000	0/0	.000	1/2	0	0	3	0	0	0	.000
Totals	200	18/63	.286	4/18	.222	13/14	.929	16/36	5	10	22	2	6	53	.265

Duke (63) Coach: Mike Krzyzewski

	Min.	Total FG/FGA	Pct.	3-Pt. FG/FGA	Pct.	FT/FTA	Pct.	Reb. O/T	A	TO	PF	S	Blk	TP	PPM
FERRY, D.	38	7/11	.636	0/3	.000	6/8	.750	2/5	4	2	2	0	1	20	.526
KING, B.	37	2/3	.667	0/0	.000	0/2	.000	1/3	4	3	3	0	2	4	.108
BRICKEY, R.	30	0/8	.000	0/0	.000	3/5	.600	3/5	0	2	2	1	2	3	.100
SNYDER, Q.	36	1/5	.200	1/4	.250	6/7	.857	0/8	3	1	3	1	2	9	.250
STRICKLAND, K.	36	9/17	.529	3/8	.375	0/1	.000	2/5	0	1	0	2	4	21	.583
KOUBEK, G.	4	1/4	.250	0/1	.000	0/0	.000	0/0	0	0	0	0	0	2	.500
ABDELNABY, A.	12	1/2	.500	0/0	.000	0/2	.000	2/3	0	0	3	1	0	2	.167
HENDERSON, P.	7	1/2	.500	0/0	.000	0/0	.000	0/1	0	0	0	0	0	2	.286
Totals	200	22/52	.423	4/17	.235	15/23	.652	10/30	11	9	13	5	11	63	.315

Team Rebounds: Duke 10; Temple 6. Disqualified: None. Technical fouls: Duke—Bench.

	1st Half	2nd Half	Final
Temple	28	25	53
Duke	25	38	63

REGIONAL FINAL WEST

Arizona (70) Coach: Lute Olson

	Min.	Total FG/FGA	Pct.	3-Pt. FG/FGA	Pct.	FT/FTA	Pct.	Reb. O/T	A	TO	PF	S	Blk	TP	PPM
COOK, A.	29	0/2	.000	0/0	.000	2/2	1.000	1/4	0	1	4	0	0	2	.069
ELLIOTT, S.	38	6/11	.545	1/3	.333	11/14	.786	0/5	3	3	3	0	0	24	.632
TOLBERT, T.	34	8/14	.571	0/0	.000	5/6	.833	1/6	0	2	3	0	0	21	.618
MCMILLAN, C.	30	4/6	.667	1/3	.333	0/0	.000	0/3	1	2	1	2	0	9	.300
KERR, S.	39	3/4	.750	3/4	.750	5/6	.833	0/3	3	1	2	1	0	14	.359
TURNER, J.	13	0/0	.000	0/0	.000	0/0	.000	0/2	0	1	2	0	1	0	.000
MASON, H.	4	0/2	.000	0/1	.000	0/0	.000	0/1	0	1	0	0	0	0	.000
BUECHLER, J.	4	0/0	.000	0/0	.000	0/0	.000	0/1	1	0	0	0	0	0	.000
LOFTON, K.	8	0/0	.000	0/0	.000	0/0	.000	0/0	1	0	1	0	0	0	.000
MUEHLEBACH, M.	1	0/0	.000	0/0	.000	0/0	.000	0/0	0	0	0	0	0	0	.000
Totals	200	21/39	.538	5/11	.455	23/28	.821	2/24	10	10	16	4	1	70	.350

North Carolina (52) Coach: Dean Smith

	Min.	Total FG/FGA	Pct.	3-Pt. FG/FGA	Pct.	FT/FTA	Pct.	Reb. O/T	A	TO	PF	S	Blk	TP	PPM
BUCKNALL, S.	21	1/1	1.000	0/0	.000	0/0	.000	0/0	2	1	4	0	0	2	.095
REID, J.	31	4/10	.400	0/0	.000	2/2	1.000	2/9	2	2	4	1	0	10	.323
WILLIAMS, S.	30	5/7	.714	0/1	.000	3/4	.750	2/6	0	1	4	0	1	13	.433
LEBO, J.	34	3/9	.333	3/8	.375	0/0	.000	0/0	4	4	3	0	0	9	.265
MADDEN, K.	17	1/9	.111	0/0	.000	0/0	.000	0/2	1	2	2	0	0	2	.118
DENNY, J.	1	0/0	.000	0/0	.000	0/0	.000	0/0	0	0	0	0	0	0	.000
HYATT, R.	1	0/2	.000	0/0	.000	0/0	.000	1/1	0	0	0	0	0	0	.000
RICE, K.	10	0/1	.000	0/0	.000	0/0	.000	1/2	0	2	0	0	0	0	.000
ELSTUN, D.	1	0/0	.000	0/0	.000	0/0	.000	0/0	1	0	0	0	0	0	.000
MAY, D.	1	0/0	.000	0/0	.000	0/0	.000	0/0	0	0	0	0	0	0	.000
CHILCUTT, P.	11	0/1	.000	0/0	.000	0/0	.000	0/1	3	0	0	0	0	0	.000
SMITH, R.	23	3/12	.250	3/10	.300	0/0	.000	1/3	0	1	1	2	0	9	.391
JENKINS, J.	1	0/0	.000	0/0	.000	0/0	.000	0/0	0	0	0	0	0	0	.000
FOX, R.	18	3/4	.750	0/0	.000	1/2	.500	1/1	0	1	2	1	0	7	.389
Totals	200	20/56	.357	6/19	.316	6/8	.750	8/25	12	12	22	4	1	52	.260

Team Rebounds: Arizona 4; N. Carolina 2. Disqualified: None. Technical fouls: None.

	1st Half	2nd Half	Final
Arizona	26	44	70
N. Carolina	28	24	52

REGIONAL FINAL SOUTHWEST

Oklahoma (78) Coach: Billy Tubbs

	Min.	Total FG/FGA	Pct.	3-Pt. FG/FGA	Pct.	FT/FTA	Pct.	Reb. O/T	A	TO	PF	S	Blk	TP	PPM
GRANT, H.	39	4/10	.400	0/0	.000	4/5	.800	2/9	2	1	2	0	0	12	.308
SIEGER, D.	33	3/9	.333	2/8	.250	0/2	.000	0/2	6	2	4	4	0	8	.242
KING, S.	36	12/20	.600	0/0	.000	4/7	.571	7/11	0	2	1	0	0	28	.778
BLAYLOCK, M.	39	5/12	.417	2/5	.400	2/2	1.000	3/5	3	1	3	4	3	14	.359
GRACE, R.	36	2/5	.400	1/4	.250	4/6	.667	0/4	5	1	4	2	0	9	.250
POLLARD, A.	1	0/0	.000	0/0	.000	0/0	.000	0/0	1	0	0	0	0	0	.000
BELL, M.	1	0/0	.000	0/0	.000	0/0	.000	0/0	0	0	0	0	1	0	.000
MULLINS, T.	8	0/2	.000	0/0	.000	0/0	.000	0/1	1	0	0	0	0	0	.000
WILEY, A.	1	2/3	.667	0/1	.000	0/0	.000	1/1	0	0	0	0	0	4	4.000
MARTIN, A.	4	0/0	.000	0/0	.000	0/0	.000	0/0	0	0	2	0	0	0	.000
SKURCENSKI, J.	1	0/1	.000	0/0	.000	2/2	1.000	1/1	0	0	1	0	0	2	2.000
JONES, T.	1	0/0	.000	0/0	.000	1/2	.500	0/0	0	0	0	0	0	1	1.000
Totals	200	28/62	.452	5/18	.278	17/26	.654	14/34	18	7	17	10	4	78	.390

Villanova (59) Coach: Rollie Massimino

	Min.	Total FG/FGA	Pct.	3-Pt. FG/FGA	Pct.	FT/FTA	Pct.	Reb. O/T	A	TO	PF	S	Blk	TP	PPM
PLANSKY, M.	38	3/11	.273	0/4	.000	0/0	.000	1/5	5	2	1	0	0	6	.158
TAYLOR, R.	30	1/5	.200	0/0	.000	0/0	.000	5/11	0	1	1	0	0	2	.067
GREIS, T.	26	4/5	.800	0/0	.000	0/0	.000	1/7	0	3	3	0	1	8	.308
WILSON, K.	38	5/14	.357	1/5	.200	4/5	.800	0/1	4	6	4	3	0	15	.395
WEST, D.	31	7/11	.636	1/2	.500	3/4	.750	1/4	1	1	4	0	0	18	.581
MASSEY, G.	24	3/4	.750	0/0	.000	0/1	.000	1/2	1	3	1	1	0	6	.250
ENRIGHT, P.	2	1/2	.500	0/2	.000	2/2	1.000	0/1	0	0	2	0	0	4	2.000
BEKKEDAM, B.	3	0/0	.000	0/0	.000	0/0	.000	0/0	0	2	0	0	0	0	.000
DOWNS, G.	2	0/0	.000	0/0	.000	0/0	.000	0/0	1	0	0	0	0	0	.000
TRIBUIANI, R.	2	0/0	.000	0/0	.000	0/0	.000	0/0	0	0	0	0	0	0	.000
MASOTTI, C.	2	0/0	.000	0/0	.000	0/0	.000	0/0	0	0	0	0	0	0	.000
MULLER, T.	2	0/2	.000	0/1	.000	0/0	.000	0/0	2	0	0	0	0	0	.000
Totals	200	24/54	.444	2/14	.143	9/12	.750	9/31	11	19	18	4	1	59	.295

Team Rebounds: Oklahoma 3; Villanova 3. Disqualified: None. Technical fouls: Villanova—Bench.

	1st Half	2nd Half	Final
Oklahoma	31	47	78
Villanova	38	21	59

FINAL FOUR

Kansas (66)   Coach: Larry Brown

	Min.	Total FG/FGA	Pct.	3-Pt. FG/FGA	Pct.	FT/FTA	Pct.	Reb. O/T	A	TO	PF	S	Blk	TP	PPM
PIPER, C.	29	3/ 4	.750	0/ 0	.000	4/ 4	1.000	0/ 6	3	2	2	1	1	10	.345
GUELDNER, J.	9	0/ 1	.000	0/ 0	.000	0/ 0	.000	0/ 1	1	2	2	0	0	0	.000
MANNING, D.	39	12/21	.571	0/ 0	.000	1/ 2	.500	4/10	2	7	3	4	6	25	.641
PRITCHARD, K.	36	2/ 6	.333	0/ 1	.000	2/ 2	1.000	1/ 7	5	2	2	2	1	6	.167
NEWTON, M.	32	8/14	.571	2/ 3	.667	2/ 3	.667	1/ 7	3	2	3	1	1	20	.625
BARRY, R.	27	1/ 2	.500	0/ 0	.000	3/ 4	.750	0/ 1	1	3	4	0	0	5	.185
MADDOX, M.	1	0/ 0	.000	0/ 0	.000	0/ 0	.000	0/ 0	0	0	0	0	0	0	.000
HARRIS, K.	15	0/ 4	.000	0/ 0	.000	0/ 0	.000	2/ 3	0	1	0	0	0	0	.000
NORMORE, C.	11	0/ 0	.000	0/ 0	.000	0/ 0	.000	0/ 1	1	1	2	0	1	0	.000
MINOR, L.	1	0/ 0	.000	0/ 0	.000	0/ 0	.000	0/ 0	0	0	0	0	0	0	.000
MATTOX, M.	0	0/ 0	.000	0/ 0	.000	0/ 0	.000	0/ 0	0	0	0	0	0	0	-
Totals	200	26/52	.500	2/ 4	.500	12/15	.800	8/36	16	21	16	9	9	66	.330

Duke (59)   Coach: Mike Krzyzewski

	Min.	Total FG/FGA	Pct.	3-Pt. FG/FGA	Pct.	FT/FTA	Pct.	Reb. O/T	A	TO	PF	S	Blk	TP	PPM
FERRY, D.	36	7/22	.318	1/ 5	.200	4/ 4	1.000	8/12	4	2	4	3	0	19	.528
KING, B.	26	1/ 4	.250	0/ 0	.000	1/ 2	.500	0/ 1	2	3	4	0	1	3	.115
BRICKEY, R.	27	2/ 9	.222	0/ 0	.000	2/ 5	.400	4/ 6	0	3	1	1	1	6	.222
SNYDER, Q.	28	4/10	.400	0/ 3	.000	1/ 2	.500	0/ 3	5	5	4	2	0	9	.321
STRICKLAND, K.	35	5/13	.385	0/ 3	.000	0/ 0	.000	3/ 6	1	0	2	1	2	10	.286
KOUBEK, G.	16	3/ 5	.600	2/ 3	.667	0/ 0	.000	1/ 4	0	1	2	0	0	8	.500
ABDELNABY, A.	12	1/ 2	.500	0/ 0	.000	2/ 4	.500	0/ 0	0	0	2	0	1	4	.333
SMITH, J.	4	0/ 0	.000	0/ 0	.000	0/ 0	.000	0/ 0	0	0	1	0	0	0	.000
HENDERSON, P.	16	0/ 2	.000	0/ 0	.000	0/ 0	.000	1/ 3	1	2	0	0	0	0	.000
COOK, J.	0	0/ 0	.000	0/ 0	.000	0/ 0	.000	0/ 0	0	0	0	0	0	0	-
Totals	200	23/67	.343	3/14	.214	10/17	.588	17/35	13	16	19	8	5	59	.295

Team Rebounds: Kansas 0; Duke 4; Disqualified: None. Technical fouls: None. Players who played 0 min. played less than 1 min. each.

	1st Half	2nd Half	Final
Kansas	38	28	66
Duke	27	32	59

Arizona (78)   Coach: Lute Olson

	Min.	Total FG/FGA	Pct.	3-Pt. FG/FGA	Pct.	FT/FTA	Pct.	Reb. O/T	A	TO	PF	S	Blk	TP	PPM
COOK, A.	37	6/13	.462	0/ 0	.000	4/ 6	.667	4/11	0	1	3	0	1	16	.432
ELLIOTT, S.	38	13/23	.565	2/ 4	.500	3/ 3	1.000	4/11	1	6	4	0	0	31	.816
TOLBERT, T.	32	5/11	.455	0/ 0	.000	1/ 2	.500	6/13	3	3	4	0	1	11	.344
MCMILLAN, C.	25	3/ 6	.500	2/ 4	.500	0/ 0	.000	0/ 0	3	0	5	0	0	8	.320
KERR, S.	40	2/13	.154	2/12	.167	0/ 0	.000	0/ 2	5	1	2	1	0	6	.150
TURNER, J.	7	0/ 0	.000	0/ 0	.000	0/ 0	.000	0/ 2	0	1	1	0	0	0	.000
MASON, H.	4	0/ 0	.000	0/ 0	.000	0/ 0	.000	0/ 0	0	0	1	0	0	0	.000
BUECHLER, J.	6	2/ 2	1.000	0/ 0	.000	0/ 0	.000	0/ 0	0	0	0	0	0	4	.667
LOFTON, K.	11	1/ 4	.250	0/ 3	.000	0/ 0	.000	1/ 2	0	3	4	1	0	2	.182
Totals	200	32/72	.444	6/23	.261	8/11	.727	15/41	12	15	24	2	2	78	.390

Oklahoma (86)   Coach: Billy Tubbs

	Min.	Total FG/FGA	Pct.	3-Pt. FG/FGA	Pct.	FT/FTA	Pct.	Reb. O/T	A	TO	PF	S	Blk	TP	PPM
GRANT, H.	36	7/14	.500	0/ 0	.000	7/10	.700	2/10	0	2	0	2	0	21	.583
SIEGER, D.	32	3/ 8	.375	1/ 6	.167	3/ 6	.500	1/ 6	3	0	3	1	0	10	.313
KING, S.	28	9/16	.563	0/ 0	.000	3/ 6	.500	3/ 6	0	3	4	1	1	21	.750
BLAYLOCK, M.	40	3/ 7	.429	0/ 0	.000	1/ 2	.500	5/ 7	6	3	1	2	0	7	.175
GRACE, R.	40	3/10	.300	2/ 7	.286	5/ 7	.714	0/ 0	8	1	3	2	0	13	.325
MULLINS, T.	7	1/ 1	1.000	1/ 1	1.000	0/ 0	.000	0/ 1	0	0	0	0	3	.429
WILEY, A.	17	4/ 8	.500	0/ 0	.000	3/ 3	1.000	2/ 4	0	1	2	0	1	11	.647
Totals	200	30/64	.469	4/14	.286	22/34	.647	13/34	18	10	13	8	2	86	.430

Team Rebounds: Oklahoma 5; Arizona 1. Disqualified: Arizona—McMillan. Technical fouls: None.

	1st Half	2nd Half	Final
Arizona	27	51	78
Oklahoma	39	47	86

NATIONAL CHAMPIONSHIP

Kansas (83)   Coach: Larry Brown

	Min.	Total FG/FGA	Pct.	3-Pt. FG/FGA	Pct.	FT/FTA	Pct.	Reb. O/T	A	TO	PF	S	Blk	TP	PPM
PIPER, C.	37	4/ 6	.667	0/ 0	.000	0/ 0	.000	1/ 7	2	5	3	3	0	8	.216
GUELDNER, J.	15	1/ 2	.500	0/ 1	.000	0/ 0	.000	0/ 2	1	0	0	1	0	2	.133
MANNING, D.	36	13/24	.542	0/ 1	.000	5/ 7	.714	7/18	2	4	3	5	2	31	.861
PRITCHARD, K.	31	6/ 7	.857	1/ 1	1.000	0/ 0	.000	0/ 1	4	5	1	1	0	13	.419
NEWTON, M.	32	6/ 6	1.000	2/ 2	1.000	1/ 2	.500	0/ 4	1	0	1	0	2	15	.469
BARRY, R.	9	0/ 2	.000	0/ 0	.000	1/ 2	.500	0/ 0	2	2	1	0	0	1	.111
MADDOX, M.	1	0/ 0	.000	0/ 0	.000	0/ 0	.000	0/ 0	0	0	1	0	0	0	.000
HARRIS, K.	12	1/ 1	1.000	0/ 0	.000	0/ 0	.000	0/ 1	0	4	2	0	0	2	.167
NORMORE, C.	16	3/ 3	1.000	1/ 1	1.000	0/ 1	.000	0/ 0	4	2	3	0	0	7	.438
MINOR, L.	11	1/ 4	.250	0/ 0	.000	2/ 2	1.000	0/ 1	1	1	1	1	0	4	.364
Totals	200	35/55	.636	4/ 6	.667	9/14	.643	8/35	17	23	16	11	4	83	.415

Oklahoma (79)   Coach: Billy Tubbs

	Min.	Total FG/FGA	Pct.	3-Pt. FG/FGA	Pct.	FT/FTA	Pct.	Reb. O/T	A	TO	PF	S	Blk	TP	PPM
GRANT, H.	40	6/14	.429	0/ 0	.000	2/ 3	.667	3/ 5	1	0	4	1	1	14	.350
SIEGER, D.	40	7/15	.467	7/13	.538	1/ 2	.500	3/ 5	7	6	2	3	0	22	.550
KING, S.	39	7/14	.500	0/ 0	.000	3/ 3	1.000	2/ 7	0	3	3	1	2	17	.436
BLAYLOCK, M.	40	6/13	.462	2/ 4	.500	0/ 1	.000	3/ 5	4	2	4	7	0	14	.350
GRACE, R.	34	4/14	.286	1/ 7	.143	3/ 4	.750	3/ 7	7	3	4	1	0	12	.353
MULLINS, T.	7	0/ 0	.000	0/ 0	.000	0/ 0	.000	0/ 1	0	1	1	0	0	0	.000
Totals	200	30/70	.429	10/24	.417	9/13	.692	14/30	19	15	18	13	3	79	.395

Team Rebounds: Kansas 1; Oklahoma 1. Disqualified: None. Technical fouls: None.

	1st Half	2nd Half	Final
Kansas	50	33	83
Oklahoma	50	29	79

○ ALL-STAR TEAMS ○

ALL TOURNAMENT
SEAN ELLIOTT	ARIZONA
STACEY KING	OKLAHOMA
★ DANNY MANNING	KANSAS
MILT NEWTON	KANSAS
DAVE SIEGER	OKLAHOMA

EAST REGIONAL
★ DANNY FERRY	DUKE
BILLY KING	DUKE
CARLTON OWENS	RHODE ISLAND
TIM PERRY	TEMPLE
KEVIN STRICKLAND	DUKE

SOUTHEAST REGIONAL
REX CHAPMAN	KENTUCKY
HARVEY GRANT	OKLAHOMA
★ STACEY KING	OKLAHOMA
DOUG WEST	VILLANOVA
KENNY WILSON	VILLANOVA

WEST REGIONAL
★ SEAN ELLIOTT	ARIZONA
STEVE KERR	ARIZONA
J. R. REID	N. CAROLINA
RUMEAL ROBINSON	MICHIGAN
TOM TOLBERT	ARIZONA

MIDWEST REGIONAL
★ DANNY MANNING	KANSAS
MILT NEWTON	KANSAS
KEVIN PRITCHARD	KANSAS
MITCH RICHMOND	KANSAS STATE
WILLIAM SCOTT	KANSAS STATE

★ Most Outstanding Player(s)

○ INDIVIDUAL RECORDS ○

SCORING

Most points in a single game
1 HERSEY HAWKINS, BRADLEY (vs. AUBURN) 44
2 GLEN RICE, MICHIGAN (vs. FLORIDA) 39
3 DANNY MANNING, KANSAS (vs. VANDERBILT) 38
4 STACEY KING, OKLAHOMA (vs. AUBURN) 37
5 CHRIS MORRIS, AUBURN (vs. BRADLEY) 36

Most total points in the tournament
1 DANNY MANNING, KANSAS 163
2 STACEY KING, OKLAHOMA 152
3 SEAN ELLIOTT, ARIZONA 116
4 HARVEY GRANT, OKLAHOMA 114
5 KEVIN STRICKLAND, DUKE 93

Highest scoring average (minimum 2 games)
1 DANNY MANNING, KANSAS (163-6) 27.17
2 CHRIS MORRIS, AUBURN (53-2) 26.50
3 CHARLES SMITH, PITTSBURGH (52-2) 26.00
4 STACEY KING, OKLAHOMA (152-6) 25.33
5 REX CHAPMAN, KENTUCKY (76-3) 25.33

FIELD GOALS

Most field goals in a single game
1 DERRICK CHIEVOUS, MISSOURI (vs. RHODE ISLAND) 16
1 DANNY MANNING, KANSAS (vs. VANDERBILT) 16
1 GLEN RICE, MICHIGAN (vs. FLORIDA) 16
4 HERSEY HAWKINS, BRADLEY (vs. AUBURN) 15
5 3 tied for fifth place.

Most total field goals in the tournament
1 DANNY MANNING, KANSAS 69
2 STACEY KING, OKLAHOMA 63
3 HARVEY GRANT, OKLAHOMA 44
4 SEAN ELLIOTT, ARIZONA 43
5 2 tied for fifth place.

Most field goal attempts in a single game
1 LAFESTER RHODES, IOWA STATE (vs. GEORGIA TECH) 32
2 MARK MACON, TEMPLE (vs. DUKE) 29
2 DANNY MANNING, KANSAS (vs. VANDERBILT) 29
4 GERALD PADDIO, UNLV (vs. IOWA) 26
5 2 tied for fifth place.

Most total field goal attempts in tournament
1 DANNY MANNING, KANSAS 125
2 STACEY KING, OKLAHOMA 111
3 MARK MACON, TEMPLE 85
4 HARVEY GRANT, OKLAHOMA 81
4 DANNY FERRY, DUKE 81

Highest field goal percentage in a single game (minimum 10 attempts)
1 STEPHEN THOMPSON, SYRACUSE (vs. N.C. A&T) (9-10) .900
2 JEROME LANE, PITTSBURGH (vs. EASTERN MICH.) (10-12) .833
2 LOWELL HAMILTON, ILLINOIS (vs. TEXAS-SAN ANT.) (10-12) .833
4 LOY VAUGHT, MICHIGAN (vs. FLORIDA) (9-11) .818
5 5 tied for fifth place.

Highest field goal percentage in the tournament (minimum 20 attempts)
1 STEPHEN THOMPSON, SYRACUSE (16-20) .800
2 WINSTON BENNETT, KENTUCKY (18-23) .783
3 TOM GREIS, VILLANOVA (19-25) .760
4 TIM PERRY, TEMPLE (26-36) .722
5 RUMEAL ROBINSON, MICHIGAN (14-20) .700

3-PT. FIELD GOALS

Most 3-pt. field goals in a single game
1 BRAD SOUCIE, EASTERN MICH. (vs. PITTSBURGH) 8
1 GERALD PADDIO, UNLV (vs. IOWA) 8
3 JEFF FRYER, LOYOLA MYMT. (vs. N. CAROLINA) 7
3 DAVE SIEGER, OKLAHOMA (vs. KANSAS) 7
3 WILLIAM SCOTT, KANSAS STATE (vs. DEPAUL) 7

Most total 3-pt. field goals in the tournament
1 WILLIAM SCOTT, KANSAS STATE 21
2 DAVE SIEGER, OKLAHOMA 19
3 STEVE KERR, ARIZONA 12
4 TROY LEWIS, PURDUE 11
4 BARRY BOOKER, VANDERBILT 11

Most 3-pt. field goals attempted in a single game
1 GERALD PADDIO, UNLV (vs. IOWA) 19
2 JEFF FRYER, LOYOLA MYMT. (vs. N. CAROLINA) 14

2 BRAD SOUCIE, EASTERN MICH. (vs. PITTSBURGH) 14
4 4 tied for fourth place.

Most total 3-pt. field goals attempted in the tournament
1 DAVE SIEGER, OKLAHOMA 46
2 RICKY GRACE, OKLAHOMA 35
3 WILLIAM SCOTT, KANSAS STATE 34
4 STEVE KERR, ARIZONA 32
5 2 tied for fifth place.

Highest 3-pt. field goal percentage in a single game (minimum 4 attempts)
1 WILLIAM SCOTT, KANSAS STATE (vs. PURDUE) (5-5) 1.000
2 WILLIAM SCOTT, KANSAS STATE (vs. DEPAUL) (7-8) .875
3 DENNIS SCOTT, GEORGIA TECH (vs. IOWA STATE) (5-6) .833
4 KENNY PAYNE, LOUISVILLE (vs. BRIGHAM YOUNG) (4-5) .800
5 HERSEY HAWKINS, BRADLEY (vs. AUBURN) (6-8) .750

Highest 3-pt. field goal percentage in the tournament (minimum 8 attempts)
1 HERSEY HAWKINS, BRADLEY (6-8) .750
2 GLEN RICE, MICHIGAN (7-11) .636
3 WILLIAM SCOTT, KANSAS STATE (21-34) .618
4 BRAD SOUCIE, EASTERN MICH. (8-14) .571
5 2 tied for fifth place.

FREE THROWS

Most free throws in a single game
1 TOM HAMMONDS, GEORGIA TECH (vs. IOWA STATE) 19
2 B.J. ARMSTRONG, IOWA (vs. FLORIDA STATE) 16
3 MIKE YOEST, LOYOLA MYMT. (vs. WYOMING) 15
4 ED DAVENDER, KENTUCKY (vs. MARYLAND) 13
5 3 tied for fifth place.

Most total free throws in the tournament
1 STACEY KING, OKLAHOMA 26
1 HARVEY GRANT, OKLAHOMA 26
3 ANTHONY COOK, ARIZONA 25
4 4 tied for fourth place.

Most free throws attempted in a single game
1 TOM HAMMONDS, GEORGIA TECH (vs. IOWA STATE)   21
2 B.J. ARMSTRONG, IOWA (vs. FLORIDA STATE) 20
3 MIKE YOEST, LOYOLA MYMT. (vs. WYOMING) 17
4 ED DAVENDER, KENTUCKY (vs. MARYLAND)   14
4 SEAN ELLIOTT, ARIZONA (vs. N. CAROLINA) 14

Most free throws attempted in the tournament
1 STACEY KING, OKLAHOMA   45
2 HARVEY GRANT, OKLAHOMA   38
3 DANNY MANNING, KANSAS   33
4 RICKY GRACE, OKLAHOMA   32
5 ANTHONY COOK, ARIZONA   31

Highest free throw percentage in a single game (minimum 7 attempts)
1 JOHN MORTON, SETON HALL (vs. UTEP) (12-12)   1.000
2 SASHA RADUNOVICH, WICHITA STATE (vs. DEPAUL) (10-10)   1.000
2 MITCH RICHMOND, KANSAS STATE (vs. LA SALLE) (10-10)   1.000
4 4 tied for fourth place.

Highest free throw percentage in the tournament (minimum 15 attempts)
1 MIKE VREESWYK, TEMPLE (18-18)   1.000
2 LABRADFORD SMITH, LOUISVILLE (15-15) 1.000
3 ED DAVENDER, KENTUCKY (19-20)   .950
4 KENNY WILSON, VILLANOVA (18-19)   .947
5 2 tied for fifth place.

REBOUNDS

Most rebounds in a single game
1 JEROME LANE, PITTSBURGH (vs. VANDERBILT)   20
2 RONNIE MORGAN, NORTH TEXAS (vs. N. CAROLINA)   19
3 DANNY MANNING, KANSAS (vs. OKLAHOMA) 18
4 JEROME LANE, PITTSBURGH (vs. EASTERN MICH.)   17
5 RONY SEIKALY, SYRACUSE (vs. N.C. A&T) 16

Most total rebounds in the tournament
1 DANNY MANNING, KANSAS   56
2 STACEY KING, OKLAHOMA   52
3 DANNY FERRY, DUKE   46
4 MILT NEWTON, KANSAS   42
5 2 tied for fifth place.

Most rebounds per game (minimum 2 games)
1 JEROME LANE, PITTSBURGH (37-2)   18.50
2 RONY SEIKALY, SYRACUSE (26-2)   13.00
3 MICHAEL SMITH, BRIGHAM YOUNG (24-2) 12.00
3 JEFF MOORE, AUBURN (24-2)   12.00
3 HANK GATHERS, LOYOLA MYMT. (24-2)   12.00

ASSISTS

Most assists in a single game
1 ROD STRICKLAND, DEPAUL (vs. WICHITA STATE)   13
2 QUIN SNYDER, DUKE (vs. SMU)   12
2 STEVE HENSON, KANSAS STATE (vs. PURDUE)   12
2 SHERMAN DOUGLAS, SYRACUSE (vs. RHODE ISLAND)   12
2 KEITH WILLIAMS, LOUISVILLE (vs. BRIGHAM YOUNG) 12

Most total assists in the tournament
1 RICKY GRACE, OKLAHOMA   41
2 MOOKIE BLAYLOCK, OKLAHOMA   38
3 DAVE SIEGER, OKLAHOMA   37
4 QUIN SNYDER, DUKE   29
5 2 tied for fifth place.

Most assists per game (minimum 2 appearances)
1 ROD STRICKLAND, DEPAUL (21-2)   10.50
2 COREY GAINES, LOYOLA MYMT. (20-2)   10.00
2 SHERMAN DOUGLAS, SYRACUSE (20-2)   10.00
4 SEAN MILLER, PITTSBURGH (16-2)   8.00
4 VERNON MAXWELL, FLORIDA (16-2)   8.00

TURNOVERS

Most turnovers in a single game
1 LYONS, TENN.-CHATT. (vs. OKLAHOMA)   10

2 CHRIS PIPER, KANSAS (vs. XAVIER [OHIO])   8
2 TERRANCE HOWARD, AUBURN (vs. OKLAHOMA)   8
4 4 tied for fourth place.

Most total turnovers in the tournament
1 DANNY MANNING, KANSAS   24
2 CHRIS PIPER, KANSAS   21
3 STACEY KING, OKLAHOMA   17
4 SEAN ELLIOTT, ARIZONA   16
5 MITCH RICHMOND, KANSAS STATE   15

SHOTS BLOCKED

Most shots blocked in a single game
1 TIM PERRY, TEMPLE (vs. LEHIGH)   8
2 RONY SEIKALY, SYRACUSE (vs. N.C. A&T) 7
3 TIM PERRY, TEMPLE (vs. DUKE)   6
3 DANNY MANNING, KANSAS (vs. DUKE)   6
5 5 tied for fifth place.

Most total shots blocked in the tournament
1 TIM PERRY, TEMPLE   20
2 DANNY MANNING, KANSAS   14
3 STACEY KING, OKLAHOMA   10
4 RONY SEIKALY, SYRACUSE   9
5 PERVIS ELLISON, LOUISVILLE   8

STEALS

Most steals in a single game
1 MOOKIE BLAYLOCK, OKLAHOMA (vs. KANSAS) 7
2 DINKINS, N.C.-CHARLOTTE (vs. BRIGHAM YOUNG)   6
2 RODNEY DOUGLAS, MEMPHIS STATE (vs. BAYLOR)   6
2 JOHN EVANS, RHODE ISLAND (vs. DUKE)   6
5 4 tied for fifth place.

Most total steals in the tournament
1 MOOKIE BLAYLOCK, OKLAHOMA   23
2 DAVE SIEGER, OKLAHOMA   16
3 RICKY GRACE, OKLAHOMA   14
4 DANNY MANNING, KANSAS   12
5 5 tied for fifth place.

❍ TEAM RECORDS ❍

SCORING

Most points in a single game
1 N. CAROLINA (vs. LOYOLA MYMT.)   123
2 LOYOLA MYMT. (vs. WYOMING)   119
3 WYOMING (vs. LOYOLA MYMT.)   115

Most total points in the tournament
1 OKLAHOMA   552
2 KANSAS   443
3 ARIZONA   421

Highest scoring average (minimum 2 games)
1 LOYOLA MYMT. (216-2)   108.00
2 IOWA (285-3)   95.00
3 OKLAHOMA (552-6)   92.00

FIELD GOALS

Most field goals in a single game
1 N. CAROLINA (vs. LOYOLA MYMT.)   49
2 WYOMING (vs. LOYOLA MYMT.)   47
3 MICHIGAN (vs. FLORIDA)   44

Most total field goals in the tournament
1 OKLAHOMA   206
2 KANSAS   172
3 ARIZONA   152

Most field goals attempted in a single game
1 LOYOLA MYMT. (vs. N. CAROLINA)   103
2 AUBURN (vs. OKLAHOMA)   84
3 SOUTHERN-B.R.(vs. KENTUCKY)   82
3 LOYOLA MYMT. (vs. WYOMING)   82
3 WYOMING (vs. LOYOLA MYMT.)   82

Most total field goals attempted in the tournament
1 OKLAHOMA   412
2 KANSAS   320
3 DUKE   308

Highest field goal percentage in a single game
1 N. CAROLINA (vs. LOYOLA MYMT.) (49-62) .790
2 KENTUCKY (vs. SOUTHERN-B.R.) (38-57)   .667
3 MICHIGAN (vs. BOISE ST.) (25-38)   .658

Highest field goal percentage in a tournament (minimum 2 games)
1 MICHIGAN (96-161)   .596
2 WYOMING (47-82)   .573
3 KENTUCKY (97-172)   .564

3-PT. FIELD GOALS

Most 3-pt. field goals in a single game
1 LOYOLA MYMT. (vs. N. CAROLINA)   13
2 FLORIDA STATE (vs. IOWA)   12
2 EASTERN MICH. (vs. PITTSBURGH)   12

Most total 3-pt. field goals in the tournament
1 OKLAHOMA   41
2 KANSAS STATE   33
3 ARIZONA   29

Most 3-pt. field goals attempted in a single game
1 LOYOLA MYMT. (vs. N. CAROLINA)   39
2 UNLV (vs. IOWA)   29
3 FLORIDA STATE (vs. IOWA)   26

Most total 3-pt. field goals attempted in the tournament

1	OKLAHOMA	105
2	ARIZONA	77
3	KANSAS STATE	65

Highest 3-pt. field goal percentage in a single game (minimum 10 attempts)

1	KANSAS STATE (vs. PURDUE) (8-10)	.800
2	KANSAS STATE (vs. DEPAUL) (10-13)	.769
3	RHODE ISLAND (vs. SYRACUSE) (7-10)	.700

Highest 3-pt. field goal percentage in the tournament (minimum 20 attempts)

1	UC SANTA BARB. (11-20)	.550
2	EASTERN MICH. (12-22)	.545
3	MICHIGAN (12-23)	.522

FREE THROWS

Most free throws in a single game

1	GEORGIA TECH (vs. IOWA STATE)	36
2	IOWA (vs. FLORIDA STATE)	32
3	IOWA (vs. UNLV)	31

Most total free throws in the tournament

1	OKLAHOMA	99
2	ARIZONA	88
3	KANSAS	80

Most free throws attempted in a single game

1	IOWA (vs. UNLV)	46
2	IOWA (vs. FLORIDA STATE)	43
3	GEORGIA TECH (vs. IOWA STATE)	42

Most total free throws attempted in the tournament

1	OKLAHOMA	156
2	DUKE	114
3	KANSAS	113

Highest free throw percentage in a single game

1	VILLANOVA (vs. KENTUCKY) (17-17)	1.000
2	BOISE ST. (vs. MICHIGAN) (13-14)	.929
2	TEMPLE (vs. DUKE) (13-14)	.929

Highest free throw percentage in the tournament (minimum 2 games)

1	AUBURN (44-50)	.880
2	MEMPHIS STATE (29-34)	.853
3	TEMPLE (76-90)	.845

Fewest free throws in a single game

1	GEORGETOWN (vs. LOUISIANA ST.)	3
1	RICHMOND (vs. TEMPLE)	3
3	2 tied for third place.	

Lowest free throw percentage in a single game

1	RICHMOND (vs. TEMPLE) (3-10)	.300
2	GEORGETOWN (vs. LOUISIANA ST.) (3-7)	.429
3	ILLINOIS (vs. VILLANOVA) (10-23)	.435

Lowest free throw percentage in the tournament (minimum 2 games)

1	SYRACUSE (19-35)	.543
2	RICHMOND (30-55)	.546
3	DEPAUL (15-26)	.577

REBOUNDS

Most rebounds in a single game

1	N. CAROLINA (vs. LOYOLA MYMT.)	54
2	KANSAS (vs. XAVIER [OHIO])	47
3	AUBURN (vs. OKLAHOMA)	45
3	SYRACUSE (vs. N.C. A&T)	45
3	PURDUE (vs. F. DICKINSON)	45

Most rebounds per game (minimum 2 games)

1	AUBURN (86-2)	43.00
2	PITTSBURGH (85-2)	42.50
3	SYRACUSE (81-2)	40.50

ASSISTS

Most assists in a single game

1	N. CAROLINA (vs. LOYOLA MYMT.)	36
2	OKLAHOMA (vs. AUBURN)	31
3	2 tied for third place.	

Most assists per game (minimum 2 games)

1	PURDUE (72-3)	24.00
2	PITTSBURGH (47-2)	23.50
3	OKLAHOMA (136-6)	22.67

TURNOVERS

Most turnovers in a single game

1	KANSAS (vs. XAVIER [OHIO])	30
2	3 tied for second place.	

Most turnovers per game (minimum 2 games)

1	BRIGHAM YOUNG (39-2)	19.50
2	UNLV (38-2)	19.00
3	KANSAS (111-6)	18.50

SHOTS BLOCKED

Most shots blocked in a single game

1	DUKE (vs. TEMPLE)	11
2	3 tied for second place.	

Most shots blocked per game (minimum 2 games)

1	SYRACUSE (13-2)	6.50
2	DUKE (27-5)	5.40
3	TEMPLE (21-4)	5.25

STEALS

Most steals in a single game

1	XAVIER (OHIO) (vs. KANSAS)	17
2	OKLAHOMA (vs. AUBURN)	16
2	LOYOLA MYMT. (vs. WYOMING)	16

Most steals per game

1	LOYOLA MYMT. (27-2)	13.50
2	OKLAHOMA (72-6)	12.00
3	DEPAUL (22-2)	11.00

1989

| FIRST ROUND | SECOND ROUND | REGIONAL SEMIFINAL | REGIONAL FINAL | FINAL FOUR | REGIONAL FINAL | REGIONAL SEMIFINAL | SECOND ROUND | FIRST ROUND |

MIDWEST

1 Illinois 77
16 McNeese St. 71
Illinois 72
8 Pittsburgh 64
9 Ball St. 68
Ball St. 60
Illinois 83
5 Arkansas 120
12 Loyola Mymt. 101
Arkansas 84
4 Louisville 76
13 Ark.-Little Rock 71
Louisville 93
Louisville 69
Illinois 89
6 Georgia Tech 70
11 Texas 76
Texas 89
3 Missouri 85
14 Creighton 69
Missouri 108
Missouri 80
7 Florida 46
10 Colorado St. 68
Colorado St. 50
2 Syracuse 104
15 Bucknell 81
Syracuse 83
Syracuse 65
Syracuse 86

Illinois 81

SOUTHEAST

1 Oklahoma 72
16 East Tenn. St. 71
Oklahoma 124
8 La Salle 74
9 Louisiana Tech 88
Louisiana Tech 81
Oklahoma 80
5 Virginia 100
12 Providence 97
Virginia 104
4 Florida St. 83
13 Middle Tenn. St. 97
Middle Tenn. St. 88
Virginia 86
Virginia 65
6 Alabama 84
11 South Alabama 86
South Alabama 82
3 Michigan 92
14 Xavier (Ohio) 87
Michigan 92
Michigan 91
7 UCLA 84
10 Iowa St. 74
UCLA 81
2 N. Carolina 93
15 Southern-B.R. 79
N. Carolina 88
N. Carolina 87
Michigan 102

Michigan 83

FINAL FOUR

Michigan 80 (ot)
Seton Hall 79

Illinois 81

Duke 78

Seton Hall 95

EAST

Georgetown 69
Georgetown 81
1 Georgetown 50
16 Princeton 49
8 Vanderbilt 65
Notre Dame 74
9 Notre Dame 81
Georgetown 77
N.C. State 102 (2 ot)
5 N.C. State 81
12 S. Carolina 66
N.C. State 61
4 Iowa 87
Iowa 96
3 Rutgers 73
Duke 78
Minnesota 80
6 Kansas St. 75
11 Minnesota 86
Minnesota 70
3 Stanford 78
Siena 67
14 Siena 80
Duke 85
7 West Virginia 84
West Virginia 63
10 Tennessee 68
Duke 87
2 Duke 90
Duke 70
15 S. Carolina St. 69

WEST

Arizona 67
Arizona 94
1 Arizona 94
16 Robert Morris 60
8 St. Mary's 70
Clemson 68
9 Clemson 83
UNLV 61
DePaul 70
5 Memphis St. 63
12 DePaul 66
UNLV 68
4 UNLV 68
UNLV 85
13 Idaho 56
Seton Hall 84
6 Oregon St. 90
Evansville 73
11 Evansville 94 (ot)
Seton Hall 78
3 Seton Hall 60
Seton Hall 87
14 SW Missouri St. 51
UTEP 69
7 UTEP 85
10 Louisiana St. 74
Indiana 65
2 Indiana 99
Indiana 92
15 George Mason 85

The 1989 championship contest between Michigan and Seton Hall—the first overtime final since 1963—capped a remarkably competitive eight-year run when the margin of victory in championship games averaged less than three points a game.

Neither of the final teams was expected to get as far as they did. Michigan was stocked with talent but had never before put it together as a team. They had struggled all year, finishing with a mediocre 12-6 Big Ten record. When coach Bill Frieder announced just before the tournament began that he had accepted the coaching job at Arizona State, it seemed like the final straw for Michigan's chances at the Final Four. For despite Frieder's stated desire to coach the team through the tournament, the Wolverines' athletic director, Bo Schembechler, insisted that he pack his bags right away. Assistant Steve Fisher, who had never been a head coach at the college level, was chosen to lead the team on an interim basis.

Michigan's opponent, Seton Hall, was even more unlikely to compete for the national championship. Just a year earlier, the school's student body, tired of having a team that was the doormat of the Big East, overwhelmingly passed a referendum demanding coach P. J. Carlesimo's ouster. And the 1988–89 season wasn't expected to be much better; the Pirates were the preseason pick of Big East coaches to finish seventh in the conference. But Seton Hall surprised everyone. Led by a group of no-name New Yorkers and an Australian import, they finished second. Then, using a tenacious, in-your-face defense as their big weapon, they bulled their way to the Final Four.

But long before Michigan's Rumeal Robinson stepped to the foul line with three seconds left in the extra session of the final game, this tournament was filled with memorable moments. Way back in the first round, mighty Georgetown barely escaped in a game against lowly Princeton of the Ivy League, a conference so out of touch with mainstream big-time hoops that it doesn't even give athletic scholarships! Coach Pete Carril's Tigers spread the floor, neutralizing the Hoyas' famous smothering D and creating open spaces from midcourt to baseline. Princeton played with precision, going backdoor, kicking the ball back out from Kit Mueller's high post whenever a lay-up didn't develop, and committing only seven turnovers all game. The Ivy Leaguers led all the way until midway through the second half. The game seesawed, until with less than three minutes to play, Alonzo Mourning blocked a lay-up that would've put Princeton up by four. With 23 seconds left Mourning hit one of two foul shots to put Georgetown up 50-49. Then another Mourning block . . . and still another as time ran out—and the Big East champs were still in the race.

In other first-round surprises, the Southeast regional's top-seeded Oklahoma had to come from 17 points back to beat feisty East Tennessee State by a point on a Mookie Blaylock lay-up. And in the same regional, 13th-seed Middle Tennessee State, behind the perfect shooting of freshman reserve guard Mike Buck (his 7 for 7 from the floor included six 3-pointers) blew out Florida State with 21 straight points in the final 5:22. "I'm a boy who likes to work hard and have fun doing it," said Buck. "Tonight I had a fantastic time." (Maybe Middle Tennessee's victory shouldn't have come as such a surprise; they were the third straight Ohio Valley Conference team—after Austin Peay in 1988 and Murray State in 1987—to upset a highly regarded opponent in tournament play.)

Perhaps the most remarkable upset of all was Siena's victory in the first round of the Eastern regional. The ECAC North Atlantic champions not only had to overcome a strong Stanford team, they also had to fight their way through a quarantine to play. Because of a measles epidemic on Siena's Loudonville, New York, campus, not a single spectator had been allowed into a Saints game for five weeks. Finally, as the tournament began, the quarantine was lifted. Saints' supporters wore T-shirts proclaiming *Siena Saints 98.6, Measles 0*, and Siena beat Stanford 80-78. Their success story ended when they lost to Minnesota in the second round.

There was no overwhelming favorite going into the tournament (No. 1–ranked Arizona lost to UNLV in the West regional semifinals, which in turn got blown out by Seton Hall), and in the end the only top seed to make it to the Final Four in Seattle was Illinois.

Arkansas coach Nolan Richardson called the Illini "a dream-type team for this time and this era. All of them can jump, run, and shoot and put the ball on the floor." They were a group of "look-alikes"; with no player over 6-7, they relied on full-court pressure to assert their athletic dominance. After his team was beaten by the Illini in the second round, Ball State coach Rick Majerus observed, "They just jumped us. They took us right out of what we wanted to do."

Before the regional semis against Louisville, Illinois coach Lou Henson, alluding to his team's height disadvantage, said, "With a lot of teams, Pervis [Ellison, Louisville's No. 3 all-time NCAA shot blocker] has to jump to block shots. With us he can stand flat footed and block them with his elbows." But Illinois, despite a knee injury to their number-two scorer, forward Kenny Battle, beat Louisville by 14. The hard-nosed play intensified in a tight-fought regional final against Syracuse. At one point the Orangemen's Matt Roe took a lead pass and drove in for what appeared to be an uncontested lay-up. From out of nowhere the Illini's Nick Anderson accelerated and caught Roe, sending him a message as he knocked him hard to the floor and blocked the shot. And Battle came back strong, scoring 18 second-half points and making both ends of a 1-and-1 to seal the victory against a taller Syracuse team. "I was in the position that everybody dreams of being in," said Battle, "at the free throw line in the final seconds with a chance to win the game. I made it come true."

Meanwhile Michigan grew stronger, looser, and more confident as the tournament progressed. They had trouble with Xavier in the first round and were rescued from their own sloppy, disorganized play in the second round against South Alabama by the deadeye shooting of Glen Rice. In the regional semis, Michigan's game came together against North Carolina, the team that had knocked them out of the previous two years' tournaments. Rice was unstoppable, shooting 13 for 19, including 8 of 12 3-pointers. "I can't believe he'll be able to do that again," said the loser's coach, Dean Smith. But in the regional finals against Virginia, Rice and his team were even better. He hit 13 of 16 overall, 4 of 5 from 3-point range, and Michigan won by 37 points. "Life's crazy," mused Fisher, the first interim coach ever to make the Final Four. "I'm just happy to be on the ride."

On the other side of the draw, P. J. Carlesimo's Seton Hall Pirates also struggled in the early rounds, then grew stronger as they faced more highly regarded foes. They chopped down Indiana in the West regional semis, handing Bobby Knight's Hoosiers their worst NCAA tournament defeat in history and holding them to 7-of-24 shooting in the second half. They destroyed UNLV (which had upset No. 1–ranked Arizona) in the West regional finals, once again using bruising defense to key a 33-8 run that turned a close game into a rout.

The favorites going into the Final Four may well have been Duke, if only because of the Blue Devils' experience. Led by the ACC's Player of the Year Danny Ferry, they made it to the national semifinals for the third time in four years. In the regional finals against Georgetown, freshman Christian Laettner outplayed Alonzo Mourning and Duke's ball movement kept the Hoyas off balance. After the game Ferry said, "I'm more confident in our team than I have been all year."

His confidence must have grown in the first 11 minutes of their national semifinal game against Seton Hall. The score was 26 to 8, Duke, and the only question appeared to be the size of the Blue Devils' final victory margin. But "We weren't going to go down like that," said Darryl Walker, the Pirates' senior center. Seton Hall fought back, and before the half ended, it was a ball game again. With 16:03 left in the game, Laettner was called for his fourth foul. His replacement, Alaa Abdelnaby, picked up his fourth just four seconds later. And Seton Hall, in one of the great turnarounds in Final Four history, won going away by 17.

The other semifinal featured two teams who knew each other very well. The Big Ten rivals had played each other twice during the regular season, and Illinois had won both—convincingly. But this was a new season. Illinois pressed full court from the first minute to the last, but Michigan, again led by the shooting of Glen Rice and the floor play of Rumeal Robinson, stayed with them. Neither team was able to pull away. With less than two minutes left, Illinois went up 79-78 and Michigan called time-out. At the bench, Steve Fisher was smiling. He told his players to calm down, and outlined their offensive options. Mark Hughes was fouled scoring on a rebound, and after he hit the foul shot, the score was 81-79 Michigan. With 31 seconds left Illinois's Kenny Battle tied the game. With time running out, Terry Mills forced up a shot from deep in the corner. Fisher, as the Michigan assistant, had been telling his players all year that long shots produce long rebounds. Sean Higgins took a step away from the basket, grabbed the ball, and put it back up. The ball went in with one second left. Michigan was playing for the championship.

The Wolverines entered the game brimming with confidence. And just as they had done against Duke, Seton Hall dug themselves into a hole. Early in the second half the Pirates' senior guard John Morton threw up a wild 3-pointer and was unceremoniously yanked by Coach Carlesimo. Michigan went on a tear, capped by a Robinson jam, and with 14 minutes left to play the lead was 12. With just over eight minutes remaining they were still up by 10. Then John Morton took over. He scored 17 points in eight minutes, finally canning a three to tie the score with 24 seconds left. When Glen Rice, on his way to 31 points and an all-time tournament scoring record, missed with two seconds to go, the game went into overtime.

With 1:35 left to go in the extra period and the Pirates up 79-76, Morton missed in the lane. Seton Hall's Gerald Greene missed the front end of a one-and-one and Michigan's Terry Mills hit on the other end to pull within one. Morton missed again, and Michigan came up with the ball. Rumeal Robinson put the ball on the floor and drove. The whistle blew. The call might have gone either way. But it was called on Seton Hall.

With a title in the balance and three seconds left in OT, Robinson, a 65 percent free-throw shooter, went to the line. Earlier in the season he had missed two in the same situation. "For two weeks straight," recalled Fisher, "he came in an hour early and shot a minimum of a hundred free throws every day." This time he did not miss. Michigan was the national champion. And Steve Fisher was undefeated as a head coach.

FIRST ROUND MIDWEST

Illinois (77)   Coach: Lou Henson

	Min.	Total FG/FGA	Pct.	3-Pt. FG/FGA	Pct.	FT/FTA	Pct.	Reb. O/T	A	TO	PF	S	Blk	TP	PPM
ANDERSON, N.	32	4/6	.667	0/0	.000	5/8	.625	5/12	2	1	1	4	2	13	.406
BATTLE, K.	32	5/13	.385	0/1	.000	8/8	1.000	1/5	2	1	1	3	0	18	.563
HAMILTON, L.	20	7/8	.875	0/0	.000	3/4	.750	0/2	0	1	3	0	1	17	.850
GILL, K.	30	5/13	.385	0/4	.000	1/1	1.000	2/3	3	1	2	4	0	11	.367
BARDO, S.	26	4/8	.500	1/3	.333	0/0	.000	1/1	3	3	1	0	0	9	.346
BOWMAN, P.	5	0/0	.000	0/0	.000	0/0	.000	0/0	1	0	1	0	0	0	.000
MANZKA, E.	1	0/0	.000	0/0	.000	0/0	.000	0/0	0	0	0	0	0	0	.000
SMITH, L.	19	3/4	.750	0/0	.000	0/0	.000	0/0	4	3	1	0	0	6	.316
SMALL, E.	13	0/2	.000	0/0	.000	1/2	.500	1/4	0	1	0	0	1	1	.077
LIBERTY, M.	18	0/7	.000	0/0	.000	2/3	.667	0/3	0	1	1	0	0	2	.111
MACDONALD, M.	3	0/0	.000	0/0	.000	0/0	.000	0/0	0	0	0	0	0	0	.000
SHAPLAND, M.	1	0/0	.000	0/0	.000	0/0	.000	0/0	0	0	0	0	0	0	.000
Totals	200	28/61	.459	1/8	.125	20/26	.769	10/30	15	12	11	11	3	77	.385

McNeese State (71)   Coach: Steve Welch

	Min.	Total FG/FGA	Pct.	3-Pt. FG/FGA	Pct.	FT/FTA	Pct.	Reb. O/T	A	TO	PF	S	Blk	TP	PPM
HARRIS, T.	24	5/10	.500	5/8	.625	0/0	.000	2/4	2	2	2	0	0	15	.625
CUTRIGHT, M.	37	12/27	.444	2/8	.250	2/2	1.000	0/2	2	5	2	3	1	28	.757
PULLARD, A.	33	6/15	.400	0/0	.000	1/1	1.000	4/8	0	6	4	0	0	13	.394
GRIGGLEY, T.	32	0/3	.000	0/0	.000	1/4	.250	1/5	3	2	5	0	0	1	.031
THOMPSON, M.	35	4/7	.571	0/0	.000	0/2	.000	5/11	0	0	4	0	1	8	.229
DAVIS, D.	19	3/4	.750	0/1	.000	0/0	.000	1/4	5	1	1	0	0	6	.316
JOHNSON, T.	15	0/0	.000	0/0	.000	0/0	.000	0/2	2	0	1	1	0	0	.000
WILLIAMS, K.	5	0/0	.000	0/0	.000	0/0	.000	0/0	0	1	1	0	0	0	.000
Totals	200	30/66	.455	7/17	.412	4/9	.444	13/36	14	17	20	4	2	71	.355

Team Rebounds: Illinois 3; McNeese State 3. Disqualified: McNeese State—Griggley. Technical fouls: None.

	1st Half	2nd Half	Final
Illinois	26	51	77
McNeese State	21	50	71

Arkansas (120)   Coach: Nolan Richardson

	Min.	Total FG/FGA	Pct.	3-Pt. FG/FGA	Pct.	FT/FTA	Pct.	Reb. O/T	A	TO	PF	S	Blk	TP	PPM
DAY, T.	22	7/12	.583	1/3	.333	5/6	.833	0/2	4	2	5	2	0	20	.909
HOWELL, L.	35	10/11	.909	0/0	.000	7/11	.636	2/12	0	3	5	1	0	27	.771
CREDIT, M.	29	14/21	.667	0/0	.000	6/9	.667	4/13	0	2	4	0	0	34	1.172
MAYBERRY, L.	36	8/14	.571	1/1	1.000	2/6	.333	1/2	8	1	0	3	0	19	.528
WILSON, K.	31	4/13	.308	0/2	.000	1/3	.333	4/11	12	2	4	3	0	9	.290
BOWERS, A.	20	2/7	.286	0/2	.000	3/4	.750	1/3	1	3	1	3	2	7	.350
HAWKINS, D.	4	1/1	1.000	0/0	.000	0/0	.000	0/1	0	0	1	1	0	2	.500
WHITBY, C.	3	1/2	.500	0/1	.000	0/0	.000	0/1	1	0	0	0	0	2	.667
MILLER, O.	19	0/0	.000	0/0	.000	0/2	.000	0/5	0	4	0	0	0	0	.000
DAVIS, S.	1	0/0	.000	0/0	.000	0/0	.000	0/0	2	2	0	0	0	0	.000
Totals	200	47/81	.580	2/9	.222	24/41	.585	12/48	30	13	26	12	0	120	.600

Loyola Marymount (101)   Coach: Paul Westhead

	Min.	Total FG/FGA	Pct.	3-Pt. FG/FGA	Pct.	FT/FTA	Pct.	Reb. O/T	A	TO	PF	S	Blk	TP	PPM
STUMER, P.	32	2/7	.286	1/3	.333	1/2	.500	3/8	1	4	4	0	0	6	.188
KIMBLE, B.	35	7/23	.304	2/11	.182	8/9	.889	5/10	3	3	4	0	0	24	.686
GATHERS, H.	38	12/24	.500	0/0	.000	4/11	.364	8/17	1	3	4	2	0	28	.737
PEABODY, T.	26	1/4	.250	0/1	.000	0/1	.000	2/4	4	3	1	0	0	2	.077
FRYER, J.	32	7/28	.250	5/22	.227	5/5	1.000	2/8	1	2	5	1	0	24	.750
MISTER	6	0/0	.000	0/0	.000	2/2	1.000	0/0	1	1	3	0	0	2	.333
O'CONNELL, J.	3	1/2	.500	0/0	.000	0/0	.000	2/2	1	1	2	0	0	2	.667
LOWERY, T.	13	2/3	.667	1/2	.500	2/2	1.000	2/2	1	2	5	0	0	7	.538
VEARGASON, J.	15	3/7	.429	0/0	.000	0/0	.000	4/7	0	1	5	0	0	6	.400
Totals	200	35/98	.357	9/39	.231	22/32	.688	28/58	13	20	33	3	0	101	.505

Team Rebounds: Arkansas 6; Loyola Mymt. 7. Disqualified: Arkansas—Day, Howell; Loyola Mymt.—Fryer, Lowery, Veargason. Technical fouls: Loyola Mymt.—Bench.

	1st Half	2nd Half	Final
Arkansas	68	52	120
Loyola Mymt.	53	48	101

Pittsburgh (64)   Coach: Paul Evans

	Min.	Total FG/FGA	Pct.	3-Pt. FG/FGA	Pct.	FT/FTA	Pct.	Reb. O/T	A	TO	PF	S	Blk	TP	PPM
PORTER, D.	38	3/12	.250	0/4	.000	2/2	1.000	0/4	4	2	3	1	0	8	.211
SHORTER, B.	20	4/5	.800	0/0	.000	5/6	.833	4/5	0	3	5	0	0	13	.650
MARTIN, B.	33	1/4	.250	0/0	.000	2/2	1.000	1/10	1	5	5	1	3	4	.121
MATTHEWS, J.	34	8/16	.500	5/9	.556	2/2	1.000	2/5	2	3	4	0	0	23	.676
MILLER, S.	39	1/9	.111	1/7	.143	3/3	1.000	0/2	8	3	0	0	0	6	.154
CAVANAUGH, P.	3	0/2	.000	0/1	.000	0/0	.000	1/1	1	0	0	0	0	0	.000
BROOKIN, R.	32	3/7	.429	2/4	.500	2/4	.500	4/9	1	3	5	1	0	10	.313
JOHNSON, G.	1	0/0	.000	0/0	.000	0/0	.000	0/0	0	0	0	0	0	0	.000
Totals	200	20/55	.364	8/25	.320	16/19	.842	12/36	17	19	22	3	3	64	.320

Ball State (68)   Coach: Rick Majerus

	Min.	Total FG/FGA	Pct.	3-Pt. FG/FGA	Pct.	FT/FTA	Pct.	Reb. O/T	A	TO	PF	S	Blk	TP	PPM
MCCURDY, P.	32	6/13	.462	0/0	.000	6/8	.750	4/7	0	1	3	3	0	18	.563
PARRISH, S.	21	4/5	.800	0/0	.000	0/0	.000	1/5	2	0	1	1	0	8	.381
KIDD, C.	39	5/15	.333	0/0	.000	5/6	.833	1/4	2	3	3	1	0	15	.385
BUTTS, B.	36	5/11	.455	3/6	.500	0/4	.000	0/1	1	3	0	0	0	13	.361
NICHOLS, S.	23	0/1	.000	0/0	.000	0/0	.000	0/2	5	2	3	1	0	0	.000
SPICER, M.	4	0/0	.000	0/0	.000	0/0	.000	0/0	0	1	0	0	0	0	.000
STALLING, K.	20	0/3	.000	0/0	.000	1/2	.500	0/3	3	0	1	4	0	1	.050
MILLER, G.	21	4/9	.444	1/5	.200	4/4	1.000	3/5	3	1	3	0	0	13	.619
MULLER, R.	4	0/1	.000	0/0	.000	0/0	.000	0/0	0	1	2	0	0	0	.000
Totals	200	24/58	.414	4/11	.364	16/24	.667	9/27	16	12	16	10	0	68	.340

Team Rebounds: Ball St. 3; Pittsburgh 2. Disqualified: Pittsburgh—Shorter, Martin. Technical fouls: Ball St.—McCurdy.

	1st Half	2nd Half	Final
Pittsburgh	31	33	64
Ball St.	37	31	68

Louisville (76)   Coach: Denny Crum

	Min.	Total FG/FGA	Pct.	3-Pt. FG/FGA	Pct.	FT/FTA	Pct.	Reb. O/T	A	TO	PF	S	Blk	TP	PPM
PAYNE, K.	36	8/17	.471	0/0	.000	1/1	1.000	2/6	2	2	3	1	1	17	.472
KIMBRO, T.	29	4/6	.667	1/2	.500	2/2	1.000	2/9	3	1	3	0	0	11	.379
ELLISON, P.	32	3/8	.375	0/0	.000	2/6	.333	3/7	3	3	5	0	3	8	.250
SMITH, T.	32	5/7	.714	0/1	.000	5/6	.833	0/1	5	5	2	1	0	15	.469
SPENCER, F.	17	3/6	.500	0/0	.000	2/4	.500	3/6	0	0	2	0	0	8	.471
HOLDEN, C.	6	0/1	.000	0/0	.000	0/0	.000	1/1	0	1	0	0	0	0	.000
SULLIVAN, E.	15	2/3	.667	0/0	.000	0/0	.000	2/4	4	0	0	0	0	4	.267
WILLIAMS, K.	33	5/11	.455	0/0	.000	3/4	.750	1/2	0	1	1	1	0	13	.394
Totals	200	30/59	.508	1/3	.333	15/23	.652	14/36	17	12	17	3	4	76	.380

Arkansas-Little Rock (71)   Coach: Mike Newell

	Min.	Total FG/FGA	Pct.	3-Pt. FG/FGA	Pct.	FT/FTA	Pct.	Reb. O/T	A	TO	PF	S	Blk	TP	PPM
OWENS, D.	38	8/13	.615	1/2	.500	2/3	.667	2/4	3	4	4	0	1	19	.500
BELL, J.	33	5/15	.333	0/0	.000	0/2	.000	5/11	1	2	3	0	0	10	.303
CUMMINGS, J.	29	2/4	.500	0/0	.000	2/5	.400	2/5	1	3	5	1	0	6	.207
SCOTT, J.	37	3/10	.300	0/2	.000	0/0	.000	4/5	3	1	4	1	0	6	.162
BROWN, C.	37	9/22	.409	6/13	.462	2/3	.667	2/3	5	3	4	1	0	26	.703
SPRINGER, P.	3	0/0	.000	0/0	.000	0/0	.000	0/1	0	0	0	0	1	0	.000
HYNES, M.	1	0/0	.000	0/0	.000	0/0	.000	1/1	0	1	0	0	0	0	.000
MORGAN, F.	5	0/0	.000	0/0	.000	0/0	.000	0/2	1	0	0	0	0	0	.000
HOGES, D.	17	1/3	.333	0/0	.000	2/2	1.000	2/3	0	2	2	0	1	4	.235
Totals	200	28/67	.418	7/17	.412	8/15	.533	18/33	15	15	22	3	3	71	.355

Team Rebounds: Louisville 5; Ark.-Little Rock 3. Disqualified: Louisville—Ellison; Ark.-Little Rock—Cummings. Technical fouls: None.

	1st Half	2nd Half	Final
Louisville	39	37	76
Ark.-Little Rock	35	36	71

Georgia Tech (70)   Coach: Bobby Cremins

	Min.	Total FG/FGA	Pct.	3–Pt. FG/FGA	Pct.	FT/FTA	Pct.	Reb. O/T	A	TO	PF	S	Blk	TP	PPM
HAMMONDS, T.	40	8/18	.444	0/0	.000	2/3	.667	2/8	0	4	2	2	0	18	.450
SHERROD, A.	31	4/11	.364	0/0	.000	0/0	.000	3/9	0	0	3	1	1	8	.258
MCNEIL, J.	7	0/1	.000	0/0	.000	0/0	.000	0/1	1	1	1	0	0	0	.000
SCOTT, D.	37	5/11	.455	1/3	.333	5/6	.833	3/3	3	0	5	3	0	16	.432
OLIVER, B.	39	10/17	.588	1/3	.333	3/4	.750	4/7	5	2	4	2	0	24	.615
BROWN, K.	19	1/4	.250	0/0	.000	0/0	.000	1/4	4	3	4	0	0	2	.105
WHITMORE, D.	18	1/4	.250	0/0	.000	0/0	.000	2/4	1	2	1	1	2	2	.111
BRITTIAN, M.	9	0/0	.000	0/0	.000	0/0	.000	1/4	0	1	2	0	0	0	.000
Totals	200	29/66	.439	2/6	.333	10/13	.769	16/40	14	13	22	9	3	70	.350

Texas (76)   Coach: Tom Penders

	Min.	Total FG/FGA	Pct.	3–Pt. FG/FGA	Pct.	FT/FTA	Pct.	Reb. O/T	A	TO	PF	S	Blk	TP	PPM
BLANKS, L.	40	5/13	.385	2/9	.222	1/4	.250	1/3	4	4	1	2	0	13	.325
HEGGS, A.	39	6/10	.600	0/0	.000	5/7	.714	2/8	2	1	1	2	1	17	.436
NASSAR, J.	23	3/5	.600	0/0	.000	0/0	.000	2/8	2	0	4	0	2	6	.261
WRIGHT, J.	39	6/12	.500	0/4	.000	5/7	.714	1/4	1	2	1	2	0	17	.436
MAYS, T.	39	8/17	.471	5/9	.556	2/4	.500	3/4	2	7	2	0	0	23	.590
JEANS, U.	1	0/0	.000	0/0	.000	0/0	.000	0/0	0	0	0	0	0	0	.000
SHEPARD, W.	1	0/0	.000	0/0	.000	0/0	.000	0/0	0	0	0	0	0	0	.000
GIPSON, T.	2	0/0	.000	0/0	.000	0/0	.000	0/0	0	0	0	0	0	0	.000
MULLER, G.	15	0/3	.000	0/0	.000	0/0	.000	3/3	0	0	5	0	0	0	.000
JONES, T.	1	0/0	.000	0/0	.000	0/0	.000	0/0	0	0	0	0	0	0	.000
Totals	200	28/60	.467	7/22	.318	13/22	.591	12/30	11	14	14	6	3	76	.380

Team Rebounds: Texas 5; Georgia Tech 0. Disqualified: Texas—Muller; Georgia Tech—Scott. Technical fouls: None.

	1st Half	2nd Half	Final
Georgia Tech	35	35	70
Texas	43	33	76

Missouri (85)   Coach: Norm Stewart

	Min.	Total FG/FGA	Pct.	3–Pt. FG/FGA	Pct.	FT/FTA	Pct.	Reb. O/T	A	TO	PF	S	Blk	TP	PPM
SMITH, D.	-	7/13	.538	1/1	1.000	3/4	.750	1/5	1	0	2	0	1	18	-
SANDBOTHE, M.	-	0/3	.000	0/0	.000	0/0	.000	1/5	2	1	4	0	0	0	-
LEONARD, G.	-	5/8	.625	0/0	.000	0/1	.000	3/6	0	2	2	2	3	10	-
COWARD, L.	-	6/11	.545	2/5	.400	1/2	.500	1/5	4	2	0	0	0	15	-
IRVIN, B.	-	9/15	.600	2/4	.500	5/6	.833	1/4	5	3	0	1	0	25	-
BUNTIN, N.	-	1/2	.500	0/1	.000	0/0	.000	1/2	0	0	0	0	0	2	-
CHURCH, G.	-	5/8	.625	0/0	.000	3/5	.600	4/5	0	2	2	0	1	13	-
PEELER, A.	-	0/4	.000	0/0	.000	2/2	1.000	0/2	2	0	1	0	1	2	-
Totals	200	33/64	.516	5/11	.455	14/20	.700	12/34	14	10	11	3	6	85	.425

Creighton (69)   Coach: Tony Barone

	Min.	Total FG/FGA	Pct.	3–Pt. FG/FGA	Pct.	FT/FTA	Pct.	Reb. O/T	A	TO	PF	S	Blk	TP	PPM
MOSER, P.	13	2/4	.500	1.1	1.000	1/1	1.000	0/0	0	2	3	1	0	6	.462
HARSTAD, B.	23	3/11	.273	0/0	.000	1/2	.500	1/5	0	1	3	0	0	7	.304
GALLAGHER, C.	39	11/16	.688	0/0	.000	1/8	.000	1/8	0	0	2	1	1	22	.564
FARR, J.	40	5/11	.455	2/5	.400	0/0	.000	3/5	5	2	2	0	0	12	.300
EISNER, T.	29	4/7	.571	3/6	.500	0/0	.000	2/3	9	6	5	1	0	11	.379
JOHNSON, K.	1	0/1	.000	0/1	.000	0/0	.000	0/0	0	0	0	0	0	0	.000
MOLITOR, T.	1	0/0	.000	0/0	.000	0/0	.000	0/0	0	0	0	0	0	0	.000
BALL, T.	1	0/0	.000	0/0	.000	0/0	.000	1/2	0	0	0	0	0	0	.000
ROGGENBURK, M.	33	2/8	.250	1/5	.200	0/0	.000	0/2	2	2	2	1	1	5	.152
WRIGHTSELL, L.	1	0/0	.000	0/0	.000	0/0	.000	0/0	1	0	1	0	0	0	.000
BELL, T.	17	1/3	.333	0/0	.000	4/4	1.000	1/3	2	0	1	0	0	6	.353
O'DOWD, B.	1	0/1	.000	0/0	.000	0/0	.000	0/1	0	0	1	0	0	0	.000
MOHR, D.	1	0/0	.000	0/0	.000	0/0	.000	0/0	0	0	0	0	0	0	.000
Totals	200	28/62	.452	7/18	.389	6/7	.857	9/29	19	13	20	4	2	69	.345

Team Rebounds: Missouri 4; Creighton 0. Disqualified: Creighton—Eisner. Technical fouls: None.

	1st Half	2nd Half	Final
Missouri	37	48	85
Creighton	39	30	69

Florida (46)   Coach: Norm Sloan

	Min.	Total FG/FGA	Pct.	3–Pt. FG/FGA	Pct.	FT/FTA	Pct.	Reb. O/T	A	TO	PF	S	Blk	TP	PPM
CHATMAN, L.	36	4/12	.333	0/1	.000	0/0	.000	3/7	2	4	2	1	0	8	.222
KERR, M.	11	1/4	.250	0/1	.000	0/0	.000	1/2	0	1	4	0	0	2	.182
SCHINTZIUS, D.	36	7/13	.538	0/0	.000	0/0	.000	1/8	3	6	3	1	1	14	.389
GARCIA, R.	26	2/4	.500	0/1	.000	0/0	.000	1/1	3	2	2	0	0	4	.154
LETT, C.	34	1/7	.143	1/5	.200	0/0	.000	1/2	4	3	2	1	0	3	.088
RAMIREZ, M.	2	0/1	.000	0/0	.000	0/0	.000	0/0	0	1	0	0	0	0	.000
TURNER, T.	2	0/0	.000	0/0	.000	0/0	.000	0/0	0	0	1	0	0	0	.000
HOGAN, B.	18	1/4	.250	0/3	.000	0/0	.000	1/2	2	0	2	2	0	2	.111
MCKINNON, K.	5	1/4	.250	0/0	.000	2/2	1.000	0/0	0	0	1	0	0	4	.800
DAVIS, D.	30	4/5	.800	0/0	.000	1/2	.500	3/6	0	1	3	2	1	9	.300
Totals	200	21/54	.389	1/13	.077	3/4	.750	11/28	14	18	20	7	2	46	.230

Colorado State (68)   Coach: Boyd Grant

	Min.	Total FG/FGA	Pct.	3–Pt. FG/FGA	Pct.	FT/FTA	Pct.	Reb. O/T	A	TO	PF	S	Blk	TP	PPM
DURHAM, P.	37	7/13	.538	0/0	.000	2/4	.500	0/4	1	4	1	1	2	16	.432
ANDERSON, A.	34	3/4	.750	1/2	.500	2/2	1.000	1/2	3	4	1	1	0	9	.265
FRIEHAUF, E.	32	1/4	.250	0/0	.000	1/5	.200	1/2	5	0	3	2	1	3	.094
TRIBELHORN, J.	35	7/12	.583	4/6	.667	2/2	1.000	1/1	2	2	0	3	0	20	.571
SHIPPEN, T.	28	2/3	.667	2/2	1.000	2/2	1.000	0/4	3	0	0	0	0	8	.286
MICHAEL, M.	2	0/0	.000	0/0	.000	0/0	.000	0/0	1	0	0	0	0	0	.000
TRYON, L.	15	1/4	.250	0/1	.000	0/1	.000	1/1	2	4	1	1	2	1	0	2	.133
MOLYNEAUX, D.	2	0/0	.000	0/0	.000	0/1	.000	0/0	0	1	0	0	1	0	.000
HINES, J.	2	0/1	.000	0/0	.000	2/2	1.000	0/1	0	0	0	0	0	2	1.000
LARSON, D.	1	1/1	1.000	0/0	.000	0/0	.000	1/1	0	0	0	0	0	2	2.000
SHARP, M.	11	1/1	1.000	0/0	.000	0/0	.000	1/4	0	2	0	0	0	2	.182
MANNA, W.	1	1/1	1.000	0/0	.000	2/2	1.000	0/0	1	0	1	0	0	4	4.000
Totals	200	24/44	.545	7/11	.636	13/21	.619	7/24	16	12	10	8	4	68	.340

Team Rebounds: Colorado State 2; Florida 3. Disqualified: None. Technical fouls: None.

	1st Half	2nd Half	Final
Florida	22	24	46
Colorado State	31	37	68

Syracuse (104)   Coach: Jim Boeheim

	Min.	Total FG/FGA	Pct.	3–Pt. FG/FGA	Pct.	FT/FTA	Pct.	Reb. O/T	A	TO	PF	S	Blk	TP	PPM
OWENS, B.	37	12/17	.706	0/0	.000	3/6	.500	7/13	1	1	2	1	1	27	.730
THOMPSON, S.	31	8/12	.667	0/0	.000	5/6	.833	2/4	4	2	2	3	0	21	.677
MANNING, R.	15	1/3	.333	0/0	.000	0/0	.000	0/2	0	0	4	0	1	2	.133
ROE, M.	32	7/14	.500	4/9	.444	1/2	.500	0/1	0	3	0	0	19	.594
DOUGLAS, S.	37	7/14	.500	2/4	.500	3/5	.600	0/1	9	5	3	3	0	19	.514
BARTELSTEIN, D.	1	0/0	.000	0/0	.000	0/0	.000	0/0	0	0	0	0	0	0	.000
JOHNSON, D.	16	2/5	.400	0/2	.000	4/4	1.000	2/4	1	0	2	1	0	8	.500
SIOCK, D.	2	0/1	.000	0/0	.000	0/0	.000	0/0	1	2	0	0	0	0	.000
HARRIED, H.	23	2/5	.400	0/0	.000	0/1	.000	2/5	2	2	2	2	0	4	.174
SCOTT, A.	5	2/3	.667	0/0	.000	0/0	.000	2/2	0	1	0	0	0	4	.800
ROGERS, E.	1	0/0	.000	0/0	.000	0/0	.000	0/0	0	0	1	0	0	0	.000
Totals	200	41/74	.554	6/15	.400	16/24	.667	16/34	17	8	20	10	2	104	.520

Bucknell (81)   Coach: Charles Woollum

	Min.	Total FG/FGA	Pct.	3–Pt. FG/FGA	Pct.	FT/FTA	Pct.	Reb. O/T	A	TO	PF	S	Blk	TP	PPM
WATSON	33	4/10	.400	0/1	.000	1/1	1.000	2/4	3	0	3	0	0	9	.273
HEIDEN	17	3/6	.500	1/3	.333	0/0	.000	2/8	0	4	3	1	0	7	.412
BUTTS	36	10/14	.714	0/0	.000	2/4	.500	2/6	0	6	4	0	0	22	.611
JOSEPH, M.	38	6/13	.462	2/7	.286	0/0	.000	0/1	9	3	4	2	0	14	.368
ACETO	34	3/9	.333	1/2	.500	4/4	1.000	0/2	3	1	2	2	0	11	.324
WOOLLUM	4	0/1	.000	0/0	.000	0/0	.000	0/0	0	0	0	0	0	0	.000
COURTNEY	2	0/0	.000	0/0	.000	2/2	1.000	1/1	1	0	1	0	0	2	1.000
FENTON	2	0/1	.000	0/0	.000	0/0	.000	0/0	1	0	0	0	0	0	.000
PFAFF, R.	3	0/1	.000	0/0	.000	1/2	.500	1/1	0	1	0	0	0	1	.333
DIVER	1	0/0	.000	0/0	.000	0/0	.000	0/0	0	0	0	0	0	0	.000
BELL	1	0/0	.000	0/0	.000	0/0	.000	0/0	0	0	0	0	0	0	.000
ALBEE	1	0/0	.000	0/0	.000	0/0	.000	0/0	0	0	0	0	0	0	.000
LEGGETT, G.	26	5/10	.500	0/0	.000	3/6	.500	3/6	3	1	2	0	0	13	.500
LESHINSKI	1	0/0	.000	0/0	.000	0/0	.000	0/0	0	0	0	0	0	0	.000
WALSH, M.	1	1/1	1.000	0/0	.000	0/0	.000	0/0	0	0	0	0	0	2	2.000
Totals	200	32/66	.485	4/13	.308	13/19	.684	11/29	19	16	20	5	0	81	.405

Team Rebounds: Syracuse 3; Bucknell 6. Disqualified: None. Technical fouls: None.

	1st Half	2nd Half	Final
Syracuse	52	52	104
Bucknell	36	45	81

FIRST ROUND SOUTHEAST

Oklahoma (72)   Coach: Billy Tubbs

	Min.	Total FG/FGA	Pct.	3-Pt. FG/FGA	Pct.	FT/FTA	Pct.	Reb. O/T	A	TO	PF	S	Blk	TP	PPM
DAVIS, W.	22	5/11	.455	0/0	.000	4/5	.800	6/9	0	0	1	0	0	14	.636
JONES, T.	27	1/2	.500	1/2	.500	0/0	.000	0/2	2	1	1	2	0	3	.111
KING, S.	40	11/21	.524	0/0	.000	6/9	.667	3/10	0	1	3	1	1	28	.700
BLAYLOCK, M.	34	5/12	.417	0/2	.000	5/8	.625	1/2	2	1	4	1	0	15	.441
MULLINS, T.	40	3/9	.333	0/1	.000	2/2	1.000	1/5	6	2	4	0	0	8	.200
HENRY, S.	14	0/2	.000	0/1	.000	0/0	.000	2/3	1	3	4	0	0	0	.000
PATTERSON, D.	13	1/2	.500	0/1	.000	0/2	.000	1/3	2	1	0	0	1	2	.154
WILEY, A.	5	1/2	.500	0/0	.000	0/1	.000	0/0	0	0	0	0	1	2	.400
BELL, M.	3	0/2	.000	0/0	.000	0/0	.000	0/0	0	0	1	0	1	0	.000
MARTIN, T.	2	0/0	.000	0/0	.000	0/0	.000	0/0	0	0	1	0	0	0	.000
Totals	200	27/63	.429	1/7	.143	17/27	.630	14/34	13	9	19	4	4	72	.360

East Tennessee State (71)   Coach: Les Robinson

	Min.	Total FG/FGA	Pct.	3-Pt. FG/FGA	Pct.	FT/FTA	Pct.	Reb. O/T	A	TO	PF	S	Blk	TP	PPM
TALFORD, C.	31	5/10	.500	0/1	.000	4/4	1.000	0/1	2	3	2	2	0	14	.452
STORY, M.	17	1/5	.200	0/0	.000	2/3	.667	2/5	0	2	4	0	1	4	.235
DENNIS, G.	37	7/17	.412	0/1	.000	6/6	1.000	6/15	1	1	4	1	1	20	.541
WEST, A.	26	4/15	.267	2/7	.286	2/4	.500	2/8	3	2	1	0	0	12	.462
JENNINGS, K.	35	3/8	.375	0/0	.000	2/2	1.000	2/5	7	1	5	0	0	8	.229
WOODS, M.	7	0/0	.000	0/0	.000	0/0	.000	0/1	0	0	1	0	0	0	.000
KELLER, C.	29	2/2	1.000	0/0	.000	3/3	1.000	3/5	1	0	2	0	0	7	.241
GREER, M.	14	2/4	.500	2/2	1.000	0/0	.000	0/1	2	0	1	0	0	6	.429
JONES, R.	4	0/0	.000	0/0	.000	0/0	.000	0/0	0	0	0	0	0	0	.000
Totals	200	24/61	.393	4/12	.333	19/22	.864	15/41	16	9	21	4	2	71	.355

Team Rebounds: Oklahoma 6; East Tenn. St. 3. Disqualified: East Tenn. St.—Jennings. Technical fouls: None.

	1st Half	2nd Half	Final
Oklahoma	31	41	72
East Tenn. St.	39	32	71

La Salle (74)   Coach: Bill Morris

	Min.	Total FG/FGA	Pct.	3-Pt. FG/FGA	Pct.	FT/FTA	Pct.	Reb. O/T	A	TO	PF	S	Blk	TP	PPM
SIMMONS, L.	40	12/28	.429	0/2	.000	2/5	.400	5/16	3	4	3	0	3	26	.650
HURD	38	8/12	.667	4/6	.667	6/6	1.000	1/3	2	1	2	4	0	26	.684
CONLIN	21	2/7	.286	0/1	.000	2/2	1.000	0/2	1	1	4	1	0	6	.286
LIEVEREST	14	0/2	.000	0/0	.000	0/0	.000	3/3	0	0	1	2	0	0	.000
OVERTON, D.	40	5/14	.357	0/2	.000	0/0	.000	2/4	3	0	1	3	0	10	.250
JOHNSON, B.	22	1/10	.100	1/6	.167	1/2	.500	2/3	4	0	3	0	1	4	.182
WRIEDT, S.	1	0/1	.000	0/0	.000	0/0	.000	0/0	0	0	0	0	0	0	.000
SHELTON, D.	24	1/1	1.000	0/0	.000	0/0	.000	1/2	0	0	4	0	1	2	.083
Totals	200	29/75	.387	5/17	.294	11/15	.733	14/33	13	6	18	10	5	74	.370

Louisiana Tech (83)   Coach: Tommy Eagles

	Min.	Total FG/FGA	Pct.	3-Pt. FG/FGA	Pct.	FT/FTA	Pct.	Reb. O/T	A	TO	PF	S	Blk	TP	PPM
NEWTON, B.	33	4/9	.444	3/5	.600	0/0	.000	1/4	1	2	5	2	1	11	.333
DADE, A.	25	5/10	.500	0/0	.000	6/9	.667	2/7	0	4	0	1	0	16	.640
WHITE, R.	35	6/13	.462	0/1	.000	10/13	.769	2/16	0	5	3	0	0	22	.629
LOUIS, K.	19	4/4	1.000	3/3	1.000	0/0	.000	0/2	1	0	2	0	0	11	.579
GUILLORY, B.	40	2/3	.667	1/2	.500	0/0	.000	0/1	11	3	1	0	0	5	.125
BROWN, P.	21	2/4	.500	0/0	.000	2/2	1.000	2/4	2	1	3	0	0	6	.286
KNIGHT, D.	26	5/8	.625	1/2	.500	1/1	1.000	0/4	2	4	5	1	0	12	.462
CRAWFORD, D.	1	0/0	.000	0/0	.000	0/0	.000	0/0	0	0	0	0	0	0	.000
Totals	200	28/51	.549	8/13	.615	19/25	.760	7/38	17	19	19	4	2	83	.415

Team Rebounds: Louisiana Tech 1; La Salle 3. Disqualified: Louisiana Tech— Newton, Knight. Technical fouls: None.

	1st Half	2nd Half	Final
La Salle	33	41	74
Louisiana Tech	41	42	83

Virginia (100)   Coach: Terry Holland

	Min.	Total FG/FGA	Pct.	3-Pt. FG/FGA	Pct.	FT/FTA	Pct.	Reb. O/T	A	TO	PF	S	Blk	TP	PPM
BLUNDIN, M.	31	1/2	.500	0/0	.000	2/3	.667	2/7	0	2	3	0	0	4	.129
STITH, B.	29	7/9	.778	0/0	.000	5/6	.833	3/7	0	1	2	1	0	19	.655
DABBS, D.	33	4/8	.500	0/0	.000	7/8	.875	1/5	1	3	3	0	2	15	.455
CROTTY, J.	37	9/10	.900	4/4	1.000	2/2	1.000	0/2	10	3	3	1	1	24	.649
MORGAN, R.	38	11/22	.500	2/5	.400	9/9	1.000	3/5	5	5	3	0	1	33	.868
OLIVER, A.	2	0/0	.000	0/0	.000	0/0	.000	0/0	0	0	0	0	0	0	.000
TURNER, K.	10	0/2	.000	0/0	.000	0/0	.000	1/1	0	0	2	0	0	0	.000
KAPSTRA, D.	6	1/1	1.000	1/1	1.000	0/0	.000	0/0	1	1	2	0	0	3	.500
DANIEL, J.	14	1/1	1.000	0/0	.000	0/1	.000	1/3	0	0	0	0	0	2	.143
Totals	200	34/55	.618	7/10	.700	25/29	.862	11/30	17	15	18	2	4	100	.500

Providence (97)   Coach: Rick Barnes

	Min.	Total FG/FGA	Pct.	3-Pt. FG/FGA	Pct.	FT/FTA	Pct.	Reb. O/T	A	TO	PF	S	Blk	TP	PPM
FOSTER, C.	14	2/2	1.000	0/0	.000	4/8	.500	2/3	0	0	2	0	0	8	.571
PALAZZI, M.	33	7/15	.467	3/6	.500	2/2	1.000	2/3	2	0	4	0	0	19	.576
CONLON, M.	29	9/15	.600	2/3	.667	3/4	.750	1/5	1	1	5	1	0	23	.793
MURDOCK, E.	30	6/12	.500	2/4	.500	2/2	1.000	0/1	6	3	4	2	0	16	.533
SCREEN, K.	29	4/9	.444	0/1	.000	2/3	.667	2/5	6	2	5	1	0	10	.345
BURTON, Q.	4	0/1	.000	0/0	.000	0/0	.000	0/0	0	0	0	0	0	0	.000
BENT, G.	6	0/0	.000	0/0	.000	0/0	.000	0/0	0	0	0	0	0	0	.000
SHAMSID-DEEN, A.	27	5/8	.625	0/0	.000	1/1	1.000	4/8	0	0	4	1	0	11	.407
WRIGHT, D.	20	4/9	.444	0/2	.000	2/2	1.000	1/1	4	2	4	2	0	10	.500
SADDLER, M.	4	0/1	.000	0/0	.000	0/0	.000	0/0	0	0	0	0	0	0	.000
WATTS, C.	4	0/0	.000	0/0	.000	0/0	.000	0/0	0	0	0	0	0	0	.000
Totals	200	37/72	.514	7/16	.438	16/22	.727	12/26	19	8	28	7	0	97	.485

Team Rebounds: Virginia 4; Providence 4. Disqualified: Providence—Conlon, Screen. Technical fouls: None.

	1st Half	2nd Half	Final
Virginia	50	50	100
Providence	49	48	97

Florida State (83)   Coach: Pat Kennedy

	Min.	Total FG/FGA	Pct.	3-Pt. FG/FGA	Pct.	FT/FTA	Pct.	Reb. O/T	A	TO	PF	S	Blk	TP	PPM
DAWSON, T.	33	10/17	.588	0/1	.000	1/1	1.000	4/8	0	2	5	1	0	21	.636
THOMAS, I.	24	2/7	.286	0/0	.000	1/2	.500	2/9	1	2	2	0	0	5	.208
HUNTER, T.	28	7/11	.636	0/0	.000	2/3	.667	5/8	1	4	1	2	1	16	.571
MAYES, T.	34	9/12	.750	1/3	.333	1/1	1.000	1/2	2	3	5	0	0	20	.588
McCLOUD, G.	40	4/15	.267	4/11	.364	0/1	.000	1/5	5	2	1	0	0	12	.300
WHITE, D.	1	0/0	.000	0/0	.000	0/0	.000	0/0	0	0	2	0	0	0	.000
HANDS, L.	2	0/1	.000	0/0	.000	0/0	.000	0/0	0	0	0	0	0	0	.000
MITCHELL, D.	34	4/10	.400	0/0	.000	0/1	.000	2/5	7	2	1	1	0	8	.235
JOHNSON, B.	4	0/0	.000	0/0	.000	1/2	.500	0/0	0	0	0	0	0	1	.250
Totals	200	36/73	.493	5/15	.333	6/11	.545	15/37	16	15	17	4	1	83	.415

Middle Tennessee State (97)   Coach: Bruce Stewart

	Min.	Total FG/FGA	Pct.	3-Pt. FG/FGA	Pct.	FT/FTA	Pct.	Reb. O/T	A	TO	PF	S	Blk	TP	PPM
VANCE, Q.	10	0/3	.000	0/0	.000	0/0	.000	3/3	1	2	0	0	1	0	.000
HAMMONDS, K.	39	5/14	.357	0/0	.000	1/2	.500	3/13	1	3	4	4	0	11	.282
RAINEY, C.	30	2/8	.250	1/5	.200	4/4	1.000	0/4	2	4	3	0	0	9	.300
HENRY, T.	36	12/18	.667	0/0	.000	2/2	1.000	3/10	1	1	3	2	0	26	.722
HARRIS, G.	36	4/9	.444	1/4	.250	0/1	.000	0/3	7	2	1	1	0	9	.250
INGRAM, C.	4	0/0	.000	0/0	.000	0/0	.000	0/1	0	0	2	0	0	0	.000
BUCK, M.	22	7/7	1.000	6/6	1.000	6/6	1.000	1/2	4	2	2	1	0	26	1.182
WALLACE, M.	7	2/3	.667	0/1	.000	1/2	.500	0/0	0	1	0	0	0	5	.714
WEBB, M.	15	4/8	.500	1/2	.500	2/2	1.000	2/2	3	0	1	1	0	11	.733
HUNTER, J.	1	0/0	.000	0/0	.000	0/0	.000	0/0	0	0	1	0	0	0	.000
Totals	200	36/70	.514	9/18	.500	16/19	.842	12/38	19	14	17	9	1	97	.485

Team Rebounds: Middle Tenn. St. 0; Florida State 3. Disqualified: Florida State—Dawson, Mayes. Technical fouls: None.

	1st Half	2nd Half	Final
Florida State	51	32	83
Middle Tenn. St.	44	53	97

Alabama (84)   Coach: Wimp Sanderson

	Min.	Total FG/FGA	Pct.	3–Pt. FG/FGA	Pct.	FT/FTA	Pct.	Reb. O/T	A	TO	PF	S	Blk	TP	PPM
HORRY, R.	26	2/3	.667	1/1	1.000	2/2	1.000	2/6	3	0	4	0	0	7	.269
ANSLEY, M.	35	12/25	.480	0/0	.000	1/2	.500	3/8	3	1	5	1	0	25	.714
BENOIT, D.	24	2/3	.667	0/0	.000	2/2	1.000	1/8	1	1	4	0	0	6	.250
WAITES, G.	34	7/13	.538	1/3	.333	2/4	.500	3/6	7	3	2	1	0	17	.500
LEE, A.	40	8/16	.500	2/4	.500	0/0	.000	0/0	2	3	2	0	0	18	.450
ASKINS, K.	23	5/8	.625	1/2	.500	0/0	.000	3/5	1	0	4	1	0	11	.478
SANDERS, J.	7	0/1	.000	0/1	.000	0/0	.000	0/1	3	0	0	0	0	0	.000
CHEATUM, M.	9	0/2	.000	0/0	.000	0/0	.000	0/1	0	0	2	0	0	0	.000
WEBB, M.	2	0/0	.000	0/0	.000	0/0	.000	0/0	0	0	1	0	0	0	.000
Totals	200	36/71	.507	5/11	.455	7/10	.700	12/35	20	8	24	3	0	84	.420

South Alabama (86)   Coach: Ronnie Arrow

	Min.	Total FG/FGA	Pct.	3–Pt. FG/FGA	Pct.	FT/FTA	Pct.	Reb. O/T	A	TO	PF	S	Blk	TP	PPM
ESTABA, G.	34	7/12	.583	0/0	.000	12/16	.750	3/7	0	0	3	1	0	26	.765
JIMMERSON, J.	26	1/4	.250	0/0	.000	1/3	.333	2/6	4	1	2	0	0	3	.115
DARDEN, P.	24	2/7	.286	0/0	.000	0/0	.000	2/3	1	0	2	0	3	4	.167
HODGE, J.	38	11/20	.550	3/7	.429	4/4	1.000	4/5	2	1	0	0	0	29	.763
LEWIS, J.	37	6/15	.400	0/0	.000	3/6	.500	4/12	5	2	1	0	0	15	.405
SMITH, N.	15	1/3	.333	0/0	.000	0/0	.000	0/3	0	0	1	0	2	2	.133
BRODNICK, T.	17	1/3	.333	0/1	.000	3/4	.750	1/1	1	0	0	1	0	5	.294
TURNER, D.	8	1/1	1.000	0/0	.000	0/0	.000	0/0	0	0	2	0	0	2	.250
NELSON, D.	1	0/0	.000	0/0	.000	0/0	.000	0/0	0	1	1	0	0	0	.000
Totals	200	30/65	.462	3/8	.375	23/35	.657	16/37	13	5	12	2	3	86	.430

Team Rebounds: South Alabama 3; Alabama 3. Disqualified: Alabama—Ansley. Technical fouls: None.

	1st Half	2nd Half	Final
Alabama	49	35	84
South Alabama	33	53	86

Michigan (92)   Coach: Steve Fisher

	Min.	Total FG/FGA	Pct.	3–Pt. FG/FGA	Pct.	FT/FTA	Pct.	Reb. O/T	A	TO	PF	S	Blk	TP	PPM
RICE, G.	40	9/22	.409	5/9	.556	0/0	.000	1/3	2	3	2	0	1	23	.575
HUGHES, M.	28	4/5	.800	0/0	.000	0/1	.000	5/10	0	0	2	0	0	8	.286
MILLS, T.	32	8/12	.667	0/0	.000	2/2	1.000	2/6	5	1	4	2	1	18	.563
GRIFFIN, M.	19	0/0	.000	0/0	.000	0/0	.000	0/0	2	0	2	1	0	0	.000
ROBINSON, R.	34	8/13	.615	1/2	.500	6/9	.667	2/4	8	6	4	2	1	23	.676
VAUGHT, L.	10	2/4	.500	0/0	.000	0/0	.000	1/3	0	0	4	0	0	4	.400
CALIP, D.	14	3/5	.600	0/0	.000	3/3	1.000	2/2	1	3	1	0	0	9	.643
HIGGINS, S.	23	3/6	.500	0/1	.000	1/1	1.000	0/3	0	4	2	1	0	7	.304
Totals	200	37/67	.552	6/12	.500	12/16	.750	13/31	18	17	21	8	3	92	.460

Xavier (Ohio) (87)   Coach: Pete Gillen

	Min.	Total FG/FGA	Pct.	3–Pt. FG/FGA	Pct.	FT/FTA	Pct.	Reb. O/T	A	TO	PF	S	Blk	TP	PPM
PARKER, C.	5	0/1	.000	0/0	.000	0/0	.000	0/0	2	0	0	0	0	0	.000
HILL, T.	33	7/12	.583	0/0	.000	7/7	1.000	3/6	2	3	4	0	0	21	.636
STRONG, D.	37	8/12	.667	0/0	.000	2/3	.667	4/10	0	8	3	1	0	18	.486
KIMBROUGH, S.	39	5/16	.313	2/4	.500	1/2	.500	2/5	6	1	4	2	0	13	.333
DAVENPORT, M.	35	6/13	.462	0/4	.000	3/4	.750	1/2	1	2	3	2	0	15	.429
WALKER, J.	34	6/9	.667	1/1	1.000	3/5	.600	2/9	9	4	3	2	0	16	.471
MINOR, D.	16	2/2	1.000	0/0	.000	0/0	.000	0/1	1	1	1	0	0	4	.250
RAEFORD, S.	1	0/0	.000	0/0	.000	0/0	.000	0/0	0	0	1	0	0	0	.000
Totals	200	34/65	.523	3/9	.333	16/21	.762	12/26	21	19	19	7	0	87	.435

Team Rebounds: Michigan 2; Xavier (Ohio) 4. Disqualified: None. Technical fouls: None.

	1st Half	2nd Half	Final
Michigan	42	50	92
Xavier (Ohio)	45	42	87

UCLA (84)   Coach: Jim Harrick

	Min.	Total FG/FGA	Pct.	3–Pt. FG/FGA	Pct.	FT/FTA	Pct.	Reb. O/T	A	TO	PF	S	Blk	TP	PPM
WILSON, T.	37	5/8	.625	0/0	.000	4/7	.571	0/11	3	3	4	1	0	14	.378
MACLEAN, D.	32	11/16	.688	0/0	.000	1/2	.500	2/6	1	4	3	1	0	23	.719
WALKER, K.	12	1/2	.500	0/1	.000	0/0	.000	1/2	1	0	3	0	0	2	.167
MARTIN, D.	38	2/7	.286	0/0	.000	4/6	.667	0/2	5	2	2	5	0	8	.211
RICHARDSON, J.	40	8/14	.571	1/2	.500	2/3	.667	0/5	14	1	1	1	1	19	.475
ROCHELIN, C.	25	8/13	.615	0/0	.000	0/0	.000	1/1	0	0	5	0	1	16	.640
OWENS, K.	16	0/1	.000	0/0	.000	2/2	1.000	0/2	1	2	3	3	0	2	.125
Totals	200	35/61	.574	1/3	.333	13/20	.650	4/29	25	12	21	11	3	84	.420

Iowa State (74)   Coach: Johnny Orr

	Min.	Total FG/FGA	Pct.	3–Pt. FG/FGA	Pct.	FT/FTA	Pct.	Reb. O/T	A	TO	PF	S	Blk	TP	PPM
URQUHART, M.	10	0/2	.000	0/0	.000	2/2	1.000	0/1	2	1	1	0	0	2	.200
BAUGH, M.	32	6/13	.462	1/3	.333	3/4	.750	4/9	4	4	3	2	0	16	.500
ALEXANDER, V.	40	7/15	.467	0/0	.000	8/12	.667	6/13	0	3	4	0	1	22	.550
WOODS, T.	37	4/11	.364	0/4	.000	1/4	.250	0/2	3	4	1	0	0	9	.243
BORN, M.	37	3/7	.429	0/3	.000	0/0	.000	2/5	2	2	3	1	0	6	.162
MACK, S.	31	3/10	.300	0/1	.000	2/2	1.000	1/8	2	3	4	2	0	8	.258
MOORE, A.	12	4/6	.667	0/0	.000	1/3	.333	3/3	0	1	2	0	0	9	.750
GOODMAN, J.	1	1/1	1.000	0/0	.000	0/0	.000	0/0	0	0	0	0	0	2	2.000
SUFFREN, H.	0	0/0	.000	0/0	.000	0/0	.000	0/0	0	0	1	0	0	0	-
Totals	200	28/65	.431	1/11	.091	17/27	.630	16/41	13	18	19	5	1	74	.370

Team Rebounds: UCLA 1; Iowa State 1. Disqualified: UCLA—Rochelin. Technical fouls: None. Player who played 0 min. played less than 1 min.

	1st Half	2nd Half	Final
UCLA	39	45	84
Iowa State	35	39	74

North Carolina (93)   Coach: Dean Smith

	Min.	Total FG/FGA	Pct.	3–Pt. FG/FGA	Pct.	FT/FTA	Pct.	Reb. O/T	A	TO	PF	S	Blk	TP	PPM
BUCKNALL, S.	33	4/6	.667	3/4	.750	2/2	1.000	0/5	7	4	2	0	0	13	.394
REID, J.	29	8/12	.667	0/0	.000	2/2	1.000	4/10	2	6	2	0	1	18	.621
WILLIAMS, S.	26	6/10	.600	0/0	.000	2/3	.667	3/11	0	1	4	1	1	14	.538
LEBO, J.	24	2/7	.286	0/4	.000	0/0	.000	2/5	5	3	3	0	0	4	.167
RICE, K.	25	1/2	.500	1/2	.500	2/2	1.000	0/0	1	7	4	1	0	5	.200
CHILCUTT, S.	10	1/3	.333	0/0	.000	1/2	.500	0/0	1	1	0	0	0	3	.300
MADDEN, K.	28	11/13	.846	0/0	.000	0/3	.000	3/7	2	1	0	0	1	22	.786
FOX, R.	23	6/14	.429	0/0	.000	0/0	.000	1/7	1	0	2	4	0	12	.522
MAY, D.	0	0/1	.000	0/1	.000	0/0	.000	0/0	0	0	0	0	0	0	-
HENSLEY, M.	1	1/1	1.000	0/0	.000	0/0	.000	1/1	0	0	0	0	0	2	2.000
DENNY, J.	1	0/0	.000	0/0	.000	0/0	.000	0/0	0	0	0	0	0	0	.000
Totals	200	40/69	.580	4/11	.364	9/14	.643	14/47	25	20	14	5	3	93	.465

Southern-B.R. (79)   Coach: Ben Jobe

	Min.	Total FG/FGA	Pct.	3–Pt. FG/FGA	Pct.	FT/FTA	Pct.	Reb. O/T	A	TO	PF	S	Blk	TP	PPM
FAULKNER, J.	36	7/17	.412	0/2	.000	0/1	.000	1/5	3	1	4	5	0	14	.389
BATTLES, D.	40	5/9	.556	0/0	.000	1/5	.200	5/10	2	2	4	1	1	11	.275
YOUNGBLOOD, R.	33	3/9	.333	0/0	.000	1/2	.500	1/5	0	1	4	0	1	7	.212
SAMPLE, C.	40	7/24	.292	6/16	.375	2/2	1.000	1/2	7	2	3	1	0	22	.550
PHILLS, B.	34	8/18	.444	4/10	.400	0/0	.000	3/6	1	3	0	4	0	20	.588
ANDERSON, D.	13	2/2	1.000	0/0	.000	1/2	.500	2/2	1	0	0	0	0	5	.385
JONES, R.	4	0/0	.000	0/0	.000	0/0	.000	0/0	0	0	1	0	0	0	.000
Totals	200	32/79	.405	10/28	.357	5/12	.417	13/30	14	9	16	11	2	79	.395

Team Rebounds: N. Carolina 2; Southern-B.R. 3. Disqualified: None. Technical fouls: N. Carolina—Williams. Player who played 0 min. played less than 1 min.

	1st Half	2nd Half	Final
N. Carolina	44	49	93
Southern-B.R.	34	45	79

FIRST ROUND EAST

Georgetown (50)   Coach: John Thompson

	Min.	Total FG/FGA	Pct.	3-Pt. FG/FGA	Pct.	FT/FTA	Pct.	Reb. O/T	A	TO	PF	S	Blk	TP	PPM
JACKSON, J.	30	2/4	.500	0/0	.000	1/2	.500	2/3	1	1	1	0	0	5	.167
TURNER, J.	8	1/1	1.000	0/0	.000	0/2	.000	0/0	0	1	1	0	1	2	.250
MOURNING, A.	38	8/11	.727	0/0	.000	5/6	.833	7/13	0	1	3	0	7	21	.553
BRYANT, D.	21	0/2	.000	0/1	.000	0/0	.000	0/3	1	2	1	1	0	0	.000
SMITH, C.	38	2/12	.167	0/5	.000	0/1	.000	0/2	2	3	4	0	0	4	.105
TILLMON, M.	29	3/9	.333	1/4	.250	1/3	.333	3/5	0	2	1	1	0	8	.276
WINSTON, B.	32	2/2	1.000	0/0	.000	4/4	1.000	3/6	3	2	1	1	0	8	.250
JEFFERSON, S.	4	1/1	1.000	0/0	.000	0/0	.000	0/1	0	0	0	0	2	.500
Totals	200	19/42	.452	1/10	.100	11/18	.611	15/32	7	13	12	3	8	50	.250

Princeton (49)   Coach: Pete Carril

	Min.	Total FG/FGA	Pct.	3-Pt. FG/FGA	Pct.	FT/FTA	Pct.	Reb. O/T	A	TO	PF	S	Blk	TP	PPM
SCRABIS, B.	40	6/13	.462	2/6	.333	1/2	.500	1/2	2	1	2	2	0	15	.375
EASTWICK, M.	6	0/0	.000	0/0	.000	0/0	.000	0/0	0	0	0	0	0	0	.000
MUELLER, K.	40	4/11	.364	0/1	.000	1/3	.333	0/3	8	2	3	2	1	9	.225
DOYLE, J.	27	4/6	.667	0/1	.000	0/0	.000	0/0	0	0	4	1	0	8	.296
LEFTWICH, G.	40	1/3	.333	0/0	.000	0/0	.000	1/5	0	1	3	1	0	2	.050
LAPIN, M.	34	5/10	.500	2/7	.286	0/0	.000	1/2	4	2	4	0	0	12	.353
HOTTENSTEIN, T.	13	1/1	1.000	1/1	1.000	0/0	.000	0/1	0	1	3	0	0	3	.231
Totals	200	21/44	.477	5/16	.313	2/5	.400	3/13	14	7	19	6	1	49	.245

Team Rebounds: Georgetown 3; Princeton 3. Disqualified: None. Technical fouls: None.

	1st Half	2nd Half	Final
Georgetown	21	29	50
Princeton	29	20	49

Vanderbilt (65)   Coach: C.M. Newton

	Min.	Total FG/FGA	Pct.	3-Pt. FG/FGA	Pct.	FT/FTA	Pct.	Reb. O/T	A	TO	PF	S	Blk	TP	PPM
BOOKER, B.	33	3/10	.300	1/3	.333	1/2	.500	1/1	1	2	2	1	0	8	.242
REID, E.	32	2/4	.500	0/0	.000	3/3	1.000	1/1	0	0	2	2	0	7	.219
KORNET, F.	33	8/14	.571	0/0	.000	1/5	.200	1/4	2	1	4	0	0	17	.515
WILCOX, J.	38	4/10	.400	1/2	.500	0/0	.000	1/2	4	4	3	1	0	9	.237
GOHEEN, B.	36	4/7	.571	1/1	1.000	9/9	1.000	2/5	3	2	1	2	0	18	.500
MAYES, C.	9	0/1	.000	0/0	.000	0/0	.000	0/4	1	0	1	0	0	0	.000
GRANT, S.	7	0/0	.000	0/0	.000	0/0	.000	0/2	0	0	0	0	0	0	.000
BALLESTRA, A.	8	1/4	.250	0/0	.000	2/2	1.000	1/2	1	1	0	0	1	4	.500
WHEAT, M.	2	0/0	.000	0/0	.000	0/0	.000	1/1	0	1	0	0	0	0	.000
BENJAMIN, F.	1	1/1	1.000	0/0	.000	0/0	.000	0/0	0	0	0	0	0	2	2.000
MILHOLLAND, T.	1	0/1	.000	0/0	.000	0/0	.000	0/0	0	0	0	0	0	0	.000
Totals	200	23/52	.442	3/6	.500	16/21	.762	8/22	12	10	14	6	1	65	.325

Notre Dame (81)   Coach: Digger Phelps

	Min.	Total FG/FGA	Pct.	3-Pt. FG/FGA	Pct.	FT/FTA	Pct.	Reb. O/T	A	TO	PF	S	Blk	TP	PPM
ELLIS, L.	25	8/14	.571	0/0	.000	1/1	1.000	6/18	1	2	4	0	3	17	.680
JACKSON, J.	35	6/19	.316	2/6	.333	2/2	1.000	2/4	6	1	1	1	0	16	.457
ROBINSON, K.	32	3/6	.500	0/0	.000	2/4	.500	4/8	0	2	1	0	0	8	.250
SINGLETON, T.	33	2/2	1.000	0/0	.000	2/2	1.000	0/2	7	0	4	1	0	6	.182
BENNETT, E.	26	3/5	.600	0/0	.000	2/2	1.000	1/1	2	2	2	1	0	8	.308
FREDRICK, J.	19	8/12	.667	4/4	1.000	0/2	.000	1/3	3	1	2	0	1	20	1.053
TOWER, K.	15	1/1	1.000	0/0	.000	0/0	.000	0/1	0	1	4	1	0	2	.133
SWEET, D.	6	1/1	1.000	0/0	.000	0/0	.000	0/0	1	0	0	0	0	2	.333
PADDOCK, S.	7	1/2	.500	0/0	.000	0/0	.000	1/1	0	0	1	1	0	2	.286
ADKINS, T.	1	0/0	.000	0/0	.000	0/0	.000	0/0	0	0	0	0	0	0	.000
CRAWFORD, T.	1	0/1	.000	0/0	.000	0/0	.000	0/0	0	0	0	0	0	0	.000
Totals	200	33/63	.524	6/10	.600	9/13	.692	15/38	20	9	19	5	4	81	.405

Team Rebounds: Notre Dame 1; Vanderbilt 2. Disqualified: None. Technical fouls: None.

	1st Half	2nd Half	Final
Vanderbilt	30	35	65
Notre Dame	34	47	81

North Carolina (81)   Coach: Jim Valvano

	Min.	Total FG/FGA	Pct.	3-Pt. FG/FGA	Pct.	FT/FTA	Pct.	Reb. O/T	A	TO	PF	S	Blk	TP	PPM
LESTER, A.	30	3/7	.429	0/0	.000	2/4	.500	4/11	0	1	5	1	1	8	.267
CORCHIANI, C.	31	2/6	.333	0/1	.000	8/10	.800	0/2	11	3	4	0	0	12	.387
MONROE, R.	40	9/17	.529	4/6	.667	0/0	.000	0/4	2	2	3	1	0	22	.550
LEE, D.	2	0/1	.000	0/0	.000	0/0	.000	0/0	0	0	0	0	0	0	.000
WEEMS, K.	17	5/7	.714	0/0	.000	2/6	.333	0/0	3	3	4	0	0	12	.706
D'AMICO, B.	3	0/0	.000	0/0	.000	0/0	.000	0/0	0	0	1	0	0	0	.000
HINNANT, M.	7	2/4	.500	0/0	.000	0/0	.000	0/0	0	0	0	1	0	4	.571
HOWARD, B.	34	3/3	1.000	0/0	.000	5/6	.833	0/6	1	3	3	1	0	11	.324
BROWN, C.	36	5/6	.833	0/0	.000	2/3	.667	2/7	2	2	1	0	3	12	.333
Totals	200	29/51	.569	4/7	.571	19/29	.655	6/30	19	14	21	4	4	81	.405

South Carolina (66)   Coach: George Felton

	Min.	Total FG/FGA	Pct.	3-Pt. FG/FGA	Pct.	FT/FTA	Pct.	Reb. O/T	A	TO	PF	S	Blk	TP	PPM
DOZIER, T.	37	8/13	.615	1/1	1.000	5/6	.833	2/5	2	1	3	1	1	22	.595
RHETT, J.	27	3/5	.600	0/1	.000	0/0	.000	2/7	0	0	0	0	0	6	.222
HUDSON, J.	33	3/11	.273	0/1	.000	7/11	.636	1/7	1	1	3	2	0	13	.394
MANNING, B.	38	3/9	.333	0/0	.000	2/4	.500	2/5	2	2	1	1	0	8	.211
ROUSLON, J.	2	0/0	.000	0/0	.000	0/0	.000	0/0	0	1	0	0	0	0	.000
ENGLISH, J.	20	3/9	.333	1/2	.500	0/0	.000	0/1	3	2	5	0	0	7	.350
McCOY, T.	6	0/4	.000	0/0	.000	1/2	.500	3/3	2	1	3	0	0	1	.167
GLOVER, M.	2	0/0	.000	0/0	.000	0/0	.000	0/0	0	0	2	0	0	0	.000
VERNEAU, B.	8	0/2	.000	0/1	.000	0/0	.000	0/4	1	1	0	0	0	0	.000
PRICE, B.	27	4/8	.500	1/3	.333	0/0	.000	1/2	2	0	5	0	0	9	.333
Totals	200	24/61	.393	3/9	.333	15/23	.652	11/31	16	9	23	4	2	66	.330

Team Rebounds: N.C. State 2; S. Carolina 3. Disqualified: N.C. State—Lester; S. Carolina—Price, English. Technical fouls: None.

	1st Half	2nd Half	Final
N.C. State	38	43	81
S. Carolina	25	41	66

Iowa (87)   Coach: Tom Davis

	Min.	Total FG/FGA	Pct.	3-Pt. FG/FGA	Pct.	FT/FTA	Pct.	Reb. O/T	A	TO	PF	S	Blk	TP	PPM
HORTON, E.	-	3/7	.429	0/0	.000	1/3	.333	2/5	2	3	4	3	0	7	-
BULLARD, M.	-	3/4	.750	2/3	.667	1/1	1.000	1/11	2	4	1	0	0	9	-
JEPSEN, L.	-	1/1	1.000	0/0	.000	0/0	.000	1/4	1	1	2	0	0	2	-
ARMSTRONG, B.	-	12/19	.632	6/9	.667	5/6	.833	0/2	5	3	1	3	0	35	-
MARBLE, R.	-	9/13	.692	1/2	.500	5/7	.714	1/4	2	4	2	0	0	24	-
MOSES, J.	-	2/4	.500	0/0	.000	0/1	.000	1/3	0	0	2	0	0	4	-
LOOKINGHILL, W.	-	1/1	1.000	0/0	.000	0/0	.000	1/2	0	1	1	1	0	2	-
GARNER, B.	-	2/3	.667	0/0	.000	0/1	.000	0/6	4	3	0	0	0	4	-
SKINNER, R.	-	0/0	.000	0/0	.000	0/0	.000	0/0	0	0	0	0	0	0	-
Totals	200	33/52	.635	9/14	.643	12/19	.632	7/31	18	20	16	7	0	87	.435

Rutgers (73)   Coach: Bob Wenzel

	Min.	Total FG/FGA	Pct.	3-Pt. FG/FGA	Pct.	FT/FTA	Pct.	Reb. O/T	A	TO	PF	S	Blk	TP	PPM
WARD, E.	18	3/3	1.000	0/0	.000	0/1	.000	2/5	1	1	2	0	0	6	.333
SALVAGE, T.	34	8/18	.444	4/9	.444	6/6	1.000	1/4	2	3	3	0	0	26	.765
DUCKETT, E.	32	6/13	.462	0/0	.000	0/0	.000	3/7	0	3	3	0	2	12	.375
DADLKA, R.	39	4/14	.286	2/9	.222	0/0	.000	0/0	4	1	5	6	0	10	.256
CARTER, C.	34	7/8	.875	0/0	.000	0/1	.000	0/1	5	5	3	3	0	14	.412
PERRY, L.	21	1/3	.333	0/1	.000	0/0	.000	3/5	0	1	3	0	0	2	.095
EVERSON, J.	3	0/0	.000	0/0	.000	0/0	.000	0/0	0	2	0	0	0	0	.000
DIXON, M.	7	1/2	.500	0/0	.000	1/2	.500	0/1	1	0	0	0	0	3	.429
SMITH, D.	2	0/1	.000	0/0	.000	0/0	.000	0/0	0	0	0	0	0	0	.000
McINNIS, J.	10	0/0	.000	0/0	.000	0/0	.000	1/2	0	1	0	0	0	0	.000
Totals	200	30/62	.484	6/19	.316	7/10	.700	10/25	13	17	19	9	2	73	.365

Team Rebounds: Iowa 1; Rutgers 2. Disqualified: Rutgers—Dadlka. Technical fouls: None.

	1st Half	2nd Half	Final
Iowa	45	42	87
Rutgers	39	34	73

Kansas State (75)   Coach: Lon Kruger

	Min.	Total FG/FGA	Pct.	3-Pt. FG/FGA	Pct.	FT/FTA	Pct.	Reb. O/T	A	TO	PF	S	Blk	TP	PPM
SIMMONS, L.	18	3/3	1.000	0/0	.000	2/2	1.000	4/4	1	1	4	1	0	8	.444
DOBBINS, M.	16	0/3	.000	0/2	.000	0/0	.000	2/5	0	1	3	0	0	0	.000
MCCOY, F.	21	5/7	.714	0/0	.000	2/5	.400	2/6	0	2	4	1	0	12	.571
HUMPHREY, L.	31	5/15	.333	1/6	.167	5/6	.833	0/3	5	5	2	5	0	16	.516
HENSON, S.	39	8/23	.348	5/15	.333	3/4	.750	1/2	1	3	2	1	0	24	.615
STANFIELD, T.	1	0/0	.000	0/0	.000	0/0	.000	0/0	0	0	0	0	0	0	.000
FRITZ, S.	1	0/0	.000	0/0	.000	0/0	.000	0/0	0	0	0	0	0	0	.000
DIGGINS, C.	10	1/7	.143	0/6	.000	0/0	.000	0/0	0	0	2	1	0	2	.200
BRITT, R.	12	2/2	1.000	0/0	.000	1/3	.333	0/1	1	0	0	0	0	5	.417
SMITH, B.	23	3/5	.600	0/0	.000	0/0	.000	1/5	1	1	4	0	0	6	.261
MASSOP, T.	27	1/1	1.000	0/0	.000	0/0	.000	1/5	0	2	3	3	1	2	.074
MAYDEW, T.	1	0/1	.000	0/0	.000	0/0	.000	1/1	0	0	0	0	0	0	.000
Totals	200	28/67	.418	6/29	.207	13/20	.650	12/32	9	15	24	12	1	75	.375

Minnesota (86)   Coach: Clem Haskins

	Min.	Total FG/FGA	Pct.	3-Pt. FG/FGA	Pct.	FT/FTA	Pct.	Reb. O/T	A	TO	PF	S	Blk	TP	PPM
BURTON, W.	34	8/15	.533	2/4	.500	11/11	1.000	4/13	2	3	4	0	0	29	.853
BOND, W.	26	3/5	.600	0/0	.000	2/2	1.000	1/5	3	1	5	2	0	8	.308
SHIKENJANSKI, J.	34	3/7	.429	0/0	.000	1/2	.500	0/1	1	1	1	0	0	7	.206
LYNCH, K.	38	6/10	.600	2/2	1.000	4/7	.571	2/6	2	2	2	1	0	18	.474
NEWBERN, M.	30	4/8	.500	2/2	1.000	2/2	1.000	1/2	3	6	5	5	0	12	.400
GREEN, M.	1	0/0	.000	0/0	.000	0/0	.000	0/0	0	0	0	0	0	0	.000
LEWIS, L.	1	0/0	.000	0/0	.000	0/1	.000	0/0	0	0	0	0	0	0	.000
GAFFNEY, R.	30	3/7	.429	2/4	.500	2/2	1.000	0/3	5	5	1	1	0	10	.333
METCALF, R.	2	0/0	.000	0/0	.000	2/4	.500	0/0	0	0	0	0	0	2	1.000
MARTIN, B.	4	0/0	.000	0/0	.000	0/0	.000	0/1	0	0	1	0	1	0	.000
Totals	200	27/52	.519	8/12	.667	24/31	.774	8/31	16	18	19	9	1	86	.430

Team Rebounds: Minnesota 7; Kansas State 1. Disqualified: Minnesota—Bond, Newbern. Technical fouls: None.

	1st Half	2nd Half	Final
Kansas State	31	44	75
Minnesota	41	45	86

Stanford (78)   Coach: Mike Montgomery

	Min.	Total FG/FGA	Pct.	3-Pt. FG/FGA	Pct.	FT/FTA	Pct.	Reb. O/T	A	TO	PF	S	Blk	TP	PPM
VLAHOV, A.	16	1/3	.333	0/1	.000	0/0	.000	0/0	1	2	1	0	0	2	.125
WRIGHT, H.	32	4/9	.444	0/0	.000	0/4	.000	3/5	1	3	4	1	1	8	.250
REVENO, E.	22	3/4	.750	0/0	.000	3/3	1.000	2/7	1	1	5	0	1	9	.409
TAYLOR, T.	37	4/7	.571	3/6	.500	0/0	.000	0/2	7	4	4	3	0	11	.297
LICHTI, T.	36	7/16	.438	3/8	.375	0/0	.000	0/5	2	1	3	1	0	17	.472
MEINERT, S.	16	2/3	.667	1/1	1.000	0/0	.000	0/0	1	5	1	1	0	5	.313
MCSWEENEY, B.	8	1/2	.500	0/0	.000	0/0	.000	1/1	0	1	0	0	0	2	.250
KEEFE, A.	26	5/6	.833	0/0	.000	12/13	.923	4/5	0	1	1	0	0	22	.846
WINGATE, D.	7	1/2	.500	0/0	.000	0/0	.000	1/3	0	1	0	0	0	2	.286
Totals	200	28/52	.538	7/16	.438	15/20	.750	11/28	13	19	19	6	2	78	.390

Siena (80)   Coach: Mike Deane

	Min.	Total FG/FGA	Pct.	3-Pt. FG/FGA	Pct.	FT/FTA	Pct.	Reb. O/T	A	TO	PF	S	Blk	TP	PPM
ROBINSON, J.	39	7/17	.412	6/10	.600	0/1	.000	0/5	3	1	0	1	0	20	.513
MCCOY, S.	28	2/4	.500	0/0	.000	1/3	.333	3/8	1	1	3	0	0	5	.179
HENDERSON, M.	25	1/1	1.000	0/0	.000	0/1	.000	1/3	0	1	5	1	4	2	.080
BROWN, B.	40	13/20	.650	4/9	.444	2/4	.500	1/1	6	6	1	0	0	32	.800
BROWN, M.	13	2/4	.500	1/1	1.000	0/0	.000	0/1	0	1	0	0	0	5	.385
HUERTER, T.	27	2/5	.400	0/3	.000	4/4	1.000	0/1	1	1	2	2	0	8	.296
SCHROEDER, B.	4	0/0	.000	0/0	.000	0/0	.000	0/0	0	0	1	0	0	0	.000
DOWNEY, T.	19	3/4	.750	0/0	.000	2/3	.667	0/0	0	5	1	0	0	8	.421
FLEURY, E.	3	0/1	.000	0/0	.000	0/0	.000	1/1	0	1	1	0	0	0	.000
GRAZULIS, A.	2	0/0	.000	0/0	.000	0/0	.000	0/0	0	0	1	0	0	0	.000
Totals	200	30/56	.536	11/23	.478	9/16	.563	6/20	11	11	18	7	4	80	.400

Team Rebounds: Siena 3; Stanford 2. Disqualified: Siena—Henderson, Downey; Stanford—Reveno. Technical fouls: None.

	1st Half	2nd Half	Final
Stanford	37	41	78
Siena	37	43	80

West Virginia (84)   Coach: Gale Catlett

	Min.	Total FG/FGA	Pct.	3-Pt. FG/FGA	Pct.	FT/FTA	Pct.	Reb. O/T	A	TO	PF	S	Blk	TP	PPM
PRUE, D.	29	5/8	.625	0/0	.000	2/3	.667	3/6	2	1	4	0	0	12	.414
BROOKS, C.	20	2/7	.286	0/0	.000	0/1	.000	0/1	0	0	4	0	0	4	.200
FOSTER, R.	34	6/7	.857	0/0	.000	7/8	.875	2/11	0	2	3	1	2	19	.559
BROOKS, H.	35	8/12	.667	0/0	.000	6/6	1.000	2/2	2	4	1	2	0	22	.629
BERGER, S.	35	4/6	.667	1/3	.333	5/7	.714	1/5	7	4	0	3	0	14	.400
SHELTON, T.	12	3/4	.750	0/0	.000	4/5	.800	0/1	2	1	0	1	0	10	.833
LEONARD, C.	1	0/0	.000	0/0	.000	0/0	.000	0/1	0	0	0	0	0	0	.000
JACKSON, S.	6	0/0	.000	0/0	.000	0/0	.000	0/1	1	1	1	0	0	0	.000
YOEST, M.	4	0/0	.000	0/0	.000	0/0	.000	0/0	0	0	1	0	0	0	.000
SMITH, W.	22	1/3	.333	0/0	.000	1/2	.500	0/4	0	2	1	0	1	3	.136
KROGER, T.	2	0/0	.000	0/0	.000	0/1	.000	0/2	0	0	0	0	0	0	.000
Totals	200	29/47	.617	1/3	.333	25/33	.758	8/34	14	15	14	7	3	84	.420

Tennessee (68)   Coach: Don Devoe

	Min.	Total FG/FGA	Pct.	3-Pt. FG/FGA	Pct.	FT/FTA	Pct.	Reb. O/T	A	TO	PF	S	Blk	TP	PPM
NIX, D.	37	10/20	.500	0/4	.000	2/4	.500	5/8	1	1	3	0	0	22	.595
GRIFFIN, M.	26	1/5	.200	1/4	.250	0/0	.000	2/3	1	2	4	1	0	3	.115
ROTH, D.	38	5/13	.385	3/6	.500	0/4	.000	4/10	1	4	4	0	1	13	.342
SWEARANGEN, C.	14	0/4	.000	0/0	.000	0/0	.000	2/3	0	2	0	0	0	0	.000
HENRY, T.	14	1/2	.500	1/1	1.000	0/0	.000	0/1	0	1	3	0	0	3	.214
PRICE, J.	1	0/0	.000	0/0	.000	0/0	.000	0/0	0	1	0	0	0	0	.000
TAYLOR, R.	17	2/9	.222	2/9	.222	1/2	.500	0/4	0	2	2	2	0	7	.412
BELL, D.	34	5/10	.500	3/6	.500	1/2	.500	0/1	5	1	4	1	0	14	.412
REESE, R.	2	0/1	.000	0/0	.000	0/0	.000	0/0	0	0	0	0	0	0	.000
LOCKHART, I.	17	2/5	.400	0/0	.000	2/2	1.000	2/2	0	1	5	0	0	6	.353
Totals	200	26/69	.377	10/31	.323	6/14	.429	15/28	12	12	26	4	1	68	.340

Team Rebounds: West Virginia 2; Tennessee 2. Disqualified: Tennessee—Lockhart. Technical fouls: None.

	1st Half	2nd Half	Final
West Virginia	35	49	84
Tennessee	23	45	68

Duke (90)   Coach: Mike Krzyzewski

	Min.	Total FG/FGA	Pct.	3-Pt. FG/FGA	Pct.	FT/FTA	Pct.	Reb. O/T	A	TO	PF	S	Blk	TP	PPM
BRICKEY, R.	25	4/6	.667	0/0	.000	0/0	.000	1/4	0	1	2	2	1	8	.320
FERRY, D.	30	6/11	.545	2/2	1.000	4/6	.667	4/8	4	1	3	1	0	18	.600
LAETTNER, C.	20	5/7	.714	0/0	.000	2/3	.667	1/2	0	3	0	0	0	12	.600
HENDERSON, P.	28	8/10	.800	1/1	1.000	5/5	1.000	0/2	2	4	3	0	0	22	.786
SNYDER, Q.	28	4/8	.500	0/2	.000	1/4	.250	1/2	8	7	2	2	0	9	.321
KOUBEK, G.	10	2/4	.500	0/1	.000	1/3	.333	0/5	0	2	0	1	0	5	.500
DAVIS, B.	10	0/0	.000	0/0	.000	0/3	.000	0/0	2	0	1	0	0	0	.000
ABDELNABY, A.	17	4/5	.800	0/0	.000	0/2	.000	0/2	1	3	4	0	1	8	.471
SMITH, J.	23	1/2	.500	0/1	.000	2/2	1.000	0/2	1	1	1	4	0	4	.174
PALMER, C.	3	0/0	.000	0/0	.000	0/0	.000	0/0	0	0	0	0	0	0	.000
BURGIN, G.	3	0/0	.000	0/0	.000	0/0	.000	0/0	0	0	0	0	0	2	.667
BUCKLEY, C.	3	0/0	.000	0/0	.000	2/2	1.000	0/0	0	0	0	0	0	2	.667
Totals	200	34/53	.642	3/7	.429	19/30	.633	7/27	18	20	19	12	2	90	.450

South Carolina State (69)   Coach: Cy Alexander

	Min.	Total FG/FGA	Pct.	3-Pt. FG/FGA	Pct.	FT/FTA	Pct.	Reb. O/T	A	TO	PF	S	Blk	TP	PPM
CALDWELL	38	6/11	.545	1/3	.333	7/8	.875	2/7	2	5	2	4	0	20	.526
MACK	33	4/7	.571	0/0	.000	2/2	1.000	3/5	0	2	4	2	0	10	.303
MAZYCK	27	3/7	.429	1/3	.333	0/0	.000	2/2	0	5	5	4	0	7	.259
GILMORE	26	2/11	.182	1/5	.200	7/8	.875	2/2	2	2	4	0	0	12	.462
JETER	27	1/6	.167	0/0	.000	0/0	.000	1/2	1	3	5	0	0	2	.074
BYRD	5	1/4	.250	0/0	.000	1/2	.500	0/0	1	0	3	0	0	3	.600
WILLIAMS	33	5/12	.417	0/0	.000	3/4	.750	5/8	0	2	3	2	0	13	.394
FELIX	3	1/2	.500	0/0	.000	0/0	.000	0/1	0	1	2	0	0	2	.667
PAULK	8	0/1	.000	0/0	.000	0/0	.000	0/2	0	0	3	1	0	0	.000
Totals	200	23/61	.377	3/11	.273	20/24	.833	14/28	7	21	29	13	0	69	.345

Team Rebounds: Duke 6; S. Carolina St. 2. Disqualified: S. Carolina St.—Mazyck, Jeter. Technical fouls: Duke—Laettner.

	1st Half	2nd Half	Final
Duke	49	41	90
S. Carolina St.	34	35	69

FIRST ROUND WEST

Arizona (94) Coach: Lute Olson

	Min.	Total FG/FGA	Pct.	3-Pt. FG/FGA	Pct.	FT/FTA	Pct.	Reb. O/T	A	TO	PF	S	Blk	TP	PPM
ELLIOTT, S.	30	8/12	.667	4/4	1.000	7/8	.875	1/7	3	6	1	1	0	27	.900
BUECHLER, J.	24	5/9	.556	0/0	.000	1/1	1.000	1/3	0	2	2	0	0	11	.458
COOK, A.	27	11/18	.611	0/0	.000	3/4	.750	2/7	0	0	2	0	1	25	.926
LOFTON, K.	28	1/2	.500	0/1	.000	0/1	.000	0/4	2	0	1	2	1	2	.071
MUEHLEBACH, M.	26	1/3	.333	0/2	.000	0/1	.000	1/2	5	1	2	2	0	2	.077
OTHICK, M.	16	0/3	.000	0/1	.000	4/4	1.000	0/2	3	2	1	1	0	4	.250
DAVID, B.	7	0/3	.000	0/0	.000	0/0	.000	1/3	0	0	0	0	0	0	.000
MASON, H.	5	2/4	.500	0/0	.000	0/0	.000	0/0	2	2	0	0	1	4	.800
ROOKS, S.	14	6/8	.750	0/0	.000	4/4	1.000	1/5	0	0	1	0	1	16	1.143
WOMACK, W.	16	1/1	1.000	0/0	.000	1/3	.333	0/5	0	0	1	1	1	3	.188
CURRY, R.	7	0/2	.000	0/0	.000	0/0	.000	1/3	1	1	1	1	0	0	.000
Totals	200	35/65	.538	4/8	.500	20/26	.769	8/41	16	14	12	8	5	94	.470

Robert Morris (60) Coach: Jarret Durham

	Min.	Total FG/FGA	Pct.	3-Pt. FG/FGA	Pct.	FT/FTA	Pct.	Reb. O/T	A	TO	PF	S	Blk	TP	PPM
STEALS	22	0/5	.000	0/0	.000	0/0	.000	2/8	1	2	4	0	0	0	.000
LUTON	26	10/21	.476	1/1	1.000	2/2	1.000	6/6	0	3	5	1	0	23	.885
DICKENS	28	2/10	.200	0/0	.000	3/4	.750	5/10	0	1	2	0	0	7	.250
BOYD, R.	30	3/12	.250	0/0	.000	2/3	.667	2/3	2	7	3	2	0	8	.267
SHEPHERD	23	2/8	.250	2/6	.333	1/2	.500	1/4	4	2	2	0	0	7	.304
COASTON	6	1/2	.500	0/0	.000	0/0	.000	0/1	0	0	1	0	0	2	.333
TIMMERSON	21	1/5	.200	0/1	.000	0/0	.000	0/1	1	0	1	2	0	2	.095
MOSS	17	1/5	.200	0/2	.000	1/2	.500	0/2	1	3	3	0	0	3	.176
FALLETTA	23	4/6	.667	0/0	.000	0/0	.000	0/4	0	0	3	0	0	8	.348
WILLIAMS	4	0/2	.000	0/0	.000	0/0	.000	0/0	0	0	0	0	0	0	.000
Totals	200	24/76	.316	3/10	.300	9/13	.692	16/39	9	18	24	5	0	60	.300

Team Rebounds: Arizona 2; Robert Morris 2. Disqualified: Robert Morris—Luton. Technical fouls: None.

	1st Half	2nd Half	Final
Arizona	54	40	94
Robert Morris	26	34	60

St. Mary's (70) Coach: Lynn Nance

	Min.	Total FG/FGA	Pct.	3-Pt. FG/FGA	Pct.	FT/FTA	Pct.	Reb. O/T	A	TO	PF	S	Blk	TP	PPM
NEWMAN	37	8/15	.533	0/0	.000	3/4	.750	6/7	3	4	3	3	0	19	.514
HAUGEN	30	3/8	.375	0/0	.000	0/0	.000	3/5	1	2	2	0	0	6	.200
CURRY	33	1/4	.250	0/0	.000	2/4	.500	1/4	2	0	3	0	0	4	.121
CARTER, J.	27	2/7	.286	1/3	.333	0/0	.000	0/1	3	0	1	1	0	5	.185
LEWIS	33	10/16	.625	5/7	.714	1/2	.500	1/2	1	2	1	2	0	26	.788
BUMS	15	1/5	.200	1/3	.333	0/2	.000	1/2	3	0	1	0	0	3	.200
DAILEY	13	0/2	.000	0/1	.000	2/2	1.000	0/3	0	2	3	0	1	2	.154
GIL	1	0/0	.000	0/0	.000	0/0	.000	0/0	0	0	0	0	0	0	.000
VONTOURE	8	2/3	.667	1/1	1.000	0/0	.000	0/0	0	0	2	0	0	5	.625
BAMBERGER	3	0/1	.000	0/0	.000	0/0	.000	0/0	0	0	0	0	0	0	.000
Totals	200	27/61	.443	8/15	.533	8/14	.571	12/24	13	10	16	8	1	70	.350

Clemson (83) Coach: Cliff Ellis

	Min.	Total FG/FGA	Pct.	3-Pt. FG/FGA	Pct.	FT/FTA	Pct.	Reb. O/T	A	TO	PF	S	Blk	TP	PPM
DAVIS, D.	27	7/8	.875	0/0	.000	4/6	.667	1/8	1	0	2	0	3	18	.667
CAMPBELL, E.	32	10/15	.667	0/0	.000	0/0	.000	4/8	0	3	2	0	4	20	.625
YOUNG, D.	28	6/10	.600	5/7	.714	2/2	1.000	0/1	2	3	4	0	1	19	.679
FORREST, D.	35	5/8	.625	1/3	.333	2/2	1.000	0/2	7	4	1	1	3	13	.371
KINCAID, T.	12	0/3	.000	0/0	.000	1/2	.500	1/1	1	2	1	1	1	1	.083
CASH, M.	34	2/5	.400	0/0	.000	4/4	1.000	2/6	7	3	2	0	0	8	.235
MITCHELL, R.	9	1/1	1.000	0/0	.000	0/0	.000	1/2	0	0	1	0	0	2	.222
PRYOR, J.	13	1/3	.333	0/0	.000	0/0	.000	1/2	0	0	0	0	0	2	.154
HOWLING	10	0/0	.000	0/0	.000	0/0	.000	0/1	0	0	1	0	0	0	.000
Totals	200	32/53	.604	6/10	.600	13/17	.765	10/31	18	15	14	2	12	83	.415

Team Rebounds: Clemson 0; St. Mary's 3. Disqualified: None. Technical fouls: St. Mary's—Bench.

	1st Half	2nd Half	Final
St. Mary's	39	31	70
Clemson	33	50	83

Memphis State (63) Coach: Larry Finch

	Min.	Total FG/FGA	Pct.	3-Pt. FG/FGA	Pct.	FT/FTA	Pct.	Reb. O/T	A	TO	PF	S	Blk	TP	PPM
DOUGLAS, R.	35	7/12	.583	0/0	.000	2/2	1.000	3/5	1	1	2	1	1	16	.457
SMITH, E.	31	4/8	.500	0/0	.000	1/2	.500	3/5	0	3	1	0	1	9	.290
BALLARD, S.	22	1/1	1.000	0/0	.000	0/0	.000	0/2	2	3	4	1	0	2	.091
GIBSON, C.	25	4/12	.333	0/3	.000	1/3	.333	0/5	3	0	2	4	0	9	.360
PERRY, E.	34	4/13	.308	1/2	.500	6/8	.750	0/5	3	0	2	2	0	15	.441
MCLAUGHLIN, J.	17	2/5	.400	0/3	.000	0/0	.000	1/1	1	0	2	2	0	4	.235
MCCLAIN, R.	1	0/0	.000	0/0	.000	0/0	.000	0/0	0	1	0	0	0	0	.000
MUNDT, T.	21	2/6	.333	0/0	.000	2/2	1.000	1/2	0	1	4	1	1	6	.286
MADLOCK, T.	14	1/2	.500	0/0	.000	0/0	.000	0/0	0	0	2	1	0	2	.143
Totals	200	25/59	.424	1/8	.125	12/17	.706	10/22	9	9	21	13	3	63	.315

DePaul (66) Coach: Joey Meyer

	Min.	Total FG/FGA	Pct.	3-Pt. FG/FGA	Pct.	FT/FTA	Pct.	Reb. O/T	A	TO	PF	S	Blk	TP	PPM
BRUNDY, S.	35	8/15	.533	0/0	.000	4/4	1.000	3/15	2	4	3	1	1	20	.571
PRICE, C.	13	0/0	.000	0/0	.000	0/0	.000	0/4	3	4	2	0	0	0	.000
HAMBY, J.	32	3/3	1.000	0/0	.000	0/0	.000	4/4	0	3	3	0	1	6	.188
MURPHY, C.	31	3/6	.500	1/2	.500	0/1	.000	0/1	3	2	2	0	1	7	.226
GREENE, T.	32	4/7	.571	2/3	.667	4/6	.667	2/4	0	1	4	1	1	14	.438
FOSTER, M.	17	0/4	.000	0/0	.000	0/0	.000	1/2	0	3	1	0	0	0	.000
HOWARD, S.	12	1/1	1.000	0/0	.000	0/0	.000	0/0	0	3	2	1	0	2	.167
BOOTH	28	5/12	.417	0/0	.000	7/7	1.000	2/5	4	3	2	1	0	17	.607
Totals	200	24/48	.500	3/5	.600	15/18	.833	12/35	12	23	19	4	4	66	.330

Team rebounds: DePaul 3; Memphis State 1. Disqualified: None. Technical fouls: None.

	1st Half	2nd Half	Final
Memphis State	30	33	63
De Paul	36	30	66

UNLV (68) Coach: Jerry Tarkanian

	Min.	Total FG/FGA	Pct.	3-Pt. FG/FGA	Pct.	FT/FTA	Pct.	Reb. O/T	A	TO	PF	S	Blk	TP	PPM
AUGMON, S.	32	7/13	.538	3/5	.600	0/0	.000	3/5	2	2	4	0	0	17	.531
SCURRY, M.	30	3/5	.600	0/0	.000	4/5	.800	3/14	0	3	2	1	0	10	.333
BUTLER, D.	34	6/13	.462	0/0	.000	4/8	.500	4/5	2	2	3	1	0	16	.471
ANTHONY, G.	26	3/8	.375	0/1	.000	6/6	1.000	1/2	2	3	4	0	0	12	.462
HUNT, A.	38	1/8	.125	1/6	.167	2/2	1.000	1/6	4	1	2	1	0	5	.132
ACKLES, G.	11	1/3	.333	0/0	.000	3/4	.750	2/2	0	0	2	1	4	5	.455
CVIJANOVICH, S.	6	0/2	.000	0/1	.000	0/0	.000	0/1	0	1	0	1	0	0	.000
ROSSUM, C.	6	0/1	.000	0/1	.000	0/0	.000	0/0	0	0	0	0	0	0	.000
YOUNG, B.	13	1/3	.333	1/3	.333	0/0	.000	0/0	2	3	0	0	2	3	.231
JONES, J.	2	0/0	.000	0/0	.000	0/0	.000	1/2	0	0	1	0	0	0	.000
JETER, C.	2	0/0	.000	0/0	.000	0/0	.000	0/1	0	1	0	0	0	0	.000
Totals	200	22/56	.393	5/17	.294	19/26	.731	15/39	10	14	20	5	4	68	.340

Idaho (56) Coach: Kermit Davis Jr.

	Min.	Total FG/FGA	Pct.	3-Pt. FG/FGA	Pct.	FT/FTA	Pct.	Reb. O/T	A	TO	PF	S	Blk	TP	PPM
FITCH, J.	33	5/12	.417	1/3	.333	3/5	.600	6/9	2	1	4	1	0	14	.424
PRELOW, C.	22	1/6	.167	0/1	.000	0/1	.000	1/3	2	2	1	1	0	2	.091
NASH, L.	37	1/3	.333	0/0	.000	0/0	.000	0/3	3	3	2	1	0	2	.054
GOMES, M.	15	2/5	.400	1/3	.333	4/4	1.000	0/0	2	1	3	0	0	9	.600
SPELLMAN, R.	3	0/3	.000	0/3	.000	0/0	.000	0/0	0	0	1	0	0	0	.000
SMITH, R.	35	9/13	.692	0/2	.000	2/4	.500	4/6	0	1	4	2	0	20	.571
BROWN, R.	36	2/10	.200	0/1	.000	0/2	.000	2/9	0	4	4	2	2	4	.111
BOYD, R.	14	1/4	.250	0/1	.000	1/2	.500	2/5	1	2	2	0	0	3	.214
CAMPBELL, A.	3	0/0	.000	0/0	.000	0/0	.000	0/0	0	0	1	0	0	0	.000
CARTER, J.	2	1/2	.500	0/1	.000	0/0	.000	0/0	0	0	0	2	0	2	1.000
Totals	200	22/58	.379	2/12	.167	10/18	.556	15/35	12	14	23	9	2	56	.280

Team Rebounds: UNLV 2; Idaho 2. Disqualified: None. Technical fouls: None.

	1st Half	2nd Half	Final
UNLV	27	41	68
Idaho	22	34	56

Oregon State (90)   Coach: Ralph Miller

	Min.	Total FG/FGA	Pct.	3–Pt. FG/FGA	Pct.	FT/FTA	Pct.	Reb. O/T	A	TO	PF	S	Blk	TP	PPM
BRANTLEY, W.	44	8/17	.471	1/1	1.000	0/0	.000	2/4	1	2	1	1	0	17	.386
MCINTOSH, L.	30	6/10	.600	0/0	.000	0/1	.000	3/7	0	2	0	1	0	12	.400
ALIBEGOVIC, T.	31	3/7	.429	1/1	1.000	3/3	1.000	2/5	2	1	4	0	0	10	.323
KNOX, E.	42	4/8	.500	1/2	.500	3/4	.750	6/11	1	2	4	0	0	12	.286
PAYTON, G.	45	11/22	.500	2/5	.400	7/8	.875	1/3	10	4	5	1	0	31	.689
MARTIN, E.	29	4/7	.571	0/0	.000	0/0	.000	3/7	3	0	4	1	0	8	.276
CAVELL, B.	2	0/0	.000	0/0	.000	0/0	.000	0/0	0	0	0	0	0	0	.000
CELESTINE, A.	1	0/0	.000	0/0	.000	0/0	.000	0/0	0	0	1	0	0	0	.000
Totals	225	36/71	.507	5/9	.556	13/16	.813	17/37	17	11	19	4	0	90	.400

Evansville (94)   Coach: Jim Crews

	Min.	Total FG/FGA	Pct.	3–Pt. FG/FGA	Pct.	FT/FTA	Pct.	Reb. O/T	A	TO	PF	S	Blk	TP	PPM
HAFFNER, S.	45	9/17	.529	6/13	.462	2/2	1.000	1/3	6	4	2	1	0	26	.578
HILL, B.	33	7/8	.875	0/0	.000	7/9	.788	4/8	0	1	4	1	0	21	.636
GODFREAD, D.	34	8/12	.667	0/0	.000	3/4	.750	3/4	2	1	5	0	2	19	.559
CRAFTON, R.	45	4/10	.400	3/6	.500	2/3	.667	0.1	10	1	1	1	0	13	.289
SHREFFLER, S.	42	4/8	.500	3/4	.750	2/3	.667	0/2	5	3	2	0	1	13	.310
MACK, C.	9	0/2	.000	0/1	.000	0/0	.000	0/0	0	0	1	0	0	0	.000
BLAB, D.	9	0/0	.000	0/0	.000	0/0	.000	0/2	0	3	3	0	1	0	.000
BOMBA, C.	9	1/1	1.000	0/0	.000	0/0	.000	0/2	0	0	0	0	0	2	.222
Totals	225	33/58	.569	12/24	.500	16/21	.762	8/24	23	10	18	3	3	94	.418

Team Rebounds: Evansville 1; Oregon State 1. Disqualified: Evansville—Godfread; Oregon State—Payton. Technical fouls: None.

	1st Half	2nd Half	1 OT	Final
Oregon State	39	39	12	90
Evansville	37	41	16	94

Seton Hall (60)   Coach: P. J. Carlesimo

	Min.	Total FG/FGA	Pct.	3–Pt. FG/FGA	Pct.	FT/FTA	Pct.	Reb. O/T	A	TO	PF	S	Blk	TP	PPM
WALKER, D.	34	3/6	.500	0/0	.000	0/0	.000	3/6	0	0	1	0	0	6	.176
GAZE, A.	34	3/4	.750	1/2	.500	2/2	1.000	0/3	4	4	4	0	0	9	.265
RAMOS, R.	24	1/6	.167	0/0	.000	0/0	.000	1/5	2	0	3	0	1	2	.083
MORTON, J.	33	9/18	.500	3/6	.500	5/5	1.000	1/2	4	2	4	2	0	26	.788
GREENE, G.	34	1/3	.333	0/0	.000	5/7	.714	1/2	1	4	3	1	0	7	.206
AVENT, A.	4	0/1	.000	0/0	.000	0/0	.000	0/1	1	1	1	0	1	0	.000
VOLCY, F.	18	3/4	.750	0/0	.000	2/2	1.000	0/1	1	0	2	0	1	8	.444
COOPER, M.	13	0/2	.000	0/0	.000	0/0	.000	1/5	1	2	2	0	0	0	.000
WIGINGTON, P.	6	1/1	1.000	0/0	.000	0/0	.000	0/1	0	0	1	0	0	2	.333
Totals	200	21/45	.467	4/8	.500	14/16	.875	7/26	12	15	19	1	3	60	.300

Southwest Missouri State (51)   Coach: Charles Spoonhour

	Min.	Total FG/FGA	Pct.	3–Pt. FG/FGA	Pct.	FT/FTA	Pct.	Reb. O/T	A	TO	PF	S	Blk	TP	PPM
STANGE, C.	14	1/2	.500	0/0	.000	0/0	.000	0/2	0	0	1	0	0	2	.143
HENDERSON, H.	37	6/12	.500	0/0	.000	6/9	.667	1/6	1	3	2	1	2	18	.486
STUCKEY, K.	32	1/8	.125	0/0	.000	3/6	.500	0/1	0	2	5	1	0	5	.156
LEWIS, D.	33	4/10	.400	0/3	.000	1/2	.500	0/2	5	3	4	2	0	9	.273
JACKSON, K.	39	3/6	.500	0/1	.000	0/2	.000	1/2	4	3	0	0	6	.154
CAMPBELL, L.	26	2/3	.667	0/0	.000	3/3	1.000	0/1	0	2	0	0	7	.269
DAVIS, C.	10	2/2	1.000	0/0	.000	0/0	.000	1/3	0	0	3	0	0	4	.400
BROWN, B.	9	0/0	.000	0/0	.000	0/0	.000	0/1	0	0	0	0	0	0	.000
Totals	200	19/43	.442	0/4	.000	13/22	.591	3/18	8	12	20	4	2	51	.255

Team Rebounds: Seton Hall 2; SW Missouri St. 6. Disqualified: SW Missouri St.—Stuckey. Technical fouls: None.

	1st Half	2nd Half	Final
Seton Hall	30	30	60
SW Missouri St.	23	28	51

UTEP (85)   Coach: Don Haskins

	Min.	Total FG/FGA	Pct.	3–Pt. FG/FGA	Pct.	FT/FTA	Pct.	Reb. O/T	A	TO	PF	S	Blk	TP	PPM
VAN, D.	15	1/3	.333	0/0	.000	0/0	.000	1/3	0	1	2	1	2	2	.133
MCCALL	15	2/5	.400	0/1	.000	0/0	.000	0/0	2	1	2	0	1	4	.267
FOSTER	32	2/7	.286	0/0	.000	0/0	.000	3/9	1	5	1	0	1	4	.125
STEWART, P.	39	7/14	.500	1/5	.200	0/0	.000	1/2	5	1	2	0	1	15	.385
HARDAWAY, T.	38	9/22	.409	3/8	.375	10/12	.833	1/4	9	3	0	3	0	31	.816
MELVIN	26	7/9	.778	0/0	.000	0/0	.000	3/4	0	1	0	0	0	14	.538
DAVIS	21	5/8	.625	0/0	.000	3/5	.600	1/9	0	1	2	1	0	13	.619
EBENWA	14	1/2	.500	0/0	.000	0/2	.000	2/5	0	0	1	2	2	2	.143
Totals	200	34/70	.486	4/14	.286	13/19	.684	12/36	17	13	9	6	7	85	.425

Louisiana State (74)   Coach: Dale Brown

	Min.	Total FG/FGA	Pct.	3–Pt. FG/FGA	Pct.	FT/FTA	Pct.	Reb. O/T	A	TO	PF	S	Blk	TP	PPM
BLANTON	40	4/17	.235	2/3	.667	1/1	1.000	5/11	4	6	3	0	0	11	.275
SIMS, W.	40	4/7	.571	0/0	.000	0/0	.000	1/3	1	2	3	1	3	8	.200
SINGLETON, V.	40	5/10	.500	0/0	.000	5/5	1.000	6/12	1	2	4	1	1	15	.375
MOUTON	39	2/9	.222	2/3	.667	1/2	.500	2/7	1	3	2	2	0	7	.179
JACKSON	31	16/32	.500	1/8	.125	0/0	.000	1/5	1	3	1	2	0	33	1.065
TRACEY, D.	9	0/0	.000	0/0	.000	0/0	.000	0/1	1	0	4	2	0	0	.000
KRAJEWSKI	1	0/0	.000	0/0	.000	0/0	.000	0/0	0	0	0	0	0	0	.000
Totals	200	31/75	.413	5/14	.357	7/8	.875	15/38	9	16	17	8	4	74	.370

Team Rebounds: UTEP 2; Louisiana St. 7. Disqualified: None. Technical fouls: Louisiana St. Bench—2.

	1st Half	2nd Half	Final
UTEP	42	43	85
Louisiana St.	29	45	74

Indiana (99)   Coach: Bob Knight

	Min.	Total FG/FGA	Pct.	3–Pt. FG/FGA	Pct.	FT/FTA	Pct.	Reb. O/T	A	TO	PF	S	Blk	TP	PPM
HILLMAN, J.	19	5/8	.625	1/1	1.000	0/0	.000	1/3	6	3	2	0	0	11	.579
ANDERSON, E.	24	5/6	.833	0/0	.000	5/5	1.000	2/4	0	1	3	0	1	15	.625
JADLOW, T.	19	5/9	.556	0/0	.000	3/4	.750	1/3	0	1	3	0	0	13	.684
JONES, L.	24	5/7	.714	0/0	.000	2/2	1.000	4/8	2	3	3	2	1	12	.500
EDWARDS, J.	20	5/10	.500	3/4	.750	0/1	.000	0/4	7	0	0	2	1	13	.650
MEEKS, J.	18	0/1	.000	0/0	.000	4/4	1.000	0/0	2	2	1	1	0	4	.222
ROBINSON, M.	21	1/2	.500	0/0	.000	3/5	.600	0/3	1	3	0	1	0	5	.238
SMITH, K.	21	3/6	.500	1/1	1.000	6/6	1.000	0/3	1	1	4	1	0	13	.619
SLOAN, B.	7	1/1	1.000	0/0	.000	1/2	.500	0/2	1	0	1	0	0	3	.429
WHITE, C.	15	4/5	.800	0/0	.000	2/2	1.000	1/3	2	1	3	0	2	10	.667
PELKOWSKI, M.	6	0/0	.000	0/0	.000	0/0	.000	1/2	0	0	0	0	0	0	.000
D'ALOISIO, M.	6	0/0	.000	0/0	.000	0/0	.000	0/0	0	3	1	0	0	0	.000
Totals	200	34/55	.618	5/6	.833	26/31	.839	10/35	22	18	21	7	5	99	.495

George Mason (85)   Coach: Ernie Nestor

	Min.	Total FG/FGA	Pct.	3–Pt. FG/FGA	Pct.	FT/FTA	Pct.	Reb. O/T	A	TO	PF	S	Blk	TP	PPM
SANDERS, K.	39	9/16	.563	1/1	1.000	4/7	.571	5/8	4	1	4	3	0	23	.590
BROADNAX, C.	27	4/11	.364	2/6	.333	0/0	.000	0/2	2	1	2	1	1	10	.370
DYKES, R.	27	3/7	.429	0/0	.000	1/2	.500	1/5	1	1	2	0	0	7	.259
SMITH, S.	39	7/13	.538	3/7	.429	0/0	.000	3/3	3	3	3	0	3	17	.436
HARGETT, M.	32	7/16	.438	5/12	.417	5/5	1.000	0/2	3	4	1	0	24	.750
MCNAMARA, K.	9	0/0	.000	0/0	.000	2/4	.500	0/1	2	3	0	0	2	.222
ABRAMS, N.	4	0/0	.000	0/0	.000	0/0	.000	0/2	0	1	0	0	0	0	.000
MOORE, E.	12	1/3	.333	0/1	.000	0/1	.000	1/1	2	1	5	2	0	2	.167
DEANE, D.	3	0/0	.000	0/0	.000	0/0	.000	0/1	0	0	0	0	0	0	.000
MORAN, S.	8	0/0	.000	0/0	.000	0/0	.000	1/1	1	0	2	0	0	0	.000
Totals	200	31/66	.470	11/27	.407	12/19	.632	8/22	17	12	26	7	4	85	.425

Team Rebounds: Indiana 2; George Mason 4. Disqualified: George Mason—Moore. Technical fouls: None.

	1st Half	2nd Half	Final
Indiana	56	43	99
George Mason	27	58	85

SECOND ROUND MIDWEST

Illinois (72)　　Coach: Lou Henson

	Min.	Total FG/FGA	Pct.	3–Pt. FG/FGA	Pct.	FT/FTA	Pct.	Reb. O/T	A	TO	PF	S	Blk	TP	PPM
ANDERSON, N.	37	10/19	.526	0/0	.000	4/7	.571	2/7	3	0	3	4	0	24	.649
BATTLE, K.	33	1/4	.250	0/1	.000	3/6	.500	4/8	3	0	0	0	0	5	.152
HAMILTON, L.	24	8/12	.667	0/0	.000	3/5	.600	2/5	0	2	4	0	2	19	.792
GILL, K.	32	6/14	.429	2/6	.333	3/3	1.000	1/2	7	3	2	5	0	17	.531
BARDO, S.	27	1/4	.250	0/0	.000	0/0	.000	1/2	4	1	1	0	0	2	.074
BOWMAN, P.	1	0/1	.000	0/1	.000	0/0	.000	0/0	0	0	0	0	0	0	.000
MANZKA, E.	1	0/0	.000	0/0	.000	0/0	.000	0/0	0	0	0	0	0	0	.000
SMITH, L.	18	2/2	1.000	0/0	.000	1/3	.333	1/2	3	3	4	0	2	5	.278
SMALL, E.	13	0/0	.000	0/0	.000	0/0	.000	0/2	0	1	1	0	0	0	.000
LIBERTY, M.	13	0/0	.000	0/0	.000	0/0	.000	0/2	1	0	1	0	0	0	.000
MACDONALD, M.	1	0/0	.000	0/0	.000	0/0	.000	0/0	0	0	0	0	0	0	.000
Totals	200	28/56	.500	2/8	.250	14/24	.583	11/30	21	10	16	9	4	72	.360

Ball State (60)　　Coach: Rick Majerus

	Min.	Total FG/FGA	Pct.	3–Pt. FG/FGA	Pct.	FT/FTA	Pct.	Reb. O/T	A	TO	PF	S	Blk	TP	PPM
MCCURDY, P.	37	6/10	.600	0/0	.000	3/4	.750	6/12	2	1	4	0	1	15	.405
PARRISH, S.	26	4/6	.667	0/0	.000	2/2	1.000	4/7	2	2	4	1	0	10	.385
KIDD, C.	34	7/13	.538	0/0	.000	2/4	.500	1/9	1	5	4	1	0	16	.471
BUTTS, B.	34	3/15	.200	2/9	.222	0/0	.000	0/1	2	7	3	0	0	8	.235
NICHOLS, S.	30	0/0	.000	0/0	.000	0/0	.000	1/1	6	1	3	3	0	0	.000
STALLING, K.	16	1/3	.333	0/0	.000	0/1	.000	0/2	1	0	0	0	0	2	.125
MILLER, G.	20	3/13	.231	2/4	.500	1/2	.500	4/6	0	1	3	0	0	9	.450
MULLER, R.	3	0/2	.000	0/0	.000	0/0	.000	1/1	0	0	1	0	0	0	.000
Totals	200	24/62	.387	4/13	.308	8/13	.615	17/39	14	17	22	5	1	60	.300

Team Rebounds: Illinois 4; Ball St. 4. Disqualified: None. Technical fouls: None.

	1st Half	2nd Half	Final
Illinois	34	38	72
Ball St.	23	37	60

Arkansas (84)　　Coach: Nolan Richardson

	Min.	Total FG/FGA	Pct.	3–Pt. FG/FGA	Pct.	FT/FTA	Pct.	Reb. O/T	A	TO	PF	S	Blk	TP	PPM
DAY, T.	27	7/20	.350	1/6	.167	5/6	.833	3/5	0	1	4	1	0	20	.741
HOWELL, L.	34	8/20	.400	0/2	.000	2/4	.500	4/9	0	2	4	1	0	18	.529
CREDIT, M.	27	3/5	.600	0/0	.000	3/8	.375	2/10	0	2	4	1	1	9	.333
WILSON, K.	27	3/6	.500	0/1	.000	0/0	.000	2/5	4	2	5	3	0	6	.222
MAYBERRY, L.	36	7/20	.350	1/2	.500	4/4	1.000	5/5	5	3	2	1	0	19	.528
BOWERS, A.	20	2/9	.222	2/5	.400	0/0	.000	0/1	3	1	1	1	0	6	.300
HAWKENS, D.	4	1/2	.500	0/0	.000	0/0	.000	1/1	1	1	0	0	0	2	.500
WHITBY, C.	4	0/1	.000	0/1	.000	0/0	.000	0/0	0	0	2	0	0	0	.000
MILLER, O.	21	1/5	.200	0/0	.000	2/3	.667	1/5	2	3	4	1	1	4	.190
DAVIS, S.	0	0/0	.000	0/0	.000	0/0	.000	0/0	0	0	0	0	0	0	-
Totals	200	32/88	.364	4/17	.235	16/25	.640	18/41	15	15	26	9	2	84	.420

Louisville (93)　　Coach: Denny Crum

	Min.	Total FG/FGA	Pct.	3–Pt. FG/FGA	Pct.	FT/FTA	Pct.	Reb. O/T	A	TO	PF	S	Blk	TP	PPM
PAYNE, K.	15	5/8	.625	0/0	.000	2/2	1.000	1/3	1	2	4	0	0	12	.800
KIMBRO, T.	28	1/6	.167	0/1	.000	1/4	.250	1/4	2	0	3	0	3	3	.107
ELLISON, P.	29	8/11	.727	0/0	.000	5/6	.833	4/15	8	4	5	1	3	21	.724
SMITH, L.	38	8/15	.533	1/3	.333	9/10	.900	0/4	8	2	3	0	3	26	.722
SPENCER, F.	21	3/4	.750	0/0	.000	3/3	1.000	0/6	0	1	2	0	1	9	.429
HOLDEN, C.	12	2/3	.667	0/0	.000	4/10	.400	0/4	0	0	1	1	0	8	.667
SULLIVAN, E.	20	2/5	.400	0/0	.000	0/1	.000	1/3	4	5	3	1	1	4	.200
BREWER, J.	4	1/2	.500	0/0	.000	0/0	.000	0/0	0	0	0	0	0	2	.500
HAWLEY, C.	0	0/0	.000	0/0	.000	0/0	.000	0/0	0	0	0	0	0	0	-
FRALEY, S.	0	0/0	.000	0/0	.000	0/0	.000	0/0	0	0	0	0	0	0	-
WILLIAMS, K.	35	4/9	.444	0/1	.000	0/1	.000	1/4	5	2	2	0	0	8	.229
Totals	200	34/63	.540	1/5	.200	24/37	.649	8/43	28	16	20	6	8	93	.465

Team Rebounds: Louisville 4; Arkansas 8. Disqualified: Louisville—Ellison; Arkansas—Wilson. Technical fouls: Arkansas—Holden. Players who played 0 min. played less than 1 min. each.

	1st Half	2nd Half	Final
Arkansas	42	42	84
Louisville	49	44	93

Texas (89)　　Coach: Tom Penders

	Min.	Total FG/FGA	Pct.	3–Pt. FG/FGA	Pct.	FT/FTA	Pct.	Reb. O/T	A	TO	PF	S	Blk	TP	PPM
BLANKS, L.	40	7/17	.412	1/6	.167	5/5	1.000	0/4	1	8	3	6	0	20	.500
HEGGS, A.	36	7/13	.538	0/0	.000	0/0	.000	2/9	2	0	4	0	0	14	.389
NASSAR, J.	32	5/7	.714	0/1	.000	0/0	.000	3/5	2	0	5	0	1	10	.313
WRIGHT, J.	40	8/16	.500	0/2	.000	3/5	.600	3/6	6	6	4	3	1	19	.475
MAYS, T.	39	8/16	.500	4/8	.500	5/6	.833	0/1	0	6	4	1	0	25	.641
JEANS, C.	1	0/0	.000	0/0	.000	0/0	.000	0/0	0	0	0	0	0	0	.000
SHEPARD, W.	7	0/0	.000	0/0	.000	1/2	.500	0/0	0	0	1	0	0	1	.143
GIPSON, D.	1	0/0	.000	0/0	.000	0/0	.000	0/0	0	0	0	0	0	0	.000
MULLER, G.	4	0/0	.000	0/0	.000	0/0	.000	0/0	0	0	0	0	0	0	.000
Totals	200	35/69	.507	5/17	.294	14/18	.778	8/25	11	20	21	10	2	89	.445

Missouri (108)　　Coach: Norm Stewart

	Min.	Total FG/FGA	Pct.	3–Pt. FG/FGA	Pct.	FT/FTA	Pct.	Reb. O/T	A	TO	PF	S	Blk	TP	PPM
SMITH, D.	33	12/19	.632	0/0	.000	8/10	.800	3/8	2	4	4	1	1	32	.970
SANDBOTHE, M.	25	3/4	.750	0/0	.000	0/0	.000	1/5	3	2	3	0	1	6	.240
LEONARD, G.	28	4/11	.364	0/0	.000	1/5	.200	2/7	3	0	2	1	1	9	.321
COWARD, L.	29	6/10	.600	3/3	1.000	1/2	.500	0/1	1	5	1	2	0	16	.552
IRVIN, B.	38	6/12	.500	0/0	.000	6/7	.857	2/5	4	1	1	5	0	18	.474
BUNTIN, N.	1	0/0	.000	0/0	.000	0/0	.000	0/0	0	0	0	0	0	0	.000
CHURCH, G.	25	5/8	.625	0/0	.000	4/4	1.000	4/9	3	3	3	1	0	14	.560
PEELER, A.	21	6/7	.857	1/1	1.000	0/1	.000	2/3	4	3	2	2	0	13	.619
Totals	200	42/71	.592	4/4	1.000	20/29	.690	14/38	20	18	16	12	3	108	.540

Team Rebounds: Missouri 3; Texas 5. Disqualified: Texas—Nassar. Technical fouls: None.

	1st Half	2nd Half	Final
Texas	41	48	89
Missouri	51	57	108

Colorado State (50)　　Coach: Boyd Grant

	Min.	Total FG/FGA	Pct.	3–Pt. FG/FGA	Pct.	FT/FTA	Pct.	Reb. O/T	A	TO	PF	S	Blk	TP	PPM
DURHAM, P.	38	3/6	.500	0/1	.000	1/4	.250	2/6	4	4	4	0	0	7	.184
ANDERSON, A.	31	5/7	.714	0/1	.000	5/6	.833	0/2	1	4	3	0	0	15	.484
FRIEHAUF, E.	19	2/6	.333	0/0	.000	0/0	.000	1/4	0	0	2	1	0	4	.211
TRIBELHORN, J.	37	3/10	.300	2/5	.400	1/2	.500	0/2	1	4	4	0	0	9	.243
SHIPPEN, T.	35	2/3	.667	1/2	.500	0/0	.000	0/3	1	1	3	0	1	5	.143
MICHAEL, M.	2	0/0	.000	0/0	.000	0/0	.000	0/0	0	0	0	0	0	0	.000
TRYON, L.	8	0/4	.000	0/1	.000	0/0	.000	0/1	0	0	1	0	0	0	.000
HINES, J.	12	1/2	.500	0/0	.000	2/2	1.000	0/1	0	2	2	1	0	4	.333
SHARP, M.	18	3/5	.600	0/0	.000	0/0	.000	0/5	3	0	2	1	0	6	.333
Totals	200	19/43	.442	3/10	.300	9/14	.643	3/24	10	15	21	3	1	50	.250

Syracuse (65)　　Coach: Jim Boeheim

	Min.	Total FG/FGA	Pct.	3–Pt. FG/FGA	Pct.	FT/FTA	Pct.	Reb. O/T	A	TO	PF	S	Blk	TP	PPM
OWENS, B.	22	2/8	.250	0/0	.000	2/2	1.000	3/6	3	1	4	3	0	6	.273
THOMPSON, S.	37	9/11	.818	0/0	.000	3/8	.375	2/3	0	1	2	0	0	21	.568
MANNING, R.	9	0/1	.000	0/0	.000	0/0	.000	0/3	0	0	1	0	0	0	.000
ROE, M.	35	4/9	.444	2/5	.400	1/2	.500	1/2	1	2	1	0	0	11	.314
DOUGLAS, S.	40	3/7	.429	0/2	.000	5/6	.833	0/2	8	5	2	3	0	11	.275
JOHNSON, D.	3	0/1	.000	0/0	.000	0/0	.000	0/0	0	0	0	0	0	0	.000
HARRIED, H.	23	2/2	1.000	0/0	.000	0/1	.000	0/1	0	1	0	2	0	4	.174
COLEMAN, D.	31	6/8	.750	0/0	.000	0/2	.000	1/7	2	0	2	0	2	12	.387
Totals	200	26/47	.553	2/7	.286	11/21	.524	7/25	14	11	14	6	2	65	.325

Team Rebounds: Syracuse 5; Colorado State 6. Disqualified: None. Technical fouls: None.

	1st Half	2nd Half	Final
Colorado State	28	22	50
Syracuse	38	27	65

SECOND ROUND SOUTHEAST

Oklahoma (124)   Coach: Billy Tubbs

	Min.	Total FG/FGA	Pct.	3-Pt. FG/FGA	Pct.	FT/FTA	Pct.	Reb. O/T	A	TO	PF	S	Blk	TP	PPM
DAVIS, W.	18	3/7	.429	0/0	.000	3/3	1.000	3/9	2	0	2	0	0	9	.500
JONES, T.	24	4/10	.400	4/6	.667	4/6	.667	1/3	2	4	2	0	0	16	.667
KING, S.	35	9/18	.500	0/0	.000	3/6	.500	5/15	0	3	2	4	4	21	.600
BLAYLOCK, M.	40	14/28	.500	4/11	.364	2/4	.500	6/7	7	2	2	4	2	34	.850
MULLINS, T.	9	1/4	.250	1/4	.250	0/0	.000	0/0	2	0	2	0	0	3	.333
HENRY, H.	31	6/11	.545	1/3	.333	4/4	1.000	2/9	3	4	3	3	2	17	.548
PATTERSON, D.	13	3/8	.375	0/0	.000	2/2	1.000	1/2	1	0	1	1	1	8	.615
WILEY, A.	8	2/2	1.000	0/0	.000	0/2	.000	1/2	0	0	4	2	0	4	.500
BELL, M.	4	1/1	1.000	0/0	.000	0/0	.000	1/2	0	0	1	0	0	2	.500
MARTIN, T.	14	4/6	.667	0/0	.000	0/1	.000	1/5	1	2	1	2	0	8	.571
SCURCENSKI, J.	1	1/2	.500	0/0	.000	0/0	.000	2/2	0	0	0	0	0	2	2.000
HOLMES, K.	3	0/1	.000	0/0	.000	0/0	.000	0/2	0	0	0	0	0	0	.000
Totals	200	48/98	.490	10/24	.417	18/28	.643	23/58	18	15	20	16	9	124	.620

Louisiana Tech (81)   Coach: Tommy Eagles

	Min.	Total FG/FGA	Pct.	3-Pt. FG/FGA	Pct.	FT/FTA	Pct.	Reb. O/T	A	TO	PF	S	Blk	TP	PPM
NEWTON, B.	22	1/6	.167	0/2	.000	2/2	1.000	2/3	1	1	2	1	0	4	.182
DADE, A.	30	7/18	.389	0/0	.000	2/3	.667	4/9	1	2	2	1	1	16	.533
WHITE, R.	29	6/12	.500	1/3	.333	5/6	.833	1/9	0	5	5	0	0	18	.621
LOUIS, K.	24	3/6	.500	2/3	.667	0/0	.000	1/3	2	3	2	0	4	8	.333
GUILLORY, B.	29	2/9	.222	0/1	.000	4/4	1.000	0/1	5	6	1	1	0	8	.276
BROWN, P.	21	3/9	.333	2/2	1.000	1/5	.200	6/13	0	2	2	3	2	9	.429
KNIGHT, D.	20	3/9	.333	2/5	.400	2/2	1.000	1/3	2	3	4	1	0	10	.500
CRAWFORD, D.	3	0/1	.000	0/1	.000	0/0	.000	0/1	0	2	0	0	0	0	.000
WATLEY, M.	16	1/3	.333	0/0	.000	2/2	1.000	1/2	2	5	1	1	0	4	.250
GOLDSMITH, J.	3	1/3	.333	0/2	.000	0/0	.000	0/0	2	0	1	0	0	2	.667
MCALISTER, R.	3	1/1	1.000	0/0	.000	0/0	.000	1/3	0	0	2	0	0	2	.667
Totals	200	28/77	.364	7/19	.368	18/24	.750	17/47	15	29	22	8	7	81	.405

Team Rebounds: Oklahoma 4; Louisiana Tech 1. Disqualified: Louisiana Tech—White. Technical fouls: Louisiana Tech—Bench.

	1st Half	2nd Half	Final
Oklahoma	55	69	124
Louisiana Tech	31	50	81

Virginia (104)   Coach: Terry Holland

	Min.	Total FG/FGA	Pct.	3-Pt. FG/FGA	Pct.	FT/FTA	Pct.	Reb. O/T	A	TO	PF	S	Blk	TP	PPM
BLUNDIN, M.	32	4/10	.400	0/0	.000	0/2	.000	3/8	0	1	2	0	0	8	.250
STITH, B.	31	7/11	.636	0/0	.000	12/12	1.000	1/4	1	1	4	0	0	26	.839
DABBS, B.	15	1/2	.500	0/0	.000	2/2	1.000	0/5	0	2	5	0	0	4	.267
CROTTY, J.	39	10/13	.769	2/3	.667	3/8	.375	0/5	14	1	3	0	0	25	.641
MORGAN, R.	33	11/22	.500	5/6	.833	6/6	1.000	3/5	0	2	3	0	0	33	1.000
TURNER, K.	15	1/2	.500	0/0	.000	4/4	1.000	1/4	0	2	3	1	0	6	.400
KAPSTRA, D.	6	0/1	.000	0/1	.000	0/0	.000	1/1	1	0	0	0	0	0	.000
DANIEL, J.	27	1/3	.333	0/0	.000	0/0	.000	2/10	0	0	2	0	0	2	.074
WILLIAMS, C.	1	0/0	.000	0/0	.000	0/0	.000	0/1	1	2	0	0	0	0	.000
COOKE, M.	1	0/0	.000	0/0	.000	0/0	.000	0/1	0	1	0	0	0	0	.000
Totals	200	35/64	.547	7/10	.700	27/34	.794	11/44	17	12	22	1	0	104	.520

Middle Tennessee State (88)   Coach: Bruce Stewart

	Min.	Total FG/FGA	Pct.	3-Pt. FG/FGA	Pct.	FT/FTA	Pct.	Reb. O/T	A	TO	PF	S	Blk	TP	PPM
VANCE, Q.	9	0/2	.000	0/0	.000	0/0	.000	1/2	1	0	0	0	0	0	.000
HAMMONDS, K.	37	8/14	.571	0/0	.000	6/7	.857	3/15	5	1	3	1	0	22	.595
RAINEY, C.	33	7/15	.467	3/5	.600	6/7	.857	0/4	5	4	5	0	0	23	.697
HARRIS, G.	23	5/7	.714	2/3	.667	0/0	.000	0/2	0	1	2	0	0	12	.522
INGRAM, G.	8	0/1	.000	0/0	.000	0/0	.000	0/0	3	0	3	0	1	0	.000
BUCK, M.	24	0/4	.000	0/4	.000	2/2	1.000	1/1	2	0	4	0	0	2	.083
WALLACE, K.	19	3/6	.500	0/2	.000	0/0	.000	2/3	2	1	3	0	0	6	.316
WEBB, M.	12	0/2	.000	0/0	.000	0/0	.000	0/0	1	1	4	0	0	0	.000
HUNTER, J.	1	0/1	.000	0/0	.000	0/0	.000	0/0	0	0	0	0	0	0	.000
HENRY, R.	34	9/20	.450	1/2	.500	4/4	1.000	1/3	2	0	2	1	0	23	.676
Totals	200	32/72	.444	6/16	.375	18/20	.900	8/31	18	8	26	3	1	88	.440

Team Rebounds: Virginia 1; Middle Tenn. St. 1. Disqualified: Virginia—Dabbs; Middle Tenn. St.—Rainey. Technical fouls: None.

	1st Half	2nd Half	Final
Virginia	49	55	104
Middle Tenn. St.	39	49	88

South Alabama (82)   Coach: Ronnie Arrow

	Min.	Total FG/FGA	Pct.	3-Pt. FG/FGA	Pct.	FT/FTA	Pct.	Reb. O/T	A	TO	PF	S	Blk	TP	PPM
ESTABA, G.	37	7/15	.467	0/1	.000	1/3	.333	4/9	2	3	4	1	0	15	.405
JIMMERSON, J.	22	3/5	.600	0/0	.000	1/2	.500	2/4	5	4	1	0	0	7	.318
DARDEN, P.	9	0/0	.000	0/0	.000	0/0	.000	0/3	0	0	4	0	1	0	.000
HODGE, J.	37	6/14	.429	3/9	.333	1/1	1.000	1/3	2	1	1	0	0	16	.432
LEWIS, J.	37	9/17	.529	0/2	.000	7/10	.700	6/9	3	4	1	0	0	25	.676
SMITH, N.	27	4/8	.500	0/0	.000	6/7	.857	5/7	0	1	4	0	0	14	.519
BRODNICK, T.	23	1/7	.143	1/4	.250	2/2	1.000	0/2	6	2	1	0	0	5	.217
TURNER, D.	7	0/4	.000	0/3	.000	0/0	.000	0/1	0	0	1	0	0	0	.000
NELSON, D.	1	0/0	.000	0/0	.000	0/0	.000	0/0	0	0	0	0	0	0	.000
Totals	200	30/70	.429	4/19	.211	18/25	.720	18/38	18	15	17	1	1	82	.410

Michigan (91)   Coach: Steve Fisher

	Min.	Total FG/FGA	Pct.	3-Pt. FG/FGA	Pct.	FT/FTA	Pct.	Reb. O/T	A	TO	PF	S	Blk	TP	PPM
RICE, G.	37	16/25	.640	3/7	.429	1/1	1.000	2/8	5	4	2	1	0	36	.973
HUGHES, M.	24	2/4	.500	0/0	.000	0/0	.000	2/4	0	0	3	1	1	4	.167
MILLS, T.	38	9/13	.692	0/0	.000	6/8	.750	2/7	5	3	3	0	0	24	.632
GRIFFIN, M.	24	2/2	1.000	0/0	.000	0/0	.000	0/1	0	2	3	0	0	4	.167
ROBINSON, R.	27	5/8	.625	1/2	.500	1/2	.500	0/3	5	3	4	3	0	12	.444
VAUGHT, L.	13	1/5	.200	0/0	.000	0/0	.000	1/7	0	0	3	0	0	2	.154
CALIP, D.	19	0/1	.000	0/0	.000	3/4	.750	0/1	5	1	2	0	0	3	.158
HIGGINS, S.	17	2/4	.500	0/1	.000	2/2	1.000	0/2	2	1	2	0	0	6	.353
PELINKA, R.	1	0/0	.000	0/0	.000	0/0	.000	0/1	0	0	0	0	0	0	.000
Totals	200	37/62	.597	4/10	.400	13/17	.765	7/31	22	15	22	5	1	91	.455

Team Rebounds: Michigan 1; South Alabama 1. Disqualified: None. Technical fouls: None.

	1st Half	2nd Half	Final
South Alabama	47	35	82
Michigan	44	47	91

UCLA (81)   Coach: Jim Harrick

	Min.	Total FG/FGA	Pct.	3-Pt. FG/FGA	Pct.	FT/FTA	Pct.	Reb. O/T	A	TO	PF	S	Blk	TP	PPM
WILSON, T.	40	6/13	.462	0/0	.000	9/15	.600	1/9	3	2	3	0	0	21	.525
MACLEAN, D.	32	7/13	.538	0/0	.000	2/4	.500	2/8	3	0	5	1	0	16	.500
WALKER, K.	30	5/8	.625	4/7	.571	3/4	.750	1/4	4	2	4	0	0	17	.567
MARTIN, D.	25	2/6	.333	0/2	.000	0/0	.000	1/2	3	1	3	1	0	4	.160
RICHARDSON, J.	40	5/13	.385	0/3	.375	1/4	.250	2/4	5	4	5	4	0	14	.350
ROCHELIN, C.	19	3/4	.750	1/2	.500	0/0	.000	0/3	1	0	4	0	0	7	.368
OWENS, K.	14	1/1	1.000	0/0	.000	0/0	.000	1/2	0	0	1	1	1	2	.143
Totals	200	29/58	.500	8/19	.421	15/27	.556	8/32	19	9	24	3	1	81	.405

North Carolina (88)   Coach: Dean Smith

	Min.	Total FG/FGA	Pct.	3-Pt. FG/FGA	Pct.	FT/FTA	Pct.	Reb. O/T	A	TO	PF	S	Blk	TP	PPM
BUCKNALL, S.	35	5/10	.500	2/6	.333	7/8	.875	1/4	11	1	3	1	0	19	.543
FOX, R.	32	6/12	.500	1/3	.333	5/6	.833	2/3	1	1	4	0	0	18	.563
WILLIAMS, S.	29	6/7	.857	0/0	.000	2/3	.667	1/8	1	0	4	1	2	14	.483
LEBO, J.	33	4/9	.444	3/8	.375	1/3	.333	0/3	4	2	3	0	0	12	.364
RICE, G.	15	1/5	.200	1/4	.250	0/0	.000	1/1	3	0	1	0	0	3	.200
MADDEN, K.	28	8/13	.615	0/0	.000	6/10	.600	1/8	2	1	4	1	0	22	.786
CHILCUTT, P.	22	0/0	.000	0/0	.000	0/0	.000	2/8	0	2	2	0	0	0	.000
DAVIS, H.	5	0/2	.000	0/2	.000	0/0	.000	0/0	0	0	0	0	0	0	.000
DENNY, J.	1	0/0	.000	0/0	.000	0/0	.000	0/0	0	0	0	1	0	0	.000
Totals	200	30/58	.517	7/23	.304	21/30	.700	8/35	22	7	21	4	2	88	.440

Team Rebounds: N. Carolina 2; UCLA 1. Disqualified: UCLA—MacLean. Technical fouls: None.

	1st Half	2nd Half	Final
UCLA	52	29	81
N. Carolina	44	44	88

SECOND ROUND EAST

Georgetown (81)   Coach: John Thompson

	Min.	Total FG/FGA	Pct.	3-Pt. FG/FGA	Pct.	FT/FTA	Pct.	Reb. O/T	A	TO	PF	S	Blk	TP	PPM
JACKSON, J.	33	4/4	1.000	0/0	.000	0/3	.000	1/7	0	1	1	2	0	8	.242
TURNER, J.	17	1/2	.500	0/0	.000	0/0	.000	0/2	0	4	2	1	0	2	.118
MOURNING, A.	37	4/5	.800	0/0	.000	9/12	.750	0/4	0	1	1	1	3	17	.459
BRYANT, D.	19	1/1	1.000	1/1	1.000	2/4	.500	1/1	2	1	2	1	0	5	.263
SMITH, C.	36	10/14	.714	4/6	.667	10/11	.909	0/1	6	3	1	3	0	34	.944
TILLMON, M.	20	1/3	.333	0/1	.000	0/0	.000	0/1	1	0	5	0	0	2	.100
WINSTON, B.	26	3/4	.750	0/0	.000	3/4	.750	0/2	3	2	1	0	0	9	.346
MUTOMBO, D.	7	1/1	1.000	0/0	.000	0/0	.000	1/2	0	0	1	0	2	2	.286
THOMPSON, R.	5	0/1	.000	0/0	.000	2/2	1.000	0/0	0	0	0	0	0	2	.400
Totals	200	25/35	.714	5/8	.625	26/36	.722	3/20	12	12	14	8	5	81	.405

Notre Dame (74)   Coach: Digger Phelps

	Min.	Total FG/FGA	Pct.	3-Pt. FG/FGA	Pct.	FT/FTA	Pct.	Reb. O/T	A	TO	PF	S	Blk	TP	PPM
ELLIS, L.	32	8/14	.571	0/0	.000	2/2	1.000	6/10	2	0	4	0	0	18	.563
JACKSON, J.	30	5/8	.625	2/4	.500	0/0	.000	0/0	1	1	4	0	0	12	.400
ROBINSON, K.	30	2/8	.250	0/0	.000	2/2	1.000	1/3	2	1	4	0	0	6	.200
SINGLETON, T.	39	2/5	.400	0/0	.000	2/2	1.000	0/2	6	5	5	1	0	6	.154
BENNETT, E.	12	1/2	.500	0/1	.000	2/2	1.000	0/0	2	0	3	1	0	4	.333
FREDRICK, J.	30	4/8	.500	2/2	1.000	6/6	1.000	2/3	2	1	4	1	0	16	.533
TOWER, K.	16	1/2	.500	0/0	.000	0/1	.000	1/2	0	1	1	0	1	2	.125
SWEET, D.	11	4/7	.571	0/0	.000	2/2	1.000	0/4	1	0	2	1	0	10	.909
Totals	200	27/54	.500	4/7	.571	16/17	.941	10/24	16	9	27	4	1	74	.370

Team Rebounds: Georgetown 1; Notre Dame 0. Disqualified: Georgetown—Tillmon; Notre Dame—Singleton. Technical fouls: None.

	1st Half	2nd Half	Final
Georgetown	32	49	81
Notre Dame	36	38	74

North Carolina State (102)   Coach: Jim Valvano

	Min.	Total FG/FGA	Pct.	3-Pt. FG/FGA	Pct.	FT/FTA	Pct.	Reb. O/T	A	TO	PF	S	Blk	TP	PPM
LESTER, A.	48	4/7	.571	0/0	.000	2/2	1.000	2/9	1	1	4	1	1	10	.208
CORCHIANI, C.	49	5/8	.625	2/2	1.000	4/6	.667	0/3	10	3	4	1	1	16	.327
MONROE, R.	41	13/21	.619	4/10	.400	10/11	.909	2/4	4	1	2	1	0	40	.976
LEE, D.	3	0/0	.000	0/0	.000	0/0	.000	0/0	0	0	1	0	0	0	.000
WEEMS, K.	9	1/1	1.000	0/0	.000	0/0	.000	0/0	2	1	1	0	0	2	.222
D'AMICO, B.	7	0/1	.000	0/0	.000	0/0	.000	0/0	0	0	1	0	0	0	.000
HINNANT, M.	4	0/0	.000	0/0	.000	4/4	1.000	0/0	0	0	0	0	0	4	1.000
BROWN, J.	43	5/7	.714	1/1	1.000	3/6	.500	2/4	0	1	5	0	1	14	.326
HOWARD, B.	46	8/12	.667	0/0	.000	0/0	.000	2/6	2	3	2	3	2	16	.348
Totals	250	36/57	.632	7/13	.538	23/29	.793	8/26	19	11	20	5	11	102	.408

Iowa (96)   Coach: Tom Davis

	Min.	Total FG/FGA	Pct.	3-Pt. FG/FGA	Pct.	FT/FTA	Pct.	Reb. O/T	A	TO	PF	S	Blk	TP	PPM
HORTON, E.	46	13/22	.591	0/1	.000	6/6	1.000	8/12	3	2	4	1	0	32	.696
BULLARD, M.	34	2/9	.222	0/3	.000	4/4	1.000	1/4	4	2	1	0	0	8	.235
JEPSEN, J.	21	2/3	.667	0/0	.000	0/0	.000	3/3	0	0	2	0	4	4	.190
ARMSTRONG, B.	46	7/13	.538	2/4	.500	4/4	1.000	1/3	5	1	3	1	1	20	.435
MARBLE, R.	44	10/23	.435	2/5	.400	2/3	.667	4/7	3	2	3	2	1	24	.545
MOSES, J.	11	0/4	.000	0/0	.000	0/0	.000	0/1	0	1	3	0	0	0	.000
GARNER, B.	31	0/0	.000	0/0	.000	2/2	1.000	1/2	5	3	2	0	0	2	.065
LOOKINGBILL, W.	17	2/2	1.000	0/0	.000	2/2	1.000	0/2	2	0	4	0	0	6	.353
Totals	250	36/76	.474	4/13	.308	20/21	.952	18/32	22	11	22	4	2	96	.384

Team Rebounds: N.C. State 1; Iowa State 3. Disqualified: N.C. State—Brown. Technical fouls: None.

	1st Half	2nd Half	1st OT	2nd OT	Final
N.C. State	41	34	8	19	102
Iowa	41	34	8	13	96

Minnesota (80)   Coach: Clem Haskins

	Min.	Total FG/FGA	Pct.	3-Pt. FG/FGA	Pct.	FT/FTA	Pct.	Reb. O/T	A	TO	PF	S	Blk	TP	PPM
BURTON, W.	34	7/13	.538	2/4	.500	3/4	.750	4/11	3	2	3	0	1	19	.559
BOND, W.	31	4/5	.800	0/0	.000	0/1	.000	1/4	2	3	2	2	0	8	.258
SHIKENJANSKI, J.	28	7/13	.538	0/0	.000	3/3	1.000	1/4	0	4	1	1	0	17	.607
LYNCH, K.	34	5/11	.455	0/2	.000	4/4	1.000	3/6	3	2	0	1	0	14	.412
NEWBERN, M.	28	7/10	.700	0/1	.000	3/6	.500	0/7	8	1	3	3	1	17	.607
GREEN, M.	1	0/1	.000	0/0	.000	0/0	.000	0/1	0	0	0	0	0	0	.000
LEWIS, C.	5	0/1	.000	0/0	.000	0/0	.000	0/0	0	0	1	0	0	0	.000
GAFFNEY, R.	19	1/3	.333	1/2	.500	0/0	.000	0/1	1	2	3	0	0	3	.158
METCALF, R.	9	0/2	.000	0/0	.000	0/0	.000	0/1	0	0	1	0	0	0	.000
MARTIN, B.	10	1/2	.500	0/0	.000	0/0	.000	0/1	0	0	1	0	0	2	.200
COFFEY, R.	1	0/0	.000	0/0	.000	0/0	.000	0/0	0	0	0	0	0	0	.000
Totals	200	32/61	.525	3/9	.333	13/18	.722	9/36	17	14	15	7	2	80	.400

Siena (67)   Coach: Mike Deane

	Min.	Total FG/FGA	Pct.	3-Pt. FG/FGA	Pct.	FT/FTA	Pct.	Reb. O/T	A	TO	PF	S	Blk	TP	PPM
ROBINSON, J.	38	8/22	.364	6/15	.400	1/3	.333	1/8	1	2	2	2	1	23	.605
McCOY, S.	27	1/3	.333	0/0	.000	0/0	.000	2/5	1	2	5	1	0	2	.074
HENDERSON, M.	23	3/7	.429	0/0	.000	1/2	.500	5/8	0	0	2	0	1	7	.304
BROWN, M.	39	4/20	.200	0/10	.000	1/1	1.000	1/2	8	4	3	3	0	9	.231
BROWN, M.	27	5/6	.833	3/3	1.000	0/0	.000	0/1	0	4	0	1	0	13	.481
HUERTER, T.	8	1/3	.333	1/2	.500	0/0	.000	0/1	2	1	0	2	0	3	.375
SCHROEDER, B.	5	0/0	.000	0/0	.000	0/0	.000	0/0	0	1	1	0	0	0	.000
DOWNEY, S.	18	3/6	.500	0/1	.000	0/2	.000	1/2	0	2	1	0	6	6	.333
FLEURY, E.	7	0/0	.000	0/0	.000	0/0	.000	0/0	0	2	0	1	0	0	.000
GRAZULIS, A.	3	0/0	.000	0/0	.000	0/0	.000	0/3	0	1	0	0	0	0	.000
FOSTER, D.	2	0/0	.000	0/0	.000	0/1	.000	1/1	0	0	0	0	0	0	.000
MIDDLETON, J.	3	2/3	.667	0/1	.000	0/0	.000	0/0	0	0	0	0	0	4	1.333
Totals	200	27/70	.386	10/32	.313	3/9	.333	12/34	11	15	19	7	3	67	.335

Team Rebounds: Minnesota 3; Siena 2. Disqualified: Siena—McCoy. Technical fouls: None.

	1st Half	2nd Half	Final
Minnesota	42	38	80
Siena	37	30	67

West Virginia (63)   Coach: Gale Catlett

	Min.	Total FG/FGA	Pct.	3-Pt. FG/FGA	Pct.	FT/FTA	Pct.	Reb. O/T	A	TO	PF	S	Blk	TP	PPM
PRUE, D.	28	4/7	.571	0/0	.000	1/3	.333	2/5	3	2	5	0	0	9	.321
BROOKS, C.	36	5/9	.556	0/0	.000	1/3	.333	3/6	2	4	4	0	0	11	.306
FOSTER, R.	33	3/7	.429	0/0	.000	1/4	.250	2/10	1	3	5	1	3	7	.212
BROOKS, H.	34	6/10	.600	1/2	.500	0/0	.000	0/3	2	7	2	1	0	13	.382
BERGER, B.	34	5/13	.385	1/3	.333	1/1	1.000	0/4	5	3	1	3	0	12	.353
SHELTON, T.	12	1/2	.500	0/0	.000	2/2	1.000	0/1	0	1	3	0	0	4	.353
JACKSON, S.	4	0/1	.000	0/0	.000	0/0	.000	0/0	1	0	1	0	0	0	.000
SMITH, W.	17	3/4	.750	0/0	.000	0/0	.000	0/3	0	2	2	0	0	6	.353
KROGER, T.	2	0/0	.000	0/0	.000	1/2	.500	0/0	0	0	0	0	1	1	.500
Totals	200	27/53	.519	2/5	.400	7/15	.467	7/32	14	22	23	5	3	63	.315

Duke (70)   Coach: Mike Krzyzewski

	Min.	Total FG/FGA	Pct.	3-Pt. FG/FGA	Pct.	FT/FTA	Pct.	Reb. O/T	A	TO	PF	S	Blk	TP	PPM
BRICKEY, R.	30	4/8	.500	0/0	.000	2/6	.333	1/6	2	1	3	0	1	10	.333
FERRY, D.	38	5/16	.313	1/3	.333	9/9	1.000	3/8	4	2	1	1	0	20	.526
LAETTNER, C.	23	6/7	.857	0/0	.000	2/2	1.000	1/3	1	3	5	0	2	14	.607
HENDERSON, P.	35	3/10	.300	1/7	.143	1/2	.500	0/2	3	5	2	1	0	8	.229
SNYDER, Q.	33	2/4	.500	0/1	.000	0/0	.000	0/3	1	2	4	3	0	4	.121
KOUBEK, G.	3	0/1	.000	0/0	.000	0/0	.000	0/0	0	1	0	0	0	0	.000
DAVIS, B.	3	0/1	.000	0/0	.000	0/0	.000	0/0	0	0	1	0	0	0	.000
ABDELNABY, A.	18	3/7	.429	0/0	.000	2/2	1.000	2/8	0	1	2	1	0	8	.444
SMITH, J.	17	2/4	.500	0/1	.000	2/2	1.000	1/1	0	0	1	0	0	6	.353
Totals	200	25/58	.431	2/12	.167	18/23	.783	8/31	11	14	19	6	3	70	.350

Team Rebounds: Duke 1; West Virginia 1. Disqualified: Duke—Laettner; West Virginia—Prue, Foster. Technical fouls: None.

	1st Half	2nd Half	Final
West Virginia	28	35	63
Duke	35	35	70

SECOND ROUND WEST

Arizona (94) Coach: Lute Olson

	Min.	Total FG/FGA	Pct.	3-Pt. FG/FGA	Pct.	FT/FTA	Pct.	Reb. O/T	A	TO	PF	S	Blk	TP	PPM
COOK, A.	37	4/9	.444	0/0	.000	6/10	.600	2/7	1	1	3	3	4	14	.378
LOFTON, K.	21	3/8	.375	2/7	.286	0/0	.000	0/2	4	2	1	2	0	8	.381
OTHICK, M.	19	2/4	.500	1/3	.333	2/3	.667	0/2	0	3	0	1	0	7	.368
MUEHLEBACH, M.	36	5/11	.455	4/10	.400	5/6	.833	0/3	4	0	1	1	0	19	.528
WOMACK, W.	2	1/1	1.000	0/0	.000	0/0	.000	0/0	0	0	0	0	0	2	1.000
ELLIOTT, S.	35	10/16	.625	1/3	.333	4/4	1.000	5/6	2	1	2	0	1	25	.714
CURRY, R.	2	0/0	.000	0/0	.000	0/0	.000	0/1	0	0	0	0	0	0	.000
DAVID, B.	2	0/0	.000	0/0	.000	0/0	.000	0/1	0	1	0	0	0	0	.000
BUECHLER, J.	30	6/9	.667	1/1	1.000	2/2	1.000	3/4	0	0	2	3	0	15	.500
MASON, H.	4	0/1	.000	0/0	.000	0/0	.000	0/0	1	1	1	0	1	0	.000
ROOKS, S.	12	2/3	.667	0/0	.000	0/0	.000	0/0	0	0	0	2	0	4	.333
Totals	200	33/62	.532	9/25	.360	19/25	.760	10/26	12	9	12	10	7	94	.470

DePaul (70) Coach: Joey Meyer

	Min.	Total FG/FGA	Pct.	3-Pt. FG/FGA	Pct.	FT/FTA	Pct.	Reb. O/T	A	TO	PF	S	Blk	TP	PPM
HOWARD, B.	10	0/1	.000	0/0	.000	0/0	.000	1/3	0	1	4	0	0	0	.000
PRICE, C.	9	1/2	.500	0/0	.000	0/0	.000	0/1	1	1	4	0	0	2	.222
BRUNDY, S.	37	3/7	.429	0/0	.000	4/8	.500	0/15	0	2	3	0	2	10	.270
HAMBY, J.	30	2/2	1.000	0/0	.000	0/0	.000	1/7	0	3	3	0	0	4	.133
MURPHY, C.	13	0/2	.000	0/0	.000	0/0	.000	0/0	1	2	1	0	0	0	.000
GREENE, T.	38	12/20	.600	0/3	.000	5/8	.625	1/7	6	3	4	1	0	29	.763
FOSTER, M.	27	5/8	.625	0/0	.000	0/0	.000	0/3	0	3	5	0	0	10	.370
BOOTH	26	6/8	.750	0/0	.000	3/4	.750	0/2	1	1	4	0	0	15	.577
NIEMANN, B.	7	0/0	.000	0/0	.000	0/0	.000	0/0	0	0	1	0	0	0	.000
SOWELL, C.	2	0/0	.000	0/0	.000	0/0	.000	0/0	0	0	0	0	0	0	.000
JACKSON, C.	1	0/0	.000	0/0	.000	0/0	.000	0/0	0	0	0	0	0	0	.000
Totals	200	29/50	.580	0/3	.000	12/20	.600	3/38	9	16	29	1	2	70	.350

Clemson (68) Coach: Cliff Ellis

	Min.	Total FG/FGA	Pct.	3-Pt. FG/FGA	Pct.	FT/FTA	Pct.	Reb. O/T	A	TO	PF	S	Blk	TP	PPM
DAVIS, D.	32	1/3	.333	0/0	.000	0/0	.000	2/5	1	3	2	1	2	2	.063
CAMPBELL, E.	33	10/17	.588	1/2	.500	3/3	1.000	2/7	0	3	4	1	1	24	.727
YOUNG, D.	23	1/4	.250	0/1	.000	0/0	.000	1/1	5	2	0	0	2	2	.087
FORREST, D.	31	8/14	.571	3/5	.600	2/2	1.000	2/4	2	3	4	0	0	21	.677
KINCAID, T.	7	0/2	.000	0/0	.000	0/0	.000	0/0	2	2	2	1	0	0	.000
CASH, M.	35	6/10	.600	1/2	.500	0/0	.000	1/3	5	5	4	0	0	13	.371
MITCHELL, R.	5	0/0	.000	0/0	.000	0/0	.000	0/1	1	0	2	0	0	0	.000
PRYOR, J.	10	1/1	1.000	0/0	.000	0/1	.000	1/3	0	1	1	0	1	2	.200
HOWLING	5	0/3	.000	0/2	.000	0/0	.000	0/1	0	1	0	0	0	0	.000
BRUCE, D.	2	0/0	.000	0/0	.000	0/0	.000	0/0	0	0	0	0	0	0	.000
JONES, R.	14	2/4	.500	0/0	.000	0/0	.000	0/2	2	2	0	0	0	4	.286
BROWN, C.	3	0/0	.000	0/0	.000	0/0	.000	0/0	0	0	0	0	0	0	.000
Totals	200	29/58	.500	5/12	.417	5/6	.833	9/25	17	22	20	3	4	68	.340

Team Rebounds: Arizona 4; Clemson 2. Disqualified: None. Technical fouls: None.

	1st Half	2nd Half	Final
Arizona	44	50	94
Clemson	35	33	68

UNLV (85) Coach: Jerry Tarkanian

	Min.	Total FG/FGA	Pct.	3-Pt. FG/FGA	Pct.	FT/FTA	Pct.	Reb. O/T	A	TO	PF	S	Blk	TP	PPM
AUGMON, S.	38	4/10	.400	1/4	.250	8/11	.727	5/11	2	1	2	0	0	17	.447
SCURRY, M.	22	4/7	.571	0/0	.000	5/9	.556	5/8	0	0	3	0	1	13	.591
BUTLER, D.	35	8/19	.421	0/0	.000	7/10	.700	2/6	0	1	3	3	0	23	.657
ANTHONY, G.	31	4/10	.400	2/4	.500	0/0	.000	0/0	6	0	4	5	0	10	.323
HUNT, A.	37	3/9	.333	1/4	.250	2/3	.667	0/0	7	1	4	3	0	9	.243
ACKLES, G.	21	3/4	.750	0/0	.000	0/0	.000	0/4	0	0	3	0	0	6	.286
CVIJANOVICH, S.	5	0/1	.000	0/1	.000	3/4	.750	0/0	0	0	0	0	0	3	.600
ROSSUM, C.	7	0/1	.000	0/1	.000	2/2	1.000	0/1	0	0	1	0	0	2	.286
YOUNG, B.	2	0/2	.000	0/2	.000	0/0	.000	0/0	0	0	0	0	0	0	.000
JONES, J.	2	1/1	1.000	0/0	.000	0/1	.000	0/0	0	0	0	0	0	2	1.000
Totals	200	27/64	.422	4/16	.250	27/43	.628	12/30	15	3	20	11	1	85	.425

Team Rebounds: UNLV 2; DePaul 1. Disqualified: DePaul—Foster. Technical fouls: None.

	1st Half	2nd Half	Final
DePaul	40	30	70
UNLV	40	45	85

Evansville (73) Coach: Jim Crews

	Min.	Total FG/FGA	Pct.	3-Pt. FG/FGA	Pct.	FT/FTA	Pct.	Reb. O/T	A	TO	PF	S	Blk	TP	PPM
HILL, B.	25	2/4	.500	0/0	.000	6/6	1.000	3/4	1	1	3	1	2	10	.400
HAFFNER, S.	37	6/19	.316	4/10	.400	4/4	1.000	1/2	3	6	1	0	0	20	.541
GODFREAD, C.	32	5/7	.714	0/0	.000	1/4	.250	2/6	0	1	3	1	2	11	.344
SCHREFFLER, G.	37	5/14	.357	3/7	.429	2/2	1.000	1/2	3	0	5	2	0	15	.405
CRAFTON, J.	39	5/12	.417	4/10	.400	3/4	.750	0/2	7	2	3	3	0	17	.436
BLAB, O.	7	0/0	.000	0/0	.000	0/0	.000	0/2	0	0	0	0	0	0	.000
BOMBA, C.	13	0/2	.000	0/0	.000	0/0	.000	2/3	1	1	3	0	0	0	.000
MACK, C.	6	0/0	.000	0/0	.000	0/0	.000	0/0	0	1	0	0	0	0	.000
JONES, T.	1	0/1	.000	0/1	.000	0/0	.000	0/0	0	0	0	0	0	0	.000
DONALD, M.	1	0/0	.000	0/0	.000	0/0	.000	0/0	0	0	0	0	0	0	.000
MORNING, J.	1	0/0	.000	0/0	.000	0/0	.000	0/0	0	0	0	0	0	0	.000
BRAND, L.	1	0/0	.000	0/0	.000	0/0	.000	0/0	0	0	0	0	0	0	.000
Totals	200	23/59	.390	11/28	.393	16/20	.800	9/21	15	11	19	7	4	73	.365

Seton Hall (87) Coach: P. J. Carlesimo

	Min.	Total FG/FGA	Pct.	3-Pt. FG/FGA	Pct.	FT/FTA	Pct.	Reb. O/T	A	TO	PF	S	Blk	TP	PPM
WALKER, D.	18	8/9	.889	0/0	.000	0/0	.000	3/10	0	2	5	1	0	16	.889
GAZE, A.	33	6/10	.600	3/6	.500	0/0	.000	1/4	4	0	3	1	0	15	.455
RAMOS, R.	29	1/4	.250	0/0	.000	3/4	.750	4/10	2	3	2	0	0	5	.172
MORTON, J.	35	3/8	.375	1/1	1.000	10/16	.625	1/2	2	2	1	2	0	17	.486
GREENE, G.	28	4/11	.364	0/4	.000	2/2	1.000	0/1	5	3	2	0	0	10	.357
AVENT, A.	10	1/6	.167	0/0	.000	2/2	1.000	2/4	1	0	0	0	1	4	.400
VOLCY, F.	18	3/3	1.000	0/0	.000	0/0	.000	1/5	0	0	2	0	3	6	.333
COOPER, M.	15	3/3	1.000	0/0	.000	1/2	.500	0/1	0	1	0	1	0	7	.467
WIGINGTON, P.	10	3/5	.600	1/2	.500	0/0	.000	0/0	5	3	2	0	0	7	.700
MONTESERIN, R.	1	0/0	.000	0/0	.000	0/0	.000	0/0	0	0	0	0	0	0	.000
KATSIKIS, N.	1	0/0	.000	0/0	.000	0/0	.000	0/0	0	0	0	0	0	0	.000
CROWLEY, T.	1	0/0	.000	0/0	.000	0/0	.000	0/0	0	0	0	0	0	0	.000
REBIMBAS, J.	1	0/0	.000	0/0	.000	0/0	.000	0/0	0	0	0	0	0	0	.000
Totals	200	32/59	.542	5/13	.385	18/26	.692	12/37	19	13	18	4	4	87	.435

Team Rebounds: Seton Hall 4; Evansville 5. Disqualified: Seton Hall—Walker; Evansville—Schreffler. Technical fouls: Evansville—Bench.

	1st Half	2nd Half	Final
Evansville	41	32	73
Seton Hall	49	38	87

UTEP (69)   Coach: Don Haskins

	Min.	Total FG/FGA	Pct.	3-Pt. FG/FGA	Pct.	FT/FTA	Pct.	Reb. O/T	A	TO	PF	S	Blk	TP	PPM
MELVIN, J.	20	3/ 5	.600	0/ 0	.000	2/ 2	1.000	0/ 3	0	3	4	0	0	8	.400
VAN, D.	16	1/ 3	.333	0/ 0	.000	0/ 0	.000	1/ 2	0	0	2	2	2	2	.125
FOSTER, G.	28	8/10	.800	0/ 0	.000	2/ 2	1.000	3/ 6	2	6	4	0	1	18	.643
HARDAWAY, T.	39	9/23	.391	2/ 9	.222	0/ 0	.000	2/ 2	4	2	2	2	0	20	.513
STEWART, P.	34	0/ 7	.000	0/ 6	.000	3/ 4	.750	0/ 0	3	3	4	1	0	3	.088
DAVIS, A.	27	1/ 3	.333	0/ 0	.000	4/ 6	.667	2/ 7	0	3	3	0	1	6	.222
MCCALL, M.	24	4/11	.364	0/ 3	.000	4/ 4	1.000	3/ 6	1	1	0	0	0	12	.500
EZENWA, F.	12	0/ 0	.000	0/ 0	.000	0/ 0	.000	0/ 1	0	0	1	0	0	0	.000
Totals	200	26/62	.419	2/18	.111	15/18	.833	11/27	10	18	20	5	4	69	.345

Indiana (92)   Coach: Bob Knight

	Min.	Total FG/FGA	Pct.	3-Pt. FG/FGA	Pct.	FT/FTA	Pct.	Reb. O/T	A	TO	PF	S	Blk	TP	PPM
HILLMAN, J.	25	4/ 7	.571	2/ 2	1.000	2/ 2	1.000	1/ 6	4	2	2	0	0	12	.480
ANDERSON, E.	34	11/17	.647	0/ 0	.000	2/ 2	1.000	4/ 7	1	3	3	0	0	24	.706
JADLOW, T.	25	4/11	.364	0/ 0	.000	6/ 7	.857	6/ 7	1	5	4	2	0	14	.560
JONES, L.	33	3/ 8	.375	0/ 0	.000	5/ 6	.833	1/ 3	6	2	1	0	0	11	.333
EDWARDS, J.	21	4/ 9	.444	3/ 5	.600	6/ 8	.750	1/ 7	3	2	3	1	0	17	.810
MEEKS, J.	19	1/ 3	.333	0/ 0	.000	0/ 0	.000	0/ 2	4	0	0	1	0	2	.105
ROBINSON, M.	10	1/ 2	.500	0/ 0	.000	0/ 1	.000	1/ 4	3	1	0	0	1	2	.200
SMITH, K.	12	1/ 2	.500	1/ 1	1.000	0/ 0	.000	0/ 1	1	1	1	0	0	3	.250
SLOAN, B.	13	1/ 2	.500	0/ 0	.000	0/ 0	.000	2/ 2	0	0	1	0	0	2	.154
WHITE, C.	4	0/ 0	.000	0/ 0	.000	0/ 0	.000	0/ 0	0	0	0	0	0	0	.000
PELKOWSKI, M.	2	2/ 3	.667	1/ 2	.500	0/ 0	.000	0/ 1	0	0	0	0	0	5	2.500
D'ALOISIO, M.	2	0/ 0	.000	0/ 0	.000	0/ 0	.000	1/ 1	0	0	0	0	0	0	.000
Totals	200	32/64	.500	7/10	.700	21/26	.808	17/41	23	16	15	4	1	92	.460

Team Rebounds: Indiana 1; UTEP 3. Disqualified: None. Technical fouls: None.

	1st Half	2nd Half	Final
UTEP	31	38	69
Indiana	45	47	92

REGIONAL SEMIFINAL MIDWEST

Illinois (83)   Coach: Lou Henson

	Min.	Total FG/FGA	Pct.	3-Pt. FG/FGA	Pct.	FT/FTA	Pct.	Reb. O/T	A	TO	PF	S	Blk	TP	PPM
LIBERTY, M.	33	7/14	.500	0/ 0	.000	0/ 0	.000	5/ 8	1	0	3	3	0	14	.424
BATTLE, K.	15	2/ 4	.500	0/ 0	.000	0/ 0	.000	0/ 4	3	3	1	0	0	4	.267
GILL, K.	38	7/17	.412	0/ 3	.000	2/ 2	1.000	1/ 3	5	4	2	2	0	16	.421
BARDO, S.	36	3/ 9	.333	1/ 2	.500	2/ 5	.400	2/ 8	6	3	2	2	0	9	.250
HAMILTON, L.	13	2/ 5	.400	0/ 0	.000	0/ 0	.000	1/ 3	0	0	2	0	1	4	.308
SMALL, E.	13	2/ 4	.500	0/ 0	.000	0/ 0	.000	2/ 2	0	0	4	0	0	4	.308
ANDERSON, N.	35	12/22	.545	0/ 0	.000	0/ 1	.000	2/ 5	3	2	1	3	1	24	.686
SMITH, L.	17	4/ 6	.667	0/ 0	.000	0/ 3	.000	1/ 2	4	0	1	1	0	8	.471
Totals	200	39/81	.481	1/ 5	.200	4/11	.364	14/35	22	12	16	11	2	83	.415

Missouri (80)   Coach: Norm Stewart

	Min.	Total FG/FGA	Pct.	3-Pt. FG/FGA	Pct.	FT/FTA	Pct.	Reb. O/T	A	TO	PF	S	Blk	TP	PPM
SANDBOTHE, M.	26	1/ 2	.500	0/ 0	.000	1/ 4	.250	2/ 6	0	2	2	0	1	3	.115
SMITH, D.	29	7/14	.500	0/ 1	.000	2/ 2	1.000	8/13	2	1	3	0	0	16	.552
LEONARD, G.	26	5/ 7	.714	0/ 0	.000	2/ 4	.500	2/ 7	0	1	4	1	1	12	.462
COWARD, L.	37	6/10	.600	0/ 2	.000	1/ 4	.250	0/ 1	6	3	3	0	0	13	.351
CHURCH, G.	20	4/11	.364	0/ 0	.000	3/ 3	1.000	1/ 2	1	2	4	1	0	11	.550
BYRON, I.	38	8/25	.320	2/ 7	.286	3/ 3	1.000	6/10	5	2	4	1	0	21	.553
BUNTIN, N.	9	1/ 1	1.000	0/ 0	.000	0/ 0	.000	2/ 2	1	0	3	0	0	2	.222
PEELER, A.	15	1/ 5	.200	0/ 1	.000	0/ 0	.000	3/ 4	2	1	1	2	0	2	.133
Totals	200	33/75	.440	2/11	.182	12/20	.545	24/45	17	12	24	5	2	80	.400

Louisville (69)   Coach: Denny Crum

	Min.	Total FG/FGA	Pct.	3-Pt. FG/FGA	Pct.	FT/FTA	Pct.	Reb. O/T	A	TO	PF	S	Blk	TP	PPM
PAYNE, K.	33	9/15	.600	1/ 3	.333	0/ 0	.000	2/ 3	1	2	1	0	0	19	.576
KIMBRO, T.	25	2/ 7	.286	1/ 4	.250	0/ 0	.000	2/ 7	0	3	2	0	4	5	.200
ELLISON, P.	35	4/ 5	.800	0/ 0	.000	4/ 6	.667	2/ 9	4	3	3	2	7	12	.343
SMITH, L.	34	2/ 8	.250	2/ 3	.667	8/ 8	1.000	0/ 1	4	2	3	1	0	14	.412
SPENCER, F.	15	0/ 2	.000	0/ 0	.000	0/ 0	.000	1/ 2	0	2	3	0	0	0	.000
HOLDEN, C.	7	0/ 1	.000	0/ 0	.000	0/ 0	.000	0/ 1	0	0	0	0	0	0	.000
SULLIVAN, E.	24	7/14	.500	1/ 3	.333	0/ 0	.000	1/ 2	1	2	2	0	2	15	.625
WILLIAMS, K.	27	2/ 6	.333	0/ 1	.000	0/ 0	.000	1/ 1	3	3	2	1	0	4	.148
Totals	200	26/58	.448	5/14	.357	12/14	.857	9/26	13	17	16	4	13	69	.345

Team Rebounds: Illinois 11; Louisville 11. Disqualified: None. Technical fouls: None.

Syracuse (83)   Coach: Jim Boeheim

	Min.	Total FG/FGA	Pct.	3-Pt. FG/FGA	Pct.	FT/FTA	Pct.	Reb. O/T	A	TO	PF	S	Blk	TP	PPM
OWENS, B.	40	10/14	.714	1/ 2	.500	4/ 7	.571	1/ 8	2	4	3	1	0	25	.625
THOMPSON, S.	37	4/ 7	.571	0/ 0	.000	3/ 5	.600	1/ 2	1	3	2	3	1	11	.297
COLEMAN, D.	29	6/15	.400	0/ 0	.000	2/ 4	.500	5/12	1	2	5	0	2	14	.483
ROE, M.	14	1/ 2	.500	0/ 0	.000	0/ 0	.000	1/ 1	0	1	3	0	0	2	.143
DOUGLAS, S.	40	8/12	.667	1/ 2	.500	10/13	.769	1/ 3	7	3	2	0	0	27	.675
JOHNSON, D.	26	1/ 2	.500	0/ 0	.000	2/ 4	.500	0/ 1	1	1	1	0	0	4	.154
MANNING, R.	2	0/ 0	.000	0/ 0	.000	0/ 0	.000	0/ 0	0	0	1	0	0	0	.000
HARRIED, H.	12	0/ 0	.000	0/ 0	.000	0/ 0	.000	0/ 0	0	1	1	1	0	0	.000
Totals	200	30/52	.577	2/ 4	.500	21/33	.636	9/27	12	14	18	5	3	83	.415

Team Rebounds: Syracuse 2; Missouri 4. Disqualified: Syracuse—Coleman. Technical fouls: None.

	1st Half	2nd Half	Final
Illinois	40	43	83
Louisville	37	32	69

	1st Half	2nd Half	Final
Missouri	42	38	80
Syracuse	40	43	83

REGIONAL SEMIFINAL SOUTHEAST

Oklahoma (80)   Coach: Billy Tubbs

	Min.	Total FG/FGA	Pct.	3-Pt. FG/FGA	Pct.	FT/FTA	Pct.	Reb. O/T	A	TO	PF	S	Blk	TP	PPM
HENRY, S.	27	4/8	.500	1/3	.333	2/2	1.000	1/3	1	2	5	2	0	11	.407
DAVIS, W.	19	5/6	.833	0/0	.000	2/2	1.000	2/3	1	2	3	0	1	12	.632
KING, S.	35	9/15	.600	0/0	.000	4/5	.800	2/6	1	2	4	1	0	22	.629
BLAYLOCK, M.	33	2/12	.167	1/6	.167	0/0	.000	0/2	5	3	2	4	0	5	.152
MULLINS, T.	37	6/12	.500	4/8	.500	0/0	.000	0/4	4	3	4	1	0	16	.432
MARTIN, A.	18	2/4	.500	0/0	.000	0/0	.000	2/3	2	1	4	0	0	4	.222
JONES, T.	19	3/5	.600	2/4	.500	0/0	.000	2/3	1	1	2	0	0	8	.421
BELL, M.	5	1/2	.500	0/0	.000	0/0	.000	0/1	0	0	0	0	0	2	.400
PATTERSON, D.	7	0/0	.000	0/0	.000	0/0	.000	0/0	0	1	2	0	0	0	.000
Totals	200	32/64	.500	8/21	.381	8/9	.889	9/25	15	15	26	8	1	80	.400

Virginia (86)   Coach: Terry Holland

	Min.	Total FG/FGA	Pct.	3-Pt. FG/FGA	Pct.	FT/FTA	Pct.	Reb. O/T	A	TO	PF	S	Blk	TP	PPM
BLUNDIN, M.	28	3/4	.750	0/0	.000	3/6	.500	5/6	2	1	2	2	0	9	.321
STITH, B.	35	9/16	.563	0/0	.000	10/11	.909	5/7	1	3	2	2	0	28	.800
DABBS, B.	35	4/11	.364	0/0	.000	2/4	.500	6/14	2	4	2	0	0	10	.286
CROTTY, J.	39	4/9	.444	0/0	.000	6/9	.667	1/3	8	3	0	1	0	14	.359
MORGAN, J.	38	7/16	.438	5/8	.625	6/6	1.000	0/4	1	3	2	2	1	25	.658
OLIVER, A.	0	0/0	.000	0/0	.000	0/0	.000	0/0	0	1	0	0	0	0	-
TURNER, K.	5	0/0	.000	0/0	.000	0/0	.000	0/1	0	1	2	1	0	0	.000
KAPSTRA, D.	3	0/0	.000	0/0	.000	0/0	.000	0/0	0	0	0	0	0	0	.000
DANIEL, J.	17	0/0	.000	0/0	.000	0/0	.000	0/1	1	1	1	0	1	0	.000
Totals	200	27/56	.482	5/8	.625	27/36	.750	17/36	15	17	10	9	2	86	.430

Team Rebounds: Virginia 2; Oklahoma 1. Disqualified: Oklahoma—Henry. Technical fouls: None.

	1st Half	2nd Half	Final
Oklahoma	37	43	80
Virginia	42	44	86

Michigan (92)   Coach: Steve Fisher

	Min.	Total FG/FGA	Pct.	3-Pt. FG/FGA	Pct.	FT/FTA	Pct.	Reb. O/T	A	TO	PF	S	Blk	TP	PPM
RICE, G.	37	13/19	.684	8/12	.667	0/0	.000	1/6	2	2	1	1	0	34	.919
MILLS, T.	33	8/11	.727	0/0	.000	0/2	.000	1/6	1	3	3	1	1	16	.485
VAUGHT, L.	23	1/3	.333	0/0	.000	2/2	1.000	0/6	0	3	5	1	2	4	.174
GRIFFIN, M.	8	0/1	.000	0/0	.000	0/0	.000	1/1	1	1	1	1	0	0	.000
ROBINSON, R.	37	7/15	.467	3/6	.500	0/2	.000	3/5	13	5	3	1	0	17	.459
HIGGINS, S.	21	5/11	.455	2/5	.400	2/2	1.000	0/2	3	1	0	1	0	14	.667
CALIP, D.	21	1/4	.250	0/1	.000	0/0	.000	0/1	0	1	1	1	0	2	.095
HUGHES, M.	20	1/2	.500	0/0	.000	3/4	.750	3/6	0	3	4	0	1	5	.250
Totals	200	36/66	.545	13/24	.542	7/12	.583	9/33	20	19	18	6	4	92	.460

North Carolina (87)   Coach: Dean Smith

	Min.	Total FG/FGA	Pct.	3-Pt. FG/FGA	Pct.	FT/FTA	Pct.	Reb. O/T	A	TO	PF	S	Blk	TP	PPM
BUCKNALL, S.	36	2/7	.286	2/4	.500	4/4	1.000	2/7	10	4	1	3	0	10	.278
MADDEN, K.	25	5/12	.417	0/2	.000	0/0	.000	1/1	0	0	1	2	1	10	.400
WILLIAMS, S.	28	4/9	.444	0/0	.000	0/0	.000	1/5	0	2	5	0	0	8	.286
LEBO, J.	32	6/10	.600	5/9	.556	2/2	1.000	1/1	7	2	3	0	0	19	.594
RICE, K.	14	1/3	.333	0/1	.000	2/2	1.000	0/1	4	2	0	2	0	4	.286
REID, J.	29	12/18	.667	0/0	.000	2/7	.286	1/6	0	2	4	0	0	26	.897
FOX, R.	27	4/5	.800	0/0	.000	0/0	.000	0/2	3	2	2	2	0	8	.296
CHILCUTT, P.	9	1/2	.500	0/0	.000	0/0	.000	0/4	0	0	2	0	0	2	.222
Totals	200	35/66	.530	7/16	.438	10/15	.667	6/27	24	14	14	11	1	87	.435

Team Rebounds: Michigan 1; N. Carolina 4. Disqualified: Michigan—Vaught. Technical fouls: None.

	1st Half	2nd Half	Final
Michigan	50	42	92
N. Carolina	47	40	87

REGIONAL SEMIFINAL EAST

Georgetown (69)   Coach: John Thompson

	Min.	Total FG/FGA	Pct.	3-Pt. FG/FGA	Pct.	FT/FTA	Pct.	Reb. O/T	A	TO	PF	S	Blk	TP	PPM
JACKSON, J.	33	7/14	.500	3/7	.429	0/0	.000	1/2	1	0	2	1	1	17	.515
TURNER, J.	25	1/5	.200	0/0	.000	5/6	.833	4/4	0	1	3	0	0	7	.280
MOURNING, A.	36	5/10	.500	0/1	.000	2/2	1.000	3/12	0	4	4	1	5	12	.333
BRYANT, D.	36	7/9	.778	5/6	.833	2/2	1.000	1/2	2	3	2	0	0	21	.583
SMITH, C.	32	0/2	.000	0/0	.000	1/3	.333	0/5	5	1	1	1	0	1	.031
TILLMON, M.	11	1/4	.250	0/1	.000	1/2	.500	1/2	0	0	5	0	0	3	.273
WINSTON, B.	17	2/3	.667	0/0	.000	2/3	.667	1/2	1	2	2	0	0	6	.353
MUTOMBO, D.	4	0/0	.000	0/0	.000	0/0	.000	0/0	0	0	0	0	0	0	.000
THOMPSON, R.	4	0/2	.000	0/1	.000	0/0	.000	0/1	0	0	0	0	0	0	.000
JEFFERSON, S.	1	0/0	.000	0/0	.000	0/0	.000	0/0	0	0	1	0	0	0	.000
EDWARDS, J.	1	1/1	1.000	0/0	.000	0/0	.000	0/0	0	0	0	0	0	2	2.000
Totals	200	24/50	.480	8/16	.500	13/18	.722	11/30	9	11	20	3	6	69	.345

North Carolina State (61)   Coach: Jim Valvano

	Min.	Total FG/FGA	Pct.	3-Pt. FG/FGA	Pct.	FT/FTA	Pct.	Reb. O/T	A	TO	PF	S	Blk	TP	PPM
LESTER, A.	35	3/5	.600	0/0	.000	1/2	.500	1/5	1	0	4	0	1	7	.200
CORCHIANI, C.	39	1/5	.200	1/2	.500	3/4	.750	0/3	4	4	5	0	0	6	.154
MONROE, R.	38	6/16	.375	3/7	.429	11/13	.846	1/4	3	2	2	1	0	26	.684
WEEMS, D.	13	2/4	.500	0/0	.000	0/0	.000	0/0	0	2	1	1	0	4	.308
D'AMICO, B.	1	0/0	.000	0/0	.000	0/0	.000	0/0	0	0	1	0	0	0	.000
HINNANT, M.	2	0/1	.000	0/0	.000	0/0	.000	0/0	0	0	0	0	0	0	.000
HOWARD, B.	33	6/9	.667	1/1	1.000	0/0	.000	4/4	1	1	4	0	1	13	.394
BROWN, C.	39	2/11	.182	0/1	.000	1/2	.500	5/12	2	1	1	0	0	5	.128
Totals	200	20/51	.392	5/11	.455	16/21	.762	11/28	11	10	18	2	2	61	.305

Team Rebounds: Georgetown 4; N.C. State 4. Disqualified: Georgetown—Tillmon; N.C. State—Corchiani. Technical fouls: None.

	1st Half	2nd Half	Final
Georgetown	42	27	69
N.C. State	28	33	61

Minnesota (70)   Coach: Clem Haskins

	Min.	Total FG/FGA	Pct.	3-Pt. FG/FGA	Pct.	FT/FTA	Pct.	Reb. O/T	A	TO	PF	S	Blk	TP	PPM
BURTON, W.	32	12/24	.500	2/7	.286	0/0	.000	-/5	0	-	4	-	-	26	.813
BOND, W.	22	2/4	.500	0/0	.000	2/2	1.000	-/6	1	-	2	-	-	6	.273
SHIKENJANSKI, J.	26	2/5	.400	0/0	.000	0/0	.000	-/2	1	-	4	-	-	4	.154
LYNCH, K.	34	5/15	.333	1/5	.200	3/4	.750	-/5	1	-	3	-	-	14	.412
NEWBERN, M.	27	1/8	.125	0/0	.000	0/0	.000	-/4	7	-	2	-	-	2	.074
GREEN, M.	1	0/0	.000	0/0	.000	0/0	.000	-/0	0	-	1	-	-	0	.000
LEWIS, C.	8	1/5	.200	0/2	.000	0/0	.000	-/2	1	-	2	-	-	2	.250
GAFFNEY, R.	14	3/5	.600	0/1	.000	0/0	.000	-/1	2	-	3	-	-	6	.429
METCALF, R.	15	1/3	.333	0/1	.000	0/2	.000	-/2	1	-	2	-	-	2	.133
COFFEY, R.	11	2/3	.667	0/0	.000	0/0	.000	-/5	0	-	5	-	-	4	.364
MARTIN, B.	10	1/2	.500	0/0	.000	2/2	1.000	-/0	0	-	2	-	-	4	.400
Totals	200	30/74	.405	3/16	.188	7/10	.700	0/32	14	15	30	0	0	70	.350

Duke (87)   Coach: Mike Krzyzewski

	Min.	Total FG/FGA	Pct.	3-Pt. FG/FGA	Pct.	FT/FTA	Pct.	Reb. O/T	A	TO	PF	S	Blk	TP	PPM
BRICKEY, R.	22	9/10	.900	0/0	.000	3/7	.429	-/7	0	-	4	-	-	21	.955
FERRY, D.	36	7/14	.500	1/2	.500	3/6	.500	-/5	4	-	3	-	-	18	.500
LAETTNER, C.	25	2/4	.500	0/0	.000	6/7	.857	-/11	1	-	4	-	-	10	.400
HENDERSON, P.	34	7/12	.583	2/3	.667	5/6	.833	-/6	3	-	1	-	-	21	.618
SNYDER, Q.	32	2/4	.500	1/3	.333	1/4	.250	-/2	8	-	2	-	-	6	.182
KOUBEK, G.	9	0/2	.000	0/0	.000	0/0	.000	-/1	2	-	0	-	-	0	.000
DAVIS, B.	4	0/0	.000	0/0	.000	3/6	.500	-/2	0	-	1	-	-	3	.750
ABDELNABY, A.	16	0/2	.000	0/0	.000	1/2	.500	-/3	1	-	1	-	-	1	.063
SMITH, J.	18	1/2	.500	0/0	.000	3/4	.750	-/4	2	-	1	-	-	5	.278
PALMER, C.	1	1/1	1.000	0/0	.000	0/0	.000	-/0	0	-	0	-	-	2	2.000
BURGIN, G.	1	0/0	.000	0/0	.000	0/0	.000	-/1	0	-	0	-	-	0	.000
BUCKLEY, C.	1	0/0	.000	0/0	.000	0/0	.000	-/0	0	-	0	-	-	0	.000
Totals	200	29/51	.569	4/8	.500	25/42	.595	0/42	21	19	16	0	0	87	.435

Team Rebounds: Duke 2; Minnesota 0. Disqualified: Minnesota—Coffey. Technical fouls: None.

	1st Half	2nd Half	Final
Minnesota	30	40	70
Duke	45	42	87

REGIONAL SEMIFINAL WEST

Arizona (67)   Coach: Lute Olson

	Min.	Total FG/FGA	Pct.	3-Pt. FG/FGA	Pct.	FT/FTA	Pct.	Reb. O/T	A	TO	PF	S	Blk	TP	PPM
ELLIOTT, S.	39	8/16	.500	1/3	.333	5/7	.714	2/14	1	5	1	2	0	22	.564
BUECHLER, J.	30	4/6	.667	0/0	.000	2/3	.667	1/7	2	1	4	0	0	10	.333
COOK, A.	33	6/9	.667	0/0	.000	0/0	.000	1/6	1	1	2	2	4	12	.364
LOFTON, K.	28	3/12	.250	2/4	.500	0/0	.000	1/2	6	2	1	0	0	8	.286
MUEHLEBACH, M.	37	3/6	.500	2/5	.400	0/0	.000	1/2	1	3	1	0	0	8	.216
OTHICK, M.	17	1/4	.250	1/4	.250	0/0	.000	0/1	2	2	0	0	0	3	.176
ROOKS, S.	14	1/3	.333	0/0	.000	2/3	.667	0/3	0	0	1	0	1	4	.286
WOMACK, W.	2	0/0	.000	0/0	.000	0/0	.000	0/0	0	0	0	0	0	0	.000
Totals	200	26/56	.464	6/16	.375	9/13	.692	6/35	13	14	10	4	5	67	.335

UNLV (68)   Coach: Jerry Tarkanian

	Min.	Total FG/FGA	Pct.	3-Pt. FG/FGA	Pct.	FT/FTA	Pct.	Reb. O/T	A	TO	PF	S	Blk	TP	PPM
AUGMON, S.	32	5/13	.385	1/4	.250	4/6	.667	1/6	4	0	2	2	2	15	.469
SCURRY, M.	23	1/3	.333	0/0	.000	0/0	.000	1/5	0	0	3	0	0	2	.087
BUTLER, D.	32	8/17	.471	0/0	.000	0/2	.000	2/2	1	4	4	0	2	16	.500
ANTHONY, G.	31	1/7	.143	0/4	.000	0/0	.000	1/1	11	2	3	1	1	2	.065
HUNT, A.	33	8/12	.667	5/8	.625	0/0	.000	0/4	3	3	3	0	1	21	.636
ACKLES, G.	25	2/3	.667	0/0	.000	0/1	.000	1/6	0	2	2	1	3	4	.160
ROSSUM, C.	16	3/4	.750	2/3	.667	0/0	.000	0/1	2	0	0	0	0	8	.500
YOUNG, B.	8	0/1	.000	0/0	.000	0/0	.000	0/0	0	0	1	0	0	0	.000
Totals	200	28/60	.467	8/19	.421	4/9	.444	6/25	21	11	18	4	9	68	.340

Team Rebounds: UNLV 6; Arizona 3. Disqualified: None. Technical fouls: None.

	1st Half	2nd Half	Final
Arizona	36	31	67
UNLV	37	31	68

Seton Hall (78)   Coach: P. J. Carlesimo

	Min.	Total FG/FGA	Pct.	3-Pt. FG/FGA	Pct.	FT/FTA	Pct.	Reb. O/T	A	TO	PF	S	Blk	TP	PPM
WALKER, D.	29	4/9	.444	0/0	.000	1/2	.500	6/10	2	3	3	2	1	9	.310
GAZE, A.	38	6/12	.500	4/7	.571	0/0	.000	1/3	2	1	2	0	0	16	.421
RAMOS, R.	22	5/12	.417	0/0	.000	2/3	.667	2/5	2	2	4	1	2	12	.545
MORTON, J.	21	4/12	.333	1/2	.500	8/9	.889	2/4	1	2	4	4	0	17	.810
GREENE, G.	29	3/6	.500	2/4	.500	7/8	.875	2/3	4	1	3	1	0	15	.517
AVENT, A.	12	0/2	.000	0/0	.000	0/0	.000	1/3	0	0	3	0	1	0	.000
VOLCY, F.	16	1/4	.250	0/0	.000	2/4	.500	3/5	1	0	3	0	1	4	.250
COOPER, M.	16	1/3	.333	0/0	.000	0/0	.000	0/1	2	1	3	0	1	2	.125
WIGINGTON, P.	12	0/0	.000	0/0	.000	0/1	.000	1/2	0	3	1	1	0	0	.000
KATSIKIS, N.	4	1/1	1.000	1/1	1.000	0/0	.000	1/1	0	0	0	0	0	3	.750
CROWLEY, T.	1	0/0	.000	0/0	.000	0/0	.000	0/0	0	0	0	0	0	0	.000
Totals	200	25/61	.410	8/14	.571	20/27	.741	19/37	14	13	26	9	6	78	.390

Indiana (65)   Coach: Bob Knight

	Min.	Total FG/FGA	Pct.	3-Pt. FG/FGA	Pct.	FT/FTA	Pct.	Reb. O/T	A	TO	PF	S	Blk	TP	PPM
HILLMAN, J.	35	4/13	.308	1/2	.500	3/4	.750	0/1	3	2	2	1	0	12	.343
ANDERSON, E.	36	4/5	.800	0/0	.000	5/6	.833	1/6	0	4	4	1	2	13	.361
JADLOW, T.	22	1/5	.200	0/0	.000	4/6	.667	3/5	0	1	3	0	0	6	.273
JONES, L.	29	1/7	.143	0/0	.000	2/2	1.000	2/4	3	3	5	0	1	4	.138
EDWARDS, J.	23	4/11	.364	1/5	.200	9/10	.900	1/3	2	2	5	0	0	18	.783
MEEKS, J.	14	2/2	1.000	0/0	.000	0/0	.000	0/1	1	0	0	0	4	4	.286
ROBINSON, M.	7	0/1	.000	0/0	.000	0/1	.000	1/2	0	0	1	1	0	0	.000
SMITH, K.	14	0/0	.000	0/0	.000	3/4	.750	0/2	1	1	1	1	0	3	.214
SLOAN, B.	11	1/1	1.000	0/0	.000	1/2	.500	0/1	1	1	2	0	0	3	.273
WHITE, C.	7	1/1	1.000	0/0	.000	0/2	.000	0/0	0	0	1	0	0	2	.286
PELKOWSKI, M.	1	0/0	.000	0/0	.000	0/0	.000	0/0	0	0	0	0	0	0	.000
D'ALOISIO, M.	1	0/0	.000	0/0	.000	0/0	.000	0/1	0	0	0	0	0	0	.000
Totals	200	18/46	.391	2/7	.286	27/37	.730	8/26	11	14	24	3	3	65	.325

Team Rebounds: Seton Hall 5; Indiana 9. Disqualified: Indiana—Edwards, Jones. Technical fouls: None.

	1st Half	2nd Half	Final
Seton Hall	42	36	78
Indiana	33	32	65

REGIONAL FINAL MIDWEST

Illinois (89)   Coach: Lou Henson

	Min.	Total FG/FGA	Pct.	3-Pt. FG/FGA	Pct.	FT/FTA	Pct.	Reb. O/T	A	TO	PF	S	Blk	TP	PPM
LIBERTY, M.	11	1/4	.250	0/0	.000	0/1	.000	1/3	0	1	2	0	0	2	.182
BATTLE, K.	34	12/17	.706	0/0	.000	4/6	.667	3/3	1	2	3	1	0	28	.824
GILL, K.	38	8/13	.615	2/4	.500	0/0	.000	4/8	5	3	1	3	0	18	.474
BARDO, S.	26	1/2	.500	0/0	.000	0/0	.000	1/3	4	4	5	0	0	2	.077
HAMILTON, L.	18	2/4	.500	0/0	.000	3/10	.300	0/2	1	0	1	1	0	7	.389
SMALL, E.	17	0/0	.000	0/0	.000	0/0	.000	0/1	2	1	3	1	0	0	.000
ANDERSON, N.	40	10/18	.556	0/0	.000	4/7	.571	9/16	2	0	2	1	0	24	.600
SMITH, L.	16	3/3	1.000	0/0	.000	2/2	1.000	0/0	5	2	4	0	0	8	.500
Totals	200	37/61	.607	2/4	.500	13/26	.500	18/36	20	13	21	7	0	89	.445

Syracuse (86)   Coach: Jim Boeheim

	Min.	Total FG/FGA	Pct.	3-Pt. FG/FGA	Pct.	FT/FTA	Pct.	Reb. O/T	A	TO	PF	S	Blk	TP	PPM
OWENS, B.	35	9/18	.500	0/1	.000	4/4	1.000	5/8	2	3	2	0	0	22	.629
THOMPSON, S.	40	8/11	.727	0/0	.000	1/2	.500	5/6	0	1	4	0	0	17	.425
COLEMAN, D.	40	5/11	.455	0/0	.000	7/10	.700	4/10	2	0	4	1	1	17	.425
ROE, M.	21	4/9	.444	4/8	.500	1/2	.500	0/0	0	2	2	0	0	13	.619
HARRIED, H.	6	0/0	.000	0/0	.000	0/0	.000	0/0	0	2	0	1	0	0	.000
DOUGLAS, S.	39	5/10	.500	1/2	.500	4/4	1.000	1/2	8	5	5	1	0	15	.385
JOHNSON, D.	19	1/3	.333	0/1	.000	0/2	.000	1/2	2	0	4	2	0	2	.105
Totals	200	32/62	.516	5/12	.417	17/24	.708	16/28	14	13	21	5	1	86	.430

Team Rebounds: Illinois 2; Syracuse 1. Disqualified: Illinois—Bardo; Syracuse—Douglas. Technical fouls: None.

	1st Half	2nd Half	Final
Illinois	39	50	89
Syracuse	46	40	86

REGIONAL FINAL SOUTHEAST

Virginia (65) Coach: Terry Holland

	Min.	Total FG/FGA	Pct.	3–Pt. FG/FGA	Pct.	FT/FTA	Pct.	Reb. O/T	A	TO	PF	S	Blk	TP	PPM
BLUNDIN, M.	21	1/ 1	1.000	0/ 0	.000	0/ 0	.000	2/ 4	2	3	1	0	0	2	.095
STITH, B.	33	3/ 6	.500	1/ 1	1.000	2/ 4	.500	0/ 3	1	2	3	1	0	9	.273
DABBS, B.	37	5/10	.500	0/ 0	.000	2/ 4	.500	3/12	0	1	2	1	0	12	.324
CROTTY, J.	36	5/13	.385	2/ 3	.667	2/ 4	.500	0/ 3	7	2	1	0	0	14	.389
MORGAN, R.	26	5/18	.278	3/ 9	.333	2/ 2	1.000	0/ 1	0	3	1	1	0	15	.577
OLIVER, A.	4	0/ 0	.000	0/ 0	.000	1/ 2	.500	1/ 2	0	2	2	0	0	1	.250
TURNER, K.	6	1/ 1	1.000	0/ 0	.000	0/ 1	.000	1/ 1	0	0	0	0	2	.333
KAPSTRA, D.	13	3/ 9	.333	1/ 6	.167	0/ 0	.000	0/ 2	1	2	2	2	1	7	.538
DANIEL, J.	13	0/ 1	.000	0/ 0	.000	0/ 2	.000	0/ 3	1	0	4	0	0	0	.000
COOKE, M.	3	1/ 3	.333	1/ 3	.333	0/ 0	.000	1/ 1	0	0	0	0	0	3	1.000
WILLIAMS, C.	8	0/ 1	.000	0/ 0	.000	0/ 3	.000	0/ 0	0	0	0	0	0	0	.000
Totals	200	24/63	.381	8/22	.364	9/22	.409	8/32	12	15	16	5	1	65	.325

Michigan (102) Coach: Steve Fisher

	Min.	Total FG/FGA	Pct.	3–Pt. FG/FGA	Pct.	FT/FTA	Pct.	Reb. O/T	A	TO	PF	S	Blk	TP	PPM
RICE, G.	32	13/16	.813	4/ 5	.800	2/ 2	1.000	0/ 6	2	3	3	2	0	32	1.000
MILLS, T.	27	4/ 9	.444	0/ 0	.000	0/ 0	.000	0/ 5	2	1	2	1	0	8	.296
VAUGHT, L.	21	4/ 6	.667	0/ 0	.000	0/ 1	.000	2/ 9	2	0	3	0	0	8	.381
GRIFFIN, M.	22	0/ 1	.000	0/ 0	.000	0/ 0	.000	0/ 0	3	0	4	1	0	0	.000
ROBINSON, R.	23	5/ 9	.556	0/ 1	.000	3/ 3	1.000	1/ 3	7	2	2	1	0	13	.565
CALIP, D.	22	2/ 3	.667	0/ 0	.000	2/ 2	1.000	0/ 5	5	2	2	0	0	6	.273
HIGGINS, S.	20	11/15	.733	7/10	.700	2/ 3	.667	1/ 3	0	2	0	0	0	31	1.550
HUGHES, M.	20	1/ 4	.250	0/ 0	.000	0/ 0	.000	0/ 7	2	1	4	0	0	2	.100
OOSTERBAAN, J.	6	1/ 3	.333	0/ 1	.000	0/ 1	.000	0/ 3	0	0	1	0	0	2	.333
PELINKA, R.	5	0/ 4	.000	0/ 3	.000	0/ 0	.000	0/ 0	0	1	0	0	0	0	.000
KOENIG, M.	2	0/ 0	.000	0/ 0	.000	0/ 0	.000	0/ 0	0	1	0	2	0	0	.000
Totals	200	41/70	.586	11/20	.550	9/12	.750	4/41	23	11	23	7	0	102	.510

Team Rebounds: Michigan 2; Virginia 1. Disqualified: None. Technical fouls: None.

	1st Half	2nd Half	Final
Virginia	25	40	65
Michigan	44	58	102

REGIONAL FINAL EAST

Georgetown (77) Coach: John Thompson

	Min.	Total FG/FGA	Pct.	3–Pt. FG/FGA	Pct.	FT/FTA	Pct.	Reb. O/T	A	TO	PF	S	Blk	TP	PPM
JACKSON, J.	22	1/10	.100	0/ 2	.000	0/ 0	.000	3/ 5	1	1	2	2	0	2	.091
TURNER, J.	17	2/ 3	.667	0/ 0	.000	0/ 2	.000	1/ 1	1	0	1	0	0	4	.235
MOURNING, A.	26	5/ 8	.625	0/ 0	.000	1/ 2	.500	3/ 5	0	2	2	0	4	11	.423
BRYANT, D.	16	0/ 4	.000	0/ 1	.000	2/ 2	1.000	0/ 2	3	1	3	1	0	2	.125
SMITH, C.	38	9/19	.474	0/ 2	.000	3/ 5	.600	2/ 5	1	2	3	0	0	21	.553
TILLMON, M.	28	6/12	.500	2/ 6	.333	2/ 5	.400	1/ 4	2	1	3	2	0	16	.571
WINSTON, K.	23	4/ 8	.500	0/ 0	.000	1/ 3	.333	1/ 1	1	0	2	1	0	9	.391
MUTOMBO, D.	5	1/ 1	1.000	0/ 0	.000	0/ 0	.000	0/ 0	0	0	2	0	1	2	.400
EDWARDS, J.	2	1/ 1	1.000	0/ 0	.000	0/ 0	.000	1/ 1	0	0	1	0	0	2	1.000
JEFFERSON, S.	23	2/ 5	.400	0/ 0	.000	4/ 4	1.000	3/ 7	1	0	5	0	0	8	.348
Totals	200	31/71	.437	2/11	.182	13/23	.565	15/31	10	7	24	6	5	77	.385

Duke (85) Coach: Mike Krzyzewski

	Min.	Total FG/FGA	Pct.	3–Pt. FG/FGA	Pct.	FT/FTA	Pct.	Reb. O/T	A	TO	PF	S	Blk	TP	PPM
BRICKEY, R.	32	2/ 6	.333	0/ 0	.000	6/ 8	.750	4/ 8	0	0	4	0	0	10	.313
FERRY, D.	39	8/17	.471	0/ 2	.000	5/ 6	.833	1/ 7	3	3	3	0	1	21	.538
LAETTNER, C.	32	9/10	.900	0/ 0	.000	6/ 7	.857	3/ 9	4	3	3	1	1	24	.750
HENDERSON, P.	36	9/15	.600	1/ 1	1.000	4/ 4	1.000	1/ 3	2	2	2	0	1	23	.639
SNYDER, Q.	34	1/ 6	.167	0/ 3	.000	2/ 4	.500	0/ 3	7	1	5	0	1	4	.118
KOUBEK, G.	4	0/ 0	.000	0/ 0	.000	0/ 0	.000	0/ 0	0	0	0	0	0	0	.000
ABDELNABY, A.	9	0/ 2	.000	0/ 0	.000	0/ 0	.000	0/ 2	0	2	3	1	0	0	.000
SMITH, J.	14	0/ 1	.000	0/ 0	.000	3/ 4	.750	1/ 3	0	0	2	0	1	3	.214
Totals	200	29/57	.509	1/ 6	.167	26/33	.788	10/35	16	11	22	2	5	85	.425

Team Rebounds: Duke 6; Georgetown 4. Disqualified: Duke—Snyder; Georgetown—Jefferson. Technical fouls: None.

	1st Half	2nd Half	Final
Georgetown	40	37	77
Duke	38	47	85

REGIONAL FINAL WEST

UNLV (61) Coach: Jerry Tarkanian

	Min.	Total FG/FGA	Pct.	3–Pt. FG/FGA	Pct.	FT/FTA	Pct.	Reb. O/T	A	TO	PF	S	Blk	TP	PPM
AUGMON, S.	33	4/12	.333	0/ 0	.000	0/ 2	.000	1/ 3	2	2	1	2	1	8	.242
SCURRY, M.	18	2/ 5	.400	0/ 0	.000	2/ 3	.667	6/14	1	0	2	1	0	6	.333
BUTLER, D.	32	6/15	.400	0/ 0	.000	3/ 5	.600	4/ 9	0	1	4	1	1	15	.469
HUNT, A.	27	1/12	.083	0/ 5	.000	5/ 6	.833	1/ 2	1	3	4	1	0	7	.259
ANTHONY, G.	31	5/15	.333	5/10	.500	1/ 2	.500	0/ 1	4	3	5	2	0	16	.516
ROSSUM, C.	22	1/ 4	.250	0/ 3	.000	0/ 0	.000	0/ 0	1	0	1	0	0	2	.091
ACKLES, G.	16	1/ 3	.333	0/ 0	.000	0/ 1	.000	2/ 4	0	0	1	0	2	2	.125
YOUNG, B.	13	1/ 6	.167	1/ 3	.333	0/ 0	.000	1/ 1	0	0	1	0	0	3	.231
JONES, J.	6	0/ 0	.000	0/ 0	.000	0/ 0	.000	0/ 0	2	0	2	0	0	0	.000
CVIJANOVICH, S.	2	1/ 1	1.000	0/ 0	.000	0/ 0	.000	0/ 0	0	2	1	0	0	2	1.000
Totals	200	22/73	.301	6/21	.286	11/19	.579	15/34	11	11	22	7	4	61	.305

Seton Hall (84) Coach: P. J. Carlesimo

	Min.	Total FG/FGA	Pct.	3–Pt. FG/FGA	Pct.	FT/FTA	Pct.	Reb. O/T	A	TO	PF	S	Blk	TP	PPM
WALKER, D.	37	5/ 9	.556	0/ 0	.000	2/ 4	.500	6/15	0	3	2	1	1	12	.324
GAZE, A.	33	6/ 9	.667	3/ 6	.500	4/ 6	.667	0/ 5	1	1	2	3	2	19	.576
RAMOS, R.	14	0/ 2	.000	0/ 0	.000	0/ 0	.000	1/ 4	2	0	2	0	1	0	.000
MORTON, J.	31	2/11	.182	0/ 3	.000	2/ 5	.400	0/ 1	2	5	2	0	0	6	.194
GREENE, G.	30	3/ 4	.750	0/ 0	.000	3/ 5	.600	0/ 4	3	4	2	1	0	9	.300
AVENT, A.	9	3/ 5	.600	0/ 0	.000	5/ 6	.833	1/ 3	0	1	2	0	0	11	1.222
VOLCY, F.	17	4/ 8	.500	0/ 0	.000	1/ 2	.500	3/ 6	1	1	1	0	3	9	.529
COOPER, M.	16	5/ 7	.714	0/ 0	.000	0/ 0	.000	2/ 5	2	1	1	0	0	10	.625
WIGINGTON, P.	9	0/ 0	.000	0/ 0	.000	3/ 4	.750	0/ 2	1	2	2	0	0	3	.333
MONTESERIN, R.	1	0/ 0	.000	0/ 0	.000	0/ 0	.000	0/ 0	0	0	0	0	0	0	.000
KATSIKIS, N.	1	1/ 1	1.000	1/ 1	1.000	0/ 0	.000	0/ 1	0	0	0	0	0	3	3.000
CROWLEY, T.	1	0/ 1	.000	0/ 1	.000	0/ 0	.000	0/ 0	0	0	1	0	0	0	.000
REBIMBAS, J.	1	1/ 1	1.000	0/ 0	.000	0/ 0	.000	0/ 0	0	0	1	0	0	2	2.000
Totals	200	30/58	.517	4/11	.364	20/32	.625	13/46	12	18	17	5	7	84	.420

Team Rebounds: Seton Hall 6; UNLV 7. Disqualified: UNLV—Anthony. Technical fouls: None.

	1st Half	2nd Half	Final
UNLV	30	31	61
Seton Hall	34	50	84

FINAL FOUR

Illinois (81) Coach: Lou Henson

	Min.	Total FG/FGA	Pct.	3-Pt. FG/FGA	Pct.	FT/FTA	Pct.	Reb. O/T	A	TO	PF	S	Blk	TP	PPM
ANDERSON, N.	-	6/14	.429	0/1	.000	5/6	.833	3/7	2	2	1	2	0	17	-
BATTLE, K.	-	10/17	.588	1/1	1.000	8/10	.800	4/7	1	1	2	0	1	29	-
HAMILTON, L.	-	5/14	.357	0/0	.000	1/2	.500	1/9	0	1	5	1	0	11	-
GILL, K.	-	5/9	.556	0/2	.000	1/1	1.000	1/4	2	1	1	3	0	11	-
BARDO, S.	-	1/7	.143	1/3	.333	4/4	1.000	2/6	8	5	3	0	1	7	-
SMITH, L.	-	3/5	.600	0/1	.000	0/0	.000	0/2	1	1	2	0	0	6	-
SMALL, E.	-	0/0	.000	0/0	.000	0/0	.000	0/0	0	0	0	2	0	0	-
LIBERTY, M.	-	0/1	.000	0/0	.000	0/0	.000	0/0	0	0	0	0	0	0	-
Totals	200	30/67	.448	2/8	.250	19/23	.826	11/35	14	11	16	6	2	81	.405

Michigan (83) Coach: Steve Fisher

	Min.	Total FG/FGA	Pct.	3-Pt. FG/FGA	Pct.	FT/FTA	Pct.	Reb. O/T	A	TO	PF	S	Blk	TP	PPM
RICE, G.	37	12/24	.500	2/4	.500	2/2	1.000	3/5	1	0	1	3	0	28	.757
HUGHES, M.	19	4/5	.800	0/0	.000	1/1	1.000	1/6	1	2	3	0	0	9	.474
MILLS, T.	31	4/8	.500	0/0	.000	0/0	.000	3/9	5	2	4	0	1	8	.258
GRIFFIN, M.	17	0/1	.000	0/0	.000	0/0	.000	0/1	3	1	2	2	0	0	.000
ROBINSON, R.	40	6/13	.462	0/1	.000	2/5	.400	1/1	12	5	4	1	0	14	.350
CALIP, D.	3	0/1	.000	0/0	.000	0/0	.000	0/0	0	0	2	0	0	0	.000
HIGGINS, S.	24	5/12	.417	1/3	.333	3/3	1.000	2/3	1	2	2	0	2	14	.583
VAUGHT, L.	29	5/13	.385	0/0	.000	0/0	.000	4/16	0	0	2	0	0	10	.345
Totals	200	36/77	.468	3/8	.375	8/11	.727	14/41	23	12	20	6	3	83	.415

Team Rebounds: Michigan 4; Illinois 4. Disqualified: Illinois—Hamilton. Technical fouls: None.

	1st Half	2nd Half	Final
Illinois	38	43	81
Michigan	39	44	83

Duke (78) Coach: Mike Krzyzewski

	Min.	Total FG/FGA	Pct.	3-Pt. FG/FGA	Pct.	FT/FTA	Pct.	Reb. O/T	A	TO	PF	S	Blk	TP	PPM
BRICKEY, R.	11	0/3	.000	0/0	.000	2/2	1.000	2/3	2	0	0	0	0	2	.182
FERRY, D.	39	13/29	.448	1/5	.200	7/11	.636	7/10	4	2	2	0	0	34	.872
LAETTNER, C.	21	4/5	.800	0/0	.000	5/7	.714	1/7	1	3	5	1	0	13	.619
HENDERSON, P.	37	4/16	.250	0/1	.000	5/6	.833	2/5	5	4	3	2	1	13	.351
SNYDER, Q.	31	3/10	.300	2/5	.400	0/0	.000	2/5	4	3	5	0	0	8	.258
KOUBEK, G.	18	0/3	.000	0/2	.000	0/0	.000	0/2	1	0	2	0	0	0	.000
DAVIS, B.	9	1/2	.500	0/0	.000	0/2	.000	0/0	0	0	1	0	0	2	.222
ABDELNABY, A.	6	0/0	.000	0/0	.000	0/0	.000	0/0	0	0	4	0	1	0	.000
SMITH, J.	23	1/4	.250	1/3	.333	3/4	.750	3/6	0	0	2	1	1	6	.261
PALMER, C.	1	0/0	.000	0/0	.000	0/0	.000	0/0	0	0	0	0	0	1	.000
BURGIN, G.	1	0/0	.000	0/0	.000	0/0	.000	0/0	0	0	0	1	0	0	.000
BUCKLEY, C.	3	0/0	.000	0/0	.000	0/0	.000	0/0	0	0	0	1	0	0	.000
Totals	200	26/72	.361	4/16	.250	22/32	.688	17/38	15	14	25	4	5	78	.390

Seton Hall (95) Coach: P. J. Carlesimo

	Min.	Total FG/FGA	Pct.	3-Pt. FG/FGA	Pct.	FT/FTA	Pct.	Reb. O/T	A	TO	PF	S	Blk	TP	PPM
WALKER, D.	29	6/9	.667	0/0	.000	7/7	1.000	2/6	0	1	4	3	1	19	.655
GAZE, A.	38	7/14	.500	4/9	.444	2/2	1.000	2/4	3	4	2	2	2	20	.526
RAMOS, R.	30	3/8	.375	0/0	.000	3/3	1.000	3/12	1	3	3	2	0	9	.300
MORTON, J.	19	4/8	.500	0/1	.000	5/6	.833	0/2	2	2	4	0	0	13	.684
GREENE, G.	39	5/9	.556	1/1	1.000	6/6	1.000	0/5	8	2	1	1	0	17	.436
AVENT, A.	10	3/4	.750	0/0	.000	0/0	.000	1/1	0	0	1	0	2	6	.600
VOLCY, F.	10	1/2	.500	0/0	.000	0/1	.000	0/1	1	0	4	0	2	2	.200
COOPER, M.	14	3/4	.750	0/0	.000	0/0	.000	1/4	0	2	3	0	0	6	.429
WIGINGTON, P.	1	0/0	.000	0/0	.000	0/1	.000	0/1	1	0	1	0	0	0	.000
MONTESERIN, R.	1	0/0	.000	0/0	.000	0/0	.000	0/0	0	0	0	0	0	0	.000
KATSIKIS, N.	7	1/1	1.000	1/1	1.000	0/1	.000	0/1	1	0	1	0	0	3	.429
CROWLEY, T.	1	0/1	.000	0/0	.000	0/0	.000	0/0	0	0	0	0	0	0	-
REBIMIAS, J.	1	0/1	.000	0/0	.000	0/0	.000	0/0	0	0	0	0	0	0	.000
LONG, K.	1	0/1	.000	0/0	.000	0/0	.000	0/0	0	0	0	0	0	0	.000
Totals	200	33/62	.532	6/12	.500	23/27	.852	9/36	16	15	23	8	7	95	.475

Team Rebounds: Seton Hall 4; Duke 5. Disqualified: Duke—Snyder, Laettner. Technical fouls: None. Players with 0 min. played less than 1 min. each.

	1st Half	2nd Half	Final
Duke	38	40	78
Seton Hall	33	62	95

NATIONAL CHAMPIONSHIP

Michigan (80) Coach: Steve Fisher

	Min.	Total FG/FGA	Pct.	3-Pt. FG/FGA	Pct.	FT/FTA	Pct.	Reb. O/T	A	TO	PF	S	Blk	TP	PPM
RICE, G.	42	12/25	.480	5/12	.417	2/2	1.000	1/11	0	2	2	0	0	31	.738
HUGHES, M.	25	1/1	1.000	0/0	.000	0/0	.000	0/2	0	0	2	0	0	2	.080
MILLS, T.	34	4/8	.500	0/0	.000	0/0	.000	3/6	2	2	2	2	3	8	.235
GRIFFIN, M.	17	0/0	.000	0/0	.000	0/0	.000	2/4	3	2	4	0	0	0	.000
ROBINSON, R.	43	6/13	.462	0/0	.000	9/10	.900	1/3	11	5	2	0	0	21	.488
VAUGHT, L.	26	4/8	.500	0/0	.000	0/0	.000	2/7	0	2	2	1	0	8	.308
CALIP, D.	11	0/2	.000	0/0	.000	0/0	.000	0/0	1	0	3	0	0	0	.000
HIGGINS, S.	27	3/10	.300	1/4	.250	3/4	.750	2/9	2	1	3	0	1	10	.370
Totals	225	30/67	.448	6/16	.375	14/16	.875	11/42	19	14	20	3	4	80	.356

Seton Hall (79) Coach: P. J. Carlesimo

	Min.	Total FG/FGA	Pct.	3-Pt. FG/FGA	Pct.	FT/FTA	Pct.	Reb. O/T	A	TO	PF	S	Blk	TP	PPM
WALKER, D.	39	5/9	.556	0/1	.000	3/4	.750	3/11	1	2	2	0	0	13	.333
GAZE, A.	39	1/5	.200	1/5	.200	2/2	1.000	2/3	3	2	3	1	0	5	.128
RAMOS, R.	33	4/9	.444	0/0	.000	1/1	1.000	0/5	1	1	2	1	1	9	.273
MORTON, J.	37	11/26	.423	4/12	.333	9/10	.900	1/4	3	3	3	0	0	35	.946
GREENE, G.	43	5/13	.385	2/5	.400	1/3	.333	0/5	5	2	3	2	0	13	.302
AVENT, A.	11	1/2	.500	0/0	.000	0/0	.000	1/3	1	0	0	0	0	2	.182
VOLCY, F.	7	0/0	.000	0/0	.000	0/2	.000	0/1	1	0	2	0	0	0	.000
COOPER, M.	14	0/0	.000	0/0	.000	0/0	.000	0/2	0	1	1	0	1	0	.000
WIGINGTON, P.	2	1/1	1.000	0/0	.000	0/0	.000	0/0	0	0	1	0	0	2	1.000
Totals	225	28/65	.431	7/23	.304	16/22	.727	7/34	14	11	17	4	2	79	.351

Team Rebounds: Michigan 3; Seton Hall 2. Disqualified: None. Technical fouls: None.

	1st Half	2nd Half	1 OT	Final
Michigan	37	34	9	80
Seton Hall	32	39	8	79

✪ ALL-STAR TEAMS ✪

ALL TOURNAMENT

DANNY FERRY	DUKE
GERALD GREENE	SETON HALL
JOHN MORTON	SETON HALL
★ **GLEN RICE**	MICHIGAN
RUMEAL ROBINSON	MICHIGAN

MIDWEST REGIONAL

★ **NICK ANDERSON**	ILLINOIS
KENNY BATTLE	ILLINOIS
SHERMAN DOUGLAS	SYRACUSE
KENDALL GILL	ILLINOIS
BILLY OWENS	SYRACUSE

EAST REGIONAL

★ **DANNY FERRY**	DUKE
PHIL HENDERSON	DUKE
CHRISTIAN LAETTNER	DUKE
ALONZO MOURNING	GEORGETOWN
CHARLES SMITH	GEORGETOWN

SOUTHEAST REGIONAL

JOHN CROTTY	VIRGINIA
SEAN HIGGINS	MICHIGAN
J. R. REID	N. CAROLINA
★ **GLEN RICE**	MICHIGAN
RUMEAL ROBINSON	MICHIGAN

WEST REGIONAL

DAVID BUTLER	UNLV
SEAN ELLIOTT	ARIZONA
★ **ANDREW GAZE**	SETON HALL
GERALD GREENE	SETON HALL
DARYLL WALKER	SETON HALL

★ Most Outstanding Player(s)

✪ INDIVIDUAL RECORDS ✪

SCORING

Most points in a single game
1	RODNEY MONROE, N.C. STATE (vs. IOWA)	40
2	GLEN RICE, MICHIGAN (vs. SOUTH ALABAMA)	36
3	B.J. ARMSTRONG, IOWA (vs. RUTGERS)	35
3	JOHN MORTON, SETON HALL (vs. MICHIGAN)	35
5	5 tied for fifth place.	

Most total points in the tournament
1	GLEN RICE, MICHIGAN	184
2	JOHN MORTON, SETON HALL	114
3	DANNY FERRY, DUKE	111
4	RICHARD MORGAN, VIRGINIA	106
5	NICK ANDERSON, ILLINOIS	102

Highest scoring average (minimum 2 games)
1	GLEN RICE, MICHIGAN (184-6)	30.67
2	RODNEY MONROE, N.C. STATE (88-3)	29.33
3	B.J. ARMSTRONG, IOWA (55-2)	27.50
4	RICHARD MORGAN, VIRGINIA (106-4)	26.50
5	TIM HARDAWAY, UTEP (51-2)	25.50

FIELD GOALS

Most field goals in a single game
1	CHRIS JACKSON, LOUISIANA ST. (vs. UTEP)	16
1	GLEN RICE, MICHIGAN (vs. SOUTH ALABAMA)	16
3	MOOKIE BLAYLOCK, OKLAHOMA (vs. LOUISIANA TECH)	14
3	MARIO CREDIT, ARKANSAS (vs. LOYOLA MYMT.)	14
5	6 tied for fifth place.	

Most total field goals in the tournament
1	GLEN RICE, MICHIGAN	75
2	NICK ANDERSON, ILLINOIS	42
3	DANNY FERRY, DUKE	39
4	RUMEAL ROBINSON, MICHIGAN	37
4	TERRY MILLS, MICHIGAN	37

Most field goal attempts in a single game
1	CHRIS JACKSON, LOUISIANA ST. (vs. UTEP)	32
2	DANNY FERRY, DUKE (vs. SETON HALL)	29
3	MOOKIE BLAYLOCK, OKLAHOMA (vs. LOUISIANA TECH)	28
3	JEFF FRYER, LOYOLA MYMT. (vs. ARKANSAS)	28
3	LIONEL SIMMONS, LA SALLE (vs. LOUISIANA TECH)	28

Most total field goal attempts in tournament
1	GLEN RICE, MICHIGAN	131
2	DANNY FERRY, DUKE	87
3	JOHN MORTON, SETON HALL	83
4	NICK ANDERSON, ILLINOIS	79
5	RICHARD MORGAN, VIRGINIA	78

Highest field goal percentage in a single game (minimum 10 attempts)
1	LENZIE HOWELL, ARKANSAS (vs. LOYOLA MYMT.) (10-11)	.909
2	ROBERT BRICKEY, DUKE (vs. MINNESOTA) (9-10)	.900
2	CHRISTIAN LAETTNER, DUKE (vs. GEORGETOWN) (9-10)	.900
2	JOHN CROTTY, VIRGINIA (vs. PROVIDENCE) (9-10)	.900
5	KEVIN MADDEN, N. CAROLINA (vs. SOUTHERN-B.R.) (11-13)	.846

Highest field goal percentage in the tournament (minimum 20 attempts)
1	CHRISTIAN LAETTNER, DUKE (26-33)	.788
2	LARRY SMITH, ILLINOIS (15-20)	.750
3	ERIC ANDERSON, INDIANA (20-28)	.714
4	BRIAN HOWARD, N.C. STATE (17-24)	.708
5	STEPHEN THOMPSON, SYRACUSE (29-41)	.707

3-PT. FIELD GOALS

Most 3-pt. field goals in a single game
1	GLEN RICE, MICHIGAN (vs. N. CAROLINA)	8
2	SEAN HIGGINS, MICHIGAN (vs. VIRGINIA)	7
3	7 tied for third place.	

Most total 3-pt. field goals in the tournament
1	GLEN RICE, MICHIGAN	27
2	ANDREW GAZE, SETON HALL	16
3	RICHARD MORGAN, VIRGINIA	15
4	JEFF ROBINSON, SIENA	12
5	2 tied for fifth place.	

Most 3-pt. field goals attempted in a single game
1	JEFF FRYER, LOYOLA MYMT. (vs. ARKANSAS)	22
2	CARLOS SAMPLE, SOUTHERN-B.R. (vs. N. CAROLINA)	16
3	JEFF ROBINSON, SIENA (vs. MINNESOTA)	15
3	STEVE HENSON, KANSAS STATE (vs. MINNESOTA)	15
5	2 tied for fifth place.	

Most total 3-pt. field goals attempted in the tournament
1	GLEN RICE, MICHIGAN	49
2	ANDREW GAZE, SETON HALL	35
3	RICHARD MORGAN, VIRGINIA	28
4	JEFF ROBINSON, SIENA	25
4	JOHN MORTON, SETON HALL	25

Highest 3-pt. field goal percentage in a single game (minimum 4 attempts)
1	MIKE BUCK, MIDDLE TENN. ST. (vs. FLORIDA STATE) (6-6)	1.000
2	JOE FREDRICK, NOTRE DAME (vs. VANDERBILT) (4-4)	1.000
2	JOHN CROTTY, VIRGINIA (vs. PROVIDENCE) (4-4)	1.000
2	SEAN ELLIOTT, ARIZONA (vs. ROBERT MORRIS) (4-4)	1.000
5	2 tied for fifth place.	

Highest 3-pt. field goal percentage in the tournament (minimum 8 attempts)
1	JOHN CROTTY, VIRGINIA (8-10)	.800
2	DWAYNE BRYANT, GEORGETOWN (6-9)	.667
3	DAVID YOUNG, CLEMSON (5-8)	.625
3	T. HARRIS, MCNEESE STATE (5-8)	.625
5	B.J. ARMSTRONG, IOWA (8-13)	.615

FREE THROWS

Most free throws in a single game
1	GABRIEL ESTABA, SOUTH ALABAMA (vs. ALABAMA)	12
1	BRYANT STITH, VIRGINIA (vs. MIDDLE TENN. ST.)	12
1	ADAM KEEFE, STANFORD (vs. SIENA)	12
4	RODNEY MONROE, N.C. STATE (vs. GEORGETOWN)	11
4	WILLIE BURTON, MINNESOTA (vs. KANSAS STATE)	11

Most total free throws in the tournament
1	JOHN MORTON, SETON HALL	39
2	BRYANT STITH, VIRGINIA	29
3	DANNY FERRY, DUKE	28
4	GERALD GREENE, SETON HALL	24
5	2 tied for fifth place.	

Most free throws attempted in a single game

1. GABRIEL ESTABA, SOUTH ALABAMA (vs. ALABAMA) 16
1. JOHN MORTON, SETON HALL (vs. EVANSVILLE) 16
3. TREVOR WILSON, UCLA (vs. N. CAROLINA) 15
4. 4 tied for fourth place.

Most free throws attempted in the tournament

1. JOHN MORTON, SETON HALL 51
2. DANNY FERRY, DUKE 38
3. BRYANT STITH, VIRGINIA 33
4. RUMEAL ROBINSON, MICHIGAN 31
4. GERALD GREENE, SETON HALL 31

Highest free throw percentage in a single game (minimum 7 attempts)

1. BRYANT STITH, VIRGINIA (vs. MIDDLE TENN. ST.) (12-12) 1.000
2. WILLIE BURTON, MINNESOTA (vs. KANSAS STATE) (11-11) 1.000
3. DANNY FERRY, DUKE (vs. WEST VIRGINIA) (9-9) 1.000
3. BARRY GOHEEN, VANDERBILT (vs. NOTRE DAME) (9-9) 1.000
3. RICHARD MORGAN, VIRGINIA (vs. PROVIDENCE) (9-9) 1.000

Highest free throw percentage in the tournament (minimum 15 attempts)

1. RICHARD MORGAN, VIRGINIA (23-23) 1.000
2. WILLIE BURTON, MINNESOTA (14-15) .933
3. LABRADFORD SMITH, LOUISVILLE (22-24) .917
4. BRYANT STITH, VIRGINIA (29-33) .879
5. RODNEY MONROE, N.C. STATE (21-24) .875

REBOUNDS

Most rebounds in a single game

1. LAPHONSO ELLIS, NOTRE DAME (vs. VANDERBILT) 18
2. HANK GATHERS, LOYOLA MYMT. (vs. ARKANSAS) 17
3. 4 tied for third place.

Most total rebounds in the tournament

1. DARYLL WALKER, SETON HALL 58
2. LOY VAUGHT, MICHIGAN 48
3. NICK ANDERSON, ILLINOIS 47
4. MOSES SCURRY, UNLV 41
4. RAMON RAMOS, SETON HALL 41

Most rebounds per game (minimum 2 games)

1. S. BRUNDY, DEPAUL (30-2) 15.00
2. K. HAMMONDS, MIDDLE TENN. ST. (28-2) 14.00
2. LAPHONSO ELLIS, NOTRE DAME (28-2) 14.00
4. R. WHITE, LOUISIANA TECH (25-2) 12.50
5. MARIO CREDIT, ARKANSAS (23-2) 11.50

ASSISTS

Most assists in a single game

1. POOH RICHARDSON, UCLA (vs. IOWA STATE) 14
1. JOHN CROTTY, VIRGINIA (vs. MIDDLE TENN. ST.) 14
3. RUMEAL ROBINSON, MICHIGAN (vs. N. CAROLINA) 13
4. RUMEAL ROBINSON, MICHIGAN (vs. ILLINOIS) 12
4. KEITH WILSON, ARKANSAS (vs. LOYOLA MYMT.) 12

Most total assists in the tournament

1. RUMEAL ROBINSON, MICHIGAN 56
2. JOHN CROTTY, VIRGINIA 39
3. SHERMAN DOUGLAS, SYRACUSE 32
4. QUIN SNYDER, DUKE 28
4. STEVE BUCKNALL, N. CAROLINA 28

Most assists per game (minimum 2 appearances)

1. JOHN CROTTY, VIRGINIA (39-4) 9.75
2. POOH RICHARDSON, UCLA (19-2) 9.50
3. RUMEAL ROBINSON, MICHIGAN (56-6) 9.33
4. STEVE BUCKNALL, N. CAROLINA (28-3) 9.33
5. CHRIS CORCHIANI, N.C. STATE (25-3) 8.33

TURNOVERS

Most turnovers in a single game

1. DEREK STRONG, XAVIER (OHIO) (vs. MICHIGAN) 8
1. LANCE BLANKS, TEXAS (vs. MISSOURI) 8
3. 5 tied for third place.

Most total turnovers in the tournament

1. RUMEAL ROBINSON, MICHIGAN 26
2. JOHN MORTON, SETON HALL 18
3. SHERMAN DOUGLAS, SYRACUSE 18
4. GERALD GREENE, SETON HALL 16
4. STEVE BARDO, ILLINOIS 16

SHOTS BLOCKED

Most shots blocked in a single game

1. AVIE LESTER, N.C. STATE (vs. IOWA) 7
1. ALONZO MOURNING, GEORGETOWN (vs. PRINCETON) 7
1. PERVIS ELLISON, LOUISVILLE (vs. ILLINOIS) 7
4. ALONZO MOURNING, GEORGETOWN (vs. N.C. STATE) 5
5. 9 tied for fifth place.

Most total shots blocked in the tournament

1. ALONZO MOURNING, GEORGETOWN 19
2. PERVIS ELLISON, LOUISVILLE 13
3. FRANTZ VOLCY, SETON HALL 10
4. 3 tied for fourth place.

STEALS

Most steals in a single game

1. RICK DADLKA, RUTGERS (vs. IOWA) 6
1. LANCE BLANKS, TEXAS (vs. MISSOURI) 6
3. 8 tied for third place.

Most total steals in the tournament

1. KENDALL GILL, ILLINOIS 17
2. NICK ANDERSON, ILLINOIS 14
3. MOOKIE BLAYLOCK, OKLAHOMA 9
4. 4 tied for fourth place.

✪ TEAM RECORDS ✪

SCORING

Most points in a single game

1. OKLAHOMA (vs. LOUISIANA TECH) 124
2. ARKANSAS (vs. LOYOLA MYMT.) 120
3. MISSOURI (vs. TEXAS) 108

Most total points in the tournament

1. MICHIGAN 540
2. SETON HALL 483
3. DUKE 410

Highest scoring average (minimum 2 games)

1. ARKANSAS (204-2) 102.00
2. MIDDLE TENN. ST. (185-2) 92.50
3. OKLAHOMA (276-3) 92.00

FIELD GOALS

Most field goals in a single game

1. OKLAHOMA (vs. LOUISIANA TECH) 48
2. ARKANSAS (vs. LOYOLA MYMT.) 47
3. MISSOURI (vs. TEXAS) 42

Most total field goals in the tournament

1. MICHIGAN 217
2. SETON HALL 169
3. ILLINOIS 162

Most field goals attempted in a single game

1. OKLAHOMA (vs. LOUISIANA TECH) 98
1. LOYOLA MYMT. (vs. ARKANSAS) 98
3. ARKANSAS (vs. LOUISVILLE) 88

Most total field goals attempted in the tournament

1. MICHIGAN 409
2. SETON HALL 350
3. ILLINOIS 326

Highest field goal percentage in a single game

1. GEORGETOWN (vs. NOTRE DAME) (25-35) .714
2. DUKE (vs. S. CAROLINA ST.) (34-53) .642
3. IOWA (vs. RUTGERS) (33-52) .635

Highest field goal percentage in a tournament (minimum 2 games)

1. WEST VIRGINIA (56-100) .560
2. CLEMSON (61-111) .550
3. SYRACUSE (129-235) .549

3-PT. FIELD GOALS

Most 3-pt. field goals in a single game

1. MICHIGAN (vs. N. CAROLINA) 13
2. EVANSVILLE (vs. OREGON STATE) 12
3. 4 tied for third place.

Most total 3-pt. field goals in the tournament

1. MICHIGAN 43
2. SETON HALL 34
3. VIRGINIA 27

Most 3-pt. field goals attempted in a single game

1. LOYOLA MYMT. (vs. ARKANSAS) 39
2. SIENA (vs. MINNESOTA) 32
3. TENNESSEE (vs. WEST VIRGINIA) 31

Most total 3-pt. field goals attempted in the tournament

1. MICHIGAN 90
2. SETON HALL 81
3. UNLV 73

Highest 3-pt. field goal percentage in a single game (minimum 10 attempts)
1 INDIANA (vs. UTEP) (7-10)   .700
1 VIRGINIA (vs. MIDDLE TENN. ST.) (7-10)   .700
1 VIRGINIA (vs. PROVIDENCE) (7-10)   .700

Highest 3-pt. field goal percentage in the tournament (minimum 20 attempts)
1 INDIANA (14-23)   .609
2 VIRGINIA (27-50)   .540
3 N.C. STATE (16-31)   .516

FREE THROWS

Most free throws in a single game
1 4 tied for first place.

Most total free throws in the tournament
1 SETON HALL   111
2 DUKE   110
3 VIRGINIA   88

Most free throws attempted in a single game
1 UNLV (vs. DEPAUL)   43
2 DUKE (vs. MINNESOTA)   42
3 ARKANSAS (vs. LOYOLA MYMT.)   41

Most total free throws attempted in the tournament
1 DUKE   160
2 SETON HALL   150
3 VIRGINIA   121

Highest free throw percentage in a single game
1 IOWA (vs. N.C. STATE) (20-21)   .952
2 NOTRE DAME (vs. GEORGETOWN) (16-17)   .941
3 MIDDLE TENN. ST. (vs. VIRGINIA) (18-20)   .900

Highest free throw percentage in the tournament (minimum 2 games)
1 MIDDLE TENN. ST. (34-39)   .872

2 NOTRE DAME (25-30)   .833
3 IOWA (32-40)   .800

Fewest free throws in a single game
1 PRINCETON (vs. GEORGETOWN)   2
2 FLORIDA (vs. COLORADO STATE)   3
2 SIENA (vs. MINNESOTA)   3

Lowest free throw percentage in a single game
1 SIENA (vs. MINNESOTA) (3-9)   .333
2 ILLINOIS (vs. LOUISVILLE) (4-11)   .364
3 PRINCETON (vs. GEORGETOWN) (2-5)   .400

Lowest free throw percentage in the tournament (minimum 2 games)
1 SIENA (12-25)   .480
2 UCLA (28-47)   .596
3 ARKANSAS (40-66)   .606

REBOUNDS

Most rebounds in a single game
1 OKLAHOMA (vs. LOUISIANA TECH)   58
1 LOYOLA MYMT. (vs. ARKANSAS)   58
3 ARKANSAS (vs. LOYOLA MYMT.)   48

Most rebounds per game (minimum 2 games)
1 ARKANSAS (89-2)   44.50
2 LOUISIANA TECH (85-2)   42.50
3 2 tied for third place.

ASSISTS

Most assists in a single game
1 ARKANSAS (vs. LOYOLA MYMT.)   30
2 LOUISVILLE (vs. ARKANSAS)   28
3 2 tied for third place.

Most assists per game (minimum 2 games)
1 N. CAROLINA (71-3)   23.67

2 ARKANSAS (45-2)   22.50
3 UCLA (44-2)   22.00

TURNOVERS

Most turnovers in a single game
1 LOUISIANA TECH (vs. OKLAHOMA)   29
2 DE PAUL (vs. MEMPHIS STATE)   23
3 2 tied for third place.

Most turnovers per game (minimum 2 games)
1 LOUISIANA TECH (48-2)   24.00
2 DEPAUL (39-2)   19.50
3 2 tied for third place.

SHOTS BLOCKED

Most shots blocked in a single game
1 LOUISVILLE (vs. ILLINOIS)   13
2 CLEMSON (vs. ST. MARY'S)   12
3 N.C. STATE (vs. IOWA)   11

Most shots blocked per game (minimum 2 games)
1 LOUISVILLE (25-3)   8.33
2 CLEMSON (16-2)   8.00
3 GEORGETOWN (24-4)   6.00

STEALS

Most steals in a single game
1 OKLAHOMA (vs. LOUISIANA TECH)   16
2 MEMPHIS STATE (vs. DEPAUL)   13
2 S. CAROLINA ST. (vs. DUKE)   13

Most steals per game
1 ARKANSAS (21-2)   10.50
2 OKLAHOMA (28-3)   9.33
3 ILLINOIS (44-5)   8.80

1990

| FIRST ROUND | SECOND ROUND | REGIONAL SEMIFINAL | REGIONAL FINAL | FINAL FOUR | REGIONAL FINAL | REGIONAL SEMIFINAL | SECOND ROUND | FIRST ROUND |

SOUTHEAST

1 Michigan St. 75 (ot)
Michigan St. 62
16 Murray St. 71
Michigan St. 80
8 Houston 66
UC Santa Barb. 58
9 UC Santa Barb. 70
Georgia Tech 93
5 Louisiana St. 70
Louisiana St. 91
12 Villanova 63
4 Georgia Tech. 99
Georgia Tech. 81 (ot)
13 E. Tennessee St. 83
Georgia Tech. 94
Georgia Tech 81
6 Minnesota 64 (ot)
Minnesota 81
11 UTEP 61
Minnesota 82
3 Missouri 71
Northern Iowa 78
14 Northern Iowa 74
Minnesota 91
7 Virginia 75
Virginia 61
10 Notre Dame 67
Syracuse 75
2 Syracuse 70
Syracuse 63
15 Coppin St. 48

WEST

1 UNLV 102
UNLV 76
16 Ark.-Little Rock 72
UNLV 69
8 Ohio St. 84 (ot)
Ohio St. 65
9 Providence 83
UNLV 131
5 Oregon St. 53
Ball St. 62
12 Ball St. 54
4 Louisville 78
Ball St. 67
13 Idaho 89
Louisville 60
9 New Mexico St. 92
Loyola Mymt. 149
UNLV 90
11 Loyola Mymt. 111
Loyola Mymt. 62
3 Michigan 76
Michigan 115
14 Illinois St. 70
Loyola Mymt. 101
7 Alabama 71
Alabama 77
10 Colorado St. 54
Alabama 60
2 Arizona 79
Arizona 55
15 South Florida 67

UNLV 103
Duke 73

UNLV 103
Arkansas 83

Georgia Tech 81
Duke 97

Duke 90
Duke 79 (ot)

UCLA 81

U. Conn. 78

U. Conn. 71

Clemson 70

N. Carolina 73

Arkansas 88

Arkansas 96

Xavier 89

Texas 85

Texas 102

EAST

U. Conn. 74
1 U. Conn. 76
16 Boston Univ. 52
California 54
8 Indiana 63
9 California 65
Clemson 79
5 Clemson 49
12 Brigham Young 47
La Salle 75
4 La Salle 79
13 Southern Miss. 63
St. John's 72
6 St. John's 81
11 Temple 65
Duke 76
3 Duke 81
14 Richmond 46
UCLA 71
7 UCLA 68
Ala.-Birmingham 56
Kansas 70
2 Kansas 79
15 Robert Morris 71

MIDWEST

Oklahoma 77
1 Oklahoma 77
16 Towson St. 68
N. Carolina 79
8 N. Carolina 83
9 S.W. Missouri St. 70
Dayton 84
5 Illinois 86
12 Dayton 88
Arkansas 86
4 Arkansas 68
13 Princeton 64
Xavier 74
6 Xavier 87
11 Kansas St. 79
Georgetown 71
3 Georgetown 70
14 Tex. Southern 52
Texas 73
7 Georgia 88
10 Texas 100
Purdue 72
2 Purdue 75
15 Northeast La. 63

In the end it was UNLV's tournament. They weren't the people's choice (that distinction went hands down to Loyola Marymount). And if truth be told, NCAA authorities would have much preferred the champion to come from a program with a cleaner, kinder, gentler image than coach Jerry Tarkanian's Runnin' Rebels.

Despite their reputation as a rough, underachieving rogue team, Nevada Las Vegas was the class act of the tournament. Before the season began, they were the top-rated team in the country, and in March they were still ranked No. 2. With all five starters back from the 29-8 team that made it to the 1989 West regional final, plus the 1989 Junior College Player of the Year, Larry Johnson, Tarkanian had finally put together the team with the talent to put him over the top.

They were simply overpowering, not just because they were the best athletes, but because they were the most highly motivated, disciplined, and intelligent *team* in the field. And they peaked at just the right time, blowing out a good Duke unit in the most one-sided championship game in history.

But 1990 was also memorable for an extraordinarily high overall level of competition, as well as for the many small moments, mostly in the early rounds, that defined grace under pressure.

In the beginning it was Hank Gathers's tournament. Gathers, Loyola Marymount's All-American center, who collapsed and died on the court just days before the first round began, was the glue that held his high-scoring team together (Gathers's teammates called him "Bankman," as in "money in the bank"), and with his death many observers counted Loyola out. Instead, his teammates took their game to a higher level. Led by Bo Kimble, Gathers's best friend since their days together in the Philadelphia playgrounds, the Lions beat New Mexico State in the first round, 111–92. In that game, and in every game Loyola played in the tournament, Bo Kimble, a right-handed shooter, took his first foul shot left handed, as his friend Hank Gathers would have done.

"It may sound corny, but it makes me believe I've got a little bit of Hank inside me. I feel his strength," said Kimble. "After that," said Loyola coach Paul Westhead, "I didn't know or care whether we won the game or not. I never wanted a shot to go in more than that left-handed shot."

It was Loyola's second round game against defending national champs Michigan that made believers out of the skeptics who felt the Lions had no chance to go anywhere without their star. Defying rationality, they broke the all-time tournament scoring record, beating the Wolverines 149-115. Jeff Fryer hit 11 of 15 from 3-point range and Kimble had 37—on an off day. Then, despite being thrown completely out of their run-and-gun game, Loyola squeaked by Alabama 62-60 to force a showdown with UNLV.

But Loyola wasn't the only underdog to give the high-profile programs a run for their money in 1990.

Ball State, for one, epitomized the unheralded, small-conference team that played the socks off the big boys. After Ball State's Cardinals beat the big-time Cardinals of Louisville, the Indiana school's coach, Dick Hunsaker, said, "It's the heart inside the jersey, not the name on the jersey, that you win with." Their hearts, like Loyola Marymount's, finally took them into a confrontation with UNLV.

Still another unknown, the University of Northern Iowa (a sign in the school's cheering section called it the University of Nothing Impossible) defeated the Big Eight's Missouri, before being eliminated by Minnesota 81-78. And when Towson State's Kurk Lee led his team to within two points of top-seeded Oklahoma late in the second half of their opening-round game, he asked a Sooner player, "Do you know where Towson State is now?" (It's in Maryland.)

Among other early-round upsets and close calls: Freshman Aaron Williams of Xavier, coming in after Musketeers' star Tyrone Hill fouled out, grabbed an offensive rebound and scored the game winner over Georgetown's Alonzo Mourning and Dikembe Mutombo. Hoyas' coach John Thompson described Xavier as "big, mobile, and flexible . . . the way we were in the old days." Murray State, powered by 37 points from a fit and trim Popeye Jones (who tipped the scales at 255 after losing 50 pounds from his roly-poly freshman season), took the Southeast Region's top-seeded Michigan State into overtime before succumbing. And, not to be overlooked, UCLA freshman Tracy Murray sank two foul shots to beat No. 2–seed Kansas 71-70, despite two time-outs called by the Jayhawks in what Murray called "a freeze-the-freshman kind of deal."

In all, nine of the top sixteen seeds lost in the first two rounds, with sixteen of the 48 first- and second-round games decided by the last shot or in overtime. The five biggest conferences got 26 bids, but they were hardly successful. Of the seven Big Ten teams, only two survived the first two rounds; all three Big Eight early season poll toppers (Missouri, Oklahoma, and Kansas) were sent home—of all the major conferences, only the ACC, which sent four teams into the round of sixteen, had anything to write home about.

Maybe it was all the action, excitement, and unpredictability at the beginning that persuaded CBS to plunk down a cool billion for the rights to televise the whole shebang for the next seven years, instead of just bidding on the Final Four, as the networks had done in the past. (ESPN, which had spent the last decade providing early-round coverage, was forced to fold its hand when they saw what CBS was putting on the table.)

But if the early rounds were enough to convince CBS, the regionals were even more seat-of-the-pants thrilling . . .

The East regional went from euphoria to heartbreak and back again in a split second: in their regional semifinal against U. Conn., Clemson fought back from an early hole to take the lead with one second to go. But the Huskies weren't ready to concede. Freshman Scott Burrell, a high school quarterback and 95-mph-fastball-pitching first-round pick of baseball's Seattle Mariners—took the ball out at his end of the court and threw an 80-foot strike to Tate George (Connecticut's only senior starter), who turned and hit a 15-foot jumper at the buzzer. The Huskies' jubilation was short lived, however, even though reserve guard Chris Smith sent their next game, against Duke, into overtime by hitting a 3-pointer with nine seconds remaining—because with four seconds left in OT and the score 78-77 U. Conn., George cut in front of the Blue Devils' Phil Henderson to steal a pass but lost it out of bounds. Christian Laettner then hit a beat-the-clock shot to send the Huskies home and the Blue Devils to the Final Four. "We're not better than Connecticut," said Duke's coach Mike Krzyzewski. "We just won."

Things got even wilder in Georgia Tech's Southeast regional semi against Michigan State. When Tech's sensational freshman Kenny Anderson hit a jumper with time running out, the referee signaled a trey and a Yellow Jacket victory. Then the officials changed the call, ruling that Anderson was on the line when he shot. The instant replay showed that indeed it was a 2-pointer, but it also showed that time had run out before the shot. The two points counted anyway—the game didn't end when the clock struck zero, only when the buzzer went off—and nobody heard the fat lady sing until after the ball left Anderson's hands. The Yellow Jackets finally won the game in overtime.

In the regional final against Minnesota, Tech's "Lethal Weapon 3" (Anderson, Dennis Scott, and Brian Oliver) scored 89 points, but the outcome remained in doubt until Minnesota's Kevin Lynch missed a 3-pointer—again at the buzzer.

In the Midwest, Arkansas dominated North Carolina and outlasted Texas to become the first Southwestern Conference school to get past the Round of Eight since Akeem Olajuwon led Houston to the title game in 1984. Razorbacks' coach Nolan Richardson, whose running style (and race) had met with a lot of opposition among school backers ever since he was hired in 1985, silenced his critics as his team moved on to Denver. By winning the regional, Richardson gained the distinction of becoming the second black coach to reach the Final Four.

And in the West there was UNLV.

As they moved toward a confrontation with Loyola Marymount, the Rebels were working to enhance their image as the meanest, baddest basketball team in captivity. The image was deliberate; they compared themselves to the NBA champion Detroit Pistons and, like the Pistons, used physical intimidation as a major part of their game. After their stiffest test of the tournament, a two-point victory over Ball State in the regional semifinals, a group of UNLV players confronted the upstart Cardinals in the hallway leading to the locker room. Afterward, Ball State coach Hunsaker called the Rebels "a bunch of thugs."

The regional final between Loyola Marymount and UNLV was a classic matchup—the forces of light against the forces of darkness. Speaking to his teammates before the game, UNLV's Greg Anthony said, "They are living a dream. It's time someone woke them up." The nation wanted to believe that the good guys would prevail, but finally Loyola's Little Engine That Could couldn't get over the big hill: they were overwhelmed by the power, precision, speed, and conditioning of the Rebels.

UNLV then went on to Denver to meet Georgia Tech in the national semifinals. In the first half the Rebels looked beatable as Lethal Weapon 3 brought Tech back from a 21-12 deficit. Scott's long-range bombing (LSU coach Dale Brown once said, "Scott shoots from the planet Jupiter"), Anderson's dishing and driving, and a steady ten points from Oliver sent the Yellow Jackets into their locker room laughing and figuring that the Rebs weren't so tough after all.

Tarkanian adjusted, and when the teams came out for the second half he abandoned the zone he had been using to stop Anderson and went back to a pressing man-to-man. In the first 3:38, UNLV outscored Georgia Tech 10-1. "They were in our jocks," said Tech forward Malcolm Mackey. With Augmon on top of Scott, Anderson Hunt hounding Anderson, and sinister sub Moses Scurry grabbing 11 rebounds in 16 second-half minutes, the Rebs stopped the Yellow Jackets' designated offense cold and finally put the game away in the last five minutes.

Meanwhile Duke outlasted Richardson's "forty minutes of hell" as Arkansas ran out of breath in Denver's high altitude and a Duke deluge took a 69-62 deficit to a 97-83 victory.

The Blue Devils thought they had escaped forty minutes of hell, but they were wrong. Against St. John's, Duke took the lead with 32 seconds left. Against Connecticut and Arkansas they clawed their way back. But finally they learned what Loyola Marymount and Georgia Tech had already found out—there was a team in the field that was just plain better than they were.

UNLV was in command from the start. They played with more intensity, more intelligence, and greater focus than Duke. They had a ferocious will to win.

With Larry Johnson fronting the post, and the Rebel

guards picking up Duke point guard Bobby Hurley at midcourt, UNLV cut off the lob. Unable to penetrate against the pressure, Hurley pulled up his dribble and threw the ball into a crowd.

Early in the second half the roof caved in on Duke as UNLV scored 18 straight points in less than three minutes. During the Rebels' devastating run, Hunt scored 12 (clinching the Final Four Most Outstanding Player award), while Duke passed sloppily, shot without conviction, and stopped running the court. As Duke's Alaa Abdelnaby said, "It was scary just watching them. They engulfed us."

The Runnin' Rebels became the first national champion to score 100 points in a title game, and their 30-point victory margin far surpassed UCLA's record 23-point win over North Carolina in 1968. After the hard-fought, highly competitive early rounds, the final was almost an anticlimax.

Tark the Shark and his rogue band finally won it all—no contest. As Duke's coach Mike Krzyzewski said, "I'm in awe of what they did tonight . . . they were great."

FIRST ROUND SOUTHEAST

Michigan State (75) Coach: Jud Heathcote

	Min.	Total FG/FGA	Pct.	3-Pt. FG/FGA	Pct.	FT/FTA	Pct.	Reb. O/T	A	TO	PF	S	Blk	TP	PPM
REDFIELD, K.	38	5/11	.455	0/1	.000	1/2	.500	4/11	1	3	3	2	0	11	.289
STEIGENGA, M.	17	0/2	.000	0/0	.000	2/2	1.000	1/3	1	2	3	0	1	2	.118
PEPLOWSKI, M.	26	1/3	.333	0/0	.000	0/0	.000	1/6	1	1	3	0	0	2	.077
SMITH, S.	40	10/16	.625	2/5	.400	0/0	.000	3/11	4	3	2	0	1	22	.550
MONTGOMERY, M.	34	2/5	.400	1/2	.500	0/1	.000	1/4	9	3	0	0	1	5	.147
MANNS, K.	26	9/18	.500	3/11	.273	0/0	.000	2/3	1	0	1	0	0	21	.808
HICKMAN, D.	14	0/3	.000	0/0	.000	0/0	.000	0/2	1	0	1	1	0	0	.000
STEPHENS, P.	29	6/9	.667	0/0	.000	0/0	.000	1/5	2	3	4	0	0	12	.414
WOLFE, T.	1	0/0	.000	0/0	.000	0/0	.000	0/0	0	0	0	0	0	0	.000
Totals	225	33/67	.493	6/19	.316	3/5	.600	13/45	20	15	17	3	3	75	.333

Murray State (71) Coach: Steve Newton

	Min.	Total FG/FGA	Pct.	3-Pt. FG/FGA	Pct.	FT/FTA	Pct.	Reb. O/T	A	TO	PF	S	Blk	TP	PPM
PRIDE, S.	13	0/0	.000	0/0	.000	0/0	.000	0/1	0	0	1	0	0	0	.000
OGDEN, C.	37	1/7	.143	0/0	.000	0/0	.000	1/5	0	0	4	1	0	2	.054
JONES, P.	45	15/36	.417	3/7	.429	4/6	.667	6/11	0	0	2	1	1	37	.822
KING, P.	45	2/6	.333	1/3	.333	2/4	.500	2/5	4	1	2	1	1	7	.156
ALLEN, F.	41	4/11	.364	2/7	.286	4/4	1.000	1/6	4	3	2	0	0	14	.341
CABLE, G.	38	4/12	.333	1/5	.200	2/2	1.000	1/2	3	0	2	1	0	11	.289
ROSARIO, I.	4	0/0	.000	0/0	.000	0/0	.000	0/1	0	0	0	0	0	0	.000
SILVILLS, S.	2	0/0	.000	0/0	.000	0/0	.000	0/0	0	1	0	0	0	0	.000
Totals	225	26/72	.361	7/22	.318	12/16	.750	11/31	11	5	13	4	2	71	.316

Team Rebounds: Michigan St. 6; Murray State 2. Disqualified: None. Technical fouls: Michigan St.—Bench.

	1st Half	2nd Half	1 OT	Final
Michigan St.	33	32	10	75
Murray State	31	34	6	71

Houston (66) Coach: Pat Foster

	Min.	Total FG/FGA	Pct.	3-Pt. FG/FGA	Pct.	FT/FTA	Pct.	Reb. O/T	A	TO	PF	S	Blk	TP	PPM
MORRIS, C.	25	3/4	.750	0/1	.000	0/2	.000	3/3	0	2	2	0	0	6	.240
UPCHURCH, C.	33	4/10	.400	0/0	.000	3/3	1.000	2/8	1	5	4	1	0	11	.333
HERRERA, C.	38	6/10	.600	0/0	.000	7/8	.875	2/9	2	2	4	1	1	19	.500
DANIELS, D.	38	3/5	.600	0/1	.000	0/1	.000	0/3	2	4	3	1	0	6	.158
SMITH, D.	36	7/14	.500	2/2	1.000	2/3	.667	1/3	1	3	4	0	0	18	.500
MICKENS, S.	20	2/2	1.000	0/0	.000	0/0	.000	0/1	3	2	5	1	0	4	.200
TEHERAN, A.	7	1/4	.250	0/0	.000	0/0	.000	0/3	1	0	0	0	0	2	.286
SMITH, K.	3	0/0	.000	0/0	.000	0/0	.000	0/1	0	0	1	0	0	0	.000
Totals	200	26/49	.531	2/4	.500	12/17	.706	8/31	10	18	23	4	1	66	.330

UC Santa Barbara (70) Coach: Jerry Pimm

	Min.	Total FG/FGA	Pct.	3-Pt. FG/FGA	Pct.	FT/FTA	Pct.	Reb. O/T	A	TO	PF	S	Blk	TP	PPM
JOHNSON, P.	37	1/4	.250	0/1	.000	5/6	.833	2/3	3	1	1	2	0	7	.189
MCARTHUR, E.	32	8/17	.471	0/0	.000	4/6	.667	6/11	1	4	4	5	2	20	.625
GRAY, G.	37	6/10	.600	0/0	.000	3/5	.600	6/9	0	2	3	1	0	15	.405
DEHART, C.	39	5/15	.333	1/5	.200	0/0	.000	0/2	6	3	0	2	1	11	.282
DAVIS, L.	28	3/4	.750	0/0	.000	2/3	.667	2/3	2	2	5	0	0	8	.286
JONES, I.	15	2/6	.333	1/4	.250	0/0	.000	1/1	0	2	1	0	0	5	.333
AKINS, U.	12	0/3	.000	0/0	.000	4/6	.667	0/2	0	1	2	0	0	4	.333
Totals	200	25/59	.424	2/10	.200	18/26	.692	16/31	12	12	16	9	6	70	.350

Team Rebounds: UC Santa Barbara 3; Houston 2. Disqualified: UC Santa Barbara—Davis; Houston—Mickens. Technical fouls: None.

	1st Half	2nd Half	Final
Houston	32	34	66
UC Santa Barbara	32	38	70

Louisiana State (70) Coach: Dale Brown

	Min.	Total FG/FGA	Pct.	3-Pt. FG/FGA	Pct.	FT/FTA	Pct.	Reb. O/T	A	TO	PF	S	Blk	TP	PPM
SINGLETON, V.	36	4/9	.444	0/0	.000	1/2	.500	2/5	1	2	3	1	1	9	.250
ROBERTS, S.	34	6/8	.750	0/0	.000	0/1	.000	1/8	0	1	3	1	3	12	.353
O'NEAL, S.	25	4/8	.500	0/0	.000	4/7	.571	3/11	1	4	4	1	4	12	.480
WILLIAMSON, M.	39	5/9	.556	4/6	.667	2/5	.400	1/3	5	13	4	3	0	16	.410
JACKSON, C.	34	6/12	.500	0/2	.000	4/4	1.000	0/2	3	5	2	1	0	16	.471
BOUDREAUX, H.	8	1/3	.333	0/0	.000	1/1	1.000	0/0	0	0	1	0	0	3	.375
DEVALL, R.	12	0/1	.000	0/0	.000	0/0	.000	1/2	2	2	0	1	0	0	.000
SIMS, W.	12	1/3	.333	0/0	.000	0/0	.000	1/5	1	1	1	0	0	2	.167
Totals	200	27/53	.509	4/8	.500	12/20	.600	9/36	13	26	18	7	8	70	.350

Villanova (63) Coach: Rollie Massimino

	Min.	Total FG/FGA	Pct.	3-Pt. FG/FGA	Pct.	FT/FTA	Pct.	Reb. O/T	A	TO	PF	S	Blk	TP	PPM
MILLER, L.	34	5/8	.625	1/2	.500	4/6	.667	1/5	2	3	3	2	1	15	.441
DOWDELL, M.	25	2/8	.250	0/0	.000	2/3	.667	3/4	1	1	4	3	0	6	.240
GREIS, T.	32	5/13	.385	0/0	.000	2/5	.400	6/9	1	4	4	0	1	12	.375
WALKER	35	6/21	.286	6/20	.300	2/2	1.000	1/2	2	1	4	2	0	20	.571
WOODARD, G.	28	1/9	.111	1/3	.333	0/0	.000	1/3	0	4	3	0	0	3	.107
BAIN, A.	20	1/7	.143	1/3	.333	0/0	.000	0/2	0	2	2	1	1	3	.150
TAYLOR, R.	16	0/2	.000	0/0	.000	0/0	.000	3/6	0	1	1	1	0	0	.000
BYRD, C.	9	1/1	1.000	0/0	.000	0/0	.000	1/4	0	0	1	0	2	2	.222
MILLER, D.	1	0/0	.000	0/0	.000	2/2	1.000	0/0	0	0	0	0	0	2	2.000
Totals	200	21/69	.304	9/28	.321	12/18	.667	16/35	6	16	21	10	4	63	.315

Team Rebounds: Louisiana St. 11; Villanova 3. Disqualified: None. Technical fouls: None.

	1st Half	2nd Half	Final
Louisiana St.	32	38	70
Villanova	23	40	63

Georgia Tech (99) Coach: Bobby Cremins

	Min.	Total FG/FGA	Pct.	3-Pt. FG/FGA	Pct.	FT/FTA	Pct.	Reb. O/T	A	TO	PF	S	Blk	TP	PPM
SCOTT, D.	39	14/22	.636	3/6	.500	5/6	.833	1/4	2	2	4	1	0	36	.923
MACKEY, M.	26	5/8	.625	0/0	.000	1/2	.500	2/7	0	1	1	1	0	11	.423
MCNEIL, J.	28	6/6	1.000	0/0	.000	2/2	1.000	1/7	1	1	1	0	0	14	.500
ANDERSON, K.	34	8/11	.727	3/4	.750	2/2	1.000	1/7	10	7	3	3	0	21	.618
OLIVER, B.	36	5/9	.556	1/3	.333	2/4	.500	0/4	2	5	2	1	0	13	.361
BROWN, K.	29	1/3	.333	0/0	.000	2/3	.667	1/3	3	0	0	0	4	4	.138
MUNLYN, J.	5	0/1	.000	0/0	.000	0/3	.000	1/2	1	1	1	1	0	2	.000
WHITE, G.	1	0/1	.000	0/0	.000	0/0	.000	0/0	0	0	0	0	0	0	.000
BARNES, D.	1	0/1	.000	0/0	.000	0/2	.000	2/3	0	0	0	0	0	0	.000
DOMALIK, B.	1	0/2	.000	0/0	.000	0/0	.000	1/1	0	1	0	0	0	0	.000
Totals	200	39/64	.609	7/13	.538	14/24	.583	10/38	19	18	12	6	2	99	.495

East Tennessee State (83) Coach: Les Robinson

	Min.	Total FG/FGA	Pct.	3-Pt. FG/FGA	Pct.	FT/FTA	Pct.	Reb. O/T	A	TO	PF	S	Blk	TP	PPM
TALFORD, C.	35	7/14	.500	3/5	.600	0/0	.000	2/2	0	2	1	2	0	17	.486
STORY, M.	13	1/2	.500	0/0	.000	0/0	.000	1/1	0	0	3	0	1	2	.154
DENNIS, G.	29	7/19	.368	0/3	.000	2/5	.400	4/8	2	2	4	0	1	16	.552
GEER, M.	28	3/13	.231	2/7	.286	2/2	1.000	1/2	2	1	1	2	0	10	.357
JENNINGS, K.	35	6/11	.545	5/8	.625	0/0	.000	1/4	5	2	2	0	0	17	.486
KELLER, C.	25	5/6	.833	0/0	.000	0/0	.000	0/4	0	1	1	2	0	10	.435
WEST, A.	25	4/8	.500	1/5	.200	0/0	.000	2/3	3	3	4	1	0	9	.360
JONES, D.	6	0/1	.000	0/0	.000	0/0	.000	0/0	0	0	0	0	0	0	.000
WOODS, M.	3	0/0	.000	0/0	.000	0/1	.000	0/1	0	0	2	1	0	0	.000
PELPHREY, J.	1	1/1	1.000	0/0	.000	0/0	.000	0/0	0	0	0	0	0	2	2.000
SPEARS, R.	1	0/1	.000	0/0	.000	0/0	.000	0/0	0	0	0	0	0	0	.000
JACOBS, J.	1	0/0	.000	0/0	.000	0/0	.000	0/1	0	0	1	0	0	0	.000
Totals	200	34/76	.447	11/28	.393	4/8	.500	11/26	12	11	19	8	2	83	.415

Team Rebounds: Georgia Tech 8; East Tenn. St. 4. Disqualified: None. Technical fouls: None.

	1st Half	2nd Half	Final
Georgia Tech	49	50	99
East Tenn. St.	24	59	83

Minnesota (64)
Coach: Clem Haskins

	Min.	Total FG/FGA	Pct.	3-Pt. FG/FGA	Pct.	FT/FTA	Pct.	Reb. O/T	A	TO	PF	S	Blk	TP	PPM
COFFEY, R.	43	3/10	.300	0/0	.000	0/1	.000	5/11	2	1	3	4	0	6	.140
BURTON, W.	35	3/11	.273	2/7	.286	6/6	1.000	2/3	3	1	4	2	0	14	.400
SHIKENJANSKI, J.	25	1/7	.143	0/0	.000	1/2	.500	1/1	0	1	4	0	0	3	.120
LYNCH, K.	38	6/13	.462	4/8	.500	2/2	1.000	2/3	3	2	2	0	0	18	.474
NEWBERN, M.	39	7/17	.412	1/4	.250	0/1	.000	1/3	2	2	3	1	0	15	.385
GREEN, M.	4	0/0	.000	0/0	.000	0/0	.000	0/0	0	1	1	0	0	0	.000
LEWIS, C.	7	1/2	.500	0/1	.000	0/0	.000	0/0	1	1	2	2	0	2	.286
METCALF, R.	2	-/0	-	0/0	.000	0/0	.000	0/0	0	0	0	0	0	0	.000
BOND, W.	28	1/5	.200	0/0	.000	2/6	.333	2/5	3	1	2	3	1	4	.143
MARTIN, B.	4	0/1	.000	0/0	.000	2/2	1.000	0/0	0	0	0	0	0	2	.500
Totals	225	22/66	.333	7/20	.350	13/20	.650	13/26	14	10	21	12	1	64	.284

UTEP (61)
Coach: Don Haskins

	Min.	Total FG/FGA	Pct.	3-Pt. FG/FGA	Pct.	FT/FTA	Pct.	Reb. O/T	A	TO	PF	S	Blk	TP	PPM
MAXEY, M.	37	6/11	.545	0/0	.000	5/6	.833	3/5	0	2	3	1	2	17	.459
DAVIS, A.	38	5/6	.833	0/0	.000	2/3	.667	3/11	1	3	2	0	1	12	.316
FOSTER, G.	34	2/6	.333	0/0	.000	0/1	.000	3/6	0	2	2	0	2	4	.118
STEWART, P.	44	3/9	.333	0/1	.000	2/3	.667	1/6	5	7	3	1	0	8	.182
HALL, H.	40	4/8	.500	3/5	.600	5/6	.833	0/3	0	4	5	0	0	16	.400
MCCALL, T.	17	0/1	.000	0/0	.000	0/0	.000	0/0	0	2	1	2	0	0	.000
EZENWA, F.	1	0/0	.000	0/0	.000	0/0	.000	0/0	0	0	0	0	0	0	.000
VAN, D.	14	0/1	.000	0/0	.000	4/4	1.000	1/5	0	3	4	2	2	4	.286
Totals	225	20/42	.476	3/6	.500	18/23	.783	11/36	6	23	20	6	7	61	.271

Team Rebounds: UTEP 3; Minnesota 5. Disqualified: UTEP—Hall. Technical fouls: None.

		1st Half	2nd Half	1st OT	Final
Minnesota		24	29	11	64
UTEP		23	30	8	61

Missouri (71)
Coach: Norm Stewart

	Min.	Total FG/FGA	Pct.	3-Pt. FG/FGA	Pct.	FT/FTA	Pct.	Reb. O/T	A	TO	PF	S	Blk	TP	PPM
MCINTYRE, J.	35	3/7	.429	3/5	.600	0/0	.000	0/2	1	1	4	2	0	9	.257
SMITH, D.	30	9/17	.529	0/0	.000	2/4	.500	5/12	2	2	5	0	1	20	.667
BUNTIN, D.	28	6/14	.429	0/0	.000	9/9	1.000	3/7	2	1	2	1	0	21	.750
COWARD, L.	29	5/11	.455	0/4	.000	0/0	.000	0/4	4	1	4	1	0	10	.345
PEELER, A.	28	1/7	.143	0/0	.000	1/2	.500	1/3	1	2	1	2	1	3	.107
FORD, T.	25	1/3	.333	1/2	.500	0/0	.000	0/0	2	0	1	0	0	3	.120
HORTON, J.	2	0/0	.000	0/0	.000	0/0	.000	0/0	0	0	1	0	0	0	.000
COLEMAN, J.	3	0/0	.000	0/0	.000	0/0	.000	0/0	0	0	1	0	0	0	.000
WARREN, J.	20	1/2	.500	0/0	.000	3/5	.600	2/3	0	0	3	0	0	5	.250
Totals	200	26/61	.426	4/11	.364	15/20	.750	11/31	12	7	22	6	2	71	.355

Northern Iowa (74)
Coach: Eldon Miller

	Min.	Total FG/FGA	Pct.	3-Pt. FG/FGA	Pct.	FT/FTA	Pct.	Reb. O/T	A	TO	PF	S	Blk	TP	PPM
MCCULLOUGH, C.	29	3/8	.375	0/0	.000	0/0	.000	3/4	0	1	3	0	0	6	.207
PHYFE, S.	25	1/2	.500	0/0	.000	0/0	.000	1/4	3	3	3	2	0	2	.080
REESE, J.	28	6/12	.500	0/0	.000	6/8	.750	4/15	2	2	5	0	0	18	.643
TURNER, D.	29	3/6	.500	1/3	.333	3/5	.600	0/3	6	1	0	0	0	10	.345
MULLENBERG, T.	33	5/9	.556	2/5	.400	4/6	.667	0/1	1	1	1	0	0	16	.485
NEWBY, M.	13	3/5	.600	3/4	.750	0/0	.000	0/0	0	2	0	0	0	9	.692
COX, J.	12	1/1	1.000	0/0	.000	0/0	.000	0/1	3	0	3	1	0	2	.167
HILL, B.	26	3/6	.500	3/3	1.000	2/4	.500	2/5	2	2	2	0	0	11	.423
PACE, N.	1	0/0	.000	0/0	.000	0/0	.000	0/0	0	0	0	0	0	0	.000
JOHNSON, C.	4	0/1	.000	0/1	.000	0/0	.000	0/0	1	0	1	0	0	0	.000
Totals	200	25/50	.500	9/16	.563	15/24	.625	10/33	18	12	18	3	0	74	.370

Team Rebounds: Northern Iowa 0; Missouri 4. Disqualified: Northern Iowa—Reese; Missouri—Smith. Technical fouls: Missouri—Smith.

		1st Half	2nd Half	Final
Missouri		31	40	71
Northern Iowa		42	32	74

Virginia (75)
Coach: Terry Holland

	Min.	Total FG/FGA	Pct.	3-Pt. FG/FGA	Pct.	FT/FTA	Pct.	Reb. O/T	A	TO	PF	S	Blk	TP	PPM
TURNER, K.	35	4/10	.400	1/2	.500	2/3	.667	3/9	2	2	2	0	0	11	.314
STITH, B.	38	7/14	.500	0/1	.000	7/9	.778	5/7	1	1	1	1	0	21	.553
JEFFRIES, T.	14	2/4	.500	0/0	.000	0/0	.000	3/6	0	2	2	1	0	4	.286
OLIVER, A.	33	1/4	.250	0/0	.000	1/2	.500	0/0	3	0	2	1	0	3	.091
CROTTY, J.	35	8/13	.615	1/6	.167	11/13	.846	1/1	5	0	3	0	0	28	.800
KIRBY, T.	7	0/0	.000	0/0	.000	0/0	.000	0/0	0	0	0	0	0	0	.000
SMITH, D.	5	1/1	1.000	0/0	.000	0/0	.000	0/0	0	0	1	0	0	2	.400
BLUNDIN, M.	33	3/6	.500	0/0	.000	0/0	.000	3/6	0	1	3	0	0	6	.182
Totals	200	26/52	.500	2/9	.222	21/27	.778	15/29	11	6	14	3	0	75	.375

Notre Dame (67)
Coach: Digger Phelps

	Min.	Total FG/FGA	Pct.	3-Pt. FG/FGA	Pct.	FT/FTA	Pct.	Reb. O/T	A	TO	PF	S	Blk	TP	PPM
ELLIS, L.	39	4/9	.444	0/0	.000	1/2	.500	3/10	0	5	5	0	3	9	.231
ELLERY, K.	14	4/7	.571	2/2	1.000	0/0	.000	2/2	0	2	3	0	0	10	.714
ROBINSON, K.	24	4/5	.800	0/0	.000	3/3	1.000	1/3	0	2	4	1	0	11	.458
BENNETT, E.	32	7/14	.500	0/2	.000	3/4	.750	0/0	9	2	4	0	0	17	.531
SWEET, D.	27	7/9	.778	0/0	.000	0/0	.000	0/1	1	1	2	0	0	14	.519
FREDERICK, J.	13	0/0	.000	0/0	.000	0/0	.000	0/2	0	0	0	0	0	0	.000
SINGLETON, T.	10	0/2	.000	0/0	.000	0/0	.000	0/0	2	0	0	0	0	0	.000
WILLIAMS, M.	26	3/5	.600	0/0	.000	0/0	.000	1/2	2	1	5	0	0	6	.231
JACKSON, J.	2	0/0	.000	0/0	.000	0/0	.000	0/0	0	0	0	0	0	0	.000
PADDOCK, S.	13	0/0	.000	0/0	.000	0/0	.000	0/0	0	0	1	0	0	0	.000
Totals	200	29/51	.569	2/4	.500	7/9	.778	7/20	14	8	24	1	3	67	.335

Team Rebounds: Virginia 4; Notre Dame 2. Disqualified: Notre Dame—Ellis, Williams. Technical fouls: None.

		1st Half	2nd Half	Final
Virginia		32	43	75
Notre Dame		18	49	67

Syracuse (70)
Coach: Jim Boeheim

	Min.	Total FG/FGA	Pct.	3-Pt. FG/FGA	Pct.	FT/FTA	Pct.	Reb. O/T	A	TO	PF	S	Blk	TP	PPM
OWENS, B.	38	6/13	.462	0/1	.000	3/3	1.000	6/10	3	3	3	4	0	15	.395
SCOTT, T.	18	2/6	.333	2/4	.500	0/0	.000	0/3	1	3	3	0	0	6	.333
COLEMAN, D.	38	5/8	.625	1/2	.500	3/4	.750	2/12	4	4	3	0	0	14	.368
EDWARDS, M.	32	2/6	.333	1/3	.333	2/2	1.000	1/2	4	2	1	0	0	7	.219
THOMPSON, S.	34	8/11	.727	0/1	.000	3/4	.750	1/4	3	3	0	1	0	19	.559
JOHNSON, D.	20	2/6	.333	0/0	.000	5/7	.714	1/5	2	1	1	0	0	9	.450
MCRAE, C.	2	0/0	.000	0/0	.000	0/0	.000	0/0	0	0	0	0	1	0	.000
ELLIS, L.	2	0/0	.000	0/0	.000	0/0	.000	0/0	0	0	0	0	0	0	.000
HOPKINS, M.	4	0/0	.000	0/0	.000	0/0	.000	0/1	0	1	0	0	0	0	.000
MANNING, R.	12	0/3	.000	0/0	.000	0/0	.000	2/6	0	2	2	0	0	0	.000
Totals	200	25/53	.472	4/11	.364	16/20	.800	13/42	18	18	14	5	1	70	.350

Coppin State (48)
Coach: Ron Mitchell

	Min.	Total FG/FGA	Pct.	3-Pt. FG/FGA	Pct.	FT/FTA	Pct.	Reb. O/T	A	TO	PF	S	Blk	TP	PPM
BOOTH, P.	33	4/12	.333	0/0	.000	1/2	.500	3/5	1	6	5	2	0	9	.273
STEWART, L.	40	7/15	.467	0/0	.000	5/7	.714	6/12	3	1	4	3	2	19	.475
MCCOLLUM, L.	19	1/2	.500	0/0	.000	0/0	.000	3/3	1	0	5	0	0	2	.105
YARBRAY, L.	37	0/3	.000	0/0	.000	2/2	1.000	0/1	2	2	1	2	0	2	.054
ISSAAC, R.	36	3/20	.150	0/8	.000	0/1	.000	1/3	2	2	4	2	0	6	.167
ORR, D.	21	1/9	.111	1/6	.167	0/0	.000	0/2	0	0	1	0	0	3	.143
WOODS, D.	1	0/0	.000	0/0	.000	0/0	.000	0/0	0	0	0	0	0	0	.000
REED, D.	8	2/2	1.000	1/1	1.000	0/0	.000	0/1	0	0	0	0	0	5	.625
HAMMOND, J.	5	1/1	1.000	0/0	.000	0/0	.000	1/1	0	0	0	0	0	2	.400
Totals	200	19/64	.297	2/15	.133	8/12	.667	14/28	9	11	20	9	2	48	.240

Team Rebounds: Syracuse 3; Coppin State 1. Disqualified: Coppin State—Booth, McCollum. Technical fouls: None.

		1st Half	2nd Half	Final
Syracuse		31	39	70
Coppin State		21	27	48

FIRST ROUND WEST

UNLV (102)　Coach: Jerry Tarkanian

	Min.	Total FG/FGA	Pct.	3-Pt. FG/FGA	Pct.	FT/FTA	Pct.	Reb. O/T	A	TO	PF	S	Blk	TP	PPM
JOHNSON, L.	23	3/4	.750	0/0	.000	7/10	.700	0/12	0	4	3	0	4	13	.565
AUGMON, S.	23	7/12	.583	0/1	.000	2/3	.667	3/7	4	4	2	2	2	16	.696
BUTLER, D.	27	5/10	.500	0/0	.000	4/5	.800	3/7	1	1	3	0	0	14	.519
HUNT, A.	21	4/10	.400	1/6	.167	2/2	1.000	0/1	4	1	0	0	0	11	.524
ANTHONY, G.	20	0/1	.000	0/1	.000	0/0	.000	2/6	4	3	3	0	0	0	.000
CVIJANOVICH, S.	18	0/1	.000	0/1	.000	0/0	.000	0/1	5	1	3	0	0	0	.000
BICE, T.	16	5/10	.500	2/6	.333	0/0	.000	1/2	5	1	3	0	0	12	.750
RICE, D.	5	1/3	.333	1/3	.333	0/0	.000	0/1	0	0	0	0	0	3	.600
YOUNG, B.	17	4/11	.364	2/5	.400	2/2	1.000	3/6	2	0	2	0	0	12	.706
JONES, J.	11	4/4	1.000	0/0	.000	5/6	.833	2/4	0	1	4	0	1	13	1.182
SCURRY, M.	14	4/5	.800	0/0	.000	0/1	.000	1/4	3	4	3	0	0	8	.571
JETER, C.	5	0/0	.000	0/0	.000	0/0	.000	0/0	0	0	1	0	1	0	.000
Totals	200	37/71	.521	6/23	.261	22/29	.759	15/51	28	20	27	2	8	102	.510

Arkansas-Little Rock (72)　Coach: Mike Newell

	Min.	Total FG/FGA	Pct.	3-Pt. FG/FGA	Pct.	FT/FTA	Pct.	Reb. O/T	A	TO	PF	S	Blk	TP	PPM
OWENS, D.	35	7/20	.350	2/8	.250	1/4	.250	3/5	3	3	3	0	0	17	.486
WOMACK, J.	19	2/7	.286	0/0	.000	2/2	1.000	2/4	0	1	5	0	0	6	.316
WADE, R.	39	3/8	.375	0/1	.000	8/14	.571	4/7	2	2	3	0	1	14	.359
SCOTT, J.	34	8/14	.571	2/2	1.000	5/6	.833	4/6	2	3	4	1	0	23	.676
BROWN, C.	38	2/17	.118	1/7	.143	0/1	.000	1/4	4	5	1	1	0	5	.132
JOHNSON, J.	1	0/0	.000	0/0	.000	0/0	.000	0/0	1	0	0	0	0	0	.000
HALL, D.	12	1/4	.250	1/4	.250	2/2	1.000	2/3	2	1	0	1	0	5	.417
HALL, D.	5	0/2	.000	0/1	.000	0/0	.000	0/0	1	0	0	0	0	0	.000
TOOLEY, T.	1	0/1	.000	0/0	.000	0/0	.000	1/1	0	0	0	0	0	0	.000
JONES, T.	16	1/2	.500	0/0	.000	0/2	.000	4/9	0	5	0	1	2	2	.125
Totals	200	24/75	.320	6/23	.261	18/31	.581	21/39	15	15	21	3	2	72	.360

Team Rebounds: UNLV 0; Ark.-Little Rock 2. Disqualified: Ark.-Little Rock—Womack, Jones. Technical fouls: Ark.-Little Rock—Coach Newell.

	1st Half	2nd Half	Final
UNLV	44	58	102
Ark.-Little Rock	25	47	72

Ohio State (84)　Coach: Randy Ayers

	Min.	Total FG/FGA	Pct.	3-Pt. FG/FGA	Pct.	FT/FTA	Pct.	Reb. O/T	A	TO	PF	S	Blk	TP	PPM
JENT, C.	35	2/8	.250	0/4	.000	0/0	.000	-/5	2	2	2	2	0	4	.114
JACKSON, J.	41	5/15	.333	0/2	.000	5/6	.833	-/5	5	4	2	0	0	15	.366
CARTER, P.	24	7/10	.700	0/0	.000	1/1	1.000	-/6	3	2	5	0	0	15	.625
BAKER, M.	44	6/9	.667	0/0	.000	5/6	.833	-/7	8	5	2	1	0	17	.386
BROWN, J.	19	0/2	.000	0/0	.000	3/4	.750	-/1	2	1	0	1	0	3	.158
DAVIS, A.	27	9/12	.750	3/4	.750	3/3	1.000	-/2	1	1	2	0	0	24	.889
LEE, T.	9	0/1	.000	0/0	.000	0/0	.000	-/3	0	0	0	0	0	0	.000
ROBINSON, B.	26	3/5	.600	0/0	.000	0/0	.000	-/9	0	2	2	1	2	6	.231
Totals	225	32/62	.516	3/10	.300	17/20	.850	-/38	21	17	15	5	2	84	.373

Providence (83)　Coach: Rick Barnes

	Min.	Total FG/FGA	Pct.	3-Pt. FG/FGA	Pct.	FT/FTA	Pct.	Reb. O/T	A	TO	PF	S	Blk	TP	PPM
BURTON, Q.	40	5/9	.556	1/3	.333	1/2	.500	-/3	3	1	3	0	0	12	.300
CONLON, M.	36	7/14	.500	0/2	.000	0/1	.000	-/8	4	3	3	1	0	14	.389
SHAMSID-DEEN, A.	31	6/10	.600	0/0	.000	0/0	.000	-/10	2	2	1	1	0	12	.387
SCREEN, C.	39	6/12	.500	2/3	.667	6/7	.857	-/1	5	4	5	0	0	20	.513
WATTS, S.	24	3/7	.429	2/5	.400	0/0	.000	-/1	2	0	0	5	0	8	.333
MURDOCK, E.	32	7/18	.389	2/5	.400	1/2	.500	-/6	4	3	2	5	0	17	.531
BENT, G.	6	0/1	.000	0/0	.000	0/0	.000	-/1	0	0	2	0	0	0	.000
BRAGG, M.	17	0/0	.000	0/0	.000	0/0	.000	-/3	1	3	4	0	1	0	.000
Totals	225	34/71	.479	7/18	.389	8/12	.667	-/33	21	16	20	12	1	83	.369

Team Rebounds: Ohio State 3; Providence 1. Disqualified: Ohio State—Carter; Providence—Screen. Technical fouls: None.

	1st Half	2nd Half	1st OT	Final
Ohio State	31	41	12	84
Providence	29	43	11	83

Oregon State (53)　Coach: Jim Anderson

	Min.	Total FG/FGA	Pct.	3-Pt. FG/FGA	Pct.	FT/FTA	Pct.	Reb. O/T	A	TO	PF	S	Blk	TP	PPM
ALIBEGOVIC, T.	27	3/7	.429	0/1	.000	1/2	.500	2/4	0	0	0	0	0	7	.259
MARTIN, E.	16	2/4	.500	1/1	1.000	1/2	.500	0/1	0	2	1	2	0	6	.375
HASKIN, S.	28	3/11	.273	0/0	.000	3/3	1.000	5/6	0	6	4	1	1	9	.321
PAYTON, G.	28	3/12	.250	1/4	.250	4/4	1.000	1/5	3	3	5	2	0	11	.393
BRANTLEY, W.	26	3/10	.300	0/0	.000	0/0	.000	1/5	1	1	2	1	0	6	.231
CAVELL, B.	12	1/3	.333	1/2	.500	0/0	.000	1/4	0	1	3	0	1	3	.250
ANDERSON, K.	13	1/3	.333	0/0	.000	0/0	.000	2/6	0	1	2	0	0	2	.154
MCKINNEY, C.	30	3/8	.375	3/5	.600	0/1	.000	0/4	1	0	3	0	0	9	.300
CELESTINE, A.	20	0/3	.000	0/1	.000	0/0	.000	1/1	6	0	1	1	0	0	.000
Totals	200	19/61	.311	6/14	.429	9/12	.750	13/36	11	14	21	7	2	53	.265

Ball State (54)　Coach: Dick Hunsaker

	Min.	Total FG/FGA	Pct.	3-Pt. FG/FGA	Pct.	FT/FTA	Pct.	Reb. O/T	A	TO	PF	S	Blk	TP	PPM
THOMPSON, C.	31	9/15	.600	0/1	.000	6/8	.750	3/13	0	1	3	2	0	24	.774
MCCURDY, P.	25	3/11	.273	0/0	.000	3/3	1.000	2/9	3	5	4	0	0	9	.360
KIDD, C.	31	3/10	.300	0/0	.000	3/4	.750	6/12	0	1	4	0	1	9	.290
NICHOLS, S.	21	0/0	.000	0/0	.000	0/0	.000	0/0	5	2	4	0	0	0	.000
BUTTS, B.	35	2/8	.250	2/6	.333	1/2	.500	0/6	2	4	0	2	0	7	.200
SPICER, M.	15	0/0	.000	0/0	.000	1/2	.500	0/0	2	0	0	0	0	1	.067
MILLER, G.	15	1/5	.200	1/3	.333	1/2	.500	1/1	1	1	1	0	0	4	.267
MULLER, S.	9	0/2	.000	0/0	.000	0/0	.000	0/0	0	0	0	0	0	0	.000
PARRISH, S.	11	0/1	.000	0/0	.000	0/0	.000	1/1	0	0	0	0	0	0	.000
CROSS, E.	7	0/1	.000	0/0	.000	0/0	.000	0/0	0	1	0	0	0	0	.000
Totals	200	18/53	.340	3/10	.300	15/21	.714	13/42	13	15	16	4	1	54	.270

Team Rebounds: Ball St. 2; Oregon State 3. Disqualified: Oregon State—Payton. Technical fouls: None.

	1st Half	2nd Half	Final
Oregon State	30	23	53
Ball St.	29	25	54

Louisville (78)　Coach: Denny Crum

	Min.	Total FG/FGA	Pct.	3-Pt. FG/FGA	Pct.	FT/FTA	Pct.	Reb. O/T	A	TO	PF	S	Blk	TP	PPM
HOLDEN, C.	18	0/2	.000	0/0	.000	0/0	.000	1/1	0	1	4	1	0	0	.000
SULLIVAN, E.	30	8/12	.667	2/4	.500	0/0	.000	2/7	4	1	0	2	0	18	.600
SPENCER, F.	35	6/11	.545	0/0	.000	5/7	.714	2/6	2	2	3	0	2	17	.486
WILLIAMS, K.	34	5/7	.714	0/1	.000	0/1	.000	0/3	5	4	2	0	0	10	.294
SMITH, L.	33	5/10	.500	0/1	.000	6/6	1.000	1/6	3	3	2	2	0	16	.485
CASE, M.	1	0/0	.000	0/0	.000	0/0	.000	0/1	0	0	0	0	0	0	.000
HAWLEY, C.	1	0/0	.000	0/0	.000	0/0	.000	0/0	0	0	0	0	0	0	.000
WEBB, D.	1	0/0	.000	0/0	.000	0/0	.000	0/0	0	0	0	0	0	0	.000
HOWARD, T.	1	0/0	.000	0/0	.000	0/0	.000	0/0	0	0	0	0	0	0	.000
SMITH, T.	1	0/1	.000	0/0	.000	0/0	.000	0/0	0	0	0	0	0	0	.000
HARMON, J.	18	6/9	.667	0/0	.000	3/4	.750	1/2	0	1	0	1	0	15	.833
KIMBRO, T.	27	1/6	.167	0/1	.000	0/1	.000	1/6	2	0	2	0	1	2	.074
Totals	200	31/58	.534	2/7	.286	14/19	.737	8/32	16	12	13	6	5	78	.390

Idaho (59)　Coach: Kermit Davis Jr.

	Min.	Total FG/FGA	Pct.	3-Pt. FG/FGA	Pct.	FT/FTA	Pct.	Reb. O/T	A	TO	PF	S	Blk	TP	PPM
MARTIN, C.	22	3/7	.429	0/0	.000	0/0	.000	2/3	3	1	5	1	1	6	.273
BOYD, R.	37	3/13	.231	0/4	.000	0/2	.000	2/4	3	1	2	0	0	6	.162
SMITH, R.	26	11/18	.611	0/0	.000	6/8	.750	4/12	0	2	5	3	0	28	1.077
LEONARD, P.	22	0/3	.000	0/0	.000	0/0	.000	1/2	1	1	1	1	0	0	.000
HENDERSON, D.	4	0/0	.000	0/0	.000	1/2	.500	0/2	0	1	0	0	0	1	.250
PRELOW, C.	2	0/1	.000	0/0	.000	0/0	.000	0/1	0	0	0	0	0	0	.000
SHEILDS, P.	16	3/6	.500	2/4	.500	0/0	.000	0/0	0	3	3	1	0	8	.500
GUSTAVEL, M.	3	0/2	.000	0/0	.000	0/0	.000	0/0	0	0	0	0	0	0	.000
FOOTE, S.	4	0/0	.000	0/0	.000	0/0	.000	1/1	0	1	1	0	0	0	.000
AKINS, D.	2	0/0	.000	0/0	.000	0/0	.000	0/0	0	0	0	0	0	0	.000
FREEMAN, S.	26	5/7	.714	0/0	.000	0/0	.000	0/6	2	1	1	0	0	10	.385
LIVINGSTON, O.	36	0/2	.000	0/0	.000	0/0	.000	0/2	12	6	5	2	0	0	.000
Totals	200	25/59	.424	2/8	.250	7/12	.583	10/33	21	17	23	8	1	59	.295

Team Rebounds: Louisville 2; Idaho 2. Disqualified: Idaho—Martin, Smith, Livingston. Technical fouls: None.

	1st Half	2nd Half	Final
Louisville	36	42	78
Idaho	19	40	59

New Mexico State (92) Coach: Neil McCarthy

	Min.	Total FG/FGA	Pct.	3-Pt. FG/FGA	Pct.	FT/FTA	Pct.	Reb. O/T	A	TO	PF	S	Blk	TP	PPM
JORDAN, R.	32	11/16	.688	0/ 0	.000	0/ 0	.000	2/ 5	2	3	3	0	1	22	.688
NEW, M.	32	5/ 6	.833	0/ 0	.000	4/ 7	.571	0/ 2	3	3	2	0	0	14	.438
ANDERSON, J.	36	6/13	.462	1/ 1	1.000	3/ 6	.500	2/ 5	2	2	3	2	0	16	.444
BROWN, R.	36	4/ 7	.571	0/ 0	.000	0/ 1	.000	1/ 6	6	7	4	4	0	8	.222
HILL, K.	26	3/ 6	.500	0/ 2	.000	3/ 4	.750	1/ 3	6	6	4	0	0	9	.346
FLUCKEY, R.	12	2/ 8	.250	1/ 7	.143	2/ 2	1.000	0/ 2	0	1	4	1	0	7	.583
BENJAMIN, W.	20	4/ 9	.444	2/ 4	.500	2/ 3	.667	2/ 5	3	2	0	3	0	12	.600
PUTZI, R.	1	0/ 0	.000	0/ 0	.000	0/ 0	.000	0/ 0	0	0	0	0	0	0	.000
IRELAND, A.	1	0/ 0	.000	0/ 0	.000	0/ 0	.000	0/ 0	1	0	0	0	0	0	.000
TRASK, J.	2	2/ 2	1.000	0/ 0	.000	0/ 1	.000	0/ 0	0	0	1	0	1	4	2.000
ACRE, M.	1	0/ 1	.000	0/ 1	.000	0/ 0	.000	0/ 0	0	0	0	0	0	0	.000
HICKMAN, C.	1	0/ 0	.000	0/ 0	.000	0/ 0	.000	0/ 0	0	0	1	0	0	0	.000
Totals	200	37/68	.544	4/15	.267	14/24	.583	8/28	23	24	22	10	2	92	.460

Loyola Marymount (111) Coach: Paul Westhead

	Min.	Total FG/FGA	Pct.	3-Pt. FG/FGA	Pct.	FT/FTA	Pct.	Reb. O/T	A	TO	PF	S	Blk	TP	PPM
STUMER, P.	33	3/ 3	1.000	1/ 1	1.000	4/ 4	1.000	1/ 7	3	3	2	0	0	11	.333
KIMBLE, B.	36	17/35	.486	5/ 9	.556	6/ 6	1.000	12/18	2	3	4	3	0	45	1.250
KNIGHT, C.	22	2/ 5	.400	0/ 0	.000	2/ 2	1.000	3/ 8	5	2	3	0	0	6	.273
WALKER, T.	28	2/ 4	.500	0/ 0	.000	0/ 2	.000	0/ 0	5	2	4	4	0	4	.143
FRYER, J.	33	8/19	.421	5/14	.357	2/ 2	1.000	2/ 6	1	0	3	3	0	23	.697
PEABODY, T.	18	2/ 3	.667	0/ 0	.000	0/ 0	.000	2/ 4	3	4	3	1	0	4	.222
LOWERY, T.	17	3/10	.300	0/ 4	.000	2/ 2	1.000	0/ 1	1	6	5	1	0	8	.471
SCOTT, C.	6	3/ 6	.500	0/ 0	.000	0/ 0	.000	2/ 4	1	0	3	0	0	6	1.000
LEE, M.	1	0/ 0	.000	0/ 0	.000	0/ 0	.000	0/ 0	0	0	0	0	0	0	.000
WALKER, G.	2	0/ 2	.000	0/ 0	.000	2/ 2	1.000	0/ 0	0	0	0	0	0	2	1.000
O'CONNELL, J.	2	0/ 0	.000	0/ 0	.000	2/ 2	1.000	1/ 1	0	0	0	0	0	2	1.000
ROSCOE, J.	1	0/ 0	.000	0/ 0	.000	0/ 0	.000	0/ 0	0	0	0	0	0	0	.000
SLATER, M.	1	0/ 0	.000	0/ 0	.000	0/ 0	.000	0/ 0	0	0	0	0	0	0	.000
Totals	200	40/87	.460	11/28	.393	20/22	.909	23/49	21	20	27	12	0	111	.555

Team Rebounds: Loyola Mymt 2; New Mexico St. 7. Disqualified: Loyola Mymt—Lowery. Technical fouls: None.

	1st Half	2nd Half	Final
New Mexico St.	46	46	92
Loyola Mymt.	46	65	111

Michigan (76) Coach: Steve Fisher

	Min.	Total FG/FGA	Pct.	3-Pt. FG/FGA	Pct.	FT/FTA	Pct.	Reb. O/T	A	TO	PF	S	Blk	TP	PPM
GRIFFIN, M.	25	1/ 5	.200	0/ 0	.000	0/ 0	.000	1/ 3	1	1	2	1	1	2	.080
VAUGHT, L.	33	6/11	.545	0/ 0	.000	6/ 8	.750	5/21	1	1	2	1	3	18	.545
MILLS, T.	34	3/15	.200	0/ 0	.000	1/ 2	.500	3/11	6	3	4	3	1	7	.206
CALIP, D.	29	6/12	.500	0/ 0	.000	1/ 3	.333	2/ 4	2	1	3	1	0	13	.448
ROBINSON, R.	37	9/17	.529	1/ 3	.333	5/ 9	.556	0/ 4	8	3	2	1	0	24	.649
TALLEY, M.	4	0/ 0	.000	0/ 0	.000	0/ 0	.000	0/ 0	0	0	0	0	0	0	.000
HIGGINS, S.	25	4/10	.400	2/ 5	.400	0/ 0	.000	1/ 2	1	2	2	0	0	10	.400
RILEY, E.	12	1/ 2	.500	0/ 0	.000	0/ 0	.000	2/ 4	0	2	4	1	2	2	.167
SETER, C.	1	0/ 0	.000	0/ 0	.000	0/ 0	.000	0/ 0	0	0	0	0	0	0	.000
Totals	200	30/72	.417	3/ 8	.375	13/22	.591	14/49	19	13	19	8	7	76	.380

Illinois State (70) Coach: Bob Bender

	Min.	Total FG/FGA	Pct.	3-Pt. FG/FGA	Pct.	FT/FTA	Pct.	Reb. O/T	A	TO	PF	S	Blk	TP	PPM
FOWLER, S.	16	1/ 4	.250	0/ 0	.000	0/ 0	.000	1/ 4	1	1	2	0	0	2	.125
JACKSON, R.	38	8/23	.348	5/12	.417	1/ 1	1.000	2/ 5	2	5	2	3	1	22	.579
COLEMAN, J.	33	8/17	.471	0/ 0	.000	2/ 4	.500	5/10	0	0	2	2	0	18	.545
THOMAS, R.	33	5/11	.455	0/ 1	.000	2/ 2	1.000	4/ 5	3	2	2	1	0	12	.364
BLAIR, R.	31	2/14	.143	0/ 3	.000	0/ 0	.000	4/12	9	0	3	1	0	4	.129
SKARICH, S.	1	0/ 0	.000	0/ 0	.000	0/ 0	.000	0/ 0	0	0	0	0	0	0	.000
HICKS, A.	7	0/ 1	.000	0/ 1	.000	0/ 0	.000	0/ 1	1	1	1	0	0	0	.000
WILLIAMS, X.	1	0/ 2	.000	0/ 0	.000	0/ 0	.000	1/ 1	0	0	0	0	0	0	.000
FLOREZ, E.	9	1/ 2	.500	1/ 2	.500	0/ 0	.000	1/ 1	0	2	0	0	0	3	.333
ROBERTS, S.	9	0/ 1	.000	0/ 0	.000	0/ 0	.000	0/ 1	0	0	3	0	0	0	.000
PEMBERTON, J.	22	3/ 7	.429	0/ 0	.000	3/ 4	.750	3/11	0	0	3	0	0	9	.409
Totals	200	28/82	.341	6/19	.316	8/11	.727	21/51	16	11	18	7	1	70	.350

Team Rebounds: Michigan 2; Illinois State 3. Disqualified: None. Technical fouls: None.

	1st Half	2nd Half	Final
Michigan	37	39	76
Illinois State	34	36	70

Alabama (71) Coach: Wimp Sanderson

	Min.	Total FG/FGA	Pct.	3-Pt. FG/FGA	Pct.	FT/FTA	Pct.	Reb. O/T	A	TO	PF	S	Blk	TP	PPM
HORRY, R.	35	10/14	.714	6/ 8	.750	1/ 3	.333	0/ 3	2	1	1	3	2	27	.771
CHEATUM, M.	36	3/ 5	.600	0/ 0	.000	0/ 0	.000	0/ 1	1	5	2	0	2	6	.167
BENOIT, D.	31	3/ 6	.500	0/ 0	.000	0/ 0	.000	1/ 7	2	1	3	0	2	6	.194
WAITES, G.	36	0/ 0	.000	0/ 0	.000	0/ 0	.000	0/ 3	4	1	0	1	0	0	.000
SANDERS, J.	35	7/10	.700	2/ 3	.667	2/ 3	.667	0/ 4	9	1	0	0	0	18	.514
ASKINS, K.	8	0/ 2	.000	0/ 0	.000	0/ 0	.000	1/ 1	0	3	4	0	0	0	.000
WEBB, M.	11	3/ 6	.500	0/ 0	.000	2/ 3	.667	2/ 2	1	0	3	0	0	8	.727
RICE, K.	1	0/ 0	.000	0/ 0	.000	2/ 2	1.000	0/ 1	0	1	0	0	0	2	2.000
BROWN, E.	2	1/ 1	1.000	0/ 0	.000	0/ 0	.000	0/ 0	0	0	1	1	0	2	1.000
LANCASTER, B.	1	1/ 1	1.000	0/ 0	.000	0/ 0	.000	0/ 0	0	1	0	0	0	2	2.000
RICH, D.	1	0/ 0	.000	0/ 0	.000	0/ 0	.000	0/ 0	0	0	0	0	0	0	.000
CAMPBELL, M.	2	0/ 0	.000	0/ 0	.000	0/ 0	.000	0/ 0	0	1	0	0	0	0	.000
LAWRENCE, A.	1	0/ 0	.000	0/ 0	.000	0/ 0	.000	0/ 0	1	1	0	0	0	0	.000
Totals	200	28/45	.622	8/11	.727	7/11	.636	4/22	20	16	14	5	6	71	.355

Colorado State (54) Coach: Boyd Grant

	Min.	Total FG/FGA	Pct.	3-Pt. FG/FGA	Pct.	FT/FTA	Pct.	Reb. O/T	A	TO	PF	S	Blk	TP	PPM
MITCHELL, M.	40	11/20	.550	1/ 4	.250	1/ 3	.333	3/ 8	5	4	2	3	0	24	.600
ANDERSON, A.	18	0/ 1	.000	0/ 0	.000	0/ 0	.000	0/ 1	4	2	1	0	0	0	.000
FRIEHAUF, E.	25	0/ 3	.000	0/ 0	.000	1/ 2	.500	2/ 4	2	1	3	1	0	1	.040
MEREDITH, M.	37	5/ 8	.625	5/ 7	.714	0/ 0	.000	0/ 1	1	2	2	0	0	15	.405
TRYON, L.	36	4/11	.364	0/ 3	.000	0/ 0	.000	2/ 4	2	1	0	1	0	8	.222
POLK, D.	4	0/ 1	.000	0/ 1	.000	0/ 0	.000	0/ 0	0	0	4	0	0	0	.000
WILSON, C.	7	0/ 0	.000	0/ 0	.000	0/ 0	.000	0/ 0	1	1	1	0	0	0	.000
JORDAN, T.	7	1/ 2	.500	0/ 0	.000	2/ 2	1.000	1/ 3	2	1	2	0	0	4	.571
MOLYNEAUX, D.	9	0/ 1	.000	0/ 0	.000	0/ 2	.000	0/ 0	1	1	1	0	0	0	.000
HINES, J.	3	0/ 1	.000	0/ 0	.000	0/ 0	.000	0/ 0	0	0	0	0	0	0	.000
SHARP, M.	14	1/ 1	1.000	0/ 0	.000	0/ 0	.000	0/ 1	1	2	2	0	0	2	.143
Totals	200	22/49	.449	6/15	.400	4/ 9	.444	8/22	19	15	18	5	0	54	.270

Team Rebounds: Alabama 6; Colorado State 1. Disqualified: None. Technical fouls: None.

	1st Half	2nd Half	Final
Alabama	33	38	71
Colorado State	22	32	54

Arizona (79) Coach: Lute Olson

	Min.	Total FG/FGA	Pct.	3-Pt. FG/FGA	Pct.	FT/FTA	Pct.	Reb. O/T	A	TO	PF	S	Blk	TP	PPM
WILLIAMS, B.	28	12/15	.800	0/ 0	.000	4/ 7	.571	2/ 7	0	0	2	0	1	28	1.000
BUECHLER, J.	39	5/ 9	.556	0/ 1	.000	6/ 7	.857	1/ 5	7	3	1	2	0	16	.410
STOKES, E.	26	2/ 7	.286	0/ 0	.000	0/ 0	.000	2/ 5	1	2	2	0	2	4	.154
OTHICK, M.	35	2/ 5	.400	2/ 3	.667	2/ 2	1.000	1/ 4	10	2	1	0	0	8	.229
MUEHLEBACH, M.	35	4/ 6	.667	1/ 2	.500	1/ 2	.500	0/ 3	4	2	3	0	0	10	.286
ROOKS, S.	24	5/11	.455	0/ 0	.000	2/ 5	.400	1/ 2	1	2	2	0	0	12	.500
SCHMIDT, C.	2	0/ 0	.000	0/ 0	.000	0/ 0	.000	0/ 0	0	1	0	0	0	0	.000
WOMACK, W.	10	0/ 1	.000	0/ 0	.000	1/ 2	.500	0/ 1	0	0	2	1	0	1	.100
DAVID, B.	1	0/ 0	.000	0/ 0	.000	0/ 0	.000	0/ 0	0	0	0	0	0	0	.000
Totals	200	30/54	.556	3/ 6	.500	16/25	.640	7/27	23	12	13	3	3	79	.395

South Florida (67) Coach: Bobby Paschal

	Min.	Total FG/FGA	Pct.	3-Pt. FG/FGA	Pct.	FT/FTA	Pct.	Reb. O/T	A	TO	PF	S	Blk	TP	PPM
LEWIS, F.	34	4/ 6	.667	0/ 0	.000	5/ 6	.833	3/ 6	1	0	4	1	0	13	.382
RUSSELL, B.	30	2/ 8	.250	0/ 0	.000	0/ 0	.000	2/ 5	3	2	3	1	0	4	.133
SHAHID, H.	30	5/ 9	.556	0/ 0	.000	1/ 3	.333	6/10	0	3	4	1	0	11	.367
TAYLOR, M.	38	4/17	.235	0/ 2	.000	0/ 0	.000	2/ 6	3	5	0	0	0	8	.211
DOBRAS, R.	37	9/19	.474	1/ 4	.250	3/ 4	.750	2/ 6	5	4	5	3	0	22	.595
SMITH, J.	1	0/ 0	.000	0/ 0	.000	0/ 0	.000	0/ 0	0	0	0	0	0	0	.000
WILLIAMS, S.	1	0/ 0	.000	0/ 0	.000	0/ 0	.000	0/ 0	0	0	0	0	0	0	.000
ARMSTRONG, T.	14	2/ 4	.500	0/ 1	.000	3/ 3	1.000	1/ 2	1	1	0	0	0	7	.500
CRENSHAW, A.	1	0/ 0	.000	0/ 0	.000	0/ 0	.000	0/ 0	0	0	0	0	0	0	.000
WEBSTER, M.	1	0/ 0	.000	0/ 0	.000	0/ 0	.000	0/ 0	0	0	0	0	0	0	.000
BISEY, C.	13	1/ 1	1.000	0/ 0	.000	0/ 0	.000	1/ 1	0	1	3	0	0	2	.154
Totals	200	27/64	.422	1/ 7	.143	12/16	.750	17/36	13	16	19	6	0	67	.335

Team Rebounds: Arizona 3; South Florida 1. Disqualified: South Florida—Dobras. Technical fouls: None.

	1st Half	2nd Half	Final
Arizona	27	52	79
South Florida	32	35	67

FIRST ROUND EAST

U. Conn. (76) Coach: Jim Calhoun

	Min.	Total FG/FGA	Pct.	3-Pt. FG/FGA	Pct.	FT/FTA	Pct.	Reb. O/T	A	TO	PF	S	Blk	TP	PPM
BURRELL, S.	28	2/6	.333	0/0	.000	5/7	.714	4/7	1	1	2	4	1	9	.321
HENEFELD, N.	28	7/16	.438	1/3	.333	4/5	.800	4/7	2	0	2	3	0	19	.679
SELLERS, R.	20	2/3	.667	0/0	.000	0/0	.000	2/7	0	1	2	1	0	4	.200
SMITH, C.	29	5/17	.294	4/7	.571	5/6	.833	3/4	3	3	2	3	0	19	.655
GEORGE, T.	37	4/10	.400	0/2	.000	1/3	.333	1/3	5	2	0	4	1	9	.243
WILLIAMS, M.	5	0/0	.000	0/0	.000	0/0	.000	0/1	0	0	0	0	0	0	.000
GWYNN, J.	19	5/12	.417	0/1	.000	0/2	.000	3/5	0	2	1	1	0	10	.526
WALKER, T.	15	1/3	.333	0/0	.000	2/2	1.000	3/5	0	0	2	1	0	4	.267
CYRULIK, D.	4	0/0	.000	0/0	.000	0/0	.000	0/0	0	0	0	0	0	0	.000
DEPRIEST, L.	14	1/2	.500	0/0	.000	0/1	.000	1/3	1	1	1	2	0	2	.143
PIKIELL, S.	1	0/0	.000	0/0	.000	0/0	.000	0/0	0	0	0	0	0	0	.000
Totals	200	27/69	.391	5/13	.385	17/26	.654	21/42	12	11	12	19	2	76	.380

Clemson (49) Coach: Cliff Ellis

	Min.	Total FG/FGA	Pct.	3-Pt. FG/FGA	Pct.	FT/FTA	Pct.	Reb. O/T	A	TO	PF	S	Blk	TP	PPM
FORREST, D.	37	3/8	.375	0/2	.000	0/1	.000	2/9	1	1	3	1	0	6	.162
DAVIS, D.	34	1/3	.333	0/0	.000	0/1	.000	6/10	0	2	3	2	0	2	.059
CAMPBELL, E.	27	5/9	.556	0/0	.000	5/10	.500	4/7	0	3	3	2	3	15	.556
YOUNG, D.	24	1/6	.167	0/3	.000	0/0	.000	1/3	4	2	2	0	1	2	.083
CASH, M.	28	1/6	.167	1/3	.333	6/8	.750	1/5	2	3	4	1	0	9	.321
HOWLING, K.	9	2/3	.667	2/3	.667	0/0	.000	0/1	0	2	1	0	0	6	.667
TYSON, S.	5	0/1	.000	0/0	.000	0/0	.000	1/3	1	1	0	0	0	0	.000
BROWN, C.	7	0/2	.000	0/0	.000	1/2	.500	1/1	0	0	0	0	1	1	.143
LASTINGER, S.	2	0/1	.000	0/1	.000	0/0	.000	0/0	0	0	0	0	0	0	.000
BUCKINGHAM, W.	14	2/6	.333	0/0	.000	1/4	.250	4/4	0	4	0	0	0	5	.357
JONES, R.	13	1/3	.333	0/0	.000	1/3	.333	1/3	1	0	1	0	1	3	.231
Totals	200	16/48	.333	3/12	.250	14/30	.467	21/46	9	18	17	6	6	49	.245

Boston Univ. (52) Coach: Mike Jarvis

	Min.	Total FG/FGA	Pct.	3-Pt. FG/FGA	Pct.	FT/FTA	Pct.	Reb. O/T	A	TO	PF	S	Blk	TP	PPM
KING, D.	6	0/2	.000	0/0	.000	0/0	.000	0/1	1	2	1	0	0	0	.000
BRIGHAM, B.	29	2/3	.667	0/0	.000	0/0	.000	3/8	0	6	5	0	1	4	.138
MOSES, R.	33	5/9	.556	0/0	.000	0/0	.000	0/8	0	4	2	1	2	10	.303
DALY, M.	25	1/4	.250	1/2	.500	0/0	.000	0/2	2	3	3	0	0	3	.120
KEY, S.	37	7/12	.583	3/3	1.000	0/0	.000	0/1	6	4	2	0	2	17	.459
DAVY, F.	31	3/11	.273	0/0	.000	2/5	.400	5/10	2	3	3	1	0	8	.258
STEWART, J.	21	2/8	.250	0/2	.000	2/2	1.000	1/2	2	3	0	0	0	6	.286
SCOTT, J.	13	1/1	1.000	0/0	.000	0/0	.000	0/1	0	2	2	0	0	2	.154
WHITE, S.	3	0/0	.000	-/0	-	0/0	.000	0/0	0	0	0	0	0	0	.000
OLMSTED, A.	1	0/0	.000	0/0	.000	0/1	.000	0/0	0	0	0	0	0	0	.000
KALITSI, F.	1	1/1	1.000	0/0	.000	0/0	.000	1/1	0	0	0	0	0	2	2.000
Totals	200	22/51	.431	4/7	.571	4/8	.500	10/34	13	27	18	4	3	52	.260

Team Rebounds: Boston Univ. 3; U. Conn. 5. Disqualified: Boston Univ.—Brigham. Technical fouls: None.

	1st Half	2nd Half	Final
U. Conn.	29	47	76
Boston Univ.	28	24	52

Brigham Young (47) Coach: Roger Reid

	Min.	Total FG/FGA	Pct.	3-Pt. FG/FGA	Pct.	FT/FTA	Pct.	Reb. O/T	A	TO	PF	S	Blk	TP	PPM
TOOLSON, A.	40	5/14	.357	2/6	.333	3/6	.500	1/7	2	2	2	3	1	15	.375
DURRANT, M.	9	1/2	.500	0/0	.000	0/0	.000	0/0	0	2	5	1	0	2	.222
SCHREINER, S.	33	3/7	.429	0/0	.000	0/0	.000	3/6	0	2	4	0	0	6	.182
HAWS, M.	35	3/13	.231	0/3	.000	5/7	.714	1/2	4	2	3	2	0	11	.314
SANTIAGO, K.	32	2/4	.500	2/3	.667	0/0	.000	2/2	4	0	4	1	0	6	.188
CROW, T.	22	3/9	.333	0/0	.000	1/2	.500	1/6	0	3	2	1	1	7	.318
MOON, S.	1	0/1	.000	0/0	.000	0/0	.000	0/0	0	0	1	0	0	0	.000
HESLOP, M.	12	0/1	.000	0/0	.000	0/0	.000	2/4	1	0	1	0	0	0	.000
ASTLE, D.	16	0/0	.000	0/0	.000	0/0	.000	0/3	0	1	2	1	0	0	.000
Totals	200	17/51	.333	4/12	.333	9/15	.600	10/30	11	12	24	9	2	47	.235

Team Rebounds: Clemson 3; Brigham Young 2. Disqualified: Brigham Young—Durrant. Technical fouls: None.

	1st Half	2nd Half	Final
Clemson	28	21	49
Brigham Young	23	24	47

Indiana (63) Coach: Bob Knight

	Min.	Total FG/FGA	Pct.	3-Pt. FG/FGA	Pct.	FT/FTA	Pct.	Reb. O/T	A	TO	PF	S	Blk	TP	PPM
NOVER, M.	11	0/0	.000	0/0	.000	0/0	.000	0/2	0	3	3	0	0	0	.000
CHEANEY, C.	39	8/18	.444	0/0	.000	1/2	.500	2/8	0	1	3	1	1	17	.436
ANDERSON, E.	36	9/14	.643	2/4	.500	0/0	.000	3/8	0	1	4	0	2	20	.556
GRAHAM, G.	28	2/7	.286	2/4	.500	5/6	.833	1/4	2	0	3	0	0	11	.393
MEEKS, J.	31	1/3	.333	1/1	1.000	0/0	.000	0/4	6	5	2	2	0	3	.097
REYNOLDS, C.	21	0/0	.000	0/0	.000	0/0	.000	0/2	2	0	2	0	0	0	.000
LAWSON, C.	8	0/2	.000	0/0	.000	0/1	.000	0/0	1	0	1	1	0	0	.000
GRAHAM, P.	25	3/6	.500	2/3	.667	4/4	1.000	0/1	5	2	0	2	0	12	.480
LEARY, T.	1	0/0	.000	0/0	.000	0/0	.000	0/0	0	0	0	0	0	0	.000
Totals	200	23/50	.460	7/12	.583	10/13	.769	6/29	16	12	18	6	3	63	.315

California (65) Coach: Lou Campanelli

	Min.	Total FG/FGA	Pct.	3-Pt. FG/FGA	Pct.	FT/FTA	Pct.	Reb. O/T	A	TO	PF	S	Blk	TP	PPM
WALTON, B.	29	3/6	.500	3/6	.500	2/2	1.000	0/2	1	1	3	1	0	11	.379
FISHER, R.	39	4/11	.364	1/1	1.000	0/0	.000	2/9	0	2	1	1	0	9	.231
HENDRICK, B.	36	3/8	.375	0/0	.000	7/10	.700	3/10	0	2	4	1	0	13	.361
SMITH, K.	40	6/11	.545	1/3	.333	6/6	1.000	0/2	4	5	1	1	0	19	.475
DREW, R.	25	2/7	.286	1/3	.333	0/0	.000	0/1	2	0	3	0	0	5	.200
ELLEBY, B.	26	1/2	.500	1/2	.500	2/4	.500	0/4	0	1	4	0	0	5	.192
REYES, A.	5	1/2	.500	0/0	.000	1/2	.500	1/1	1	0	0	0	1	3	.600
Totals	200	20/47	.426	7/15	.467	18/24	.750	6/29	8	11	16	4	1	65	.325

Team Rebounds: Indiana 2; California 0. Disqualified: None. Technical fouls: None.

	1st Half	2nd Half	Final
Indiana	26	37	63
California	27	38	65

La Salle (79) Coach: Bill Morris

	Min.	Total FG/FGA	Pct.	3-Pt. FG/FGA	Pct.	FT/FTA	Pct.	Reb. O/T	A	TO	PF	S	Blk	TP	PPM
SIMMONS, L.	39	13/26	.500	3/5	.600	3/5	.600	7/16	3	2	2	3	2	32	.821
HURD, J.	19	3/6	.500	1/4	.250	0/0	.000	1/2	1	0	3	3	0	7	.368
LIEVERST, L.	18	0/1	.000	0/0	.000	0/1	.000	1/3	0	3	0	3	0	0	.000
OVERTON, D.	38	5/12	.417	3/5	.600	3/4	.750	0/5	6	3	3	1	0	16	.421
WOODS, R.	34	3/14	.214	2/11	.182	2/2	1.000	3/4	2	2	2	5	0	10	.294
JOHNSON, B.	28	4/12	.333	1/8	.125	5/8	.625	3/6	1	0	2	2	0	14	.500
HOLLAND, D.	20	0/0	.000	0/0	.000	0/0	.000	1/3	1	1	1	0	0	0	.000
MORRIS, K.	1	0/0	.000	0/0	.000	0/0	.000	0/0	0	0	0	0	0	0	.000
BERGIN	1	0/0	.000	0/0	.000	0/0	.000	0/0	0	0	0	0	0	0	.000
SHELTON, D.	1	0/1	.000	0/0	.000	0/0	.000	0/0	0	0	0	0	0	0	.000
STOCK, M.	1	0/0	.000	0/0	.000	0/0	.000	0/0	1	0	1	0	0	0	.000
Totals	200	28/72	.389	10/33	.303	13/20	.650	16/40	14	8	16	14	2	79	.395

Southern Mississippi (63) Coach: M.K. Turk

	Min.	Total FG/FGA	Pct.	3-Pt. FG/FGA	Pct.	FT/FTA	Pct.	Reb. O/T	A	TO	PF	S	Blk	TP	PPM
WEATHERSPOON, .	38	6/11	.545	0/0	.000	4/7	.571	7/14	1	3	3	1	1	16	.421
CROWELL, M.	21	2/10	.200	0/0	.000	0/0	.000	3/7	2	1	3	0	0	4	.190
JENKINS, D.	35	3/10	.300	0/0	.000	2/2	1.000	3/9	1	2	3	0	1	8	.229
JOHNSON, R.	39	5/12	.417	4/10	.400	0/0	.000	2/5	7	2	1	2	0	14	.359
CHANCELLOR, D.	38	6/16	.375	1/5	.200	1/4	.250	1/4	3	5	5	1	0	14	.368
LACEY, J.	6	1/1	1.000	0/0	.000	0/0	.000	0/2	0	1	0	0	0	2	.333
JONES	4	2/4	.500	1/3	.333	0/0	.000	0/1	0	1	0	0	0	5	1.250
DALE, D.	9	0/1	.000	0/1	.000	0/0	.000	0/1	2	2	0	0	0	0	.000
REMBERT, R.	8	0/4	.000	0/4	.000	0/0	.000	0/2	0	2	1	1	0	0	.000
SULLIVAN, C.	1	0/0	.000	0/0	.000	0/0	.000	0/1	0	1	0	0	0	0	.000
MEALER	1	0/0	.000	0/0	.000	0/0	.000	1/1	0	0	0	0	0	0	.000
Totals	200	25/69	.362	6/23	.261	7/13	.538	17/47	16	18	18	5	2	63	.315

Team Rebounds: La Salle 5; Southern Miss. 4. Disqualified: Southern Miss.—Chancellor. Technical fouls: None.

	1st Half	2nd Half	Final
La Salle	36	43	79
Southern Miss.	29	34	63

St. John's (81)   Coach: Lou Carnesecca

	Min.	Total FG/FGA	Pct.	3-Pt. FG/FGA	Pct.	FT/FTA	Pct.	Reb. O/T	A	TO	PF	S	Blk	TP	PPM
SEALY, M.	40	6/10	.600	0/1	.000	6/9	.667	1/7	3	0	2	0	2	18	.450
SINGLETON, B.	35	3/6	.500	0/0	.000	0/2	.000	0/9	1	2	2	0	0	6	.171
WERDANN, R.	35	4/7	.571	0/0	.000	6/7	.857	3/7	1	5	3	0	4	14	.400
HARVEY, B.	39	6/9	.667	1/3	.333	4/4	1.000	0/1	6	3	1	2	0	17	.436
BUCHANAN, J.	29	4/7	.571	4/5	.800	4/4	1.000	0/1	3	2	3	1	0	16	.552
MUTO, S.	10	2/2	1.000	0/0	.000	2/2	1.000	1/1	0	0	2	0	0	6	.600
SPROLING, C.	11	0/1	.000	0/0	.000	2/2	1.000	0/1	2	1	2	0	0	2	.182
CAIN, D.	1	1/1	1.000	0/0	.000	0/0	.000	1/1	0	0	0	0	0	2	2.000
Totals	200	26/43	.605	5/9	.556	24/30	.800	6/28	16	13	15	3	6	81	.405

Temple (65)   Coach: John Chaney

	Min.	Total FG/FGA	Pct.	3-Pt. FG/FGA	Pct.	FT/FTA	Pct.	Reb. O/T	A	TO	PF	S	Blk	TP	PPM
STRICKLAND, M.	39	3/4	.750	0/0	.000	0/0	.000	2/5	0	1	5	2	1	6	.154
KILGORE, M.	29	0/8	.000	0/5	.000	1/2	.500	3/5	3	2	5	1	0	1	.034
HODGE, D.	36	5/10	.500	0/0	.000	3/5	.600	2/8	0	3	4	1	0	13	.361
HARDEN, M.	40	4/11	.364	3/9	.333	0/0	.000	0/0	6	0	2	2	0	11	.275
MACON, M.	40	11/24	.458	6/9	.667	4/4	1.000	4/6	1	4	4	1	0	32	.800
LOVELACE, C.	4	0/0	.000	0/0	.000	0/0	.000	1/1	0	0	0	0	0	0	.000
RANDOLPH, S.	6	0/0	.000	0/0	.000	0/0	.000	0/0	0	0	1	1	0	0	.000
CONIC, J.	5	1/2	.500	0/1	.000	0/0	.000	1/2	0	0	1	0	0	2	.400
POLLARD, E.	1	0/0	.000	0/0	.000	0/0	.000	0/0	0	0	0	0	0	0	.000
Totals	200	24/59	.407	9/24	.375	8/11	.727	13/27	10	10	22	8	1	65	.325

Team Rebounds: St. John's 3; Temple 1. Disqualified: Temple—Strickland, Kilgore. Technical fouls: None.

	1st Half	2nd Half	Final
St. John's	35	46	81
Temple	17	48	65

Duke (81)   Coach: Mike Krzyzewski

	Min.	Total FG/FGA	Pct.	3-Pt. FG/FGA	Pct.	FT/FTA	Pct.	Reb. O/T	A	TO	PF	S	Blk	TP	PPM
BRICKEY, R.	22	3/5	.600	0/0	.000	0/0	.000	1/5	0	3	3	0	3	6	.273
LAETTNER, C.	28	1/4	.250	0/0	.000	5/6	.833	3/7	4	2	1	2	0	7	.250
ABDELNABY, A.	22	9/14	.643	0/0	.000	4/5	.800	4/12	1	2	1	1	3	22	1.000
HENDERSON, P.	27	7/14	.500	2/5	.400	3/5	.600	1/3	5	2	0	6	0	19	.704
HURLEY, B.	35	2/3	.667	0/1	.000	0/0	.000	0/4	6	4	1	1	0	4	.114
HILL, T.	21	3/6	.500	0/0	.000	0/0	.000	1/2	3	1	3	2	0	6	.286
DAVIS, B.	7	2/2	1.000	0/0	.000	2/4	.500	0/0	1	0	0	0	0	6	.857
MCCAFFREY, B.	13	2/6	.333	0/0	.000	0/1	.000	0/1	1	0	0	0	0	4	.308
KOUBEK, G.	11	2/3	.667	0/0	.000	0/0	.000	1/3	0	1	2	0	0	4	.364
PALMER, C.	6	0/0	.000	0/0	.000	2/2	1.000	1/2	0	0	1	0	0	2	.333
BUCKLEY, C.	4	0/0	.000	0/0	.000	0/0	.000	1/1	0	0	0	0	0	0	.000
COOK, J.	4	0/1	.000	0/0	.000	1/2	.500	0/0	0	0	1	1	0	1	.250
Totals	200	31/58	.534	2/6	.333	17/25	.680	13/40	21	15	13	13	6	81	.405

Richmond (46)   Coach: Dick Tarrant

	Min.	Total FG/FGA	Pct.	3-Pt. FG/FGA	Pct.	FT/FTA	Pct.	Reb. O/T	A	TO	PF	S	Blk	TP	PPM
STAPLETON, S.	38	5/13	.385	0/0	.000	0/1	.000	4/7	5	1	4	1	1	10	.263
WOOD, K.	27	1/6	.167	0/1	.000	0/0	.000	1/1	0	3	3	0	0	2	.074
CONNOLLY, T.	21	4/9	.444	0/1	.000	1/2	.500	3/3	1	3	4	2	1	9	.429
ATKINSON, K.	32	5/14	.357	1/2	.500	1/2	.500	4/8	3	2	1	2	0	12	.375
BLAIR, C.	27	3/14	.214	1/4	.250	0/0	.000	1/3	2	4	3	2	0	7	.259
SPRINGER, J.	17	0/6	.000	0/0	.000	0/0	.000	2/3	0	1	2	0	0	0	.000
WEATHERS, T.	19	2/3	.667	0/0	.000	0/0	.000	0/2	2	0	1	1	0	4	.211
BRYANT, J.	8	0/1	.000	0/0	.000	0/0	.000	0/1	1	0	1	0	0	0	.000
SHIELDS, J.	5	0/0	.000	0/0	.000	0/0	.000	1/2	0	1	1	0	0	0	.000
MULDOWNEY, B.	2	0/0	.000	0/0	.000	0/1	.000	0/0	0	1	1	0	0	0	.000
MCDONALD, J.	2	1/1	1.000	0/0	.000	0/0	.000	0/0	0	0	0	0	0	2	1.000
JOHNSON, E.	2	0/0	.000	0/0	.000	0/0	.000	0/0	0	1	0	0	0	0	.000
Totals	200	21/67	.313	2/8	.250	2/6	.333	16/30	14	16	22	8	2	46	.230

Team Rebounds: Duke 6; Richmond 3. Disqualified: None. Technical fouls: None.

	1st Half	2nd Half	Final
Duke	42	39	81
Richmond	26	20	46

UCLA (68)   Coach: Jim Harrick

	Min.	Total FG/FGA	Pct.	3-Pt. FG/FGA	Pct.	FT/FTA	Pct.	Reb. O/T	A	TO	PF	S	Blk	TP	PPM
WILSON, T.	35	9/17	.529	0/0	.000	5/9	.556	3/9	0	2	4	3	1	23	.657
MACLEAN, D.	34	3/14	.214	0/0	.000	4/4	1.000	1/7	2	2	3	1	0	10	.294
MURRAY, T.	29	7/13	.538	0/2	.000	0/0	.000	5/7	0	1	4	3	1	14	.483
MADKINS	31	2/3	.667	0/0	.000	3/4	.750	1/2	2	1	0	2	0	7	.226
MARTIN, T.	36	2/7	.286	0/0	.000	4/4	1.000	0/2	8	4	1	1	0	8	.222
BUTLER, M.	21	2/3	.667	0/0	.000	0/0	.000	0/4	3	0	0	0	0	4	.190
WALKER, K.	14	1/4	.250	0/3	.000	0/0	.000	2/3	0	1	1	0	0	2	.143
Totals	200	26/61	.426	0/5	.000	16/23	.696	12/34	15	11	13	10	2	68	.340

Alabama-Birmingham (56)   Coach: Gene Bartow

	Min.	Total FG/FGA	Pct.	3-Pt. FG/FGA	Pct.	FT/FTA	Pct.	Reb. O/T	A	TO	PF	S	Blk	TP	PPM
KENNEDY	33	2/9	.222	1/5	.200	4/4	1.000	1/8	2	2	5	1	0	9	.273
REMBERT, L.	20	3/5	.600	0/0	.000	0/0	.000	1/3	0	1	1	0	0	6	.300
OGG	25	4/8	.500	0/0	.000	0/0	.000	4/8	0	1	1	0	2	8	.320
BEARDEN	35	3/10	.300	2/6	.333	0/0	.000	1/2	2	3	3	0	0	8	.229
KRAMER	34	4/16	.250	2/12	.167	0/0	.000	0/5	4	5	4	1	0	10	.294
ROGERS, E.	21	4/9	.444	0/0	.000	3/4	.750	2/4	0	3	4	0	0	11	.524
WILKERSON	10	0/2	.000	0/0	.000	0/0	.000	0/0	1	0	1	0	0	0	.000
DEVAUGHN	14	2/4	.500	0/0	.000	0/0	.000	2/3	1	0	2	0	3	4	.286
JACKSON	8	0/0	.000	0/0	.000	0/0	.000	0/0	0	1	0	0	0	0	.000
Totals	200	22/63	.349	5/23	.217	7/8	.875	11/33	9	17	20	3	5	56	.280

Team Rebounds: UCLA 7; Ala-Birmingham 7. Disqualified: Ala-Birmingham—Kennedy. Technical fouls: None.

	1st Half	2nd Half	Final
UCLA	30	38	68
Ala.-Birmingham	27	29	56

Kansas (79)   Coach: Roy Williams

	Min.	Total FG/FGA	Pct.	3-Pt. FG/FGA	Pct.	FT/FTA	Pct.	Reb. O/T	A	TO	PF	S	Blk	TP	PPM
CALLOWAY, R.	27	9/10	.900	0/0	.000	4/4	1.000	3/5	4	2	1	0	2	22	.815
RANDALL, M.	27	4/6	.667	0/0	.000	2/2	1.000	0/4	2	1	2	1	1	10	.370
MARKKANEN, P.	18	1/3	.333	0/0	.000	3/4	.750	1/1	0	1	1	0	0	5	.278
PRITCHARD, K.	35	4/9	.444	3/7	.429	2/2	1.000	1/4	9	2	3	3	0	13	.371
GUELDNER, J.	30	3/8	.375	2/7	.286	2/3	.667	0/5	4	0	2	0	0	10	.333
MADDOX, M.	23	5/6	.833	0/0	.000	0/0	.000	1/1	1	2	2	0	0	10	.435
BROWN, T.	10	1/5	.200	1/5	.200	0/0	.000	0/0	1	1	1	0	1	3	.300
JORDAN, A.	7	0/0	.000	0/0	.000	0/0	.000	0/1	2	2	0	0	0	0	.000
WEST, F.	16	2/2	1.000	0/0	.000	0/0	.000	1/3	2	0	0	0	1	4	.250
JAMISON, A.	7	1/1	1.000	0/0	.000	0/1	.000	0/0	0	2	1	0	0	2	.286
Totals	200	30/50	.600	6/19	.316	13/16	.813	7/24	25	13	13	5	2	79	.395

Robert Morris (71)   Coach: Jarret Durham

	Min.	Total FG/FGA	Pct.	3-Pt. FG/FGA	Pct.	FT/FTA	Pct.	Reb. O/T	A	TO	PF	S	Blk	TP	PPM
MOSS	26	3/8	.375	0/1	.000	0/0	.000	1/1	4	4	3	0	0	6	.231
DICKENS	38	3/5	.600	0/1	.000	3/4	.750	2/5	3	3	4	1	0	9	.237
FALLETA	34	4/8	.500	0/0	.000	1/2	.500	2/6	1	0	2	0	0	9	.265
BOYD	35	7/15	.467	1/4	.250	2/3	.667	1/4	4	5	1	2	0	17	.486
SHEPHERD	18	3/6	.500	3/5	.600	1/1	1.000	0/1	1	0	0	0	0	10	.556
STEALS	16	1/3	.333	0/0	.000	0/0	.000	1/1	0	0	2	1	0	2	.125
VINCENT	9	1/4	.250	1/3	.333	0/0	.000	0/0	0	2	0	0	0	3	.333
CANNON	14	6/9	.667	0/0	.000	1/2	.500	2/2	0	0	4	1	0	13	.929
TIMMERSON	10	1/1	1.000	0/0	.000	0/0	.000	0/1	2	0	0	1	0	2	.200
Totals	200	29/59	.492	5/14	.357	8/12	.667	8/20	15	12	18	6	0	71	.355

Team Rebounds: Kansas 6; Robert Morris 6. Disqualified: None. Technical fouls: None.

	1st Half	2nd Half	Final
Kansas	37	42	79
Robert Morris	36	35	71

FIRST ROUND MIDWEST

Oklahoma (77)   Coach: Billy Tubbs

	Min.	Total FG/FGA	Pct.	3–Pt. FG/FGA	Pct.	FT/FTA	Pct.	Reb. O/T	A	TO	PF	S	Blk	TP	PPM
JONES, J.	35	9/21	.429	0/2	.000	1/2	.500	5/9	5	4	3	0	2	19	.543
PATTERSON, D.	34	3/5	.600	0/0	.000	2/2	1.000	2/10	2	3	1	0	0	8	.235
DAVIS, W.	25	3/7	.429	0/0	.000	4/8	.500	2/8	0	4	4	0	1	10	.400
MCCOVERY, S.	27	2/6	.333	1/2	.500	2/4	.500	3/4	5	4	4	1	0	7	.259
HENRY, S.	30	4/7	.571	2/4	.500	2/4	.500	3/6	1	1	3	1	0	12	.400
EVANS, T.	21	3/9	.333	2/6	.333	0/1	.000	2/2	1	1	0	0	0	8	.381
MULLINS, T.	6	1/1	1.000	1/1	1.000	0/2	.000	0/0	1	1	1	0	0	3	.500
HOLMES, K.	3	0/3	.000	0/1	.000	0/2	.000	1/2	0	0	0	0	0	0	.000
MARTIN, T.	17	4/6	.667	0/0	.000	2/2	1.000	3/4	0	3	3	0	0	10	.588
HARRIS, M.	2	0/0	.000	0/0	.000	0/0	.000	0/0	0	2	0	0	0	0	.000
Totals	200	29/65	.446	6/16	.375	13/27	.481	21/45	15	20	19	2	3	77	.385

Towson State (68)   Coach: Terry Truax

	Min.	Total FG/FGA	Pct.	3–Pt. FG/FGA	Pct.	FT/FTA	Pct.	Reb. O/T	A	TO	PF	S	Blk	TP	PPM
WILLIAMSON, K.	32	3/10	.300	0/0	.000	1/4	.250	1/2	2	2	4	0	0	7	.219
JONES, K.	35	5/5	1.000	0/0	.000	1/4	.250	3/10	3	4	3	0	0	11	.314
MORIN, M.	25	2/4	.500	0/0	.000	0/0	.000	3/5	0	1	2	0	0	4	.160
BOYD, D.	29	0/6	.000	0/2	.000	0/0	.000	2/2	3	3	3	0	0	0	.000
LEE, K.	38	10/28	.357	0/7	.000	10/11	.909	5/7	5	2	4	3	0	30	.789
WALLER, L.	13	4/5	.800	1/1	1.000	0/0	.000	0/0	0	1	1	2	0	9	.692
GRIFFIN, W.	7	0/0	.000	0/0	.000	0/0	.000	0/0	0	0	3	0	1	0	.000
LIGHTENING, C.	18	2/7	.286	0/0	.000	2/2	1.000	2/4	1	3	1	0	1	6	.333
BROWN, L.	3	0/1	.000	0/0	.000	1/2	.500	1/1	0	0	0	0	1	1	.333
Totals	200	26/66	.394	1/10	.100	15/23	.652	17/31	14	16	21	8	2	68	.340

Team Rebounds: Oklahoma 1; Towson State 8. Disqualified: None. Technical fouls: Oklahoma—Henry; Towson State—Lee, Truax.

	1st Half	2nd Half	Final
Oklahoma	45	32	77
Towson State	33	35	68

North Carolina (83)   Coach: Dean Smith

	Min.	Total FG/FGA	Pct.	3–Pt. FG/FGA	Pct.	FT/FTA	Pct.	Reb. O/T	A	TO	PF	S	Blk	TP	PPM
CHILCUTT, P.	28	4/10	.400	0/0	.000	0/1	.000	3/7	1	1	1	0	1	8	.286
FOX, R.	35	7/11	.636	2/4	.500	1/3	.333	2/2	2	1	2	0	1	17	.486
WILLIAMS, S.	27	9/14	.643	0/0	.000	0/1	.000	1/6	1	3	5	1	2	18	.667
RICE, K.	35	2/9	.222	0/1	.000	2/3	.667	1/4	7	3	2	3	0	6	.171
MADDEN, K.	26	6/6	1.000	0/0	.000	0/0	.000	0/2	0	0	1	2	0	12	.462
HARRIS, K.	5	3/3	1.000	0/0	.000	0/0	.000	0/1	0	0	0	0	0	6	1.200
RODL, H.	13	2/2	1.000	0/0	.000	2/5	.400	2/3	3	0	4	2	0	6	.462
LYNCH, G.	19	3/7	.429	0/0	.000	2/2	1.000	5/8	2	2	4	0	0	8	.421
DAVIS, H.	10	0/2	.000	0/1	.000	2/2	1.000	0/1	0	0	0	0	0	2	.200
WENSTROM, M.	2	0/0	.000	0/0	.000	0/0	.000	0/1	0	0	1	0	0	0	.000
Totals	200	36/64	.563	2/6	.333	9/17	.529	14/35	16	10	20	8	4	83	.415

SW Missouri State (70)   Coach: Charles Spoonhour

	Min.	Total FG/FGA	Pct.	3–Pt. FG/FGA	Pct.	FT/FTA	Pct.	Reb. O/T	A	TO	PF	S	Blk	TP	PPM
STANGE, C.	23	4/4	1.000	0/0	.000	0/1	.000	0/0	1	0	1	0	0	8	.348
FORD, J.	32	8/15	.533	4/9	.444	5/6	.833	6/11	2	1	4	0	0	25	.781
CAMPBELL, L.	37	3/7	.429	0/0	.000	0/1	.000	2/8	0	3	2	0	0	6	.162
BERNARD, A.	35	3/9	.333	1/4	.250	0/2	.000	0/4	6	3	3	2	0	7	.200
REID, D.	40	3/13	.231	0/5	.000	7/9	.778	0/2	3	4	3	1	1	13	.325
REDMOND, L.	17	2/3	.667	1/1	1.000	0/0	.000	0/0	1	0	2	1	0	5	.294
BREWER, D.	11	3/4	.750	0/0	.000	0/0	.000	2/2	0	0	4	0	0	6	.545
RIBBLE, D.	5	0/0	.000	-/0	–	0/0	.000	0/0	0	2	0	0	0	0	.000
Totals	200	26/55	.473	6/19	.316	12/19	.632	10/27	13	13	19	4	1	70	.350

Team Rebounds: N. Carolina 2; SW Missouri St. 5. Disqualified: N. Carolina—Williams. Technical fouls: None.

	1st Half	2nd Half	Final
N. Carolina	41	42	83
SW Missouri St.	40	30	70

Illinois (86)   Coach: Lou Henson

	Min.	Total FG/FGA	Pct.	3–Pt. FG/FGA	Pct.	FT/FTA	Pct.	Reb. O/T	A	TO	PF	S	Blk	TP	PPM
LIBERTY, M.	34	6/17	.353	0/0	.000	6/7	.857	2/7	0	0	5	0	1	18	.529
BARDO, S.	37	4/12	.333	0/6	.000	1/2	.500	3/9	2	6	4	0	1	9	.243
SMALL, E.	27	2/4	.500	0/0	.000	0/0	.000	4/14	2	3	3	2	0	4	.148
BOWMAN, P.	19	0/6	.000	0/4	.000	0/0	.000	0/1	4	3	2	0	0	0	.000
GILL, K.	39	9/15	.600	5/7	.714	5/8	.625	4/7	0	4	4	2	0	28	.718
TAYLOR, B.	3	0/0	.000	0/0	.000	0/0	.000	0/1	2	0	2	0	0	0	.000
JONES, R.	17	5/7	.714	0/0	.000	2/2	1.000	1/5	0	0	2	0	0	12	.706
KAUFMANN, A.	22	4/8	.500	1/4	.250	6/7	.857	2/4	6	3	1	0	0	15	.682
KPEDI, A.	2	0/0	.000	0/0	.000	0/0	.000	0/0	0	0	0	0	0	0	.000
Totals	200	30/69	.435	6/21	.286	20/26	.769	16/48	16	19	23	4	2	86	.430

Dayton (88)   Coach: Jim O'Brien

	Min.	Total FG/FGA	Pct.	3–Pt. FG/FGA	Pct.	FT/FTA	Pct.	Reb. O/T	A	TO	PF	S	Blk	TP	PPM
CORBITT, A.	35	7/15	.467	1/1	1.000	8/11	.727	2/9	1	1	3	4	1	23	.657
ROBINSON, N.	24	3/8	.375	1/2	.500	0/0	.000	2/7	1	2	0	0	0	7	.292
COFFEE, W.	13	2/3	.667	0/0	.000	0/1	.000	2/4	0	1	4	1	0	4	.308
SPRINGER, R.	31	4/13	.308	3/7	.429	0/1	.000	0/3	4	1	0	3	0	11	.355
KNIGHT, N.	36	6/14	.429	4/8	.500	11/13	.846	1/5	8	3	4	1	0	27	.750
UHL, B.	22	1/5	.200	0/4	.000	3/4	.750	2/3	0	0	3	3	1	5	.227
GREVEY, N.	10	1/2	.500	1/1	1.000	0/0	.000	0/0	0	1	1	1	0	3	.300
ROBERTSON, A.	19	1/3	.333	0/0	.000	4/4	1.000	1/2	1	0	5	2	1	6	.316
HOWARD, S.	10	1/2	.500	0/1	.000	0/0	.000	0/2	0	2	1	0	0	2	.200
Totals	200	26/65	.400	10/25	.400	26/34	.765	10/35	15	11	21	15	3	88	.440

Team Rebounds: Dayton 5; Illinois 2. Disqualified: Dayton—Robertson; Illinois—Liberty. Technical fouls: None.

	1st Half	2nd Half	Final
Illinois	36	50	86
Dayton	41	47	88

Arkansas (68)   Coach: Nolan Richardson

	Min.	Total FG/FGA	Pct.	3–Pt. FG/FGA	Pct.	FT/FTA	Pct.	Reb. O/T	A	TO	PF	S	Blk	TP	PPM
DAY, T.	38	4/12	.333	1/5	.200	0/1	.000	0/6	3	1	1	3	0	9	.237
HOWELL, L.	33	3/6	.500	0/0	.000	4/4	1.000	1/3	2	2	2	0	0	10	.303
CREDIT, M.	18	3/5	.600	0/0	.000	5/7	.714	2/2	0	1	4	0	1	11	.611
MAYBERRY, L.	39	7/8	.875	2/2	1.000	1/2	.500	2/4	4	2	4	2	0	17	.436
BOWERS, A.	35	0/1	.000	0/0	.000	4/5	.800	1/1	4	1	1	1	0	4	.114
MURRY, E.	3	0/0	.000	0/0	.000	0/0	.000	0/0	0	0	1	0	0	0	.000
HAWKINS, D.	7	1/2	.500	0/0	.000	0/0	.000	0/0	0	1	1	0	0	2	.286
MILLER, O.	22	5/9	.556	0/0	.000	0/1	.000	1/8	3	4	3	2	1	10	.455
HUERY, R.	5	2/2	1.000	0/0	.000	1/1	1.000	1/1	1	0	2	0	5	1.000
Totals	200	25/45	.556	3/7	.429	15/21	.714	8/25	17	12	19	12	2	68	.340

Princeton (64)   Coach: Pete Carril

	Min.	Total FG/FGA	Pct.	3–Pt. FG/FGA	Pct.	FT/FTA	Pct.	Reb. O/T	A	TO	PF	S	Blk	TP	PPM
LAPIN, M.	29	3/8	.375	1/5	.200	0/0	.000	4/7	2	0	5	0	0	7	.241
EASTWICK, M.	40	5/8	.625	3/4	.750	4/6	.667	1/4	1	3	2	1	0	17	.425
MUELLER, K.	40	8/12	.667	0/0	.000	3/4	.750	1/6	8	5	4	0	0	19	.475
JACKSON, S.	40	2/8	.250	2/6	.333	3/5	.600	1/3	1	3	4	1	0	9	.225
LEFTWICH, G.	40	4/4	1.000	1/1	1.000	1/3	.333	0/2	1	4	4	1	0	10	.250
HENSHON, M.	11	1/2	.500	0/1	.000	0/0	.000	0/0	1	0	1	0	0	2	.182
Totals	200	23/42	.548	7/17	.412	11/18	.611	7/22	14	15	20	3	0	64	.320

Team Rebounds: Arkansas 1; Princeton 3. Disqualified: Princeton—Lapin. Technical fouls: Arkansas—Day.

	1st Half	2nd Half	Final
Arkansas	40	28	68
Princeton	37	27	64

Xavier (Ohio) (87)   Coach: Pete Gillen

	Min.	Total FG/FGA	Pct.	3-Pt. FG/FGA	Pct.	FT/FTA	Pct.	Reb. O/T	A	TO	PF	S	Blk	TP	PPM
BRANTLEY, M.	26	2/ 3	.667	0/ 0	.000	4/ 4	1.000	1/ 3	1	0	2	0	0	8	.308
HILL, T.	35	6/12	.500	0/ 0	.000	17/18	.944	4/14	0	0	4	1	0	29	.829
STRONG, D.	37	4/10	.400	0/ 0	.000	9/11	.818	4/11	1	4	4	0	2	17	.459
WALKER, J.	39	5/11	.455	1/ 3	.333	0/ 1	.000	0/ 2	6	4	1	1	1	11	.282
GLADDEN, J.	37	5/ 9	.556	0/ 1	.000	2/ 2	1.000	1/ 2	1	0	4	0	0	12	.324
DAVENPORT, M.	18	1/ 4	.250	1/ 2	.500	5/ 7	.714	2/ 3	1	2	2	0	0	8	.444
WILLIAMS, A.	8	1/ 2	.500	0/ 0	.000	0/ 0	.000	0/ 4	0	0	2	0	1	2	.250
Totals	200	24/51	.471	2/ 6	.333	37/43	.860	12/39	10	10	19	2	4	87	.435

Kansas State (79)   Coach: Lon Kruger

	Min.	Total FG/FGA	Pct.	3-Pt. FG/FGA	Pct.	FT/FTA	Pct.	Reb. O/T	A	TO	PF	S	Blk	TP	PPM
JONES, A.	-	6/13	.462	1/ 1	1.000	0/ 2	.000	1/ 3	1	0	4	0	0	13	-
SIMMONS, L.	-	2/ 5	.400	0/ 0	.000	0/ 0	.000	3/ 4	0	1	5	0	1	4	-
MASSOP, T.	-	1/ 5	.200	0/ 0	.000	0/ 0	.000	4/ 6	1	1	4	0	0	2	-
HENSON, S.	-	11/19	.579	6/11	.545	7/ 7	1.000	0/ 2	2	2	4	4	0	35	-
DEROUILLERER, J.	-	4/13	.308	0/ 1	.000	4/ 7	.571	1/ 5	5	1	3	1	1	12	-
WIRES, J.	-	0/ 0	.000	0/ 0	.000	0/ 0	.000	0/ 0	0	0	0	0	0	0	-
MALHAM, J.	-	0/ 0	.000	0/ 0	.000	0/ 0	.000	0/ 0	0	0	0	0	0	0	-
AMERSON, K.	-	1/ 1	1.000	0/ 0	.000	0/ 0	.000	0/ 0	0	0	3	1	0	2	-
WEIGEL, N.	-	0/ 0	.000	0/ 0	.000	0/ 0	.000	0/ 0	0	0	0	0	0	0	-
SAMS, P.	-	0/ 0	.000	0/ 0	.000	0/ 0	.000	0/ 0	0	0	0	0	0	0	-
BRITT, R.	-	2/ 3	.667	0/ 0	.000	0/ 0	.000	0/ 2	0	1	3	0	0	4	-
SMITH, B.	-	0/ 1	.000	0/ 0	.000	3/ 4	.750	0/ 2	0	0	0	1	0	3	-
HOWARD, W.	-	0/ 0	.000	0/ 1	.000	0/ 0	.000	0/ 0	0	0	0	0	0	0	-
RETTIGER, J.	-	1/ 2	.500	0/ 0	.000	2/ 4	.500	1/ 3	0	0	5	0	0	4	-
Totals	200	28/63	.444	7/14	.500	16/24	.667	10/27	9	6	31	7	2	79	.395

Team Rebounds: Xavier 1; Kansas State 0. Disqualified: Kansas State—Simmons, Rettiger. Technical fouls: None.

	1st Half	2nd Half	Final
Xavier (Ohio)	42	45	87
Kansas State	32	47	79

Georgetown (70)   Coach: John Thompson

	Min.	Total FG/FGA	Pct.	3-Pt. FG/FGA	Pct.	FT/FTA	Pct.	Reb. O/T	A	TO	PF	S	Blk	TP	PPM
ALLEN, A.	2	0/ 0	.000	0/ 0	.000	0/ 0	.000	0/ 0	0	0	0	1	0	0	.000
MOURNING, A.	26	6/ 6	1.000	0/ 0	.000	0/ 2	.000	1/ 8	1	4	4	0	1	12	.462
MUTOMBO, D.	40	8/ 9	.889	0/ 0	.000	2/ 3	.667	4/16	0	5	2	1	3	18	.450
BRYANT, D.	38	6/14	.429	3/ 7	.429	1/ 4	.250	0/ 2	6	2	1	2	0	16	.421
TILLMON, M.	37	6/15	.400	1/ 6	.167	9/10	.900	2/ 6	2	6	2	1	0	22	.595
EDWARDS, D.	22	0/ 2	.000	0/ 0	.000	2/ 3	.667	1/ 5	4	1	3	0	0	2	.091
STOUDAMIRE, A.	15	0/ 2	.000	0/ 1	.000	0/ 0	.000	0/ 3	2	1	1	1	0	0	.000
JEFFERSON, S.	20	0/ 4	.000	0/ 0	.000	0/ 0	.000	0/ 3	0	0	1	0	0	0	.000
Totals	200	26/52	.500	4/14	.286	14/22	.636	8/45	15	19	13	7	4	70	.350

Texas Southern (52)   Coach: Bob Moreland

	Min.	Total FG/FGA	Pct.	3-Pt. FG/FGA	Pct.	FT/FTA	Pct.	Reb. O/T	A	TO	PF	S	Blk	TP	PPM
WEST, F.	40	7/23	.304	2/12	.167	1/ 3	.333	3/ 7	2	2	1	2	1	17	.425
PRICE, C.	33	2/ 9	.222	1/ 5	.200	0/ 0	.000	4/10	3	3	4	2	0	5	.152
BROOKS, M.	17	2/ 4	.500	0/ 0	.000	0/ 0	.000	0/ 2	1	2	2	0	0	4	.235
APPLEWHITE, J.	37	3/10	.300	2/ 5	.400	0/ 0	.000	2/ 5	1	3	1	2	0	8	.216
YOUNGER, R.	29	5/19	.263	2/ 9	.222	0/ 0	.000	2/ 7	2	2	4	2	0	12	.414
GATLIN, T.	19	0/ 2	.000	0/ 0	.000	0/ 0	.000	0/ 3	3	0	4	0	0	0	.000
ARMWOOD, K.	4	0/ 1	.000	0/ 0	.000	0/ 0	.000	0/ 0	0	1	0	0	0	0	.000
COLLINS, R.	12	0/ 2	.000	0/ 0	.000	2/ 2	1.000	2/ 2	0	0	1	0	0	2	.167
PARKER, C.	9	1/ 4	.250	0/ 0	.000	2/ 2	1.000	1/ 3	0	0	4	0	0	4	.444
Totals	200	20/74	.270	7/33	.212	5/ 7	.714	14/36	12	13	21	8	1	52	.260

Team Rebounds: Georgetown 1; Texas Southern 4. Disqualified: None. Technical fouls: Texas Southern—Younger.

	1st Half	2nd Half	Final
Georgetown	32	38	70
Texas Southern	23	29	52

Georgia (88)   Coach: Hugh Durham

	Min.	Total FG/FGA	Pct.	3-Pt. FG/FGA	Pct.	FT/FTA	Pct.	Reb. O/T	A	TO	PF	S	Blk	TP	PPM
KESSLER, A.	37	12/17	.706	0/ 0	.000	9/10	.900	-/17	1	3	4	1	0	33	.892
WILSON, M.	31	6/16	.375	1/ 2	.500	3/ 3	1.000	-/ 9	1	3	4	1	2	16	.516
AUSTIN, N.	25	1/ 3	.333	0/ 0	.000	0/ 0	.000	-/ 4	1	3	2	1	2	2	.080
GREEN, L.	33	6/17	.353	1/ 4	.250	4/ 9	.444	-/ 0	4	5	4	0	1	17	.515
COLE, R.	36	5/11	.455	1/ 4	.250	0/ 0	.000	-/ 5	2	4	5	1	1	11	.306
GOLDEN, S.	12	0/ 2	.000	0/ 0	.000	2/ 2	1.000	-/ 2	2	4	5	0	1	2	.167
PATTON, J.	12	2/ 6	.333	0/ 3	.000	1/ 1	1.000	-/ 2	1	1	4	0	0	5	.417
RHINE, K.	5	0/ 0	.000	0/ 0	.000	0/ 0	.000	-/ 0	0	0	1	0	0	0	.000
HOWARD, L.	9	1/ 1	1.000	0/ 0	.000	0/ 0	.000	-/ 2	0	0	2	0	1	2	.222
HARRON, M.	0	0/ 0	.000	0/ 0	.000	0/ 0	.000	-/ 0	0	0	0	0	0	0	-
Totals	200	33/73	.452	3/13	.231	19/25	.760	-/41	12	23	31	4	8	88	.440

Texas (100)   Coach: Tom Penders

	Min.	Total FG/FGA	Pct.	3-Pt. FG/FGA	Pct.	FT/FTA	Pct.	Reb. O/T	A	TO	PF	S	Blk	TP	PPM
BLANKS, L.	34	9/14	.643	3/ 8	.375	0/ 2	.000	-/ 2	3	2	5	4	0	21	.618
COLLIE, L.	19	3/ 5	.600	0/ 0	.000	0/ 1	.000	-/ 5	0	0	4	0	0	6	.316
MYERS, G.	32	4/ 9	.444	0/ 0	.000	1/ 5	.200	-/14	0	3	0	4	9	.281
WRIGHT, J.	33	5/14	.357	0/ 2	.000	2/ 6	.333	-/ 4	4	6	3	4	2	12	.364
MAYS, T.	33	10/17	.588	1/ 4	.250	23/27	.852	-/ 6	1	5	3	0	1	44	1.333
WILLIAMS, B.	14	3/ 7	.429	0/ 0	.000	0/ 0	.000	-/ 3	0	1	3	1	0	6	.429
DUDEK, H.	13	0/ 1	.000	0/ 0	.000	0/ 0	.000	-/ 3	0	0	2	0	0	0	.000
MULLER, G.	1	0/ 0	.000	0/ 0	.000	0/ 0	.000	-/ 0	0	0	0	0	0	0	.000
JEANS, C.	6	0/ 0	.000	0/ 0	.000	0/ 2	.000	-/ 0	0	0	1	0	0	0	.000
SHEPARD, W.	12	1/ 1	1.000	0/ 0	.000	0/ 0	.000	-/ 0	0	0	0	1	0	2	.167
HOUSTON, G.	1	0/ 0	.000	0/ 0	.000	0/ 0	.000	-/ 0	0	0	0	0	0	0	.000
FOWLER, A.	1	0/ 0	.000	0/ 0	.000	0/ 0	.000	-/ 0	0	0	0	0	0	0	.000
HALL, M.	1	0/ 0	.000	0/ 0	.000	0/ 0	.000	-/ 0	0	0	0	0	0	0	.000
Totals	200	35/68	.515	4/14	.286	26/45	.578	-/37	8	14	21	13	7	100	.500

Team Rebounds: Texas 2; Georgia 4. Disqualified: Texas—Blanks; Georgia—Cole, Golden. Technical fouls: None. Played who played 0 min. played less than 1 min. each.

	1st Half	2nd Half	Final
Georgia	41	47	88
Texas	40	60	100

Purdue (75)   Coach: Gene Keady

	Min.	Total FG/FGA	Pct.	3-Pt. FG/FGA	Pct.	FT/FTA	Pct.	Reb. O/T	A	TO	PF	S	Blk	TP	PPM
BERNING, R.	36	5/ 7	.714	3/ 4	.750	4/ 4	1.000	1/ 6	0	0	1	0	1	17	.472
WHITE, C.	18	3/11	.273	0/ 0	.000	1/ 1	1.000	4/ 8	4	1	3	1	0	7	.389
SCHEFFLER, S.	35	7/11	.636	0/ 0	.000	9/10	.900	1/10	2	2	2	0	1	23	.657
AUSTIN, W.	31	4/ 9	.444	1/ 3	.333	0/ 0	.000	1/ 7	3	3	2	0	1	9	.290
JONES, T.	40	6/10	.600	0/ 0	.000	3/ 4	.750	0/ 2	3	2	1	2	0	15	.375
MOUNT, R.	0	0/ 0	.000	0/ 0	.000	0/ 0	.000	0/ 0	0	0	0	0	0	0	-
PAINTER, M.	3	0/ 0	.000	0/ 0	.000	0/ 1	.000	0/ 0	0	0	0	0	0	0	.000
CLYBURN, L.	6	0/ 1	.000	0/ 0	.000	0/ 0	.000	0/ 2	1	1	0	0	0	0	.000
BARRETT, D.	4	0/ 0	.000	0/ 0	.000	0/ 0	.000	0/ 1	1	1	0	0	0	0	.000
OLIVER, J.	27	1/ 2	.500	0/ 0	.000	2/ 4	.500	1/ 4	3	1	3	1	1	4	.148
SCHOETTELKOTTE, T.	0	0/ 0	.000	0/ 0	.000	0/ 0	.000	0/ 1	0	1	0	0	0	0	-
RILEY, C.	0	0/ 0	.000	0/ 0	.000	0/ 0	.000	0/ 0	0	0	0	0	0	0	-
Totals	200	26/51	.510	4/ 7	.571	19/24	.792	8/38	18	12	14	4	4	75	.375

Northeast Louisiana (63)   Coach: Mike Vining

	Min.	Total FG/FGA	Pct.	3-Pt. FG/FGA	Pct.	FT/FTA	Pct.	Reb. O/T	A	TO	PF	S	Blk	TP	PPM
VINCENT, L.	-	0/ 2	.000	0/ 0	.000	0/ 0	.000	1/ 3	0	3	0	1	1	0	-
FUNCHESS, C.	-	2/ 8	.250	1/ 3	.333	0/ 0	.000	2/ 5	0	0	4	1	1	5	-
CRAIG, P.	-	7/11	.636	0/ 0	.000	3/ 4	.750	2/ 6	0	1	3	1	0	17	-
COBB, T.	-	3/10	.300	0/ 1	.000	0/ 0	.000	0/ 2	6	0	1	1	0	6	-
THOMPSON, F.	-	3/ 9	.333	3/ 7	.429	3/ 4	.750	0/ 2	0	1	4	0	0	12	-
JONES, A.	-	5/12	.417	2/ 5	.400	2/ 2	1.000	0/ 2	2	2	2	1	0	14	-
JONES, J.	-	1/ 4	.250	1/ 2	.500	0/ 0	.000	0/ 0	1	1	2	0	0	3	-
JEFFERSON, E.	-	0/ 4	.000	0/ 0	.000	0/ 0	.000	0/ 0	0	0	0	0	0	0	-
JACOBS, C.	-	3/ 5	.600	0/ 0	.000	0/ 0	.000	1/ 4	0	1	5	0	1	6	-
BYRD, J.	-	0/ 2	.000	0/ 0	.000	0/ 0	.000	0/ 0	1	0	1	0	0	0	-
PORTER, M.	-	0/ 0	.000	0/ 0	.000	0/ 0	.000	0/ 0	0	0	1	0	0	0	-
Totals	200	24/67	.358	7/20	.350	8/10	.800	6/25	13	7	23	6	3	63	.315

Team Rebounds: Purdue 4; Northeast La. 1. Disqualified: Northeast La.—Jacobs. Technical fouls: None. Players who played 0 min. played less than 1 min. each.

	1st Half	2nd Half	Final
Purdue	33	42	75
Northeast La.	34	29	63

SECOND ROUND SOUTHEAST

Michigan State (62)   Coach: Jud Heathcote

	Min.	Total FG/FGA	Pct.	3-Pt. FG/FGA	Pct.	FT/FTA	Pct.	Reb. O/T	A	TO	PF	S	Blk	TP	PPM
REDFIELD, K.	32	2/5	.400	0/0	.000	3/8	.375	2/7	2	4	1	1	0	7	.219
STEIGENGA, M.	21	3/4	.750	0/0	.000	2/2	1.000	1/4	2	1	3	3	0	8	.381
PEPLOWSKI, M.	30	3/6	.500	0/0	.000	2/4	.500	2/11	0	2	3	1	1	8	.267
SMITH, S.	37	6/15	.400	0/2	.000	9/10	.900	2/6	4	4	2	2	0	21	.568
MONTGOMERY, M.	31	1/4	.250	0/1	.000	0/1	.000	0/3	2	0	3	0	0	2	.065
MANNS, K.	17	1/5	.200	0/2	.000	1/1	1.000	1/2	0	2	1	0	0	3	.176
HICKMAN, P.	11	2/2	1.000	0/0	.000	1/1	1.000	0/2	0	2	0	1	1	5	.455
STEPHENS, D.	21	3/3	.667	0/0	.000	4/5	.800	0/3	1	1	1	0	0	8	.381
Totals	200	20/44	.455	0/5	.000	22/32	.688	8/38	11	16	14	8	2	62	.310

UC Santa Barbara (58)   Coach: Jerry Pimm

	Min.	Total FG/FGA	Pct.	3-Pt. FG/FGA	Pct.	FT/FTA	Pct.	Reb. O/T	A	TO	PF	S	Blk	TP	PPM
JOHNSON, P.	20	2/5	.400	1/2	.500	1/1	1.000	1/3	2	1	5	0	0	6	.300
MCARTHUR, E.	28	3/8	.375	0/0	.000	2/4	.500	3/7	2	2	4	2	2	8	.286
GRAY, G.	36	3/12	.250	0/0	.000	0/0	.000	3/5	1	4	3	0	0	6	.167
DEHART, C.	40	8/20	.400	3/12	.250	4/4	1.000	0/1	1	2	4	0	1	23	.575
DAVIS, L.	34	2/6	.333	1/1	1.000	1/2	.500	2/5	2	3	5	0	0	6	.176
JONES, I.	17	1/7	.143	1/5	.200	2/2	1.000	2/6	1	0	3	2	0	5	.294
AKINS, U.	11	2/4	.500	0/0	.000	0/0	.000	1/2	0	1	3	1	0	4	.364
MEYER, M.	9	0/0	.000	0/0	.000	0/0	.000	0/4	0	1	0	0	1	0	.000
ERBST, B.	5	0/1	.000	0/0	.000	0/0	.000	1/1	0	0	0	1	0	0	.000
Totals	200	21/63	.333	6/20	.300	10/13	.769	13/34	9	14	27	6	4	58	.290

Team Rebounds: Michigan St. 3; UC Santa Barb. 4. Disqualified: UC Santa Barb.—Davis, Johnson. Technical fouls: Michigan St.—Stephens.

	1st Half	2nd Half	Final
Michigan St.	25	37	62
UC Santa Barbara	20	38	58

Louisiana State (91)   Coach: Dale Brown

	Min.	Total FG/FGA	Pct.	3-Pt. FG/FGA	Pct.	FT/FTA	Pct.	Reb. O/T	A	TO	PF	S	Blk	TP	PPM
SINGLETON, V.	37	9/13	.692	0/1	.000	2/7	.286	7/8	1	0	5	0	0	20	.541
ROBERTS, S.	35	10/17	.588	0/0	.000	1/4	.250	4/15	2	2	4	0	4	21	.600
O'NEAL, S.	38	5/10	.500	0/0	.000	9/12	.750	4/14	2	1	4	0	4	19	.500
WILLIAMSON, M.	27	6/15	.400	2/6	.333	2/2	1.000	2/3	5	1	4	0	0	16	.593
JACKSON, C.	36	5/15	.333	3/9	.333	0/0	.000	0/3	3	3	5	0	1	13	.361
BOUDREAUX, H.	5	0/2	.000	0/0	.000	0/0	.000	2/4	0	0	2	0	0	0	.000
DEVALL, R.	17	1/3	.333	0/2	.000	0/0	.000	0/1	3	0	1	0	0	2	.118
SIMS, W.	5	0/2	.000	0/1	.000	0/0	.000	0/2	0	0	0	0	1	0	.000
Totals	200	36/77	.468	5/19	.263	14/25	.560	19/50	16	7	25	0	10	91	.455

Georgia Tech (94)   Coach: Bobby Cremins

	Min.	Total FG/FGA	Pct.	3-Pt. FG/FGA	Pct.	FT/FTA	Pct.	Reb. O/T	A	TO	PF	S	Blk	TP	PPM
SCOTT, D.	40	10/32	.313	5/12	.417	5/8	.625	5/11	4	1	3	1	0	30	.750
MACKEY, M.	33	3/6	.500	0/0	.000	3/5	.600	7/14	1	0	4	0	1	9	.273
MCNEIL, J.	19	2/4	.500	0/0	.000	3/4	.750	2/5	0	1	5	0	1	7	.368
ANDERSON, K.	40	10/21	.476	3/6	.500	3/4	.750	2/8	4	2	1	2	0	26	.650
OLIVER, B.	37	4/16	.250	2/7	.286	8/10	.800	4/7	2	0	0	0	0	18	.486
BROWN, N.	30	1/2	.500	0/0	.000	2/2	1.000	0/0	3	0	4	0	0	4	.133
MUNLYN, J.	1	0/0	.000	0/0	.000	0/0	.000	0/0	0	0	0	0	0	0	.000
Totals	200	30/81	.370	10/25	.400	24/33	.727	20/45	14	4	17	3	2	94	.470

Team Rebounds: Georgia Tech 7; Louisiana St. 1. Disqualified: Louisiana St.—Singleton, Jackson; Georgia Tech—McNeil. Technical fouls: None.

	1st Half	2nd Half	Final
Louisiana St.	41	50	91
Georgia Tech	40	54	94

Minnesota (81)   Coach: Clem Haskins

	Min.	Total FG/FGA	Pct.	3-Pt. FG/FGA	Pct.	FT/FTA	Pct.	Reb. O/T	A	TO	PF	S	Blk	TP	PPM
COFFEY, R.	18	2/3	.667	0/0	.000	0/0	.000	2/2	0	2	4	1	0	4	.222
BURTON, W.	31	13/17	.765	1/2	.500	9/12	.750	5/12	0	1	3	1	1	36	1.161
SHIKENJANSKI, J.	29	3/8	.375	0/0	.000	3/6	.500	0/1	0	0	4	0	0	9	.310
LYNCH, K.	37	5/13	.385	1/3	.333	1/1	1.000	1/3	3	3	3	0	1	12	.324
NEWBERN, M.	34	3/10	.300	2/4	.500	0/0	.000	1/5	9	1	3	2	0	8	.235
LEWIS, C.	7	0/1	.000	0/1	.000	0/0	.000	0/0	1	0	1	0	0	0	.000
METCALF, R.	2	0/0	.000	0/0	.000	0/0	.000	1/1	0	1	1	0	0	0	.000
BOND, W.	28	4/6	.667	0/0	.000	4/4	1.000	3/5	5	4	1	2	0	12	.429
MARTIN, B.	10	0/1	.000	0/0	.000	0/0	.000	1/4	0	0	1	0	0	0	.000
TUBBS, N.	4	0/0	.000	0/0	.000	0/0	.000	0/1	0	0	0	0	1	0	.000
Totals	200	30/59	.508	4/10	.400	17/26	.654	14/34	18	12	18	7	3	81	.405

Northern Iowa (78)   Coach: Eldon Miller

	Min.	Total FG/FGA	Pct.	3-Pt. FG/FGA	Pct.	FT/FTA	Pct.	Reb. O/T	A	TO	PF	S	Blk	TP	PPM
MCCULLOUGH, C.	21	1/2	.500	0/0	.000	0/0	.000	1/3	1	0	3	0	0	2	.095
PHYFE, S.	19	2/4	.500	0/0	.000	1/2	.500	0/5	1	0	3	0	0	5	.263
REESE, R.	35	12/15	.800	0/0	.000	5/7	.714	3/10	1	2	4	1	0	29	.829
TURNER, D.	36	3/8	.375	3/5	.600	0/0	.000	0/4	9	3	2	2	0	9	.250
MULLENBERG, T.	35	7/17	.412	4/11	.364	2/2	1.000	0/2	1	1	4	3	0	20	.571
NEWBY, M.	19	3/11	.273	2/9	.222	0/0	.000	3/3	2	4	1	2	0	8	.421
COX, J.	12	0/0	.000	0/0	.000	0/0	.000	0/0	2	2	2	0	0	0	.000
HILL, B.	20	1/3	.333	0/1	.000	3/4	.750	2/3	3	1	5	0	1	5	.250
PACE, N.	3	0/1	.000	0/0	.000	0/0	.000	1/1	0	0	0	0	0	0	.000
Totals	200	29/61	.475	9/26	.346	11/15	.733	10/31	20	13	24	8	1	78	.390

Team Rebounds: Minnesota 3; Northern Iowa 1. Disqualified: Northern Iowa—Hill. Technical fouls: None.

	1st Half	2nd Half	Final
Minnesota	46	35	81
Northern Iowa	40	38	78

Virginia (61)   Coach: Terry Holland

	Min.	Total FG/FGA	Pct.	3-Pt. FG/FGA	Pct.	FT/FTA	Pct.	Reb. O/T	A	TO	PF	S	Blk	TP	PPM
TURNER, K.	39	4/10	.400	1/4	.250	0/0	.000	2/8	1	1	2	0	0	9	.231
STITH, B.	38	11/21	.524	5/7	.714	3/4	.750	0/2	0	3	3	0	0	30	.789
JEFFRIES, T.	19	1/2	.500	0/0	.000	2/4	.500	0/1	0	0	0	0	0	4	.211
OLIVER, A.	18	0/5	.000	0/0	.000	0/0	.000	1/2	2	1	2	4	1	0	.000
CROTTY, J.	40	4/11	.364	0/2	.000	2/2	1.000	1/2	12	3	0	2	0	10	.250
KIRBY, T.	2	0/1	.000	0/1	.000	0/0	.000	0/0	0	0	0	0	0	0	.000
BLUNDIN, M.	26	2/2	1.000	0/0	.000	0/0	.000	5/6	1	1	4	0	0	4	.154
DANIELS, J.	18	2/3	.667	0/0	.000	0/0	.000	1/6	2	0	1	0	0	4	.222
Totals	200	24/55	.436	6/14	.429	7/10	.700	10/27	18	9	12	6	1	61	.305

Syracuse (63)   Coach: Jim Boeheim

	Min.	Total FG/FGA	Pct.	3-Pt. FG/FGA	Pct.	FT/FTA	Pct.	Reb. O/T	A	TO	PF	S	Blk	TP	PPM
OWENS, B.	40	7/18	.389	0/4	.000	2/3	.667	4/8	1	1	1	1	0	16	.400
SCOTT, T.	21	4/7	.571	1/4	.250	0/0	.000	2/2	0	1	2	0	0	9	.429
COLEMAN, D.	40	4/8	.500	1/2	.500	10/12	.833	3/10	9	3	3	0	2	19	.475
EDWARDS, M.	28	2/5	.400	1/2	.500	0/0	.000	0/2	3	0	0	0	0	5	.179
THOMPSON, S.	40	7/16	.438	0/0	.000	0/0	.000	3/6	2	2	3	0	0	14	.350
JOHNSON, D.	12	0/1	.000	0/0	.000	0/0	.000	0/2	0	0	0	0	0	0	.000
ELLIS, L.	19	0/1	.000	0/0	.000	0/0	.000	2/3	0	0	3	1	0	0	.000
Totals	200	24/56	.429	3/12	.250	12/15	.800	14/33	15	7	12	2	2	63	.315

Team Rebounds: Syracuse 2; Virginia 1. Disqualified: None. Technical fouls: None.

	1st Half	2nd Half	Final
Virginia	28	33	61
Syracuse	41	22	63

SECOND ROUND WEST

UNLV (76)   Coach: Jerry Tarkanian

	Min.	Total FG/FGA	Pct.	3-Pt. FG/FGA	Pct.	FT/FTA	Pct.	Reb. O/T	A	TO	PF	S	Blk	TP	PPM
JOHNSON, L.	28	10/14	.714	0/0	.000	3/7	.429	7/16	1	4	4	0	2	23	.821
AUGMON, S.	36	2/5	.400	0/2	.000	2/2	1.000	2/8	2	3	1	2	2	6	.167
BUTLER, D.	29	6/14	.429	0/0	.000	2/3	.667	2/7	2	3	4	1	0	14	.483
HUNT, A.	37	4/12	.333	0/7	.000	2/3	.667	0/3	2	2	3	4	1	10	.270
ANTHONY, G.	34	3/7	.429	1/2	.500	7/8	.875	0/0	5	1	2	1	0	14	.412
CVIJANOVICH, S.	7	0/2	.000	0/1	.000	0/0	.000	1/2	0	1	1	0	1	0	.000
BICE, T.	2	0/0	.000	0/0	.000	0/0	.000	0/0	0	0	0	0	0	0	.000
YOUNG, B.	4	0/1	.000	0/1	.000	2/2	1.000	0/0	0	0	0	2	0	2	.500
SCURRY, M.	23	3/7	.429	0/0	.000	1/2	.500	2/5	1	1	2	1	0	7	.304
Totals	200	28/62	.452	1/13	.077	19/27	.704	14/41	13	15	17	11	6	76	.380

Ohio State (65)   Coach: Randy Ayers

	Min.	Total FG/FGA	Pct.	3-Pt. FG/FGA	Pct.	FT/FTA	Pct.	Reb. O/T	A	TO	PF	S	Blk	TP	PPM
JENT, C.	25	1/9	.111	1/6	.167	0/0	.000	1/5	1	3	3	1	0	3	.120
JACKSON, J.	34	5/15	.333	0/1	.000	1/2	.500	4/6	4	5	0	1	0	11	.324
CARTER, P.	29	5/11	.455	0/0	.000	5/7	.714	3/8	2	6	3	1	0	15	.517
BAKER, M.	29	4/8	.500	0/0	.000	1/2	.500	1/7	0	2	4	1	0	9	.310
BROWN, J.	29	3/9	.333	0/2	.000	5/5	1.000	5/7	2	2	2	1	0	11	.379
DAVIS, A.	18	2/8	.250	0/2	.000	0/0	.000	0/1	1	2	0	0	0	4	.222
LEE, T.	19	4/10	.400	0/0	.000	2/2	1.000	4/4	0	1	2	0	2	10	.526
ROBINSON, B.	17	0/0	.000	0/0	.000	2/2	1.000	1/6	1	0	4	0	2	2	.118
Totals	200	24/70	.343	1/11	.091	16/20	.800	19/44	11	21	18	5	4	65	.325

Team Rebounds:UNLV 1; Ohio State 3. Disqualified: None. Technical fouls: UNLV—Johnson.

	1st Half	2nd Half	Final
UNLV	39	37	76
Ohio State	37	28	65

Ball State (62)   Coach: Dick Hunsaker

	Min.	Total FG/FGA	Pct.	3-Pt. FG/FGA	Pct.	FT/FTA	Pct.	Reb. O/T	A	TO	PF	S	Blk	TP	PPM
THOMPSON, C.	30	6/10	.600	0/0	.000	3/4	.750	3/6	2	4	2	0	1	15	.500
MCCURDY, P.	26	2/4	.500	0/0	.000	2/2	1.000	2/7	1	7	3	1	0	6	.231
KIDD, C.	35	3/10	.300	0/0	.000	5/6	.833	1/6	0	3	4	0	0	11	.314
NICHOLS, S.	25	0/0	.000	0/0	.000	0/0	.000	0/1	2	3	5	3	0	0	.000
BUTTS, B.	33	4/8	.500	3/7	.429	4/5	.800	0/4	4	1	1	1	0	15	.455
SPICER, M.	11	0/2	.000	0/0	.000	0/0	.000	1/2	0	0	0	0	0	0	.000
MILLER, G.	7	3/4	.750	1/2	.500	0/0	.000	2/5	1	0	1	0	1	7	1.000
MULLER, R.	5	1/2	.500	0/0	.000	0/0	.000	1/2	0	2	0	0	0	2	.400
PARRISH, S.	18	2/4	.500	0/0	.000	0/0	.000	1/3	0	1	3	2	0	4	.222
CROSS, E.	10	1/4	.250	0/1	.000	0/0	.000	0/0	0	1	1	0	0	2	.200
Totals	200	22/48	.458	4/10	.400	14/17	.824	11/36	10	20	21	8	1	62	.310

Louisville (60)   Coach: Denny Crum

	Min.	Total FG/FGA	Pct.	3-Pt. FG/FGA	Pct.	FT/FTA	Pct.	Reb. O/T	A	TO	PF	S	Blk	TP	PPM
HOLDEN, C.	19	1/4	.250	0/0	.000	2/2	1.000	1/3	0	0	2	0	0	4	.211
SULLIVAN, E.	25	1/8	.125	0/0	.000	0/0	.000	0/1	1	2	2	1	0	2	.080
SPENCER, F.	36	5/8	.625	0/0	.000	4/6	.667	4/12	1	6	2	2	1	14	.389
WILLIAMS, K.	40	2/9	.222	1/4	.250	4/4	1.000	0/3	8	0	3	0	0	9	.225
SMITH, L.	34	4/12	.333	1/5	.200	2/2	1.000	3/3	1	2	4	3	0	11	.324
HARMON, J.	26	7/11	.636	0/0	.000	0/0	.000	1/2	0	1	0	2	0	14	.538
KIMBRO, T.	20	2/6	.333	1/3	.333	1/1	1.000	1/3	0	1	5	0	1	6	.300
Totals	200	22/58	.379	3/12	.250	13/15	.867	10/27	11	12	15	11	2	60	.300

Team Rebounds: Ball St. 2; Louisville 0. Disqualified: Ball St.—Nichols; Louisville—Kimbro. Technical fouls: None.

	1st Half	2nd Half	Final
Ball St.	36	26	62
Louisville	23	37	60

Loyola Marymount (149)   Coach: Paul Westhead

	Min.	Total FG/FGA	Pct.	3-Pt. FG/FGA	Pct.	FT/FTA	Pct.	Reb. O/T	A	TO	PF	S	Blk	TP	PPM
STUMER, P.	30	6/9	.667	5/8	.625	4/4	1.000	1/8	2	3	4	0	1	21	.700
KIMBLE, B.	37	11/29	.379	1/8	.125	14/17	.824	3/7	4	2	5	2	0	37	1.000
KNIGHT, J.	18	2/5	.400	0/0	.000	0/0	.000	1/6	3	0	5	0	0	4	.222
WALKER, T.	27	0/2	.000	0/0	.000	5/7	.714	3/9	3	3	1	0	0	5	.185
FRYER, J.	32	15/20	.750	11/15	.733	0/0	.000	0/4	3	2	4	2	0	41	1.281
PEABODY, T.	19	4/5	.800	0/0	.000	6/6	1.000	2/3	5	0	3	3	0	14	.737
LOWERY, T.	23	10/17	.588	3/8	.375	0/0	.000	3/3	6	5	2	3	0	23	1.000
SCOTT, C.	9	0/1	.000	0/0	.000	0/0	.000	1/2	1	1	0	1	2	0	.000
LEE, M.	1	1/1	1.000	1/1	1.000	0/0	.000	1/2	0	0	0	0	0	3	3.000
WALKER, G.	1	0/0	.000	0/0	.000	1/2	.500	0/0	0	0	0	0	0	1	1.000
O'CONNELL, J.	1	0/0	.000	0/0	.000	0/0	.000	0/0	0	0	0	0	0	0	.000
ROSCOE, J.	1	0/0	.000	0/0	.000	0/0	.000	0/0	0	0	0	0	0	0	.000
SLATER, M.	1	0/0	.000	0/0	.000	0/0	.000	0/0	0	0	0	0	0	0	.000
Totals	200	49/89	.551	21/40	.525	30/36	.833	13/38	33	16	26	12	3	149	.745

Michigan (115)   Coach: Steve Fisher

	Min.	Total FG/FGA	Pct.	3-Pt. FG/FGA	Pct.	FT/FTA	Pct.	Reb. O/T	A	TO	PF	S	Blk	TP	PPM
GRIFFIN, M.	13	2/4	.500	0/0	.000	0/0	.000	0/1	5	1	5	1	0	4	.308
VAUGHT, L.	30	9/15	.600	0/0	.000	1/3	.333	8/17	0	4	3	0	0	19	.633
MILLS, T.	33	11/16	.688	0/0	.000	1/2	.500	5/10	1	8	2	0	0	23	.697
CALIP, D.	31	2/8	.250	0/0	.000	6/8	.750	1/5	3	3	2	1	0	10	.323
ROBINSON, R.	35	7/14	.500	2/6	.333	7/10	.700	1/3	8	5	4	0	1	23	.657
TOLBERT, T.	11	7/11	.636	1/2	.500	1/1	1.000	2/2	1	1	3	1	0	16	1.455
TALLEY, M.	13	1/3	.333	0/1	.000	1/2	.500	1/2	1	2	3	1	0	3	.231
HIGGINS, S.	23	5/13	.385	1/4	.250	4/4	1.000	2/3	2	1	5	1	1	15	.652
RILEY, E.	9	1/1	1.000	0/0	.000	0/0	.000	0/3	0	2	2	0	3	2	.222
VOSKUIL, J.	1	0/0	.000	0/0	.000	0/0	.000	0/0	0	0	0	0	0	0	.000
SETER, C.	1	0/0	.000	0/0	.000	0/0	.000	0/0	0	0	0	0	0	0	.000
Totals	200	45/85	.529	4/13	.308	21/30	.700	20/46	21	27	29	5	5	115	.575

Team Rebounds: Loyola Mymt. 1; Michigan 5. Disqualified: Loyola Mymt.—Kimble, Knight; Michigan—Griffin, Higgins. Technical fouls: Michigan—Vaught.

	1st Half	2nd Half	Final
Loyola Mymt.	65	84	149
Michigan	58	57	115

Alabama (77)　Coach: Wimp Sanderson

	Min.	Total FG/FGA	Pct.	3-Pt. FG/FGA	Pct.	FT/FTA	Pct.	Reb. O/T	A	TO	PF	S	Blk	TP	PPM
HORRY, R.	26	3/7	.429	2/5	.400	0/0	.000	3/8	3	1	3	0	0	8	.308
CHEATUM, M.	26	5/13	.385	0/0	.000	2/2	1.000	4/5	1	4	3	0	0	12	.462
BENOIT, D.	36	9/13	.692	0/0	.000	2/2	1.000	4/13	1	3	3	0	0	20	.556
WAITES, G.	23	3/4	.750	2/2	1.000	2/3	.667	0/2	2	0	1	1	0	10	.435
SANDERS, J.	36	5/11	.455	0/2	.000	2/2	1.000	0/2	13	2	2	0	0	12	.333
ASKINS, K.	28	3/8	.375	2/6	.333	2/4	.500	1/1	3	1	1	0	0	10	.357
WEBB, M.	19	2/5	.400	0/0	.000	0/0	.000	4/4	0	1	2	0	0	4	.211
RICE, K.	1	0/1	.000	0/1	.000	0/0	.000	0/0	0	0	0	0	0	0	.000
BROWN, E.	1	0/1	.000	0/1	.000	0/0	.000	0/0	0	0	0	0	0	0	.000
LANCASTER, B.	1	0/0	.000	0/0	.000	0/0	.000	0/1	0	0	0	0	0	0	.000
RICH, D.	1	0/0	.000	0/0	.000	0/0	.000	0/0	0	0	0	0	0	0	.000
CAMPBELL, M.	1	0/0	.000	0/0	.000	1/2	.500	0/1	0	0	0	0	0	1	1.000
LAWRENCE, A.	1	0/0	.000	0/0	.000	0/0	.000	0/0	0	0	0	0	0	0	.000
Totals	200	30/63	.476	6/17	.353	11/15	.733	16/37	23	12	15	1	0	77	.385

Arizona (55)　Coach: Lute Olson

	Min.	Total FG/FGA	Pct.	3-Pt. FG/FGA	Pct.	FT/FTA	Pct.	Reb. O/T	A	TO	PF	S	Blk	TP	PPM
WILLIAMS, B.	14	0/3	.000	0/0	.000	0/0	.000	1/2	0	2	0	0	0	0	.000
BUECHLER, J.	39	2/8	.250	0/2	.000	2/3	.667	2/11	3	4	2	0	1	6	.154
STOKES, E.	37	5/6	.833	0/0	.000	7/10	.700	4/5	0	2	4	0	2	17	.459
OTHICK, M.	33	1/7	.143	1/6	.167	2/2	1.000	1/2	5	4	2	1	0	5	.152
MUEHLEBACH, M.	39	6/15	.400	4/11	.364	0/0	.000	0/2	5	1	2	3	0	16	.410
ROOKS, S.	25	5/8	.625	0/0	.000	1/2	.500	1/2	0	2	5	0	1	11	.440
SCHMIDT, C.	1	0/0	.000	0/0	.000	0/0	.000	0/1	0	0	0	0	0	0	.000
WOMACK, W.	11	0/0	.000	0/0	.000	0/0	.000	0/1	0	2	0	0	0	0	.000
DAVID, B.	1	0/0	.000	0/0	.000	0/0	.000	0/0	0	0	0	0	0	0	.000
Totals	200	19/47	.404	5/19	.263	12/17	.706	9/26	13	15	17	4	4	55	.275

Team Rebounds: Alabama 4; Arizona 3. Disqualified: Arizona—Rooks. Technical fouls: None.

	1st Half	2nd Half	Final
Alabama	38	39	77
Arizona	33	22	55

SECOND ROUND EAST

U. Conn. (74)　Coach: Jim Calhoun

	Min.	Total FG/FGA	Pct.	3-Pt. FG/FGA	Pct.	FT/FTA	Pct.	Reb. O/T	A	TO	PF	S	Blk	TP	PPM
BURRELL, S.	31	4/9	.444	0/0	.000	5/6	.833	5/7	2	1	3	1	0	13	.419
HENEFELD, N.	30	4/7	.571	1/1	1.000	1/2	.500	0/3	2	1	3	4	0	10	.333
SELLERS, R.	14	1/4	.250	0/0	.000	0/0	.000	2/3	1	1	2	1	0	2	.143
SMITH, C.	33	6/17	.353	5/13	.385	7/8	.875	1/3	2	3	2	0	0	24	.727
GEORGE, T.	35	4/9	.444	0/1	.000	2/2	1.000	1/3	3	2	2	3	0	10	.286
WALKER, T.	13	1/1	1.000	0/0	.000	0/0	.000	1/3	1	0	3	0	0	2	.154
GWYNN, J.	15	3/10	.300	1/2	.500	2/3	.667	1/4	0	0	1	1	0	9	.600
WILLIAMS, J.	7	0/1	.000	0/0	.000	0/0	.000	0/0	0	2	0	0	0	0	.000
CYRULIK, D.	2	0/0	.000	0/0	.000	0/0	.000	0/0	0	0	2	0	0	0	.000
DEPRIEST, L.	18	1/4	.250	0/0	.000	1/2	.500	1/3	0	1	3	4	0	3	.167
PIKIELL, S.	1	0/0	.000	0/0	.000	1/2	.500	0/0	0	0	0	0	1	1	1.000
MACKLIN, O.	1	0/1	.000	0/0	.000	0/0	.000	0/0	0	0	0	0	0	0	.000
Totals	200	24/63	.381	7/17	.412	19/25	.760	12/29	11	11	21	16	0	74	.370

California (54)　Coach: Lou Campanelli

	Min.	Total FG/FGA	Pct.	3-Pt. FG/FGA	Pct.	FT/FTA	Pct.	Reb. O/T	A	TO	PF	S	Blk	TP	PPM
WALTON, B.	32	3/7	.429	1/4	.250	0/0	.000	0/8	0	4	4	0	0	7	.219
FISHER, R.	39	6/7	.857	0/1	.000	5/8	.625	1/6	2	10	3	0	1	17	.436
HENDRICK, B.	35	5/7	.714	0/0	.000	2/4	.500	1/6	0	5	4	1	1	12	.343
SMITH, K.	37	3/6	.500	0/0	.000	3/3	1.000	0/3	5	7	3	0	0	9	.243
DREW, R.	23	2/6	.333	1/4	.250	0/2	.000	1/2	2	0	0	0	5	.217
ELLEBY, B.	18	0/4	.000	0/2	.000	2/2	1.000	0/0	0	1	1	1	0	2	.111
REYES, A.	4	0/0	.000	0/0	.000	0/0	.000	0/0	1	0	0	0	0	0	.000
HARRELL, S.	8	0/1	.000	0/0	.000	2/3	.667	1/1	1	1	3	0	1	2	.250
MCDONOUGH, E.	1	0/0	.000	0/0	.000	0/0	.000	0/0	0	0	0	0	0	0	.000
CARTY, J.	1	0/0	.000	0/0	.000	0/0	.000	0/0	0	0	0	0	0	0	.000
BRANHAM, R.	1	0/1	.000	0/1	.000	0/0	.000	0/0	0	0	0	0	0	0	.000
BRIGHAM, A.	1	0/0	.000	0/0	.000	0/0	.000	0/0	0	0	1	0	0	0	.000
Totals	200	19/39	.487	2/12	.167	14/22	.636	4/26	11	28	19	2	3	54	.270

Team Rebounds: U. Conn. 3; California 7. Disqualified: None. Technical fouls: U. Conn.—Campanelli.

	1st Half	2nd Half	Final
U. Conn.	42	32	74
California	26	28	54

Clemson (79)　Coach: Cliff Ellis

	Min.	Total FG/FGA	Pct.	3-Pt. FG/FGA	Pct.	FT/FTA	Pct.	Reb. O/T	A	TO	PF	S	Blk	TP	PPM
FORREST, D.	32	6/14	.429	0/2	.000	0/2	.000	6/9	3	3	3	3	1	12	.375
DAVIS, D.	39	8/12	.667	0/0	.000	10/14	.714	7/17	0	1	1	3	2	26	.667
CAMPBELL, E.	30	3/8	.375	0/0	.000	1/1	1.000	0/5	0	3	5	0	2	7	.233
YOUNG, D.	11	1/4	.250	0/2	.000	0/0	.000	0/0	1	0	1	0	0	2	.182
CASH, M.	38	4/8	.500	1/2	.500	5/10	.500	0/4	5	7	3	0	0	14	.368
HOWLING, K.	7	0/4	.000	0/2	.000	1/2	.500	1/1	0	1	0	0	1	.143
TYSON, S.	36	8/16	.500	0/0	.000	1/4	.250	7/11	4	2	1	2	0	17	.472
BROWN, L.	2	0/0	.000	0/0	.000	0/0	.000	0/1	1	0	1	0	0	0	.000
BUCKINGHAM, W.	2	0/0	.000	0/0	.000	0/0	.000	0/0	0	0	0	0	0	0	.000
JONES, R.	2	0/0	.000	0/0	.000	0/0	.000	0/1	0	1	0	0	0	0	.000
Totals	200	30/66	.455	1/8	.125	18/33	.545	21/50	13	19	14	8	5	79	.395

La Salle (75)　Coach: Bill Morris

	Min.	Total FG/FGA	Pct.	3-Pt. FG/FGA	Pct.	FT/FTA	Pct.	Reb. O/T	A	TO	PF	S	Blk	TP	PPM
SIMMONS, L.	39	12/21	.571	1/6	.167	3/3	1.000	1/6	3	2	5	2	2	28	.718
HURD, J.	19	4/10	.400	2/7	.286	0/1	.000	1/5	0	2	4	1	0	10	.526
LIEVERST, M.	20	2/2	1.000	0/0	.000	0/1	.000	0/0	1	1	4	1	1	4	.200
OVERTON, D.	40	4/14	.286	0/6	.000	0/0	.000	2/4	6	2	4	3	1	8	.200
WOODS, R.	38	6/18	.333	4/13	.308	2/3	.667	4/6	4	1	4	3	0	18	.474
JOHNSON, B.	24	3/7	.429	1/3	.333	0/0	.000	4/7	1	2	2	1	0	7	.292
HOLLAND, B.	18	0/1	.000	0/0	.000	0/0	.000	0/1	1	2	4	0	0	0	.000
MORRIS, K.	1	0/0	.000	0/0	.000	0/0	.000	0/0	0	0	0	0	0	0	.000
SHELTON, D.	1	0/0	.000	0/0	.000	0/0	.000	0/1	0	0	0	0	0	0	.000
Totals	200	31/73	.425	8/35	.229	5/8	.625	12/30	16	12	27	11	4	75	.375

Team Rebounds: Clemson 5; La Salle 6. Disqualified: Clemson—Campbell; La Salle—Simmons. Technical fouls: La Salle—Team.

	1st Half	2nd Half	Final
Clemson	27	52	79
La Salle	43	32	75

St. John's (72) Coach: Lou Carnesecca

	Min.	Total FG/FGA	Pct.	3-Pt. FG/FGA	Pct.	FT/FTA	Pct.	Reb. O/T	A	TO	PF	S	Blk	TP	PPM
SEALY, M.	40	8/13	.615	0/0	.000	3/4	.750	1/3	3	1	3	4	2	19	.475
SINGLETON, B.	38	3/5	.600	0/0	.000	2/2	1.000	1/4	1	1	3	1	0	8	.211
WERDANN, R.	21	4/6	.667	0/0	.000	0/0	.000	2/4	2	3	4	2	1	8	.381
HARVEY, B.	39	4/18	.222	3/6	.500	6/8	.750	1/2	9	3	3	5	0	17	.436
BUCHANAN, J.	34	5/12	.417	0/2	.000	0/0	.000	0/0	7	3	0	1	0	10	.294
MUTO, S.	16	3/6	.500	0/0	.000	0/1	.000	4/10	0	1	5	0	0	6	.375
SPROLING, C.	11	2/3	.667	0/0	.000	0/0	.000	0/1	0	0	3	1	0	4	.364
CAIN, D.	1	0/0	.000	0/0	.000	0/0	.000	0/0	0	0	0	0	0	0	.000
Totals	200	29/63	.460	3/8	.375	11/15	.733	9/24	22	12	21	14	3	72	.360

Duke (76) Coach: Mike Krzyzewski

	Min.	Total FG/FGA	Pct.	3-Pt. FG/FGA	Pct.	FT/FTA	Pct.	Reb. O/T	A	TO	PF	S	Blk	TP	PPM
BRICKEY, R.	34	7/13	.538	0/0	.000	8/12	.667	5/9	2	6	2	2	1	22	.647
LAETTNER, C.	27	0/7	.000	0/0	.000	6/9	.667	2/7	0	2	3	0	1	6	.222
ABDELNABY, A.	26	6/8	.750	0/0	.000	5/6	.833	2/7	1	3	1	0	0	17	.654
HENDERSON, P.	29	5/8	.625	1/3	.333	2/2	1.000	1/4	2	4	4	0	0	13	.448
HURLEY, B.	40	4/9	.429	2/2	1.000	0/3	.667	1/3	7	5	4	0	0	10	.250
HILL, T.	12	2/2	1.000	0/0	.000	0/0	.000	0/0	1	0	1	0	0	4	.333
DAVIS, B.	17	2/3	.667	0/0	.000	0/0	.000	0/1	0	1	0	1	0	4	.235
MCCAFFREY, B.	10	0/2	.000	0/0	.000	0/0	.000	0/1	0	0	1	1	0	0	.000
KOUBEK, G.	5	0/0	.000	0/0	.000	0/0	.000	0/1	1	0	0	0	0	0	.000
Totals	200	25/50	.500	3/5	.600	23/32	.719	11/33	13	20	17	4	2	76	.380

Team Rebounds: Duke 6; St. John's 5. Disqualified: St. John's—Muto. Technical fouls: St. John's—Muto.

	1st Half	2nd Half	Final
St. John's	32	40	72
Duke	36	40	76

UCLA (71) Coach: Jim Harrick

	Min.	Total FG/FGA	Pct.	3-Pt. FG/FGA	Pct.	FT/FTA	Pct.	Reb. O/T	A	TO	PF	S	Blk	TP	PPM
WILSON	38	8/19	.421	0/0	.000	2/4	.500	4/12	3	3	3	4	1	18	.474
MACLEAN, D.	35	3/8	.375	0/0	.000	4/4	1.000	1/5	1	1	1	3	1	10	.286
MURRAY, T.	27	5/12	.417	0/3	.000	2/3	.667	4/8	0	0	2	2	0	12	.444
MADKINS	32	1/3	.333	1/2	.500	0/0	.000	0/0	6	3	5	1	0	3	.094
MARTIN	33	7/12	.583	0/0	.000	4/5	.800	0/6	6	5	3	5	0	18	.545
BUTLER, M.	19	1/5	.200	0/1	.000	6/6	1.000	0/0	0	0	1	0	0	8	.421
WALKER, K.	12	0/0	.000	0/0	.000	2/2	1.000	0/1	1	0	1	0	0	2	.167
OWENS, K.	4	0/0	.000	0/0	.000	0/0	.000	0/2	0	2	0	1	1	0	.000
Totals	200	25/59	.424	1/6	.167	20/24	.833	9/27	17	12	17	16	2	71	.355

Kansas (70) Coach: Roy Williams

	Min.	Total FG/FGA	Pct.	3-Pt. FG/FGA	Pct.	FT/FTA	Pct.	Reb. O/T	A	TO	PF	S	Blk	TP	PPM
CALLOWAY, R.	24	4/8	.500	0/0	.000	6/7	.857	1/3	2	2	3	3	0	14	.583
RANDALL, M.	26	2/5	.400	0/0	.000	0/0	.000	1/7	3	3	4	1	0	4	.154
MARKKANEN, P.	27	0/2	.000	0/0	.000	0/0	.000	1/2	1	0	0	0	2	0	.000
PRITCHARD, K.	34	5/8	.625	1/2	.500	4/5	.800	0/1	3	7	4	0	1	15	.441
GUELDNER, J.	17	3/8	.375	1/4	.250	0/0	.000	2/8	3	0	1	1	0	7	.412
MADDOX, M.	12	4/7	.571	0/0	.000	2/2	1.000	1/5	1	4	3	0	2	10	.833
BROWN, T.	19	5/8	.625	5/6	.833	0/0	.000	2/4	0	2	1	1	0	15	.789
JORDAN, A.	8	0/1	.000	0/0	.000	0/0	.000	0/0	0	1	2	1	0	0	.000
WEST, F.	15	2/4	.500	0/0	.000	1/2	.500	0/2	0	1	1	0	0	5	.333
JAMISON, A.	18	0/1	.000	0/0	.000	0/0	.000	0/1	2	1	0	0	0	0	.000
Totals	200	25/52	.481	7/12	.583	13/16	.813	8/33	16	22	18	6	5	70	.350

Team Rebounds: UCLA 3; Kansas 2. Disqualified: UCLA—Madkins. Technical fouls: None.

	1st Half	2nd Half	Final
UCLA	35	36	71
Kansas	36	34	70

SECOND ROUND MIDWEST

Oklahoma (77) Coach: Billy Tubbs

	Min.	Total FG/FGA	Pct.	3-Pt. FG/FGA	Pct.	FT/FTA	Pct.	Reb. O/T	A	TO	PF	S	Blk	TP	PPM
JONES, J.	33	6/13	.462	3/6	.500	0/2	.000	0/0	2	3	2	0	2	15	.455
PATTERSON, D.	19	1/2	.500	0/0	.000	1/1	1.000	0/1	1	3	4	1	0	3	.158
DAVIS, W.	36	8/14	.571	0/1	.000	6/7	.857	3/14	0	3	2	3	0	22	.611
MCCOVERY, S.	34	4/8	.500	2/5	.400	3/4	.750	2/4	7	1	3	1	0	13	.382
HENRY, S.	40	4/9	.444	2/5	.400	2/2	1.000	2/4	6	5	3	3	0	10	.300
EVANS, T.	18	0/2	.000	0/2	.000	2/2	1.000	0/0	4	1	1	2	0	2	.111
MARTIN, T.	20	5/10	.500	0/0	.000	0/0	.000	1/1	1	1	3	0	0	10	.500
Totals	200	28/58	.483	7/19	.368	14/18	.778	8/24	21	17	18	10	2	77	.385

North Carolina (79) Coach: Dean Smith

	Min.	Total FG/FGA	Pct.	3-Pt. FG/FGA	Pct.	FT/FTA	Pct.	Reb. O/T	A	TO	PF	S	Blk	TP	PPM
CHILCUTT, P.	34	6/10	.600	0/0	.000	5/5	1.000	1/5	2	1	1	1	2	17	.500
FOX, R.	33	9/16	.563	5/7	.714	0/0	.000	1/3	2	1	4	3	0	23	.697
WILLIAMS, S.	17	1/8	.125	0/0	.000	0/0	.000	0/3	2	1	5	1	0	2	.118
RICE, K.	38	5/8	.625	1/1	1.000	1/4	.250	0/2	7	7	2	3	0	12	.316
MADDEN, K.	29	4/4	1.000	0/0	.000	6/7	.857	1/2	2	1	2	0	0	14	.483
HARRIS, P.	2	0/0	.000	0/0	.000	0/0	.000	0/0	1	0	0	0	0	0	.000
RODL, H.	10	1/1	1.000	1/1	1.000	0/0	.000	0/1	0	0	0	0	0	3	.300
LYNCH, G.	23	2/5	.400	0/0	.000	2/2	1.000	3/8	1	5	5	2	5	6	.261
DAVIS, H.	13	1/2	.500	0/1	.000	0/0	.000	0/1	1	0	0	0	0	2	.154
WENSTROM, M.	1	0/0	.000	0/0	.000	0/0	.000	0/0	0	0	1	0	0	0	.000
Totals	200	29/54	.537	7/10	.700	14/19	.737	6/24	18	17	20	10	7	79	.395

Team Rebounds: N. Carolina 8; Oklahoma 4. Disqualified: N. Carolina—Williams, Lynch. Technical fouls: Oklahoma—Martin.

	1st Half	2nd Half	Final
Oklahoma	38	39	77
N. Carolina	40	39	79

Dayton (84) Coach: Jim O'Brien

	Min.	Total FG/FGA	Pct.	3-Pt. FG/FGA	Pct.	FT/FTA	Pct.	Reb. O/T	A	TO	PF	S	Blk	TP	PPM
CORBITT, A.	32	8/15	.533	0/0	.000	2/3	.667	3/6	1	4	4	0	0	18	.563
ROBINSON, N.	24	9/14	.643	0/3	.000	2/4	.500	4/10	1	2	2	1	0	20	.833
COFFEE, W.	18	2/2	1.000	0/0	.000	2/6	.333	2/5	1	1	2	0	3	6	.333
SPRINGER, R.	36	7/12	.583	3/6	.500	0/0	.000	0/4	3	3	3	2	0	17	.472
KNIGHT, N.	38	3/12	.250	2/5	.400	8/10	.800	0/3	10	5	1	1	0	16	.421
UHL, B.	16	0/2	.000	0/0	.000	0/0	.000	0/1	0	2	3	0	1	0	.000
ROBERTSON, A.	17	1/6	.167	1/2	.500	0/0	.000	2/5	3	1	0	0	0	3	.176
HOWARD, S.	14	1/4	.250	0/1	.000	0/0	.000	3/3	1	2	0	0	0	2	.143
BRADDS, D.	5	1/2	.500	0/0	.000	0/0	.000	0/0	0	0	0	1	0	2	.400
Totals	200	32/69	.464	6/19	.316	14/23	.609	14/37	20	20	15	5	4	84	.420

Arkansas (86) Coach: Nolan Richardson

	Min.	Total FG/FGA	Pct.	3-Pt. FG/FGA	Pct.	FT/FTA	Pct.	Reb. O/T	A	TO	PF	S	Blk	TP	PPM
DAY, T.	33	11/17	.647	2/4	.500	1/1	1.000	3/9	2	6	3	2	0	25	.758
HOWELL, L.	34	7/12	.583	2/3	.667	7/8	.875	1/5	3	2	2	1	1	23	.676
CREDIT, M.	17	4/10	.400	0/0	.000	4/5	.800	4/6	1	0	2	2	1	12	.706
MAYBERRY, L.	34	2/10	.200	0/5	.000	0/0	.000	0/2	1	2	0	0	0	4	.118
BOWERS, A.	19	0/3	.000	0/0	.000	0/0	.000	0/0	1	1	3	1	0	0	.000
MURRY, E.	14	2/4	.500	0/2	.000	0/0	.000	0/2	2	1	1	0	1	4	.286
HAWKINS, D.	11	1/2	.500	0/0	.000	1/2	.500	2/5	0	2	2	1	0	3	.273
MILLER, R.	22	3/7	.429	0/0	.000	1/2	.500	1/7	2	4	4	2	3	7	.318
HUERY, R.	16	3/10	.300	1/4	.250	1/1	1.000	3/6	4	1	2	0	1	8	.500
Totals	200	33/75	.440	5/18	.278	15/19	.789	14/42	16	19	19	13	7	86	.430

Team Rebounds: Arkansas 2; Dayton 5. Disqualified: None. Technical fouls: Arkansas—Bench.

	1st Half	2nd Half	Final
Dayton	42	42	84
Arkansas	42	44	86

Xavier (Ohio) (74)   Coach: Pete Gillen

	Min.	Total FG/FGA	Pct.	3-Pt. FG/FGA	Pct.	FT/FTA	Pct.	Reb. O/T	A	TO	PF	S	Blk	TP	PPM
BRANTLEY, M.	22	3/4	.750	1/1	1.000	0/1	.000	3/6	1	3	3	2	1	7	.318
HILL, T.	25	5/9	.556	0/0	.000	3/3	1.000	4/8	1	5	5	1	1	13	.520
STRONG, D.	36	5/12	.417	0/0	.000	9/10	.900	3/12	1	3	4	1	0	19	.528
WALKER, J.	38	4/13	.308	0/4	.000	7/8	.875	2/4	9	5	4	1	0	15	.395
GLADDEN, J.	36	6/10	.600	0/1	.000	1/2	.500	1/2	1	2	0	0	0	13	.361
DAVENPORT, M.	21	2/5	.400	1/4	.250	0/0	.000	0/1	2	1	2	0	0	5	.238
PARKER, C.	3	0/0	.000	0/0	.000	0/0	.000	0/0	0	0	0	0	0	0	.000
WILLIAMS, A.	16	1/3	.333	0/0	.000	0/1	.000	3/5	0	0	2	1	1	2	.125
WILSON, D.	3	0/0	.000	0/0	.000	0/0	.000	0/0	0	1	1	0	0	0	.000
Totals	200	26/56	.464	2/10	.200	20/25	.800	16/38	15	20	21	6	3	74	.370

Georgetown (71)   Coach: John Thompson

	Min.	Total FG/FGA	Pct.	3-Pt. FG/FGA	Pct.	FT/FTA	Pct.	Reb. O/T	A	TO	PF	S	Blk	TP	PPM
ALLEN, A.	16	0/2	.000	0/0	.000	0/0	.000	1/2	0	0	2	1	1	0	.000
MOURNING, A.	34	5/8	.625	0/0	.000	5/7	.714	4/10	1	6	5	0	2	15	.441
MUTOMBO, D.	23	4/7	.571	0/0	.000	1/3	.333	5/12	1	0	3	1	2	9	.391
BRYANT, D.	28	3/9	.333	0/3	.000	0/0	.000	0/4	3	4	3	4	2	6	.214
TILLMON, M.	36	6/17	.353	1/5	.200	3/4	.750	1/1	1	0	2	0		16	.444
EDWARDS, D.	32	7/13	.538	4/8	.500	1/5	.200	2/2	2	5	2	4	0	19	.594
TATE, M.	5	1/2	.500	0/0	.000	0/0	.000	2/2	0	0	0	0	0	2	.400
STOUDAMIRE, A.	15	0/3	.000	0/3	.000	0/0	.000	1/1	0	0	0	0	0	0	.000
JEFFERSON, S.	11	2/4	.500	0/0	.000	0/1	.000	1/1	0	0	1	0	0	4	.364
Totals	200	28/65	.431	5/19	.263	10/20	.500	17/35	10	14	19	8	5	71	.355

Team Rebounds: Xavier (Ohio) 2; Georgetown 3. Disqualified: Xavier (Ohio)—Hill; Georgetown—Mourning. Technical fouls: Georgetown—Bryant.

	1st Half	2nd Half	Final
Xavier (Ohio)	42	32	74
Georgetown	26	45	71

Texas (73)   Coach: Tom Penders

	Min.	Total FG/FGA	Pct.	3-Pt. FG/FGA	Pct.	FT/FTA	Pct.	Reb. O/T	A	TO	PF	S	Blk	TP	PPM
BLANKS, L.	36	6/16	.375	3/7	.429	4/4	1.000	0/2	1	3	5	2	0	19	.528
COLLIE, L.	16	1/6	.167	0/0	.000	0/0	.000	1/3	0	1	2	0	0	2	.125
MYERS, G.	33	1/2	.500	0/0	.000	0/0	.000	4/13	0	1	3	1	4	2	.061
WRIGHT, J.	38	9/16	.563	1/3	.333	1/1	1.000	1/5		2	1	1	0	20	.526
MAYS, T.	40	5/14	.357	1/4	.250	5/5	1.000	2/4	2	2	2	0	0	16	.400
WILLIAMS, B.	21	5/6	.833	0/0	.000	2/2	1.000	2/2	1	1	3	2	0	12	.571
COURTNEY, J.	6	0/0	.000	0/0	.000	0/0	.000	0/0	0	0	1	0	0	0	.000
DUDEK, H.	5	1/2	.500	0/0	.000	0/1	.000	1/2	0	1	1	0	0	2	.400
MULLER, G.	5	0/0	.000	0/0	.000	0/0	.000	0/1	1	1	0	2	0	0	.000
Totals	200	28/62	.452	5/14	.357	12/13	.923	11/32	7	11	20	6	4	73	.365

Purdue (72)   Coach: Gene Keady

	Min.	Total FG/FGA	Pct.	3-Pt. FG/FGA	Pct.	FT/FTA	Pct.	Reb. O/T	A	TO	PF	S	Blk	TP	PPM
BERNING, R.	35	2/4	.500	1/1	1.000	2/3	.667	2/7	0	1	2	2	2	7	.200
WHITE, C.	24	3/5	.600	0/0	.000	2/2	1.000	2/4	2	3	1	1	0	8	.333
SCHEFFLER, S.	36	6/17	.353	0/0	.000	6/6	1.000	2/8	1	1	1	1	0	18	.500
AUSTIN, W.	27	6/12	.500	1/4	.250	2/2	1.000	0/2	2	2	2	1	0	15	.556
JONES, T.	40	3/7	.429	0/1	.000	2/3	.667	1/3	8	2	3	0	0	8	.200
CLYBURN, L.	10	2/2	1.000	1/1	1.000	0/1	.000	0/1	0	1	2	0	0	5	.500
BARRETT, D.	5	0/0	.000	0/0	.000	0/0	.000	0/0	1	1	1	0	0	0	.000
OLIVER, J.	23	5/7	.714	1/2	.500	0/0	.000	0/2	3	2	1	0	0	11	.478
Totals	200	27/54	.500	4/9	.444	14/17	.824	7/27	17	13	13	5	2	72	.360

Team Rebounds: Texas 1; Purdue 4. Disqualified: Texas—Blanks. Technical fouls: None.

	1st Half	2nd Half	Final
Texas	33	40	73
Purdue	35	37	72

REGIONAL SEMIFINAL SOUTHEAST

Michigan State (80)   Coach: Jud Heathcote

	Min.	Total FG/FGA	Pct.	3-Pt. FG/FGA	Pct.	FT/FTA	Pct.	Reb. O/T	A	TO	PF	S	Blk	TP	PPM
REDFIELD, K.	36	3/6	.500	0/1	.000	1/2	.500	2/5	2	2	4	1	1	7	.194
STEIGENGA, M.	25	2/9	.222	0/0	.000	0/0	.000	1/4	3	3	4	1	0	4	.160
PEPLOWSKI, M.	19	4/5	.800	0/0	.000	1/1	1.000	1/4	1	0	1	0	0	9	.474
SMITH, S.	44	13/22	.591	3/5	.600	3/4	.750	1/5	6	4	0	2	0	32	.727
MONTGOMERY, M.	29	2/5	.400	1/1	1.000	0/0	.000	1/1	2	3	5	1	1	5	.172
MANNS, K.	12	0/3	.000	0/1	.000	0/0	.000	0/1	0	1	1	0	0	0	.000
HICKMAN, P.	25	6/9	.667	0/0	.000	1/1	1.000	1/10	0	1	2	0	2	13	.520
STEPHENS, D.	35	3/6	.500	0/0	.000	4/4	1.000	3/5	2	0	0	0	0	10	.286
Totals	225	33/65	.508	4/8	.500	10/12	.833	10/35	16	14	17	5	4	80	.356

Georgia Tech (81)   Coach: Bobby Cremins

	Min.	Total FG/FGA	Pct.	3-Pt. FG/FGA	Pct.	FT/FTA	Pct.	Reb. O/T	A	TO	PF	S	Blk	TP	PPM
SCOTT, D.	45	7/22	.318	2/10	.200	2/2	1.000	1/9	1	3	3	1	0	18	.400
MACKEY, M.	25	3/6	.500	0/0	.000	0/2	.000	4/7	0	0	3	0	2	6	.240
MCNEIL, J.	37	4/6	.667	0/0	.000	4/4	1.000	1/6	0	1	5	0	0	12	.324
ANDERSON, K.	45	13/23	.565	3/8	.375	2/3	.667	3/4	3	2	0	3	0	31	.689
OLIVER, B.	43	4/10	.400	0/4	.000	3/4	.750	0/1	1	2	4	1	0	11	.256
BROWN, K.	29	1/2	.500	1/1	1.000	0/0	.000	1/1	1	1	3	2	0	3	.103
BARNES, D.	1	0/0	.000	0/0	.000	0/0	.000	0/0	0	0	0	0	0	0	.000
Totals	225	32/69	.464	6/23	.261	11/15	.733	10/28	6	9	18	7	2	81	.360

Team Rebounds: Georgia Tech 6; Michigan St. 4. Disqualified: Georgia Tech—McNeil; Michigan St.—Montgomery. Technical fouls: None.

	1st Half	2nd Half	1 OT	Final
Michigan St.	35	40	5	80
Georgia Tech	39	36	6	81

Minnesota (82)   Coach: Clem Haskins

	Min.	Total FG/FGA	Pct.	3-Pt. FG/FGA	Pct.	FT/FTA	Pct.	Reb. O/T	A	TO	PF	S	Blk	TP	PPM
COFFEY, R.	32	5/8	.625	0/0	.000	2/2	1.000	4/12	3	1	4	0	1	12	.375
BURTON, W.	29	4/8	.500	1/2	.500	3/6	.500	2/4	1	1	4	1	0	12	.414
SHIKENJANSKI, J.	19	3/5	.600	0/0	.000	0/0	.000	0/0	0	1	2	1	0	6	.316
LYNCH, K.	35	7/10	.700	2/2	1.000	2/3	.667	0/3	4	3	4	1	0	18	.514
NEWBERN, M.	33	9/15	.600	0/1	.000	2/3	.667	0/3	4	3	2	4	0	20	.606
GREEN, M.	3	0/1	.000	0/0	.000	0/0	.000	0/1	0	1	1	0	0	0	.000
LEWIS, C.	9	0/0	.000	0/0	.000	0/0	.000	0/0	1	0	0	0	0	0	.000
BOND, W.	24	1/4	.250	0/1	.000	2/3	.667	0/4	1	3	3	1	2	4	.167
MARTIN, B.	16	4/5	.800	0/0	.000	2/2	1.000	1/3	0	0	2	0	0	10	.625
Totals	200	33/56	.589	3/6	.500	13/19	.684	7/29	13	14	19	8	3	82	.410

Syracuse (75)   Coach: Jim Boeheim

	Min.	Total FG/FGA	Pct.	3-Pt. FG/FGA	Pct.	FT/FTA	Pct.	Reb. O/T	A	TO	PF	S	Blk	TP	PPM
OWENS, B.	40	8/16	.500	2/3	.667	0/2	.000	6/9	1	2	5	1	0	18	.450
SCOTT, T.	25	3/16	.188	2/11	.182	2/2	1.000	2/4	0	1	3	0	0	10	.400
COLEMAN, D.	40	5/13	.385	2/4	.500	3/8	.375	4/11	4	4	4	2	1	15	.375
EDWARDS, M.	9	3/6	.500	1/4	.250	0/0	.000	0/2	0	0	1		0	7	.778
THOMPSON, S.	39	8/10	.800	0/1	.000	0/0	.000	5/7	6	5	1	0	0	16	.410
JOHNSON, D.	18	1/2	.500	0/0	.000	0/2	.000	2/3	3	0	3	0	0	2	.111
ELLIS, L.	29	2/6	.333	0/0	.000	3/6	.500	3/7	0	1	2	1	1	7	.241
Totals	200	30/69	.435	7/23	.304	8/20	.400	22/40	16	13	18	5	2	75	.375

Team Rebounds: Minnesota 3; Syracuse 3. Disqualified: Syracuse—Owens. Technical fouls: Syracuse—Coleman.

	1st Half	2nd Half	Final
Minnesota	35	47	82
Syracuse	39	36	75

REGIONAL SEMIFINAL WEST

UNLV (69) Coach: Jerry Tarkanian

	Min.	Total FG/FGA	Pct.	3-Pt. FG/FGA	Pct.	FT/FTA	Pct.	Reb. O/T	A	TO	PF	S	Blk	TP	PPM
JOHNSON, L.	33	8/18	.444	1/2	.500	3/3	1.000	4/13	2	1	3	0	1	20	.606
AUGMON, S.	35	8/14	.571	1/3	.333	3/5	.600	2/9	4	1	3	2	3	20	.571
BUTLER, D.	35	5/10	.500	0/0	.000	3/4	.750	2/7	3	0	2	1	0	13	.371
HUNT, A.	23	1/2	.500	1/1	1.000	0/0	.000	0/1	2	0	4	0	1	3	.130
ANTHONY, G.	35	2/5	.400	2/5	.400	1/4	.250	0/3	9	3	1	1	2	7	.200
CVIJANOVICH, S.	5	0/1	.000	0/0	.000	0/0	.000	0/1	0	0	1	1	0	0	.000
BICE, T.	14	1/5	.200	1/5	.200	0/0	.000	0/0	0	2	0	0	0	3	.214
YOUNG, B.	7	1/3	.333	1/3	.333	0/0	.000	0/0	0	0	2	0	0	3	.429
JONES, J.	2	0/0	.000	0/0	.000	0/0	.000	0/0	0	0	0	0	0	0	.000
SCURRY, M.	11	0/1	.000	0/0	.000	0/0	.000	0/0	0	1	2	1	0	0	.000
Totals	200	26/59	.441	7/19	.368	10/16	.625	8/34	20	8	18	6	6	69	.345

Ball State (67) Coach: Dick Hunsaker

	Min.	Total FG/FGA	Pct.	3-Pt. FG/FGA	Pct.	FT/FTA	Pct.	Reb. O/T	A	TO	PF	S	Blk	TP	PPM
THOMPSON, C.	26	9/19	.474	2/3	.667	1/5	.200	5/9	2	2	3	0	0	21	.808
MCCURDY, P.	30	6/15	.400	1/1	1.000	4/4	1.000	8/11	1	1	4	4	0	17	.567
KIDD, C.	33	4/9	.444	0/0	.000	3/4	.750	3/12	1	0	3	0	1	11	.333
NICHOLS, S.	28	0/1	.000	0/0	.000	0/0	.000	0/1	10	1	5	0	0	0	.000
BUTTS, B.	28	2/9	.222	2/7	.286	0/0	.000	0/1	2	3	1	0	0	6	.214
PARRISH, S.	15	3/7	.429	0/0	.000	1/1	1.000	3/4	1	0	2	0	0	7	.467
MILLER, G.	10	1/4	.250	1/4	.250	2/3	.667	2/3	0	1	0	0	5	5	.500
SPICER, M.	5	0/1	.000	0/0	.000	0/0	.000	0/0	0	1	1	0	0	0	.000
CROSS, E.	20	0/4	.000	0/2	.000	0/0	.000	1/3	1	2	0	0	0	0	.000
MULLER, R.	5	0/2	.000	0/0	.000	0/0	.000	1/3	0	0	1	0	0	0	.000
Totals	200	25/71	.352	6/17	.353	11/17	.647	23/47	18	11	19	5	6	67	.335

Team Rebounds: UNLV 2; Ball St. 4. Disqualified: Ball St.—Nichols. Technical fouls: None.

	1st Half	2nd Half	Final
UNLV	41	28	69
Ball St.	33	34	67

Loyola Marymount (62) Coach: Paul Westhead

	Min.	Total FG/FGA	Pct.	3-Pt. FG/FGA	Pct.	FT/FTA	Pct.	Reb. O/T	A	TO	PF	S	Blk	TP	PPM
STUMER, P.	35	3/8	.375	1/4	.250	0/0	.000	6/12	2	2	3	1	0	7	.200
KIMBLE, B.	38	9/25	.360	1/5	.200	0/0	.000	1/6	0	2	3	4	0	19	.500
KNIGHT, C.	16	0/2	.000	0/0	.000	0/0	.000	0/3	1	0	0	0	1	0	.000
WALKER, T.	18	0/5	.000	0/0	.000	0/0	.000	0/0	1	1	1	1	0	0	.000
FRYER, J.	36	4/13	.308	3/10	.300	2/2	1.000	5/7	2	0	3	4	0	13	.361
PEABODY, T.	25	3/6	.500	0/1	.000	1/2	.500	2/5	1	3	4	2	0	7	.280
LOWERY, T.	27	6/15	.400	2/8	.250	2/5	.400	3/3	1	2	2	1	0	16	.593
SCOTT, C.	5	0/0	.000	0/0	.000	0/0	.000	0/0	0	0	1	0	0	0	.000
Totals	200	25/74	.338	7/28	.250	5/9	.556	17/36	8	10	17	13	1	62	.310

Alabama (60) Coach: Wimp Sanderson

	Min.	Total FG/FGA	Pct.	3-Pt. FG/FGA	Pct.	FT/FTA	Pct.	Reb. O/T	A	TO	PF	S	Blk	TP	PPM
HORRY, R.	36	8/16	.500	0/3	.000	5/7	.714	3/5	3	8	2	2	3	21	.583
CHEATUM, C.	36	10/18	.556	0/0	.000	1/2	.500	3/9	1	2	0	1	2	21	.583
BENOIT, D.	20	2/5	.400	0/0	.000	0/0	.000	0/5	0	0	1	1	0	4	.200
WAITES, G.	39	1/1	1.000	1/1	1.000	0/0	.000	0/2	3	3	1	0	1	3	.077
SANDERS, J.	40	3/7	.429	0/3	.000	2/3	.667	1/5	5	5	2	0	0	8	.200
ASKINS, K.	28	1/4	.250	0/0	.000	1/2	.500	3/9	1	6	5	0	2	3	.107
WEBB, M.	1	0/0	.000	0/0	.000	0/0	.000	0/0	0	0	0	0	0	0	.000
Totals	200	25/51	.490	1/7	.143	9/14	.643	10/35	13	24	11	3	9	60	.300

Team Rebounds: Loyola Mymt. 3; Alabama 5. Disqualified: Alabama—Askins. Technical fouls: Loyola Mymt—Kimble.

	1st Half	2nd Half	Final
Loyola Mymt.	22	40	62
Alabama	21	39	60

REGIONAL SEMIFINAL EAST

U. Conn. (71) Coach: Jim Calhoun

	Min.	Total FG/FGA	Pct.	3-Pt. FG/FGA	Pct.	FT/FTA	Pct.	Reb. O/T	A	TO	PF	S	Blk	TP	PPM
BURRELL, S.	32	2/9	.222	0/0	.000	5/6	.833	6/15	1	1	3	2	0	9	.281
HENEFELD, N.	22	1/3	.333	0/1	.000	0/3	.000	0/3	3	4	4	0	0	2	.091
SELLERS, R.	19	2/3	.667	0/0	.000	0/1	.000	2/3	0	0	1	0	0	4	.211
SMITH, C.	33	8/14	.571	4/6	.667	3/3	1.000	2/3	5	3	2	1	0	23	.697
GEORGE, T.	30	5/12	.417	0/1	.000	2/2	1.000	0/1	4	1	2	1	1	12	.400
WILLIAMS, M.	9	0/1	.000	0/0	.000	0/0	.000	0/0	1	0	2	0	0	0	.000
GWYNN, J.	17	4/13	.308	0/2	.000	1/2	.500	1/1	0	3	1	0	0	9	.529
WALKER, T.	14	1/2	.500	0/0	.000	0/0	.000	0/2	0	5	4	1	0	2	.143
CYRULIK, D.	6	1/1	1.000	0/0	.000	0/1	.000	0/0	0	1	2	1	0	2	.333
DEPRIEST, L.	17	4/6	.667	0/0	.000	0/0	.000	2/2	2	1	2	1	0	8	.471
MACKLIN, O.	1	0/0	.000	0/0	.000	0/0	.000	0/0	0	0	0	0	0	0	.000
Totals	200	28/64	.438	4/10	.400	11/15	.733	13/30	16	19	23	7	1	71	.355

Clemson (70) Coach: Cliff Ellis

	Min.	Total FG/FGA	Pct.	3-Pt. FG/FGA	Pct.	FT/FTA	Pct.	Reb. O/T	A	TO	PF	S	Blk	TP	PPM
FORREST, D.	27	2/4	.500	0/2	.000	2/2	1.000	0/1	2	3	1	2	0	6	.222
DAVIS, D.	37	6/10	.600	0/0	.000	3/5	.600	7/17	0	3	2	0	1	15	.405
CAMPBELL, E.	33	5/11	.455	0/0	.000	5/7	.714	2/8	1	5	3	1	3	15	.455
YOUNG, D.	9	1/2	.500	1/2	.500	0/0	.000	1/1	0	3	1	2	0	3	.333
CASH, M.	33	2/9	.222	1/1	1.000	3/5	.600	2/3	4	1	3	2	0	8	.242
HOWLING, K.	24	2/8	.250	1/6	.167	2/3	.667	0/1	1	0	2	0	0	7	.292
TYSON, S.	22	5/8	.625	0/0	.000	1/3	.333	2/4	2	2	2	0	1	11	.500
BROWN, C.	1	0/0	.000	0/0	.000	0/0	.000	0/0	0	0	0	0	0	0	.000
LASTINGER, S.	4	1/2	.500	1/1	1.000	0/0	.000	0/1	1	0	1	0	0	3	.750
BUCKINGHAM, W.	8	1/2	.500	0/0	.000	0/0	.000	1/2	0	0	2	0	0	2	.250
JONES, R.	2	0/0	.000	0/0	.000	0/0	.000	0/0	0	0	1	0	0	0	.000
Totals	200	25/56	.446	4/12	.333	16/25	.640	15/38	11	17	16	9	4	70	.350

Team Rebounds: U. Conn. 6; Clemson 2. Disqualified: None. Technical fouls: Clemson—Davis.

	1st Half	2nd Half	Final
U. Conn.	38	33	71
Clemson	29	41	70

Duke (90) Coach: Mike Krzyzewski

	Min.	Total FG/FGA	Pct.	3–Pt. FG/FGA	Pct.	FT/FTA	Pct.	Reb. O/T	A	TO	PF	S	Blk	TP	PPM
BRICKEY, R.	33	3/8	.375	0/0	.000	1/3	.333	0/3	3	2	3	2	1	7	.212
LAETTNER, C.	32	8/12	.667	0/0	.000	8/8	1.000	4/14	0	1	4	0	0	24	.750
ABDELNABY, A.	20	5/7	.714	0/0	.000	4/5	.800	2/7	1	1	4	0	2	14	.700
HENDERSON, P.	38	10/22	.455	6/11	.545	2/2	1.000	3/5	2	1	3	1	0	28	.737
HURLEY, B.	36	3/6	.500	1/4	.250	5/6	.833	1/4	9	4	3	2	0	12	.333
MCCAFFREY, B.	12	0/4	.000	0/0	.000	3/4	.750	0/1	2	1	0	0	0	3	.250
DAVIS, B.	12	1/1	1.000	0/0	.000	0/0	.000	0/0	1	2	3	0	0	2	.167
HILL, T.	11	0/3	.000	0/1	.000	0/0	.000	0/1	0	0	2	1	0	0	.000
KOUBEK, G.	4	0/1	.000	0/0	.000	0/0	.000	0/1	0	0	3	0	0	0	.000
PALMER, C.	2	0/0	.000	0/0	.000	0/0	.000	0/0	1	0	0	0	0	0	.000
Totals	200	30/64	.469	7/16	.438	23/28	.821	10/36	19	12	25	6	3	90	.450

UCLA (81) Coach: Jim Harrick

	Min.	Total FG/FGA	Pct.	3–Pt. FG/FGA	Pct.	FT/FTA	Pct.	Reb. O/T	A	TO	PF	S	Blk	TP	PPM
WILSON	39	5/18	.278	0/1	.000	6/10	.600	1/6	3	3	5	2	0	16	.410
MACLEAN, D.	36	9/17	.529	0/0	.000	3/5	.600	6/15	0	1	3	2	0	21	.583
MURRAY, T.	35	6/12	.500	3/5	.600	0/2	.000	4/9	0	1	3	0	0	15	.429
MADKINS	30	5/6	.833	2/3	.667	2/2	1.000	2/2	6	1	4	1	0	17	.567
MARTIN	34	1/9	.111	0/4	.000	2/2	1.000	1/3	8	3	2	1	0	4	.118
BUTLER, M.	16	1/4	.250	0/1	.000	4/4	1.000	4/5	1	0	4	0	0	6	.375
WALKER, K.	7	1/2	.500	0/0	.000	0/1	.000	1/1	0	1	1	0	0	2	.286
OWENS, K.	2	0/0	.000	0/0	.000	0/0	.000	0/0	0	0	1	0	0	0	.000
MASON, Z.	1	0/1	.000	0/0	.000	0/0	.000	0/0	0	0	1	1	0	0	.000
Totals	200	28/69	.406	5/14	.357	20/32	.625	19/41	18	11	24	6	0	81	.405

Team Rebounds: Duke 6; UCLA 6. Disqualified: UCLA—Wilson. Technical fouls: None.

	1st Half	2nd Half	Final
Duke	47	43	90
UCLA	38	43	81

REGIONAL SEMIFINAL MIDWEST

North Carolina (73) Coach: Dean Smith

	Min.	Total FG/FGA	Pct.	3–Pt. FG/FGA	Pct.	FT/FTA	Pct.	Reb. O/T	A	TO	PF	S	Blk	TP	PPM
CHILCUTT, P.	35	5/10	.500	1/3	.333	0/0	.000	3/11	3	2	1	0	0	11	.314
FOX, R.	33	4/10	.400	1/5	.200	0/0	.000	3/8	3	3	4	0	0	9	.273
WILLIAMS, S.	28	6/15	.400	0/1	.000	8/8	1.000	4/8	0	5	4	2	2	20	.714
RICE, K.	30	3/5	.600	1/2	.500	3/6	.500	1/4	5	3	4	1	0	10	.333
HARRIS, K.	7	1/1	1.000	0/0	.000	0/0	.000	0/0	0	1	0	1	0	2	.286
RODL, H.	16	0/2	.000	0/0	.000	0/2	.000	0/1	1	0	1	0	0	0	.000
LYNCH, G.	15	3/4	.750	0/0	.000	4/7	.571	0/3	1	2	2	0	0	10	.667
DAVIS, H.	27	4/12	.333	2/4	.500	1/2	.500	2/3	0	0	2	0	0	11	.407
WENSTROM, M.	2	0/0	.000	0/0	.000	0/0	.000	0/0	0	0	0	0	0	0	.000
DENNY, J.	6	0/3	.000	0/2	.000	0/0	.000	1/1	0	2	0	0	0	0	.000
GREENE, J.	1	0/0	.000	0/0	.000	0/0	.000	0/0	0	0	0	0	0	0	.000
Totals	200	26/62	.419	5/17	.294	16/25	.640	14/39	12	19	17	5	2	73	.365

Arkansas (96) Coach: Nolan Richardson

	Min.	Total FG/FGA	Pct.	3–Pt. FG/FGA	Pct.	FT/FTA	Pct.	Reb. O/T	A	TO	PF	S	Blk	TP	PPM
DAY, T.	20	6/13	.462	3/6	.500	3/4	.750	1/4	3	2	3	2	0	18	.900
HOWELL, L.	36	12/18	.667	1/1	1.000	0/0	.000	5/8	0	1	3	2	0	25	.694
CREDIT, M.	15	0/0	.000	0/0	.000	2/2	1.000	0/3	0	0	4	0	0	2	.133
MAYBERRY, L.	35	7/14	.500	4/7	.571	1/2	.500	1/6	7	2	3	3	0	19	.543
BOWERS, A.	30	1/5	.200	0/2	.000	2/2	1.000	0/0	3	1	1	2	0	4	.133
MURRY, E.	4	0/2	.000	0/1	.000	0/0	.000	0/0	0	1	0	0	0	0	.000
HAWKINS, D.	10	1/2	.500	0/0	.000	0/0	.000	0/2	3	0	0	0	0	2	.200
MILLER, O.	25	7/7	1.000	0/0	.000	5/5	1.000	0/4	1	3	4	0	1	19	.760
HUERY, R.	20	2/8	.250	0/0	.000	0/0	.000	2/6	3	2	3	1	0	4	.200
WHITBY, C.	3	0/2	.000	0/1	.000	1/2	.500	0/0	0	0	0	0	0	1	.333
LINN, W.	1	1/1	1.000	0/0	.000	0/0	.000	0/0	0	0	0	0	0	2	2.000
MARKS, L.	1	0/0	.000	0/0	.000	0/0	.000	0/0	0	0	0	0	0	0	.000
Totals	200	37/72	.514	8/18	.444	14/17	.824	9/33	20	12	21	10	1	96	.480

Team Rebounds: Arkansas 3; N. Carolina 1. Disqualified: None. Technical fouls: N. Carolina—Coach Smith.

	1st Half	2nd Half	Final
N. Carolina	34	39	73
Arkansas	39	57	96

Xavier (Ohio) (89) Coach: Pete Gillen

	Min.	Total FG/FGA	Pct.	3–Pt. FG/FGA	Pct.	FT/FTA	Pct.	Reb. O/T	A	TO	PF	S	Blk	TP	PPM
BRANTLEY, M.	26	5/6	.833	0/0	.000	2/3	.667	1/2	0	0	4	0	0	12	.462
HILL, T.	34	8/14	.571	0/1	.000	6/9	.667	2/15	5	2	4	0	2	22	.647
STRONG, D.	34	11/17	.647	0/0	.000	5/5	1.000	6/14	4	3	5	2	0	27	.794
WALKER, J.	33	6/14	.429	0/2	.000	2/2	1.000	0/3	3	6	3	1	0	14	.424
GLADDEN, J.	36	2/7	.286	0/0	.000	0/2	.000	0/0	1	3	4	1	0	4	.111
DAVENPORT, M.	16	1/7	.143	0/5	.000	0/0	.000	0/1	1	0	4	0	0	2	.125
PARKER, C.	7	1/2	.500	0/1	.000	0/0	.000	0/0	0	2	0	0	0	2	.286
WILLIAMS, A.	9	1/1	1.000	0/0	.000	2/3	.667	0/1	0	2	1	0	0	4	.444
WILSON, D.	1	0/0	.000	0/0	.000	0/0	.000	0/0	0	0	0	0	0	0	.000
KOESTER, B.	1	0/0	.000	0/0	.000	0/0	.000	0/0	0	0	0	0	0	0	.000
BUTLER, J.	1	1/1	1.000	0/0	.000	0/0	.000	0/0	0	0	1	0	0	2	2.000
POYNTER, M.	1	0/0	.000	0/0	.000	0/0	.000	0/0	0	0	0	0	0	0	.000
MINOR, D.	1	0/0	.000	0/0	.000	0/0	.000	0/0	0	0	0	0	0	0	.000
Totals	200	36/69	.522	0/9	.000	17/24	.708	9/36	14	16	28	4	2	89	.445

Texas (102) Coach: Tom Penders

	Min.	Total FG/FGA	Pct.	3–Pt. FG/FGA	Pct.	FT/FTA	Pct.	Reb. O/T	A	TO	PF	S	Blk	TP	PPM
BLANKS, L.	38	9/21	.429	0/7	.000	10/11	.909	1/5	3	1	5	2	0	28	.737
COLLIE, L.	33	3/8	.375	0/0	.000	3/6	.500	6/16	0	4	1	1	0	9	.273
MYERS, G.	28	1/2	.500	0/0	.000	1/2	.500	4/7	0	0	4	1	1	3	.107
WRIGHT, J.	31	9/12	.750	2/2	1.000	6/8	.750	0/4	3	0	4	1	0	26	.839
MAYS, T.	39	9/21	.429	3/9	.333	11/12	.917	1/2	2	2	1	3	0	32	.821
WILLIAMS, B.	5	0/1	.000	0/0	.000	0/0	.000	0/0	0	0	3	0	0	0	.000
DUDEK, H.	9	2/3	.667	0/0	.000	0/0	.000	1/2	0	1	3	1	0	4	.444
MULLER, G.	5	0/0	.000	0/0	.000	0/0	.000	0/0	0	0	1	0	0	0	.000
JEANS, C.	10	0/0	.000	0/0	.000	0/0	.000	0/0	0	1	1	1	0	0	.000
HOUSTON, G.	1	0/0	.000	0/0	.000	0/0	.000	0/0	0	0	0	0	0	0	.000
SHEPARD, W.	1	0/0	.000	0/0	.000	0/0	.000	0/0	0	0	0	0	0	0	.000
Totals	200	33/68	.485	5/18	.278	31/39	.795	13/36	8	10	23	10	1	102	.510

Team Rebounds: Texas 7; Xavier (Ohio) 4. Disqualified: Texas—Blanks; Xavier (Ohio)—Strong. Technical fouls: None.

	1st Half	2nd Half	Final
Xavier (Ohio)	53	36	89
Texas	41	61	102

REGIONAL FINAL SOUTHEAST

Georgia Tech (93)   Coach: Bobby Cremins

	Min.	Total FG/FGA	Pct.	3-Pt. FG/FGA	Pct.	FT/FTA	Pct.	Reb. O/T	A	TO	PF	S	Blk	TP	PPM
SCOTT, B.	40	12/22	.545	7/12	.583	9/10	.900	1/4	0	2	3	3	0	40	1.000
MACKEY, M.	24	0/0	.000	0/0	.000	0/2	.000	2/6	0	2	2	0	3	0	.000
MCNEIL, J.	26	1/1	1.000	0/0	.000	0/0	.000	2/3	0	1	4	0	0	2	.077
ANDERSON, K.	39	10/15	.667	1/2	.500	9/11	.818	0/8	3	5	1	0	0	30	.769
OLIVER, B.	38	5/15	.333	0/1	.000	9/12	.750	3/5	1	2	2	1	0	19	.500
BROWN, K.	30	1/3	.333	0/1	.000	0/0	.000	1/2	2	2	3	1	0	2	.067
MUNLYN, J.	1	0/0	.000	0/0	.000	0/0	.000	0/0	0	0	0	0	0	0	.000
BARNES, D.	2	0/0	.000	0/0	.000	0/0	.000	1/1	0	0	0	0	0	0	.000
Totals	200	29/56	.518	8/16	.500	27/35	.771	10/29	6	14	15	5	3	93	.465

Minnesota (91)   Coach: Clem Haskins

	Min.	Total FG/FGA	Pct.	3-Pt. FG/FGA	Pct.	FT/FTA	Pct.	Reb. O/T	A	TO	PF	S	Blk	TP	PPM
COFFEY, R.	32	2/4	.500	0/0	.000	0/0	.000	6/9	0	2	4	0	0	4	.125
BURTON, W.	33	15/23	.652	5/10	.500	0/0	.000	5/7	3	3	3	1	1	35	1.061
SHIKENJANSKI, J.	31	9/14	.643	0/0	.000	1/1	1.000	1/5	0	1	2	1	0	19	.613
LYNCH, K.	29	3/8	.375	2/3	.667	4/8	.500	2/3	3	0	4	2	0	12	.414
NEWBERN, M.	32	8/17	.471	1/2	.500	0/2	.000	2/5	6	3	4	3	1	17	.531
GREEN, M.	1	0/0	.000	0/0	.000	0/0	.000	0/0	0	0	1	0	0	0	.000
LEWIS, C.	10	1/3	.333	0/1	.000	0/0	.000	0/3	2	1	2	0	0	2	.200
METCALF, R.	1	0/0	.000	0/0	.000	0/0	.000	0/0	0	0	0	0	0	0	.000
BOND, W.	28	1/6	.167	0/2	.000	0/0	.000	0/2	3	2	3	0	0	2	.071
MARTIN, B.	3	0/0	.000	0/0	.000	0/0	.000	0/0	0	0	0	0	0	0	.000
Totals	200	39/75	.520	8/18	.444	5/11	.455	16/34	17	12	23	7	2	91	.455

Team Rebounds: Georgia Tech 4; Minnesota 3. Disqualified: None. Technical fouls: Minnesota—Burton.

	1st Half	2nd Half	Final
Georgia Tech	47	46	93
Minnesota	49	42	91

REGIONAL FINAL WEST

UNLV (131)   Coach: Jerry Tarkanian

	Min.	Total FG/FGA	Pct.	3-Pt. FG/FGA	Pct.	FT/FTA	Pct.	Reb. O/T	A	TO	PF	S	Blk	TP	PPM
JOHNSON, L.	31	10/14	.714	0/0	.000	0/1	.000	4/18	5	3	2	0	2	20	.645
AUGMON, S.	30	13/20	.650	0/0	.000	7/7	1.000	3/11	6	4	2	2	1	33	1.100
BUTLER, D.	25	4/7	.571	0/0	.000	1/5	.200	1/8	2	4	5	0	0	9	.360
HUNT, A.	34	11/23	.478	4/12	.333	4/6	.667	0/4	13	2	1	6	1	30	.882
ANTHONY, G.	30	8/10	.800	3/4	.750	2/3	.667	0/1	8	3	3	3	0	21	.700
CVIJANOVICH, S.	10	0/0	.000	0/0	.000	2/2	1.000	0/2	0	4	1	0	0	2	.200
BICE, T.	6	0/4	.000	0/2	.000	1/2	.500	0/1	1	0	1	0	0	1	.167
RICE, D.	1	0/0	.000	0/0	.000	0/0	.000	0/1	0	0	0	0	0	0	.000
YOUNG, B.	9	0/0	.000	0/0	.000	0/0	.000	0/2	0	2	1	2	0	0	.000
JONES, J.	9	2/3	.667	0/0	.000	3/4	.750	1/3	0	1	1	0	1	7	.778
SCURRY, M.	14	3/4	.750	0/0	.000	2/2	1.000	2/4	0	0	0	0	1	8	.571
JETER, C.	1	0/1	.000	0/0	.000	0/0	.000	1/1	0	1	0	0	2	0	.000
Totals	200	51/86	.593	7/18	.389	22/32	.688	12/56	35	24	17	13	8	131	.655

Loyola Marymount (101)   Coach: Paul Westhead

	Min.	Total FG/FGA	Pct.	3-Pt. FG/FGA	Pct.	FT/FTA	Pct.	Reb. O/T	A	TO	PF	S	Blk	TP	PPM
STUMER, P.	28	2/4	.500	0/2	.000	0/0	.000	1/5	2	5	4	0	0	4	.143
KIMBLE, B.	37	14/32	.438	8/11	.727	6/6	1.000	2/11	3	6	4	3	0	42	1.135
KNIGHT, C.	19	4/8	.500	0/0	.000	0/0	.000	1/2	2	1	3	2	2	8	.421
WALKER, T.	22	1/1	1.000	0/0	.000	2/3	.667	0/4	3	3	3	3	0	4	.182
FRYER, J.	36	7/24	.292	4/16	.250	3/3	1.000	4/6	2	0	2	1	0	21	.583
PEABODY, T.	22	0/2	.000	0/2	.000	0/1	.000	0/2	4	2	3	2	0	0	.000
LOWERY, T.	23	6/16	.375	4/9	.444	2/2	1.000	0/6	5	3	3	0	0	18	.783
SCOTT, C.	3	0/2	.000	0/0	.000	0/0	.000	1/1	1	1	2	0	0	0	.000
LEE, M.	1	1/2	.500	1/1	1.000	0/0	.000	0/0	0	0	1	0	0	3	3.000
WALKER, G.	1	0/1	.000	0/0	.000	0/0	.000	0/1	0	0	0	0	0	0	.000
O'CONNELL, J.	6	0/0	.000	0/0	.000	1/2	.500	1/2	0	0	2	0	0	1	.167
ROSCOE, J.	1	0/0	.000	0/0	.000	0/0	.000	0/1	0	0	0	0	0	0	.000
SLATER, M.	1	0/2	.000	0/0	.000	0/0	.000	1/1	0	0	0	0	0	0	.000
Totals	200	35/94	.372	17/41	.415	14/17	.824	11/34	23	23	27	14	2	101	.505

Team Rebounds: UNLV 8; Loyola Mymt. 9. Disqualified: UNLV—Butler. Technical fouls: Loyola Mymt.—Kimble, Coach Westhead.

	1st Half	2nd Half	Final
UNLV	67	64	131
Loyola Mymt.	47	54	101

REGIONAL FINAL EAST

U. Conn. (78)   Coach: Jim Calhoun

	Min.	Total FG/FGA	Pct.	3-Pt. FG/FGA	Pct.	FT/FTA	Pct.	Reb. O/T	A	TO	PF	S	Blk	TP	PPM
BURRELL, S.	22	6/10	.600	0/0	.000	0/0	.000	4/5	1	1	5	1	0	12	.545
HENEFELD, N.	44	5/10	.500	1/4	.250	4/4	1.000	2/6	4	4	3	1	1	15	.341
SELLERS, R.	24	0/1	.000	0/0	.000	1/2	.500	0/5	0	1	3	0	4	1	.042
SMITH, C.	42	4/16	.250	1/4	.250	2/2	1.000	0/4	5	7	1	2	0	11	.262
GEORGE, T.	27	4/8	.500	1/2	.500	0/0	.000	0/2	4	0	4	0	0	9	.333
WILLIAMS, M.	1	0/0	.000	0/0	.000	0/0	.000	0/0	0	0	0	0	0	0	.000
GWYNN, J.	28	6/15	.400	0/4	.000	3/3	1.000	0/4	0	2	3	0	0	15	.536
WALKER, T.	21	4/5	.800	0/0	.000	1/1	1.000	3/5	1	1	3	1	1	9	.429
CYRULIK, D.	5	2/2	1.000	0/0	.000	0/0	.000	1/1	0	0	0	0	4	.800
DEPRIEST, L.	11	1/1	1.000	0/0	.000	0/0	.000	1/3	0	3	4	1	0	2	.182
Totals	225	32/68	.471	3/14	.214	11/12	.917	11/35	15	19	26	6	6	78	.347

Duke (79)   Coach: Mike Krzyzewski

	Min.	Total FG/FGA	Pct.	3-Pt. FG/FGA	Pct.	FT/FTA	Pct.	Reb. O/T	A	TO	PF	S	Blk	TP	PPM
BRICKEY, R.	14	1/4	.250	0/0	.000	0/0	.000	1/1	1	4	2	1	0	2	.143
LAETTNER, C.	38	7/8	.875	0/0	.000	9/11	.818	1/5	2	1	3	2	1	23	.605
ABDELNABY, A.	37	9/16	.563	0/0	.000	9/12	.750	5/14	0	1	2	1	2	27	.730
HENDERSON, P.	42	7/20	.350	4/10	.400	3/3	1.000	0/3	1	1	2	0	0	21	.500
HURLEY, B.	43	0/9	.000	0/2	.000	3/4	.750	0/2	8	2	3	4	0	3	.070
HILL, T.	17	0/2	.000	0/0	.000	0/0	.000	1/3	1	0	0	0	0	0	.000
DAVIS, B.	23	1/2	.500	0/0	.000	0/0	.000	1/3	1	1	4	1	0	2	.087
MCCAFFREY, B.	5	0/2	.000	0/0	.000	1/2	.500	0/1	1	1	0	0	0	1	.200
KOUBEK, G.	6	0/1	.000	0/1	.000	0/0	.000	1/2	0	1	0	0	0	0	.000
Totals	225	25/64	.391	4/13	.308	25/32	.781	10/34	15	12	16	9	3	79	.351

Team Rebounds: Duke 4; U. Conn. 10. Disqualified: U. Conn.—Burrell. Technical fouls: None.

	1st Half	2nd Half	1 OT	Final
U. Conn.	30	42	6	78
Duke	37	35	7	79

REGIONAL FINAL MIDWEST

Arkansas (88)   Coach: Nolan Richardson

	Min.	Total FG/FGA	Pct.	3-Pt. FG/FGA	Pct.	FT/FTA	Pct.	Reb. O/T	A	TO	PF	S	Blk	TP	PPM
DAY, T.	34	5/17	.294	0/4	.000	2/5	.400	3/6	1	3	4	4	1	12	.353
HOWELL, L.	25	7/13	.538	0/2	.000	7/10	.700	5/9	2	3	4	2	0	21	.840
CREDIT, M.	22	5/8	.625	0/0	.000	4/5	.800	2/5	0	3	5	2	1	14	.636
MAYBERRY, L.	39	8/15	.533	1/2	.500	1/2	.500	2/5	7	1	2	4	0	18	.462
BOWERS, A.	23	0/5	.000	0/2	.000	2/3	.667	1/3	0	0	4	0	0	2	.087
MURRY, E.	5	0/2	.000	0/1	.000	0/0	.000	0/0	0	0	0	0	0	0	.000
HAWKINS, D.	12	3/3	1.000	0/0	.000	0/0	.000	0/1	0	1	3	0	0	6	.500
MILLER, O.	22	2/3	.667	0/0	.000	5/11	.455	3/9	2	3	4	1	2	9	.409
HUERY, R.	15	2/3	.667	0/0	.000	2/2	1.000	0/2	1	1	0	2	0	6	.400
MARKS, L.	3	0/0	.000	0/0	.000	0/0	.000	0/0	0	0	0	0	0	0	.000
Totals	200	32/69	.464	1/11	.091	23/38	.605	16/40	13	15	26	15	4	88	.440

Texas (85)   Coach: Tom Penders

	Min.	Total FG/FGA	Pct.	3-Pt. FG/FGA	Pct.	FT/FTA	Pct.	Reb. O/T	A	TO	PF	S	Blk	TP	PPM
BLANKS, L.	40	4/12	.333	3/6	.500	6/6	1.000	2/6	4	4	1	2	0	17	.425
COLLIE, L.	28	4/6	.667	0/0	.000	8/11	.727	3/9	0	3	2	0	0	16	.571
MYERS, G.	20	3/5	.600	0/0	.000	0/2	.000	2/4	0	1	5	1	1	6	.300
WRIGHT, J.	38	5/15	.333	2/3	.667	8/10	.800	2/6	0	5	4	1	0	20	.526
MAYS, T.	39	6/15	.400	4/8	.500	4/4	1.000	0/2	5	6	5	0	1	20	.513
WILLIAMS, B.	20	1/2	.500	0/0	.000	0/1	.000	0/6	2	3	2	0	0	2	.100
DUDEK, H.	7	1/1	1.000	0/0	.000	0/0	.000	1/2	0	0	5	0	0	2	.286
MULLER, G.	5	0/1	.000	0/0	.000	0/0	.000	0/0	0	0	3	0	0	0	.000
JEANS, C.	1	0/2	.000	0/0	.000	0/0	.000	0/0	0	0	1	0	0	0	.000
SHEPARD, W.	1	1/1	1.000	0/0	.000	0/0	.000	1/1	0	0	0	0	0	2	2.000
HOUSTON, G.	1	0/0	.000	0/0	.000	0/0	.000	0/0	0	0	0	0	0	0	.000
Totals	200	25/60	.417	9/17	.529	26/34	.765	11/36	11	22	28	4	2	85	.425

Team Rebounds: Arkansas 12; Texas 7. Disqualified: Arkansas—Credit; Texas—Myers, Mays, Dudek. Technical fouls: None.

	1st Half	2nd Half	Final
Arkansas	43	45	88
Texas	36	49	85

FINAL FOUR

Georgia Tech (81)   Coach: Bobby Cremins

	Min.	Total FG/FGA	Pct.	3-Pt. FG/FGA	Pct.	FT/FTA	Pct.	Reb. O/T	A	TO	PF	S	Blk	TP	PPM
SCOTT, B.	39	8/17	.471	7/14	.500	6/9	.667	0/4	0	4	3	2	0	29	.744
MACKEY, M.	26	2/3	.667	0/0	.000	0/0	.000	1/5	0	0	3	0	0	4	.154
MCNEIL, J.	29	2/4	.500	0/0	.000	0/1	.000	1/9	0	2	2	1	1	4	.138
ANDERSON, K.	34	7/14	.500	1/4	.250	1/2	.500	1/8	8	4	4	1	0	16	.471
OLIVER, B.	37	9/18	.500	0/3	.000	6/9	.667	1/8	4	3	3	0	0	24	.649
BROWN, K.	29	2/3	.667	0/0	.000	0/0	.000	2/2	3	1	5	0	0	4	.138
BARNES, D.	6	0/0	.000	0/0	.000	0/0	.000	0/0	0	0	0	0	0	0	.000
Totals	200	30/59	.508	8/21	.381	13/21	.619	5/31	15	15	20	4	1	81	.405

UNLV (90)   Coach: Jerry Tarkanian

	Min.	Total FG/FGA	Pct.	3-Pt. FG/FGA	Pct.	FT/FTA	Pct.	Reb. O/T	A	TO	PF	S	Blk	TP	PPM
JOHNSON, L.	26	5/11	.455	1/1	1.000	4/4	1.000	3/5	3	3	5	0	1	15	.577
AUGMON, S.	37	9/16	.563	1/1	1.000	3/3	1.000	4/9	3	0	3	2	0	22	.595
BUTLER, L.	31	6/10	.600	0/0	.000	1/3	.333	1/10	1	3	4	2	0	13	.419
HUNT, A.	38	7/15	.467	5/9	.556	1/2	.500	0/2	7	1	1	1	1	20	.526
ANTHONY, G.	39	4/9	.444	3/4	.750	3/7	.429	0/1	5	4	2	1	0	14	.359
CVIJANOVICH, S.	1	0/0	.000	0/0	.000	0/0	.000	0/0	0	2	1	0	0	0	.000
BICE, J.	2	0/0	.000	0/0	.000	0/0	.000	0/0	1	0	0	0	0	0	.000
YOUNG, B.	3	0/0	.000	0/0	.000	0/0	.000	0/0	0	0	0	0	0	0	.000
JONES, J.	2	0/0	.000	0/0	.000	0/0	.000	0/0	0	0	0	0	0	0	.000
SCURRY, M.	21	3/4	.750	0/0	.000	0/0	.000	2/11	0	2	4	0	0	6	.286
Totals	200	34/65	.523	10/15	.667	12/19	.632	10/38	20	15	20	6	2	90	.450

Team Rebounds: UNLV 2; Georgia Tech 4. Disqualified: UNLV—Johnson; Georgia Tech—Brown. Technical fouls: None.

	1st Half	2nd Half	Final
Georgia Tech	53	28	81
UNLV	46	44	90

Duke (97)   Coach: Mike Krzyzewski

	Min.	Total FG/FGA	Pct.	3-Pt. FG/FGA	Pct.	FT/FTA	Pct.	Reb. O/T	A	TO	PF	S	Blk	TP	PPM
BRICKEY, R.	24	8/10	.800	0/0	.000	1/3	.333	4/11	3	3	3	1	0	17	.708
LAETTNER, C.	32	5/7	.714	0/0	.000	9/12	.750	4/14	1	1	4	2	1	19	.594
ABDELNABY, A.	27	8/12	.667	0/0	.000	4/5	.800	0/5	0	0	3	3	1	20	.741
HENDERSON, P.	37	10/21	.476	3/7	.429	5/5	1.000	3/8	3	3	2	1	1	28	.757
HURLEY, B.	36	0/2	.000	0/1	.000	3/6	.500	0/1	6	6	0	1	0	3	.083
HILL, T.	4	0/0	.000	0/0	.000	0/0	.000	0/1	0	0	1	0	0	0	.000
DAVIS, B.	23	1/4	.250	0/0	.000	3/4	.750	2/4	2	2	3	0	0	5	.217
MCCAFFREY, B.	5	0/1	.000	0/0	.000	3/4	.750	0/0	1	1	1	1	0	3	.600
KOUBEK, G.	10	1/4	.250	0/1	.000	0/0	.000	0/0	0	0	2	0	0	2	.200
BUCKLEY, C.	1	0/0	.000	0/0	.000	0/0	.000	0/0	0	0	0	0	0	0	.000
COOK, J.	1	0/0	.000	0/0	.000	0/0	.000	0/0	0	0	0	0	0	0	.000
Totals	200	33/61	.541	3/9	.333	28/39	.718	13/44	16	16	19	9	3	97	.485

Arkansas (83)   Coach: Nolan Richardson

	Min.	Total FG/FGA	Pct.	3-Pt. FG/FGA	Pct.	FT/FTA	Pct.	Reb. O/T	A	TO	PF	S	Blk	TP	PPM
WHITBY, C.	2	0/2	.000	0/2	.000	0/0	.000	0/0	0	0	0	0	0	0	.000
LINN, E.	1	0/1	.000	0/0	.000	0/0	.000	0/0	0	0	0	0	0	0	.000
MARKS, L.	3	0/0	.000	0/0	.000	0/0	.000	0/1	0	0	2	0	0	0	.000
DAY, T.	30	8/17	.471	4/8	.500	7/7	1.000	3/7	1	4	4	0	0	27	.900
HOWELL, L.	30	5/9	.556	1/2	.500	7/8	.875	3/6	0	2	3	1	0	18	.600
CREDIT, M.	19	2/3	.667	0/0	.000	1/4	.250	1/3	0	0	5	1	0	5	.263
MAYBERRY, L.	33	6/18	.333	0/4	.000	0/0	.000	2/2	6	4	1	3	0	12	.364
BOWERS, A.	20	1/6	.167	0/1	.000	0/0	.000	1/2	2	0	0	0	2	2	.100
MURRY, E.	11	2/5	.400	1/3	.333	0/0	.000	1/1	1	0	3	0	0	5	.455
HAWKINS, D.	15	2/4	.500	0/0	.000	2/2	1.000	0/2	0	1	1	0	1	6	.400
MILLER, O.	20	1/3	.333	0/0	.000	1/2	.500	0/6	1	2	5	1	3	3	.150
HUERY, R.	16	2/5	.400	0/1	.000	1/3	.333	1/3	3	1	1	1	0	5	.313
Totals	200	29/73	.397	6/21	.286	19/26	.731	12/33	14	14	25	7	4	83	.415

Team Rebounds: Duke 6; Arkansas 7. Disqualified: Arkansas—Credit, Miller. Technical fouls: None.

	1st Half	2nd Half	Final
Duke	46	51	97
Arkansas	43	40	83

NATIONAL CHAMPIONSHIP

UNLV (103) Coach: Jerry Tarkanian

	Min.	Total FG/FGA	Pct.	3-Pt. FG/FGA	Pct.	FT/FTA	Pct.	Reb. O/T	A	TO	PF	S	Blk	TP	PPM
JOHNSON, L.	30	8/12	.667	2/ 2	1.000	4/ 4	1.000	2/11	2	3	3	4	1	22	.733
AUGMON, S.	26	6/ 7	.857	0/ 0	.000	0/ 1	.000	2/ 4	7	3	5	2	2	12	.462
BUTLER, D.	27	1/ 4	.250	0/ 0	.000	2/ 2	1.000	0/ 3	3	0	3	1	0	4	.148
HUNT, A.	31	12/16	.750	4/ 7	.571	1/ 2	.500	0/ 2	2	1	0	0	0	29	.935
ANTHONY, G.	30	5/11	.455	0/ 1	.000	3/ 4	.750	1/ 1	6	3	3	5	0	13	.433
CVIJANOVICH, S.	10	1/ 2	.500	1/ 1	1.000	2/ 2	1.000	1/ 1	2	0	2	2	0	5	.500
BICE, T.	9	0/ 1	.000	0/ 0	.000	0/ 0	.000	0/ 0	2	3	2	1	0	0	.000
RICE, D.	2	0/ 2	.000	0/ 1	.000	0/ 0	.000	0/ 1	0	0	0	0	0	0	.000
YOUNG, B.	12	2/ 2	1.000	1/ 1	1.000	0/ 0	.000	0/ 0	0	0	1	0	0	5	.417
JONES, J.	8	4/ 5	.800	0/ 0	.000	0/ 0	.000	0/ 2	0	1	2	0	0	8	1.000
SCURRY, M.	12	2/ 5	.400	0/ 0	.000	1/ 2	.500	3/ 6	0	2	2	1	0	5	.417
JETER, C.	3	0/ 0	.000	0/ 0	.000	0/ 0	.000	0/ 0	0	1	0	0	0	0	.000
Totals	200	41/67	.612	8/14	.571	13/17	.765	9/31	24	17	23	16	3	103	.515

Duke (73) Coach: Mike Krzyzewski

	Min.	Total FG/FGA	Pct.	3-Pt. FG/FGA	Pct.	FT/FTA	Pct.	Reb. O/T	A	TO	PF	S	Blk	TP	PPM
BRICKEY, R.	24	2/ 4	.500	0/ 0	.000	0/ 2	.000	1/ 3	2	2	2	0	0	4	.167
LAETTNER, C.	29	5/12	.417	0/ 0	.000	5/ 6	.833	5/ 9	5	3	4	1	0	15	.517
ABDELNABY, A.	24	5/ 7	.714	0/ 0	.000	4/ 6	.667	4/ 7	0	1	3	0	2	14	.583
HENDERSON, P.	32	9/20	.450	1/ 8	.125	2/ 2	1.000	1/ 2	0	6	2	1	0	21	.656
HURLEY, B.	32	0/ 3	.000	0/ 2	.000	2/ 2	1.000	0/ 0	3	5	3	1	0	2	.063
HILL, T.	8	0/ 2	.000	0/ 0	.000	0/ 0	.000	1/ 3	1	1	0	1	0	0	.000
DAVIS, B.	21	2/ 5	.400	0/ 0	.000	2/ 3	.667	1/ 1	0	0	1	1	1	6	.286
McCAFFREY, B.	9	1/ 3	.333	0/ 0	.000	2/ 2	1.000	0/ 2	0	2	1	0	0	4	.444
KOUBEK, G.	14	1/ 4	.250	0/ 1	.000	0/ 0	.000	2/ 2	0	1	0	0	0	2	.143
PALMER, C.	2	0/ 0	.000	0/ 0	.000	3/ 4	.750	0/ 3	0	0	0	0	0	3	1.500
BUCKLEY, C.	3	0/ 0	.000	0/ 0	.000	0/ 0	.000	0/ 1	0	1	0	0	0	0	.000
COOK, J.	2	1/ 1	1.000	0/ 0	.000	0/ 0	.000	0/ 0	0	1	0	0	0	2	1.000
Totals	200	26/61	.426	1/11	.091	20/27	.741	15/33	11	23	16	5	3	73	.365

Team Rebounds: UNLV 2; Duke 6. Disqualified: UNLV—Augmon. Technical fouls: None.

	1st Half	2nd Half	Final
UNLV	47	56	103
Duke	35	38	73

○ ALL-STAR TEAMS ○

ALL TOURNAMENT

STACEY AUGMON	UNLV
PHIL HENDERSON	DUKE
★ ANDERSON HUNT	UNLV
LARRY JOHNSON	UNLV
DENNIS SCOTT	GEORGIA TECH

EAST REGIONAL

ALAA ABDELNABY	DUKE
TATE GEORGE	UCONN
PHIL HENDERSON	DUKE
★ CHRISTIAN LAETTNER	DUKE
CHRIS SMITH	UCONN

SOUTHEAST REGIONAL

★ KENNY ANDERSON	GEORGIA TECH
WILLIE BURTON	MINNESOTA
MELVIN NEWBERN	MINNESOTA
DENNIS SCOTT	GEORGIA TECH
STEVE SMITH	MICHIGAN ST.

WEST REGIONAL

★ STACEY AUGMON	UNLV
ANDERSON HUNT	UNLV
LARRY JOHNSON	UNLV
BO KIMBLE	LOYOLA MYMT.
CHANDLER THOMPSON	BALL ST.

MIDWEST REGIONAL

LANCE BLANKS	TEXAS
★ LEN HOVELL	ARKANSAS
LEE MAYBERRY	ARKANSAS
TRAVIS MAYS	TEXAS
OLIVER MILLER	ARKANSAS

★ Most Outstanding Player(s)

○ INDIVIDUAL RECORDS ○

SCORING

Most points in a single game

1. BO KIMBLE, LOYOLA MYMT. (vs. NEW MEXICO ST.) — 45
2. TRAVIS MAYS, TEXAS (vs. GEORGIA) — 44
3. BO KIMBLE, LOYOLA MYMT. (vs. UNLV) — 42
4. JEFF FRYER, LOYOLA MYMT. (vs. MICHIGAN) — 41
5. DENNIS SCOTT, GEORGIA TECH (vs. MINNESOTA) — 40

Most total points in the tournament

1. DENNIS SCOTT, GEORGIA TECH — 153
2. BO KIMBLE, LOYOLA MYMT. — 143
3. PHIL HENDERSON, DUKE — 130
4. KENNY ANDERSON, GEORGIA TECH — 124
5. ALAA ABDELNABY, DUKE — 114

Highest scoring average (minimum 2 games)

1. BO KIMBLE, LOYOLA MYMT. (143-4) — 35.75
2. DENNIS SCOTT, GEORGIA TECH (153-5) — 30.60
3. LIONEL SIMMONS, LA SALLE (60-2) — 30.00
4. TRAVIS MAYS, TEXAS (112-4) — 28.00
5. BRYANT STITH, VIRGINIA (51-2) — 25.50

FIELD GOALS

Most field goals in a single game

1. BO KIMBLE, LOYOLA MYMT. (vs. NEW MEXICO ST.) — 17
2. WILLIE BURTON, MINNESOTA (vs. GEORGIA TECH) — 15
2. JEFF FRYER, LOYOLA MYMT. (vs. MICHIGAN) — 15
2. POPEYE JONES, MURRAY STATE (vs. MICHIGAN ST.) — 15
5. 2 tied for fifth place.

Most total field goals in the tournament

1. DENNIS SCOTT, GEORGIA TECH — 51
1. BO KIMBLE, LOYOLA MYMT. — 51
3. PHIL HENDERSON, DUKE — 48
3. KENNY ANDERSON, GEORGIA TECH — 48
5. STACEY AUGMON, UNLV — 45

Most field goal attempts in a single game

1. POPEYE JONES, MURRAY STATE (vs. MICHIGAN ST.) — 36
2. BO KIMBLE, LOYOLA MYMT. (vs. NEW MEXICO ST.) — 35
3. BO KIMBLE, LOYOLA MYMT. (vs. UNLV) — 32
3. DENNIS SCOTT, GEORGIA TECH (vs. LOUISIANA ST.) — 32
5. BO KIMBLE, LOYOLA MYMT. (vs. MICHIGAN) — 29

Most total field goal attempts in tournament
1 BO KIMBLE, LOYOLA MYMT. 121
2 DENNIS SCOTT, GEORGIA TECH 115
3 PHIL HENDERSON, DUKE 105
4 KENNY ANDERSON, GEORGIA TECH 84
5 ANDERSON HUNT, UNLV 78

Highest field goal percentage in a single game (minimum 10 attempts)
1 RICK CALLOWAY, KANSAS (vs. ROBERT MORRIS) (9-10) .900
2 BRIAN WILLIAMS, ARIZONA (vs. SOUTH FLORIDA) (12-15) .800
2 JASON REESE, NORTHERN IOWA (vs. MINNESOTA) (12-15) .800
4 3 tied for fourth place.

Highest field goal percentage in the tournament (minimum 20 attempts)
1 JOHNNY MCNEIL, GEORGIA TECH (15-21) .714
2 JASON REESE, NORTHERN IOWA (18-27) .667
3 ALAA ABDELNABY, DUKE (42-64) .656
4 JEROME HARMON, LOUISVILLE (13-20) .650
5 STEPHEN THOMPSON, SYRACUSE (23-37) .622

3-PT. FIELD GOALS

Most 3-pt. field goals in a single game
1 JEFF FRYER, LOYOLA MYMT. (vs. MICHIGAN) 11
2 BO KIMBLE, LOYOLA MYMT. (vs. UNLV) 8
3 DENNIS SCOTT, GEORGIA TECH (vs. UNLV) 7
3 DENNIS SCOTT, GEORGIA TECH (vs. MINNESOTA) 7
5 5 tied for fifth place.

Most total 3-pt. field goals in the tournament
1 DENNIS SCOTT, GEORGIA TECH 24
2 JEFF FRYER, LOYOLA MYMT. 23
3 PHIL HENDERSON, DUKE 17
4 BO KIMBLE, LOYOLA MYMT. 15
4 ANDERSON HUNT, UNLV 15

Most 3-pt. field goals attempted in a single game
1 CHRIS WALKER, VILLANOVA (vs. LOUISIANA ST.) 20
2 JEFF FRYER, LOYOLA MYMT. (vs. UNLV) 16
3 JEFF FRYER, LOYOLA MYMT. (vs. MICHIGAN) 15
4 JEFF FRYER, LOYOLA MYMT. (vs. NEW MEXICO ST.) 14
4 DENNIS SCOTT, GEORGIA TECH (vs. UNLV) 14

Most total 3-pt. field goals attempted in the tournament
1 JEFF FRYER, LOYOLA MYMT. 55
2 DENNIS SCOTT, GEORGIA TECH 54
3 PHIL HENDERSON, DUKE 44
4 ANDERSON HUNT, UNLV 42
5 BO KIMBLE, LOYOLA MYMT. 33

Highest 3-pt. field goal percentage in a single game (minimum 4 attempts)
1 TERRY BROWN, KANSAS (vs. UCLA) (5-6) .833
2 JASON BUCHANAN, ST. JOHN'S (vs. TEMPLE) (4-5) .800
3 ROBERT HORRY, ALABAMA (vs. COLORADO STATE) (6-8) .750
4 7 tied for fourth place.

Highest 3-pt. field goal percentage in the tournament (minimum 8 attempts)
1 MARK MACON, TEMPLE (6-9) .667
2 BRYANT STITH, VIRGINIA (5-8) .625
2 KEITH JENNINGS, EAST TENN. ST. (5-8) .625
4 KEVIN LYNCH, MINNESOTA (9-16) .563
5 2 tied for fifth place.

FREE THROWS

Most free throws in a single game
1 TRAVIS MAYS, TEXAS (vs. GEORGIA) 23
2 TYRONE HILL, XAVIER (OHIO) (vs. KANSAS STATE) 17
3 BO KIMBLE, LOYOLA MYMT. (vs. MICHIGAN) 14
4 3 tied for fourth place.

Most total free throws in the tournament
1 TRAVIS MAYS, TEXAS 43
2 CHRISTIAN LAETTNER, DUKE 42
3 ALAA ABDELNABY, DUKE 30
4 BRIAN OLIVER, GEORGIA TECH 28
5 DENNIS SCOTT, GEORGIA TECH 27

Most free throws attempted in a single game
1 TRAVIS MAYS, TEXAS (vs. GEORGIA) 27
2 TYRONE HILL, XAVIER (OHIO) (vs. KANSAS STATE) 18
3 BO KIMBLE, LOYOLA MYMT. (vs. MICHIGAN) 17
4 DALE DAVIS, CLEMSON (vs. LA SALLE) 14
4 ROD WADE, ARK-LITTLE ROCK (vs. UNLV) 14

Most free throws attempted in the tournament
1 CHRISTIAN LAETTNER, DUKE 52
2 TRAVIS MAYS, TEXAS 48
3 BRIAN OLIVER, GEORGIA TECH 39
3 ALAA ABDELNABY, DUKE 39
5 DENNIS SCOTT, GEORGIA TECH 35

Highest free throw percentage in a single game (minimum 7 attempts)
1 NATHAN BUNTIN, MISSOURI (vs. NORTHERN IOWA) (9-9) 1.000
2 CHRISTIAN LAETTNER, DUKE (vs. UCLA) (8-8) 1.000
2 SCOTT WILLIAMS, N. CAROLINA (vs. ARKANSAS) (8-8) 1.000
4 3 tied for fourth place.

Highest free throw percentage in the tournament (minimum 15 attempts)
1 STEPHEN SCHEFFLER, PURDUE (15-16) .938
2 BO KIMBLE, LOYOLA MYMT. (26-29) .897
3 TRAVIS MAYS, TEXAS (43-48) .896
4 CHRIS SMITH, U. CONN. (17-19) .895
4 PHIL HENDERSON, DUKE (17-19) .895

REBOUNDS

Most rebounds in a single game
1 LOY VAUGHT, MICHIGAN (vs. ILLINOIS STATE) 21
2 BO KIMBLE, LOYOLA MYMT. (vs. NEW MEXICO ST.) 18
2 LARRY JOHNSON, UNLV (vs. LOYOLA MYMT.) 18
4 4 tied for fourth place.

Most total rebounds in the tournament
1 LARRY JOHNSON, UNLV 75
2 CHRISTIAN LAETTNER, DUKE 56
3 ALAA ABDELNABY, DUKE 52
4 STACEY AUGMON, UNLV 48
5 DALE DAVIS, CLEMSON 44

Most rebounds per game (minimum 2 games)
1 LOY VAUGHT, MICHIGAN (38-2) 19.00
2 DALE DAVIS, CLEMSON (44-3) 14.67
3 DIKEMBE MUTOMBO, GEORGETOWN (28-2) 14.00
4 LARRY JOHNSON, UNLV (75-6) 12.50
5 2 tied for fifth place.

ASSISTS

Most assists in a single game
1 ANDERSON HUNT, UNLV (vs. LOYOLA MYMT.) 13
1 JAMES SANDERS, ALABAMA (vs. ARIZONA) 13
3 JOHN CROTTY, VIRGINIA (vs. SYRACUSE) 12
3 OTIS LIVINGSTON, IDAHO (vs. LOUISVILLE) 12
5 4 tied for fifth place.

Most total assists in the tournament
1 BOBBY HURLEY, DUKE 39
2 GREG ANTHONY, UNLV 37
3 ANDERSON HUNT, UNLV 30
4 KENNY ANDERSON, GEORGIA TECH 28
5 JAMES SANDERS, ALABAMA 27

Most assists per game (minimum 2 appearances)
1 JAMES SANDERS, ALABAMA (27-3) 9.00
2 NEGELE KNIGHT, DAYTON (18-2) 9.00
3 JOHN CROTTY, VIRGINIA (17-2) 8.50
4 RUMEAL ROBINSON, MICHIGAN (16-2) 8.00
5 3 tied for fifth place.

TURNOVERS

Most turnovers in a single game
1 MAURICE WILLIAMSON, LOUISIANA ST. (vs. VILLANOVA) 13
2 ROY FISHER, CALIFORNIA (vs. UCONN) 10
3 ROBERT HORRY, ALABAMA (vs. LOYOLA MYMT.) 8
3 TERRY MILLS, MICHIGAN (vs. LOYOLA MYMT.) 8
5 9 tied for fifth place.

Most total turnovers in the tournament
1 BOBBY HURLEY, DUKE 26
2 ROBERT BRICKEY, DUKE 20
2 KENNY ANDERSON, GEORGIA TECH 20
4 TERRELL LOWERY, LOYOLA MYMT. 18
4 LARRY JOHNSON, UNLV 18

SHOTS BLOCKED

Most shots blocked in a single game
1 GEORGE LYNCH, N. CAROLINA (vs. OKLAHOMA) 5
1 ERIC MCARTHUR, UC SANTA BARB. (vs. HOUSTON) 5
3 8 tied for third place.

Most total shots blocked in the tournament
1 LARRY JOHNSON, UNLV 11
2 GUILLERMO MYERS, TEXAS 10
2 OLIVER MILLER, ARKANSAS 10
2 STACEY AUGMON, UNLV 10
2 ALAA ABDELNABY, DUKE 10

STEALS

Most steals in a single game
1 PHIL HENDERSON, DUKE (vs. RICHMOND) 6
1 ANDERSON HUNT, UNLV (vs. LOYOLA MYMT.) 6
3 6 tied for third place.

Most total steals in the tournament
1 LEE MAYBERRY, ARKANSAS 18
2 BO KIMBLE, LOYOLA MYMT. 12
2 STACEY AUGMON, UNLV 12
4 3 tied for fourth place.

⚙ TEAM RECORDS ⚙

SCORING

Most points in a single game
1	LOYOLA MYMT. (vs. MICHIGAN)	149
2	UNLV (vs. LOYOLA MYMT.)	131
3	MICHIGAN (vs. LOYOLA MYMT.)	115

Most total points in the tournament
1	UNLV	571
2	DUKE	496
3	GEORGIA TECH	448

Highest scoring average (minimum 2 games)
1	LOYOLA MYMT. (423-4)	105.75
2	MICHIGAN (191-2)	95.50
3	UNLV (571-6)	95.17

FIELD GOALS

Most field goals in a single game
1	UNLV (vs. LOYOLA MYMT.)	51
2	LOYOLA MYMT. (vs. MICHIGAN)	49
3	MICHIGAN (vs. LOYOLA MYMT.)	45

Most total field goals in the tournament
1	UNLV	217
2	DUKE	170
3	GEORGIA TECH	160

Most field goals attempted in a single game
1	LOYOLA MYMT. (vs. UNLV)	94
2	LOYOLA MYMT. (vs. MICHIGAN)	89
3	LOYOLA MYMT. (vs. NEW MEXICO ST.)	87

Most total field goals attempted in the tournament
1	UNLV	410
2	DUKE	358
3	LOYOLA MYMT.	344

Highest field goal percentage in a single game
1	ALABAMA (vs. COLORADO STATE) (28-45)	.622
2	UNLV (vs. DUKE) (41-67)	.612
3	GEORGIA TECH (vs. EAST TENN. ST.) (39-64)	.609

Highest field goal percentage in a tournament (minimum 2 games)
1	NOTRE DAME (29-51)	.569
2	PRINCETON (23-42)	.548
3	NEW MEXICO ST. (37-68)	.544

3-PT. FIELD GOALS

Most 3-pt. field goals in a single game
1	LOYOLA MYMT. (vs. MICHIGAN)	21
2	LOYOLA MYMT. (vs. UNLV)	17
3	2 tied for third place.	

Most total 3-pt. field goals in the tournament
1	LOYOLA MYMT.	56
2	UNLV	39
2	GEORGIA TECH	39

Most 3-pt. field goals attempted in a single game
1	LOYOLA MYMT. (vs. UNLV)	41
2	LOYOLA MYMT. (vs. MICHIGAN)	40
3	LA SALLE (vs. CLEMSON)	35

Most total 3-pt. field goals attempted in the tournament
1	LOYOLA MYMT.	137
2	UNLV	102
3	GEORGIA TECH	98

Highest 3-pt. field goal percentage in a single game (minimum 10 attempts)
1	ALABAMA (vs. COLORADO STATE) (8-11)	.727
2	N. CAROLINA (vs. OKLAHOMA) (7-10)	.700
3	UNLV (vs. GEORGIA TECH) (10-15)	.667

Highest 3-pt. field goal percentage in the tournament (minimum 20 attempts)
1	NORTHERN IOWA (18-42)	.429
2	ALABAMA (15-35)	.429
3	N. CAROLINA (14-33)	.424

FREE THROWS

Most free throws in a single game
1	XAVIER (OHIO) (vs. KANSAS STATE)	37
2	TEXAS (vs. XAVIER [OHIO])	31
3	LOYOLA MYMT. (vs. MICHIGAN)	30

Most total free throws in the tournament
1	DUKE	136
2	UNLV	98
3	TEXAS	95

Most free throws attempted in a single game
1	TEXAS (vs. GEORGIA)	45
2	XAVIER (OHIO) (vs. KANSAS STATE)	43
3	2 tied for third place.	

Most total free throws attempted in the tournament
1	DUKE	183
2	UNLV	140
3	TEXAS	131

Highest free throw percentage in a single game
1	TEXAS (vs. PURDUE) (12-13)	.923
2	U. CONN. (vs. DUKE) (11-12)	.917
3	LOYOLA MYMT. (vs. NEW MEXICO ST.) (20-22)	.909

Highest free throw percentage in the tournament (minimum 2 games)
1	OHIO STATE (33-40)	.825
2	LOYOLA MYMT. (69-84)	.822
3	KANSAS (26-32)	.813

Fewest free throws in a single game
1	RICHMOND (vs. DUKE)	2
2	MICHIGAN ST. (vs. MURRAY STATE)	3
3	EAST TENN. ST. (vs. GEORGIA TECH)	4
3	COLORADO STATE (vs. ALABAMA)	4
3	BOSTON UNIV. (vs. U. CONN.)	4

Lowest free throw percentage in a single game
1	RICHMOND (vs. DUKE) (2-6)	.333
2	SYRACUSE (vs. MINNESOTA) (8-20)	.400
3	COLORADO STATE (vs. ALABAMA) (4-9)	.444

Lowest free throw percentage in the tournament (minimum 2 games)
1	CLEMSON (48-88)	.546
2	GEORGETOWN (24-42)	.571
3	LOUISIANA ST. (26-45)	.578

REBOUNDS

Most rebounds in a single game
1	UNLV (vs. LOYOLA MYMT.)	56
2	ILLINOIS STATE (vs. MICHIGAN)	51
2	UNLV (vs. ARK.-LITTLE ROCK)	51

Most rebounds per game (minimum 2 games)
1	MICHIGAN (95-2)	47.50
2	CLEMSON (134-3)	44.67
3	LOUISIANA ST. (86-2)	43.00

ASSISTS

Most assists in a single game
1	UNLV (vs. LOYOLA MYMT.)	35
2	LOYOLA MYMT. (vs. MICHIGAN)	33
3	UNLV (vs. ARK.-LITTLE ROCK)	28

Most assists per game (minimum 2 games)
1	UNLV (140-6)	23.33
2	LOYOLA MYMT. (85-4)	21.25
3	KANSAS (41-2)	20.50

TURNOVERS

Most turnovers in a single game
1	CALIFORNIA (vs. U. CONN.)	28
2	BOSTON UNIV. (vs. U. CONN.)	27
2	MICHIGAN (vs. LOYOLA MYMT.)	27

Most turnovers per game (minimum 2 games)
1	MICHIGAN (40-2)	20.00
2	CALIFORNIA (39-2)	19.50
3	OHIO STATE (38-2)	19.00

SHOTS BLOCKED

Most shots blocked in a single game
1	LOUISIANA ST. (vs. GEORGIA TECH)	10
2	ALABAMA (vs. LOYOLA MYMT.)	9
3	4 tied for third place.	

Most shots blocked per game (minimum 2 games)
1	LOUISIANA ST. (18-2)	9.00
2	MICHIGAN (12-2)	6.00
3	UNLV (33-6)	5.50

STEALS

Most steals in a single game
1	U. CONN. (vs. BOSTON UNIV.)	19
2	3 tied for second place.	

Most steals per game
1	LOYOLA MYMT. (51-4)	12.75
2	LA SALLE (25-2)	12.50
3	U. CONN. (48-4)	12.00

PART 2

Twenty Tournament Greats

Profiles and Analyses of the Men Behind the Statistics

THE PLAYERS

Great players are artists with the ball, inventors of the game every time they step onto the court. They improvise, experiment, and continually discover new ways to play and new ways to win. They take over close contacts with bravura solo performances, and subtly raise the level of play of everyone around them. They find ways of doing things that nobody has ever thought of, or done so well before.

More often than not a great player first appears in the national spotlight in the NCAA tournament. It is *the* initial showcase for the stars.

The ten men profiled here are *among* the greatest performers in NCAA tournament history. Many others have also performed brilliantly and deserve recognition. Many have been selected tournament Most Outstanding Players or placed on All-Tournament Teams (see Part 1). Era by era, they have lifted the standards of excellence and changed the way the game of basketball is played and perceived.

In the forties: Two innovative little men, Johnny Adams and Kenny Sailors, discovered that the easiest way to get an open shot was to put the ball up one-handed at the top of a jump. They invented the jump shot and changed the game forever.

In the fifties: Tom Gola combined a big man's size with a small man's quickness; Elgin Baylor displayed a remarkable repertoire of offensive moves that almost carried his small college to a national championship; Wilt Chamberlain brought an awesome new dimension to pivot play; Oscar Robertson proved he was not only one of the greatest scorers of all time but also a peerless passer who sacrificed his own point production to help his team win; and Jerry West showed that he was an electrifying defensive player as well as an explosive scorer in the clutch.

In the sixties: Jerry Lucas was a one-man Mr. Outside and Mr. Inside, hitting from the top of the key, rebounding and hurling outlet passes to start the devastating Ohio State fast break; and Elvin Hayes was a one-man gang, almost unstoppable as a scorer and a rebounder.

In the seventies: David Thompson went airborne, carrying North Carolina State past UCLA to the national championship; Jack Givens banged in crushing barrages of line-drive jumpers; and Larry Bird redefined the standard for front-court play with his incomparable court sense.

In the eighties: Isiah Thomas, Patrick Ewing, Akeem Olajuwon, David Robinson, Michael Jordan, Danny Manning, and Glen Rice all sparkled in tournament play.

The ten men profiled here are not necessarily the greatest players ever, although a number of them would certainly appear on anybody's ten best list. Some of them never again approached the levels of excellence they attained in the NCAAs. They all have one thing in common, however. They rose to the occasion, seized the moment, and made a difference in college basketball's supreme showcase.

Bob Kurland

Oklahoma A&M

Bob (Foothills) Kurland was the first of the great 7-foot centers. Kansas coach Phog Allen railed against him as a freak who was likely to destroy the game of basketball and avoided scheduling the Aggies and their "Glandular Goon." Indeed, Kurland was awkward and ungainly when he arrived at Oklahoma A&M in 1942. But by the time he finished, he changed the popular perception of the big man as an uncoordinated oddity of nature. And along with George Mikan, his 6-9 contemporary at DePaul, Kurland ushered in a new era in basketball.

By the end of Kurland's freshman year, A&M coach Henry Iba had developed a zone defense that took advantage of the rule allowing a player to block a shot on its downward arc to the basket. With the narrow lane then in use, Kurland would plant himself under the hoop and leap to swat away (or catch) opponents' shots. After his sophomore season, the rules committee outlawed goaltending, but it didn't stop the domination of the big, well-coordinated boy from St. Louis.

As an All-American in 1944, Kurland led his team into a memorable NIT game against DePaul and Mikan. Both the powerful Mikan and the quick, agile Kurland were still learning the game; they would both get even better the next year. Still the NIT matchup was a battle of titans, among the most exciting games ever seen in college basketball. After taking a 17-point lead the Aggies stopped moving. They turned the ball over again and again as De Paul cut into the lead. Finally, with two minutes remaining, Kurland fouled out. A&M had already lost a player on personals and another with an injury. Since college basketball at the time allowed only limited substitutions (and A&M had reached its limit), the Aggies were forced to finish the game with only four players on the floor. The game ended with a three-point DePaul victory.

The next season A&M qualified for the NCAA tournament. In the Aggies' first-round victory over Utah, Kurland scored 28 points. "His specialty," *The Denver Post* reported, "was a 'duffer' shot in which he leaped into the air and pushed the ball downward thru the netting with a terrific swish." The shot, of course, would later have a variety of different names—dunk, slam, jam, and more— but it was as electrifying in 1945 as it would be nearly half a century later.

Next, Kurland led the Aggies past Arkansas and into the tournament finals against NYU. In the title game in Madison Square Garden, Kurland shot, passed, played defense, ran the floor, and rebounded—he was the complete big man. He made the difference and was voted the tournament's Most Outstanding Player.

After winning the NCAA title, the Aggies played against DePaul, the NIT champs, in a Madison Square Garden benefit for the Red Cross. The game would determine the national champions, once and for all. Again it was Kurland versus Mikan. But this time Kurland challenged Mikan in the post. "I had this shot called a 'scoop sucker shot,'" said Kurland, "where I spun and came in low with a scoop shot." The DePaul star fouled out in the first half and Kurland went on to dominate the game, won by A&M, 52-44.

Kurland was even better in his senior year. After leading his team to a 28-2 regular-season record (one of the two losses was to DePaul), Kurland and the Aggies returned to the NCAA tournament. In the first round against Baylor, the big redhead had an unspectacular game (for him), shooting 7 for 13 (53.8 percent) and scoring 20 points. Today, those statistics would be nothing special. When put in the perspective of the mid-1940s, however, they are nothing short of miraculous. In Harvard's first round game against Ohio State, the entire Crimson *team* shot 10 for 72. And for the 1946 tournament as a whole, the average team shooting percentage was only around 25 percent.

In the Western championships against California, Kurland was even better, scoring 17 points in the first half. Then, when North Carolina made a second-half run on A&M in the finals, *The Denver Post* reported that "The big fellow dunked in a pair of field goals from the mezzanine level and the Aggies were on their way again." In leading his team to the title Kurland scored 72 points, more than half his team's total of 139. He was of course the unanimous choice for tournament Most Outstanding Player for the second straight season.

By averaging over 25 points a game for the last 12 games of his college career, Kurland breezed to the nation's scoring title. Coach Iba said big Bob had just learned the art of tipping in rebounds while in the air. "I consider that now, at the end of his college career, he has just reached the height of his ability," Iba declared.

While George Mikan signed with the National Basketball League and immediately became pro basketball's dominant center, Bob Kurland graduated with honors and turned down a lucrative ($11,000) offer from Ned Irish and the New York Knickerbockers, opting instead to play in the AAU industrial league (a company-sponsored pro-caliber amateur league) with the Phillips Oilers. As an amateur, Kurland played for both the 1948 and 1952 Olympic gold medal winners.

Once, two years after graduation, Kurland had second thoughts and figured he might want to turn pro after all. The St. Louis native stopped at the office of the home-team Bombers, a sub-.500 team in the newly merged professional league. "I left my name with the secretary," he said, but "nobody called me. A few weeks later I visited the Bombers again and this time I talked with some of the officials. They didn't seem too interested in me, so I gave up the idea." After the 1952 Olympics Kurland retired from basketball and became a Phillips 66 executive.

Clyde Lovellette

University of Kansas

He was 6-9 and upwards of 235 pounds. Sportswriters called him "the beast." "I was the biggest baby ever born in Pike County, Indiana," said Clyde Lovellette, "and the record still stands."

As a Terre Haute, Indiana, high-school star, Lovellette was actively recruited by the Indiana Hoosiers, for whom his brother had already played. North Carolina State flew him down to Raleigh. And Adolph Rupp actively pursued him for Kentucky. So how did he get to Kansas? Phog Allen explained:

"The poor boy was asthmatic. He couldn't play a full game in high school. I assured his mother that I would give him personal medical attention [Dr. Allen is an osteopathic physician] . . . and that Kansas University was situated on a mountain with the finest type of breathing air." (KU indeed sits atop Mount Oread, a breathtaking 75 feet above the city of Lawrence.)

In 1952, Lovellette broke the record for points in the NCAA tournament. But he didn't just break it; as he often did to his opponents in the paint, he battered it. Opposing coaches tried zones, double-teams, collapsing man-to-man defenses, but nothing could stop Kansas's three-time All-American from making his hook shots, and nobody could move him away from the boards (he also broke the all-time tourney rebound mark). The first player to even approach the century mark in points in the NCAAs, Big Clyde scored an incredible 141 in four games. When Lovellette was selected tournament MVP, finishing first on 27 of 29 ballots, one Seattle writer called it "an understatement."

At one point during the final against St. John's (in which he scored 33 points), the Kansas skyscraper, upset by the Redmen's physical play, stormed over to the bench and shouted to Coach Allen, "Dammit, Doc, I'm going to kill the ——." When Clyde's mother, who was sitting nearby, reminded her son that he was raised to be "a good Christian," he replied, "Okay, Mom. I won't kill him, but I'm sure going to mark him up." (And he could have, too; the big guy was a Golden Gloves boxer before he turned to hoops.)

After his Kansas team won the NCAA title, Allen called Lovellette "the greatest player ever produced by the game of basketball." Even though Allen was well known for hyperbole, there were few who would argue. Lovellette was the only national scoring leader ever to play for an NCAA champion, he owned the all-time major college career scoring record, and he dominated the NCAA's championship tournament more completely than anyone had ever done before.

In the eight-team Olympic trials that followed immediately on the heels of the NCAA tournament, Clyde scored 40 in leading Kansas to victory over NIT titlist La Salle. He finally showed he was human in the final seconds of the final game of the Olympic trials, when, playing against the AAU champion Peoria Cats, he missed a game-winning lay-up that would have made Phog Allen the U.S. Olympic team coach. Instead Allen became assistant coach of the American squad, and Lovellette was selected as the starting center. Clyde's human frailty continued into the games themselves, however, until finally coach Warren Womble benched him for lackluster play and a lack of "enthusiasm."

But he rebounded with a distinguished NBA career, and during his eleven seasons in the league he averaged 17 points a game. He also maintained his reputation for being an ornery cuss. Not only was he tough around the boards, he was also well known for carrying a pair of six-shooters around with him on the road.

One night, after getting whistled out of a game by Ref Jim Duffy, Clyde growled, "Just for making all those blind calls against me, I'm gonna blow daylight through you." He then parked himself outside the ref's motel room, waiting for him to go to bed. "About one o'clock in the morning," Lovellette said, "when everything was deathly quiet, I loaded my guns with blanks and talked my roomie, Hub Reed, into knocking on Duffy's door. When he finally dragged himself out of bed, drowsily opening the door, I let fly—both barrels blazing." Clyde laughed. "It scared the devil out of him."

After Lovellette retired from the pros, he was elected sheriff of Vigo County, Indiana. On the night he was voted into the Basketball Hall of Fame, he lost a tight election for the final at-large spot on the Republican ticket for the Wabash County Council. But in March 1952 the Kansas Skyscraper, the Leaning Tower of Lawrence, Cumulous Clyde Lovellette took on the nation's best basketball players and came out the ultimate winner.

Bill Russell

University of San Francisco

Nobody ever played the game of basketball like Bill Russell. He wasn't much of a shooter. He couldn't put the ball on the floor. He was often criticized for not being a complete ballplayer. But he turned defense into an art and rebounding into a science. He was the great intimidator, the most imposing defensive player the game has ever known.

And he was a winner. In college, playing for the San Francisco Dons, he led his team to 55 straight wins and two NCAA titles (in 1955 and 1956). When Russell first joined the Boston Celtics, they had never even reached the NBA finals. With him they won 11 league titles in 13 years. In an era when Elgin Baylor once averaged over 38 points per game, and Wilt Chamberlain averaged 50 for an entire season, Russell never even got close to 20 a game. Yet in 1980 he was voted the greatest NBA player of all time.

What made Russell so great?

He was quick, with lightning reflexes. He was competitive, and always thinking on the court. And he could leap. While starring for USF, Big Bill related a startling experience: "It scared me the first time it happened," he said. "I leaped for a jump shot and was—well, shocked to find myself looking down into the basket." Today an above-the-rim game is not unusual, but in Russell's day it was unique. He even entertained thoughts of being an Olympic high jumper, having gone over the bar at 6-feet, 8-inches while a relative neophyte in the event.

Russell began his career "as the sixteenth man on a fifteen-man junior varsity squad" at McClymonds High School in Oakland, California. "I was third string varsity center as a junior," he said, "and when the other two fellows graduated, I inherited the job. Many a time I wanted to quit, but the coach [George Powles] was my friend and wouldn't let me." Although Russell said Powles "may not have known too much about basketball, he taught me a lot of other things, how important your heart and your attitude is."

When Russell was ready for college, no major college coach would take a chance on him. But Phil Woolpert, whose Dons represented a small (2,500-student) Jesuit school and had no home court, gave the tall, gangly black player a scholarship. In his memoirs Russell said Woolpert wanted him to play like a 6-5 center and did not stress shot blocking. But Woolpert was quoted in San Francisco's second championship season as having told Russell, "If they can't shoot, they can't score."

And nobody could shoot against Bill Russell. In one game against California he blocked twenty-five shots. In a Madison Square Garden game he convinced East Coast skeptics by dominating Holy Cross's Tom Heinsohn; Heinsohn had scored 36 points in his previous game but against Russell he got only 12—all on outside shots. Russell, meanwhile, scored 24, grabbed 22 rebounds, and blocked a half a dozen shots.

Russell's principal offensive weapons were unique in the college game. He scored off offensive rebounds and on what was called "the steer shot," timing his leap to grab teammates' off-target shots and redirecting them into the hoop.

The New York Times, in describing Big Bill's "amazing display of all-around court skill" in the 1955 title game against La Salle, said, "Anytime the ball neared the Don goal Russell was there to (1) assist the ball through the meshes, (2) grab the rebound and score or (3) pass to a teammate."

After the 1955 season, exasperated rival coaches wrote a new "Russell rule," widening the lane to keep Big Bill from basket hanging. It didn't help. Again the Dons went undefeated, and against Iowa in the 1956 championship game Russell was just as dominating as he had been against La Salle the year before; he clogged the middle, controlled the boards, and led all scorers with 26 points.

After Big Bill graduated, the NCAA acted to limit Russell-style defensive domination with a revised goaltending rule. But it wasn't the rules that made Russell dominant—it was the man. He was quite simply the greatest defensive player who ever put on sneakers. And year after year, in college with the Dons and in the pros with the Celtics, he did something else better than any other player in the history of the game—he won.

Bill Bradley

Princeton

In 1965, Bill Bradley lived up to his advance billing by carrying a group of Ivy Leaguers into the Final Four, and turning the third-place game into his personal show with one of the greatest shooting performances in the history of the NCAA tournament.

Then he took his Rhodes Scholarship and went to Oxford.

Bradley always followed his own muse. From the moment the son of the president of the Crystal City (Missouri) State Bank decided to play the game of basketball, he single-mindedly dedicated himself to mastering it. He spent hours on end practicing his moves and shooting at the hoop in his backyard, and by his senior year in high school he was everybody's All-American. In his final high school game, he led his small-town team into the state championships against the big city boys from St. Louis

University High. With eight seconds left in the game and his team losing by a point, Bradley, who already had 33 points, pulled down a rebound, saw a teammate downcourt, gave him a perfect feed, and watched him miss the winning lay-up.

Bradley was recruited by 75 colleges, including many big-time basketball powers, but he confounded them all by choosing Princeton, a school whose rich tradition had nothing at all to do with basketball.

To Bradley, the game was important, but it wasn't everything. And since he didn't need an athletic scholarship to attend college, he chose a school that he thought would allow him to be both a scholar and an athlete. He played for the love of the game, and in doing so virtually single-handedly turned the Tigers into a competitive basketball team.

In his sophomore year, Bradley was selected as an All-American as he led Princeton to the Ivy League title and an automatic bid to the NCAA tournament. In the first round, against St. Joseph's, he scored 40 points and took down 16 rebounds, but it wasn't quite enough—Princeton lost in overtime.

Then, in the opening round of the 1964 tournament, he had 34 points, 10 rebounds, and 8 assists (despite his teammates missing a number of easy shots) to lead Princeton over VMI. In the second round, he finished with 22 points and 10 rebounds, but he had the ball stolen from him in the last seconds of a 2-point loss to Connecticut.

Bradley's senior year would turn out to be the most eventful of all. During the summer, he served as a Capitol Hill intern, and then went on to play for the gold-medal-winning American Olympic basketball team. After the Olympic victory, he returned to Princeton for another year of school and basketball.

The Tigers and Bradley were better than ever. In an early-season battle against Michigan in Madison Square Garden, Princeton was actually leading the nation's top-ranked team by 12 points when Bradley fouled out with four minutes to go. After his teammates lost the game, Bradley stood up in front of them and said he expected them to win the Ivy League, and to keep on winning until they reached the Final Four, where he expected them to meet Michigan again. Only the next time, he said, Princeton would win.

Despite winning their last ten games, the Tigers were unranked going into the 1965 tournament. They soon proved to everyone that they belonged.

In the first round, against Penn State, the Nittany Lions' superb zone effectively contained Bradley for 32 minutes. But when he drove for a lay-up and was fouled with eight minutes left, the complexion of the game changed. Within minutes he'd scored 8 points in a row. He finished with 10 of the Tigers last 14—and Princeton won by a basket.

Next the Tigers took on heavily favored North Carolina State and beat them easily. Bradley scored 27 points and his passing, according to *The New York Times,* "left the Wolfpack stunned." Bradley's coach Bill Van Breda Kolff dismissed it as "an average game" for his star.

What happened next proved Van Breda Kolff right. In the regional final against fourth-ranked Providence, Bradley and the Tigers ran wild, overwhelming the Friars by 40 points as their star scored 41 on 14 of 20 from the floor, while adding 9 assists and 10 rebounds.

Princeton had become the first Ivy League team in more than two decades to reach the Final Four. "Except for my schoolwork," Bradley said, "basketball is the most important thing I've done in college, and this is the climax." His prediction that Princeton would meet Michigan again in the semifinals had come true.

When the game began, "the Big Man," as Van Breda Kolff called Bradley, seemed to be intent on making his prediction of victory a reality too, as he scored 13 of Princeton's first 15 points. But with the Tigers ahead 34-29, Bradley was whistled for his third foul; the tide turned and Michigan stormed into the lead. Then, just a minute into the second half, Bradley picked up his fourth foul. When he finally fouled out with 29 points and five minutes remaining, it was still a game. But after he left, it turned into a rout, as the Wolverines stretched an 8-point lead to 17.

The consolation game against Wichita State was Bradley's ultimate one-man show, one of the greatest individual performances in basketball history. Every time he handled the ball it seemed Princeton scored two points. The Tigers had an insurmountable lead when, with less than four minutes to go, Van Breda Kolff called for a timeout. In the huddle he told his star, who had already scored 46 points, to go for Oscar Robertson's all-time tournament record of 56. For the next three minutes, with the crowd roaring in appreciation of his every move, Bradley bombed from all over the court. Lay-ups, hooks, long jumpers, it didn't matter what he put up—he couldn't miss. When he finally came out of the game with 30 seconds left, the crowd was in a frenzy. Bradley had scored 58 points, 39 in the second half, and he had not only broken Robertson's single-game record, but the record for a tournament as well.

Bradley's 58 points could have easily been 70 if he had played selfishly; but he played the way he always did, setting up his teammates for lay-ups instead of taking 15-footers himself (which is not to say that there were no mortar shots among his points—he hit from as far out as 30 feet). He also dominated the boards, pulling down just six fewer rebounds than the entire Wichita State team.

Referee Bob Korte, who had called the fouls which put Bradley out of the Michigan game, came into the Princeton locker room after his record performance. "That was the greatest exhibition I ever saw," he told Bradley. "It was a pleasure to watch, and I wanted to thank you."

After graduation, Bradley once again did exactly what he wanted to do. He turned down the pro basketball windfall that was waiting for him and instead went to England's venerable Oxford University as a Rhodes Scholar. Two years later, the story goes, he was alone in an English gym dribbling a basketball when he decided that once again he would not do what was expected of him. He wouldn't go into business or law after all—he wanted to play basketball. He returned to America, where his big contract with the New York Knicks earned him the nickname Dollar Bill. As a professional, he was a consummate team man, an unspectacular role player on a team of role players. And although his stats and stardom never approached his college achievements, he was the starting small forward on a team that won two NBA championships. After ten years of moving without the ball, he retired.

Less than a year later, Bradley announced another unusual decision. He wanted to return to Capitol Hill, where he had spent the summer before his senior year at Princeton. Today, Bill Bradley, the senior senator from New Jersey, is widely regarded as a potential president of the United States.

Gail Goodrich

UCLA

Gail Goodrich was the point man on the UCLA fast break, the trigger man on the press, the epitome of the Southern California fair-haired boy.

The son of the captain of Southern Cal's 1939 basketball team, he grew up in North Hollywood with a basketball in his hands. And although he was small and slight (as a high school sophomore he was just 5-4 and 99 pounds), by the time he reached his teens his left-handed jump shot boggled the mind of his father (who was a pretty fair set-shooter in his day). He was so good that as a 5-9, 135-pound senior, he led his school to a city championship and was selected as the Los Angeles high school Player of the Year. Despite his exceptional play, the only college coach willing to take a chance on the diminutive guard was John Wooden.

After starring for UCLA's first undefeated freshman team, Goodrich moved on to the varsity, where he became a sometime starter at off-guard and occasionally even played forward, even though he was still just 6 feet tall.

In his junior year—1963–64—he and All-American Walt Hazzard formed the backcourt tandem that sparked UCLA to its first undefeated season and its first NCAA championship. It was during that season that Wooden, in an effort to utilize his small, quick team to its fullest potential, unveiled his famous full-court zone press. Goodrich, with his tremendous speed, was an essential part of the new, devastating defense. He was also the team's high scorer, but the play-making duties were handled by Hazzard, who was generally acknowledged to be the best guard in the country. Goodrich showed flashes of brilliance, but he was still inconsistent at times.

In the 1964 NCAAs, he was selected as a tournament all-star. Even though he had three subpar games, he was dazzling in the final, leading the Bruins in scoring with 27 points.

After Hazzard graduated, Goodrich assumed the leadership of the team. As a senior, he was All-American—selected as co–Player of the Year (along with Princeton's Bill Bradley) by the Helms Athletic Foundation. He inspired his team to run, press, fast break, crash the boards, and wear down the opposition game after game, all season long.

He was the quickest member of an astonishingly quick UCLA team that averaged 100 points per game during the NCAA tournament. (The previous high team-scoring average was the 1964 UCLA team's 89-plus points per game.) In each of his 1965 tournament games, he was far and away the best player on the floor. Against Brigham Young, he scored 16 of UCLA's first 18 second-half points to lead a Bruin blitz that turned the game into a rout. Then, in a close game against regional rival San Francisco, he destroyed the Dons' hopes by scoring 8 points in the final five minutes.

The Final Four was more of the same. UCLA ran away with their semifinal against Wichita State, as Goodrich led them to a 17-point halftime lead. Playing barely over half the game (he left for good with over twelve minutes left), the little lefty scored 28 points. If Wooden hadn't decided to rest him for the finals, he might have scored 50.

In the championship game, the small, swift Bruins faced big, bad Michigan. And UCLA went into the game against the top-ranked Wolverines with their top defensive player, Keith Erickson, sidelined by an injury. For UCLA even to have a chance, Goodrich had to have a spectacular game.

He was nothing less than brilliant. He dribbled past the bigger Michigan players as though they weren't there, driving in for lay-ups and pulling up for long jumpers which invariably found nothing but net. He led the fast break, and with Erickson out, Goodrich was the glue that held the zone press together. He held his man to 4 points, and took the second half tip out of a Michigan player's hands and dashed in for a lay-up.

According to *The New York Times*, he was "a singular magician masquerading as a guard." He wound up scoring 42 points, and left the game with 1:22 left to play holding a new championship game scoring record, and only 1 point shy of Clyde Lovellette's four-game tournament scoring record. And in the final minutes, in a superb display of ball-handling, he dribbled around and through the Wolverines as the game ticked away, forcing Michigan to foul out three of their starters in a desperate effort to stay in the game. The little man did it all.

Despite his record 42 points and 18 free throws, Goodrich wasn't selected tournament MVP; Bill Bradley was. But Goodrich's performance still ranks as one of the finest in tournament history. It even prompted Wooden to call him "the greatest all-around basketball player I've ever coached."

After graduating from UCLA, Gail Goodrich went into pro basketball, where in his fourteen seasons, he was a five time all-star, a member of two Los Angeles Laker NBA championship teams, and the captain of the Lakers from 1974 to 1976. He retired in 1979 having scored over 19,000 points in his pro career.

Lew Alcindor (Kareem Abdul-Jabbar)

UCLA

Long before Kareem Abdul-Jabbar became the highest scorer in NBA history, Lew Alcindor was the player who turned John Wooden's UCLA into a dynasty.

Three times Alcindor led his team to the NCAA title, and three times he was the tournament's Most Valuable Player. The NCAA changed the rules because of him, but the change only forced him to make his all-around game better, and he became an even more dominating player.

He had a rare combination of size and agility, quickness and strength that fostered comparisons on offense with Chamberlain, and on defense with Russell. He was the complete big man: an intimidating shot-blocker, an outstanding rebounder, and an offensive force of fluid grace and awesome power. And he was a team player, always ready to recognize the contributions and enhance the performances of his teammates.

He could put the ball on the floor when need be, or kick it out to a cutting teammate when double-teamed. And he could shoot: he hit almost sixty-four percent throughout his college career with an arsenal that included a soft-touch jump shot, an exclamation-point dunk (until the NCAA banned the shot in response to him), an effective variety of inside moves, and that amazing, unstoppable sky hook, which, when shot from outside the lane, invariably floated softly down from the ceiling into the hoop.

When Big Lew arrived on the UCLA campus in the fall of 1965, he was the most ballyhooed player to come along in nearly a decade—since Wilt Chamberlain left Philadelphia for the plains of Kansas. The 7-foot 1-inch Alcindor, from New York's Power Memorial Academy, was one of

five high-school All-Americans in his freshman class. He arrived just in time for UCLA's new fieldhouse, Pauley Pavilion, to open for business.

The first game ever played in Pauley Pavilion was an all-UCLA affair, the Alcindor-led freshman team against the defending national champion varsity. It was no contest; the varsity may have been No. 1 in the nation, but they were No. 2 in Westwood—the freshman won by 15 points.

After an undefeated freshman season, Alcindor and his teammates moved up to a higher level of competition. In his first varsity game, playing alongside three sophomore classmates and one junior, Lew scored 56 points against the Bruins' crosstown rivals from USC. "Great start," UCLA Coach John Wooden told him. "Keep it up." He did—during the three years of the Alcindor era, UCLA had a record of 88-2.

Lew was the first really big man ever to play for Wooden. Because of his presence in the lineup, the coach was able to modify the UCLA style of play, so that along with the devastating Bruin fast break, there were more set plays to take advantage of Lew's post-up abilities. Alcindor also gave Wooden's pressing defense a new dimension. Because of his quickness, mobility, and shot-blocking ability, his teammates were able to gamble more without fearing that their men would penetrate to the hoop.

In 1966–67, Alcindor led UCLA to an undefeated season. Then, in the NCAA tournament, UCLA won every game decisively as Big Lew was named the most outstanding player in both the West regional and the Final Four. When Houston collapsed three men around him in the semis, he didn't see the ball much, but the special defense designed to stop him left his teammates open and they took up the scoring slack. On the other end of the floor, Alcindor's intimidation and shot-blocking completely took away the Cougars' strong inside game. Despite the easy UCLA victory, the Big E—Elvin Hayes—said he was "unimpressed" by Alcindor and his team. His words would come back to haunt him a year later.

In the 1967 NCAA final against Dayton, Alcindor was again double- and triple-teamed. He responded by kicking the ball out to his teammates and dominating the boards. After the tournament, Wooden spoke about his big center's effect on the opposition's offense. The coach called him "a tremendous force defensively," saying, "He sets the tone for us. He is a tremendous psychological advantage for us. He blocks shots and he keeps down the other team's shooting average."

Even though they lost once, to Houston and Hayes in the Astrodome, the following year's UCLA team is generally considered to be the best of the Alcindor era. A week before the loss to Houston, Alcindor was scratched in the cornea in a game against Cal and he spent most of the week in bed with a patch over his eye. When he returned for the nationally televised game, he was out of condition and suffering from double vision. Despite his injury, Alcindor played and UCLA lost by only two points. Nonetheless, Houston took over the No. 1 ranking. After the game, which Hayes dominated, he talked about how Alcindor was overrated.

When the rematch finally came, in the NCAA semis, The Big E flatly predicted an easy victory. It was—but not for Houston. UCLA was on fire. In a total team effort, the Bruins built a lead of 44 points before the starters came out. Hayes was held to 10 points and 5 rebounds, while Alcindor was one of five UCLA players in double figures with 19 points, 18 rebounds, and several blocked shots. At one point he also intercepted a Houston pass, drove downcourt like a 6-foot guard, and softly laid it in.

The final against North Carolina was almost as easy as the Houston blowout. The tone was set in the first few minutes as Big Lew blocked half a dozen shots; he finished with 34 points and 16 rebounds, far and away the highest totals on the floor. After the tournament, Dean Smith said, "This is the best team of all time and Alcindor is the greatest who ever played college basketball."

In Alcindor's senior year he matured as a man, but he and the team were under tremendous pressure to repeat as champions, and he was booed everywhere he went outside of the friendly confines of Pauley Pavilion. Despite the pressure, he was able to maintain an even keel. His teammates Lucius Allen, Mike Lynn, and Edgar Lacey all got into academic or legal trouble at various times in their college careers, but he kept rolling along.

Even in college, Alcindor was a sophisticated, well-read, insightful young man. Nonetheless, Wooden always tried to protect him by shielding him from the press. At times this caused conflict between the coach and his star player.

Just before the 1969 tournament, an article in the *Los Angeles Times West Magazine,* written by a former Black Student Union leader, portrayed Alcindor as a separatist and a racist. He did, in fact, strongly associate himself with black nationalist consciousness, but he felt there was a difference between the positive message of black pride and the struggle for equal rights, and the negative message of racial hatred. Alcindor wanted to respond to the article on television; he felt he had been made to appear illiterate and bigoted. But Wooden canceled his TV appearance, thus increasing the friction between the two. Later, however, the coach relented, and Alcindor went on TV to praise Wooden and refute the article.

In Alcindor's senior season, UCLA again lost one game, the last one of the regular season against USC. In the tournament, the Bruins barely got by a hustling, underdog Drake team in the semis before taking Purdue apart in the finals. Alcindor went out in style, scoring 37 points (24 in the first half) and taking down 20 rebounds. He finished his college career by leading UCLA to a record-breaking

three straight NCAA titles and was voted the most valuable player in the tournament for the third straight time.

After the tournament, he was wooed by both the New York Nets of the ABA and the Milwaukee Bucks of the NBA. He set ground rules for the two leagues: he would accept only sealed bids, with no bargaining. The ABA owners believed that signing the UCLA superstar would make their league both more visible and more viable, and they were prepared to underwrite the Nets and spend through the roof to land him. But the offer Commissioner George Mikan finally approved was, inexplicably, far below the owners' figure. Alcindor went with the Bucks and the NBA.

In the summer before his senior year, Alcindor, who had been deeply influenced by the ideas of Malcolm X, converted to the Muslim faith. And it was with a new name, Kareem Abdul-Jabbar, that he followed his stupendous college career with an equally extraordinary professional basketball career. He was a member of six NBA championship teams and was the playoff MVP twice. He was named to the NBA all-star team 19 times, and was the league's MVP a record six times. He holds NBA career records in numerous categories, including playoff and regular season games and minutes played, scoring, field goals, and blocked shots. He retired in 1989, at the age of 42.

Austin Carr

Notre Dame University

In 1970 Austin Carr had the best tournament of any player who never made it to the Final Four. By far. The Notre Dame junior All-American was on fire from the moment he stepped on the court in Dayton, Ohio, for a first-round game against Ohio University, and he didn't stop shooting the eyes out of the basket until the Irish went home to South Bend a week later.

Notre Dame operated out of what was called a "double-stack" offense. With two large bodies setting picks on either side of the key, point guard Jackie Meehan would handle the ball until Carr's constant movement sprung him for an open shot. It was quite effective; Carr got free often enough to finish the regular season with an average of 38.1 points per game, second in the nation to Pistol Pete Maravich. (He did, however, hit a far higher percentage of his shots than the LSU star.)

In the 1970 tourney opener, Ohio's John Canine was assigned to guard Carr in a box-and-one. "At one point," Canine told *The National* two decades later, "he came across half-court, and he didn't come across but four or five steps, and he just pulled up and shot it through. I thought to myself, *Well, John. We know whose side the Lord's on today."*

Carr had 35 points at the half and finished with 61, a record that still stands as the most ever by a player in a tournament game. Hitting from as far out as 35 feet, Carr shot 25 of 44 shots in the game. But he wasn't finished. The next time out, he again scored more than half his team's points as Notre Dame lost to Kentucky 109-99. Finally, in the regional consolation game, he scored 45 more against Iowa. His three game totals: 68 of 118 from the floor, 22 of 26 from the line, and a total of 158 points (52.7 per game).

The next year, when Notre Dame was upset in the second round by Drake, Carr again averaged over 40 points per game. His career tournament scoring total (for three years) was 289 points in seven games, again the best record in history. His career average was more than five points per game more than anyone else's *single tournament* best. He had the best single tournament scoring average ever . . . and he had the second best. He had four of the top ten single-game scoring performances in NCAA tourney history. And he did it all before the advent of the 3-point shot.

Austin Carr went on to become the NBA's top draft pick in 1971. In his first three years in the league, before an injury slowed him down, he led the Cleveland Cavaliers in scoring. Still, he averaged fifteen points a game for his ten-year pro career.

Carr graduated from Notre Dame with a degree in economics, and he went into business after he retired from basketball. "My parents always preached, 'You won't be able to do this forever. You have to get an education,'" he recalled in a 1986 interview with *The Indianapolis Star.* But he said he'd "never forget those days" when he was the greatest scorer in the history of college basketball's greatest show.

Bill Walton
UCLA

When Denny Crum, John Wooden's top assistant and the chief recruiter for UCLA, first saw Bill Walton play, he returned to Westwood and told his boss, "I've just seen the greatest high school prospect ever." When Wooden reminded Crum that he had recruited Lew Alcindor, Crum replied, "Yeah, but this kid is better."

Huck Finn in sneakers didn't know how to lose. As a high school boy in La Mesa, California, the gangling, free-spirited redhead with the toothy grin scored 50 points and grabbed 34 rebounds (both records) in leading his team to a tournament championship and their 31st straight victory.

But the best was yet to come. No team with Bill Walton at center lost a single game between his junior year at Helix High and his senior year at UCLA.

The comparisons between Walton and Kareem Abdul-Jabbar were inevitable, because of all the great centers, the one Walton most resembled was his predecessor at UCLA. They are quite possibly the two greatest *all-around* centers in college basketball history. Each could do everything—shoot, rebound, pass, and play defense. And their coach, John Wooden, called them both "completely team oriented, totally unselfish basketball players."

Walton was a genius of the hardwood, who, as much as any big man in history, made everyone around him better. He was a defensive intimidator and a devastating rebounder whose outlet passes keyed one of the greatest fast breaks ever seen in college basketball.

After leading his UCLA freshman team to an undefeated season, he joined the Bruins' defending national champions and immediately became the team's most important player. As a sophomore, he led UCLA to an undefeated season and was named college player of the year. During the NCAA tournament (in which he was named Most Outstanding Player of both the West regionals and the Final Four), he dominated quietly but effectively. In four games he shot 28 of 41 (68.3%), and averaged 20 points and 16 rebounds a game. And he was at his best in situations when he was most needed. In the opening game, a 32-point victory over Weber State, he played only 20 minutes and took only one shot. But in the Final Four against Louisville, he turned a tight game into a UCLA romp by scoring eight straight points in less than three minutes in the first half. And in the finals, although he expressed bitter disappointment with both his team's and his own performance, he lead the Bruins in scoring and pulled down twice as many rebounds as anyone else on the court.

The 1973 season started out as more of the same. UCLA once again went through the regular season undefeated, and Walton was voted player of the year for the second straight time. In the tournament that followed, he was selected West regional MOP after shooting 17 for 25 (68 percent) and grabbing 14 rebounds per game. In the Final Four against Indiana, he shot 7 for 12, had 17 rebounds (no other player on either team had more than six), and was also the game's leading playmaker with nine assists. He also benefited from a disputed call when, playing with four fouls, he collided with Indiana center Steve Downing on a drive and the whistle went against the Hoosier.

Everything Walton did to that point, however, was just a prelude. In the 1973 national championship contest against Memphis State, he played the perfect game—and he made it look easy. In the most brilliant individual performance in the history of the tournament title game, he shot 21 of 22 from the floor, scored 44 points, and was far and away the leading rebounder on the court. Without him, UCLA would have been hard pressed to win. Even with him, the Bruins didn't break the game open until midway through the second half, when Wooden left Walton in the game with four fouls and the big redhead responded by moving smoothly across the lane for score after score despite his opponents' desperate attempts to foul him out. By the time he left the game with an injury in the last three minutes, he had broken Gail Goodrich's championship game scoring record and UCLA was far out in front.

After the season, Walton was reportedly offered as much as four million dollars by the Philadelphia 76ers to turn pro. He was clearly miffed by the college rules that forbade the dunk and allowed the stall, and he was tired of being constantly triple teamed and zoned. Nonetheless, he turned down the money for one more year at UCLA.

Bill Walton was devoted to John Wooden, loved playing basketball for him, and was a great competitor within the team concept Wooden taught. But by the time he was a senior, he and his teammates had begun to chafe under the Wooden philosophy that demanded haircuts, ties, discipline, and decorum. As one teammate said about the Walton gang, "We have this great UCLA image, and nobody suspects we are a bunch of wonderful lawbreaking degenerates." Walton himself was a child of his time, passionately and publicly against the war in Vietnam, aware of racial prejudice, and involved in youth culture. The single-mindedness, the killer instinct that was necessary to maintain perfection, began to break down.

Nothing lasts forever, not even the streak. Midway through Walton's senior season, after amassing 88 consecutive victories, far and away the most in major college history, UCLA finally lost. And then they lost again. By tournament time 1974, the Bruins had proven to the world that they were mortal—once and for all.

From the beginning of the tournament, it was clear that UCLA could be taken. In their first game, against Dayton, Walton scored 27 and pulled down 19 rebounds, but he and his teammates allowed Dayton to come back from a 17-point first-half deficit to extend the Bruins to the limit. It took three overtimes before the Bruins could beat the 20th-ranked Flyers. Finally, in the national semifinals in Greensboro, North Carolina, the Walton gang was ambushed by a talented, pumped-up North Carolina State team. Walton played every minute and led all scorers and rebounders—but this time it wasn't quite enough; UCLA lost in double overtime.

UCLA had won seven consecutive NCAA tournaments—30 straight tournament games—but even with Bill Walton they couldn't bring home the eighth title. Walton was the centerpiece of a terrific team. He was surrounded by great players. (Even his seldom-used backup, Swen Nater, eventually had a long and distinguished NBA ca-

reer.) And they played great team ball. But even the Walton gang couldn't win them all.

Walton dominated—baseline to baseline—as few other players ever have. He had the highest career field goal percentage (68.6 percent) in NCAA tournament history, while averaging over 13 rebounds per game. He blocked shots, started the fast break, and hit the open man. And he was the leading player on a UCLA team that didn't lose a game for two and a half seasons.

As a pro, Walton showed flashes of his collegiate brilliance, but he was slowed by a series of injuries that prevented him from becoming one of the all-time greats. In his third season in the league (one of the few in which he was more or less completely healthy), he led his Portland Trail Blazers to the NBA title. When he wasn't hurting, Huck Finn in sneakers remembered how to win.

Earvin (Magic) Johnson

Michigan State

From the moment he arrived on the Michigan State campus in 1977, Earvin Johnson was Magic.

He was a local boy from Lansing, one of ten children of hardworking parents. As a freshman, there were great expectations for him: it was hoped that he would help turn the Spartans—who had been consistent losers for nine of the previous ten years—into a respectable team. Instead he led them to a 25-5 record. What was most remarkable was the way he did it, by putting the ball in his teammates' hands at just the right time and in just the right place for them to do the most with it.

His new teammate Terry Donnelly knew about Magic's gift as soon as he stepped onto the court with him. "It didn't really hit me until I got in the backcourt with him, on the first day of practice," Donnelly said. "You're running down the floor and you're open and most people can't get the ball to you through two or three people, and all of a sudden the ball's in your hands and you've got a lay-up."

As the tallest man on the Michigan State team, Johnson was a combination forward/point guard. He controlled the ball, called out instructions to his teammates, and despite a multitude of zones designed to stop his pinpoint passing, he invariably hit the open man.

By the end of the season, Michigan State had won the Big Ten title (their first in 19 years) and reached the NCAA regional finals, where they gave the eventual national champions from Kentucky their stiffest test of the tournament. Although Johnson shot poorly throughout the 1978 tournament, he still earned raves for his brilliant passing.

In Johnson's sophomore year, he went beyond brilliance; his sleight of hand transformed an otherwise fair-to-middling Spartan team into national champions. And he had fun doing it every step of the way. To Magic, basketball wasn't work, it was a game. It was show time, party time, and he was the life of the party, laughing and talking and slapping five as he got his teammates—especially the high-flying, high-scoring forward Gregory Kelser—into the act too.

During the 1979 tournament, Indiana coach Bobby Knight said of Magic, "Anyone who judges that guy strictly on physical ability is making the biggest mistake in the world. You judge him here," he said, touching his heart. "He does so many things for you that it is amazing. He is one player who plays strictly for the team. He is one player who thinks of everybody else before he thinks of himself. He is one player who makes everyone else around him better."

Magic's effect on the game was not reflected in his statistics, which were ordinary (he averaged only 16.5 points and 7.2 rebounds per game for the season, second on the team in both categories to Kelser). And he was still being criticized as a poor shooter (his field goal percentage was much lower than most of his teammates'). But he wasn't getting the passes they were. And he wasn't concerned. "I'll take zero [points]," he added, "as long as I get the assists."

In the 1979 tournament, Magic got the points and the assists. In the regional semi against LSU, he scored 24 and had 12 assists; then in the regional final against Notre Dame, he had 13 assists, including three perfect alley-oops to Kelser.

In the semis, Magic led the charge as Michigan State ran Penn off the floor. Johnson shot 9 of 10 from the field on his way to 29 points. He also led the Spartans in rebounding and had 10 assists before he came out of the game with five minutes remaining.

The finals promised a dream matchup: Johnson and Michigan State against unbeaten Indiana State and their star forward Larry Bird. The game, and the charismatic presence of Magic and Bird, catapulted college basketball to new heights of popularity. Each of the two stars had the ability to raise the level of play of everyone around him. Of course, they would meet again, many times, in NBA championship competition, but their first meeting—in their last collegiate game—had a storybook quality about it.

It turned out to be Magic's game. He had the run of the court, leading his team in scoring and keeping the ball on a string. Meanwhile his teammates double-teamed Bird; they kept him away from the ball in the open court and took away the effectiveness of his great passing game.

During the tournament, Al McGuire called Magic the best player in the game—college or pro. But there was a great deal of skepticism as to whether he could do in the pros what he did for the Spartans. Some said he couldn't jump well, others suggested he couldn't play defense or

score. One NBA executive declared, "He will not turn around a franchise." But the Lakers, who had traded for the first pick, still chose the 19-year-old with the Magic hands. And when Magic and Bird arrived in the NBA, they gave the league the shot in the arm it so desperately needed.

When Magic joined the Lakers, they were a solid veteran unit led by one of the league's greatest players, Kareem Abdul-Jabbar. But as Johnson had done at Michigan State, he immediately put his imprint on the Laker franchise. Magic took a good team and made it *the* team of the 80s. In his rookie year, when Abdul-Jabbar, who had been dominating the play-offs, was forced to the sidelines with an injury in the fifth game of the finals, it was Magic who came out to play center for the next game against the 76ers in Philadelphia. Here was a 20-year-old 6-9 rookie point guard, playing the position for the first time since high school, and he came onto the court giggling at the very thought of taking Abdul-Jabbar's place. At the end—after he had scored 42 points, pulled down 15 rebounds, passed off for 7 assists, picked off 3 steals, and blocked a shot—he was still giggling. Three years out of high school, he had come through in the NBA finals with one of the greatest individual performances in the history of the game. He was, as Julius Erving put it, "unreal."

Laker coach Paul Westhead shook his head and marveled at his prodigy. Johnson, he said, "thinks every season goes like that. You play some games, win the title, and get named MVP." Just like Magic.

James Worthy
University of North Carolina

On March 30, 1982, James Worthy rose to the occasion. He was *the man* for North Carolina, gracefully racing downcourt for jam after jam in a performance his front-court partner, Sam Perkins, called "the most explosive he's ever been." And though freshman Michael Jordan hit the game winner, it was Worthy who intercepted George-town guard Fred Brown's errant pass and started dribbling the night away to victory.

Worthy was fouled with two seconds left and missed both shots. Which proved that, after all, he was only human.

It was a long, hard road back for Worthy. Three years earlier his combination of size, speed, leaping, and ball-handling ability made the Gastonia, North Carolina, native one of the most sought-after high-school players in the nation. When he chose North Carolina, Dean Smith made no promises about playing time. But he became only the third freshman in Smith's twenty years at Chapel Hill to earn a spot on the Tar Heel starting five.

In January of his freshman year, Worthy shattered his ankle. It was a serious break, requiring the surgical placement of two metal screws and a rod in the ankle. When James came back as a sophomore, with the screws and rod still in place, he no longer had the same mobility and strength he'd had previously. Despite playing in severe pain all year, Worthy started alongside Al Wood and Sam Perkins in the front court, and Carolina made it to NCAA Finals before losing to Indiana.

After the season was over, the hardware was removed. The next year, James was finally able to play again without pain.

Throughout the 1981–82 season, he was the Tar Heels' big-game player. And in the 1982 post-season, he was voted the Most Outstanding Player of the ACC tournament, the NCAA East regional, and the Final Four. Worthy did it all within Coach Smith's team concept; not by piling up stats, but by taking over at crunch time.

In the first eleven minutes of the ACC tournament final against Ralph Sampson and Virginia, he went seven for seven from the floor and also contributed an assist and a steal.

In the NCAA regional semis against Alabama, he fouled out 'Bama's star forward Eddie Phillips, boxing him out and keeping him off the boards. And when the Tar Heels went into their four corners stall, it was Worthy who held back the Tide with his spectacular ball handling. 'Bama coach Wimp Sanderson bemoaned, "We couldn't keep the ball off him."

In the regional finals the tandem of Worthy and Perkins, alternately posting and cutting, gave Villanova fits. Against Houston in the Final Four, North Carolina went into the four corners with a four-point lead and seven minutes left. When the Cougars came out to challenge the ball, James cut from the wing toward the basket. The ball and Worthy both went up, and James stuffed home the pass with an electrifying leap that broke the back of Houston. Teammate Chris Brust marveled, "That's the highest I've ever seen James jump."

But James Worthy was saving the best for last.

It was Georgetown against North Carolina in the finals, two great teams at the top of their game. At first it looked like Georgetown freshman Patrick Ewing would swat the ball away from the hoop all night. Then, midway through the first half, with Carolina down by four, Dean Smith recognized that his best chance to beat the Hoyas was to beat Ewing downcourt. He abandoned his half-court offense and told the Tar Heels to run. Worthy led the charge, almost single-handedly bringing his team back to tie the game.

In the second half, with Georgetown again nursing a small lead, Worthy took over again. The Tar Heels came back with three of their next four baskets coming on spectacular Worthy dunks.

By the time he picked off the pass that clinched Carolina's 63-62 victory, James Worthy had scored 28 points on 13 for 17 shooting. He had brought his club back twice when Georgetown threatened to blow the game open. He had come through when he was needed—and he had put up the numbers.

After his junior year, Worthy left school with Smith's blessing to become the NBA's No. 1 draft choice (ahead of Terry Cummings and Dominique Wilkins). He fit right into the Laker team concept, coming off the bench as a rookie at three positions: power forward, small forward, and off guard.

He's been a Laker mainstay ever since. And, as Magic Johnson says about his teammate: "James is a money man." In the 1987 final against the Celtics Worthy made a spectacular play his teammates credited with turning the sixth game around. The next year against the Pistons he was the play-off MVP, this time coming up big with a triple double when his team needed him to put up the numbers. As usual, James Worthy got the job done.

THE COACHES

College basketball is a coaches' game. Unlike the pros, where star players define a franchise, the college coach decides the direction, creates the team concept, and provides the continuity for a school's basketball program. He is a recruiter and a teacher, and he stamps his teams with his personality from one year to the next. Just as we think of the Los Angeles Lakers of the 1980s as the team of Magic Johnson and Kareem Abdul-Jabbar, the Boston Celtics as Larry Bird's team, or the Chicago Bulls as the Michael Jordan franchise, we can't imagine North Carolina without Dean Smith, Georgetown without John Thompson, or Indiana coached by anyone other than Bob Knight.

There have been dozens of brilliant, innovative, and successful coaches during the 52 years of the NCAA tournament. Ten of the greatest are profiled here. Other coaches who have made an indelible mark on the game include:

The formidable Henry Iba, the prophet of ball control, who was among the first to recognize the value of a coordinated big man and who led his disciplined Oklahoma A&M Aggies to the national championship twice.

Fred Taylor, who brought his smoothly running Ohio State Buckeyes to the tournament finals three straight times.

Ed Jucker of Cincinnati, who molded a team without superstars into a defensive juggernaut, and just missed winning three championships in his first three years as a coach.

Phil Woolpert of San Francisco, who put together one of the greatest teams in basketball history around his concept of "if they can't shoot, they can't score."

Pete Newell of Cal, whose teams played beyond their potential and won because they hardly ever made mistakes.

Frank McGuire, the master of psychology, who built nationally ranked teams at three different schools.

Ray Meyer of DePaul, who amassed over 700 victories in his long and illustrious career.

Among today's top coaches are Mike Krzyzewski, Rollie Massimino, Billy Tubbs, Larry Brown, Lou Carnesecca, Lute Olsen, and Dale Brown, each of whom, year in and year out, has built strong, successful basketball programs that bear the unmistakable mark of their personalities.

Following is a closer look at ten of the greatest coaches of today and of the past.

Phog Allen

University of Kansas

Coaching Record:	W	L	Pct.
At Kansas	590	219	.730
At Central Missouri State	107	7	.938
At Baker	46	2	.958
At Haskell	27	5	.843
Totals	770	233	.768

NCAA Tournament Record: Four appearances (1940, 1942, 1952, 1953).
Won-Lost Record: 10-3.
National Second Place: 1940, 1953.
National Championship: 1952.

When Forrest C. Allen was a student at the University of Kansas in 1908, he told his teacher, Dr. James Naismith, that he wanted to be a basketball coach. "You don't coach this game, Forrest, you play it," said Naismith, who, not too many years before, had nailed two peach baskets to the rails of 10-foot balconies, handed his students a soccer ball, and told them to look up, thus inventing the game of basketball. "Well," replied young Allen, "you can teach them to pass at angles and run in curves."

While Naismith invented basketball, Phog Allen can be called the game's first coach. From 1908 until he was forced to retire as the University of Kansas coach 48 years later, he accumulated more victories than any other coach—ever—and his record stood until his own star pupil, Adolph Rupp, surpassed it in 1968.

Phog was a master at teaching his players to pass at angles and run in curves. He told his players to "guard as if your arms were cut off at the elbows" (translation, keep your hands up on defense). He taught a "stratified transitional man-for-man defense with zone principles." (Explained Tus Ackerman of the Jayhawks' 1923 national championship: "Phog loved to double-talk those writers back East. It was a zone, that's all.") Although he was an unwavering advocate of a strict ball control offense—even going so far as to claim victory in the 1940 championship game lost by Kansas to Indiana 60-42 because *his team had the ball most of the game*—his two most illustrious students (Adolph Rupp, substitute guard, Kansas '23, and Dean Smith, substitute guard, Kansas '53) both based their offenses around the fast break. And Rupp even

attributed that innovation to Allen. "Basically it was very simple," said the Kentucky coach at the 45th reunion of the 1923 Kansas team, "the middle man just went as far as he could, then passed off. Each man stayed in his lane, because criss-crossing just slowed things down. I made a few modifications."

Allen had other visionary ideas:

Starting in the late 1920s, he fought a one-man crusade to include basketball in the Olympic games. His efforts finally paid off when the game Dr. Naismith invented was added to the 1936 Berlin Olympics.

And as a founding member and the first president of the National Association of Basketball Coaches, he pushed for a national championship event that would be run by the coaches and the schools, and would compete with New York's NIT. In 1940 he brought the new post-season event to Kansas City, and was responsible for the NCAA tournament turning its first profit.

A list of Allen's students reads like a who's who of college coaches: Rupp, the Kentucky Baron, who finished his career with more wins than any other coach in history; Smith, who, by the end of the 1990 season, had brought his North Carolina team into twenty tournaments and was rapidly approaching 700 career victories; Ralph Miller, who had over 650 career victories and coached three different schools in the NCAA tournament; Dick Harp, who succeeded Allen and took the Kansas team (with Wilt Chamberlain) to a triple overtime thriller for the national championship; and Frosty Cox, who led Colorado to a third-place NCAA finish in 1941.

Dr. Allen (he was an osteopath) was always ready to venture forth with an opinion, which he generally pronounced in the stentorian tones that earned him his nickname. (A student sportswriter once heard him umpiring a baseball game and immediately christened him "Foghorn." Another writer changed it to "Phog," and that was the name that stuck.)

Many of Phog's ideas were controversial, and today some appear ludicrous:

He spent much of his career fighting against the dominance of big men and fought for decades for the adoption of 12-foot (instead of 10-foot) baskets in order to neutralize their advantage. But after he recruited 7-foot, 1-inch Wilt Chamberlain to play for Kansas, he declared: "Twelve-foot baskets? What are you talking about? I've developed amnesia."

He also charged that political maneuvering led to the

abolition of the center tap after each score and advocated its return as late as 1950.

In 1941 he predicted that college football—a "high-pressured big business"—would die within a decade.

In 1945 he called for the appointment of a czar, along the lines of Major League baseball's Judge Kenesaw Mountain Landis, to police college basketball. The czar's job would be to prevent professionalism and recruiting abuses and stop the spread of gambling.

Phog said, "We might as well face the fact that other schools are spending money for players." However, when he got Philadelphia high-school student Wilt the Stilt Chamberlain to attend Kansas in what most outside observers saw as a cash-on-the-table bidding war for America's greatest prospect, the Jayhawk coach said, "If anybody, any alumni, are contributing for Chamberlain, I know not a thing, not by wink or nod." And when asked for his comment about Chamberlain's decision to attend Kansas, he remarked, "That's wonderful news. I hope he'll come out for the team." (Later, in a moment of greater candor, he said, "No team that has won a championship can look back and say it has kept the real letter of the law.")

"The Foghorn of the Prairies" generally directed his blasts at the sins of others, and his extraordinary ability to point his innocent finger at someone else infuriated many opponents, as well as the fraternity of East Coast—and particularly New York—sportswriters. As the *New York Post*'s Milton Gross once wrote, "It's about time someone cut the clay feet from under this corn country pop-off, who has befogged his own people as much as he has bulldozed the rest of the country."

After a 1950 speech in which Allen vilified pro basketball, Eastern basketball, the Big Ten, the Pacific Coast Conference, the AAU, and the NCAA's Joint Rules Committee, CCNY coach Nat Holman called Phog's performance "A lot of unmitigated hooey, lips that quiver and say nothing."

Allen's feelings about Eastern basketball and its officials went very deep: he once referred to Frank McGuire's St. John's five as a bunch of "alley fighters." And in 1952 he refused to allow his NCAA champions to play in the Olympic trials against NIT titlist La Salle unless a Western referee was there to co-officiate the game.

Despite what his detractors had to say about him, Phog Allen was more than a "corn country pop-off," more than a blast of hot air. After all, his teams won 770 games. In 39 years at Kansas his Jayhawks won 24 conference championships. They won the NCAA title in 1952 and placed second in both 1940 and 1953. Between 1908 and 1956 his teams had only two losing campaigns. He was voted Coach of the Year in 1950 and was inducted into the Naismith Hall of Fame in 1959.

Rupp spoke simply and eloquently at his funeral service. "He will go down in history," said the Baron of Lexington,

"as the greatest basketball coach of all time." Phog Allen was there at the beginning, when basketball was still in the process of being invented, and he was still there—winning—a half century later.

Branch McCracken

Indiana University

Coaching Record:	W	L	Pct.
At Ball State	93	41	.694
At Indiana	364	174	.676
Totals	457	215	.680

NCAA Tournament Record: Four appearances (1940, 1953, 1954, 1958).
Won-Lost Record: 9-2.
National Championships: 1940, 1953.

When Branch McCracken coached Indiana, the greatest goal a boy from Terre Haute (or Muncie, Evansville, or Sunman) could have was to run the fast break for the Big Bear's Hoosiers.

McCracken was a Hoosier himself, brought up in the collective basketball mania that built a big gym in every small town and emptied Main Street on basketball night all over the state of Indiana. Though his first basketball was an inflated pig's bladder and his first hoop an old peach basket nailed to the side of a barn, the farm boy from Monrovia (pop. 406) grew to a strapping 6-3 and became the star of his high-school county champs. (Monrovia lost in the statewide tournament to neighboring Martinsville, whose star, Johnny Wooden, went on to have a pretty fair coaching career of his own.) As an all-state player, McCracken entered Indiana University, where he became an All-American in 1929 and 1930 (again competing against Wooden, who played for Purdue). A great all-around athlete, he was also an all–Big Ten football player, even though football was a sport he had never seen before he arrived on the Bloomington campus.

After graduation, McCracken briefly played pro ball (this was long before the NBA and its big money). In 1931, he accepted a job as coach of the Ball State Cardinals.

At Ball State he started to develop a coaching philosophy that valued speed on offense, pressure on defense, and excellent physical conditioning. He also married the college president's daughter. ("It's one way to get tenure," he said. "Besides, she was the prettiest girl in town.") After he was named Indiana's Small College Coach of the Year in his eighth season with the Cardinals, McCracken was picked to succeed the Hoosiers' beloved Everett Dean, and he moved to Bloomington.

McCracken was just 30 when he became the Indiana coach in 1939, and if there were some with doubts who felt he was simply too young to handle such a big job, it didn't take him long to prove them wrong. In his first season at Indiana the Hoosiers finished with a 17-3 record; in his second year they won the NCAA championship and he was named National Coach of the Year.

Big Mac's Hurryin' Hoosiers lived and died by the fast break. "Sure, we'd make mistakes when we'd be running and firing the ball up," he said. "But we'd get the people yelling and throw off the patterns of the teams we'd be playing. That's why my clubs were always in shape. We'd run the other guy right into the floor."

He was tough, too—on himself, his players, and especially the officials. After a game against Purdue (and its fiery coach, "Piggy" Lambert) in the early forties, one Big Ten official told McCracken, "This league ain't big enough for two of your kind." But McCracken never stopped storming off the bench to question a call or shouting at his boys to hit the boards for a rebound. (In the 1953 title game against Kansas his jumping up and arguing with refs cost him two technicals, and almost the game.)

McCracken used his network of Indiana high school coaches to bring him the best players in the state. The system worked like a charm. Among the schoolboy stars he molded into All-Americans were Marvin Huffman (from the 1940 national champs), Don Schlundt and Bob Leonard (of the 1953 title team), plus future pro standouts like Walt Bellamy and Tom and Dick Van Arsdale. He also recruited Bill Garrett, a first-team All-American in 1951. (McCracken was extremely proud of the award he received from the NAACP in recognition of breaking the color line at Indiana with Garrett.)

Branch was called "the Sheriff of Monrovia" because he ran his players hard and enforced strict discipline on stars and scrubs alike. He boasted that his players told him "the game is a lot easier than our practices." He believed that if a player proved his mettle by surviving his tough training regimen, he would respond better in game situations and eventually wear the other team down.

Most of the time McCracken was right. In his 24 years of coaching, the two-time Coach of the Year finished with a record of 457-215. As a coach, he was enshrined in the Helms Hall of Fame in 1957, and as a player in the Naismith Basketball Hall of Fame in 1960.

Branch McCracken was a tough act to follow. His successor, Lou Watson, brought the Hoosiers into the NCAA tournament only once, and it wasn't until Bob Knight arrived that Indiana began to regain the glory of the McCracken years.

Adolph Rupp

University of Kentucky

Coaching Record:	W	L	Pct.
At Kentucky	875	190	.822

NCAA Tournament Record: Twenty appearances (1942, 1945, 1948, 1949, 1951, 1952, 1955, 1956, 1957, 1958, 1959, 1961, 1962, 1964, 1966, 1968, 1969, 1970, 1971, 1972).
Won-Lost Record: 30-18.
National Third Place: 1942 (tie).
National Second Place: 1966.
National Championship: 1948, 1949, 1951, 1958.

The Baron of Bluegrass Country, the Man in the Brown Suit, Old Rupp and Ready was charming and brilliant—or cantankerous and cruel—depending on your point of view.

His supporters might have elected him governor of the great state of Kentucky, except that the job he already held, as the basketball coach at the U of K, was more important.

His detractors would have consigned him to oblivion, had they had the power. But nobody could depose Rupp, not even the NCAA, not even a respected member of the United States federal judiciary.

To Adolph Rupp, every game was a vendetta. Winning was everything. In December 1958, months after gaining his fourth NCAA title, he wrote, "Defeat and failure to me are enemies. Without victory, basketball has little meaning. I would not give one iota to make the trip from the cradle to the grave unless I could live in a competitive world."

Rupp won more games than any other college basketball coach in history. His success spanned nearly half a century, from the time he arrived at the University of Kentucky in 1930 until his enforced retirement at the age of 70 in 1972. He was a Kansas farm boy who learned to play basketball by stuffing a feedsack and throwing it around the barnyard. After playing for the legendary Phog Allen at the University of Kansas, he adopted the Bluegrass State and surpassed all his teacher's great records. And he turned his own mentor's lessons upside down, for unlike Allen, who preached ball-control basketball, Rupp revolutionized the game with a precision fast break.

"Championships are not won by wishing and hoping," the Baron said, "they are won by hard work and willingness on the part of the boys to sacrifice." Rupp was an autocrat who demanded that his players either do things the right way (his way) or face the consequences. He ran his practices like a drill-sergeant, working his players through the same regimens over and over until, through constant repetition, they developed near-flawless execution of fundamentals. "Perfection," he said, "can be achieved in no other way."

A boy who received a basketball scholarship to the University of Kentucky was expected to do one thing only—play ball and win for Adolph Rupp. For decades, as far as recruiting basketball talent went, Rupp virtually owned the state, and much of the rest of the South as well. And he was not averse to going ever farther afield to sign up the best players for UK. Opposing coaches, particularly those in the Midwest, accused him of being a carpetbagger who raided their territories of quality talent. In 1941, for example, he brought in 35 top high school players from all over the country to try out for the privilege of playing for the Wildcats. After almost a week of intense workouts and scrimmages, he chose the best of the lot and offered them scholarships. The rest were free to go elsewhere.

Rupp often joked that "the door of my office is six feet two inches high. If the boy doesn't bump his head coming in, I don't even shake hands with him." The statement was only a slight exaggeration; if a boy was exceptional enough, like All-American Ralph Beard of UK's 1948–49 National Champions (the "Fabulous Five"), the Baron might give him special dispensation.

There was one category of players, however, who couldn't get in the door no matter how good they were. Although black players came into town with visiting teams as far back as 1951, when Solly Walker played for St. John's against the Wildcats in Lexington, Rupp's own teams remained segregated for virtually his entire career; he didn't challenge Jim Crow until the color line had been successfully broken by many other schools throughout the South.

With his unerring focus on victory, Rupp developed one standard of ethics for the rest of the world and another for himself. It was almost as if he thought he had a franchise on morality and was himself above the law.

In 1951, in the midst of the college basketball game-fixing scandal that had already affected all the top New York and other nationally prominent teams, Rupp pronounced his judgment on the issue. "Everybody concerned should protect the kids from people who might corrupt them," he declared. "One of the most important things to do is to punish all the guilty parties." Then, as rumors started to fly that Kentucky players would soon be implicated, he declared, "Gamblers couldn't get at my boys with a ten-foot pole." Within days of Rupp's statement, Alex Groza, Ralph Beard, and Dale Barnstable—three of Kentucky's Fabulous Five—were indicted for point-shaving. Although Rupp no longer called them "my boys," he did excuse them. "The Chicago Black Sox threw games," he declared gravely, "but these kids only shaved points."

In testimony concerning the point-shaving charges before Federal Judge Saul Streit, Rupp admitted that he gave money to players when they performed well (including money raised to support the 1948 Olympic team), and that he had a close relationship with Lexington's most notorious gambler, Ed Curd. Testimony revealed that Curd occasionally traveled with the Kentucky team, and Beard swore to the court that Rupp once entered the Kentucky locker room before a game and told his players, "I just called Curd to get the points. Now these guys will be tough tonight so I want you to pour it on."

The investigation ended with the conviction of all three Kentucky players. In 1952, the NCAA banned Kentucky from participating in intercollegiate basketball for a year. Rupp was indignant. "The NCAA is trying to play God," he declared. "They have finally found a way to beat Kentucky. They have cancelled our schedule." He vowed that he would not retire until the person who handed down the suspension handed him another championship trophy.

In referring to the Kentucky basketball program, Judge Streit "found covert subsidization of players, ruthless exploitation of athletes, cribbing at examinations, 'illegal' recruiting, a reckless disregard for their [the players'] physical welfare, matriculation of unqualified students, demoralization of the athletes by the coach, alumni and townspeople, and the most flagrant abuse of the athletic scholarship." He further observed that "in view of his conduct Rupp's sanctimonious attitude before me becomes ludicrous and comic," and recommended both de-emphasis of the Kentucky basketball program and strong sanctions against the coach.

The University administration responded that "our policies will not be dictated by Judge Streit." And Rupp added, "I'm in favor of de-emphasizing de-emphasis."

After sitting out a year, Rupp's Wildcats came back with an undefeated season in 1953–54. Although they were the top-ranked team in the country they didn't get to play in the NCAAs because of a rule that made the team's stars (who were in their fifth year at UK) ineligible for post-season play. The rule against fifth-year seniors was subsequently changed, but at the time it deprived Rupp of his chance to win another national championship.

Whether or not you were a fan of the Baron, it was hard to argue with Rupp's record. During his time, he was probably the game's greatest teacher of fundamentals. He always got the best out of his players. But he demanded even more—he wanted absolute perfection. Once the Fabulous Five ran up a 38-4 halftime lead, but Rupp was furious—a single player had scored all the opponent's points, and the Baron wanted him stopped. "Somebody guard that man," Rupp bellowed. "Why, he's running wild!"

Rupp's particular genius was his ability to mold teams out of groups of individuals. Decade after decade, he taught his players to put team goals first. They learned how to run the fast break, how to play a man-to-man defense, how to execute a game plan better than anyone. And because of their superior execution, they won. As North Carolina coach Frank McGuire put it, "Kentucky has found the secret of basketball, that it's five guys playing together."

During the Rupp era, Kentucky won 27 S.E.C. championships and four national championships. Rupp won the NCAA title with the 1948 Fabulous Five, and again in 1949. He coached a new core of players to the 1951 championship, and yet another group—the "Fiddlin' Five"—won in 1958. His 1954 team was unbeaten and top-ranked, and his 1966 "Rupp's Runts" made it to the title game before being defeated. In the history of college basketball, only John Wooden had a better championship record.

Rupp felt that winning was its own reward, and that his players should accept any degree of sacrifice to ensure victory. Most of them did. And many of them played better than anyone could have expected: Rupp once wrote that the players on his 1958 squad were considered average in ability. "However," he said, "you cannot measure the desire in a boy, you cannot measure the heart in a boy. I told them that if we would all work together as a unit, we could win. I told them, 'Boys, it is just this simple; individually, we will not go anywhere, as a unit, we can.' " His boys did what the Baron asked. And by executing his strategic game plans perfectly, they were able to defeat physically superior teams and go on to take the national championship.

Some people grow more rigid and irascible as they grow older; in many ways Rupp seemed to do the opposite. In his thirty-ninth season as the Wildcat coach he finally broke down and taught a zone defense (although in his inimitable style he refused to admit it, instead referring to it as "a stratified, transitional, hyperbolic paraboloid").

He also became more understanding and sympathetic to his players. Whereas Alex Groza of the "Fabulous Five" remarked, "With us there was no joking, no laughing, no whistling, no singing, no nothing—just basketball," Pat Riley, one of the stars of "Rupp's Runts" of 1966, said, "I really want to win this thing for him. We all do. We're very close. It seems like we've all grown this year, and he's just grown into us."

Of course, the Baron didn't give up his ornery streak altogether. In 1967, with UK playing poorly, Rupp began to ride a player named Bob Tallent, calling him "no-talent Tallent," Finally, in a game against Tennessee, Tallent, who had been playing with an injured ankle for a month, made a pass to Louie Dampier that went out-of-bounds and was immediately yanked by Rupp. "Oh, hell," muttered Tallent as he left the floor. Rupp challenged him, "What did you say?" Tallent repeated it, and after being lambasted by the Baron, replied, "I'm tired of being a puppet." The next day he came to practice to find his locker cleared out; he was off the squad. Rupp also threatened to take away his scholarship (he was a B student in engineering), but the Baron finally relented when Tallent apologized, and he allowed the player to retain his grant.

Circumstances also forced Rupp to change his long-standing racial policy. After his all-white squad lost in the 1966 NCAA finals to Texas Western (whose seven top players were all black), it began to become clear—even to Rupp—that a championship caliber program could no longer be built with a whites-only recruiting policy. The following year, when UK was only the third best team in Kentucky (the top two, Louisville and Western Kentucky, were both built around black stars), it became even more evident that something would have to change. But because of all the years of benign neglect, Rupp had little to offer black players. Eventually, though, Kentucky integrated in 1970.

In the end, Adolph Rupp went out a winner. Even as he reached the mandatory retirement age of seventy, he brought another Southeastern Conference championship to Lexington and led his team into one more NCAA tournament. And although a petition campaign to keep Coach Rupp spread across the state, the state law was not amended and he was finally forced to step down.

Once, upon hearing Grantland Rice's famous words, "When the Great Scorer comes to mark against your name, He writes not that you won or lost, but how you played the game," the Baron of Bluegrass remarked, "Well now, I just don't know about that. If winning isn't so important, why do they keep score?"

John Wooden

UCLA

Coaching Record:	W	L	Pct.
At Indiana State	47	14	.770
At UCLA	620	147	.808
Totals	667	161	.805

NCAA Tournament Record: (At UCLA) Sixteen appearances (1950, 1952, 1956, 1962, 1963, 1964, 1965, 1967, 1968, 1969, 1970, 1971, 1972, 1973, 1974, 1975).
Won-Lost Record: 47-10.
National Fourth Place: 1962. National Third Place: 1974. National Championship: 1964, 1965, 1967, 1968, 1969, 1970, 1971, 1972, 1973, 1975.

John Wooden's life would be an improbable American fable if it weren't true.

Basketball's greatest coach grew up on a farm in Indiana and became the star athlete of his four-room small-town grade school. One time the school's basketball coach and principal made him sit on the bench for an entire losing game to teach him a lesson about behaving. Afterward, Wooden remembered, "he put an arm on my shoulder and said, 'Johnny, we could have won with you in there, but winning just isn't that important.'"

In 1924, Wooden's family lost their farm and moved to Martinsville (pop. 5,200), where the town gym held 5,520. He soon became the best player on the Martinsville High School state championship basketball team.

Wooden then went to Purdue, where he became a three-time All-American and, as a senior, the College Player of the Year. With his brilliant ball handling and slashing, wild drives, he bounced off the floor so often that he became known as the "India Rubber Man." And even though he was the basketball playing idol of every kid in Indiana, Purdue didn't give him a free ride; it was the depths of the Great Depression and he had to work hard to pay his way through school.

After graduation Wooden played semipro and pro ball and saved, as he later recalled, $909 and a nickel. Two days before he was to marry his high school sweetheart, the bank he had deposited his money in failed—and all his money was gone.

The Woodens managed, with John getting a job as a high school coach in Dayton, Kentucky (his first year there would turn out to be the only losing season of his career). He also worked part-time as a barnstorming professional basketball player and was once credited with making 138 consecutive free throws.

He left Dayton for South Bend Central High School, where he coached basketball, baseball, and tennis, taught English, and was the school athletic director and controller. After 11 years at South Bend Central, his overall coaching record was an extraordinary 218-42.

During World War II, Wooden was a navy lieutenant and an instructor at a pre-flight training school for combat pilots. After the war he returned to South Bend only to find that because he had not kept up with his mortgage payments he had lost his house. And although the school wanted him back in his old job(s), many of his fellow faculty members from before the war had been unceremoniously replaced.

Under the circumstances, he was ready to leave South Bend. And when Indiana State Teachers College in Terre Haute asked him to become their team's basketball coach, he took the job. Since it was right after the war, many of Wooden's former players at South Bend Central were also just getting out of the service. These men—14 freshmen and a sophomore—formed the core of Wooden's first Indiana State team, and went 18-7. The next year Wooden's team's record improved to 29-7. But when the National Association of Intercollegiate Athletics wouldn't let

him bring a black player to its championship tournament in Kansas City, Wooden refused to play.

The young coach's accomplishments did not escape the attention of major college athletic directors. In fact, after his second successful season at Indiana State, both UCLA and Minnesota tried to lure him away. Minnesota made a better offer, and Wooden preferred to stay in the Midwest. But a detail of the contract remained unresolved. On the day he said he would make his final decision, the Minnesota athletic department promised to telephone him at a specified hour to work out the last remaining detail of their offer. But as fate would have it, an unexpected snowstorm knocked down phone lines and delayed the call. A disappointed Wooden accepted the UCLA job.

When he arrived in California in 1948 he told a UCLA banquet, "The fast break is my system and we'll win 50 percent of our games by outrunning the other team in the last five minutes." His prediction turned out to be true. In his first season at UCLA, his fast-breaking, superbly conditioned team, which had been expected to finish last in the Coast Conference, went 22-7.

At the age of 39, when Wooden was in his second season at UCLA, he was offered a chance to come home as the head coach of Purdue. He was still a small-town Hoosier at heart, not terribly comfortable with the fast pace and big-city atmosphere of L.A., and besides Purdue was offering him more money and better benefits than UCLA. But he'd signed a three-year contract. UCLA officials agreed to release him from his agreement, but they also reminded him that it was he who insisted on the three-year term. "I decided if I'm going to be honest with my own beliefs," Wooden said, "I'll stay."

For the next 15 years Wooden had excellent, competitive teams, but it wasn't until the early sixties, when the quicksilver guards Walt Hazzard and Gail Goodrich arrived in Westwood, that Wooden's future, the fortunes of UCLA, and the entire course of college basketball changed forever. During the 1963–64 season, Wooden, making maximum use of his small but speedy personnel, introduced the full-court zone press, known as the "Glue Factory." It was his greatest strategic innovation, and it lifted the Bruins, who had no player over 6-5, to an undefeated season.

For the next dozen years, from 1964 to 1975, John Wooden and UCLA were virtually unbeatable. The Bruins were so successful that Wooden became known as "the Wizard of Westwood" and the NCAA tournament became "the UCLA Invitational."

His first champs, in 1964, were the quickest, the most adept at the full-court press. The 1965 team, with Goodrich taking over Hazzard's starring role, continued to win with speed and conditioning against bigger, stronger teams.

During the Alcindor era—1967–69—Wooden took advantage of his first great big man's dominating presence by introducing a strong set offense to go with his traditional fast-breaking attack. And he turned the press loose to gamble more on steals, because the brilliant shot-blocker parked in the lane was always there to cover mistakes and discourage penetration.

After Lew Alcindor (Kareem Abdul-Jabbar) and his classmates graduated, a new crew took over and UCLA continued to win. The 1970 and 1971 squads, led by forwards Sidney Wicks and Curtis Rowe, were less physically dominating, but they still had the mental toughness to come back from deficits time and again to invariably win the close ones.

Next came the Walton gang, which won the 1972 and 1973 championships and didn't lose a game for two and a half years. This Bruin squad, keyed by Bill Walton's rebounding and outlet passes and Jamaal Wilkes' smooth-as-silk floor play, was UCLA's greatest fast-breaking team.

Wooden's last team, the 1975 national champions, entered the season minus four graduated starters (including Walton and Jamaal Wilkes). But with Dave Meyers and Marques Johnson leading the way they eventually became the perfect Wooden team, playing better than anyone expected them to because they played so well *together*.

During UCLA's ten title seasons only one thing remained constant—the coach, John Wooden. Throughout one of the most troubled, divided times in American history, this small-town Hoosier, a deacon of his church, almost stereotypically old-fashioned and unhip in style and in temperament, molded disparate groups of black nationalists, hippies, antiwar activists, fraternity men, surfers, and ROTC officers into winning teams. And in the end, the vast majority of his players—stars and scrubs alike—left UCLA with feelings of respect, admiration, and even love for their coach.

"What we do is simple," he told *Sports Illustrated* in 1972 when he was honored as the magazine's Sportsman of the Year, "[we] get in condition, learn fundamentals and play together."

He was a teacher who preferred practices to games. He spent hours planning each day's practice, breaking down each session into ten or twelve brief drills of five to fifteen minutes each (thus avoiding monotony). For two hours every afternoon he stressed movement, physical conditioning, and fundamental skills. And every day he finished up with an intrasquad scrimmage.

He believed, as his college coach "Piggy" Lambert taught him, that the team making the most mistakes would win, because that was inevitably the team that took the initiative and forced the action. He said he used the press, not to steal the ball, but to "get to the emotions of the other team." As for his own squad, he taught balance—

never getting too high or too low—as a principle of basketball and of life. "Just remember," he told his players after winning his second title, "when you win, it's a temporary thing. It's not going to affect anything in the future. Don't let it go to your head."

Wooden believed in preparing his teams to play their own game to perfection. And although he rarely scouted the opposition, when he did adjust his game plan in response to another team the results could be devastating. Wooden's strategic preparation to combat Houston and their star Elvin Hayes in the 1968 semifinals paved the way to what is widely regarded as a UCLA team's greatest performance. He devised a new diamond-and-one defense—with Alcindor in the lane and Lynn Shackelford on Hayes—against the previously undefeated Cougars. The defense stopped Hayes cold, and UCLA ran away with a 32-point victory.

Wooden never let his remarkable record go to his head. Homespun homilies, like "failure to prepare is preparing to fail," and "the journey is better than the end," remained part of his speech throughout his career. And his "Pyramid of Success," a combination self-improvement formula and code of conduct he first developed in 1939 while he was an Indiana high school coach, was sent to players before every season.

Also, despite his record, Wooden was not perfect and not everyone loved him. Opposing coaches frequently found his needling of officials to be so effective that it gave him an unfair advantage. And some players rebelled at being put into the Wooden "machine," where each lost his individuality in the interest of the team.

In a 1973 interview in *The Cleveland Plain Dealer,* Steve Patterson, the starting center for the 1971 and 1972 champs, said that Wooden's conservatism often conflicted with the players' attitudes, and that his grandfatherly approach was at times resented. He also said the team "had quite a bit of internal dissension. There were team meetings. But we had so much respect for him [Wooden] that we never let it get out to the press." During the Walton years a player joked that "We have this great UCLA image, and nobody suspects we are a bunch of wonderful law-breaking degenerates." Walton himself once requested Wooden's permission to smoke marijuana (because of his bad knees); the coach reminded his star center it was against the law. And when Patterson and Sidney Wicks asked to be excused from practice to join an antiwar protest, Patterson said "He asked us if this reflected our convictions, and we told him it did. He told us he had his convictions, too, and if we missed practice it would be the end of our careers at UCLA." Yet despite their off-the-court attitudes and behavior, the UCLA players invariably maintained discipline when it involved the team.

At times players like Abdul-Jabbar and Mike Warren had differences with Wooden about racial issues, but years after his UCLA career ended Kareem remained friends with his coach, referring to Wooden in his two autobiographies in respectful, almost reverential tones. And Curtis Rowe, another of UCLA's great black stars, said "Coach Wooden doesn't see color. He sees players."

At times Wooden simply chose not to look at things that were against his principles. He often expressed his distaste for high-pressured recruiting, and was fundamentally opposed to red-shirting and freshman-eligibility. He spoke of abolishing recruiting altogether, ignoring the fact that his team's success and his own larger-than-life reputation made his job as a recruiter infinitely easier than the opposition's.

Wooden's recruiting was also made easier by the largesse of UCLA's powerful alumni boosters, particularly the wealthy Los Angeles contractor Sam Gilbert. Wooden avoided confronting the obvious questions about Gilbert's relationship with UCLA's players. The coach himself promised the players nothing, was not involved in the financial details of their scholarships, and ignored the actions of boosters.

Wooden told his players they were at UCLA for an education first, and for basketball second. He felt the university's reputation for excellence was a strong inducement to come to UCLA, and he had an old-fashioned idea of education that went beyond getting a degree and making a living. "Education is more than the means of acquiring possessions," he said. "It must help man live harmoniously with his fellow man."

Statistically, John Wooden's accomplishments as a coach are unparalleled. Four times his teams finished undefeated; they won 10 NCAA championships and 38 straight tournament games. The list of records goes on and on.

But John Wooden would not want to be remembered just for his victories. More important is how he won them: with hard work and old-fashioned values. Despite being the biggest winner in the history of American sport, winning was just not that important to him. His priorities have never varied: "Family, Lord, profession. And that's not the order it should be," he said, "but I think No. 2 understands."

Al McGuire

Marquette University

Coaching Record:	W	L	Pct.
At Belmont Abbey	109	64	.630
At Marquette	295	80	.787
Totals	404	144	.737

NCAA Tournament Record: Nine appearances (1968, 1969, 1971, 1972, 1973, 1974, 1975, 1976, 1977).
Won-Lost Record: 20-9.
National Second Place: 1974. National Championship: 1977.

Al McGuire was always the tough guy, the fiery Irishman with the quick quip, but as the clock ticked off the final seconds and his Marquette team held on to beat North Carolina for the 1977 national championship, he broke down and cried. "After all the wet jocks and socks," he said, "driving the car at Belmont Abbey, freshman coach at Dartmouth, all the PALs and CYOs, all the odors in the locker room. All the fights in the gyms. Just the wildness of it all. And now to have it end like this . . ."

The Al McGuire story began on the streets of New York. He was born in The Bronx and grew up in the Rockaway Beach section of Queens, where his family owned a bar. Alongside his brother Dick, he learned to play an in-your-face style of city basketball. And he carried his pugnaciousness from the schoolyard to college ball at St. John's and to every subsequent stage of his career.

After college he played for the New York Knicks. He called himself "the worst player ever to last three years in the big time" and claimed to be personally responsible for the first sellout crowd in Boston Garden history, when Celtics fans paid to see him make good on his boast that he could stop the great Bob Cousy. In fact, McGuire claims, Cousy didn't score a point against him, but only because every time Bob got the ball, Al was whistled for a foul—away from the ball—on the guy who set the picks. McGuire fouled out in the first quarter, but while he was in the game, Cousy never got off a shot.

McGuire averaged 3.9 points per game in his 190-game pro career. "Every coach coaches the way he played," he said. "I couldn't shoot when I played, so I teach defense."

And all of McGuire's teams were known for playing *great* defense. They slowed the game down, got back quickly, forced turnovers by attacking the offense, and took away the fast break. Offensively, he played a deliberate, set-up game, and his teams only used the fast break when it was there for the taking. McGuire wasn't much for *x*'s and *o*'s. "I've never blown a whistle, looked at a film, worked at a blackboard, or organized a practice in my life," he said. His style drove his more scientific colleagues crazy. But what made them even crazier was that he could be both so unorthodox and so successful.

His coaching career started at Dartmouth in 1954, as an assistant to Alvin "Doggie" Julian. In 1956, he became head coach of tiny Belmont Abbey (a 500-student Catholic institution in rural North Carolina). Almost overnight, he turned this unlikely school into a small-college powerhouse by recruiting New York kids. Without a decent gym of their own, they had to play most of their games on the road, and it was hard to find competition—no major college wanted to take a chance on being embarrassed by the likes of Belmont Abbey!

Eventually the limitations of his program caused it to disintegrate. His teams went 6-19 and 6-18 in his last two years, and he was ready to leave coaching altogether. But then, almost on a whim, he interviewed for the vacant job at Marquette . . .

Needless to say, he got it.

When McGuire arrived in Milwaukee in the fall of 1964 he took over a floundering program in desperate need of a turnaround. He was no miracle worker; his first team won only eight games. But his ability to communicate with inner-city kids soon began to pay off. "I can't recruit a kid who has a front lawn," he said. "Give me a tenement and a sidewalk."

McGuire had a unique way of communicating with his players. He allowed them to air their differences—they fought with each other and yelled at their coach. They were involved, aggressive, even angry—an extension of McGuire's own personality. "My teams are arrogant and obnoxious," he once declared.

He also never sidestepped the issue of race. Point guard Lloyd Walton, who often shouted at McGuire to sit down during games, said, "He figures your problems are his problems. Hey, I've had a black coach in summer ball, but I never had the rapport with him I had with Al."

He cared about the kids who played for him, and in return they cared about him. Believing that "sports is a coffee break," he wanted his players to get their degrees, even if it took longer than the four years they were eligible to play basketball. "I'd hate to have it ever said that I was running a plantation here," he said, "taking athletes and using them and never giving anything back."

McGuire's Marquette teams qualified for postseason play every year from 1967 until his retirement in 1977 (in 1970 he rejected an NCAA bid in favor of the NIT because he was offended by his squad's placement outside the Mideast region). He was voted Coach of the Year in both 1971 and 1973, and in the last ten years of his career his Warriors went 252-41.

In December of 1976 he announced he would retire at the end of the season: "I'm not doing the job anymore," he said. He believed that young players need young coaches, and that at the age of 48, his time was past.

On February 20, 1977, in Marquette's last home game with Al McGuire as coach, the Warriors were overpowered by Wichita State. It was their third straight loss and their seventh in 23 games, and it appeared to cost them a bid to the NCAAs. McGuire blamed himself for having lost his composure (he was hit with two technicals when Jim Boylan was called for a foul in the middle of a Marquette comeback). It wasn't the first time his fights with officials had hurt his team, either. He had two crucial technicals called on him in both the 1974 title game and in the 1976 Mideast regionals, and believed that both times his temper cost Marquette a victory.

After the game against Wichita State, though, McGuire never lost another game as a coach.

In the 1977 tournament, Marquette squeaked by Kansas State despite another costly McGuire technical. They barely survived in the semis against North Carolina–Charlotte. Then they played Dean Smith and North Carolina for the championship.

McGuire was McGuire. Early in the game he kicked the scorer's table in frustration and limped the rest of the night. When North Carolina made a run on Marquette in the second half, he started ranting on the sidelines. His wife, Pat, stood in the stands, begging him to sit down. This time he did, and he didn't blow it.

Al McGuire finally won the big one. His team didn't have the greatest natural talent, but no one could ever accuse them of being short on heart. And when they won the game—a game they weren't supposed to win—McGuire showed the world how much it meant to him.

Butch Lee, the Most Outstanding Player on Marquette's championship team, described what it was like to play for Al McGuire: "You needed good earplugs. There was a lot of hollering. We love him, I think."

Since his retirement, Al McGuire has been a business executive and one of the most successful and colorful announcers in network sports history. The gift of blarney remains.

Dean Smith

University of North Carolina

Coaching Record (through 1990):	W	L	Pct.
At North Carolina	688	203	.771

NCAA Tournament Record: 20 appearances (1967, 1968, 1969, 1972, 1975, 1976, 1977, 1978, 1979, 1980, 1981, 1982, 1983, 1984, 1985, 1986, 1987, 1988, 1989, 1990).
Won-Lost Record: 43-21.
National 4th Place: 1967, 1969.
National 3rd Place: 1972.
National 2nd Place: 1968, 1977, 1981.
National Championship: 1982.

Before 1982, Dean Smith was always the bridesmaid, never the bride. Six times he went to the Final Four, six times he came away without the title.

The rap against Smith, that he couldn't win the big one, was finally laid to rest in 1982's epic final between North Carolina and Georgetown. Never mind that Smith had coached the Olympic squad that regained the gold medal for the United States in 1976. Forget his 1971 NIT championship, all his ACC titles, and the six times he brought North Carolina to the NCAA Final Four. None of that mattered until the Tar Heels beat Georgetown in New Orleans on March 29, 1982. That was the date Dean Smith became, finally, unquestionably, the Dean of College Basketball.

His first years at Chapel Hill were not so auspicious. The story is told that when Tar Heel coach Frank McGuire was looking for an assistant, his predecessor, Ben Carnevale, recommended a young Air Force assistant who had played for Phog Allen's NCAA champion Kansas Jayhawks a few years earlier. "I come from New York where there a lot of Smiths," said McGuire. "But they're Bill Smith, Sam Smith, Frank Smith. What is this name—Dean? Can't we change it?" McGuire hired him anyway.

As a basketball man, the new Tar Heel assistant was always thinking. He was also serious, plain spoken, and religious. And he was guided by a strong, almost absolute, sense of right and wrong.

One of Smith's most important contributions in his first years at North Carolina had nothing to do with basketball, but it had a lot to do with Dean Smith the man. In the summer of 1959 Reverend Robert Seymour, the pastor of the Baptist church Smith attended, asked the 28-year-old assistant coach to join him and a visiting black theology student in an attempt to desegregate a restaurant in Chapel Hill where Carolina teams ate many of their training meals. Smith went, and the restaurant manager—knowing his livelihood depended on the continuing patronage of Tar Heel teams—consented to serve the three men.

When Frank McGuire decided to leave Chapel Hill in 1961, he recommended that Dean Smith take his place. Not everybody was happy about the choice. "The successor to Frank McGuire, one of the most dynamic men in sports," noted one local paper, "is not overpowering in personality." And it was true: where the New Yorker always had a colorful anecdote to relate, the Kansan was serious, almost solemn in demeanor; and where McGuire was a master of psychology, the new coach was far more comfortable diagraming x's and o's.

When Dean Smith took over the reins, North Carolina basketball was under NCAA probation and its program was severely restricted, both in recruiting and in its ability to schedule opponents. Along with the probation, however, McGuire had bequeathed Smith one last recruit of his famed New York to Chapel Hill underground railroad—Billy Cunningham. But Cunningham was a freshman, ineligible to play on the varsity. And without him, Smith's first roster had so little basketball talent that it eventually produced more lawyers (9) than wins (8).

The next year, Cunningham, at 6-4, moved up to the varsity. But the team was still sorely lacking in both talent and size, and Smith had no choice but to use his star sophomore at center. Early in the season the Tar Heels were blown out by Indiana. The next game was in Lexington, against Adolph Rupp's powerful Kentucky Wildcats and their All-American Cotton Nash. Before the game, Carolina guard Larry Brown (who would later become a coach of some note himself) broke out in hives just at the thought of what was going to happen once the game began. Coach Smith was not ready to concede, however. In a pregame meeting he told his team to use a box and one defense, with one man hounding Nash while the other four played a zone. On offense, he said he wanted to try a special formation the squad had been working on in practice, with Brown dribbling into the middle while his teammates spread out in four corners. The first time Smith signaled the spread offense, Brown beat his man for a layup. The second time, when one of the Kentucky players came over to help out, Brown fed a teammate for another lay-up. Meanwhile, Nash was being taken so far out of Kentucky's offensive flow that by the end of the game he was reduced to standing by and watching the action. Carolina beat Kentucky, 68-66. And Dean Smith's players knew they had a coach.

Not everyone else was convinced, however. During a four game losing streak in the 1964–65 season, the team arrived back in Chapel Hill after a bad loss to Wake Forest and saw an effigy of Smith hanging on campus. Cunningham ran off the team bus in a rage, tore it down, and kicked it aside. But even with the support of his star player, it seemed only a matter of time before Smith would be forced to leave.

Despite the success of his strategic ideas, many of his

of, but getting outhustled is," started using a full-court zone press, as much for the sake of morale as for its more tangible benefits. He recalled Wooden saying "the by-products of the press were more important than the press itself. Things like hustle, enthusiasm, and intimidation."

The following year Crum's Cardinals won their first title, beating UCLA for the championship. It was the beginning of a seven-year run in which Louisville reached the national semifinals four times. It was also the last time UCLA reached the Final Four.

Ever since he scouted the likes of Lew Alcindor and Bill Walton for John Wooden, Crum has been a great recruiter. At Louisville he looks for athletes more than players—runners, leapers, tall, strong guards and quick, ball-handling forwards. ("That's why a lot of our forwards have been able to play guard in the NBA," he said. "They have a lot of versatility.") Like Wooden, he puts together teams that excel at a running game. But unlike Wooden, in his nineteen years at Louisville he's only had one bona-fide star at center, 6-9 Pervis Ellison, MVP of the 1986 national championships.

Crum goes after players who can take care of themselves, who are responsible and dedicated, and who can learn. He is an exceptional teacher, in the Wooden mold. As Al McGuire told the *Sporting News,* "his players improve, month-wise and year-wise. A lot of players improve, but not like Denny's do."

Crum enforces few rules, insisting only that his players attend class and get to practice on time. (When the 1989–90 Cardinals' second-leading scorer, Jerome Harmon, cut classes, he was suspended from the team.)

The Louisville coach prides himself on running a clean program. In 1990, however, he was accused for the first time of a recruiting violation when Dwayne Morton, a 6-7 forward from Louisville Central High, was barred from attending his hometown college. An NCAA rule prohibits meetings between coaches and families of recruits at certain times of year, and Morton's mother and his high school coach met with Crum on campus during one of those periods. Although Crum pleaded that he didn't know about the rule and reported the violation as soon as he was aware of it, the NCAA decided against Louisville.

Crum has a reputation for keeping cool under pressure. "I don't worry about things I can't control," he said. According to former Louisville coach John Dromo, "Denny always plays the percentages, never loses control of a game, never pushes the panic button. He's the best in the country at conversing during time-outs. He might get beat, but he never beats himself."

In the 1986 final, his team was losing to Duke in the second half and guard Milt Wagner was in the middle of a horrendous game. "He just took me aside and told me that I was a senior leader and I was playing like a freshman," said Wagner. "He doesn't throw chairs or anything like that—he's Cool Hand Luke—but he knows how to get his message across." As Louisville players usually do, Wagner heard the quiet man's message loud and clear. He stepped up his game a notch and came through in crunch time.

Denny Crum is the perfect college basketball coach. He's a great judge of talent and a great teacher, a man who motivates without fear and without inducements that would compromise the integrity of his players or his program. He's everything a disciple of John Wooden might hope to be. Everything UCLA could want in a coach. And nearly two decades after he left sunny southern California, he's still carrying on the John Wooden tradition. He's winning—in Louisville.

Bob Knight

Indiana University

Coaching Record:	W	L	Pct.
At Army	102	50	.671
At Indiana	430	148	.744
Totals	532	198	.729

NCAA Tournament Record: (At Indiana) Fourteen appearances (1973, 1975, 1976, 1978, 1980, 1981, 1982, 1983, 1984, 1986, 1987, 1988, 1989, 1990).
Won-Lost Record: 29-11.
National Third Place: 1973.
National Championship: 1976, 1981, 1987.

Bob Knight is an enigma. He's the only active coach to win as many as three NCAA titles, yet he is perpetually dissatisfied and rarely able to savor his triumphs. He demands total discipline on the part of his players, yet he is himself prone to outbursts and indiscretions that tarnish his successes and keep him in constant trouble.

He's a tough guy who cries.

A man with an obsession for winning who points to his players' graduation rate as one of his proudest achievements.

A father figure who abuses and humiliates the young men he most loves.

A person who never forgives a slight and never forgets a friend.

He's one of the most written about, talked about, analyzed, and misunderstood men in American sports.

Knight's players talk about their college experience almost as if it was combat. Steve Alford, one of Knight's favorite players, was asked before the 1987 NCAA championship game what misconceptions the public might have about his coach. The quiet, devout Alford, who was selected by Knight for the 1984 U.S. Olympic Team while still a freshman, but who was also repeatedly thrown out of practice, demoted to the second unit, and publicly berated by his coach during his time at Indiana, replied, "I've survived for four years, and I've only got one more game left." A fellow Olympian, Jeff Turner, when asked whether he could live with four years of Bob Knight, tactfully responded, "I have a lot of respect for Steve Alford."

Knight has always taught his teams to play not just against their opponents, but against themselves, as he pushes them to reach the limit of their potential. "He wants to play that perfect basketball game," said Alford. "He would love to win 100 to nothing." Hard work, dedication, and the sacrifice of individual goals for the team are all part of Knight's prescription for perfection. He also insists on his own absolute control—both mental and physical—of his teams and players. And he is willing to go to extraordinary lengths to maintain that control.

When Knight was coaching Army during the 1969 NIT against South Carolina, he told his point guard Mike Krzyzewski, "If you shoot, it'll be the last thing you do on this earth." Krzyzewski remembers that he found himself all alone with the ball, went up for the shot, hung there for a minute . . . and passed off. (Knight and Krzyzewski, now the successful Duke coach, are still friends.)

In 1976, Knight benched Quinn Buckner, one of his most hard-nosed, disciplined, and dedicated players ever, to get a point across. After an Indiana loss in 1984, he ordered his players out of the locker room and back onto the court for practice. He once sat down an entire starting five—on national TV—because they weren't disciplined enough. And he kicked his best freshman off the team in 1990, and then refused to let him transfer to the school of his choice.

He has never accepted any deviation from his instructions. Even when he coached one of the greatest collections of players in basketball history—the 1984 Olympic team—he made it clear it was his ball. Patrick Ewing sat for long stretches and when he played he was under strict orders to stay with his man rather than float underneath to block shots. Chris Mullin and Alvin Robertson didn't get enough playing time to allow them to unleash their particular offensive and defensive talents. Even Michael Jordan was kept largely under wraps, averaging just 17 points per game.

Even more than the 1984 Olympic team, the 1976 Indiana Hoosiers were Bob Knight's perfect team. Not just because of their record (they were the last major college team to finish undefeated), but because of their collective personality as well. Individually, they were excellent players (every member of the starting five went on to play in the NBA), but none of them had the ability to dominate a game by himself. Instead they dominated as a team. They were a group of supremely disciplined role players who knew their jobs and did them with single-mindedness and dedication. They did exactly what the coach ordered them to do.

In some ways, Knight is even harder on himself than he is on his players. He's so driven that he couldn't even take the time to enjoy the 1976 championship. Immediately after winning the tournament, he told the press, "I'm not paid to relax. I'll be on the train tomorrow morning. Recruiting."

Despite his perfectionism, Knight does not always hold himself to the same high standards that he demands from team members. While he insists on total discipline from his players, he himself is known almost as much for his erratic behavior as for his victories. His temper, his indiscretion, and his lack of judgment are all as much a part of the public's perception of him as are his strategic brilliance and talent for getting the most out of his players.

Time and again his obscene language and violent temper have gotten him into trouble. He's been known to use physical force on team members, including one documented instance of throwing a ball in a player's face in practice and another of grabbing a player off the floor during a game and yanking him into his seat.

He was arrested for assaulting an officer while serving as the U.S. Pan American Games coach in 1979 in Puerto Rico; witnesses said the incident was the policeman's fault, but Knight aggravated it by insulting local fans.

In 1980 he pointed a gun and fired a blank at a reporter. In 1981 he shoved an LSU fan into a trash can after a contentious tournament game. The following season he cursed Big Ten commissioner Wayne Duke at midcourt while complaining about the officiating at conference games. In 1985, he threw a chair across the court during a game against Purdue in Bloomington. In 1987, he smashed a telephone on the scorer's table during a tournament game.

Sometimes there's even an element of self-parody in Knight's outbursts: once during an Indiana exhibition against a Soviet team he objected to a call by taking off his shoe and banging it on a table (a la the former Coach Nikita K. of the U of SSR). But in a much more serious incident, he pulled his team off the court in the middle of a game against the Soviets when he didn't like the officials' calls.

It's a shame that Knight draws so much negative attention to himself, because in so many ways his accomplishments are truly remarkable. The Orrville, Ohio, native, a substitute guard on Ohio State's 1960 NCAA champions, became the Army coach in 1965 at the age of 24. In six years at West Point, the Cadets made four NIT appearances while leading the nation in scoring defense three times. In 1971, he moved to Bloomington to become coach of Indiana.

At Indiana, he immediately implemented his coaching

philosophy, scrapping the run-and-gun style that was prevalent in the Big Ten at the time and replacing it with an aggressive pressing defense that contested every shot, every pass, and nearly every move by the opposition, along with a precision motion offense that relied on picks, passing, and moving without the ball. In 1975, at the age of 34, he won his first national Coach of the Year award after leading the Hoosiers to a 31-1 record. The following year his undefeated team won the national championship. He has since won two more NCAA titles, in 1981 and 1987.

In 1984 Knight became the youngest coach in history to post 400 major college victories, and in 1989, at the age of 48, he became the second youngest ever to win 500 games. He has the best winning percentage and the most Big Ten conference wins of any coach ever. He's coached NIT, Pan American Games, and Olympic champions, and has produced six Olympians in his own programs, including Olympic captains Mike Silliman of Army in 1968 and Quinn Buckner of Indiana in 1976.

At the age of 40, however, after winning his second NCAA title, Knight almost called it quits. There were no more hurdles to overcome, no more challenges to face. And CBS, which had just acquired the rights to televise the NCAA tournament, was offering him major money to handle the tournament coverage. But when Landon Turner, one of the stars of his 1981 championship team, was paralyzed in a car crash, he threw himself heart and soul into setting up a fund to care for Turner and help provide him with the necessities of his new life. Knight realized that it wasn't just the money, and it wasn't just the winning that made him a coach—he turned down the CBS job.

He stands by his friends—his teachers as well as his students. After the U.S. Olympic victory in 1984, when team members tried to lift him onto their shoulders and celebrate, he waved them off and ordered them to first pick up an old man sitting courtside. The old man, Henry Iba, had been the coach of several winning U.S. Olympic teams, but his last experience in the international arena had been a bitter one. After Iba's 1972 team lost a disputed championship game to the Soviets, he was widely castigated for his archaic ideas, both in the press and among his coaching peers. Knight felt the victory was stolen from him, that the criticism was unwarranted, and that Iba deserved better. So he ordered his players to make Iba's last Olympic experience a memorable one. The old man was lifted onto their shoulders in celebration.

Knight is a brilliant strategist and is unsurpassed in his attention to detail. Give him time to prepare and his strategic adjustments will generally take his opponents out of their game. He's also a teacher in the best sense of the word: a man who's able to impart his fundamental knowledge of the game to others. Numerous current head coaches started out as his assistants, including Mike Krzyzewski of Duke, Don DeVoe of Florida, Tom Miller of Colorado, Jim Crews of Evansville, and Dave Bliss of New Mexico—no other coach in modern times even comes close to Knight as a teacher of basketball.

In recent years, Knight has shown himself to be capable of adjusting his basic strategies as the game changes and rules and recruiting practices evolve. The rule changes—particularly the institution of the 45-second clock and the 3-point shot—have made Knight's mainstay set-up offense less effective than it was in the past; he's responded by pushing the ball downcourt and taking advantage of fast-break opportunities and quick 3-pointers and by utilizing a three-guard offense to create matchup problems for the opposition. He's also made his defenses harder to read, as he now mixes up his man-to-man with a zone.

Knight's also changed his recruiting practices to maintain his competitive edge. The top schoolboys in Indiana no longer become automatic Hoosiers, and even if they did it might not be enough to ensure victory in today's game. As a result he's now making personnel moves he once rejected as unnecessary, even unethical. He's begun to follow his friend Jerry Tarkanian's example and use junior college transfers. (Two of his first jucos, Keith Smart and Bill Garrett, were instrumental in bringing the NCAA championship back to Bloomington in 1987.) In addition, he's started to red-shirt players. (Red-shirting is a practice whereby a player sits out a year and gains an extra year of eligibility as a fifth-year senior. Coaches often red-shirt a player to bolster a future team when a current team is stocked with talented upperclassmen.)

Despite his adjustments, though, there are some things that don't change. He still won't let his teams quit—the 1987 champions came back from sizable deficits four times in the tournament. And he still insists on maintaining academic standards—when the other three Final Four teams were in New Orleans preparing for the championship rounds, Knight's players were in Bloomington attending class.

As Bob Knight approaches the age of 50, he is no longer the enfant terrible of the coaching profession. But he's still a tough guy, hard to understand at times and even harder to take at others. His temper still gets him in trouble. His inflexibility is still at times astonishing. But he's also the knight errant of the coaching profession, a Don Quixote tilting at windmills.

In the end, he'll probably be remembered as he'd like to be, as "a guy who got the most out of what he had to work with." "The greatest compliment to a coach," Knight says, "is that he is worth a few points sitting on the bench." He proved it in '76, in '81, in '87. And he's likely to prove it again.

John Thompson

Georgetown

Coaching Record (through 1990):	W	L	Pct.
At Georgetown	423	142	.749

NCAA Tournament Record: Fourteen appearances (1975, 1976, 1979, 1980, 1981, 1982, 1983, 1984, 1985, 1986, 1987, 1988, 1989, 1990).
Won-Lost Record: 26-13.
National Second Place: 1982, 1985.
National Championship: 1984.

John Thompson is an imposing man by any standards.

He is self-defining, complex, charming, and exasperating. He's 6-feet, 10-inches tall and weighs 300 pounds, and carries every inch and every pound with the courage of his convictions. He is also one of the most successful coaches of our era, and is, as a result, a pioneer.

When Thompson first took Georgetown to the Final Four, he bristled when asked how it felt to be the first black coach to reach that pinnacle of success. "I resent the hell out of that question," he said. "The implication is that I was the first black capable of coaching a team to the Final Four. That's just stupid."

The fact is, however, that Thompson's success has enabled other black coaches, like Arkansas's Nolan Richardson, Temple's John Chaney, Minnesota's Clem Haskins, and USC's George Raveling, to get the opportunity to prove they can coach at predominantly white schools with major college basketball programs. Like Jackie Robinson, Thompson was not the first black man capable of excelling in his field. But also like Robinson, when he got the chance he made the best of it, and blazed a trail for everyone who came after.

When John Thompson was hired by Georgetown, an elite Catholic university in Washington, the school president said, "Get us to the NIT every once in a while, and I'll be happy." Instead Thompson built a program that's gone to the NCAA every year since 1979; he won the championship in 1984 and finished second—by an eyelash—twice.

Who Thompson is, and what he stands for, is inextricably tied to where he came from. His father was illiterate, and in his early years at a Washington Catholic school, Thompson also had trouble learning to read. Although he had bad eyes, some of his teachers thought he was retarded, and after fifth grade, the nuns asked his parents to take their difficult son out of school. He then went to segregated public schools, where he became both a good student and an exceptional basketball player. He returned to a Catholic high school, John Carroll, and led his team to two city championships. "It was a very positive thing," he said, "not being successful in Catholic school, going to public school, and then returning to Catholic school and being very successful. It gave me a great deal of self-confidence."

In 1960 he carried his self-confidence to Providence, where, after an exceptional season on the freshman team, he was touted as the next Bill Russell. But during his unextraordinary sophomore year, he learned by personal experience that young athletes need to be shielded from their own hype.

Eventually Thompson had a fine college career, and was drafted by the Boston Celtics. But since Bill Russell was still in his prime, he saw little playing time, and after two years he was selected by the Chicago Bulls in the expansion draft. Although he was assured he would start for the new franchise, he chose not to go and instead returned to Washington. There he studied for his master's in guidance and counseling from the University of the District of Columbia, directed the city's 4-H Club, and became the basketball coach at St. Anthony's, a small Catholic high school, which he soon transformed into a local power. Six years later he was offered the job at Georgetown.

Before accepting the offer, he turned to Dean Smith for advice. The North Carolina coach spoke with him about recruiting, about the business of college basketball, and about how coaches could either exploit their players or work to meet their academic needs. His discussions with Smith helped Thompson clarify his own thinking. He decided to take the job.

The year before Thompson arrived, Georgetown was 3-23. He knew he would have to build his program from scratch, and he committed himself to doing it without sacrificing his players' education.

He hired Mary Fenlon, a fellow teacher at St. Anthony's, as his "academic coordinator," his conscience. Her job was to ensure that players went to class, kept up with their work, and graduated. Thompson also installed a deflated basketball on his desk as a constant reminder to his players that the air can go out of a basketball career at any time.

In 1975, three years after he arrived at the university, Georgetown was still a program in transition. But that season, a banner directing a racial slur against Thompson was raised in Georgetown's gym. After the incident, his team caught fire and made the NCAA's for the first time. Georgetown has been selected for a postseason tournament every year since.

By 1980, when Georgetown played its way to the regional finals, Thompson's program had become so attractive that the nation's top recruit, Patrick Ewing, chose to become a Hoya. With Ewing as the anchor, Georgetown became even more successful—as close to a dynasty as college basketball has seen since the end of UCLA's reign in the mid-70s. During Ewing's four years they were a fiercely competitive, balanced team, known for their smothering, pressing defense and a bruising, physical style of play.

They also became known as a coach and a team with an attitude problem.

Throughout the decade of the 80s, Georgetown's physically intimidating style has been blamed for the fighting that frequently mars Hoyas' games. Some, including Pittsburgh coach Paul Evans, feel unequivocally that Georgetown crosses the line between competitive fire and uncontrolled aggression. In 1984, Dayton's Sedric Toney accused the Hoyas' freshman intimidator Michael Graham of dirty, dangerous play and said, "He's deliberately trying to hurt me." Addressing the issue of fighting in *The Washington Post,* Thomas Boswell wrote, "No coach in basketball has more virtues than Thompson. That's why it's so important for him to face his faults. Especially the temper he's never conquered."

Thompson's temper and distrust were also blamed for another controversy that surrounded Georgetown during the Ewing years. When Ewing arrived at Georgetown amid allegations that he was academically unprepared, Thompson moved to shield his teenage star from the intense scrutiny of the media—thus "Hoya Paranoia" was born. Thompson, who only months before was being hailed as "St. John," was suddenly roundly criticized for his refusal to allow the press access to his players. *Sports Illustrated*'s Curry Kirkpatrick blasted the "preposterous paramilitary atmosphere surrounding the team." But Red Auerbach, Thompson's Boston Celtic coach, put the protection of Ewing in a different light, comparing it to what John Wooden did when Lew Alcindor played at UCLA. Hoya Paranoia reached its apex in 1982, when Ewing received a death threat and Thompson billeted his team in Biloxi, Mississippi, ninety miles from the Final Four site in New Orleans.

Despite all the criticisms and the talk of Georgetown's attitude problem, Thompson was quietly teaching his players to be personally responsible for their actions, both on and off the court. He was not only protecting Ewing, he was also carving out the space he needed to teach *all* his students about basketball and life. Ed Spriggs, who was a postal worker for three years before being recruited to play at Georgetown, discussed Thompson's approach and the effect it had on him. "The team could be practicing and then he would sit us down and talk to us," Spriggs said. "You would think it would be a lecture about basketball, but then he'll start talking about current-events issues and how to deal with people in real-life situations. At the end of the lecture he would tie it all in to basketball. I learned a lot from those talks."

Even Thompson's lessons about competition went far beyond winning and losing. After Fred Brown made the pass into James Worthy's hands that gave North Carolina the 1982 championship, the coach wrapped his arms around his player and, as Carolina coach Dean Smith cut the net, whispered, "Fred, this is what it's all about." Two years later, Brown said, Thompson's advice helped him concentrate on his studies and "feel safe." It also helped him maintain the perspective he needed to play a major role in Georgetown's championship season. Brown said, "Coach Thompson teaches you how to deal with adversity. He's made me realize you can't sit and pout and worry about it. I dealt with it and went on my way."

After winning the 1984 title, the Hoyas were being hailed everywhere as one of the greatest teams ever. Thompson, however, went into the locker room and told his players to keep that moment, too, in perspective. Then, after the Hoyas' 1985 championship game loss to Villanova, he led his team in applauding the victors. "We know how to win basketball games, and how to lose them," he said with pride.

John Thompson's players know they are expected to excel on the court, but they also know their responsibilities and opportunities at Georgetown go far beyond basketball. Thompson makes it clear that, for most of them, playing basketball is a means to an end. Their athletic scholarships provide them with an opportunity to receive an education and earn a degree from a respected university. Despite Thompson's stated concern for academics and the presence of Mary Fenlon on his staff, he has been accused of recruiting players "who shouldn't have been in college" in the first place. Critics of the Georgetown program pointed to Michael Graham, a hero of the 1984 championship team, as evidence of Thompson's lack of standards.

A 1990 *Washington Post* article by Michael Wilbon tracing the subsequent achievements of the 1984 Georgetown team provides an unequivocal answer to the questions about Thompson's program: as of 1990, Ralph Dalton had earned his MBA, Fred Brown was a law student, Horace Broadnax a grad student, Michael Jackson had been a Rhodes Scholar candidate, and Patrick Ewing, Bill Martin, Gene Smith, David Wingate, and Reggie Williams all earned their degrees. The chance Thompson took on Michael Graham certainly helped Georgetown win the national championship. But so did the chance he took on Ewing and others. And when Graham didn't "develop greater responsibilities and eliminate inconsistencies in his approach to academics," as Thompson put it, he was gone.

Thompson's opposition to NCAA Proposition 42 (which bars scholarships to student athletes who do not meet certain minimum academic standards) is an extension of his own recruiting policies. When he walked off the court and boycotted two games in protest, he dramatized the issue and virtually demanded attention to what he had to say. He felt Proposition 42 was racist and class-based, and that the standardized tests used to make the decisions are discriminatory and do not accurately predict readiness for a college curriculum. Thompson said he himself could not have gone to college under Proposition 42, which expanded the provisions of a previous NCAA bylaw (Proposition 48) that bars eligibility, but not scholarships, to freshmen whose test scores fall below the standard. (Rumeal Robinson, the hero of Michigan's 1989 championship, is an example of a Proposition 48 student who would have been effectively barred from attending college by Proposition 42.)

The controversies surrounding John Thompson are not all political. For example, as head coach of the 1988 United States Olympic team, he built a squad in the Georgetown mold and included only one high-scoring outside shooter, Hersey Hawkins. When Hawkins was injured, the team was left without a legitimate outside threat, and the Soviet Union defeated the United States to win the gold.

The moral, of course, is that everyone makes mistakes, even John Thompson. "I know I'm not perfect," Thompson admitted to William Rhoden of *The New York Times,* "and as I've gotten older I suppose I've come to accept the fact that life isn't perfect and players are not perfect. I realize all of this," he concluded, "and I resent the hell out of it."

Jerry Tarkanian

Long Beach State/University of Nevada at Las Vegas

Coaching Record (Major College):	W	L	Pct.
At Long Beach State	116	17	.872
At UNLV	449	102	.815
Totals	565	119	.826

NCAA Tournament Record: With Long Beach State—four appearances (1970, 1971, 1972, 1973); with UNLV—eleven appearances (1975, 1976, 1977, 1983, 1984, 1985, 1986, 1987, 1988, 1989, 1990).
Won-Lost Record: 33-15.
National Third Place: 1977, 1987 (tie).
National Championship: 1990.

His name—Tark the Shark; his looks—bald and short and unrefined, with dark rings under his eyes; his place of business—sin city, Las Vegas. His image may be questionable, but there's no question about his work—Jerry Tarkanian knows how to win.

After his UNLV team ran away with the 1990 NCAA championship, Tarkanian had the second-highest winning percentage of any major college coach in history (and he's only .0006 percent behind Clair Bee's all-time high percentage). With 565 victories he ranks second among active

coaches in wins (after Dean Smith). And that doesn't even include his 212-26 record in seven years as a junior college coach.

Tarkanian wins by molding what appear to be undisciplined, unmotivated, and self-centered kids—many of them players other coaches wouldn't touch—into highly focused, disciplined teams. He demands dedication, and teaches a style of play that uses superior conditioning to wear down the opposition.

"The way we play the game," says Tarkanian, is to "get up and down the court fast, shoot quick, play pressure defense." UNLV broke several all-time tournament scoring records in 1990, but it was the Rebels' unrelenting defensive pressure that broke the backs of their opponents. "Very few teams take the ball where they want it against UNLV," says Tark. "We deny them the spot they want, we deny them the ball."

The way Tarkanian has built his powerful teams—first at Long Beach State and later at UNLV—has gone against the longstanding wisdom of his peers. While most coaches believed you couldn't win with junior college and other transfer students, Tark did it. He's been known to quip that he liked jucos "because their new cars have already been paid for," but his record is no joke. And his success with players who either (1) didn't fit into other programs, (2) entered college academically ineligible for four-year schools, or (3) were not heavily recruited by major powers, has taken him to the top of his class. It's also led other coaches—even those like Indiana's Bob Knight who coach traditional powers—to follow his example.

His recruiting practices, and the makeup of his teams, have also contributed to making him one of the most controversial figures in American sports. To put it bluntly: Tark the Shark and the NCAA have been at war for nearly twenty years.

On January 6, 1974, just months after Tarkanian left Long Beach State for Nevada–Las Vegas, his old school was placed on probation by the NCAA for basketball and football violations that included excessive financial aid and fraudulent test scores. Tarkanian was implicated, but his penalty—suspension of his coaching rights at Long Beach State—was unenforceable since he was no longer at the California college.

A year later the NCAA enacted its "Tarkanian Rule," stating that a coach who has been suspended may not shift to another member school without the new school losing its post-season eligibility.

In 1977 the NCAA informed UNLV that its basketball team would be put on probation for two years for violations that included fraudulent grades and illegal payments; in addition they recommended that Tark be barred from participating in the school's athletic program for the duration of the probation. Tark refused to go down; he claimed the NCAA was carrying out a vendetta with trumped-up charges and was denying him due process. "Ever since I wrote a column blasting the NCAA while I was at Long Beach State, they've been after me," he asserted.

Backed by affidavits from players and former players citing harassment by NCAA investigators, Tarkanian filed suit. Soon after, he was offered a lucrative contract to coach the Los Angeles Lakers, but he turned it down to stay with UNLV. "If I took the pro job," he said later, "the case would become moot. . . . I just got to the point where winning the case was more important to me than anything else. When you try to destroy a man's life, I think you should have some kind of evidence to back it up."

After hearing the arguments, District Court Judge James Brennan agreed with Tarkanian, ruling that the NCAA's case against him could be "reduced to one word: *incredible.*" The NCAA appealed, and after Tarkanian won at the first appellate stage, the case was finally heard by the United States Supreme Court in 1988. The Court ruled 5-4 that, since the NCAA is a private organization, it is not bound by the constitutional requirement of due process; Tarkanian's constitutional rights were not violated by the NCAA ruling demanding his suspension.

Even now Tark rejects every allegation of impropriety, of buying players, and of bringing in student-athletes who in reality have no business being in college.

He says that as a kid, he was tough himself, a lot like many of his own players. His father died when he was young, and his mother remarried, moving the family west to California. Tark says he was wild, the type who never missed a party—not exactly the kind of kid you'd expect to make something of himself. Yet he attended Pasadena City College, graduated from Fresno State, and earned a master's from Redlands University.

"The way I look at it," he argued in 1989, "if you bring a kid in that can't read and write, somebody nobody will touch, and you keep him here four or five years, teach him to follow the rules, make him responsible for what he does, at the end if he can read and write a little, you've done him a favor. Even if he doesn't have a piece of paper you've given him a chance to straighten out. I don't see anything wrong with that."

In 1987 he took on two difficult reclamation projects: Lloyd Daniels and Clifford Allen. Allen, at 6-10, was considered the best young center in California—but he was also completing high school in El Paso Robles detention home. Daniels, who hailed from Brooklyn, was being compared to Magic Johnson, but he tested at a third grade reading level after going to five high schools and a California junior college. Soon after he arrived in Las Vegas for remediation, Daniels was busted for attempting to buy cocaine from an undercover cop. Neither Daniels nor Allen ever played a minute for UNLV, but their names come up constantly in discussions of Tark's recruiting practices.

Tarkanian prefers to point to Ricky Sobers as an example of a kid who turned his life around when given a chance at UNLV. Sobers was from The Bronx, and like Daniels he never graduated high school—but he did finish junior college before enrolling at Vegas. Sobers graduated from UNLV with a degree in business, went on to play 11 years in the NBA, and is now in real estate. He considers his college coach an important influence on him: "You can talk to him," said Sobers. "And he listens." Tarkanian asserts that the possibility of changing dead-end kids by giving them a chance is rooted in the reality of his own life and in the cases of kids, like Ricky Sobers, who did succeed.

The fact remains, however, that in his first thirteen years in the desert, the vast majority of his players left without degrees. And that his players' graduation rates were even more dismal at Long Beach State. Dwight Taylor was one of several former Long Beach State players who spoke bitterly about their ex-coach to *People* magazine. He said Tarkanian persuaded him to change his major from art to physical education, "because they said they could 'control' things better if I majored in phys ed. . . . I think I'd be a hell of an artist today if they had just helped me in the thing I really liked and wanted to do." He did not graduate, did not play pro ball, and now makes a bare living working in temporary jobs.

In recent years, possibly because of NCAA scrutiny, most certainly as a result of an increasing focus on academic achievement at UNLV, Tarkanian has become more committed to seeing that his players attend class and earn degrees. "I've been hearing about some of you guys missing class," he reportedly told his team early in the 1990 championship season. "Anybody misses class, we're going to run you at six A.M., run you till you vomit. There's no excuse for this . . . you miss class, you lose your scholarship. You miss class, you can't play. You can't play, and there goes our depth."

Tarkanian's wife, Lois, even brought in Dr. Harry Edwards to help upgrade the academic program for UNLV basketball players. And in 1987 two full-time tutors and a part-timer were hired to help ensure that the Rebels would be academically up to par. That same year, five of his six senior players were scheduled to graduate with their class, and the sixth, point guard Mark Wade, was behind only because he had changed his major.

Despite Tark's seemingly suspect attitude toward education, his program has brought money, visibility, and vitality to the school once known as "Tumbleweed Tech." So much so that *U.S. News and World Report* recently called UNLV one of only three "up-and-coming" universities in the 15 Western states. In the case of UNLV, basketball success has begun to breed academic success.

Tarkanian's UNLV players have expressed fierce loyalty to him. He gives them the credit for a win and shoulders the blame himself for a loss. "These are kids," he says, "you're grown up." It's an attitude that helped create a superb sense of team cohesiveness and loyalty during UNLV's 1990 run to the national championship.

In 1991, though, Tark and his rebels won't be back to defend the title. The NCAA has banned UNLV from tournament play for a year in furtherance of its 1977 penalty. And more trouble may lie ahead for Tarkanian and UNLV. When the NCAA investigation into the 1987 recruitment of Lloyd Daniels is finally wrapped up, there are likely to be further sanctions. Peace between the NCAA and Tarkanian is still a long way off.

PART 3

All-Time Tournament Records

COMPLETE SCHOOL-BY-SCHOOL RECORDS

Coaches are listed alphabetically under each school name. Next to the coaches names are the years they coached in the tournament, and, in parentheses, their tournament finishes in the regional final round or beyond. To the right are the composite tournament records for each coach and each school.
Following are the abbreviations used in this section:

Yrs	Years
W	Games Won
L	Games Lost
Ch.	Championships
2nd	2nd Place
F-4	Final Four Appearances
F-8	Round of 8 (Regional Final) Appearances

NOTE:
F-8 in the left-hand column (School/Coach/Years) indicates that the team lost in the Round of 8.

F-8 in the right-hand column (Tournament Totals) indicates appearances (both wins and losses) in the Round of 8.

ALL TIME RECORDS—SCHOOL BY SCHOOL

AIR FORCE

	Yrs	W	L	Ch.	2nd	F-4	F-8
Spear, Bob—1960, 1962	2	0	2	0	0	0	0
TOTAL	2	0	2	0	0	0	0

AKRON

	Yrs	W	L	Ch.	2nd	F-4	F-8
Huggins, Bob—1986	1	0	1	0	0	0	0
TOTAL	1	0	1	0	0	0	0

ALA.-BIRMINGHAM

	Yrs	W	L	Ch.	2nd	F-4	F-8
Bartow, Gene—1981, 82 (F-8), 1983, 1984, 1985, 1986, 1987, 1990	8	6	8	0	0	0	1
TOTAL	8	6	8	0	0	0	1

ALABAMA

	Yrs	W	L	Ch.	2nd	F-4	F-8
Newton, C.M.—1975, 1976	2	1	2	0	0	0	0
Sanderson, Wimp—1982, 1983, 1984, 1985, 1986, 1987, 1989, 1990	8	9	8	0	0	0	0
TOTAL	10	10	10	0	0	0	0

ALCORN STATE

	Yrs	W	L	Ch.	2nd	F-4	F-8
Whitney, Davey—1980, 1982, 1983, 1984	4	3	4	0	0	0	0
TOTAL	4	3	4	0	0	0	0

APPALACHIAN STATE

	Yrs	W	L	Ch.	2nd	F-4	F-8
Cremins, Bobby—1979	1	0	1	0	0	0	0
TOTAL	1	0	1	0	0	0	0

ARIZONA

	Yrs	W	L	Ch.	2nd	F-4	F-8
Enke, Fred—1951	1	0	1	0	0	0	0
Olson, Lute—1985, 1986, 1987, 88 (F-4), 1989, 1990	6	7	6	0	0	1	1
Snowden, Fred—76 (F-8), 1977	2	2	2	0	0	0	1
TOTAL	9	9	9	0	0	1	2

ARIZONA STATE

	Yrs	W	L	Ch.	2nd	F-4	F-8
Wulk, Ned—1958, 61 (F-8), 1962, 63 (F-8), 1964, 1973, 75 (F-8), 1980, 1981	9	8	10	0	0	0	3
TOTAL	9	8	10	0	0	0	3

ARK.-LITTLE ROCK

	Yrs	W	L	Ch.	2nd	F-4	F-8
Newell, Mike—1986, 1989, 1990	3	1	3	0	0	0	0
TOTAL	3	1	3	0	0	0	0

ARKANSAS

	Yrs	W	L	Ch.	2nd	F-4	F-8
Lambert, Eugene—45 (F-8), 1949	2	2	2	0	0	0	1
Richardson, Nolan—1988, 1989, 90 (F-4)	3	5	3	0	0	1	1
Rose, Glen—41 (F-8), 1958	2	1	3	0	0	0	1
Sutton, Eddie—1977, 78 (F-4), 79 (F-8), 1980, 1981, 1982, 1983, 1984, 1985	9	10	9	0	0	1	2
TOTAL	16	18	17	0	0	2	5

AUBURN

	Yrs	W	L	Ch.	2nd	F-4	F-8
Smith, Sonny—1984, 1985, 86 (F-8), 1987, 1988	5	7	5	0	0	0	1
TOTAL	5	7	5	0	0	0	1

AUSTIN PEAY

	Yrs	W	L	Ch.	2nd	F-4	F-8
Kelly, Lake—1973, 1974, 1987	3	2	4	0	0	0	0
TOTAL	3	2	4	0	0	0	0

BALL STATE

	Yrs	W	L	Ch.	2nd	F-4	F-8
Brown, Al—1986	1	0	1	0	0	0	0
Hunsaker, Dick—1990	1	2	1	0	0	0	0
Majerus, Rick—1989	1	1	1	0	0	0	0
Yoder, Steve—1981	1	0	1	0	0	0	0
TOTAL	4	3	4	0	0	0	0

BAYLOR

	Yrs	W	L	Ch.	2nd	F-4	F-8
Henderson, Bill—1946, 48 (2), 50 (F-8)	3	3	5	0	1	0	2
Iba, Gene—1988	1	0	1	0	0	0	0
TOTAL	4	3	6	0	1	0	2

BOISE STATE

	Yrs	W	L	Ch.	2nd	F-4	F-8
Connor, Bus—1976	1	0	1	0	0	0	0
Dye, Bob—1988	1	0	1	0	0	0	0
TOTAL	2	0	2	0	0	0	0

BOSTON COLLEGE

	Yrs	W	L	Ch.	2nd	F-4	F-8
Cousy, Bob—67 (F-8), 1968	2	2	2	0	0	0	1
Davis, Tom—1981, 82 (F-8), 1989	3	5	2	0	0	0	1
Martin, Donald—1958	1	0	1	0	0	0	0
Williams, Gary—1983, 1985	2	3	2	0	0	0	0
Zuffelato, Bob—1975	1	1	2	0	0	0	0
TOTAL	9	11	9	0	0	0	2

BOSTON UNIV.

	Yrs	W	L	Ch.	2nd	F-4	F-8
Jarvis, Mike—1988, 1990	2	0	2	0	0	0	0
Pitino, Rick—1983	1	0	1	0	0	0	0
Zunic, Matt—59 (F-8)	1	2	1	0	0	0	1
TOTAL	4	2	4	0	0	0	1

BOWLING GREEN

	Yrs	W	L	Ch.	2nd	F-4	F-8
Anderson, Harold—1959, 1962, 1963	3	1	4	0	0	0	0
Fitch, Bob—1968	1	0	1	0	0	0	0
TOTAL	4	1	5	0	0	0	0

BRADLEY

	Yrs	W	L	Ch.	2nd	F-4	F-8
Albeck, Stan—1988	1	0	1	0	0	0	0
Anderson, Forddy—50 (2), 54 (2)	2	6	2	0	2	0	2
Vanatta, Bob—1955	1	2	1	0	0	0	0
Versace, Dick—1980, 1986	2	1	2	0	0	0	0
TOTAL	6	9	6	0	2	0	2

BRIGHAM YOUNG

	Yrs	W	L	Ch.	2nd	F-4	F-8
Anderson, Ladell—1984, 1987, 1988	3	2	3	0	0	0	0
Arnold, Frank—1979, 1980, 81 (F-8)	3	3	3	0	0	0	1
Reid, Roger—1990	1	0	1	0	0	0	0
Watts, Stan—1950, 1951, 1957, 1965, 1969, 1971, 1972	7	4	10	0	0	0	0
TOTAL	14	9	17	0	0	0	1

BROWN

	Yrs	W	L	Ch.	2nd	F-4	F-8
Allen, George—1939	1	0	1	0	0	0	0
Cingiser, Mike—1986	1	0	1	0	0	0	0
TOTAL	2	0	2	0	0	0	0

BUCKNELL

	Yrs	W	L	Ch.	2nd	F-4	F-8
Woollum, Charles—1987, 1989	2	0	2	0	0	0	0
TOTAL	2	0	2	0	0	0	0

BUTLER

	Yrs	W	L	Ch.	2nd	F-4	F-8
Hinkle, Tony—1962	1	2	1	0	0	0	0
TOTAL	1	2	1	0	0	0	0

CAL. ST. FULLERTON

	Yrs	W	L	Ch.	2nd	F-4	F-8
Dye, Bob—78 (F-8)	1	2	1	0	0	0	1
TOTAL	1	2	1	0	0	0	1

CAL. STATE LA

	Yrs	W	L	Ch.	2nd	F-4	F-8
Miller, Bob—1974	1	0	1	0	0	0	0
TOTAL	1	0	1	0	0	0	0

CALIFORNIA

	Yrs	W	L	Ch.	2nd	F-4	F-8
Campanelli, Lou—1990	1	1	1	0	0	0	0
Newell, Pete—57 (F-8), 58 (F-8), 59 (Ch.), 60 (F-4)	4	10	3	1	0	1	4
Price, Nibs—46 (F-8)	1	1	2	0	0	0	1
TOTAL	6	12	6	1	0	1	5

CANISIUS

	Yrs	W	L	Ch.	2nd	F-4	F-8
Curran, Joseph—1955, 56 (F-8), 1957	3	6	3	0	0	0	1
TOTAL	3	6	3	0	0	0	1

CATHOLIC

	Yrs	W	L	Ch.	2nd	F-4	F-8
Long, John—1944	1	0	2	0	0	0	0
TOTAL	1	0	2	0	0	0	0

CCNY

	Yrs	W	L	Ch.	2nd	F-4	F-8
Holman, Nat—47 (F-8), 50 (Ch.)	2	4	2	1	0	0	2
TOTAL	2	4	2	1	0	0	2

CENTRAL MICHIGAN

	Yrs	W	L	Ch.	2nd	F-4	F-8
Coles, Charles—1987	1	0	1	0	0	0	0
Parfitt, Dick—1975, 1977	2	2	2	0	0	0	0
TOTAL	3	2	3	0	0	0	0

CINCINNATI

	Yrs	W	L	Ch.	2nd	F-4	F-8
Baker, Tay—1966	1	0	2	0	0	0	0
Catlett, Gale—1975, 1976, 1977	3	2	3	0	0	0	0
Jucker, Ed—61 (Ch.), 62 (Ch.), 63 (2)	3	11	1	2	1	0	3
Smith, George—1958, 59 (F-4), 60 (2)	3	7	3	0	1	1	2
TOTAL	10	20	9	2	2	1	5

CLEMSON

	Yrs	W	L	Ch.	2nd	F-4	F-8
Ellis, Cliff—1987, 1989, 1990	3	3	3	0	0	0	0
Foster, Wm. C. (Bill)—80 (F-8)	1	3	1	0	0	0	1
TOTAL	4	6	4	0	0	0	1

CLEVELAND STATE

	Yrs	W	L	Ch.	2nd	F-4	F-8
MacKey, Kevin—1986	1	2	1	0	0	0	0
TOTAL	1	2	1	0	0	0	0

COLORADO

	Yrs	W	L	Ch.	2nd	F-4	F-8
Cox, Frosty—1940, 42 (F-8), 1946	3	2	4	0	0	0	1
Lee, Bebe—1954, 55 (F-8)	2	3	3	0	0	0	1
Walseth, Sox—62 (F-8), 63 (F-8), 1969	3	3	3	0	0	0	2
TOTAL	8	8	10	0	0	0	4

COLORADO STATE/A&M*

	Yrs	W	L	Ch.	2nd	F-4	F-8
Grant, Boyd—1989, 1990	2	1	2	0	0	0	0
Strannigan, Bill—1954	1	0	2	0	0	0	0
Williams, Jim—1963, 1965, 1966, 69 (F-8)	4	2	4	0	0	0	1
TOTAL	7	3	8	0	0	0	1

COLUMBIA

	Yrs	W	L	Ch.	2nd	F-4	F-8
Ridings, Gordon—1948	1	0	2	0	0	0	0
Rohan, Jack—1968	1	2	1	0	0	0	0
Rossini, Lou—1951	1	0	1	0	0	0	0
TOTAL	3	2	4	0	0	0	0

COPPIN STATE

	Yrs	W	L	Ch.	2nd	F-4	F-8
Mitchell, Ron—1990	1	0	1	0	0	0	0
TOTAL	1	0	1	0	0	0	0

CORNELL

	Yrs	W	L	Ch.	2nd	F-4	F-8
Dement, Mike—1988	1	0	1	0	0	0	0
Greene, Royner—1954	1	0	2	0	0	0	0
TOTAL	2	0	3	0	0	0	0

CREIGHTON

	Yrs	W	L	Ch.	2nd	F-4	F-8
Apke, Tom—1975, 1978, 1981	3	0	3	0	0	0	0
Barone, Tony—1989	1	0	1	0	0	0	0
Hickey, Eddie—1941	1	1	1	0	0	0	0
McManus, Red—1962, 1964	2	3	3	0	0	0	0
Sutton, Eddie—1974	1	2	1	0	0	0	0
TOTAL	8	6	9	0	0	0	0

DARTMOUTH

	Yrs	W	L	Ch.	2nd	F-4	F-8
Brown, Earl—44 (2)	1	2	1	0	1	0	1
Cowles, Ozzie—1941, 42 (2), 1943	3	4	3	0	1	0	1
Julian, Doggie—1956, 58 (F-8), 1959	3	4	3	0	0	0	1
TOTAL	7	10	7	0	2	0	3

*Colorado State was known as Colorado A&M in 1954.

DAVIDSON

	Yrs	W	L	Ch.	2nd	F-4	F-8
Driesell, Lefty—1966, 68 (F-8), 69 (F-8)	3	5	4	0	0	0	2
Holland, Terry—1970	1	0	1	0	0	0	0
Hussey, Bobby—1986	1	0	1	0	0	0	0
TOTAL	5	5	6	0	0	0	2

DAYTON

	Yrs	W	L	Ch.	2nd	F-4	F-8
Blackburn, Tom—1952	1	1	1	0	0	0	0
Donoher, Don—1965, 1966, 67 (2), 1969, 1970, 1974, 84 (F-8), 1985	8	11	10	0	1	0	2
O'Brien, Jim—1990	1	1	1	0	0	0	0
TOTAL	10	13	12	0	1	0	2

DEPAUL

	Yrs	W	L	Ch.	2nd	F-4	F-8
Meyer, Joey—1985, 1986, 1987, 1988, 1989	5	6	5	0	0	0	0
Meyer, Ray—43 (F-8), 1953, 1956, 1959, 1960, 1965, 1976, 78 (F-8), 79 (F-4), 1980, 1981, 1982, 1984	13	14	16	0	0	1	3
TOTAL	18	20	21	0	0	1	3

DETROIT

	Yrs	W	L	Ch.	2nd	F-4	F-8
Calihan, Robert—1962	1	0	1	0	0	0	0
Gaines, Dave Smokey—1979	1	0	1	0	0	0	0
Vitale, Dick—1977	1	1	1	0	0	0	0
TOTAL	3	1	3	0	0	0	0

DRAKE

	Yrs	W	L	Ch.	2nd	F-4	F-8
John, Maurice—69 (F-4), 70 (F-8), 71 (F-8)	3	5	3	0	0	1	3
TOTAL	3	5	3	0	0	1	3

DREXEL

	Yrs	W	L	Ch.	2nd	F-4	F-8
Burke, Eddie—1986	1	0	1	0	0	0	0
TOTAL	1	0	1	0	0	0	0

DUKE

	Yrs	W	L	Ch.	2nd	F-4	F-8
Bradley, Harold—1955	1	0	1	0	0	0	0
Bubas, Vic—60 (F-8), 63 (F-4), 64 (2), 66 (F-4)	4	11	4	0	1	2	4
Foster, Wm. E. (Bill)—78 (2), 1979, 80 (F-8)	3	6	3	0	1	0	2
Krzyzewski, Mike—1984, 1985, 86 (2), 1987, 88 (F-4), 89 (F-4), 90 (2)	7	21	7	0	2	2	4
TOTAL	15	38	15	0	4	4	10

DUQUESNE

	Yrs	W	L	Ch.	2nd	F-4	F-8
Cinicola, John—1977	1	0	1	0	0	0	0
Davies, Chick—40 (F-8)	1	1	1	0	0	0	1
Manning, Red—1969, 1971	2	2	2	0	0	0	0
Moore, Dudey—1952	1	1	1	0	0	0	0
TOTAL	5	4	5	0	0	0	1

EAST CAROLINA

	Yrs	W	L	Ch.	2nd	F-4	F-8
Quinn, Tom—1972	1	0	1	0	0	0	0
TOTAL	1	0	1	0	0	0	0

EAST TENN. STATE

	Yrs	W	L	Ch.	2nd	F-4	F-8
Brooks, J. Madison—1968	1	1	2	0	0	0	0
Robinson, Les—1989, 1990	2	0	2	0	0	0	0
TOTAL	3	1	4	0	0	0	0

EASTERN KENTUCKY

	Yrs	W	L	Ch.	2nd	F-4	F-8
Baechtold, Jim—1965	1	0	1	0	0	0	0
Byhre, Ed—1979	1	0	1	0	0	0	0
McBrayer, Paul—1953, 1959	2	0	2	0	0	0	0
Strong, Guy—1972	1	0	1	0	0	0	0
TOTAL	5	0	5	0	0	0	0

EASTERN MICHIGAN

	Yrs	W	L	Ch.	2nd	F-4	F-8
Braun, Ben—1988	1	0	1	0	0	0	0
TOTAL	1	0	1	0	0	0	0

EVANSVILLE

	Yrs	W	L	Ch.	2nd	F-4	F-8
Crews, Jim—1989	1	1	1	0	0	0	0
Walters, Dick—1982	1	0	1	0	0	0	0
TOTAL	2	1	2	0	0	0	0

FAIRLEIGH DICKINSON

	Yrs	W	L	Ch.	2nd	F-4	F-8
Green, Tom—1985, 1988	2	0	2	0	0	0	0
TOTAL	2	0	2	0	0	0	0

FAIRFIELD

	Yrs	W	L	Ch.	2nd	F-4	F-8
Buonaguro, Mitch—1986, 1987	2	0	2	0	0	0	0
TOTAL	2	0	2	0	0	0	0

FLORIDA

	Yrs	W	L	Ch.	2nd	F-4	F-8
Sloan, Norm—1987, 1988, 1989	3	3	3	0	0	0	0
TOTAL	3	3	3	0	0	0	0

FLORIDA STATE

	Yrs	W	L	Ch.	2nd	F-4	F-8
Durham, Hugh—1968, 72 (F-8), 1978	3	4	3	0	0	0	1
Kennedy, Pat—1988, 1989	2	0	2	0	0	0	0
Williams, Joe—1980	1	1	1	0	0	0	0
TOTAL	6	5	6	0	0	0	1

FORDHAM

	Yrs	W	L	Ch.	2nd	F-4	F-8
Bach, John—1953, 1954	2	0	2	0	0	0	0
Phelps, Digger—1971	1	2	1	0	0	0	0
TOTAL	3	2	3	0	0	0	0

FRESNO STATE

	Yrs	W	L	Ch.	2nd	F-4	F-8
Grant, Boyd—1981, 1982, 1984	3	1	3	0	0	0	0
TOTAL	3	1	3	0	0	0	0

FURMAN

	Yrs	W	L	Ch.	2nd	F-4	F-8
Holbrook, Eddie—1980	1	0	1	0	0	0	0
Williams, Joe—1971, 1973, 1974, 1975, 1978	5	1	6	0	0	0	0
TOTAL	6	1	7	0	0	0	0

GEORGIA SOUTHERN

	Yrs	W	L	Ch.	2nd	F-4	F-8
Kerns, Frank—1983, 1987	2	0	2	0	0	0	0
TOTAL	2	0	2	0	0	0	0

GEO. WASH.

	Yrs	W	L	Ch.	2nd	F-4	F-8
Reinhart, Bill—1954, 1961	2	0	2	0	0	0	0
TOTAL	2	0	2	0	0	0	0

GEORGE MASON

	Yrs	W	L	Ch.	2nd	F-4	F-8
Nestor, Ernie—1989	1	0	1	0	0	0	0
TOTAL	1	0	1	0	0	0	0

GEORGETOWN

	Yrs	W	L	Ch.	2nd	F-4	F-8
Ripley, Elmer—43 (2)	1	2	1	0	1	0	1
Thompson, John—1975, 1976, 1979, 80 (F-8), 1981, 82 (2), 1983, 84 (Ch.), 85 (2), 1986, 87 (F-8), 1988, 89 (F-8), 1990	14	26	13	1	2	0	6
TOTAL	15	28	14	1	3	0	7

GEORGIA

	Yrs	W	L	Ch.	2nd	F-4	F-8
Durham, Hugh—83 (F-4), 1985, 1987, 1990	4	4	4	0	0	1	1
TOTAL	4	4	4	0	0	1	1

GEORGIA TECH

	Yrs	W	L	Ch.	2nd	F-4	F-8
Cremins, Bobby—85 (F-8), 1986, 1987, 1988, 1989, 90 (F-4)	6	10	6	0	0	1	2
Hyder, Whack—60 (F-8)	1	1	1	0	0	0	1
TOTAL	7	11	7	0	0	1	3

HARDIN-SIMMONS

	Yrs	W	L	Ch.	2nd	F-4	F-8
Scott, Bill—1953, 1957	2	0	2	0	0	0	0
TOTAL	2	0	2	0	0	0	0

HARVARD

	Yrs	W	L	Ch.	2nd	F-4	F-8
Stahl, Floyd—1946	1	0	2	0	0	0	0
TOTAL	1	0	2	0	0	0	0

HAWAII

	Yrs	W	L	Ch.	2nd	F-4	F-8
Rocha, Red—1972	1	0	1	0	0	0	0
TOTAL	1	0	1	0	0	0	0

HOFSTRA

	Yrs	W	L	Ch.	2nd	F-4	F-8
Gaeckler, Roger—1976, 1977	2	0	2	0	0	0	0
TOTAL	2	0	2	0	0	0	0

HOLY CROSS

	Yrs	W	L	Ch.	2nd	F-4	F-8
Blaney, George—1977, 1980	2	0	2	0	0	0	0
Julian, Doggie—47 (Ch.), 48 (F-8)	2	5	1	1	0	0	2
Leening, Roy—1956	1	0	1	0	0	0	0
Sheary, Buster—1950, 1953	2	2	3	0	0	0	0
TOTAL	7	7	7	1	0	0	2

HOUSTON

	Yrs	W	L	Ch.	2nd	F-4	F-8
Foster, Pat—1987, 1990	2	0	2	0	0	0	0
Lewis, Guy—1961, 1965, 1966, 67 (F-4), 68 (F-4), 1970, 1971, 1972, 1973, 1978, 1981, 82 (F-4), 83 (2), 84 (2)	14	26	18	0	2	3	5
Pasche, Alden—1956	1	0	2	0	0	0	0
TOTAL	17	26	22	0	2	3	5

HOUSTON BAPTIST

	Yrs	W	L	Ch.	2nd	F-4	F-8
Iba, Gene—1984	1	0	1	0	0	0	0
TOTAL	1	0	1	0	0	0	0

HOWARD

	Yrs	W	L	Ch.	2nd	F-4	F-8
Williamson, A. B.—1981	1	0	1	0	0	0	0
TOTAL	1	0	1	0	0	0	0

IDAHO

	Yrs	W	L	Ch.	2nd	F-4	F-8
Davis Jr., Kermit—1989, 1990	2	0	2	0	0	0	0
Monson, Don—1981, 1982	2	1	2	0	0	0	0
TOTAL	4	1	4	0	0	0	0

IDAHO STATE

	Yrs	W	L	Ch.	2nd	F-4	F-8
Belko, Steve—1953, 1954, 1955, 1956	4	2	4	0	0	0	0
Boutin, Jim—1987	1	0	1	0	0	0	0
Evans, John—1960	1	0	1	0	0	0	0
Grayson, John—1957, 1958, 1959	3	4	5	0	0	0	0
Killingsworth, Jim—1974, 77 (F-8)	2	2	2	0	0	0	1
TOTAL	11	8	13	0	0	0	1

ILLINOIS

	Yrs	W	L	Ch.	2nd	F-4	F-8
Combes, Harry—49 (F-8), 51 (F-8), 52 (F-8), 63 (F-8)	4	9	4	0	0	0	4
Henson, Lou—1981, 1983, 84 (F-8), 1985, 1986, 1987, 1988, 89 (F-4), 1990	9	11	9	0	0	1	2
Mills, Doug—1942	1	0	2	0	0	0	0
TOTAL	14	20	15	0	0	1	6

ILLINOIS STATE

	Yrs	W	L	Ch.	2nd	F-4	F-8
Bender, Bob—1990	1	0	1	0	0	0	0
Donewald, Bob—1983, 1984, 1985	3	2	3	0	0	0	0
TOTAL	4	2	4	0	0	0	0

INDIANA

	Yrs	W	L	Ch.	2nd	F-4	F-8
Knight, Bob—73 (Ch.), 75 (F-8), 76 (Ch.), 1978, 1980, 81 (Ch.), 1982, 1983, 84 (F-8), 1986, 87 (Ch.), 1988, 1989, 1990	14	29	11	4	0	0	6
McCracken, Branch—40 (Ch.), 53 (Ch.), 1954, 1958	4	9	2	2	0	0	2
Watson, Lou—1967	1	1	1	0	0	0	0
TOTAL	19	39	14	6	0	0	8

INDIANA STATE

	Yrs	W	L	Ch.	2nd	F-4	F-8
Hodges, Bill—79 (2)	1	4	1	0	1	0	1
TOTAL	1	4	1	0	1	0	1

IONA

	Yrs	W	L	Ch.	2nd	F-4	F-8
Kennedy, Pat—1984, 1985	2	0	2	0	0	0	0
Valvano, Jim—1979, 1980	2	1	2	0	0	0	0
TOTAL	4	1	4	0	0	0	0

IOWA

	Yrs	W	L	Ch.	2nd	F-4	F-8
Davis, Tom—87 (F-8), 1988, 1989	3	6	3	0	0	0	1
Miller, Ralph—1970	1	1	1	0	0	0	0
O'Connor, Bucky—55 (F-8), 56 (2)	2	5	3	0	1	0	2
Olson, Lute—1979, 80 (F-4), 1981, 1982, 1983	5	7	6	0	0	1	1
Raveling, George—1985, 1986	2	0	2	0	0	0	0
TOTAL	13	19	15	0	1	1	4

IOWA STATE

	Yrs	W	L	Ch.	2nd	F-4	F-8
Menze, Louis—44 (F-8)	1	1	1	0	0	0	1
Orr, Johnny—1985, 1986, 1987, 1988, 1989	5	2	4	0	0	0	0
TOTAL	6	3	5	0	0	0	1

JACKSONVILLE

	Yrs	W	L	Ch.	2nd	F-4	F-8
Locke, Tates—1979	1	0	1	0	0	0	0
Wasdin, Tom—1971, 1973	2	0	2	0	0	0	0
Wenzel, Bob—1986	1	0	1	0	0	0	0
Williams, Joe—70 (2)	1	4	1	0	1	0	1
TOTAL	5	4	5	0	1	0	1

JAMES MADISON

	Yrs	W	L	Ch.	2nd	F-4	F-8
Campanelli, Lou—1981, 1982, 1983	3	3	3	0	0	0	0
TOTAL	3	3	3	0	0	0	0

KANSAS

	Yrs	W	L	Ch.	2nd	F-4	F-8
Allen, Phog—40 (2), 1942, 52 (Ch.), 53 (2)	4	10	3	1	2	0	3
Brown, Larry—1984, 1985, 86 (F-4), 1987, 88 (Ch.)	5	14	4	1	0	1	2
Harp, Dick—57 (2), 60 (F-8)	2	4	2	0	1	0	2
Owens, Ted—66 (F-8), 1967, 71 (F-4), 74 (F-4), 1975, 1978, 1981	7	8	9	0	0	2	3
Williams, Roy—1990	1	1	1	0	0	0	0
TOTAL	19	37	19	2	3	3	10

KANSAS STATE

	Yrs	W	L	Ch.	2nd	F-4	F-8
Fitzsimmons, Cotton—1970	1	1	1	0	0	0	0
Gardner, Jack—48 (F-8), 51 (2)	2	4	3	0	1	0	2
Hartman, Jack—72 (F-8), 73 (F-8), 75 (F-8), 1977, 1980, 81 (F-8), 1982	7	11	7	0	0	0	4
Kruger, Lon—1987, 88 (F-8), 1989, 1990	4	4	4	0	0	0	1
Winter, Tex—1956, 58 (F-4), 59 (F-8), 61 (F-8), 64 (F-4), 1968	6	7	9	0	0	2	4
TOTAL	20	27	24	0	1	2	11

KENTUCKY

	Yrs	W	L	Ch.	2nd	F-4	F-8
Hall, Joe—73 (F-8), 75 (2), 77 (F-8), 78 (Ch.), 1980, 1981, 1982, 83 (F-8), 84 (F-4), 1985	10	20	9	1	1	1	6
Rupp, Adolph—42 (F-8), 1945, 48 (Ch.), 49 (Ch.), 51 (Ch.), 1952, 1955, 56 (F-8), 57 (F-8), 58 (Ch.), 1959, 61 (F-8), 62 (F-8), 1964, 66 (2), 68 (F-8), 1969, 70 (F-8), 1971, 72 (F-8)	20	30	18	4	1	0	13
Sutton, Eddie—86 (F-8), 1987, 1988	3	5	3	0	0	0	1
TOTAL	33	55	30	5	2	1	20

LA SALLE

	Yrs	W	L	Ch.	2nd	F-4	F-8
Ervin, Lefty—1980, 1983	2	1	2	0	0	0	0
Harding, Jim—1968	1	0	1	0	0	0	0
Loeffler, Ken—54 (Ch.), 55 (2)	2	9	1	1	1	0	2
Morris, Bill—1988, 1989, 1990	3	1	3	0	0	0	0
Westhead, Paul—1975, 1978	2	0	2	0	0	0	0
TOTAL	10	11	9	1	1	0	2

LAFAYETTE

	Yrs	W	L	Ch.	2nd	F-4	F-8
Davidson, George—1957	1	0	2	0	0	0	0
TOTAL	1	0	2	0	0	0	0

LAMAR

	Yrs	W	L	Ch.	2nd	F-4	F-8
Foster, Pat—1981, 1983	2	2	2	0	0	0	0
Tubbs, Billy—1979, 1980	2	3	2	0	0	0	0
TOTAL	4	5	4	0	0	0	0

LEBANON VALLEY

	Yrs	W	L	Ch.	2nd	F-4	F-8
Marquette, Rinso—1953	1	1	2	0	0	0	0
TOTAL	1	1	2	0	0	0	0

LEHIGH

	Yrs	W	L	Ch.	2nd	F-4	F-8
McCaffery, Fran—1988	1	0	1	0	0	0	0
Schneider, Tom—1985	1	0	1	0	0	0	0
TOTAL	2	0	2	0	0	0	0

LIU-BROOKLYN

	Yrs	W	L	Ch.	2nd	F-4	F-8
Lizzo, Paul—1981, 1984	2	0	0	0	0	0	0
TOTAL	2	0	0	0	0	0	0

LONG BEACH STATE

	Yrs	W	L	Ch.	2nd	F-4	F-8
Jones, Dwight—1977	1	0	1	0	0	0	0
Tarkanian, Jerry—1970, 71 (F-8), 72 (F-8), 1973	4	7	5	0	0	0	2
TOTAL	5	7	6	0	0	0	2

LOUISIANA STATE

	Yrs	W	L	Ch.	2nd	F-4	F-8
Brown, Dale—1979, 80 (Ch.), 81 (F-4), 1984, 1985, 86 (F-4), 87 (F-8), 1988, 1989, 1990	10	14	11	1	0	2	4
Rabenhorst, Harry—53 (F-8), 1954	2	2	4	0	0	0	1
TOTAL	12	16	15	1	0	2	5

LOUISIANA TECH

	Yrs	W	L	Ch.	2nd	F-4	F-8
Eagles, Tommy—1987, 1989	2	1	2	0	0	0	0
Russo, Andy—1984, 1985	2	3	2	0	0	0	0
TOTAL	4	4	4	0	0	0	0

LOUISVILLE

	Yrs	W	L	Ch.	2nd	F-4	F-8
Crum, Denny—72 (F-8), 1974, 75 (F-4), 1977, 1978, 1979, 80 (F-4), 1981, 82 (F-4), 83 (F-4), 1984, 86 (Ch.), 1988, 1989, 1990	15	32	15	1	0	4	6
Dromo, John—1968	1	1	1	0	0	0	0
Hickman, Peck—1951, 59 (F-4), 1961, 1964, 1967	5	5	7	0	0	1	1
TOTAL	21	38	23	1	0	5	7

LOYOLA MARYMOUNT

	Yrs	W	L	Ch.	2nd	F-4	F-8
Arndt, John—1961	1	1	1	0	0	0	0
Jacobs, Ron—1980	1	0	1	0	0	0	0
Westhead, Paul—1988, 1989, 90 (F-8)	3	4	3	0	0	0	1
TOTAL	5	5	5	0	0	0	1

LOYOLA N.O.

	Yrs	W	L	Ch.	2nd	F-4	F-8
Harding, Jim—1958	1	0	1	0	0	0	0
McCafferty, Jim—1954, 1957	2	0	2	0	0	0	0
TOTAL	3	0	3	0	0	0	0

LOYOLA-CHICAGO

	Yrs	W	L	Ch.	2nd	F-4	F-8
Ireland, George—63 (Ch.), 1964, 1966, 1968	4	7	3	1	0	0	1
Sullivan, Gene—1985	1	2	1	0	0	0	0
TOTAL	5	9	4	1	0	0	1

MANHATTAN

	Yrs	W	L	Ch.	2nd	F-4	F-8
Norton, Ken—1956, 1958	2	1	3	0	0	0	0
TOTAL	2	1	3	0	0	0	0

MARIST

	Yrs	W	L	Ch.	2nd	F-4	F-8
Furjanic, Matt—1986	1	0	1	0	0	0	0
Magarity, Dave—1987	1	0	1	0	0	0	0
TOTAL	2	0	2	0	0	0	0

MARQUETTE

	Yrs	W	L	Ch.	2nd	F-4	F-8
Hickey, Eddie—1959, 1961	2	1	3	0	0	0	0
McGuire, Al—1968, 69 (F-8), 1971, 1972, 1973, 74 (2), 1975, 76 (F-8), 77 (Ch.)	9	20	9	1	1	0	4
Nagle, Jack—1955	1	2	1	0	0	0	0
Raymonds, Hank—1978, 1979, 1980, 1982, 1983	5	2	5	0	0	0	0
TOTAL	17	25	18	1	1	0	4

MARSHALL

	Yrs	W	L	Ch.	2nd	F-4	F-8
Huckabay, Ricky—1984, 1985, 1987	3	0	3	0	0	0	0
Rivlin, Jule—1956	1	0	1	0	0	0	0
Tacy, Carl—1972	1	0	1	0	0	0	0
TOTAL	5	0	5	0	0	0	0

MARYLAND

	Yrs	W	L	Ch.	2nd	F-4	F-8
Driesell, Lefty—73 (F-8), 75 (F-8), 1980, 1981, 1983, 1984, 1985, 1986	8	10	8	0	0	0	2
Millikan, Bud—1958	1	2	1	0	0	0	0
Wade, Bob—1988	1	1	1	0	0	0	0
TOTAL	10	13	10	0	0	0	2

MCNEESE STATE

	Yrs	W	L	Ch.	2nd	F-4	F-8
Welch, Steve—1989	1	0	1	0	0	0	0
TOTAL	1	0	1	0	0	0	0

MEMPHIS STATE

	Yrs	W	L	Ch.	2nd	F-4	F-8
Bartow, Gene—73 (2)	1	3	1	0	1	0	1
Finch, Larry—1988, 1989	2	1	2	0	0	0	0
Kirk, Dana—1982, 1983, 1984, 85 (F-4), 1986	5	9	5	0	0	1	1
Lambert, Eugene—1955, 1956	2	0	2	0	0	0	0
Vanatta, Bob—1962	1	0	1	0	0	0	0
Yates, Wayne—1976	1	0	1	0	0	0	0
TOTAL	12	13	12	0	1	1	2

MERCER

	Yrs	W	L	Ch.	2nd	F-4	F-8
Bibb, Bill—1981, 1985	2	0	2	0	0	0	0
TOTAL	2	0	2	0	0	0	0

MIAMI (FLA.)

	Yrs	W	L	Ch.	2nd	F-4	F-8
Hale, Bruce—1960	1	0	1	0	0	0	0
TOTAL	1	0	1	0	0	0	0

MIAMI (OHIO)

	Yrs	W	L	Ch.	2nd	F-4	F-8
Hedric, Darrell—1971, 1973, 1978, 1984	4	1	4	0	0	0	0
Irson, Jerry—1985, 1986	2	0	2	0	0	0	0
Locke, Tates—1969	1	1	2	0	0	0	0
Rohr, Bill—1953, 1955, 1957	3	0	3	0	0	0	0
Shrider, Dick—1958, 1966	2	1	3	0	0	0	0
TOTAL	12	3	14	0	0	0	0

MICHIGAN

	Yrs	W	L	Ch.	2nd	F-4	F-8
Cowles, Ozzie—1948	1	1	1	0	0	0	0
Fisher, Steve—89 (Ch.), 1990	2	7	1	1	0	0	1
Freider, Bill—1985, 1986, 1987, 1988	4	5	4	0	0	0	0
Orr, Johnny—74 (F-8), 1975, 76 (2), 77 (F-8)	4	7	4	0	1	0	3
Strack, Dave—64 (F-4), 65 (2), 66 (F-8)	3	7	3	0	1	1	3
TOTAL	14	27	13	1	2	1	7

MICHIGAN STATE

	Yrs	W	L	Ch.	2nd	F-4	F-8
Anderson, Forddy—57 (F-4), 59 (F-8)	2	3	3	0	0	1	2
Heathcote, Jud—78 (F-8), 79 (Ch.), 1985, 1986, 1990	5	11	4	1	0	0	2
TOTAL	7	14	7	1	0	1	4

MIDDLE TENN. STATE

	Yrs	W	L	Ch.	2nd	F-4	F-8
Earle, Jimmy—1975, 1977	2	0	2	0	0	0	0
Simpson, Stan—1982	1	1	1	0	0	0	0
Stewart, Bruce—1985, 1987, 1989	3	1	3	0	0	0	0
TOTAL	6	2	6	0	0	0	0

MINNESOTA

	Yrs	W	L	Ch.	2nd	F-4	F-8
Dutcher, Jim—1982	1	1	1	0	0	0	0
Haskins, Clem—1989, 90 (F-8)	2	5	2	0	0	0	1
Musselman, Bill—1972	1	1	1	0	0	0	0
TOTAL	4	7	4	0	0	0	1

MISS. VALLEY STATE

	Yrs	W	L	Ch.	2nd	F-4	F-8
Stribling, Lafayette—1986	1	0	1	0	0	0	0
TOTAL	1	0	1	0	0	0	0

MISSISSIPPI

	Yrs	W	L	Ch.	2nd	F-4	F-8
Weltlich, Bob—1981	1	0	1	0	0	0	0
TOTAL	1	0	1	0	0	0	0

MISSISSIPPI STATE

	Yrs	W	L	Ch.	2nd	F-4	F-8
McCarthy, Babe—1963	1	1	1	0	0	0	0
TOTAL	1	1	1	0	0	0	0

MISSOURI

	Yrs	W	L	Ch.	2nd	F-4	F-8
Edwards, George—1944	1	1	1	0	0	0	0
Stewart, Norm—76 (F-8), 1978, 1980, 1981, 1982, 1983, 1986, 1987, 1988, 1989, 1990	11	7	11	0	0	0	1
TOTAL	12	8	12	0	0	0	1

MONTANA

	Yrs	W	L	Ch.	2nd	F-4	F-8
Heathcote, Jud—1975	1	1	2	0	0	0	0
TOTAL	1	1	2	0	0	0	0

MONTANA STATE

	Yrs	W	L	Ch.	2nd	F-4	F-8
Breeden, John—1951	1	0	1	0	0	0	0
Starner, Stu—1986	1	0	1	0	0	0	0
TOTAL	2	0	2	0	0	0	0

MOREHEAD STATE

	Yrs	W	L	Ch.	2nd	F-4	F-8
Laughlin, Robert—1956, 1957, 1961	3	3	4	0	0	0	0
Martin, Wayne—1983, 1984	2	1	2	0	0	0	0
TOTAL	5	4	6	0	0	0	0

MURRAY STATE

	Yrs	W	L	Ch.	2nd	F-4	F-8
Luther, Cal—1964, 1969	2	0	2	0	0	0	0
Newton, Steve—1988, 1990	2	1	2	0	0	0	0
TOTAL	4	1	4	0	0	0	0

NORTH CAROLINA

	Yrs	W	L	Ch.	2nd	F-4	F-8
Carnevale, Ben—46 (2)	1	2	1	0	1	0	1
Lange, Bill—1941	1	0	2	0	0	0	0
McGuire, Frank—57 (Ch.), 1959	2	5	1	1	0	0	1
Smith, Dean—67 (F-4), 68 (2), 69 (F-4), 72 (F-8), 1975, 1976, 77 (2), 1978, 1979, 1980, 81 (2), 82 (Ch.), 83 (F-8), 1984, 85 (F-8), 1986, 87 (F-8), 88 (F-8), 1989, 1990	20	43	21	1	3	2	11
TOTAL	24	50	25	2	4	2	13

N.C. A&T

	Yrs	W	L	Ch.	2nd	F-4	F-8
Corbett, Don—1982, 1983, 1984, 1985, 1986, 1987, 1988	7	0	7	0	0	0	0
TOTAL	7	0	7	0	0	0	0

N.C. STATE

	Yrs	W	L	Ch.	2nd	F-4	F-8
Case, Everett—50 (F-8), 1951, 1952, 1954, 1956	5	6	6	0	0	0	1
Maravich, Press—1965	1	1	1	0	0	0	0
Sloan, Norm—1970, 74 (Ch.), 1980	3	5	2	1	0	0	1
Valvano, Jim—1982, 83 (Ch.), 85 (F-8), 86 (F-8), 1987, 1988, 1989	7	14	6	1	0	0	3
TOTAL	16	26	15	2	0	0	5

N.C.-CHARLOTTE

	Yrs	W	L	Ch.	2nd	F-4	F-8
Mullins, Jeff—1988	1	0	1	0	0	0	0
Rose, Lee—77 (F-4)	1	3	2	0	0	1	1
TOTAL	2	3	3	0	0	1	1

NAVY

	Yrs	W	L	Ch.	2nd	F-4	F-8
Carnevale, Ben—1947, 1953, 1954, 1959, 1960	5	4	6	0	0	0	0
Evans, Paul—1985, 86 (F-8)	2	4	2	0	0	0	1
Hermann, Pete—1987	1	0	1	0	0	0	0
TOTAL	8	8	9	0	0	0	1

NEBRASKA

	Yrs	W	L	Ch.	2nd	F-4	F-8
Iba, Moe—1986	1	0	1	0	0	0	0
TOTAL	1	0	1	0	0	0	0

NEVADA-RENO

	Yrs	W	L	Ch.	2nd	F-4	F-8
Allen, Sonny—1984, 1985	2	0	2	0	0	0	0
TOTAL	2	0	2	0	0	0	0

NEW MEXICO

	Yrs	W	L	Ch.	2nd	F-4	F-8
Ellenberger, Norm—1974, 1978	2	2	2	0	0	0	0
King, Bob—1968	1	0	2	0	0	0	0
TOTAL	3	2	4	0	0	0	0

NEW MEXICO STATE

	Yrs	W	L	Ch.	2nd	F-4	F-8
Askew, Presley—1959, 1960	2	0	2	0	0	0	0
Hayes, Ken—1979	1	0	1	0	0	0	0
Henson, Lou—1967, 1968, 1969, 70 (F-4), 1971, 1975	6	7	7	0	0	1	1
McCarthy, George—1952	1	0	2	0	0	0	0
McCarthy, Neil—1990	1	0	1	0	0	0	0
TOTAL	11	7	13	0	0	1	1

NEW ORLEANS

	Yrs	W	L	Ch.	2nd	F-4	F-8
Dees, Benny—1987	1	1	1	0	0	0	0
TOTAL	1	1	1	0	0	0	0

NIAGARA

	Yrs	W	L	Ch.	2nd	F-4	F-8
Layden, Frank—1970	1	1	2	0	0	0	0
TOTAL	1	1	2	0	0	0	0

NORTH TEXAS

	Yrs	W	L	Ch.	2nd	F-4	F-8
Gales, Jimmy—1988	1	0	1	0	0	0	0
TOTAL	1	0	1	0	0	0	0

NORTHEAST LA.

	Yrs	W	L	Ch.	2nd	F-4	F-8
Vining, Mike—1982, 1986, 1990	3	0	3	0	0	0	0
TOTAL	3	0	3	0	0	0	0

NORTHEASTERN

	Yrs	W	L	Ch.	2nd	F-4	F-8
Calhoun, Jim—1981, 1982, 1984, 1985, 1986	5	3	5	0	0	0	0
Fogel, Karl—1987	1	0	1	0	0	0	0
TOTAL	6	3	6	0	0	0	0

NORTHERN ILLINOIS

	Yrs	W	L	Ch.	2nd	F-4	F-8
McDougal, John—1982	1	0	1	0	0	0	0
TOTAL	1	0	1	0	0	0	0

NORTHERN IOWA

	Yrs	W	L	Ch.	2nd	F-4	F-8
Miller, Eldon—1990	1	1	1	0	0	0	0
TOTAL	1	1	1	0	0	0	0

NOTRE DAME

	Yrs	W	L	Ch.	2nd	F-4	F-8
Dee, Johnny—1965, 1969, 1970, 1971	4	2	6	0	0	0	0
Jordan, John—1953, 1954, 1957, 58 (F-8), 1960, 1963	6	8	6	0	0	0	1
Phelps, Digger—1974, 1975, 1976, 1977, 78 (F-4), 79 (F-8), 1980, 1981, 1985, 1986, 1987, 1988, 1989, 1990	14	15	16	0	0	1	2
TOTAL	24	25	28	0	0	1	3

NYU

	Yrs	W	L	Ch.	2nd	F-4	F-8
Cann, Howard—1943, 45 (2), 1946	3	3	4	0	1	0	1
Rossini, Lou—60 (F-4), 1962, 1963	3	6	5	0	0	1	1
TOTAL	6	9	9	0	1	1	2

OHIO

	Yrs	W	L	Ch.	2nd	F-4	F-8
Nee, Danny—1983, 1985	2	1	2	0	0	0	0
Snyder, James—1960, 1961, 64 (F-8), 1965, 1970, 1972, 1974	7	3	8	0	0	0	1
TOTAL	9	4	10	0	0	0	1

OHIO STATE

	Yrs	W	L	Ch.	2nd	F-4	F-8
Ayers, Randy—1990	1	1	1	0	0	0	0
Dye, Tippy—1950	1	1	1	0	0	0	0
Miller, Eldon—1980, 1982, 1983, 1985	4	3	4	0	0	0	0
Olsen, Harold—39 (2), 44 (F-8), 45 (F-8), 46 (F-8)	4	6	4	0	1	0	4
Taylor, Fred—60 (Ch.), 61 (2), 62 (2), 68 (F-4), 71 (F-8)	5	14	4	1	2	1	5
Williams, Gary—1987	1	1	1	0	0	0	0
TOTAL	16	26	15	1	3	1	9

OKLAHOMA

	Yrs	W	L	Ch.	2nd	F-4	F-8
Bliss, Dave—1979	1	1	1	0	0	0	0
Drake, Bruce—39 (F-8), 1943, 47 (2)	3	4	3	0	1	0	2
Tubbs, Billy—1983, 1984, 85 (F-8), 1986, 1987, 88 (2), 1989, 1990	8	15	8	0	1	0	2
TOTAL	12	20	12	0	2	0	4

OKLAHOMA CITY

	Yrs	W	L	Ch.	2nd	F-4	F-8
Lemons, Abe—56 (F-8), 57 (F-8), 1963, 1964, 1965, 1966, 1973	7	7	8	0	0	0	2
Parrack, Doyle—1952, 1953, 1954, 1955	4	1	5	0	0	0	0
TOTAL	11	8	13	0	0	0	2

OKLAHOMA STATE/A&M*

	Yrs	W	L	Ch.	2nd	F-4	F-8
Hansen, Paul—1983	1	0	1	0	0	0	0
Iba, Henry—45 (Ch.), 46 (Ch.), 49 (2), 51 (F-8), 1953, 1954, 58 (F-8), 65 (F-8)	8	15	7	2	1	0	6
TOTAL	9	15	8	2	1	0	6

OLD DOMINION

	Yrs	W	L	Ch.	2nd	F-4	F-8
Webb, Paul—1980, 1982, 1985	3	0	3	0	0	0	0
Young, Tom—1986	1	1	1	0	0	0	0
TOTAL	4	1	4	0	0	0	0

ORAL ROBERTS

	Yrs	W	L	Ch.	2nd	F-4	F-8
Acres, Dick—1984	1	0	1	0	0	0	0
Trickey, Ken—74 (F-8)	1	2	1	0	0	0	1
TOTAL	2	2	2	0	0	0	1

OREGON

	Yrs	W	L	Ch.	2nd	F-4	F-8
Belko, Steve—60 (F-8), 1961	2	2	2	0	0	0	1
Hobson, Howard—39 (Ch.), 1945	2	4	1	1	0	0	1
TOTAL	4	6	3	1	0	0	2

OREGON STATE

	Yrs	W	L	Ch.	2nd	F-4	F-8
Anderson, Jim—1990	1	0	1	0	0	0	0
Gill, Amory "Slats"—1947, 49 (F-8), 1955, 62 (F-8), 63 (F-8), 1964	6	8	8	0	0	0	3
Miller, Ralph—1975, 1980, 1981, 82 (F-8), 1984, 1985, 1988, 1989	8	3	9	0	0	0	1
Valenti, Paul—66 (F-8)	1	1	1	0	0	0	1
TOTAL	16	12	19	0	0	0	5

PACIFIC

	Yrs	W	L	Ch.	2nd	F-4	F-8
Edwards, Dick—1966, 67 (F-8), 1971	3	2	4	0	0	0	1
Morrison, Stan—1979	1	0	1	0	0	0	0
TOTAL	4	2	5	0	0	0	1

PENN STATE

	Yrs	W	L	Ch.	2nd	F-4	F-8
Egli, John—1955, 1965	2	1	3	0	0	0	0
Gross, Elmer—1952, 54 (F-8)	2	4	3	0	0	0	1
Lawther, John—1942	1	1	1	0	0	0	0
TOTAL	5	6	7	0	0	0	1

PENNSYLVANIA

	Yrs	W	L	Ch.	2nd	F-4	F-8
Dallmar, Howie—1953	1	1	1	0	0	0	0
Daly, Chuck—72 (F-8), 1973, 1974, 1975	4	3	5	0	0	0	1
Harter, Dick—1970, 71 (F-8)	2	2	2	0	0	0	1
Littlepage, Craig—1985	1	0	1	0	0	0	0
Schneider, Tom—1987	1	0	1	0	0	0	0
Weinhauer, Bob—1978, 79 (F-4), 1980, 1982	4	6	5	0	0	1	1
TOTAL	13	12	15	0	0	1	3

PEPPERDINE

	Yrs	W	L	Ch.	2nd	F-4	F-8
Colson, Gary—1976, 1979	2	2	2	0	0	0	0
Dowell, Duck—1962	1	1	1	0	0	0	0
Duer, Al—1944	1	0	2	0	0	0	0
Harrick, Jim—1982, 1983, 1985, 1986	4	1	4	0	0	0	0
TOTAL	8	4	9	0	0	0	0

PITTSBURGH

	Yrs	W	L	Ch.	2nd	F-4	F-8
Carlson, Harold—41 (F-8)	1	1	1	0	0	0	1
Chipman, Roy—1981, 1982, 1985	3	1	3	0	0	0	0
Evans, Paul—1987, 1988, 1989	3	2	3	0	0	0	0
Ridl, Buzz—74 (F-8)	1	2	1	0	0	0	1
Timmons, Bob—1957, 1958, 1963	3	1	4	0	0	0	0
TOTAL	11	7	12	0	0	0	2

PORTLAND

	Yrs	W	L	Ch.	2nd	F-4	F-8
Negratti, Al—1959	1	0	1	0	0	0	0
TOTAL	1	0	1	0	0	0	0

PRINCETON

	Yrs	W	L	Ch.	2nd	F-4	F-8
Cappon, Franklin—1952, 1955, 1960	3	0	5	0	0	0	0
Carril, Pete—1969, 1976, 1977, 1981, 1983, 1984, 1989, 1990	8	3	8	0	0	0	0
McCandless, Jake—1961	1	1	2	0	0	0	0
Van Breda Kolff, B.—1963, 1964, 65 (F-4), 1967	4	7	5	0	0	1	1
TOTAL	16	11	20	0	0	1	1

PROVIDENCE

	Yrs	W	L	Ch.	2nd	F-4	F-8
Barnes, Rick—1989, 1990	2	0	2	0	0	0	0
Gavitt, Dave—1972, 73 (F-4), 1974, 1977, 1978	5	5	6	0	0	1	1
Mullaney, Joe—1964, 65 (F-8), 1966	3	2	3	0	0	0	1
Pitino, Rick—87 (F-4)	1	4	1	0	0	1	1
TOTAL	11	11	12	0	0	2	3

*Oklahoma State was known as Oklahoma A&M in 1954 and before.

PURDUE

	Yrs	W	L	Ch.	2nd	F-4	F-8
Keady, Gene—1983, 1984, 1985, 1986, 1987, 1988, 1990	7	5	7	0	0	0	0
King, George—69 (2)	1	3	1	0	1	0	1
Rose, Lee—80 (F-4)	1	5	1	0	0	1	1
Schaus, Fred—1977	1	0	1	0	0	0	0
TOTAL	10	13	10	0	1	1	2

RHODE ISLAND

	Yrs	W	L	Ch.	2nd	F-4	F-8
Calverley, Ernie—1961, 1966	2	0	2	0	0	0	0
Kraft, Jack—1978	1	0	1	0	0	0	0
Penders, Tom—1988	1	2	1	0	0	0	0
TOTAL	4	2	4	0	0	0	0

RICE

	Yrs	W	L	Ch.	2nd	F-4	F-8
Brannon, Buster—1940, 1942	2	1	3	0	0	0	0
Knodel, Don—1970	1	0	1	0	0	0	0
Suman, Don—1954	1	1	1	0	0	0	0
TOTAL	4	2	5	0	0	0	0

RICHMOND

	Yrs	W	L	Ch.	2nd	F-4	F-8
Tarrant, Dick—1984, 1986, 1988, 1990	4	4	4	0	0	0	0
TOTAL	4	4	4	0	0	0	0

RIDER

	Yrs	W	L	Ch.	2nd	F-4	F-8
Carpenter, John—1984	1	0	1	0	0	0	0
TOTAL	1	0	1	0	0	0	0

ROBERT MORRIS

	Yrs	W	L	Ch.	2nd	F-4	F-8
Durham, Jarret—1989, 1990	2	0	2	0	0	0	0
Furjanic, Matt—1982, 1983	2	1	2	0	0	0	0
TOTAL	4	1	4	0	0	0	0

RUTGERS

	Yrs	W	L	Ch.	2nd	F-4	F-8
Wenzel, Bob—1989	1	0	1	0	0	0	0
Young, Tom—1975, 76 (F-4), 1979, 1983	4	5	5	0	0	1	1
TOTAL	5	5	6	0	0	1	1

S'WESTERN LA.

	Yrs	W	L	Ch.	2nd	F-4	F-8
Paschal, Bobby—1982, 1983	2	0	2	0	0	0	0
Shipley, Beryl—1972, 1973	2	3	3	0	0	0	0
TOTAL	4	3	5	0	0	0	0

SOUTH CAROLINA

	Yrs	W	L	Ch.	2nd	F-4	F-8
Felton, George—1989	1	0	1	0	0	0	0
McGuire, Frank—1971, 1972, 1973, 1974	4	4	5	0	0	0	0
TOTAL	5	4	6	0	0	0	0

S. CAROLINA STATE

	Yrs	W	L	Ch.	2nd	F-4	F-8
Alexander, Cy—1989	1	0	1	0	0	0	0
TOTAL	1	0	1	0	0	0	0

SAN DIEGO

	Yrs	W	L	Ch.	2nd	F-4	F-8
Brovelli, Jim—1984	1	0	1	0	0	0	0
Egan, Hank—1987	1	0	1	0	0	0	0
TOTAL	2	0	2	0	0	0	0

SAN DIEGO STATE

	Yrs	W	L	Ch.	2nd	F-4	F-8
Gaines, Dave "Smokey"—1985	1	0	1	0	0	0	0
Vezie, Tim—1975, 1976	2	0	2	0	0	0	0
TOTAL	3	0	3	0	0	0	0

SAN FRANCISCO

	Yrs	W	L	Ch.	2nd	F-4	F-8
Barry, Peter—1981, 1982	2	0	2	0	0	0	0
Belluomini, Dan—1979	1	1	1	0	0	0	0
Gaillard, Bob—1972, 73 (F-8), 74 (F-8), 1977, 1978	5	4	5	0	0	0	2
Peletta, Peter—1963, 64 (F-8), 65 (F-8)	3	3	3	0	0	0	2
Woolpert, Phil—55 (Ch.), 56 (Ch.), 57 (F-4), 1958	4	13	2	2	0	1	3
TOTAL	15	21	13	2	0	1	7

SAN JOSE STATE

	Yrs	W	L	Ch.	2nd	F-4	F-8
Berry, Bill—1980	1	0	1	0	0	0	0
McPherson, Walter—1951	1	0	1	0	0	0	0
TOTAL	2	0	2	0	0	0	0

SANTA CLARA

	Yrs	W	L	Ch.	2nd	F-4	F-8
Feerick, Bob—52 (F-8), 1953, 1954, 1960	4	6	6	0	0	0	1
Garibaldi, Dick—68 (F-8), 69 (F-8), 1970	3	3	3	0	0	0	2
Williams, Carroll—1987	1	0	1	0	0	0	0
TOTAL	8	9	10	0	0	0	3

SEATTLE

	Yrs	W	L	Ch.	2nd	F-4	F-8
Boyd, Bob—1964	1	2	1	0	0	0	0
Brightman, Al—1953, 1954, 1955, 1956	4	4	6	0	0	0	0
Buckwalter, Morris—1969	1	0	1	0	0	0	0
Castellani, John—58 (2)	1	4	1	0	1	0	1
Cazzetta, Vince—58 (2), 1961, 1962	3	4	3	0	1	0	1
Markey, Clair—63 (F-4)	1	0	1	0	0	1	0
Purcell, Lionel—1967	1	0	1	0	0	0	0
TOTAL	12	14	14	0	2	1	2

SETON HALL

	Yrs	W	L	Ch.	2nd	F-4	F-8
Carlesimo, P. J.—1988, 89 (2)	2	6	2	0	1	0	1
TOTAL	2	6	2	0	1	0	1

SIENA

	Yrs	W	L	Ch.	2nd	F-4	F-8
Deane, Mike—1989	1	1	1	0	0	0	0
TOTAL	1	1	1	0	0	0	0

SMU

	Yrs	W	L	Ch.	2nd	F-4	F-8
Bliss, Dave—1984, 1985, 1988	3	3	3	0	0	0	0
Hayes, E.O. "Doc"—1955, 56 (F-4), 1957, 1965, 1966, 67 (F-8)	6	7	8	0	0	1	2
TOTAL	9	10	11	0	0	1	2

SOUTH ALABAMA

	Yrs	W	L	Ch.	2nd	F-4	F-8
Arrow, Ronnie—1989	1	1	1	0	0	0	0
Ellis, Cliff—1979, 1980	2	0	2	0	0	0	0
TOTAL	3	1	3	0	0	0	0

SOUTH FLORIDA

	Yrs	W	L	Ch.	2nd	F-4	F-8
Paschal, Bobby—1990	1	0	1	0	0	0	0
TOTAL	1	0	1	0	0	0	0

SOUTHERN ILLINOIS

	Yrs	W	L	Ch.	2nd	F-4	F-8
Lambert, Paul—1977	1	1	1	0	0	0	0
TOTAL	1	1	1	0	0	0	0

SOUTHERN MISS.

	Yrs	W	L	Ch.	2nd	F-4	F-8
Turk, M.K.—1990	1	0	1	0	0	0	0
TOTAL	1	0	1	0	0	0	0

SOUTHERN-B.R.

	Yrs	W	L	Ch.	2nd	F-4	F-8
Hopkins, Robert—1985	1	0	1	0	0	0	0
Jobe, Ben—1987, 1988, 1989	3	0	3	0	0	0	0
Stewart, Carl—1981	1	0	1	0	0	0	0
TOTAL	5	0	5	0	0	0	0

SPRINGFIELD

	Yrs	W	L	Ch.	2nd	F-4	F-8
Hickox, Ed—1940	1	0	1	0	0	0	0
TOTAL	1	0	1	0	0	0	0

ST. BONAVENTURE

	Yrs	W	L	Ch.	2nd	F-4	F-8
Donovan, Eddie—1961	1	2	1	0	0	0	0
Statlin, Jim—1978	1	0	1	0	0	0	0
Weise, Larry—1968, 70 (F-4)	2	4	4	0	0	1	1
TOTAL	4	6	6	0	0	1	1

ST. JOHN'S

	Yrs	W	L	Ch.	2nd	F-4	F-8
Carnesecca, Lou—1967, 1968, 1969, 1976, 1977, 1978, 79 (F-8), 1980, 1982, 1983, 1984, 85 (F-4), 1986, 1987, 1988, 1990	16	14	18	0	0	1	2
Lapchick, Joel—1961	1	0	1	0	0	0	0
McGuire, Frank—1951, 52 (2)	2	5	2	0	1	0	1
Mulzoff, Frank—1973	1	0	1	0	0	0	0
TOTAL	20	19	22	0	1	1	3

ST. JOSEPH'S

	Yrs	W	L	Ch.	2nd	F-4	F-8
Boyle, Jim—1982, 1986	2	1	2	0	0	0	0
Lynam, Jim—81 (F-8)	1	3	1	0	0	0	1
McKinney, Jack—1969, 1971, 1973, 1974	4	0	4	0	0	0	0
Ramsay, Jack—1959, 1960, 61 (F-4), 1962, 63 (F-8), 1965, 1966	7	8	11	0	0	1	2
TOTAL	14	12	18	0	0	1	3

ST. LOUIS

	Yrs	W	L	Ch.	2nd	F-4	F-8
Hickey, Eddie—1952, 1957	2	1	3	0	0	0	0
TOTAL	2	1	3	0	0	0	0

ST. MARY'S

	Yrs	W	L	Ch.	2nd	F-4	F-8
Nance, Lynn—1989	1	0	1	0	0	0	0
Weaver, James—59 (F-8)	1	1	1	0	0	0	1
TOTAL	2	1	2	0	0	0	1

STANFORD

	Yrs	W	L	Ch.	2nd	F-4	F-8
Dean, Everett—42 (Ch.)	1	3	0	1	0	0	1
Montgomery, Mike—1989	1	0	1	0	0	0	0
TOTAL	2	3	1	1	0	0	1

SW MISSOURI STATE

	Yrs	W	L	Ch.	2nd	F-4	F-8
Spoonhour, Charles—1987, 1988, 1989, 1990	4	1	4	0	0	0	0
TOTAL	4	1	4	0	0	0	0

SYRACUSE

	Yrs	W	L	Ch.	2nd	F-4	F-8
Boeheim, Jim—1977, 1978, 1979, 1980, 1983, 1984, 1985, 1986, 87 (2), 1988, 89 (F-8), 1990	12	18	12	0	1	0	2
Danforth, Roy—1973, 1974, 75 (F-4), 1976	4	5	5	0	0	1	1
Guley, Marc—57 (F-8)	1	2	1	0	0	0	1
Lewis, Fred—66 (F-8)	1	1	1	0	0	0	1
TOTAL	18	26	19	0	1	1	5

TCU

	Yrs	W	L	Ch.	2nd	F-4	F-8
Brannon, Buster—1952, 1953, 1959	3	3	3	0	0	0	0
Killingsworth, Jim—1987	1	1	1	0	0	0	0
Swaim, Johnny—68 (F-8), 1971	2	1	2	0	0	0	1
TOTAL	6	5	6	0	0	0	1

TEMPLE

	Yrs	W	L	Ch.	2nd	F-4	F-8
Casey, Don—1979	1	0	1	0	0	0	0
Chaney, John—1984, 1985, 1986, 1987, 88 (F-8), 1990	6	7	6	0	0	0	1
Cody, Josh—1944	1	1	1	0	0	0	0
Litwack, Harry—56 (F-4), 58 (F-4), 1964, 1967, 1970, 1972	6	7	6	0	0	2	2
TOTAL	14	15	14	0	0	2	3

TENN.-CHATT.

	Yrs	W	L	Ch.	2nd	F-4	F-8
Arnold Murray—1981, 1982, 1983	3	1	3	0	0	0	0
McCarthy, Mack—1988	1	0	1	0	0	0	0
TOTAL	4	1	4	0	0	0	0

TENNESSEE

	Yrs	W	L	Ch.	2nd	F-4	F-8
Devoe, Don—1979, 1980, 1981, 1982, 1983, 1989	6	5	6	0	0	0	0
Mears, Ray—1967, 1976, 1977	3	0	4	0	0	0	0
TOTAL	9	5	10	0	0	0	0

TENNESSEE TECH

	Yrs	W	L	Ch.	2nd	F-4	F-8
Oldham, Johnny—1958, 1963	2	0	2	0	0	0	0
TOTAL	2	0	2	0	0	0	0

TEXAS

	Yrs	W	L	Ch.	2nd	F-4	F-8
Black, Leon—1972, 1974	2	1	3	0	0	0	0
Bradley, Harold—1960, 1963	2	2	3	0	0	0	0
Gilstrap, H.C. "Bully"—43 (F-8)	1	1	1	0	0	0	1
Gray, Jack—1939, 47 (F-8)	2	2	3	0	0	0	1
Lemons, Abe—1979	1	0	1	0	0	0	0
Penders, Tom—1989, 90 (F-8)	2	4	2	0	0	0	1
TOTAL	10	10	13	0	0	0	3

TEXAS A&M

	Yrs	W	L	Ch.	2nd	F-4	F-8
Floyd, John—1951	1	0	1	0	0	0	0
Metcalf, Shelby—1964, 1969, 1970, 1975, 1980, 1987	6	3	6	0	0	0	0
TOTAL	7	3	7	0	0	0	0

TEXAS SOUTHERN

	Yrs	W	L	Ch.	2nd	F-4	F-8
Moreland, Bob—1990	1	0	1	0	0	0	0
TOTAL	1	0	1	0	0	0	0

TEXAS TECH

	Yrs	W	L	Ch.	2nd	F-4	F-8
Gibson, Gene—1962	1	1	2	0	0	0	0
Myers, Gerald—1973, 1976, 1985, 1986	4	1	4	0	0	0	0
Robinson, Polk—1954, 1956, 1961	3	1	3	0	0	0	0
TOTAL	8	3	9	0	0	0	0

TEXAS-SAN ANTONIO

	Yrs	W	L	Ch.	2nd	F-4	F-8
Burmeister, Ken—1988	1	0	1	0	0	0	0
TOTAL	1	0	1	0	0	0	0

TOLEDO

	Yrs	W	L	Ch.	2nd	F-4	F-8
Bush, Jerry—1954	1	0	1	0	0	0	0
Nichols, Bob—1967, 1979, 1980	3	1	3	0	0	0	0
TOTAL	4	1	4	0	0	0	0

TOWSON STATE

	Yrs	W	L	Ch.	2nd	F-4	F-8
Truax, Terry—1990	1	0	1	0	0	0	0
TOTAL	1	0	1	0	0	0	0

TRINITY

	Yrs	W	L	Ch.	2nd	F-4	F-8
Polk, Bob—1969	1	0	1	0	0	0	0
TOTAL	1	0	1	0	0	0	0

TUFTS

	Yrs	W	L	Ch.	2nd	F-4	F-8
Cochran, Richard—1945	1	0	2	0	0	0	0
TOTAL	1	0	2	0	0	0	0

TULSA

	Yrs	W	L	Ch.	2nd	F-4	F-8
Barnett, J. D.—1986, 1987	2	0	2	0	0	0	0
Iba, Clarence—1955	1	1	1	0	0	0	0
Richardson, Nolan—1982, 1984, 1985	3	0	3	0	0	0	0
TOTAL	6	1	6	0	0	0	0

UC SANTA BARBARA

	Yrs	W	L	Ch.	2nd	F-4	F-8
Pimm, Jerry—1988, 1990	2	1	2	0	0	0	0
TOTAL	2	1	2	0	0	0	0

UCLA

	Yrs	W	L	Ch.	2nd	F-4	F-8
Bartow, Gene—76 (F-4), 1977	2	5	2	0	0	1	1
Brown, Larry—80 (2), 1981	2	5	2	0	1	0	1
Cunningham, Gary—1978, 79 (F-8)	2	3	2	0	0	0	1
Farmer, Larry—1983	1	0	1	0	0	0	0
Harrick, Jim—1989, 1990	2	3	2	0	0	0	0
Hazzard, Walt—1987	1	1	1	0	0	0	0
Wooden, John—1950, 1952, 1956, 62 (F-4), 1963, 64 (Ch.), 65 (Ch.), 67 (Ch.), 68 (Ch.), 69 (Ch.), 70 (Ch.), 71 (Ch.), 72 (Ch.), 73 (F-4), 74 (F-4), 75 (Ch.)	16	47	10	9	0	3	12
TOTAL	26	64	20	9	1	4	15

U. CONN.

	Yrs	W	L	Ch.	2nd	F-4	F-8
Calhoun, Jim—90 (F-8)	1	3	1	0	0	0	1
Greer, Hugh—1951, 1954, 1956, 1957, 1958, 1959, 1960	7	1	8	0	0	0	0
Perno, Dom—1979	1	0	1	0	0	0	0
Rowe, Dee—1976	1	1	1	0	0	0	0
Shabel, Fred—64 (F-8), 1965, 1967	3	2	3	0	0	0	1
Wigton, George—1963	1	0	1	0	0	0	0
TOTAL	14	7	15	0	0	0	2

U. MASS.

	Yrs	W	L	Ch.	2nd	F-4	F-8
Zunic, Matt—1962	1	0	1	0	0	0	0
TOTAL	1	0	1	0	0	0	0

UNLV

	Yrs	W	L	Ch.	2nd	F-4	F-8
Tarkanian, Jerry—1975, 1976, 77 (F-4), 1983, 1984, 1985, 1986, 87 (F-4), 1988, 89 (F-8), 90 (Ch.)	11	26	10	1	0	2	4
TOTAL	11	26	10	1	0	2	4

USC

	Yrs	W	L	Ch.	2nd	F-4	F-8
Barry, Sam—40 (F-8)	1	1	1	0	0	0	1
Boyd, Bob—1979	1	1	1	0	0	0	0
Morrison, Stan—1982, 1985	2	0	2	0	0	0	0
Twogood, Forrest—54 (F-8), 1960, 1961	3	3	5	0	0	0	1
TOTAL	7	5	9	0	0	0	2

UTAH

	Yrs	W	L	Ch.	2nd	F-4	F-8
Archibald, Lynn—1986	1	0	1	0	0	0	0
Gardner, Jack—1955, 56 (F-8), 1959, 1960, 61 (F-4), 66 (F-4)	6	8	9	0	0	2	3
Peterson, Vadal—44 (Ch.), 1945	2	3	2	1	0	0	1
Pimm, Jerry—1977, 1978, 1979, 1981, 1983	5	5	5	0	0	0	0
TOTAL	14	16	17	1	0	2	4

UTAH STATE

	Yrs	W	L	Ch.	2nd	F-4	F-8
Anderson, Ladell—1962, 1963, 1964, 70 (F-8), 1971	5	4	7	0	0	0	1
Belnap, Dutch—1975, 1979	2	0	2	0	0	0	0
Romney, Dick—1939	1	1	1	0	0	0	0
Tueller, Rod—1980, 1983, 1988	3	0	3	0	0	0	0
TOTAL	11	5	13	0	0	0	1

UTEP/TEXAS WESTERN*

	Yrs	W	L	Ch.	2nd	F-4	F-8
Haskins, Don—1963, 1964, 66 (Ch.), 1967, 1970, 1975, 1984, 1985, 1986, 1987, 1988, 1989, 1990	13	12	12	1	0	0	1
TOTAL	13	12	12	1	0	0	1

VA. COMMONWEALTH

	Yrs	W	L	Ch.	2nd	F-4	F-8
Barnett, J. D.—1980, 1981, 1983, 1984, 1985	5	4	5	0	0	0	0
TOTAL	5	4	5	0	0	0	0

VANDERBILT

	Yrs	W	L	Ch.	2nd	F-4	F-8
Newton, C.M.—1988, 1989	2	2	2	0	0	0	0
Skinner, Roy—65 (F-8), 1974	2	1	3	0	0	0	1
TOTAL	4	3	5	0	0	0	1

VILLANOVA

	Yrs	W	L	Ch.	2nd	F-4	F-8
Kraft, Jack—62 (F-8), 1964, 1969, 70 (F-8), 71 (2), 72 (2)	6	11	7	0	2	0	3
Massimino, Rollie—78 (F-8), 1980, 1981, 82 (F-8), 83 (F-8), 1984, 85 (Ch.), 1986, 88 (F-8), 1990	10	19	9	1	0	0	5
Severance, Alex—39 (F-8), 1949, 1951, 1955	4	4	4	0	0	0	1
TOTAL	20	34	20	1	2	0	9

VIRGINIA

	Yrs	W	L	Ch.	2nd	F-4	F-8
Holland, Terry—1976, 81 (F-4), 1982, 83 (F-8), 84 (F-4), 1986, 1987, 89 (F-8), 1990	9	15	9	0	0	2	4
TOTAL	9	15	9	0	0	2	4

VIRGINIA TECH

	Yrs	W	L	Ch.	2nd	F-4	F-8
DeVoe, Don—1976	1	0	1	0	0	0	0
Moir, Charles—1979, 1980, 1985, 1986	4	2	4	0	0	0	0
Shannon, Howard—67 (F-8)	1	2	1	0	0	0	1
TOTAL	6	4	6	0	0	0	1

VMI

	Yrs	W	L	Ch.	2nd	F-4	F-8
Blair, Bill—76 (F-8)	1	2	1	0	0	0	1
Miller, Weenie—1964	1	0	1	0	0	0	0
Schmaus, Charlie—1977	1	1	1	0	0	0	0
TOTAL	3	3	3	0	0	0	1

WAKE FOREST

	Yrs	W	L	Ch.	2nd	F-4	F-8
Greason, Murray—1939, 1953	2	1	2	0	0	0	0
McKinney, Bones—61 (F-8), 62 (F-4)	2	6	2	0	0	1	2
Tacy, Carl—77 (F-8), 1981, 1982, 84 (F-8)	4	5	4	0	0	0	2
TOTAL	8	12	8	0	0	1	4

WASHINGTON

	Yrs	W	L	Ch.	2nd	F-4	F-8
Dye, Tippy—1951, 53 (F-8)	2	5	2	0	0	0	1
Edmunson, Hec—1943	1	0	2	0	0	0	0
Harshman, Marv—1976, 1984, 1985	3	2	3	0	0	0	0
McLarney, Art—1948	1	1	1	0	0	0	0
Russo, Andy—1986	1	0	1	0	0	0	0
TOTAL	8	8	9	0	0	0	1

WASHINGTON STATE

	Yrs	W	L	Ch.	2nd	F-4	F-8
Friel, Jack—41 (F-8)	1	2	1	0	0	0	1
Raveling, George—1980, 1983	2	1	2	0	0	0	0
TOTAL	3	3	3	0	0	0	1

WAYNE STATE

	Yrs	W	L	Ch.	2nd	F-4	F-8
Mason, Joel—1956	1	1	2	0	0	0	0
TOTAL	1	1	2	0	0	0	0

WEBER STATE

	Yrs	W	L	Ch.	2nd	F-4	F-8
Johnson, Phil—1969, 1970, 1971	3	2	3	0	0	0	0
McCarthy, Neil—1978, 1979, 1980, 1983	4	1	4	0	0	0	0
Motta, Dick—1968	1	0	1	0	0	0	0
Visscher, Gene—1972, 1973	2	1	3	0	0	0	0
TOTAL	10	4	11	0	0	0	0

WEST TEXAS STATE

	Yrs	W	L	Ch.	2nd	F-4	F-8
Mill, Gus—1955	1	0	1	0	0	0	0
TOTAL	1	0	1	0	0	0	0

WEST VIRGINIA

	Yrs	W	L	Ch.	2nd	F-4	F-8
Catlett, Gale—1982, 1983, 1984, 1986, 1987, 1989	6	3	6	0	0	0	0
King, George—1962, 1963, 1965	3	2	3	0	0	0	0
Schaus, Fred—1955, 1956, 1957, 1958, 59 (F-8), 1960	6	6	6	0	0	0	1
Waters, Bucky—1967	1	0	1	0	0	0	0
TOTAL	16	11	16	0	0	0	1

WESTERN KENTUCKY

	Yrs	W	L	Ch.	2nd	F-4	F-8
Arnold, Murray—1987	1	1	1	0	0	0	0
Diddle, Ed—1940, 1960, 1962	3	3	4	0	0	0	0
Haskins, Clem—1981, 1986	2	1	2	0	0	0	0
Keady, Gene—1980	1	0	1	0	0	0	0
Oldham, Johnny—1966, 1967, 1970, 71 (F-4)	4	6	4	0	0	1	1
Richards, Jim—1976, 1978	2	1	2	0	0	0	0
TOTAL	13	12	14	0	0	1	1

*The University of Texas at El Paso was known as Texas Western before 1967.

WESTERN MICHIGAN

	Yrs	W	L	Ch.	2nd	F-4	F-8
Miller, Eldon—1976	1	1	1	0	0	0	0
TOTAL	1	1	1	0	0	0	0

WICHITA STATE

	Yrs	W	L	Ch.	2nd	F-4	F-8
Fogler, Eddie—1987, 1988	2	0	2	0	0	0	0
Miller, Harry—1976	1	0	1	0	0	0	0
Miller, Ralph—64 (F-8)	1	1	1	0	0	0	1
Smithson, Gene—81 (F-8), 1985	2	3	2	0	0	0	1
Thompson, Gary—65 (F-4)	1	2	2	0	0	1	1
TOTAL	7	6	8	0	0	1	3

WILLIAMS

	Yrs	W	L	Ch.	2nd	F-4	F-8
Shaw, Alex—1955	1	0	1	0	0	0	0
TOTAL	1	0	1	0	0	0	0

WISCONSIN

	Yrs	W	L	Ch.	2nd	F-4	F-8
Foster, Bud—41 (F-8), 1947	2	4	1	0	0	0	1
TOTAL	2	4	1	0	0	0	1

WYOMING

	Yrs	W	L	Ch.	2nd	F-4	F-8
Brandenburg, Jim—1981, 1982, 1987	3	4	3	0	0	0	0
Dees, Benny—1988	1	0	1	0	0	0	0
Shelton, Everett—1941, 43 (Ch.), 1947, 1948, 1949, 1952, 1953, 1958	8	4	12	1	0	0	1
Strannigan, Bill—1967	1	0	2	0	0	0	0
TOTAL	13	8	18	1	0	0	1

XAVIER (OHIO)

	Yrs	W	L	Ch.	2nd	F-4	F-8
Gillen, Pete—1986, 1987, 1988, 1989, 1990	5	3	5	0	0	0	0
McCafferty, Jim—1961	1	0	1	0	0	0	0
Staak, Bob—1983	1	0	1	0	0	0	0
TOTAL	7	3	7	0	0	0	0

YALE

	Yrs	W	L	Ch.	2nd	F-4	F-8
Hobson, Howard—1949	1	0	2	0	0	0	0
Vancisin, Joe—1957, 1962	2	0	2	0	0	0	0
TOTAL	3	0	4	0	0	0	0

This section is divided into two parts, the first covering players' records and the second concerning team records. These records have been derived from the box score data found in Part 1 (except for team won-lost and appearance records, which are based on the first section of Part 3). As in the Part 1 Year-by-Year Records, the All-Time Records found here have been compiled to be as accurate and complete as possible. However, since they are based on *available* information, they do not include, for example: Bill Russell's rebounds per game, Oscar Robertson's assists, Lew Alcindor's blocked shots, and other performances of individuals and teams that would, in all likelihood, be among all-time leading performances *if statistics were available*.

INDIVIDUAL PERFORMANCES

⭐ SCORING

Most points in a game
1. AUSTIN CARR, NOTRE DAME (vs. OHIO, 1970)61
2. BILL BRADLEY, PRINCETON (vs. WICHITA STATE, 1965) 58
3. OSCAR ROBERTSON, CINCINNATI (vs. ARKANSAS, 1958) 56
4. AUSTIN CARR, NOTRE DAME (vs. KENTUCKY, 1970) 52
4. AUSTIN CARR, NOTRE DAME (vs. TCU, 1971) 52

Most points in a Final Four game
1. BILL WALTON, UCLA (vs. MEMPHIS STATE, 1973) 44
2. GAIL GOODRICH, UCLA (vs. MICHIGAN, 1965) 42
3. JACK GIVENS, KENTUCKY (vs. DUKE, 1978) 41
4. AL WOOD, N. CAROLINA (vs. VIRGINIA, 1981)39
5. 3 tied for fifth place.

Most points in a championship game
1. BILL WALTON, UCLA (vs. MEMPHIS STATE, 1973) 44
2. GAIL GOODRICH, UCLA (vs. MICHIGAN, 1965) 42
3. JACK GIVENS, KENTUCKY (vs. DUKE, 1978) 41
4. LEW ALCINDOR, UCLA (vs. PURDUE, 1969) 37
5. JOHN MORTON, SETON HALL (vs. MICHIGAN, 1989) 35

Most points in a tournament
1. GLEN RICE, MICHIGAN (1989) 184
2. BILL BRADLEY, PRINCETON (1965) 177
3. ELVIN HAYES, HOUSTON (1968) 167
4. DANNY MANNING, KANSAS (1988) 163
5. 2 tied for fifth place.

Most points in a career
1. ELVIN HAYES, HOUSTON 358
2. DANNY MANNING, KANSAS (1965) 328
3. OSCAR ROBERTSON, CINCINNATI (1961) 324
4. GLEN RICE, MICHIGAN (1951) 308
5. LEW ALCINDOR, UCLA (1981, 1982, 1983) 304

Highest scoring average in a tournament
1. AUSTIN CARR, NOTRE DAME (1970) (158-3) 52.67
2. OSCAR ROBERTSON, CINCINNATI (1958) (86-2) 43.00
3. AUSTIN CARR, NOTRE DAME (1971) (125-3) 41.67
4. OLLIE JOHNSON, SAN FRANCISCO (1965) (72-2) 36.00
4. DAN ISSEL, KENTUCKY (1970) (72-2) 36.00

Highest scoring average in a career
1. AUSTIN CARR, NOTRE DAME (1984) (289-7) 41.29
2. BILL BRADLEY, PRINCETON (1985) (303-9) 33.67
3. OSCAR ROBERTSON, CINCINNATI (1961) (324-10) 32.40
4. JERRY WEST, WEST VIRGINIA (1958, 1959, 1960) (275-9) 30.56
5. BOB PETTIT, LOUISIANA ST. (1953, 1954) (183-6) 30.50

⭐ FIELD GOALS

Most field goals in a game
1. AUSTIN CARR, NOTRE DAME (vs. OHIO, 1970)25
2. AUSTIN CARR, NOTRE DAME (vs. KENTUCKY, 1970) 22
2. BILL BRADLEY, PRINCETON (vs. WICHITA STATE, 1965) 22
2. DAVID ROBINSON, NAVY (vs. MICHIGAN, 1987) 22
5. 3 tied for fifth place.

Most field goals in a Final Four game
1. BILL WALTON, UCLA (vs. MEMPHIS STATE, 1973) 21
2. JACK GIVENS, KENTUCKY (vs. DUKE, 1978) 18
3. DON MAY, DAYTON (vs. N. CAROLINA, 1967) 16
3. LARRY BIRD, INDIANA STATE (vs. DEPAUL, 1979) 16
5. 4 tied for fifth place.

Most field goals in a championship game
1. BILL WALTON, UCLA (vs. MEMPHIS STATE, 1973) 21
2. JACK GIVENS, KENTUCKY (vs. DUKE, 1978) 18
3. LEW ALCINDOR, UCLA (vs. PURDUE, 1969) 15
3. LEW ALCINDOR, UCLA (vs. N. CAROLINA, 1968) 15
5. 4 tied for fifth place.

Most field goals in a tournament
1. GLEN RICE, MICHIGAN (1989) 75
2. ELVIN HAYES, HOUSTON (1968) 70
3. DANNY MANNING, KANSAS (1988) 69
4. AUSTIN CARR, NOTRE DAME (1970) 68
5. JOHNNY DAWKINS, DUKE (1986) 66

Most field goals in a career
1. ELVIN HAYES, HOUSTON (1966, 1967, 1968) 152
2. DANNY MANNING, KANSAS (1985, 1986, 1987, 1988) 140

3. GLEN RICE, MICHIGAN (1986, 1987, 1988, 1989) 128
4. OSCAR ROBERTSON, CINCINNATI (1958, 1959, 1960) 117
4. AUSTIN CARR, NOTRE DAME (1969, 1970, 1971) 117

Most field goal attempts in a game
1. AUSTIN CARR, NOTRE DAME (vs. OHIO, 1970)44
2. DWIGHT LAMAR, S'WESTERN LA. (vs. LOUISVILLE, 1972) 42
2. LENNIE ROSENBLUTH, N. CAROLINA (vs. MICHIGAN ST., 1957) 42
4. AUSTIN CARR, NOTRE DAME (vs. HOUSTON, 1971) 40
5. AUSTIN CARR, NOTRE DAME (vs. IOWA, 1970) 39

Most field goal attempts in a Final Four game
1. LENNIE ROSENBLUTH, N. CAROLINA (vs. MICHIGAN ST., 1957) 42
2. RICK MOUNT, PURDUE (vs. UCLA, 1969) 36
2. ERNIE DIGREGORIO, PROVIDENCE (vs. MEMPHIS STATE, 1973) 36
4. JIM DUNN, WESTERN KY. (vs. VILLANOVA, 1971) 33
5. ELGIN BAYLOR, SEATTLE (vs. KENTUCKY, 1958) 32

Most field goal attempts in a championship game
1. RICK MOUNT, PURDUE (vs. UCLA, 1969) 36
2. ELGIN BAYLOR, SEATTLE (vs. KENTUCKY, 1958) 32
3. KEVIN GREVEY, KENTUCKY (vs. UCLA, 1975) 30
4. ARTIS GILMORE, JACKSONVILLE (vs. UCLA, 1970) 29
4. BILL SPIVEY, KENTUCKY (vs. KANSAS STATE, 1951) 29

Most field goal attempts in a tournament
1. JIM MCDANIELS, WESTERN KY. (1971) 138
2. ELVIN HAYES, HOUSTON (1968) 137
3. GLEN RICE, MICHIGAN (1989) 131
4. DANNY MANNING, KANSAS (1988) 125
5. LENNIE ROSENBLUTH, N. CAROLINA (1957) 124

Most field goal attempts in a career
1. ELVIN HAYES, HOUSTON (1966, 1967, 1968) 310
2. DANNY MANNING, KANSAS (1985, 1986, 1987, 1988) 257
3. OSCAR ROBERTSON, CINCINNATI (1958, 1959, 1960) 235

4 AUSTIN CARR, NOTRE DAME (1969, 1970,
1971) 225
5 GLEN RICE, MICHIGAN (1986, 1987, 1988,
1989) 224

Highest field goal percentage in a game (minimum 10 attempts)
1 KENNY WALKER, KENTUCKY (vs. WESTERN KY.,
1986) (11-11) 1.000
2 MARVIN BARNES, PROVIDENCE (vs.
PENNSYLVANIA, 1973) (10-10) 1.000
3 BILL WALTON, UCLA (vs. MEMPHIS STATE,
1973) (21-22) .955
4 DENNY HOLMAN, SMU (vs. CINCINNATI, 1966)
(12-13) .923
5 PEMBROKE BURROWS, JACKSONVILLE
(vs. IOWA, 1970) (11-12) .917

Highest field goal percentage in a Final Four game (minimum 10 attempts)
1 BILL WALTON, UCLA (vs. MEMPHIS STATE,
1973) (21-22) .955
2 JERRY LUCAS, OHIO STATE (vs. ST. JOSEPH'S,
1961) (10-11) .909
2 BILLY THOMPSON, LOUISVILLE (vs.
LOUISIANA ST. 1986) (10-11) .909
4 EARVIN JOHNSON, MICHIGAN ST. (vs.
PENNSYLVANIA, 1979) (9-10) .900
5 BILL WALTON, UCLA (vs. LOUISVILLE, 1972)
(11-13) .846

Highest field goal percentage in a championship game (minimum 10 attempts)
1 BILL WALTON, UCLA (vs. MEMPHIS STATE,
1973) (21-22) .955
2 OLIVER DARDEN, MICHIGAN (vs. UCLA, 1965)
(8-10) .800
3 JAMES WORTHY, N. CAROLINA (vs.
GEORGETOWN, 1982) (13-17) .765
4 LEW ALCINDOR, UCLA (vs. PURDUE, 1969)
(15-20) .750
5 ANDERSON HUNT, UNLV (vs. DUKE, 1990)
(12-16) .750

Highest field goal percentage in a tournament (minimum 25 attempts, since 1963)
1 CHRISTIAN LAETTNER, DUKE (1989) (26-33)
.788
2 HEYWARD DOTSON, COLUMBIA (1968) (22-28)
.786
3 KEVIN GAMBLE, IOWA (1987) (32-41) .781
4 M. DRESSLER, MISSOURI (1980) (27-35) .771
5 REGGIE LEWIS, NORTHEASTERN (1984) (23-30)
.767

Highest field goal percentage in a career (minimum 50 attempts, since 1963)
1 STEVE SCHALL, ARKANSAS (1977, 1978, 1979)
(41-58) .707
2 JOHN SHUMATE, NOTRE DAME (1974) (35-50)
.700
3 BILL WALTON, UCLA (1972, 1973, 1974)
(109-159) .686
4 STEPHEN THOMPSON, SYRACUSE (1987, 1988,
1989, 1990) (78-114) .684
5 ROBERT MILLER, CINCINNATI (1975, 1976,
1977) (34-50) .680

❂ 3-PT. FIELD GOALS

Most 3-pt. field goals in a game
1 JEFF FRYER, LOYOLA MYMT. (vs. MICHIGAN,
1990) 11
2 FREDDIE BANKS, UNLV (vs. INDIANA, 1987) 10
3 GARDE THOMPSON, MICHIGAN (vs. NAVY, 1987)
9
4 4 tied for fourth place.

Most 3-pt. field goals in a Final Four game
1 FREDDIE BANKS, UNLV (vs. INDIANA, 1987) 10
2 3 tied for second place.

Most 3-pt. field goals in a championship game
1 DAVE SIEGER, OKLAHOMA (vs. KANSAS, 1988) 7
1 STEVE ALFORD, INDIANA (vs. SYRACUSE, 1987)
7
3 GLEN RICE, MICHIGAN (vs. SETON HALL, 1989)
5

Most 3-pt. field goals in a tournament
1 GLEN RICE, MICHIGAN (1989) 27
2 FREDDIE BANKS, UNLV (1987) 26
3 DENNIS SCOTT, GEORGIA TECH (1990) 24
4 JEFF FRYER, LOYOLA MYMT. (1990) 23
5 2 tied for fifth place.

Most 3-pt. field goals in a career
1 JEFF FRYER, LOYOLA MYMT. (1988, 1989,
1990) 38
2 GLEN RICE, MICHIGAN (1986, 1987, 1988,
1989) 35
3 DENNIS SCOTT, GEORGIA TECH (1988, 1989,
1990) 33
4 WILLIAM SCOTT, KANSAS STATE (1987, 1988) 26
4 FREDDIE BANKS, UNLV (1984, 1985, 1986,
1987) 26

Most 3-pt. field goal attempts in a game
1 JEFF FRYER, LOYOLA MYMT. (vs. ARKANSAS,
1989) 22
2 WALKER, VILLANOVA (vs. LOUISIANA ST., 1990)
20
3 GERALD PADDIO, UNLV (vs. IOWA, 1988) 19
3 FREDDIE BANKS, UNLV (vs. INDIANA, 1987) 19
5 2 tied for fifth place.

Most 3-pt. field goal attempts in a Final Four game
1 FREDDIE BANKS, UNLV (vs. INDIANA, 1987) 19
2 DENNIS SCOTT, GEORGIA TECH (vs. UNLV, 1990)
14
3 DAVE SIEGER, OKLAHOMA (vs. KANSAS, 1988)
13

Most 3-pt. field goal attempts in a championship game
1 DAVE SIEGER, OKLAHOMA (vs. KANSAS, 1988)
13
2 JOHN MORTON, SETON HALL (vs. MICHIGAN,
1989) 12
2 GLEN RICE, MICHIGAN (vs. SETON HALL, 1989)
12

Most 3-pt. field goal attempts in a tournament
1 FREDDIE BANKS, UNLV (1987) 65
2 JEFF FRYER, LOYOLA MYMT. (1990) 55
3 DENNIS SCOTT, GEORGIA TECH (1990) 54
4 GLEN RICE, MICHIGAN (1989) 49
5 DAVE SIEGER, OKLAHOMA (1988) 46

Most 3-pt. field goal attempts in a career
1 JEFF FRYER, LOYOLA MYMT. (1988, 1989,
1990) 97

2 DENNIS SCOTT, GEORGIA TECH (1988, 1989,
1990) 76
3 ANDERSON HUNT, UNLV (1989, 1990) 65
3 PHIL HENDERSON, DUKE (1988, 1989, 1990) 65
5 GERALD PADDIO, UNLV (1987, 1988) 64

Highest 3-pt. field goal percentage in a game

1 MIKE BUCK, MIDDLE TENN. ST. (vs. FLORIDA
STATE, 1989) (6-6) 1.000
2 WILLIAM SCOTT, KANSAS STATE (vs.
DEPAUL, 1988) (7-8) .875
3 6 tied for third place.

Highest 3-pt. field goal percentage in a Final Four game (minimum 6 attempts)
1 STEVE ALFORD, INDIANA (vs. SYRACUSE, 1987)
(7-10) .700
2 ANDERSON HUNT, UNLV (vs. DUKE, 1990) (4-7)
.571
3 ANDERSON HUNT, UNLV (vs. GEORGIA TECH,
1990) (5-9) .556

Highest 3-pt. field goal percentage in a championship game (minimum 6 attempts)
1 STEVE ALFORD, INDIANA (vs. SYRACUSE, 1987)
(7-10) .700
2 ANDERSON HUNT, UNLV (vs. DUKE, 1990) (4-7)
.571
3 DAVE SIEGER, OKLAHOMA (vs. KANSAS, 1988)
(7-13) .538

Highest 3-pt. field goal percentage in a tournament (minimum 12 attempts)
1 GARDE THOMPSON, MICHIGAN (1987) (12-16)
.750
2 BILLY DONOVAN, PROVIDENCE (1987) (14-22)
.636
3 WILLIAM SCOTT, KANSAS STATE (1988) (21-34)
.618
3 STEVE ALFORD, INDIANA (1987) (21-34) .618
5 B.J. ARMSTRONG, IOWA (1989) (8-13) .615

Highest 3-pt. field goal percentage in a career (minimum 20 attempts)
1 WILLIAM SCOTT, KANSAS STATE (1987, 1988)
(26-40) .650
2 BILLY DONOVAN, PROVIDENCE (1987) (14-22)
.636
3 STEVE ALFORD, INDIANA (1984, 1986, 1987)
(21-34) .618
4 T. McCALISTER, OKLAHOMA (1984, 1985, 1986,
1987) (13-22) .591
5 GLEN RICE, MICHIGAN (1986, 1987, 1988,
1989) (35-62) .565

❂ FREE THROWS

Most free throws in a game
1 BOB CARNEY, BRADLEY (vs. COLORADO, 1954)
23
1 TRAVIS MAYS, TEXAS (vs. GEORGIA, 1990) 23
3 DAVID ROBINSON, NAVY (vs. SYRACUSE, 1986)
21
4 TOM HAMMONDS, GEORGIA TECH (vs. IOWA
STATE, 1988) 19
5 3 tied for fifth place.

Most free throws in a Final Four game
1 GAIL GOODRICH, UCLA (vs. MICHIGAN, 1965) 18
2 JERRY WEST, WEST VIRGINIA (vs. LOUISVILLE,
1959) 14

3 VERNON HATTON, KENTUCKY (vs. SEATTLE, 1958) 12
3 PAUL HOGUE, CINCINNATI (vs. UCLA, 1962) 12
3 JIM SPANARKEL, DUKE (vs. NOTRE DAME, 1978) 12

Most free throws in a championship game
1 GAIL GOODRICH, UCLA (vs. MICHIGAN, 1965) 18
2 VERNON HATTON, KENTUCKY (vs. SEATTLE, 1958) 12
3 4 tied for third place.

Most free throws in a tournament
1 BOB CARNEY, BRADLEY (1954) 55
2 DON SCHLUNDT, INDIANA (1953) 49
3 BILL BRADLEY, PRINCETON (1965) 47
4 JERRY WEST, WEST VIRGINIA (1959) 46
5 CEDRIC MAXWELL, N.C.-CHARLOTTE (1977) 45

Most free throws in a career
1 OSCAR ROBERTSON, CINCINNATI (1958, 1959, 1960) 90
2 BILL BRADLEY, PRINCETON (1963, 1964, 1965) 87
3 ED PINCKNEY, VILLANOVA (1982, 1983, 1984, 1985) 83
4 JERRY WEST, WEST VIRGINIA (1958, 1959, 1960) 81
5 LEN CHAPPELL, WAKE FOREST (1961, 1962) 77

Most free throw attempts in a game
1 TRAVIS MAYS, TEXAS (vs. GEORGIA, 1990) 27
1 DAVID ROBINSON, NAVY (vs. SYRACUSE, 1986) 27
3 BOB CARNEY, BRADLEY (vs. COLORADO, 1954) 26
4 DONNIE GAUNCE, MOREHEAD STATE (vs. IOWA, 1956) 24
5 3 tied for fifth place.

Most free throw attempts in a Final Four game
1 JERRY WEST, WEST VIRGINIA (vs. LOUISVILLE, 1959) 20
1 GAIL GOODRICH, UCLA (vs. MICHIGAN, 1965) 20
3 BOB CARNEY, BRADLEY (vs. LA SALLE, 1954) 17
3 PAUL HOGUE, CINCINNATI (vs. UCLA, 1962) 17
5 2 tied for fifth place.

Most free throw attempts in a championship game
1 GAIL GOODRICH, UCLA (vs. MICHIGAN, 1965) 20
2 BOB CARNEY, BRADLEY (vs. LA SALLE, 1954) 17
3 WILT CHAMBERLAIN, KANSAS (vs. N. CAROLINA, 1957) 16
4 VERNON HATTON, KENTUCKY (vs. SEATTLE, 1958) 15
5 ED WARNER, CCNY (vs. BRADLEY, 1950) 14

Most free throw attempts in a tournament
1 JERRY WEST, WEST VIRGINIA (1959) 71
2 BOB CARNEY, BRADLEY (1954) 70
3 DON SCHLUNDT, INDIANA (1953) 63
4 LEN CHAPPELL, WAKE FOREST (1962) 62
4 WILT CHAMBERLAIN, KANSAS (1957) 62

Most free throw attempts in a career
1 LEW ALCINDOR, UCLA (1967, 1968, 1969) 119
2 OSCAR ROBERTSON, CINCINNATI (1958, 1959, 1960) 116
3 ED PINCKNEY, VILLANOVA (1982, 1983, 1984, 1985) 115
4 JERRY WEST, WEST VIRGINIA (1958, 1959, 1960) 114
5 LEN CHAPPELL, WAKE FOREST (1961, 1962) 105

Highest free throw percentage in a game (minimum 10 attempts)
1 BILL BRADLEY, PRINCETON (vs. ST. JOSEPH'S, 1963) (16-16) 1.000
1 FENNIS DEMBO, WYOMING (vs. UCLA, 1987) (16-16) 1.000
3 MIKE MALOY, DAVIDSON (vs. ST. JOHN'S, 1969) (13-13) 1.000
3 BILL BRADLEY, PRINCETON (vs. PROVIDENCE, 1965) (13-13) 1.000
3 AL GOODEN, BALL ST. (vs. BOSTON COLLEGE, 1981) (13-13) 1.000

Highest free throw percentage in a Final Four game (minimum 10 attempts)
1 JIM SPANARKEL, DUKE (vs. NOTRE DAME, 1978) (12-12) 1.000
2 RON KING, FLORIDA STATE (vs. N. CAROLINA, 1972) (10-10) 1.000
3 DICK ESTERGARD, BRADLEY (vs. LA SALLE, 1954) (11-12) .917
3 BILL WALTON, UCLA (vs. LOUISVILLE, 1972) (11-12) .917
3 EARVIN JOHNSON, MICHIGAN ST. (vs. PENNSYLVANIA, 1979) (11-12) .917

Highest free throw percentage in a championship game (minimum 10 attempts)
1 DICK ESTERGARD, BRADLEY (vs. LA SALLE, 1954) (11-12) .917
2 GAIL GOODRICH, UCLA (vs. MICHIGAN, 1965) (18-20) .900
3 JOHN MORTON, SETON HALL (vs. MICHIGAN, 1989) (9-10) .900
3 RUMEAL ROBINSON, MICHIGAN (vs. SETON HALL, 1989) (9-10) .900
5 LARRY FINCH, MEMPHIS STATE (vs. UCLA, 1973) (11-13) .846

Highest free throw percentage in a tournament (minimum 20 attempts, since 1960)
1 RICHARD MORGAN, VIRGINIA (1989) (23-23) 1.000
2 SIDNEY MONCRIEF, ARKANSAS (1979) (26-27) .963
3 JEFF LAMP, VIRGINIA (1981) (25-26) .962
4 DWAYNE MCCLAIN, VILLANOVA (1985) (24-25) .960
5 STEVE ALFORD, INDIANA (1984) (21-22) .955

Highest free throw percentage in a career (minimum 30 attempts, since 1960)
1 OLIVER ROBINSON, ALA.-BIRMINGHAM (1981, 1982) (29-30) .967
2 LABRADFORD SMITH, LOUISVILLE (1988, 1989, 1990) (45-47) .957
3 PHIL FORD, N. CAROLINA (1975, 1976, 1977, 1978) (37-39) .949
4 WAYNE ESTES, UTAH STATE (1963, 1964) (29-31) .936
5 DERRICK MCKEY, ALABAMA (1985, 1986, 1987) (28-30) .933

✪ REBOUNDS

Most rebounds in a game
1 FRED COHEN, TEMPLE (vs. U. CONN, 1956) 34
2 NATE THURMOND, BOWLING GREEN (vs. MISSISSIPPI ST., 1963) 31
3 JERRY LUCAS, OHIO STATE (vs. KENTUCKY, 1961) 30
4 THOMAS KIMBALL, U. CONN. (vs. ST. JOSEPH'S, 1965) 29
5 ELVIN HAYES, HOUSTON (vs. PACIFIC, 1966) 28

Most rebounds in a Final Four game
1 BILL RUSSELL, SAN FRANCISCO (vs. IOWA, 1956) 27
2 ELVIN HAYES, HOUSTON (vs. UCLA, 1967) 24
3 BILL RUSSELL, SAN FRANCISCO (vs. SMU, 1956) 23
4 4 tied for fourth place.

Most rebounds in a championship game
1 BILL RUSSELL, SAN FRANCISCO (vs. IOWA, 1956) 27
2 BILL SPIVEY, KENTUCKY (vs. KANSAS STATE, 1951) 21
3 BILL WALTON, UCLA (vs. FLORIDA STATE, 1972) 20
3 LEW ALCINDOR, UCLA (vs. PURDUE, 1969) 20
5 3 tied for fifth place.

Most rebounds in a tournament
1 ELVIN HAYES, HOUSTON (1968) 97
2 ARTIS GILMORE, JACKSONVILLE (1970) 93
3 SAM LACEY, NEW MEXICO ST. (1970) 90
4 CLARENCE GLOVER, WESTERN KY. (1971) 89
5 LEN CHAPPELL, WAKE FOREST (1962) 86

Most rebounds in a career
1 ELVIN HAYES, HOUSTON (1966, 1967, 1968) 226
2 LEW ALCINDOR, UCLA (1967, 1968, 1969) 201
3 JERRY LUCAS, OHIO STATE (1960, 1961, 1962) 197
4 BILL WALTON, UCLA (1972, 1973, 1974) 176
5 PAUL HOGUE, CINCINNATI (1960, 1961, 1962) 160

Most rebounds per game in a tournament (minimum 3 games)
1 NATE THURMOND, BOWLING GREEN (1963) (70-3) 23.333
2 HOWARD JOLLIFF, OHIO (1960) (65-3) 21.667
3 ELVIN HAYES, HOUSTON (1968) (97-5) 19.400
4 JOHN GREEN, MICHIGAN ST. (1957) (77-4) 19.250
5 PAUL SILAS, CREIGHTON (1964) (57-3) 19.000

Most rebounds per game in a career (minimum 6 games)
1 JOHN GREEN, MICHIGAN ST. (1957, 1959) (118-6) 19.667
2 ARTIS GILMORE, JACKSONVILLE (1970, 1971) (115-6) 19.167
3 ELVIN HAYES, HOUSTON (1966, 1967, 1968) (226-13) 17.385
4 LEN CHAPPELL, WAKE FOREST (1961, 1962) (137-8) 17.125
5 LEW ALCINDOR, UCLA (1967, 1968, 1969) (201-12) 16.750

✪ ASSISTS

Most assists in a game
1 MARK WADE, UNLV (vs. INDIANA, 1987) 18
2 JACKIE MEEHAN, NOTRE DAME (vs. OHIO, 1970) 17
3 BERT BERTELKAMP, TENNESSEE (vs. MARYLAND, 1977) 16
4 4 tied for fourth place.

Most assists in a Final Four game
1 MARK WADE, UNLV (vs. INDIANA, 1987) 18
2 GREG LEE, UCLA (vs. MEMPHIS STATE, 1973) 14
2 ANDRE MCCARTER, UCLA (vs. KENTUCKY, 1975) 14
4 LUCIUS ALLEN, UCLA (vs. HOUSTON, 1968) 12
4 RUMEAL ROBINSON, MICHIGAN (vs. ILLINOIS, 1989) 12

Most assists in a championship game
1 GREG LEE, UCLA (vs. MEMPHIS STATE, 1973) 14
1 ANDRE MCCARTER, UCLA (vs. KENTUCKY, 1975) 14
3 REX MORGAN, JACKSONVILLE (vs. UCLA, 1970) 11
3 RUMEAL ROBINSON, MICHIGAN (vs. SETON HALL, 1989) 11
5 CHRIS FORD, VILLANOVA (vs. UCLA, 1971) 10

Most assists in a tournament
1 MARK WADE, UNLV (1987) 61
2 RUMEAL ROBINSON, MICHIGAN (1989) 56
3 EARVIN JOHNSON, MICHIGAN ST. (1979) 50
4 SHERMAN DOUGLAS, SYRACUSE (1987) 49
5 3 tied for fifth place.

Most assists in a career
1 SHERMAN DOUGLAS, SYRACUSE (1986, 1987, 1988, 1989) 106
2 MARK WADE, UNLV (1986, 1987) 93
2 RUMEAL ROBINSON, MICHIGAN (1988, 1989, 1990) 93
4 ANDRE TURNER, MEMPHIS STATE (1983, 1984, 1985, 1986) 87
5 KENNY SMITH, N. CAROLINA (1984, 1985, 1986, 1987) 86

Most assists per game in a tournament (minimum 3 games)
1 MARK WADE, UNLV (1987) (61-5) 12.20
2 MARK WADE, UNLV (1986) (32-3) 10.67
3 EARVIN JOHNSON, MICHIGAN ST. (1979) (50-5) 10.00
4 OSCAR ROBERTSON, CINCINNATI (1959) (39-4) 9.75
4 JOHN CROTTY, VIRGINIA (1989) (39-4) 9.75

Most assists per game in a career (minimum 6 games)
1 MARK WADE, UNLV (1986, 1987) (93-8) 11.63
2 EARVIN JOHNSON, MICHIGAN ST. (1978, 1979) (76-8) 9.50
3 JOHN CROTTY, VIRGINIA (1989, 1990) (56-6) 9.33
4 RUMEAL ROBINSON, MICHIGAN (1988, 1989, 1990) (93-11) 8.46
5 PHILIP BOND, LOUISVILLE (1975, 1977) (49-6) 8.17

✪ BLOCKED SHOTS

Most blocked shots in a game
1 DAVID ROBINSON, NAVY (vs. CLEVELAND ST., 1986) 9
2 TIM PERRY, TEMPLE (vs. LEHIGH, 1988) 8
2 ROOSEVELT BOUIE, SYRACUSE (vs. WESTERN KY., 1978) 8
2 AKEEM OLAJUWON, HOUSTON (vs. LOUISVILLE, 1983) 8
2 AKEEM OLAJUWON, HOUSTON (vs. VILLANOVA, 1983) 8

Most blocked shots in a Final Four game
1 AKEEM OLAJUWON, HOUSTON (vs. LOUISVILLE, 1983) 8
2 TOM BURLESON, N.C. STATE (vs. MARQUETTE, 1974) 7
2 AKEEM OLAJUWON, HOUSTON (vs. N.C. STATE, 1983) 7

Most blocked shots in a championship game
1 TOM BURLESON, N.C. STATE (vs. MARQUETTE, 1974) 7
1 AKEEM OLAJUWON, HOUSTON (vs. N.C. STATE, 1983) 7
3 PAT EWING, GEORGETOWN (vs. HOUSTON, 1984) 4

Most blocked shots in a tournament
1 AKEEM OLAJUWON, HOUSTON (1983) 28
2 DAVID ROBINSON, NAVY (1986) 23
3 TIM PERRY, TEMPLE (1988) 20
4 ALONZO MOURNING, GEORGETOWN (1989) 19
5 AKEEM OLAJUWON, HOUSTON (1984) 18

Most blocked shots in a career
1 AKEEM OLAJUWON, HOUSTON (1982, 1983, 1984) 56
2 PAT EWING, GEORGETOWN (1982, 1983, 1984, 1985) 37
3 TIM PERRY, TEMPLE (1985, 1986, 1987, 1988) 34
4 RONY SEIKALY, SYRACUSE (1985, 1986, 1987, 1988) 33
5 PERVIS ELLISON, LOUISVILLE (1986, 1988, 1989) 32

✪ STEALS

Most steals in a game
1 GARY GARLAND, DEPAUL (vs. USC, 1979) 10
2 ALVIN ROBERTSON, ARKANSAS (vs. PURDUE, 1983) 8
2 ALVIN ROBERTSON, ARKANSAS (vs. VIRGINIA, 1984) 8
4 8 tied for fourth place.

Most steals in a Final Four game
1 MOOKIE BLAYLOCK, OKLAHOMA (vs. KANSAS, 1988) 7
1 TOMMY AMAKER, DUKE (vs. LOUISVILLE, 1986) 7
3 2 tied for third place.

Most steals in a championship game
1 MOOKIE BLAYLOCK, OKLAHOMA (vs. KANSAS, 1988) 7
1 TOMMY AMAKER, DUKE (vs. LOUISVILLE, 1986) 7
3 ROD FOSTER, UCLA (vs. LOUISVILLE, 1980) 6

Most steals in a tournament
1 MOOKIE BLAYLOCK, OKLAHOMA (1988) 23
2 GARY GARLAND, DEPAUL (1979) 22
3 MARK WADE, UNLV (1987) 18

3 LEE MAYBERRY, ARKANSAS (1990) 18
5 KENDALL GILL, ILLINOIS (1989) 17

Most steals in a career
1 MOOKIE BLAYLOCK, OKLAHOMA (1988, 1989) 32
2 CLYDE DREXLER, HOUSTON (1981, 1982, 1983) 29
3 RICKY GRACE, OKLAHOMA (1987, 1988) 28
4 OTHELL WILSON, VIRGINIA (1981, 1982, 1983, 1984) 27
5 2 tied for fifth place.

✪ TURNOVERS

Most turnovers in a game
1 MAURICE WILLIAMSON, LOUISIANA ST. (vs. VILLANOVA, 1990) 13
2 ED FOGLER, N. CAROLINA (vs. DRAKE, 1969) 11
2 LARRY BIRD, INDIANA STATE (vs. DEPAUL, 1979) 11
2 GARY GARLAND, DEPAUL (vs. UCLA, 1979) 11
5 5 tied for fifth place.

Most turnovers in a Final Four game
1 LARRY BIRD, INDIANA STATE (vs. DEPAUL, 1979) 11
2 HERBERT CROOK, LOUISVILLE (vs. DUKE, 1986) 9
3 REX MORGAN, JACKSONVILLE (vs. UCLA, 1970) 8
3 AKEEM OLAJUWON, HOUSTON (vs. VIRGINIA, 1984) 8
3 SIDNEY LOWE, N.C. STATE (vs. GEORGIA, 1983) 8

Most turnovers in a championship game
1 HERBERT CROOK, LOUISVILLE (vs. DUKE, 1986) 9
2 REX MORGAN, JACKSONVILLE (vs. UCLA, 1970) 8
3 5 tied for third place.

Most turnovers in a tournament
1 RUMEAL ROBINSON, MICHIGAN (1989) 26
1 BOBBY HURLEY, DUKE (1990) 26
1 LARRY BIRD, INDIANA STATE (1979) 26
4 SHERMAN DOUGLAS, SYRACUSE (1987) 25
5 4 tied for fifth place.

Most turnovers in a career
1 SHERMAN DOUGLAS, SYRACUSE (1986, 1987, 1988, 1989) 54
2 DANNY MANNING, KANSAS (1985, 1986, 1987, 1988) 51
3 ANDRE TURNER, MEMPHIS STATE (1983, 1984, 1985, 1986) 45
3 KENNY SMITH, N. CAROLINA (1984, 1985, 1986, 1987) 45
3 DANNY FERRY, DUKE (1986, 1987, 1988, 1989) 45

TEAM PERFORMANCES

⭐ SCORING

Most points in a game—one team
1	LOYOLA MYMT. (vs. MICHIGAN, 1990)	149
2	UNLV (vs. LOYOLA MYMT., 1990)	131
3	ST. JOSEPH'S (vs. UTAH, 1961)	127
4	OKLAHOMA (vs. LOUISIANA TECH, 1989)	124
5	N. CAROLINA (vs. LOYOLA MYMT., 1988)	123

Most points in a game—both teams
1	LOYOLA MYMT. (vs. MICHIGAN, 1990)	264
2	ST. JOSEPH'S (vs. UTAH, 1961)	247
3	LOYOLA MYMT. (vs. WYOMING, 1988)	234
4	UNLV (vs. LOYOLA MYMT., 1990)	232
5	IOWA (vs. NOTRE DAME, 1970)	227

Most points in a half—one team
1	LOYOLA MYMT. (vs. MICHIGAN, 1990)	84
2	IOWA (vs. NOTRE DAME, 1970)	75
3	OKLAHOMA (vs. LOUISIANA TECH, 1989)	69
4	ARKANSAS (vs. LOYOLA MYMT., 1989)	68
5	UNLV (vs. LOYOLA MYMT., 1990)	67

Most points in a half—both teams
1	LOYOLA MYMT. (vs. MICHIGAN, 1990)	142
2	IOWA (vs. NOTRE DAME, 1970)	139
3	LOYOLA MYMT. (vs. WYOMING, 1988)	126
4	N. CAROLINA (vs. LOYOLA MYMT., 1988)	122
5	2 tied for fifth place.	

Largest winning margin in a game
1	LOYOLA-CHICAGO (vs. TENNESSEE TECH, 1963)	69
2	UCLA (vs. WYOMING, 1967)	49
2	SYRACUSE (vs. BROWN, 1986)	49
4	DUKE (vs. U. CONN, 1964)	47
4	DEPAUL (vs. EASTERN KY., 1965)	47

Most points in a game by a losing team
1	UTAH (vs. ST. JOSEPH'S, 1961)	120
2	WYOMING (vs. LOYOLA MYMT., 1988)	115
2	MICHIGAN (vs. LOYOLA MYMT., 1990)	115
4	UNLV (vs. ARIZONA, 1976)	109
5	2 tied for fifth place.	

Fewest points in a game—one team
1	N. CAROLINA (vs. PITTSBURGH, 1941)	20
2	SPRINGFIELD (vs. INDIANA, 1940)	24
3	PITTSBURGH (vs. N. CAROLINA, 1941)	26
4	KENTUCKY (vs. DARTMOUTH, 1942)	28
5	2 tied for fifth place.	

Fewest points in a game—both teams
1	PITTSBURGH (vs. N. CAROLINA, 1941)	46
2	DUQUESNE (vs. WESTERN KY., 1940)	59
3	WISCONSIN (vs. PITTSBURGH, 1941)	66
4	INDIANA (vs. DUQUESNE, 1940)	69
5	USC (vs. COLORADO, 1940)	70

Most points in a Final Four game—one team
1	UCLA (vs. WICHITA STATE, 1965)	108
2	UNLV (vs. DUKE, 1990)	103
3	UCLA (vs. HOUSTON, 1968)	101
3	MICHIGAN ST. (vs. PENNSYLVANIA, 1979)	101
5	2 tied for fifth place.	

Most points in a Final Four game—both teams
1	UCLA (vs. WICHITA STATE, 1965)	197
2	INDIANA (vs. UNLV, 1987)	190
3	MEMPHIS STATE (vs. PROVIDENCE, 1973)	183
4	KENTUCKY (vs. DUKE, 1978)	182
5	2 tied for fifth place.	

Largest winning margin in a Final Four game
1	CINCINNATI (vs. OREGON STATE, 1963)	34
1	MICHIGAN ST. (vs. PENNSYLVANIA, 1979)	34
3	UCLA (vs. HOUSTON, 1968)	32
4	UNLV (vs. DUKE, 1990)	30
5	PURDUE (vs. N. CAROLINA, 1969)	27

Most points in a Final Four game by a losing team
1	UNLV (vs. INDIANA, 1987)	93
2	WICHITA STATE (vs. UCLA, 1965)	89
2	WESTERN KY. (vs. VILLANOVA, 1971)	89
4	DUKE (vs. KENTUCKY, 1978)	88
5	NOTRE DAME (vs. DUKE, 1978)	86

Most points in a championship game—one team
1	UNLV (vs. DUKE, 1990)	103
2	UCLA (vs. DUKE, 1964)	98
3	KENTUCKY (vs. DUKE, 1978)	94

Most points in a championship game—both teams
1	KENTUCKY (vs. DUKE, 1978)	182
2	UCLA (vs. DUKE, 1964)	181
3	UCLA (vs. KENTUCKY, 1975)	177

Largest winning margin in a championship game
1	UNLV (vs. DUKE, 1990)	30
2	UCLA (vs. N. CAROLINA, 1968)	23
3	UCLA (vs. MEMPHIS STATE, 1973)	21

Fewest points in a championship game—one team
1	OHIO STATE (vs. OREGON, 1939)	33
2	GEORGETOWN (vs. WYOMING, 1943)	34
2	WASHINGTON ST. (vs. WISCONSIN, 1941)	34

Fewest points in a championship game—both teams
1	WISCONSIN (vs. WASHINGTON ST., 1941)	73
2	OREGON (vs. OHIO STATE, 1939)	79
3	WYOMING (vs. GEORGETOWN, 1943)	80

Most total points in a tournament—one team
1	UNLV (1990)	571
2	OKLAHOMA (1988)	552
3	MICHIGAN (1989)	540
4	INDIANA (1987)	535
5	LOUISVILLE (1986)	513

Most points per game in a tournament (minimum 3 games)
1	LOYOLA MYMT. (1990) (423-4)	105.75
2	NOTRE DAME (1970) (317-3)	105.67
3	UNLV (1977) (505-5)	101.00
4	UCLA (1965) (400-4)	100.00
5	S'WESTERN LA. (1972) (296-3)	98.67

Largest average winning margin in a tournament (minimum 3 games)
1	UCLA (1967) (95-4)	23.75
2	LOYOLA-CHICAGO (1963) (115-5)	23.00

3	INDIANA (1981) (113-5)	22.60
4	UCLA (1968) (85-4)	21.25
5	NOTRE DAME (1974) (63-3)	21.00

Fewest points per game in a tournament (minimum 3 games)
1	WISCONSIN (1941) (126-3)	42.00
2	UTAH (1944) (127-3)	42.33
3	CALIFORNIA (1946) (130-3)	43.33
3	DARTMOUTH (1942) (130-3)	43.33
5	OKLAHOMA STATE (1949) (131-3)	43.67

Most opponents' points per game in a tournament (minimum 3 games)
1	NOTRE DAME (1970) (312-3)	104.00
2	LOYOLA MYMT. (1990) (398-4)	99.50
3	NOTRE DAME (1971) (292-3)	97.33
4	IOWA (1988) (283-3)	94.33
5	ST. BONAVENTURE (1968) (279-3)	93.00

Fewest opponents' points per game in a tournament (minimum 3 games)
1	INDIANA (1940) (96-3)	32.00
2	OKLAHOMA STATE (1946) (104-3)	34.67
3	UTAH (1944) (106-3)	35.33
4	OREGON (1939) (111-3)	37.00
5	WISCONSIN (1941) (114-3)	38.00

⭐ FIELD GOALS

Most field goals in a game—one team
1	IOWA (vs. NOTRE DAME, 1970)	52
2	UCLA (vs. DAYTON, 1974)	51
2	UNLV (vs. LOYOLA MYMT., 1990)	51
4	3 tied for fourth place.	

Most field goal attempts in a game—one team
1	MARSHALL (vs. S'WESTERN LA., 1972)	112
2	INDIANA (vs. MIAMI [OHIO], 1958)	106
3	WESTERN KY. (vs. VILLANOVA, 1971)	105
4	3 tied for fourth place.	

Highest field goal percentage in a game—one team
1	N. CAROLINA (vs. LOYOLA MYMT., 1988) (49-62)	.790
2	VILLANOVA (vs. GEORGETOWN, 1985) (22-28)	.786
3	NORTHEASTERN (vs. VA COMMONWEALTH, 1984) (33-44)	.750
4	GEORGETOWN (vs. OREGON STATE, 1982) (29-39)	.744
5	N.C. STATE (vs. UTEP, 1985) (30-41)	.732

Fewest field goals in a game—one team
1	SPRINGFIELD (vs. INDIANA, 1940)	8
2	PITTSBURGH (vs. N. CAROLINA, 1941)	9
2	N. CAROLINA (vs. PITTSBURGH, 1941)	9
2	OKLAHOMA STATE (vs. KENTUCKY, 1949)	9
5	3 tied for fifth place.	

Fewest field goal attempts in a game—one team
1	BOSTON COLLEGE (vs. U. CONN. 1967)	26
2	KANSAS (vs. OHIO, 1985)	28
2	VILLANOVA (vs. GEORGETOWN, 1985)	28
4	BOSTON COLLEGE (vs. PRINCETON, 1983)	29
4	WICHITA STATE (vs. OKLAHOMA STATE, 1965)	29

Lowest field goal percentage in a game—one team
1	SPRINGFIELD (vs. INDIANA, 1940) (8-63)	.127
2	HARVARD (vs. OHIO STATE, 1946) (10-72)	.139
3	CREIGHTON (vs. CINCINNATI, 1962) (14-72)	.195
4	N.C. STATE (vs. BAYLOR, 1950) (15-77)	.195
5	ARKANSAS (vs. OREGON STATE, 1949) (13-63)	.206

Most field goals in a game—two teams
1	IOWA (vs. NOTRE DAME, 1970)	97
2	KENTUCKY (vs. AUSTIN PEAY, 1973)	96
3	ST. JOSEPH'S (vs. UTAH, 1961)	95
4	LOYOLA MYMT. (vs. MICHIGAN, 1990)	94
5	UCLA (vs. DAYTON, 1974)	91

Most field goal attempts in a game—two teams
1	ST. JOSEPH'S (vs. UTAH, 1961)	204
2	KENTUCKY (vs. AUSTIN PEAY, 1973)	196
3	IOWA (vs. NOTRE DAME, 1970)	195
4	INDIANA (vs. MIAMI (OHIO), 1958)	194
4	HOUSTON (vs. PACIFIC, 1966)	194

Fewest field goals in a game—two teams
1	PITTSBURGH (vs. N. CAROLINA, 1941)	18
2	WISCONSIN (vs. PITTSBURGH, 1941)	22
3	DUQUESNE (vs. WESTERN KY., 1940)	24
3	INDIANA (vs. DUQUESNE, 1940)	24
5	2 tied for fifth place.	

Fewest field goal attempts in a game—two teams (since 1960)
1	N.C. STATE (vs. NEVADA-RENO, 1985)	56
2	BOSTON COLLEGE (vs. U. CONN., 1967)	59
3	GEORGETOWN (vs. WYOMING, 1982)	69
3	FRESNO STATE (vs. WEST VIRGINIA, 1982)	69
5	KANSAS (vs. OHIO, 1985)	70

Lowest field goal percentage in a game—two teams
1	OHIO STATE (vs. HARVARD, 1946) (27-135)	.200
2	INDIANA (vs. SPRINGFIELD, 1940) (27-132)	.205
3	N.C. STATE (vs. BAYLOR, 1950) (31-137)	.226
4	INDIANA (vs. DUQUESNE, 1940) (24-103)	.233
5	N. CAROLINA (vs. OHIO STATE, 1946) (42-180)	.234

Most field goals in a Final Four game—one team
1	UCLA (vs. WICHITA STATE, 1965)	44
2	UCLA (vs. HOUSTON, 1968)	43
3	4 tied for third place.	

Most field goal attempts in a Final Four game
1	WESTERN KY. (vs. VILLANOVA, 1971)	105
2	PURDUE (vs. UCLA, 1969)	92
3	UCLA (vs. WICHITA STATE, 1965)	89
4	TEMPLE (vs. IOWA, 1956)	88
4	N. CAROLINA (vs. MICHIGAN ST., 1957)	88

Highest field goal percentage in a Final Four game
1	VILLANOVA (vs. GEORGETOWN, 1985) (22-28)	.786
2	OHIO STATE (vs. CALIFORNIA, 1960) (31-46)	.674
3	UCLA (vs. MEMPHIS STATE, 1973) (40-62)	.645
4	KANSAS (vs. OKLAHOMA, 1988) (35-55)	.636
5	2 tied for fifth place.	

Fewest field goals in a Final Four game—one team
1	OKLAHOMA STATE (vs. KENTUCKY, 1949)	9
2	KENTUCKY (vs. GEORGETOWN, 1984)	13
2	N. CAROLINA (vs. OKLAHOMA STATE, 1946)	13
4	3 tied for fourth place.	

Fewest field goal attempts in a Final Four game
1	VILLANOVA (vs. GEORGETOWN, 1985)	28
2	VILLANOVA (vs. MEMPHIS STATE, 1985)	38

3	GEORGETOWN (vs. LOUISVILLE, 1982)	41
4	HOUSTON (vs. VIRGINIA, 1984)	42
4	ST. JOHN'S (vs. GEORGETOWN, 1985)	42

Lowest field goal percentage in a Final Four game
1	WASHINGTON ST. (vs. WISCONSIN, 1941) (14-65)	.215
2	BAYLOR (vs. KENTUCKY, 1948) (15-64)	.234
3	KENTUCKY (vs. GEORGETOWN, 1984) (13-53)	.245
4	WISCONSIN (vs. WASHINGTON ST., 1941) (16-63)	.254
5	LOYOLA-CHICAGO (vs. CINCINNATI, 1963) (23-84)	.274

Most field goals in a Final Four game—two teams
1	UCLA (vs. WICHITA STATE, 1965)	80
2	MEMPHIS STATE (vs. PROVIDENCE, 1973)	79
3	VILLANOVA (vs. WESTERN KY., 1971)	75

Most field goal attempts in a Final Four game—two teams
1	VILLANOVA (vs. WESTERN KY., 1971)	178
2	N. CAROLINA (vs. MICHIGAN ST., 1957)	168
3	SAN FRANCISCO (vs. IOWA, 1956)	167

Highest field goal percentage in a Final Four game—two teams (since 1960)
1	VILLANOVA (vs. GEORGETOWN, 1985) (51-81)	.630
2	INDIANA STATE (vs. DEPAUL, 1979) (71-122)	.582
3	GEORGETOWN (vs. HOUSTON, 1984) (65-116)	.560

Fewest field goals in a Final Four game—two teams
1	KENTUCKY (vs. OKLAHOMA STATE, 1949)	25
2	OKLAHOMA STATE (vs. N. CAROLINA, 1946)	29
3	WISCONSIN (vs. WASHINGTON ST., 1941)	30

Fewest field goal attempts in a Final Four game—two teams (since 1960)
1	VILLANOVA (vs. GEORGETOWN, 1985)	81
2	VILLANOVA (vs. MEMPHIS STATE, 1985)	88
3	GEORGETOWN (vs. LOUISVILLE, 1982)	89

Lowest field goal percentage in a Final Four game—two teams
1	WISCONSIN (vs. WASHINGTON ST., 1941) (30-128)	.235
2	KENTUCKY (vs. BAYLOR, 1948) (38-147)	.259
3	N. CAROLINA (vs. MICHIGAN ST., 1957) (51-168)	.304

Most field goals in a championship game—one team
1	UNLV (vs. DUKE, 1990)	41
2	UCLA (vs. MEMPHIS STATE, 1973)	40
3	KENTUCKY (vs. DUKE, 1978)	39

Most field goal attempts in a championship game—one team
1	PURDUE (vs. UCLA, 1969)	92
2	SAN FRANCISCO (vs. IOWA, 1956)	87
3	KENTUCKY (vs. UCLA, 1975)	86
4	LOYOLA-CHICAGO (vs. CINCINNATI, 1963)	84
5	2 tied for fifth place.	

Highest field goal percentage in a championship game—one team
1	VILLANOVA (vs. GEORGETOWN, 1985) (22-28)	.786
2	OHIO STATE (vs. CALIFORNIA, 1960) (31-46)	.674
3	UCLA (vs. MEMPHIS STATE, 1973) (40-62)	.645

Fewest field goals in a championship game—one team
1	OKLAHOMA STATE (vs. KENTUCKY, 1949)	9
2	N. CAROLINA (vs. OKLAHOMA STATE, 1946)	13
3	OHIO STATE (vs. OREGON, 1939)	14
3	GEORGETOWN (vs. WYOMING, 1943)	14
3	WASHINGTON ST. (vs. WISCONSIN, 1941)	14

Fewest field goal attempts in a championship game—one team
1	VILLANOVA (vs. GEORGETOWN, 1985)	28
2	MICHIGAN ST. (vs. INDIANA STATE, 1979)	43
3	2 tied for third place.	

Lowest field goal percentage in a championship game—one team
1	WASHINGTON ST. (vs. WISCONSIN, 1941) (14-65)	.215
2	BAYLOR (vs. KENTUCKY, 1948) (15-64)	.234
3	WISCONSIN (vs. WASHINGTON ST., 1941) (16-63)	.254

Most field goals in a championship game—two teams
1	UCLA (vs. KENTUCKY, 1975)	71
2	UCLA (vs. DUKE, 1964)	68
2	KENTUCKY (vs. DUKE, 1978)	68

Most field goal attempts in a championship game—two teams
1	SAN FRANCISCO (vs. IOWA, 1956)	167
2	UCLA (vs. KENTUCKY, 1975)	164
3	SAN FRANCISCO (vs. LA SALLE, 1955)	151

Highest field goal percentage in a championship game—two teams
1	VILLANOVA (vs. GEORGETOWN, 1985) (51-81)	.630
2	GEORGETOWN (vs. HOUSTON, 1984) (65-116)	.560
3	UCLA (vs. MICHIGAN, 1965) (66-122)	.541

Fewest field goals in a championship game—two teams
1	KENTUCKY (vs. OKLAHOMA STATE, 1949)	25
2	OKLAHOMA STATE (vs. N. CAROLINA, 1946)	29
3	WISCONSIN (vs. WASHINGTON ST., 1941)	30

Fewest field goal attempts in a championship game—two teams
1	VILLANOVA (vs. GEORGETOWN, 1985)	81
2	N. CAROLINA (vs. KANSAS, 1957)	92
3	INDIANA (vs. N. CAROLINA, 1981)	95

Lowest field goal percentage in a championship game—two teams
1	WISCONSIN (vs. WASHINGTON ST., 1941) (30-128)	.235
2	KENTUCKY (vs. BAYLOR, 1948) (38-147)	.259
3	KENTUCKY (vs. KANSAS STATE, 1951) (51-149)	.342

Most field goals in a tournament
1	UNLV (1977)	218
2	UNLV (1990)	217
2	MICHIGAN (1989)	217
4	OKLAHOMA (1988)	206
5	LOUISVILLE (1986)	203

Most field goal attempts in a tournament
1	WESTERN KY. (1971)	442
2	UNLV (1977)	441
3	HOUSTON (1968)	418
4	OKLAHOMA (1988)	412
5	UNLV (1990)	410

Highest field goal percentage in a tournament (minimum 3 games, since 1963)
1	N. CAROLINA (1975) (113-187)	.604
2	MICHIGAN (1988) (96-161)	.596
3	MICHIGAN ST. (1978) (92-156)	.590
4	ALABAMA (1987) (99-169)	.586
5	ARKANSAS (1979) (83-143)	.581

Most field goals per game (minimum 3 games)
1	UNLV (1977) (218-5)	43.600
2	NOTRE DAME (1970) (130-3)	43.333
3	NOTRE DAME (1974) (128-3)	42.667
4	UCLA (1965) (162-4)	40.500
5	S'WESTERN LA. (1972) (119-3)	39.667

Lowest field goal percentage in a tournament (minimum 3 games)
1	CREIGHTON (1962) (71-235)	.302
2	N.C. STATE (1951) (74-230)	.322
3	BOWLING GREEN (1963) (73-222)	.329
4	OKLAHOMA STATE (1951) (76-228)	.334
5	N.C. STATE (1950) (73-218)	.335

Highest opponents' field goal percentage in a tournament (minimum 3 games, since 1963)
1	WAKE FOREST (1977) (101-174)	.581
2	GEORGETOWN (1980) (91-159)	.572
3	VILLANOVA (1978) (105-187)	.562
4	OREGON STATE (1982) (67-121)	.554
5	ST. BONAVENTURE (1968) (112-204)	.549

Most opponents' field goals per game (minimum 3 games)
1	NOTRE DAME (1970) (131-3)	43.67
2	NOTRE DAME (1971) (120-3)	40.00
3	LOYOLA MYMT. (1990) (158-4)	39.50
4	BOSTON COLLEGE (1975) (116-3)	38.67
5	3 tied for fifth place.	

✪ FREE THROWS

Most free throws in a game—one team
1	UTAH (vs. SANTA CLARA, 1960)	41
1	NAVY (vs. SYRACUSE, 1986)	41
3	SEATTLE (vs. UTAH, 1955)	39
3	UTEP (vs. TULSA, 1985)	39
5	2 tied for fifth place.	

Most free throw attempts in a game—one team
1	UTEP (vs. TULSA, 1985)	55
2	MOREHEAD STATE (vs. PITTSBURGH, 1957)	54
3	MOREHEAD STATE (vs. IOWA, 1956)	53
4	4 tied for fourth place.	

Highest free throw percentage in a game—one team
1	FORDHAM (vs. S. CAROLINA, 1971) (22-22)	1.000
2	DAYTON (vs. VILLANOVA, 1985) (17-17)	1.000
2	VILLANOVA (vs. KENTUCKY, 1988) (17-17)	1.000
4	TCU (vs. NOTRE DAME, 1987) (12-12)	1.000
5	2 tied for fifth place.	

Lowest free throw percentage in a game—one team (minimum 5 attempts)
1	UNLV (vs. N. CAROLINA, 1977) (1-5)	.200
2	UCLA (vs. ARKANSAS, 1978) (2-8)	.250
2	N. CAROLINA (vs. PITTSBURGH, 1941) (2-8)	.250
4	LOUISIANA ST. (vs. DEPAUL, 1987) (2-7)	.286
5	WASHINGTON ST. (vs. CREIGHTON, 1941) (4-14)	.286

Most free throws in a game—two teams
1	PITTSBURGH (vs. MOREHEAD STATE, 1957)	69
2	OKLAHOMA CITY (vs. KANSAS STATE, 1956)	68
2	IOWA (vs. MOREHEAD STATE, 1956)	68
4	BRADLEY (vs. COLORADO, 1954)	64
5	3 tied for fifth place.	

Most free throw attempts in a game—two teams
1	IOWA (vs. MOREHEAD STATE, 1956)	105
2	PITTSBURGH (vs. MOREHEAD STATE, 1957)	97
3	UCLA (vs. SEATTLE, 1956)	92
4	OKLAHOMA CITY (vs. KANSAS STATE, 1956)	92
5	MANHATTAN (vs. WEST VIRGINIA, 1958)	91

Fewest free throws in a game—two teams
1	ILLINOIS STATE (vs. ALABAMA, 1984)	3
2	ALABAMA (vs. ILLINOIS, 1986)	6
3	GEORGETOWN (vs. SMU, 1984)	7
3	VA COMMONWEALTH (vs. NORTHEASTERN, 1984)	7
3	UCLA (vs. SAN FRANCISCO, 1973)	7

Fewest free throw attempts in a game—two teams
1	ILLINOIS STATE (vs. ALABAMA, 1984)	4
2	ALABAMA (vs. ILLINOIS, 1986)	9
2	UCLA (vs. SAN FRANCISCO, 1973)	9
4	ST. JOSEPH'S (vs. DEPAUL, 1981)	12
5	2 tied for fifth place.	

Most free throws in a Final Four game—one team
1	JACKSONVILLE (vs. ST. BONAVENTURE, 1970)	37
2	BRADLEY (vs. LA SALLE, 1954)	32
2	DUKE (vs. NOTRE DAME, 1978)	32

Most free throw attempts in a Final Four game—one team
1	JACKSONVILLE (vs. ST. BONAVENTURE, 1970)	45
2	3 tied for second place.	

Highest free throw percentage in a Final Four game—one team
1	OHIO STATE (vs. CINCINNATI, 1961) (15-16)	.938
2	IOWA (vs. LOUISVILLE, 1980) (14-15)	.933
3	MARQUETTE (vs. N. CAROLINA, 1977) (23-25)	.920

Fewest free throws in a Final Four game—one team
1	UNLV (vs. N. CAROLINA, 1977)	1
2	DEPAUL (vs. INDIANA STATE, 1979)	2
2	DARTMOUTH (vs. UTAH, 1944)	2

Fewest free throw attempts in a Final Four game—one team
1	DEPAUL (vs. INDIANA STATE, 1979)	5
1	UNLV (vs. N. CAROLINA, 1977)	5
1	DARTMOUTH (vs. UTAH, 1944)	5

Lowest free throw percentage in a Final Four game—one team
1	UNLV (vs. N. CAROLINA, 1977) (1-5)	.200
2	OKLAHOMA STATE (vs. NYU, 1945) (5-15)	.333
3	TEMPLE (vs. IOWA, 1956) (6-17)	.353

Most free throws in a Final Four game—two teams
1	JACKSONVILLE (vs. ST. BONAVENTURE, 1970)	52
2	LA SALLE (vs. BRADLEY, 1954)	50
3	2 tied for third place.	

Most free throw attempts in a Final Four game—two teams
1	KENTUCKY (vs. SYRACUSE, 1975)	70
2	3 tied for second place.	

Fewest free throws in a Final Four game—two teams
1	INDIANA STATE (vs. DEPAUL, 1979)	8
2	STANFORD (vs. DARTMOUTH, 1942)	9
3	UCLA (vs. INDIANA, 1973)	11

Fewest free throw attempts in a Final Four game—two teams
1	INDIANA STATE (vs. DEPAUL, 1979)	14
1	STANFORD (vs. DARTMOUTH, 1942)	14
3	HOUSTON (vs. VIRGINIA, 1984)	19
3	UCLA (vs. INDIANA, 1973)	19
3	UTAH (vs. DARTMOUTH, 1944)	19

Most free throws in a championship game—one team
1	BRADLEY (vs. LA SALLE, 1954)	32
2	DUKE (vs. KENTUCKY, 1978)	30
3	2 tied for third place.	

Most free throw attempts in a championship game—one team
1	BRADLEY (vs. LA SALLE, 1954)	44
2	UCLA (vs. PURDUE, 1969)	41
3	KENTUCKY (vs. SEATTLE, 1958)	36

Highest free throw percentage in a championship game—one team
1	OHIO STATE (vs. CINCINNATI, 1961) (15-16)	.938
2	MARQUETTE (vs. N. CAROLINA, 1977) (23-25)	.920
3	DUKE (vs. LOUISVILLE, 1986) (19-21)	.905

Fewest free throws in a championship game—one team
1	DARTMOUTH (vs. UTAH, 1944)	2
2	DARTMOUTH (vs. STANFORD, 1942)	4
3	OHIO STATE (vs. OREGON, 1939)	5
3	STANFORD (vs. DARTMOUTH, 1942)	5
3	OKLAHOMA STATE (vs. NYU, 1945)	5

Fewest free throw attempts in a championship game—one team
1	DARTMOUTH (vs. UTAH, 1944)	5
2	DARTMOUTH (vs. STANFORD, 1942)	6
3	GEORGETOWN (vs. VILLANOVA, 1985)	8
3	STANFORD (vs. DARTMOUTH, 1942)	8
3	JACKSONVILLE (vs. UCLA, 1970)	8

Lowest free throw percentage in a championship game—one team
1	OKLAHOMA STATE (vs. NYU, 1945) (5-15)	.333
2	DARTMOUTH (vs. UTAH, 1944) (2-5)	.400
3	GEORGETOWN (vs. WYOMING, 1943) (6-14)	.429

Most free throws in a championship game—two teams
1	LA SALLE (vs. BRADLEY, 1954)	50
2	3 tied for second place.	

Most free throw attempts in a championship game—two teams
1	LA SALLE (vs. BRADLEY, 1954)	68
2	KENTUCKY (vs. SEATTLE, 1958)	66
3	UCLA (vs. PURDUE, 1969)	65

Fewest free throws in a championship game—two teams
1	STANFORD (vs. DARTMOUTH, 1942)	9
2	UTAH (vs. DARTMOUTH, 1944)	12
3	WISCONSIN (vs. WASHINGTON ST., 1941)	13

Fewest free throw attempts in a championship game—two teams
1	STANFORD (vs. DARTMOUTH, 1942)	14
2	UTAH (vs. DARTMOUTH, 1944)	19
3	WISCONSIN (vs. WASHINGTON ST., 1941)	22

Most free throws in a tournament
1	BRADLEY (1954)	146
2	UCLA (1980)	136
2	DUKE (1990)	136
4	SMU (1956)	130
5	WEST VIRGINIA (1959)	129

Most free throw attempts in a tournament
1	BRADLEY (1954)	194
2	WEST VIRGINIA (1959)	192
3	DUKE (1990)	183
4	PURDUE (1980)	178
5	SYRACUSE (1987)	175

Highest free throw percentage in a tournament (minimum 3 games, since 1960)
1	ST. JOHN'S (1969) (47-54)	.870
2	NOTRE DAME (1987) (47-55)	.855
3	ALABAMA (1987) (50-59)	.848
4	TEMPLE (1988) (76-90)	.845
5	WESTERN KY. (1962) (51-61)	.836

Most free throws per game (minimum 3 games)
1	MOREHEAD STATE (1956) (91-3)	30.33
2	BRADLEY (1954) (146-5)	29.20
3	UTAH (1960) (85-3)	28.33
4	ALA.-BIRMINGHAM (1981) (84-3)	28.00
5	SEATTLE (1964) (83-3)	27.67

Lowest free throw percentage in a tournament (minimum 3 games)
1	DARTMOUTH (1944) (11-25)	.440
2	WASHINGTON ST. (1941) (22-45)	.489
3	CALIFORNIA (1946) (24-46)	.522
4	WYOMING (1943) (23-44)	.523
5	TEMPLE (1958) (49-93)	.527

Most opponents' free throws per game (minimum 3 games)
1	SEATTLE (1964) (121-3)	40.33
2	SEATTLE (1956) (120-3)	40.00
3	BRADLEY (1954) (194-5)	38.80
4	UTAH (1960) (116-3)	38.67
5	WEST VIRGINIA (1959) (192-5)	38.40

✪ 3-PT. FIELD GOALS

Most 3-pt. field goals in a game—one team
1	LOYOLA MYMT. (vs. MICHIGAN, 1990)	21
2	LOYOLA MYMT. (vs. UNLV, 1990)	17
3	PROVIDENCE (vs. ALABAMA, 1987)	14
4	3 tied for fourth place.	

Most 3-pt. field goal attempts in a game—one team
1	LOYOLA MYMT. (vs. UNLV, 1990)	41
2	LOYOLA MYMT. (vs. MICHIGAN, 1990)	40
3	LOYOLA MYMT. (vs. N. CAROLINA, 1988)	39
3	LOYOLA MYMT. (vs. ARKANSAS, 1989)	39
5	2 tied for fifth place.	

Highest 3-pt. field goal percentage in a game—one team (minimum 10 attempts)
1	ALABAMA (vs. N.C. A&T, 1987) (9-11)	.818
2	KANSAS STATE (vs. PURDUE, 1988) (8-10)	.800
3	KANSAS STATE (vs. DEPAUL, 1988) (10-13)	.769
4	DUKE (vs. INDIANA, 1987) (8-11)	.727
4	ALABAMA (vs. COLORADO STATE, 1990) (8-11)	.727

Most 3-pt. field goals in a game—two teams
1	LOYOLA MYMT. (vs. MICHIGAN, 1990)	25
2	UNLV (vs. LOYOLA MYMT., 1990)	24
3	PROVIDENCE (vs. ALABAMA, 1987)	21
4	MICHIGAN (vs. N. CAROLINA, 1989)	20
5	2 tied for fifth place.	

Most 3-pt. field goal attempts in a game—two teams
1	UNLV (vs. LOYOLA MYMT., 1990)	59
2	LA SALLE (vs. SOUTHERN MISS., 1990)	56
3	LOYOLA MYMT. (vs. MICHIGAN, 1990)	53
4	N. CAROLINA (vs. LOYOLA MYMT., 1988)	48
4	ARKANSAS (vs. LOYOLA MYMT., 1989)	48

Highest 3-pt. field goal percentage in a game—two teams (minimum 15 attempts)
1	SYRACUSE (vs. GA. SOUTHERN, 1987) (11-16)	.688
1	KANSAS STATE (vs. GEORGIA, 1987) (11-16)	.688
3	KANSAS STATE (vs. PURDUE, 1988) (17-26)	.654
4	GEORGETOWN (vs. NOTRE DAME, 1989) (9-15)	.600
5	UCLA (vs. CENTRAL MICH., 1987) (12-21)	.571

Most 3-pt. field goals in a Final Four game—one team
1	UNLV (vs. INDIANA, 1987)	13
2	OKLAHOMA (vs. KANSAS, 1988)	10
2	UNLV (vs. GEORGIA TECH, 1990)	10

Most 3-pt. field goal attempts in a Final Four Game—one team
1	UNLV (vs. INDIANA, 1987)	35
2	OKLAHOMA (vs. KANSAS, 1988)	24
3	2 tied for third place.	

Highest 3-pt. field goal pct. in a Final Four game—one team (minimum 10 attempts)
1	UNLV (vs. GEORGIA TECH, 1990) (10-15)	.667
2	INDIANA (vs. SYRACUSE, 1987) (7-11)	.636
3	UNLV (vs. DUKE, 1990) (8-14)	.571

Most 3-pt. field goals in a Final Four game—two teams
1	UNLV (vs. GEORGIA TECH, 1990)	18
2	INDIANA (vs. UNLV, 1987)	15
3	KANSAS (vs. OKLAHOMA, 1988)	14

Most 3-pt. field goal attempts in a Final Four game—two teams
1	INDIANA (vs. UNLV, 1987)	39
1	MICHIGAN (vs. SETON HALL, 1989)	39
3	OKLAHOMA (vs. ARIZONA, 1988)	37

Highest 3-pt. field goal pct. in a Final Four game—two teams (minimum 15 attempts)
1	INDIANA (vs. SYRACUSE, 1987) (11-21)	.524
2	UNLV (vs. GEORGIA TECH, 1990) (18-36)	.500
3	KANSAS (vs. OKLAHOMA, 1988) (14-30)	.467

Most 3-pt. field goals in a championship game—one team
1	OKLAHOMA (vs. KANSAS, 1988)	10
2	UNLV (vs. DUKE, 1990)	8
3	2 tied for third place.	

Most 3-pt. field goal attempts in a championship game—one team
1	OKLAHOMA (vs. KANSAS, 1988)	24
2	SETON HALL (vs. MICHIGAN, 1989)	23
3	MICHIGAN (vs. SETON HALL, 1989)	16

Highest 3-pt. field goal pct. in a championship game—one team (minimum 10 attempts)
1	INDIANA (vs. SYRACUSE, 1987) (7-11)	.636
2	UNLV (vs. DUKE, 1990) (8-14)	.571
3	OKLAHOMA (vs. KANSAS, 1988) (10-24)	.417

Most 3-pt. field goals in a tournament
1	LOYOLA MYMT. (1990)	56
2	PROVIDENCE (1987)	45
3	UNLV (1987)	43
3	MICHIGAN (1989)	43
5	OKLAHOMA (1988)	41

Most 3-pt. field goal attempts in a tournament
1	LOYOLA MYMT. (1990)	137
2	UNLV (1987)	132
3	OKLAHOMA (1988)	105
4	UNLV (1990)	102
5	GEORGIA TECH (1990)	98

Highest 3-pt. field goal percentage in a tournament (minimum 20 attempts)
1	INDIANA (1989) (14-23)	.609
2	UC SANTA BARB. (1988) (11-20)	.550
3	EASTERN MICH. (1988) (12-22)	.545
4	VIRGINIA (1989) (27-50)	.540
5	MICHIGAN (1987) (18-34)	.529

Most 3-pt. field goals per game in a tournament (minimum 3 games)
1	LOYOLA MYMT. (1990) (56-4)	14.00
2	PROVIDENCE (1987) (45-5)	9.00
3	UNLV (1987) (43-5)	8.60
4	KANSAS STATE (1988) (33-4)	8.25
5	GEORGIA TECH (1990) (39-5)	7.80

✪ REBOUNDING

Most rebounds in a game—one team
1	NOTRE DAME (vs. TENNESSEE TECH, 1958)	83
2	TEMPLE (vs. U. CONN, 1956)	76
3	UCLA (vs. SEATTLE, 1956)	72
3	HOUSTON (vs. N. CAROLINA, 1967)	72
5	HOUSTON (vs. TCU, 1968)	67

Largest rebound differential in a game (since 1963)
1	N.C. STATE (vs. NEVADA-RENO, 1985)	34
2	UCLA (vs. WEBER ST., 1972)	29
3	INDIANA STATE (vs. OKLAHOMA, 1979)	28
4	5 tied for fourth place.	

Fewest rebounds in a game—one team
1	U. CONN (vs. BOSTON COLLEGE, 1967)	11
2	WEST VIRGINIA (vs. FRESNO STATE, 1982)	12
2	FRESNO STATE (vs. GEORGETOWN, 1982)	12
4	PRINCETON (vs. GEORGETOWN, 1989)	13
4	BOSTON COLLEGE (vs. U. CONN, 1967)	13

Most rebounds in a game—two teams
1	UCLA (vs. SEATTLE, 1956)	128
2	S'WESTERN LA. (vs. MARSHALL, 1972)	126
3	HOUSTON (vs. PACIFIC, 1966)	124
4	3 tied for fourth place.	

Fewest rebounds in a game—two teams (since 1963)
1	BOSTON COLLEGE (vs. U. CONN, 1967)	24
2	FRESNO STATE (vs. WEST VIRGINIA, 1982)	28
3	NORTHEASTERN (vs. FRESNO STATE, 1981)	30
4	VILLANOVA (vs. GEORGETOWN, 1985)	31
5	MEMPHIS STATE (vs. WAKE FOREST, 1982)	33

Most rebounds in a Final Four game—one team
1	WESTERN KY. (vs. VILLANOVA, 1971)	61
2	SAN FRANCISCO (vs. IOWA, 1956)	60
3	MICHIGAN ST. (vs. N. CAROLINA, 1957)	58

Largest rebound differential in a Final Four game
1	UCLA (vs. WICHITA STATE, 1965)	21
1	SYRACUSE (vs. PROVIDENCE, 1987)	21
3	2 tied for third place.	

Fewest rebounds in a Final Four game—one team
1	VILLANOVA (vs. GEORGETOWN, 1985)	14
2	GEORGETOWN (vs. VILLANOVA, 1985)	17
3	2 tied for third place.	

Most rebounds in a Final Four game—two teams
1	VILLANOVA (vs. WESTERN KY., 1971)	111
2	SAN FRANCISCO (vs. IOWA, 1956)	108
3	N. CAROLINA (vs. MICHIGAN ST., 1957)	107

Fewest rebounds in a Final Four game—two teams
1	VILLANOVA (vs. GEORGETOWN, 1985)	31
2	N. CAROLINA (vs. GEORGETOWN, 1982)	48
3	INDIANA STATE (vs. DEPAUL, 1979)	51

Most rebounds in a championship game—one team
1	SAN FRANCISCO (vs. IOWA, 1956)	60
2	UCLA (vs. PURDUE, 1969)	56
3	2 tied for third place.	

Largest rebound differential in a championship game
1	UCLA (vs. MEMPHIS STATE, 1973)	19
2	KENTUCKY (vs. KANSAS STATE, 1951)	15
2	LOUISVILLE (vs. DUKE, 1986)	15

Fewest rebounds in a championship game—one team
1	VILLANOVA (vs. GEORGETOWN, 1985)	14
2	GEORGETOWN (vs. VILLANOVA, 1985)	17
3	MEMPHIS STATE (vs. UCLA, 1973)	19

Most rebounds in a championship game—two teams
1	SAN FRANCISCO (vs. IOWA, 1956)	108
2	UCLA (vs. PURDUE, 1969)	99
3	UCLA (vs. KENTUCKY, 1975)	95

Fewest rebounds in a championship game—two teams
1	VILLANOVA (vs. GEORGETOWN, 1985)	31
2	N. CAROLINA (vs. GEORGETOWN, 1982)	48
3	CINCINNATI (vs. OHIO STATE, 1961)	54
3	MARQUETTE (vs. N. CAROLINA, 1977)	54
3	UCLA (vs. MICHIGAN, 1965)	54

Most total rebounds in a tournament
1	HOUSTON (1968)	265
2	WESTERN KY. (1971)	260
3	UNLV (1990)	251
4	NEW MEXICO ST. (1970)	243
5	2 tied for fifth place.	

Most rebounds per game in a tournament (minimum 3 games)
1	NOTRE DAME (1958) (174-3)	58.00
2	MICHIGAN ST. (1957) (222-4)	55.50
3	S'WESTERN LA. (1972) (165-3)	55.00
4	IOWA (1956) (214-4)	53.50
5	HOUSTON (1968) (265-5)	53.00

Largest average rebound differential in a tournament (minimum 3 games)
1	MARQUETTE (1971) (52-3)	17.333
2	CINCINNATI (1960) (61-4)	15.250
3	UCLA (1972) (59-4)	14.750
4	CLEMSON (1990) (44-3)	14.667
5	CINCINNATI (1961) (57-4)	14.250

⭐ ASSISTS

Most assists in a game—one team
1	N. CAROLINA (vs. LOYOLA MYMT., 1988)	36
2	UNLV (vs. LOYOLA MYMT., 1990)	35
3	LOYOLA MYMT. (vs. MICHIGAN, 1990)	33
4	LOUISVILLE (vs. SYRACUSE, 1975)	32
5	4 tied for fifth place.	

Most assists in a game—two teams
1	LOUISVILLE (vs. SYRACUSE, 1975)	59
2	UNLV (vs. LOYOLA MYMT., 1990)	58
3	MICHIGAN (vs. FLORIDA, 1988)	55
4	LOYOLA MYMT. (vs. MICHIGAN, 1990)	54
5	2 tied for fifth place.	

Most assists in a Final Four game—one team
1	UCLA (vs. HOUSTON, 1968)	26
1	UCLA (vs. MEMPHIS STATE, 1973)	26
1	LOUISVILLE (vs. LOUISIANA ST., 1986)	26

Most assists in a Final Four game—two teams
1	KENTUCKY (vs. SYRACUSE, 1975)	41
2	5 tied for second place.	

Most assists in a championship game—one team
1	UCLA (vs. MEMPHIS STATE, 1973)	26
2	UNLV (vs. DUKE, 1990)	24
3	UCLA (vs. KENTUCKY, 1975)	23

Most assists in a championship game—two teams
1	UCLA (vs. KENTUCKY, 1975)	39
1	GEORGETOWN (vs. HOUSTON, 1984)	39
3	UCLA (vs. VILLANOVA, 1971)	38

Most assists in a tournament
1	UNLV (1990)	140
2	OKLAHOMA (1988)	136
3	MICHIGAN (1989)	125
4	LOUISVILLE (1986)	120
5	KANSAS (1988)	115

Most assists per game in a tournament (minimum 3 games)
1	PURDUE (1988) (72-3)	24.00
2	N. CAROLINA (1989) (71-3)	23.67
3	UNLV (1990) (140-6)	23.33
4	OKLAHOMA (1988) (136-6)	22.67
5	LOUISVILLE (1988) (68-3)	22.67

⭐ BLOCKED SHOTS

Most blocked shots in a game—one team
1	HOUSTON (vs. VILLANOVA, 1983)	13
1	LOUISVILLE (vs. ILLINOIS, 1989)	13
3	CLEMSON (vs. ST. MARY'S, 1989)	12
4	5 tied for fourth place.	

Most blocked shots in a Final Four game—one team
1	HOUSTON (vs. LOUISVILLE, 1983)	10
2	KANSAS (vs. DUKE, 1988)	9
3	2 tied for third place.	

Most blocked shots in a championship game—one team
1	N.C. STATE (vs. MARQUETTE, 1974)	8
1	HOUSTON (vs. N.C. STATE, 1983)	8
3	UCLA (vs. KENTUCKY, 1975)	7
3	SYRACUSE (vs. INDIANA, 1987)	7
3	LOUISVILLE (vs. DUKE, 1986)	7

Most blocked shots in a tournament
1	HOUSTON (1983)	43
2	UNLV (1990)	33
3	SYRACUSE (1987)	30
4	SETON HALL (1989)	29
5	LOUISVILLE (1986)	28

Most blocked shots per game in a tournament (minimum 3 games)
1	HOUSTON (1983) (43-5)	8.60
2	LOUISVILLE (1989) (25-3)	8.33
3	S. CAROLINA (1973) (23-3)	7.67
4	MEMPHIS STATE (1984) (20-3)	6.67
5	2 tied for fifth place.	

⭐ STEALS

Most steals in a game—one team
1	OREGON STATE (vs. MIDDLE TENN. ST, 1975)	19
1	PROVIDENCE (vs. AUSTIN PEAY, 1987)	19
1	U. CONN. (vs. BOSTON UNIV., 1990)	19
4	XAVIER (OHIO) (vs. KANSAS, 1988)	17
5	7 tied for fifth place.	

Most steals in a Final Four game—one team
1	UNLV (vs. DUKE, 1990)	16
2	OKLAHOMA (vs. KANSAS, 1988)	13
2	DUKE (vs. LOUISVILLE, 1986)	13

Most steals in a championship game—one team
1	UNLV (vs. DUKE, 1990)	16
2	OKLAHOMA (vs. KANSAS, 1988)	13
2	DUKE (vs. LOUISVILLE, 1986)	13

Most steals in a tournament
1	OKLAHOMA (1988)	72
2	PENNSYLVANIA (1979)	64
3	ARKANSAS (1990)	57
4	UNLV (1990)	54
5	HOUSTON (1982)	53

Most steals per game in a tournament (minimum 3 games)
1	LOYOLA MYMT. (1990) (51-4)	12.75
2	OKLAHOMA (1988) (72-6)	12.00
3	U. CONN. (1990) (48-4)	12.00
4	ARKANSAS (1990) (57-5)	11.40
5	MICHIGAN (1977) (34-3)	11.33

⭐ PERSONAL FOULS

Most personal fouls in a game—one team
1	DAYTON (vs. ILLINOIS, 1952)	41
2	KANSAS (vs. NOTRE DAME, 1975)	39
3	UCLA (vs. SEATTLE, 1956)	36
3	N. CAROLINA (vs. TEXAS A&M, 1980)	36
5	5 tied for fifth place.	

Most personal fouls in a Final Four game—one team
1	ST. JOHN'S (vs. KANSAS, 1952)	35
2	PROVIDENCE (vs. SYRACUSE, 1987)	33
3	ST. BONAVENTURE (vs. JACKSONVILLE, 1970)	32
3	BRADLEY (vs. CCNY, 1950)	32
5	2 tied for fifth place.	

Most personal fouls in a championship game—one team
1	ST. JOHN'S (vs. KANSAS, 1952)	35
2	BRADLEY (vs. CCNY, 1950)	32
3	PURDUE (vs. UCLA, 1969)	30

Most personal fouls in a tournament

1 PENNSYLVANIA (1979)   150
2 PROVIDENCE (1987)   135
3 KENTUCKY (1975)   128
4 MICHIGAN (1989)   124
5 UNLV (1977)   123

Most personal fouls per game in a tournament (minimum 3 games)

1 PROVIDENCE (1987) (135-5)   27.00
2 OKLAHOMA STATE (1951) (108-4)   27.00
3 PITTSBURGH (1957) (79-3)   26.33
4 ST. JOHN'S (1952) (105-4)   26.25
5 KENTUCKY (1975) (128-5)   25.60

★ TURNOVERS

Most turnovers in a game—one team

1 N. CAROLINA (vs. DRAKE, 1969)   36
2 JACKSONVILLE (vs. WESTERN KY., 1971)   33
2 LOUISVILLE (vs. SYRACUSE, 1975)   33
4 SAN FRANCISCO (vs. UNLV, 1977)   32
5 2 tied for fifth place.

Fewest turnovers in a game—one team

1 ST. JOHN'S (vs. WICHITA STATE, 1987)   2
2 UNLV (vs. DEPAUL, 1989)   3
2 CINCINNATI (vs. OHIO STATE, 1961)   3
2 LOYOLA-CHICAGO (vs. CINCINNATI, 1963)   3
5 11 tied for fifth place.

Most turnovers in a game—two teams

1 DRAKE (vs. N. CAROLINA, 1969)   59
2 OREGON STATE (vs. MIDDLE TENN. ST, 1975)   55
3 FLORIDA STATE (vs. N. CAROLINA, 1972)   53
4 KANSAS STATE (vs. HOUSTON, 1970)   52
4 ARIZONA (vs. UNLV, 1976)   52

Most turnovers in a Final Four game—one team

1 FLORIDA STATE (vs. N. CAROLINA, 1972)   27
2 N. CAROLINA (vs. FLORIDA STATE, 1972)   26
2 N. CAROLINA (vs. PURDUE, 1969)   26
2 UCLA (vs. N. CAROLINA, 1968)   26
2 SYRACUSE (vs. KENTUCKY, 1975)   26

Most turnovers in a Final Four game—two teams

1 FLORIDA STATE (vs. N. CAROLINA, 1972)   53
2 UCLA (vs. N. CAROLINA, 1968)   49
2 KENTUCKY (vs. SYRACUSE, 1975)   49

Most turnovers in a championship game—one team

1 UCLA (vs. N. CAROLINA, 1968)   26
2 DUKE (vs. UCLA, 1964)   24
2 LOUISVILLE (vs. DUKE, 1986)   24

Fewest turnovers in a championship game—one team

1 CINCINNATI (vs. OHIO STATE, 1961)   3
1 LOYOLA-CHICAGO (vs. CINCINNATI, 1963)   3
3 PURDUE (vs. UCLA, 1969)   4

Most turnovers in a championship game—two teams

1 UCLA (vs. N. CAROLINA, 1968)   49
2 UCLA (vs. DUKE, 1964)   43
3 2 tied for third place.

Most turnovers in a tournament

1 PENNSYLVANIA (1979)   115
2 KANSAS (1988)   111
3 SYRACUSE (1975)   110
4 UCLA (1980)   102
4 PURDUE (1980)   102

Most turnovers per game in a tournament (minimum 3 games)

1 N. CAROLINA (1969) (98-4)   24.50
2 SYRACUSE (1975) (110-5)   22.00
3 N. CAROLINA (1975) (66-3)   22.00
4 HOUSTON (1970) (63-3)   21.00
5 2 tied for fifth place.

Largest turnover differential in a game

1 S. CAROLINA (vs. FORDHAM, 1971)   20
1 N. CAROLINA (vs. LOYOLA MYMT., 1988)   20
3 4 tied for third place.

Largest turnover differential in a Final Four game

1 UCLA (vs. PURDUE, 1969)   15
2 INDIANA STATE (vs. DE PAUL, 1979)   14
3 2 tied for third place.

Largest turnover differential in a championship game

1 UCLA (vs. PURDUE, 1969)   15
2 CINCINNATI (vs. LOYOLA-CHICAGO, 1963)   13
3 LOUISVILLE (vs. DUKE, 1986)   10

Largest average turnover differential in a tournament (minimum 3 games)

1 ARIZONA (1976) (25-3)   8.33
2 N. CAROLINA (1969) (31-4)   7.75
3 GEORGIA TECH (1986) (23-3)   7.67
4 N.C. STATE (1985) (30-4)   7.50
5 COLORADO STATE (1969) (18-3)   6.00

★ APPEARANCES/WINS

Most Tournament Appearances

1 Kentucky   33
2 UCLA   26
3 N. Carolina   24
4 Notre Dame   24
5 Louisville   21

Most Consecutive Tournament Appearances

1 N. Carolina   16
2 UCLA   13
3 Georgetown   12
4 Marquette   10

5 Arkansas   9
5 Kentucky   9

Most Tournament Games Won

1 UCLA   64
2 Kentucky   55
3 N. Carolina   50
4 Indiana   39
5 Louisville   38
5 Duke   38

Most Consecutive Tournament Games Won

1 UCLA   38
2 Cincinnati   11
2 San Francisco   11
2 Kentucky   11
5 Georgetown   10

Highest Tournament Winning Percentage (min. 25 games)

1 UCLA (64-20)   .762
2 Indiana (39-14)   .736
3 UNLV (26-10)   .722
4 Duke (38-15)   .717
5 Cincinnati (20-9)   .690

Most Final Four Appearances

1 UCLA   14
2 N. Carolina   9
2 Kentucky   9
4 Duke   8
4 Kansas   8
4 Ohio State   8

Most Consecutive Final Four Appearances

1 UCLA   10
2 Cincinnati   5
   5 tied for 3rd

Most Championships

1 UCLA   10
2 Kentucky   5
2 Indiana   5
   7 tied for 4th

Most Consecutive Championships

1 UCLA (1967–1973)   7
2 UCLA (1964–1965)   2
2 Cincinnati (1961–1962)   2
2 San Francisco (1955–1956)   2
2 Kentucky (1948–1949)   2
2 Oklahoma A&M (1945–1946)   2